The Avenel Companion to English & American Literature

The Avenel Companion to English & American Literature

Volume One
Britain and the Commonwealth
Edited by David Daiches

Volume Two
United States of America
Edited by Malcolm Bradbury
and Eric Mottram

Avenel Books
New York

CONTENTS

Volume One: Britain and the Commonwealth

Volume Two: United States of America

BRITAIN AND THE COMMONWEALTH

EDITORIAL FOREWORD

The main function of this work is to enable the reader to find out quickly exactly what the significance of a writer is, the kind of interest his work possesses, the main facts of his career, and where further knowledge can be obtained. This volume is concerned with writers (whatever their language) in the British Isles and with writers who use the English language in Commonwealth countries except that we include French Canadian writers. The organization of a work of this kind is bound to involve some inconsistencies and even contradictions. French Canadian literature in French might have been included in the European volume, but in the end it was found more convenient to have it in this. No profound questions of cultural history or demarcation are involved, but here as elsewhere there were arguments on all sides of the question and in the end the decision had to be made largely in terms of editorial convenience. Similarly, there is the insoluble question of what borderline figures to include. English literature is particularly rich in writers who are not 'creative' or 'imaginative' writers in the full sense but whose work can be considered 'literature'. If we had included every historian, philosopher, scholar, essayist and writer on general subjects whose work had some cultural significance of interest to the student of literature, this volume would have grown to quite unrealistic proportions. Then there is the question of quality. There are enormous numbers of minor writers—especially of the last hundred years or so—who might with some justice claim a place here but whose inclusion would again swell the volume to a preposterous size. On both these issues the editor has had to make decisions which others might consider arbitrary. A writer tends to have a better chance of being included the further back in time he is, if only because the numbers are fewer the further back we go and an Anglo-Saxon scholar is a rarer and more significant phenomenon than a nineteenth-century one. Many who were first included were later excised (on the grounds, 'If we include A, then we must logically have B, C, D, . . .') and some who were at first rejected were later admitted (on the grounds, 'But we have X, therefore we must logically have Y'). But in the end it was found impossible to be wholly consistent and logical with borderline cases and minor writers. As for the question of length of entry, though in general length is proportionate to importance there is no mathematical precision here, nor could there be. Individual contributors tended to work with different degrees of expansiveness or compression, and though the editor did have to curtail or expand in particular cases in order to see that all entries conformed to the general pattern laid down for the book, no attempt was made to remove differences in flavour and kinds of emphasis which reflected the critical personality of the contributor. At the same time it must be emphasized that this is a reference book, not a collection of personal critical essays. Its aim is to lead the reader beyond itself and to help him to decide just where he wants to go and why.

3

I have to thank Dr Nikita Lary for his help in correcting the final text of the work, Miss Brenda Magurran for long-continued assistance in typing, filing, corresponding and organizing, and Miss Stella Anderson for painstaking reading of proofs.

University of Sussex   DAVID DAICHES

PUBLISHER'S NOTE

Bibliographies

The bibliographies in small type which generally follow an entry are arranged as follows. The first paragraph lists editions of texts and of translations of texts not already given in the entry itself. The second paragraph lists critical works concerning the subject of the entry. In cases where only one paragraph is given, it will be clear from the titles of the works listed whether they are texts or criticism.

The list of critical works is deliberately selective – further bibliographical information can usually be found in the listed works themselves.

Places of publication are not given for texts or critical works published in the British Isles.

Abbreviated titles are explained in the List of Abbreviations on page 9.

Bibliographies have been compiled by the contributors of the relevant articles – their initials are placed before the bibliographies only for convenience.

Cross-references

Cross-references (◇ = see, ◈ = see also) from one article to another are made in the following cases: (a) when relevant information can be found in the articles cross-referred to; (b) when the writer cross-referred to is comparatively minor and the reader may wish to know who he is, even though he has not much relevance to the article in which cross-reference occurs.

5

CONTRIBUTORS

AG	The late Antony Gibbs
AI	A. A. H. Inglis, Lecturer in English, University of Sussex
AR	Angus Ross, Reader in English, University of Sussex
CO	Charles Osborne, Assistant Literature Director, Arts Council
CRPM	Cedric R. P. May, Lecturer in French, University of Birmingham
DD	David Daiches, Professor of English, University of Sussex
DDG	David D. Galloway, Associate Professor of Modern Literature, Case Western Reserve University, Cleveland, Ohio
DELC	D. E. L. Crane, Lecturer in English, University of Durham
DL	Diane Lary, Assistant Professor, Department of History, York University, Toronto
DT	Derick S. Thomson, Professor of Celtic, University of Glasgow
FG	Frederick Grubb, Tutor, The Open University
FM	F. V. Morley
G	Arnold Goldman, Lecturer in American Literature, University of Sussex
GC	Glen Cavaliero, Research Fellow, St Catharine's College, Cambridge
GDJ	G. D. Josipovici, Lecturer in English, University of Sussex
GG	Giles Gordon
GS	Gāmini Salgādo, Reader in English, University of Sussex
GSF	G. S. Fraser, Reader in English, University of Leicester
JH	John Hewish
JK	John Kelly, Lecturer in English and American Literature, University of Kent at Canterbury
JM	Mrs Jan Marsh
JC	Jenni Calder
JRFP	J. R. F. Piette, Lecturer in Welsh Language and Literature, University College of Wales, Aberystwyth
JWB	J. W. Blench, Senior Lecturer in English, University of Durham
KC	Kellow Chesney
MJ	Michael Jamieson, Lecturer in English, University of Sussex
MR	Melville Richards, Professor of Welsh, University College of North Wales, Bangor
NL	Nikita Lary, Assistant Professor, Division of Humanities, York University, Toronto
PJK	P. J. Keating, Lecturer in English Literature, University of Leicester
PM	Peter Malekin, Lecturer in English, University of Durham
PR	Peter Riley
PT	Peter Thomson, Lecturer in Drama, University of Manchester
RB	Ronald Blythe
RH	Rodney M. Hillman, Lecturer in English, University of Sussex
RM-G	R. R. Milner-Gulland, Lecturer in Russian, University of Sussex
SB	Seán de Búrca, Lecturer in Celtic Languages, University College, Galway

Contributors

SM   Stephen Medcalf, Lecturer in English, University of Sussex
SO   Sybil Oldfield, Lecturer in English, University of Sussex
TG   Tea Gang
TV   Teresa Verschoyle
WAG   W. A. Griffith

ABBREVIATIONS OF TITLES

CBEL. *Cambridge Bibliography of English Literature*.
CHEL. *Cambridge History of English Literature*.
DNB. *Dictionary of National Biography*.
E&S. *Essays and Studies*.
EC. *Essays in Criticism*.
EETS. Early English Text Society.
ELH. *English Literature History*.
JEGP. *Journal of English and German Philology*.
JHI. *Journal of the History of Ideas*.
MLQ. *Modern Languages Quarterly*.
MLR. *Modern Languages Review*.
MP. *Modern Philology*.
N&Q. *Notes and Queries*.
PEL. Penguin English Library.
PMLA. *Publications of the Modern Languages Association*.
PMP. Penguin Modern Poets.
PQ. *Philological Quarterly*.
RES. *Review of English Studies*.
SP. *Studies in Philology*.
STS. Scottish Text Society.
TLS. *Times Literary Supplement*.
WTW. Writers and Their Work (Supplements to *British Book News*).

BRITAIN AND THE COMMONWEALTH

A

Abercrombie, Lascelles (1881–1938). Poet and critic. Born at Ashton-on-Mersey, Cheshire, son of a stockbroker, Abercrombie was educated at Malvern College and at Manchester University. After a period of literary journalism and reviewing (and a job as munitions inspector during the First World War), he became Lecturer in Poetry at the University of Liverpool, 1919–22. He was Professor of English Literature, University of Leeds, 1922–9, and Goldsmith's Reader in English at Oxford, 1935–8. Abercrombie was one of those who gave to Georgian poetry a sense of being embarked on radically new things. 'To any man with brain and spirit active and alert in him,' he wrote in 1912, 'the present is a time wherein the world, and the destiny of man in the world, are ideas different from anything that has ever been before. . . . They are exciting but fearfully exacting times for the poet.' But though possessing intellectual vigour and a powerful imagination, Abercrombie never really developed a style commensurate with his ambitions and his sense of historical opportunity. His verse plays, notably *The Sale of St Thomas* (1911, 1930) and *The End of the World* (1915), show an intensely thoughtful, close-packed verse, but he was no more successful than other Georgian poets were in achieving the effective new realism he sought. He admired 17th-century poetry, and his own showed some attempt to be 'metaphysical', but the impression remains that certain irrelevant Victorian traditions kept too strong a hold on him. Of his many cogently argued critical works, *The Idea of Great Poetry* (1925) and *Principles of Literary Criticism* (1932) are the most impressive, though today both seem very dated, very pre-Eliot, pre-Richards and pre-Leavis. His *Collected Poems* (1930) includes most of the plays. [D D]

Robert H. Ross, *The Georgian Revolt: Rise and Fall of a Poetic Ideal 1910–1920* (1967).

Abrahams, Peter Henry (1919–). Coloured South African novelist. Born in Vrederdorp, a Johannesburg slum district, as a scholarship boy he had better schooling than most poor Africans, but satisfactory jobs were hard to get, and he developed Communist sympathies. After publishing a volume of poems, *A Black Man Speaks of Freedom* (1940), he escaped to England by enlisting on a British ship. Since then he has supplemented his writing by journalism and broadcasting. In 1955 he visited Jamaica in connexion with a documentary book, *Jamaica* (1957). Attracted by the island's beauty and its reduced racial tensions, he left England to live there. Abrahams' writings have been almost exclusively concerned with Africa's problems. The love of history that enlivens *Jamaica* informs such novels as *Wild Conquest* (1951) and the accomplished *A Wreath for Udomo* (1956). This novel's complex sympathies are an advance on the anger of *Mine Boy* (1946) and the stories of *Dark Testament* (1942). *A Night of Their Own* (1965) concerns the Indians' part in the South African underground's struggles. Abrahams has a lively, angled understanding of the Western mind and a strong control of narrative. [P T]

Tell Freedom (1954) (autobiography); *This Island Now* (1966).
Michael Wade, '*The Novels of P.A.*' *Critique*, XI, 1 (1968).

Achebe, Chinua (1930–). Nigerian novelist. His father was a mission teacher in Ogidi. He was among the first to follow a full degree course at the University College of Ibadan. Having toured in Africa and America, he joined the Nigerian Broadcasting Corporation in 1954 and later became Director of External Broadcasting.

His first novel, *Things Fall Apart* (1958), deals with the impact on tribal life of the white man's arrival. It is a book of impressive neutrality. Achebe makes no decisions for us. His cool, terse prose, illuminated in the dialogues by the proverbial imagery of the Ibo language, distances the author, leaving room for irony and a meaningful ambiguity. *No Longer at Ease* (1960) turns to modern Lagos and the temptations confronting a young Nigerian with a Western education when given responsibility in his own country. Again the excessive demands made on the individual in an uneasy society are presented without bias and economically. *Arrow of God* (1964) returns to the theme of civilization's threat to traditional village life. The detailed documentation of tribal customs, gay and sinister, gives an equivocal dignity to the hero, the chief priest of Ulu, whose means of life they are. [P T]

A Man of the People (1966).

G. Moore, *Seven African Writers* (1962); A. G. Stock, 'Yeats and A.', *Journal of Commonwealth Literature*, 5 (July 1968); Abiola Itele, 'The Tragic Conflict in A.'s Novels', *Black Orpheus*, 17 (June 1965).

Acton, Sir John Emerich Edward Dalberg (1st Baron Acton of Aldenham) (1834–1902). Historian. He was born of an ancient Roman Catholic Shropshire family at Naples, where his grandfather had been chief minister, and educated at Oscott, Birmingham, under Wiseman (later cardinal) and thereafter privately at Edinburgh and Munich; at the latter town (1848–54) under Döllinger, the scholarly and ecumenical leader of the Old Catholics. Acton was M.P. for Carlow (1859–65), and became a friend of Gladstone. He was made a peer in 1869. He wrote a great number of periodical articles and founded the *English Historical Review*. He edited the Roman Catholic *Rambler*, changing its title to the *Home and Foreign Review*, but discontinued publication under threat of ecclesiastical censure on account of his opposition to the dogma of papal infallibility and of his other 'liberal' views (also displayed in his 4 famous letters to *The Times*, 1875, attacking the ultramontane Vatican decrees). Acton produced no single work equal to his vast erudition (which brought him the friendship of most of the great scholars of the day, and the chair of modern history at Cambridge). His work was, however, influential enough to be collected after his death (*Lectures on Modern History*, 1906; *Historical Essays and Studies*, 1907; and *Lectures on the French Revolution*, 1910); and he laid down the lines of the *Cambridge Modern History*, which in turn long influenced the development of English historiography. He was primarily a historian of politics, in which he saw the conscious struggle for power as the main human activity. He worked all his life on a history of liberty, but died without writing it; he left a library largely bearing on this, which, through the generosity of an American benefactor, is now in the Cambridge University Library. [A R]

Lord A. and His Circle, ed. F. A. Gasquet (1906) (letters).

G. P. Gooch, *History and Historians in the Nineteenth Century* (1913); D. Ogg, *Herbert Fisher* (1947); L. Kochan, *A. on History* (1954); H. Butterfield, 'A.: His Training, Methods and Intellectual System', in *Studies in Diplomatic History and Historiography in Honour of G. P. Gooch*, ed. A. O. Sarkisian (1961); D. Mathew, *Lord A. and His Times* (1968).

Adamnan, St (*c.* 624–704). Chronicler. A native of Donegal; Abbot of Iona in 679 and one of the greatest scholars at that community. His Latin prose life of its founder, St Columba (*Vita S. Columbae*, ed. J. T. Fowler, 1894; tr. J. T. Fowler, 1895; tr. W. Hyshe, 1905, repr. 1908, 1922), gives a vivid portrait of the saint and is one of the finest examples of medieval hagiography extant. He also wrote an account of a pilgrim's visit to the Holy Land, *De locis sanctis* (ed. P. Geyer, Corpus Scriptorum Ecclesiasticorum Latinorum, 39, Vienna, 1898; tr. J. R. Macpherson, *The Pilgrimage of Arculpus in the Holy Land*, 1895).

E. S. Duckett, *Anglo-Saxon Saints and Scholars* (New York, 1947).

Addison, Joseph (1672–1719). Poet, moralist, essayist and politician. He was the son of the Dean of Lichfield and educated at Charterhouse and Magdalen College, Oxford, where he was a Fellow. He abandoned his intention of becoming a parson when in 1699 he obtained through his patrons the annual government pension of £300 to travel abroad as a training for the diplomatic service. He visited Italy, but lived chiefly in France until 1703, when, on the death of William III, his patron Halifax fell. He first appeared as a Latin poet at Oxford, and later contributed verse translations of Ovid to a publication of Dryden's. While he was abroad he wrote a couple of poems, one addressed to Halifax, the other a typical 18th-century 'topographical' poem, *Several Parts of Italy*. Addison was never really a poet, but he could produce the kind of verse intelligent men wrote in an age when they were expected to try their hand at it. In 1704, in *The Campaign*, he commemorated in respectable but dull verse the battle of Blenheim, pleasing his political sponsors (and being made a Commissioner of Excise).

His other successful poem is an ode based on Psalm 19, 'The Spacious Firmament on High' (*Spectator*, 465). He was also the author of a celebrated neo-classical blank-verse tragedy, *Cato* (1713), which had some vogue during the century for political reasons. Though not without some fine touches it seems unlikely ever to be revived. *Rosamond: An Opera* appeared in 1707, and a comedy *The Drummer, or, The Haunted House* in 1716, reprinted with a preface by his old school-fellow ⬦ Steele in 1722. In April 1709, Steele started the *Tatler, by Isaac Bickerstaff Esq.*, a thrice-weekly periodical which ran until January 1711. Addison became an early contributor of 'hints', and wrote 46 complete papers. On 1 March 1711 appeared the first number of their successor periodical, the *Spectator*, which appeared daily until 6 December 1712. It was revived by Addison alone in 1714, when a further 80 numbers appeared. Addison contributed 274 numbers (signed C., L., I. or O.) to the first series and 24 numbers to the second. He also wrote a few essays in the *Whig Examiner* (1710), the *Guardian* (1713) and other periodicals.

It was as an essayist that Addison expressed his genius for *haute vulgarisation*, being entirely in tune with the contemporary development of ideas and expanding intellectual interests of the middle classes. Moving on from the lighter themes of the *Tatler*, the essays in the *Spectator* on conduct, morals, political doctrine, philosophy, science and literature were designed to be light in tone but weighty in influence, and show Addison to be a master of the Augustan idea of prose style – well-bred, clear and useful. As a stylist, however, he lacks the sympathy and humanity of Steele. Addison's chief importance was as an educator and popularizer of Augustan culture (including ideas which in his considerable reading he had gleaned from Descartes, Locke, Newton and the French critics). He was not original in discovery but a powerful synthesizer. His view of social behaviour as a shield and protection is abhorrent to many modern readers, as is his patronage of women, though his standards of polite behaviour were in some ways an advance on the brutality of the previous age. He has been called the 'first Victorian'. In his series of *Spectator* essays, 'The Pleasures of the Imagination' and 'Milton', he developed the (partly social) notion of 'taste' as a critical touchstone in place of

inherited doctrine, and a primitive formulation of the psychological problems of literary judgement. His rationalized religious moralizing, which sometimes has an unpleasant flavour of 'enlightened self-interest', was long popular. He was one of the first, and most successful, exponents of the typically English form of political argument which takes up a position of 'impartiality' and suggests that any opposition comes from people engaged in the political hurly-burly. He was thus a powerful Whig political writer. His writings often contain, however, a kind of common sense which commands respect independent of their indisputable historical importance. [AR]

The Miscellaneous Works in Verse and Prose, ed. A. C. Guthkelch (1914); *The Tatler*, ed. G. A. Aitken (4 vols., 1898–9); *The Spectator* (complete essays), ed. D. F. Bond (5 vols., 1965); ed. G. Gregory Smith (8 vols., Everyman, 1897–8, 1907); ed. G. A. Aitken (8 vols., 1898).
P. Smithers, *The Life of J. A.* (1954); C. S. Lewis, 'A.', in *Essays Presented to D. Nichol Smith* (1945); C. D. Thorpe, 'A.'s Contribution to Criticism', in *The Seventeenth Century: Studies by R. F. Jones and Others in His Honour* (Stanford, Calif., 1951); B. Dobrée, *English Literature in the Early Eighteenth Century* (1959); L. A. Elioseff, *The Cultural Milieu of A.'s Literary Criticism* (Austin, Texas, 1963) (bibliography).

'AE' (Æ or A.E.) (pseud. of George William Russell) (1867–1935). Irish poet, painter and journalist. He was born at Lurgan, Co. Armagh, of an Irish Protestant family. Moving later to Dublin, he attended Rathmines School and evening classes at the Metropolitan School of Art, where in 1886 he met W. B. Yeats, who introduced him to theosophy. He then abandoned painting as a career, though he continued as an amateur for the rest of his life. Theosophical mysticism was successfully combined with Irish mythology in his first volume of poems, *Homeward: Songs by the Way* (1894). This and his play *Deirdre* (1906) gained him a place in the Irish literary revival, but his interests widened to public affairs when he joined the Irish Agricultural Organization Society and in 1905 became editor of its journal, *The Homestead*, dedicated to land reform. From then until 1930 he combined the roles of poet and journalist, earning for himself a prominent position in Irish affairs. His most important volumes of poetry are *The Divine Vision* (1904) and *Voices of the Stones* (1925); of politics *Co-operation and*

Nationality (1912) and *The National Being* (1916). His poetry followed Yeats's development from Celtic Twilight romanticism to a tougher style, but without Yeats's genius. AE's most successful poem, 'On Behalf of Some Irishmen Not Followers of Tradition', is a fine public lyric. *The Homestead*, later the *Irish Statesman*, was a moderately reformist and cultured newspaper; Russell was a good editor and attractive personality; in the last years of his life he left Ireland, saddened and disgusted by what his country had become. He was affectionately regarded as a saint and mystic, and is a characteristic figure in the Irish revival, but as a poet he is notable chiefly as a pale copy of Yeats rather than as an individual writer. [JM]

Collected Poems (1926); *The Living Torch: Selected Prose*, ed. Monk Gibbon (1937).
Alan Denson, *Bibliography* (1961); William I. Thompson, *The Imagination of an Insurrection* (1967).

Aelfric (*c*. 955–*c*. 1020). Grammarian and homilist. Abbot of Eynsham from 1005. Educated under Bishop Aethelwold at the monastic school at Winchester, Aelfric became novice-master at the monastery of Cernel in 987. Here, with the encouragement of the powerful Alderman Aethelweard, he wrote much of his most important work, notably the 2 series of *Catholic Homilies* (ed. B. Thorpe, 1843–6) between 989 and 992, and the *Lives of Saints* (ed. W. W. Skeat, 1881–1900), completed 996–7. These works illustrate his cultured style and range, unsurpassed in Old English prose. In the homilies, which comprise 2 complete sets of sermons for the ecclesiastical year, Aelfric aims to instruct an intelligent audience; his style, though relatively plain, reveals his classical learning and rhetorical mastery, notably in the passages of exegesis. In the *Lives of Saints* admiration for the heroes of the Church is aroused by the use of an ornate, highly rhythmical prose, influenced by late Latin, and also, perhaps, by native epic style. His large output also includes works on mathematics, a grammar, a glossary, and historically important translations from the Old Testament which display his prose at its best. [AG]

The Old English Version of the Heptateuch, ed. and intr. S. J. Crawford (1922).
R. W. Chambers, *On the Continuity of English Prose* (1932); G. H. Gerould, 'Abbot A.'s Rhythmical Prose', in *Modern Philology* (1925);

P. A. M. Clemoes, 'The Chronology of A.'s Work', in *The Anglo-Saxons: Studies Presented to Bruce Dickins* (1959), and 'A.', in *Continuations and Beginnings: Studies in Old English Literature*, ed. E. G. Stanley (1966).

Agate, James (Evershed) (1877–1947). Dramatic critic. A product of Manchester Grammar School, he trained on the *Manchester Guardian* and was drama critic from 1907 till 1914. He was dramatic critic of the *Sunday Times* from 1923 until his death. He broadcast on the theatre in the years 1925–32, and under pseudonyms wrote the theatre columns of *John O' London's* and *Country Life*. He regularly made collections of his notices which form an accessible and idiosyncratic record of London theatrical activities. He was film critic on the *Tatler* and book reviewer to the *Daily Express*. In 1935 he published an autobiography, *Ego*, and issued 8 further instalments of his diary. He wrote, edited or compiled some 60 books, and calculated that between 1921 and 1944 he had written over six million words and earned £70,000.

A provincial, a Francophil, a champion of the art of Bernhardt and Irving, he wrote pugnaciously about the theatre in a brisk, allusive style and was a better critic of acting than of plays. His world revolved round Shaftesbury Avenue, the Café Royal and the Savage Club, and his diaries reveal equal gusto for great acting, good living, Hackney ponies, golf and gossip. [MJ]

Ego–Ego 9 (1935–48); *A Shorter Ego* (3 vols., 1946–9); *J.A.: An Anthology*, ed H. van Thal, intr. A. Dent (1961).
A. Dent, 'Footnote' to *Ego 9* (1948).

Ainsworth, William Harrison (1805–82). Journalist and historical novelist. Born in Manchester, the son of a solicitor, and educated at the Grammar School there, he jibbed at the law and went went to London, where he married the daughter of John Ebers, a publisher, who introduced him to writers and the frequenters of the London Opera House, which Ebers managed. Ainsworth edited *Bentley's Miscellany* (1840–2), *Ainsworth's Magazine* (1842–53) and the *New Monthly Magazine*. His first novel, *Rookwood* (1834), about Dick Turpin, was an immediate success, and thereafter he wrote 38 others, of which the best known are *Old St Paul's* (1841), *Windsor Castle* (1843) and *The Lancashire Witches* (1848). In these books the main interest is sensational and archaeological: there is little intrinsic interest in the characters or action. Cruickshank's illustrations turned the lurid passages, especially in *The Tower of London* (1840), to good account. [A R]

Collected Works (12 vols., 1923).
S. M. Ellis, *W. H. A. and His Friends* (2 vols., 1911); H. Locke, *Bibliographical Catalogue of A.* (1925); B. Bevan, 'H.A.', in *Contemporary Review*, August 1955.

Akenside, Mark (1721–70). Poet. The son of a butcher of Newcastle-upon-Tyne, he was educated at Edinburgh for the dissenting ministry, but studied medicine at Leyden and later practised in London. He wrote some rather tame *Odes* (1745) and an 'anti-Tory' poem of political principle, *Epistle to Curio* (i.e. Pulteney) (1744). His main work was the blank-verse didactic poem, *The Pleasures of Imagination* (1744; revised edn, 1772), one of the most influential 18th-century works on aesthetic theory. It is an imprecise but powerful synthesis of ideas derived from Longinus, ◊ Addison, ◊ Shaftesbury and ◊ Hutcheson, and was a popular source of notions about the sublime and beautiful seasoned with political doctrine ('Whig Aesthetics'), religious beliefs, psychological speculation and moral teaching. [A R]

Works, ed. A. Dyce (Aldine Poets, 1894).
Johnson, *Lives of the Poets*; C. T. Houpt, *A.: A Bibliographical and Critical Study* (Philadelphia, 1944); W. L. Renwick, in *Essays Presented to David Nichol Smith* (1945).

Alabaster, William (1567–1640). Poet. Educated at Westminster and at Trinity College, Cambridge, of which he became a Fellow, he wrote numerous Latin and occasional Greek poems, including *Eliseis*, an unfinished, still unprinted Latin epic on Queen Elizabeth known to Spenser, and *Roxana*, a Latin verse-tragedy later commended by Dr Johnson. He was chaplain to Essex on his Cadiz expedition in 1596, and became a Catholic on his return. During the period of his conversion he wrote a series of divine sonnets, which survive in 6 manuscripts and which were first edited only in 1959 (*The Sonnets of W.A.*, ed. Helen Gardner and G. M. Story). After a period abroad (and some trouble with the Inquisition), he returned to England and reverted to Protestantism, married and became a country clergyman. He continued the studies of mystical theology which had led

to his break with Rome, and published cabbalistic works. The 60 or so divine sonnets, little known in his own day, are interesting examples by a minor poet of devotional writing and anticipate the work of the great Metaphysicals. [M J]

Alcuin or **Ealhwine** (735–804). Scholar and poet. Born at York, he was educated in the cloister school under Archbishop Egbert, and became master of it in 778. Although he pays eloquent tribute to the library and teachers there, and although his career bears striking witness to 8th-century English culture, Alcuin's real importance is European. Returning from Rome in 781, he met Charlemagne, and, persuaded to stay in France, became his teacher and friend and guiding force of the Carolingian renaissance. Except for a two-year visit to England (790–2), he spent the rest of his life there, and was made Archbishop of Tours. Alcuin's considerable output (*Opera*, ed. J. P. Migne, *Patrologia Latina* C–CI, 1851) includes liturgical, grammatical, philosophical and hagiological works, and he was also an accomplished Latin poet. He popularized the dialogue for teaching purposes, and encouraged a humanistic attitude towards classical culture. [A G]

E. S. Duckett, *A., Friend of Charlemagne* (1952); M. L. Laistner, *Thought and Letters in Western Europe, A.D. 500–900* (1957); W. Levison, *England and the Continent in the Eighth Century* (1946).

Aldington, Richard (1892–1962). Poet, novelist and biographer. He was born in Hampshire and educated at Dover College and the University of London, although he left without taking a degree. He had a precocious talent and in the years before 1914 he made his name as a promising young poet, and as an exponent of the ◊ Imagist school. He also worked as assistant editor of the *Egoist* in 1913. By 1916 he was in the army and in France, from where he returned in 1918, penniless, with a bad case of shell-shock and war neurosis. For several years, until he recovered his health, he earned a living of sorts by translations and literary journalism, and when he eventually began creative writing again, it was in prose. His early novels, such as *Death of a Hero* (1929) and *The Colonel's Daughter* (1931), are outpourings of the immense anger and hatred created in him by his war experiences – he felt 'that the whole war had been declared against him personally'. Less balanced than the work of Graves or Sassoon, *Death of a Hero* is none the less a fearful indictment of civilian smugness. As his anger evaporated his novels became duller and less interesting, but during the Second World War, when he had moved to the U.S.A., he emerged as a competent biographer with *Wellington* (1946), although his portraits of D. H. Lawrence, *Portrait of a Genius, But . . .* (1950), and *Lawrence of Arabia* (1955) aroused controversy. Essentially, Aldington's life was a disappointment: robbed of his youthful promise by the war, he never fully recovered nor fully forgave the world. He remained for the rest of his life bitter and disillusioned, and his writing reflected this. [JM]

Life for Life's Sake (1968) (autobiography).
Bernard Bergonzi, *Heroes' Twilight* (1965).

Alexander, Sir William (Earl of Stirling) (*c.* 1577?–1640). Scottish courtier and poet. Educated at Glasgow and Leyden, Alexander travelled on the continent as tutor to the young Earl of Argyle. In 1607 he received a mining patent from King James, and was knighted in 1608 on becoming permanently attached to the court in the retinue of Prince Henry; he became secretary of state for Scotland in 1626 and was created Earl of Stirling in 1633. His patent to settle and exploit Nova Scotia and Canada, granted by James in 1621, was nullified by French expansion and he died insolvent. Alexander wrote much minor verse in the regular Jacobean modes – 4 *Monarchic Tragedies* on rulers destroyed by ambition (1603–7), a long moralistic poem *Doomsday* (1614), and a sequence of songs and sonnets (*Aurora*, 1604) which he omitted from his collected *Recreations with the Muses* (1637). Alexander was largely or wholly the author of the version of the psalms published as King James's in 1631, and inherited the copyright; his American interests led him to publish *An Encouragement to Colonies* (1624). [AI]

Poetical Works, ed. L. E. Kastner and H. B. Charlton (2 vols., STS, 1921–9); 'Anacrisis; or, A Censure of Some Poets Ancient and Modern', in *Critical Essays of the Seventeenth Century*, ed. J. E. Spingarn (3 vols., 1908–9).
T. H. McGrail, *Sir W. A.* (1940).

Alexander, William (1826–94). Scottish fiction writer. Educated at a parish school in Aberdeenshire, Alexander was successive-

ly a farm boy and a ploughman in the county. On losing a leg in his early twenties he turned to journalism and became eventually the editor of the *Aberdeen Free Press*. His novel *Johnny Gibb of Gushetneuk* (1871) gives a sympathetic but unsentimental and realistic account of life in a Scots village about the time of the Disruption of the Church of Scotland in 1843. [AI]

Sketches of Life among My Ain Folk (1875); *Twenty-Five Years: A Personal Retrospect* (1878).

Alfred (849–99). King of the West Saxons and national hero. He succeeded to the throne of Wessex in 870, and so much of his life was spent in warring against the Danish invaders that it is a wonder that he found time to fulfil his great literary and educational projects. The motive for them is consistent with his whole career: to profit his people by making available those works vital to his plan of re-education. The first translation to survive is of Gregory the Great's *Cura pastoralis* (ed. H. Sweet, 1871–2), a primer of instruction for the clergy. The preface, in Alfred's own efficient and unadorned prose style, set out his aims as a translator. Next came the standard work of history and geography of Orosius (ed. H. Sweet, 1883), in which he included contemporary accounts of voyages to the White Sea by Ohthere, and to the Baltic by Wulfstan. The translation (after 897) of the *De consolatione philosophiae* of Boethius (ed. W. J. Sedgefield, 1899) shows him at a loss for philosophical vocabulary, and somewhat baffled by his original, but it was a useful popularization of a very influential work. His last work, the version of St Augustine's *Soliloquies* (ed. H. L. Hargrove, 1902), the magnificent preface in particular, reveals his gift of eloquence. Alfred inspired the Old English translations of Bede and Gregory's *Dialogues*, but his greatest monument is the *Anglo-Saxon Chronicle* (tr. G. N. Garmonsway, 1953), begun at his command at Winchester in 890. This is the most notable achievement of vernacular prose in the whole of Western Europe in this period. [AG]

The Parker Chronicle, ed. A. H. Smith (1935).
C. Plummer, *The Life and Times of A. the Great* (1902); R. W. Chambers, *On the Continuity of English Prose* (1932); D. Whitelock, 'The Prose of Alfred's Reign', in *Continuations and Beginnings: Studies in Old English Literature*, ed. E. G. Stanley (1966).

Allen, Walter (Ernest) (1911–   ). Novelist and critic. Born in Birmingham, he was educated at King Edward's Grammar School, Aston, and Birmingham University. On graduating from university he worked as a schoolmaster, university lecturer and journalist. His early novels, *Innocence is Drowned* (1938), *Blind Man's Ditch* (1939) and *Living Space* (1940), are studies of working-class life in the North of England which retain an interest today primarily for their sociological content. His other novels are *Rogue Elephant* (1946), *Dead Man Over All* (1950) and his best work of fiction, *All in a Lifetime* (1959), a shrewd examination of the changing structure of working-class life in the 20th century as seen through the eyes of an ageing radical. He has also written the studies *Arnold Bennett* (1948), *Joyce Cary* (WTW, 1953) and *George Eliot* (1964); and 2 wide-ranging critical histories of English and American fiction, *The English Novel* (1954) and *Tradition and Dream* (1964). [PJK]

Allingham, William (1824–89). Poet. He was born at Ballyshannon in Ireland, the son of a banker, of an English family. He became a Civil Servant (in the Customs) and wrote for Leigh ◊ Hunt's *London Journal*. Hunt introduced him to Carlyle; he was also a member of the ◊ Rossetti circle. Between 1850 and 1887, he produced about a dozen volumes of verse. He was not an Irish nationalist, but had a feeling for the Irish ethos, and his main interest now is perhaps the influence he had on Yeats, who gave him more space in his anthology *A Book of Irish Verse* (1894) than he gave Thomas ◊ Moore. Allingham had a certain lyric gift and fancy (which he also displayed in editing *The Ballad Book* in the Golden Treasury series, 1864). His best-known poem is 'Up the Airy Mountain'. His most ambitious work was *Laurence Bloomfield in Ireland* (1864), but he cannot support extended argument. His *Collected Poems* were published in 6 volumes (1888–93). [AR]

W. A., *A Diary*, ed. H. Allingham and D. Radford (1907) (selections).
W. B. Yeats, 'W. A.', in *Poets and Poetry of the Century*, ed. A. H. Miles, 5 (1892); P. S. O'Hegarty, *A Bibliography of W. A.* (1945).

Amis, Kingsley (1922–   ). Poet and novelist. Educated at the City of London School and St John's College, Oxford, he was in the army (1942–5) and taught English at University College, Swansea, from 1949 to 1961, and then at Peterhouse, Cambridge, from 1961 until he resigned in 1963. He has published 3 volumes of poems: *A Frame of Mind* (1953), *A Case of Samples* (1956) and *A Look around the Estate* (1967). His verse writing has considerable variety, and he sometimes cultivates a flat 'nonpoetical' tone which characterizes the poetry of 'the movement' (he is one of the poets represented in Robert Conquest's anthology *New Lines*, 1956). What has been called a 'militant philistinism' is also found in his work, as well as wit and a kind of muffled moral statement. His first novel, *Lucky Jim* (1954; filmed 1957), has been seen as presenting in its hero Jim Dixon, a provincial university teacher, one of the original protest figures of the fiction produced by the 'Angry Young Men' generation. He is, however, more one of the put-upon inhabitants of Amis's comic world. The targets of satire in all Amis's fiction are social pretence (Jim finds that his university education does not really give him entrée to the worlds of social grace, power or true intellectual endeavour) and the sexual trap which lies waiting for the male. *That Uncertain Feeling* (1955; filmed as *Only Two Can Play*, 1962) moves the scene to a Welsh public library. In his later novels, *I Like It Here* (1958), set in Portugal, *Take a Girl Like You* (1960), *One Fat Englishman* (1963) and *I Want It Now* (1968), set in America, he is less farcical and writes with a more sombre touch. The single 'point-of-view' which damages some of the sharpness of *Lucky Jim* is absent. The problems are less simplified socially and more complex morally. The writing is more truly comic. Amis has always shown great verbal cleverness and accomplishment. In *The Green Man* (1969) he has produced a mixture of sex and the supernatural spiced with his increasing irascibility. He has also written a volume of short stories, *My Enemy's Enemy* (1962), and a good deal of literary journalism. This includes *New Maps of Hell* (1960), in which the science fiction genre is given a full-scale 'Eng. Lit.' critical treatment, and *The James Bond Dossier* (1965), in which he develops his 'militant philistinism' by a sociological discussion of the current popularity of the spy thriller hero of Ian ◊ Fleming. [AR]

J. Gindin, *Postwar British Fiction* (U. of California P., 1962); G. S. Fraser, *The Modern Writer and His World* (1964); Walter Allen, *The Modern Novel* (1964).

Anand, Mulk Raj (1905–   ). Indian novelist. Born in Peshawar, he was at university in Lahore, London and Cambridge, and has spent much of his life in England, but his main concern is the Indian scene, social, cultural and political. His early novels were the contribution of a left-wing progressive to India's struggles. After the war he returned to India, settled in Bombay, and became editor of the artistic journal *Marg*. Only in *Private Life of an Indian Prince* (1953) has he added notably to his early fiction. In his first novels, *Coolie* (1933), *Untouchable* (1935) and *Two Leaves and a Bud* (1937), Anand expresses an angry sympathy for those who suffer in the complex snobberies of Indian society. The Lalu Singh trilogy, *The Village* (1939), *Across the Black Waters* (1940) and *The Sword and the Sickle* (1942), follows the career of a young Sikh from before the First World War through the restless period that succeeded it. *Across the Black Waters* is among the best novels to come out of the war. Anand's understanding of the revolutionary temperament is again apparent in *The Big Heart* (1945), whose theme is the crushing of craftsmanship by capitalism. [P T]

Seven Summers (1951) (Autobiography).
K. R. Srinivasa Iyengar, *Indian Writing in English* (1962); Satos Cowasiee, 'Princes and Proletarians', *Journal of Commonwealth Literature*, 5 (July 1968).

'Ancrene Riwle, The' (*c*.1200 ?). A devotional manual. Written originally for the guidance of three young women who had embraced the anchoress's life, it is the most important prose work of the early Middle English period. The evidence of the sources used, and of the dialect, indicates a date of composition after 1160, in the west Midlands. It was revised early on, as the *Ancrene Wisse* (ed. J. R. Tolkien, 1962; selection ed. G. Shepherd, 1959), for the use of a larger community, and versions in French and Latin were also made; its influence was great and long-lived. Though the thought and doctrine are fairly standard, the author is a cultured and well-read man, who provides an enlightened rule for his charges. There is much sound advice about externals, but his main concern is the inner life, though he does not encourage a search for mystical experience. The apparent simplicity of the prose is the careful work of a skilled rhetorician. His analogies are developed from a very solid material world. Though he recalls ⋄ Aelfric

and ⋄ Wulfstan, he is consciously and perceptibly modern. [A G]

Ed. M. Day (1952); tr. J. Morton, intr. F. A. Gasquet, *The Nun's Rule* (1905); tr. M. B. Salu, intr. G. Sitwell, *The Ancrene Riwle* (1955). R. W. Chambers, *On the Continuity of English Prose* (1932); E. J. Dobson, 'The Date and Composition of the *Ancrene Wisse*', *Proceedings of the British Academy*, 52 (1966); M. D. Knowles, *The English Mystics* (1927); R. M. Wilson, *Early Middle English Literature* (1939).

Andrewes, Lancelot (1555–1626). Preacher and scholar. Educated at Merchant Taylors' School under Mulcaster, and at Cambridge, he took holy orders in 1580 and was Master of Pembroke College from 1589 to 1605. He was chaplain to Archbishop Whitgift and to Queen Elizabeth, in whose last years he was Dean of Westminster. Prominent and favoured at the court of James VI and I, he was successively Bishop of Chichester, of Ely and of Winchester. He attended the Hampton Court Conference in 1604 and his name leads the list of divines appointed in 1607 to make the Authorized Version. He was a great patristic and biblical scholar, and preached eloquent, impassioned, closely reasoned and condensed sermons (intended for a select and theologically educated auditory), some of which were published posthumously in *XCVI Sermons* in 1629. His *Preces Privatae* or *Devotions* were translated and published in 1647. Andrewes contributed to the philosophic foundations of the Church of England. His death was mourned in poems by Milton and Crashaw. [M J]

Sermons, selected and ed. G. M. Story (1967).
D. Bush, *English Literature in the Earlier Seventeenth Century* (revised edn, 1962); T. S. Eliot, *For L. A.* (1928; essay reprinted in *Selected Essays*, 1932, revised edn, 1951); M. F. Reidy, s.J., *Bishop L. A.* (Chicago, 1955); P. A. Welsby, *L. A.* (1958).

Aneirin (fl. 6th cent.). Welsh poet. His poetry, preserved in *Llyfr Aneirin* ('Book of Aneirin'), a manuscript of *c*.1250 at Cardiff Free Library, consists of a long poem of 103 stanzas called *Y Gododdin*. The theme of the poem is an expedition by 300 warriors from Dineidyn (Edinburgh) to Catraeth (Catterick) to do battle with the Saxons. This is heroic poetry of a similar eulogistic and elegiac character to that of ⋄ Taliesin. The language is direct and simple, and good artistic use is made of the mead which was drunk by the young heroes and which proved to be fatal, for only one man survived this débâcle in which the flower of champions from other British territories as well as from Manaw Gododdin (Edinburgh –Stirling area) perished. Economy of expression and contrast of descriptions and lack of sentimentality are notable virtues of these elegiac stanzas. In the second stanza the hero is 'breathless [shy] before a maiden, although he was worthy of his mead'.

As for the authenticity of the Aneirin poem the same reservations have been expressed as in the case of Taliesin. The 13th-century manuscript was certainly copied from an exemplar of the Old Welsh period (8th to 10th centuries), as is clearly manifest from internal evidence. The balance of probability is that most of the poems attributed to Aneirin are genuinely contemporary with him. [MR]

Canu Aneirin, ed. I. Williams (1938).
I. Williams, *Lectures on Early Welsh Poetry* (1944); R. Bromwich, 'The Character of the Early Welsh Tradition', in *Studies in Early British History*, ed. N. L. Chadwick (1954); K. H. Jackson, *The Gododdin* (1969).

'Anglo-Saxon Chronicle, The'. A series of annals written in Old English (or Anglo-Saxon), probably begun in the reign of King ◊ Alfred. It starts with an outline of English history from Julius Caesar's invasion to the mid 5th century and – in one of its 7 manuscripts – continues till 1154. Each of the different manuscripts was kept in a different place and, after the beginning of the 10th century, they differ considerably, each one including material of local interest. Notable among examples of Old English prose narrative in the *Chronicle* is the story of Cynewulf and Cyneheard (755), which shows a well-developed narrative style at a surprisingly early period. The *Chronicle* illustrates to a unique degree the development and continuity of Old English prose, although the quality of the prose is not consistent. Especially vivid are passages written at the end of the 10th century describing the ravages of the second great wave of Danish invasions. Manuscript *D* is important for its account of Anglo-Scandinavian relations in the reign of Edward the Confessor (1043–66) and for its first-hand account of the Norman Conquest; manuscript *C* (ending in 1066) describes vividly conflicts with the Danes in the reign of Ethelred the Unready (978–1016). The latest entry is for the year 1154, in a manuscript which was continued at Peterborough. By now the language had developed from its Old English to its Middle English stage. The Norman Conquest set back the development of English prose (French historical prose was at this time less well developed), which did not emerge significantly again till the 15th century. Six of the 7 texts (*A–F*) were edited by B. Thorpe, with translations (2 vols., Rolls Series, 1861). Texts *A* and *E* in parallel were edited by John Earle (revised by C. Plummer) (2 vols., 1952). [DD]

Translations: G. N. Garmonsway (Everyman, 1953); D. Whitelock, in *English Historical Documents, c. 500–1042* (1955).
R. W. Chambers, *On the Continuity of English Prose* (1932).

Angus, Marion (1866–1946). Scots poet. The daughter of a United Presbyterian minister at Arbroath, she later lived at Aberdeen and began to write shortly after the First World War, publishing her first volume of poems, *The Lilt*, in 1922. Her poetry is more sensitive and more private than the robust Scots work of her contemporary Violet ◊ Jacob, and is narrower in range and more nostalgic than the poems of Hugh ◊ MacDiarmid, with whose Scottish Renaissance movement she was nevertheless associated. Marion Angus writes wryly, in a consciously minor key, about frustrated love and unhappy marriages; echoes of ballad and folksong strengthen and sharpen her work by distancing the feeling and extending its reference beyond the immediate situation she dramatizes. [AI]

Selected Poems, ed. M. Lindsay, with a memoir by H. B. Cruikshank (1950).
C. M. Grieve, *Contemporary Scottish Studies* (1926).

Anselm of Aosta (1033–1109). Saint, logician and spiritual writer. Born in northern Italy, he went to France to study in his youth and finally settled at Bec under Lanfranc. He took monastic vows there in 1060, became prior after Lanfranc and then abbot. Made Archbishop of Canterbury by William Rufus in 1093, the investiture contest twice caused his exile but it was in England that he died in 1109. Rapid developments in Aristotelian logic and the widespread admiration for the spiritual writings of St Bernard curtailed Anselm's influence in these fields in the century after his death, particularly on the continent, but there was a revival of interest in the late 13th century.

Of his many writings, the best known are the *Monologion, Proslogion* and *Cur Deus Homo*. Of these, the *Proslogion* contains the expression of his well-known ontological argument for the existence of God, later criticized as involving a logical fallacy, while the *Cur Deus Homo* undertakes to prove the necessity of the Incarnation. His main importance perhaps lies in his acceptance and development of the methods of rational inquiry into the mysteries of faith. [ATH]

Opera omnia, ed. F. S. Schmitt (Rome, 1940–51). R. W. Southern, *St Anselm and His Biographer: A Study of Monastic Life and Thought 1059–c. 1130* (1963).

Anstey, Christopher (1724–1805). Poet. Educated at Eton and King's College, Cambridge, author of a number of works but now only known for his pleasant, satirical, anapaestic poem, *The New Bath Guide* (1766), arranged as a series of letters illustrating the Blunderhead family's visit to Bath, and said to have given ◊ Smollett material for his *Humphry Clinker*. [AR]

The Poetical Works (1808). R. A. Hesselgrave, *Lady Miller and the Batheaston Literary Circle* (Yale U.P., 1927).

'Apocalypse, The'. A vaguely defined and short-lived literary movement that arose in reaction to the politically committed literature of the thirties. The principal leaders were Henry ◊ Treece, J. F. Hendry and G. S. ◊ Fraser, who proclaimed themselves hostile to the machine age and organized politics. They were in favour of a utopian form of anarchism, freedom from all political and literary ideologies and a revival of myth, seeing their literary ancestors as including the Book of Revelations, Webster, Blake and Kafka. More directly, they were influenced by Surrealism, the poetry of Dylan ◊ Thomas and the critical writings of Sir Herbert ◊ Read. Three Apocalypse anthologies were published: *The New Apocalypse* (1939), *The White Horseman* (1941) and *The Crown and the Sickle* (1944). [PJK]

Francis Scarfe, *Auden and After* (1942); Henry Treece, *How I See Apocalypse* (1946).

Arbuthnot, John (1667–1735). Wit, satirist, miscellaneous, medical and scientific writer. Born at the Manse of Arbuthnott in Kincardineshire, he was the son of a cadet member of the noble family of that place.

He was educated at Marischal College, Aberdeen, and abroad (probably studying mathematics under Christian Huygens). On his return to Britain, he studied medicine at Oxford while acting as bear-leader to a youth at University College, and took an M.D. at the University of St Andrews. He acted briefly as Assistant Secretary to the Royal Society (F.R.S., 1704) and was Physician Extraordinary to Queen Anne (1705), then Physician-in-Ordinary (1709), and became a Fellow of the College of Physicians (1710). Arbuthnot's stimulating talents, chiefly exerted in mathematics, medicine, science, literature, music and politics, were very great, but perhaps too fragmentary to produce any single work that did them justice. An intimate of Swift and Pope, he was the central figure in the Scriblerus Club, and the breadth of satire in the *Memoirs of Martinus Scriblerus* (1741; ed. Charles Kerby-Miller, Yale U.P.,1950) is probably due to him. His best-known work is the *History of John Bull* (5 pamphlets which appeared in 1712), a deft and powerful political satire advocating an end to the Marlborough wars which is often attributed to Swift and in which John Bull makes his first appearance. Arbuthnot wrote a number of other political pieces and *jeux d'esprit*, as well as medical works which were much valued in their day. The latter are characterized by conservative common sense and close observation: *An Essay Concerning the Nature of Aliments* (1731) and *An Essay Concerning the Effects of Air on Human Bodies* (1733). His nobility of character and amiable honesty made him an emblem of good social behaviour in (for example) the poems of Pope. [AR]

G. A Aitken, *Life and Works* (1892); L. M. Beattie, *J. A., Mathematician and Satirist* (Harvard U. P., 1935).

Archer, William (1856–1924). Dramatic critic. Born in Perth, with Norwegian connexions, Archer was already earning money as a journalist while he was an undergraduate at Edinburgh. He was co-author of *The Fashionable Tragedian: A Criticism*, an anonymous polemic on the mannered and affected style of Henry Irving, published in 1877. The following year Archer went to London and became dramatic critic of the *World*, a post he held for twenty-one years. The official translator of the plays of Ibsen and an early advocate of a National Theatre for Britain, Archer was a publicist of the New Drama, and did much to promote performances of important European and English plays in London. He secured for his friend, Bernard Shaw, the post of art and music critic on the *World*. Later, by proposing that they collaborate on a play, he interested Shaw, till then an unsuccessful novelist, in playwriting. Archer's own taste was for the well-made play. In 1923 he published an influential book, *The Old Drama and the New*, in which he attacked some of the Elizabethan dramatists. Archer's only success in the theatre was with the soundly planned, far-fetched melodrama, *The Green Goddess*. [MJ]

The Theatrical 'World' (5 vols., 1894–8); Three Plays (1927).
C. Archer, *W. A.* (1931); G. B. Shaw, *Pen Portraits and Reviews* (1931; repr. 1949).

Arden, John (1930–   ). Dramatist. After studying at Cambridge and at Edinburgh (where fellow-students performed a play of his), he practised architecture but continued to write plays for radio, television and the stage. He held a fellowship in drama at Bristol University (1960–1) and gave the Judith Wilson Lecture at Cambridge in 1965. Although he has never had a commercial success in the theatre, in critical circles he is more admired than such playwrights as ◊ Osborne and ◊ Wesker. His closely written plays are usually experimental in form, and use prose, verse and ballad. Arden makes great demands on his audience, often refusing to take sides in the moral and political issues raised in his work. His stageplays include *Live like Pigs* (London, 1958), *Serjeant Musgrave's Dance* (London, 1959), *The Happy Haven* (London, 1961), *The Workhouse Donkey* (Chichester, 1963), *Armstrong's Last Goodnight* (Glasgow, 1964; Chichester and London, 1965) and *Left-Handed Liberty* (London, 1965). An apparent dissatisfaction with the professional theatre has led him to stage his most recent (and less successful) works himself with fringe groups under improvised conditions. [MJ]

Ed. W. A. Armstrong, *Experimental Drama* (1963); ed. J. R. Brown, *Modern British Dramatists* (New Jersey, 1968); R. Hayman, *J.A.* (1968); ed. C. Marowitz, *Theatre at Work* (1967); ed. Tom Milne, *The Encore Reader* (1965); J. Russell Taylor, *Anger and After* (revised edn, 1969).

Arlen, Michael (1895–1956). Novelist. Born in Roustchouk, Bulgaria (he changed his name by deed-poll from Dikrān Kuyumjian), he came to England as a boy and was educated at Malvern College. He became a naturalized British subject in 1922. In 1928, he married Countess Atalanta Inarcati. They lived on the French Riviera, where Arlen was a celebrated, elegant, man-about-town in the 1930s. His first novel, *The London Venture*, appeared in 1920, but he became famous with the publication of *The Green Hat* (1924; he later dramatized it, and it was the basis for a famous Greta Garbo film). His novels, mixtures of sex, farce and melodrama set in a fantasy London society, lightly and flippantly written, continued to be popular evocations of the twenties. The novels of ◊ Ouida are probably the closest prototypes of his fiction; he added a strong infusion of naïve cynicism. Other titles included *Mayfair* (1925) (short stories), *Young Men in Love* (1927), *Babes in the Wood* (1930) (short stories), *Hell! Said the Duchess* (1934) and *The Flying Dutchman* (1939). He was a Civil Defence public-relations officer during the Second World War, and served in Coventry during the blitz. Invalided out, he went to Hollywood to write film scripts, and died in America. [AR]

Armstrong, Dr John (1709–79). Poet. The son of a Roxburghshire minister, he practised medicine in London and wrote poems, essays and a play, of which the only dim survivor is *The Art of Preserving Health* (1744), a competent (in places ingenious) didactic work in a style and diction derived from the work of his friend James ◊ Thomson. [AR]

Poems, ed. R. Cohen (Augustan Reprint Society, 1951).
H. R. Smith, 'Medicine and Poetry', *N & Q* (September 1952).

Arnold, Matthew (1822–88). Poet and critic. Son of Thomas ◊ Arnold, headmaster of Rugby, he made up for the constrained atmosphere of Rugby by his liveliness and his gay and idle time at Oxford, where he gained a reputation as a dilettante. He graduated with second-class honours in 1844, and the following year was elected to a fellowship at Oriel. After a period of travel and unsettled experiment he became an inspector of schools in 1851, which was his life's career, except for ten years as Professor of Poetry at Oxford (1857–67). His

23

job, though often dull and pedestrian, brought direct experience of educational methods (not only in England but in France and other European countries to which he was sent on special missions) and this influenced his larger involvement with the quality of culture and the responsibility of the cultured. In 1883–4 he went on a lecture tour of America.

His first poems, which surprised his friends and family by their concern with moral issues, were published in 1849. It was a third volume, *Poems: A New Edition* (1853), that made his reputation. Arnold held that poetry should be 'a criticism of life', but his own poetry was withdrawn in tone, and it was perhaps this, and his parallel emphasis on the educational importance of criticism, that led him to turn to prose as a more efficient analytical instrument. He regarded the spiritual death of Victorian England with a mind that was scorchingly critical but humanist and sympathetic. He was confident that culture, which he saw as classless and universal, was the power that could save modern society from materialism. *Culture and Anarchy* (1869) and *Friendship's Garland* (1871) were the crucial essays in this discussion. His uncompromising analysis is sharpened by an ironic sense of humour and a brilliantly apt use of reference and quotation. He characterizes the upper, middle and working classes as Barbarians, Philistines and Populace, and shows how each is inadequate in its consciousness of proper actions and attitudes. He calls for 'sweetness and light', humanist sensitivity combined with intellectual toughness, and although he condemns middle-class complacency he sees that class as being the most competent to guide the nation's progress.

Arnold was the first to emphasize, in *Essays in Criticism* (1st series, 1865, 2nd series, 1888), the poet's position in society rather than his position in the artistic world. He closely associated the function of religion with that of the poet and in *Literature and Dogma* (1873) and *God and the Bible* (1875) he attacked dogmatism and conventional orthodoxy. He considered that the Bible was important as poetry, as a means of combating spiritual paralysis. His own poetry expresses less aggressively his sense of a widening gulf between the possibilities of belief and the facts of the modern world, although it is coloured by didacticism. His rhythms are solemn and often lax, and his language restrained and reflective. His poetry was a means of relating in more personal terms his own responses to the society he examined so vigorously in prose. The dominant mood is elegiac, a controlled and pulsing melancholy. 'Dover Beach' (1867), in which private happiness is woven with the calm relentlessness of the natural world and the large confusions of humanity, is an eloquent expression of this. Two of Arnold's best-known poems, 'The Scholar Gypsy' (1853), about a 17th-century student who leaves Oxford to live amongst gypsies, and 'Thyrsis' (1866), written in memory of his close friend Arthur Hugh ◊ Clough, are a characteristic blend of an introspective contemplation of the countryside, personal doubts and a transcendent sadness. In the former Arnold, as he did frequently, used the bones of a traditional story to carry his own speculations. He often slowed his poems down to a grave and composed conclusion, even in the case of his major narrative poem 'Sohrab and Rustum' (1853), but it is the doubts and quiet pain that linger. There is a contradiction between Arnold's belief that poetry should deal with 'human actions', that situations in which 'the suffering finds no vent in action' are inadmissible and his own brooding, elegiac verse, and this contradiction is another reason for his giving up poetry for critical prose.

Arnold's refusal to compromise his absolute values is both the strength and the weakness of his thought. Critically, this provided a relentless weapon, but it rendered his constructive proposals imprecise. The reasons for his faith in culture were not always presented with absolute logic and clarity. Nevertheless he produced what was perhaps the most articulate expression of the Victorian malaise, and in his investigation of the intimate relationship between the arts, criticism and society he broke new ground and provided an influence that has been felt far into this century. [JRC]

Complete Prose Works, ed. R. H. Super (U. of Michigan P., 1960–); *Poetical Works*, ed. C. B. Tinker and H. L. Lowry (1950); *The Poems*, ed. and annotated K. Allott (1965); *Poetry and Prose*, ed. J. Bryson (1954) (selection); *Selected Essays*, ed. N. Annan (1964).
G. Tillotson, *Criticism and the Nineteenth Century* (1951); L. Trilling, *M.A.* (1939, 1955); E. K. Brown, *M.A.* (1948); V. Buckley, *The Poetry of Morality* (1959); W. Johnson, *The Voices of M.A.* (1961); P. J. MacCarthy, *A. and the Three Classes* (1964); W. D. Anderson, *A. and the Classical Tradition* (1965).

Arnold, Dr Thomas (1795–1842). Educationist and historian. Father of Matthew ◊ Arnold. He was born in the Isle of Wight, the son of a Customs' collector, and was educated at Winchester and Corpus Christi College, Oxford. He was a Fellow of Oriel, then developing into the leading teaching college of the university, and a lively intellectual centre. ◊ Newman was elected just as Arnold left (1828) to become headmaster of Rugby. He was a broad churchman, and as an educational and ecclesiastical reformer frequently embroiled himself in controversies. He may be said to have founded the English public (private) school system (he was brought in to rescue Rugby from the doldrums). He drew from Rousseau's ideas, not always directly, and from the prevailing Romantic emphasis on education, all that could be used by a ruling caste coming to terms with new doctrines of the self ('the child is father of the man '). Thus Arnold emphasized virtue, honesty, honour, personal duty, fusing these old concepts with a typical 19th-century 'personal' religion. The power of his influence on upper-class English intellectual life may be seen in the violence of the caricature of him in *Eminent Victorians* (1918) by Lytton ◊ Strachey, which is obviously an unsuccessful exorcism. Arnold was a historian, but his *History of Rome* (3 vols., 1838–42, unfinished) has long since been superseded. He was appointed Regius Professor of Modern History at Oxford (1841). [A R]

Dean A. P. Stanley, *Life and Correspondence of A.* (1844); N. Wymer, *Dr A. of Rugby* (1953); T. W. Bamford, *T. A.* (1960); E. L. Williamson, *The Liberalism of T. A.* (U. of Alabama P., 1964).

Ascham, Roger (1515–68). Scholar. Educated at St John's College, he became Reader in Greek, a subject only recently revived, at Cambridge in 1540 and later Public Orator. This great humanist, believing in the doctrine of imitation of classical models, wrote his poems and letters in Latin and felt that Greek was easier for him to write than English, but adopted his native tongue for his most important works. His *Toxophilus* (1545) consists of 2 charming, vivid and prejudiced platonic dialogues on the virtues of the English long-bow as against crossbows, and was dedicated to Henry VIII, from whom he received a pension. From 1548 he was briefly tutor to Princess Eliza-

beth. He was Latin secretary to Edward VI and, though well known as a Protestant, served Queen Mary also in this capacity, and later Elizabeth. At his death he left unfinished his greatest work, *The Schoolmaster* (ed. L. V. Ryan, 1968), published in 1570, a humane, practical treatise on education, showing a lively understanding of the young. His English style, admired by Gabriel ◊ Harvey, was plain and he avoided anglicizing Romance words at a time when there was no agreement about writing English prose. [M J]

Whole Works, ed. J. A. Giles (3 vols., 1864–5). C. S. Lewis, *English Literature in the Sixteenth Century* (1954); L. V. Ryan, *R. A.* (Stanford, Calif., 1963).

Ashford, Daisy (1881–). Child authoress and unconscious humorist. At the age of 9 she wrote in pencil in a twopenny notebook a romantic novel, *The Young Visiters, or Mr Salteena's Plan*. Many years later, in 1919, through the influence of Frank Swinnerton, it was published in its original childish spelling with a preface by J. M. Barrie. It immediately went through some 20 editions and remains a cult book. It gives a remarkable and amusing child's eye view of high life derived from hearsay, imagination and (possibly) the novels of ◊ Ouida, Marie ◊ Correlli, and Mrs Henry ◊ Wood. *Daisy Ashford: Her Book* (1920) consists of 3 earlier stories dictated to her father, and another by her sister, Amanda. [M J]

Ashton-Warner, Sylvia (*c.* 1905–). New Zealand novelist. Born in Stratford, New Zealand. She attended the Auckland Teachers' Training College. After her marriage she taught, with her husband, in Maori schools. In retirement she devotes much time to painting and music. Her extraordinary first novel, *Spinster* (1958), makes poetic use of personal experience. Its central character and narrator is a hard-drinking, passionately intuitive, unbalanced and inspired teacher of a mainly Maori infant class. The story is less important than its narrator. The book is a presentation of the teacher as artist ('Communication is so fiery . . .'). A second novel, *Incense to Idols* (1960), is less successful, though it also has a memorable woman as its central character. *Greenstone* (1966) is her latest novel. [P T]

Myself (1967) (autobiography).

25

Asser (850–909). Welsh monk at St David's and later Bishop of Sherborne. His reputation for learning caused him to be invited to the court of King ◊ Alfred, with whom he spent a great part of his time until the King's death in 899. Doubts have been thrown (by V. H. Galbraith, for instance, in *Historical Research in Medieval England*, 1951) on Asser's right to be considered the author of the earliest biography of an English layman, Alfred, commonly attributed to him.

Annales rerum gestarum Alfredi Magni, ed. W. H. Stevenson (1904; new edn, 1959, with a note by D. Whitelock, supporting A.'s authorship); tr. J. A. Giles, *Six Old English Chronicles* (1896); tr. A. S. Cook, *A.'s Life of King Alfred* (1906).
D. Whitelock, *The Genuine A*. (1968).

Aubrey, John (1626–97). Antiquary and country gentleman. He was educated at Trinity College, Oxford, lost his estates through litigation, and spent his life avoiding creditors and compiling the manuscript collections which, published long after his death, make him a pioneer of the development of English biographical writing. During his lifetime he published only *Miscellanies* (1696), a collection of folklore. Anthony à ◊ Wood made use of his biographical collections. Aubrey put down everything he heard, however trivial it seemed, which has made his work more, not less, valuable. He is a master of vivid phrases. [AR]

Brief Lives, ed. O. L. Dick (1960); *Brief Lives and Other Selected Writings*, ed. Anthony Powell (1949; revised edn, 1965).

Auden, W(ystan) H(ugh) (1907–). Poet. English-born, he acquired American citizenship in middle life. He was born in York but his parents moved to Birmingham when he was a year old, and the landscape of the industrial Midlands had a considerable effect on his poetry. At his public school, Gresham's School, Holt, Norfolk, he specialized in biology but discovered his vocation as a poet in his fifteenth year. Between 1925 and 1928 he was at Oxford, where he read English, showing a special interest in Anglo-Saxon literature, and began to make a reputation. He twice edited the anthology *Oxford Poetry*, and his friend Stephen ◊ Spender hand-printed a limited edition of his early poems. His public reputation, however, began with the publication of *Poems* (1930), which included the verse play *Paid on Both Sides: A Charade*. Earning his living as a schoolmaster Auden published poetry copiously throughout the 1930s, and also collaborated with his friend Christopher ◊ Isherwood in writing Brechtian topical plays with songs and choruses, with his friend Louis ◊ MacNeice in a travel book about Iceland (*Letters from Iceland*, 1937), and with Christopher Isherwood in a travel book about China (*Journey to a War*, 1939). He was regarded as the leading radical, anti-Fascist, and at least near-Marxist poet of the English 1930s, the major figure of a group of whom the other members were Stephen Spender, Louis MacNeice and C. ◊ Day Lewis. The degree of shared opinion and active collaboration between this group has, however, been exaggerated. Two other of his more important volumes of the 1930s were *Look, Stranger!* (1936) and *Spain* (1937).

In January 1939 Auden left England with Isherwood to settle permanently in the United States, but the volume *Another Time* (1940) collected most of his later 1930s poems with an English relevance and bearing. In America he supported himself by stints of college teaching and some reviewing and acquired American citizenship in 1946. His poems now began to lose their radical political flavour and became at first hesitantly and then overtly Christian. The transitional poem is *New Year Letter* (in America *The Double Man*) published in 1941. Auden's work of the 1940s included *For the Time Being* – two long poems, one a set of variations on Shakespeare's *Tempest*, the other a Christmas oratorio – and *The Age of Anxiety: A Baroque Eclogue*. In the 1950s his most important new volumes of poems were *The Shield of Achilles* (1955) and *Homage to Clio* (1960). His *Collected Shorter Poems 1930–44* were published in 1950 (revised edn, 1966), his *Collected Longer Poems* in 1968, and a collection of his critical writing, *The Dyer's Hand*, in 1962. Two important new volumes of poems, growingly personal in tone, of the 1960s were *About the House* (1967) and *City without Walls* (1970). His Eliot memorial lectures of 1968, *Secondary Worlds*, had fascinating chapters on the passion play, opera and the sagas. Auden has also written opera libretti, the most famous of which is the text for Stravinsky's *The Rake's Progress* (in collaboration with Chester Kallman), and has edited and introduced, alone or in collaboration, numerous anthologies of verse and prose.

Auden is generally recognized as the most copious, versatile and intellectually vigorous poet writing in English and born in this century. Some critics have been worried by his transition from a near-Marxist to a Christian position, others by his unevenness, which, like his copiousness, suggests a Victorian rather than a modern poet, and others again by what they take as an undergraduate flippancy and a lack of personal emotional engagement in his poems. Many of these criticisms can be met by considering that, like Dryden, to whom one of his best critics compares him, he is an intellectual poet, more poetically excited by ideas than by sensations or things; that he views poetry as a 'serious game' which ought not directly to affect men's political and religious choices, though it should deepen their self-awareness; that the seeds of his later religious attitudes can be found even in very early poems (such as the sonnet beginning 'Sir, no man's enemy . . .'); and that a certain unevenness and occasional coarseness of texture is the price most poets of Auden's abundance must pay for their range. It would be generally agreed that Auden is a major figure in 20th-century Anglo-American poetry; there is still some hesitation about whether he is, more simply, a 'great poet'. [GSF]

Richard Hoggart, *A.: An Introductory Essay* (1951); J. Warren Beach, *The Making of the A. Canon* (1957); M. K. Spears, *The Poetry of W. H. A.: The Disenchanted Island* (1963); B. Everett, *A.* (1964).

Austen, Jane (1775–1817). Novelist. Born at Steventon near Basingstoke, the seventh child of the rector of the parish. Of the family: James died in 1819; Edward took the name Knight from a cousin whose property he inherited; Henry became a clergyman; Francis William and Charles became admirals in the navy. Jane Austen's sister, Cassandra, died unmarried in 1845. The novelist lived with her family at Steventon until they moved to Bath when her father retired in 1801. After his death in 1805, she moved around with her mother; in 1809, they settled in Chawton, near Alton, Hampshire. Here she remained, except for a few visits to London, until in May 1817, she moved to Winchester to be near her doctor. There she died.

As a girl she wrote stories, including burlesques of popular romances. She wrote an epistolary novel, 'Elinor and Marianne', after the fashion of ◊ Richardson and Fanny ◊ Burney, and in 1796–7 a narrative called 'First Impressions'. She read these productions aloud, and her father thought only the latter worth publishing. Her works were published only after much revision, and the relation between the chronology of the composition and the chronology of the publication is difficult to establish. Four works were published during her lifetime. They are: *Sense and Sensibility: A Novel. By a Lady* (1811; 1813 with minor corrections: this is 'Elinor', twice rewritten in 1797 and 1809–10); *Pride and Prejudice: A Novel by the Author of Sense and Sensibility* (1813, twice; 1817: this is a drastic revision of 'First Impressions', which her father had unsuccessfully offered to Cadell the publisher in 1797, even offering to pay for the printing); *Mansfield Park* (1814; 1816 with minor corrections); and *Emma* (1816). Two other novels, *Northanger Abbey* and *Persuasion*, were published posthumously in 1818, with a biographical notice by Henry Austen (the first announcement of the open secret of her authorship). The former is probably comprised for the most part of more immature work than the other novels; the publisher to whom it was first sold in 1803 failed to bring it out; in 1809 Jane Austen attempted to get him to publish it; in 1816 she bought the book back again but after starting to revise it, she decided to put it aside. *Persuasion* was written in a race against failing health in 1815–16. It is on this handful of 6 novels that her great but often challenged reputation rests. Besides juvenilia she has left us two compositions dating from the years before she dedicated herself to writing for a public: a short epistolary novel, *Lady Susan,* and an unfinished novel, *The Watsons*; in comparison with the later novels, their characters, themes and situations are rather bare-boned. At the time of her death she was working on a new novel, *Sanditon,* a fragmentary draft of which survives.

Jane Austen's novels deal in the main with groups of small landed gentry, and their ramifications in the professions, chiefly the church and the navy, all living in the country. There are occasional glimpses of town life. The dramatic situations involve young girls who are about to marry. The interest in *Northanger Abbey* is satiric; the naïve heroine is introduced first to the pleasures and confusion of Regency Bath and then to the splendid home of some friends. Her adventures are used to poke fun at the conventions of 18th-century novelists, the gothic fiction of Mrs ◊ Radcliffe being a particular target. *Sense and Sensibility* offers a clear (not necessarily convincing) statement of Jane Austen's most characteristic theme: in the interest of oneself and of others, behaviour if not feeling should be regulated in accordance with the demands of society. Marianne Dashwood believes in a Romantic display of feeling and is jilted. For a time her prudent elder sister Elinor finds no greater happiness in her suitor, the sober Edward Ferrars, but the moral of the story is asserted when the obstacle to Edward's proposal is removed – he had been honour-bound by an engagement to another girl – while Marianne learns to value sincerity, understanding, generosity, caution and a solid fortune. *Pride and Prejudice* is outstanding for dramatic dialogue and for comedy turning on the deceptiveness of appearance. Elizabeth Bennet, a heroine in the line of Beatrice in *Much Ado About Nothing*, and Mr Darcy start by disliking one another, but wit turns dislike into love and leads them to a greater understanding of themselves and of others.

The last phase of Jane Austen's work has won most attention from modern critics; some value her as a forerunner of James' experiments in point of view; Marxists note the detailed exploration of economic realities in her little world; others look for hidden meanings going against the surface moral of her works. *Mansfield Park* contains her most sustained examination of family life. The consciousness of the quiet, self-effacing Fanny Price becomes the medium through which life at the home of the heroine's rich aunt and uncle is viewed. Everybody's peace and complacency is shattered with the arrival of the witty and worldly Mary Crawford and her brother Henry. Jane Austen saw this work as an attempt to engage in a more serious kind of novel, but in places the seriousness looks very like sententiousness – in the view she adopts of amateur theatricals and in the handling of Mary Crawford. *Emma* is probably the modern favourite. In the little world of Highbury, Emma, the daughter of Mr Woodhouse and the heiress to 30,000 pounds, occupies a position of great authority, but so many of her actions are based on misguided motives and on misconceptions that her power proves an illusory one. Whereas in the beginning we are principally aware of her as snobbish and headstrong, by the end she emerges as a woman who can love and feel. The novel is rich in dramatic irony; the use of Emma's consciousness to present the action is masterly; and there is a greater realism of plot (inasmuch as Jane Austen's previous heroines were gentlemen's daughters in modest circumstances, whose true worth was recognized by suitors much richer than themselves). And yet there is probably too easy an acceptance of the social order and the quiet life of Highbury for the novel to be wholly satisfying. In *Persuasion* (ed. D. W. Harding, 1965) Jane Austen does greater justice to the demands of impulse and feeling than she does elsewhere, and here, in writing of her families of naval officers and country squires, she conveys a richer sense of life. The heroine Anne Eliott had yielded some years before the story opens to the claims of family and duty in breaking off an engagement with a penniless naval captain. The sense of a wasted existence, the oppressive family and social order, and the rebirth of hope are among Jane Austen's finest achievements. To the extent, however, that *Persuasion* opens up a series of new questions, it demands a new investigation of the nature of happiness and life, of a kind its author possibly could not have given.

Jane Austen's novels are a valuable record of the manners and snobbery of a section of English society. Jane Austen was moreover a creator of great comic figures – among others, Lady Catherine de Bourgh and Mr Collins in *Pride and Prejudice* and Mr Woodhouse and Miss Bates in *Emma*. They are the more real for not being presented simply for our amusement: in the confined society portrayed by Jane Austen they have to be treated seriously; they make enormous demands on the people who must live with them. But she is a classic because she writes about a central area of human experience – the ways in which individuals deal with social, familial and traditional pressures. To those who accept that ultimately men must accept restrictions, she can give understanding and even enjoyment of the social prison they inhabit. That the restrictions imposed by society need present no bar to the individual's expressing himself, Elizabeth Bennet in *Pride and Prejudice* bears eloquent witness. And if throughout Jane

Austen's work there can be detached a hesitation to engage in life unless every calculation has been made and every reasonable condition for happiness exists, nonetheless her ideals of civilization – comprising tolerance, intelligence, sensibility, order, self-knowledge – were high ones and are still relevant today. [NL]

The Novels of J.A., ed. R. W. Chapman (6 vols., 1923–54); *Letters*, ed. R. W. Chapman (1932). R. W. Chapman, *J.A.: A Critical Bibliography* (revised edn, 1955), and *J.A.: Facts and Problems* (1948); J. E. Austen-Leigh, *Memoir. By Her Nephew* (enlarged edn, 1871; ed. R. W. Chapman, 1926); G. W. and R. A. Austen-Leigh, *J.A., Her Life and Letters* (1913); E. Jenkins, *J.A.* (1938); M. Lascelles, *J.A. and Her Art* (corrected edn, 1941); Q. D. Leavis, 'A Critical Theory of J.A.'s Novels', *Scrutiny*, x (1942–3) and xiii (1944), reprinted in *A Selection From Scrutiny*, ed. F. R. Leavis, ii (1968); M. Mudrick, *J.A.: Irony as Defence and Discovery* (Princeton, 1952); A. H. Wright, *J.A.'s Novels: A Study in Structure* (1953); L. Trilling, 'Mansfield Park', in *Pelican Guide to English Literature*, 5 (1957); ed. I. Watt, *J.A.: A Collection of Critical Essays* (Englewood Cliffs, N.J., 1963) (with bibliography).

Austin, Alfred (1835–1913). Journalist and Poet Laureate. He was born at Headingley of a Roman Catholic family, and educated at Stonyhurst and Oscott College. He became a barrister, but gave up the law for journalism and politics (as a supporter of Disraeli). He was editor of the *National Review* (jointly with W. J. Courthope, 1883–7; on his own 1887–95). For these services to Tory journalism, he was made Poet Laureate by Lord Salisbury (1896). Austin had written 20 volumes of bad verse, trying most forms, including 2 dreary narratives, *The Human Tragedy* (1862; revised 1876) and *England's Darling* (Alfred the Great) (1896). Austin was a 'follower' of Byron. He wrote a very popular prose piece, *The Garden That I Love* (Swinford Old Manor) (1894). His *Autobiography* (2 vols., 1911) is impossibly pompous. [AR]

N. B. Crowell, *A. A., Victorian* (New Mexico U.P., 1953); 'The Banjo Byron', *TLS* (13 November 1953) and reply by V. G. Milner (27 November); K. Hopkins, *The Poets Laureate* (1954).

Ayton or **Aytoun, Sir Robert** (1570–1638). Poet. Ayton, a Scotsman educated at St Andrews and Paris, followed James I to London and was made a gentleman of the bedchamber and private secretary to the Queen, positions which he retained under Charles I. His verses in English, French, Latin and Greek were much admired in his own time; he was a friend of Ben Jonson and advised Hobbes on his translation of Thucydides. Ayton was one of the first Scotsmen to write competently in Southern English. A handful of his best poems survives in the anthologies, and an early version of 'Auld Lang Syne' is often ascribed to him. The bulk of his English verse, however, merely exemplifies the tradition of minor amorous verse that flowed unbroken from the lesser Tudors to the lesser Cavaliers, unaffected by the characteristically Elizabethan or Metaphysical modes. [AI]

English and Latin Poems, ed. C. Gullans (STS, 1963).
H. M. Shire, *Song Dance and Poetry at the Court of Scotland under King James VI* (1969).

Aytoun, William Edmondstoune (1813–65). Scottish nationalist, verse-writer and professor. An Edinburgh lawyer, the son of another, and the son-in-law of Christopher ◊ North he was connected throughout his adult life with *Blackwood's Magazine*, whose robust Tory Philistinism appears in various forms in his fluent, facile, Macaulayesque *Lays of the Scottish Cavaliers* (1849), in his mock-tragedy *Firmilian* (1854, a parody of the ◊ 'Spasmodic' poets ◊ Bailey, ◊ Dobell and Alexander ◊ Smith), in his miscellaneous parodies *The Bon Gaultier Ballads* (with T. Martin, 1855) and in his prose sketches. His conventional pieces, a dramatic poem and a novel, are worthless, lacking the boisterous but crude vigour of the rest of his work. As Professor of Rhetoric and Belles Lettres at Edinburgh University from 1845 (a post which he combined with a sinecure sheriffdom bestowed in 1852 for political services to the Tories) Aytoun published little academic work, but the popularity of his teaching led to the inclusion of English Literature as a regular part of the Scottish M.A. degree from 1858, and thus to its development elsewhere as a university study. Aytoun was the leading spirit in the Association for the Vindication of Scottish Rights (1853), the first organized Scottish movement for revision of the Act of Union of 1707. [AI]

Poems, ed. F. Page (1921); *Stories and Verse*, ed. W. L. Renwick (1963).
T. Martin, *Memoir* (1867); E. Frykman, *W. E. A.* (1963); M. A. Weinstein, *W. E. A. and the Spasmodic Controversy* (1968).

B

Bacon, Francis (Baron Verulam and Viscount St Albans) (1561–1626). Philosopher and scientist. The son of Sir Nicholas Bacon, Lord Keeper of the Great Seal, he studied at Cambridge and was enrolled at Gray's Inn in 1576 to study law, before going to Paris with the English Ambassador to train in diplomacy; he was recalled by his father's death. Sir Nicholas had made no provision for his gifted and precocious son who, unable to pursue his studies, applied in vain to the Government for an official post. He finally entered Parliament in 1584, thanks to the Duke of Buckingham. His policy of moderation and tolerance is outlined in the *Temporis partus masculus* (1584), though his *Letter of Advice to Queen Elizabeth* a few years later urged strong measures against the Catholics. Bacon, who took a keen and active interest in politics all his life, became Lord Chancellor in 1618, after having been Solicitor-General, Attorney-General and Lord Keeper. His main preoccupations, however, were philosophical and scientific. Already as a 16-year-old-boy at Cambridge Bacon was critical of Aristotle, whose works were then the basis of all philosophical instruction. Later he strove to replace Aristotelianism by a new system of philosophy, described in the *New Organon and Related Works* (1622), first published in Latin as the *Novum organum* in 1620. *The Advancement of Learning* (1605), subsequently enlarged in the Latin edition published under the title *De augmentis scientiarum*, was included in the *Instauratio magna* or great renewal of the sciences. It was in fact the first work in this series and was to be an exposition of the present state of learning, enabling the seekers of tomorrow to start out on their quest for true knowledge without loss of time. Bacon saw the 'mechanical' arts as the model for all scientific research. He considered that all learning should be based on experiment rather than on theory. He believed that primitive man had possessed the true wisdom which he had expressed in myths and fables; but that the Greek philosophers, starting with Plato and Aristotle, had strayed from the truth through an arrogance which had led them to elaborate systems out of their own heads instead of studying the world before them. This notion, which underlies most of Bacon's philosophy, is made explicit in the *Redargutio philosophiarum* (1608) and the *De sapientia veterum* (1609). Bacon wrote mostly in Latin, and his great familiarity with this language left its mark on his English prose style, which is terse and Senecan rather than elaborate and Ciceronian. His main literary work is the collection of *Essays* first published in 1597 and much expanded in later editions. He also wrote the *Maxims of the Law* and *Reading on the Statute of Uses* as a result of his legal and diplomatic training. In 1621 Bacon was accused of 'corruption and neglect', deprived of the Great Seal, fined, imprisoned in the Tower and disabled from sitting in Parliament. The sentence, though promptly mitigated by the intervention of the King, inevitably had a lasting effect on the man and on his writings, and the works of his last years show him to have been disappointed and embittered. His health declined and he wrote feverishly in the hope of concluding what he considered to be his mission: the great renewal or reform of science. The *Sylva silvarum*, finished just before his death and published posthumously in 1627, bears witness to the anguish and haste attending its composition: the examples supporting his theories are borrowed uncritically from writers he had previously dismissed as untrustworthy. Bacon's *History of Henry VII* was published in 1622.

Recognition only came a quarter of a century after his death. The founders of the Royal Society recognized Bacon as one of their most important precursors; indeed, his description of Solomon's house in the *New Atlantis* (1626) seemed to them to be a premonition of their own Society. Though Bacon wrote continuously for over forty years, his works are often repetitive, as he was always expanding and translating what he had written. [G D J]

Works, ed. R. L. Ellis, J. Spedding and D. D. Heath (7 vols., 1890).

F. Anderson, *The Philosophy of F. B.* (Chicago,

1948); B. Farrington, *F. B.: Philosopher of Industrial Science* (New York, 1949); P. M. Schuhl, *La pensée de B.* (Paris, 1949); P. Rossi, *F. B., dalla magia alla scienza* (Bari, 1957; tr. 1968); J. G. Crowther, *F. B., the First Statesman of Science* (1960); B. Farrington, *The Philosophy of B., an Essay on Its Development from 1603 to 1609* (1964).

Bacon, Roger (*c.* 1220–*c.* 1292). Scholar and scientist. He may well have studied at Paris, where we find him lecturing in the 1240s on Aristotelian and pseudo-Aristotelian works. While teaching at Oxford between 1247 and 1257 he became interested in the experimental sciences and in languages. In 1257 he became a Franciscan, but his relations with the order seem early to have become very poor, probably at least in part as a result of his studies. He was in fact imprisoned for a time by the order for 'suspected novelties in his teaching'. He attempted to produce encyclopedias of science (*Opus maius, Opus minus, Opus tertium*) as well as scientific treatises. He tried to substitute for what he regarded as an over-emphasis on logic the use of a combination of mathematical demonstration and experimental investigation. His researches were thus undertaken as an illustration of the validity of his methodological theory as well as for their own sakes. Though the dominant influence on his thought is Aristotelian, neo-platonic elements are also present in it. [ATH]

Opus maius, ed. J. H. Bridges (3 vols., 1897–1900); *Opera hactenus inedita,* ed. R. Steele (16 vols., 1909–   ); *Compendium studii theologiae,* ed. H. Rashdall (1911).
Ed. A. G. Little, *R. B.: Essays* (1914); E. Heck, *R. B. Ein mittelalterlicher Versuch einer historischen und systematischen Religionswissenschaft* (Bonn, 1957); A. C. Crombie, *Robert Grosseteste* (1955).

Bagehot, Walter (1826–77). Businessman, economist, historian, journalist and literary critic. Born at Langport in Somerset, and educated at Bristol and University College, London. He was called to the bar, but joined his father's banking and shipping business. He wrote for a number of periodicals; from 1855 he was joint-editor of the *National Review* and from 1860 until his death was editor of the *Economist.* In *The English Constitution* (1867; ed. A. J. Balfour, World's Classics, 1928; ed. and intr. R. H. S. Crossman, 1963) he advances a theory of the benefits of combining legislative and executive power based on

an examination of recent English history and the contemporary political scene. He also published a work of some economic importance in its time, *Lombard Street. A Description of the Money Market* (1873; several later 'revised' editions until 1915). His *Physics and Politics, or Thoughts on the Application of the Principles of Natural Selection and Inheritance to Political Society* (1872; ed. J. Barzun, New York, 1948) was an early attempt at a psychology of social behaviour. A collection of his papers which had originally appeared in the *National Review* was published as *Literary Studies,* edited by his co-editor, R. H. Hutton (2 vols., 1879; 3 vols., 1895; selections in Everyman, 1911); these include notable discussions of Wordsworth and Shakespeare (where he represents the best contemporary informed opinion); he is much poorer on authors then unfashionable, such as Sterne. His interest in psychology, the 'man behind the writing', was widely influential. [AR]

Works and Life, ed. E. Barrington (10 vols., 1915); *Collected Works,* ed. N. A. F. St J. Stevas (9 vols., 1965–   ; vols. 1 and 2, *The Literary Essays,* 1965).
William Irvine, *W.B.* (1939); N. A. F. St J. Stevas, *W. B.* (1959), and *W. B.* (WTW, 1963); G. M. Young, 'Victorian Psychology'. *TLS* (25 January 1936).

Bailey, Philip James (1816–1902). Poet. He was born in Nottingham, went to Glasgow University, but abandoned his intention of the Presbyterian ministry and became a barrister. He travelled abroad and was greatly influenced by Goethe's *Faust* (though never a master of German, he used Part II, not translated at the time) in his poem *Festus* (1839; enlarged edns 1845 etc.; final edn, of 40,000 lines, 1889). This was a poem of cosmic significance, written in blank verse, interspersed with songs. Festus (a Faust figure) is tempted by Lucifer, with God's permission; and in the semi-dramatic 52 scenes there are long conversations with spirits and mortals. Festus's aim is universal salvation (which accounts for the contemporary popularity of the poem), but when he succeeds in his desires the Last Judgement comes, bringing the hero his merited reward. Tennyson thought there were 'very grand things' in *Festus,* but it seems unreadable now. Bailey belongs to Aytoun's ◊ 'Spasmodic school' of 'grand' themes and incoherent

31

writing. He packed the later editions with work from his other books of poems. [AR]

A. D. McKillop, 'A Victorian Faust', *P M L A*, XL (1925); G. A. Black, 'B.'s Debt to Goethe's *Faust* in his *Festus*', *MLR*, XXVIII (1933); R. Birley, in *Sunk Without Trace* (1962).

Baillie, Lady Grizel or **Grisell** (*née* Hume) (1665–1746). Scottish song-writer. Her only surviving song, 'Werena my heart licht I wad die', was published in Allan ◊ Ramsay's *Tea Table Miscellany* (1724) and helped to set the 18th-century Scottish fashion for affecting ballad-like verses composed by the gentry about incidents in common life. Lady Grizel spent her youth adventurously shielding, and later in exile with, persecuted Covenanting relatives; and the *Household Book* (ed. R. Scott Moncrieff, 1911) which she kept after her homecoming and marriage contains interesting details of domestic life and management on a large Border estate between 1692 and 1733. [AI]

S. Tytler and J. Watson, *The Songstresses of Scotland* (1871).

Baillie, Joanna (1762–1851). Poet and dramatist. Born in Scotland, she published *Fugitive Verses* in 1790, 3 volumes of *Plays on the Passions* in 1798, 1802 and 1812, *Miscellaneous Plays* in 1804, and *Dramas* in 1836. Of her 26 plays only 5 were ever staged. Her ambitious aim in *Plays on the Passions* was to write parallel comedies and tragedies on the same emotions. Mrs Siddons appeared in *De Montfort* (a tragedy on hate) at Drury Lane in 1800. The plays have only a historical interest today: they illustrate the divorce between literature and theatre in the 19th century, and their language typically echoes Shakespeare and the Elizabethans. She is a minor figure through her affinity with Scott in the history of Romanticism and the Gothic in Britain. [MJ]

The Dramatic and Poetical Works (1851). M. S. Carhart, *The Life and Work of J. B.* (1923); G. Wilson Knight, *The Golden Labyrinth: A Study of British Drama* (1962); A. Nicoll, *A History of English Drama, 1660–1900*, iii and iv (revised edn, 1960).

Balchin, Nigel (Martin) (1908–). Novelist. Born at Potterne in Wiltshire and educated at Dauntsey's School and Peterhouse, Cambridge (where he studied Natural Science). He became a fruit farmer, and during the Second World War he was a scientific adviser to the Army Council. His 2 early satires, *How to Run a Bassoon Factory* (1934) and *Business for Pleasure* (1935), are collections of *Punch* articles based on his commercial experience. He began writing fiction in 1933 and became famous with his satire on Civil Service bureaucracy, *The Small Back Room* (1943), dealing in a speedy narrative with wartime research. *Mine Own Executioner* (1945) is a psychological thriller which became a successful film; he wrote the screen-play also. Later fiction includes *The Fall of a Sparrow* (1955) and *Seen Dimly before Dawn* (1962). [AR]

Bale, John (1495–1563). Dramatist, antiquary and religious controversialist. Educated at a Carmelite convent in Norwich, and at Jesus College, Cambridge, where he took holy orders, he was converted to Protestantism and became the fiercest of anti-Catholic, anti-monastic controversialists. His 21 plays (mostly lost) include *King John* – whose hero opposes Usurped Power (the Pope) – and *The Three Laws of Nature, Moses, and Christ*. They were written as a means of exposing Catholic abuses to as wide an audience as possible. Between 1537 and 1540 his itinerant troupe performed in various parts of England at the request of Thomas Cromwell, Henry VIII's chief anti-clerical adviser. After Cromwell's fall he lived in Germany (1540–7). He became vicar of Swaffham in Norfolk in 1551, and Bishop of Ossory in 1553, but had to flee to the continent. Later he was prebendary of Canterbury. His ambitious antiquarian project *Illustrium majoris Britanniae scriptorum summarium* (1548), later revised as *Scriptorum illustrium majoris Britanniae catalogus* (1557), was a dictionary of British writers listing their works and giving some biographical information. His polemical writings in English are scurrilous and venomous (Fuller called him 'bilious Bale') and include *Brief Chronicle Concerning Sir John Oldcastle* (1544) and *Acts of English Votaries* (1546).

Bale's importance in the evolution of English drama is that, unlike authors of courtly morality plays, he wrote for itinerant professional troupes, and brought a degree of literary sophistication to popular entertainment. By emphasizing topical allusion, he contributed to the secularization of moralities and interludes. [MJ]

Dramatic Writings, ed. J. S. Farmer (1907).
D. M. Bevington, *From 'Mankind' to Marlowe* (1962) and *Tudor Drama and Politics* (1968); J. W. Harris, *J. B.: A Study in the Minor Literature of the Reformation* (Urbana, Ill., 1940); H. McCusker, *J. B., Dramatist and Antiquary* (Bryn Mawr, Pa, 1942); A. P. Rossiter, *English Drama from Early Times to the Elizabethans* (1950); F. P. Wilson, *The English Drama, 1485–1585* (1969).

Ballantyne, Robert Michael (1825–94). Writer of boys' stories. Born in Edinburgh and related to the family of printers, in his youth he spent six years working for the Hudson's Bay Company (*Hudson's Bay; or Every-Day Life in the Wilds of North America*, 1845; repr. 1902) and later worked for Constable, the publishers (*Personal Reminiscences in Bookmaking*, 1893). He was a pioneer writer of adventure stories, specially written for boys; these sustained interest by adventures in exotic places and kept off dangerous topics, which made them more 'acceptable' than the tales of Captain ◊ Marryat. His 80 or so stories were very popular, and are still found in public libraries. *Martin Rattler, or A Boy's Adventures in the Forests of Brazil* (1858) is his best; others are *The Young Fur Traders* (1856), *The Coral Island* (1858; ed. E. Rhys, Everyman, 1907; intr. James Barrie, 1913), *The Dog Crusoe* (1860), *The Gorilla Hunters* (1861) and *The Iron Horse, or Life on the Line* (1871). [AR]

E. Osborne, 'B. the Pioneer', *Junior Bookshelf*, VIII (1944); C. Meigs et al., *A Critical History of Children's Literature* (New York, 1953); E. Quayle, *B. the Brave: A Victorian Writer and His Family* (1967).

Bannatyne, George (*c.* 1545–*c.* 1608). A burgess of Edinburgh whose manuscript anthology of over 800 pages, compiled in 1568 and preserved in the National Library of Scotland, is the only source for much of the poetry of ◊ Dunbar, ◊ Henryson, ◊ Lindsay, Alexander ◊ Scott and other Middle Scots poets. The Bannatyne Manuscript provided most of the material in Allan ◊ Ramsay's *The Ever Green* (1724), an early and important influence on the revival of interest in older Scottish literature. The Bannatyne Club, founded by Sir Walter Scott in 1823 and named in Bannatyne's honour, edited and published much Scottish literature and history, including a memoir of Bannatyne by Scott (1829).

Bannatyne's own verses, also preserved in his manuscript, are of little interest. [AI]

The Bannatyne Manuscript, ed. W. T. Ritchie (4 vols., STS, 1928–34). H. M. Shire, *Song Dance and Poetry of the Court of Scotland under James VI* (1969).

Barbauld, Mrs Anna Laetitia (1743–1825). Poet and authoress. Born the daughter of Aikin, a schoolmaster, who educated her with his pupils, she was the author of a collection of miscellaneous poems (*Poems*, 1773). She married (1774) a French Protestant schoolmaster, and became involved in his work, producing devotional and educational works of some reputation, such as *Hymns in Prose for Children* (1781, and many editions well into the 19th century), and *Selections from the Spectator, Tatler, Guardian, and Freeholder* (3 vols., 1804). She collected the letters of Samuel Richardson in 6 volumes with a Life (1804), and edited *British Novelists* (50 vols., 1810), a widely read selection. [AR]

A. L. Le Breton, *A Memoir of Mrs B.* (1874); G. A. Ellis, *A Memoir, Letters, and a Selection from the Works of A. L. B.* (2 vols., Boston, 1874).

Barbour, John (1316?–95). Author of *The Bruce, or The Metrical History of Robert I King of Scots*. Little is known of Barbour's life: he became Archdeacon of Aberdeen in 1357, travelled to Oxford several times and to Paris at least once, held court offices in Scotland in the 1370s and 1380s and was awarded a royal pension in old age. Other histories and translations have been ascribed to Barbour, in particular *The Buik of Alexander* (ed. R. L. G. Ritchie, STS, 4 vols., 1921–9).

The Bruce (ed. W. W. Skeat, EETS, 1870–89; repr. with corrections, STS, 1894; selection ed. A. M. Kinghorn, 1960), a poem of some 7,000 octosyllabic couplets, glorifies Bruce, Douglas and their supporters by embroidering the history of the Scottish War of Independence with traditional anecdotes and with episodes and atmospheres drawn from French romances. Barbour nevertheless organized the poem as a continuous and exhaustive narrative, forgoing the artistic advantages of arrangement and selection. Much of *The Bruce*, therefore, is pedestrian – the vigour and directness that mark its best passages, such as the praise of freedom and the account of Bannockburn, are not sustained. In contrast with the *Wallace* of ◇ Henry the Minstrel, *The Bruce* subordinates purely national feeling to veneration for the international code of chivalry. Although the poem is in a sense the 'national epic' of Scotland, it functions not as a living classic but as the ultimate source of widely accepted historical beliefs. [AI]

Barclay, Alexander (c. 1475–1552). Poet. Probably of Scottish birth, he was priest to the College of Ottery St Mary in Devon when in 1508 he made his translation or adaptation of Sebastian Brant's *Narrenschiff* into English verse as *The Ship of Fools* (ed. T. H. Jamieson, 2 vols., 1874) a satirical work with many interpolated contemporary allusions. He became a Benedictine monk at Ely and later a Franciscan at Canterbury and was rector of All Hallows, London, at the time of his death. He also made a prose translation of Sallust's *Bellum Jugurthinum* and wrote a manual, *The Introductory to Write and to Pronounce French* (1521), which is of historical interest. His poetry has no literary merit, is mainly translation, and includes 5 *Eclogues*. [MJ]

C. S. Lewis, *English Literature in the Sixteenth Century* (1954).

Barclay, John (1582–1621). Poet and prose satirist. The son of a Scottish jurist, he was born in France, spent a considerable part of his life in England, and died at Rome. He wrote poems and prose satires in admirable Latin. His best works are *Satyricon* (1603–7), a satire on the Jesuits, and *Argenis* (Paris, 1621), a satirical romance in the style of Petronius. Fénelon and Calderón were greatly indebted to his work and it has been translated into many languages.

Apologia (1610); *Sylvae* (1606); *Poemata* (1615). Sir David Dalrymple, Lord Hailes, *Sketch of the Life of J. B.* (1786); A. Dupond, *L'Argenis de J.B.* (Paris, 1875); J. Dukas, *Bibliographie du Satyricon de J.B.* (Paris, 1880); C. F. Schmid, *B.s Argenis* (Munich, 1903).

Baring-Gould, Sabine (1834–1924). Writer of hymns, religious and miscellaneous works, and novelist. Educated at Clare College, Cambridge, he became rector of Lew Trenchard in Devon. He wrote a great deal, exploiting the antiquities and folklore of that region in fiction, which makes him in some ways similar to Hardy. His best-known works are *The Gaverocks: A Tale of*

the *Cornish Coast* (1887) and *The Pennycomequicks: A Novel* (1889). He also wrote books for children, historical works (fictional and semi-fictional), books of sketches, guide books, and several theological works. Among his hymns, 'Onward Christian Soldiers' is the best known. [AR]

Early Reminiscences: 1834–64 (1923); *Further Reminiscences: 1864–94* (1925).
S. M. Ellis, *Mainly Victorian* (1925); L. Powys, 'A Devonshire Gentleman', *North American Review*, CCXXI (1925); W. Purcell, *Onward Christian Soldiers* (1957) (life); W. J. Hyde, 'B.-G. as a Novelist', in *Nineteenth-Century Fiction*, 15 (1961).

Barker, Sir Ernest (1874–1960). Political philosopher. Born in Cheshire, he attended Manchester Grammar School and Balliol College, Oxford, where he studied modern history and classics. He taught history as a Fellow of various Oxford colleges, and was Principal of King's College, London (1921–7), and Professor of Political Science at Cambridge until he retired in 1939. He published much on political theory and ideology, in which his historical scholarship and philosophical reflection take the place of any actual political experience. His chief works are: *Greek Political Theory* (Plato and Aristotle) (1918); *Political Thought in England from Herbert Spencer to the Present Day* (1915); *The National Character and the Factors in Its Foundation* (1927); *Ideas and Ideals of the British Empire* (1941); *Principles of Social and Political Theory* (1951). [AR]

Father of the Man (1948); *Age and Youth* (1953) (autobiographies).

Barker, George (Granville) (1913–   ). Poet. Born in Loughton, Essex, educated at an L.C.C. school and Regent Street Polytechnic, which he left at 14, he worked at a variety of jobs before turning to writing for a living. In 1939 he was appointed Professor of English Literature at the University of Tokyo but in 1940 went to America and returned to England three years later. Although some of his early poetry, *Thirty Preliminary Poems* (1933), *Poems* (1935) and *Calamiterror* (1937), one of the finest long poems inspired by the Spanish Civil War, deal with political themes, in style and feeling he remained an individual, seemingly uninfluenced by the mainstream of English poetry in the thirties. Barker's poetry is curiously uneven in quality. Intensely emotional and sensual, it appears at times to be merely an outpouring, a continual play with words in which surrealistic images, terrible puns, irrelevant archaisms and convoluted sentences stand side by side with passages of tragic grandeur and visionary lyricism. His later volumes of poetry, *Lament and Triumph* (1940), *Eros in Dogma* (1944), *News of the World* (1950), *The True Confession of George Barker* (1950), *A Vision of Beasts and Gods* (1954), *Collected Poems* (1957), *The View from a Blind I* (1962), *Dreams of a Summer Night* (1966) and *The Golden Chains* (1968), show the same mixture of artistic naïvety and lyrical beauty. He has also published *Two Plays* (*The Seraphina* and *In the Shade of the Old Apple Tree*, 1958), and a tortuously symbolic novel, *The Dead Seagull* (1950). [PJK]

Francis Scarfe, *Auden and After* (1942); Erik G. Schwimmer, 'G. B., An Exploration', *Numbers*, IX (1959); Patrick Swift, 'Prolegomenon to G. B.', *X, A Quarterly Review*, I (1960); A. J. Farmer, 'Aspects de la poésie de G. B.', *Études anglaises*, XIV (July 1961).

Barker, Harley Granville (Granville-Barker) (1877–1946). Man of the theatre, dramatist and Shakespearean scholar. With little formal education, Barker trained as an actor, and twice acted under William Poel, the reformer of Shakespearean production. He was associated with the New Drama, and a valued friend of Shaw, William ◊ Archer and Gilbert ◊ Murray. In 1900 he played the first of his many Shavian parts, Marchbanks in *Candida*. In 1902 his own play, *The Marrying of Ann Leete*, was produced. In 1904 he directed his first Shakespearean production, and, with Archer, published a plan for a National Theatre (which secured Government sanction only in 1962). Between 1904 and 1907 he directed the historic seasons at the Court Theatre which set new standards for the acting and production of modern European and British drama, and established Shaw as a popular playwright. His own *The Voysey Inheritance* was produced there in 1905. His modern political tragedy *Waste* was seen in London in 1907, and *The Madras House* in 1910. His position as the leading English man of the theatre was confirmed by his three Shakespearean productions in which his actress wife Lillah McCarthy appeared at the Savoy Theatre – *The Winter's Tale* and *Twelfth Night* in 1912 and *A Midsummer Night's Dream* in 1914.

These productions, with their quick pace, respect for Shakespeare's text, and light and brilliant décors, revolutionized Shakespearean presentation in Britain.

In any other European country Barker would have been given his own subsidized theatre. He directed two of Murray's translations of Euripides on open Greek stages in America in 1915, and met the rich American whom he later married. Thenceforth Granville-Barker (*sic*) was almost exclusively a writer. In a notable series, *Prefaces to Shakespeare*, he brought his unique experience as a director and his great scholarship of the Elizabethan stage to bear upon Shakespeare's texts. The *Prefaces* led to a fresh understanding of Shakespeare as a dramatist by both academics and producers. [MJ]

The Collected Plays, intr. I. Brown (3 vols., 1967). W. Bridges-Adams, *The Lost Leader* (1954); C. B. Purdom, *H. G. B.* (1955); M. M. Morgan, *A Drama of Political Man* (1961); J. Dover Wilson, 'Memories of H. G. B.', in *Elizabethan and Jacobean Studies Presented to F. P. Wilson* (1959).

Barnard, Lady Anne (*née* Lindsay) (1750–1825). Scots authoress. She composed in 1772 the sentimental Scots ballad 'Auld Robin Gray' (ed. W. Scott, 1825; ed. J. L. Weir, 1938) to preserve the air of an older Scots song whose words were too indelicate for contemporary ears. Lady Anne's song was immensely popular in the later 18th century, but she revealed her authorship only in 1823 in a letter to Sir Walter Scott, whose own novels were still anonymous. Lady Anne had meantime been a confidante of the Prince of Wales and Mrs Fitzherbert in the 1790s, and had lived in South Africa from 1797 until 1802, writing letters which describe colonial life at that period (collected in *South Africa a Century Ago*, ed. W. H. Wilkins, 1901). [AI]

A. W. C. Lindsay, Earl of Crawford and Balcarres, *Lives of the Lindsays* (1849); M. Masson, *Lady A. B.* (1948).

Barnes, Barnabe (*c.* 1569–1609). Poet and dramatist. Son of the Bishop of Durham, he was educated at Brasenose College, Oxford. A prolific poet, he published in 1593 *Parthenophil and Parthenophe*, a sonnet-sequence influenced by Sidney, and in 1595 100 sonnets on religious themes, *A Divine Century of Spiritual Sonnets*. He has been a candidate for 'rival poet' in Shakespeare's *Sonnets*. His tragedy *The Devil's Charter or Pope Alexander VI* (1607) deals with Lucrezia Borgia, and his other play, *The Battle of Hexham*, is lost. [MJ]

Poems, ed. A. B. Grosart (1875).
C. S. Lewis, *English Literature in the Sixteenth Century* (1954); C. J. Sisson, *Thomas Lodge and Other Elizabethans* (1933).

Barnes, William (1801–86). Clergyman, poet and local historian. Born at Rushey in Dorset, the son of a farmer, he was variously a solicitor's clerk and a schoolmaster, but went to St John's College, Cambridge (1838), and took orders. In 1862, he became rector of Came in Dorset, where he died. He published poems in local papers, collected as 3 series of *Poems of Rural Life in the Dorset Dialect* (1844, 1859, 1863; *Collected Poems*, 1879). These love-poems, short nature pieces and verses on local events, beliefs and customs show a strong feeling for deeply rooted regional life and familiar natural scenes (in this, as in the region he wrote of, he was a significant forerunner of Thomas ◊ Hardy, who made a selection of his verse, *Select Poems*, 1908). Barnes also wrote various works on the Dorset dialect, and local Dorset history; he was a prolific journalist and contributed to *Macmillan's* and *Frazer's Magazines*. [AR]

Poems, ed. B. Jones (1962); *Selected Poems*, ed. G. Grigson (Muses' Library, 1950).
L. Baxter, *Life of W. B.; by His Daughter* (1887) (with bibliography); G. Grigson *Harp of Aeolus* (1947); W. D. Jacobs, *W. B.*, *Linguist* (New Mexico U.P., 1952); G. Dugdale, *W. B. of Dorset* (1953).

Barnfield, Richard (1574–1627). Poet. He took his B.A. at Brasenose College, Oxford, in 1592 and at the age of 20 published anonymously *The Affectionate Shepherd, Containing the Complaint of Daphnis for the Love of Ganymede* (1594), a poem influenced by Shakespeare's *Venus and Adonis*, which was followed by *Cynthia, with Certain Sonnets and the Legend of Cassandra* (1595). The 20 sonnets, pederastic in theme, also show Shakespearean influence; *Cynthia* is a panegyric on Queen Elizabeth in Spenserean stanzas in imitation of *The Faerie Queene*. In 1598 his comic poem *The Encomion of Lady Pecunia* included the first verse-tribute to Shakespeare, and of the 21 poems printed as Shakespeare's in *The Passionate Pilgrim* (1599) 2 are by Barnfield, including

the lyric 'As it fell upon a day', often judged his most delightful poem. He retired to Staffordshire, and wrote nothing in later life. [MJ]

Poems, ed. A. B. Grosart (1876).
C. S. Lewis, *English Literature in the Sixteenth Century* (1954).

Barrie, Sir James (Matthew) (1860–1937). Dramatist and novelist. Born in Kirriemuir, Forfarshire, the ninth child of a weaver, he was educated at Glasgow Academy, Dumfries Academy and Edinburgh University. He worked as a journalist in Nottingham and moved to London in 1885. He sold many stories about 'Thrums' (Kirriemuir) in the manner of the ◊ Kailyard School, exploiting a sentimental image of life in Scotland, and had an immense success in 1891 with his first novel, *The Little Minister*. He soon turned to the theatre and an early hit was *Walker, London* in 1892. He wrote an affectionate life of his mother, *Margaret Ogilvy*, in 1896. His last novels, *Sentimental Tommy* and *Tommy and Grizel*, had Scots settings, the latter appearing in 1900, from which time he devoted himself to the theatre. A dramatization of *The Little Minister* had done well in America and Britain, and eventually earned him £80,000. Other successes included the sentimental period comedy *Quality Street*, and his most Shavian piece, *The Admirable Crichton*. In 1904 was produced his celebrated fantasy *Peter Pan* about The Boy Who Would Not Grow Up, long a perennial children's play and book. *What Every Woman Knows* (1908) contains one of his omni-competent heroines, who knows what is best for her husband. *Dear Brutus* (1917) is a play on the idea of a second chance offered to a group of people most of whom repeat their mistakes. Another success, *Mary Rose*, is about a child-bride who disappears on a Hebridean magic island. In 1936 the biblical play *The Boy David*, elaborately mounted and cast, was a failure.

Barrie was greatly honoured. He was Rector of St Andrews University in 1919 and Chancellor of Edinburgh University from 1930. He was made a baronet and appointed to the Order of Merit. His plays show great technical cunning but are marred by coyness, sentimentality and whimsy. A psychological analysis of them would be revealing. Successful, melancholy and timid, he admired courage, and helped to sponsor Scott's Antarctic exploration. [MJ]

Plays, ed. A. E. Wilson (1942); *Works* (11 vols. 1913–32); *Letters*, ed. V. Meynell (1942). G. Blake, *B. and the Kailyard School* (1951); W. A. Darlington, *J. M. B.* (1938); J. A. Hammerton, *B.: The Story of a Genius* (1929); Denis Mackail, *The Story of J. M. B.* (1941); H. M. Walbrook, *J. M. B. and the Theater* (New York, 1922); C. Asquith, *Portrait of Barrie* (1954); J. Dunbar, *J.M.B.: The Man Behind the Image* (1970).

Bates, H(erbert) E(rnest) (1905–   ). Short-story writer and novelist. He was born at Rushton in Northamptonshire, and educated at Kettering Grammar School. He worked on a local newspaper and as a clerk before he published his first story, a fantasy, *The Two Sisters*, in 1926. Thereafter he has written more than 18 novels, including *Catherine Foster* (1929), a Maupassant-like 'simple story'; a naturalistic novel of industrial life, *Charlotte's Row* (1931); and novels of rural conditions in the vein of Hardy like *The Fallow Land* (1932), *The Poacher* (1935), *A House of Women* (1936). During the Second World War, he was a Squadron Leader in the R.A.F. and some of his stories of service life, published in such collections as *The Greatest People in the World* (1942), *How Sleep the Brave* (1943) and *The Face of England* (1952), were written under the pseudonym of 'Flying Officer X'. Towards the end of the war he was sent to write about the Burma theatre of operations, from which sprang his novels *The Purple Plain* (1947) and *The Jacaranda Tree* (1949). His most famous long work of fiction is the best-seller *Fair Stood the Wind for France* (1944), about a British bomber crew forced down over France. Bates has always been an exponent of the well-made story, told with an economical narrative line, an expertise that has been perhaps undervalued. His collections of stories include *My Uncle Silas* (1939), *An Aspidistra in Babylon* (1960) and *Now Sleeps the Crimson Petal* (1961), and recent novels include *The Sleepless Moon* (1956), *The Darling Buds of May* (1958) and *Oh! To Be in England* (1963). He has written a play, *The Day of Glory* (1945), and *The Modern Short Story* (1941), as well as miscellaneous works on gardening. [AR]

The Vanished World (1969) (autobiography).

Bates, Ralph (1899–   ). Novelist. Born in Swindon, Wiltshire; after serving in the army during the First World War he worked in the Great Western Railway workshops there. He lived in Spain from 1923 until he went to America when Franco assumed power in 1937. He was a captain in the Loyalist Army and a member of the International Brigade, and Spain is the setting of his earliest fiction, *Sierra* (1933), *Rainbow Fish* (1932) and *The Olive Field* (1936). Mexico where he has travelled much, is the setting of *The Fields of Paradise* (1941). *The Undiscoverables* (1942) is a collection of short stories. He has also written a biography, *Schubert* (1934), and an autobiographical volume, *The Dolphin in the Wood* (1950), which is an interesting account of regional life in the West of England at the beginning of the century. He has taught literature at New York University. [AR]

'Battle of Maldon'. A fine epic poem describing an incident during the fierce Scandinavian raids against England in 993, when a gallant Essex ealdorman, Byrhtnoth, chose to fight rather than bribe the enemy, the latter method of obtaining peace having become the custom under King Ethelred. It is the story of one of those heroic defeats in British history in which honourable conduct and high valour bring greater spiritual rewards than victory.

On 11 August 993 a mainly Norwegian force (called Danes) under Anlaf attempted to enter the Blackwater estuary after harrying Ipswich. Byrhtnoth, an old man who personified the courage and ideals of Alfred's reign, proudly opposed the great raiding army of over 3,000 men with an improvised defence force drawn mainly from local patriots. The armies parleyed for a while with the river in full tide separating them. When the tide went out the raiders attempted to rush Byrhtnoth across a narrow causeway. The English used their famous shield-wall tactics – to be later employed at Stamford Bridge and Hastings. The full engagement, when it came, was appallingly violent. Byrhtnoth fell and was beheaded by the enemy. This part of the battle has been compared with the classical story of the struggle over the body of Patroclus during the Trojan War.

The poem contains nine brave speeches spoken by seven heroes. These reach high tragedy as the hopelessness of the situation makes itself felt.

It is believed that the courage of these Mercian 'Few' was one of the chief reasons for the postponement of the Scandinavian

Baxter

conquest of Britain. The poem appears in the ◊ *Anglo-Saxon Chronicle* under the date 991 (993) and is a superb example of Old English alliterative writing. [RB]

E. Laborde, *Byrhtnoth and Maldon* (1936); B. Mitchell, *The Battle of Maldon* (1965).

Baxter, James Keir (1926–). New Zealand poet. Born in Dunedin, he broke off his studies at the University of Otago and took a variety of jobs, many of them manual, before returning to university. Since graduating he has been mainly concerned in the practice and administration of teaching in Wellington. He visited India in 1958. In addition to his poetry he has published a book of parodies, *The Iron Breadboard* (1957), 2 plays and 2 short critical works, *Recent Trends in New Zealand Poetry* (1951) and *The Fire and the Anvil* (1955).

Baxter is perhaps too prolific and too proficient, but he has a strong sense of poetry's moral responsibilities. The title-piece of *The Fallen House* (1953) is characteristic in its poignant presentation of waste. Baxter's opposition to social restrictions with their inevitable train of lost opportunities is an aspect of what he considers the poet's therapeutic delinquency. His obvious lyrical gift, his allusiveness and his coherence enrich such collections of his verse as *In Fires of No Return* (1958), *Howrah Bridge* (1961) and *Pig Island Letters* (1966). [PT]

The Band Rotunda (1965) (play); *The Man on the Horse* (1967) (lectures); *Aspects of Poetry in New Zealand* (1967).
W. Hart-Smith, 'The Poetry of J. K. B.', in *Meanjin*, II, 4 (Summer, 1952).

Baxter, Richard (1615–91). Preacher, theologian and controversialist. He became an eminent scholar, though never at a university. Ordained at Worcester (1638), he became a leader of the Presbyterian party in the Church and was ejected from his ministry at Kidderminster (1642). During the Civil War, although an army chaplain, he opposed the execution of the King, and Charles II made him a royal chaplain at the Restoration. He refused the offer of the see of Hereford and left the Church of England (1662), thereafter suffering persecution and imprisonment. He was the author of many works, the best known being 'practical' religious works, e.g. *The Saint's Everlasting Rest* (1650) and *A Call to the Unconverted* (1657). He was bullied by Jeffreys when prosecuted for seditious libel. His autobiography, *Reliquiae Baxterianae* (1696; Everyman, 1931, selections), was admired by Dr Johnson and Coleridge. [AR]

Practical Works, ed. W. Orme (23 vols., 1830).
F. J. Powicke, *A Life of the Reverend R. B.* (1924); G. F. Nuttall, *R. B.* (1966); R. B. Schlatter, *R. B. and Puritan Politics* (Rutgers U.P., 1959) (essays and selections).

Baylebridge, William (pseud. of Charles William Blocksidge) (1883–1942). Australian poet. Born in Brisbane and educated mainly privately, in 1908 he began extensive travels in England, Europe and the Middle East. Back in Brisbane, he published a selection from his 9 previous books of verse (*Selected Poems*, 1919). Living on adequate private means, he continued to publish volumes regularly. Among the best are the sonnets of *Love Redeemed* (1934) and the epigrammatic *Sextains* (1939). *An Anzac Muster* (1921) is a collection of stories about Australians in the Gallipoli campaign, told in unattractive epic prose and ending with a long passage of Nietzschean nationalism. Blocksidge's large collection *This Vital Flesh* (1939) sets itself out as the work of a philosopher-poet. His poetry too often becomes the vehicle of a philosophical fascism that draws on Bergson, Nietzsche and Hegel more consistently than his verse draws on Shakespeare and the English 17th-century poets; but an uncompromising celebration of the life-force, couched in awkward but persevering poetic diction, distinguishes him from his sources of ideas and techniques. [PT]

T. Inglis Moore, *Six Australian Poets* (1942); *Southerly*, 3 (1955) (special Baylebridge issue).

Beattie, James (1735–1803). Scottish poet. The son of a small farmer, Beattie rose through schoolmastering to the chair of Moral Philosophy and Logic in Marischal College, Aberdeen. His verse and his interests mark him as one of the ineffectual but ambitious Scottish *literati* characteristic of the period; his principal poem, *The Minstrel* (unfinished: Book I, 1771; Book II, 1774), relates in Spenserean stanzas the development of an imaginary Scottish shepherd-poet of 'Gothic days'. It was received with a shower of compliments, patronage and honorary degrees that really rewarded the *Essay on Truth* (1770), a violent, superficial and widely welcomed attack on ◊ Hume. Beattie shares some 'Romantic' characteristics – primitivism and responsiveness to Nature – but is fatally genteel: 'Here pause, my gothic lyre, a little while. / The leisure hour is all that thou canst claim.' In 1779 he published a volume of *Scoticisms* which he urged his countrymen to avoid. Samuel Johnson found something to admire in Beattie's seriousness and decency. [AI]

Poetical Works, ed. A. Dyce (1831); *The Poetical Works of B., Blair, and Falconer*, ed. and intr. G. Gilfillan (1854); *London Diary, 1773*, and *Daybook 1773–98*, ed. R. S. Walker (1946, 1948); *Dissertations* (1783); *Elements of Moral Science* (1790–3).
M. Forbes, *B. and His Friends* (1904).

Beaumont, Francis (1584–1616). Dramatist. The son of a judge, he went to Oxford in 1597 and entered the Inner Temple in 1600. His poem *Salmacis and Hermaphroditus*, based on Ovid, was published in 1602. For some five or six years, from about 1607 till his marriage to an heiress and withdrawal to Kent, he collaborated as a playwright with John ◊ Fletcher, who outlived him and who wrote, either unaided or in collaboration with Philip ◊ Massinger and others, most of the 52 plays published as Beaumont's and Fletcher's. He is thought to be the sole author of *The Woman Hater* (1606) and the ever-popular burlesque of contemporary drama, *The Knight of the Burning Pestle* (1607). The 12 or so plays written with Fletcher include tragi-comedies which have affinities with Shakespeare's last plays and which may have influenced them. [MJ]

C. M. Gayley, *B.: Dramatist* (1914).

Beckett, Samuel (1906–   ). Irish novelist and playwright. Born in Dublin, Beckett has long lived in Paris, where for a time he was secretary to James Joyce. He writes in both English and French. The novels *Murphy* (1938) and *Watt* (1953), written in English, show his characteristic concern with the helpless individual consciousness. More and more Beckett's subject came to be the appalling yet somehow ridiculous situation of the impotent individual trapped in a decaying body and confined to a single consciousness. 'I'm working with impotence, ignorance,' he once wrote. 'I don't think impotence has been exploited in the

past. . . . My little exploration is that whole zone of being that has always been set aside by artists as something unusable – as something by definition incompatible with art.' His trilogy of novels, written in French, *Molloy* (1951; tr. P. Bowles and Samuel Beckett, 1955), *Malone meurt* (1951; tr. Beckett, *Malone Dies*, 1956) and *L'Innommable* (1953; tr. Beckett, *The Unnameable*, 1958), manipulate language so as to project a process of search for self-identification: the confused thoughts and imaginings of the isolated and helpless self produce words which, in a bizarre kaleidoscopic way, try to come to terms with chronology, identity, expectation, objective reality. The characteristic posture of a hero of a Beckett novel is immobility, reduction on the physical level to a mere object while still uncertain of identity on the mental level. *Comment c'est* (1961; tr. Beckett, *How It Is*, 1964) uses a deliberately formless language to present the meaningless void of experience as encountered by the naked, helpless, struggling characters Bom and Pim. Beckett's plays develop further the character of the naked, poor, helpless, immobile character, yet by introducing dialogue of almost music-hall comic patter, as well as by a shifting and disquieting symbolism, manage both to inject comedy into despair and a curious ritual note if not of hope at least of some further meaning somewhere. His greatest success, *En attendant Godot* (1952; tr. Beckett, *Waiting for Godot*, 1954), with its two tramps forever waiting in a bare symbolic landscape for the arrival of the unidentified Godot and their encounter with the disturbingly symbolic rich man and his slave, is saved from bleak nihilism by the vulgar colloquial humour and sometimes the deliberately ironical nonsense of the dialogue and the ritualistic overtones of the situation. *Krapp's Last Tape* (1958) and *Happy Days* (1961) reveal in different ways Beckett's obsession with reducing characters to immobile objects who recognize their own existence only by talking or listening. *Fin de partie* (1957; tr. Beckett, *Endgame*, 1958) has three of its four characters who appear on stage paralysed; the senile couple Nagg and Nell have been discarded to dustbins; the meaningless, grotesque, nightmare dialogue, which is nevertheless touchingly human, dies away in the end and yields to silence and immobility. In the end Beckett seems to rescue his meanings precariously from the far side of

Beckford

No's Knife: Collected Shorter Prose 1945–1966 (1967); *Eli Joe and Other Writings* (1967); *Come and Go* (1967).
R. N. Coe, *B.* (1964); R. Cohn, *S.B.: The Comic Gamut* (1962); F. J. Hoffman, *S.B.: The Language of Self* (1962); J. Jacobson and W. R. Mueller, *The Testament of S. B.* (1964); L. Janvier, *Pour S. B.* (Paris, 1966); P. Mélèse, *B.* (Paris, 1966).

Beckford, William (1759–1844). Miscellaneous writer. The prototype of the English millionaire eccentric, he was the son of William Beckford, the Lord Mayor of London who supported Wilkes. William, the younger, inherited an immense fortune largely derived from the West Indies. As a writer he is remembered for his fantastic romance, *Vathek: An Arabian Tale* (1786; tr. S. Henley, Everyman, 1930; tr. H. B. Grimsditch, 1953), written in French and translated into English under his supervision, which contains some passages of theatrical, but impressive, sombre power, particularly the account of the subterraneous halls of Eblis and the death of the hero. Beckford was the builder of the costly 'gothick' mansion of Fonthill, but his undoubted intellectual ability makes his eccentricity and extravagance of real interest. He was also the author of 2 excellent travel books, *Dreams, Waking Thoughts and Incidents* (1783; revised 1834) and *Recollections of an Excursion to the Monasteries of Alcobaça and Batalha* (1835), which contain some brilliant and sympathetic sketches of Portugal, where he also built a palace. He was an M.P., and when he died had dissipated his vast fortune. [AR]

The Journal of W. B. in Portugal and Spain, 1787–88, ed. B. Alexander (1954); *Life at Fonthill 1807–1822*, tr. and ed. B. Alexander (1957) (letters).
S. Sitwell, *B. and Beckfordism* (1930); H. A. N. Brockman, *The Caliph of Fonthill* (1956); F. M. Mahmoud, *W. B. Bicentenary Essays* (Cairo, 1960).

Beddoes, Thomas Lovell (1803–49). Poet and playwright. Born at Clifton, Somerset, he was a nephew of Maria ◊ Edgeworth. Beddoes was educated at Bath Grammar School, Charterhouse and Oxford and later went on to study medicine at Göttingen and Würzburg. He spent much of his short life on the continent, becoming involved in revolutionary politics. Some of his work is in German. Beddoes visited England for the last time in 1846 and three years later committed suicide in Basle. Beddoes' first publication was a collection of three verse tales entitled *The Improvisatore* (1821), though at school he had already written a Gothic romance which indicated the line of his interests. He also wrote *The Bride's Tragedy* (1822), based on the murder of an undergraduate, and *Death's Jest Book, or The Fool's Tragedy* (1850). Beddoes had no conspicuous dramatic gift and his chief interest lies in the tortured intensity of some of the passages in which he reflects on the obsessive theme of death. [GS]

Plays and Poems, ed. H. W. Donner (Muses' Library, 1950).
H. W. Donner, *T. L. B.: The Making of a Poet* (1935).

Bede or **Baeda** (673–735). Historian and chronologer. Born in Monkwearmouth, Bede lived and died in the monastery at Jarrow. He was a pupil of Benedict Biscop, and acquired a knowledge of Greek and Hebrew, as well as Latin. He also composed in the vernacular, but only one of his English poems survives, the *Death Song* (ed. A. H. Smith, *Three Northumbrian Poems*, 1933), which is preserved in a letter by his pupil, Cuthbert. His outstanding work is the *Historia ecclesiastica gentis Anglorum* (ed. C. Plummer, 1896; tr. L. Shirley Price, *A History of the English Church and People*, Penguin Classics, 1954), completed in about 731. In any age, this would be recognized as a great work of history. Alfred had it translated into English, and much of it has passed into the national consciousness – the stories of Caedmon or of Gregory the Great and the English slaves, for example. Compared with the Latin style of earlier English and British writers, Bede's shows a lack of affectation, and great narrative power.

His large output includes popular ecclesiastical biography, such as the *Martyrology*, a chronological work like the *De temporibus*, and the *De natura rerum*, a compendium of such physical science as was then known. His most important Latin poem is the *Life of St Cuthbert*. The title of 'Venerable' was given to him soon after his death. [AG]

A. H. Thompson, *B., His Life, Times, and Writings* (1935); C. J. Godfrey, *The Church in Anglo-Saxon England* (1962).

40

Beerbohm, Sir Max (1872–1956). Caricaturist and wit. Born in London, the younger half-brother of Sir Herbert Beerbohm-Tree, the actor manager, he was educated at Charterhouse and Merton College, Oxford, where he first gave his character full play. In the *fin-de-siècle* London of the 'decadents', he was a busy figure, caricaturing, knowing everybody and writing dramatic criticism for the *Saturday Review* (where he succeeded ◊ Shaw). His writing has the care and 'style' which was cultivated and admired in that age. He exhibited and issued collections of his caricatures signed 'Max'; collections of his written pieces include *A Christmas Garland* (parodies) (1895); *The Works of Max Beerbohm* (1896); *The Happy Hypocrite* (1897); *Seven Men* (1919); and *Around Theatres* (1930; 1953). His fantastic Oxford romance, *Zuleika Dobson* (1911), is a fine example of his irony, ridicule and skill. The wit is based on the arrogant Edwardian sense of rich achievement, spiked with resentment at the solemnity of the previous age. It is not entirely self-aware. He went to live in Rapallo in 1911, and visited London only briefly in 1936, though he spent the Second World War in England, where he broadcast on the B.B.C. (*Mainly on the Air*, 1947). He was knighted in 1939, perhaps for his role of official *enfant terrible*. [AR]

Letters to Reggie Turner, ed. R. Hart-Davis (1964).
A. E. Gallatin, *Bibliography* (revised 1952); S. N. Behrman, *Conversation with Max* (1960); Lord David Cecil, *Max: A Biography* (1964).

Behan, Brendan (1923–64). Dramatist. Born in Dublin, he became a member of the I.R.A. at 14, and was sent to a British borstal for three years in 1939. In 1942 he received from a military court a fourteen-year sentence for political offences, and served six years of it. He has described his formative years in an autobiography, *Borstal Boy* (1958). His first play, *The Quare Fellow* (1956), depicts the life of an Irish prison in the hours immediately preceding a hanging; it is a compassionate play, rich in macabre comedy and vivid Irish conversations. Presented by Theatre Workshop, the play owed some of its success to the cast's improvisation under the sympathetic director, Joan Littlewood, whose methods were even more crucial to a second success, *The Hostage*, in 1959. Looser in structure, this often hilarious entertainment centred on an English hostage held by the I.R.A. in a Dublin bawdy-house, and exploited music-hall and revue techniques.

From 1956 Behan was lionized, televised and publicized; his Dublin drinking-bouts were headlined in the yellow press, which seemed to find in him a figure to rival in wit, conviviality and self-destructiveness the late Dylan Thomas. He left *Richard's Cork Leg*, an unfinished script. Ulick O'Connor's critical biography (1970) stresses Behan's early links with poets in Erse. [MJ]

J. Russell Taylor, *Anger and After* (revised edn, 1969); K. Tynan, *Curtains* (1961); D. Behan, *My Brother Brendan* (1966).

Behn, Mrs Aphra or **Afra** (1640–89). Romance writer and dramatist. The details of her life are obscure. For long her own account was believed. It is set out in 'The Life and Memoirs of Mrs Behn, Written by One of the Fair Sex' (in *Histories and Novels of the Late Ingenious Mrs Behn*, published by Charles Gildon in 1696 and often reprinted). But it has been plausibly argued that this is complete fiction. The question is not entirely decided, and she certainly lived through many bizarre (and probably disreputable) experiences. She wrote plays for many years, but is now remembered for her prose romances, which combine realism with improbable coincidence, sex and sentimentality. Two of her stories are worth preserving, *Oroonoko, or the Royal Slave* and *The Fair Jilt*, both published in *Three Histories* (1688). *Oroonoko* is the best of her works. It shows all her faults of formlessness, but she makes the Negro slave, despite the story's sentimental and primitivistic trappings, something of a tragic hero. The story shows another feature which made her writings popular, a strong touch of the exotic. [AR]

Works, ed. Montague Summers (6 vols., 1915); *Selected Writings*, intr. R. Phelps (New York, 1950).
G. Woodcock, *The Incomparable A.* (1948); H. Hahn, *A. B.* (1951).

Bell, Clive (1881–1964). Critic of politics, literature and art. Born into a 'county family' which provided him with independent means, he was educated at Marlborough College and Trinity College, Cambridge. In 1907 he married Vanessa, the elder daughter of Sir Leslie ◊ Stephen and sister of Virginia ◊ Woolf. Bell was a member of the

◊ Bloomsbury Group; he was a regular contributor to the *New Statesman and Nation*. In his art criticism he propounded a kind of 'pure' aestheticism, and was one of the best practitioners of the difficult ('Bloomsbury') art of writing intelligently about the powerful feelings evoked by visual art. He set out to develop a complete theory of visual art in *Art* (1914; 1915; repr. 1930). In this book he invented the term 'significant form' as a term of value, the purely aesthetic quality that exists to some degree in all visual art and which comes from the endeavour to express an idea rather than create a pleasing object. It is the pattern imposed by the artist. Other works of his include *Peace at Once* (1915); *Poems* (1921); *Since Cézanne* (1922); *On British Freedom* (1923); *Landmarks in Nineteenth-Century Painting* (1927); *Civilisation* (1928); *Proust* (1928); *An Account of French Painting* (1931). [AR]

J. K. Johnstone, *The Bloomsbury Group* (1954); L. Woolf, *Beginning Again: Autobiography, 1911–18* (1964); Q. Bell, *Bloomsbury* (1968).

Bell, Gertrude (Margaret Lowthian) (1868–1926). Traveller and archaeologist. Born in County Durham, the daughter of an ironmaster, and educated at Queen's College, Harley Street, and Lady Margaret Hall, Oxford, she was the first women to get a first-class degree in modern history. For ten years from 1888 she combined social activities with travel to Persia and Bulgaria, learning Persian and translating (*Poems from the Divan of Hafiz*, 1897). Then in 1899 she went to Jerusalem to learn Arabic; visits to Petra and Baalbek aroused her interest in archaeology, but her first expedition did not take place until 1905, when she travelled to Konya in Asia Minor. She wrote a vivid account of this in *The Desert and the Sown* (1907), and of her later explorations in the Middle East in *The Thousand and One Churches* (1909) and *The Palace and Mosque at Ukhaidir* (1914). Her ambition was to penetrate into Central Arabia, at that time a daring exploit for a solitary woman, and although her first attempt in 1913 was a failure, she was called to Cairo by the military authorities in 1915 and asked to collect information about the Arab tribes. In this capacity she travelled across the whole of Arabia, and at the end of the war she was in Baghdad, helping the British authorities to establish the Arab kingdom of Iraq. A staunch liberal by upbringing, she was a firm believer in early independence for the Arabs, and was influential in bringing it about. Both her fame and her writing helped to create public interest in the problems and romance of Arabia, in a way similar to the achievement of T. E. ◊ Lawrence. [JM]

Letters, ed. Lady Bell (1927).
Elizabeth Burgoyne, *G. B.* (2 vols., 1958, 1961).

Bell, John Joy (1871–1934). Scottish writer of fiction, farces, travel-books and reminiscences. The newspaper sketches of Glasgow family life collected in *Wee MacGreegor* (1902) sold half a million copies in Bell's lifetime; though a lively and plausible rendering of Glasgow speech, they are essentially an urban counterpart of the ◊ 'Kailyard' novels of Barrie and his imitators. [AI]

I Remember (1932) (autobiography).

Bell, Julian (1908–37). Poet and essayist. Son of Clive ◊ Bell and Vanessa Bell, he was educated at Cambridge, and later taught at a Chinese university. He served as an ambulance driver on the Republican side in the Spanish Civil War, and fell before Madrid in 1937. A memorial volume containing letters, essays and poems was published in 1938 (*Essays, Poems and Letters*, ed. Q. Bell). It is clear from his essays that his liberalism was too complex to be uncritical of the left-wing orthodoxies of his period. He attacks the 'irresponsible' enthusiasm of the poets of the Auden group, pleading for classical restraint, common sense and foresight, examining such questions as how standards are to operate in the egalitarian society of the future. For Bell the matter of taste was involved in the question of conduct; a touch of the moralist made him reject the private, aesthetic values of the free-thinking circle in which he had been brought up. His volumes of verse, *Winter Movement* (1930) and *Work for the Winter* (1936), contain pastoral poems in lucid, flexible patterns. They are adventurous in form, near-sighted in vision; their exact vitality, their feeling for the life of the land, their affirmation of roots are native without being nationalistic. [FG]

P. Stansky and W. Abrahams, *Journey to the Frontier: John Cornford and J. B.* (1966); F. Grubb, *A Vision of Reality* (1965).

Bellenden, John (*c.* 1495–1548?). Scottish translator and poet. Bellenden matriculated at St Andrews in 1508 and later became a Doctor of Divinity at the Sorbonne. He held minor court offices under James V of Scotland, at whose command, in the early 1530s, he translated into Scots Hector ◊ Boece's *Historia gentis Scotorum*, (1527) and the first 5 books of Livy's history of Rome (*Livy's History of Rome Translated into Scots*, ed. W. A. Craigie, STS, 2 vols., 1901–3). The Livy, one of the first British translations of the classics, remained in manuscript until 1822, but the free translation of Boece, the first considerable prose work in Scots, was printed (*The History and Chronicles of Scotland by Hector Boece*, *c.* 1536; repr. 1821; ed. R. W. Chambers, E. C. Batho and H. W. Husbands, from early manuscripts which differ considerably from the printed volume, 2 vols., STS, 1938–41) and became the basis of later histories, including part of Holinshed. Bellenden was later made Canon of Ross, Archdeacon of Moray, resident Precentor of Glasgow Cathedral and Rector of Glasgow University (1542–4). The verse prologues attached to his translations are among the last examples of Chaucer's influence in Scotland. [AI]

Belloc, (Joseph) Hilaire (Pierre) (1870–1953). Essayist, historian, novelist and poet. Born in Saint-Cloud of an English mother ånd a French father, and educated at the Oratory School, Birmingham, and Balliol College, Oxford, Belloc was a most prolific as well as skilful essayist and propagandist for his Catholic faith. He frequently collaborated with G. K. ◊ Chesterton in the production of satirical novels which Chesterton illustrated, thus giving his contemporary and opponent Bernard Shaw the opportunity to conceive a monstrous animal called the Chesterbelloc, whose ideas were in direct opposition to the socialism of Shaw and Wells. He was a Liberal M.P. from 1906 to 1910, but found the House of Commons uncongenial and gave up the political life in order to take charge of the English Department of East London College from 1911 to 1913.

Belloc's earlier works such as *The Path to Rome* (1902), *Esto Perpetua* (1906) and *The Servile State* (1912) are written in an agreeably lucid prose. Later, his style was to harden until it became weightily impenetrable. His first published volumes were of poetry, *Verses and Sonnets* (1896) being followed by the pleasantly enjoyable and immensely popular *Bad Child's Book of Beasts* (1896). A later collection of his gruesome and ferocious rhymes for children, *Cautionary Tales* (1908), represents Belloc's talents at their finest and most sympathetic. The novels, owing something to those of ◊ Disraeli, are lesser achievements. The most considerable are *Mr Clutterbuck's Election* (1908), *A Change in the Cabinet* (1909) and a comparatively late work, *The Postmaster-General* (1932). As a historian, Belloc's principal achievements are his biographies, *Danton* (1899), *Robespierre* (1901), *Napoleon* (1932) and *Cromwell* (1934). His travel books include *The Four Men* (1912) and *The Cruise of the 'Nona'* (1925). To some extent Belloc was the victim of his own versatility. Today his reputation survives mainly on his light verse. [CO]

R. Speaight, *The Life of H. B.* (1957).

Bennett, (Enoch) Arnold (1867–1931). Journalist, novelist and playwright. Born at Hanley in Staffordshire (in the 'Potteries'), the eldest of six children of a Methodist solicitor, he was educated at Burslem Endowed School, and the Middle School in Newcastle-under-Lyme. He worked first in his father's office, and then went to London as an articled clerk in a firm of solicitors there. His family was strict, but musical and cultivated, and he learned French well. He had a short story published in the ◊ *Yellow Book* (July 1895), and his first novel, *A Man from the North* (under the influence of George ◊ Moore), appeared in 1898. In 1893, he became a professional writer as assistant editor (editor 1896) of the weekly journal *Woman*. He also wrote reviews for the more exalted *Academy*. Some of the pulp fiction he wrote as editor reappeared in later life to plague him when he was famous. In 1900, he gave up his editorial work, but all his life continued to write reviews, columns of advice and miscellaneous articles. From 1902 to 1912, he lived in Paris, and was familiar with Turgenev and other European masters.

His reputation rests, out of a mass of work of very uneven quality and many plays now forgotten, on several novels of provincial life, based on close, even ruthless observation and set chiefly in the industrial district of his birth: *Anna of the Five Towns* (1902); *The Old Wives' Tale*

(1908), which placed him with Galsworthy in the leading rank of English novelists; and *Clayhanger* (1910), the first part of a trilogy, which contains some of his best writing; the sequels *Hilda Lessways* (1911) and *These Twain* (1916), however, show the failure that prevented Bennett ever quite realizing the promise of his masterpiece, *The Old Wives' Tale*. The general plan of the trilogy is too mechanically articulated. The 2 final volumes are monuments more to industry and perseverance than to an organizing idea or sensibility. The copious documentation, which was Bennett's strong point, and which, at his best, he could suffuse with remarkable sardonic imagination, drags the novel down. Of all his later work, only *Riceyman Steps* (1923) is notable. His last ambitious work, *Imperial Palace* (1930), has always been the target for detractors of Bennett. He was fascinated by highly developed, opulent organizations, and here wrote a novel round a luxury hotel, incurring the charge that he was mesmerized (and since it was not very good, corrupted) by wealth and power. His life in London 'society' after the First World War (in which he was engaged in propaganda) gave some support to this line of attack. A reading of his best books qualifies it. He was a mixture of puritanism, love of luxury, savage judgement and liberal views. His writing reflects this: sometimes in the difference of kind between books; sometimes by variations of tone within the same work. In *The Old Wives' Tale* he has given as good a picture as any of life moulded and compressed by sheer experience, the inexorable onset of age and the facts of death in a family. His vision is pathetic rather than tragic. His qualities of craftsmanship strengthen rather than offset the failure of his art, a failure of imagination. [AR]

Journals: *1896–1928*, ed. N. Flower (3 vols., 1932–3); *Letters*, ed. J. Hepburn (vol. 1, to J. B. Pinkes, 1966; vol. 2, 1968).
R. Pound, *A. B.* (1952); F. Swinnerton, article in *DNB*, and *A. B.* (WTW, 1950) (with bibliography); J. Hall, *A. B.: Primitivism and Taste* (U. of Washington P., 1959); J. G. Hepburn, *The Art of A. B.* (Indiana U.P., 1963) (both with bibliographies).

Benson, Arthur Christopher (1862–1925). Essayist. Born at Wellington College, the son of the headmaster, E. W. Benson (afterwards Archbishop of Canterbury), and elder brother of E. F. ◊ Benson, he was educated at Eton and King's College,

Cambridge, returning to teach at Eton, where he was influential as a housemaster from 1892. In 1903, he resigned a post he hated (though he wrote a book on teaching, *The Schoolmaster*, 1902). With Viscount Esher, he edited *Selections from the Correspondence of Queen Victoria* (1907); he had known the Queen, who admired his verse and hymns (he wrote 'Land of Hope and Glory'). In 1915 he was elected Master of Magdalene College, Cambridge. He was the author of a number of biographies of churchmen and writers, such as *William Laud* (1887), *Tennyson* (1904) and *Walter Pater* (English Men of Letters, 1906). He also wrote an account of the lives of his father and Rossetti. He was best known in his day for volumes of chatty, belletristic essays: *The Upton Letters* (1905); *From a College Window* (1906); *Beside Still Waters* (1907); and also for several mediocre novels. His diary, in 180 manuscript volumes (selections ed. P. Lubbock, 1926), presents quite another picture of the melancholic side of an industrious great Victorian. [AR]

Benson, Edward Frederick (1867–1940). Novelist. Born at Wellington College, younger brother of A. C. ◊ Benson, and educated at Marlborough and King's College, Cambridge, where he studied classics. He spent 1892–5 at the British School of Archaeology in Athens. His first novel, *Dodo*, appeared in 1893, and created the sensation to be expected from an Archbishop of Canterbury's son writing indiscreet society fiction. The book had 2 sequels, and during the nineties and the early part of this century Benson wrote a mass of light fiction (such as *The Babe, B.A.*, 1897; *Mammon and Co.*, 1899, and *David Blaize*, 1916), as well as many sketchy biographies (*Alcibiades*, 1928; *Charlotte Brontë*, 1932). He also developed something of a corner in royal biography through his access to Windsor papers (*Queen Victoria*, 1935; *The Kaiser and English Relations*, 1936; *Daughters of Queen Victoria*, 1938). He lived for many years in Henry James's house, Lamb House, Rye (where he was mayor, 1934–7). [AR]

As We Were: A Victorian Peep Show (1930); *As We Are* (1932) (autobiographies).

Benson, Stella (1892–1933). Novelist. Born at Lutwyche Hall, Much Wenlock, Shropshire. She was educated privately and in

France, Germany and Switzerland. Her first novel, *I Pose* (1915), was based on a trip to the West Indies which she had made three years earlier and was written while she kept a shop in Hoxton, as a basis for social work among the poor. She worked on the land during the First World War, and for her health went to California in 1918; there she had various jobs. Two years later, she returned to Europe by way of China (where she taught in a mission school). She married J. O'G. Anderson of the Chinese Custom Service in 1921, and for her honeymoon travelled across the U.S.A. in a Ford (*The Little World*, 1925, describes her adventures). She lived most of her remaining life in China. Among her works are *Living Alone* (1919), *The Poor Man* (1922) and *Goodbye, Stranger* (1926), a retelling of myths and stories. Her last novel, *Tobit Transplanted* (1931), about a group of White Russians in Manchuria, was rather successful, and won the Fémina Vie Heureuse Prize. [AR]

Collected Stories (1936); *Poems* (1935).
R. Ellis Roberts, *Portrait of S. B.* (1939).

Bentham, Jeremy (1748–1832). Philosopher and theorist of jurisprudence. Born in London, the son of a prosperous attorney, he was educated at Westminster School and Queen's College, Oxford, called to the bar at Lincoln's Inn, but never practised. He dabbled in various scientific and intellectual pursuits, but settled down to study the theory of law; the first work he started on was the *Introduction to the Principles of Morals and Legislation*, his most influential book (published 1789), but his first published work was his *Fragment on Government* (1776), a critique of the theory of the legal *Commentaries* of Blackstone. The *Fragment* introduced Bentham to Lord Shelburne and other politicians, lawyers and intellectuals. In 1785, he went to Russia, where his brother was in the Tsar's service, and there wrote his *Defence of Usury* (1787) and the *Panopticon* (1791), a series of letters on the value of supervised activity in prison reform, an obsessive project. He worked hard on reforms of the Poor Law, problems of taxation, government finance, a *Discourse on Civil and Penal Legislation* (1802), religion and religious tests, and problems of evidence. In 1792 his father died and left him a fortune. His ideas and sketches were often written up and finished by disciples, such as James ◊ Mill. Bentham came of a Tory family, but became, under pressure of his thinking and of events, a 'philosophical radical'. As a moralist and theorist of ethics, he is best known for his 'utilitarian' ideas, the test of 'the greatest good of the greatest number'. These he inherited as perhaps one of the last descendants of the Enlightenment. In the development of English law, his works are of great importance. He also grappled, less successfully, with specific problems of economics and education, fields in which his 19th-century successors were more effective. When he died he left his body for dissection, and his skeleton, clad in his ordinary clothes, is preserved in a glass case in University College, London, which he helped to found; he also helped to start the *Westminster Review*. [AR]

Works, ed. with a Life by Sir J. Bowring (11 vols., 1838–43; reprinted New York, 1962); *The Correspondence*, ed. L. S. Sprigge (2 vols., 1968).
A. V. Dicey, *Law and Public Opinion in England* (1905); E. Halévy, *The Growth of Philosophic Radicalism* (1901, tr. 1928; 1955); Sir L. Stephen, *The English Utilitarians* (1900; 1950); *Mill on Bentham and Coleridge*, ed. and intr. F. R. Leavis (1950); M. Mack, *J. B.* (1962); S. R. Letwin, *The Pursuit of Certainty* (1965).

Bentley, Phyllis (Eleanor) (1894–). Novelist. Born in Halifax, Yorkshire, the daughter of a textile manufacturer, she was educated at Cheltenham Ladies' College and London University. She taught briefly, and in 1922 published her first novel, *Environment*. Her favourite and most successful fictional form is the chronicle covering several generations of one or more families, set in her native Yorkshire West Riding textile country. The historical range is broad and her optimism produces neatly arranged plots rather than deeply probed characters. Her novels include *The Spinner of the Years* (1928), a tale of an arranged marriage; *The Partnership* (1928), a story of passionate love; *Carr* (1929), which deals with Victorian industrialism; *Inheritance* (1932), a wide-ranging historical tale dealing with the struggle of 'capital and labour' from the early 19th century to 1931; *A Modern Tragedy* (1934), set in the slump; and 2 novels of local dynastic history, *Sleep in Peace* (1938) and *Take Courage* (1940). Her latest stories are *Crescendo* (1958), *Kith and Kin* (1960) and *Ned Carver In Danger* (1967). She has also published a useful survey, *The English Regional Novel*

(1941), *Some Observations on the Art of Narrative* (1946) and 2 volumes on the Brontës (she is the editor of the Heather Edition of their works). [AR]

O Dreams, O Destinations (1962) (autobiography).

Bentley, Richard (1662–1742). Classical scholar and theologian. Born in Yorkshire of peasant stock, he was educated at St John's College, Cambridge, and appointed tutor to the son of Stillingfleet, Dean of St Paul's and Bishop of Worcester. Bentley took orders and came to notice as the first holder of the lectureship founded by Robert Boyle, to combat error and maintain good Christian doctrine. Bentley's lectures drew on the 'new philosophy' of Newton to confute atheism and bolster up the Christian cause. He became Keeper of the Royal Library (1694) and Master of Trinity College, Cambridge (1700). His arrogant behaviour in the latter office (electing himself Regius Professor of Divinity) kept him for twenty years defending himself against suits of deposition, in which he demonstrated one of the finest legal brains in England. He came to notice as a classical scholar with his treatise on the Greek dramatists in his *Epistola* in John Mills's edition of Malelas (a medieval chronicler). His *Dissertation* (1699) proving the *Letters of Phalaris* to be spurious won him a European reputation, and he showed himself to be one of the greatest English classical scholars in works which followed, including editions of Horace, Manilius and Terence, which are marked by powerful comparison from a copious memory, daring and brilliant emendation and a prose style which crackles with neat and devastating sarcasm. Bentley's destruction of accepted opinion about the classics, and his dismissal of amateur scholars, put him among the 'moderns' in *The Battle of the Books* (◊ Swift). As a magisterial critic he figures in the *Dunciad* (IV, 201 ff.). His emendations to the text of *Paradise Lost*, edited 1732, and his theory of its composition are bizarre but not without shrewdness. [AR]

J. H. Monk, *Life of R. B.* (2 vols., 1833); R. C. Jebb, *B.* (English Men of Letters, 1902); R. J. White, *Dr B.* (1965).

'Beowulf' (late 8th cent.?). The only surviving Old English heroic epic and the greatest poetic achievement of Anglo-Saxon times. Over 3,000 lines long, it treats a basically folk-tale subject in an exalted, epic style. Most of the characters are historical; the scene is laid in Denmark and southern Sweden, and England is never mentioned. The poem relates the deeds of Beowulf, a Geatish (S. Swedish) hero, who frees the court of the Danish king, Hrothgar, from the ravages of the monster, Grendel, and of his equally monstrous mother. He eventually becomes king of the Geats, and rules for 50 years until he is called on to rescue his country from a fire-breathing dragon, in slaying which he is mortally wounded. The poem ends with his cremation on a gigantic funeral pyre amid the lamentations of his people.

Though *Beowulf* describes a pagan society, it contains elements of Christian feeling; nevertheless, what is celebrated above all is human endurance in a transient world, and the consolation offered is heroic, not Christian. The poet uses a richly allusive technique, relying on his audience's knowing a host of other heroic legends. Balance and parallelism dominate the whole, as well as the single alliterative line, and the language displays the finest qualities of Old English poetic style. [AG]

Beowulf and the Fight at Finnsburg, ed. F. Klaeber (1922); tr. J. R. Clark Hall (1940); tr. E. Morgan (1962); tr. D. Wright (Penguin Classics, 1957).

A. Bonjour, *The Digressions in 'Beowulf'* (1950); A. G. Brodeur, *The Art of 'Beowulf'* (1960); R. W. Chambers, *'Beowulf', An Introduction to the Study of the Poem* (1932); K. Sisam, *The Structure of Beowulf* (1965); E. G. Stanley, 'Beowulf', in *Continuations and Beginnings: Studies in Old English Literature* (1966); J. R. R. Tolkien '"Beowulf", The Monsters and the Critics', *Proceedings of the British Academy,* XXII (1936); D. Whitelock, *The Audience of 'Beowulf'* (1951).

Berkeley, George (1685–1753). Philosopher and bishop. Born near Kilkenny in Ireland, like Swift he was of a family of English immigrants. He was educated at Kilkenny School and Trinity College, Dublin, where he was ordained priest and gained a reputation as a mathematician; he became a Fellow, and his first book, *An Essay Towards a New Theory of Vision* (Dublin, 1709), propounded a psychological theory of perception as the creative act of the beholder in interpreting the relations between phenomena which might also be mathematically demonstrated; the process presupposed a corresponding rational arrangement by the Creator. Thus Berkeley hinted at the ontological theory of physics which he beautifully developed in *A Treatise Concerning the Principles of Human Knowledge* (1710; rev. edn, 1734; ed. A. J. Ayer and R. Winch, in *British Empirical Philosophers*, 1952), and defended in *Three Dialogues between Hylas and Philonous* (1713). This is the famous idealist theory of matter: '*esse est percipi*', i.e. 'being is being perceived'. Berkeley intended thus ingeniously to combat the materialism which had developed the split forced by Descartes between soul and matter, by internalizing or idealizing material arrangements; he thus unwittingly gave an opening to sceptics like ♢ Hume, who stressed the unreliability of human reason and judgement. In 1713, he visited England and became an intimate of the writers there, particularly Swift and Pope; he wrote essays for the *Guardian* edited by ♢ Steele. In 1721, he became a D.D., and three years later Dean of Derry. Berkeley spent much time trying to win support for a project to found a college in Bermuda to train Anglican clergy for service in the New World; 'Westward the Course of Empire takes its Way', he wrote in a celebrated poem. He left for America, failed to get the money, and while he lived in Rhode Island (1728–31) wrote *Alciphron: or the Minute Philosopher*, in 7 dialogues (2 vols., 1732), which contains some of his liveliest writing as well as observations on life in the New World. This was the work, combating the deism of ♢ Shaftesbury, that brought him his contemporary fame as a defender of the Christian religion. Another popular work was *Siris: A Chain of Philosophical Reflections and Inquiries Concerning the Virtues of Tar-Water* (1744); here 'philosophical' is taken in its widest sense. The book shows Berkeley's neo-platonism deepening, and deals with the action and reaction of the soul and the body; his ideas were stimulated by certain obsessive physiological and medical theories he had developed in America. In 1734 he had been made Bishop of Cloyne, where he spent the rest of his life, until in 1752 he retired to Oxford. He died a few months later. One of his most interesting miscellaneous works is *The Querist* (1735–7), which pleads for toleration of differences, and in several hundred queries raised by a consideration of life in Ireland initiates a number of religious, political and economic ideas. Berkeley was an extremely clear and graceful writer. [AR]

Works, ed. A. A. Luce and T. E. Jessop (9 vols., 1948–57); *Philosophical Writings*, ed. T. E. Jessop (1952) (selections).
A. A. Luce, *Life of B.* (1949); G. J. Warnock, *B.* (1953); T. E. Jessop, *G. B.* (WTW, 1959) (with short bibliography); T. E. Jessop, *Bibliography* (1934) (supplemented by J. Lawrence, etc., in *Revue Internationale de Philosophie*, VII, 1953).

Berners, Lord. ♢ Bourchier, Sir John.

Besant, Sir Walter (1836–1901). Historian, social reformer and novelist. Born in Portsmouth, and educated at King's College, London, and Christ's College, Cambridge, he taught for some time in Mauritius, but returned when his health broke down, and became Secretary of the Palestine Exploration Fund (1868–86). From his academic work came *Studies in Early French Poetry* (1868) and *The French Humourists* (1873); he also published *Jerusalem* (1871), a historical work. Besant began writing novels in collaboration with James Rice (1844–82), and they produced several best-sellers: *Ready-Money Mortiboy* (1872), *The Golden Butterfly* (1876) and *Chaplain of the Fleet* (1881). Thereafter he continued on his own, writing historical fiction, such as *For Faith and Freedom* (1888), but also using his fiction as the direct expression of social thought. In *All Sorts and Conditions of Men* (1882) he wrote about the East End of London, and he also dealt with the appalling conditions of industrial workers. He might be called a low-powered Gissing. Besant was also a practical social worker and helped to found the People's Palace, Mile End, containing concert and lecture halls, a swimming bath and other facilities for education and recreation; he was a founder-member of the Society of Authors (1884). He wrote a number of straight historical works, including *Rabelais* (1879) and *Captain Cook* (1890), though he specialized in the history of London (material he also used in fiction). He began a *Survey of London* (1902–12), unfinished at his death, and published several separate volumes on different parts of the city. [AR]
Autobiography (1902).
'Lewis Melville', *Victorian Novelists* (1906); F. W. Boege, 'B. Novelist', in *Nineteenth-Century Fiction*, 10 and 11 (1956, 1957).

Bethell, Mary Ursula (1874–1945). New Zealand poetess. She wrote her best poetry after her return to New Zealand, her girlhood home, in 1924. The poems in her most accomplished collection, *From a Garden in the Antipodes* (1929), begin with the realistic description of objects in her Christchurch garden, but move on into the religious and devotional themes that increasingly occupied her as she grew older. *Collected Poems* (1950) contains all her best work. [P T]

M. H. Holcroft, *Discovered Isles* (1950); L. Baigent, 'The Poetry of U. B.', *Landfall*, 17 (March 1951).

Betjeman, John (1906–   ). Poet and authority on, particularly, English Victorian railway stations and church and chapel architecture. Educated at Marlborough School and Magdalen College, Oxford, he came from a business family of Dutch ancestry, but as a young man preferred teaching and literature to entering the family firm. His early volumes of poems, *Mount Zion* (1933), *Continual Dew* (1937) and *Old Bats in New Belfries* (1940), with their parodies or imitations of minor Victorian poets, their interest in grotesque oddities of character and nuances of the English social scene, attracted a select highbrow audience, but – partly because many of his poems lend themselves to comic recitation, partly because they reflect a widely shared nostalgia for Edwardian and Victorian England – his reputation grew and *Collected Poems* (1958) was a runaway best-seller. His books on architecture and topography include *Ghastly Good Taste* (1933), *First and Last Loves* (1952) and a number of guide-books to English counties. Some critics consider Betjeman a trivial, snobbish and sentimental poet, but he has a uniquely individual flavour, and his admirers include W. H. Auden and Philip Larkin. [G S F]

Collected Poems (1970).

W. H. Auden, intr. to *Slick but Not Streamlined* (New York, 1947) (selection of B.'s poems); *Poetry* (*Chicago*), December 1947.

Bible Translation. The great age of English Bible translation begins with William ◊ Tyndale in 1523 and culminates in the publication of the so-called Authorized Version (A.V.) in 1611. In 1523 Tyndale vainly tried to persuade the Bishop of London to take him into his service in order to translate the Bible. Disillusioned with the Bishop's response, Tyndale left London in 1524 and went first to Hamburg, where he completed his translation of the New Testament (N.T.) by the end of 1525, then to Cologne, where printing of the translation

commenced, then to Worms, where he had to flee with the incompletely printed translation as he had been informed against for heretical activities. In Worms in 1525 he prepared 2 editions of his English New Testament, a quarto (of which no copy survives) and an octavo. Copies reached England the following year, and attempts to suppress it did not prevent it from circulating widely. Meanwhile Tyndale went on to translate the Pentateuch, published in 1531 ostensibly at Marburg but actually at Antwerp. This was followed by his separate translation of the Book of Jonah (date and place of publication uncertain). A revised edition of Tyndale's N.T. (Antwerp, 1534) included a translation of 'The Epistles taken out of the olde testament, which are red in the Church after the vse of Salsburye upon certen dayes of the yere'. Further revisions of Tyndale's N.T. appeared in 1535 and 1536. Tyndale's motivation in Bible translation was the old Lollard ideal of making the Bible, as the Word of God, available in the vernacular to the common people. He was a considerable Greek and Hebrew scholar, and a conscious stylist much of whose vocabulary and many of whose phrases were carried through to the Authorized Version. The humanist development of Greek and Hebrew scholarship in the 16th century combined with the new Protestant attitude to the Bible as the one true source of Christianity which should be made available to all Christians to produce the spate of Bible translation of which Tyndale was the pioneer.

Tyndale's translation of N.T. had been prohibited in England by a royal proclamation of 1530, but Henry VIII's break with the Pope led him to develop a more tolerant attitude towards Bible translation. Miles ◊ Coverdale's translation of the complete Bible (Zurich, 1535) is dedicated to the King and was not prohibited. Coverdale did not have Tyndale's scholarship in Hebrew and Greek, but drew on the Vulgate, Pagninus's Latin version of 1528, Luther's German Bible, the Zurich Bible of Leo Juda, Zwingli, Conrad Pellican and others, and Tyndale's N.T. and Pentateuch. Coverdale sometimes went in for diffuse paraphrase where Tyndale had been more succinct, but he had a fine sense of prose rhythm which helped to determine the style of Bible translation we find in A.V. The 1537 quarto edition of Coverdale's Bible (James Nycholson, Southwark) is described as 'set foorth with the Kynges moost gracious licence', and is thus the first 'authorized' version of the English Bible. Meanwhile, Archbishop Cranmer was anxious to promote an official 'bishops'' Bible, which appeared in 1537, attributed to Thomas Matthew and actually edited and arranged by John Rogers. This version, the so-called 'Matthew's Bible', was a composite, made up of Tyndale's O.T. and his hitherto unpublished translation of O.T. from Joshua to II Chronicles, Coverdale's translation of the rest of O.T. including the Apocrypha, and Tyndale's N.T. (1525 edition). 'Matthew's Bible' provided the basis for the series of revisions that culminated in A.V. An independent translation outside this line of descent was Richard Taverner's Bible of 1539: Taverner's N.T. shows evidence of original Greek scholarship, but his O.T. shows no independent knowledge of Hebrew. The 'Great Bible' of 1539 was a revision of 'Matthew's Bible' undertaken by Coverdale with the help of a variety of new secondary sources including Sebastian Munster's Latin translation of O.T. from the Hebrew. The second edition of the 'Great Bible', 1540, together with subsequent editions, has a prologue by Archbishop Cranmer and is thus sometimes known as 'Cranmer's Bible'. Bible translation in England lapsed during the reign of Mary, but the Protestant exiles in Geneva produced during her reign the great Geneva Bible (1560), the most important and the most accurate of all pre-A.V. translations: its O.T. was a thorough revision of G.B. after the original Hebrew and its N.T. was a revision of Tyndale after Theodore de Beze's Greek and Latin N.T. of 1565. The Geneva translators worked in close consultation with the translators of the French Geneva Bible of 1558. Their translation is scholarly and literal, but stylistically inferior to the 'Great Bible'. Its superior accuracy, and its handy quarto size (as opposed to the heavy folios of most previous translations), made it immensely popular in England, even after the publication of A.V.; 96 editions appeared between 1560 and 1640, 8 after publication of A.V. It was the translation used by Shakespeare. But the 'Great Bible' remained the authorized version, and early in Elizabeth's reign a revision of this was commissioned by Archbishop Parker. This, the 'Bishops' Bible', appeared in 1568, but, though 22 editions appeared between 1568 and 1602 (when the last edition appeared) it never ousted the Geneva Bible, which reigned unchallenged between 1602 and 1611. The 'Bishops' Bible' is an erratically carried out revision of the 'Great Bible' with the help of a variety of European translations.

Soon after King James I ascended the English throne he called the Hampton Court Conference to discuss the religious situation and it was this conference which put forward definite proposals for a new translation. The King approved, and translators in six groups (two each from Westminster, Oxford and Cambridge) split up the Bible between them. There were 54 translators in all, including most of the ablest scholars in semitic languages and Greek in the country. They worked from 1604 until 1611, when A.V. was published. Though ostensibly a revision of the 'Bishops' Bible', A.V. is in some respects more dependent on the Geneva Bible than on the Bishops', though in tone and style it is much more like the latter. It is in fact a critical revision of both the Geneva Bible and the 'Bishops' Bible' in the light of the translators' own scholarship in the original languages and with the help of a great variety of secondary sources and linguistic aids which had been made available over the preceding century. It deliberately uses a 'biblical' style, already old-fashioned as English but long associated with the liturgical use of the language. It was produced at a time when the English language was in one of its most creative periods, when it was being stretched and exercised by a great variety of poets, dramatists and translators. A happy combination of the linguistic traditions started by Renaissance humanism, the Protestant feeling for the Bible as the one source of Christianity, the Elizabethan literary efflorescence, and a peak moment in the history of the English language, A.V. is the only great literary work in English to have been produced by a committee. A Catholic translation of the Bible, out of the mainstream of English Bible translation and made from the Vulgate and not from the original Hebrew and Greek, appeared in Rheims in 1582 (N.T.) and at Douai in 1509–10 (O.T.). [D D]

Charles C. Butterworth, *The Literary Lineage of the King James Bible* (Philadelphia, 1941); D. Daiches, *The King James Version of the English Bible* (Chicago, 1941); A. W. Pollard, *Records of the English Bible* (1911); B. F. Westcott, *A General View of the History of the English Bible* (3rd edn, 1905).

Binyon, Robert Laurence (1869–1943). Poet and expert on Far Eastern art. Born in Lancaster and educated at St Paul's School and Trinity College, Oxford, from 1913 to 1932 he was first an assistant in and later Keeper of the Department of Oriental Prints and Drawings in the British Museum. In 1933 he was for a year visiting Professor of Poetry at Harvard. He was a poet of fine taste and pure diction but too remote and academic for wide popularity, though one poem, 'For the Fallen', was widely acclaimed after the First World War and another, 'The Burning of the Leaves', expresses with a more personal poignancy the sense both of destruction and hope that accompanied the Second World War. Binyon's major achievement, however, was his magnificently lucid and dignified version of Dante's *Divine Comedy*, published between 1933 and 1943. His books and essays on Far Eastern art are pioneer works of appreciation, and *English Poetry in its Relation to Painting and the Other Arts* (1919) brings together very interestingly his two major enthusiasms. [GSF]

The Penguin Book of Contemporary Verse, ed. K. Allott (revised edn, 1962); *Modern American Poetry and British Poetry*, ed. L. Untermeyer (enlarged edn, 1962).

Birney, Earle (1904–   ). Canadian poet, novelist and critic. Born in Calgary, he spent his childhood in the mountainous regions of Alberta and British Columbia, where the violence of nature made a lasting impression. After graduating from the University of British Columbia he turned to university teaching, and is now a Professor of English at his former university. He responded whole-heartedly to the socialism of the thirties, writing little poetry until he became literary editor of *The Canadian Forum* in 1936. *David*, a mountaineering narrative, was published in 1942. Birney's distinguished war service with the Canadian army enlarged his capacity as a chronicler of the Canadian experience. Its direct effects are evident in the poems of *Now is Time* (1945) and the humorous picaresque novel *Turvey* (1949). Familiarity with the idiosyncrasies of Canadian speech, a pervasive humanity tested by a mistrust of social expedients, and imagic clarity in the presentation of ominous nature are all present in the radio play *Trial of a City* (1952). A technical *tour de force*, it describes the trial of modern Vancouver before the Minister of History. Later volumes of poetry are *Ice Cod Bell or Stone* (1962) and *Near False Creek Mouth* (1964). *Down the Long Table* (1955) is a semi-autobiographical novel set in Canada during the depression. [PT]

Selected Poems (1966).
D. Pacey, *Ten Canadian Poets* (1958); B. R. Elliott, 'E. B.: Canadian Poet', *Meanjin*, XVIII, 3 (1959).

Birrell, Augustine (1850–1933). Essayist and statesman. Born near Liverpool the son of a Baptist minister, Birrell read law at Cambridge and was called to the bar in 1875. In 1889 he entered Parliament as a Liberal and was President of the Board of Education, 1905–7, and Chief Secretary for Ireland, 1907–16, resigning from the latter post during a stormy debate on the Easter Rising in Dublin. In 1884 he published, anonymously and at his own expense, a collection of literary essays called *Obiter Dicta*. The book was an immediate popular success. A second series of *Obiter Dicta* was published in 1887 and a third in 1924. Birrell also wrote biographies of Andrew Marvell, Charlotte Brontë and William Hazlitt, and a volume of autobiography, *Things Past Redress* (1937). Birrell's essays owed their popularity to his broad knowledge, gentle philosophizing and casual, conversational style. [PJK]

Collected Essays and Addresses (3 vols., 1922).
A. P. Ryan, 'Augustine Birrell: A Lucky Mid-Victorian', *Listener* (17 August 1950).

Blacklock, Thomas (1721–91). Scottish verse-writer. Blacklock was blind from infancy and knew only the literature that had been read aloud to him by others. Patronized by ◊ Hume and by other Scottish intellectuals, he studied divinity at Edinburgh University and in 1746 published a volume of poems which was used by ◊ Burke to support the view that a poet need not have any detailed vision of the objects he describes. Blacklock's fortitude and amiability made him an honoured figure in the Edinburgh of Henry ◊ Mackenzie; his early recognition and encouragement of Burns now seem much more important than any of his own verse. [AI]

Poems, ed. with a Life by H. Mackenzie (1793).

Blackmore, Sir Richard (*c*. 1650–1729). Poet, Physician-in-ordinary to William III and Queen Anne, author of several medical and political works. Best-known for his enormous heroic and epic poems, e.g. *King Arthur* (1697), whose dullness earned him several references in the *Dunciad* ('Blackmore's endless line'). His unreadable *The Creation: A Philosophical Poem* (1712) was admired by Addison. One or two of his critical essays have been reprinted (see *Critical Essays of the 17th Century*, iii, ed. J. E. Spingarn, 1909; *Essay on Wit*, ed. R. C. Boys, Augustan Reprint Society, 1946). [AR]

Johnson, *Lives of the Poets*; A. Rosenberg, *B.* (Lincoln, Neb., 1953).

Blackmore, Richard Doddridge (1825–1900). Novelist. Born at Longworth in Berkshire, and educated at Blundell's School, Tiverton, and Exeter College, Oxford. He began his writing career as a poet (*Poems by Melanter*, 1854; *Epullia*, 1855; *The Bugle of the Black Sea; or the British in the East*, 1855), but turned to fiction and with his third novel, *Lorna Doone: A Romance of Exmoor* (1869; World's Classics, 1914; ed. R. O. Morris, 1920), produced a best-seller, which is still filmed, dramatized, televised and read. (He appears to have invented the name Lorna.) He thought *The Maid of Sker* (1871–2 in *Macmillan's Magazine*; 1872) his best novel; others are *Christowel: A Dartmoor Tale* (in *Good Words*, 1881; 1882) and *Springhaven: A Tale of the Great War* (1886–7 in *Harper's Magazine*; 1887), about the Napoleonic war. In his rather melodramatic historical fashion, Blackmore follows Scott in setting an action involving interesting minor characters against a backcloth of historical events and figures (the Restoration and Judge Jeffreys in *Lorna Doone*), and was also influenced latterly by Hardy. Periodical publication made his fiction rather shapeless, but he is strong on descriptions of nature. [AR]

Q. G. Burris, *R. D. B., His Life and Novels* (Urbana, Ill., 1930); K. Budd, *The Last Victorian* (1960).

Blackwood, Algernon (1869–1951). Novelist and short-story writer. Born in Kent of an upper-class Evangelical family, he was educated at a variety of public schools and Edinburgh University. At 20 he left home and for ten years led a wandering life in Canada and America, later described in a lively volume of autobiography, *Episodes before Thirty* (1923). He returned to England in 1899, but did not publish his first book, a collection of ghost stories, *The Empty House*, until 1906. This was followed by several ambitious novels on psychic and supernatural themes, the best of which are *Jimbo* (1909), *The Human Chord* (1910), *The Centaur* (1911) and *A Prisoner in Fairyland* (1913). He also wrote at this time one of the finest of his long short-stories, 'The Man Whom the Trees Loved', in *Pan's Garden* (1912). In later life he concentrated mainly on the short story and published many collections including *Wolves of God* (1921), *The Dance of Death* (1927), *Shocks* (1935) and *Tales of the Uncanny and Supernatural* (1949). A writer of great subtlety and skill, with a clear, distinctive style and a profound love and understanding of nature, Blackwood always rejected the description of himself as a writer of horror stories, and claimed, rightly, that he was concerned with 'questions of extended or expanded consciousness'. For a long time he earned little money from his books, and it is ironic that during the closing years of his life he attained, through the medium of television, great popularity. His work still remains curiously neglected. [PJK]

Derek Hudson, *Essays and Studies* (1961).

'Blackwood's Magazine'. *Blackwood's*, or 'Maga' to its intimates, was a monthly first published in Edinburgh in 1817 and called then the *Edinburgh Monthly Magazine*. Tory in politics, it was edited by a brilliant trio of journalists whose invective scourged the literary scene. Under John Gibson ◊ Lockhart, later editor of the *Quarterly* and biographer of Sir Walter Scott, John Wilson, who signed himself 'Christopher ◊ North' and James ◊ Hogg, the 'Ettrick Shepherd', the new magazine drew scandalized attention on itself by satirizing Edinburgh's celebrities in a mock 'Chaldee MS' and then proceeded to set itself up as the mortal enemy of the 'Cockney School'. In the latter role it savaged John Keats after the publication of *Endymion* (1818) and hounded Hazlitt with the most extraordinary vindictiveness. William Maginn (1793–1842) joined 'Maga' in 1819, his first contribution being a banal parody of Coleridge's *Christabel*. Between 1822 and 1835 *Blackwood's* published a series of 71 witty conversation pieces entitled *Noctes Ambrosianae* which broadened its popularity and introduced a greater element of reasonableness into its fighting columns. [RB]

Mrs Oliphant, *Annals of a Publishing House* (1897); M. Lochhead, *John Gibson Lockhart* (1954).

Blair, Eric. ◊ Orwell, George.

Blair, Hugh (1718–1800). Scottish sermon-writer and critic. Blair, an Edinburgh minister who was also Professor of Rhetoric and Belles-Lettres at Edinburgh University from 1762, published several volumes of pretentiously written and very successful *Sermons* (1777–1801) and by his early encouragement of James ◊ Macpherson was virtually the promoter of Macpherson's 'translation' of ◊ Ossian as well as Ossian's chief defender in a loosely argued *Critical Dissertation on the Poems* (1763). Blair's *Lectures on Rhetoric and Belles-Lettres* (1783) vulgarize the critical approach of Henry ◊ Home, Lord Kames, by tamely philosophizing about 'taste' and 'sublimity', and his early, anonymous Scottish edition of Shakespeare (1753) slavishly follows the English edition of William ◊ Warburton. [AI]

J. Hill, *Life and Writings of H. B.* (1807); R. M. Schmitz, *H.B.* (New York, 1948).

Blair, Robert (1700?–1746). Scottish poet. Minister of Athelstaneford in East Lothian, he wrote a blank-verse didactic poem, *The Grave* (1743), which tapped the vein of rhetorical pietism opened by ◊ Young's *Night Thoughts*. Blair's verse is a curious and ungainly blend of pulpit exhortation with reminiscences of the phrases and cadences of Jacobean drama. *The Grave* was illustrated by William Blake in 1808 and remained popular in the serious and slightly morbid middle-class dissenting circles until well into the 19th century. [AI]

Poetical Works of Beattie, B. and Falconer, ed. G. Gilfillan (1854).

Blake, George (1893–1961). Scottish novelist. A native of Greenock, he served in the First World War before succeeding Neil ◊ Munro as literary editor of the *Glasgow Evening News*, and held other appointments in journalism, publishing and (during the Second World War) in the Ministry of Information. His many novels of Glasgow and Clydeside life, from *Mince Collop Close* (1923) to *The Shipbuilders* (1935) and *Down to the Sea* (1937), disseminated on the popular level of Scottish fiction the reaction initiated by George ◊ Douglas against the rural stereotypes of the ◊ 'Kailyard' novelists. Blake's strength lies in an easy naturalistic treatment of Clydeside work and environment, but his essential conventionality is betrayed by his bland acceptance of industrial civilization at a time when more sensitive contemporaries felt it as a problem to be grappled with. Blake's works include plays, a descriptive volume *The Firth of Clyde* (1952) and a critical study, *Barrie and the Kailyard School* (1951). [AI]

Blake, William (1757–1827). English artist and poet. Born in London, the son of a haberdasher, Blake had no formal education except in art. He attended the Royal Academy of Art, and at 14 was apprenticed to an engraver. In 1781 he married the illiterate daughter of a market gardener, whom he taught to read and to help with his engraving. In 1800 Blake moved to the Sussex coast under the patronage of William Hayley, but he rebelled against Hayley's attempts to make him more conventional, and therefore more popular, in his art, and three years later he returned to London. Blake always had to struggle as an artist. In 1809 he held a one-man exhibition of his work, but it failed, and it was not until the end of his life that he achieved the recognition of a small group of people. Blake was much influenced by the American and French Revolutions, but unlike many other prominent writers his disillusion with events in France did not turn him towards conservatism but confirmed him in a more individual and millenarian vision.

Blake remained virtually unknown as a poet in his lifetime. His first volume, *Poetical Sketches*, was published in 1783. He was attempting to work out a poetic language and form that broke away from the dominant neo-classicism of the 18th century. He found his inspiration in the Elizabethan lyrical poets, Ossian and those 18th-century poets who were outside the mainstream of writing. The result in this first volume was a collection of largely imitative lyrics and ballads. Later his experimentation with rhyme, rhythm and symbol produced poetry that was entirely his own. With the publication of *Songs of Innocence* (etched 1789) Blake combined poetry and pictorial design. Both poem and illustration were etched and painted with water colours. These poems – they include the famous 'The Lamb' – are fresh and simple, yet they have a depth of imagination and directness that avoids all sentimentality. Many are vital but finely controlled expressions of the enjoyment of simple things; at the same time as celebrating spontaneity Blake is illustrating the necessity of discipline.

The *Songs of Experience* were etched five years later. In them Blake describes with a simplicity that is now grim and stark the shattering of innocence by man and society. (They are also indications of his disillusion with France.) These poems present man as selfish, institutions as destructive, society as unconcerned. Blake built the *Songs of Experience* out of the harsh details of poverty and destitution that he witnessed. While he saw corruption in images of beauty – 'The Sick Rose' – he could present 'The Tyger' as a symbol of both beauty and terror, of a force that was both destructive and regenerative.

Subsequent poetry showed more obscure influences from a variety of mystical and visionary thinkers. In *The Book of Thel* (1789), in which Blake begins to develop his personal mythology, he experimented with a long free verse line that occasionally rhymed almost incidentally and was rhythmically unpronounced. This became the style of the prophetic books that form the bulk of Blake's writing. This kind of verse, crammed with rhetoric and symbol, could be sombre and powerful, but it sometimes allowed the speed of the narrative to lapse. In the prophetic books Blake used mythological figures, of his own devising but corresponding to the standard mythopoeic versions of the creation and redemption of the world, as vehicles for presenting a closely worked out system of belief. The particularities of his symbolism are often complex, but the tone and texture of his verse suggestively reinforce the meaning. His language combines the lyric, the colloquial and the rhetorical. His figures are both massively larger than life and rooted in elemental concerns. *The Marriage of Heaven and Hell* (1793) is perhaps the richest and clearest of the prophetic books, but they are all elaborations of a vast theme drawn from the Book of Revelation describing man's self-destruction and apocalyptic redemption. His vision, though so complexly and lengthily presented in a manner that was sometimes breathless and stumbling, still retained the

basic elements of the *Songs of Experience* and incorporated his immediate reactions to the world around him – the distortions of middle-class religion, the crimes of the state, the cruelties of society – as well as presenting the necessary means of the world's salvation. Even at his most difficult Blake remained in touch with the ordinary realities of life.

All Blake's prophetic books were etched with illustrations and decorative designs. Though better known as an artist than as a poet his etchings, almost all illustrative – perhaps the most famous are those for the Book of Job (1825) – were of such startling originality that they had little contemporary appeal. He condemned the conventional style of painting that depended on the artificial arrangement of selected details and tried to arrive at a reality of spirit and human development. Apart from the illustrations of his own writing many of his subjects were biblical. The Pre-Raphaelites rediscovered him in the 1850s and acknowledged his influence on their own work, and by the sixties his skill and originality were cautiously recognized. But his art, even more than his poetry, remains unique. [JRC]

The Complete Writings, ed. Geoffrey Keynes (1966); *The Poetry and Prose*, ed. D. V. Erdman and H. Bloom (New York, 1965); *Selected Poems*, ed. F. W. Bateson (1957).
S. Foster Damon, *W. B.: His Philosophy and Symbols* (1924); M. Wilson, *Life of W. B.* (1927; revised edn 1948); Northrop Frye, *Fearful Symmetry* (1947); H. M. Margoliouth, *W.B.* (1951); D. V. Erdman, *B. Prophet against Empire* (Princeton, 1954); Sir A. Blunt, *The Art of W. B.* (1959); P. Fisher, *The Valley of Vision: B. as Prophet and Revolutionary* (1961); H. Bloom, *B.'s Apocalypse* (1963); E. Hirsch, *Innocence and Experience: An Introduction to W. B.* (1964).

Blixen, Karen (Baroness Blixen-Finecke) (1885–1962). Danish authoress who also wrote in English. Born at Rungsted into an aristocratic family, after studying art at Copenhagen, Paris and Rome she married her cousin, Baron Bror Blixen-Finecke, in 1914. Together they went to Kenya to manage a coffee plantation. The marriage was dissolved in 1921. After their divorce she continued to run the plantation until a collapse in the coffee market forced her back to Denmark in 1931. Though she had written occasional contributions to Danish periodicals since 1905 (under the *nom de plume* of Osceola) her real debut took place in 1934 with the publication under the name Isak Dinesen of *Seven Gothic Tales*, written in English. Set largely in 19th-century Europe, their atmosphere is exaggeratedly Gothic. Ornate prose and plots heavy with ritual and mystery combine to produce these exotic, self-parodying melodramas. Most of her subsequent books were published in English and Danish simultaneously, including *Out of Africa* (1938), a warm-hearted and deeply moving epitaph of a period which has now become remote history, and a novel, *The Angelic Avengers* (1947, under the name Pierre Andrezel). *Winter's Tales* (1942), *Last Tales* (1957), and *Anecdotes of Destiny* (1958) and *Shadows on the Grass* (1960) are further collections of stories in which a sophisticated wit is put to work on a tradition of writing that has suffered from the lack of it.

Blocksidge, Charles William. ◊ Baylebridge, William.

Bloomsbury Group. Bloomsbury began as an address for Vanessa and Virginia Stephen, when they moved from Hyde Park Gate to Gordon Square after the death of their father, Sir Leslie ◊ Stephen, and later came to mean a statement of literary and personal values. The establishment of the celebrated coterie (active from about 1907) began when Thoby Stephen introduced his sisters to their future husbands, Clive Bell and Leonard Woolf. Woolf was a member of the exclusive Cambridge society, the 'Apostles', whose bible was G. E. Moore's *Principia Ethica* (1903), although E. M. Forster, a peripheral supporter of Bloomsbury, recently confessed never to have read it. The essence of what Bloomsbury drew from Moore is contained in his statement that 'one's prime objects in life were love, the creation and enjoyment of aesthetic experience and the pursuit of knowledge'. Bloomsbury consisted of Virginia ◊ Woolf and E. M. ◊ Forster (the novel); Vanessa Bell and Duncan Grant (painting); Clive ◊ Bell and Roger Fry (art criticism); Lytton ◊ Strachey (biography); John Maynard Keynes (economics); and Leonard ◊ Woolf (political theory). Both David ◊ Garnett and Desmond ◊ MacCarthy later became closely associated with the group. Bloomsbury was an intellectual aristocracy which could trace itself back to the Clapham Sect – the great-grandparents of

Forster, Strachey and the Stephens had all been members of the Sect – and to the exclusive 19th-century liberal humanists of Cambridge University. One of its members, Clive Bell, denied the existence of Bloomsbury and said that it was just a tag used, mainly in mockery, by outsiders to describe a group of painters and writers bound together by the natural ties of blood and friendship. At no time did the group issue a manifesto or declare its object in the socio-literary manner so common at the time. The approach of the Second World War both justified Bloomsbury's beliefs and threatened them. Keynes had long ago discovered that 'civilization was a thin and precarious crust erected by the will and personality of the very few', and the group was forced to see that it was the abyss, and not merely 'vulgarity', 'convention', etc., which lay beneath this crust. Bloomsbury was really Cambridge in London. [R B]

J. K. Johnson, *The Bloomsbury Group* (1954); Virginia Woolf, *Roger Fry* (1940); Leonard Woolf, *Sowing: An Autobiography of the Years 1880 to 1904* (1960); *Growing, 1904 to 1911* (1961); *Beginning Again, 1911 to 1918* (1964); *Downhill All the Way, 1918 to 1939* (1967); Lionel Trilling, *The Liberal Imagination* (1951); E. M. Forster, *Two Cheers for Democracy* (1951); Clive Bell, *Art* (1914); Quentin Bell, *Bloomsbury* (1968).

Blunden, Edmund Charles (1896–). Poet and critic. Brought up in the Kentish countryside, Edmund Blunden served as a young man throughout the First World War, at the same time publishing his early poems in Sir Edward ◊ Marsh's *Georgian Anthologies*. There are two main strands in his poetry, a deep love for the traditional sights, sounds and customs of the English countryside, deriving much from poets like Hardy, whom he knew, and John Clare, whom he edited, and a feeling of deep malaise deriving from his experience in the First World War. Through much of the 1920s and again in the late 1940s, he taught in Japan and from 1953 to 1964 was Professor of English Literature at Hong-Kong University. He was the Oxford Professor of Poetry in 1967–8. His sympathy with the Far East comes out in a number of his later poems and prose essays. *Undertones of War*, prose memories interspersed with poems, is one of the classic books to come out of the First World War. As a critic and essayist Blunden has been largely concerned with the more elusive figures of the Romantic period, like Leigh Hunt, and with the delights of cricket and country life and landscape. [GSF]

R. C. K. Ensor, intr. to *Selected Poems of E.B.* (1957); H. L'Anson Fausset, article in *Nineteenth Century* (June 1941).

Blunt, Wilfrid Scawen (1840–1922). Poet, travel writer and pamphleteer. Born into an aristocratic Roman Catholic family of Sussex landowners, Blunt entered the diplomatic service at 18 and served as an attaché at embassies in Athens, Constantinople, Frankfurt, Madrid and Paris. In 1863 in Paris he met 'Skittles', a famous courtesan, who inspired much of his best love poetry, published later as *Sonnets and Songs of Proteus* (1875, 1881, 1892) and *Esther* (1892). In 1869 he married Lady Anne Noel and resigned from the diplomatic service. Blunt's poetry is a frank, free-flowing record of his life. Lacking any kind of self-consciousness, it is remarkable for its vigorous colloquial tone and lyrical tenderness, a combination of qualities more often found in Elizabethan than Victorian poetry. In 1875 he paid his first visit to Egypt and two years later he travelled widely in Central Arabia. Always a man of strong temperament and idiosyncratic views, Blunt's travels produced in him a violent reaction against British Imperialism, and the second half of his life was spent in publishing a stream of poems, books and pamphlets championing the nationalist cause in Egypt, India, Arabia and Ireland. He twice tried to enter Parliament but was defeated on both occasions; and in 1887 he spent two months in prison after speaking at a meeting in favour of Irish nationalism, during which time he wrote a sonnet sequence *In Vinculis* (1889). His prose works include *The Future of Islam* (1882), *Ideas about India* (1885), *The Secret History of the English Occupation of Egypt* (1907), *Gordon at Khartoum* (1910) and *My Diaries 1888–1914* (2 vols., 1922). He also wrote many interesting translations of Arabic poetry and a novel in verse, *Griselda* (1893). [PJK]

Edith Finch, *W.S.B.* (1938); M. J. Reinehr, *The Writings of W.S.B.* (Wisconsin, 1940); V. de Sola Pinto, *Crisis in English Poetry 1880–1914* (1951); The Earl of Lytton, *W.S.B.: A Memoir* (1961); Thomas J. Assad, *Three Victorian Travellers* (1964); William T. Going, 'W. S. B.: Victorian Sonneteer', *Victorian Poetry*, II (Spring, 1964).

Boece or **Boethius, Hector** (1465?–1536). Scottish humanist and historian. Boece, a native of Dundee, was successively a student and a teacher of philosophy at Paris, where in the 1490s he formed a lifelong friendship with Erasmus. At the turn of the century he returned to Scotland as a canon of Aberdeen Cathedral and Principal of the new university there, at the request of its founder, Bishop Elphinstone, whom Boece commemorates in elegant humanist Latin in his *Murthlacensium et Aberdonensium episcoporum vitae* (1522; ed. and tr. J. Moir, *Lives of the Bishops of Mortlach and Aberdeen*, 1894). His *History of the Scottish Nation* (1527; prose tr., *The Mar Lodge translation of the History of Scotland*, ed. G. Watson, vol. 1 only, STS, 1946) published like his earlier work at Paris, was promptly translated into Scots prose by John ◊ Bellenden and into verse by William Stewart (ed. W. B. Turnbull, *The Book of the Chronicles of Scotland*, 1858); based on the earlier chronicles of ◊ Fordun and ◊ Wyntoun, it subordinates fact and fable indiscriminately to the overriding aim of glorifying the Scottish monarchy and its ancestry. Boece was awarded a royal pension in 1527. [AI]

W. D. Simpson and J. B. Black, *Quatercentenary of the Death of H. B.* (1937).

Boldrewood, Rolf (pseud. of Thomas Alexander Browne) (1826–1915). Australian novelist. Born in London, he was taken to Australia in 1830 and educated in Sydney. After some years as a squatter in Victoria, he became a Goldfields Commissioner and a magistrate. He was over 40 before he began writing, but was already prolific by 1882, when *Robbery under Arms* was serialized in the *Sydney Mail*. It is a story of bush-ranging, narrated by a convicted and repentant bushranger. His distractingly phoney respect for the law gives room for moralizing, and his admiration for the gang's aristocratic English leader, Captain Starlight, whose exploits, performed with humour in the service of daring, are the book's highlights, allows also the celebration of splendid crime. Browne took his pseudonym, 'Rolf Boldrewood', from Scott who is behind his narrative technique and his romantic characterization. The goldfields novel, *The Miner's Right* (1890), and *Nevermore* (1892), a book about penal life in Australia, are among his better novels. [PT]

C. Roderick, *An Introduction to Australian Fiction* (1950); C. Hamer, 'B. Reassessed', *Southerly*, XXVI, 4 (1966).

Bolingbroke, Henry St John, First Viscount (1678–1751). Politician and political philosopher. Born at his family's seat of Battersea, the son of Sir Henry (later Lord) St John, a Restoration rake, he was educated at Eton. After a grand tour he became an M.P. (1701) and rose by his skill as a speaker and his support of Harley. He was Secretary-at-War (1704–8) and when Harley became Treasurer (1710) he was made Secretary of State, and a peer (1712). In 1714, on the collapse of Harley's ministry, Bolingbroke leading the extreme Jacobite section of the Tories formed a ministry, but the next day Queen Anne died. He was unable to bring in the Stuarts and when George I landed he was impeached, fled to France and foolishly became Secretary of State to the Pretender. He was soon dismissed. From 1716 he lived in France, studying and writing, and was pardoned in 1723, his estates, but not his seat in the Lords, being restored in 1725. Thereafter he lived at his villa of Dawley, near Uxbridge, and produced his most considerable writings. His conversation was said to be most impressive (the original 'Feast of Reason, and the Flow of Soul') and he was a valued companion of ◊ Swift and ◊ Pope. He had considerable ascendancy over the thought of the latter, who based the long philosophical poem, *The Essay on Man*, in part on Bolingbroke's hints. Bolingbroke wrote much for the anti-Walpole periodical *The Craftsman*. His active politics never prospered (he was never personally trusted), and in 1735 he returned to France to live on an estate of his French wife's, near Touraine. His philosophical ideas are a more or less neat, 'gentleman-like' and every-day expression of deism and rational behaviour. His style, once admired, strikes the modern reader as unimpressively rhetorical. His political thinking (the ancestor of some modern Tory ideas) minimizes the clash of principles, and advances a kind of essential 'harmony of interests' between different classes of society. His chief works (anonymously published) were *A Dissertation upon Parties* (essays from *The Craftsman*) (1735); *Remarks on the History of England* (repr. from *Craftsman*, 1743); *Letters on the Spirit of Patriotism: On the Idea of a Patriot King: On the State of the Parties* (1749); *Letters on the Study and Use of History* (1752): *Reflections Concerning Innate Moral Principles* (1752). He left his manuscripts to David Mallet, who published his *Works* (5 vols., 1754; several reissues). [AR]

Walter Sichel, *B. and His Times* (1901; sequel with a bibliography, 1902); Sir C. Petrie, *B.* (1937); D. G. James, *The Life of Reason* (1949); J. Hart, *Bolingbroke: Tory Humanist* (1965); S. W. Jackman, *Man of Mercury* (1965); H. C. Mansfield, *Statesmanship and Party Government: A Study of Burke and Bolingbroke* (1965).

Bolitho, (Henry) Hector (1898–). Historian, biographer and miscellaneous writer. Born in Auckland, New Zealand, as a journalist he roamed the South Seas in 1919, and in 1920 travelled with the Prince of Wales (*With the Prince of Wales in New Zealand*, 1920). In 1921 he became editor of the Sydney *Sunday Times* and the next year came to England. He travelled widely, producing a number of travel books and giving lectures in America. He wrote 2 novels, *Solemn Boy* (1927) and *Judith Silver* (1929), and thereafter became well known as a kind of court biographer of the British royal family, with access to the royal archives and apartments in Windsor Castle. During the Second World War he served as a Squadron Leader in the R.A.F.V.R., publishing various works on the war like *Task for Coastal Command* (1946); his war reminiscences are contained in *A Penguin in the Eyrie* (1955). His biographical and historical work includes *The Letters of Lady Augusta Stanley* (1927; *Later Letters* 1929); *Albert the Good, a Life of the Prince Consort* (1932; a second book, *The Prince Consort*, appeared in 1964); *Victoria, the Widow and Her Son* (1934). His *Edward VIII, His Life and Reign* (1937) was his most popular work and he continued to write about the royal family after the war, with *A Century of British Monarchy* (1951) and *Their Majesties* (1951). [AR]

My Restless Years (1962) (autobiography).

Bolt, Robert (1924–). Dramatist. Educated at Manchester Grammar School and at the Universities of Manchester and Exeter, he was a public-school master before he achieved fame and commercial success with *Flowering Cherry* (1957), a realistic domestic play with symbolic overtones, and with *The Tiger and the Horse* (1960), a drama of moral conflicts set in an Oxford college. His historical play *A Man* *for All Seasons* (1960) presented the story of Sir Thomas More in restrained Brechtian terms. For a time he wrote for the cinema, notably the screen-play of *Lawrence of Arabia*, before writing *Gentle Jack* for production in 1963. This furiously ambitious symbolic play on the conflicting claims of passion and restraint in modern life was outside Bolt's range. *Vivat! Vivat Regina!* (1970) was a popular play about Elizabeth I and Mary Queen of Scots. [MJ]

R. Hayman, *R.B.* (1969); J. Russell Taylor, *Anger and After* (revised edn, 1969); K. Tynan, *Curtains* (1961).

Borrow, George (1803–81). Miscellaneous writer, linguist, bohemian and eccentric traveller. Born in East Dereham, Norfolk, the son of a recruiting officer, Borrow was educated chiefly at Edinburgh High School and in Norwich, where he was articled to a solicitor, but took to writing (contributing to the *Celebrated Trials, New Newgate Calendar*, 6 vols., 1825; revised edn E. H. Beierstadt, 1928) and travelled widely in England, France, Germany, Russia, Spain and the East. His original writings are chiefly formless books, an indeterminate mixture of highly coloured autobiographical fact and equally romantic fiction, based on these travels. In Russia and Spain he was an agent for the British and Foreign Bible Society, an interest which adds a strain of shrill anti-popery and somewhat bogus piety to his work. Borrow's travels allowed him to develop his considerable talents as a linguist, but the 'originality' of his philological speculations does not make up for their lack of systematic observation and thought.

His unorthodox approach did, however, allow him to meet gypsies and other off-beat people with sympathy and write about them with knowledge, zest and understanding. This is the best quality in his writing, together with a fine love of the open road, and has made some of his works long popular. The best known of his books are: *The Zincali; or, An Account of the Gypsies of Spain with a Collection of Their Songs and Poetry – and a Copious Dictionary of Their Language* (2 vols., 1841; several other edns, the best in 1901); *The Bible in Spain*, an account of his travels distributing Bibles in 1835–40 (3 vols., 1843; World's Classics, 1906; intr. Walter Starkie, Everyman, 1961; *Lavengro; The Scholar – The Gypsy – The Priest*, a semi-novel of picaresque adventure, interspersed with strange erudition about gypsies, languages and low life (3 vols., 1851; World's Classics, 1904; Everyman, 1906); and *The Romany Rye* (the title means 'The Gypsy Gentleman'), which is a sequel to *Lavengro* (2 vols., 1857; World's Classics and Everyman, 1906; ed. W. Starkie, 1949). He also produced many translations of ballads, songs and stories from a number of languages, many of which have been reprinted in collections by themselves. [AR]

Complete Works, ed. C. Shorter (16 vols., 1923–4); *The Pocket George Borrow*, ed. Edward Thomas (1912); *Selections*, ed. and intr. H. S. Milford (1924).
W. I. Knapp, *Life, Writings and Correspondence* (2 vols., 1899) (with bibliography); M. D. Armstrong, *G. B.* (1950); B. Vesey-Fitzgerald, *Gypsy B.* (1953); R. R. Myers, *G. B.* (New York, 1966).

Boswell, James (1740–95). Advocate, biographer and miscellaneous writer. Born in Edinburgh, the son of Alexander Boswell of Auchinleck (who as Lord Auchinleck was a judge of the Court of Session of Scotland), James was educated at the High School in Edinburgh, and studied law at the university there, as well as at Utrecht. Under the domineering insistence of his father he practised as an advocate, but he had powerful if vague interests in politics, writing and cutting a dash. This family conflict had a maiming effect on Boswell's personality, manifested as occasional hysteria, melancholy, temporary impotence, lack of resolution, bouts of drunkenness and other uncomfortable traits; but out of the stress grew certain gifts, of perception, frank and sympathetic interest in abnormal behaviour, ability to dramatize scenes of conflict of character, which he put to good use in his writings. Boswell was a man of considerable cultivation and had an intense interest in the human spirit in all its (sometimes bizarre) aspects. He travelled widely in Europe (1764–6), and for complex reasons thrust himself on men of note (such as Voltaire and Rousseau), who yet received him well. In this way, he went to Corsica, then seldom visited, in 1765 and thereafter championed General Paoli, the patriot leader of 'the Brave Corsicans' in their fight for freedom; his *Account of Corsica* (1768) and a less successful sequel (1769) gave 'Corsica' Boswell the European fame he hankered for. He published some juvenile correspondence with the Hon. Andrew

Erskine (1763) and was the author of many anonymous squibs, articles and ephemera, as well as several widely read pamphlets (including an allegorical Spanish tale, *Dorando*, 1767) on the Douglas cause, in which he was retained. Boswell also wrote *The Hypochondriack*, 70 essays (1771–83) written for the *London Magazine*, which are not without interest for their expression of various moods (ed. Margery Bailey, 2 vols., Stanford U.P., 1928; selected as *Boswell's Column*, 1951). All Boswell's other work, however, has tended unjustly to be overshadowed by his masterpiece, *The Life of Johnson* (2 vols., 1791; see below). Thus he has often ignorantly seemed a puzzling case of a man of one very good book. Boswell met ◊ Johnson in 1763, and between 1772 and 1784 he cultivated this friendship on frequent visits to London chiefly in the spring vacations from his advocacy in Edinburgh. In 1788, six years after the death of his father, he removed to London and gave himself up to publishing his great work. Far from producing the great work by accident, he seems to have known very well what he was doing, and his methods of working and writing were elaborate. He sought to give a complete picture of Johnson's life, and to this end he used a remarkable creative art to reduce a mass of material to order and shape. This material is very various: his own conversations with Johnson (often deliberately stimulated to draw Johnson out); documents and letters; and statements from friends. The voluminous journals and papers of Boswell's which survive (now collected at Yale) show the meticulous care, accuracy and ideals which govern his work. They also show that Johnson is frequently more 'Johnsonian' when Boswell has got him into the *Life* than he was in the first notes made after the meeting. Thus Boswell's art and personality joined to produce a work of biography which is a classic of the language. A by-product of the friendship was a remarkable and entertaining travel-book, *The Journal of the Tour to the Hebrides* (1785; ed. from the original manuscript by F. Pottle and C. Bennett, revised edn, 1963; ed. L. F. Powell, Everyman, 1958), which followed a journey made by Johnson at Boswell's prodding, when Johnson was 64. Boswell's last years were unhappy as his character decayed under the stress of melancholy and alcoholism. [A R]

The Life of Samuel Johnson, LL.D. (2 vols., 1791;

'revised and augmented', 3 vols., 1793); revised edn by Edward Malone (4 vols., 1804) (Malone was a strong prompter of Boswell); ed. and annotated G. Birkbeck Hill, revised L. F. Powell (6 vols., 1934–50); ed. R. W. Chapman (Oxford Standard Authors, 1953); ed. S. C. Roberts (2 vols., Everyman, 1949); *Letters*, ed. C. B. Tinker (2 vols., 1924); *The Private Papers* (*B.'s London Journal, 1762–63; B. on the Grand Tour; B. in Search of a Wife; B. for the Defence*; etc., ed., in a 'trade' edn, F. A. Pottle et al., 1950 ff.) (in a 'research' edn, vol. 1, *The Correspondence of J. B. and Johnston of Grange*, ed. R. S. Walker, 1966 etc.).

F. A. Pottle, *The Literary Career of J. B.* (1929; new edn 1966) (with bibliography); P. C. Quennell, *Four Portraits* (1945); F. Brady, *B.'s. Political Career* (1965); F. A. Pottle, *J.B. The Earlier Years, 1740–1769* (1966) (a second vol. to follow).

Bottome, Phyllis (1884–1963). Novelist. Born at Rochester, Kent, the daughter of a New York clergyman and his English wife, she was privately educated in England and America, and attended drama school. In 1917 she married Captain A. E. Forbes Dennis and lived in Austria and England. Her first novel was published by Andrew ◊ Lang in 1901, and she published many others, including *Raw Material* (1905); *Wind in His Fists* (1931; republished in 1948 as *The Devil's Due*), a romantic tragedy set in the Tyrol; *The Mortal Storm* (1937), a violent and dramatic story dealing with the Nazis' rise to power; *London Pride* (1941); *Against Whom?* (1954); and *Eldorado Jane* (1956). Her novels were popular in America, and have been filmed and translated. She was a successful short-story writer, and her collections include *Man and Beast* (1953), 5 stories about the 'relationships between men and animals', and *Walls of Glass* (1958). Her miscellaneous works include *Alfred Adler, Apostle of Freedom* (1939); she drew on personal knowledge of post-war Vienna, and her study of psychology helped to shape her fiction. [A R]

Search for a Soul (1947); *The Goal* (1962) (autobiographies).

Bottomley, Gordon (1874–1948). Poet and dramatist. Born in Yorkshire and intended for a career in banking, he was forced by ill health to adopt a quiet, rural life. An admirer of Rossetti, Morris and Swinburne, he became a minor late Romantic poet. His plays were acted, in the main, by amateurs and by small experimental professional groups. His later short plays on Scottish and supernatural themes were influenced by the Japanese Nō plays and have affinities with Yeats's drama. Bottomley's plays are an offshoot of the Celtic Twilight, and are the work of a genuine, if limited, talent. He wrote a modest defence of his plays in letters and essays (*A Stage for Poetry: My Purposes with My Plays*, 1948), and was co-editor in 1937 of Isaac Rosenberg's *Complete Works*. [MJ]

Poet and Painter: The Correspondence between G. B. and Paul Nash, ed. C. C. Abbott (1955).
C. C. Abbott, Introduction to B.'s *Poems and Plays* (1953); G. Wilson Knight, *The Golden Labyrinth* (1962); K. Wittig, *The Scottish Tradition in Literature* (1958).

Bottrall, Ronald (1906–). Poet. Born in Cornwall of working-class parentage, he went to Cambridge, where he was considered one of the most brilliant poets of a generation which included William ◊ Empson, Charles ◊ Madge and Kathleen ◊ Raine. He contributed prose criticism (including a very interesting article on Ezra Pound's first 30 *Cantos*) to the famous Cambridge critical magazine *Scrutiny* and was hailed by F. R. ◊ Leavis, its chief editor, as one of the most promising younger poets of the early 1930s. Working for the British Council, Bottrall has been its representative in Sweden, Italy, Brazil and Japan, and has also taught for the Council in Helsingfors, Singapore, Florence and Greece. His poetry reflects his wide experience and cosmopolitan sophistication. The earlier poems were much influenced by Pound. [GSF]

Collected Poems (1946); *Palisades of Fear* (1949); *Adam Unparadised* (1954).
F. R. Leavis, *New Bearings in English Poetry* (1935).

Boucicault, Dion (Lardner) (originally Bourcicault) (*c.* 1820–90). Dramatist and man of the theatre. A Dubliner, he was educated at London University, and became an actor. When only 21 he achieved a huge success with *London Assurance* (1841), a 'modern' comedy presented at Covent Garden by Madame Vestris with meticulous and revolutionary attention to realistic detail. He wrote further comedies, and many adaptations from the French of such melodramatic hits as *The Corsican Brothers* and *Louis XI*. He later devised a profitable form of spectacular melodrama in which he combined elaborate mechanical effects with Irish settings: *The Colleen Bawn* (1860) had a cave scene in which the hero saves the heroine from death by drowning at the villain's hands. Like *Arrah-na-Pogue, or The Wicklow Wedding* (1864), and *The Shaughraun* (1875), the play had an effective part for himself in which he gave realism and charm to the stage Irishman. From 1853 he appeared increasingly in New York, where he eventually settled. There he staged *The Octoroon* (1859), which featured the explosion of a Mississippi steamboat; *The Poor of New York* (1857), which showed a house burning down; and his adaptation of *Rip Van Winkle* (1865), long a favourite in the American theatre. *The Shaughraun* was sympathetically revived with charm, wit and pathos by the Abbey Players (Dublin 1967; London 1968). [MJ]

The Dolmen B., ed. D. Krause (1964).
T. Walsh, *The Career of D. B.* (New York, 1915).

Bourchier, Sir John (Lord Berners) (1467–1533). Statesman and author. Grandnephew of the 1st Earl of Sussex, he was probably at Balliol College, Oxford. He succeeded his grandfather as Lord Berners in 1474 and was knighted in 1477. He was concerned in an attempt to put Richmond on the throne, and fled to Brittany, but entered the service of Henry VII in 1492. He was marshal of Surrey's army in Scotland, 1513, and Chancellor of the Exchequer in 1516. He helped to negotiate an alliance between Henry VIII and Charles V in 1518, and two years later was present at the Field of the Cloth of Gold. He was Deputy of Calais from 1520 until his death. A diplomat and courtier, he was also the last translator in the great medieval tradition of chivalric romance and history (an appropriate literary interest for someone who attended the Field of the Cloth of Gold), and he has been judged the equal of Sir Thomas Malory on the strength of his version of Froissart's *Chronicles*, which was issued in 1523 and 1525 (ed. W. P. Ker, 6 vols., 1901–3; reprinted, 8 vols., 1927–8). He also translated the romance *The Boke of Duke Huon of Burdeux* and the less distinguished *Hystorie of Arthur of Lytell Brytayne*. He also made an English version (from the French) of a forged life of Marcus Aurelius. [MJ]

C. S. Lewis, *English Literature in the Sixteenth Century* (1954).

Bourne, Vincent (1695–1747). English Latin poet. He was a Fellow of Trinity College, Cambridge, and afterwards a master at Westminster School. His verse shows a wonderful command of Latin, combined with real poetic feeling. William Cowper, who was a pupil of Bourne at Westminster, admired his poems greatly and translated a number of them into English.

Poemata, ed. J. Mitford (1840) (with a memoir).

Bowen, Elizabeth (Dorothea Cole) (1899–). Novelist. Born in Dublin, the daughter of an Irish lawyer and landowner (her *Bowen's Court*, 1942, is a history of her family and their house in Co. Cork and *Seven Winters*, 1942, contains reminiscences of her Dublin childhood). She was educated at Downe House School, Downe, Kent. She left home in 1918, and lived in London and abroad until in 1923 she married Alan Charles Cameron, thereafter settling near Oxford. She is considered by many to be one of the most distinguished novelists of the present age. As a writer she is tentative, a theorist of fiction, and in her consciousness as an artist has been compared with Jane Austen. She sees the object of a novel as 'the non-poetic statement of a poetic truth' and adds that 'no statement of it can be final'. Her chief characters are women, and the centre of many of her novels is the 'death of the heart' of a sensitive girl or young woman. She is less interested in social observation and more in personal relationships and feeling. The scrupulous care of her writing challenges comparison with Henry James, and with Virginia Woolf, with whom she shares several preoccupations. Her first novel, a tale of loneliness and post-war ennui, *The Hotel*, appeared in 1927. It was followed by *The Last September* (1929), in which the young girl is Anglo-Irish, attempting to cope with the violent world which preceded the 1922 Treaty and with the problems of class. Personal relationships, incomplete and unsatisfying, are the centre of *Friends and Relations* (1931). In *The House in Paris* (1935), she first developed a deeper, tragic sensibility; *The Death of the Heart* (1938), set in London, examines the struggle of the heroine, Portia Quayne, to be a person. *The Heat of the Day* (1949) is a 'war' novel, set in blitzed London, with a rather melodramatic plot. In *A World of Love* (1955), she returns to Ireland; *A Time in Rome*

appeared in 1960. Her latest book is *Eva Traut* (1969), a novel of ironical fantasy, subtitled *Changing Scenes*, told in her usual involved and static style. Elizabeth Bowen is also a very skilful short-story writer and has published 6 collections, including *Look at All Those Roses* (1941) and *The Demon Lover* (1945). *Collected Impressions* (1950) and *Afterthought* (1962) are two books of essays. [AR]

Jocelyn Brooke, *E.B.* (WTW, 1952); W. W. Heath, *E.B.: An Introduction to Her Novels* (U. of Wisconsin P., 1961).

Bowles, William Lisle (1762–1850). Poet and critic. Born at Kings Sutton, Northamptonshire, where his father was the vicar, and educated at Winchester (a pupil of Joseph ◊ Warton) and Trinity College, Oxford. He was made vicar of Bremhill, Wiltshire (1804); prebendary of Salisbury (1804); canon residentiary (1828). His first work, fourteen *Sonnets* (1789; 8 edns by 1805), made him well known. He follows up the melancholy and sentiment of Warton, Goldsmith, and Cowper, though in a watered-down, self-pitying picture of himself as 'the wanderer'. His sonnets, the most accomplished handlings of the form for many years, influenced Coleridge and Wordsworth. Thereafter there was a rash of sonneteering. In 1806 Bowles produced an edition of Pope's works with a Life and critical preface, the patronizing tone of which started a controversy over Pope's merit. ◊ Byron was provoked by Bowles's *Invariable Principles of Poetry* (1819) to write his celebrated *Letters* in defence of the earlier master. Bowles's other poems, some of great length, e.g. *The Battle of the Nile* (1799) and *St John in Patmos* (1833), are now forgotten. He became chaplain to the Regent (1818). [AR]

A Wiltshire Parson and His Friends: The Correspondence of W.B., ed. G. Greeve (1926).

J. J. Van Rennes, *B., Byron and the Pope Controversy* (1927).

Boyd, Mark Alexander (1563–1601). Scottish humanist and poet. Boyd left Glasgow University after trouble with the authorities, fought a duel at court, went to France in 1581 and divided the following ten years between study at Paris, Orleans, Bourges, Lyons and Toulouse and fighting in the confused French civil wars of the time. At Antwerp in 1592 he published a volume of Latin poems and letters and attracted attention by conversing in Greek; he returned to Scotland in 1595, went abroad again as a tutor, and died of fever in Ayrshire. His manuscripts in Latin and French on legal and political topics are in the National Library of Scotland; his only surviving poem in Scots is the sonnet 'Cupid and Venus', notable for treating a Petrarchan theme with unusual sharpness and intensity. A text, with comment, appears in J. Speirs, *The Scots Literary Tradition* (1962). [A I]

DNB; Sir David Dalrymple, Lord Hailes, *Life of M. A. B.* (1786; reprinted in Hailes's *Annals of Scotland*, iii, 1819).

Boyd, Martin A'Beckett (pseud. Martin Mills) (1893–   ). Australian novelist, born in Lucerne, but brought up in Melbourne. His family was distinguished socially and artistically, and in dividing his life and loyalties between Australia and England, Boyd has followed a hereditary pattern. Without completing his architectural studies in Melbourne he enlisted in the British Army at the outbreak of the First World War and was later transferred to the Royal Flying Corps. In 1921 he returned to England, first as a journalist and later as a member of a Franciscan community. He describes his restlessness at this period in the autobiographical *A Single Flame* (1939).

Boyd published his first 3 novels as 'Martin Mills'. Among them *The Montforts* (1928) already presents him as the fascinated chronicler of his family's history. This has been the pattern of his best work, beginning with *Lucinda Brayford* (1946), an Anglo-Australian family saga. In *The Cardboard Crown* (1952), *A Difficult Young Man* (1955), *Outbreak of Love* (1957) and *When Blackbirds Sing* (1962), he restricts himself to describing single areas of the Langton family's history. His main interest is in character. The plots move forward unhurriedly, while the mannered eccentricity of the narrator's style and point of view is modified by the individual eccentricities of his informants, so that attention is artfully divided between story and tellers. Boyd writes elegiacally and with gentle irony about a social class now in decline. [P T]

Day of My Delight (1966) (autobiography).
G. A. Wilkes, 'The Achievement of M. B.', *Southerly*, 2 (1958); Brian Elliott, 'M.B.: An Appreciation', *Meanjin*, XVI, 1 (Autumn, 1957); A. French, 'M.B. An Appraisal', *Southerly*, XXVI, 4 (1966).

Boyd, Zachary (1585?–1653). Scottish Presbyterian divine. Boyd studied at Glasgow, St Andrews and the Huguenot college at Saumur, declining the principalship there to become a minister in Glasgow (1623), where he was later rector and vice-chancellor of the University. An active Covenanter and anti-Royalist during the Civil Wars, he later denounced Cromwell to his face. He produced many sermons, pamphlets and scripture paraphrases, notably *The Last Battle of the Soul in Death* (1629; ed. G. Neil, with biographical sketch of Boyd, 1831), *Four Letters of Comforts* (1640), *The Garden of Zion* (1644) and *The Psalms of David in Metre* (1646), and he was an important member of the committee that in 1648 produced the metrical version of the psalms used ever since in the Scottish churches. [A I]

DNB.

Bradley, Andrew Cecil (1851–1935). Literary critic. Born in Cheltenham, the son of a clergyman, he was educated at the College there and at Balliol College, Oxford, where he studied classics. He was elected a Fellow of Balliol in 1874, and lecturer in English, and later in philosophy. Bradley's work was in line with the platonism, Hegelianism and idealism (both philosophical and general) of Jowett, who was Master of the college, and of T. H. ♢ Green, whose *Prolegomena to Ethics* Bradley edited in 1883. Bradley was appointed to the new chair of Literature and History at Liverpool University College, and in 1889 became Professor of English Language and Literature at Glasgow. He retired in 1900 to London, to write. In 1901, he was elected Professor of Poetry at Oxford, so that his great work *Shakespearean Tragedy* (1904) is a series of lectures; he also published *Oxford Lectures on Poetry* (1909). The book on Shakespeare was long one of the most influential works of criticism in English education. Modern critics frequently use it as a starting point for discussing the framework of Shakespearean criticism, particularly in arguments about whether a theory of tragedy is necessary, or whether the Aristotelian discourse instinctively accepted by Bradley is appropriate and, more recently, in arguments about the true nature and function of a dramatic 'character'. Bradley's position (based on a close reading of the plays) is a romantic, subjective one, carrying on from Coleridge; he treats the dramatic characters as persons, 'human beings with an existence of their own'. This fits in well with his idealist conception of literary art and made his book a powerful teaching instrument. His works have not received close scrutiny (apart from polemic) as an interesting growth of late Romantic literary, philosophical and even political thought. [A R]

Bradley, Katharine Harris. ◊ Field, Michael.

Braine, John (Gerard) (1922–   ). Novelist. Born in Bradford and educated at St Bede's Grammar School there, he had a number of jobs in shops, a laboratory and a factory. During the Second World War he served in the navy (1940–3), and worked in the Bingley Public Library (1943–51), and in the libraries of Northumberland (1954–6) and the West Riding of Yorkshire (1956–7). In the latter year he became a professional writer. His first novel, *Room at the Top*, appeared in 1957, and gained wide popularity (it was successfully filmed in 1959). It is perhaps the classic 'angry young man' novel. The hero, Joe Lampton, is a good illustration of Braine's good and bad qualities as a writer. In the book he is offered a rather schematic choice between 'true' love with an older woman and 'false' love with Susan (through whom Lampton is able to enter the world of wealth and power). Braine surrounds this story with a narrow but deadly accurate account of contemporary northern small-town life, and its preoccupation with money, status and class. The hero chooses success, but the author's point of view is wavering, and this softens the impact of the book. His other novels are *The Vodi* (1959), an account of a tubercular sanatorium patient who has a private delusion of being 'condemned' by alien beings; *Life at the Top* (1962; filmed 1965); *The Jealous God* (1964); and *The Crying Game* (1968). Braine's fiction is important in giving an anti-pastoral view of working-class life (in opposition to that of Richard Hoggart and Raymond Williams): it accentuates the individual will and attacks the 'togetherness' of the crowd. [A R]

Brasch, Charles Orwell (1909–   ). New Zealand poet. Born in Dunedin and educated at Oxford University, after graduating he worked as an archaeologist in Egypt before becoming a teacher of problem children. He was a Civil Servant in England during the war. He returned to New Zealand, and in 1947 founded the important literary quarterly, *Landfall,* which he edited until 1966. *Landfall Country* (1962) is his selection from its first 15 volumes. Brasch is a painstaking poet whose search for a harmony between individual men and their context is openly stated in the allegorical 'words for a mime play' *The Quest* (1946). *Disputed Ground* (1948) collects the tentative poems he wrote during the war. It is a less relaxed book than *The Estate* (1957), in which several poems seem to have resolved the too immediate tensions of his earlier work. Later poems are collected in *Ambulando* (1964). [P T]

Brennan, Christopher John (1870–1932). Australian poet. Born in Sydney into an Irish Catholic family, he attended a Jesuit school and Sydney University, where he took a degree in philosophy. From 1892 to 1894 he studied philosophy and classics in Germany, where he first felt the influence of Mallarmé and other European poets. After his return to Australia he worked at the Sydney Public Library, marrying in 1897 and publishing his first book of verse the same year. Until the appearance of the definitive *The Verse of Christopher Brennan* (1958) his poetry was largely available only in *Poems* (1914). In 1908 he joined the Modern Languages Department at Sydney University, later becoming Associate Professor of German and Comparative Literature. His dismissal in 1925 was partly the result of his growing alcoholism and partly a reaction to the scandal of the divorce proceedings instigated by his wife. During his last desperate years Brennan returned to the Roman Church.

Brennan has strong claims to recognition as a major poet. Appreciation of the complex architectonics of *Poems* demands an understanding of his aesthetic principles and his idiosyncratic use of myth and symbol. Such an understanding has been facilitated by a considerable body of critical commentary and by the publication of *The Prose of Christopher Brennan* (1960). The tensions of his poetry arise from the momentary successes and the overall failure of his search for a poetic and a philosophy able to unify a diversity of actual and imaginative experience. 'The Wanderer' is partly a blank-verse meditation arising from the failed romantic mood of imaginative dejection, and partly the record of a necessary, terrible pilgrimage towards nothing certain. [PT]

G. A. Wilkes, 'New Perspectives on B.'s Poetry', *Southerly*, XII, 1–4 (1952) and XIII, 3 (1953); H. M. Green, *C.B.* (1939); *Southerly*, IX, 4 (1949) (special Brennan issue).

Breton, Nicholas (*c.* 1545–*c.* 1626). Poet, pamphleteer and prose-writer. Son of a London merchant, he was educated at Oxford. He wrote in a variety of genres, and his work included satirical, religious, pastoral and romantic poetry and prose. His best lyrics appear in distinguished company in the finest Elizabethan miscellany, *England's Helicon* (1600), and in his own collection of pastorals, *The Passionate Shepherd* (1604). His verse writings included such volumes as *A Small Handful of Fragrant Flowers* (1575), *The Pilgrimage to Paradise, Joined with The Countess of Pembroke's Love* (1592), *Pasquil's Madcap* (1600; printed 1626), *A Divine Poem: The Ravished Soul and the Blessed Weeper* (1601), *The Soul's Immortal Crown* (1605) and *The Honour of Value* (1605). Among his prose works were *Wit's Trenchmour* (1597), a dialogue on angling which influenced Isaak ◊ Walton, *A Post with a Packet of Mad Letters* (1602), *A Dialogue Full of Pith and Pleasure: between Three Philosophers* (1603), *An Old Man's Lesson and a Young Man's Love* (1605), *The Good and the Bad, or Descriptions of the Worthies and Unworthies of This Age* (1616) and *Fantasticks Serving for a Perpetual Prognostication* (1626), an anthology of observations arranged by seasons and times. [MJ]

Works in Prose and Verse, ed. A. B. Grosart (2 vols., 1879); *Poems Not Hitherto Reprinted*, ed. Jean Robertson (1952).

Bridges, Robert (Seymour) (1844–1930). Poet, critic, editor, anthologist and (until he abandoned his practice in 1870) surgeon. Born in Walmer, Kent, he became British Poet Laureate in 1913 and was awarded the Order of Merit in 1925 but is now best known for his friendship and correspondence with Gerard Manley Hopkins, whose poems, or a selection of them, he edited in 1918, some thirty years after Hopkins's death. Differing deeply in their religious beliefs, the two men were drawn together by their common love of experiment in metrics and their fastidious taste in poetry. A certain remote and literary quality in Bridges' poems has distracted attention from their technical excellence, as has the sane and wholesome but rather tepid and academic attitude to life which they convey. The important volumes are *Shorter Poems* (1890), *New Poems* (1929) and *The Testament of Beauty* (1929). The latter is a long poem in a metre which Bridges invented as something like an English equivalent of Lucretian hexameters, and draws a great deal on the philosophy of Santayana, whom Bridges greatly admired. Bridges also wrote many essays on literature and language in a scholarly and incisive style. He chose, however, to print them in a phonetic script he had invented, which makes them difficult of access to the common reader. He was one of the greatest metrical scholars among English poets, and wrote an important book on Milton's prosody, as well as making many experiments, ingenious if never wholly convincing, in writing classical quantitative metres in English. Standing aside from most of the main currents of change in his age, he is a poet whose technical mastery and honesty of thought and feeling may win him new admirers if a neo-conservative trend in poetic taste sets in. One or two poems, like the famous and beautiful 'London Snow', are anthology favourites. [GSF]

Poetical Works (1953); *Collected Essays* (10 vols., 1927–36); *Poetry and Prose*, ed. J Sparrow (1955) (selection).
W. B. Yeats, Introduction to *The Oxford Book of Modern Verse* (1936); H. W. Garrod, *Poetry and the Criticism of Life* (1931); Francis Brett Young, *R. B.* (1914); J. G. Ritz, *R.B. and G. Hopkins* (1960).

Bridie, James (pseud. of Osborne Henry Mavor) (1888–1951). Dramatist. A Glaswegian by birth and education and a physician by profession, he took to writing plays as 'Mary Henderson' and, from 1929, as 'James Bridie'. His early plays were presented by the Scottish National Theatre, but from 1931, when his play on Dr Knox, Burke and Hare, *The Anatomist*, was produced in London, his pseudonym was also familiar in the West End. He wrote charming, robust biblical and apocryphal plays like *Tobias and the Angel* (1930) and *Jonah and the Whale* (1932) as well as 'plays of ideas' like *A Sleeping Clergyman* (1933), on the theme of heredity, in which a murderess's child becomes a great doctor. *Mr Bolfry* (1943), a debate between a 'Wee Free' Highland minister and the Devil, is one of a series of Scots plays with which Alastair Sim was brilliantly associated as actor and director. The others include *Dr Angelus* (1947), a study of a hypocritical murderer, and *Mr Gillie* (1950), the hero of which is a failed dominie. *Daphne Laureola* (1949), a great commercial success, starred Dame Edith Evans as an eccentric alcoholic. *The Queen's Comedy* (1950) was written for the Edinburgh Festival and is an ambitious work on the Homeric wars.

Bridie wrote over 40 plays and was the first modern indigenous playwright Scotland has produced, Barrie belonging to the London theatre. His outlook, his love of argument, his preoccupation with good and evil were essentially Scots. As a dramatist he was fertile of ideas, and adept at presenting quirky and eccentric characters, and at writing dialogue. He used to say 'Only God can write last acts', and his construction was sometimes wayward. He never established a reputation outside Britain. Bridie was a spokesman on artistic affairs in Scotland, and the founder of the Glasgow Citizens' Theatre. [MJ]

One Way of Living (1939) (autobiography).
W. Bannister, *J. B. and His Theatre* (1955); Eric Linklater, 'B.', in *The Art of Adventure* (1947); H. L. Luyben, *J.B. Clown and Philosopher* (1965); K. Wittig, *The Scottish Tradition in Literature* (1958).

Brittain, Vera (Mary) (1896–1970). Novelist. Born in Newcastle-under-Lyme, Staffordshire, the only daughter of a Cheshire paper manufacturer, she was educated at St Monica's, Kingswood, and Somerville College, Oxford. Her autobiographical volume *Testament of Youth* (1933) records her experiences as a nurse in the First World War and develops her pacifist views; thereafter she lived in London as a freelance writer, marrying G. E. Catlin, the political philosopher, in 1925. She travelled widely in Europe, and lectured extensively in the United States and Canada. She wrote some 25 books. Her first novel, an Oxford story, *The Dark Tide*, was published in 1923 and later fiction includes *Account Rendered* (1945) and *Born 1925: A Novel of Youth* (1948). She is also the author of *Lady into Woman: A History of Women from Victoria to Elizabeth II* (1953). Her autobiographical volumes include *Testament of Friendship* (1940), a tribute to her friend Winnifred Holtby, *Testament of Experience* (1957) and *On Becoming a Writer* (1947). [AR]

Brome, Richard (*c*. 1590–*c*. 1653). Dramatist. He was Ben Jonson's servant before becoming his dramatic disciple in the Caroline theatre. He wrote over 20 plays, which included *The Northern Lass* (1629), *The Weeding of Covent Garden* (1632), *The Late Lancashire Witches* with Thomas Heywood (1634), *The Sparagus Garden* (1635), *The Antipodes*, a clever and entertaining comedy (1638; ed. A. Haaker, 1967), and *The Jovial Crew, or The Merry Beggars*, a gay and romantic play written within two years of the closing of the theatres by the Puritans in 1642 (ed. A. Haaker, 1968). Brome's plays were either romantic comedies or comedies of actual London life with the accent on local colour, social conduct and place-realism, their plots based on intrigue. [MJ]

Dramatic Works (3 vols., 1873; repr. 1966).
R. J. Kaufmann, *R.B.* (1961).

Brontë, Anne (1820–49). Novelist. Born in Thornton, she lived at Haworth, in Yorkshire, and was the sister of Charlotte Brontë. She had only a few months' formal education in 1835, at the school in Roehead, and held two posts as a governess (in both of which she had bad luck with her employers); first in 1839 with the Ingrams at Blake Hall, and later from 1845 with the Robinsons at Thorp Green. She gives a fictionalized account of her experiences in *Agnes Grey* (1847, published with *Wuthering Heights*). Her other novel (*The Tenant of Wildfell Hall, by Acton Bell*, 1848; ed. M. Sinclair, Everyman, 1914) has more interest, but though marked by the Brontë imagination, is more 'literary' and derivative, and has never been very widely read. She contributed verse to the sisters' volume of *Poems, by Currer, Ellis and Acton Bell* (1846). ($\Diamond$ Brontë, Charlotte.) [AR]

Poems, ed. C. K. Shorter and C. W. Hartford (1923).
W. Gémi, *A. B.* (1959) (with bibliography); A. M. Harrison and D. Stanford, *A. B., Her Life and Work* (1959); P. Bentley, *The B. Sisters* (W T W, 1950). ($\Diamond$ Brontë, Charlotte.)

Brontë, Charlotte (1816–55). Novelist. Born at Thornton in Yorkshire, the third child of Patrick Brontë, the eccentric perpetual curate of that parish, and Maria Branwell. An only son, Patrick Branwell Brontë was born in 1817. The family moved to Haworth, a small bleak town in the moors, nine miles from Bradford; the population was partly employed in the local woollen manufacture, and the arrogant parson was kept busy battling strong dissent from the Church of England. The mother died in 1821, and the household was run by her sister, something of a recluse. In 1824, Maria, Elizabeth, Charlotte and Emily went to a school for daughters of the clergy at Cowan Bridge; Maria and Elizabeth died of tuberculosis the same year, and Charlotte and Emily returned home to be educated. Charlotte Brontë incorporates a fictionalized account of the rigours of her school life at the beginning of *Jane Eyre*, and attributes the deaths of her sisters to ill-management at the school. The children were left much on their own. Charlotte, with some assistance from Branwell, chronicled the strange land of Angria, and Emily (at first with Anne) produced the many notebooks of the *Gondal Chronicle*, another romance cycle. The children also wrote plays and magazines. From 1831 to 1832, Charlotte was at school at Roehead, between Leeds and Huddersfield; there she made one or two life-long friends, who appear in various guises in her novels. The Brontës' early education was bizarre. They read newspapers and their father's books, and obviously discussed many topics that interested their elders. The influence of the wild moors where they wandered also gave character to their circumscribed lives but powerful imaginations. Their fiction grew out of this background, but now is often thought a question for the psychologist rather than the literary critic: the problem has had the attention of both. The Brontës had some acquaintance with the arts, in the form of drawing lessons; Branwell, who afterwards died of tuberculosis and drink, was interested in painting and writing. In 1835, Charlotte returned to Roehead as a teacher, and Emily was also there, but could only stand it for a few months; she was succeeded by Anne. In 1836, Emily lived as a teacher for six months at a school in Halifax. The girl's health was poor from incipient tuberculosis. In 1839, Charlotte and Anne tried to make a living as governesses. Branwell and Charlotte wrote to ◊ Wordsworth and ◊ Southey about becoming writers, but got discouraging replies. In

February 1842, Charlotte and Emily went to study at the Pensionnat Héger in Brussels, to prepare themselves to run a school. They returned in November. In 1843, Charlotte taught at the Héger establishment. Her experiences abroad form autobiographical strands in her fiction. She accidentally came across some poems of Emily's in 1845, which she greatly admired. She found out that Anne also had written verse, and at their own expense the three of them published *Poems, by Currer, Ellis and Acton Bell* (1846); it was reviewed in the *Athenaeum*, but sold few copies. Charlotte offered her novel *The Professor* to various publishers in vain. She had taken her father to Manchester to have an operation for cataract; there she received another refusal of *The Professor* and started *Jane Eyre, An Autobiography by Currer Bell*. Smith and Elder refused *The Professor*, but invited her to send *Jane Eyre*, which they published in October 1847; it was at once very successful (repr. 1848, with the dedication to Thackeray; ed. M. Sinclair, Everyman, 1908). In July 1848, Charlotte visited London; in September Branwell died, and in December Emily died; Anne died at Scarborough the following year. *Shirley, A Tale, by Currer Bell* appeared in October 1849. Charlotte lived alone with her father, though in 1849, 1850, 1851 and 1853 she visited London and became known to various writers such as Mrs ◊ Gaskell and ◊ Thackery. *Villette, by Currer Bell* appeared in 1853. *The Professor, A Tale, by Currer Bell* was finally published posthumously in 1857. Charlotte Brontë refused at least three offers of marriage, but in 1854 she overcame her father's objections and married the Reverend A. B. Nicholls, who had been his curate.

Charlotte Brontë's chief difficulty is her urge to force straight autobiography into situations rather implausibly realized. *The Professor* contains a poorly disguised account of her love for M. Héger, and its main interest is biographical. *Jane Eyre* is saddled with stiff dialogue and a melodramatic plot, but it works as a novel because of the force of the author's imagination; it displays the irresistible sweep of passion without any rationalization. The love of Rochester, a married man, for Jane is the focus of almost cosmic significance. The novel had a certain value in introducing the novel-reading public in England to certain human situations such as this, not

Brontë

hitherto used by fiction writers. In *Shirley*, she tries to shift to new ground, and sets her story against the Luddite riots of 1807–12 in the Yorkshire textile industry. There is much discussion of women's rights, though she is not very successful as a novelist of ideas. *Villette* is again more strongly autobiographical; Lucy Snow is a girl consumed by hopeless love, and Paul Emanuel is another Héger-figure. The plot is complicated. Much of the psychological material, too, can be found in the early Angria stories, which are spiritually autobiographical, rather than based on specific events. A sense of the power of dream wishes is found in all the Brontës' writing. Passionate personal integrity is the theme of Charlotte's novels and the fierceness of her insight makes her characterizations succeed against all the penalties of home-made construction. [A R]

The Shakespeare Head Brontë, ed. T. J. Wise and J. A. Symington (20 vols., 1932–40; novels; life and letters; miscellaneous and unpublished writings; poems; bibliography); *Works*, ed. P. Bentley (6 vols., 1949) ('The Heather Edition' of the works of the B. sisters); *Jane Eyre*, ed. J. Jack and M. Smith (Clarendon Edition of the B. novels, 1969–).
Mrs Gaskell, *The Life of C. B.* (1857; ed. M. Sinclair, 1908); M. Lane, *The B. Story: A Reconsideration of Mrs Gaskell's Life of C. B.* (1953); M. Crompton, *The Passionate Search: A Life of C. B.* (1955); Phyllis Bentley, *The B. Sisters* (W T W, 1950) (with bibliography); F. E. Ratchford, *The B.s' Works of Childhood* (1941); R. B. Martin, *The Accents of Persuasion: C. B.'s Novels* (1966); W. Gérin, *C. B.: The Evolution of Genius* (1967); W. A. Craik, *The Brontë Novels* (1968); P. Bentley, *The B.s and Their World* (1969) (pictures); see also *Brontë Society Transactions*.

Brontë, Emily Jane (1818–48). Poet and novelist. Born at Thornton in Yorkshire, the sister of Charlotte ◊ Brontë. In the girls' childhood writings, Emily was the author of the 'cycle' of Gondal. She contributed to *Poems, by Currer, Ellis and Acton Bell* (1846), and hers are by far the best. Her poems are personal and passionate, even mystical. Her imagination resembles that of Blake in power and freedom, but she lacked skill and craftsmanship. Her novel *Wuthering Heights* (ed. and intr. D. Daiches, P E L, 1966) appeared in 1847, attracting little success, but modern criticism would probably rank this most unclassifiable of novels above those of her sister Charlotte, which were more famous in their day, and

have more obvious historical importance. If *Wuthering Heights* is not approached as a 'morbid romance' it can be seen to have a very skilful arrangement. She deals in evil and good, not right and wrong, and the wildness and fierceness of her vision gives her one long work a kind of elemental power not matched in any other novel. The brilliant shifts in focus in the narration, by employing narrators who are themselves engaged in the events, add to the impact of the book. While the reader is involved in the rather claustrophobic atmosphere of the story his attention is securely gripped. There is a powerful allegorical possibility in the work. Heathcliff and Catherine Earnshaw often seem drawn to each other in some non-earthly way. Lockwood is an outsider in some dynamic, occult world. The grim and ever-present Yorkshire moors are a perfect theatre for the action. (◊ Brontë, Charlotte.) [A R]

Complete Poems, ed. P. Henderson (1951); *Gondal Poems* (ed. H. Brown and J. Mott 1938). (◊ Brontë, Charlotte.)
K. W. Maurer, 'The Poetry of E. B.', *Anglia*, 51 (1937); H. Brown, 'The Influence of Byron on E. B.', *MLR*, 34 (1939); M. Willy, 'E. B., Poet and Mystic', *English*, 6 (1946); M. Spark and D. Stanford, *E. B., Her Life and Work* (1953; new edn, 1966); N. Crandall, *E. B. : a Psychological Portrait* (1957); F. R. and Q. D. Leavis, *Lectures in America* (1969); F. Goodridge, *E. B. 'Wuthering Heights'* (1964); J. Hewitt, *E.B.* (1969). (◊Brontë, Charlotte.)

Brooke, Henry (1703–83). Poet, novelist and dramatist. Born in Co. Cavan and educated at Trinity College, Dublin. After a period in London, he retired to Dublin on his private income and produced among other things *Universal Beauty* (1735), a once-admired 'philosophical poem' in couplets, dealing with design in the universe from a Deist, scientific, moralistic angle, and a translation of Tasso's *Gerusalemme liberata* (1738 ff.). His only work to survive in any way is *The Fool of Quality* (5 vols., 1765–70; ed. and abridged John Wesley, 1780; intr. Charles Kingsley, 1859; ed. E. A. Baker, 1906). This is a formless novel, with a somewhat uninteresting 'plot', but it contains curious passages of Rousseauesque discussion, which deal with suffering and constraint, as well as Christian mysticism. [A R]

H. M. Scurr, *H.B.* (Minneapolis, 1927); E. Gillett, 'The Fool of Quality', *London Mercury* xxx (1934).

Brooke, Rupert (Chawner) (1887–1915). Poet, prose-writer, and critic. He acquired a legendary fame because of his good looks, his charm, and the wide appeal of his patriotic poems, particularly the sonnet, 'If I should die, think only this of me . . .', at the beginning of the First World War; his unusual personal beauty and charm had already acquired him a wide circle of friends, including the aged Henry James, Edward ◊ Marsh and through him Winston ◊ Churchill, and the poets of the Georgian school, particularly Lascelles ◊ Abercrombie, John ◊ Drinkwater and Wilfrid ◊ Gibson. Born at Rugby, and educated there and at Cambridge, he seemed an incarnation of everything that was fresh and wholesome in English youth. His death in a hospital ship in the Aegean in 1915, before he had been exposed to the harsh realities of war, as ◊ Blunden, ◊ Sassoon, ◊ Owen and ◊ Rosenberg were, set a seal on his reputation. Later there was an inevitable critical reaction against what seemed an excessive youthful renown and a naïve and sentimental attitude to war, and to life in general.

The critical reaction went too far. Brooke anticipated T. S. Eliot both in his interest in Elizabethan drama, reflected in *John Webster and Elizabethan Drama* (1916), and in his admiration, reflected in some of his own verse, for the passion and ingenuity of Donne and the Metaphysicals. 'Grantchester', one of his most famous poems, verges on sentimental pastoral but saves itself by a delicately poised wit and fantasy. A poem like 'A Channel Passage', with its vivid evocation of sea-sickness, is an experiment in a new kind of poetic realism. He was a much more intelligent, and less naïve, man and poet than those who idealized him thought, and had he survived the war would probably have been numbered among the 'moderns' rather than the 'Georgians'. He was a member of the Fabian Society, with serious social and political as well as literary interests. As a critic, he welcomed new and experimental work, like the poems of Ezra Pound and the paintings of the Post-Impressionists. [GSF]

Georgian Poetry, ed. E. Marsh (1913) (for early poems); *1914 and Other Poems* (1915); *Letters from America* (1916); *Collected Poems*, intr. Sir Edward Marsh (1918); *Prose*, ed. C. Hassall (1956); *Letters*, ed. G. Keynes (1968).
C. Hassall, *R. B.: A Biography* (1964).

Brooke, Stopford Augustus (1832–1916). Theologian, popular critic and miscellaneous writer. Born in Co. Donegal and educated at Trinity College, Dublin, he took orders in 1857 and held various Church of England cures in London, becoming a Royal Chaplain (1867); in 1880 he joined the Unitarians. He published many sermons and theological works, but is now chiefly known for a very influential handbook, *English Literature* (1876; 1896; revised 1901, with additions covering English literature 1832–92, and American literature, by G. R. Carpenter; 1924, with a chapter on literature since 1832 by G. Sampson). This book appeared when English literature was hardly a formal study, yet interested the growing number of adult students. Hence its influence. Brooke saw his study in a 'romantic' light, as being an 'improving' and 'inspiring, national' one (see his *The Development of Theology as Illustrated in English Poetry from 1780–1830*, 1893, and *English Literature from the Beginning to the Norman Conquest*, 1898). [AR]

L. P. Jacks, *Life and Letters of B.* (1917).

Brougham, Henry Peter (1st Baron Brougham and Vaux) (1778–1868). Lawyer, judge, journalist and popular educator. Born in Edinburgh, the son of Henry Brougham of Brougham Hall, Westmorland, and educated at Edinburgh High School and University, he was called to the bar in Scotland (1800) and in England (1808). He gained early notice as a legal and parliamentary orator, and made himself an expert on the slave-trade (as an abolitionist), economics, legal reform and popular education. He was Queen Caroline's Attorney-General (1820) and thanks to his brilliant conduct of her defence in the King's divorce plea, she became a successful martyr (and her triumph a valuable political asset to the Whigs). In the landslide of 1830, Brougham was made Lord Chancellor, but he fell out with his political colleagues and never again held office, though during his term he brought about valuable reforms. He was a man of astonishing energy and diversity of interests, but as far as literature goes, he is best known as the co-founder (1802) with Sydney ◊ Smith and Francis ◊ Jeffrey of the independent Whig ◊ *Edinburgh Review*, for which he displayed his omni-competence in voluminous articles.

He was the author of the article (January 1808) on *Hours of Idleness*, Byron's first publication, in which his deservedly tough handling of the lord's youthful poems provoked *English Bards and Scotch Reviewers*. He was also a leading member of the Society for the Diffusion of Useful Knowledge, a movement which promoted popular education and led to the founding of the Mechanics' Institutes. For the libraries in the latter, he wrote a vast number of popular scientific and historical works, now of no value. Brougham was also one of the founders of London University, for which he campaigned against powerful religious, social and political opposition. His enthusiasm for popular causes made him an easy butt for satire (in part deserved); the best-known caricature of him is as 'the learned friend' in ◊ Peacock's *Crotchet Castle*. His autobiography, *The Life and Times of Lord Brougham* (1871), is his only writing which is now read. [AR]

Works (11 vols., 1855–61; 2nd edn, 1872–3, with bibliography by R. Thomas); *Contributions to the Edinburgh Review* (1856).
F. Hawes, *H.B.* (1957); C. W. New, *The Life of H.B. to 1830* (1961).

Broughton, John Cam Hobhouse, 1st Baron (1786–1869). Politician and miscellaneous writer. The eldest son of a country gentleman of Redland, near Bristol, he was educated at Westminster School and Trinity College, Cambridge, where he became a friend of ◊ Byron's, whom he accompanied on his first travels in the Peninsula and the Levant, publishing *A Journey through Albania and Other Provinces of Turkey* (1813, twice; 2 vols., 1855). He was best man at Byron's wedding, and stuck to him after the separation (see his *A Contemporary Account of the Separation of Lord and Lady Byron*, privately printed, 1870; reprinted in *Recollections*, 2nd edn, see below). He also published *Historical Illustrations of the IVth Canto of Childe Harold* (which had been dedicated to him) (1818), and was Byron's executor. He entered politics in the Reform interest (being briefly imprisoned in Newgate, 1819, for a pamphlet he had written), and later sat for Westminster. When the Whigs came to power he was in the cabinets of Grey, Melbourne and Russell, and was created a peer. His lively memoirs, *Recollections of a Long Life* (5 vols., privately printed, 1865; 6 vols., 1909–11), contain much of interest

about Byron and about the struggle for Parliamentary reform. [AR]

Brown, George Douglas. ◊ Douglas, George.

Brown, Ivor (John Carnegie) (1891–   ). Journalist and writer on language. Born in Penang, the son of a physician, and educated at Cheltenham College and Balliol College, Oxford. He entered the Home Civil Service in 1913, but took up writing and was London dramatic critic and a leader-writer for the *Manchester Guardian* (1919–35), dramatic critic on the *Saturday Review* (1923–30), for the *Observer* (1929–54; Editor of the paper, 1942–8; and Associate Editor, 1948–54), for the *Week-End Review* (1930–4), the *Sketch* (1935–9) and *Punch* (1940–2). He was Shute Lecturer in the Art of the Theatre at Liverpool University in 1926, and Royal Society of Literature Professor of Drama in 1939; in 1940–2 he was Director of Drama for the Council for the Encouragement of Music and the Arts. He has written 4 novels: *Years of Plenty* came out in 1915, and *Marine Parade* in 1932. He is, however, best known as a witty writer on words and their eccentricities. His collections of essays on this topic include *A Word in Your Ear* (1942), and the latest, *Chosen Words* (1955), *Words in Season* (1961) and *Mind Your Language!* (1962). He has also written works on politics, and on Shakespeare, in *Shakespeare* (1949), *Shakespeare in His Time* (1960) and *How Shakespeare Spent the Day* (1963). [AR]

Brown, John (1810–82). Scottish essayist. An Edinburgh doctor and a blameless and attractive character, he published 3 series of *Horae Subsecivae* (1858, 1861, 1882), pleasant enough musings about Scottish characters and places, children and dogs whose immense reputation in their own day now seems difficult to account for. Brown's connexion with the Free Church of Scotland (his father was a famous Lowland minister and some of his essays appeared in Hugh ◊ Miller's paper the *Witness*) and the provincialization of Scottish taste at the time help to explain his local success; his national influence (his friendship with Ruskin and Thackeray and the impetus he gave to the cult of the child-prodigy Marjory Fleming) reflect the vogue of the essay and the (unconscious) relaxed dilettantism of much of the Victorian literary public. [AI]

Letters, ed. J. Brown and D. W. Forrest (1909). J. T. Brown, *Dr J.B.* (1903).

Browne, Sir Thomas (1605–82). Prosewriter. Born in London, he was educated at Winchester and Oxford, and studied medicine at Montpellier, Padua and Leyden, where he took his doctor's degree in 1633. He may have practised medicine briefly near Oxford, where he took the M.D. degree in 1637, the year in which he settled in Norwich. He married, raised a large family, was a distinguished doctor, and became famous in England and abroad as an antiquary and a man of science. The early draft of *Religio Medici* was circulated in manuscript for some seven years before it appeared, twice in pirated editions in 1642 and in the authorized text in 1643. It is a personal, reflective book on religious and philosophical themes. The conclusions are Christian and orthodox, and Browne delights in the paradoxes and mysteries of Christianity. It is in a characteristic prose, occasionally simple, in grander passages elaborately wrought, and often pairing synonyms of classical and Saxon derivation for sonorous or rhythmic effects. *Pseudodoxia Epidemica* (1646), usually known as *Vulgar Errors,* is a contribution to scientific thought, and critically scrutinizes a variety of suppositions and delusions. After an interval he published together in 1658 2 works: *Hydriotaphia, Urn Burial* and *The Garden of Cyrus.* The first is a treatise on burial methods in ancient times, and the second considers the quincunx and the number five in various phenomena. In *Urn Burial* the theme is the transitoriness of the world of man – a traditional theme suited to Browne's learning and to his style. In *The Garden* his concern with analogies and hieroglyphics creates difficulties for the modern reader. *Christian Morals* was not printed till 1716.

Browne corresponded with many of the leading thinkers and scientists of his age. Sir Kenelm ◊ Digby published *Observations upon Religio Medici* in 1643, and John ◊ Evelyn travelled to Norwich 'having a desire to see that famous scholar and physician Dr T. Browne'. Why he never became a Fellow of the Royal Society is a mystery – he may have preferred his seclusion in East Anglia, where in 1671 he was knighted as Norwich's most distinguished citizen. [MJ]

Works, ed. Sir Geoffrey Keynes (4 vols., revised 1964).
Joan Bennett, *Sir T. B.* (1962); Peter Green, *Sir T. B.* (1959); F. L. Huntley, *Sir T. B.* (1962); G. Keynes, *A Bibliography of Sir T.B.* (revised 1968); L. Nathanson, *The Strategy of Truth: A Study of Sir T.B.* (1967); Basil Willey, *The Seventeenth Century Background* (1934); F. P. Wilson, *Seventeenth Century Prose* (1960).

Browne, Thomas Alexander. ◊ Baldrewood, Rolf.

Browning, Elizabeth Barrett (1806–61). Poet. Born at Coxhoe Hall in County Durham, the eldest daughter of Edward Moulton, who assumed the name Barrett when he inherited considerable holdings in the West Indies slave plantations, she was well educated at her father's country house, Hope End, in Herefordshire, learning Greek with a tutor. She began to write verse early, and *The Battle of Marathon* was privately published by her father in 1820. Her father suffered some financial reverses and sold his country estate, and in 1835 the family moved to London. She had injured her spine in a riding accident, which in some way produced an invalid condition that imprisoned her off and on for eight years. She published *Prometheus Bound* (a translation of Aeschylus's play) *and Miscellaneous Poems* (1833; ed. A. Meynell, 1896) and *The Seraphim and Other Poems* (1838). By the time *A Drama of Exile: and Other Poems* appeared in New York in 1845, she was very famous. In this year she met Robert Browning, and on 12 September she married him against her father's will, and they fled to Pisa. She was never reconciled with her family. This was the climax of her legend, which had been growing for years. She was much more famous in her own day than her husband, and her story has passed into common knowledge – the sole companionship of her dog, Flush, her aloofness from literary visitors, her heroine-like debility. From 1847, she lived in Florence. In 1850 her *Poems,* in a new and enlarged edition, appeared in 2 volumes. This issue contained her masterpiece, *Sonnets from the Portuguese,* 44 love poems which she had written in secret before and after she married Browning, who had once called her 'his Portuguese'. This circumstance suggested the title, a slight disguise to cloak the publication of such personal sonnets. In 1851 appeared *The Casa Guidi Windows, A Poem* (the Casa Guidi was where she lived), and in 1856, her long narrative poem, *Aurora Leigh*. She also published, in *Poems before Congress* (1860) and other works, enthusiastic praise of the *Risorgimento*, as well as verse about liberal and humanitarian causes of social protest. These might sometimes have been the subject of prose pamphlets, with more effect. Mrs Browning cultivated spontaneity, after the fashion of the ◊ 'Spasmodics'. Her intensity of emotion is rather grimly exhibited in the treatment she gave her son (born 1849). This emotional pressure leads her into false freedom of technique, empty facility and sloppy thinking. (Napoleon III was a bad bet as a saviour of Italy even as she was writing.) In her *Sonnets from the Portuguese*, however, she achieved a discipline of expression, allied with a profound power of feeling and thinking, which have kept these poems alive. She also wrote miscellaneous essays and critiques, some of which were not published until after her death. A spurious edition of '*Sonnets by E.B.B.* (privately printed, Reading, 1847)' is one of the key issues in the unmasking of T. J. Wise, the bibliophile forger (see J. Carter and G. Pollard, *Thomas J. Wise in the Original Cloth*, revised edn, 1946). (◊ Browning, Robert.) [AR]

Works (Oxford Complete Poets, 1904); *The Poetry of the Brownings*, ed. C. Bax (1947).

R. Hagedorn, 'E. Gosse and the *Sonnets from the Portuguese*', *Papers of the Bibliographical Society of America*, 46 (1952); A. Hayter, *Mrs B.* (1963) and *E.B.B.* (W T W, 1965).

Browning, Robert (1812–89). English poet. Born in Camberwell, the son of a bank clerk, Browning had a sporadic education, mostly acquired at home, where he lived until his marriage. In 1846 he married Elizabeth Barrett ◊ Browning, who at that time was better known. They went to Italy, where Browning lived until his wife's death in 1861. It was not until his return to England that he was widely read, but his reputation finally came to rival Tennyson's. He lived an enthusiastic and relatively untroubled life, as he was able to overlook the social ills of Victorian society and avoided the worried moral concern of more typical Victorian writers.

Browning experimented both in form and content. In 1833 he published 'Pauline', an autobiographical poem influenced by Shelley that was severely criticized. He deliberately abandoned the poetry of direct self-expression, and turned to the dramatic monologue, which he established as a powerful means of poetic statement and investigation of personality. Browning used the dramatic monologue to implant his own ideas and opinions in the context of historical personality and a period atmosphere. He presented both real and imagined characters – painters, musicians, nobility – and manipulated their voices to express the social and domestic flavour of historical reality. He created his own kind of colloquialism not in itself authentic, but convincing in its rhythm and vocabulary as an imitation of speech and action. The result is that Browning's characters have a direct toughness while much of each monologue's background and meaning is only hinted. In 'My Last Duchess' (1842) the fate of the duchess, her personality, the character of the duke, are indicated by brief, vigorous phrases that are unequivocal without being explicit. At his best Browning can present a complicated and convincing explanation of character and action, failure and success, as in 'Andrea del Sarto' (1855) and 'Bishop Blougram's Apology' (1855).

Browning ignored the lush imagery and the imprecision of the Romantics and injected a new vigour into the language of poetic expression. He developed strenuous metres that could accommodate his characters' energetic and irregular bursts of speech. In some ways his excellence in metric innovation and control equalled Tennyson's, and although he did not use such a wide variety of metre, he often used it with more appropriateness. Browning's situations are inevitably static, but his rhythms suggest activity. Although he is at his best in *Dramatic Lyrics* (1842), *Dramatic Romances* (1845), *Men and Women* (1855) and *Dramatis Personae* (1864), he wrote a number of longer poems and verse dramas. His best known, *The Ring and the Book* (1868–9), is in fact composed of a series of long dramatic monologues constructed around a criminal trial of Renaissance Italy presenting the varying points of view of the characters involved. It is a mammoth achievement, but suffers from the verbosity that tainted Browning's late poetry.

Browning found his chief source of inspiration in the late Renaissance in Italy. The combination of luxurious opulence and vicious jealousies with a genuine appreciation and encouragement of art and a prideful religion intrigued him. In later life he gained a reputation as a propounder of calm and optimistic religious belief. When popularity came to him his public enjoyed his untroubled optimism rather than his creative experiments. His interest in the Renaissance had provided channels for the exploration of timeless problems of faith as well as contemporary problems of the position of the artist, but modern discoveries and thought did not interfere with his conviction of the existence of heavenly perfection. Browning's stylistic achievements, his vitality and his boldness, made him a major influence on modern writers. Almost every 20th-century poet who uses the dramatic monologue form, notably Eliot and Pound, owe something to him. His technical innovations and his very real psychological understanding of minds and motives override his vein of complacency and make him perhaps the most extrovertly impressive of the Victorian poets. (◊ Browning, Elizabeth Barrett.) [JRC]

Complete Works, ed. C. Porter and H. A. Clarke (12 vols., New York, 1898); *Complete Poetical Works*, ed. A. Birrell and F. G. Kenyon (1945); *Selected Poems*, ed. James Reeves (1955); *Selected Poems*, ed. K. Allott (1967).
Walter Pater, *B.* (1901); Betty Miller, *R.B.: A Portrait* (1952); J. M. Cohen, *R.B.* (1952); Roma A. King, *The Bow and the Lyre* (1957); R. Langbaum, *The Poetry of Experience* (1957); Park Honan, *B.'s Characters* (1961); P. Drew, *B.: A Collection of Critical Essays* (1966); R. D. Altick and J. F. Loucks, *B.'s Roman Murder Story: A Reading of the Ring and the Book* (Chicago, 1968).

Bruce, Michael (1746–67) and **Logan, John** (1748–88). Minor Scottish verse-writers. They were subjects of a disproportionately prolonged controversy about the authorship of a negligible ode, 'To the Cuckoo'. Bruce, the son of a poor weaver in Kincardineshire, struggled through Edinburgh University and died of consumption at 21 while training for the ministry of the Secession Church. Logan, his college friend and a Church of Scotland minister in Leith, edited and published Bruce's manuscripts in 1770, and in 1781 published under his own name poems which Bruce's relations asserted were by Bruce. The question is unlikely to be settled, but has evoked one book or rival edition every decade for the past century; a full and fair, though still

inconclusive, discussion can be found in T. G. Snoddy's *Michael Bruce* (1947). Logan's talents, certainly, lay in editing and amending; he wrote some of the best of the metrical paraphrases now used by the Church of Scotland (although those too have been claimed for Bruce) and his best poem, 'The Braes of Yarrow', is a pastiche of popular ballads. His tragedy *Runnamede*, presented in Edinburgh in 1783, indicates his comparatively advanced political opinions; less fortunate than John ◊ Home, Logan was driven from his charge at Leith under a cloud of scandalous allegations, and spent the rest of his life in London as a pamphleteer and historical writer. [AI]

DNB.

Bryce, James, 1st Viscount (1838–1922). Politician and historian. Born in Belfast and educated at the High School and the University of Glasgow, Trinity College, Oxford and Heidelberg. He was called to the bar (1867), but in 1880 entered politics and became one of Gladstone's chief lieutenants in his third (Home Rule) ministry. Bryce later held various offices, including Chief Secretary for Ireland (1905–6) and Ambassador to the U.S.A. (1907–13). He made an impression early with his clever *Holy Roman Empire* (1864), a piece of orthodox 'political' history: he was Regius Professor of Civil Law at Oxford (1870–93). His classical 'institutional' study *The American Commonwealth* first appeared in 1888. Bryce wrote a number of other works which show alert observation and wide interests, including *Trans-Caucasia and Ararat* (1877); *Impressions of South Africa* (1897); *South America: Observations and Impressions* (1912); *Modern Democracies* (1921). [AR]

H. A. L. Fisher, *J. B.* (2 vols., 1927); A. J. Toynbee, *Acquaintances* (1967); E. S. Ions, *J. B. and American Democracy, 1870–1922* (1968).

Brydges, Sir Samuel Egerton (1762–1837). Bibliographer, antiquarian and novelist. Educated at the King's School, Canterbury, and at Cambridge, he was called to the bar (1787) but never practised. He was created a baronet (1814) and died in Geneva. The author of many poems, moral romances and miscellaneous works, he is best known for his bibliographical works such as *Censura Literaria: Containing Titles, Abstracts and Opinions of English Books* (10 vols., 1805–9; and 1815) and *The British Bibliographer* (4 vols., 1810–14). He reprinted and edited or excerpted many rare early books from his collections, and was the author of several genealogical works. [A R]

M. Woodworth, *The Literary Career of Sir S. E. B.* (1935) (with bibliography).

Buchan, John (1st Baron Tweedsmuir) (1875–1940). Imperial statesman and writer of adventure stories. Born in Perth, the son of the Rev. John Buchan, a minister in the Free Kirk. He was educated at Hutcheson's Boys School, Glasgow, Glasgow University, and Brasenose College, Oxford, where he was President of the Union and won prizes for poetry and history. He failed to gain a fellowship, and was called to the bar at the Middle Temple (1901), but spent the next two years in South Africa as secretary to Lord Milner, who was reorganizing the administration after the Boer War. As one of Milner's young men, Buchan became a convinced imperialist. His career as a writer was begun as a student, and continued seriously as a member of the publishing firm of Nelson. Two autobiographical novels of African adventure were his first tries at fiction. *Prester John* (1910) began the long series of the adventure stories for which he is now famous; others are *The Thirty-Nine Steps* (1915; the basis of an early, influential Hitchcock film), a story of German spies in England; *Greenmantle* (1916), involving portentous anti-imperial movements and their frustration in the Near East during the war; *The Power-House* (1916); *Mr Standfast* (1919); *Huntingtower* (1922), an adventure yarn set in the Scottish countryside and introducing his group of Glasgow boys; and *The Three Hostages* (1924). Many of these books are still in print. During the First World War he was a newspaper correspondent in France, an intelligence officer, and later Director of Information; he wrote a lengthy history of the war. Buchan was a lively and tendentious historical writer, best in dealing with a single man who captured his rather sentimental imagination but also writing vividly about military campaigns: his *Marquis of Montrose* (1913; revised 1928), *Walter Scott* (1932) and *Cromwell* (1934) are examples. Buchan was an athletic man who delighted in climbing and walking. This gives his adventure stories well-realized settings and physical excite-

ment. He tells a yarn with economy. The implications of his social and political ideas, conscious and unconscious, are less admirable, and for all his intelligence connect his fiction with that of writers of popular stereotypes like Sax ◊ Romer. In 1927, he was elected (Conservative) M.P. for the Scottish Universities, and in 1935 was given a peerage on being appointed Governor-General of Canada, the summit of his imperial activities. His life of George V, *The King's Grace: 1910–1935*, appeared in 1935. [A R]

Memory Hold-the-Door (1940) (autobiography). 'O. Douglas' (Anna Buchan), *Unforgettable, Unforgotten* (1945); J. Adam Smith, *J.B.* (1965); Susan C. Buchan, *J.B.: By His Wife and Friends* (1947); A. Hanna, *J.B.: A Bibliography* (1953); R. Usborne, *Clubland Heroes: A Nostalgic Study of Some Recurrent Characters in the Romantic Fiction of Dornford Yates, B. and 'Sapper'* (1953).

Buchanan, George (1506–82). Scottish humanist and historian. As a student at St Andrews, Buchanan revolted against the traditional philosophical teaching of John ◊ Major. After ten years of teaching at Paris (1526–36) he returned to Scotland as tutor to a bastard son of James V, but his satires on the Franciscans forced him to flee again to the continent, where he spent the following twenty years as a university teacher and a private tutor. At Bordeaux he taught Montaigne (1540–3) and at Coimbra in Portugal he was imprisoned by the Inquisition for heresy (1550–2). During this period he wrote most of his Horatianizing Latin verse paraphrase of the Psalms, long a standard text in Scottish schools. In 1561 he turned Protestant and returned to Scotland, where for some time he contrived to be simultaneously Poet Laureate to the Catholic queen and an important ally of John ◊ Knox in Church affairs and educational reform. After the murder of Darnley, Buchanan's polemic *Detectio Mariae Reginae* was of decisive importance in the dethronement of Mary Queen of Scots. From 1570 to 1578 Buchanan was tutor to the infant ◊ James VI, and in his last years he compiled a voluminous and partisan *History of Scotland* (1582; selections tr. and ed. W. A. Gatherer, *The Tyrannous Reign of Mary Stuart,* 1958). In spite of his political offices, he died penniless.

Apart from a few pamphlets and letters (*Vernacular Writings,* ed. P. H. Brown, S T S,

1892) all Buchanan's work is in Latin, and much of it demonstrates the inhumanity which the secondary 'humanist' culture, based exclusively on mastery of Latin style and Ciceronian rhetoric, manifested under the stresses of the Reformation. Even Buchanan's poetry, the most attractive and lasting part of his Latin writings, seldom quite avoids the taint of the conventional exercise; in his 'biblical tragedies' *Baptistes* and *Jephtha* (both written about 1541 but published in 1554 and 1578 respectively; Scots tr. R. G. Sutherland, 1959; tr. A. Brown, 1906) Buchanan's own temperament helps him to exploit the grim and statuesque effect inherent in his material. Buchanan's prestige helped to establish his austerity and authoritarianism as a pattern for Scottish education and culture down to the 19th century. [A I]

Opera omnia, ed. T. Ruddiman (1715); *The Powers of the Crown in Scotland*, tr. C. F. Arrowood (Austin, Texas, 1949) and *The Art and Science of Government among the Scots*, tr. with commentary by D. H. McNeill (1965) (versions of B.'s chief political work, *De jure regni apud Scotos*, 1579); *The Sphera of G.B.*, tr. with commentary by J. R. Naiden (1952) (an anti-Copernican poem on astronomy).
P. H. Brown, *G.B.*, *Humanist and Reformer* (1890); *G.B.: Glasgow University Quatercentenary Studies* (1907) (reprints a translation of *Baptistes* attributed to Milton).

Buchanan, Robert Williams (1841–1901). Poet, novelist, critic and playwright. Born in Staffordshire, the son of a Scottish socialist, and educated at Glasgow. He had some success with his poems, particularly his third volume, *London Poems* (1866), and (among later volumes) *Ballads of Life, Love and Humour* (1882). In *The Outcast, A Rhyme for the Time* (1891) and *The Wandering Jew, A Christmas Carol* (1893), he developed his anti-Christian views; and altogether had some power in expressing contemporary feelings of religious and social revolt. He wrote more than a score of novels, none of which have lived, and some plays, of which *Alone in London* (1884) had some success. Buchanan held strong views on the poet's role as a seer (he was an early admirer of Whitman) and is best known for involving himself in a quarrel with ◊ Rossetti (and Swinburne), through writing a cruel critique on Rossetti's *Poems* in the *Contemporary Review* for October 1871 (reprinted separately as *The Fleshly School of Poetry*, 1871). Buchanan's talent was

thought to be spoiled by a cantankerous temper. [A R]

Complete Poetical Works (2 vols., 1901).
H. Jay, *R.B.* (1903) (with bibliography); J. A. Cassidy, 'B. and the Fleshly Controversy' *PMLA*, LXVII (1952).

Buckingham, Duke of. ◊ Villiers, George.

Buckle, Henry Thomas (1821–62). 'Philosophical' historian. Born at Lee in Kent, the son of a wealthy shipowner, he was privately educated, and devoted himself to a life of travel and study. His leisure, knowledge of languages and cast of mind led him to attempt a vast *History of Civilization in England*, of which only the first two volumes were completed (1857–61; World's Classics, 1903–4; ed. J. M. Robertson, 1904). In this introduction to his projected work, Buckle attempts the difficult task of making historical generalizations from his vast reading (in the manner of Toynbee) along the lines of a belief in impersonal 'laws', and a 'more scientific approach' to the part played by physical surroundings in the 'progress' of human development. The first volume is a preliminary consideration of different nations and ages to illustrate his principles; and the second volume includes an application of these principles to a history of 18th-century Scottish culture. Buckle had considerable influence as a historian. [A R]

J. M. Robertson, *B. and His Critics* (1895); G. St Aubyn, *A Victorian Eminence* (1958).

Buckley, Vincent (1925–   ). Australian poet and critic. Born in Victoria, he was educated at a Jesuit school in Melbourne and at Melbourne University, where he is a lecturer in English. During the war he served with the Australian Air Force. His Roman Catholicism directs the choice of imagery and subject in his predominantly religious poetry. Formally and thematically he makes great demands on himself, lapsing into obscurity, particularly in *The World's Flesh* (1954), when he fails to meet them. *Masters in Israel* (1961) is much less uneven than the earlier collection, though the longer meditative poems continue the tendency to achieve depth at the cost of momentum. Buckley is an incisive and influential critic of Australian literature. In addition to many articles in periodicals he has written *Essays in Poetry: Mainly*

Australian (1957) *Poetry and Morality* (1959), and *Poetry and the Sacred* (1968). [P T]

Arcady and Other Places (1966).
P. Curtis, 'V. B. as Poet', *Quadrant*, 24 (Spring, 1962).

Budgell, Eustace (1686–1737). Essayist. He contributed over 30 essays to the *Spectator*, rather in the style of his cousin, Addison; among his other miscellaneous writing was a successful translation of Theophrastus. After he lost his government job in Ireland, considerable losses in the South-Sea Bubble unsettled his wits and caused him to behave outrageously. After long lawsuits he drowned himself in the Thames. [A R]

Bulwer Lytton, Edward George. ◊ Lytton of Kenilworth.

Bunyan, John (1628–88). Allegorist. Born at Elstow, near Bedford, the son of a tinker; after a brief education he was apprenticed to his father's trade. He served in the Parliamentary army, 1644–6, and in the latter year married a poor woman, among whose few possessions were two popular Puritan religious works: Dent's *The Plain Man's Pathway to Heaven,* and *The Practice of Piety*. Thereafter followed for Bunyan a time of spiritual torment and oppression of guilt; he had been formerly a swearer and causeless ringer of the church bell. After the death of his wife in 1656, he experienced a spiritual enlightenment and became an itinerant preacher, finally settling as the leader of a Baptist meeting in Bedford. At the Restoration, he was imprisoned for contumaciously preaching without the bishop's licence, and spent the next twelve years in prison. He had married a second time, and he supported his family by making metal lace tags. In prison he constantly studied the Bible, ◊ Fox's *Book of Martyrs* and other Puritan literature; he himself wrote many books and pamphlets, such as *A Few Sighs from Hell* (1658). His first substantial work was a spiritual autobiography of a kind common among his co-religionists, *Grace Abounding to the Chief of Sinners: or, A Brief and Faithful Relation of the Exceeding Mercy of God in Christ to his Poor Servant, John Bunyan* (1666; ed. E. Venables, revised M. Peacock, 1900; Everyman, 1928). In 1675, while again imprisoned for six months, he wrote his most famous book, *The Pilgrim's Progress from This World, To That Which Is to* Come; *Delivered under the Similitude of a Dream. Wherein is Discovered, the Manner of His Setting Out, His Dangerous Journey, And Safe Arrival at the Desired Country* (1678, and a second part, 1684; ed. J. B. Wharey, revised R. Sharrock, 1960; with an afterword by F. R. Leavis, New York, 1964; ed. R. Sharrock, P E L, 1966). Christian, the pilgrim, Mr Worldly Wiseman, Giant Despair, Hopeful and Ignorance are engaged in powerfully dramatic movement against a solidly realized background of town and country, spiced with Bunyan's acute and satirical perceptions of the 'Vanity Fair' of his own society. The book has been read in many ways; for its religious doctrine, for the power of its narrative episodes, for the realism of its dialogue and as a historical document. For more than two hundred years almost every English writer read Bunyan's plain, pithy prose, and the influence of the book, direct and indirect, on English fiction was great, though impalpable. *The Life and Death of Mr Badman* (1680) is a series of narrative episodes, again utilizing the popular fiction of the day and skilfully handled, set in a long-winded dialogue between Mr Wiseman and Mr Attentive. *The Holy War . . . or, The Losing and Taking Again of the Town of Mansoul* (1682) treats salvation in an allegorical structure more complicated than *The Pilgrim's Progress*, with political and social overtones; it develops an interesting account of the psychology of religious conversion. Bunyan's writings, for all their complexity, were very popular, and, with the Authorized Version, almost the sole reading matter for many over a long period. He uses the ingenious allegorizing of the popular preachers, and to a tough theological mind unites one of the greatest talents in English literature. Many 19th-century pundits wrote on Bunyan (see, for instance, Macaulay's *Biographical Sketches*). [A R]

Works (1692) (vol. 1 only; no more printed); *Works*, ed. G. Offor (3 vols., 1852); ed. H. Stebbing (4 vols., 1859).
G. B. Harrison, *J.B.: A Study in Personality* (1928); H. Talon, *B.: l'homme et l'œuvre* (1948; tr. *B., the Man and His Works*, 1951); R. Sharrock, *B.* (1954); F. M. Harrison, *Bibliography of the Works of B.* (Bibliographical Society, 1932).

Burgess, Anthony (1917–   ). Novelist and journalist. Born John Burgess Wilson in Manchester, he was educated at Xaverian

College and Manchester University, served in the army 1940–6, and has held various teaching jobs, lecturing mainly in English literature and phonetics. From 1954 to 1959 he served as an education officer in Malaya and Borneo, during which time he wrote a trilogy of novels set in Malaya, *Time for a Tiger* (1956), *The Enemy in the Blanket* (1958) and *Beds in the East* (1959). An incredibly prolific novelist with a fertile imagination and an obsessive interest in word-play, speech patterns and religious symbolism, his novels are often very funny, but deeply felt, criticisms of contemporary society. They include, *The Doctor is Sick* (1960), *The Worm and the Ring* (1961), *Devil of a State* (1961), *A Clockwork Orange* (1962), *The Wanting Seed* (1962), *Honey for the Bears* (1963), *The Eve of St Venus* (1964) and *Inside Mr Enderby* (1966). He has also written *Nothing like the Sun* (1964), a fictional re-creation of Shakespeare's love life; *Here Comes Everybody* (1965), an introduction to James Joyce for the ordinary reader; and *The Novel Now* (1967), a student's guide to contemporary fiction. He is as prolific a journalist as novelist and contributes articles and book reviews to many periodicals. [P J K]

Christopher Ricks, 'The Epicene', *New Statesman*, LXV (5 April 1963); Julian Mitchell, 'Anthony Burgess', *London Magazine*, III (February 1964).

Burke, Edmund (1729–97). Political writer and orator. Born in Dublin, the second son of an Irish Protestant lawyer and his Catholic wife, he was educated at the Quaker school in Balitore kept by Abraham Shackleton, whom all his life after he revered. Without doubt the breadth of his early education strongly influenced him towards the toleration, humanity and generous sympathy which can be seen in his later championing of the Irish Catholics, American colonists and native inhabitants of British India; to the same source may be traced part of the caution he displayed in his long struggle with the problem of the French Revolution. On 14 April 1744 he entered Trinity College, Dublin, and in 1750 he was admitted to the Middle Temple in London, where his father sent him to study law, but he was never called to the bar, and he later attacked the narrowing tendency of contemporary legal education. He was much more interested in writing. In 1756 appeared his first 2 works: *A Philosophical*

Enquiry into the Origin of Our Ideas of the Sublime and the Beautiful (ed. and intr. J. T. Boulton, 1958) and *A Vindication of Natural Society*. The *Enquiry*, which Burke had been writing for some years, is a rather jejune work, yet, carrying on the shift of critical interest into the psychological cause (in the author) and effect (in the audience) of a work of art that was characteristic of the age, it was a work of considerable influence on such writers as Kant. It also shows one of the permanent considerations of Burke's political thought, the study of the nature of man himself. The *Vindication* is a parody of what Burke considered the too-schematic political theories of ◊ Bolingbroke, whose works had appeared in 1754. Burke married in 1757, and to support his family became the editor of Dodsley's new project, *The Annual Register* (1758; still in progress), designed to give a review of important events and the writing of each year. In this, until he gave up contributing in 1788, Burke indulged his wide-ranging curiosity and vast knowledge, for which Dr Johnson, ◊ Reynolds and the other members of the Club valued him; he was a founder member of this group in 1764. He became secretary to the Marquis of Rockingham (then briefly Prime Minister), who brought him into Parliament that year as M.P. for Wendover. He was a leading member of the 'constitutionalist' opposition group known as the 'Rockingham Whigs', who considered themselves the upholders of the Glorious Revolution of 1688. Apart from a few months' office as Paymaster General in 1782 (when Rockingham was again for a short time in power), Burke spent his parliamentary career (1765–94) in opposition. His first speech, in 1766, was characteristically on America; he consistently opposed the fatal American policies of Lord North's administration; and this topic was the subject of 2 of his greatest political writings, *Speech on American Taxation* (1774) and *On Conciliation with the Colonies* (1775). Another (but related) concern was his opposition to the growing influence of the crown under George III, which culminated in the King's unsuccessful attempt at 'personal government'. Burke's views on parties and the legalistic side of his theories are developed in his first major political work, *Thoughts on the Present Discontents* (1770). His support for the Americans, even after they took up arms, coupled with his views on the nature of parliamentary

75

representation and his plea for practical and expedient measures, is again the subject of his *Speech on the Address to the King* (1777) and his *Letter to the Sheriffs of Bristol* (1777). He had been M.P. for Bristol since 1774, but the merchants of that western port objected to his American views and wished to throw him out. Other political questions (all Bristol concerns) which exercised him were Irish trade (where he thought the parliamentary majority's views oppressive of the Irish) and the slave trade (which he thought inhumanely conducted). His conservatism was displayed in his conduct in the controversy over parliamentary reform; he advocated a plan for the reform of the civil establishment to prevent corruption (i.e. bribery by the crown) but opposed Fox's bill (1782) as being too radical and too rushed. A great part of his political career was devoted to the problem of India. The East India Company, an organization set up for profit, was being forced to play a political role by the collapse of the Moghul empire. Burke and others thought that a more responsible way ought to be found of dealing with the 'governed' in India. This vast and complex subject (geographical, political, sociological, financial, religious and administrative) fascinated Burke.

He was master of almost all accessible writing on it, and his own works show in this instance perhaps his greatest powers of digestion and comprehension. His *Speech on Mr Fox's East India Bill* (printed 1784) advocated the transfer of the Company's powers to the Government, and his *Speech on the Nabob of Arcot's Debts* (1785) continued his campaign. Burke also took the lead in the impeachment of Warren Hastings (*Articles against Warren Hastings*, 1786); during the long-drawn-out trial (Hastings was acquitted on 23 April 1795), Burke spoke interminably and his summing-up lasted nine days. The final great political theme of his public career, which obsessed him for the rest of his life, was his opposition to the doctrines of the French Revolution. The famous *Reflections on the Revolution in France* (1790; ed. and intro. Conor Cruise O'Brien, P E L, 1968) is a formal explanation at some length of his own views, and it suffers, as does all his writing on this topic, from too much rhetorical sail, and too little ballast of information. Thus he fails just where he succeeded most brilliantly in his earlier writing. By this time he was not really arguing for practical ends, but developing

a wide-ranging theory and defending his own beliefs. Other writings that succeeded the *Reflections* (answered in Tom ◊ Paine's *Rights of Man*) were the *Letter to a Member of the National Assembly* (1791); *Appeal from the New to the Old Whigs* (1791), which acknowledges his political isolation; and *Letters on a Regicide Peace* (1796). The value of his conservative thinking on the Revolution is the attention paid to the psychological facts of man's existence in societies; this concern springs from his powerful moral imagination. The failure is a lack of consciousness of his own point of view. He sees himself a 'legislator' with people to legislate 'for'. His doctrine of history as 'the tragic past' lies behind all his views. Burke as a political theorist is always stimulating; his oratory, the 'classic eloquence' so beloved of his own day, does not read so persuasively now. It is most successful in the famous *Letter to a Noble Lord* (the Duke of Bedford) (1796), a personal apologia, where it appears frankly as what it is, a theatrical act. The self-indulgence is decorative and amusing. Burke grapples with the great moral questions of power and subjection, and illuminates them with humanity and imagination, whatever may be thought of his own views. The sprawling body of particular knowledge which he brought to these questions was of great immediate political value, but is now somewhat forbidding. It is the bulk, detail and breadth of his writing that prevents him being successfully taken over as the mouthpiece of unthinking conservatism. [A R]

Works, ed. F. Laurence and W. King (8 vols., 1792–1827); ed. W. Willis and F. W. Raffety (6 vols., World's Classics, 1906–7); *Burke's Politics* (New York, 1949) (selections); *Selected Writings*, ed. and intr. W. J. Bate (Modern Library, 1960); *Correspondence*, ed. T. W. Copeland et al. (10 vols., 1958 ff.).

T. W. Copeland, *Our Eminent Friend E. B.* (1949); C. B. Cone, *B. and the Nature of Politics* (2 vols., 1957, 1964); F. P. Canavan, *The Political Reason of E. B.* (Duke U.P., 1960); F. L. Lucas, *The Art of Living* (1959); H. C. Mansfield, *Statesmanship and Party Government: B. and Bolingbroke* (Chicago, 1965); G. W. Chapman, *E.B.: The Practical Imagination* (1967); W. B. Todd, *Bibliography* (1964).

Burnet, Gilbert (1643–1715). Cleric and historian. The son of an Edinburgh advocate, he was educated at Aberdeen, Paris and Amsterdam and influenced by meeting the Cambridge platonists. He was ordained in the Church of Scotland; became Divinity Professor at Glasgow (1669) and a royal chaplain. He refused the bishopric of Edinburgh and went to London, working to reconcile Presbyterians and Episcopalians, but lost Charles II's favour by remonstrating with the King about his dissolute life; he fled to Holland (1683–8), where he became intimate with William of Orange, who on becoming king made him Bishop of Salisbury. Among Burnet's works, the most important are: an edifying 'rationalist' account of the death-bed repentance of Rochester, *Some Passages in the Life and Death of . . . Rochester* (1680); a 3-volume 'latitudinarian' *History of the Reformation in England* (1679, 1682, 1714); and *History of His Own Time* (posthumously by direction; 1724, 1734; ed. M. J. Routh, 1833; ed. O. Airy, vols. 1 and 2 only, 1897–1900). The latter is valuable as a lively eye-witness account, written with a quaint egotism by a quick rather than a profound mind. [A R]

T. E. S. Clarke and H. C. Foxcroft, *Life* (1907).

Burnet, Thomas (*c.* 1635–1715). Prosewriter. Educated at Clare Hall, Cambridge, and Fellow of Christ's College, he travelled abroad as a tutor and became Master of the Charterhouse (1685). His chief work is his *Sacred Theory of the Earth* (Latin, 1681; English 1684; ed. and intr. B. Willey, 1965). This book, with its sequel *De conflagratione* (1689; tr. 1690), is a fanciful, romantic cosmogony, organized with the Flood as the great past event, and the conflagration as the great future. It is interesting as an attempt to combine a style which affected the great magnificence of the obsolescent manner of Sir Thomas ◊ Browne, with the scientific discoveries and speculations (particularly in physics, astronomy and geology) of the later 17th century. He also published *Remarks* on Locke's *Essay Concerning Human Understanding*. [A R]

D N B; H. V. S. Ogden, 'B.'s *Telluris theoria sacra* and Mountain Scenery', *E L H*, 14 (1947).

Burnett, Frances Hodgson (1849–1924). Novelist and children's writer. Frances Hodgson was one of the five children of a Manchester manufacturer. The family became very much poorer when the father died, and the poverty of a family that had once been well-to-do later became one of her favourite themes. In 1865 the Hodgsons emigrated to America, where Frances earned all she could by writing poems, novelettes and stories. Her first novel, *That Lass o' Lowrie's* (1877), is about working-class life in Manchester, for she had a capacity for noting details quickly and remembering them for long periods. She married Dr Swan Burnett in 1873, and their second son, Vivian, a remarkably graceful, well-mannered child, was the original for the character of Fauntleroy in *Little Lord Fauntleroy* (1885). She returned to England after this book had made her reputation, but suffered strokes of personal ill-fortune in her divorce from Dr Burnett, the failure of her second marriage with Stephen Townsend, and the death of her elder son in 1890. After 1901 she lived in Bermuda and Long Island, occupied in turn by gardening, Christian Science, theosophy and spiritualism.

Her reputation depends on 3 children's books, *Little Lord Fauntleroy*, *A Little Princess*, which appeared in its final form in 1905, after being published in a short serial form in 1887 and in 1903 as a play, and *The Secret Garden* (1910). The theme of all these books is the value of personal dignity and pride, however one is circumstanced, but this message is presented with less didactic force in each book. So it is that Cedric Erroll moves from back street to castle without becoming puffed up, and Sara Crewe behaves like a princess even when reduced to the status of a drudge. The principle achieves its most complete and artistic expression in *The Secret Garden*, where Mary and Colin gain a more constructive independence (and health) as they fall under the spell of Dickon and the garden. The garden here is both a means of health and a symbol of the growing personality. [T V]

V. Burnett, *The Romantic Lady* (1927); Marghanita Laski, *Mrs Ewing, Mrs Molesworth and Mrs H. B.* (1960).

Burnett, James (Lord Monboddo) (1714–99). Scottish judge and pioneer anthropologist. Educated at Aberdeen, Edinburgh and Groningen, and raised to the bench in 1767, Monboddo collected and analysed travellers' tales of savage societies in the first volume of his *Essay on the Origin and Progress of Language* (1773); his work, long superseded, suffers from the limitations of his 'armchair' method and of his witnesses, but was a serious exploration along lines that later proved fruitful. Monboddo's speculations on the relation between man and the anthropoid apes, especially the orang-outang, made him an eccentric in the eyes of Samuel Johnson and other contemporaries and inspired the character of Sir Oran Haut-ton in ◊ Peacock's *Melincourt*. Monboddo's devotion to Greek philosophy is expressed in his *Ancient Metaphysics* (1779–99); his projected *History of Man* was never written. [A I]

W. Knight, *Lord M. and Some of His Contemporaries* (1900); Hugh MacDiarmid, *Scottish Eccentrics* (1936); A. O. Lovejoy, *Essays in the History of Ideas* (Baltimore, 1948).

Burney, Fanny (Mrs Frances Burney D'Arblay) (1752–1840). Novelist and diarist. The daughter of Dr Charles Burney, the historian of music, who left her to educate herself. She published her first novel, *Evelina, or The History of a Young Lady's Entry into the World* (1778), unaided and anonymous (ed. E. A. Bloom, 1968). It immediately made her famous and introduced her to Mrs ◊ Thrale's circle and to the friendship of Johnson. She followed this success with a comedy (never staged, on the advice of her father) and a novel, *Cecilia* (1782), which was also a great success. She was appointed second keeper of the robes to Queen Charlotte (1786), but finding this uncongenial and oppressive obtained permission to retire (with an annual pension of £100) in 1791. In 1796, she published her third novel, *Camilla*, which was very profitable (though of no great interest), and *The Wanderer* (1814), her last, was a failure. Meanwhile, she had married (1793) General D'Arblay, a French *émigré*. She was interned in France (1802–12). Her last work was a rather pompous edition of her father's *Memoirs* (1832). All her life she kept a diary, and a vast quantity of her interesting letters have survived (and are being edited at McGill University). Her *Early Diary: 1768–78* (1889) contains useful sketches of Johnson, Garrick, Reynolds and others. *Diary and Letters: 1778–1840* (7 vols., 1842–6; ed. C. F. Barrett and Austin Dobson, 6 vols., 1904; selection ed. L. Gibbs, Everyman, 1940) gives an account of her life in the stuffy court atmosphere, and of the later years with D'Arblay. In her most original work, *Evelina*, she more or less invented the social novel of domestic life, associating it with comedy and using loosely connected formal letters with some rather stiff reported conversation. She

stands rather dimly at the back of Jane Austen and is of more historical than intrinsic interest as a writer of fiction. Her journals show more imaginative quality. [A R]

Joyce Hemlow, *The History of F. B.* (1958); P. A. Scholes, *The Great Dr Burney* (2 vols., 1948) (bibliography).

Burns, Robert (1759–96). Scottish poet. His father, a struggling tenant-farmer in Ayrshire, nevertheless joined with neighbours to employ a university-trained tutor for their children. When very young Burns read the Bible, the English Augustans and Gray; later he learned some French and a little Latin. The surrounding countryside was rich in folk-lore, but Scots literature came his way only by chance; in boyhood he read William ◊ Hamilton of Gilbertfield's version of the *Wallace*, and much later ◊ Fergusson's poems opened his eyes to the possibility of contemporary literature in Scots. Meanwhile the privation and over-work of subsistence farming began the rheumatic heart-disease that was to cause his premature death. When his father died bankrupt in 1784, Burns, as head of the family, himself leased a farm at Mossgiel.

Ayrshire, Covenanting country in the 17th century, was a stronghold of the Calvinist party in the Church disputes of the 18th. Burns circulated verse satires on such Calvinist extremists as the Rev. John Russel, of 'The Twa Herds' and other poems, and the Kirk elder William Fisher of 'Holy Willie's Prayer'. In July 1786 the Church avenged itself by exacting public penance from Burns and Jean Armour, who was with child by him. His plan to emigrate with Mary Campbell ('Highland Mary') ended when she died, apparently in childbirth, in October, and Burns acknowledged Jean Armour as his wife in 1788, when she had already borne him two pairs of twins. *Poems Chiefly in the Scottish Dialect* (Kilmarnock, 1786) omitted the Church satires, offering instead the general social satire of 'The Twa Dogs' and the shrewd verse-epistles, some mock-elegies in the tradition of ◊ Ramsay, the 'nature' verse of 'To a Mouse' and 'To a Mountain Daisy', and the pious idealization of family life in 'The Cotter's Saturday Night'. Thomas ◊ Blacklock and Dugald ◊ Stewart praised the poems, Henry ◊ Mackenzie reviewed the volume enthusiastically, and Burns's Edinburgh admirers subscribed to his augmented Edinburgh edition of 1787, which on Hugh Blair's advice still suppressed the best of the satires and the boisterous radical Villonesque 'The Jolly Beggars'.

Burns spent the winters of 1786–7 and 1787–8 in Edinburgh, acting out with increasing unease the role of child of nature and untutored poet of the plough in which the Edinburgh gentry had cast him, and seeking relief and stimulus in the city's hard-drinking low life to the detriment of his standing with his aristocratic patrons. An admirer leased him a farm at Ellisland and in 1789 he was appointed to the Excise Division in nearby Dumfries. His farm failed; he had insufficient capital, his excise duties required him to travel about the district in all weathers, and his real energy was going into the collection and rewriting of Scots songs for *The Scots Musical Museum* (1787–1803; ed. J. Johnson, but mainly Burns's work) and for G. Thomson's *Select Scotish Airs* (1793–1818). Giving up Ellisland in 1791 he moved to Dumfries, where, after official investigation of his declared sympathy for the American and French Revolutions, he was promoted in the Excise and helped to organize local Volunteer units. His health gave way and bad medical advice hastened his end.

Except for the triumphantly impersonal 'folk' songs of his last years and the irrelevant mass of election ballads and other occasional verse that he turned out as Scotland's unofficial laureate, Burns's poetry shows a division similar to those in his education and in his social life in Edinburgh. On the one hand, in the poetry of social observation, the admirer of Pope somehow merges with the ranting Scots village daredevil; on the other, the admirer of Henry Mackenzie blends the sententious piety of James Thomson, Edward Young and Robert Blair with the moral and social optimism of the ' Enlightenment. The former figure – the Burns of the satires and epistles, of 'The Jolly Beggars' and other 'radical' poems and of 'Tam o' Shanter' – is now preferred, but Burns has had several reputations. Read in innumerable chapbook editions or passed on by word of mouth, his poems gave a voice to the ordinary Scotsman of his day; later, for radical Scots and Englishmen of the Peterloo period and for the Chartists, his anti-clericalism and his egalitarian songs offered a cultural alternative to the conservatism of Wordsworth and Scott, an aspect reflected in his high reputa-

tion in modern Russia. Among the 19th-century middle class the 'Edinburgh' interpretation of Burns as ploughman poet, modified by Jeffrey's essay (1809), by the tributes of Wordsworth and Keats and by the reaction against industrialism, prevailed, with 'To a Mountain Daisy' as the representative poem, until Matthew Arnold unexpectedly spoke out for 'The Jolly Beggars'. Meanwhile, nostalgic emigrant Scots in England and the Empire had vulgarized Burns into a symbolic super-patriot; at home, the 'ploughman' reputation released a spate of inept imitators. Of Burns's biographers the first was a moralizing teetotaller and the most widely read was the genteel J. G. ◊ Lockhart; with his sexuality hushed up and his drinking exaggerated Burns the man became a saint of mawkish hearth and maudlin club. Biography and editions of the 1890s first assailed the accumulated cant; later research and criticism, and the complete reassessment of Scottish Victorianism conducted by Hugh ◊ MacDiarmid and his followers, have revealed the Burns sketched here. [A I]

Poems and Songs, ed. J. Kinsley (3 vols., 1968) (with the airs); *The Life and Works*, ed. R. Chambers, revised W. Wallace (1896) (life, poems and letters in chronological sequence); *The Letters of R. B.*, ed. J. D. Ferguson (1931); *Selected Letters*, ed. J. D. Ferguson (1953) (with material omitted from the standard edition above); *The Merry Muses of Caledonia*, ed. J. Barke, J. D. Ferguson and S. G. Smith (1965) (bawdy folk-song used as the basis for published songs, and bawdry written on his own account). C. Carswell, *R. B.* (1930); F. B. Snyder, *R. B.* (1932); D. Daiches, *R. B.* (1952); T. Crawford, *B.* (1960); *The Burns Chronicle* (1892–   ) (annually); J. W. Egerer, *A Bibliography of R.B.* (1964).

Burton, John Hill (1809–81). Scottish historian. Burton was qualified as an advocate although he did not practise. One of the few men in the Scotland of his day to be interested in philosophical radicalism, Burton contributed to the *Westminster Review* and other periodicals; he wrote the introductory Life in Bowring's edition of ◊ Bentham's works (1838–43), edited a selection of *Benthamiana* (1843) and wrote and edited the *Life and Correspondence of David Hume* (1846). His *History of Scotland* (1853–70; revised 1873) was the fullest and most substantially based work on its subject when it appeared. Burton was Secretary of the Prison Board for Scotland from 1854, and a Commissioner of Prisons from 1877; he produced a stream of legal and political pamphlets, biographies and bibliographical essays. [AI]

The Bookhunter (1882 edn) (with a memoir by his widow).
DNB.

Burton, Sir Richard Francis (1821–90). Explorer, travel writer and translator. Born at Torquay, the son of an army officer. He matriculated at Trinity College, Oxford, but after five terms joined the Indian Army, seeing service under Sir Charles Napier, which he described in *Scinde, or the Unhappy Valley* (1851). Thereafter he spent a life of adventurous exploration. He is the epitome of the Victorian explorer, fearless, eccentric and literate; he learned over thirty languages and wrote many books on his travels. Burton's style was famous at the time. It is very complicated, with a pseudo-Elizabethan richness of vocabulary and luxuriance of opinion, full of 'local colour' and shot through with a swashbuckling tone. He travelled in Africa, publishing *First Footsteps in East Africa* (1856; ed. G. Waterfield, 1966) and *The Lake Regions of Central Africa* (1859). In disguise, he was one of the first Englishmen to make the pilgrimage to Mecca (1853), which led to his popular *Personal Narrative of a Pilgrimage to Al-Medinah and Mecca* (1855; ed. Lady Burton and S. Lane-Poole, 1898; reprinted 1965). He also travelled in South America and published *Exploration of the Highlands of Brazil* (1869) and *Letters from the Battlefields of Paraguay* (1870). He served in the Crimean War, and was British Consul in Damascus (1869–71) and at Trieste until his death; he was knighted in 1885. Burton produced the first unexpurgated translation of *The Thousand Nights and a Night* (1885–8), which has been praised by Arabic scholars, and here his elaboration works well in realizing the tone of the work. He wrote an unreadable 'antique' translation of Camões' epic *The Lusiads* (1880). [AR]

N. M. Penzer, *Bibliography* (1923); H. J. Schonfield, *R.B., Explorer* (1936); Sir Arnold Wilson, *R.B.* (1937); A. Edwardes, *Death Rides a Camel: A Biography of Sir R. B.* (New York, 1964); B. Farwell, *B.* (New York, 1963).

Burton, Robert (1577–1640). Scholar. Born in Leicestershire, he was educated at Oxford, where he became a student of Christ Church in 1599. He remained a don all his life, amassing a considerable library and never travelling 'but in Map or Card'. By profession a divine, he produced in 1621 his great compendium *The Anatomy of Melancholy* (ed. A. R. Shilleto, 3 vols., 1926–7) under the pseudonym 'Democritus Junior' but with a signed postscript. This encyclopedic, analytic work surveys and catalogues those psychological states for which the Elizabethans used the blanket-term 'melancholy'. Burton's marshalling of authorities and examples show great learning and familiarity with a diverse range of material, including medical and philosophical treatises by Greeks, Arabs and Renaissance Europeans, superstitious and literary as well as 'scientific' writings, and forgotten medieval love. The book was much read, and Burton revised it five times, adding copiously to it. It remains a treasurehouse of Jacobean ideas on human behaviour and of recondite knowledge. Though Burton wanted to present his analytic treatise in Latin, his English prose style, colloquial, discursive, seemingly extemporaneous and bristling with quotations and donnish asides expresses his own personality. [MJ]

L. Babb, *Sanity in Bedlam: A Study of R.B.'s 'Anatomy of Melancholy'* and *The Elizabethan Malady: A Study of Melancholia in English Literature 1580–1642* (East Lansing, Michigan, 1959, 1951); D. Bush, *English Literature in the Earlier Seventeenth Century* (revised edn, 1962); B. Evans, *The Psychiatry of R.B.* (New York, 1944); W. R. Mueller, *The Anatomy of R.B.'s England* (Berkeley, Calif., 1952); F. P. Wilson, *Seventeenth Century Prose* (1960).

Bury, John Bagnell (1861–1927). Historian. Born at Monaghan, Co. Monaghan, in Ireland, and educated at Foyle College, Londonderry, and Trinity College, Dublin, where he became a Fellow (1885) and Professor of Modern History (1893); he succeeded Acton in 1903 as Regius Professor at Cambridge. Bury had a vast range of knowledge in languages and classical learning. He edited several Greek texts, and wrote much on later Roman imperial and Byzantine history. He is remembered by students of English literature for his useful edition of ◊ Gibbon's *Decline and Fall of the Roman Empire* (7 vols., 1896–1900). He also wrote an optimistic, obviously pre-First World War *History of Freedom of Thought* (1913). [AR]

Butler

Butler, Frederick Guy (1918–). South African poet, playwright and critic. Born in Cape Province, he spent his youth in the Karoo. He was educated at Rhodes University and Oxford. He did war service in 1940–5, lectured at Witwatersrand University from 1948 to 1950, then joined the staff of Rhodes University, where he has been Professor of English since 1952. His *Stranger to Europe* (1952) was republished with additional poems in 1960. Butler is sometimes an unshowy commentator on the impact of nationality on attitudes and sometimes a showily sensuous descriptive poet. His verse plays, *The Dam* (1953) and *The Dove Returns* (1956), are more ambitious and more uneven. In the latter the Bible is interestingly used as background to a Boer War incident, but the departures from the normative, almost perfunctory blank verse, jar as often as they please. Butler's contribution as a critic is considerable. He became English editor of *Standpunte* in 1956, and is an advisory editor of the newer literary periodical *Contrast*. For the Oxford University Press he edited *A Book of South African Verse* (1959), and he has been a visiting lecturer in England (1954) and the U.S.A. (1958). [P T]

Butler, Joseph (1692–1752). Theologian and moral philosopher. Although the son of a dissenter, he went to Oriel College, Oxford, and was ordained in the state Church (1718). He became Bishop of Bristol (1738) and in addition Dean of St Pauls (1740). In 1750 he was translated to the see of Durham. He published some 20 solid sermons (1726, 1749, etc.; ed. W. R. Mathews, 1914), in which he discussed in an anti-optimistic manner the difficulties men have in judging what is right conduct, and the primary role of conscience (not happiness) in the search. His most famous book, however, is his *Analogy of Religion, Natural and Revealed, in the Constitution of Nature* (1736 ff.; ed. R. Bayne, Everyman, 1906; World's Classics, 1907). In this rather austere but impressive work, he attempts far from dogmatically to dissuade the Deists, on their own grounds of rational argument, not to reject the traditional Christian beliefs and the evidence of the scriptures. [A R]

Leslie Stephen, *English Thought in the Eighteenth Century* (1876); C. D. Broad, *Five Types of Ethical Theory* (1930); E. C. Mossner, *B. and the Age of Reason* (1936); A. Duncan-Jones, *B.'s Moral Philosophy* (1952).

Butler, Samuel (1612–80). Satirist. The son of a Worcestershire yeoman. Little is known of his early life, but he may have been a member of Gray's Inn. He was certainly a very learned man. He was steward of Ludlow Castle for Carbery, Lord President of Wales, and for a time (in the seventies) secretary to George Villiers, Duke of Buckingham. He was a friend of ◊ Hobbes, Sir William ◊ Davenant and John ◊ Aubrey. Butler's fame as a writer rests on his long mock-heroic poem *Hudibras* (part I, 1663; part II, 1664; part III, 1678), which ridicules the Puritans and Independents, chivalry, heroism, argument, poetic imagery, new doctrines in the church, intellectual self-sufficiency, as well as scientific investigation and its concomitant, the idea of 'progress'. The loosely constructed, episodic, narrative line, describing the adventures of Hudibras, a pedantic Presbyterian and his Independent squire, Ralpho, is boring, but the poem contains passages of brilliant, sceptical satire, in the long grotesque character-sketches. The rough octosyllabic measure, used in this burlesque manner, has given the word 'hudibrastics' to the language. The poem is learned, realistic, scurrilous, anti-pedantic; it uses travesty, as well as all kinds of popular writing; and is in the tradition that includes Rabelais, Scarron and Swift. Butler wrote an 'anti-scientific' poem, *The Elephant on the Moon* (the elephant is a mouse which has fallen into a telescope), as well as some famous *Characters* (not published until 1759). [A R]

Poetical Works, ed. R. B. Johnson (2 vols., 1893); *Collected Works*, i, *Hudibras*, ed. A. R. Waller (1905), ii, *Characters, etc.* (1908), iii, *Satires and Miscellaneous Writings*, ed. R. Lamar (1928); *Hudibras*, ed. J. Wilders (1968).
Johnson, *Lives of the Poets*; E. A. Richards, *Hudibras in the Burlesque Tradition* (New York, 1937).

Butler, Samuel (1835–1902). Speculative writer, satirist and novelist. Born at Langar in Nottinghamshire, the son of the rector (later a canon of Lincoln), and grandson of Bishop Samuel Butler, whose *Life and Letters* he published in 1896. He was educated at Shrewsbury and St John's College, Cambridge. A product of the ecclesiastical establishment, he was himself destined for the Church by his over-bearing father on whom he was financially dependent, but rebelled, offering doubt in the efficacy of infant baptism as his stumbling-

81

block. The experience of breaking out of his family, caste and religious expectations and pressures marked Butler for life; it is the making of his greatest book, the auto-biographical novel *The Way of All Flesh*, long in writing, but not published until 1903 (ed. R. A. Streatfeild; ed. G. B. Shaw, World's Classics, 1936; ed. R. Hoggart, PEL, 1966). After a five-year spell as a sheep-farmer in Rangitata, New Zealand (his letters home were printed by his father as *A First Year in Canterbury Settlement*, 1863; ed. R. A. Streatfeild, 1914), he returned to England with a small fortune. A man of many talents, he tried a career as an artist, exhibiting pictures in the Royal Academy. His work was slight and derivative, just as his taste in musical composition led him to write Handelian *pastiches*. Thereafter he settled down to a literary career. Ironically, his rebellion (perhaps out of timidity) follows the same lines as conformity would have done, apart from abortive painting and musical attempts, and his novel. He detested his father's beliefs, so he does not ignore them or flout them, but tries to argue them down. He opposes his erstwhile co-religionists by writing anti-Christian theology. His opposition to opinions because they are received often makes him for all his intelligence simply a high-class crank. He wrote an excellent spoof, of limited interest: '*The Fair Haven. A Work in Defence of the Miraculous Element in Our Lord's Ministry upon Earth, both against Rationalistic Impugners and Certain Ortho-dox Defenders. By the late J. P. Owen. Edited by W. B. Owen, with a Memoir of the Author*' (1873; ed. R. A. Streatfeild, 1913; ed. G. Bullett, 1938). In two cases this argumentative spleen produced works of satirical art: *Erewhon: or Over the Range* (1872; revised 1872, 1901) and *Erewhon Revisited, Both by the Original Discoverer of the Country and His Son* (1901). Mr Higgs finds among the new people in New Zealand a true utopia, containing bad and good features satirizing Butler's own society. The worship of the Goddess Ydgrun (Mrs Grundy) and the Musical Banks attack respectability and pharisaical church-going, but the inhabitants are praiseworthy in admiring physical health and well-being. Higgs's escape passes into the Erewhonian religious mythology, and 'Sunchildism' is the centre of the sequel, which is livelier and more humane among all its paradoxes. Butler was a good scholar, but used his talents in

promoting theories because they were un-orthodox, such as that the *Odyssey* was written by a woman. His writing, however, contains much good sense, especially on the Homeric poems. In *Shakespeare's Sonnets Reconsidered and in Part Rearranged* (1899), he claimed they were addressed to a man of low birth. He intervened in the evolution controversies, characteristically as a clever amateur; he inspected the theories of Darwin and suggested the intelligent modification that the variations which help survival are not necessarily chance, but that will and 'memory' might be considered; his works in this line include *Life and Habit* (1877), *Unconscious Memory* (1880) and *Luck or Cunning* (1887). He thought himself slighted by Darwin, who had accidentally failed to acknowledge his work and though generally accepted theory came round to some of his views, it cannot be said that his speculations, unsupported by any observation, were crucial. *The Way of All Flesh* is of some importance in the history of the novel and perhaps (if life imitates art) in the development of English society. In it his familial, social, theological and evolutionary views meet, and the whole work, a marvellous document of Victorian sensibility, is alive with passionate bitterness. It set the style for decades of anti-father books, but has somewhat lost its force now that the commonsensical, propertied, healthful solutions it advocates to family dissensions are not only in doubt psychologically, but politically impossible. Butler also wrote some of the then fashionable Alpine description as in *Alps and Sanctuaries of Piedmont and the Canton Ticino* (1882, 1913, 1931). [AR]

Works, 'Shrewsbury Edition', ed. H. F. Jones and A. T. Bartholomew (20 vols., 1923–6); *The Essential S. B.*, ed. G. D. H. Cole (1950; revised 1961).

H. Festing Jones, *S. B., Author of Erewhon: A Memoir* (1917); M. Muggeridge, *The Earnest Atheist: A Study of S. B.* (1936); P. N. Furbank, *S. B.* (1948); G. D. H. Cole, *S.B.* (WTW, 1952; revised 1961); R. P. Blackmur, *The Double Agent* (1935); V. S. Pritchett, *The Living Novel* (1946); W. Allen, *The English Novel* (1954); M. D. Zabel, *Craft and Character in Modern Fiction* (New York, 1951); S. B. Harkness, *The Career of S. B.: A Bibliography* (1955); B. Willey, *Darwin and B.: Two Versions of Evolution* (1960).

Byrom, John (1692–1763). Poet, physician and inventor of a short-hand system. He was a Fellow of Trinity College, Cambridge, but lived in Manchester. He was inclined to mysticism, and a fervent Jacobite, and the considerable bulk of his verse, in which he is fond of anapaestic measures, reflects these interests. 'Christians awake! Salute the happy morn' is his only work to survive popularly. He also kept a voluminous diary of considerable interest. [A R]

Poems, ed. A. W. Ward (Chetham Society, 3 vols., 1894–1912); *The Private Journals*, ed. R. Parkinson (Chetham Society, 4 vols., 1854–7); *Selections from the Journal and Papers* ed. H. Talon (1950).

Byron, George Gordon, Lord (1788–1824). English poet. Descended from a violent and lawless family, Byron suffered in early life from a mother whom he described as 'diabolical' and from a vicious nurse. He had a club foot which made him self-consciously determined to excel at physical activities. On inheriting the barony he went to Harrow and Cambridge, after which he rapidly gained a reputation in London society for his startling good looks and extravagant behaviour. His first collection of poems, *Hours of Idleness* (1807), was not well received, but with the publication of the first 2 cantos of *Childe Harold's Pilgrimage* he took London by storm and challenged Scott as the most popular writer of romantic melodrama. He was lionized by society and pursued by women; in 1812 he married Annabel Milbanke, although her personality – she was determined to reform him – was the antithesis of Byron's. He left her after a year, and shocked his public by his relationship with his half-sister Augusta, which, if unnatural, was genuine and lasting. He left England in 1816, and after a number of involvements settled into a relatively stable relationship with Teresa Guiccioli in Italy. By this time, 1819, he had been working on *Don Juan* (ed. L. A. Marchand, Boston, 1958; ed. T. G. Steffan and W. W. Pratt, 4 vols., 1957), the poem on which his modern reputation is based, for two years. Finally, Byron identified himself with the Greek fight for independence from Turkey, and died while he was training troops for the cause.

Although Byron was contemporarily popular for his dark romances, in which the mysterious and misanthropic Byronic hero wanders and overcomes every variety of hazard and obstruction, it is such works as *Beppo* (1817), *The Vision of Judgment* (1822) and *Don Juan* that represent his most sophisticated and accomplished work. The earlier melodramatic tales, such as *The Giaour* (1813), *The Bride of Abydos* (1813) and pre-eminently *Childe Harold*, were exotic and full of a gloomy passion that appealed to the bored and romantic imagination of the time, but although there is immense speed and attractive vitality in these verse narratives there are patches of careless rush and times when the grandiosity carries him away. His language is moody and vivid, and he covers vast areas, both geographically and emotionally, and the fact that he hints at, without explicitly or offensively presenting, conventionally unacceptable passions heightens his appeal.

In *Beppo* Byron worked with the stanza form, *ottava rima*, that he perfected in *Don Juan*. Its rapid flexibility accommodated light irony, stinging malice and the delicately lyrical. Byron undertook *Don Juan* in a light-hearted mood, but he also intended it to be a serious criticism of society, and to represent real life – 'is it not *life*, is it not *the thing*?' he wrote. The poem relates Byron's own version of the adventures of the legendary Juan in a tone far different from the sombre earlier tales. His Juan is the continually seduced rather than the seducer – a mild, charming young man who cannot resist his irresistibility. *Don Juan* was published in instalments, the first 2 cantos in 1819. The sixteenth canto was never finished. The incidents are a compound of the ridiculous and the melodramatic, with moments of gentle illumination and critical comment. But the predominant tone is that of sophisticated and lively irony, maintained by the countering of the biting and humorous satire of the narrator and the easy extravagance of Juan's activities, and this is what appeals to the modern reader.

Byron's contemporary influence was extensive, but although he was so popular in England and the news of his death was received with a sense of personal loss it was in Europe that this influence was most widely expressed. It was the tormented, homeless hero of the melodramas, who came to be identified with Byron himself, that appealed rather than his deeply felt criticisms or the charming immorality of Juan. The Byronic hero was a prototype frequently imitated and embraced as a living myth in European literature – in Pushkin's *Evgeny Onegin*, for example – and was all the more powerful for the fact that Byron's own life, which had such an aura of guilty mystery about it, became a part of the myth. In England the rapturous idealism of Shelley tended to supplant Byron's gloomy nobility as a significant influence. [J R C]

Works, ed. E. H. Coleridge and R. E. Prothero (13 vols., 1898–1904) (includes 6 vols. of letters and journals); *Correspondence*, ed. Sir J. Murray (1922); *Selections from Poetry, Letters and Journals*, ed. P. Quennell (1949).

L. Marchand, *B.: A Biography* (1957); P. Quennell, *The Years of Fame* (1935); W. W. Robson, *B. as Poet* (British Academy Lecture, 1957); P. West, *B. and the Spoiler's Art* (1960); A. Rutherford, *B.: A Critical Study* (1961); W. Marshall, *The Structure of B.'s Major Poems* (1962).

C

Caedmon (d. 670–80). Poet. ◊ Bede's story (bk iv, ch. xxiv) is the only source for Caedmon's biography, and it contains a Latin paraphrase of his *Hymn*. We cannot ·be sure whether the English versions (*Three Northumbrian Poems*, ed. A. H. Smith) are transcripts of the original or translations of Bede. Caedmon entered the monastery of Whitby during the rule of Abbess Hild (658–80). He was, says Bede, then advanced in years, and had lived as an untaught herdsman until, one night, he was divinely inspired in a dream to compose a hymn on the Creation. After being received into the monastery, he went on to make many verse paraphrases of biblical narratives. The basic facts are probably reliable, but the story contains familiar folk-tale elements, and modern criticism has pointed out that Caedmon's *Hymn* is a very conventional poem, in the Old English tradition of oral composition, and Caedmon is not likely to be the first religious poet in English. Of the poems in the *Junius Manuscript* (ed. G. P. Krapp, 1931), once thought to be his, 'Genesis', 'Exodus' and 'Daniel' deal with subjects that Caedmon treated, but they are later in date, and have no common authorship. There is some point, however, in terming them 'Caedmonian', since, in comparison with 'Cynewulfian' verse, they correspond more nearly to the dense, epic, formulaic style, rich in 'kennings', which Caedmon seems to have used. [A G]

C. W. Kennedy, *Early English Christian Poetry* (1960); G. Shepherd, 'Scriptural Poetry', in *Continuations and Beginnings: Studies in Old English Literature*, ed. E. G. Stanley (1966); C. L. Wrenn, *The Poetry of C.* (1947); F. P. Magoun, 'Bede's Story of C.', *Speculum*, xxx (1955).

Callaghan, Morley (Edward) (1903–   ). Canadian novelist and short-story writer. Born in Toronto, he went to university and law school there. He was called to the bar in 1928, but by that time was already a reporter, with Ernest Hemingway, on the Toronto *Daily Star*. Hemingway encouraged him to write, and his first novel,

Strange Fugitive, was published in 1928. He spent that year in Paris (described in *That Summer in Paris*, 1963), where he met Scott Fitzgerald and Gertrude Stein. Since 1929 he has lived mainly in Toronto, where he has become well known on radio and television.

Callaghan is a Roman Catholic and a city dweller. In his best novels, *Such Is My Beloved* (1934), *They Shall Inherit. the Earth* (1935), *More Joy in Heaven* (1937) and *The Loved and the Lost* (1951), the importance of these two facts is evident. He tests moral values by placing detailed urban observation in a framework of Christian symbolism. The need for a revaluation is enforced by an insistent irony set to work on a fallen world, in which real goodness in one man precipitates vice in others. Callaghan's novels are extended inquiries into the implications of a single situation, a fact which has been used to show the primacy of his talent as a short-story writer (*Collected Stories*, 2 vols., 1959). That one 'genre' has easy access to the other is apparent in the case of *The Many Colored Coat* (1960), which was originally a short story. [P T]

A Passion in Rome (1961); *That Summer in Paris* (1963) (memoirs).
H. McPherson, 'The Two Worlds of M. C.', *Queen's Quarterly*, LXIV, 3 (1957); F. W. Watt, 'M. C. as Thinker', *Dalhousie Review*, XLIX, 4 (1959); B. Conron, *M.C.* (1966).

Calverley, Charles Stuart (1831–84). Poet. Born at Martley in Worcestershire, the son of a clergyman, and educated at Marlborough, Harrow, Balliol College, Oxford (where he was sent down), and Christ's College, Cambridge (where he became a Fellow). He was called to the bar at the Inner Temple in 1865, but the next year was seriously injured while skating and became a permanent invalid. His *forte* was wit and parody (of Browning, Macaulay and ◊ Tupper) in the vein of Andrew ◊ Lang, Austin ◊ Dobson and Edmund ◊ Gosse. His *Verses and Translations* appeared in 1862 and *Fly Leaves* (parodies and light verse) in 1872. [A R]

Complete Works, ed. and intr. W. J. Sendal (1901). R. B. Ince, *Calverley and Some Cambridge Wits of the Nineteenth Century* (1929).

Camden, William (1551–1623). Historian and antiquary. Educated at one great London school, St Paul's (and at Magdalen College, Oxford), he became headmaster of another, Westminster, earning the gratitude of a famous pupil, Ben Jonson. The Greek grammar he prepared for his pupils (1595) remained long in use. His great compendium of British pre-history and history in Latin, the *Britannia*, first appeared in 1586, reaching its eighth edition in 1616. Philemon Holland's translation into English was published in 1610, and new translations with added materials continued to appear as late as the 19th century. His history of his own times, *Annales rerum anglicarum et hibernicarum*, was first published in Latin in 1615 and extended in 1625 to cover the years 1558–1603; several English versions were published. His assembling of materials, particularly on the Arthurian legends, made his *Britannia* a source-book for poets, and he is generally regarded as the greatest of the Elizabethan antiquaries. *The Camden Miscellany* of the Royal Historical Society, which prints historical source-materials, commemorates him. [MJ]

D. Bush, *English Literature in the Earlier Seventeenth Century* (revised edn, 1962).

Campbell, Roy (Dunnachie) (1901–57). South African poet. Born in Natal. From childhood his life was divided between study and outdoor activity: 'I have always known that the non-bookish existence underlies and precedes the bookish one.' After abandoning the intention of entering Oxford University, he travelled in France and Spain in 1920. *The Flaming Terrapin* (1924), a long symbolic poem, was enthusiastically received in England. Returning to South Africa, Campbell became co-editor of *Voorslag* (1926–7), an outspoken journal forced into silence by 'respectable' hostility. Leaving the country, he wrote *The Wayzgoose* (1928), an angry satire on South Africa's leading figures. He became a professional lancer and bullfighter in Provence. *Adamastor* (1930) is a boisterously romantic and frankly self-vaunting collection of lyrics, and *The Georgiad* satirizes in heroic couplets the Georgian literary world that tried to lionize him on his return to England. Back in Spain he turned Roman Catholic, and an excited feeling for ritual and mystery is prominent in the lyrics of *Mithraic Emblems* (1936). In the Spanish Civil War he fought for Franco, and, despite a wound, fought again in the Second World War. Invalided out of the army, he was given a life pension. He lived for a few years in England, then went back to Spain. He was killed in a car crash in Portugal.

Campbell's poems celebrate danger, beauty and energy, in language that reflects the intensity with which he measured life. He was also a translator of genius (see *Collected Poems*, vol. 3, 1960), among others of Lorca and St John of the Cross. He never lost, though he learnt to control, the verbal prodigiosity of *The Flaming Terrapin*. [PT]

Collected Poems (vol. 1, 1949; vol. 2, 1957); *Light on a Dark Horse* (1951) (autobiography). H. Sergeant, 'Restive Steer: A Study of the Poetry of R. C.', *Essays and Studies*, New Series, x (1957); David Wright, *R.C.* (WTW, 1961).

Campbell, Thomas (1777–1844). Poet, critic and journalist. Born in Glasgow, the son of a merchant, and educated at the university there. He became known for a discursive poem in couplets, *The Pleasures of Hope* (1799), a 'literary' and derivative exercise with some neat turns, such as the often quoted line: "'Tis distance lends enchantment to the view.' He was also the author of *Gertrude of Wyoming* (1809), in Spenserian stanzas, which tells the story of the destruction in 1778 of a settlement of that name in Pennsylvania by Mohawk Indians, and of the death of Gertrude and her family. The poem, which seeks to exploit an exotic American setting, never rises above a rather timid pathos. Campbell also wrote swinging war songs, some of which are still remembered (if only as school recitation pieces), such as 'Ye Mariners of England' and 'Hohenlinden'; his ballad 'Lord Ullin's Daughter' was once a favourite drawing-room piece. Campbell, a lover of liberty, never really realized his potential as a poet, though he was admired by his friends ◊ Byron and ◊ Scott. He is buried in Westminster Abbey. [AR]

Collected Poems (1907).
W. Beattie, *Life and Letters* (1849); G. Saintsbury, *Essays in English Literature*, 2nd series

(1895) (deals with the songs); H. H. Jordan, *English Romantic Poets and Essayists: A Review of Research and Criticism* (revised 1966).

Campion, Thomas (1567–1620). Songwriter. He was the child of well-to-do parents who died in his childhood. In 1581, he was entered at Peterhouse, Cambridge, as a gentleman pensioner, but there is no evidence either that he matriculated in the university or that he took a degree. He appears to have left Cambridge in 1584, and was admitted to Gray's Inn in 1586. He remained there, without being called to the bar, until about 1595, although it seems that in 1591 he served briefly as a volunteer in the expedition led by the Earl of Essex to Dieppe to assist Henri IV. Shortly after 1595, he apparently began the studies which led to a degree in medicine some time between 1602 and 1606, probably from a continental university. For the rest of his life he practised as a doctor. The first collection of songs published by Campion was a collaboration with his friend Philip Rosseter, *A Book of Ayres* (1601), the first part of which contained songs with words and music by Campion. In 1602 there appeared the first of Campion's 2 prose works, *Observations in the Art of English Poesie*, which disparaged the use of rhyme and occasioned ◊ Daniel's famous reply the *Defence of Rhyme* (1603). Campion himself continually used rhyme in his ayres and it seems that he intended only to criticize rhyme as encouraging less than perfection in poetry, because it could camouflage the coarse modulations of bad verse, and could entail distortion of sense; unrhymed verse was likely to demand more sensitive metrical control, and less distortion of the matter. He attempted to demonstrate in this treatise, like other of his contemporaries, how certain unrhymed classical metres could fit naturally into English, and, unlike them, to assert the value both of accent and position in determining the length of English syllables. He also asserted a similarity between musical notes and poetic words, thinking of the foot as equalling the semi-breve, and thus concluding that each foot could be broken up into syllables of varying values, so long as the time-value of each foot equalled that of each other foot in the line. In 1607 Campion composed the first of his 3 masks, known as *Lord Hayes' Mask*. In 1613, he

produced the others, known as the *Lords' Mask* and the *Squires' Mask* (the latter establishes a connexion between Campion and the gruesome affair of the murder of Sir Thomas Overbury, but it seems that Campion was not culpably involved). In the same year there appeared his *Songs of Mourning* on the death of Prince Henry, Campion providing the words and John Coperario, or Cooper, the music; and probably in 1613 also the *Two Books of Ayres*, for which he wrote both words and music. In 1617 he published the *Third and Fourth Book of Ayres*, and possibly in the same year his second prose work, the *New Way of Making Four Parts in Counterpoint*, a technical musical treatise. The next year were published the *Ayres that were Sung and Played at Brougham Castle*, with music by George Mason and John Earsden, and words fairly certainly by Campion, which had been produced for the entertainment of James I by the Earl of Cumberland at Brougham Castle. It is neither as a writer of masks nor as a theorist in poetry or music that Campion is remembered, but as a writer of songs, which are distinctive among other songs of the time both for their excellence and because one man composed words and music. They are ayres and not madrigals, so that the musical element tends not to dominate and reduce entirely the verbal, the words of the songs being to a degree independent of the music. It is clear that the entire predominance of sound in the music of the songs has encouraged in the words a certain similar predominance of verbal sound over sense content, a verbal sound very often exquisitely modulated, including rhyme not as a camouflage but as an extra adornment, but depending upon a devaluation of the sense content which could be described as essentially the kind of distortion that Campion criticizes in the *Observations*. Accordingly, the songs are a slight achievement, if judged by the standards of poetry, although a delightful one. And even if a different standard be demanded for songs, it might be said that the greatest songs achieve their effects by exploiting the struggle between words and music functioning fully in character, and not by the partial submission of one element to the other. [DELC]

Campion's Works, ed. P. Vivian (1909) (excluding music); *The English School of Lutenist Song Writers*, ed. E. H. Fellowes (1st series, vols. 4 and 13, 1920–2, *A Book of Ayres*; 2nd series, vols. 2, 3, 10, 11, 1925–6, *Two Books of Ayres* and *Third and Fourth Book of Ayres*).

M. M. Kastendieck, *England's Musical Poet, T. C.* (1938); A. H. Bullen, *Elizabethans* (1924); E. H. Fellowes, *Grove's Dictionary of Music and Musicians*, 5th edn., ed. E. Blom (1954).

'Caradar'. ◊ Cornish Literature.

Carew, Thomas (?1594–1640). Poet. The son of Matthew (later Sir Matthew) Carew, D.C.L., and Master in Chancery, he was descended on his mother's side from two Lord Mayors of London. In 1608 Carew went to Merton College, Oxford, took his B.A. in 1611, was incorporated B.A. at Cambridge in 1612, and in that year moved to the Inner Temple to study law. On his father's suffering heavy financial losses, he went out to Venice as secretary to Sir Dudley Carleton, the English ambassador there, and retained his position when the latter became ambassador to the Netherlands in 1616. However, Carew fell foul of his employer, apparently by writing a satirical character-sketch of him and his wife, and was sent back to England; here his disgrace and his profligate way of living seem to have caused a break between him and his family. In 1619 he entered the employment of Sir Edward Herbert, the ambassador to Paris, finally returning to England in 1624. His reputation as a wit and poet earned him recognition in court, and in 1630 he became a Gentleman of the Privy Chamber Extraordinary, and, at about the same time, Sewer in Ordinary to the King.

In his earlier years Carew's sensual love poetry, especially 'The Rapture', gained wide circulation in manuscript. While he borrowed extensively from Donne (to whose posthumous collected poems he contributed an elegy), Carew is at his most successful in the lighter style of the courtly followers of Ben Jonson. Lacking profundity of emotion or thought, he often achieves grace and cynical charm, while at his very best he rises to a fragile delicacy of form, as in the much quoted 'Ask me no more where Jove bestows'. His most substantial achievement is the delightful masque *Coelum Britannicum* (1634), written for performance before the King; while the thought is borrowed, the pleasing combination of humour and grace is Carew's own. [P M]

Poems, ed. R. Dunlap (1949).

E.I. Selig, *The Flourishing Wrath: A Study of T.C.'s Poetry* (Yale U.P., 1958).

Carey, Henry (*c.* 1687–1743). Dramatist and writer of burlesques and songs. He has a place in 18th-century literary and musical history as an exploiter of the taste for ballad opera which developed after *The Beggar's Opera* by ◊ Gay. His *Namby Pamby* (1726), attacking the mawkish poems of Ambrose ◊ Philips, added a new word to the language. He is best known as the author of the words and music of 'Sally in Our Alley', and is often, but probably wrongly, credited with 'God Save the King'. [A R]

The Poems, ed. and intr. F. T. Wood (1930).
F. W. Bateson, *English Comic Drama: 1700–1750* (1929).

Carlyle, Alexander (1722–1805). Scottish prose-writer. Nicknamed 'Jupiter', he was minister of Inveresk near Edinburgh from 1748 to 1805 and was a leader of the 'Moderate' party in the Church of Scotland, a champion of John ◊ Home in the controversy over his *Douglas*, and the author of an *Autobiography* (ed. J. H. Burton, 1860, and reprints) which provides one of the best contemporary accounts of the atmosphere of literary and intellectual Edinburgh in the 18th century. [A I]

Carlyle, Thomas (1795–1881). Philosopher, critic and historian. Born at Ecclefechan in Annandale, the eldest son of a prosperous mason and small farmer, a member of the extreme dissident Presbyterians called the 'burghers'. The son was educated at the village school, at Annan Grammar School, and in 1809 went to the University of Edinburgh. He was destined for the Church, but at first his taste was for mathematics, and in 1814 he began to teach that subject at Annan, and later taught at Kirkcaldy. In 1818, he abandoned teaching, which he hated; and also, with the development of his views, all hope was lost of completing the divinity course he was engaged in. He taught private pupils, and studied law unsuccessfully in Edinburgh; he began to write articles for the *Edinburgh Encyclopaedia*. His private reading, fits of depression and dyspepsia (from which he suffered all his life), as well as a close study of German Romantic writers, all began to form his characteristic picture of the world, and hence his own style of writing. *Sartor*

Resartus (II, 7–9) gives an account of his spiritual crisis, and his emergence with a conscious, but precarious, positive doctrine, his 'everlasting Yea'. In 1821, he met Jane Baillie Welsh, the remarkable daughter of a small laird and doctor, and fell in love with her. He started to publish a *Life of Schiller* in the *London Magazine* (1823–4), and in 1824 translated the first part of Goethe's *Wilhelm Meister*. This brought him the esteem of the great German writer he so much admired; but Carlyle's Goethe, whom he considered to have contributed so much, is more a creation of Carlyle's own imagination and feeling than the classical writer others have discerned. In that year he visited London as a private tutor and met Coleridge, who also greatly influenced him; he thought nothing of Lamb and the other literary men active in the capital.

He was married in 1825, and for ten years the Carlyles lived a precarious and lonely life in Edinburgh and at his wife's isolated farm at Craigenputtock in Dumfriesshire. Carlyle tried unsuccessfully to write a novel, *Wotton Reinfred*. He met ◊ Jeffrey, who, claiming kinship with his wife, accepted articles for the *Edinburgh Review*; these included 'Jean Paul Richter' (1827), 'The Present State of German Literature' (1828), 'Burns' (1828) and 'The Signs of the Times' (1829), in which he began to discuss contemporary problems. This was the role in which he was perhaps most influential. 'Characteristics' (1831) is one of his most important essays, and surveys the intellectual trends of the time. Carlyle wrote with agonizing difficulty, and all his magazine articles were substantial enough to be reprinted either in the *Miscellaneous and Critical Essays* section of his collected works (1839), or expanded as separate books. He typifies the writer who supported, and was supported by, the great 19th-century periodicals. It is also obvious that this method of publication exaggerated his discursiveness, allusiveness, argumentativeness and his sense of playing the prophet's part. In the *Foreign Review* he published 8 essays on German literature, such as 'Goethe's Helena', 'Goethe' and another essay on Richter, and a paper on Voltaire. Jeffrey's successor on the *Edinburgh Review*, Macvey Napier, disapproved of Carlyle's increasingly intransigent radicalism, but J. S. Mill took essays in the *Westminster Review*, and *Fraser's Magazine* published (1833–4) his most successful long work up to this time, *Sartor Resartus* (*The Life and Opinions of Herr Teufelsdröckh*; published as a book by Emerson, Boston, 1836; ed. C. F. Harrold, New York, 1937; ed. W. H. Hudson, Everyman, 1908). In the two parts of this work, Carlyle shows his contorted, 'German' style in full flower: in his view, language, institutions and laws are the 'garments' of man's thought; the body is the 'garment' of the soul; the universe is the 'garment' of God. Under the influence of his own theological education, and Fichte's destructive critique of 18th-century rationalism, Carlyle was driven into a 'transcendental' philosophy. In his consideration of social problems, the apparently inexorable effects of the industrialization of Europe also cornered him there. The tailor (man) needs to be 're-tailored'; this is Carlyle's job, which explains the autobiographical cast of sections of this book. In 1834, the Carlyles moved to London and settled in 5 (now 24) Cheyne Row, Chelsea, now a Carlyle museum.

Carlyle was well known in some circles, but a puzzling writer to many. He began work on his *French Revolution* (3 vols., 1837; Everyman, 2 vols., 1906), which consolidated his reputation. The heavy labour was made heavier by J. S. Mill's unfortunate accidental destruction of the first manuscript. Carlyle was interested in revolutions, because they showed the divine idea breaking through in societies which had become fossilized, more and more out of touch with the informing truth. He never argued that revolution is the best form of change, nor was he a democrat. He was on the watch for the emergence of a 'hero', a human leader truly in touch with divine power, acting his part in society. At this time, he gave 4 series of lectures, of which 3 are important: *Lectures on the History of Literature* (1838; ed. J. R. Greene, 1892); *Six Lectures on Revolutions in Modern Europe* (delivered in 1839; reported in Shepherd, *Memoirs*, i); and *On Heroes, Hero-Worship, and the Heroic in History* (6 lectures delivered in 1840; published in extended and revised form, 1841; ed. W. H. Hudson, Everyman, 1908; World's Classics, 1935). A writer could be a 'hero', just as a soldier, a political leader, a priest, a king. The 'hero' transcended ordinary men by having to a transcendent degree the faculty of apprehending the 'Divine Idea'

89

which informs everything, though all souls possess this faculty in a greater or less measure. Hence Carlyle's 'knotty' writing is personal, because he himself as a seer was a hero; his history, too, has to be biographical, as does his criticism. Carlyle's other major historical works are an attempt to deal with the Puritan revolution in England, *Oliver Cromwell's Letters and Speeches: With Emendations* (2 vols., 1845; ed. W. A. Shaw, Everyman, 1907), and *The History of Friedrich II of Prussia, called Frederick the Great* (6 vols., 1858–65). On the latter he lavished the most careful research, but since his 'idea' of Frederick the Great is not really borne out by the evidence, his mythopoeic effort partially fails; he did however receive the Prussian Order of Merit from Bismarck. Carlyle's method of writing history was to work hard on research (for the *French Revolution* he read almost everything available) and then to allow his imagination to make the synthesis that would re-interpret the subject for the modern reader. This poetic effort, which he held to be required in every age, was itself heroic, and more valuable than the cold pedantry of Dryasdust.

In his political thought, Carlyle became more and more radically anti-democrat in his search not for elected but for transcendent heroes or leaders. *Past and Present* (1843; ed. A. M. D. Hughes, 1918; ed. D. Arnold, Everyman, 1960) is a work in which his attack on the contemporary failure of democracy, as he saw it, was presented poetically as an account of the ordered life at the medieval abbey of St Edmund's, Bury. Labour and duty are the true ends of life (the 'gospel of work'), and the many voluntarily submit to the leadership of the superior few, such as Abbot Sampson. *Latter Day Pamphlets* (8 essays) (1850) deals with the contemporary scene and is more savage in its gloomy socioeconomic prognostications, more violent in its anathemas, and a failure as a persuasive document. The *Life of John Sterling* (his friend, the editor of *The Times*) (1851) is his best piece of straight biography. Carlyle became one of the most celebrated literary figures in London, and his wife after some years of unhappy isolation also gathered a circle of brilliant friends. Jane Welsh Carlyle died on 21 April 1866, and this event plunged Carlyle into a state of miserable remorse. He felt, with some justice, that he had neglected her: he arranged the *Letters and Memorials of Jane Welsh Carlyle* (controversially edited by J. A. ◊ Froude, 3 vols., 1883) as a kind of expiation. In 1867, he attacked the second Reform Bill, which further extended the parliamentary franchise, in 'Shooting Niagara, and After?' (in *Macmillan's Magazine*). He defended Governor Eyre, the suppressor of the Morant Bay rebellion in Jamaica; and supported the Prussians in the Franco–German War. In 1874, Carlyle refused a baronetcy from Disraeli, and also refused burial in Westminster Abbey. Froude wrote that 'Carlyle (like the Jewish prophets) believed that he had a special message to deliver to the present age. Whether he was correct in this belief, and whether it was a true message, remains to be seen.' This is too simple. Carlyle's reputation shrank as his 'message' was believed to be 'untrue'; it is rising again as his truly poetic attempt to diagnose the ills of his society is appreciated without any necessity to 'assent' to his answers. [A R]

Collected Works, 'Library Edition' (34 vols., 1869–71); 'People's Edition' (37 vols., 1871–4); 'Centenary Edition', ed. H. D. Traill (30 vols., 1896–9); *C. An Anthology*, ed. G. M. Trevelyan (1953); *Selected Works, Reminiscences and Letters*, ed. J. Symons (1955); *Letters to His Wife*, ed. T. Bliss (1953); *Correspondence of Emerson and C.*, ed. J. Slater (New York, 1964) (with important bibliography); *Correspondence between Goethe and C.*, ed C. E. Norton (1887); *Letters* (1814–36), ed. C. E. Norton (1886, 1888); *Letters of C. to J. S. Mill, J. Sterling and Robert Browning*, ed. A. Carlyle (1923).

D. A. Wilson, *Life of C.* (6 vols., 1923–4); J. A. Froude, *T.C.* (4 vols., 1882, 1884) (on the controversy over Froude's biographical approach see W. Dunn, *Froude and C.*, 1930); L. and E. Hanson, *Necessary Evil: The Life of Jane Welsh C.* (1952) (contains unpublished letters); J. Symons, *C., the Life and Ideas of a Prophet* (1952); C. F. Harrold, *C. and German Thought* (Yale U.P., 1934); L. M. Young, *C. and the Art of History* (Philadelphia, 1939); Basil Willey, *Nineteenth Century Studies* (1949); J. Holloway, *The Victorian Sage* (1953); E. R. Bentley, *A Century of Hero-Worship . . . C. and Nietzsche, with Notes on Wagner, Spengler, Stefan George and D. H. Lawrence* (Boston, 2nd edn, 1957); R. K. P. Pankhurst, *The Saint Simonians: Mill and C.* (1957); D. Daiches, 'C. and the Victorian Dilemma', Carlyle Society Lectures, 4 (1963); A. J. LaValley, *C. and the Idea of the Modern* (Yale U.P., 1968); D. Gascoyne, *T. C.* (WTW, 1952) (select bibliography); C. Moore, 'C., a Critical Bibliography', in *English Romantic Poets and Essayists*, ed. C. W. and L. H. Houtchens (revised 1966).

Carman, Bliss (1861–1929). Canadian poet. Born at Fredericton, he attended the universities of New Brunswick, Edinburgh and Harvard. In America he lived precariously as a journalist and public lecturer. His first book, *Low Tide on Grand Pré* (1893), was his best. Friendship with Mrs Mary King, begun in 1897 and continuing with increasing intimacy until his death, added to his monist transcendentalism a fatal quasi-philosophical unitrinianism. With the exception of the popular but undistinguished 'Vagabondia' volumes, his 20th-century verse is marred by prolixity, didacticism and vagueness masking as clarity. After 1908 Carman lived mainly with Dr and Mrs King at New Canaan, Connecticut. Despite the doctrinaire optimism of his philosophical poetry, he suffered from ill health and recurrent depressions aggravated by fear of poverty and death. His books of essays, especially *The Kinship of Nature* (1906), make clear his basically romantic, intuitional poetic. Much of his enormous output reveals a mind at odds with a creative instinct. *Selected Poems* was published in 1954. Carman only rarely does justice to an unusual feeling for the precisely evocative word. He is at his best when he re-creates the sources of regret, as in his first volume, or when formal demands restrict his wordiness, as in the unrhymed sonnets of *Sanctuary* (1929). [P T]

D. Pacey, *Ten Canadian Poets* (1958); H. D. C. Lee, *B. C.: A Study in Canadian Poetry* (1912); D. Stephens, 'A Maritime Myth', *Canadian Literature*, 9 (Summer, 1961).

Carolan, T. ◊ Ó Caerbhalláin, Toirdhealbhach.

Carpenter, Edward (1844–1929). Socialist and moral reformer. Born at Brighton and educated at Trinity Hall, Cambridge, he became a Fellow and took orders, but lost his faith and resigned them (Leslie ◊ Stephen had a similar crisis of conscience). His religious change was followed by a political development when in 1883 he became a socialist and published a long poem, *Towards Democracy* (1883 and later revisions). Carpenter had a nostalgic vision of a primitive, free, moral society based on the ideas of a number of writers, including Whitman (whom he visited), Thoreau and Tolstoy. He thought much on ethics (particularly of sexual behaviour),

aesthetics and sociology, and developed some of his ideas in *Civilisation: Its Cause and Cure* (1889), *Love's Coming of Age* (1896) and *The Intermediate Sex* (1908). He also published an autobiography, *My Days and Dreams* (1916), with a bibliography. [A R]

E. Lewis, *E.C.* (1915); ed. G. Beith, Lowes Dickinson, Havelock Ellis and others, *E. C.: In Appreciation* (1931); F. Vanson, 'C.: The English Whitman', *Contemporary Review*, June 1958.

Carr, John Dickson (pseud. Carter Dickson) (1905–). Prolific detective-story writer. He was born in Uniontown, Pennsylvania, the son of a politician who later became a U.S. Congressman; he went to school in Washington (1913–15). He became a journalist and lived in England and on the continent. The first of his detective novels were set in France and related the adventures of Inspector Bencolin of the Paris police. He became a popular writer when John Dickson Carr began writing about Dr Gideon Fell and 'Carter Dickson' created Sir Henry Merrivale. The eccentricities of these unconventional characters owe much to Carr's own wide experience. His stories are lively and the two main characters full of colour; he favours 'puzzle' plots of the 'locked room' variety and is master of a swift story-telling line. His own peculiar talent lies perhaps in a knack for the macabre; it was the 'tinge of black magic' which saved his story *The Burning Court* from Edmund Wilson's all-inclusive condemnation of detective fiction in the *New Yorker* (14 October 1944 and 20 January 1945). His works include, as John Dickson Carr, *The Emperor's Snuff Box* (1942), *The Devil in Velvet* (1951), and (with A. Conan Doyle) *Exploits of Sherlock Holmes*; and as, Carter Dickson, *She Died a Lady* (1943) and *The Cavalier's Cup* (1953). Carr has also written a biography, *Sir Arthur Conan Doyle* (1949). He has wide-ranging historical interests which often figure in his fiction, and *The Murder of Sir Edmund Godfrey* (1937) offers an ingenious solution of a famous 17th-century mystery. [A R]

'Profile', *New Yorker* (8 and 15 September 1951); H. Haycraft, *Murder for Pleasure: The Life and Times of the Detective Story* (1941).

Carroll, Lewis (pseud. of Charles Lutwidge Dodgson) (1832–98). Mathematician and writer of nonsense. Born at Daresbury in Cheshire, the son of a clergyman, he was educated at Rugby and Christ Church, Oxford, where he became a Student (Fellow) and taught mathematics. He took orders (1861) but held no benefice and rarely preached. Carroll published mathematical works under his real name, on Euclid, algebra and mathematical logic. He had a turn for mathematical puzzles. As a man he was eccentric and withdrawn, finding peace only with little girls (with whom he had many friendships and to whom he wrote whimsical letters). This trait has led the psychologists to find various hidden patterns (more or less unsavoury) in his books of nonsense for children (written under his pseudonym). These also contain rather complex patterns of logical play, parody and satire, that have made them long popular, too, with adult readers. The first of them, *Alice's Adventures in Wonderland* (1865), was written to entertain Alice Liddell, daughter of the Dean of Christ Church; it was originally called 'Alice's Adventures Underground'. He produced a sequel, *Through the Looking Glass* (1872). The illustrations made for these 2 books by Sir John Tenniel are now inseparable from the text. Carroll had a marvellous ear for the associative power of the sound of words, which led him to produce some of the best nonsense verse in English, including the fantasy *The Hunting of the Snark* (1876). *Sylvie and Bruno* (1889) and *Sylvie and Bruno Concluded* (1890) also have some good nonsense verse in them, but are otherwise laboured and unsuccessful attempts to unite a children's story with Christian teaching. He wrote many other shorter pieces of varying interest. [A R]

Collected Verse (1932); Complete Works, ed. A. Woollcott (revised edn, 1949) (not fully comprehensive); Works, ed. R. L. Green (1965).
R. L. Green, L.C. (1960); C. J. Woollen, 'L. C., Philosopher', in Hibbert Journal, XVI (1947); E. Sewell, The Field of Nonsense (1952); A.L. Taylor, The White Knight: A Study of C. L. D. (1952); D. Hudson, L.C. (1954); R. Sutherland, Language and L.C. (The Hague, 1970); M. Gardner, The Annotated Alice (1964), The Annotated Snark (New York, 1962); S. H. Williams and F. Madan, The L.C. Handbook (1962) (bibliography); D. Hudson, L.C. (WTW, 1958).

Carswell, Catherine Roxburgh (1870–1946). Scottish novelist and biographer. The daughter of a Glasgow businessman, Mrs Carswell supported herself by reviewing

for the *Glasgow Herald* from the annulment of her first marriage in 1905 until the paper dropped her in 1915 over a favourable review of D. H. Lawrence's *The Rainbow*. She was one of Lawrence's most loyal and perceptive friends from 1914 until his death, and her biography *The Savage Pilgrimage* (1932, after the original version had been withdrawn under threat of legal action by J. M. ◊ Murry) is the fullest and most sympathetic of the accounts of Lawrence by his friends. Her interpretative biography of Robert Burns (1930, reprinted 1951) affronted adherents of the sentimental 19th-century view of Burns but is now respected as a sound pioneering work. [A I]

Open the Door! (1920) (autobiographical novel); Lying Awake, ed. J. Carswell (1950) (autobiography).

Cartwright, William (1611–43). Poet and dramatist. From Westminster School he went up to Christ Church, Oxford, in 1628, and remained there for the rest of his life. In 1636 his play *The Royal Slave*, with designs by the great Inigo Jones, was successfully acted for the King and Queen at Oxford. He took orders in 1638, and was noted for florid, rhetorical sermons. In 1642 he became Reader in Metaphysic to the University, was briefly imprisoned for his Royalist activities, and preached at Oxford before King Charles after the Battle of Edgehill. Over 50 commendatory verses prefixed his *Works* in 1651. His 4 plays were intended for academic or private performances, though 3 later reached the London stage. *The Lady-Errant*, *The Royal Slave* and *The Siege* are fashionable Cavalier dramas on the cult of platonic love favoured by Queen Henrietta Maria. *The Ordinary* is an imitation of Ben Jonson's 'comedy of humours'. Cartwright's poems include occasional verse, love poetry, humorous verses and translations, and are influenced by Jonson and Donne. [M J]

The Plays and Poems, ed. and intr. G. Blakemore Evans (U. of Wisconsin P., 1951).
A. Harbage, Cavalier Drama (1936).

Cary, (Arthur) Joyce (Lunel) (1888–1957). Poet and novelist. Born in Londonderry, Northern Ireland, the son of an Anglo-Irish family. The 'Joyce' is his mother's family name. He was educated at Tunbridge Wells and Clifton College, and in 1904 went to Edinburgh and Paris to study art; painting, particularly the impressionist imagination, is an important influence on his writing. From 1909 to 1912, he was at Trinity College, Oxford, and from 1912 to 1913 he fought with the Montenegrins in the Balkan War. In 1913, he went to Nigeria in the colonial political service, and during the First World War fought with the Nigeria Regiment in the Cameroons, where he was wounded. Ill-health forced his retirement from Africa in 1920, and he lived in Oxford, devoting his time to writing. His first book, which he worked on for years, was *Aissa Saved* (1932), a story of an African girl converted by missionaries. In 1936, his second novel, *The African Witch*, was a Book Society choice. In 1939 appeared the best of his early works, *Mister Johnson*. In this story of an African clerk Cary raises the main preoccupations of his later fiction, the difficulty of establishing moral judgement, the need for tolerance. In his early work he uses the consciousness of Africans to jolt the reader into examining European clichés. Cary shows great power of understanding other sensibilities (Africans', women's, etc.). He is also a master of considerable comic invention. His other fiction consists of two trilogies, and two separate novels. The first trilogy, about art, is a triptych, which uses the technique of triple representation to develop his thesis, that 'we are alone in our worlds'. *Herself Surprised* (1941) is presented through the eyes of Sara Monday, *To Be a Pilgrim* (1942) through Tom Wilcher and *The Horse's Mouth* (1944) through the artist, Gulley Jimson. The second trilogy deals with politics, and the technique is more complex. In *A Prisoner of Grace* (1952), Naomi Latter is far more articulate than Sara; the main focus of the book is the politician Chester Nimmo, who is the narrator of *Except the Lord* (1953); Jim Latter is the narrator of *Not Honour More* (1955) in which, however, the main emphasis moves back to Nimmo. Love is the theme of one of the detached novels (*A Fearful Joy,* 1945) and the other, *The Captive and the Free* (1959; left unfinished and skilfully edited), deals with a faith-healer; it is the vestige of Cary's plan to devote a third trilogy to religion, later abandoned. He left a mass of manuscript drafts and unpublished material, which a generous benefactor has placed in the Bodleian Library. Cary is a writer whose power is now more fully being recognized. As the titles of the novels show, his views are the product of much reading and reflection. *The Case for African Freedom* (1941) is a political book; *Marching Soldier* (1945) and *The Drunken Sailor* (1947) are volumes of poems. [AR]

Works ('Carfax Edition') (1951 ff.) (fiction only). Walter Allen, *J.C.* (WTW, 1953); A. H. Wright, *J.C.: A Preface to His Novels* (1958) (deals largely with his manuscripts); R. Bloom, *The Indeterminate World: A Study of the Novels of J.C.* (Philadelphia, 1962); C. G. Hoffmann, *J.C.: The Comedy of Freedom* (Pittsburgh U.P., 1965); M. M. Mahood, *J.C.'s Africa* (1964); B. Hardy, 'Form in J. C.'s Novels', *Essays in Criticism*, IV (1954); W. van O'Connor, *J.C.* (Columbia Essays on Modern Writers, New York, 1966); J. Wolkenfeld, *J.C.: The Developing Style* (1968) (with bibliography).

Caudwell, Christopher (pseud. of Christopher St John Sprigg) (1907–37). Marxist critic and theorist, novelist and poet. Born in Putney, he earned his living in London by turning out detective novels and books on aviation very rapidly, wrote sincere and imperfect poems (*Poems*, 1939), but is best remembered for his two works of Marxist criticism, *Studies in a Dying Culture* (1938) and *Illusion and Reality: A Study of the Sources of Poetry* (1939), both published after his death as a soldier in the International Brigade in Spain in 1937. He was a clever, over-productive, rapidly absorptive writer, converted to Marxism in the last two or three years of his short life. His two Marxist critical works lack a solid historical sense, and lack any fine and detailed sense of literary quality, but have a very engaging intuitive eagerness, and aim at a libertarian interpretation of Marxist theory fairly unusual in his own time and rather anticipating the emphasis of modern 'New Left' critics with the young Marx's theories of 'alienation'. He oversimplifies, and yet spots very acutely elements of self-contradiction in writers so different as H. G. Wells, D. H. Lawrence and T. E. Lawrence; and he has a remarkably generous attitude towards the positive merits of the writers with whom he is polemically engaged. [GSF]

Caxton, William (*c.* 1421–91). Printer and translator. Born in the Weald of Kent, he was apprenticed to a London merchant, and was himself a wool trader in the Low Countries for many years, serving as governor of the English Merchant Adventurers at Bruges, 1463–9. Retiring in middle age, he entered the service of

Edward IV's sister, the Duchess of Burgundy, where he indulged his taste for reading and literary work and became interested in the revival of chivalric ideas which influenced the choice of books he was later to print in England. In Cologne around 1472 he first saw a printing-press at work, and there learned the art of printing. He soon established his own press in Bruges, producing 2 works in French before setting up the first book printed in English, his translation of Raoul le Fevre's *The Recuyell of the Historyes of Troye* (1475). In 1476 he crossed to London, where he set up his press at the Red Pale in Westminster, and in the ensuing fourteen industrious years printed and published some 80 works, of which he was himself translator of 21, mainly the French romances that he particularly enjoyed. Early volumes included Lydgate's *Temple of Glass* (1477), Chaucer's *Anelida and Arcite* and *The Parliament of Foules* (1478), and Boethius; and his first big books were *The History of Jason* (1477) and *The Canterbury Tales* (1478 and 1484). Amongst the most important were John of Trevisa's *Polychronicon* of 1387 continued by Caxton (1482); Gower's *Confessio Amantis* (1483); Caxton's major translation, *The Golden Legend* (1483); and Malory's *Morte d'Arthur* (1485).

As a translator Caxton sometimes used curious, old-fashioned and awkward English, but his prefaces and epilogues suggest a vivid, enthusiastic and sensible personality, and his influence as a writer of English was considerable. He has been called the greatest literary figure of the 15th century in Britain – not as author or translator but as technologist, arbiter of literary taste and champion of English (rather than Latin) as the language of the English printed book. He made possible the wide dissemination of books throughout England, and was a key-figure in the history of communication. [M J]

W. Blades, *The Life and Typography of W.C.* (2 vols., 1861–3); G. P. Winship, *W.C. and His Work* (1937) and *W.C. and the First English Press* (1938); M. McLuhan, *The Gutenberg Galaxy: The Making of Typographic Man* (1962).

Cecil, Lord (Edward Christian) David (Gascoyne) (1902–). Literary critic. The youngest son of the 4th Marquess of Salisbury, he was educated at Eton and Christ Church, Oxford, and became a Fellow of Wadham College (1924–30). In 1930 he became a Fellow of New College, Oxford, and in 1948 was elected Goldsmith's Professor of English Literature at that university. He is an urbane and *belletrist* critic. His books read well, and propound no particular scheme or overt doctrine. *The Stricken Deer*, a life of Cowper, perhaps concentrating too heavily on that unfortunate man's unhappy illness to the neglect of his writing, appeared in 1929. This was followed by *Sir Walter Scott* (1933); and other titles include *Early Victorian Novelists* (1934); *Jane Austen* (1935); *The Young Melbourne* (1939; a sequel, *Lord M.*, 1954); *Hardy, The Novelist* (1943); *Poets and Story-Tellers* (1949) and *Max* (Beerbohm) (1964). Much of his writing comes from his popular university lecturing. He edited the *Oxford Book of Christian Verse* (1940) and *The Fine Art of Reading* (1957). [A R]

Ceiriog. ◊ Hughes, John.

Céitinn, Séathrún (Geoffrey Keating (1570–c. 1650). Irish poet and historian. Born in Co. Tipperary, he was the author of devotional works, including *Trí Biorghaoithe an Bháis* ('Three Shafts of Death'), a collection of short essays and meditations. His magnum opus is *Foras Feasa ar Éirinn* ('Outline of Irish History'). As a historian, he deemed it his duty to undertake the defence of Ireland against such writers as Davies, Hanmer, Spenser and Giraldus Cambrensis. The circumstances of the day hardly favoured scholarly objectivity, in Ireland or elsewhere. Not infrequently, his literary sense outweighed his critical faculty: he included tales on their artistic, rather than historical, merits; usually, however, with the caution *más fíor* ('if it be true'). His book became a firm favourite and established his fame in Irish literature. Among his poems is the well-known 'Mo bheannacht leat, a sgríbheann/go hInis aoibhinn Ealga' ('My blessing with thee, missive, to pleasant Inis Ealga'), written probably while he was a young student in France: and 'Óm sgeól ar Ardmhaigh Fháil ní chodlaim oidhche' ('With the tidings from Fál's great plain I sleep not nightly'), a fine piece, full of patriotic indignation. [S B]

D. Comyn and P. S. Dinneen, *Foras Feasa ar Éirinn* (1902, 1908); E. C. Mac Giolla Eáin, *Dánta, amhráin is caointe S.C.* (1900).

Chambers, Sir E(dmund) K(erchever) (1866–1954). Scholar. A brilliant undergraduate, he failed to carry off a fellowship at Oxford. He entered the Civil Service in 1892, and when he retired in 1926 was Second Secretary to the Board of Education. He contrived to be often in the British Museum, was a founder-member of the Malone Society in 1906, and in his spare-time scholarship far exceeded in output and comprehensiveness that of many professional academics. From the nineties he had planned 'a little book about Shakespeare and the conditions, literary and dramatic, under which he wrote', but felt he must thoroughly explore Shakespeare's antecedents. The result was that he published in 1903 *The Medieval Stage* in 2 volumes, and in 1923 *The Elizabethan Stage* in 4. In 1930 the 2-volume *William Shakespeare: Facts and Problems* appeared. He edited many texts, and wrote on medieval and 19th-century works. Chambers's great service was to gather together and assess the many documents relating to the drama, and his *Elizabethan Stage*, though it will eventually need revision, will remain the standard work of scholarly reference. [M J]

F. P. Wilson and J. Dover Wilson, 'Sir E. C.', *Proceedings of the British Academy*, XLII (1956).

Chambers, Robert (1802–71). Scottish publisher, editor and miscellaneous writer. He acquired an intimate knowledge of Scottish folklore during his childhood in Peebles, a Scottish Border town. He began selling books from a street stall in Edinburgh in 1818, and with his elder brother William (1800–83) soon ventured into jobbing printing and the issue of a small magazine. The popular education movement of the 1820s, associated with ◊ Brougham, Birkbeck, Constable's *Miscellany* and the Society for the Diffusion of Useful Knowledge, encouraged the brothers to launch in 1832 *Chambers's Edinburgh Journal*, a three-halfpenny weekly magazine which almost at once attained the unprecedented circulation of fifty thousand copies, creating technical problems solved only by the introduction of the steam press. William managed the *Journal*, while Robert's essays, 'moral, familiar and humorous', pitched at just the right level for an uneducated but aspiring audience and avoiding the relentless informativeness of the S.D.U.K. publications, determined its character and its success in the great

19th-century diffusion of culture. The Chamberses published many other educational works, most notably their *Encyclopaedia* (from 1859). Robert himself wrote most of the *Cyclopaedia of English Literature* (1842–4; new editions down to 1938) and of the *Biographical Dictionary of Eminent Scotsmen* (1833–5, etc.): he wrote a still valuable *Life of Robert Burns* (1851; revised by W. Wallace, 1896) and collected *Traditions of Edinburgh* (1824), *Popular Rhymes of Scotland* (1826), *The Songs of Scotland Prior to Burns* (1862) and *Domestic Annals of Scotland* (1859–61). In *Vestiges of the Natural History of Creation*, published anonymously in 1844, Robert contributed to the intellectual life of his time by arguing a popular case for evolution. Although not strictly a scientific work, *Vestiges* prepared the way for *The Origin of Species* by accustoming the public to discussion and controversy about the issues with which Darwin was to deal. [A I]

W. Chambers, *Memoir of William and Robert C.* (1872); A. A. Cruse, *The Victorians and Their Books* (1935); M. Millhauser, *Just Before Darwin* (Middletown, Conn., 1959); J. Lehmann, *Ancestors and Friends* (1962).

Chambers, William. ◊ Chambers, Robert.

Chapman, George (*c*. 1560–1634). Poet, dramatist and translator. Little is known of the early and later life, or of the education, of this major Elizabethan author. Born of yeoman stock in Hertfordshire, he emerged as a poet in 1594 with the publication of *The Shadow of Night*, and as a playwright a year later when Philip ◊ Henslowe presented his very popular comedy *The Blind Beggar of Alexandria*. His later plays were acted by the boy players at Blackfriars. An early associate of Marlowe, Ralegh, the mathematician Matthew Roydon, the astronomer Thomas Harriot, and the free-thinking 'school of night', he was the *protégé* of Prince Henry from 1603 to 1612, and subsequently of the Earl of Somerset. After 1616, the year of his most massive Homeric publication, he wrote no major poems and only occasional plays (always in collaboration). His long friendship with Jonson ended in vituperative quarrels, and he was constantly bedevilled by debt. On his death a monument by Inigo Jones was erected to his memory in St Giles-in-the-Fields.

Chapman's first volume consisted of 2

obscure, highly intellectual poems on contrasting themes, *Hymnus in Noctem* and *Hymnus in Cynthiam*, which combine semi-serious wit with philosophical speculation. His next book (1595) contained the Ovidian erotic epyllion *Ovid's Banquet of Sense*, one of the most striking examples of this Elizabethan genre, as well as *A Coronet for His Mistress* (10 sonnets), and an *Amorous Zodiac* translated from the French. In 1596 he made a blank-verse contribution to Lawrence Keymis's *Second Voyage to Guiana*, and in 1598 there appeared his brilliant completion of Marlowe's *Hero and Leander*. Scholars have called his *Euthymiae Raptus, or The Tears of Peace* (1609) the best poetic exposition of his difficult philosophy, which combined Christian, Platonist and Stoic strands, and which is embodied in both his epic translations and his conception of the tragic hero.

The year 1598 also saw the publication of *Seven Books of the Iliads of Homer, Prince of Poets*, the first instalment of his great poetic translation, which was followed by *Achilles' Shield* (1598), by a further collection in 1608, by the complete *Iliads* (1611), by 12 of the 24 *Homer's Odysses* (1964) and by *The Whole Works of Homer, Prince of Poets, In his Iliads and Odysses* (1616). His translation (with its frequent interpolations and moralizations) is Renaissance in spirit and has usually been admired: Keats's first reading of it was the occasion of a famous sonnet (1816). Six of Chapman's comedies, written between 1595 and 1605, are extant. They combine the Jonsonian 'comedy of humours' with romance, and include *A Humorous Day's Mirth*, *The Gentleman Usher* and *Monsieur D'Olive*. *Eastward Ho!*, the excellent city comedy, done in collaboration with Jonson and Marston, resulted in prison sentences for the authors because of a moderate jibe about King James. *The Widow's Tears* (c. 1609) is a version of the perennially popular Widow of Ephesus theme. Chapman's most characteristic works are the tragedies, which have their basis in his philosophic speculations and classical learning. Each is centred on a strong-willed and powerful hero, Marlovian in ambition, who has affinities with Hercules. *Bussy D'Ambois* (1604) and its sequel *The Revenge of Bussy D'Ambois* (1610) were both based on recent French history. A second 2-part play was *The Conspiracy and Tragedy of Charles Duke of Byron* (1608), again treating a Herculean figure, but exposing weakness as well as strength. A third play was *The Tragedy of Chabot Admiral of France* (c. 1613). No actor or director has made the effort to bring to life in the modern theatre Chapman's unique fusion of strong situations, commanding hero, rhetorical speech and philosophic exploration. [M J]

The Poems, ed. P. Bartlett (1941; reissued 1962); *C.'s Homer: The Iliad, The Odyssey, and the Lesser Homerica*, ed. A. Nicoll (2 vols., 1957); *The Plays*, ed. T. M. Parrott (4 vols., reissued 1961). M. C. Bradbrook, *The School of Night* (1936); G. de F. Lord, *Homeric Renaissance: The Odyssey of G.C.* (1956); M. MacLure, *G.C.: A Critical Study* (Toronto, 1966); E. Rees, *The Tragedies of G.C.: Renaissance Ethics in Action* (1954); E. Waith, *The Herculean Hero in Marlowe, C., Shakespeare and Dryden* (1962); J. W. Wieler, *G.C.: The Effect of Stoicism on His Tragedies* (New York, 1949).

Chatterton, Thomas (1752–70). Poet. Born in Bristol, the posthumous son of a schoolmaster, he was educated at Colston's Hospital (1760–7), a charity school, and in 1767 apprenticed to a local attorney as a clerk. His family were practically hereditary sextons of the church of St Mary Redcliffe, and the young Chatterton spent time studying the ancient archives of the parish. His literary talent developed precociously and showed itself during his brief life in enough satire, lyric, dramatic and narrative poetry to fill 3 volumes. His peculiar education, however, united his genius with a talent for literary imitation, a union which he was rarely given an opportunity to break. He created from the muniments and tombs of St Mary Redcliffe an imaginary 15th-century world of Bristol, in which he set the poems of 'Thomas Rowley, a Secular Priest of St John's'. The context came from his imaginative re-creation of the ancient history and architecture of Bristol; Chatterton's imaginative act is related to the general interest in the past which developed all through the 18th century (◊ Gray, Macpherson and Walpole, Horace), but there is to be found in Chatterton's work an intensity of imagination, an interest in the past for its own sake, which is perhaps the most remarkable concomitant of his genius. The language which Chatterton devised for his writings (he seems to have 'translated' his compositions) is to a modern reader an obvious hodge-podge of different periods and dialects, but Rowley himself, as a creation, is 'real' enough. The literary inspiration of Chatterton's poems is not, however, medieval (he seems to have known little of 15th-century poetry outside Chaucer), but comes from Shakespeare, Spenser and the 16th-century poets chiefly. In 1763 he published his first poem, 'On the Last Epiphany', in *Farley's Bristol Journal*. In 1768, he began publishing his 'forged' documents, and offered a series of several 'ancient poems' to James Dodsley, the publisher, who refused them. The case of Macpherson's *Ossian* was perhaps an inhibition. The main contemporary interest in Chatterton lay in discussing the 'authenticity' of his poems. He offered some of his work to Horace Walpole, hoping for patronage; Walpole at first took him up, but dropped him when William Mason, Gray and others said he was a 'forger'. Chatterton had been publishing in London periodicals since early 1769, and in 1770 began writing political verse satire in support of 'Wilkes and Liberty'. He went to London in April of the latter year. He made something of a living by writing topical poems and comic opera libretti, but grew despondent through lack of recognition, and killed himself with arsenic.

Three aspects of Chatterton's career have engaged attention. His qualities as a poet of genius are now obvious (perhaps best seen in 'An Excelente Balade of Charitie', often anthologized). His passionate interest in history has been interpreted as a Romantic state of mind, escaping from the harsh reality of the present into a dream world; there may be something in this, but his valuing of the past for its own sake appeals to the modern reader. To the Romantic poets who followed him, he became the emblem of the native genius (an 18th-century preoccupation) who died young; to this, though, they added the notion of the artist at odds with his society, who scornfully took his own life. He thus became Wordsworth's 'marvellous Boy, The sleepless Soul, who perished in his Pride'; and Keats (in some ways another version of the emblem) dedicated *Endymion* to his memory. [A R]

Works (*Rowley Poems*) (1777); *Works*, ed. R. Southey and J. Cottle (3 vols., 1803); *Poetical Works*, with an essay on the Rowley Poems by W. W. Skeat (2 vols., 1875); *The Poems*, ed. Sidney Lee (2 vols., 1906–9); *The Complete Poetical Works*, ed. H. D. Roberts (2 vols., Muse's Library, 1906) (modernized spelling).

E. H. W. Meyerstein, *A Life of T. C.* (1930); F. S. Miller, 'The Historic Sense of T. C.', in *ELH*, XI (1944); F. A. Hyatt and W. Bazeley, *The Bibliographer's Manual of Gloucester Poetry* (1895–7).

Chaucer, Geoffrey (1340?–1400). Poet. Born in London, son of John Chaucer, a prosperous wine-merchant, and his wife Agnes. He was in the household of Prince Lionel, Duke of Clarence, by 1357, fought in France 1359–60, was taken prisoner and ransomed. During the 1360s he probably studied at the Inner Temple and may have visited Spain. About 1366 he married Philippa, whose sister Katherine Swynford was mistress and later third wife of Lionel's brother, John of Gaunt. An esquire of the royal household in 1367, in 1368 he went to France and in 1372–3 to Italy (where he may have met Petrarch) on diplomatic missions which brought him into contact with continental and Renaissance culture. He had probably begun to write with a translation (some of which survives) of the great French model of psychological allegory, *Le Roman de la Rose*: but his earliest certainly dateable work is *The Book of the Duchess*, an elegy for John of Gaunt's beloved first wife Blanche, who died in 1369. Italian influence appears in *The House of Fame* (?1379–80). Living in London over Aldgate in 1374–86, he was first Controller of the customs for wool, and in 1382 also Controller of the petty custom on wines, with a permanent deputy. In 1386 he lost these posts, but represented Kent in Parliament. During these years he translated the classic medieval work on free will and predestination, time and eternity, Boethius's *Consolation of Philosophy*, and wrote a number of works, including *Troilus and Criseyde* and *The Parliament of Fowls*, and some drafts of stories later to appear in *The Canterbury Tales* – whose prologue he seems to have begun in 1387, when it was probably first conceived as a single work. In 1387 he was in trouble for debt, but in 1389 he was appointed (perhaps by the direct influence of King Richard II, who assumed control of affairs in that year) Clerk of the King's Works, a post in which he was active, and in the performance of which he was assaulted and twice robbed. In 1390, he composed for his 10-year-old son Lewis (a student at Oxford) a scientific work, his *Astrolabe*. In 1391 he resigned the Clerkship, but was made deputy forester in the royal forest of Petherton in Somerset. He was in some trouble for debt between then and his death, but also received a number of grants from Richard II and from John of Gaunt's son Henry IV. He probably died on 25 October 1400, in a house leased by him in the gardens of Westminster Abbey, and he was buried in the Abbey. His son Thomas was also later a distinguished public servant.

Chaucer's interests were all-embracing: he knew the world and read omnivorously. Among his personal friends were such great men as John of Gaunt, poets such as the Frenchman Eustace Deschamps, John Gower and the philosopher-poet Ralph Strode, probably also Strode's friend Wycliffe the reformer, and the great architect Henry Yevele. His face in a contemporary portrait seems shrewd, benevolent and quizzical. He portrays himself in his books as shy, naïve, a lover of solitude and daisies, bookish and unhappy in love and marriage. But, though this may represent an aspect of him, the very techniques he uses in self-mockery reveal underlying it a sophisticated artist, a subtle psychologist and a brilliant thinker and master of words. To understand the irony with which he treats himself is to begin to appreciate the humility, sympathy and humour with which he treats the rest of humanity, and indeed the whole universe. As in other books of his time (e.g. *Sir Gawain and the Green Knight*) this vision has a religious basis in the theology of penitence and self-knowledge: and it issues ultimately in a kind of humour of the sublime.

These qualities are already present in *The Book of the Duchess*, a charming elegy which, although in the tradition of the dream-allegories of Machaut and Froissart, breaks from that tradition in dealing more immediately with a dialogue between two real people, the sympathetic but stupid Chaucer and the heartbroken John of Gaunt, in a wood during a May morning hunt. The sorrow which the poem aims to console is, by its inclusion in comedy of character and sweetness of natural description, transcended in a comprehensive world-view.

This unity by inclusion appears again in *The House of Fame*, in which however humour is dominant, going so far as deliberate parody of Dante and his Beatrice in the again comically incapable Chaucer and his heavenly guide the Eagle. In the delightful *Parliament of Fowls*, a Valentine's-day council of birds over a love-dispute, he carries out an inquiry into love in the orders of society and in the universe which anticipates the ethical and social observation of *The Canterbury Tales*. The relationship of earthly love to the universe is again at the centre of *Troilus and Criseyde*, and, together with the Boethian theme of the relation of man's freewill to God's foreknowledge, enables Chaucer to deepen and humanize his source, Boccaccio's *Il filostrato*. The comedy, tragedy and charity with which he draws Pandarus, Troilus and Criseyde, his mastery of dialogue and psychological analysis (including dream-psychology) and the varied music of the rhyme-royal stanza which he perfected for this poem, support C. S. Lewis's judgement that, although one passage, Troilus's betrayal, 'is so painful that perhaps no one without reluctance reads it twice', yet in the whole Chaucer 'shows himself our supreme poet of happiness'. 'Anelida and Arcite', 'The Complaint to Pity', *The Legend of Good Women* and other shorter poems are less remarkable, though the *Legend* illustrates Chaucer's growing skill in narrative, and gives us both his most delightful self-portrait and one of his best lyrics, the balade 'Hyd, Absolon, thy gilte tresses clere'. Two independent lyrics also illustrate his genius, 'Merciless Beauty', a roundel of 39 lines which covers the gamut from broken-hearted pathos to serene comedy, and the noble balade 'Truth'. Whether a couplet from this last – 'Forth, pilgrim, forth! Forth, beste, out of thy stal! Know thy contree, look up, thank God of al' – conveys the unifying theme of *The Canterbury Tales* may be regarded as the central interpretative problem of that book. Chaucer seems to have begun it with a few tales independently written, set them in the framework of a pilgrimage and story-telling contest, and gradually developed a grand design, which, however, although he marked its beginning and end with the 'Prologue' and 'The Parson's Tale', is scarcely half completed. Some readers feel that in the book as we have it, although the tales are memorable individually for their variety and stylistic brilliance, only those of the Pardoner and the Wife of Bath can be seen as 'dramatic extensions of personality', while the framework has a purely mechanical function and only intermittent life, there being no central theme to which all the tales subscribe. This view seems unnecessarily purist. While the tales of the dominating, affectionate and worldly Wife of Bath and the corrupted Pardoner, 'the one lost soul among the Canterbury Pilgrims' (Kittredge), do most to reveal their tellers, still the already antique nobility of the Knight, the Squire's romantic fantasy, the Miller's joyful bawdry, the Franklin's balance between class-sensitivity and good-heartedness, and the presence of the Prioress's femininity in her devotion to a child-saint, qualities hinted at in the descriptions of the Pilgrims in the 'Prologue' and partly developed in their conversations, do unfold in their tales. The Nun's Priest's witty beast fable of Chanticleer and the fox, the Canon's Yeoman's diatribe against alchemy, and other excellent stories, are either related by characters not developed in the 'Prologue' or are only very generally appropriate, yet they do help to form a series of dialogues between the Pilgrims on humanity's various attitudes to living. Chaucer, as ever, directs his simplest joke at himself by making his own tale the gauchest of all: and this helps the impression that he intends throughout to jolt his readers into self-awareness by seeing that they themselves are described. His perennial themes of freewill and fate, and the relationship of kinds of love to kinds of marriage, with, underlying them, his hunt for a harmony between God's view of the world and man's, run through the book; and it has a logical conclusion in the Parson's sermon on penitence as the glorious pilgrimage to Jerusalem celestial. The Miller's tale of how a student seduced his landlord's wife and was branded in the bottom, the Knight's of the rivalry of two prisoners of war for Emelye, and the Pardoner's of the young men who set out to kill death, are perhaps the finest. But the book as a whole is the masterpiece, forming (except that it lacks the intensity of *Troilus and Criseyde*) the consummation of everything Chaucer had written hitherto, so much so that its incompleteness seems only necessary tribute to its indefinite variety. His style keeps up the pace: he will move from an unforced sublimity ('O martir, sowded to virginitee') to a brutal physicality ('My throte is cut unto my nekke-boon') in a few verses. The language has a straight-forwardness and force lost to later English (cf. Dryden's translations: compare, e.g., 'Now with his love, now in his colde grave / Allone, withouten any compaignye' with

'Now warm in love, now withering in the grave / Never, O never more to see the sun / Still dark, in a damp vault, and still alone'). Chaucer's eye for significant detail is most noteworthy in caricature (as with the lawyer, 'Nowhere so bisy a man as he ther was / And yet he semed bisier than he was') but it is equally present in the aureate diction for which his own age prized him.

His disciple ◊ Lydgate praised him as the first to 'rain the gold dewdrops of speech and eloquence' into English. Hoccleve compared him to Virgil and Aristotle. In the 16th and 17th centuries, loss of the medieval final *e* and broad vowels spoilt his music, and he was then patronized a little, though still admired for commonsense and good story-telling. Dryden could not say less of his character-drawing than 'here is God's plenty', and Blake followed him in saying 'Chaucer's characters live age after age. Every age is a Canterbury Pilgrimage; we all pass on, each sustaining one of these characters; nor can a child be born who is not one or other of these characters of Chaucer.' Once the nature of Chaucer's dialect and metre was recovered (primarily by Thomas Tyrwhitt, in his edition of *The Canterbury Tales*, 1775–8) his style was more and more admired. Matthew Arnold allowed him 'liquid diction, fluid movement, largeness, freedom, shrewdness, benignity' but denied him 'high seriousness'; modern scholars, attending to his philosophic and religious themes, have restored him that also. His modern popular audience is again realizing his dramatic gifts. The tendency is once more towards recognizing him as second among English writers only to Shakespeare. [S M]

Works, ed. F. N. Robinson (2nd edn, 1957). H. S. Bennett, *Chaucer and the Fifteenth Century* (1947); G. K. Chesterton, *Chaucer* (1932); M. M. Crow and C. C. Olson, *Chaucer Life Records* (1966); N. Coghill, *Geoffrey Chaucer* (WTW, 2nd edn, 1959); G. G. Coulton, *Chaucer and His England* (1930); G. L. Kittredge, *Chaucer and His Poetry* (Cambridge, Mass., 1915); J. L. Lowes, *Geoffrey Chaucer* (1934); J. Speirs, *Chaucer the Maker* (1951); J. A. W. Bennett, *The Parlement of Foules* (1957) and *Chaucer's Book of Fame* (1968); M. Bowden, *A Commentary on the General Prologue to The Canterbury Tales* (1949); W. Clemen, *Chaucer's Early Poetry* (1963); C. S. Lewis, *The Allegory of Love* (1936); G. Muscatine, *Chaucer and the French Tradition* (1957); R. O. Payne, *The Key of Remembrance* (1963); D. W. Robertson, Jr, *A Preface to Chaucer* (1963).

Chaudhuri, Nirad Chandra (1897–). Indian writer. Born into a liberal Hindu family in Bengal, he was forced by failing health to abandon his postgraduate studies in history at the University of Calcutta, and he spent several years in retirement. He was active among Tagore's literary following in Calcutta during the twenties. He has been an editor, journalist, broadcaster and government employee in Delhi. Chaudhuri began writing *The Autobiography of an Unknown Indian* (1951) in 1947. It is a fascinating, discursive account of his own life, disciplined by a knowledge of the historical forces at work in India, full of challenging perceptions and written with the educated Indian's characteristic delight in English words. A visit to England in 1955, sponsored by the B.B.C., led to the writing of *A Passage to England* (1959), a book distinguished by the graceful articulation of unique insights into the English way of life. *Continent of Circe* (1965) is an attack on the Indian way of life. [P T]

The Intellectual in India (1967).

Cheke, Sir John (1514–57). Classical scholar and prose writer. Born in Cambridge, he was a don at St John's College, a notable centre of Protestantism and classical humanism. In 1540 he was made the first Regius Professor of Greek at Cambridge: he taught Roger ◊ Ascham, who succeeded him; he introduced a new pronunciation of Greek; and he vigorously promoted Greek studies in England. From 1544 he was tutor to the future Edward VI and occasionally also to Elizabeth. He flourished politically under Henry VIII and Edward VI, receiving a royal pension, monastic lands, the provostship of King's College, Cambridge, and, in 1552, a knighthood. He became Secretary of State in 1553, but his Protestantism and his support of Lady Jane Gray forced him to leave England on the accession of Mary. A treacherous safe conduct led to his arrest in Brussels, to imprisonment in the Tower and to a forced recantation of his Protestant beliefs. Never primarily an English writer, Cheke published Greek texts, translations into Latin and works of theology. He had strong views on English spelling reform and on keeping English in its native purity, unmixed with Romance words, as his curious translation of St Matthew shows. His *Hurt of Sedition* (1549) is a political pamphlet in a more normal prose. [M J]

C. S. Lewis, *English Literature in the Sixteenth Century* (1954).

Chester Cycle. ◊ Miracle Plays.

Chesterfield, Philip Dormer Stanhope, 4th Earl of (1694–1773). Diplomatist, statesman, letter and miscellaneous writer. Educated at Trinity College, Cambridge, he was ambassador to The Hague (1728–36), Secretary of State in 1744 and Lord Lieutenant of Ireland (1745–6). An able parliamentarian and speaker, he also dabbled in political journalism (in the *Craftsman* and the *World*), and was renowned for his wit. His literary fame rests on *Characters of Eminent Persons* (1777, 1778) and his famous *Letters*, polished and worldly, written almost daily to his bastard son Philip Dormer Stanhope, to direct his education (published by his son's widow in 1774; ed. and intr. B. Dobrée, 6 vols., 1932; Everyman, 1929). They are an 18th-century version of the old conduct books, and in the manner of their kind concentrated on the inculcation of polished and sophisticated social behaviour, subordinating moral and intellectual improvement to that end. For this they have been censured; and they do often seem to be unpleasantly calculating. Ironically, the boy was awkward and inarticulate. A second series, published by Lord Carnarvon (1890), was addressed to Chesterfield's godson, who succeeded to the title. Chesterfield was the unfortunate recipient of Samuel ◊ Johnson's devastating letter charging him with neglect and then exploitation on the appearance of the Dictionary – unfortunate, because he seems to have been a man of cultivation and wide reading and genuinely interested in the project. [A R]

Miscellaneous Works, with 'Memoirs of His Life' by Dr M. Maty (2 vols., 1777).
W. Connely, *The True C.* (1939); R. Coxon, *C. and His Critics* (1925).

Chesterton, Gilbert Keith (1874–1936). Essayist, novelist, poet. Born in London, son of an estate agent, he was educated at St Paul's and the Slade School of Art. He began his career as a literary journalist, and it is in this genre that his most successful work was done. His first book of poems, *The Wild Knight* (1900), was published in the year he met ◊ Belloc, some of whose work he later illustrated. *The Napoleon of Notting Hill* (1904) was the first of his several novels. Chesterton was, however, primarily an essayist, and his novels of ideas are to a large extent fictionalized polemical essays. More successful were his works of literary criticism, which include *Robert Browning* (1903), an excellent straightforward guide, *Dickens* (1906), an enthusiastic study, and *Bernard Shaw* (1909). *Orthodoxy* (1908) is Chesterton's exposition of the Christian religion, and *What's Wrong with the World* (1910) sets out his political and social beliefs. Already he was greatly intrigued by Catholicism, and he wrote a number of detective stories in which the detective is a Catholic priest. The first volume of these to appear was *The Innocence of Father Brown* (1911). His critical volume *The Victorian Age in Literature* (1913) is a model of its kind, strangely followed by the inaccurate and one-sided *Short History of England* (1917).

Chesterton was received into the Roman Catholic Church in 1922 by his friend Father O'Connor, the original of 'Father Brown'. From then on, he became predominantly a Catholic apologist, producing the studies *St Francis of Assisi* (1923) and *St Thomas Aquinas* (1933) as well as other theological works. His published works run to over 100 volumes. Amongst the fiction, *The Club of Queer Trades* (1905) and the Father Brown stories are excellent light entertainment. *The Man Who Was Thursday* (1908) starts out as a detective-story involving anarchists, secret agents and a revolutionary plot, and turns into a parable about God, in which Chesterton presents some of his favourite ideas about life, ordinary man, happiness and the wisdom of the heart. [C O]

The Man Who Knew Too Much (1922); *The Flying Inn* (1914); *Collected Poems* (1933); *The Club of Queer Trades* (1905); *Selected Essays*, ed. J. Guest (1936); *Essays*, ed. K. E. Whitehorn (1953).
M. Ward, *G.K.C.* (1944) (biography); H. Belloc, *The Place of C. in English Letters* (1940); F. A. Lea, *The Wild Knight of Battersea: G.K.C.* (1945); Hugh Kenner, *Paradox in C.* (1948).

Chettle, Henry (*c.* 1560–*c.* 1607). Dramatist and pamphleteer. The son of a dyer, he was apprenticed to a London printer in 1577, and was partner in a printing firm for three years from 1591. He edited Robert Greene's *Groatsworth of Wit* for posthumous publication in 1592, and wrote 2 undistinguished narrative pamphlets in the style of Greene and Nashe – *Kind-Heart's Dream* (1593)

and *Pierce Plainnes Seven-Years' Prenticeship* (1595). In the preface to the first he regretted not having moderated Greene's jealous attack on Shakespeare. Between 1598 and *c.* 1603 he was sole author of 13 plays and joint author of some 35 plays, mainly for Philip ◊ Henslowe's theatre. This prolific output, and the fact that he was imprisoned for debt, suggest that he was constantly under financial hardship. He worked in a wide variety of Elizabethan dramatic genres, but only 5 plays survive in print. They are 2 plays on English history, *The Downfall* and *The Death of Robert, Earl of Huntingdon* (both with ◊ Munday, 1598); *The Blind Beggar of Bednal-Green* (with J. ◊ Day, 1600); *The Pleasant Comedy of Patient Grissill* (with ◊ Dekker and Haughton, 1600); and his most important play *The Tragedy of Hoffman, or A Revenge for a Father* (1602), in which, for the first time, a revenger-*villain* replaced Kyd's revenger-*hero* as the central figure of a typical tragedy of blood. [M J]

F. Bowers, *Elizabethan Revenge Tragedy, 1587–1642* (1940); H. Jenkins, *The Life and Work of H.C.* (1934).

Christie, Agatha (Mary Clarissa) (1891–). Detective-story writer. Born at Torquay, the daughter of F. A. Miller of New York, she was educated at home and studied singing in Paris. She was married in 1914, divorced in 1928, and subsequently married the archaeologist Max Mallowan; thereafter she spent several months each year in Syria and Iraq (the setting of *Death on the Nile*, 1937, *Murder in Mesopotamia*, 1936, and *They Came to Baghdad*, 1951, as well as her autobiographical volume *Come Tell Me How You Live*, 1946). She is the author of over 50 very popular detective stories, with wide sales in Europe and America, and extensively translated. Her first novel, *The Mysterious Affair at Styles*, appeared in 1920, and perhaps the most famous, *The Murder of Roger Ackroyd*, in 1926. Since 1953 she has enjoyed another run of success with West End theatre adaptations of her fiction. She follows the English detective-story formulae of intricate (sometimes highly implausible) plots and an 'eccentric' private detective (such as the Belgian Hercule Poirot, who speaks a kind of schoolboy imitation Anglo-French). Her idealized English bourgeois settings may contribute to her popularity. She was created D.B.E. in 1971. She has also written 'straight' fiction as 'Mary West-macott'. Some of her stories have been filmed, and her latest titles include *Cat among the Pigeons* (1959), *The Pale Horse* (1961), *The Mirror Crack'd from Side to Side* (1962) and *Endless Night* (1967). [AR]

H. Haycraft, *Murder for Pleasure* (1941); Edmund Wilson, 'Who Cares Who Killed Roger Ackroyd?', *New Yorker* (20 January 1945); Raymond Chandler, 'The Simple Art of Murder', in *The Art of the Mystery Story*, ed. H. Haycraft (1946); G. C. Ramsey, *A.C., Mistress of Mystery* (1968) (bibliography).

Church, Richard (Thomas) (1893–   ). Poet, novelist, autobiographer and essayist. The son of a London postman, he made a career in the Civil Service and later as a publisher's adviser, while devoting most of his real interests and energies to writing. As a poet, he is in a homely and pastoral tradition, owing something to the Georgians and, beyond them, to his favourite poet, Wordsworth. His 2 volumes of auto-biography, *Over the Bridge* (1955) and *The Golden Sovereign* (1957), were awarded the *Sunday Times* gold medal in 1955. The first in particular is a fascinating account of a humble London childhood, transfigured by a passion for poetry. [GSF]

Twentieth-Century Psalter (1943); *Collected Poems* (1948); *The Porch* (1937) (first of a trilogy of novels).

Churchill, Charles (1731–64). Satirist and political writer. He was born in Westminster, the son of the curate of St John's there, and later also rector of Rainham in Essex. After a brilliant career at Westminster School, he spent a brief period at St John's College, Cambridge, but at 17 an unfortunate, clandestine marriage with a young girl (they later separated) terminated his academic career, forcing him, however, into the uncongenial necessity of taking holy orders. He held a poor country curacy but in 1758 succeeded his father in the scarcely more profitable curacy in Westminster. Together with his school friend ◊ Colman, the elder, he was greatly interested in the theatre, and made his reputation with a satire praising Garrick and attacking other actors and managers, as well as public figures, *The Rosciad* (1761, 5 edns). As a celebrated writer, he became intimate with John Wilkes and other opposition political figures; he took a major part in the writing of the

former's influential periodical, the *North Briton*, and wrote the famous unpublished no. 45, which was one of the pretexts for the warrant for Wilkes's arrest. Churchill shows himself a skilled prose writer. His satire makes very effective use of ironical eulogy and wounding personal portraits; his vehement tone of superiority has been more easily imitated by undergraduates than his skill. His best sustained work is found in 3 poems: *An Epistle to William Hogarth* (1763, 3 edns), attacking the painter for the anti-Wilkes views of his political caricatures; *The Prophecy of Famine: A Scots Pastoral* (1763, 5 edns), an attack on the chief minister Lord Bute and his fellow-countrymen; and an onslaught on 'Jemmy Twitcher', Lord Sandwich, *The Candidate* (1764). An unfinished fragment, the ironical *Dedication to Dr W. Warburton Bishop of Gloucester*, is a powerful piece of vindictive hostility, short enough to avoid Churchill's common fault of disconnected fullness. After Dryden and Pope, Churchill is probably the greatest master of the polemical use of the heroic couplet. His own hallmark is a combination of sharp personalities and complex syntax. In the couplet, his longest work, *Gotham*, in 3 separately published books (1764), contains hints of other interests which his very brief writing career gave no time for development; *The Times* (1764) is a more generalized attack on the 'vices' of the time and shows a tiresome tendency in Churchill's work towards a lack of sympathy with the complexities of human character. He also dealt extensively with the contemporary problem of authorship and independence. *The Ghost* (1762–3), in 4 separately published books, contains a famous attack on Johnson and together with *The Duellist* (1764) shows him as a less successful writer of octosyllabic couplets. Financial independence allowed Churchill to abandon his career in the Church and give rein to his taste for drink and women. The contrast between his declarations of principles as a satirist and an apparently 'abandoned' personal life earned him much contemporary abuse and a poor critical reception in the last century. With a certain powerful rhetoric, he rises in places to a considerable height as a poet. His poems, however, like those of Swift, with whom they may profitably be compared, require considerable annotation to explain the oblique and frequent personal references which are a constant feature of his wit, so that he has rarely been successfully anthologized. He thus tends to remain unread. [AR]

The Poetical Works, ed. W. Tooke (3 vols., 1804; revised Aldine edn, 2 vols., 1892); *The Poetical Works*, ed. and intr. D. Grant (1956); *Poems*, ed. J. Laver (2 vols., 1933); *Correspondence of Wilkes and C.*, ed. E. H. Weathersley (New York, 1934).
W. C. Brown, *C.: Poet, Rake and Rebel* (Kansas, 1953); G. Nobbe, *The North Briton* (New York, 1939); I. A.Williams, *Seven Eighteenth Century Bibliographies* (1924).

Churchill, Sir Winston (Leonard Spencer) (1874–1965). Statesman, journalist, rhetorician, historian. Born at Blenheim Palace, son of Lord Randolph Churchill and his American wife Jennie Jerome, Churchill was educated at Harrow and Sandhurst and entered the army in 1895. He served, among other theatres, on the north-west frontier of India. As special correspondent (1899–1900) of the *Morning Post* in the Boer War he was taken prisoner but escaped and was later present at a variety of important actions. His South African experiences provided the material for *The Story of the Malakand Field Force* (1898), *The River War* (1899) and *London to Ladysmith via Pretoria* (1900). Churchill's political career began in 1900 with his election as Conservative M.P. for Oldham. He subsequently represented a variety of constituencies – North-West Manchester (as a Liberal) 1905–8, Dundee (as a Conservative, as always henceforth) 1908–22, Epping Division of Essex 1924–45, Woodford 1945–67. Among the governmental offices he held were: President of the Board of Trade, 1908–10; Home Secretary, 1910–11; First Lord of the Admiralty, 1911–15; Minister of Munitions, 1917; Secretary of State for War and Air, 1919–21; Chancellor of the Exchequer, 1924–9; First Lord of the Admiralty, 1939–40; Prime Minister, 1940–5, 1951–5.

Churchill's erratic political career reflects his character both as man and as writer. His imaginative sponsorship of the Gallipoli campaign in 1915 led to his resignation as First Lord of the Admiralty on its collapse and his service for a period as a lieutenant-colonel in France. In 1918–21 he championed the use of British troops against the Bolshevist regime in Russia. Basically a romantic conservative with a deep emotional attachment to Britain and to the idea of British history as a story of unfolding glory, he was at his worst when challenged with problems of social change and econom-ic reorganization and at his best when confronted with an ethically simple problem of grand dimensions and great national implications. History was kind to him in giving him the opportunity to become Prime Minister in Britain's 'finest hour'; it was certainly his own finest hour. He was able to voice, in his characteristically rhetorical manner, sentiments of resolution and conviction of ultimate victory in a way that created as much as it reflected such sentiments in the nation. It was Churchill who enabled Britain to survive undefeated when she stood alone against Hitler in 1940. His post-war political history was less impressive: he never accepted the loss of India to the British Empire and never fully understood the modern world. His remarkable command of language came largely from his reading of Gibbon and other 18th- and early 19th-century historians and stylists. His relatively frequent periods out of office gave him the opportunity to cultivate his gift for biography (*Lord Randolph Churchill*, 1906, *Marlborough*, 4 vols., 1933–8) and for contemporary history (*The World Crisis*, 4 vols., 1923–9). His speeches, often moving and highly effective at the time of delivery, read less well and out of their temporal context sometimes seem flamboyant and over-strained: they can be found in *Into Battle* (1941); *The Unrelenting Struggle* (1942); *The End of the Beginning* (1942); *Onwards to Victory* (1944); *The Dawn of Liberation* (1945). His masterpiece is his history, written from the inside, of the Second World War (6 vols., *The Gathering Storm*, 1948; *Their Finest Hour*, 1949; *The Grand Alliance*, 1950; *The Hinge of Fate*, 1951; *The Close of the Ring*, 1952; *Triumph and Tragedy*, 1954). Here his gift of phrase and mastery of the unfolding periodic sentence join with his dramatic sense of history and a deep feeling of personal involvement to produce a remarkable narrative. His *History of the English Speaking Peoples* (4 vols., 1956–8) shows something of the same narrative sweep and gift for dramatic generalization, but in dealing with such a wide stretch of time and space Churchill's gifts often become drawbacks, eloquence producing grandiose over-simplification and a sense of destiny producing superficial pronouncements which ignore the realities of the life and culture of the period under discussion. His achievement remains nonetheless remarkable: he was a combination of statesman, soldier and writer that could only have been produced at a particular moment in English history and which is not likely to recur. [DD]

Savrola (1900) (novel); *My Early Life* (1930). Randolph Churchill, *W.S.C.* (2 vols., 1966–7) (the official life, to be completed by M. J. Gilbert); C. L. Broad, *W.C.* (1953); John Connell, *W.C.* (1956).

Churchyard, Thomas (*c.* 1520–1604). Poet. Variously described today as a 'miscellaneous writer' and as a 'hack poet', Churchyard, throughout a long and very unrewarding career, sought favour as a soldier, a hanger-on at court, and as a writer working mechanically in a variety of styles. His *Mirror for Man* was issued before 1553; and he contributed *The Legend of Shore's Wife* to *The Mirror for Magistrates* in 1563. He published many broadsheets and small volumes of prose and verse, sometimes topical and autobiographical, including *Churchyard's Chips* (1575). In 1587 appeared *The Worthiness of Wales*. He began life as a page to the Earl of Surrey and lived to celebrate King James's accession, but seems to have impressed contemporaries by his longevity and his versatile copiousness rather than by any literary achievement. [MJ]

C. S. Lewis, *English Literature in the Sixteenth Century* (1954).

Cibber, Colley (1671–1757). Man of the theatre. The son of Caius Gabriel Cibber, a Danish sculptor settled in England, he became an actor under Thomas Betterton at Drury Lane in 1690. A failure in tragedy, he had a flair for comedy, and in 1696, soon after his marriage, he wrote *Love's Last Shift* with a view to providing himself with a good part as the fop. It was the first of the new sentimental comedies, but had sufficient of the old Restoration spirit to get him reprimanded for immorality by Jeremy ◊ Collier. Vanbrugh wrote *The Relapse* as a sequel, and Cibber again played Lord Foppington. In 1700 he made his famous melodramatic adaptation of Shakespeare's *Richard III* which held the boards until Irving's day; some of Cibber's lines were retained in Laurence Olivier's film. He wrote over 30 plays and adaptations, and was the leading actor of eccentric parts. In 1710 he became a part sharer in Drury Lane, and proved a great manager. Steele joined him on the board, and in 1717 he produced *The Non-Juror*, an adaptation of *Tartuffe*

directed against the Tories. In 1730 he became Poet Laureate, in which capacity he produced worthless verses, and the appointment, together with his high-handed management of Drury Lane, called down upon him the enmity of Fielding and of Pope, who altered *The Dunciad* in 1743, replacing Theobald with Cibber as the hero. Cibber published in 1740 *An Apology for the Life of Mr Colley Cibber Comedian*, a brilliant inside story of the theatre in his time and the best of English theatrical autobiographies. [MJ]

The Dramatic Works, ed. D. E. Baker (5 vols. 1777).
F. W. Bateson, *English Comic Drama 1700–1750* (1929); R. H. Barker, *Mr C. of Drury Lane* (New York, 1939); F. D. Senior, *The Life and Times of C.C.* (1928).

Clare, John (1793–1864). Poet. Born at Helpstone between Peterborough and Stanford. His father was a labourer on parish relief; his mother was illiterate. He was a precocious though 'waukly' child and had little formal education, but learned songs and read chap-books and the Bible. He bought a copy of the *Seasons* and tried his hand at verses and songs while working here and there on the land. He had a number of love affairs, all frustrated by his poverty. He unsuccessfully tried to print a volume of poems by subscription, but finally *Poems Descriptive of Rural Life and Scenery. By John Clare a Northamptonshire Peasant* was published in 1820 (3 edns; 1821). It can be seen by the title that Clare was a prisoner of the current admiration of the 'peasant poet' that had earlier crippled Burns; but quite rightly the title also stresses Clare's great genius for describing the countryside. The volume was very successful, and Clare was taken up by various magnates. He married in 1820, and after a visit to London his second volume, *The Village Minstrel and Other Poems* (2 vols., 1821; reissued 1823), appeared and did not sell quite so well. The title poem is autobiographical and the book bears marks of the pressure that would be brought on Clare to make his work 'characteristic' and human. The best things in it, however, are again the straight descriptions, such as 'Rural Morning' and especially 'Rural Evening'. He paid three other visits to London and became acquainted with Coleridge, Hazlitt and others. Lamb, who had no notion of what Clare could do, advised him to imitate ◊ Shenstone and made other foolish suggestions. A third volume, *The Shepherd's Calendar; with Village Stories and Other Poems*, containing some of Clare's very best descriptive work, appeared in 1827. The publishers were complaining that the poems were too often 'merely descriptive', and obviously wanted human interest, reflection and the usual concomitants of contemporary poetry. Clare did his best to provide this in parts of his book, like the 'stories', but the *Calendar* is quite beautifully just a series of pictures and sounds. He was helpless before impertinent and useless suggestions because his life in Helpstone, with a wife and seven children, was impoverished and sometimes even without food. He occasionally had labouring employment, and was patronized by several people. In 1823, he was given a cottage in Northborough, and in 1835 appeared the last volume of poems he published, *The Rural Muse*, in which (like Burns again) he apparently tried to show that he could be as good as others in the expected forms and conventions. His health collapsed and in 1837 delusions and mental disorder forced his removal to Dr Allen's private asylum at Fairmead House in Epping Forest: there he was intelligently treated and allowed to wander in the forest. He escaped back to Northamptonshire in July 1741 to see his old girl-friends, and at the end of the year had to be placed in the Northampton Lunatic Asylum, where he lived quietly, suffering from delusions that he was Byron or Napoleon, until he died. During the latter part of his life he wrote much, including a few visionary poems of value, such as 'Song's Eternity' and '*Now* is past'. Clare's work has been increasingly esteemed in the last fifty years. Some of this admiration comes no doubt from the fact that he is a symbol of the deprivation of genius by the social structure, but he has very great qualities that make some of his poems as fine as any descriptive passages in the language. He has a real, rooted knowledge of the countryside; he shows signs that he would have been a flexible and inventive user of his own rural language, and some of the poems succeed by the accuracy and solidity of these country words. His love of plants and animals can produce new and illuminating images; so, too, the honesty of his imagination reminds the reader of Blake. As a poet of the English countryside that was passing with the advance of industrialization, he has also of course attracted attention, and the sense of social change and the disappearance of immemorial customs imbues his descriptions with poignant feeling. Connexions are often made between Clare's poems and the verse of W. H. ◊ Davies and Edward ◊ Thomas. [A R]

Sketches in the Life of J. C. Written by Himself, ed. E. Blunden (1931); *Life and Remains* (1873); *Poems*, selected and intr. N. Gale (1901) (bibliography); *The Poems*, ed. J. W. Tibble (2 vols., 1935) (incomplete); *Poems of J.C.'s Madness*, ed. G. Grigson (1949) (with new material); *Later Poems*, ed. E. Robinson and G. Summerfield (1964); *The Shepherd's Calendar*, ed. E. Robinson and G. Summerfield (1964); *Poems*, ed. A. Symons (1908) (selection); *Selected Poems*, ed. G. Grigson (Muses' Library, 1950); *Selected Poems*, ed. J. Reeves (1954); *Selected Poems and Prose*, ed. E. Robinson and G. Summerfield (1966); *The Prose*, ed. J. W. and A. Tibble (1951); *The Letters*, ed. J. W. and A. Tibble (1951). J. W. and A. Tibble, *J.C.: His Life and Poetry* (1956) (with bibliography); J. M. Murry, *Unprofessional Essays* (1956); E. Robinson and G. Summerfield, 'J. C.: An Interpretation of Certain Asylum Letters', *RES*, n.s. 13 (May 1962).

Clarendon, Edward Hyde, Earl of (1609–74). Lawyer, politician, memoir writer and historian. Born in Wiltshire of a family of country gentry, and educated at Magdalen Hall, Oxford, he studied law in London, and was M.P. in the Short and Long Parliaments. He was at first against the King, but on the outbreak of the Civil War became one of Charles's chief advisers and wrote in his support. He became in turn one of Charles II's chief counsellors and in 1658 was made Lord Chancellor and chief minister, offices which he retained after the Restoration. In 1667, after the failure of the Dutch war, he was dismissed and exiled to France, where he lived at Montpellier; he died in Rouen. During his years in France he completed his *History of the Rebellion and Civil Wars in England*, begun in 1641 (ed. W. D. Macray, 6 vols., 1888; selections ed. G. Huehns, World's Classics, 1955), one of the great monuments of English historical writing. It is a noble piece of neo-classical building though marked with the idiosyncrasies that characterize English art of this kind. It contains disparate materials and passages of different degrees of credibility. Clarendon shows the lawyer's interest in constitutional problems, but keeps the English historian's view that men rather than 'issues' only were at the root of the Civil War. Thus the 'character-sketches' are among the best things in the book (D. Nichol Smith, *Characters of the Seventeenth Century*, 1918, reprints some of them). Clarendon's style is formal and elaborate, in contrast to the kind of prose coming into fashion at the end of the century (◊ Sprat, Thomas), and sometimes the complexity of his sentences, while adding to their stateliness, increases their obscurity. Clarendon bequeathed his manuscripts to the University of Oxford, where he was Chancellor (1660–7). The profits of printing the history (1702–4) were used by the university to build the Clarendon Press building. He left other writings. [AR]

H. Craik, *The Life of E.E. of C.* (2 vols., 1911); L. C. Knights, 'Reflections on C.'s *History*', Scrutiny 15 (1948); B. H. G. Wormald, *C., 1640–60* (1951); F. Fogle and H. R. Trevor-Roper, *Milton and C.* (Los Angeles, 1965).

Clarke, Marcus (Andrew Hislop) (1846–81). Australian journalist and novelist. Born in London, Clarke emigrated in 1863 and made his name as the writer of a weekly column in the *Australasian* (1867–70). He spent most of his journalistic life in Melbourne. In 1868 he serialized his first novel, *Long Odds*, in the *Colonial Monthly*, which he owned. The failure of this journal and of the comic weekly *Humbug*, which he founded in 1869, together with his marriage in that year and the subsequent birth of six children, left Clarke in financial straits from which he never escaped. His second novel, *For the Term of His Natural Life* (PEL, 1970), was serialized in the *Australian Journal* (1870–72). A third novel, *Felix and Felicitas*, begun in 1876, was unfinished at his death. Harassed by moneylenders Clarke squandered his talent on pantomimes, burlesques and the melodramas too well suited to his temperament. *For the Term of His Natural Life* grew from commissioned research into Tasmania's penal history. Its brisk prose rises to savagery in attacks on society's outlawry of humanity. Clarke's celebration of the human spirit is hampered by a sub-plot that occupies more space than interest, and by a heroine whom he lets grow from girlhood into priggishness, but his insights into the criminal mind, his eerie evocation of the Tasmanian coast and his ferocity turn a melodrama into a masterpiece. [PT]

A M. C. Reader, ed. Bill Wannan (1963).
B. R. Elliott, *M.C.* (1958); R. G. Howarth, 'M. C.', *Southerly*, 4 (1954).

Cleveland, John (1613–58). Poet. Born in Loughborough, Leicestershire, where his father was usher at Burton's Charity School, Cleveland moved to Hinckley, Leicestershire, in 1621, his father having been presented to the living, and his education was there entrusted to Richard Vynes, a Presbyterian divine famous for his learning. In 1627 Cleveland went up to Christ's College, Cambridge, taking his B.A. in 1631 and his M.A. in 1635. In 1634 he was made Fellow of St John's College and in 1642 began to study law. Like Milton he officiated as father of the Cambridge revels, and he was twice chosen to give Latin orations welcoming distinguished visitors. He also contributed a mediocre poem to the volume of elegies on Edward King which contained 'Lycidas'. In 1643, after the occupation of Cambridge by a Parliamentary garrison, Cleveland, a Royalist, left for Oxford, and subsequently joined the garrison at Newark, serving as judge-advocate until the town's surrender in 1646. In 1647 he arrived destitute in London, having sold his books and clothes. He subsisted partly on charity, and until about 1650 engaged in writing for and editing the Royalist Mercuries. About 1654 he left for Norwich, where he was arrested in 1655 as a dissident Royalist and imprisoned for three months at Yarmouth; he wrote a personal appeal of some dignity to Cromwell, saying that though poor and a Royalist he was no criminal, and Cromwell ordered his release. He moved to Gray's Inn, where he seems to have been an intimate friend of Samuel ◊ Butler; there he died in 1658.

Celebrated as a poet in his own day, Cleveland is underrated in ours. His flamboyantly developed conceits exhilarated contemporaries, but often seem misplaced or even repugnant to modern readers, whose sense of decorum and of the ludicrous owes a great deal to the standards of the 18th century. However, some of Cleveland's lighter pieces retain the appeal of a virtuosity which dares to tread the edge of bathos without sliding over the brink (even 'The Hecatomb to His Mistress' has this appeal if its images are taken in context). His satires, having greater simplicity and directness, have worn best: 'The Rebel Scot', in forceful heroic couplets, is a fine and early example of the type of vigorous personal satire on particular individuals and events which came into full flower at the Restoration. Cleveland's satires almost certainly influenced Butler's.

His poems were collected and edited by his pupils Dr Drake and Bishop Lake in 1677. [P M]

The Poems, ed. J. M. Berdan (New Haven, 1911); *Poems*, ed. B. Morris and E. Withington (1966). S. V. Gapp, 'Notes on J.C.', *PMLA*, XLVI (1931).

Clough, Arthur Hugh (1819–61). Poet and educational administrator. He was born in Liverpool, but his father emigrated to Charleston, Carolina, when he was 4. He was sent back to be educated, and in 1829 went to Rugby, where he became legendary as scholar and athlete. His seriousness was enhanced by Thomas ◊ Arnold, with whose family Clough spent many vacations. Matthew ◊ Arnold became a close friend and later contributed to the enduring idea of Clough's failure by his portrait in *Thyrsis*. Clough gained a Balliol scholarship in 1836, when the theological disputes resulting from ◊ Newman's *Tracts* and sermons and from the new biblical criticism were at their height. He encountered German philosophy, Goethe, Carlyle and the Romantics partly through the influence of friends such as J. C. Shairp (Oxford poetry professor, 1877), Arnold and Froude. In 1842–8 he held a fellowship at Oriel, but the necessity to subscribe to the Thirty-Nine Articles produced a crisis. His resignation of his fellowship was a pattern-setting decision. The *Bothie of Toper-na-Fuosich* (1848), his 'long-vacation pastoral' using the classical hexameter with great facility, was produced soon afterwards. It was Clough's best-liked work, in his age. Its characters (some based on his pupils), satire and versatility make it still one of the most readable of Victorian narrative poems, but one may agree with Shairp, who told Clough that 'the hexameter has always a feeling of parody'. An Oxford pamphlet in the Carlyle manner, 'Retrenchment' (1847), deals with the human cost of economic growth. His early poems (1840–7) were published as *Ambarvalia* (1849). The deep integrity of 'The Higher Courage' and 'Blank Misgivings of a Creature . . .' now seems more impressive than some of his anthology pieces.

Clough's friends obtained for him the headship of University Hall, London (a non-sectarian university residence), in 1849.

His summer in Italy the same year coincided with the siege of Rome, and resulted in *Amours de Voyage* (1849). The theme is failure to be committed, either socially or politically. The setting of his most profound and disturbing poem, *Dipsychus*, is Venice, where Clough went in 1850, but he wrote and revised the poem over a long period and it was published posthumously in 1865. Influenced by Goethe's *Faust* and by *Don Juan* it is a dialogue in various verse forms between the Spirit, who represents partly *l'homme moyen sensuel* in Clough, and Dipsychus, his moral and speculative nature. A half-expressed awareness of sexuality plays an important part in his poetry; sometimes the writing seems to dissociate at the frontiers of instinct.

During 1851–2 Clough became engaged to Blanche Smith. He resigned from University Hall and went to Emerson in Cambridge, Massachusetts. He considered making enough to marry on by journalism, but welcomed a chance to return to London to an Examinership at the Education Office. In 1854 he married.

He became closely involved with the work of his wife's cousin, Florence Nightingale. Their temperaments, somewhat hypochondriac and mystical, had something in common. Clough became ill while travelling in 1861, and died in Florence. His formally most accomplished works are perhaps the short, satirical lyrics such as 'The Latest Decalogue', but he is continually interesting as an essentially modern sensibility at work in the mid-19th century. [J H]

Poems, ed. A. L. P. Norrington (1968); *Correspondence*, ed. F. L. Mulhauser (1957). K. Chorley, *A.H.C., The Uncommitted Mind* (1962); W. E. Houghton, *The Poetry of C.* (1963) and *The Prose Works of A. H. C., A Checklist* (New York Public Library Bulletin 64, 1960); W. Bagehot, 'C.'s Poems', *National Review*, 15 (1862); F. E. Faverty, *The Victorian Poets* (Cambridge, Mass., 1956); H. Sidgwick, *Miscellaneous Essays* (1904); S. Waddington, *A.H.C., A Monograph* (1883).

Clouston, Joseph Storer (1870–1944). Scottish prose writer. The son of a Cumberland doctor, he first attracted attention with *The Lunatic at Large* (1899) and its successors, works in the Edwardian satirical vein deriving from Samuel ◊ Butler. Later he drew on his family's Orkney background to become a sort of local John ◊ Buchan, writing thrillers (*The Spy in Black*, 1917) and

Cobbett

historical and topographical works about Orkney. [AI]

Cobbett, William (1762–1835). Political controversialist. Born at Farnham in Surrey, the son of an agricultural labourer, he was a soldier (1784–91), rising to be a sergeant-major. When he bought himself out, his charges of dishonesty laid against his officers brought him into trouble and he fled to France, and then to America, where he became (as 'Peter Porcupine') a pro-British, anti-French political satirist and was fined for libelling. On his return to England he gradually switched from being a monarchist Tory, until by 1804 he was writing in the Radical interest. In 1809 he was imprisoned for writing against flogging in the army. He farmed in Surrey and Hampshire, and fled again to America as a debtor (1817–19); he was elected M.P. for Oldham in the first Reform Parliament, but made no mark. Cobbett's changes of opinion were violent, but his obvious sincerity, the power of his observation and the vigour of his writing made him influential as a political journalist. He produced the popular *Cobbett's Weekly Political Register* (88 vols., 1802–35) and many varied essays, 'sermons' and practical economic works, as well as a famous *English Grammar for the Use of Schools* (New York, 1818; many editions) and a *History of the Protestant 'Reformation' in England and Ireland* (1826–7). His most famous work is his *Rural Rides ... with Economical and Political Observations* (1830; ed. J. H. Lobban, Everyman, 1914; ed. G. D. H. and M. Cole, 3 vols., 1930; ed. G. Woodcock, PEL, 1967). Cobbett disapproved of the landowners' suggestions for dealing with the distress of the agricultural workers following the Napoleonic Wars, and he travelled the country to refute these statements by the on-the-spot observation that the peasants did not get their fair share of the wealth produced by the land. The frequent violence of his language adds a spice to his magnificently realized picture of English country life, already passing, but his tendency to idealize peasant life should have made him less influential as a source. [AR]

The Progress of a Ploughboy to a Seat in Parliament, ed. W. Reitzel (1933) (autobiographical passages from his writings, revised as *The Autobiography of C.*, 1947).
G. D. H. Cole, *Life of W. C.* (1924); G. D. H. Cole and M. Cole, *The Opinions of C.* (1944);

W. Pemberton, *W.C.* (1949); M. L. Pearl, *C.: A Bibliographical Account of His Life and Times* (1953).

Cockburn, Alison or **Alicia** (1713–94). Scottish poets. The wife of an Edinburgh advocate, correspondent of David Hume, and kinswoman and friend of Sir Walter Scott, she wrote to the tune of 'The Flowers of the Forest' the set of words beginning 'I've seen the smiling of Fortune beguiling'. It has been asserted that these words refer not to the Battle of Flodden but to a wave of bankruptcies among gentlemen speculators in Selkirkshire. (♢ Elliott, Jean.) [AI]

Letters and Memoirs of Her Own Life, ed. T. Craig-Brown (1900).

Cockburn, Henry Thomas (1779–1854). Scottish Whig judge. Educated in Edinburgh and called to the Scottish bar in 1800, Cockburn, like his friend Francis ♢ Jeffrey, suffered professionally for his political views and had ample leisure to write for the *Edinburgh Review*. When Jeffrey became Lord Advocate under the Reform administration, Cockburn became Solicitor-General for Scotland (1830) and was made a judge in 1834. Unlike Jeffrey's, Cockburn's contributions to the *Edinburgh Review* were confined to legal topics; more important than these or than his *Life of Jeffrey* (1852) are his posthumous volumes of reminiscences – *Memorials of His Time* (1856), *Journal 1831–54* (1874) and *Circuit Journeys* (1888). Together they form an intimate and perceptive account of Scottish life from Cockburn's boyhood to his old age, written with a shrewd judicious wit that is very attractive. [AI]

Coimín, Mícheál (Michael Comyn) (1688–1760). Irish author. Coimín was a native of Co. Clare. Unlike the majority of his contemporaries, he showed no sense of involvement in the great problems and struggles of the day. His work includes a prose tale in the Romantic manner, entitled *Eachtra Thoroilbh Mhic Stairn*, and the better-known *Laoidh Oisín ar Thír na nóg* ('Lay of Ossian in the Land of Youth'). The latter is a typical example of Fenian or Ossianic verse, simple in diction and design. The hero of the story is Ossian. Once, while hunting with the other Fiana, he is visited by a fair princess called Niamh of the Golden Hair, who wants him to be her husband. He consents, and accompanies her to her

108

father's kingdom, the Land of Youth. After many blissful years, he is seized by a longing to see his former companions again. Reluctantly, his wife agrees to this, but enjoins him not to touch the soil of Ireland. On his arrival, he is amazed to learn that he has been away for three hundred years. Like Rip Van Winkle, he finds everything utterly changed. His friends are dead and gone. In dejection, he heads homewards again; but is accidentally thrown from his horse, and on touching the ground becomes a helpless old man, fated never to return to the Land of Youth.

It is interesting to note that James ◊ Macpherson in Scotland was working along similar lines at the same time as Coimín; for in 1760, the year of the latter's death, appeared *Fragments of Ancient Poetry*, the first of a series based on Fenian or Ossianic lore from the Highlands of Scotland. [SB]

T. Ó Flannghaile. *Lay of Oisín in the Land of Youth* (1896).

Colenso, John William (1814–83). Mathematician, biblical critic and miscellaneous writer. Born in Cornwall and educated at St John's College, Cambridge, where he became a tutor for the usual heavily mathematical course of study, he was appointed first Bishop of Natal (1853) and wrote a grammar, dictionary and school books in the language of the Zulus (see his *Ten Weeks in Natal*, 1855, and *First Steps of the Zulu Mission*, 1860). He also wrote mathematical works, but is best known for his *Commentary on the Epistle to the Romans* (1861), attacking sacramentalism, and *A Critical Examination of the Pentateuch and the Book of Joshua* (7 parts, 1862–79). These are not important works in themselves, but when they were published they roused the High Church party against what seemed their extreme 'critical' views. The latter book, which suggested that arithmetical calculation demonstrated large portions of the Mosaic narrative to be 'unhistorical', caused Colenso to be deposed and excommunicated by Gray, Bishop of Capetown, but restored by the English courts of law. This established (among other things) the nature of colonial ecclesiastical tenure. The theological controversy had political overtones. [AR]

A. W. Benn, *The History of English Rationalism in the Nineteenth Century* (2 vols., 1906); *DNB*.

Coleridge, Hartley (1796–1849). Journalist and miscellaneous writer. Born at Clevedon,

Somerset, the eldest son of S. T. ◊ Coleridge; Southey brought him up after his parents had separated, and he was educated at Ambleside and Merton College. He was made a Fellow of Oriel, but later lost his fellowship following a charge of intemperance. After journalism in London and unsuccessful schoolmastering at Ambleside, he lived in seclusion at Grasmere. His career was one of brilliant promise but little achievment. His best poems are found in a handful of sonnets, melancholy and in places touched with deep religious feeling; he also wrote some good criticism, particularly an edition of *The Dramatic Works of Massinger and Ford* (1840), and a *Life of Marvell* (1835), as well as *Biographia Borealis, or, Lives of Northern Worthies* (1833; 1856). [AR]

Complete Poems, ed. D. Coleridge (1851) (with a memoir); *New Poems, Including a Selection from His Published Poetry*, ed. E. L. Griggs (1942); *Letters*, ed. G. E. and E. L. Griggs (1936).

E. L. Griggs, *H.C.* (1929) (with bibliography); H. Hartman, *H.C.* (1931) (with bibliography).

Coleridge, Samuel Taylor (1772–1834). Poet and critic. Born in Devon, Coleridge went to school in London and in 1791 to Jesus College, Cambridge. His precocity and learning were such that the university had little to offer him, and after idling his time and getting into debt he enlisted in the 15th Dragoons under the name of Silas Tomkyn Comberbacke. He returned to Cambridge but never completed his degree. In 1794 Coleridge met Robert ◊ Southey, later to become Poet Laureate, and the two were enthusiastic about the French Revolution. They planned to found a community in America, to which Coleridge gave the name 'Pantisocracy', but the scheme collapsed. The following year he married Sara Fricker, but it was not a happy marriage. At this time Coleridge was a strong nonconformist with an interest in preaching. In 1797, when Wordsworth came to live a few miles from Nether Stowey, Somerset, where Coleridge was living, the close association between the two poets began. Coleridge had already published *Poems on Various Subjects* (1796), which had been well received. In 1798 he and Wordsworth published *Lyrical Ballads*, a volume of poetry put together as a conscious break with 18th-century traditions. Most of the work was Wordsworth's, but the volume included one of Coleridge's greatest poems, 'The Rime of the Ancient

Mariner', a narrative of the nightmarish effects of a sailor's offence against nature, whose simplicity of form accommodated a variety of movement and moods. Coleridge's language is simple and stark, presenting the ordinary in terms of the outlandish, and vice versa, with a glaring energy that no other poet of the Romantic movement achieved.

Coleridge was given an annuity by the Wedgwood brothers which enabled him to concentrate on writing. In 1798 and 1799 he was in Germany and came into contact with the thought of the German transcendentalist philosophers. In 1800 he settled near Wordsworth in Cumberland, and fell deeply in love with Sarah Hutchinson, Wordsworth's sister-in-law. By this time Coleridge had been taking opium for some years. Many of his poems, notably 'Kubla Khan' (1816), the product of an opium dream, show the influence of this. Coleridge travelled, lectured, wrote articles, founded and edited *The Friend* (see below), all in the midst of growing financial difficulties and an increasing reliance upon opium. He was known and admired throughout the literary world as an inspiring intellect and a brilliant talker. In 1816 he put himself in the care of Dr James Gillman in Highgate, who helped him to control his opium consumption, and in that year also he published another volume of poetry. In 1817 *Biographia Literaria*, in which his literary and philosophical theories are presented, was published. By the end of his life Coleridge had moved from his early radical nonconformism and died a Tory and an Anglican according to his own somewhat Burkean working out of the meaning of these terms.

Coleridge's poetic styles vary considerably. He wrote sometimes in the vein of Cowper or Gray, but could achieve within this style the rhythmic interest of, for instance, 'This lime-tree bower my prison' (1800), in which he combines colloquial simplicity and meditative perception of nature, or the powerful linking of scene, mood, remembrance and reflection of 'Frost at Midnight' (1798), where the realization of particular details grows into the exploration of morality and the universe and a quiet end to the contemplation of the poet's sleeping child. In 'Kubla Khan' and 'Christabel' (1816) Coleridge uses exotic images to conjure an atmosphere that is both bright and sinister. 'Kubla Khan'

presents with a rich, dark clarity and rhythmic intensity symbols of the warmth and pleasure of art and the cold forces that threaten it. Often considered to be merely a brilliant but confused outburst the poem is in fact meticulously and meaningfully constructed. 'Christabel' was never finished, but the combined elements of the transmuted medievalism that appealed so much to the Romantic poets and hints of terror and the grotesque have an intriguing strength. 'Dejection: An Ode' (1802), which arose from Coleridge's marital difficulties and his impossible love for Sarah Hutchinson, describes, in language that weaves together sombre passion and desperate directness, the destruction of his response to the natural world and his poetic inspiration. He moves from positioning his feelings philosophically to the almost abrupt plain statement of his distress. The result, embodied in a variety of metres and stanza-forms, is a controlled and modulated statement of an almost violent uncontrol.

Coleridge's drug addiction, his estrangement from his wife, his quarrel with Wordsworth in 1810, all contributed to reduce him to something of a wreck, but he managed to continue with literary work, however irregularly. He gave public lectures in London on literary and philosophical subjects and published *The Friend*, 'a literary, moral and political weekly paper', over a period of 14 months from January 1809 (the essays in it, enlarged and revised, appeared in book form in 1818). In spite of his intimacy and collaboration with Wordsworth (there was in fact a long separation owing to disagreements and quarrels) Coleridge developed his own philosophical theories of art and the artist. They are mainly contained in *Biographia Literaria*. These theories were only a part of the universal philosophical scheme that Coleridge never completed. He explained the art of creation through his theory of the imagination – the primary imagination which sifts the details of experience and enables perception, and the secondary imagination that consciously interprets and creates. This was an integral part of his concept of unity, the blending together of disparate elements to form a unified whole and the growth from this of mutual explanation. This he felt to be the aim of the poet. Coleridge believed that pleasure was the object of artistic creation, and distinguished between imagination, the fundamental unifier, and fancy, which merely elaborates on the products of the imagination. Coleridge's complex theories have been variously interpreted and widely influential. Especially influential was his concept (derived from German philosophy) of the organic nature of literary form. But it is clear that his striving to provide a philosophic system for poetic art, while it brought a wealth of striking applications of stimulating analyses, was complicated and even confused by the very attempt to schematize. [JRC]

Complete Poetical Works, ed. E. H. Coleridge (2 vols., 1912); Complete Poems, ed. M. Bishop (1954); Biographia Literaria, ed. J. Shawcross, revised G. Watson (1956); Letters, ed. E. L. Griggs (1956 ff.); Shakespearian Criticism (2 vols., 1960) and Miscellaneous Criticism (1936), ed. T. M. Rayson.
J. L. Lowes, The Road to Xanadu (1927; revised 1930) (on the sources of 'The Ancient Mariner' and 'Kubla Khan'); E. K. Chambers, S.T.C. (1938) (a factual biography); H. House, C. (1953) (on the poetry); H. M. Margoliouth, Wordsworth and C. 1795–1834 (1953); J. Beer, C. the Visionary (1959); J. Colmer, C.: Critic of Society (1959); M. H. Abrams, The Mirror and the Lamp (1953).

Collier, Jeremy (1650–1726). Pamphleteer. Educated at his father's school in Ipswich and at Cambridge, he became a clergyman, and in 1685 was appointed to Gray's Inn. A non-juror who spent some time in prison, he published sermons and pamphlets against William III, and was outlawed for absolving on the scaffold two would-be assassins of the King. His place in the annals of English letters was earned by his pamphlet A Short View of the Immorality and Profaneness of the English Stage (1698), in which he attacked the Restoration dramatists for licentiousness and the encouragement of vice, supporting his charges with detailed analyses of plays by Dryden, D'Urfey and Vanbrugh. Dryden did not reply, but Congreve, Vanbrugh and others did, and Collier made rejoinders. He remained an adherent of the Stuart cause, and a pamphleteer on religious and other matters, his later controversies splitting the non-juring communion. [MJ]

Sister Rose Anthony, The J.C. Controversy 1698–1726 (Milwaukee, 1937); J. W. Krutch, Comedy and Conscience after the Restoration (New York, 1924).

Collingwood, Robin George (1889–1943). Historian, archaeologist and philosopher. Born at Cartmel Fell in Lancashire, the son of W. G. Collingwood, a painter and secretary to Ruskin, he learned to draw well, a talent he used as an archaeologist. He was educated at Rugby and University College, Oxford. Collingwood published much on the history of Roman Britain, particularly the archaeology and epigraphy, and with J. N. L. Myres was responsible for the first volume of the Oxford History of England, which deals with that period and appeared in 1936. He became a Fellow of Pembroke College and was Professor of Metaphysical Philosophy at Oxford from 1934 to 1941. As a philosopher his best-known work is an Essay on Philosophical Method (1933), an attempt somewhat characteristic of its time to develop English idealism on sceptical principles. He was most original in the area between philosophy and history, where he allowed his great erudition and expertise in both fields to produce new ideas. Perhaps his greatest work is his Idea of History (ed. and intr. T. M. Knox, 1946). Here he shows a change in his philosophical views and came to think that as natural philosophy was once, so history was now, the most fruitful model for the development of philosophy, and in fact that philosophy as a separate discipline is liquidated by being 'converted into history'. He stands out from other British philosophers in having an intelligent interest in aesthetics. The Principles of Art (1938) is informed by a wide knowledge of painting, music, and literature and by a concern for the role of art in the modern world. In his later years under the influence of a paralytic disease, his work became increasingly erratic and dogmatic. His last work was The New Leviathan (1942), a defence of the Western liberal view of civilization which had become an obsession with him in the face of the Nazi attack on it. [AR]

An Autobiography (1939).
Obituary in Proceedings of the British Academy, 29 (1943) (with bibliography).

Collins, Tom. ⟡ Furphy, Joseph.

Collins, William (1721–59). Poet. One of the best 18th-century lyric poets, he was born in Chichester, the son of a hatter and educated at Winchester and Magdalen College, Oxford. While still a student he published a series of Persian Eclogues (1742; reprinted as Oriental Eclogues, 1757), in the conventional pretty 'orientalizing' taste of

Collins

the day. His worthwhile work, slender in bulk, was produced in less than a decade. With Joseph ◊ Warton he planned, but published separately, *Odes on Several Descriptive and Allegoric Subjects* (1746). These gained no popular success at once, which deeply hurt him. He planned a number of other works, a *Review of the Advancement of Learning* and a commentary on Aristotle's *Poetics*, but in 1750 fell ill of a mental depression and, after a period of misery, died insane in the town of his birth. His work (which was developing until he ceased writing) shows a powerful imagination informing a classical form, giving an impression of intense heat within a cool container. His 2-stanza 'Ode Written at the Beginning of the Year 1746' ('How sleep the brave') is one of the few satisfactory poems in English addressed to men who have been killed in a war, because of its tough suggestion of the passing of all human memory and celebration. The syntax of his later odes sometimes seems to break under the concise development of his ideas. His taste lay not only in Greek, but in medieval art, and he is often considered a 'pre-Romantic' (in the last poem he wrote, the touching 'Ode on the Death of Mr Thomson', the dead poet appears as a Druid). Collins also wrote an 'Ode on the Popular Superstitions of the Highlands of Scotland, Considered as a Subject of Poetry' (published only in 1777, by Alexander Carlyle). Collins used the ode form as a strictly classical form, not the irregular 'pindaricks' of the earlier English sort; his most famous are the odes 'To Evening' and 'To the Passions'. [AR]

The Poems of Gray and C., ed. C. Stone and A. L. Poole (revised edn, 1937); *The Poems*, ed. and intr. E. Blunden (1929); *Poems of Gray, C., and Goldsmith*, ed. and intro. R. Lonsdale (1969) (annotated).
Johnson, *Lives of the Poets*; J. M. Murry, *Countries of the Mind* (1922); E. G. Ainsworth, *Poor C.* (Cornell U.P., 1937); P. L. Carver, *W.C.: The Life of a Poet* (1967).

Collins, (William) Wilkie (1824–89). Novelist and dramatist. Eldest son of the landscape painter William Collins, he was born in London. In 1837 the family went to Italy, where they lived for 18 months. Despite Wilkie's wish to be a writer, his father placed him in the tea business in 1841, but in 1846 he was entered to read for the bar at Lincoln's Inn: his knowledge of legal affairs was to provide him with considerable material for his writings. His first published work was the *Memoirs* (1848) of his father's life. *Antonina; or The Fall of Rome*, a historical novel after the fashion of Bulwer Lytton, on which Collins had been working for several years, finally appeared in 1850. From the early fifties he was a friend and companion of Dickens, acting with him, contributing to *Household Words*, travelling with him on the Continent, and writing works in collaboration with him. Dickens produced and acted in two melodramas written by Collins, *The Lighthouse* in 1855 and *The Frozen Deep* in 1857. The attention Dickens paid to plot and construction in his later novels is attributed to Collins' influence. It is for the novels he wrote in the following decade that Collins is remembered. *The Woman in White* (1860, in *All the Year Round*) is a thriller revolving round two nearly identical women, who turn out to be sisters. The narrative is pieced together out of accounts by the various participants. Collins used this method to ever greater effect in *The Moonstone* (1868); with its masterly plot it is worthy to rank as the first English detective novel, while in range and depth of characterization it outclasses its successors. *No Name* (1862, in *All the Year Round*) has a social theme – illegitimacy. *Armadale* (1866, in *The Cornhill*) is an intricate melodrama, in which the son of a murderer becomes obsessed with the idea that he is doomed to reenact his father's crime. In his later novels Collins is concerned with social problems but the abuses he attacks do not always sufficiently account for the sensational qualities he seeks to evoke. Among his targets are: the divorce laws, in *Man and Wife* (1870); the Jesuits, in *The Black Robe* (1881); and experimentation and vivisection, in a good thriller *Heart and Science* (1883). Collins braved Victorian morals by living with a mistress who kept house for him; he maintained another mistress in a separate establishment. But though his experience may explain his vivid female characters, he never seriously challenged social conventions in his novels. [NL]

Basil: A Story of Modern Life (1852); *Poor Miss Finch* (1872); *The New Magdalen* (1873); *The Lazy Tour of Two Idle Apprentices and Other Stories* (by C. Dickens and W.C.) (1890).
S. M. Ellis, *W.C., Le Fanu and Others* (1931); K. Robinson, *W.C.* (1951); R. Ashley, *W.C.* (1952); N. P. Davis, *The Life of W.C.* (U. of

112

Illinois P., 1956); T. S. Eliot, *Selected Essays 1917–1932* (1932).

Colman, George, the Elder (1732–94). Dramatist. After training for a legal career he was drawn into theatre management and playwriting through his friendship with the greatest actor of the day, David ◊ Garrick. He wrote some 30 stage entertainments in a variety of genres, and published translations from Terence (1765) as well as an edition of Beaumont and Fletcher, 2 of whose plays he adapted for performance. His real talent was for 'laughing comedy', a form in which the emerging sentimental comedy was tempered with the older tradition of the Restoration. *Polly Honeycombe* (1760), a satirical afterpiece on the current vogue of sentimental novels, anticipates Sheridan's *The Rivals*. Its success led to Colman's adapting Fielding's *Tom Jones* in loose partnership with Garrick as *The Jealous Wife* (1761), and to their collaborating on the highly successful *The Clandestine Marriage* in 1766. A synthesis of the new comedy with the old, it holds the stage today, chiefly on account of the character of Lord Ogleby, an elderly fop whom actors are still delighted to play. [M J]

Dramatic Works (4 vols., 1777).
R. B. Peake, *Memoirs of the C. Family* (2 vols., 1841); E. R. Page, *G.C., the Elder* (New York, 1935).

Colman, George, the Younger (1762–1836). Dramatist. The son of Garrick's friend and collaborator, George ◊ Colman, the Elder, he grew up in a theatrical household, and was himself a competent contriver of farces and melodramas, including *Blue Beard, or Female Curiosity!* staged at Drury Lane in 1798. His most famous melodrama, *The Iron Chest* (1796), based on William ◊ Godwin's novel *Caleb Williams*, was for long a popular vehicle with such great actors as Edmund Kean and Sir Henry Irving. [M J]

Dramatic Works, ed. J. W. Lake (4 vols. Paris, 1827); *Random Records* (2 vols., 1830).
J. F. Bagster-Collins, *G. C., the Younger* (New York, 1946).

Colum, Padraic (1881–   ). Poet. One of the senior surviving poets of the Irish Renaissance, poet, story-teller and memorialist, he was the son of the master of a workhouse in Co. Longford. As a young man he was associated with ◊ Yeats, Lady ◊ Gregory, ◊ AE and ◊ Synge, as well as with writers of a younger generation like James ◊ Joyce, about whom, with his wife Mary Colum, he published a collection of reminiscences, *Our Friend James Joyce*, in 1959. His own slight but true lyrical gift has a good deal in common with Joyce's gift in *Pomes Penyeach*. One of his loveliest lyrics, 'She Passed Through the Fair', has become an Irish folk-song in Colum's own lifetime; it is sung everywhere, but few who sing it in Ireland could name its author, partly because Colum has passed the later part of his life in the United States. Colum changed the English spelling of his name, Patrick Colm, into a Gaelic spelling out of enthusiasm for the Celtic revival. In 1914 he went to America and in 1923 visited Hawaii and wrote a study of Hawaiian myth and folklore. His interest in Irish folklore came out in *A Treasury of Irish Folklore* (1955). In 1916 he founded the *Irish Review* with Thomas MacDonagh, later that year one of the leaders of the Easter Rebellion. [G S F]

Broken Soil (1901) (drama); *Wild Earth* (1907) (poems); *Dramatic Legends and Other Poems* (1922); *Creatures* (1927); *Old Pastures* (1930); *Flower Pieces* (1939); *Collected Poems* (1954); *An Anthology of Irish Verse* (1948); *The Roads Round Ireland* (1927) (travel); *A Half Day's Ride* (1932) (essays); *The Flying Swans* (1960) (novel).

Columba, St (c. 520–97). Christian missionary to the Picts and Scots, and founder of the monastery of Iona. He is the reputed author of an eschatological poem, *Altus prosator vetustus* (ed. J. H. Bernard and R. Atkinson, in *The Irish Liber Hymnorum*, 1898, with translation), of nearly 300 lines, in stanzas of 12 lines each, with 8 syllables to the line. The lines rhyme in couplets. The stanzas begin with the letters of the alphabet in turn, from A to Z – a favourite device with early Irish poets.

Poems, ed. C. Blume (*Analecta Hymnica*, 51, 1908).
W. D. Simpson, *The Historical St C.* (1927; 3rd revised edn 1963); E. S. Duckett, *The Wandering Saints of the Early Middle Ages* (New York, 1959).

Columbanus, St (c. 550–615). Irish missionary. The founder of monasteries at Luxeuil and Bobbio, he was a prolific writer of Latin prose and verse, and shows a considerable knowledge of classical Latin writers.

Patrologia Latina, ed. J. P. Migne, 80 (1844); *Poems*, ed. W. Gundlach (*Monumenta Germaniae Historica, Epistolae*, iii).

E. Martin, *Saint C.* (Paris. 1905); G. Metlage, *Life and Writings of St C.* (Philadelphia, 1914); G. Domenici, *S. C.* (Rome, 1923); E. S. Duckett, *The Gateway to the Middle Ages* (New York, 1938) and *The Wandering Saints of the Middle Ages* (New York, 1959).

Comfort, Alexander (1920–   ). Poet, novelist, doctor of medicine, writer on social psychology and gerontologist. He refused military service during the Second World War because of pacifist and anarchist beliefs which he has expressed in poems, novels and discursive prose. During the Second World War, he was regarded as the leading figure in a broad movement sometimes called 'the New Romanticism', deeply influenced by the writings of Herbert ◊ Read. Like other poets of this movement he emphasized the importance of the image in poetry and of the unconscious mind in the production of images. Since the end of the 1940s, he has been more notable as an essayist than as a poet or novelist. [G S F]

France and Other Poems (1942); *A Wreath for the Living* (1943); *The Signal to Engage* (1947); *The Power House* (1944) (novel).

Compton-Burnett, Ivy (1892–1969). Novelist. Born in London, she was educated at home and London University, where she graduated in classics. Her first novel, *Dolores* (1911), was uncharacteristic, but *Pastors and Masters* (1925) began the series of 17 novels in which is created a chilling world of late-Victorian upper-class people. The stories are told in a highly characteristic manner. She said that she held a grudge against life because there is no plot, so she supplied the lack in her novels with ingenious constructions of violent happenings, coincidences and contrived patterns. The subject-matter of the jungle of these large family groups, the dangerous struggles of malice, cruelty, greed and dissimulation, of children versus parents (both destructive), of tyranny and tragedy, is contrasted with the manner of telling the story, the slowly unfolding narrative almost wholly in stylized and formal dialogue, the deadly wit, the reticence. Her whole creation makes up a narrow but powerful critique of the idea of society. *Brothers and Sisters* appeared in 1929 and was followed among others by *Men and Wives* (1931), a story of a tyrannical family head, attempted suicide, blackmail and murder; *More Women than Men* (1933); *Elders and Betters* (1944),

about a destroyed will (all the quarrels in this world are about power and property); *Manservant and Maidservant* (1947), in which children allow their father to be killed; *Mother and Son* (1955), which won the James Tait Black Memorial Prize; *The Mighty and Their Fall* (1961); and *A God and His Gifts* (1963). [A R]

P. Hansford Johnson, *I.C.-B.* (WTW, 1953); F. Baldanza, *I.C.-B.* (New York, 1964); C. Burkhart, *I.C.-B.* (1965).

Comyn, M. ◊ Coimín, M.

Congreve, William (1670–1729). Playwright and poet. Born at Bardsey, near Leeds, he spent his early youth in Ireland, where his father served as a military officer. He was educated at Kilkenny School and Trinity College, Dublin, at both of which he was a contemporary of Swift. He came back to England in 1688, and after a return visit to Ireland two years later enrolled as a law student in the Middle Temple in London, though he does not seem to have practised law. He retired from the stage after the production of his third comedy, *The Way of the World*, in 1700, though in 1704 he collaborated with Vanbrugh in *Squire Trelooby*, a farce adapted from Molière. About this time he was briefly joint manager with Vanbrugh of the new Haymarket Theatre, but gave this up for the sinecure of Commissioner of Wine Licences obtained for him by his patron Charles Montague, later Lord Halifax. Ten years later he secured two more sinecures, Undersearcher of Customs and Secretary for Jamaica. In 1720, Pope dedicated his version of Homer's *Iliad* to Congreve and Voltaire visited him in 1726. At his death he left the substantial sum of £10,000, most of it to Henrietta, Duchess of Marlborough, by whom he had a daughter in 1723. He died in London and is buried in Westminster Abbey.

As an undergraduate, Congreve wrote a prose romance, *Incognita* (published 1692), of which Dr Johnson said that he would rather praise it than read it. In addition to 4 comedies and a tragedy, he also wrote some miscellaneous verse, a reply to Jeremy ◊ Collier's attack on the stage, an essay *Concerning Humour in Comedy* (published 1695), an opera, *Semele*, and a masque, *The Judgment of Paris*. His comedies, on which his fame now rests, were all written before he had reached 30.

Perhaps the most curious fact about Congreve's reputation as a playwright is that his tragedy, *The Mourning Bride* (1697), was the most popular of his plays in his own day (Dr Johnson found in it 'the most poetical paragraph in all English poetry'), while his last comedy, *The Way of the World* (1700), was received by his contemporaries with comparative coolness. Today *The Mourning Bride* is hardly ever acted and not much read, while *The Way of the World* is recognized as one of the supreme achievements of the comedy of manners. Mirabell and Millamant are the outstanding example of 'the gay couple' of this kind of comedy, and the final scene where the conditions for a mutually satisfying marriage contract are laid down is representative in outlook at the same time as it is unique in wit and insight.

Neither of Congreve's first 2 comedies, *The Old Bachelor* and *The Double Dealer* (both produced in 1693), has much to distinguish it from the ordinary run of Restoration comedy, though the character of Maskwell in the latter is an interesting if unsuccessful attempt at something unusual. But *Love for Love* (produced in 1695) is a very different matter. This has always been the most popular of Congreve's comedies, achieving two (bowdlerized) productions even in the 19th century, when Restoration comedies were virtually banned from the stage. Sir John Gielgud's 1942 production ran for 471 performances, a record for a classic revival on the London stage. The popularity seems wholly justified. Congreve is loosely classified as a 'Restoration' dramatist, though he was born ten years after the Restoration. In this play he writes for a wider audience than that of the original court circle, an audience that includes the wits of the coffee-house as well as 'the mob of gentlemen who wrote with ease'. One result is that the portrait of the gallant hero is more acute and less flattering than usual. The minor characters of the play have a vivid life of their own while the complications of the plot never become bewildering, being always adequate to the working out of the familiar comic oppositions between love and money, youth and age and above all spontaneity and 'affectation'. [GS]

Complete Works of W. C., ed. M. Summers (4 vols., 1924); *Works*, ed. B. Dobrée (2 vols., World's Classics, 1925–8); *Representative English Comedies*, ed. C. M. Gayley (vol. 4, 1936) (includes *The Way of the World*); *The Way of the World*, ed. K. M. Lynch (1966) and *Love for Love*, ed. E. L. Avery (Regents Restoration Drama Series, 1967); *Three Restoration Comedies*, ed. G. Salgādo (PEL, 1968) (includes *Love for Love*).
J. C. Hodges, *C. the Man* (New York, 1941); B. Dobrée, *Restoration Comedy 1660–1720* (1924); K. M. Lynch, *The Social Mode of Restoration Comedy* (1926).

Connolly, Cyril (Vernon) (1903–). Writer and critic. Born in Coventry, the son of an army major, he was educated at Eton and Balliol College, Oxford, where he was a companion of Graham Greene. He became a regular contributor to the *New Statesman*, and in 1939 (together with Stephen ◊ Spender) founded the eclectic literary magazine *Horizon*. This was an important periodical which published an astonishing variety of writing; he edited it until it folded up, perhaps for lack of a 'policy' or an 'audience', in 1950. He was literary editor of the *Observer* (1942–3) and contributes a weekly book review to the *Sunday Times*. He published a novel, *The Rock Pool* (1935), which portrays the decline and fall of a smug young Englishman in a Riviera art colony. His best work is to be found in 2 collections of essays, the partly autobiographical *Enemies of Promise* (1938), and *Ideas and Places* (1953). *The Unquiet Grave* (1944) is a collection of quotations and melancholy *pensées*. It was issued by Connolly under the pseudonym of 'Palinurus', the ill-fated Trojan steersman who fell overboard and was later killed. Palinurus typifies the 'will-to-failure' in which Connolly is much interested, for historical and cultural reasons. Some of his reviews are collected in *Previous Convictions* (1963). [AR]

G. Ewart, 'C. C.', *London Magazine* (December 1963).

Conrad, Joseph (1857–1924). Novelist. Born in Poland, his real name was Teodor Józef Konrad Nałęcz Korzeniowski. His second language was French, and he did not learn English until he was 20, yet he was to become one of the greatest English novelists. Conrad's father was a Polish writer and nationalist who suffered exile in Russia for his political activities, together with his wife and son. Conrad was orphaned at 11, and his uncle became his guardian and mentor. In 1874 he went to Marseilles to become a sailor and after four unsettled years, involving gun-running, a passionate love affair and attempted suicide, he joined a British freighter. He subsequently served in eastern seas and elsewhere, gaining his Master's Certificate in 1886, the year he became a naturalized British subject. Many of his novels draw on his experience in the East. In 1890 he went to the Belgian Congo to command a river steamer. *Almayer's Folly* was published in 1895, and Conrad subsequently devoted himself to writing. In 1896 he married Jessie George. It was not until the publication in 1913 of *Chance* that Conrad gained wide popularity. In his later years he suffered much from ill-health, though he continued writing until his death in 1924.

Conrad's best work is to be found in *The Nigger of the 'Narcissus'* (1898), the first 20 chapters of *Lord Jim* (1900), 'Heart of Darkness' (1902, in *Youth and Two Other Stories*), *Typhoon* (1902), *Nostromo* (1904), *The Secret Agent* (1907), *Under Western Eyes* (1911), 'The Secret Sharer' (1912, in *'Twixt Land and Sea*) and *The Shadow-Line* (1917). It is generally agreed that in Conrad's earliest fiction, e.g. *An Outcast of the Islands* (1896), he is still feeling his way, and that the work of Conrad's later years, e.g. *The Arrow of Gold* (1919), shows a marked decline. There is disagreement about when this decline starts and critical opinion of *Chance* (1913) and *Victory* (1915) varies enormously.

There are weaknesses in Conrad's work, notably his inability to handle a love relationship convincingly and a recurrent tendency to lapse into a vague and wordy romanticism. In contrast Conrad's best work has remarkable solidity, for it is written to appeal 'primarily to the senses'. Another of his strengths is the skill with which he uses time-shifts and the contrasted perspectives of his narrator and characters to explore the complex significance of his material. Again, one admires the coherence of his best work, in which every detail has its place and is relevant. When he writes in his important preface to *The Nigger of the 'Narcissus'* that a work of art 'should carry its justification in every line', he sets himself a standard which his best work fulfils.

Conrad's art is not primarily concerned with evocations of eastern settings or even with what he impatiently referred to as 'the damned sea'. Man is at the centre of his work and Conrad is recurrently concerned to test him in extreme situations. What, he asks, do the moments of searching stress, of danger, of darkness and of isolation tell us about men and what they live by? Communities and individuals are both tested in Conrad's works. The ship's crew in *The Nigger of the 'Narcissus'* is menaced from without by the storm, and from within by Wait's fear of death. In *Typhoon*, under the threat of the typhoon and the rioting coolies, the faithful, unimaginative MacWhirr and the vulnerable young Jukes are tested and the positive communal values emerge against the storm: 'builders . . . good men'. The testing can focus on a single person and if he passes his test it acts as his initiation into understanding. The young captain in 'The Secret Sharer' has to recognize in Leggett a possibility of his own inner self. Similarly the young captain in *The Shadow-Line* grows beyond his initial brash arrogance to recognize our common physical and moral frailty. Conrad also explores the situation of those who fail their testing. In 'Heart of Darkness', Kurtz in the solitude of the wilderness is found 'wanting', for he is 'hollow at the core'. In *Lord Jim* Conrad holds his own inquiry into Jim's case, probing the causes of weakness in Jim, the 'idealized selfishness' of his romanticism, and the implications for us all of Jim's jump – 'the doubt of the sovereign power enthroned in a fixed standard of conduct', the recognition that 'nobody is good enough'.

Conrad's exploration of politics and society has commanded growing respect. His presentation of the colonial enterprise in 'Heart of Darkness' is devastatingly effective. In *The Secret Agent* he examines the uncomprehending conventionalities of revolutionaries and representatives of the law alike and shows destructive violence breaking out in both public and domestic contexts. The secret agent of the title is ultimately no single person but something working unseen within society – anarchy itself. In *Under Western Eyes* Conrad is primarily concerned with Razumov's isolation, betrayal and guilt, but he is also concerned to show 'the lawlessness of autocracy' and 'the lawlessness of revolution'. There is an interesting ambiguity in the novel's title for 'under' suggests not only the distance of perspective, but also – and more disturbingly – *proximity*. In *Nostromo* Conrad presents a widely representative range of different personal and political viewpoints, exploring both the variety of personal motives, and the discrepancy between men's aspiration's and self-idealizations and their actual achievements. The political line of this novel of revolution and counter-revolution culminates in Monygham's denunciation of 'material interest'; they have achieved a kind of justice, yet this, being founded on 'expediency', lacks 'rectitude'. Yet *Nostromo* is more than a political novel. The ultimate testing in Conrad comes in solitude and at the heart of the novel we find Nostromo and Decoud alone in the darkness of the Placid Gulf.

Conrad suggested that 'the world . . . rests on a few very simple ideas . . . notably . . . on the idea of Fidelity'. Yet in his best work he is also aware of ethical complexities, psychological depths and elemental forces before which the 'simple ideas' of the seaman's code seem at best but very frail supports. Two recurrent images focus the conflict in his work: the steersman and the darkness. The steersmen represent the values of 'a community of inglorious toil' and 'fidelity to a certain standard of conduct'. The darkness that surrounds his steersmen represents not only the elemental forces of nature but also by analogy the darker forces within man himself. One admires the courage with which Conrad confronted the darkness and the strength of his commitment to the small lighted area of human solidarity and order, to 'mind, will and conscience'. [R H]

Collected Edition (21 vols., 1946–55).
G. Jean-Aubry, *J.C.: Life and Letters* (2 vols., 1927); J. Baines, *J.C.: A Critical Biography* (1960); A. Fleishman, *C.'s Politics* (1967); A. Guerard, *C. the Novelist* (1958); T. Moser, *J. C.: Achievement and Decline* (1957); ed. M. Mudrick, *C.: A Collection of Critical Essays* (Englewood Cliffs, N. J., 1966); N. Sherry, *C.'s Eastern World* (1966); J. I. M. Stewart, *J.C.* (1968); I. Howe, *Politics and the Novel* (1957); F. R. Leavis, *The Great Tradition* (1948); J. H. Miller, *Poets of Reality* (1966); M. D. Zabel, *Craft and Character in Modern Fiction* (1957).

Conry, F. ⟡ Ó Maoil Chonaire, Flaithrí.

Constable, Henry (1562–1613). Poet. Educated at St John's College, Cambridge, he became a Roman Catholic and settled in Paris. He published a volume of 23 sonnets in the manner of Sidney, *Diana, the Praises of His Mistress*, in 1592, which his publisher enlarged to contain 77 (not all by Constable) in 1594. His hopes of returning to England in 1595 were not fulfilled, and he served as papal envoy to Edinburgh from 1599, and later secured a pension from the French

King. He returned to England in 1603, and was briefly imprisoned in the Tower; he died abroad at Liège. [M J]

Diana, Sonnets and Other Poems of H. C., ed. W. C. Hazlitt (1859); *Poems*, ed. J. Grundy (1960).
C. S. Lewis, *English Literature in the Sixteenth Century* (1954).

Cooper, Edith Emma. ⟡ Field, Michael.

Cooper, William (1910–). Novelist. Born Harry Summerfield Hoff in Crewe, Cooper was educated at Crewe Secondary School and Cambridge University, and was for a while a schoolmaster in Leicester before joining the Civil Service in 1945. Since 1958 he has been Personnel Consultant to the U.K. Atomic Energy Authority. His first distinctive novel (he had published 4 earlier novels under his real name), *Scenes From Provincial Life* (1950), with its provincial setting, flat narrative style, and amoral anti-hero, was a direct forerunner of the kind of novel to be made popular later in the fifties by John ⟡ Wain and Kingsley ⟡ Amis. This was followed by *The Struggles of Albert Woods* (1952), *The Ever-Interesting Topic* (1953), *Disquiet and Peace* (1956) and his most successful novel, *Young People* (1958), which explores with sympathy and understanding the ambitious dreams of four lower-middle-class undergraduates at a provincial university in the 1930s. His more recent novels are *Scenes From Married Life* (1961) and *Memoirs of a New Man* (1966). He has also written the critical study *C. P. Snow* (1959), and has dramatized *The Tale of Genji* for radio. [P J K]

James Gindin, *Postwar British Fiction* (U. of California P., 1963).

Coppard, A(lfred) E(dgar) (1878–1957). Short-story writer and poet. Born at Folkestone, the son of a tailor and a housemaid, Coppard spent his early years in Brighton, where he attended a Board School until the age of 9. He was then sent to the East End of London to learn the tailoring trade but after three years returned to Brighton. Until 1919 when he became a full-time writer he earned his living as a clerk, educating himself by reading poetry. In 1907 he took a clerical job at Oxford where his contact with university life, mainly through extra-mural activities, encouraged him to write with more seriousness of purpose, and he began to contribute short stories and poems to periodicals. His first collection of short stories, *Adam and Eve and Pinch Me* (1921), was followed by many others, including *Clorinda Walks in Heaven* (1922), *Fishmonger's Fiddle* (1925), *The Field of Mustard* (1926), *Silver Circus* (1928) and *Dunky Fitlow* (1933). Although the influence of Chekhov and Maupassant is discernible in some of Coppard's stories, he himself saw his work as belonging to the English tradition of folk tales and ballads, and there is much justice in this view. A master of rural dialogue and lyrical description and a profound analyst of human behaviour, he belongs, at best, with the handful of outstanding English exponents of the short story. His volumes of poems, *Hips and Haws* (1922), *Pelagea* (1926), *Yokohama Garland* (1926) and *Collected Poems* (1928), possess little distinction. Coppard's finest poetry is to be found in his short stories. He also wrote a lively and amusing autobiography, *It's Me, O Lord* (1957). [PJK]

Jacob Schwartz, *The Writings of A. E. C.* (1931); H. E. Bates, *The Modern Short Story* (1941); Frank O'Connor, *The Lonely Voice* (1963).

Corbet, or Corbett, Richard (1582–1635). Poet. Son of a gentleman-gardener, he was educated at Westminster School and went to Oxford in 1598 to Broadgates Hall, transferring the following year to Christ Church, with which he was associated for the next thirty years. When he took his M.A. in 1605, he was already adept at light verse, which has not survived, and his Latin poems on Queen Elizabeth's death and King James's visit to Oxford were printed in Oxonian collections. He had a local reputation as a ballad-singer and a practical joker. A supporter of Laud, Corbet assiduously sought and won influential friends at James's court, including Buckingham. He also entertained Ben Jonson at Oxford. He became Chaplain to King James, and Dean of Christ Church in 1620. *Iter Boreale*, a long poem, describes a journey through the Midlands; and he sycophantically addressed many verse epistles and poems to his patron Buckingham. In 1628 his careerist zeal was rewarded in the nick of time: he was appointed to the bishopric of Oxford, and installed ten days after his patron's assassination. Four years later Laud translated him to the bishopric of Norwich, but found him to be over-tolerant of Puritans and administratively lax. Two posthumous

gatherings of poems are *Certaine Elegant Poems, Written by Dr Corbet, Bishop of Norwich* (1647) and *Poëtica Stromata* (1648).

An interesting figure in the academic and ecclesiastical life of his time, Corbet is essentially a minor poet whose song 'Farewell, Rewards & Faeries' expresses nostalgic regrets at the passing of the old England and the advent of Puritanism. [MJ]

The Poems, ed. and intr. J. A. W. Bennett and H. R. Trevor-Roper (1955).

Corelli, Marie (1854–1924). Novelist. The daughter of an Italian father and Scottish mother, she was educated in a convent in France as a musician, but the first of her many works of fiction, *A Romance of Two Worlds* (1886), partly autobiographical, was so successful that she began a career as a best-selling novelist. Her work is marked by 'earnestness' and an attempt to make the fruits of scientific discovery more palatable to readers who still wished uncritically to be left with their old comfortable moral, ethical and cosmological pictures. Though she has no place in serious literary history, she is still read with attention, especially on the fringes of Western culture (in the West Indies, for example). Her best-known works are: *Thelma* (1887), *Barabbas* (1893), *Sorrows of Satan* (1895), *The Mighty Atom* (1896), *The Master Christian* (1900), *God's Good Man* (1904) and *The Secret Power* (1921). She settled in Stratford-on-Avon. [AR]

G. Bullock, *M.C.: The Life and Death of a Best-Seller* (1940); E. Bigland, *M.C.: The Woman and the Legend* (1953).

Cornford, Frances Crofts (*née* Darwin) (1886–1960). Poet. A grand-daughter of Charles Darwin, she was born at Cambridge, where both of her parents were university lecturers. She was encouraged in her early writing of poetry by the young Rupert ◊ Brooke, then an undergraduate at Cambridge, whom she later described in a famous phrase as the 'young Apollo golden-haired'. In 1909 she married Francis M. Cornford, the classicist, and published her first book, *Poems*, in the following year. Later volumes of poetry include *Spring Morning* (1915), *Autumn Midnight* (1923), *Mountains and Molehills* (1935), *Collected Poems* (1954) and *On a Calm Shore* (1960). A poet of small but unpretentious talent, whose work is firmly in the lyrical tradition of ◊ *Georgian Poetry*, she is best known for the much anthologized poem 'To a Fat Lady Seen from the Train'. [PJK]

P. Stansky and W. Abrahams, *Journey to the Frontier: John Cornford and Julian Bell* (1966).

Cornford, Rupert John (1915–36). Poet and essayist. Son of the poetess Frances ◊ Cornford and Professor F. M. Cornford, he was named after Rupert Brooke. At the L.S.E. and Cambridge he was a Marxist, a history scholar and a political leader. On the outbreak of the Spanish War he joined the anarchist militia, writing his poems in lulls between the fighting. Later he fought at Madrid University, behind a barricade of philosophy books, and was killed near Cordoba. A memorial volume containing letters, essays and poems was published in 1938 (*J. C. A. Memoir*, ed. P. Sloan). Cornford's essays condemn those whose radicalism is caused by maladjustment rather than conviction. Generous and a lover of life, he wished to express values in action. He had too many interests to be primarily a poet, but his best poems will survive because they are part of history as well as individual statements. 'Heart of the heartless world', a love poem, mingles practical resolve with human concern. 'Before the Storming of Huesca' faces up to the reality of fear. 'Letter from Aragon' is an assertion of courage and hope in a context of horror. 'Keep Culture out of Cambridge', an early poem, is not to be despised as invective. [FG]

P. Stansky and W. Abrahams, *Journey to the Frontier: J. C. and Julian Bell* (1966); F. Grubb, *A Vision of Reality* (1965).

'Cornhill Magazine'. Created by the publishers Smith and Elder in 1860, the *Cornhill* set both a new fashion and standard for shilling magazines of illustrated fiction. ◊ Thackeray was its first editor. It contained his complete novel, *The Adventures of Philip* (1862), and the unfinished *Denis Duval* (1864). Sir Leslie ◊ Stephen became editor in 1871 and used the magazine to encourage young writers, among them R. L. Stevenson, Thomas Hardy, W. E. Henley and Henry James. In 1881 the publishers suggested to Stephen that he should resign the editorship in order to head a great literary project they had in mind, the *Dictionary of National Biography* (1886 ff.). The *Cornhill* proceeded under the successive editorships of James Payn (1830–98), J. St Loe Strachey (1860–1927) and R. J. Smith (1857–1916). The latter had to fight fierce competition from the new sixpenny magazines which entered the market during the early 1900s. Among modern writers to have notably assisted at the adaptive process which all old-established journals have to undergo from time to time is Peter ◊ Quennell, who edited the *Cornhill* from 1944 to 1951. [RB]

Cornhill Gallery of Illustrations (1865); *Sheaves from the Cornhill*, ed. L. Huxley (1926).

Cornish Literature. The history of Cornish divides itself into three periods: Old Cornish (to the 12th century), Middle Cornish (12th–16th centuries), Late Cornish (16th–18th centuries), to which 'New Cornish' or the resurrected language should be added. The only extant documents of Old Cornish are a few glosses, some proper names (e.g. in the Domesday Book), and a Cornish–Latin vocabulary, adapted from Aelfric's Anglo-Saxon vocabulary, which dates from the early 12th century and is therefore on the border of Middle Cornish. This is not to say, of course, that there was no Cornish literature during those centuries. Cornwall played a part in the creation and diffusion of the Arthurian cycle, in particular of the legend of Tristan and Isolde. But, as in the case of Brittany, most of this literature remained probably oral.

The oldest literary text in Middle Cornish is a fragment (41 lines of verse) from a comic play or a comic interlude in a miracle, copied about 1400 on the back of a Latin charter preserved in the British Museum. Apart from this, all extant Middle Cornish literature is religious. It consists of a long poem, *Pascon agan Arluth* ('The Passion of Our Lord'), and a trilogy of miracle plays known as *Ordinalia* (*Origo Mundi, Passio Domini Nostri Ihesu Christi* and *Resurrexio Domini Nostri Ihesu Christi*). The *Pascon* seems somewhat older than the *Ordinalia*; it is written in strophes of 8 lines of 7 syllables, while the metre of the *Ordinalia* is quite varied, but Middle Cornish had lost the Celtic system of prosody so well preserved in Welsh and Breton. From a literary point of view, the *Ordinalia* deserve more attention than they have hitherto been given. They represent an older, more liturgical type of miracles than the Coventry Plays, and they are perhaps unique in European medieval literature for their use of the 'Legend of the Rood', i.e. the legend of the three seeds from the Tree of Knowledge put by Seth in Adam's grave and eventually becoming the Tree of the Cross (see F. E. Halliday, *The Legend of the Rood*, 1955; R. M. Longsworth, *The Cornish Ordinalia*, 1967).

Another miracle play, *Beunans Meriasek* ('The Life of St Meriadec'), was written (or copied) in 1504; it deals with the life of St Meriadec, Bishop of Vannes (Brittany) in the 7th century, curiously mixed up with that of St Silvester, the 4th-century Pope. The only important Cornish text in prose dates from 1555; it is a part translation of Bishop Bonner's homilies, known as the *Tregear MS*, from the translator's name.

The Cornish people long resisted the Reformation, and at least one miracle play was still performed in the 17th century; it is *The Creacon of the World*, the manuscript of which is dated 1611 but is almost certainly a copy of an older text. It is longer and more theatrical than *Origo Mundi*, from which it has borrowed many passages. The language is rather corrupt, but very lively and often humorous. The title and stage directions are in English and not in Latin as in the older mysteries.

The Cornish language declined very rapidly during the 18th century, and the last native speaker is said to have died in 1777. During the last stages of its existence it became more and more corrupt and the few people who could still write it had forgotten the traditional orthography and spelled it phonetically as best they could. The Welsh scholar Edward Lhuyd inserted in his *Archæologia Britannica* (1707) an account of Cornish with a folk-tale and a preface in the language, in a phonetic script of his own. Another document of the period is a short bilingual treatise, *Nebbaz gerriau dro tho Carnoack* ('A Few Words about Cornish'), by John Boson. Some prayers, proverbs and fragments of folk-songs remained in oral knowledge, in a more or less mutilated form, until quite late in the 19th century.

Cornish texts were edited, and dictionaries composed, by 19th-century Celtic scholars (E. Norris, W. Stokes, R. Williams, etc.), and their work made possible the revival of Cornish in the 20th century, initiated mainly by Henry Jenner (1848–1934). In 1903 he made a speech in Cornish at a congress in Brittany, and in 1904 published a *Handbook of the Cornish Language*, intended as a practical rather than a scholarly work, with an attempt at rationalization of the grammar and unification of the spelling. His work was completed by his disciples, Robert Morton Nance (1873–1959) and A. S. D. Smith ('Caradar') (1883–1950). Cornish is now studied by a fair number of persons (it is even taught in some schools) and has become again, if not an everyday language, at least a literary medium. The Cornish Gorsedd was established in 1928 with Welsh and Breton help, and its annual competitions are a great help to the fostering of a new literature. Among the most important modern productions are the long poem *Trystan hag Ysolt*, by Caradar, and *Bewnans Alysaryn* ('The Life of St Alizarin') by Peggy Pollard, a witty parody of the medieval miracles. Many other works remain in manuscript owing to the difficulties of publication. There have been two all-Cornish literary journals, *Kernow* ('Cornwall') in 1934–6, and *An Lef Kernewek* ('The Cornish Voice') since 1952; articles in Cornish appear also in the review *Old Cornwall*. [JRFP]

Thomas Jones, 'Cornish Literature', in *Chambers' Encyclopaedia*; Henry Jenner, *A Handbook of the Cornish Language* (1904); A. S. D. Smith, *The Story of the Cornish Language* (1947).

Corvo, Baron. ◊ Rolfe, Frederick William.

Coryate, Thomas (1577–1617). Travel-writer. Son of George Coryate, the divine, he was educated at Oxford, and was an entertaining courtier in Prince Henry's household. In 1608 he travelled extensively in Europe, mainly on foot, going through France to Venice and returning via Switzerland, Germany and Holland. In 1611 he published *Coryat's Crudities Hastily Gobled up in Five Moneths Travells* (2 vols., Glasgow, 1905), an amusing account of his continental sojourn, enlivened with descriptions of great buildings, and much incidental information about women stage-players and Venetian courtesans. In 1612 Coryate travelled to India via Constantinople, Greece, Egypt, Palestine, Mesopotamia and Persia. He visited the court of the Great Mogul, whom he addressed in Persian, but died at Surat on his way home. Some fragments of his eastern travels were published posthumously. [MJ]

D. Bush, *English Literature in the Earlier Seventeenth Century* (revised edn, 1962); M. Strachan, *The Life and Adventures of T.C.* (1962).

Cotton, Charles (1630–87). Poet and translator. Born in Derbyshire, which he celebrated in his popular, long poem, *The Wonders of the Peak* (1681). He was an early writer of humorous verses in the travesty or burlesque form, later very fashionable, on Virgil (1664) and Lucian (1685). He translated Montaigne's *Essays* (1685), but is best known to the general reader as the author of the second part of his friend Izaak ◊ Walton's *The Compleat Angler* (1676). [A R]

Poems, ed. J. Beresford (1923); ed. and selected J. Buxton (1958).
C. J. Sembower, *The Life and Poetry of C. C.* (New York, 1911); G. G. P. Heywood, *C. C. and His River* (1928).

Coventry Cycle. ◊ Miracle Plays.

Coverdale, Miles (1488–1568). Translator. Educated at Cambridge, he took holy orders in 1514, and lived at the Austin Friary in Cambridge until 1526. He became a Lutheran, and defended Robert Barnes on a charge of heresy in 1526. He soon went abroad to Antwerp, where he made the first complete translation into English of the ◊ Bible. Lacking the scholarship in Greek and Hebrew of his predecessor ◊ Tyndale, he worked from German and Latin translations – mainly Zwingli's Zürich Bible (1524–9), Luther's German Bible, Paginus's Latin Bible (1528), and the Vulgate – as well as Tyndale's New Testament. His fluent, melodious style was enormously influential; one authority claims 'it was he more than any other single translator whose sense of rhythm produced that musical quality which is particularly evident in the Authorized Version of 1611'. His translation, probably printed at Zürich, was issued in England in 1535 with a dedication to the King. Coverdale became the quasi-official supervisor of biblical translations supported by the King and the bishops. In 1537 there appeared a new edition of his bible and also the composite 'Matthew's Bible', which contained Tyndale's incomplete Old Testament translation made up from Coverdale's version together with Tyndale's New Testament. In 1539 Coverdale went to Paris to superintend the printing of his sumptuous 'Great Bible' which was sponsored by Thomas Cromwell, the King's minister; the second edition in 1540 was 'appointed to the use of the churches' and had a preface by Thomas Cranmer, Archbishop of Canterbury. After a sojourn in England, Coverdale returned to the continent until 1548. He became Bishop of Exeter in 1551, but three years later was allowed to leave England during the reign of the Catholic, Mary. He returned and helped to consecrate Archbishop Parker in 1559. In 1563 he was made a D.D. of Cambridge and rector of St Magnus, London Bridge, a post which he shortly gave up for puritanical reasons, and preached privately in London until his death.

Coverdale translated various theological tracts, and around 1540 he published *Goostly Psalmes and Spirituall Songs*, verse-translations of German hymns. His great literary achievement, however, was to influence the style of the Authorized Version, itself the biggest single influence on English literature and the English language. [M J]

C. C. Butterworth, *The Literary Lineage of the King James Bible* (1941); David Daiches, *The King James Bible: Its Development and Sources* (1941); C. S. Lewis, *English Literature in the Sixteenth Century* (1954); J. F. Mozley, *C. and His Bibles* (1954).

Coward, Noël (1899–   ). Man of the theatre. He made his stage *début* in 1911 and was Slightly in *Peter Pan* at Christmas in 1913. He has long had a glittering international reputation as an actor, playwright, stage and film director, composer of light music, and cabaret performer. His most characteristic successes were in the twenties and thirties. His best comedies have won themselves the status of minor classics in the theatre and are known for their gay and impudent dialogue. They include *Hay Fever* (1925), *Private Lives* (1930), *Blithe Spirit* (1941) and *Present Laughter* (1943). Believing that 'it is still a pretty exciting thing to be English', Coward devised the sentimental patriotic pageant-play *Cavalcade* at Drury Lane in 1931, and his jingoistic successes in the Second World War include *This Happy Breed* (1943) and the film *In Which We Serve* (1942). His many musical plays and revues include *Bitter Sweet* (1929) and *Words and Music* (1932), which contained the song 'Mad Dogs and Englishmen'.

A prodigious worker, Coward has since the war written straight and musical plays which have been staged in London and New York, but, although his public remains loyal, none has had much *critical* success. In 1953 he gave a notable performance in Shaw's *The Apple Cart*. Since 1956, for taxation and health reasons, he has lived mainly abroad. On his seventieth birthday the theatrical profession toasted 'the Master'; Sheridan Morley's biography *A Talent to Amuse* was published; and soon afterwards Coward was knighted. [MJ]

Present Indicative (1937); *Middle East Diary* (1944); *Future Indefinite* (1954); Prefaces to *Play Parade: The Collected Plays* (in progress). P. Braybrooke, *The Amazing Mr N. C.* (1933); R. Greacen, *The Art of N. C.* (1953); R. Mander and J. Mitchenson, *A Theatrical Companion to C.* (1957); G. J. Nathan, *Passing Judgments* (New York, 1935); Sean O'Casey, *The Flying Wasp* (1937); J. Russell Taylor, *The Rise and Fall of the Well-Made Play* (1967).

Cowley, Abraham (1618–67). Poet. The son of a wealthy London stationer, he was educated at Westminster School, and Trinity College, Cambridge, where he took his B.A. in 1639, was made a minor Fellow in 1640 and became an M.A. in 1643. He was ejected from Cambridge as a result of the Civil War and removed to Oxford. In 1646 he left for France, where he became cipher-secretary to Queen Henrietta Maria, and was employed on various diplomatic missions. In 1655 he returned to England to act as a Royalist spy. He was arrested and interrogated by Cromwell. He was released on bail, but remained under suspicion in England as a Royalist, while the Royalists themselves suspected him of being a turn-coat. To ingratiate himself with Cromwell's government he wrote a conciliatory paragraph in the preface to his 1656 volume of poems, for which the Royalists never entirely forgave him; moreover his poems 'Destiny' and 'Brutus' were interpreted as political allegories justifying the rebellion and even the execution of Charles I. Cowley then took to the study of medicine, being created M.D. at Oxford in 1657. After the Restoration he failed to obtain the mastership of the Savoy, which he considered his right, but obtained a favourable lease of some of the Queen's lands through the patronage of the Earl of St Albans and the Duke of Buckingham. He retired to the country, died at Chertsey, and was buried with great pomp beside Spenser and Chaucer in Westminster Abbey.

Cowley was in the intellectual forefront of his time. His conception of poetry was profoundly influenced by Hobbes (an influence which has often been misinterpreted). He was exceedingly well informed on contemporary scientific discoveries, and was closely associated with the Royal Society. His numerous works included English and Latin poetry, plays, essays and prose works. His essays are accepted masterpieces of their kind.

In his own lifetime Cowley was reckoned the greatest poet of his age and one of the glories of English literature. Shortly after his death a change of taste resulted in some dissatisfaction with his wit and some qualification of the general praise, but his work remained close enough to the ideals of the succeeding period for him to continue to be accounted a great poet during the 18th century. In the 19th century he was largely forgotten, and whereas Donne's reputation was revived in the earlier 20th century, Cowley continued in obscurity. There are, however, at last signs of a long-overdue reassessment of his work and of his being reinstated in his just position as a major English poet.

The first characteristic of Cowley's achievement is its extreme range; he wrote elegies, poems on love, anacreontics, translations, Pindaric odes and part of an epic. His greatest limitation is a lack of powerful passion; his greatest virtues the brilliant, controlled music of his versification, and a wise and witty insight into the predicaments of life; his greatest poetic misfortune has been the constant comparison of his work with that of Donne, a poet with whom he has fundamentally little in common. His most important work is contained in *The Mistress* (1647), in the 1656 volume of *Poems*, which contained a critical preface, the *Miscellanies*, the *Pindaric Odes* and the *Davideis*. *The Mistress* is not love poetry in the ordinary sense, being directed to the reason rather than the heart of the reader. Like a sonnet sequence it is based on certain conventional formulations and metaphors for the love relationship, but instead of using these as vehicles of passion it examines them in the light of an acute and sensitive intelligence, and thus explores the predicament of being in love; the love relationship is seen throughout from the outside and the result is a poetry quite different from, for instance, the love poetry of Donne.

The Pindaric ode, an enthusiastic poem written in irregular verses and stanzas irregularly rhymed, and permitting a greater freedom of imagination than other kinds, was introduced into English by Cowley and was much copied throughout the following century. Sometimes Cowley overreaches himself and descends to the ludicrous, but the flights of his imagination are usually controlled by a sure judgement. The ode 'To Mr Hobbes', a noble tribute, is among the best of them. The *Davideis*, published before *Paradise Lost*, is the first attempt at a genuine, neo-classical, biblical epic in English. The epic was not suited to Cowley's genius, and the *Davideis* lacks the grandeur and power necessary to such a poem, but it does show a superb mastery of the heroic couplet from which Dryden learnt and developed his skill. Of the other poems the elegies on Crashaw and Hervey deserve mention, the latter especially being a controlled and powerful expression of mourning which is only excelled by the greatest of its kind in English. The ode 'To the Royal Society', besides being a fine poem, is also indicative of Cowley's attitude to science and philosophy.

Cowley is usually thought of as a Metaphysical poet, a judgement which requires careful qualification. While he does rely on argument and indulge in excesses of wit, his poetry is seldom obscure and his sentiments are usually general. He owes as much to Ben Jonson as to Donne. Deeply interested in philosophy and the natural sciences, he looked upon scientific knowledge as a prop and confirmation of biblical truth; for this reason, just as he favoured a biblical subject for his projected epic, so he drew greatly on scientific discovery for his imagery. Many things which seem to a modern reader wild exaggerations (such as the hardening of ice into crystal under geological pressure) were the established scientific theories of his time. In his rational approach, his emphasis on good sense, his inheritance of the classical tradition and his skill in versification, Cowley stands in the tradition that descends from Ben Jonson to Dryden and the 18th century. As an introduction to his work Cowley's own preface to the 1656 volume, *Poems*, is important. [P M]

Works, ed. T. Sprat (1668) (with *Life of Cowley*); *English Writings*, ed. A. R. Waller (2 vols., 1905–6); *Essays*, ed. J. R. Lumby, revised A. Tilley (1923); *Poetry and Prose, with Sprat's Life*, ed. L. C. Martin (1949) (selection).

Johnson, *Lives of the Poets*; J. Loiseau, *C.: sa vie, son œuvre* (Paris, 1931); A. H. Nethercot, *C.: The Muse's Hannibal* (1931); R. B. Hinman, *C.'s World of Order* (Cambridge, Mass., 1960); U. Suerbaum, *Die Lyrik der Korrespondenzen: C.'s Bildkunst und die Tradition der Englischen Renaissancedichtung* (Bochum-Langendreer, 1958).

Cowley, Mrs Hannah Parkhurst (1743–1809). Poet and dramatist. She wrote a number of comedies, of which *The Belle's Stratagem* (1780) survived well into the 19th century. She also wrote magazine verse (e.g. 'Anna Matilda' in *The World*). [A R]

Works: *Poems and Dramas*, with Life (2 vols., 1841). R. C. Rhodes, 'The Belle's Stratagem', *R E S*, 5 (1929).

Cowper, William (1731–1800). Poet and letter writer. Born at Great Berkhampstead in Hertfordshire, the son of the rector, and well connected. He was educated first at a private school, then at Westminster; he finally entered the Middle Temple, and was called to the bar (1754). The death of his mother when he was 6, severe bullying at his first school, and the termination of his love affair with a cousin, Theodora Cowper, by her father, left him with severe mental problems. Family interest found him the valuable office of Clerk of the Journals in the House of Lords, but the prospect of his approaching (purely formal) examination drove him to a fit of suicidal mania. After a year in an asylum in St Albans, his malady receded, and he retired to Huntingdon to live on a small private income in the household of Morley and Mary Unwin. On the former's death, Cowper retired to Olney with the widow, who had become his closest friend. There he fell under the influence of the Olney curate, the Rev. John Newton, an evangelical. A recurrence of his mania in 1773, involving a conviction of his own damnation, prevented his marriage with Mrs Unwin; he calmed down some years later, but had recurrent fits of mania. In 1779 appeared the well-known collection of *Olney Hymns* (281 by Newton; 67 by Cowper). Cowper's contributions are a notable addition to English hymnody, and include 'Oh! for a closer walk with God' and 'God moves in mysterious ways'. Cowper's poetry was a therapeutic interest, strongly encouraged by Mrs Unwin after his illness of 1773. His *Poems* (1782) contained a few lyrics and 8 reflective essays in couplets: 'The Progress of Error'; 'Truth'; 'Table Talk' (containing some interesting comments on contemporary poetry); 'Expostulation' (on anti-semitism); 'Hope'; 'Charity'; 'Conversation'; and 'Retirement'. The book was well received, because of its tone (serious and pious) as well as its neatness and interest. He became friendly with a new neighbour, Lady Austin, who gave him the story for his masterly comic ballad, *John Gilpin's Ride* (1782). She also gave him the suggestion which led to the 5,000 blank-verse lines of *The Task: A Poem in Six Books* (1785), in which Cowper indulges his interest in rural scenes, country life and moral teaching (attacking blood sports among other things). He sees natural beauty as the innocence into which, as an escapist, he wishes to immerse himself: 'God made the Country, and Man made the Town'. The poem is simply written (to the point of flatness in places), but is precise and 'natural'. Cowper's blank verse is more accomplished than his couplets. He also had a true, if restrained, lyric gift, which is illustrated in his famous lines 'On the Loss of the Royal George' (1782; but not published until after his death along with 'Yardley Oak', the famous sonnet 'To Mrs Unwin', and the lines 'To Mary'). The success of *The Task* encouraged him to produce a not very successful translation of Homer into blank verse (started 1785; published 1791). After Mrs Unwin died in 1794, Cowper (who received a pension in that year) relapsed into silence, except for the fine, melancholy, personal poem of despair 'The Castaway', written just before his death. He was one of the best letter-writers of the century, a deft and interesting master of this form of literary expression. [A R]

Poetical Works, ed. H. S. Milford (1934); *Correspondence*, ed. T. Wright (4 vols., 1904; additional vol., 1925); *W. C.: Poetry and Prose*, ed. and intr. B. Spiller (1968) (selection).
Lord David Cecil, *The Stricken Deer* (1928) (biography); G. Thomas, *W. C. and the Eighteenth Century* (1935); N. Nicholson, *C.* (1951); C. Ryskamp, *W.C. of the Inner Temple Esq.* (1959) (bibliography).

Crabbe, George (1754–1832). Poet. Born at Aldeburgh in Suffolk, the son of a collector of the salt-tax. After a period of apprenticeship and unsuccessful practice as a surgeon, in 1780 Crabbe went to London to make his way as a writer. Two unimportant anonymous poems *Inebriety* and *The Candidate* had no success and in desperation he sent some of his work to Edmund ⟡ Burke, who took him up, lodged him in his own house, and introduced him to his circle. In 1781 Crabbe took orders and published anonymously *The Library* (acknowledged 1783), an uninteresting ramble through his read-

ing which, however, became quite popular. Crabbe was chaplain to the Duke of Rutland at Belvoir (1782–5), and published in 1783 one of his best-known poems, *The Village* (according to Boswell revised by Johnson), which is an anti-pastoral, realistic treatment of rural misery; and in 1785, *The Newspaper* (a somewhat disjointed reflective poem in couplets). He married in 1783 and published nothing of importance until his *Poems* (1807), which contains *The Parish Register*, 'principally the Annals of the Poor', divided into Baptisms, Marriages, Funerals, and intermingled with reflections on gardening, the state of the peasantry, and the like. Thereafter followed *The Borough* (1810), a poem in 24 letters, including the famous story of Peter Grimes, one of 'the Poor of the Borough'; 21 *Tales in Verse* (1812); and *Tales of the Hall* (in 22 books) (1819). By 1814 he had become Vicar of Trowbridge in Wiltshire. He was never much liked as a parish priest, and had a liking for opium, which affected some of his later work (for the better in *Sir Eustace Grey*, 1807, an account in 8-line stanzas by a mad-house patient).

In his technique, his use of the couplet and a fondness for satire, Crabbe was a conservative, an admirer and follower (at a distance) of Pope and Johnson. In his choice of subject, the obscure lives of the poor, the debilitating and pervasive effects of human weakness, he was a forerunner of the realistic novelists. The juxtaposition of these apparently ill-matched elements of his art, added to a grim, but genuine humour and a dogged disillusion, invest many of his poems with a queer power, which many have noticed but which is very difficult to characterize. His framework of positive doctrine is a commonplace Christianity, but this leaves free play to his power of feeling, which seems to spring from a deep-seated hatred of the helplessness of small-town and rural life. Attacked for being morbid and ignoring the 'higher flights of poetry', and praised for realism (and a humanitarianism frequently in fact absent from his work) the ups and downs of his reputation give an interesting picture of critical sensibility. 'Peter Grimes', 'The Patron', 'The Frank Courtship', 'Silford Hall' and 'The Equal Marriage' are among the best of his work.

His son, also the Rev. George Crabbe, produced a *Life* (1834; intr. E. M. Forster, World's Classics, 1932; intr. E. Blunden,

1947). This is one of the classics of reticent English biography. [A R]

Poems, ed. A. W. Ward (3 vols., 1905–7); *The Poetical Works*, ed. A. and R. Carlyle (1908); *Poems*, selected and intr. P. Henderson (1946); *Selected Poems*, ed. G. Grigson (1950); *New Poems*, ed. A. Pollard (1960); *A Selection*, ed. and intr. J. Lucas (1967).

E. M. Forster, 'C. and Peter Grimes', in *Two Cheers for Democracy* (1951); J. H. Evans, *The Poems of G. C.: A Literary and Historical Study* (1933); L. Haddakin, *The Poetry of C.* (1955); R. Huchon, *G. C. and His Times* (1907) (with bibliography).

Craig, Edward Gordon (1872–1966). Man of the theatre. The illegitimate son of the architect E. W. Godwin and the great actress Ellen Terry, he was brought up by his mother and had a promising career as an actor in Henry Irving's company. He was also known as an artist and wood-engraver. Between 1900 and 1903 he directed and designed six productions in out-of-the-way theatres which represented a challenge to the sumptuous realism of the Victorian theatre. From 1904 he lived a nomadic life on the continent, expressing his vision of a new theatre in a series of books, articles, drawings, woodcuts, engravings and models. He participated in only four productions, including his famous *Hamlet* at the Moscow Art Theatre. His detractors claimed that his designs were impractical, but to others he was a romantic figure of persecuted genius. His most influential writings include essays in his periodical *The Mask* (1908–29) and *On the Art of the Theatre* (1911). *Scene* (1923), a series of etchings, envisages a great, adaptable performing area, while *A Production – 1926* (1930) commemorates in folio his designs for *The Pretenders* in Copenhagen. An idolatrous memoir *Henry Irving*(1930), *Ellen Terry and Her Secret Self* (1931) and *Index to the Story of My Days* (1957) show Craig as an evocative prose-writer and historian. His great European influence was through his publications. He was made a Companion of Honour in 1958. The fine biography by his son Edward Craig (1968) shows Craig as one of the last bohemian writer-artists of the 19th century – gifted, misunderstood, demanding, wayward, improvident. [M J]

I. K. Fletcher and A. Rood, *E.G.C.: A Bibliography* (1967).

Cranmer, Thomas (1489–1556). Archbishop of Canterbury (1533–6), theologian and liturgist. Cranmer went to Cambridge University in 1503, and was elected Fellow of Jesus College some eight years later. It is possible that the young Cranmer was influenced by the reforming ideas of Erasmus, who became Lady Margaret Lecturer in Divinity at Cambridge in 1511. We may date from this period his intensive study of the Scriptures and Fathers. Shortly before 1520 he was ordained priest, and in 1529 it came to the notice of Henry VIII that Cranmer had suggested that the question of Henry's divorce from Catherine of Aragon, not satisfactorily settled by Rome, should be submitted instead to the theologians of the English and continental universities. By 1533, he was Archbishop of Canterbury. The major details of the progress of reform during the remainder of Cranmer's life are well known, as are the facts, perhaps, that on the accession of Queen Mary he refused to take refuge abroad, and after some weakness and vacillation affirmed his belief in the re-formed doctrine in St Mary's Church in Oxford, and was immediately afterwards burnt at the stake. Cranmer's major concerns in his published work were theological, and his theological insights underlay his work as a liturgist, which itself has proved to be of more widespread and enduring influence. Cranmer had the major hand in the production of the Edwardian prayer books of 1549 and 1552, which became the basis of the *Book of Common Prayer* (1662), one of the two foundation stones of the Church of England (the other being the Authorized Version of the ⋄ Bible) and one of the 2 books whose rhythms and phrasing have been most deeply absorbed into the English language. Cranmer's achievement was to make of English a liturgical language comparable in dignity and beauty with Latin, and yet comprehensible to the common man as Latin was not. His liturgical prose style is fundamentally utilitarian, intended to be clear and accurate, and its memorable effect is at least in part the result of so much matter compacted in an orderly fashion into so brief a space. It was in large part the achievement of Cranmer also that the theology and worship of the Church of England were so firmly based upon the Scripture. Not only was he mainly responsible for the Forty-Two Articles of Religion finally drawn up in 1552, and revised and abbreviated into the Thirty-Nine Articles in 1563, but he was principally involved in the royal order for the Great Bible of 1539, to be available in every church. In the Preface included with the second edition of the Great Bible in 1540, he argued that the Bible should be more widely read. Cranmer's central theological position is set forth in 3 homilies, from the official volume of 12, issued in 1547, *Of Salvation, Of Faith* and *Of Good Works*, which are generally attributed to him. His faith regarding the Sacrament of the Altar is expounded chiefly in his most important theological work, *A Defence of the True and Catholic Doctrine of the Sacrament* (1550). [A G]

Works, ed. J. E. Cox (2 vols., Parker Society, 1844–6); *Work*, ed. G. E. Duffield, intr. J. I. Packer (Courtenay Library of Reformation Classics, 2, 1964) (selection); *Selected Writings*, ed. C. S. Mayer (1961).
A. F. Pollard, *T.C. and the English Reformation* (1904); F. E. Hutchinson, *C. and the English Reformation* (1951); J. Ridley, *T.C.* (1962); G. W. Bromiley, *T.C. Theologian* (1956); N. Sykes, E. C. Ratcliff and A. T. P. Williams, *T.C.* (1956) (3 commemoration lectures).

Crashaw, Richard (1612 or early 1613–1649). Poet. Born in London and orphaned while still a child, Crashaw went to Pembroke College, Cambridge, as an exhibitioner in 1631, and in 1635 was elected to a fellowship at Peterhouse, Cambridge. He was curate of Little St Mary's, the church adjoining Peterhouse, in 1639. The college was at this time the centre of Laudianism in Cambridge, and in other ways also Crashaw was connected with the high church movement in the Church of England. Crashaw suffered in the reaction against Laudianism as the Parliamentary side triumphed in the Civil War, and in 1644 was formally deprived of his fellowship, although he seems to have left Cambridge already the previous year. By 1645, in exile on the continent, he had been received into the Catholic Church; in 1647, as the delayed result of the exiled Queen Henrietta Maria's intercession on his behalf, he was given a post in the entourage of Cardinal Palotto; and in 1649, after making enemies among the Cardinal's followers, he was sent away to be out of danger and admitted to a minor office in the gift of the Cardinal at the Cathedral of the Santa Casa at Loreto, where the same year he died and was buried *in tumulo sacerdotum*. In October 1631, Crashaw had been elected to the Greek Scholarship at Pembroke, whose duties included the composition of Latin and Greek verses on scriptural themes, and a good many in the collection of Latin epigrams which he published in 1634 as *Epigrammatum Sacrorum Liber* were probably written to meet the requirements of the scholarship. The collection was enlarged, notably with the inclusion of some Greek verses, in a later edition of 1670. In reality, however, like Herbert, Crashaw is the poet of one book, *Steps to the Temple . . . with . . . Delights of the Muses*, published in 1646, its title an acknowledgement of Herbert's achievement. The volume was published in a revised and enlarged form in 1648. In 1652, Miles Pinkney (alias Thomas Car), confessor to the English Augustinian nuns at Paris and a friend of Crashaw's, edited a volume of his poetry under the title *Carmen Deo Nostro*, which was made up chiefly of poems from the 1648 collection, but with some important additions, notably the last part of *The Flaming Heart*. Crashaw is best known, perhaps notorious, as the major exponent of the baroque style in English poetry, reflecting the influence notably of the Italian poet Marino. The baroque, as it appears in Crashaw, is difficult to define but easy to illustrate, most obvious in its more tasteless manifestations, as when the Magdalene's eyes, in *The Weeper*, are described as: 'Two walking baths; two weeping motions; / Portable, & compendious oceans.'

Such extravagant, sensuous, intellectually curious conceits result all too frequently in the materialization of the spiritual in the religious poetry which is the major part of Crashaw's achievement, and he is rather often to be described, in Quiller-Couch's memorable phrase, as 'terribly at his ease in Sion'. In his best work, however, such poems as the *Hymn to the Name and Honour of the Admirable Saint Teresa* and *The Flaming Heart*, what is achieved is rather the spiritualization of the material, as the rich and complex material content of image and metaphor is directed away from an opaque selfconsciousness towards its proper spiritual object by a focused intellectual movement, and an underlying simplicity of intent becoming explicit at times in lines surprisingly reminiscent of Herbert in their plain and genuinely unselfconscious ease in Sion. The following lines addressed to St Teresa in *The Flaming Heart* are an example of Crashaw at his best, the material riches concentrated upon the spiritual object here, for instance, by the simplicities of the syntax: 'By thy larg draughts of intellectuall day, / And by thy thirsts of loue more large then they; / By all thy brim-fill'd Bowles of feirce desire / By thy last Morning's draught of liquid fire; / By the full kingdome of that finall kisse / That seiz'd thy parting Soul, & seal'd thee his. . . .' [DELC]

The Poems, English, Latin and Greek, ed. L. C. Martin (2nd edn, 1957).
A. Warren, *R.C.* (Baton Rouge, Louisiana, 1939; repr. 1957); R. C. Wallerstein, *R.C.* (Madison, Wisconsin, 1959); M. E. Rickey, *Rhyme and Meaning in R.C.* (U. of Kentucky P., 1961); G. W. Williams, *Image and Symbol in the Sacred Poetry of R.C.* (Chapel Hill, S. Carolina, 1963); M. Praz, *The Flaming Heart* (1958); H. C. White, *The Metaphysical Poets* (New York, 1936); E. I. Watkin, *Poets and Mystics* (1953); M. Willy, *Three Metaphysical Poets* (WTW, 1961); J. Bennett, *Five Metaphysical Poets* (1964).

'Criterion, The'. A literary quarterly, edited by T. S. ◊ Eliot, which ran from October 1922 to January 1939. It appeared monthly for a brief period in 1927–8. *The Waste Land* made its initial appearance, without notes, in the first number. It was the first British magazine to print the work of Paul Valéry, Jacques Rivière, Marcel Proust, Charles Maurras and many other contemporary European writers and critics, thus demonstrating its editor's belief in the unity of European culture. *The Criterion* published new poetry and new doctrines about poetry. Central to its intention was Eliot's insistence on the minority understanding of literature proper: 'Those . . . who affirm an antinomy between literature, meaning any literature which can appeal only to a small and fastidious public, and "life", are not only flattering the complacency of the half-educated, but asserting a principle of disorder.' [RB]

The Criterion Miscellany (1929).

Crockett, Samuel Rutherford (1860–1914). Scottish ◊ 'Kailyard' novelist. Crockett, the illegitimate son of a Galloway farm girl, won a bursary to Edinburgh University (1876). While a Free Church of Scotland minister near there (1886–95) Crockett exploited the vogue of Sir James Barrie's sketches of Scottish provincial life with the short stories in *The Stickit Minister* (1893) and followed up R. L. Stevenson's historical tales with *The Raiders* (1894), a tale of smuggling in 18th-century Galloway. En-couraged by his rapid financial success and by the dying Stevenson's recognition of his work, Crockett abandoned his ministry to become a professional author. His later work, chiefly in the sentimental vein of *The Lilac Sunbonnet* (1894), is prolific but feeble, as though he had ruined his limited talent by overworking it. [AI]

M. M. Harper, *C. and Grey Galloway* (1907); G. Blake, *Barrie and the Kailyard School* (1951).

Crofts, Freeman Wills (1879–1957). Detective-story writer. Born in Dublin, the son of a British Army doctor, he was educated at the Methodist College and Campbell College in Belfast, and became a railway engineer, work which he finally gave up in 1929. In 1920, he began his literary career with *The Cask*; the success of this stimulated him to write *The Ponson Case* (1921), and he completed some 40 books as well as short stories and radio plays: his works are popular and have been widely translated. Some of his titles are: *Inspector French's Greatest Case* (1925), *Inspector French and the Cheyne Mystery* (1926), *The 12.30 from Croydon* (1934), *Circumstantial Evidence* (1941), *French Strikes Oil* (1952) and *Murderers Make Mistakes* (1947) (short stories). Crofts wrote 'puzzle' stories in which all the evidence – the train time-tables, the tides, the weather – is presented and discussed. His hero is a hard-working policeman, and his *forte* is the absolutely flat use of meticulous detail. He is a most restful writer. [AR]

H. Haycraft, *Murder for Pleasure* (1941).

Croker, John Wilson (1780–1857). Satirist, historian, editor and politician. Educated at Trinity College, Dublin, he was a very party-minded Tory M.P. and behind-the-scenes politician (reputed to be the original of the venal Rigby in ◊ Disraeli's *Coningsby*). Croker held various offices, and was Secretary of the Navy for twenty years. He contributed to the Tory *Quarterly Review* and was the author of the notorious slashing attack (typical of his reviewing style) on Keats's *Endymion*. Croker edited Boswell's *Johnson* (1831; revised 1848) with some useful notes. He also edited *Royal Memoirs of the French Revolution* (1823) and wrote *Essays on the Early Period of the French Revolution* (1857); the latter were enlarged versions of *Quarterly* essays. His views were anti-revolutionary, and in general historical controversy he crossed swords with Macaulay. [A R]

Croker Papers (correspondence and diaries), ed. with a memoir by L. J. Jennings (3 vols., 1884; revised 1885); 1808-1857, ed. B. Pool (1967). M. F. Brightfield, *J.W.C.* (California U.P., 1940).

Cronin, A(rchibald) J(oseph) (1896–   ). Novelist. Born at Cardross, Dunbartonshire, and educated at Dumbarton Academy and Glasgow University Medical School. After a career in hospitals, as a medical inspector of mines and as a general practitioner in South Wales and London, he gave up medicine in 1930 after the success of his first novel, *Hatter's Castle* (1931), enabled him to devote all his time to writing. This novel put him among the popular middle-of-the-road, commonsense, realist writers such as Priestley. It does not compare well with George ◊ Douglas's *The House with the Green Shutters* on a similar theme, but was much more successful. *Hatter's Castle*, like many of Cronin's novels, is a mixture of a naturalistic treatment of social problems (backed by considerable knowledge and experience) with sentiment; the plots are often melodramatic to allow (by coincidence, or other means) optimistic endings. His works include: a story of possessive love, *Three Loves* (1932); *The Stars Look Down* (1935), set in the Northumberland mining country and dealing with an ambitious miner's rise to be a Member of Parliament; the best-seller, *The Citadel* (1937), a tale of a mining company doctor's struggle to balance scientific integrity with social obligations (the book also contains powerful propaganda for a national health service); *The Keys of the Kingdom* (1942); *The Green Years* (1945); *The Spanish Gardener* (1950); *The Judas Tree* (1961); and *A Question of Modernity* (1966). Some of Cronin's novels made very successful films, and characters from his fiction have been adopted by television serial writers. [A R]

Adventures in Two Worlds (1952) (autobiography).

Cross, Ian (1925–   ). New Zealand novelist. Born and educated in Wanganui, he became a journalist with the Wellington *Dominion*, and in 1954 studied journalism at Harvard. In 1959 he was elected to a year's fellowship in literature at the University of Otago. He now works as a public relations officer in Wellington. Cross's first novel, *The God Boy* (1957), was widely acclaimed. Its narrator is a convent schoolboy 'pretty good at religion', whose wild-blooded description of the events preceding his father's murder is the unusual casebook history of his probable future delinquency. Cross's other novels include *The Backward Sex* (1960) and *After Anzac Day* (1961), a picture of New Zealand's class-ridden suburban society. [P T]

Cross, Mary Ann. ◊ Eliot, George.

Crowne, John (*c.* 1640–*c.* 1712). Dramatist. A hard-working run-of-the-mill author, he produced nothing of permanent literary value or even of commercial success in his own day. He wrote 11 tragedies in the heroic Restoration mode, including the 2-part *Destruction of Jerusalem by Titus Vespasian* (1677 and 1693) and *Thyestes* (1681), as well as 5 comedies of intrigue, of which *Sir Courtly Nice, or It Cannot Be* (1685) is the best known. Crowne's derivative plays are so completely in the prevailing styles of his time that one critic has granted them the historical interest of being 'textbooks of late Restoration playwriting'. [M J]

The Dramatic Works (4 vols., 1873–4). A. F. White, *J.C.* (Cleveland, Ohio, 1922); L. N. Chase, *The English Heroic Play* (New York, 1903); K. E. Wheatley, *Racine and English Classicism* (Austin, Texas, 1956).

Cruikshank, Helen B. (1896–   ). Scots poet. Her slender output (*Up the Noran Water*, 1934; *Sea Buckthorn*, 1954) is fairly represented by the well-known title-piece of her first volume. Her work owes as much to her fellow-townswoman Violet ◊ Jacob as it does to Hugh ◊ MacDiarmid's early poems. Her role in the Scottish Renaissance of the 1920s and 1930s is indicated by her 'Personal Reminiscences' in *Hugh MacDiarmid: A Festschrift* (ed. K. D. Duval and S. G. Smith, 1962). [A I]

Cumberland, Richard (1732–1811). Dramatist and author. A member of a distinguished ecclesiastical and academic family, he was educated at Westminster School and at Trinity College, Cambridge (of which he became a Fellow). He spent much of his long life in administrative and diplomatic posts, but was also a prolific dramatist, writing tragedy, comedy and comic opera, and an adaptation of *Timon of Athens*. His biggest success (never to be repeated) was with *The West Indian*, which ran for 30 nights in 1771. It is an example of sentimental comedy which had a great vogue. His 40-odd plays included *The Fashionable Lover* (1772), *The Choleric Man* (1774), *The Mysterious Husband* (1783), *The Jew* (1794), *The Wheel of Fortune* (1795) and *The Days of Yore* (1796). He was satirized as Sir Fretful Plagiary in Sheridan's *The Critic* (1779), but continued writing undaunted. He published a translation of *The Clouds* of Aristophanes, 3 novels, *Arundel* (1789), *Henry* (1795) and *John de Lancaster* (1809), and collaborated with Sir James Bland Burgess, the politician, on an epic, the *Exodiad* (1808). His *Memoirs* (1806–7) are very revealing of the 18th-century theatre at work. [MJ]

Memoirs of R.C. Written by Himself (2 vols., 1806–7).
W. Mudford, *The Life of R. C.* (1812); S. T. Williams, *R. C., His Life and Dramatic Works* (1917).

Cunningham, Allan (1784–1842). Scottish miscellaneous writer. A Dumfriesshire stone-mason, he wrote himself, or concocted from traditional fragments, most of Robert Cromek's 'collected' *Remains of Nithsdale and Galloway Song* (1810). Moving to London at Cromek's invitation, he became secretary and superintendent of works to Chantrey the sculptor, editing in his spare time a collection of songs and an edition of Burns, and writing 3 worthless novels and a dramatic poem. Cunningham's work, although ultimately unimportant, includes several of the more attractive Regency and sentimental-Jacobite songs, among them 'A wet sheet and a flowing sea'. His *Lives of Eminent British Painters, Sculptors and Architects* (1829–33) was a pioneer work, and he wrote the standard Life of the Scottish painter Wilkie (1842). [AI]

Traditional Tales of the English and Scottish Peasantry (1822); *Poems and Songs*, ed. P. Cunningham (1847; 1875).
D. Hogg, *Life of A.C.* (1875); J. A. Fairley, *A.C.* (1907).

Curnow, Thomas Allen Monro (1911–   ). New Zealand poet and playwright. Born at Timaru and educated at the Universities of Canterbury and Auckland, he was associated with the group that produced the radical quarterly *Phoenix* (1932–3), was a journalist with the Christchurch paper *The Press* (1935–48), joined the *News Chronicle*

in London in 1949 and visited America the following year. In 1951 he became a lecturer in the English Department of the University of Auckland. He has edited New Zealand poetry anthologies, including *The Penguin Book of New Zealand Verse* (1960), to which he added a long critical introduction. Curnow's early verse satires score rather too easily on their obvious targets. With *Not in Narrow Seas* (1939) he finds his richest theme in the descriptions of his country as the sublimely beautiful death-bed of the 'pilgrim dream'. In 5 subsequent collections, the most recent being *A Small Room with Large Windows* (1962), Curnow's interest in New Zealand history and his evocative childhood reminiscences are often mythopoeic. *The Axe* (1949) and *Moon Section* (1959) are ambitious, experimental verse plays. Technically he is New Zealand's most versatile poet, as the humorous and satirical poems of *Whim Wham Land* (1967) have further shown. [PT]

Cynddelw Brydydd Mawr (fl. 1155–1200). Welsh poet. He is the major figure among those Welsh professional poets who flourished from about 1100, and who are known as *Gogynfeirdd* or *Beirdd y Tywysogion*, i.e. the court poets of the independent Welsh princes. Their poetry was a continuation of the themes of eulogy and elegy found in the works of the *Cynfeirdd* (◊ Aneirin and ◊ Taliesin), and this earlier tradition was studied in such great detail that words and phrases which were archaic and even obsolete in the 12th century were being reproduced like variations on a theme. The special diction of the *Gogynfeirdd* made abundant use of compound nouns and adjectives, the verb-noun, hyperbole and exaggeration, all bound up in a very tight and compressed syntax which must have been extremely difficult to understand even in the halls of the medieval Welsh princes. The metres most often used were those of the *awdl*, although the short *englyn* was sometimes employed for certain specific purposes. These poets laid special emphasis on sound and rhythm rather than on immediate verbal understanding. They were now a professional class who received long and arduous training in bardic schools, and were accorded a legal status in the princely courts. There were three grades: *Pencerdd*, 'chief of song', *Bardd Teulu*, 'poet of the prince's guard', and *Cerddor*, 'minstrel'. Their eulogy of the princes and their families was based on the Augustinian platonism of the Middle Ages which held that society was logical, fore-ordained and beautiful, and that God had so fashioned it (there is much religious poetry to God and the saints in the work of the *Gogynfeirdd*). The aim of professional poetry was therefore the glorification of the ideal leader in society.

Cynddelw was a notable exponent of this creed. He gained the title of Pencerdd at the court of Madog ap Maredudd, prince of Powys (d. 1160), after a poetic contention with Seisyll Bryffwrch. He also sang to the other princes of Gwynedd in North Wales and Deheubarth in the South. He is renowned for the strength and majesty of his poetry, and he revelled in stark descriptions of battles. He seems to have fulfilled the function of Bardd Teulu on occasion. The slaying of Llywelyn ap Gruffydd in 1282 and the final Edwardian settlement of Wales in 1284 resulted in the gradual loosening of the bardic order, although the later poets continued to ply their craft for another hundred years, in a simpler language and with more regular use of *cynghanedd* (internal consonance and rhyme) as an adornment. [MR]

The Poetry of the Red Book of Hergest, ed. J. Gwenovvryn Evans (1911); Llawysgrif Hendregadredd, ed. J. Morris-Jones and T. H. Parry-Williams (1933); The Myvyrian Archaiology of Wales (2nd edn, 1870).
J. Vendryes, La poésie galloise des XIIᵉ –XIIIᵉ siècles (1930); J. Lloyd-Jones, The Court Poets of the Welsh Princes (1948); H. Idris Bell, The Nature of Poetry as Conceived by the Welsh Bards (1955).

Cynewulf (late 8th–9th cent.). Poet. About half of extant Old English religious poetry has been attributed to Cynewulf at various times, but only the 4 poems containing his runic signature are certainly his. Two, the saint's life, *Juliana* (ed. R. Woolf, 1955), and the second section of the tripartite *Christ*, 'The Ascension', are in the Exeter Book. The Vercelli Codex contains the short *Fates of the Apostles*, and Cynewulf's masterpiece, *Elene* (ed. P. O. E. Gradon, 1958). Though the copies are West Saxon, Cynewulf was of Mercian or Northumbrian origin. His style demonstrates his admiration for the clarity and order of Latin syntax, as opposed to the profusion of Caedmonian poetry (◊ Caedmon), and all the poems except the *Fates of the Apostles* can be traced to Latin sources. His concern for form and his occasional use of rhyme are rare in Old English, and the choice of devotional subjects rather than biblical narrative also points to an advance in Christian culture. *Elene* is the story of St Helena's finding of the Holy Cross. It includes, besides an interesting autobiographical passage, some fine descriptions, notably a splendid storm-piece, but Cynewulf impresses above all as a poet concerned with ideas and emotions. He has not the power of the best Caedmonian poetry, but is more consistently readable. Out of the poetry attributed to him, one would like to claim the magnificent *Dream of the Rood* (ed. B. Dickins and A. S. C. Ross, 1934); unacceptable to experts, this is a deserved compliment to the poet. [AG]

The Poems of C., tr. C. W. Kennedy (1910) (prose).
G. Shepherd, 'Scriptural Poetry', in Continuations and Beginnings: Studies in Old English Literature, ed. E. G. Stanley (1966); K. Sisam, Studies in the History of Old English Literature (1953).

D

Dafydd ap Gwilym (fl. 1340–70). Welsh poet. He belonged to an influential gentry family which had connexions in Pembrokeshire, Carmarthenshire and Cardiganshire. Dafydd was probably born at Brogynin in north Cardiganshire, and he is supposed to have spent much time with his uncle, Llywelyn ap Gwilym, constable of Newcastle Emlyn. He was not dependent on poetry for his support, and this may explain why he felt able to elaborate on new themes and forms. He was buried at the abbey of Strata Florida in Cardiganshire under the yew which bears his name. Dafydd ap Gwilym had undergone the training of a professional poet and could compose poetry in the intricate and obscure style and medium of the later *Gogynfeirdd* (◊ Cynddelw). He chose however as his main verse form the short *cywydd* metre of 7 syllables which had come into vogue by his day, but even he still used the traditional modes of expression, with an archaic vocabulary and parenthetical constructions. He travelled ˏwidely in Wales, was well acquainted with the new Norman boroughs, and was certainly aware of the continental *trouvères*, many of whose stock themes, the aubade, serenade, etc. are found in his work.

His great achievement was in using the *cywydd* for the twin themes of love and nature, themes which had already appeared in the work of his predecessors. He made great use of the device of the love-messenger, *llatai*, but his treatment of love was far removed from the artificial conventions of *amour courtois*. Many of his poems are extremely earthy and are relieved by great good humour and a readiness to laugh at himself, particularly when he finds himself involved in embarrassing situations. Many of the persons and places named in his poetry are readily identifiable. The two women to whom he addressed much of his attention were called Morfudd and Dyddgu. As a nature poet he stands supreme in his meticulously detailed and accurate descriptions of living creatures and in his love for them.

Dafydd ap Gwilym has always been regarded as the master of Welsh poetry, an opinion which is supported by the technical excellence of his language and poetic craft. His extensive vocabulary and astonishing virtuosity in the handling of *cynghanedd* as a metrical adornment are controlled by a genuine poetic awareness of man and nature. [MR]

Gwaith D. ap G., ed. T. Parry (1952); *Dafydd ap Gwilym, Fifty Poems*, tr. H. Idris Bell (*Y Cymmrodor*, XVLIII, 1942).
T. M. Chotzen, *Recherches sur la poésie de D. ap G.* (Amsterdam, 1927).

Dafydd Nanmor (fl. 1420–85). Welsh poet. Born at Nanmor near Beddgelert, he moved from there *c.* 1450 after finding himself in trouble for addressing love poetry to a married woman, Gwen o'r Ddôl (Dolfrïog), and found patrons in Rhys ap Maredudd and his family at Tywyn near Cardigan. He was a supporter of the Lancastrian cause and addressed poems to Edmund and Jasper Tudor and to the young Henry Tudor (Henry VII).

His early love poetry, melodious and charming as it is, is still the work of an immature bard. It was not until his move to South Wales and acceptance in the gentry houses of Cardiganshire, Pembrokeshire and Carmarthenshire that he evolved a philosophy of poetry which was in accordance with the accepted canons of his day. His well-known poems to the generosity and amplitude of the feasting at the house of Rhys ap Maredudd are full of the delight of one who has himself a secure place in his small society. Dafydd Nanmor lay great stress on the idea of *perchentyaeth*, the ownership of a great house, with all its responsibility and obligations. He was obsessed, as were his fellow bards for that matter, with *bonedd* or good stock and breeding, which he likens to a great oak which shelters and sustains with its spreading branches. His greatest poem is undoubtedly the one addressed to Rhys ap Rhydderch ap Rhys, the grandson of his first patron, in which he sets out the principles of *noblesse oblige* in a masterly and dignified form: 'it is good blood which nourishes a prince'. [MR]

The Poetical Works, ed. T. Roberts and I. Williams, (1923).

Dalling and Bulwer, William Henry Lytton (1801–72). Diplomatist and miscellaneous writer. He was born in London, the eldest brother of Lord ◊ Lytton. He served in various embassies, including Madrid (where he was an object of Queen Victoria's suspicion) and Washington. Lytton was made a peer in 1871. He wrote a number of travel books and biographies, of which a *Life of Byron* (1835) is useful. [AR]

Dampier, William (1652–1715). Buccaneer, discoverer and writer. Born near Yeovil, in the course of a seafaring and semi-piratical career he voyaged to South America, the Spanish Main (where he cut log-wood), the Pacific and Australia (on a government voyage of survey and discovery, 1699–1700), as well as the Indies, East and West. He published plain but interesting and vigorous accounts of his travels: *A New Voyage Round the World* (1697; ed. Sir A. Gray, 1927); *Voyages and Descriptions* (1699; ed. C. Wilkinson, 1931); *Voyage to New Holland* (1703, 1709; ed. J. A. Williamson, 1939). All these are reprinted in *Dampier's Voyages* (ed. John Masefield, 2 vols., 1906). [AR]

C. Lloyd, *W.D.* (1966); C. Wilkinson, *W.D.* (1939).

Daniel, Samuel (1562/3–1619). Poet and man of letters. Born in Somerset, Daniel matriculated at Magdalen Hall, Oxford, in 1581. He stayed at the university for about three years, but apparently left without a degree. In about 1592, he came under the patronage of the Countess of Pembroke, the sister of Sidney and the leading figure in a literary circle which included Spenser. The association with the Pembroke circle came to an end in 1594, and Fulke Greville and Lord Mountjoy replaced the Countess of Pembroke as Daniel's patrons. In 1604 he was accorded the patronage of the court of James I, with the appointment as licenser to the Children of the Queen's Revels. The brief and apparently not very successful period as licenser for this company ended in 1605, although not the court patronage. About 1605, he found in the Earl of Hertford an additional patron, and in about 1609 the connexion with Lady Pembroke was restored. He retired to a farm at Beckington

in Somerset soon afterwards, although until his death he retained some connexion with the court. That the details of Daniel's life become so easily the details of his various patrons is of some significance; he was a professional poet very much dependent upon patronage for a living. Though not a poet of outstanding genius, Daniel wrote well and sometimes very well in the accepted Elizabethan manner. He is best remembered for the sonnet sequence, *Delia*, which was continually revised for successive editions between 1592 and 1601. It is one of the finest of the Elizabethan sonnet sequences and reaches a climax in perhaps the best known of his poems, 'Care-charmer Sleep, son of the sable Night'. The narrative poem *The Complaint of Rosamund* (1592) is a reworking of the *Mirror for Magistrates* kind of poetry. *The Tragedy of Cleopatra*, written in 1594 and much revised in 1607, was a not very successful attempt to write a play conforming to the classical ideas of structure, as expounded by Sidney at the end of his *Apology for Poetry*, written about 1580. The influence of the Pembroke circle seems clear. *Musophilus* (1599), a poem in defence of the poet's vocation, is cast in the form of a debate between Musophilus, the defender of poetry, and Philocosmus, his opponent. Its finest parts possess a weight that seems produced by a poet writing from the established centre of a tradition rather than from any rare height of inspiration, and represent Daniel at his best. A similar quality is to be found in the 2 verse epistles, *To the Countess of Bedford* and *To the Countess of Cumberland* (1599). In 1603 Daniel published *A Defence of Rhyme* to counter Campion's advocacy, in his *Observations in the Art of English Poesie* (1602), of the classical quantitative metres as most suitable for English poetry. In 1605, *The Tragedy of Philotas* brought Daniel under suspicion of an undue sympathy for the recently executed Essex, the friend of his patron Mountjoy, and the trouble over this play was probably an important factor in the confusing circumstances which led to his losing the position as licenser to the Children of the Queen's Revels. *The Queen's Arcadia* (1605), a pastoral drama in the Italian manner, is interesting mainly as an early adaptation of this form to English; Daniel also wrote a second pastoral drama, *Hymen's Triumph*, published in 1615. He was not very successful in this genre, nor indeed in the masque form, which he attempted on occasion for the entertainment of the court. In 1609, the final though still unfinished version of *The Civil Wars* was published. Daniel considered this the most important of his poems, and he had been writing it since 1594. In 8 books, he recounted the history of England from the Norman Conquest to Edward IV, and this interest in chronicling the history of England may remind us of Drayton's similar interest, and of the general Elizabethan concern to record the antiquities of Britain which produced such works as Camden's *Britannia* (1586). The prose history of England, which appeared in its final form in 1618 as *The Collection of the History of England*, was a more substantial attempt at recording the past than *The Civil Wars*. [DELC]

The Complete Works in Verse and Prose, ed. A. B. Grosart (5 vols., 1885–96); *Poems and A Defence of Ryme*, ed. A. C. Sprague (Harvard U. P., 1930) (selection); *The Tragedie of Cleopatra nach dem Drucke von 1611*, ed. M. Lederer (Louvain, 1911); *The Tragedy of Philotas*, ed. L. Michel (Yale U.P., 1949); *The Civil Wars*, ed. L. Michel (Yale U.P., 1958).
J. Rees, *S.D.* (1964).

D'Arblay, Mrs Frances Burney. ♦ Burney, Fanny.

Darley, George (1795–1846). Poet, mathematician and novelist. Born in Dublin and educated at Trinity College there, he came to England and worked for the *London Magazine* and the *Athenaeum*, to which he contributed chiefly dramatic criticism (he also edited *The Works of Beaumont and Fletcher*, 1840), and prose tales in the manner of Washington Irving (collected as *The Labours of Idleness*, 1862, which includes his most famous story, *Lilian of the Vale*). The latter he turned into a lyrical drama, prettily reviving the fairy-tale stage properties of the Elizabethans in the Romantic fashion. His skill in a pastiche Cavalier song, 'It is not beauty I demand', deceived F. T. ♦ Palgrave, who put it in his *Golden Treasury*. Darley wrote 2 tragedies and some fine songs, as well as 3 mathematical works. [AR]

Complete Poetical Works, ed. R. Colles (Muses' Library, 1908).
C. C. Abbott, *The Life and Letters of G.D., Poet and Critic* (1928); J. Heath Stubbs, *The Darkling Plain: A Study of the Later Fortunes of Romanticism in English Poetry from G.D. to*

W. B. Yeats (1950); Graham Greene, *Lost Childhood and Other Essays* (1951).

Darwin, Charles (Robert) (1809–82). Biologist. Born in Shrewsbury, the grandson of Erasmus ♦ Darwin. He was educated at home and with a Unitarian clergyman and, in 1818, sent to Shrewsbury School. From 1825 to 1827, he studied medicine at Edinburgh, concentrating on zoology. Abandoning medicine in 1828, he went to Christ's College, Cambridge, to prepare himself for the Church; the *Evidences* of ♦ Paley and social life were his chief study, though he became a *protégé* of Henslow, Professor of Botany, who advised him to study geology. From 1831 to 1836, he sailed as a naturalist with H.M.S. *Beagle*, on a survey of South America; this was the greatest formative experience of his life, as a collector, zoologist and geologist. His work with fossils, and his comparative study of South American life, particularly the birds on the Galapagos Islands, with animals and birds in other continents, first gave him ideas for a theory of evolution. The official accounts of the scientific findings on the voyage were published by Darwin and his assistants in 8 volumes (1840–6). His *Journal of Researches into the Geology and Natural History of the Countries Visited by H.M.S. Beagle* was published in 1839; a celebrated classic of scientific travel, it was several times reprinted (ed. N. Barlow, 1934). During the voyage, Darwin had read Charles Leyell's *Principles of Geology* (1830), an important work which advanced the 'uniformitarian' scientific position, arguing that all geological changes and observations can be accounted for by natural causes and asking why the same is not true in biology.

Geology was the sensitive study in the fight (extending back into the 18th century) between the creationists and the evolutionists. La Marck (and Erasmus Darwin) had constructed theories of evolution suggesting alterations in form, the mutability of species, caused by changes in environment. Darwin also made intensive studies of artificial selection by deliberately chosen differences (particularly the breeding of fan-tailed and pouter pigeons). In 1830, he read the *Essay on the Principle of Population* (1798), by ♦ Malthus, and made his revolutionary theory unique by utilizing Malthus's notion of the struggle for existence to explain why evolution occurs. No

Darwin

two living beings are quite alike; the chance differences are transmitted to their progeny; variations favourable to the struggle for life are strengthened. Others had argued for evolution, but in his *Origin of Species by Means of Natural Selection, or the Preservation of Favoured Races in the Struggle for Life* (1859; many later editions with corrections and additions; variorum edn, ed. M. Peckham, Philadelphia, 1959; World's Classics, 1963), Darwin not only assembles all the *arguments* previously advanced for evolution with examples from his own excellent experience, he provides in the notion of advantageous chance variation a reason why evolution occurs and species develop. Darwin does not speculate on the origin of life, or on why there are countless variations (many of which cannot be explained in terms of use). In fact, he did not clearly see the complex implications of his theory, though it was not he but popular writers who fastened on to Natural Selection as the only factor in his theory. The rest of the century resounded with argument over Darwinism, and its theological and social consequences. Darwin phrased the theory positively and progressively, with a notion of the rising swell of the Great Chorus of Being, but the theory really works destructively. The 'fittest' survive because the others (by far the majority) are destroyed. Darwinian theories, applied by analogy to social, national and racial conflict, can produce rationalization of destructive plans of action. The danger of endowing survival with moral worth has been seen by later thinkers and writers (cf. the treatment of Neanderthal Man in William ◊ Golding's novel *The Inheritors*, 1955). Darwin, in *The Descent of Man and Selection in Relation to Sex* (2 vols., 1871), extended his theory to the more theologically problematic ground of human development, but this book stirred less controversy than the *Origin of Species*. His work also stimulated all kinds of collecting, and comparative studies; demonstrated the inadequacy of the palaeontological record; and produced the quest for the 'missing link'. Many writers, such as Arnold, Browning, Byron and Tennyson, were interested in using evolutionary ideas in discussing the condition of man, and the theory had great influence on the writing of fiction. It strengthened the tendency to naturalistic description, the notion of 'character', and the tendency to length, to give material and scope enough to show

change at work. Modern genetic study, and the investigations into the physico-chemical make-up of DNA are modifying evolutionary theories swiftly. [A R]

A *Darwin Reader*, ed. M. Bates and P. S. Humphrey (1957); *Autobiography*, ed. N. Barlow (1958).
Sir F. Darwin, *Life and Letters of C.D.* (3 vols., 1887); J. Barzun, *D., Marx, Wagner* (2nd edn, New York, 1958); S. E. Hyman, *The Tangled Bank: D., Marx, Frazer and Freud as Imaginative Writers* (New York, 1962); Sir G. R. de Beer, *C.D.: Evolution by Natural Selection* (1963); J. Huxley, *Evolution, the Modern Synthesis* (1942); W. Irvine, *Apes, Angels and Victorians: D., Huxley and Evolution* (1961); L. Stevenson, *D. among the Poets* (Chicago U.P., 1932); L. J. Henkin, *Darwinism in the English Novel: 1860–1910* (1940); J. Huxley and H. B. D. Kettlewell, *C.D. and His World* (1965); A. Moorehead, *D. and the Beagle* (1969).

Darwin, Erasmus (1731–1802). Physician and scientist. Educated at St John's College, Cambridge, and the University of Edinburgh (M.D.), he settled in Lichfield, where he was in good practice and pursued his botanical studies. He wrote several long poems, chiefly a set of didactic couplets, which in tortuously ingenious verse discussed the Linnaean system of plant classification, *The Botanic Garden: I, The Economy of Vegetation* (1791); *II, The Loves of the Plants, with Philosophical Notes* (1789) (extracts in *The Stuffed Owl: An Anthology of Bad Verse*, ed. D. B. Wyndham Lewis and C. Lee, 1930, reprinted 1960). This work was popular in its day, and also immediately ridiculed. The latter view has prevailed. Darwin also wrote several scientific works in prose, the most notable being *Zoonomia, or the Laws of Organic Life* (1794–6, etc.), in which he advances an early form of the evolutionary theory (Charles ◊ Darwin was his grandson). Darwin combined broad, speculative, 'philosophical' interests with an almost complete lack of literary tact. He was a member of the intellectual coterie that surrounded Anna ◊ Seward. [A R]

J. V. Logan, *The Poetry and Aesthetics of E.D.* (Princeton U.P., 1936); D. K. Hele, *E.D.* (1963); Hesketh Pearson, *Doctor D.* (1930).

Davenant or **D'Avenant, Sir William** (1606–68). Poet and dramatist. The son of an Oxford inn-keeper who seems to have been on friendly terms with Shakespeare, he may have been the Bard's god-child, and, in later life, he never denied the rumours that he was Shakespeare's illegitimate son. He went to grammar school in Oxford and possibly to the University. In London Fulke ⋄ Greville was briefly his patron, and by the time the tragedy *Albovine*, never acted, was published in 1629, Davenant's *The Cruel Brother* had been staged by the King's Men. His numerous complimentary verses at this period suggest that he was in search of a new patron. In the early thirties he almost died of syphilis, and his disfigured nose was the subject of much satirical comment. His comedy *The Wits* (1634), revised and revived in the Restoration, held the stage till 1726. *Love and Honour, or The Courage of Love*, a tragi-comedy, was produced in 1634. The following year the masque *The Temple of Love* was presented at court before the Queen, and Davenant was made chief author of such entertainments for the rest of Charles I's reign. Most of his work for the theatre and the court, including the tragi-comedy *The Platonic Lovers* (1635), reflects Henrietta Maria's cult of platonic love and preciosity, and the Queen broke tradition by seeing his work in the playhouse as well as at court. *Madagascar, with Other Poems* was published in 1638, when he was made Poet Laureate. After an abortive effort to start his own troupe, he was briefly manager of the King's and Queen's Young Company before the Puritans closed the theatres in 1642. He was knighted in 1643, and was active in the Royalist cause throughout the Civil War. In 1649 he was appointed Lieutenant Governor of Maryland, and in 1650 before sailing for America published in Paris the *Discourse upon Gondibert*, his projected heroic poem, along with Thomas Hobbes's *Answer*. He was captured at sea and imprisoned until 1654, when Cromwell pardoned him. *Gondibert*, unfinished and partly written in prison, was published in 1651. By 1656 he was organizing clandestine theatrical performances of an operatic and spectacular nature, including his *First Days Entertainment at Rutland House* and *The Siege of Rhodes Made a Representation by the Art of Prospective in Scenes, and the Story Sung in Recitative Music* (Part 1, 1656; Part 2, 1659). This paved the way for his appointment at the Restoration as the head of one of the two legitimate (i.e. officially licensed) theatres in London, the Duke's or Lincoln's Inn Playhouse. There he presented further heroic tragedies of Love and Honour as well as his

own 'improvements' of Shakespeare, which included *Hamlet, Macbeth* and – with Dryden – *The Tempest, or the Enchanted Island*, which were revised according to neoclassic doctrines and the new fashions for spectacle and music. He was buried in Westminster Abbey, and in 1673 there appeared in folio *The Works of Sir William D'avenant Kt.*

A minor poet, he is important in the history of critical theory through *Gondibert* and the controversy it created. A minor dramatist who influenced Caroline taste, he is much more important in English stage history as the author-impresario who ensured the continuity of courtly theatre throughout the Commonwealth period and as the innovator who made heroic tragedy and opera fashionable in the Restoration and who revolutionized stage scenery and spectacular effects. [MJ]

The Dramatic Works, ed. J. Maidment and W. H. Logan (5 vols., 1872–4).
H. S. Collins, *The Comedy of Sir W.D.* (The Hague, 1967); A. Harbage, *Sir W.D., Poet, Venturer, 1608–1668* (1935); L. Hotson, *The Commonwealth and Restoration Stage* (1928); A. H. Nethercot, *Sir W.D., Poet Laureate and Playwright-Manager* (1938); Hazelton Spencer, *Shakespeare Improved* (1927).

Davenport, Robert (fl. 1624–40). Dramatist. Nothing is known of this minor figure, to whom 10 plays can be attributed, save that he must have begun writing for the theatre around 1624 and that he lived in Ireland around 1635. *The City Nightcap* (1624) and *A New Trick to Cheat the Devil* (c. 1639) are his best-known comedies; the latter has, like his tragedy *King John and Matilda* (date uncertain), been judged old-fashioned and technically crude by the few critics who have examined it. [MJ]

Works, ed. A. H. Bullen (1890).
F. E. Schelling, *Elizabethan Drama, 1558–1642* (1908).

Davidson, John (1857–1909). Poet. Born at Barrhead, Renfrewshire, the son of an Evangelical minister, he was educated at Greenock Academy, worked as a chemist and a pupil teacher, and studied briefly at Edinburgh University. He spent from 1876 to 1884 teaching in schools, and began his career as a writer with *Bruce* (1886), a pastiche chronicle-play. *Smith, A Tragic Farce* (1888), his first real work, already showed hints of his Nietzschean view of the world – 'Obey your nature, not authority'. Other 'literary' dramas followed; in 1889, Davidson went to London to make his way as a journalist and writer of fiction: his novel *Perfervid* (1890) was moderately successful. *In a Music Hall and Other Poems* (1891) and *Fleet Street Eclogues* (1893) established his reputation as a poet of city life. His best work appeared in *Ballads and Songs* (1894), *New Ballads* (1897) and *The Last Ballad and Other Poems* (1899). Davidson nurtured his egotism, the sacredness of his desires and the fierceness of his resistance to hardship. He also voiced some of the current worship of the 'super-man' and some imperialist thinking. Towards the end of his life, in 5 incoherent *Testaments* (1901–8), illumined by flashes of powerful writing, he developed a kind of satanism, and showed signs of psychological disturbance. He disappeared from the cliffs near Penzance, and some months later his body was found at sea. [AR]

Selected Poems (1905); *Poems and Ballads*, ed. R. Macleod (1959); *Selected Poems*, intr. T. S. Eliot (1961).
J. B. Townsend, *J.D., Poet of Armageddon* (Yale U.P., 1961).

Davies, John, of Hereford (1565?–1618?). Poet. Born in Hereford, he lived for a time n Oxford and afterwards in London. His first work was a philosophical poem, *Mirum in Modum, A Glimpse of God's Glory and the Soul's Shape* (1602). This was followed by other prolix treatises in verse – for instance, the physiological and psychological *Microcosmos* (1603), and *Humours Heav'n on Earth* (1605), a description, occasionally vivid, of the plague of 1603. *The Scourge of Folly* (1610?) contains complimentary epigrams addressed to Shakespeare, Ben Jonson, Donne, Daniel, Marston, Hall, J. Fletcher and other contemporary figures. [NL]

Complete Works, ed. and intr. A. B. Grosart (2 vols., 1878).
R. B. McKerrow, *Review of English Studies*, 1 (1925).

Davies, Sir John (1569–1626). Poet. A Wiltshire man, Davies was educated at Winchester and Queen's College, Oxford, and became a barrister at the Middle Temple in 1595. His political career involved him much in Irish affairs; he was M.P. at various times for both English and Irish constituencies and was Attorney-General for Ireland, 1606–19. He was Speaker of the Irish Parliament in 1613, and was appointed Chief Justice just before his death. Like Fulke Greville and George Chapman, Davies was one of those Elizabethan poets who found effective ways of giving poetic expression to their philosophical reflections. His *Orchestra* (1596; ed. R. S. Lambert, 1922; ed. E. M. W. Tillyard, 1945), 'a poem of dancing', in rhyme royal, presents the dance as the principle of order and pattern in the universe and is interesting for its picture of the Elizabethan view of universal order. *Nosce Teipsum* (1599; ed. E. Arber in *English Garner*, v, 1882; ed. A. H. Bullen in *Some Longer Elizabethan Poems*, 1903; ed. G. Bullett in *Silver Poets of the 16th Century*, 1947) is a long didactic poem in quatrains discussing the vanity of human knowledge and the importance of cultivating the individual soul. His *Hymns of Astraea* (1599) are a series of 26 acrostic poems to Astraea, who is Queen Elizabeth. He published his *Epigrams* in a puzzling undated volume which also contained 'All Ovid's Elegies' by Marlowe (ed. C. Edmonds, 1870, 1925; and in C. F. Tucker Brooke's edn of Marlowe's works, 1910). *A Discovery of the True Causes Why Ireland was Never Entirely Subdued until the Beginning of His Majesty's Happy Reign* (1612; ed. G. Chalmers, *Historical Tracts*, 1786, and H. Morley in *Ireland under Elizabeth and James I*, 1890) gives vividly his view of the Irish question. [DD]

Poetical Works (1773); *The Works in Verse and Prose*, ed. A. B. Grosart (3 vols., 1869–76); *The Complete Poems*, ed. A. B. Grosart (2 vols., 1876); *Works*, ed. H. Morley (1889).
M. Seemann, *Sir John Davies, sein Leben und seine Werke* (Vienna, 1913); M. D. Holmes, *The Poet as Philosopher: A Study of Nosce Teipsum* (1921); E. M. W. Tillyard, 'Sir John Davies' *Orchestra*', in *Five Poems, 1470–1870* (1948).

Davies, Rhys (1903–). Novelist and short-story writer. Born at Porth, Glamorgan, and educated at the County School, he had several jobs and then lived abroad (staying at one point with D. H. Lawrence in Paris). During the Second World War, he worked in the War Office in London. His writing is chiefly on Welsh themes, and his stories are told in an evocative and lyrical writing of great beauty. He has published several collections of short stories including *A Pig in a Poke* (1931) and *Collected Stories* (1955). *No Escape* (1954) is a play. His first novel, *The Withered Root* (1927), is about a religious revival in a Welsh coal valley like his native Rhondda. Other novels include *Count Your Blessings* (1932), *A Time to Laugh* (1937), *The Perishable Quality* (1957) and *Girl Waiting in the Shade* (1960). [A R]

R. L. Mégroz, *R. D.: A Critical Sketch* (1932); G. F. Adam, *Three Contemporary Anglo-Welsh Novelists* (Bern, 1944).

Davies, Robertson (1913–). Canadian novelist and playwright. Born at Thamesville, Ontario, the son of a journalist, he was educated at Queen's University and Oxford. His Canadian journalistic experience includes editorship of the Peterborough *Examiner* and a successful term as literary editor of *Saturday Night* in Toronto. The sophisticated, dilettante humour of *The Table Talk of Samuel Marchbanks* (1949) has its origin in an editorial column. Davies was for a while a professional actor, and taught at the Old Vic Drama School shortly after the war. He is a Governor of the theatre at Stratford, Ontario, and wrote annual accounts of its early Shakespeare seasons. His own plays have a characteristic epigrammatic wit, presided over by a cultured hedonism. He was recently appointed head of the Department of Graduate Studies at the University of Toronto. Davies's novels are mildly ribald satires of Canadian manners, particularly of a national puritan sobriety. *Leaven of Malice* (1955) and *A Mixture of Frailties* (1958) are better sustained than *Tempest-Tost* (1952). His urbanity and elegance are unique in Canadian fiction. [P T]

Marchbanks' Almanack (1967).
H. McPherson, 'The Mask of Satire', *Canadian Literature*, 4 (Spring, 1960); I. Owen, 'The Salterton Novels', *Tamarack Review*, 9 (Autumn, 1958).

Davies, W(illiam) H(enry) (1871–1940). Poet. The son of a poor Welsh inn-keeper who had little money to educate him, the young Davies drifted from casual labour to the life of a tramp and lost his leg boarding a fast-moving freight train in America. When he came back to London, he found that a small allowance had been saved up for him. Living in doss-houses at sixpence a night, he spent his time writing poems and also a prose book, *Autobiography of a Super-Tramp* (1907). Bernard Shaw discovered Davies, through little privately printed pamphlets of verse Davies had been selling, and wrote an introduction to the autobiography. From then on, Davies had a ready public for his poetry, which he produced much too prolifically. He was granted a Civil List pension, married, and retired to the country. He published 36 volumes in the last 34 years of his life. The poetry is uneven but always unaffectedly sincere. At its best, it has a simplicity, a directness and an eye for country things which recalls John Clare. There are touches also of a less 'literary' Herrick, a more simple-minded Blake. [G S F]

Complete Poems (1943).
R. J. Stonesifer, *W. H. D.: A Critical Biography* (1963); L. Untermeyer, *Lives of the Poets* (1960); E. Sitwell, *Aspects of Modern Poetry* (1934).

Davin, Dan (1913–). Novelist. Born in New Zealand and educated at the University of Otago and at Oxford. He served in the Mediterranean campaigns during the war, and is the author of a volume in the New Zealand Official War History. He lives in Oxford, where he is on the advisory board of the Clarendon Press. *Cliffs of Fall* (1945) was his first novel. Like *Roads from Home* (1949) and *No Remittance* (1959), it is set in New Zealand in a cliquish immigrant Irish Catholic community. Davin is a discursive novelist, always ready to talk through his introspective characters, both in the New Zealand novels and in *For the Rest of Our Lives* (1947; reissued 1965), a war novel set in Cairo, and its thematic sequel, *The Sullen Bell* (1956). The characteristic movement of his books is towards mildly cynical acceptance of necessary disaster. The stories of *The Gorse Blooms Pale* (1947) gain in tautness from their enforced compression. They are his best work. [P T]

Daviot, Gordon. ◊ Mackintosh, Elizabeth.

Davis, Thomas Osborne (1814–45). Poet of the Irish Revival. Born at Mallow in Co. Cork, the son of an army surgeon, he was educated at Trinity College, Dublin, and called to the bar (1838). With Charles Gavan ◊ Duffy he was one of the founders (1842) of the *Nation*, a newspaper which was important in assisting the forerunners of the Irish literary renaissance. He was also a founder of the Young Ireland Party, which, though it had little immediate political effect, yet stimulated Irish pride and patriotism to provide a basis for later action. Davis wrote patriotic ballads, a *Life of the Right Hon J. P. Curran* (the Irish lawyer) (1845, 1846), and literary and historical essays. [A R]

Poems (Dublin, 1846); *Selection from His Prose and Poetry*, ed. T. W. Rolleston (1914); *Essays and Poems, with a Centenary Memoir* (Dublin, 1945); *Songs, Ballads and Poems* (Dublin, 1945). T. W. Moody, *T.D.* (1945).

Day, John (*c.* 1574–1640). Dramatist. While an undergraduate at Caius College, Cambridge, he was sent down for stealing a book, and became one of the many authors employed by Philip ◊ Henslowe as a hackwriter. In four years he wrote 24 playscripts (mostly lost), often in collaboration with Chettle, Hathway, Haughton, Smith, or – occasionally – Dekker. *The Blind Beggar of Bednal-Green* (1600), with Chettle, belongs to this period, but does not add to the reputation of either author. More distinguished are 3 independent plays, written to be acted by boys, including *Law Tricks, or Who Would Have Thought It* (1604), *The Isle of Gulls* (1606), and a romantic comedy in the vein of Lyly, *Humour out of Breath* (1608), which some critics have admired. *The Parliament of Bees* (*c.* 1608–16) is not a play for the stage but a charming series of six 'characters' in dialogue form. Day was one of several minor Elizabethan journeymen-playwrights whose work, competent in its way, lacked the personal or original quality to interest posterity. Ben Jonson classed him with 'rogues' and 'base fellows', and although Day was writing plays as late as 1623 none have survived. [MJ]

Works, ed. A. H. Bullen (2 vols., 1881). M. C. Bradbrook, *The Growth and Structure of Elizabethan Comedy* (1955).

Day, Thomas (1748–89). Writer, eccentric and social reformer. Educated at Charterhouse and Corpus Christi College, Oxford, he was called to the bar (1775) but lived as a gentleman of private means, producing several miscellaneous works. He was a friend of Erasmus ◊ Darwin. He is remembered for his once popular novel-like discussion of Rousseauesque educational principles, *The History of Sandford and Merton* (i, 1783; ii, 1787; iii, 1789), in which

'naturalism' is 'harmonized' with a more orthodox Christianity. [A R]

D N B; Hesketh Pearson, *Doctor Darwin* (1930); Sir S. H. Scott, *The Exemplary Mr Day* (1935).

Day Lewis, Cecil (1904–). Poet and critic. Born in Ballintogher, Ireland. Educated at Sherborne and Wadham College, Oxford, Day Lewis was one of that group of poets (which included his Oxford contemporaries Auden and Spender) who were at their most active in the thirties, and whose concern for social justice led them to espouse several left-wing causes including the Republican side in the Spanish Civil War. Though they shared common concerns, however, their talents were disparate. Day Lewis is a lyric poet of great distinction. His first volume, *Beechen Vigil* (1925), was followed by *Country Comets* (1928), but it was with *Transitional Poem* (1929) that he made his name. The theme of the poem adumbrates the subjects which were to engage the poet's interest throughout the following decade: the contending allegiances to the social and the personal. Day Lewis's next volume, *From Feather to Iron* (1931), concentrates on the personal, being the description of a love affair. This was followed by *The Magnetic Mountain* (1933), in which the poet's voice is at its most individual. *A Time to Dance* (1935) contains much purely topical verse which has not worn well, but by the time of *Overtures to Death* (1938) the poet had reached a maturity of technique and vision. And in the poems of his more recent years, although there is little technical experiment, Day Lewis has consolidated his position as one of the finest and most civilized lyric poets of his age.

His most important critical work is *The Poetic Image*, which combines excellent practical criticism with a discussion in depth of the nature of poetic experience. Day Lewis has written 3 novels, *The Friendly Tree* (1936), *Starting Point* (1937) and *Child of Misfortune* (1939), and under the pseudonym of 'Nicholas Blake' has produced nearly a score of murder mysteries whose witty, urbane detective Nigel Strangeways bears a distinct resemblance in manner and temperament to his author.

C. Day Lewis is a greatly admired speaker of verse, and has also made excellent translations of Virgil and Paul Valéry. In January 1968 he was appointed Poet Laureate. [C O]

Collected Poems (1954); *The Gate and Other Poems* (1962); *The Room and Other Poems* (1965); *The Buried Day* (1960) (autobiography). C. Dyment, *C.D.L.* (1955).

Deeping, (George) Warwick (1877–1950). Novelist. Born at Southend, Essex, the son of a doctor, he was educated at Merchant Taylors' School and Cambridge. He studied medicine and practised as a doctor for a year until his success with a series of romantic historical novels, of which the most popular was *Love among the Ruins* (1904), enabled him to abandon medicine for writing. Thenceforth his output was large and consistently mediocre, until the publication of his best-known book, *Sorrell and Son* (1925), which drew on his war experiences in the R.A.M.C. Of this book Deeping wrote: 'One realised that a nice culture was less important than courage and character. One set out to see life and its realities, its pathos and heroism, and I have managed to find it more splendid than sordid.' *Sorrell and Son* provides an interesting period contrast to the bitterness of most First World War writing, but has little intrinsic merit. Annually to the end of his life Deeping continued to produce a nice story with a happy ending – 69 books in all, of which *Old Pybus* (1928) is typical. His virtues were described by the *New York Times* as 'British solidity, a gentlemanly goodness and fun, and well-woven plots'. [JM]

Defoe, Daniel (1660–1731). Merchant, economist, journalist, spy and novelist. The son of James Foe, a London tallow chandler, he was educated for the Presbyterian ministry at the excellent Newington Dissenting Academy, but quickly abandoned this intention. He thereafter embarked on a life of several careers and great complexity, of which many details remain obscure. His early engagement in commerce, which involved wide travel in Britain and Europe and operations as a stocking wholesaler and tile manufacturer, ended in bankruptcy. He later dealt in ship-insurance, wool, oysters and linen. His mercantile experience led him to write on economics, which led in turn to an intimacy with William III, for whom he wrote pamphlets. The most famous of these was the best-selling set of verses, *The True Born Englishman* (1701), a satire in support of the Dutch king against xenophobia. As a writer, Defoe early

took the habit of adopting a mask; it is his chief characteristic, but in 1703 it landed him in the pillory (though he never stood '*earless* on high') for his satire against High Church tyranny, *The Shortest Way with the Dissenters*. In this pamphlet he was only too successful in his irony of putting forward the opposition case; but perhaps his political alignment was also to blame for his prosecution. He was pardoned from a very severe prison sentence by the intervention of Robert Harley, whose confidant, spy and publicist he became. He acted as Harley's secret agent in Edinburgh during the negotiations for the Union of the Scottish and English Parliaments (1707). He wrote the thrice-weekly *Review* practically single-handed from 1704 until its death in 1713; as a journalist he was connected with about 26 different periodicals. The *Review* develops many of Defoe's interests and theories, in economics, politics and foreign affairs, providing valuable information on the period. After the Queen's death and Harley's fall (1714), Defoe wrote on behalf of whatever ministry was in power and acted as a government double agent by writing for Mist's Jacobite *Weekly-Journal*. He died 'of a lethargy' and was buried in Bunhill Fields.

Defoe was the author of some 500 works, and there are some puzzles of attribution. Apart from his journalism, his main interests are reflected in the following works: POLITICS: *A General History of the Union of Great Britain* (1709); *The Secret History of the White Staff* (1714); ECONOMICS: *An Essay on the South Sea Trade* (1712); *A General History of Trade* (1713); *A Tour Thro' the Whole Island of Great Britain. Divided into Circuits or Journeys* (i, 1724; ii, 1725; iii, 1727), which contains a great deal of what would now be thought of as sociological observation; *The Complete English Tradesman* (i, 1726; ii, 1727); *A Plan of the English Commerce* (1728); MORALIZING: *The Family Instructor* (i, 1715; ii, 1718); *Religious Courtship* (1722); SUPERNATURAL: *A True Relation of the Apparition of One Mrs Veal* (1706); *The Political History of the Devil* (1726); *A System of Magic* (1727); HISTORY and BIOGRAPHY: *A History of the Wars of Charles XII* (1715); *Memoirs of the Duke of Shrewsbury* (1718); *The History of Peter the Great* (1723); CRIME: *The King of Pirates* (1719); *A General History of the Most Notorious Pirates* (1724 and 1728); *A*

139

Narrative of All the Robberies, Escapes, etc. of John Sheppard (1724); NOVELS: *Robinson Crusoe* (1719; ed. A. Ross, PEL, 1966); *Memoirs of a Cavalier* and *Captain Singleton* (1720); *Moll Flanders, A Journal of the Plague Year* (ed. A. Burgess, PEL, 1966) and *Colonel Jacque* (all 1722); *The Fortunate Mistress, or Roxana* (1724).

Defoe is now best known as a writer of fiction, but his novels must be viewed against his career and other interests. He is a ready and sometimes rambling writer, who often relies on the inspiration of the moment to carry his shapeless tales along. This 'unpremeditated art', however, has its strength in the air of truth to detail which it can give, in a kind of 'poetry of the everyday'. He surrounds exotic and fantastic events with a domestic air of documentation. His economic and sociological interests, powerful imagination and inquisitive mind, combined with the practical skill of a journalist and vast experience of all varieties of life, enabled him to give in fiction an unparalleled account of 18th-century life, and to convey its flavour. A non-Augustan, even anti-Augustan writer, he has been undervalued as an artist by those who take the noble ideals of Pope, Swift and Addison at their face value, without perceiving the struggle that seethed behind the classical serenity.

Many of Defoe's works have never been reprinted, but there is a complete facsimile of the *Review* (ed. A. W. Secord, 22 vols., Columbia U.P., 1938) and of the *Index* (ed. W. L. Payne, 1948), anthologized by Payne in *The Best of Defoe's Review* (1951). [AR]

Letters, ed. G. H. Healey (1955); *Romances and Narratives*, ed. G. A. Aitken (16 vols., 1895); *Novels and Selected Writing* (14 vols., Shakespeare Head, 1927–8).
P. Dottin, *D. et ses romans* (1924); J. Sutherland, *D.* (1935; 2nd edn 1950); J. R. Moore, *D.D., Citizen of the Modern World* (Chicago U.P., 1958); M. E. Novak, *Economics and the Fiction of D.D.* (California U.P., 1962); W. D. Mackillop, *The Early Masters of English Fiction* (Kansas U.P., 1956); I. Watt, *The Rise of the Novel* (1963); G. A. Starr, *D. and Spiritual Autobiography* (1965); M. Shinagel, *D.D. and Middle-Class Gentility* (1968).

De hÍde, Dubhghlas (Douglas Hyde) (1860–1949). Irish author and scholar. He was born in Co. Roscommon, the son of a clergyman, and educated at Trinity College, Dublin. A copious writer, both in Irish and in English, much of his work was done under the pseudonym 'An Craoibhín Aoibhinn'.

De hÍde did more than any other writer of his time to draw attention to the literature and traditions of the Gaeltacht or Irish-speaking areas of Connacht, much of which he himself recorded and published in such volumes as *Leabhar Sgéalaigheachta* (1889), *Beside the Fire* (1890), *The Love Songs of Connacht* (1893), *The Religious Songs of Connacht* (1906). In these the Irish texts are usually accompanied by English renderings: he had a singular talent for this type of interpretation. In 1893, he became president of the newly founded *Connradh na Gaeilge* ('Gaelic League'), an organization for the revival of the Irish language. In 1904, he took part in founding the Abbey Theatre, with Lady ◊ Gregory, Edward Martyn and Yeats. His own work, *Casadh an tSúgáin* (1901), was the first Gaelic play to be produced in a theatre. In addition, he composed several Irish poems, some of which have considerable artistic merit; and, although his bent was creative and literary rather than scholarly, he published learned editions of several medieval Irish texts. His *Literary History of Ireland* appeared in 1899. In 1931, he retired from the Professorship of Modern Irish in University College, Dublin, and seven years later became the first President of Ireland. [SB]

D. Coffey, *D. H.* (1938).

Dekker, Thomas (*c.* 1572–1632). Dramatist and pamphleteer. Though he was evidently born and brought up in the London he celebrated in his plays and pamphlets, nothing is known of Dekker until 1597, when he had already started working under the theatre-manager Philip ◊ Henslowe, for whom he wrote, mainly in collaboration with others, 44 plays, mostly lost, between 1598 and 1602. He worked in a variety of genres over a period of thirty years, and Professor Bowers' great edition prints the texts of 19 entertainments, plus 2 Lord Mayor's pageants and 3 plays usually attributed to Dekker. His early, popular comedies included his masterpiece *The Shoemakers' Holiday, or The Gentle Craft*, a play still revived in the theatre, and *Old Fortunatus* – both unaided works – as well as *Patient Grissill* (1599), written with Henry Chettle and William Haughton. The last was ridiculed by Ben Jonson in *Poetaster* (1601), and in the so-called War of the

Theatres Dekker replied with *Satiro-Mastix, or The Untrussing of the Humorous Poet*, acted by the Lord Chamberlain's Men (Henslowe's rivals) in 1602. Dekker's somewhat primitive technique, lack of critical rigour, and readiness to engage in hackwork and get-penny entertainments earned him the contempt of Jonson. He collaborated with Thomas Middleton on *The Honest Whore*, Part I (1604), and himself produced a second part (1605). The conventional story of a reformed courtesan is presented against a vivid and realistic background. To this period also belong the city comedies *Westward Ho!* and the poorer *Northward Ho!* written in collaboration with John Webster for a boys' company, as well as a contemporary political allegory, *The Whore of Babylon* (unaided and in Marlovian blank verse). His first pamphlet appeared in 1603, and by 1610 he had published over a dozen, which may have freed him from hack-work for Henslowe. *The Roaring Girl, or Moll Cut-Purse*, another London comedy collaboration with Middleton, took a real woman, Moll Frith, as its heroine. After *If This Be Not a Good Play, the Devil Is in It* (1612) and *Match Me in London* (c. 1613) were performed, Dekker seems to have spent six or seven years in prison until 1619, when he recommenced writing – for a variety of companies. In 1621 he collaborated on an impressive play, *The Witch of Edmonton*, with John Ford, and around 1624 they worked on four entertainments, including a masque, *The Sun's Darling*, and the lost 'thriller' *The Late Murder of the Son upon the Mother, or Keep the Widow Waking*. In 1628 and 1629 he wrote the Lord Mayor's entertainments, *Britannia's Honour* and *London's Tempe*. Bowers also credits to him *Lust's Dominion, The Noble Spanish Soldier* and *The Welsh Ambassador*.

Dekker's pamphlets are successful examples of a distinctively Elizabethan form: such journalism by early denizens of Grub Street combined reportage of contemporary events with moral instruction, story-telling, invention and social criticism. In a series of pamphlets beginning with *The Wonderful Year* (1603) Dekker described the London plagues. *The Seven Deadly Sins of London* (1606) enumerated the vices and follies of London citizens, and *The Bellman of London* (1608), derived from earlier pamphlets by Greene and others, catalogued the various kinds of roguery and confidence-trickery which fascinated Elizabethans. *The Gull's Hornbook* (1609) is a satirical manual for the young-man-about-town.

As a dramatist Dekker excelled at portraying London life. Some of his plays are valuable social documents as his pamphlets also are. Although only *The Shoemakers' Holiday* merits revival, some other works have attractive qualities of geniality, spontaneity and local colour. [M J]

Dramatic Works, ed. F. Bowers and C. Hoy (1953 ff.; *Selected Prose Writings*, ed. E. D. Pendry (1967).
M. C. Bradbrook, *The Growth and Structure of Elizabethan Comedy* (1955); M. T. Jones-Davies, *T.D., un peintre de la vie londonienne* (Paris, 1958).

De La Mare, Walter (1873–1956). Poet, writer of tales and fantasies, essayist and anthologist. Born in Kent of an old Huguenot family, at 18 he became a clerk with the Standard Oil Company, where he remained for twenty years. His first book, *Songs of Childhood*, was published under the pseudonym of Walter Ramal. At 36, he received a Civil List pension which allowed him to retire to the country and devote all his time to writing. He published some 50 volumes of poetry, short stories, essays and novels. He was made a Companion of Honour at 75 and given the Order of Merit at 80.

Both as a writer of poetry and of fiction Walter de la Mare had a flavour uniquely his own, a gift for suggesting eeriness, ghostliness, mystery, a visionary or uncanny quality in actual experience. He had also a gift for the gay and grotesque and was the most gifted writer of truly imaginative verse and stories for children of his time. All his work is preoccupied with dreams, but neither in a Freudian sense, nor in a sense tied to Christian dogma. If he has ancestors in the Anglo-American tradition they are probably the Coleridge of 'The Ancient Mariner', the Edgar Allan Poe of poems like 'Romance' and 'The City under the Sea' and writers like Lewis Carroll and Edward Lear, who disguised the romantic agony behind the mask of nonsense writing. But a vivid and exact feeling for natural beauty, including its homelier sides, also gives him some affinity with Hardy and the better Georgians. At their best, his most famous poems, like 'The Listeners', poignantly state the riddle of existence without attempting to solve it. He is an extremely individual writer, who belonged to no school or group, and never engaged in literary controversies. [GSF]

Collected Poems (1970); *Collected Rhymes and Verses* (1944); *Collected Stories for Children* (1947); *A Choice of de la M.'s Work*, ed. W. H. Auden (1963).
F. Reid, *W. de la M.: A Critical Study* (1929); R. L. Mégroz, *W. de la M.* (1924).

Delaney, Shelagh (1939–). Dramatist. A working-class girl from Salford, Lancashire, with a chequered secondary schooling, she turned to the theatre at 17 in the confidence that she could achieve something better than Terence Rattigan's *Variations on a Theme*, which she had just seen. Her script *A Taste of Honey* (1959) was sent to Theatre Workshop and accepted by Joan Littlewood, under whose creative, improvisatory direction it was very successfully staged in East London and in the West End. It is a study, sometimes realistic and occasionally idyllic, of the emotional growth of an unloved schoolgirl in the industrial North. It was the basis of Tony Richardson's film, shot in Lancashire. A second play, *The Lion in Love*, failed to succeed with the public but won a prize. An autobiography, *Sweetly Sings the Donkey*, appeared in 1964. [MJ]

J. Russell Taylor, *Anger and After* (revised edn, 1969).

De La Roche, Mazo (1885–1961). Canadian novelist. Born in Toronto of mixed English, French and Irish descent. Her easy Ontario girlhood encouraged in her a love, prominent in her novels, of animals and country life. She spent much time in England, Italy and the United States as well as Canada. With the publication of *Jalna* in 1927, she was suddenly famous. Books about the Whiteoak family continued to appear with astonishing regularity until her death. Among the best are *The Building of Jalna* (1945) and *The Whiteoak Brothers* (1954). The first 6 Jalna novels were collected in 1940 as *Whiteoak Chronicles*, and her play, *Whiteoaks*, was first performed in 1936. De la Roche describes with charm the eccentric vision of the very old and the very young, but her domestic dramas suffer from romantic distortion. [PT]

Ringing the Changes (1957) (autobiography).

Delius, Anthony Ronald St Martin (1916–). South African poet and prose writer. He was born in Simonstown and attended Rhodes University. After completing war service in the Intelligence Corps he worked as a journalist in Port Elizabeth before becoming a leader writer on the *Cape Times*. He was English editor of the quarterly *Standpunte* (1952–6), and later joined the editorial board of the literary magazine *Contrast*. Among his publications are travel books and a play about Rhodes, *The Fall* (1960), as well as the poems of *An Unknown Border* (1954), the verse satire *The Last Division* (1959), a number of short stories and a satirical novel, *The Day Natal Took Off* (1964). [PT]

Deloney, Thomas (*c.* 1543–1600). Author of ballads and prose fiction. Nothing is known of his education and little of his life. Originally a silk-weaver by trade, he became the prolific author of journalistic ballads collected in such volumes as *The Garland of Good Will* (*c.* 1593), *Strange Histories of Kings, Princes, Dukes, Lords,* etc. (1602) and *Canaan's Calamity, Jerusalem's Misery* (1618). His prose fictions were aimed at the Elizabethan bourgeoisie whose values and qualities are glorified and exaggerated, and the rarity of surviving copies of early editions suggests that they were much read. These 'novels' are episodic narratives, often with historical backgrounds. They include *Jack of Newbury, the Famous and Worthy Clothier of England* (1597), *The Gentle Craft, . . . Showing what Famous Men have been Shoemakers in Time Past in This Land* (1597–1600) and *Thomas of Reading, or The Six Worthy Yeomen of the West* (*c.* 1598). [MJ]

Works, ed. F. O. Mann (1912).
C. S. Lewis, *English Literature in the Sixteenth Century* (1954).

Delta (Δ). ▷ Moir, David Macbeth.

De Morgan, William Frend (1839–1917). Craftsman and novelist. Born in London and educated at the University there, where his father, Augustus de Morgan, was the first Professor of Mathematics, William later studied art and as a potter and stained-glass worker was employed by William Morris in his firm of 'Fine Art Workmen'. On retiring at 67, de Morgan started producing long, old-fashioned novels, combining the techniques of Dickens (whom he greatly admired) and Trollope. The first 2, *Joseph Vance* (1906), *Alice-for-Short* (1907), had a brief popularity. There were 4 more.

Old Man's Youth (1921), completed by his wife, is largely autobiography. [AR]

Denham, Sir John (1615–69). Poet and playwright. Born in Dublin and educated at Oxford, Denham was called to the bar in 1639, but did not earn his living as a lawyer. During the Civil War he served the Royalist cause and after its defeat he spent some time at the court of the exiled Queen Henrietta Maria in Paris. He returned to England in 1652 and went back to the continent in 1659. After the Restoration he was rewarded by Charles II with a knighthood in 1661 and the office of Surveyor of the Royal Works (architect), an appointment for which his qualifications could be charitably described as theoretical. While at Oxford he had begun translating the first 6 books of the *Aeneid*, but he first attracted attention as a writer with his blank-verse play *The Sophy* (1642). In the same year he published *Cooper's Hill*, a long topographical poem describing the scenery near his home at Egham, near Windsor. This set the pattern for a minor genre which remained popular throughout the succeeding century. He later revised and enlarged it. Denham was also one of the early members of the Royal Society and served as M.P. for Sarum for a short time, distinguishing himself by praising *Paradise Lost* immediately on publication, in the House of Commons. He is buried in Poets' Corner in Westminster Abbey.

In spite of *Cooper's Hill*, which is a poem of charm and distinction, Denham's literary interest today is historical rather than intrinsic. Together with Edmund ◊ Waller he was responsible for making the heroic couplet the standard poetic form of the 18th century. Both Dryden and Pope acknowledged their debt to him, and in his elegant and agreeable end-stopped couplets it is possible to recognize something of the sweetness if not the strength and subtlety of the later masters. [GS]

Poems and Translations (1668); *The Poetical Works*, ed. T. H. Banks, Jr (New Haven, 1928). Johnson, *Lives of the Poets*; R. A. Aubin, *Topographical Poetry in 18th Century England* (New York, 1936).

Dennis, John (1657–1734). Critic and dramatist. Born in London, the son of a prosperous saddler, he was educated at Harrow and Cambridge, first at Caius College, then, after his expulsion for stabbing a fellow-

scholar, at Trinity Hall. He travelled in France and Italy, and as a young man was an intimate member of Dryden's circle. Never a very good verse-writer, he wrote occasional poems and controversial political pamphlets in the 'Whig' interest of William III and Halifax, which earned him a small Customs House sinecure. He was always financially embarrassed and lived out a poverty-stricken old age. He wrote 8 plays, including 2 adaptations of Shakespeare, all acted with varying degrees of ill-success except for his tragedy *Liberty Asserted* (1704), which for extra-literary reasons ran well. In the first decade of the 18th century, Dennis was the leading theoretical critic in London, but as he grew older his views became out of date; he became cantankerous, and his squabbles with Addison, Steele, Swift and Pope (who pilloried him in the *Dunciad*) have obscured with ridicule his earlier genuine achievements. His chief critical works are: an attack on ◊ Rymer, *The Impartial Critick* (1693; reprinted in *Critical Essays of the Seventeenth Century*, ed. J. E. Spingarn, 3 vols., 1909); *The Advancement and Reformation of Modern Poetry* (1701; reprinted in *Critical Essays: 1700–1725*, ed. W. H. Durham, Yale U.P., 1915); and his most important work, the sketch for a longer book which failed to attract subscribers, *The Grounds of Criticism in Poetry* (1704; also reprinted in Durham); he also wrote *An Essay on the Genius and Writings of Shakespeare* (1712; reprinted in *Eighteenth Century Essays on Shakespeare*, ed. Nichol Smith, 1903). Lacking in humour and tact, Dennis was a learned and pertinacious arguer who makes some good points in developing neo-classical didactic theories; he was interested in the emotional and religious response to art, as well as the social background to literature. His *Original Letters, Familiar, Moral and Critical* (2 vols., 1721) is an interesting document of the writer's world of the time. [AR]

Critical Works, ed. and intr. N. Hooker (2 vols., Baltimore, 1939–43) (with bibliography). H. G. Paul, *J. D.: His Life and Criticism* (New York, 1911); R. S. Crane, 'English Neo-Classical Criticism: An Outline Sketch', in *Critics and Criticism*, ed. R. S. Crane (Chicago, 1952).

Dennis, Nigel (Forbes) (1912–   ). Novelist, playwright and journalist. Born in Surrey, Dennis spent his childhood in

Rhodesia and was partly educated at the Odenwaldschule in Austria. In 1934 he went to America and worked as a journalist there until 1949, when he was transferred to the London office of *Time* magazine. Since then he has lived in England. His first novel was *Boys and Girls Come Out to Play* (1949), but he did not become well known until the appearance of *Cards of Identity* (1955). A brilliantly original novel, it explores, with a great deal of social satire, black humour and fantasy, 20th-century man's inability to establish a sense of personal identity which is meaningful both to himself and society as a whole. This was followed by *A House in Order* (1966), a less ambitious but still impressive novel on a similar theme. *Cards of Identity* was produced as a play in 1956 and *The Making of Moo*, a religious satire, appeared in the following year. They have been published as *Two Plays and a Preface* (1958). His most successful play is *August for the People* (1961), a very funny satirical examination of the power of the press in a rapidly changing society. In 1960 Dennis became the dramatic critic for *Encounter* and he has published a collection of his writings, *Dramatic Essays* (1962). At best his particular brand of aggressive intellectualism recalls the work of Bernard Shaw and Wyndham Lewis. [PJK]

Gavin Ewart, 'Nigel Dennis – Identity Man', *London Magazine*, III (November 1963).

De Quincey, Thomas (1785–1859). Journalist and autobiographical writer. Born in Manchester, the son of a well-to-do merchant of literary interests. He was sent to Manchester Grammar School at 15, but eighteen months later ran away, wandered through Wales, and went to London. There he led a beatnik life, and associated with a prostitute, Ann, who figures in a celebrated sequence in his *Confessions*. His guardians sent him to Worcester College, Oxford, where he began the life of solitude which was to be a feature of his career. He gradually amassed a stock of recondite classical and other knowledge, but becoming addicted to opium, which he had taken to allay a toothache, he left the university without taking a degree. He became acquainted with Coleridge and Wordsworth, having been an admirer of the latter's poetry. Though he lost touch with Wordsworth, these contacts influenced him for the rest of his life. From Wordsworth he developed an interest in the growth of the mind and sensibility. Passages in the *Confessions* may justly be paralleled with *The Prelude*, and the digressions and curious proportions of his later work in part rise from this interest. With Coleridge, he shared the mental difficulties resulting from habitual drug-taking, as well as the consequent insight into the values of the dream inscape of man's life. As a kind of understudy of this much greater thinker and writer, his comments on the Romantic poets from an informed and sympathetic point of view are of great interest and value. His *Reminiscences of the Lake Poets* are collected and edited by J. E. Jordan (Everyman, 1961) and by D. Wright (PEL, 1970). Like Coleridge too, he was greatly interested in German writing, and was one of the intermediaries through whom the works of Kant and others filtered to the English reader.

He decided to follow a literary career, and rented Dove Cottage in Grasmere from 1809 to 1821. He became financially embarrassed through bad luck and carelessness, and edited an unimportant paper, the *Westmoreland Gazette*. In 1821, he moved to London, and through the kindness of ◊ Lamb he started writing for the *London Magazine* (though he was a difficult and very dilatory contributor). In the October and November numbers appeared his *Confessions of an English Opium Eater* (in book form 1822; 1823), which made him famous. This work was rewritten in a longer form and printed in 1856. The autobiographical sketches are much expanded; the writing is more florid; and though there are interesting passages, the earlier book is the crisper and better work (both versions in *Confessions*, ed. M. Elwin, 1956). The *Confessions*, though adopting an exemplary tone, is not in fact an apologetic work at all.

De Quincey wrote voluminously for magazines. Of his vast output, sometimes disfigured by irrelevance, digression and peculiarly flat facetiousness, there survives a small corps of essays which gives him permanent fame. His talents were curiously unsuited to the periodical writing by which he lived, particularly his desire to display his learning. As a critic, he wrote some passages of very great value not for their connected argument or analysis, but because of his grasp of the importance of the unconscious movements of the spirit in writer and reader and the psychological insights this gave him. The best example of this is his essay 'On the Knocking at the Gate in Macbeth'. His pieces on actual dreams are also good, such as *The English Mail Coach* (ed. J. E. Jordan, Everyman, 1961), not so much as providing grist for the mills of abnormal psychology as because the dream connexions and values liberate the writer from his more common and often foolish prejudices. When De Quincey is allowed to create a dream world he presents to the readers their own judgements, preconceptions, habits, reflected and distorted in a way that gives them real insight into their own minds. Powerful dream experiences make his elaborate prose set-pieces work. Perhaps the best instance is the rhetoric of the 'Dream Fugue' following the 'Vision of Sudden Death' in the *Mail Coach*. When the inspiration flags, the labour becomes hard and dull.

From 1828 until his death, De Quincey lived in various lodgings in and around Edinburgh. He moved out of and into the bosom of his family; his tastes were those of a recluse, and when his quarters were snowed under with accumulated papers, he simply moved on. His work, for which there was a steady market, appeared in *Blackwood's*, *Tait's Edinburgh Magazine*, the *Encyclopædia Britannica*, 7th edition (on Goethe, an unbalanced appreciation; on Schiller and on Shakespeare), and in many other places. A sequel to the *Confessions*, *Suspiria de Profundis* ('Sighs from the Depths'), came out partly (4 instalments) in *Blackwood's* (1845; ed. M. Elwin in *Confessions*, 1956), and more were published in *Posthumous Works* (ed. A. H. Japp, 2 vols., 1891–3). These pieces, on the relevance of misery and grief to the soul's development, exploit his notions on the creativity of dreaming, a drug-taker's experience, defence and delusion. *Savannah-la-Mar* carries his writing into the very difficult genre of the 'prose poem', and its artifice runs counter to much modern taste. De Quincey himself linked his ideas on this kind of associative prose with ideas about music.

There is no complete edition of his works; there are several extensive collections, of which *Selections Grave and Gay from Thomas De Quincey*, published by J. Hogg (14 vols., 1853–60) contains revisions by the author; the *Collected Writings* (ed. D. Masson, 14 vols., 1889–90) is the best so far, but needs supplementing from later volumes. [AR]

De Q.'s Literary Criticism, ed. H. Darbishire (1909) (selections); *T. de Q.*, ed. B. Dobrée (1965); *Selected Essays on Rhetoric*, ed. F. Burwick (U. of S. Illinois P., 1967).

H. A. Eaton, *T. De Q.* (1936); E. Sackville-West, *A Flame in Sunlight: The Life and Work of T. De Q.* (1936); J. E. Jordan, *T. De Q.: Literary Critic* (1952) and *De Q. to Wordsworth* (1962); A. Hayter, *Opium and the Romantic Imagination* (1968); H. S. Davies *T. de Q.* (WTW, 1964).

De Vere, Aubrey Thomas (1814–1902). Poet. Born at Adare, Co. Limerick, the son of Sir Aubrey de Vere (1788–1846), who also wrote poetry. De Vere, the younger, was educated at Trinity College, Dublin. As a young man he was strongly influenced by his acquaintance with Coleridge and Wordsworth. His verse has a rather pale Wordsworthian ambience, which with the wide variety of his subject matter places it rather apart from the work of the other 'Irish Revival' poets like T. O. ⟡ Davis. He was also a friend of Tennyson, Landor and Browning, and under the influence of Newman became a Roman Catholic (1851). His first works were *The Waldenses, or the Fall of Rora: A Lyrical Sketch, with Other Poems* (1842) and *The Search after Proserpine, Recollections of Greece, and Other Poems* (1843). Later he turned to Irish subjects, such as *Inisfail, a Lyrical Chronicle of Ireland* (1862) and *The Legends of St Patrick* (1872), but never confined himself to this. He also wrote literary and political essays. [AR]

The Poetical Works (6 vols., 1884–98); *Selections*, ed. G. E. Woodberry (New York, 1894); *Poems*, selected and ed. Lady Margaret Domvile (1904).

M. P. Reilly, *A. de V.: Victorian Observer* (Lincoln, Nebr., 1953).

Dickens, Charles (1812–70). Novelist. Born in Portsea, Portsmouth, the second child of John Dickens, a clerk in the Navy Pay Office; in 1816, the family moved to Chatham, and in 1823 to Camden Town in London. His father was in serious financial difficulties, and, though affectionate, totally neglected Charles's education. His mother unsuccessfully tried to start a school and his father was imprisoned as a debtor. The family furniture was pawned, and Dickens himself was sent to work as an odd-job boy in a blacking factory at Hungerford Stairs. The family lived with the father in the Marshalsea Prison; finally on John Dickens's release as an insolvent debtor they moved to Somers Town. Dickens's unsettled early life, his feeling of being unjustly neglected and degraded from middle-class respectability, and his early wanderings through the streets of London were the formative experiences from which came much of his fiction, and on which his social theories finally rest. He was sent to private schools for three years, and in 1827 articled as a solicitor's clerk; he worked as a shorthand court reporter, moving to parliamentary reporting; this he finally did for the *Morning Chronicle.* He also travelled. Such, together with reading in the British Museum, was his education. It gave him a wide knowledge of some aspects of contemporary life as well as varied practice in writing. He began to publish sketches, first in the *Monthly Magazine,* and then in the *Evening Chronicle, Bell's Life in London* and other periodicals. These pieces were collected and published as *Sketches by 'Boz', Illustrative of Everyday Life and Everyday People. Illustrations by George Cruikshank* (1836; and a second series, also 1836). These prose sketches come from his keen observation, and they introduce the episodic, opportunist, improvisatory side of his literary art, which persisted even in his great, mature works. They owe much to Leigh Hunt, Hazlitt and other writers who developed the English essay into an art of personal impressions. The *Sketches* were quite successful, and they were followed by *The Posthumous Papers of the Pickwick Club ... Edited by 'Boz'* (20 monthly parts, March 1836 to October 1837). This has a more connected (though still loose) structure. It was conceived in a form then popular with ◊ Surtees and other humorists, a succession of prose pieces to accompany a series of engravings. Seymour, the original artist, committed suicide after the second number was prepared. Thackeray wanted to draw for the enterprise, but Hablot Knight Browne ('Phiz') produced the plates, and Dickens became the driving force. 'Phiz' thenceforth illustrated all the novels but the last four. The deepening and broadening of the conception of *Pickwick* can be seen in the development from the Cockney club of 'humours' at the beginning, to the really powerful, comic combination of Pickwick and the Wellers. The serial idea of the work indulges Dickens's prodigality; here is the Dickens gallery, but without the shaping imagination shown in the later novels. It has been in the past the most admired of his works, perhaps for this reason, and is now rather unjustly neglected.

The first numbers excited no great interest, but it gradually became a remarkable success, with many imitations and 'sequels'; it launched Dickens into his career as a star entertainer.

While *Pickwick* was still running, he began to print another serial in *Bentley's Miscellany,* which he was editing: this was the much more sombre *Oliver Twist: or, The Parish Boy's Progress* (February 1837 to March 1838; 1838). It introduces, with Fagin and Bill Sykes, Dickens's great preoccupation with crime as a violent disorder of a loveless society, and murder as the act of man become a monster. The propaganda intention of the novel's 'exposure' of workhouses and the Poor Law is also obvious, as well as the sentimentalized treatment of childhood. Social satire is also to be found in *Nicholas Nickleby* (20 monthly parts, April 1838 to November 1839; 1839), in the picture of Mr Squeers and his school, Dotheboys Hall, both on the grounds of bad education and (autobiographically) the exploitation of children. This novel is more episodic and disorganized, but ran well; the improvisation does not always keep the reader's interest, and the sentiment of the Cheeryble brothers, which Dickens advances as admirable, is not admired as much now as this pathetic vein once was. Dickens then projected a series of essays and stories which he called *Master Humphrey's Clock,* but a club and the other parts of the essay framework disappeared as sales declined, and the 88 weekly parts contain chiefly *The Old Curiosity Shop* (April 1840 to February 1841; 1841) and *Barnaby Rudge. A Tale of the Riots of 'Eighty,* (February to November 1841; 1841). *The Old Curiosity Shop* contains some of Dickens's best and most powerful 'caricature' figures, such as Quilp, the dwarf, as well as his most sentimental creation, Little Nell, whose death exceeds anything he ever did in contrived pathos; it stimulated vast audience reaction, an important influence on Dickens's art. The debtors' prison scenes are somewhat sentimentalized realizations of childhood memories. *Barnaby Rudge* is an unsuccessful and un-imagined historical novel, set in the period of the Gordon Riots, with a routine love story embedded in it. Dickens was by then a famous and financially successful writer.

In 1842 he visited America, where his attacks on the publishers' piracy of British copyrights (which was costing him a

146

fortune) rather disenchanted the American public, who were prepared to adulate the modern man of feeling. This was not alleviated by his *American Notes for General Circulation* (1842), in which he is critical of the American scene, though not unduly so to foreign eyes. He used American colour, and more hostile but rather flat satire, in *The Life and Adventures of Martin Chuzzlewit* (20 monthly parts, 1843–4; 1844). Mrs Gamp and Mr Pecksniff appear here from the world of fantasy, and Tom Pinch from the world of pathos: this novel was not so successful, the sales of any one number never exceeding 23,000 copies, whereas *The Old Curiosity Shop* had bettered 70,000. *A Christmas Carol* came out in December 1843, followed by *The Chimes* (1844), *The Cricket on the Hearth* (1845), and 2 others in the following years. The use of the supernatural, caricature, social allegory and sentiment made these Christmas stories extremely popular; they are perhaps most responsible for fixing a Dickens stereotype.

From 1844 to 1845, Dickens and his wife lived in Italy, and on his return he took up amateur dramatics, in which he showed great (at times manic) interest. He was a lover of melodrama, and the contemporary theatre influenced the form of his novels to a high degree. His novels were dramatized, and the dramatic possibilities in them were exploited in his later career, reading his own works in public. He briefly edited the *Daily News*, and went to Switzerland in 1846; at Lausanne he began to write *Dealings with the Firm of Dombey and Son, Wholesale, Retail, and for Exportation* (20 monthly numbers, 1846–7; 1848). This is the first of his great novels, more carefully worked out than the previous ones, and with a powerful convergence of imagery. The fantasy is more controlled, and in this case subordinated to a strongly realistic programme. In the next novel, however, the autobiographical impulse broke out more strongly than ever: *David Copperfield* (20 monthly parts, 1849–50; 1850; etc.). The opening chapters of personal reminiscence, in which his father appears as Mr Micawber, provide the moving picture of Dickens's early life, so much prized by some readers. The novel, however, is also a masterpiece of technical arrangement of the 'point-of-view' in the narration. Uriah Heep is a powerful caricature. In the treatment of Steerforth, Dickens shows the failure of his genteel picture of

ideal society, but with the Peggotys and their boat-house he equally displays the extraordinarily suggestive power of his organizing imagination.

On 30 March 1849 appeared the first number of *Household Words* (with the opening of a story by Mrs ♢ Gaskell), the weekly periodical he edited until 1859, when he incorporated it into *All the Year Round*: this he ran until he died. In his periodicals, Dickens was able to carry out his ambitions as a social reformer, essayist, public commentator and moral teacher. He also published much fiction from other (particularly young) writers, whom he befriended and helped (e.g. Wilkie ♢ Collins). *Bleak House* (20 monthly parts, 1852–3; 1853) has also a closely knit structure and controlled imagery. The attack on legal obfuscation was part of the movement that led to legal reforms in the sixties, but Dickens's attack goes deeper, without his perhaps being aware of the implications. *Bleak House* has strong traces of the imaginative anarchism that impelled his poetic powers; this is often in tense conflict with his far more orthodox, conservative, conscious solutions for the moral and social problems he explores. Such tension is a feature of his last and greatest novels. In *Hard Times* (published as a serial in *Household Words*, 1 April to 12 August 1854) his diagnosis of the ills of industrialized society is the centre of interest: the novel is dedicated to Thomas Carlyle. The book is passionate, introducing a powerful argument that education is an area of human endeavour that can save by love, but kill by greed. *Little Dorrit* (20 monthly parts, 1855–6; 1857) really begins Dickens's final phase of carefully structured novels with a brilliant symbolic treatment of characters, objects and incidents. Its concern with the destructive and dehumanizing power of money is characteristic of much of his later writing (cf. *Our Mutual Friend*). In *A Tale of Two Cities* (serialized in *All the Year Round* and issued in 8 monthly parts, 1859; 1859), Dickens returned for the second and last time to the historical novel, this time combining an account of a rather poorly imagined past with elaborately contrived melodrama. The novel is also over-written; because of its failure in true moral and imaginative engagement, its rhetoric is empty. Unfortunately, this novel, probably because of its 'educational' historical content, has for years been kept

Dickens

on school reading-lists, and is the only novel by Dickens that many people have experienced. In 1858-9, Dickens gave his first important series of readings from his works.

He had given a few readings since 1853, and his enthusiasm for dramatics gave scope for his acting. Now, however, this desire for intimate confrontation with an audience was well satisfied. His novels show the same need in the way they are constructed, with personal intervention by the writer; his editorial work is another instance. Three other reading tours followed, 1861-3, 1866-7 (including a successful return visit to America) and 1868-70. These performances earned Dickens much money, but the physical and nervous strain hastened his death; in April 1869, for example, he had a stroke at Preston.

His two greatest works, *Great Expectations* (serialized in *All the Year Round*, 1860-1; 1861) and *Our Mutual Friend* (20 monthly parts, 1864-5; 1865), carry on his development as an artist. The writing of *Great Expectations* is careful and studied. The imagery and imagination carry out a profound exploration of modern society's most haunting problem, that of identity: how do men know who they are? The fantasy of Miss Havisham, the caricatures like Joe Gargery, are all compellingly connected to Dickens's belief that greed and the demands of society kill the individual, living soul. *Our Mutual Friend* has an intricate plot, replete with deliberate coincidences, unreality and powerful symbolism. Crime, one of the dark preoccupations that Dickens handles so well on the poetic level, so badly on the consciously practical level, is the nexus that binds together the several apparently unrelated circles of characters. The humour is grim and satirical; the caricatures, like Silas Wegg, are complex. Crime is bred by 'money, money, money', the corrupting solvent of social life. What money makes of life is the theme of the book, and of Dickens's best fiction. Money stands for the iron social laws; life is found in the free movement of love. While he was in the middle of *The Mystery of Edwin Drood* (6 monthly parts, 1870; 1870), he died. The novel was running extremely successfully, and there have been numerous attempts (none convincing) to finish it.

Dickens has never been completely in eclipse as a novelist; his work appeals to too many different kinds of readers. He has, however, come to be treated with more and more respect as a diagnostician of his (and our) society. He is less often seen as an imperfect, 'vulgar' writer of natural genius, and more often as a writer of great poetic power whose work has a complex development. He said and did many foolish things, but the penetration of his insight is of first-rate value. His imagination is subterranean and on occasions apparently in opposition to his conscious doctrine. He is also a violent writer, whose linguistic innovations and virtuosity have been disastrous in the hands of feeble imitators. Dickens wrote much journalism, many short stories; he printed reading versions of episodes from his novels. He also wrote plays and farces, as well as poetry.

The bibliography of Dickens's works is extremely complex and in places uncertain, because of the size and nature of the printings in monthly parts. Since Dickens has for long been an interest of wealthy collectors, there is a number of bibliographies and catalogues (see *CBEL*). *The Dickensian* (1905 – in progress), now quarterly, contains bibliographical information, especially 39-41 (1943-5), and other discussion. There are numerous collected editions of his works and novels. [A R]

'The Gadshill Edition', ed. and intr. Andrew Lang and B. W. Matz (36 vols., 1897-1908) (fullest edn, with original and other illustrations); 'The Charles Dickens Library', ed. Sir J. A. Hammerton (18 vols., 1910) (with original and other illustrations); 'The New Oxford Illustrated Edition', (1947 ff.) (with introductions); 'The Clarendon Dickens', ed. K. Tillotson and J Butt (vol. 1, *Oliver Twist*, 1967); *The Uncollected Writings of C.D. Household Words. 1850-1859*, ed. H. Stone (2 vols., 1969); *Letters*, ed. M. House and G. Storey (1965 ff.).

J. Forster, *Life of D.* (3 vols., 1872-4; ed. G. K. Chesterton, 2 vols., Everyman, 1927; ed. with notes, J. W. T. Ley, 1928; ed. A. J. Hoppé, 1966); U. Pope-Hennessy, *C.D.* (1945); H. Pearson, *C.D.* (1949); J. Lindsay, *C.D.* (1950); K. J. Fielding, *C.D.* (WTW, 1953); *The D. Critics*, ed. G. H. Ford and L. Lane, Jr (Cornell U.P., 1961); E. Johnson, *C. D. His Tragedy and Triumph* (2 vols., 1952) (relies heavily on symbolical interpretation); G. H. Ford, *D. and His Readers* (Princeton U.P., 1955); J. Hillis Miller, *C.D. The World of His Novels* (1958); A. O. J. Cockshut, *The Imagination of C.D.* (1961); K. J. Fielding, *C.D.: A Critical Introduction* (2nd edn, enlarged, 1965); M. Steven, *D. from Pickwick to Dombey* (1965); H. House, *The Dickens World* (1941); K. Tillotson,

Novels of the 1840s (1954); M. Spilka, *D. and Kafka* (Indiana U.P., 1963); J. Butt and K. Tillotson, *D. at Work* (1957); P. A. W. Collins, *D. and Crime* (1962) and *D. and Education* (1963; reprinted with alterations, 1966); R. Garis, *The Dickens Theatre* (1965); R. H. Dabney, *Love and Property in the Novels of D.* (1967); B. Hardy, *The Moral Art of D.* (1970); F. R. Leavis and Q. D. Leavis, *D. the Novelist* (1970); ed. S. Wall, *C.D.: A Critical Anthology* (1970); Angus Wilson, *The World of C.D.* (1970).

Dickens, Monica (Enid) (1915–). Novelist. Born in London, the daughter of a lawyer (the grandson of Charles Dickens). She was educated at St Paul's Girls School, Hammersmith. In 1951 she married Commander Roy O. Shallon of the U.S. Navy, and now lives in Massachusetts. She wrote amusing popular autobiographical accounts of various jobs she held: as a cook, *One Pair of Hands* (1939); as a nurse, *One Pair of Feet* (1942) and *My Turn to Make the Tea* (1951). Her first novel was *Mariana* (1940), and others include *The Fancy* (1943); *No More Meadows* (1953); *The Angel in the Corner* (1956); *Man Overboard* (1958); *The Heart of London* (1961); *Cobbler's Dream* (1963) and *The Room Upstairs* (1966). [AR]

Digby, Sir Kenelm (1603–65). Writer and diplomatist. His father was executed in 1606 for his share in the Gunpowder Plot. He was educated at Oxford, supported the Catholic cause, was knighted in 1623, and defeated a French and Venetian fleet in Scanderoon harbour in 1628. A man of charm, versatility and genuine philosophic and scientific curiosity, he wrote in 1628 his *Private Memoirs* (printed only in 1827) to defend from scandal his wife, Venetia Stanley, whom he had known from childhood. He briefly professed Protestantism, but again declared himself for Catholicism, publishing in 1638 *Conference with a Lady about Choice of Religion*. He was an active supporter of the King in the Civil War, pleading his cause in 1645 with the Pope, was banished in 1649, and lived in Paris, where he knew Descartes. In 1660 he resumed office as chancellor to Queen Henrietta Maria and was a member of the council of the Royal Society at its inception. He published works on religious and scientific subjects including a criticism of Sir Thomas ◊ Browne (1643), *Of the Immortality of Man's Soul* (1644), *Discourse on Vegetation*, on the necessity of oxygen to the life of plants (1660), and *On the Cure of Wounds* (1658). [MJ]

E. W. Bligh, *Sir K.D. and His Venetia* (1932); D. Bush, *English Literature in the Earlier Seventeenth Century* (revised edn, 1962); J. F. Fulton, *Sir K.D.* (New York, 1937); R. T. Petersson, *Sir K.D.* (1956).

Disraeli, Benjamin (1st Earl of Beaconsfield) (1804–81). Imperialist statesman and novelist. Born in London, the son of Isaac ◊ D'Israeli; he was educated at home, and in 1821 was articled to a firm of solicitors. He was entered at Lincoln's Inn in 1825, but later withdrew. He started his literary career by writing poetry, and his first novel, *Vivian Grey*, appeared with great success in 1826–7 (ed. L. Wolf, 1904). The book has a strong flavour of politics (which was to become his consuming passion), and needed a 'key' in later editions; as might be expected from a man of Disraeli's so far slender experience, the chief interest lies in its wit and extravagant writing. *The Voyage of Captain Popanilla* (1828) and *The Young Duke* (1831) are also densely political fantasies, carried on in Peacock-like conversation. Disraeli had spent three years travelling in Spain, Italy and the Near East. *Contarini Fleming: A Psychological Autobiography* (1832) is interesting because it reveals something of Disraeli's ambitions and an evaluation of himself; the setting, in the Levant, is congenially exotic. This enjoyment of foreign *locales* is also the main interest in *The Wondrous Tale of Alroy* and *The Rise of Iskander* (1833). In *Henrietta Temple* (1837), he tried his hand at a love story, unsuccessfully. Disraeli is never a convincing writer when he is dealing with sexual feeling. *Venetia* (1837) makes free use of then little known biographical details about Byron and Shelley. Having stood for Parliament unsuccessfully, Disraeli was finally elected M.P. for Maidstone in July 1837. His subsequent parliamentary and political career is mostly outside the bounds of literature. The bombast of his first speech was a failure, but with increasing political power he came to be a persuasive and admired speaker without much changing his style. In the House of Commons, he came to lead the Young England party of the Conservatives against Peel. This was a radical group that sought to keep power by initiating change on their own terms. He supported the Chartists in 1839 and de-

149

fended the Corn Laws in 1843. His two best novels are an imaginative statement of his political creed: *Coningsby: or, The New Generation* (1844; ed. A. Maurois, World's Classics, 1931) and *Sybil: or, The Two Nations* (1845; ed. W. Sichel, 1925; World's Classics, 1925; ed. V. Cohen, 1934). Disraeli's views are a blend of genuine response to the industrial unrest that was producing the Chartist movement, together with a kind of opportunist, mystical belief in a solution in which the monarchy and an awakened aristocracy seized their 'true place' as leaders of the masses from wicked agitators and self-seeking industrialists. Disraeli had first-hand experience of the industrial north through visits, and the genuine reportage of conditions there sits oddly with the rather naïvely unbounded imagination he deploys in celebrating exaggerated aristocratic grandeur. In *Tancred: or, The New Crusade* (1847) the wise, mystical uplift of the East is hinted at as being a possible solution to English doubt and political despair. The doctrine is vague and gets out of hand. In 1852 he was briefly Chancellor of the Exchequer, and again in 1858–9 and in 1866–7. He became Prime Minister for a few months in 1868. His last serious attempt at fiction was *Lothair* (1870), another novel dealing with a wealthy English aristocrat's quest for his true role in a modern industrialized society and finding it in religious duty. The atmosphere is suggested by the upheavals of the Tractarian Movement (◊ Newman, J. H.). He was again Prime Minister from 1874 to 1880; during his term of office he made Queen Victoria 'Empress' of India; he was made Earl of Beaconsfield in 1876; and carried out an expansionist imperial policy. His government also enacted useful domestic legislation, including badly needed Factory Acts. His last novel, *Endymion*, appeared in 1880 and is a medley of politics, economics (the Railway Bubble), Tractarianism, autobiography and adulatory glorification of English aristocratic society and opulence. Disraeli's novels are fascinating to read in the light of his own extraordinary and influential political career. Only *Sybil* and *Coningsby* really stand on their own as live works of art. In them, Disraeli creates a lively sense of political action and idealistic dreams. They are also witty, but the analysis of the true effects of industrialization on English life is much less convincing than, for example, the more impractical ◊

150

Ruskin's. Disraeli also wrote a number of poems, and political works, such as a *Vindication of the English Constitution* (1835), and a political biography, *Lord George Bentinck* (1852). Many of his speeches were published. [A R]

Novels and Tales (Bradenham Edition), ed. and intr. P. Guedalla (12 vols., 1926–7); *Whigs and Whiggism; Political Writings*, ed. W. Hutcheon (1913).
W. F. Monypenny and G. E. Buckle, *The Life of B.D.* (6 vols., 1910–20; revised edn, 2 vols., 1929); A. Maurois, *Life of D.* (tr. 1928); R. Blake, *D.* (1969); M. E. Speare, *The Political Novel* (1924); R. Hamilton. 'D. and the Two Nations', *Quarterly Review*, 288 (1950); J. Holloway, *The Victorian Sage* (1953); P. Bloomfield, *D.* (W T W, 1961) (with select bibliography); E. D. Feuchtwanger, *D., Democracy and the Tory Party* (1968); M. Sadleir, *Excursions in Victorian Bibliography* (1922) (bibliography); C. Dahl, in *Victorian Fiction: A Guide to Research*, ed. L. Stevenson (Harvard U.P., 1964).

D'Israeli, Isaac (1766–1848). Literary antiquarian and miscellaneous writer. Born at Enfield of a family of Sephardic Jews who had fled from Spain to Venice and thence to England, he was educated at Amsterdam and Leyden. His chief claim to fame is probably as the father of Benjamin ◊ Disraeli, but he also had a great store of learning and wrote several curious collections of essays and anecdotes, which are sometimes of value (particularly on 18th-century literature) because he, and his extensive circle, had access to traditions and documents now lost. The earliest of these collections was *Curiosities of Literature; Consisting of Anecdotes, Characters, Sketches and Dissertations, Literary, Critical and Historical* (Series 1, 2 vols., 1791–3, 1798, 3rd vol., 1817; Series 2, 1823; whole work, 6 vols., 1834, etc., 3 vols., 1927). There were 3 others: *Calamities of Authors, Including Some Inquiries Respecting their Moral and Literary Characters* (2 vols., 1812); *Quarrels of Authors* (including material on Addison, Pope, Curll, Cibber, etc.) (3 vols., 1814); *Amenities of Literature* (a history of English literature) (3 vols., 1841). D'Israeli also wrote biographies of James VI & I and of Charles I, as well as poetry and novels. [A R]

Works, ed. with a memoir by Benjamin Disraeli (7 vols., 1858–9).
W. Maginn, *A Gallery of Illustrious Characters*, ed. W. Bates (1873); W. F. Monypenny and

G. E. Buckle, *Life of B.D.* (1929); S. Kopstein, *D.* (Jerusalem, 1939).

Dobell, Sydney Thompson (1824–74). Poet. Born at Cranbrook in Kent, he lived chiefly in Cheltenham. His father, a rich wine-merchant, had him educated privately. His first work, *The Roman: A Dramatic Poem* (1850, under the pseudonym of Sydney Yendys), was an enormously popular expression of sympathy with the Italian revolt against tyranny. His second 'dramatic poem', *Balder, Part the First* (1854), was much less popular, an incoherent rhapsody based on a thin, mystical story. Part II was never completed, some of it being printed in *Thoughts on Art, Philosophy and Religion, selected from the Unpublished Papers of Sydney Dobell* (with an introductory note by J. Robertson Nicoll, 1876). Dobell was a member of the so-called ◊ 'Spasmodic School' (and satirized by Aytoun in his *Firmilian: A Spasmodic Tragedy*, 1854); with the other chief member, Alexander Smith, he printed *Sonnets on the War* (the Crimean) (1855). Dobell's work was incohate, derivative (from the Authorized Version, Milton and other lofty writers) and overheated, lapsing badly into inflated ideas, bathos and a confusion of imagery. His best poem is a literary ballad, 'Oh, Keith of Ravelston'. [AR]

Poetical Works, intr. J. Robertson Nicoll (2 vols., 1875); *Home in War Time*, selected by W. G. Hutchison (1900).
G. Gilfillan, *Third Gallery of Literary Portraits* (1854; Everyman selection, 1927); E. Jolly, *The Life and Letters of S.D.* (2 vols., 1878).

Dobson, Henry Austin (1840–1921). Poet and critic. Born the son of a Plymouth engineer, he was educated there and at the French school in Strasbourg. Thereafter he combined a career as a Civil Servant at the Board of Trade (1856–1901) with writing. Dobson was an accomplished practitioner of the light verse, imitations (rondeaux, triolets, etc.), parodies and translations fashionable in the seventies and eighties in the work of writers like ◊ Lang and ◊ Gosse. His chief books of verse were *Vignettes in Rhyme* (1873), *Proverbs in Porcelain* (1877) and *At the Sign of the Lyre* (1885). Such writing (shadows of shades) needed learning to underpin its effect of effortlessness. This Dobson had. He specialized in the literary history of the 18th century, producing biographies of writers and artists, including *Goldsmith* (1888), *Horace Walpole* (1890), *Hogarth* (1891), *Richardson* (1902). His 3 series of essays, *Eighteenth Century Vignettes* (1892; 1894; 1896), have often been reprinted in various combinations. Although he has a tendency to the 'Beau Brocade' kind of writing, Dobson had a close knowledge of some aspects of 18th-century society and writing, and considerable sympathy. Several volumes of his essays are reprinted in the World's Classics. [AR]

Complete Poetical Works, ed. A. T. A. Dobson (1923); *Selected Poems*, ed. A. T. A. Dobson (World's Classics, 1924).
A. T. A. Dobson, *A.D.: Some Notes* (1928) (includes chapters by Gosse and Saintsbury); B. I. Evans, *English Poetry in the Later Nineteenth Century* (1933); A. T. A. Dobson, *Bibliography* (1925) (much of his poetry was privately printed).

Doddridge, Philip (1702–51). Independent dissenting minister, theologian and devotional writer. He was born in London, the son of a well-to-do merchant. His family, which had produced a line of distinguished non-conformist divines, lost their property while he was a boy. He was educated at non-conformist schools, including the well-known dissenting academy founded by his grandfather at Kingston-on-Thames. He was prepared for the ministry, for which he had an early inclination, by Samuel Clark of St Albans and at Jennings' Independent Academy at Kibworth in Leicestershire. Doddridge began to teach at Kibworth in 1723, moving in 1725 to Market Harborough, where he opened his famous theological academy under the auspices of Isaac ◊ Watts and other influential non-conformist ministers. He moved in 1729 with his Academy to Northampton, where he became ordained as pastor in 1730. Doddridge was well-read without being learned, an excellent, popular and influential teacher, if not an original theologian. His earliest work *Free Thoughts on the Most Probable Means of Recovering the Dissenting Interest* (1730) is an expression of his life-long attempts at unifying the dissenters and uniting the liberal, 'cultured' side of non-conformist thought with the evangelism that was its most 'popular' manifestation. He was a Calvinist who tried to bend this hard religious current into the channel of rational or moderate dissent. He started to keep a diary in 1716 and had a voluminous correspondence in which he prosecuted his many interests, educational, missionary, charitable, organizational. His best known work was *On the Rise and Progress of the Soul* (1745; etc.) and his addresses collected as *The Family Expositor* (1739; etc.). He also wrote hymns, of which 'O God of Bethel' is still widely sung. [A R]

Works, ed. J. D. Humphreys (10 vols., 1802–5; 1811); *Diary and Correspondence* (5 vols. 1829–31); *Hymns* (1839).
C. Stanford, *P.D.* (1880); ed. G. F. Nuttall, *D. His Contribution to English Religion* (1951).

Dodgson, Charles Lutwidge. ⟡ Carroll, Lewis.

Donn, Rob (pseud. of Robert Mackay) (1714–78). Scottish Gaelic poet. His poetry is almost all concerned with the life of his home region, Strathnaver in north-west Scotland. His work gives us a vivid picture of the life of this community, its pastoral occupations, its social structure, the impingement of emigration and of military service on the society. Wit and subtle humour add a sparkle and gleam to the many facets of this complex picture. In Rob Donn, and in part of the work of his contemporary John MacCodrum, we find a true reflection of the lively intelligence and gay disposition of the mercurial Gaelic Celts. This reflection is only slightly clouded by Evangelical gloom, but the gathering evil of alien landlordism throws a rather longer shadow over Rob Donn's sunny world.

He gives an interesting and full account of the family of his tacksman patron Iain Mac Eachainn, playfully teasing the daughter Iseabail, describing the father's and son's business activities, composing a moving elegy on the death of Iain. He describes the thrill of the deer-hunt and the drudgery of routine farm work, the pin-up girl of the Officers' Mess, dubious goings-on in Lady Reay's household, a sea trip, the killing of a bull, the sad mishap of a man who lost his trousers, the death of two miserly bachelor brothers, and various romantic and unromantic predicaments.

Rob Donn's language is sinuous and economical. Many of his poems, although deceptively simple at a first reading, are complex in expression and imagery, and subtle in thought. [D T]

Orain le R. D., ed. Hew Morrison (1899); *Songs and Poems*, ed. A. Gunn and M. Macfarlane (1899); 'Elegy for Iain Mac Eachainn', tr. Iain C. Smith, *An Gaidheal.* LIII, 6 (1958).
Alex J. MacAskill, 'R.D.', *An Gaidheal*, L, 5 and 6 (1955); Ian Grimble, 'Emigration in the Age of R.D.', *Scottish Studies*, VII, pt 2 (1963); Donald J. MacLeod, 'The Poetry of R. D. Mackay', *Scottish Gaelic Studies*, XII, pt 1 (1970).

Donne, John (1572–1631). Poet and divine. Donne was born in London, son of a prosperous ironmonger. His mother was the daughter of the poet and dramatist John Heywood and a descendant of the family of Sir Thomas More. His childhood education was solidly Roman Catholic. Between 1584 and 1594 Donne studied at Oxford, Cambridge and the Inns of Court in London and before 1596 he travelled in France, Spain and Italy. During these years his adherence to the Roman Catholic Church lapsed, and he seriously studied the claims of the rival Churches (see *Satyre* III).

In 1596 he took part in the naval expedition to Cadiz and in 1597 to the Azores (described in the verse letters 'The Calme' and 'The Storm'). He was appointed secretary to Sir Thomas Egerton, the Lord Keeper, in 1598, and, seemingly set for a career in the public service, entered Parliament in 1601; but in that year he secretly married Anne More, a niece of Lady Egerton's. Furious at this breach of convention, Anne's father secured his dismissal and imprisonment, and though Donne was released after a few days and reunited with Anne after some months, he was not taken back into Egerton's employment. His career in ruins and his private means exhausted, Donne was now forced to depend on the generosity of friends (such as Sir Francis Woolley, in whose house at Pyrford the couple lived 1602–6). To prepare himself for a resumption of his career, Donne studied canon and civil law, and travelled on the continent as companion to Sir Walter Chute (1605–6); and when with his growing family the poet moved into a small, damp house at Mitcham in 1606, he took lodgings in the Strand so as to be able to spend more time in London. His growing circle of influential friends (which came to include Mrs Magdalen Herbert, Lucy Harrington Countess of Bedford, and the Countess of Huntingdon) were, however, powerless to secure him the state employment he hoped for, while scruples concerning his vocation and worthiness made him refuse Dean Morton's offer of a living in the Church of England. These were years of debt, ill-health, frustration and inner conflict (reflected in his semi-serious treatise in partial justification of suicide, *Biathanatos*) but also of a growing devoutness.

About 1609 Donne became interested in Dean Morton's pamphleteering controversy with the Jesuits, and in 1610 he published his own contribution to it, *Pseudo-Martyr*, a treatise urging English Catholics to take the oath of allegiance to the crown. The more polemical anti-Jesuit pamphlet, *Ignatius his Conclave*, followed in 1611. These works won the King's favour, but seem to have persuaded him that Donne should serve the Church rather than the state. That Donne's interest in religion at this stage was mainly a matter of intellect is suggested by his *Essayes in Divinity* (1612–14?) which consist of learned discussions of the opening verses of each of the first two books of the Bible. Where his career was concerned, Donne still had secular hopes. He had attached himself to a new patron, Sir Robert Drury, in 1611, and moved with his family into the Drurys' London mansion in 1612. However, a diplomatic mission to the continent, on which Donne accompanied Sir Robert and Lady Drury, failed to further the career of either patron or poet, and Donne left his service. More dependent than ever on gifts from the great, he now had the good fortune to win the favour of Viscount Rochester who proved a generous patron. In April 1614 Donne entered Parliament, which the King dissolved within two months. Donne now made one more bid for an appointment of state. With the support of his patron (now Earl of Somerset), as well as the Lord Hay and his former employer Egerton (now Lord Ellesmere), he petitioned the King, who, without actually refusing the petition, made it clear that he wished Donne to enter the Church. Submitting to what he now accepted as the will of God, Donne took orders in 1615.

As a priest Donne found himself closer to affairs of state than ever before, for he was appointed a royal chaplain, and not only preached to the King and the court but was entrusted with diplomatic correspondence. In 1619 he accompanied Viscount Doncaster on a mission to Germany. His fame as a preacher grew. In 1621 he was appointed Dean of St Paul's, and his duties multiplied. A serious illness in 1623 brought him,

as he thought, to the verge of death; but as soon as he began to recover he embarked on the composition of his *Devotions*, a work in which the experience of disease and the expectation of death are made starting points for contemplation and prayer. He now returned to a strenuous life of preaching, pastoral care and ecclesiastical administration. In 1630 his health again began to fail; and on the first Friday in Lent, 1631, he preached what he knew was his last sermon. In March he engaged an artist to sketch him in his shroud, to provide the sculptor of his funeral monument with a design from which to work. He died on 31 March 1631.

Though few of Donne's poems can be dated with complete certainty, their approximate chronology is becoming clearer. The *Satyres* were written over the years 1593–8. Applying the form and matter of Roman satire to contemporary theme and balancing the conventional satiric indignation with a tone of rueful self-mockery, Donne views London life in town and at court. It is not always easy to tell which are the main and which the subsidiary targets of his attack, for the *Satyres* burst at the seams with characters brought on momentarily to point out what are often incidental morals. (*Satyre* III, with its clear-cut theme of the poet's search for the true church, possesses a unity lacking in the others.) Numerous elisions and startling departures from normal word-order create an impression of roughness and violence.

It would seem that the majority at least of the *Elegies* belong likewise to the 1590s. Smoother than the *Satyres* in rhythm, but loaded with paradox and verbal wit, they surpass their models (Ovid's *Amores*) in intellectual complexity as well as emotional power, and present an extraordinary range of tone, from tenderness to brutal cynicism, and from happy sensuality to disgust. They are closely related in approach and subject-matter to the *Songs and Sonets*, many of which undoubtedly belong to the same period, but some of which (e.g. those which, like 'The Relique' and 'A Nocturnall upon St Lucies Day', seem to allude to his noble patronesses Mrs Herbert and the Countess of Bedford) are evidently from a much later period in the poet's life. The *Songs and Sonets* are for the most part arguments about love; and while the tone is direct and passionate (be the emotion love or lust, despair or delight, scorn or adoration) the argument is always conducted in a sophistical manner, proceeding from obviously false premises, by way of audaciously false analogies, to a surprising conclusion which on entirely different grounds we may accept as true. The balance between passionate directness and intellectual play varies from poem to poem and often results in a teasing emotional ambiguity; but the arresting opening lines, the sudden shifts in the poet's attitude to his subject, and the pretence, in many poems, that they are being spoken in the midst of an unfolding situation, all contribute to give them an air of intensity and excitement unrivalled in English poetry. Donne's images are drawn from many spheres of human thought and activity – geography, astronomy, law, alchemy, scripture, scholastic philosophy (hence the term 'metaphysical poet' which was attached to Donne and his followers by later critics) and even everyday life; on the whole, however, he shuns the conventional images of love-poetry. No doubt the persona that emerges from these poems – the lover as a bold, cynical, unconventional intellectual – has held a particular attraction for the 20th century, and readers have not always observed that some of the most startling poems convey attitudes that are basically highly conventional – 'platonick' compliments or 'Petrarchan' despair.

In 1601, before his marriage, Donne started and left unfinished a brilliant and bitter poem, *The Progresse of the Soule*, which purports to trace the metempsychosis of the soul of the apple of the Tree of Knowledge, through the bodies of plants, beasts, and then human deceivers, and heretics, down to those of his own day. (Donne broke off at stanza 52 with the soul embodied in the sister and wife of Cain.) Among the other poems written before 1601 are the *Epithalamion Made at Lincolnes Inne*. Criticism has not so far done justice to Donne's verse letters, which span the whole of his poetic career and in which his development as a poet can be studied. The *Epicedes and Obsequies*, almost all of them written between his marriage and his ordination, display Donne at his most fantastic; it is here that we find some of his most exaggerated displays of scientific and philosophical learning. These are 'public' poems, in which the poet pretends to speak for mankind as a whole. Donne's funerary manner reaches its greatest brilliance in the two *Anniversaries*, which praise the dead Elizabeth Drury in terms that even Donne's contemporaries found excessive. But it is evident that Donne used her simply as a symbol for human perfection, for his principal subjects in these two profoundly religious poems are the corruption of the physical universe and the liberation of the soul by death.

Donne's religious poetry, most of which is now known to have been composed long before he took orders, is more heterogeneous than his love-poetry. 'The Crosse' seems a mere exercise in ingenuity; 'La Corona' (1607?) is an impersonally beautiful celebration of Christian mysteries; 'A Litanie' (1608) is a prayer and has a sober grandeur seldom found in Donne's verse. The most striking of the religious poems are the 'Holy Sonnets' (mostly 1609–11). These tend to open with magnificent gestures ('Death, be not proud', 'Batter my heart, three-person'd God', 'At the round earth's imagined corners blow Your trumpets, Angels'), but what follows is usually in a lower key, and the poet's attempts to close as impressively as he opened seem forced or hollow: thus the paradoxes 'Death, thou shalt die' and 'Nor ever chaste unless thou ravish me' are purely verbal. Donne's main concern in these poems seems to be not so much to express faith as to induce or strengthen it; and although he writes in the first person, he tends to cast himself in various more or less conventional roles, e.g. as the Chief of Sinners. In contrast, the three Holy Sonnets found only in the Westmoreland MS ('Since she whom I loved', 'Show me dear Christ' and 'Oh to vex me' – all written after 1617) are poems of self-revelation and confession; free from self-dramatization and unforced in tone they have an air of frankness which is found again in the three 'Hymnes' ('To Christ at the Authors last going into Germany', 1619?; 'To God the Father', 'To God my God, in my sicknesse', probably 1623).

None of Donne's earlier prose can compare in interest with his poetry of the same period. It is in the prose-works written after his ordination – the *Devotions* and the *Sermons* – that the richness of his mind is revealed. The only orthodox thing about the sermons is his theology. Here we have all the intellectual daring, subtlety and self-knowledge that we know from the poems; but without their ambivalence of attitude. He elaborates on words and phrases of scripture with passionate ingenuity. Donne uses prose in a conspicuously rhetorical manner, his sentences now curt, now trailing, symmetrical or asymmetrical, according to the requirements of the moment. Perhaps however it is the *Devotions*, with their acute self-observation, that are most likely to attract the modern reader.

Donne's reputation as a poet stood very high in his lifetime; for though he did not allow any of his poems (except the *Anniversaries* and one or two trifles) to be printed, they circulated widely in manuscript. His manner of writing was imitated both by good and by less good poets. An edition of his poems appeared in 1633, within two years of his death: 6 further editions followed before 1670. Of his prose-works, *Pseudo-Martyr, Ignatius his Conclave*, the *Devotions* and a number of sermons were published in his lifetime. After his death, his last sermon (*Deaths Duell*) reached 4 editions, and in 1640 a collection (*LXXX Sermons*) was published, complete with a *Life* of Donne by Izaak Walton. Further collections were issued in 1649 and 1660. *Paradoxes and Problems* were published as *Juvenila* in 1633. *Biathanatos*, which Donne did not want published, was first printed in 1646; *Essays in Divinity* in 1651. Most interesting of all, Donne's son printed a large collection of the poet's letters in 1651 (*Letters to Severall Persons of Honour*) and a further, smaller collection (*A Collection of Letters, Made by Sir Tobie Mathews*) in 1660. There was a fairly abrupt change in taste round about 1660, and Donne went out of fashion. He was not totally forgotten in the 18th century: Pope translated two of his *Satyres* into the idiom of his day; there was an edition of his poems in 1719, and another in 1779; and Dr Johnson wrote about him in his *Life of Cowley*. Donne's poems were available in 8 editions or selections published between 1793 and 1840; Lamb speaks of him approvingly, and Coleridge commented on him. His sermons and some poems were published by Dean Alford in 1839. However, he was very little read until the 1870s, when interest in him gradually began to revive (e.g. Grosart's edition, 1872–3). In the 1890s the revival was in full swing on both sides of the Atlantic, with complete editions of the poems by J. Russell Lowell (1895) and E. K. Chambers (1896), as well as various selections. The publication in 1912 of Grierson's edition at last made Donne's poetry available in a reliable, well-annotated

text; canon and approximate dating were established; and Donne criticism and scholarship were placed on a firm foundation. (The Oxford Standard Authors 1920 edition prints virtually the same text with a new introduction.) A new major edition, by Helen Gardner and W. Milgate (in progress) supplements and in part supersedes Grierson. [TG]

Complete Poetry and Selected Prose, ed. J. Hayward (Nonesuch, 1929); *Paradoxes and Problemes*, ed. R. E. Bennett (1936); *Biathanatos*, ed. J. W. Hebel (1930); *Ignatius His Conclave*, intr. C. M. Coffin (1941) (facsimiles); *A Courtiers Library*, ed. E. M. Simpson (1930); *Paradoxes and Problemes*, ed. G. Keynes (1923); *Essays in Divinity*, ed. E. M. Simpson (1952); *Devotions*, ed. J. Sparrow (1923); *Sermons*, ed. E. M. Simpson and G. R. Potter (10 vols., 1953–62); *Letters to Severall Persons of Honour*, ed. C. E. Merrill (1910).

R. C. Bald, *J.D. A Life* (1970); E. Gosse, *Life and Letters* (1899); E. M. Simpson, *Study of the Prose Works* (2nd edn, much revised, 1948); I. Walton, *Life* (1640, enlarged 1658, 1670, 1675); G. Keynes, *D. Bibliography* (3rd edn, 1958); H. C. Combs and Z. R. Sullens, *Concordance to D.* (1940); M. P. Ramsay, *Les doctrines médiévales chez D.* (2nd edn, 1924); C. M. Coffin, *D. and the New Philosophy* (1937); Ben Jonson, *Conversations with Drummond of Hawthornden*; Thomas Carew, 'Elegie on the Death of Dr D.'; Johnson, *Life of Cowley*; T. S. Eliot, 'The Metaphysical Poets' (1921; in *Selected Essays*, 1932) and 'D. in Our Time' (in *A Garland for J.D.*, 1931); H. Gardner, *J.D.: A Collection of Critical Essays* (1962); J. Bennett, *Five Metaphysical Poets* (1963); J. B. Leishman, *The Monarch of Wit* (1951); L. Martz, *The Poetry of Meditation* (1954); K. W. Gransden, *J.D.* (1954); L. Unger, *The Man in the Name* (1956); A. Stein, *D.'s Lyrics* (1962); J. Webber, *Contrary Music* (1963) (analyses the prose style); W. R. Mueller, *J.D., Preacher* (1962); F. Kermode, *J.D.* (WTW, 1957).

Dorset, Charles Sackville, Lord Buckhurst and later 6th Earl of (1638–1706). Wit and poet. One of the dissolute group of Restoration courtiers which included ◊ Sedley. He was a patron of writers and was praised for his poetry by Dryden and Prior. His poems are chiefly personal satires, and some pleasant songs (among the latter is the famous ballad, 'To All You Ladies now at Land'). [AR]

Collected Poems (1714; 1718) (with Rochester and Roscommon); R. Anderson, *The Poets of Great Britain* (1793 ff.); *The Works of the English Poets*, ed. A. Chalmers, viii (21 vols., 1810).

155

B. Harris, *S.: Patron and Poet* (Illinois U.P., 1940); Johnson, *Lives of the Poets.*

Doughty, C(harles) M(ontagu) (1843-1926). Explorer, travel-writer and poet. Born at Theberton Hall, Suffolk, the son of a clergyman. He failed the medical examination for entry to the navy, and went to Caius College, Cambridge, where he studied geology, but was chiefly interested in the poetry of Chaucer and Spenser and English philology. In 1870, as 'God's wanderer, who not looking back to his worldly interest, betakes himself to the contemplative life's pilgrimage', he went to North Africa, Syria and Arabia. In 1835-6 he learned Arabic and for the next two years made the pilgrimage from Damascus to Mecca and lived among the Bedouin. He wrote this up during the next ten years in his famous *Travels in Arabia Deserta* (2 vols., 1888; 2 vols., intr. T. E. Lawrence, 1921; abridged as *Wanderings in Arabia* by Edward Garnett, 2 vols., 1908; selections by Garnett published as *Passages from Arabia Deserta*, 1931). The appearance of T. E. Lawrence in the history of this book is no accident. Doughty is the greatest exponent of the peculiarly English practical and philosophical admiration for the bleak country of the Arabs and for their special way of life. His writing, which is a complex mixture of archaism, dialect lore, arabisms and philological virtuosity, has been the subject of a Doughty cult. To his difficult language, he added a queer kind of metaphysical questing. This is more strongly marked in his poetry, which he considered his principal work. Chief among this is *The Dawn in Britain* (6 vols., 1906; *Selected Passages*, ed. B. Fairley, 1935), a 30,000-line epic with an allegorical-mystical-patriotic message. Other poems are *Adam Cast Forth: A Sacred Drama* (1908), *The Cliffs* (1909), and *The Clouds* (1912), written to arouse England against Germany. His last poem was *Mansoul, or The Riddle of the World* (1920; revised 1923). These poems have had a few enthusiastic admirers. He was a Doctor of Letters of Oxford and Cambridge. [A R]

B. Fairley, *C.M.D.: A Critical Study* (1927); A. Treneer, *C.M.D.: A Study of His Prose and Verse* (1935) (with bibliography); Sir R. Storrs, 'D. and T. E. Lawrence', *Listener* (25 December 1947); J. Holloway, 'Poetry and Plain Language: The Verse of D.', *Essays in Criticism*, iv (1954); J. Bishop, 'The Heroic Ideal in D.'s Arabia Deserta', *M L Q*, 21 (1960); T. J. Assad, *Three Victorian Travellers: Burton, Blunt, D.* (1964).

Douglas, Lord Alfred Bruce (1870-1945). Poet. Born at Ham Hill, near Worcester, the son of the Marquis of Queensberry, he was educated at Winchester and Magdalen College, Oxford. In 1891, he met Oscar ◊ Wilde; Queensberry, his father, objecting to the association, accused Wilde of homosexual practices. Wilde had to sue for libel, lost, and as a result of the trial was successfully prosecuted by the police. Douglas edited the *Academy* (1907-10). His best poetry is found in his sonnets; he also tried his hand at satire and nonsense. His first book of *Poems* (in English and French) appeared in Paris in 1896; *The City of the Soul* appeared in 1899; *Sonnets* in 1909 and *In Excelsis* (a sonnet sequence) in 1924. [A R]

Complete Poems, Including the Light Verse (1928); *Lord A.D.* (Augustan Books of Modern Poetry, 1926) (selection).
P. Braybrook, *Lord A.D., His Life and Work* (1931); M. C. Stopes, *Lord A.D.: His Poetry and Personality* (1949); R. Croft-Cooke, *Bosie* (1963).

Douglas, Gavin (1475?-1522). Scottish poet. His rhymed-couplet version of the *Aeneid*, completed in 1513, is the most sustained poetic achievement in Scots and the first actual translation of any major classical poem into an 'English' language. A son of the Earl of Angus, Douglas studied for the Church at St Andrews University (1490-94) and perhaps at Paris; from 1501 he was Provost of St Giles' Cathedral in Edinburgh. After 1513 he plunged into the political intrigue and dynastic feuds that followed the death of James IV at Flodden; he became Bishop of Dunkeld in 1515 but enemies made it difficult for him to take possession of his see, and after the overthrow of the Douglases in 1521 he died in exile in London.

Douglas stands squarely between the Middle Ages and the Renaissance. *The Palice of Honour* (c. 1501) uses the old convention of courtly love allegory to treat typically Renaissance matters – statecraft and the conduct of a courtier; its extraordinarily difficult form (stanzas of 9 lines, all rhyming on only two sounds) displays Douglas's technical virtuosity, and he solves some of his difficulties by freely introducing foreign words and coining new ones. Having extended the range of his native language in this original poem, he goes on in his translation to vindicate it as a medium capable of rendering classical epic; he is the first writer to call the language 'Scots' (as distinct from English) rather than 'English' (as distinct from the Gaelic of the Highlanders). In his Prologue to Book I of Virgil's poem, Douglas scornfully attacks ◊ Caxton's rendering (derived from a French summary) of part of the *Aeneid* as a prose romance; he declares his respect for Virgil and for the original text, whose *meaning* he promises to render (not necessarily word for word) as accurately as the limitations of his native language will allow him. Douglas honestly carried out this intention, yet the finished work is largely medieval both in intellectual procedure and in sensibility. Douglas retains the spurious Book XIII, and in his pursuit of clarity he interweaves passages from the (humanist) commentary of Ascenius as though they were parts of the original. The detail of the poem is rendered into contemporary and local terms; ships sink 'among blind crags', the roadstead at Tenedos is 'but a firth in the sea flood', Dido lives in a 'castle'. This effect is not really dispelled by the reminder (true though it is) that Douglas's Scots was a courtly language, less homely than it now seems; the 'medieval' ingenuousness extends into incident and characterization as well. The tension between Douglas's Scots and the Latin of his original is by no means entirely a handicap; he avoids the rhetoric of Surrey and the self-conscious decorum of Dryden's version, and his freedom from the explicit post-humanist 'classicism' allows him really to confront the foreign poem without preconceptions and to re-create it in terms of his own sensibility and language. The prologues prefixed to each book (some in rhyme royal and alliterative verse, instead of couplets) now moralize on the action in a medieval manner, now draw out symbolic interpretations or discuss the theory of translation in a typically humanist way. Three of them describe the seasons; again, the range of Douglas's sensibility is apparent, for Spring (Prologue XII) is a fairly traditional 'May morning', Summer (XIII) an elegiac and classicized June evening, and Winter (VII) a naked and sustained evocation of Scottish scenery rendered with a directness that did not reappear until Thomson's *Winter* two hundred years later. The traditional moral allegory *King Hart*, sometimes printed as Douglas's, is no longer confidently attributed to him. [AI]

Poetical Works, ed. J. Small (1874); *Virgil's Aeneid Translated into Scottish Verse*, ed. D. F. C. Coldwell (STS, 1957–64); *Shorter Poems of G.D.*, ed. P. J. Bawcutt (STS, 1967); *G.D.: A Selection* ed. S. G. Smith (1959); *Selections from G.D.*, ed. D. F. C. Coldwell (1964).
L. M. Watt, *D.'s Aeneid* (1920); C. S. Lewis, *English Literature in the Sixteenth Century* (1954); E. Pound, *The A B C of Reading* (1934).

Douglas, George (pseud. of George Douglas Brown) (1869–1902). Scottish novelist. The illegitimate son of an Ayrshire farmer, he won a bursary to Glasgow University, where he was befriended by Gilbert ◊ Murray and took a first in Classics; proceeding to Balliol as an exhibitioner he nursed his dying mother instead of working for Finals, and so got a third-class degree. Debarred from an academic career, he settled in London and lived by writing magazine fiction and boys' books until the success of *The House with the Green Shutters* (1901). He died suddenly of pneumonia leaving other novels and stories in draft.

The title of Brown's novel is a phrase from Balzac, although he emphasizes his debt to Turgenev. Brown's mordant rendering of the malicious gossip and the brutal futility of life in the small Scots town of Barbie shattered the cosy ◊ 'Kailyard' picture of Scotland made current during the nineties by 'the sentimental slop of ◊ Barrie and ◊ Crockett and ◊ Watson ('Maclaren')', as Brown put it. Brown later thought that this polemic aim had distorted his book, distracting attention from its central theme of tragedy in family life – the discovery by Gourlay, the domineering cock-of-the-village who built the symbolic 'House', that his conduct in his years of success had made his wife and children too feeble to give him any support when, his carrier's business collapsing in face of competition from the railways and from cleverer men whose hatred he had courted, he sought in them ultimate justification for his pride. The novel moves out of Barbie to include a vivid account of the Scottish university from which Gourlay's son, a reluctant student, returns home in disgrace to precipitate the Strindbergian climax. [AI]

J. Veitch, *G.D.B.* (1952).

Douglas, Keith Castellain (1920–44). Poet. Born in Tunbridge Wells and educated, on scholarships, at Christ's Hospital and Oxford. His first published poem appeared when he was 16, and at Oxford he took an active part in the literary life there until the outbreak of war cut short his time as a student. By 1941 he was serving as a tank commander in North Africa, where many of his mature poems were written; his experience of desert fighting is recorded in *Alamein to Zem-Zem* (1946). By 1944 he was back in Britain, preparing for the D-Day landings, and he was killed in Normandy on his third day there, in June 1944. His *Collected Poems* was first published in 1951, but his reputation remained that of a war-poet until the 1960s, when Ted Hughes edited *Selected Poems* (1964) and Douglas's importance as a poet became established. His early work is accomplished but immature. War brought a greater candour and urgency to his poetry, especially in his recurrent image of death; perhaps his best poem is 'Simplify me when I'm dead' in which the vision, detached and powerful, is of his own death. [JM]

Douglas, (George) Norman (1868–1952). Novelist and essayist. Born in Falkenhorst, Austria, of a Scottish father and a Scottish-German mother, he was educated at Uppingham and Karlsruhe. He joined the Foreign Office and served in St Petersburg from 1894 to 1896 before going to live in Italy, where he eventually settled in Capri. He was bilingual in German and English. In 1901 he published *Unprofessional Tales*, a volume of short stories written in collaboration with his wife, under the joint pseudonym of 'Normyx'; but his first important published work was *Siren Land* (1911), an account of his travels in Southern Italy. *Old Calabria* (1915) is often regarded as Douglas's masterpiece. It is a unique and stylishly written compound of travel book, history, philosophy and autobiography. His classical erudition, engagingly cheerful pagan outlook and his limpidity of style have caused these and his other travel books such as *Fountains in the Sand* (1912), *Alone* (1921) and *Together* (1923) to obscure his individual virtues as a novelist, although his best-known work is the novel *South Wind* (1917).

Douglas is said to have concocted *South Wind* in order to give the public what he thought it wanted, and to have deliberately included in the book all the known sins as well as some previously unknown ones. Though hardly likely to shock the reader today, *South Wind* remains an entertaining account of the flora and fauna of Capri before the days of mass tourism, and of the liberating effects of southern temperament and temperature upon Anglo-Saxon puritanism.

Douglas's other novels, like *South Wind*, are serious in intent: serious in their propagation of the hedonistic enjoyment of life. *They Went* (1920) and *In the Beginning* (1928) did not, however, achieve the success of *South Wind*. As a novelist, Douglas was concerned to give expression to his ideas about life. Consequently, characterization is not his strong point. Yet his personality pervades the novels as surely as it does the travel books. He was the prototype of the Englishman infatuated with Italy, and can almost be considered the founder of the modern Anglo-Italian colony. [CO]

How About Europe? (1929); *Looking Back* (1933); *Late Harvest* (1946).
H. M. Tomlinson, *N.D.* (1931); I. Greenlees, *N.D.* (1957); R. M. Dawkins, *N.D.* (1933); N. Cunard, *Grand Man* (1954).

Dowden, Edward (1843–1913). Scholar and critic. Born in Cork, the son of a landowner and merchant, he was educated at Queen's College, Cork, and at Trinity College, Dublin, where in 1867, four years after he graduated, he was appointed to the new chair of English; he remained there until his death. Dowden edited several of Shakespeare's plays, and is now remembered for his once influential Shakespeare criticism, particularly *Shakespeare: His Mind and Art* (1875). He is a representative of the 19th-century 'psychologizing' school of critics, who saw literary works as biographical records of their authors' feelings and judgements and sought to interpret them by establishing the temperament of the writers. He also published several other volumes of essays and studies covering a wide range, as well as a rather unsuccessful *Life of Shelley* (1886). The 'sages', Wordsworth, Browning and Whitman, fascinated him. He wrote several volumes of verse. *Letters of E. Dowden and His Correspondents* (ed. E. D. and H. M. Dowden, 1914) is an interesting record of his life: he was an anti-nationalist. [AR]

Dowson, Ernest (Christopher) (1867–1900). Poet. Born in Kent but partly educated in France, where (in Paris and Dieppe) he passed much of his life; he was associated with the writers of the 'decadence' and was much influenced by Verlaine and Swinburne. His poetry is narrow in scope and technically expert, dealing with renunciation of the 'world', hopeless love, and death. Before moving to France in 1894 he was an active member of the Rhymer's Club, together with Lionel ⟡ Johnson, W. B. Yeats and others of what Yeats called 'the tragic generation'. His brief life, ended by poverty, drink and consumption, was in tune with this aestheticism. His best-known piece is the touching and passionate *Non sum qualis eram bonae sub regno Cynarae*: Cynara was according to Yeats the daughter of the keeper of an Italian eating house in London. Dowson contributed to Beardsley and Symons's *The Savoy* (1896), to *The Books of the Rhymers' Club* (1892 and 1894) and published several books of verse. *Dilemmas* (1893), *Verses* (1896) and *Poems* (posthumous, 1905). He also wrote essays, and a poetic drama, *The Pierrot of the Minute* (1897). [A R]

Poems, ed. J. M. Longaker (Philadelphia, 1962; revised 1968); *Poetical Works*, ed. D. Flower (1934; reissued 1967); *Stories*, ed. J. M. Longaker (Philadelphia, 1947); *Letters*, ed. D. Flower and H. Maas (1967).

J. M. Longaker, *E.D.* (Philadelphia, 1945); T. B. Swann, *E.D.* (New York, 1965); W. B. Yeats, *The Trembling of the Veil* (1927).

Doyle, Sir Arthur Conan (1859–1930). Novelist and controversialist. Born in Edinburgh, the son of a Civil Servant, he was educated by the Jesuits (though later leaving the Catholic Church) at Stonyhurst and for a year in Austria; he studied medicine at Edinburgh, graduating as an M.D. in 1885. Conan Doyle practised in Southsea, and to supplement his small income wrote a detective story, *A Study in Scarlet* (1887). This, not otherwise remarkable, forms the first appearance of Sherlock Holmes, the creation that earned him wide fame. He wrote several other novels and tales of adventure, for which brief periods of practice at sea gave him material; these included *The Sign of Four* (1890), another Holmes adventure. Starting in July 1891 with 'A Scandal in Bohemia', Conan Doyle contributed Sherlock Holmes stories regularly to the *Strand Magazine*. In December 1893, he killed off Holmes (together with the arch-criminal Professor Moriarty) in an Austrian drama. The stories were collected as *The Adventures of Sherlock Holmes* (1892) and *Memoirs of Sherlock Holmes* (1894). A longer story, *The Hound of the Baskervilles* (1902), first appeared as a serial in the *Strand*, after popular demand had forced Conan Doyle to announce that Holmes had escaped destruction in the mountain crevasse. A second series of stories appeared in the magazine from August 1901 to April 1902, and was collected as *The Return of Sherlock Holmes* (1905). Conan Doyle admired the ingenious detective stories of Émile Gaboriau (who was also read by Stevenson), and drew on his memories of Dr Joseph Bell and his teachers at Edinburgh, to create his famous practitioner of deductive 'methods' and 'scientific' collector and user of information. The provision of a worthy, experienced, but slow-thinking medical friend, Dr Watson, was a stroke of genius in constructing a narrative formula. The popularity of the incisive and successful detective is understandable, but the cult of Sherlock Holmes (a club in London, the Baker Street Irregulars in New York, the pseudo-scholarly papers and so on) presents an interesting problem in the sociology of literature.

Conan Doyle writes clearly; his narrative is also clear; his stories convey a wonderfully stylized late-Victorian world, which attracts nostalgia, and has proved its possibilities in film and television; Holmes's omniscience, both social and scientific, is also very soothing. Conan Doyle wrote romances and historical novels (which he valued highly) after the manner of Stevenson, Rider Haggard and Quiller-Couch, and also employed another useful stereotype, the eccentric but physically powerful scientist-explorer, Professor Challenger, in early 'science fiction' such as *The Lost World* (1912) and *The Poison Belt* (1913). Professor Challenger (and Sherlock Holmes) or their surrogates still live in comic strip art. Conan Doyle wrote on a number of imperial and political topics of his day; he was knighted in 1902 for his defence of British policy in the South African war (*The Great Boer War*, 1900, and *The War in South Africa: Its Cause and Conduct*, 1902). He wrote *The British Campaign in Flanders* (6 vols., 1916–19), and after the death of his son, as the result of a wound in the First World War, he became a spiritualist, and his later work, books, lectures and even fiction, is concerned with this (see *The Wanderings of a Spiritualist*, 1921, and *The History of Spiritualism*, 2 vols., 1926). [AR]

Collected Poems (1922); *Historical Romances* (2 vols., 1931-2); *The Annotated Sherlock Holmes*, ed. and intr. W. S. Baring-Gould (1968) (with bibliography).
J. D. Carr, *The Life of Sir A.C.D.* (1949); Hesketh Pearson, *C.D.: His Life and Art* (1943; revised 1961); A. Conan Doyle, *The True C.D.* (1945); P. Nordon, *C.D.* (tr. from French, 1966) (bibliography).

Drayton, Michael (1563–1631). Poet and man of letters. Born in Hartshill, Warwickshire, Drayton seems to have received the normal Elizabethan grammar school education, possibly in the school at Coventry. There is other evidence that he was a page in the service of Henry, later Sir Henry, Goodere of Polesworth in Warwickshire, a friend of Sidney's, and that his master was responsible for his education. Much of Drayton's life was intimately bound up with the Goodere family, and his early love for Sir Henry's youngest daughter, Anne, later wife of Sir Henry Rainsford, was recorded, for instance, in the sonnets which appeared in 1594 under the title *Idea's Mirror*. It was a love which lasted his whole life, and he never married. Sir Henry Goodere died in 1595 and, in Drayton's words, 'bequeathed' him to Lucy Harington, Countess of Bedford, so that she should continue to foster and protect his Muse, that otherwise 'had been by his death left a poor orphan to the world'. In 1602, Drayton acquired a new patron, Walter, later Sir Walter, Aston and we may date from this time an estrangement from the Countess of Bedford. He had many other patrons, in the early years and later, and it is clear that he relied very much upon them. So, not surprisingly, Drayton was one of those who in 1603 addressed congratulatory poems to the new King, in the hope of royal patronage. His hope was disappointed, and he remained outside the circle of poets, such as Jonson and Donne, who enjoyed the court favour and the friendship of the Countess of Bedford. An Elizabethan long after the death of Elizabeth, Drayton lived on until 1631.

Forty years earlier, he had made a late start as a poet with *The Harmony of the Church* (1591), an uninspired collection of verse paraphrases of scripture. In 1593 there appeared *Idea, The Shepherd's Garland*, a collection of pastoral poems in imitation of Spenser. The sonnet sequence *Idea's Mirror*, like the previous work, had Anne Goodere as its inspiration. Like much of his other work, the sonnets were continually revised, and his best sonnet, 'Since there's no help, come let us kiss and part', appeared first in the final revision of what was by then the sonnet sequence *Idea*, in 1519. *Endimion and Phoebe* (1595), a narrative treatment of the classical myth, recast in 1606 as *The Man in the Moon*, was probably written on the occasion of the marriage of the Countess of Bedford. *Mortimeriados* (1596) was one of Drayton's many attempts at historical poetry. Written in rhyme royal, it was recast into *ottava rima*, lengthened and divided into 6 cantos, to re-appear in 1603 as *The Barons' Wars*. Other historical poems of this period were the 4 legends, cast in the *Mirror for Magistrates* mould, *Peirs Gaveston* (1593), *Matilda* (1594), *The Tragical Legend of Robert, Duke of Normandy* (1596) and *The Legend of Great Cromwell* (1607), the first 3 of these much revised when they re-appeared in 1619. *England's Heroical Epistles* (1597), the most popular of Drayton's works with his contemporaries, consisted of a series of love letters passing between famous pairs of English lovers, and was clearly modelled upon Ovid's *Heroides*. From 1597, he worked for the theatrical businessman Philip ◊ Henslowe, producing plays in collaboration with other writers. He wrote periodically for Henslowe until 1602, but of all the plays on which he collaborated only *The First Part of Sir John Oldcastle* (1599) remains. In 1606, there appeared his most famous ode, *To the Virginian Voyage*, and the same year *The Ballad of Agincourt*. The first part of his most ambitious work, *Poly-Olbion* was published in 1612, and the second not until 1622. This enormous poem, much of its information derived from ◊ Camden's *Britannia* (1586), was a topographical and historical description of the wonders of Britain, conceived in the mood of patriotic love and pastoral myth that we associate with Spenser. In his old age, Drayton wrote the kind of poetry that ought to belong to his youth – *Nimphidia*, a cross between Chaucer's *Sir Thopas* and the fairy lore of *A Midsummer Night's Dream* and the most attractive of his poems, and 2 other delightful and still belatedly Elizabethan poems,

The Quest of Cinthia and *The Shepherd's Sirena*, all published together in 1627. *The Muses' Elysium* (1630) was also a delightful compound of Elizabethan pastoral and fairy lore.

Like ◊ Daniel, Drayton was a professional poet, and so more conventional and conservative than such amateur poets as Donne. He turned his hand to almost every kind of poetry and the themes and attitudes of the Elizabethan age were always those that found expression. [DELC]

Works, ed. J. W. Hebel, K. Tillotson and B. H. Newdigate (5 vols., 1931–41); *Poems*, ed. J. Buxton (2 vols., 1953) (selection).
B. H. Newdigate, *M.D. and His Circle* (1941); O. Elton, *M.D.* (1905); M. Praz, 'M.D.', *ES*, XXVIII (1947).

Drinkwater, John (1882–1937). Poet and dramatist. Born at Leytonstone, Essex, Drinkwater went to live with his grandfather in Oxford when his father forsook school-teaching for acting. He attended Oxford High School and in vacations he spent much time with farming relatives in North Oxfordshire, where he acquired a permanent love of rural life. He left school at 15 to work in an insurance office in Nottingham and in 1901 was transferred by the company to Birmingham. He began writing poetry as a relief from office drudgery and also became involved first with amateur acting and eventually with the founding of the Birmingham Repertory Theatre in 1913. In 1910 he left insurance to become manager of Barry Jackson's Pilgrim Players. His *Poems of Men and Hours* appeared in 1911, the year of *Cophetua*, his first of many verse plays, notably the history plays *Abraham Lincoln* (1918), *Mary Stuart* (1921), *Oliver Cromwell* (1921) and *Robert E. Lee* (1923). Drinkwater's friendship with Lascelles ◊ Abercrombie brought him into association with other Georgian poets and he became a contributor to ◊ *Georgian Poetry* as well as a member of the group which produced the short-lived poetry periodical *New Numbers* in 1914. Of some interest in the history of modern verse drama, Drinkwater is a tame and undistinguished Georgian in his non-dramatic verse. He wrote 2 rather reticent volumes of autobiography, *Inheritance* (1931) and *Discovery* (1932), and critical studies of *William Morris* (1912) and *Swinburne* (1913). [DD]

R. H. Ross, *The Georgian Revolt* (Southern Illinois U.P., 1965).

Drummond, William, of Hawthornden (1585–1649). Scottish poet. Educated at Edinburgh University, Drummond visited London and studied law at Bourges and Paris (1607–8) before settling in 1610 on his estate near Edinburgh. There he read and imitated other literature (especially Italian) with equal diligence, and also studied history, genealogy and mechanical invention. Like his seniors ◊ Ayton and ◊ Alexander he wrote in English, and his Italianate poetry is elegant, derivative, and slightly uneasy and lacking in idiom. A melancholy, doubtless connected with his fiancée's premature death in 1615, colours his best sonnets and madrigals (published in *Poems*, 1616) and his chief prose work, *The Cypress Grove, or Philosophical Reflections against the Fear of Death* (1630). His most energetic poem is *Forth Feasting*, which congratulates James I on his visit to Scotland in 1617. Drummond also wrote a history of Scotland from 1423 to 1524 (printed 1655) and a number of Royalist pamphlets. He entertained Ben Jonson at Hawthornden, making notes of their table-talk, and corresponded with Drayton. [AI/MJ]

Poetical Works, ed. L. E. Kastner (STS, 1913); *Conversations of Ben Jonson with W.D.*, ed. R. F. Patterson, 1923 (also in Jonson's *Works*, ed. C. H. Herford and P. and E. Simpson, 1925–52, vol. i).
F. R. Fogle, *A Critical Study of W.D.* (1952).

Dryden, John (1631–1700). Poet, critic and playwright. Born of Puritan stock at Aldwinkle in Northamptonshire, Dryden was educated at Westminster School and while there published in 1649 an elegy 'Upon the Death of Lord Hastings'. In 1654 he took his B.A. degree from Trinity College, Cambridge. In 1658 appeared an elegy on the death of Cromwell, followed two years later by early poems to the King and Sir Robert Howard, whose sister Dryden married in 1663. He was elected to the Royal Society in 1660, but was dropped for non-payment of dues six years later.

Dryden's first play, a comedy called *The Wild Gallant*, appeared in the year of his marriage and marked the beginning of a long and successful theatrical career. Indeed, he was so successful that only four years after this, in 1667, he was able to lend £500 to Charles II, a loan which he renewed

Dryden

when he became Poet Laureate the following year. In this role he is lampooned in the character of Mr Bayes in ◊ Buckingham's *The Rehearsal* (1671–2), a satire of heroic plays, particularly Dryden's *The Conquest of Granada* (1671). In 1670 Dryden was appointed Historiographer Royal with an annual pension of £200. His chronicle poem *Annus Mirabilis* had appeared in 1666, and his *Essay of Dramatic Poesy* in 1668. In 1673–4 he wrote *The State of Innocence*, an opera on the theme of *Paradise Lost*. His best and best-known play, *All for Love*, adapted from Shakespeare's *Antony and Cleopatra*, appeared in 1677. Among his other plays are *Marriage à la Mode* (1673), *Aurangzebe* (1676), a tragi-comedy called *The Spanish Fryar* (1680) and his last play *Love Triumphant* (1693). In 1677 Dryden's pension was increased to £300, but the advantages accruing from this increment were somewhat diminished by the fact that over the next seven years he received only half of it. In 1679, possibly as a result of being suspected of writing Mulgrave's *An Essay on Satire*, which attacks Rochester and two of the King's mistresses, Dryden was beaten up by thugs in Rose Alley, Covent Garden.

Dryden's most famous non-dramatic work, *Absalom and Achitophel*, was published in 1681 and was followed the next year by *The Medal*, an even more direct attack on Shaftesbury. In this year too came the first of Dryden's 2 poems on religion, *Religio Laici*, a somewhat uneasy plea for a 'commonsensical' compromise, based on reverence for biblical and patristic authority and the need for social stability, between the twin excesses of Catholic dogmas of infallibility and Protestant reliance on private judgement. With the accession of James II, Dryden became a Roman Catholic and in 1687 wrote *The Hind and the Panther*, a defence of his new Church. The dethronement of James II in 1688 did nothing to shake his faith and he remained a Catholic to the end of his life, though he was dismissed from both his posts when William III succeeded to the throne. *MacFlecknoe*, a satirical attack on his fellow-poet and playwright Thomas ◊ Shadwell, was Dryden's answer to the latter's *The Medal of John Bayes*, which was itself one of the numerous counterattacks provoked by *The Medal*. Its first, unauthorized, edition appeared in 1682 after the poem had been circulating in manuscript for some time. It attacks Shadwell's

pretensions to be the true heir of Ben Jonson and makes him instead the son of Richard ◊ Flecknoe, the true father of dullness.

Dryden's last years were mainly taken up with translations from the classics, including a collaborative translation of Ovid's *Epistles*. He continued to write plays, but felt increasingly mistrustful of his dramatic talent, or perhaps of his capacity to cater to the new taste in drama. In 1684 he published *Miscellany Poems*, containing satires and translations and the elegy 'To the Memory of Mr Oldham', and the following year *Sylvae, or the Second Part of Poetical Miscellanies*, which included the famous ode 'To the Memory of Anne Killigrew'. His translation of the *Satires of Juvenal and Persius* appeared in 1692, and was followed five years later by his version of *The Works of Vergil*. In the same year Dryden wrote 'Alexander's Feast'. In the year of his death was published his *Fables*, being translations from Chaucer, Boccaccio and Ovid, together with a preface which has become one of Dryden's most celebrated pieces of critical writing. He died on the first of May and is buried in Westminster Abbey.

Both intrinsically and historically, Dryden is the major literary figure of the latter part of the 17th century. He turned his hand to almost all the available varieties of literary expression – non-dramatic verse, heroic tragedy and Restoration comedy, translation and critical essays – and excelled in all of them. Even in the drama, where his claim to distinction is shakiest, he produced, in *All for Love*, the most distinguished example of an all but impossible form, while a comedy such as *Amphitryon* has more wit (albeit of a coarse and unsubtle variety) and dramatic gusto than any but the very best Restoration comedy. As a poet, his historical importance is sufficiently indicated in Johnson's comment in his *Life of Dryden*: 'To him we owe the improvement, perhaps the completion of our metre, the refinement of our language, and much of the correctness of our sentiments.' But Dryden's greatness as a poet does not by any means reside wholly in the fact that he paved the way for Pope, though he did this too. He is Pope's equal, and sometimes his superior, in the public mode of ceremonial celebration and panegyric. Even a comparatively early poem such as 'Annus Mirabilis' illustrates this aspect of Dryden's strength. The ostensible subject of the poem is the

162

Anglo-Dutch naval war and the Fire of London, but its real concern is a triumphant affirmation of the values of Augustan culture in terms of a panegyric on England's commercial greatness, scientific achievement and naval power. His 'Ode on St Cecilia's Day' and 'Alexander's Feast' have perhaps been overrated, though there is no doubt of their sustained, if somewhat flashy, technical virtuosity; but 'To the Memory of Anne Killigrew' is undoubtedly one of the great Augustan poems. *Absalom and Achitophel*, his great satiric masterpiece, transcends the satiric mode; how much is implied in Johnson's phrase 'the refinement of our language' may be seen by comparing this poem to the satire of Marvell, Oldham and Butler. As a poet, what finally needs stressing is the sheer variety of Dryden's achievement, in metrical form, in flexibility of tone, range of diction and choice of theme; he is a much more various poet than the poetic theories of his day would lead one to imagine.

As a critic, Dryden is distinguished by his capacity for lucid generalization but also for the sturdy empiricism which was one result of the fact that his critical writings invariably grew out of his creative concerns. His *Essay of Dramatic Poesy* is perhaps his best-known critical work, and Neander's discussion of Jonson's *The Silent Woman* in this work has some claim to be the earliest sustained specimen of close analytic criticism in the language. Dryden's respect for literary tradition and precedent went hand in hand with a vigorous independence of mind (as his deflation of Shadwell's Jonsonian pretensions, among other things, illustrates), and, both in his criticism and in his creative writing, his classicism is tempered by a rich and warm humanity which reminds us that for the age he lived in one of the key words was 'social'. [GS]

Poetical Works, ed. J. Kinsley (4 vols., 1958); *Essays*, ed. G. Watson (2 vols., 1962); *Plays*, ed. M. Summers (6 vols., Nonesuch, 1931–3); *Letters*, ed. C. Ward (1942); The '*California*' Edition of the Works of J.D., general ed., H. T. Swedenberg, Jr (1956 ff., 2 vols. published so far).
C. E. Ward, *The Life of J.D.* (1961); M. van Doren, *The Poetry of J.D.* (1920; revised edn, 1931); L. Bredvold, *The Intellectual Milieu of J.D.* (1934); T. S. Eliot, *J.D.: The Poet, the Dramatist, the Critic* (1932); H. MacDonald, *J.D.: A Bibliography* (1939); S. H. Monk, *J.D.: A List of Critical Studies – 1895–1948* (1950); J. M. Osborn, *J.D.: Some Biographical Facts and Problems* (1940).

Duffy, Sir Charles Gavan (1816–1903). Irish nationalist journalist. Born in Monaghan, the son of a tradesman, he was self-educated. He was one of the founders (1842) of the nationalist newspaper the *Nation* (◊ Davis, T. O.) and of the group known as 'Young Ireland', who opposed the gradualism of Daniel O'Connell's parliamentary struggle, but were more a group of cultural activists than revolutionaries. After the suppression of the paper in 1849, he went to Victoria, Australia, where he took a leading part in politics, becoming Premier of that state. He started a cheap series of books, *The Library of Ireland*, and published a historically important collection, *Ballad Poetry of Ireland* (1843). [AR]
My Life in Two Hemispheres (1898) (autobiography).

Du Maurier, Daphne (1907–). Novelist. Born in London, the second daughter of the actor Sir Gerald du Maurier (who was in turn the son of George ◊ du Maurier), she was privately educated in Paris, and in 1925 started writing articles and short stories of suspense (a collection of which, *The Apple Tree*, appeared in 1925). Her first novel, *The Loving Spirit*, was published in 1931. In 1932 she married Sir F. A. M. Browning. Her successful novels are romantic tales, often set on the wild coast of Cornwall, where she lives. She has also written interesting, but perhaps less popular, historical fiction. Her books include *Jamaica Inn* (1936); *Rebecca* (1938), her most successful title; *The King's General* (1946); *My Cousin Rachel* (1951), another popular romance; *The Breaking Point* (1959); *Castle Dor* (1962), a continuation of a manuscript left by ◊ Quiller-Couch; and *The Flight of the Falcon* (1965). She has written on the Brontës, as well as several plays, the most successful of which is *The Years Between* (1945). *Gerald: A Portrait* (1934) is a life of her father; and her family is also the subject of *The Du Mauriers* (1937); *The Young George du Maurier* (1951) is a collection of letters. *Vanishing Cornwall* (1967) contains reminiscences. [AR]

Du Maurier, George (Louis Palmella Busson) (1834–96). Illustrator, cartoonist and novelist. Born in Paris, the son of a naturalized Englishman, he was educated in Paris and at University College, London, where he studied chemistry. On his father's death, he studied his real *métier*, art, in

Paris and Antwerp. In 1860, he came to England, and made a living illustrating books and providing periodicals with cuts of famous drawings; in October 1861 he began contributing to *Punch*, in 1864 becoming a permanent member of the staff, though he contributed to other periodicals, chiefly illustrations in the *Cornhill* for stories by Meredith, Hardy and others. He produced satirical drawings in *Punch*, which are of great value to students of the society, fashions and manners of the time. Du Maurier also wrote verse and prose. *Peter Ibbetson*, a fantastic romance about dreams, appeared in the American *Harper's Magazine*, and was published as a book in 1892 (ed. D. du Maurier, 1969); its best parts are excellent descriptions of the Paris of his childhood. In 1894, he began another serial in *Harper's*: this was his most famous work, *Trilby*, again based on his experiences, this time as an art student, with his English companions in romanticized, bohemian Paris. Trilby herself is a variety of the harlot with the heart of gold. The story has a famous supernatural character, the sinister Svengali, exploiting the then popular interest in hypnotism. The book was a best-seller, and was successfully staged at the Haymarket in 1895 by Beerbohm Tree. A last serial, *Martian*, based on his schooldays, started in 1896. [A R]

The Young G.D.M.: A Selection of His Letters, 1860–67, ed. D. du Maurier (1951).
D. P. Whiteley, D.M.: His Life and Work (1948); L. Ormond, G.D.M. (1969).

Dunbar, William (*c*. 1460–*c*. 1520). Scots poet. Dunbar probably took degrees at St Andrews University in 1477 and 1479, and was probably a Franciscan novice, if not a friar. By 1500 he was well enough established at the Scottish court to receive a royal pension, which increased during his subsequent years of literary activity and diplomatic employment until, after the death of James IV at Flodden in 1513, Dunbar's name disappears from the records. (J. W. Baxter's *William Dunbar: A Biographical Study*, 1952, gives reasons for rejecting many additional biographical speculations based on statements in the poems.)

Less profound, serious and humane than Robert ◊ Henryson and always working on a less ambitious scale than Gavin ◊ Douglas, Dunbar is nevertheless more vigorous, diverse and technically accomplished than either. The 80-odd poems which survive in

the manuscript collections of ◊ Bannatyne, ◊ Maitland and others show no obvious line of development, although a few can be dated by external events from 1503, when the courtly allegory 'The Thrissil and the Ros' celebrated the King's marriage to Margaret, daughter of Henry VII of England, to as late as 1517. Dunbar concludes another allegory, 'The Goldyn Targe', by declaring his respect for Chaucer and his direct debt to the 'angel mouthis most mellifluate' of ◊ Gower and ◊ Lydgate. The 5 poems that accompany it in one of the first productions of a Scottish printing-press (*c*. 1508) show that this conventional tribute acknowledges only one of the traditions to which Dunbar had access. 'The Flyting of Dunbar and Kennedy' – a duel of virtuoso scurrility in which Dunbar, from the stance of a civilized metropolitan speaker of English, affects to abuse the literary pretensions of the ragged Celtic peasant Kennedy, who replies in kind – parallels and probably draws upon the Gaelic convention of scolding bardic contests; 'The Testament of Master Andro Kennedy' is a comically blasphemous mingling of Scots and Latin that shows command of the manner of Villon's French imitators, if not of Villon himself; and Dunbar uses liturgical Latin in a quite different spirit when he weaves the refrain *Timor mortis conturbat me* into the serious and moving 'Lament for the Makaris', his dead fellow-poets. 'The Tretis of the Tua Mariit Women and the Wedo' again plays off two traditions against each other; the conversation is set in a courtly garden, but its content – cynical and uninhibited discussion by the three women of the sexual deficiencies of their husbands – is 'folk' material presented through farmyard imagery. This poem, like the many shorter ones that attack the abuses of the law, the corruption of the friars, the pretensions of the lower classes and the stench and squalor of the Edinburgh streets, is in some sense satiric; but Dunbar's grotesque imagery, boisterous dance-rhythms and general extravagance blunt the edge of the satire and convert it to virtuoso comic performance like the 'Flyting'. All Dunbar's work in this vein tends towards, and is summed up in, the lurid and macabre 'Dance of the Sevin Deidly Synnis'. Other short poems present the more intimate humour of life at court through attacks on various officials (and an alchemist), parodies of the rituals of dances and masques, and wry self-mocking appeals to the King for money. Another group, perhaps but not necessarily written in old age, movingly develops the sober moralizing vein of the 'Lament' (although some critics find these poems conventional). A group of religious poems celebrates the Virgin Mary and the events of the Christian year – 'Don is a battell on the dragon blak', a treatment of the Resurrection, is the most immediately attractive of these.

In recent years ◊ MacDiarmid and others have stressed Dunbar's European range, technical boldness and freedom from sentimentality as a corrective to the stereotyped Scottish admiration for Burns. [A I]

Poems. ed. J. Small and W. Gregory (STS, 3 vols., 1884–9); ed. W. M. Mackenzie (1932, 1961). J. Kinsley, *Scottish Poetry* (1955); J. Speirs, *The Scots Literary Tradition* (1940); K. Wittig, *The Scottish Tradition in Literature* (1958); C. S. Lewis, *English Literature in the Sixteenth Century* (1954); E. Morgan, 'D. and the Language of Poetry', in *Essays in Criticism*, ii (1952); T. Scott, *D.* (1966).

Dunsany, Lord (Edward John Moreton Drax Plunkett) (1878–1957). Irish dramatist and short-story writer. Born in London of an Irish family, son of the 17th Baron Dunsany, Dunsany was educated at Cheam, Eton and Sandhurst and succeeded to the baronetcy in 1899. He served with the Coldstream Guards in the Boer War and with the Royal Iniskilling Fusiliers in the First World War. His first published book was *The Gods of Pegana* (1905), in which he invented his own idiosyncratic mythology. This was followed by *Time and the Gods* (1906), *Fifty-One Tales* (1915), *Travel Tales of Mr Joseph Jorkens* (1931), *The Curse of the Wise Woman* (1933) and many other volumes of short stories which possess the qualities of folk or fairy tales. They are brief, simple, occasionally evoking an indefinable atmosphere of menacing power, and written in an easy, fluent style. His first play, *The Glittering Gate* (1909), was written, at Yeats's request, for the Abbey Theatre, Dublin. A characteristically bizarre work, it treats of two burglars trying to get into Heaven, in a manner that at times anticipates the later 'absurd' school of dramatists. Other plays include *King Argimenes and the Unknown Warrior* (1911), *The Gods of the Mountain* (1911), *The Golden Doom* (1912) and *The Lost Silk Hat* (1913), published

together as *Five Plays* (1914). In complete contrast to the dream world he created in his books, Dunsany was ferociously aristocratic, a big-game hunter, cricketer, crack pistol shot and a master at chess. He also published *Fifty Poems* (1929) and a volume of autobiography, *Patches of Sunlight* (1938). [PJK]

E. Bierstadt, *D. the Dramatist* (Boston, 1917); Hazel G. Littlefield. *Lord D., King of Dreams* (New York, 1959); G. B. Saul, 'Strange Gods and Far Places: The Short Stories of Lord D.', *Arizona Quarterly*, XIX, 19 (1963).

D'Urfey, Thomas (Tom Durfey) (1653–1723). Dramatist and song writer. Descended from a Huguenot family, he wrote Loyalist satires, 30 plays and some wretched odes, but was one of the most successful (and prolific) song writers of the Restoration period, the 'poet-laureate of the country squires'. He used old tunes and had his words set by contemporary composers such as Purcell. His career is best described in the *ben trovato*: 'The Town may da-da-damn me for a Poet, but they si-si-sing my Songs for all that.' He was a familiar of Charles II and James II, and published an important collection of songs and ballads, *Wit and Mirth, or Pills to Purge Melancholy* (6 vols., 1719–20; ed. C. L. Day, 3 vols., New York, 1959). [AR]

The Songs, ed. C. L. Day (Harvard U.P., 1933). R. Forsythe, *A Study of the Plays of T.D.* (2 vols., Cleveland, Ohio, 1916–17); K. M. Lynch, *PQ*, 9 (1930).

Durrell, Lawrence (George) (1912–   ). Poet and novelist. Born in India, the son of an engineer, and educated at the College of St Joseph, Darjeeling, and St Edmund's School, Canterbury. With his family he lived for some time on the Greek island of Corfu and during and after the war held a number of jobs as a government press officer and attaché in the Levant. He has also been Director of the British Council Institutes in Athens and Cordoba, Argentina. He has published 6 books of poems, including *Private Country* (1943), *Cities, Plains and People* (1946), *The Tree of Idleness* (1955) and *Collected Poems* (1960). His poetry is characterized by elaborate syntax and his inspiration is most often the Mediterranean; he has 'the sad heart of Horace' as he watches the diseased and amoral culture of this region and thinks of the classical values. His writing is sensuous and often

165

concerned with the nature of knowledge and love. He has published a volume of translations, *From Greek Poets* (1946). His first 2 novels, *Pied Piper of Lovers* and *Panic Spring*, appeared in 1935, but with *The Black Book* (1938) he began his individual career as a writer. This book, with its stream of jokes, and lack of plot, has been considered as one instance of the influence of James Joyce. In the personal nature of its association, it is reminiscent of Henry Miller's writing. *Prospero's Cell* (1945) is a story of Corfu, and *Bitter Lemons* (1957), set in Greece, won the Duff Cooper Prize. Durrell's most ambitious work, however, is 'The Alexandria Quartet': *Justine* (1957), *Balthazar* (1958), *Mountolive* (1958) and *Clea* (1960). Durrell has written on the theory of novel-writing, and novel-writing, or art, could be said to be the theme of this work. The narrator of the first 2 volumes, Darley, is himself a novelist, as are two other characters. Copious use is made of journals, letters and other written experience. The world, Alexandria, is again the amoral landscape which appears in his poetry, and the characters often seem to exist as part of that landscape. The shifting points of view (Darley, the narrator of *Justine* and *Balthazar*, is a character in *Mountolive*) and the relativistic treatment of time (only in *Clea* does the action advance in a regular narrative) develop Durrell's view of fiction as presenting layers of reality. This is another Joycean conception, and Durrell has himself linked his novel, in what he thinks of as a new departure, with modern scientific developments. The novel is also about the nature of love, a theme which the Alexandrian setting, ancient, cosmopolitan and amoral, renders complex. Durrell sometimes seems to be implying that sex is itself love, and that sexual experience is the only true knowledge. The writing is elaborate, and is occasionally luscious. The most powerful ideas in the novel are connected with time and the nature of experience, and in this work Durrell deliberately challenges comparison with Proust and Eliot. Other modern writers who have been working along the same lines are Anthony ◊ Powell in his 'Music of Time' series, and C. P. ◊ Snow. Durrell has also published a series of lectures, *A Key to Modern Poetry* (1952). [AR]

Tunc (1968) (novel).
H. T. Moore, *The World of L.D.* (Illinois U.P. 1962, new edn, 1964); F. R. Karl, *The Contemporary English Novel* (New York, 1962); G. S. Fraser, *The Modern Writer and His World* (1964); Walter Allen, *The Modern Novel* (1964); J. E. Unterecker, *L.D.* (Columbia Essays on Modern Writers, 6, 1964); J. A. Weigel, *L.D.* (New York, 1965).

Dutt, Toru (1856–77). Indian poetess. Born in Calcutta. Her father, an influential convert to Christianity, took his daughters, Toru and Aru, to Europe in 1869. At school in Nice they began translating French lyrics into English. After Aru's death Toru published these as *A Sheaf Gleaned in French-Fields* (1875). The Dutts returned to Calcutta in 1873, and Toru and her father studied Sanskrit together. The year after Toru's death her father prepared an English edition of the *Sheaf*, and in 1882 her translations from Sanskrit were published as *Ancient Ballads and Legends of Hindustan*. This extraordinary girl also wrote a novel in French, and an unfinished one in English. Extravagant claims need not be made for her poetry. [PT]

H. Das, *Life and Letters of T.D.* (1921); K. R. Srinivasa Iyengar, *Indian Writing in English* (1962).

Dyer, John (1700–58). Poet and painter. Born in Carmarthenshire and educated at Westminster School, he studied painting with Jonathan Richardson and practised in South Wales as an itinerant painter. About this time he printed the work for which he is famous, *Grongar Hill* (1727), a short descriptive poem in octosyllabics on the valley of the Towy, written with some stylistic uncertainty, but an impressive freshness of observation of the country and a living use of words. The Romantics kept the fame of this poem alive for its content, and it has been several times reprinted (ed. R. C. Boys, Baltimore, 1941). Dyer also wrote 2 long poems, *The Ruins of Rome* (1740), the fruit of a professional visit to Rome, and *The Fleece* (1757), a dullish descriptive-didactic poem about sheep-raising. He was ordained, and died the incumbent of the Lincolnshire villages of Coningsby and Kirkby. [AR]

Poems, ed. E. Thomas (1903); *The Minor Poets of the Eighteenth Century* (Everyman, 1930). Johnson, *Lives of the Poets*; R. M. Williams, 'Thomson and D.: Poet and Painter', in *The Age of Johnson: Essays Presented to C. B. Tinker* (New Haven, 1949).

E

Ealwhine. ◊ Alcuin.

Earle, John (*c.* 1600–65). Bishop and 'character' writer. Born in York, the son of Thomas Earle(s), an ecclesiastical functionary, he was educated at Merton College, Oxford. He wrote poems on various Royalist worthies, and on taking orders was made a Fellow of his college. He became a tutor to Prince Charles, and when the latter became King in exile, Earle was made Clerk of the Closet and a chaplain. At the Restoration he was preferred to the Deanery of Westminster, to the Bishopric of Worcester in 1662, and translated to Salisbury a year later. Earle was a man of toleration and benevolence who sought to mitigate the rigours of the laws concerning dissenters, for example. His famous collection of 'characters', *Micro-cosmographie* ('Description of the Little World'): *or, a Peece of the World Discovered, in Essays and Characters*, appeared in 1628, with 54 'characters'; the fifth edition of 1629 added 23 pieces; a further character was added in 1633 (ed. G. Murphy, 1928; ed. H. Osborne, 1933). The work was anonymous in all of the 12 editions before 1700, but the authorship was well known. Earle is the most interesting, humane and deft of the Theophrastan 'character' writers in English (◊ Hall, Joseph, for a discussion of the genre). Earle has also an excellent touch of original observation of everyday life, and an ironical wit. [AR]

A Book of 'Characters', ed. R. Aldington (1924); D. Nichol Smith, *Characters of the Seventeenth Century* (1918); C. N. Greenough, *A Bibliography of the Theophrastan Character in English* (Harvard U.P., 1947).

Edgeworth, Maria (1767–1849). Novelist. Born in England, the daughter of Richard Edgeworth of Edgeworthstown, Co. Longford. Her father was an 18th-century *amateur* and low-pressure *philosophe*, in whose houses in London, Ireland and France, however, she met a wide variety of people. Aside from acting as stepmother to his various sets of children, she was his assistant in several writing projects, particularly his *Practical Education* (influenced by Rousseau's educational notions). To illustrate this work, under strict parental tutelage (perhaps in the long run fatal to the full development of her own remarkable powers), she first wrote tales: *The Parent's Assistant* (6 vols., 1796), *Early Lessons* (1801, 1814), *Moral Tales for Young People* (1801), etc. She also wrote 2 series of *Tales of Fashionable Life* (1809, 1812); the second contains one of her best short novels, *The Absentee* (Everyman, 1906). This story continues her treatment of Irish life which she started in her first real novel, *Castle Rackrent* (1800; Everyman, 1906) and which made her an innovator. Scott acknowledged that she suggested to him the possibilities of regional manners and community life in fiction. Edgeworth, however, though she knew the whole range of Irish life well through her practical work in managing her father's estates, never identified herself with the natives. She was always the rational, improving, Anglo-Irish observer. This tone spoils her otherwise keenly observed and lively writing. In *Castle Rackrent* she also pioneered another kind of writing, later to become a staple of fiction: the chronicles of a family over some period of time. Maria Edgeworth's third remarkable success is her understanding, and use in her writing, of the economic drives within society. She has suffered by being compared with Jane Austen. She does not have quite the same subtle insights and personal judgements, but Jane Austen (for her own purposes) ignores the acquisition of the income so necessary for life in her world. *Patronage* (1814) deals with political power, and *Ormond* (1817) is also worth reading. Her work is spoiled for some by its 'purposefulness'. [AR]

Tales and Novels (12 vols., 1893).
P. H. Newby, *M.E.* (1950); E. Inglis-Jones, *The Great Maria* (1959).

'Edinburgh Review'. A quarterly, founded in 1802 by Sydney ◊ Smith, with Francis ◊ Jeffrey, Henry ◊ Brougham and the political economist Francis Horner. The first number had so great a success that the survival of the venture was ensured. In 1803 Jeffrey became sole editor, and under him the circulation rose to 7,000 in 1807, to 13,000 in 1812, and to a peak of 14,000 in 1818. The *Edinburgh Review* introduced the principle of selectivity in reviewing, and with the high rates of pay it offered was able to set new standards of professional criticism. The traditions of the Scottish enlightenment, which had survived in clubs in the latter part of the 18th century, were continued in its pages. It was signalled in politics by opposition to the slave trade and to flogging in the army and navy, and by support for Catholic Emancipation (however, James Mill was to charge in the first number of the ◊ *Westminster Review*, in 1824, that the *Edinburgh* was essentially a Whiggish instrument for aristocratic predominance). In literature it was famous for its criticisms – many of them well considered – of the Romantic poets. Despite a decline in quality towards the end of Jeffrey's editorship in 1829, the journal survived for one hundred years more. Except in its last few years, reviews were anonymous. Jeffrey and Brougham were the principal reviewers during the early period; other famous contributors included T. R. Malthus, T. J. Hogg, F. Palgrave, Macaulay, Carlyle, Thomas Arnold, McCulloch, Bulwer, Lytton, Monckton Milnes, and Gladstone. [NL]

W. Graham, *English Literary Periodicals* (1930); J. Clive, *Scotch Reviewers: The Edinburgh Review 1802–1815* (1957); Lord Cockburn, *Memorials of His Time* (1856).

Eliot, George (pseud. of Marian, or Mary Ann, Evans) (1819–80). English novelist. Daughter of a Warwickshire farmer, she spent her early life cut off from cultural activity. She was greatly influenced by a pious and evangelical teacher, who appears in various forms in several of her novels, but her later contact with Charles Bray, the sceptical philosopher, led her to question orthodox beliefs. She completed a translation of Strauss's *Life of Jesus* (1846) and Feuerbach's *Essence of Christianity* (1853). She looked after her father until his death in 1849, and then went to London to become (1850) contributor to and then (1851–3) assistant editor of the *Westminster Review*. In the home of John Chapman, the editor, she met contemporary literary figures, including the philosopher Herbert ◊ Spencer, and George ◊ Lewes, with whom she fell in love. Lewes was already married, but

separated from his wife, and in 1854 she made the decision, not without doubts, to live with him, which she did until his death in 1878. He dedicated himself to helping and encouraging her. In 1880, six months before her own death, she married J. W. Cross, who had long been a friend and admirer.

Marian Evans did not begin to write fiction, although she had been writing articles and reviews, until after she met Lewes. Her first 3 stories, afterwards brought together to form *Scenes of Clerical Life* (1858), were published in *Blackwoods* in 1857 under the name of George Eliot. These were sketches of provincial life in which, although the solidarity of her later novels was lacking, her powerful character drawing and uncannily sensitive ear for conversation were already present. She was recognized at once as a writer of significance. *Adam Bede* (1859) was her first novel proper, and in it rich pastoral, simple dignity, violence and weakness are interwoven with a sure touch and a shrewd understanding of motive. If the theme is constructed from well-worn elements – the seduction by the squire of the innocent country girl, for instance – the treatment is finely balanced and the action is rooted in the realities of daily life. The unhesitant grasp of the texture of life formed by the fusion of commonplace detail and shocking drama counteracts the tendency, to which George Eliot was often prone, to allow one or two of her characters to harden into symbols.

With the publication of *The Mill on the Floss* (1860) George Eliot's concern with the moral problems of personality and human relationships became clearly dominant. The novel is partly based on her own life – the heroine, Maggie Tulliver, and her brother Tom are in many respects Marian and her brother – and there is present at times a note of strained intensity which disturbs the novel's development. But there is a profound understanding in the portrayal of Maggie's childhood, hemmed in by provincial middle-class narrow-mindedness, which has rarely been equalled in English fiction. The second half of the novel, Maggie's relationship with the handsome but shallow Stephen Guest and the death of herself and Tom, is less satisfactory. *Silas Marner* (1861) is a slighter work, though technically almost unflawed. It is constructed around a simple legend-like theme, the story of the change brought about in the life and character of the miserly Silas by a child mysteriously left on his doorstep. There is no great resonance in *Silas Marner*, but the lack of complexity is attractive.

Her next 2 novels, *Romola* (1863) and *Felix Holt the Radical* (1866), were less well worked out. In setting the former in the Florence of Savonarola she relinquished the opportunity to exploit one of her richest veins – the natural speech of midland country and provincial life. *Felix Holt*, though often tense and vigorous, is a little raw and clumsy. The moments of human contact are sensitive, the overall plot unconvincing. Her major achievement, and one of the greatest achievements of English fiction, is *Middlemarch* (1871-2). Here George Eliot presents her richest and most detailed picture of English provincial life and personalities, focused by confrontations of idealism, painstaking materialism and benevolent insensitivity. She presents the social, personal and professional intercourse of her characters on a wide variety of levels, and shows how petty jealousies and major conflicts make up the moral texture of society. Idealist and egotist can be equally blundering, but her characters are never wholly weak or wholly vicious. They learn from their mistakes, even if it is too late to rectify them. Dorothea, her sensitive, idealistic, determined heroine, has a second chance, which itself constitutes the least satisfactory element of the novel. It is her most admirable qualities that lead her into her agonizing marriage with Dr Cassaubon (◊ Pattison, Mark), but, though her second husband, the nebulous Will Ladislaw, is presented as the perfect counterpart of her generosity and dedication, there is no evidence that she finds what she seeks. Yet the portrayal of Dorothea is remarkable in its depth, its delicacy and its gentle but razor-edged humour.

In *Middlemarch* George Eliot drew together all those aspects of life that she knew best. Her final novel, *Daniel Deronda* (1876), clearly seeks new areas of concern. It contains some of the best and worst of her writing. Its two main themes, unsatisfactory in their relation to one another, lead her in different directions. The story of Gwendolyn Harleth, who over-confidently marries for money and security and is desperately unhappy, is as finely handled as anything in her work, but the exotic attractiveness of Daniel himself, and the mystery and melodrama that he brings to the novel, is less surely apprehended. In her attempt to portray Daniel's Zionism and other aspects of Jewish life she is not sufficiently sure of her ground.

George Eliot did not only express her vision of personality and society through fiction. Her articles are on a wide variety of subjects – religion, philosophy, history, in fact all those areas that troubled so many writers in the period. She wrote in a tone of consistent critical inquiry and a confident scepticism. She herself occupied an almost unique position in Victorian society, being a woman with the courage to conduct her life unconventionally while being intensely respected by those who knew her and her work for the clarity and power of her moral comment. Her unpretentious ambition in the choice of material for her fiction widened the horizons of the novel, and her psychological insights influenced the approach to fictional character. She is now considered to be, with Dickens, a key figure in the development of the 19th-century novel. [J R C]

Essays, ed. T. Pinney (1963); *Essays and Leaves from a Notebook*, ed. C. L. Lewes (1884); *Letters*, ed. G. S. Haight (7 vols., 1954-5); *G.E.'s Life, as Related in Her Letters and Journals* ed. J. W. Cross (1885).
G. S. Haight, *G.E.: A Biography* (1968); *G.E.: Her Mind and Her Art* (1948); F. R. Leavis, *The Great Tradition* (1948); Barbara Hardy, *The Novels of G.E.* (1959); W. J. Harvey, *The Art of G.E.* (1961); David Daiches, *G.E.: Middlemarch* (1963); Basil Willey, *Nineteenth Century Stories* (1949) (on E.'s relation to Heppell, Strauss and Feuerbach).

Eliot, T(homas) S(tearns) (1888–1965). Poet, critic, verse dramatist, editor and publishing executive. Eliot came from a business family in St Louis, Missouri, but had strong family connexions with Harvard, Massachusetts, where he received his first university training. At Harvard, the teaching of Irving Babbitt gave his mind a classical, authoritarian and anti-romantic bent, but his main interest was philosophy. He came to Europe intending to complete a dissertation on F. H. ◊ Bradley, the late Victorian neo-Hegelian idealist, and attended the Sorbonne, Merton College, Oxford, and Marburg University in Germany, but his interests had shifted from philosophy to poetry. First drafts of some of his best early poems, like 'The Love Song of J. Alfred Prufrock', were completed while Eliot was still at Harvard, but the style and tone were so new that he did not manage to get anything published (and then through the help of his friend Ezra Pound) till 1915. His first volume, *Prufrock and Other Observations* (1917), was too much unlike the run of English war poems and Georgian poems of country life to attract wide attention outside a discriminating few. Eliot was at this time working in a bank, having previously worked in a school, and also reviewing copiously for *The Times Literary Supplement* and for little magazines like *The Egoist*. His first volume of criticism, *The Sacred Wood* (1920), was quietly influential and his long poem, *The Waste Land* (1922), though it infuriated conservative critics, made him famous. It had been drastically revised and shortened with the help of Ezra Pound. The first draft, together with many unpublished drafts and fragments of early poems, became available to the public in 1968 when the manuscript collections of the New York patron of art and literature, John Quinn, were made available to scholars. The drafts and fragments, however, have still to be edited and published. *The Waste Land* was an evocation of the desiccation of modern civilization by means of a kaleidoscopic use of symbolic imagery and a carefully organized proliferation of references to a variety of myths and literary works, both occidental and oriental; the binding theme was the failure and sterility of the sexual relationship, and the suffering of women, presented against a vividly phantasmagoric London scene. Eliot became a director of the publishing firm Faber and Gwyer (later Faber and Faber) and in the later 1920s became both a British subject and a member of the Anglican Church. For Faber and Faber he edited till the outbreak of the Second World War the ◊ *Criterion*, a quarterly of European literature, and also during the 1930s as a publisher gave much encouragement to young poets at an opposite political and religious pole from himself, ◊ Auden, ◊ MacNeice and ◊ Spender.

Ash Wednesday (1930), a poem of religious self-abnegation, was in some ways Eliot's most personal poem, though the *Four Quartets*, 4 long poems of meditation on the mysterious relationship between time and eternity, were, particularly the last of them, *Little Gidding*, the crown of his achievement. In his religious play, *Murder in the Cathedral* (1935), and in his 4 modern tragi-comedies with religious overtones, *The Family Reunion, The Cocktail Party, The Confidential Clerk* and *The Elder Statesman*, Eliot

reached and held a much wider audience than he had done with his non-dramatic poems at the cost of simplifying his mode of exposition and flattening his language. he believed that the verse of modern drama should be transparent, not drawing attention to itself, and when he wants a deliberately poetic effect in *The Cocktail Party* he has one character quote a long passage from Shelley. His plays with a modern setting drew in plot and structure on classical Greek tragedy but in texture and manner on West End drawing-room comedy. Honours, including the Order of Merit and the Nobel Prize, came thickly upon Eliot in his later years and his death in 1965 was recognized as the end of an era in poetry and criticism over which he had largely presided. Unlike Yeats, his great contemporary, Eliot avoided, except in the religious meditations of *Ash Wednesday* and perhaps in the tone of desperation of *The Hollow Men* (1925), bringing his personal experiences and emotions directly into poetry. Indeed, one of his most important critical tenets was the Flaubertian one of the separation of the man who suffers and the artist who creates. True poetry, he thought, is impersonal, not an expression of the artist's personal feelings. The poet's mind, rather, is a catalyst which causes disparate elements of experience to fuse into new wholes. F. R. ◊ Leavis is one of several critics who have felt that Eliot protested too much about his impersonality and that in spite of his use of the *persona* in his earlier poems the quality of his poetry is a 'heroic sincerity', an actual identity of the man who suffers and the artist who creates.

Certainly, it is possible to see the poems as the record of a spiritual pilgrimage. Eliot's poetic development was broadly one from scepticism, near-despair, a terrible sense of sterility and isolation, to acceptance of Christian belief and affirmation of an often rather bleak and stoical, but also noble and sincere, Christian vision of life. Certainly key images, the suffering woman, spring flowers like hyacinth and lilac, loss and quest, link the earlier poems with the later. Technically, Eliot's great achievement was to create rhythms and images corresponding to the tensions and stresses of modern urban life. Apart from the flowers, nearly always associated with frustrated sexual passion, and the river in *The Waste Land* and the desert there, also, there are few images from nature in his poems up to *Ash*

Wednesday. Like Baudelaire, one of his masters, he is creating the terrible image of the modern city. But after *Ash Wednesday* images especially from his boyhood memories of New England, granite shores, pine trees, sea mists, gulls, the noise of the sea and its salt smell, recur frequently. It was as if Christian belief had rebaptized nature for him. He never, however, lost his love for the London scene, which is as vividly present in the passages about the Underground and the bombing-raids in *Four Quartets* as it is throughout that great London panorama, *The Waste Land.*

Eliot is not a poet with an extraordinarily broad range of interests and sympathies, but he is extraordinarily piercing, deep and compassionate, though the master also occasionally of a Dantesque scorn. The element that will last least well in his poems – at its most ostentatious in *The Waste Land* and in the comparatively unsuccessful poems in Gautierian quatrains which immediately preceded *The Waste Land* – is a compulsive polyglot allusiveness, which is, however, much muted and mitigated in his later work. As a critic, he largely created in academic circles the fashion for the Metaphysicals and the darker Jacobean dramatists, and also wrote magnificently on Pascal, Baudelaire and above all Dante, his chief master in poetry. He invented one or two phrases like 'the objective correlative' and 'a certain dissociation of sensibility' which subsequent critics found extremely suggestive, and was one of the pioneers of the method of making a critical point not by vague generalization but by the exactly pertinent quotation. He had also a gift for sharp attack and a dry sardonic wit. His prose (modelled very much on that of F. H. Bradley) has a Johnsonian weight, with more flexibility of manoeuvre behind it than Dr Johnson possessed, and occasionally with a very un-Johnsonian bland evasiveness. Pound's nickname for Eliot, 'Old Possum', referred to Eliot's circuitous critical tactics, his avoidance of the headlong attack. Both in prose and verse, Eliot is a pregnant and concrete writer, who says things that are concentrated and vivid and might bear indefinite expansion, and who gives the sense of huge powers held in reserve. [G S F]

Collected Poems (1963); *Complete Poems and Plays* (1969).
H. Gardner, *The Art of T.S.E.* (1949); F. R. Leavis, *New Bearings in English Poetry* (re-vised edn, 1950); F. O. Matthiessen, *The Achievement of T. S. E.* (revised C. L. Barber, 1958); Grover Smith, *T.S.E.'s Poetry and Plays: A Study in Sources and Meaning* (revised edn, Chicago, 1960); ed. L. Unger, *T.S.E. A Selected Critique* (New York, 1948); G. Williamson, *A Reader's Guide to T.S.E.* (1955).

Elliot, Jean or **Jane** (1727–1805). Scots poetess. Daughter of a Scottish judge, she wrote to the tune of 'The Flowers of the Forest' the earlier and better set of words – the one beginning 'I've heard the lilting at our yowe-milking' (1756). (◊ Cockburn, Alison.) [A I]

S. Tytler and J. L. Watson, *The Songstresses of Scotland* (1871); *DNB.*

Elliott, Ebenezer (1781–1849). Poet. Known as the 'Corn Law Rhymer', he was born at Masborough in Yorkshire and became an iron-founder in his father's works; later he was his own master. His first poem, *A Vernal Walk* (1801), was in the vein of James ◊ Thomson and the meditative poets of the previous century, as was *Night* (1818), but under the influence of his own life in Sheffield, and the rhetoric of Byron, the early Southey and other Romantics, he became a very successful poet of social protest on behalf of the poor against the Corn Laws, which he saw as the grand national evil. *Corn Law Rhymes* (1831, 3 edns) were fierce, popular poems which had some political effect. *The Village Patriarch* (1829, 1831) is in the vein of ◊ Crabbe at his grimmest and hardest. [A R]

Poetical Works (1840; revised E. Elliott, 2 vols., 1876); T. H. Ward, *English Poets*, 4 (1911).
T. Carlyle, 'Corn Law Rhymes', *Edinburgh Review*, LV (1832; reprinted in his *Critical Essays*, 1839) (review article); 'January Searle' (G. S. Phillips), *The Life of E.E.* (1850, 1852); Asa Briggs, 'E. E., the Corn Law Rhymer', *Cambridge Journal*, III (1950); L. James, *Fiction for the Working Man* (1963) (Appendix 1: 'Working Class Poets and Poetry').

Ellis, George (1753–1815). Satirist and antiquarian. The son of a West Indian planter, he began by publishing some topical satirical pieces, of which *Poetical Tales by Sir Gregory Gander, Knt* (Bath, 1778) was popular. He contributed to the Whig anti-Pitt satires *The Rolliad* (1784, etc.; collected 1791). Thereafter he was one of the founders of, and satirical contributor to, the Tory, pro-Pitt newspaper *The Anti-Jacobin* (1791-8) (◊ Frere, J. H.). He is also remembered for his influential antiquarian studies. He was a friend of Sir Walter Scott's, who dedicated the fifth canto of *Marmion* to him. Ellis also wrote a *History of the Late Revolution in the Dutch Republic* (1789), with which he was personally familiar. [A R]

Specimens of Early English Poets (1790; enlarged 1801; 3 vols., 1803); *Specimens of Early English Metrical Romances* (3 vols., 1805; ed. J. O. Halliwell-Phillipps, 1847).

Elyot, Sir Thomas (*c.* 1490–1546). Prose writer, diplomat and scholar. The only son of a famous jurist, he learned Latin and Greek at home, was the pupil of Sir Thomas ◊ More and probably of Thomas ◊ Linacre, and entered the Middle Temple in 1510. He was made Clerk of the Privy Council by Cardinal Wolsey in 1523, was knighted in 1530, and later served in Parliament and as Sheriff of Cambridgeshire. A man of learning and of practical affairs, he played a full part in making the Humanist inheritance accessible in English. *The Boke Named the Governor* was published in 1531, dedicated to King Henry VIII (who made the author ambassador to the Emperor Charles V), and was 7 times reprinted by 1580 (ed. H. H. S. Croft, 2 vols., 1880). The book's aim was the complete training of a gentleman of the governing class in leadership and responsibility according to classical precedents. He also wrote a health manual, *The Castle of Health*, and a series of platonic dialogues, *Of the Knowledge Which Maketh a Wise Man*. He translated works by Isocrates, Plutarch and Pico della Mirandola, amongst others. *The Dictionary of Sir Thomas Elyot* (1538), also dedicated to the King, gave an English vernacular equivalent for each Latin word included, and, along with Elyot's own mastery of English prose, this work helped to establish his native tongue as the language of learned and practical discourse. [M J]

S. E. Lehmberg, *Sir T.E., Tudor Humanist* (Austin, Texas, 1959); C. S. Lewis, *English Literature of the Sixteenth Century* (1954).

Empson, William (1906–   ). Poet and critic. Empson made his earlier reputation mainly as a critic but from about 1953 on his poetry exercised a strong technical influence on the group of young poets known as 'the Movement'. Born in Yorkshire, of a squire's family, he went to Winchester and Cambridge, where he studied both mathematics and literature, and came under the influence of I. A. ◊ Richards, who supervised the dissertation which turned into Empson's first critical book, *Seven Types of Ambiguity* (1930). The theme of this book – brilliantly if sometimes erratically illustrated by detailed quotation – was that many striking effects in poetry come from conscious or unconscious double meanings, that reflect tensions or confusions in the poet's mind. Empson's first volume of *Poems* (1935), much influenced in tone and technique by his favourite poet, John Donne, deliberately exploited as many ambiguities as possible, and had prose notes to work out the poet's riddles. His second volume, *The Gathering Storm*, which came out in 1940, was written in a clearer style, owing something to Rochester and Dryden, and was concerned to inculcate a tough but realistic attitude to the menace of Fascism and the coming of the Second World War. Empson wrote only a handful of new poems after 1940, though his *Collected Poems* did not come out till 1955. Some of the poems in *The Gathering Storm* draw vividly on his experiences of Japan and China, in both of which countries he had been teaching during the 1930s. He worked on Far Eastern broadcasting for the B.B.C. during the Second World War, returned to teach in Peking for some years afterwards, and since 1953 has been Professor of English Literature at Sheffield.

Empson's second volume of criticism, *Some Versions of Pastoral* (1935), pursued the idea of ambiguity through larger-scale literary structures, like the double plot in Elizabethan tragedies, the use of classical imagery in Milton's Christian epic *Paradise Lost*, burlesque and fantasy. His third critical volume, *The Structure of Complex Words* (1951), was a more technical study of how the social use of words like 'native' and 'honest' can give them a derogatory tone which does not seem to be implied in their sense. More recently, Empson has written appreciative articles on writers including Shakespeare, Fielding and Joyce, and has become much concerned with what he regards as the latent cruelty and wickedness of the Christian moral and theological tradition. This was one main thread running through his vivid and powerful study of *Paradise Lost: Milton's God* (1961).

Few writers of our time with so comparatively small an output have had such a large effect on both poetic and critical practice, and the reading of Empson tends to be a crucial stage in the development of any young poet or critic of poetry: though as time goes on this enthusiasm may cool. The criticism is weakened, though not fatally, by over-ingenuity and a carelessness about accurate quotation; the poetry sometimes blinds both reader and poet with its own fireworks; and Empson's range of human sympathy, though not of intellectual curiosity, both in his criticism and poetry is narrow. He also tends, as in his recent concern with Christianity, to become an obsessional writer. He remains a seminal figure of very great importance, from whom, for instance, very much in the American 'New Criticism' derives. [G S F]

The Review (1964) (special Empson issue); G. S. Fraser, *Vision and Rhetoric* (1959); G. S. Fraser, *The Modern Writer and His World* (revised edn, 1964).

'England's Helicon'. One of 3 miscellanies published in 1600, the others being *England's Parnassus* and *Belvedere*. It is a magnificent anthology of Elizabethan lyric poetry containing, among others, works by Shakespeare, Sidney, Drayton, Spenser and Lodge. It succeeded ◊ Tottel's *Miscellany* (1557) and a comparison of the 2 works reveals the brilliant development of English poetry during the last quarter of the 16th century. The *Helicon* includes poems signed 'Ignoto' which are attributed to Sir Walter Ralegh and also contains examples of the curious pastoral fantasies of Richard ◊ Barnfield. Neither the anthologist nor the owner of the initials L.N., to whom the book is dedicated, is known. Many of the poems have been taken from the song-books of Byrd, Morley and Dowland. The sureness behind the choice and the splendour of what has been chosen make *England's Helicon* one of the finest of anthologies. [R B]

Ed. H. MacDonald (1949).

Enright, D(ennis) J(oseph) (1920–). Poet, novelist and critic. Born at Leamington and educated at Leamington College and Downing College, Cambridge. He taught English at the University of Alexandria (1947–50) and has also held chairs at Konan in Japan, Berlin and Bangkok. He was until recently Professor of English in the University of Singapore. He has been publishing poems since the early 1950s; his collections are *The Laughing Hyena* (1953), *Bread Rather Than Blossoms* (1956), *Some*

Men are Brothers (1960) and *Addictions* (1962). In his 'unsentimental impressions of sentimentalized places' such as Japan, Egypt and the Mediterranean, the tone of his poems has been compared to that of Kingsley ◊ Amis, but he is more 'committed', more resiliently tough, underneath his controversial, sometimes flippant, writing. In his novels, too, the same flexible comic judgement is found (*Academic Year*, 1955; *Heaven Knows Where*, 1957; *Insufficient Poppy*, 1960). He is well known as a witty literary journalist; *The Apothecary's Shop* (1957) and *Conspirators and Poets* (1966) are collections of critical essays. [A R]

Memoirs of a Mendicant Professor (1969) (autobiography).

Ervine, St John (1883–). Dramatist, novelist, biographer and dramatic critic. Born in Belfast, he had several plays produced and 2 novels published before the First World War, in which he was seriously wounded. He had also worked briefly as manager of the Abbey Theatre, Dublin, and had contributed a political biography, *Sir Edward Carson and the Ulster Movement* (1915), to the important series 'Irishmen of Today'. When the Irish Academy was created in 1932 he became with AE, Shaw, Yeats and others one of the first members. His long career has been that of an all-round man-of-letters, but he is best known as a dramatist.

His early plays were influential, socially realistic 'problem dramas': *Mixed Marriage* (1911) dealt with the bitterness between Catholics and Protestants in Ulster, and *Jane Clegg* (1913) suggested that a woman should not suffer to preserve an unhappy marriage. *John Ferguson* (1915) chronicled the struggles of a middle-class hero to cope with family misfortunes. The plays were staged by such pioneering groups as Miss Horniman's Gaiety Theatre, Manchester, and are linked with the Mancunian realists. Ervine's later plays include such successful but conventional West End domestic comedies as *The First Mrs Fraser* (1928) and *Robert's Wife* (1937); a fanciful sequel to *The Merchant of Venice* called *The Lady of Belmont* (1924); and a robust Irish comedy, *Boyd's Shop* (1936). His post-war output includes a reactionary play on nationalization, *Private Enterprise* (1947). Ervine was for many years dramatic critic of the *Observer* and has written such general books on drama as *The Organised Theatre*

(1925), which puts the case for national and civic theatres, and *The Theatre in My Time* (1933).

He is the author of 7 novels – including *Francis Place, the Tailor of Charing Cross* (1912) and *Alice and a Family: A Story of South London* (1915) – many essays, political studies of the Ulster movement, and a biography of General Booth, *God's Soldier* (1934). His *Oscar Wilde: A Present-Time Appraisal* (1951) is a hostile study, revealing a Puritan's and an Ulsterman's prejudice against the peacocking Dubliner. *Bernard Shaw: His Life, Work, and Friends* (1956) is a massive and adulatory biography of the Irishman who so greatly influenced Ervine's generation. [MJ]

Allardyce Nicoll, *British Drama* (revised edn, 1962).

Etherege, Sir George (?1635–91). Playwright and poet. Little is known of Etherege's life until the production of his first play *The Comical Revenge, or Love in a Tub* in 1664 beyond the fact that he came from an Oxfordshire family of modest means. His intimate knowledge of France and its literature suggests that he spent some part of his youth there. (His father died in France in 1649.) In 1668, Etherege travelled to Constantinople as secretary to the English ambassador to Turkey, returning to London three years later. About the year 1679 he was knighted and married 'a rich old widow'. He was appointed envoy to Ratisbon (Regensburg) by James II in 1685 and created something of a sensation there by conducting, more or less openly, an affair with a visiting actress. At the Revolution of 1688 he remained loyal to James II and fled to Paris in 1689, after the accession of William III. He died in Paris.

In addition to *The Comical Revenge, or Love in a Tub*, Etherege wrote 2 other comedies, *She Would If She Could* (1668) and his best and best-known play *The Man of Mode, or Sir Fopling Flutter* (1676). He also wrote some agreeable light verse and was an amateur musician, while his published correspondence shows him to have been a shrewd and perceptive observer of the social scene with a vivid and racy idiom. (Dryden regarded him as the leading prose stylist of the age.) In his life as well as in his work, Etherege is a typical Restoration figure. He was a great dandy (a contemporary thought that the figure of Sir Fopling Flutter was based on Etherege

himself), a man-about-town who had to hide from the law at least once after a tavern brawl, and was also distinguished by that 'noble laziness of mind' which characterized the wits of the day.

Love in a Tub was an immediate and sensational success and was recognized by contemporaries as inaugurating 'the modern way' in comedy. It has three plots, of which the 'high' plot, in rhyming couplets, recalls the absurdities of heroic tragedy, while the 'low' plot dealing with the intrigues of two confidence tricksters is plainly connected with the comedy of the Jacobean era. It is in the 'middle' plot, dealing with an amorous gallant's pursuit of a rich widow, that we can see the beginnings of the Restoration comedy of manners. Etherege's second comedy, *She Would If She Could*, was also a great success, despite an apparently indifferent production. This is much more recognizably a Restoration comedy, with two contrasting pairs of lovers instead of the double or treble plot of the older comedy. Here, too, we have a vivid glimpse of fashionable London life which is to be one of the features of Restoration comedy. Nearly ten years were to elapse before Etherege's last play was produced. *The Man of Mode, or Sir Fopling Flutter* is undoubtedly Etherege's masterpiece and one of the outstanding comedies in English. The figure of Sir Fopling Flutter is one of the great comic creations, but it is seen in its full power not as an independent characterization but in relation to the theme, which is an exploration of the uses and abuses of 'affectation' in social life and the implications of libertinism. In the glitter of its language, the liveliness of its situations and the shrewdness of its social vision, *The Man of Mode* deserves to rank with the best Restoration comedies, such as *The Country Wife* and *The Way of the World*. [GS]

The Dramatic Works, ed. H. F. B. Brett-Smith (2 vols., 1927); *Three Restoration Comedies*, ed. G. Salgádo (PEL, 1968) (includes *The Man of Mode*).
Dale Underwood, *E. and the Seventeenth-Century Comedy of Manners* (New Haven, Conn., 1957).

Eusden, Laurence (1688–1730). Poet Laureate (1718). Ordained in 1724, he became rector of Coningsby, Lincolnshire, in 1730. One of the 'nucleus of nobodies' in the *Dunciad*, open to attack because of his contemptible verse, and as a 'Parson, much be-mus'd in Beer'. [AR]

G. Nicholson, 'E.', *TLS* (18 May 1946).

Evans, Mary Ann. ◊ Eliot, George.

Evans, Theophilus (1693–1767). Welsh prose writer. He was born at Penywennallt near Newcastle Emlyn, of a minor gentry family, and spent his life in the Church, being successively curate, vicar and rector of livings mainly in Brecknock – Llanlleonfel, Defynnog, Llandyfrïog (Cardiganshire), Llanynys, Llangamarch and Llanfaes. He is said to have discovered the healing properties of the waters at Llanwrtyd Wells. As a staunch Churchman, he detested Nonconformists and published a scarifying account of their activities in *A History of Modern Enthusiasm* (1752; 2nd edn., 1757). A prolific author, his best work is *Drych y Prif Oesoedd* (1716; ed. G. Hughes, 1961; 2nd edn, 1740; ed. S. J. Evans, 1902; ed. D. Thomas, 1955). There were about 18 editions of this during the 19th century, proof that it was widely read, not merely for its factual content (for this was the only work on Welsh history in Welsh which was available) but also for the intimacy and liveliness of its style.

Evans considered himself a serious historian. He had read widely in Geoffrey of Monmouth, Polydore Virgil, Sir John Price, William Camden, Humphrey Lhuyd, David Powel, Pezron and Edward Lhuyd. He endeavoured to make a synthesis of the early history of the Welsh people by ingeniously reconciling the various traditions and theories which had gained favour from time to time, i.e. that the Welsh (*Cymry*) were descended from Gomer son of Japhet son of Noah, that these were the Britons who had crossed to Britain from Gaul, and that they were later joined by Brutus the Greek at the end of his wanderings from Troy.

There are significant differences between the edition of 1716 when Evans was a young man in his early twenties and that of 1740, the product of his maturer judgement. In the second edition he gave currency to the legend of Madog's discovery of America, and he has more to say of Arthur and the Round Table. Style and presentation were much more carefully considered. Evans abjured the bare factual manner of historical writing which had developed during the 17th century and

returned to the classical tradition of Cicero. He owed much to a close study of Virgil, and it has been held that we must consider the *Drych* as a prose epic in Welsh. The metaphors are very striking and serve to render the already lively narrative more dramatic. [MR]

Evelyn, John (1620–1706). Diarist, dilettante and miscellaneous writer. Born of a Surrey family of country gentry and educated at Balliol College, Oxford. He interrupted his extensive travels abroad to serve briefly as a Royalist volunteer (1642), and married the daughter of Sir Richard Browne. On his return in 1652, he settled at Sayes Court, Deptford, where he cultivated his famous gardens, and helped to found the Royal Society, serving for a time as Secretary (1672). He published a number of (chiefly practical) works, e.g. *Fumifugium* (1661), on air-pollution in London; *Sylva* (1664), an influential book on the cultivation of trees; and *Navigation and Commerce* (1674). His most famous work is his *Diary*, covering the years 1641 to 1706 (first published 1818), which contains invaluable detailed references to political and social events, as well as sketches of his contemporaries. It is a readable work by a somewhat inflexible man in opposition to the tone of Charles II's court. The only complete edition is the monumental *Diary of John Evelyn*, edited by E. S. de Beer (1956), with valuable introduction and notes. [AR]

W. G. Hiscock, *J.E. and His Family Circle* (1955); G. Keynes, *J.E.: A Study in Bibliophily* (1937).

'Everyman' (*c.* 1500). Medieval English morality play. It survives in single copies of 4 separate editions, 2 of them fragmentary, dating from the first half of the 16th century. It is closely related to the Flemish play *Elkerlye* ('Everyman'), first printed in 1495, and a flourishing scholarly-critical controversy centred on which came first; the weight of critical opinion appears to have decided in favour of the Flemish play.

Though *Everyman* is unmistakably English in the details of its characterization and the rhythms of its language, its concerns – death, the last things and the *contemptus mundi* – are the universal concerns of late medieval Catholicism. Its dramatic form, that of the morality play, is a later form of the miracle play, in fact the last stage before the emergence of a completely secular drama. Instead of dealing directly with biblical incident, the play dramatizes the Christian view of man's nature and destiny on earth. Everyman, the protagonist, is summoned to his last journey by Death, acting on God's orders. (God himself appears at the beginning of the play.) Everyman seeks help from his former friends, who include Kindred Knowledge, Beauty and Five Wits (Senses), but none of them will keep him company now. Only Good Deeds, faint and feeble at first but growing stronger as Everyman gathers resolution, abides with him to the last. The play ends with Everyman commending his spirit to God as he sinks into his grave.

Everyman triumphantly overcomes the inherent tendency of this form of drama towards a dull and lifeless didactic allegory. The plot, while obviously not naturalistic, has a genuinely dramatic movement in the hero's progression from complacency through panic and despair to Christian regeneration. Everyman himself is as much an individual dramatic voice as a universal symbol while the minor characters are sharply observed, with the occasional unexpected and telling detail (such as Cousin's excuse of cramp in her toe for not going with Everyman). The play uses rhymed couplets as well as a variety of stanza forms, and the very awkwardness and untidiness of the rhythms seems hauntingly appropriate. The openness of the theatrical form, with its direct address to the audience and its highly stylized language, is likely to impress today's audience by its modernity rather than its archaism. Indeed, *Everyman* remains in the active repertoire of the modern theatre, both in its original version and in numerous adaptations, notably that of Hugo von Hofmannstahl. [GS]

Everyman, ed. A. C. Cawley (1961); *Everyman and Mediaeval Miracle Plays*, ed. A. C. Cawley (1956); *Chief Pre-Shakespearian Dramas*, ed. J. Q. Adams (1924).

F

Fairburn, Arthur Rex Dugard (1904–57). New Zealand poet. He published his first book of verse, *He Shall Not Rise* (1930), in England, but returned to New Zealand and became a spokesman for the important radical writers of the *Phoenix* group in Auckland (1932–3), where he spent most of his life. Fairburn would have delighted in selecting for mention among his many jobs his secretaryship of a Farmers' Union and his editorship of a compositing society's magazine, but he was also a journalist, script-writer, university tutor in English and finally a lecturer in the history and theory of art at the University of Auckland. He was a man of wide interests and catholic learning, a lover of New Zealand and a tireless critic of its faults, a hedonist and a humanist.

Fairburn did not lose the lyric grace of his first volume, but *Strange Rendezvous* (1952) is a much better collection, dignified by an easy eloquence, treating human and personal experience often in the context of love or death. The long poems in *Three Poems* (1952) range from the vitriolic vigour of the satire 'Dominion' to the meditative humanism of 'To a Friend in the Wilderness'. He is at his best in the control of argument by an interweaving of lyrical and colloquial language. *The Rakehelly Man* (1946) and *The Disadvantages of Being Dead* (1958) contain further examples of his comic and satiric writing. [P T]

R. A. K. Mason, *R.F.* (1962).

Fairfax, Thomas (1612–71). Soldier and poet. The 3rd Baron Fairfax of Cameron was born in Denton, Yorkshire, and educated at Cambridge. He fought in the Netherlands from 1629 to 1631. His early sympathies were with the Parliamentarians and in June 1642 he presented a petition against the raising of troops to Charles I. On the outbreak of the Civil War he was appointed General of Horse under his father and rose to be Commander-in-Chief of the Commonwealth Army, showing great personal courage at the battles of Marston Moor and Naseby. At 33 he was Captain-General of the New Model Army and was chiefly responsible for its organization and training. He fought and won the battle of Naseby with Oliver Cromwell.

Although he was appointed one of the judges at the trial of Charles I, he opposed the King's execution. He served as a member of the Commonwealth Council of State for a short time, but resigned his military office in 1650 because he refused to march against the Scots who had proclaimed Charles II king. He was instrumental in the Restoration of Charles II and served as a Member of Parliament in 1660.

As a man, Fairfax was known to be gentle and mild, though his activity as a general was marked by great aggressiveness. From his retirement as Commander-in-Chief in 1650, his life was devoted to growing roses, translating psalms and writing indifferent verse in his house at Nunappleton which he had moved into after his marriage in 1637, and which was the subject of a celebrated poem by Andrew Marvell. Fairfax died there in his sixtieth year. [G S]

Poems, ed. E. R. Bliss (1909); *Correspondence*, ed. G. W. Johnson and R. Bell (4 vols., 1848–9); *Memorials* (1699) (defending F.'s conduct in the Civil War).
M. A. Gibb, *The Lord-General* (1938); M. Ashley, *Cromwell's Generals* (1954).

Fairfield, Cicily Isabel. ◊ West, Rebecca.

Falconer, William (1732-69). Scottish poet. A ship's purser from Edinburgh, he was wrecked off Greece in his youth and made the experience the basis of *The Shipwreck* (1762, and, with extensive revision, 1764 and 1769; ed. with Life, R. Carruthers, 1858). The poem was immediately successful, and remained popular for nearly a century with the class of readers who admired Young and Cowper; its curious mixture of nautical vocabulary with the techniques and diction of 18th-century couplet verse has a certain technical interest today, but the content of the poem, save for some short and energetic passages of description, is insipid. Falconer was patronized and promoted into the navy, compiled a nautical dictionary (1769) and was lost at sea. [A I]

Poems, ed. J. Mitford (1836); *Poetical Works of Beattie, Blair and F.*, ed. G. Gilfillan (1854).
J. Friedrich, *W.F.: The Shipwreck* (Vienna, 1901); M. K. Joseph, 'F.', *Studies in Philology*, XLVII (1950).

Fanshawe, Sir Richard (1608–66). Diplomatist and translator. Born at Ware Park in Hertfordshire of a family of country gentry, he was educated at Cambridge, and after the Grand Tour he became a Royalist Party activist; he was Charles II's secretary during his exile in Holland. After the Restoration, Fanshawe was given various offices, and was sent as ambassador to Portugal, and later Spain. He produced several translations in rather old-fashioned verse – Guarini's *Il pastor fido* (1647), reprinted in 1648 with *Aeneid IV* translated into passionate Spenserian stanzas (ed. A. L. Irvine, 1924) – as well as original verse. In 1652, he published selections from Horace, but his most considerable achievement was his quaint and fanciful version, the first in English, of Camões' Portuguese epic *The Lusiads* (1655; ed. J. D. M. Ford, 1940). [AR]

Lady Fanshawe, *Memoirs*, ed. H. C. Fanshawe (1907) (contains some letters from Sir R.F.).
J. W. Mackail, *Studies of English Poets* (1926); J. D. M. Ford, 'The First Translator of Camoens', *Annual Bulletin of the Modern Humanist Research Association*, XLII (1938).

Farjeon, Herbert (1887–1945). Dramatic critic and revue writer. At one time an actor, he worked for thirty years as dramatic critic on a succession of London newspapers and magazines, and his perceptive and knowledgeable reviews of Shakespearean productions have been collected in *The Shakespearean Scene*. He contributed the preface to the Nonesuch Shakespeare. He was co-author of *Advertising April*, a skit on the star system, and wrote other comedies, but was best known as a witty contributor of sketches and parodies to the Farjeon revues, which set new standards for intimate revue in the thirties and forties. Some of these were presented at the Little Theatre, which he managed. [MJ]

Farmer, Richard (1735–97). Prose writer. Now known chiefly as a Shakespeare scholar, he was born at Leicester and educated at Emmanuel College, Cambridge, becoming Master in 1775; he took orders and was a prebendary of St Paul's. Farmer wrote an *Essay on the Learning of Shakespeare* (1767; in *Eighteenth-Century Essays on Shakespeare*, ed. D. Nichol Smith, 1903). This discusses the 'errors' which Shakespeare displays in his use of Greek and Latin classics, hence arguing that he was dependent on translations. This was part of a complicated argument of long standing about Shakespeare's status as a writer, stemming from Jonson's aside about his 'small Latin and less Greek', and developing to discuss either Shakespeare's innate ability, 'warbling wood-notes wild', or the possibility that some other justification (nationality, genius or the like) could be found for the 'lack' of classical basis for his work. [AR]

Farquhar, George (1678–1707). Dramatist. The son of an Irish clergyman, he spent a year as a sizar at Trinity College, Dublin, and some years in the army before becoming an actor. He gave up acting after accidentally wounding a fellow-player, and, on Wilkes's advice, turned to writing comedy with *Love and a Bottle* (1698). *The Constant Couple* (1700) was a box-office success; its sequel, *Sir Harry Wildair*, was not. Farquhar's best comedies were *The Recruiting Officer* (1706) and *The Beaux' Stratagem* (1707). Both are vigorous, entertaining pieces, set in the country rather than in London, and they mark a significant stage in the evolution of English comedy from the courtly, hedonistic style of the Restoration to the 'laughing', more sentimental mode of Goldsmith. The young blades of *The Beaux' Stratagem* are more genial than their rakish counterparts in Etherege or Wycherley, and the heroine Mrs Sullen escapes an adulterous liaison by being granted a divorce. Farquhar died in penury, without learning of his comedy's success. The play has remained popular on the stage: the John Clements–Kay Hammond production in London in 1949–50 ran for 532 performances. Bertold Brecht's *Trumpets and Drums* (Berlin, 1956) was a free adaptation of *The Recruiting Officer*. Its influence was seen in the brilliant, anti-military production of Farquhar's original at the National Theatre in 1964. [MJ]

The Complete Works, ed. Charles Stonehill (2 vols., 1930).
W. Connely, *Young G.F.: The Restoration Drama at Twilight* (1949); E. Rothstein, *G.F.* (New York, 1967).

Farrar, Frederick William (1831–1905). Novelist, sermon and theological writer. Born in Bombay and educated at London University and Trinity Hall, Cambridge, where he succeeded Leslie ◊ Stephen as tutor, Farrar was one of the stream of muscular Christian teachers just appearing at this time under the impetus of the Evangelical and Oxford movements. He was a master at Harrow, and Headmaster of Marlborough School (1871–6), much under the influence of Thomas ◊ Arnold. He became canon of Westminster, Archdeacon of Westminster and Dean of Canterbury. A voluminous writer of sermons and theological works (of which *The Life of Christ*, 1874, was very popular), he is remembered as the author of school stories with a very high content of Arnoldian virtue and religion (*Eric, or Little by Little*, 1858; *Julian Home, A Tale of College Life*, 1859; *St Winifred's, or The World of School*, 1862). Through these stories (and many tales by imitators) a debased form of Arnold's ideas was made known to tens of thousands who knew nothing else of the closed world of upper-class education. [AR]

R. Farrar, *The Life of F.W.F.* (1904); 'Hugh Kingsmill', *After Puritanism: 1850–1900* (1929).

Fenton, Elijah (1683–1730). Poet. He was educated at Cambridge, but left without a degree because he would not swear allegiance. He lived for a time as secretary to Lord Orrery in Flanders, and was later a schoolmaster, finally a steward. His original poetic production, mainly contributions to miscellanies (collected 1707), was small. He wrote a successful tragedy, *Mariamne* (1723), and edited *Paradise Lost* (1725), 'restoring' the punctuation and contributing a Life of Milton. He also edited the poems of ◊ Waller (1729) with notes and a life. He is best known as one of Pope's auxiliaries in the translation of the *Odyssey* (1725–6), of which he translated Books I, IV, XIX and XXII. [AR]

Johnson, *Lives of the Poets;* E. Harlan, *E.F.* (Philadelphia, 1937).

Ferguson, Sir Samuel (1810–86). Gaelic scholar and antiquary. Born of a Scottish-Irish family in Belfast, he was educated at Trinity College, Dublin, was called to the bar and became Q.C. in 1859, and Deputy Keeper of the Irish Records (1867). He was knighted in 1878. Ferguson was one of the most important workers who provided the 'traditional' material (often to Irishmen with a scanty knowledge of the ancient language) that made the Irish literary renaissance possible (◊ O'Grady, Standish). His own verse was not outstanding, but he handled the old tales well (*Lays of the Western Gael*, 1865; *Congal*, 1872; *Epic Poem*, 1872). A collection of his better prose tales was published by his wife as *Hibernian Nights' Entertainments* (1887); she also published a *Life* (2 vols., 1896). Ferguson's chief work of scholarship was *Ogham Inscriptions in Ireland, Wales and Scotland* (1887). [AR]

M. Ferguson, *F. in the Ireland of His Day* (2 vols., 1896); G. Taylor, in *Irish Poets of the 19th Century* (1951) (introduction and selection).

Fergusson, Robert (1750–74). Scots poet. He attended schools in his native Edinburgh and in Dundee and then studied for four years at St Andrews University (1765–8), where he was befriended by the eccentric William ◊ Wilkie. On his father's death in 1767 he gave up his intention of reading divinity, and in 1769 took a poorly paid job as a copyist in a legal office in Edinburgh. He contributed some songs to the Edinburgh theatre in 1769, and after a series of poems in English appeared in the *Weekly Magazine and Edinburgh Amusement* (1771) he was hailed as successor to Allan ◊ Ramsay. He attended meetings of the convivial Cape Club with David Herd and the painters and actors of the town, published a volume of poems, including 9 in Scots, in early 1773, and went on to exploit the Scots vein that he had struck. Under the impact of poverty, religious tensions, and a series of illnesses and accidents he broke down, and died in the public asylum in Edinburgh.

Before his early death Fergusson, educated and a townsman, had transmuted and enriched the pastoral, genteel and diffident gamut of Scots poetry inherited from Ramsay. His urban themes are those of a crude town-life recognizably not very different from the Edinburgh of Dunbar, and his attitude – satiric, yet with a humane acceptance of human weakness and a readiness to elaborate it into boisterous caricature – also recalls Dunbar's; yet comparison of Fergusson's 'Auld Reikie' with Swift's 'A City Shower' will show that Fergusson had learned from the English Augustans as well. Assimilating the

179

Augustan modes rather than imitating them, he is more confidently and pointedly Scottish than Ramsay and his satire on certain intellectual and cultural fashions of the day is launched from a secure base. Some of his criticism, political and moral as much as social, is conveyed through verse-dialogues, forms which, like the verse epistles, point forward to Burns, and Fergusson's celebrations of urban feasts and fairs – 'Leith Races' and 'Hallow Fair' – provided both the form and the convention for some of Burns's most telling satire. Acquaintance with Fergusson's work encouraged Burns to resume writing at a time when he had given it up, and in 1787 he placed a stone over the neglected grave of his 'elder brother in the muses and in misfortune'. It is arguable, indeed, that Fergusson's range of sensibility and reference and his confident relation to English literature show up, by comparison, the limitations of Burns's achievement. [AI]

Poems, ed. M. P. McDiarmid (STS, 2 vols., 1954–6) (with biography); *Scots Poems*, ed. B. Dickins (1925); *Scots Poems*, ed. J. Telfer (1948); *Selections from the Scottish Poems*, ed. A. Law (1947).
Ed. S. G. Smith, *Robert Fergusson, 1750–74* (1952); J. Kinsley, *Scottish Poetry* (1955); A. H. MacLaine, *R.F.* (New York, 1965).

'Fianaigheacht' ('Fenian or Ossianic lore'). The name given to the hundreds of Irish tales and poems relating to the Fiana. Originally these Fiana were bands of hunters or warriors (compare Latin *uenari*, 'to hunt', or Slavonic *vojna*, 'war'), but in the literature they appear as an armed organization capable of such roles as the defence of Ireland against invasion. Of the various literary cycles, mythological, heroic or Red Branch, kingly or historical, Fenian or Ossianic, the latter was easily the most popular.

Although not prominent in the earliest extant records, *Fianaigheacht* can be traced back at least to the 8th century. Among the chief characters are Fionn Mac Cumhaill, Goll Mac Morna, Oisín son of Fionn, Diarmaid Ó Duibhne, Caoilte Mac Rónáin; and Gráinne, daughter of Cormac Mac Airt. (The 'Pursuit of Diarmaid and Gráinne' has been dramatized in our day by Mícheál Mac Liammóir.) About A.D. 1200 an unknown author linked many of the existing episodes together, by assuming that Oisín and Caoilte survived their comrades and lived until the coming of St Patrick, whom they accompanied around Ireland, while his scribe recorded their reminiscences on the way. This is the *Agallamh na Seanórach* ('Colloquy of the Ancient Men'), a kind of frame pattern, like *The Arabian Nights* or *The Decameron*.

While the real authors are virtually all anonymous (a late exception is Micheál ◊ Coimín), much of the poetry is attributed to Fionn, or Caoilte; but especially to Oisín, whose lively dialogues with St Patrick often develop into a war of words between old and new, as Oisín, like Llywarch Hen, wistfully recalls the days of his youth. As it happened, Oisín's name loomed larger as time went by, and the name 'Ossianic' was sometimes applied to the cycle, particularly in Gaelic Scotland, whence it reached the main stream of European literature owing to the work of MacPherson in the 18th century.

A striking fact about *Fianaigheacht* is its longevity. Robin Flower writes (*The Irish Tradition*, 1947): 'This matter in one form or another is older than the Anglo-Saxon *Beowulf*, and yet it lives still upon the lips of the peasantry, a real and vivid experience, while, except to a few painful scholars, *Beowulf* has long passed out of memory.' [SB]

G. Murphy, *The Ossianic Lore and Romantic Tales of Medieval Ireland* (1955).

Field, Michael. Under this pseudonym, Katharine Harris Bradley (1846–1914) and her niece, Edith Emma Cooper (1862–1913), wrote many (unacted) verse plays, and poems. *Selections* from their work were compiled by T. Sturge Moore (1923) and there are some in the *Oxford Book of Modern Verse*. [AR]

C. Alexander, *Catholic Literary Revival* (Milwaukee, 1935).

Field, Nathan (1587–1620). Dramatist. Although he was the son of John Field, preacher, pamphleteer and puritanical denouncer of the theatre, Nat Field began as a child-actor, appearing in several plays by Ben Jonson, who seems to have tutored him in Horace and Martial. As an adult player with Queen Elizabeth's Men he appeared in *Bartholomew Fair* (in which Jonson pays him a compliment), and he acted for various companies, but left the stage in about 1619 – possibly because of a scandal involving him and the Countess of Argyll. He wrote 2 coarse London comedies, *A Woman is a Weathercock* (*c.* 1609) and *Amends for Ladies* (*c.* 1611), both acted by boys' companies. He also collaborated with Massinger in *The Fatal Dowry* (*c.* 1618), and possibly was part-author of several plays in the Beaumont and Fletcher canon, including *Bonduca, Cupid's Revenge, The Knight of Malta, Thierry and Theodoret* and *Four Plays in One*. A competent and experienced man of the theatre, he had some gifts for writing dialogue and devising action, but his characterization and verse were not distinguished. [MJ]

Nero and Other Plays, ed. A. Wilson Verity (1888); *The Plays*, ed. W. Peery (Austin, Texas, 1950).
R. F. Brinkley, *N.F , the Actor-Playwright* (1928).

Fielding, Henry (1707–54). Dramatist and novelist. Born at Sharpham Park, near Glastonbury, Somerset, the son of General Fielding, of a family descended from the Earls of Denbigh. He was educated at Eton, and from 1724 to 1728 spent his time as a wit and man-about-town in London. On 16 February 1728, his first play, *Love in Several Masques. A Comedy*, was acted, and the next month he set out for Leyden, where he studied law until his return to London just under a year later. For the next seven years, Fielding pursued his career as a dramatist. Had he never written a novel, he would still have been one of the most considerable writers of the age. Between 1730 and 21 June 1737 (when, largely as a result of his own political satire, the Stage Licensing Act was passed and he was excluded from the stage), he wrote some 25 dramatic pieces.

Recent criticism of his novels has made more use of these plays (as well as of the vast mass of his essays, pamphlets and other writing) than was common even fifty years ago, when the novels themselves overshadowed all his other work. His drama includes several different kinds of writing. The comedies (of manners, in the fashion of the Restoration writers, by that time sadly faded) were never very successful, partly because, despite his background, he believed that 'high life' was very dull. His talents, too, developed more in the line of satire and argument, which found better scope in his brilliant mingling of burlesque,

farce and social and political satire. His comedies include *The Modern Husband* (1732) and *The Universal Gallant* (1735); but only his *Miser* (1733), a version of Molière's *L'avare*, kept the stage long. His best play is *The Tragedy of Tragedies; or The Life and Death of Tom Thumb the Great* (published 1730, with elaborate spoof notes by Scriblerus Secundus; ed. J. T. Hillhouse, Yale, 1918). This is a complex attack on rhetorical dishonesty, worldly 'greatness' and unthinking literary convention. Several of his pieces are in the literary-critical tradition of the 'Rehearsal' plays (◊ Villiers, George), for example *The Author's Farce* (1730). Fielding also developed these unconventional dramatic techniques to produce topical political satires such as *Pasquin* (1736) and *The Historical Register for 1736* (1737). As a dramatist he shows growing impatience with the restrictions of stage technique, great verbal dexterity, and a powerful satirical drive that the theatre could not easily serve.

Silenced as a dramatist, he again took up law in November 1737, and on 20 June 1740 was called to the bar at the Inner Temple. He also pursued a very active career as a journalist, editing the anti-Walpole *Champion, or, British Mercury* 'by Captain Hercules Vinegar' from 15 November 1739 to June 1741; after the fall of Walpole he edited the pro-government, anti-Jacobite *True Patriot, and History of Our Own Time* (5 November 1745 to 17 June 1746, during the Rebellion); and a similarly oriented burlesque *Jacobite's Journal* 'by John Trott-Plaid' from 5 December 1747 to 5 November 1748. Towards the end of his career he ran a satirical, anti-dunce periodical, in the vein of his Augustan mentor Pope, called *The Covent-Garden Journal* 'by Sir Alexander Drawcansir, Knt, Censor of Great Britain' (4 January to 25 November 1752). Besides his *Miscellanies* (1743), which contain poems, essays, a fantastic *Journey from This World to the Next* and *Jonathan Wild*, this mass of journalism includes many pieces characteristic of Fielding's character, ideas, feelings and belief, and the mode of writing obviously influenced his fiction, with its constantly intruded 'essays'. In 1748 Fielding was commissioned as a Justice of the Peace for Westminster, as part of a government plan to provide some police security in London, where a chaotic situation was rapidly developing as the violent growth of the city out-stripped the capability of the ancient legal machinery, which never had been very efficient. Fielding and his brother, the blind Justice (John) Fielding, took a prominent part in developing the police force, the celebrated Bow Street Runners, and Henry Fielding wrote a good deal on the social problems of the time: *A Charge Delivered to the Grand Jury* (1749); *An Enquiry into the Causes of the Late Increase of Robbers, with Some Proposals for Remedying This Growing Evil* (1751) and *A Proposal for Making an Effectual Provision for the Poor, To Which is Added, A Plan of the Buildings Proposed* (1753). He also wrote accounts of several celebrated criminal cases.

Amid all this activity he produced the 4 works of fiction on which his fame solidly rests. His novel-writing career had a preliminary try-out with *Shamela* (1741). It is significant that this work was provoked by what Fielding thought a wrong conception of virtue, or a smug overvaluation of a certain notion of untried virtue, in *Pamela*, the novel by ◊ Richardson. This had been published the year before. It is equally significant that the form Fielding's disapproval took should be a burlesque on Richardson's work. Fielding's fiction always challenges the reader to make some comparison or connexion with some other literary work (Richardson, Homer, Horace, the historians and so on). In February 1742, however, appeared *The History of the Adventures of Joseph Andrews, and His Friend Mr Abraham Adams Written in the Manner of Cervantes* (G. Saintsbury, Everyman, 1910; ed. L. Rice-Oxley, World's Classics, 1929; ed. and intr. M. Mack, 1948; ed., with *Shamela*, M. C. Battestin, 1961). *Joseph Andrews* is again lightly attached to the previous burlesque at the beginning and the end (Joseph is Pamela's brother), but the book itself operates on two related but quite different bases: a theory of the comic-epic, elaborated in a long introduction, by which Fielding gives the book a 'literary' structure; and powerful satire (involving judgements of human relationships, class, sexual ethics and religious belief) which is the characteristic mode of Fielding's moralistic mind. In the fiction, though, Fielding for the first time allows his imagination a free and untrammelled run, and he creates in Parson Adams a magnificent and original comic

character. Fielding's political and sociological interests (present in *Joseph Andrews*) are bent into a powerful book by his mastery of irony in *The Life of Mr Jonathan Wild the Great* (1743), in which he uses Wild, a criminal hanged in 1725, as a symbol of political corruption through the ironical confusion of 'greatness' and 'success'. His greatest work, *The History of Tom Jones, A Foundling*, appeared in 1749 (2 edns that year; revised the same year; ed. G. Saintsbury, Everyman, 2 vols., 1909; ed. R. P. C. Mutter, PEL. 1966). This is a masterpiece of the story-teller's art. The plot is extremely elaborate and this, together with the satirical implications of the idea of history and the interspersed essay-comments of the author (or at least the narrator), provides a rich and devious comic masterpiece. One again, the structure of the book depends on the links carefully made with other literary works and conventions, as well as the central doctrines of virtue and reason which Fielding develops in his satire. The pace of the story and the force of the comedy also keep *Tom Jones* alive. *Amelia* (4 vols., 1752; reprinted 1914) is his last important work. Here he is interested in domestic tragedy, and perhaps (allowing his increasing involvement with the problems of his office) in a more realistic rendering of the world. The uncertainty about his own 'point of view', which is uncomfortably present in his earlier works, occurs again here, and forces a comic conclusion to what seems a tragic work. Fielding seeks to attack the social structure of his day, but does not see that his view is so destructive as to be anarchic. He draws back into the protection of comedy. This works well in *Joseph Andrews*, less well in the more complex *Tom Jones*, and least well in the sombre world of *Amelia*. In 1754 his health began to fail rapidly, and on 7 August he set out for Lisbon, where he died on 8 October and lies buried. His *Journal of a Voyage to Lisbon* (1755) was published by his second wife. Fielding had an incalculable influence on the 18th- and 19th-century English novel, particularly through his use of free authorial comment – the presentation of the 'story' in a slightly deprecatory way for some purpose of the author's. [AR]

The Complete Works, ed. W. E. Henley et al. (16 vols., 1902) (the fullest collection of works, plays and writings); *The Covent-Garden Journal*, ed. G. E. Jensen (2 vols., Yale U.P., 1915) (not in *Complete Works*); *Shamela*, ed.

I. Watt (Augustan Reprint Society, 1956) (not in *Complete Works*).
W. Cross, *The History of H.F.* (3 vols., Yale U.P., 1918); F. Homes Dudden, *H.F., His Life, Works and Times* (2 vols., 1952); J. Butt, *F.* (W T W, 1954, revised 1959) (with bibliography); A. D. McKillop, 'H.F.', in *The Early Masters of English Fiction* (U. of Kansas P., 1956); I. Watt, *The Rise of the Novel* (1957); ed. R. Paulson, *F.: A Collection of Critical Essays* (1962); A. Wright, *H.F., Mask and Feast* (1965).

Fielding, Sarah (1710–68). Novelist and translator. Sister of Henry ◊ Fielding, who had a high opinion of her talents. She was the author of various forgotten romances of which the best known was *The Adventures of David Simple in Search of a Faithful Friend* (1744), the story of a young man wronged by his brother, who sets out to look for real friendship and finds it with another deprived youth and two wronged girls. He regains his inheritance and the two couples live on it happily ever after. The moralizing is not much to modern taste, but the book contains some close observations of the London scene. Sarah Fielding also wrote a famous book for educating girls called *The Governess, or Little Female Academy* (1749, often reprinted and recast, well into the 19th century). She translated Xenophon's *Memorabilia and Apologia* (1762). [AR]

Firbank, (Arthur Annesley) Ronald (1886–1926). Novelist. Born in London and educated at Trinity Hall, Cambridge, he sat for no examinations and took no degree, but was received, while at Cambridge, into the Catholic Church, whose ritual held great aesthetic appeal for him. The son of wealthy parents, he spent much of his time travelling in France, Italy, North Africa and the West Indies. He was always delicate in health, but probably precipitated his early death by heavy drinking.

Firbank's is the most unusual talent amongst 20th-century novelists. That he is a minor novelist cannot be denied, that he will remain a minority taste is probable, but that his novels are superb works of art and of artifice is beyond question. He can almost be regarded as a subterranean link between Oscar ◊ Wilde and Ivy ◊ Compton-Burnett. His first book was *Odette d'Antrevernes* (1905), a feeble piece of *fin-de-siècle* sentimentality which gives no hint of the direction in which he was to develop ten

years later. Next to be written, though it was not published until after his death, was *The Artificial Princess* (1934), in which his treatment of narrative is still traditional, though the fantastic humour of the later Firbank is recognizably present.

With *Vainglory* (1915) begins the series of novels whose plots are wispy, whose dialogue is fragmentary and as though imperfectly overheard, and whose characterization is, to say the least, impressionistic. Firbank's wit is difficult to define. Artificial and fantastic, it evaporates quickly when taken out of context. The author's homosexual sensibility allied with his *fin-de-siècle* aestheticism creates a kind of pre-absurdist approach to the novel. Firbank's genius was as fragile as his health. *Vainglory* is, for him, a long novel. *Inclinations* (1916), which followed it, is slighter in every way and is written almost entirely in dialogue. *Caprice* (1917) is one of Firbank's finest and most characteristic achievements. *Valmouth* (1919) exploits its author's fascination with the trappings of Catholicism. It overflows with priests, incense, choir-boys and an occasional nun. *Concerning the Eccentricities of Cardinal Pirelli* (1926) is set in Spain. The Cardinal, whose eccentricities include the baptism of dogs in his cathedral, dies a typically Firbankian death, collapsing while pursuing a choir-boy around the altar. [CO]

The Flower Beneath the Foot (1923); *Sorrow in Sunlight* (1925); *The Complete R.F.*, intr. Anthony Powell (1961).
Jocelyn Brooke, *R.F.* (1951); M. J. Benkowitz, *Bibliography of R.F.* (1963).

Fitzgerald, Edward (1809–83). Poet and translator. Born at Bredfield House, near Woodbridge, Suffolk, the son of a country gentleman, he was educated at Bury St Edmunds Grammar School and Trinity College, Cambridge, where he was intimate with Thackeray; later he became a friend of Tennyson. He lived most of his rather secluded life in various parts of Suffolk. He was a voluminous letter-writer and travelled about enjoying the company of his friends (who also included Carlyle). Fitzgerald published *Euphranor: A Dialogue on Youth* (1851; ed. F. Chapman, 1906), criticizing English education for, as he thought, neglecting exercise and practical matters, and *Polonius: A Collection of Wise Saws and Modern Instances* (1852), an anthology of quotations. Under the influence of E. B. Cowell of Ipswich, a dilettante linguist, he studied Spanish and Persian. His methods of dealing with other writers' work are illustrated in *Poems and Letters of Bernard Barton* (1849), 200 pages of dovetailing and distillation from his Quaker friend's 9 volumes of writing. In 1853 appeared his *Six Dramas of Calderón*, which are paraphrased rather than translated and because of this were not very well received. In 1856, he published his first version of the Persian poet Jāmī's mystical allegory, *Salāmán and Absāl* (the second version, freed from Cowell's supervision, was even freer). Also in 1856, he was reading the quatrains (*rubáiyát*) of 'Omar Khayyám (who died about 1122), and found in them some consolation for his unhappy marriage and recent separation. He collected manuscripts of 'Omar's poems, and started to 'translate' them. He published *The Rubáiyát of 'Omar Khayyám, the Astronomer Poet of Persia* in 1859 (2nd edn, revised and enlarged, 1868; 3rd edn, revised, 1872; 4th edn, revised, and this text commonly reprinted, 1879). 'Omar's quatrains are spontaneous, occasional, short poems; Fitzgerald makes them a continuous sequence, sometimes compressing more than one poem by 'Omar into one of his own quatrains. The Fitzgerald stanza, with its unrhymed, poised third line, is an admirable invention to carry the sceptical irony of the work and to accommodate the opposing impulses of enjoyment and regret. Fitzgerald's poem has a kind of dramatic unity, starting with dawn and the desire to seize the enjoyment of the passing moment, moving through the day until, with the fall of evening, he laments the fading of youth and the approach of death. Several interests of the time, divine justice versus hedonism, science versus religion and the prevailing taste for eastern art and bric-à-brac, were united in the poem and it became enormously popular. The *Rubáiyat* appeared in the same year as the *Origin of Species*, and 'Omar was a sceptical astronomer. Fitzgerald's version of another allegory, 'Attâr's *Matik-ut-Tair, the Bird Parliament*, which appeared in 1859, contains some of his best writing. He is one of the most charming English letter writers, whimsically commenting on the developments of the day from a detached and nostalgic vantage point. He writes to his intimate friends of music, poetry, his enjoyment of nature and himself. [AR]

Works (2 vols., New York, 1887); *Letters and Literary Remains*, ed. W. Aldis Wright (3 vols., 1889); *Letters*, ed. W. Aldis Wright (4 vols., 1902–3); *Variorum and Definitive Edition of Poetical and Prose Writing*, G. Bentham (7 vols., New York, 1902); *Selected Works*, ed. J. Richardson (1962); *Letters*, ed. J. M. Cohen (1960).
A. J. Arberry, *F.'s Sālāman and Absāl: A Study* (1956), and *Omar Khayyám and Fitzgerald* (1959); A. M. Terhune, *Life of E.F.* (Yale U.P., 1947) (standard biography); J. Richardson, *E.F.* (WTW, 1960) (with bibliography); A. G. Potter, *Bibliography of the Rubáiyat of Omar Khayyám* (1929); T. G. Ehversam and R. H. Deity, *Bibliographies of 12 Victorian Authors* (New York, 1936) and J. C. Fucilla, 'Supplement' in *MP*, 38 (1938).

Fitzgerald, G. ◊ Mac Gearailt, G.

FitzGerald, Robert David (1902–). Australian poet. Born and educated in Sydney, he abandoned his scientific studies at the University of Sydney, qualified as a land surveyor in 1925 and later spent several years in Fiji as a government surveyor. During the war he worked on airfield construction, and was afterwards appointed a senior surveyor in the Department of the Interior. As well as writing poetry, he has lectured on it and contributed a number of critical essays to Australian periodicals. His influence on recent Australian poetry has increased its confidence in philosophical statement.

FitzGerald's best-known poem, 'Essay on Memory', appears in the collection *Moonlight Acre* (1938). It is his fullest treatment of a favourite theme, the dependence of the present on the past. The meditative development of this and other poems is contained in the broken rhythms of serious conversation and reinforced by persuasively appropriate visual imagery. Many of the poems in *This Night's Orbit* (1953) celebrate action as man's finest resource in his uneasy poise between meaning and absurdity. The long narrative poem *Between Two Tides* (1952) describes the experiences of the only survivor of a massacre at sea, touching on another favourite theme, the responsibilities of choice and opportunity. With *The Wind at Your Door* (1959) FitzGerald returned to reflective poetry. Further (mainly lyrical) poems were published as *Southmost Twelve* (1962). [PT]

R.D.F. (1965) (selection).
V. Buckley, *Essays in Poetry: Mainly Australian*

(1957); H. J. Oliver, 'The Achievement of F.', *Meanjin*, XIII, 1 (Autumn, 1954); G. Wilkes, 'The Poetry of R.F.', *Southerly*, XXVII, 4 (1967).

Fitzpatrick, Sir James Percy (1862–1931). South African statesman and writer. Author of *Jock of the Bushveld*. Born in King William's Town and sent to school in England, back in South Africa he spent a number of adventurous years in the Eastern Transvaal before joining Lord Randolph Churchill's 1891 expedition through the unmapped region that became Southern Rhodesia. His first book, *Through Mashonaland with Pick and Pen* (1892), was the outcome of this expedition. The publication of *The Transvaal from Within* was delayed until 1899 by the Jameson Raid of 1895. As Secretary of the Reform Committee, Fitzpatrick was arrested, found guilty of treason, fined £2,000 and forced to keep out of politics for four years. Before the outbreak of the Boer War he worked hard to reconcile Britain and the Transvaal, and was later a loyal member of the Unionist Party and a member of the Union Parliament.

Jock of the Bushveld (1907) was intended for children. It is the story of a dog which accompanies its master on his transport-riding trips across the Transvaal. The book is firmly placed in the era of empire building, but its re-creation of the low veld landscape and its confident handling of a simple narrative have made it a South African classic. [P T]

South African Memories (1932) (autobiography).

Flecker, (Herman) James Elroy (1884–1915). Poet and playwright. Born in Lewisham, Flecker was educated at Uppingham, Oxford and at Cambridge, where he studied Persian and Arabic as a preparation for entry into the Foreign Service. His first volume of poems, *Bridge of Fire*, written while he was an undergraduate, was published in 1907. In June 1910, Flecker was posted to Constantinople but returned in a few months because of illness. He was transferred to Smyrna and later became Vice-Consul at Beirut. He died of tuberculosis in a sanatorium at Davos.

Flecker's travel in the Middle East intensified the strain of exoticism which is present even in his earliest poems. He strove, not always successfully, to combine this with a classical lucidity and detach-ment. His best-known works are *The Golden Journey to Samarkand*, in which a vaguely evocative lyricism and a compulsive rhythm create an almost hypnotic effect, and the verse play *Hassan*, produced posthumously in 1922 with music by Delius and choreography by Fokine and enthusiastically received at the time as the harbinger of a new wave of poetic drama. Flecker's other verse play, *Don Juan* (published 1925), had to wait till 1946 for its first production. His genuine feeling for the exotic coexisted with the kind of intense patriotism which Rupert Brooke made famous and which comes out in Flecker's last poems, written on the outbreak of the First World War. [G S]

Collected Poems (revised edn, 1946).
G. Hodgson, *The Life of J.E.F.* (1925).

Flecknoe, Richard (c. 1600–78). Playwright and poet. The exact date and place of Flecknoe's birth is not known, but he may have been of Irish extraction, a Catholic by religion and later a Jesuit priest. He travelled widely and the chief source of information about him is his own *Relation of Ten Years' Travels in Europe, Asia, Affrique and America* (1654?), a compilation of letters to famous people. Of his 5 plays, only *Love's Dominion* (1654) was publicly performed. His *Short Discourse on the English Stage* (1664), in which he disapproved of the contemporary theatre, may have been partly responsible for Dryden's attack on him, *MacFlecknoe* (1682), in which he is immortalized as the epitome of Dullness. Andrew Marvell also wrote a lampoon on Flecknoe entitled *An English Priest at Rome*. His non-dramatic works, apart from those already mentioned, include a collection of prose sketches, *Enigmaticall Characters* (1658), and a verse miscellany, *Epigrams of All Sorts* (1670). Though both Lamb and Southey defended him vigorously, it is not unfair to say that Flecknoe's main contribution to literature lay in serving as a target for Dryden's satirical masterpiece. [G S]

G. Langbaine, *Dramatic Poets* (1691); P. H. Doney, *Life and Works of R.F.* (1938).

Fleming, Ian (Lancaster) (1908–65). Novelist and journalist. He was born in London, the son of a rich private banker and M.P. who was killed in the First World War. He was educated at Eton and briefly at the

Royal Military College, Sandhurst, and spent four years in Munich and Geneva preparing for a Foreign Service career. Having failed to gain an appointment, he began a career as a foreign correspondent with Reuters, and worked as a merchant banker and stockbroker. During the Second World War, he was Personal Assistant to the Director of Naval Intelligence. From 1945 to 1959, he was Foreign Manager of Kemsley Newspapers, organizing a foreign news service. Fleming is chiefly known for the series of best-selling suspense novels which he wrote around an imaginary British Secret Service agent, 007, James Bond, who has been assigned the double 0 prefix to his number by being 'allowed' to kill. Bond, handsome, omnicompetent, is to some degree a fantasy wish-fulfilling figure for Fleming himself. The adventures take place in exotic places like Japan or the Caribbean, allowing Fleming to deploy a good deal of travel writing, which he is good at, though such detail can become intrusive. Fleming's books are well-paced, crisply narrated. They differ from the novels of Sax ◊ Rohmer and earlier practitioners of the genre chiefly in containing more explicit descriptions of sexual activity, violence and torture, as well as in greater care and realism in details. Part of the peculiar and successful effect of the books lies in Fleming's ability to powder his confections with out-of-the-way details about food, cars, guns, gadgets, sex, travel, gambling, fish and plants. A corollary of this is the intolerable knowingness of sometimes bogus judgements. There are 12 Bond novels, 11 of them 'spy' stories and one, *The Spy Who Loved Me* (1962), an unsuccessful attempt at expanding Bond as a 'character'. The titles are: *Casino Royale* (1953), *Live and Let Die* (1954), *Moonraker* (1955), *Diamonds are Forever* (1956), *From Russia with Love* (1957), *Dr No* (1958), *Goldfinger* (1959), *Thunderball* (1961), *On Her Majesty's Secret Service* (1963), *You Only Live Twice* (1964) and *The Man with the Golden Gun* (1965). *For Your Eyes Only* (1960) contains 5 short stories, of which 'Riscio' and 'The Hildebrand Rarity' are the best. [AR]

Kingsley Amis, *The James Bond Dossier* (1965); J. Pearson, *The Life of I.F.* (1966).

Fleming, (Robert) Peter (1907–　). Travel writer. Brother of Ian ◊ Fleming. Born in London, he was educated at Eton and

Christ Church, Oxford. He became a journalist, and travelled widely in Eastern and Central Asia, as well as Mexico and Brazil (writing as a special correspondent for *The Times*). He had a distinguished record during the Second World War in the Grenadier Guards, and retired as a colonel. He was the *Spectator*'s theatre critic. His books are chiefly on travel and war history. They include: *Brazilian Adventure* (1933), an account of an expedition in search of Colonel Fawcett; *News from Tatary* (1936) an account of a journey in China; *The Forgotten Journey* (1952); *Invasion 1940* (1957); *The Siege at Peking* (1959); *Bayonets to Lhasa* (1961), an account of the British invasion of Tibet in 1904; and *The Fate of Admiral Kolchak* (1963), an episode in the Russo-Japanese War. [AR]

Fletcher, Andrew, of Saltoun (1655–1716). Scots political writer. An early Scottish Whig who opposed the terms of the Anglo-Scottish Union of 1707, arguing for an open, federal relationship instead of the 'incorporating' one that was preferred, Fletcher is remembered for his epigram on the social influence of literature – 'if a man were permitted to make all the ballads, he need not care who should make the laws of a nation'. [AI]

Political Works (1732).
W. C. Mackenzie, *A.F.* (1935).

Fletcher, Giles, the Elder (1546–1611). Poet and prose-writer. Son of a clergyman, he was educated at Eton and at King's College, Cambridge, where he held a fellowship and a succession of college offices (including a lectureship in Greek) until he resigned in order to marry. He took the degree of Doctor of Civil Law in 1581, and the following year became chancellor of the diocese of Sussex. From 1584 he sat in Parliament for Winchelsea, and in 1585 was appointed Remembrancer of the City of London. A zealous Protestant, he served on committees, and undertook diplomatic missions to Scotland, Hamburg and Holland. In 1588 he was sent as Elizabeth's ambassador to Russia, where he effected a favourable trade treaty. He presented *Of the Russe Commonwealth* in manuscript to the Queen in 1589. The Russia Company sought to suppress the first edition in 1561, but part was reprinted by ◊ Hakluyt in his *Voyages* of 1598. It was republished in 1643, 1656 and 1657. It long influenced the Britisher's view of Russia, and its literary importance stems from the fact that it was certainly used by Ralegh, Webster, Jonson and Milton – and possibly by Bacon, Spenser and Shakespeare. Fletcher's proposed Latin history of Queen Elizabeth's time did not materialize, since he failed to secure Burghley's support, and the subsequent patronage of Essex almost proved his undoing. Dr Fletcher's claim to literary fame is that he fathered two English poets, Phineas ◊ Fletcher and Giles ◊ Fletcher, the Younger, and aside from his Latin works, he wrote a sonnet-sequence which was published anonymously in 1593 along with an ode, 3 elegies, and 'A Lover's Maze' in the same volume as *The Rising to the Crown of Richard III*, a monologue in the style of *A Mirror for Magistrates*. [MJ]

The English Works of G.F., the Elder, ed. L. E. Berry (Madison, 1964).

Fletcher, Giles, the Younger (1585–1623). Poet. The son of Giles ◊ Fletcher, the Elder, poet, traveller and public servant, and brother of Phineas ◊ Fletcher. From Westminster School he went up to Cambridge in 1603, where his distinguished academic career culminated in a readership in Greek grammar (1615). In 1617 he was appointed to a college living, which cannot have entailed prolonged absence from the university as in 1618 he was elected reader in Greek language. In 1619 he left the university and became rector of Alderton, Suffolk, where he lived (unappreciated, it is said, by his 'clownish parishioners') until his early death in 1623.

Fletcher's best-known work is his short epic, *Christs Victorie and Triumph in Heaven and Earth, over and after Death* (1610). The first section depicts the debate between Justice and Mercy over fallen man: Mercy (a blend of Alain of Lille's Natura and Spenser's Mercilla) wins the debate by pointing to the humanity of Christ, as manifested in his birth and childhood. The second section is a vastly elaborated account (owing much to Spenser's Bower of Bliss) of the temptation of Christ in the wilderness. The third narrates the Passion story, while the fourth describes the Resurrection, Ascension and triumphal entry of Christ into heaven, and culminates in the mystical marriage of Christ and the Church ('fair Egliset'). The poem combines great descriptive richness (of a fairly conventional kind) with passages of witty didacticism, prettiness with rhetoric, religiosity with erotic imagery: in short, it is a 'baroque' work. It is a very competent piece of writing, but it does not compel attention. Though much of the detail is closely imitated from Spenser, the allegory lacks his richness of meaning, nor is the movement of the verse ever Spenserian.

Christs Victorie and Triumph must have enjoyed a measure of success in its day, for it was reprinted in 1632 and 1640. Its influence on Milton, particularly on *Paradise Regained*, is well known, and has been studied by H. E. Cory, in *Spenser, the School of the Fletchers, and Milton* (Berkeley, Calif., 1912). [TG]

Complete Poems, ed. and intr. A. B. Grosart (1868, revised edn, 1876); *The Poetical Works of Giles and Phineas Fletcher*, ed. F. S. Boas (2 vols., 1908–9).
J. D. Wilson, *MLR* (1910); H. M. Belden, *SP* (1929).

Fletcher, John (1579–1625). Dramatist. Son of Richard Fletcher, who became Bishop of London in 1594, and a cousin of Giles ◊ Fletcher and Phineas ◊ Fletcher, he is thought to have been at Corpus Christi College, Cambridge. For five years from about 1607 or 1608 he collaborated with Francis ◊ Beaumont in writing plays for the boy companies at the small private theatres. In 1609 Shakespeare's company, the King's Men, took over one of these theatres, the Blackfriars, for adult performances and the collaborators' experience of writing for select, courtly audiences meant that their services were in demand. Fletcher wrote on for another twelve years after Beaumont's death in 1616, sometimes alone, often in collaboration with Philip ◊ Massinger, or others. He succeeded Shakespeare as principal writer to the King's Men. Beaumont was sole author of a few of the 52 plays described as theirs and a dozen or so were written by the collaborators, but the majority were written by Fletcher aided or unaided. The tragi-comedies with Beaumont, *Philaster, or Love Lies a-Bleeding* and *A King and No King*, probably influenced Shakespeare in his last plays, his first for Blackfriars. Fletcher's comedies include *The Woman's Prize* (a sequel to *The Taming of the Shrew*), *Monsieur Thomas*, *The Humorous Lieutenant*, *The Chances* and *The Wild Goose Chase*. The

187

Maid's Tragedy was written with Beaumont; and among his other tragedies were *Valentinian* and *Thierry and Theodoret* (with Massinger). He collaborated with Shakespeare in *The Two Noble Kinsmen*, the lost *Cardenio*, and *Henry VIII*. Fletcher was a courtly dramatist, capable of satiric thrusts, skilled in plotting and adept at putting unusual and extravagant emotional situations into convincing settings and natural blank verse. He often manipulated plot, character and audience-response to obtain maximum effect, and has been charged with decadence and salaciousness. Beaumont and Fletcher were, with Jonson and Shakespeare, the only writers to have their plays collected in folio, and throughout the 17th century were consistently ranked third after Jonson and Shakespeare, though several other Jacobean dramatists rate more highly today. [MJ]

The Dramatic Works in the Beaumont and Fletcher Canon, general ed. F. Bowers (1966–); The Works of Francis Beaumont and J.F., ed. A. H. Bullen, P. A. Daniel etc. (4 vols., incomplete, 1904–12).
W. W. Appleton, *Beaumont and F.: A Critical Study* (1956); J. F. Danby, *Poets on Fortune's Hill* (1952); Clifford Leech, *The J.F. Plays* (1962); B. Maxwell, *Studies in Beaumont, F., and Massinger* (1939); A. H. Thorndike, *The Influence of Beaumont and F. on Shakspere* (Worcester, Mass., 1901); E. W. Waith, *The Pattern of Tragicomedy in Beaumont and F.*, (1952); L. B. Wallis, *F., Beaumont and Company: Entertainers to the Jacobean Gentry* (New York, 1947).

Fletcher, Phineas (1582–1650). Poet. The son of Giles ◊ Fletcher, the Elder, and brother of Giles ◊ Fletcher, the Younger. He was born at Cranbrook, Kent. From Eton he went to King's College, Cambridge, in 1600. Between this date and 1611 he wrote a substantial quantity of verse, which he seems to have hoped would bring him advancement, but in 1611 he left Cambridge, embittered and disillusioned, and with no regular employment to go to. At some point between 1612 and 1614 he enjoyed the hospitality of the Willoughby family at Hilgay (Norfolk). A last attempt to make a name for himself in the world (or at least at Cambridge) was with his piscatory drama *Sicelides*, presented at King's College for King James's visit in March 1614/15; but the King departed before the play was put on. Fletcher promptly left Cambridge, married, took orders and

became chaplain to Sir Henry Willoughby at his seat at Risley, Derbyshire. In 1621 the living at Hilgay became vacant, and he was appointed rector of that parish, where he spent the remainder of his life.

Most of Phineas Fletcher's poems were published long after he wrote them; thus *Brittains Ida* (also known as *Venus and Anchises*), one of his earliest productions, was published (anonymously) in 1628; the Latin *Locustae* (written before 1611), together with its expanded English version *The Apollyonists*, had been printed at Cambridge in 1627; *Sicelides* (before 1615) was published in 1631; while a volume printed at Cambridge in 1633 contained *The Purple Island* (commenced before 1610), *Piscatorie Eclogues* (some of them earlier than 1611) and *Elisa* (an elegy on Sir Anthony Irby, who died in 1610). In addition to these, and various shorter English and Latin poems, Phineas Fletcher wrote 3 prose tracts – *The Way to Blessedness* (1632), *Joy in Tribulation* (1632) and *A Father's Testament* (published posthumously, 1670); the latter contains a number of interesting poems.

Brittains Ida is a standard 'Ovidian' erotic narrative poem. *The Apollyonists* (his best poem) is far more original: an account of a Satanic conspiracy to check the growth of piety in the world by the launching of a Catholic counter-offensive headed by the Jesuits and culminating in the Gunpowder Plot. (Ignatius de Loyola figures in the debate in Hell as the foul fiend Equivocus.) The poem is shrill and grotesque, but dramatic and powerfully imagined. It provided Milton with a clear model for his Hell scenes. *The Purple Island* is an allegorical description of the human body, the human psyche, and the fight between vices (led by Satan) and the virtues (ultimately led by Christ) over man's rational soul. The anatomical and physiological lore contained in the first 5 cantos is of considerable interest. Fletcher knew of the pulmonary circulation, but not of the peripheral circulation of blood.

Sicelides is a competent piscatory–pastoral play (i.e. it mixes fishermen and shepherds, complete with a sea-monster, a wicked temptress, and some comic characters); but as it is generally impossible to guess what will happen next (and not always easy to understand what is going on) no dramatic suspense is generated. The *Piscatorie Eclogues* provide an elaborately coded account of the activities of the poet, his father and various of his friends.

Although Phineas has interesting things to say, and a considerable visual imagination, his powers of verbal invention are limited. His favourite poetic device is verbal repetition in one form or another. He often re-uses his own material. It is not surprising that in an age that valued tight-knit argument and verbal cleverness Phineas Fletcher should have failed to make a great name for himself as a poet. [TG]

Collected Poems, ed. A. B. Grosart (4 vols., 1869); *Poetical Works of Giles and P.F.*, ed. F. S. Boas (2 vols., 1908–9). A. B. Langdale, *P.F.* (New York, 1937).

Flint, Frank Stewart (1885–   ). Poet and translator. Born in London, the son of a commercial traveller, Flint left school at 13 and worked at various temporary jobs. At 17 he became interested in literature and two years later he took a post as typist in the Civil Service, at the same time attending night school to study languages. His first volume of poetry, *In the Net of the Stars* (1909), consisted mainly of love lyrics which clearly showed the influence of Keats and Shelley, but his extensive knowledge of the work of the French symbolist poets, and his friendship with T. E. Hulme and Ezra Pound, helped him to develop a distinctive poetic style. He became a leading member of the Imagists (◊ Imagism) and contributed to *Des Imagistes* (1914) and *Some Imagist Poets* (1915). He published only 2 further volumes of poetry, *Cadences* (1915) and *Otherworld: Cadences* (1920), which contain some of the finest and most typical Imagist poems. In later life Flint published a great number of translations, mainly from French, and rose to a high position in the Ministry of Labour. [PJK]

Glenn Hughes, *Imagism and the Imagists* (1931); Stanley K. Coffman, *Imagism* (Norman, Okla., 1951); C. Le Roy Breunig, 'F. S. Flint, Imagism's Maître d'école', *Comparative Literature*, IV (Spring, 1952); A. R. Jones, *Thomas Ernest Hulme* (1960).

Florence of Worcester (d. 1118). Chronicler. A monk, he compiled a *Chronicon ex chronicis* (ed. B. Thorpe, 2 vols., 1848–9; tr. J. Stevenson, in *Church Historians of England*, ii, 1853; tr. T. Forester, 1854), beginning with the creation of the world and ending in the year 1117. It is based on a lost part of the *Anglo-Saxon Chronicle*, on Bede,

Asser and other writers. Florence begins to write independently about 1030.

Florio, Giovanni or **John** (*c.* 1553–1625). Translator and lexicographer. The son of Michael Angelo Florio (Protestant refugee and preacher to the Italian Protestant congregation in London), he grew up abroad, but, at 28, entered Magdalen College, Oxford, and became a university teacher of French and Italian. Already he had published his *First Fruits* (1578), a miscellany of translations, proverbs and linguistic instruction, dedicated to his patron, the Earl of Leicester. He also secured the patronage of Southampton and Pembroke. In 1580 he published a translation of Cartier's *Navigations*, and in 1583 entered the service of the French Ambassador to London. *Second Fruits* appeared in 1591, at a time when he was preparing his magnum opus, *A World of Words*, a huge folio Italian–English dictionary embracing 46,000 words which was published in 1598, dedicated to the Earls of Rutland and Southampton and the Countess of Bedford. He then engaged in translating the *Essays* of Montaigne (the definitive edition of which had appeared in Paris only in 1595) and it appeared in 1603 in magnificent folio as *The Essays, or Moral, Politic, and Military Discourses of Lo. Michael de Montaigne*, dedicated to six aristocratic patronesses. On King James's accession Florio was appointed tutor to Prince Henry and reader in Italian to the Queen. A passionate delighter in words, Florio wrote in a Euphuistic style, using compound words and doubling, and showing the influence of Du Bartas. Shakespeare may have satirically portrayed him as Holofernes in *Love's Labour's Lost*, but, like other Elizabethans, was greatly influenced by Florio's *Montaigne*, which was several times reprinted. The Italian–English dictionary remained a landmark in the history of English scholarship, and, with English–Italian added by Terriano in 1657, was a standard work throughout the 17th century. [MJ]

F. O. Matthiessen, *Translation: An Elizabethan Art* (1931); F. A. Yates, *J.F.: The Life of an Italian in Shakespeare's England* (1934), and *A Study of 'Love's Labour's Lost'* (1936).

Foote, Samuel (1720–77). Actor and dramatist. He dissipated a fortune while an undergraduate at Oxford, studied law in London, and quickly established himself (at first in

Ford

amateur entertainments) as a cruel mimic and wit. He ridiculed the leading actors of the day (especially Colley Cibber), the stars of the Italian opera, and celebrated figures in society like the Duchess of Kingston, but he cannily avoided lampooning politicians. His many short plays, farces and topical skits were designed as vehicles for his own talents as a mimic; their contemporary satire and reference meant that they were ephemeral, occasional pieces. *The Minor* (1760) satirized the Methodists. *The Mayor of Garrett* (1763) is generally reckoned his best play. Foote was involved in theatre management, and in 1766, when he lost a leg as the result of a practical joke, he secured through the Duke of York a licence for a theatre in the Haymarket, where he presented a farce exploiting his disability. A great entertainer, he kept alive the spirit of laughter at a time when the English theatre was surfeited with sentimental comedy. [MJ]

M. M. Belden, *The Dramatic Work of S.F.* (1929) (with bibliography).

Ford, Ford Madox (1873–1939). Novelist. Born in Surrey, son of Dr Francis Hueffer, a music critic, he changed his name to Ford after the First World War. His grandfather was Ford Madox Brown, the painter. Ford was educated privately in Folkestone, and at University College School, London. He was received into the Roman Catholic Church as a youth of 18. *Poems for Pictures* (1900) was followed by 2 novels in the writing of which he collaborated with Joseph Conrad: *The Inheritors* (1901) and *Romance* (1903). In 1908, Ford founded the *English Review* and edited it for a year. His first independently written novels were *The Fifth Queen* (1906) and *The 'Half Moon'* (1909), but it was not until *The Good Soldier* (1915) that he began to attract critical attention. After the war, in which he served and in which he was gassed, he wrote a novel-tetralogy *Parade's End*, whose 4 separate components are *Some Do Not* (1924), *No More Parades* (1925), *A Man Could Stand Up* (1926) and *Last Post* (1928). His subject was Western civilization as it led up to the First World War, and he treats it with great skill and imaginative power. His ability to give significance to the minutiae of physical experience and the richness of his narrative prose combine to make him one of the finest 20th-century English novelists. He was consistently underrated in his own lifetime, but has found greater critical favour posthumously.

In addition to his masterpiece, *Parade's End*, Ford wrote several volumes of reminiscence which are fascinating, informative and often amusing: *Ancient Lights* (1911), *Thus to Revisit* (1921), *Return to Yesterday* (1931), *It was the Nightingale* (1934) and *Mightier Than the Sword* (1938). These volumes contain first-hand accounts of literary life and characters in Edwardian London and elsewhere, and are a valuable pendant to Ford's fiction. [CO]

Letters, ed. R. M. Ludwig (Princeton, 1965).
D. Goldring, *The Last Pre-Raphaelite* (1948); P. L. Wiley, *Novelist of Three Worlds: F.M.F.* (Syracuse, N.Y., 1962); F. MacShane, *The Life and Work of F.M.F.* (Princeton, 1965).

Ford, John (1586–c. 1640). Dramatist. Little is known of his life save that he was born in Devonshire and may have been briefly at Oxford before being admitted to the Inner Temple as a law student. He probably practised law in London. No record survives of his death or burial. Two early, occasional works were an elegy on the death of the Earl of Devonshire, *Fame's Memorial* (1606), and *Honour Triumphant or, The Peer's Challenge*, a chivalric prose pamphlet. Ford's earliest known work for the theatre was around 1621–4, when he collaborated with the experienced ◊ Dekker on 5 plays. Two survive: *The Witch of Edmonton* (on which William ◊ Rowley was a third collaborator) and a masque, *The Sun's Darling*. One of the lost plays was *The Late Murder of the Son upon the Mother, or Keep the Widow Waking*, a get-penny entertainment based on two recent London crimes hastily put together by Dekker, Ford, Rowley and Webster. Between 1625 and 1630 Ford wrote 3 plays acted by the King's Men, the leading company of the time, including *The Lover's Melancholy* (1628), a quiet tragi-comedy, and *The Broken Heart* (c. 1630), a tragedy about a forced marriage that brings grief to a group of characters. Both plays show the influence of the psychological theories set out in Burton's *Anatomy of Melancholy* (1621). Ford then wrote 5 plays for the theatre manager Christopher Beeston, including *'Tis Pity She's a Whore* (published 1633, staged earlier), his celebrated, sympathetic tragedy on the incestuous love of a brother and sister, and *Love's Sacrifice* (1633), a courtly tragedy of love and jealousy. *Perkin Warbeck* (c. 1634) was

190

a late example of an English history-play, and *The Fancies Chaste and Noble* (*c.* 1635), an unsuccessful comedy. Ford's last recorded play was *The Lady's Trial* (1638), a tragi-comedy, but he is nowadays credited also with *The Queen* (printed 1653). Writing at a time when the Elizabethan–Jacobean dramatic impulse was becoming exhausted, Ford was both aided and inhibited by the example of Shakespeare, but his imaginative sympathy, skill with blank verse and dramatic instinct make him the leading writer of tragedy in the reign of Charles I, and ensure that *'Tis Pity She's a Whore* and *The Broken Heart* are occasionally revived in the modern theatre, and frequently reprinted in anthologies. [MJ]

The Dramatic Works, ed. W. Gifford (2 vols., 1827; revised A. H. Bullen, 3 vols., 1895).
T. S. Eliot, 'J.F.', in *Selected Essays* (1932; revised edn, 1954); S. B. Ewing, *Burtonian Melancholy in the Plays of J.F.* (1940); C. Leech, *J.F. and the Drama of His Time* (1957) and *J.F.* (1964); H. J. Oliver, *The Problem of J.F.* (Melbourne, 1955); M. J. Sargeaunt, *J.F.* (1935); G. F. Sensabaugh, *The Tragic Muse of J.F.* (Palo Alto, 1944); M. Stavig, *J.F. and the Traditional Moral Order* (1968).

Fordun, John (d. 1384?). Scottish annalist. A secular priest and canon of Aberdeen Cathedral, he travelled through Scotland and England in the 1360s and 1370s in quest of materials for his history. He completed Latin annals of Scotland down to 1153 (*Chronica gentis Scotorum*, ed. W. F. Skene, 1871; tr. F. J. H. Skene, *Chronicle of the Scottish Nation*, 1872), and left notes and material for a continuation to the 1380s; after his death Walter Bower (d. 1449), Abbot of Inchcolm, continued his annals as the *Scotichronicon* (ed. W. Goodall, 1759) to the death of James I in 1437. Fordun tidied and to some extent rationalized the legendary early history, and becomes more credible and reliable as his narrative approaches his own time. For the 14th and 15th centuries the joint work is a contemporary authority. [AI]

Forster, E(dward) M(organ) (1879–1970). Novelist and essayist. Born in London, the son of an architect, he was educated at Tonbridge School as a day boy, and studied classics and history at King's College, Cambridge (where he was an honorary Fellow). There he came under the influence of Goldsworthy ◊ Lowes Dickinson, whose *Life* he published in 1934. He lived in Italy

and Greece, and these classical and Mediterranean countries form the background for some of his short stories (particularly 'The Story of the Siren' and 'The Eternal Moment') and for 2 of his novels, *Where Angels Fear to Tread* (1905) and *A Room with a View* (1908). Cambridge is the setting for the first part of his third novel, *The Longest Journey* (1907); and *Howards End* (1910) is placed in pre-First World War London and its countryside. In 1912 he travelled to India with Lowes Dickinson, and this experience (together with a later stay there in 1922 for six months, as secretary to the Maharaja of Dewas) produced *A Passage to India*, begun before the First World War but appearing in 1924. During the war itself, Forster was in Alexandria, and he later wrote *Alexandria: A History and Guide* (1922; reissued 1961), a book worth reading on its own account and an amusing exposition of Forster's Hellenism and antipathy to Anglo-Saxon Christianity; these years also went into a volume of historical essays, *Pharos and Pharillon* (1923). In 1927 he delivered the Clark Lectures at Trinity College, Cambridge, and published them as *Aspects of the Novel* (1927). His short stories are collected in 2 volumes, *The Celestial Omnibus* (1911) and *The Eternal Moment* (1928). He published 2 volumes of personal, critical, travel and political essays: *Abinger Harvest* (1936), which takes its title from a Surrey village where he lived; and *Two Cheers for Democracy* (1951), containing some of the broadcasts he delivered during the Second World War. *The Hill of Devi* (1953) is an account of his life in India, and his biographical work includes the Rede Lecture for 1941 *Virginia Woolf* (published in 1942) and *Marianne Thornton, 1797–1887: A Domestic Biography* (1956), on his great-aunt.

With 5 novels (all but one published before the First World War), 2 volumes of short stories and some essays, Forster established a reputation as one of the greatest modern English writers. By family descent he was the inheritor of the moral concern of the evangelical 'Clapham Sect'; by education, he was one of the Cambridge intellectuals excited by G. E. ◊ Moore's *Principia Ethica*; and by temperament a member of the ◊ 'Bloomsbury Group', he lived in an intellectual atmosphere that continued the old evangelical moral concern but with a detachment permitted by inherited wealth and secularized beliefs. His study of the classics added a feeling for the power of myth, the attraction of magic. His own gifts and tastes, in which some of those values were at war, added sharp observation of life, wit, irony and a poet's power of writing. His stories and novels contrast the freedom of paganism with the restraint of (English) civilization; the personal delight in the body, with the impersonal, social inhibition of behaviour. In *Where Angels Fear to Tread*, the vitality of disreputable, violent, pitiable Gino is contrasted with the different kinds of narrowness and lifelessness of the English visitors. In *The Longest Journey*, the pagan Wiltshire of the third section of the book is juxtaposed with the deadly village of Sawston of the second. Forster's Indian experiences broadened and deepened his half-prophetic probing into the dilemma of European civilization. The Hindu 'openness' to feeling, to experience, to religious awe (with its dangerous concomitant of indecision) is contrasted with the 'practical' English inflexibility, which is necessary to maintain and exercise power. As a humanist, Forster's vision was individual, almost anarchic. 'Only connect' is the theme of *Howards End*, where Mrs Wilcox is the individual person drawing her power from the country, and the male Wilcoxes are the social beings, the inhabitants of the world of 'telegrams and anger', the world of modern civilization, of organization. Forster's great gift, moreover, was to organize his view of the world in comedy. His stories, too, contain violent happenings, coincidences, unrealities, which serve to further his concern with life, feelings and acceptance, at war with useless effort, lack of communication and death-like rejection. [A R]

L. Trilling, *E.M.F.* (1944); J. B. Beer, *The Achievement of E.M.F.* (1962); A. Wilde, *Art and Order: A Study of E.M.F.* (New York, 1964); ed. M. Bradbury, *F. A Collection of Critical Essays* (1966); F. C. Crews, *E.M.F. The Perils of Humanism* (1962); B. K. Kirkpatrick, *A Bibliography of E.M.F.* (1965).

Forster, John (1812–76). Journalist and biographer. Born in Newcastle, and educated at the Grammar School there and University College, London, he was called to the bar at the Inner Temple, but became a professional writer, contributing biographical articles to Lardner's *Cyclopaedia* (1836–9). In 1834 he had become assistant

editor of the *Examiner*, to which he contributed dramatic reviews; he was later editor (1847–55). He was also editor of the *Foreign Quarterly Review* (1842–3) and the *Daily News* (1846). He was Secretary to the Commissions of Lunacy and a Commissioner (1861–72). Forster was an opinionated and peremptory man, but had the friendship of two men of genius, whose lives he wrote: *W. S. Landor* (1868) and *Charles Dickens* (1872–4). He collected valuable materials for a *Life of Swift* (only one volume of which appeared, in 1875), which he bequeathed to the Victoria and Albert Museum. He was also the author of several other works, informative but not critically distinguished, e.g. *Life of Goldsmith* (1848) and *Historical and Biographical Essays* (1858). [A R]

M. Elwin, *Victorian Wallflowers* (1934).

Foulis, Hugh. ◊ Munro, Neil.

Fowler, H(enry) W(atson) (1858–1933). Philologist and lexicographer. Born at Tonbridge, Kent, and educated at Rugby and Balliol College, Oxford, he taught at Sedbergh from 1882, until he retired in 1899 because he refused to prepare boys for confirmation. Fowler wrote literary essays for periodicals, which were collected in 4 volumes, but is best known for the works which he prepared for the Oxford University Press in collaboration with F. G. Fowler, his brother: *The King's English* (1906 etc.) and *The Concise Oxford Dictionary of Current English* (1911 etc.), an abridgement of the *Oxford English Dictionary*, and after his brother's death, the well-known *Dictionary of Modern English Usage* (1926; revised Sir E. Gowers, 1965). Fowler's work is in support of 'pure English', the middle-class 'mandarin' conception of language. The illustrations and quotations which he produces in connexion with the points of correct style show much entertaining, quiet wit. [A R]

G. G. Coulton, *H.F.* (Society for the Preservation of English, 1934).

Foxe, John (1517–87). Religious writer and martyrologist. A Lincolnshire man, he was educated at Brasenose College, Oxford, and had to relinquish his fellowship at Magdalen in 1545 because of his Protestant beliefs. He was tutor to several noble families, and was ordained in 1550. At the accession of Mary in 1555 he took refuge in Europe, at first at Frankfurt with John Knox and other Protestants. His literary work was far more important than his ministry, and was for long second only to the Bible as a force in British Puritanism. He published in exile at Strassburg a first Latin account of the Christian martyrs, *Commentarii rerum in ecclesia gestarum*, in 1554, enlarged it in 1559, and in 1563 issued a massive, double-columned folio volume in English, *The Acts and Monuments of the Church*, in which the history of martyrs was brought up to date to include Tyndale, Latimer and others. *The Book of Martyrs*, as his work became called, went into 3 further editions before his death (ed. S. R. Cattley and G. Townsend, 8 vols., 1837–41). It is a passionate, partisan, detail and vivid compendium of persecutions and suffering, and the accounts of recent martyrs under Bloody Mary often included the testimony of witnesses. [MJ]

C. H. Garrett, *The Marian Exiles* (1938); C. S. Lewis, *English Literature in the Sixteenth Century* (1954); J. F. Mozley, *J.F. and His Book* (1940).

Frame, Janet (1924–   ). New Zealand novelist. Born near Dunedin and educated at Otago University, she taught for a while, then became a nurse-companion in Dunedin. The short stories of *The Lagoon* (1951) were mainly written at this time. She spent several years in a mental hospital after suffering a breakdown, and there wrote *Faces in the Water* (1962). The novel's narrator is a young woman in whom sensitivity has reached the point of madness. Frame sees two insanities, the world's and the madman's. The book is disturbing because she is not sure which she prefers. She left New Zealand in 1956 and now lives in London.

Frame thinks of her books as 'explorations' rather than novels. Their main development is verbal and reflective. In both *Owls Do Cry* (1957) and *The Edge of the Alphabet* (1962) she is concerned with the private vision of three people, all of them outside the area of simple 'normality'. In the first they are three children, in the second three New Zealand emigrants. Among the subjects of her exploration are the meaning of personality and the possibility of self-fulfilment in communication. Dialogue and description are generally used in the context of interior monologue. Her most recent novels are *Scented Gardens for the*

Blind (1963), *The Adaptable Man* (1965), *A State of Siege* (1966) and *The Rainbirds* (1968). [PT]
The Reservoir and Other Stories (1966).

Frankau, Pamela (1908–   ). Novelist, short-story writer and journalist. The daughter of Gilbert Frankau, she was educated at the P.N.E.U. School in Burgess Hill, Sussex, and became a journalist, working for the *Woman's Journal*. She served in the A.T.S. during the Second World War, and in 1942 became a Roman Catholic. She now lives in the United States and has written under the name 'Eliot Naylor'. Her first novel, a piece of light fiction, *Marriage of Harlequin*, was published in 1927. Her many other novels include *Willow Cabin* (1949), a love story; *The Winged Horse* (1953); *A Wreath for the Enemy* (1954), a tale of a girl growing up on the French Riviera; *Road through the Woods* (1960); *Slaves of the Lamp* (1965); and *Over the Mountains* (1967). [AR]

Fraser, G(eorge) S(utherland) (1915–   ). Poet and critic. Born in Glasgow, he was educated at Aberdeen Grammar School and St Andrews University. In the late thirties he was closely associated with the ◊ Apocalypse movement. From 1939 to 1945 he served in the army and contributed to several anthologies of forces poetry. Until 1958, when he became a lecturer in English Literature at Leicester University, he worked as a freelance writer and in 1950 visited Japan as Cultural Adviser to the U.K. Liaison Mission. Written mainly under the impact of war, Fraser's poetry, in *Home Town Elegy* (1944), *The Fatal Landscape* (1948) and *The Traveller Has Regrets* (1948), explores personal and local themes in a mood of gentle, restrained lyricism. In recent years he has concentrated mainly on literary criticism and has published studies of Dylan Thomas, Ezra Pound and W. B. Yeats. He is best known for *The Modern Writer and His World* (1953; revised 1964) and *Vision and Rhetoric* (1959), a perceptive examination of modern poetry.

Frazer, Sir James (George) (1854–1941). Social anthropologist. Born in Glasgow, the son of a businessman, and educated there and in Helensburgh, at the University of Glasgow, and at Trinity College, Cambridge, of which he became a Fellow in classics, he was called to the bar at the

Freeman

Middle Temple, of which he became an Honorary Bencher in 1931, but he never practised. Frazer became interested in anthropology by writing 2 articles, on 'Totemism' and 'Taboo', for the *Encyclopædia Britannica*. He moved from a historical study of religion, by way of the evolutionary theory of human development from savagery to civilization, towards a quasi-scientific set of theories about the development of religious beliefs and rituals. He started with a discussion of the riddle of the King of the Wood in Diana's Grove in Aricia, and from this investigation of the ancient Italian succession in the priesthood he evolved a universal concept of religion as the ritual killing of a divine king by his successor as part of man's attempt to control nature. He followed this theory up by investigations of magical practices, religious beliefs and observances, and myths in many societies; his great work *The Golden Bough*, which began appearing in 1890, is an accretion in several volumes of such discussions; the original volume was followed by *The Magic Art and Evolution of Kings*; *Taboo and the Perils of the Soul*; *The Dying God*; *Adonis, Attis and Osiris – Studies in the History of Oriental Religion*; *Spirits of the Corn and of the Wild*; *The Scape-goat*; *Balder the Beautiful – The Fire Festivals of Europe – The Doctrine of the External Soul* (the 2nd edn began appearing in 1900 and a 3rd, enlarged and revised, appeared in 1915; a supplement was added in 1936; the work was issued in an abridged single volume version in 1922). The thread of theory at times fails under the strain and the work is now valuable as a repository of Frazer's investigations presented with powerful imagination and literary skill. His substructure of 'laws' of development was attacked at the time by other workers in the field (◇ Lang, Andrew) and is now largely discredited, but individual parts of his investigations are of great interest. His work, with that of Freud, which he opposed, has had considerable influence on the analysis of literary texts in terms of archetypal themes and motifs. He was the author of many other works based on his extensive study of classical literature and primitive history. His interests were, however, largely literary, ignoring the work of sociologists and linguists. [AR]

R. A. Downie, *J.G.F.: The Portrait of a Scholar* (1940); B. K. Malinowski, 'Biographical Appreciation', in *A Scientific Theory of Culture*

(Chapel Hill, 1944); S. E. Hyman, *The Tangled Bank: Darwin, Marx, F. and Freud as Imaginative Writers* (New York, 1962); T. Besterman, *A Bibliography of F.* (1934).

Freeman, Edward Augustus (1823–92). Historian. Born at Harborne, Staffordshire, and privately educated, he went on to Trinity College, Oxford, where he became a Fellow. Freeman wrote much for periodicals, chiefly for the *Saturday Review*, and published many of his essays separately. In 1884, he succeeded ◇ Stubbs as Regius Professor of Modern History at Oxford. Like Stubbs, he was interested in the Middle Ages (his chief work was *The History of the Norman Conquest of England. Its Causes and Results*, 6 vols., 1867–79), and he was also interested in the 'development' of institutions, but worked more or less solely from secondary material, so that his ideas (like some of Stubbs's) have often been superseded. Other substantial historical works were: *History of Federal Government* (in Ancient Greece) (1863; ed. J. B. Bury, 1893); *The Growth of the English Constitution from the Earliest Times* (1872): *The Historical Geography of Europe* (2 vols., 1881, etc.) and *The History of Sicily from the Earliest Times* (4 vols., 1891–4). He was an ardent controversialist (his earliest work was a contribution to the then dangerous Gothic Revival bickering, *Principles of Church Restoration*, 1846), and he put a strong infusion of ethical judgement in his history. A union of these two tendencies produced his violently anti-Turkish *The Ottoman Power in Europe* (1877) and led him to adopt a view of European history as a kind of illustration of England's 'manifest destiny' (◇ Seeley, Sir J. R.). He was widely travelled (and wrote about his travels), dying of smallpox while rambling in Spain. [AR]

W. R. W. Stephens, *The Life and Letters of E.A.F.* (2 vols., 1895) (with bibliography); J. Bryce, *Studies in Contemporary Biography* (1903); H. A. Cronne, 'E.A.F.', *History*, XXVIII (1943).

Freeman, John (1880–1929). Poet and critic. An interesting example, in both his literary and business careers, of the successful self-made man. Born at Dalston, the son of a commercial traveller, his boyhood was chequered by scarlet-fever, which left him with a permanently weakened heart. He left his school, Hackney Academy, at 12 to become a junior clerk in a Friendly Society

194

of which he ultimately became general secretary and director. Passionately fond of literature, he taught himself Greek. He wrote much poetry, criticism and critical biography, contributing frequently to Sir John ◊ Squire's *London Mercury* (Squire, with Freeman's widow, later edited his letters). A facile and pleasant writer both in prose and verse, he lacked the individuality that would have given him a permanent posthumous reputation, but, unlike many writers who have lasted better, had a successful and enjoyable literary life. [GSF]

Twenty Poems (1909); *Fifty Poems* (1911); *Presage of Victory* (1916); *The Moderns* (1916); *Portrait of George Moore* (1922); *English Portraits* (1924); *Herman Melville* (1926); *Solomon and Balkis* (1926); *Letters*, ed. G. Freeman and Sir J. Squire (1931).

French Canadian Literature. The French Canadians of the St Lawrence valley and the mining and rural communities of the Laurentian Shield are the descendants of the French settlers who came to Canada in the 17th century. This people, some five millions in number, surrounded by the two hundred million English-speaking North Americans, offers a striking example of cultural vitality in the face of opposition, and their literature can best be seen as a literature of survival, finding expression in a search for identity and the assertion of national values.

French Canadian society before the British conquest of 1763 was that of a benign form of feudalism and it was not until 1800 that a middle class, capable of giving rise to a literary culture, emerged. Up to 1800 there was a wealth of writing, though nothing that could be considered indigenous – the annual reports of the Jesuit missions, travellers' tales and correspondence addressed to France by settlers for the most part born and educated in France.

The 19th century opened with the founding of the first French-language newspaper of note, creating a tradition of journalism, conservative in the main, but with brief periods of lively protest that caused newspapers to be suppressed and journalists to be imprisoned. French Canadian writers were for the first time really stung into action by the conclusions of Lord Durham's Report of 1839 which found in the French Canadians a people 'without history and without a literature' and who could only benefit from assimilation to a British way of life. A reply came from the group of men who created the 'mouvement littéraire et patriotique de Québec' in the fifties. The make-up of this group, which met in a backroom of the bookshop owned by the poet Octave Crémazie and his brother, gives a fair idea of the mood of the cultural life of the time – newspaper editors Taché and Cauchon, poets Crémazie, Lemay and Fréchette, and historians Ferland and François-Xavier Garneau, whose *Histoire du Canada* (1845–52) first took up the challenge presented by the Durham Report.

Garneau's history marks the beginning of a traditional predilection for history which in the 20th century has become the domain of university teachers and archivists. Canon Lionel Groulx, an ardent nationalist, has rewritten Garneau's work, with titles such as *Notre grande aventure* (1958), *Nos luttes constitutionnelles* (1915–16) and *Notre maître le passé* (1936), while younger men like Frégault, Trudel, Brunet and Lanctot have begun the task of demythologizing the history of New France in works based on scrupulous research but occasionally illumined by flashes of national fervour.

Garneau's history directly inspired one of the early novels, Aubert de Gaspé's *Les anciens Canadiens* (1863), which won great popular acclaim for its author who had conveyed perfectly in his long historical romance, set in 18th-century Quebec, the nostalgia felt by Canadians for the 'golden age' before the national tragedy of the Conquest. The novel fared less well than the other genres, perhaps for want of a novel-reading public, perhaps because poetry, history and journalism required a less sustained effort of the imagination on the writer's part, most probably because the lyricism and eloquence of poetry and polemics best suited the French Canadian's mixed mood of nostalgia and resigned fortitude.

François-Xavier Garneau was a source of inspiration for the writer of the other novel of note in the 19th century. Félicité Angers (1845–1924), who wrote under the name of Laure Conan, published in 1881 French Canada's first novel of psychological analysis, *Angéline de Montbrun*. This novel in letter-form describes the first stirrings of love and then, with great perception, the torments of unrequited passion, closing with the portrayal of a devout life of melancholy contemplation and reverence for the past lived in the seclusion of rural Quebec; the life, in fact, of its author.

The influence of the French Romantics on 19th-century poetry in French Canada has been painstakingly demonstrated by L. A. Bisson in his thesis *Le Romantisme littéraire au Canada français* (Paris, 1932). In Louis Fréchette's *Légende d'un peuple* (1887) the influence of Hugo and the patriotic inspiration of Garneau join forces. Octave Crémazie (1827–79), another admirer of Hugo, devoted more energy to reading and writing than to selling books and had to flee his creditors into what Gilles Marcotte has called a second exile in France, the first being the self-imposed exile of the French Canadian poet who chose to alienate himself by his imitation of his French models ('Une poésie d'exil', in *Mercure de France*, May 1958, and *Une littérature qui se fait*, 1962, a valuable collection of essays by this consistently reliable Canadian critic).

Imitation finds its highest expression in the works of the first of French Canada's 'poètes maudits', Émile Nelligan (1879–1941). After a burst of precocious poetic creation (180 poems written between the ages of 15 and 19) when his poetry was received with wild enthusiasm at the meetings of the École Littéraire de Montréal, he lost his reason and spent the rest of his life in an asylum. Fifty years of Nelligan studies, the best of French Canadian academic criticism, have shown what the poet owed to Verlaine, Baudelaire, Rodenbach, Rollinat and Coppée, but also the extent of his own original genius.

Hector de ◊ Saint-Denys-Garneau was the first French Canadian poet to write truly original and intensely personal poetry, tortured free verse that translates his own fundamental disharmony and his nostalgia for the freedom of the spacious world of the child's imagination. His poetry, too, is written in the space of three years or so (1935–9) during which he is gradually reduced to silence, in his case the silence of lucid despair and a premature death. His friends were to say, after his death, that he was killed by the stifling, narrowly conformist society of Quebec in the thirties. The cultural vacuum of this period is mirrored in a novel of the time, Jean-Charles Harvey's *Les demi-civilisés* (1934; tr. *Sackcloth for Banner*, Toronto, 1938), a satirical work reminiscent of Anatole France which fails as a novel because it tries to be too many things at once, but is important as a social document and because of Harvey's courageous attempt to break new ground by

setting his novel in the city, encouraging a free discussion of love and attempting to introduce psychological realism.

The French Canadian novel, for most people, means *Maria Chapdelaine* (1916; tr. W. H. Blake, Toronto, 1921). This novel was in fact written by a Frenchman, Louis Hémon, for a French public. In Canada, it had the unfortunate result of setting the pattern for the novel that was to persist until the Second World War. The 'roman du terroir' is seen at its most lyrical in Félix-Antoine Savard's *Menaud, maître-draveur* (1937; revised 1944; tr. A Sullivan, *Boss of the River*, Toronto, 1947). More realistic treatments of the theme, presenting without sentimentality the decline of the traditional rural life, are to be found in Ringuet's *30 Arpents* (pseud. of Doctor Philippe Panneton, Paris, 1938; tr. F. and D. Walter, *Thirty Acres*, 1940), one of the finest novels to come from French Canada, Germaine Guèvremont's *Le survenant* (1945; tr. *The Outlander*, New York, 1950), and Claude-Henri Grignon's bitter portrait of a peasant miser, *Un homme et son péché* (1933).

The Second World War helped the Canadian writer by stopping temporarily the flow of books from Europe and by waking him up to the rapid urbanization and industrialization that had taken place almost unnoticed. With the prize-winning novel of Gabrielle ◊ Roy, *Bonheur d'occasion* (1945), and the gentle satire of Roger Lemelin's *Au pied de la pente douce* (1944; tr. S. Putnam, *The Town Below*, New York, 1948), urban life established its place in the novel, and the theme was explored, often in more cutting terms, by the novelists of the fifties, André Langevin (1927–   ), Eugène Cloutier (1921–   ) and Jean Simard (1916–   ), all of whom have been criticized for the debt they owe to the French novel from Mauriac and Proust through Bernanos to Camus and Robbe-Grillet.

Yves ◊ Thériault, the most prolific of French Canadian writers, escapes this criticism by his highly individual style and by his courageous rehandling of modern themes in Canadian terms, the drama of the minority group, the status of women, the search for identity and the varied human interest provided by life in a small community. The last ten years has seen an ever greater diversification of themes as novels appear in increasing numbers (over two per month in 1961) but certain themes can be seen to recur, all of them facets of the crisis of human values in the age of the machine: the self-analysis of the hero confronted with the absurdity of existence (Réal Benoit, *Quelqu'un pour m'écouter*, 1964), freedom and self-affirmation (Claude Jasmin, *Ethel et le terroriste*, 1964), the mystery that lies behind the mask of routine, insignificant existence of middle-class life (Jean Simard, *Les sentiers de la nuit*, 1959), and the exploration of the traumatic universe that lies at the limits of consciousness (Marie-Claire Blais, *Une saison dans la vie d'Emmanuel*, 1965; Prix Medicis, 1966).

In spite of the flourishing state of the live theatre in Montreal, French Canada cannot boast a large number of published dramatic works, perhaps because of the strong temptation to write for television amongst would-be dramatists.

Again it is poetry which has achieved the greatest success in recent times. A revolution in French poetry similar to that of geometrical abstraction in painting has suddenly made the writing of poetry accessible to almost anyone with a feeling for the poetry of words. This poetry consists in the semi-formal arrangement of words, of nouns in particular which take on the force of ciphers, choice and arrangement being justified by the coherence, the sincerity and the artistic necessity of the impression created. It is a form of poetry which, at its best, whatever the purist may say, captures the elusive sensitivity of the age. The best examples of the poetry in French Canada are to be found in the work of Alain ◊ Grandbois and Anne ◊ Hébert, both of whom, in their very different ways, manage to assimilate their experience of French poetry and to write original verse. Inspired by them a succession of able young poets have, in the last fifteen years, turned this new poetry to their own purposes: political protest, the affirmation of a Canadian identity or the celebration of the union of man with the earth (see Alain Bosquet's anthology, *La poésie canadienne*, Paris and Montreal, 1962).

Anne Hébert, in the brief prose preface to a collection of her poems, has given us two lyrical definitions of poetry, which, with the simple beauty of great writing, sum up the Canadian poet's patient endeavours to capture and to give voice to 'cette seconde vie que la poésie peut signifier à la beauté surabondante du monde', 'l'effort de la vie qui cherche sa nourriture et son nom'. This effort takes on its true meaning when set against the scale of the continent in which the experience is taking place. Its achievements bring Quebec close to deserving the title one of its own poets gave it in a recent essay, 'pays de poésie'. [CRPM]

The Oxford Book of Canadian Verse, ed. A. J. M. Smith (1960); *La poésie canadienne*, ed. A. Bosquet (Paris, 1962; revised edn, 1966); volumes devoted to Alain Grandbois, Anne Hébert, Rina Lasnier, Felix Leclere, Saint-Denys-Garneau, Gilles Vigneault in the Collection 'Poètes d'aujourd'hui'.
G. Tougas, *Histoire de la littérature canadienne-française* (Paris, 1960; revised edn, 1964); P. de Grandpré, *Histoire de la Littérature française du Québec* (4 vols., Montreal, 1967–9).

Frere, J(ohn) H(ookham) (1769–1846). Diplomatist, translator and satirist. Born in London and educated at Eton and Caius College, Cambridge, he had a clerkship in the Foreign Office, and was an M.P. and under-secretary for that department. He was envoy to Portugal (1800–2), ambassador at Madrid (1802–4) and with the Junta during the war (1808–9). Frere retired to Malta, where he entertained British travellers like Byron and Scott. His wide interests lay in ancient and foreign poetry. While at school, he translated the Old English poem *Brunanburh* and contributed to the *Specimens of the Early English Poets* (enlarged edition, 1801) published by George ◊ Ellis; he collaborated with Southey in his translation of *The Chronicle of the Cid* (1808). Frere, on his own, published lively verse translations (still among the most readable renderings) of Aristophanes (*Aristophanes' Plays*, 1839, 1840, etc.; World's Classics, 1907). He was an active journalist in the Tory interest; one of the founders of *The Microcosm* (1786–7) and a contributor to *The Anti-Jacobin*, in which he wrote most of the *Loves of the Triangles* (ridiculing Erasmus ◊ Darwin) and collaborated with Canning in sending up Southey in *The Friend of Humanity* and *The Knife Grinder* (see *Parodies and Other Burlesques by Canning, Ellis and Frere, with the Whole Poetry of the Anti-Jacobin*, ed. H. Morley, 1890). Frere was also one of the founders of the *Quarterly Review*. His place in the history of English literature, however, rests on his *Prospectus and Specimen of an Intended National Work by William and Robert Whistlecraft Intended to Comprise the Most Interesting Particulars Relating to King Arthur and His Round Table* (cantos i

197

and ii, 1817; iii and iv, 1818); extended as *The Monks and the Giants* (1818, etc.; ed. R. D. Waller, 1926). This mock-heroic poem, witty and learned, inspired Byron to take up this kind of writing, which he excelled in (e.g. *Beppo* and *Don Juan*), by sending him to read the Italian masters used by Frere, Luigi Pulci (who burlesques the Charlemagne legend in an old Italian genre) and Francesco Berni. [AR]

G. Festing, *J.H.F. and His Friends* (1899); H. Walker, *English Satire and Satirists* (1925).

Froude, James Anthony (1818–94). Historian and miscellaneous writer. Born near Totnes in Devon (of which his father was Archdeacon), and educated at Westminster and Oriel College, Oxford. His eldest brother, R. H. Froude, was one of the leading Tractarians and J. A. came briefly under the influence of J. H. ◊ Newman, contributing to the latter's *Lives of the English Saints* (1844–5). This work gave the final jolt to his weakening belief and he thereafter turned away from Christianity, chronicling his loss of faith (in the contemporary manner) in works of semi-fictional autobiography, *Shadows of the Clouds* (1847) and *The Nemesis of Faith* (1849, etc.). He became a disciple of Carlyle and turned to writing historical and other essays in the *Westminster Review, Fraser's Magazine* (which he edited, 1860–74) and elsewhere. Some of these essays were later reprinted as *Short Studies on Great Subjects* (2 vols., 1867; 2nd series, 1871; 3rd series, 1877; 4th series, 1883, etc.; 1st series reprinted in World's Classics, 1924). As a historian, Froude was best known for his *History of England from the Fall of Wolsey to the Death of Elizabeth* (12 vols., 1856–70; revised, 1870; Everyman, 10 vols., 1909–12). Froude believed (with his 'hero' Carlyle) that great men initiate and control events, and that the 'art' of history was to enter dramatically and imaginatively into what the historian thought was the successful 'force' of the time. The dangers of this polemical approach are obvious, and to them Froude united a quite individual inaccuracy. Both his long work and his book *The English in Ireland in the Eighteenth Century* (3 vols., 1872–4; 1881) were the centres of bitter controversy. Froude was the literary executor of Carlyle and his edition of the letters of Carlyle and his wife, with biographical reminiscences, was thought to be injurious to his friend

because of their 'indiscretion'. Froude visited Africa, Australia and the West Indies in various capacities (sometimes as a government commissioner), and the books he wrote as a result – *Oceana, or England and Her Colonies* (1886) and *The English in the West Indies* (1888) – are of some interest and entertainment to the modern reader. He was appointed Regius Professor of History at Oxford (1892), and published several books of his lectures: *Life and Letters of Erasmus* (1893); *Lectures on the Council of Trent* (1893); *English Seamen in the Sixteenth Century* (1895, etc.; ed. A. A. Froude, 1923). [AR]

A. Cecil, *Six Oxford Thinkers* (1909); W. H. Dunn, *F. and Carlyle* (New York, 1930); L. Strachey, *Characters and Commentaries* (1933); B. Willey, *More Nineteenth Century Studies* (1956).

Fry, Christopher (1907–). Dramatist. Originally a schoolmaster, he directed repertory companies at Tunbridge Wells and Oxford, and his early religious plays were written for religious festivals. A tragedy on Moses, *The Firstborn*, was completed at the end of the war when Fry became known in the London theatre coterie after the production of his sprightly verse-play *A Phoenix Too Frequent*. His spring-time comedy *The Lady's Not for Burning*, first seen at a club theatre, was successfully staged on Shaftesbury Avenue in 1949 by Sir John Gielgud, a success repeated on Broadway. *Venus Observed*, its autumnal counterpart, commissioned by Sir Laurence Olivier, followed in 1950, and in 1954 Fry wrote for Dame Edith Evans his winter comedy on a pacifist theme, *The Dark Is Light Enough*. Greatly in vogue around 1950, when journalists predicted a revival of the poetic drama, Fry has since been neglected. He has translated plays by Anouilh and Giraudoux and written screenplays. A history-play on Henry II, *Curtmantle*, was not produced in Britain till 1962. The comedies show a brilliant verbal gift and a warm celebration of life, but the poetry does not always advance or clarify the action. Fry was awarded the Queen's Medal for poetry. [MJ]

Marius Bewley, 'The Verse of C.F.', *Scrutiny*, XLII (1951); D. Donoghue, *The Third Voice* (1959); D. Stanford, *C.F.: An Appreciation* (1951), *C.F. Album* (1952), and *C.F.* (revised edn, 1962).

Frye, H(erman) Northrop (1912–). Canadian literary critic. Born in Sherbrooke, Quebec, and educated at the University of Toronto. On completing graduate studies in theology in 1936, he was ordained a minister of the United Church of Canada. In 1939 he became a lecturer in English at the University of Toronto, where he is now a Professor and Principal of Victoria College. As teacher, as editor of the *Canadian Forum* (1948–54) and as annual reviewer of Canadian poetry in the *University of Toronto Quarterly* (1951–60), he has had considerable influence on modern Canadian writing, encouraging a creative interest in myth, careful self-criticism and wide reading in older literatures. His own remarkable breadth of reading is evident in *Fearful Symmetry* (1947), his exegesis of William Blake's work, and in *Anatomy of Criticism* (1957), an original and provocative interpretation of the critic's task based on the classification of literary types according to archetypal themes and modes, which has had wide influence. He has also written *T. S. Eliot* (1963), *A National Perspective* (1966) and *Fools of Time* (1967). [PT]

Fulke, Greville, Lord Brooke. ◊ Greville, Fulke.

Fuller, Roy (Broadbent) (1912–). Poet and novelist. Born in Lancashire, Fuller left school at 16 and was articled to a solicitor. Throughout his life he has been a practising member of the legal profession and he was solicitor to the Woolwich Equitable Building Society. During the thirties, influenced by the poetry of Auden and Spender, he was closely associated with left-wing literary movements and contributed to *New Writing* and *New Verse*. He published his first volume of poetry, *Poems*, in 1940. From 1941 to 1945 he served in the Royal Navy and during this period published *The Middle of a War* (1942) and *A Lost Season* (1944), in which he consciously set out to portray the reality of service life. Notable for his keen sense of observation, strong humanitarian conscience and dry, occasionally prolix style, he is one of the finest poets of the Second World War. The poems in his next 2 volumes, *Epitaphs and Occasions* (1949) and *Counterparts* (1954), were markedly different from his earlier work. Very simple in form and sardonic in tone,

they express a deeply felt discontent with post-war English society. The publication of *Brutus's Orchard* (1957), *Collected Poems 1936–1961* (1962) and *Buff* (1965), in which personal bitterness has been replaced by profound self-analysis, has placed Roy Fuller among the most important living English poets. Although he had earlier written 2 novels for children, his first adult novel, *The Second Curtain*, a fast-moving, highly intelligent thriller in the tradition of Graham Greene's 'entertainments', was not published until 1953. This was followed by *Fantasy and Fugue* (1954), *Image of a Society* (1956), an outstanding portrayal of middle-class suburban life, *The Ruined Boys* (1959), *The Father's Comedy* (1961), *The Perfect Fool* (1963) and *My Child, My Sister* (1965). [PJK]

New Poems (1968).
R. N. Currey, *Poets of the 1939–45 War* (WTW, 1960); Frank McGuinness, 'The Novels of Roy Fuller', *London Magazine*, III (November 1963).

Fuller, Thomas (1608–61). Historian and preacher. Born in Aldwinkle in Northamptonshire, Fuller was educated at Cambridge and at 20 was the youngest M.A. of the university. In 1635 he received the degree of Bachelor of Divinity and preached at Cambridge, Salisbury, Dorset and Bristol before being appointed Preacher at the Chapel Royal in London in 1641. Although he was opposed to military solutions of the political conflict between King and Parliament, his sympathies were definitely Royalist, and Parliamentary opposition made him leave London for Oxford. From 1643 to 1644 he was Chaplain to the Royal Army. He married twice, in 1638 and again in 1652, and died at Covent Garden after being taken ill while preaching a sermon.

In his own day Fuller had a great reputation as a preacher. He was enormously prolific as a writer and his output included, besides poems, translations and occasional pamphlets such as a satire against Cromwell entitled *Andronicus or the Unfortunate Politician* (1646), a history of the Crusades, *A History of the Holy War* (1639), and *The Worthies of England* (1662). This last, a series of lives of celebrated Englishmen arranged by counties, was published posthumously by Fuller's elder son and is perhaps the work by which he is best known today. It displays the vigorous intelligence, the unsubtle but engaging wit and the passion for detail which are characteristic of Fuller. [GS]

Poems and Translations in Verse, ed. A. B. Grosart (1868).
Anon., *Life* (1661); J. E. Bailey, *Life of T.F.* (1874); *Bibliography*, ed. S. Gibson (Oxford Bibliographical Society, 1936); S. C. Roberts, *T.F.* (1953).

Furphy, Joseph (1843–1912). Australian novelist. Born near Melbourne of Northern Irish parents. A slight formal education, farming, road-building and goldfield labour were followed by several years in the Riverina district as a teamster. It was these years which provided the material for his writing. In 1884 he was forced to sell his bullock-teams and take work at a Shepparton foundry. His first story reached the *Bulletin* in 1889, and the unwieldy manuscript of *Such is Life* was trimmed for publication in 1903. The omitted sections formed 2 further books, published long after Furphy's death. He died at Claremont three years after he and his wife had joined their sons in Western Australia.

Such Is Life pretends to be random extracts from the diary of Tom Collins, a Government Deputy-Assistant-Sub-Inspector. This slight structure allows Furphy to present the variety of his remarkable personality. His love of the camp-fire tall story spills over into *The Buln-Buln and the Brolga* (1948), and his socialism into *Rigby's Romance* (1946), but these books do not match the page by page surprises of *Such Is Life*. 'Temper democratic; bias offensively Australian', wrote Furphy. As the title suggests, the book shows his stylized vernacular realism, but its genius is comic. [PT]

M. Franklin and K. Baker, *J.F.* (1944); *Southerly*, 3 (1945) (special Furphy issue); B. Sutherland, 'J.F., Australian', *University of Toronto Quarterly*, XX, 2 (January 1951).

G

Galsworthy, John (1867–1933). Novelist and dramatist. Born in Coombe, Surrey, and educated at Harrow and New College, Oxford, he studied law and was called to the bar in 1890, but instead of practising went on a trip to the Far East where, on a merchant ship, he met Joseph Conrad, who became a lifelong friend. *From the Four Winds* (1897), a volume of short stories, was followed by the novels *Jocelyn* (1898) and *Villa Rubein* (1900), and a further collection of stories, *Man of Devon* (1901), none of which made much impression. All were published under the pseudonum 'John Sinjohn'.

In 1906 Galsworthy achieved his first successes with a play, *The Silver Box*, and with the first part of what was to become the 'Forsyte Saga', *The Man of Property*. The earlier works had been written under the influence, if not in direct imitation, of Turgenev, and something of the Russian novelist's manner remains in the work of the mature Galsworthy. The 'Forsyte Saga' was continued with *In Chancery* (1920) and *To Let* (1921), and two further trilogies were devoted to an account of the fortunes of the Forsyte family, Galsworthy's representatives of the Edwardian moneyed classes. The cycle is notable more for its painstaking completeness than for any specific literary virtues. Galsworthy wrote several non-Forsyte novels, including *The Dark Flower* (1913), *The Freelands* (1915) and *Saint's Progress* (1919).

As a playwright, Galsworthy was concerned with moral issues. Conrad described him as a humanitarian moralist, and it is true that he champions the victim of injustice, albeit in a rather cold and aloof judicial manner. *Strife* (1909) is a study of industrial relations; *Justice* (1910) deals with prison life and was, in fact, instrumental in effecting some reforms. The plays, which include *The Skin Game* (1920), *Loyalties* (1922) and *Escape* (1926), are never less than solidly constructed, though not especially striking in dramatic effect.

Galsworthy's other mature work consists of several volumes of short stories, and a book of essays, *Castles in Spain* (1927). His *Collected Poems* (1934) were published posthumously. [co]

H. V. Marrot, *Life and Letters of J.G.* (1935); H. Ould, *J.G.* (1934); R. Mottram, *J.G.* (1953); D. Barker, *The Man of Principle* (1963).

Galt, John (1779–1839). Scottish novelist. The son of a sea-captain, he grew up in the Clyde ports of Irvine and Greenock, where as a young clerk he carried on his education through local libraries and discussion societies. In 1804, moving to London, he published some poems and set up as a merchant; bankrupt in 1808, he travelled through the Mediterranean with Byron and on through Turkey into the Balkans. He published accounts of these travels, a life of Wolsey and some plays. Settling again in London after a spell in Gibraltar (1813) he combined various administrative and business posts with further literary hackwork. As early as 1813 Constable rejected Galt's proposal for a Scots novel (compare the fate of *Waverley*) but in 1820 Galt began to write for *Blackwood's Magazine* and rapidly produced the fiction for which he is remembered – *Annals of the Parish* and *The Ayrshire Legatees* (1821), *The Provost* and *Sir Andrew Wylie* (1822) and *The Entail* (1823). Already he was deeply concerned in promoting a company for the settlement and development of Upper Canada, now Ontario, and in 1826 he went out to manage affairs on the spot. During a panic in 1829 he was dismissed and on his return to England he was imprisoned for debt. His fiction and other writing of the thirties, produced during a constant struggle against poverty and ill-health, is much inferior to his earlier work.

Galt, clearly, was not a dedicated artist, but his businessman's interest in the contemporary, in social change and economic development, makes his Scottish novels a useful supplement to the more generalized and historically based analyses of Scott. The *Annals* and *The Provost* chronicle successive episodes of the later 18th century in, respectively, an Ayrshire country parish, seen through the eyes of its minister, and a burgh (Galt's native Irvine) recorded by its provost. Aware (perhaps over-aware) of the limitations of these societies, working through the consciousness of characters who do not themselves transcend those limitations, and deprived by his chronicle form of any dramatic central issue, Galt often seems to be patronizing his material, displaying it for the mere amusement of a more sophisticated audience. Typically, his provost's name is 'Pawkie'. In Galt's more ambitious fiction, too, incoherent plot, stock characterization and over-exploitation of quaintness of character and dialect rather outweigh the careful observation and shrewd humour that appear here and there. [A I]

Works, ed. D. S. Meldrum and W. Roughead (1936) (selected novels); *Autobiography* (1833); *Literary Life* (1844); *Poems: A Selection*, ed. G. H. Needler (Toronto, 1954).
J. W. Aberdein, *J.G.* (1936); E. Frykman, *J.G.'s Scottish Stories* (1959).

Garnett, Constance (*née* Black) (1861–1946). Translator. She translated into English almost the entire corpus of classic Russian prose fiction, and was perhaps the only translator from Russian of significance to English literature. Daughter of the Brighton coroner (a Scotsman whose father had been Naval Architect to Tsar Nicholas I) she was precociously brilliant – at 17 a scholar of Newnham College, Cambridge, where she headed the Classical Tripos list. Subsequently librarian to the People's Palace, she met (at 24) and married Edward Garnett, six years her junior; they moved in intellectual, notably Fabian Socialist, company. Edward Garnett's acquaintance with various European political exiles brought her into contact with the London circle of Russian revolutionary-minded *émigrés* (including Kropotkin). She learnt Russian from them with extraordinary speed while awaiting the birth of her only child (David ◊ Garnett); six months later (winter of 1892-3) she went alone to Russia, carrying funds for famine relief but also as the revolutionists' secret courier; she met Korolenko and Tolstoy. As soon as she learnt Russian she had begun to translate its literature; her first volumes (e.g. Turgenev's *Rudin*) appeared in 1894. She devoted herself to translation for the rest of her working life, rendering all the major fiction of Turgenev, Goncharov, Dostoevsky, Tolstoy, Gogol and Chekhov: most of these had been previously trans-

lated, but inadequately. The Social Democrat party conference in London (1907) disillusioned her with Lenin's Bolshevik faction (though she supported the Reds in the Civil War) and after the Revolution she befriended a new wave of Russian *émigrés*.

Her translations have been criticized, and are sometimes inaccurate: yet they have style enough to outlive their period. They largely instigated the Russomania which spread outwards from ◊ Bloomsbury into English literary life before the First World War (cf. the reception of *The Brothers Karamazov*, 1912). Her Turgenev, Chekhov and Dostoevsky were probably her most influential successes, yet her versions of the almost-untranslatable Gogol perhaps show up best against her rivals: recent attempts to refurbish her work are disappointing (which witnesses to her inimitable qualities). [R M-G]

David Garnett, *The Golden Echo* (1953); C. G. Heilbrun, *The Garnett Family* (1961); G. Phelps, *The Russian Novel in English Fiction* (1956).

Garnett, David (1892–   ). Novelist and publisher. Born in Brighton, the son of Edward and Constance ◊ Garnett, he was educated at the Royal College of Science in Kensington, where he studied botany. In 1919, with Francis Meynell, he set up a book shop in Soho, and in 1923 became a publisher; he has been connected with Meynell's Nonesuch Press, and with Rupert Hart-Davis. He has been book-critic for the *New Statesman*, and in 1956 was elected a Fellow of the Imperial College of Science and Technology. His first book, the deliberate and mannered fantasy *Lady into Fox*, appeared in 1922 and had considerable success; this was followed by *A Man in the Zoo* (1924), an amusing tale of a man who offers himself as a specimen of *homo sapiens*. *Go She Must!* (1927) is a more realistic story set in the Fens. His most recent novel is *Ulterior Motives* (1966), a comedy with a touch of dry sobriety. *The Grasshoppers Come* was published in 1931. Garnett learned to fly and wrote an account of this experience in *A Rabbit in the Air* (1932). He has edited *Letters of T. E. Lawrence* (1938) and *The Essential T. E. Lawrence* (1951), as well as *The Novels of Thomas Love Peacock* (1948). [A R]

Autobiography: *The Golden Echo* (1953) (to 1914); *The Flowers of the Forest* (1955) (to 1922); *The Familiar Faces* (1962) (to 1940).

Garnett, Richard (1835–1906). Miscellaneous writer. Born in Lichfield; his father, a learned philologist, became an assistant keeper at the British Museum Library and Garnett was largely educated at home, where he read widely in ancient and modern literatures. In 1851, after his father's death, he himself became an assistant in the Library, an assistant keeper, and Supervisor of the Reading Room, and later Keeper of Printed Books; he is responsible after Panizzi for many of the benefits of the present library; he retired in 1899. While at the British Museum, he began the printed catalogue, and also (as well as after his retirement) wrote much for periodicals; he contributed articles to the *Encyclopædia Britannica* and to such works as Gosse's *Illustrated Record of English Literature* (1903–4) and the *DNB*. He also wrote introductions for many reprints of English classics and of European literature. His biographies have now been mostly superseded and his verse is forgotten. The latter, much indebted to Shelley, is written in the graceful, derivative, 'literary' fashion then common; a series of classical and oriental fables, *The Twilight of the Gods* (1888; enlarged 1903; ed. T. E. Lawrence, 1926), remained popular. The tales are amusing and cynical. [AR]

Garrick, David (1717–79). Actor and dramatist. Born in Lichfield, he was the pupil of Samuel Johnson, with whom he walked to London in 1737. He quickly established himself as an actor, became the greatest figure of the 18th-century stage, and made Drury Lane the foremost theatre in Europe during the twenty-nine years of his management (1747–76). Himself a player of genius, he revolutionized production techniques, lighting and scene-design. His literary fame rests more on his playing of the main Shakespearean parts than on his sponsorship of new dramatists, but by organizing the Shakespeare Jubilee celebrations at Stratford-upon-Avon in 1769 he can be said to have inaugurated the Shakespeare tourist industry. His original writing for the theatre consists mainly of prologues, epilogues, brief farces like *Miss in Her Teens* (1747) and adaptations of Shakespeare (whose plays he acted in the Restoration 'improved' texts) and other dramatists. His collaborations with George ◊ Colman, the Elder, have more enduring interest, especially *The Clandestine Marriage*

(1766), but his greatness was as a man of the theatre rather than as a writer. His correspondence (now sumptuously edited) shows the high place he won in his society, and his business acumen. [MJ]

The Letters, ed D. M. Little and G. M. Kahrl (3 vols., 1963).
Thomas Davies, *Memoirs of D.G.* (2 vols., 1780); Carola Oman, *D.G.* (1958); E. P. Stein, *D.G., Dramatist* (1938); Hazleton Spencer, *Shakespeare Improved* (1927).

Garth, Sir Samuel (1661–1719). Physician and poet. A member of the Kit-Kat club, he became physician-in-ordinary to George I (knighted 1714), and physician-general to the army. He was an early encourager of Pope, and a friend of Addison. He intervened to secure an honourable burial for Dryden and pronounced a eulogy at the funeral. Garth wrote a burlesque poem (an ancestor of Pope's *Rape of the Lock*), *The Dispensary* (1699; later editions with additions until 1715), in support of the physicians in their quarrel with the apothecaries over a free medical aid scheme. He also edited a translation of Ovid's *Metamorphoses* (1717), to which Addison, Pope and others contributed. [AR]

Johnson, *Lives of the Poets*; *DNB*.

Gascoigne, George (c. 1530–77). Poet and playwright. Born in Cardington, Bedfordshire, and educated at Cambridge and Gray's Inn, Gascoigne typified both in his literary output and his personal life the energy and diversity of the early phase of the English Renaissance. He was a Member of Parliament for Bedford for two years (1557–9) and a soldier in the Low Countries for two more (1572–4). For some time he was a fashionable courtier and a friend of some of the leading literary figures of his time, including Edmund Spenser. In 1561 he married a widow, Elizabeth Breton, and thus became stepfather to the poet Nicholas ◊ Breton. He led the life of a country gentleman for a while, but also had a considerable reputation for loose living and was once imprisoned for debt. He died near Stamford and is buried there.

In 1573, Gascoigne produced *A Hundred Sundry Flowers* (ed. C. T. Prouty, Columbia, Miss., 1942), noteworthy not only for anticipating, in its groups of connected sonnets, the form of the sonnet-sequence which was to become so popular in the

Elizabethan period, but also because 'The Adventures of Master F.J.' which it contains can claim to be the first original prose narrative in the language. In *The Posies*, published two years later, Gascoigne included 'Certain Notes of Instruction', the first English critical treatise on poetry. *The Steel Glass* (1576), a satire on the corrupting influence of Italianate manners, shows him introducing non-dramatic blank verse into English, while his *Complaint of Philomene* (1576) provides the pattern of Ovidian narrative verse which Shakespeare followed in *Venus and Adonis* and *Lucrece*. Of Gascoigne's plays, *Jocasta* (performed 1566), written in collaboration with Francis Kinwelmersh, is derived, via Latin and Italian, from Euripides' *Phoenissae* and was the first Greek tragedy on the English stage, while *Supposes* (performed 1566?), a comedy adapted from Ariosto, provided the sub-plot for *The Taming of the Shrew*. Gascoigne's account of *The Spoil of Antwerp* (1577) gives him some claim to be called the first English war correspondent.

While he achieved some distinction in all the varieties of literary expression which he attempted, Gascoigne's chief importance to literature is as a pioneer of the English Renaissance, a man who adapted foreign modes into English in such a way that they could be used by the greater figures who were to follow him. [GS]

Complete Works, ed. J. W. Cunliffe (2 vols., 1907–10).
C. T. Prouty, *G.G. Elizabethan Courtier, Soldier and Poet* (New York, 1942); S. A. Tannenbaum, *A Concise Bibliography* (New York, 1942).

Gascoyne, David (Emery) (1916–   ). Poet. He was educated at Salisbury Cathedral Choir School and the Regent Street Polytechnic, and published his first volume of poetry, *Roman Balcony*, when he was 16 and a novel, *Opening Day*, in the following year. One of the few English poets profoundly influenced by continental Surrealism, he wrote many articles and translations publicizing the movement and in 1935 published *A Short Survey of Surrealism*. This was followed by a volume of obscure but tightly controlled surrealist verse, *Man's Life Is This Meat* (1936) and *Hölderlin's Madness* (1938), which consisted of an essay on Hölderlin, translations of some of his poems and 4 of Gascoyne's own poems. His preoccupation with Sur-

realism did not place him outside the mainstream of English poetry in the thirties. He was a regular contributor to *New Verse*, served in Spain during the Civil War and wrote many poems on social and political themes, one of which, 'Farewell Chorus', is an impressive commentary on the intellectual atmosphere of the thirties. With his more recent work, *Poems 1937–1942* (1943), which was illustrated by Graham Sutherland, *A Vagrant* (1950) and *Night Thoughts* (1956), he has emerged as one of the finest religious poets writing in England today. His *Collected Poems*, with an excellent introduction by Robin Skelton, appeared in 1965. [PJK]

Claude Legangneux, 'Le poète anglais D.G.', *Le Journal des Poètes* (October 1951); Anthony Cronin, 'Poetry and Ideas: D.G.', *London Magazine*, IV (July 1957); Elizabeth Jennings, 'The Restoration of Symbols : The Poetry of D.G.', *Twentieth Century*, CLXV (June 1959); Ann Atkinson, 'D.G.: A Checklist', *Twentieth Century Literature*, VI, 1961; Derek Stanford, 'D.G. and the Unacademics', *Meanjin*, XXIII (1964); Gavin Ewart, 'A Voice from the Darkness', *London Magazine*, V (November 1965).

Gaskell, Mrs Elizabeth Cleghorn (1810–65). Novelist. Born in Chelsea, the daughter of William Stevenson, a Civil Servant formerly a Unitarian minister. She was brought up by an aunt in Knutsford, a small country town near Manchester, and in her teens went to a school for two years in Stratford-upon-Avon. She stayed with relatives here and there in England, and in 1832 she married the Reverend William Gaskell, a Unitarian minister in Manchester, where she lived with him happily for the rest of her life. Her first published work was a poem in the vein of Crabbe (in collaboration with her husband), *Sketches among the Poor*, which appeared in *Blackwood's Magazine* (41, 1837). This theme, 'the social question', was one of which she had much personal experience. It formed the centre of several of her works, such as *Life in Manchester* (by Cotton Mather Mills, Esq.) (1848), a volume of short stories originally published in Howitt's *Journal of Literature and Popular Progress* (1–3, 1847–8); *Mary Barton, A Tale of Manchester Life* (2 vols., 1848; Everyman, 1912; dramatized as *The Long Strike*); and *North and South* (2 vols., 1855; Everyman, 1914). Her fiction of this kind has a pleasant warmth of feeling but a scanty theoretical understanding of the economic issues involved. She gives a first-hand picture and seeks to be 'impartial' and 'fair', showing the hardships of 'both sides' of employers and employed. Though her tendency to melodramatic plots is annoying, she gives an honest, uncomplicated, middle-class, 'humane' approach. Her work was admired by Dickens; *North and South* and other stories and articles first appeared in *Household Words*. From the same outraged, rather unaware feeling, came her most famous book, *Cranford*, the first of her contributions to Dickens's magazine (1853). This is a series of country town sketches, based on her childhood in Knutsford; it was a way of life under sentence of death; the nostalgia for poor gentility, the quiet of rural happenings, described with excellent understatement and slightly ironic humour, ensure the book's survival (cf. the work of the American Sarah Orme Jewett). Other works of this kind are *Cousin Phyllis* (published in the *Cornhill Magazine*) (1864; Everyman, 1912) and *Wives and Daughters. An Everyday Story* (*Cornhill*) (1866). It is inevitable that Wordsworthian echoes should be found in these pastoral tales, told in fear of and feeling for the tremors of the industrial age. There is a fair amount of autobiography in Mrs Gaskell's stories; the childhood reminiscences in these novels work well enough. The 'question' of women is the subject of *Ruth* (3 vols., 1853) and *Sylvia's Lovers* (3 vols., 1863). Here again she responds with naïve and open feeling to the conflict between social *mores* and personal passion, and to the 'double standard' of morality of men in Victorian society, without being able to see that her own attitude of Christian forgiveness was itself a 'position' in the struggles. She met Charlotte Brontë in 1850, and wrote a *Life* (1857), with imaginative enthusiasm, two years after her death. The book is still a starting point in the study of the Brontës, but it here and there fell foul of Victorian ideas of reticence. [A R]

Works (Knutsford Edition), intr. A. W. Ward (8 vols., 1906) (omits verse); *Novels and Tales*, ed. C. K. Shorter (11 vols., World's Classics, 1906–19) (including verse and *Life of Charlotte Brontë*); *Letters*, ed. J. A. V. Chapple and A. Pollard (1966).

A. B. Hopkins, *Mrs G. Her Life and Work* (1952) (with bibliography); A. Pollard, *Mrs G. Novelist and Biographer* (1965); M. Allott, *E.G.* (WTW, 1960); G. de W. Sanders, *E.G.: A Bibliography* (Yale U.P., 1929); A. B. Hopkins, *E.G. Her Life and Work* (1952) (bibliography); M. Lane, *The Brontë Story: A Reconsideration of Mrs G.'s Life* (1953); E. Wright, *Mrs Gaskell: Basis for Reassessment* (1965); D. Howard, J. Lucas and J. Goode, *Tradition and Tolerance in Nineteenth Century Fiction* (1966).

'Gawain Poet, The' (fl. 1370). The name given to the author of the alliterative romance, *Sir Gawain and The Green Knight* (ed. J. R. R. Tolkien and E. V. Gordon, 1936; ed. R. A. Waldron, York Mediaeval Texts, 1970; tr. K. Hare, 1948; tr. B. Stone, Penguin Classics, 1959), who may have written the other poems contained in the manuscript, *Pearl* (ed. Gordon, 1953), *Patience* (ed. J. J. Anderson, 1969) and *Purity* (ed. J. Gollancz, 1921). This seems probable on linguistic grounds, and the technical mastery apparent in *Sir Gawain* and *Pearl* supports the notion. All 4 are in alliterative verse. *Patience* and *Purity* are homilies – the former based on the story of Jonah – but the moral preoccupation extends even to the chivalric romance, *Sir Gawain*, the climax of the alliterative style. Combining a complex stanza-form with regular alliteration, it is a consciously literary poem written for a sophisticated audience. Though it has been a happy hunting-ground for literary anthropologists, it is best approached as an example of chivalric romance, whose theme is the knightly quest for perfection and self-knowledge, here illustrated in the testing of Gawain's courage through the 'Beheading Game' proposed by the mysterious Green Knight, and of his courtesy and chastity by the Lady of the castle. The poet combines humour and a light touch with a powerful evocation of the grotesque and savage.

Pearl is technically even more ambitious; an intricate stanza, coupled with all the devices of rhyme and alliteration. It is a dream-vision, cast in an elegiac form. The Dreamer mourns for the death of a child, the Pearl of the title, but in his dream he is led to understanding and acceptance of his loss by the maiden herself. This progression is carefully shaped, and conveyed with great delicacy and insight, though it may be thought that the highly wrought style obscures the meaning occasionally. [A G]

D. Everett, *Essays on Middle English Literature* (1955); M. W. Bloomfield, 'Sir G. and the Green Knight; an Appraisal', *PMLA*, LXXVII

(1961); J. A. Burrow, *A Reading of Sir Gawain and the Green Knight* (1965); I. Bishop, *Pearl in Its Setting* (1968); P. M. Kean, *The Pearl: An Interpretation* (1967); A. C. Spearing, 'Symbolic and Dramatic Development in "Pearl"'; *Modern Philology*, LX (1962); J. Speirs, 'Sir G. and the Grene Knight', *Scrutiny*, XVI (1949).

Gay, John (1685–1732). Poet and writer for the stage. Born in Barnstaple in Devon, the youngest son of a Nonconformist burgess of an old family in middling circumstances. His father died when he was 10, and after an education at the free grammar school in his town he was apprenticed to a silk mercer in London, but returned to his family and began to write verse. Back in London, he became acquainted with writers such as his fellow-townsman Aaron Hill and the contributors to the latter's pompous question-and-answer sheet, *The British Apollo*. Gay's first published poem, which he did not include in his collected works, was the anonymous *Wine* (1708; several printings; facsimile 1926), written in Miltonics rather slackly connected with *Cyder* by John ◊ Philips. Gay was well-read in the periodicals of the time, and with *The Present State of Wit, in a Letter to a Friend in the Country* (1711 ; reprinted in Arber's *English Garner*, 1903; ed. D. F. Bond, Augustan Reprint Society, 1947) he became known to Pope, and the Scriblerus circle then forming. This friendship was of crucial social importance to Gay, who also produced most of his later work in this ambience. It also meant that criticism of Gay's work was formed by the remarks of Pope, a younger man who survived Gay. Pope chose to present Gay as an artless poet, childlike and good-natured. However true to Gay's personality, this stereotype obscures two sides of Gay's work: one is a serious imaginative interest in the odd, the off-beat, which was more characteristic of other Scriblerians like ◊ Arbuthnot than Pope; the other is a powerful and able grasp of poetic forms and forces other than the admired norms of the classical Augustan myth, such as ballads, real burlesque, farce and the 'low Style'. He also had a remarkable sense of what would appeal to the changing tastes of the town, as may be seen in the success of his essay *An Argument Proving that the Present Mohocks and Hawkubites are the Gog and Magog of Revelation* and a play on the same theme of upper-class teenage hooliganism, *The Mohocks. A Tragi-Comical Farce*, which

both appeared in 1712. In the manner of the time, Gay also sought an assured income. In 1712 he became secretary to the half-crazy Duchess of Monmouth, and in 1714 his friends got him the post of secretary to the Earl of Clarendon on his diplomatic mission to Hanover, an opportunity abruptly ended by the death of Queen Anne two months later. Thereafter he lived much in the houses of patrons, particularly the Duke of Queensbury, whose wife was his particular champion. He unwisely invested his money by buying South Sea stock at its height, and saw it seriously diminished when the bubble burst. From 1722 to 1751 he was a Commissioner for the Public Lottery and had apartments in Whitehall until he was thrown out for political reasons in 1728. After dancing attendance on the Prince of Wales's family, when George II succeeded, Gay refused the long-awaited offer of being Gentleman-Usher to an infant princess. He died at the Queensberrys', and is buried in Westminster Abbey.

Gay's first substantial poem, *Rural Sports*, appeared in 1713, dedicated to Pope; *The Fan* (3 books, 1713) is too long for a *jeu d'esprit*. In 1714 he published *The Shepherd's Week*, designed to parody the pastorals of Ambrose ◊ Philips; this became his first major success on its own merit, in drolly presenting the country swains of Gay's own experience. Along with a sharply observant eye, Gay had developed the control of the couplet which by its ease and finish has led to his being greatly underrated as a poet. His best poem, to modern taste, is the town-eclogue *Trivia: or The Art of Walking the Streets of London* (1716), distinguished by close social observation, nice management of tone and skilful humour. He wrote a good deal of other miscellaneous poetry, but his *Fables* (2 vols.: 1727, 50 pieces; 1738, 16 pieces; over 50 editions in various combinations before 1800) was the work by which he was known as a poet for the rest of the century. The modern reader does not always relish the moralizing and gentle satire of these didactic poems written for the edification of Prince William, later the butcher Duke of Cumberland.

It is as a writer for the stage that Gay is most original and most difficult to type. *The What d'ye Call It: A Tragi-Comi-Pastoral Farce* (played and published 1715) injects the tragedies and grotesque chances of everyday life into a pastoral scene. *Three Hours after Marriage*, in which Pope and Arbuthnot collaborated (played and published 1717; Augustan Reprint Society, 1961), is a complex work of satire on false learning and technical guying of the conventions of stage comedy. These plays had appeal, but the flouting of conventional modes prevented their theatrical success. This changed, however, with *The Beggar's Opera* (first played at Lincoln's Inn Fields on 29 January 1728; published twice in 1728; ed. F. W. Bateson, 1934). This ballad opera, arising out of a suggestion of Swift's for a Newgate prison pastoral, swept the town. It is built up of political satire, travesty of the fashionable Italian opera, deft use of old English and Scottish songs and airs, and a serious philosophical statement about human nature. Its rather 'prettyfied' revival by Nigel Playfair in 1926 at the Lyric Theatre, Hammersmith, showed the piece had dramatic vitality. Benjamin Britten has made a version of the music, and the film (1953) with Sir Laurence Olivier used a version by Arthur Bliss. The real possibilities of the work, however, are suggested by Brecht's, adaptation in *The Threepenny Opera*. The production of a sequel, *Polly* (1729; ed. O. Doughty, 1922), was banned by Walpole, and consequently was a financial success. Gay was a great song writer and adapter, a delicate and subtle art, for which, like Burns, he has never really received adequate tribute, since it is difficult to say anything about it. [A R]

Poems on Several Occasions (2 vols., 1720; revised 1731); *Poetical Works*, ed. J. Underhill (2 vols., Muses' Library, 1893); ed. G. Faber (1926) (including selections from his dramatic works); *Selected Poems*, ed. A. Ross (1950); *Letters*, ed. C. S. Burgess (1966).
W. H. Irving, *J.G., Favourite of the Wits* (North Caroline U.P., 1940); S. Armens, *J.G., Social Critic* (New York, 1954); A. Forsgren, *J.G., Poet 'Of a Lower Order'* (Stockholm, 1964); B. H. Bronson, *The Beggar's Opera* (California U.P., 1941); J. R. Sutherland, 'J.G.', in *Pope and His Contemporaries*, ed. J. L. Clifford and L. A. Landa (1949).

Geoffrey of Monmouth (1100?–54). Chronicler. Author of one of the most influential books of the Middle Ages, the *Historia Regum Britanniae* (ed. A. Griscom, 1929). Born at Monmouth, probably of Breton parents, Geoffrey lived near Oxford between 1129 and 1151. The *Historia* was completed in about 1136, and Geoffrey was made Archdeacon of Monmouth before 1140. In 1152, he was named Bishop of St Asaph, but died before assuming office.

The *Historia* purports to be a serious history of Britain from its foundation by Brutus, grandson of Aeneas, to the death of Cadwallader, the last independent British king. Geoffrey used the British histories of ◊ 'Gildas' and Nennius, but also claimed to have a 'British book', lent him by Walter, the Archdeacon of Oxford. Whether or not this book existed, he drew very heavily on his own invention, particularly for the Arthurian story which is the core of the work. The intention may have been to counter the French epic cycles of Charlemagne, and also to give some kind of precedent for the policies of the Norman kings. There were always those who recognized its fictional quality, but the *Historia* governed ideas about British history well into the 17th century. Its literary importance is greater still. It supplied the base for the Arthurian cycles, and produced vulgarized versions in French (Wace and Gaimar) and English (◊ Laȝamon, Robert of Gloucester, and Mannyng). It was a mine of material for generations of English poets, for Lear, Locrine, Cymbeline and Gorboduc, to name a few, all make their first significant appearance here. To a lesser degree, Geoffrey's other major work, the *Vita Merlini* (ed. J. J. Parry, Urbana, Ill., 1925), has a similar importance. [A G]

J. S. P. Tatlock, *The Legendary History of Britain* (1950).

'Georgian Poetry'. An anthology of verse designed to show that in the early years of George V's reign English poetry was 'putting on a new strength and beauty'. Five volumes were published between the years 1912 and 1922. It was edited by Edward ◊ Marsh, who was mainly responsible for making it a commercial success, and its poetic tone was established by Rupert ◊ Brooke. It was published by Harold ◊ Monro from The Poetry Bookshop, Bloomsbury. The contributors included ◊ Lascelles ◊ Abercrombie, Edmund ◊ Blunden, Gordon ◊ Bottomley, W. H. ◊ Davies, John ◊ Drinkwater, Wilfrid ◊ Gibson, Ralph ◊ Hodgson, Robert ◊ Graves and D. H. ◊ Lawrence. Although the quality and range of verse presented in *Georgian Poetry* varied greatly, and although the earliest volumes were criticized for their 'realism', the adjective 'Georgian' is customarily used in a pejorative sense, implying slack conventional poetry that celebrates rural English society. After the demise of *Georgian Poetry*, J. C. ◊ Squire became the unofficial leader of the Georgian poets, publishing their work in *The London Mercury*, which he edited. [P J K]

Georgian Poets, ed. James Reeves (1962); *Georgian Poets*, ed. Alan Pryce-Jones (1959).

Herbert Palmer, *Post-Victorian Poetry* (1938); Frank Swinnerton, *The Georgian Literary Scene* (1935); Robert H. Ross, *The Georgian Revolt 1910–1922* (Southern Illinois U.P., 1965).

Gerald of Barry. ◊ Giraldus Cambrensis.

Gerard, Alexander (1728–95). Scottish philosopher and literary critic. While Professor of Moral Philosophy and Logic at Marischal College, Aberdeen, from 1750, Gerard published a pamphlet advocating reforms in curriculum and administration in the interest of higher intellectual standards. His aesthetic theory, influential in its day and expounded in an *Essay on Taste* (1759) and an *Essay on Genius* (1774; ed. B. Fabian, Munich, 1966), widens the definition of 'taste' to include what would now be called creative imagination, and finds the essential process of literary creation in the *association of ideas*; his essays suffer from the undirected discursive rationalizing so common in lesser 18th-century criticism. Professor Divinity from 1760, Moderator of the General Assembly of the Church of Scotland in 1764, and Professor of Divinity in the richer and more important King's College from 1771, Gerard was a leading 'moderate' churchman and with his friends ◊ Beattie and ◊ Reid formed the Aberdeen group of Hume's opponents. [A I]

W. J. Bate, *From Classic to Romantic* (1946); *DNB*.

Ghose, Sri Aurobindo (1872–1950). Indian poet and philosopher. Born in Calcutta and educated in England, he graduated from Cambridge in 1893, and entered the service of the Maharaja of Baroda, remaining in Baroda till 1906. He became involved in political agitation, was arrested in 1908 and put in prison and there had the mystical experience which led to total commitment to his Yoga. His uninterrupted residence in Pondicherry began in 1910. Most of his philosophical writings were originally published in *Arya*, a journal founded in 1914 to satisfy a growing number of disciples. The most important is *The Life Divine* (vol. 1, 1939; vol. 2, 1940), an account of his 'world-transforming Yoga' which aims by cultivation of the spirit to move through mind into 'supermind' and a direct apprehension of Being.

Aurobindo was a prolific poet of considerable range. He experimented with hexameters and quantitative verse as well as adapting traditional English forms to accommodate the attitudes of Vedic spirituality. In his blank verse-plays (in *Collected Poems and Plays*, 1942) he finds mythical correlatives for his philosophy in the legends of Greece, Scandinavia and Syria as well as India. His major work is the vast blank-verse epic, *Savitri*, on which he had worked intermittently for fifty years before the first volume appeared in 1946. It is indebted, formally and stylistically, to English epics, but can be read only in the context of Aurobindo's Yoga. The Savitri legend of the *Mahabharata* is transformed to embody the teaching of *The Life Divine*. It is unambiguously an epic of the soul. [P T]

A. B. Purani, *Life of S.A.* (1960); P. Nandakumar *A Study of 'Savitri'* (1961); K. R. Srinivasa Iyengar, *Indian Writing in English* (1962).

Ghose, Sudhindra Nath (1899–). Indian novelist and art critic. Born at Burdwan, the son of a High Court Judge, he attended school and university in Calcutta, graduating in 1920. He studied art history in Europe, finally taking a doctorate at Strasbourg in 1929. He has worked as a journalist, with the League of Nations, and as a lecturer to H.M. Forces and at Nottingham University. Since 1946, with the exception of a year as visiting professor at Visva-bharati University, he has been a part-time lecturer at L.C.C. Institutes for Adult Education.

Ghose's fictional style blends the grotesque and the naturalistic under the licence of the picaresque. In 4 books he pursues, with humerous gusto, the natural and supernatural quest of an eager, sometimes petulant, hero, setting it against the traditional spiritual background of India. *And Gazelles Leaping* (1949) describes the hero's childhood, *Cradle of the Clouds* (1951) his adolescence, and *The Vermilion Boat* (1953) and *The Flame of the Forest*

(1955) follow the young man's adventures in search of a career. [PT]

H. Ghoshal, 'An Indian Tetralogy', *Books Abroad* (Summer, 1956).

Gibbon, Edward (1737–94). Historian. Born at Putney, the son of Edward Gibbon, a wealthy Tory M.P. A delicate, precocious child, he was educated privately and at a school in Kingston-on-Thames; and lived with an aunt when his father went into seclusion. He went to Westminster School, and Magdalen College, Oxford. He had begun his wide reading in classical history earlier, and said he learned nothing at Oxford, steeped in port and prejudice; but while there he was converted to Roman Catholicism. His father, in alarm, sent him to board with a Calvinist minister in Lausanne. There he learned French well, pursued his studies and finally renounced his conversion. He travelled in Switzerland and fell in love with Suzanne Curchod, later Madame Necker, and the mother of Madame de Staël. His father disapproved, and in 1758 Gibbon 'sighed as a lover' but 'obeyed as a son': they became friends later after some coldness on Gibbon's part. He began to work seriously at his reading, and published an *Essai sur l'étude de la littérature* (1761; tr. 1764). From 1759 to 1763 he was a captain in the Hampshire militia, an experience he felt useful in writing his great work; by 1770, though not permanently serving, he had become a colonel. Considering, and rejecting, several subjects for a great historical work, he read much in preparation for a visit to Italy (April 1764 to May 1765), and while musing among the ruins of the Roman Capitol decided to write the history of the decline and fall of the city. He published several miscellaneous works, and settled in London from 1768, after selling his estate. In 1774 he joined Johnson's 'Club'. He was an M.P. for a Cornish rotten borough and took part in the debates and politics of the time.

The first volume of *The Decline and Fall of the Roman Empire* was published in 1776. It speedily became famous; the 'infidel' chapters on the rise of Christianity provoked controversy, and Gibbon dealt quite successfully with the attacks (*Vindication*, 1779; rept. 1961). In 1779, he was appointed a Commissioner of Trade and Plantations. In 1781, volumes II and III of his work appeared, and more slowly gained acceptance. The Board of Trade

was abolished in 1782, and Gibbon failed in his desire to be Secretary of the Embassy in Paris. In 1783, he moved to Lausanne to live with a friend and on 17 June 1787, between 11 and 12 at night, he wrote the last words of the sixth and last volume of *The Decline and Fall* (volumes IV, V and VI were published in 1788). He lived quietly in Lausanne until 1793, when amid the bustle of the French Revolutionary Wars he returned to England, where he died on 16 January 1794.

Gibbon's work is 18th-century history in the grand manner: a drama carried on in incomparably disciplined and measured prose. Gibbon's Rome is an ideal city, and the tale of its decline is developed with matchless cynical observation and nostalgia. He was a learned man, and though modern research can correct him, his history as a work of art cannot be replaced any more than Shakespeare's history plays can. *The Decline and Fall* was many times reprinted, annotated, translated and condensed (see particularly J. B. Bury's edition, 7 vols., 1896–1900; 1909–14; and a revised text, 1926–9; Everyman, 1903–4 and 1910). [AR]

Miscellaneous Works (2 vols., 1796, etc.); *Autobiographies* (6 drafts), ed. J. Murray (1896); ed. J. B. Bury (World's Classics, 1907); ed. G. A. Bonnard (1966); *Letters*, ed. J. E. Norton (3 vols., 1956).

P. Quennell, *Four Portraits* (1945); G. M. Young, *G.* (1948); C. V. Wedgwood, *G.* (1954); H. L. Bond, *The Literary Art of E.G.* (1960); G. de Beer, *G. and His World* (1968); J. E. Norton, *Bibliography of the Works of G.* (1940); F. Cordasco, *G.: A Handlist of Critical Notices and Studies, 1878–1950* (New York, 1950).

Gibbon, Lewis Grassic (pseud. of James Leslie Mitchell) (1901–35). Scottish novelist. He grew up on farms in Aberdeenshire and Kincardineshire, worked on local newspapers in his teens, and between 1918 and 1929 was a clerk first in the army and later in the R.A.F. He then lived by freelance journalism until his early death. The novels, short stories and works on South American archaeology published under his own name are virtually forgotten; his reputation rests on his work as 'Gibbon' (his mother's maiden name) – the trilogy of novels about his native countryside and the essays and short stories in *Scottish Scene* (with Hugh ◊ MacDiarmid, 1934) and *A Scots Hairst* (1967).

The 3 novels (*Sunset Song*, 1932; *Cloud Howe*, 1933; *Grey Granite*, 1934; in one

209

Gibbons

volume as *A Scots Quair,* 1946) follow a single character through her country childhood and marriages before and after the First World War and on to town life (in Aberdeen?) during the thirties of the depression and the hunger-marches. Secondary characters expand the books' range to three generations of Scots in transition from a country culture based on the land and on Victorian religion to modern secular and political living, and then, in reaction, back to the land again. For the first time since Dougal ◊ Graham and John ◊ Galt the characteristic rhythm and vocabulary of Scots speech are used in the body of the narrative and not confined to a mere dressing of colourful dialogue in the Scott tradition. The town-life of *Grey Granite* is the least successful part of the trilogy, and Gibbon does not always keep a plangent nostalgia under control in the 'country' sections. [AI]

G. Wagner, 'The Greatest since Galt', *Essays in Criticism,* II (1952) and 'The Other G.G.', *Saltire Review,* 5 (1955); I. S. Munro, *Leslie Mitchell: L.G.G.* (1966).

Gibbons, Stella (Dorothea) (1902–). Novelist and short-story writer. Born in London, the daughter of a doctor, and educated at the North London Collegiate School for Girls. After studying journalism at University College, London, she worked for ten years on various papers, including the *Evening Standard.* In 1933 she married Alan Webb, the actor. She has published several volumes of verse, and *Collected Poems* (1950). As a novelist she became successful with *Cold Comfort Farm* (1932), a burlesque of country-life fiction which won the Fémina Vie Heureuse prize. It was followed by *Bassett* (1934), and other fiction includes *Enbury Heath* (1935), *The Shadow of the Sorcerer* (1955), *A Pink Front Door* (1959), *The Wolves Were in the Sledge* (1964) and *The Charmers* (1965). *Christmas at Cold Comfort Farm* (1940), *Conference at Cold Comfort Farm* (1949) and *Beside the Pearly Water* (1954) are volumes of short stories. [AR]

Gibson, Wilfrid Wilson (1878–1962). Poet. Born at Hexham, Northumberland, and educated privately, he published his first volume of verse, *Mountain Lovers,* in 1902. He was one of the poets whose work was published by Edward ◊ Marsh in the 5 volumes of ◊ Georgian Poetry. He wrote

prolifically on subjects drawn from nature, as well as about ordinary villagers and industrial workers in their daily lives or in wartime or at moments of crisis (e.g. *Daily Bread,* 1910). But there is not enough pressure behind his verse for it to be compelling, and uncertainty of diction impairs his attempts to render individual viewpoints. His *Collected Poems 1905–25* appeared in 1926; subsequent volumes of verse include *Hazards* (1930), *The Outpost* (1944) and *The Island Stag* (1947). [NL]

F. A. Swinnerton, *The Georgian Literary Scene, 1910–35* (1950).

Gilbert, Sir William Schwenck (1836–1911). Humorous playwright and poet. Born in London, the son of a well-known author of children's books and a direct descendant of Sir Humphrey Gilbert, the Elizabethan explorer. He was educated at Boulogne and London, joined the Inner Temple in 1855 and was called to the bar eight years later. For some time after this he served as a captain in the volunteers and a magistrate in Middlesex. In 1861, Gilbert began to contribute comic verse to the periodical *Fun* under the pseudonym of 'Bab'. These contributions were published in a volume in 1869 under the title *Bab Ballads* and first brought their author to public attention; *More Bab Ballads* followed in 1873.

In 1866, at the suggestion of the playwright T. W. Robertson, Gilbert had written, in ten days, a burlesque drama, *Dulcamara, or the Little Duck and the Great Quack,* as a Christmas entertainment for the St James's Theatre. It proved very popular and indicated clearly the direction in which his talents lay. In the next seven years, he wrote 4 plays, among them *Pygmalion and Galatea* (1871) and an adaptation of a novel by Madame de Genlis, *The Palace of Truth* (1870). There followed several undistinguished and typically Victorian plays such as *Broken Hearts* (1875) and *Engaged* (1877).

In 1870, Gilbert met Sullivan and in the following year began the collaboration which has made the two names inseparable household words, the earliest example of a words-and-music partnership whose latter-day exemplars include Rodgers and Hammerstein and Lerner and Loewe. Gilbert wrote the librettos and Sullivan provided the music for 14 comic operas, beginning with *Thespis, or the Gods Grown Old* (1871), which was only moderately

210

successful. But four years later *Trial by Jury* was enormously popular, and most of the others ran for at least a year, first at the Opéra Comique and later at the Savoy Theatre, specially built for the Gilbert and Sullivan comic operas by Richard D'Oyly Carte in 1881. *Patience*, a burlesque on the aestheticism of the pre-Raphaelites, transferred to the Savoy in 1881, and was followed by such perennial favourites as *Iolanthe, or the Peer and the Peri* (1882), *The Mikado, or the Town of Titipu* (1885), and *Ruddigore, or the Witch's Curse* (1887). To this period also belongs *Princess Ida, or Castle Adamant*, an adaptation of Tennyson's *The Princess* (written in 1870 but not performed for fifteen years) which Gilbert himself called 'a respectful perversion'.

The collaboration between writer and composer lasted for nearly a quarter of a century, though there was a temporary estrangement after *The Gondoliers* (1889), when Gilbert felt he had not been supported by Sullivan in a business argument with D'Oyly Carte. After Sullivan's death in 1900, Gilbert continued to write operas and plays but did not achieve anything of lasting value. His last opera, *Fallen Fairies* (1909), had music by Edward German and his last play, *The Hooligan*, was performed in the year of his death. Gilbert was knighted in 1907 and died four years later as a result of a heart attack following his efforts to save a woman from drowning.

Over fifty years after his death, Gilbert's fame seems secure, if only because of the unabated popularity of the Savoy operas among amateur operatic circles. He had a genuine gift for writing lyrics that lent themselves easily to music and was fortunate to find in Sullivan a talent so exactly complementary to his own. Though his satire is at times savager than his audiences have generally noticed, on the whole he accepted the values of his audience and directed his shafts either at specifically literary and artistic conventions – the aesthetes, the vogue for 'Cornish seamen' plays (*The Pirates of Penzance or Slaves of Duty*, 1880) and so on – or at topics such as education for women which seemed self-evidently funny to most Victorians. But he also attacked Victorian ritual and self-importance in the worlds of politics, society and the law. Further, he tapped the vein of fantasy which lay just below the surface of Victorian realism and earnestness and he had a verbal ingenuity, particularly a sense of the comic possibilities of rhyme, which not infrequently reminds one of Byron. In addition, he managed, in figures such as Pooh Bah, Lord High Everything Else, to achieve, if not the intensity, at least something of the universality of satire. [G S]

Collected Poems and Plays (1947).
S. Dark and R. Grey, *W.S.G. His Life and Letters* (1924); H. Pearson, *G. and Sullivan* (1935); T. Searle, *A Bibliography of Sir W.S.G.* (1931).

Gildas (*c.* 510–70). Chronicler. A Briton, born in Strathclyde, he is said to have lived in Wales, Ireland and Brittany. His *De excidio et conquestu Britanniae* (ed. and tr. G. H. Williams, *The Ruin of England*, and other works by Gildas, 2 vols., 1899–1901) professes to be a history of Britain from the Roman conquest to his own time, followed by a lament on the evils of his day. But, as G. M. Trevelyan says, 'There are no authentic chronicles of the Saxon Conquest. The Britons in their refuge among the Welsh mountains lapsed into Celtic barbarism, and if the priest Gildas wrote for them a Book of Lamentations in Latin, it answers few of the purposes of history.'

Migne, *Patrologia Latina*, 69 (1844–64); *De excidio* ed. T. Mommsen (*Monumenta Germaniae Historica, Auctores Antiquissimi, xiii*, 1896), followed by his other works, ed. J. Stevenson (1838); Eng. tr. J. A. Giles in *Six Old English Chronicles* (1878 and numerous reprints).
I. Cazzaniga, *Le prime fonti letterarie dei popoli d'Inghilterra: G. e la Historia Brittorum* (1961); E. S. Duckett, *The Gateway to the Middle Ages* (New York, 1938).

Giraldus Cambrensis, or **Gerald of Barry** (*c.* 1147–1223). Chronicler. A native of Pembrokeshire, he became an archdeacon but did not achieve his ambition of becoming a bishop. In 1185 he accompanied Prince (afterwards King) John on his expedition to Ireland, recording his experiences in *Topographia hiberniae*. His *Expugnatio hiberniae*, prejudiced, like all his writings, gives an account of the conquest of Ireland by Henry II. His *Itinerarium Cambriae* records a journey through Wales and contains a number of good stories and folk tales. His *Gemma ecclesiastica* is a kind of handbook for the instruction of the ignorant Welsh clergy. Towards the end of his life he wrote an autobiography, *De rebus a se gestis* (tr. H. E. Butler, 1937). Giraldus is a learned and entertaining writer, with a gift for description and character painting, but is partial and vain.

Works, ed. J. S. Brewer et al. (8 vols., Rolls Series, 1861–91); *Historical Works*, tr. T. Forester et al. (1863; repr. 1892).
H. Owen, *G. the Welshman* (1889; revised 1904).

Gissing, George (Robert) (1857–1903). Novelist. Born in Wakefield, the son of a pharmacist, he was educated there and at a Quaker school at Alderley Edge, Cheshire. In 1872, he went on a scholarship to Owens College (now the University of Manchester). His academically brilliant career there, where he specialized in Greek and Latin, was cut short when he stole money in an attempt to reform a young prostitute, Marianne Harrison. He was briefly imprisoned, and went to America where he had various jobs, but ended up on the verge of starvation in Chicago. He sold some short stories to the *Tribune* and other papers there, but wrote himself out. This episode in his life forms one of the best sections in his novel *New Grub Street* (1891; intr. G. W. Stonier, World's Classics, 1938; ed. B. Bergonzi, PEL, 1968). He returned to Europe, and married Marianne Harrison, a desperate action that turned out badly for both. When she died, after living with him in poverty while he drudged at various tasks, he married another uneducated working-class girl, finally separating from her in acrimony in 1897. Between 1880, when he published his first novel, *Workers in the Dawn* (ed. R. Shafer, New York, 1935), and his death, Gissing published over 20 books. He lived for a time in London, teaching, writing and reading in the British Museum. He became known to other writers, such as Henry James, H. G. Wells and Frederick ⬦ Harrison, who admired his books. These never sold well, but he was able by scrimping to make a visit to Greece and three journeys to Italy. As a result of his travels in these classical lands, in which he was passionately interested, he published one of his best pieces of writing, *By the Ionian Sea: Notes of a Ramble in Southern Italy* (1901; intr. Virginia Woolf, Travellers' Library, 1933; ed. Frank Swinnerton, 1958). In 1898 he met Gabrielle Fleury, and from 1899 lived in France with her in a bigamous marriage, because he could not obtain a divorce.

With the exception of his last two or three works, Gissing's novels were published in the conventional 3-volume format,

with melodramatic plots of a routine kind. He has two qualities which make him of great interest as a writer, but which do not work well together, and which spoil the novels as wholes. They are also indicative of his personal dilemma. He is considered as the straightforward describer of the miseries of poverty, a naturalist in the style of Zola, who would place the emphasis on environment in conditioning human sensibility. This is, of course, partly true. In his unsentimentalized portrayal of the poor he is a new kind of writer in English; it marks him off from Dickens, of whom he wrote a *Critical Study* (1898; often reprinted), which says more about Gissing than Dickens. His view of the poor is very much a 'class' one; he constantly wants to 'serve' them but constantly finds that this is no solution. He feels the destructive effect of environment on the human spirit, but then mostly implies that the working class are being swindled out of middle-class values, a situation that would be improved if they were simply better off. He feels, as Dickens did, that he was himself, by being poor, unjustly *déclassé*. Unlike Dickens, he has no poetic power to present an alternative view of the human situation that might transcend his own conscious evaluation. Gissing's other talent is for a kind of psychological exploration, but to exert this he feels obliged to choose middle-class characters as being more familiar and 'richer' in possibility. It is this latter quality that makes *The Private Papers of Henry Ryecroft* (published in the *Fortnightly Review*, 1903; often reprinted) his best book, because it is a kind of autobiographical reminiscence, exploring various states of mind with successful candour. Among his other novels are: *A Life's Morning* (1888; ed. W. Plomer, 1947); *Demos: A Story of English Socialism* (1886); *Born in Exile* (1892); *The Odd Women* (1893); *In the Year of the Jubilee* (1894; ed. W. Plomer, 1947). *Human Odds and Ends* (1898), *The House of Cobwebs* (1906) and *A Victim of Circumstances and Other Stories* (1927, with a preface by A. C. Gissing, his younger son) from among the collections of his short stories. In *New Grub Street*, the class and economic circumstance of writers, which from the subject of the novel, crystallized some of Gissing's best insights (and this produces also some of his best writing). In his response to sex (both in fiction and in his life) Gissing was also a prisoner of his class. He nearly always has an 'idealized' woman in a novel. Gissing, not Lucky Jim, is the prototype of the modern English lower-middle-class intellectual. He is not, however, conscious of the complexities of his situation.

There are important collections of manuscripts in the Berg Collection of the New York Public Library and the Adams Gissing Collection in the Yale University Library. [AR]

Selections, ed. A. C. Gissing (1929); *Letters to Members of His Family*, ed. A. Gissing (his elder son) and E. Gissing (sister) (1927) (unreliable); *George Gissing and H. G. Wells: Correspondence*, ed. R. A. Gettmann (1961).
M. Roberts, *The Private Life of Henry Maitland* (1912) (fictionalized biography by a close friend); F. Swinnerton, *G.G.: A Critical Study* (revised edn, 1924); G. D. Leavis, 'G. and the English Novel', *Scrutiny*, 7 (1938); M. C. Donnelly, *G.G.: Grave Comedian* (Harvard U.P., 1954) (with bibliography); J. Korg, *George Gissing* (1963); O. H. Davis, *G. A Study in Literary Leanings* (1966); ed. P. Coustillas, *Collected Articles on G.* (1968).

Glanvill, Joseph (1636–80). Writer on philosophy and religion. Son of a Puritan merchant in Plymouth, he turned towards neoplatonism and the beginnings of science while at Exeter and Lincoln Colleges, Oxford (1652–8), becoming somewhat the type of modernist Anglican clergyman. His first book, *The Vanity of Dogmatizing* (1661), strongly influenced by Henry More and Descartes, urges the insignificance of man's knowledge (anticipating at one point Hume's critique of causation) and the need for a humble scepticism and wonder before the mystery of things. One of his illustrations is the story of a man who left Oxford to learn the gypsies' secret of controlling other men's minds, which inspired ◊ Arnold's *Scholar Gypsy*. Beautifully written in the image-laden style of Browne, the book was later twice recast (*Scepsis Scientifica*, 1665: *Essay against Confidence in Philosophy*, 1676) into the plain prose of later times. This change was probably connected with Glanvill's membership of the Royal Society (from 1664) which advocated such prose, and of which he wrote 2 defences, *Plus Ultra* (1668; ed. Jackson Cope, Gainsville, Fla, 1958) and *Philosophia Pia: or a Discourse of the Religious Temper and Tendencies of the Experimental Philosophy, which is Profest by the Royal Society* (1671). His constant desire for a unified approach to religion and science had a curious offspring in *Saducismus Triumphatus* (1681, from an original essay of 1666), an attempt to prove the existence of witches and hence of a spiritual world from empirical evidence, which he reasonably alleged to be strong: this included his own investigation of a poltergeist, the drummer of Tedworth. Other works of his defend pre-existence of souls (*Lux Orientalis*, 1661), the application of reason to religion (Λογου Θρησκεια, 1670), the establishment of the Church of England (*The Zealous and Impartial Protestant*, 1681) and plain preaching (*An Essay Concerning Preaching*, 1678) – all in opposition to Puritanism and Calvinism, from whose professors he seems to have suffered at Bath, where he was rector from 1666 and where he died. Some of his views resemble those of Locke, whom he may possibly have influenced. [SM]

The Vanity of Dogmatizing: The Three Versions, intr. Stephen Medcalf (1970).
Jackson Cope, *J.G., Anglican Apologist* (1956); Basil Willey, *The Seventeenth Century Background* (1934); Margaret Wiley, *The Subtle Knot* (1952).

Glapthorne, Henry (1610–42?). Dramatist. Born in Cambridgeshire and educated at Corpus Christi College, Cambridge, this minor dramatist probably went to London under a nobleman's patronage before writing some 11 plays in about ten years, probably beginning around 1633 with the tragedy *Argalus and Parthenia*, derived from Sidney's *Arcadia*. *The Hollander* (1635) reflects the vogue for Jonsonian realism at that time, and with *Wit in a Constable* (revised 1639) ranks highly among Caroline comedies. *The Lady's Privilege* is an absurd example of the love-and-honour theme, doubtless calculated to please devotees of Henrietta Maria's cult of platonic love. *Albertus Wallenstein* (produced 1639) is a tragedy on European events of only five years before, later to be the subject-matter of a play by Schiller. [MJ]

The Plays and Poems, ed R. H. Shepherd (2 vols., 1874).
F. E. Schelling, *Elizabethan Drama, 1558–1642* (1908).

Glover, Denis James Matthews (1912–). New Zealand poet. Born in Dunedin and

213

educated at the University of Canterbury where he won a boxing blue. After a brief spell in journalism he returned to the university to lecture in English (1936–8 and again 1946–8). In 1938 he founded the important Caxton Press, using excellent typography to publish many of the best New Zealand writers. He had a distinguished war record in the navy, and is now production manager of a Wellington printing and publishing firm.

Glover's poetic touch is light, and there is an attractive good humour in his early satire on New Zealand's literary 'puffing', *The Arraignment of Paris* (1937), which continues in later satires and lampoons. He has also preserved from the thirties his democratic sympathies and his admiration for independence and devotion to one's craft. The central figure of the linked lyrics of *Arawata Bill* (1953) is an indefatigable gold prospector with folk-hero overtones. Like the bard of *Sings Harry* (1951) Bill is realistic in his assessment of society and looks finally to nature for his sense of values. Here, as well as in the main early collection *The Wind and the Sand* (1945) and the more recent *Since Then* (1957), Glover favours the short line and simple, largely unadorned language. [P T]

Hot Water Sailor (1962) (autobiography).
J. E. P. Thomson, 'Time and Youth in the Poetry of D.G.', *Landfall*, 82 (1967).

Godley, Alfred Denis (1856–1925). Classical scholar and writer of college verse. Born in Co. Leitrim and educated at Harrow and Balliol College, Oxford, he was a Fellow and tutor of Magdalen College and appointed university orator (1910). Godley was joint editor of the *Classical Review* (1910–20) and edited Tacitus's *Histories* (1887, 1890). He translated Horace's *Odes* (1898) and Herodotus's works (Loeb, 1921–3). For samples of his light verse, see *Lyra Frivola* (1899), *Echoes from the Oxford Magazine* (1896) and *Reliquiae A. D. Godley* (1926). Single pieces (like 'Motor Bus') are sometimes anthologized. He also edited the works of Praed (1909) and Thomas Moore (1910). [A R]

Godwin, Mary Wollstonecraft (1759–97). Educationist and miscellaneous writer. She made a living keeping school with her sister, at Newington, and as a governess with Lord Kingsborough. Then she lived by her pen, as a translator and as a reader for Johnson, a London publisher. She was a member of a group of Radicals which included William ◊ Godwin, Tom Paine, Priestley and Fuseli, the painter. In 1793 she had an affair in Paris with Captain Gilbert Imlay, an American, who deserted her. Godwin lived with her following her attempted suicide at Putney Bridge. He married her shortly before the birth of a child (which proved fatal), a daughter, the Mary Wollstonecraft Godwin who became Shelley's second wife. Godwin wrote an interesting and touching *Memoir* of her (1798; ed. J. Middleton Murry, 1928). Her best-known work is *Vindication of the Rights of Women* (1792; ed. J. M. Murry, 1930), in which, drawing on her educational experiences and revolutionary ideas, she attacked contemporary society. [A R]

H. R. James, *M.W.* (1932); Virginia Woolf, *The Second Common Reader* (1932); R. M. Wardle, *M.W.* (Kansas U.P., 1952); M. George, *One Woman's 'Situation'* (U. of Illinois P., 1970).

Godwin, William (1756–1836). Philosopher and novelist. Born in East Anglia, the son of a Presbyterian minister, he was himself educated at Hoxton Academy for that calling. He exercised it for five years near London, but gave it up on losing his faith in God, and took to writing. In 1797, to safeguard his coming child's rights, he married Mary Wollstonecraft ◊ Godwin. In 1801, he married a Mrs Clairmont, whose daughter by her first marriage (Jane 'Claire' Clairmont) was the mother of Byron's Allegra. Godwin published a good deal of journalism and historical writing, as well as a few tragedies, but is remembered now only for a philosophical work and a novel. In 1793, he published the work which made him famous, and which he never equalled, *An Enquiry Concerning Political Justice* (revised 1796; ed. F. E. L. Priestley, Toronto U.P., 1946). When he abandoned his ministry, Godwin seems to have transferred the rigorous Calvinist thought he inherited, away from a religion based on the power of the inner light of private judgement derived from God, to a belief in the inner light of reason, the doctrine of the 'enlightenment'. Developing Locke's sensationalist theory of knowledge, he held that reason if properly heeded never betrays; it will always lead a man to make right political decisions. Since the world can, and must, be regenerated on rational principles, Godwin found himself arguing that the political doctrines then canvassed were anti-rational, therefore oppressive and wicked. The most rational, therefore best, society was a group of rational individualists whose aims, since rational, would be the same. He was a kind of Puritanical anarchist. This train of thought is still found in British trade unionism and in such movements as the Campaign for Nuclear Disarmament. If the *Enquiry* merely dealt with such abstract and cold doctrines, it would now be dead, but Godwin brought to his arguments a kind of impassioned personal commitment (perhaps also inherited from his dissenting past) which has kept the book alive. He is also fearless in following his argument to its logical conclusion. His novel, *Caleb Williams, or Things as They Are* (1794), which is an early 'propaganda' novel, manages perhaps for the same reasons to be fascinating, despite its clumsiness and unreality. The story concerns the individual and social consequences of crime, with a very early example of the 'good man' being 'framed'. [A R]

C. K. Paul, *W.G.: His Friends and Contemporaries* (1876) (prints a good deal of original material); H. N. Brailsford, *Shelley, G. and Their Circle* (1926); M. R. G. Grylls, *W.G. and His World* (1953).

Gogarty, Oliver St John (1878–1957). Irish poet and wit. He was born in Dublin, the son of a successful Catholic doctor, and was educated at Stonyhurst, Trinity College, Dublin, Oxford and Vienna before he qualified as a surgeon. During his student days he established himself as a boisterous Dublin personality, composer of unprintable limericks and superb mimic. His friends included George ◊ Moore, W. B. ◊ Yeats, and ◊ 'AE', although his classical training and ribald wit made him unsympathetic to the mystical aspects of the Irish revival and his friendship with James Joyce was more characteristic. He became a successful surgeon and in 1922 was nominated a Senator in the Irish Parliament; this made him a target for Republican terrorism and after an assassination attempt he spent a year in London. His first book of poems, *An Offering of Swans*, was published in 1924 and until the Senate was abolished in 1936 he was active in political life, especially with housing schemes to replace the slums. In the thirties he published a book of reminiscences, *As I Was Going*

Down Sackville Street (1936) and 3 more books of poetry. During and after the Second World War he spent much of his time in America, writing and lecturing. In his lifetime his poetry was overrated – Yeats gave him disproportionate space in the *Oxford Book of Modern Verse* – and it has since been neglected; his best poems are those on classical themes, such as 'Leda' and 'Europa', and his more public odes and elegies. Gogarty is perhaps most importantly remembered as a personality – the original of Joyce's 'stately plump Buck Mulligan' – and as a raconteur whose wit 'flowed from him like fresh water', but his achievements in medicine, poetry and politics together are impressive and characteristic of the best Irish writers of his time. [J M]

Collected Poems (1952).
Ulick O'Connor, *O. St J. G.* (1964).

Golding, Arthur (1536–1606). Translator. Son of John Golding, gentleman of Essex. Golding was educated at Jesus College, Cambridge, and entered the service of the Protector Somerset. His most important work was his translation of Ovid's *Metamorphoses, The Fyrst Fower Bookes of P. Ovidius Nasos Worke, intitled Metamorphosis translated into English meeter* (1565), and *The XV Bookes of P. Ovidius Naso, entytuled Metamorphosis* (1567). The translation, in clumsy 'fourteeners', nevertheless has movement and does get the stories told; it was very popular and was known to Shakespeare. The verse introduction to this translation gives his view of the *Metamorphoses* as a work of edification as it teaches the mutability of all things. Among Golding's other translations were versions of Caesar's *Commentaries*, Calvin's commentaries on the Psalms, Theodore Beza's *Tragedie of Abraham's Sacrifice* (1577; ed. M. W. Wallace, Toronto, 1906), Seneca's *De Beneficiis* (1578) and a completion of Sir Philip Sidney's translation of Philippe de Mornay, *A Worke concerning the Trewenesse of the Christian Religion* (1604). [D D]

C. S. Lewis, *English Literature in the Sixteenth Century* (1954); L. T. Golding, *An Elizabethan Puritan: A.G.* (New York, 1937).

Golding, William (Gerald) (1911–   ). Novelist. Educated at Marlborough Grammar School and Brasenose College, Oxford, he spent some time as a schoolmaster, and his first novel, *Lord of the Flies* (1954; filmed 1963), is about a group of boys, or at least uses boys for 'characters'. It is partly a science-fiction tale, partly a desert island story. The general effect, however, as in all Golding's fiction, is of a symbolical moral fable. The story, apparently simple, is loaded; it can be, and has been, interpreted in several ways. In part it is a commentary on the 'falsity' of the moral world, the middle-class clichés, of ◊ Ballantyne's *Coral Island*, which comfortably externalizes evil into savages and external nature (the boys' names are the same, for example). Golding 'internalizes' the power of darkness, as a function of each soul. The book thus touches deeply on the nature of society, of courage and of the self. *The Inheritors* (1955) is another moral fable about the extermination by *homo sapiens* of Neanderthal man. It is written from the point of view of the latter, a brilliant imaginative feat. Starting from H. G. Wells, who endows the doctrine of evolution with a moral content very gratifying to the holder of it, Golding overturns Wells's easy rationalism, which had again externalized evil into Neanderthal man, the unsuccessful species. *Pincher Martin* (1956) is a novel about a naval officer blown off his ship by a torpedo. Like a crab, he clings to a barren rock; the novel relates his tenacious and ingenious attempts to survive, interspersed with flashbacks of his life. The last few chapters, however, suggest the possibility that his actions may have been hallucinations; he loses his grip figuratively and actually, in disintegration. *Free Fall* (1959) is a more realistic work; a long reflection on his past life by a man consumed by greed. The story is difficult to work out because the man himself is searching for a pattern of meaning and is in constant argument about freedom and the will. *The Spire* (1964) is set in 14th-century England, obviously in Salisbury Cathedral close, though it is not a historical novel. The symbolism is vested in the spire, the life's work of Dean Jocelin; the author's point seems to be: 'There is no innocent work. God knows where God may be.' Beauty, pride, religion, sex, sin and redemption are all parts of the dean's vision. The honesty of Golding's head-on attempts to grapple with his intractable ideas command respect and admiration. [AR]

The Pyramid (1967).

S. Heynes, *W.G.* (Columbia Essays on Modern Writers, 1964) (with bibliography); Peter Green, 'The World of W.G.', *Review of English Literature*, 1 (April 1960); J. Peter, 'Fables of W.G.', *Kenyon Review*, 19 (Fall, 1957); M. Walters, 'The Fabulists: G. and Camus', *Melbourne Critical Review*, 4 (1961); F. W. Nelson, *Source Book on 'Lord of the Flies'* (New York, 1963); C. B. Cox, '*Lord of the Flies*', *Critical Quarterly*, 2 (Summer 1960); M. Kinkhead-Weakes and J. Gregor, *W.G.* (1967).

Goldsmith, Oliver (1730–74). Poet, essayist, dramatist and miscellaneous writer. The second son of Charles Goldsmith, curate of the parish of Kilkenny West in West Meath in Ireland, he lived at his family's house in Lissoy (now called Auburn). He went to school in Elphin, Athlone and Edgeworthstown, and in 1745 was admitted as a sizar (a poor student who worked for a stipend) at Trinity College, Dublin, graduating as a B.A. in 1750, after an undistinguished career and some disciplinary trouble. Being rejected as an ordinand in the Church of Ireland, he took a post as a tutor in Co. Roscommon. He dissipated his savings by gambling, a vice he never freed himself from, on a visit to Cork and later in Dublin *en route* to London to study law; in 1752, he settled to the study of medicine at Edinburgh, where he remained for two years, followed by a year at the University of Leyden. He spent 1755–6 travelling in Paris, Germany, Switzerland and Italy. At Padua or elsewhere he may have obtained the doctorate in medicine with which he later dignified himself. He is reputed to have eked out a living by playing the flute (or the violin) and disputing doctrinal points at monasteries and universities. In February 1756, he landed at Dover without a penny, and worked as an assistant in a London apothecary's shop, as a doctor in the poor district of Southwark, and as an usher in a school at Peckham.

He began his career as a writer with 25 reviews and essays, and nearly 40 short notices for Ralph Griffiths' *Monthly Review*, and gradually extended his scope as a hack writer to translations; as the pseudonymous James Willington he published J. Marteilhe's *Memoirs of a Protestant Condemned to the Galleys of France* (1758). His ability and range as a professional writer should be noticed. He also wrote for the *Critical Review* of ◊ Smollett, *The Busy Body*, and other periodicals; his career as a writer was sealed when he was found 'not qualified' for a medical post on the coast of Coromandel. *An Enquiry into the Present State of Polite Learning in Europe* (1759) was his first considerable work. This sketch of man's intellectual history develops the myth, dear to Goldsmith's heart, of an original golden age which can be recaptured by naturalness on the part of the poet. He sees his own age as characterized by a destructive pedantry. In the same year the 8 numbers of his periodical *The Bee* appeared, immediately reprinted as a book; these included some of his most famous essays, such as 'A City Night Piece' and 'An Account of the Augustan Age in England'. Among his extensive periodical writing, in 1761 he contributed a series of 'Chinese Letters' to Newbery's *Publick Ledger*. At this time, he met Dr Johnson and became a founder member of 'The Club'. After the republication as a volume of *The Citizen of the World, or Letters from a Chinese Philosopher, Residing in London to his Friends in the East* (2 vols.; many reprintings; ed. A. Dobson, 1891–1900), he turned to more substantial hack work such as biographies, anthologies, translations, and compilations like his *History of England in a Series of Letters from a Nobleman to His Son* (1764; many reprintings), a *History of the Fathers* (1764), *A History of England* (1771), prefatory and connective matter in Brooke's *Natural History* (1763–4), the *History of the Earth and Animated Nature* (8 vols., 1774), and digests of Greek and Roman history. In Boswell's *Life of Johnson*, Goldsmith fills the role of a childishly vain, goodnatured man, unready of wit, a butt for the brilliant conversation, yet a man whom the grand Cham somewhat eccentrically admired and loved. The picture is more effective dramatically than plausible on closer examination. Goldsmith was fairly obviously a self-mocker, a conscious user of Irish Bulls. While he no doubt wrote better than he spoke, his miscellaneous work is always marked by experience, balance and wide, though not always accurate, information.

Scattered throughout his essays is a thought-out poetic theory, rejecting pedantry, the bric-à-brac of the new school of ◊ Gray, and affirming the didactic function of art. As a poet, he wrote slowly and carefully. *The Traveller: or A Prospect of Society* appeared in 1764 (many reprintings; ed. G. B. Hill, 1888) and *The Deserted Village* in 1770 (many reprintings and translations). In these 2 major works written in couplets and riding the main stream from Dryden and Pope, Goldsmith proves himself a poet with an individual voice. *The Traveller* is a panoramic poem powerfully developing a central 18th-century concern with the comparative study of human life, and written with a genuine and deep note of feeling. *The Deserted Village* is more pathetic and may be seen as an outcry, using rhetoric, myth and tradition, against the changes he felt to be upon the face of Britain.

The Vicar of Wakefield: A Tale (1766; ed. A. Dobson, 1885, with bibliography; ed. C. F. Doble, 1909; ed. O. Doughty, 1928) is probably the best known of Goldsmith's works. It is often wrongly read as a novel of sentiment, though Goldsmith abhorred the growing cult, and it naturally seems weak as a realistic novel. Read as a tale, in the light of Goldsmith's poetry – it contains for example his best-known lyric, 'When lovely Woman stoops to Folly' – it appears as a traditional work of considerable art which sends up some of the literary conventions of his time. Its didacticism is irradiated with humour and it might be placed alongside *Rasselas* by Johnson. In 1768 was performed *The Good Natur'd Man* (published 1768) and in 1773 his most famous play, *She Stoops to Conquer: or, The Mistakes of a Night* (published 1773; several reprintings and translations). Both comedies are founded on the incongruity between good feeling and experience. Goldsmith once more affirms his belief that what is most natural is most admirable and its enemy is pedantry, of sentiment, behaviour, belief and social conformity. In March 1774 Goldsmith fell seriously ill, and a combination of poor self-treatment and worry (he had committed himself to more work than he could manage) hastened his death. An unfinished poem, *Retaliation*, was provoked by Garrick's proposed epitaph, which made fun of him, and shows that Goldsmith had a keen eye for the worth of his friends. It is interesting to note the frequent appearance in his work of the figure of a homeless traveller, who listens to his own feelings and views with wary alienation the societies, countries and scenes he visits. [AR]

Collected Works, ed. A. Friedman (5 vols., 1966); Works, ed. J. W. M. Gibbs (5 vols., 1884–6); The Miscellaneous Works, ed. D. Masson (Globe Edition, 1869); Poems and Plays, ed. A. Dobson (Everyman, 1910); Poetical Works, ed. A. Dobson (1927) (with notes); *Gray, Collins and G.*, ed. and intr. R. Lonsdale (1969); *Plays*, ed. A. Dobson (Temple Classics, 1901); ed. C. E. Doble (1909); *Collected Letters*, ed. K. C. Balderston (1928).

R. M. Wardle, *O.G.* (Kansas U.P., 1957); J. Forster, *Life of G.* (2 vols., 1854); E. L. Mc-Adam, 'G. the Good-Natured Man', in *The Age of Johnson*, ed. F. W. Hilles (Yale U.P., 1949); W. C. Brown, *Triumph of Form* (U. of N. Carolina P., 1948); A. N. Jeffares, *O.G.* (WTW, 1959); R. S. Crane, in *CBEL*, iii (1940) and *Supplement* (1957).

Goodall, Walter (*c.* 1706–66). Scottish historian, assistant librarian of the Advocates' Library, Edinburgh, from 1735. His *Examination of the Letters Said to Have Been Written by Mary Queen of Scots* (1754) challenged the accepted Presbyterian account of 16th-century Scottish affairs and opened the way for the romantic rehabilitation of the Queen; other pioneering work included an edition of the *Scotichronicon* of John ◊ Fordun and an *Introduction to the History and Antiquities of Scotland* (1769). [AI]

DNB.

Gordimer, Nadine (1923–   ). South African novelist and short-story writer. Born in Springs near Johannesburg, she left the University of the Witwatersrand without taking a degree and has since contributed widely to periodicals. The first of 3 short-story collections was *The Soft Voice of the Serpent* (1953). She is married to Reinhold Cassirer and lives in Johannesburg. Her eye for precise emotional discrepancy and her nervous prose are concentrated in numerous short stories on the slight shifts of mood or attitude that constitute domestic crises. Her novels *The Lying Days* (1953), *A World of Strangers* (1958) and *Occasion for Loving* (1963) show the same skilled penetration of the complex moment, but there is a falling away of intensity in their narrative passages that weakens them structurally. She explores the psychology of boredom, observing the restless introversion of people who live at a loose end. Statement is characteristically qualified by subordinate clauses, as if uncertain of its accuracy. Her most recent novel is *The Late Bourgeois World* (1966), and the latest collection of stories, *Not for Publication* (1965). [PT]

L. Abrahams, 'N.G.: the Transparent Ego', *English Studies in Africa*, III, 2 (September 1960); A. Woodward, 'N.G.', *Theoria*, 16 (1961); W. H. Gardner, 'Moral Somnambulism', *The Month* (September 1957).

Gordon, Adam Lindsay (1833–70). Australian poet. Born in the Azores. Having left England under a cloud in 1853, he was variously a mounted policeman, horse-breaker, famous jockey and parliamentarian in Australia. He published 2 books of verse in 1867, and continued for two years to win steeplechases and write poems in and around Melbourne. In 1870 financial pressure forced him out of retirement and he had a serious racing fall from which he never fully recovered. He saw his final book through the press, and shot himself. Gordon became the object of literary adulation in Australia, but his pre-eminence was widely doubted by 1913, when his *Poetical Works* were published, and dismissed by 1934, when a bust was placed in Poet's Corner in Westminster Abbey. His jingling horse-riding poems are better than those in which Swinburnian rhythms obscure a flaccid melancholy. [PT]

E. Humphris, *The Life of A.L.G.* (1933); A. J. Coombes, *Some Australian Poets* (1938).

Gosse, Sir Edmund (1849–1928). Critic, verse-writer and essayist. Born in London the son of Philip Gosse, a distinguished zoologist and member of the Plymouth Brethren. Gosse's account of the sombre religious fanaticism surrounding his youth is the subject of his best book, *Father and Son* (published anonymously, 1907), a brilliant and moving document of Victorian social and intellectual history. Gosse was educated privately and spent a leisured life as an assistant librarian in the British Museum (1867), translator at the Board of Trade (1874) and librarian at the House of Lords (1904–14). Among his linguistic interests, Gosse included a knowledge of the Scandinavian tongues, and published *The Ethical Condition of Early Scandinavian Peoples* (1874). His critiques of Ibsen, reprinted in *Northern Studies* (on Danish, Swedish, Norwegian and Dutch poets) (1879 and 1890), translations of his plays, and *Life* (1908) were important in introducing the 'new drama' to England, and earned him a Norwegian knighthood (1901). Gosse was also widely read in French literature, which gave his writing on English literature a wide and civilized scope; he was a Commander of the Legion of Honour. Gosse's most important critical work was his *Life and Letters of John Donne*, which appeared as early as 1899, giving him an important role in the revaluation of the Metaphysical poets which has marked the critical sensibility of the last fifty years. Gosse's interests were wide, but his scholarship was often inaccurate, and his casual, belletristic judgements, though masked by humanity and feeling, often seem stuffy to a modern reader less prone to accept his society's values. He wrote well, however, and was influential with such volumes as lives of Gray (1882), Jeremy Taylor (1904) and Sir Thomas Browne (1905) for Henry Morley's Men of Letters series, as well as Congreve (1888) and Swinburne (of whom he was a close friend) (1917). His man-of-the-world, *causerie* type of criticism, best illustrated in his Clark Lectures at Cambridge, *From Shakespeare to Pope* (1885), and in his volumes of essays and vignettes like *Gossip in a Library* (1891), annoyed more vigorous historical scholars such as Churton Collins. Gosse wrote much on the contemporary French and English literary scene and on many of the important writers of his day. He was an accomplished pastiche verse writer, translator and parodist. [AR]

Collected Poems (1911); *Collected Essays* (12 vols., 1912–27).
E. Charteris, *The Life and Letters of Sir E.G.* (1931).

Gosson, Stephen (*c*. 1554–1624). Pamphleteer. Born in Canterbury, he attended the King's School there, and went to Corpus Christi College, Oxford. He wrote pastorals and plays before turning moralist and pamphleteer and using inside knowledge to attack the theatrical profession. In 1579 he published *The School of Abuse, Containing a Pleasant Invective against Poets, Pipers, Players, Jesters, and such like Caterpillers of a Commonwealth . . .*, a piece of invective written in a Euphuistic style, which he dedicated, without permission, to Sir Philip Sidney; and followed it the same year with *The Ephemerides of Phialo and a Short Apologie for the School of Abuse*. In 1582, as part of a continuing debate, he published a more sustained attack, *Plays Confuted in Five Actions, Proving That They Are Not to Be Suffered in a Christian Common Weal*, in which he marshalled classical authors to make his anti-theatrical points, and argued that acting was a form of lying. Gosson, never a puritan, became an Anglican clergyman, first in the country and later in London, where he preached a Paul's Cross sermon in 1598, *The Trumpet of War*. [MJ]

W. Ringler, *S.G.*, *A Biographical and Critical Study* (1942); C. S. Lewis, *English Literature in the Sixteenth Century* (1954).

Gower, John (1330?–1408). Poet and friend of Chaucer. A Londoner of good family and considerable means, he was a notable benefactor of churches. He was in the service of Henry of Lancaster (later Henry IV) and shared in his patron's good fortune, though he went blind before his death. He combined a social conscience with his lively personal ambition, and his works in three languages (ed. G. C. Macaulay, 4 vols., 1899–1902) all have a moral and didactic purpose. The French *Mirour de l'homme* (1376–9) illustrates the effects of sin on society. Gower was the leading political poet of his time, and the Latin *Vox clamantis* (*c*. 1382) is an attack on the government of Richard II and includes a terrified vision of the violence and destruction wrought by the Peasants' Revolt of 1381. His major English work, *Confessio amantis* (1390), written at the request of and dedicated to Richard II (ed. R. A. Peck, 1968; tr. T. Tiller, Penguin Classics, 1963), was revised and rededicated to Henry IV in 1392. It is a well-constructed though rather mechanical allegory, using the device of a lover's confession to examine the relative claims of courtly love and Christianity. In the stories which illustrate the argument, Gower appears as a lucid narrator and a pioneer of a plain English style. Though his smooth octosyllabic couplets often become monotonous, he can convey an atmosphere of strangeness, and romance which is foreign to Chaucer, together with whom he brings French literary culture into English. [AG]

D. Pearsall, *G and Lydgate* (WTW, 1969), and 'G's Narrative Art', *PMLA* (1966); W. P. Ker, *Essays on Medieval Literature* (1905); C. S. Lewis, *The Allegory of Love* (1936).

Graham, Dougal (1724–79). Town crier of Glasgow, author of a verse *History of the Rebellion of 1745* and reputed author of several chapbooks containing earthy tales and traditional jests in colloquial Scots speech of the mid 18th century – virtually the only surviving examples of the dialect. [A I]

Collected Writings, ed. G. MacGregor (2 vols. 1883).

Graham, James (1st Marquess of Montrose) (1612–50). Poet and soldier. He fought for the Scottish Covenanters in 1638–9 but then, repelled by the conduct of the victorious Presbyterian leaders, transferred his loyalty to Charles I. A soldier at the mercy of indecisive politicians, Graham found that his brilliant guerrilla campaign in the Highlands (1644–5) had been authorized too late to affect the outcome of the Civil War. After years of exile and intrigue he was defeated, betrayed and executed while leading an abortive invasion of Scotland for Charles II in 1650. Graham's anthology-piece 'My dear and only love . . .' fairly represents the spirit of his handful of poems; the brilliance, glamour and pathos of his career provided material for a novel by Scott and biographies by John Buchan (1928) and C. V. Wedgwood (1952). [A I]

Poems, ed. J. L. Weir (1938).
C. V. Wedgwood, 'The Poems of M.', in *Essays and Studies by Members of the English Association* (1960).

Graham, Robert Bontine Cunninghame (1852–1936). Scottish traveller, patriot, socialist, short-story writer and historian of South America. Born in London of a Scottish landed family and educated at Harrow, Cunninghame Graham learned Spanish in childhood and spent most of the 1870s ranching and horse-and-cattle-dealing in the Argentine and Texas. Succeeding to the family estate and debts in 1884, he sat as Radical M.P. for North-West Lanarkshire (1886–92), was imprisoned after the 'Bloody Sunday' riots in Trafalgar Square (1887) and helped Keir Hardie to found the Scottish Parliamentary Labour Party. *Mogreb-el-Acksa* (1898) describes a visit to the interior of Morocco the previous year, and supplied Shaw with the setting and some of the incidents for *Captain Brassbound's Conversion*. Cunninghame Graham again visited South America during and after the First World War, and in 1928 was the first President of the Scottish National Party. His many stories and sketches, mostly published between 1899 and 1914, are based on his experiences in Scotland and the

Argentine; like the essays and minor work of his friend Joseph ◊ Conrad, they are good reflective *rapportage* rather than original creation. Cunninghame Graham's histories of the exploration and conquest of South America appeared chiefly in the 1920s. [A I]

Thirty Tales and Sketches, ed. E. Garnett (1929); *The Essential R.B.C.G.*, ed. P. Bloomfield (1952).
H. F. West, *A Modern Conquistador* (1932); A. F. Tschiffely, *Don Roberto* (1937).

Grahame, Kenneth (1859–1932). Essayist and children's writer. Born in Edinburgh, the third child of an advocate and a cousin of Anthony ◊ Hope. His mother died when he was 5, and the children went to live with their grandmother, spending the first two years at Cookham Dene by the Thames. Kenneth went to St Edward's School, Oxford, and wanted to go on to the university, but his family pushed him into a clerkship at the Bank of England. He was encouraged in writing prose by Dr Frederick Furnivall, through whom he joined the New Shakespeare Society, and met among others Tennyson, Browning, Ruskin and William Morris. He contributed to the *St James's Gazette* and the ◊ *Yellow Book*, and published a collection of essays, *Pagan Papers*, in 1893. Much of this writing records his desire to escape from cities, noise and the demands of regular work. He became Secretary of the Bank of England in 1898, and married Elspeth Thomson in 1899. Their only child, Alastair, was born the following year.

Two books of essays or stories, *The Golden Age* (1895) and *Dream Days* (1898), brought him increased recognition. The stories concern the same family of children, whose games and response to their surroundings and adult mentors are told with Wordsworthian freshness and clarity. *The Wind in the Willows* (1908) began with a series of bedtime stories told to his son in 1904–7, and was continued in letters when the child went away. When the book was to be published, the first half of the story had to be recaptured and written down, a painful struggle for an author who always found writing hard. This book holds great appeal for children and adults, because of its delightful characterization and idyllic riverside setting. The familiar theme of escape reappears in the characters of Mole, who turns his back on domestic chores, and

Portly and the Seafaring Rat, but home has a strong pull too. Mole, Rat and Badger's comfortably shipshape homes are all minutely described, and though Toad's pile seems less cosy, he makes up for it in pride. It is a beautiful and benevolently ordered world. [T V]

Peter Green, *K.G.* (1959).

Grandbois, Alain (1900–). French Canadian poet. Born in Saint-Casimir, between Quebec and Three Rivers, Grandbois received a university education and then inherited a sum of money which allowed him to travel widely, between the wars, in North America, Europe, Asia and Africa. From 1930 to 1938, when not travelling, Grandbois spent much of his time at Port-Cros on the Mediterranean, where he met Supervielle. Like Supervielle, Grandbois is a French-language poet from the Americas whose cosmic perspectives add a visionary quality to a strong physical sense of the textures of a world of concrete objects. This sense of reality appears in Grandbois' poetry as an intense love of life and this is given urgency by the fear of death and animated by a sense of adventure (besides poetry he has written biographies of Marco Polo, 1942, and of the 17th-century Canadian explorer, Louis Jolliet, 1933). His 3 volumes of poems, including some published in Hankow (China) in 1934, reappeared collectively in Montreal in 1963. Grandbois only rarely uses conventional verse-forms. The tone of his poetry is often declamatory, making it grave and aristocratic, but this quality is relieved by the pervasive presence of powerful though unostentatious erotic imagery. [C R P M]

Jacques Brault, *A.G.* ('Poètes d'Aujourd'hui', Paris. 1968).

Granville-Barker, Harley. ◊ Barker, Harley Granville.

Graves, Robert Ranke (1895–). Poet, novelist, critic, mythographer and translator. One of the most notably versatile all-round men of letters in English literary history, he came from a literary and scholarly family and was educated at Charterhouse, from the O.T.C. of which he went straight to the First World War in his late teens. He began to publish poetry very early and, being wrongly supposed to have been killed by the blast of a shell in France, read his own obituary in *The Times* before he was 21. He wrote a number of harshly realistic poems about the First World War, most of which he rejected from his later volumes, and after the war went to Oxford, where he was allowed to work for a B.Litt. with a thesis on dreams and poetry. He suffered from shell-shock for about ten years after the First World War and his poems of the 1920s reflect his sense of stress as well as the growing unhappiness of his first marriage. After an unhappy experience of teaching in Egypt, he determined to earn his living entirely by writing. The success of his harsh and candid autobiography, *Good-Bye to All That* (1929) enabled him to emigrate to Majorca, accompanied by the poetess Laura Riding, who had a great influence on his work at this time. Later Miss Riding went back to her native United States, and Graves, who had never married her and had been divorced from his first wife, Nancy Nicholson, married a second wife, much younger than himself. The stress of difficult love on a constitution and temperament intrinsically tough and resilient, but much shaken by the First World War, is a thread that runs through all Graves's poetry.

The success of historical novels like *I, Claudius* (1934) enabled Graves, during the years of the Second World War, to devote himself to mythography, *The White Goddess* (1948; amended and enlarged 1952, 1961). The theory behind this book is that all true poetry is in subjection to a Muse, who represents both Nature and the primitive traditions of a matriarchal religion and society, and who is both creative and destructive, both to be loved and feared. Though Graves is in a sense turning his private stresses into a myth, in doing so he gives them, and is later able to give his poetry a greater universality. He has published several volumes of *Collected Poems* – the most recent in 1965 – in each of which he has fastidiously revised poems he has left to stand and rejected poems that have come to displease him. Partly because of his classical training and interests, his poetry has a terseness and rotundity hard to match among contemporary poets. He is never clumsy, though his passion for revision shows that he knows he runs the risk of being facile. The deep melancholy and almost neurotic sense of fear and anxiety in much of his poetry is counterbalanced by a robust and irreverent sense of humour, sometimes bawdy, and by moments of very pure lyrical tenderness. As a critic, a tendency to trail his coat and ridicule poets he dislikes has prevented him from being taken wholly seriously, but he is much more readable than many soberer critics, and always worth listening to when he writes about verse as a craftsman. In his earlier years, he was thought of as a very true and scrupulous minor poet. The increasing amount and the consistent high quality of his work has led many critics more recently to claim major rank for him, but Graves himself is interested in being a 'good' rather than a 'great' poet. [GSF]

The Crowning Privilege. Collected Essays on Poetry (1959); *Oxford Addresses on Poetry* (1962); *Beyond Giving* (privately printed, 1969); *Poems about Love* (1969).
M. S. S., *R.G.* (1956); J. M. Cohen, *R.G.* (1960); G. S. Fraser, *Vision and Rhetoric* (1959); *Shenandoah* (Winter, 1962) (special Graves issue).

Graveyard School. So called by the lugubrious vogue set by Edward ⋄ Young in his best-selling poem *The Complaint, or Night Thoughts on Life, Death and Immortality* (1742–4). Young's soliloquies on the deaths of his wife and of his step-daughter and her husband take place during nine nights and in each one gloom is manipulated with all the artistry of an amorist stroking a shroud. It ran through many editions in the poet's lifetime and was translated into most of the European languages. A similar poem, *The Grave* (1743) by Robert ⋄ Blair, joined it in popularity and frequently between the same covers. And in 1817 a bumper edition of misery appeared, when *Night Thoughts* was accompanied by a paraphrase on the Book of Job, *The Grave* and a homily by Bishop Porteous on *Death*. This popular reading led to extravagant mourning customs and a vast quantity of amateur funereal verse in 19th-century annuals. [RB]

Gray, Thomas (1716–71). Poet and letter-writer. Born in Cornhill, London, the son of a mentally unbalanced exchange broker (11 other children did not survive), he was sent to Eton by his mother in 1725, where with Horace ⋄ Walpole, Richard West and Thomas Ashton he formed a quadrumvirate known as the 'Quadruple Alliance'. In October 1734, he was admitted to Peterhouse, Cambridge; he left in September 1738 without taking a degree, but with a reputation for writing Latin verse. In March 1739, he set out on the Grand Tour (of

France and Italy) with Walpole, but they quarrelled at Reggio in May 1741 and Gray returned alone to England. On the death of his father in that year, his mother and aunts retired to a country house in Stoke Poges, Buckinghamshire. Gray stayed in London studying law, and wrote *Agrippina*, a tragedy, but spent the summer of the next year at Stoke Poges; there he wrote his 'Ode on the Spring', which he sent to his close friend West on the day the latter died. This event shook Gray into a burst of creativity, and later that summer he wrote his 'Sonnet: On the Death of Richard West', the 'Ode on a Distant Prospect of Eton College' (printed 30 May 1747) and the *Ode to Adversity*; he also began the 'Elegy Written in a Country Churchyard'. He worked on the latter intermittently until he sent it to Walpole (with whom he had become reconciled) in June 1750. Walpole and Dodsley published the poem on 15 February 1751. It instantly became popular, and there were 11 editions in a short time. Meanwhile, Gray returned to law studies at Cambridge in October 1742 (LL.B., 1743), and lived there for the rest of his life, with brief summer excursions to Scotland, the Lakes, or to other historical, picturesque or sublime scenes. In March 1747, he wrote his famous 'Ode on the Death of a Favourite Cat' (Walpole's); this, with the 'Spring' and the 'Eton' odes, was printed in Dodsley's *Collections* (1748). On 5 March 1756, as a result of an undergraduate practical joke, Gray crossed the street to live in Pembroke College. The kind of studies (varied and profound) pursued by Gray during these years are reflected in the 2 poems 'The Progress of Poesy' and 'The Bard', published by Dodsley on 8 August 1757 as *Odes by Mr Gray* (the first book issued from Walpole's Strawberry Hill press). On the strength of the few works he had published, Gray was already acknowledged as a great formative poet. He refused the offer of the laureateship in December 1757. In March 1768, Dodsley published the first collected edition of his work, *Poems by Mr Gray* (this first printed 'The Fatal Sisters', 'The Descent of Odin' and 'The Triumphs of Owen'). From 1759 to 1761 he had lived in London, reading in the newly opened British Museum, and on 28 July 1768 he was elected Regius Professor of Modern History at Cambridge (though he never lectured). Between December 1769 and March 1770 he enjoyed his brief but powerful friendship with a young Swiss scholar, C.-V. de Bonsetten. Gray is buried in the churchyard of Stoke Poges beside his mother.

Despite the traditional and neo-classical origins of many of his ideas, he is a curiously modern kind of poet; his work springs from a learned and scrupulous aestheticism. He is the most important representative poet of the mid 18th century. His production was slender: it is the tip of a vast iceberg of study, which covered historical and other fields of growing importance during the century. His knowledge of Celtic and Old Norse writing, while derivative, was a valuable imaginative stimulus. He was also a close and competent student of natural history, the classics and the history of English (including medieval English) writing. His 'Elegy' has been shown to contain many complexities of thought and feeling, yet it is still the most widely known English poem because of its handling of two deep human preoccupations: death and history. It is a masterly example of Gray's peculiar poetic qualities, perfect harmony of disciplined personal feeling and wide experience of traditional art. His more idiosyncratic and violent flights of imagination are equally disciplined and suggestive. In an age of great correspondents, his witty and observant letters are outstanding. [AR]

Poems, ed. A. Lane Poole, revised edn, L. Whibley, in *Poems of G. and Collins* (1937); *Complete Poems, English, Latin and Greek*, ed. H. W. Starr and J. R. Hendrickson (1966); *Poems*, ed. and intr. R. Lonsdale, in *G., Collins and Goldsmith* (1969); *G.'s English Poems*, ed., with notes, D. C. Tovey (1898; several times reprinted); *Works*, ed. T. J. Mathias (2 vols., 1814) (contains selections from 'Commonplace Books'); *Correspondence*, ed. P. Toynbee and L. Whibley (3 vols., 1935).

R. W. Ketton Cremer, *T.G.: A Biography* (1955); Lord David Cecil, *Two Quiet Lives* (1948); W. Empson, *Some Versions of Pastoral* (1935); C. Brooks, *The Well Wrought Urn* (1947); M. Golden, *T.G.* (New York, 1964); C. S. Northup, *A Bibliography of T.G.* (Yale U.P., 1917); H. W. Starr, *A Bibliography of T.G.: 1917–1951* (1953).

Green, Henry (pseud. of Henry Vincent Yorke) (1905–   ). Novelist. Born near Tewkesbury and educated at Eton, he joined his family business of food engineers, of which he is now managing director. While still at Oxford, he wrote his first novel, *Blindness* (1926); the narrator, a novelist, has been blinded in boyhood in a pointless accident. Green is thus already exploring two of the things he has made his own province: the nature of sensation, the quality of the flotsam and jetsam on the surface of experience; and the power of language (the blind writer develops a sharpened sense for this). It is perhaps significant that Henry Green suffers from partial deafness. His second novel, *Living* (1929), is set in a foundry. The story involves a clash between the working-class group and the upper-class owners. But, though Green renders the industrial context accurately, from experience, the novel is far more than a social documentary. His other 8 novels are: *Party Going* (1939), set in a railway station and involving a strange group of futile upper-class figures who are (in a rather Kafkaesque way) frustrated by fog from pursuing their journey (the title is thus suggestively ambiguous); *Pack My Bag* (1940); *Caught* (1943), a 'war' novel about the Auxiliary Fire Service – in which Green served – in blitzed London; *Loving* (1945), set in an Irish castle, while the blitz is going on, with an elaborate parallel between the servants' life and the owners'; *Back* (1946), dealing with the resettlement of a prisoner-of-war; *Concluding* (1948); *Nothing* (1950) and *Doting* (1952), his last 2 novels, told almost entirely by dialogue. Green is a highly conscious writer, whose strange stories, which try to suppress the novelist's point of view, present a highly individual achievement. The titles of the novels, suggestive, open, are one indication of the kind of impressionistic writer he is. His comic gift, however, prevents the novels from being as portentous as a title like *Concluding* might suggest. His prose, too, is mannered and has affinities with James Joyce (in its indirection) and Hemingway. He is one of the few modern English novelists who seems able to make sex a natural element in human experience. He has discussed his art in a radio broadcast he made in 1950, and in an essay he wrote in 1951. His reputation seems to be growing, and there is a fair body of commentary on his sometimes puzzling works. His novels defy ready categorization. [AR]

E. Stokes, *The Novels of H.G.* (1959); J. Russell, *H.G.: Nine Novels and an Unpacked Bag* (1960).

Green, John Richard (1837–83). Journalist and historian. Born in Oxford, the son of a tradesman, and educated there at Magdalen College School and Jesus College. He took orders and held various curacies in London. Under pressure of ill-health, he gave his work up in 1869 to become librarian at Lambeth Palace, where he was able to follow his taste for historical research. He contributed frequently to the *Saturday Review*, republishing some of his contributions in *Stray Studies from England and Italy* (1876), but is best known for his *Short History of the English People* (1874; revised Mrs Alice Stopford Green, 1888; Everyman, 2 vols., 1915), which he expanded as a *History of the English People* (4 vols., 1877–80). Green's work, long popular with adult education students, was justly valued for its clear and straightforward narrative, and for the way in which it does not dwell exclusively on political and military history, but tries to give some idea of scientific, intellectual and social facts of importance. He further expanded certain parts of his main work in *The Making of England* (1881) and *The Conquest of England* (1883). [AR]

J. Bryce, *Studies in Contemporary Biography* (1903); W. G. Addison, *J.R.G.* (1946); R. L. Schuyler, 'G. and His Short History', *Political Science Quarterly*, LXIV (1949).

Green, Matthew (1696–1737). Poet, Civil Servant. Remembered in his brief obituary as a 'facetious companion', he is now known only for his octosyllabic poem *The Spleen* (1737, posthumously; ed. with other poems, R. K. Wood, 1925; ed. H. Fausset in *Minor Poets of the Eighteenth Century*, Everyman, 1930), so called from the contemporary use of the word to denote depression and *ennui*, the 'English disease'. His original and lively verses (admired by Pope and Gray) discuss the prevention and cure (particularly by living the simple life) of this condition, with a pleasant mixture of satire and raillery. [AR]

Green, T(homas) H(ill) (1836–82). Metaphysician and social philosopher. Born at Birkin, Yorkshire, the son of the rector, and educated at Rugby and Balliol College, Oxford. In 1878, he became White's Professor of Moral Philosophy. His main works were: a critique of the English empiricists, Locke, Berkeley and Hume, in his commentary on Hume's *Treatise* in *Philosophical Works of Hume*, which he edited with T. H. Grose (4 vols., 1874–8); *Prolegomena to Ethics* (1883); *Lectures on the Principles of Political Obligation* (posthumous, 1895).

Green was a member of the group that introduced Hegelian systematizing of thought, feeling and experience ('the real world is essentially a spiritual world') in Oxford philosophy. His kind of philosophical synthesis is the basis of the aesthetics of Walter ⋄ Pater. This, combined with a strong social commitment, made him influential among the students of his day (including many future administrators). [AR]

Works, with a memoir by R. L. Nettleship (3 vols., 1885–8).

W. D. Lamont, *Introduction to G.'s Moral Philosophy* (1934); M. Richter, *The Politics of Conscience: G. and His Age* (Harvard U.P., 1964); J. H. Randall, 'G. The Development of English Thought from Mill to Bradley', *JHI*, XXVII (1966).

Greene, (Henry) Graham (1904–   ). Novelist and dramatist. Born at Berkhamstead in Hertfordshire, the son of a schoolmaster, and educated at his father's school and Balliol College, Oxford, he was on the editorial staff of *The Times*, and was literary editor of the *Spectator* from 1940 until he joined the Foreign Office in 1941. He worked there until 1944. He has publishing interests. In 1927 he married and was converted to Roman Catholicism; in the thirties he travelled in Africa, giving an account of Liberia in *Journey without Maps* (1936), and of Mexico in *The Lawless Roads* (1939): both experiences were significant in his career as a novelist. Graham Greene's fiction is divided into serious novels and 'entertainments' (his own words). His first novel, *The Man Within* (1929), is a piece of historical fiction about betrayal among a group of early 19th-century smugglers. The theme of betrayal, and other preoccupations of the thirties, frontiers, spies and the police, are the chief centres of interest in the entertainments. These are: *Stamboul Train* (1932); *A Gun for Sale* (1936), which introduces Greene's interest in the villain-hero; *The Confidential Agent* (1939), set in the Spanish Civil War; *The Ministry of Fear* (1943); *The Third Man* (1950; the film script of this story of post-war Vienna was written in 1949); *Loser Takes All* (1955); and *Our Man in Havana* (1958; film script 1960; opera 1963), almost a burlesque of British Intelligence operations in pre-Castro Cuba. These stories have been called 'symbolic melodrama' and 'literary thrillers'; they contain many ideas and problems worked out more elaborately (not always more successfully) in his novels. He has also published several volumes of short stories along similar lines, most of them collected in *Twenty-One Stories* (1954). His early novels are *The Name of Action* (1930), *It's a Battlefield* (1934) and *England Made Me* (1935), a story of ruthless international finance and English expatriates in Scandinavia. With *Brighton Rock* (1938; film script 1948), Greene wrote his first explicitly 'Catholic' novel; Pinkie, the ex-Catholic criminal 'hero', because of his religious upbringing is in contact with the 'possibility' of grace; Ida, the whore, kindly, helpful, is not. She values the distinction between right and wrong (with no means of judging except experience); Pinkie has access to the means of distinguishing between good and evil. *The Power and the Glory* (1940) is based on a story Greene relates in his Mexican travel book; the novel, however, is vastly more complex. The 'whisky priest' is the 'hero'; a man who seems to be closest to God because of his sin. The action takes place during a revolution, so that Catholic doctrine and Marxist doctrine are introduced into the problem of judging individual human action; Greene's view seems to be that the violence and decay of the whisky priest will, in a way, produce his resurrection as a man. (This novel won the Hawthornden Prize.) Scobie, the main character of *The Heart of the Matter* (1948), is another failed hero (he commits adultery, connives at murder, takes communion without absolution and finally commits suicide), yet all the while, as a Catholic, has the possibility of judging his own actions and is truly the hero. *The End of the Affair* (1951) allows a lover to see himself supplanted in his mistress's heart by God. *The Quiet American* (1955) takes place in Vietnam during the war of liberation against the French; again the theme is betrayal. *A Burnt Out Case* (1961), set in a Congo leprosarium before the Belgians withdrew from the country, is another moral parable. *Travels with My Aunt* (1969) introduces an 'innocent abroad' in a less vigorous moral fable.

Greene grapples with the problem of providing, in the middle of the 20th century, a 'final solution' to the question of the nature of morality. Criticism of his fiction has been mainly concerned either with his handling of 'heroes' in terms of Greek tragedy or with his Catholic doctrine. He often seems to suggest the view that Grace is the necessary condition for true and meaningful life, and that without it even virtues are contemptible. He is a skilful narrative writer and his technique has been influenced by the films; he often works by means of 'shots' or 'scenes'. He has written several successful plays, which deal mostly with marital infidelity as the setting for his moral questing: *The Living Room* (1953) and *The Complaisant Lover* (1959) are examples. He is also the author (and coauthor) of volumes of children's stories. [A R]

Collected Essays (1969).
K. Allott and M. Farris, *The Art of G.G.* (1951); M. D. Zabel, *Craft and Character in Modern Fiction* (New York, 1957); J. A. Atkins, *G.G.* (1957; 2nd edn, 1966); ed. R. O. Evans, *G.G.: Some Critical Considerations* (U. of Kentucky P., 1963) (with bibliography); P. Stratford, *Faith and Fiction* (U. of Notre Dame P., 1964).

Greene, Robert (*c*. 1558–92). Poet, playwright and pamphleteer. Born at Norwich, Greene was educated at Cambridge, where he received his Master of Arts degree in 1583. Five years later he received a degree from Oxford, and made a point of parading his academic titles in some of his published works. Some time before this he travelled in France and Italy, drawn thither, if we are to believe him, by the persuasions of the 'lewd wags' who were his university friends, such as ◊ Nashe and ◊ Peele. He married in 1585, but soon left his wife for London and a life of resolute dissipation prodigious even by the impressive standards of his day. He died in great poverty a month after he had dined in the company of his friend Thomas Nashe, on pickled herring washed down with Rhenish wine. After his death he was the subject of a pamphlet controversy between Nashe and Gabriel ◊ Harvey.

Greene is an outstanding example of the literary man who deliberately and determinedly set out to provide exactly what the public wanted. In an age of prolific writers he was more prolific than most, producing some 35 works in twelve years. Beginning with imitations of the Euphuistic mode made fashionable by ◊ Lyly, he went on to produce pastoral romances modelled on Sidney's *Arcadia*. Of these, *Pandosto* (1588) is notable not only for the charming lyrics scattered throughout it, but also because it was the direct source of Shakespeare's *The Winter's Tale*. In the 1590s Greene, by

his own account, abandoned Chaucer for
the more moral Gower and produced a
series of serious didactic works such as
Greene's Vision (written 1590, published
posthumously). In many of these the moral
purpose is purely formal. His plays include
Alphonsus, King of Aragon (1588), an ill-
advised attempt to match Marlowe's
mighty line; an attack on contemporary
corruption, *A Looking Glass for London and
England* (c. 1590), written in collaboration
with Thomas Lodge; and *Friar Bacon and
Friar Bungay* (c. 1591), his best play, a
romantic comedy which handles the necro-
mantic theme of *Dr Faustus* rather more
lightly than Marlowe.

But Greene's intrinsic interest as a literary
figure rests on the most explicitly autobiographical of his writings. These can be
roughly divided into those in which Greene
casts himself in the role of an abjectly
penitent sinner confessing his evil deeds and
those in which he gives a more detached
account of some of the activities of the
London underworld he knew so well. To the
first group belongs *Greene's Groatsworth of
Wit* (published posthumously in 1592), in
which he repents, among other things, of
the evil example afforded by the lives of his
former friends, Marlowe, Nashe and Peele.
This pamphlet is also noteworthy because it
contains the first clearly identifiable reference to Shakespeare as 'an upstart crow,
beautified with our feathers, that with his
tiger's heart wrapped in a player's hide,
supposes he is as well able to bombast out
a blank verse as the best of you; and being an
absolute *Johannes factotum*, is in his own
conceit the only Shake-scene in a country'.
The best of the more objective portrayals
of contemporary low life are the *Cony-
catching* pamphlets and *A Notable Discovery of Cosenage*, written in the last year
of his life. [G S]

Complete Works, ed. A. B. Grosart (15 vols.,
1881–6); *Plays and Poems*, ed. J. C. Collins (2
vols., 1905).
J. C. Jordan, *R.G.* (1915).

Greenwood, Walter (1903–   ). Novelist
and dramatist. Born at Salford, Lancashire,
the son of a hairdresser, he was educated at
Langworthy Road Council School. His
first book was a novel, *Love on the Dole*
(1933), based on his experiences in various
unskilled jobs, and in unemployment. This
book (together with the successful stage
version in collaboration with Roland Gow,

1934) had considerable social impact in
publicizing the suffering of the working
class. His subsequent books (some of which
were dramatized) placed him in a leading
position as a proletarian writer, but he has
never rivalled the success of his first book.
During the Second World War he wrote the
screenplay for a documentary on the
Merchant Navy. His novels, written with
pessimistic realism, include *His Worship the
Mayor* (1934), *Standing Room Only* (1936),
Only Mugs Work (1938) and *How the Other
Man Lives* (1939). *The Cleft Stick* (1937) is a
volume of short stories, and he has written
film scripts and television scripts such as the
B.B.C. serial *The Secret Kingdom* (1960).
[A R]

There Was a Time (1967) (autobiography).

Greg, Sir Walter Wilson (1875–1959).
Scholar and bibliographer. In 1900 the
Bibliographical Society published his preliminary finding-list of English plays to
1643, eventually developed into his greatest
work, *A Bibliography of the English Printed
Drama to the Restoration* (4 vols., 1939–59).
Principally interested in the Elizabethan
drama and all that pertains to the transmission of theatrical texts, he also extended
knowledge of the working conditions of
Elizabethan dramatists by his editions of ◊
Henslowe's *Diary* and other theatrical documents. In 1906 he founded the Malone
Society for the meticulous reprinting of rare
plays, and was general editor till 1939. His
books include *The Editorial Problem in
Shakespeare* (1942, revised 1951), *The
Shakespeare First Folio* (1955), and the
magnificent 2-text edition *Marlowe's 'Dr
Faustus', 1604–1616*, published in 1950,
the year in which he was knighted 'for
services to the study of literature'. Greg
made English bibliographical studies, hitherto disorganized and often amateurish, into
a rigorous, scientific discipline. [MJ]

F. Bowers and others, 'W.W.G.', *The Library*,
Fifth Series, xiv (1959); F. P. Wilson, 'Sir
W.W.G.', *Proceedings of the British Academy*,
xlv (1959), and 'Shakespeare and the "New
Bibliography"', *The Bibliographical Society*,
1892–1942 (1945).

Gregory, Isabella Augusta (Lady Gregory)
(1852–1932). Dramatist. An aristocrat, she
was educated privately, and in 1880
married Sir W. H. Gregory, whose estate
at Coole Park bordered her father's. Her
husband died in 1892. She came under the

influence of Yeats, who encouraged her researches into Irish folklore, and in 1899, with Edward Martyn, they founded the Irish Literary Theatre. She, Yeats and J. M. Synge founded the Abbey Theatre in Dublin, one of the great creative companies of the century, which produced both fine plays and fine players. Coming late to the theatre, she yet had a talent for construction and for rural Irish dialogue, and wrote some lively comedies including *The Workhouse Ward*, as well as making versions of Molière (*L'Avare* transposed to Ireland) and Goldoni, and translating Irish sagas. She was an able administrator, keeping the affectionate respect of the disillusioned Sean O'Casey. By her firm diplomacy she helped to bring about twenty-seven years after her own death the return from London on semi-permanent loan to Dublin of half the great collection of paintings assembled by her nephew, Sir Hugh Lane. It was at her house, Coole Park, that Yeats gained his admiration for the aristocratic attitudes, and in the death on active service of her son, the greatly gifted Major Robert Gregory, a modern Renaissance man, he found one of his finest subjects for poetry. [M J]

Our Irish Theatre (1914); *Lady G.'s Journals*, ed. Lennox Robinson (1946); *Selected Plays*, ed. E. Coxhead, intr. S. O'Casey (1962).

E. Coxhead, *Lady G.: A Literary Portrait* (1961); U. Ellis-Fermor, *The Irish Dramatic Movement* (1939); G. Fay, *The Abbey Theatre* (1958).

Grenfell, Julian (1888–1915). Soldier and poet. The eldest son of Lord Desborough, educated at Eton and Balliol, he chose the Regular Army as a career and served in India and South Africa. His regiment sailed for France in October 1914 and Grenfell soon excelled himself as a courageous, romantic figure of a soldier. He died of wounds in May 1915 and on the day of his death his poem 'Into Battle' appeared in *The Times*. This was the poem that made his reputation: he became the personification of youthful sacrifice and triumph, and his popular appeal equalled that of Rupert Brooke. The poem glorifies the action of battle and the soldier's sense of sacrifice; almost immediately after it was written this attitude became an anachronistic obscenity amid the realities of trench warfare, but it was a genuine and natural expression of feeling for Grenfell, and representative of the response of many young men to the outbreak of war. 'Into Battle' survives be-cause it is infused with Grenfell's own energetic exhilaration and almost mystical sense of his own destiny. [J M]

Bernard Bergonzi, *Heroes' Twilight* (1965).

Greville, Fulke (Lord Brooke) (1554–1628). Poet and biographer. Born into a powerful Warwickshire family, he went to Shrewsbury School at the same time as his exact contemporary Philip ◊ Sidney, whose life-long friend and biographer he was destined to be. He went to Cambridge and Sidney to Oxford, but they entered Elizabeth's court together and shared political and literary interests. In 1584 Greville entertained Giordano Bruno in England, and in 1586 he was pall-bearer at Sidney's untimely funeral. His long public career under Elizabeth and James combined prudence and subservience with loyalty to fallen favourites like Essex and Bacon. He was a Member of Parliament for Warwickshire, a statesman and a diplomat. He was also a gentleman of letters, whose poems (save for a few in miscellanies) and prose were never printed in his lifetime. He was knighted in 1597, was Treasurer of the Navy from 1589 to 1604, and Chancellor of the Exchequer from 1614 to 1622. King James gave him Warwick Castle, then a ruin, which he splendidly rebuilt and in 1621 he was made a peer. He was fatally stabbed by one of his servants, who harboured an imagined grudge against him, in 1628.

Caelica, begun under Sidney's guidance, is a collection of poems in varying metres on conventional love-themes, though the later ones are religious and philosophical. Around 1600 he wrote closet-plays in the manner of Seneca, *Mustapha* and *Alaham*, but destroyed a third on Antony and Cleopatra since it embodied his feelings about Essex's fall. His 'treaties' (treatises or philosophical poems) are concerned with religion and government – and with the conflict between man's nature and his destiny ('Created sick commanded to be sound'). *The Treaty of Monarchy* was followed by other treaties: *Wars, Fame and Honour, Humane Learning* and *Religion*. His most famous work, written around 1610–14 but printed only in 1652, was *The Life of the Renowned Sir Philip Sidney*, both a memoir of his friend and an autobiographical re-creation of the greatness of Elizabeth's age compared with what came after. It is not a detailed biography in the modern sense, but a memorial to the most attractive and dazzling English courtier of the Renaissance. [M J]

Poems and Dramas, ed. G. Bullough (2 vols., 1939); Works, ed. M. W. Croll (Philadelphia, 1903); The Remains, ed. G. A. Wilkes (1965).
C. S. Lewis, English Literature in the Sixteenth Century (1954).

Grierson, Sir Herbert (John Clifford) (1866–1960). English scholar. Born at Queendale in Shetland, the son of a small landowner, he was educated at King's College in Aberdeen University, and at Christ Church, Oxford, where he studied classics. In 1894, he was appointed to the chair of English at Aberdeen, and in 1915 became Professor of Rhetoric and English Literature at Edinburgh University. Grierson was a very popular and influential teacher; on his retirement, the students elected him Rector of the university. The 2 most important works he published are *The Poems of John Donne*, edited with an introduction and commentary (2 vols., 1912), and an anthology, *Metaphysical Lyrics and Poems of the Seventeenth Century: Donne to Butler* (1921). His *Donne* was the first real edition of this difficult poet, and is still a standard work. Together with the anthology it made the Metaphysical poets available; Grierson thus had an important part in the revaluation of these poems which has been one of the most noticeable features of the development of English studies since the First World War. His work was also used by T. S. Eliot and other formative poets in developing the art of poetry, but the nature of Grierson's anthology led them to stress certain of the intellectual features of the poems at the expense of the other traditional aspects which might have been seen in a different collection. Grierson published many editions of other authors, and volumes of literary studies including *Cross Currents in the Literature of the Seventeenth Century* (1929). He edited the *Letters of Sir Walter Scott* (12 vols., 1932–7). [A R]

D. Daiches, Proceedings of the British Academy, XLVI (1960) (obituary).

Grieve, Christopher Murray. ◊ MacDiarmid Hugh.

Grigson, Geoffrey (Edward Harvey) (1905–). Poet, editor, anthologist, topographer, critic of painting and poetry, and journalist. Grigson edited *New Verse*, a slim periodical which between 1933 and 1937 published and publicized the poets of the ◊ Auden group and attacked other poets of an older generation, notably Dame Edith ◊ Sitwell. Grigson's own poems have a vivid, painterly quality and reflect his keen interest in natural history. His interests after the late 1930s shifted from recent poetry to the roots of the Romantic movement, painters (Samuel Palmer), and poets (Christopher Smart and John Clare). His autobiography, *The Crest on the Silver* (1950), is an indispensable book for the understanding of cross-currents of taste and literary politics in the 1930s. His best collection of critical articles is probably *The Harp of Aeolus* (1947), which contains a slashing attack on what he considers the unnatural diction and idiom of Dylan Thomas, George Barker and Edith Sitwell, but *Poems and Poets* (1969) was notable for fine appreciative essays on Hopkins, Landor and Clare. [G S F]

Collected Poems (1963).

Grosseteste, Robert (c. 1168–1253). Scholar and reforming bishop. Little is known of his early life; he may well have studied and/or taught at Oxford or Paris. After 1215 he was teaching at Oxford and became the university's first Chancellor. In 1235 he became a very active Bishop of Lincoln, and in the same year begins a new period in his literary work. He was a prolific writer, many of whose works are still unpublished, while others, such as his Pauline commentaries, are now lost. Up to 1235 he wrote commentaries on Aristotle and the Bible and some treatises; his commentary on the *Posterior Analytics* is probably the most important and influential of these works. He was a reasonable and possibly a good Greek scholar, with at least a smattering of Hebrew, and after 1235 organized and participated in the making of translations from Greek, among which those of Pseudo-Dionysius and of the *Nichomachean Ethics* stand out. He produced no important work on speculative theology, but the translation and commentary on Pseudo-Dionysius were influential on mystical theology and his letters and sermons on pastoral. He is however chiefly remembered as a scientist. Deeply imbued with the Augustinian platonist tradition, his own bent was mathematical rather than experimental, but his investigation of the role of experiment in scientific inquiry was of the greatest importance. [ATH]

Ed. D. A. Callus, *R.G., Scholar and Bishop: Essays in Commemoration on the Seventh Centenary of his Death* (1955); A. C. Crombie, *R.G. and the Origins of Experimental Science* (1953); S. Harrison Thomson, *The Writings of R.G., Bishop of Lincoln* (1940).

Grossmith, George (1847–1912) and **Weedon** (1854–1919). Entertainers and authors. Born in London, the sons of a law reporter. George worked as a reporter for some years, before becoming a singer and entertainer; his connexion with the operas of Gilbert and Sullivan began in 1877, and during his twelve years with them he 'created' many of the chief roles. He then toured Britain and the U.S.A. and also wrote music for shows. His brother Weedon studied to be a painter at the Slade but in 1885 embarked on an acting career, which he successfully combined with management and playwriting. As an actor he was famous for his playing of small, unhappy men who stand on their dignity and thus make fools of themselves – the type epitomized by Mr Pooter in *Diary of a Nobody*. This book, written in collaboration by the brothers and illustrated by Weedon, first ran as a serial in *Punch*, and was then published in 1892. It was a tremendous success and has continued to be so, for the saga of a lower-middle-class clerk, his wife and their misfortunes is written in a prim, straight-faced style which brings out all the humour and pathos in the situation. It foreshadows H. G. Wells's treatment of the same theme. [JM]

George Grossmith, *A Society Clown* (1888); Weedon Grossmith, *From Studio to Stage* (1913).

Grote, George (1794–1871). Banker, politician and historian. Born at Beckenham in Kent, the son of a rich banker, he was educated at the Charterhouse and entered his father's business, becoming manager (1830). He was greatly influenced by Bentham and Mill, becoming a 'philosophic Radical'; he was M.P. for the City of London (1832–41). In 1843, Grote retired from business, and he published his great work, *A History of Greece* (12 vols.) in 1846–56. Grote possessed both learning and a firm grasp of a useful set of principles: this enabled him with the aid of a strong clear style to produce a history which is not easily superseded by modification or extension of mere information. Naturally there are losses as well as gains from his identification with an active political life. Grote also wrote several pieces on Greek philosophy, including *Plato, and the Other Companions of Sokrates* (3 vols., 1865) and *Aristotle* (ed. A. Bain and G. C. Robertson, 2 vols., 1872). He refused a peerage (1869) and is buried in Westminster Abbey. [AR]

H. Grote, *The Personal Life of G.G.* (1873); A. Momigliano *G. and the Study of Greek History* (1952); M. L. Clarke, *G. A Biography* (1962).

Grove, Frederick Philip (1871–1948). Canadian novelist. Born into a wealthy family in Sweden, after travelling and studying in Europe he went to Canada, where, in 1892, he heard of his family's financial collapse. Twenty years as a nomadic farmhand (*A Search for America*, 1927) were followed by twelve as a schoolmaster in Manitoba. His vast literary ambitions were constantly thwarted, even after the move to Ontario in 1930. At the end of his life, continuing poverty forced him to manual labour and hack writing.

Grove's first published book, though by no means the first written, was *Over Prairie Trails* (1922), a group of linked essays inspired by frequent trips across the Manitoba prairies to snatch time with his family. His first novel, *Settlers of the Marsh* (1925), was strangely branded obscene. Together with the other novels of Canada's pioneering west, *Our Daily Bread* (1928), *The Yoke of Life* (1930) and *Fruits of the Earth* (1933), and his most ambitious novel, *The Master of the Mill* (1944), it forms Canada's most painstakingly serious contribution to realism in fiction. With scant humour to balance it, Grove's sense of tragedy becomes obsessive, but his strength is his obstinacy of purpose in the pursuit of high literary ideals. [PT]

In Search of Myself (Toronto, 1946) (autobiography).
D. Pacey, *F.P.G.* (1945); W. Eggleston, 'F.P.G.', in *Our Living Tradition*, ed. C. T. Bissell, Series 1 (1957).

Gruffydd, William John (1881–1954). Welsh poet, critic and scholar. Born at Bethel, Llanddeiniolen, Caernarvonshire, he was educated at the County School, Caernar-

Guest

von, and Jesus College, Oxford. In 1909 he was appointed lecturer in Welsh at Cardiff, and later professor. He represented the University of Wales in Parliament from 1945.

In his earlier days Gruffydd had been influenced by the English Romantic poets, and his Eisteddfod Crown poem 'Trystan ac Esyllt' (1902) shows undoubted touches of Swinburne. After he moved to Cardiff he became increasingly aware of the contrast between an anglicized area of South Wales and his own essentially Welsh background in Llanddeiniolen, so much so that he spoke of himself as an exile in his own country. He was deeply sensitive to the lives, emotions and fears of other people and very conscious that the stuff of poetry often lies in everyday things. His 'Ynys yr Hud' ('Isle of Enchantment'), romantic though it is, with its descriptions of far-off lands, makes us realize that the 'miracles of the Lord' can be seen and experienced without moving from home. In his masterly poem on the yew-tree of Llanddeiniolen, the little village and his native heath become the pattern for the whole of Wales, and Gruffydd had enough genuine sympathy and faith to realize that life is not entirely a matter of drab uncertainty but that mankind can find time for happiness even under the shadow of inevitable misfortune and death.

Professionally he was deeply interested in the composition of the Four Branches of the ◊ Mabinogion and published penetrating studies. He also wrote on the history of Welsh literature. He was best known perhaps for his editorship of the quarterly magazine Y Llenor for thirty years. This reached the highest standard of any Welsh periodical which has ever appeared. His editorial notes were eagerly read, for in them he raged against cant and hypocrisy and injustice particularly in Welsh public life. As a prose writer he was at his best in depicting the society of the late 19th century, and interpreted it brilliantly in his own unfinished autobiography Hen Atgofion (1936) and his biography of the earlier part of the life of Sir Owen M. Edwards (1937). [M R]

Telynegion, W. J. Gruffydd and Silyn Roberts (1900); Caneuon a Cherddi (1906); Ynys yr Hud (1923); Caniadau (1932).

Guest, Lady Charlotte Elizabeth (1812–75). Collector and amateur of Welsh literature. Born at Uffington, Lincolnshire, the

230

daughter of the 9th Earl of Lindsey, in 1835 she married Sir Josiah Guest, a wealthy South Wales ironmaster. She learned Welsh, and with the aid of Tegid, Carnhuanawc and other Welsh scholars she published (1838–49) an expurgated and genteel translation of the 11 stories from The Red Book of Hergest as well as the Hanes Talresin, to which she gave the incorrect title of ◊ Mabinogion (plural of Mabinogi, 'instruction for young bards') (Everyman, 1906). This title has stuck to her varied collection of ancient Welsh writing (retranslated and ed. G. and T. Jones with intr., 1949). She also published a boy's Mabinogion containing tales of King Arthur' [A R]

Journals (2 vols., 1911).

Gunn, Neil (Miller) (1891–). Scottish novelist. A crofter-fisherman's son from Latheron in Caithness, he spent some of his boyhood in Galloway and worked as an exciseman from 1906 until 1937; since then he has lived in the Highlands and devoted himself to writing. Gunn's earlier novels offer sensitive but naturalistic presentation of his social experience – The Grey Coast (1926), Morning Tide (1931) and Highland River (1937) all deal with childhood and adolescence among the Caithness crofting communities, and The Drinking Well (1946) portrays Edinburgh life at the height of the Scottish Nationalist movement in the 1930s. Butcher's Broom (1934) and The Silver Darlings (1941) re-create earlier periods of Highland history. The plots and themes of Gunn's later novels subserve a post-Christian mysticism that invites comparison with the poetry of Edwin ◊ Muir and that does not compensate for the attenuation of feeling and loss of sharp social detail that it brings; the best of the later novels is probably The Key of the Chest (1945). [A I]

The Atom of Delight (1956) (autobiography).
K. Wittig, The Scottish Tradition in Literature (1958); F. R. Hart, 'The Hunter and the Circle: N.G.'s Fiction of Violence', Studies in Scottish Literature (July 1963).

Gunn, Thom (1929–). Poet. The son of a successful Fleet Street journalist, Herbert Gunn, educated at University College School in London and at Trinity College, Cambridge. The Fantasy Press published his first pamphlet of verse in 1953, when he was still an undergraduate, and his first volume, *Fighting Terms*, in 1954, shortly after he had taken his degree. His second volume, *The Sense of Movement*, came out in 1957, and won him a Somerset Maugham award, which he used to visit Italy. Between 1954 and 1957 he had been teaching and studying in Stanford University in California and was much influenced there by the critical theories and poetic practice of Yvor Winters. He has since spent more time in the United States than in England and might be called a mid-Atlantic or Anglo-American poet. He has been a pioneer among English poets in the use of syllabics or syllable-count metrics which on the whole suits the prosody of American more than English speech-patterns. He is a poet of will and intellect, concerned with separateness, self-sufficiency, energy, a Sartrean sense that value is not to be found lying inertly in outer nature or passively accepted tradition but in movement, risk and choice. Perhaps the poem which most completely expresses his philosophy is 'On the Move' from *The Sense of Movement*, a poem about young men, black-jacketed James Dean characters, roaring through American small towns on motorcycles, disturbing birds and suburbanites, but in a paradoxical way seeking an absolute. His third volume, *My Sad Captains* (1961), is notable for its syllabic experiments and for a non-symbolic yet very moving treatment of landscape as mere space and air. Not a lyrical poet, nor a humorous one, he is notable for wit, in the sense of intellectual adroitness, clear syntactical shaping of the stanza, and a clean-cut exactness of rhythm and diction. *Positives* (1966), a collection of short poems about London people based on photographs by his brother Ander Gunn, has less bite than the earlier work but perhaps a gentler and more diffused human sympathy. He is generally considered, with Philip ◊ Larkin (who is in fact rather older) and Ted ◊ Hughes, as one of the three most distinguished English poets of his generation. The other two, in different ways, might claim to have richer sensibilities, but of the three Gunn has certainly the most incisive intellect. [G S F]

G. S. Fraser, 'The Poetry of Thom Gunn', *Critical Quarterly* (Winter, 1961); J. Press, *Rule and Energy* (1963); F. Grubb, *A Vision of Reality* (1965).

H

Hackett, P. ◊ Haicéad, P.

Haggard, Sir Henry Rider (1856–1925). Romance writer. Born at Bradenham, Norfolk, the son of a lawyer, and educated at Ipswich. He went to South Africa (1875) as secretary to the Governor of Natal, Sir Henry Bulwer, returned to England in 1880 and was called to the bar in 1884, at Lincoln's Inn. On the great success of his first work of fiction, *King Solomon's Mines* (1885), he retired to a country house in Norfolk and thereafter wrote a series of vastly popular, extravagant romances with African settings, such as *She* (1887) and *Allan Quatermain* (1887). Haggard's mixture of the exotic background with rather finely paced adventure filled the prescription for romance-writing set by the influential reviewer Andrew ◊ Lang, with whom Haggard collaborated in *The World's Desire* (1890). He may be considered a much coarser and less talented writer in the vein of Stevenson. Haggard also wrote on farming and country life. [AR]

M. Elwin, in *Old Gods Falling* (1939); L. R. Haggard, *The Cloak that I Left* (1951) (biography); J. E. Scott, *A Bibliography of the Works of R.H.* (1947); M. N. Cohen, *R.H.: His Life and Works* (1960).

Haicéad, Pádraigín (Patrick Hackett) (1600–54). Irish poet. Born in Co. Tipperary, he joined the Dominican order, studied on the continent, was ordained at Louvain, and then returned to Ireland. He resembles ◊ Céitinn in several respects: both were priests, each wrote patriotic and elegiac verse, love poetry and poems of exile. Much of his work relates to the war which began in 1641, in which he himself played an active part. On the outbreak of hostilities he composed a stirring poem, arousing his countrymen to fight; and again in 1646 he wrote 'Musgail do mhisneach, a Bhanbha' ('Take courage, O Banbha'), a poem full of hope and encouragement for the followers of Eoghan Ruadh O'Neill. After the Cromwellian catastrophe he retired to Louvain.

Many of his poems were written abroad, like 'Cuirim séad suirghe chum seise' ('I send my sweetheart a love-token'), in which he says he has been away from Ireland for seven long winters, and hopes to visit it soon. Some of them are very short, such as the quatrain beginning 'Isan bhFraingc im dhúsgadh damh / I nÉirinn Chuinn im chodladh' ('Though in France I awake / In Ireland is my slumber'), in which the exile's longing for home is epigrammatically expressed. A skilled metrist, he occasionally succumbs to formalism: to an art luxuriant in ornateness, and lines overgrown with alliteration. [SB]

M. Ní Cheallacháin, *Filíocht Phádraigín Haicéad* (1962).

Hakluyt, Richard (1553–1616). Geographer and translator. Educated at Westminster School and Christ Church, Oxford, he was at one time chaplain to the English Ambassador at Paris. Even while an undergraduate he read widely in records of travel and exploration in several languages, and he became the greatest compiler of first-hand narratives of voyages. *Divers Voyages Touching the Discovery of America*, dedicated to Sidney, appeared in 1582; but his greatest work, of which a foretaste appeared in 1589, is the 3 volumes called *The Principal Navigations, Voyages, Traffics, and Discoveries of the English Nation, Made by Sea or Overland to the Remote and Farthest Distant Quarters of the Earth at Any Time within the Compass of These 1600 Years* (Hakluyt Society Publications, 12 vols., 1903–5). The narratives are of varying literary merit and come from various sources: printed volumes, log-books, accounts in foreign tongues, Hakluyt's own interviews with seafarers. The prose writers include Sir Walter ◊ Ralegh, as well as unlettered sailors. The volumes are a monument to Hakluyt's industry, patriotism and editorial skill, and include one hundred eye-witness accounts. It is the greatest Elizabethan compendium of English adventures, and stimulated and inspired many 16th- and 17th-century writers. Hakluyt never went to sea. [MJ]

R. R. Cawley, *The Voyagers and the Elizabethan Drama* (Boston, Mass., 1938) and *Unpathed Waters: The Influence of the Voyagers on Elizabethan Literature* (1940); G. B. Parks, *R.H. and the Elizabethan Voyages* (1928); ed. E. W. Lynam, *R.H. and His Successors* (1946).

Haliburton, Thomas Chandler (1796–1865). Canadian satirist. Born and educated in Windsor, Nova Scotia. After practising law for a time, he was elected to the provincial House of Assembly. He was a Tory, a firm opposer of any limitation of British sovereignty. Resigning from active politics, he published a *Historical and Statistical Account of Nova Scotia* (1829). Further association with his publisher, Joseph Howe, led to the appearance in Howe's liberal paper, the *Novascotian*, of the first Sam Slick sketches, collected as *The Clockmaker* (1836). Four more collections were published before 1853, but none excelled the first. In 1841 he became a judge of the Supreme Court. He left for England in 1856, and was M.P. for Launceston for six years. He died in England. *The Old Judge* (1849) is the best of his other books.

The aim of *The Clockmaker* was to provoke the lethargic Novascotians to useful action. The method – that of presenting lethargy exploited by an energetic Yankee clockmaker – allowed incidental mockery of America and Britain. Sam Slick became part of the British image of the American. Haliburton's genius is comic rather than satiric. Each sketch is a narrative monologue of prodigious colloquial inventiveness. The characteristic movement through fable to a ludicrously inadequate resolution in proverb, results in a rare combination of tall story and political satire. [P T]

V. L. O. Chittick, *T.C.H.* (1924); Robert McDougall, 'T.C.H.', in *Our Living Tradition*, ed. R. McDougall, Series 2 and 3 (1959).

Halifax, George Savile, Marquess of (1633–95). Politician and pamphleteer. The eldest son of a Yorkshire country gentleman, his education after two years at Shrewsbury School took the form of travel in France and Italy. A man of independent mind and very great ability, he eagerly sought power but scorned the day to day personal deals by which it is retained. He was an M.P. in the Convention parliament that restored Charles II; created Viscount Halifax in 1668, and thereafter he formed part of the King's administration from time to time. He was created Marquess of Halifax in 1682. His cool interest in political principle united with a cynical, witty, elegance of style make the few pamphlets he wrote towards the end of his life both interesting in themselves and characteristic of the new Restoration style of writing and thinking. His best known pieces are 'The Character of a Trimmer' by the Honourable Sir W(illiam) C(oventry) (1688, etc.) and 'Advice to a Daughter' (1684, etc.). 'Trimmer' sums up his religious and political views, which he suggested did not indicate a lack of principle, but a principled refusal to follow the herd. [A R]

D. G. James, *The Life of Reason: Hobbes, Locke, Bolingbroke* (1949).

Hall, Edward (1498–1547). Historian. From Eton he went to King's College, Cambridge, and later read law at Gray's Inn. After holding various political appointments, he became a judge and an M.P. His active career fell within Henry VIII's reign, but he survived to dedicate the second edition of his chronicle-history to Edward VI in 1548. As a historian, Hall gave the official Tudor version of the Wars of the Roses, drawing upon Polydore Vergil and on Sir Thomas More's (unfinished) *Richard III*. His importance is that he moralized English history, tracing a pattern of cause and effect, and his intentions and emphasis are shown in the long title: *The Union of the Two Noble and Illustre Families of Lancaster and York, Being Long in Continual Dissension for the Crown of this Noble Realm, with all the acts done . . . beginning at the Time of King Henry the Fourth, the First Author of this division and so successively proceeding to the Reign of the High and Prudent Prince: King Henry the Eighth, the undubitate flower and very heir of both the said Lineages.* The reign of Henry VIII comprises about half of the whole book, and Hall's Protestant bias ensured that the first edition (1542) was burned in the reign of the Catholic Mary. Hall's influence was not only on subsequent historians; his doctrine that history teaches by example impressed the authors of *The Mirror for Magistrates* and he helped to shape and popularize the view of history which Shakespeare adopted in the play-sequence *Richard II–Richard III*. [M J]

L. B. Campbell, *Shakespeare's 'Histories'* (San Marino, Calif., 1947); E. M. W. Tillyard, *Shakespeare's History Plays* (1944).

Hall, Joseph (1574–1656). Bishop, satirist, 'character' and miscellaneous writer. Born at Ashby-de-la-Zouch, he was educated at Emmanuel College, Cambridge, and, taking orders, became chaplain to Prince Henry, the eldest son of James VI & I. In 1618 the King sent him as a Deputy to the Synod of Dort, and he became successively Bishop of Exeter in 1627 and of Norwich in 1641. A low churchman, but a stout defender of episcopacy against Milton and 'Smectymnuus', he was imprisoned and in 1643 sequestrated; finally in 1647 he was expelled from his palace to a small farm nearby. Hall was an inventive, pioneering and influential writer, a friend of Donne and of Sir Thomas ◊ Browne. As well as poems, he published sermons, works of controversy and devotional volumes. His chief works were: *Virgidemiarum sex libri* ('Six Books of Lashes') (1597–8), an attack in rough couplets on contemporary abuses after the fashion of Juvenal, which was condemned to be burned; a prose satire, *Mundus alter et idem* (1605), in the platonic and utopian genre of imaginary worlds; and *Characters of Virtues and Vices* (1608). Just as in the first work he was one of the earliest writers of verse 'satire', so in the latter Hall was virtually the first English 'character' writer. Obviously such short sketches had always been used by English writers such as Chaucer and medieval preachers, but generally as parts of larger works, or in sermons. The 'character' as he used it became fashionable (◊ Earle and Overbury) as a short piece which in informality and length was related to the 'essay' (◊ Bacon). The writer took a virtue or a vice and 'illustrated' this in a well-defined moral-rhetorical way – hence the link with the pulpit – from contemporary life. The fashion was no doubt also related to the 16th- and 17th-century development of scientific observation and classification. Theophrastus, from whom the form took its name, was the classical exemplar whose 'characters' date from the 3rd century B.C.; he was a botanist and pupil of Aristotle. The form persisted in English into the 18th century and was an important forebear of the periodical essay, the short story and the novel. Hall's own prose, too, was an important and influential 'Senecan' mode of writing; his temper of mind was largely 'Stoic'. His 'characters' are didactic examples and moral abstracts. [A R]

Works, ed. P. Wynter (10 vols., 1863); *Collected Poems*, ed. A. Davenport (1949); *Character Writings of the Seventeenth Century*, ed. H. Morley (1891); *A Book of 'Characters'*, ed. R. Aldington (1924); D. Nichol Smith, *Characters of the Seventeenth Century* (1918) (selection).

T. F. Kinloch, *The Life and Works of H.* (1951); A. Chew, 'H. and Neo-Stoicism', *PMLA*, 65 (1950); C. N. Greenough, *A Bibliography of the Theophrastan Character in England to 1642* (Harvard U.P., 1947).

Hall, Willis. ◊ Waterhouse, Keith.

Hallam, Henry (1777–1859). Historian. Born at Windsor, son of the Dean of Wells, he was educated at Eton and Christ Church, Oxford, called to the bar at the Inner Temple, and appointed to the sinecure of a Commissioner of Stamps. He was a Whig and wrote for the *Edinburgh Review*, incurring an unfavourable mention in Byron's *English Bards and Scottish Reviewers* for a paper not by him. In 1818 appeared his long-awaited book *A View of the State of Europe during the Middle Ages*, followed by *The Constitutional History of England from the Accession of Henry VII to the Death of George II* (1827). These works are chiefly of interest to the historiographer, as part of the Whig rewriting of history as a drama of principle versus royal or feudal tyranny. His last important work was an *Introduction to the Literature of Europe in the Fifteenth, Sixteenth and Seventeenth Centuries* (4 vols., 1837–9). Hallam read much, knew his way around historical records and was never afraid of generalizing. [A R]

Hamilton, William, of Bangour (1704–54). Scottish poet. Hamilton contributed to Allan ◊ Ramsay's *Tea-Table Miscellany* (1724), became a Jacobite, went into exile after Culloden and died abroad. Most of his verse is in ornate but otherwise undistinguished English; his most successful poem, 'The Braes of Yarrow' ('Busk ye, busk ye, my bonny bonny bride'), draws very heavily on the ballad of the same name but refines and anglicizes the material in a way characteristic of minor Scottish writers of the period. [A I]

Poems and Songs, ed. J. Paterson (1850).
N. S. Bushnell, *W.H. of Bangour, Poet and Jacobite* (1957).

Hamilton, William, of Gilbertfield (1665?–1751). Scottish verse-writer. His 'Last Dying Words of Bonnie Heck', published in

James Watson's *Choice Collection* (1706), transmitted from Robert ◊ Sempill to Allan ◊ Ramsay (and onwards to Burns) the form of the 'Habbie Simpson' stanza and the genre of the mock-bucolic elegy – the verse-epistles which Hamilton exchanged with Ramsay also supplied a genre to ◊ Fergusson and Burns. Hamilton's anglicized abridgement and paraphrase of ◊ Henry the Minstrel's *Wallace* (1722) had great popular success in its own century and was part of Burns's childhood reading; it is a symptom, however, of the declining potentialities of Scots as a literary medium. [A I]

DNB.

Hanley, James (1901–). Novelist, essayist and short-story writer. Born in Dublin of a poor family, he left school at 13 and was ten years a seaman. Thereafter he had various jobs and became a journalist. *Men in Darkness* (1931) is a collection of stories, but his best work (and most successful) is a series of novels about the squalor and despair of the Dublin of his boyhood: it includes *The Furys* (1935), *The Secret Journey* (1936), *Our Time is Gone* (1940) and *An End and a Beginning* (1958). *Say Nothing* (1962) continues his probing of the problem of communicating with other people. He is a naturalistic writer of power, and writes well about his main obsession, the sea. Other novels are *The Maelstrom* (1935) and *Hollow Sea* (1938). *The Closed Harbour* (1952), one of his best novels, is a story set in Marseilles of a French captain who lost his ship. He has also published volumes of essays: *Soldiers Wind* (1938) and *Don Quixote Drowned* (1953). [A R]

'Broken Water', in *London Mercury* (July 1937) (autobiography).

Hansford-Johnson, Pamela (1912–). Novelist and critic. Born in London and educated at Clapham County Secondary School. She worked for some years in a bank and published her first novel, an account of South London working-class life, *This Bed Thy Centre*, in 1935, with some critical success. Her novels are solidly competent fiction, and her general tone seems to be acceptance of life, but an informed acceptance springing from a real knowledge of the complexities of everyday experience. To present this she masses detail, but in a well-digested structure. She

has quite reasonably been compared with George Eliot in this. She is also intelligent and aware (she has presented several excellent B.B.C. programmes on Proust). Among her novels are: *Too Dear for My Possessing* (1940); *An Avenue of Stone* (1947); *A Summer to Decide* (1948); *Catherine Carter* (1952); *The Last Resort* (1956). *The Unspeakable Skipton* (1959) is an accomplished work set in Bruges; the central character, a paranoid author (not unlike Frederick ◊ Rolfe, 'Baron Corvo'), is devastatingly revealed, yet in such a way as to halt judgement and force consideration. Her latest novels include *Night and Silence Who is Here* (1963) and *Cork Street, Next to the Hatter's* (1965). *On Iniquity* (1968) deals with the Yorkshire 'Moors Murders', an instance of sadistic behaviour which she believes was partly caused by reading De Sade. Her critical work includes, besides much literary journalism, *Thomas Wolfe* (1947) and an interesting pamphlet, *Ivy Compton-Burnett* (1951). In 1950 she married the novelist C. P. ◊ Snow. [A R]

Hardy, Thomas (1840–1928). Poet and novelist. Hardy was born in Upper Bockhampton, Dorset, the son of a master mason. His mother had intellectual ambitions for him and encouraged him to pursue his education. He continued his studies even after being apprenticed to a Dorchester architect at 16. Hardy was trained in the architecture of the Gothic revival and retained throughout his life his great knowledge of, and interest in, stonework and architecture, particularly of the country church of the south-west. In 1862 he went to London to pursue his profession. At this time he began writing, greatly stimulated by his close friendship with Horace Moule, a Cambridge graduate whose later suicide affected Hardy and his writing deeply. After criticism from George Meredith, Hardy withdrew his first novel from the publishers and it has never since been published, but his second, *Desperate Remedies* (1871), was fairly well received. It was his third novel, *Under the Greenwood Tree* (1872), which indicated the area of life in which Hardy was to find his greatest inspiration. This is a delicately ironic picture of Dorset country life without the ominous undertones of his later work.

Hardy returned to Dorset and continued as an architect while maintaining his literary contacts in London. He was advised to write for serial publication to enable him to devote himself to writing. This he did, and *A Pair of Blue Eyes* (1873), again set in the 'Wessex' which became the territory of all Hardy's fiction, was his first serialized novel. The following year he married Emma Gifford, a Dorset girl, but their marriage was not entirely happy, partly because of her mental instability. The same year saw the publication of the first of the 5 novels that represent his greatest work. *Far from the Madding Crowd* sets Hardy's vision of the fatefulness of human life against the ruthless authority of the seasons which governed so absolutely the agricultural round. In this novel the conflicts are resolved almost happily. In later fiction the implications were uncompromisingly tragic.

Hardy concentrated in single characters all the evidence of a way of life trapped in the inescapable decay which the agricultural depression of the 1870s and 1880s forced on his mind. Britain's industrial prosperity sacrificed farming and those who worked on the land to an irrecoverable extent. In *The Mayor of Casterbridge* (1886) and what is usually regarded as his greatest novel, *Tess of the D'Urbervilles* (1891), the relentless conflict between Hardy's profoundly nostalgic picture of the old rural ways and the tyranny of modern efficiency is at the root of the human tragedies he portrays. Behind this lay what Hardy saw as the devastating source of human destruction: rigid codes of behaviour which could push someone like the selfless and courageous Tess to her death.

In *The Return of the Native* (1878) and *The Woodlanders* (1887) Hardy pictured the agricultural cycle as a source of both comfort and imprisonment. While his heroes and heroines often respond deeply and lovingly to the work they do, to nature and to the traditions of the country, they are doomed by the rigidity that inevitably comes from the power of tradition and routine. Ambition, whether social or intellectual, or for quiet personal happiness as in the case of Marty South in *The Woodlanders*, has no chance of achievement. Hardy's last novel, *Jude the Obscure* (1896), frequently criticized for the uncompromising tone which sometimes topples incidents over the edge of credibility, is his most devastating statement of the uselessness of trying to break from the chains of convention, tradition and the accepted confines of rural life.

The novel is relentless in its handling of the doomed Jude and the neurotically high-principled Sue. Even what in other novels emerges as an elegiac picture of the countryside offers no relief.

Hardy was troubled throughout his fiction-writing career by the narrow-minded response of his public. He frequently had to mutilate his fiction, refine it almost to the point of nonsense, for serial publication. He was always extremely sensitive towards his readers, and there are frequent touches of misplaced artificiality in his prose where the thought of his reader proves stronger than his imaginative grasp of his fiction. But even without this his style would be uneven and undisciplined. The same paragraph can contain both breathtaking fluidity of expression and jarring awkwardness. The force of what he wanted to say tended to overwhelm the manner in which it was said. This, while being his most frequently criticized fault, is also the source of his unique achievement. He was uncompromising in his pessimistic view of humanity, both within a simple rural life and in its attempts to break out, but at the same time his concern for humanity was sensitive and passionate.

Hardy did not begin to publish poetry until 1898, but he always considered himself primarily a poet. His first volume, *Wessex Poems*, was poorly received, and it was the publication of his ambitious epic verse drama based on the Napoleonic Wars, *The Dynasts* (1903–8), which brought him widespread public acclaim. Suddenly his reputation was immense, and for the rest of his life he was revered throughout the country. Hardy published more than 10 volumes of poetry, and much of it is second-rate. But at his best he wrote with a controlled nostalgia about personal experience which is unrivalled. He was much influenced by country traditions of ballad and folk-song, and often incorporated into his poetry anecdotes of country life, but it is his poetry of personal reflection based on the sudden awakening of memory that most impresses. Although his verse forms are usually simple, he experimented frequently with rhythm, often deliberately breaking its regularity. His life-long love of music is very important here. At times Hardy's simplicity can be mundane, at other times it is immensely and movingly powerful, and reflects in a gentler and sadder mood the fierce climate of the novels.

In the last years of his life Hardy rarely moved from his house, Max Gate, near Dorchester, which he had designed himself. His wife died in 1912 and two years later he married Florence Dugdale. He continued to write poetry until his death, and his last volume was published posthumously. [J R C]

Collected Poems (1960); *The Hand of Ethelberta* (1876); *The Trumpet Major* (1880); *A Laodicean* (1881); *Two on a Tower* (1882); *The Well-Beloved* (1897). Short stories: *Wessex Tales* (1888); *A Group of Noble Dames* (1891); *Life's Little Ironies* (1894); *A Changed Man* (1913). F. E. Hardy, *The Early Life of T.H. 1840–91* (1928) and *The Later Years of T.H. 1892–1928* (1930) (virtually Hardy's autobiography as dictated to his second wife); C. J. Weber, *H. of Wessex. His Life and Literary Career* (1965); E. Hardy, *T.H.* (1954) (biography and criticism); W. R. Rutland, *T.H. A Study of His Writings and Their Background* (1938); H. C. Webster, *On a Darkling Plain* (1947); George Wing, *H.* (1963); F. R. Leavis, *New Bearings in English Poetry* (1932); R. P. Blackmur, *Language as Gesture* (1954); D. Brown, *T.H.* (1954).

Harington, Sir John (1561–1612). Poet, translator and wit. Son of the treasurer to Henry VIII's camps and buildings, Harington was a godson of Queen Elizabeth, with whom his father had been imprisoned in the Tower in 1554. He was born at Kelston, near Bath, and educated at Eton and Christ's College, Cambridge, and then, after a spell at Lincoln's Inn, embarked on a career as a courtier. His translation of Ariosto's *Orlando furioso* (1591), a vigorous verse paraphrase, was according to tradition done as a penance imposed on him by Queen Elizabeth for having translated the indiscreet story of Giocondo from Ariosto and shown it to her ladies. There was a strong Rabelaisian strain in Harington, evidenced in *The Metamorphosis of Ajax* (pun on 'a Jakes'), *An Anatomie of the Metamorphosed Ajax* and *Ulysses upon Ajax* (all 1596). He served under Essex in Ireland in 1598 and was knighted by Essex on the field, to Elizabeth's annoyance. He tried unsuccessfully to reconcile Elizabeth to Essex, and never regained the Queen's favour (he had been banished from court after his Rabelaisian publications in 1596), but on James I's accession he obtained the position of tutor to Prince Henry. Several volumes of his *Epigrams* were published between 1615 and 1618 (ed. N. E. McClure, with letters, U. of Pennsylvania, P., 1930). His preface to his translation of Ariosto is reprinted in G. G. Smith, *Elizabethan Critical Essays* (1904). *Nugae Antiquae* (ed. H. Harington, 2 vols., 1769–75; ed. T. Park, 2 vols., 1804) contains letters and miscellaneous writings. [D D]

Sir Walter Raleigh, *Some Authors* (1923); G. Rehfeld, *Sir J.H.* (Halle, 1914); Huntington Brown, *Rabelais in English Literature* (Harvard, 1933); T. Rich, *H. and Ariosto* (New Haven, 1940).

Harrington (or Harington), James (1611–77). Political theorist. Born at Upton, Northamptonshire, he went to Trinity College, Oxford, in 1629, but did not take a degree, and after leaving spent several years travelling on the continent. Despite his refusal to take part in the Civil War, he attended Charles I on the Scottish expedition and in captivity. He held that the government of England was bound to reflect a social system in which the bulk of the land was no longer owned by the King and the Church but by the gentry. *The Commonwealth of Oceana* (1656; ed. S. B. Liljegren, 1924), a tract in the guise of a political romance, has a certain historical interest as a reply to Hobbes's *Leviathan* and for the attention it drew from political thinkers as important as Hume, Montesquieu and Burke. He depicted Oceana (England) in the hands of a Protector, Olphaus Megalator (Oliver Cromwell), who endowed the country with a constitution adapted to the needs of an agrarian democracy (Cromwell did not receive the hint kindly). Elections were to be indirect: each year the citizens (property owners) would choose a certain number of electors, and they in turn would elect new members to the Senate and to the House of Deputies, to replace those who had completed their term of office. Laws would be discussed by the Senators and then put to the Deputies for approval or rejection. The Senators also appointed Magistrates responsible for the execution of the law. Primogeniture and the accumulation of property were subject to limitation (the income yielded by a man's estate could not exceed £3,000 a year). Harrington is important for his advocacy of the principle of rotation in office. The Rota Club, formed in 1659 for the discussion of his ideas, was visited by well-known figures, including John Aubrey, Andrew Marvell and Pepys. After the Restoration, Harrington was for a time imprisoned. [N L]

The Oceana of J.H. and His Other Works, ed. with an account of his life by John Toland (1700).

Z. Fink, *The Classical Republicans* (1945); R. H. Tawney, 'Harrington's Interpretation of His Age', *Proceedings of the British Academy*, XXVII (1941).

Harris, Frank (1856–1931). Journalist and miscellaneous writer. Born at Galway, the son of a naval commander in the revenue service, he was educated there, at Armagh, and briefly in England. At 15 he emigrated to America and after a variegated career, including two years as a cow-puncher, studied at the University of Kansas and was called to the bar in that state. He travelled about and studied at Heidelberg until he began his journalistic career in London by successfully editing the ailing *Evening News* (1883–7); after his dismissal, he successively edited the *Fortnightly Review* (1887–94); the *Saturday Review* (as owner) (1894–9); the *Candid Friend*, a weekly which he founded (1901–2; revived 1905–6); the *Automobile Review*; the *Motorist and Traveller*; and *Hearth and Home* (1911–12). Thereafter his ventures were less widely successful and profitable. He managed the weekly *Modern Society* (1913–14), and was imprisoned for contempt of court in a libel suit; during the war he returned to America and took over *Pearson's Magazine*, which he edited with declining ability from 1916 to 1922. Harris wrote volumes of short stories and novels, such as *Montes the Matador and Other Stories* (1900) and *Bomb: The Haymarket Riot* (1908; intr. J. Dos Passos, Chicago, 1963). Two of his plays, *Mr and Mrs Daventry* (1900) and *Shakespeare and His Love* (1910), were very successful. Harris knew everybody of importance in the public life of letters in London at the end of the century (perhaps better than they knew him). Wells and Shaw, who admired his panache, wrote for his *Saturday Review* and his best work is about another friend, *Oscar Wilde: His Life and Confessions* (1918; reprinted by Michigan State U.P., 1959). His 5 series of *Contemporary Portraits* (1915–30), for all their patronizing tone, give some lively sketches. He was a fearless if arrogant journalist, as his pro-Boer sentiments show. His own favourite book, *The Man Shakespeare* (1909), gave Shakespeare 'back to the people' and is a gross example of biographical criticism. Harris's strong suit as

a writer was his range of exotic experiences, sometimes valuable, sometimes delusive as a standard of judgement, and sometimes pushed into exaggeration or untruth. He is probably best known for the 5 volumes of 'candid' autobiography, *My Life and Loves* (1923–7; ed. and intr. J. F. Gallagher, 1963), which fell foul of the censors in Britain and the U.S.A. This, despite the conceit, self-justification and barely credible sexual athletics, gives an amusing picture of the strange juxtapositions of personalities and ideas in the raffish Edwardian era, seen by a somewhat insensitive intelligent man on the make. [A R]

A. I. Tobin and Elmer Gertz, *F.H.: A Study in Black and White* (Chicago, 1931); E. M. Root, *F.H. A Biography* (New York, 1947); V. Brome, *F.H. The Life and Loves of a Scoundrel* (1949).

Hartley, David (1705–57). Philosopher. Educated at Bradford Grammar School and Jesus College, Cambridge, he abandoned reading for the Church on account of theological difficulties and practised as a doctor. His important work is *Observations on Man, His Frame, His Duty, and His Expectations* (1749; reprinted as *Hartley's Theory of the Human Mind, with Essays by J. Priestley*, 1775). In this work he carries Locke's attack on the theory of innate ideas further, maintaining (against ◊ Shaftesbury and Francis ◊ Hutcheson) that 'the moral sense' was also the product of the association of ideas. This psychological theory, in its moral and aesthetic aspects, had some influence on Coleridge and Wordsworth (see A. Beatty, *William Wordsworth, His Doctrine and Art*, 1922; but this view has been opposed). Hartley also advanced a physical theory of brain vibrations, now of only historical interest, but his psychology had considerable value for a long time and perhaps still has. [A R]

G. S. Bower, *H. and James Mill* (1881); N. Moore, 'D.H.', *Hibbert Journal*, XLVIII (1949).

Hartley, L(esley) P(oles) (1895–   ). Novelist. Born in Peterborough, and educated at Harrow and Balliol. Although a writer of somewhat limited range, Hartley is a superb craftsman, and a stylist comparable to Henry James or Jane Austen. He is a novelist of sensibility, of quietness rather than power, of civilization rather than passion. His tone of voice is completely his own.

Hartley's first novel, *Simonetta Perkins*

(1925), did not appear until its author was 30. Its plot has Jamesian overtones: a girl from Boston, on a visit to Venice in the company of her mother, becomes infatuated with a handsome gondolier. But already the flavour is Hartley's own, and his sophisticated caricatures of characters are expertly judged. A volume of stories, *The Killing Bottle*, appeared in 1932. Then, twenty years after the first, came another novel, *The Shrimp and the Anemone* (1944), the beginning of a trilogy completed by *The Sixth Heaven* (1946) and *Eustace and Hilda* (1947). The 'Eustace and Hilda' trilogy is the account of a relationship between brother and sister from childhood until adult life. In *The Shrimp and the Anemone* they are seen as children, and indeed the book ranks amongst the classical studies of childhood. The saga of this middle-class couple's lives embraces the entire English social scene between the two wars. In *The Sixth Heaven* the children have grown up, and in *Eustace and Hilda* they are mature and ready to be struck down, but gently. If the trilogy has not the stature of tragedy, it has its own compelling and individual quality. It is a unique achievement within its limits.

The *Boat* (1949) is, in the beauty of its style and the subtlety of its construction, one of Hartley's finest achievements. He is, for all his cunning penetration of the child's world, an extremely adult writer, and an exact chronicler of his time and class. *The Brickfield* (1964) continues his exploration of an inner world of sensibility. His art is necessarily delicate and, to that extent, vulnerable. But that he is a verbal artist of rare talent is indisputable. [C O]

My Fellow Devils (1951); *The Go-Between* (1953); *Facial Justice* (1960); *Two for the River and Other Stories* (1961); *Collected Stories* (1968); *Poor Clare* (1968); *The Novelist's Responsibility* (1968).

P. Bloomfield, *L.P.H.* (1962).

Harvey, Gabriel (1545?–1630). Scholar and critic. The son of a ropemaker at Saffron Walden, Essex, he became a Fellow of Pembroke Hall, Cambridge, in 1570, where ♢ Spenser was in his second year. A friendship developed between them, but Harvey's influence on Spenser was slight, their views on poetry being fundamentally unlike. In 1578 he became a Fellow of Trinity Hall, and in 1579 published some satires which caused considerable displeasure at court because of their allusions. In 1585 he was elected to the Mastership of Trinity Hall, but the election was set aside by royal mandate. He was drawn into a prolonged quarrel with Thomas ♢ Nashe, who had abused Harvey and his brothers in *Pierce Peniless His Supplication to the Devil* (August 1592). The Harveys had been attacked also by Robert ♢ Greene in his *Quip for an Upstart Courtier* (July 1592), and when Greene died before a prosecution could be brought against him, Gabriel, who was the eldest of the brothers, vilified Greene's character in *Four Letters and Certain Sonnets, Especially Touching Robert Greene and Other Parties by Him Abused* (September 1592). This caused Nashe to reply in a pamphlet whose title contains a scurrilous *double entendre*; *Strange News of the Intercepting Certain Letters and a Convoy of Verses as They Were Going Privily to Victual the Low Countries* (January 1593). Harvey retaliated with *Pierce's Supererogation* (1593), while after minor skirmishing Nashe riposted with the devastating *Have with You to Saffron Walden, or Gabriel Harvey's Hunt is Up* (1596). The attribution to Harvey of yet another reply, *The Trimming of Thomas Nashe* (1597), is doubtful, but the continuation of the quarrel was forbidden by a decree of the censors on 1 June 1599, which declared: 'that all Nashe's books and Dr Harvey's books be taken, wheresoever they may be found, and that none of their books be ever printed hereafter.' Harvey's last years seem to have been spent in retirement in his native Saffron Walden.

Although he was arrogant and opinionated and had the touchiness of a disappointed man, Harvey was not merely the 'Gorboduc Huddleduddle' of Nashe's satire; he was a considerable scholar (cf. his *Rhetor* and *Ciceronianus*, 1577) and he had some acuteness as a critic. Also, it is unlikely that without at least some amiable qualities he would have enjoyed the friendship of Spenser. [J W B]

Works, ed. A. B. Grosart (3 vols., 1884–5; *Three ... Letters* and *Two ... Letters* (1580), in E. de Selincourt's edn of Spenser (1912); *Foure Letters* (1592), ed. G. B. Harrison (1922); *Elizabethan Critical Essays,* ed. G. G. Smith (1904) (extracts from letters).

C. S. Lewis, *English Literature in the Sixteenth Century* (1954); C. Sanders, *Robert Greene and the H.s*(Bloomington, Ind.,1931); H. S. Wilson, 'The Humanism of G.H.', in *J. Q. Adams Memorial Studies* (Washington, D.C., 1948). See also R. B. McKerrow's edn of Nashe.

Hawes, Stephen (?1474–?1523). Poet. Educated at Oxford, Hawes became Groom of the Chamber to Henry VII. His major works are the long moral allegories, *The Example of Virtue* (1504) and *The Pastime of Pleasure* (1505; ed. W. E. Mead, 1928). Though Hawes acknowledges ◊ Lydgate as his master and his style is old-fashioned, his combination of extended moral allegory and chivalric romance is new in English. It is a dim prefiguring of *The Faerie Queene* and Spenser probably read the *Pastime*. This is an allegory of human life as a whole, weakest when education is the theme, strongest when Hawes evokes love and death. A curiously modern romanticism distinguishes him from earlier allegorists, but his metrical inadequacies and earnest didactic purpose war against his imagination. [A G]

English Verse between Chaucer and Surrey, ed. E. P. Hammond (1927) (selection).

J. M. Berdan, *Early Tudor Poetry* (1920); C. S. Lewis, *English Literature of the Sixteenth Century* (1954); D. Pearsall, 'The English Chaucerians', in *Chaucer and Chaucerians*, ed. D. S. Brewer (1966).

Hay, George Campbell (Deorsa Caimbeul Hay) (1915–   ). Scottish Gaelic poet. Hay is not a native-speaker of Gaelic, although this is his main literary medium. He is a versatile linguist, and has translated into Gaelic from Italian, modern Greek, French, Spanish, Welsh, Finnish and Arabic, besides writing both original poems and translations from Gaelic in French and Norwegian. He has also written in Scots. His work has widened the horizons of contemporary Gaelic poetry, and enriched the poetic vocabulary.

His first collection, *Fuaran Sléibh* (1947), consists largely of original poems: love-lyrics (strongly influenced by the Irish *dánta grádha*), Scottish Nationalist verse, nature poetry, humorous verse and satire. He is still feeling his way to an individual style in this collection. There is a marked increase in philosophical and dramatic power, foreshadowed by the earlier 'Tilleadh Uiliseis' ('The Return of Ulysses') in his second collection, *O na Ceithir Airdean* (1952): this is apparent in the love poems and in the nationalist and war poetry. *Bisearta* has great pictorial clarity, and emotional and intellectual urgency. His translations are skilfully assimilated to the Gaelic tradition, so that his Finnish love song, *Oran Gaoil Finneach*, reads like a 17th-century Gaelic folk-song.

Hay is deeply interested in traditional Gaelic metrics, and it seems true to say that his work shows greater technical skill and variety than the work of any Gaelic poet since the 18th century. [D T]

Wind on Loch Fyne (1948).

Haywood, Eliza Fowler (c. 1693–1756). Novelist, dramatist and writer of scandalous memoirs. After an unhappy marriage, Mrs Haywood tried to make her way by writing. As was often the case with 18th-century women writers (◊ Manley, Mary), she produced several novels with thinly disguised scandalous passages about her contemporaries, as well as plays in the same vein. She worked in collaboration with the infamous Curll, and is severely mentioned in the *Dunciad*. She also wrote poetry, but finally joined the growing numbers of periodical writers, publishing among others the *Tea Table* (35 numbers, 1724) and the best known, *The Female Spectator* (24 numbers, 1744–6; selected and intr. J. B. Priestley, 1929). Her last 2 novels, *The History of Miss Betty Thoughtless* (1751) and *The History of Jemmy and Jenny Jessamy* (1753), were widely read. [A R]

G. F. Whicher, *The Life and Romances of Mrs E.H.* (New York, 1915).

Hazlitt, William (1778–1830). Critic and essayist. Born at Maidstone, the son of a Unitarian minister. His first publication was a letter in the *Shrewsbury Chronicle* (1791), denouncing the persecution at Birmingham of Joseph Priestley, who was connected with Hackney College, where Hazlitt was sent to study for the ministry in 1793. He gave this idea up in 1797, but heard Coleridge's last sermon, delivered in his father's church in Shropshire. His political courage in subscribing to minority views and his intellectual honesty, which sometimes turned into cantankerousness, were shown early in his career and characterized Hazlitt's writing. Coleridge encouraged him to pursue his early interest in philosophy, and he published several such works, e.g. *An Essay on the Principles of Human Action* (1805), which shows a good grasp of all the main 18th-century currents of thought and their relationships, and *An Abridgement of 'The Light of Nature pursued by Abraham Tucker'* (1807); and he also wrote against Malthus because of what he considered the moral apathy of his work on population. This early philosophical train-

ing gives Hazlitt's criticism a sound foundation of deft and tough argument, and
enables him to base the history of English
literature, which he later sketched, on the
development of ideas. He went to Paris
in 1802, as part of an abortive course of
study in painting; his talent did not match
his ambition, but the training left its mark in
his writing on the fine arts, and in attractive
painterly touches in his essays and biographical sketches. In 1798 Coleridge had
introduced him to Wordsworth, whose
poetry he greatly admired. In 1803 a
rupture took place with the Wordsworths,
partly because of Hazlitt's conduct and
partly for political reasons. Hazlitt is one
of the English writers upon whom the
French Revolution had a great impact, but
unlike many he held by his early enthusiasm
for it. He viewed the change of heart of
Wordsworth, Coleridge and Southey as
black apostasy.

Hazlitt's criticism was (in the best sense)
personal and prejudiced – the strength and
beauty of his writing on Wordsworth's
poetry lies not least in the struggle between
his sure and generous appreciation of
literary achievement and the disfavour with
which he views the poet's political beliefs.
With the help of Lamb and others, he gradually launched himself on a career of writing
and lecturing; his first public appearance
was a series of 10 lectures on 'The Rise and
Progress of Modern Philosophy' (from
Hobbes to the 18th-century followers of
Locke); he reported parliamentary debates
and wrote political articles for the *Morning
Chronicle*. He also contributed essays to
Leigh ◊ Hunt's *Examiner* in a feature
called *The Round Table* (2 vols., 1817;
mostly by Hazlitt). The plan was to follow
'the old *Spectator* manner', and as an
essayist Hazlitt was a follower of the earlier
writers, particularly Steele – not in the
pastiche manner of Lamb's use of early
writers, however, but rather in temper,
professional competence as a writer, and
brilliance in handling the form. Hazlitt's
essays are longer, though – more elaborate
and less didactic. They show a considerable
range of styles, from the easy handling of
abstract and formal ideas in 'On Reason
and Imagination', to the colloquialism of
the much later piece, 'The Fight', published
in *Table Talk, or Original Essays* (2 vols.,
1821–2), mostly reprinted from the *New
Monthly Magazine* and *London Magazine*.
A third collection of reprints from the same

periodicals, *The Plain Speaker: Opinions
on Books, Men, and Things* (2 vols.),
appeared in 1826. Hazlitt's essays are
also marked by a tough, independent
view of the world; this toughness is shown
in the essays on literary matters, but the
critical writing which has given him his
important place in 19th-century thought
appears in several separate works. *Memoirs
of the late Thomas Holcroft* (3 vols.,
1816; ed. E. Colby, 2 vols., 1925) is an
important contemporary study of a man
who, though not very eminent as a writer,
is a representative figure in English intellectual life during the French Revolution.
Characters of Shakespeare's Plays (1817) is
not unlike the *Dramatic Specimens* of ◊
Lamb, to whom it is dedicated; it is in the
form of a collection of 'beauties' with
comments. It stresses the characters as
'pictures' of human life. Hazlitt writes with
insight and obvious enjoyment, as well as
with the theatrical knowledge shown in
another collection of his periodical essays,
A View of the English Stage (1818). His
best criticism is to be found in 3 series of
lectures delivered at the Surrey Institution.
In these, Hazlitt, writing when the work of
Thomas ◊ Warton was the only attempt at a
history of English literature, covered the
central body of writing from the Elizabethans to his own day. *Lectures on the
English Poets* (1818) deals chiefly with the
18th century: Spenser and Shakespeare are
discussed, but the Metaphysicals practically
omitted. His comments on the Romantic
poets then living (in fact chiefly Wordsworth) are of the greatest interest, as giving
an intelligent, sympathetic view by a
contemporary, before the assumptions of
the new writers had hardened into dogma.
The English Comic Writers (1819) includes
comment on several genres, and is most
interesting on the 18th-century novelists;
Cervantes is included as a kind of honorary
Englishman. Hazlitt writes well on Fielding, with whose 'exact' painting and
philosophical assumptions he was largely in
sympathy. *Lectures Chiefly on the Dramatic
Literature of the Age of Elizabeth* (1820) is
rather more perfunctory – a kind of Cook's
tour – and not so well thought out; it is
important, though, in developing a growing
interest in the earlier dramatists. Hazlitt's
scheme of division, however, helped to
ossify criticism of Elizabethan tragedy for a
long time. *The Spirit of the Age: or, Contemporary Portraits* (1825; 2nd enlarged

edn, 1825), partly reprints of essays, is a lively and intelligent comment on the contemporary literary and intellectual scene.

Hazlitt's criticism, like that of Johnson, whom he often much resembles, rises passionate and sharp from his own life and education; he often relates the writing and ideas he talks about to the life of the time by masterly character sketches. He very often forestalls modern comment and evaluation, and writes with wit and humanity. He spent several years writing his *Life of Napoleon Buonaparte* (4 vols., 1828–30), which is unhistorical without the compensation of living experience. Napoleon, the destroyer of the old rotten order, was one of his heroes, and his work is a failed attempt at justification, without apparently much appreciation of the problems (intellectual, social and humanitarian) such a view involves. His interest in the arts is shown in *Sketches of the Principal Picture Galleries in England* (1824), *Notes of a Journey through France and Italy* (1826) and *Conversations of James Northcote, Esq., R.A.* (reprinted periodical essays) (1830; ed. F. Swinnerton, 1949). *Liber Amoris, or, The New Pygmalion* (1823; ed. R. Le Gallienne and W. C. Hazlitt, 1894, with additional matter) is a pathetic book of conversations and letters about an infatuation with a landlord's daughter, which has the tedium of obsession without the interest of real confession, though he meant it to be compared with Rousseau's *Confessions*. Hazlitt was not a learned man, but held tenaciously to what he had read and experienced. He is comparable to Wordsworth in his interest in early formative experience. He joins intelligent judgement with the faculty of detecting the significant trends in his age. [A R]

Collected Works, ed. A. R. Waller and A. Glover (12 vols., 1902–6); *Complete Works*, ed. P. P. Howe (20 vols., 1930–4); *Selected Essays*, ed. G. Keynes (1930); *Hazlitt on Literature*, ed. and intr. J. Zeitlin (New York, 1913); *The Essays: A Selection*, ed. C. M. MacLean (1949). P. P. Howe, *Life of W.H.* (revised edn, 1947); H. Baker, *W.H.* (Harvard U.P., 1962); E. W. Schneider, *The Aesthetics of W.H.* (Philadelphia, 1933; 1952); C. I. Patterson, 'W.H. as a Critic of Fiction', *PMLA*, IIL (1953); G. D. Klingopulos, 'H. as Critic', *EC* VI (1956); A Whitley, 'H. and the Theatre', *Texas Studies in English* (1955); K. Coburn, 'Hazlitt on the Disinterested Imagination', in *Some British Romantics*, ed. J. V. Logan (Columbus, Ohio, 1966); G. Keynes, *Bibliography of W.H.* (1931); E. W. Schneider, Bibliography, in *English Romantic Poets and Essayists*, ed. C. W. and L. H. Houtchens (revised 1966).

Hearn, Lafcadio (1850–1904). Travel writer and lover of the exotic. Born on the Ionian island of Santa Maura (Leucas or Lefcada), the son of a British army surgeon and his Greek wife, he was educated by the Jesuits in Yorkshire and in France. In 1869 he emigrated to America and, struggling against the loss of an eye in youth, made a precarious living as a peddlar and later as a journalist in Cincinnati and New Orleans. He slowly made his way as a writer, however, and was admired for his style in a macabre newspaper series of 'Fantastics', and for his translations of Gautier's short stories *One of Cleopatra's Nights* (1882). He also wrote *Stray Leaves from Strange Literature* (1884), *Gombo Zhêbes* (a collection of French Creole proverbs) (1885) and a volume of highly wrought oriental legends, *Some Chinese Ghosts* (1887). Hearn lived in St Pierre in Martinique (1887–9) and wrote of this experience in *Two Years in the French West Indies* (1890) as well as locating his rather feeble novel *Youma* (1890) there. Thence he went to Japan, marrying the daughter of a family of samurai and becoming a Japanese subject under the name of Koizumi Yakumo. He was Professor of English at Tokyo University (1896–1903). Hearn catered to the avid Western interest in Japan with a series of impressionist essays and studies dealing with the flora, fauna, supernatural beliefs and old customs of his adopted country. The best of these are *Glimpses of Unfamiliar Japan* (1894); *Out of the East* (1895); *In Ghostly Japan* (1899); and his last work, which attempts a summary of his views and interests, *Japan: An Attempt at Interpretation* (1904). [A R]

E. Stevenson, *L.H.* (1961).

Hearne, John (1926–   ). West Indian novelist. Born of upper-middle-class parents in Canada and educated in Jamaica. After war service and a brief return to Jamaica, he read history at Edinburgh University and took a Diploma of Education at London University before becoming a teacher. Hearne's first novel, *Voices under the Window* (1955), describes a Kingston riot, after which the injured and dying hero relives his past in a series of flashbacks. It reveals Hearne's deliberate association with

Caribbean poverty rather than with the colonial upper-middle-class minority. *Stranger at the Gate* (1956) began a series of novels set on the mythical island of Cayuna. It has been followed by *The Faces of Love* (1957), *Autumn Equinox* (1959) and *Land of the Living* (1961). Written with great narrative skill in taut prose reinforced by the accurate evocation of a Caribbean island, they explore the complex social relations of Jamaica. Hearne has written plays for television and feature articles for the press. In 1962 he became a lecturer at the University of the West Indies. [WAG]

Hearne, Thomas (1678–1735). Scholar and eccentric antiquary. He lived all his life in Oxford, where he became second keeper in Bodley's library in 1712, but was deprived of this office for refusing to take the oath of allegiance to George I in 1716. He refused other places and remained a strong Jacobite partisan until he died. He wrote much in Latin and English, and possessed great learning, which, following the fashion of the day, Pope and other wits thought mere pedantry. Still useful are his editions of Leland's *Itinerary* (1710–12) and Camden's *Annales* (1717): he was the editor of medieval chronicles and other collections of documents. He left an autobiography and a journal full of private interest and Oxford gossip (*Remarks and Collections*, ed. C. E. Doble, D. W. Rannie et al., Oxford Historical Society, 11 vols., 1885–1921). [AR]

D. C. Douglas, *English Scholars* (1939).

Heber, Reginald (1783–1826). Hymnodist. Born at Malpas in Cheshire, the son of the rector (and half-brother of Richard Heber, the bibliophile), he was educated at Brasenose College, Oxford, where he wrote the Newdigate Prize poem, *Palestine* (1807), and was a Fellow of All Souls (1805). He travelled widely in Europe, and took orders (1807), to qualify himself for the family living of Hodnet in Shropshire. In 1822, he became Bishop of Calcutta, dying in his bath of an apoplexy at Trichinopoly four years later. He is best known as the author of several still-popular hymns, devout, tuneful, dignified and neat in the 18th-century Anglican tradition, such as 'From Greenland's icy mountain', 'Holy, holy, holy' and 'Brightest and best of the Sons of the morning'. (They may be contrasted with the hymns of ◊ Keble.) His *Poetical Works* (which contain a fragment of a romance in the style of his friend Sir Walter Scott) appeared in 1841. He is the author of an interesting *Narrative of a Journey through the Upper Provinces of India: 1824–5* (ed. A. Heber, 2 vols., 1828).[AR]

G. Smith, *Bishop H., Poet and Missionary* (1895).

Hébert, Anne (1916–). French Canadian poetess. Anne Hébert occupies a special place in French Canadian literature. She has succeeded in expressing in poetry the sense of dispossession and of spiritual solitude, threatened by silence, that was immediately familiar to the French Canadian literary public. She seems to have been through a crisis of maturity almost identical with that of her cousin Hector de ◊ Saint-Denys-Garneau and, unlike him, came through it and achieved a qualified victory, which she described in perceptive words of great beauty in an address of 1958, *Poésie, solitude rompue*, the best of which was used in 1960 as preface to her poems *Mystère de la parole*. Her poetry and her example have inspired several of the best poets of the present generation. She has been acclaimed in France – Albert Béguin and André Rousseaux amongst others wrote of her with enthusiasm and Pierre Emmanuel prefaced poems by her published in 1953 – and this interest has been sustained, something rare in the overcrowded world of modern poetry in France, as is demonstrated by the fact that the Éditions du Seuil have continued to publish her work: *Les chambres de bois*, a novel, in 1958; *Poèmes*, in 1960; and in 1965, *Le torrent*, a collection of short stories, written mainly before 1950. Her novel is a poetic transcription in three phases, of the experience also described in her poetry: the long calm days of childhood occasionally transfigured by a moment of magic; the temptation in adolescence to pursue this magic into the autonomous world of dreams, a world of alienation and self-immolation; the return in maturity to a world of humble joys, viewed with quietly sustained passion. [CRPM]

René Lacôte, *A.H.* (Poètes d'Aujourd'hui, Paris, 1969).

Hemans, Mrs (Felicia Dorothea Browne) (1793–1835). Poet. She was born in Liverpool, where her father was a merchant and consul, and where her first collection of poems was published when she was 15. In 1812 she married Captain Hemans, and published *The Domestic Affections*. Six years later they separated for good. From 1809 to 1831 she lived at Bronwylfa, near St Asaph, in North Wales and at Rhyllon in the same district. She later moved to Dublin, where she became a well-known literary figure. Throughout her life Mrs Hemans produced a steady stream of verse, and her collected works run to 7 volumes. She was well liked – 'that holy Spirit, sweet as the spring' of Wordsworth's *Extempore Effusion* – and was a friend of Scott, who promoted her play *The Vespers of Palermo*, put on in Edinburgh in 1824. Her *Restoration of the Works of Art to Italy* was praised by Byron in 1816. The piety and liberalism of her verse seem, indeed, to have been the bases of her vanished reputation. She often chose fashionable heroic subjects which encouraged a fatal inflation. 'Too many flowers and too little fruit,' said Scott. Her best-known poem, *Casabianca*, is also one of her most concise. [J H]

Works, ed. with a memoir by her sister (7 vols., 1839); *The Poetical Works*, ed. W. M. Rossetti (1873; repr. 1912); *The Poets and Poetry of the Nineteenth Century*, vii, ed. A. H. Miles (11 vols., 1905–7).
A. T. Ritchie, 'Felicia Felix', *Blackstock Papers* (1908); E. Duméril, *Une femme poète au déclin du romantisme anglais, Felicia Hemans* (Toulouse, 1929).

Henderson, Mary. ⟡ Bridie, James.

Hendry, James Findlay. ⟡ Apocalypse.

Henley, William Ernest (1849–1903). Poet, playwright, critic and journalist. Born at Gloucester, the eldest son of a bookseller, he was educated at the Crypt Grammar School there. When he was 12, he suffered a severe tubercular illness which required the amputation of a foot. His other leg was saved after twenty months in Edinburgh Infirmary, where he wrote 'Hospital Verses' (published in the *Cornhill Magazine*, 1875) about his feelings and moods. In Edinburgh he also became a friend of R. L. Stevenson, though he tended to disparage him later. Henley wrote miscellaneous articles for the *Encyclopædia Britannica* and for London periodicals. In 1887 he became editor of *London*, and published Stevenson's stories, the *New Arabian Nights* there, as well as his own poetry. He also edited other

journals such as the Edinburgh *Scots Observer*, which became the *National Observer* on moving to London; it was anti-Gladstone and imperialist in tone. Henley gathered a group of young writers (including Kipling) who were imbued with his ideas (Henley's young men). He versified the policy in 'England, My England', a poem in *The Song of the Sword* (1892) and *For England's Sake: Verses and Songs in Time of War* (the South Africa war) (1900). His misfortunes perhaps force the tone of patriotic *braggadocio* on him: but he also wrote interesting poems combining the fashion for elaborate old verse forms developed by Austin ⟡ Dobson and ⟡ Gosse with realistic social observation and description, in volumes like *London Voluntaries and Other Verses* (1893) and *London Types* (1898). His *Poems* (1898) collected these works. *A Song of Speed* (1903) celebrates the thrill of 'motoring'; he also wrote verse in a more lyrical mode in *Hawthorn and Lavender: Songs and Madrigals* (1899, 1901). Henley had a keen interest in the 'Englishness' of the English language, and consequently projected the 'Tudor Translations' (by Elizabethan prose writers) and compiled a *Dictionary of Slang* (1894–1904). Like Kipling again, he used slang and popular speech in his poems. He wrote a number of unoriginal critical essays attacking 'aesthetes' and 'socialist' writers, and produced many introductory essays for volumes of reprints. One of the collections he edited, *Lyra Heroica* (1892), poems about heroism, was long popular in the educational system. [A R]

Works (7 vols., 1908; 5 vols., 1921); *Selected Poems* (1931).
L. C. Cornford, *W.E.H.* (1913); J. H. Buckley, *W.E.H.* (Princeton U.P., 1945); 'John Connell' (J. H. Robertson), *H.* (1949); K. F. Thompson, 'Beckford, Byron, H.', *Études Anglaises*, 14 (1961).

Henry the Minstrel (Blind Harry) (fl. 1470–92). Reputed author of a poem, *Wallace*, narrating in some 6,000 couplets the exploits of the Scottish popular leader William Wallace (1272?–1305). The *Wallace* (ed. J. Moir, STS, 1885–9) purports to be based on a narrative by Wallace's chaplain, but is patently a collection of traditional tales in which history, exaggeration, rumour, propaganda and legend mingle indiscriminately. Echoes and allusions in the poem suggest that the author knew courtly

Chaucerian literature as well as the popular romances, but the dominant note is a zestful, bloodthirsty hostility to the English which makes the *Wallace* seem much more primitive than its counterpart the *Bruce*, written by John ◊ Barbour a century before. Nothing is known of Henry save his blindness, his occupation and a few payments recorded in the accounts of the Scottish court. W. H. Schofield (in *Mythical Bards and 'The Life of William Wallace'*, 1920) explains the literary allusions and the repeated sharp visual descriptions in the poem by treating 'Blind Harry' as a traditional *persona* assumed by a courtly writer intent on encouraging Scottish national feeling. The *Wallace* had much more popular success than Barbour's *Bruce*; first printed in 1508 and reprinted frequently in the 16th and 17th centuries, it was modernized by William ◊ Hamilton of Gilbertfield in 1722 and this version, a boyhood influence on Burns, remained in popular circulation until the early 19th century. [A I]

G. Neilson, 'Blind Harry's *Wallace*', *Essays and Studies*, i (1910).

Henryson, Robert (fl. 1480). Middle Scots poet. He is best known to English readers for *The Testament of Cresseid* (ed. D. Fox, 1968), a pendant to Chaucer's *Troilus and Criseyde*. After recalling the end of Chaucer's poem Henryson recounts (on the alleged authority of 'ane uther quair', although no source has been found) how Criseyde, deserted by Diomede, blasphemes against Cupid and Venus and is punished with leprosy. Outcast and deformed, begging her bread with other lepers at 'the tounis end', she meets Troilus; neither recognizes the other but, somehow reminded of 'fair Cresseid sumtyme his awin darling', he gives unusually generous alms. When Cresseid learns his identity she dies penitent. Henryson has been condemned for replacing Chaucer's urbanity and detachment with an insistent moralizing severity, and also praised for his tragic interpretation of the story – Cresseid finally recognizes that she betrayed Troilus because, knowing her own 'unstabilnes', she expected nothing better of him.

The *Testament* runs to some 600 lines of rhyme royal and its language tends towards the aureate manner of Chaucer's successors. Each of the 13 *Morall Fabillis of Esope the Phrygian* is much shorter, avoiding any risk of structural looseness, and in them Henryson braces and counterpoints his Chaucerian stanza with native alliteration and racy popular speech; the stories, too, owe as much to the popular Reynard fabliaux as to the Aesopian material of medieval school-books. Brief as they are, the *Fables* offer much more than a series of illustrative anecdotes with conventional morals attached. The animal actors are characterized and humanized, motivated, made capable of deception and self-deception and set in a framework of social relationships to one another, and Henryson often qualifies the conventional secular moral that arises out of a fable by insisting, in his own explicit 'Moralitas', on a religious interpretation. Several of the fables show an awareness of the abuse of power, the psychology of domination and the perversion of justice and religion in the interests of the powerful; Henryson's attitude is one of sardonic disapproving comprehension of such situations. These preoccupations, his control of tone and the wealth of detailed observation of Scots country life that he offers combine to make the *Fables* seem to be more deeply felt, and to embody more experience, than the *Testament*.

Nothing is known of Henryson's life save that he probably taught in the school of Dunfermline Abbey in Fife and that he was dead by about 1506. The *Testament* and the *Fables* survive in 16th-century editions but *Orpheus and Eurydice* (notable for the blend of ballad and Dantean material in its description of Hell) and several short poems, including the attractive pastoral *Robene and Makyne*, are known only from the manuscript of George Bannatyne. [A I]

Poems, ed. G. G. Smith (S T S, 3 vols., 1906–14); *Poems and Fables*, ed. H. H. Wood (1933, 1958); *Selections*, ed. D. Murison (1952); *Poems*, selected and ed. C. Elliott (1963).
M. W. Stearns, *R.H.* (Columbia, 1949); S. Rossi, *R.H.* (1955); E. Muir, *Essays on Literature and Society* (1949); ed. J. Kinsley, *Scottish Poetry* (1955); J. Speirs, *The Scots Literary Tradition* (1940); K. Wittig, *The Scottish Tradition in Literature* (1958); J. MacQueen, *R.H.* (1967).

Henslowe, Philip (?–1616). Theatre manager and proprietor. Born at Lindfield in Sussex (date unknown) Henslowe had settled at Southwark some time before 1577. He married a rich widow and as a result was able to acquire considerable property in the Southwark area, mainly inns and lodging houses. He became financially involved in several forms of small business, including dyeing and starch manufacture, and was also a thriving pawnbroker and money-lender. He also held some minor court offices.

It is in 1587 that Henslowe becomes a figure of interest to the student of literature, for in that year he built, in collaboration with a partner, the Rose Theatre, near Southwark Bridge. A few years after this, he acquired an interest in the provincial theatre at Newington Butts as well as in the Swan Theatre at the west end of Bankside. For some time he had also been concerned in the bull- and bear-baiting shows presented on a piece of open ground near the Swan Theatre and in 1610 he built on this site the Hope Theatre, intended for the presentation of plays as well as for bull-and bear-baiting. In this venture his partner was Edward Alleyn, who married Henslowe's stepdaughter; with Richard Burbage, Alleyn is commonly considered the greatest actor of the period. The most lavishly appointed of all the theatres with which Henslowe was associated was the Fortune (1600), where Edward Alleyn appeared with the Admiral's Men.

The chief source of information about Henslowe is his famous *Diary* (ed. W. Greg, 2 vols., 1904–8; ed. R. A. Foakes and R. T. Rickert, 1961), now in the library of Dulwich College (founded by Henslowe's son-in-law Alleyn). This is the single most important source-book for the theatrical history of this period, and is especially rich in information about the organization and workings of the London theatre in the last few years of the 16th century and the opening of the 17th. The *Diary* is actually a mixture of theatre accounts, payments to playwrights, personal memoranda and comment, and Henslowe emerges from it as a shrewd and not too scrupulous businessman, chiefly concerned to keep the playwrights with whom he was involved – and these included most of the leading figures in the Elizabethan theatre, such as Dekker, Chapman and Heywood – more or less permanently indebted to him. In 1615, a year before his death, his players charged him with 'oppression'; the evidence of the diary suggests that the charge may not have been without substance.

Henslowe's *Diary* was first referred to by the great 18th-century Shakespearean editor Edmond ◊ Malone, but its full publication

did not take place till 1845, when John Payne Collier edited it for the Shakespeare Society. This edition was not only full but over-full, as Collier, following his usual practice, interpolated several forged entries. The first accurate edition was that of Walter Greg (2 vols., 1904–8). The fact that two-thirds of the plays mentioned by Henslowe are now lost gives some indication of the unique importance of this document for the theatrical history of the period. [G S]

The H. Papers: Documents Supplementary to H.'s Diary, ed. W. Greg (1907).
E. K. Chambers, *The Elizabethan Stage*, i (4 vols., 1923).

Henty, George Alfred (1832–1902). Writer of boys' stories and novelist. He wrote about 90 boys' stories of adventurous incident, rather following on from R. M. ◊ Ballantyne, but perhaps more nationalistic, e.g. *Out on the Pampas, or The Young Settlers* (1868), *Under Drake's Flag* (1883), *The Lion of St Mark, A Tale of Venice* (1889) and *With Roberts to Pretoria* (1902). He edited *The Union Jack* (1880–3) and contributed to other periodicals. Henty also wrote a dozen novels, of which the best known is *Colonel Thorndyke's Secret* (1898). [A R]

G. M. Fenn, *G.A.H.: The Story of an Active Life* (1907); G. Trease, 'G.A.H.: Fifty Years After', *The Junior Bookshelf*, 16 (1952); *D N B; TLS* (28 November 1952); R. S. Kennedy and B. J. Farmer, *Bibliography* (1956).

Heppenstall, Rayner (1911–   ). Novelist, poet and critic. Born in Huddersfield and educated in Yorkshire, Calais, and at the Universities of Leeds and Strasbourg. For most of his life Heppenstall has worked for the B.B.C. as a producer. Among his early published volumes are *Patins* (1932), *Middleton Murry: A Study in Excellent Normality* (1934) and *First Poems* (1935). His first novel, *The Blaze of Noon* (1939), is one of the finest novels of its time, and was singled out for acclaim twenty-seven years later when its author was awarded an Arts Council Literature Prize of £1,000.

Heppenstall's more recent novels are closely linked up with his critical writings on the modern French school of anti-novelists. He has written perceptively of the work of such writers as Butor, Robbe-Grillet and Sarraute. Such novels of his own as *The Woodshed* (1962) and *The Connecting Door* (1962) could be considered as English offshoots of the French school. A work of criticism, *The Fourfold Tradition* (1961), also reveals the influence of French models. This is the kind of serious philosophical-literary criticism which is rarely met with in English literature. Heppenstall is a lively and contentious thinker, and possesses a first-rate critical mind. *The Intellectual Part* (1963) is a volume of autobiography. [C O]

The Lesser Infortune (1953); *Four Absentees* (1960); *The Greater Infortune* (1960).

Herbert, Sir A(lan) P(atrick) (1890–   ). Verse writer, dramatist and humorist. Born in London, the son of a Civil Servant, he was educated at Winchester and New College, Oxford. After service in Gallipoli and France, he resumed his legal studies and was called to the bar at the Inner Temple, but has never practised. He had begun writing for *Punch* in 1910, and in 1924 joined its staff. From 1935 he represented Oxford University as an Independent M.P., until the university seats were abolished in 1950. He has two special interests: reform of the marriage laws (in which he partially succeeded by an Act of 1937, and of which he wrote in *Holy Deadlock*, 1934); and the improvement of authors' legal rights and remuneration. He is also a lover of London's river and his book, *The Thames* (1966), is a pleasant volume. He has published many volumes of amusing articles and essays (many first appeared in *Punch*), including *Light Articles Only* (1921). One of his most successful forms of humour, stemming from his legal training, was *Misleading Cases in the Common Law* (3 series, 1927, 1930, 1933; *Codd's Last Case*, 1952; and *Bardot M.P.? and other Modern Misleading Cases*, 1964); these were burlesques of the reported cases, but the points they made were often of substance. He has also published several collections of light verse (successful because of his dexterity); these include *Laughing Anne* (1925), *She Shanties* (1926) and *Less Nonsense!* (1944). He is the author of the books of some highly successful musicals, such as *Big Ben* and *Bless the Bride*. He has also published a novel, *The Water Gipsies* (1930); sailing has been one of his interests and he lives beside the river at Hammersmith. He was knighted in 1945. [A R]

Independent Member (1950) (autobiography); *Look Back and Laugh* (1960) (selection).

Herbert, Alfred Francis Xavier (1901–   ). Australian novelist and short-story writer. Born at Port Hedland in Western Australia, he abandoned his scientific studies at Melbourne University and shortly afterwards began a long residence in the Northern Territory. He took a variety of jobs, among them the post of Protector of Aborigines. During the Second World War he undertook dangerous reconnaissance duties in the Pacific. *Seven Emus* (1959), *Soldiers' Women* (1961) and *Larger Than Life* (1964) are less outstanding than his first book, *Capricornia* (1938), in which Herbert exploits exuberantly his familiarity with the Northern Territory. It is a long book whose inclusiveness indulges his sense of discrepancy. High comedy and grotesque violence are set in a context of social and descriptive realism. Herbert had witnessed the degeneration of responsibility into bullying, and this book's ironic distortions aim to discredit undue pride in human achievement. Corruption, racial discrimination and brutality are zestfully isolated, and they form a disquieting background of disorder for the dominant exaggerated comedy. [P T]

Vincent Buckley, 'Capricornia', *Meanjin*, XIX, 1 (Autumn, 1960).

Herbert of Cherbury, Lord Edward (1583–1648). Philosopher, autobiographer and poet. The eldest son of Richard and Magdalen Herbert of Montgomery, and brother of George ◊ Herbert. In 1596 he went to University College, Oxford. After his marriage in 1598/9 to his cousin Mary, he pursued his studies with unflagging zeal, and also begot 'divers' children. He moved to London (*c.* 1606) where he was introduced to life at court, and gradually entered on a career of public service. Tired of domesticity, he left his family in 1608, and went to France. He spent much of the next ten years abroad, getting to know the French aristocracy and court, participating in battles and sieges, indulging in a variety of gallantries, but also pursuing his studies. In 1619 he was appointed ambassador to the French court, a post he filled admirably.

In 1624 he completed his philosophical treatise, *De veritate*. In the same year he was dismissed from his post – probably on account of an excess of candour. The arrears of his salary were not paid, his sole reward from James I being the barony of Castle-Island, a place in Ireland that was already his property. In 1629 Charles I made him

Baron Herbert of Cherbury, and in 1632 he was appointed to the Council of War; but he was systematically passed over for public office or substantial honour. In 1639 and again in 1640 he reluctantly travelled north at the King's command, but when the Civil War broke out he withdrew to Montgomery Castle and tried to avoid getting involved. In 1644 he allowed a besieging Parliamentary force to occupy and garrison the castle (in exchange for the preservation of his books in London, which had been seized). Herbert moved to London, offered his services to Parliament, and petitioned for a pension. This was granted, but payments soon fell into arrears.

During the early 1640s he was probably working on his autobiography. He also added an appendix (*De causis errorum*, 1645) to the *De veritate*. In 1647 he visited Gassendi in Paris; and in 1648 he died in London, impoverished and alone.

Herbert's chief claim to fame, in the 17th century, was the *De veritate* (tr., ed. and intr. M. H. Carré, 1937). Disagreeing both with those who held that reason could tell us nothing about the truth, and those who believed that all truths could be discovered by reason, Herbert sets out to define different kinds of truth, and establish the mechanism by which we recognize it. He posits an analogy between the external world and the human mind, and sees truth of perception as the situation obtaining when a faculty of the mind is in contact with the corresponding item in the world. As for non-sensory matters such as good and evil, value and its reverse, the mind has *a priori* intuitions about them.

De veritate ran into 4 Latin editions and a French one. It was read by Mersenne. Gassendi and Descartes, who took it seriously enough to disagree with it. Orthodox Christian comment was naturally unfavourable; on the other hand, Locke, in Book I of the *Essay on Human Understanding*, demolished the theory of innate ideas. (But he found common ground with Herbert in his opposition to priests and their dogmatism.) The work continued to be read and disagreed with throughout the 18th century, and Herbert is held to have anticipated some much later developments in philosophy.

Herbert's *Autobiography* (which breaks off in 1624) (ed. Sir Sidney Lee, 1886, revised 1906) was first published by Horace Walpole (Strawberry Hill, 1764). Much of the amusement that he and other readers have derived from this work seems to have been at the author's expense. The work is certainly full of striking instances of self-praise and self-deception; but if it is remembered that it records the auspicious beginnings of a career that was to be suddenly blighted, and that it was written after years of conspicuous failure, we may well attribute the apparent boastfulness of the work to motives other than vanity. Whichever way we read it, the work is a picture of the times.

Lord Herbert wrote poetry throughout his life. Superficially his verses bear some resemblance to Donne's. There are numerous echoes; and in a general way Herbert is difficult, metrically rough, and indulges in conceits. Yet his difficulty arises, chiefly, from grammatical overcomplication or imprecision; the roughness turns out to be feebleness; and the conceits do not shock or surprise. As a poet and as a prose-writer, in English and (if the Latin is his) in Latin, Herbert shows a lack of command over his medium. The poems were first published as *Occasional Verses* in 1665. [T G]

Collected Works, ed. G. C. Moore Smith (1923); *Minor Poets of the Seventeenth Century*, ed. R. G. Howarth (Everyman, 1931); *De religione laici* (1645; ed. and tr. H. R. Hutcheson, 1944). C. de Rémusat, *Lord H. de C.* (Paris, 1874); B. Willey, 'H. of C.: A Spiritual Quixote of the Seventeenth Century', *Essays and Studies* (1941); M. Bottrall, *Every Man a Phoenix* (1958) (for *Autobiography*).

Herbert, George (1593–1633). Poet. The fifth son of Richard Herbert of Montgomery, an Anglo-Welsh gentleman of ancient family, and the beautiful and learned Magdalen Herbert, the patroness of John Donne. (George's eldest brother, Edward, was later created Lord ◊ Herbert of Cherbury.) After Richard Herbert's death in 1596, Mrs Herbert devoted herself to supervising the education of her sons, and her influence on George remained powerful to the end of her life (1627), being apparently unimpaired by her marriage in 1607/8 to Sir John Danvers, a man twenty years her junior.

George had a distinguished career at Westminster School (?1605–9). Shortly after going to Trinity College, Cambridge (December 1609), he sent his mother a New Year's letter consecrating his abilities to God's glory, and 2 sonnets in praise of religious poetry. In 1612 (the year he took his B.A.) he contributed 2 Latin elegies on the death of Prince Henry to a Cambridge memorial volume. By 1615 he had become a close friend of Donne's, to whom he sent a short Latin poem with its English translation.

By accepting a Fellowship of his college (1615/16, the year of his M.A.) he became subject to a statute requiring him to take orders within seven years. In 1618 he was appointed Reader in Rhetoric, while in 1620, after considerable lobbying, he was appointed to the important office of Public Orator. His correspondence of that period suggests that he was a gay and somewhat vain young man, pleased with the greatness of his office. He was on friendly terms with the great (for example with Francis Bacon, whom he honoured in Latin verse, and to whom he remained faithful after his fall) and the appointment led him to mix in court circles and even provided him with an introduction to the King. Before he was appointed he protested that he did not mean the Oratorship to deflect him from his religious vocation, but his failure to take orders in 1623 (the year appointed by his college statutes), his increasing withdrawal from Cambridge (where his work was largely done by deputy), and his election to Parliament as member for Montgomery (1624–5) show him virtually committed to a secular career. (The portion of the living of Llandinam, bestowed on him in 1624, was a sinecure that could be held by a layman.) Walton however records that his mother was opposed to his abandonment of his earlier plans.

Then Herbert suddenly changed course. All that we know for certain is that in 1626 Herbert debarred himself from civil employment by taking minor orders. Appointed to the prebend of Leighton Ecclesia (virtually a sinecure) he set about raising money to rebuild the ruinous church at Leighton Bromwold. In the event he found most of it from his own pocket. In 1627 his mother died and we learn something of George's feelings for her from the set of Latin poems he wrote in her memory (*Memoriae Matris Sacrum*, published in the same year together with Donne's funeral sermon on her). In 1628 he resigned his Public Oratorship.

In March 1629 Herbert married Jane Danvers, a young kinswoman of his stepfather's. A year later he was instituted as rector of Bemerton, near Salisbury (April 1630), while the taking of full orders followed in the autumn. As a country parson he soon gained a reputation for piety, zeal and charity. His correspondence shows that this last quality was allied to tact and good sense: he took two of his nieces (recently orphaned) into his family and justified this action in terms that totally avoid self-righteousness.

Early in 1633, Herbert, whose health had never been robust, recognized that he was dying of consumption and sent a copy of his book *The Temple* to his friend Nicholas Ferrar at Little Gidding, requesting him to print it or burn it as he saw fit. On 1 March 1633 Herbert died; 2 editions of *The Temple* were published before the end of the year.

The Temple (on which Herbert's fame rests) comprises almost all his surviving English poems. Of his Latin verses, apart from those already mentioned, there have survived a handful of short occasional poems, 2 sets of sacred poems (*Lucus* and *Passio Discerpta*), and *Musae Responsoriae*, a defence of the Church of England against Andrew Melville's *Anti-Tami-Cami-Categoria* (1621?). His surviving prose consists of *A Priest to the Temple* (the character and rules of conduct of a country parson), notes on *The Hundred and Ten Considerations* by Juan de Valdés (Valdesso), the translation of Luigi Cornaro's *Treatise of Temperance and Sobrietie*, and at least the core of the *Outlandish Proverbs* (a collection of foreign proverbs in translation). Some of his Latin letters and orations and a portion of his private correspondence have survived.

The Temple is a miscellany of short and shortish sacred poems introduced by a longer, rather severe didactic piece on virtuous living ('The Church Porch') and followed by a witty and almost bitter account of Church history ('The Church Militant'). The miscellany itself (sub-titled *The Church*) consists of hymns and prayers, meditations on the great mysteries of the faith, explanations of doctrine, emblematic and epigrammatic pieces, and above all direct appeals to God and pieces of spiritual autobiography. (It is these, no doubt, that Herbert referred to when he spoke of his poems containing 'a picture of the many spiritual conflicts that have passed betwixt God and my soul'.) The arrangement of the poems is neither haphazard nor systematic.

The order of the first and of the last few pieces is significant: from 'The Altar' Herbert proceeds to 'The Sacrifice' (i.e. the Crucifixion), and there follows a series of poems appropriate to Good Friday and Easter Sunday; the last poems are 'Death', 'Doomsday', 'Judgment', 'Heaven' and 'Love'. In between, however, the arrangement seems rather to be based on principles of association and contrast than on an overall scheme (though traces of such a scheme are to be found).

Herbert employs a very wide variety of verse-forms, yet his tone is remarkably uniform. The manner is informal, yet concise and clear. On the other hand, each poem is distinctive and differs from all the others; for in each poem a situation is imagined and brought to life. Each poem, moreover, contains some surprising thought or image; and Herbert's surprises (unlike some of Donne's) are not interchangeable. The raw materials of a Herbert conceit may be commonplaces of religious language; from these he creates an unexpected picture, which on second thoughts we see to be appropriate.

The appeal to the imagination is not always through the conceit. Thus in 'The Sacrifice', a dramatic monologue spoken by Christ on the Cross, each detail of the Crucifixion is considered, and then invested with a terrible irony. In the sonnet 'Sinne' the forces of virtue are shown crowding in relentlessly, so that their defeat by 'one cunning bosome-sinne' creates an effect of shock (and perhaps secret rejoicing). All Herbert's poems have a clear, logically developed argument. But he makes less play with his reasoning processes than does Donne.

The spiritual conflict which many of the poems describe arises neither from doubt nor (mainly) from the temptations of the world, but in part at least from Herbert's passionate longing for a direct awareness of God. Such an awareness he must have known early in life ('ev'n in the midst of youth and night'); and it seems to have returned intermittently. But its absence left him desolate, and even (as in 'The Collar') rebellious. The resolution to the conflict lies in the acceptance of suffering, and utter submission to God's will. The struggle is described with a candour and a clarity that renders it comprehensible even to the irreligious reader.

There were 13 editions of *The Temple*

between 1633 and 1679; after that Herbert's popularity began to wane, though there was a certain amount of interest in him (for his piety) in the early 18th century. Later in the century John ⋄ Wesley adapted some 40 of his poems to conform with 18th-century notions of sacred poetry, but also published a small selection in an unamended version (1773). The edition of *The Temple* of 1799 heralded a revival, to which Coleridge's appreciation of Herbert, in *Biographia Literaria* (1817), gave a considerable boost. About 30 editions of *The Temple* were published during the 19th century. The main objection that 19th-century critics raised against Herbert – the 'artificiality' of his conceits – ceased to be an objection after the great Donne revival of the early 20th century. The first detailed *Life* of Herbert is that by Izaak Walton (1670; the 1674 and 1675 editions contain significant changes); the deficiencies of Walton have been thoroughly explored by David Novarr (*The Making of Walton's Lives*, 1958). [T G]

Complete Works, ed. F. E. Hutchinson (1941); *G.H.*, ed. H. Gardner (1961); (selection).
J. Bennett, *Four Metaphysical Poets* (1934; republished in 1953 as *Five Metaphysical Poets*); J. B. Leishman, *The Metaphysical Poets* (1934); F. E. Hutchinson, in *Seventeenth Century Studies Presented to Sir Herbert Grierson* (1938); M. Bottrall, *G.H.* (1954); J. H. Summers, *G.H.* (1954) (most thorough study so far published); R. Tuve, *A Reading of G.H.* (1952); I. Husain, *The Mystical Element in the Metaphysical Poets* (1948); L. Martz, *The Poetry of Meditation* (1954); C. Mann, *H. Concordance* (1927); G. H. Palmer, *H. Bibliography* (1911).

Herd, David (1732–1810). Collector and editor of *Ancient and Modern Scots Songs* (1769; 2nd edn, 1776). The son of a farmer in Kincardineshire, he includes some of the earliest printed versions of the Scottish ballads and a selection of Scots songs in which the native traditions of bawdry and absurdity, later transmuted by Burns and bowdlerized by Lady ⋄ Nairne, are fairly represented. Herd neither modernized his texts nor made them genteel, and he printed many fragments and odd stanzas in the hope of being sent complete versions. Many of these were worked up and completed afresh by Burns, who owned both editions of Herd's book. Herd's large collection of manuscripts, divided between the libraries of the British Museum and the University of Edinburgh, has been of use to scholars and editors from Scott's time to the present day. [A I]

Songs from D.H.'s Manuscripts, ed. Hans Hecht (1904).

Herrick, Robert (1591–1674). Poet. Born in London in 1591, Herrick was apprenticed to his uncle, a prosperous goldsmith, in 1607. In 1613 he abandoned this career and at the mature age of 22 went up to Cambridge (St John's College; before graduating B.A. in 1617 he changed to Trinity Hall). In 1620 he took his M.A., and he was ordained priest in 1623. It seems likely that throughout these years, and indeed until 1630, he moved in London literary circles, making the acquaintance of such figures as Ben Jonson, Endymion Porter, and William and Henry Lawes. In 1627 he accompanied the Duke of Buckingham as chaplain on his expedition to the Isle of Rhé, and in 1628–9 he was appointed to the living of Dean Prior in Devonshire, though he did not take up residence there until 1630. There he remained, though apparently not in total isolation from the world of London, until 1647, when he was ejected from his living. It seems that he then lived in London, possibly on his relatives' charity, until the Restoration, when he was reinstated.

Herrick may have started on his career as a poet before he reached the age of 20; and there is no evidence of his having written any poems after 1649 (when 'The New Charon' was published in *Lachrymae Musarum*, a volume lamenting the death of Lord Hastings). A handful of his poems were published during the 1630s and 1640s but the great bulk of his output was first printed in *Hesperides* (1648), a volume that contains both his secular poems and, with a separate title-page describing them as *His Noble Numbers*, his religious verse. Those poems of which a pre-1648 version is extant show Herrick to have been a meticulous reviser, who worked towards greater compression and smoothness of versification.

In form, Herrick's poems range from the epigrammatic couplet to the Horatian ode, the epithalamium and the verse epistle; but the majority of them are short lyrics, of a more or less epigrammatic terseness, and modelled on such classical examples as the lyrics of Catullus and pseudo-Anacreon, Martial's epigrams, and the so-called epigrams of the Greek Anthology (or their Renaissance Latin imitations), and on such native patterns as the lyrics of Ben Jonson, English popular ballads and carols, rhyming proverbs, or Thomas Tusser's versified country-lore. In subject-matter, there is a great deal of variety – compliment to friends, erotic fantasy, love, religion, politics, morality, country lore, the festivals of the countryman's year, the poet's fame, death – yet the variations in tone and manner are slighter than the diversity of genre and content would suggest.

Although Herrick is careful to give his poems an argument and a rhetorical structure, he is essentially a poet of local effects: surprising transitions from one line to the next, ingeniously pointed or sensuously suggestive tropes, odd but apt lexical combinations, new twists to old phrases. It is just because his basic repertory of images, and his basic diction, are so conventional that minute variations produce so telling an effect. The simile comparing the mistress's complexion to milk or cream is a standard Elizabethan cliché; but to compare her cheeks to 'creame Enclarited', as Herrick does, is to make the image more visually convincing and yet at the same time more gastronomically enticing. Often the effects are more complex, and arrived at by even more delicate variations from the stock formula. There is frequently a deliberate, though mild, *indecorum* of imagery, as when Julia's leg is praised for being 'as white and hairless as an egg'; and this helps to create a kind of pastoral effect even in poems in which there is no overt reference to country life. Although Herrick's poetry is by no means devoid of conceits, these are never developed in the manner of Donne: it is their more obvious implications that are explored.

The poet presents us with more than one persona: sometimes he pictures himself as the wild, drunken, inspired Anacreontic poet; at other times as the admiring lover, delighted by the physical beauty of a mistress (but never, apparently, doing anything to obtain any mistress's favours – so that one often infers that he is already in possession); at other times, again, as the rustic householder, the worshipper of country deities, the supporter of ancient custom. To offset the prevailing blandness of tone, Herrick intersperses *Hesperides* with short didactic and satiric epigrams – the former flat, the latter gross but oddly unamusing. *His Noble Numbers* contains very few poems that are in any way remarkable.

Herrick seems to have achieved fame quite early in his career, but by the time *Hesperides* appeared he had fallen out of fashion, and the book sold very slowly indeed. There are few references to him in the century after his death, but interest revived in the 19th century, when numerous selections appeared. Swinburne called Herrick the 'greatest song-writer ever born of English race'. Among 19th-century complete editions, that of W. C. Hazlitt (1869) deserves mention for being the first to include Herrick's letters. A. W. Pollard's first Muses' Library edition of 1891 has an introduction by Swinburne, while the second (1898) contains valuable additional notes.

In the present century the reputation of Herrick has been greatly overshadowed by those of Donne and other 17th-century lyric poets, but editions and selections have continued to appear. [T G]

Works, ed. F. W. Moorman (1919 ff.); ed. L. C. Martin (1956).
F. Delattre, *R.H.* (1912); F. W. Moorman, *R.H.* (1910); Emily Easton, *Youth Immortal: A Life of R.H.* (1934); Kathryn A. McEuen, *Classical Influence on the Tribe of Ben* (1939); S. Musgrove, *The Universe of R.H.* (Auckland, 1950); E. E. Hale, *Die Chronologische Anordnung der Dichtungen R.H.* (1892); S. A. and D. R. Tannenbaum, *H., A Concise Bibliography* (New York, 1949).

Hervey, John (Baron Hervey of Ickworth, known by his courtesy title of Lord Hervey) (1696–1743). Memoir writer and pamphleteer. Born at Ickworth in Suffolk, the son of the Earl of Bristol, he was educated at Westminster School, and Clare Hall, Cambridge. In 1716, he went on the Grand Tour and visited Hanover, where he became a friend of Prince Frederick (Prince of Wales and later George II). In 1720, he married Mary Lepell, a Maid of Honour to the princess, who figures as a toast in the verses of Pope, Gay and others. He was elected M.P. for Bury St Edmunds in 1725. On joining the supporters of Walpole, he became vice-chamberlain and a privy councillor in 1730. Thereafter he wrote numerous, effective pamphlets in support of Walpole's policies, attacking Bolingbroke and his former political chief, Pulteney, with whom he fought a duel on 25 January 1731. In 1733, he was called to the Lords by writ for his father's barony. He had great court influence as a favourite of Queen Caroline's. In 1740 he became Lord Privy Seal. He supported Walpole to the end, and was dismissed some months after the minister's fall. He was a clever, knowledgeable and cynical observer of the political scene. His *Memoirs of the Reign of George II* (ed. J. W. Croker, 2 vols., 1848; ed. R. Sedgwick, 3 vols, 1931, revised 1952) are among the best examples of that branch of 18th-century historical writing. Acid, prejudiced but also at times curiously fair, spiced with epigrams, they give a vivid and dramatic account of power and personality struggles. Hervey was a feeble but unscrupulous satirist in verse; and, with Lady Mary Wortley ◊ Montague, embroiled himself with Pope, who, in his finest cutting style, attacked him as 'Sporus' in the *Epistle to Dr Arbuthnot*. Hervey was an affected man of effeminate appearance. [A R]

Earl of Ilchester, *Lord H. and His Friends, 1726–38* (1950) (correspondence).

Hewlett, Maurice (1861–1923). Novelist and poet. He was born in Weybridge, Surrey, the son of a senior Civil Servant, and educated at several different private schools. At 17 he entered the family law firm, was called to the bar in 1890 and three years later succeeded to his father's post in the Record Office. In 1898 he published his first novel, *The Forest Lovers* – a medieval Arthurian romance in the style of the period – which was an immediate success and enabled him to become a full-time writer. During the years up to 1904 his output consisted mainly of historical or Italian romances, such as *Richard Yea-and-Nay* (1900); from 1905 to 1914 he turned to novels of Regency and contemporary times, of which the best known is *Rest Harrow* (1910); and from 1914 onwards he regarded himself as a poet and essayist. In his later work he expounds his belief in the English peasantry as the only hope for the future of the nation, notably in his nostalgic would-be epic poem and chronicle of the common history of England, *The Song of the Plow* (1916) – originally entitled *The Hodgiad*. But his poetry was not distinctive enough and his name was indissolubly linked with romantic fiction, so the public refused to take his work seriously. [J M]

Letters, ed. Laurence Binyon (1926).

Heywood, John (*c.* 1497–*c.* 1580). Dramatist and author. Educated at Oxford, he married the daughter of John Rastell, printer, writer of interludes, and son-in-law of Sir Thomas ◊ More. Through More's influence and his own skill as a musician, minstrel and wit, he became a court favourite of Henry VIII and of Mary. He published versified collections of proverbs and epigrams such as *Dialogues Containing the Number of Proverbs* (1546) and the anthologies of 1555, 1556 and 1560. Like his long allegorical poem in rhyme royal *The Spider and the Fly*, which contrasts Protestantism with Catholicism, his work as epigrammatist and proverb-collector is of interest only to specialists.

He wrote a number of short dramatic interludes which, in a simple and lively way, mark the transition from medieval moralities to the earliest Elizabethan comedies. His decorous disputations for a courtly audience included *The Play of the Weather* (printed 1533), *The Play of Love* (*c.* 1533) and *Witty and Witless* (*c.* 1520–33). Farce and comedy are more developed, and dialogue more vigorous, in 3 brief and coarser pieces usually attributed to Heywood: *The Pardoner and the Friar* (*c.* 1519), *The Four PP* (*c.* 1520) and the 3-character playlet (modelled on a French farce) *John John the Husband, Tib his Wife, and Sir John the Priest* (*c.* 1520). These more popular works seem designed both for the court and the country audiences of strolling players. Heywood, a staunch Catholic, went abroad on Elizabeth's accession. [MJ]

Works, ed. B. A. Milligan (Urbana, 1956).
R. W. Bolwell, *The Life and Works of J.H.* (1921); R. de la Bère, *J.H., Entertainer* (1937); David M. Bevington, *From 'Mankind' to Marlowe* (1962); M. C. Bradbrook, *The Growth and Structure of Elizabethan Comedy* (1955); F. P. Wilson, *The English Drama, 1485–1585* (1969).

Heywood, Thomas (*c.* 1574–1641). Dramatist and poet. Born in Lincolnshire, he may have studied at Cambridge; by 1596 he was an actor and playwright for various companies in London. He claimed to have had a hand, as author or part-author, in 220 plays, of which over 20 survive. He wrote in various genres: popular English chronicle-histories like *Edward IV* (2 parts) and *If You Know Not Me, You Know Nobody*, low comedy in *The Wise Woman of Hogsdon*, classical and mythological plays like his dramatization of Greek mythology in 5 plays (*The Golden Age, The Silver Age, The Brazen Age*, and the 2 parts of *The Iron Age*) and *The Rape of Lucrece*, rollicking comedies of adventure like *The Fair Maid of the West, or A Girl Worth Gold* (2 parts) and *Fortune by Land and Sea*, domestic tragedies like *The English Traveller* and his masterpiece *A Woman Killed with Kindness* (ed. and intr. R. W. van Fossen, 1961), as well as the scripts of city pageants and masques. From 1608 he was prolific in non-dramatic work also: his translation of Sallust appeared in 1608 and 1609, *Troia Britannica*, a heroic poem of some 13,000 lines on the story of Troy, in 1609, and an *Apology for Actors*, an eloquent defence of the stage against the Puritans' attacks, in 1612. He published a lament for Prince Henry and an epithalamium for Princess Elizabeth, and worked on *The Lives of the Poets Modern and Foreign*, which never appeared. Queen Henrietta's players had a striking success at court with his *Love's Mistress, or The Queen's Masque*, in 1634, and *England's Elizabeth* was published in 1631. In 1635 his poem with prose sections, *The Hierarchie of the Blessed Angels*, appeared in a splendid illustrated edition. In his last years he wrote and directed annual civic pageants for the Lord Mayor's day. A phenomenally productive author, Heywood nowadays have become a successful screen-writer. *A Woman Killed with Kindness* is regarded as the finest example of Elizabethan domestic tragedy. An edition of the plays by A. Brown is in progress. [MJ]

Dramatic Works, ed. R. H. Shepherd (6 vols., 1874).
F. S. Boas, *T.H.* (1950); A. M. Clark *T.H.: Playwright and Miscellanist* (1931); O. Cromwell, *T.H., A Study in the Elizabethan Drama of Everyday Life* (New Haven, 1928).

Hickey, William (1749–1830). Journal writer. Born in Westminster, the son of Joseph Hickey, a solicitor. After some time he too became an attorney and travelled widely, to China, Portugal, the West Indies and the Cape Colony. He spent most of his life in Bengal as a lawyer practising before the Supreme Court, and held a number of public offices. He was addicted to women, wine and convivial society. His acquaintance was catholic, extending from Burke and other men of note to the fringes of the underworld. His *Memoirs: 1749–1809* (selected, ed. and intr. A. Spencer, 4 vols., 1913–25; selected and ed. P. Quennell, 1960) are kaleidoscopic papers of great minuteness and indiscriminate interest, though not always accurate. [A R]

Higden, Ranulf (d. 1364). Chronicler. Born in the west of England, Higden entered the Benedictine abbey of St Werburgh, Chester, in 1299. His major work, the *Polychronicon*, is a universal history in Latin down to his own times. In its day, it was the most exhaustive of such works, and maintained its popularity for nearly two centuries. Over 100 manuscripts survive, and there are 2 English translations, one by ◊ Trevisa (ed. C. Babington and J. R. Lumby, 1865–86; ed. J. Taylor, *The Universal Chronicles of R.H.*, 1967), and an anonymous 15th-century one. Higden's original historical value is small, but the *Polychronicon* serves as an index of the historical, geographical and scientific knowledge of the 14th century. It was completed in 1327, but there are several continuations and reductions, the earlier of which Higden probably made himself. He produced other historical and religious works and has been thought, on somewhat flimsy evidence, to be the author of the Chester Cycle of mystery plays. [A G]

Hilton, James (1900–54). Novelist. Born in Lancashire, the son of a schoolmaster, he was educated at the Leys School and Cambridge University. His first novel, *Catherine Herself* (1920), was published while he was an undergraduate. He then went into journalism and later became fiction reviewer on the *Daily Telegraph* while continuing to write his own novels. The fifth of these, *Lost Horizon* (1933) – a story of dreamlike excitement and suspense at a secret Tibetan monastery called Shangri-La – was immediately popular, and Hilton followed up this success in 1934 with his most famous best-seller, *Good-Bye, Mr Chips*. This tale of a schoolmaster's life, old age and death at an ancient public school, with its complacent assumptions about English tradition and education expressed in jokes and understatements, had an even greater popular appeal, and was dramatized, filmed and translated. From then on Hilton continued his regular output of novels until his death; in 1935 he went to live in Hollywood, where he wrote film screenplays. [J M]

Hilton, Walter (d. 1396). Mystical writer. Probably of midland stock, Hilton was an Augustinian canon at Thurgarton, near Newark. As a young man, he may, like ◊ Rolle, have lived as a hermit, and he may have ended his life as a Carthusian, with whose ideals he certainly sympathized. His best-known work, *The Scale of Perfection* (ed. E. Underhill, 1923, modernized text; tr. L. Sherley-Price, *The Ladder of Perfection*, Penguin Classics, 1957), was written late in life. Its theme is man's search for God, and it reveals Hilton's Victorine insistence on self-knowledge – God is best known in the soul He made in His image. Written ostensibly for a female recluse, it reached a much wider audience, and long remained influential. Though Hilton employs the vivid and homely images characteristic of the earlier mystic, Richard Rolle, there are in the *Scale* no comparable descriptions of raptures and ecstasy. Together with Rolle, ◊ Juliana of Norwich and the unknown author of *The Cloud of Unknowing* (ed. P. Hodgson, 1958), Hilton represents the finest in medieval English prose.

His other well-known work, *An Epistle on Mixed Life* (*Minor Works*, ed. D. Jones, 1929, modernized text), may have influenced Langland; at least, there is some similarity of thought. [A G]

R. W. Chambers, *On the Continuity of English Prose* (1932); M. D. Knowles, *The English Mystics* (1927), and *The English Mystical Tradition* (1961); H. L. Gardner, 'W.H. and the Mystical Tradition in England', *Essays and Studies*, XXII (1937); P. Hodgson, *Three Fourteenth Century Mystics* (WTW, 1967); J. E. Milosh, *The Scale of Perfection and the English Mystical Tradition* (1966).

Hobbes, Thomas (1588–1679). Philosopher and man of letters. Hobbes was born at Westport, near Malmesbury, Wiltshire, the son of a country parson. After a solid grammar school education he went up to Magdalen Hall, Oxford, in 1603, but found the scholastic curriculum unrewarding. He graduated in 1608 and was appointed tutor, and later secretary and companion, to William Cavendish, who was to become the 1st Earl of Devonshire. At Chatsworth and Welbeck Abbey, the homes of the highly intelligent Cavendish family, he mingled with their distinguished guests (including such figures as Lord Herbert of Cherbury, Lucius Cary and Ben Jonson), had access to good libraries, and in his capacity as tutor accompanied his pupil on the grand tour in 1610. At some date before 1626 Hobbes acted as secretary to Francis Bacon. In 1628 William Cavendish died, and Hobbes took a position as travelling companion to the son of Sir Gervase Clinton on a tour of France and Switzerland. On this tour Hobbes first read Euclid, and fell in love with mathematics. Returning to the Cavendish household in 1630, he became tutor to the Earl of Devonshire's son, and made a third grand tour. This time his mind was filled with meditations on physics and philosophy. He met Galileo and Mersenne. On his return to England he set about constructing his philosophical system, which was to deal with Body, with Man and with Citizenship. His writings on the first of these topics culminated in the *De corpore* (published in 1655); but he was soon drawn to the third, and in 1640 wrote *Humane Nature; or the Fundamentals of Policie*, and *De corpore politico, or The Elements of Law* (ed. F. Tönnies, 1889).

These treatises circulated widely in manuscript. His next essay on the same topics, *De cive* (published in 1642; ed. S. P. Pamprecht, New York, 1949), was written in Paris, for Hobbes had felt it prudent to emigrate before his support for absolute monarchy involved him in trouble with Parliament. In Paris Mersenne encouraged him to return to the subject of natural philosophy, and he at once became involved in a controversy with Descartes, publishing his *Objections* to Descarte's *Meditations* in 1641. A treatise on optics followed in 1644.

A fellow exile in Paris, Bishop Bramhall, engaged in private debate with Hobbes over his materialism and determinism. Hobbes's part of the argument was published in London without his consent some nine years later (*Of Libertie and Necessitie*, 1654; ed. C. von Brockdorff, Kiel, 1938), and the controversy, thus revived, was carried on intermittently until the end of Hobbes's life.

In 1645 Hobbes was appointed tutor in mathematics to Prince Charles, though it was feared that his 'atheistic' notions might corrupt the Prince. (Whether they did or not, Charles did not govern by Hobbesian principles when he became king. On the other hand, he was well disposed towards Hobbes and awarded him a pension after the Restoration.) The publication of *Leviathan* in 1651 scandalized the exiled court to such an extent that Hobbes was banished from it, and he returned to England in 1652.

In 1653 Hobbes returned to the Cavendish family, and with them he spent much of the remainder of his life. His chief preoccupation now was with mathematics, but his belief in his own powers as a mathematician was something of a delusion. He read mathematical papers to the Royal Society and was disappointed not to be elected a Fellow. Over his attempts to square the circle and duplicate the cube he became involved in a long-drawn-out and acrimonious personal controversy with the eminent mathematician John Wallis.

Long before Hobbes wrote any works of philosophy he had been a man of letters. Thus in 1629 he had published an excellent translation of Thucydides, which was to run into numerous editions; in 1636 his Latin poem on the marvels of the Peak District, *De mirabilibus pecci*, was published, while a brilliant (and still useful) English condensation of Aristotle's *Rhetoric* appeared in 1637 under the title of *A Briefe of the Art of Rhetorique*. When his friend Davenant's epic *Gondibert* was published in Paris (1650), the prefatory Discourse was followed by an 'Answer' by Hobbes (in *Critical Essays of the Seventeenth Century*, ed. J. E. Spingarn, 1908), in which the nature of epic poetry was discussed.

In his old age, Hobbes returned to literature: he translated Homer (*Odyssey*, 1673; *Iliad*, 1676) and again discussed the properties of epic in his preface to the 1675 edition of his *Odyssey* (in *Critical Essays of the Seventeenth Century*, ed. J. E. Spingarn, 1908). More important, perhaps, was his account of the Civil Wars, *Behemoth* (published posthumously, 1680; ed. F. Tönnies, 1889). He also produced a Latin verse autobiography (published 1680 with English translation), and left an incomplete one in Latin prose (published in 1681). He died peacefully, and apparently a devout Christian, in 1679.

Hobbes's great work, *Leviathan* (ed. M. Oakeshott, 1946; ed. J. Plamenate, 1962), is a theory of society founded on a theory of man, based in its turn on an *a priori* materialism. Although Hobbes did not deny the existence of God, he utterly denied the existence of any divinely instituted moral laws in the universe. Laws are man-made, and they were made to protect man against the consequence of his own rapaciousness and aggressiveness. Where organized society does not exist, there is a war of every one against every one; society is the result of a contract by which men give up a great measure of their natural liberty in order that they may have security. The ideal state is that in which there exists the greatest degree of security and stability, and this Hobbes believed to be the state ruled by an absolute ruler. Such a doctrine could not fail to offend both sides in the Civil War, since both sides believed human law to be the carrying out of God's will on earth. Long before the appearance of *Leviathan* it had become apparent that Hobbes's views were utterly destructive of Christian morality. *Leviathan* itself, with its grandly dogmatic dismissal of the very terminology of Christian theology as so much 'insignificant sound', caused a great deal of scandal. At the same time it was a book that demanded to be argued with: and its influence lay, not in the establishment of a 'Hobbist' school of English philosophers, but in its power to force Christian philosophers to re-examine their own doctrines. The Cambridge Platonists, notably More, Whichcote, and Culverwell, as well as Joseph Glanville, all wrote, directly or indirectly, to refute Hobbes, and in the process they learnt from him. A very entertaining attack from a different angle was launched by John Eachard in *Mr Hobbs's State of Nature Considered* (1672), and *Some Opinions of Mr Hobbs Considered* (1673). (There is a list of anti-Hobbes literature in England, 1650–1700, in S. I. Mintz, *The Hunting of Leviathan*, 1962.)

Leviathan stands out from the great body of English philosophical prose by its simplicity, its compactness and its aggressiveness. Hobbes avoids technical terminology, or, where he does use technical terms of his own, uses words which have familiar meaning and strong emotional connotation; thus he defines *memory* as 'decaying sense'. His sentences are often curt and epigrammatic; occasionally they are of the trailing type, but they do not often trail for very long: and though devices of symmetry are used to give sentences shape and order, they are never used predictably. His diction is grave, yet simple and concrete: visual imagery abounds. The argument is spiced with a good deal of incidental and often very amusing sarcasm at the expense of theology, scholastic philosophy and the clergy. But the real power of the book lies not only in its stylistic brilliance but also in its constant appeals to human experience and to common sense. His picture of man may be appallingly one-sided and his view of human relations altogether too pessimistic, but as far as they go they are truthful.

Hobbes's literary criticism, such as it is, has received a certain amount of attention in the present century, partly because Hobbes's psychological interest in the operation of the imagination presents certain analogies with later theories of poetic activity, and partly as a consequence of the recent wave of interest in the influence of the anti-scholastic Frenchman Peter Ramus – an influence which can perhaps be detected both in the *Answer to the Preface to Gondibert* and in the Preface to the translation of the *Odyssey*. However, he says little that is illuminating or startling. For the student of literature, as for the philosopher, Hobbes remains interesting, principally, as the author of *Leviathan*.

In his lifetime Hobbes published a collected edition of his Latin works (including a translation of *Leviathan*) at Amsterdam (1668). [T G]

Works, ed. W. Molesworth (16 vols., 1839–45); *Body, Man and Citizen*, ed. R. S. Peters (New York, 1962) (selections).
John Aubrey, *Brief Lives*; Leslie Stephen, *H.* (English Men of Letters, 1904); R. S. Peters, *H.* (1956); Leo Strauss, *The Political Philosophy of H.: Its Basis and Its Genesis* (1952); Howard Warrender, *The Political Philosophy of H.* (1957); F. C. Hood, *The Divine Politics of H.* (1964); C. D. Thorpe, *The Aesthetic Theory of T.H.* (1940); H. Macdonald and M. Hargreaves, *H.: A Bibliography* (1952).

Hobhouse, John Cam. ◊ Broughton, John Cam Hobhouse.

Hoby, Sir Thomas (1530–66). Translator. Born in Leominster and educated at St John's College, Cambridge, he became famous as a linguist and a traveller in Italy and in France. At the time of his death in Paris he was English ambassador. His literary achievement was to make available in English the great Renaissance handbook on the fashioning of a courtier, *Il cortegiano* by Baldassare Castiglione. *The Courtier Done into English by T. Hoby* first appeared in 1561, was three times reprinted by 1603, and was widely influential in courtly and literary circles, although not itself a memorable translation (ed. W. Raleigh, 1900). [M J]

C. S. Lewis, *English Literature in the Sixteenth Century* (1954); F. O. Matthiessen, *Translation, An Elizabethan Art* (1931).

Hoccleve or **Occleve, John** (1370?–1450?). Poet and Civil Servant. Hoccleve himself tells us that he was a clerk in the Privy Seal office, and more biographical information can be gathered from his work. In 1415, he suffered temporarily from madness, and he gives an interesting and skilful account of his experience in *La Male Regle* (*Minor Poems*, ed. F. J. Furnivall and Sir I. Gollancz, 1892–7). Though not in orders, he was granted a benefice, perhaps for his literary work, in 1424. Like ◊ Lydgate, he was a follower of Chaucer, and his long work *The Regement of Princes* (ed. F. J. Furnivall, 1897) contains a famous elegy on his master. The *Regement* is a work of moral instruction directed to Prince Henry (Henry V). Hoccleve uses the rhyme royal stanza, but in him ease descends very readily into slackness. A syllable-counter, he does not compare with Lydgate as a master of the 'aureate style', but there are some good narrative poems. Except when he is being personal in works like *La Male Regle* and the *Complaint*, he is dull, and the chief remaining interest of his work is a fairly full picture of his times. [A G]

H. S. Bennett, *Chaucer and the Fifteenth Century* (1947); J. Mitchell, *T.H.: A Study in Early Fifteenth Century Poetic* (1968).

Hodgson, Ralph (1871–1962). Poet. Born in Yorkshire. By temperament a recluse, he was extremely reticent about his personal background and little of a biographical nature is known about him. He was for several years editor of *Fry's Magazine* and at other times earned his living by breeding bull-terriers and drawing cartoons. In 1924 he went to Japan and lived most of his later life in America. He was a contributor to ◊ *Georgian Poetry* and throughout his long lifetime published only 4 volumes of poetry, *The Last Blackbird* (1907), *Poems* (1917), *The Skylark and Other Poems* (1958) and *Collected Poems* (1961). A nature poet with a deep love and understanding of animals, which provided the subject matter for much of his work, he is best known for the often anthologized poem 'Time you Old Gipsy Man'. [P J K]

John Sparrow, 'R.H.'s New Poetry', *Listener*, L X I (12 March 1959): L. A. G. Strong, *Green Memory* (1961).

Hoff, Harry Summerfield. ◊ Cooper, William.

Hogg, James (1770–1835). Poet and novelist. Nick-named 'The Ettrick Shepherd', he was famous as a poet and character in his own day but is now remembered chiefly for *The Private Memoirs and Confessions of a Justified Sinner* (1824; ed. J. Carey, 1969), a supernatural tale in which the Calvinist doctrine of predestination allows a self-consciously devout young man to rationalize and acquiesce in the Devil's promptings to murder his 'worldly' brother. Hogg balances a narrative (often grimly humorous) by an objective 'editor' against a vivid and haunting first-person account by the deluded murderer. Although Hogg, like Hawthorne, sets his tale in a remote Calvinist past, it reflects moral and religious tensions of the society in which he lived.

Hogg, the son of an unsuccessful farmer, grew up as a shepherd in the oral culture of a remote Border valley. He taught himself to write, published some poems in magazines and helped Walter Scott to collect material for the *Minstrelsy of the Scottish Border* (1802–3). In later life Hogg farmed, not very successfully, in the Borders, save for an attempt to live by journalism in Edinburgh (1810–17). He was a prolific and slapdash writer of tales, all virtually worthless save for the *Justified Sinner*. His verse appeared in *The Mountain Bard* (1807), *The Queen's Wake* (1813), and, masquerading as collected material, in much of *The Jacobite Relics of Scotland* (1819–21): 'Bonny Kilmeny' and some of the songs are still worth reading. The travesty of 'The Shepherd' in Christopher ◊ North's 'Noctes Ambrosianae' exaggerates, but does not merely invent, Hogg's brashness and hard-drinking pugnacity. His *Domestic Manners and Private Life of Sir Walter Scott* (1834) offended J. G. Lockhart and led to prolonged controversy. [A I]

Works, ed. T. Thomson (1865) (selection; prose altered and cut); *Selected Poems*, ed. J. W. Oliver (1940).

E. C. Batho, *The Ettrick Shepherd* (1927) (with bibliography); L. Simpson, *J.H., A Critical Study* (1962); D. Craig, *Scottish Literature and the Scottish People* (1961).

Hogg, Thomas Jefferson (1792–1862). Biographer of Shelley. Born at Stockton-on-Tees, he was educated at Durham

Grammar School and in 1810 went to University College, Oxford, where he became intimate with Shelley. In 1811, he collaborated with the latter in a volume of burlesque, anti-monarchical and gothick verse, *Posthumous Fragments of Margaret Nicholson* (who had tried to assassinate George III in 1785). He remonstrated with the authorities who expelled Shelley, and was in turn sent down. He was put to study law; tried to seduce Harriet Westbrook, Shelley's first wife, placed under his protection in York (October 1811); and was more or less reconciled by 1813. He was called to the bar, and held various minor offices in the north. His reminiscences of Shelley's life at Oxford appeared in the *New Monthly Magazine* during 1832 (ed. R. A. Streatfeild, 1904) and 2 volumes of a *Life of Shelley* appeared in 1858 (ed. E. Dowden, 1906). He published a novel, travels and miscellaneous pieces. Hogg is obviously eccentric, and a great egotist; but he did have first-hand knowledge of some of what he writes. He also had access to Shelley's papers, but is extremely unreliable, though amusing and often lively. [AR]

F. L. Jones, 'Shelley and H.', *TLS* (23 June 1945). ◊Shelley (biographies).

Holinshed, Raphael (d. *c.* 1582). Historian. Little is known of this Warwickshire man except that he was employed by a printer called Reginald Wolfe, who planned a great history of the world. Wolfe died in 1573, leaving the work unfinished, and Holinshed became coordinating editor of that part dealing with England, Scotland and Ireland, which appeared in 2 volumes in 1577. Holinshed's *Chronicles of England, Scotland and Ireland* were revised and expanded in 3 volumes by a team of compilers in 1587. The importance of this second edition is that it formed the principal source for Shakespeare's plays on English history and for *Macbeth*. Beginning with Noah, Holinshed gave in a plain style a compilation from previous chroniclers and historians, including ◊ Geoffrey of Monmouth and those scholars like Polydore Vergil and Edward ◊ Hall who propagated the official 'Tudor Myth' which portrayed Henry VII as restoring peace to a troubled and divided England. [MJ]

Shakespeare's H.: An Edition of H.'s Chronicles, selected and ed. R. Hoseley (New York, 1968).
L. B. Campbell, *Shakespeare's 'Histories'* (San Marino, Calif., 1947); C. S. Lewis, *English Literature in the Sixteenth Century* (1954); A. and J. Nicoll, *H.'s Chronicle as Used in Shakespeare's Plays* (1927); E. M. W. Tillyard, *Shakespeare's History Plays* (1944).

Home, Alexander. ◊ Hume, Alexander.

Home, Henry (Lord Kames) (1696–1782). Scottish judge, critic and philosopher. Privately educated, called to the Scottish bar in 1723 and raised to the bench in 1752, Kames was a friend and patron of Hume and a friend of Adam ◊ Smith, Hugh ◊ Blair, Lord Monboddo, Thomas ◊ Reid, Boswell and Benjamin Franklin. His attempted refutation of Hume (*Essays on the Principles of Morality and Natural Religion*, published anonymously in 1751) provoked a Church campaign against them both. Kames's most influential work, the *Elements of Criticism* (1762), tries to establish an aesthetic based on reason and the facts of human nature rather than on authority; he demonstrates the consequences of his theoretical position by much detailed discussion of passages by Shakespeare. Kames also published historical and educational essays, legal works, and (a typical interest among Scottish intellectuals of his time) *The Gentleman Farmer* (1776). [AI]

A. F. Tytler, Lord Woodhouselee, *Memoirs of the Honourable H.H. of Kames* (1807); E. C. Mossner, *The Life of David Hume* (1954); H. W. Randall, *The Critical Theory of Kames* (Northampton, Mass., 1944); G. Saintsbury, *History of English Criticism* (1911); J. W. H. Atkins, *English Literary Criticism: Seventeenth and Eighteenth Centuries* (1951).

Home, John (1722–1808). Scottish minister and *littérateur*. His blank-verse tragedy *Douglas*, neo-classic in form and based on an old Scots ballad, was produced with great success in Edinburgh in 1756 and at Covent Garden in 1757. It was overestimated by his cousin David ◊ Hume and by many Scottish contemporaries. Evangelical objections to the stage, however, forced him to resign his Berwickshire parish and for a time to move to London, where he wrote other, diminishingly successful plays and was tutor to the Prince of Wales, later George III. In retirement in Edinburgh from 1779, Home was an important social influence in the Edinburgh of Henry ◊ Mackenzie and the young Scott. [MJ]

Works, ed., with Life, H. Mackenzie (1822).
A. E. Gipson, *J.H.* (Caldwell, Idaho, 1917); W. J.

Bate, *From Classic to Romantic* (1946); E. C. Mossner, *The Life of David Hume* (1954).

Hood, Thomas (1799–1845). Poet, humorist and journalist. Born in London, the son of a bookseller, he had a brief period as a clerk and engraver, but during a stay with relatives in Dundee for his health he began writing for local journals. He combined engraving with journalism on his return to London, becoming the sub-editor of the *London Magazine* (1821–3). All his life Hood (often in financial trouble) continued this journalistic hack-work, editing and contributing to *The Gem* (1829), the *Comic Annual* (1830–9), the *New Monthly Magazine* (1841–3) and *Hood's Magazine* (1843). He was a poet of real power, but too much of his work failed in the end because of the rush of writing. He was a friend of Lamb, Hazlitt and De Quincey, and can exploit their kind of fantastic humour, though he often disappoints with their 'quaintness'. His comic poetry, more to modern taste than his serious work (and now valued more fairly than it once was), is marked by extreme competence in the use of funny verbal play for (sometimes) serious purposes, in the tradition of Swift. Of his serious poems, the best known are *The Dream of Eugene Aram* (in *The Gem*, 1829; 1831, etc.) and the bitter *The Song of the Shirt* (1843), a protest against sweated labour, which made *Punch* (in which it appeared) a successful periodical. Hood also wrote an unsuccessful novel, *Tylney Hall* (1834, etc.), and a series of sketches, *Up the Rhine* (1840), satirizing English tourists. His works include *Odes and Addresses* (1825), *The Plea of the Midsummer Fairies* (1827) and *Whims and Oddities* (1826, 1827). [AR]

Works, ed., with notes by his son, T. Hood (7 vols., 1862; 10 vols., 1869–73); *Poetical Works*, ed. W. Jerrold (1906; 1907); *Poems*, ed. C. Dyment (1948) (selection).
W. Jerrold, *T.H., His Life and Times* (1907); L. A. Marchand, *Letters of T.H.* (1945); 'H.; the Language of Poetry', *TLS* (19 September 1952); J. C. Reid, *T.H.* (1963).

Hooker, Richard (c. 1554–1600). Anglican divine. Born at Heavitree, near Exeter, Hooker went to Corpus Christi, Oxford, in 1568, becoming a Fellow of the college in 1577. He married in 1581, and was then presented to the living of Drayton Beauchamp, near Aylesbury in Buckinghamshire. In 1585 he was appointed Master of the Temple, but in 1591, having begun his most important work, *Of the Laws of Ecclesiastical Polity*, he asked to be given a country living in order to have time to complete it. He was accordingly presented to the living of Boscombe near Salisbury, and in 1595 to the living of Bishopsbourne in Kent. Hooker's massive defence of the *via media* represented by the Church of England between the Roman Catholic position on the one hand and the Puritan position on the other appeared in several stages. The first 4 books of the *Ecclesiastical Polity* were published in 1593; the long fifth book in 1597; the sixth and eighth books first appeared in an edition of 1648, and the seventh in an edition of 1662. Hooker appears to have completed all 8 books of the *Ecclesiastical Polity* before his death, and though the history of the 3 books published posthumously is obscure, it seems that they are substantially Hooker's work. The most distinguishing quality of the greatest of all apologias for the Church of England is its moderation. The book is directed primarily against the Puritan extremists, since by the time it appeared the Roman Catholic threat to the Church of England was all but past. Hooker denied the Puritan belief in the sole authority of Scripture, and asserted in modification of it the value of human reason and the natural law. He did not reject the authority of Scripture, and indeed criticized the Roman position for its insufficient reliance upon it, but he would not be drawn into the opposite extreme in reaction against Rome. The balance of Catholic and reformed elements in the Anglican position suited precisely the balance of his mind. The balance and reasonableness of the *Ecclesiastical Polity* is reflected in its style: in general grave and lucid with no marked mannerism, but on occasion rising to a climax of power. The most important biography of Hooker is Izaak Walton's *Life* (1665), printed with notes, in Keble's edition of the works. Indispensable biographical and textual information is provided by C. J. Sisson, *The Judicious Marriage of Mr Hooker and the Birth of The Laws of Ecclesiastical Polity* (1940). Sisson disposes of the myth of Hooker's unfortunate marriage and the destruction of the manuscripts of the last 3 books of the *Ecclesiastical Polity* by his wife after his death – the principal inaccuracies of Walton's *Life*. [DELC]

Works, ed. J. Keble (3 vols., 1836; revised edn, R. W. Church and F. Paget, 1888); *H.'s*

Ecclesiastical Polity, ed. R. Bayne (2 vols., Everyman, 1907) (first 5 books); *H.'s Ecclesiastical Polity*, viii, ed. R. A. Houk (Columbia U.P., 1931).
L. S. Thornton, *R.H. A Study of His Theology* (1924); G. Hillerdal, *Reason and Revelation in R.H.* (Lund, 1962); J. S. Marshall, *H. and the Anglican Tradition* (1963); E. T. Davies, *The Political Ideas of R.H.* (1946); F. J. J. Shirley, *R.H. and Contemporary Political Ideas* (1949); P. Munz, *The Place of H. in the History of Thought* (1952).

Hope, Alec Derwent (1907–   ). Australian poet. Born at Cooma, New South Wales, he attended Sydney University, from which he won a scholarship to Oxford. Back in Australia, he became a practising psychologist as well as a lecturer in English at Melbourne University. In 1951 he was appointed Professor of English at Canberra University College. After the war Hope published poems in magazines, and his calculatedly impolite attacks on contemporary values were already influential before the appearance of *The Wandering Islands* (1955). In his critical writing he has refused to make allowances for home-grown products, and he helped towards Australia's emergence as the first of the Commonwealth countries to reject double values in its literary judgements. A second collection, *Poems*, was published in 1960.

Much of Hope's originality lies in his presentation of themes of 20th-century disintegration in polished, traditional verse-forms. Many readers were shocked by his treatment of sex, which he sees as one of the remedies for a growing sense of isolation. Another remedy is an involvement in artistic creation. Hope's work is unified by a recognizably individual tone of voice. He achieves his vivid visual and aural effects by an exact placing of the unexpected word, and his satirical astringency by the surprising juxtaposition of verifiable aspects of experience. [P T]

Collected Poems (1966).
V. Buckley, *Essays in Poetry, Mainly Australian* (1957); W. A. Suchting, 'The Poetry of A.D.H.', *Meanjin*, XXI, 2 (Winter, 1962); B. Argyle, 'The Poetry of A.D.H.', *Journal of Commonwealth Literature*, 3 (July 1967).

Hope, Anthony (pseud. of Sir Anthony Hope Hawkins) (1863–1933). Novelist. He was born at Clapton, son of a clergyman schoolmaster, educated at Marlborough

and Balliol, and launched upon adult life with three careers open to him: politics, law and literature. Within six years he was an up-and-coming barrister, had stood as a Liberal parliamentary candidate, and published 5 novels. But in 1894 he achieved overnight fame with *The Prisoner of Zenda*, the classic swashbuckling Ruritanian romance, and later in the same year with *Dolly Dialogues*, a delicately witty satire on the London season; thereafter he concentrated on writing. Of his many subsequent novels, the best-known are *Rupert of Hentzau* (1898), *Sophy of Kravonia* (1906) and *The Great Miss Driver* (1908). *The Prisoner of Zenda* was dramatized in 1896 and Hope then wrote other plays, full of event and melodrama in the style of the period. He joined the Ministry of Information in 1914, was knighted in 1918 and retired to Surrey, where he played the part of squire. Other novels include *Simon Dale* (1898) and *Tristram of Blent* (1901). His work was immensely popular, and widely borrowed and copied in other media, especially films and television, where action is more important than character. [J M]
Memories and Notes (1927).
Sir Charles Mallett, *A.H. and His Books* (1935).

Hopkins, Gerard Manley (1844–89). English poet. The eldest child of a prosperous middle-class family, Hopkins was educated at Highgate School and Balliol College, Oxford, where the influence of J. H. ◊ Newman and the Oxford Movement led him to the Roman Catholic Church in 1866. Two years later he joined the Society of Jesus. In 1877 he was ordained, and was priest in a number of parishes including a slum district of Liverpool, an experience which affected his poetry. In 1884 he became Classics Professor at University College, Dublin. In his lifetime Hopkins was hardly known as a poet, except to one or two friends. His poems were not published until 1918, in a volume edited by his friend Robert ◊ Bridges. He felt that the publication of his poems would have been contrary to his duty as a Jesuit (he also feared the disapproval of his superiors) and in fact his startling experiments in rhythm and language would probably not have been appreciated by his contemporaries.

The tension between Hopkins's religious faith and his poetic genius is reflected in his poetry. It is a poetry of strain and excitement, of elated response and tortured interpretation. Its precision and intensity were such that Hopkins often found it necessary to fashion new words and new associations of words to express his meaning. He revived archaic and dialect words – he was influenced by medieval and Welsh traditions of verse – and combined and hyphenated words in order to suggest new possibilities of meaning and feeling through ordinary overworked language. He used devices such as alliteration and internal rhyme with an acutely sensitive ear for the sound texture of his poems, and arranged his words not according to the demands of conventional syntax but according to the pulse and tone of their meaning. Hopkins was a skilled draughtsman and had a deep interest in painting. This went with his concern for fundamental beauty and the form and pattern that established it. From his feeling for the essential quality that lay behind what the eye perceived Hopkins developed his theory of 'inscape' and 'instress'. 'Inscape' described the unique intrinsic pattern of objects and experiences, while 'instress' described the energy that generated 'inscape'. Hopkins was always trying to throw new light on reality, suddenly to focus the reader's attention on a fundamental quality or relationship that had not been illuminated before.

Hopkins's involvement with the arrangement of language in the richest and most meaningful way brought a new approach to rhythm and metre. He evolved a rhythmic system, which he called 'sprung rhythm', in which language, syntax and sound were geared to the natural qualities of the experience described and the emotional response to it. In 'The Windhover' the heaving movement of the rhythm imitates not only the strong rise and fall of the bird but the precarious elation of the poet, and the rhyme and repetition of sounds are rhythmically bound together in mutual support and association. 'Sprung rhythm' dispensed with conventional metrical feet and allowed the words themselves to create the rhythmic pattern. It therefore had a flexibility and a quality of movement that was quite new to English poetry, although it echoed the medieval alliterative poets. Hopkins frequently used stress-marks to indicate emphasized and unaccented syllables – the latter he termed 'outriders' – and these also influenced the speed of the verse. Intrinsic to 'sprung rhythm' were the almost abrupt variations of line length, the splitting of words between lines and the running together of lines. These in their turn were part of Hopkins's conception of 'inscape' – they helped to bind and unify the poem. There were times, however, when his rhythms come near to disaster. 'The Wreck of the Deutschland', his first sustained use of 'sprung rhythm', has some strained patches, and in 'The Loss of the Euridice' Hopkins's rather prosaic language refuses to be forced into the rhythmic patterns required of it.

Hopkins was much influenced by Duns Scotus, who emphasized the unique quality that characterizes each individual and object. Hopkins felt that poetry was the result of the mutual reaction of the poet's individualism and that of some particularity of external nature. Many of his poems were concerned with the response to nature, and with the investigation of associations between nature, God and man. There is frequently a tormented doubt and a harsh ruthlessness in Hopkins's poetry, particularly in the late 'terrible' sonnets, that produces a creative clash with the confidence of faith. Hopkins deals with emotional and spiritual complexities with an immediacy which is itself startling. Nature seems to quicken and grow as one reads him. Christ becomes a solid and human reality whom the poet addresses with a colloquial directness. Most of Hopkins's poems reveal layers of meaning which his extraordinarily original language and metric innovations sustain and elucidate – God can be simultaneously a living detail and a universal presence. The fusion of nature and religious faith results in qualities that are both toughly sensuous and inspirationally spiritual. Hopkins was in many ways a 'modern' poet writing before his time and, once discovered, his poetry was profoundly influential, particularly on the poets writing in the 1930s. [J R C]

Poems, 4th edn, ed. W. H. Gardner and N. H. Mackenzie (1967); *Letters and Correspondence*, ed. C. C. Abbott (2 vols., 1935; revised 1955), and *Further Letters* (1938; revised 1956); *Notebooks and Papers*, ed. H. House (1937); *Journals and Papers*, ed. H. House and G. Storey (1959); *Sermons and Devotional Writings*, ed. C. Devlin (1959); *A. H. Reader*, ed. J. Pick (1953); *G.M.H.*, ed. W. H. Gardner (Penguin Poets, 1953).
W. H. Gardner, *G.M.H.* (2 vols. 1944–9); A. Heuser, *The Shaping Vision of G.M.H.* (1958); The Kenyon Critics, *G.M.H.* (1949).

Houghton, Lord. ◊ Milnes, Richard Monckton.

Housman, A(lfred) E(dward) (1859–1936). Classical scholar and poet. The finest textual critic among classical scholars of his time, and also the fiercest controversialist. As a poet, his range is extremely narrow in subject matter, mood and form, and his total production of poems in a long life was very small, but the intensity and sincerity of his pessimistic view of life and his meticulous verse craftsmanship made him one of the most widely read poets of his time. Housman had expected as an undergraduate to take a First in Greats at Oxford but concentrated so much on textual scholarship that he was ill-equipped in ancient history and philosophy and did not even obtain a Pass degree. This failure, which was followed by ten years of obscure work in the Civil Service in London, soured his nature, though his contributions to classical journals eventually earned him a professorship at London University, which was followed by one at Cambridge. With great gifts for affection and friendship, he was constitutionally a homosexual, and this fact, combined with his early failure, made him painfully shy and reserved. He was an atheist in religion, but a patriotic Tory in politics. His classical training, apart from one or two translations and poems on historical themes, does not show itself in his English poems, except in a certain fastidiousness of vocabulary and regard for terseness and sometimes for epigrammatic point. The setting of the poems is an English countryside in which young men lament the passing of time, curse the contrary nature of the universe, rejoice sadly in transient beauty or pleasure, are sometimes hanged and often enlist in the army and are killed. Housman's obsessed fascination with soldiers is a trait often shown by homosexuals of a repressed kind.

His periods of poetic productivity were intermittent, but intense. In his famous lecture, 'The Name and Nature of Poetry' (1933), he shocked many of his Cambridge hearers by denigrating the then very fashionable 'difficult' poetry of the Metaphysicals and by asserting that the excitement felt both in the composition of poetry and its recognition, is something physical and has almost no connexion with a poem's 'meaning'. I. A. ◊ Richards, coming out of the lecture, is reported to have said: 'Housman has put the clock back thirty years!' His theory in this lecture seems to apply at least very well to his own works. These lend themselves easily to parody and it is easy enough to point out that their world is an artificial one and their pessimism so wilful as to seem at times petty and even sentimental. Yet Housman's best poems have a thrilling and haunting quality, a memorableness, not easily conveyed by any description of their intellectual content; perhaps his poems, taken as a whole, are most significant when read as an expression, all the more intense for being indirect and impersonal, of one man's lifelong wistfulness and frustration. The mood which Housman felt consistently most readers feel at some time; and no English poet has expressed that mood more individually than Housman. In the aggressiveness, indeed savagery, of his prefaces to his editions of Juvenal and Manilius the frustration found another, very different outlet. [G S F]

A Shropshire Lad (1896); *Last Poems* (1922); *The Name and Nature of Poetry* (1933); *More Poems* (1936); *Complete Poems* (Penguin Poets, 1956); *Selected Prose*, ed. J. Carter (1961).
A. S. F. Gow, *A.E.H., A Sketch* (1936); Grant Richards, *H. 1897–1936* (1941); Ian Scott-Kilvert, *A.E.H.* (WTW, 1955).

Housman, Laurence (1865–1959). Dramatist and novelist. Brother of A. E. ◊ Housman and born at Bromsgrove, Worcestershire, he was educated at a local school and later studied painting in London. His earliest work consisted of fairy tales and poems illustrated by himself; his first popular success was *An Englishwoman's Love Letters,* published anonymously in 1900. A prolific writer of novels, plays, poems and fantasies, often on religious or political themes, he is remembered today for his royal pageants *Victoria Regina* (1934) and *Happy and Glorious* (1945). Once considered rather daring, they now appear completely innocuous. He published his autobiography, *The Unexpected Years,* in 1937. [P J K]

Howard, Henry, Earl of Surrey (1517–47). Poet. Born into one of the great families of England, he was educated at the Tudor and the French courts as friend and companion of the Duke of Richmond, bastard son of Henry VIII. In 1532 he married the daughter of the Earl of Oxford. He was present at Anne Boleyn's trial, and served under his father, the Duke of Norfolk, against the Pilgrimage of Grace in 1536. Briefly imprisoned in 1537, he distinguished himself three years later in the tournament in honour of Henry's fourth queen, Anne of Cleves, and was made Knight of the Garter in 1541. He witnessed the execution of his cousin, Catherine Howard, Henry's fifth wife. In 1542 and again in 1543 he was briefly imprisoned – for striking a courtier and for riotous behaviour during Lent. He was wounded at the siege of Montreuil in 1545 and was given command of Boulogne. The following year he lost a battle at St Étienne, was recalled to England, soon arrested on trumped-up charges of treason and beheaded.

Barely 30 at the time of his execution, Surrey now commands interest for his small poetic output rather than his dashing public career. In 1589 George ◊ Puttenham called him and Sir Thomas ◊ Wyatt 'the two chieftains' in 'a new company of courtly makers' of Henry VIII's reign. Both poets' work appeared posthumously in the same collection, and Surrey, the younger man by fourteen years, is usually regarded as Wyatt's disciple in the Petrarchan tradition. He was, in fact, the first English poet to react fully to the new teaching of classical literature by humanists like Erasmus and Colet as continued by such men as Roger ◊ Ascham and Sir John ◊ Cheke. Surrey's classical imitations and his translation of Books II and IV of Virgil's *Aeneid* are now thought to be the foundations of his literary development. In blank verse he strove to find English equivalents for Virgil's syntax, rhetoric, figures of speech and occasionally word-order, and his pioneering aim is more important for the history of English poetry than the unevenness of the translation itself.

As a 'courtly maker' the Elizabethans seem to have preferred Surrey to the greater poet, Wyatt; he was the only poet named on the title-page of ◊ Tottel's *Miscellany* (1557), the important and much-printed anthology in which the first 36 poems and 4 later ones were by Surrey. His amatory sonnets, Petrarchan in influence and theme, often use the rhyme-scheme now known as 'Shakespearean'. His poetry is smoother and more graceful than Wyatt's but less strong; some poems seem exercises rather than declarations of love.

Surrey's poems, mainly imitations or translations of Latin or Italian poets, were influential in the later 16th century through their metre, syntax and diction. His virtues included urbanity, control, clarity and precision. His most recent editor, Emrys Jones, has shown that, though a lesser poet than Wyatt, he was indeed – as Thomas Warton claimed in 1781 – 'the first classical English poet'. [MJ]

Poems, ed. E. Jones (1964); *The Poems*, ed. F. M. Padelford (revised edn, Seattle, 1928). E. Casady, *H.H., Earl of Surrey* (New York, 1938); H. W. Chapman, *Two Tudor Portraits* (1960).

Hudson, W(illiam) H(enry) (1841–1922). Naturalist and writer. Born near Buenos Aires in Argentina, of an American farming family. His schooling was haphazard, and he roamed freely on the pampas, watching the bird life with fascinated interest. A serious illness prevented him from ever doing outdoor work, and depression followed. In 1869 he left South America and went to live in London, where he survived for some years in poverty and loneliness. During the next thirty years he wrote much, but won little attention; his books included *The Purple Land* (1885) and some works of natural history such as *Argentine Ornithology* (1889) and *Birds in a Village* (1893). In 1901 he was awarded a Civil List pension, which enabled him to travel round Britain observing wild life, but it was not until the publication of *Green Mansions* (1904) that he won any measure of success. The haunting creation of Rima, the bird-girl, in this novel, became a much-loved literary figure, and helped to revive interest in Hudson's earlier work. His sensitive perception of the natural world, combined with a touch of the exotic from his alien background, aroused the admiration of a wide range of people, including Conrad. Hudson himself was a cold, sober man, who regarded himself more as a scientist than as a popular novelist. In the last years of his life he was too ill to do much writing, but he did publish an account of his childhood: *Far Away and Long Ago* (1918). [JM]

G. F. Wilson, 'A Bibliography of W.H.H.', *The Bookman* (July 1929).

Hughes, John or **Ceiriog** (1832–87). Welsh poet. Born in Llanarmon Dyffryn Ceiriog, Denbighshire, he moved to Manchester in 1849 where he became a railway clerk, and member of a literary society which had great influence on him. He returned to Wales in 1865 and was stationmaster at Llanidloes,

Towyn and Caer-sws. Inspired by the singer Idris Fychan, Ceiriog became a devotee of Welsh traditional airs and collected all he could find, together with their history and that of the harpists who played them. Much of his poetic work in fact consists of words composed with great virtuosity for a particular tune or air. They therefore satisfied a great popular demand for light entertainment of the sort which was fashionable in his day.

It would be a mistake, however, to dismiss Ceiriog merely as a popular entertainer. He has an important place in the development of the Welsh lyric of the 19th century, although he did also compose some poetry in the strict metres. He realized that setting words to music demands a special and exacting application, and he established an appropriate diction which was fluent, simple and melodious without being undignified. This is seen at its best in his 3 major lyrics 'Y Gwcw' ('The Cuckoo'), 'Nant y Mynydd' ('Mountain Brook') and 'Aros mae'r mynyddau mawr' ('The great mountains remain'). His pastoral poem 'Alun Mabon', though full of mawkish sentimentality, is still capable of moving us with its simplicity, its wedding of words and music, and its proof that poetry may be found in the ordinary life of a Welsh countryman and in his reaction to Nature. The Welsh lyric became a recognized literary form which was imitated by many versifiers, but which was to be revitalized by John ♢ Morris-Jones. [MR]

Collected Works (vols. i and ii, n.d.; vol. iii, 1888).

Hughes, Richard (Arthur Warren) (1900–). Novelist and poet. Born in Weybridge, Kent, of a Welsh family and educated at Charterhouse and Oriel College, Oxford. While he was a student his 1-act play *The Sister's Tragedy* was produced in London (1922; printed with other plays, 1924) and praised by Shaw. In the same year he published *Gipsy Night and Other Poems*; a second volume of collected poems, *Confessio Juvenis*, appeared in 1926. He travelled in America and the Caribbean and contributed to British and American literary journals. His best-known novels are *A High Wind in Jamaica* (also known as *The Innocent Voyage*) (1929; filmed 1965), a story of malevolent children and amiable pirates, and *In Hazard* (1938): he has also published

short stories (collected in *A Moment of Time*, 1926), and children's tales, such as *Gertrude's Child* (1966). During the Second World War he served in the Admiralty, and with J. D. Scott is the author of a volume in the official history of the war (on the Civil Service), *The Administration of War Production* (1956). [AR]

Hughes, Ted (1930–). Poet. Born in Yorkshire, though brought up in the West Country, he has said that the West Riding dialect, 'eloquent and emphatic', is the basis of his poetic tone. At Cambridge, where he was the slightly older contemporary of poets like Philip Hobsbaum and Peter Redgrove, he showed a special interest in anthropology and folklore, and a special admiration for the poems of D. H. Lawrence, whose *Birds, Beasts and Flowers* volume is the most obvious positive influence on him. He also admired Hopkins, as a nature poet rather than a religious poet, and the later Yeats. His great intuition as a poet is that, in an era of complex industrial and urban organization, nature continues to exist. His view of nature, however, is not a Wordsworthian one, but rather an admiration of the animal cunning and brutal single purpose that enables otters, thrushes and even snowdrops to survive. His poems on human topics similarly celebrate not human rationality and subtlety but a certain grim animal persistence. He was married to the very distinguished American woman poet, Sylvia Plath. The strength of his poems is in empathy, and a certain rough impatient energy, rather than in subtlety or balance. He is generally considered, along with Thom ♢ Gunn and Philip ♢ Larkin, as one of the three most distinguished English poets of his generation. He has greater force than either Larkin or Gunn but a much more uneven mastery of technique and, for all his surface vivacity, a much narrower range of human understanding and sympathy. [GSF]

The Hawk in the Rain (1957); *Lupercal* (1960); *Wodwo* (1968).
J. Press, *Rule and Energy* (1963); F. Grubb, *A Vision of Reality* (1965).

Hughes, Thomas (1822–96). Novelist and miscellaneous writer. Born at Uffington in Berkshire, the son of a country gentleman, he was educated at Rugby and Oriel College, and called to the bar (1848). He is best known as the author of the once enormously popular propagandist story *Tom Brown's Schooldays: By an Old Boy* (1857; ed. F. Sidgwick, 1913), in which he expounded the doctrine of 'muscular' Christianity, the beneficial effects on the soul of outdoor exercise, public-school 'discipline' and the sermons of Dr T. ◊ Arnold. Charles ◊ Kingsley was another expounder. The book certainly influenced adults by its romantic view of boarding school life (at Rugby), whatever effect it had on the children to whom they frequently presented it. Hughes produced a slightly less successful sequel, *Tom Brown at Oxford* (1861), and another well-known fictional work, *The Scouring of the White Horse, or the Long Vacation Ramble of a London Clerk* (1859), a discursive tale of rustic humours and topographical nostalgia about his birthplace. Hughes was an apostle of F. D. ◊ Maurice, contributing an introduction to the latter's *Christian Socialism* (1898), and writing a number of other works, including the biographies *Alfred the Great* (1869), *David Livingstone* (1889) and *A Layman's Faith* (1868). He was a Liberal M.P. (1865–74), an early proponent of the Cooperative movement and a County Court judge from 1882. [A R]

S. Selfe, *Chapters from the History of Rugby School. Together with Notes on the Characters and Incidents Depicted in 'Tom Brown's Schooldays'* (1910); E. C. Mack and W. H. G. Armytage, *T.H.* (1953).

Hulme, T(homas) E(rnest) (1883–1917). Philosopher and literary critic. Born at Endon, North Staffordshire, Hulme was educated at Newcastle-under-Lyme High School and St John's College, Cambridge. He was sent down for brawling in 1904. After two years studying independently in London he went to Canada for three months, then, in 1907, spent seven months in Brussels teaching English and learning French and German. His interests had now turned to philosophy. In 1911 he attended the Philosophical Congress at Bologna and travelled for three months in Italy. In 1812 he was re-admitted to Cambridge, largely through the intervention of Henri Bergson, whom he had impressed by his philosophical acumen. But his temperament was not academic and he soon left Cambridge, first for nine months in Berlin and then to settle in London. By now he was known as an admirer and translator of Bergson (*Introduction to Metaphysics*, 1913) and a friend of Ezra Pound

and other pioneering writers, artists and critics in the years immediately preceding the outbreak of the First World War. He translated Georges Sorel's *Réflexions sur la violence* (*Reflections on Violence*, 1916) and wrote frequently for the political and literary weekly the *New Age* under the stimulating editorship of A. R. ◊ Orage. Five of his poems, under the title 'Complete Poetical Works of T. E. Hulme', appeared in 1915 as an appendix to Ezra Pound's *Ripostes*. These are very short poems in which the precision and ordering of the images are all-important (◊ Imagism). Hulme continued his periodical articles after he joined up and went to France late in 1914. He was killed near Nieuport on 28 September 1917.

Hulme was a leader of the anti-romantic movement which has had such an effect on modern poetry and criticism. In his *New Age* articles he tried to establish a number of correlations and a set of oppositions: classicism, discipline, belief in original sin, 'the religious attitude', and hard, dry, precise writing were all recommended and were contrasted unfavourably with their opposites – romanticism ('spilt religion'), emotional self-indulgence, belief in human perfectibility, humanism, and 'the bringing in of some of the emotions that are grouped round the word infinite'. He declared himself as antipathetic to 'the *Weltanschauung* . . . of all philosophy since the Renaissance', exalted abstract and geometrical art over naturalistic art, and championed royalism against democracy. This elaborate set of correlations and oppositions was not generally accepted, though echoes of it are found often in T. S. Eliot's criticism. But in his insistence on clarity and precision of imagery he fathered Imagism and in his belief that 'it is the business of every honest man to clean the world of these sloppy dregs of the Renaissance' he helped to canalize certain anti-Romantic attitudes and to change poetic taste. Hulme's philosophy now seems confused and in some aspects sinister. But in rejecting any traditional definition of an appropriate poetic subject matter (such as Arnold's 'high seriousness'), in emphasizing craft rather than inspiration, in pointing to imagery and metaphor as the essential elements in poetry, and in stressing the absolute difference between mechanical form and the organic complexity of artistic form, he has had an influence on the criticism and the practice of poetry out of all proportion to the consistency and conclusiveness of his arguments.

Hulme's essays on art, literature and philosophy were collected and edited by Herbert Read as *Speculations* (1924). A less rewarding further gleaning is *Further Speculations* (ed. S. Hynes, 1955). [D D]

Alun R. Jones, *The Life and Opinions of T.E.H.* (1960); Michael Roberts, *T.E.H.* (1938); Raymond Williams, *Culture and Society 1780–1950* (1958); W. K. Wimsatt and Cleanth Brooks, *Literary Criticism: A Short History* (1957).

Hume or Home, Alexander (*c.* 1557–1609). Scots poet. Hume, the son of a Scottish judge, studied for the Scottish bar at St Andrews and in France, held some court appointments, turned to religion and in 1598 became minister of Logie, near Stirling. His *Hymns or Sacred Songs* (1599) include 'Of the Day Estivall', a sharp, lucid description of a summer day, virtually secular and Brueghelesque in effect, that is one of the few Scots poems which are at once fine and distinctively of the Renaissance. His other verse is less interesting, but his prose work *Ane Treatise of Conscience* (1594) is an early discussion of a theme which became increasingly important in Scottish literature. [A1]

Poems, ed. A. Lawson (S T S, 1902) (includes *Ane Treatise of Conscience*).
R. M. Fergusson, *A.H.* (1899).

Hume, David (1711–76). Philosopher and historian. Younger son of a small Berwickshire laird, Hume was born at Edinburgh and brought up on the family estate at Ninewells. Two or perhaps three years at Edinburgh University were followed by some dabbling in law and much private reading in classical and modern literature. A few months as a clerk in Bristol in 1734 were followed by three happy and productive years in France, where he composed his *Treatise of Human Nature* (1739–40) which was either ignored or misunderstood. Settling in Ninewells in 1740 to start afresh, he decided that the best way to put his ideas across to the public was in the lighter form of essays (*Essays Moral and Political*, 1741, 1742, 1748). *Philosophical Essays Concerning Human Understanding* (1748), which became in later editions *An Enquiry Concerning Human Understanding*, was followed by *An Enquiry Concerning the Principles of Morals* (1752; both ed. L. A. Selby-Biggs,

2nd edn 1902). Hume's reputation as a sceptic led to his failure to obtain the chair of Ethics and Pneumatical Philosophy at Edinburgh University in 1744; he spent a year in 1745–6 as companion to the mad young Marquess of Annandale, then two years as secretary to General St Clair on his military missions in Europe. He returned to Edinburgh in 1749 having saved enough to be henceforth financially independent. He was keeper of the Advocates' Library, Edinburgh (1751–7), access to whose 30,000 books enabled him to work on his *History of Great Britain* (1754–6), the major task of his later years, of which the later volumes (1759, 1762, 8 vols., 1763) dealt only with England. He paid visits to London, but was more at home in Paris, where he was private secretary to the British ambassador (1763–5), Embassy Secretary (1763–5) and chargé d'affaires (July–November 1765), and where he found friendship and adulation. He was in London as Under-Secretary of State, Northern Department, briefly in 1767–8, and in 1768 settled down in Edinburgh 'Body & Soul without casting the least Thought of Regreat to London, or even to Paris', to spend his last years living among his friends with epicurean ease and to die with that heroic tranquillity which so astonished the religious. Hume was a good and kind man, considered by Adam Smith 'as approaching as nearly to the idea of a perfectly wise and virtuous man, as perhaps the nature of human frailty will admit', but such virtues in a religious sceptic outraged the orthodox, such as James ◊ Beattie. Hume's *Dialogues on Natural Religion*, a suavely ironic dialogue between a sceptic, a deist and an orthodox Christian, and a classic destruction of the traditional 'argument from design' for the existence of God, was published posthumously in 1779 (ed. N. Kemp Smith, 1935; 2nd edn 1947).

Hume's examination of the consequences of Locke's doctrine of ideas led him to provide a different basis for belief. The origin of morality Hume, like Francis ◊ Hutcheson before him, found in the sentiments of approval and disapproval which naturally arise in men on contemplating particular actions, but he went on to extend this basing of belief on feeling to *all* value judgements and further still to all reasoning that is not 'abstract reasoning concerning quantity and number'. Such reasoning (which, in Hume's view, involves belief rather than knowledge) is referable to human feelings, instincts, emotions (all of which are included in Hume's term 'passions'). 'Reason is and ought to be the slave of the passions.' On causation, for example, Hume remarked: 'This connexion which we *feel* in the mind, this customary transition of the imagination from one object to its usual attendant, is the sentiment or impression from which we form the idea of power or necessary connexion. Nothing farther is in the case.' Belief for Hume was a passion, dependent on the nature of the human mind. 'All *probable* reasoning is nothing but a species of sensation. 'Tis not solely in music and poetry, we must follow our taste and sentiment, but likewise in philosophy.' If belief is a passion, it is none the less real for Hume. We believe that the sun will rise tomorrow, and rightly act on this belief, even though the proposition 'the sun will not rise tomorrow' cannot be shown to be false. Since for Hume natural beliefs are not dependent on rational knowledge, they cannot be destroyed by rational doubt. 'Nature breaks the force of all sceptical arguments in time.' Thus for Hume the problem of truth in questions of fact and existence (as opposed to abstract questions of number and relationship) is referable to psychology rather than to logic. He saw himself as the prophet of a new science of human and general nature grounded on psychological fact. [D D]

The Philosophical Works (4 vols., 1826, 1836, 1854); The Letters, ed. J. Y. T. Grieg (2 vols., 1932); New Letters, ed. R. Klibansky and E. C. Mossner (1954).
J. Laird, H.'s Philosophy of Human Nature (1932); N. Kemp Smith, The Philosophy of D.H. (1941); E. C. Mossner, The Life of D.H. (1954; revised 1971); T. E. Jessop, A Bibliography of D.H. and of Scottish Philosophy (1938); J. V. Price, The Ironic H. (Austin, Texas, 1965).

Hunt, (James Henry) Leigh (1784–1859). Poet and journalist. Born at Southgate, Middlesex, the son of an improvident preacher and tutor from Barbados. He was educated at Christ's Hospital, where he learned Italian and started to write pastiche verse, following Gray, Collins, Thomson and Spenser; some of these *Juvenilia* were published in 1801. His career as a journalist is distinguished. He was one of the first to produce balanced and comprehensive drama criticism based on regular attendance at the theatres (for his brother's *News*, 1805–7; and for the quarterly *Reflector*, 1810–11). In these and in other essays, he shows a delight in music and the visual arts which was missing from much of the age's criticism. The hundreds of essays which he published in several periodicals that he conducted himself, as well as in other magazines, year books, collections and keepsakes, are chatty, written with obvious enjoyment to give enjoyment, but, though influential in promoting interest in Italian and other foreign literature and in enthusiastically introducing new poets (his span reaches from Keats to Tennyson), they survive now only in passages or an occasional piece. From 1813 to 1815, he and his brother were imprisoned for attacking the Prince Regent in the *Examiner*, his brother's Sunday paper with which he was connected from 1808 to 1821. Leigh Hunt was not really a political figure: his political writing was symptomatic rather than causative. His occasional essays, observing and reflecting, resemble those of Steele or Goldsmith rather than suggesting any political action or programme. As a poet, Hunt is best known for the influence, not very fortunate, which he exercised over Keats at the beginning of the younger man's career. Hunt was widely attacked for political reasons in the Tory organs like the *Quarterly Review*, and Keats was associated with him in these sallies. Hunt had some interesting technical talents: his use of run-on couplets; his pleasant facility for adapting Italian poetry to English uses; and his light fanciful imagination. He suffered, however, from a failure of feeling and imagination in carrying out his ideas. This comes out in his unsureness in handling language and is often quaintly called his 'vulgarity', with interesting implications about the 'ownership' of language. Keats soon became aware that his own tremendous genius had far more linguistic power and sureness and left the 'lovely woman in a rural spot' to Hunt, but not before he had been labelled a 'Cockney poet'.

The Story of Rimini (1816; revised 1817; unrevised again 1819) is based on Dante's story of Paolo and Francesca, but deals with it in a pathetic rather than tragic fashion. His other works included: *The Descent of Liberty: A Masque* (1815), celebrating the fall of Napoleon; *Foliage, or Poems Original and Translated* (1818); and *Captain Sword and Captain Pen* (1835), his most vigorous verse, written 'to show the horrors of War' and to attack its leaders. Of his work, 'Abou ben Adhem' and 'Jenny Kissed Me' are sometimes anthologized. He also published, translated, modernized, selected and anthologized the poems of others. In 1822, he went to Italy at the invitation of Shelley and Byron, to assist with a projected periodical, *The Liberal*. Shelley was drowned soon after; Hunt was present at his cremation. In Italy Byron lost interest, and Hunt almost starved. In 1828, he published a volume of useful notes, and not unjustified recriminations, *Lord Byron and Some of His Contemporaries*. Hunt lived and wrote well into the Victorian era. One of his best works is his *Autobiography* (3 vols., 1850; revised by the author 1860; ed. E. Blunden, World's Classics, 1928; ed. J. Morpurgo, 1949). [AR]

The Poetical Works, ed. H. S. Milford (1923); *Essays and Poems*, ed. R. B. Johnson (2 vols., 1891); *Dramatic Essays*, ed. W. Archer and R. W. Lowe (1894); *Dramatic Criticism* (New York, 1949), *Literary Criticism* (1956), and *Political and Occasional Essays* (New York, 1962), ed. L. H. and C. Houtchens; *Essays*, ed. J. B. Priestley (Everyman, 1929); *Correspondence*, ed. T. Hunt (his eldest son) (2 vols., 1862).

E. Blunden, *L.H.* (1930); A. Landré, *L.H.* (2 vols., Paris, 1935–6); I. Jack, *English Literature, 1815–1832* (1963) (bibliography); *Cambridge Bibliography of English Literature* (for periodicals edited by L.H.).

Hunt, Violet (1866–1942). Novelist and short-story writer. Born in Durham, the daughter of W. A. Hunt, one of the pre-Raphaelite group of painters and a member of Rossetti's circle. She was educated with the daughters of William Morris and Burne-Jones. She gave up her study of art and became a successful novelist. Her best novels are *Unkist, Unkind!* (1897), *The Wife of Altamont* (1910), *The House of Many Mirrors* (1910) and *The Tiger Skin* (1924). Her short stories appeared in 2 series of *Tales of the Uneasy* (1911 and 1925). She wrote a biography of the ever-controversial *Wife of Rossetti* (1932) and published a volume of gossipy memoirs, *The Flurried Years* (1926). [AR]

Hurd, Richard (1720–1808). Miscellaneous writer and cleric. Educated at Emmanuel College, Cambridge; his edition of Horace's *Ars poetica* (1749) introduced him to ◊ Warburton and he thereafter became known as a divine and a critic. In his clerical career, his publications include an essay opposing David Hume, 3 volumes of *Sermons, Moral and Political Dialogues* (1759) and a complete edition of Warburton's works (1788); he

became Bishop of Lichfield (1775), Preceptor to the Prince of Wales (1776) and Bishop of Winchester (1781); he refused an offer of the Primacy from his friend George III in 1783. Hurd is best known for his *Letters on Chivalry and Romance* (1762), in which he discusses medieval writing with some attempt to understand its differences from the admired classical models of his day. He thus takes his part in the growing interest in the 'gothick', with such writers as Gray, ◊ Percy, and Horace ◊ Walpole. [AR]

Correspondence (with William Mason and Thomas Gray), ed. L. Whibley (1932); Horace Walpole, *Letters*, ed. W. Lewis (Yale U.P., in progress).

F. Kilvert, *Memoirs of the Life and Writings of Bishop H.* (1860).

Hutcheson, Francis (1694–1746). Philosopher. An Ulster Scot educated at Glasgow University, he conducted a Protestant Academy in Dublin before returning to Glasgow in 1729 as Professor of Moral Philosophy; he was the first Scottish philosophy professor to teach in English instead of in Latin. His principal works are *An Inquiry into the Original of Our Ideas of Beauty and Virtue* (1725), *An Essay on the Nature and Conduct of the Passions* (1728) and *A System of Moral Philosophy* (1755). Hutcheson developed ◊ Locke's concept of 'inner senses' in a much more literal way and in particular transmutes ◊ Shaftesbury's metaphor of 'moral sense' into a technical 'sense' which perceives good and evil as directly as the eye perceives colour and proportion. Hutcheson retreats into moral optimism and theological orthodoxy, but ◊ Hume pursued the consequences of Hutcheson's view that, in effect, moral judgements are non-rational. Hutcheson equates the moral sense with a tendency to approve actions that make for the common good; he is thus an early Utilitarian, and in fact coined the phrase usually attributed to Bentham, 'the greatest happiness of the greatest number'. [AI]

W. R. Scott, *F.H.* (1900); J. Bonar, *Moral Sense* (1930); L. Stephen, *History of English Thought in the Eighteenth Century* (1876); N. Kemp Smith, *The Philosophy of David Hume* (1941); D. D. Raphael, *The Moral Sense* (1947).

Huxley, Aldous (Leonard) (1894–1963). Novelist and miscellaneous writer. Born at Godalming, Surrey, the son of the biologist Thomas Henry ◊ Huxley and a great-nephew of Matthew Arnold, he was educated at Eton and Balliol College, Oxford. A serious disease of the eye causing virtual blindness (which profoundly influenced his life) interrupted his preliminary medical studies, and on his partial recovery he completed his degree in English in 1915. He became a journalist on the staff of the *Athenaeum* (1919–20) and drama critic of the *Westminster Gazette* (1920–21). For most of the 1920s he lived in Italy writing fiction, and there became a friend of D. H. Lawrence (who appears as Rampion in *Point Counter Point*). In 1934, Huxley travelled in Central America, and he settled permanently in California in 1937. His early novels, *Crome Yellow* (1921), *Antic Hay* (1923) and *Those Barren Leaves* (1925), are gay, clever and cynical novels of conversation; the characters are of no great importance amid the ideas bombinating in a vacuum.

The intelligent handling of *ideas* of good and evil (which Huxley was always interested in) is detached and effective: these are typical twenties works. Later, however, Huxley seems to have felt more need of being a serious proponent of some of the ideas, and then the puppet-like types become less acceptable; the characters in the later novels speak 'detachable essays' with the discomfort to the reader of feeling that the author is trying too hard. Huxley was greatly fascinated by the idea of psychological 'conditioning' and this is the fear that underlies much of his fantasy writing about the future. His later novels include *Point Counter Point* (1928); *Brave New World* (1932), with its horrible picture of the results of controlled reproduction (he published a less pessimistic supplement, *Brave New World Revisited*, 1959); and *Eyeless in Gaza* (1936). In *After Many a Summer* (1939), the search for an elixir produces 200-year-old recessive apes and Mr Propter gives Huxley's comment. Huxley had the typical English intellectual's irreconcilable dilemma of idealizing art and seeing reality as an experience of physical and physiological disgust. This state of mind finally led him to the study of mysticism as the source of the true good (e.g. in *The Perennial Philosophy*, 1946), and it predictably led him into some rather violent sensationalist writing in his later fiction. Huxley as an essayist has a wide and exotic range of information, and became greatly concerned with the possibilities of mental release offered by narcotics, such as mescalin and peyote and other non-habit-forming drugs. His collections of essays include: *On the Margin* (1923); *Proper Studies* (1927); *Ends and Means* (1937); *Collected Essays* (1960); *Literature and Science* (1963). *The Devils of Loudun* (1952) is a deservedly famous study of a medieval case of mass-hysteria. [AR]

Letters, ed. G. Smith (1969).
L. A. Huxley, *This Timeless Moment* (1969) (account of last years and survival after death); J. Brooke, *A.H.* (WTW, 1954); J. A. Atkins, *A.H.: A Literary Study* (1956); A. Henderson, *A.H.* (1964) (with bibliography); P. Bowering, *A.H.: A Study of the Major Novels* (1969).

Huxley, Sir Julian (Sorell) (1887–   ). Biologist, humanist and writer. The elder brother of Aldous ◊ Huxley and son of T. H. ◊ Huxley, he was born in Godalming, Surrey, and educated at Eton and Balliol College, Oxford, where he studied zoology (and won a poetry prize). He taught this subject at Oxford, the Rice Institute, Texas, and King's College, London (professor, 1925–7), and was director of the London Zoo (1935–42). He has lectured at institutions all over the world, and travelled widely as a member of government committees and commissions. His appointment as Director-General of UNESCO (1946–8) caused some uproar because of his atheism. He was made an F.R.S. in 1938 and knighted in 1958. Huxley has edited many publications; he is a lucid and prolific writer. Among his best-known works of more general interest are: *Essays of a Biologist* (1923); *Essays in Popular Science* (1926); *At the Zoo* (1936); *Evolution: The Modern Synthesis* (1942; revised 1963); *Soviet Genetics and World Science* (1949), a well-documented attack on Lysenko and a passionate demand for freedom of scientific investigation; *Evolution in Action* (1953), a series of lectures given on the B.B.C.; *Conservation of Wild Life in Central and East Africa* (1961); *Essays of a Humanist* (1964); and *Charles Darwin and His World* (1965). [AR]

Huxley, T(homas) H(enry) (1825–95). Biologist and controversialist. Born at Ealing, the son of a schoolmaster there, he was educated at his father's school, then in Coventry, and at London University, where he studied medicine at Charing Cross Hospital. His interest was in comparative anatomy. He was a doctor in the navy, and his work in observing sea organisms made him an F.R.S. in 1851. During the next few years he published much, and lived by teaching. He was a pioneer in scientific education and a brilliant popularizer: he incurred Arnold's displeasure for enthusiastically promoting science in place of more traditional humane subjects. When Darwin's *Origin of Species* appeared in 1859, Huxley, though he had reservations about the theory, defended the book in many violent controversies against Gladstone and others, often in the columns of the *Nineteenth Century* and other periodicals. Huxley was an energetic fighter, a baiter of orthodox religionists (he invented the term 'agnosticism'), and operated as a champion of free investigation and speech. He used his biological knowledge as a basis for excursions into philosophy. He was more speculative and eloquent than Darwin, who left much of the controversy to him. Huxley believed that natural processes could not be endowed with moral ends; and that man's moral sense is unique and comes from his conscious struggle against necessity. His chief non-technical works are *Man's Place in Nature* (1863), *Lay Sermons, Addresses and Reviews* (1870), which includes his celebrated paper, 'The Physical Basis of Life' (1868), and *Evolution and Ethics* (1893). [A R]

Collected Essays (9 vols., 1894).
L. Huxley, *Life and Letters of T.H.H.* (2 vols., 1900); H. C. Bibby, *T.H.H.: Scientist, Humanist, Educator* (1959); W. Irvine, *Darwin, H. and Evolution* (1961); *T.H.H.* (WTW, 1960) (with bibliography); A. O. J. Cockshutt, *in Unbelievers: English Agnostic Thought, 1840–90* (1964); R. W. Clark, *The Huxleys* (1918).

Hyde, D. ◊ de hIde, D.

Hyde, Edward. ◊ Clarendon, Edward Hyde, Earl of.

I

Imagism. A poetic movement begun in England in 1912 largely under the direction of Ezra Pound and drawing for its principles (though not always directly) on the ideas of T. E. ⟡ Hulme, especially on Hulme's insistence on the precise and disciplined use of visual images in order to produce a 'dry and hard' poetry. Pound, reporting the English poetic scene for *Poetry* (Chicago) in January 1912, described the *Imagistes* (the final 'e' was soon dropped and they became simply Imagists) as 'in opposition to the numerous and unassembled writers who busy themselves with dull and interminable effusions, and who seem to think that a man can write a good long poem before he learns to write a good short one, or even before he learns to produce a good single line'. An article on the critical position of the Imagists by F. S. ⟡ Flint in the March 1913 issue of *Poetry* stated the three basic Imagist rules: '1. Direct treatment of the "thing", whether subjective or objective. 2. To use absolutely no word that did not contribute to the presentation. 3. As regards rhythm: to compose in sequence of the musical phrase, not in sequence of a metronome.' The Imagists in England published their poetry first in the *New Freewoman* and then in its successor the *Egoist*. But the movement was Anglo-American. Poets contributing to the *Egoist* included, in addition to Pound, Richard Aldington, H. D. (Hilda Doolittle), F. S. Flint, John Gould Fletcher, Amy Lowell and (though he was never formally an Imagist) D. H. Lawrence. In 1914 appeared *Des Imagistes: An Anthology*, a project of Pound's which included, besides substantial representation of the poetry of Aldington and H.D., poems by Pound and Flint and one poem each by seven other writers including Amy Lowell and James Joyce. Pound then lost interest in the movement and the leadership was assumed by the American Amy Lowell, who brought out 3 Imagist anthologies (each entitled *Some Imagist Poets*) in the U.S.A. in 1915, 1916 and 1917. Selections from all 4 volumes were included in a retrospective *Imagist Anthology* (1930). The Imagists were influenced by French Symbolism, by Chinese and Japanese poetry and Japanese pictorial art, and (in Aldington's case) by Greek lyric poetry. They aimed at a combination of precision and suggestiveness in language and at freer rhythms. Their revolt against post-Romantic vagueness and lushness had a permanent effect on the poetry of Eliot and his generation, but their lack of interest in poetic form suggested by their concentration on the very short poem limited their own achievement. They were, however, one of the streams which flowed into the revolution in poetic taste which exalted Donne at the expense of Spenser and Milton and placed Hopkins above Tennyson. Limited in practice and inadequate in theory, Imagism nevertheless has a significant place in the development of modern poetry both in Britain and in the United States. [D D]

Stanley K. Coffman, *Imagism: A Chapter for the History of Modern Poetry* (Norman, Oklahoma, 1951); D. Daiches, *Poetry and the Modern World* (Chicago, 1940); Glenn Hughes, *Imagism and the Imagists: A Study in Modern Poetry* (Stanford, Calif., 1931); Robert H. Ross, *The Georgian Revolt: Rise and Fall of a Poetic Ideal 1910–1922* (1967).

Inchbald, Mrs Elizabeth Simpson (1753–1821). Novelist and dramatist. Born the daughter of a Suffolk farmer, she ran away to London when she was 16 and married Inchbald, an actor, who died in 1797. She was on the stage for ten years, then made her living by writing plays. She afterwards tried the profitable novel form. Two of her stories have been frequently reprinted: *A Simple Story* (1791) and *Nature and Art* (1796), which though poorly constructed do contain some real feeling and some realism in the dialogue, perhaps a legacy from her plays. She translated Kotzebue's *Lovers' Vows* (1798), the vehicle of improper private theatricals in Jane Austen's *Mansfield Park*, and edited 3 collections of plays: *The British Theatre* (25 vols., 1808); *Farces* (7 vols., 1809); *The Modern Theatre* (10 vols., 1809). [A R]

S. R. Littlewood, *E.I. and Her Circle* (1921); W. McKee, *E.I., Novelist* (Baltimore, 1935).

Ingelow, Jean (1820–97). Novelist and poetess. Born at Boston, Lincolnshire, she lived in London as a writer. She wrote several very popular series of poems; the 1863 volume of *Poems* had gone into 23 editions by 1880. Her most popular single poem is most probably 'The High Tide on the Coast of Lincolnshire, 1571', a frequently anthologized 'literary ballad' (1863), but 'A Story of Doom' is also sometimes found. She published several novels and shorter stories (some as contributions to *Good Words*) as well as children's stories (*Mopsa the Fairy*, 1869, is remembered). [A R]

Poems (1913).
H. B. Forman *Our Living Poets* (1871); G. Singers-Biggar, 'J. I.', *English*, III (1940).

Innes, Michael. ♢ Stewart, John Innes Mackintosh.

Isherwood, Christopher (William Bradshaw) (1904–   ). Novelist. Born at High Lane, Cheshire, the son of an army officer, he was educated at Repton School and Corpus Christi College, Cambridge. From 1928 to 1929 he was a tutor in London and during this time published his first novel, *All the Conspirators* (1928), a story about an artist's conflict between his individualism and his family (the kind of novel reminiscent of Samuel ♢ Butler). As early as this, however, he was experimenting with techniques derived from the cinema – flashbacks, 'shots'– and in his next novel, *The Memorial* (1932), he worked an elaborate time-shift movement. During some years in London as a journalist (1934–6), he worked as a film-script writer (♢ Greene, Graham, for the influence cinematic technique had on fiction of this period). From 1930 to 1933 he lived in Berlin by teaching English, and the fiction he wrote based on that experience is among his best work. *Mr Norris Changes Trains* (1935) and *Goodbye to Berlin* (1939) are collections of 'episodes' rather than elaborately worked-out novels (and perhaps for this reason are rather undervalued now). The technique of the observer ('Issyvoo'), 'I am a camera', fits the method of telling the story and also provides a powerful moral element in the books. This period saw the rise of the Nazis to power, but the detached narrator of the 'documentary' carefully abstains from any superior moral position; and the handling of all the thirties themes, such as betrayal, homosexuality and the development of tyranny, is rendered moving and truthful. In 1938 he travelled to China with his school-fellow, W. H. ♢ Auden, publishing with him *Journey to a War* (1939); they had already collaborated in 3 plays, in which the influence of the German expressionist theatre is strong: *The Dog beneath the Skin, or Where is Francis?* (1935), *The Ascent of F.6* (1937) and *On the Frontier* (1938). In 1940, Isherwood went to California, where he resumed film-script work and became a U.S. citizen. A visit to South America produced *The Condor and the Cows* (1949). Isherwood's later fiction has not, in general estimation, lived up to his early promise. *Prater Violet* (1946) is about the film industry; the central figure, an interesting portrait of a director, is a little sentimentalized. His other works are *The World in the Evening* (1954), *Down There on a Visit* (1962) and *A Single Man* (1964). All his work is marked, however, by good, neat writing. He has translated a number of books on Yoga (with the collaboration of a Swami), such as the *Bhagavadgita* (with an introduction by Aldous Huxley, 1953), and written such volumes as *Vedanta for Modern Man* (1951) and *Ramakrishna and His Disciples* (1965). Yoga and homosexuality are prominent themes in his later fiction. [A R]

Lions and Shadows (1938) (autobiography).

Islwyn. ♢ Thomas, William.

J

Jabavu, Nontando ('Noni') (*c.* 1921–   ). South African writer. Born into the Xosa tribe in Eastern Cape Province. Her father, D. D. Jabavu, was the first African to obtain a British degree. He later became Professor of Latin and Bantu Languages at Fort Hare University and an influential moderator of coloured opinion in South Africa. Nontando completed her schooling in England and was a student at the Royal Academy of Music on the outbreak of the Second World War. She left the Academy and trained as a semi-skilled engineer and acetylene welder. After the war she stayed in London but continued to pay long visits to South Africa until her marriage to an English film-director broke the Union's miscegenation laws. *Drawn in Colour* (1960) is an account of Bantu life in South Africa, put in its historical and political setting and given an autobiographical orientation. Jabavu and her husband lived for five years in Uganda. She is still a frequent visitor to Africa, and *The Ochre People* (1963) is a second book on that continent and its people. [P T]

Jacob, Naomi (**Ellington**) (1884–1964). Novelist. Born at Ripon, Yorkshire, of a Jewish father and a mother descended from local yeomen, she was educated at Middlesborough High School. She taught for some years, and after a time as a secretary was a supervisor of a munitions factory during the First World War. She spent three years in a sanatorium recovering from tuberculosis, and was thereafter on the stage for eleven years. Her first novel (a great success) was *Jacob Ussher* (1926). She had to live in Italy for reasons of health, and thereafter wrote about two books a year. In 1939, she returned to Britain and during the Second World War worked for E N S A. Her novels (optimistic and breezy light fiction) include *The Loaded Stick* (1934), *The Cap of Youth* (1941) and *The Morning Will Come* (1953). She also wrote a series of still popular, gossipy autobiographical volumes with titles beginning '*Me*' – the first was *Me: A Chronicle about Other People* (1933) and the last *Me – Likes and Dislikes* (1954). [A R]

Jacob, Violet (1863–1946). Scottish poetess. A native of Montrose, Mrs Jacob married a hussar officer and lived for some years in India. In her forties she published novels and children's stories, bringing out *Songs of Angus*, the first of her several volumes of poetry, as late as 1915. Although her work in Scots was appearing simultaneously with the early work of Hugh ◊ MacDiarmid, and was one of the impulses behind the Scots Renaissance of the 1920s, none of it is modernist in feeling, as MacDiarmid's always is; Mrs Jacob offers adequate explorations within the modes fixed by the poetic tradition of Victorian Scotland – the exile's, or the landlord's, view of rural life and landscape. She wrote a racy, humorous, critical Scots, fluent enough but shallower and earthier than the work of Marion ◊ Angus, the natural comparison to make. [A I]

The Scottish Poems (1944).
C. M. Grieve, *Contemporary Scottish Studies* (1926).

Jacobs, W(illiam) W(ymark) (1863–1943). Short-story writer. He was born in London, the son of a wharf manager, and grew up in the dockland area of Wapping. In 1879 he entered the Civil Service as a clerk; although he was soon having stories and sketches accepted by magazines (in particular by Jerome K. ◊ Jerome on the *Idler* and *Today*) he did not leave his job until he had published several books and felt secure enough to earn his living as a writer. His first collection of stories, *Many Cargoes*, appeared in 1896 and was an immediate popular success, as were most of the 20 volumes which followed in the succeeding years until 1926 – these include *Light Freights* (1901), *The Lady of the Barge* (1902), which contained the classic horror story 'The Monkey's Paw', *Short Cruises* (1907) and *Night Watches* (1914). Jacobs is best known for his stories of longshoremen, sailors and other dockland characters, and for his tales of the macabre, but he also wrote about country village life, and produced several one-act plays. His humour is quiet and traditional, and his narrative control faultless, but there is no development in his work: the later stories are much the same as the early ones. Although public demand continued, Jacobs appears to have tired of devising new variations on the same themes, and in his later years he wrote little and published less. [J M]

Cruises and Cargoes: A W.W.J. Omnibus (1934); *Selected Short Stories*, ed. D. K. Roberts (1959).

Jacobson, Dan (1929–). South African novelist. Born in Johannesburg and educated at the University of the Witwatersrand. After jobs in teaching, journalism and business and a short period in an Israeli agricultural settlement, he came to England. His short novel *The Trap* (1955) illuminates his decision to emigrate. Its treatment of colour prejudice shows how South Africa can incapacitate even the best intentioned. In *The Price of Diamonds* (1957) he again underlines the collaboration of men in their own degradation. The award of a Fellowship in Creative Writing at Stanford University furnished him with material for his book about California, *No Further West* (1959). With *The Evidence of Love* (1960) he returned to the novel and to the theme of colour conflicts. Since his arrival in England Jacobson has contributed to a number of papers and magazines including *Encounter*. He has published 3 books of short stories, *A Long Way from Home* (1958), *Beggar My Neighbour* (1964) and *Through the Wilderness* (1968), and a collection of essays and reminiscences, *Time of Arrival* (1963). *The Beginners* (1966) is a long, ambitious novel. [P T]

M. Decter, 'Novelist of South Africa', *Commentary*, XXV, 6 (June 1958).

James I, King of Scotland (1394–1437). Reputed author of the Chaucerian *Kingis Quair* and, less plausibly, of the boisterous short poems in Scots, 'Peblis to the Play' and 'Christis Kirk on the Green'. Captured at sea in childhood, James was detained in England for nineteen years, educated there, and married an English lady in 1424 before being ransomed and restored to Scotland. In the *Kingis Quair* (ed. W. W. Skeat, STS, 1884; revised 1911) James's first sight of Lady Jane Beaufort is described in a manner that recalls Palamon's glimpse of Emily from his prison window in Chaucer's 'Knight's Tale'; then follows a dream-vision of love and marriage in which

Venus's commands to the poet are qualified by the wise advice of Minerva, and a final vision of Fortune launches him on his courtship. Scholarly disputes about the date and authorship of the poem are fairly summarized in the editions of A. Lawson (1910) and W. M. Mackenzie (1939), and the late-medieval change in attitudes and sensibility which the poem manifests has been discussed by C. S. Lewis (*The Allegory of Love*, 1936) and John Speirs (*The Scots Literary Tradition*, 1962). The other 2 poems traditionally ascribed to James are utterly different – each describes a rural holiday-festival in the lively swinging rhythm of a country dance, and their popularity established a very attractive, though not profound, genre of Scots poetry. [A I]

E. W. M. Balfour-Melville, *James I King of Scots* (1936).

James VI of Scotland and I of England (1566–1625). Son of Mary Queen of Scots and her murdered husband Lord Darnley, and successor to Queen Elizabeth I, he contributed by his personality and policies to a shift from the England of Elizabeth to the England of the Civil War. James nominally succeeded to the Scottish throne in infancy, when his mother was forced to abdicate; for years, in the aftermath of the Reformation and the anarchy of a royal minority, the King was a mere token at the mercy of rival factions of noblemen. His character, formed in these conditions under the stern tutorship of the aged George ⟡ Buchanan, developed as a blend of hypochondria, pedantry and homosexuality that impaired his human dignity and prevented his considerable intellectual power from emerging as effective political judgement.

In his youth, James published typically moralistic 16th-century poems, with a critical introduction; later he wrote a *Daemonologie* (1597; ed. G. B. Harrison, 1924), in which he argued for the existence of witches; *A Counter Blast to Tobacco* (1604); a translation of some of the Psalms, although the one published posthumously under his name was really by William ⟡ Alexander, Earl of Stirling; and a defence of absolute monarchy (*Basilicon Doron*, 1599; ed. J. Craigie, STS, 2 vols., 1944–50). For James as patron and collaborator, see H. M. Shire, *Song, Dance and Poetry of the Court of Scotland under King James VI* (1969). [A I]

Poems, ed. J. Craigie (STS, 1955–8); *Political Works*, ed. C. H. McIlwain (1918).
D. H. Willson, *King James VI and I* (1956); W. L. McElwee, *The Wisest Fool in Christendom* (1958); H. M. Chew, 'King James I', in *Social and Political Ideas of Some Great Thinkers of the Sixteenth and Seventeenth Centuries*, ed. F. J. C. Hearnshaw (1926).

James, Henry (1843–1916). Novelist, dramatist and critic. The second of five children and brother of the scientist-philosopher William James, he was prepared, almost from birth, to assume the role of 'Master' of the cosmopolitan novel. His patrician father, an idiosyncratic philosopher-theologian, was anxious that his children's education should not prejudice them towards any particular religion, political system or ethical code. Although he was first taken to Europe as an infant, James spent most of his childhood in New York City, where he was born, and in Albany, New York, where his Irish immigrant grandfather had amassed one of the state's largest commercial fortunes. From an early age he was, in his father's words, a 'devourer of libraries' – particularly of French and English novels. From 1855 to 1860 the James family lived in Paris, Geneva, London, Boulogne and Bonn, returning to America on the eve of the Civil War and settling briefly in Providence, Rhode Island. While helping to fight a fire James injured his back and was physically prevented from volunteering for service in the war; what he later termed his 'obscure hurt' became symptomatic of the role he was to play in life as in art – that of the detached but concerned observer.

Having made brief attempts at developing his talents in mathematics and in painting, James entered the Harvard Law School at 19, shortly after his family made their permanent home in Cambridge, Massachusetts. He soon withdrew, however, and devoted himself entirely to literature – a vocation in which he was encouraged by Charles Eliot Norton and William Dean Howells, as he had been earlier by the American painter John LaFarge. James's earliest piece of fiction was published in 1864, and for more than fifty years he sought with increasing subtlety and complexity to reach his own aesthetic goals, producing 20 full-length novels, 12 novellas, and more than 100 short stories, as well as plays, travel sketches, essays and reviews. His work won a steadily increasing audience and soon assured his

financial independence. In 1869–70 James made his first adult visit to Europe and in his absence his favourite cousin, Mary Temple, died of tuberculosis. Her magnificent fight for life and the dreams which she had never fulfilled fixed themselves forever in James's imagination, and her memory inspired two of his most intriguing heroines, Isabel Archer in *The Portrait of a Lady* and Milly Theale in *The Wings of the Dove*.

James's earliest fiction was set in America, but he later disowned most of the early tales, as well as his first novel, *Watch and Ward* (1871), with its unreal Boston setting. His visits to Europe in 1869–70 and 1872–4 inspired him to become the chronicler of the international *comédie humaine*, and his first novel of consequence, *Roderick Hudson* (1875), illustrated a dilemma which confronted the young novelist himself – the feeling that American society offered little inspiration for the artist, but the concomitant fear that the American innocent might be corrupted and destroyed by the richer culture of Europe. Determined, however, that Europe would yield up more material for him as a novelist of manners, and that it brought into play aspects of consciousness that might never be revealed in a milder social climate, James settled in Paris in 1875; there he met Turgenev, and through him Flaubert, Zola, Edmond de Goncourt, Daudet and Maupassant. To Turgenev he was indebted for the technique of permitting the structure of his fiction to grow directly from the psychological composition of his characters, and to the French realists for what Flaubert called the 'chiselled' style. In 1875 James published *The American*, the story of a New World innocent who discovers at once the cultural richness of Europe and its underlying depravity; in *The Europeans* (1878) he reversed the international pattern in his witty, meticulously controlled study of the way in which two 'Europeanized' Americans readjust to the life of staid and quiet Boston. With *Daisy Miller* (1879) James's international reputation was assured: 'the American girl' made her naïve debut before an eagerly receptive public. *Daisy Miller* also marked the beginning of one of the most prolific periods in an astonishingly prolific career; it was followed later in 1879 by a collection of tales, the short novel *Confidence* and James's brilliant study, *Hawthorne*. *Washington Square* was being prepared for publication early in 1880, and the first instalments of *The Portrait of a Lady* were soon to appear. That novel marks the climax of what is generally regarded as James's first period; the melodrama and exaggeration of his earlier 'international' tales and novels has yielded almost entirely to the ambiguous vision of the interplay of ethical and aesthetic values which characterizes all his major fiction.

In 1876 James had settled in London, where most of the fiction of his middle period was written. He returned to America in 1881 and was recalled there the following year by the death of his father, but thenceforth he ceased to be a wanderer and remained abroad for twenty years – chiefly in England. His second period as a novelist began with 2 financially unsuccessful novels about reformers, *The Princess Casamassima* (1886) and *The Bostonians* (1886); *The Tragic Muse* (1889), a more critical glimpse of the world of fashion, heralded, in its attention to the stage, James's own abortive flirtation with the theatre. While some of his most distinctive short fiction belongs to this period, his plays are almost entirely without merit except as preparation for the masterful control of dialogue and scene in his late novels. In 1898 James purchased Lamb House in Rye, Sussex, and withdrew there to produce, in sociable retreat, the rich works of his 'major phase' – *The Wings of the Dove* (1902), *The Ambassadors* (1903) and *The Golden Bowl* (1904), as well as a perceptive book on America and 2 volumes of autobiography. From 1907 to 1909 James revised his novels for the collected 'New York edition', adding to them the prefaces which, taken together, constitute one of the most provocative and authoritative treatises on the art of the novel. In 1915, annoyed by America's reluctance to enter the First World War and as a gesture of gratitude to and sympathy for England, James became a British subject; he received the Order of Merit in the New Year Honours of 1916 – only a month before his death. Among his manuscripts were 2 unfinished novels, *The Ivory Tower* and *The Sense of the Past*, and the unfinished third volume of his autobiography.

James was a brilliant novelist of manners, but more importantly he was an international writer who by critical statement and creative example showed to succeeding generations of English novelists the wide range of aesthetic and psychological considerations the form might encompass: within the confines of an old tradition he

created a new one. His own style, relatively simple and unadorned in the early fiction, became increasingly ambiguous and elliptical as he himself became more aware of the obscure and subtle forces ruling human conduct. While he recognized that 'The house of fiction had . . . not one window but a million', his own preference was always for a 'psychological reason'. In relentlessly probing the motives of his characters and placing the 'central consciousness' in the mind of an innocent child or an ingenuous girl or a middle-aged man attempting to recapture the possibilities of youth, he moved toward the stream-of-consciousness technique; Virginia ◊ Woolf, Dorothy ◊ Richardson and James ◊ Joyce are among the many novelists who acknowledged their indebtedness to the Master. [DDG]

The Novels and Tales of H.J. (24 vols., New York, 1907–9); *The Novels and Stories of H.J.*, ed. P. Lubbock (35 vols., 1921–3); *A Small Boy and Others* (1913), *Notes of a Son and Brother* (1914) and *The Middle Years* (1917) (autobiographical); *The Notebooks of H.J.*, ed. F. O. Matthiessen and K. B. Murdock (New York, 1947); *Selected Literary Criticism*, ed. M. Shapira (1963).
Q. Anderson, *The American H.J.* (1958); O. Cargill, *The Novels of H.J.* (1961); F. W. Dupee, *H.J.* (revised edn, 1956); L. Edel, *H.J.: The Untried Years* (1953), *The Conquest of London* (1962) and *The Middle Years* (1962); D. Krook, *The Ordeal of Consciousness in H.J.* (1962); F. O. Matthiessen, *H.J. The Major Phase* (1944); S. G. Putt, *The Fiction of H.J.* (1968).

James, M(ontague) R(hodes) (1862–1936). Scholar and short-story writer. Born at Goodnestone in Kent, the son of a clergyman, he was educated at Eton and King's College, Cambridge, and became assistant in classical archaeology at the Fitzwilliam Museum there; he also dug in Cyprus. He was elected a Fellow of King's for a dissertation *The Apocalypse of St Peter*, and lectured in divinity, becoming Dean of the college in 1889. His interests turned to palaeography and from 1895 onwards he produced very learned, detailed and useful catalogues of the Western manuscripts in Cambridge colleges, Eton, Lambeth, Westminster Abbey, Aberdeen and private collections. He also edited volumes for the specialized bibliographical and historical societies. James had an unusually retentive memory as well as great industry, and his single-handed work, though in places requiring correction, pioneered in many directions. He wrote on the Apocrypha, and on medieval and other literary topics. He is best known now to the general reader for his ghost-stories, neat and creepy works, which still please because of the union of malignant purpose on the part of the spirits, chilling atmosphere and flat descriptions of the contemporary life of the upper middle class. The stories appeared in several collections: *Ghost Stories of an Antiquary* (1904; second volume 1911); *A Thin Ghost and Others* (1919); *Twelve Mediaeval Ghost Stories* (1922); *The Five Jars* (1922); *Collected Ghost Stories* (1931). [A R]

S. G. Lubbock, *A Memoir of M.R.J., with a List of His Writings* (1939); M. Richardson, 'The Psychoanalysis of Ghost Stories', *Twentieth Century*, 166 (December 1956).

Jameson, (Margaret) Storm (1897–). Novelist and critic. Born at Whitby, Yorkshire; her family were shipbuilders. She was educated at Leeds University and has been an advertising writer, journalist and drama critic. She married the historian Guy Chapman. She is one of the leading modern writers of the English 'family chronicle' novel, with elaborate entangled relationships, and (because of a tendency of the genre to dullness) a penchant for 'heightening' the characters. She is concerned with the change in *mores* from pre-First World War England to more recent times, but has been described as 'sympathetic' with this change. Mary Hervey is the main character of her first 3 novels, a trilogy about a Yorkshire shipbuilding family, *The Lovely Ship* (1927), *The Voyage Home* (1930) and *A Richer Dust* (1931) (all reprinted under the title *The Triumph of Time*, 1932). A second trilogy relates the life of Mary's granddaughter, Hervey Russell: *That Was Yesterday* (1932), *Company Parade* (1934) and *Love in Winter* (1935). Among her other novels are *The Green Man* (1952), a Galsworthy-like family chronicle covering the years 1930–45, and *A Month Soon Goes* (1962). *The Early Life of Stephen Hind* (1966) is the chronicle of a man on the make. She did much work for refugee European intellectuals with P.E.N. from 1938 on, and has written about this interest in *The Writer's Situation* (first published in 1947) *and Other Essays* (1950). Among her critical works is *Morley Roberts, the Last Eminent Victorian* (1961). [A R]

No Time Like the Present (1933) (autobiography); *Journey from the North* (1969) (autobiography to 1939).
J. Gray, *On Second Thought* (Minneapolis, 1946).

Jefferies, (John) Richard (1848–87). Novelist and essayist. Born at Coate, Wiltshire, the son of a farmer, Jefferies was educated locally and at a school in Sydenham. In 1866 he became a journalist on the *North Wilts Herald* and began writing the descriptive sketches of rural life that were later to make him famous. At this stage of his life he was ambitious to make his name writing fiction, but his early novels, *The Scarlet Shawl* (1874), *Restless Human Hearts* (1875) and *World's End* (1877), on aristocratic and melodramatic themes, were not successful. In 1877 he moved from Wiltshire to London, the first of many temporary homes, and achieved a popular success with *The Gamekeeper at Home*, a collection of articles reprinted from the *Pall Mall Gazette*. This was followed by *Wild Life in a Southern County* (1879), *The Amateur Poacher* (1879), *Hodge and His Masters* (2 vols., 1880; intr. Raymond Williams, 1966), and *Round about a Great Estate* (1880), which are notable for their intensely detailed descriptions of natural scenes and objects, keen social observation and pure, lyrical style. In addition to these qualities his later books, *Wood Magic* (2 vols., 1881), *Bevis: The Story of a Boy* (3 vols., 1882) and *The Story of My Heart* (1883), are imbued with an idiosyncratic mystical philosophy. He continued to write novels and from *Greene Ferne Farm* (1880) onwards turned to rural life for his subject matter. His best novels are *After London* (1885) and *Amaryllis at the Fair* (1887). For the last six years of his life he suffered from a crippling disease and he died at Goring-on-Sea, Worthing. Two collections of essays, *Field and Hedgerow* (1889) and *The Toilers of the Field* (1892), were published posthumously. [P J K]

Works, ed. C. H. Warren (1948); *The J. Companion*, ed. S. J. Looker (1948).
Walter Besant, *The Eulogy of R.J.* (1888); H. S. Salt, *R.J.* (1894); Edward Thomas, *R.J.: His Life and Work* (1909); A. F. Thorn, *The Life Worship of R.J.* (1920); T. R. Arkell, *R. J.* (1933); W. J. Keith, *R.J.* (1965); Samuel Looker and Crichton Porteous, *R.J.: Man of the Fields* (1965).

Jeffrey, Francis, Lord (1773–1850). Lawyer, critic and political writer. Born in Edinburgh, the son of an advocate, and educated at the High School, Glasgow University and (briefly) at Oxford, he studied law at Edinburgh University and was called to the bar in 1794. Jeffrey was a typical product of the Scottish educational system and lawyer caste: clever, with wide interests, a keen arguer and didact. He became a member of the group of young Edinburgh lawyers who supported Whig reforming ideas, against the immovable, powerful Tory regime of the Dundases. He was never a revolutionary, but sought to reform the system according to rational principles to give the middle classes a voice in government. He was elected Dean of the Faculty of Advocates in 1829 (a sign of the retreat of the old order), and in the 1830 Reform ministry was Lord Advocate, with a large say in drafting the Scottish Reform Bill. In 1832 he was M.P. for Edinburgh, and in 1834 became a Lord of Session, as Lord Jeffrey (though he was not a leading lawyer). His literary interest lies in his editorship (1802-29) of the ◊ *Edinburgh Review*, which he helped to found. As a descendant of the Edinburgh Athenians, Jeffrey did not really give a high place to imaginative writing. Also he was a rather dogmatic exponent of the old classical school of criticism, placing his reliance on reason and established judgements, as against the coming Romantic dogmatism of personal feeling. None the less, he struggled to be fair to the new poets (Wordsworth, Southey, Coleridge etc.), the 'Lakists', though naturally appearing sharp and aridly intellectual in dealing with them. His article on Wordsworth is remembered now as a wrong judgement, but it should be realized that there was an arguable case behind it. Jeffrey wrote much on many topics, offending some by a characteristic tone of superior levity, but he is a good example of a kind of mind and a kind of judgement important in its day. [AR]

Contributions to the Edinburgh Review (4 vols., 1844) (collected essays); *J.'s Literary Criticism* ed. D. Nichol Smith (1910) (selection).
Lord Cockburn, *Life of Lord J.* (2 vols., 1852); J. A. Greig, *J.* (1948); J. Clive, *Scotch Reviewers* (1957).

Jeffrey, William (1896–1946). Scottish poet. Jeffrey, the son of a Lanarkshire colliery manager, attended Glasgow and Edinburgh Universities and, after being gassed in France, worked as leader-writer and drama critic for the *Glasgow Evening Times* and the *Glasgow Herald*. Between 1921 and 1933 he published several volumes of verse, but his best work is contained in the posthumous *Sea Glimmer* (1947). A mystic and an admirer of Yeats and Blake, Jeffrey relied too readily on his undoubted gravity and the weightiness of his subject-matter; if one responds to his work at all, one reacts to his cumulative statements rather than to a distinctively creative mastery of structure or expression. In his work in Scots, likewise, he is heavily dependent on the modes of Hugh ◊ MacDiarmid and on the cadence and vocabulary of 16th-century Scots, rather academically exploited; 'The Galleys', a monologue supposedly spoken by John Knox, shows his slightly uneasy manner at its best. [AI]

Selected Poems, ed. A. Scott (1951).

Jenner, Henry. ◊ Cornish Literature.

Jennings, Elizabeth (1926–). Poetess. A doctor's daughter, she took an English degree at Oxford, worked for a time in the Oxford public library, and later in London in publishing and literary journalism. Her first pamphlet of poems, *Poems* (1953), won an Arts Council Prize and her second volume, *A Way of Looking* (1955), a Somerset Maugham Award, with which she paid a visit to Italy, a country which has deeply influenced her subsequent poems (she published a translation of Michelangelo's sonnets in 1961). She was the only woman poet included in Robert Conquest's 'Movement' anthology, *New Lines*, and shares with the other 'Movement' poets traditional metrics, plainness of diction and a clear expository line. She differs from the others in being profoundly religious (she is a Roman Catholic) and in having a primarily lyrical impulse. Some of her recent poems have made a moving use of hospital experiences, following a nervous breakdown. She is probably the most gifted English woman poet of her generation. [GSF]

A Sense of the World (1958); *Song for a Birth or a Death* (1961); *Recoveries* (1964); *Collected Poems* (1967); *The Animals' Arrival* (1969).
R. Conquest, Introduction to *New Lines* (1955).

Jenyns, Soame (1704–87). Poet and miscellaneous writer. Educated at St John's College, Cambridge, he sat in the House of Commons for Cambridgeshire and Dunwich (1742–80). He was the author of a number of forgotten poems, such as *The Art of Dancing* (1729), which were collected in the *Works* (ed. with a memoir by C. N. Cole, 1790). Not a very profound thinker, he wrote *A Free Enquiry into the Nature and Origin of Evil* (1757), which prompted a bitter review by Dr Johnson, stung in some way by the book's flaccid 'free-thinking'. He also wrote an orthodox *View of the Internal Evidence of the Christian Religion* (1776), which had an extravagant reception, as well as some political tracts. [A R]

J. Boswell, *Life of Johnson*, ed. B. Hill, revised L. F. Powell (1934–50).

Jerome, Jerome K(lapka) (1859–1927). Novelist and playwright. Born in Walsall, Staffordshire, the son of a poor tradesman and evangelical preacher. Klapka, an exiled Hungarian general, was a friend of his father. The family moved to London, and he was sent to Marylebone Grammar School. He worked as a clerk, reporter and schoolmaster. His life as a theatrical super with touring companies is the subject of *On the Stage and Off* (1885). A series of sketches, *Idle Thoughts of an Idle Fellow* (1889), did well, and this induced him to try writing and journalism. In the same year, his most famous humorous work, a series of loosely connected, farcical sketches, with slangy conversation, *Three Men in a Boat*, was a great success; a sequel, *Three Men on the Bummel*, appeared in 1900. *Paul Kelver* (1902) is autobiographical fiction, and *My Life and Times* (1926) is straight autobiography. In 1892, he founded his own paper, the *Idler*, in which Stevenson's *Ebb-Tide* was serialized. When the paper folded he became quite a successful playwright. *The Passing of the Third Floor Back* (1908), a sentimental moral fable set in Bloomsbury, was one of Forbes-Robertson's very successful productions, and is occasionally revived by amateurs. [A R]

A. Moss, *J.: His Life and Works* (1929).

Jerrold, Douglas (William) (1803–57). Dramatist and humorist. Originally a child actor, he served in the British fleet and became the resident dramatist at the Surrey Theatre, a home of spectacular melodrama. He wrote several pieces featuring local, domestic settings and the stock characters and situations of Victorian popular theatre – the Jolly Jack Tar, the extortionate landlord and the drunkard. His popular successes

were *Black-ey'd Susan* (1829), *The Rent Day* (1832) and *Fifteen Years of a Drunkard's Life* (1828). He subsequently attempted to write sophisticated comedy, but failed to win an audience, and became from 1846 a regular contributor of essays and character-sketches (the most famous being 'Mrs Caudle's Curtain Lectures') to *Punch*, in whose columns he denounced the British stage. He also ran from 1845 *Douglas Jerrold's Shilling Magazine* and from 1846 *Douglas Jerrold's Weekly Newspaper*. [M J]

Works, ed. W. B. Jerrold (4 vols., 1863–4).
Walter Jerrold, *D.J., Dramatist and Wit* (2 vols. 1914).

Jewsbury, Geraldine Endsor (1812–80). Novelist and journalist. Born at Measham in Derbyshire, she was a member of the Carlyle circle (a friend of Jane Welsh). She wrote several novels, including *Zoë* (3 vols., 1845), *The Half Sisters* (2 vols., 1848) and *The Sorrows of Gentility* (1856). She is probably best remembered because of her appearance in a famous controversial essay on women writers by Virginia Woolf, 'Geraldine and Jane' (*T L S*, 28 February 1929). [A R]

S. Howe, *G.J., Her Life and Errors* (1935).

Jocelin of Brakelond (fl. 1170–1200). Chronicler. Born at Bury St Edmunds, Suffolk, he entered the great Benedictine monastery there in 1173 and wrote a most interesting chronicle of life in the abbey during his own time. It is particularly valuable for the picture it gives of relations between the monks and the townsmen. Its striking portrait of the Abbot Samson has led to Jocelin being called a medieval Boswell. His account of Samson's election to the abbacy is especially interesting and even entertaining.

Cronica, ed. T. Arnold in *Memorials of St Edmund's Abbey*, i (Rolls Series, 1890); ed. and tr. H. E. Butler, *The Chronicle of Jocelin of Brakelond* (1949; repr. 1951, 1962); tr. L. C. Jane, *The Chronicle of Jocelin of Brakelond* (1907; repr. 1922, 1925, 1931).

John of Howden or Hoveden (d. 1275). Scholar and poet. Chaplain to Eleanor, the widow of Henry III of England, for whom he wrote a Norman French paraphrase of his Latin poem, *Philomena* (ed. C. Blume, Leipzig, 1930). This is a mystical poem, in over a thousand stanzas, on the passion of Christ, and is its author's masterpiece. Howden was both a scholar of outstanding importance and also a poet of great originality.

Poems, ed. F. J. E. Raby (Surtees Society, 1939).
F. J. E. Raby, *Christian Latin Poetry* (2nd edn, 1953).

John of Salisbury (*c.* 1115–80). Philosopher. A native of Salisbury, he was a pupil of Abelard at Paris. After further study at Chartres, where he absorbed the humanism in vogue, he returned to England to be secretary to Thomas Becket, Archbishop of Canterbury. With him he went into exile and returned to England, and he was present when Becket was murdered in Canterbury Cathedral. During the last four years of his life he was Archbishop of Chartres. A lover of knowledge for its own sake, he was the most learned man of his time; he had a keen appreciation of classical literature and wrote in polished Latin. His two chief works are *Policraticus* (ed. C. C. J. Webb, 2 vols., 1909; selections tr. J. Dickinson, New York, 1927; J. B. Pike, Minneapolis, 1938), which, after desultory remarks on varied subjects, goes on to its main themes – politics and ethics; and *Metalogicon* (ed. C. C. J. Webb, 1929; tr. D. D. McGarry, 1955, repr. 1962), which is concerned mainly with logic and the philosophical problems of his time.

Historia Pontificalis, ed. R. L. Poole (1927); tr. and ed. M. Chibnall (1956); *Letters*, ed. W. J. Millor and H. E. Butler, revised C. N. L. Brooke (1955).
C. C. J. Webb, *J. of S.* (1932).

John of Trevisa (d. before 1402). Scholar and translator. Born at Carados in Cornwall, he was a Fellow of Exeter College, Oxford (1362–5), and subsequently of Queen's. He was expelled from there in 1379 for 'unworthiness', which may mean that he had Wyclifite sympathie, and he became vicar of Berkeley. His best-known work is the English translation of ◊ Higden's *Polychronicon*, which he finished in 1378. His other major translation was of Bartholomæus Anglicus's *De Proprietatibus Rerum*, the great medievial encyclopedia of natural science, completed in 1398. As a translator, he is fairly literal, though not always accurate, and apart from the interest of the material he is chiefly important in the historical development of English secular prose, his style being plain and efficient. His rare additions, notably the account of the reform of teaching at Oxford, are of great historical value.

Though the thesis that Trevisa had a large hand in the writing of 'Piers Plowman' is hardly tenable, D. C. Fowler's *Piers the Plowman: Literary Relations of the A and B Texts* (Seattle, 1961) collects much valuable information on him. [A G]

Shorter Works, ed. and intr. A. J. Perry (EETS, 1925).
D. C. Fowler, 'New Light on J. of T.', *Traditio*, XVIII (1962), and 'J. of T. and the English Bible', *MP*, LVIII (1960).

Johnson, Lionel Pigot (1867–1902). Poet and critic. Born at Broadstairs in Kent, the son of an Irish army officer, he was educated at Winchester and New College, Oxford. He became a literary journalist, writing in the *Spectator*, *Academy*, *Athenaeum* and other journals, for which he was equipped with considerable learning and an enthusiastic interest in medieval life and thought. His chief critical works are *Postliminium* ('the right to return home and resume lost privileges'), which consists of essays on Pater, Charlotte Brontë, Savonarola, Blake, Bacon, Pascal, Newman, etc. (ed. T. Whittemore, 1911), and *The Art of Thomas Hardy* (1894; 1923). Johnson's poetry was largely inspired by his classical learning, a close following of the Irish literary revival and the strong influence of Walter Pater. He was converted to Roman Catholicism in 1891. Johnson contributed to the ◊ *Yellow Book* and the *Book of the Rhymer's Club*, and his poems are characterized by a spare beauty as well as an occasional *fin-de-siècle* remorse caused (in his case genuinely) by overmastering alcoholism. His best poems are probably 'By the Statue of King Charles at Charing Cross' and his meditation on his own ruined life, 'The Dark Angel'. *Poems* (1895) and *Ireland and Other Poems* (1897) contain most of his best work. [A R]

Poetical Works, ed. and intr. Ezra Pound (1915); *The Complete Poems*, ed. I. Fletcher (1953); *Selections*, ed. C. K. Shorter (1908); *A New Selection*, ed. H. V. Marrot (1927).
B. I. Evans, *English Poetry in the Later Nineteenth Century* (1933); C. Alexander, in *Catholic Literary Revival* (Milwaukee, 1935).

Johnson, Samuel (1709–84). Poet, lexicographer, critic and moralist. Born in Lichfield, Staffordshire, the son of a bookseller. In his infancy he contracted scrofula (and was taken to London in 1712 to be 'touched' by the Queen). As a result of his disease, though a man of powerful physique, he suffered all his life from damaged eyesight. He was educated by reading in his father's shop and at Lichfield Grammar School. He spent 1728 to 1729 at Pembroke College, Oxford, where his poverty, pride, and intellectual ability made him live in bitterness, 'a mad and violent life'. He returned to Lichfield without a degree and lived at home reading and writing verse. After the death of his father, he taught for some months at Market Bosworth, until he quarrelled with the school's patron. In 1731, his Latin translation of Pope's *Messiah* had been published by Oxford friends, and in 1732 he spent some time working for a Birmingham printer, for whom he translated *A Voyage to Abyssinia* (1735) by Father Lobo, a Portuguese Jesuit. In the latter year he married Elizabeth Jervis or Porter, a widow of 45, and with her money opened a boarding academy at Edial, near Lichfield. This attracted only three scholars, so with his tragedy *Irene* (unsuccessfully acted, and printed in 1749) he went to London in March 1737, accompanied by his most hopeful pupil, David ◊ Garrick. Johnson's early life in London is obscure. He worked for Edward Cave, the publisher of the *Gentleman's Magazine*, to which he contributed many pieces: reviews, essays, biographies, translations and, in particular, illegal reports (1738–43) of the parliamentary debates, under the title 'Debates in the Senate of Lilliput'. Among other miscellaneous writing at this time are contributions to *James's Medical Dictionary* and a learned *Catalogue of the Harleian Library*. Some idea of his life in the shady circumstances of Grub Street may be found in his *Life of Richard Savage* (1744). In 1738 had appeared his *London: A Poem in Imitation of the Third Satire of Juvenal*, which attracted attention, though anonymous; *The Vanity of Human Wishes: The Tenth Satire of Juvenal Imitated* appeared (with the author's name) in 1749. Johnson also wrote verse prologues and epilogues for the theatre, of which that for the opening of Garrick's season at Drury Lane in 1747 is an important work. As a poet, Johnson is a master of a noble and sententious style; his couplets are less flexible than Pope's, but well suited to the gravity and pith of his thought. His lines 'On the Death of Robert Levet' show that his restraint and generalized application make the expression of personal grief more, not less, poignant.

In 1746, he had signed a contract with the booksellers for his *Dictionary*, work on which continued with half a dozen assistants over the next nine years. *The Plan of an English Dictionary*, addressed to the Earl of ◊ Chesterfield, appeared in 1747. The Earl, one of the secretaries of state, failed to give any assistance, until he belatedly wrote a puff of the work after it appeared. Natural disappointment and pride made Johnson write the famous letter to Chesterfield on 7 February 1755, on patronage. Boswell first published the letter in 1790, since when it has been the centre of much sentimental comment on Johnson's independence and Chesterfield's bad behaviour. *A Dictionary of the English Language: in Which the Words are Deduced from Their Originals, and Illustrated in Their Different Significations by Examples from the Best Writers* appeared in 2 folio volumes (1755; last revised by Johnson 1773; abstracts and abridgements were also printed). This was the work that gave 'Dictionary' Johnson the intellectual reputation he enjoyed in his own day. In this year, he was awarded an honorary Oxford M.A. His customary title comes from honorary doctorates awarded him by Trinity College, Dublin, in 1765 and Oxford in 1775. Johnson's *Dictionary* was neither the first in English nor even in his own day the most comprehensive; the etymologies, too, are naturally unsatisfactory, being based on the defective knowledge of the time. It was most remarkable for showing the power and grasp of his mind and of his reading, especially in Elizabethan and 17th-century literature, and, in more than a hundred thousand quotations, it develops philosophical and moral thinking, and ideas of all kinds. It also displayed the range of the English vocabulary and helped to fix the spelling of English.

From 20 March 1750 to 17 March 1752 (the year of his wife's death) Johnson almost single-handed wrote the essays for a twice-weekly periodical, the *Rambler* (208 numbers; essays reprinted in 4 vols., 1751; 6 vols., revised by Johnson, 1752). He consolidated his reputation as a notable moral essayist with some 25 essays in John Hawkesworth's periodical the *Adventurer* (1753) and from 1758 to 1760 he wrote about 100 weekly essays for a newspaper, the *Universal Chronicle*; the latter were called the *Idler* (essays reprinted in 2 vols., 1761). His prose is more massive than that of ◊

Addison and the earlier group of essayists, so that his essays are more didactic and less purely entertaining, though the *Idler* pieces are lighter. He develops many of his characteristic ideas on a variety of topics in these pieces, moral and critical. His reflections on life and writing are characterized by practicality and are constantly shown tested against his own experience. In eight days in January 1759, he wrote *Rasselas* (*The Prince of Abyssinia: A Tale*) (2 vols., 1759; ed. R. W. Chapman, 1927; ed G. J. Kolb, New York, 1962), an oriental apologue about the nature of happiness, the 'choice of life', the vanity of human wishes and the terrible power of imagination that preys on life. Read as a novel, this work is static and the conversation is 'unrealistic'. The real imaginative power lies in the forceful thinking, in the wit and vigour of the controlled writing.

In 1762, the government awarded him a Civil List pension of £300 a year, and in 1763 he first met ◊ Boswell. In 1745, at a time when he was still making his way, he had published *Proposals* for an edition of the works of Shakespeare, along with a specimen *Miscellaneous Observations on Macbeth*; in 1765, he finally published *The Plays of William Shakespeare* (8 vols., reprinted 1765 and 1768; several times reissued with the notes augmented and revised by various scholars). Johnson's Shakespearean criticism is marked by his imaginative and sensitive reading, controlled by intelligent use of his neo-classical critical theory. Stressing as always the *use* of literature, he sees Shakespeare as a 'moralist'. The notes abound in individual insights and contain some absurdities.

In 1764, he was introduced to the wealthy brewer, Henry Thrale, with whom and his talented wife (◊ Piozzi) Johnson spent much time in London and at their country house at Streatham. In the same year was founded 'The Club' of literary men, later called 'The Literary Club', which met weekly at the Turk's Head in Gerrard Street, Soho. This group included Bishop Percy, Garrick, the Wartons, Gibbon, Fox, Burke and Adam Smith. In 1773, Boswell finally squeaked in. In this group, Johnson had free play for exercising his conversational art, an important aspect of contemporary life and one which, necessarily ephemeral, Boswell's *Life* is invaluable in preserving. From August to November 1773, he toured Scotland with Boswell, and in 1775 published *A Journey to the Western Islands of Scotland* (3 editions that year; ed. R. W. Chapman, 1924). Johnson from time to time wrote political pamphlets to support his conservative 'Tory' views on English politics; in 1775 appeared his famous anti-American tract *Taxation no Tyranny*. In 1777 he agreed with a syndicate of booksellers to write introductions for a collection of English poetry. This, his last great work, appeared as *Prefaces, Biographical and Critical, to the Works of the English Poets* (vols. 1–4, 1779; 5–10, 1781; revised and corrected as *The Lives of the Most Eminent English Poets with Critical Observations on Their Works*, 4 vols., 1783; ed. G. Birkbeck Hill, 3 vols., 1905). In many of these pieces, Johnson has given judgements and readings that appeal to modern readers who value not necessarily a 'system' but an argued position. In particular his comments on Dryden, Pope and the Metaphysical poets (in the *Life of Cowley*) are suggestive: with Milton and Gray, writers whose imagination is less tractable to his kind of reading, he is less successful. In 1781, Henry Thrale died and Johnson, sinking into melancholy and physical debility, pathetically quarrelled with Mrs Thrale over her marriage with Piozzi, an Italian musician. In 1783 he suffered a stroke; the next winter he fell fatally ill, and died in his house in Gough Square off Fleet Street. He is buried in Westminster Abbey.

There are two Johnsons. The 'sage' of Boswell's work is an imaginative creation who occasionally gets in the way of the Johnson, writer and poet, who can be most satisfactorily seen by reading his own writings. The Boswellian 'character' for long dominated the study of Johnson's work. It has been the task of modern scholarship to establish what he actually wrote and to give it a fair and careful reading. Thus emerges something that only overlaps in places with Boswell's conception; not the quaint figure and dull writer of the stereotype, but a fascinating mind and sensibility, and one of the great writers of his century.

Few English writers except Shakespeare have been more fully written about and commented on than Johnson. A guide through the maze of more recent works is J. L. Clifford, *Johnsonian Studies: 1887–1950* (Minneapolis, 1951) supplemented by J. L. Clifford and D. Greene ('A Bibliography of Johnsonian Studies: 1950–1960', in *Johnsonian Studies*, ed. M. Wahba, Cairo, 1962). [AR]

Works, ed. Sir John Hawkins (11 vols., 1787) (all later complete editions more or less reprint this defective collection); *The Yale Edition of the Works* (in progress), ed. A. T. Hazen and J. H. Mitzendorf (comprehensive edn, taking advantage of work during the last half century in extending the list of Johnson's writings): I, *Diaries, Prayers, Annals* (1958); II, *The Idler and the Adventurer* (1963); VI, *The Poems* (1966); VII and VIII, *J. on Shakespeare* (1966); *Poems*, ed. D. Nichol Smith and E. L. McAdam (1941); *Letters*, ed. R. W. Chapman (3 vols., 1952); *Selected Prose and Poetry*, ed. B. H. Bronson (1924); *Prose and Poetry*, ed. M. Wilson (1950) (Reynard Library); *Selected Writings*, ed. P. Grutwell (PEL, 1968); *The Political Writings*, ed. J. P. Hardy (1968).

Sir John Hawkins, *Life* (1787), ed. B. H. Davis (New York, 1961) (a valuable contemporary corrective to Boswell); J. Boswell, *Life*, ed. G. B. Hill, revised L. F. Powell (6 vols., Oxford 1934–50); J. L. Clifford, *Young Sam J.* (New York, 1955) (corrects the biographical inaccuracies in the early part of Boswell's work); A. L. Reade, *Johnsonian Gleanings* (11 vols., 1909–52); W. J. Bate, *The Achievement of S. J.* (New York, 1955); J. H. Hagstrum, *S.J.'s Literary Criticism* (Minneapolis, 1952); J. W. Krutch, *S.J.* (New York, 1944); W. K. Wimsatt, *The Prose Style of S.J.* (Yale U.P., 1941); F. R. Leavis, 'J. and Augustanism' and 'J. as a Poet' in *The Common Pursuit* (1952) (reprinted from *Scrutiny*); *The Age of J.: Essays Presented to C. B. Tinker* (Yale U.P., 1949; new edn, 1964); F. W. Hilles, *New Light on Dr J.* (Yale U.P., 1959); *Johnsonian Studies*, ed. M. Wahba (Cairo, 1962); *S.J. A Collection of Critical Essays*, ed. D. J. Greene (Twentieth Century Views, 1965); W. P. Courtney and D. Nichol Smith, *A Bibliography of S.J.* (1915; repr. 1925); D. J. Greene, 'The Development of the Johnson Canon', in *Restoration and Eighteenth Century Literature: Essays in Honour of A. D. McKillop*, ed. C. Camden (Chicago U.P., 1963); A. Sachs, *Passionate Intelligence* (1968).

Jones, David (1895–   ). Painter, engraver, illustrator, novelist. Born at Brockley, Kent, he studied at Camberwell and Westminster Schools of Art. In 1924 he worked with Eric Gill at Ditchling, subsequently producing many illustrations, including copper engravings for Douglas Cleverdon's edition of *The Ancient Mariner*. In 1937 he was awarded the Hawthornden Prize for his autobiographical war novel *In Parenthesis*, a *tour de force* in prose and free verse, having some affinities with the work of Joyce, the later Pound and Eliot. *The Anathemata*, an equally remarkable work, equally difficult to classify, was published in 1952. [GG]

Agenda, v, 1–3 (1967) special David Jones issue).

Jones, Henry Arthur (1851–1929). Dramatist. He began his career as resident dramatist for Wilson Barrett, for whom he helped to devise the spectacular melodrama *The Silver King* in 1882, but he had a high notion of the playwright's calling. Like Pinero he wrote 'Society drama' and like him was considered 'daring' in his day. His problem plays include *The Masqueraders* (1894) and *Michael and His Lost Angel* (1896), in which a young priest is seduced by a rich married woman. It was not well received and he later concentrated on comedies of intrigue, well made and with some mild pretensions to social criticism, including *The Liars* (1897) and the more serious *Mrs Dane's Defence* (1900), yet another Society play on the theme of 'the woman with a past'. Jones wrote almost a hundred plays, but, though he rightly prophesied a renaissance in English drama, he did not really contribute to it himself. [MJ]

Representative Plays (4 vols., 1925); *The Renascence of English Drama* (1895); *The Theatre of Ideas* (1915).

D. J. Jones, *The Life and Letters of H.A.J.* (1930); R. A. Cordell, *H.A.J. and the Modern Drama* (New York, 1932); G. Rowell, *The Victorian Theatre* (1956); J. Russell Taylor, *The Rise and Fall of the Well-Made Play* (1967).

Jones, John Morris. ◊ Morris-Jones, John.

Jones, Thomas Gwynn (1871–1949). Welsh poet and writer. Born at Betws-yn-Rhos, Denbighshire, he was educated locally and at Denbigh and Abergele. Ill-health forced him to spend some time in Egypt. In 1909 he was appointed a cataloguer at the National Library of Wales, and four years later he became a lecturer in Welsh at the University College of Wales, Aberystwyth, and later Professor of Welsh Literature.

Gwynn Jones was a very prolific writer and his works include novels, short stories, a play, a travel book, children's books and essays, together with translations, especially his *Awen y Gwyddyl* (from Irish) and Goethe's *Faust* (both 1922). It is his poetry, however, which makes him an outstanding figure in the 20th century. His *awdl* 'Ymadawiad Arthur' ('The Passing of Arthur') gained him the chair at Bangor Eisteddfod in 1902. The content is 19th-century romantic medievalism with Welsh nationalist undertones and is not particularly new, but distinguished from the general run of Eisteddfodic *awdl* by its choice vocabulary and narrative skill. His other chair *awdl*, 'Gwlad y Bryniau' ('Country of the Hills') (1909), is filled with the same longing for a romantic Welsh past, and this is presented by generalized characters like the soldier, the poet, etc. The synthesis of idealistic nationalism and romantic medievalism which characterizes his early poetry gradually yielded to a rationalization of the difference between idealism and actuality, so that his later poetry is melancholic. In his 6 major poems, 'Madog', 'Tir na-nOg', 'Broseliawnd', 'Anatiomaros', 'Argoed' and 'Cynddilig', he returned to the past for his inspiration, to medieval Wales and ancient Gaul. His characters are creatures of his imagination and represent those virtues which he found so rare in his own world.

Gwynn Jones was an artist in his command of language, with a wealth of felicitous phrasing to clothe his imaginative recreations of the past. This led him sometimes to play on words and he tended to become the victim of his own style. But he also explored the possibilities of adapting *cynghanedd* to accentual metres rather than to the traditional syllabic ones in which it had been evolved. He also used the old *englyn* (4-line stanza) as a couplet, particularly in 'Madog', with phenomenal success. [MR]

Ymadawiad Arthur a Chaniadau Ereill (1910); *Detholiad o Ganiadau* (1926); *Manion* (1932); *Caniadau* (1934); *Y Dwymyn* (1944).

Jonson, Ben (1572–1637). Dramatist, poet and man of letters. The posthumous son of a clergyman, he was educated at Westminster School, where the headmaster was William ◊ Camden. He worked briefly and humiliatingly as a bricklayer under his stepfather, served as a soldier in the Low Countries, married, and was an actor before 1597 when he wrote plays for ◊ Henslowe's company. He was part-author with ◊ Nashe of the satire *The Isle of Dogs* and was imprisoned. He wrote, or helped to write, get-penny entertainments like *Hot Anger Soon Cold*, *Robert the Second*, *King of Scots* and *Richard Crookback*, as well as the excellent additions to ◊ Kyd's *The Spanish Tragedy*. In 1598 he fought a duel with, and killed, an actor called Gabriel

Spencer, was imprisoned, but pleaded benefit of clergy. Essentially a learned man who drew sustenance from the classical writers, he allowed none of his early work to be printed. His first truly Jonsonian comedies were *Everyman in His Humour*, in which Shakespeare acted in 1598, and *Every Man out of His Humour*. Both are 'comedies of humours' in which each character is a type dominated by a ruling passion or obsession. *Poetaster* (1601), an allusive, topical satire on literary life, was his contribution to the War of the Theatres; ◊ Dekker (and possibly ◊ Marston) returned the attack in *Satiromastix, or The Untrussing of the Humorous Poet*, but he soon collaborated with Marston and ◊ Chapman on a lively London comedy *Eastward Ho!*, in which an anti-royal joke caused all three writers to be imprisoned. His run of great comedies consists of *Volpone*, a savage satire on human cupidity set in Venice (1606), *The Silent Woman* (1609), *The Alchemist*, another piece about confidence tricksters and their dupes vividly set in London (1610), and the looser, panoramic *Bartholomew Fair* (1614). His Roman tragedies, correct by classical standards, *Catiline His Conspiracy* and *Sejanus His Fall*, were never theatrical successes, and his later comedies, *The Devil Is an Ass* (1616), *The Staple of News* (1626), *The New Inn* (1629), *The Magnetic Lady* (1632) and *A Tale of a Tub* (1633), show a steady falling-off. His great comedies are lucidly planned, executed with classical precision, and often enriched by a superb command of low speech and local usage.

Jonson was the greatest English writer and contriver of court masques, producing 33 royal entertainments for King James, and inventing the grotesque or comic interlude of the anti-masque, his first success being *The Masque of Blackness* in 1605. In 1616 he was made Poet Laureate. He was also an honorary graduate of both Cambridge and Oxford. Between 1618 and 1619 he walked to Edinburgh, where he was acclaimed and made a burgess; his pithy, opinionated and revealing table-talk was taken down by William ◊ Drummond of Hawthornden. In Charles I's reign the great deviser of masques quarrelled with the great designer of them, Inigo Jones, whose increasingly elaborate spectacles eclipsed Jonson's words and songs. Jonson was replaced by Aurelian ◊ Townshend, and wrote embittered satires on Jones.

As a poet Jonson was a devotee of the plain style and wrote epistles, epigrams and satires, as well as superb songs in masques and plays and some moving elegies. *Timber* is a commonplace book on literary theory, supporting the classical doctrine of imitation of the masters. Jonson was himself the model for 'the tribe of Ben'. Throughout the 17th century William Shakespeare (to whom he had paid generous critical tribute in prose and verse) was placed next after Jonson among English dramatists. [MJ]

Ben Jonson, ed. C. H. Herford and P. and E. Simpson (11 vols., 1925–52).

M. Chute, *B.J. of Westminster* (1954); J. J. Enck, *J. and the Comic Truth* (Madison, Wisconsin, 1958); B. Gibbons, *Jacobean City Comedy* (1968); L. C. Knights, *Drama and Society in the Age of J.* (1937); E. Linklater, *B.J. and King James* (1931); J. C. Meagher, *Methods and Meaning in J.'s Masques* (1966); S. Orgel, *The Jonsonian Masque* (1965); E. B. Partridge, *The Broken Compass: A Study of J.'s Major Comedies* (1958); W. Trimpi, *B.J.'s Poems: A Study of the Plain Style* (Stanford, Calif., 1962).

Joyce, James (1882–1941). Irish novelist and short-story writer. He was born in Dublin, and educated at Clongowes Wood College, Belvedere College and University College, Dublin. At Belvedere he began to distinguish himself academically, winning a number of national scholastic prizes, and for a time, under Jesuit tutelage, he considered a priestly vocation. First that and then the Roman Catholic Church itself were abandoned by him, and the rejection was closely allied to his choice of an artistic career. In 1900, while he was still an undergraduate, his long review of Ibsen's last play was published in the *Fortnightly Review* (London). At this time he wrote a play which has not survived, did translations, wrote some literary criticism, collected his 'epiphanies' – prose-poetic and realistic sketches – and began writing the lyric poems later collected in *Chamber Music* (1907).

After graduation from university in 1902, Joyce lived for a time in Paris. During this time he contributed book reviews to Dublin newspapers, and in 1903 returned to Dublin for the fatal illness of his mother. In October 1904, he again left for the continent, this time taking with him Nora Barnacle, a Galway girl he had met in Dublin that summer. (Joyce and Nora were married only in 1931, to protect the legal rights of their two children.) From 1905 until 1915,

with minor exceptions, the Joyces lived in Trieste and Joyce worked as a teacher of English. There he completed *Dubliners*, a collection of 15 short stories he had begun in Dublin in 1904. In 1909 and 1912, Joyce made his last two trips to Ireland, to arrange the publication of *Dubliners*, over which he experienced much difficulty. (The satirical broadside 'Gas from a Burner' expresses his views.) The book was finally published, in England, in 1914, by which time he had nearly completed the final version of the quasi-autobiographical novel *A Portrait of the Artist as a Young Man*, which he had begun in 1904. This novel was published serially in the magazine *The Egoist* in 1914–15, through the help of Ezra Pound (whom Joyce had met in 1913), and in New York and London in 1916–17.

By this time Joyce had begun a 'sequel' (as he wrote to H. G. Wells) to the *Portrait*, developing an idea he had had for an additional short story in *Dubliners* into a comic novel of epic proportions, *Ulysses*. During 1915, Joyce also wrote his one published play, *Exiles*. In June, the Austrians in Trieste allowed Joyce to move with his family to neutral Switzerland, and for the duration of the war they lived in Zürich, where Joyce worked steadily at *Ulysses*. From March 1918, the American magazine *The Little Review* began to serialize *Ulysses* until prosecution suspended publication in 1920. The kind of difficulties which beset Joyce over *Dubliners* seemed to be recurring.

After the cessation of hostilities the Joyces returned for a time to Trieste, but in 1920 moved to Paris, which was to remain their home in the years between the two world wars. There *Ulysses* was completed and published in 1922. In 1923 Joyce began the composition of *Finnegans Wake*, a cosmic epic in a punning 'little language' which was to engross the remaining seventeen years of his life. Throughout these years Joyce was dogged by prolonged periods of eye trouble which were excruciatingly painful, required multiple operations, and resulted in a serious diminution of vision. From 1932, the increasing gravity of his daughter Lucia's mental condition, eventually diagnosed as schizophrenia, exacted more and more of Joyce's solicitous attention. *Finnegans Wake* was finally published in 1939, the Joyces once again left for neutral Switzerland in 1940, and two months later Joyce was dead of a perforated ulcer.

Joyce's writing incorporates extremes of

literary realism and symbolism. Each can be seen, precipitated out, in the posthumously published *Epiphanies*, where the realistic depiction of snatches of conversation is alternated with poeticizing passages of a *fin de siècle* intensity. His early poetry, in the sequence *Chamber Music*, 36 short lyrics written about various stages of a love-relationship, is mainly in the more romantic and impressionist style, though the quasi-Jacobean simplicity is cross-grained with a certain modern sophistication of vocabulary, rhythm and idea. ⟡ AE, the Irish mystic and poet, told Joyce that his poems proved he did not have 'enough chaos' in him – the literary understatement of the century.

Dubliners developed from the more realistic side of the *Epiphanies*. Though there are few reappearances of characters, the stories have continuity in a recognizably stable Dublin milieu and deal progressively with youth, adolescence, young manhood and maturity. In theme they are often about rebellion and revolt from the Dublin environment and entrapment within it. A young boy dreams of romance and the exotic but arrives at the church bazaar only as it is closing ('Araby'); a girl meditates elopement with her sailor boyfriend but is held back in her dingy shop-girl life by the memory of her mother's death-bed wish ('Eveline'); a man, meeting the London journalist he thinks he might have become, sees the extent of his own loss of manhood as his wife bullies him at home ('A Little Cloud'). The forms of submission to the milieu – and possibly even of triumph within it – become progressively more sophisticated in the collection. The final story, 'The Dead', is the longest and most complex, even to the point of ambiguity, as the acknowledgement of failure becomes itself a possible triumph. Despite the 'realism' of the working- and lower-middle-class milieus both the aspirations of the characters and a certain stylistic narrative delicacy preserve a more formal discipline in the stories.

Attempts to escape the demands of environment, successful and unsuccessful, provide the rhythmical basis of *A Portrait of the Artist as a Young Man*. The quasi-autobiographical figure of Stephen Dedalus moves from childhood to university in a series of selective tableaux reported, as it were, from the inside: Joyce's prose mimes Stephen's impressions at each stage of his growth. This is not yet the fully developed 'stream-of-consciousness'-exposing tech-

nique of parts of *Ulysses*, as we are not inside Stephen's mind, but events are seen as he would see them. These variable points of view control the realistic basis of the biographical story and account for a certain combination of sympathy and irony in the presentation: if things are shown as Stephen sees them, it is *only* as he sees them. We take leave of Stephen after his rejection of the Church, his vision of an artistic vocation and the careful, scholastic self-education in aesthetics by which he prepares himself for an artistic career. The definitive success or failure of his aims is not given us.

Nor is it given us when he reappears in *Ulysses*, though his hopes are severely deflated. Indeed all through the single day during which *Ulysses*' action takes place, he is occupied with the 'family, church and state' whose appeals he has not yet succeeded in throwing off and even with philosophical problems of his own potential development as an artist. In the *Portrait* he was confident, in *Ulysses* he is near-despondent, maintaining only a certain forced gaiety. In comparison to Stephen's 'day' we are given that of a type antithetical to him, an advertising canvasser of Jewish extraction named Leopold Bloom. If Stephen is thinking of making it a day of choice – perhaps to break with his friends and leave Ireland once again – Bloom has a crisis and choice thrust upon him: he knows that his wife Molly has arranged a tryst for that very afternoon with her concert-manager, 'Blazes' Boylan ('the worst man in Dublin', thinks Bloom).

In nearly alternating sections, we watch Stephen and Bloom's problems unfolded and developed. Will Bloom prevent the tryst? Will he go back home afterwards? Eventually, at midnight, Bloom rescues Stephen from an affray outside a brothel and takes him home, but Stephen refuses the kindly, if romantic, offer of lodgings and goes off into an unknown future. Bloom goes to bed.

Ulysses has an astounding technical virtuosity; it is a *tour de force* of literary styles. Joyce came to say that he wrote each chapter in a different style, stream-of-consciousness, literary and journalistic pastiches, surrealist fantasy, catechism, so that we not only have a story, but a large number of ways that story can be told and viewed. The notorious Homeric parallels, by which Bloom's wanderings approximate the *Odyssey*, have a similar, if dual effect, suggesting both Bloom's ennoblement to a kind of Odysseus and the distance he is from the heroic Greek world. That dual view, domestic and heroic, is rigorously codified in *Finnegans Wake* (1939; printed with author's corrections in text, 1964), the multivalence of whose punning language permits reference to many worlds simultaneously. Domestically about a Dublin publican with a wife and three children, the allegory has a number of wider worlds, where the publican becomes Everyman and his wife the quintessential Woman, or geographically the River Liffey that flows through Dublin. There is a cosmological (and eschatological) epic dimension and one in which the novel is our world, and the publican's artistic son (Shem) not only the eternal artist but James Joyce, author of the 'Blue Book of Eccles', *Ulysses*. If the difficulties of reading *Finnegans Wake* restrict it to a small audience, there is no doubt that the novel's scope is not similarly bounded. The artist-figure may no longer be presented, as he was in the *Portrait*, as a heroic, priestly figure, but the range of his interests has widened to the uttermost limits of human activity and knowledge.

There were several editions of *Ulysses* published before an edition was legally permitted in the U.S. (1934) and in the U.K. (1936). Of these the first was published by Shakespeare & Co., Paris, 1922. The edition published by The Odyssey Press, Hamburg, 1932, is textually the most accurate. [G]

Collected Poems (1936); *Letters*, i, ed. S. Gilbert (1957), ii and iii, ed. R. Ellmann (1966); *Critical Writings*, ed. E. Mason and R. Ellmann (1959); *The Essential J.J.*, ed. H. Levin (1948, 1963) (includes *Chamber Music*, *Dubliners*, *A Portrait of the Artist as a Young Man*, other poems and selections from *Ulysses* and *Finnegans Wake*).
R. Ellmann, *J.J.* (New York, 1959) (biography); H. Blamires, *The Bloomsday Book* (1966); S. Gilbert, *J.J.'s Ulysses* (1930, 1952); Seon Givens ed., *J.J.: Two Decades of Criticism* (New York, 1948, 1963); A. Glasheen, *A Census of Finnegans Wake* (1956), *A Second Census* (Northwestern U.P., 1963); S. L. Goldberg, *The Classical Temper* (1961); A. Goldman, *The J. Paradox* (1966); C. Hart, *Structure and Motif in Finnegans Wake* (1962); R. M. Kain, *Fabulous Voyager* (1959); H. Kenner, *Dublin's J.* (1955); H. Levin, *J. J.: A Critical Introduction* (revised edn, 1960).

Juliana or **Julian of Norwich**, Dame (1342–after 1416). Mystic. Juliana had the first of her mystical experiences or 'shewings' in 1373, following an illness, when she was still living in her mother's house. The shorter account of the revelations (*A Shewing of God's Love*, ed. A. M. Reynolds, 1958) was perhaps written soon after the event. The *Revelations of Divine Love* (ed. G. Warwick, 1901, repr. 1958; ed. R. Hudleston, 1952, modernized text; ed. C. Walters, Penguin Classics, 1966) is a fuller account of the same experience, seen in the light of twenty years' meditation and further mystical insight. It was completed before 1400, by which time Juliana was established in a cell at St Julian's Church, Norwich. She was connected with the Benedictine community at Carrow, though probably not a member of it. She was sought out as a spiritual counsellor, and there is a record of a visit paid to her by Margery ◊ Kempe some time between 1400 and 1410. She describes herself as 'a simple creature vnlettyrde' though she is clearly a woman of keen intellect and some learning. Like ◊ Rolle, she recounts her own mystical experiences, but adopts a much stricter standard of self-criticism, so that the accounts are impressively trustworthy. They are notable for their great freshness and simplicity and have the stylistic virtues of the other English mystics – compactness and particularity, with a sparing but effective use of imagery. [AG]

P. Molinari, *J. of N.* (1958); D. Knowles, *The English Mystics* (1927), and *The English Mystical Tradition* (1961); R. W. Chambers, *On the Continuity of English Prose* (1932).

Junius. Pseudonym of the writer of a series of 70 letters which appeared at irregular intervals in Woodfall's *Public Advertiser*, from 21 January 1769 to 21 January 1772. The letters, which were enormously popular and widely reprinted in London and provincial newspapers and periodicals, strongly attacked the ministries of the Duke of Grafton and Lord North, and the 'personal government of George III'. Letter 35 (19 December 1769) was an 'Address to the King' and caused Woodfall to be prosecuted in 1770 before Lord Mansfield for seditious libel; the City of London jury refused on a technical point to find him guilty. Woodfall published a collected edition of the *Junius Letters* (1772) with a preface by the writer; there are many other piracies and collections. The writer of the letters was master of a rather stiff invective, and exercised great influence on political and newspaper writing for a hundred years. His attacks on the Dukes of Grafton and Bedford and others are distinguished by violent, personal savagery. About 40 people have at one time or another been suggested as the writer. Sir Philip Francis (1740–1818), on no conclusive grounds, is most often cited; Lord Shelburne is another candidate.

The Letters of Junius were edited in 1927 by C. W. Everett from the 1772 text; he also prints the letters from Junius to his printer which are in the British Museum and gives much useful information. The literature of speculation on the writer's identity is vast. [AR]

F. Cordasco, *A J. Bibliography* (New York, 1949) (with an essay); T. H. Bowyer, *A Bibliographical Examination of the Earliest Editions of the Letters of J.* (U. of Virginia P., 1957) (with selection of sources and references).

K

Kailyard School. A moderately derisive title (from the Scottish kailyard, cabbage patch) given to a group of Scottish writers which exploited the sentimental aspects of Lowland life during the period 1880–1914. It derives from the motto of the poem *Beside the Bonnie Brier Bush* by John ◊ Watson, 'Ian Maclaren' – 'There is a bonnie briar bush in our kailyard'. J. M. ◊ Barrie contributed to the school with his *Auld Licht Idylls* (1888) and *A Window in Thrums* (1889), the rustic coyness in both of these books being tolerably redeemed by wit. But novels by S. R. ◊ Crockett and others in this vein pursued Scottish country quaintness into whimsical middens which were less endurable. [R B]

J. H. Millar, *A Literary History of Scotland* (1903); G. Blake, *Barrie and the Kailyard School* (1951).

Kames, Lord. ◊ Home, Henry.

Kavanagh, Patrick (1905–67). Poet. The son of an Irish cobbler, Kavanagh was born in Co. Monaghan, and was self-educated. As a young man he was a small farmer, and also worked for a time as a shoe-maker. In 1939 he made his way to Dublin and to free-lance literary journalism, by which time his first volume of verse, *Ploughman and Other Poems* (1936), and an autobiography, *The Green Fool* (1938), which he later dismissed as 'stage-Irish rubbish', had already been published. For some years, Kavanagh continued to support himself precariously by writing gossip columns and film criticism for Irish newspapers, until in 1955 he joined the staff of the Board of Extra-Mural Studies of University College, Dublin. His publications include a long poem, *The Great Hunger* (1942), a collection of verse, *A Soul for Sale* (1947), and a novel, *Tarry Flynn* (1948; re-issued 1965). The novel was a failure, but the quality of Kavanagh's verse remained constant over the years, though he appears not to have undergone any significant poetic development. A comparatively recent collection, *Come Dance with Kitty Stobling* (1960), revealed the poet's usual somewhat dry fluency to be function-

ing as capably as it had always done. He is a master of the lively rhythm rather than of the striking phrase, for his language is inclined to be ordinary, and his thought frequently verges on the trite. The best of his verse, however, is undoubtedly entertaining; lyrically musical rather than intellectually stimulating. [C O]

Collected Poems (1964); *Collected Prose* (1967).

Kaye-Smith, Sheila (1887–1956). Novelist. Born at Hastings, Sussex, the daughter of a doctor, and educated at the Hastings and St Leonards Ladies' College. To alleviate the boredom of 'a world of afternoon calls, at homes, and subscription dances' she began writing novels. Her first, *The Tramping Methodist*, was published in 1908, and used as its background the Sussex countryside, which was the main feature of her work. From then until her death she published nearly 50 books, of which the best known are the novels *Starbrace*, *The Hidden Son* and *Joanna Godden*. Marriage in 1924 and conversion to the Catholic Church filled the threatening emptiness of her life, but her writing showed little or no development. Stories of rural Sussex, often set back historically, such as *Green Apple Harvest*, with its hero a young farmer caught up in the Evangelical movement, are characteristic of her work. She also wrote 2 volumes of autobiographical sketches, *Three Ways Home* (1937) and *All the Books in My Life* (1956), some poetry and religious biography. Later novels include *The Lardners and the Laurelwoods* (1948) and *Mrs Gailey* (1951). [J M]

Keating, G. ◊ Céitinn, S.

Keats, John (1795–1821). Poet. The son of a livery stable keeper, he trained as a medical student after an education at private school. He became determined to support himself as a poet, gave up his training, and was taken under the wing of Leigh ◊ Hunt, who sponsored his first publication. In spite of this Keats's work never belonged to the kind of writing, that of the 'Cockney school' of poetry, that Leigh Hunt represented. By 1816 Keats was writing mature and controlled poetry. His first published volume (1817), which included 'On First Looking into Chapman's Homer' and 'Sleep and Poetry', revealed the imaginative and energetic appreciation of life which was to be an important part of his later poetry. His second volume, *Endymion* (1818), was less controlled, a wandering and extravagant succession of rich imagery and lush descriptive passages. The allegory of the search for beauty which the poem presents is vague and undirected, but there are sure signs of the delicacy of phrasing and firmness of rhythm that came later. Keats was attacked by the Tory ⟡ *Blackwood's Magazine*, which associated him with Hunt's radicalism, and *Endymion* was savaged in the *Quarterly Review*.

Towards the end of 1818 Keats fell in love with Fanny Brawne, whom he was never able to marry. Under the emotional strain of this unhappy and tormenting love affair Keats produced his greatest work. 'Isabella; or the Pot of Basil' (1820) followed *Endymion*. Written in *ottava rima* there is a bright but stark balladic strain in the poem which guides its emotional grimness. In language and tone it hints at the achievement of 'The Eve of Saint Agnes' (1820), which brilliantly displays the more conventional characteristics of Romanticism that automatically associated Keats with the Romantic movement. In Spenserian stanzas it binds together sparkling heraldic symbols of love and cold threatening symbols of hostility to form a rich and clear-cut version of medievalism. 'La Belle Dame Sans Merci' (1820) is nightmarish in its apparent simplicity and chilling suggestiveness. But it is Keats's odes that represent the peak of his achievement. In these the impression of his senses responding to experience with a painful intensity is at its most powerful, and provides the root of his contradictory feelings and aspirations. In 'Ode to a Nightingale' and 'Ode on a Grecian Urn' (both 1820) Keats explores the relationship between the static but immortal lifelessness of art and the vital but condemned experiences of life. Keats himself longs for death as an escape from decay, but embraces life with all his senses. The everlasting beauty of the figures on the urn is compelling, but experience is reduced to a cold, unfulfilled instant. The 'Ode to Autumn' is a less complex poem, creating a more optimistic mood out

of a sympathetic identification with season and landscape. In these odes Keats's closely woven sensuous imagery, the deeply felt, precise and suggestive language, the flowing but measured rhythms combine to produce poetry that is full of impact and unforgettable.

'Lamia' (1820) continued the exploration of the conflict between art and life, but in a more confused and diffusive manner. The lack of clarity and cohesion prevents its success, although there are passages of immense sinister power. Keats's final work was a rewritten version of an earlier poem, *Hyperion*, originally written in deliberately Miltonic blank verse. Dissatisfied with the results of Milton's influence Keats attempted in his second version, *The Fall of Hyperion*, to adopt a less restrictive and more accommodating style. As with *Endymion* and 'Lamia' he tries to inject a story from Greek mythology with an allegorical meaning, but neither version was finished. In February 1820, the tuberculosis that had already killed his mother and brother became unmistakeable, and Keats died in Rome a year later.

Much of our appreciation of Keats comes from reading his many letters, which contain, as well as the lively, humorous descriptions of people and places, discussions of his feelings and theories about poetry. These are important critically both in our approach to Keats's own poetry and in our reading of the poetry of the Romantic movement. [J R C]

The Poetical Works and Other Writings, ed. H. B. and M. B. Forman (8 vols., 1938); *Poetical Works*, ed. H. W. Garrod (1956); *The Letters*, ed. H. E. Rollins (1958); *Selected Poems and Letters*, ed. R. Sharrock (1964); ed. R. Gittings (1966).
A. Ward, *J.K.: The Making of a Poet* (1963); R. Gittings, *J.K.* (1968); Sir Sidney Colvin, *J.K.* (1917); M. R. Ridley, *K.'s Craftsmanship* (1933); R. H. Fogle, *The Imagery of K. and Shelley* (1949); E. Pettet, *On the Poetry of K.* (1957); W. J. Bate, *The Stylistic Development of K.* (1958); B. Blackstone, *The Consecrated Urn* (1959).

Keble, John (1792–1866). Hymnodist and founder of the Oxford Movement. Born at Fairford in Gloucestershire, the son of the Rev. John Keble, vicar of Coln St Aldwyn, he was educated by his father and at Corpus Christi College, Oxford, where he was elected Fellow and tutor of Oriel College (becoming a colleague of J. H. ⟡ Newman and Pusey). He took orders (1817) and became his father's curate. During this country retirement, he wrote his enormously popular collection of sacred verse, *The Christian Year* (2 vols., anonymous, 1827; Everyman, 1914). His verse is a mixture of watered-down Wordsworthian 'love of nature' and sentimental piety. Although written to steal the fire of the Evangelicals' imagination, his work is difficult to distinguish now from theirs. He was elected Professor of Poetry at Oxford (1831), and published more verse, *Lyra Innocentium* (1846); a posthumous *Miscellaneous Poems* appeared in 1869. In July 1833, Keble preached an intolerant Assize sermon at Oxford on 'national apostasy', in which he attacked the Erastian and latitudinarian tendencies (as he thought them) of the contemporary Anglican Church and government. This caught the mood of many members of the university, and of the Church in general. Keble, Newman (who quickly overshadowed the rest in ability) and others, building on the enthusiasm generated, started a generally 'Catholic' and 'traditional' series of *Tracts for the Times*, short essays on the liturgy, Church history and doctrinal points. Keble wrote 8 of these, taking a rather high line on 'submission to authority', the rights of priests and the dangers of free-thinking. He became vicar of Hursley, near Winchester, where he died. Keble published various other ecclesiastical works, including a translation of Irenaeus and an edition of the works of Hooker. His *Lectures on Poetry: 1832–41* appeared in 1844 (2 vols.; tr. from the Latin by E. K. Francis, 1912). Keble College, Oxford, is named in his memory. [A R]

Sir J. T. Coleridge, *A Memoir of J.K.* (1869); W. Lock, *J.K.* (1893) (with bibliography); E. F. L. Wood, *J.K.* (1909; 1932); G. Faber, *Oxford Apostles* (1936; 1954).

Kempe, Margery (1373?–1440?). Mystic. The daughter of a former Mayor of Lynn, in Norfolk, she married the burgess John Kempe in 1393, and carried on business, unsuccessfully, as a brewer and miller. After her first child was born, she suffered from madness, but was restored to sanity by an apparition of Christ and experienced religious conversion. Eventually, in 1413, she persuaded her husband to take vows of chastity, and embarked on a series of pilgrimages, about England, and to Rome, Santiago and the Holy Land. Her auto-biography (*The Book of Margery Kempe*, ed. S. B. Meech, H. E. Allen, 1940; abridged edn W. Butler-Bowden, 1936), set down in old age (1432–6) with the help of two clerks, since she was illiterate, records these journeys, and the many religious experiences she claimed to have had.

Her testimony regarding these is not reliable, for though earnest and pious she was a neurotic and hysterical personality. However, she was taken seriously by many, including ◊ Juliana of Norwich, whom she visited, and her beliefs were orthodox. She knew ◊ Hilton's work, but there are more fruitful parallels to her piety in female European mystics like St Bridget of Sweden, whom she consciously imitated. King's Lynn's trading connexions are significant here. As a social document, and the record of a formidable personality, the book is immensely rich. The style suggests her dictation – it is homely and vivid, very close to the rhythms of speech, and studded with proverbial and idiomatic expressions. [A G]

D. Knowles, *The English Mystics* (1927), and *The English Mystical Tradition* (1961); H. S. Bennett, *Chaucer and the Fifteenth Century* (1947); L. Collis, *The Apprentice Saint* (1964).

Kennedy, Margaret (1896–1967). Novelist. Born in London, the elder daughter of a barrister, she was educated at Cheltenham and Somerville College, Oxford, where she read history. Her first book was a commissioned history, *A Century of Revolution* (1922). In 1923, her novel *The Ladies of London* was published. Of her fiction, the best known is her story with a sentimental heroine, *The Constant Nymph* (1924; dramatized with Basil Dean, 1926; later filmed). Other novels are *Red Sky at Morning* (1927); *Together and Apart* (1936); *The Feast* (1950); *Troy Chimneys* (1953), which won the James Tait Black prize; and *A Night in Cold Harbour* (1960). She had a gift for humorous characterization of odd or minor foibles. She wrote several plays (e.g. *Escape Me Never!*, 1934) and a study, *Jane Austen* (English Novelists Series, 1950). [A R]

Ker, W(illiam) P(aton) (1855–1923). Scholar. Born in Glasgow and educated there at the Academy and University, from which he went on a Snell exhibition to Balliol College, Oxford, he was elected Fellow of All Souls in 1879 and continued to be active in that college until he died. His life was spent teaching, and he was one of those who guided the early development of English studies as an academic discipline, along historical and linguistic lines. He was assistant in humanity (Latin) at the University of Edinburgh; in 1883, he was appointed Professor of English Literature and History at the newly founded University College in Cardiff; and in 1889 he succeeded Henry ♢ Morley as Professor of English Language and Literature at University College, London. He was an active academic politician in London University, and also became Director of Scandinavian Studies, which he organized. Ker's linguistic and literary interests covered all Europe, particularly in the medieval period, and he was one of the authorities in England on genre criticism and the history of literary forms. His chief works, which were very influential, were: *Epic and Romance* (1897); *The Dark Ages* (1904); *English Literature: Medieval* (1912). He was Professor of Poetry at Oxford (1920–2) and published *The Art of Poetry: Seven Lectures* (1923); he edited medieval and other texts and was a well-known Alpinist. [AR]

D. J. Palmer, *The Rise of English Studies* (1965); B. Ifor Evans, *W.P.K. as a Critic of Literature* (W.P. Ker Lectures 16, 1955); J. H. P. Pafford, *W.P.K., a Bibliography* (1950).

Keyes, Sidney (1922–43). Poet. A lonely childhood caused him to acquire much 'rustic innocence and antique wisdom'. Most of his poems were written between his arrival at Oxford in 1940 and his death in the Tunisian campaign. His friend, John Heath-Stubbs, enlarged Keyes's knowledge of technique, and gave his romanticism point by tracing the origins of romanticism in legend, in medieval verse and even in the Augustans. In *The Iron Laurel* (1942) and *The Cruel Solstice* (1943) Keyes avoided the neo-romantic fashion, trying to express 'some inkling of the fusion of finite with infinite, spiritual and physical, which is our world'. Pain, death and guilt are his preoccupations, but his gift was for the rendering of sense impressions, apt similes and quiet lyrical effects. He was skilled in dramatic monologue and blank verse. In his ambitious poems 'The Foreign Gate' and 'The Wilderness' he aims to unify his erudition, his hopes of love, and his anticipation of death. [FG]

Collected Poems, ed. and intr. M. Meyer (1945).

King, Henry (1592–1669). Poet and preacher. Son of John King (Vice-Chancellor of Oxford, later Bishop of London, a favourite preacher of King James I and friend of John Donne), he was educated at Westminster School, where Lancelot ♢ Andrewes taught, and at Christ Church, Oxford, of which his father was then Dean. He was known as a writer at the university where he took his M.A. in 1614 and subsequently his D.D. in 1625. With his family connexions his early rise in the Church was rapid: he was successively Canon of St Paul's (where Donne was Dean), Archdeacon of Colchester, chaplain to the Court, and Canon of Christ Church, Oxford, but became Dean of Rochester only in 1638, possibly losing influential friends at the time of his father's death in 1621. He became Bishop of Chichester in 1642, defended his diocese, unsuccessfully, against the Puritan army, and was forced to take refuge with recusants. He published a translation of the Psalms in 1651 and a pirated edition of the poems appeared in 1657. In 1659 he conspired with the Bishop of Oxford to organize clandestine consecration of bishops, but failed. At the Restoration he was restored to his bishopric; he preached Jacobean sermons at Charles II's court, and denounced Puritanism in Sussex. He hoped to be translated to the Archbishopric of York, but died at an advanced age in 1669.

As a poet King was influenced both by Ben Jonson and by Donne, and he wrote elegies on both poets. His amorous poems show a Donnean wit, while other poems have a Jonsonian discipline and precision. Most of his poetry was occasional and almost half consisted of funeral elegies on public and literary men, including one on Sir Walter Ralegh and the memorable 'Upon the Death of My Ever Desired Friend Doctor Donne Dean of Pauls', whose literary executor he was. His most famous work is 'The Exequy', a great and personal poem on the early death of his young wife in 1624, and one of the finest poems of its century. Less complex than Donne, King drew strength from the Metaphysical tradition. [MJ]

The Poems, ed. J. R. Baker (Denver, Col. 1960); *The Poems*, ed. M. Crum (1965); *The Poems*, ed. J. Sparrow (1925).

R. Berman, *H.K. and the Seventeenth Century* (1964); D. Bush, *English Literature in the Earlier Seventeenth Century* (1962).

Kinglake, Alexander William (1809–91). Traveller and historian. Born in Somerset and educated at Eton and Trinity College, Cambridge, he was called to the bar (1837) and was a successful lawyer, but is known for 2 non-legal works. The first, *Eothen* (1844; Everyman, ed. H. Sponder, 1908, 1954; World's Classics, 1900; ed. F. Baker, 1964) (Greek $E\omega\theta\varepsilon\nu$ = towards the dawn), a description of his travels in Egypt and the Levant, is one of the minor classics of travel-writing. It is full of historical insight and sympathy with the places visited, the product of the typical 19th-century English love of the East. In 1856 he gave up the law for writing. He accompanied the British army in the Crimea and, at the request of Lady Raglan (widow of the Commander-in-Chief), produced his elaborate work of art, *The Invasion of the Crimea* (8 vols., 1863–87). This is biased in favour of Raglan, but generally acknowledged to be (if somewhat long) one of the best war histories in English. [AR]

W. Tuckwell, *A.W.K.*, *A Biographical and Critical Study* (1902); F. T. Wood, 'An English Traveller of the Nineteenth Century'. *Anglica* (1946); R. Fedden, 'Towards the Dawn and the Sun-rising', *Nineteenth Century*, CXLIV (1948)

Kingsley, Charles (1819–75). Clergyman, novelist, historian and miscellaneous writer. Born at Holne Vicarage, near Dartmoor, and educated at King's College, London, and Magdalene College, Cambridge. He took orders and became curate of Eversley in Hampshire (1842), rector (1844), canon of Chester (1869) and of Westminster (1873). He was a chaplain to the Queen. Kingsley's voluminous literary work was varied: he was something of a poet, publishing a verse semi-drama about St Elizabeth of Hungary, *The Saint's Tragedy* (1848), and a small volume of poems, *Andromeda and Other Poems* (1858), which includes among the songs and ballads his best poem 'The Sands of Dee' (often anthologized). Kingsley was a Christian deeply concerned about social reform, though (as might be expected of a 'Christian socialist' at this time, influenced by F. D. ◊ Maurice and ◊ Carlyle) he 'believed in the people' but preached against violent change, in favour of moral persuasion. He wrote pamphlets under the name 'Parson Lot'. His fiction was broadly speaking written as propaganda. *Yeast* (*Fraser's Magazine*, 1848; 1850) – the title is symbolic of the 'ferment of new ideas' – deals powerfully but superficially with the bad conditions of the country poor. *Alton Locke* (1850), in a similar way, treats of the squalor in towns; it is also aimed against the Chartists' direct-action tactics. Kingsley advocated 'saner' policies, the country life, cheerful religion. He did succeed in arousing the middle-class conscience. His most popular work, *Westward Ho!* (1855), a tale of Elizabethan adventure, is made unreadable now by its uncritical nationalism (the popular wave of Crimean War enthusiasm influenced its writing) and its transference of Victorian morals to the 16th century. Other stories were *Hereward the Wake* (1866) and a once-popular children's book, *The Water Babies* (1863). This was written to foster the love of nature but its uncertain tone, neither adult parable nor fantasy for children, has prevented its survival. Kingsley was made Professor of Modern History at Cambridge (1860–9) and, over a review of some volumes of the *History of England* by ◊ Froude, got into controversy with ◊ Newman. The controversy drew the latter's *Apologia*. Kingsley was a biased and not very well-read historian, and as a debater no match for the Catholic champion. His historical works include a volume of lectures *The Roman and the Teuton* (1864). He also wrote *The Heroes* (1856), a retelling of classical myths for children, and *Prose Idylls* (1873), rather over-written for modern taste. Throughout his life he published sermons written in a straightforward, effective style. [AR]

Life and Works (19 vols., 1901–3).
S. E. Baldwin, *C.K.* (Cornell U.P., 1934); M. F. Thorp, *C.K.* (Princeton, 1937); V. Pope-Hennessy, 'K. as a Children's Writer', *TLS* (15 June 1951); R. B. Martin, *The Dust of Combat* (New York, 1960); J. B. Barry, Bibliography, in *Victorian Fiction*, ed. L. Stevenson (Cambridge, Mass., 1964).

Kingsley, Henry (1830–76). Journalist and novelist. Brother of Charles ◊ Kingsley, he was at Worcester College, Oxford, but as a result of some trouble went without a degree to Australia (1853–8). Experiences in the bush, in the gold-diggings and in the Sydney Mounted Police gave him material for some of his novels, which are rather rambling; but the poor narrative line is redeemed by the author's generous sympathy and insight into character. The best known of his novels are *The Recollections of Geoffrey Hamlyn* (1859), an adventure story of the old settlers in Australia; *Ravenshoe* (1862; World's Classics, 1925), containing a melodramatic narrative of family secrets, seduction and the wronged heir restored; and *The Hillyars and the Burtons* (1865), another Australian story. Some keen observation of slum life is interesting. Kingsley joined the Edinburgh *Daily Review* (1869) as editor, but abandoned this post to become the paper's correspondent during the Franco-Prussian War. [AR]

S. M. Ellis, *H.K.: Towards a Vindication* (1931) (bibliography); R. B. Martin, *The Dust of Combat* (New York, 1960); A. Thirkell, 'H.K.', *Nineteenth Century Fiction*, v (1959).

Kinsella, Thomas (1928–). Irish poet. Kinsella was born in Dublin and educated by the Christian Brothers; he works as a Civil Servant for the Government of Eire. An intensely introspective poet, he has published several slim volumes of tightly controlled elemental verse, including *The Starlit Eye* (1952), *Another September* (1958), *Moralities* (1960), *Poems and Translations* (New York, 1961), *Downstream* (1962) and *Nightwalker* (1967). He has also published translations of early Irish poetry. [PJK]

Kipling, (Joseph) Rudyard (1865–1936). Poet, short-story writer, journalist and imperialist. Born in Bombay, the son of John Lockwood Kipling, a talented man who taught sculpture at the school of art there and was later curator of the museum at Lahore. His mother was the sister of Lady Burne-Jones, and another sister was Stanley Baldwin's mother. In 1871, Kipling was sent home to England, first to an elderly, evangelical relative's at Southsea, where his lonely and unhappy life was later the material for a story, *Baa, Baa, Black Sheep*. A series of schoolboy stories, *Stalky and Co.* (1899), in which Beetle is something of a self-portrait, is based on his life at the United Services College, Westward Ho!, a minor public school for the sons of service officers, to which he was sent in 1878. Here he began writing verse, and his first publication was a privately printed volume, *Schoolboy Lyrics* (1881). From 1882 to 1889, he was on the staff of the Lahore *Civil and Military Gazette*, and also wrote for the Allahabad *Pioneer*. The discipline,

observation and information he acquired as a journalist, as well as the wide experience of all kinds of activity on the varied Indian scene, formed Kipling. The observation was raised to great art in some of his stories, where the surface of life is the medium he works with. The information, treated with skilful empathy in the animal stories at his best, often becomes a kind of knowingness that can infuriate readers, a kind of 'in' talk about the army or steam-engines that parallels his 'inside information' on political, national and racial questions. He produced a body of work in India, stories, sketches and poems, which becoming known in England, made him already famous when he arrived to live in London in 1889, and introduced him to the leading writers of the time. *Departmental Ditties*, a volume of verse, had appeared in 1886, and in 1888 several volumes of stories such as *Plain Tales from the Hills*, *Soldiers Three* and *Wee Willie Winkie*. These early stories introduce the immortal privates Ortheris, Mulvaney and Learoyd, and show much that is characteristic of his later work. The stories are brilliantly and economically related and sometimes placed within a framework (though this is commoner later) that enforces and enhances the point of the tale. They introduce the concept of the 'Law', outside which stand the other breeds, and which is basic to Kipling's imperialism. The idea, however, is not without a hard application that Kipling's detractors too often attempt to shout down rather than argue down. The stories romanticize the life of soldiers at war, but are harsh, too, and attack the English public's indifference to what he considered their military and imperial commitments; they praise violence as a former of character, and similarly value highly the efficiency of the technicians of empire, the soldiers and Civil Servants who fight the problems. They are also permeated with a strange, at times hysterical, humour not without a repulsive fascination.

In 1891, Kipling published his only novel, *The Light that Failed*, not quite successful as a whole; it contains the seeds of a strange prejudice against women, as a kind of vampire. On one level, the 'light' is an artist's eye-sight, and Kipling's idea of art is dedicated and efficient craftsmanship (often spoiled by the 'rag and a bone and a hank of hair' of one of his poems). In 1892, he published his second volume of poems,

Barrack Room Ballads, which contains some of his most popular work, such as 'The Road to Mandalay', 'Gunga Din' and 'If'. Kipling was a real, if rhetorical, poet, just as Macaulay was a rhetorical writer. Sometimes the rhetoric is empty, and masks vague ideas being used as counters, but sometimes it works. Hymns, music-hall songs, ballads, the public poetry, lie behind his verse. He also experiments with form and language, especially the language of his soldier-poems, a kind of literary cockney. Throughout his life he was fascinated by regional and class dialect as a tool of his art. He can turn a neat idea into a neat verse, but most often, as in his fiction, failure comes from technique being betrayed by narrow and inadequate ideas, such as notions of 'blood', 'race' and unquestioning obedience. Kipling assumed the role of national bard with some seriousness, and published verses like 'Recessional' (1897) in *The Times*, without fee; however, in 1895 he refused the laureateship, offered to him after the death of Tennyson. Kipling married an American, and from 1892 to 1896 he lived on his wife's property in Vermont; the experiment was not a success, and perhaps underlies some of his at times extreme anti-Americanism, though there were good doctrinal and commonsense reasons for this.

A book of stories, *Many Inventions* (1893), contains 'His Private Honour' and 'Love O' Women', and also introduces the wild boy, Mowgli (though grown up here), one of his most successful creations, who figures in his books for children. The latter contain some of his most lasting writing, though the 'Laws of the Jungle' closely resemble the 'Law' of the white man's burden. They are made up of the two 'Jungle Books' (*The Jungle Book*, 1894, and *The Second Jungle Book*, 1895); *Captains Courageous* (1897), a somewhat inferior adventure story of character-building hardship and the sheltered young; *Kim* (1901), his best long work, a secret service story of a boy's dream world (both Kim's and Kipling's) in a British India taken for granted; and the *Just So Stories* (1902), which with the 'Jungle Books' are not really beast fables in the usual sense, but depend on Kipling's empathy with the variety of animals. His narrative technique was never more masterly. Two other books for children, *Puck of Pook's Hill* (1906) and *Rewards and Fairies* (1910), show two other

sides to Kipling, which appear in his fiction generally: his interest in the supernatural, and his sense of the continuity of English history, particularly as seen in the ancient Sussex countryside and among its queer and taciturn peasants. The Roman legionaries are again the efficient technicians of an empire not altogether usefully directed; the peasants, like their Indian brethren, go stubbornly about their affairs regardless of rulers.

In 1902, Kipling retired to Burwash, where he lived for the rest of his life (his house, Bateman's, is opened to the public by the National Trust). During the Boer War, he attacked the imperialists, not for being wrong, but for being inefficient. In 1900, he went to South Africa and wrote some brilliant war-correspondent reports. His imperialist ideas strengthened. His prophecies, first against the Russians, then against the Germans, grew sterner and gloomier. Thereafter, Kipling, though always successful and rich, never quite enjoyed the wide popularity of his earlier years. His books became too polemical for great audiences; he had never been accepted by the 'leaders' of literature. His volumes of stories at this time, like *Traffics and Discoveries* (1904) and *Actions and Reactions* (1909), include accompanying poems. During the First World War, he wrote much journalism for the war effort, and after the war continued his preoccupation with imperial themes. His continued anti-German sentiments put him increasingly out of touch with a wide public, nor did he adjust to any viable political consideration of the labour movement, the important post-war domestic concern. His son had been killed in 1915, and Kipling's stories became more sombre. From themes of ordeal, which tried and proved the efficiency and spirit of the soldier or administrator, he moved to tales of strains that went beyond the breaking point. A parallel development (perhaps in reaction to his being typed as a 'popular writer') took place in his technique; the stories became more allusive, obscure and difficult to interpret. These last stories, with themes of healing and a deepening appreciation of the power of art, appeared in *Debits and Credits* (1926), *Thy Servant a Dog* (1930) and *Limits and Renewals* (1932). Modern criticism has generally held these to contain some of his very finest writing, such as 'Mrs Bathurst', one of the greatest short stories in the language. The stories often work by a kind of unconscious, subterranean movement of symbolism, and are not susceptible of any 'explanation'. He refused the Order of Merit, and is buried in Westminster Abbey.

Something of Myself (1937) is an autobiography. The 'Sussex Edition' of his collected works (35 vols., 1937–9) is definitive, incorporating later revisions; the American 'Burwash Edition' (28 vols., New York, 1941) prints this text: there are several other English and American collections. English first publication was usually in the 'Uniform Edition' (28 volumes, 1899–1938). [A R]

A Choice of K.'s Verse (1941) (with important introduction by T. S. Eliot); A Choice of K.'s Prose, intr. Somerset Maugham (1952).
C. Carrington, R.K.: His Life and Work (1955); C. H. Brown, K.: A New Appreciation (1945); J. M. S. Tompkins, The Art of R.K. (1959); C. A. G. Bodelsen, Aspects of K.'s Art (1964) (on later stories); ed. A. Rutherford, K.'s Mind and Art (1964); B. Dobrée, R.K. (WTW, 1951; revised 1965) (with select bibliography and an index to the short stories); T. R. Henn, K. (1967); Edmund Wilson, The Wound and the Bow (New York, 1941); George Orwell, in Critical Essays (1946); L. Trilling, The Liberal Imagination (1951); N. Annan, 'K.'s Place in the History of Ideas', Victorian Studies, III (1960); J. I. M. Stewart, Eight Modern Writers (1963); F. V. Livingston, Bibliography of the Works of R.K. (New York, 1927) and Supplement (Harvard U.P., 1938); J. I. M. Stewart and A. W. Yeats, K.: A Bibliographical Catalogue (Toronto U P., 1959); English Fiction in Transition, iii, 3, 4, and 5 (1960); Kipling Journal (1927 ff).

Kirkup, James (1923–   ). Poet and prose writer. Born in South Shields, he has given a vivid account of an unusually happy proletarian boyhood in his autobiography, *The Only Child* (1957). His poems are noted for a combination of exact observation of detail with a traditional taste in metrics and diction. He was Gregory Fellow at Leeds for some years and later taught in Japan and Hawaii. His most famous poem is probably 'A Correct Compassion', a detailed account of an operation involving the removal and replacement of a human heart. Latterly many of his poems have had Far Eastern settings. His descriptive and autobiographical prose has the same vividness of detail as his poems. [G S F]

The Cosmic Shape (1947); The Drowned Sailor (1947); The Creation (1951); The Submerged Village (1951); A Spring Journey (1954); The Prodigal Son (1959); These Horned Islands (1962); The Love of Others (1962); Refusal to Conform (1963).

Klein, Abraham Moses (1909–   ). Canadian poet. Born in Montreal and educated at McGill University and the French-speaking University of Montreal, he first published poetry in 1929 and was represented in the important *New Provinces* anthology (1936). He practised law from 1933 until his health broke down in 1954, and on recovering turned to public relations work in Montreal. He is a student of Joyce, has edited Jewish journals, has lectured in support of Zionism and is a prominent Talmudist. His first collection, *Hath Not a Jew* (1940), is a brilliant exploitation of the riches of Jewish culture. In 1944 he published *Poems* and the savage couplets of *The Hitleriad*. His fourth volume, *The Rocking Chair* (1948), treats of the mixed cultures of French Canada, but he returns to Jewish themes in the symbolic novel *The Second Scroll* (1951). The passion of the Zionist pilgrimage is here recreated in vivid, allusive prose. Klein's often humorous poetry is erudite and rhetorical without becoming obscure or verbose. The conflict between rejection and celebration of life is reflected in a presiding irony. [P T]

D. Pacey, Ten Canadian Poets (1958); M. W. Steinberg, 'A Twentieth Century Pentateuch (The Second Scroll)', in Canadian Literature, 2 (Autumn, 1959).

Knight, George Wilson (1897–   ). Literary critic. Born in Surrey and educated at Dulwich College and Oxford, he began his career as a schoolmaster (1920–31), and then became Professor of English at Toronto University, where his main interest was in Shakespeare, and where, as well as writing criticism, he produced and acted in many of the plays. His critical works, such as *Myth and Miracle* (1929), *The Wheel of Fire* (1930) and *The Imperial Theme* (1931), traced new lines of Shakespearean criticism, emphasizing the poetic themes and symbols which run through the plays. In 1941 he returned to Britain and in 1946 went to teach at Leeds University, where he was Professor of English in 1956–62. His later books include *The Starlit Dome* (1941), on the vision of the Romantic poets, and *The Crown of Life* (1947), on the last plays of Shakespeare, as well as work on the staging of Shakespeare. Knight has been influential in the critical movement which considers Shakespeare's plays as symbolic poems and pays close attention to their pattern of imagery. He has also championed Byron both as poet and as moral personality (*Lord Byron: Christian Virtues*, 1952) and, in his later years, developed and applied in various ways a highly original theory of the bisexuality of genius. [JM]

Knights, L(ionel) C(harles) (1906–   ). Critic. Educated at Selwyn and Christ's College, Cambridge. He taught English at Manchester University (1933–47), Sheffield (Professor, 1947–53) and Bristol (Professor, 1952–63). He is now Edward VII Professor of English at Cambridge. He was a member of the editorial board of ◊ *Scrutiny* until it ceased publication in 1963. He belongs to that group of Cambridge critics, which included F. R. ◊ Leavis and Q. D. Leavis, who in the 1930s sought to develop close reading and an emphasis on the social setting of literature as profitable ways to develop a complete response to a work of art. His book *Drama and Society in the Age of Jonson* (1937) was a valiant attempt to relate economic activities and general culture in a period which had traditionally been the province of more old-fashioned Shakespeare scholars. Knights showed a brilliant analytical mind in discussing the dramatic poems, but his book does not really unite this with the preliminary economic history summary. In addition this summary needs revision in the light of more modern knowledge of the economic facts. *Explorations: Essays in Criticism* (1946), mainly on the 17th century, has a wide range of reference and moves away in an original fashion from the analysis of critical clichés like 'character' to a more strenuous unified sensibility as the reader's response. His other books include *Some Shakespearean Themes* (1959), *An Approach to Hamlet* (1960) and *Further Explorations* (1965). Knights is one of the most influential modern historical critics. [AR]

Knox, John (*c.* 1514–72). The architect of the Scottish Reformation. Born at Haddington and educated probably at St Andrews University under John ◊ Major, Knox began to preach after the burning of his Reforming friend George Wishart in 1546 and was himself condemned to the French galleys after the failure of the Protestant revolt at St Andrews in 1547. On his release he preached in England, declining a bishopric from Edward VI and leaving for Geneva on the accession of Mary Tudor; his attack on Mary Tudor and on the Scottish Queen Regent, Mary of Lorraine, published in 1558 as *The First Blast of the Trumpet against the Monstrous Regiment of Women*, misfired by embroiling him with both Queen Elizabeth of England and Mary Queen of Scots. Returning to Scotland in 1559, Knox was co-author of *The First Book of Discipline* (1559) and sole author of a *Treatise on Predestination* (1560), works which decisively influenced the organization and the theology, respectively, of the Scottish Churches for the next 300 years and more. *The First Book of Discipline* also proposes the scheme of national education which, introduced by the Church with considerable though incomplete success, contributed so much to the scientific and philosophical achievements of 18th-century Scotland. Knox's political activity in the early 1560s securely established the Reformation in Scotland; his own tendentious account of this period, published posthumously, dominated historical interpretation of the Scottish Reformation until recently. The content of Knox's works has affected in one way or another virtually all subsequent Scottish literary, intellectual and artistic activity, and his decision to write in English, and to encourage English rather than Scots versions of the Bible, helped to prevent the development of an adequate Scots prose medium. [AI]

Works, ed. D. Laing (6 vols., 1846–64; repr. 1895); *History of the Reformation of Religion in Scotland*, ed. W. C. Dickinson (1949) (complete, with modernized spelling); ed. R. S. Walker (1957) (selections reprinted exactly from the 1584 edition).
P. Hume Brown, *J.K.* (1895) (the standard biography); J. D. Mackie, *J.K.* (1951) (Historical Association Pamphlet, 1951); W. C. Dickinson, *Andrew Lang, J.K. and Scottish Presbyterianism* (1952); G. MacGregor, *The Thundering Scot* (1958).

Koestler, Arthur (1905–   ). Novelist, political and scientific writer. Hungarian-born, Koestler spent most of his childhood in Vienna. At the end of his second year at that city's university, in 1925, he went to Palestine, inspired by his contact with Vladimir Jabotinsky, the Zionist leader. After a brief spell in a collective settlement

Koestler began his career in journalism which finally led him to the position of foreign editor of Berlin's *B.Z. am Mittag* in 1932. At this time he joined the German Communist Party, and worked for the Party in various capacities until 1938, when he left it. When Hitler came to power he had to leave Germany, and he lived in France until 1940. In 1936 and 1937 he was in Spain to report the Civil War.

It was only when he was growing away from Communism that Koestler began to write fiction, and most of his novels are concerned with demonstrating the progress and failure of revolution. His first, *The Gladiators* (1939), discusses revolution in a historical perspective; but it is his second novel, *Darkness at Noon* (1940), which is now his most famous. It presented and analysed with dramatic effect the Moscow Purges as a part of the degeneration of the Russian Revolution. A third novel, *Arrival and Departure* (1943), investigated the motives behind revolutionary action. In 1940 Koestler had to leave France as Hitler's armies advanced, but not before he had been interned as a suspect alien by the French authorities. He described his experiences in *Scum of the Earth* (1941), the first of 3 volumes of autobiography.

Koestler came to England and after 1940 all his writing was done in English (his first two novels had been written in German, but were first published in English translations). At the end of the war he produced a collection of essays, *The Yogi and the Commissar* (1945), analysing the contemporary political situation, particularly the position of Russia and the nature of Communism. He continued his commentary on contemporary politics and society in *The Trail of the Dinosaur* (1955). Koestler retained his Zionist sympathies and wrote both a historical account of the Jews in Palestine, *Promise and Fulfilment* (1949), and a novel about the Jewish fight for independence, *Thieves in the Night* (1946). In the fifties Koestler turned to an examination of the role of science and scientific ideas in history in *The Sleepwalkers* (1959) and the parallels between scientific invention and artistic creation in *The Act of Creation* (1964).

Koestler's style is clipped, at time almost bullying, antithetical and vigorous, but the urgency behind his fiction and his predominantly intellectual approach are sometimes responsible for flaws of char-acterization and construction. He tended to present individuals as examples of the power of events, but it was precisely because of this that he played an almost unique role in presenting and interpreting the European political struggle for the English reader. His rapid response to political forces, his varied experiences in the political arena of the thirties and his acute intellectual grasp of facts and ideas made him an impressive and attention-demanding writer. He has retreated from politics and no longer writes fiction, but his work continues to be illuminating and challenging. [JRC]

Drinkers of Infinity. Essays 1955–67 (1968); *The Ghost in the Machine* (1967).
J. Atkins, *A.K.* (1956); R. Garaudy, *Literature of the Graveyard* (1947); J. Nevada, *A.K.* (1948); J. Calder, *Chronicles of Conscience* (1968).

Krige, Uys (1910–   ). Bilingual South African poet, playwright, novelist and critic. He went to England as a journalist in 1931, and later travelled widely in France and Spain (see *Sol y Sombra*, 1948). During the war he was a correspondent in North Africa and Europe, and a prisoner in Italy. Since then he has devoted himself to writing.

Krige's best work is in Afrikaans. A sense of ephemeral beauty dominates his early poetry, notably *Rooidag* (1940). In the war years, the conflict between brutal force and the joy of living prompted some of his best writings, while *Die Groue Kring* (1956) contrasts the glowing warmth of life and the omnipotence of death. Krige's insight into foreign literatures is considerable, his translation of Lorca's lament being probably the finest translation in Afrikaans (*Vir die Luit en die Kitaar*, 1950). He has edited collections of the poetry of Roy ◊ Campbell and Guy ◊ Butler. Among Krige's English writings, the war novel *The Way Out* (1946) and the stories of *The Dream and the Desert* (1953) share a strangely sensuous and poetic prose style. He has also published *The Sniper and Other One Act Plays* (1962).

Oorlogsgedigte (1942); *Alle Paaie Gaan na Rome* (1949); *Ballade van die Groot Begeer* (1960); *Gedigte 1927–40* (1961).
R. MacNab and C. Gulston, *South African Poetry* (1948); D. J. Operman, *Digters van Dertig* (1953); R. Antonissen, *Die Afrikaanse Letterkunde* (Pretoria, 1955).

Kyd, Thomas (1558–94). Dramatist. Probably educated at Merchant Taylors' when Mulcaster was headmaster and Spenser a pupil there, he may have worked as a scrivener. A most capable man of the theatre, he wrote several plays, including *The Spanish Tragedy*, a sensational melodrama with a play-within-the-play finale which was enormously popular in its day and inaugurated the vogue of the Elizabethan Revenge Tragedy. He also wrote an early version of *Hamlet*, now lost, which preceded and probably influenced Shakespeare's. He handled rhetoric effectively and had a good sense of theatre, so that his plays were influential beyond their worth. [MJ]

Works, ed. F. S. Boas (1901).

F. Bowers, *Elizabethan Revenge Tragedy* (1940); M. C. Bradbrook, *Themes and Conventions of Elizabethan Tragedy* (1935); W. Clemen, *English Tragedy before Shakespeare* (1961); A. Downer, *The British Drama: A Handbook and Brief Chronicle* (New York, 1950); Philip Edwards, Introduction to *The Spanish Tragedy* (1959); A. Freeman, *T.K.: Facts and Problems* (1967); M. Prior, *The Language of Tragedy* (1947).

L

Lamb, Charles (1775–1834). Essayist, poet and letter writer. Born in Crown Office Row, in the Inner Temple, London, where his father was the confidential clerk of a bencher, he was educated on a scholarship at Christ's Hospital, and there became friendly with Coleridge. In 1789, he started work as a clerk, first with a city merchant, then in 1791 at the South Sea House, finally in 1792 with the accountant's office of the East India Company. He retired on 29 March 1825 with a pension of £450 per annum.

He began as a writer of poetry, and in 1794 he and Coleridge wrote sonnets for the *Morning Post*; he also had 4 sonnets in Coleridge's volume, *Poems on Various Subjects* (1796; and more poems in the second edition, 1797). Through Coleridge, he came to know the Wordsworths, but later moved away from Coleridge's domination, and his later writing is quite different in character from the melancholy of his first attempts, which he found too agitating. Perhaps his later heavy drinking is connected with this tension. Only one or two of Lamb's poems, such as 'Hester' and 'The Old Familiar Faces', are still read, and these because of a skill in dealing with tight forms, and a pleasing sentiment or easy nostalgia. The members of Lamb's family were subject to mental disturbance, and he was himself briefly confined in 1795. In 1796, his sister, Mary, in a mad seizure stabbed their mother to death. Charles Lamb thereafter assumed complete responsibility for his sister, who was liable to fits of insanity, but was also a useful companion to him; he never married. In 1801, he settled in Mitre Court Buildings in the Inner Temple, and wrote for the newspapers. He published a sentimental-pathetic *Tale of Rosamund Gray and Old Blind Margaret* (1798) in prose heavily indebted to Richard ◊ Burton, and tried his hand unsuccessfully at the drama. *John Woodvil* (published in 1802 but written earlier) was a pastiche Elizabethan tragedy in blank verse; *Mr H.*, a farce, was hissed off the stage at Drury Lane in 1806. Lamb wrote several children's books: *Tales from Shakespeare* (in

collaboration with his sister) appeared in 1807; others are *The Adventures of Ulysses* (1808) and *Beauty and the Beast* (1811). His first work of criticism was *Specimens of the English Dramatic Poets who Lived about the Time of Shakespeare* (1808). This collection of the 'beauties' of Middleton, Webster, Tourneur, Ford, with the much more important essays of Coleridge and Hazlitt, stimulated the growing interest in the old English dramatic authors. Lamb's views are implicit in his selection, not worked out in argument. In 1818, he published 2 volumes of *Collected Works*, which included 'Recollections of Christ's Hospital', and essays on Hogarth and 'The Tragedies of Shakespeare'. The latter essay illustrates the strength and weakness of Lamb as a critic; he is for modern taste absurdly subjective and disregards the form of what he is talking about. He wants to develop his own meditations, not to let the play work in its own way. He also has a thoroughly extreme view of the 'characters' as entities. Lamb's social life was important; his Wednesday and Thursday evenings at this time were important gathering places for his literary friends. In August 1820, he started contributing essays signed 'Elia' to the *London Magazine*; the first was 'The South Sea House', and in 1823 he collected them as the *Essays of Elia*; a subsequent less successful volume, *The Last Essays of Elia*, appeared in 1833. Lamb's essays are thoroughly 'literary'. They are elaborately constructed to present Lamb's 'personality' and are heavily dependent on old prose writers of the 17th century (and on Sterne, dependence twice removed), as well as on knowledge on the reader's part of these writers. Thus, while enjoyed by readers who like to exercise their knowledge, they are not admired by critics who are anti-historical. When a Lamb essay works well, as in 'Witches and Other Night Fears', 'The Super-annuated Man' and 'Old China', it can be brilliant and penetrating, and stir up moods and feelings in the reader: when it works badly, it is annoyingly overdone pastiche. Some of the best of Lamb's writing is to be found in his *Letters* (2 vols., ed. Sir T. N. Talfourd, 1848; ed. E.V. Lucas, 3 vols., 1935; selected by G. Pocock, Everyman, 1945). [AR]

Works, ed. E. V. Lucas (7 vols., 1903–5; 6 vols., 1912); *Lamb's Criticism*, ed. E. M. W. Tillyard (1923); *The Portable Lamb*, ed. J. M. Brown (New York, 1949); *Essays of Elia*, ed. M. Elwin (1952); *A Lamb Selection*, ed. F. B. Pinion (1965).
E. V. Lucas, *The Life of L.* (revised edn, 1921); E. Blunden, *L.* (WTW, 1954) (with bibliography); L. Trilling, 'The Sanity of True Genius', in *The Liberal Imagination* (1951).

Lamming, George (1927–). West Indian novelist. Born and educated in Barbados, he describes the peasant village of his birth in *In the Castle of my Skin* (1953). Seeking a less restricted environment, though eager to retain his peasant consciousness, he went to teach in Trinidad in 1946 and began to submit poems to Caribbean magazines. Still in search of freedom, he went to England in 1950. After various factory jobs he became a regular contributor to the B.B.C.'s 'Caribbean Voices'. *The Emigrants* (1954) gives the background and reasons for the West Indian migration. It begins where his first novel ends – in the colonial's flight. This impulse is considered at length in the discursive autobiography, *The Pleasures of Exile* (1960). Lamming lives mainly in London, but he has travelled extensively in Europe, America and Africa. His most recent trip was to Canada, and he followed it with a lecture tour in the West Indies.

Of Age and Innocence (1958) is set on a mythical Caribbean island, and, like *Season of Adventure* (1960), it explores the search for a new multi-racial West Indian ethos. Both novels are essentially poetic experiences, employing allegory and phantasy and written in allusive prose dense with images and heightened by passages of superb dialogue. Lamming is deeply concerned with the problems of the Negro writer and the cultural needs of a new West Indian society. Relentlessly political and relentlessly introspective, he is a major 20th-century writer. [WAG]

Lampman, Archibald (1861–99). Canadian poet. Born in Ontario, the son of an Anglican clergyman, he spent much of his boyhood near Lake Rice. In 1882 he graduated in classics from Trinity College, Toronto. After failing as a schoolmaster, he moved to Ottawa to become a Post Office Department clerk. He spent much of his time in the beautiful surrounding country. His first book, *Among the Millet*, was published in 1888. Only one other volume, *Lyrics of Earth* (1896), appeared before his early death of a heart ailment, but in 1943 his friend Duncan Campbell ◊ Scott helped bring out a volume of unpublished work called *At the Long Sault*. The title poem is Lampman's best narrative. Scott also edited *Selected Poems* (1947).

Lampman was at his best as a landscape poet, recording a sensuous and well-informed response to nature. A strong tendency to melancholy, increased by the growing mechanization of city life, was subdued by the discipline of description. Even so, precise scene-painting is often marred by language which grows vaguer as it aims at evocativeness. His sonnets ('Here after all is my best work') and those lyrics in which dream and nightmare are in tension – 'Heat' and 'The City of the End of Things' – achieve an attractive balance of detachment and involvement. [PT]

D. Pacey, *Ten Canadian Poets* (1958); C. Y. Connor, *A.L.: Canadian Poet of Nature* (1929).

Landon, Letitia Elizabeth (1802–38). Poet, journalist and novelist. Born in London, the daughter of an army contractor, she became, as 'L.E.L.', a prolific and very popular writer of verse, and contributor to the 'annuals' then popular. She had a taste for pretty and romantic sentiment, shown in *The Fate of Adelaide: A Swiss Romantic Tale, and Other Poems* 1821) and *Flowers of Loveliness: Twelve Groups of Female Figures Emblematic of Flowers* (1838). She wrote several novels, of which the '3-decker', *Ethel Churchill; or the Two Brides* (1837), was most popular. She married a Mr MacLean, a colonial governor in West Africa, and died there of an overdose of prussic acid, which she was treating herself with. [AR]

Poetical Works, ed. W. B. Scott (1873).
D. E. Enfield, *L.E.L.: A Mystery of the Thirties* (1928); M. M. H. Thrall, *Rebellious Frazer's* (1934); H. Ashton, *Letty Landon* (1951).

Landor, Walter Savage (1775–1864). Poet and prose stylist. Born at Ipsley Court in Warwickshire, the son of a doctor and the daughter of an old county family, he was educated at Rugby and, as the 'mad Jacobin', was expelled from Trinity College, Oxford; this was the first serious appearance of the ungovernable temper and Whiggish, 'aristocratic' eccentricity which forced him to leave his country house in Monmouthshire in 1814, and after a libel action drove him out of English Society in 1858. He served briefly against Napoleon in the Peninsula in 1808; later he became one of the colony of cultivated 'literary' Britons who lived abroad, in his case chiefly in Florence. His first book of *Poems* (1795; suppressed) was a collection written in the manner of Pope, but *Gebir: A Poem in Seven Books* (1798; revised 1803), in Miltonic blank verse, is his real beginning. This is one of the elaborate, exotic, 'epic' poems so admired then, so tedious to read now; parts of it attracted ♢ Southey, who practised the same form. After trying his hand at verse based on Arabic, Persian and of course classical writing, with *Count Julian* (1812) Landor started to produce the non-dramatic tragedies and 'scenes' then fashionable; the kind of subject was also handled by Southey in *Roderick*. Landor's *Andrea of Hungary, Giovanna of Naples* (1827) and *Fra Rupert* (1840) form a historical trilogy. He wrote several books of idylls, dramatic fragments, lyrics, epigrams and occasional pieces; *Hellenics* (1847; revised 1859; ed. A. Symons, 1907); *Italics* (1848); *Heroic Idylls* (1863). From these about a dozen poems survive in anthologies. These include 'Ianthe', 'The Dragon-fly', 'Rose Aylmer' and the famous quatrain 'Finis', presenting his own picture of his life. Landor's verse, heavily indebted to classical forms and themes (he often drafted poems in Latin), is at its best neat and clear; he also has at times a deft satirical touch.

Perhaps his best-known work, however, is to be found in his *Imaginary Conversations of Literary Men and Statesmen* (3 vols., 1824–8; second series, 2 vols., 1829; *Greeks and Romans*, 1853; ed. G. C. Crump, 6 vols., 1891–3; selected and ed. E. de Sélincourt, World's Classics, 1915; selected and ed. T. Welby, 1934). These 150 prose pieces, like the poems, are varied in style and tone. Interspersed with action, the best of them are lively and entertaining. Like his life, they are undisciplined and sometimes fail through wayward riding of hobby-horses: they include 'Alcibiades and Xenophon', 'Dante and Beatrice' and 'Romilly and Wilberforce'. His other prose works include similar but extended pieces: *The Citation and Examination of William Shakespeare Touching Deer-Stealing, to*

Which is Added a Conference of Edmund Spenser with the Earl of Essex (1834) and *Pericles and Aspasia* (1836). These illustrate his parasitic 'literary' imagination. There are critical essays on Landor by de Quincey and Swinburne. [A R]

Complete Works, ed. T. E. Welby and S. Wheeler (1927–36) (with bibliography); *Poems and Conversations*, ed. H. Ellis (Everyman, 1933) (selections); *Poetry and Prose*, with critical essays, ed. E. K. Chambers (1946) (selection); *The Shorter Poems*, ed. J. B. Sidgwick (1946); *The Sculptured Garland*, ed. R. Buxton (1948) (selected poems); *Letters*, ed. S. Wheeler (1897, 1899).
J. Forster, *W.S.L.: A Biography* (2 vols., 1869); S. Colvin, *L.* (English Men of Letters, 1881); M. Elwin, *L.* (1941, revised 1958); R. H. Super, *L.* (1957); G. R. Hamilton, *W.S.L.* (1960); P. Vitoux, *L'œuvre de L.* (Paris, 1964); D. Davie 'Shorter Poems of Landor', *EC*, I (1951), II (1952).

Lang, Andrew (1844–1912). Historian, poet and journalist. Born at Selkirk, and educated at the High School there, Edinburgh Academy, St Andrews University and Balliol College, Oxford, he was a Fellow of Merton College. In his literary career, Lang's wide interests in many fields led him to produce good (even distinguished) work in most, but the dissipation of his energies prevented him from dominating any. He began as a poet: *Ballads and Lyrics of Old France* (1872), *Ballades in Blue China* (1880 and 1881) and *Grass of Parnassus* (1888; 1892) show him to be accomplished in handling verse forms. His inspiration is literary, in the manner of ♢ Rossetti (translations of Villon), Austin ♢ Dobson, ♢ Praed and other 'men of letters' who wrote *vers de société*. Lang also had printed an ambitious narrative *Helen of Troy* (1882); his *Collected Poems* were printed in 1923.

His most influential work was done as an anthropologist (though dealing with literary texts), in *Custom and Myth* (1884), *Myth, Ritual and Religion* (1887; much revised, 1889) and *The Making of Religion* (1898). In these works he fused his Greek scholarship, literary sensibility and interest in the sociology of religion. He had an influential place in the discussion of totemism, folklore as the 'basis' of religion and literary culture, rather than a debased form of them. He was also an early critic of ♢ Frazer's theorizing in *The Golden Bough*. He translated Homer (Butcher and Lang, *Odyssey*, 1879; Lang, Leaf and Myers, *Iliad*, 1883) into rather 'biblical' prose, as well as Theocritus (1880). His work on 'the Homeric question', *Homer and the Epic* (1893), is now outdated by archaeological research and changed literary taste.

Lang was a good historian, with a very readable narrative style and mastery of original sources (*History of Scotland*, 1900–7; *James VI and the Gowrie Mystery*, 1902; *Sir George Mackenzie*, 1909 – his best single biography). He had a dilettante's predilection for historical mysteries and Jacobite puzzles. Lang's imaginative works were off-shoots of his scholarship, like his multi-coloured *Fairy Books* (long popular). In his rather uninteresting novels, he cultivated 'romance' and collaborated with Rider ◊ Haggard in *The World's Desire* (1890) and A. E. W. ◊ Mason in *Parson Kelly* (1900). Lang was a voluminous periodical journalist, book-reviewer and controversialist. His judgement on new novels (which he sometimes reviewed more than once under different names) was important, and is worth serious study. [AR]

R. L. Green, *A.L.: A Critical Biography* (with bibliography) (1946); ed. A. Blyth Webster, *Concerning A.L.* (1949) (lectures); R. L. Green, 'Descriptions from the Darlington Collection of L.'. *Indiana University Bookman*, 7 (1965).

Langland or **Langley, William** (*c*. 1331–99?). Poet. There is no reliable information on the author of *Piers Plowman* (ed. W. W. Skeat, 1886; modernized versions: H. W. Wells, New York, 1935; J. F. Goodridge, Penguin Classics, 1959), the most ambitious and perhaps the greatest poem in Middle English. A 15th-century manuscript says that he was born near Malvern, where the poem begins, the (illegitimate?) son of Stacy de Rockayle, a member of the powerful Despencer family of Shipton-under-Wichwood in Oxfordshire. The poem itself tells us a little; the name Longe Wille ('I have lived in *londe*', quod I, 'my name is Longe Wille'), and the fact that the Dreamer (the main character), at any rate, was in minor orders, though married, and scraped a living in London by singing psalms for the souls of his benefactors. There are 3 versions of *Piers Plowman* represented by the surviving manuscripts, indicating successive redactions, all, it is thought, by Langland. The shortest, Version A, is dated 1362 (ed. G. Kane, 1960), while B (1376–7) develops and expands the original to 7,000 lines. The C version is about as

long, but shows many changes. It was made after 1390 (selections ed. E. Salter and D. Pearsall, York Medieaval Texts, 1969).

In 11 dream-visions, Langland explores the shape and meaning of the human predicament in relationship to God. In the first vision, the Dreamer falls asleep on Malvern Hills and sees a picture of the earthly commonwealth as 'A fair field ful of folke' set between Heaven and Hell. This sinful society is brought to penitence, and is directed on a pilgrimage to Truth by Piers the Plowman, a symbol of the divine element in man. The rest of the poem is an account of this pilgrimage as it takes place in the mind of the Dreamer. In the course of it, he witnesses the Crucifixion and the Harrowing of Hell, the building of Holy Church and the assault of Antichrist, while at the same time we witness the progress of his life on earth. Thus 'huge fluidity' (Coghill) is Langland's first poetic gift, but the poem has an organic shape in the search, which is the instinctive apprehension of the truth of Christianity known by the intellect.

As an allegorist, Langland does not work to a set pattern; he rather relies on an allegorical habit of mind which led him to exploit, and his audience to accept, a multiplicity of significance. In his hands, the alliterative line becomes capable of an astonishing range of effects, from the 'terse, dramatic, conversational . . . to those of great rhetorical splendour' (Salter). But for all his poetic genius, Langland is moved above all by religious feeling, and cannot be adequately judged by aesthetic criteria alone. [AG]

M. W. Bloomfield, *Piers Plowman as a Fourteenth Century Apocalypse* (1962); E. T. Donaldson, *Piers Plowman; The C-Text and Its Poet* (1949), N. K. Coghill, 'God's Wenches and the Light that Spoke', in *English and Medieval Studies Presented to J. R. R. Tolkien*, ed. N. Davis and C. L. Wrenn (1962); G. Kane, *Piers Plowman: The Evidence for Authorship* (1965); J. Lawlor, *Piers Plowman, An Essay in Criticism* (1962); E. Salter, *Piers Plowman, An Introduction* (1962; repr. 1970).

Larkin, Philip (1922–). Poet. He established himself, with a remarkably small production of verse, as the most distinguished and typical new English poet of the 1950s and 1960s. Born in Coventry he went to Oxford in the 1940s as a brilliant but shy scholarship boy, an experience vividly recaptured in his novel *Jill* (1946). This novel, like Larkin's first volume of poems, *The North Ship* (1945), attracted comparatively little notice, but Larkin had already secured the friendship and admiration of such Oxford contemporaries of his as Kingsley ◊ Amis and John ◊ Wain. On leaving Oxford, he worked as a university librarian in Belfast, Leicester, and then Hull. After ten years of comparative obscurity, he became famous partly through Robert Conquest's 'Movement' anthology, *New Lines* (1956), and his own volume, *The Less Deceived*, brought out in 1955 by an enterprising small publisher, the Marvell Press. Larkin was seen as the most distinguished voice of a new generation, reacting equally against what seemed to them the confused romanticism of Dylan Thomas and his imitators, and the naïve political enthusiasm and idealism of such poets of the 1930s as Auden, Spender and Day Lewis. One poem in this volume, 'Church Going', an expression of an agnostic's reluctant respect for what the Churches have done in giving meaning to the three crucial moments of human life, birth, marriage and death, soon became a classic anthology piece and a stand-by for lecturers on the 'new poetry'. Larkin's skill and sensitivity were immediately recognized, though some critics disliked what they felt to be a note of excessive caution, timidity and unadventurousness in confronting life. An acceptance of life's various kinds of defeat certainly runs through Larkin's poetry, but there is also recognition of beauty and praise of certain moral qualities, above all staunchness. His more positive responses to life come out in a poem like 'Arundel Tombs' or in the title poem of his second important volume, *The Whitsun Weddings* (1964).

Larkin is above all a very English poet, interested in the local feel and texture of life, in scene and anecdote, reticent and unrhetorical, though capable at times of a fine, properly earned eloquence. In the family of English poets, he belongs with Hardy, with Edward Thomas, and perhaps a little, in his lighter pieces, with his own favourite contemporary poet, John Betjeman. He is one of those writers who, in a not obviously dramatic way, give one a closer and truer sense of the moral and physical world in which one is living, and who thus effect a certain transformation in the general sensibility. Larkin, it might be said, has made us aware of the holiness of the drab, of the quiet passion and persist-

ence of submerged lives, of the heroism of compromise with frustration. He has recently been commissioned by the Oxford University Press to edit an *Oxford Book of Modern Verse* which will take the place of the brilliantly introduced, but eccentrically selected, anthology of the same title edited by W. B. Yeats. [GSF]

A Girl in Winter (1947) (novel).

Laver, James (1899–   ). Verse writer, novelist and art historian. Born in Liverpool and educated at the Liverpool Institute and New College, Oxford; there in 1921 he won the Newdigate Prize for a poem on Cervantes, and his volumes of published verse include *His Last Sebastian* (1922); a philosophical poem, *Macrocosmos* (1929); and *Ladies' Mistakes* (1933). He also wrote several plays (and his novel *Nymph Errant*, 1932, was produced by C. B. Cochran as a musical comedy at the Adelphi in 1933). His fiction includes a volume of short stories, *The Laburnum Tree* (1935). In 1922, he joined the staff of the Print Room at the Victoria and Albert Museum, and was Keeper of the Departments of Engraving, Illustration, Design and Paintings (1938–59). He has written much on the history of art, particularly costume (*Eighteenth Century Costume*, 1931; *Tudor Costume*, 1951) and on décor and costume in the theatre (*Stage Designs by Oliver Messel*, 1933; *Costume in the Theatre*, 1964). He has also written, in the course of his duties, on painters such as Titian and Whistler and is the author of a very useful biography of Huysmans: *The First Decadent: The Strange Life of J. K. Huysmans* (1954). [AR]

Lawler, Raymond Evenor (1921–   ). Australian playwright. Born into a large working family in Melbourne, he left school at 13 and worked with an engineering firm till the end of the war. His theatrical experience began in Brisbane in 1948 when he joined a variety show. The following year he joined the national theatre company in Melbourne as actor and producer and later became a director of the Melbourne University repertory company.

Lawler's early plays were mainly inferior comedies set in England. *The Summer of the Seventeenth Doll* was first produced in Melbourne in 1955. Lawler himself acted in this production and in the London production in 1957. It is a realistic play about the inability of two cane-cutters to cope articulately with an emotional crisis during the seventeenth of their yearly summer liaisons. The dialogue is colloquial and excitingly violent, tautening at the precise theatrical moment. The same explosive technique is used in *The Piccadilly Bushman* (performed in 1959, published in 1961), but in a situation not strong enough to bear it. In the earlier play Roo is forced suddenly and dramatically to confront himself with the attitudes of other people, whereas the self-recognition of Alec Ritchie in the later one is too long delayed and too sulky to sustain interest. *The Unshaven Cheek* was produced at the 1963 Edinburgh Festival. *A Breech in the Wall* was produced on B.B.C. television in March 1967. [P T]

Lawrence, D(avid) H(erbert) (1885–1930). Novelist and poet. Born at Eastwood, Nottinghamshire, the fourth child of a miner and his wife (a former school-teacher). The conflicting interests of his parents, his father's powerful working-class character and his mother's restless aspirations to refinement, coloured Lawrence's imaginative life. The interplay in the family of class and sex was also important. The area in which his childhood was spent, mingling industrialization (coal-mining) with the older agricultural life, was also an important formative influence. In 1898, Lawrence won a scholarship to the Boys' High School in Nottingham, and in 1901 he briefly worked for a firm of surgical appliance makers there. He then became an uncertified teacher for four years; first at Eastwood, then at Ilkeston. In 1906, he began the two-year teacher training course at the University College in Nottingham, and in 1908 started teaching at Davidson Road Boys School in Croydon. In 1909, he had some poems accepted by Ford Madox ◊ Ford in the *English Review*, and in 1910, *The White Peacock* (1911), a novel he had started in 1907, was accepted by Heinemann. Two other novels, *The Trespasser* (1912) and *Sons and Lovers* (1913), make up the preliminary period of his writing career. These 3 works introduce a number of themes which he later developed more impressively: adolescent sexuality, unfulfilled ambition, the feeling of English provincial life. They were rewritten and revised, and show a strong realism in dealing with his own experience and a more derivative, romantic urge in the writing itself.

The Trespasser is set in the Isle of Wight and London, and deals with love outside marriage. Helena cannot respond to physical passion; and the erotic involvement destroys Siegmund.

Lawrence's mother had died in 1910, and in *Sons and Lovers*, his best work up to then, and one of the important books of the time, there is an indication that he is swinging away from an earlier partisanship for her, towards a truer understanding of his father; this is stronger in intention than in realization. The family tensions are convincingly set in a realistic local setting. Lawrence introduces the denunciation of what he considers destructive effects of industrialization that characterizes his thought; the book can be read as a solid evocation of working-class life. In April 1912, Lawrence had met Frieda von Richthofen, the wife of the Professor of French at Nottingham University College, and in May they eloped to Europe and spent the next year in the Alps and Italy. In 1913, a book of verse, *Love Poems and Others*, appeared and in 1917 another collection, *Look! We Have Come Through!* These early poems are largely autobiographical, somewhat self-consciously literary in form yet of great interest.

While he was abroad in 1913, he started work on a novel, *The Sisters*, which later became two books: *The Rainbow* (September 1915; suppressed in November) and *Women in Love* (privately printed, New York, 1920; 1921). *The Rainbow* takes in three generations of the Brangwen family; it centres on marriage, under the urgency of his relationship with his own wife (they were married in July 1914, on Frieda's divorce), and on the relationship between man and woman. This he thought was now '*the* question'. The passage of time develops a kind of 'paradise, fall, quest for regeneration' movement in the book, as a commentary on modern society; Ursula, the educated woman, is the seeker for wholeness, for the rainbow. The book shows Lawrence's originality in construction, and in using symbols – Lincoln Cathedral and the frightening horses at the end. Its withdrawal was caused by the descriptions of physical intercourse, but Lawrence's presentation of sex is far wider than this. *Women in Love* takes up the quest for ultimate marriage again with Ursula and Gudrun Brangwen. Lawrence's elaboration of a vocabulary to encompass his vision of sex, and his constant exploratory striving in his writing to experience, and make the reader experience, this vision leads to difficulties in this book. There are more than a few impenetrable passages, and some turgid writing. The book itself, though, is completely original and pioneering, grimly honest, and greatly influential. The general doctrine is that love is made impossible, or killed, by the exercise of the conscious will, just as life or art is killed by mere knowledge. Lawrence and his wife were in England when the First World War broke out and Lawrence opposed it. They were subjected to local persecution in Cornwall because of his wife's nationality, and finally, in October 1916, expelled from the county. Lawrence was medically examined for the army and found unfit; but he took the process as personal persecution.

After 1919, he travelled about looking for a place to settle in. These changes of locale are incorporated in his later fiction, some of which had been begun earlier. *The Lost Girl* (1920; James Tait Black Prize) is set in a beautifully realized Abruzzi, contrasted with the English midlands: it similarly contrasts the attitude to love and 'intelligence' of Alvina Houghton, uprooted from English bourgeois life, with the attitudes of her husband, Cicio, and his community. Lawrence wrote many of his best poems out of his observations in Italy, breaking away from the straight autobiography of his earlier verse, and developing a new voice using natural things – fruit, insects animals – to create his picture of man and nature. A visit to Sardinia produced his beautiful travel book, *Sea and Sardinia* (1921). *Aaron's Rod* (1922) is interesting in its place in the development of Lawrence's doctrines, but fails as a novel because of its incoherent structure and a tendency on the author's part to shout at the reader. In 1922, Lawrence travelled to Ceylon and then to Australia. He stayed four months in New South Wales, where he wrote *Kangaroo* (1923). This novel, never one of the more popular of Lawrence's books, reflects the way he had been forced to argue his ideas, in face of public hostility (see particularly 'The Nightmare' chapter which relates to his Cornish experiences) and ridicule of his art. The novel is largely autobiographical and is concerned with Lawrence's own problems; it is fundamentally the working-out of something like a new religion. The speculative side of Lawrence, which became

increasingly important in his later fiction, is shown in *Fantasia of the Unconscious* (New York, 1922), and later works among his considerable journalistic output; in writings such as *Studies in Classic American Literature* (New York, 1923), his 'Introduction' to *The Paintings of D. H. Lawrence* (1929), *Pornography and Obscenity* (1929), and his letters, he can be a resourceful, witty and knowledgeable controversialist.

At the end of 1922, he went to Taos in New Mexico, where he stayed, with visits to Mexico itself, New York and London, until 1925. The main work of this period is *The Plumed Serpent* (published 1926). In this book his search for the meaning of human life associates the whole sexual life of man with an archaic, dark consciousness underlying civilized, educated minds. The story is set against a deliberate revival by Don Ramón and Don Cipriano of the 'indigenous' Aztec religion in the form of a 'Plumed Serpent' cult, to oust Christianity. Kate Leslie, a divorced Irishwoman, is the European observer and participant. Lawrence seems to identify himself with the violence in the book, and his line or argument can be given a fascist interpretation. In 1925, after a serious illness which was the development of a consumptive condition, Lawrence returned to Europe. In this year, one of the greatest of his tales (or short stories), *St Mawr*, was published. Lawrence is a master of the form which is half way between a short story and a novel. These shorter works are not imperfect novels, or trial sketches, but true dramatic works with a strong touch of the parable. It is truer to say that there are tales embedded here and there in the novels. St Mawr, the horse, for whom a wife gives up her husband, takes on a strong symbolic tint, as a being that fulfils his true nature. Another of his greatest tales also comes out of his American experience, *The Woman Who Rode Away* (published 1928), which deals with 'truth' possessed by the despised Indians who are yet in touch with ancient powers of darkness. They can tap these powers in resisting the incursions of the white civilization. In *The Escaped Cock* (Paris, 1929; published in England as *The Man Who Died*, 1931), he strives to reinterpret Christianity in his own terms; on the level of art, this works well.

From 1926, Lawrence lived mainly in Italy, and he died in a sanatorium at Vence, in the south of France. His last novel,

Lady Chatterley's Lover, was written in 1926–7; it exists in 3 versions. The first draft was published as *The First Lady Chatterley* (New York, 1944); the final version was privately printed in Florence in 1928 (reprinted in Penguin Books, 1961). In this novel, Lawrence returns to the industrialized land of his birth to place another story of sexual questing. Sir Clifford Chatterley, Mellors (his gamekeeper) and Connie (his wife) are the main characters. The sterility of the established social order and the natural life of the working man are the contrasted worlds. In some respects, this is a return to *Sons and Lovers*, but the drive in the book is less intense. The explicit descriptions of Connie's intercourse with Mellors caused official trouble, but a more dangerous weakness is Lawrence's propagandist use of four-letter words in the third version. Even a great writer ignores at his peril the social patina which words acquire. Lawrence's attempt to rehabilitate these words as written forms is theoretically justifiable, but in practice, in the cooperative art of literature, it fails. He himself joined the controversy over the book with *À Propos of Lady Chatterley* (1930).

His short stories appeared in several collections, including: *The Prussian Officer and Other Stories* (1914); *England, My England, and Other Stories* (New York, 1922); *The Lady Bird* (1923); and a posthumous volume, *The Lovely Lady, and Other Tales* (1932). He published several volumes of poetry which include: *Birds, Beasts and Flowers* (New York, 1923); *Collected Poems* (2 vols., 1928); and *Last Poems* (Florence, 1932), in which he faces death. He also wrote plays, which have recently been revived on the stage with great success. An exhibition of his paintings was raided by the London police in July 1929, an event he celebrated in his poem 'Innocent England'.

Lawrence has become a very influential writer, not so much in actual writing technique as in vision and method. His art arises from the instinctive rejection of the industrial civilization by a profoundly sensitive man educated in traditional ways and living at a particular moment in English history. His negative, conscious view may be a partial one, but any future development of English sensibility will have been heavily influenced by him. He was forced into an illuminating exploration of important areas of human experience. Despite the incoherent doctrine of some of his work, his sensibilities are formed into a powerful art; or perhaps the doctrine is simply irrelevant. [AR]

Works ('Phoenix Edition') (21 vols., 1954–7); *Complete Poems*, ed. V. de Sola Pinto and W. Roberts (2 vols., 1964); *Complete Plays* (1965); *Collected Letters*, ed. H. T. Moore (2 vols., 1962); *Phoenix*, ed. E. D. McDonald, and *Phoenix II*, ed. W. Roberts and H. T. Moore (1936; 1968) (uncollected and other prose works); *Selected Literary Criticism*, ed. A. Beal (1956); *Poetry and Prose*, ed. T. R. Barnes (1957) (selection).

R. Aldington, *Portrait of a Genius But . . .* (1950); E. Nehls, *D.H.L. A Composite Biography*, (3 vols., U. of Wisconsin P., 1957–9) (a mine of information); H. T. Moore, *The Intelligent Heart* (revised edn, 1960); G. Hough, *The Dark Sun: A Study of D.H.L.* (1956; 1961); F. R. Leavis, *D.H.L., Novelist* (1955; new edn, 1964); A. Beal, *D.H.L.* (1961; and paperback) (introduction with a short bibliography); *Modern Fiction Studies*, 5 (1959) (special Lawrence issue with check-list of studies in periodicals); J. Moynahan, *The Deed of Life: The Novels and Tales of D.H.L.* (1963); ed. M. Spilka, *D.H.L.: A Collection of Critical Essays* (Englewood Cliffs, N.J., 1963); H. M. Daleski, *The Forked Flame, a Study of D.H.L.* (1965); G. H. Ford, *Double Measure: A Study of the Novels and Stories of D.H.L.* (1965); C. H. Rolph, *The Trial of Lady Chatterley* (1961) and *A Propos of Lady Chatterley*; P. Rieff, *The Triumph of the Therapeutic: Uses of Faith after Freud* (1966); W. Roberts, *A Bibliography of D.H.L.* (1963).

Lawrence, T(homas) E(dward) (1888–1935). Writer. Born in Tremadoc, Caernarvonshire, and educated at Oxford High School and Jesus College. he became known as Lawrence of Arabia. He first went to the Middle East as an archaeologist. In the First World War he worked for British Intelligence, and was instrumental in organizing the revolt of the Arab tribesmen against the Turks, becoming an almost legendary figure. His principal literary work is *Seven Pillars of Wisdom* (1926), a lengthy account of the Arabian campaign which took seven years to write. The initial publication was private. In 1927 an abridged edition called *Revolt in the Desert* was published commercially. In 1932 Lawrence's prose translation of the *Odyssey* appeared. *The Mint* was published posthumously in 1955.

Lawrence was, of course, as much man of action as writer, and his name survives more for the myth of his personality and exploits than for any intrinsic literary excellence. Yet *Seven Pillars of Wisdom* is more than merely a soldier's account of his campaign. It is both a valid piece of military history and a revealing self-portrait of a highly unusual and complex personality. Lawrence was highly conscious of the fact that he was not a professional writer, and it is true that his prose lacks style: before it was edited by his friend Bernard Shaw, it apparently lacked punctuation as well. He has not even the virtue of simplicity, for he over-writes in the belief that adornment is improvement. Nevertheless, he tells his story clearly. The book's effect may be due as much to its subject's fascination as to its creator's skill, but it is assuredly a classic of its kind.

Disillusioned with British official policy in the Middle East, Lawrence buried himself in the ranks of the Royal Air Force under the name of Shaw. He was killed in a motor-cycle accident. [CO]

R. Graves, *L. and the Arabs* (1927); R. Aldington, *L. of Arabia* (1955); ed. A. W. Lawrence, *T.E.L. by His Friends* (1937).

Lawson, Henry (1867–1922). Australian short-story writer. Born at Mudgee, New South Wales, the son of a Norwegian gold-digger. An irregular and unhappy education and home life did nothing to alleviate his innate solitariness, which was intensified by deafness at the age of 9. He was 13 when he took the first of his innumerable jobs. When his parents separated he followed his mother to Sydney and contributed socialist articles to her magazine, *The Republican*. In 1892 he began an eighteen-month residence in the outback around Bourke which had far-reaching effects on his writing. The melancholy that led to his over-drinking was not relieved by his marriage in 1896, nor by trips to New Zealand and England. His best work was done by 1901. Later stories too often succumb to sentimentality.

Lawson was better known during his life as a balladist, expressing popular democratic sentiments in bounding rhythms; but it is the brilliantly off-hand sketches and stories, many of them contributed to the Sydney *Bulletin* in the nineties, that show his quality. *Prose Works* (1937) includes stories from his 3 best volumes, *While the Billy Boils* (1896), *On the Track and over the Sliprails* (1900) and *Joe Wilson and His Mates* (1901). Lawson was already an accomplished writer when he first exploited his insights into the world of the in-domitable bushmen whose thought and language he characterized with reticent humour. He is a central influence in three Australian literary traditions: the bias towards the working man; 'Mateship', though to the pessimistic Lawson mateship is companionship in endurance, a resource against the relentless movement from bad to worse; and reliance on a restrained, anti-climactic prose style. [PT]

D. Prout, *H.L.* (1963); S. Murray-Smith, *H.L.* (Australian Writers and Their Work, 1962); T. Inglis Moore, 'The Rise and Fall of H.L.', *Meanjin*, XVI, 4 (Summer, 1957).

Layton, Irving (1912–). Canadian poet. Born in Rumania but taken to Canada in 1913, he completed a course of agricultural studies before entering McGill University from which he graduated in 1936. He served with the Canadian Army in the Second World War, and on being discharged taught in a Montreal school. He is now a lecturer in modern poetry at Sir George Williams College in Montreal. Layton's early poetry was designed to shock by its flamboyant self-advertisement and sexuality. He has continued to oppose the austerity of one of Canada's schools of poetry, but his collections, *Improved Binoculars* (1956) and *A Red Carpet for the Sun* (1959), show a deepening sensitivity and social concern. In these books and *The Swinging Flesh* (1961) he exploits the traditional duality of mind and body to the mind's dismay. *The Shattered Plinth* (1967) was the nineteenth book of his poems to be published. His influence on the younger Canadian poets has been profound. [PT]

Collected Poems (1965).
W. Francis, 'I.L.', *Journal of Commonwealth Literature*, 3 (July 1967); G. Woodcock, 'A Grab at Proteus', *Canadian Literature*, 28 (1966).

Laȝamon (fl. *c.* 1200). Chronicler. All that we know of Laȝamon comes in the proem to his long verse-chronicle, *The Brut* (ed. F. Madden, 1847; ed. G. L. Brook and R. F. Leslie, 1963; sels: J. Hall, 1924; C. S. Lewis, 1963), written between 1189 and 1205. He was a priest at King's Areley, in Worcestershire, near Restone Ferry. It came into his mind, he says, to make a record of the rulers of Britain, and he travelled about the country to collect material. Though he mentions three authorities, the only one he really made use of was the *Roman de Brut* by ◊Wace, of which his poem is a free paraphrase but much longer because of natural diffuseness and artistic elaboration. Laȝamon does add some new material especially on Arthur. Stylistically the poem is midway between the old alliterative poetry and the new syllabic rhymed verse of his model. Though Laȝamon aimed at a historical pattern in *The Brut* most of its beauties are incidental – some fine descriptions in the native vein, some well-handled narratives such as the first vernacular version of *Lear*, and some spirited epic similes. The poem centres around Arthur, as the representative national hero, and the Britons are seen as the instruments of the Divine Will. Without Wace's grace and neatness, Laȝamon's work has a dignity and seriousness lacking in Wace. [A G]

D. Everett, *Essays in Middle English Literature* (1955); W. F. Schirmer, 'Laȝamon's *Brut*', in *Bulletin of the Modern Humanities Research Association* (1957); J. S. P. Tatlock, *The Legendary History of Britain* (1950); H. C. Wyld, 'Laȝamon as an English Poet', *RES*, VI (1930).

Leacock, Stephen (Butler) (1869–1944). Canadian humorist. He was born in the Isle of Wight, but when he was 6 his parents emigrated to Canada and he 'decided to go with them'. Educated in Toronto, he taught for eight years at his old school before being appointed a lecturer at McGill University in 1901. From 1908 until his retirement in 1936 he was head of the Department of Economics and Political Science. His earliest writings were on economics and Canadian history, but *Literary Lapses* (1910) was the first of over 30 humorous books ('I would sooner have written *Alice in Wonderland* than the whole *Encyclopædia Britannica*'). *My Discovery of England* (1922) was the outcome of one of his numerous and highly successful lecture tours.

Leacock excels in the drawing out to absurdity of likely situations. His humour is based on exaggeration and a quasi-logical pursuit of the inappropriate implication. He lacks the commitment of a satirist and the constancy of a novelist. *Nonsense Novels* (1911) and *Frenzied Fiction* (1917) show his skill as a parodist, but his best books, *Sunshine Sketches of a Little Town* (1912) and *Arcadian Adventures with the Idle Rich* (1914), are the product of an ambiguous treatment of economics and the paraphernalia of success. [P T]

The Boy I Left Behind Me (1947) (autobiography). G. Mikes, *Eight Humorists* (1954); G. G. Sedgewick, 'S.L. as a Man of Letters', *University of Toronto Quarterly*, XV, 1 (October 1945); *Canadian Literature*, 5 (Summer, 1960) (2 articles).

Lear, Edward (1812–88). Artist and poet. He was born in London of Danish descent, the youngest son of a stockbroker's family of fifteen surviving children. After being educated mainly by his elder sister Anne, at the age of 15 his father's imprisonment for debt forced him to earn his own living by jobbing drawing and colouring, for which he was developing some talent. He was hired by the Earl of Derby to produce the illustrations for a description of the menagerie at Knowsley Hall, where he lived for some years. This patronage brought him social connexions and enough commissions to finance his extensive travels in Italy, the Mediterranean, the Levant, Egypt, India and Ceylon. From 1880, he lived completely abroad at San Remo in the Italian Riviera, where he died. As a painter, Lear specialized in large landscapes, which are often rather fussy, but satisfied a demand for big pictures. The drawings and sketches he made on his travels as notes for his larger works are, however, very varied, fresh and original. His water-colours are also prized as accurate geological, botanical and topographical records; his ornithological water-colours are esteemed and were made for such volumes as *Illustrations of the Family of Psittacidae* (1832). Lear dashed off nonsense drawings, to which James Thurber's work is obviously allied, but is most famous as a writer of nonsense verses. These he first produced for the Stanley children at Knowsley. In them his melancholy and alienation from Victorian society, deepened by depression and epilepsy (or some nervous complaint), are given a haunting expression. It is not too much to say that Lear is a powerful poet in his world of nonsense. He favours a form of the limerick, anti-climactic, which by repeating the first line at the end (frequently after allusions to violence, oppression or social tyranny) falls away into a stammering repose of mute withdrawal. He is also an inventive punster and neologist: such poems as *The Jumblies* are worth serious study. *A Book of Nonsense* first appeared in 1846 (enlarged, 1861; further enlarged, 1863); it was followed by *Nonsense Songs, Stories, Botany and Alphabets* (1871), *More Nonsense Pictures, Rhymes, Botany etc.* (1872) and *Laughable Lyrics. A Fresh Book of etc.* (1877). Lear also wrote and illustrated books on natural history, and several good travel books such as his *Illustrated Excursions in Italy* (4 vols., 1846). His *Letters* (ed. Lady C. Strachey, 1907–11) are worth reading as human documents illustrative of his age. [AR]

L. Omnibus, ed. R. L. Megroz (1938); *Complete Nonsense*, ed. H. Jackson (1947).

Angus Davidson, *E.L.* (1938; reprinted 1968); E. Sewell, *The Field of Nonsense* (1952); J. Richardson, *E.L.* (WTW, 1965); V. Noakes, *E.L.: The Life of a Wanderer* (1968); P. Hofer, *E.L. as a Landscape Draughtsman* (1968); W. B. O. Field, *L. on My Shelves* (New York, 1935) (bibliography).

Leavis, Frank Raymond (1895–   ). Literary critic. Born in Cambridge and educated at the Perse School and Emmanuel College, Cambridge, in 1936 he became a Fellow of Downing College, and taught English. He retired from his college position and university readership in 1962. In 1929 he married Queenie Dorothy Roth, who is herself a distinguished literary critic. In the thirties, Leavis made himself one of the most influential university teachers in England. This influence was exerted on Cambridge, partly through his teaching, and at large through the periodical ◊ *Scrutiny* (1932–53, reissued 1963), of which he was one of the founders. Some valuable essays from this periodical, not elsewhere reprinted and including some important criticism by his wife, have been collected by him in *A Selection from Scrutiny* (2 vols., 1968). Perhaps the centre of his approach to literary art is his preoccupation with English literature as the subject of academic study which has replaced the classics in the universities, and which should thus provide the traditional and moral orientation of the young élite intellectuals. He has discussed the problems involved in *Mass Civilisation and Minority Culture* (1930) and *Education and the University* (1943). Though, as the title of his periodical indicates, he is concerned with close study of texts, he is not concerned primarily with explaining texts (unlike many of the American 'new critics', with whom he is often erroneously linked). He has indeed personally provided little

in the way of technical scholarship. Rather he is concerned with treating a text, a poem, a novel as a 'complex and balanced structure' which demands for reading a grasp of the world and a moral perspective which it is the business of education to provide. Thus it can be seen that his view of literature is ideological, demanding discipline and vigour of personal response. His vigorous insistence that only the writers he considers great or truly serious are worth academic study, his passion for the creation and ruthless application of standards, his contempt for gentlemanly dilettantism in criticism and for the literary Establishment in all its forms and the harsh and uncompromising manner in which he has sometimes expressed himself won him enemies among the orthodox, but his reputation is now firmly established.

In his insistence on moral feeling and moral taste he is perhaps a descendant of Arnold and the Arnoldian critics: such views are traditionally linked with a historical response to the industrial revolution. His work has been valuable in demanding a clearly realized point of view, but has been less valuable in prompting on occasion a parochial response, and a narrowness of interest. Among his publications are *D. H. Lawrence* (1930) and *New Bearings in English Poetry* (T. S. Eliot, Pound, Hopkins) (1932). He was influential in developing academic study of Lawrence and Eliot in England. He has also published *For Continuity* (1933); *Culture and Environment* (with Denys Thompson) (1933); *Revaluation: Tradition and Development in English Poetry* (1936); a book on the English novel, *The Great Tradition* (Jane Austen, George Eliot, James, Conrad, D. H. Lawrence) (1948); *The Common Pursuit* (1952); *D. H. Lawrence, Novelist* (1955); *Anna Karenina and Other Essays* (1967); *English in Our Time and the University* (1969); he is co-author with his wife of *Lectures in America* (1969); he has edited *Determinations* (1934), a book of critical essays, and *Mill on Bentham and Coleridge* (1950). [AR]

Ed. E. Bentley, *The Importance of Scrutiny* (1948); S. E. Hyman, *The Armed Vision* (1948); L. Trilling, *A Gathering of Fugitives* (1957); V. Buckley, *Poetry and Morality: Studies in the Criticism of Arnold, Eliot and L.* (1959); G. Watson, *The Literary Critics* (1962); G. S. Fraser, *The Modern Writer and His World* (1964); D. F. McKenzie and M. P. Allum, *F.R.L.: A Check List, 1924–64* (1966).

Lecky, William Edward Hartpole (1838–1903). Historian. Born near Dublin, the son of an Anglo-Irish landowner, he was all his life an opponent of Home Rule, though at the same time of strong pro-Irish sympathies. He was educated at Cheltenham and Trinity College, Dublin (for which he sat in Westminster as M.P. from 1895). Brought up for a career in the Church of Ireland, Lecky turned to writing, though his first works caused little interest: *The Religious Tendencies of the Age* (anonymous, 1860) and *The Leaders of Public Opinion in Ireland* (Swift, Flood, Grattan and O'Connell) (anonymous, 1861; revised 1871). He travelled in Europe, and in 1863 published an arresting essay 'The Declining Sense of the Miraculous', which subsequently formed part of his famous *History of the Rise and Influence of the Spirit of Rationalism in Europe* (1865). This was followed by a *History of European Morals from Augustus to Charlemagne* (1869). Under the influence of ◊ Buckle, Lecky became a controversial historian of civilization, and caught the spirit of the age (in which he was aided by the circumstances of his birth and politics) by treating beliefs, morals and ethics in a comparative or 'evolutionary' manner. Objecting to the work on the history of the 18th century by ◊ Froude, Lecky produced his most useful work, *A History of England in the Eighteenth Century* (8 vols., 1878–90; and 7 vols. on England and 5 on Ireland, 1892). In this, Lecky tries to place the history of the 'development' of institutions and political ideas in a social and economic context. He also published *Democracy and Liberty* (1896; revised, with an essay on Gladstone, 1899) and collections of essays. He was one of the original members of the Order of Merit (1902). His letters (1859–78) were edited by H. Montgomery Hyde under the title *A Victorian Historian* (1947). [AR]

J. J. Auchmuty, *L.: A Biographical and Critical Essay* (1945).

Lee, Laurie (1914–). Poet. Born in Gloucestershire, Lee was educated at a local village school and Stroud Technical School and for many years worked as a writer of documentary film scripts. He visited Spain during the Civil War and some of his best lyrics were written on this subject. A nature poet with an attractively simple style, he has published 3 very brief volumes of poetry, *The Sun My Monument* (1944), *The Bloom of Candles* (1947) and *My Many-Coated Man* (1955); a verse play, *The Voyage of Magellan* (1948); a record of his travels in Andalusia, *A Rose for Winter* (1955), and a best-selling autobiography, *Cider with Rosie* (1959), in which he describes, with great charm and restraint, his childhood in a village isolated from the mainstream of 20th-century English life. [PJK]

Lee, Nathaniel (c. 1649–92). Dramatist. After studying at Trinity College, Cambridge, and failing as an actor, he became a writer of tragedies. His work is in the prevailing Restoration neo-classical mode of rhetorical, rhyming tragedy in which the protagonist is torn between Love and Honour. Nat Lee has been called 'the most completely "heroic" of all the outstanding heroic writers'. His principal plays, mostly based on classical subjects or on French versions of classical themes, were *Nero* (1674), *Sophonisba, or Hannibal's Overthrow* (1675), *The Rival Queens, or The Death of Alexander the Great*, his most popular play (1677), *Oedipus*, in collaboration with John Dryden (1679), *Mithridates, King of Pontus* (1678), *Lucius Junius Brutus, Father of His Country* (1680), *The Princess of Cleve* (1681) and *The Massacre of Paris* (written c. 1679, acted 1689). Unlike the best work of his contemporary ◊ Otway, none of his plays have survived on the stage. They are representative examples of a high-flown and artificial form of tragedy; their reading is an acquired taste which Bonamy Dobrée has striven to encourage. [MJ]

Works, ed. T. B. Stroup and A. L. Cooke (2 vols. New Jersey, 1968).
B. Dobrée, *Restoration Tragedy, 1660–1720* (1929); R. G. Ham, *Otway and L.* (New Haven, Conn., 1931).

Lee, Sir Sidney (1859–1926). Biographer. Born in London as Solomon Lazarus, and educated at the City of London School and Balliol College, Oxford, he was a member of the editorial staff of the *Dictionary of National Biography* under Leslie ◊ Stephen from its beginning (1883) and became joint-editor (1890) and then sole editor (1891). In all, he wrote over 800 articles. Some of his entries he expanded into solid and useful books, for example his life of *Queen Victoria* (1902) and his *Life of William Shakespeare* (1898; 1915; enlarged, 1925), long a standard work recommended to students. He was greatly interested in the Elizabethan period, producing *Great Englishmen of the Sixteenth Century* (Sir Thomas More, Sidney, Ralegh, Spenser, Bacon and Shakespeare), and particularly in Shakespeare (and Shakespeareana), on which he wrote and published much, including a valuable facsimile of the first folio (1902). He planned and partly edited the useful compendium *Shakespeare's England* (1916). Lee was knighted in 1911, and wrote a biography of King Edward VII (2 vols., 1925–7). [AR]

C. H. Firth, *Sir S.L.* (1931).

Le Fanu, Joseph Sheridan (1814–73). Novelist. Born in Ireland, the great-grand-nephew of ◊ Sheridan and the son of a Church of Ireland dean, he was educated at Trinity College, Dublin, called to the bar (1839), but took to writing after he had become known by publishing his Irish ballads, *Phandrig Croohoore* and *Shamus O'Brien* (1836). He wrote about a dozen novels; some of them appeared in the *Dublin University Magazine*, which he afterwards bought. He was a master of the story of mystery and occult suspense (the ingenious construction of his novels and his exploitation of the uncanny connect him with Wilkie ◊ Collins and to a lesser degree ◊ Ainsworth); he combined this with a power of telling Irish stories that places him second only to Charles ◊ Lever. Le Fanu's best-known stories are *The House by the Church-yard* (1863), *Uncle Silas* (1864; reprinted with an introduction by Elizabeth Bowen, 1947), and a collection, *In A Glass Darkly* (1872), which contains his most chilling story, 'The Watcher'. [AR]

S. M. Ellis, *Wilkie Collins, Le F. and Others* (1931); N. Browne, *S. Le F.* (1951).

Le Gallienne, Richard (1866–1947). Poet and essayist. Born in Liverpool, the son of a businessman, he was educated at Liverpool College and apprenticed to a firm of accountants, but in 1888 he fled from both office and family to seek his fortune as a writer in London, having already (1887) had privately printed his first poems, *My Ladies' Sonnets*. By 1891 he had become an established figure of the London literary scene: he had a regular column of book reviews in the *Star*; he was one of the founder-members of the poetic Rhymers' Club, together with W. B. Yeats, Lionel Johnson, Ernest Rhys and others; he knew Oscar Wilde, Aubrey Beardsley and John Lane, and contributed

to the ◊ *Yellow Book*. He published a stream of verse and criticism throughout the nineties (of which the standard criticism is that it was 'largely Wilde-and-water'), also a romantic novel, *The Quest of the Golden Girl* (1896), which contains a search for the poet's Ideal Woman and a great many 'naughty' allusions to petticoats. But the dragon-fly years of the nineties passed, and with them Le Gallienne's fame; increasingly troubled by drink and debts, he went to America to escape his creditors and scraped a living there with journalism and lecturing. He also wrote *The Romantic '90s* (1925) and after many years achieved a measure of security and returned to Europe in 1927, spending the last years of his life in the South of France. [JM]

Richard Whittington-Egan and Geoffrey Smerdon, *The Quest of the Golden Boy: Life and Letters of R. Le G.* (1960).

Lehmann, John (Frederick) (1907–   ). Editor, publisher, man of letters and poet. Perhaps better known as a public-spirited literary *entrepreneur* than for his own literary achievements, he was educated at Eton and Trinity, and began work as a publisher assisting Leonard and Virginia Woolf on the Hogarth Press and, during the Second World War, as editor of *Penguin New Writing*. Both gave a platform for established writers of the younger generation and encouraged new and unknown war poets and documentary prose writers in the forces. After the war, as editor of the *London Magazine*, he kept up the same high standards. His interest in new and experimental writing is shown in his critical work, *New Writing in Europe* (1940), but his own poetry, though its thought is often difficult and intricate, tends to be clear and traditional, and often a little cold and rhetorical, in form and feeling. His autobiographies are an indispensable source for the literary historian of the 1930s. He was a close friend and associate of Isherwood, Auden and Spender. [GSF]

A Garden Revisited (1931); *Down River* (1939); *Forty Poems* (1942); *Sphere of Glass* (1944); *The Age of the Dragon* (1951); *The Open Night* (1952) (criticism); *Edith Sitwell* (1952) (criticism); *The Whispering Gallery* (1955) (memoirs); *Collected Poems* (1963); edited: *The Year's Work in Literature* (1949 and 1950); *Poems from New Writing* (1946); *English Stories from New Writing* (1951); *The Craft of Letters in England* (1956).

Lehmann, Rosamund (Nina) (1903–).
Novelist. Born in London, the sister of
John ◊ Lehmann, she was privately educated, and went to Girton College, Cambridge, where she set part of her first novel,
Dusty Answer (1927). It is about the childhood and adolescence of a sensitive girl (a
subject which has remained her prime concern as a novelist). The children in the first
half of the novel are rendered in a way
which gave her an immediate reputation as
a writer. She is a novelist of the inner life
and personal relations: in her interest in
the middle and upper class and in the care
and deliberation of her prose she is often
compared with Virginia ◊ Woolf. Her slow
narratives, however, rarely generate much
passion. *Invitation to the Waltz* (1932) is a
short work about a girl's apprehensive
facing of a social situation; *The Weather
in the Streets* (1936) is a sequel. Her next
novel, *The Ballad and the Source* (1944), is a
longer and more sombre work; the narrator
of this story about a domineering old
woman is a child, and the indirect narrative,
in which the child listens, comments, asks
and half understands, is reminiscent of
Henry James. Her best book is perhaps
The Echoing Grove (1953), in which she
sets her chosen theme of a girl's awakening
consciousness in a love triangle and surrounds it with her most sustained attempt
at realizing political and social life; in technique the novel is also her most elaborate.
She has written an interesting essay on
fiction, 'The Future of the Novel', in
Britain Today (June 1946). *No More Music*
(1939) is a play; and she has published
a volume of short stories, *The Gypsy's
Baby* (1946). [A R]

The Swan in the Evening (1968) (autobiography).
E. Bowen, *Collected Impressions* (1950).

Lennox, Mrs Charlotte (1720–1804). Novelist, translator and playwright. Born
Ramsay, in New York, where her father was
Lieutenant-Governor. Dr Johnson wrote a
dedication to her romance *The Female
Quixote; or The Adventures of Arabella*
(1752), an imitation of Cervantes' work
which had some vogue. She became a
member of the Johnson–Thrale circle and
obtained another preface to her *Shakespeare
Illustrated* (1753–4), the first collection of
source material for some 22 of the plays.
[A R]

M. R. Small, *C.M.L.* (New Haven, Conn., 1935).

Lessing, Doris (May) (1919–). Novelist
and playwright. Born in Persia, she was
brought up on a Southern Rhodesian farm.
After being twice married, she left for
England in 1949 with the manuscript of her
first novel, *The Grass is Singing* (1950). For
many years she was an active Communist.
A characteristically strong element of
psychological autobiography is evident in
the Martha Quest novels, *Martha Quest*
(1952), *A Proper Marriage* (1954) and *A
Ripple from the Storm* (1958). *The Habit of
Loving* (1957) was a second collection of
short stories. Much of her work is on three
themes: the necessity for active interest in
political issues, the psychology of ageing
women, and the conflict of generations from
which the young emerge as less ambitious
than their elders. *The Golden Notebook*
(1962) is an ambitious and impressive
attempt to illuminate these themes by
repeating them with variations in a single
book. Her play, *Play with a Tiger* (1962), is
an extension of one of the novel's episodes.
As a journalist she revisited the Rhodesias
and wrote an angry account in *Going Home*
(1957). She has always been active in political and social agitation.

Lessing's challenging books are often
overloaded with documentary detail and a
casebook thoroughness of psychological
exposition. The stories, and some of the
short novels in *Five* (1953), are less flawed,
but her best sustained work is her description of her early months in London, *In
Pursuit of the English* (1960). *A Man and
Two Women* (1963) and *African Stories*
(1964) contain much of her best work in the
field of the short story. *Landlocked* (1965) is
the fourth of the Martha Quest novels,
which were published in two volumes under
the title *Children of Violence* (1965–6). [P T]

D. Brewster, *D.L.* (1965); S. R. Burkom, 'Form
and Content in the Work of D.L.', *Critique*,
XI, 1.

L'Estrange, Sir Roger (1616–1704). Journalist, pamphleteer and translator. He played
an important part in the history of censorship. He fought for the King in the Civil
War, and after being condemned to death,
escaped to Holland and took service with
Charles II. Before and after the Restoration
he was an active pamphleteer in support of
the King. Of an authoritarian disposition, in
1663 he published *Considerations and Proposals in Order to the Regulation of the Press*,

advancing the usual arguments for censorship, and quoting legal precedents; thus he had himself appointed Surveyor of Printing Presses and Licenser of the press, as well as being given the sole privilege of printing public news. Under the latter patent, he published the weekly *Intelligencer* (31 August 1663–29 January 1666), and *The Newes* (3 September 1663–29 January 1666), a Thursday supplement. These were ousted by printers willing to print more information and more lively news. He fled the country again during the Popish plot, and on his return published *The Observator* (13 April 1681–9 March 1687), supporting the court and attacking the dissenters. He was knighted in 1685. He lost his appointments (which had become dead letters) in the Revolution and was several times imprisoned. L'Estrange published a number of useful translations, among them *The Visions of Quevedo* (1667, and later editions), some *Colloquies of Erasmus* (1680), *The Fables of Aesop and Other Eminent Mythologists* (1692), Terence's *Comedies* (1694) and *The Works of Josephus* (1702). [A R]

G. Kitchin, *Sir R. L'E.* (1913).

Lever, Charles James (1806–72). Novelist. Born in Dublin of an Anglo-Irish family, he studied medicine at Trinity College there and at Göttingen. He turned professionally to literature on the very favourable reception of his first novel, *The Confessions of Harry Lorrequer* (intr. 'Lewis Melville', Everyman, 1907), first published in 1837 in the *Dublin University Magazine* (which Lever edited, 1842–5). Thereafter he published a novel a year, beginning by exploiting the developing 'provincial novel' (◊ Edgeworth and Le Fanu), which Walter Scott's success had made respectable, and producing breezy, loosely organized stories of hard-drinking Irish squires, the English garrison, sporting life and Irish peasants, e.g. *Charles O'Malley, the Irish Dragoon* (2 vols., 1840); *Our Mess* (3 vols., 1843–4). He also had an interest in history, in realistic portrayal of the Napoleonic wars, and in romance, e.g. *The Knight of Gwynne* (1847). His realism is sometimes mingled with rather trying sentiment. In his later work, written largely abroad (he lived in Brussels, and in 1845 settled in Italy), he turned his clever talent to considering Irish social questions, poverty and the decline of the great estates. [A R]

Works (Harry Lorrequer Edition) (34 vols., 1876–8); *The Novels*, ed. by his daughter (37 vols., 1897–9).
L. Stevenson, *Dr Quicksilver: The Life of C.L.* (1939).

Lewes, George Henry (1817–78). Journalist and miscellaneous writer. Born in London, he was educated there as well as abroad. His career was as varied as his writing; he experimented with the law, business and medicine, travelled in Germany and was briefly on the London stage. Thereafter he became a journalist, writing for the *Morning Chronicle* and the *Penny Encyclopaedia*, and editing (with Leigh ◊ Hunt) *The Leader* (1851–4); he was one of the founders and first editor (1865–6) of the influential *Fortnightly Review*. He wrote much on philosophy, including a *Biographical History of Philosophy* (4 vols., 1845–6; several expanded editions), and was important in introducing to England the positivist ideas of Comte (*Comte's Philosophy of the Sciences*, 1853). His most important literary work was a 2-volume book on *The Life and Works of Goethe* (1855). George Eliot formed an irregular union with him (he could not obtain a divorce), and it is against this background of interest in philosophy and psychology (see his *Problems of Life and Mind*, 5 vols., 1874–9) and his acute and persuasive theories of fiction that she produced her novels. They lived part of the time in Germany. Lewes also tried his hand at play-writing under the pseudonym of 'Lawrence Slingsby'; his book *On Actors and the Art of Acting* (1875) is a knowledgeable study. [A R]

Literary Criticism, ed. A. R. Kaminsky (U. of Nebraska P., 1964); *The George Eliot Letters*, G. S. Haight (7 vols., New Haven, Conn., 1954–6).
A. T. Kitchel, *G.L. and George Eliot* (1933); M. Greenhut, 'L. as a Critic of the Novel', in *Studies in Philology*, XV (1948); R. L. Brett, 'L.: Dramatist, Novelist and Critic', *E & S*, n.s. II (1958).

Lewis, Alun (1915–44). Poet and short-story writer. He was born at Aberdare, South Wales, the son of a schoolmaster; his family had country roots and his humane, egalitarian values were due to his dislike of the effects of industrialism. He was educated at Aberystwyth University. His stories, collected in *The Last Inspection* and *In the Green Tree*, are ironically factual about army life, or evoke the philosophical strangeness of active service in India. His poems, collected in *Raider's Dawn* (1942) and *Ha, Ha, Among the Trumpets* (1945), suffered in reputation from the reaction against 'neo-Romanticism', but are now recognized as the finest of the Second World War. Robert Graves defined their quality as 'both illuminating and healing'. Sometimes romantic in diction, they are wholly thought through and built up, while sounding natural. Lewis's power is to marry fact with feeling, to divine in reality an essential, often new emotion. He brings action and inwardness, the immediate and the lasting, and, in his love poems, the anguish of separation and enduring hope ('timeless love') into a harmony which is a vital repose ('a robustness at the core of sadness'). Lewis was killed in Arakan in 1944. [FG]

Selected Poetry and Prose, intr. Ian Hamilton (1966).

Lewis, C. Day. ◊ Day Lewis, C.

Lewis, C(live) S(taples) (1898–1963). Novelist and critic. Born in Belfast, the son of a solicitor, and educated at Malvern College and privately. His career at University College, Oxford, in which he studied classics and English, was interrupted by service in the First World War with the Somerset Light Infantry (1918–19). He was a Fellow and tutor of Magdalen College, Oxford, from 1925 to 1954, when he was elected Professor of Medieval and Renaissance English at Cambridge, and transferred to Magdalene College there. He published his first book, *Dymer* (1926; 1950), an allegorical poem in rhyme royal, under the pseudonym 'Clive Hamilton'. As a critic he was a master of well-digested learning. *The Allegory of Love* (1936), which won the Hawthornden Prize, is a discussion of the interrelation in the Middle Ages between literary form and the development of passionate and romantic love. The attempt to unite these two matters is daring, but specialists in either study may perhaps find the union less satisfactory. *A Preface to Paradise Lost* (1942) is an attempt to defend Milton's poem as a Christian epic. *English Literature in the Sixteenth Century* (1954) is an intelligent attempt at literary history (a genre of writing seldom practised with so much distinction). *Studies in Words* (1960) and *Experiment in Criticism* (1961) perhaps best show Lewis's qualities of presenting wide information and argument in readable form. He has practised two

other kinds of writing, both linked to his Christian beliefs. With *Out of the Silent Planet* (1938), in which two wicked scientists abduct a 'good' Cambridge philologist to the planet Mars, he started writing allegorical fantasy fiction. This has seldom interested the science fiction fanciers, but readers with religious views find them pleasing. *Perelandra* (1943) shows a new Eve tempted by a new Devil, this time on Venus. *That Hideous Strength* (1945) foreshadows the explosion of the atomic bomb, and raises the ethical questions which have forced themselves into common notice since then. Lewis also wrote a number of religious works: *The Problem of Pain* (1940) and *The Screwtape Letters* (1942) are perhaps the best known. The latter is another fantasy – a series of letters from a devil called Screwtape to his nephew, Wormwood, giving advice on how to tempt a human to sin. *Beyond Personality* (1944) were lectures he gave on the B.B.C., and a volume of apologetics, *Mere Christianity*, appeared in 1952. He wrote a number of books for children. [AR]

Surprised by Joy (1955) (autobiography).

Lewis, D(ominic) B(evan) Wyndham (1894–). Journalist. The son of a Welsh clergyman. Army service in the First World War cut short his university career at Oxford. He made his name in the twenties and thirties as a humorous columnist: as 'Beachcomber' on the *Daily Express* (1919–24); 'At the Sign of the Blue Moon' on the *Daily Mail* (1925–30); and as 'Timothy Shy' on the *News Chronicle*. Many of his nonsense pieces were published in collections: *A London Farrago* (1922), *At the Green Goose* (1923) and *On Straw and Other Conceits* (1927). With Charles Lee, he published *The Stuffed Owl, an Anthology of Bad Verse* (1930). He has also published translations from the French, such as Barbey d'Aurevilly's *The Anatomy of Dandyism* (1928), and several useful biographies of Frenchmen: *Villon* (1928), *King Spider, Louis XI* (1930), *Ronsard* (1944), *The Soul of Marshal Gilles de Raiz* (1952), *Rabelais* (1957) and *Molière* (1959). His life of Boswell, *The Hooded Hawk* (1946; 1952), is a defence which the alteration of taste and literary fashion has in a measure rendered unnecessary. [AR]

Lewis, John Saunders (1893–). Welsh critic, dramatist, prose writer. Born in Wallasey, son of a Methodist minister, he graduated in English at the University of Liverpool. After war service from 1914 to 1919 he was appointed lecturer in Welsh at University College, Swansea. In 1937 he was dismissed as a result of his participation in burning the Bombing School near Pwllheli and his subsequent imprisonment. He was later appointed lecturer in Welsh at University College, Cardiff.

One of the most prolific of modern Welsh writers, the main influence on Saunders Lewis's writing are his Roman Catholicism (he received acceptance in 1933) and his identification with the Welsh Nationalist Party (he was president from 1925 to 1938). He stands apart from many modern Welsh men of letters in his receptiveness to continental influences, in particular from France, in whose literature he is extremely well read. This lends his literary criticism a rather more objective appearance than is usual in Wales, and certainly gives his work a more individual character. In his account of Welsh literature ending in 1535 this fresh standpoint is particularly notable, but its value is decreased by his over-enthusiastic acceptance of debatable hypotheses. His volume of essays, *Canlyn Arthur* (1938), raises propaganda and political writing to a high artistic level. His study, *Williams Pantycelyn* (1927), is a highly individual and penetrating psychological analysis of a complex character. The novel *Monica* (1930) is a study of the shallow romantic view of love with which Lewis himself has little sympathy because of his rather austere views on love in general.

Saunders Lewis's major contributions to creative Welsh literature have been in drama. *Blodeuwedd* (1948), in blank verse, is based on the ◊ Mabinogi, but he recreates the problems of illicit and unrecognized love in the tightly knit society of medieval Wales. The metrical drama *Buchedd Garmon* (1937) in *vers libre* is mainly concerned with the unity of Christendom, and has many fine passages of passionate patriotism. *Amlyn ac Amig* (1940), mostly in *vers libre*, is based on the medieval Charlemagne story *Vita Amici et Amelii*. Since then Lewis has written a number of plays of great variety of style and merit, including *Dwy Gomedi* (2 comedies) (1952), *Siwan* (the betrayal of Llywelyn by his wife Siwan (Joan)), *Gymerwch chi sigaret?* (1956) (set in Eastern Europe and Vienna on a contemporary theme of political expedience), *Brad* (1958) (on the Paris

putsch against Hitler), *Esther* (on the biblical theme), and *Serch yw'r Doctor* (a light opera) (both 1960). [MR]

Cymru Fydd (1967); *Probleman Prifysgol* (1968).

Lewis, Matthew Gregory 'Monk' (1775–1818). Novelist, playwright and miscellaneous writer. The son of a Civil Servant, he was educated at Westminster School and Christ Church, Oxford. He became attaché at the British Embassy in Weimar where, under the influence of his reading in early German romantics like Tieck, he wrote his romance, *The Monk* (1796; ed. E. A. Baker, 1907; text of first edition ed. L. F. Peck, New York, 1952), a gothic tale of rape, murder, sorcery, incest and the supernatural which combines several literary traditions in an extravagant but powerful mixture. It had many imitators. The eloquent monk Ambrosio (the ancestor of *The Italian* of Mrs ◊ Radcliffe), is a kind of Faust figure. Lewis was also the author of some verse tales. Scott admired these, and contributed to Lewis's anthology, *Tales of Terror* (1799). *The Journal of a West Indian Proprietor* (1834; ed. M. Wilson, 1929) is a very readable account of Lewis's visit to the estates in Jamaica which he inherited. It shows him to be a deft writer and good-humoured, sympathetic observer. [AR]

L. F. Peck, *A Life of M.G.L.* (Harvard U.P., 1961); A. M. Killen, *Le roman terrifiant* (Paris, 1923); M. Summers, *The Gothic Quest* (1938).

Lewis, (Percy) Wyndham (1884–1957). Painter, novelist and essayist. Lewis was born off the North American coast in his father's yacht. With his parents separated, his childhood was unsettled, and he was educated at several schools, the last of which was Rugby. He then studied at the Slade School of Art and afterwards travelled for some years in Europe, with a period of bohemian living in Paris. By 1914 he had emerged as a leader of the Vorticist movement, founding and editing with Ezra Pound the periodical *Blast: Review of the Great English Vortex* (2 issues, 1914 and 1915) which published the Vorticist manifestos of Pound and the French sculptor Henri Gaudier-Brzeska. The flamboyant aggressiveness of the Vorticist group of young modernists did not produce any very clear account of their principles, which were related to those of ◊ Imagism in poetry: definiteness of line and structure, a sharp awareness of the arrangement of planes, bright contrasting colours arranged in clearly defined patterns – these were characteristics both of Vorticist ideals and Lewis's own painting. Lewis's satirical and polemical writing was largely directed against the cultural patterns and literary movements of the 1920s, especially the surrender to the Bergsonian concept of time represented by the 'stream of consciousness' novel and to the 'dark forces' of sex and the unconscious as represented by D. H. Lawrence, the 'mirthless formal acrobatics' of Joyce, and the Bloomsbury combination of liberal humanism and high culture. To fashionable theories of temporal flux and surrender to inward feeling he opposed 'conceptual quality, hard exact outline, grand architectural proportion'. His first novel, *Tarr* (1918), which drew on his life in Paris, gave evidence of the polemical stance which later manifested itself in his editing of the angry periodicals *The Tyro* (1924) and *The Enemy* (1927, 1929), and, most impressively, in his massive ironic novel *The Apes of God* (1930), an attack on the cultural life of the 1920s done with immense comic gusto and reaching far beyond the immediate objects of its satire. His opposition to what he considered the flabby exhibitionism of the liberal culture of his day led him to an intense flirtation with fascism (*Hitler*, 1931), but he later changed his mind radically (*The Hitler Cult and How It Will End*, 1939).

Lewis managed to put across his views in a great variety of ways: *The Lion and the Fox* (1927), ostensibly a study of 'the role of the hero in the plays of Shakespeare', is really a polemic on behalf of individual consciousness and will against the unconscious and the mass. *Time and Western Man* (1927), a key work in the interpretation of Lewis's thought, mounts a frontal attack on all the forces of subjectivism and surrender to inwardness which he considered had corrupted modern literature. *Men without Art* (1934) attacks some of the heroes of modern literature, including the 'dumb ox' Hemingway and the 'pseudo-believer' Eliot. But his most remarkable work is *The Human Age*, a trilogy of which the first part, *The Childermass*, appeared in 1928 and 2 subsequent parts, *Monstre Gai* and *Malign Fiesta*, appeared in 1955. The scene of the trilogy is a waste land outside heaven, where the 'emigrant mass' of humanity awaits examination by the Bailiff. The hallucinatory atmosphere, the grotesquerie, the

power and conviction of the narrative, the ritualistic and symbolic overtones of meaning, together make this novel sequence something unique in modern literature. [DD]

Blasting and Bombardiering (1937); *Rude Assignment* (1950) (autobiographies); *Letters*, ed. W. K. Rose (1963).
G. Grigson, *A Master of Our Time: A Study of W.L.* (1951); ed. C. Handley-Read, *The Art of W.L.* (1951); Hugh Kenner, *W.L.* (1954); E. W. F. Tomlin, *W.L.* (1955); Geoffrey Wagner, *W.L.* (Norfolk, Conn., 1957); John R. Harrison, *The Reactionaries* (1966).

Leyden, John (1775–1811). Scottish poet, ballad-collector and orientalist. Leyden, the son of a Border shepherd, attended Edinburgh University (1790–7) and acquired a remarkably wide knowledge of languages. He collected, and wrote, ballads for Scott's *Minstrelsy of the Scottish Border* (1802–3), and edited *The Complaint of Scotland* (1801) and *Scottish Descriptive Poems* (1803), which includes his own 'Scenes of Infancy'. Leyden worked for the East India Company as a judge and doctor in Madras, Sumatra and Calcutta, publishing important works on Indian and Malayan language, literature and institutions before his premature death from fever in Java. [AI]

Poetical Works, ed. T. Brown (1875); *Poems and Ballads*, ed. R. White (1858) (with memoir by Scott from his *Miscellaneous Prose Works*, 1834–6, vol. iv).
J. Sinton, *Dr J.L.* (1907); J. Reith, *Life of Dr J.L.* (1923).

Lillo, George (1693–1739). Dramatist. Little is known of his life, but he is thought to have been of Flemish descent and a jeweller by profession. He produced at least 5 tragedies, deliberately violating the precepts of neoclassicism by writing in prose about middle-class characters. *The London Merchant, or The History of George Barnwell*, acted in 1731, was based on an Elizabethan ballad, and was approved by Pope. His other plays included *The Christian Hero* (1735) and *Fatal Curiosity* (1736). He showed his awareness of his predecessors in the genre by adapting the anonymous Elizabethan domestic tragedy *Arden of Feversham* for performance in 1736. He had little influence in England, though his continental followers included Lessing (*Miss Sara Sampson*, 1755) and Diderot (*Le fils naturel*, 1757). [MJ]

The London Merchant and *Fatal Curiosity*, ed. A. W. Ward (Boston, 1906); ed. W. H. McBurney (2 vols., 1965 and 1967).

Lindsay or Lyndsay, Sir David (1490?–1555). Scottish poet and Reformation satirist. A childhood companion to James V of Scotland and later a royal herald, he was knighted and made Lyon King at Arms, the chief herald of Scotland, in 1542. Later he sat in the Scottish Parliament and took part in diplomatic missions; he joined the popular and reforming party, and was one of the group who urged Knox to begin preaching in public. His poems are a series of outspoken attacks on the 'unthrift, sweirness [sloth], falsehood, poverty and strife' of contemporary Scottish politics, society and religion, carried out through the medieval conventions of *The Dream* (1528) and *The Complaint of the Papyngo* (parrot) (1530), a conversation between two dogs about preferment at court (1536) and the admonitory narrative *Tragedy of the Cardinal* (1547). *Squire Meldrum*, written after 1550, is a vigorous poem combining chivalric ideas with contemporary narrative.

Lindsay's most effective and interesting work is the morality-play *Ane pleasant satire of the thrie estaitis* (1540; ed. J. Kinsley, 1954), produced before the court three times in his lifetime and successfully revived in 1948 at the Edinburgh Festival (ed. R. Kemp, 1951). It is a rich, sprawling, panoramic satire in which King Humanity is assailed by flatterers and sycophants, while John the Commonweal suffers at the hands of the Church. Lindsay used allegory to present not only an ethical debate but a political moral and his satire is savage, compassionate and anti-clerical. The comedy is much broader, more naturalistic and more lively than the abstract names of the characters suggest. Many of Lindsay's lines and phrases became proverbial, and he was common reading in Scotland until the end of the 18th century. [AI/MJ]

Works, ed. D. Hamer (STS, 4 vols., 1931-6); *Poems*, selected M. Lindsay (1948).
W. Murison, *Sir D.L.* (1938); J. Speirs, *The Scots Literary Tradition* (1940); K. Wittig, *The Scottish Tradition in Literature* (1958).

Lindsay, John Maurice (1918–). Scottish poet, editor and journalist. Lindsay grew up in Glasgow; while serving in the army in England (1940–6) he 'discovered' Hugh ◊ MacDiarmid's *Sangschaw* and changed his poetic style from the fashionable Apocalypticism to Lallans. From his early Scots work (*Hurlygush*, 1948 – virtually an accomplished pastiche of early Mac-

Diarmid) to his dramatically explicit abandonment of Scots for the ironic English of ◊ Larkin and ◊ Davie in *Snow Warning* (1962), Lindsay has appeared as a serious and intelligent writer who has always just failed to develop a satisfactory personal idiom. He has given real service to Scottish literature as an editor – first of the wartime Poetry Scotland series; later, with Douglas ◊ Young, of the Saltire Modern Poets; of *Modern Scottish Poetry* (1946; revised edn, 1966), still the most adequate anthology of the Scottish Renaissance; and of selections from David ◊ Lindsay, Marion ◊ Angus and John ◊ Davidson. His other works include *Robert Burns* (1954), a useful *Burns Encyclopaedia* (1959) and 2 volumes on the Scottish Lowlands in the County Books (1953–56). He held an Atlantic Award for Literature in 1947–8, and now lives by freelance broadcasting and journalism. [AI]

The Exiled Heart, ed. G. Bruce (1957) (selected poems); *One Later Day and Other Poems* (1964).

Lindsay, Norman (1879–). Australian artist and novelist. The best known of a family that has produced five artists and three novelists in two generations. He was born at Creswick, a small town in Victoria renamed 'Redheap' in his novels. From 1896 to 1901 he was a struggling illustrator in Melbourne. He recalls these high-spirited years in his first novel, *A Curate in Bohemia* (1913). In 1901 he moved to Sydney as a *Bulletin* cartoonist. His capacity – and willingness – to offend puritan sensibilities soon revealed itself. His 'supreme gods', he has said, are Rabelais and Nietzsche. He has spent much of the last fifty years at Springwood in the Blue Mountains.

Lindsay writes best of the Australia of his childhood, entertaining by an unembittered awareness of human nature as no better than it should be. The Redheap books, *Redheap* (1930), *Saturdee* (1933) and *Halfway to Anywhere* (1947), are observant, sometimes caustic and often hilarious. The last two show his unusual insight into the child's mind. Other novels include *Miracles by Arrangement* (1932), *Age of Consent* (1938) and *The Cousin from Fiji* (1945). In 1918 he wrote and illustrated *The Magic Pudding*, a children's book of high quality. [PT]

J. Hetherington, *N.L.* (Australian Writers and Their Work, 1961); *Southerly*, XIX, 1 (1959) (special Lindsay issue).

Lindsay, Robert, of Pitscottie in Fife (1500?–78?). Nothing is known of his life. He wrote the first history of Scotland to be written both in Scots and in prose – a racy account, from a Protestant point of view, of events between 1437 and 1575. The opening is a translation and expansion of Hector ◊ Boece's Latin history and the middle a compilation from other writers, but Pitscottie writes as a contemporary and sometimes as an eyewitness during the last thirty years of his account. Although often wrong or vague about precise dates and names, Pitscottie had an eye for anecdote and circumstance that has made him useful to and admired by many later writers, including Sir Walter Scott. His work remained in manuscript until 1728. [AI]

The History and Chronicles of Scotland, ed. A. J. G. Mackay (STS, 3 vols., 1899–1911).

Linklater, Eric (Robert Russell) (1899–   ). Scottish novelist. A native of Orkney, he served as a private in the First World War; at Aberdeen University he abandoned medicine for English literature, which he taught for a time, visiting the United States on a fellowship from 1928 to 1930 and producing the picaresque *Juan in America* (1931), the forerunner of a whole genre of 'innocent in America' novels. An attractive, sharp, intellectual wit, uncommitted and perhaps evading commitment, runs through his light fiction of the 1930s and later and suggests a parallel with his fellow-countryman James ◊ Bridie; the early novels *White Maa's Saga* (1929), *The Men of Ness* (1932) and *Magnus Merriman* (1934) show Linklater's original purely Scottish documentary interests rapidly yielding to his lighter vein. He has also worked on official war histories and has published 2 volumes of autobiography, *The Man on My Back* (1941) and *A Year of Space* (1953). [AI]

K. Wittig, *The Scottish Tradition in Literature* (1958).

Llwyd, Morgan (1619–59). Welsh man of letters. Born at Cynfal in Maentwrog, Merioneth, he was educated at Wrexham and Brompton Bryan. He was influenced by Walter Cradoc and the early Dissenters. He served with the Parliamentary forces as a chaplain during the Civil War and settled at Wrexham in 1647 as a minister and itinerant preacher. He was intimately concerned with Commonwealth politics, and disapproved strongly of Cromwell's acceptance of the title 'Lord Protector'. He was a prolific author in English and Welsh in both prose and verse. His most important (and most popular and widely read) book was his *Dirgelwch i rai iw ddeall ac i eraill iw watwar* ('A mystery for some to understand and for others to mock'), more familiarly known as *Llyfr y Tri Aderyn* ('Book of the Three Birds') (1653). The birds who converse with each other are the Eagle (representing civil authority), the Raven (organized and established religion) and the Dove (the voice of inner conscience which has no allegiance to civil or religious authority).

Morgan Llwyd was greatly influenced by the ideas of his period. He had worked out the concept of individual conscience, the 'inner light', as a standard by which men should live, independently of the Quakers. He was greatly indebted to the mysticism of Jacob Boehme (two of whose works he translated into Welsh) according to which Christ's sacrifice takes place within the believer, heaven and hell are states of mind and not actual places, and the whole creation is moving to a predetermined salvation. These ideas permeate Llwyd's work but do not submerge his own very individual personality. He was an intensely religious man who wished to convince and convert his fellow countrymen, and his style is rather that of a preacher and prophet than of a consciously literary man. When he was deeply moved his language became a rushing torrent of eloquence and white-hot sincerity, which owes little to literary sophistication, but which does reflect the high standard of his native dialect. [MR]

Gweithiau Morgan Llwyd, i, ed. T. E. Ellis (1899); ii, ed. John H. Davies (1908).

Llywarch Hen. A 6th-century British prince from the old North and cousin of Urien Rheged (◊ Taliesin). A cycle of poems about the deeds of Llywarch and his twenty-four sons and Urien was for long attributed to Llywarch Hen himself. Recent research however has evolved the convincing theory that these poems were composed in Powys at a time of disaster in the mid 9th century when Mercia was pressing on the borders of Wales. They may well be the verse portions of a long prose saga in which Llywarch Hen and his sons, from the 6th century, and Cynddylan King of Powys and his sister Heledd, from the 7th century, have become characters in a drama of resistance and death. The scene is set in eastern mid-Wales on the borders of the present Montgomeryshire and Shropshire.

The form and content of this cycle of poems are quite different from those of ◊ Aneirin and Taliesin. The metre used is a short stanza of 3 or 4 lines (*englyn*) as opposed to the longer lines of the earlier poems, and the mood is one of regret and despair. Llywarch himself is the major character in the first cycle, which consists of elegiac stanzas on his twenty-four sons who were killed in battle, and with this is interwoven the perennial theme of the old man who laments the passing of his contemporaries until he is left alone to face harsh realities. Fate (*tynged*) and his own pride and boastfulness have played a large part in his undoing.

Intermixed with the 2 cycles are stanzas of nature poetry which are very similar in their very compressed style, and their use of nature and human gnomes, to that found in Ireland. [MR]

Canu L. H., ed. I. Williams (2nd edn, 1953).
I. Williams, *The Poems of L.H.* (1933) and *Lectures on Early Welsh Poetry* (1944); K. Jackson, *Early Celtic Nature Poetry* (1935) and *Early Welsh Gnomic Poetry* (1935).

Locke, John (1632–1704). Philosopher. Born at Wrington in Somerset, the son of a country attorney, he was educated at Westminster School and Christ Church, Oxford. He lectured on Greek and rhetoric, but his interests lay not in the Aristotelianism of the current teaching but in medicine and the new experimental science being developed by Robert Boyle and others. In 1666, he became physician and secretary to Anthony Ashley Cooper, later 1st Earl of Shaftesbury. In the same year he wrote (in Latin, for publication in Holland, where he had been) his first *Letter for Toleration* (published 1689). Under Shaftesbury's influence Locke developed his characteristic ideas on politics, property, trade, monarchy and the mind. Shaftesbury, the opponent of Charles II and James II, the Achitophel of ◊ Dryden's *Absalom and Achitophel*, gave practical expression to these modern developments, Locke supplied the theory of limited monarchy, the social contract; with the accession of William and Mary, he published his vastly influential *Two Treatises of Civil Government* (1690; ed.W. F. Carpenter, Everyman, 1924). In the same year appeared the work which made Locke famous, and

which has had the greatest influence on subsequent thought: *An Essay Concerning Humane Understanding* (1690; ed. A. C. Fraser, 1894; ed. A. S. Pringle-Pattison, abridged, 1924; best edn (abridged) by A. J. Ayer and R. Winch in *British Empirical Philosophers*, 1952). In the first book, Locke argued against the theory of innate ideas; then propounded a theory of ideas which depended on a simple mechanistic psychology of perception; from this he evolved a discussion of language as a series of counters put in motion by associative ideas; all this led, in the fourth book, to his final series of arguments about the limitations of knowledge, as coming only from sense impressions and from reflections on the experience of them. The influence of the new science was paramount, as was the rejection of ancient, traditional metaphors and metaphysics. Locke's metaphysical thinking of course supported his anti-monarchical, property-oriented political philosophy. Ideas become a sort of personal property, for example. He also intended his arguments to strengthen a greatly shortened line of defence of religion, a much simplified creed, but they were used by the deists, and later the rationalists who followed him, to get rid of most of the idea of God which he wished to keep. The effect of his ideas on aesthetic theory, on poetry, fiction and the writing of history was immense. Locke had shared Shaftesbury's brief exile before the Revolution; after 1688 he prospered. In 1696 he became a Commissioner for Trade and in 1698 was consulted about the re-coinage. He retired from London life because of asthma, and died at his retreat, Oates in Essex, where he had lived with Sir Ralph and Lady Masham. Apart from the works cited, Locke wrote on educational problems and in defence of religious toleration for all except Roman Catholics. [AR]

M. Cranston, *L.* (1957); D. J. O'Connor, *J. L.* (1952); K. MacLean, *J.L. and English Literature of the Eighteenth Century* (1936).

Lockhart, John Gibson (1794–1854). Journalist and biographer. Editor of the *Quarterly Review* from 1825 to 1853 and biographer of Sir Walter Scott, whose daughter he married in 1820. Son of a Lanarkshire minister, Lockhart went from Glasgow University to Balliol with a classical exhibition and later qualified as an advocate in Edinburgh. With John ◊ Wilson he revived *Blackwood's Magazine* (1817), apparently rejoicing in the violence of its literary and political comment and being chiefly responsible for its notorious review of the dying Keats's *Endymion* (1818). His *Peter's Letters to his Kinsfolk* (1819) contains a witty and penetrating account of Edinburgh and Glasgow society of the time, and of his novels *Adam Blair* (1822; intr. D. Craig, 1963) and *Matthew Wald* (1824) explore the same dark areas of Calvinist religious consciousness as the comparable works of James ◊ Hogg and Nathaniel Hawthorne (for *Adam Blair*, see D. Craig, *Scottish Literature and the Scottish People*, 1961). Lockhart's *Life of Burns* (1828), which drew a famous dismissive comment from D. H. Lawrence, avoided the moralistic disapproval of earlier biographers at the cost of glossing over details of the poet's life and adapting him to the genteel standards of Lockhart's own class and time; F. B. Snyder, in his definitive *Life of Robert Burns* (1932), calls Lockhart's work 'inexcusably inaccurate, at times demonstrably mendacious'. Even Lockhart's great *Life of Scott* (1837–8; several edns including a 2-vol. abridgement, 1848; 5 vols., 1900, 1902) must be used with caution; Lockhart tones down Scott's moodiness and impulsiveness, manipulates the text and dates of letters for convenience or for dramatic effect, retails a partisan version of the intricate financial manoeuvres that led to Scott's ruin, and perhaps fabricated the edifying last words that he attributes to Scott. Nevertheless Lockhart had lived in daily contact with Scott for five years, knew his milieu, and shared many of his friends and acquaintances; the *Life* places Scott squarely in the setting of his interest in Scottish life and history and of his aspirations as laird of Abbotsford.

As editor of the *Quarterly* Lockhart maintained the review's Toryism in politics, and in religious matters moved with the times towards qualified approval of the Oxford Movement. Perhaps overshadowed by his chief contributor, J. W. ◊ Croker, he did not impose any more distinctive personal stamp during his long editorship. [A I]

Lockhart's Literary Criticism, ed. M. C. Hildyard (1931).

A. Lang, *Life and Letters of J.G.L.* (1897); M. Lochhead, *J.G.L.* (1954).

Lodge, Thomas (1558–1625). Poet, dramatist, writer of prose romances. Second son of Sir Thomas Lodge – grocer, Lord Mayor of London in 1563, and subsequently a bankrupt – he was educated at Merchant Taylors' School under Richard Mulcaster, at Oxford, and at Lincoln's Inn. He had a career of remarkable variety, and attempted, for pressing financial reasons, a variety of literary forms. He quitted his legal studies to become a man about town and a pamphleteer, his first publication (1579) being a defence of the stage in reply to Stephen ◊ Gosson. *An Alarum against Userers* appeared in 1584. He made a voyage as a gentleman-soldier to the Canaries and the Azores in 1588, and killed time by writing a leisurely pastoral prose-romance in the style of ◊ Lyly, *Rosalynde, Euphues Golden Legacie*, which was published in 1590, was the basis of *As You Like It* by Shakespeare, and went through 12 editions by 1642. A second romance, *Euphues Shadow*, was published in 1592, while he was making a disastrous voyage in the South Seas and writing a third, *A Margarite of America* (printed 1596). At this time he also published 2 historical romances, a sonnet-sequence entitled *Phillis, Honored with Pastorall Sonnetts*, and a narrative love-poem, *Scillaes Metamorphosis*, as well as writing one play, *The Wounds of Civill War*, and collaborating with Robert ◊ Greene on another, *A Looking Glass for London and England*. He was converted to Catholicism and wrote a devotional book, *Prosopopeia the Teares of the Holy, Blessed and Sanctified Marie, the Mother of God*, in 1596, when he also published a treatise on the Seven Deadly Sins, *Wits Miserie and the Worlds Madnesse*.

Early in 1597, aged 39, he abandoned Grub Street for Avignon to study medicine, taking his M.D. there in 1598 and at Oxford by incorporation in 1604, by which time he was practising, mainly amongst Catholic recusants, in London. His Catholic sympathies forced him to live abroad in Brussels from 1606, where he worked as medical officer to a regiment in the pay of Spain, but was on friendly terms with the English ambassador. He was admitted to the College of Physicians in 1610, and by the following year was once more in England, where he succeeded to his brother's estate in 1612. In his years as medical practitioner, he wrote *A Treatise of the Plague* (1603) and published translations – *The Famous and Memorable Workes of Josephus* (1602), *The Workes both Morrall and Natural of Lucius*

Annaeus Seneca (1614) and Simon Goulart's commentary.

Lodge was one of the original 'University Wits' and used his education to win a living in the Elizabethan literary, journalistic, and theatrical worlds, before adopting a new career in medicine. [MJ]

Complete Works, ed. E. Gosse (4 vols., 1883).
N. B. Paradise, *T.L.: The History of an Elizabethan* (1931); C. J. Sisson, *T.L. and Other Elizabethans* (1935); E. A. Tenney, *T.L.* (1935).

Logan, John. ◊ Bruce, Michael.

Lom, Iain (pseud. of John MacDonald) (*c.* 1620–*c.* 1707). Scottish Gaelic poet. He played an important part in Montrose's campaigns and in clan politics in the mid 17th century, and survived to comment pungently in verse on the battle of Killiecrankie, the sovereignty of William and Mary, and the Union of the Parliaments of Scotland and England.

Approximately 40 of his poems (some 3,000 lines) survive. Almost all his verse is on public themes, whether at a local or a national level: the battle of Inverlochy, the coronation of Charles II, the Keppoch murder of 1663. He seems very well informed; there is much material for historians in his verse. There is a strange mixture of piety and mercilessness in his poetry: the touching and intimate lament for Montrose is in sharp contrast to the scathing and scurrilous poem on William and Mary. His poetry of exhortation and exultation is not excelled by Mac Mhaighstir Alasdair (◊ MacDonald, Alexander), whom he influenced strongly.

His language has a vivid immediacy; it is hard and brilliant, with no otiose phraseology. His imagery is precise, direct, always graphic and effective, and it is more varied than that of most Gaelic poets. He used strophic metres, and the largest early corpus of verse in these metres is ascribed to him. He is the earliest considerable figure in the history of vernacular Scottish Gaelic poetry, and one of the most vital poets in Gaelic. [DT]

The Poems, ed. Annie M. Mackenzie (1964).

Love, Nicholas (d. 1424). Religious writer. Nothing is known of Love before 1409, but in 1410 he was appointed Prior of the Carthusian House of Mount Grace, in Yorkshire. He resigned the office in 1421, and died as an ordinary monk. In 1410, his

Mirror of the Blessed Life of Jesu Christ (ed. L. F. Powell, 1908; modernized edn by a Monk of Parkminster, 1926) was approved by the Archbishop of Canterbury. This is a translation of the devotional work, *Meditationes Vitae Christi*, once thought to be by St Bonaventure. Love aims at a wide and non-specialist audience, and his success is evidenced by a large manuscript survival; he also aimed to refute Lollard teaching. He knew the ◊ *Ancrene Riwle* and may have known Walter ◊ Hilton personally, so warm are his references to him. His prose is good, benefiting from a study of the techniques of his Latin original; elegant, but more subdued than the highly wrought, semi-poetic prose characteristic of the devotional writings from the west of the country. [AG]

R. W. Chambers, *English Literature at the Close of the Middle Ages* (1947); E. Zeeman, 'N.L.– A Fifteenth-Century Translator', *RES*, n.s. 6 (1955).

Lovelace, Richard (1618–56/7). Cavalier poet. The son of Sir William Lovelace, a gentleman of an old Kentish family, who was killed in the wars in Holland, Richard went to school at Charterhouse, and to Gloucester Hall, Oxford, in 1634. In 1636 he was granted an honorary M.A. He moved among wits and courtiers. In 1639 and 1640 he served as an ensign in the Bishops' Wars, during the second of which he wrote a tragedy called *The Soldier* (now lost). He became involved in the political turmoil of the time when, in April 1642, he presented to Parliament the Kentish petition (for the retention of bishops and the Prayer Book) when Parliament had already once declared such a petition seditious. To punish this act of defiance, he was imprisoned in the Gatehouse. This was the occasion of his lyric 'To Althea, from Prison'. After seven weeks he was released on bail, having undertaken to engage in no further anti-Parliamentary activities, but although he could not now personally participate in the Civil War he set about providing his brothers with money and men for the King's cause. Living in London, he associated with other authors and wits (including ◊ Davenant, ◊ Cotton, Stanley, and the musician Henry Lawes); but his movements from this time onwards are hard to trace. He visited Holland (probably on more than one occasion); but he was in England in 1648, when, perhaps as a precautionary measure, he was again imprisoned, this time for ten months. In 1649 he published *Lucasta*, which contains the majority of his best poems. The remainder of his life is not very well documented. He was certainly in financial straits at one time, but Wood's assertion that he died in extreme poverty is not generally credited. The exact date of his death is unknown, but it must have occurred in 1656 or 1657.

The label 'cavalier lyrist' suggests preoccupations more courtly, or more political, than we find in many of Lovelace's poems. His range is in fact remarkably wide – from epigram and song to verse essay and pastoral *roman-à-clef* ('Aramantha'), from funeral elegies to comic trivia. The poems on animal subjects vary from the emblematic treatment of 'The Snail' to the almost mock-epic of 'The Toad and the Spider'.

There is a good deal of *préciosité* about Lovelace's complimentary pieces and the conceits are generally appropriate to the subject. Quite often, however, Lovelace makes use of deliberately 'inappropriate' imagery, in the Metaphysical manner. Very occasionally Lovelace assumes a 'libertine' stance, but in general he writes of love and longing in a singularly unfleshly manner.

Lovelace is a lively and intelligent poet, but very few of his poems have a compelling argument or a clear-cut shape. Brilliant patches are interspersed with stretches of verse that are neither interesting in their own right nor contribute to a larger whole. The obscurity for which Lovelace has sometimes been blamed seems sometimes to be due merely to corruptions of the text, but is often the result of his slapdash way of writing.

His best-known poems, 'To Lucasta, Going to the Wars' and 'To Althea, from Prison', use the vehicle of courtly compliment to make points of a far wider applicability. It is on these two poems that his reputation rests; but it is misleading to use them as a yardstick for measuring the excellence of his other works.

It is surmised that Lovelace supervised the printing of *Lucasta* in 1649. His remaining works were published as *Posthume Poems* (1659). He was virtually forgotten in the earlier part of the 18th century, but the publication of 'To Althea from Prison' in Percy's *Reliques* (1765) re-established his reputation. [TG]

Lucasta, The Poems of R.L., ed. S. W. Singer (2 vols., 1817–18); ed. C. H. Wilkinson (2 vols., 1925; issued as 1 vol. 1930); *Minor Poets of the Seventeenth Century*, ed. R. G. Howarth (Everyman, 1931).

C. H. Hartmann, *The Cavalier Spirit* (1925); *Cambridge History of English Literature*, VII, 1 (1911); R. Skelton, *The Cavalier Poets* (WTW, 1960); H. M. Richmond, *The School of Love* (1964).

Lover, Samuel (1797–1868). Irish miniature painter, playwright, song writer and novelist. He was born in Dublin, and wrote and sang songs somewhat in the manner of Tom ◊ Moore, and some of them, such as 'The Angel's Whisper' and 'Molly Brown', were very popular. His novels, in their dependence on burlesque and farce, are (though a long way behind) related to the work of Charles ◊ Lever; in knowledge of and sympathy with the native Irish he has merit, but is the inferior of the underrated William Carleton. His best-known works in this vein are *Rory O'More. A National Romance* (originally a ballad) (1836; revised 1839; ed. D. J. O'Donoghue, 1898) and *Handy Andy* (1842; ed. C. Whibley, 1896; ed. D. J. O'Donoghue, 1898). The latter is a rollicking whimsical story of the 'humours' of Irish servants and 'squires'. His *Songs and Ballads* appeared in 1839, and *The Poetical Works* in 1880. Lover was associated with Dickens (who was the editor) in founding *Bentley's Miscellany*. [AR]

Collected Writings, ed. J. J. Roche (10 vols., Boston, 1901–13).

W. B. Bernard, *The Life of S.L., Artistic, Literary, and Musical, with Selections from His Unpublished Papers and Correspondences* (2 vols., 1874); A. J. Symington, *S.L.* (1880) (with selections).

Lowes Dickinson, Goldsworthy (1862–1932). Historian, scholar and man of letters. His father was Cato Lowes Dickinson, well-known portrait painter, friend of Charles Kingsley, Frederick Denison Maurice and members of the Christian Socialist movement. Dickinson ceased to be a churchman but the dominant purpose of his life was to assert the spiritual values as expressed in all great religions, and he regarded his work mainly in the light of its direct social utility. He was in the first class of the Classical Tripos at Cambridge in 1884 and was Fellow of King's College (1887–1932), where most of his books were written. Opponent of 'compulsory' Greek (as equally of 'compulsory' chapel), he expressed in an early book, *The Greek View of Life* (1896), his abiding feeling for 'the Greek spirit'; it achieved wide circulation. A more startling response attended publication of his *Letters* *from John Chinaman* (1901), an attack on squalor and ugliness as then perceived in modern industrialism; when republished in America as *Letters from a Chinese Official*, the supposed Chinaman was hotly attacked by the politician William Jennings Bryan. The outbreak of war in 1914 represented to Dickinson the destruction of all that he valued; before the end of 1914 he was working actively with Lord Bryce on planning which contributed later to the formation of the League of Nations. The study made by Dickinson of all the then available documents about diplomacy of the years 1904–14 led to his largest book, *The International Anarchy* (1926). Dickinson also produced many writings reflecting the character of a man sensitive to beauty in all forms and rich in hope and faith, though as he said in one of his poems he would not name his hope nor label it faith. Among his works, in addition to those mentioned, are *A Modern Symposium* (1905), *Appearances* (*Notes of Travel, East and West*) (1914), and *Goethe and Faust* (with F. M. Stawell) (1928). [FM]

Roger Fry and J. T. Sheppard, *G.L.D., Fellow of King's* (1933) (with bibliography); E. M. Forster, *G.L.D.* (1934).

Lowry, (Clarence) Malcolm (1909–57). Novelist and poet. Born near Liverpool, he left his public school and enlisted as a deckhand on a ship bound for China. *Ultramarine* (reissued 1963), a novel based on this experience, was published in 1933, the year after he graduated from Cambridge. Restless and ambitious, he went to the continent. He took his wife to Mexico, where he drank and wrote more. They were divorced in 1939. With his second wife he lived at Dollarton, in a squatter's shack on the British Columbia coast, from 1940 to 1954, his most productive years. There he wrestled into shape the relentless torrent of atmospheric prose that forms his disquieting confessional novel *Under the Volcano* (1947; reissued 1962). It is a dense, demented book, set in Mexico and describing the last days of a former British Consul whose desperate lucidity is weirdly dependent on his alcoholic delirium. After its completion Lowry continued to intersperse bouts of furious drinking and intensive writing. During a visit to England in 1957 he choked to death in his sleep. Some of Lowry's stories were collected in 1961 as *Hear us O Lord from Heaven Thy Dwelling Place*. From a mass of unpublished material his

editors have so far produced *Selected Poems* (1962), a short novel, *Lunar Caustic* (1963), and *Dark as the Grave Wherein my Friend is Laid* (1968). They promise an important novel, *October Ferry to Gabriola*. [PT]

Selected Letters (1965).
George Woodcock, 'M. L.'s *Under the Volcano*', *Modern Fiction Studies*, 4 (1958); *Canadian Literature*, 8 (Spring, 1961) (special Lowry issue); D. Edmonds, 'The Short Fiction of M.L.', *Tulane Studies in English*, 15 (1967).

Lubbock, Percy (1879–1965). Miscellaneous writer. Born in London and educated at Eton and King's College, Cambridge. He was librarian of Magdalene College, Cambridge (1906–8), and used the Pepys library there for his book *Pepys* (1909); he edited the *Diary* of the master of the college, A. C. ◊ Benson, in 1926. He is best known for his influential book *The Craft of Fiction* (1921; new edn, 1954), a historical analysis of great novels, which indicated the trend of academic interest towards fiction. He also wrote a book, *Edith Wharton* (1947), on the American novelist, which is quite valuable for its personal recollections and 2 books of reminiscences, *Earlham* (1922), about his Norfolk childhood, and *Shades of Eton* (1929). [AR]

Lucas, E(dward) V(errall) (1868–1938). Essayist. He was born at Eltham, Kent. His education was interrupted by continual changes of school, and at 16 he was apprenticed to a Brighton bookseller. He was working for the *Sussex Daily News* in 1892, when a gift from an uncle enabled him to spend several months at University College, London, attending lectures and reading widely. After this he supported himself by journalism and literary work. His essays (on paintings, books, street-scenes, etc.) were popular in their day, and numerous collections of them appeared. He also brought out a dozen books on travel (e.g. *Highways and Byways in Sussex*, 1904), edited anthologies, contributed to *Punch*, and tried his hand at novels (*Over Bemerton's*, 1908). He produced the standard editions of Charles ◊ Lamb's *Works* and *Letters*, as well as the standard *Life*. His reminiscences, *Reading, Writing and Remembering* (1932), probably hold greater interest for the modern reader than do the essays, which are often sentimental and quaint. [NL]

A. Lucas, *E.V.L.: A Portrait* (1939).

Lyly

Lucas, F(rank) L(aurence) (1894–1967). Critic and writer. Born at Hipperholme in Yorkshire and educated at Rugby and Trinity College, Cambridge. His classical studies at the university were interrupted by service in the army during the First World War; in the Second World War he worked in the Foreign Office. In 1920 he was elected a Fellow of King's College, Cambridge, and became a university Reader in English. Lucas was a traditionalist critic, grounded in the classics and with wide interests in European literature. Although making a valiant attempt to keep abreast of psychological studies, he was hostile to new movements in literary taste, preferring his own established 'commonsense views'. His works include *Seneca and Elizabethan Tragedy* (1922); *Euripides and His Influence* (1924); many translations from the Greek, including Euripides' *Medea*; *Authors Dead and Living* (1926); the informative *Tragedy in Relation to Aristotle's 'Poetics'* (1927), revised and enlarged as *Tragedy, Serious Drama in Relation to Aristotle's Poetics* (1957); and *The Decline and Fall of the Romantic Ideal* (1936), more useful as a document of the intellectual history of England in the 1930s than as a critical work. Lucas also edited a *Complete Works* of John Webster (1927), an old-fashioned but accurate and learned edition within its limits. His wider European interests are shown in *Ibsen and Strindberg* (1962) and *The Drama of Chekhov, Synge, Yeats and Pirandello* (1963), and he wrote two general works, *Literature and Psychology* (1951) and *Style* (1955). His approach to literature is indicated in *The Search for Good Sense; Four Eighteenth-Century Characters: Johnson, Chesterfield, Boswell, Goldsmith* (1958). He also wrote books of verse, novels and plays. [A R]

Lydgate, John (?1370–1452). Poet. The 'Monk of Bury' spent all his life in the monastery of Bury St Edmunds, except for eleven years as prior of Hatfield. Nevertheless he came to fulfil the function of a court poet, and received a royal pension. His great reputation in his day and for some time afterwards now puzzles us. He wrote vast quantities of occasional verse, but was mainly a translator and compiler. *The Fall of Princes* (ed. H. Bergen, 1918), a version in rhyme royal at the second remove of Boccaccio's *De casibus virorum illustrium*, was a valuable source-book for the Tudors, but is oppressively dull. *The Troy Book* (ed. H. Bergen 1906–35), a verse paraphrase of Guido delle Colonne's history of the Trojan War, has many good things, but its couplet form indulges Lydgate's fatal garrulity. He also translated Déguileville's *Pilgrimage of the Life of Man*, together with various other moral and psychological allegories. The *Minor Poems* (ed. H. N. MacCracken and M. Sherwood, 1934) include personal reminiscence and some good satire as well as florid devotional verse. There are also some attractive decorative effects in the love-visions and complaints. His curse is his prolixity. [A G]

Poems, ed. J. Norton-Smith (1966) (selection).
H. S. Bennett, *Chaucer and the Fifteenth Century* 1947: D. Pearsall, *J.L.* (1970): W. F. Schirmer, *J.L.* (1961); A. Renoir, *The Poetry of J.L.* (1967).

Lyly, John (*c.* 1554–1606). Dramatist and author of prose romance. Grandson of the author of a much-used Latin Grammar, he came of an educated family, and probably went to the King's School, Canterbury, before going to Magdalen College, Oxford, a centre of humanist culture. He probably moved to London around 1576 to seek literary or academic advancement through a great patron. In 1578 he published *Euphues, the Anatomy of Wit* and in 1580 a sequel, *Euphues and His England*. Less a novel than an exemplary treatise on the education of a gentleman, the didactic first part follows a student from Athens (Oxford) to Naples (London), where he errs, repents and begins a new life. The sequel, dedicated to his hedonistic patron, the Earl of Oxford, is primarily a narrative centred on love, and has been regarded by some critics as a recantation of the *Anatomy*'s highly moral conclusion. Both parts were hugely successful and totalled 26 editions by 1630. 'Euphuism' has come to stand for a style (itself pre-dating Lyly's own work) which is self-consciously elaborate and rhetorical, and rich in antitheses, allusion and alliteration. In 1584–5, Oxford, possibly to regain the Queen's favour, presented at court 2 entertainments by Lyly, *Alexander and Campaspe* and *Sapho and Phao*, played by a company of well-trained boys. Other comedies, acted by the Boys of Paul's, were the pastoral *Gallathea* (1588), *Endimion, the Man in the Moon* (1588) and *Midas* (1589). Artificial, delicate and courtly, Lyly's

325

comedies were usually either mythological or pastoral romances; sophisticated prose dialogue was mingled with songs; and the cast of the sub-plot included pert and witty page-boys. This characteristic formula was abandoned in 3 later, more experimental pieces – *Mother Bombie* (*c.* 1590), an un-courtly native version of Terentian comedy in which the pages control the plot, his shortest play *Love's Metamorphosis* and *The Woman in the Moon*, his only play in verse, which seems to have been written for adult actors. Lyly seems to have held a minor court appointment, and probably hoped to be made Master of the Revels. He became a Member of Parliament, and he defended, in at least one pamphlet, the bishops of the ◊ Marprelate controversies. The last years were bitter, and he addressed 2 unsuccessful petitions, still in his ornate and even play-fully witty prose, to Queen Elizabeth.

Lyly's importance is chiefly as a stylist. He influenced a school of euphuistic prose-romancers, and, in the theatre, his courtly and mannered dialogue achieved a transi-tion from the prevailing low comedy to the romantic comedy of courtship, verbal wit and high life. Shakespeare may have burl-esqued Euphuism in *Love's Labour's Lost*, but Shakespearean comedy developed out of Lyly's courtly entertainments, and Lyly has been seen as a precursor of Congreve also. [MJ]

Complete Works, ed. R. Warwick Bond (3 vols., 1902; reprinted 1967); *Works*, ed. G. K. Hunter (in preparation).

G. K. Hunter, *J.L.: The Humanist as Courtier* (1962); J. Dover Wilson, *J.L.* (1905); C. S. Lewis, *English Literature in the Sixteenth Century* (1954); P. Saccio, *The Court Comedies of J.L.* (1969).

Lyndsay, Sir David. ◊ Lindsay, Sir David.

Lyttelton, George (Baron Lyttelton) (1709–73). Politician and poet. Educated at Eton and Christ Church, Oxford; after taking a seat in the Commons he eventually became a leader of the opposition to Walpole. He was in this way made Secretary to the Prince of Wales, and to improve his master's image persuaded him to grant pensions to a few writers (of whom Lyttelton was himself a generous patron), such as ◊ Mallet and James ◊ Thomson. He was a friend of Pope and Henry Fielding. Lyttelton was a voluminous but insuperably dull writer,

whose works provided 'nothing to be despised and little to be admired' (Johnson). His publications include *Letters from a Persian in England* (1735) (a genre fast be-coming fashionable), *Dialogues of the Dead* (1760), which enjoyed some vogue, and a *History of Henry II*. He was briefly Chancellor of the Exchequer in 1756. [AR]

Collected Works, ed. G. E. Ayscough (1774); *Memoirs and Correspondence*, ed. R. J. Philli-more (1845).

S. C. Roberts, *An Eighteenth-Century Gentleman* (1930).

Lytton of Knebworth, Edward George Earle Lytton Bulwer-Lytton, 1st baron (1803–73). Novelist, playwright, poet, journalist and politician. Born in London, the third son of General Earle Bulwer, and educated at Trinity College and Trinity Hall, Cam-bridge. As a dandy and man-about-town, his marriage (1825; separation 1836) to Rosina Wheeler, an Irish beauty, alienated his wealthy mother, Elizabeth Lytton of Knebworth, and the consequent loss of in-come forced him into his successful career as a prolific writer. When he inherited Kneb-worth, he took the additional name of -Lytton. While continuing to write, he turned his opportunistic talents to politics (M.P., 1831), and changing his party became Colonial Secretary (1858–9) in the second administration of the Tory, Lord Derby. He was knighted, and made a peer (1866). Lytton was chiefly successful, and still has a precarious fame, as a novelist. He tried all the kinds of fiction then being written, and, though not an innovator, he very quickly got on to new ideas, and his success was influential on better writers. The titles that now, in any way, survive, range from the satirical *Pelham* (1828), about fashionable society, to *Paul Clifford* (1830) and *Eugene Aram* (1832), which deal with the injustices in society's reaction to crime. Lytton is perhaps now known chiefly for his series of historical romances, full of solid archaeo-logical information, and fictionalizing well-known historical figures: *The Last Days of Pompeii* (1834), which also has the Christian message that the eruption was well deserved; *Rienzi* (1835), set in medieval Rome; *The Last of the Barons* (1843), about the Wars of the Roses; and *Harold* (1848). He also wrote a realistic series of stories about contemp-orary life, which includes *The Caxtons* (3 vols., 1849), *My Novel* (1853) and *Kenelm Chillingly* (1873), reminiscent of the work of

Charles ◊ Kingsley. Lytton's novels are clever and serious works, but vitiated by their peculiar English contempt for the imagination in its own right. This also appears as irritating and pompous authorial comment (as in *My Novel*). He has 2 rather good short stories of the supernatural (sometimes anthologized), 'The Haunted and the Haunters' (1859) and 'A Strange Story' (1862). [A R]

Works (38 vols., 1874; 26 vols., 1877–8); *Novels* (29 vols., 1895–8).
M. Sadleir, *B.*, *A Panorama* (1931); The Earl of Lytton, *B.L.* (1948); C. Dahl, bibliography in *Victorian Fiction: A Guide to Research*, ed. L. Stevenson (Harvard U.P., 1964).

M

'Mabinogion' (early medieval Welsh tales). This has come to be accepted as a composite title for a number of prose tales. The more correct form, *mabinogi* ('youth, tale of youth') occurs in *Pedair Cainc y Mabinogi* ('Four Branches of the Mabinogi'), probably redacted in the 11th century, but containing much ancient mythological material and representing the result of centuries of oral story-telling by the *cyfarwyddiaid*. Their form is that of the typical hero-tale as found in early Irish literature in which the hero's career is divided into 'branches' or chapters which deal with his birth, his youthful adventures, his courtship, his exile or imprisonment and his death. The main hero is Pryderi son of Pwyll, prince of Dyfed, but the Children of Llŷr take a prominent place in the second and third branches, and the account of the death of Pryderi in the fourth branch is overlaid by the much abridged story of another hero, Lleu Llaw Gyffes. The addition of folklore elements, onomastic tales and originally unrelated characters complicate the basic pattern. The locale is the western seaboard of Wales, and in the second branch ('Branwen ferch Lŷr') there is considerable Irish influence. The unknown author showed considerable if uneven skill in fusing this mixture of incidents and themes, but his great virtue lies in his style and presentation. He was a master of the narrative art and made telling and effective use of dialogue, an accomplishment which would accord with the traditional oral mastery of the *cyfarwyddiaid*.

Culhwch and Olwen is a single story which tells of the wooing of Olwen by Culhwch in spite of the difficult and virtually impossible tasks set by Ysbaddaden, Olwen's father. Culhwch succeeds in his quest, aided by Arthur, his cousin, and his men. This story too is a fusion of mythology and folklore motifs, the chief of which is 'The Giant and his prophesied death'. The whole story is related with tremendous zest and good humour in which little account is taken of incredible doings. There is much exaggerated description in which the author pokes as much fun at himself as at the characters. His glowing description of Olwen's beauty, however, is rightly accounted a literary gem in its sense of style and perfect balance of rhythm. This tale occupies a very important position in the development of the Arthurian legend.

Three shorter stories in a different genre and of much greater literary sophistication are (1) *Lludd and Llefelys*, in which Lludd, King of Britain (cf. *Lud* in *Ludgate*), gains the aid of his brother Llefelys, King of France, in ridding Britain of three pests, the Coraniaid (or Fairies), fighting and screeching dragons, and a black man who filches the king's food; (2) *Breuddwyd Macsen* ('Dream of Maxen'), in which the historica Roman Emperor dreams of Elen, whom he eventually finds in Caer Saint, i.e. Caernarvon. He travels from Rome to Caernarvon to woo and win her, thereby endangering his authority in Rome which he regains with the help of his British allies. The story is well told with many tender touches and balanced descriptions; (3) *Breuddwyd Rhonabwy* ('Dream of Rhonabwy'), a very consciously literary piece based on historical events in Powys in which the dream form is used as political propaganda to contrast the glorious days of Arthur and the present sorry plight of Powys (*c.* 1200?). The tale is simply told but with a wealth of detailed descriptions of horses and arms. The picture of Arthur is not the usual one either of a puissant chieftain or a world-emperor, but is mixed with certain satirical elements. These 3 stories are notable, because they betray the influence of a literary source like ◊ Geoffrey of Monmouth's *Historia regum Britanniae.*

The 3 Arthurian romances, *Geraint ac Enid, Owain a Luned* (*Iarlles y Ffynnon,* 'The Countess of the Fountain') and *Peredur fab Efrog*, correspond in many ways to the 3 poems of Chrétien de Troyes, *Erec et Enid, Yvain* and *Perceval*. But the Welsh tales and Chrétien's poems are quite different in many important respects, and neither is a translation or adaptation of the other. The Welsh tales are a native product, albeit influenced by the growth and development of the Arthurian legend on the continent. In contrast with the earlier hero-tales there is much greater unity in their concern with a single central character. Arthur has changed from a warrior-chief and a helping magician to a dignified emperor with his court at Caerllïon and not at Gelli-wig. The precision and topographical detail of the Four Branches and Culhwch have yielded to a vague geography where the characters wander in search of one another, and chivalry has of course thrown its blanket of courtesy and good manners over all. [MR]

The White Book Mabinogion, ed. J. Gwenogvryn Evans (1907); *The Text of the Mabinogion . . . from the Red Book of Hergest*, ed. J. Rhŷs and J. Gwenogvryn Evans (1887); *Pedeir Keinc y Mabinogi*, ed. I. Williams (1930); *Breuddwyd Maxen*, ed. I. Williams (1928); *Cyfranc Lludd a Llevelys*, ed. I. Williams (1932); *Breudwyt Ronabwy*, ed. M. Richards (1948); G. Jones and T. Jones, *The Mabinogion* (1949); *Pwyll Pendenic Dynet*, ed. R. L. Thomson (1957); *Branwen Uerch Lyr*, ed. D. S. Thomson (1961); *Owein*, ed. R. L. Thomson (1968). W. J. Gruffydd, *Rhiannon* (1953); W. J. Gruffydd, *Math vab Mathonwy* (1928); Proinsias Mac Cana, *Branwen* (1958); R. S. Loomis, *Arthurian Tradition and Chrétien de Troyes* (New York, 1950); ed. R. S. Loomis, *Arthurian Literature in the Middle Ages* (1959); R. S. Loomis, *Wales and the Arthurian Legend* (1956).

Mac an Bhaird, Eoghan Ruadh (E. R. Ward) (*c.* 1540–1609). Irish poet. As implied by his surname, meaning 'son of the bard', he belonged to a learned literary family; and he was himself attached to the court of Red Hugh O'Donnell, prince of Tír Chonaill or Donegal. The defeat of O'Neill and O'Donnell at Kinsale in 1601 marked the final victory of Tudor policy in Ireland. With it the era of independent native princes came virtually to an end, and because these had been the patrons of native literature and learning, the poets, too, felt the impact of the disaster. Eoghan Ruadh is remarkable chiefly for the poems he composed during those early years of the 17th century. Among them is a poem to Red Hugh O'Donnell as he sailed for Spain. When Red Hugh was poisoned by an English agent, his brother Rory succeeded him; but he soon had to flee to the continent, and died in Rome, where he was buried. It was this which inspired 'A bhean fuair faill ar an bhfeart' ('O woman who didst find the tomb forlorn'), in which the poet contemplates O'Donnell's sister mourning at his grave, lonely in a foreign land. The poem is known to English readers in Mangan's adaptation, 'O woman of the piercing wail'. In a happier vein on the occasion of receiving a letter from Rory's youthful son, Hugh. Eoghan Ruadh composed a reply in *deibhidhe*, a type of syllabic verse, in which he concluded, 'It was a scholar who wrote thee, O letter!' [SB]

T. O. Raghallaigh, *Duanta Eoghain Ruaidh Mhic an Bhaird* (1930).

Macaulay, Rose (1881–1958). Novelist. Born in Cambridge, she spent most of her childhood in Italy, and was educated at Oxford. Her first published novel was *The Valley Captives* (1911). She was a witty and intelligent writer whose novels were written from an essentially Christian viewpoint. This is not to say that she was unable to create character, but that she occasionally used the novel for moral and critical purposes connected with her religious beliefs. She first began to receive critical attention with a satirical novel, *Potterism* (1920). In *Told by an Idiot* (1923) she describes the lives of an entire family of three generations over a period of half a century. *Orphan Island* (1924) is a skilfully conceived and constructed satirical novel. *They Were Defeated* (1932) is a historical romance set in 17th-century Cambridge. Her most successful novel is *The Towers of Trebizond* (1956), in which she makes brilliant use of high comedy to convey a meaning which is anything but comic. Ostensibly an adventure story in which the young narrator goes to Turkey in the company of an aunt and an Anglican Canon, *The Towers of Trebizond* is, in reality, a backward look at the subjects which had been the novelist's primary concerns throughout most of her life: the Church, travel, love and human relationships.

Rose Macaulay was the author of several travel books, including *They Went to Portugal* (1946) and *Fabled Shore* (1949), as well as 3 books of verse, somewhat mystical in tone: *The Two Blind Countries* (1914), *Three Days* (1919) and *Poems* (1927). She was a member of the ◊ Bloomsbury Group during the thirties, and published a study of E. M. Forster (1938). [CO]

Milton (1934).

Macaulay, Thomas Babington (1st Baron Macaulay of Rothley) (1800–59). Historian and essayist. Born at Rothley Temple,

Leicestershire, the son of Zachary Macaulay, the philanthropist. T. B. Macaulay's precocity as a child was encouraged by Hannah ◊ More and other members of the evangelical 'Clapham Sect' among whom the family lived. He read assiduously from the age of 3, had a photographic memory, and began to write history at 7. He was educated by an evangelical schoolmaster, and in 1818 entered Trinity College, Cambridge. He spoke in the Union, and held strong Whig views, with a few radical notions. His academic career was brilliant, including writing a prize essay on William III; he was elected a Fellow of the college in 1824. In 1826, his father's hitherto prosperous affairs becoming straitened, Macaulay was called to the bar, but never practised. In 1823, he had begun his literary career by contributing essays to Knight's *Quarterly Review*, and began to contribute to the *Edinburgh Review*, for which all of his most famous essays were written. His first paper was on Milton (1825). He soon became one of the chief, and most popular, contributors; on the retirement of ◊ Jeffrey, he was invited to become editor, but refused. As a reviewer and periodical essayist, he had several great advantages: a firm and unqualified belief in his own strong opinions; a large stock of miscellaneous information; a brilliant and slashing style; and considerable insensitivity. His essays (and conversational fame) brought him political advancement. In 1830, Lord Lansdowne gave him the parliamentary seat for Calne in Wiltshire. Though never a good debater, he made several influential speeches in support of the Reform Bill. Rising fast in social reputation, in 1832 he was appointed Secretary of the Board of Control (of India), and from 1834 to 1838 he lived in India as a member of the Supreme Council. There, his most important work was in setting up an education system, with English as the language of instruction, and the organization of a commission (which he chaired) to establish a criminal code; he did most of the latter work himself.

Macaulay's politics naturally influenced his writing, and his reviews grew more brutal. He was never very competent in dealing with philosophy, as his essay on Bacon (1837) shows. Most of these essays are framed as reviews of books. His historical sketches are lively, but often skewed and wrong-headed, as for example his famous paper on Warren Hastings (1841)

though here he certainly knows what he is talking about. His influential position caused his opinions to be echoed and re-echoed, and finally to provoke very justifiable annoyance at the 'Whig view of history' and the tendentiousness of 'all right-thinking men'. His influence on literary criticism has been more disastrous. He represents a very English kind of mind; enormously able, highly political, well read, and almost devoid of any sense of the power and variety of art. He treats all literary works as exercises in social and moral thinking, and judges writers as a J.P. would. This can be seen in his ludicrous sketch of Boswell (1831), which riveted a stereotype for years on that most interesting and skilful writer. Macaulay was the master of an obvious, rhetorical verse, with which he created several long-famous poems such as 'Horatius' (in *Lays of Ancient Rome*, 1842; World's Classics, 1903). The *Essays* were published as a collection in 1843 and produced an important part of his income. His most solid achievement is the *History of England from the Accession of James II* (to the death of William III) (vols. 1 and 2, 1849; 3 and 4, 1855; 5, ed. by his sister, 1861). He began this work in 1839, on his return from India, and worked on it while at the same time continuing his political career.

He was Secretary-at-War, 1839–41; Paymaster-General, 1846–7. In 1847, he failed to gain re-election for his constituency of Edinburgh, and devoted his time to writing. He was returned for Edinburgh, without campaigning, in 1852, but seldom spoke. In 1857, Palmerston offered him a peerage; he continued to write his history in retirement, and died in his study. He is buried in Westminster Abbey. Macaulay is *par excellence* the historian of the 'Glorious Revolution'; his good Whigs constantly battle with the wicked and stupid opposition. Unlike ◊ Gibbon's, Macaulay's vision is not tragic or paradisial, only contemporary and opinionated. The book lives, however, because of the power of his writing. In his sweep, he rivals the best novelists as narrators. He read much, and though his brilliance is at times tiresome and overpowering, the reader still reads. It is good argumentative history, not cosmopolitan, nor really dealing with the economic forces that modern historians have seen as important in the period (imperialism and colonial trade). Macaulay's thesis is that the best of all possible worlds was made possible in 1688, and that the continued prosperity of English oligarchy will maintain it; this is not so persuasive now. There were many critiques of his work even in his own day. [AR]

Works, ed. Lady Trevelyan (his sister) (8 vols., 1866); *Critical and Historical Essays,* F. C. Montague (3 vols., 1903; 2 vols., Everyman, 1907); *The History of England* (Everyman, 3 vols., 1906; ed. T. F. Henderson, World's Classics, 5 vols., 1931); *Prose and Poetry,* ed. G. M. Young (1953) (selection).
Sir G. O. Trevelyan, *Life and Letters of Lord M.* (2 vols., 1876); A. Bryant, *M.* (1932); J. W. Thompson and B. J. Holm, 'M., Carlyle and Froude', in *A History of Historical Writing* (New York, 1942); G. R. Potter, *M.* (WTW 1959) (with bibliography); J. R. Griffith, *The Intellectual Milieu of M.* (Ottawa, 1964); *REL,* 1 (1960) (essays).

McAuley, James (1917–   ). Australian poet. Born in Sydney and educated at Sydney University, he was a schoolteacher until the outbreak of the Second World War. His educational experience with the Australian army in the East Indies led to a long-lasting post-war appointment as Senior Lecturer in Government at the Australian School of Pacific Affairs. Since 1956 he has been editor of the political and literary quarterly, *Quadrant.* In 1944 he was one of the perpetrators of the famous 'Ern Malley' hoax, a startling protest against what he felt to be inadequate poetic criteria. An outspoken convert to Roman Catholicism, he is now Professor of English at the University of Tasmania. McAuley is a careful craftsman with a terse, often caustic wit. In *Under Aldebaran* (1946) and *A Vision of Ceremony* (1956) elegant lyrics are balanced by uncompromising satires. He is also the author of a challenging book of essays, *The End of Modernity* (1959), and of *Versification: A Short Introduction* (1966). [PT]

V. Buckley, *Essays in Poetry, Mainly Australian* (1957); L. J. Kramer, 'J.M.' (*Commonwealth Literary Fund Lecture,* 1957).

MacCaig, Norman (1910–   ). Poet. Born in Edinburgh, where he still lives, MacCaig is a schoolmaster by profession. His books of verse include *Far Cry* (1943), *The Inward Eye* (1946), *Riding Lights* (1955), *The Sinai Sort* (1957), *A Common Grace* (1960), *A Round of Applause* (1962), *Measures* (1965) and *Surroundings* (1967). MacCaig's poetry is both metaphysical and distinctly Scottish.

At his best, he is a highly skilled technician with an ability to evoke town or landscape skilfully and economically. It is when he uses his undoubted feeling for nature to convey a metaphysical point of some complexity that he is not entirely convincing. There are times when his language, usually restrained, appears over-elaborate, tending to obscure his argument. He is not a poet whose personality is apparent in every line, but his incisive intelligence and technical command have combined to produce a good deal of excellent verse. From *Riding Lights* onwards, he has steadily progressed, and the poems in *The Sinai Sort* are particularly impressive, both for their subtlety and their power. [CO]

MacCarthy, Sir Desmond (1877–1952). Critic and literary journalist. He was educated at Eton and Cambridge, where he was one of the brilliant group of Trinity intellectuals – G. E. Moore, Bertrand Russell, Lytton Strachey, Leonard Woolf and others – whose work was later to be the inspiration of the ◊ Bloomsbury Group. When he left Cambridge, MacCarthy was thought by his friends 'to have the world at his feet. . . . Here is in the making a writer or novelist of the highest quality.' But in the years before 1914 his output was mainly journalistic, including an intellectual magazine, *The New Quarterly* (1907), to which Moore and others contributed, and theatre reviewing for the newborn *New Statesman.* A warm friend and enchanting conversationalist, MacCarthy appears to have lacked concentration, but he proved to be a brilliant literary editor of the *New Statesman* during the twenties, and in this capacity, as well as a critic of books and plays, his influence (which has not yet been thoroughly assessed) was probably as great as that of some of his better-known friends. In the later years of his life he became a weekly contributor to the *Sunday Times,* and some of his critical writings were published, including *Drama* (1940), *Shaw* (1951) and *Humanities* (1953). His position in that network of friendship which comprised Bloomsbury remains slightly elusive. He was knighted in 1951. [JM]

Memories, ed. R. Kee (1953).
L. Woolf. *Sowing* (1960) and *Beginning Again* (1964); E. Hyams, *New Statesman* (1963).

McCarthy, Justin (1830–1912). Irish politician, historian, novelist and journalist.

Mac Conmidhe

Educated at London University, he was an M.P. (1884–92). He wrote, in a popular style, *A History of Our Own Times* (4 vols., 1879–80; with continuations, 1905); *A History of the Four Georges and of William IV* (4 vols., 1884–1901). He also wrote novels (some in collaboration with Mrs Campbell Praed); the best known of his own are *Dear Lady Disdain* (1875) and *Miss Misanthrope* (1878). He was also one of the editors of *Irish Literature* (an anthology) (10 vols., Chicago, 1904). [A R]

Mac Conmidhe, Giolla Brighde Albanach (G. MacNamee) (*c.* 1180–*c.* 1260). Irish poet. Born in Co. Tyrone, his work provides some fine specimens of Irish court poetry. Among the princes he celebrated, in addition to his own immediate chief, Niall O'Gormley (d. 1261), were Cathal O'Connor (d. 1224), called *Croibhdhearg* ('Red-hand'), who was King of Connacht after the death of his brother, the last High-King of Ireland, Roderick; Donnchadh O'Brien (d. 1242), prince of Thomond, whose sister was the wife of Cathal Red-hand; Brian O'Neill (d. 1260) of Tyrone; Domhnall Óg O'Donnell (d. 1281) of Donegal, whose mother was Cathal Red-hand's daughter. O'Donnell had marriage connexions with Gaelic Scotland; while the poet himself was called *Albanach* ('Scottish'), on account of his Scottish associations. At this time the whole of Gaeldom was a single coherent cultural entity.

Apart from his eulogies and historical poems, Giolla Brighde wrote an interesting piece in praise of poetry: through it, he asserts, man's renown is enhanced and perpetuated; without it, however, society would soon become ignorant of its past. Similar thoughts have been expressed by poets such as Horace and Spenser. More personal is a poem in which, left childless, he asks the Almighty to grant him a son. His approach to the problem is quite professional: just as human patrons rewarded him for his poetry with land, horses or cattle, he now asks for 'A son in payment for my poem, O God'. [S B]

A. de Blácam, *Gaelic Literature Surveyed* (1933); ed. J. Carney *Early Irish Poetry* (1965).

McCrae, Hugh Raymond (1876–1958). Australian poet. Born in Melbourne, the son of George Gordon McCrae, he was a notable Australian literary figure (cf. *My Father and My Father's Friends*, 1935).

Influenced by Norman ◊ Lindsay, whose mischievous vitality he shared, McCrae abandoned his architectural studies to contribute verse and drawings to the Sydney *Bulletin*, a characteristically cavalier flaunting of security. He was variously an actor, public lecturer, wartime censor, dramatic critic and magazine editor. After 1930 he lived at Camden and later in Sydney. He published many short stories and other prose works, in which reminiscence mingles with fantasy.

McCrae's first book of poems was published in 1909 (republished as *Satyrs and Sunlight*, 1911). Its descriptions of pagan frolics in a golden landscape are light and melodic, so that their precision of imagery is easily missed. In *Poems* (1939) this visual precision is unmistakeable. Without losing his love of fantasy – his narrative extravaganza 'The Mimshi Maiden' came out in 1938 – he developed the ironic relationship between a pantheistic world and the real Australia. Among his later books are *Forests of Pan* (1944), *Voice of the Forest* (1945) and *The Ship of Heaven* (1951), a fairy opera. [P T]

Story-Book Only (1948) (memoirs).
Southerly, no. 3, 1956 (special McCrae issue); T. Inglis Moore, *Six Australian Poets* (1942).

Mac Cuarta, Séamus (1647–1732). Irish poet. In Irish syllabic verse, a poem normally ended with a *dúnadh* ('closing'), but sometimes the author added a postscript; thus, for example, to a eulogy for his patron the poet might append a supplementary stanza or more in praise of the patron's wife or other relative. These extra stanzas might be less elaborate, metrically, than the poem itself; and later on, as stressed metres were coming into vogue, such stanzas were composed according to the new measures. From this a distinct genre, called *Trí rann agus amhrán*, 'three stanzas (in simplified syllabic verse) and a quatrain (in stressed metre)', came into being and was widely cultivated by Northern Irish poets, especially in the 18th century.

The best-known of these poets was Mac Cuarta, who was born in Co. Louth and used the *Trí rann agus amhrán* in much the same manner as poets in other languages use the sonnet. He was particularly fond of nature: one of his poems is a welcome to the cuckoo, in true Wordsworthian style, while another, on the death of a pet blackbird, recalls a series of parallels reaching back to

332

Catullus himself. Of his longer poems, one is a debate between the personified seasons of the year. This last theme may be an imported one: the seasons loom large also in English and in Scottish Gaelic verse of the 18th century. In general, his work is characterized by sobriety, restraint and a quiet note of homely patriotism. [SB]

Ua Muireadhaigh, *Amhráin Shéamais Mhic Chuarta* (1925).

MacDiarmid, Hugh (pseud. of Christopher Murray Grieve) (1892–   ). Scottish poet and begetter of the 'Scottish Renaissance'. He grew up in the Dumfriesshire weaving town of Langholm, where he was taught by the composer F. G. Scott, an important influence and later collaborator of whom he wrote a memoir (1955). He abandoned teacher-training in Edinburgh for journalism, joined the I.L.P., worked for the Fabian Research Department and contributed to A. R. ◊ Orage's *New Age*; after war service in the R.A.M.C. (1915–19) he worked as a journalist in Montrose and later in London and Liverpool, retreating in poverty, after a second marriage and a breakdown in health, to a croft on Whalsay in the Shetland. (1933–41). After war work as an engineer on the Clyde he settled at Biggar, Lanarkshire, where he now lives; he received a Civil List pension in 1950.

From Montrose in the early twenties MacDiarmid assailed, through periodicals and through books, poems and articles under several pen-names, the existing cultural situation in Scotland – a country, he asserted, resignedly provincial, out of touch alike with the mind of Europe and with its own past, lost in a fog of ◊ 'Kailyard' fiction and the cult of a sentimentalized Burns. MacDiarmid's campaign took three forms. He wrote and fostered a Scots poetry which drew, for tone and convention, on the ballads and the Middle Scots poets (especially ◊ Dunbar) rather than on Burns, and which tried to reconstitute a metropolitan and adequately expressive national language from the regional dialects into which the older literary Scots had disintegrated. On this level MacDiarmid's highly individual blend of acrid and poignant, of 'folk' and literary sensibility, in the lyrics of *Sangschaw* (1925) and *Penny Wheep* (1926) was at once accepted and widely admired. Second, he tried to assimilate the distinctive attitudes and techniques of the Modern Movement into a truly contemporary Scots poetry; his

very fine long poem *A Drunk Man Looks at the Thistle* (1926), a phantasmagoric meditation on his identity as a creative writer and on the relation of this function to his sexuality, his social setting and his place in the universe, was accessible to a much smaller public than the lyrics and threw their Scottish admirers into disarray. Thirdly, his bitter onslaughts on Scottish bourgeois culture-figures of the times, and his sometimes over-optimistic attempts at setting up in their places such 'modern' figures as R. B. Cunninghame ◊ Graham, A. S. Neill, Edwin ◊ Muir, Neil ◊ Gunn and many others (*Contemporary Scottish Studies*, 1926), antagonized the greater part of conventional public opinion in Scotland. None the less this period of MacDiarmid's work has had greatest influence, both directly on Lewis Grassic Gibbon, W. ◊ Soutar, S. G. ◊ Smith and others, and more generally on the increased liveliness and openness of Scottish culture today.

Since 1930, discrepancies, which he provocatively defends, have appeared among MacDiarmid's intellectual positions and within his literary creed. He found it possible to support Social Credit and, in 1934, to join the Communist Party; the Party however expelled him in 1938 because of his continued membership of the Scottish National Party, which he had helped to found (1928). He rejoined in 1957. Advocating a political and cultural alliance of the Celtic nations, he urged compulsory Gaelic in Scottish schools and called for a 'genuine and thorough-paced revival of Scots' to the exclusion, in Scotland, of literature in English; yet almost simultaneously he turned first to a much diluted Scots and then to English to write, in *Scots Unbound* (1932), *Stony Limits* (1934), and the *First* (1931) and *Second Hymn to Lenin* (1935), poetry whose realism and integrity compares very well with the romantic English left-wing verse of the period. Meantime MacDiarmid began to write (also in English) a 'poetry of pure fact', an inclusive mode less allusive and experimental than Pound's *Cantos* but like them incorporating catalogues, quotations and long didactic meditations. Only fragments of these long poems have appeared (in his autobiography *Lucky Poet*, 1943; as *In Memoriam James Joyce*, 1955; and in *Collected Poems*, 1962) and their quality is disputed; the customary dismissal as 'formless' clearly fails to take account of the rhythmical subtlety and strong local life of the verse,

333

but none of the sympathetic accounts – rapturous, arcane or apologetic – is particularly cogent. The revised edition of *Collected Poems* (ed. J. C. Weston, 1967), though by no means complete, is much more accurate and helpful than the original edition (1962). [A1]

The Company I've Kept (1966) (autobiography); *The Uncanny Scot*, ed. K. Buthlay (1968) (selected prose); *Selected Essays*, ed. D. Glen (1969).
D. Glen, *H.M. and the Scottish Renaissance* (1964) (with bibliography); K. Buthlay, *H.M.* (1964); ed. K. D. Duval and S. G. Smith, *H.M., a Festschrift* (1962).

Mac Domhnaill, Seán Clárach (S. C. Mac-Donald) (1691–1754). Irish Jacobite poet. During much of the 18th century, Irish literature reflected a lively interest in the fortunes of the House of Stuart. Strangely enough, Stuart sympathies were strongest, not in the region nearest to Scotland, but in Munster, where quite a number of Jacobite poets flourished, chief among them being Seán Clárach Mac Domhnaill, a native of Co. Cork.

Like his Scottish namesakes, Iain Lom Mac Dhomhnaill and Alasdair Mac Dhomhnaill, he was a keen student of contemporary politics. Following a convention widespread among Jacobite poets, he generally refers to the Prince in figurative terms only: *Ní mhaoidhfead féin cé hé mo stór* ('I shall not betray my darling's name') he writes, comparing his hero to various characters in Irish and classical tradition, and hoping for his speedy and triumphant return. Coexistent with and closely allied to Irish Jacobite verse was the *aisling* or vision poem, of which MacDonald composed quite a number. His work also includes a caustic satire on the death of a certain unpopular local landlord, Colonel James Dawson, of the glen of Aherlow in Co. Tipperary: *In Eatharla fhosaigh in oscail idir dhá shliabh/ Gur cheangail an gorta den phobal dá gcur fá riaghail* ('In sheltered Aherlow between two hills/he tethered the famine, to harass the people'). [SB]

R. Ó Foghludha, *Seán Clárach* (1934).

MacDonald, Alexander (*c*. 1695–*c*. 1770). Scottish Gaelic poet. Known as Alasdair Mac Mhaighstir Alasdair. Nothing is known for certain of his activities before 1729; from then until 1745 he appears as a teacher and catechist in the west Highlands. In 1741

he published a Gaelic *Vocabulary*. In 1745 he left his school to recruit for Prince Charles Edward, and served as an officer in the Prince's army; he had to lie low after the '45, but in 1751 he published a collection of his poems (*Ais-eiridh*), said to have been burned by the common hangman in Edinburgh because of the fierce anti-Hanoverian sentiments in it.

His pre-1745 work includes a short series of Nature poems, slightly influenced by Thomson's *Seasons*, and in their turn influencing all the Gaelic Nature poets of the century. It also includes the initial poems in his political series, continued between 1745 and 1751. This public verse often has a propagandist purpose: it is exhortatory verse of great eloquence and verve, with mesmeric rhythms. He wrote scathingly bitter poems about the Hanoverians, and about the Campbells, and several satires which are extremely lewd but show a remarkable linguistic virtuosity. This virtuosity appears in his greatest poem, *Birlinn Chlann Raghnaill* ('Clanranald's Galley'), which is hard and brilliant verse, metrically ornate, full of technical detail and close observation, but relieved by elements of extravaganza borrowed from Gaelic folk-tales. In this poem MacDonald's hard, exact intellectual power and his rich exuberance are both amply demonstrated.

MacDonald was well versed in the Gaelic traditions, both bardic and vernacular. He assimilated influences from English and classical poetry, and radiated influence to his contemporary Gaelic poets. Forceful, craggy, dynamic, bawdy, disciplined, his contradictory nature and achievements form a vivid landmark in 18th-century Gaelic poetry. [DT]

The Poems, ed. A. and A. MacDonald (1924).
D. S. Thomson, 'A. M. A.', *An Gaidheal*, LVI, 10 and 11 (1961); H. MacDiarmid, verse translation of the *Birlinn*, in *The Golden Treasury of Scottish Poetry* (1940).

MacDonald, George (1824–1905). Scottish novelist. Born in rural Aberdeenshire and educated at Aberdeen University (1840–5), MacDonald worked as a tutor in London before becoming Congregational minister at Arundel (1850–3). Dismissed for heresy, he lived by journalism and lecturing in Manchester and elsewhere until, aided financially by Byron's widow and appointed to a professorship of English Literature at Bedford College, he settled in London in 1859. He had already published volumes of verse and the allegorical *Phantastes, a Faerie Romance for Men and Women* (1858). In his first 3 novels (*David Elginbrod*, 1863, *Alec Forbes*, 1865, and *Robert Falconer*, 1868), set in the Aberdeenshire countryside which he knew, MacDonald attacks the rigours of Calvinist ethics and theology from a position close to that of his friend F. D. ◊ Maurice; his 20-odd later novels retreat into a moralistic vein, less deeply felt and less controversial, but still sometimes blending religious material with Scottish rural manners in a way that points forward to ◊ Barrie and the other ◊ 'Kailyard' novelists of the nineties.

MacDonald was a friend of Lewis ◊ Carroll, and *Alice's Adventures in Wonderland* was tried out on the MacDonald children before Carroll decided to publish it; MacDonald's own books for children (*At the Back of the North Wind*, 1871; *The Princess and the Goblin*, 1872) are still read. These fairy tales, *Phantastes*, and the later allegorical fantasy *Lilith* (1895) contributed themes and techniques to the fiction of C. S. ◊ Lewis and his circle, in which MacDonald was also much admired for his religious insights. [A I]

Poetical Works (1893); *G.M.: An Anthology*, ed. C. S. Lewis (1946); *The Visionary Novels* (*Phantastes* and *Lilith*), ed. A. Fremantle, intr. W. H. Auden (New York, 1954); *Phantastes and Lilith*, intr. C. S. Lewis (1962). J. M. Bulloch, *A Centennial Bibliography of G.M.* (1925); G. MacDonald, *G.M. and His Wife* (1924); R. L. Wolff, *The Golden Key, a Study of the Fiction of G.M.* (New Haven, 1961).

MacDonald, John. ◊ Lom, Iain.

MacDonald, S. C. ◊ Mac Domhnaill, S. C.

Mac Éil, Seán (John MacHale) (1791–1881). Irish writer. During much of the 19th century, until the revival initiated by the Gaelic League in 1893, Irish literature was at a very low ebb. While there were plenty of folk poets and story-tellers, the only author of more than local repute was Dr Seán Mac Éil, a native of Co. Mayo, who became Archbishop of Tuam in 1834.

Like Flaithrí Ó Maoil Chonaire, his great 17th-century predecessor in the see of Tuam, he laboured in the cause of his native language and translated several books of Homer into Irish, together with various devotional works, including part of the Old Testament and a number of liturgical hymns. He was also the author of an Irish catechism which long remained in use. Unlike the great Louvain writers, however, he was out of touch with the classical genius of the language, and his literary efforts are not particularly successful: the style is rather stilted, and the Irish itself shows signs of wrenching both in grammar and vocabulary. What assures him a place in Irish literary history is not his own achievements, but the encouraging example which he gave to others at a critical period: thus Canon Peadar Ó Laoghaire states in his autobiography that it was Archbishop MacHale who first induced him to embark on his literary career. [S B]

N. Costello, *J.M.* (1939).

Mac Gearailt, Gearóid (Gerald Fitzgerald) (d. 1398). Irish poet. By the middle of the 14th century the Norman aristocracy in Ireland had become largely assimilated to the native population in language and customs. Like native chieftains, foreign lords fostered Irish poets; and, in turn, the native *literati* became acquainted with new aspects of the European literary tradition, such as the sophisticated love-poetry of Provence.

Gearóid Mac Gearailt, Earl of Desmond, is typical of Norman noblemen who became, as it were, more Irish than the Irish themselves. He mastered the art of poetry, and is the author of perhaps the earliest love-poem of its kind in the language, *Mairg adeir olc ris na mnáibh* ('Woe to him who defameth women'). It is a short piece, light and witty in treatment, and expresses typical troubadour sentiments. The composition of this artful love-poetry was subsequently practised by other gentlemen poets like Riocard a Búrc or Maghnas Ó Domhnaill, by professional poets such as Eochaidh Ó hEódhusa, and by anonymous authors. Over one hundred pieces, ranging in date from the 14th to the 17th century, still survive in manuscripts.

Mac Gearailt's fame extended to Gaelic Scotland, and several of his poems appear in the Book of the Dean of Lismore. [S B]

T. F. Ó Rathile, *Dánta Grádha* (1926).

Mac Giolla Meidhre, Brian (Brian Merriman) (*c.* 1740–1805). Irish poet. Born in Co. Clare, he worked as a schoolmaster both there and in Limerick city, where he died. His claim to literary recognition rests on *Cúirt an Mheadhon-Oidhche* ('The Midnight

McGonagall

Court'), an unusual poem of over a thousand lines, written in 1780.

Since its publication by Stern in the *Zeitschrift für celtische Philologie* in 1904, the poem has attracted considerable attention at home and abroad. Several English translations of it have appeared. Briefly, it concerns a controversy of the sexes, held at the court of Aoibheall, a local queen of the fairies. Despite its faery trappings, however, the poem is hard, realistic, and sometimes Rabelaisian in tone. One of the main protagonists is a comely young lady, who dilates on the shortcomings of men and the difficulties of finding a suitable husband; she herself having tried all her wiles and charms in vain. The other speaker is a gaunt, fierce, elderly man, who sets forth the faults of women in general and of his opponent in particular, and concludes by advocating the complete abolition of matrimony.

Some passages seem to indicate that Mac Giolla Meidhre was familiar with the work of the English poet Richard Savage, author of *The Wanderer* and *The Bastard*. All in all, the poem well portrays the customs, superstitions and general atmosphere of the Clare countryside in the late 18th century. [SB]

R. Ó Foghludha, *Cúirt an Mheadhon-Oidhche* (1912).

McGonagall, William (1830–1902). Scottish versifier. Born in Edinburgh of an Irish father and trained as a weaver in Dundee, McGonagall recognized his poetic vocation in 1877, the year in which he published his first collection of verse and began his life as an itinerant versifier and reciter. In 1878 he walked to Balmoral to try (unsuccessfully) to present personally a copy of his second edition (price 2d) to the Queen. He visited London and even New York, vainly confident of being acclaimed a great poet. Edinburgh University students rather cruelly encouraged him to believe in his genius with various practical jokes. McGonagall was a master of unconscious bathos and the unintentionally ludicrous rhyme. The sublime badness of his doggerel gives it a certain charm. Anything was poetry to him if it rhymed; his lines could run to any length provided the end word rhymed with the end word of the preceding line, and his vocabulary ranged easily from the pretentious to the ludicrous. His verse is still savoured by connoisseurs of doggerel. [DD]

Poetic Gems Selected from the Works of W.M., with biographical sketch and reminiscences by the author (1890, 1954); *More Poetic Gems* (1962); *Last Poetic Gems* (1968).
H. MacDiarmid, 'The Great McG.', in *Scottish Eccentrics* (1936), reprinted in *The Uncanny Scot*, ed. K. Buthlay (1968); W. Power, *My Scotland* (1934).

MacHale, S. ◊ Mac Eil, S.

Machen, Arthur (Llewellyn) (1863–1947). Novelist. Born into a family of Welsh clergymen and scholars at Carleon-on-Usk, he was a lonely child and voracious reader. In 1874 he was sent to Hereford Cathedral School. In 1880 the income yielded by his father's living had become so inadequate that Arthur left school and went to London to take the examination for the Royal College of Surgeons, although in fact he was to devote himself to the study of literature. He produced a few translations from the French, including the *Memoirs of Casanova* (1894; many subsequent editions). A legacy gave him sufficient independence to embark on creative work in the 1890s. *The Great God Pan* (1894) was brought out by John Lane, the publisher of the ◊ *Yellow Book*. Another novel, *The Hill of Dreams* (1907), which he started to write in 1895, is a characteristic piece of autobiographical escapism: visions of the Celto-Romanic past or of evil in a London street become the raw material of the hero's artistic efforts, and art is seen as the self-justifying attempt to recapture and to embody these moments of ecstasy. Machen had to rely on journalism rather than fiction for the bulk of his income. After the death of his first wife in 1899, he travelled with a company of actors for a few years. In the twenties he was suddenly discovered and his writings to date (comprising his principal works) were collected (Carleon edn, 9 vols.). From 1933 he was supported by a Civil List pension from the King. He has become something of a cult figure among devotees of the occult and the sensational; several of his exercises in the genre – among them *The Inmost Light* (1894) and *The White Powder* (1896) – are reprinted in *Tales of Horror and the Supernatural* (1964). [NL]

Hieroglyphics (1902) (essays); *Far-Off Things* (1922) and *Things Near and Far* (1923) (autobiographical).

336

A.M.: Essay, ed. Fr Brocarn Sewell (1960); A. Reynolds and W. Charlton, *A.M.* (1963); W. D. Sweetser. *A.M.* (1964); *Bibliography*, W. D. S. and A. Goldstone (1965).

Macinnes, Colin (1914–   ). Novelist. Macinnes was born in London and educated in Australia, the son of the novelist Angella Thirkell. During the Second World War he served as a Sergeant in the Intelligence Corps and on leaving the army worked as a free-lance journalist, and as a script writer for the B.B.C. His first book, *To the Victors the Spoils* (1950), was a fictionalized account of his wartime experiences. This was followed by a rather melodramatic novel of life in Australia, *June in Her Spring* (1952), but with the publication of *City of Spades* (1957), which explored the unknown world of coloured immigrants in Britain, he emerged as a distinctive and original novelist. His work is notable for its keenly observed sociological content, free-flowing style and vociferous sympathy for the under-dog. Later novels are *Absolute Beginners* (1959), *Mr Love and Justice* (1960) and *All Day Saturday* (1966). He has also published a collection of essays, *England, Half English* (1961), and a study of the music hall, *Sweet Saturday Night* (1967). [PJK]

Macintyre, Duncan Bàn (Donnchadh Bàn Mac an t-Saoir) (1724–1812). Scottish Gaelic poet. Macintyre was a forester (*c.* 1746–66), thereafter serving in the Edinburgh City Guard and for a brief period in the Breadalbane Fencibles. He died in Edinburgh in 1812.

His central theme is wild nature, in particular the appearance, habits and nature of the deer. No Gaelic poet has excelled him in his detailed, loving observation of these animals and the Argyllshire–Perthshire landscape in which he had observed them. The hard core of his recorded poetic output of some 6,000 lines is in this descriptive poetry, especially in *Oran Coire a' Cheathaich*, a description of a mountain corrie in which the poet deploys a very rich vocabulary and a galaxy of assonantal and rhyming effects to bring the scene vividly to life; and in *Moladh Beinn Dobhrain* ('The Praise of Ben Doran'), which is both the most ambitious and the greatest of Macintyre's poems. In this latter poem descriptive power and wealth of vocabulary are joined to technical mastery and sound construction: by a strange chance of genius the poet achieved a work that can be set beside the great examples of *ceòl-mór* (classical bagpipe music) and of Celtic illumination. His powers must have been at their height, the circumstances congenial to him, and the subject was one he was supremely interested in, and trained by nature and calling to treat.

Macintyre also composed elegies and eulogies for members of the Clan Campbell, love-songs, songs about drinking and hunting, and satires. He was influenced in many ways by his older contemporary Alexander ◊ MacDonald, but in his nature poetry he surpassed his master. [DT]

The Songs, ed. A. MacLeod (1952).
D. S. Thomson, 'Gaelic Poets of the 18th Century', *An Gaidheal*, LIII, 6 (1958); I. C. Smith, *Ben Dorain* (1969) (translation).

Mackay, Robert. ◊ Donn, Rob.

McKenna, Stephen (1888–   ). Novelist. Born in London and educated at Westminster School and Christ Church, Oxford, he travelled widely in all continents and during the First World War was in the War Trade Intelligence Department; during the Second World War he worked for the Ministry of Economic Warfare (1939–40). His first novel, *The Reluctant Lover*, appeared in 1912. His great success was *Sonia* (1917). He has written many other novels, which include *Sonia Married* (1919), *An Affair of Honour* (1925), *The Shadow of Guy Denver* (1928), *Last Confession* (1937), *That Dumb Loving* (1957) and *A Place in the Sun* (1962). His territory is upper-class London society, with which, as a rich man, he is familiar; and his interest is in the details and minutiae of that group as they impinge on personal life. He has also written a life of his father, a well-known financier: *Reginald McKenna, 1863–1943: A Memoir* (1948). [AR]

While I Remember (1921) (autobiography).

Mackenzie, Sir (Edward Montague) Compton (1883–   ). Novelist and miscellaneous writer. Born at West Hartlepool and educated at Oxford, he is a prolific and many-faceted novelist and miscellaneous writer. His early novels *Carnival* (1912) and *Sinister Street* (1913) were praised by Henry James. After a colourful war career (described in several volumes of *Memories*, one of which was suppressed under the Official Secrets Act in 1932) and conversion to Roman Catholicism (1914) he moved in the Mediterranean set of Norman ◊ Douglas and D. H. ◊ Lawrence, breaking with Lawrence when he felt himself satirized by Lawrence's tale 'The Man Who Loved Islands'. During the twenties Mackenzie's literary interests shifted from the serious novel to the novel of sophisticated entertainment; in 1928 he settled in Barra in the Hebrides and helped to found the Scottish National Party, and in 1929 he started *Vox*, an independent (and short-lived) magazine of radio criticism; the chief work of this middle period is *The Four Winds of Love* (1937–45). Since the war Mackenzie has assumed ever more frankly the role of entertainer, publishing a series of amusing light novels of which the first and best was *Whisky Galore* (1947) and exploiting his remarkable memory and his wide acquaintance with figures of the Edwardian period and the 1920s in broadcasting, articles and volumes of reminiscence. His autobiography, to be completed in several volumes, has been in progress since 1963. [AI]

Henry James, 'The New Novel', in *Notes on Novelists* (1914); L. Robertson, *C.M., an Appraisal* (1954).

Mackenzie, Henry (1745–1831). Scottish novelist and essayist. An Edinburgh lawyer who had worked in London, he was best known in his own day for his tale *The Man of Feeling* (1771), which established a brand of sentiment barely distinguishable from sentimentality as a fashionable literary quality in its own right, independent of the psychological realism and moral emphasis with which sentiment had previously been combined in the works of Samuel ◊ Richardson. The key word of the new mode, which flourished rankly for fifty years, was *sensibility*. Mackenzie himself outgrew the mode of *The Man of Feeling* and its sequels *The Man of the World* (1773) and *Julia de Roubigné* (1777). His papers in the *Mirror* (1779–80) and the *Lounger* (1785–7) – Edinburgh periodicals in imitation of the *Spectator*, which Mackenzie founded and in the main wrote – show him developing a humour based on much sharper and more accurate observation of human character and conduct, and his work in this direction provided an impulse for some of the Scottish comedy of Scott, John ◊ Galt,

D. M. ◊ Moir and William ◊ Alexander; it shares their weakness of springing from mere interest rather than deep impulse, and of slipping too readily into patronizing its material. In no. 97 of the *Lounger* Mackenzie published the first influential favourable review of Burns's poems, and in 1805 he drew up the report of the committee of inquiry into the authenticity of ◊ Ossian's supposed poems. His life of John ◊ Home, prefixed to Home's *Works* (1822), is a valuable record of the literary circles of mid-18th-century Edinburgh, and in old age Mackenzie was venerated by Scott, ◊ Jeffrey and their contemporaries as a last survivor of that period. *Waverley* is dedicated to Mackenzie as 'Our Scottish Addison'. [AI]

Anecdotes and Egotisms, ed. H. W. Thompson (1927); *Letters to Elizabeth Rose of Kilravock*, ed. H. W. Drescher (1967).
H. W. Thompson, *A Scottish Man of Feeling* (1931).

Mackintosh, Elizabeth (1897–1952). Dramatist and novelist. Born and educated in Inverness, she worked as a physical training teacher. From 1929, under the pseudonym Gordon Daviot, she wrote several novels and the historical play *Richard of Bordeaux*, in which in 1933 the young John Gielgud made a great impression as Richard II. She wrote several other plays on historical themes. As Josephine Tey she published one novel in 1936 and resumed that pseudonym for her later very successful mystery-stories, which include *Miss Pym Disposes* (1946), *The Franchise Affair* (1948) and *The Daughter of Time* (1951), in which her detective hero re-examines the sources and vindicates Richard III from the villainies cast upon him by the historians who created the Tudor Myth. [MJ]

Maclean, Sam (Somhairle MacGhill-Eathain) (1911–). Scottish Gaelic poet. Maclean is a key figure in the mid-20th-century renaissance of Gaelic poetry. His main published work, *Dàin do Eimhir agus Dàin Eile* (1943), contains a series of 48 love poems, written mainly between 1937 and 1939, and 31 other poems, on autobiographical, literary and political topics. His thought ranges widely, over music and politics, Gaelic, Irish, English and French literature. His politics here are radical: his Communism, like Hugh ◊ MacDiarmid's, is modified by Scottish Nationalism. His poetry is deeply personal, emotionally tense, frank and subtle, and at times both lyrical and obscure. It is rich in imagery, especially imagery connected with stars, light and jewels. He alternates between spare, terse statement and exuberant word-play, showing a wide mastery and fine discrimination in his use of Gaelic.

Maclean's metrical technique is fairly traditional. In subject-matter, however, he innovates freely, and his work has greatly widened the horizons of Gaelic verse, bending the vocabulary and the metrical norms of the Gaelic poetic tradition to new purposes. For the adequate appreciation of his poetry, a double awareness, of Gaelic and English poetry, is needed. His work, together with that of his younger contemporaries, has wrenched Gaelic poetry from its traditional course, and opened up new and exciting possibilities. [D T]

S. M. and Robert Garioch, *17 Poems for Six-pence* (1940).
Iain C. Smith, 'Modern Gaelic Poetry', *Scottish Gaelic Studies*, VII (1953); I. Grimble and D. S. Thomson, *The Future of the Highlands* (1968).

MacLennan, Hugh (1907–   ). Canadian novelist and essayist. Born in Nova Scotia, the son of a Scottish Canadian doctor. Childhood memories enrich his fourth novel, *Each Man's Son* (1951). He graduated from Dalhousie in 1929, going on first to Oxford as a Rhodes Scholar, then to graduate work on Roman History at Princeton. He was a schoolteacher for several years before he joined the English Department at McGill University in 1951.

MacLennan is not an innovator in the technique of the novel, but no Canadian has more seriously confronted the theme of nationality. *Barometer Rising* (1941), his first novel, centres round the Halifax explosion of 1917, though history here reads like coincidence. The same austere fatalism and the search for a national myth reappear in the later novels, *Two Solitudes* (1945) and *The Precipice* (1948). MacLennan's gift as a story-teller is sometimes overburdened by extra-narrative comment even in his best novel, *The Watch that Ends the Night* (1959), and his psychological penetration, though often profound, is erratic. His most recent collection of essays, *Seven Rivers of Canada* (1961), is further evidence of a considerable descriptive talent. *Return of the Sphinx*

(1967)) is a novel based on separatist tensions in Quebec. [P T]

G. Woodcock. 'A Nation's Odyssey: The Novels of H. M.', *A Review of English Literature*. II, 4 (October 1961); H. McPherson, 'The Novels of H.M.', *Queen's Quarterly*, LX, 2 (Summer, 1953).

MacLeod, Mary (Màiri Nighean Alasdair Ruaidh) (*c.* 1615–*c.* 1706). Scottish Gaelic poetess. She was born in Harris, but her closest connexions were with the chiefs of the MacLeods, who lived at Dunvegan in Skye. She was nurse to several members of the MacLeod family, and composed poems in their honour, reserving her warmest attachment for Sir Norman MacLeod of Bernera. She also composed elegies for Mackenzie of Applecross (d. 1646) and MacLeod of Raasay (d. 1671), and a song of welcome to MacDonald of Sleat (*c.* 1695). Her songs are lyrical evocations of the chiefs' prowess and character, and of the grandeur of their residence and equipment. They give a vivid account of this small sector of society, showing how the ideals of a heroic age had survived in the 17th-century Highlands. Her verse is very rich in vowel music: like the majority of early modern Gaelic poems, hers were meant to be sung. She used strophic rather than syllabic metres, but despite this metrical independence her imagery is often closely allied to that of the professional bards: she is a vernacular poet usurping some of the traditional functions of the court poets. [D T]

The Gaelic Songs on M.M., ed. James C. Watson (1965).

MacMhuirich, Niall (*c.* 1637–*c.* 1726). Gaelic poet and historian. Great historical interest attaches to this poet, the last considerable figure in the long line of Mac-Mhuirich bards descended from a 13th-century poet Muireadhach Albanach. This family of bards and historians had served the MacDonalds of the Isles, and later the Clanranald branch of the MacDonald family, their total service extending to over 500 years. They retained literary ties with their bardic colleagues in Ireland, but also conducted bardic schools in Scotland. By the 18th century, with the steady erosion of Gaelic independence and the anglicizing of their Clanranald patrons, their status became diminished, until in 1800 the representative of the family could not write.

Niall's work survives mainly in the so-called *Red Book of Clanranald*, to which he contributed a prose account of the Montrose Wars and of subsequent 17th-century Mac-Donald history, as well as poetry, and in Gaelic manuscripts in the National Library of Scotland. Among his poems are an elegy for Donald MacDonald of Clanranald (d. 1686), and poems on the birth of Allan of Clanranald (1673), on his assuming the chiefship, and on his death after Sherriff-muir in 1715. He also composed some verse of a philosophical and religious nature. The greater part of his surviving work is in the bardic language common to Scottish and Irish bards, but at least two poems also survive in the Gaelic vernacular, on the wounding and death of Allan, these are in stressed metre. He made his concession to the current revolution in Gaelic verse, but proudly plied his more learned craft to the end. [D T]

Alexander Cameron, *Reliquiae Celticae*, ii (1894).

MacNamee, G. ◊ Mac Conmidhe, G. B. A.

MacNeice, Louis (1907–63). Poet, verse dramatist, translator and prose writer. Born in Belfast, the son of a Church of Ireland clergyman who became a bishop, he was educated at Marlborough and at Merton College, Oxford, where he read Greats. Unlike his Oxford contemporaries Auden and Spender, he had the gifts of an exact scholar, and between 1930 and 1936 was a lecturer in Classics at Birmingham, and between 1936 and 1940 a lecturer in Greek at Bedford College, University of London. A fine translation of the *Agamemnon* of Aeschylus appeared in 1936. From 1940 to 1949 and again, after a year with the British Institute in Athens, till the end of his life, MacNeice was a feature-writer and producer for the B.B.C. and was one of the mainstays of the Third Programme in its great days. He was twice married, the second time (after a first marriage had ended in divorce) to the well-known singer Hedli Anderson, and had one son and one daughter. He was made a C.B.E. in 1957.

MacNiece's first volume, *Blind Fireworks* (1929), was published when he was still at Oxford and reflects the rather dandified pose which he assumed there and his fondness for vivid and highly coloured imagery and for dancing rhythms and clashing and surprising rhymes. In his sensuousness and gaiety combined with a sort of epicurean melancholy he stood apart from the group of poets with whom his name was most often associated in the 1930s, Stephen ◊ Spender, C. ◊ Day Lewis and W. H. ◊ Auden. His Irish roots were important to him, and in the 1940s he published a useful short book on W. B. Yeats. Four kinds of poem which attracted him were the nursery rhyme, the riddle or puzzle poem, the Horatian ode (he wrote some good translations of Horace) and allegory (most of his radio plays, of which the best is *The Dark Tower*, 1947, are allegorical). He had also a gift, in prose and verse, for reportage, which reflected itself in his vivid description, in the weekly magazine *Picture Post*, of the German fire-raids on London in late 1940 and early 1941, and in travel books like *I Crossed the Minch* (1938) and *Letters from Iceland*, a collaboration with W. H. Auden (1936). He travelled widely, visiting India for the B.B.C. as well as teaching in Athens, and his 2 long poems, *Autumn Journal* (1939) and *Autumn Sequel* (1954), are remarkable for their vivid evocations of place.

Of his friends of the 1930s, MacNeice resembled Auden in his intelligence, his wide range of intellectual and practical interests and capacities, and his technical versatility and virtuosity as a poet. Never so far to the left as Auden, Spender or Day Lewis in the 1930s (though a staunch anti-Fascist, he was temperamentally antipathetic to Communism and, admiring the Irish peasantry, had no strong or intimate feelings for the English working classes), he did not retreat from a liberal social commitment after 1940. A lack of easy sentiment or of the 'common touch' made him a less popular poet than the other three, a poet whose ironies and loyalties were always consciously ambivalent. In the 1950s, his reputation slumped a little, for a series of long poems for broadcasting, *Ten Burnt Offerings*, published in 1952, and the very long poem in *terza rima*, *Autumn Sequel*, published in 1954, seemed to display a gift for improvisation, a willed determination to produce poems of some length, rather than an inner compulsion. Two later volumes, *Visitations* (1957) and *Solstices* (1961), had a much more authentic ring, and the poems had a compulsive tightness of construction. In a strange way, it might be said that MacNeice, like Thomas Gray in Matthew Arnold's phrase, 'never spoke out'. A polarity between a brilliant and gay outer impact and the sense that certain final intimacies are being refused, certain basic arguments are being evaded, can be felt in his poems as it was seen in his life, and explains both their distinction and their limitations. He was always a true craftsman and never a mere spokesman of the *Zeitgeist*, his submerged doubts and depressions lay a solid foundation for the glittering iceberg surfaces that appear on his page, and he is probably a poet whose reputation will grow when it becomes less closely associated with the political and social ideas, and the literary groupings, of his period. A study of MacNeice's poetry by D. B. Moore is due for publication in 1971. [GSF]

Poems (1935); *Out of the Picture* (1937); *The Earth Compels* (1938); *Modern Poetry* (1938); *The Poetry of W. B. Yeats* (1941); *Plant and Phantom* (1941); *Christopher Columbus* (1944); *Springboard* (1944); *Holes in the Sky* (1948); *Collected Poems* (1949); *Goethe's Faust, Parts 1 and 2* (1951) (verse translation); *Eighty-Five Poems* (1959); *Collected Poems* (1967).
G. S. Fraser, *Vision and Rhetoric* (1959).

Macpherson, James (1736–96). Poet. Born in Invernesshire, the son of a small farmer, he was educated at the Universities of Aberdeen and Edinburgh, with the intention of becoming a minister. He had some literary talent, and some knowledge of the Gaelic poetry which still circulated orally in his native parish, where he briefly kept school. He produced first an ambitious but unsuccessful heroic poem in 6 cantos, *The Highlander* (1758), but in 1760, with the assistance of the Rev. John ◊ Home and others, he published *Fragments of Ancient Poetry Collected in the Highlands of Scotland, and Translated from the Gallic or Erse Language* (1760). This was an instant success and poetic stimulant in Scotland, England and Europe generally, though at the same time bitter controversy immediately started over the genuineness of the poems (doubts still exist). The success came because the book appeared to provide the poetry demanded by several contemporary developments: an interest in poetic traditions outside the Greek and Roman (explored in the work of ◊ Gray); the cult of the imagination and the sublime; and the modish vein of primitivism in Augustan culture. From all this, of course, sprang the literary material for various Romantic

preoccupations. Macpherson also appeared to satisfy the needs of nationalistic aspirations, which exacerbated the literary quarrels. As a result of this success, a subscription was raised to pay for further searches, and Macpherson published *Fingal: An Ancient Epic Poem* (1762); *Temora: An Ancient Epic Poem* (1763); and *The Works of Ossian* (2 vols., 1765; 3rd edn with a critical dissertation by the Rev. Hugh Blair; ed. W. Sharp, Edinburgh, 1896) Goethe (among others) much admired these works, and with J. H. Merck published *The Works of Ossian* (Frankfurt, 1773–7). Macpherson claimed that he had translated these epic poems from the Gaelic of ◊ Ossian (Oisin, a legendary warrior and bard, the son of Fingal, or Finn), who was said to have lived in the 3rd century A.D. Macpherson's poems are related to the Feinian cycle of Irish Celtic romance, but he seems to have 'translated' them in a way common enough at the time, by altering, amending and inserting passages of his own. His heavily poetic prose is a perfect vehicle for the 'sublime', a mixture of the idiom of the Authorized Version, Homer, Milton, Pope's translation of the *Iliad* and other writers. He could not produce, when challenged, the 'ancient, authentic MSS' to support his claims and in fact did some faking of 'evidence', not being a sophisticated enough scholar to discuss satisfactorily the oral tradition to which he undoubtedly had some access. He was also a writer of history and pamphlets in the interest of the Government, which increased the number of attacks on him. He held various offices in America (*in absentia*) and at home, and is buried in Westminster Abbey. [AR]

E. D. Snyder, *The Celtic Revival in English Literature* (Harvard U.P., 1923); D. S. Thomson, *The Gaelic Sources of Macpherson's 'Ossian'* (1952).

Macpherson, Jay (1932–). Canadian poetess. She attended Carleton College, Ottawa and the University of Toronto, where she now studies and teaches. Her publication of poetry chapbooks has helped a number of unknown poets into print. Macpherson's lively prose retelling of the classical myths in *The Four Ages of Man* (1962) reflects her poetic interests. *The Boatman* (1957), her third collection, is her best. Familiarity with mythopoeic poetry regulates her use of symbol and extends the

341

reference of her short, subjective lyrics. By a meticulous refusal to overcrowd her poems, she achieves her intended effects without any sense of strain. [P T]

J. Reaney, 'The Third Eye', *Canadian Literature*, 3 (Winter, 1960).

Macpherson, Mary (Màiri Mhór nan Oran) (1821–98). Scottish Gaelic poet. Almost half her life was spent in Inverness and Glasgow, where she identified herself with the radical movement for land reform in the Highlands (*c.* 1870–90). Many of her poems are commentaries on the events and personalities in that acrimonious campaign. As a personality she had enormous zest and a huge presence (she weighed seventeen stone). She lacked self-criticism, so that her verse is uneven, and some of her subject-matter is trivial. It provides, however, a pithy commentary on an interesting period in Highland social history, throwing much light on Gaelic thought and customs in a time of rapid change. Some of her finest and most popular verse is descriptive, building up a picture of life in her native island of Skye in the mid 19th century. Here nostalgia is tempered by realism. A similar dualism can be seen in her style: the metrical serenity of her verse often explodes in caustic comment or in the country-woman's directness of speech. [D T]

Dàin agus Orain Ghàidhlig (1891) (collected poems).
M. Murray 'Màiri Nighean Iain Bhàin', *Transactions of the Gaelic Society of Inverness*, XXXVII (1946).

Mac Piarais, Pádraig (Patrick H. Pearse) (1879–1916). Irish author. He was born in Dublin, qualified as a barrister, but worked mainly as a teacher, writer and organizer. Active in the Gaelic League, and later in the Irish Volunteers, he played the leading role in the Easter Rising of 1916, for which he and a number of others were executed.

Recognizing the importance of the Irish language, Mac Piarais devoted himself to furthering the development of a modern literature, and wrote plays, short stories, essays and a number of poems. As a short-story writer, his work is marked by the sudden opening, simplicity of plot and economy in style. One of his best stories concerns an aged recluse, Sean-Mhaitias, who had lapsed from practising his religion, but was visited and consoled by the Infant

Jesus before his death. His poetry manifests a certain intensity and pervasive idealism, as in *Fornocht do chonnac thú* ('Stark-naked I saw thee'); verses of dedication to heroic sacrifice in the cause of freedom: *Do thugas mo ghnúis | Ar an ród so romham | Ar an ngníomh do-chím | 'S ar an mbás do-gheobhad* ('I set my face | To the road afore | To the deed foreseen | And the death foretold'). He also composed a number of pieces in English, like *The Wayfarer*, written in Kilmainham Barracks as he awaited execution. [S B]

L. N. Le Roux, *Patrick H. Pearse* (tr. D. Ryan, 1932).

Madge, Charles (1912–   ). Sociologist and poet. Born in South Africa, the son of English parents, he was educated at Winchester and Cambridge, where he was a pupil of I. A. ◊ Richards. Later T. S. Eliot helped him to publish his early poems and to get a job as a reporter on the *Daily Mail*. He left that job to start Mass-Observation, a sociological investigation unit, and from this work produced a number of books in collaboration with Tom Harrisson. During the Second World War he directed a survey of wartime spending habits, and later edited the reconstruction series *Target for Tomorrow*. In 1947 he was appointed social development officer at Stevenage New Town, but found the job frustrating and in 1950 he became Professor of Sociology at Birmingham University. Throughout his sociological work he continued to write poetry, and has published 2 books, *The Disappearing Castle* (1937) and *The Father Found* (1941). [J M]

Society in the Mind (1964).

Mais, Roger (1905–55). West Indian novelist. Born and educated in Jamaica, on leaving school he became a journalist. Although near white, he identified himself with Jamaica's poor. In 1944 he was sentenced to six months' imprisonment for attacking the British Government in an article called 'Now We Know'. Painter, poet and dramatist, he was an important contributor to Jamaica's cultural development. Despite his prolific output, he could not find the right vehicle for his talent. He went to London in 1953, and in the same year published his first novel, *The Hills Were Joyful Together*, a profoundly disturbing evocation of Kingston's degrading poverty.

Brother Man (1954), illustrated by himself, *Black Lightning* (1955), and *Face and Other Stories* (1955) are further passionate protests against conditions in Jamaican slums. Mais never produced a technically accomplished work, but his passionate idealism and the intense pity behind the almost crudely realistic portraits of poverty and misery give his awkward prose a peculiar strength. *Brother Man* especially is an important work. From 1953 to 1955 Mais lived in England and France, but when his cancer was discovered he returned to Jamaica to die. [WAG]

Maitland, Sir Richard (1496–1586). Scottish satirist and compiler of 2 manuscript collections of Scottish verse. Educated at St Andrews and Paris, Maitland successively served James V, Mary Queen of Scots and James VI as judge and privy counsellor and in other legal and diplomatic offices. His satires, written in old age, mingle tart comment on contemporary practices with elegiac regret for the passing of the courtly civilization of his youth; his denunciation of the Border raiders, 'Aganis the theivis of Liddisdaill', similarly mingles bitterness and zest. The Maitland Manuscripts, now at Magdalene College, Cambridge, are the second main source, after the collection of George ◊ Bannatyne, of texts of Middle Scots poetry; the Maitland Club, a publishing society, was named in Maitland's honour in 1828. [AI]

The Maitland Quarto Manuscript, ed. W. A. Craigie (STS, 1920); *The Maitland Folio Manuscript*, ed. W. A. Craigie (STS, 1919–27).

Major or **Mair, John** (1467–1550). Philosophical teacher and historian. Major was educated at St Andrews, Cambridge and Paris, where he led the last stand of medieval philosophy (1526–31) before returning to St Andrews for the rest of his career. His chief philosophical works are *Commentaries* on Peter Lombard (1509–17) and on Aristotle's *Ethics* (1530); his typically medieval political theory influenced later Scottish history through his pupils John ◊ Knox and George ◊ Buchanan, and his coolness towards the Renaissance may account for other characteristics of Knox's thought. His Latin *History of Greater Britain, both England and Scotland* (1521; last reprinted in Latin, 1740; tr. A. Constable, with Life by A. J. G. Mackay, STS, 1892) is more substantial than the early Scottish chronicles of ◊ Fordun and ◊ Wyntoun and is less credulous and more critical than the contemporary 'humanist' history of Hector ◊ Boece. [AI]

T. G. Law, 'J.M.: Scottish Scholastic', in *Collected Essays* (1904); R. G. Cant, 'J.M.', in *Veterum Laudes*, ed. J. B. Salmond (1950); J. H. Burns, 'New Light on John Maior', *The Innes Review: Scottish Catholic Historical Studies*, V (1954).

Mallet or **Malloch, David** (1705?–65). Scots poet. A minor poet whose career shows what a compliant and ambitious Scotsman could hope for in the early 18th century. Educated at Edinburgh University, Malloch came to London as a tutor in 1723, purged his speech of Scotticisms, anglicized his name to Mallet, and proceeded to ingratiate himself with Pope's set and with the Prince of Wales. He imitated and collaborated with James ◊ Thomson, whose 'Rule Britannia' he tried to claim as his own; he accepted a legacy from the Duchess of Marlborough, but did not fulfil his undertaking to write a life of her late husband, the famous general; he was employed by ◊ Bolingbroke to attack Pope after his death, and published the posthumous edition of Bolingbroke's works that provoked Johnson's famous asperity about the blunderbuss fired for hire by a beggarly Scotchman; dedications to the Prince of Wales (later George III) and Lord Bute brought him sinecures late in life. Mallet nevertheless remained on good terms with Hume, Gibbon and Smollett. His tragedies and blank-verse poems are forgotten: his ballad-pastiche 'William and Margaret' (1724) shows the first hints of the process by which the material and apparatus of the traditional ballad degenerated into the frissons of the 'Gothic'. [AI]

Works (1759); *Ballads and Songs*, ed. F. Dinsdale (1857).
Johnson, *Lives of the Poets*.

Mallock, William Hurrell (1849–1923). Novelist. He was born at Cheriton Bishop in Devonshire, where his father was rector. His maternal uncle was James Antony ◊ Froude. Mallock was educated privately and at Balliol College, Oxford, where he read classics. *The New Republic* (1877; ed. J. M. Patrick, U. of Florida P., 1954), which he began at Oxford, is an accomplished exercise in the manner of Peacock, set in a country house where a group of characters discuss God, the Church, culture, and the social élite. Through the fictional disguises certain leading personalities of the day are recognizable: ◊ Huxley (Storks), ◊ Tyndall (Stockton), Matthew ◊ Arnold (Luke), ◊ Pater (Rose), W. K. Clifford (Saunders), Jowett (Jenkinson), and ◊ Ruskin (Herbert). In *The New Paul and Virginia* (1878) Mallock turns to Voltaire's *Candide* for a model; here an atheistic but very moral professor (Tyndall) is shipwrecked on a desert island with a precariously reformed *demi-mondaine* married to a High Church colonial bishop. Mallock exposes some of the unwarranted generalizations and uncomfortable compromises his contemporaries arrived at, and detects complacency or timid conservatism in the outlook of many of them. But he seems to regard the social forms and standards they were reluctant to discard as the essential part of civilization, and suggests that without a belief in divine retribution civilized life is impossible. Because of the fundamental Toryism of his own outlook he is unable to appreciate the real force of the social criticism of a Ruskin or an Arnold. In his later novels the issues remain the same, and have an outdated air. *Social Equality* (1882) inaugurated a series of social and political writings in which he made himself an apologist for inequality and wealth (his views hardly stood up to Bernard ◊ Shaw's attack on them in *Socialism and Superior Brains* in 1910). *Memoirs of Life and Literature* (1920) is the disappointing record of a man whose life had been increasingly given over to such fashionable society as he had access to in London and here and there on the continent. [NL]

A. B. Adams, *The Novels of W.H.M.* (U. of Maine, 1934); C. R. Woodring, 'Notes on M.'s *New Republic*', *Nineteenth Century Fiction*, VI (1951).

Malone, Edmond (1741–1812). Scholar and editor. Born of Irish legal stock, he was educated in Dublin and London, and abandoned a promising career at the Irish bar to lead an industrious, productive life as a literary scholar in London, where he was the friend of Johnson, Boswell, ◊ Reynolds and ◊ Burke. He published editions of Goldsmith (1777 and 1780), Reynolds (1797) and Dryden (1800), but his massive learning was centred on Shakespeare. His early researches, prompted by the 1773 edition of Johnson and George Steevens,

were embodied in his *Attempt to Ascertain the Order in Which the Plays of Shakespeare Were Written* (1778), and in a 2-volume supplement to the Johnson–Steevens edition which dealt with Elizabethan stage-history, Shakespeare's sources and the apocryphal plays. In 1790 was published his great edition of Shakespeare in 10 volumes; the introductory matter included the 'Historical Account of the English Stage', a landmark in theatrical and dramatic scholarship. In 1796 he exposed the notorious William Henry Ireland's Shakespearean forgeries. His papers passed to Boswell's son, and were the basis of the Boswell–Malone edition of Shakespeare in 21 volumes (1821).

Malone, the greatest of 18th-century editors, passionately and diligently sought to establish Shakespeare's text as accurately as possible, and to make Elizabethan materials available to the reader. He turned Shakespeare studies (till then the province of poets and men of letters) into a demanding scientific discipline. His memory is honoured by the Malone Society, which issues dramatic texts, documents and records meticulously and rigorously edited. [MJ]

A. Brown, *E.M. and English Scholarship* (1963); Sir J. Prior, *Life of E.M.* (1860).

Malory, Sir Thomas (d. 1471). Author of *Le Morte Darthur*. This history of King Arthur was finished in 1469–70, while Malory was in prison, and printed by Caxton in a slightly edited form in 1485. The modern text is based on a comparison of Caxton's with that of a manuscript found in Winchester College Library in 1934. G. L. Kittredge's identification with Sir Thomas Malory of Newbold Revel in Warwickshire (d. 1471), M.P. in 1445, and eight times imprisoned for rape, armed robbery and cattle-lifting (twice followed by dramatic escapes), has troubled admirers of the book's noble ethics, and W. Matthews has advanced plausible arguments (e.g. that the author's language points further north than Warwickshire) for Thomas Malory of Studley and Hutton in Yorkshire. Internal evidence suggests only that the author was a member of the gentry and a Lancastrian who deeply mourned the prevalence of civil war and the decay of the aristocratic ideals of chivalry, that he was for long periods in prison, and perhaps ill in prison, and that he had seen service in south-western France. He may indeed have written some of his book as a prisoner of war with Jacques d'Armagnac, owner of a large Arthurian library.

But he does not obtrude himself, and it is easy to underestimate his originality in reshaping his material. He seems to have begun by transmuting a north English alliterative verse *Morte Arthure* into the muscular prose of what was eventually his second part, then to have continued this from French sources. Here, by unravelling the complex cycles which appealed to medieval taste into single tales, by playing down symbolic patterns in favour of emotion and motive, and by paring the theological elaborations of the *Queste del Saint Graal* so as to accentuate the felt mystical force of the Grail appearances, he ensured the continuing appeal of the Arthurian story to modern taste. His final book, new-created out of several sources, shows him at his full mastery in its concentration on the tragic conflict of loyalties which destroyed Arthur's kingdom.

It is debated whether the whole work is a unity. There is enough of a theme (the nature, rise and fall of the Round Table) and enough interconnexions to make it so, but the variety of the stories within is so great as to constitute an entire world, capable of containing Galahad's ruthlessly austere religiousness and Gawain's secularity, Tristram's high-flown chivalry and Dinadan's sardonic comments on it. Because Malory desires only to give his own sense to a matter built up before him, the stories of millennia, from pre-Christian goddesses to the Wars of the Roses, echo in it, dominated by his remarkably unified Christian and chivalric vision. Malory's down-to-earthness (he scarcely troubles with the medieval dilemma of heavenly versus earthly love – normally to him all honourable and stable love is God-given) and his sense of the bitterness of contrition preserve it from being a dream-world. Its centre in the end is Lancelot, great, flawed, unstable and contrite, incapable because of his disloyal love for the king's wife of the Grail which his bastard son achieves, but dying a holy priest.

Malory's style, particularly delicate in courtly usage (e.g. the uses of the familiar 'thou' and the ceremonial 'you' in the interchanges of Lancelot and Guinevere), varies according to the needs of the narrative from eerie beauty to sturdy colloquialism;

perhaps its only limitation is its scorn for anyone not of the gentry. But even allowing for this, its appeal is wide: every century has been enthralled by some aspect of it and provided its own interpretation, down to the 2 modern renditions of its extreme aspects – as a novel without the Grail of emotion and politics by T. H. ◊ White, and as a cycle of richly symbolic poems centring on the Grail by Charles ◊ Williams. This popularity, in contrast to the disappearance for everyone but scholars of most other Arthurian histories, is enough to attest the genius of Malory's union of medievalism and modernity, and the originality of his handling of tradition. [SM]

Le Morte Darthur (Everyman, 1906) (Caxton's text); *Works*, ed. E. Vinaver (3 vols., 1947; 1 vol., 1954).

Ed. J. A. W. Bennett, *Essays on M.* (1963); D. S. Brewer, *Morte Darthur* (1968); ed. R. M. Lumiansky, *M.'s Originality* (Baltimore, 1964); W. Matthews, *The Ill-Framed Knight* (U. of California P., 1966); E. Reiss, *Sir T.M.* (New York, 1966); E. Vinaver, *M.* (1929).

Malthus, Thomas Robert (1766–1834). Political and economic theorist. Born near Guildford, Surrey, the son of a country gentleman, he was educated at Jesus College, Cambridge, where he was a Fellow. He took orders and in 1798 became curate of Albury in Surrey. His interest in political economy was stimulated by extensive European travel, during which he collected much valuable economic information, when hard facts were at a premium. In 1798 he published his famous book, *An Essay on the Principle of Population as it Affects the Future Improvements of Society*. His main thesis was based on what he considered he had proved as an axiom, that population increases in geometrical progression, whereas the means of subsistence increase only in arithmetical progression; therefore, he argued, some check on population growth was required, otherwise starvation or pestilence would restore the equilibrium. In a second edition of his essay, he modified his conclusions and called the enlarged work *The Principles of Population, A View of Its Past and Present Effects on Human Happiness* (1803); he professed to find a slackening of the pressures of population growth, due, he thought, partly to the operation of morality on the working class (a sort of voluntary birth control). His views caused much controversy and influenced much 19th-century thought. In recent times his nightmare has come to look less remote than it once did. He wrote several other works on economics, on rent and value, and a general work, *The Principles of Political Economy* (1820). [A R]

K. Smith, *The Malthusian Controversy* (1951); G. F. MacCleary, *The Malthusian Population Theory* (1953); ed. D. V. Glass, *Introduction to M.* (1953).

Mandeville, Bernard de (1670–1733). Physician, satirist and novelist. Born at Dort in Holland, he studied medicine at Leyden, coming to England to practise. He is the author of some Latin and English medical treatises and miscellaneous works, but is best known for a collection of satirical writing which began with an octosyllabic poem, *The Grumbling Hive, or Knaves Turned Honest* (1705), and was several times reissued with added prose commentaries as *The Fable of the Bees: or Private Vices, Publick Benefits* (1714; 1723: Part II, 1728; both parts, 1734; ed. F. B. Kaye, 2 vols., 1924; repr. 1957; ed. P. Harth, PEL, 1970). The accompanying prose essays included 'An Enquiry into the Origin of Moral Virtue', and his other works included *A Modest Defence of Publick Stews* (1724) and *An Enquiry into the Origin of Honour, and the Usefulness of Christianity in War* (1732). Mandeville's concern is with man in society (the fable of the hive of bees) and his temper is cynical, anti-benevolent and inimical to the optimistic outlook often found in religio-social writing of the time. He is, within his limits, a masterly colloquial writer, full of hudibrastic vigour, and no mean arguer. So much so, that his chief work got under the skin of most orthodox thinkers of his day, and provoked replies from, among others, ◊ Berkeley, ◊Hutcheson and Law (of the *Serious Call*). Mandeville argues that men are good from the worst of motives, and consequently that vice produces good results, 'when it's by Justice lop't and bound'; he also develops an expansionist economic doctrine (that waste promotes prosperity) and propounds other paradoxes annoying to orthodox (and particularly Puritan) thinking. Few readers at the time penetrated to the heart of his paradoxes and he was carelessly viewed as simply a scoffing irreligious writer. His books were attacked as blasphemous libels (e.g. by the Middlesex Grand Jury). [A R]

L. Stephens, *History of English Thought in the Eighteenth Century* (1902); J. C. Maxwell, 'Ethics and Politics in M.', *Philosophy*, X X V I (1951).

'Mandeville, Sir John' (fl. 1350). The *Travels* of Sir John Mandeville (ed. P. Hamelius, 1919; ed. M. C. Seymour, *The Bodley Version of M.'s Travels*, EETS, 1965), as well as being the most popular travel book of the Middle Ages, is one of its most successful frauds. 'Sir John Mandeville', who claims in his preface to be an Englishman from St Albans, probably never existed, and certainly never wrote the book. The English version, made, it seems, before 1500, is a translation from the French of Jehan de Bourgogne, a physician of Liège, who wrote it in 1356–7 without ever having left home. The first half is a pilgrim's guide to the Holy Land, based on authentic accounts; the second, a description of the Orient, draws partly on Odoric of Pordenone's account of an Eastern voyage, written in 1330, and, for the rest, on a vivid imagination. It was immensely popular, and by 1500 had been translated into most western languages.

Apart from the fascination of the material, the English version offers a clear, simple prose. Its author is not always a reliable French scholar, but he has a good ear for cadence, and though he can no longer be regarded, as he once was, as 'The Father of English Prose', still ranks high among the writers of secular prose. [A G]

M. Letts, *Sir J.M.: The Man and His Book* (1949).

Mangan, James Clarence (1803–49). Poet. Born in Dublin, the son of a poor shopkeeper, he was educated by a priest and learned several languages. He was employed as a lawyer's clerk and in the library of Trinity College, Dublin. He contributed poems and translations to the *Dublin University Magazine* and the patriotic newspaper *The Nation*. His brief and very promising life was ended by cholera in circumstances of alcoholism and opium addiction that have led him to be compared with Poe (F. J. Thompson, 'Poe and M.', *Dublin Magazine*, X X V, 1950). Mangan knew no Gaelic, but working from prose translations furnished by friends he wrote versions of old Irish songs: his patriotic hymn to Ireland, 'My Dark Rosaleen', is still remembered, as well as a powerful confessional piece, 'The Nameless One'. [AR]

Poems, intr. J. Mitchel (New York, 1903); *Poems* (1931); *The Prose Writings*, ed. D. J. O'Donoghue (1904).
James Joyce, 'J.C.M.', in *St Stephens*' (May 1902; reprinted, 1930); J. Sheridan, *J.C.M.* (Dublin, 1937); M. Magalanev, 'M. and Joyce's Dedalus Family', *PQ*, xxxi (1952).

Manley, Mrs Mary de la Rivière (1663-1724). Novelist, dramatist and writer of scandalous memoirs. Escaping from a bigamous marriage with her cousin, she tried to make a living by her pen and was forced into rather successful libellous writing (◊ Haywood, Eliza). She began as a playwright in 1696 with a comedy, *The Lost Lover*, and a tragedy, *The Royal Mischief*. Her most famous works of prose scandal are *The Secret History of Queen Zarah* . . . (1705) and *Secret Memoirs and Manners of Several Persons of Quality of Both Sexes. From the New Atlantis* . . . (1709). She was arrested for reflecting on 'persons of quality' but released. She succeeded Swift as editor of the political *Examiner* in 1711. [AR]

P. B. Anderson, 'Mistress Delarivière M.'s Biography', *MP*, xxxiii (1936); J. J. Richetti *Popular Fiction before Richardson* (1969).

Mannin, Ethel Edith (1900–). Novelist and miscellaneous writer. Born in London, she left school at 15 to become a typist in an advertising agency. She has also been a journalist, and her first novel, *Martha*, appeared in 1923; her many novels, often left-wing (first Marxist, then anarchist), include *Sounding Brass* (1925), a successful satire on the advertising world; *Children of the Earth* (1930); *The Pure Flame* (1936); *Darkness My Bride* (1938); *Comrade, O Comrade* (1947); *The Living Lotus* (1956); *The Road to Beersheba* (1963); *The Night and Its Homing* (1966). She uses exotic backgrounds in her fiction, and has also written several straight travel books such as *Forever Wandering* (1934); *South to Samarkand* (1936); *German Journey* (1948); and *Moroccan Mosaic* (1953). She has published several volumes of short stories, and writes on education and 'child psychology' (*Commonsense and the Child*, 1931, and *Commonsense and the Adolescent*, 1937). Her children's books include *Ann and Peter in Sweden* (1959) and sequels. Her

experiences have furnished 3 autobiographical volumes: *Confessions and Impressions* (1930), *Privileged Spectator* (1939) and *Brief Voices* (1959). [AR]

Manning, Olivia (? –). Novelist and journalist. Born in Portsmouth, the daughter of a naval officer. Her first novel, *The Wind Changes*, appeared in 1937. Others include *Artist Among the Missing* (1949), a story of complex personal relationships set in the Middle East, and *School for Love* (1951), the story of a 16-year-old boy in wartime Jerusalem. She is publishing a vast panorama of modern history in fictional form: *The Great Fortune* (1960) is set in Bucharest in the first year of the 1939-45 war; the story is taken up again in *The Spoilt City* (1962) and continued down to the occupation by German troops after the fall of France. Against this complex background is told the story of the changing and complex relations between Pringle, a British cultural representative, and his wife. *Growing Up* (1948) is a volume of (often satirical) short stories; and *My Husband, Cartwright* (1956) is a collection of humorous sketches. She writes for many periodicals. [AR]

Mannyng of Brunne, Robert (fl. 1288-1338). Poet. Born at Bourne (Brunne) in Lincolnshire, he belonged to the Gilbertine order, whose headquarters were at Sempringham. Biographical information about him derives from his 2 works, *Handlyng Synne* (ed. F. E. Furnivall, 1901), which he started in 1303, and the *Chronicle of England* (ed. F. E. Furnivall, 1887), completed in 1338 at Sixhill Priory. Of lesser importance is the *Chronicle*, a close translation of the Norman-French works of ◊ Wace and Langtoft. The first half, where Wace is the source, is in the accepted form for popular history, the short couplet, but Mannyng later moves on to a longer line. His breezy approach is attractive, and there are many interesting references to current traditions and popular legends, but the *Chronicle* has little literary merit. *Handlyng Synne*, also in couplets, is a very free translation of the 13th-century French *Manuel des pechiez*, a handbook written to aid the layman at confession. Mannyng deals systematically with the commandments, sins and sacraments, but it is the illustrative stories which show him at his best. These *exempla* combine sound doctrine with good entertainment, in an easy, unaffected style, and his gusto conveys itself readily to his reader. [AG]

R. Crosby, 'R. M. of B.: A New Biography', *PMLA*, LVII (1942).

Mansfield, Katherine (pen-name of Kathleen Mansfield Beauchamp) (1888–1923). New Zealand short-story writer. Daughter of a prominent Wellington businessman, she came to London in 1908 to embark on a literary career. In revolt against her father's middle-class ethics, she embarked on an unfortunate marriage which soon broke up. A period of unhappiness and disillusion in Germany resulted in the bitter sketches of German life that make up *In a German Pension* (1911). She returned to London and wrote stories for *The New Age* and other periodicals. In 1912 she began her association with J. Middleton ◊ Murry, critic and editor whom she was unable to marry until 1918, when her first husband divorced her.

The death of her brother in the war in 1915 turned her thoughts and emotions back to her New Zealand childhood, the result being a series of stories with New Zealand settings – *Prelude* (1918), *Bliss and Other Stories* (1920), *The Garden Party and Other Stories* (1922), *The Dove's Nest and Other Stories* (1923) – which contain her best work. She developed tuberculosis in 1917, stopped writing in 1922, and died suddenly in January 1923 at Fontainebleau, where she was following Gurdjieff's course of 'spiritual discipline'.

The quiet clarity of detail, the symbolic use of objects and incidents presented with extraordinary physical accuracy, the cunning distillation of atmosphere, are the outstanding features of her stories, which have something in common with those of Chekhov. [DD]

Letters, ed. J. Middleton Murry (2 vols., 1928); *Journal*, ed. J. Middleton Murry (new edn, 1954).
S. Berkman, *K.M., a Critical Study* (1951); A. Alpers, *K.M., A Biography* (1954); I. A. Gordon, *K.M.* (1954) (with bibliography).

Map (Mapes), Walter (*c.* 1140–*c.* 1209). Satirical writer. After studying in Paris (*c.* 1154–62), he became clerk to Henry II and an itinerant justice until the King's death ended his connexion with court life, and after holding various canonries he became Archdeacon of Oxford in 1197. He was probably the author of the first Latin versions of the Arthurian legends, and

certainly of the *De nugis curialium*, written between 1181 and 1193 (ed. M. R. James, in Latin 1914, in an English translation 1923). This is erudite and amusing, filled with biblical, scholastic and classical allusions and with attacks on the monastic orders, particularly the Cistercians. His authorship of Latin Goliardic verse (ed. T. Wright, *The Latin Poems Commonly Attributed to Walter Map*, 1841) is contested (e.g. by F. J. E. Raby, *Secular Latin Poetry*, ii, 1957), since the attribution is late and the only well-authenticated scraps of verse of his are in classical metre. [ATH]

Markhandeya, Kamala (1924–). Indian novelist. Born in South India. Her travels in India and Europe interrupted her schooling. On leaving Madras University she worked as a journalist. She did liaison and staff work for the army in India during the war, but returned to journalism shortly after it ended. She is married to an Englishman and lives in London. Markhandeya's first novel, *Nectar in a Sieve* (1954), is her best known. It is the restrained chronicle of an Indian peasant woman's life, divided between love for her family and a desperate search for money to fend off starvation. *Some Inner Fury* (1956) describes the loves of a group of young people in India during the violent days of the 'Quit India' campaigns. She has also written *A Silence of Desire* (1960), *Possession* (1963), *A Handful of Rice* (1966) and *The Coffer Dams* (1969). [PT]

Marlowe, Christopher (1564–93). Poet and dramatist. Born at Canterbury, he was the son of a fairly prosperous shoemaker. His social origins are comparable with those of his exact contemporary William Shakespeare, but his formal education was more extensive. At 17 he went from the King's School, Canterbury, to Corpus Christi College, Cambridge. He took his B.A. in 1584 and the M.A. in 1587 – but only after the Privy Council intervened with the University authorities (who suspected him of wishing to enrol as a Catholic convert at the English seminary at Rheims) and disclosed that Marlowe had been employed abroad in some kind of secret political mission. Although his education seemed to point to a career in the Church, he did not take holy orders, but moved to London to live, apparently, on his literary and dramatic earnings. He was rumoured to hold atheistic, blasphemous and seditious opinions, and was called before the Privy Council for investigation. He was stabbed to death at a tavern in Deptford by Ingram Frizer in the company of two men known to be government spies.

Marlowe's literary and dramatic career was tragically short, and the exact chronology of his work can never be determined. While still at Cambridge he translated parts of Ovid's *Amores* and wrote the famous lyric 'Come live with me and be my love'. He may also have written there *Tamburlaine the Great* (performed with great acclaim by the most impressive declamatory actor of the age, Edward Alleyn, *c*. 1587). The 'general welcome' of *Tamburlaine* demanded an immediate sequel, Part Two, and these 'two tragical discourses' proved to be, with ◊ Kyd's *Spanish Tragedy*, the two seminal works of Elizabethan tragedy. More a panoramic pageant than a play, the 2-part *Tamburlaine* influenced later writers both through its portrayal of a single, Herculean hero and through its masterly use of blank verse, which Marlowe virtually established as the Elizabethan norm of dramatic expression. Marlowe's tragic heroes are humbly born, self-asserting men and 3 plays have a common theme: the limits of human power. *Tamburlaine* deals with military and territorial conquest; the Oriental hero is invincible save by death. *The Jew of Malta* (*c*. 1590), sometimes called a sardonic farce, centres on wealth and on the Machiavellian, acquisitive Jew, Barabbas. Marlowe's greatest, and possibly final, play, *Dr Faustus*, dramatizes the compulsions the Renaissance intellectual felt to explore all regions of knowledge, including regions forbidden by the Church. *Edward II* (*c*. 1592), a sympathetic biographical tragedy, is personal rather than political; possibly influenced by Shakespeare's *Henry VI* plays, it certainly influenced his *Richard II*. *Dido, Queen of Carthage* and *The Massacre at Paris*, early and late works, are minor dramas. Most of Marlowe's plays survive in corrupt and mutilated texts (for an example of the difficulties involved see Sir Walter Greg's great parallel-text edition of *Faustus*, 1950). *Edward II*, *The Jew* and an adaptation of *Tamburlaine* have all been successfully staged in recent years; *Dr Faustus* has been more frequently produced.

Marlowe's best work in non-dramatic poetry was the two sestiads of *Hero and Leander* (a fragment later continued by George Chapman), generally judged to be the finest English epyllion of the 16th century. It is in the Italianate Ovidian tradition of erotic narrative, decorative and exuberant in style and tone. The blank-verse translation of part of Lucan's *Pharsalia* (posthumously published as *Lucan's First Book*, 1600) has never been satisfactorily dated.

Marlowe was stabbed to death at an age when most dramatists (including Shakespeare) have done only apprentice-work, a fact which invites critics to speculate on the great plays he might have gone on to write. Calvin Hoffman's hypothesis in *The 'Murder' of the Man Who Was Shakespeare* that Marlowe did not die at Deptford but lived to write in secret the plays attributed to Shakespeare is not based on any verifiable fact. [MJ]

Works and Life, general ed. R. H. Case (6 vols., 1930–3); *The Revels Edition of the Works*, general ed. C. Leech (1962– ; in progress). D. Cole, *Suffering and Evil in the Plays of C.M.* (1962); P. Kocher, *C.M.: A Study of His Thought, Learning, and Character* (1946); ed. C. Leech, *Marlowe: A Collection of Critical Essays* (1964); H. Levin, *The Overreacher: A Study of C.M.* (1954); J. B. Steane, *C.M.: A Critical Study* (1961); F. P. Wilson, *M. and the Early Shakespeare* (1953).

Marprelate Tracts (1588–9). A series of 7 satiric, anti-episcopal tracts, issued variously under the pseudonyms of Martin Marprelate and his two 'sons', Martin Junior and Martin Senior. These left-wing Puritan productions were printed on a secret press which moved about the country to avoid the pursuit of the authorities. Five of them appeared in the name of Martin Marprelate, and they are generally known by the following abbreviated titles: the *Epistle*, printed in Mrs Crane's house at East Molesey in October 1588; the *Epitome*, printed in Sir Richard Knightley's house, Fawsley House, Northamptonshire, in November 1588; *Mineral and Metaphysical Schoolpoints*, printed in John Hales's house, White Friars, Coventry, in February 1589; *Hay any Work for Cooper*, printed also at White Friars in March 1589; and the *Protestation*, printed in Roger Wigston's house, Wolston Priory, without his knowledge but with his wife's connivance, in September 1589. The remaining 2 of the Marprelate Tracts, issued respectively in the names of each of Martin's 'sons', appeared between *Hay any Work for Cooper* and the *Protestation*. They are generally known as *Theses Martinianae* (Martin Junior), printed at Wolston Priory in July 1589; and the *Just Censure and Reproof* (Martin Senior), printed also at Wolston Priory at the end of the same month. The tracts are a mixture of theological argument against episcopacy in the reformed Church of England and scurrilous abuse of individual bishops and defenders of the established ecclesiastical order, abuse difficult to counter because often based upon regrettable fact and because so racily written as to undermine the dignity of the defenders of the establishment. The immediate occasion, for instance, of the appearance of the tracts was the publication of a learned *Defence of the Government Established in the Church of England for Ecclesiastical Matters* (1587) by John Bridges, Dean of Salisbury, and the Dean's style evoked Martin's damaging merriment, 'His stile is as smooth as a crabtree cudgell.' The best of the answers to the Marprelate Tracts, in fact, was not the work of any scholar but of Thomas ◊ Nashe, almost certainly the author of the anti-Martinist tract, *An Almond for a Parrot* (1590), in which the typically Martinist invective is turned against Martin.

There has been much speculation as to the identity of the author or authors who influenced Nashe's mature style and who can claim to rank very high among Elizabethan satirists. The major contenders for the honour have been John Penry, the Welsh Puritan apologist; Job Throckmorton, Puritan, Member of Parliament for East Retford, 1572–83, and for Warwickshire, 1586–7; and Sir Roger Williams, a Welshman, friend of Essex, and one of the most famous soldiers of the time. A collection of documents bearing on the Marprelate Controversy, consisting notably of testimonies before the authorities by various people suspected of being implicated in the affair, and vital for any examination of the authorship problem, has been made by E. Arber (*An Introductory Sketch to the Martin Marprelate Controversy*, 1875). Arber supports the candidature of Penry and Throckmorton as authors of the tracts. The claim for Throckmorton alone is made by W. Pierce (*An Historical Introduction to the Marprelate Tracts*, 1908), who also deals at length with their historical context.

An interesting argument for a divided authorship and an attempt to identify Martin Marprelate with Sir Roger Williams, Martin Junior with Penry and Martin Senior with Throckmorton occurs in 2 articles by J. Dover Wilson ('Martin Marprelate and Shakespeare's Fluellen', *The Library*, 3rd ser., vol. 3, 1912). The most recent defence of Penry's sole authorship is by D. J. McGinn (*John Penry and the Marprelate Controversy*, Rutgers U.P., 1966). [DELC]

The M. Tracts, ed. W. Pierce (1911).
The Works of Thomas Nashe, ed. R. B. McKerrow (1910) (vol. 5 for introduction to tracts and the M. affair); A. F. Scott Pearson, *Thomas Cartwright and Elizabethan Puritanism* (1925); T. L. Summersgill, 'The Influence of the M. Controversy upon the Style of Thomas Nashe', *SP*, XLVIII (1951).

Marryat, Captain Frederick, R.N. (1792–1848). Naval writer and novelist. Born in London, the son of a West India merchant. After a career in the navy he retired in 1830 as a post-captain and C.B. Many of Marryat's novels are largely autobiographical, dealing with the 'old navy' in tales of adventure, set in the various parts of the world in which he served, with some historical matter added. In this he follows on from ◊ Smollett. Marryat writes a competent, sometimes loose prose and tells a tale straightforwardly with a plain moral message (*The Lord of the Flies* by William ◊ Golding might be considered an antidote to his kind of fiction). He has a taste for the grotesque and gruesome, and a broad humour which made his works survive as boys' stories after they had declined from being considered serious fiction. In some of them he advocated several serious reforms in the naval service. The best-known of his sea-stories are *The King's Own* (1830), *Peter Simple* (1834), *Jacob Faithful* (1834), *Mr Midshipman Easy* (1836) and *Masterman Ready* (1841, etc.). Marryat also had an old-fashioned, rather 'gothick' interest in the supernatural (*The Dog Fiend, or Snarley-yow*, 1837; *The Phantom Ship*, 1839). He wrote a long-famous historical children's story, *The Children of the New Forest* (1847). His *Diary in America* (1839; ed. J. Zanger, 1960), published after quite extensive travel, is an interesting (if critical) picture of early American manners and society. Marryat's novels are found in many editions. [AR]

Novels, ed. R. B. Johnson (26 vols., 1929–30).
C. Lloyd, *Captain M. and the Old Navy* (1939);
V. Woolf, 'The Captain's Death Bed', in *The Captain's Death Bed and Other Essays* (1950);
O. Warner, *Captain M.: A Rediscovery* (1953).

Marsh, Sir Edward (1872–1953). Editor of ◊ *Georgian Poetry*. Educated at Westminster and Cambridge, Marsh entered the Civil Service and in 1905 became Sir Winston Churchill's private secretary. He developed an interest in modern poetry mainly through his friendship with Rupert ◊ Brooke, with whom he planned the first volume of *Georgian Poetry* (1912). A wealthy man, he used his money and influence to publicize the anthology, sharing the profits among the contributors. His paternal attitude and his narrow, dogmatic view of literature helped to earn him, not unjustly, D. H. Lawrence's description 'a policeman of poetry', and a knighthood in 1937. His published works include *Rupert Brooke: A Memoir* (1918) and *A Number of People* (1939). [PJK]

Christopher Hassall, *E.M.* (1959); Robert H. Ross, *The Georgian Revolt 1910–1922* (Southern Illinois U.P., 1965).

Marston, John (1576–1634). Dramatist and poet. The son of a prosperous lawyer, he went from Brasenose College, Oxford, to the Middle Temple in 1595, at a period of great intellectual brilliance in the life of that institution. He was in residence there throughout his brief literary and theatrical career, which coincided with the deliberate rejection of the Elizabethan and Petrarchan poetic traditions in favour of a mode derived from the Roman satirists. In 1598 he published *The Metamorphosis of Pygmalion's Image, and Certain Satires*, the title-poem of which is a burlesque (possibly unintentional) of the conventional Ovidian love-poem. *The Scourge of Villanie* (1598, enlarged 1599) consists of 10 fiercer verse-satires which express genuine philosophical convictions. Even before the Order of the Conflagration of 1599 legally suppressed the writing of verse-satires Marston had probably already turned to the theatre, for his didactic comedy *Histrio-mastix, or the Player Whipped* (possibly revised from an older play) was performed about this time by the child actors of St Paul's. Its satirical portrayal of Jonson is supposed to have enraged Ben himself and intensified the dramatic feud known as 'The War of the Theatres'.

Jack Drum's Entertainment and *Antonio and Mellida* (both acted by the boys of Paul's, c. 1600) are burlesques of standard lovers-in-distress plays, but *Antonio's Revenge* (1601), though a sequel, is a first attempt at tragedy, a revenge play somewhat akin to ◊ Kyd. The comedy *What You Will* preceded Marston's most famous and popular play, *The Malcontent*, acted by boys in 1603 and by the adult company at the Globe in a revised text in 1604. Though comic in its outcome, the action centres on revenge themes, and the play is notable for its sardonic, even grotesque tone. Marston's other plays are *The Fawn* (1604), the vivid London comedy *Eastward Ho!* (written in 1605 in collaboration with Chapman and the now reconciled Jonson), the bawdy *Dutch Courtesan* (1605), and *The Tragedy of Sophonisba* (1606), a play uncharacteristic of its author, and much admired by T. S. Eliot. He seems also to have been part-author with William Barksted of *The Insatiate Countess*, as well as sole writer of occasional entertainments like the City's pageant for King James and the King of Denmark in 1606.

Marston was briefly imprisoned for unknown reasons in 1608 but may already have renounced the theatre. He returned to Oxford in 1609 to study for the priesthood, was ordained, and was a country clergyman for twenty-five years, before retiring to London in 1631. The difficulties of Elizabethan satire for the modern reader (see the books below by Kernan and Peter) are such as to make him little read today, but *The Malcontent* remains important and *The Dutch Courtesan* has been acted by the National Theatre (1964). [MJ]

The Plays, ed. H. H. Wood (3 vols., 1934–9); *The Poems*, ed. A. Davenport (1961).
A. Caputi, *J.M.*, *Satirist* (1961); T. S. Eliot, 'J.M.', in *Selected Essays* (enlarged edn, 1951); P. J. Finkelpearl, *J.M. of the Middle Temple* (1969); B. Gibbons, *Jacobean City Comedy* (1967); A. Kernan, *The Cankered Muse: Satire of the English Renaissance* (1959); J. Peter, *Complaint and Satire in Early English Literature* (1956).

Martin, Violet. ◊ Ross, Martin.

Martineau, Harriet (1802–76). Moralist, economist, journalist and novelist. Born in Norwich, the daughter of a manufacturer of Huguenot extraction and the sister of the Rev. Professor James Martineau, a well-known Unitarian minister and scholar. As a child she was deaf and very delicate, and started to write at a young age. When her father's affairs became embarrassed, she turned professional, as a writer of religious works: *Devotional Exercises for the Use of Young Persons* (1823; enlarged 1832) and *Addresses with Prayers and Original Hymns for the Use of Families* (1826). She became interested in the developing science of economics, and became well known as the writer of popular fiction to illustrate her theories (and propound her notions of social reform); *Illustrations of Political Economy* (9 vols., 1832–4), for instance, contains stories, sometimes lively, under titles like 'Life in the Wilds', 'A Manchester Strike' and 'Sowers not Reapers'; *Poor Laws and Paupers Illustrated* (4 parts, 1833–4) was a similar collection. She followed the ideas of James ◊ Mill and Ricardo. Martineau wrote travel books, e.g. *Society in America* (1837), which has interesting passages on slavery; *Retrospect of Western Travel* (1838); and *Eastern Life, Present and Past* (1848); as well as 2 novels, less didactic than her stories, *Deerbrook* (1839) and *The Hour and the Man* (1841), a historical romance about Toussaint L'Ouverture. Later in life she lost her Christian faith, and published a translation and abridgement of Comte's *Philosophie positive* (1853) as well as anti-religious periodical articles. The only works now read of her output are some children's stories from the collection *The Play Fellow* (1841), chiefly 'Feats on the Fiord'. Her whiggish *History of England during the Thirty Years' Peace* (1815–45) (1849) is still consulted, as is an *Autobiography* (published posthumously by M. Chapman, 1877). [A R]

T. Bosanquet, *H.M.* (1927) (with bibliography); R. K. Webb, *H.M.: A Radical Victorian* (1960); J. B. Rivlin, 'H.M.: A Bibliography of Separately Printed Books', *Bulletin of the New York Public Library*, L (1946).

Marvell, Andrew (1621–78). Poet, parliamentarian and pamphleteer. He was the son of a moderately conformist clergyman. From Hull Grammar School he proceeded to Trinity College, Cambridge (1633), where he took his B.A. in 1638/9; but (after, it is said, a short-lived conversion to Roman Catholicism) he went down from Cambridge in 1641 without a higher degree. At the outbreak of the Civil War in 1642 he did not commit himself to either side, and he spent four out of the next seven years travelling on the continent. The commendatory verses he contributed to ◊ Lovelace's *Lucasta* (published 1649), and his elegy on Lord Hastings (in *Lachrymae Musarum*, 1649) suggest that round about the year of the execution of Charles I, Marvell was keeping Royalist company and entertaining Royalist sympathies. By the summer of 1650, however, he was able to see Cromwell as an instrument of divine justice, and possibly a good man ('An Horatian Ode upon Cromwell's Return from Ireland'), and within a year he had been appointed tutor to Mary, daughter of the recently retired Parliamentary general Lord ◊ Fairfax. Marvell spent two years in Fairfax's house at Nun Appleton (Yorkshire), and undoubtedly wrote a number, perhaps many, of his poems there. In 1653 he was being recommended by Milton for the post of Assistant Latin Secretary to the government; and though he did not obtain this appointment until 1657, he spent the intervening years as tutor to a ward of Cromwell's. His political sympathies were now entirely with Cromwell and the Commonwealth (see his poem 'The First Anniversary of the Government under Oliver Cromwell', 1655). In 1659 he was elected to Parliament as member for Hull, a seat which he held until the end of his life. We do not know whether he supported the Restoration (though we know that in 1659 he was opposed to the republicans); at all events he exerted some influence to obtain Milton's release from prison, and he was sufficiently reconciled to the new regime to act as secretary to an embassy to Russia, Sweden and Denmark. His correspondence with his constituents shows him as a conscientious Member of Parliament, but does not reveal much about the way he voted; but he spoke repeatedly, and strongly, in favour of religious toleration, and this was the cause that most preoccupied him in his later years. His main political activity, however, was outside Parliament: he became a writer of satires and controversial tracts. He had already displayed satiric talent earlier ('Fleckno, an English Priest at Rome', 1645 or 1646; 'Tom May's Death', 1650; 'The Character of Holland', probably 1653); now his most elaborate verse satire, 'Last Instructions to a Painter' (1667), depicts financial and sexual corruption at court and in Parliament, the country's unpreparedness for war, and its general mismanagement. A later satire, 'A Dialogue between the Two Horses' (1675; not proved to be by Marvell), comes close to advocating armed rebellion. In prose, Marvell's first major publication, *The Rehearsall Transprosed* (1672), supports the King's policy of religious toleration and violently attacks Samuel Parker for opposing the toleration of dissent. (*The Second Part of the Rehearsall Transprosed*, 1673, is a more purely personal attack on Parker.) Another enemy of toleration, Francis Turner, is held up to ridicule in *Mr Smirke: or the Divine in Mode* (1676), while the increasing absolutism of the King's rule, and indeed the whole political history of England since the Restoration, is bitterly described in *An Account of the Growth of Popery, and Arbitrary Government* (1677). It was as a champion of liberty and a master of controversial prose (he influenced Swift, for example) that Marvell was remembered in the 18th century.

The great majority of Marvell's poems however remained unpublished until 1681, three years after his death, when they appeared in folio as *Miscellaneous Poems*. This volume contains, in the main, shorter pieces, including love lyrics or poems about love, complimentary pieces, pastorals and near-pastorals such as the 'Damon the Mower' poems on the one hand and 'The Garden' on the other, dialogue poems on secular and religious topics, and religious lyrics. Though these poems are difficult to classify exactly, the genres to which most belong are of the less serious kind, and their forms generally suggest that they are a fairly 'light' or at any rate informal though elegant kind of poetry. Yet even the 'slightest' of Marvell's lyrics consists of a carefully composed argument, where new points are raised and controverted, line by line. It is this 'dialectical' rigour that provides Marvell's link with Donne and Jonson. Unlike Donne, however, Marvell seldom makes his argument depend on sophistries; his paradoxes and hyperboles generally serve only to give additional complexity to an argument that can actually stand up without them. 'The Definition of Love', which is an exception to this generalization, is Marvell's most Donne-like poem in its imagery too (astronomy, cartography and geometry provide the vehicles of his conceits here); in general, however, Marvell's images are drawn from those realms in the physical world which poets have conventionally utilized – the world of flowers, gardens, birds and so on (see, for example, the roses and lilies of 'The Nymph Complaining for the Death of her Fawn'). Yet one of the pleasures Marvell's poetry provides is the teasing complexity of meaning which he manages to impart to quite simple, even conventional, images. Although the surface 'argument' of most of Marvell's poems can generally be worked out without too much difficulty it is not always easy to be sure just what point of view Marvell is actually advancing; this is partly because of his habit of using expressions with powerful religious and other associations. In 'The Nymph Complaining' for example there seem to be allusions to the crucifixion; and the 'Mower' poems allude to the biblical phrase 'All flesh is grass'. The question arises how exactly one is to take such hints. Do they imply the existence of a coherent allegorical meaning in the poem? Do they have a locally symbolic significance without implying anything about the meaning of the remainder of the poem? Or do they merely serve to enrich the poem by being, in a general way, mysteriously suggestive? These questions have exercised the more recent critics of Marvell. All critics, however, would agree that Marvell manages to combine passion with formality, lightness of touch with seriousness, and lyric beauty with intelligence of argument. [TG]

The Poems and Letters, ed. H. M. Margoliouth (2nd edn, 2 vols., 1952); *Poems*, ed. H. Mac-Donald (Muses' Library, 1952) (with 1681 poems but not the satires); *Poetry and Prose*, ed. J. H. Summers (New York, 1961); *Complete Works*, ed. A. B. Grosart (4 vols., 1872–5) (contains collected prose).
P. Legouis, *A.M., Poet, Puritan and Patriot* (1965; abridged and revised edn of French original, Paris, 1928); M. C. Bradbrook and M. G. Lloyd Thomas, *A.M.* (1940); J. B. Leishman, *The Art of M.'s Poetry* (1966); R. Wallerstein, *Studies in Seventeenth-Century Poetic* (Madison, 1950); M.-S. Røstvig, *The Happy Man*, i (Oslo, 1954); H. E. Toliver, *M.'s Ironic Vision* (New Haven and London, 1965).

Masefield, John (1878–1967). Poet, critic and romantic novelist. He was awarded the Order of Merit in 1935 and was Poet Laureate from the death of Robert Bridges in 1930 up to his own death. Masefield's reputation suffered a little because of the extreme copiousness of his production, with its concomitant risks of unevenness and looseness of form, but at his best he was a remarkably vigorous and inventive writer both in prose and verse, and was probably the only poet of this century who has made a serious attempt at the realistic long narrative poem. He was particularly fascinated by the sea, of which he had practical experience as a young man, and a poem like *Dauber* (1913) is remarkable both for its realistic detail of life at sea and its acute probing into the psychology of the frustrated artist, with the true urge, but without the technical gift. *The Everlasting Mercy* (1911) attracted much attention when it was first published by its frankness of speech and its sympathetic but unglamourized picture of the life of the country labourer, and *Reynard the Fox* (1919) is a vivid and often surprisingly successful attempt to revive the manner, and the series of character portraits, of Chaucer's prologue to *The Canterbury Tales*. Among Masefield's plays, *The Tragedy of Nan* (1909) is a distinguished essay in poetic naturalism and *The Tragedy of Pompey the Great* (1910) a gallant effort to carry on from the tradition of Shakespeare's great Roman plays. Masefield's short book on Shakespeare, in the Home University Library, is, incidentally, one of the best short studies. Masefield was less successful in the short poem, and after he became Poet Laureate was too conscientious in celebrating royal and official occasions; but a number of his short poems, like 'Sea Fever', are favourite anthology pieces, and in their simplicity and directness make a particular appeal to young readers. [GSF]

Salt-Water Ballads (1902); The Daffodil Fields (1913); Good Friday and Other Poems (1916); Lollingdon Downs and Other Poems (1917); King Cole and Other Poems (1923); A Tale of Troy (1932); Pontus and Other Verse (1936).

Mason, A(lfred) E(dward) W(oodley) (1865–1948). Novelist. Born at Dulwich and educated at Dulwich College and Oxford, Mason began his career as an actor, but soon became an author. From 1895 to 1901 he wrote mainly historical novels, in the style of the nineties, such as *Miranda of the Balcony* (1899), but he followed these with two successes: *Four Feathers* (1902), about Egypt, and *The Broken Road* (1907), about India. From 1906 to 1910 he was M.P. for Coventry, and then he began his classic detective stories, starting with *At the Villa Rose* (1910). The main feature of these stories, besides their wit and ingenuity, is the character of one of the earliest fictional detectives, Hanaud of the Sûreté. Mason served in Naval Intelligence during the First World War and continued writing for the rest of his life, producing over 30 books

and several dramatizations of his own work. One of his later books was *Fire over England* (1936), a successful historical novel for teenagers. [JM]

R. L. Green, *A.E.W.M.* (1952).

Mason, Ronald Allison Kells (1905–   ). New Zealand poet. Born near Auckland, he graduated in Classics from the University of Auckland and has spent most of his life in that city. He was a trade union official from 1945 to 1955, and has otherwise held jobs varying from schoolteaching to landscape gardening. He is a student of Far Eastern politics, the author of an angry study of New Zealand administration in the Cook Islands (*Frontier Forsaken*, 1946), and a frequent contributor to left-wing periodicals.

Mason's earliest poetry had a negligible audience. His insistent sense of community is not unexpected in a poet whose brief editorship of the short-lived periodical *Phoenix* (1932–3) brought out its Marxist sympathies. Mason's unwillingly cynical social poetry takes into account the style and mood of Horace and of A. E. Housman. His recurring use of Christ as a symbol of God's betrayal of man shows an unyielding, often stoical awareness of man's need to 'go it alone'. After the publication of *No New Thing* (1934), Mason's poetry became more strident and less controlled. He has written very little since 1940. He is an accomplished technician who writes with austerity in mainly traditional verse forms, often heightening his effect through the witty adjustment of poetic stress by conversational stress. *Collected Poems* (1962) recalled critical attention to his considerable talent. [PT]

Massinger, Philip (1583–1640). Dramatist. Son of a former don and Member of Parliament in the service of the powerful Herbert family, he left Oxford without taking a degree, and may have been an actor before working from 1613 as a collaborative playwright for Philip ◊ Henslowe. From around 1616 he collaborated with John ◊ Fletcher on some dozen plays later published as Beaumont's and Fletcher's work, as well as writing unaided *The Fatal Dowry, The Woman's Plot, The Duke of Milan, The Unnatural Combat, The Maid of Honour, A New Way* *to Pay Old Debts, The Bondman, The Parliament of Love* and *The Renegado.* He collaborated with Dekker on *The Virgin Martyr.* For fifteen years after Fletcher's death in 1625 he was the principal playwright to Shakespeare's old company, the King's Men, the leading troupe in England, and wrote at least a play a year, sometimes 2, and once 4. These include *The Roman Actor, The Picture, The Emperor of the East, Believe As You List, The City Madam, The Guardian, A Very Woman* and several plays now lost. *The Great Duke of Florence* was played by a rival company. Massinger never approached Fletcher's popularity or success. A prolific and workmanlike author, he wrote in various genres, but his serious plays are nowadays found drab and have not been re-staged. *The City Madam* has some lively satirical comedy at the expense of social pretensions and has a soundly middle-class moral. *A New Way to Pay Old Debts* (1964) contains the villainous extortioner Sir Giles Overreach, a part that strong actors from Edmund Kean to Sir Donald Wolfit have greatly relished, and its popularity as a histrionic vehicle kept it long on the boards of British theatres. P. Edwards has undertaken a full edition. [MJ]

The Plays, ed. W. Gifford (4 vols., 1805; revised 1813, 1840).
R. H. Ball, *The Amazing Career of Sir Giles Overreach* (1939); T. W. Craik, Introductions to *The City Madam* and *A New Way to Pay Old Debts* (1964); A. H. Cruickshank, *P.M.* (1920); T. A. Dunn, *P.M.: The Man and the Playwright* (1957); T. S. Eliot, 'P.M.', in *Selected Essays* (enlarged edn, 1951).

Masson, David (1822–1907). Journalist and biographer of Milton. Educated at Aberdeen and Edinburgh Universities, Masson considered entering the Church, and studied theology under Thomas Chalmers. After some years of hackwork in Scotland, he was introduced to the higher journalism of Victorian London by Carlyle, and became the founder and editor of *Macmillan's Magazine* (1859–67). He succeeded A. H. ◊ Clough at University College, London (1853), and W. E. ◊ Aytoun at Edinburgh University (1865) as Professor of English Literature. His monumental *Life of John Milton* (7 vols., 1859–94), which places Milton in his contemporary context in great detail, remains unsurpassed for exhaustiveness, and his study of William ◊ Drummond

(1873) is also a uniquely full and thorough account. His editions of Milton, Goldsmith and De Quincey, and his literary criticism, have been superseded, but the volumes of reminiscence written in his old age (*Edinburgh Sketches and Memories*, 1892; *Memories of London in the Forties*, 1908; *Memories of Two Cities*, 1911) contain useful information about literary circles in Scotland and London at mid-century. Masson was a champion of women's higher education, and was made Historiographer Royal for Scotland in 1893 in recognition of his work as editor of the *Register of the Privy Council of Scotland* (1880–99). [AI]

Maturin, Charles Robert (1782–1824). Novelist. Born of Huguenot stock in Dublin, where he was educated at Trinity College and took holy orders. He wrote a number of tragedies, of which the most famous was *Bertram, or the Castle of St Aldobrand* (1816), which was admired by Scott and Byron and produced by Kean. He is, however, best known for his novels, combining Irish nationalism (of the kind derived from Maria ◊ Edgeworth), which gives a relish to his pictures of desolation, and a vein of rather chilling gothic horror in the style of Mrs ◊ Radcliffe and 'Monk' ◊ Lewis. *Fatal Revenge* appeared in 1807; others are *The Milesian Chief* (1812) and *Women* (1818). The only survivor is *Melmoth, the Wanderer* (1820) (ed. D. Grant, 1968), which adds to the interests outlined above a neat reworking of the wandering Jew theme (Melmoth sold his soul to the devil in the 17th century, and is still alive), anti-Catholicism and an exotic Indian scene. The novel consists of 6 episodes, in which a human being at the extremity of suffering refuses Melmoth's offer of relief in return for assuming his eternal life. The novel had a powerful European influence: Baudelaire and Poe admired it; Balzac wrote a sequel, *Melmoth réconcilié.* Oscar Wilde after his conviction assumed the pen name of 'Sebastian Melmoth', the martyr and doomed wanderer. [AR]

W. Scholten, *C.R.M. The Terror Novelist* (Amsterdam, 1933); E. Birkhead, *The Tale of Terror* (1921); M. E. Hammond, 'M. and Melmoth the Wanderer', *English* 11 (1956).

Maugham, W(illiam) Somerset (1874–1965). Novelist, short-story writer and playwright. Born in Paris, he was the son of a solicitor at the British embassy. His very early life in a French-speaking society gave him a mastery of that language and he lived in the South of France from 1930. On the death of his parents he was educated by a relative at Whitstable, Kent, and went to King's School, Canterbury, and Heidelberg University. He studied medicine at St Thomas's Hospital, but though he qualified never practised. His experiences as a student in London, his medical training, and the influence of the French naturalistic writers are all seen in his first novel, *Liza of Lambeth* (1897), a naturalistic account of the slums of London; Liza and Jim are factory workers and the story of their unmarried love starts the development of Maugham's anti-chivalric heroes and 'warm-hearted' heroines. In *Of Human Bondage* (1915), Philip, club-footed, failed artist turned medical student is trapped in a triangle with the idealistic Fanny Price (who hangs herself) and the waitress, Mildred. Philip finally settles for whatever life offers. Maugham's view of women here, and with Rosie in *Cakes and Ale* (1930), another picture of early 20th-century London, seems essentially a male fantasy of the ideal lover and mother. Maugham was the master,however, of a sharp observation and anti-romantic pen; he was also opposed to using the novel for 'ventilating every sort of point of view' or 'any theory', so that his social observation was at the mercy of his gifts as a writer. His novels include *The Moon and Sixpence* (1919; opera, 1957), where to Strickland, the artist, love is a disease; *The Painted Veil* (1925), set in China, amid whose health problems the idealistic heroine is allowed to sublimate her power feelings; *The Razor's Edge* (1944) and *Catalina* (1948). Maugham had a considerable success in the 1920s with comedies of manners, derived from Oscar Wilde's gayer and more finished pieces; among Maugham's plays are *The Circle* (1921), *East of Suez* (1922), *The Letter* (1925) and *The Sacred Flame* (1928). Two qualities of Maugham as a writer brought him mastery of the short story: an economical and exact means of fixing the sense of place, often exotic places; and an equally economical skill in realizing the crisis of a story. He has written much magazine fiction and his *Complete Short Stories* appeared in 1951 in 3 volumes. Several films (*Quartet, Trio, Encore*) have been made from combinations of his brilliant tales. *A Writer's Notebook*

(1949) is an interesting glimpse of his travels and an insight into his mind. [A R]

J. Brophy, *S.M*.(WTW, 1952); R. Cordell, *S.M.: A Biographical and Critical Study* (Indiana U.P., 1961); L. Brander, *S.M.: A Guide* (new edn, 1965) (the two latter have bibliographies); R. Maugham, *Somerset and all the Maughams* (1965).

Maurice, (John) Frederick Denison (1805–72). Christian socialist. Born near Lowestoft, the son of a Unitarian minister, he was educated at Trinity Hall, Cambridge. He joined the Church of England, however, and after studying at Oxford took orders in 1834. He was devoted to Christian unity (urged in his *The Kingdom of Christ*, 1837), and attacked any views which he thought divisive. His other main tenet was a belief in a kind of Christian socialism, 'true socialism'. Both these views, put forward eloquently and sincerely, gained him many followers, and his social thinking greatly influenced Charles ◊ Kingsley. Maurice was chaplain to Guy's Hospital and held other London benefices. In 1840 he was appointed Professor of English Literature and History (and later theology) at King's College, London, but was dismissed in 1853 for his unsatisfactory views on the doctrine of Eternal Punishment. His chief theological works were *Theological Essays* (1853 and 1871). He helped to found the Working Men's College, and was its first principal. He was elected Professor of Moral Philosophy at Cambridge (1866). His social views are contained in *Social Morality* (1869) and in articles in *The Christian Socialist* (a periodical which he briefly edited). There is a considerable literature on Maurice and his views. [A R]

Sir J. F. Maurice, *Life and Letters* (1884) (with a bibliography); H. G. Wood, *M*. (1950); A. R. Vidler, *F. D. M. and Company* (1967); S. Rothblatt, in *The Revolution of the Dons* (1968).

Mavor, Osborne Henry. ◊ Bridie, James.

Mayhew, Henry (1812–87). Journalist and social investigator, humorist, dramatist, novelist, author of works of travel and popular instruction. The son of a London solicitor, educated at Westminster School, whence he eventually ran away, Mayhew went to sea and travelled to India before entering his father's office, which, however, he soon quitted to embark on a long, prolific, often penurious, literary career. In

1831 with his old schoolfellow Gilbert à Beckett he started *Figaro in London*, a pungent illustrated weekly that had numerous imitators. In 1834 his *Wandering Minstrel*, a farce enlivened by the famous cockney ballad 'Villikins and his Dinah' – still enormously popular twenty years later – was staged at the Fitzroy Theatre. In 1841, with a group of coadjutors, Mayhew founded *Punch*, but changed financial control quickly led to his being ousted from his co-editorship and in 1846 he severed connexion with the journal, which assumed an increasingly conformist complexion. Mayhew's fame rests on his detailed, intimate and copious reports on the lowest strata of London society, the fruit of innumerable inquiries carried out with remarkable tact, perseverance, acuity and, at times, physical hardihood. The voluminous survey known as *London Labour and the London Poor* began publication in 1849 in the *Morning Chronicle*; the following year it was appearing independently in weekly (two-penny) and monthly (ninepenny) parts and in 1851–2 bound volumes of the collected, uncompleted work were issued. Further publication was interrupted by litigation (though in 1856 Mayhew was issuing a series of similar studies in monthly numbers entitled *The Great World of London*). The first full edition came in 1861–2 in 4 volumes, the first 3 being chiefly reprints of already published work, but the fourth, devoted to professional delinquents, consisting largely of new material. A further edition, more abundantly illustrated, appeared in 1864–5. Meantime *The Criminal Prisons of London*, which he considered his most important contribution, had been published in 1862. In general these socio-logical studies are notably, sometimes confusingly, ill-organized and often betray careless haste. Important sections are explicitly attributed to assistants; yet in some of these it is hardly possible to mistake outcroppings of Mayhew's own characteristically vivid reportage, while there are passages manifestly by other hands in what is supposedly his own composition. At his frequent best his unsentimental sympathy, humour, eye for circumstantial detail, appetite for odd information and, especially, marvellous power of eliciting confidences leave him without rival among contemporary recorders of the facts of urban low-life. His great work remains a chaotic treasure-house for the student of social history. Apart from his London researches Mayhew's most noteworthy book would seem to be his highly readable *German Life and Manners* (1864).

Mayhew was an outspoken advocate of social reform and a trenchant critic of *laissez-faire* doctrine. Even before his death his work had sunk into obscurity and evidently it for long remained almost unknown save to specialists, some of whom were not above pillaging it without acknowledgement. Its revived, enhanced celebrity dates from the later 1940s. [K C]

The Street Trader's Lot, ed. S. Rubinstein, intr. M. D. George (1947) (from *London Labour and the London Poor*); *M.'s London* (1949), *London's Underworld* (1950), *M.'s Characters* (1951), all ed and intr. P. Quennell (extensive selections from *London Labour and the London Poor*); *H.M.*, ed. and intr. J. L. Bradley (World's Classics, 1965) (selections from first 3 vols. of *London Labour and the London Poor*).

Meredith, George (1828–1909). Novelist and poet. Born in Portsmouth, the son of a naval outfitter, Meredith was educated at St Paul's Church School, Southsea, and the Moravian School at Neuwied, Germany. Largely owing to the extravagance of his father, who moved to London in 1841 and to Cape Town in 1849, Meredith did not receive his expected inheritance and in 1845 he was articled to a London solicitor. Soon disappointed with the legal profession he began to earn money as a journalist, publishing poems and articles in various magazines and using his spare time to read widely in classical, German, French and English literature. In 1849 he married Mary Ellen Nicolls, the widowed daughter of Thomas Love ◊ Peacock, and for several years they lived with or near Peacock. It was soon clear that the marriage had been a mistake and in 1858 Mary Ellen left Meredith to bring up their son and went abroad with the painter Henry Wallis. Meredith fully realized that he was unlikely to make a living from literature and for most of his life his basic income came from sources other than his creative writing. In 1860 he began to contribute weekly leading articles to the *Ipswich Journal*, a Tory newspaper holding political views very different from his own, and in the same year he became a reader for Chapman and Hall, in which capacity he encouraged many young authors, most notably Thomas Hardy and George Gissing. During the early sixties he was a close friend of Swinburne and Rossetti and for a while shared a flat with them in London. Meredith's first wife died in 1861 and three years later he married Marie Vulliamy, with whom, after a period spent in Italy as a war correspondent for the *Morning Post*, he moved to Flint Cottage, Box Hill, Surrey, where he lived for the rest of his life.

His first published book, *Poems* (1851), possessed little distinction save for the lyrical beauty of his most famous single poem, 'Love in the Valley', which was rewritten and expanded in 1878. This was followed by 2 prose fantasies, *The Shaving of Shagpat* (1856) and *Farina* (1857). His first characteristic novel, *The Ordeal of Richard Feverel*, which tells the story of an idyllic love affair that is brought to a tragic conclusion by blind adherence to social and educational 'systems', appeared in 1859. It was followed by a more light-hearted, largely autobiographical novel, *Evan Harrington* (1861), which featured two of Meredith's most famous comic characters, 'the great Mel' and the Countess de Saldar. His second volume of poetry, *Modern Love* (1862), was an original and impressive work. Possessing a strength and vigour that is unencumbered by the abstruse philosophizing of his later poetry, it consists of 50 interlocking 16-line 'sonnets' describing the break-up of an unhappy marriage. For the next twenty years Meredith concentrated mainly on fiction, publishing *Emilia in England* (1864), later reprinted as *Sandra Belloni* (1886), *Rhoda Fleming* (1865), *Vittoria* (1867), *The Adventures of Harry Richmond* (1871) and *Beauchamp's Career* (1876), one of the finest political novels in English. Although Meredith longed for popularity he refused to adapt his high intellectual and literary standards to the dictates of the commercial market (a determination strongly re-inforced by his experiences as a publisher's reader), and his novels appealed, then as now, to only a very small public. Few English novelists have been so aggressively poetic as Meredith. A profusion of mythological allusions, elliptical sentences, metaphors and epigrams, and a too-conscious pre-occupation with forming theories (on evolution, masculine egoism, feminism, and the all-embracing power of Nature) often tends to obscure rather than heighten his unique, idiosyncratic genius. All of his novels are notable for their occasional brilliance of wit and social satire,

but only *The Egoist* (1879), the most completely integrated of his novels, can be regarded as an unqualified artistic success. His one critical work, *An Essay on Comedy and the Uses of the Comic Spirit* (1897), first published in the *New Quarterly Magazine*, April 1877, is a classic study of the role of comedy in literature.

With the appearance of *The Egoist* critical opinion turned sharply in Meredith's favour and his home at Box Hill became a literary shrine where young aspiring writers paid homage to the lonely, dedicated artist who had so steadfastly held out against the corrupting forces of commercialism. His next novel, *The Tragic Comedians* (1880), was based on the life of Ferdinand Lasalle, the German Socialist, and in 1885 Meredith achieved his first popular success with *Diana of the Crossways*. Not without a certain amount of deliberate scorn for the reading public that had so long ignored him Meredith allowed full rein to his love of epigram, convoluted sentences, social satire and involved plot patterns, with the result that *One of Our Conquerors* (1891), *Lord Ormont and his Aminta* (1894) and *The Amazing Marriage* (1895) are his most obscure and least satisfactory novels. *Celt and Saxon* was published posthumously in 1910. His later volumes of poetry include, *Poems and Lyrics of the Joy of Earth* (1883), *Poems and Ballads of Tragic Life* (1887), *A Reading of Earth* (1888), *A Reading of Life* (1901) and *Last Poems* (1909). A collected edition of the letters is at present being prepared by C. L. Cline. [PJK]

The Mickleham Edition (19 vols., 1922–4) (novels); *Poetical Works*, ed. G. M. Trevelyan (1912); *Letters*, ed. W. M. Meredith (2 vols., 1912).

R. Le Gallienne, *G.M.: Some Characteristics* (1890); G. M. Trevelyan, *The Poetry and Philosophy of G.M.* (1906); M. B. Forman, *G.M.: Some Early Appreciations* (1909); J. Moffat, *G.M.: A Primer to the Novels* (1909); C. Photiades, *G.M.: His Life, Genius and Teaching* (Paris, 1910; tr. 1913); J. W. Beach, *The Comic Spirit in G.M.* (1911); S. M. Ellis, *G.M.: His Life and Friends* (1919); G. R. Milnes *M. and the Cosmic Spirit* (1925); J. B. Priestley, *G.M.* (1926); A. Woods, *G.M. as Champion of Women and Progressive Education* (1937); S. Sassoon, *M.* (1948); L. Stevenson, *The Ordeal of G.M.* (1954); Walter F. Wright, *Art and Substance in G.M.* (Nebraska, 1953); J. Lindsay, *G.M.* (1956); N. Kelvin, *A Troubled Eden: Nature and Society in the Works of G.M.* (1961); Phyllis Bartlett, *G.M.* (WTW 1963);

M. B. Forman, *Bibliography* (1922); H. Lewis Sawin, 'G.M.: A Bibliography of Meredithiana, 1920–1953', *Bulletin of Bibliography*, XXI (Boston, 1955–6).

Meres, Francis (1565–1647). Antiquarian. Educated at Cambridge, this otherwise obscure clergyman and schoolmaster published in 1598 *Palladis Tamia. Wit's Treasury* (ed. D. C. Allen, New York, 1938), essentially a common-place book in which he had assembled under headings a series of observations, quotations, anecdotes and other lore, running to some 600 pages. In one brief section he lists the great authors of antiquity and patriotically attempts to find English equivalents for each. Shakespeare appears in the listings, and several plays are mentioned by name, as well as 'his sugared sonnets among his private friends'. Meres thus gives valuable proof that the plays named were written by 1598, which helps scholars to determine their dates more accurately. His *critical* comments are quite undiscriminating, and he lumps together as British tragic authors Dr Legge of Cambridge, Dr Edes of Oxford, Marlowe, Shakespeare and many others. [MJ]

G. E. Bentley, *Shakespeare: A Biographical Handbook* (1961).

Merriman, B. ◊ Mac Giolla Meidhre, B.

Mew, Charlotte (1869–1928). Poetess. She had a tragic life and destroyed most of her poems but remains one of the most poignant and true poets of the Georgian period. She was born in Bloomsbury, the daughter of an architect who died young, leaving his four children to struggle with poverty. Two of them spent most of their lives in insane asylums. Her life was a long struggle with poverty, and one of its few happy occasions was a visit to Thomas Hardy, who spoke of her as 'undoubtedly the best woman poet of our day'. She was granted a small Civil List pension in 1923 but the death of a sister whom she had spent much of her energy in nursing destroyed her will to live and, after collapsing and being admitted to hospital, she took poison in 1928. The title poem of her first book, 'The Farmer's Bride', and the best poems of her posthumous volume *The Rambling Sailor* have a detailed exactness that recalls Hardy and a poignancy of feeling which her executor,

Sir Sidney Cockerell, compared to that of Emily Brontë. [GSF]

L. Untermeyer, *Lives of the Poets* (1960).

Meynell, Alice (Christiana Gertrude) (1847–1922). Poet and essayist. She was born in London and spent most of her childhood in Italy. As a young woman she suffered from the female complaint of 'having nothing to do', which led to her conversion to Roman Catholicism at 25 and her first book of verse, *Preludes* (1875). She married Wilfred Meynell in 1877 and their house was always full – of children, friends such as Tennyson, Patmore and Meredith, magazines, articles, poems, and the unhappy poet Francis ◊ Thompson, whom the Meynells had rescued from destitution and drug-addiction. Alice Meynell's work mainly consisted of critical journalism which she wrote for various periodicals including those edited by her husband, for example the Catholic *Merry England* (1883–95); these essays were republished, e.g. in *The Colour of Life* (1896). She also found time to produce 6 books of poetry. After the proclamation of her 'genius' by Patmore, and at the height of her fame in the 1890s, her style changed. Previously it had been the style of a refined, religious, slightly melancholy Victorian lady, but later it became tougher, expressing her distaste for modern life, though still liable to sentimental excesses. Her appeal came largely from the image she presented of poetess and saint: 'Ethereal, rather than very real, she seemed to live with a nimbus of adoration around her', but her essays, which are lively, independent-minded and feminist, go some way towards correcting this impression of sickening piety. [JM]

The Poems (1940); *Prose and Poetry*, intr. V. Sackville-West (1947).

Michael of Northgate (fl. 1340). Scholar. A monk of St Augustine's, Canterbury, and a considerable scholar, to judge by the 25 manuscripts he donated to the library, both religious and scientific. One of them was the holograph of his *Ayenbite of Inwit*, or 'Prick of Conscience' (ed. R. Morris, 1866), a translation in prose of Lorens of Orleans' *Somme des vices et des vertues* (1279). The subject-matter is conventional moral teaching, the translation flat, barren and inaccurate. A few lines of doggerel at the end express Michael's intention to edify 'lewede men'. However, as a precisely dated (27 October

1340) autograph manuscript, with well-marked dialect features, its value to students of the language is obvious. [A G]

Mickle, William Julius (1735–88). Translator and verse-writer. Mickle, a bankrupt Edinburgh brewer, attempted to support himself in London by his writing but had to become a proof-reader for the Clarendon Press. His translation into heroic couplets of the Portuguese national epic, Camões's *Lusiad*, was published by subscription (1771–5) and was very successful financially; a share in the prize-money of a naval expedition and a lucrative marriage enabled Mickle to retire in comfort. Mickle, too, almost certainly wrote the fresh and spirited Scots song 'There's nae luck aboot the house', and his ballad pastiche 'Cumnor Hall' suggested to Scott the subject of *Kenilworth*. [A I]

Poetical Works, ed. J. Sim (1806).

M. E. Taylor, *W.J.M., A Critical Study* (Washington, 1937).

Middleton, Thomas (1580–1627). Dramatist. Son of a quite prosperous bricklayer, he was educated at Queen's College, Oxford, and his early poems, *The Wisdom of Solomon Paraphrased* (1597), *Micro-Cynicon* (1599) and *The Ghost of Lucrece* (1600), are juvenile productions. Like many Elizabethan writers he began his work in the theatre (around 1602) as a writer for Philip ◊ Henslowe, for whom he wrote *The Chester Tragedy* and part of *Caesar's Fall*, as well as a fresh prologue and epilogue for *Friar Bacon and Friar Bungay*. He also wrote scripts for boy companies between 1602 and 1608, mostly comedies with London settings, and his successes included *A Mad World, My Masters, Michaelmas Term* and *A Trick to Catch the Old One*. He collaborated with Dekker on *The Roaring Girl, or Moll Cut-Purse*, and with Rowley on *A Fair Quarrel* (*c.* 1617). He wrote many plays for the adult companies, including the leading troupe of the day, the King's Men, which produced amongst others, *The Witch, Anything for a Quiet Life*, and the phenomenally successful *A Game at Chess*, which in 1624 had the longest initial run of any Jacobean play. A topical anti-Catholic and anti-Spanish piece, the last-named play satirized recent politics in the guise of a chess game, and was suppressed on the Spanish Ambassador's complaint. *A Chaste Maid in Cheapside* (*c.* 1615) is a masterly comedy. *The Changeling*, the work of Middleton's most admired

by modern critics, was written in collaboration with Rowley and acted in 1622. Like his tragedy *Women Beware Women* (*c.* 1625) it vividly dramatizes in blank verse the progressive moral deterioration of a woman who yields to temptation, but its special distinction lies also in the way in which the comic sub-plot enhances and parallels the tragic action. Middleton wrote civic entertainments for the Lord Mayor of London and was appointed City Chronologer.

His best London comedies deserve revival in the modern theatre, and the high placing of his tragedies by critics in the thirties and forties has led to productions of *The Changeling* by Tony Richardson (London, 1961) and Elia Kazan (New York, 1964) and of *Women Beware Women* by the Royal Shakespeare Company (London, 1962). He is sometimes credited with the authorship of *The Revenger's Tragedy*, usually thought of as by Cyril ◊ Tourneur, *The Second Maid's Tragedy*, which survives, without title, in manuscript, and *Hengist, King of Kent*, a tragedy of Saxon times. [M J]

Works, ed. A. H. Bullen (8 vols., 1885).

R. H. Baker, *T.M.* (1958); M. C. Bradbrook, *Themes and Conventions of Elizabethan Tragedy* (1935); T. S. Eliot, 'Thomas Middleton', in *Selected Essays* (enlarged edn, 1951); B. Gibbons, *Jacobean City Comedy* (1967); L. C. Knights, *Drama and Society in the Age of Jonson* (1937); G. Salgādo, Introduction to *Three Jacobean Tragedies* (P E L, 1965) (includes *The Changeling*); S. Schoenbaum, *M.'s Tragedies: A Critical Study* (1955); P. Thomson, Introduction to *The Changeling* (1964).

Mill, James (1773–1836). Historian and utilitarian philosopher. Born at Northwater Bridge in the parish of Logie Pert, in the county of Angus, Scotland, the son of a poor country shoemaker, he was educated at his parish school and Montrose Academy. Under the patronage of a neighbouring landowner, Sir John (Belsches) Stuart of Fettercairn, he studied for the Church of Scotland ministry at the University of Edinburgh and was actually licensed to preach (1798), but, sceptical by temperament and intellectually unfitted for the calling, he went to London in 1802 and became a professional writer. He edited the weekly *London Journal* (1803–5) and was also editor of the *St James's Chronicle*; he published pamphlets, and articles in the *Edinburgh Review* and other dissident intellectual and political journals. At this time commenced his close friendship with and discipleship of Jeremy ◊ Bentham, which was the most important influence on his life. In 1806 he began his *History of British India* (3 vols., 1817; 4th edn, 9 vols., 1948; 5th edn ed. and continued by H. H. Wilson, 10 vols., 1858). This categorical work, with its social and economic speculation, gained him the office of Assistant to the Examiner of Correspondence in the India Office (1819), and by 1830 he was head of the department, exerting some influence on official policy drafting dispatches but keeping his radical views for his English activities. His other works, expounding Bentham's utilitarian ideas, included the *Elements of Political Economy* (1821) and the *Analysis of the Phenomena of the Human Mind* (1829; ed. J. S. Mill, 1869). He was also, with ◊ Brougham and others of a Benthamite group, one of the founders of the London University, and of the *Westminster Review*. His son, John Stuart ◊ Mill, developed many of his ideas by thinking himself out of his father's positions. [AR]

Essays on Government, ed. P. Wheelwright (New York, 1935) (originally written for the *Encyclopædia Britannica*).
A. Bain, *J.M.: A Biography* (1882); M. St J. Packe, *Life of J. S. Mill* (1954); L. Stephen,*The English Utilitarians* (1900; repr. 1950); J. S. Mill, *Autobiography*, ed. J. J. Coss (1924) (contains much about J. M.).

Mill, J(ohn) S(tuart) (1806–73). Philosopher. Born in London, the son of James ◊ Mill, he was a precocious child and was subjected by his father to an education of frightening rigour and extent, following Benthamite principles; by the time he was 14 he had studied most of the important Greek and Latin authors as well as logic, economics and history. His literary tastes were quite ordinary. In 1823, he formed a Utilitarian Society for debating. In the same year, he was given a clerkship at India House, under his father, and he pursued this career, which gave him leisure to write, with success; he retired in 1858 as chief of the Examiners' Office, with a salary of £2,000 a year. In 1824, he started publishing articles in the *Westminster Review*, the organ of the Utilitarians, and his father pressed him into service in writing, editing and publishing the works of Bentham and others of that circle, chores which he did not get rid of until his father's death in 1836. In 1826, Mill had suffered a mental (and spiritual) crisis, involving severe depression. This recurred

in 1836. After the first of these experiences, he gradually moved away from the narrow 'calculating' speculation of the old Utilitarians. He became interested in the feelings, and in Wordsworth, Coleridge, Saint-Simon and Auguste Comte. Mill is a key figure in the change from the old rationalism of the Enlightenment (personified by ◊ Bentham) to the Romantics' renewed interest in mysticism and the emotions. He phrases the conflict neatly in 2 essays published in the *Westminster Review*, on Bentham (1838) and on Coleridge (1840) (see F. R. Leavis, *M. on Bentham and Coleridge*, 1950). In 1830, the year of the revolution in France, Bentham visited Paris. His observations further modified his philosophical and political principles. He wrote much for newspapers, and a series of essays *The Spirit of the Age* (ed. F. A. Hayek, Chicago U.P., 1942) in *The Examiner* brought him the friendship of ◊ Carlyle, but the two men were uncongenial, quite apart from Mill's celebrated accidental destruction of the manuscript of Carlyle's *French Revolution*. After the Reform Bill was passed and the Whigs became conservative, Mill worked to establish a real radical party. He helped to run the *London and Westminster Review* for this purpose and owned the paper from 1836 to 1840. In 1843 he published his *System of Logic, Ratiocinative and Inductive* (reprinted 1930), in which he theorized on the construction of scientific 'laws' and theories. In 1844 appeared his *Essays on Some Unsettled Questions of Political Economy* (reprinted 1949), which had been written about 1830 out of discussions with his father; it was followed in 1848 by his influential *Principles of Political Economy*, which is based on the work of Ricardo, and is in part an attempt to discuss the growth in size and importance of the working class. In 1851 he married his friend, the invalid Harriet Taylor, on the death of her husband; this friendship, which he valued highly in his intellectual development, had the sanction of Harriet's husband but caused scandal. It obviously influenced one of Mill's most important works, *The Subjection of Women* (1869; World's Classics, 1912). His other chief writings are: *On Liberty* (1859); *Considerations on Representative Government* (1860); and *Utilitarianism* (1863) (all published in Everyman, 1950). There is much of interest, not all of a technical nature, in *Dissertations and Discussions* (I and II, 1859; III, 1867; IV, 1875).

Mill's greatness lies in the power and

eloquence with which he fuses political and social thought. The power comes from his old sense of the tension between rationalism and the feelings. *On Liberty* is the fine flower of the noble liberalism which the 19th-century thinkers developed. His works were of vital importance in enhancing the value placed on individual action and judgement, a value affirmed by the century's poets and novelists. Mill was sharp in analysis and lucid in exposition. He had a prophetic power in nosing out the issues that have become important. In 1865 he was elected to Parliament for Westminster, but was defeated in 1868, because he could not please enough of his supporters by his actions. He died at Avignon. [A R]

Collected Works, ed. F. E. L. Priestley (Toronto, 1963–).
M. St J. Packe, *Life of J.S.M.* (1954); F. A. Hayek, *J.S.M. and Harriet Taylor: Their Correspondence and Subsequent Marriage* (U. of Chicago P., 1957); M. Cranston, *J.S.M.* (W T W, 1958) (with bibliography); R. P. Anschutz, *The Philosophy of J.S.M.* (1953); K. Britton, *J.S.M.* (1953); R. L. Heilbroner, *The Worldly Philosopher* (New York, 1953) (on his economics); W. L. Davidson, *Political Thought in England: The Utilitarians from Bentham to J.S.M.* (Home University Library, 1915); T. Woods, *Poetry and Philosophy: A Study in the Thought of J.S.M.* (1961); M. Cowling, *M. and Liberalism* (1963); E. Alexander, *Matthew Arnold and J.S.M.* (1965) (with bibliography); E. Halévy, *The Growth of Philosophic Radicalism* (New York, 1953); L. Stephen, *English Utilitarians* (3 vols., 1900); J. Plamenatz, *English Utilitarians* (1949); B. Willey, *Nineteenth Century Studies* (1949); J. Hamburger, *Intellectuals in Politics: J.S.M. and the Philosophic Radicals* (New Haven, 1965); S. R. Letwin, *The Pursuit of Certainty: Hume, Bentham, M. and Beatrice Webb* (1965); D. Hascall and J. M. Robson, 'Bibliography of Writings on M.', *Mill News Letter*, 1 (1965–).

Miller, Hugh (1802–56). Scottish essayist and geologist. A seaman's son, Miller grew up in the Highland port of Cromarty and, rejecting formal education, was apprenticed to a stonemason and worked in many parts of the Highlands and in Edinburgh. His descriptive newspaper articles led to his being employed by a bank in Cromarty (1834) and having attracted nation-wide attention with a pamphlet arguing the case for the popular election of ministers in the Church of Scotland (1839) Miller settled in Edinburgh in 1840 to edit the *Witness*, the newspaper of the anti-patronage party and later (when the dispute had split the Church of Scotland) of

the Free Church. His newspaper pursued a moderate policy during the bitter fanaticism of the later 1840s, and in particular Miller argued against perpetuating sectarian differences by the introduction of denominational schools. Worn out by ecclesiastical squabbles and by pneumoconiosis contracted while he was a stonemason, he broke down and shot himself. Miller's autobiography, ironically called *My Schools and Schoolmasters* (1854), his *First Impressions of England and Its People* (1847) and his *Scenes and Legends of the North of Scotland* (1835) are still of considerable interest, while the collected volumes of *Essays* (1862) and *Leading Articles* (1870) represent the political, social and religious attitudes of an independent-minded Scottish Whig of the period. *The Old Red Sandstone* (1841), based on first-hand observation in Highland quarries and glens, was a substantial contribution to the developing science of geology. In the related controversy over evolution Miller's attempt at reinterpreting the biblical account of the Creation to fit the geological evidence (*Footprints of the Creator*, 1849, in reply to R. ◊ Chambers's *Vestiges of Creation*) satisfied neither party but disseminated the terms of scientific discussion among orthodox churchmen, raising the level of later argument. [A I]

P. Bayne, *Life and Letters of H.M.* (1871); W. M. Mackenzie, *H.M., a Critical Study* (1905).

Millin, Sarah Gertrude (1889–1968). South African novelist and historian. Born in Cape Province. Failing eyesight prevented an academic career, and she became a music teacher. Her first novel, *The Dark River* (1920), was followed more significantly by *Adam's Rest* (1922), *God's Stepchildren* (1924) and *Mary Glenn* (1925), to form the first considerable body of realistic fiction in South African English literature. Millin's husband, a Judge of the Supreme Court of South Africa, died in 1952, and in the same year she was awarded an Honorary D. Litt. by Witwatersrand University for her work in the field of history. She is the author of a history of South Africa, *The South Africans* (1934), and the biographies, *Rhodes* (1933) and *General Smuts* (1936), about whom she also wrote 13 short radio plays and a full-length one. The 6 volumes of her war diaries came out between 1944 and 1948.

Of the rest of her work *No Longer Mourn*, produced in London in 1935, is a play based on *Mary Glenn*, and *Two Bucks Without*

Hair (1957) a collection of short stories. The last of her 16 novels was *The Wizard Bird* (1962). It shows a continuing interest in and knowledge of the byways of African customs, but there is a marked decline in narrative strength. [PT]

The Measure of My Days (1955) (autobiography). J. P. L. Snyman, *The Works of S.G.M.* (1955).

Mills, Martin. ◊ Boyd, Martin A'Beckett.

Milman, Henry Hart (1791–1868). Poet and historian. Born in London, the son of Sir Francis Milman, the fashionable physician, and educated at Eton and Brasenose College, Oxford. He took orders and was successively incumbent of St Mary's, Reading, Rector of St Margaret's, Westminster (1835), and Dean of St Paul's (1849). Milman's verse tragedy, *Fazio* (1815), in the then popular 'Elizabethan' vein, had some success at Covent Garden in 1816. He followed this with 3 'dramatic poems' on Bible stories, of which the most popular was *The Fall of Jerusalem* (1820), and a fourth, *Anne Boleyn* (1826). He is chiefly remembered as a historian, for his *History of the Jews* (3 vols., 1829; 2 vols., Everyman, 1909); *The History of Christianity to the Abolition of Paganism in the Roman Empire* (3 vols., 1840) and *The History of Latin Christianity . . . to Nicholas V* (6 vols., 1854–5). Milman wrote a readable prose, and possessed adequate learning for his task; he was in addition a 'liberal' in theology, and his attempts to 'rationalize' the miracles led him into hot water with his co-religionists, and difficulties in harmonizing his views with the Jews' notions of their own history. His *Annals of St Paul's Cathedral* appeared in 1868. [AR]

C. H. E. Smyth, *Dean M.* (1949).

Milne, A(lan) A(lexander) (1882–1956). Essayist, versifier and children's writer. He was the third son of John Vine Milne, a hardworking schoolmaster who ran a private school, Henley House, which his sons attended, in Mortimer Road, Kilburn, now Mortimer Crescent, St John's Wood. Alan was inseparable from his elder brother Kenneth, who was considered to be the writer of the family. H. G. Wells taught science for a time at their father's school. In 1893 Kenneth, and later Alan, who was the youngest recorded Queen's Scholar, went to Westminster School, and their father's school

moved to Westgate-on-Sea. Alan, who had been a precocious mathematician, now took things easy.

On leaving school Alan went to Trinity College, Cambridge, where he edited *Granta* and took a third-class degree. He spent the next three years writing freelance in London, and had had articles and verses accepted by *Punch* and the *St James' Gazette*, when in 1906 he became assistant editor of *Punch*, to which he now contributed every week. His first book of essays, *The Day's Play*, appeared in 1910, and was followed by *Not That It Matters* (1919) and *The Sunny Side* (1921). During the war he fought in France, and also wrote 2 comedies, *Wurzel-Flummery* (1917) and *Belinda* (1918). His first big success was with the play *Mr Pim Passes By* (1919). He also published 2 novels, *The Red House Mystery* (1922) and *Two People* (1931). His son Christopher Robin was born in 1920, and Milne showed a new talent for writing verse for children in *When We Were Very Young* (1924) and *Now We Are Six* (1927). These, and the 2 books he wrote about his son's toy animals, *Winnie-the-Pooh* (1926) and *The House at Pooh Corner* (1928), are nursery classics. Pooh and his friends are gentle caricatures of human character and habits of mind. The mood, as in all Milne's work, is relaxed and happy; his verses for children have none of the clouds or apprehensions that creep into Robert Louis Stevenson's poems, nor do his essays mirror the struggles of their times. Milne was no serious writer, but excelled in using words with light, nimble grace and joyous craftsmanship. [TV]

It's Too Late Now (1939) (autobiography)
R. L. Green, *Tellers of Tales* (1946) (short section only).

Milnes, Richard Monckton (Lord Houghton) (1809–85). Poet and patron. Born into a wealthy Yorkshire family, Milnes was educated at Trinity College, Cambridge, where he became a member of the 'Apostles' together with ◊ Tennyson and ◊ Hallam. Ambitious for literary or political fame, he published his first volume of poetry, *Memorials of a Tour in Some Parts of Greece* (1833), and became Tory M.P. for Pontefract in 1837. By 1844 he had published a further 4 volumes of poetry, including *Poetry for the People* (1840) and *Palm Leaves* (1844). In 1846 on the fall of Peel's government he changed his political allegiance and served Pontefract for a further seventeen years as a

Whig. His one remembered literary work, *Life, Letters and Literary Remains of John Keats* (1848), was the first published biography of Keats, and was influential in reviving interest in the poet's work during the second half of the 19th century. It was now apparent to Milnes that he was unlikely to succeed as either a poet or politician and he turned his attention to cultivating friendships with the great and aspiring literary men of his time. The parties he held at Fryston Hall, his Yorkshire home, became famous for bringing together distinguished English, European and American writers. Milnes himself was justly renowned for his wit, kindness to struggling writers and vast collection of erotica. His intense yearning for a peerage was finally rewarded in 1863, but not before Swinburne had dubbed him 'Baron Tattle of Scandal'. [PJK]

Sir Thomas Wemyss Reid, *Life, Letters and Friendships of R.M.M.*, *Lord Houghton* (2 vols., 1890); James Pope-Hennessy, *M.M.* (2 vols., 1949).

Milton, John (1608–74). Poet and pamphleteer. Born in London, son of a prosperous scrivener who, Milton later claimed, 'destined [him] from a child to the pursuits of literature'. He attended St Paul's School, where he was much influenced by the Christian humanist curriculum originally devised by Colet and Erasmus and where the headmaster, Alexander Gill, illustrated his explanations of the structure of English by quotations from English poets. He was thoroughly trained in Latin and Greek and in addition had private tuition in Hebrew from a Scottish divine, Thomas Young. He proceeded to Christ's College, Cambridge, in 1625, where he rebelled against the conservative curriculum and pleaded for the study of history, geography, 'the manners of men', physics and astronomy. He was already dedicated to poetry, and produced both skilful Latin elegiacs in Ovidian style and a number of English poems including paraphrases of Psalms, partly in the style of Joshua Sylvester's *Divine Weeks and Works*, and an 'Ode on the Death of a Fair Infant', in an Elizabethan rhetorical style which echoed Phineas Fletcher as well as Ovid. He also wrote Latin poems in Horatian metres, and a mock-epic Latin poem on the gunpowder plot. In 1627 he concluded a Latin 'vacation exercise' delivered before the young men of his college with an eloquent English poem in rhymed couplets hailing his native English language and asserting his resolution to become an English rather than a Latin poet. The following year he produced a group of sonnets in Italian apparently professing his love for an Italian singer called Emilia. He took his B.A. in 1629, but stayed at Cambridge until 1632. He celebrated Christmas 1629 with his first really important poem, 'On the Morning of Christ's Nativity', a brilliant baroque account of the Nativity and its significance consisting of an introduction followed by a hymn. A companion poem, 'The Passion', was left uncompleted, and a third in this religious group, 'Upon the Circumcision', while technically interesting as deriving from a Petrarchan form of *canzone*, is of no great merit. More significant is the sonnet on Shakespeare prefixed to the Second Folio of 1632, which combines Jonsonian formality, personal feeling and a sustained metaphysical conceit. A poem (1631) on the death of Hobson, the university Carrier, shows a mild metaphysical wit, and the 'Epitaph on the Marchioness of Winchester' of the same year shows a controlled lapidary style of real charm. The companion poems 'L'Allegro' and 'Il Penseroso', probably written during a vacation before he finally left Cambridge after taking his M.A. in 1632, are skilfully stylized pictures (in octosyllabic couplets) of the cheerful man and the contemplative man set in appropriate scenery.

After Cambridge, Milton retired to his father's estate in Horton, Buckinghamshire, to prepare himself by a comprehensive course of study and contemplation for the career of poet to which he had long been dedicated. The obvious career in the Church for a man of his parts was perhaps declined by him as a result of his already highly critical views of the Anglican clergy. The short poems 'On Time' and 'At a Solemn Musick' (the product of either his late Cambridge or early Horton days) show the influence on his poetic technique of his reading of Italian poetry. The latter reflects Milton's life-long interest in music and a fascination with the Pythagorean and Platonic notion of the harmony of the spheres. This musical interest led to Milton's being asked to produce *Arcades*, 'part of an entertainment presented to the Countess Dowager of Derby at Harefield' for which Henry Lawes wrote the music. The Elizabethan tone of courtly compliment which Milton captured with great elegance and beauty in these songs and verse recitations shows him master of an aristocratic form of entertainment, though, on his second such commission, the masque *Comus* presented at Ludlow Castle in 1634 on the occasion of the Earl of Bridgewater's inauguration as Lord President of Wales, he gave the masque form a deeper ethical content than was usual in this kind of formal art. A dramatic poem in the Elizabethan masque tradition, Christian in feeling with Platonic overtones, having as its main theme the praise of chastity, *Comus* modulates through a variety of keys and shows real skill in the mutual confrontation of different attitudes. The evil enchanter Comus, whose hedonistic philosophy is expressed in some of Milton's most attractive verse, is in some respects a first sketch for Satan in *Paradise Lost*. Milton already knew that evil can be persuasive. The final English poem of Milton's early period is 'Lycidas', a pastoral elegy written in 1637 on the death of his former fellow-student Edward King. This cunningly wrought, careful-mannered poem reworks an old European tradition and succeeds in combining the objective demands of a special kind of set piece, an attack on the corrupt Anglican clergy, the Christian conclusion of confidence in heavenly consolation, and a deep personal feeling about the predicament of dedicated and talented youth (like himself) in an uncertain world.

In April 1638 Milton set off on a journey intended to be the climax of his long self-preparation as a poet. He intended to visit both Italy and Greece, but he never got to Greece as he was recalled to England in August 1639 by the outbreak of the English Civil War. His stay in Italy left a deep and permanent impression on him; he charmed the Italians by his learning and his desire for literary friendships; among the Italian friends he made was Giovanni Batista Manso (who had been Tasso's patron), to whom he wrote a Latin poem in which he discussed his own high poetic ambitions. On arriving home he found that his old schoolfellow and close friend Charles Diodati had died. He had looked forward to talking with Diodati about his Italian experience and confiding in him about his plans to write poetry; the deep frustration produced by his death led him to write the Latin elegy *Epitaphium Damonis*, a more directly personal elegy than 'Lycidas' and an important source for our knowledge of Milton's state of mind at this time.

The Civil War drastically changed Milton's career. He became involved in the great controversy about Church government, as his old tutor Thomas Young had been one of the Puritan preachers engaged in anti-episcopal pamphleteering; it was in Young's defence that Milton published, anonymously, his first prose pamphlet, *Of Reformation Touching Church-Discipline in England* (1641). This was soon followed by other anti-episcopal pamphlets, including *Of Prelatical Episcopacy, The Reason of Church-Government Urg'd against Prelaty* (the first to be published under his own name) and *An Apology against . . . Smectymnuus* (1642). The main thought running through these pamphlets is the incompleteness of the English Reformation and the necessity of now bringing it to glorious completion. A sense of high personal excitement is conveyed in the urgent and sometimes passionate prose, and occasionally, especially in a notable passage in *Of Reformation in England*, Milton broke out of the historical and theological argument to present an excited picture of his own ambitions as the poet of a new, great, truly reformed England. The special kind of Protestant patriotism that flashes out from these pamphlets, though highly personal in expression and feeling, is in a tradition of English Protestant thought.

On his return from Italy Milton had settled in 'a pretty garden-house' in Aldersgate Street, London, and took in pupils. In 1645 he published his first volume of poems, containing most of what he had written so far. Probably in the spring of 1642 he precipitately married Mary Powell, 16-year-old daughter of an Oxfordshire royalist family. For long dedicated to chastity because of his high ideal of marriage as providing both intellectual, spiritual and sexual companionship, Milton quickly discovered the basic incompatibility between himself and this flighty young girl; Mary soon returned to her parents, though in 1645 a reconciliation was effected and she came back to Milton; they lived together until her death in 1652. The tremendous emotional shock of the failure of his marriage led Milton to examine the whole Christian doctrine of marriage and divorce and to write a series of pamphlets on divorce (1643–5) in which he argued that the function of marriage was true companionship in every sense and if it failed to serve that function divorce should be allowed. He was more successful in this argument than in proving that it represented traditional Christian doctrine. The divorce pamphlets brought Milton into conflict with the censorship imposed by Parliament in 1643, and this in turn produced his *Areopagitica* (1644), one of the most eloquent and passionately urged pleas for the freedom of the press ever written. In 1644 he published his treatise *Of Education*, a humanist programme for the training of an élite. Milton's increasing disillusion with the Presbyterians and sympathy with the Independents brought him closer to the group whose political thinking was radically anti-monarchist. *The Tenure of Kings and Magistrates* (1649) defended the rebellion against Charles I by means of an argument about the rights of the people against tyrants: kings and magistrates were put in authority over the people to enforce justice and the keeping of covenants; if they failed in this, their power could and should be revoked by the people for whom they held it in trust. Milton's later pamphlets in defence of Cromwell's government, written in Latin for a European audience, eventually involved him more and more in fierce personal abuse with pamphleteers abroad who had been horrified by Charles's execution and increasingly looked on Milton as its chief public defender. The result was a new vein of spiteful personal abuse in Milton's prose (giving back what he got) as well as a number of important personal passages in which he defends himself by citing his own autobiography and ambitions. In the middle 1640s Milton also began an elaborate Latin work, *De Doctrina Christiana*, developing his often somewhat original views on Christian doctrine, but this was not published until 1825.

In March 1649 Milton was appointed Latin Secretary to the Council of State (or Secretary of State for Foreign Tongues), so that his Latin pamphlets defending those who executed Charles were in a sense official publications. He had already begun to grow blind, and by 1652 was totally blind. In that year he was deprived of his official chambers in Whitehall but given an assistant; he moved to a house in Petty France, Westminster. On Cromwell's death in 1658 Milton resumed his pamphleteering with *A Treatise of Civil Power in Ecclesiastical Causes* (1659), arguing against any kind of supreme religious authority. A further pamphlet on the same subject followed. Just before the Restoration, with the political

situation fluid again, Milton wrote his last political pamplet, *The Readie and Easie Way to Establish a Free Commonwealth* (1660), using for the last time 'the language of that which is not called amiss *The Good Old Cause*'. Thirteen years later he turned again to pamphleteering to argue, in *Of True Religion*, in favour of individual freedom of interpretation of God's word.

Milton wrote sonnets at intervals during the period of his political pamphleteering, and these sometimes reveal an attractive, informal side of his character. Verses of compliment, invitation or advice show him using the sonnet form with great skill and versatility with techniques he had learned from Italian sonneteers, especially Della Casa. Among his sonnets are also poems of personal indignation and of public protest, the notable example of the latter being 'On the Late Massacre in Piedmont' (1655). In the middle and later 1640s Milton also worked on a *History of Britain*, in which we can trace his change of mood from one of national celebration to one of indignation and frustration. His frustration was complete with the Restoration; all his political hopes were now ended for ever and the great new reformed England to which he had dedicated his life had now to be found only in the 'Paradise within', not in the world of public affairs. The disillusion with public life is reflected in everything that Milton subsequently wrote.

At the Restoration Milton escaped the vengeance of the returned Royalists and returned to private life to work on the epic of man's fall which he had long meditated and which at one time he had considered writing not as an epic but as a tragedy. He married again in 1656, happily, Catherine Woodcock, who died in 1658; in 1662 he married Elizabeth Minshull and moved to what is now Bunhill Row, where he spent his remaining years a distinguished but isolated figure though not without friends and visitors from both home and abroad. *Paradise Lost* appeared in 10 books in 1667 and in a revised edition in 1674 divided into 12 books. It is the only completed successful epic in English, a treatment of the Fall ostensibly so as to 'justify the ways of God to men' but in fact so as to illuminate the paradoxes and contradictions of man's condition and the currents of hope, despair and chastened resolve that stirred in Milton's own breast. It is written in a blank verse which is not the sustained 'organ voice' traditionally ascribed to Milton but is rather a flexible and often dramatic medium in which conflicting attitudes and points of view can be powerfully projected. It is true that Milton's Latinized language and his preference for suggesting scenes and situations by massively abstract terms have been criticized by those who believe that the best poetic language should not be stylized and that all good poetic imagery must be precisely visualized and 'imagist'. It is true also that his special kinds of stylization had an unfortunate effect on the language of some more ambitious kinds of poetry in the 18th century, notably in certain kinds of 'Miltonizing' poets. But Shakespeare, too, had a paralytic effect on those who tried to imitate him, and a poet's greatness is not judged by his successful imitability. The portrait of Satan, the great debate in Hell in Book II, the picture of the prelapsarian Adam and Eve in the primeval garden, the beautifully managed changes in tone and language when Adam and Eve converse *after* the Fall and the equally beautifully managed account of their moral recovery, are some of the finest things in the epic. More traditional epic properties, such as the war in Heaven, are less successful, and Michael's account of future world history in the final books is sometimes tedious. Milton does not succeed in resolving the theological questions he thought he was resolving – man's responsibility for the Fall and God's benevolence and justice in punishing it with such dire consequences – and his picture of the Christian scheme of redemption is perfunctory and quite incapable of countering the mood of gloom about human destiny which creeps into the later books. The true, if unadmitted, hero of the epic is not God, still less Christ, and not Satan, in spite of the romantic view that Milton was really 'of the Devil's party': it is Adam, man, who faces a world he never made amid all the horrors involved in his own nature with dignity and resolution. The final lines of the poem express with peculiar beauty this combination of gloom and chastened hope – despair mutating into resolution.

Paradise Regained (published together with *Samson Agonistes* in 1671) is an altogether slighter work, often deliberately spare in language. The theme is Satan's temptation of Christ. Satan is given the high, rhetorical language and Christ the simple sometimes almost deliberately bathetic speech: the temptation to public life, rhetorical and political success, and external power is set against the virtues of patience, private life and the cultivation of an inward confidence in God's ultimate purpose. The last line of the poem, 'Home to his Mother's house private return'd', shows Jesus resisting all temptation to dedicate himself to showy public gestures and reflects Milton's own complete disillusion with public life, of which he once had such high hopes. *Samson Agonistes* is the final phase of the biblical story of Samson and Dalila cast in the form of a Greek tragedy. It opens with Samson already blind and a prisoner of the Philistines, and the action is simply a series of confrontations between Samson and various visitors in the course of which his state of mind turns from near-despair to resignation to God's will for him, culminating in his allowing himself to be taken to the Philistine festival where, acting under divine inspiration, he pulls down the temple and destroys the audience and himself. The final action, shown off-stage, is reported to Samson's father who sees 'no time for lamentation' in the news, asserts that 'all is best, though we oft doubt', and concludes in 'calm of mind all passion spent'. The true theme of the play is Samson's moral recovery. Comment on God's justice in spite of the difficulty of reconciling it with man's fate is made at intervals by the chorus, who also comment on Samson's state of mind. Samson's visitors in prison are first his father, who does not help Samson by taking up an 'I told you so' attitude, then his treacherous wife Dalila, who in a scene of great sexual tension convincingly argues that she delivered Samson to the Philistines not so that he should be hurt and imprisoned but that he should be delivered back to her, shorn of his hair and supernatural strength, for her to love and cherish as 'mine and love's prisoner, not the Philistines''. Samson's agonized repudiation of this degenerate version of the Courtly Love view of the lover's bondage to his mistress is a high point of the play. Then the Philistine champion Harapha comes to taunt Samson and exult over him, in an effectively rendered swaggering speech; Samson replies with calmness and dignity, a sign of his progress towards moral recovery. Finally, the Philistine officer enters to summon Samson to come before the Philistine lords at their pagan feast; after contemptuously declining, Samson realizes that this must be God's plan for him, and consents. The return of Samson's father fatuously confident that he can secure his son's release brings a note of false hope into the tragedy before the news of Samson's heroic death brings it to its appropriate conclusion. Milton's original and flexible handling of a kind of free verse in this play in scenes of doubt or passion or choric questioning is very impressive: Samson's great lyric cry 'O dark, dark, dark, amid the blaze of noon' is one of the high spots of English poetry. The movement from chant to cry to speech and back to chant in Samson's language is skilfully handled. Among the models for the play are the Book of Job, Sophocles's *Oedipus at Colonus* and Aeschylus's *Prometheus Bound*.

The attack on Milton as a fatal influence in English verse, begun by T. S. Eliot and continued by F. R. Leavis, has produced a great deal of argument pro and con, little of which gets down to the reality of Milton's kind of poetry and his use of language. The argument has been complicated by the introduction of the question of Milton's Christian orthodoxy and of the viability of his views about God.

Among the innumerable editions of Milton, the most complete is the 'Columbia Milton' (general ed. F. A. Patterson, 20 vols., 1931–40) and the most fully annotated the 'Yale Edition' of the prose (general ed. Don M. Wolfe, 1953 ff.; still in progress). H. Darbishire's 'Oxford Edition' (2 vols., 1952) of the poems aims at providing the text that Milton would have given us if he had not gone blind; her 1-volume edition of the poems (1961) is a reprint from the printed copies produced in Milton's lifetime. Meritt Y. Hughes's 1-volume *Complete Poems and Major Prose* (1957) is helpfully annotated for students, while F. A. Patterson's *Student's Milton* (revised edn, 1936) collects in one volume all the poetry (in the original spelling), much of the prose, text and translations of the Italian, Latin and Greek poems, early biographies of Milton, and an introduction and notes. Another useful student's edition of the poetry is H. F. Fletcher's 'New Cambridge Edition' of 1941. [DD]

J. H. Hanford, *J.M.*, *Englishman* (1950) (biography); W. R. Parker, *M.: A Biography* (2 vols., 1966) (standard modern Life); J. H. Hanford, *M. Handbook* (4th edn, 1946); E. M. W. Tillyard, *M.* (1930) (good introductory account); D. Daiches, *Milton* (1957, 1961) (primarily a critical study of the works in chronological order); F. R. Leavis, *Revaluation* (1936) (contains an attack on M.); C. S. Lewis, Preface to *Paradise Lost* (1942) (in some degree an answer to Leavis); A. J. A. Waldock, *Paradise Lost and Its Critics* (1947) (attacks both Lewis and Tillyard); B. Rajan, *Paradise Lost and the Seventeenth Century Reader* (1947), J. B. Broadbent, *Some Graver Subject* (1960), W. Empson, *M.'s God* (1961) (represent three different modern approaches to M.'s epic, the last highly idiosyncratic and immensely provocative); C. Ricks, *M.'s Grand Style* (1963) (a defence of his use of language); E. M. Pope, '*Paradise Regain'd': The Tradition and the Poem* (1947), F. M. Krouse, *M.'s Samson and the Christian Tradition* (1949) and C. A. Patrides, *M. and the Christian Tradition* (1966) (helpfully show some of the traditional materials M. was working with); F. T. Prince, *The Italian Element in M.'s Verse* (1954) (a model study of its kind); *The Living M.*, ed. F. Kermode (1960) (collection of modern essays on M. which shows the range and interests of modern Milton critics); D. H. Stevens, *Reference Guide to M.* (1930) and Calvin Huckabay, *J.M.: A Bibliographical Supplement 1929–1957* (1960) (on Milton scholarship and criticism).

Minot, Laurence (fl. 1330–50). Poet. Eleven poems in a northern dialect by Minot are extant in which he mentions himself twice. Probably contemporary with the events they describe, they celebrate Edward III's victories over the Scots and French in unashamedly jingoistic fashion and with a notable anti-Scots bias. Though this nationalistic feeling is characteristic of the period, Minot is a political hack, and his effusive praise of Edward may not always reflect popular sentiment. He handles various stanza forms in a brisk and forthright style, in spite of a fondness for superfluous tags. [AG]

Poems, ed. J. Hall (1914).

Miracle Plays. Plays presenting saints' lives and biblical events which flourished in later medieval Europe. Known of in England from the 12th century, they flowered during the 14th and 15th centuries in the cycles presenting the whole biblical scheme and developing as a communal activity in certain towns, of which 4 survive: the Chester, York and Wakefield cycles, and the N. town cycle, often called (from a mistaken attribution to Coventry) *Ludus Coventriae*.

Their origins are liturgical. The Mass,

dramatic in itself since involving a community in the recalling of Christ and His life, was by the 5th century associated with the annual sequence commemorating His birth and acts. Ceremonies presenting the events of the festival days developed (e.g. the 10th-century amplification or trope, *Quem quaeritis*, at the Easter introit, which presents the three women meeting the angel at Christ's tomb). These gave rise to little plays performed independently of the services, at first in Latin, later in English. Possibly their increasing popularity is connected with the tendency in western Europe to exclude the laity from active participation in the drama of the Mass: their urge to participate in, place themselves in relation to, celebrate and witness the events of redemption found this other expression. The confirmation in 1311 of the Feast of Corpus Christi seems to have given the cycles an impetus: they were normally performed on that day, and much has been made by some scholars of its importance as celebrating not one redeeming event, but the whole act of salvation mediated by the Mass, and hence suggesting the drawing together of the plays from their separate festivals. As a summer festival it also gave opportunity of good weather for open-air performance: and in the procession of the Host, with which the plays were associated, it gave an example of elaborate pageantry. The cycles were sometimes performed at Whitsun also. Each play was the responsibility of a guild. At York, for example, these guilds included the Tanners, Plasterers, Card-makers, Fullers, Gaunters or glovers, Shipwrights, Fishers and Mariners – responsible for *Noah and the Ark*; Bookbinders, Goldsmiths – *The Three Kings*; Butchers – *The Crucifixion*; Mercers, Ostlers, etc.). They were presented each on a separate pageant wagon at various stations in the town. But the cycles (except perhaps the N. town) were written for the whole community: they are colloquial, simple at least on the surface, and deliberately unsophisticated, though the very sophisticated King Richard II went to York to see its cycle in 1397.

Their origins give them certain peculiar features. They present the whole of time in its significance as the establishment of salvation and epiphany of God's scheme through the battle of good and evil, from the Creation and Fall of the angels till judgement day: but (as with the Mass) they centre on the great epiphany of the incarnation in Christ, Old Testament events being anticipations, preparations and figures of this, and they have a dual dramatic time and place – the historical and the present. The union between the two is expressed, sometimes clearly deliberately, by anachronisms and spatial displacements (the Wakefield *Nativity* takes place both at Bethlehem and near Wakefield): their true time and place is that of the ever present act and offer of salvation. They have thus five aims: to entertain and instruct simply: to represent the events they depict as histories; to be transparent to them as epiphanies; and to involve the audience in them as always relevant. They therefore unite the sublime and heavenly with the secular and everyday. Good, as the manifestation of God (e.g. in the Creation), has archetypal grandeur and the fate of Christ is presented with agonizing pity and appeal. Evil, with its root in pride, is violent, chaotic and comic (compare their Lucifer, Cain and Herod with Milton's Satan, Byron's Cain and Marlowe's Tamburlaine). Ordinary people (e.g. Joseph, or the shepherds of Bethlehem) are realistic, often incapable, but always involved (to their own amazement) in the infinite designs of God.

Of the four cycles, Chester's is the earliest, dating traditionally from 1327–8, though much worked over later: it survives in a number of manuscripts of the late 16th century. It is also the cycle most simply concerned to be a 'servant of the Word', straightforwardly outlining the whole scheme. It occupied three days, and was last played in 1575.

York's is the fullest. First mentioned in the city's memorandum book in 1387, it contains 48 plays listed in a manuscript of *c*. 1475. All were performed on a single day, the first, appropriately containing God's creation of light, at 4.30 a.m. They are by various hands, roughly in three periods of construction. The middle period is dominated by a distinguished metrist playwright and also by a realist author who has something in common with the Wakefield Master, although not such a great writer. The cycle was last presented in 1569 and the register was later confiscated by Archbishop Grindall. It was triumphantly revived in 1951 as part of the Festival of Britain, when its relevance to the mortal comedy proved timeless.

The Wakefield or 'Towneley' plays (so

called because the manuscript was preserved in the library of John Towneley, 1731–1813, of Towneley Hall, Lancs.), 32 in number, are contained in a register dated *c.* 1485, and are closely connected with the York cycle. They are remarkable for the contributions of the single great playwright known as the 'Wakefield Master', who added *Noah*, *Pastores I* and *II*, *Magnus Herodes*, the *Buffeting* and perhaps part of *Cain and Abel*: all are written in swift, exciting two-stressed lines which hurry the action along. The author's outlook is harsh and realistic, and both pietistic flummery and social pomp are threatened by his satire. *Pastores II* is the famous comedy of Mak, who steals a sheep and persuades his wife Gill to hide it in a cradle disguised as a new-born child. The shepherds discover the deception, laugh at the hoax and toss Mak in a blanket. Their romping over, they hear angels telling of another strange birth – the Redeemer's. (Both children are addressed as *little daystar*, probably an example of figural symbolism: the daystar signifies the time of salvation.)

The N. town cycle survives in a single manuscript, perhaps of 1468. It is more overtly learned and theologically conscious than the other three, and is possibly the reworking of an earlier cycle for private reading.

A number of individual plays from other sources survive (e.g. *Abraham and Isaac* in a commonplace book from Brome Manor in Suffolk, and two genuinely from Coventry). Alongside the cycle plays grew up other forms, such as the *Play of the Sacrament*, concerning miracles performed by the Host on a Jew who tries to destroy it, and notably the allegorical morality, of which the most striking examples are ◊ *Everyman* and *The Castell of Perseverance*. All disappeared during the 16th century, partly under governmental pressure as being popishly associated, partly from such causes as a Puritan dislike of acting God or Christ, the waning of the sense of the figural pattern of history, and the restoration of the laity Bible-reading and a part in the liturgy. Old Testament plays (e.g. Milton's *Samson Agonistes*) continued to be written; and Jacobean drama probably inherits from the miracle plays its concern to see justice prevail and its free combination of the sublime and the everyday. But all four of the cycles will stand on their own merits as religious expression and as drama. [RB]

E. K. Chambers, *The Medieval Stage* (2 vols., 1903); H. Craig, *English Religious Drama of the Middle Ages* (1955); V. A. Kolve, *The Play Called Corpus Christi* (1966); M. Roston *Biblical Drama in England* (1968); K. Young, *The Drama of the Mediaeval Church* (1933). *Everyman and Medieval Miracle Plays*, ed. A. C. Cawley (1956); *The Chester Plays*, ed. H. Deimling and G. W. Matthews (2 vols., 1892, 1916); *The York Plays*, ed. L. Toulmin Smith (1885); *The Wakefield Cycle of Mystery Plays*, ed. and tr. M. Rose (1961); *The Wakefield Pageants in the Towneley Cycle*, ed. A. C. Cawley (1958); *Ludus Coventriæ*, ed. K. S. Block (1922); *The Non-Cycle Mystery Plays*, ed. O. Waterhouse (1909); *The Macro Plays*, ed. F. J. Furnivall and A. W. Pollard (1904); *Ten Miracle Plays*, ed. R. G. Thomas (Northwestern U.P., 1968).

Mitchell, James Leslie. ◊ Gibbon, Lewis Grassic.

Mitchison, Naomi Margaret (Lady) (1897–1964). Novelist. Born in Edinburgh, the daughter of Professor J. S. Haldane, an eminent physiologist, she married G. Richard (Baron) Mitchison, a barrister and Labour politician. She was educated at the Dragon School, Oxford, and (as a private student of science) at the University there. In 1937, she went to live at Carradale in Kintyre, where she was active in local politics. She abandoned her scientific interests for novel writing, and wrote various kinds of fiction. Among her most popular novels were historical tales (chiefly of ancient Greece and Rome) marked by rather detailed domestic particularity, such as *The Conquered* (1923), *When the Bough Breaks* (1924), *Cloud Cuckoo Land* (1925) and *Black Sparta* (1928). She also wrote romances of Viking times, such as *The Swan's Road* (1954) and *Karensgaard* (1961), and fantasies of the past and future: *The Corn King and the Spring Queen* (1931) and *Memoirs of a Space Woman* (1962). She was the author of political works, poems (*The Laburnum Branch*, 1926), a play (*Spindrift*, for the Glasgow Citizens' Theatre, 1951), biographies (*Socrates*, 1937, with R. H. S. Crossman; and *Anna Comnena*, 1928) and stories and history-books for children. [AR]

Mitford, Mary Russell (1787–1855). Poet and novelist. Born at Alresford, Hampshire, the daughter of a country doctor whose extravagance ruined the family. She supported them by writing. She is remembered for her fiction, principally *Our Village: Sketches of Rural Life, Character and Scenery* (those in the first volume first appeared in the *Lady's Magazine*) (5 vols., 1824–32; ed. Lady Ritchie, 1893). These are early examples of the amiable, detailed, loosely connected, dryly humorous sketches of country life so successfully exploited by women writers such as Mrs ◊ Gaskell in England and Sarah Orne Jewett in America. Other tales include *Belford Regis, or Sketches of a Country Town* (3 vols., 1835) and *Atherton, and Other Tales* (3 vols., 1854). She also wrote tragedies such as *Julian* (1823), *Foscari* (1826) (reminiscent of Byron's) and *Rienzi* (1828), which was fairly popular on the stage. Her poems (some narrative) are forgotten, but her *Recollections of a Literary Life* (3 vols., 1852) and various volumes of letters contain some handy information pleasantly put down. [AR]

W. J. Roberts, *M.R.M.*, *The Tragedy of a Blue Stocking* (1913); V. G. Watson, *M.R.M.* (1949).

Mitford, Nancy (Freeman) (1904–   ). Novelist and biographer. Born in London, the daughter of the second Baron Redesdale. The family is related to that of Swinburne. She was educated privately and in 1933 married Peter Rodd, brother of the second Baron Rennell. She has written several novels: after a few 'indifferent' books in the thirties, *The Pursuit of Love* (1945) became extremely successful. She went to live in Paris and wrote *Love in a Cold Climate* (1949) and *The Blessing* (1951). She is a master in rendering the conversation of upper-class English eccentrics which, presented in dialogue (without comment), gives a picture of the society she has made her territory. Her farcical situations show her a comic writer of some expertise. With A. S. C. Ross, she edited a volume of essays, *Noblesse Oblige: An Enquiry into the Identifiable Characteristics of the English Aristocracy* (1956). This volume contained excellent illustrations by Osbert Lancaster, and though far too slight to be of more than humorous value, provoked a tedious (and snobbish) cult of labelling (chiefly speech) characteristics as 'U' (upper class) and 'non-U'. Miss Mitford's own contribution (like her essays in *The Water Beetle*, 1962) was enhanced by skilful and fresh personal recollection or observation. The comments, however, do not bear generalization. She has also written lively biographies, such as *Mme de Pompadour* (1954), *Voltaire in Love*

(1957) and *The Sun King* (1966); and published several translations from the French. Her version of André Roussin's *The Little Hut* was a West End theatrical success in 1953. [AR]

Mittelholzer, Edgar Austin (1909–65). West Indian novelist. Born in British Guiana of Swiss, German and Negro extraction. He reacted strongly against the cultural restrictions of his middle-class colonial environment. In the discursive *With a Carib Eye* (1958) he relates the fear of confinement that lies behind his restlessness. He joined the Trinidad Royal Navy in 1941. His first novel, *Corentyne Thunder* (1941), was largely destroyed in the blitz, and, because of publishing difficulties and active discouragement of his writing, he left for England in 1948 to work for the British Council.

Morning at the Office (1950) began the great decade of the West Indian novel. It is a realistic picture of routine life in a Trinidadian society divided by subtle gradations of race and colour. Mittelholzer's output was varied and prolific. *Shadows Move Among Them* (1951), with its sense of the oppressive Guianese forest, was dramatized and produced in New York as *Climate in Eden*. The Guianese trilogy, *Children of Kaywana* (1952), *The Harrowing of Hubertus* (1954) and *Kaywana Blood* (1958), is a detailed family chronicle of early colonial life. He portrayed both urban and peasant life, wrote thrillers (*Tinkling in the Twilight*, 1959; *Eltonsbrody*, 1966), exploited the macabre and the comic and explored a Wagnerian 'leitmotif' theory of drama, narrative and poetry in the novel (*Latticed Echoes*, 1960; *Thunder Returning*, 1961). His own stated prerequisites for the novel are 'theme, characterization, atmosphere with the over-shadowing sovereignty of "Story Interest"'. [WAG]

A Swarthy Boy (1963) (autobiography).

Moir, David Macbeth, known as Delta (Δ) (1798–1851). Scottish fiction and verse writer. A doctor near Edinburgh, he contributed voluminously in prose and verse to *Blackwood's Magazine*, edited the poems of Mrs ◊ Hemans and wrote on local antiquities. His *Life of Mansie Wauch, Tailor in Dalkeith* (ed. T. F. Henderson, 1902) was printed as a series of sketches in *Blackwood's* from 1824, and as a volume, with extra material and with its Scots passages considerably anglicized, in 1828. It coarsens the humorous realism of John ◊ Galt's fiction into a ludicrous caricature of Scottish small-town life, and begins the dissociation between Scottish writers and the day-to-day life of the country that culminates in the work of the ◊ 'Kailyard' novelists at the end of the 19th century. [A1]

Poetical Works, ed. with a memoir by T. Aird (1852).

Monro, Harold Edward (1879–1932). Poet. Better known as an editor and anthologist than for his own minor, though occasionally distinguished, work in verse. As a poet, he was on the whole typically 'Georgian', subdued and conversational in tone, dealing pleasantly and vividly with slight topics, like a cat's lust for milk. T. S. Eliot, however, in his introduction to Monro's *Collected Poems*, posthumously published in 1933, noted an unusual depth and painfulness in some late poems written out of experience in hospital. As editor of *Poetry Review* and later of *Poetry and Drama* and as owner of the Poetry Bookshop, Monro showed an admirable catholicity of taste and a wide human sympathy in encouraging and bringing together all sorts of poets, many of them, like Eliot and Pound, not at all of his own sort. His disinterested care for poetry as such militated, as often happens, against his own poetic reputation, and he lost a good deal of money over the Poetry Bookshop, where he often provided free quarters for poor poets. [GSF]

Poems (1906); *Children of Love* (1914); *Trees* (1916); *Real Property* (1922); *Elm Angel* (1930). Jay Grant, *H.M. and the Poetry Bookshop* (1967).

Montagu, Mrs Elizabeth (1720–1800). Prose writer. The original blue-stocking. She was born Robinson, the daughter of a Yorkshire country gentleman, and married Edward Montagu, the grandson of the 1st Earl of Sandwich. The *salons* which she held at her London houses in Hill Street and Portman Square brought her fame as a patron of the arts, without biting too deeply into her vast fortune. These gatherings, and similar meetings held by Mrs Vesey, Mrs Ord, and Mrs Chàpone, were rather pale imitations of the French society women's *salons* (see Boswell, *Life of Johnson*, under 1781, for a description of a meeting). Dr Johnson admired her conversation. She

'defended' Shakespeare against the strictures of Voltaire in her *Essay on the Writings and Genius of Shakespeare* (1769), but unfortunately for her influence and reputation as a critic she backed the poetry of James ◊ Beattie and Lord ◊ Lyttelton. The latter allowed her to add 3 pieces to his *Dialogues of the Dead* (1760). She wrote letters (ed. M. Montagu, 4 vols., 1809–13; ed. J. Doran, 1873; ed. E. Climenson, 2 vols., 1906; ed. M. Wyndham, 2 vols., 1924) which illustrate various literary fashions of the time, such as an interest in 'scenery'. Her own opinion of her influence was high. [AR]

Mrs M., '*Queen of the Blues*'. *Her Letters and Friendships from 1762 to 1800*, ed. R. Blunt (2 vols., 1923).
R. Huchon, *Mrs M.* (1906); C. B. Tinker, *The Salon and English Letters* (1915); K. G. Hornbeak, 'New Light on Mrs M.', in *The Age of Johnson: Essays Presented to C. B. Tinker* (New Haven, Conn., 1949).

Montagu, Lady Mary Wortley (1689–1762). Letter-writer. Born in London, the eldest daughter of Evelyn Pierrepont, 5th Earl and 1st Duke of Kingston, she received a good education at home. She was elected a toast of the Kit-Cat Club. In 1712, against her father's refusal of permission, she married Edward Wortley Montagu, the brother of a friend, an M.P., and a friend of Addison. On the accession of George I, Montagu held various political offices, and with his wife frequented the court. She also cultivated the friendship of wits and writers, including Pope, who eagerly accepted her flattering offers of acquaintance on terms of equality. In 1716, Montagu was appointed Ambassador to the Sublime Porte. She accompanied him to Constantinople, travelling overland by way of Vienna. She stayed in Turkey until June 1718, returning by sea. Her letters provide an excellent and lively account of what she observed there, including the Sultan's harem. In England, she was a prominent 'society' woman and engaged in intellectual pleasures and struggles. She fell out with Pope about 1723 over a cause which is obscure, and she thereafter turns up, not in complimentary verses, but as 'Sappho' in the *Dunciad* and in other satires. After an unhappy love affair, though still on friendly terms with Montagu (who became a miser), she lived abroad from 1739, in various Italian cities and in Avignon, until urged by her daughter, the Countess of

Bute, she returned to England in 1762. She died of cancer at her daughter's house in that year. As a letter-writer, she deals with a great variety of subjects: her feelings; her travels; scientific investigations, including the value of innoculation, which she introduced to England from Turkey; literature; and politics. She is alert, witty on occasion, and intelligent; an easy and fluent writer. With Lord ◊ Hervey she collaborated in some flat satirical verse. [AR]

The Complete Letters, ed. R. Halsband (3 vols., 1966); *Letters*, ed. R. B. Johnson (Everyman, 1906); *The Letters and Works*, ed. Lord Wharncliffe, revised with a memoir by W. May Thomas (2 vols., 1861).
R. Halsband, *The Life of Lady M.W.M.* (1956).

Montague, C(harles) E(dward) (1867–1928). Journalist and novelist. Montague was born in London of an Irish family, and was educated at the City of London School and Oxford University. In 1890 he joined the staff of the *Manchester Guardian*, and, except for a period of war service, remained there for thirty-five years, becoming chief leader-writer and dramatic critic. On the outbreak of war in 1914 he dyed his hair to help conceal his age and enlisted as a private soldier. He was commissioned in 1916 and served in France as an Intelligence Officer. Like so many other writers Montague's early enthusiasm for the First World War was rendered bitter by personal experience, and the books which made his name – *Disenchantment* (1922), war memoirs; *Fiery Particles* (1923), short stories; and *Rough Justice* (1926), a novel – explore, with impressively restrained cynicism, the changing structure of English society before and during the war. Other published works include, *A Hind Let Loose* (1910), *Dramatic Values* (1911), *The Right Place* (1924) and *A Writer's Notes on His Trade* (1930). [PJK]

Oliver Elton, *C.E.M.* (1929); Frank Swinnerton, *The Georgian Literary Scene* (1935); Henry Nevinson, *Last Changes, Last Chances* (1928).

Montgomerie, Alexander (1545?–1598?). Scots poet. Distantly related to King James VI, in whose literary education he took part. Later Montgomerie travelled abroad and was imprisoned, apparently as an ineffectual Roman Catholic political agent; embroiling himself in conspiracy, he lost favour at court and died an outlaw. He is best known as the author of (and the probable inventor of the characteristic stanza-form popular-

ized by) *The Cherrie and the Slae* (1597; ed. H. H. Wood, 1937), a tepid and belated example of medieval allegorical modes which nevertheless remained popular in Scotland throughout the 17th century and received new life in the 18th from its inclusion in the anthologies of James Watson and Allan Ramsay. The stanza, too, was popular and was used by Burns in the 'Epistle to Davie' and in 'The Jolly Beggars'. Montgomerie also wrote satires, a 'flyting' (a set-piece of virtuoso abuse), some elaborate but insipid love-poems, minor religious pieces, and intermittently striking translations of the Psalms. His work marks the decline of Scottish courtly literature as the country became impoverished and provincialized by religious strife and diminishing political importance. [AI]

Poems, ed. J. Cranstoun (STS, 1887); *Supplement*, ed. G. Stevenson (STS, 1910); *A Selection*, ed. H. M. Shire (1960).
H. M. Shire, *Song Dance and Poetry of the Court of Scotland under King James VI* (1969).

Montgomery, James (1771–1854). Poet. Born at Irvine in Ayrshire, and educated at the school in Fulneck near Leeds kept by the Moravian Brethren, of whom his father was a missionary, he had various jobs, but in 1792 began practising journalism in Sheffield. He was editor and proprietor of the *Sheffield Iris* (1795–1825) and was twice imprisoned for seditious libel because he published articles against the war (1796). His first book of verse was *Prison Amusements* (1797). His long poems, chiefly descriptive, such as *Greenland* (1819) and *The Pelican Island* (1828), are now forgotten, except that *The World before the Flood* (1812) is sometimes noted because it might have been a source for Byron's speculative poem *Heaven and Earth* (1823). One of Montgomery's poems of social protest, *The Chimneysweeper's Friend* (1824), is sometimes reprinted. He is, however, still remembered for his fervent hymns, particularly 'For Ever with the Lord' and 'Hail to the Lord's Anointed'. [AR]

Poetical Works (4 vols., 1850).
J. Holland and J. Everett, *Memoirs of the Life and Writings of J.M.* (7 vols., 1854–6); A. S. Holbrook, 'The Life and Work of M.', *London Quarterly*, 179 (1954).

Montgomery or Gomery, Robert (1807–55). Poet and minister in the Scottish Episcopal Church. Born at Bath and educated at Oxford, he wrote several very popular, bad, religious poems, 2 of which, *The Omnipresence of the Deity* (1828; 11th edn, 1830) and *Satan* (2 edns, 1830), were the subject of a vituperative review essay by Macauley in the April 1830 issue of the *Edinburgh Review*, which has long delighted schoolboys. [A R]

K. Hopkins, 'Reflections on Satan Montgomery', *Texas Studies in Literature and Language*, 4 (1962).

Montrose, 1st Marquess of. ◊ Graham, J.

Moore, Brian (1921–   ). Novelist. Born and educated in Belfast, he was sent to Algiers by the Ministry of War Transport in 1943, and this began five years of extensive travelling, ended in 1948 by his entry into Canada as an immigrant. He lived for many years in Montreal.

Like *The Feast of Lupercal* (1958), *The Lonely Passion of Miss Judith Hearne* (1955) is set in Belfast. With a brilliant combination of high comedy and pathos it describes the fears and fantasies of an ageing spinster, which reach a hysterical crisis when religious doubt is added to the torments of sex and drink. Moore's comic world is the undignified one of dingy respectability. The hero of *The Luck of Ginger Coffey* (1960) is an Irish citizen of Montreal as resourceless in the material world as Judith Hearne. Colourfully accurate dialogue, an Irish love of the rhetorical set piece and a delight in the ludicrous distinguish all Moore's work. *An Answer from Limbo* (1963), describes the crisis that develops when a determined writer brings his devout mother from Ireland to New York to look after his children while his wife works. It follows Moore's own move to New York. *The Emperor of Ice Cream* (1965) returns to Belfast, and *I Am Mary Dunne* (1968), Moore's best work since his first, to New York. [P T]

J. Ludwig, 'A Mirror of M.', *Canadian Literature*, 7 (Winter 1961); R. Fulford interviews B.M., *Tamarack Review*, 23 (Spring, 1962).

Moore, George (1852–1933). Novelist and playwright. Born at Moore Hall, Co. Mayo, he was educated at Oscott College, Birmingham. In his twenties he studied painting in Paris, and during this time his only 2 books of verse were published: *Flowers of Passion* (1878) and *Pagan Poems* (1881). His early novels sought to bring into English fiction a new naturalism, influenced by Zola and the French realists. The first, *A Modern Lover* (1883), was a not very well-written account of the adventures of an artist. This was followed by *A Mummer's Wife* (1885), a study of life in a theatrical touring company. *A Drama in Muslin* (1886) was an intricate social novel about the decaying Irish gentry. After several weak novels, and a fascinating account of his Paris years, *Confessions of a Young Man* (1888), in which Moore championed aestheticism and French impressionist painting, he achieved a popular success with *Esther Waters* (1894). Here Moore defied Victorian conventions in his treatment of the heroine, a servant who gives birth to an illegitimate son; her life is difficult, but she is not punished for her failing, and her boy grows into a fine young man. Another theme is the disastrous effect of gambling upon the 'lower orders'. The novels which followed *Esther Waters* were less successful, and in 1901 Moore returned from London, where he had lived for some years, to Ireland, becoming associated with the Celtic revival. He turned Protestant, and became High Sheriff of Mayo. *The Lake* (1905) brought into prominence another aspect of Moore's gift: no longer a challenging naturalism, but a sensual refinement expressed in symbolism. He wrote several volumes of autobiography and reminiscence in which the best of his writing is to be found. These include *Memoirs of My Dead Life* (1906), *Ave* (1911), *Salve* (1912) and *Vale* (1914). In 1911 he had returned to London, where he spent the rest of his life. He wrote some historical novels in an elaborate, melodious style; among them were *The Brook Kerith* (1916) (about Christ) and *Héloise and Abelard* (1921). Apart from *Esther Waters* and the autobiographical volumes, he is remembered for a book of meandering essays, *Conversations in Ebury Street* (1924), whose subjects range from Balzac, George Eliot and Hardy to the painters Sickert, Tonks and Steer. [C O]

Collected Works (20 vols., 1937).
J. Hone, *The Life of G.M.* (1936); N. Cunard, *Memories of G.M.* (1956); A. N. Jeffares, *G.M.* (W T W, 1965); J. C. Noël, *G.M. L'homme et l'œuvre* (Paris, 1966).

Moore, Thomas (1779–1852). Song-writer and poet. Born in Dublin, the son of a grocer, he was educated at Whyte's School there, and at Trinity College, where Catholics were by then being admitted. In 1799, he went to London, and was entered at the Middle Temple. He had begun to write verse at college; and in London he developed his talents as a drawing-room singer and good companion, becoming well known in the great houses. He published 2 volumes of adolescent erotic verse – rather bad, vulgarized classical songs and pieces of Regency conventional verse: a version of the *Odes of Anacreon* (1800) and *The Poetical Works of the Late Thomas Little Esq.* (1801) (both ran to many editions). In 1803, he was given an appointment in Bermuda and went there, but turning his work over to a deputy, toured America and Canada. He returned to England and published *Epistles, Odes and Other Poems* (1806), which was severely handled by ◊ Jeffrey in the *Edinburgh Review*; but Moore later contributed to this journal, and refused the editorship. The best verse of Moore appeared in *Irish Melodies* (in 10 parts with various prefatory matter, 1808–34). Love of Irish music and Irish patriotism (mostly of a sentimental kind) were Moore's inspiration in those songs, and in such volumes as *National Airs* (1815). Among the songs are the only things of Moore's now remembered, such as 'The Harp That Once through Tara's Halls', 'The Minstrel Boy' and 'Oft in the Stilly Night'. The 'best Original Irish Melody' is largely in 18th-century form, but contain something of older Irish art. Moore's words are written for the music and lose by being read as 'poems'. There is sometimes an interesting counterpointing of English metre with another spirit arising from the music's Irish rhythm and movement. The slightness of his political commitment, however, has perhaps led to neglect of his mastery of the art of song writing; his work is often tawdrily ornamented. The enterprise was financially very successful, as was his most famous single poem, *Lalla Rookh; an Oriental Romance* (1817, six edns). This is really a set of 4 stories exploiting the oriental fashion in verse tales which had been popularized by Byron. Moore also wrote satire: when ephemeral and lighthearted, it had its day; his more serious attempts, such as *Corruption and Intolerance* (1808) and *The Sceptic: A Philosophical Satire* (1809), never took. *Intercepted Letters, etc.* (1813) were lampoons on the Prince Regent and his associates, and another success was *The Fudge Family in Paris* (1818), a series of jolly verse letters, not unlike The

New Bath Guide by ◊ Anstey. Responsibility for embezzlement by his Bermudan deputy forced Moore to live abroad for some years after 1819. In Venice he met Byron, who gave him his manuscript *Memoirs*. Moore later consented to the weird scene of destruction of this valuable document in Murray the publisher's room. He did, however, print *Letters and Journals of Lord Byron, with Notices of His Life* (2 vols., 1830). Moore wrote much for periodicals, and published several volumes of ephemera. [AR]

Poetical Works (10 vols., 1840–1; ed. A. D. Godley, 1910); *Prose and Verse, 'with Suppressed Passages from the "Memoirs of Lord Byron"'*, ed. R. H. Shepherd (1878); *Lyrics and Satires*, ed. S. O'Faoláin (1929) (selections); *Memoirs, Journal and Correspondence*, ed. Lord John Russell (8 vols., 1853–6); *Diary*, selected J. B. Priestley (1925); *Journal: 1818 to 1841*, ed. P. Quennell (revised, 1964); *Letters*, ed. W. S. Dowden (1964).

H. M. Jones, *The Harp that Once – : a Chronicle of the Life of T.M.* (New York, 1937); D. J. O'Sullivan, 'The Bunting Collection of Irish Folk Music and Songs', *Journal of the Irish Folk Song Society* (1926–32); H. H. Jordan, 'Byron and M.', *MLQ*, 9 (1948); R. Birley, *Sunk without Trace* (1962) (on *Lalla Rookh*); H. H. Jordan, bibliography, in *English Romantic Poets and Essayists: A Review of Research*, ed. C. W. and L. H. Houtchens (New York, revised 1966).

Moore, Thomas Sturge (1870–1944). Poet, art historian, aesthetic theorist and graphic artist. He is perhaps better known for his friendship with Yeats than for his work in poetry, though Yeats, who greatly admired him, quotes his poem 'The Dying Swan' in full in the notes at the back of his own *Collected Poems* and the American critic Yvor Winters, often very original in his judgements, thinks Moore a better poet than Yeats. Moore was the brother of the famous Cambridge philosopher, G. E. Moore, and in a long correspondence with Yeats defended his own understanding of his brother's epistemological realism against Yeats, who wished to use G. E. Moore's arguments to prop his belief in the reality of visionary experience. He also designed the dust-covers for some of Yeats's best volumes of poetry, including *The Tower* and *The Winding Stair*. His poetry, which makes much use of classical mythology, is notable for its clarity and fluidity of line and its chastity of diction, but may seem, to modern tastes, to lack concentration and tension.

Moore wrote prose books on Correggio and Dürer, and in Hampstead, where he lived much of his life, was the centre of a circle interested in poetry and the arts. [GSF]

The Vinedresser and Other Poems (1899); *Poems* (1906); *Poems* (1931–3); *Selected Poems* (1934); *The Unknown Known and a Dozen Odd Poems* (1939).

Moraes, Dom (1938–   ). Indian poet. Born in Bombay, the son of Frank Moraes, a leading Indian journalist. As a child he travelled widely with his father. His first published poems appeared in *Encounter* when he was 16. After a wandering year in Europe, he entered Oxford University in 1956. His first book of verse, *A Beginning* (1957), won him the Hawthornden Prize. A second, *Poems*, was published in 1960. A self-indulgent eroticism mars some poems, but at his best Moraes is graceful and controlled, with a tactile sensuality of image and language. [PT]

PMP, 2 (1962); *Gone Away. An Indian Journal* (1960); *John Nobody* (1966) (poem); *My Son's Father* (1968) (autobiography).

More, Hannah (1745–1833). Playwright, miscellaneous and tract writer, philanthropist and poetess. A good representative of a lady of 'culture', that is the literary, moralistic, didactic, practical side of 18th-century civilization (which she embodied in very competent prose). She was the youngest of five sisters of a Gloucestershire schoolmaster, and was educated at a boarding school they kept at Bristol. She began by writing plays which brought her to the attention of Garrick, who when she moved to London in 1774, introduced her to Johnson, Reynolds, Burke and that circle, and she became a friend of Mrs ◊ Montagu and the Blue Stockings. Garrick successfully produced her tragedy *Percy* (1777), which characteristically turns on the ethical dilemma of a woman torn between passion for a lover and duty to a husband she has been forced to marry. Turning from the theatre and a series of poems (now forgotten) she began her long series of ethical and religious works with *An Estimate of the Religion of the Fashionable World* (1791). She was the author of 2 series of tracts which were valued highly, at least by the distributors: *Village Politics by Will Chip* (1793) and *Cheap Repository Tracts* (1795–8), which included the very well-known 'The Shepherd of Salisbury Plain'. The Religious

Tract Society was formed as a result of this encouragement. She also wrote several works on the education of women and a semi-novel of ethical instruction, *Coelebs in Search of a Wife* (1808). As a result of her literary success, she and her sisters were able to retire to a life of philanthropy and educational good works in Cheddar. [AR]

Letters, selected and intr. R. B. Johnson (1925). William Roberts, *Memoirs of the Life and Correspondence of H.M.* (1834); M. G. Jones, *H.M.* (1952).

More, Henry (1614–87). Poet and philosopher. He was born at Grantham, Lincs., and educated at Eton and at Christ's College, Cambridge. In 1639 he became a Fellow of Christ's, and thenceforth led a happy and active life within the college gates, avoiding all offers of preferment. In spite of Calvinist leanings inherited from his parents, he was not a Puritan, and remained loyal to the monarchy and to the Church of England during the Civil War. His first published work was a collection, *Psychozoia Platonica: or a Platonical Song of the Soul*, which appeared in 1642 (a fuller collection appeared under the title *Philosophical Poems* in 1647). The title-piece, 'Psychozoia', sets out to show the spiritual nature of reality; the stanza form, allegorical method and archaic diction are all derived from ◊ Spenser. More hardly succeeds in imparting his mystic vision; his system – the neoplatonism of Plotinus combined with Christianity – is not transmuted into poetry. Nonetheless some of the struggles of the soul as it strives to merge with the World-Soul are vividly dramatized, and there are a few telling satires on contemporary religious excesses. Some of More's minor poems celebrating the benevolence of the universe do reveal a true lyrical gift. After 1647 More's writings were in prose; they include *An Antidote against Atheism* (1653), devoted to spiritualistic phenomena, and *Divine Dialogues* (1668), which set forth More's religious ideal. He also wrote in Latin and translated his English writings into that language. He was interested in Descartes's philosophy and corresponded with him, but finally saw that his system rested on an essentially materialistic basis. [NL]

Complete Poems, ed. A. B. Grosart (1878); *Philosophical Poems: Psychozoia and Minor Poems*, ed. and intr. G. Bullough (1931);

Philosophical Writings, ed. F. I. Mackinnon (New York, 1925); Descartes, *Correspondance avec Arnaud et M.*, ed. G. Lewis (Paris, 1953).
F. J. Powicke, *The Cambridge Platonists* (1926); A. Lichtenstein, *H.M. The Rational Theology of a Cambridge Platonist* (1962).

More, Sir Thomas (1478–1535). Prose writer. The son of a barrister, he was brought up in the household of Cardinal Morton, Archbishop of Canterbury. He went to Oxford, and seemed destined for a Church career, but studied law in London. He became the friend of Erasmus and of John Colet, studied Greek under Grocyn, and entered Parliament. At this period he lectured on Augustine's *De civitate Dei*, translated from the Greek, made an English version of the Life of Pico della Mirandola, composed Latin epigrams, and wrote several poems in English – including humorous pieces and a lament for Queen Elizabeth. He became an Under Sheriff of the City in 1510, and in 1513–14 wrote in Latin the *Historia Ricardi Tertii*, but left unfinished his own English version of it. More's well-told history is Lancastrian in sympathy, dwelling on the monstrosity of Richard; Edward Hall drew on it heavily, so that Shakespeare's handling of Richard was ultimately influenced by More. The satire *Utopia* (tr. R. Robinson, 1551; R. Steele, 1908; P. Turner, Penguin Classics, 1965), written in Latin, appeared in 1516 in Louvain and in 1517 in Paris. Book II, written in Flanders while More was on a diplomatic mission for Henry VIII, describes an ideal island in the New World. Book I, written later, concerns the imaginary traveller and his criticism of social conditions in England. More became a servant and friend of Henry VIII. He was employed on embassies, knighted in 1521, and succeeded Wolsey as Lord Chancellor in 1529. He advised Henry on the writing of the attack on Luther which earned the King the title Defender of the Faith, and engaged, at the Bishop of London's request, in religious polemic, mainly directed against William Tyndale, including *The Supplication of Souls* (1529), *Confutation of Tyndale's Answer* (1532), *Debellation of Salem and Byzance* (1533) and the *Answer of the Poisoned Book* (1533). Such works have historical interest only, but are enlivened by comic techniques and by scurrility. His devotional pieces include the *Dialogue of Comfort against Tribulation* (1534), judged his noblest work in English, which was written in the Tower of London where, having refused the oath on the Act of Supremacy (which made the King not the Pope head of the Church in England), he awaited barbaric tortures – commuted in 1534 to beheading. More was canonized by the Roman Catholic Church in 1935.

A great figure in public life and religious controversy, More was, in youth, a minor court poet; as the humanist author of the *Utopia* and friend of Erasmus he rose to European eminence; and in the history of English prose he has an important place.

The St Thomas More Project at Yale University (Chairman L. L. Martz) is issuing the *Complete Works* (14 vols., 1965–) and a modernized series (about 7 vols., 1961–). [MJ]

The English Works, ed. R. W. Chambers and A. W. Reed (2 of a planned 7 vols., 1931); *Selections*, ed. P. S. and H. M. Allen (1924).
W. Roper (M.'s son-in-law), *The Life of Sir T.M.* (new edn, 1935); R. W. Chambers, *Sir T.M.* (1935); R. A. Knox and others, *The Fame of Blessed T.M.* (1929); C. S. Lewis, *English Literature in the Sixteenth Century* (1954); E. E. Reynolds, *Sir T.M.* (1954).

Morgan, Charles (1894–1958). Novelist and playwright. Born in Kent, and educated at the naval colleges of Osborne and Dartmouth, he served in the Navy during the First World War, after which he studied at Oxford where he became president of the university dramatic society. His early novels *The Gunroom* (1919) and *My Name is Legion* (1925) were unremarkable. In 1921 he became drama critic of *The Times*. *Portrait in a Mirror* (1929) won the Fémina–Vie Heureuse Prize: thus began his critical popularity on the continent, which was often to seem excessive to English literary critics. Morgan's 3 plays are *The Flashing Stream* (1938), *The River Line* (1952) and *The Burning Glass* (1954). While his seriousness of purpose has never been in doubt, he was not always fortunate enough to find the appropriate manner of expression for it. The dialogue in the plays is heavy, characterless and determinedly literary. Each play high-mindedly concerns itself with a specific problem. The novel is better equipped to function in this way, and it is as a novelist that Morgan is more likely to be remembered. *The Fountain* (1932) won the Hawthornden Prize. Its narrative of an English officer interned in Holland in wartime is interspersed with the novelist's philosophical reflections. Morgan was not the most exciting or imaginative of novelists, but he was a devoted and serious practitioner of the art. [CO]

Reflections in a Mirror (1944); Challenge to Venus (1957); Selected Letters, ed. E. Lewis (1967). H. C. Duffin, The Novels and Plays of C.M. (1959).

Morley, Henry (1822-1894). Literary journalist, editor and inventor of 'Eng. Lit.'. Born in London, he studied medicine at King's College there. After a dispute with a dishonest partner, he ceased practising medicine and turned to journalism. He wrote for Dickens' Household Words, then for All the Year Round, and finally edited the Examiner. Morley wrote a number of biographies, including a Life of Cardano, Physician of Milan (2 vols., 1854) and of the Hermeticist Cornelius Agrippa (1856). He became Professor of English at University College, London (1865). His educational interests also took him into adult education, and he lectured to audiences (often of working men) outside the universities. He was indefatigable and very influential through this work, and also in the development of English as an academic study. To further these interests he began his vast (20-volume) history of English literature, English Writers, of which he lived to write only half (1887-95), carrying the narrative down to Shakespeare. He was also of incalculable influence with his editions of cheap reprints of English classics, notably Cassell's Library of English Literature (annotated extracts) (5 vols., 1875-81) and Cassell's National Library (similar to the previous work) (205 vols., 1886 ff.). Few readers of English even today can have escaped Morley's judgement on some writer. His criticism was largely 'historical' and biographical. [AR]

Early Papers and Some Memories (1891) (some autobiographical chapters). H. S. Solly, The Life of H.M. (1898); D. J. Palmer, The Rise of English Studies (1965).

Morley, John (1st Viscount Morley of Blackburn) (1838-1923). Journalist, politician and biographer. Born at Blackburn in Lancashire, the son of a doctor, he was educated at Cheltenham College and Lincoln College, Oxford; he was called to the bar but never practised. He became a journalist in London, writing chiefly for the Saturday Review, and was a friend of J. S. Mill, Meredith and other writers and

thinkers; he edited the Fortnightly Review (1867-82) and also the Pall Mall Gazette (1881-3). He published many of his Fortnightly essays as Critical Miscellanies (on Carlyle, Byron, Macaulay, George Eliot, etc.) (1871-7). Morley also wrote many biographies in a useful, straightforward, narrative manner, including Burke (1867), Voltaire (1872, revised), Rousseau (1873), Cobden (1881; abridged 1882), Cromwell (1900) and Gladstone (1903), as well as editing the English Men of Letters series. In 1883 he was elected Liberal M.P. for Newcastle, and became a close supporter and aide of Gladstone. His interests were India (Speeches on India, 1908; 1917), education (The Struggle for National Education, 1873) and Ireland. He was Chief Secretary for Ireland (1886 and 1892-5), Secretary of State for India (1905-10) and Lord President of the Council (1910-14, resigning in protest at the declaration of war). [AR]

Works (15 vols., 1921; 12 vols., 1923); Select Essays, ed. and intr. H. G. Rawlinson (1923); Recollections (1917) (autobiography). J. D. MacCallum, Lord M.'s Criticism of English Poetry and Prose (Princeton, N.J., 1921); P. Braybrooke, Lord M. (1924); E. M. Everett, The Party of Humanity: The Fortnightly Review and its Contributors, 1865-74 (Chapel Hill, N.C., 1939); W. Staebler, The Liberal Mind of J.M. (Princeton, N.J., 1943); D. A. Hamer, J.M. (1968).

Morris, William (1834-96). Poet, designer and political writer. Morris had a comfortable middle-class childhood in the fashionable London suburbs and was educated at Marlborough and Oxford. His first ambition was to be a clergyman, but his meeting with Burne-Jones, the painter, and his reading of ◊ Ruskin turned him to architecture. A later meeting with ◊ Rossetti encouraged him to abandon architecture for painting. In 1859 he married his model, Jane Burden, the daughter of an Oxford groom, but their marriage was a difficult one. Morris developed his interest in design. His friend Philip Webb designed the Red House at Upton (Bexleyheath) for him, and Morris himself founded a company – Morris, Marshall, Faulkner and Webb – to design and make the furniture and decorations. This was the start of a long career of fabric and furniture designing, church and house decorating. His main concern was to combine the aesthetic and the useful and to make hand-workmanship an integral part of everyday life. This was at the root of his socialism, which was to take up more of his life later. His hatred of capitalism and the effects of the industrial revolution led him to a utopian vision that overcame the tyranny of the machine and the division of labour and allowed both men and labour to be organized according to need and ability. This vision was embodied in *A Dream of John Ball* (reprinted from the *Commonweal* in 1888) and *News from Nowhere* (1891), and also in a great quantity of shorter essays and lectures which are more specifically critical of contemporary society. *News from Nowhere* now seems to have more charm than persuasiveness, but it remains an important contribution to utopian literature. In 1883 Morris joined the Democratic Federation and founded his own Socialist League the following year. He edited the League's journal, the *Commonweal*, but later broke away from it with a small group who continued to meet together. In 1890, with the founding of the Kelmscott Press, Morris's interests became focused on experiments in printing and book design.

Morris had begun writing poetry when he was at Oxford, and in 1858 he published his first volume, *The Defence of Guenevere*. This was not well received – critics found his rhythms irregular and perverse, while the medieval subject-matter led them to expect smooth Tennysonian metres – but there now seems to be a certain power in Morris's slightly jagged transmutations of medieval themes. Morris's brief association with the Oxford Movement and his contacts with the Pre-Raphaelites encouraged a love of medievalism which he had always had. In 1868 he published *The Earthly Paradise*, an immensely long poem which was an instant success with the middle-class public who found its soothing handling of Greek and Norse legend undemanding reading. In 1869 Morris visited Iceland and his attempts to translate the Icelandic sagas influenced his *Sigurd the Volsung* (1876), which although his use of artificial archaic devices disturbs the narrative has an intriguing strength. Later verse was more directly inspired by Morris's socialism. The short propagandic verse in *Chants for Socialists* (1885) are simply phrased and unremarkable but have an effective energy.

Morris's socialism derived in the first instance from the same kind of disgust with the horrors of industrial England that had moved Ruskin, but he was a more systematic political thinker than Ruskin and, while his aesthetic sensibilities and his love of individual craftsmanship led him to project his ideal vision of England in quasi-medieval terms, his activity in the Democratic Federation and (later) the Social Democratic Federation was often vigorous and hard-headed.

Although Morris's career ranged so widely and gives an impression of restlessness he was never hasty in his work. We now remember him most for his work as designer and social critic, but his poetry, even when artificial and at a distance from reality, is always careful and controlled. [JRC]

Collected Works, ed. M. Morris (24 vols., 1965); *W.M.*, ed. G. D. H. Cole (1934) (stories, poems, lectures and essays); *Selected Writings and Designs*, ed. Asa Briggs (1963); *A Choice of W.M.'s Verse*, ed. G. Grigson (1969).
J. W. Mackail, *The Life of W.M.* (1899; World's Classics, 1950); A. Vallance, *W.M., His Art, His Writings and His Public Life* (1897); H. H. Sparling, *The Kelmscott Press and W.M.* (1924); J. Ormerod, *The Poetry of W.M.* (1938); G. Hough, *The Last Romantics* (1949); E. P. Thompson, *W.M., Romantic to Revolutionary* (1955).

Morris-Jones, John (1864–1929). Welsh scholar, poet and critic. He was born at Llandrygarn, Anglesey, and educated at Friars School, Bangor, Christ College, Brecon, and Jesus College, Oxford. Ostensibly a student of mathematics he spent much of his time reading Welsh books and manuscripts in the Bodleian, and attended the lectures of John Rhys, Professor of Celtic at Jesus. In 1889 he was appointed lecturer in Welsh at University College of North Wales, Bangor, and later professor. He was knighted in 1918.

John Morris-Jones showed a remarkable consistency in all his work. His wide reading in the prose and verse classics of Welsh literature had made him realize how debased the standards of Welsh scholarship had become during the 19th century, and how greatly literature depends on certain canons of good taste and refinement. His early poetry, collected and published as *Caniadau* in 1907, included original lyrics, translations from Heine and other continental poets, and the stanzas from the original Persian of Omar Khayyám. These poems for their period were marvels of clarity and good diction and sureness of touch. They had great influence on the development of modern Welsh poetry and set a standard for the lyric form. Morris-Jones was appalled by the pompous, turgid and pseudo-philosophical poems of well-known 19th-century poets and he found that the National Eisteddfod could provide him with a stage from which to lay about him. Audiences were captivated by his performances as a critic and adjudicator, and gradually he was able to raise the standards of entry for the main poetry competitions. As editor of the quarterly *Y Beirniad* (1911–19) he influenced literary opinion. He had also studied the works of the classical Welsh poets in great detail in order to discover what *cynghanedd* and Welsh prosody really meant (*Cerdd Dafod*, 1925).

Morris-Jones was mainly responsible for two major revisions of Welsh orthography in 1893 and 1928. But his outstanding work was his Welsh Grammar (1913). The etymological portion is the weakest, but the descriptive section remains a monument to Morris-Jones's unerring judgement and complete lucidity. A few pedantries here and there do nothing to mar this massive achievement, and it remains the standard grammar of literary Welsh. [MR]

Thomas Parry. *J. M.-J.* (1958).

Mortimer, Penelope (Ruth) (*née* Fletcher) (? –). Novelist and journalist. Born in Rhyl, North Wales, she was educated at London University and wrote book reviews, short stories and poetry before publishing her first novel, *A Villa in Summer* (1954). This was followed by *The Bright Prison* (1956), *With Love and Lizards* (1957), written in collaboration with her husband John Mortimer, *Daddy's Gone A-Hunting* (1958), *The Pumpkin Eater* (1962), *Saturday Lunch with the Brownings* (1960) (short stories) and *My Friend Says It's Bullet-Proof* (1967). Written with great intensity, psychological penetration and an incisive sense of social behaviour, her novels bring vividly alive a world of domesticity, child-bearing and broken marriages, a world that hovers continually on the edge of nightmare. She is at present film critic for the Sunday *Observer*. [PJK]

Mottram, R(alph) H(ale) (1883–). Novelist. Born in Norwich, the son of a bank manager, and educated there and in Lausanne. He started as a clerk in the local bank his family had long served, and in 1904 became known to Galsworthy (he wrote an intimate portrait of Galsworthy, *For Some We Loved*, 1956, and is the author of the British Council pamphlet *John Galsworthy*, WTW, 1963), who encouraged his literary ambitions. He published 2 volumes of poetry under the pseudonym 'J. Marjoram', *Repose* (1907) and *New Poems* (1909). In the First World War he served as an interpreter with the Norfolk Regiment, and in 1924 he scored a great success with his novel of war reminiscences, *The Spanish Farm* (filmed as *Roses of Picardy*), which gained the Hawthornden Prize, and its sequels *Sixty-Four Ninety-Four* (1925) and *The Crime at Vanderlynden's* (1926); all were republished as *The Spanish Farm Trilogy* in 1927, when he abandoned banking and devoted himself to writing. He is chiefly known as a regional novelist with a strong interest in the tenacity of provincial tradition. *Our Mr Dormer* (1927) is perhaps the best known of his books in this vein; it is based on his own family history. Other novels include *The English Miss* (1928), *Flower Pot End* (1935), *The Gentleman of Leisure* (1948), *Over the Wall* (1955), *Musetta* (1960) and *Happy Birds* (1964). He has also written on banking, and on Norwich and his own countryside, *The Broads* (1952). [AR]

Autobiography with a Difference (1938); *The Window Seat, or Life Observed* (2 vols., 1954, 1957) (also autobiography).

Mphahlele, Ezekiel (1919–). South African writer. Born in Pretoria. His autobiography, *Down Second Avenue* (1959), combines documentary precision with the structure and style of a novel. Inevitably it is a story of struggle and setback. In 1932 Mphahlele was brought to live in a Pretoria slum. He went through High School, then Teaching Training College in Natal. In 1941–5 he worked at an institute for the African blind. Seven years as a school-master ended in 1952 when he was dismissed and banned from teaching in the Union as a result of agitation against the Bantu Education Act. In 1955 he joined the staff of *Drum*, but disliked journalism. His Syndicate of Artists was formed to meet higher cultural standards among Africans. In 1957 he went to teach in Nigeria. His book *The African Image* (1962) is partly an explanation of his voluntary exile, partly a record of a visit to England and partly a reworking of a degree thesis on the non-white in fiction. He is now senior lecturer in

English at the University of Zambia.

Mphahlele has an easy mastery of prose style, but has not so far written fiction to equal his autobiography. His second collection of stories, *The Living and Dead* (Ibadan, 1961), is erratic, but in at least two stories he has found the balance he seeks – 'the ironic meeting between protest and acceptance in their widest terms'. A further collection of short stories, *In Corner B*, appeared in 1967. He had edited *Modern African Stories* (with E. A. Komey, 1964) and *African Writing Today* (1967). [PT]

Man Must Live (1946).
G. Moore, *Seven African Writers* (1962).

Muir, Edwin (1887–1959). Poet. Generally recognized as the most distinguished poet to have come out of Scotland in this century with the exception of the much more, vehemently nationalist Hugh ◊ MacDiarmid. He was also a literary critic of fine talent and, with his wife, the novelist Willa Muir, the translator of a number of important German writers, including Kafka and Broch. Muir was born in the Orkneys, the originally Norse-speaking islands to the north of Scotland, the son of a small tenant farmer. When he was in his early teens, his father was evicted from his farm, and the family transferred to the slums of Glasgow, where the unhealthy air and grim surroundings rapidly depleted their numbers. The contrast between the ballad-like, pastoral setting in which he had been first brought up and modern industrial civilization at its worst haunted Muir and is the main theme of his *Autobiography* (1954), a revision of *The Story and the Fable* (1940), and is also expressed allegorically in one of his finest long poems, *The Labyrinth*. In spite of grim surroundings and disagreeable jobs, the young Muir managed to give himself a very thorough education. He learned German, and was deeply influenced both by Nietzsche and Heine. Heine, with the Scottish ballads, is the main influence behind his first volume of poems, *First Poems*, published in his middle thirties in 1925. With his wife Willa, a fine German scholar, born in the Shetlands, Muir settled in London in the 1920s and lived by translating and reviewing. In the 1930s, he settled for a time in St Andrews, worked for the British Council in Edinburgh during the Second World War, and later worked for the Council in Prague between 1945 and 1948, and in Rome between 1948 and 1950.

Later, he was head for some time of a residential adult education college, Newbattle Abbey near Edinburgh, and towards the end of his life was Charles Eliot Norton Professor for a year at Harvard. His critical works included a thoughtful work on the novel, an attack on the romantic and genteel Scottish tradition called *Scott and Scotland*, and a volume of essays, *Literature and Society*. He also wrote a biography of John Knox, but his *Autobiography*, an indispensable companion to his poems, is his most memorable prose work. His prose, like his poetry, had always a memorable clarity and measure.

As a poet, Muir was hardly influenced at all by the 'modernist' movement, by Pound or Eliot. He admired such poets but felt that there was a traditional poetic mode of diction, rhythm and feeling, a comparatively 'timeless' mode, which would always reassert itself. There are some echoes of Yeats in his poetry, in cadences, and in his fascination with mythology, but he is a much less dramatic writer. The mood of his best poetry is sometimes coloured by sadness but in the end it is always calm, serene and sustained by a sense of timeless pattern, 'the fable', underlying 'the story', the worrying changes of time. He liked blank verse which, as in *The Labyrinth*, he could use with great originality, in long parenthetical sentences, and stanzas, sometimes ballad stanzas, written in a strict traditional metre, but with much subtlety of rhythm. Both in his prose and verse, a very distinctive voice, quiet and gentle but with a strong note of authority, can be heard. Full recognition of his poetic gifts came to him rather late in life and he was late, also, having started off as a Nietzschean and a socialist, in recognizing that his point of view was essentially that of a Christian visionary and, socially, of a humane traditionalist. His reputation has grown steadily since his death. [GSF]

Variations on a Time Theme (1934); *Journeys and Places* (1937); *The Narrow Place* (1943); *The Voyage* (1946); *The Labyrinth* (1949); *New Poems, 1949–51* (1951); *Collected Poems*, ed. J. C. Hall (1952).
J. C. Hall, *E.M.* (WTW, 1956); P. Butter, *E.M.* (1962).

Mulcaster, Richard (1530?–1611). Education theorist. Educated at Eton under the headmastership of Nicholas ◊ Udall, he

381

studied at Cambridge and Oxford, and became in 1561 the first headmaster of Merchant Taylors' School, where his pupils included Thomas Kyd, Thomas Lodge, Edmund Spenser and Launcelot Andrewes. He resigned the headship in 1586, and was clergyman to several parishes before becoming high master of St Paul's School in 1596. In 1581 he published *Positions wherein those Circumstances be Examined Necessarie for the Training Up of Children* (ed. R. H. Quick, 1888), which embodied a philosophy of education in advance of its time. His importance to English literature rests not only on glory reflected from his former pupils but on his own championship of English as a written language superior to any other, ancient or modern. His book *The First Part of the Elementarie which Entreateth Chefelie of the Right Writing of Our English Tung* (1582; ed. E. T. Campagnac, 1925) contains such significant pronouncements as 'I love *Rome* but *London* better, I favour *Italy* but *England* more, I honour the *Latin* but I worship the *English*' and 'I do not think that any language, be it whatsoever, is better able to utter all arguments either with more pith or greater plain-ness than our *English* tongue is'. Himself a notable stylist, he helped to make English the accepted literary language of Elizabethan times. [MJ]

C. S. Lewis, *English Literature in the Sixteenth Century* (1954).

Munday or **Mundy, Anthony** (1560–1633). Dramatist and author. Son of a freeman of the Merchants' and Drapers' companies, he was orphaned about 1570 and was a boy-actor before becoming apprenticed to a printer. In 1578 he travelled in Europe, spying upon the English Catholic refugees in France and Italy and entering the English College at Rome under an assumed name. *The English Roman Life* (1582), an account of his experiences, was the first of his anti-Catholic pamphlets. About the time he published *A Watchword to England* (1584), which warned against the possible assassination of Queen Elizabeth, he was made a minor court official and later a Messenger of the Chamber. He was unusually prolific. He wrote political and religious pamphlets, lyrics and ballads; he translated 12 volumes of *Amadis de Gaule* and other romances (*Zelanto*, a prose-romance of 1580, has analogies with ◊ Lyly's *Euphues*); he revised ◊ Stow's *Survey of London* (1618);

and he produced a profusion of play-scripts for Philip ◊ Henslowe, many of them in collaboration and mostly now lost. In 1584 *Fedele and Fortunio*, an adaptation from the Italian, was acted at court. In 1589 he was lampooned as Post-haste in the satirical play *Histriomastix*, and recent research has established that by 1590 he had already written his comedy *John a Kent and John a Cumber* which seems to have suggested to Shakespeare the love-plot for *A Midsummer Night's Dream* (*c*. 1595) as well as the characters of Puck, Bottom and the 'mechanicals'. Few of Munday's other plays have survived, but his plays on Robin Hood, *The Downfall of Robert Earl of Huntingdon* (1598) and *The Death of Robert Earl of Huntingdon* (in collaboration with Henry Chettle; also 1598), may have influenced Shakespeare in *As You Like It* (1599). He was part-author, with Drayton, Hathway and Wilson, of the first play on Sir John Oldcastle (*Sir John Oldcastle*, 1599). In 1913 it was proved that the manuscript of *Sir Thomas More* is in Munday's hand, and it is certain that he was at least part-author, and possibly sole author, of the early version (*c*. 1593); Shakespeare may have had a hand in the revision. It is a biographical play, sympathetic to More, drawing on the history in Edward ◊ Hall and William ◊ Roper. I. A. Shapiro, whose research on Munday still awaits full publication, has pointed out that 'the tolerant and broad-minded appreciation of More' is magnanimous in 'a formerly active and convinced anti-Catholic agent'. Francis ◊ Meres called Munday 'our best plotter', and Shapiro believes that often Munday provided other dramatists with scenarios but that earlier he may have introduced into England the sort of extemporary playing he had seen by the *commedia dell'arte* troupes in Italy. [MJ]

C. Turner, *A.M., An Elizabethan Man of Letters* (Berkeley, Calif., 1928); G. Hayes, *A.M.'s Romances of Chivalry* (1925); I. A. Shapiro, 'The Significance of a Date' and 'Shakespeare and Mundy', *Shakespeare Survey*, 8 (1955) and 14 (1961).

Munro, H(ector H)ugh((pseudonym 'Saki') (1870–1916). Short-story writer. 'Saki' is the female cup-bearer in the last stanza of the *Rubá'iyát of Omar Khayyám*. He was born at Akyab in Burma, the son of a senior official in the Burma police. It is tempting to see the cruelty of some of his stories springing from his education from the age of 2 in the strict and oppressive household of two maiden aunts at Pilton near Barnstaple in Devonshire. He went to school in Exmouth and at Bedford Grammar School; later his father retired and took over his education by travelling with him widely in Europe. He joined the Burma police, but resigned because of ill-health after a year's service and began contributing fanciful, Tory, political sketches, 'The Westminster Alice' (in Wonderland), to the *Westminster Graphic*. He wrote *The Rise of the Russian Empire* (1900) and became a foreign correspondent (1902–8) in the Balkans and Paris for the right-wing 'society' paper, the *Morning Post*. On his return he continued as a journalist. adding the *Daily Express* to his outlets. His first short stories appeared in the *Westminster Gazette* and as a book, *Reginald* (1904); this was followed by *Reginald in Russia* (1910), and other collections are 28 stories in *The Chronicles of Clovis* (1912) and *Beasts and Super-Beasts* (1914). *The Unbearable Bassington*, a novel, was published in 1912 and *When William Came* (1914) is a pro-war fantasy of England under German occupation. His 'patriotic' sketches from the Western Front were collected as *The Square Egg and Other Sketches* (1924). He enlisted as a private in 1914, refused a commission, went to France and was killed as a sergeant in the Royal Fusiliers at Beaumont Hamel. Munro's stories are masterpieces of economy. His wit and tone are often that of an upper-class schoolboy carried to the extreme of talent. At his best he is concerned to show the triumph of the human beast (often in children) over the seemingly powerful but really impotent control of Edwardian society. His horror is the correlative of P. G. ⋄ Wodehouse's humour and is apt to be similarly undervalued. [AR]

The Complete Short Stories (1930) (with a biography by E. M. Munro, his sister); The Bodley Head Saki, ed. J. W. Lambert (1963); The Unbearable Bassington and Other Stories, selected J. W. Lambert (1965).

R. Drake, 'Saki: Some Problems and a Bibliography', English Fiction in Transition, v, 1 (1962).

Munro, Neil (pseud. Hugh Foulis) (1864–1930). Scottish novelist and journalist. Munro's career, from his Gaelic childhood on a farm near Inveraray, Argyll, to his editorship of the *Glasgow Evening News* (1918–27), gives a painful impression of a real though minor talent frustrated by the need to earn a living in the Scotland of his day. His early work (*The Lost Pibroch*, 1896, and *Gilian the Dreamer*, 1899) presents Highland life through the concepts of the then fashionable 'Celtic twilight' popularized by Yeats and William ⋄ Sharp; after treating Highland history in a Stevensonian vein (*John Splendid*, 1898; *The New Road*, 1914) he turned to realistic novels, now forgotten, about Glasgow life. Ironically, Munro is remembered today chiefly for the amusing and energetic, but relatively trivial, tales of a Clyde 'puffer' (coaster) and its crew collected in *The Vital Spark* (1906) and several later volumes. [AI]

The Poetry, intr. John Buchan (1931).

Murdoch, Iris (1919–). Novelist. Born in Dublin of Anglo-Irish parents, and educated at Badminton School, Bristol, and Somerville College, Oxford, she was for some years a tutor in philosophy at St Anne's College. As a novelist, she began late, publishing her first novel, *Under the Net* (1954), when she was in her mid-thirties, having already written an excellent critical work, *Sartre* (1953). *Under the Net*, pleasantly picaresque, was followed by *The Flight from the Enchanter* (1956), a more highly organized and elaborate piece of machinery, whose ambiguity of tone is cunningly maintained. With *The Sandcastle* (1957) it seemed likely that Iris Murdoch would settle into becoming a conventional middle-brow novelist, but the directions her work has taken since then make it clear that her position is by no means so simple. A real division of critical opinion exists concerning her more recent novels. If, to some tastes, they appear to be of a humourless formality too arid to be of interest, to others they present a different and much more significant aspect. *The Bell* (1958) boasts a formidable cast of characters including reformed homosexual, schizophrenic monk, drunken pervert and a highly overwrought theme: the struggle between the sexual and the religious impulses. In *A Severed Head* (1961) Iris Murdoch puts intrinsically dull or antipathetic characters into a Schnitzler-like sexual minuet in an attempt to shake them into life. *An Unofficial Rose* (1962) is a more engaging work, intelligently planned, beautifully written and technically assured.

Miss Murdoch's world might be said to be that of Virginia Woolf observed with a somewhat less indulgent eye. Her frequent use of symbolism can appear over-deliberate: as a consequence her symbols sometimes lack poetic resonance. *The Unicorn* (1963) suffers from this defect. *The Italian Girl* (1964) manipulates its characters and their motivations so deliberately that it becomes clear that the author is in the process of formulating a new kind of *roman à thèse*, and that the suspension of disbelief is irrelevant to her purpose. *The Red and the Green* (1965), which followed it, however, seems a return to the old ambivalence. She is one of the most complex and interesting of contemporary novelists. [CO]

The Time of the Angels (1966); The Nice and the Good (1968); Bruno's Dream (1969); A Fairly Honourable Defeat (1970).
A. S. Byatt, Degrees of Freedom: The Novels of I.M. (1965).

Murray, Charles (1864–1941). Scottish verse-writer. Murray spent his childhood in an Aberdeenshire village and his youth as an apprentice surveyor in Aberdeen; emigrating to South Africa in 1888, he became manager of a mining company, fought in the Boer War, was made Director of Public Works to the new Dominion in 1910 and retired in 1924. His verses in Aberdeenshire dialect on village matters (*Hamewith*, 1900; enlarged edn, 1909) are too strongly tinged with the nostalgia of the Scottish exile and the literary attitudes of the ◊ 'Kailyard' period to appear very interesting today; the best is the best known, 'The Whistle', a lively tale of a country boy's holiday. The dialect movement which formed around Murray's work was one of the sources of the Scottish literary renaissance associated with Hugh ◊ MacDiarmid. [AI]

C. M. Grieve, Contemporary Scottish Studies (1926); C. Christie, Some Memories of C.M. (1943).

Murray, (George) Gilbert (Āime) (1866–1957). Classical scholar and controversialist. Born in Sydney, New South Wales, the son of a senior colonial Civil Servant, he left Australia in 1867 and was educated at the Merchant Taylors' School and St John's College, Oxford. He became a classics Fellow of New College in 1888, and in 1889 Professor of Greek at Glasgow University. From 1908 to 1936, he was Regius Professor of Greek at Oxford. As a Greek scholar, Murray's work was mostly in the drama. Through his verse translations, published from 1902 to 1951, the works of Aristophanes, Sophocles, Euripides and Aeschylus were made familiar to contemporary English-speaking audiences. The late-Romantic cast of his verse dates his work and makes it rather emptily rhetorical and 'poeticized'. This change of taste in translation from the ancient Greek is partly the result of his own work, for in such influential works as *Four Stages of Greek Religion* (1912; *Five Stages*, 1935) and *Euripides and his Age* (1913) he drew on the new work of anthropologists and familiarized the English reader with the religious, political and social background of ancient Greek writing, making a purely 'literary' treatment of the texts unsatisfactory. His own poetic gifts did not match this insight. Murray wrote much on philosophy, and had a long career as a proponent of the League of Nations, which he supported with great idealism (see his *The Problem of Foreign Policy*, 1921, and *Liberality and Civilisation*, 1938). He is one of the best examples of the powerful effect phil-hellenism has had on British intellectual life. [AR]

Autobiography, ed. J. Smith and A. Toynbee (1960) (unfinished; with contributions by his friends).

Murry, John Middleton (1889–1957). Critic. Born in Peckham, he was educated at Christ's Hospital and Brasenose College, Oxford. As a young journalist he worked for the *Westminster Gazette* and the *Nation*. In 1913 he met Katherine ◊ Mansfield and later married her. During the First World War he worked in the Intelligence Department of the War Office and became Chief Censor. In 1923 he founded the literary magazine *Adelphi*. After Katherine Mansfield's death he married again in 1924, and later wrote a biography of his first wife, *The Life of Katherine Mansfield* (1933). He also edited much of her work for publication.

Murry's own first publications were novels and collections of verse, but these are of less importance than his criticism. *Keats and Shakespeare* (1925) is an excellent study of Keats, marred only by Murry's stylistic shortcomings which were to disfigure much of his work. His imperfections as a prose stylist are, however, compensated for by his enthusiasm for the subjects he writes about. He is intrinsically a creative critic, in the sense that he is concerned mainly with communicating his delight in literature. A Christian Marxist, he wrote a *Life of Jesus* (1926) and several other religious books. His solemn, almost completely humourless cast of mind prevented him from becoming a really first-rate critic, but *Son of Woman, the Story of D. H. Lawrence* (1931) and *William Blake* (1933) are by no means without interest. His experiments in community living, based on naïve and pre-Freudian assumptions, were not an unqualified success. During the Second World War, Murry was the editor of *Peace News*. [co]

The Problem of Style (1922); *Between Two Worlds* (1935) (autobiography); *Select Criticism 1916–1957* (1960).
P. Mairet, *J.M.M.* (1958); F. A. Lea, *The Life of J.M.M.* (1959).

Myers, L(eo) H(amilton) (1881–1944). Philosophical novelist. He came of a family well known in the scientific and religious thought of the 19th century. His father, F. W. H. Myers, was a leading exponent of late Victorian scientific spiritualism as well as an essayist and poet, and a founder-member of the Society for Psychical Research. Myers went to Eton, where his inner rebellion against its *mores* was an early sign of his critical attitude to society. He continued his education first in Germany, then briefly at Cambridge, leaving in 1901 when his father died. In 1906 a legacy left him well off, and he followed no profession but that of writer, except briefly during the First World War. Myers went with his mother to America in 1901 for what was hoped would be a posthumous meeting with his father, and there met Elsie Palmer, whom he married in 1908. Myers was not a facile writer, and could afford to be, in the best sense, unprofessional. After an unimportant verse play, *Arvat* (1908), he worked at his first novel, *The Orissers*, for more than thirteen years. It was published in 1922 and was immediately recognized as a work of distinction. *The Clio* (1925) was influenced by – or was a response to – the vogue for Aldous Huxley. Myers subjected his socialite characters on a jungle-bound yacht to the test of the primeval, and went rather deeper than entertainment or light satire. (Lightness was not his vein.) His masterpiece, an Indian tetralogy set in the time of Akbar, the Great Mogul, in the late 16th century, was written between 1929 and 1940. It consists of *The Near and the Far* (1929), *Prince Jali* (1931), *The Root and the Flower* – the first two plus an extra book, 'Rajah Amar' – (1935) which won the James Tait Black and Femina prizes, and *The Pool of Vishnu* (1940). The 4 were published as a single volume in 1940, as *The Near and the Far*. Between the last 2 volumes came a separate work, *Strange Glory* (1936).

His leftish conscience is evident in *The Pool of Vishnu* especially, with its paternalist, Tolstoyan characters such as Mohan, and he shared the enthusiasm of the thirties for Communism. Myers is said to have become increasingly embittered and misanthropic towards the end of his life: as with Lawrence, who certainly influenced him, the quest for ideal relationships in his work was counterpart to a frustrated 'societal' instinct. His acutely depressive temperament is evident in the novels, where the prevailing weather is close, and he became another artist victim of the war period, committing suicide at Marlow in 1944. Little is publicly known of his private life and its relation to his work: he destroyed his autobiographical writing, and asked his friends to burn his letters.

In a period of experiment in the novel Myers, like Forster, was not a technical innovator. The concern with the chaos and vulgarity of modern life which he shared with Lawrence is not expressed through realist treatment: the emphasis is on inner or visionary experience, so to this extent he is a romantic writer. An agnostic, he anticipated contemporary interest in the relevance of Eastern mysticism and detachment to modern problems. Myers held that spiritual experience is as compelling a part of life as sex but his themes are not those easiest treated in fiction. His creative life was a search for adequate formal rendering of them: uneasy in the melodramatic *The Orissers*, he was more successful in *The Clio*, which showed his powers of exotic invention and symbolic setting. *The Near and the Far* is of a scale and social complexity that permits interaction of the personal-spiritual and political sectors. Its importance as a modern novel may be limited by the remote, aristocratic society portrayed and it sometimes lacks the impact and inevitability of the very greatest novels (Myers admitted his interest waned) but it is a major work. The sheer amplitude and splendour of his re-creation of Akbar's India and – in his brief appearances – its tycoon-like emperor is a *tour de force*. Myers focused all his sense of corruption, and condemnation of sensibility divorced from moral values, in the despotic Daniyal and his Pleasaunce of the Arts – said to be partly based on Bloomsbury. His spiritual refinement involved no lack of sophistication and psychological insight. But novelistic 'life' in Myers is less compelling than his account of the inner spiritual climate and tragic sense of man. Two decades have increased the interest of his work, but he has proved too austere for the common reader. [J H]

G. H. Bantock, *L.H.M.*, *A Critical Study* (1956); Irène Simon, *The Novels of L.H.M.* (1956); R. Bottrall, in *A Review of English Literature* (1961); L. P. Hartley, *DNB Supplement*; D. W. Harding et al., *Scrutiny*, III, IV, V, VI, VII, and IX.

Mystery Plays. ♢ Miracle Plays.

Naidu, Sarojini (1879–1949). Indian poet. Born into a wealthy family in Hyderabad. Her parents sent her to England at 15. She studied at London and Cambridge, met Edmund Gosse and Arthur Symons and felt the influence of the Rhymers' Club. Returning to India in 1898 she made the impossible marriage her parents had hoped to prevent. The intensities of love and motherhood are present in her first book of poetry, *The Golden Threshold* (1905). Sickness and a near-mysticism drove her inwards. Growing sadness is apparent in *The Bird of Time* (1912) and dominant in *The Broken Wing* (1917). This was her last book of poetry. Her involvement with Indian politics, particularly with the status of women, began in 1906 and increasingly occupied her energies. Her support of Gandhi was influential and unwavering. The vogue for Mrs Naidu's poetry has passed; nevertheless, in occasional lyrics, and in the fine sequence 'The Temple' in her last volume, she rids her work of the throb that England in the nineties had taught her and allows an obvious gift for words to make its effect without over-straining. *The Feather of the Dawn* (1961) is a collection of her poetry. [PT]

P. E. Dustoor, *S.N.* (1961); K. R. Srinivasa Iyengar, *Indian Writing in English* (1962).

Naipaul, V(idiadhur) S(urajprasad) (1932–). West Indian novelist. Born into an Indian family in Trinidad and educated in Trinidad and at Oxford. His birthplace forms the background of his early novels, which reveal the profound influence of his Hindu extraction. His work is conspicuously Indian in its orientation, and clearly influenced by an English education. After graduating, he became a freelance colonial broadcaster and began writing his finely disciplined farces about the life of the Trinidad poor. *The Mystic Masseur* (1957), *The Suffrage of Elvira* (1958) and *Miguel Street* (1959), in which he uses the street as a stage for an amusing or wryly moving succession of stories, were the first. Immaculately lucid prose combines with an incisive grasp of the comic and a sharp irony in the dispassionate observation of human behaviour. *A House for Mr Biswas* (1961), his most ambitious work, is also his best. A total sensory recall of environment informs its description of a man's life and death in poverty. A fourth novel, *Mr Stone and the Knights Companion*, written after a visit to India, was published in 1963, and *The Mimic Men* in 1967. Naipaul is also the author of two travel books, *The Middle Passage* (1962), the outcome of a commissioned return to the Caribbean in 1960, and *An Area of Darkness* (1964), a brilliant account of a visit to India. *The Loss of El Dorado* (1969) concerns the history of Trinidad. Now settled in London, he is a frequent contributor to magazines and periodicals and makes regular television appearances. [WAG]

A Flag on the Island (1967) (short stories).
K. Miller, 'V.S.N. and the New Order', in *Kenyon Review*, XXIX, 5.

Nairne, Carolina Oliphant, Baroness (1766–1845). Scottish song-writer. Born of a Perthshire Jacobite family, Lady Nairne wrote nearly all her songs pseudonymously for *The Scottish Minstrel* (1821–4), an enterprise intended to refine and in effect to bowdlerize the current repertoire of Scottish popular song. Some of her best songs and adaptations – 'Caller Herrin'', 'The Laird o' Cockpen', 'The Hundred Pipers' and 'Will Ye No Come Back Again', for example – are as good as Burn's earlier, more robust reshaping of traditional songs, but much of Lady Nairne's work (including such pieces as the once famous 'The Land o' the Leal') merely contributed to the sentimental pietism and the genteel falsification of working-class life that overtook Scottish culture in the early 19th century. [AI]

Life and Songs, ed. C. Rogers (1869).
G. Henderson, *Lady N. and Her Songs* (1900).

Nance, Robert M. ◊ Cornish Literature.

Narayan, Rasipuram Krishnaswami (1907–). Indian novelist. Born in Madras and educated in South India. The influence of journalistic experience is already visible in the documentation of his first novel *Swami and Friends* (1935). Like its successor, *The Bachelor of Arts* (1937), it is set in the town of Malgudi which Narayan's descriptive art has localized at the same time as his unruffled irony has made it representative of urban India. Other 'Malgudi' novels are *The Dark Room* (1938), *The English Teacher* (1945), *Mr Sampath* (1949), *The Financial Expert* (1952), *The Man-Eater of Malgudi* (1962) and *The Sweet Vendor* (1967). *Waiting for the Mahatma* (1955) is his most political work. During the war Narayan edited the short-lived *Indian Thought*. He lives now in Mysore, where he continues to write as a columnist.

Narayan's stature as a novelist is best seen in *The Guide* (1958). The unobtrusive meeting of seriousness and hilarity is here contained in an interplay of past and present. The hero is among the finest of Narayan's energetic frauds. An undemonstrative, purposeful prose and a sharp eye for situations in which humanity confronts its own absurdity are Narayan's main weapons. His incidents and characters are at once realistic and grotesque. He finds in the tentative commitments of the Indian middle class the best chance for a profoundly humorous exploration of the dilemma of being normal. His first two volumes of short stories, *An Astrologer's Day* (1947) and *Lawley Road* (1956) are similar in style to the novels. The third, *Gods, Demons, and Others* (1964), retells Indian myths and legends. [P T]

My Dateless Diary (1960) (travelogue).
W. Walsh, 'The Novels of R.K.N.', in *A Review of English Literature*, II, 4 (October 1961); K. R. Srinivasa Iyengar, *Indian Writing in English* (1962); V. P. Rao, 'The Art of R.K.N.', *Journal of Commonwealth Literature*, 5 (July 1968).

Nashe, Thomas (1567–c. 1601). Pamphleteer, poet and dramatist. Born in Lowestoft, the son of a preacher, he was educated at St John's College, Cambridge, where Robert ◊ Greene, the first and most prolific of Elizabethan professional writers, had preceded him. His earliest printed work (1589) was a preface to Greene's *Menaphon* defending his late friend against an attack by Gabriel ◊ Harvey, who was long to remain a sparring partner in satirical pamphleteering. The preface is a confident young man's review of the state of literature at the time. Later in 1589 he published *The Anatomie of Absurditie* as a reply to Philip ◊ Stubbes' *Anatomie of Abuses* (1583). His hatred of Puritanism and his natural combativeness drew Nashe into the ◊ Marprelate controversy: *An Almond for a Parrot* (1590) is usually attributed to him along with a series of pseudonymous pieces. His most successful and wide-ranging pamphlet, *Pierce Penniless his Supplication to the Devil*, went through 3 editions in 1592: this vivid social satire revealed Nashe as a brilliant reporter of the follies and vices of his day who also undertook a defence of the theatres against the Puritan moralists. *Strange News of the Intercepting Certain Letters . . . as They Were Going Privily to Victual the Low Countries* (1593) contains an enthusiastic, generous defence of Greene against a fresh attack by Harvey, a controversy which was still raging in 1596 when Nashe included a pseudo-biography of Harvey in *Have With You to Saffron Walden*.

Nashe's *The Unfortunate Traveller, or the Life of Jack Wilton* (1594) is an important example of picaresque fiction and a keywork in the evolution of the English novel. Set in the reign of Henry VIII, it recounts the knaveries of a page in plague-ridden England, the Low Countries, Germany, France and Italy. It was – and is – frequently reprinted.

Nashe was part-author (with Ben Jonson amongst others) of *The Isle of Dogs* (1597), which was prosecuted for its slanderous and seditious content, but his most inventive dramatic work is outside the mainstream of Elizabethan commercial drama. *Summer's Last Will and Testament* (1592) was acted at Croydon by members of Archbishop Whitgift's staff. The principal character was Will Summers, Henry VIII's court fool, and punningly the entertainment took as its theme the cycle of the seasons with Summer yielding to Autumn. The famous lyric 'Adieu, farewell, earth's bliss' (especially the stanza beginning 'Beauty is but a flower') has been much anthologized.

Nashe was a brilliant and lively writer of prose and excelled in several modes while ultimately lacking control and organization. His influence was considerable. Readers and scholars of Nashe are well served by the fine edition *The Works of*

Thomas Nashe, edited by R. B. McKerrow (1904–10; revised by F. P. Wilson, 1958). [MJ]

G. R. Hibbard, *Thomas Nashe* (1962); ed. Stanley Wells, *Thomas Nashe* (1964).

Neilson, John Shaw (1872–1942). Australian poet. Born of Scottish parents in Penola, South Australia, he received a little over two years' formal education before beginning a life of manual labour in the bush, which lasted, despite his defective eyesight, until 1922. Under these conditions he wrote his delicate lyrics. His first collection was published in 1919. In 1922 he was given a small literary pension, and in 1928 was offered a sinecure in a Melbourne government department. *Collected Poems* was published in 1934, and *Unpublished Poems* in 1947. Neilson's best verse has an inconspicuous harmonic discipline. It is poetry of incomplete statement, relying on its subdued emotional activity to involve the reader. A delight in natural beauty is often set against a sense of loss. [PT]

T. Inglis Moore, *Six Australian Poets* (1942); *Southerly*, 1 (1956) (special Shaw Neilson issue).

Nesbit, E(dith) (1858–1924). Children's writer. The daughter of a well-known agricultural chemist in Kennington; her father died in 1862, and the family lived on the continent until 1870, when they returned to live in Halstead in Kent and later in London. She was an impetuous, generous and enthusiastic creature all her life. She had poetic ambitions, and later regretted that she had to spend so much time writing prose, although in fact there was nothing remarkable about her verses. She married Hubert Bland, and she took to writing commercially soon after when her husband's business partner absconded with the capital. For some years she wrote copiously, stories, novels, verses and even some children's stories. The work was undistinguished, but she learnt to tell a story. The Blands were founder members of the Fabian Society, and kept open house for Bernard Shaw, H. G. Wells and their other friends. Her husband was a political journalist and moulded her political views for her, while she flung herself into social work. Hubert Bland died in 1914, and she married Thomas Tucker, a marine engineer, in 1917.

She found her true balance as a comic prose writer when the first Bastable stories appeared in 1898. They were published in book form the following year. E. Nesbit wrote all her best-known work over the next fourteen years. The best books fall into two groups: first, the family adventures, 3 books about the Bastables, *The Story of the Treasure Seekers* (1899), *The Wouldbegoods* (1901) and *New Treasure Seekers* (1904), and *The Railway Children* (1906); second, the magic stories, especially *Five Children and It* (1902), and its sequels *The Phoenix and the Carpet* (1904) and *The Story of the Amulet* (1906). She is noted for her lack of whimsy (she satirizes the convention of romantic story-telling for children) and for vivid representations of family life. She much preferred inventing characters to plots. She was outstanding in her handling of magic themes, and tart, unpredictable magic creatures such as the Psammead and the Phoenix, and her power to re-create the past if her characters travelled in time. [TV]

D. Moore, *E.N.: A Biography* (1967).

Newbolt, Sir Henry (John) (1862–1938). Poet and man of letters. He became well known for his nautical ballads and patriotic verse during the Edwardian and First World War periods. Many were inspired by Devonshire heroes but he was born at Bilston, Staffordshire, where his father was vicar. His school, Clifton, is part of the satiric consciousness of English readers from *Vitai Lampada* and *Clifton Chapel* (1908). After Oxford, he practised at the Chancery Bar 1887–9, and made his name with *Admirals All* – 21 impressions (1898) – and *Songs of the Sea* (1904). While editor of the *Monthly Review*, from 1900 to 1904, he introduced the work of De la Mare. *Drake's Drum*, published in the *St James' Gazette* in 1897, elicited from Bridges the comment that 'It isn't given to man to write anything better'. Newbolt was Comptroller of Telecommunications during the First World War and an official naval historian. He was knighted in 1915 and made a C.H. in 1922. He lived for much of his life at Netherhampton, in Wiltshire, and died in London. His reputation has deservedly suffered. Once valued above Kipling's, his weakly Kiplingesque poetry does not tell the truth either about public schools or war. Nevertheless Newbolt was a craftsman in the short narrative ballad, for instance *He Fell among Thieves*, though it is marred by sentimentality. He was at his best in a dialect monologue such as the poacher's in *Master and Man*. [JH]

Selected Poems, ed. John Betjeman (1940); *A Perpetual Memory and Other Poems*, with memoirs by W. de la Mare and R. Furse (1939); *My World as in My Time* (1932) (autobiography).
C. K. Stead, *The New Poetic* (1964); M. Newbolt, *The Later Life and Letters of Sir H.N.* (1942).

Newcastle, Margaret Cavendish, Duchess of (1624?–94). A daughter of Sir Thomas Lucas, she became the devoted second wife (1645) of William Cavendish, Marquis (later first Duke) of Newcastle, whose *Life* (1667; ed. C. Firth, 1886; Everyman's Library, 1915) she wrote. She was a quasi-learned, fantastic and undisciplined writer of a minor but genuine talent. Her works (with a little collaboration from her husband) run to a dozen volumes; of her verses, the *Past-times of the Queen of Fairies* is remembered; her plays are unreadable; but in prose, she was an early biographer in the Restoration manner, and also published an interesting autobiography (one of the first), in *Nature's Pictures Drawn by Fancie's Pencil to the Life* (1655). She also wrote, in imitation of Lucian, a 'philosophical voyage', *The Blazing World* (1668?), as well as essays, notably the not uninteresting, fictional *CCXI Sociable Letters* (1664) which give some idea of the private life of the time. Though Pepys thought her mad, she is a queer instance of the difficulty that women then had in developing any intellectual life. [AR]

H. T. E. Perry, *The First Duchess of Newcastle and Her Husband* (Boston, 1918).

Newman, John Henry, Cardinal (1801–90). Theologian, Christian apologist and miscellaneous writer, prominent in the Oxford Movement. Born in London, the eldest son of an evangelical banker, and privately educated at Ealing and at Trinity College, Oxford, he became a Fellow of Oriel College (1822), where he was a colleague of Pusey and ◊ Keble. Two years later he took orders, becoming curate of St Clement's, and in 1828 vicar of St Mary's Oxford. After 1830, Newman became more and more 'High Church', and on a visit (1832) to Rome and the south of Europe with ◊ Froude wrote most of his short poems, including 'Lead Kindly Light', published in the collection by Keble and others, *Lyra Apostolica* (1836). Following Keble's Assize sermon in 1833, Newman was the principal organizer of the *Tracts for the Times* (hence the title of the 'Tractarian Movement'), to which he contributed 24, including the celebrated Tract XC (1841; frequently reprinted separately; ed. A. W. Evans, 1933). In this essay, Newman attempted to show that the admittedly ambiguous 39 Articles of the Church of England could be given a 'Catholic' meaning, though refusing obedience to the See of Rome. His fine-drawn (not to say sophistical) arguments gave offence to many, and incurred official censure. His sermons in St Mary's gave full play to his brilliant gifts of preaching and personality. His doctrine of the *Via Media* of the Anglican Church (adumbrated in various works between 1830 and 1841, and published under that title in 1877) sought to show that his Church avoided the errors of authoritarian Rome and the vagaries of the inner-light of the Puritans. This, together with his powerful, unsettling influence caused him (and the Tractarian Movement) to be accused of 'Romanizing'. He found himself that the distinctions between his position and the Roman Church melted away, and after a period of prayer and fasting he resigned his living (1843) and entered the Roman Church (1845). He became a Roman priest and D.D. (1846) in Rome, returning to England (1847) to found the Oratory in Birmingham and in 1850 that in the Brompton Road, London. He published fiercely polemical *Lectures on the Present Position of the Catholics in England* (1851) and in 1854 became Rector of the Catholic University in Dublin, which he had helped to found and the British Government financed. His work in this connexion prompted various discourses, which make up one of the most famous of his works, *The Idea of a University* (ed. A. R. Waller, 1903; Everyman, 1915). In this he champions the notion that a university itself exists to develop the mind rather than to hand out information, and that all fields of human investigation are to be unified by the organizing concepts of theology, which is a 'science' of its own kind. Newman was unable to put his ideas into practice in the Irish situation, however, and soon resigned. Charles ◊ Kingsley, in a stupid aside, incautiously accused Newman of intellectual prevarication and thus involved himself in a battle which prompted Newman's *Apologia pro Vita Sua* (1864; 1865, with the savaging of Kingsley omitted; Everyman, 1912).

This work is partly polemical, in the sense that Newman clearly hopes to convince and influence the reader by his sincerity and persuasive powers, but also partly a powerful justification of his action and beliefs to himself. It holds a high place as a spiritual autobiography. Newman's verse account of the Soul's journey through judgement to purgatory, *The Dream of Gerontius* (1866), is the text of Elgar's powerful oratorio of that title (1900). His last important work, and perhaps the most interesting, though difficult to read, is *An Essay in Aid of a Grammar of Assent* (1870; ed. C. F. Harrold, New York, 1947), an account of the springs of religious belief. He also wrote 2 bad novels. Newman was made Cardinal of St George in Velabro in 1879; he died and was buried in Birmingham. He is of great importance in the history of English religious thought in the last century. He was a man of brilliant and persuasive personality, and the master of a lucid and fine prose style, as well as of a powerful, argumentative cast of mind. He stands as a supreme rhetorician, in the best sense of that word.

There is a vast body of writing about Newman and the Oxford Movement. His works were collected in 40 volumes (1874–1921) and (the fullest edition) in 41 volumes (1908–18); there are many different volumes of selections (e.g. *Prose and Poetry*, ed. G. Tillotson, 1957). [AR]

The Letters and Correspondence of N., ed. A. Mozley (1891). W. Ward, *The Life of J. H. Cardinal N.* (2 vols., 1912); M. Trevor, *N.* (2 vols., 1962); *N. Centenary Essays* (1945); G. Faber, *Oxford Apostles* (1936; 1944), W. E. Houghton, *The Art of Newman's Apologia* (Yale U.P., 1945); A. O. J. Cockshut, *Anglican Attitudes: A Study of Victorian Religious Controversies* (1959); A. Läple, bibliography, *Newman Studien*, 1, ed. H. Fries and W. Becker (Nuremberg, Passau, 1948).

Nicholson, Norman (Cornthwaite) (1914–). Poet, critic and topographical writer. Born in Millom, Cumberland, where he still lives. A close knowledge of the geography, and indeed geology, of Cumberland underlies his poems and verse dramas, which are also firmly Christian in the attitudes and beliefs expressed. His Christian beliefs come out, also, in the *Pelican Anthology of Modern Religious Verse*, which he edited, and in his critical book, *Man and Literature*. Aiming at accuracy and honesty rather than brilliant or experimental effects in his poetry, he might be described as a poet in the Wordsworthian tradition. He was made a Fellow of the Royal Literary Society in 1945, and was awarded the Heinemann Prize for his first volume of poems, *Five Rivers* (1944). [GSF]

Rock Face (1948); *The Pot Geranium* (1954); *Selected Poems* (1956); verse dramas: *The Old Man of the Mountains* (1946); *A Match for the Devil* (1955); *Birth by Drowning* (1960); criticism and topography: *Man and Literature* (1943); *William Cowper* (1951); *Cumberland and Westmorland* (1949); *The Lakers* (1955); *Provincial Pleasures* (1959); *Portrait of the Lakes* (1963).

Ní Chonaill, Eibhlín Dubh (*c.* 1750–1800). Irish poetess. Poems of love and lamentation, attributed to women such as Créide, Liadan and Deirdre, have survived from the early Irish period; and the modern period provides similar instances, like *Caoineadh Uí Raghallaigh* ('O'Reilly's Lament') and *Caoineadh Airt Uí Laoghaire* ('Lament for Art O'Leary'), which was composed by his widow, Eibhlín Dubh Ní Chonaill, a native of Co. Kerry.

The 'Penal Code' discriminated heavily against the native Irish: thus, Art O'Leary, being the owner of a prize horse which he refused to part with for a nominal sum, was waylaid and shot. His body lay beside a whin bush, covered with an old shawl. In her lament, the author's consciousness flows freely, as it were, along the course of her life with Art; from the time she fell in love with him: 'Your mien attracted me / You stole my heart from me / I fared afar with thee / From my father's hearth with thee'. She remembers the wedding reception, and their years together, to the day of his last fatal journey. How is she to tell the children when they call for their father? Her mind lights on his enemy, and she curses fervently. At last she ends, on a quiet note; having attained, like Milton, 'Calm of mind, all passion spent'.

Technically, the poem is simplicity itself, consisting of short swift phrases, strung together by final assonances, of a type already known in Old Irish as *rosc*. Here, indeed, feeling overcomes artlessness. [SB]

O. J. Bergin, 'Caoineadh Airt Uí Laoghaire', in *Gaelic Journal* (1896); S. O. Tuama, *Caoineadh Airt Uí Laoghaire* (1961).

Nicolson, Harold (1886–1968). Critic and diplomat. Born in Teheran, where his father was *chargé d'affaires*, and educated at

Nigel

Wellington College and Oxford, Nicolson joined the Diplomatic Service and held posts in Madrid, Istanbul, Teheran and Berlin. Resigning in 1929, he began a career in journalism on the staff of the *Daily Express*. From 1935 to 1945 he was a Member of Parliament. He married Victoria Sackville-West in 1913, and was knighted in 1953.

Nicolson's first published work was a novel, *Sweet Waters* (1921), but although he wrote one or two more novels it was as a critic of literature that he became known. He published an excellent monograph, *Paul Verlaine*, as early as 1921, and followed it with *Tennyson* (1923), *Byron: The Last Journey* (1924) and *Swinburne* (1926). *Tennyson* did a great deal to turn the tide of critical favour which had been running against the poetry of Tennyson. *Curzon: The Last Phase* (1934) was a serious study of the statesman. More recently Nicolson has published his diaries which give a fascinating picture of political life in the years between the wars as it was seen by a well-to-do diplomat and critic who was something of a dilettante in the best sense of the word. *The English Sense of Humour* (1946) is an agreeably civilized collection of articles, lectures and addresses. [CO]

Public Faces (1932); *Small Talk* (1937); *Journey to Java* (1957); *Diaries and Letters, 1930–39, 1939–45*, and *1945–62* (3 vols., 1966–8).

Nigel Longchamps (*c.* 1130–*c.* 1200). Latin poet. Sometimes erroneously called Nigel Wireker, he was probably born at Longchamps in Normandy. He became a Benedictine at Christ Church, Canterbury, and spent the rest of his life there. His chief work, *Speculum stultorum* (ed. with tr. J. H. Mozley and R. R. Raymo, Stanford, 1960; tr. in verse J. H. Mozley, *A Mirror for Fools*, 1961; tr. G. W. Ragenos, *The Book of Dan Burnel the Ass*, Austin, Texas, 1959), is a satire on the clergy, written in elegiacs. Its hero is an ass, Burnellus, who is dissatisfied with his tail, which he considers too short. His physician gives him a prescription for a longer tail, to be made up at Salerno, but he fails to get it. After various misadventures he is recaptured by his former master and returns to servitude. Burnellus represents the priest or monk who is discontented with getting no preferment in the church and the various classes of the clergy are satirized in turn, particularly the Cistercians and the secular canons.

392

F. J. E. Raby, *Secular Latin Poetry*, ii (2nd edn, 2 vols., 1957).

North, Christopher (pseud. of John Wilson) (1785–1854). Scottish essayist and editor. The son of a Paisley factory-owner, he was educated at Glasgow and Oxford Universities; he bought an estate in Westmorland, lost it, studied for the Scottish Bar, and attracted attention with a poem. *The Isle of Palms* (1812), in the manner of Thomas ◊ Campbell. In 1817 Wilson became chief contributor and adviser to *Blackwood's Magazine*, whose first number contained the notorious 'Chaldee Manuscript' – a joint production by Wilson, ◊ Hogg and ◊ Lockhart – in which Edinburgh notables were satirized under a thin disguise of biblical language and names. In 1820 the unreformed Tory Town Council of Edinburgh appointed Wilson Professor of Moral Philosophy in Edinburgh University. Although not wholly unqualified by the standards of the time, he published no original work during his thirty years' tenure of the chair and was supplied with material for his lectures, especially in his early years, by an obliging and well-informed friend near Birmingham. Wilson's delivery, manner and moral tone nevertheless made a great impression on his students. He contributed voluminously to *Blackwood's*, writing most of the series of 'Noctes Ambrosianae' (1822–35), convivial conversation-pieces in which literary, social and political issues of the day were handled with a mixture of robust good sense and scurrilous philistinism by 'Christopher North' (Wilson himself), 'The Ettrick Shepherd' (Hogg) and 'Timothy Tickler' (Wilson's uncle, Robert Sym). Wilson also published some sentimental tales, forerunners of the ◊ 'Kailyard' Scottish fiction of the late 19th century. [AI]

Works, ed. J. Ferrier (1855–8).
M. Gordon, *C.N., a Memoir* (1862); E. Swann, *C.N.* (1934).

North, Sir Thomas (*c.* 1535–*c.* 1601). Translator. The younger son of the 1st Baron North, he may have gone to Peterhouse, Cambridge, before taking up residence in Lincoln's Inn in 1557. He was given the freedom of Cambridge in 1568. He travelled to France in 1574, was knighted in 1591, made J.P. for Cambridgeshire in 1592, and received a royal pension from Elizabeth in 1601. He translated Guevara's *Dial of*

Princes from a French version in 1557, and the *Moral Philosophy of Doni* in 1570, both of which were reprinted and widely read. In France he perhaps met Amyot, from whose version he worked in making his greatest translation, Plutarch's *Lives of the Noble Grecians and Romans* (1579; reprinted 1595, 1603, 1612, 1631 and 1657; ed. G. Wyndham, 6 vols., 1895). North's distinction as a translator is enhanced by the fact that Shakespeare found greater artistic stimulus in North than in any other source. He gave Shakespeare plots, conceptions of characters, and actual words. He was not a scholarly translator, but a lively and idiomatic prose-writer, who made the lives of the heroes of antiquity vividly available to his contemporaries; in English literature he is important as a prose stylist and as a potent influence on Shakespeare. [MJ]

C. S. Lewis, *English Literature in the Sixteenth Century* (1954); F. O. Matthiessen, *Translation: An Elizabethan Art* (1931); ed. T. J. B. Spencer, *Shakespeare's Plutarch* (1964).

Norton, Mrs Caroline Elizabeth Sarah (1808–77). Verse-writer, novelist and social worker. Born a Sheridan, the granddaughter of Richard Brinsley ◊ Sheridan. Her first book, *The Sorrows of Rosalie: A Tale*, with other poems (1829), was well received and she published several other long poems, and a book of children's ballads. She also wrote 3 novels. In 1827 she had married the Hon. C. G. Norton, who later sued her for her earnings from her writings. As a result she separated from him and produced several short works to better the conditions of married women, including a pamphlet, *English Laws for Women in the Nineteenth Century* (1854), which was part of her successful agitation for the Married Women's Property Act. George ◊ Meredith in part based the plot of *Diana of the Crossways* (1885) on Mrs Norton's career. In 1871 she married Sir William Stirling-Maxwell. [AR]

J. G. Perkins, *The Life of Mrs N.* (1909); A. S. Acland, *C.N.* (New York, 1948).

Norton, Thomas (1532–84). Poet and dramatist. A member of the Grocers' Company, he was admitted to the Inner Temple in 1555 and was successively Member of Parliament for Galton, Berwick and London. He was made an M.A. of Cambridge in 1570 and Remembrancer of the City of London in 1571. Son-in-law of Cranmer and a zealous anti-Catholic in Parliament, he went to Rome to procure information against English Catholics. He conducted investigations of suspected recusants under torture. Sonnets by him appeared in ◊ Tottel's *Miscellany* (1557) and he made an English version of Calvin's *Institution of the Christian Religion*. His chief claim to literary fame is his part-authorship with Thomas ◊ Sackville of the first English tragedy in blank verse, *Gorboduc*. Originally called *The Tragedy of Ferrex and Porrex*, it is an academic, formalized entertainment, modelled on Seneca, and was first presented at the Inner Temple in 1562 and later before the Queen at Whitehall. Based on an episode in the legendary pre-history of England, it tells in blank-verse set speeches of the fatal division of Gorboduc's kingdom between his sons and of the resulting civil war. It points a political moral, and the actions tend to be reported rather than staged. [MJ]

A. P. Rossiter, *English Drama from Early Times to the Elizabethans* (1950); F. P. Wilson, *The English Drama, 1485–1585* (1969).

Noyes, Alfred (1880–1958). Poet, critic and biographer. A fervent Roman Catholic convert, he is chiefly remembered for ballad-like poems like 'The Highwayman' or 'Come to Kew in Lilac-Time' which still survive in the more old-fashioned British school anthologies. He set a higher value himself on long narrative poems like *Drake* (1906–8) and *The Torchbearers* (3rd edn, 1937), the second of which dealt with some of the great British scientists. He was a fierce opponent of all 'modernist' movements in art and poetry, and these prejudices are expressed, often in a lively way, in *Some Aspects of Modern Poetry* (1924) and even more in his autobiography, *Two Worlds for Memory* (1953). His work, both in prose and verse, lacks distinction of style or subtlety of feeling, but has a certain strenuousness, which reflected itself both in his biography of Voltaire (1936), a remarkably sympathetic study which shocked some of his co-religionists, and, in his later years, in his courageous defence of the memory of the Irish patriot, executed during the First World War, and later accused of having kept a scandalous homosexual diary, Sir Roger Casement. [GSF]

The Watchers of the Sky (1922); *Ballads and Poems* (1928).

O

Ó Bruadair, Dáibhidh (1625–98). Irish poet. The second half of the 17th century was a period of stirring events in Ireland: the rising of 1641 and its aftermath, the Cromwellian confiscations, the Williamite war, the battle of the Boyne, the siege of Athlone and the fall of Limerick. These are mirrored in the work of Ó Bruadair, who was a native of Co. Cork.

Confining himself to a strictly limited range of themes, he was a very voluble writer. He was not a lyrist, like Aodhagán Ó Rathaille; in fact, much of his work could be described simply as a versified commentary on current affairs, as seen from the Irish side. For example, in verses beginning *Nach ait an nós so ag mórchuid d'fhearaibh Éireann* ('How strange this craze among many men of Erin'), he rails against those who were straining to imitate alien ways and learn the English language. Few authors could wield such an extensive vocabulary as Ó Bruadair, but, even in poems addressed to his friends, the style is almost invariably ponderous and pedantic. His best work was written towards the end of his life, in the years following the peace treaty of Limerick (1691). In his time most poets were discarding the classical syllabic metres in favour of *amhrán* or accented verse, but Ó Bruadair regretted the change, and referred to the new metres as *sráidéigse* ('street poetry'). His heart was with the old bardic order. [SB]

J. C. Mac Erlean, *Duanaire Dháibhidh Uí Bhruadair* (I, 1910; II, 1913; III, 1917).

Ó Cadhain, Máirtín (1914–   ). Irish novelist and short-story writer. He was born in Co. Galway and works as a lecturer in Trinity College, Dublin. Hitherto he has published several volumes of short stories, *Idir Shúgradh is Dáiríre* (1939), *An Braon Broghach* (1948), *Cois Caoláire* (1953); and a novel, *Cré na Cille* (1953).

Like Pádraig ◊ Ó Conaire, he shows a high degree of originality, in both thought and expression; but his mastery of the language is far superior to that of the older author. Keenly observant and frankly realistic, Ó Cadhain does not hesitate to portray the less pleasant aspects of existence: in this he differs from a number of other writers. By comparison with Séamus ◊ Ó Grianna, for example, his style shows a certain lack of terseness in description and verbosity in dialogue; and some of his short stories suffer from loose construction. His talent is rather for psychological exposition and the creation of atmosphere. His most ingenious work is undoubtedly *Cré na Cille* ('Churchyard Dust'), portraying the careers, opinions, intrigues and petty jealousies of a rural community, as represented by its deceased members in the local cemetery. These souls still retain the characteristics of their earthly existence, and they freely express their personalities in luxuriant and racy Irish: exhorting and admonishing each other, conversing and gossiping in huge stretches of exuberant dialogue. The book has a kind of Slavic flavour. [SB]

J. E. C. Williams, *Traddodiad Llenyddol Iwerddon* (1958).

Ó Caiside, Tomás (Thomas O'Cassidy) (*c*. 1710–*c*. 1770). Irish author. Irish literature in the 18th century was adversely affected by the prevailing social and political conditions. Prose was particularly handicapped: there was no outstanding writer, and indeed few works of any kind were produced; among the more notable was the autobiography of Friar Tomás Ó Caiside, who was born in Co. Roscommon, and descended from an old Ulster family, who had been physicians to the Maguires of Fermanagh.

According to his own account, he joined the Augustinian Order at an early age; but, finding life dull and discipline intolerable, he left the monastery and thenceforward led a roving, freelance existence. Like numerous Irishmen of those days, he went abroad as a soldier of fortune, and joined the French army. Soon, however, he and another trooper absconded, 'like two blackbirds from a bush'. After a further period spent in the Prussian forces of Frederick I, he again escaped, 'by the help of God and powerful St Patrick', and left for Bristol, where he enlisted in the English army before finally arriving back in Ireland, where he ended his days in poor circumstances. He recounts these adventures in a headlong, tumultuous style.

Ó Caiside was also the author of several songs, mostly amorous in content, which still survive among Irish-speaking people in Connacht. [SB]

M. Nic Philibín, *Na Caisidigh agus a gCuid Filidheachta* (1938).

O'Casey, Sean (1880–1964). Dramatist. Born into a poor, Protestant family in the slums of Dublin, he was largely self-educated and became the greatest of the second generation of Abbey Theatre dramatists with a series of realistic tragedies written after the First World War. *The Shadow of a Gunman* (1923), *Juno and the Paycock* (1924) and *The Plough and the Stars* (1926) are set in the tenements O'Casey had known during the 'Troubles'. *Juno*, with its almost photographic setting, mingles the vulgar, the comic and the tragic; its entertaining braggarts and parasites are contrasted with the women who suffer and endure. In 1926 O'Casey moved to England, where he lived in exile. In 1928 Yeats precipitated an Irish literary feud by rejecting for performance at the Abbey the 'expressionist' anti-war play *The Silver Tassie*, staged in London the following year. O'Casey's bold attempts at an experimental form of drama were not well received, and in 1934 criticism of *Within the Gates*, a play about the Depression, embittered him. In 1934 he published *The Flying Wasp*, attacking reviewers for indifference to new work. His later plays include *Red Roses for Me* (1943), *Cock-a-Doodle Dandy* (1949) and the anti-clerical *The Bishop's Bonfire*, produced in Dublin in 1955. In 1958 the Archbishop of Dublin refused to inaugurate the Dublin Festival by celebrating Mass if O'Casey's *The Drums of Father Ned* was included. O'Casey withdrew his play, and discouraged professional performances of any of his plays in Ireland.

In 1939 he published *I Knock At the Door*, the first of 6 volumes of autobiography. Other volumes are: *Pictures in the Hallway* (1942); *Drums under the Windows* (1945); *Inishfallen, Fare Thee Well* (1949); *Rose and Crown* (1952); *Sunset and Evening Star* (1954), all reprinted as *Autobiographies* (2 vols., 1963). [M J]

Collected Plays (4 vols., 1949–51).
Ed. R. F. Ayling, *S.O'C.: Modern Judgments* (1969). S. Cowasjee, *S. O'C.: The Man behind the Plays* (1963) and *O'C.* (1966); G. Fallon, *S. O'C.: The Man I Knew* (1965); R. G. Hogan, *The Experiments of S. O'C.* (1960); D. Krause, *S. O'C., the Man and His Work* (1960).

Occleve. ♢ Hoccleve.

Ó Cearbhalláin, Toirdhealbhach (T. Carolan) (1670–1738). Irish poet and musician. He was born in Co. Meath, but the family migrated to North Connacht, where the boy – who had been blinded by small-pox – was trained as a harpist under the patronage of the Mac Dermott Roe family. Thenceforward, he lived by the harp, and for nearly fifty years he travelled the Irish countryside, staying at the big houses and entertaining the local gentry with music and song. His principal patrons were the Mac Dermotts and O'Conors of North Roscommon. His was a sociable, convivial character, whose popularity brought him to the notice of the English-speaking public at an early stage: e.g. an essay by Oliver Goldsmith entitled 'Carolan, the Last Irish Bard' appeared in the *British Magazine* for July 1760.

Fundamentally, he was a musician who could devise verse to fit music. His literary technique was limited, and the content of his verse is trivial enough: songs in praise of ladies and gentlemen, of whiskey and good cheer; and even one in praise of himself, full of jesting hyperbole, *Ní fheicfear mo leitheid go bráth* ('My compeer will never be seen'). He met and was friendly with many Irish authors of his day, such as Séamus ♢ Mac Cuarta, and Cathaoir Mac Cába, who composed his elegy: *Ní tréan mo labhairt 's ní mheasaim gur cúis náire / Óir is éan bocht sgaite mé ó chaill mé mo chúl báire* ('Feeble my speech, and I think it no shame / For I am a poor, lonely bird since I lost my companion'). [SB]

T. Ó Máille, *Amhráin Chearbhalláin* (1916); D. O'Sullivan, *Carolan*, I, II (1958).

Ó Conaire, Pádraig (1883–1928). Irish essayist and story writer. He was born in Galway city, but spent much of his early life in Connemara. It was the Oireachtas, or annual literary festival organized by the Gaelic League, which attracted his first literary efforts, such as the prize-winning essay of 1908, in which he outlined his ideas on Irish literature and showed a marked appreciation of contemporary trends in European writing.

He was especially successful as a writer of sketches and short stories, of which several collections appeared, including *Seacht mBuaidh an Éirghe Amach* (1918), *An Crann Géagach* (1919) and *Síol Éabha* (1922). He liked to ramble through the countryside, and wrote a series of essays on the joys and events of open-air life – the whims of his little dark donkey, the sounds of wind among the trees, the smells of burning wood – generally reminiscent of Stevenson's *Travels with a Donkey*. On the other hand, he was quite at home in depicting city life: he had an urbanity rare among contemporary Irish writers. In 1910 appeared his *Deoraidheacht*, a novel about Irish emigrants in London.

Ó Conaire was one of the outstanding pioneers of Irish literature in the present century. At his best, he showed considerable psychological insight. His work has the mild and subtle shades of a Connemara skyscape. [SB]

A. Ní Chnáimhín, *P. Ó C.* (1947).

O'Connor, Frank (pseud. of Michael O'Donovan) (1903–66). Irish writer and critic. Born in Cork of a poor family and largely self-educated, he took the Republican side in the civil war, which led to his meeting with Séan ◊ O'Faoláin, and a spell of imprisonment in 1923 which he used to fill the gaps left in his literary education. In response to the nationalist fervour of the time, his early writing was in Gaelic, and he later published some good verse translations from the Irish, in particular *The Wild Bird's Nest* (1932) and *Lords and Commons* (1938). His first stories were published in the *Irish Statesman* by ◊ AE and his first book of stories, *Guests of the Nation*, appeared in 1931. He made a name for himself in the group of younger writers in Ireland who included O'Faoláin and Liam ◊ O'Flaherty and for a time he worked as Director of the Abbey Theatre in Dublin, in close contact with Yeats during the last years of his life. O'Connor eventually resigned from the Abbey on the issue of censorship, and for the latter part of his life he lived and worked mostly in America. He published several more collections of short stories, 3 books about Ireland, and 2 readable and acute books of criticism: *The Mirror in the Roadway* (1957), on the modern novel, and *The Lonely Voice* (1963), on the short story, which he describes as 'the literature of submerged population groups'. His stories all have an Irish background: even tales which he collected elsewhere he rewrote with an Irish setting, thus perfecting what Muriel Spark called 'a miraculous technique which universalizes the stories without impairing their local virtue' – although sometimes a certain sweetness in the conception of the stories may be felt to qualify this statement. [JM]

Stories of Frank O'Connor (1953); *My Oedipus Complex* (1963); *An Only Child* (1961) and *My Father's Son* (1968) (autobiography).

Ó Dálaigh, Donnchadh Mór (D. O'Daly) (*c.* 1170–1244). Irish poet. Donnchadh Ó'Dálaigh (the adjective *mór* means 'great') was the most famous religious poet of medieval Ireland. In the Annals of the Four Masters he is described as a poet that never was and never will be surpassed. He was traditionally reputed to have been Abbot of Boyle, Co. Roscommon, but may have actually been a layman, employed by that monastery to write religious verse, in the same way as his brother, Muireadhach Albanach ◊ Ó Dálaigh, wrote verse for secular patrons.

His work consists of long, polished syllabic poems on such subjects as the Holy Cross, the transience of life, the signs that will precede the Day of Judgement. In *Truagh mo thuras ar Loch Dearg* ('Alas, for my journey to Lough Derg'), he tells of his disappointment, on arriving at St Patrick's Purgatory on a penitential pilgrimage, to find that he had no tears to shed. Another piece clearly reflects the professional attitude: just as any artist depends on the reward of his art, so Donnchadh Mór offers God a poem, for which he expects heaven in return. It may be compared with ◊ MacNamee's prayer for a son. Full of conceits and quaint turns of expression, these poems differ from the short religious lyrics of the Old Irish period.

Owing to his prestige, later scribes tended to ascribe religious verse of doubtful authorship to Donnchadh Mór; and poems attributed to him were current in Connacht folklore down to the present century (see D. Hyde, *A Literary History of Ireland*, 1899). [SB]

L. McKenna, *Dán Dé* (1922).

Ó Dálaigh, Muireadhach Albanach (*c.* 1180–*c.* 1250). Irish poet. The Ó Dálaigh brothers, Donnchadh Mór ◊ Ó Dálaigh and Muireadhach Albanach, were probably the most colourful Irish literary personalities of their time. In the year 1213, according to the Annals of the Four Masters, Muireadhach was living at Lisadell, Co. Sligo, when a steward of O'Donnell's came from Donegal to levy taxes there. A dispute arose, and the poet killed the agent with an axe.

Fearing O'Donnell's vengeance, he fled .southwards and took refuge with de Burgo, then travelled to Limerick, later to Dublin, and finally across the sea to Scotland, whence the agnomen *Albanach* ('Scottish'). He married – probably a Scottish lady – and founded the famous bardic family of Mac Mhuirich ('son of Muireadhach'), who maintained their literary heritage in Scotland down to the end of the 18th century (see Watson, *Rosg Gàidhlig*, 139). He also visited the Holy Land, and addressed a poem to Cathal Croibhdhearg O'Connor while on board ship in the Adriatic. In addition to eulogistic and religious verse, he composed a touching personal poem, a lament for his dead wife. It survives in a single copy in the Scottish Book of the Dean of Lismore, from which it has been edited and translated by Osborn Bergin: 'My soul parted from me last night; a pure body that was dear is in the grave; a gentle stately bosom has been taken from me with one linen shroud about it.' [SB]

R. Flower, *The Irish Tradition* (1947).

Ó Domhnaill, Maghnas (M. O'Donnell) (?–1563). Irish poet and hagiographer. Of the princely house of O'Donnell, he became lord of Tír Chonaill or Donegal in 1537, and was quite prominent in the political affairs of his time.

As a man of letters, he was the author of love-poems in the Provencal manner, several of which have survived. He had a sharp wit, and appears to have enjoyed composing satirical quatrains; those still extant relate to matters such as a bad harper, or the friars of Donegal. His greatest work is the prose *Betha Colaim Chille* ('Life of Colum Cille'), written in 1532. The choice of subject was a happy one, St Colum Cille being esteemed in Irish tradition, not only as a successful missionary, but also as a scholar and a friend of the literati. His earliest biographer had been Adamnan (d. 704). Moreover, a wealth of miscellaneous lore relating to St Colum Cille was still current in the 16th century among the people of his native Donegal. All these sources were utilized by Ó Domhnaill. He collated and reorganized the material, modernized it and recounted it all in his own words. The result is an attractive and highly readable work, remarkably free from the twin faults of Irish prose, namely archaism and over-ornateness, and bearing the imprint of its author's decided literary taste. [SB]

A. O'Kelleher and G. Schoepperle, *Betha Colaim Chille* (Chicago, 1918); T. F. O'Rahilly, *Dánfhocail* (1921); *Dánta Grádha* (1926).

O'Faoláin, Seán (1900–). Irish novelist and biographer. Born in Dublin and educated at the National University Dublin, and Harvard, he fought on the Republican side in the Civil War and was Director of Publicity for the I.R.A. in 1922. He then went to America, where he studied and taught in Massachusetts, before returning to Ireland in 1933. He was a teacher in Co. Wicklow until the success of his books enabled him to live by writing. His earliest work, as became a patriot, was in Gaelic. A collection of short stories, *Midsummer Night Madness* (1932), was followed by his best-known novel, *A Nest of Simple Folk* (1933), with its quiet power of suggestive vagueness. But, on his own admission, these books were written in a romantic daze, and their successful qualities could not be recaptured. His writing therefore diversified: biographies of Irish heroes, such as *Daniel O'Connell* (1938) and *The Great O'Neill* (1942); travel books such as *South to Sicily* (1953); and miscellaneous writings. O'Faoláin's work has been increasingly critical of Ireland, in particular of what he regards as its false religiosity and insularity; he felt that 'Ireland had not adjusted herself to the life about her in the least little bit', and his later stories are more satirical. This made him unpopular in Ireland, but elsewhere he has been widely praised as a realistic and sympathetic writer. [JM]

Vive Moi! (1965) (autobiography); *The Stories of S. O'F.* (1958).
M. Harmon, *S.O'F.: A Critical Introduction* (1966).

O'Flaherty, Liam (1897–). Irish novelist. Born on the Aran Islands, off the coast of Galway, and intended for the priesthood, he was educated at Catholic schools and the National University, Dublin. From an early age he had been attracted by violence and after abandoning his vocation he enlisted in the Irish Guards in the First World War and fought in France until he was invalided out in 1917. For the next three years he travelled the world, working his passage. In 1922 he returned to Dublin to fight with the Republicans in the Civil War, although he appears to have been more interested in fighting for socialism at that time. A year later he went to London to write. Of his first (unpublished) novel he said 'At least two million people were killed in it'. His next book, *The Neighbour's Wife* (1923), set in Aran, was published on the advice of Edward Garnett; 2 more books followed without great success until the lurid and violent *The Informer* (1925) was hailed as a masterpiece for its portrayal of the confused and ugly Republican terrorism. It was made into a successful film by John Ford, and has inspired many subsequent books about the Irish 'Troubles'. O'Flaherty's other novels, which include *The Puritan* (1931), *Famine* (1937) and *Insurrection* (1950), have similar settings of violence and poverty, but his short stories, *Spring Sowing* (1924) and *The Tent* (1926), for example, are quiet and peaceful. He is an uneven and uneasy writer; his neurotic autobiography, *Shame the Devil* (1934), indicates some of the tensions which have beset him, but is factually unreliable. Since 1935 he has lived mainly in America and written little. [JM]

O'Grady, Standish James (1846–1915). Folklorist and antiquarian. Born at Castletown Berehaven, Co. Cork, the son of a clergyman, and educated at Tipperary Grammar School and Trinity College, Dublin, he was called to the bar, but took to writing. His works made available much information about ancient Irish history and legend; this was capitalized later by the Irish revival writers (◊ Yeats). Among his works were *Early Bardic Literature, Ireland* (1879) and *History of Ireland*: i, *the Heroic Period*: ii, *Cuculain and his Contemporaries* (1880). He wrote several historical romances including *The Flight of the Eagle* (1874), and a volume of short stories, *The Bog of Stars* (1893). [AR]

H. O'Grady, *O., the Man and the Writer* (Dublin, 1929).

Ó Grianna, Séamus (1891–1969). Irish novelist and short-story writer. Many Irish writers of the revival era have used pseudonyms, but none is better known to readers of the language than 'Máire', the name used by Séamus Ó Grianna, a native of Co. Donegal, and one of the most prolific prose writers of recent years.

His career began with 2 romantic novels, the best-known being *Caisleán Óir* (1924). In these, he displayed his mastery of the vigorous and racy dialect of Donegal; but, as regards plot construction, his genius did not seem to favour the inherent ramifications of a novel. He turned to short-story writing with more conspicuous success, his first collection, *Cioth is Dealán* (1926), already showing considerable familiarity with the art of the short story. Later he produced a more or less continuous stream of short stories, mostly portraying the lives and characters of the people of his native Donegal. Many of his plots suggest the influence of Maupassant: precise, well planned and economical; at times they are almost mechanical, when one gets the impression that characters have been pressed into service for the occasion. Romantic rather than realistic, he treats the ups and downs of fortune and life with a kind of ironic humour. In addition to his novels and short stories, he published an autobiography, and translated works of fiction from English and French. His style is perhaps the most self-conscious and polished in contemporary Irish literature. [SB]

S. Ó Grianna, *Saol Corrach* (1946).

Ó hUiginn, Tadhg Dall (1550–91). Irish poet. He lived in Co. Sligo, and belonged to one of the most distinguished of the medieval Irish bardic families. His brother, Maolmhuire Ó hUiginn, was Catholic Archbishop of Tuam.

Most of his extant work consists of encomiastic poems, composed in syllabic metres and addressed to Irish or Norman noblemen of his time. One of the earliest is in praise of Shane O'Neill, prince of Tyrone. Other poems were addressed to O'Donnell, O'Connor, O'Hara, Maguire; and several to the de Burgos, among them William Burke, with whom the poet was united by 'a bond of art' in learning, music and the improvisation of poetry. One piece, in praise of Hugh O'Byrne of Co. Wicklow, is interesting as an example of the *amhrán* or accented metre which gradually ousted the syllabic verse in the course of the next century. Among his less formal, more personal poems, one refers to young friends of his who had gone to London, while others are vision-poems, of a type that underwent further development during the 18th century.

The style, ideas, virtues and shortcomings of Irish court poetry are excellently exemplified in the work of Tadhg Ó hUiginn. (The adjective *dall* – 'blind' – appears in the names of several Irish poets.) His work is that of the trained craftsman, exquisitely finished according to professional canons, but little influenced by personal feeling. [SB]

E. Knott, *The Bardic Poems of Tadhg Dall Ó hUiginn* (i, 1922; ii, 1926).

Ó Laoghaire, Peadar (Peter O'Leary) (1839–1920). Irish prose writer. From the end of the 19th century, one great problem facing the Irish revival movement was the establishment of a suitable literary style: one school of writers favoured a return to 17th-century standards, while another advocated the use of living speech as represented in the spoken dialects. Among the latter, the leading figure was Canon Peter O'Leary. Boldly adopting his native dialect of West Cork as his medium, he became the author of an impressive array of literary works. The most famous of these is *Séadna*, a kind of novel with a traditional background, concerning a man who has sold himself to the devil: it is cognate with Goethe's *Faust* and Marlowe's *Dr Faustus*. O'Leary also made modernized versions of several early Irish classical tales. The best known of these is *An Craos-Deamhan*, an adaptation of the 'Vision of Mac Conglinne', a 12th-century tale of a scholar poet from Connacht, who went to Munster and succeeded in ridding its gluttonous king of a hunger-demon. It is somewhat analogous to *The Land of Cokaygne* in English. In addition to the foregoing, he published a number of devotional works, including a new translation of the *Imitatio Christi*; and an autobiography, entitled *Mo Sgéal Féin*.

Following Canon O'Leary's example, each Irish author wrote in his own dialect; and it was not until 1945 that a literary standard at last began to evolve, actively encouraged by the national government. [SB]

R. de Hae, agus B. Ní Dhonnchadha, *Clár Litridheacht na Nua-Ghaedhilge, I* (1938).

Old English Poetry. Some 30,000 lines of Old English (or Anglo-Saxon) poetry survive, the great bulk of it in four manuscripts: MS Cotton Vitellius XV in the British Museum, which contains ◊ *Beowulf, Judith*, and 3 prose works; the Junius Manuscript in the Bodleian Library, Oxford (MS Bodleian Junius 11), containing *Genesis, Exodus, Daniel*, and *Christ and Satan*; the Exeter Book, given by Bishop Leofric to Exeter Cathedral, containing *Christ, Juliana, The Wanderer, The Seafarer, Widsith, Deor*, and a variety of short pieces; the Vercelli Book, preserved in the cathedral library at Vercelli, in northern Italy, containing *Andreas, The Fates of the Apostles, Address of the Soul to the Body, The Dream of the Rood*, and *Elene*. It is impossible to determine what proportion of the poetry produced is represented by what has survived, especially with non-religious poetry where there was little clerical motive for copying and preserving.

In spite of the fragmentary nature of what survives of Old English poetry, it represents a body of literature earlier in date than any extant poetry of the other Germanic literatures. Much of it reflects the old Germanic heroic world whose literature was primarily an oral court minstrelsy. *Widsith*, which purports to be an autobiographical poem by a *scop* (itinerant minstrel), consists of an older core with some later additions and reflects the old heroic view of the bard's function as well as giving us the Old English view of the history of their own Germanic past. The text preserved in the Exeter Book is 10th-century West Saxon, though the poem originated in Northumbria in the late 7th or early 8th century.

Beowulf has its unique place in Germanic heroic poetry, the only complete surviving epic in an ancient Germanic language. Two fragments – one describing the attack on Hnaef's hall by Finn's followers and the other an Old English version of the story of Waltharius, well known on the continent – complete the body of existing Old English heroic poetry. The conversion of the Anglo-Saxons to Christianity produced a distinctive religious poetry which flourished in Northumbria in the 8th century but which has survived only in late-10th-century West Saxon transcriptions. ◊ Caedmon, who wrote in the late 7th century, is known only through ◊ Bede's reference and quotation. *Genesis, Exodus* and *Daniel* are later poems, the product of the 'Caedmonian School'. A remarkable interpolated passage in *Genesis*

('*Genesis* B') shows great dramatic vigour, especially in its depicting of Satan. *Exodus* is older (early 8th century?) and shows the old heroic style adapted to religious purposes. *Christ and Satan* may show the influence of ◊ Cynewulf, the most self-consciously craftsmanlike of the Old English poets. *Christ, Juliana, Elene* and *The Fates of the Apostles* are signed by Cynewulf by means of acrostics woven into the poems. The finest of the poems written under Cynewulf's influence is *The Dream of the Rood*, of which an early version is carved in runic characters on the Ruthwell Cross in Dumfriesshire. *Judith* is a verse rendering of the Vulgate text of the apocryphal book of Judith: it survives only in the concluding part, which tells of Judith's beheading of Holofernes, the defeat of the Assyrians, and Judith's triumphant song of praise to God.

A quite distinct kind of poetry is represented by *The Wanderer* and *The Seafarer*, in both of which a lyrical elegiac note (as distinct from the heroic note) dominates. *The Wanderer* is the lament of a lonely man once happy in the service of his lord and now after his lord's death, a journeying exile: the speaker looks back on departed joys and contrasts the past with the present. In *The Seafarer* an old sailor speaks, recalling the hardships of a sailor's life: here too the tone is elegiac, though the mood alternates between weariness of the sea and fascination with it. A note of personal passion emerges in the lyric poem generally entitled *The Wife's Lament*, another monologue, this time of a wife separated from her husband. *The Husband's Message* and *Wulf and Eadwacer* are also dramatic monologues, the latter of which sounds a curiously modern note of romantic passion.

Old English poetry comes to an end with a revival of the old heroic note in two poems about real battles. *The Battle of Brunanburh* (in *The Anglo-Saxon Chronicle* under the year 937) is a victory poem in which the note of patriotism (as opposed to emphasis on an individual hero in a wide Germanic setting) is first sounded; *The Battle of Maldon* (*Anglo-Saxon Chronicle*, 991) is a poem of defeat under hopeless odds ending with a famous expression of stoical courage enduring until the inevitable end. Old English poetry thus went down fighting. By the time the next known significant English poems appear, they are written in the next phase of the English language, Middle English, after the Norman Conquest had accelerated some

linguistic changes and originated others. [DD]

G. P. Krapp and E. van K. Dobbie, *The Anglo-Saxon Poetic Records* (5 vols., New York, 1931–53) (definitive texts of the Old English poems); W. J. Sedgefield, *An Anglo-Saxon Verse-Book* (Manchester, 1922) (an anthology of Old English poetry, with historical and explanatory notes); R. K. Gordon, *Anglo-Saxon Poetry* (Everyman, 1927, 1954) (the whole corpus of Old English poetry, in translation).
C. W. Kennedy, *The Earliest English Poetry* (New York, 1943); G. K. Anderson, *The Literature of the Anglo-Saxons* (Princeton, 1949); S. B. Greenfield, *A Critical History of Old English Literature* (New York U. P., 1965); C. L. Wrenn, *A Study of Old English Literature* (1967).

Oldham, John (1653–83). Poet, satirist and translator. Born at Shipton-Moyne in Gloucestershire, the son of a non-conformist minister, he was educated at St Edmund Hall, Oxford, and became a member of the literary scene of the time. Dryden's poem to his memory after his untimely death of small-pox is only one of many tributes to the promise of his genius. He published 'pindaric' odes in the manner of the time (◊ Cowley), but is best remembered for his popular and influential translations and imitations of Horace, Juvenal and Boileau. His chief works were *A Satyr against Virtue* (1679) and 4 severe *Satyrds upon the Jesuits* (1681; 1682; 1685) relating to the 'Popish plot'. Oldham combines a forthright cynicism with a considerable mastery of a solid couplet form. *Poems and Translations* appeared in 1683 (reprinted 1684). Oldham has fallen under the shadow of Dryden, and there is no good modern edition or critical essay. [AR]

Works (1684; several reprintings); *Poetical Works*, ed. R. Bell in Bell's *English Poets* (1854; reprinted 1871; intr. B. Dobrée, 1960).
D. M. Vieth, 'Oldham, the Wits and A Satyr Against Virtue', *PQ*, XXXII (1953); C. R. Macklin, 'O.'s Satirical Technique in the *Satyrs*', *SP* LXII (1965); H. F. Brooks Bibliography in the *Proceedings of the Oxford Bibliographical Society*, V (1936) (lists his various contributions to contemporary *Miscellanies*).

Oldys, William (1696–1761). Antiquary, editor and Norroy King-of-Arms. The author of numerous works including some early and important biographical work, such as his *Life of Sir Walter Raleigh* prefixed to an edition of ◊ Ralegh's *History of the*

World (1736) and a number of lives in the first edition of the *Biographia Britannica* (1747–60). He collaborated with Dr Johnson in editing *The Harleian Miscellany* (8 vols., 1744–6), a reprint of tracts from the library of the Harleys, Earls of Oxford. Oldys is most often encountered as the author of a frequently anthologized lyric, 'Busy, curious, thirsty fly!'. [AR]

DNB.

Oliphant, Laurence (1829–88). Novelist, journalist, miscellaneous writer and traveller. Born in South Africa, he afterwards became a barrister in Ceylon, where his father, Sir William, was Chief Justice. His education was irregular and he travelled extensively, being given occasional diplomatic employment (secretary to Lord Elgin in North America and China) and acting as *The Times* correspondent. His adventures took him to the Crimean War and the Indian Mutiny; he plotted with Garibaldi and with Polish revolutionaries; he wrote dispatches from the Franco-Prussian War. After a spell in Parliament (1865–7), he became a follower of an American mystic, T. C. Harris, gave him his property and went to America to join the Brotherhood of the New Life. In the eighties he founded a community of Jewish immigrants at Haifa, where he wrote several of his works. His many varied writings include travel-books, *Journey to Katmandu* (1852), *The Russian Shores of the Black Sea* (1853), *Minnesota and the Far West* (1855) and a *Narrative of the Earl of Elgin's Mission to China and Japan* (1859); novels such as *Piccadilly* (a satire which appeared in *Blackwood's*, 1865; reprinted 1870); *Altiora Peto* (1883), a religious work; and poetry. He also produced (with his first wife) *Sympneumata or Evolutionary Forces now Active in Man* (1885), but this he claimed was dictated by a spirit. [AR]

Mrs Margaret Oliphant, *Memoir of L.O.* (2 vols., 1891); P. Henderson, *The Life of O.* (1959); M. Kent, 'An Errant Genius', *Cornhill Magazine*, CLIV (1936).

Oliphant, Mrs Margaret (1828–97). Prolific novelist and miscellaneous writer. Born a Wilson near Edinburgh, she married her cousin, William Oliphant, an artist. As a writer of fiction she published sketches in *Blackwood's Magazine* (with which she had a long connexion, writing over 200 articles), under the title *The Chronicles of Carling-*ford (1863–6; and separately published); the series included *Salem Chapel, The Perpetual Curate* and *Miss Marjoribanks.* In her vast output of fiction, she treats of Scottish life and dissenting communities, trying competently to 'use' fiction for a serious (sometimes a religious) end; she was also interested in the occult. Mrs Oliphant was a George Eliot with talent instead of genius, and blunt observation instead of subtle insight. As well as fiction, she wrote historical studies (*The Makers of Florence*, 1876, is often encountered on bookstalls), and biographies. Her *Annals of a Publishing House: William Blackwood and His Sons* (1897) is useful. [AR]

R. B. Johnson, *The Women Novelists* (1918); L. Stebbins, *A Victorian Album* (New York, 1946); V. and R. A. Colby, *The Equivocal Virtue: Mrs O. and the Victorian Literary Market Place* (1966).

Ó Maoil Chonaire, Flaithrí (F. Conry) (1560–1629). Irish writer and scholar. This remarkable man belonged to a learned family of hereditary poets and historians, and was born in Co. Roscommon. He joined the order of Friars Minor, and pursued his studies in Salamanca. He accompanied the Spanish forces of Don Juan del Aguila to Ireland in 1601, but after the defeat of the Irish princes at Kinsale, he returned to the continent, and spent the remainder of his life in exile.

In 1606, through his influence, Philip III founded the College of St Antony at Louvain in the Spanish Netherlands, which became in some respects the greatest of the Irish colleges abroad. In 1609, Conry was appointed Archbishop of Tuam, but never visited his see. He was an international authority on the works of St Augustine, on which he published several treatises in Latin. In Irish, his principal publication is *Desiderius* or *Sgáthán an Chrábhaidh*, a version of *El Desseoso*, an allegorical work of the *Pilgrim's Progress* type, first published in Barcelona in 1515 and subsequently translated into several European languages. The Irish version was published at Louvain in 1616. Its aim was to provide Irish Catholics with reading matter in their own language: this and the fact that much of the original is in dialogue form favoured a relatively simple, easy style. The book is an interesting landmark in the history of Irish prose. [SB]

T. F. O'Rahilly, *Desiderius* (1941).

Ó Neachtain, Seán (John Naughton) (1655–1728). Irish author. Dublin in the early 18th century was not merely the home of Swift and other Anglo-Irish writers: it also held a school of Irish authors, which might be described as the Naughton Circle (on the analogy of the somewhat later Morris Circle in Wales) because its principal figure was Seán Ó Neachtain or Naughton, who was born in Co. Roscommon.

He composed Jacobite and other verse, his best-known poem being *Rachainn fö'n gcoill leat, a mhaighdean na n-órfholt* ('I would go to the wood with thee, golden-haired maiden'), in which (as often in the poetry of Dafydd ap Gwilym) the love-motif yields pride of place to the pleasures and delights of the greenwood. In addition, he wrote prose romances. The most popular of his prose works is *Stair Éamoinn Uí Chléirigh* ('Story of Edmund O'Clery'), depicting the spiritual progress of its central character, through successive failures and disappointments, to final triumph. It is mock-heroic in tone, satirical rather than serious, and sometimes trivial; nevertheless, it affords an insight into the contemporary scene; thus, for example, the increasing awareness of the English language is indicated in humorous passages, referring to Irish speakers' attempts to learn English and the resultant clash of idiom. Ó Neachtain was well educated, a competent writer, and a man of humane character. [SB]

Ú. Ní Fhaircheallaigh, *Filidheacht Sheáin Uí Neachtain* (1908); E. Ó Neachtain, *Stair Éamoinn Uí Chléirigh* (1918).

Orage, Alfred Richard (1873–1934). Journalist and editor. Although the death of his father left the family in poverty, Orage completed his studies at a village school at Fenstanton in Huntingdonshire and went to a teachers' training college at Culham, Oxfordshire. While working as an elementary-school teacher in Leeds, he became interested in socialism and in the possibility of effecting a revolution in culture and taste. This interest took a practical form when he founded the Leeds Art Club with a friend, Holbrook Jackson. In 1906 he went to London as a free-lance journalist, and with Jackson set up an arts group within the Fabian Society. With the backing of Bernard Shaw the two men bought a weekly review, the *New Age*, in 1907. Under Orage's editorship the aims and nature of socialism became an important topic of discussion in the journal, and contributions were drawn from Shaw, G. K. Chesterton, Belloc, H. G. Wells, Havelock Ellis, and Arnold Bennett. Orage published a number of young writers, among them Katherine ◊ Mansfield, J. M. ◊ Murry, J. C. ◊ Squire, T. E. ◊ Hulme, Herbert ◊ Read, and Edwin ◊ Muir. Criticism and reviews were contributed by Ezra Pound and Arnold Bennett. A lively concern for the state of literature informed his own critical writings, part of which have been collected in *Readers and Writers (1917–21)* (1922) and *The Art of Reading* (1930). At the same time he was concerned to find an organization of society where men could find a better outlet for their creative energies and a more genuine freedom than was likely to result from the State Socialism championed by the Fabians under Sidney and Beatrice Webb. Thus for a time he became an advocate of Guild Socialism, based on worker-ownership and worker-management of the different industries. After 1918 he became a convert to the Douglas social credit system – a scheme for abolishing wages and replacing them. with universal dividends. He was consistently opposed to the Bolshevik government in Russia. In 1922 he gave up the editorship of the *New Age* in order to devote himself to the work of Gurdjieff, a teacher of occultism. In 1932 he took charge of the *New English Weekly*, where he returned to the advocacy of social credit. [NL]

Political and Economic Writings, ed. Montgomery Butchart (1936); *Selected Essays and Critical Writings*, ed. Herbert Read and Denis Saurat (1935).
Philip Mairet, *A.R.O. A Memoir* (1935).

Ó Rathaille, Aodhagán (1670–1726). Irish poet. He was a native of Co. Kerry, and composed elegies, satires, and other poems, but excelled as a lyrical poet.

He gave a new impetus to the *aisling* 'vision', a type of poem in which Ireland is personified as a beautiful lady awaiting the return of her true lover from beyond the sea. His best-known visions, *Gile na Gile* ('Splendour of Brightness'), and *Mac an Cheannaidhe* ('The Merchant's Son'), served as models for later poets: they were often imitated, but never surpassed. In such poems as *Is atuirse ghéar liom créachta crích' Fodla* ('Bitter to me are the wounds of Fodla's realm'), he expresses in sombre music the pent-up feelings of a sensitive and defiant people at a time of great crisis in their history. His personality is perhaps best displayed in his last poem, composed on his deathbed, *Cabhair ní ghoirfead go gcuirtear mé i gcruinn-chomhrainn* ('I shall not cry for help ere I am placed in a closed coffin'). Having referred, Lear-like, to his vexations and misfortunes, he concludes: 'I will cease now, death is nigh unto me without delay / Since the warriors of the Laune, of Lein, and of the Lee have been laid low / I will follow the beloved among heroes to the grave / Those princes under whom were my ancestors before the death of Christ.' His best work has a splendour of its own. [SB]

P. S. Dineen and T. O'Donoghue, *Dánta Aodhagáin Uí Rathaille* (1911); D. Corkery, *The Hidden Ireland* (1925).

Ó Reachtabhra, Antoine (A. Raftery) (1784–1835). Irish poet. Raftery, the last notable poet of pre-Famine Ireland, was born in Co. Mayo. Blinded by smallpox in his youth, he became a travelling fiddler, lacked education in the formal sense, and was in effect a folk-poet like Robert Burns.

Vigorous, simple, fluent and direct in style, his verse abounds in homely metaphors and strong local colour. Some of his songs refer to contemporary developments such as local elections or the Catholic emancipation movement, others were composed in honour of generous individuals or in praise of skilful craftsmen. One of the best concerns a boating tragedy on the River Corrib near Galway in 1828, when a number of people lost their lives. Another, in praise of his native Co. Mayo, abounds in the enthusiastic hyperbole so common in popular poetry. His most ambitious effort is *Seanchas na Sceiche* ('Lore of the Thorntree'), a long metrical history of Ireland, showing a considerable knowledge of native tradition, including written sources such as Keating's *History of Ireland*, which the author had acquired through oral transmission. Although unwritten, Raftery's own poems lived on in the vernacular; until, with the newly awakened interest in oral Irish literature towards the end of the 19th century, they were finally recorded and preserved, mainly through the efforts of Lady Gregory and Dr Douglas Hyde. [SB]

D. de híde, *Abhráin agus Dánta an Reachtabhraigh* (1933).

Orrm or **Orrmin** (fl. 1170?–1210?). Poet. All that we know of Orrm comes from the dedication of his long poem, *Orrmulum* (ed. R. Holt, 1878), written for his brother Walter, an Augustinian canon like himself. The manuscript is dated *c.* 1210, and the dialect is north Lincolnshire, with a strong Norse admixture, as the name 'Orrm' suggests. He may have been a canon of Elsham Priory, or possibly he can be identified with Orm, brother of Walter, Augustinian prior of Carlisle from 1150–70.

Orrmulum is a collection of homilies, in verse of strict syllabic regularity and conspicuous clarity, designed to give a complete course of instruction for the Church year, though only about an eighth of the intended work survives. Each gospel for the day is followed by an interpretation and application. Its importance is less literary than linguistic. Orrm developed a very original system of orthography to help the reading of the work aloud. [AG]

H. C. Matthes, *Die Einheitlichkeit das Ormulum* (1933); R. Stevick, 'Plus Juncture and the Spelling of the *Ormulum*', *JEGP*, LXIV (1966).

Orwell, George (pseud. of Eric Blair) (1903–50). Novelist and political writer. Orwell, son of a Civil Servant, was born in India in 1903. He was sent to a private school in the south of England, which he describes in his essay 'Such, such were the joys . . .', and won a scholarship to Eton. At Eton, although he seems to have been happy and to have done well, he was acutely conscious of the difference between his own moneyless middle-class background and his richer companions. When he left school he joined the Imperial Police in Burma. He was there from 1922 to 1927, and it gave him a searing experience of oppressive colonialism. He returned to England with a guilty conscience which he felt he must in some way expiate. By this time he was sure that he wanted to write, and he went to Paris trying to earn money by teaching while he made his first attempts. His experiences of near-destitution in Paris and later as a tramp in England provided the material for his first book, *Down and Out in Paris and London* (1933).

Orwell had shared the lives of some of the worst-off members of society and these he described with a detached directness which was throughout his career the keynote of his style. His response to social injustice led him inevitably to political commitment, but it was a very individual commitment, guided by his own conscience rather than by any political creed. He never joined a political party. In *The Road to Wigan Pier* (1937) he investigated the conditions of the unemployed in the North of England. He makes his socialist belief quite clear, but the book also contains a biting if rather crude attack on the left-wing intellectuals of the time, who took up theoretical postures without coming close to the facts that inspired them. He was criticized by many sections of the left, and his next book, *Homage to Catalonia* (1938), in many ways his most finely written, was virtually ignored. This was an account of his part in the Spanish Civil War. He had gone to Spain as a journalist in December 1936, and true to his compulsion to act according to his beliefs he at once joined the Republican army. *Homage to Catalonia* was an important book politically, for it gave the only first-hand account of the Communist Government's suppression of Trotskyist and Anarchist elements and gave a fair picture of the Trotskyist role. As most of the British left-wing joined in the Communist condemnation of the Trotskyists, Orwell's unpopularity and his isolation from the main body of left opinion was increased.

By 1936 Orwell had written 3 novels, which reflect his own revolt against the middle class. His characters are trapped in a decaying middle-class environment against which they make ineffectual, and sometimes self-destructive, attempts to rebel. The drab atmosphere and hopeless tone of these novels is an indication of the difficulties in Orwell's own life at this time. Although his characterization is often flawed, Orwell's early fictional writing is gloomily powerful. *Coming Up for Air* (1939) is perhaps his best pre-war novel. It reveals Orwell's nostalgia for some of the features of pre-First World War England, which was an important aspect of his socialism, and a sense of doom at the inevitability of war.

When war broke out Orwell shared the belief amongst the left wing that the fight against Hitler would necessitate some kind of social revolution in Britain. His articles at the time, which appeared in several newspapers and periodicals, and his book *The Lion and the Unicorn* (1941), an analysis of the English character and the likely nature of this revolution, reflect this feeling. But by 1942 it was clear that this would not occur, and the last years of the war, and victory itself with its promise of cold war, confirmed Orwell's pessimism about the situation both at home and abroad. Throughout the war years Orwell's journalistic output was immense, and many of his most interesting ideas are contained in short articles and reviews, particularly in his weekly column in *Tribune*.

In 1945 Orwell suddenly received widespread public acclaim with his allegorical novel *Animal Farm*. This described with piercing simplicity and a quiet affection for the animals of his allegory the degeneration of the Russian Revolution. For the first time Orwell coincided with public opinion. He had always attacked Stalin, but 1945 was the time when Britain, after approving Stalin as an ally, condemned him when his post-war ambitions became clear. In the years after the war Orwell, whose health had never been good since his years of privation and the severe wound he received in Spain, suffered increasingly from tuberculosis. His illness intensified his pessimism. In 1949, just before his death, his most famous novel, *Nineteen Eighty-four*, was published. In it Orwell visualizes an authoritarian state of the future, but the book is most remarkable for his political predictions, some of which have come true, and his logical development of features of post-war Britain. The book demonstrated how the logic of totalitarianism was that the individual consciousness would eventually be entirely obliterated. It was welcomed by the right wing as a condemnation of Communism and the authoritarian tendencies of socialism, but in fact *Nineteen Eighty-Four* condemned totalitarianism of every kind and, just as strongly, the sterility of modern life, a sterility which Orwell believed until his death could be best countered by socialism.

In his writing Orwell covered almost every aspect of modern life from major political issues to tiny details of daily living. He was always swift and direct in his responses. His honesty sometimes led to an impulsiveness which marred the clarity of his style, but generally his writing is taut, lucid, detached and with a striking tendency for effective and sometimes shocking understatement. One of his most impressive essays, 'Politics and the English Language', reveals his striving to use language with a complete understanding of its precise meaning. Few modern writers have such a distinctive and exact command of words.

His most important works, other than those mentioned above, are: Fiction:

Burmese Days (1935); *Keep the Aspidistra Flying* (1936). Essays: *Inside the Whale* (1940); *Critical Essays* (1946); *Shooting an Elephant* (1950); *England Your England* (1953); *Such, Such Were the Joys* (New York, 1953). [JRC]

J. Atkins, *G.O.* (1954); I. Howe, *O.'s 'Nineteen Eighty-Four'* (New York, 1963); R. Rees, *G.O. – Fugitive from the Camp of Victory* (1961); R. J. Voorhees, *The Paradox of G.O.* (1960); G. Woodcock, *The Crystal Spirit* (1967); J. Calder, *Chronicles of Conscience* (1968).
Collected Essays, Journalism, and Letters, ed. S. Orwell and I. Angus (1968).

Osborne, John (1929–   ). Dramatist. A Londoner, he became an actor in 1948, and, while acting in provincial repertory companies, he was part-author of 2 plays produced in 1950 and 1955 at Huddersfield and Harrogate. In 1956 his *Look Back in Anger* was directed in London (like much of his subsequent work) by Tony Richardson for the newly founded English Stage Company, and proved to be a seminal work. Set in a Midlands attic flat, the play centres on Jimmy Porter, the archetypal 'angry young man' – classless, rebellious, disillusioned with contemporary Britain. *Epitaph for George Dillon* (London, 1958; written earlier, in collaboration with Anthony Creighton) is a study of a parasitic young writer, a failure by his own standards. In *The Entertainer* (1957), Sir Laurence Olivier appeared memorably as the failed comedian, Archie Rice; the fading music-hall setting symbolized the ebbing of Britain's imperial self-confidence.

Osborne's own social attitudes are expressed in 'They Call it Cricket', his contribution to the symposium *Declaration* (1957), and in a notorious article in *Tribune*, 'Damn you, England'; they intrude into his satirical musical on gossip-columnists *The World of Paul Slickey*, a failure in 1959, and a ponderous one-act skit on royal weddings, *The Blood of the Bambergs*, presented in a double-bill with a novel comedy on fetishists, *Under Plain Cover*, in 1962. *Luther* (1961), a psychological study of the German reformer, provided great scope for the talents of Albert Finney, who starred in the film of *Tom Jones* on which Osborne and Tony Richardson collaborated in 1962, following their films of *Look Back in Anger* and *The Entertainer*. *Inadmissible Evidence* (1964), ostensibly about a failing middle-aged solicitor, again self-indulgently explored Osborne's personal preoccupations and antipathies, but with some objectivity. *A Patriot for Me* (1965), a long chronicle-play about a scandal in the Austrian army in 1890–1913, was performed under theatre club auspices on account of its depiction of homosexual activities. In 1968 were produced 2 'plays for the meantime', *Time Present* and *The Hotel in Amsterdam*. Both were static conversation-pieces about comfortably-off people in show business.

Seldom experimental in form, Osborne's plays are usually dominated by a compulsive talker with a flair for invective and social criticism. In 1969 three academic studies of Osborne (by M. Banham, A. Carter and S. Trussler) were published. [MJ]

K. Allsop, *The Angry Decade* (1958); ed. W. A. Armstrong, *Experimental Drama* (1963); ed. J. R. Brown, *Modern British Dramatists* (New Jersey, 1968); ed. C. Marowitz, *Theatre at Work* (1967); R. Hayman, *J.O.* (1968); J. Russell Taylor, *Anger and After* (revised edn, 1969), and ed. *Look Back in Anger: a Casebook* (1968); K. Tynan, *Curtains* (revised edn, 1964).

O'Shaughnessy, Arthur William Edgar (1844–81). Poet. Born in London and privately educated, he worked in the British Museum Library and later in the Natural History Museum, where he specialized in reptiles and fish. O'Shaughnessy was a peripheral member of the circle of D. G. ◊ Rossetti. His first book, *An Epic of Women* (1870), is a rather satirical work, but he afterwards produced more characteristic pre-Raphaelite work in *Lays of France* (1872) and *Music and Moonlight: Poems and Songs* (1874). His poetry is skilful and musical, but thin. With his wife (E. O'Shaughnessy) he wrote *Toyland* (1875), a book of poems for children. [AR]

Poems, selected and ed. W. A. Percy (New Haven, 1923).
L. C. Moulton, *A.O'S. His Life and Work. With Selections from His Poems* (1894); B. I. Evans, *English Poetry in the Later Nineteenth Century* (1933; revised 1966).

Ossian. The near-legendary 3rd-century Gaelic bard whose 'rediscovered' works were the literary sensation of the 1760s. The discoverer was James ◊ Macpherson, a handsome romantic of 26, who claimed to have found extensive oral and manuscript remains of Ossian's poetry in the Highlands. The authenticity of *Fragments of Ancient Poetry Collected in the Highlands of*

Scotland, and Translated from the Gaelic or Erse Language (1760), Fingal, an Ancient Epic Poem in Six Books (1762) and Temora (1763) was at once denied by Dr Johnson as 'impudent forgeries'. In Europe it was a very different story. Ossian was a triumph, a strange Celtic sun which suddenly forced the first blossom of European Romanticism. The Germans placed him next to Homer, and Goethe made Werther and Charlotte weep over his ballads. The Scottish nation, previously regarded as near-barbarian, enthralled the literary world, who chose to regard it as the Greece of the North.

Macpherson's forgeries were made up of a mixture of small but true talent and vast (and lying) energy. He was emotionally involved in the Highland collapse during 1745, which he had seen when he was a boy, and such real feeling as existed in his clumsy Ossianics derived from this and other genuine experiences. He also knew some of the few genuine Ossianic poems. He covered this honest basis for a re-evaluation of the Celtic soul with thick layers of the sentimentality which the age demanded, incidentally taking his place at the head of a procession of literary mummers which include 'Monk' ◊ Lewis, Mrs ◊ Radcliffe, Horace ◊ Walpole and Mary ◊ Shelley. Twenty years later the world demanded the Ossian originals, forcing Macpherson into miserably laborious activity, for he was sick of the whole business and was more concerned with writing official apologetics for the British Government after the American colonies had proclaimed their independence. He demanded burial in Westminster Abbey, and received it.

Thomas ◊ Chatterton's suicide at 18 can be partly traced to Macpherson's Ossian. Those who repudiated this discovery were in no mood to see in The Rowley Poems (1765–8) their genuine 'Gothic' virtues and the 'marvellous boy' who anticipated the ballad feeling of The Ancient Mariner was made to see himself as yet another hoaxer. [RB]

D. S. Thomson, *The Gaelic Sources of Macpherson's 'Ossian'* (1952).

Otway, Thomas (1652–85). Dramatist. Educated at Winchester and Christ Church, Oxford, he made an unsuccessful debut as an actor in 1671. He became a dramatist, and wrote in the prevailing Restoration mode of heroic tragedy. Alcibiades (1675) and Don Carlos, Prince of Spain (1676) are

in rhyme, and good examples of that limited genre, Drydenesque tragedy. Otway also made English versions of Racine (Titus and Berenice, 1676) and of Molière (A Farce Called the Cheats of Scapin, 1676) and undertook an 'improvement' of Romeo and Juliet (The History and Fall of Caius Marius, 1679) before finding his real form with 2 blank-verse tragedies, The Orphan, or The Unhappy Marriage (1680) and Venice Preserv'd, or A Plot Discover'd (1682), both of which he designed for the actress Mrs Barry. They are essentially domestic tragedies, rich in pathos; they show that the influence of Shakespeare and the Elizabethans was not always inhibiting. As they provided strong acting parts they almost rivalled Shakespeare's tragedies on the stage throughout the 18th and 19th centuries. They represent the finest work in tragedy of their period, and Venice Preserv'd was memorably staged in London in 1953 by Peter Brook and John Gielgud. His three Restoration comedies, including The Soldier's Fortune (successfully produced in 1680), have fared less well. [MJ]

The Complete Works, ed. M. Summers (3 vols., 1926); Works, ed. J. C. Ghosh (2 vols., 1932).
A. Mackenzie Taylor, *Next to Shakespeare: Venice Preserv'd and The Orphan and Their History on the London Stage* (Durham, N.C., 1950).

'Ouida' (Marie Louise de la Ramée) (1839–1908). Popular novelist and journalist. Born in Bury St Edmund's, the daughter of a Frenchman and an Englishwoman, she became known as a writer of short stories in Bentley's Miscellany. Her many novels were escapist works, set in a larger-than-life fashionable world, but her unbridled imagination was genuinely in revolt against the stuffiness of much of the moral thinking of the time. Her good characters (especially the men) are too virtuous, handsome and courageous to live, but she told a good story and was in consequence read by all, though criticized for her bad tone. This now seems innocuous enough. She was also open to attack by the 'realists', as an emotional drug-peddler. Her pen-name is a child's pet form of 'Louise'. Her most famous book is Under Two Flags (1867); others are Held in Bondage (1863); Strathmore (1865); A Dog of Flanders (1872), an animal story of which she wrote several; Moths (1880). She also wrote Bimbi: Stories for Children (1882). After 1875 she lived in Italy. [AR]

E. Bigland, *O.: The Passionate Victorian* (1950).

Overbury, Sir Thomas (1581–1613). Courtier, wit and 'character' writer. Born at Compton-Scorpion, Warwickshire, of a family of gentry, he was educated at Queen's College, Oxford, and the Middle Temple. He became a friend and hanger-on of Robert Carr, the King's favourite later created Earl of Somerset. When he opposed his patron's marriage to Frances Howard, the divorced Countess of Essex, he succumbed to the intrigue of the Howards; the King imprisoned him in the Tower, where he died of poison. Carr and his countess were convicted of murder, but received a royal pardon, and the affair has always been a celebrated historical puzzle (see C. Whibley, *Essays in Biography*, 1913, and Sir E. A. Parry, *The Overbury Mystery*, 1925). Just after Overbury's death appeared his poem *A Wife now the Widow of Sir T. Overbury* (1614) and 21 'characters' by Overbury, and several of his gentlemen friends were added to the second edition of *A Wife* in the same year. The number of these additional pieces was increased in later printings. These are Theophrastan 'characters' (◊ Hall, Joseph), but the emphasis is on witty conceits and epigrams: a few are idealized, such as 'A Fayre and Happy Milkmaid', but most are flippant attacks. Of the final 82 'Overburian characters', 35 are usually assigned to John ◊ Webster, and are printed in the edition of his works by F. L. Lucas (1927); 9 'characters from a debtors' prison' added to the 9th edition (1615) are usually assigned to ◊ Dekker; and 2 pieces, *The Dunce* and an *Essay on Valour*, added to the edition of 1622, are given to Donne. [AR]

The Overburian Characters, ed. W. J. Paylor (Percy Reprints, 1936).
CBEL (under 'Character Books').

Owen, Daniel (1836–95). Welsh novelist. Born at Mold, Flintshire, of a coal-mining family, he received little formal education, and was apprenticed to a tailor. In 1865 he went to the Bala theological college but did not complete his course, and he returned to Mold to look after his mother and sister. He continued to work as a tailor, and commenced business on his own, combining this with preaching until 1876. During a period of ill-health he began his literary career.

At that time in Wales novels were regarded as at best a sheer waste of time and at worst as directly contrary to the practice of piety and godly living. Fiction could only be tolerated if it performed some religious or reforming function. Thus it was only possible for Daniel Owen's forerunners to produce novels which were propaganda for the temperance movement or in some way aired the radical views of the state of society. No wonder that Daniel Owen's first book was called *Offrymau Neilltuaeth* ('Offerings of Seclusion', 1876, 1879), and that his first major novel was termed an autobiography, *Hunangofiant Rhys Lewis*. Most of the novels too were published as serials in Welsh denominational magazines and periodicals. And this is perhaps part of the reason why they can be criticized for their lack of planning and construction. But Daniel Owen had a real gift for straightforward storytelling and for character drawing. His novels are invaluable social records but they depict the society which he knew so well through the eyes of a literary artist. *Y Dreflan* (1879, 1881) is a description of a small country town; *Rhys Lewis* (1882–4; tr. J. Harris, 1888) and *Enoc Huws* (1890, 1891; tr. anon., 1894–5) introduce us to the effects of the industrial revolution on that town and the society of which the chapel was the centre. *Gwen Tomos* (1893, 1894; tr. T. Ceiriog Williams, 1963) presents us with rural life earlier in the century. A galaxy of characters who are familiar figures in the Welsh consciousness remind us of his ability to delineate faithfully and accurately: Mari Lewis, Abel Huws, Tomos Bartley, Will Bryan and many others. Daniel Owen's Welsh is not free from the very general fault of 19th-century writers, those of longwindedness and stereotyped phrasing, but when he forgot to write 'correctly' he could produce strong idiomatic Welsh exactly suited to the character or incident which he was portraying. Added to this he had the rare (for his period) and saving grace of humour which still appeals to a modern reader. [MR]

Straeon y Pentan (1895).

Owen, Goronwy (1723–69). Welsh poet. Born in the parish of Llanfair Mathafarn Eithaf (Anglesey) of a poor but intellectual family, he was educated at Pwllheli, Bangor, and for a pitifully short period at Oxford (a fortnight in June 1744). He became a school usher and then entered the Church, serving as schoolmaster and curate in his native parish, in Oswestry, Uppington and

Donnington (Salop) and Walton near Liverpool, and finally as curate at Northolt (Middlesex). In 1758 he emigrated to Virginia as headmaster of William & Mary College, Williamsburg. In 1760 he obtained the living of St Andrew's in Virginia, and ended his life as the owner of a tobacco and cotton plantation. He owed a good deal to some staunch friends (particularly those of the so-called 'Morris' circle, and the London Welshmen) who recognized his natural genius.

Goronwy Owen was an accomplished classical scholar, steeped in biblical knowledge, and an earnest student of early Welsh poetry, particularly of the *Gogynfeirdd* (11th–13th centuries). Added to these attainments was his wide reading of contemporary English poetry and literary criticism. His choice medium was the *cywydd* (the favourite metre of the classical poets, 1350–1650), which he used not for the old themes of eulogy and elegy, but for 'occasional' verse of the current English type, on such subjects as 'The Wish', 'The Search for Happiness', 'The Garret'. In his use of this strict metre and his mastery of Welsh he represents, together with his friends of the 'Morris' circle, a classical revival in the mid 18th century. But he was very receptive to the literary theories of his age and desired most fervently to produce a Christian epic in Welsh. His 'Day of Judgement' is an early attempt in this direction, but he never realized his dream. In his letters may be traced the evolution of his ideas and the gradual realization that the *cywydd* metre would not suffice. These ideas were widely diffused in the late 18th century and early 19th century and greatly influenced the emergence of the Eisteddfodic *awdl* and later *pryddest*. [MR]

The Poetical Works: With His Life and Correspondence, ed. R. Jones (1876); *The Letters*, ed. J. H. Davies (1924).
J. Saunders Lewis, *A School of Welsh Augustans* (1924).

Owen, John (*c.* 1560–1622). Poet. A Welshman, he was for several years a Fellow of New College, Oxford, and then a schoolmaster. He was famous for his Latin poems, particularly for his brilliant epigrams, which brought him the name of 'the British Martial' on the Continent of Europe.

Epigrammata, ed. A. A. Renouard (2 vols., Paris, 1794; tr. T. Vicars, *Epigrams*, 1619).

Owen, Wilfred (1893–1918). Poet. Born in Oswestry, Shropshire, and educated at the Birkenhead Institute and London University. From 1913 to 1915 he lived near Bordeaux as tutor to a French family. He enlisted in the First World War, but was invalided out in 1917 and sent to a war hospital where a fellow patient, Siegfried Sassoon, encouraged him to write poetry. Sent back to the front, he was killed a week before armistice. His posthumously published *Poems* (1920) were collected by Sassoon. Owen's was one of the new voices to come out of the war, new in technique, and new in attitude to war. The romantic heroic approach of Rupert Brooke, who glorified war as a healthy release, is at the farthest remove from Owen's feelings of humanity and pity at the horror of war. In most of the poems his technical experiments are revealing and of great interest. It is probable that had he lived Owen would have developed into a notable peace-time poet. He made fine use of assonance and internal rhyme. His bitterness is not that of self-pity, nor is there any trace of irony in the poems. His meaning is concentrated, his metaphors striking. Owen exercised a deep influence on the generation of poets which followed him. [CO]

Collected Letters, ed. H. Owen and J. Bell (1967).
D. S. R. Welland, *W.O.*, *A Critical Study* (1960); H. Owen (brother), *Journey from Obscurity: W.O.*, *1893–1918* (3 vols., 1963–5).

'Owl and the Nightingale, The' (*c.* 1200). Early English poem. Internal references suggest a date between 1189 and 1216 for this poem. The author may have been a certain Nicholas of Guildford, who is mentioned, though the poem may be a compliment to him by an admirer. Verse-form and subject show continental influence, for this is the first competent English handling of the French 4-stress couplet, and the first English debate poem. The contestants are the Owl and the Nightingale; the issue is their personal worth, especially in relation to mankind. Though allegory is present, the particular terms of reference cannot be defined – perhaps the conflict between 'solemn and joyous ways of life' (Stanley) is as inclusive as any. There is no resolution, and the contestants, accompanied by the other birds, go off to ask Nicholas to arbitrate.

The argument is realistically presented, and shaped by legal procedure, to produce a much more conscious work of art than anything else in early Middle English. The poet uses alliterative technique occasionally, but he adopts not only the French verse-form, but the French 'light ironic and humorous tone' (Wilson).

Ed. J. W. H. Atkins (1922) (with translation); ed. E. G. Stanley (1960).
R. M. Wilson, *Early Middle English Literature* 1939).

P

Paine, Thomas (1737–1809). Political writer. Born at Thetford in Norfolk, the son of a Quaker artisan-farmer, he was given an education, but put to his father's trade of stay-making at 13. He served at sea, and in 1761 became an exciseman and led a chequered career. On his discharge in 1772, he went to London, thence on Franklin's advice to Philadelphia, where he ran a magazine. He supported republican independence and wrote a number of pamphlets, including *Common Sense* (1776). His pamphlets published under the title of *The Crisis* were important propaganda during the war of independence. In 1777 he was appointed by Congress as Secretary to the Committee on Foreign Affairs, but was forced to resign two years later. In 1781, he went to France as secretary to the American envoy. In 1787, he returned to London, where he published *Prospects on the Rubicon*, advocating the anti-Pitt policy of friendship with France. In 1790, when ◊ Burke's *Reflections on the Revolution* appeared, Paine answered it by his most famous work, the first part of *The Rights of Man* (Everyman, 1915; ed. H. Collins, PEL, 1969), immediately published in America and translated into French. He went backwards and forwards to France, and began the second part (published in 1792). That year he was indicted for treason and fled to France in September. He became a member of the Convention, served on the constitution committee, but lost influence with the fall of the Girondists. He spoke and wrote against the King's execution and was imprisoned by Robespierre. His last considerable work was *The Age of Reason* (I, 1794; II, 1795; ed. J. M. Robertson, 1905), more successful as an attack on the Church than as a defence of rational deism. In 1802, he returned to America, and died there in political isolation, obscurity and neglect. His success lay in simplistic bluntness, rough readiness and a mastery of all the usual democratic arguments. He is not an original thinker, but his direct energy (reminiscent of popular preaching) is contrasted with Burke's complexity and Macintosh's vacillation. [AR]

Complete Writings, ed. P. S. Foner (2 vols., New York, 1945); *Selections*, ed. H. Fast (1948); *T.P.: Representative Selections*, ed. H. H. Clark (1965).
H. Pearson, *T.P., Friend of Mankind* (1937); A. O. Aldridge, *Man of Reason. Life of T.P.* (1960); R. R. Fennessy, *Burke, P. and the Rights of Man* (The Hague, 1963).

Painter, William (*c.* 1540–94). Translator and story-teller. After leaving St John's College, Cambridge, without a degree, he became first a schoolmaster in Kent, and later, under the patronage of the Earl of Warwick, Clerk of Ordnance in the Tower of London. He was charged with embezzling government property with the Earl's connivance, but was not prosecuted. In 1566 and 1567 he issued, in 2 volumes dedicated to his patron, a huge collection of about a hundred exciting and amorous tales which he had translated or re-told from Latin, Greek and especially contemporary French and Italian originals. These volumes, *The Palace of Pleasure Beautified, Adorned, and Well Furnished with Pleasant Histories, and Excellent Novelles Selected out of Divers Good and Commendable Authors* (ed. H. Miles, 4 vols., 1929) included English versions of Livy and Plutarch as well as of *novellieri* like Bandello, Boccaccio, Cinthio and Queen Margaret of Navarre. Painter thus made the erotic *novella* available in English, and his compendious volumes were regarded by ◊ Ascham as dangerous reading for young people. His work became a treasure-house for Elizabethan dramatists seeking plots, including Shakespeare. *The Palace of Pleasure* inaugurated a series of such compilations by Geoffrey Fenton, George ◊ Pettie and others. [MJ]

C. S. Lewis, *English Literature in the Sixteenth Century* (1954).

Paley, William (1743–1805). Theologian. He became a Fellow of his college (Christ's, Cambridge) and Archdeacon of Carlisle. A master of lucid exposition, Paley systematized economic and social thought and the hitherto chaotic ideas of utilitarian pioneers, and applied the synthesis to theological exposition, producing 4 works which survived as influential textbooks in universities well into the 19th century: *Principles of Moral and Political Philosophy* (1785), *Horae Paulinae* (1790), *View of the Evidences of Christianity* (1794) and *Natural Theology* (1802). In the latter 2 books, he also dealt with new developments in science, particularly biology and physiology, in a way useful for contemporary Christian apologists, and was a particularly cogent exponent of the 'argument from design' (ignoring the fact that the argument had already been exploded in David Hume's *Dialogues on Natural Religion*). His arguments were also somewhat outflanked by Darwin and later evolutionary theory. [AR]

DNB; L. Stephen, *History of English Thought in the Eighteenth Century* (2 vols., 1902).

Palgrave, Francis Turner (1824–97). Poet and critic. Born at Great Yarmouth, the son of Sir Francis Palgrave the historian, he was educated at Charterhouse and Balliol College, Oxford, where he knew Matthew ◊ Arnold and A. H. ◊ Clough. After holding a fellowship at Exeter College, he became a Civil Servant and was briefly an assistant secretary to Gladstone. He was Vice-Principal of Kneller Hall Training College from 1850 to 1855, then moved to the Education Department, where he retired as Assistant Secretary. Palgrave published several volumes of now forgotten and highly derivative verse, including *Idylls and Songs* (1854) and *Amenophis, and Other Poems* (1892), but is best known for his anthology (compiled under the influence of his close friend Tennyson), *The Golden Treasury*, 'selected from the best songs and lyrical poems in the English language' (1861; revised and enlarged, 1896). This volume, once widely used in schools and sometimes the only poetry book ever read, has many merits of selection, but has been of incalculable effect in rivetting a mid-Victorian sensibility on to English readers of poetry, for Palgrave was nothing if not backward-looking. It might be said to be an account of a certain tradition of English poetry (presented for the whole), according to the editor's belief that 'passion, colour and originality cannot atone for serious imperfections of clearness, unity or truth'. Palgrave produced other anthologies and a good deal of art criticism of a tradionalist kind, as well as publishing *Landscape in Poetry, from Homer to Tennyson* (1897), lectures delivered when he was Professor of Poetry at Oxford (1885–95). [AR]

G. F. Palgrave, *F.T.P.: His Journals and Memories of His Life* (1899); J. C. Horne, 'P.'s *Golden Treasury*', *English Studies*, II (1949); N. Lewis, 'P. and His Golden Treasury', *Listener* 4 January 1962.

Palmer, Vance Edward (1885–1959). Australian writer. Born at Bundaberg and brought up in Queensland. Newspaper work in Brisbane and two spells in London preceded his army service during the First World War. He was actively concerned with the Pioneer Players, an Australian Little Theatre group, during the twenties. Such plays as *The Black Horse* (1924) were written with a view to creating a specifically Australian theatre. They are not his best work. With his wife, Nettie Palmer, he continued as an influential critic and promoter of Australian literature until his death. He served for eleven years after 1942 on the board of the Commonwealth Literary Fund, contributed to Australian periodicals and wrote a number of critical books including the important revaluation, *The Legend of The Nineties* (1954).

In his novels and short stories Palmer uses a flat, objective approach, accumulating material for psychological inference. The late trilogy, *Golconda* (1948), *Seedtime* (1957) and *The Big Fellow* (1960), traces the rise of Macy Donovan from the Queensland minefields to leadership of the State Parliament. As in others of his 12 novels and in such story collections as *The Rainbow Bird* (1957), Palmer persistently investigates the primacy of normal priorities by placing moral problems firmly in the context of daily work. [PT]

Meanjin, XVIII, 2 (Winter, 1959) (special Palmer issue); A. D. Hope, 'V. P. Reconsidered', *Southerly*, 4 (1955).

Pantycelyn. ◊ Williams, William.

Paris, Matthew (*c.* 1200–59). Medieval historian. One of the greatest of medieval historians, he was probably of English birth but educated at Paris. He became a Benedictine at St Albans Abbey in 1217 and spent the rest of his life there, except for two visits to France and one to Norway. His great *Chronica majora* (ed. H. R. Luard, Rolls Series, 7 vols., 1872–80; tr. J. A. Giles, *Matthew Paris's English History*, 3 vols.,

1852–4) begins with Creation and extends to 1259. Until 1235 it is merely a new edition of the works of John de Cella, Abbot of St Albans until 1214, and Roger of Wendover, a contemporary of Matthew at St Albans, where he died in 1236. From that point it is Matthew's original work, based partly on letters from leading men of the time and partly on conversations with participants in the events which he chronicles, particularly King Henry III and his brother Richard, Earl of Cornwall. Matthew paints a vivid picture of his time, excelling in narrative and description, but is not a good judge of character, and is not always accurate in his chronology.

R. Vaughan, *M.P.* (1958).

Parnell, Thomas (1679–1718). Poet. Born in Dublin of a landed Anglo-Irish family and educated at Trinity College. He took orders in 1700 and became Archdeacon of Clogher. Coming to London in 1712, he first contributed 2 allegorical papers to the *Spectator,* but shortly after, he was taken up by Swift, under whose stimulation and that of the other members of the Scriblerus Club, he gave rein to his humour, wit and powers of poetry. He tried a number of forms, and in several reflective poems of a religious cast (which were long popular) he shows a genuine poetic talent – e.g. *The Night-Piece on Death, The Hymn to Contentment* and *The Hermit.* He also produced imitations and graceful poetical translations, such as his accomplished version of *Pervigilium Veneris.* Little of his poetry was printed during his lifetime, except for *An Essay on the Different Styles of Poetry* (1713). His friend Pope, to whose *Iliad* he had contributed an 'Essay on the Life of Homer', brought out a carefully edited selection of his work, *Poems on Several Occasions* (1722). Parnell returned unwillingly to Ireland (1716) and gave himself up to a congenital melancholy. [AR]

The Poetical Works, ed. G. A. Aitken (1894); *Poems,* selected by L. Robinson (Dublin, 1927); *Minor Poets of the Eighteenth Century* (Everyman, 1930) (contains most of his poems). O. Goldsmith, *The Life of T.P.* (1770); Johnson, *Lives of the Poets*; R. W. Jackson, 'P. the Poet', *Dublin Magazine,* xx (1945).

Parry, Robert Williams (1884–1956). Welsh poet. Born at Tal-y-sarn, Caernarvonshire, he was educated at the County School, Caernarvon, and Pen-y-groes, and University College of Wales, Aberystwyth, later

for periods at Bangor. He was a schoolteacher for many years until he was appointed lecturer in Welsh at Bangor in 1921, retiring in 1944.

As with many other poets of his generation Williams Parry first came into prominence with a prizewinning poem, in this case the *awdl* 'Yr Haf' ('The Summer') at the Eisteddfod of Colwyn Bay in 1910. This was an extremely sensuous poem on the theme of *carpe diem,* the young man's realization of the impermanence both of love and hate, happiness and grief, summer and winter, all expressed with a singular charm and melody of *cynghanedd* and metre. The years of the First World War (in which he served) brought a gravity and maturity to his poems, especially in his elegiac stanzas to his friends and contemporaries who died. These memorial *englynion* represent the summit of the virtues of brevity, sincerity and concision, the like of which had not been possible since the days of ◊ Llywarch Hen. Williams Parry was little moved by voices from the past (except in his poem 'Drudwy Branwen'), and his was not the idealistic nationalism of other poets of his period. He was very sensitive to the beauties of nature and many lyrics reflect not only the accuracy and loving care of his descriptions (as in his famous sonnet to the fox), but also his vision of what lies behind the actual appearance of a flower or a bird or an animal. In 1936 and 1937 he was greatly moved by the events connected with the burning of the Bombing School near Pwllheli, and his poems 'Cymru, 1937' and 'Y Dieithryn' are a bitter condemnation of what he considered to be apathy and Laodiceianism in Welsh public life. This critical aspect of his poetry became more evident in his later years. He was disturbed too by the equivocal nature of his appointment at Bangor. He became concerned with the function of the poet in the modern world, and he has several poems on this theme. [MR]

Yr Haf a Cherddi and *Eraill* (1924); *Cerddi 'r Gaeaf* (1952).

Parry-Williams, Thomas Herbert (1887–   ). Welsh poet and essayist. Born at Rhyd-ddu, Caernarvonshire, the son of the local schoolmaster, he was educated at the County School, Porthmadog, University College of Wales, Aberystwyth, Jesus College, Oxford, the Universities of Freiburg and Paris. He was Professor of Welsh at Aberystwyth from 1920 to 1952. As a young man Parry-

Williams won ooth Chair and Crown at the Eisteddfodau of Wrexham (1912) and Bangor (1915). Although he was obviously at home in the strict classical metres, in his later poetry he chosé to compose in two forms of free metres, the sonnet and what he calls 'Rhigymau' or series of rhyming couplets. He delights in words for their own sake, and takes great but not too obvious pains to find the exact word to express his intention. A marked feature of his vocabulary is his extensive use of dialect words (many of them of English origin) especially in his Rhigymau. This represents partly perhaps a reaction against the too rigid standards of poetic diction laid down by John ◊ Morris-Jones but more particularly his own awareness of the whole significance of current colloquialisms. A by-product of this is the demonstration of how literary Welsh can be nourished and enriched from dialect sources. Parry-Williams's poetry is the result of deep meditation by an extremely sensitive and diffident personality. His sonnets are perfectly fashioned and balanced, and the greatest care is taken to express in them the exact nuance which is often one of cynicism, verging at times on despair.

Parry-Williams was also an accomplished essayist. He was the first to make extensive use of the essay form in Welsh. As with his poetry, each essay is brilliantly balanced, although he has no set plan, and here too he makes great and effective use of colloquial words. His themes are all very subjective and he expresses them in an intimate and familiar way. Academically, Parry-Williams has always been interested in Welsh borrowings from English (*The English Element in Welsh*, 1923), and this may provide a clue to his use of local dialect words. His main concern in the history of Welsh literature has been with the development of the free metre poetry and with poetic diction (*Llawysgrif Richard Morris o Gerddi*, 1931, *Carolau Richard White*, 1931, *Canu Rhydd Cynnar*, 1932, *Welsh Poetic Diction*, 1947). [M R]

Ysgrifau (1928); *Cerddi* (1931); *Olion* (1935); *Synfyfyrion* (1937); *Lloffion* (1942); *O'r Pedwar Gwynt* (1944); *Ugain o Gerddi* (1949); *Myfyrdodau* (1957); *Pensynnu* (1966).

'Paston Letters, The' (1422–1509). An invaluable social document giving a detailed record of the doings of three generations of the Pastons, a wealthy Norfolk family (ed. J. Gairdner, 4 vols., 1901; selection ed. N. Davis, 1964). They contain, as well as business matters – the Pastons were inveterate litigants – a wealth of information on the education, leisure habits and domestic life of the period. Their literary value is incidental, though there is much to be learnt about the reading habits of the middle classes from the lists of books mentioned and discussed, and, being in English, they illustrate a stage in the ascendancy of the vernacular. The letters are written in a simple unaffected style, and their tone is personal and homely. [A G]

H. S. Bennett, *The Pastons and Their England* (1922).

Pater, Walter (Horatio) (1839–94). Essayist, critic and prose stylist. Born in London, the son of an ex-Roman Catholic doctor, he was educated at King's School, Canterbury. In 1855 he came under the influence of John ◊ Keble, one of the leaders of the ◊ Oxford Movement. In 1858, he went to Queen's College, Oxford, where he enthusiastically studied Plato under Benjamin Jowett. As a student, he twice visited Germany and developed an interest in German philosophy; he became something of a sceptic, and his friends dissuaded him from entering the Church. He was elected a Fellow of Brasenose in 1865, and in the same year a tour of Ravenna, Pisa and Florence with a pupil stimulated his growing interest in the Renaissance. Thus he laid the foundation for his aestheticism: Platonic and Hegelian currents of thought united with an admiration for the humanist art (as he conceived it to be) of the Italian Renaissance gave him a substitute for the religion which his scepticism had made unpalatable. At this time the controversies instigated by the 'art-for-art's-sake' school – Gautier, Swinburne etc. – were in full swing. Though he never directly engaged in controversy, or even adverse criticism, confining himself in his work to favourable appreciation, Pater adopted many of the views of this group. His essays on Winckelmann and on Botticelli and other humanist artists were collected in 1873 in *Studies in the History of the Renaissance* (the second edition, *The Renaissance: Studies in Art and Poetry*, 1877, omits the 'Conclusion', which came under attack; ed. K. Clark, 1961). He had also published an essay, 'Aesthetic Poetry', in 1868, dealing with the early work of William ◊ Morris. Pater published several collections of his periodical essays, which often took the form of 'portraits', either based on history or more or less fictitious: *Imaginary Portraits* (1887), *Appreciations* (1889) and *Plato and Platonism* (1893). He turned his attention to Greek literature and art, travelled in France and Germany, and lived in Oxford, where he gathered a group of young men around him and his views on art gained considerable prestige. In 1887, a satire on him (as Mr Rose) and his views, *The New Republic*, was published by W. H. ◊ Mallock. Pater resigned his fellowship in 1882, and went to live first in Rome, then in London, devoting his time to writing.

He produced *Marius the Epicurean* (2 vols., 1885; revised 1888; revised 1892; ed. O. Burdett, 1934) as a responsible defence of the doctrines which had had so great an effect on his pupils. It is in the form of a highly wrought 'historical' fiction portrait, in which Marius, the detached observer, is offered as a kind of self-portrait of Pater transferred to the Rome of Marcus Aurelius, allowing him to develop and qualify his views on art and life. Specifically, at the end of the first version of the *Renaissance*, the 'love of art for its own sake' is recommended as being the only true wisdom. In Marius, a moral obligation is outlined for the man who wishes to lead the good life, an obligation to lead a comely and ordered life. The wisely pagan Marius is brought in contact with Christianity to show the conflict of two possible attitudes. A similar but inferior work, *Gaston de Latour* (1888), was abandoned after several chapters. The attention Pater paid to different historical and social contexts may be considered as an unsuccessful variation of ◊ Ruskin's awareness of the problems of English industrialized society; he had importance though in stimulating the recovery of interest in the art of the Renaissance, after the attacks of Ruskin and other 'medievalists'.

Pater also wrote essays on English poetry and prose, among others on Wordsworth, Sir Thomas Browne, Rossetti, and several of Shakespeare's plays. He is an elaborately subjective critic, but beneath his personal attitudes so carefully worked out in the essays lies quite a powerful base of philosophical thought. Oscar Wilde in *The Critic as Artist* carries this kind of criticism to its extreme conclusion, Wilde being devoid of Pater's austerity and discrimination. Wilde (with encouragement from Pater) treats the work of art as 'simply a starting point for a new creation'. Pater has certain preoccupations that make his fiction unpleasant: his coy fascination with violence, for example, and his somewhat furtive suggestions of supernatural sin (in *Apollo in Picardy*, a portrait published in 1893). He is important for his part in the dissemination of that nostalgic humanism which (in Arnold and others) was important in 19th-century English thought. He was also greatly admired as a stylist, a fastidious virtuoso whose unmethodical insights retain considerable power of inward life. His views and practice have had influence on modern criticism of poetry. [A R]

Works (9 vols., 1900–1; 10 vols., 'New Library Edition', 1910); *Selected Works*, ed. R. Aldington (1948); *Selected Prose*, ed. D. Patmore (1949).
A. C. Benson, *W.P.* (English Men of Letters, 1906); I. Fletcher, *W.P.* (WTW, 1959) (with select bibliography); R. C. Child, *The Aesthetic of P.* (New York, 1946); G. Hough, *The Last Romantics* (1949); F. Kermode, *The Romantic Image* (1957); S. Fishman, *The Interpretation of Art* (Berkeley, Calif., 1963).

Paterson, Andrew Barton ('The Banjo') (1864–1941). Australian balladist who was in great vogue at the turn of the century. He was born into a landowning family in New South Wales, was educated in Sydney and practised law there. As 'The Banjo' he wrote ballads for the *Bulletin*, and his collection *The Man from Snowy River* (1895) became a best-seller. In 1899 Paterson abandoned law for journalism, becoming a war correspondent in the Boer War. In 1904 he edited a Sydney paper. After six years as a pastoralist he did distinguished war service, before settling in Sydney. Paterson and ◊ Lawson were the great exponents of the bush ballad revival, celebrating Australian manhood in swinging metres and slangy language. Paterson collected and anthologized (*The Old Bush Songs*, 1905). His *Collected Verse* (1921) includes heroic and idealistic accounts of an active past, among them 'Waltzing Matilda'. [P T]

B. R. Elliott, *Singing to the Cattle* (1947); A. J. Coombes, *Some Australian Poets* (1938).

'Patience' ◊ 'Gawain Poet, The'.

Patmore, Coventry (Kersey Dighton) (1823–96). Poet. Born in Woodford, Essex, he was educated privately. His early *Poems* (1844), though they attracted the attention of

Rossetti and Holman Hunt, were not well received. He worked for nearly twenty years in the Printed Book Department of the British Museum, during which time he published the 4 separate volumes of *The Angel in the House* (1854–62), his poetic celebration of conjugal love, in which he describes his own first courtship and marriage. Though his verse technique is occasionally clumsy, the poem has a certain naïve honesty of intention which impresses. In 1864 Patmore became a Roman Catholic, and his subsequent poems, mainly on religious subjects, underwent a change from his earlier manner. *The Unknown Eros* (1877) is a series of 42 odes ostensibly on the metaphysics of love, which betray a thoughtless nostalgia and a naïve political attitude as well as, occasionally, too great a discursiveness. Patmore was a friend of Tennyson and Ruskin, and a contributor to the Pre-Raphaelite magazine, *The Germ*. [co]

Amelia (1878); *Rod, Root and Flower* (1895).
J. C. Reid, *The Mind and Art of C.P.* (1957).

Paton, Alan Stewart (1903–   ). South African novelist. Born in Pietermaritzburg and educated at the University of Natal, he taught in Natal schools for eleven years, before becoming principal of an African reformatory in 1935. He resigned in 1948 to devote himself to writing. In the same year *Cry, the Beloved Country* was published. It is a passionately propagandist novel about a black man's country and the white man's laws. Its prose is an ambitious attempt to enlarge the suggestiveness of English by the addition of Zulu lyricism. Paton is not afraid to shout, or to preach. *Too Late the Phalarope* (1953) is slighter but better controlled in its treatment of South African problems.

In 1956 Paton was elected National Chairman of the Liberal Party. Government mistrust of his influence reached a head after his visit to New York in 1960 to receive the Freedom Award, and his passport was impounded on his return. *Debbie Go Home* (1961) is a collection of short stories based mainly on his Reformatory experience. Among his non-fictional writings are *South Africa in Transition* (1956) and *Hope for South Africa* (1958). [PT]

Hofmeyr (1964) (biography); *The Long View* (1967) (essays).
E. Callan, *A.P.* (1968); S. Baker, 'P.'s Late

Phalarope', *English Studies in Africa*, III 2 (September 1960); H. Davies, 'Pilgrims, Not Strangers', in *A Mirror of the Ministry in Modern Novels* (1959).

Pattison, Mark (1813–84). Scholar, critic and biographer. Son of the rector of Hauxwell, Yorkshire, Pattison went to Oriel College, Oxford, in 1832 and was disappointed in not obtaining a fellowship on graduation in 1836. He obtained a fellowship at Lincoln College in 1839; at this time he was a Puseyite and strongly under the influence of J. H. ◊ Newman, and Lincoln was an anti-Puseyite college. Though ordained in 1843 he subsequently lost his faith, but becoming tutor of Lincoln College in the same year he found his métier as a brilliant teacher and a friend and helper of the young. He was at that time the only real scholar in the college and this fact, together with his administrative talents, made him the obvious candidate for the rectorship of Lincoln when it became vacant in 1851. He failed to obtain the post because of jealousy and intrigue, and the failure permanently embittered him and endangered his health. He was finally elected rector in 1861, the year in which he married Emilia Francis Strong (afterwards Lady Dilke). But by this time he had become a dry and bitter character, and the marriage was such as to prompt George Eliot to depict it (or at least to provide some echoes of it) in her account of Casaubon and Dorothea in *Middlemarch*. In later life Pattison showed his contempt for normal university routine as well as for awards, lectures, examinations and degrees and preached a doctrine of the free pursuit of knowledge for its own sake. Pattison's literary activities include writing for the *Quarterly* and other periodicals, biographical articles for the 9th edn of the *Encyclopædia Britannica*, a life of Isaac Casaubon (1875; ed. H. Nettleship, 1892), and a bio-critical study of Milton in the English Men of Letter series (1879). His educational ideas are to be found in *Oxford Essays*, 1855; *Suggestions on Academical Organization*, Edinburgh, 1868; 'Review of the Situation' (in *Essays on the Endowment of Research*, 1876). [DD]

Memoirs, ed. Mrs Pattison (1885; reprinted, intr. J. Munton, 1970); *Essays*, ed. H. Nettleship (2 vols., 1889, 1903).
V. H. H. Green, *Oxford Common Room: A Study of Lincoln College and M.P.* (1957); J. Sparrow *M.P. and the Idea of a University* (1967).

Peacock, Thomas Love (1785–1866). Poet, satirist and wit. Born at Weymouth, the son of a London glass-merchant, he went to school at Englefield Green, and at 16 he moved with his mother to London. He studied on his own and became proficient in Greek, Latin, French and Italian. He began to write poetry in 1801 and published a good deal of verse, including *Palmyra, and Other Poems* (1806), *The Genius of the Thames: A Lyrical Poem* (1810) and *Rhododaphne: or, the Thessalian Spell. A Poem* (1818). He showed no sustained poetic talent, but in his tales he intersperses neat parodies, clever *pastiches* and sometimes quite beautiful verses. In 1812, he was introduced to Shelley, and in 1813 accompanied him and Harriet Westbrook to Edinburgh. Peacock was a confidant of Shelley during the separation from Harriet and spent the winter of 1815 in close intimacy with him. These conversations were a stimulus to Peacock's imagination all his life. His essay *The Four Ages of Poetry* (1820) has its own importance as well as the interest of baiting Shelley to write his brilliant *Defence of Poetry* (both essays ed. H. F. B. Brett-Smith, 1921). Peacock had a traditional education, a wide knowledge of French and Italian literature of the past, and an acute, conservative mind; his reaction to the literary trends of his time produces good argument. Peacock never wrote a life of Shelley, which by his personal knowledge, sympathy and critical ability he was well qualified to do, but he did publish the important 'Memoirs of Percy Bysshe Shelley' in *Fraser's Magazine* (July 1858; January 1860; March 1892) (ed. H. F. B. Brett-Smith, 1909). In 1819, he had joined the staff of the East India Company at the same time as James ◊ Mill, and he became an important man in the Company's service; from 1836 to 1856, he was chief examiner of correspondence.

Peacock is best known for his 7 novels or satirical tales. In these books which have mostly very tenuous, romantic stories, the important feature is talk. A house-party of 'humours', representing various contemporary obsessions and preoccupations is assembled; the figures talk at each other, mostly, and satire is allowed free play. Peacock's wit generally succeeds in making his own conservative, normative point of view plausible and acceptable. The form, which has also been used by Aldous Huxley and (without the wit) by H. G. Wells, owes something to drama; such action as there is in a Peacock novel is usually farcical. The figures are sometimes loosely identified with various proponents of the ideas which are being satirized. Mr Foster in *Headlong Hall* (1816), the first and weakest of the satires, is the mouthpiece for some of Shelley's views. This is also the least unified book, because Peacock is trying out a number of ideas. *Melincourt, or, Sir Oran Haut-ton* (3 vols., 1817; 1856, with a new preface) satirizes an uncritical belief in progress; it is more serious (and too long) and is headed by an epigraph from Rousseau about the dangers of mocking the Romances. The ideas of Southey (Mr Feathernest) and Malthus (Mr Fax) are among the targets, and the political overtones these ideas have; the oran-outang is as fine a gentleman as may be, and becomes a satisfactory Member of Parliament. The 'dark lantern of the spirit' of Samuel ◊ Butler's satire presides over *Nightmare Abbey* (1818), which attacks factitious melancholy; Coleridge (Mr Flosky) and Byron (Mr Cypress) are among the *dramatis personae*. This novel has a more carefully worked out plot, involving Mr Scythrop (Shelley). As his poems show, Peacock had a vein of rather stagey Romanticism, and this is employed in *Maid Marian* (1822), a re-working of the Robin Hood story to guy Jacobin doctrines of the 'social order', and in *The Misfortunes of Elphin* (1829); the latter is a regional novel, perhaps under the influence of Walter Scott, set in Wales, which Peacock loved. The 6th-century Celtic *bric-à-brac* provides some entertainment, and there are some good songs. The fantasy and satire work harmoniously in neither of these books. *Crotchet Castle* (1831) is similar to the first 3 stories, and introduces Dr Folliott, one of his most successful sybaritic clergymen. ◊ Brougham, the pioneer of adult education, and 'the march of mind' are the main targets: throughout, the corruptions of the present are unfavourably contrasted with the vanishing virtues of the old English, hierarchical, rural society. *Gryll Grange* (*Fraser's Magazine*, 1860 and 1861) is the last and best. Mr Falconer's obsession with the ancient Greeks is a splendid farcical and intellectual invention. Butler again presides: 'Opinion governs all mankind / Like the blind leading of the blind'. The book opens with his best character, the learned Dr Opinian, on 'Palestine soup', and concludes with marriages all round and the same cleric on the traditional Greek definitions of the good life. In between, the talk is inspired, the point of view mellow and the background peaceful. [A R]

Works ('Halliford Edition'), ed. H. F. B. Brett-Smith and C. E. Jones (10 vols., 1924–34) (including a *Life* and *Letters*); *Novels*, ed. D. Garnett (1948); *The Pleasures of P.*, ed. B. R. Redman (New York, 1947) (selection); *Selection*, ed. H. L. B. Moody (1966).

J.-J. Mayoux, *Un Épicurien anglais: T.L.P.* (Paris, 1933); J. B. Priestley, *T.L.P.* (English Men of Letters, 1927; 1966); J. I. M. Stewart, *T.L.P.* (WTW, 1963); H. Mills, *P., His Circle and His Age* (1969).

'Pearl'. ◊ 'Gawain Poet, The'.

Pearse, P. H. ◊ Mac Piarais, P.

Pecham, Peckham or **Patcham, John** (d. 1292). Anglo-Latin poet. Supposed to have been born at Patcham in Sussex, he was educated at Lewes by Cluniacs, became a Franciscan and read in the Franciscan houses at Oxford and Paris under Bonaventura. From 1279 until his death he was Archbishop of Canterbury. Pecham was one of the few Anglo-Latin poets of the 12th and 13th centuries. He was the author of a number of hymns full of Franciscan emotion, of a rhythmical Office of the Holy Trinity, and of the beautiful poem, *Philomena Analecta Hymnica*, 50; ed. with tr. W. Dobell, 1924), in which the nightingale represents the human soul longing for its heavenly home.

Registrum epistolarum, ed. C. T. Martin (Rolls Series, 3 vols., 1882–5); *Tres tractatus de paupertate*, ed. C. L. Kingsford, etc. in *British Society of Franciscan Studies* (1910); *De anima*, ed. H. Spettman (1919).

D. L. Douie, *Archbishop P.* (1952); F. J. E. Raby, *Christian Latin Poetry* (2nd edn, 1953).

Pecock, Reginald (?1395–?1460). Scholar and polemicist. A Welshman, Pecock attracted the attention of Humphrey, Duke of Gloucester, while a Fellow of Oriel College, Oxford, and taught for a while under his patronage in London. Pecock was already well known as a writer against the Lollards when he was made Bishop of St Asaph in 1444. His great vanity, and also his tolerance towards opponents, were resented by the hierarchy, who saw in his defence of the ecclesiastical system by the appeal to reason, a negation of authority. As a member of the court party, he was also hated by the mob, though he gained prefer-

ment to the see of Chichester. Archbishop Bourchier, a Yorkist partisan, denounced *The Repressor of Over Much Blaming of the Clergy* (ed. C. Babington, 2 vols., 1860) as heretical. Pecock recanted but his works were suppressed and he was confined to Thorney Abbey where he eventually died.

Pecock is an important innovator in English prose, being the first to argue theology in set forms in the vernacular. He writes elegant, balanced prose, using illustrations well, but it is marred by a fondness for legal jargon and a pleonastic tendency. [A G]

The Donet and *The Follower to the Donet*, ed. E. V. Hitchcock (1921–4); *The Reule of Crysten Religion*, ed. W. C. Greet (1927).

V. H. H. Green, *R.P.* (1945); J. F. Patrouch, 'Reginald Pecock and the Laity', *DA*, xxv (1966).

Peele, George (1556–96). Dramatist and poet. Born in London, he was educated at Christ's Hospital and at Christ Church, Oxford. He continued to live in Oxford until 1581, when he moved to London to win a living as a 'University wit' by writing poetry, plays and civic pageants. His first play, *The Arraignment of Paris*, acted by a boy company around 1582, combines mythological and pastoral elements. It was followed by *The Hunting of Cupid*, of which only fragments survive. He turned to the popular theatre of adult players and between 1592 and 1593 wrote a loose-structured chronicle-play, *Edward I* or *Longshanks*, for ◊ Henslowe's Admiral's Men, who scored a hit with it. Around 1589 he wrote *The Battle of Alcazar*, a Senecan revenge-play – influenced by Marlowe's *Tamburlaine* and Kyd's *Spanish Tragedy* – with patriotic and anti-Spanish sentiments. To this period also belong his effective, jingoistic pamphlet, *A Farewell, Entitled to the Famous and Fortunate Generals of Our English Forces: Sir John Norris and Sir Francis Drake*, and a poem welcoming home a nobleman who had accompanied these two men on their Portuguese expedition, *An Eclogue Gratulatory, Entitled: To the Right Honorable, and Renowned Shepherd of Albion's Arcadia: Robert Earl of Essex and Ewe*. The poem is an imitation of Spenser's *Shepherd's Calendar*, in the archaic pastoral mode. Peele, who seems to have had financial difficulties, continued to write plays, some of which are now lost. *The Old Wives' Tale* (printed 1595) combines two fairy tales in an effective entertainment, notable for its songs and dream-like tone, and *David and Bethsabe* (printed 1599), a play on the theme of retribution, skilfully condenses its scriptural material into a unified, mature work, containing some memorable poetry. Peele wrote 3 occasional poems – *Polyhymnia* (1590), *The Honour of the Garter* (1593) and *Anglorum Feriae* (1595). The first commemorates the annual tournament marking the anniversary of Elizabeth's accession; the second is a complimentary poem in blank verse to the Earl of Northumberland; the third a tribute to Queen Elizabeth on the thirty-seventh anniversary of her accession.

In 1607 there appeared *The Merry Conceited Jests of George Peele, Sometimes a Student of Oxford*, a work which earned Peele a posthumous reputation as a roistering, thriftless character, given to prankish swindling and confidence tricks – a reputation exaggerated by later commentators who have portrayed Peele as the François Villon of England. Peele may have been just such a rogue – but at least half the escapades attributed to him are traditional and hackneyed and figure in Elizabethan jest-collections or in other jest-biographies. [MJ]

The Life and Works of G.P., ed. C. T. Prouty (1952 ff.) (including the *Life* by D. H. Horne). P. H. Cheffaud, *G.P.* (Paris, 1913); G. Wilson Knight, *The Golden Labyrinth: A Study of British Drama* (1962); F. E. Schelling, *Elizabethan Drama 1558–1642* (2 vols., 1908).

Pepys, Samuel (1633–1703). Diarist. Born in London, the son of John Pepys, a London tailor. He was a scholar of St Paul's School in London and also of Magdalene College, Cambridge; he became a B.A. in 1654 and an M.A. in 1660. In 1655 he married Elizabeth le Marchant de St Michel, the 15-year-old daughter of a Huguenot inventor. In 1654 he had entered the household of a distant relative, Sir Edward Montagu (later 1st Earl of Sandwich), as a secretary, a position he again filled in 1660 when Montagu took command of the fleet which brought Charles II back to England. Having been a Roundhead, he now became, and remained, an ardent Royalist. Montagu saw to Pepys's advancement as an administrator in the naval service, and (a diligent and astute man) he held several important posts: Clerk of the Acts, Surveyor General of the Victualling Office and, through the favour of the Duke of York, Secretary to the Commissioners of the Admiralty (1673). He was a Justice of the Peace, Member of Parliament, and, as a leading 'virtuoso' and technical expert, President of the Royal Society. In 1679 he was imprisoned in the Tower and charged with complicity in the Popish Plot, but discharged and reinstated. He resigned on the flight of his patron, then James II, in 1688. Pepys was a notable collector and on his death he left his library, containing interesting ballad books, to Magdalene College (*Bibliotheca Pepysiana*, ed. J. R. Tanner et al., 4 parts, 1914–40). There, among his papers (which include the *Account of the Preservation of Charles II after the Battle of Worcester* dictated to him by the king; ed. W. Rees-Mogg, 1954), was discovered in the 19th century his famous *Diary*, which he kept in a secret shorthand until he thought his eyesight was failing in 1669. His varied background of travel, intellectual interests, public office and experience make this an important document in the study of affairs and manners of his day, but his personal, candid revelations of aspects of his life which most men keep secret, or push from contemplation, make it a first-rate human document of great psychological interest. In the last century, such 'indiscretion' earned him the same censure as that heaped on ◊Boswell, as a coxcomb and foolish, if quaint, babbler, but modern readers are not apt to be so censorious or categorical. The *Diary* was deciphered by the Rev. John Smith and first published,·with notes and considerable excisions, by Lord Braybrook (1825). The fullest, but not complete, edition is by H. B. Wheatley (1893–9; revised and with an introduction by J. Warrington, 3 vols., Everyman, 1953) (various abridgements are available, for example that by J. P. Kenyon, 1963). The first three volumes of a complete edition by R. Latham and W. Matthews appeared in 1970. Pepys has been the subject of plays, novels and a number of interesting books. [AR]

Memoires Relating to the State of the R.N. (1690; ed. J. R. Tanner, 1906); *Letters*, ed. H. T. Heath (1955). A. Bryant, *S.P.* (3 vols., 1933–9); J. H. Wilson, *The Private World of Mr P.* (1959); M. Willy, *English Diarists: Evelyn and P.* (WTW, 1963); R. Barber, *S. P. Esq.* (1970) (catalogue of National Portrait Gallery exhibition).

Percy, Thomas (1729–1811). Poet, antiquary and cleric. Born the son of a grocer, he was educated at Christ Church, Oxford, and became Dean of Carlisle (1778) and Bishop of Dromore (1782). He was interested in the exotic in literature, producing in 1761 a 'Chinese novel', and in 1763 joined the new wave of interest in Ossianic (◊ Ossian) poetry by producing 5 'runic poems' from a Latin version of the Icelandic texts. He then transferred his interest to his own country's literary past and produced the work by which he is best known, *Reliques of Ancient English Poetry* (1765, 1767, 1775 and 1794; ed. H. B. Wheatley, 1876), a collection of ballads, sonnets, songs and metrical romances ranging from very early date to the 17th century. Most of them were drawn from a 17th-century manuscript which he acquired (now known as the *Percy Folio* in the British Museum; ed. F. J. Furnivall and J. W. Hales, 1867–8) and which formed the basis of Child's collection of ballads. Percy's collection, though by later standards badly edited and 'adulterated', was an important stage in the revival of interest in the ballads, and formed an important stimulus to writers such as Scott and Wordsworth. Percy's own poetry is turgid and stilted. There is no single adequate study of Percy. A number of papers has been published on aspects of his life and work (see the *Cambridge Bibliography of English Literature*). [AR]

Letters, ed. Cleanth Brooks et al. (Louisiana State U.P., Baton Rouge) (1944–).

Peter of Blois (Petrus Blesensis) (*c.* 1135–*c.* 1205). Medieval theologian. Born at Blois, he read law at Bologna and theology at Paris. After spending some time in Sicily he entered the service of Henry II of England and became Archdeacon of Bath and London successively. He is best known for his letters, addressed to Henry II, Becket, ◊ John of Salisbury and others, and for his verse.

Works, ed. J. A. Giles (4 vols., 1846–7); Migne, *Patrologia Latina* (207–10).

Pettie, George (*c.* 1548–89). Story-teller. Educated at Christ Church, Oxford, he travelled abroad as a soldier. His literary activity was possibly inspired by William ◊ Painter's *Palace of Pleasure*, and in 1576 his compilation of 12 tales which had circulated in manuscript was issued by a piratical publisher under the punning title *A Petite Palace of Pettie his Pleasure*. It went into 6 editions. Pettie's stories were classical in origin, coming mainly from Ovid and Livy, but he retold them in contemporary guise, in an artful and mannered style which anticipated ◊ Lyly's Euphuism. *The Civil Conversation* (1581) was a translation of the first 3 books of Stefano Guazzo's popular dialogues, which formed an instructive handbook on polite conversation; the final book was translated by Bartholomew Young in 1586. [MJ]

C. S. Lewis, *English Literature in the Sixteenth Century* (1954).

Philips, Ambrose (*c.* 1675–1749). Poet and playwright. A fellow of St John's College, Cambridge, and a member of Addison's circle, he held various government places in Ireland after 1714. Pope thought Philips was 'capable of writing very nobly' but believed he had been encouraged to abuse him in coffee-houses, and so destroyed Philips's *Pastorals* (1706 onwards, collected 1710) by praising them in comparison with his own in an ironical *Guardian* article, and subsequently lampooned him elsewhere. Philips's mawkish, short-lined poems praising young children of the nobility earned him the *soubriquet* Namby-Pamby from Henry ◊ Carey, providing a new English word. In imitation of his patron's *Spectator*, Philips wrote for the *Grumbler* (1715) and edited the *Freethinker* (1718–21). [AR]

Poems, ed. with a Life by M. G. Segar (1937).
Johnson, *Lives of the Poets*.

Philips, John (1676–1709). Poet. Educated at Winchester and Christ Church, Oxford, where he was a keen botanist. Harley and St John encouraged him to write a poem (published 1705) on Blenheim, probably as a counter to Addison's *Campaign*. He is best known for *The Splendid Shilling* (1701, 1705 and other editions), a very popular poem in burlesque Miltonic verse, contrasting the happiness of the possessor of the shilling with the difficulties of the poet. He also published *Cyder* (1708), in 2 books of blank verse, an imitation of Virgil's *Georgics*, full of information about apples and the technology of cider-making, with some fine passages of country description. The latter appealed to the Romantics. [AR]

The Poems of J.P., ed. M. G. Lloyd-Thomas (1927) (with a biographical introduction).
H. de Maar, *A History of Modern English Romanticism*, i (1924); Johnson, *Lives of the Poets*.

Phillips, Stephen (1864–1915). Dramatist and poet. At one time a member of the Shakespearean acting company of his cousin Frank Benson, he had published several volumes of poetry, including *Orestes and Other Poems* (1884), *Eremus* (1894) and *Christ in Hades* (1897), when his *Poems* (1898) proved successful enough for him to abandon tutoring and become a professional writer. One leading Edwardian actor-manager, Sir George Alexander, commissioned in 1898 a poetic tragedy, *Paolo and Francesca*, which he staged with great success in 1902, by which time another, Sir Herbert Tree, had won financial and artistic success for Phillips by producing, in characteristically spectacular manner, his play *Herod* (1901). Tree later produced *Ulysses* (1902) and *Nero* (1906), in both of which scenic effects were expensive and elaborate. Tree's production of *Faust* (1908), the joint work of Phillips and J. Comyns Carr, submerged the play in spectacle. Early success spoiled Phillips; his later years were penurious and unhappy, and his plays were unsuccessful. The great vogue of *Paolo and Francesca* coincided with a short-lived resurgence of poetic drama, but the rebirth was soon seen to be abortive. Overpraised in his own day and compared to Sophocles and Shakespeare, Phillips survives now only as a name in the history of English poetic drama at a time when prose was the medium of the truly contemporary theatre. All Phillips's plays were historical, and his brief period of acclaim shows the nostalgia for Shakespeare and the Elizabethans which perennially deceives critics and public into welcoming a renaissance of verse-drama. [MJ]

A. Nicoll, *British Drama* (5th edn, 1962); H. Pearson, *The Last Actor-Managers* (1950) and *Herbert Tree* (1956).

Pindar, Peter. ◊ Wolcot, John.

Pinero, Sir Arthur Wing (1855–1934). Dramatist. At one time an actor in Sir Henry Irving's company, from 1877 he wrote farces and comedies which showed an actor's sense of the theatre. Amongst the most successful were *The Magistrate* (1885), *The Schoolmistress* (1886), and *Dandy Dick* (1887), in all of which farcical eruptions in staid Victorian drawing-rooms are superlatively stage-managed. He was a devotee of Eugène Scribe and of the well-made play. In his 4 celebrated 'problem plays', *The Second Mrs Tanqueray* (1893), *The Notorious Mrs Ebbsmith* (1895), *Iris* (1901) and *Mid-Channel* (1909), he wrote effective and eminently playable scenes in the manner of the Society melodramas of Dumas *fils*, but with just a hint of Ibsen's serious social concern. *The Second Mrs Tanqueray* was daring and epoch-making in its day, but it is contrived and specious as social criticism, though still actable. *Trelawney of 'The Wells'* (1898) is a nostalgic play about the older theatre in which Pinero had grown up. [MJ]

H. Hamilton Fyfe, *Sir A.W.P.'s Plays and Players* (1930); W. D. Dunkel, *Sir A.P.* (Chicago, 1941); A. Nicoll, *British Drama* (5th edn, 1962); G. Rowell, *The Victorian Theatre* (1956); J. Russell Taylor, *The Rise and Fall of the Well-Made Play* (1967).

Pinter, Harold (1930–   ). Dramatist. Born in the East End of London, he was educated at Hackney Downs Grammar School, and became an actor under the name of David Baron. *The Room* (1957) was performed by the University of Bristol's Drama Department. His first full-length play, *The Birthday Party*, baffled reviewers in 1958 and ran only three nights in London. It later made a strong impression on television and was successfully restaged in 1964, by which time Pinter's reputation had been established by *The Caretaker* (1959), which was also filmed. Several one-act plays – *The Dumb Waiter, A Slight Ache, The Collection* and *The Lover* – originally written for B.B.C. radio or television, have been produced in the theatre. A third full-length play, *The Homecoming*, was presented by the Royal Shakespeare Company in 1965. He has also contributed highly characteristic sketches to West End revues and has adapted 3 novels for the screen: *The Servant* (by R. Maugham), *The Pumpkin Eater* (by P. ◊ Mortimer) and *Accident* (by N. Moseley). His plays (which are classed as 'comedies of menace') have claustrophobic settings, drab and occasionally sinister; the characters fail to communicate with one another, and the truth about their situations is not always clear. Pinter has an uncanny ear for dialogue, investing prosaic conversations with intensity, suggestiveness and ambiguity. His ultimate importance as a dramatist has yet to be critically established, but his reputation in Britain and abroad is high. He was made a C.B.E. in 1967. [MJ]

Ed. W. A. Armstrong, *Experimental Drama* (1963); ed. J. R. Brown, *Modern British Dramatists* (New Jersey, 1968); R. Hayman, *H.P.* (1968); W. Kerr, *H.P.* (1967); ed. C. Marowitz, *Theatre at Work* (1967); J. Russell Taylor, *Anger and After* (revised edn, 1969).

Piozzi, Hester Lynch (1741–1821). Miscellaneous writer and friend of Dr ♢ Johnson. Born at Bodvel, near Pwllheli, Caernarvonshire, the daughter of John Salusbury, a small, impoverished landowner who went to Canada to make his fortune. She had a private education and married Henry Thrale, the son of a rich brewer, an arrangement made by her paternal uncle and her mother. Thrale was a respectable man with nothing in common with his wife; she, a clever woman, spent her time with her five daughters and in reading. Dr Johnson became an intimate of the family in 1765 and lived much in their house (now destroyed) at Streatham Park (now a public park in South London). Johnson also accompanied the Thrales to Brighton and on visits to Wales (1774) and France (1775). Thrale suffered from apoplexy, and Mrs Thrale took over his business before his death in 1781; the brewery was then sold to Barclay's. In 1780, she had been introduced to Gabriel Piozzi, an Italian musician; she resolved to marry him, but under family pressure sent him away. The strain was too much for her and they were married in Roman Catholic and Anglican ceremonies in July 1784. They then lived in Italy until 1787. The marriage caused a family rupture and an estrangement from the ailing Johnson, whom she had felt burdened with. While in Italy, she wrote *Anecdotes of the Late Samuel Johnson during the last Twenty Years of His Life* (1786; ed. S. C. Roberts, 1925) and also published *Letters to and from the Late Samuel Johnson LL.D.* (1788; and see Johnson's *Letters*, ed. R. W. Chapman, 1952) as well as travels and other unimportant pieces. [A R]

Autobiography, Letters and Literary Remains, ed. A. Hayward (2 vols., revised and enlarged, 1861); *Piozziana . . . Recollections by a Friend* (E. Maugin) (1833); *Diary*, edited as *Thraliana*, J. L. Clifford, *H.L.P., Mrs Thrale* (2nd edn, 1952).

Pitscottie. ♢ Lindsay, Robert.

Pitter, Ruth (1897–). Poetess. Born at Ilford in Essex, the daughter of an elementary schoolmaster, she was herself educated at an elementary school. During the First World War, she held a small job in the War Office. She has published volumes of poems at intervals of several years since 1920, and, though she has led a retired life and has never been a member of any literary movement or group, has attracted the admiration of fellow poets from Hilaire Belloc to John Wain. She was the recipient of the Heinemann Foundation Award in 1954 and of the Queen's Gold Medal for Poetry in 1965. Her verse, basically religious in feeling, is decorative and fantastic in texture, and she has a talent for grotesque and humorous as well as for serious poetry. [G S F]

First Poems (1920); *First and Second Poems* (1927); *A Mad Lady's Garland* (1934); *A Trophy of Arms* (1936) (Hawthornden Prize); *The Spirit Watches* (1939); *The Rude Potato* (1941); *The Bridge* (1945); *Pitter on Cats* (1947); *Urania* (1951); *The Ermine* (1953); *Collected Poems* (1960).

Plomer, William (Charles Franklyn) (1903–). South African poet and novelist. Born in Northern Transvaal. After schooling at Rugby, he returned to South Africa as a farmer and trader and wrote there his first, angry novel, *Turbott Wolfe* (1925). As joint-editor with Roy ♢ Campbell of the monthly *Voorslag* he again expressed his scorn for racial discrimination. Attempts were made to silence the journal and Plomer left for Japan in 1927. He came to England in 1929, and has since lived mainly in London and Sussex. He has been a reviewer, broadcaster, editor and for many years, interrupted by wartime Admiralty service, a publisher's adviser. He is the editor of *Kilvert's Diary* (1938–40) and has also written short stories and biographies.

Plomer has always been interested in the kinship of violence and absurdity. This is particularly apparent in the ballad-satires which form half of his *Collected Poems* (1960). There is a Japanese restraint in some descriptive pieces and a precision in the creation of character through circumstance that also enlivens his prose work. The novels *The Case Is Altered* (1932) and *The Invaders* (1934) describe the reactions of widely varying people to London's changing conditions, and *Museum Pieces* (1952) the tragic and humorous results of the refusal of two Edwardians, mother and son, to move with the times. Plomer's wit and humour often complement an irony that undermines man's self-importance. He has worked with Benjamin Britten on *Curlew*

River (1964), *The Burning Fiery Furnace* (1966) and *The Prodigal Son* (1968). [PT]

Double Lives (1943); *At Home* (1958) (autobiographies); *Taste and Remember* (1966) (poems).

J. R. Doyle, 'The Poetry of W.P.', *Sewanee Review*, 75 (Autumn, 1967).

Plunkett, Edward John Moreton Drax. ◊ Dunsany, Lord.

Pollard, A(lfred) W(illiam) (1859–1944). English scholar and bibliographer. Born in London, the son of a physician, he was educated at King's College School and St John's College, Oxford, where he studied classics. In 1883 he joined the Department of Printed Books of the British Museum. He wrote for the *Guardian* and edited several of Chaucer's *Canterbury Tales* (1886–7; long in print and used in schools), a Chaucer primer and *The Canterbury Tales* in the Globe *Chaucer* (1898). He also printed *English Miracle Plays, Moralities and Interludes* (1890), a selection, and, in collaboration, the *Towneley Plays* (1897) and the *Macro Plays* (1904). These pioneering works, which long stood alone, had an influential effect, for good or ill, on the development of the study of medieval writing within English studies. He was co-editor of *The Library* from 1904 and was secretary of the Bibliographical Society (1893–1933). He gradually became an experienced bibliographer, and devoted much of his attention to Shakespeare's works; his *Shakespeare's Folios and Quartos: 1594–1685* (1909) is the foundation of the vast improvements made in the last fifty years in the textual criticism of Shakespeare's plays. *Shakespeare's Fight with the Pirates and the Problems of the Transmission of His Text* (1917; revised 1920) may be cited as an example of his originality. He became Keeper of the Printed Books in the British Museum in 1919, and retired in 1924, when he took over the Bibliographical Society's project for *A Short Title Catalogue of Books Printed in England, Scotland and Ireland and of English Books printed Abroad: 1475–1650* (the *STC*), which appeared in 1926. [AR]

Ed. H. Thomas, *A Select Bibliography of the Writings of A. W. Pollard* (1938) (autobiographical preface).

Pollard, Peggy. ◊ Cornish Literature.

Pomfret, John (1667–1703). Poet. Educated at Queens' College, Cambridge, he became Rector of Maulden in Bedfordshire. He is the author of a number of poems, but the only real survivor is *The Choice or Wish* (1700), a meditative poem which was popular for a long time. In it the poet outlines the happy country life, on a competence, which he would choose: 'Near some fair Town, I'd have a private Seat . . .'. [AR]

Johnson, *Lives of the Poets*; E. E. Kellett, *Reconsiderations* (1928).

Pope, Alexander (1688–1744). Poet. Born in Lombard Street in London, the son of elderly parents. His father, Alexander Pope, a Roman Catholic, was a merchant and linen-draper; in 1700, the family moved to Binfield in Windsor Forest where there was a Catholic colony, probably in conformity with the anti-Catholic legislation to depart from London. Pope inherited a small income from his father. A precocious boy, he was briefly at one or two Catholic schools, but mostly studied at home. When he was about 12, he had the first of several illnesses which left him with ruined health, and finally a tubercular spine, though he continued his intensive reading and writing. He was taken up and encouraged as a prodigy by several retired men of letters in the neighbourhood, particularly William ◊ Walsh, and about 1705 he began to know something of the London writers through William ◊ Wycherley. In May 1709, Pope's *Pastorals* were published in Tonson's *Miscellany* (vol. VI) and gained him some fame. The opening of Pope's career is marked by ambition, consciousness of genius, narrow but intensive education, obtrusive help from older men of which he was vain but understandably felt imprisoning, and ill-health. The *Pastorals* are assured exercises in an almost dead poetic kind, marked by virtuoso writing. His next work, *An Essay on Criticism* (May 1711), is a brilliant epigrammatic statement of codified neo-classical critical doctrine, particularly defining the critic's social function. Pope's conception of the function of the poet and his most profound critical insights are best seen in his own practice, and conclusions based on this early work must be modified; it was, however, very influential and praised in the *Spectator*, in which Pope printed *Messiah*, an imitation of Virgil's fourth *Eclogue*. ◊ Steele published essays by Pope in the *Guardian*.

In May 1712, Pope published the first, shorter, version of *The Rape of the Lock*, and enlarged it in 1714. This masterpiece of mock-heroic technique starts as a joke arising from an actual incident, but contains some very powerful, even tragic, poetry. It shows several themes and attitudes characteristic of Pope's later work: his attack on his society for not realizing its potentialities; his half-unwilling admiration for English opulence; his moral concern with leading the good life; and, in Belinda, his awareness of the predicament of women, creatures of nearly irresistible passion living in a man's world of reason and reputation. In 1713 Pope issued proposals for a translation of the *Iliad* (6 vols., 1715–20). For ten years he laboured on this; and for a further three (with assistants) on the *Odyssey* (5 vols., 1725–6). In 1717, he published a collection of his *Works*, preserving all he thought worthy of his earlier poetry. This includes 'Windsor Forest', which had appeared in 1713, a topographical poem uniting natural description (he was then studying painting) with historical and social reflections; 2 interesting romantic poems, 'Lines to the Memory of an Unfortunate Lady', and a heroical epistle, *Eloisa to Abelard*. It also includes translations from Chaucer and an interesting reworking, *The House of Fame: A Vision*. This early volume shows the breadth of Pope's reading; his apprenticeship in imitation of Chaucer, Spenser, Crashaw and the Metaphysicals; and the extent of his virtuosity outside satire. The *Iliad* and *Odyssey* have great poetry in them; Pope seeks to 'realize' Homer for the contemporary reader and the labour of translation undoubtedly deepened his art. From the proceeds of the enterprise, he added considerably to his financial independence, and from 1719 lived in the pretty house at Twickenham, where he spent his life improving the garden he often refers to in his writing. At this time he was writing a fair amount of miscellaneous verse, and in 1725 published his edition of *The Works of Shakespeare*. His work is rather perfunctory, though not without insights prompted by his genius. The Homer and the Shakespeare embroiled Pope in the literary infighting of the time; and in 1728, the first *Dunciad*, with Theobald the detractor of his editorial competence as the 'hero', heralded his later career as the principal satirist of the age. Many fugitive pieces and squibs as well as later works are associated with these poems (the *Dunciad* was reprinted with an elaborate anti-pedantic apparatus of notes as *The Dunciad Variorum* in 1729; a fourth book, *The New Dunciad*, appeared in 1742; and the poem was rewritten with Colley ◊ Cibber in Theobald's place, appearing in 1743). Pope took enormous care over the elaboration of this poem; in it the mock-heroic is more than a mere device, it becomes the vehicle for a powerful vision of English society (or at least its literary and intellectual structure). By using reminiscences of Homer, Virgil, Dante, Milton and other great constructors of visions, he unifies (more or less successfully) individual attacks on Grub Street hacks into a denunciation of the betrayal of the deepest human values. The extraordinary power of the writing allows him to imply his own view of the poet as seer, the bard who is needed to keep society healthy. The closing passage of Book iv is one of the noblest statements of this ancient and generous view of art. It gains in power, perhaps, from a prophetic sense which Pope has but never argues out, that his humanist culture is doomed by intellectual and social forces then gaining strength. The poem is eventually tragic rather than epic.

Associated with the satirical (witty and personal) passages in the *Dunciad* are Pope's *Imitations of Horace*. These are translations and happy adaptations to the contemporary scene of passages from Horace's *Epistles*, *Satires* and *Odes*. They are relaxed in tone, but contain some of Pope's most concentrated wit and virtuoso writing in conversational and other varied couplets. There are 11 poems of this kind. ◊ Bolingbroke gave Pope the idea, and 'The First Satire of the Second Book of Horace Imitated' appeared in February 1733. Several other works are associated with the *Imitations*. In 1735, Pope dedicated to his dying friend 'An Epistle from Mr Pope to Dr Arbuthnot' (◊ Arbuthnot), and this was altered, given the title of 'The Prologue to the Satires' and placed at the beginning of the 'Satires' as the *Imitations* section was called in the *Works* (1751) edited by ◊ Warburton. 'One Thousand Seven Hundred and Thirty Eight: A Dialogue something like Horace' was published in May 1738 (*Dialogue II* in July) and the title altered to 'Epilogue to the Satires' in the *Works* (8vo, 1740), edited by Pope. Literary criticism, autobiography and politics are the themes of these poems; Pope is constantly making his judgements and justifying his positions. They do not, however, really form a homogeneous series. At times, they shade into the second great division of his later work, the poems in which he 'moralized his song' and made the positive statements of values which underlie his satire. This division comprises the *Essay on Man* (four 'Epistles' addressed to Bolingbroke; I–III, 1733; IV, 1734) and the 4 poems known variously as *Epistles to Various Persons*, *Ethic Epistles* or *Moral Essays* (I, 'To Cobham: Of the Knowledge and Characters of Men', 1733–4; II, 'To a Lady [Martha Blount]: Of the Characters of Women', 1734–5; III, 'To Bathurst: Of the Use of Riches', 1732–3; IV, 'To Burlington: Of the Use of Riches' (and taste), 1731). Pope toyed with the idea that the *Essay on Man* was the first book of a work which would include the *Epistles* as, illustrations, but the idea was very tentative. Warburton in his editing tinkered to make it clearer and more rigid. The *Essay on Man* is a philosophical (or reflective) poem in the epistolary form, the middle style – not dramatic like *Paradise Lost*, but relaxed and not rigidly argued. Books I and III are concerned with a Theodicy; that is, with what part evil plays in the world of God's dispensation and in the social order he has made for man. Whatever is, is right; man cannot know God's purposes, and cannot, therefore, complain about the existence of evil. Books II and IV are concerned with an Ethic; that is, how man must act in this world given his psychological make up. He must oppose evil. The poem makes use of traditional Christian and humanist materials: the great chain of being; the conflict of reason and passion; the argument from design. The poem is often attacked as unoriginal, but its beauty lies in the poetic tension (within the work) which Pope produces to hold the disparate, traditional materials together, since they cannot be synthesized by reason. It was attacked as unorthodox by a Swiss theologian, Crousaz, and Warburton gained his ascendancy over the old poet by coming to his rescue. Much of the defence, as well as the attack, is beside the point. The poem also serves to justify, however, the satirist's social role.

Pope also wrote influential criticism in prose that is worth studying, particularly the Prefaces to the *Iliad* and *Odyssey*. He was practically the first English writer to publish his own letters, and perhaps it was partly the novelty of the action that made necessary the complicated series of manoeuvres, false piracies and complex arrangements by which this was done between 1735 and his death. He altered the text of letters to secure 'artistic' truth, a procedure that has gained him much abuse. His letters are analyses of his own thoughts and feelings rather than accounts of his society. They were considered models of elegant writing. Later reaction against the technical domination of Pope in the poetry of the century obscured many of his noblest qualities of sympathy, humanity and passion; 19th-century critics were generally content to accept the stereotype of a brilliantly malicious, prosaic technician. Byron made significant objection to this faulty judgement, and in the last forty years Pope has reappeared as the great poet he is.

There are many collected *Works*. Pope himself issued editions in 1717 and 1735, etc.; Warburton's edition appeared in 9 volumes (1751) and was frequently reprinted; the annotation of the edition by W. Elwin and W. J. Courthope (10 vols., 1871–89), though often hostile, is not yet superseded; the text is corrupt. [AR]

Works ('The Twickenham Edition'), general ed. J. Butt, I, *Pastorals* and *Essay on Criticism*, etc., 1961; II, *The Rape of the Lock* and other poems, revised, 1962; III. i, *An Essay on Man*, 1950; III.ii, *Epistles to Several Persons (Moral Essays)*, 1951; IV, *Imitations of Horace*, corrected, 1961; V, *The Dunciad*, 3rd edn, revised, 1963; VI, *Minor Poems*, 1954; VII and VIII, *Iliad*, 1967; IX and X, *Odyssey*, 1967; XI, Index, 1970; *Prose Works*, I, ed. N. Ault (1936) (incomplete, but the only modern volume of prose); *Correspondence*, ed. G. Sherburn (5 vols., 1956).
G. Sherburn, *The Early Career of A.P.* (1934); N. Ault, *New Light on P.* (1949); B. Dobrée, *A.P.* (1951); A. Warren, *P. as Critic and Humanist* (Princeton U.P., 1929); G. Tillotson, *On the Poetry of P.* (2nd edn, 1962), *The Moral Poetry of P.* (1946) and *P. and Human Nature* (1958); D. M. Knight, *P. and the Heroic Tradition: A Critical Study of His Iliad* (Yale U.P., 1951); G. Wilson Knight, *Laureate of Peace* (1954); A. L. Williams, *P.'s Dunciad* (1955); R. W. Rogers, *The Major Satires of P.* (Illinois U.P., 1955); F. R. Leavis, *Revaluation* (1936) (on *The Dunciad*); I. Jack, *Augustan Satire* (1951); *Essays in the Eighteenth Century Presented to D. Nichol Smith* (1945); ed. J. L. Clifford and L. A. Landa, *P. and His Contemporaries. Essays Presented to G. W. Sherburn* (1949); *The Seventeenth Century. Essays Presented to R. F. Jones* (Stanford U.P.. 1951); ed. M. Mack, *Essential Articles for the Study of A.P.* (Hamden, Conn., 1964); R. Griffith, *A.P. A Bibliography* (1 vol. in 2 pts, Austin, Texas, 1922, 1927) (incomplete); R. Griffith, *CBEL*;

E. Abbott, *A Concordance to the Works of P.* (1875) (needs revision).

Postgate, Raymond William (1896–   ). Historian, novelist and miscellaneous writer. Born in Cambridge, the son of J. P. Postgate, the Professor of Latin, and educated at the Perse School, Cambridge, Liverpool College and St John's College, Oxford. During the First World War he was a conscientious objector and was imprisoned in 1916. After the war he was a journalist for eight years, chiefly as foreign sub-editor on the *Daily Herald*; he also edited left-wing political papers. In 1918 he married the daughter of George Lansbury, whose *Life* he published in 1951. He has been an editor on the *Encyclopædia Britannica*, a publisher and a Civil Servant (1942–50). Since 1950, he has been president of the Good Food Club and has written various works on wine. He founded and edited the annual *Good Food Guide* (1951–   ). He is the author of several political works, such as *The Bolshevik Theory* (1920) and *What to Do with the B.B.C.* (1935), as well as historical works. The latter include *Revolution from 1789 to 1906* (1920), *A Pocket History of the British Workers* (1937) *Karl Marx* (1933) and (with his brother-in-law G. D. H. Cole) *The Common People: 1746–1946* (1946). He has also written several works of fiction: *Verdict of Twelve* (1940); *Somebody at the Door* (1943); *The Ledger is Kept* (1953). [A R]

Potter, Beatrix (1866–1943). Children's writer and illustrator. Born in Bolton Gardens, Kensington, the child of moneyed and restrictive parents, she had an uneventful childhood, with one younger brother, and she grew up slightly old fashioned, obstinate and unsentimental. Her observation of human character, scenery and animal nature was all the closer for her quiet life, broken only by family holidays in Scotland, Wales and the Lake District. She sketched and painted very accurately, and became a knowledgeable illustrator of flowers and fungi. She kept many pets, some of which were the originals of animals in her stories; they included a rabbit named Mr Bouncer, a Mrs Tiggy-Winkle and a favourite mouse called Hunca Munca. In 1893 she sent the first draft of the story of Peter Rabbit as an illustrated letter to Noel Moore, the son of her former governess. *The Tale of Peter Rabbit* was

printed privately in 1900, and by F. Warne and Co. in 1902; the editorial association with Norman Warne ended in 1905 in an engagement, which was broken by his death in the same year. Also in 1905 she bought a small farm in Sawrey in the Lake District, to which she escaped when she could. In after years she added to this property, and eventually left it to the National Trust. Her best books were written by 1913, when she married her solicitor William Heelis and settled down to sheep farming.

Her best-known books include *The Tailor of Gloucester* (1903), *The Tale of Benjamin Bunny* (1904), *The Tale of Two Bad Mice* (1904), *The Tale of Mrs Tiggy-Winkle* (1905), *The Tale of Mr Jeremy Fisher* (1906), *The Tale of Tom Kitten* (1907), *The Tale of Jemima Puddle-Duck* (1908), *The Roly-Poly Pudding* (1908), *The Tale of Mrs Tittlemouse* (1910) and *The Tale of Mr Tod* (1912). Each creature in her stories fits into a complete and consistent world. Her illustrations of domestic settings are superb; each house or rabbit hole has its own exquisitely appropriate interior. She knew her animals so well that they were like people to her; she was taking no liberties when she dressed them and equipped them with kitchens, larders and four-poster beds. She never associated creatures in her books unless this might happen naturally. Her dialogue is crisp and natural, the narrative style clean and economical. There is nothing in excess. [T V]

The Journals, 1881–97, ed. L. Linder (1966).
Margaret Lane, *The Tale of B.P.* (1946; revised edn, 1968).

Potter, Stephen (1900–70). Humorist and critic. Educated at Westminster School and Merton College, Oxford, he was a lecturer in English at London University and wrote several critical and historical works such as *D. H. Lawrence: A First Study* (1930), *Coleridge and S.T.C.* (1935) and *The Muse in Chains* (1937); the latter is a light-hearted but useful study of the development of English literature as a subject of university study in England. He also wrote a novel, *The Young Man* (1929), but is best known for his 'gamesmanship' series of humorous books: *The Theory and Practice of Gamesmanship, or The Art of Winning Games without Actually Cheating* (1947); *Lifemanship* (1950); *One-Upmanship* (1952); *Supermanship* (1958); *Anti-Woo* (1965). His brand of humour, quite original, is a blend of flat and serious tone (reminiscent of a gentlemanly sports handbook) united with a sceptical judgement of the values of the English middle-class social scene. He has also written (rather disappointingly) on humour itself in *Sense of Humour* (1954). [AR]

Powell, Anthony (Dymoke) (1905–   ). Novelist. Born in London, the son of an army colonel, he was brought up in various army posts, and educated at Eton and Balliol College, Oxford. He has been a publisher, a journalist and a film-script writer. In the Second World War, he served in his father's regiment, the Welch Regiment, and became a major in the Intelligence Corps. He wrote a biography, *John Aubrey and His Friends* (1948), but is best known as a novelist of neat skill and considerable satirical power. His novels fall into two groups. The early ones are concerned with London's bohemia, Chelsea and Bloomsbury, a seedy area depicted with dry wit. The stories are often farcical, reminiscent of the early fiction of Evelyn ◊ Waugh, but the life they deal with is much more closely documented and much more clearly explained. This group of works includes *Afternoon Men* (1931), *Venusberg* (1932) and *What's Become of Waring* (1939). The second group is projected as a considerable series under the general title 'The Music of Time'. This began with a public school–university novel, *A Question of Upbringing* (1951), and it, too, deals with the same upper-middle-class world of the earlier novels, but the elaboration of the series, the way in which characters appear, disappear and reappear, provides a solidly imagined web-like structure of social life. The narrator is Nicholas Jenkins, himself a novelist and a compulsive observer and verbalizer of experience. The shifts of view are (as is the title) reminiscent of Proust, though the shared social experience and ageing takes the place of personal memory. Comparison is also to be made with 'The Alexandria Quartet' of ◊ Durrell and C. P. Snow's series fiction. The companions of Jenkins are also 'new men' (◊ Snow), but not scientists, rather businessmen, writers, contact men. The representative is the insensitive, plodding, successful Widmerpool. The later titles in the series are to date: *A Buyer's Market* (1952); *The Acceptance World* (1955); *At Lady Molly's* (1957;

James Tait Black prize); *Casanova's Chinese Restaurant* (1960); *The Kindly Ones* (1962); *The Valley of Bones* (1964); *The Military Philosophers* (1968). With the last three, the account of the ageing process has assumed a grimmer and more sombre tone. [AR]

B. Bergonzi, *A.P.* (WTW, 1962).

Powys, John Cowper (1872–1963). Novelist. Eldest son of the Rev. C. F. Powys, and brother of T. F. and Llewelyn ◊ Powys, he was educated at Sherborne School and Corpus Christi College, Cambridge. In 1896 he married Margaret Alice Lyon, by whom he had one son. Between 1905 and 1929 he lectured in the United States to popular audiences on the major European and American writers. His first major novel, *Wolf Solent* (1929), was published when he was 57. He then retired to up-state New York, where he wrote *A Glastonbury Romance* (1932) and *Weymouth Sands* (1934). These novels together with *Maiden Castle* (1936) are set in the scenes and world of his boyhood, and are works of self-exploration and studies in the relationship between environment and personality. In 1934 Powys settled in Wales, where he wrote the lengthy historical novels *Owen Glendower* (1940) and *Porius* (1951), in which perhaps the fullest expression of his philosophy can be found, as well as a number of fantasies, of which *Atlantis* (1954) is the most considerable. He was an Honorary Doctor of Letters of the University of Wales, and his work has been translated into several languages.

Powys was a prolific and highly individual writer; but although he wrote poetry philosophy and criticism, his reputation is likely to rest upon the novels and upon the *Autobiography* (1934), a self-portrait quite exceptional in its thoroughness and candour. His powerful personality pervades all his books, which are complex, romantic, humorous, frequently extravagant, and in their combination of 19th-century prolixity and 20th-century introspection quite unlike others of their time. Powys's view of life owes much to Wordsworth in its close response to nature, and its emphasis on the creative power of the imagination; while his treatment of aesthetic experience recalls the work of Proust and ◊ Pater. The novels, however, have a Dickensian exuberance in their feeling for physical actuality and idiosyncrasies of character. Powys combines an awareness of the power of spiritual forces with a feeling for the normal and matter-of-fact, and an understanding of the complexities of sexual and romantic feeling with a sympathetic knowledge of the very young and the very old. For a confessional novelist he has a wide imaginative range, although he was more interested in individuals than in society as such, and was outspoken in his distrust of the developments in modern science and technology. His novels, uneven in style and inspiration, have a Blake-like veneration for life; and although they have divided the opinions of critics, their remoteness from the literary world of their time gives them a singular integrity. [G C]

Ducdame (1925), *The Brazen Head* (1956) (fiction); *Visions and Revisions* (1915), *Rabelais* (1948) (criticism); *The Meaning of Culture* (1930); *Letters to Louis Wilkinson* (1958); G. Wilson Knight, *The Saturnian Quest* (1964); H. J. Collins, *J.C.P.* (1966); D. Langridge, *J.C.P.: A Record of Achievement* (1966) (bibliography).

Powys, Llewelyn (1884–1939). Essayist and miscellaneous writer. Born in Dorset, younger brother of the more famous J. C. ◊ Powys and T. F. ◊ Powys, he was educated at Sherborne and at Corpus Christi, Cambridge, from which he graduated in 1906. He followed his brother J. C. to America in 1909 and lectured there. When he returned home later that year he was struck with tuberculosis. After stays in Switzerland, he went in 1914 to East Africa to farm with his youngest brother William. The first work of his to be published – extracts from diaries – appeared with some autobiographical reflections by J. C. Powys in *Confessions of Two Brothers* in 1916. He returned to England in 1920 and went to America the following year. After leaving America in 1925, he settled in Dorset, but continued to travel. Still suffering from tuberculosis, he finally went to Switzerland, where he spent his last three years. His sketches of African life in *Ebony and Ivory* (1923) and *Black Laughter* (1925) are among his better writings. His other books include an 'imaginary autobiography', *Love and Death* (1939), and 2 volumes of reminiscences, *Skin for Skin* (1926) and *The Verdict of Bridlegoose* (1927); a novel, *Apples be Ripe* (1930); and several books of travel. His work – a celebration of nature, of country folk and of life – is strangely (and perhaps damagingly) unmarked by his own experience of suffering. [N L]

Dorset Essays (1935); *Somerset Essays: A Pagan's Pilgrimage* (1937); *Selection*, ed. K. Hopkins (New York, 1961) (with introduction). M. Elwin, *The Life of L.P.* (1946). (◊ Powys, John Cowper.)

Powys, Theodore Francis (1875–1953). Fiction-writer. One of the eleven children (including J. C. ◊ Powys) of an Evangelical clergyman, and scantily educated, he did not start writing until he was nearly 30, first attempting (disastrously) to be a farmer. He then abandoned work and settled in a remote Dorset village, where he lived more or less as a hermit (though married) and produced his entire output between c. 1902 and 1933. During the first fifteen of these years he produced many works (mostly unpublished) which evince strongly his long struggle with Christian ideas; combined with a rather melancholic disposition these resulted in a sense of doom-laden fatality mitigated by transcendental release at death and in moments of vision and love. These concerns remained throughout his career but were increasingly tempered and eventually transformed by a bitterly ironic sense of humour. He began writing fiction about 1915 and moved from a Hardy-esque fatalism (seen at its best in *Mark Only*, 1924) towards a very individual style of dream-like grotesquery and ambiguous symbolism. His novels show little interest in realism or characterization, and are like intellectual puppet-plays. The best of them is *Mr Weston's Good Wine* (1927), a fable of God as a travelling wine-salesman visiting the benighted world of a small Dorset village and enacting there, in a time-suspended action, his judgement on the representative humours of humanity. The symbolism is both complex and ambiguous, relying on a structural network of comic interplay and bathos. The characteristic feature is a Swift-like irony thrust into a rich texture of signification, action, and feeling, which finally leaves intact a detached but strongly upheld sense of ultimate values, and of real hope. While being detached and tightly structured, the writing is emotionally intense – almost euphoric. *Kindness in a Corner* (1930) is a more serene and light-hearted comedy; *Unclay* (1931) is a much darker version of the visitation myth, in which 'Death', as a travelling journeyman

Praed

with a scythe, descends on another village-microcosm to bring release (which is ambiguously figurized as both passion and extinction). Powys's clipped, incisive style was suited to the short story, of which there are 7 books, notably *Fables* (1929), a set of very strange parables, beast-fables etc. *The Left Leg* (1923) is the best of several novellas. It features God as 'Old Jar', an aged and destitute wandering tinker who reappears many times in Powys's later stories, always pathetically outside the world, a representation of the Void. *Soliloquies of a Hermit* (1915) is Powys's only published non-fiction – a meditation on his secluded life and an exposition of his quasi-religious ideas. He 'retired' from writing in 1933. His work has never reached a large public and most of his major works are now out-of-print. [P R]

Mr Tasker's Gods (1925); *Mockery Gap* (1925); *Innocent Birds* (1926); *The Market Bell* (unpublished); *The White Paternoster* (1930) (stories); *The Two Thieves* (1932) (3 novellas); *Captain Patch* (1935) (stories); *Bottle's Path* (1946) (stories and novellas); *Come and Dine* (1967); *Rosie Plum and Other Stories* (1968).
W. Hunter, *The Novels and Stories of T.F.P.* (1930); F. Kermode, 'The Art of T.F.P., Ironist', in *The Welsh Review*, VI, 3 (1947); H. Coombes, *T.F.P.* (1960).

Praed, Winthrop Mackworth (1802–39). Poet. Born in London, the son of a lawyer, and educated at Eton (where he edited the *Etonian*) and Trinity College, Cambridge (where he twice won the Chancellor's medal for English verse). He was called to the bar (1829), and entered Parliament, where he supported the Reform Bill. In 1834, he was Secretary of the Board of Control in Peel's government and at his premature death seemed likely to hold higher office. His social position and political connexion allied to a skilful hand at versification enabled Praed to produce some clever *vers-de-société*, such as 'The County Ball', 'Goodnight to the Season' and 'The Vicar', though the point of his rather benign political satire has now mostly evaporated ('Stanzas on Seeing the Speaker Asleep' was famous). He wrote romantic tales in verse, spiced with irony, and his best-known poem is in a grotesque vein (rather like Hood's), 'The Red Fisherman'. His odd rhymes and stanzas are rather like Barham's in the *Ingoldsby Legends*. [A R]

Poems, with a Memoir by D. Coleridge (2 vols.

1864 etc.); *Selected Poems*, ed. K. Allott (Muses' Library, 1953).
D. Hudson, *A Poet in Parliament* (1939) (additions in *N. & Q.*, 3 January 1942).

Pratt, Edwin John (1883–1964). Canadian poet. Born in Newfoundland where he observed the anxieties of life in a fishing community. Like his father, he became an ordained Methodist minister. In 1907 he entered the University of Toronto to study theology and psychology – his poetry shows the influence of Wundt's mechanistic psychology. Instead of entering the active ministry he became a lecturer in psychology and, in 1919, Associate Professor of English at Toronto. He retired in 1953, continuing to live in Toronto.

Pratt's first collection was published in 1923. *The Witches' Brew* (1925) was his second. It is a rhetorical, irreverent celebration of alcohol that marks his rejection of his upbringing's strictest limitations, and announces the narrative power confirmed by *Titans* (1926). The 2 poems in this volume introduce the recurrent theme of gigantic struggle, balanced between heroism and cataclysm. In 'The Cachalot' a whale is pitted against the mechanical cunning of man, while 'The Great Feud' is subtitled 'A Dream of a Pleiocene Armageddon'. 'The Titanic' (1935) and 'Brébeuf and His Brethren' (1940) are Pratt's best poems. He adapts a variable iambic pentameter to accommodate exactly calculated areas of sound, giving strong narrative the full reinforcement of an impressive poetic armoury. Later poems include 'Dunkirk' (1941), 'Behind the Log' (1947) and 'Towards the Last Spike' (1952). *Collected Poems* (1958) constitutes perhaps the finest body of 20th-century narrative poetry in English. [P T]

J. Sutherland, *The Poetry of E.J.P.* (1956); H. W. Wells and C. F. Klinck, *E.J.P. The Man and His Poetry* (1947); Earle Birney, 'E.J.P. and His Critics', *Our Living Tradition* (Series 2 and 3, 1959, ed. Robert McDougall); 'A Garland for E.J.P.', *Tamarack Review*, 6 (Winter, 1958).

Prichard, Katharine Susannah (1884–   ). Australian novelist. Born in Fiji, the daughter of a journalist, she spent her early childhood in Tasmania, but was educated in Melbourne and took her first newspaper job there. She spent six years as a freelance journalist in London, where she wrote *The Pioneers* (1915). She married in 1919.

As a novelist Prichard has always preferred a broad canvas, and a real knowledge of her subject. To achieve these aims she travelled all over Australia, writing her regional novels only when she had familiarized herself with the local relations of men to nature and to their work. *Working Bullocks* (1926) is a typical product of this method. Before writing *Haxby's Circus* (1930) she travelled with a circus troupe. *Coonardoo* (1929) is a cruel and beautiful novel about the relationship of an aboriginal girl and the cattle-station owner who fathers her child. Unflawed by her typical over-inclusiveness, this is Prichard's finest novel. During the thirties Communist sympathies led her to write *The Real Russia* (1935) and a number of pamphlets. She has not abandoned her extremist championing of working humanity. The goldfields trilogy, *The Roaring Nineties* (1946), *Golden Miles* (1948) and *Winged Seeds* (1950), is its finest literary expression. The books are set in the tough country of Western Australia where she now lives. [P T]

Southerly, 4 (1953) (2 articles); M. Holburn, 'K.S.P.', *Meanjin*, x, 3 (Spring, 1951).

Priestley, J(ohn) B(oynton) (1894–   ). Novelist, dramatist and miscellaneous writer. Born in Bradford, the son of a schoolmaster, he was educated in his native city, and after army service in the First World War returned to study at Trinity Hall, Cambridge. He went to London in 1922, and worked as a reviewer, essayist and literary journalist. In the variety of his writings, he may best be described as a 'man of letters' in the old sense of the term: this also best describes his resources of character, the old-fashioned radicalism of his political views, and the career he has had as a public figure – as a patriotic broadcaster during the Second World War (see *Postscripts*, 1940); as a publisher; as a theatre experimentalist. His very extensive list of published works includes some literary history: *Figures in Modern Literature* (1924); *The English Comic Characters* (1925); *George Meredith* (English Men of Letters, 1926); *Peacock* (English Men of Letters, 1927); *The English Novel* (1927); and *Literature and Western Man* (1960). He started writing novels with *Benighted* (1927), a nightmare story of horror. In 1929 appeared *The Good Companions*, which was awarded the James Tait Black

Prize and was an instant popular success. Deliberately old-fashioned in the picaresque style, it is optimistic, hearty and pathetic – a deliberate exercise on Priestley's part in 'the clean, open air of the genuine tale'. He has little time for the 'committed' novel and is an admirer of the older English novelists, who are in his opinion less complicated than modern writers are trying to be. *Angel Pavement* (1930) is a story of London business, and other titles are *They Walk in the City* (1936), *Let the People Sing* (1939), *Festival at Fairbridge* (1951) and *The Magicians* (1954). His novels have been, and still are, best-sellers. Recent titles include *Salt is Leaving* (1966). In the 1930s he started a new and equally successful career as a playwright, with a dramatization of *The Good Companions* (1931); he followed this with many plays on diverse topics. For some time he was interested in Dunne's theory of time, and *Dangerous Corner* (1932) and *Time and the Conways* (1937) are concerned with this. He has also written comedies, such as *Laburnum Grove* (1933), plays about northern provincial life, such as *When We Are Married* (1938), and middle-class 'documentaries', such as *Eden End* (1934), with elements of farce. *An Inspector Calls* (1945), a kind of modern morality play, shows one reason for his popularity and success. His writing is thoughtful but not too demanding. In 1953, he married Jacquetta Hawkes, the archaeologist, with whom he had collaborated in writing a play, *The Dragon's Mouth* (1952). His work for the stage (he has had much production experience too) is craftsmanlike, and like all his writing highly competent. He has been involved in dramatizing other writers' work, such as Iris ◊ Murdoch's *A Severed Head* (1963). He has written film scripts and radio programmes as well as many volumes of essays, such as *Apes and Angels* (1928), *Delight* (1949) and *The Moments – and Other Pieces* (1966). He has published several volumes of autobiographical pieces, of which *Margin Released: A Writer's Reminiscences* (1962) is the most recent. [A R]

Essays of Five Decades (1969).
I. J. C. Brown, *J.B.P.* (W T W, 1957); D. Hughes, *J.B.P.: An Informal Study of His Work* (1958); G. L. Evans, *P. the Dramatist* (1964).

Pringle, Thomas (1789–1834). Poet. He was born near Kelso and educated at Edinburgh University. A childhood accident left him a cripple. In 1817 he founded and edited the *Edinburgh Monthly Magazine*. Financial setbacks followed his marriage in the same year, and he emigrated to South Africa with his family in 1819. During his six-year residence he opened a school and founded the *South African Journal*, a periodical which aimed to unite the country's cultural groups. His serious humanity is apparent in the prose *Narrative of a Residence in South Africa* (1835). Back in England, he became secretary of the Anti-Slavery Society in 1827, and died in London shortly after the passing of the Act of Abolition.

Pringle was among the first English poets to respond to the African scene. The nostalgia of 'Afar in the Desert' is less typical of his work than the combination of humanity and sentimentality in 'The Bechuana Boy'. Neither great nor original, he was open-minded and observant enough to let Africa remake him. He is an early exemplar of the South African tendency to obscure the distinction between social prescription and literature. [PT]

Poetical Works, with a Memoir by L. Ritchie (1838).
G. M. Miller and H. Sergeant, *A Critical Survey of South African Poetry in English* (1957).

Prior, Matthew (1664–1721). Poet and diplomatist. Born (according to tradition) near Wimborne Minster in Dorset, the son of a joiner. He worked in his uncle's Rhenish Tavern, near Charing Cross, London, where the Earl of Dorset (◊ Dorset, Charles) discovered his literary ability and helped to send him first to Westminster School and then to St John's College, Cambridge. While an undergraduate, he collaborated with Charles Montague, Earl of Halifax, in burlesqueing Dryden's religio-political poem as *The Hind and the Panther transvers'd to the Story of the Country Mouse and City Mouse* (1687; 1709). The influence of Dorset and his circle is present in Prior's light and truly elegant use of neo-classical bric-à-brac in his poems. He also wrote political and autobiographical verse, while pursuing a career as an M.P., Civil Servant (he was an Under-Secretary of State and a Commissioner for Trade and Plantations) and diplomatist in Holland and France. His public life culminated in his being made Plenipotentiary (he was not noble enough to be Ambassador) to France. He helped to draft the Treaty of Utrecht (1713), 'Matt's Peace', and as a result on the death of Queen Anne spent two years in the Tower of London. As a poet he is in the first flight of writers of *vers de société*; intelligent, tactful, a master of colloquial grace, and a follower of Horace. A handful of his poems, epigrams and amorous verses, such as 'The Merchant to Secure his Treasure' or *The Lady Who Offers her Looking-Glass to Venus*, are part of the solid achievement of Augustan England. He also wrote witty poems for children, like the attractive verses *To a Child of Quality Five Years Old* and *Cupid Turn'd Stroller*. Prior was a deft metrical experimenter and, like Swift, with whom he can be named, a master of octosyllabics, chiefly in broad, occasionally tedious, tales. His verse appeared in miscellanies, but after a pirated volume of his work appeared in 1707 Tonson published a collected *Poems on Several Occasions* (1709). The subscription folio edition of his *Poems* brought out by his friends in 1718 contains 2 more pretentious poems: *Alma: or the Progress of the Mind*, a sceptical and learned treatment in light octosyllabic couplets of Lockeian and Cartesian notions, and *Solomon on the Vanity of Human Wishes*, in heroic couplets. These have interesting passages, but have never excited enthusiasm. Lord Harley gave him Down Hall in Essex, near Harlow, and he died at Wimpole, Harley's seat. He is buried in Poets' Corner, Westminster Abbey. [AR]

The Literary Works ed. H. Bunker Wright and M. K. Spears (2 vols., 1959) (with bibliography and commentary); *Poems on Several Occasions* (1905) and *Dialogues of the Dead and Other Works* (1907), ed. A. R. Waller.
F. Bickley, *Life* (1914) and *M.P.: A Study of His Public Career and Correspondence* (1921); C. K. Eves, *P., Poet and Diplomatist* (1939).

Pritchett, V(ictor) S(awdon) (1900–   ). Novelist, short-story writer and critic. Born in Ipswich and educated at Alleyns School. Although he has written several novels, his reputation rests mainly on his short stories and his literary criticism. His first published work was a book about the Spanish character and landscape, *Marching Spain* (1928). The novels he published in the thirties, though eminently respectable achievements, give little indication of the success he was later to achieve with the short story. His first novel, *Clare Drummer* (1929), was followed by a volume of stories,

The Spanish Virgin (1930), and another novel, *Shirley Sanz* (1932). The titles suggest a preoccupation with female characters, and it is true that Pritchett is a particularly shrewd observer of feminine behaviour. *Nothing like Leather* (1935) suffered from the lack of interest of its subject-matter, but *Dead Man Leading* (1937) was an original and compelling work. It was at about this time that Pritchett's attention appears to have directed itself more seriously to the writing of short stories, which were collected in such volumes as *You Make Your Own Life* (1938), *It May Never Happen* (1945) and *When My Girl Comes Home* (1961).

Pritchett's eye is for the bizarre incident, but his ear is for the natural rhythms of dialogue and narrative. The juxtaposition gives his stories a creative tension and individuality which greatly distinguish them from the majority of stories. To the imaginative eye and the realist ear Pritchett adds the mind of a poet: though his prose is never 'poetic' it is quick with the instincts of poetry. On the surface, his characters are not in themselves unusual: he reveals the unusual under the ordinary and, at his best, the universal in the particular. He has been compared with D. H. Lawrence, than whom he is a considerably more careful and thoughtful artist. *Mr Beluncle* (1951), a novel, owes more to, or is certainly more reminiscent of, Wells.

Pritchett is an admirable critic of literature, particularly of fiction. His knowledge is extensive, his taste unfailing, and his essays always manage to convey the texture and flavour of the work under discussion. Those in *The Living Novel* (1946) offer many insights. He has always been strongly drawn to Spain. *The Spanish Temper* (1954) sums up his complex feelings about that country. He has also written with affection of London in *London Perceived* (1962). *The Working Novelist* (1965) is a collection of his longer fiction reviews. [CO]

Collected Stories (1956); *The Key to My Heart* (1963); *Foreign Faces* (1964).

Prynne, William (1600–69). Pamphleteer and politician. He was born in Somerset and educated at Bath Grammar School, Oriel College, Oxford, and Lincoln's Inn. In 1628 he was called to the bar. His *Histriomastix* (1632), a pamphlet more than 1,000 pages long, played a part in the long struggle waged by the Puritans and culminating in the closure of the playhouses by the Long Parliament in 1642. Its scope is indicated by the subtitle: *The Players' Scourge . . . Wherein it is Largely Evidenced . . . by the Concurring Authorities and Resolutions of Sundry Texts of Scripture; of the Whole Primitive Church, both under the Law and Gospell; of 55 Synodes and Councels; of 71 Fathers and Christian Writers; . . . of above 150 Foraigne and Domestique Protestant and Popish Authors . . .; of 40 Heathen Philosophers, Historians, Poets; . . . and of Our Own English Statutes, Magistrates, Universities, Writers, Preachers, That Popular Stage-Plays* (*the Very Pompes of the Divell Which We Renounce in Baptisme if We Believe the Fathers*) *are Sinful, Heathenish, Lewde, Ungodly Spectacles, and Most Pernicious Corruptions. . . .* Wilfully construing the pamphlet as an attack on Queen Henrietta Maria for taking part in a masque, Archbishop Laud contrived to have Prynne committed to the Tower. Prynne lost the upper part of his ears in the pillory in 1634, but undaunted he managed to write and publish more pamphlets during his imprisonment, and in 1637 he was sentenced to lose what remained of his ears. The rest of his life was spent sometimes in Parliament and sometimes under arrest, and always in the heat of controversy. His fierce independence rested on a belief in tradition, monarchy, an established Puritan Church, and Parliament. Thus he was actively concerned in the prosecution of Laud, but was opposed to the trial and execution of Charles I, as well as to the Commonwealth Army, the Rump Parliament, and Milton's doctrine of 'divorce at pleasure'. After the Restoration he was appointed Keeper of the King's Records in the Tower. In all he wrote some 200 lengthy pamphlets. The term 'marginal Prynne' appears to be a reference to the copious notes larding his publications. [NL]

E. W. Kirby, *W.P.* (1931); W. M. Lamont, *Marginal P.* (1963).

Pudney, John (1909–   ). Poet and writer. He was born in Langley, Bucks., and educated at Gresham's. After leaving school he worked in real estate and then at the B.B.C. until the Second World War, when he served in the R.A.F. He had been publishing volumes of verse since 1933, but he now achieved a certain popularity. Such poems as 'For Johnny', which celebrated

431

the lives and deaths of the boys fighting to save Britain, met a need of the time. Since the war John Pudney has earned a living in publishing and by the pen, and has produced biographical, historical and aeronautical works, as well as books for children (the 'Fred and I' adventure series). His *Collected Poems* appeared in 1957; *Spill Out* (1967) and *Spandrels* (1969) are, however, noteworthy for his attempt to find a more contemporary idiom and to explore new themes. [NL]

Home and Away (1960) (autobiography); *Who Only England Know* (1943) (wartime reminiscences); *Jacobson's Ladder* (1938) (novel).

'Purity'. ◊ 'Gawain Poet, The'.

Puttenham, George (*c.* 1529–90). Literary critic. Nephew of Sir Thomas ◊ Elyot, Puttenham matriculated at Christ's College, Cambridge, in 1546, at the age of 17 but seems to have left without taking a degree. In 1556 he entered the Middle Temple at a time when the Inns of Court were, as his editors put it, 'the chief centre of literary activity'. In 1589 there appeared anonymously the most important of his productions, *The Arte of English Poesie* (ed. G. D. Willcock and A. Walker, 1936). There has been some doubt whether Puttenham was its author, but, after reviewing the available evidence, the editors of the *Art* reach the conclusion, which we may accept, that he was. Some difficulty attaches also to its dating; it seems likely it was begun as early as the mid-1560s. *The Arte of English Poesie* is the most elaborate piece of Elizabethan criticism, although not the most influential. It has not the fire or the energy of Sidney. It is after all an *Art* and not a *Defence* of poetry, but at a lower level it asserts an importance for poetry by assuming that it will be one of the ordinary interests of the gentleman to acquire some skill at verse. [DELC]

P. J. Traci, 'The Literary Quality of P.'s *Arte of English Poesie*', in *Renaissance Papers*, ed. A. H. Gilbert (Duke U.P., 1957); W. L. Rushton, *Shakespeare and 'The Arte of English Poesie'* (1909); B. M. Ward in *RES*, I (1925) and R. L. Eagle, M. H. Dodds and N. H. Graham in *N & Q*, CCI (1956) (on problem of authorship).

Q

'Q'. ⟡ Quiller-Couch, Sir Arthur.

Quarles, Francis (1592–1644). Poet and prose writer. Born at Romford in Essex, Quarles took his B.A. at Christ's College, Cambridge, in 1609 and subsequently entered Lincoln's Inn. He was of a good family and had some connexion with the court, being a strong supporter of the Royalist cause. No doubt as a consequence, his fortunes declined during the Civil War period, and he died in poverty. Quarles was a very prolific writer, but only a few of his works really claim attention. The best known of them, *Emblems* (1635), is the most famous of the English emblem books (books of symbolic pictures with a text and a verse exposition). It was followed shortly by another book of emblems, *Hieroglyphics* (1638), reprinted in one volume with *Emblems* in 1639. The 2 books were published together in many subsequent editions, and they became the most popular verse of the 17th century. Also popular was Quarles's most important prose work, *Enchiridion* (1640), a collection of moral aphorisms. [DELC]

The Complete Works, ed. A. B. Grosart (3 vols. 1880–1); *Hosanna and Threnocles*, ed. J. Horden (English Reprints Series, 1960).
E. N. S. Thompson, *Literary Bypaths of the Renaissance* (New York, 1924); F. E. Schelling, 'Devotional Poetry', in *Shakespeare and Demi-Science* (U. of Pennsylvania P., 1927); J. R. B. Horden, *F.Q., 1592–1644. A Bibliography of His Works to the Year 1800* (Oxford Bibliographical Society Publications, new series, vol. 2, 1953).

Quennell, Peter (Courtney) (1905–   ). Poet and biographer. Born in London, the son of an architect and of Marjorie Quennell, a well-known writer and illustrator of children's books. He was educated at Berkhamsted Grammar School and Balliol College, Oxford. He became a journalist in London, writing for the *New Statesman*, the *Criterion* and other periodicals, before spending a year (1930–1) as Professor of English at Tokyo University. He wrote about the latter experience in *A Superficial Journey through Tokyo and Peking* (1932).

He was editor of the *Cornhill Magazine* (1944–51) and now edits *History To-day* as well as being a free-lance literary journalist. He began publishing poems in the 1920s (and is represented in the last volume of ⟡ *Georgian Poetry*); his collections of verse include *Masques and Poems* (1922), *Poems* (1926) and *Inscription on a Fountain Head* (1929). He has also published a novel, *The Phoenix Kind* (1931), and a book of short stories, *Sympathy* (1933). He is best known as the author of quite learned and very readable biographies. These are strong in the analysis of character (perhaps partly deriving from the 'psychography' of Lytton ⟡ Strachey) and include: *Byron: The Years of Fame* (1935); *Byron in Italy* (1941); *Four Portraits* (Boswell, Gibbon, Sterne, Wilkes) (1945); *Ruskin* (1949); and *A. Pope: The Education of Genius, 1688–1728* (1968). He has also published a volume of essays, *The Singular Preference* (1952); translations from the French; and useful editions of selections from ⟡ Mayhew's *London Labour and the London Poor* (original edition 1851) and *Memoirs of William Hickey* (1960). [AR]

Quiller-Couch, Sir Arthur ('Q') (1863–1944). Critic and fiction writer. Born at Bodmin in Cornwall, the eldest son of a doctor, he was educated locally, at Clifton College and at Trinity College, Oxford, where he studied classics. In the *Oxford Magazine*, to which he contributed parodies, he first adopted his later well-known pseudonym, 'Q'. He became a journalist in London, and helped to edit the Liberal weekly *Leader*. He wrote novels and short stories, and in 1892 he retired to Fowey and for twenty years lived as a freelance writer. Quiller-Couch also edited several anthologies, of which the *Oxford Book of English Verse* (1900) had the vast influence which the inclusions and exclusions of such 'authoritative' works often have (⟡ Palgrave). In 1910, he was knighted for political services and in 1912 the Liberal Government appointed him first King Edward VII Professor of English Literature at Cambridge. His lectures (published in such volumes as *On the Art of Writing*, 1916, and *On the Art of Reading*, 1920) were extremely popular. He presented literature as something for the hearty enjoyment of ordinary human beings, and helped to organize the English tripos (honours school) at Cambridge. His conventional critical response has not earned him unmixed admiration; he was ignorant of medieval or linguistic studies, but was a practising and successful writer. His novels were mostly romances in the style of Stevenson; the best are *The Splendid Spur* (1889) and *The Ship of Stars* (1899); many of them use his picturesque sense of his Cornish background. His *Tales and Romances* appeared in 30 volumes (1928–9). He wrote several literary studies. [A R]

'*Q*' *Anthology*, ed. F. Brittain (1948).

F. Brittain, *Q.-C.: A Biographical Study of '*Q*'* (1947).

R

Radcliffe, Mrs Ann Ward (1764–1823). Novelist. The wife of William Radcliffe, journalist and antiquary. Her 'gothick' novels are of some importance in the history of literary taste and the development of English fiction. *The Castles of Athlin and Dunbayne* (set in Scotland) appeared in 1789, but the 5 novels that followed, in which she changed her setting to the more 'frightful' and exotic Alps and Pyrenees, made her famous. They are *A Sicilian Romance* (1790), *The Romance of the Forest* (1791), *The Mysteries of Udolpho* (1794; ed. R. A. Freeman, Everyman, 1931 ed. B. Dobrée, 1966), and *The Italian* (1797; ed. F. Garber, 1968). A posthumous work, *Gaston de Blondeville*, was published in 1826, and is full of rather undigested antiquarianism. Mrs Radcliffe's imaginative power lay in the exploitation of pictures of 'sublime' landscape, in the manner of Salvator Rosa, with whose work she was long familiar (see also her descriptive *Journey through Holland and the Western Frontier of Germany*, 1795). Her characters are wooden and their dialogue stilted, but by keeping the reader's curiosity and apprehension taut she strings her tenebrous pictures together, until at the end her rationalism forces a disappointing 'explanation' of the horrors. In *The Mysteries of Udolpho* (her master work), the scene is a gloomy castle, with attendant secular misdeeds of brigands and wicked lords; in *The Italian*, the malevolence is provided by the Inquisition, and the scene is that 18th-century symbol of dark secrets, a monastery. She had a number of imitators, but clumsy as her constructions are they contain real imagination and a certain freedom. [AR]

Novels, intr. Walter Scott (1824).
J. M. S. Tompkins, *The Popular Novel in England* (1932); M. Summers, *The Gothic Quest* (1938); A. Grant, *A.R.* (Denver, Colo., 1951).

Raftery, A. ◊ Ó Reachtabhra, Antoine.

Raine, Kathleen (Jessie) (1908–   ). Poet, translator and Blake scholar. Born in 1908, the daughter of George Raine, a schoolmaster, and his wife Jessie. She studied natural science at Girton College, Cambridge, of which she was later to become a Fellow. She was married first to the Cambridge English don, Hugh Sykes Davies, and later to the poet Charles Madge, by whom she has two children. Both marriages ended in divorce. Miss Raine began writing poems in the 1930s, and her work in Geoffrey ◊ Grigson's *New Verse* and, during the Second World War, in M. J. Tambimuttu's *Poetry London* attracted much attention. Her first volume, *Stone and Flower*, was brought out by Editions Poetry London in 1943, and is today a collector's item, both because of its rarity and because of its striking illustrations by Barbara Hepworth. It is notable for its use of botanical and geological imagery, for its pure and transparent diction, and its lyrical poise. Subsequent volumes leading up to the *Collected Poems* (1956) showed a growing preoccupation with the visionary and mythmaking role of the poet, and with poetry as the expression of a traditional spiritual philosophy, a preoccupation which culminated in ten years of intensive scholarly work on the thought of William Blake, some of whose results are summarized in *William Blake and Traditional Mythology*, the Andrew Mellon lectures, delivered in Washington in 1962. Miss Raine has written widely in English and American periodicals on the thesis that all true poetry is the expression of a traditional mythology, which is itself an allegorical statement of profound spiritual truths. Her poems have the austere, intense and elevated quality, perhaps to some degree also the narrowness, that goes with a Blakean impatience with the 'vegetative universe'. Their distinction of rhythm, clear imagery and transparency of diction makes them, however, attractive even to those who cannot share her platonic or neo-platonic idealism; and her interest in natural science, the precision of her thinking about and observation of outer nature, gives the poems a grip on the outer world, and prevents her mysticism from becoming merely mystifying. [GSF]

Living in Time (1946); *The Pythoness* (1949); *The Year One* (1952); *Collected Poems* (1956); *The*

Hollow Hill (1965); *Defending Ancient Springs* (1967); *Blake and Tradition* (1968).

Ralegh, Sir Walter (*c.* 1552–1618). Poet and historian. Born in Devon, he left Oriel College, Oxford, without taking a degree and had a spectacular career as a courtier, sailor, soldier, explorer, poet and amateur scientist. A special favourite of Queen Elizabeth in the eighties, he was knighted in 1584, granted a monopoly in wine-trading, and given a patent to conquer and colonize far-off lands in her name. He is the author of some 40 poems preserved in manuscript or in anthologies, the short ones being amongst the finest. They are the work of a gifted amateur poet, and some are deservedly famous. Replaced in Elizabeth's favour by Essex, he was imprisoned in 1592 for an intrigue with one of the maids of honour, Elizabeth Throgmorton. In 1595 he led an expedition to Orinoco and Guiana, and his *Discovery of Guiana* (1597) describes that voyage. He took part in expeditions to Cadiz and to the Azores. For thirteen years King James had him imprisoned in the Tower, where he conducted scientific experiments and wrote the huge fragment of a *History of the World*, reaching 130 B.C. in three-quarters of a million words. He aimed to show the workings of Providence from the Creation to his own day, and the lengthy preface embodies his view of history. The book was published from prison in 1614, and two years later Ralegh undertook to sail to Orinoco and bring back to King James vast quantities of gold. The voyage was disastrous, and a promise not to attack Spaniards was not kept. He was executed in 1618, partly for piracy against Spain. [MJ]

Poems, ed. and intr. A. M. C. Latham (revised edn, 1951).
W. Oakeshott, *The Queen and the Poet* (1960); E. A. Strathmann, *Sir W.R.: A Study in Elizabethan Skepticism* (New York, 1951); E. Thompson, *Sir W.R.: The Last of the Elizabethans* (1935); W. M. Wallace, *Sir W.R.* (1959); N. L. Williams, *Sir W.R.* (1962).

Ramsay, Allan (1685?–1758). Scottish poet and editor. Father of the portrait-painter of the same name. Ramsay came from his native Lanarkshire to Edinburgh as a wig-maker's apprentice, and founded the Easy Club (1712), a mutual improvement society modelled on the 'Club' of the *Spectator*. He published poems in broadsheets and periodicals from 1713 and in successive collected editions from 1720. About 1718 he took to bookselling; in 1728 he founded what may well have been the first circulating library in Great Britain; in 1736 he founded the first regular theatre in Edinburgh and managed it until it was closed by the Licensing Act of 1737. Ramsay's work symbolizes (and actually contributed to) the cultural confusion of 18th-century Scotland. On the one hand are the Addisonian ambition of the Easy Club, the English and Scots social verse in the manner of ◊ Prior, the *Fables* (from 1722) and pastorals in explicit imitation of his friend ◊ Gay; on the other, the sentimental Jacobitism, the Scots patriotism (sometimes covert, sometimes strident), the comic broadsheet elegies in Scots ('Lucky Wood', 'Johnny Cowper') in the form and manner of Robert ◊ Sempill's 'Habbie Simpson' and the 'Familiar Epistles', again in Scots, exchanged with William ◊ Hamilton of Gilbertfield. The two strains mingle with unintentional comic discrepancy in the English couplets of 'Tartana, or The Plaid', and to rather better effect in *The Gentle Shepherd* (as pastoral comedy, 1725; re-written as ballad opera, 1728) where the attenuated Scots and the pastoral convention do not completely belie the daily realities of Scottish country life. Ramsay's broadside editions of *Christis Kirk on the Green* reputedly by ◊ James I (1718), his collection of Scots songs and ballads in *The Tea Table Miscellany* (1724–37 – texts, but no music), his printing of poems by Henryson, Dunbar and many others from the ◊ Bannatyne manuscript in *The Ever Green* (1724) and his *Collection of Scots Proverbs* (1736) revived an awareness of Scottish national culture which had been overlaid by the turbulence of the preceding century and, among the gentry and intellectuals, by the prestige of the English Augustans. Ramsay is no less culturally confused as editor than he is as poet. He 'completes' 'Christis Kirk' with two inferior cantos of his own, he feels no loyalty to his manuscript text if its difficulties can be removed or its rhythms Augustanized by emendation, he rather patronizes his *Proverbs* and, worst of all, he often substitutes for the rustic or coarse words of a folk-song a genteel 18th-century pastoral vision of nymphs and swains; by the time of David ◊ Herd, the first serious collector, many sets of the traditional words were irrecoverably lost. For all its limitations, however, his work helped to provide Herd – and Fergusson and Burns – with a starting-point and a public. [AI]

Works, ed. B. Martin, J. W. Oliver, A. M. Kinghorn, and A. Law (STS, 1951–61).
A. Gibson, *New Light on A.R.* (1927); B. Martin, *A.R.* (1931); J. Kinsley, *Scottish Poetry* (1955); J. Speirs, *The Scots Literary Tradition* (1962); K. Wittig, *The Scottish Tradition in Literature* (1958).

Randolph, Thomas (1605–35). Poet and playwright. Born near Daventry, Northamptonshire, Randolph was educated at Westminster School and Trinity College, Cambridge, at both of which places he acquired a reputation as an accomplished maker of both English and Latin verses. He became a Fellow of Trinity in 1629 and wrote 2 plays for performance at Cambridge, *The Conceited Pedlar* (1631) and *Aristippus, or The Jovial Philosopher* (1631). In 1632 he left Cambridge for London and was adopted as one of 'the sons of Ben' by Jonson, to whom he addressed several poems. He was soon involved in the dissolute London life of his day and died a short time after contracting smallpox. Randolph's other plays include *Amyntas* (performed 1631; ed. J. J. Parry, New Haven, Conn., 1917) and *Hey for Honesty* (published 1651), a comedy adapted from Aristophanes. He also wrote a good deal of miscellaneous verse showing a slight but genuine lyric gift. [GS]

Poetical and Dramatic Works, ed. W. C. Hazlitt (2 vols., 1875); *Poems*, ed. G. Thorn-Drury (1929).
S. A. and D. R. Tannenbaum, *T.R.* (Cambridge, Mass., 1947); C. G. M. Smith, *Proceedings of the British Academy*, XIII (1927).

Ransome, Arthur (1884–1967). Journalist, essayist and children's writer. Son of a history professor at Leeds University, he went to Rugby School, and then became an office boy in Grant Richards' publishing firm. He published various sketches and reminiscences while he was a young man, including *Bohemia in London* (1907), but his first full-length book was *A History of Storytelling* (1909). He also published studies of Edgar Allan Poe and Oscar Wilde. He travelled in China, Egypt and the Sudan, and paid several visits to Russia as a newspaper correspondent before and after the Revolution. A by-product of these was *Old Peter's Russian Tales* (1916). *Racundra's First Cruise* (1923) tells how he sailed the Baltic Sea in a boat he built on its shores.

He was always happiest by water, especially in the Lake District or in East Anglia, where he could sail and fish, and these places are the settings for 8 of the 12 *Swallows and Amazons* books, which appeared between 1930 and 1947. These, his best-known books (although he had been writing for adults for thirty years before the series began), are remarkable for detailed and accurate writing about outdoor projects such as building a bird-watching hide, sailing or camp cooking, and for lively characterization and good plots. The style is concise and direct, though the books are considerably longer than most children's novels of this date. The main interest goes to the child characters, who mature perceptibly from book to book, although they seem to have no personal problems; the adults are simple background figures. Two of the books, *Peter Duck* (1932) and *Missee Lee* (1941), differ in that they are adventures imagined by the child characters as having happened to themselves. [TV]

H. Shelley, *A.R.* (1960).

Rao, Raja (1909–   ). Indian novelist. Born into an old Brahmin family in Mysore, he graduated from Madras University in 1928 and continued his studies in Europe, at Montpellier and the Sorbonne. His earliest appearance in print was as a short-story writer, but his first book was the novel *Kanthapura* (1938), which describes the impact of Gandhi on a South Indian village. Its narrator is a village grandmother whose idiomatic language and effortless story-telling involve politics in domesticity. Rao's stories were collected in *Cow of the Barricades* (1947), but by that time he had already returned to India in the search for spiritual peace which produced, after a long silence, *The Serpent and the Rope* (1960).

The hero and narrator of *The Serpent and the Rope* is a cultivated young Brahmin whose sensitivity is heightened by the effects of tuberculosis. His choice is between the serpent – unreality masquerading as reality, seductive because it is apparently verifiable – and the rope – reality hidden because man sees through the serpent's eyes. It is the spiritual quest that links this long novel's widely varying characters and episodes, but the book is sustained by the authenticity of its psychological comment.

Raja Rao's third novel, *The Cat and Shakespeare* (1965), is no less spiritual but more hopeful. [PT]

K. R. Srinivasa Iyengar, *Indian Writing in English* (1962).

A. Ali, 'Illusion and Reality: The Art and Philosophy of R.R.', *Journal of Commonwealth Literature*, 5 (July 1968).

Rattigan, Terence (Mervyn) (1911–   ). Dramatist. Educated at Harrow and Oxford, he made his name as a contriver of light comedies, and is the only author to have written 2 plays each of which ran for over a thousand consecutive performances in London – *French without Tears* (1936) achieved 1,039 performances and *While the Sun Shines* (1943) 1,154. Both were farcical comedies about high-spirited upper-class young people. As a serious dramatist Rattigan has successfully kept abreast of public taste, and claims to write for a mythical, middle-class member of the audience 'Aunt Edna', a lady of conventional outlook. *The Winslow Boy* (1946), a workmanlike dramatization of the Archer-Shee case, ran for 476 performances in London, and won the New York Drama Critics' Award for the best foreign play on Broadway in 1947. The 1-act play *The Browning Version* (1948) was a study of an unpopular schoolmaster. *The Deep Blue Sea* (1952) attempted to present a psychological drama of personal relationships. *Ross* (1960), based on the career of Lawrence of Arabia, employed a more experimental technique. Almost all Rattigan's plays have been filmed, and he has written original scripts for films and television.

His lucrative career in the theatre testifies to the public's continuing demand for agreeable West End comedies and for well-made, well-told narrative plays which make little demand on the intellect or the imagination. A craftsman, Rattigan is the Pinero of our day. [MJ]

Collected Plays (3 vols., 1954 ff.) (with Prefaces by the author).

J. Russell Taylor, *The Rise and Fall of the Well-Made Play* (1967); K. Tynan, *Curtains* (1961).

Rau, Santha Rama (1923–   ). Indian writer. Born in Madras, the daughter of a diplomat. Her father's official appointments brought her wide experience of many countries. She was at school in England and university in America. *Home to India* (1945) is an account of her feelings and experiences on returning from ten years in the West. Her novel, *Remember the House* (1956), has a similarity of theme. Herself married to an American, she is a perceptive chronicler of the impact of alien traditions on the Indian mind. In 1947 she went to Tokyo as a diplomatic hostess. This period and her later travels in Asia are the subject of *East of Home* (1951). Other travel books are *View to the Southeast* (1958) and *My Russian Journey* (1959). Her accomplished dramatization of E. M. Forster's *A Passage to India* had its first London performance in 1960 and was published the same year. She now lives in America. [PT]

Gifts of Passage: An Informal Autobiography (1961).

Read, Sir Herbert (Edward) (1893–1968). Poet, critic and publisher. Born at Muscoates Grange, Kirbymoorside, in Yorkshire, the son of a farmer, and educated at Crossley's School, Halifax, and Leeds University. During the First World War he served with the Yorkshire Regiment and earned the D.S.O. and M.C. From 1919 to 1922 he was an assistant principal in the Treasury, and transferred to the Victoria and Albert Museum as an assistant keeper. Thereafter he briefly held the chair of Fine Art at Edinburgh and lectured at Liverpool University. He edited the *Burlington Magazine* (1933–9). He also lectured extensively abroad on poetry and art. *Naked Warriors* (1919) was a collection of realistic war poems, and thereafter he published several collections of verse. He influenced the group of poets known in the 1940s as the 'New-Apocalypse', who reacted against the 'topicality' of poetry written under the influence of Auden, and he was also interested in a kind of imagist writing. His *Collected Poems* appeared in 1946 and 1966. *In Retreat* (1925) and *Ambush* (1930) use brief fictional accounts of war experiences. As an art and literary critic Read was a consistent champion of avant garde work; his own position is eclectic, romantic (even anarchist) and distinguished by open-mindedness. Of his many books of critical essays, *Reason and Romanticism* (1926) contains a very well-balanced essay, 'Psycho-analysis and Art' (later expanded into his essay 'The Nature of Art' in *Collected Essays in Literary Criticism*, 1938); other collections are *To Hell with Culture* (1963) and *Poetry and Experience* (1966). Though perceptive, he never really used any psycho-analytical insights in his criticism. In his *Wordsworth* (1930; the Clark Lectures) he turns the prevalent biographical criticism out-side-in. In his art criticism he was much concerned with the function of art in education. The critical books are *The Meaning of Art* (1931); *The Philosophy of Modern Art* (1952); *Icon and Idea; The Function of Art in the Development of Human Consciousness* (1955). *Selected Writings* appeared in 1963. He has been influential as a publisher of new writers. [AR]

The Innocent Eye (1933); *Annals of Innocence and Experience* (1940) (autobiographies).
F. Berry, *H.R.* (WTW, 1953).

Reade, Charles (1814–84). Dramatist and novelist. Born of a family of gentry in Oxfordshire and educated at Magdalen College, Oxford, where he was a Fellow, he entered Lincoln's Inn and was called to the bar (1843) but never practised. He began his literary career as a quite successful dramatist. The influence of this apprenticeship can be seen in the strong dialogue, rather crude presentation and tendency to melodrama of his novels; his melodrama, *The Courier of Lyons* (1854), was a favourite of Sir Henry Irving's. He rewrote his comedy, *Masks and Faces* (first performed at the Haymarket in 1852), as a popular novel, *Peg Woffington* (1853). Some of Reade's novels were propagandist, based (like Zola's) on ledgers of classified material from newspapers, government publications and his own observation. He dramatized the French realist's *L'assommoir* as *Drink* (1879). *It's Never Too Late to Mend* (1856) deals with prison reform; *Hard Cash* (1863) with the private lunatic asylum racket; *Foul Play* (1869), written in collaboration with Dion ◊ Boucicault, with ship insurance; *Put Yourself in His Place* (1870) is an attack on trade unions. Other novels are less 'purposeful', but Reade's own violent opinions sometimes lessen the impact of powerful character presentation. His best single book is probably *The Cloister and the Hearth* (1861), the only title by which he is now remembered. This historical romance, set in the Reformation, is based on Reade's wide acquaintance with the writings of all kinds of that age, and gives a very broad sweep of European life in a tale of a wandering scholar whose son is hinted at the end to be the future Erasmus. Historical detachment seems to have modified Reade's cantankerous involvement with problems of his own day and gave an impressive spaciousness to his work. [AR]

Complete Works (17 vols., 1895 ff.); M. Elwin, *C.R.: A Biography* (1931) (with bibliography); W. C. Phillips, *Dickens, R. and Collins, Sensational Novelists* (1919); A. M. Turner, *The Making of the Cloister and the Hearth* (Chicago U.P., 1938); W. Burns, *C.R.* (New York, 1961); E. G. Sutcliffe in *SP* and *PMLA* (several articles on R.).

Reaney, James (1926–   ). Canadian poet and playwright. Born in Stratford, Ontario, and educated at the University of Toronto, from which he graduated in 1948. Before joining the staff of the University of Toronto he was for several years a lecturer at the University of Manitoba. He now lives in London, Ontario, where he lectures in English at the University of Western Ontario. Reaney is one of a group of Canadian mythopoeic poets. His first collection, *The Red Heart* (1949), proved his eye for the grotesque by its concatenation of felt horror and rationalized boredom. His technical assurance was confirmed by the 12 pastoral eclogues of *A Suit of Nettles* (1958), in which his excited erudition leads sometimes to obscurity. Among his other publications is *The Killdeer and Other Plays* (1962). The title play was acclaimed on its presentation at the Dominion Drama Festival in Vancouver in 1960. Reaney is a leading opponent of 'Canadianism' in Canadian writing, and some of this distaste for parochialism informs the connected poems of *Twelve Letters to a Small Town* (1962). [PT]

A. A. Lee, *J.R.* (1968).

Reeve, Clara (1729–1807). Novelist. Her best-known work is *The Champion of Virtue: A Gothick Story* (1777), renamed in the second edition (and many subsequent printings) *The Old English Baron*. It was often printed with the *Castle of Otranto* by Horace ◊ Walpole and exploits his 'gothick' vein of historical fiction, but plays down the supernatural happenings. Similar interests are also shown in her historical work, *The Progress of Romance through Times, Centuries and Manners* (1785). [AR]
DNB.

Reeves, James (1909–   ). Poet. Born in Middlesex and educated at Stowe and Cambridge, he has lived mainly in southern England and, until he became a full-time writer in 1952, taught English in schools and teachers' training colleges. His first book of poems, *The Natural Need*, appeared in 1936 and was followed at intervals by 3 others, and then, in 1960, by *Collected Poems 1929–1959*. Since then he has published two further collections, *The Questioning Tiger* (1964) and *Subsong* (1966). Poems by Reeves were included in Michael Roberts's *Faber Book of Modern Verse* (1936). He is also well known as a writer of poems and stories for children, and as an editor, notably of English folk-song texts from the original manuscripts of Cecil Sharp and others. The qualities which his poems aim at are principally clarity, compression and emotional intensity. His chief themes are those of human relations and the problem of maintaining private integrity and individuality in the modern world, and the frustration and ironies which this entails.

The Idiom of the People (1958); *The Everlasting Circle* (1960); *A Short History of English Poetry* (1961); *Understanding Poetry* (1965).

Reginald of Canterbury (fl. 11th cent.). Anglo-Latin poet. Born and educated in France, he became a Benedictine monk at Canterbury towards the close of the 11th century. He was a writer of hymns and of a life of St Malchus in nearly 6,000 lines of Latin verse. This poem is inspired by a life of the same saint (a masterpiece of prose narrative) by St Jerome.

Anglo-Latin Satirical Poets, ed. T. Wright (vol. 2, 1872); *Analecta Hymnica*, 50; *Vita S. Malchi*, ed. L. R. Lind (Urbana, Ill., 1942).

F. J. E. Raby, *Secular Latin Poetry* (2nd edn, 2 vols., 1957).

Reid, Thomas (1710–96). Scottish philosopher. Founder of the Scottish or Common Sense School in philosophy. Reid was Professor of Moral Philosophy at King's College, Aberdeen (1752–64), and at Glasgow University (1764–81), where he succeeded Adam Smith. His chief works are *An Inquiry into the Human Mind on the Principles of Common Sense* (1764) and *Essays on the Intellectual Powers of Man* (1785; ed. and abridged, A. D. Woozley, 1941; intr. B. A. Brody, Massachusetts, 1969). Unable to reject the reasoning of David Hume or to accept his sceptical conclusions (which Reid, a good churchman and loose thinker, found disturbing in religious and moral matters as well as in philosophy) Reid proposed to refute Hume by attacking his starting-points in Cartesian

dualism and Locke's theory of perception. Reid's contention that the unit of knowledge is not the act of perception but the act of judgement bridges the gap between matter and mind; this granted, the objects of perception are real, and not mere mental images. These and other axioms of the Common Sense of mankind – not of course the views of the man in the street, but 'beliefs common to all rational beings as such' – are, Reid adds, 'the natural outcome of those faculties which God hath given them'. Hume treated Reid with grave irony, but Reid's views, popularized by James ◊ Beattie and developed and disseminated by Dugald ◊ Stewart and Sir William Hamilton in Scotland and Victor Cousin in France, long rivalled Kant's as the accepted refutation of Hume. [AI]

Works, ed. Sir William Hamilton (1846–63); *British Empirical Philosophers*, ed. A. J. Ayer and R. Winch (1952) (excerpts).

D. Stewart, *Account of the Life and Writings of T.R.* (1802); A. C. Fraser, *T.R.* (1898); S. A. Grave, *The Scottish Philosophy of Common Sense* (1960).

Reid, Victor Stafford (1913–   ). West Indian novelist. Born in a working-class area of Kingston, Jamaica, and educated there, he entered journalism and became leading feature writer for Jamaica's *Daily Gleaner*. He was an original contributor to and co-editor of *Focus*, a strongly nationalist publication of social protest, which appeared in 1943 and 1948 and initiated the modern literary movement in Jamaica.

Reid published several short stories before producing the first full-scale Jamaican novel, *New Day* (1949), an old man's highly patriotic account of Jamaican history between the Morant Bay rising of 1865 and the new constitution of 1944. In it he sustains the stylized dialect of Jamaican speech rhythms which he had first used in earlier experimental folk stories, attempting a transposition from oral to written form. Canada Council and Guggenheim awards allowed him to travel in Canada, the United States and Mexico. The manuscripts of his novels were rejected, and it was not until 1958 that *The Leopard*, a phantasy of race-hatred in Kenya's Mau-Mau revolt, was published. The novel's use of flashbacks is almost cinematic and it makes use of detailed symbolism and recurrent imagery. In 1960 the Jamaican Ministry of Education commissioned *Sixty-Five*, a children's version of *New Day*, for use in secondary schools; Reid lives in Kingston, where he is editor of *Spotlight*. [WAG]

Reitz, Deneys (1882–1944). South African soldier, statesman and writer. Born in Bloemfontein. His father was President of the Orange Free State and Secretary of State for the Transvaal under President Kruger on the outbreak of the Boer War. Reitz joined the Boer forces at 17, and wrote an excited, boyish account of his war experiences during a residence in Madagascar as an irreconcilable opponent of British rule. This book, *Commando* (1929), has become a South African classic. Long before its publication Reitz's friendship with General Smuts had led him to return to South Africa. He fought with Smuts against the Germans, later writing an account of his campaigns in *Trekking On* (1933). Between the wars he continued his practice as a lawyer in Johannesburg, but became increasingly occupied with politics. He entered the South African Parliament in 1920 and served in Smuts's cabinets. He was sent to London as Union High Commissioner in 1942 and died there two years later. [PT]

Reynolds, Sir Joshua (1723–92). Painter and aesthetic theorist. Born at Plympton-Earl's in Devonshire, the son of a clergyman, who was master of the grammar school there, and educated his son. He was apprenticed to Hudson, the portrait painter. He studied in Italy (1750–2), and on his return to London, his retentive mind stored with material he used all during his life, his ambition was to raise the status of the painter in England. This he did, by helping to found the Royal Academy, of which he was the first President, but also by deliberately uniting learning, the literary culture, with painting. Reynolds was the most celebrated portrait painter of his day, but also painted 'historical' (i.e. allegorical) and other works, in a constant struggle with the fashionable indifference in England to anything but portraiture. He was an intimate friend of Dr Johnson, and one of the founders of the 'Club'. From 1769 to 1790, he delivered 15 *Discourses* before the Royal Academy in which he eloquently expounded the traditionalist theory of the mimetic or imitative function of art, the 'grand style' and other neo-classic conceptions. The *Discourses*, indispensable for

a study of aesthetic theory in England, were issued in varying combinations as they were delivered (also ed. A. Dobson, World's Classics, 1907; ed. R. R. Wark, Huntington Library, 1959, with plates; ed. R. Lavine, 1961). Reynolds also wrote for Johnson's *Idler* and produced other miscellaneous works. [AR]

Works, with an Account of the Life and Writings, ed. E. Malone (1797); *Portraits*, ed. F. W. Hilles (1952) (biographical pieces by R. found among Boswell's papers).
F. W. Hilles, *The Literary Career of Sir J.R.* (1936) (with bibliography); D. Hudson, *Sir J.R. A Personal Study* (1958); W. J. Bate, *From Classic to Romantic* (1946).

Rhys, Jean (? –). Novelist. She was born and brought up in Dominica; her father was Welsh, her mother Creole. She came to Europe when she was 16, and her first 5 books (*The Left Bank*, 1927; *Postures*, 1928; *After Leaving Mr Mackenzie*, 1931; *Voyage in the Dark*, 1934; and *Good Morning, Midnight*, 1939) are set against the background of her drifting life in Paris and London during the 1920s and 1930s. Their central theme is the struggle of a woman alone against isolation, poverty and lack of appreciation. There is a controlled contempt for the dilettante bohemian world of Paris, and for the thin-blooded Anglo-Saxons. These books enjoyed a critical but not a popular success. After 1939, nothing more was heard of Jean Rhys for nearly twenty years, when she was discovered in Cornwall. A novel which she was then working on, *Wide Sargasso Sea*, was published in 1966. The novel, set in the lush but menacing world of Jean Rhys's native West Indies, tells the story of Antoinette Cosway, the mad first wife of Mr Rochester in *Jane Eyre*. It owes little beyond its heroine to Charlotte Brontë and is told entirely without sentimentality. Jean Rhys has since published 2 collections of short stories. [DL]

Richards, I(vor) A(rmstrong) (1893–). Poet and literary critic. Born at Sandbach in Cheshire and educated at Clifton. At Magdalene College, Cambridge, he studied moral sciences, becoming a college lecturer in English and Moral Sciences in 1922, and a Fellow in 1926. He was a visiting professor at Tsing Hua University, Peking (1929–30). He visited Harvard in 1931, and from 1939 to 1944 he was director of the

Harvard Commission on English Language Studies. In this he carried out work he had begun as Director of the Orthological Institute of China, where he was one of the developers of the possibilities of the 850-word system, 'Basic English'. His first work (which he produced with a psychologist, C. K. Ogden, and an art historian, James Wood) was *Foundations of Aesthetics* (1922) and illustrates the trend of some of his criticism, which covers problems raised by considering the nature of experience (from a psychological view-point) and its relation to communication, and *vice versa*. *The Meaning of Meaning* (with C. K. Ogden) (1923) is a study of the influence of language upon thought, the nature of signs and their interpretation, symbolism, and a pioneering study of much now discussed in the discipline of semantics. In the influential volume *Principles of Literary Criticism* (1925), Richards attempts to grapple with the problems the developing study of psychology presents to the evaluation of literature; it is a suggestive rather than an exhaustive work. *Practical Criticism* (1929) is a companion volume, designed to show actual instances of critical evaluation produced anonymously by Richards' pupils, and to present the chaotic disorganization of their critical procedures. *Science and Poetry* (1926) consists of 7 essays on specific topics; *Mencius on the Mind* (1932) deals with Chinese modes of meaning and the two-way relationship between the Chinese language and culture patterns. Richards also published *Interpretation in Teaching* (1938), *Basic English and Its Uses* (1943), *Nations and Peace* (1947) and *So Much Nearer, Essays Toward a World English* (New York, 1969). He is widely respected as a poet for volumes such as *Goodbye Earth and Other Poems* (1958), *The Screens and Other Poems* (1960) and *Tomorrow Morning, Faustus!* (1962). He has been influential in a limited way as a critic involved in the general improvement of reading (◊ Leavis), but few have felt competent enough to work at the general synthesis of elaborate disciplines in which Richards has ventured. [AR]

S. E. Hyman, *The Armed Vision* (1948); D. G. James, in *Critiques and Essays in Criticism*, ed. R. W. Stallman (U. of Minnesota P., 1950); H. W. N. Hotopf, *Language, Thought and Comprehension: A Study of the Writings of I.A.R.* (1965); J. P. Schiller, *I.A.R.'s Theory of Literature* (Yale U.P., 1969).

Richardson, Dorothy (Miller) (1873–1957). Novelist. She was born at Abingdon in Berkshire and partly brought up in London. After leaving school she worked as a teacher and clerk until her marriage to a painter. She began writing her mammoth work, *Pilgrimage*, with the volume *Pointed Roofs* in 1915 and continued over the next thirty years, producing 13 novels in all, which were collected into 4 volumes and republished as *Pilgrimage* (1938). This work presents the impressions, feelings and thoughts (rather censored) of a young Englishwoman, who teaches in Germany and England, then becomes a governess and later a secretary, explores society, falls in love with a Russian Jew, becomes the mistress of a literary figure, and ends up living in a Quaker family. Her real identity is found in moments of mystical illumination arising from the beauty of sense experience. Dorothy Richardson also wrote historical works such as *The Quakers: Past and Present* (1914) and *John Austen and the Inseparables* (1930). Her work in fiction is important because it represents the first use of the interior monologue in the modern novel, antedating both Virginia Woolf and James Joyce in this. Her vision of reality, as a rich and continually changing confusion of thought and image, was influenced by Bergson's philosophy, but her work lacks discipline, selection and structure, so that it is, in the end, boring and difficult to read, although important in the history of technique. [JM]

C. R. Blake, *Dorothy Richardson* (U. of Michigan P., 1960).

Richardson, Ethel Florence or Henry Handel Richardson (1870–1946). Australian novelist. Born in Melbourne. After the crisis of her father's madness and death in poverty, she was sent to the Melbourne Presbyterian Ladies' College. Her adolescence there is behind the writing of *The Getting of Wisdom* (1910). Her musical talent led to her being entered at the Leipzig Conservatorium round which she sets her first novel, *Maurice Guest* (1908). Aware of temperamental inadequacies, she abandoned the intention of becoming a concert pianist. In Leipzig she met J. G. Robertson, whom she married in 1895. After 1903 she lived in London, where her husband was Professor of German Literature, and, after his death, in Sussex.

Richardson is among the best naturalistic

novelists. Her trilogy, *The Fortunes of Richard Mahony* (*Australia Felix*, 1917; *The Way Home*, 1925; *Ultima Thule*, 1929), was completed in 1929. Its account of the mental degeneration of a brilliant doctor begins during the Australian gold rush and centres on his marriage. In both design and detail it draws heavily on her father's life. Her determined confrontation of the facts does not hide the insistent melancholy that turns psychological realism into case history, an aspect ordered into disturbing significance in the fine last volume. As in *Maurice Guest* meaningful life and the means of life are mutually hostile, and, as in the earlier novel, a Nietzschean stress is laid on the prerogatives of genius. [PT]

Myself When Young (1948) (autobiography).
N. Palmer, *H.H.R., A Study* (1950); V. Buckley, *H.H.R.* (Australian Writers and Their Work, 1961).

Richardson, Henry Handel. ◊ Richardson, Ethel Florence.

Richardson, Samuel (1689–1761). Novelist. Born in Derbyshire, the son of a joiner, he received a somewhat sketchy education; his father's intention of bringing him up for the Church was frustrated by poverty. In 1706 he was apprenticed to a London stationer and also gained a knowledge of printing. In 1719 he set up for himself as a stationer and printer and became one of the leading men in the London business. As a printer his output included political writing such as the high-flying Tory periodical *The True Briton*; the newspapers *Daily Journal* (1736–7) and *Daily Gazeteer* (1738); the *Journals* of the House of Commons (26 vols.); and law printing. Richardson was a friend and patron of writers (he assisted Johnson, when the latter was imprisoned for debt), and in 1754 was Master of the Stationers' Company. His house, shop and printing office were first in Fleet Street, and then in Salisbury Court, where he built himself large premises. He was twice married and had six children by each wife. He died of an apoplexy and is buried in St Bride's Church.

In his business life he is the epitome of the industrious London apprentice and successful tradesman. In 1739, however, two book-sellers proposed that Richardson should compile a volume of model letters for unskilled writers; this appeared as *Letters to and for Particular Friends, Directing the Requisite Style and Forms to be Observed in Writing Familiar Letters* (1741; ed. B. W. Downs, 1928). While he was preparing it, however, he recollected a story he had heard and developed that into a series of letters; this was published as *Pamela: or, Virtue Rewarded* (2 vols., 1740; 4 edns in 1741; 4 vols., adding *Pamela in Her Exalted Condition*, 1742; ed. G. Saintsbury, 2 vols., Everyman, 1914). The great success of this work (it was translated, and dramatized in Italy by Goldoni, as well as in England) led him to begin his master-piece, *Clarissa: or, The History of a Young Lady* (7 vols., 1747–8; with the addition of a volume of restored passages, 1749; 4 vols., Everyman, 1932). His last novel, intended to display a good man (in distinction to Lovelace in *Clarissa*), was begun in 1751, and appeared as *The History of Sir Charles Grandison* (7 vols., 1754, 3 edns; ed. G. Saintsbury, 1895).

Thus Richardson had a second career as one of the fathers of the novel. His writing brought him great personal *éclat*, and a coterie of devoted admirers, mostly women, gathered round him or corresponded with him, discussing the moral aspects of the actions in the novels. These works were abridged, gutted of moral sentiments and otherwise passed into wide circulation in the 18th century. Richardson is a great and influential novelist; his epistolary method (though he handled it rather loosely under the pressure of his greatest conceptions) fathered many works in this fashion, such as *Evelina*, by Fanny Burney; and Saul Bellow's *Herzog* (1965) shows that the idea has unexplored possibilities. By making his characters write letters, Richardson concentrates on his great area of investigation, the complex nature of judgement. He is the novelist of mental and emotional struggle. The enormously detailed scope of his works, and their repetitiousness, also work in this direction. Of course, Richardson uses the language of the cult of sentiment to define his perceptions, and the clash of feeling issues in *Pamela* in an ungainly economic reward. This is only incidental. In *Clarissa*, Richardson shows a darker side of his imagination. Both Clarissa and Lovelace are tragic victims of a sexuality which is obsessive and destructive, one of the demonic forces in human nature. Richardson also shows a remarkable grasp of the pervasive effect of economic and political forces on human feelings and character.

His works were more valued in France and abroad than in England, where for long he was admired, but with severe reservations because of his apparently clumsy handling of narrative. [A R]

Works, ed. L. Stephen (12 vols., 1883–4); *The Novels*, ed. A. Dobson and W. L. Phelps (18 vols., 1901–3; 19 vols., New York, 1902); *Selected Letters*, ed. J. Carroll (1964).

J. W. Krutch, *Five Masters* (1930); A. D. Mac-Killop, *S.R.*, *Printer and Novelist* (Chapel Hill, 1936) and *The Early Masters of English Fiction* (U. of Kansas P., 1956); J. Kermode, 'R. and Fielding', *Cambridge Journal*, IV (1950); W. M. Sale, *S.R.*, *Master Printer* (New York, 1950); R. F. Brissenden, *S.R.* (W T W, 1958) (with select bibliography); M. Golden, *R.'s Characters* (Michigan U.P., 1963).

Richler, Mordecai (1931–   ). Canadian novelist. Born in Montreal, he left Sir George Williams College without a degree in 1951 and spent two years in Europe. He did various jobs in Canada in 1953 before returning to live in France and Germany. He has contributed stories, essays and reviews to several periodicals. For several years he has lived mainly in London.

The novels *The Acrobats* (1954) and *A Choice of Enemies* (1957) explore areas of world guilt. The second, set among Jews and expatriates in London, is about a post-war society that has made its choice of enemies, and about the way those who have not, the young or the conscientiously non-committal, are made to suffer, and even to feel that they deserve to. *The Apprenticeship of Duddy Kravitz* (1959), like *Son of a Smaller Hero* (1955), is set in Jewish Montreal. In its hero Richler has found an ideal vehicle for his colloquial gusto. Duddy Kravitz sets out to beat society at its own materialistic game by rejecting the cant of cooperation and engaging in passionate private enterprise. The prose is brash and exuberant, and the larger-than-life episodes sometimes comic and sometimes sombre. The air of improvisation is deceptive. The book is controlled by Richler's vigorous understanding of the pressures of modern society. The same is true of *The Incomparable Atuk* (1963), which is a cynical and outrageous charting of a naïve eskimo's corruption by materialistic exploiters. Richler's latest novel, *Cocksure* (1968), is not his best. [P T]

Hunting Tigers under Glass (1969) (essays).

N. Cohen, 'Heroes of the R. View', *Tamarack Review*, 6 (Winter, 1958); P. Scott, 'A Choice of Certainties', *Tamarack Review*, 8 (Summer, 1958); W. Tallman, 'Wolf in the Snow', *Canadian Literature*, 6 (Autumn, 1960); *Canadian Literature*, 29 (1966).

Robert of Gloucester (fl. late 13th cent.). Chronicler. *The Metrical Chronicle of Robert of Gloucester* (ed. W. A. Wright, 2 vols., 1887) is a composite work, by three monks of Gloucester. The surviving manuscripts suggest two separate revisions and continuations of the original, and Robert is the earlier reviser, working at about 1300. The original is a verse history of Britain, combining rhyme and loose alliterations, from the destruction of Troy to the death of Henry I. Robert adds about 3,000 lines, expanding the earlier parts and continuing the chronicle to the death of Henry III. The authors used a wide variety of sources, notably ◊ Geoffrey of Monmouth and ◊ Laȝamon as well as responsible historians like ◊ William of Malmesbury. There is much traditional material and some first-hand testimony, especially in Robert's vivid accounts of the civil wars of Henry III. Though Arthur is the central figure, a stand is made against the wilder legends. Even by the standards of the genre, the chronicle reveals little artistic ambition. Verse and the vernacular are adopted as the popular forms. There are, however, some sharp descriptions, and the simple and sincere patriotism makes an attractive impression. [A G]

Roberts, Sir Charles George Douglas (1860–1943). Canadian poet and short-story writer. Born near Fredericton. After graduating from the University of New Brunswick, he was a schoolteacher, a journalist and, from 1885 to 1895, a professor at Kings College, Windsor. His first book, *Orion and Other Poems* (1880), though influenced by the Romantics and by Greek legends and verse-forms, was an important step towards the independence of Canadian poetry; but it was with the sonnets of *Songs of the Common Day* (1893) that he established his talent for indigenous descriptive poetry. In 1897 Roberts left his family and country for New York. There his stories of animal life became popular. Though marred by sentimentality and melodrama, they show the same gift for detailed observation as his poems. Distinguished war service in the Canadian army was followed by residence mainly in London. Not until 1925 did he return to Canada, but his reputation as a national poet was still alive. Heartened by this, Roberts broke a long poetic silence, publishing 4 volumes of verse before 1941. Knighted for services to Canadian letters in 1935, he spent his last years in Toronto. Roberts is consistently good when he limits himself to description, sometimes good when he describes his own restlessness, but only rarely so when he sets out to philosophize. *Selected Poems* (1955) effectively balances the three styles. [PT]

E. Pomeroy, *Sir C.G.D.R.* (1943); D. Pacey, *Ten Canadian Poets* (1958).

Roberts, Kate (1891–   ). Welsh short-story writer and novelist. Born at Rhosgadfan, Caernarvonshire, she was educated at the County School, Caernarvon, and University College, Bangor. She commenced teaching at Llanberis and moved to South Wales to Ystalyfera and Aberdare. After her marriage to Morris T. Williams in 1928 she lived in Rhiwbina and Tonypandy. In 1935 she returned to North Wales to Denbigh and continued with the work of the Gee Press after her husband's death.

Kate Roberts published her first, extremely promising, collection of short stories *O Gors y Bryniau* in 1926. A second volume followed in 1929 and a third in 1937. She had already experimented with the novel as early as 1926, and followed this up in 1930 (*Laura Jones*) and 1936 (*Traed mewn Cyffion*). Since then she has concentrated on the long short story or short novel with her *Stryd y Glep* (1949), the diary of an invalid, *Te yn y Grug* (1959), life through the eyes of a child, and *Tywyll Heno* (1962), a study of a minister's wife in a mental institution.

She has confessed herself to be extra sensitive , easily hurt, and a rebel by nature. This explains her reactions to the hard, bare subsistence level of the quarry areas of Caernarvonshire, and the despairing, grim and drab existence of the coal-mining villages of Glamorgan during the depression of the twenties and thirties. She has a very sharp ear for the nuances of conversation, and her style is a felicitous combination of classical Welsh prose infused with the strength and vitality of her own native dialect. Her gift for pregnant compression is seen at its best, perhaps, in her novel *Tysyll Heno*, in which the central character recalls her loss of faith. Her autobiography *Y Lôn Wen* (1960) is valuable for the light it throws on her family and her early home. [MR]

O Gors y Bryniau (1926); *Deian a Loli* (1926); *Laura Jones* (1930); *Rhigolau Bywyd* (1929); *Traed mewn cyffion* (1936); *Ffair Gaeaf* (1937; tr. *A Summer Day*, 1946); *Y Byw sy'n cysgu* (1956); *Hyn o Fyd* (1963); *Tegwch y Bore* (1967); *Prynn Dol* (1970).

Robertson, Angus (Aonghas MacDhonnchaidh) (1870–1948). Scottish Gaelic poet and novelist. Robertson was born in the island of Skye, and spent most of his life in Glasgow, where he had extensive business interests, and took a prominent part in Gaelic affairs, becoming President of An Comunn Gaidhealach.

He wrote only one novel, *An t-Ogha Mor* (1913), a historical novel set in the period 1715 to 1745. Its plot is over-involved, and the novel's main interest lies in its creation of atmosphere and its rich, eccentric use of language. A similar, at times grotesquely overloaded use of vocabulary can be seen in his collection of English essays on Celtic themes, *The Children of the Fore-World* (1933).

Robertson composed many songs, and set them to airs of his own composition, as in *Orain na Céilidh*. His most lasting literary work is in the collection of poetry *Cnoc an Fhradhairc* (1940). The title poem, which Robertson called a Gaelic eclogue, describes the progress of the seasons in rural Skye. The society depicted is idyllic, and many of the characters are those of Gaelic myth and saga. But he also depicts realistically the society he knew in his youth, and he includes a powerful indictment of the State which has treated Gaelic society either with hostility or with cynical indifference. This poem has much wisdom in it, a vivid pictorial quality, and imagination which is sometimes expressed with an excess of linguistic virtuosity. [DT]

Robertson, John Mackinnon (1856–1933). Politician, rationalist and literary critic. Robertson, a native of Arran who had left school at 13 and educated himself, made his name as a leader-writer on the liberal *Edinburgh Evening News* from 1878. Brought to London by Charles Bradlaugh in 1884 to edit the free-thinking and radical *National Reformer*, he carried on the paper after Bradlaugh's death and then ran the *Free Review* (1893–5). Robertson sat as Liberal member for Tyneside (1906–18), becoming Parliamentary Secretary to the Board of Trade and a Privy Counsellor. His rationalist writings include 'short histories' of free thought (1899), Christianity (1902) and morals (1920); lives or criticisms of Bradlaugh, Buckle, Gibbon, Renan, Voltaire and Whitman; *Christianity and Mythology* (1900); *The Historical Jesus* (1916); and a *History of Free Thought in the Nineteenth Century* (1929). Much of his Shakespeare criticism is vitiated by his irrational determination to distribute the plays among a large number of supposed collaborators, and has been superseded by later scholarship in any case, but his *Montaigne and Shakespeare* (1897; revised edn, 1909) remains a valuable and suggestive study in literary relationships. In *Essays towards a Critical Method* (1889), *Modern Humanists* (1891), *Criticisms* (1903) and their various sequels Robertson turns one of the most intelligent of contemporary eyes on Carlyle, Mill, Arnold, Ruskin and other writers of the period; *Criticisms* includes one of the most perceptive accounts that has been offered of literary conditions in Victorian Scotland. [A I]

New Essays Towards a Critical Method (1897); Modern Humanists Reconsidered (1927). DNB.

Robertson, William (1721–93). Scottish historian and churchman. Educated at Edinburgh University, and himself the son of a minister, Robertson became a minister in the country near Edinburgh in 1743, and moved to a charge in the city in 1758. Meantime, he had become known both in the General Assembly of the Church of Scotland and in the Edinburgh 'Select Society' (the set which included Adam ◊ Smith, Henry ◊ Home of Kames and Adam Ferguson) and he had begun his *History of Scotland during the Reigns of Queen Mary and of King James VI* (published 1759), a rational and urbane treatment of a fanatical period which achieved wide and instant success. Robertson was made Principal of Edinburgh University and historiographer-royal for Scotland; he later wrote a *History of Charles V* (1769) and a *History of America* (1777) which, like his Scottish volumes, have been superseded by later research but which have the virtues of their period. Robertson formed and led the 'moderate' party in the 18th-century Church of Scotland – the group of classically educated, urbane, rational clergymen who defended both David Hume and

John ◊ Home from harassment by the Evangelical or Popular party. [A I]

Works (1817).
J. B. Black, *The Art of History* (1926); R. Birley, *Sunk without Trace* (1962).

Robinson, Henry Crabb (1775–1867). Diarist, journalist and letter-writer. Born in Bury St Edmunds, the son of a tanner, he was articled to a solicitor, and practised in London (1796–1800), but then travelled in Germany, studying at Jena. He met Goethe, Schiller, Herder and other writers. In 1807 he became foreign correspondent (and later foreign editor) of *The Times*, then rising fast by its attention to obtaining accurate news quickly; he was also sent as special correspondent to the Peninsula (1808–9). He was called to the bar (1813), as a member of the Middle Temple, and became leader of the Norfolk circuit until his retirement in 1823. Thereafter his great powers of conversation, wide interests and ingratiating temper made him a popular member of society, who knew everybody in London literary circles. His diaries and correspondence are thus invaluable for the intellectual and social history of the time, particularly through his intimacy with Wordsworth, Coleridge, Lamb and Hazlitt. Extracts from his voluminous papers (which are preserved in Dr Williams's Library in London) were edited by T. Sadler as *The Diary, Reminiscences and Correspondence of Henry Crabb Robinson* (3 vols., 1869; 2 vols., 1872, with Augustus de Morgan's 'Recollections' of Robinson). [A R]

Blake, Coleridge, Wordsworth, Being Selections from the Remains of H.C.R., ed. E. J. Morley (1922); The Correspondence of H.C.R. with the Wordsworth Circle: 1808–66, ed. E. J. Morley (2 vols., 1927); H.C.R. on Books and Their Writers, ed. E. J. Morley (3 vols., 1938).
J. M. Baker, H.C.R. (1937); I. Elliott, Index to the H.C.R. Letters in Dr Williams's Library (1960); D. G. Larg, H.C.R. and Madame de Staël (1929).

Rochester, John Wilmot, 2nd earl of (1647–80). Poet, intellectual and wit. Born at Ditchley, near Woodstock in Oxfordshire, he succeeded his father when he was 11. He was educated at Wadham College, Oxford. After a Grand Tour, he returned to England and became a member of the group of dissolute courtiers that included ◊ Sedley and ◊ Dorset. He was a favourite of Charles II's. The best of his poetry is satire and in this he shows himself a powerful master of the couplet. He also has a command of phrasing that gives him a high rank as a poet, now that his immoral and pointless life does not seem the disqualification for exercising his art that it once did. He also had the misfortune to be on the wrong side in a quarrel with Dryden, which damaged his reputation. As a patron he was unreliable, being subject to fits of capricious malice. His 2 best works are *A Satyr against Mankind* (1675) and *Upon Nothing*, in which he shows strong poetical intelligence and an effective sceptical (even anti-rational) attitude. His literary and political satires (e.g. his *Allusion to Horace's 10th Satyr of the First Book*, and *The Commons Petition to King Charles II*, attacking the King), though not without considerable merit, are never so good. Rochester also wrote competent songs. He made an edifying death, reported by Bishop Gilbert ◊ Burnet.

His *Poems* (Muses' Library, 1953; revised 1964) are edited by V. de Sola Pinto with notes and a good introduction, in which the editor has compared him with Byron. He had the same kind of aristocratic arrogant intelligence, which is not attractive to everybody. [AR]

V. de Sola Pinto, *R* (1935; rewritten 1962); K. B. Murdock, 'A Very Profane Wit', in *The Sun at Noon* (1939).

Rodgers, W(illiam) R(obert) (1909–68). Northern Irish poet. Born in Belfast, educated at Queen's University, Belfast, between 1939 and 1946 he was minister of Loughgall Presbyterian Church, Co. Armagh. From 1946 to 1952 he worked in London as a producer for the B.B.C., being especially associated with Third Programme productions on Ireland and Irish literary characters. His 2 volumes of verse, *Awake! and Other Poems* (1941) and *Europa and the Bull* (1952), have a bouncing, muscular rhythm, vivid imagery and an Irish raciness of idiom which comes out also in his articles in periodicals like the *New Statesman*. He was elected to the Irish Academy of Letters in 1951. [GSF]

Ireland in Colour (1957) (prose).

Rogers, Samuel (1763–1855). Banker, poet, traveller and connoisseur. Born at Stoke Newington, the son of a dissenting banker and capitalist. His wealth enabled him to apply the fruits of a careful education to dilettante writing. He made some mark with 2 poems in the discursive and meditative 18th-century fashion in the vein of ◊ Akenside: *Ode to Superstition* (1786); and *The Pleasures of Memory* (1792), which elaborated the 'association of ideas' theory derived from Locke through ◊ Hartley and Archibald Alison. He also wrote an *Epistle to a Friend* (1798) on 'taste' in art-collecting. Under the impact of Wordsworth and other Romantic writers, Rogers produced *Columbus* (1810), a fragment of epic narrative, in which he attempts to give a Romantic colour to essentially old-fashioned ideas. *Jacqueline* (1814) is a domestic tale in verse, and the moralizing *Human Life* (1819) is more like his first poems. His most famous poem is *Italy* (1822-8), a collection of impressions and stories (5 in prose, 47 in blank verse) in which, following Childe Harold's Italian wanderings, Rogers (in a tribute to Byron) again attempts to combine his classical literary instincts with rather sentimentalized expressions of personal feeling. In later editions of the poem (privately printed) he employed Turner as an illustrator. Rogers declined the Laureateship on the death of Wordsworth, and advocated Tennyson. His main importance is perhaps as a patron, and social *littérateur*: his famous 'breakfasts' provided a meeting place for writers, artists and 'celebrities' of all kinds. [AR]

Poetical Works, ed. Bell (Aldine Poets, 1875); *Italy* (1830) and *Poems* (1834) (illustrated by Turner and T. Stothard); *Reminiscences and Table Talk of S.R.*, ed. G. H. Powell (1903).
R. E. Roberts, *R. and His Circle* (1910); J. R. Hale, *The Italian Journal of S.R.* (1956); C. P. Barbier, *R. and Gilpin* (1959).

Rohmer, Sax (pseud. of Arthur Sarsfield Ward, Warde or Wade). (1886- 1959). Novelist. Born in Birmingham of Irish parents, as a schoolboy he was interested in Egyptology and the literature of the occult. He failed a Civil Service examination for a post in the East, and was briefly in the City, followed by a period as a rather unsuccessful journalist. He began writing very popular mystery stories, and with *Dr Fu Manchu* (1913) he hit on one of the most successful exotic 'thriller' formulae ever devised. Rohmer's imagination was crude and colourful; his writing simple and full of *clichés*. Dr Fu Manchu, the inscrutable oriental villain, battles against a tight-lipped, suave Englishman, Nayland Smith, through countless adventures involving religion, dope and, after the Second World War, communism. Like the novels of Ian ◊ Fleming, the Fu Manchu stories exploited and satisfied some wide-spread imaginative hunger (and possibly fear). In 1955 Rohmer sold the television film and radio rights in the Doctor for $4,000,000. Among Rohmer's titles, which include other characters and situations, are *The Yellow Claw* (1915), *Dope* (1919), *Tales of Chinatown* (1922), *Daughter of Fu Manchu* (1931), *Fu Manchu's Bride* (1933), *The Trail of Fu Manchu* (1934), *President Fu Manchu* (1936), *The Drums of Fu Manchu* (1939), *Shadow of Fu Manchu* (1949) and *Sinister Madonna* (1956). There have been several film versions of some of these adventures and they have also been widely translated. [AR]

Rolfe, Frederick William (Serafino Austin Lewis Mary, also known as Baron Corvo) (1860–1913). Novelist and historian. Born in London, the son of a dissenting piano manufacturer, he left school at 15, studied briefly at Oxford, acted as a tutor and lived by badly paid hack writing. He was frequently taken up by patrons, but his life-long attempts to convince the Roman Catholic Church, to which he had become a convert, that he had been called to the priesthood developed (or strengthened) a disturbed state of mind that came close to paranoia, and led inevitably to rupture. His delusive, self-justifying, spiritual dreams of a rejected convert who became the noblest Pope were the stuff of his best work of fiction, spiced with malicious sketches of his 'enemies', in *Hadrian the Seventh* (1904). Containing remarkable passages of wit and learning, the book peters out in anti-socialist melodrama. A commission he undertook to make money, the *Chronicles of the House of Borgia* (1901), shows again his curious knowledge, vivid but undisciplined imagination and considerable writing skill. He contributed six *Stories Toto Told Me* (1898) to *The ◊ Yellow Book*; these legends of the saints with 26 more were printed as *In His Own Image* (1901; ed. Shane Leslie, 1924). He died as a sponger in Venice, where he claimed to have been given the title of Baron; his last years are idealized and his 'enemies' vilified in *The Desire and Pursuit of the Whole* (ed. A. J. A. Symons, 1934; intr. W. H. Auden, 1953), which again has its beauties and originalities.

There has been something of a cult of Corvo, stimulated by A J. A. Symons' very readable biography, *The Quest for Corvo* (1934). [AR]

Letters (3 vols., 1959–62).
Ed. C. Woolf, *C.: 1860–1960* (1961) (essays); C. Woolf, *Bibliography* (1957).

Rolle, Richard (*c.* 1300–49). Mystical writer. Born in Pickering, Yorkshire, Rolle studied at Oxford, but seems to have been repelled by scholasticism. He returned home without taking orders and lived as a hermit in a cell on the Dalton estates, where he developed his mystical religion and began to write in Latin and English. He had a wide popularity among female religionists; the *Form of Perfect Living* and possibly the important *Ego dormio et cor meum vigilat* were written for his disciple, Margaret Kirkby. Towards the end of his life, he retired to Hampole, living in close contact with the nuns there, for whom he wrote the *Commandment of Love to God*. An unsuccessful attempt to canonize him was made after his death. As a religious thinker, Rolle cannot match the intellect and depth of ◊ Hilton, and his appeal is almost entirely emotional, inspired by belief in the personal bond of ardent love between man and God. His sincerity is unquestioned, but an occasional striving for effect is apparent. As a devotional writer and stylist, his reputation is deserved. His rhythmical and melodious prose and verse (lyrics like 'Love Is Life' and 'A Song of Love-Longing to Jesus', for example) have all the virtues of the English tradition. The simpler 'teaching style' he adopts in pieces like *The Bee and the Stork* may now be found more attractive than his more exalted style. [AG]

English Writings of R.R., ed. H. E. Allen (1931, revised 1963).
H. E. Allen, *Writings Ascribed to R. and Materials for His Biography* (1927); R. W. Chambers, *On the Continuity of English Prose* (1932); P. Hodgson, *Three Fourteenth Century Mystics* (WTW. 1967); D. Knowles, *The English Mystics* (1927), and *The English Mystical Tradition* (1961).

Roper, William (1496–1578). Biographer. Born in Kent, he was the son of a friend of Sir Thomas ◊ More, and, like his father, was a member of Lincoln's Inn. He was a member of More's household, and in 1521 married his eldest daughter, Margaret. Briefly attracted by Luther's teachings, he became, under More's influence, a firm

Catholic, was elected to the bench, and was active in local Kentish and in parliamentary affairs. Under Elizabeth he fell into disfavour. His one literary work was his reminiscences of his father-in-law, *Life of Sir Thomas More*, circulated in manuscript from about 1557 and printed only in 1626 at Paris (ed. E. V. Hitchcock, 1935). This attractive, modest and pious memoir has been judged to be 'probably the most perfect little biography in the English language'; the dialogue is especially good. [MJ]

R. W. Chambers, *Thomas More* (1935).

Ros, Amanda McKittrick (1861–1939). Novelist. After training as a teacher in Dublin, she married a country stationmaster, Andy Ross (*sic*), in 1887. Her romantic snobbishness and enthusiasm for the writing of Marie ◊ Correlli are apparent in 2 novels she wrote in an alliterative Euphuistic prose and published in Belfast at her own expense. *Irene Iddlesleigh* (1897) and *Delina Delaney* (1898) subsequently became the object of a cult at Oxford and elsewhere, being republished (at the instigation of Aldous Huxley and others) in London in 1926 and 1935 respectively, and later reprinted. Men like Lord Beveridge and Desmond MacCarthy called upon Mrs Ros professing their admiration for her style, and, although adverse criticism provoked angry broadsides in verse, she never realized that her books had given rise to affectionate laughter and even derision. [MJ]

A. Huxley, 'Euphues Redivivus', in *On the Margin* (1923); J. Loudan, *O Rare Amanda!* (1954).

Roscommon, Wentworth Dillon, 4th Earl of (1633?–85). Critic and courtier. Born in Ireland, nephew and godson of Wentworth, the great Earl of Strafford. He was educated at the University of Caen and travelled on the continent, returning to England at the Restoration. Roscommon enjoyed a somewhat inflated reputation, no doubt because of his rank, based on a blank-verse translation of Horace's *Art of Poetry* (1680) and a stiff, didactic *Essay on Translated Verse* (1684; revised 1685; ed. J. E. Spingarn, in *Critical Essays of the Seventeenth Century*, iii, 1909). He also tried to set up a society (based on the French Academy) to 'fix' the English language. Roscommon is commended by Pope because '... in all Charles's

Days, / Roscommon only boasts unspotted Lays'. [AR]

Poems (1717).
Johnson, *Lives of the Poets.*

Rosenberg, Isaac (1890–1918). Poet and artist. Of Russian Jewish ancestry, his parents had worked in South Africa before settling in London. He was brought up mainly in Whitechapel, where his close friends included young Jewish artists and writers, such as John Rodker and Mark Gertler, but he also had contacts with Pound's 'forgotten group', T. E. ◊ Hulme and other precursors of ◊ Imagism, around 1909. He attended the Slade School, and his surviving paintings and drawings have an affinity with the French post-Impressionists, notably Gauguin; he was also an admirer of the 19th-century French neo-classicist painter, Puvis de Chavannes. His poems, like those of Ezra Pound, with whom he has notable affinities in his development, show in the beginning a strong influence from the Pre-Raphaelites and the Decadents of the 1890s, in rhythm, diction and subject matter, and, though there is little evidence of contact, his development makes more sense if his poems are read alongside the early poems of Pound, Eliot, Hulme, Richard ◊ Aldington and Herbert ◊ Read than if read alongside those of the Georgians. Two very strong influences were Blake as artist, poet and creator of myths and the Hebrew scriptures. His treatment of Hebrew mythology is, however, by no means orthodox; he was suspicious of the rigid Father–God image of traditional Judaism and wrote a poem about a female god, as well as a poem about Valkyrie-like Amazon figures, gathering men into unity through death in battle, who resemble Blake's 'Daughters of Albion'. This interest in the mythical and the gigantesque is typical of the artistic growing points of his time. The poems best remembered, however, are non-mythical, growing out of Rosenberg's experiences as a private in the trenches in the First World War. These have an extraordinary honesty, complexity and concrete directness, avoiding the touches of rhetoric and sentiment that tend to flaw even the best poems of ◊ Owen. Rosenberg is an extremely uneven poet, uncertain about tone and diction, but compensating for these weaknesses by direct emotional strength and a plastic and pictorial quality. His early poems appeared in privately printed pamphlets and magazines. Sir Edward ◊ Marsh gave him some encouragement and printed a fragment from his play *Moses* in ◊ *Georgian Poetry*.

A collected volume, edited by Gordon Bottomley, whose verse plays Rosenberg greatly admired, came out in 1922: Bottomley unfortunately destroyed many fragments and variant drafts, but a definitive volume, including some very interesting letters, edited nominally by Bottomley and D. W. Harding, but with Harding doing the textual work, first came out in 1937. Unlike Owen, Rosenberg did not believe that the 'Poetry is the Pity'. Though his poems are full of compassion, especially the trench poems, the desire to shape a poem properly, making poetic not logical order out of the chaos of experience, is always primary. Of all the poets who fought in the First World War, he has, even more than Owen, the makings of a major figure; his development through a rather faded literariness to a living handling of myth and finally to a sharp and complex awareness of reality shows extraordinary parallels to Ezra Pound's development from *A Lume Spento* to *Hugh Selwyn Mauberley*. [GSF]

D. W. Harding, *Experience into Words* (1963); F. Grubb, *A Vision of Reality* (1965); B. Bergonzi, *Heroes' Twilight* (1965); J. Cohen, *Tulane Studies in English*, x (1960); M. Bewley, 'The Poetry of Isaac Rosenberg', *Commentary* (1949); J. Silkin, 'Isaac Rosenberg 1890–1918', *Leeds University Catalogue* (1959).

Ross, Martin (pseud. of Violet Martin) (1862–1915). Novelist. Born at Ross House, Co. Galway, whence she derived her pseudonym under which she collaborated in tales of Irish life with her cousin Edith Oenone ◊ Somerville. She also wrote 2 volumes of pleasant, reminiscent essays, *Some Irish Yesterdays* (1906) and *Strayaways* (1920). [AR]

Ross, William (1762–91). Scottish Gaelic poet. The popular image of Ross is that of a romantic lover, whose rejection by his sweetheart Mòr Ros was responsible for a number of sweet and plaintive songs, and later for a decline in health which resulted in an early death. The truth is somewhat different. After spending some time as a travelling packman, Ross became a schoolmaster at Gairloch in Wester Ross. He was delicate, sensuous and addicted to whisky; he had had a classical education, and was also well versed in the Gaelic poetic tradi-

tion. His wit was keen, and his sense of humour was sometimes ribald. This intellectual and scholastic equipment appears in his nature poetry (as in *Oran a t-Samhraidh*), his bacchanalian and his satirical verse. His pastoral poems are influenced by his knowledge of the classics, but elsewhere he uses nature imagery more subjectively than his 18th-century Gaelic contemporaries.

His best poetry is that closest to the popular legend, and centres on his unhappy love for Mòr Ros, who married and settled in Liverpool in 1782. Although these poems are a mere handful (the most important being *Feasgar Luain*, *Oran Cumhaidh* and *Oran Eile*) their combination of lyricism with controlled art and hard unsentimental realism give them great distinction, and give some point to Sam ◊ Maclean's linking of the names of Ross and Yeats. [DT]

Songs, ed. G. Calder (1937).
D .S. Thomson, 'William Ross', *An Gaidheal*, LIV, 2 and 3 (1959).

Rossetti, Christina Georgina (1830–94). Poet. Born in London, the sister of Dante Gabriel ◊ Rossetti, she was a precocious child and, like her brother, was educated at home and was bilingual in Italian and English. Her first verses, *To My Mother, on the Anniversary of Her Birth* (1842), were privately printed by her grandfather, who also printed a collection of imitative pieces in 1847. From her childhood she suffered ill-health, and spent much of her life as an invalid within her family circle; as a model for some of her brother's paintings, her thin face has become one of the typical Pre-Raphaelite spiritual symbols. She was a devoutly religious Anglican, and much of her poetry is marked by her ascetic, self-denying faith. Because of religious differences, she refused to marry the painter, John Collinson, a member of the Pre-Raphaelite Brotherhood, with whose artistic aims she was in sympathy. Her first volume of published poems, *Goblin Market and Other Poems* (1862), was in fact the first great literary success for the Pre-Raphaelites. It contained poems she had contributed to the *Athenaeum*, *Macmillan's Magazine* and the Pre-Raphaelite organ, *The Germ*. She was a voluminous writer and this, together with the nature of her religious beliefs and her love of simplicity, may have contributed to the thin texture of much of her verse. She wrote sonnets, carols, ballads and much religious verse, of which her carol 'In the Bleak Mid-Winter' is one of the most successful and characteristic. She is the best poet inspired by the ◊ Oxford Movement, better than ◊ Keble, and in some poems to be ranked with George Herbert. Her volumes of poems included *The Prince's Progress and Other Poems* (1866); a collection of children's poems and nursery rhymes, *Sing Song* (1872); *A Pageant and Other Poems* (1881); and *Verses* (reprinted from several prose works in which they had been interspersed) (1893). *A Pageant* included a sonnet-sequence, *Monna Innominata*, which is one of the places in which she celebrates her denial of love for religious purity, in her rejection in 1866 of a proposal of marriage from Charles Cayley. Christina Rossetti wrote religious tracts, and in *The Face of the Deep: A Devotional Commentary on the Apocalypse* (containing also more than 200 poems and verse fragments) (1892) she shows her concern with contemporary social problems such as prostitution, vivisection, unemployment and destitution. To help support her family, she wrote biographical articles on Italians, read proofs and translated. *Goblin Market* is one of her best poems, and shows how she can capture eerie symbolic suggestions and make them further her beliefs; it is also very successful in counterpointing a light measure with serious, even grim, intentions. She is a poet of devotion and seeking, rather than mystical experience. [AR]

Poetical Works, ed. W. M. Rossetti (brother), with unpublished work and memoirs and notes (1904); *Poems*, selected and intr. R. Ironside (1953); *Poems*, selected K. Jarvis (1955); *Family Letters*, ed. W. M. Rossetti (1908); *The R.–Macmillan Letters*, ed. L. M. Packer (U. of California P., 1963).

M. Zaturenska, *C.R.* (New York, 1949); L. M. Packer, *C.R.* (U. of California P., 1963) (bibliography); J. C. Troxell, *Three Rossettis* (Harvard U.P., 1955) (contains additional letters); G. Battiscombe, *C.R.* (WTW, 1965); V. Woolf, *The Common Reader*, 2 (1932); M. Bowra, *The Romantic Imagination* (1950); W. E. Fredeman, *Pre-Raphaelitism: A Biblio-Critical Study* (Harvard U.P., 1965) (bibliography).

Rossetti, Dante Gabriel (Gabriel Charles Dante Rossetti) (1828–82). Painter and poet. Born in London, the second child of Gabriele Rossetti, a royalist exile from Naples, who later became Professor of Italian at King's College, London. Like his sister,

Christina ◊ Rossetti, he was bilingual in Italian and English. His education was at home and rather scrappy. He abandoned his father's political and economic ideals, and hated the science which was then altering his society. He imbibed a love of Dante and the earlier Italian poets who heavily influenced his own work. From King's College School, he was sent to a small art school, and then to the Antique School of the Royal Academy, but he was out of sympathy with the conventional instruction there. With two other rebellious students, William Holman Hunt and John Everett Millais, he helped to found the Pre-Raphaelite Brotherhood, which was enlarged to include several other artists and sympathizers. The name came partly from Keats's claim that the earlier Italian painters were greater than Raphael (whose technique was the model of the academicians), and partly from the study at that very time of certain medieval frescoes which were thought to show greater intellectuality and nobler accuracy. Hunt's view of the movement was as a renewal of moral uplift, felt to be lacking in traditional classical art. Rossetti's interests were quite different. His revolt against the Academy had technical aims which they all subscribed to, greater detail in painting, naturalism and romantic symbolism; but it had no moral content. He valued freedom for itself. His imaginative power made him the leader, as Ruskin soon saw. Through Rossetti, the influence of the Pre-Raphaelites penetrated to literature, and their painting became highly literary. Rossetti founded their organ, *The Germ: Thoughts towards Nature in Poetry, Literature and Art* (two numbers, January 1850–May 1851; 2 numbers as *Art and Poetry*), and in it started publishing his own poetry, including the first version of *The Blessed Damozel*, a decoratively sentimental piece of Dantesque imagery, as well as one or two of his tales. During the fifties the original force of the Brotherhood waned, but took new life with help from Ruskin; and Rossetti started to collaborate with Burne-Jones, Swinburne and William Morris; the famous murals in the Oxford Union were painted in 1856, and the movement began making converts amongst the 'daring' young people.

In 1860, he at last married Elizabeth Siddal, who had been his model in several paintings, in certain of the sonnets in *The House of Life* and in *Love's Nocturne*. She died in 1862 of an overdose of laudanum, which she was taking to offset tuberculosis.

In remorse for fancied neglect, he buried with her the manuscript volume of poems he was preparing for the press. In 1861, he published a book of translations, *The Early Italian Poets from Ciullo d' Alcamo to Dante* (revised as *Dante and His Circle*, 1874; ed. E. G. Gardner, 1904; 1924). This gave him a small but sure literary reputation as the leader of a new movement. He moved to Chelsea, where he pursued his career as a painter, first in the water colours of mythological or symbolical subjects which are now greatly admired, and then returning to the oils of beautiful 'women and flowers'. In 1869 he consented to the recovery of his *Poems,* which were printed in 1870 (reprinted in re-arranged form, excluding *The House of Life,* 1881); this volume established him as a leading poet. It contains most of his best poems. A later volume, *Ballads and Sonnets,* appeared in 1881. From 1871 to 1874, he lived at Kelmscott Manor with Morris, to try to improve his health, which had seriously broken down. For insomnia, he started taking the newly discovered drug, chloral; this finally ruined his already quite disorganized life. Suffering from delusions of persecution, he lived more or less under the care of Watts-Dunton. In 1871, too, a virulent attack on his work, *The Fleshly School of Poetry,* was published by a journalist, Robert ◊ Buchanan. In his last years he wrote sonnets and 3 long 'ballads', *Rose Marv, The White Ship* and *The Ballad of Jan Van Hunks.*

There is an obvious connexion between Rossetti's poetry and painting; his painting is often allegorical, mythological and 'literary'; his poems are highly visual, and use words in a way that suggests an original colourist. He tried many different forms, including the elaborated · 'ballad' of the Romantics. Gothick tales and the works of Edgar Allen Poe are obvious influences. His imagination, like his language, was 'physical', and some of his very best poems are about women and love. The unfinished *Bride's Prelude* introduces the 'wicked Damozel' with the unblessed, clandestine passion, that was also an interest of his. Browningesque poems are also found, such as *A Last Confession. The House of Life* sonnet-sequence (ed. P. F. Baum, Harvard U.P., 1928) is a good instance of the care that Rossetti took with his poems; by personal experience and revisions of the writing, between 1870 and 1881, it was gradually

shaped into one of his greatest works, though it also contains some rather thin poetry. The title is astrological; the 'forces' that Rossetti thought influenced life are love and death; these are mirrored in the two halves of the collection, 'Youth and Change' and 'Change and Fate'. The sequence is not connected and not autobiographical, except that the changing moods are the poet's. It is perhaps one of the greatest 'painterly' poems by a Pre-Raphaelite. [AR]

Works, ed. W. M. Rossetti (brother) (1911); *Poems,* ed. O. Doughty (1957); *D.G.R., An Anthology,* ed. F. L. Lucas (1933); *Letters,* ed. O. Doughty and J. R. Wahl (5 vols., 1965–7).

Max Beerbohm, *R. and His Circle* (1922) (historically valuable caricatures); O. Doughty, *D.G.R. A Victorian Romantic* (Yale U.P., 1949) (with valuable bibliography) and *D.G.R.* (WTW, 1957); G. Pedrick, *Life with R.* (1964); W. Gaunt, *The Pre-Raphaelite Tragedy* (1942); G. H. Fleming *R. and the Pre-Raphaelite Brotherhood* (1967); G. Hough, *The Last Romantics* (1949); J. Heath-Stubbs, *The Darkling Plain* (1950); H. M. Jones, bibliography in *Victorian Poets,* ed. F. E. Faverty (Harvard U.P., revised 1968); W. E. Fredeman, *Pre-Raphaelitism: A Biblio-Critical Study* (Harvard U.P., 1965) (bibliography).

Rowe, Nicholas (1674–1718). Dramatist. Originally a lawyer, he wrote his first play, *The Ambitious Stepmother,* in 1700, but it was his third, *The Fair Penitent,* adapted from Massinger, which in 1703 established his reputation as the leading Augustan tragedian. Like his later success, *The Tragedy of Jane Shore* (1714), it is a 'she-tragedy', melodramatic in plot and affording great opportunities of pathos to a strongly emotional actress. Both plays long held the stage. In 1709 he brought out an edition of Shakespeare's plays, *The Works of Mr William Shakespeare, Revis'd and Corrected,* dividing them into acts and scenes, and giving each scene a location, a process which blinded succeeding generations of readers to the conventions of the Elizabethan stage. [MJ]

Three Plays, ed. J. R. Sutherland (1929).

B. Dobrée, *English Literature in the Early Eighteenth Century* (1959); A. Nicoll, *British Drama* (revised edn, 1962) and *A History of English Drama, 1660–1900,* ii (revised edn, 1952).

Rowley, William (*c.* 1585–1626). Actor and dramatist. Nothing is known of his birth, education or death. He had a considerable reputation in his own day as an actor (specializing in fat clown parts) and as a man of the theatre. He wrote a prose pamphlet, *A Search for Money* (1609), and several unaided plays, including *All's Lost by Lust* (1619), *A Shoemaker a Gentleman* (1608) and the lost *Hymen's Holiday, or Cupid's Vagaries* (1612). He had a talent for melodrama and for the comedy of low life. His chief work was in collaboration with some of the leading dramatists of the day: with Thomas Heywood he wrote *Fortune by Land and Sea* (1609); with Dekker and Ford *The Witch of Edmonton* (1621); with Dekker, Ford and Webster the lost crime-play *The Late Murder of the Son upon the Mother* (1624); with Webster *A Cure for a Cuckold* (1625). He worked with Thomas Middleton on several plays, amongst which were *A Fair Quarrel* (1617), *The World Tossed at Tennis* (1620) and *The Spanish Gypsy* (1623), as well as one masterpiece of Jacobean drama – the tragedy *The Changeling* (acted 1621). Rowley is usually assumed to have devised the comic plot which ironically parallels the main action. [MJ]

R. H. Barker, *Thomas Middleton* (1958); G. E. Bentley, *The Jacobean and Caroline Stage,* v (1956).

Roy, Gabrielle (1909–). French Canadian novelist. Born in Saint-Boniface (Manitoba), Gabrielle Roy trained as a teacher at the Winnipeg Normal School. Her early interest in the theatre led her in 1937 to Europe, where she studied in London and Paris. At the outbreak of war she returned to Canada and lived in Montreal. She has lived in Quebec City since marrying in 1947. Gabrielle Roy published 4 works in the ten years following 1945. A novel, *La petite poule d'eau* (1950; tr. H. Binsse, *Where Nests the Waterhen,* New York, 1951), and a book of stories, *Rue Deschambault* (1955; tr. H. Binsse, *Street of Riches*), were inspired by her childhood in Manitoba. Her father was employed by the Federal Government and travelled the prairie provinces, settling immigrants who came to Canada from many parts of Europe. These 2 books draw on his experiences, describe the mosaic of cultures, the extremes of climate, the vast perspectives and the often cruel natural forces of the prairies, as well as giving a picture of childhood and family life. *Bonheur d'occasion* (1945; tr. *The Tin Flute,* New York, 1947) and *Alexandre Chenevert* (1954; tr. *The Cashier,* Toronto, 1955) were amongst the first to introduce the problems of urban life into the French Canadian novel and the former was something of a national event because it was awarded in France the Prix Fémina in 1947. *Bonheur d'occasion* describes, with what Gabrielle Roy calls 'une économie de tendresse', the depreciation of human values as a result of urbanization. *Alexandre Chenevert* is a portrait with the same constrained sympathy, perfectly sustained, of the pathos of much of the average man's self-imposed anguish and misery. A fourth novel, *La montagne secrète* (1961; tr. H. Binsse, *The Hidden Mountain,* Toronto, 1962), follows the heroic efforts of a painter to wrest from Canada's vast north lands the spiritual reality which they hide and mirrors the urgent problem the Canadian artist has of defining in Canadian terms the reality which is his raw material. A collection of stories, *La route d'Altamont* (1966), returns to the author's childhood and the inspiration of *La petite poule d'eau.* [CRPM]

Royde-Smith, Naomi Gwladys (d. 1964). Novelist and playwright. Born at Llanwrst in Wales and educated at Clapham High School and in Geneva, she was literary editor of the *Westminster Gazette* from 1912 to 1922, and just after the First World War held a literary *salon* with her friend Rose ◊ Macaulay. In 1926, she married Ernest Milton, the actor. She is the author of over 40 novels, sentimental, well-told and readable. *The Tortoiseshell Cat* (1925) is perhaps her most successful; *In the Wood* (1928) deals with her childhood; others are *The Delicate Situation* (1931), *The Unfaithful Wife* (1941), *Mildensee* (1943), *She Always Caught the Post* (1953) and *Love and a Bird Cage* (1960). She has written several plays, including *A Balcony* (1926) and *All Night Sitting* (1954). Her biographies include *The Private Life of Mrs Siddons* (1933). [AR]

Ruskin, John (1819–1900). Art and social critic. Son of a prosperous wine merchant, Ruskin was educated privately, with much opportunity for foreign travel, and at Christ Church, Oxford, which he entered in 1836, winning the Newdigate Prize in 1839. A year of foreign travel, for his health, delayed his graduation till 1842. He had already studied drawing and had derived from his mother (whose over-protectiveness persisted well into his manhood and permanently affected his character) a love of the

Authorized Version of the Bible which was to have great influence on his prose style. His foreign travels (which were to continue throughout most of his life) had given him the opportunity to observe and appreciate painting and architecture all over Europe. Thus a lively interest in the visual arts, a prophetic prose style, and a deeply religious upbringing combined to produce an art critic with profound ethical and social pre-occupations. *Modern Painters* (5 vols., 1843–60) grew out of his resentment of attacks on the landscape painter J. M. W. Turner and developed into a comprehensive discussion of the principles of painting, especially land-scape painting. The first 2 volumes, which were anonymous, discuss the problem of truth in art and the function of the imagi-nation; the third discusses the Grand Style and gives a history of landscape painting; the fourth deals with colour and illumination (and includes a famous passage on the tower of Calais church); the fifth deals with the four orders of landscape painters (heroic, classical, pastoral and contemplative) with detailed examples. The whole gave a new dimension to English art criticism and aroused great interest. Ruskin set himself from the beginning against the Joshua ◊ Reynolds view that great painting was simply technical excellence plus a poetical imagination. 'In all high ideas of beauty, it is more than probable that much of the pleasure depends on delicate and untrace-able perceptions of fitness, propriety and relation, which are purely intellectual, and through which we arrive at our noblest ideas of what is commonly and rightly called "in-tellectual beauty".'

Turning from painting to architecture, Ruskin produced *The Stones of Venice* (3 vols., 1851–3), in which he explained the development and the beauty of Gothic architecture in terms of the moral virtue of the society that produced it and attacked 'the pestilent art of the Renaissance' as arising from an immoral society. 'You cannot paint or sing yourselves into being good men; you must be good men before you can either paint or sing, and then the colour and sound will complete in you all that is best.' This insistence on a direct relation between moral and artistic value led to some confusions and some self-delusion, but it also provided a base from which Ruskin could launch a supremely eloquent attack on the Philistines of his day. The effects of industrialism both on the face of England and on the lives and attitudes of its inhabitants led Ruskin to eco-nomics and to attack (like ◊ Carlyle, who influenced him) *laissez-faire* economics and the Victorian business ethic. He set 'the reckless luxury, the deforming mechanism, and the squalid misery of modern cities' against his own vision of the city beautiful, and in doing so expressed more eloquently than any other English writer has done the aesthetic and moral case against uncon-trolled industrial development. In *Unto This Last* (4 essays on economics, 1860–62), *Munera Pulveris* (*Fraser's Magazine*, 1862–3, unfinished because of popular clamour against it), *The Crown of Wild Olive* (4 lec-tures, 1866) and *Fors Clavigera* (letters to workmen of Britain, 1871–84) he mounted his attack and preached his own social and economic gospel sometimes obscurely and sometimes with great eloquence and, even when he developed into his latest and too wordy style, with flashes of wit and irony or invective or visionary splendour that remain memorable. This side of his thought had great influence not only in developing a neo-medieval conception of life, work and the community but also in more practical ways, on Fabian Socialism and concepts of town planning. In his unfinished autobiography, *Praeterita* (1885–9), Ruskin tells of the early influences on him, of his childhood, and of his early travels.

Ruskin's marriage in 1848 to Euphemia Chalmers Gray was annulled in 1855 (Euphemia subsequently married the painter Millais). Ruskin continued with his life of lecturing, writing, travelling. In 1871 he founded the Guild of St George to act out his view that 'food can only be got out of the ground and happiness out of honesty' and he was subsequently involved in a number of activities related to the revival of handi-crafts. He was first Slade Professor of Fine Art at Oxford in 1870–9, and held the post again in 1883–4. His last years were clouded by mental vagueness.

Ruskin's extraordinary visual percep-tiveness is the main reason for the continu-ing appeal of his art criticism. While his cor-relation of art and morality now seems naïve, and his economics impossibly amateurish, his views of the relation between values in art, work and community are still relevant, so that his later work, though often arousing hostility at the time, is still esteemed, particularly those witty and eloquent attacks on Philistinism such as his lecture on 'Traffic' delivered at the Bradford Town Hall in 1864 (it is in *The Crown of Wild Olive*). [D D]

Works, ed. E. T. Cook and A. D. O. Wedderburn (39 vols., 1903–12); *R. as Literary Critic: Selections*, ed. A. H. R. Ball (1928); *Selections*, ed. K. Clark (1964).

E. T. Cook, *The Life of J.R.* (2 vols., 1911); Peter Quennell, *J.R.: The Portrait of a Prophet* (1949); Admiral Sir William James, *The Order of Release* (1947) (on Ruskin and Euphemia Gray and the disaster of Ruskin's unconsummated marriage); R. H. Wilenski, *J.R.* (1933); F. W. Roe, *The Social Philosophy of Carlyle and R.* (1921); Graham Hough, *The Last Romantics* (1949; 1961); J. D. Rosenberg, *The Darkening Glass* (1961).

Russell, Bertrand (Arthur William), 3rd Earl (1872–1970). Mathematician and philosopher. Born at Trelleck in Wales, the grandson of the 1st Earl Russell, he succeeded his brother in the earldom in 1931. Bertrand Russell was educated privately and at Trinity College, Cambridge, where he studied mathematics and moral sciences, and became a Fellow in 1895. He made considerable contributions to mathematics, but was best known for the way he tried to apply the clarity and definition he admired in mathematical reasoning to the solution of problems in other fields, particularly ethics and politics. To a strenuous intellectual life, Russell also brought the fervour of a reformer's active zeal, though informed by humanism and philosophical materialism and opposed to dogmatism (political, moral and religious). The two movements in which his activities had most effect were education and pacifism. He ran a progressive school in Sussex from 1927 to 1932. For the development of the human creative faculties which he considered the principle of growth, Russell demanded total freedom of thought and speech, and the scope of his educational reform thus encompassed social, ethical and sexual considerations. In following his logical, pacifist conduct, Russell was (temporarily) deprived of his fellowship at Trinity and briefly imprisoned during the First World War. He was one of the leading figures in the pacifist opposition to the development of nuclear weapons since the Second World War.

Russell was a voluminous writer and his works are marked by a clarity and wit which have gained many of them wide popular circulation. He was made an O.M. in 1949 and in 1950 was awarded the Nobel Prize for Literature. His first two books were in two fields in which he excelled: *German Social Democracy* (1896) and *Essay on the Foundations of Geometry* (1897). Russell was a brilliant expounder of other philosophers' work; his *Philosophy of Leibnitz* (1900) is an instance of this, as are *Problems of Philosophy* (1912), *The A.B.C. of Relativity* (1925) and the *History of Western Philosophy* (1945). *Principia Mathematica* (with A. N. Whitehead) (1910) is one of his greatest works and other books in the same field are *Our Knowledge of the External World as a Field for Scientific Method in Philosophy* (1915) and *The Analysis of Mind* (1921). Some of his other works are: *Marriage and Morals* (1929); *The Amberley Papers* (with Patricia Russell) (1937); *The Impact of Science on Society* (1952); *Satan in the Suburbs* (5 short stories) (1953); *Human Society in Ethics and Politics* (1954); an interesting book of reminiscences, *Portraits from Memory* (1956); *Has Man a Future?* (1961); and *Unarmed Victory* (1963). The first two volumes of his *Autobiography* appeared in 1967, the third in 1969. [A R]

A. Wood, *B.R., the Passionate Sceptic* (1957); J. Feibleman, *Inside the Great Mirror* (1958) (R. Wittgenstein and their followers in 20th-century philosophy); L. W. Aitken, *B.R.'s Philosophy of Morals* (New York, 1963); J. Park, *B.R. on Education* (Ohio State U.P., 1963).

Rutherford, Mark (pseud. of William Hale White) (1831–1913). Novelist and miscellaneous writer. Born in Bedford, the son of a dissenting printer and bookseller, William White (later door-keeper of the House of Commons, and author of *The Inner Life of the House of Commons*, 2 vols., 1897), he studied at a dissenting theological college, but had to leave because he developed heretical views. He became a Civil Servant in Somerset House and later in the Admiralty, becoming assistant director of contracts. His first literary works were anonymous personal confessions of his loss of faith in Calvinist certainty, written with a tough irony and knowledge of London low life, *The Autobiography of Mark Rutherford, Dissenting Minister* (1881; ed. and intr. H. W. Massingham, 1936) and *Mark Rutherford's Deliverance: The Second Part of His Autobiography* (1885; together, with Pt 2 expanded, 1888). His novels are loosely put together, but give rather sympathetic and powerful accounts of the world of dissenters (mostly small tradesmen), and the stresses and strains set up by the prevailing crisis of religious doubt as it affects these shabby-genteel citizens. His fiction, now being revalued, is worthwhile both for its religious content and for a certain solid achievement as social comment. The best-known is *The Revolution in Tanner's Lane* (1887), set in the post-Napoleonic period and pervaded by a discussion of Romantic and Wordsworthian ideas and feelings. Others are *Miriam's Schooling and Other Papers* (1890) and *Catharine Furze* (2 vols., 1893). He also wrote 3 series of miscellanies, *Pages from a Journal* (1900; 1910; 1915, posthumous; 1st series in World's Classics, 1930). Under his own name he published translations of Spinoza's *Ethics* (1883) and *Tractatus* (1895), as well as volumes of literary comment. [AR]

S. Nowell Smith, *M.R.: A Bibliography of First Editions* (1930); M. Praz, 'The Autobiography of M.R.', in *Anglica*, I, 2 (1946) (in Italian); C. M. Maclean, *M.R.* (1955); J. Stone, *M.R.* (1955); I. Stock, *W.H.W.* (1956).

Rymer, Thomas (?1643–1713). Critic and historian. Born at Yafforth in Yorkshire, the son of Ralph Rymer, a Puritan country gentleman executed in 1664 for treasonable conspiracy. He was educated at the Free School in near-by Northallerton and at Sidney Sussex College, Cambridge, and was called to the bar at Gray's Inn. His critical theories were first advanced in the Preface to his translation of Rapin's *Reflections on Aristotle's Treatise of Poesie* (1674) and *The Tragedies of the Last Age Consider'd and Examined by the Practice of the Ancients and by the Common Sense of All Ages* (1678); his work was admired and praised by Dryden, Mulgrave and others. In *A Short View of Tragedy* (1693 for 1692), however, which contains a long hostile critique of *Othello*, his principles seemed to be pressed to extremes in attacking Shakespeare, and he was thereafter often ridiculed, particularly by abusing his own unsuccessful tragedy *Edgar, or the English Monarch* (1678). Rymer was the leading exponent in England of the French, systematic neo-classical criticism, though he employed these foreign ideas for progressivist, nationalistic ends. His critical writing is somewhat disconnected, colloquial and destructive: it raises awkward problems of moral teaching and technique which must be taken seriously, but which are never solved by his own positive views. In 1692, Rymer was appointed historiographer-royal, and he painstakingly edited the first 15 volumes of the great collection of English treaties and related matter known as Rymer's *Foedera* (20 vols., 1704–35; revised by G. Holmes, 20 vols., 1727–35; enlarged, 10 vols., The Hague, 1739–45; edited, incomplete, by J. Caley and F. Holbrooke, 4 vols., 1816–69). [AR]

Critical Works, ed. and annotated C. Zimansky (Yale U.P., 1956); *Critical Essays of the Seventeenth Century*, ed. J. E. Spingarn (3 vols., 1908–9).

C. Zimansky, Introduction to *Critical Works* (Yale U.P., 1956); F. Gallaway, *Reason, Rule and Revolt in English Classicism* (New York, 1940); R. S. Crane, in *Critics and Criticism*, ed. Crane (Chicago, 1952); D. C. Douglas, *English Scholars: 1660–1730* (2nd edn, 1951) (marred by erroneous biographical information).

S

Sackville, Charles. ◊ Dorset, Charles Sackville.

Sackville, Thomas (1st Earl of Dorset and Baron Buckhurst) (1536–1608). Poet, dramatist and statesman. Son of Sir Richard Sackville, lawyer and statesman, Thomas attended both Oxford and Cambridge before becoming a barrister at the Inner Temple, where he planned and wrote his contributions to the 1563 edition of *A Myrroure for Magistrates* (ed. L. B. Campbell, 1938). This is a composite didactic work originally designed as a continuation of ◊ Lydgate's *Falls of Princes*, in the form of monologues spoken by the ghosts of eminent persons who had suffered drastic reversals of fortune. Sackville's contributions were an 'Induction', noted for its elegiac cadences and poised gravity of movement and imagery, and the 'Complaint of Henry Duke of Buckingham'. He also collaborated with Thomas Norton in writing the Senecan tragedy *Gorboduc* (ed. J. Cunliffe, in *Early English Classical Tragedies*, 1912), produced in 1561 both at the Inner Temple and before the Queen at Whitehall. *Gorboduc*, a tragedy of civil war and divided authority, is historically significant as an early attempt at a 'regular' form of tragedy and as the first English play in blank verse: it has 5 acts, follows the classical manner of avoiding violence on the stage, and is sententious and rhetorical. The latter part of Sackville's life was devoted to affairs of state. He sat as Member of Parliament for a number of constituencies between 1558 and 1563 and was knighted and raised to the peerage in 1567. Among the offices he held were commissioner at state trials (it was he who announced to Mary Queen of Scots her death sentence in 1586), commissioner for ecclesiastical causes (1588), ambassador to the Low Countries (1589) and Lord Treasurer from 1599 until his death. He was created Earl of Dorset in 1604. [DD]

The Complaint of Henry Duke of Buckingham, ed. M. Hearsey (New Haven, 1936); *Works*, ed. R. W. Sackville-West (1859) (includes letters and Sackville's part of *Gorboduc*).

W. F. Trench, *A Mirror for Magistrates* (1898); J. Swart, *T.S.* (Groningen, 1948); P. Bacquet, *T.S., L'homme et l'œuvre* (1966).

Sackville-West, Edward (Charles) (5th Baron Sackville) (1901–65). Novelist and music critic. Educated at Eton and Christ Church, Oxford, he studied the piano, and wrote music criticism for the *Spectator* in 1924, and for the *New Statesman* (1926–7); with Desmond Shawe-Taylor, he edited *The Record Guide* (1951). His novels include *Piano Quintet* (1925); *The Ruin* (1926), a 'gothic novel' which he wrote while at Oxford; *The Sun in Capricorn* (1934) and *The Rescue* (1945). He wrote a book on De Quincey, *A Flame in Sunlight* (1936). *Inclinations* (1949) is a book of critical essays. [AR]

Sackville-West, Victoria (Mary) (1892–1962). Poet and novelist. Daughter of the 3rd Baron Sackville, she was born at Knole, the ancestral home of the family, in Kent, and educated there. In 1913 she married Harold ◊ Nicolson, then a diplomat, and they spent some years in Teheran, which resulted in her first book, *Poems of West and East* (1917), and later in a prose work, *Passenger to Teheran* (1926). She published several other books, poetry and novels, but she was known and appreciated only by a small audience – mostly composed of friends from the ◊ 'Bloomsbury group' – until 1927, when her long poem *The Land* won the Hawthornden Prize, and her work reached a larger public. Her best novels were *The Edwardians* (1930), about Knole, and *All Passion Spent* (1931), a study in old age. She knew Virginia Woolf well and, with her aristocratic family, was the model for the hero/heroine in *Orlando*. An affection, tending to obsession, for Knole and her ancestry (which can be seen in detail in her work of devotion *Knole and the Sackvilles*, 1922) limited her work, but it also gave her the subtlety and poise which are her greatest assets as a writer. Her other passion was for gardening, which she both practised, at Sissinghurst, her married home, and wrote about, in her poem *The*

Garden (1946) and as gardening correspondent of the *Observer* in the later years of her life. [JM]

Leonard Woolf, *Downhill All the Way* (1967).

Sadleir, Michael (1888–1957). Novelist and bibliographer. Born in Oxford, the son of Sir M. E. Sadleir, the educationist, he was educated at Rugby and Balliol College, Oxford. Sadleir worked in publishing with Constable and Co., of which firm he became a director; he was a member of the British delegation to the peace conference in 1919 and of the League of Nations secretariat. His interest in book collecting centred in 19th-century fiction at a time when that was an unexplored field. His vast and important collection is in the library of the University of California at Los Angeles, and his *Nineteenth Century Fiction: A Bibliographical Record* (2 vols., 1951) is a pioneering work. Sadleir wrote novels, as well as studies and biographical pieces, generally in less well-known 19th-century fields: among these are *Trollope* (*A Commentary*, 1927; *A Bibliography*, 1928) and *Bulwer: A Panorama* (1931). [AR]

Passages from the Autobiography of a Bibliomaniac (1962).

Saint-Denys-Garneau, Hector de (1912–43). French Canadian poet. Born in Montreal, he was the great-grandson of the 19th-century historian F.-X. Garneau. He spent his childhood on the family estate twenty-five miles north of Quebec city. Educated by the Jesuits in Montreal, he interrupted his studies on medical advice in 1934. A handsome, athletic youth, passionately interested in poetry, music and painting, he was surrounded by friends with some of whom he founded a review, *La Relève*, in 1934. However, an attack of rheumatism in 1928 had left him with a heart complaint which sparked off a series of psychological and religious crises. His *Journal* (published posthumously, 1954) follows closely this crisis from January 1935 to January 1939. Pages of moral introspection follow pages which relate his experience of music and art to general aesthetic theories about the artist's possession of reality, but these are complementary aspects of a very articulate treatment of the crisis of maturity. The adult world of responsibility demands a different courage from that which the child needs to explore and possess the world through his imagination. The last pages of the *Journal* are a meditation on the suicide of Mouchette, the stubborn and rebellious adolescent heroine of Georges Bernanos. Saint-Denys-Garneau envies this purification in death, 'the escape from any connivance with mediocrity' but there is evidence that he saw in suicide – and the total silence of the last four years of his life can be seen as a spiritual suicide – the other aspect of the suicide of Mouchette, an ultimate, desperate appeal to the grace of God. His *Poésies complètes* (1949) contain some nature poetry, but at their best are an eloquent if halting gloss, in tortured free verse, on his spiritual career. [CRPM]

'Le mauvais pauvre', presented by Albert Béguin, *Esprit* (September 1953).
Eva Kushner, *S.-D.-G.* (Poètes d'Aujourd'hui, Paris, 1967).

Saintsbury, George Edward Bateman (1845–1933). Journalist and literary critic. Born at Southampton, where his father was dock superintendent, he was educated at King's College School, London, and Merton College, Oxford, where he failed to gain a fellowship. He became a schoolmaster at Manchester Grammar School, in Guernsey and finally in Elgin. He began to write reviews for the *Academy* and in 1876 became a professional writer in London, where he was at first known for his work on French writers. In October 1875, he published an influential article on Baudelaire followed by 8 pieces on contemporary French novelists, many articles for the *Encyclopaedia Britannica* and several books, including *A Short History of French Literature* (1882; often reprinted and long used by British students). As a critic he remains known, if at all, for his writing on English literature. Beginning with a volume on *Dryden* (English Men of Letters, 1881), he began to publish voluminously. He produced a valuable re-editing of Scott's *Works of Dryden* (1882–93; only now being superseded) and wrote numberless essays which he later selected in *Essays in English Literature: 1780–1860* (1890) and *Miscellaneous Essays* (1892); he also edited and wrote introductions for many works. During this time he worked hard as a journalist on the *Daily News* and the *Manchester Guardian*; and contributed largely, with Andrew Lang and R. L. Stevenson, to W. E. ◊ Henley's *London* as well as to the *Pall Mall Gazette* and the *St James's Gazette*. From

1883 to 1894, he was assistant editor of the *Saturday Review*, the 'independent' Tory line of which (irresponsible and argumentative) was his own inclination. In September 1895, Saintsbury was appointed by the Secretary of State in Scotland to the chair of Rhetoric and English Literature at Edinburgh University and in time became an influential teacher. His years in the university produced his largest-scale works: his famous *Short History of English Literature* (1898; last reprinted 1960) was followed by a *History of Criticism and Literary Taste in Europe from the Earliest Texts to the Present Day* (3 vols., 1900–4), still valuable and in places a unique survey, and *Loci Critici* (1903), a supporting collection of passages which pioneered a kind of university teaching aid now highly developed. Another work in a field still neglected in English scholarship is the *History of English Prosody from the Twelfth Century* (3 vols., 1906–10) with an associated *Historical Manual of English Prosody* (1910) and *A History of English Prose Rhythm* (1912). His edition of *Minor Poets of the Caroline Period* (3 vols., 1905–21) is still valuable. As a straightforward 'historian' of English literature, he produced 4 volumes: *A History of Elizabethan Literature* (1887), *The Flourishing of Romance and the Rise of Allegory* (1897), *The Earlier Renaissance* (1901) and *The Later Nineteenth Century* (1907). He also wrote books on individual writers, such as *Scott* (1897) and *Arnold* (1899), and continued his editorial work. He contributed 21 chapters to the *Cambridge History of English Literature* (1907–16) and celebrated his retirement from his chair by *The Peace of the Augustans: A Survey of Eighteenth Century Literature as a Place of Rest and Refreshment* (1916; World's Classics, 1946). Saintsbury had read everything, so that his taste (that of the time) for narrative history of 'trends' and developments in writing is based on enormous knowledge. He had no real critical theory; his critical values were rooted in a perception of style (not really form) rather than subject. As a romantic, personal 'taster' of literature he was a strong influence on the conversational style of English criticism and as such is now out of favour. His own writing is best in essays, where eccentricity of manner and excessive parenthesis add amusement to his often original and suggestive insights. He remains a monument of Victorian taste and diligence, and portions of his work are useful. Saintsbury has a second reputation as a wine-taster and ritualist: his *Notes on a Cellarbook* (1920) has never lacked readers. [A R]

Scrapbooks (3 vols., 1922–4)(reminiscences); *G.S. The Memorial Volume* and *G.S. The Last Vintage*, ed. A. Muir, J. W. Oliver and A. M. Clark (1945; 1950) (essays).
D N B (entry by his pupil D. Nichol Smith); A. B. Webster, *G.S.* (1934); R. Wellek, 'S.', *English Miscellany*, 12 (1961).

Saki. ◊ Munro, Hector Hugh.

Salesbury, William (*c.* 1520–84). Welsh scholar and man of letters. Notable for his immense learning and contributions to Welsh prose. Born at Llansannan (Denbighshire) of a gentry family and educated at Oxford, he spent most of his life at Plas Isa, Llanrwst. He was a typical example of the Renaissance scholar and gentleman. His works include a dictionary of English and Welsh (1547), a collection of Welsh proverbs (1547) and a herbal (composed between 1568 and 1574). He was well versed in the traditional Welsh learning and scholarship of the classical poets and wished to make this more readily available to the outside world. His chief service, however, was in the translation of the Welsh Bible. In 1551 he published a translation of the Church Communion Service. In 1563 he was invited to assist Richard Davies, Bishop of St Davids, to translate the whole Bible and Book of Common Prayer. The New Testament and Prayer Book were published in 1567, and Salesbury must be credited with the larger part of the work. His collaboration with Davies on the Old Testament came to an abrupt end, and it was left for William Morgan to publish a translation of the whole Bible in 1588. Salesbury was a rather pedantic scholar and was obsessed with the debt of Welsh to Latin. His translations were rightly criticized at the time because of their orthographical peculiarities (*eccles* instead of *eglwys* because of Latin *ecclesia*, etc.). But this is a minor blemish compared with the very real qualities of his prose, and it is certain that Salesbury laid the foundations on which Morgan was later to build. These translations provided a standard of written Welsh of paramount benefit to the preservation of the language, and were to be a source of inspiration and example for literary style for four centuries. [M R]

A Dictionary in Englyshe and Welshe (1547; 1877); Oll Synnwyr pen Kembero ygyd (1547; 1902); Kynniver Llith a ban (1551; ed. J. Fisher, 1931); Testament Newydd (1567; 2nd edn, 1850), Lliver gweddi gyffredin (1567; new edn, M. Richards and G. Williams, 1953, 1965).
D. R. Thomas, Life and Work of Bishop Davies and W.S. (1902); Isaac Thomas, W.S. and His Testament (1967).

Salkey, Andrew (1928–). West Indian novelist. Born in Panama of Jamaican parents, he was sent to Jamaica for secondary education and came to London in 1951. He taught English in a London comprehensive school and began freelance broadcasting on 'Caribbean Voices'. The award of a Poetry Prize in 1956 for his *Jamaican Symphony* encouraged him to make a career of writing. In 1959 he resigned his teaching post and published his first novel. *A Quality of Violence* is a historical novel of Jamaican peasants in 1900, their existence threatened by drought and their Christianity confused by voodoo Pocomania. *Escape to an Autumn Pavement* (1960) describes a middle-class Jamaican immigrant's attempt to resolve his perplexed sexuality. Both novels are distinguished by an expert control of prose movement. The narrative of the first, infused with Jamaican dialect, attains a quiet, lyrical dignity. The cosmopolitan London milieu of the second is described in the first person, in staccato, idiomatic prose, coloured by Caribbean rhythms, which moves into measured restraint as the protagonist's mind and problems approach resolution. *The Late Emancipation of Jerry Stover* (1968) returns to Jamaica. *The Adventures of Catullus Kelly* (1969) is a humorous novel concerning a Jamaican immigrant's predicament in London. Salkey edited and introduced *West Indian Stories* (1960), an important first collection in England. He has also written books for children. [WAG]

Sansom, William (1912–). Novelist and short-story writer. Born in Dulwich, and educated at Uppingham School. His first published works were short stories which were collected under the title *Fireman Flower* (1944). These are stories of strange Kafka-like power, and individual tone. *The Body* (1949) was Sansom's first novel. He is adept at creating an atmosphere of unease, and at implying the not easily described malaise of his characters. Underneath a sometimes comical surface, the lives he describes are those lived in quiet desperation. At the same time, Sansom is an accomplished travel writer. The deliberately jaded tone of much of his fiction has not affected the freshness of approach or the lively imagery of the best of his travel books, such as *The Icicle and the Sun* (1958). *Goodbye* (1966), in which he depicts a disintegrating relationship, is the most powerful of his more recent novels. [CO]

A Bed of Roses (1954); Among the Dahlias (1957); The Last Hours of Sandra Lee (1961).

Sargeson, Frank (1903–). New Zealand short-story writer and novelist. Born in Hamilton, he qualified and practised as a solicitor in Auckland where he has also been a Civil Servant and a market gardener. During the depression years of the thirties his radical sympathies found expression in sketches contributed to *Tomorrow* and collected as *Conversations with My Uncle* (1936).

Sargeson's dislike of bourgeois values is sometimes presented in the guise of a boy's revolt against a respectable background. *I Saw in My Dream* (1949) lengthens a story on this theme into a novel. The postlude of revolt is acquaintance with the hand-to-mouth proletariat whose pared-down existence Sargeson describes with colloquial realism in numerous stories. He makes skilled use of the artless monologue, which concentrates as much on the narrator as his narration, in such stories as the title-piece of *That Summer* (1946). He has also written a fine short novel, *I For One* (1954), in which comedy and hostile suburban realism are ironically united. [PT]

Collected Stories (1965).
Ed. H. Shaw, The Puritan and the Waif (1955); H. Winston Rhodes, 'The Moral Climate of S.'s Stories', Landfall, 33 (March 1955).

Sassoon, Siegfried (1886–1967). Poet, autobiographer and biographer of Meredith. His father was a member of a distinguished Sephardic Jewish family, which was to make its mark in English politics and finance, but his mother, a sister of Sir Hamo Thorneycroft, the famous Victorian sculptor, separated from her husband and the young Sassoon was brought up as an English country gentleman. There is no sign of influence from his paternal ancestry either in his poetry or his prose. He was educated at Marlborough Grammar School and then went to Clare College, Cambridge, of which he became an Honorary Fellow, but from which he was sent down without taking a degree, being more interested in tennis, hunting and writing poetry than in academic studies. In the years before the war his interests were divided between country sports, particularly hunting, and a rather solitary life in London, meeting men of letters, and publishing small pamphlets of poetry. His uncle's friendship with Sir Edmund ◊ Gosse gave him an *entrée* into London literary circles, and there is a vivid account in his memoirs of such characters as Robbie Ross and T. W. H. Crosland. At the outbreak of the First World War, he enlisted and was sent abroad as a second lieutenant. He served gallantly, being wounded twice, and winning the M.C. His humane reaction against the monotony and horror of trench warfare was the making of him as a poet. Wounded in 1917, and invalided home, he decided, as a protest against the inhumanity of war, to announce publicly his refusal to serve again. He expected to be court-martialled, but instead was sent to a sanatorium, reconsidered his decision and was posted to Palestine and then went back to France again, where he was wounded once more, and ended up the war as a captain. After the war, he flung himself into Labour Party politics, assisting Philip Snowden in his election campaign and writing literary columns for the *Daily Herald*. He also went on a lecture tour in America, giving frank accounts of the horrors of trench warfare.

In the end, however, his fondness for country life proved deeper and stronger than his political enthusiasms. In 1928 he published anonymously his *Memoirs of a Fox-Hunting Man*, an account of his upbringing and early war experiences in a thinly disguised fictitious form. It won the James Tait Black and Hawthornden Prizes and with its successor, *Memoirs of an Infantry Officer*, is probably the classic personal account of the First World War in English, better proportioned and more carefully worked than Robert ◊ Graves's *Good-Bye to All That*, less subjective than Edmund ◊ Blunden's *Undertones of War*. The memoirs of George Sherston were completed in 1936 in *Sherston's Progress* and later Sassoon filled in gaps and completed his personal story in 3 memoirs written with Sassoon, not Sherston, as the hero, *The Old Century and Seven More Years, The Weald of Youth* and *Siegfried's Journey, 1916–1920*. Sassoon continued to write

poems, growingly religious in feeling (he was a Roman Catholic convert), but, sensitive and true in feeling though these are, the poems by which he will be remembered are those shocked into existence by the First World War; and he is probably a greater master of prose, a prose suffused with poetic feeling and insight, but never crudely 'poetical', than of verse. [GSF]

The Old Huntsman (1917); *Counterattack* (1918); *Satirical Poems* (1926); *Vigils* (1930); *The Old Century and Seven More Years* (1938); *Rhymed Ruminations* (1940); *Collected Poems* (1947); *Meredith: A Biography* (1948); *Sequences* (1956); *Collected Poems, 1908–1956* (1961). Edmund Blunden, *War Poets 1914–18* (1958); D. J. Enright, 'The Literature of the First World War', in *The Modern Age* (Penguin Companion to English Literature, 7, 1961); Edmund Blunden, 'S. S.'s Poetry', in *E. Blunden: A Selection of His Poetry and Prose*, ed. K. Hopkins (1950) (first published in *The Mind's Eye*, 1934); Michael Thorpe, *S.S.* (1966).

Saunders Lewis, John. ◊ Lewis, John Saunders.

Savage, Richard (*c.* 1696–1742). Poet. According to his own account, the bastard son of Earl Rivers and the Countess of Macclesfield, though modern investigation has shown more or less conclusively that he was of humble birth. Savage, however, made a career of being rejected by his 'mother', 'father', patrons and society. Johnson, in his younger days, was an intimate of the bohemian Savage, and wrote a long life of him (1744, and in *Lives of the Poets*), discussing his problems of personality with the greatest humanity and penetration. According to Johnson, Savage had remarkable powers of intellect, memory, strong feelings and wide experience of life, but his performances seem to the modern reader in general second-rate, with only a few rather striking passages. He is best known for a comedy, *Love in a Veil* (1718); a tragedy, *Sir Thomas Overbury* (1723); and 2 long satirico-reflective poems, *The Wanderer* (1729) and *The Bastard* (1728). The latter contains the often-quoted line 'No tenth transmitter of a foolish face'. Savage was found guilty of the murder of a man in a tavern brawl (1727), but pardoned. He died in a debtors' prison in Bristol, having outlasted many attempts to help him. [AR]

C. Tracy, *The Artificial Bastard* (1953).

Sayers, Dorothy L(eigh) (1893–1957). Novelist and playwright. Born in Oxford and educated at Somerville College, she was one of the first women to get an Oxford degree. Her first novels are detective stories of an unusual kind. They are scrupulously well written and generously littered with classical quotation, and their detective, Lord Peter Wimsey, is both erudite and aristocratic. He was modelled on an Oxford don of the author's acquaintance. *Whose Body?* (1923), *Clouds of Witness* (1926) and *Strong Poison* (1930) are among the most popular of the early volumes. *Murder Must Advertise*(1933) makes use of the author's experience as a copy writer in an advertising agency. *The Nine Tailors* (1934) was followed by *Gaudy Night* (1935), which has a background of Oxford academic life, and *Busman's Honeymoon* (1937), which, in collaboration with M. St Clare Byrne, she later turned into a play.

Her original plays are not thrillers, but religious works. She was a devout Christian, and concerned with propagating a specifically Christian drama. *The Zeal of Thy House* (1937), a verse play, was written for production at Canterbury. It has sensitivity of expression, and a fine dramatic sweep. Other religious plays include *The Devil to Pay* (1939) and *Just Vengeance* (1946). Her sequence of plays for radio, *The Man Born to be King* (1941), was considered controversial at the time, but reads now as pious but not unlively religious drama.

Dorothy L. Sayers's early training was as a medieval linguist, and she wrote a number of critical essays on medieval literature, as well as the Penguin Classics translation of Dante's *Divine Comedy: Hell* (1949), *Purgatory* (1955), *Paradise* (completed by Barbara Reynolds, 1962). Her religious views were expressed in a collection of essays and addresses, *Creed or Chaos?* (1940), in which she defined Christianity as a religion for adult minds. [CO]

Scarfe, Francis (Harold) (1911–   ). Poet, novelist and translator. Born at South Shields, County Durham, he was educated at the Royal Merchant Seamen's Orphanage (his father was lost at sea) and at the universities of Durham, Cambridge and Paris. He taught French at Trinity College, Cambridge, and the University of Glasgow (senior lecturer 1947–59), and has been Professor of French in the University of London since 1965. During the Second World War, he served in the army and became a colonel in the Education Corps. He was a director of the British Institute in Paris from 1959. His poetry appeared in *Inscapes* (1940), *Poems and Ballads* (1941) and *Underworlds* (1950). His works of criticism include *Auden and After* (1942), *W. H. Auden* (1949) and *The Art of Paul Valéry* (1954). Some translations from the French appear in his *Reflections on the World To-day* (1951); and he has edited *Baudelaire* (Penguin Poets, 1961) and *Chénier* (1961). His novels are *Promises* (1950), *Single Blessedness* (1951) and *Unfinished Woman* (1954). [AR]

Schreiner, Olive (Emilie Albertina) (1855–1920). South African novelist. Born in Cape Colony. After several years as a governess, she went to England in 1881 with the manuscript of *The Story of an African Farm*, which she published in 1883 under the pseudonym 'Ralph Iron'. Schreiner returned to South Africa in 1889, and in 1894 married Samuel Cronwright, a politician. Her own interest in politics, especially in the place of women in society, was expressed in such tracts as *Woman and Labour* (1911). A second novel, *Trooper Peter Halket of Mashonaland* (1897), was widely attacked for its criticism of early Rhodesian settlers. An unfinished novel, on which she worked intermittently for many years, was published posthumously as *From Man to Man* (1926).

The Story of an African Farm is confessionally uninhibited. There is sadism and sentimentality in its description of the lives of the occupants, particularly the children, of a remote ostrich farm in the veld. Schreiner is apt to preach free-thinking sermons when revolt is already embodied in the action, but this is a result of the passion that is the novel's greatest quality. It is dense with a dream-occultism and an almost sacrificial plea for the emancipation of woman's soul. Despite the splendour of its descriptive passages, its vision is obsessively gloomy. [PT]

Letters, 1876–1920, ed. S. C. Cronwright-Schreiner (1924).
D. L. Hobman, *O.S.* (1955); M. V. Friedmann, *O.S.: A Study in Latent Meanings* (1954).

Scott, Alexander (1525?–1584?). Scottish poet. The best of the Scottish school of courtly lyric poets which succeeded ◊Dunbar, ◊ Douglas and ◊ Lindsay in the later

16th century. Little is known of Scott's life; trained in law and skilled in music, he probably lived in Edinburgh. His 36 short poems are preserved in the manuscript of George ◊ Bannatyne. Many of his poems are trivial songs about unsuccessful love, in the 'true – rue – pursue – adieu' tradition of so much of ◊ Wyatt's poetry. Like Wyatt, however, Scott sometimes attains a real depth of feeling and energy of expression, particularly in the poems 'Up, helsum hairt', 'Return thee, hairt, hamewart agane' and 'To luve unluvit it is ane pane'; and like Wyatt, Scott translated some of the psalms and wrote moral 'satires', of which his best is 'Ane New Yeir Gift to the Quene' (1562). In 'The Slicht Remeid of Luve' and several other poems Scott voices a cold cynicism absent in Wyatt; it recalls Dunbar's 'Tua Mariit Wemen and the Wedo' and may reflect the coarser civilization of the insecure Scottish court. [AI]

The Poems, ed. J. Cranstoun (STS, 1896); *The Poems*, ed. A. K. Donald, (EETS, 1902); *The Poems*, ed. A. Scott (1952).
H. M. Shire, *Song Dance and Poetry of the Court of Scotland under King James VI* (1969).

Scott, Duncan (Campbell) (1862–1947). Canadian poet and short-story writer. The son of a Methodist minister, he spent his boyhood in various towns in Ontario and Quebec, acquiring a lasting interest in music and painting. In 1879 he joined the Department of Indian Affairs in Ottawa – his interest in the Canadian Indians is evident in his work. For the last eighteen of his fifty-two years in this department he was its administrative head. ◊ Lampman encouraged him to write, and his first book, *The Magic House*, was published in 1893. *In the Village of the Viger*, the first of 2 short-story collections, followed in 1896. A further 7 volumes of verse were published in his lifetime. *The Green Cloister* (1935) followed his retirement and includes many poems inspired by his travels with his second wife in Europe. *Selected Poems* was published in 1951.

Apart from occasional dramatic and humorous pieces, Scott's poetry is of three kinds. His descriptive verse is often sumptuous but always accurate. His ballads, like his stories, recount sensational events in poignantly unemphatic language. Sometimes, as in 'The Piper of Arll', he uses the emotiveness of lyric diction to draw

narrative towards fantasy. It is in these poems with their simultaneity of passion and restraint that he is at his best. [PT]

D. Pacey, *Ten Canadian Poets* (1958); A. J. M. Smith, 'D.C.S.', in *Our Living Tradition* (Series 2 and 3, 1959, ed. R. McDougall).

Scott, Francis Reginald (1899–). Canadian poet. Born in Quebec. His father was a clergyman and minor poet. Scott was an Oxford Rhodes Scholar (1920–3), but his interest in poetry was not confirmed until his meeting with A. J. M. ◊ Smith at McGill University. Together they edited the short-lived *McGill Fortnightly Review* (1925–6). Scott has been both an academic and a practising lawyer, has been concerned, actively and as a writer, with national Socialism and international affairs, has been closely associated with many Canadian literary ventures, and has helped to compile 2 important anthologies, *New Provinces* (1936) and the satirical collection *The Blasted Pine* (1957). Both politically and poetically he has aimed to discredit Canadian shibboleths.

Wit is the distinguishing mark of his best poetry. *Overture* (1945) contains pungent, unadorned social and satirical poems and clear-cut lyrics of nature and love. *Events and Signals* (1954) has a greater generosity of technique and less anger, but in *The Eye of a Needle* (1957) Scott collects and augments his satirical work. He and his wife, the painter Marian Scott, have had an important influence on the growth of experiment in Canadian arts. [PT]

D. Pacey, *Ten Canadian Poets* (1958).

Scott, Sir Walter (1771–1832). Scottish novelist, ballad-collector, poet, critic and man of letters. The son of an Edinburgh lawyer, educated at the High School and University of Edinburgh, and practising there as an advocate from 1792 to 1806, Scott passed his formative years in the lull between the generation of David ◊ Hume and the reign of Francis ◊ Jeffrey and the *Edinburgh Review*. His family roots were in the Borders, where, weakened by infantile paralysis that left him lame for life, he spent many convalescent months at Kelso, assimilating oral tradition from relatives and servants and meeting as schoolmates the Ballantyne brothers, who later managed printing and publishing businesses for which Scott provided both capital and literary material. In the 1790s Scott translated German Romantic dramas and travelled in the Highlands, conceiving a passionate love for a girl who preferred to marry a rising banker – an experience which perhaps left its mark on his novels. Within a year he married someone else. From 1799 until his death he was Sheriff of Selkirkshire and from 1806 to 1830 he held another well-paid office as a Clerk to the Court of Session. The procedures of Scots law and characters and incidents from the courts of course recur in the novels, and his territorial title may have fanned the expensive ambition to live as a landed magnate at Abbotsford (purchased 1811) that contributed to his ruin when, in 1826, the Ballantynes and other firms in which Scott was concerned proved to have insufficient reserves to meet a financial crisis. As is well known Scott spent the close of his life working at an extraordinary pace to repay his creditors, who were paid in full by the posthumous sale of his copyrights. He had been created baronet in 1820, and in 1822 had acted as master of ceremonies for George IV's state visit to Scotland – the occasion on which the kilted Highland piper supplanted the frugal Lowland peasant and the hungry émigré intellectual as the national stereotype. Scott's personal qualities and traits are recorded in the biography by his son-in-law J. G. ◊ Lockhart and revealed in his *Letters* (12 vols., ed. H. J. C. Grierson and others, 1932–7) and in his *Journal* (ed. J. G. Tait and W. M. Parker, 1950).

In his first important work, *The Minstrelsy of the Scottish Border* (1802–3; ed. T. F. Henderson, 1902), Scott collated, adapted and arranged ballad versions obtained from peasant recitation by James ◊ Hogg and other helpers or from existing collections such as those of David ◊ Herd and Bishop ◊ Percy. The authenticity of Scott's texts has been questioned; almost certainly Scott rearranged, conflated and 'improved' his texts to some extent, but he was not interested in forging texts and he carefully checked the authenticity of those sent in to him. Since there is no definitive text of a folk-ballad his improvements are acceptable as activity just within the limits of the folk tradition. Thereafter Scott edited important editions of Dryden (1808) and Swift (1814) and many minor works; he contributed to the *Edinburgh Review* and helped to launch the rival Tory *Quarterly* (1809). His Romantic narrative poems set in the past of his be-

loved Borders (*The Lay of the Last Minstrel*, 1805; *Marmion*, 1808) and in the Highlands (*The Lady of the Lake*, 1810) were very successful commercially, but Byron soon offered more titillating material to the public that Scott had created and in 1813 the Ballantynes burned their fingers by advancing Scott £3,000 for the comparatively unsuccessful *Rokeby*. These poems lingered into 20th-century schoolrooms but are little read today (although D. Davie makes a case for them in *Proceedings of the British Academy*, XLVII, 1961). The lyrics that keep up Scott's reputation as a poet were dramatically conceived for their original settings in these narrative poems or in the novels, and may lose a dimension when anthologized out of context. The Waverley novels – initially anonymous, perhaps because of gentlemanly embarrassment (not confined to Scott) about writing fiction for the market, although the prolonged mystification over the identity of the Great Unknown was 'good publicity' even after its acknowledgement in 1827 – start with *Waverley*, begun in 1805 and twice abandoned for more obviously marketable work. It went through 4 editions in the year of publication, 1814. Its successors were unprecedentedly (though not invariably) successful; Scott played various publishers off against one another for the later Scottish novels, tapping a new and inferior vein with *Ivanhoe* (1819) and the later romances. The still weaker fiction produced after the 1826 disaster coincides with a return to more general authorship with a *Life of Napoleon Buonaparte* (1827), the child's history of Scotland, *Tales of a Grandfather* (1828–30) and *Letters on Demonology and Witchcraft* (1830).

The 'medieval' romances, in which Scott's Romantic awareness of the particularity of the past comes out in details of furniture, accoutrements, ceremonial and archaic speech, are antiquarian rather than historical. The Scottish novels set in the century before Scott's birth reveal an awareness of social and political change as a process entailing gain and loss; Scott concentrates on the tragic irrelevance of the older 'heroic' qualities as civilization becomes increasingly prosperous, secure and orderly. Hence the predicaments of Bradwardine in *Waverley*, of Rob Roy (1818) and of the fanatical Jacobite Redgauntlet (1824) when the Government emissary urbanely announces that the conspirators are free men – provided they disperse at once to their homes. Interest on this level, discussed without examination of Scott's local realization of his material, may seem rather generalized and mechanical; Scott transcends this type of 'historical' conflict when he presents, in *The Heart of Midlothian* (1818), Jeanie Deans's rejection of the chance to save her sister's life by giving perjured evidence, but even here Jeanie's more inward and personal predicament, seen as part of the moral life of a community and its codes, is firmly set in a historical dialectic. Scott fathered, in one sense or another, the Scots novels of ◊ Galt, ◊ Hogg and ◊ Lockhart, and is responsible for the Victorian tradition of vulgarized historical romance that runs down through ◊ Ainsworth and Charles ◊ Reade. The handling of social process in his novels apparently influenced Cooper, and Pushkin acknowledges direct debts to Scott. He never attained Jane Austen's subtlety in the handling of relationships and situations however, and despite striking particular debts (in *Barnaby Rudge*, *Wuthering Heights*, *Adam Bede*) the great Victorian novelists really owed little to him. As a writer of picturesque novels of chivalry and romance he remained popular, if not influential, until the end of the 19th century; thereafter his reputation outside Scotland declined. Recently Scott's historical grasp and the particular richness of the 'Scotch novels' – *Waverley*, *Old Mortality*, *The Heart of Midlothian*, among others – have again been acknowledged by serious critical attention. [AI]

J. C. Corson, *A Bibliography of Sir W. S.* (1943); H. J. C. Grierson, *Sir W.S., Bart. A New Life Supplementary to and Corrective of Lockhart's Biography* (1938); J. T. Hillhouse, *The Waverley Novels and Their Critics* (1936); G. Lukacs, *The Historical Novel* (1962); A Welsh, *The Hero of the Waverley Novels* (1963); T. Crawford, *S.* (1965); F. R. Hart, *S.'s Novels* (U. of Virginia P., 1966); A. O. J. Cockshut, *The Achievement of W.S.* (1969); *W.S.*, ed. D. Devlin (1968); *S.'s Mind and Art: Essays Old and New*, ed. A. N. Jeffares (1969); Edgar Johnson, *W.S.: The Great Unknown* (1970).

'Scrutiny'. A literary quarterly review published in Cambridge 1932–53 and edited by L. C. ◊ Knights, F. R. ◊ Leavis and others, but always dominated by Leavis's critical programme. Leavis was from the outset dedicated to the restoration of true critical standards in literature. The tone of the magazine was always astringent and often belligerent. It took sharp issue with both the academic and the more popular 'middle-brow' critical assessments of its day and concentrated on (successfully) advancing the claims of certain writers to greatness, notably George Eliot and D. H. Lawrence. Although often caustic and embattled in tone, *Scrutiny* was a venture of the highest critical courage and importance, and it is essential to any deep comprehension of the literary ideas of its time. It has left a permanent mark on literary criticism on both sides of the Atlantic. It was republished complete in 20 volumes in 1963 with an essay by Dr Leavis. [RB]

Seafarer, The. ◊ Old English Poetry.

Sedley, Sir Charles (1639?–1701). Poet and wit. One of the dissolute band of Restoration courtiers which included Sackville, Earl of ◊ Dorset. Sedley was the chief of the three rakes who showed their aristocratic contempt for the 'mob' by exhibiting themselves in indecent postures after an orgy at the Cock in Covent Garden, and were nearly lynched by the burghers. He was the author (or part author) of 2 feeble tragedies, and 3 comedies, of which the best are *Bellamira* (1687), taken from Terence, and *The Mulberry Garden* (1668), based on Molière's *L'école des maris*. He also wrote some satirical poems and prose, but was most successful with gay love-poems. [AR]

The Poetical and Dramatic Works, ed. V. de Sola Pinto (2 vols., 1928).
V. de Sola Pinto, *Sir C.S.* (1927).

Seeley, Sir John Robert (1834–95). Historian and publicist. Born in London, the son of a publisher, and educated at the City of London School and Christ's College, Cambridge, where he was a fellow student of Walter Besant. He was Professor of Latin at University College, London (1863–9), and Professor of Modern History at Cambridge from 1869. Seeley was really interested in ethics, and his literary and historical works are designed to further this study (as in his London inaugural lecture, *Classical Studies as an Introduction to the Moral Sciences*, 1864). In 1866, his anonymous life of Christ, *Ecce Homo*, caused much controversy (5 edns in 1866; 1895; Everyman, 1908). Seeley was a strong proponent of Christian ethical teaching, and his historical works are written to advance that view by demonstrating what he considered the inevitability of British assumption of imperial power for Christian, ethical reasons ('the White Man's Burden'). Thus he saw the past, in rather an old-fashioned way, as full of 'lessons', and considered his educational work as a historian to be that, partly, of training statesmen (one of the purposes indeed behind the founding in the 18th century of the chair he held at Cambridge). His chief works were *The Expansion of England in the Eighteenth Century* (1883), *The Life and Times of Stein* (an architect of the rise of Prussia) (1878) and *The Growth of British Policy* (1895). German scholars of the 1930s were much interested in Seeley's imperialist ideas. [AR]

J. Gazeau, *L'impérialisme anglais, son évolution*; *Carlyle, S., Chamberlain* (Paris, 1903); B. E. Lippincott, *Victorian Critics of Democracy* (1938); H. G. Powell, 'Ecce Homo: The Historical Jesus in 1865', *London Quarterly*, 191 (1966).

Selden, John (1584–1654). Scholar and jurist. Born at Salvington, Sussex, Selden matriculated at Hart Hall, Oxford, in 1600, and after a brief period at Clifford Inn entered the Inner Temple in 1604. He was called to the bar in 1612, and from 1623 onwards was many times a Member of Parliament, becoming deeply involved in affairs of state before and during the Civil War, in which he supported the Parliamentary party. He associated with many poets of the day, notably Ben Jonson, and provided notes for the first 18 cantos of ◊ Drayton's *Polyolbion*, the first part of which was published in 1612. Only one of Selden's many works, however, is of interest to literary students. This, *Table Talk*, first published in 1689, is not in fact the product of his pen but a collection of his spoken opinions on many subjects made over the last twenty years of his life by his secretary, Richard Milward. *Table Talk* is free of the difficulty of style for which Selden is known in his other work, and is an indication that he spoke more directly than he wrote. [DELC]

Opera omnia, ed. D. Wilkins (3 vols., 1725); *The Table Talk of J.S.*, ed. F. Pollock (Selden Society, 1927).
A. W. Ward, *CHEL*, VIII (1912).

Selvon, Samuel (1924–   ). West Indian novelist. Born in a Trinidad village, he received a secondary education, served as a telegraphist on a minesweeper (1941–6) and entered journalism after the war, submitting poems and short stories to West Indian magazines and to the B.B.C.'s 'Caribbean Voices'. He went to England in 1950, with the manuscript of his first novel almost completed, and worked for the B.B.C. and as a freelance journalist. *A Brighter Sun* (1952) presents the prejudices and mutual distrust of the unintegrated Negro and Indian communities in Trinidad. Selvon's Indian background is again behind *An Island is a World* (1955), written after his recovery from a serious illness, in which he portrays the drawing of Indian peasants into complex urban life. *The Lonely Londoners* (1956) describes the West Indian community in London. The short stories of *Ways of Sunlight* (1957) range in setting from rural Trinidad to urban Britain. *Turn again Tiger* (1958) is a sequel to his first novel.

Selvon's genius is comic, but it reveals itself in sympathetic humour rather than detached irony. A master of stylized Trinidad dialect, he retains the dialect influence on prose rhythm and syntax in conventional narrative, where it gives his work the vigour of improvisation. *I Hear Thunder* (1963) takes as the starting point of a high-spirited investigation of Trinidad's pleasures, the return of an English-trained doctor with a white wife to his native island. *The Housing Lark* (1965) is another novel about immigrants in London. [WAG]

Sempill, Francis (*c*.1625–82). Scots poet. Son of Robert ◊ Sempill (1595?–1665?). Contact with Cromwellian officers in Glasgow led to his early recognition in England and to the appearance of some of his songs in Restoration anthologies. Sempill spent his mature years, however, trying to restore the family fortunes exhausted during the Civil Wars; he became Sheriff-Depute of Renfrewshire before 1677 and took part in action against the Covenanters. His best poem, 'The Banishment of Poverty', is an allegorical description of his struggles and an expression of gratitude to the Duke of Albany (later James II), who had saved him from his creditors. [AI]

The Poems of the Sempills of Beltrees, ed. J. Paterson (1849).
D. Craig, *Scottish Literature and the Scottish People* (1961); *DNB*.

Sempill, Sir James (1566–1625). Scottish Reformation controversialist. Sempill was educated, with James VI, by George

Buchanan, and later attended St Andrews University. He assisted James in writing the *Basilicon Doron* (1595) and was employed as James's ambassador in London and later in Paris. He defended Calvinism and Presbyterianism in pamphlets in Latin and English, and wrote *The Packman's Paternoster*, an anti-Roman Catholic satire in English which was later augmented and published by his son Robert ◊ Sempill (1595?–1665?). [AI]

DNB.

Sempill, Robert (1530?–95). Scottish Reformation satirist. Sempill was present at the siege of Leith (1559–60) and while at Paris escaped the massacre of St Bartholomew (1572). In the 1570s and 1580s he circulated vigorous, though violent and brutal, broadsheets attacking Queen Mary, Bothwell and their supporters; these are reprinted in *The Sempill Ballates* (ed. T. G. Stevenson, 1872), and in *Satirical Poems of the Time of the Reformation* (ed. J. Cranstoun, STS, 2 vols., 1891–3). There is no proven connexion between this writer and the other Sempills of the same period. [AI]

DNB.

Sempill, Robert (1595?–1665?). Scots poet. Educated at Glasgow University, Sempill apparently lived on his estate in Renfrewshire; he fought on the side of Charles I and was active in promoting the Restoration. He is remembered for 'The Life and Death of the Piper of Kilbarchan, or The Epitaph of Habbie Simpson', a burlesque elegy on a village piper which supplied the tone and form for much later Scots verse. Allan ◊ Ramsay's elegies are direct imitations, and the stanza, used elsewhere by Ramsay and by Robert ◊ Fergusson, is the 5-lined 'wheel-and-bob' verse regularly and characteristically used by Robert Burns. Other popular Scots poems have been inconclusively attributed to Sempill, whose only other known work is the revision and perhaps publication of *The Packman's Paternoster* by his father Sir James ◊ Sempill (printed by 1669). [AI]

The Poems of the Sempills of Beltrees, ed. J. Paterson (1849).
DNB.

Service, Robert William (1874–1958). Canadian poet. Born in Preston and brought up in Glasgow, he worked for a Scottish bank before emigrating to Canada. After taking various jobs along the Pacific coast, he returned to banking in 1905 and spent eight years in the Yukon. The impact of this 'man's country' conditioned his verse. He travelled extensively outside and inside Canada. *Collected Verse* (1960) consists largely of ballads spiced with rhyme, melodrama and sentimentality, and lyrics of homely piety. Service is aggressively muscular and self-consciously anti-intellectual. He boasted that he made poetry pay. [PT]

Ploughman of the Moon (1945) and *Harper of Heaven* (1948) (autobiographies).

Settle, Elkanah (1648–1724). Dramatist. A prolific author of tragedy in the ranting, heroic Restoration style, he had a great success in 1673 with his *The Empress of Morocco* and was critically attacked by John Dryden. He replied by attacking *The Conquest of Granada*, and he is now remembered only as the satirized Doeg in *Absalom and Achitophel*. [MJ]

F. C. Brown, *E.S.* (Chicago, 1910); A. Nicoll, *British Drama* (revised edn, 1962) and *A History of English Drama, 1660–1900*, ii (revised edn, 1952); J. Sutherland, *English Literature in the Late Seventeenth Century* (1969).

Seward, Anna (1747–1809). Poet and letter-writer. The centre of a provincial literary coterie in Lichfield which included Erasmus ◊ Darwin. As her literary editor, Walter Scott published her dull poems with a memoir (1810). She kept up literary correspondences and her *Letters*, which she frequently re-wrote for publication, appeared in 1811. She was not an admirer of Dr Johnson's but frequently met him and knew the local tradition about him. Boswell used her as an informant. [AR]

M. Ashmun, *The Singing Swan* (Yale U.P., 1931); S. Mont, 'S. and the Romantic Poets', in *Studies in Honor of G. M. Harper* (Princeton U.P., 1939).

Shadwell, Thomas (c. 1642–92). Dramatist. Educated at Cambridge, and a member of the Middle Temple, he scored his first success in the theatre in 1668 with *The Sullen Lovers* and contributed a play to almost every season for the next fourteen years. A disciple of Ben Jonson's he revived the comedy of humours, but also wrote pastoral, tragedy and opera, including *The Enchanted Island*, an adaptation of *The Tempest*. His best work was in comedy and included *The Humorists* (1670), *Epsom Wells* (1672), *The Virtuoso* (1676) and *Bury Fair* (1689). All are vigorous plays of Restoration life with a gallery of eccentric, humorous characters and a love-plot typical of the times. It is unjust that he is only remembered now as MacFlecknoe, the butt of Dryden's wit. Their quarrel was political as well as literary, and their exchange of satires included his *The Medal of John Bayes* and Dryden's *MacFlecknoe*. When the Whigs triumphed in 1688, he succeeded Dryden as Poet Laureate. [MJ]

Complete Works, ed. Montague Summers (5 vols., 1927).
A. S. Borgman, *T.S.* (New York, 1928).

Shaffer, Peter (1926–). Dramatist. Educated at St Paul's and Trinity College, Cambridge, he has worked in music publishing and book-reviewing. His well-constructed domestic drama, *Five-Finger Exercise*, was directed by Sir John Gielgud (London, 1958; New York, 1960), and established Shaffer's reputation as a playwright. It was followed by a double-bill, *The Private Ear* and *The Public Eye* (London, 1962; New York, 1963). *The Royal Hunt of the Sun*, an ambitious and spectacular entertainment on the conquest of Peru, was successfully produced by the National Theatre in 1964, and in the following year the company staged his farcically adroit and amusing after-piece *Black Comedy*. Shaffer has won awards for the best new play of the season both in London and in New York, and has written television-plays and the script of a Joan Littlewood pantomime. His work shows a mastery of stage technique and an ability to work in a variety of genres (domestic drama, chronicle-play, extended revue-sketch) which is rare in the British theatre. *The Battle of Shrivings*, an ambitious contemporary play presenting the confrontation between a pacifist-philosopher and an atheist-poet, had a mixed critical reception in 1970. [MJ]

J. Russell Taylor, *Anger and After* (revised edn, 1969); K. Tynan, *Curtains* (revised edn, 1964).

Shaftesbury, Anthony Ashley Cooper, 3rd Earl of (1671–1713). Philosopher. Born in London, the grandson of the 1st Earl, the Achitophel of Dryden's poem. His education was supervised by his grandfather's *protégé*, John ◊ Locke, whose ideas he

combatted. He studied at Winchester College and travelled on the continent. He was an M.P. (1695–8), and succeeded to the title in 1700, thereafter taking part in the Lords' debates until ill-health forced him to retire to private life. He died in Naples, where he had gone in 1711. Between 1698 and his death, he wrote a number of philosophical essays, including *An Inquiry Concerning Virtue* (unauthorized printing by Toland, the deist, 1699); *Letter Concerning Enthusiasm* (1708); *Sensus Communis: An Essay on the Freedom of Wit and Humour* and *The Moralists* (1709); and *Soliloquy, or Advice to an Author* (1710). All these were collected with *Miscellaneous Reflections on the Preceding Treatises, and Other Critical Subjects* as *Characteristicks of Men, Manners, Opinions, Times* (3 vols., 1711; revised text 1714; ed. J. M. Robertson, 1900). In 1914 B. Rand published Shaftesbury's incomplete work *Second Characters, or the Language of Forms*. An elegant writer, and hater of systems, Shaftesbury was the 'gentlemanly' writer his age demanded. He worked hard at creating some intellectual position that would require neither the dogma of religion nor the mathematical universe of Hobbes or Locke's mechanistic psychology. His writings, on which the earlier English neo-platonists had considerable influence, were widely read and used. His organic view of nature as God's art, and his notion of the innate moral sense implanted in man to appreciate this was taken up by ◊ Hutcheson and other Scottish philosophers. The 'Moral Sense' or 'Moral Sentiment' also throve by contemplating the '*beautiful* in Nature', so that his writings are of great importance in the development of 18th-century aesthetic theory. In this way the useful and the beautiful in art were satisfactorily united, and the sentimental trend towards stressing the audience's reaction as the most important subject for theoretical inquiry was given respectable, if not very rigorous, philosophical underpinning. He supported ridicule as a test of truth (thus admitting genteel satire), but only some ridicule; Swift's *A Tale of A Tub* he abhorred. Bernard ◊ Mandeville was his chief opponent. [AR]

J. Bonar, *Moral Sense* (1930); R. L. Brett, *The Third Earl of S.* (1951); F. H. Heinemann, 'The Philosopher of Enthusiasm', *Revue Internationale de Philosophie*, VI (Paris, 1952); E. Tuveson, 'The Importance of S.', *ELH*, XX (1953).

Shakespeare, William (1564–1616). Poet and dramatist. The greatest of English writers was born at Stratford-upon-Avon, Warwickshire, the son of John Shakespeare, glove-maker and leather-dresser, who in 1568 was bailiff (i.e. mayor) of Stratford. The exact day of his birth is unknown, but he was baptized in Holy Trinity Church on 26 April 1564, and scholars have assumed he was born on 23 April, St George's Day. He almost certainly went to the Stratford Grammar School, where he would have received a decent education in the classics under masters trained at Oxford. In 1582 he married Ann Hathaway, eight years his senior, and they had three children, including one son who died in boyhood. How Shakespeare spent the years till 1592 is a mystery – he may have been a country school-master or a provincial actor. By 1592 he was established in London, while still maintaining property in his home town.

Shakespeare seems to have entered the theatre as an actor, for the first record of his London career is the resentment expressed by one of the University wits, Robert ◊ Greene, that a mere player should presume to write plays. Between 1590 and 1591 Shakespeare wrote the second and third parts of *Henry VI* and followed them with the first part and with *Richard III*. The 4 plays form a tetralogy of English history from 1422 to 1485, and *Richard III* contains Shakespeare's most powerful characterization to date, Richard Crookback.

The theatres were closed because of plague for part of 1592 and most of 1593, and when the play-producing companies were reorganized Shakespeare was engaged as an actor in one of the two leading troupes of the day, the Lord Chamberlain's Men, which became the King's Men in 1603, and was for a further forty years the pre-eminent troupe in England. Almost from the outset of his career as a playwright, therefore, Shakespeare was associated with the best company of his time – the one which had the most continuous and prosperous existence – and with the age's leading actor, Richard Burbage. He became one of the 'company sharers', i.e. the senior actors who controlled the policy of the company, commissioned the plays and paid the other actors. His status within the company gave him much more authority and influence than a mere dramatist usually enjoyed in Elizabethan times. He grew rich, and by 1597 had bought New Place, a fine house in Stratford. In 1598 he became one of the theatre landlords also, owning a tenth share in the Globe Theatre, which was the new headquarters of the King's Men.

In 1593 was published the long non-dramatic poem *Venus and Adonis*, and a year later *The Rape of Lucrece*. Both poems were carefully seen through the press, and both were dedicated by Shakespeare to Henry Wriothesley, Earl of Southampton. Around this time the 'sugared sonnets amongst his private friends' were being circulated and read in manuscript; the greatest of Elizabethan sonnet-sequences did not appear in print until the unauthorized edition of 1609. The *Sonnets* may contain Shakespeare's early reactions to the sophisticated and metropolitan world of London, but, at this date, it is impossible to extricate the real from the conventional and fictitious situations, or to identify either the handsome young man addressed in the early sonnets or the Dark Lady of the later ones.

Shakespeare's early comedies (1593–5) were *The Two Gentlemen of Verona*, *Love's Labour's Lost* and *The Taming of the Shrew*. The second is a young man's play, witty, verbally ornate and packed with topical, literary allusions. The third is a robust comedy of unorthodox courtships which has always proved highly stage-worthy. More mature comedies (1595–9) are *A Midsummer Night's Dream*, whose action involves young Athenian lovers, rustics and the fairy world; *The Merchant of Venice*, where the happy outcome of courtship is threatened by the Jew, Shylock; and *Much Ado About Nothing*. Shakespeare's comedies always centre on love and are often characterized by the resourcefulness of the heroine. *Twelfth Night* and *As You Like It*, both written around 1600, are his masterpieces in this genre.

Romeo and Juliet (*c*. 1595), the lyrical story of young lovers doomed to separation and premature death by family feud and by Fate, is Shakespeare's first notable tragedy; its style is often literary and artificial. *Richard II*, which gains in meaning by being taken as part of the second tetralogy of historical plays, can be seen as a further experiment in tragedy dealing with the fall of an incompetent but not unsympathetic King; *Julius Caesar* (1599), the first of the Roman plays, marks another stage in Shakespeare's tragic development. The 2 parts of *Henry IV* are his most distinctive achievements in the history play; the antithesis of the worlds of tavern and court, and the inclusion of Falstaff as commentator, critic and satirist of the high, chivalric action enrich this history. Prince Hal, whose moral and political education is dramatized in both parts, emerges as the ideal King in the spectacular heroics of *Henry V*. The second tetralogy deals with the history preceding the first, and the sequence *Richard II* to *Richard III* embodies in dramatic form the official Tudor view of history.

Around the time Shakespeare was writing his greatest work in tragedy, King James came to the throne and took the Chamberlain's Men under his patronage as the King's Men. To this period belong the supreme artistic achievements, *Hamlet* (*c*. 1600), *Othello* (*c*. 1604), *King Lear* (*c*. 1605) and *Macbeth* (*c*. 1605), the Scottish setting of the last possibly being to interest James himself. These tragedies contain Shakespeare's most celebrated protagonists and, with *Antony and Cleopatra* (which is both a political and personal tragedy), his greatest dramatic poetry. Like the military tragedy *Coriolanus* the last play has its origins in the translation of Plutarch's *Lives* by Sir Thomas ⟡ North which stimulated Shakespeare more than any other single source.

Between *Hamlet* and *Othello* came 3 comedies difficult to classify and often grouped together as 'problem plays' or 'dark comedies' because of their sardonic, disillusioned tone – the satire *Troilus and Cressida* and *Measure for Measure* (both of which have been understood better since their critical re-assessment in the 1920s and 1930s) as well as a play which has no obvious links with them, *All's Well That Ends Well*. *Timon of Athens*, whose spendthrift hero becomes a life-hating malcontent, has never found general favour.

In 1608 the King's Men acquired a second house, Blackfriars, where (in the winter) they played indoors by candle-light to a more select, courtly audience than at the open-air Globe Theatre. Beaumont and Fletcher proved adept at satisfying this coterie audience, and Shakespeare, possibly under their influence, wrote *Pericles* and *Cymbeline*, 2 experimental romances or tragi-comedies, for this new kind of audience and stage, before going on to write his 2 masterpieces in the genre – *The Winter's Tale*, a pastoral romance based on Greene's *Menaphon*, and *The Tempest*, set on an enchanted island.

By 1611 Shakespeare had retired to Stratford, but he collaborated with John Fletcher on 2 plays – the spectacular chronicle-play *Henry VIII* and *The Two Noble Kinsmen* – and on the lost play *Cardenio*. Many records testify to his investments and property transactions in Stratford and London. He died, on St George's Day 1616, a prosperous figure in his home town. He was buried in Holy Trinity Church, in a place of prominence, and a monument by Gheerhart Janssen was erected there.

At the time of his death some 18 of his plays had been published, mostly in unauthorized, pirated quartos, but Shakespeare had evidently taken no pains to get his plays (which belonged to the King's Men) into print. In 1616 Ben ⟡ Jonson was ridiculed for including among his own works in folio the scripts of stage-plays, but his action probably inspired two of Shakespeare's fellow company-sharers and householders, the actors John Heminge and Henry Condell, to issue *Mr William Shakespeares Comedies, Histories, & Tragedies. Published according to the True Original Copies* (1623). This great collection – the First Folio – includes besides better texts of plays previously printed by pirates 18 plays never published before (such as *Macbeth, Antony and Cleopatra, Twelfth Night* and *As You Like It*), a preface by Heminge and Condell, and a long and warm poetic tribute from Jonson. It thus preserved for posterity plays which might easily have been lost.

Throughout the 17th century Shakespeare was usually placed second amongst English dramatists to Ben Jonson, and sometimes third after Beaumont and Fletcher, but early in the 18th century he moved to first place in the pantheon of English writers, a position he has long held. Stratford-upon-Avon, his birth-place, has become a place of pilgrimage and a centre of tourism. Its annual Festival is dedicated to performing his plays. Several theatres in the United States and one in Canada are devoted to Shakespearean performances. The quatercentenary of his birth in 1964 was celebrated throughout the world with productions of the plays, exhibitions, the issue of commemorative postage-stamps and other institutional honours.

Some commentators have refused to grant that the plays of Shakespeare could, in fact, have been written by someone who went to a grammar school in the English midlands, and they have attempted to prove that the plays were written by a member of the aristocracy or at least a graduate of Oxford or Cambridge. The Earl of Oxford, Christopher ◊ Marlowe, Francis Bacon, an Elizabethan nun, and even the Society of Jesus have been credited with authorship of the plays by a variety of anti-Stratfordians (see R. C. Churchill, *Shakespeare and His Betters*, 1958).

Books on Shakespeare are so numerous as to make a brief bibliography impossible. New books are regularly listed and reviewed in the British annual *Shakespeare Survey* and in the American *Shakespeare Quarterly*. Gordon Ross Smith's *Classified Shakespeare Bibliography, 1936–1958* (University Park, Pennsylvania, 1963) is a useful, curiously organized check-list. [MJ]

The First Folio: The Norton Facsimile, prepared by C. Hinman (1969); *The Complete Works* ed. P. Alexander (1961); *The Complete Works*, ed. C. J. Sisson (1953); *The Complete Pelican S.*, general ed. A. Harbage (1969); *The New Arden S.*, general eds. U. Ellis-Fermor and H. F. Brooks (1951–ξ); *The New Cambridge S.*, general ed. J. Dover Wilson (1921–62).
E. K. Chambers, *W.S., Facts and Problems* (1930); E. K. Chambers and C. Williams, *A Short Life of S.* (1933); G. E. Bentley, *W.S.: A Biographical Handbook* (1961); ed. H. Granville-Barker and G. B. Harrison, *A Companion to S. Studies* (1934); K. J. Holzknecht, *The Backgrounds of S.'s Plays* (1950); M. C. Bradbrook, *S. and Elizabethan Poetry* (1951); G. I. Duthie, *S.* (1951); H. Fluchère, *S.* (1953); E. Partridge, *S.'s Bawdy* (1947); T. Spencer, *S. and the Nature of Man* (1943); ed. D. Nicoll Smith, *S. Criticism: A Selection, 1623–1840* (1916); ed. A. Bradby, *S. Criticism: 1919–1935*; ed. A. Ridler, *S. Criticism, 1935–1960* (1963); ed. L. Lerner, *Shakespeare's Tragedies: A Selection of Modern Criticism* (1963) and *Shakespeare's Comedies* (1967); C. L. Barber, *S.'s Festive Comedy* (1959); A. C. Bradley, *S. Tragedy* (1904); S. T. Coleridge, *S. Criticism*, ed. T. M. Raysor (1930); B. Evans, *S.'s Comedies* (1960); H. Granville-Barker, *Prefaces to S.* (5 series, 1927–48); J. Holloway, *The Story of the Night* (1961); E. Hubler, *The Sense of S.'s Sonnets* (1952); G. Wilson Knight, *The Wheel of Fire* (revised edn, 1949); L. C. Knights, *Some Shakespearean Themes* (1959); C. Leech, *S.'s Tragedies and Other Studies in Seventeenth Century Drama* (1950); J. B. Leishman, *Themes and Variations in S.'s Sonnets* (1961); A. Righter, *S. and the Idea of a Play* (1962); C. Spurgeon, *S.'s Imagery* (1935); E. M. W. Tillyard, *S.'s History Plays* (1944); D. A. Traversi, *An Approach to S.* (revised edn, 1957); J. Dover Wilson, *The Fortunes of Falstaff* (1943); J. Bartlett, *A Complete Concordance to S.* (1895); ed. O. J. Campbell and E. G. Quinn *A Shakespeare Encyclopaedia* (1966).

Sharp, William (1855–1905). Scottish miscellaneous writer. He published his most distinctive work under the assumed female personality of 'Fiona Macleod'. A native of Paisley, Sharp attended Glasgow University and worked in a law office there before turning to journalism in London, where during the 1880s he edited a cheap series of 'selected poems', and wrote both boys' yarns and, for a popular series, lives of Shelley, Heine and Browning. Like W. B. Yeats, Sharp had spent much of his boyhood in Celtic peasant districts (the Scottish Highlands in his case) and like Yeats he was much influenced by the Pre-Raphaelites, publishing verse in their manner and a life of D. G. Rossetti (1882). 'Fiona Macleod's' *Pharais, a Romance of the Isles* (1894) appeared immediately after Yeats's stories of *The Celtic Twilight* (1893), and other novels, poems, essays and plays by the mysterious Highland authoress, supposedly a cousin of Sharp's, were published during the following ten years. They show the blend of mysticism with romanticization of peasant life typical of the 'Celtic twilight' movement. Sharp, who during Fiona Macleod's career published under his own name some minor novels and essays, a Celtic anthology (*Lyra Celtica*, completed jointly with his wife, 1896) and an edition of ◊ Ossian (1896), concealed his identity with his 'cousin' by elaborate stratagems, including a bogus entry for Fiona Macleod in *Who's Who*. [AI]

Writings (1909–10; 1927).
E. A. Sharp, *W.S., a Memoir* (1910).

Shaw, George Bernard (1856–1950). Dramatist, controversialist, critic and wit. Born into genteel poverty in Dublin, he worked as a land agent's junior clerk. In 1876 he moved to London, and for ten years he lived mainly on his mother. He wrote 5 unsuccessful novels, including *The Irrational Knot* and *Cashel Byron's Profession*, became an active Socialist and brilliant platform speaker, and undertook his own education in the British Museum. He wrote art and music criticism, and from 1895 as drama critic on the *Saturday Review* conducted a brilliant attack on the old-fashioned, intellectually arid London theatre. He publicized the works of Marx, Wagner and Ibsen. William Archer, who helped to get him journalist's jobs, suggested they should collaborate on a play. The collaboration foundered, but

Shaw's *Widowers' Houses*, attacking slum landlordism, was the result, and had two performances in 1892. Discouraged as too daring by the commercial theatres, Shaw sought readers for his early plays by giving full and discursive stage-directions, and by writing polemical prefaces on the social, political and moral implications of the plays. His early problem-plays ('Plays Unpleasant') included *Mrs Warren's Profession*, on prostitution; among 'Plays Pleasant' were the dazzling light comedies *Arms and the Man* and *You Never Can Tell*, and the more serious *Candida*. From 1904, when *Candida* was acted in London by Harley ◊ Granville-Barker, Shaw was closely associated with the intellectual revival of the British theatre, and even scored popular successes with such plays as the sardonic and dashing melodrama *The Devil's Disciple*. *Caesar and Cleopatra* was acted in 1906, though written before his marathon high comedy on the Life Force *Man and Superman*, with its Socialist intellectual hero and its persistent, predatory heroine. *John Bull's Other Island*, set in Ireland, and *Major Barbara* belong to this period. *The Doctor's Dilemma* (1906) combines satire on medical men with a romantic view of art. *Getting Married* (1908) and *Misalliance* (1910) are discussion plays and *Androcles and the Lion* (1913) an entertaining, but not unserious, charade. The high comedy *Pygmalion* (also 1913) was his greatest commercial success, endlessly revived in the theatre, and the basis of a film and the long-running musical *My Fair Lady* (Broadway, 1955). *Heartbreak House*, 'a fantasia in the Russian Manner on English themes' written during the First World War, shows with mingled poetry and farce the decline of Edwardian England. In his sixties Shaw wrote his 'metabiological Pentateuch', *Back to Methuselah*, a series of plays giving his view of Man's past and future, and the other perennial in the modern repertory, the chronicle-play *St Joan* (1923), his greatest play. The 'political extravaganzas' of his seventies were conversation-pieces, even debates, of which *The Apple Cart* (1929) is a lively static comedy on constitutional monarchy. The others were *On the Rocks*, *Too True to Be Good*, *Geneva*, and '*In Good King Charles's Golden Days*'. The post-war *Buoyant Billions* and *Farfetched Fables* are dewdrops from the lion's mane. Shaw wrote brilliant dialogue, was fertile of ideas and had a great sense of theatre; in his early years he ventilated all sorts of problems; and his comic vitality ensures regular revival of his plays.

As a Socialist pamphleteer, and controversialist, Shaw wrote the same lucid expository prose as in his prefaces. In 1889 he edited *Essays in Fabian Socialism*; and his voluminous output included *Commonsense about the War* (1914), *How to Settle the Irish Question* (1917), *The Intelligent Woman's Guide to Socialism and Capitalism* (1928) and *What I Really Wrote about the War* (1931). His reviews were collected in several volumes: *Music in London 1890–1894* (3 vols., 1932) and *London Music in 1888–9* (1937); *Dramatic Opinions and Essays 1895–98* (2 vols., 1907) and *Our Theatres in the Nineties* (3 vols., 1932); *Pen Portraits and Reviews* (1931).

Shaw's marriage in 1895 to the wealthy Charlotte Payne-Townsend saved him from ill-health and financial worries; his subsequent literary earnings were great. His love-affairs with the actresses Ellen Terry and Mrs Patrick Campbell were on paper only. Essentially shy, he created the persona of G.B.S., showman, satirist, pundit and intellectual buffoon. He declined both the Order of Merit and a peerage from the first Labour Government, and reluctantly accepted the Nobel Prize in 1925. In coining a term to embody his brilliant qualities, commentators brought a new adjective into English, Shavian. [MJ]

Works (36 vols., 1930–50); *The Complete Plays* (1934); *The Complete Prefaces* (1934); *Selected Prose*, ed. D. Russell (1953); *Collected Letters*, ed. D. H. Laurence (1965–); *Sixteen Self Sketches* (1949).
G. B. Shaw, *Sixteen Self Sketches* (1949); E. Bentley, *B.S.* (1950); St John Ervine, *B.S.: His Life, Work, and Friends* (1956); A. Henderson, *G.B.S.: Man of the Century* (1956); D. MacCarthy, *S.* (1951); R. Mander and J. Mitchenson, *A Theatrical Companion to S.* (1955); M. Meisel, *S. and the Nineteenth Century Theatre* (1963); ed. R. J. Kaufmann, *G.B.S.: a Collection of Critical Essays* (1965); B. Patch, *Thirty Years With S.* (1951); Hesketh Pearson, *B.S.: His Life and Personality* (complete edn, 1961); M. Shenfield, *B.S.: A Pictorial Biography* (1962); Edmund Wilson, 'B.S. at Eighty', in *The Triple Thinkers* (revised edn, 1952).

Shelley, Mary Wollstonecraft (Godwin) (1797–1851). Novelist and miscellaneous writer. Born in London, the only daughter of William ◊ Godwin, the philosopher, and Mary ◊ Wollstonecraft, the author of a

Vindication of the Rights of Women. Her mother died almost immediately, and she was brought up by her father, who had married Mrs Clairmont. She became acquainted with Shelley in May 1814 and went to Europe with him in July, accompanied by Jane Clairmont. Shelley heard of his wife's suicide in December, and he married Mary Godwin shortly after. She devoted herself to her husband, and studied hard during the next six years. After his death she remained in Italy with their son and with Byron and Leigh Hunt. She returned to England in 1823. After a time her son, who had become heir to the baronetcy, was better treated by the poet's father, and thereafter she lived more comfortably.

In 1816, Byron suggested to Shelley and his wife, who were staying nearby in Switzerland, that they should each write a 'ghost' story. Byron produced the *Vampyre* fragment; Mrs Shelley wrote *Frankenstein, or the Modern Prometheus* (1818), an excellent story in the contemporary tradition of 'gothick' horror. It is a judicious blend of sentimental humanitarianism and 'scientific' notions such as 'galvanism', the idea of the 'vital spark'. In this philosophic romance, Frankenstein creates a monster, who reads the scientist several lectures. The hideous creation has been reading *The Sorrows of Werther*, and has a number of Godwinian and Shellean ideas, but is maddened because his benevolence is not returned. Frankenstein is driven insane by the monster's vengeance, and destroyed; the sorrowing monster seeks to destroy its own 'vital spark' which it no longer wants. Mrs Shelley wrote other romances, of which *The Last Man* (3 vols., 1826; reprinted 1954; ed. J. Luke, Nebraska U.P., 1965) is a tale of the destruction of mankind by a plague, in the 21st century, leaving a single survivor. Two of her novels, *Lodore* (1835) and *Falkner* (1837), are defences of Shelley. She wrote a good deal of journalism, and published an idiosyncratic edition of Shelley's poems. [AR]

Tales and Stories, ed. R. Garnett (1891); *Letters* (2 vols., 1944) and *Journal* (1947), ed. F. L. Jones (U. of Oklahoma P.).
Muriel Spark, *Child of Light: A Reassessment* (1951); E. Bigland, *M.S.* (1959); K. N. Cameron, *Shelley and His Circle*; *1773–1822* (8 vols., 1961 ff.) (in progress); W. E. Peck, 'The Biographical Element in the Novels of M.W.S.', *PMLA*, XXXVI (1923).

Shelley, Percy Bysshe (1792–1822). Poet. The son of Sussex aristocracy, Shelley went to Oxford, but was sent down because of his publication of atheistic beliefs. In 1811 he married Harriet Westbrook, but three years later left her to elope with Mary, daughter of William Godwin, whose brand of anarchic rationalism influenced Shelley's thought. His suggestion at this time that Harriet should live with Mary and himself illustrates his social and moral eccentricity. After he married Mary Godwin (Harriet committed suicide) he developed a number of idealized relationships with women which he celebrated in his poetry. He lived in Italy, where he was the focal point of a group of English writers, from 1818 to 1822, when he was drowned under curious circumstances which suggest that he made no attempt to save himself.

For many years Shelley's poetry was considered almost unmentionable. He published his first important poem, *Queen Mab*, a demonstration of the corruption of humanity by institutions and conventional morality, in 1813, and this set the tone of much of his succeeding writing. It is characterized by a lack of concrete development and logical reasoning. Shelley was concerned with social and political issues but never evolved a specific philosophy of action. His tendency to translate his beliefs into large, sublimated visions of utopia, and to inject them with self-pity and a moral outlook that was selfish in effect if not in motive, leads the reader away from the particular content to the general tone of his poetry. At times he reveals a very modern sophistication, at times a childish petulance, but he invariably uses language with a startling though at times unenergetic, ease.

Some of his poems, such as 'The Masque of Anarchy' (1819), have an unequivocal and grim power, and manipulate allegory with a stark effectiveness. But, as is often the case, he cannot curb the inclination to rely ultimately on symbolic rhetoric. Later he turned more persistently to symbolism and a poetry of mood rather than of overt didacticism. In *Alastor, or the Spirit of Solitude* he develops at some length a characteristic theme. The poem's hero, pure and uncorrupted, is led by his idealistic imagination to seek a living symbol of his vision. He is destroyed by his own failure and disappointment. Here, Shelley combines a visionary and a self-absorbed attitude, and the expression of failed idealism becomes a vehicle for self-indulgence. The poem is in blank verse, which helps to dissipate any concrete reality, and the language is a combination of vast passion and imprecise pallor. Yet the poem's intensity, its lack of restriction, the very absence of connexion in its leaps from image to image, are deeply impressive.

The influence of Godwin's *Inquiry Concerning Political Justice* did not transmit itself with any great precision to Shelley's poetry. His mature poems reveal the influence of the neo-platonists. The lack of solidity, the glimpses of shifting, luminous forms, show Shelley striving to express the possibility of a world of eternal perfection. *Prometheus Unbound* (1820), a verse drama, iterates the redeeming victory of love, which Shelley saw as the means of man's moral salvation. *Epipsychidion* (1821) is his fullest statement of his theory of Platonic love, but self-pity intrudes, and the poem ends in a kind of fury at being unable to achieve the high flights his imagination offered him. *Adonais* (1821), an elegy on the death of Keats, takes Shelley away from himself (although he has a strangely prophetic vision of death at sea) and he uses language and symbol with greater energy than his careless languor often allows. But Shelley is best known for his shorter lyrics, and in these his poetic imagination combines with more controlled use of language, although he still achieves a tremulous ecstasy. In 'Ode to the West Wind', 'To a Skylark' and 'The Cloud' (1820) his customary self-concern and a vigorous use of the pathetic fallacy are present, but they are steadily directed by firm rhythm and vividly pictorial language.

Shelley's *A Defence of Poetry* (written in 1821 but not published until 1840), a prose work that shows some of his most mature and sophisticated thinking, argues the essential validity of the creative imagination. He attacks narrow-minded utilitarianism, and upholds poetry as an unequalled instrument of moral teaching and legislation. In his poetry Shelley was frequently technically careless, naïve and perverse. His achievement lies in the fact that in spite of these defects many of his poems are profound and brilliant articulations of a warm-hearted and wide-ranging idealism. [JRC]

Complete Poetical Works, ed. T. Hutchinson (1934); *S.'s Prose*, ed. D. L. Clark (1954); *Selected Poems and Prose*, ed. G. M. Matthews (1964); *Letters*, ed. F. L. Jones (2 vols., 1964). Edmund Blunden, *S.: A Life Story* (1946); P. H. Butter, *S.'s Idols of the Cave* (1954); N. Rogers, *S. at Work* (1956); H. Bloom, *S.'s Mythmaking* (1959); D. Perkins, *The Quest for Permanence* (1959); M. T. Wilson, *S.'s Later Poetry* (1959); D. Hele, *S.: His Thought and Work* (1960).

Shenstone, William (1714–63). Poet and miscellaneous writer. Born at The Leasowes in Worcestershire, the eldest son of a country gentleman who farmed his own estate, he was educated at Solihull Grammar School, near Birmingham, and Pembroke College, Oxford (1732–6), but as was often the fashion left without taking his degree. In 1735 he inherited The Leasowes and a small income. He exhausted the latter in turning his miniature estate into a *ferme ornée* that, as a show place, rivalled the near-by much grander Hagley Park, the seat of Lord ◊ Lyttelton. Shenstone was one of the most famous and influential exponents of the 'picturesque' style in landscape gardening. His views on taste (and much else) are developed in his letters to Lady Luxborough (a country neighbour), Dodsley the publisher and others; he is a representative, if not outstanding, 18th-century letter writer, who himself considered his correspondence of main importance in his literary production. As a correspondent, he is rather excessively self-conscious, a fault which permeates his poems; he quite deliberately views his writing as that of an amateur. *Poems upon Various Occasions Written for the Entertainment of the Author, and Printed for the Entertainment of a Few Friends Prejudiced in his Favour* was published anonymously (1737); as was his *Judgement of Hercules, A Poem* (1741). His most famous poem is *The Schoolmistress* (first published in the 1737 volume; re-cast and separately published anonymously, 1742; revised, expanded and re-published in Dodsley's *Collection*; 2nd edn, 1748). This began as a mock-Spenserian poem, but ended up as a minor classic, containing an admirable balance of sentiment, observation, real love of Spenser and humour, with the burlesque acting as a kind of defence of Shenstone's personal uncertainty. Shenstone admired his friend James ◊ Thomson's work, but more particularly the real genius of *The Castle of Indolence* rather than the more Miltonic moments of *The Seasons*. Shenstone had over 40 poems (odes, songs, moral pieces and ballads) in various metres included in that representative treasury of mid-century work, Dodsley's *Collection*; he later helped to choose poems for it. As an amateur of the ballad, he corresponded with Bishop ♢ Percy about the contents of *The Reliques*. His own pastoral ballad, *Jemmy Dawson*, was long popular. His 26 pentameter *Elegies* were only published after his death, but circulated widely in manuscript. From these, and his 'Prefatory Essay on Elegy', he has been given credit (with James Hammond) for being a pioneer in the 'moral elegy', genre which Gray in his *Country Churchyard* raised to the height of one of the greatest English forms. Shenstone also wrote interesting essays on literary topics. Johnson's account of him in *Lives of the Poets* should be read to counteract the idea that Shenstone was completely admired. [A R]

Verse and Prose, ed. R. Dodsley (2 vols., 1764); *Poetical Works*, ed. C. C. Clarke (1868); *The Schoolmistress* (facsimile of 1742 edition) (1924); *S.'s Miscellany, 1759–63*, ed. I. A. Gordon (1954); *Letters*, ed. M. Williams (1939).

A. R. Humphreys, *W.S.* (1937); G. Tillotson, *Essays in Criticism and Research* (1942); M. Williams, *W.S.* (1935); I. A. Williams, *Seven Eighteenth-Century Bibliographies* (1924).

Sheridan, Richard Brinsley (1751–1816). Dramatist and orator. The son of Thomas Sheridan, the actor and elocutionist, and his novelist-playwright wife Frances, he was educated at Harrow, married the singer Miss Linley under romantic circumstances in 1773, and at the age of 24 had in 1775 his first play, *The Rivals*, produced. A high-spirited comedy of intrigue which comes at times close to farce, it both burlesques and endorses romantic love, and contains that proverbial character Mrs Malaprop. Within the same year he wrote a farce, *St Patrick's Day*, and a comic opera, *The Duenna*. In 1776 he purchased David Garrick's share in Drury Lane and became manager. His initial years there were brilliant, and in 1777 he brought out *A Trip to Scarborough*, a refined version of Vanbrugh's bawdier *The Relapse*, and his greatest play *The School for Scandal*, which was tailored to suit the best actors in the company. In the comedy, a scandalous *salon* of hypocrites imperil a marriage of Age and Youth. The witty dialogue and the theatricalism of 'the screen scene' have ensured the play's regular revival. In 1779 Sheridan revised Buckingham's *The Rehearsal* as *The Critic*, a superb burlesque of heroic tragedy, and in 1799 he wrote a tragedy, *Pizarro*, from Kotzebue.

In 1780 he entered Parliament, and Drury Lane suffered. He was a noted wit and a great parliamentary orator, making a celebrated speech of over five hours supporting the impeachment of Warren Hastings, and was on intimate terms with the Prince of Wales. Party leadership eluded him, and Drury Lane had twice to be rebuilt during his régime, so that his last years brought disappointment and debt. He was buried with full honours in Westminster Abbey. [M J]

The Plays and Poems, ed. R. C. Rhodes (3 vols., 1928); *Letters*, ed. L. Price (3 vols., 1966).

T. Moore, *Memoirs of the Life of R.B.S.* (1825); R. C. Rhodes, *Harlequin S.* (1933); W. Sichel, *The Life of R.B.S.* (1909).

Sherriff, R(obert) C(edric) (1896–   ). Novelist, playwright and film-script writer. Born at Kingston-on-Thames and educated at the grammar school there, he entered his father's business of insurance, but shortly after, on the outbreak of the First World War, he joined the army, and served as a captain in the East Surrey Regiment. He rejoined his business in 1918, and spent ten years as a claims adjuster. An interest in amateur theatricals led him to try his hand at writing. In 1929, Shaw was instrumental in having his play *Journey's End* produced at the Savoy Theatre. This was based on his thoughts and experiences as a soldier, a realistic treatment of trench life, and was an immediate success in Europe and America. After two years at New College, Oxford, he became a professional writer, and for a time worked in Hollywood. His film-scripts include *The Invisible Man* (1933), *Goodbye Mr Chips* (1936), *The Four Feathers* (1938), *Lady Hamilton* (1941), *Odd Man Out* (1945) and *The Dam Busters* (1955). None of his plays has been as successful as his first. They include: *Badger's Green* (1930), *Windfall* (1933), *Home at Seven* (1950), *The White Carnation* (1953), and *Shred of Evidence* (1960). Among his novels are *The Fortnight in September* (1931), *Another Year* (1948), *King John's Treasure* (1954) and *The Wells of St Mary's* (1962). *No Leading Lady* (1968) is an autobiography. [A R]

Shirley, James (1596–1666). Dramatist. Born in London, he went to the Merchant Taylors' School and possibly to Oxford (where Archbishop Laud is said to have dissuaded him from becoming a clergyman on account of a large mole on his cheek) before going to Cambridge University in 1615. His narrative poem *Echo and Narcissus* may date from his undergraduate days. He entered the Church, married, and was head-master of the grammar school at St Albans, a post he relinquished in 1624 when he be-came a Roman Catholic. From this date Shirley was a very prolific playwright, sound and craftsmanlike rather than original, and working in a variety of genres. For some ten years he wrote mostly for the Cockpit Theatre; in the plague year 1636 he followed the Earl of Strafford to Dublin and for four years wrote for the St Werburgh Street Theatre; and back in London in 1640 he succeeded Philip Massinger as principal dramatist to the leading company of the age, the King's Men. After the closing of the theatres in 1642, when he probably returned to school-teaching, he supported the Royalist cause, and in 1646 published his non-dramatic verse and later several masques.

Shirley is credited with 31 plays, most of which reflect Caroline courtly taste, and none of which has been professionally revived in the modern theatre. The plot of *The Gamester* (1633) is said to have been suggested by Charles I, and Shirley's other successful comedies included *The Witty Fair One* (1628) and *The Lady of Pleasure* (1635), both of which are interesting and vivid fore-runners of Restoration comedy. He also wrote masques, tragi-comedies, tragedies, including *The Maid's Revenge* and *Love's Cruelty*, and several dramas such as *The Duke's Mistress*. His serious plays are imita-tive and derivative, and he represents, in a worthy way, the end of the Elizabethan dramatic tradition. *The Cardinal* (1641) is a revenge-tragedy exactly in the mode of Kyd's *The Spanish Tragedy* (c. 1587). Today Shirley has a textbook reputation only. [MJ]

The Dramatic Works and Poems, ed. W. Gifford, revised A. Dyce (6 vols., 1833).

M. C. Bradbrook, *Themes and Conventions of Elizabethan Tragedy* (1935); R. S. Forsythe, *The Relations of S.'s Plays to the Elizabethan Drama* (1914); A. Harbage, *Cavalier Drama* (New York, 1936); A. H. Nason, *J.S., Drama-tist* (1915).

Shorthouse, Joseph Henry (1834–1903). Novelist. Born in Birmingham, he worked as a chemist in the business of his father, a Quaker. He became an Anglican and carried his interest in mysticism and the contemporary tensions (at the root of the Tractarian troubles) between Anglicanism and Roman Catholicism into his first and most famous novel, *John Inglesant* (2 vols., privately printed, 1880; 1881). This he set in the 17th century, and his hero encounters Jesuits, the Little Gidding community, Charles I (who turns out a treacherous employer), and a papal election, all mingled with lofty ethical sentiment. There is a lot of quite good pastiche writing in the book, and a mosaic of unacknowledged quotation and reminiscence from 17th-century writing. The religious content of the fiction of Mrs Humphrey ◊ Ward is part of the same 19th-century vogue, as is the fiction of Walter Pater. Shorthouse wrote 3 or 4 other much less successful novels, a paper *The Platonism of Wordsworth* (1882), and edited Herbert's *Temple* and other works of devotion. [AR]

The Life and Letters of J.H.S., ed. by his wife (Sarah) (2 vols., 1901).

J. Durham, *Marius the Epicurean and John Inglesant* (1905); M. Polak, *The Historical, Philosophical and Religious Aspects of John Inglesant* (1934); H. Anson, 'The Church in Nineteenth-Century Fiction: II, S.', *Listener*, 4 May 1939; ed. M. Bishop, *John Inglesant and Its Author* (1958).

Shute, Nevil (pseud. of Nevil Shute Norway) (1899–1960). Novelist. He was born in Ealing, the son of a senior Civil Servant, and educated at Shrewsbury and Oxford, where he went after serving in the army in the latter part of the First World War. He then be-came an aeronautical engineer, building first airships and later aircraft, a job he combined with writing popular novels. During the Second World War he served in the R.N.V.R. Afterwards he settled in Australia. His first book, *Marazan*, was published in 1926 and he wrote a total of 24 over the next thirty years; they include *So Disdained* (1928) and *What Happened to the Corbetts* (1939), a vivid anticipation of the plight of bombed-out families. His later novels were set in Australia; the most famous are *A Town like Alice* (1950), about the war in the Far East, and *On the Beach* (1957), about the effect of nuclear war and radiation on the people of Australia. All Shute's novels have a high moral purpose and happy endings, and are written in an easy style which practically reads itself. His autobiography, *Slide Rule* (1954), is mostly about his life as an engineer. [JM]

Sidgwick, Henry (1838–1900). Philosopher. Born at Skipton, Yorkshire, the son of a schoolmaster, and educated at Rugby and Trinity College, Cambridge, where he was a Fellow, and from 1883 university Professor of Moral Philosophy. Sidgwick, as a political thinker (and probably as an educator of administrators and politicians), followed the 'utilitarian' fusion of ethics, economics and politics developed by ♢ Bentham and J. S. ♢ Mill; at the same time, as a philosopher, he sought to provide these views with a better and tighter theoretical substructure by developing certain 'intuitional' notions of the Scottish 'common sense' thinkers ♢ Hamilton and ♢ Reid. Hence his interest in ethics based on an empirical evaluation of goodness (utilitarian) and an intuitional notion of prudence, benevolence and justice. Sidgwick also sought by this attempted fusion of ideas to establish his position in the contemporary arguments about the existence of God, arguing for a divine order from the conflict between intuition and experience. His chief works were *Methods of Ethics* (1874), *The Principles of Political Economy* (1883), *The Elements of Politics* (1891), and 'The Ethics of Religious Conformity', in the *International Journal of Ethics* (1896). [AR]

'An Auto-Historical Fragment', *Mind*, n.s., xx (1901).
A. S(idgwick) and E. M., *Memoir* (1906); C. D. Broad, *Five Types of Ethical Theory* (1930) and *Ethics and the History of Philosophy* (1952); S. Rothblatt, *The Revolution of the Dons* (1968); T. Y. Mullins, 'S.'s Concept of Ethical Science', *JHI*, xxiv (1963).

Sidney, Sir Philip (1554–86). Poet and author of prose romance. Eldest son of Sir Henry Sidney, three times Lord Deputy of Ireland, he was born at Penshurst, Kent, and entered Shrewsbury School at the same time as his friend and biographer, Fulke ♢ Greville. He went to Christ Church, Oxford, but left without taking a degree, and from 1572 to 1575 travelled in Europe in the train of his uncle, the Earl of Leicester, being made Gentleman of the Bedchamber to Charles IV in Paris. He met Ramus at Frankfurt, was painted by Veronese at Padua, and was influenced by Hubert

Languet, scholar and Protestant. He became a brilliant member of Elizabeth's court, and in 1578 wrote a masque, *The Lady of May*, in her honour; he also went on diplomatic missions to Europe. After a quarrel with the Earl of Oxford, he quitted the court for the country where he stayed with his sister, the Countess of Pembroke, for whose entertainment he wrote the first, cancelled, version of *Arcadia*. Almost none of his work was printed in his lifetime, but his poetry and prose was widely circulated in manuscript. Hakluyt's *Voyages* and Spenser's *Shepherd's Calendar* were dedicated to him, and he became to the Elizabethans the *beau idéal* of the Renaissance courtier, combining the chivalric virtues of the man of action with the learning and poise of the man of letters. He became a Member of Parliament, was knighted in 1582, married Frances Walsingham, and became Joint Master of Ordnance. He was contemplating sailing with Ralegh and Drake to the West Indies in 1585 when he was sent to serve the Protestant cause in the Low Countries as Governor of Flushing. In 1586 he was mortally wounded at Zutphen, and died twenty-six days afterwards. He was buried with great honour in St Paul's Cathedral.

His greatest achievement in poetry was the sonnet-sequence *Astrophel and Stella*, which showed his mastery of the Petrarchan tradition. He remains one of the finest of Elizabethan sonneteers, in addition to having been an important influence on those who followed him. His pastoral-chivalric romance, the *Arcadia*, exists in 3 versions. The earliest, written before 1580, is in 5 prose books, which contain within them sonnets and lyrics, and between the books are long connecting 'eclogues', part verse, part prose. Later, Sidney began to rewrite the *Arcadia*, complicating the narrative in the manner of Ariosto or Spenser, weaving a complex web of stories into the new structure. The revision, which stopped in the middle of Book III, was posthumously published in quarto in 1590; three years later it was republished in folio completed, but with alterations, by the Countess of Pembroke from the old version. This is the version familiar to most critics, but in the 20th century manuscripts of the cancelled version have been discovered and the full old text published. The later *Arcadia* is less romance than prose epic, written in a heightened style, and is comparable to Spenser's unfinished poem *The Faerie*

Queene, in that it offers instruction and moral enlightenment as well as entertainment. Sidney's critical theories are contained in his *Defence of Poesy*, which, though neo-classical in tone, sees the rules as useful and valid but does not elevate them into dogma. *The Defence* is still one of the best introductions to Renaissance literature. [MJ]

The Complete Works, ed. A. Feuillerat (4 vols., 1912–26; *The Prose Works* only reissued in 4 vols., 1962); *The Poems*, ed. W. A. Ringler, Jr (1962).
E. J. Buxton, *Sir P.S. and the English Renaissance* (1954); K. Muir, *Sir P.S.* (1960); N. L. Ruden-stine, *S.'s Poetic Development* (1967).

Sillitoe, Alan (1928–). Novelist. Born in Nottingham, and educated at the Radford Boulevard Secondary Modern School, Sillitoe was one of the regional working-class novelists who emerged in the 1950s and who were widely thought to have enlarged the scope, subject matter and concerns of the modern English novel. His first book, *Saturday Night and Sunday Morning* (1958), is, to date, his most successful. Its protagonist, Arthur Seaton, became the prototype of the young factory-worker, hedonistic, alienated from society, violent and unthinking, who was frequently met with in the fiction of the next few years. Although, in *Saturday Night and Sunday Morning*, the novelist's attitude to his hero is more than usually indulgent, the authenticity of the Nottingham setting helps to lend credence to the story of Arthur's adventures, which is thinly veiled picaresque.

In a volume of short stories, *The Loneliness of the Long Distance Runner* (1959), particularly in the title-story, it becomes apparent that within the realist regional novelist there lurks an ironic romanticist struggling for release. The praises of the selfish, anti-social life are again sung, and the writer's approval of his characters' actions is even less ambiguous than in the novel. In *The General* (1960), Sillitoe attempts to break new ground by writing a political fable, but the result is unsuccessful. Not only does it not convince on any level, it is also noticeably less well written than the earlier works. A book of verse, *The Rats* (1960), served merely to confirm the suspicion aroused by his earlier volume of poems, *Without Beer or Bread* (1957), that the author's literary talent was exclusively a prose one.

With *Key to the Door* (1961), Sillitoe returned to his familiar Nottingham background to examine the Seaton family in the thirties. This time he judged his distance from his characters with a real novelist's precision, and wrote with passion and integrity of proletariat life in time of depression. *Key to the Door* may lack shape, and some of the writing in it may be clumsy; nevertheless it is a novel of some power. *The Death of William Posters* (1964) concerns a 27-year-old Nottingham factory worker who, at the start of the book, has walked out on wife, children, marriage. The progress of a man deadened by the cacophony of modern industrialism is flamboyantly and loosely recorded. Sillitoe in mid-career remains the most interesting of the regional novelists of his generation. [CO]

The Ragman's Daughter (1963); *Road to Volgograd* (1964); *Guzman Go Home* (1968) (short stories).

Simeon of Durham (d. c. 1130). Chronicler. A Benedictine at Jarrow, from which he moved with the other members of his community to Durham. His *Historia ecclesiae Dunelmensis*, based on Bede, traces the history of the see of Durham to the year 1096. His *Historia regum Anglorum et Danorum* is drawn from earlier writers, except for the years 1119–29. Simeon shows considerable narrative ability in many places.

Opera omnia, ed. T. Arnold (Rolls Series, 2 vols., 1882–5); *Historical Works*, tr. J. Stevenson, in *Church Historians of England*, III, 2 (1855).

Singh, Khushwant (1915–). Indian novelist and historian. Born at Hadali in the Punjab, he attended the universities of Delhi, the Punjab and London, returning to practise as a lawyer in Lahore. For several years he was a lecturer in Hindu law at the University of the Punjab, but he joined the Ministry of External Affairs when India achieved its independence. The first product of his interest in the history of the Sikhs was *The Sikhs* (1951). Since then he has edited *The Sacred Writings of the Sikhs* (1960), and written *The Fall of the Kingdom of the Punjab* (1962), the biography of *Ranjit Singh* (1963 –6) and the 2-volume *History of the Sikhs* (1963). The research for this book took him to many countries, and he lectured at several universities. After attending the 1962 Edinburgh Writers' Conference he returned to his home in New Delhi. Singh's fictional work includes the short stories of *The Mark of Vishnu* (1949), and his best-known novel, *Train to Pakistan* (1955), which probes the violence that surrounded the partition of India. A second novel, *I Shall Not·Hear the Nightingale* (1961), centres on a Sikh family in the Punjab during the pre-partition tensions. Recent stories are collected in *A Bride for the Sahib*. [PT]

Sitwell, Edith (1887–1964). Poet, anthologist and prose-writer. Born at Scarborough, the eldest child and only daughter of Sir George Sitwell, a baronet of ancient family, an English eccentric immortalized in his son Osbert's memoirs, and a very difficult, because egotistic and unsympathetic father. Her mother disliked a daughter whose good looks were not of a conventional type and who had no taste for fashionable frivolities. Renishaw Hall, in Derbyshire, gave both Edith and her brothers Osbert and Sacheverell Sitwell a lasting taste for the grand and picturesque. *The Sleeping Beauty* (1924) is indirectly an autobiographical poem, suggesting both the beauty of the young Edith's surroundings at Renishaw and the loneliness and neglect she endured, except from kindly servants. A governess, Helen Rootham, a translator of Rimbaud's prose poems, aroused in Edith an interest in French symbolist poetry and in the idea of synaesthesia, or the transmutation, in poetic imagery, of the impressions of one sense into the key of another. In her late twenties, she attracted attention by her anthology *Wheels* (1916), which was in principle opposed to the flat naturalism of much Georgian poetry, and encouraged poets, like the young Aldous Huxley, influenced by Rimbaud and Mallarmé. Edith Sitwell's interest in her earlier poems, like *Façade* (set to music by Sir William Walton, one of the many artists in music, paint or verse whom she and her brothers encouraged), was in gaiety of rhythm, near-nonsense verse and a tapestry-like richness of texture in sound and imagery. The Sitwell family set themselves out to shock middle-class stodginess and philistinism, though from an aristocratic rather than a proletarian stance. *Gold Coast Customs* (1929) moved away from this playful aestheticism to a denunciation of the frivolity and corruption of fashionable Mayfair life, set in juxtaposition with the savage rites of West African tribes, and showed a religious and social sense which became deepened in Miss Sitwell's 3 wartime volumes of poetry, *Street Songs* (1942), *Green Song* (1944) and *Song of the Cold* (1945), volumes in which, in poems of long lines, with many recurrent images, Miss Sitwell expressed her horror at the suffering and inhumanity of modern war, at the miseries of poverty, combined with an exultant faith in the power of God and the plenitude of nature. Her prose works, though uneven, and sometimes drawing heavily on other people's books, and often written rapidly for money, have richness and zest. Her study of Alexander Pope (1930) was a pioneer rehabilitation of a great poet, academically ignored in her time, whom one would not have expected her to appreciate. [GSF]

The Mother (1915); *Twentieth Century Harlequinade* (with Osbert Sitwell) (1916); *Clowns' Houses* (1918); *Façade* (1922); *Troy Park* (1925); *Elegy on Dead Fashion* (1926); *Collected Poems* (1930 and 1957); *The Canticle of the Rose* (1949); *Gardeners and Astronomers* (1953).
L. Untermeyer, *Lives of the Poets* (1960).

Sitwell, Sir Osbert (1892–1969). Poet, essayist and novelist. Born in London and educated at Eton, he held a commission in the Grenadier Guards from 1912 to 1919 and during this period wrote poems for the publications of his sister Edith ◊ Sitwell. With her, and his brother Sacheverell ◊ Sitwell, he was a self-described fighter against the 'philistine'. He retired (1965) to live in his Italian castle. Osbert Sitwell was one of the century's most professional writers. He published volumes of poetry all his life, distinguished by grace and wit: these include *Argonaut and Juggernaut* (1919), *Collected Satires and Poems* (1931), *Selected Poems* (1943), *Wrack at Tidesend* (1952) and *On the Continent* (1958). He was also a graceful short-story writer with a strong sense of atmosphere; *Triple Fugue and Other Stories* was published in 1924 and his *Collected Stories* appeared in 1953. As a novelist, with *Before the Bombardment* (1926) he produced a minor masterpiece in the realization of period, the end of the Edwardian age in the destructiveness of the First World War; other titles are *The Man Who Lost Himself* (1929) and *Miracle on Sinai* (1933). Sitwell was a lucid critic who skilfully used his aristocratic poise in neat essays (*Discursions on Travel, Art and Life*, 1925; *Sing High! Sing Low!*, 1944; *Pound Wise*, 1963), but perhaps most successfully in his very popular autobiographical volumes, which mingle personal reminiscence, a fine sense of social style and shrewd judgement (*Left Hand, Right Hand!*, 1944; *The Scarlet Tree*, 1946; *Great Morning*, 1948; *Laughter in the Next Room*, 1949; and *Noble Essences*, 1950). [A R]

J. Lehmann, *A Nest of Tigers* (1968).

Sitwell, Sacheverell (1897–   ). Poet and essayist. Born at Scarborough, the brother of Edith ◊ Sitwell and Osbert ◊ Sitwell, and educated at Eton, during the First World War he served in the Grenadier Guards. He has published 15 volumes of poetry characterized by a subtle mystery and clever informality; these include *The People's Palace* (1918), *The Hundred and One Harlequins* (1922) and *The Cyder Feast* (1927). He is perhaps best known now, however, as a learned and sensitive critic of culture with a dash of dilettante aestheticism and has written a number of lively books, including *Southern Baroque Art* (1924), *German Baroque Art* (1927), *Spanish Baroque Art* (1931), *British Architects and Craftsmen* (1945), *The Red Chapel of Banteai Srei* (1962) and *Monks, Nuns and Monasteries* (1965). He also writes intelligent travel books (*The Netherlands*, 1948, and *Spain*, 1950). *Truffle Hunt with Sacheverell Sitwell* (1953) is a collection of essays, and he is publishing reminiscences. [A R]

J. Lehmann, *A Nest of Tigers* (1968).

Skeat, Walter William (1835–1912). Scholar and philologist. Born in London, the son of an architect, he was educated there at King's College School, Highgate School, and at Christ's College, Cambridge, where he became a Fellow in 1860. After some years as a curate, in 1864 ill-health forced his return to his college as a lecturer in mathematics. Skeat privately pursued the study of early English texts under the impetus of historical reading and also turned his attention to the history of the language. In 1878, he was elected to the Elrington and Bosworth chair of Anglo-Saxon at Cambridge. He produced a large number of editions, such as *Lancelot of the Laik* (E E T S, 1865); *Piers Plowman* (E E T S, 1867–85, for long the authoritative printing); ◊ Barbour's *Bruce* (E E T S, 1870–89); *The Anglo-Saxon Gospels: Northumbrian and Old Mercian* (1871–87); and ◊ Aelfric's *Lives of the Saints* (E E T S, 1881–

1900). His great edition of the *Complete Works of Geoffrey Chaucer* (7 vols., 1894–7; the basis of the Oxford Standard Authors text and other printings) is still in many respects standard. Much of Skeat's work formed the basis of editions used in schools and universities, though it is gradually being superseded by more accurate texts intended for different purposes. Skeat's approach is largely a 'historical', philological one, which imposes severe limitations on his work (however admirable) as the basis for the study of old texts in a full social and imaginative context. He founded the English Dialect Society in 1873, and published a number of etymological works such as the *Etymological Dictionary of the English Language Arranged on an Historical Basis* (1882; revised and enlarged 1910). He was a prolific writer of reviews, essays and notes in journals, and interested himself in spelling reform and the developing systematic study of place-names. His *Primer of Classical and English Philology* (1905) and *The Science of Etymology* (1912) were the kind of works which gave direction to the 'scientific', yet historical, study of the language, which was then held to be the stiffening required in the newish university English courses. [A R]

A Student's Pastime (1896) (includes autobiographical essay); *D N B*.

Skelton, John (1464?–1529). Poet. Educated at both Oxford and Cambridge, Skelton took orders in 1498, and at about that time went to court as tutor to Prince Henry (Henry VIII). His earliest poetry is typically late-medieval and heavily aureate, but the *Bouge of Court* (1498–9) uses the dream-allegory as the vehicle for a lively satire of court intrigue. His period as Rector (1502–11?) of Diss in Norfolk, his home county, contains much of his most distinctive and attractive work – poems like *Philip Sparrow*, *Ware the Hawk*, and *The Tunning of Eleanor Rumming*, written in 'Skeltonics' (short lines, usually 3-stress, with irregular but persistent rhyme). *Philip Sparrow*, treating a child's grief at the loss of her pet in mock-heroic tones, is light, tender and artless, while in *The Tunning of Eleanor Rumming*, low-life comedy depicting the ale-wife and her customers, the disorder of the verse is in keeping with the crudeness of the setting. From 1512, Skelton starts describing himself as *Orator Regius*, and many of the works in this period are semi-official in purpose – the political ballads against the Scots, or the vast morality play *Magnificence* (1515). Perhaps the lampoons on Cardinal Wolsey, *Colin Clout* and *Why Come Ye Not to Court?* (1522), could be classed with them. These are good invective, and made an effect, for Skelton had to seek sanctuary from the Archbishop's anger at Westminster. He soon found a new protector in the Countess of Surrey, to whom he addressed *The Garland of Laurel* (1523), a dull reversion to formal allegory, partly redeemed by a few short 'Skeltonic' lyrics. The cryptic *Speke Parot* (1521) is probably another attack on Wolsey; though the meaning is lost, it can be read with pleasure now, almost as inspired nonsense poetry.

Skelton impresses more as a personality than as a poet, and, in spite of the great enjoyment to be derived from him, not as a particularly pleasant one, for he is a trimmer and a time-server. As a poet, his strength and his limitation is his artlessness, which is basic and not assumed. The relationship of style to subject matter is quite hit-or-miss. Historically he is difficult to place. He used medieval forms throughout his life, and his 'humanism', though there are signs of it in, say, *Magnificence*, is superficial. He is an arch-individualist. [A G]

Complete Poems, ed. P. Henderson (1931).
H. L. R. Edwards, *S.: The Life and Times of an Early Tudor Poet* (1949); S. Fish, *J.S.'s Poetry* (1965); I. A. Gordon, *J.S.* (1943); C. S. Lewis, *English Literature in the Sixteenth Century* (1954); J. Holloway, *The Charted Mirror* (1960).

Skinner, John (1721–1807). Poet and song writer. An Episcopalian minister in Aberdeenshire, he wrote an *Ecclesiastical History of Scotland* (1788) but is remembered as the writer of 'Tullochgorum' and some other of the raciest and most genial Scots songs before the time of Burns, to whose own collections Skinner contributed. [A I]

Songs and Poems, ed. H. G. Reid (1859).
W. Walker, *Life and Times of J.S.* (1883).

Slater, Francis Carey (1876–1959). South African poet. Born near Grahamstown. In 1899 he began a banking career, taking a job in Port Elizabeth. It took him to many parts of the Eastern Districts, including the bleak Karroo, which he came to love. He retired from the managership of a Grahamstown bank in 1930, and devoted himself to writing.

Slater's *Collected Poems* (1957) divides naturally into 4 parts. In 'Drought' (1929) he uses a favourite structural technique of linked lyrics – in this case closely linked and written in irregular, unrhymed verse. The poems align drought, the land's sickness, with hate, the sickness of South African society. In 'Dark Folk' (1935) he re-creates in English the language and feelings of the Xhosas, again in a series of linked lyrics. 'The Trek' (1938) is a long narrative poem about the Great Trek. Constant metrical variation and the frequent introduction of lyrics prevent monotony at the expense of a sustained level of achievement. However, the poem is a fine combination of undercharged narration and imaginative structure. The extended symbolic lyric, 'The Dead Eagle', is the finest of his other poems. [P T]

G. M. Miller and H. Sergeant, *A Critical Survey of South African Poetry in English* (1957).

Slessor, Kenneth (1901–). Australian poet. Born at Orange, New South Wales, and educated in Sydney. His long journalistic experience began in 1920 in Sydney with the *Sun*. His early poems carried into words some of the decorative daring of Norman ◊ Lindsay, with whom he worked on the magazine *Vision* (1923–4). After two years on Melbourne papers Slessor returned to Sydney in 1927 to join *Smith's Weekly*, which he later edited. He published 3 further volumes of poetry before 1939, in which verbal energy became increasingly tempered by irony. During the war he was Official War Correspondent with the Australian Army. Since then he has written virtually no poetry. *One Hundred Poems* (1944) was a collection of all he wished to preserve. *Poems* (1957) has only 3 additions. After the war he returned to journalism in Sydney. He edited the literary quarterly *Southerly* (1956–61), and was one of the editors of *The Penguin Book of Australian Verse* (1958).

Slessor's technique is dramatic. In poems like 'Captain Dobbin' he preserves his early eloquence and eye for eccentricity, but with overtones of unease. Time and the sea, favourite themes in Slessor, are ominous in the fine elegy 'Five Bells'. In much of his work, concern leads disquietingiy quickly to disenchantment. [P T]

V. Buckley, *Essays in Poetry, Mainly Australian* (1957); T. Inglis Moore, 'K. S.', *Southerly*, 4 (1947).

Smart, Christopher (1722–71). Poet. Born at Shipborne in Kent, the son of a steward on the estate of Lord Vane. When he was 11, his father died and he went to live in Durham, where he became the *protégé* of another member of the Vane family, Lord Barnard, of Raby Castle. In October 1739, he was admitted to Pembroke College, Cambridge, where he became well known for his Latin verses (he published a famous Latin version of Pope's 'Ode on St Cecilia's Day' in 1743). He took his B.A. in 1744, and was elected Fellow of the college in 1745. At this time he began publishing English verse, but in 1747, when he took his M.A., he seems to have begun to lose control of his affairs and was arrested for debt. With the aid of his friends he was back at the college in 1748. In 1749, he went to London and made a meagre living as a miscellaneous writer for John Newbery's periodicals *The Student, or Oxford and Cambridge Monthly Miscellany* and *The Mid-Wife, or The Old Woman's Magazine*. Smart produced with success all the usual contributions expected at that time in magazines: essays, satires and witty pieces. His *Poems on Several Occasions* (1752) contains his georgic, *The Hop-Garden*, which with its Miltonizing is related to such poems as *Cyder* by John ◊ Philips but also contains some touching, direct realization of childhood memories. In 1756 he published a prose translation of the *Works of Horace* ('Satires' and 'Epistles', Everyman, 1911) and also wrote his *Hymn to the Supreme Being on Recovery from a Dangerous Fit of Illness*. This was the onset of his mental disease, which took the form of religious mania and from which he suffered severely for the next seven years, being at intervals forcibly confined in St Luke's Hospital. Here he wrote such poems, not published until 1939, as *Rejoice in the Lamb, A Song from Bedlam*, which he called *Jubilate Agno* (ed. W. H. Bond, 1954). In 1763 he published *A Song to David*, which had probably been written a year or two earlier. This made no impact at the time, and his later writing, now highly valued, passed almost unnoticed. Browning admired the *Song*, and since then Smart's reputation (developed by Sir Edmund ◊ Gosse) has grown steadily. Some of his other works are: *A Translation of the Psalms of David* (1765); *The Works of Horace Translated into Verse* (1767) and *Parables of Our Lord and Saviour, Jesus Christ, Done into Familiar Verse*. On 26 April 1770 he entered prison for debt; there he completed his *Hymns for the Amusement of Children* (1770; edited in 1947 for the Luttrell Society) and died in the next year. *A Song to David* (ed. E. Blunden, 1924; ed. J. B. Broadbent, 1960) is one of the most splendid poems of the century, full of direct writing, great verbal dexterity and beauty, wide-ranging imagery (familiar and exotic). His mania, a command 'to pray without ceasing', is transmuted by genius in his poems into a piercing honesty and a truly happy piety. The simplicity of his nature is, however, matched with a technique and authority which more recent closer study of his works is slowly unfolding. [AR]

Collected Poems, ed. N. Callan (Muses' Library, 2 vols., 1949) (excluding translations); *Poems by C.S.*, ed. R. E. Brittain (Princeton U.P., 1950) (selection with introductory essay). G. Grigson, *C.S.* (WTW, 1961) (with bibliography); C. Devlin, *Poor Kit S.* (1961).

Smiles, Dr Samuel (1812–1904). Biographer, miscellaneous writer and popular moralist. Born near Edinburgh and educated at Haddington High School and Edinburgh University, where he studied medicine. After practising in Scotland, he took up journalism, and later business (as secretary to several of the fast-developing railway companies). In the midst of these various occupations, and drawing material from them, he produced biographies of successful industrialists like Josiah Wedgwood and self-taught men such as Robert Dick, the baker of Thurso. He used these works to put forward ideas of political and social reform blended with the more orthodox economic and ethical doctrine of 'self-interest' which he derived from the 'Manchester School', for example *Life of George Stephenson* (1857), *Lives of the Engineers* and *Industrial Biography* (1863). His most famous work was the enormously popular *Self-Help: With Illustrations of Character and Conduct* (1859; centenary edn intr. Asa Briggs, 1958; translated into many languages). [AR]

Asa Briggs, *Victorian People* (1954); A. Smiles, *S.S. and His Surroundings* (1956).

Smith, Adam (1723–90). Scottish economist. Smith, educated at Glasgow University and Balliol, attracted the attention of the Edinburgh 'Select Society' of Hume and Robertson by his lectures on literature, and so obtained the Chairs of Logic (1751) and of Moral Philosophy (1752) at Glasgow. His eloquent, optimistic and shallow *Theory of Moral Sentiments* (1759), deriving from ◊ Shaftesbury and ◊ Hutcheson, forms an intellectual counterpart to the literary movement associated with Henry ◊ Mackenzie. Its immediate fashionable success brought Smith a tutorship to a young duke, and, consequently, a European tour and the pension that enabled him to retire for ten years to his native Kirkcaldy and compose his masterly *Inquiry into the Nature and Causes of the Wealth of Nations* (1776), the foundation of classical economics and still a standard textbook. Its impact came from Smith's comprehensiveness and the range and particularity of his illustrations rather than from actual originality of thought; many of Smith's theories and arguments had been anticipated by ◊ Hobbes, ◊ Mandeville and the French physiocrats. Smith's emphasis on the free market underlies Victorian liberalism, the Free Trade movement, and much later capitalist doctrine; he disapproves of price-rings as strongly as he does of government intervention, remarking that 'People of the same trade seldom meet together even for merriment or diversion but the conversation ends in some conspiracy against the public, or in some contrivance to raise prices'. Smith has been criticized for stressing mere exchange at the expense of production, and for regarding the 'free market' with a facile optimism resembling his philosophical position. [AI]

Lectures on Rhetoric and Belles Lettres, ed. J. M. Lothian (1963).
J. Rae, *Life of A.S.* (1895); G. Morrow, *The Ethical and Economic Theories of A.S.* (1923); C. R. Fay, *A.S. and the Scotland of His Day* (1956) and *The World of A.S.* (1960).

Smith, Alexander (1830–67). Scottish poet. Smith, a designer of patterns for lacework in Glasgow, enjoyed a brief success in the 1850s with his *Life-drama* (published in a periodical in 1851, in a volume in 1853) and his *City Poems* (1857). 'Literary', extravagant, technically coarse and ultimately naïve, Smith's verse recalls his American contemporary Poe's. Nicknamed (with his collaborator ◊ Dobell and his critical patron Gilfillan) ◊ 'Spasmodic', satirized by ◊ Aytoun and entangled in controversy over his alleged plagiarism from Tennyson, Smith turned to prose. His novels (chiefly *Alfred Hagart's Household*, 1866) and the

once very popular essays in *Dreamthorp* (1863) are less readable today than his Highland sketches, *A Summer in Skye* (1865). Smith was appointed Secretary to Edinburgh University; otherwise his career of early 'discovery' and excessive patronage followed by neglect and premature death follows the general pattern for Scottish working-class poets from Burns and Fergusson down to such obscure figures as William Thom and David Gray. [AI]

Poetical Works, ed. W. Sinclair (1909).
P. P. Alexander, Memoir in Smith's *Last Leaves* (1868); T. Brisbane, *The Early Years of A.S.* (1869).

Smith, Arthur James Marshall (1902–   ). Canadian poet. Born in Montreal and educated at McGill University, he founded the *McGill Fortnightly Review* and published in it his earliest poetry and criticism (1925–6). After doing graduate work at Edinburgh University, he taught in a Montreal school. A long association with the English Department of the Michigan State University began in 1936, the year in which some of his poems appeared in the *New Provinces* anthology.

Although he has spent much of his life outside Canada, Smith has had a great influence on Canadian poetry. He is the editor of 2 crucial anthologies, *The Book of Canadian Poetry* (1943, 1948, 1957) and *The Oxford Book of Canadian Verse* (1958), and the author of a number of essays on Canadian poetry. His own output is surprisingly meagre – some of the poems from his slim first book, *News of the Phoenix* (1943), are included in his slim second, *A Sort of Ecstasy* (1954) – but this is the result of rigorous self-criticism. He is an austere poet who deploys a carefully selected diction in taut, syntactical groupings. He has been open to various recognizable influences, most of them leading him towards the still centre of poetic craftsmanship rather than out into a world ominous of chaos. His refusal to indulge a passion for 'poetry' in his poems has made him a leader of Canadian 'academic' poetry. [PT]

Collected Poems (1962); *Poems New and Collected* (1967).
D. Pacey, *Ten Canadian Poets* (1958); F. R. Scott, 'A.J.M.S.', *Leading Canadian Poets*, ed. W. P. Percival (1948).

Smith, Mrs Charlotte Turner (1749–1806). Poet and novelist. She took to writing when her husband, a West Indian merchant, ruined himself. Apart from her sonnets (following the fashion set by ♢ Bowles) and other poems, she is known for 2 rather formless novels, *Emmeline* (1788) and *The Old Manor House* (1793), which exploit in a lively way the interests of the time, such as tourism and the French Revolution; and for her observation of contemporary manners. She also wrote educational works. [AR]

F. M. A. Hilbish, *C.S.*, *Poet and Novelist* (Philadelphia, 1941).

Smith, Horatio or **Horace** (1779–1849). Stockbroker, poet and novelist. Born in London, the son of a solicitor, and educated at Chigwell, Smith was the author of a number of novels (mostly historical) and short stories, the most popular of which was *Brambletye House, or Cavaliers and Roundheads* (3 vols., 1826). He also wrote 2 comedies (one, *Amarynthus, the Nympholept*, 1821, a verse pastoral) as well as comic poems (in which he was most successful) and serious verse; he was a friend of Shelley and Keats. Smith is best known as the co-author, with his elder brother James ♢ Smith, of *Rejected Addresses, or, The New Theatrum Poetarum* (anonymous, 1812; 18th edn, carefully revised, 1833; ed. with a bibliography by A. Boyle, 1928). This clever and popular series of parodies purported to be poems unsuccessfully submitted for the prize offered by the proprietors of the New Drury Lane Theatre for an address to be recited at the opening. (Byron in fact finally did write the prologue.) Horace Smith did Walter Scott and Moore. The brothers also wrote *Horace in London* (imitations of the *Odes*, Books I and II) (1813), reprinted from the *Monthly Mirror*. [AR]

A. H. Beavan, *James and H.S.* (1899).

Smith, Iain Crichton (Iain Mac a' Ghobhainn) (1928–   ). Scottish Gaelic poet and short-story writer. Smith uses English mainly as his medium for verse, and Gaelic for his short stories. He teaches English at Oban High School.

In his Gaelic verse, which is small in quantity, he tends to use traditional forms to discuss contemporary subjects, as when he echoes cosy 20th-century songs in a cynical appraisal of personal relations in the nuclear age. His chief contribution to modern Gaelic literature is as a writer of short stories. He has published 2 collections, *Burn is Aran* (1960) and *An Dubh is an Gorm* (1963), besides writing regularly for the Gaelic quarterly *Gairm*. Many of his stories are psychological explorations of single characters, such as Abraham or Napoleon, or of two characters caught in some close or tense situation, e.g. the Ground Officer and the old Lady he is evicting from her land, a British and a German soldier confronting each other in the mud of France, a Calvinistic minister attempting an eleventh-hour conversion of a young boy dying of T.B. His best stories are spare, tense and stark. His sense of dialogue is finely developed.

A translation and adaptation of one of his best long-short stories, 'An Dubh is an Gorm', appeared in *New Saltire*, 7, under the title 'The Black and the Red'. [DT]

Biobuill is Sanasan-reice (1965).

Smith, James (1775–1839). Humorous writer. Elder brother of Horace ♢ Smith, he was also at school in Chigwell and became a solicitor, succeeding his father as Solicitor to the Board of Ordnance. He contributed the parodies of Wordsworth, Coleridge and Crabbe to the very popular *Rejected Addresses* (1812). [AR]

A. H. Beavan, *J. and Horace S.* (1899).

Smith, (Lloyd) Logan Pearsall (1865–1946). Essayist and critic. Born in Millville, N.J., the son of a Quaker glass manufacturer of an eminent Philadelphia family (Walt Whitman stayed with them; Smith's cousin was president of Bryn Mawr College; his sisters married Bernard Berenson and Bertrand Russell). He was educated at Haverford College and Harvard. Giving up his father's business, he went to study at Balliol College, Oxford, and settled in England. He was a friend of Matthew Arnold and Whistler, the painter. His mind and temperament, and the tone of his writing, are American expatriate of a certain kind: finicky, neutral, 'ironic' in the sense of rather colourlessly detached. He became well known to a select circle by his collection of essays and aphorisms, *Trivia* (1902; at first privately printed), and he wrote much in this short form (*More Trivia*, 1922; *Afterthoughts*, 1931; *Last Words*, 1933; collected as *All Trivia*, 1933). His self-mocking, defensive intellectual withdrawal was accompanied by an admiration of

English 'society' and wealth. He published historical and critical works which, within their narrow scope, showed learning and sensitivity: among these are *The Life and Letters of Sir Henry Wotton* (1907), *On Reading Shakespeare* (1933) and *Milton and His Modern Critics* (1940). His once-influential writings on language are characterized by mandarin notions of 'authority' and 'taste' as elements in choice writing (see *The English Language*, 1912, and *Words and Idioms*, 1925). He also published volumes of verse.

Unforgotten Years (1938) is autobiographical and R. Gathorne-Hardy in *Recollections of Logan Pearsall Smith* (1949) gives a close, sad account of his last sixteen years of life. [A R]

Ed. J. Russell, *A Portrait of L.P.S. Drawn from His Letters and Diaries* (1950).

Smith, Sydney (1771–1845). Wit, parson and journalist. Born in Essex in a family of small country gentry, he was educated at Winchester and New College, Oxford, where he was a Fellow (1791). He was in Edinburgh as a tutor to Michael Hicks Beach and joined the group, including ◊ Jeffrey and ◊ Brougham, that founded the ◊ *Edinburgh Review*. Smith contributed articles to this periodical, which gave scope for his liberalism, urge for reform and liking for satire. He went to London in 1803, and his personal address secured him a place in the brilliant Holland House Whig set. His best-known and longest work is *The Letters of Peter Plymley* (1807; ed. G. C. Heseltine, 1929), a good-humoured tract in support of Catholic emancipation. His *Works* were collected (1839–40) and include lectures on moral philosophy, given at the Royal Institution, and sermons. Smith's celebrated conversational wit is difficult to enjoy and discuss at this distance of time. His churchmanship was broad (he would have preferred to have been a lawyer) but he adequately performed pastoral duties in Yorkshire and Somerset, and in 1831 a canonry of St Paul's gave him more scope for his great energy in good works. [A R]

Works (3 vols., 1854; 2 vols., 1859); *Selected Writings*, ed. W. H. Auden (1953); *Letters*, ed. N. C. Smith (2 vols., 1953; selection, World's Classics, 1956).
Hesketh Pearson, *The Smith of Smiths* (1934).

Smith, Sydney Goodsir (1915–). Scots poet and leading member of the second generation of Hugh ◊ MacDiarmid's 'Scottish Renaissance'. Smith, a native of New Zealand, settled in Edinburgh in his early twenties and began to publish poems in Scots about 1940. During the 1940s his poetry showed an increasingly successful assimilation of the rhythm and contractions of spoken Scots to a literary vocabulary gathered from the Middle Scots poets and from MacDiarmid himself. Smith used this medium directly, in various ironic modes, and in creative conjunction with a range of reference to Latin, German, French, Russian and Scots literature surpassed among the 'Renaissance' writers, if at all, only by Grieve. His early volumes (*Skail Wind*, 1941; *The Wanderer*, 1943; *The Deevil's Waltz*, 1946) include some political and elegiac verse, but the best work in them is the love-lyrics which, in the main, appear to chronicle one particular developing relationship. A breach in this, and the narrator's consequent breakdown into a state of regretful lethargy, is the theme of Smith's finest work, the 'XXIV Elegies' of *Under the Eildon Tree* (1948). Here, celebratory short lyrics alternate with longer poems that reflect on the whole affair and examine it sometimes from a viewpoint of harsh yet comic realism (with a debt to Propertius) and sometimes through exalted mythical masks – Aeneas, Orpheus (both influenced by the comparable work of Gavin ◊ Douglas), Antony, Tristan, Cuchulain, Thomas the Rhymer. The speaker delicately and seriously explores the mixed emotions, including undiminished love for the woman he has, perhaps, let down, that the affair has left in him. Smith's less ambitious later poetry (*So Late into the Night*, 1952; *Figs and Thistles*, 1959; pamphlet collections, and poems in magazines) might be summed up as Scots lyric in the mode of Robert Graves. Smith has turned increasingly to editing – of small periodicals, of collections of essays (on Robert ◊ Fergusson and MacDiarmid), and of editions or selections of Douglas and Burns. He has published a verse-play, *The Wallace* (1960), and a comic novel, *Carotid Cornucopius* (1947; augmented 1964), a Joycean extravaganza in which Smith's bawdy and outrageous playing about with his manufactured language predominates. [A I]

N. MacCaig, 'The Poetry of S.G.S.', *Saltire Review*, I (1954).
J. Speirs, *The Scots Literary Tradition* (1962);

K. Wittig, *The Scottish Tradition in Literature* (1958).

Smollett, Tobias George (1721–71). Novelist, poet, satirist and miscellaneous writer. Born at Dalquhurn, Cardross, in Dumbartonshire, he claimed descent from a local family of landowners. He went to school in Dumbarton, studied at the University of Glasgow and was apprenticed to a surgeon. In 1739 he set out for London to make his fortune with an unlucky tragedy, *The Regicide: or, James the First of Scotland*. Having failed to get it acted (it was no more successful when he printed it at his own expense in 1749), he shipped in 1741 as a surgeon's mate on H.M.S. *Chichester* with Ogle's West India Squadron. He was present at the attack on Cartagena, and lived for some years in Jamaica, where he married. He returned to London in 1744 and practised as a physician, rather unsuccessfully.

Smollett wrote much as a journalist, translator and hack writer, but he is most famous as a novelist. The qualities that he put to use as a controversialist – anger, spite, opportunism, particularity and energy – give his novels a solidity and vitality which prevent them from being dismissed; at the same time, however, they prevented Smollett from excelling in some of the qualities now admired in fiction. His reputation has declined from the time when liveliness and rough humour were admired, through a period (in the last century) when his comments on his society were thought to be too savage, indiscreet, 'low' and outspoken. Now he is sometimes undervalued on the ground that his fiction has little formal structure or obvious coherence, and appears unruly and sprawling. His first novel, *The Adventures of Roderick Random* (2 vols., 1748), appeared in the same year as Richardson's *Clarissa* and the year before *Tom Jones. Roderick Random* (Everyman, 1927) is a loosely linked series of vivid episodes, joined in a picaresque fashion by the travels of the partly autobiographical Scottish hero. These travels allow realistic descriptions of life in the 18th-century royal navy and of manners in the West Indies, and a satirical *exposé* of London life, before the novel's happy ending. Smollett was much interested in the picaresque and in writing satire. He translated *Gil Blas* (1749; ed. J. Fitzmaurice Kelly, World's Classics, 1907) and *Don Quixote* (1755; often reprinted as a standard version until the early 19th century), and the influence of Le Sage and Cervantes is seen throughout his writing. His second novel, *The Adventures of Peregrine Pickle* (4 vols., 1751; Everyman, 1930; ed. and intr. J. L. Clifford, Oxford English Novels, 1964), contains one of the best examples of Smollett's art of caricature, in the eccentric Commodore Hawser Trunnion. Under the influence of modern trends in fiction, his expertise in this art (reminiscent of Hogarth or Daumier) gains Smollett more respect than formerly. The swollen chapter 81, 'Memoirs of a Lady of Quality', shows Smollett's surprising lack of local structural tact. *In The Adventures of Ferdinand, Count Fathom* (2 vols., 1753), Smollett pioneers the gothick horrors which became popular later in the century. *The Adventures of Sir Launcelot Greaves* (first published in Smollett's periodical, the *British Magazine*, 1760–2; 2 vols., 1762) is a rather clumsy, modernized version of Don Quixote's adventures. Greaves, though mad, misses the tragic force and powerful ambiguity of the Spanish hero. The last novel, *The Expedition of Humphry Clinker* (3 vols., 1771; Everyman, ed. H. Mumford Jones and C. Lee, 1943; ed. and intr. A. Ross, PEL, 1967), told in an ingenious series of overlapping correspondences, is Smollett's best book. The writers of the letters are brilliantly individualized both by their different observation of life in Bath and London and on a journey through the island of Britain, and by an inventive use of different styles of letter-writing. The book is held together by the composite picture formed of a more mellow Smollett, an acute judge of the British scene exploiting his knack for detail, sensitivity to class-differences and preoccupation with national and religious differences. Smollett was a voluminous miscellaneous writer, which may account for the long-winded passages in his fiction. He was co-editor and translator of the *Works of Voltaire* (5 vols., 1761–5); his long-popular *Complete History of England* (4 vols., 1757–8; continuation 4 vols., 1760–1) was often printed with the *History* of David Hume; 7 volumes of a *Compendium of Authentic and Entertaining Voyages* appeared in 1756. Smollett edited the *Critical Review* (1756–63) and *The Briton*, in support of Lord Bute, from 29 May 1762 to 12 February 1763. His violent political, literary and personal partisanship often landed him in trouble and he spent a brief period in prison for libel. [A R]

Works, ed. D. Herbert (1870; etc.); ed. W. E. Henley and T. Seccombe (12 vols., 1899–1901); ed. G. Saintsbury (12 vols., 1895) (prose fiction only); *Travels through France and Italy* (1766; ed. T. Seccombe, World's Classics, 1907); *Letters*, ed. E. S. Noyes (1926).

L. M. Knapp, *T.S.: Doctor of Men and Manners* (1949); L. L. Martz, *The Later Career of T.S.* (1942); G. M. Kahrl, *T.S.: Traveller-Novelist* (1945); R. Giddings, *The Tradition of S.* (1967); A. D. McKillop, *The Early Masters of English Fiction* (1956).

Snow, C(harles) P(ercy) (Baron Snow of Leicester) (1905–   ). Novelist, publicist and scientist. Born in Leicester and educated there at Alderman Newton's School and the University College. He went to Christ's College, Cambridge, and after taking a Ph.D. for research in physics he became a Fellow of the college in 1930 and was a tutor (1935–45). He joined the Government service as a scientific expert during the Second World War, and was a Civil Service Commissioner (1945–60). From 1938 to 1940 he edited *Discovery*. Snow's first work of fiction was a detective story, *Death under Sail* (1932); his first serious novel, *The Search* (1934; reprinted with slight revision 1958), contains some allusions to most of the preoccupations found in his later work – ethics (particularly of scientific honesty), politics and power. The story (like later works) is told by an autobiographical narrator. Since 1935, he has been writing a sequence of novels under the general title of 'Strangers and Brothers', dealing over an extended period of time (from the early 1930s to the present day) with the life of a lawyer, Lewis Eliot – who is sometimes an autobiographical narrator – his brother Martin Eliot, a physicist; and various friends and colleagues in business, the University of Cambridge, scientific endeavour and the public service (which Snow views as the situation of 'power'). *Strangers and Brothers* (1940) was the first to appear. The others are *The Light and the Dark* (1947); *Time of Hope* (1949), in which Eliot is the narrator; *The Masters* (1951), which won the James Tait Black Prize and has been successfully dramatized by Ronald Miller; *The New Men* (1954), in which Martin Eliot first appears as a major character, and which deals with the clash of power in wartime scientific research; *Homecomings* (1956), another Lewis Eliot autobiography; *The Conscience of the Rich* (1958), which goes back into Lewis

Eliot's life and deals with the family of his Jewish friend, Charles March; *The Affair* (1960; dramatized by Ronald Millar), another treatment of the ethics of scientific discovery; and *Corridors of Power* (1963); which gains a certain interest because in 1964 Snow was made a life peer and an Under-Secretary of State in the Ministry of Technology in the Labour government (resigned, 1966). The latest title in the series is *In Pursuit of Reason* (1968). In 1950 Snow married the novelist Pamela ◊ Hansford-Johnson and he was knighted in 1957. He has written *The Two Cultures and the Scientific Revolution* (Cambridge, Rede Lecture, 1959), and offers himself, on the strength of his scientific interests, 'political' career and career as a novelist, as a bridge between the 'literary' traditional culture and the culture of science. In *Science and Government* (Harvard, Godkin Lecture, 1961) he discusses his other main interest, the interplay of power involved in large-scale government-sponsored scientific research. The programme for his series of novels involves an imaginative treatment of the scientific culture and attitude, but this is not really worked out. He presents an often fascinating, quite orthodox ethical study in a scientific setting, just as Trollope did in a political setting. [A R]

W. Cooper, *C.P.S.* (WTW, 1959); R. Gorham Davis, *C.P.S.* (Columbia Essays on Modern Writers, 1965) (both with bibliographies); F. Karl, *C.P.S.: The Politics of Conscience* (S. Illinois U.P., 1963); B. Bergonzi, 'The World of Lewis Eliot', *Twentieth Century*, CLXVII (February 1960); F. R. Leavis, 'The Significance of C. P. Snow', *Spectator*, CCVIII (16 March 1962) (a private lecture which being made public provoked an interesting controversy); *Two Cultures* (1963) (containing Leavis's lecture and M. Yudkin, 'Sir Charles Snow's Rede Lecture'); ed. D. K. Cornelius and E. St Vincent, *Cultures in Conflict: Perspectives in the Snow–Leavis Controversy* (1964).

Somerville, Edith Anna Oenone (1858–1949). Novelist and miscellaneous writer. Born in Corfu, the daughter of an Irish land owner, she was educated abroad, in Paris. She was a Master of Foxhounds (1903–19) and published *Notes of the Horn* (1934), a hunting anthology. She is best known for the novels she wrote with her cousin Violet Florence Martin (◊ Ross, Martin), under the names 'Somerville and Ross', the best of which are *The Real Charlotte* (1894), *Some Experiences of an Irish R.M.* (Resident Magistrate)

(1899), *Further Experiences of an Irish R.M.* (1908) and *In Mr Knox's Country* (1915). These tales are well written, humorous and competent pictures of a now vanished Irish rural society under the Anglo-Irish ascendancy, seen from the upper-class point of view. [AR]

Soutar, William (1898–1943). Scots poet. Soutar, the son of a Perth joiner, contracted a spinal infection while serving on the lower deck in the navy (1916–19) and became an invalid shortly after he graduated from Edinburgh University with third-class honours in English in 1923; all the poems he is remembered by were written after he became totally bedridden in 1929. Like other followers of Hugh ◊ MacDiarmid, Soutar worked to revitalize Scots as a literary language by extending its range and applying its traditional modes to modern experience and feelings; he wrote some haunting poems about the psychological effects of his illness, and his epigrams and children's verses are also touched sharply with feeling for the life he was losing. His English poems and his diaries confirm his vitality and intelligence. [AI]

Collected Poems, ed. H. MacDiarmid (1948) (incomplete); *Poems in Scots and English*, selected W. R. Aitken (1961); *Diaries of a Dying Man*, ed. A. Scott (1954).
A. Scott, *Still Life* (1958).

Southerne, Thomas (1660–1746). Dramatist. Born near Dublin and educated at Trinity College, Southerne was entered at the Middle Temple in 1678 and subsequently lived in London. His first play, *The Persian Prince, or The Loyal Brother* (1682), had contemporary political references, but his first real popular success was his sentimental drama *The Fatal Marriage, or The Innocent Adultery* (1694) based on Mrs Aphra ◊ Behn's novel *The Nun*. After a number of undistinguished comedies he produced another great success in his tragedy *Oroonoko, or The Royal Slave* (1695), based on Mrs Aphra Behn's novel of the same name (with the addition of a comic sub-plot). *Oroonoko* – both the play and the novel – is a strong if implied protest against the oppression of the Negro and against the slave trade and embodies the concept of the 'noble savage' which was to be of importance in the 18th century. Southerne was a successful practical man of

the theatre and retired rich. His collected works, edited by T.E(vans) with a biography, were published in London in 1774. [DD]

J. W. Dodds, *T.S.*, *Dramatist* (New Haven, 1933).

Southey, Robert (1774–1843). Poet, historian and man of letters. Born at Bristol, the son of a linen-draper, he was a precocious boy, and was educated locally and at Westminster School, from where, however, he was expelled after four years for attacking flogging in an article in the school magazine. He was sent to Balliol College, Oxford, but left without a degree, and having become a friend of ◊ Coleridge joined the group of 'Pantisocrats' in Bristol, who were mustering for the journey to the banks of the Susquehanna river, to found the ideal society. In 1795, Southey abandoned the group (causing a rupture with Coleridge, his future brother-in-law), and went to Lisbon. He stayed in the Peninsula for two years, an important experience in his life, and published *Letters Written in Spain and Portugal* (1797). With Coleridge, Wordsworth and others, Southey was an enthusiastic supporter of the Jacobins, and the Revolution, in France. In 1797, however, he changed his political opinions; this 'apostasy' caused him personal trouble for the rest of his life, and makes him historically important in charting the significant alterations which were taking place then in the English views of the French Revolution. Southey was gradually pushed into the Tory ranks, and became a principal contributor and reviewer in the *Quarterly Review*. As a prose writer, Southey was competent, but spoiled his work by diffuseness and unselectiveness.

Among his voluminous works are a *History of Brazil* (1810–19); *The Life of Nelson* (1813), which was very popular and went through scores of editions (ed. Sir Henry Newbolt, 1925); a *History of the Peninsular War* (1823–32), distinguished by his knowledge of and love for the countries concerned; works in 'defence' of the Anglican Church; many biographies, such as *Lives of the British Admirals* (5 vols., 1833–40). *Sir Thomas More, or Colloquies on the Progress and Prospects of Society* (1829) shows his conservatism, and the impossible historicism of his ideas and expression, a strand in English thinking that was given far more powerful voice by later writers, as were many of Southey's notions: in this case by Ruskin.

It is wrong to think of Southey as a Romantic poet, though his early relationship with Coleridge and his friendship with Wordsworth encourage the connexion. He lived in Keswick, but suffers in being yoked by ◊ Jeffrey into the 'Lake School of Poetry'. He had the misfortune to work in a low-powered way in areas, such as ballad-writing, history poems, exotic romances and narratives, all quite common in the previous age in the work of Gray, the Wartons and less well-known writers, but which were suddenly taken over by really great poets. 'I have a dislike of all strong emotion', he wrote; he was a diligent and erudite writer, who planned excellent poems, but simply never had the imagination to make them work well, though there are things worth reading in the mass of his verse. He was too bookish to let himself go. His long poems are: *Thalaba the Destroyer* (2 vols., 1801 ff.), in 'the Mohammedan taste'; *Madoc* (1805 ff.), in the 'Celtic taste', though Madoc emigrates to the Aztecs; *The Curse of Kehama* (1810 ff.; ed. H. Morley, 1888), perhaps the most readable, in the 'Hindoo taste'; these illustrate his interest in mythologies. *Roderick, the Last of the Goths* (1814) is set in Spain. *A Vision of Judgement* (1821) is remembered only for Byron's savage rejoinder. Southey experimented with irregular, unrhymed lines, blank verse and quantitative measures. He did some things for the first time, but eventually someone did them better. His prose compilations, like *The Doctor* (7 vols., 1834–47), contain more of interest. From his curious reading he often extracted something of value, and sometimes it made a passable short poem, like 'The Inchcape Rock'. As a poet he is historically important as a middleman rather than as an original artist. [A R]

Poetical Works (10 vols., 1837–8) (with his own Prefaces); *Poems*, ed. M. H. Fitzgerald (1909) (prints the longer poems and selects others); *Select Prose*, ed. J. Zeitlin (1916); *Life and Correspondence*, ed. C. C. Southey (6 vols., 1849–50).

W. Haller, *Early Life of S.* (New York, 1917) (bibliography); G. Carnall, *R.S. and His Age: The Development of a Conservative Mind* (1960. and *R.S.* (WTW, 1964) (bibliography); A Cobban, *Edmund Burke and the Revolt against the Eighteenth Century: A Study of the Political and Social Thinking of Byron, Wordsworth, Coleridge and S.* (2nd edn, 1960).

Southwell, Robert (1561–95). Poet and prose-writer. A member of an old Norfolk family, he was educated abroad at Douai (by English Jesuits) and at Paris, where he underwent a spiritual crisis and firmly resolved to enter the Society of Jesus. He became a novice at Rome in 1578 and was ordained priest in 1584. Two years later he set out with Father Henry Garnet on the perilous English mission. He was received by Catholic families who had kept the faith, and for six years, though hounded by the authorities, he pursued his priestly task, moving secretly around London by night, and also published prose devotional works from his secret printing-press. In 1592 Father Southwell was arrested and imprisoned; he was repeatedly racked and tortured at the direction of the notorious Richard Topcliffe. Executed at Tyburn in February 1595, he was beatified and was one of the forty English martyrs canonized in 1970.

He wrote a number of surreptitious works, such as *An Epistle of Comfort to the Reverend Priests* (1587). His prose meditation *Mary Magdalen's Funeral Tears* was openly published in 1591 and went through 7 editions by 1636. In the year of his martyrdom 6 editions of works by him appeared in London – 3 editions of *Saint Peter's Complaint, with Other Poems*, 2 of *Mœoniae, or Certain Excellent Poems and Spiritual Hymns*, and the prose work *The Triumphs over Death. A Short Rule of Good Life* followed after his death (*c.* 1598). *Saint Peter's Complaint* was printed 11 times in England, twice in Scotland, and twice in Europe before 1636.

By circumstance an independent religious poet, Southwell belongs with the later Metaphysicals more through his subtle conceits and imagery than through his metrical qualities. Professor Martz sees him as the first writer of a new kind of English poetry, blending the continental practice of religious 'meditation' with the Elizabethan lyric, and he finds five strands in his work influential on subsequent poets: his poetical 'meditations' on the lives of Christ and Mary, his effort to convert the devices of profane poetry to the service of God, his strong affinities with George Herbert (and with John Donne), his contrasting self-analysis, and his introduction to England of the continental 'literature of tears' – especially Mary Magalden's tears. [M J]

The Poems, ed. J. H. McDonald and N. Pollard Brown (1967); *The Complete Poems*, ed. A. B. Grosart (1872).
C. Devlin, S.J., *The Life of R.S., Poet and Martyr* (1956); ed. L. I. Guiney, *Recusant Poets* (1938); P. Janelle, *R.S. the Writer: A Study in Religious Inspiration* (1935); L. L. Martz, *The Poetry of Meditation: A Study in English Religious Literature of the Seventeenth Century* (1954).

Soyinka, Wole (1934–   ). Nigerian playwright and poet. Born in Abeokuta, the son of a schools' supervisor, he attended the universities of Ibadan and Leeds. He then spent eighteen months studying the theatre in London. He was attached to the Royal Court Theatre, where his play *The Invention* was produced experimentally. In 1960 he returned to Ibadan to study indigenous drama forms at University College. Until his imprisonment shortly after the outbreak of the Nigerian Civil War he was a lecturer in English at the University of Ife, and manages a touring company of players in his spare time.

Soyinka's ambition to develop a Nigerian theatre is apparent in his own plays, several of which have been produced in Nigeria. *The Trials of Brother Jero*, *The Swamp Dwellers* and *The Strong Breed* were collected in *Three Plays* (Ibadan, 1963), and he has also published *A Dance of the Forests* (1963) and a satirical comedy, *The Lion and the Jewel* (1963), in which he presents the imposition of modern civilization on Africa as a threat to the African villagers' individuality. Soyinka's proverbial style, and the strong rhythmic rather than visual quality of his prose as well as his poetry, share with many of his themes a source in Nigerian folklore. His recent work includes a novel, *The Interpreters* (1965), a book of poems, *Idakre* (1967), and 2 plays, *The Road* (1965) and *Kongi's Harvest* (1967). [PT]

Anthologie africaine et malgache, ed. L. Hughes and C. Reygnault (Paris, 1962); *Modern, Poetry from Africa*, ed. G. Moore and U. Bieir (1963). J. Povey, 'West African Drama in English', *Comparative Drama*, I, 2.

Spark, Muriel (1918–   ). Novelist. Born in Edinburgh, she was educated at Gillespie's School for Girls, Edinburgh. Her first published works gave no indication that she would later make her mark as a novelist. *Child of Light* (1951), a reassessment of Mary ◊ Shelley, was run-of-the-mill criticism, and the poems of *The Fanfarlo* (1952) were conventional. The publication of *Emily Brontë* (1953), written in collaboration with Derek Stanford, and *John Masefield* (1953) did little to alter the situation, and it was not until 1957 that *The Comforters* appeared and was favourably reviewed. *Memento Mori* (1959), a gruesome account of life in an old people's hospital is a *tour de force* of a kind, though it is difficult to discern any artistic purpose in it. *The Bachelors* (1960) presents an amusing picture of suburban spiritualism.

Muriel Spark's talent is for fairly loosely directed satire. Though she may lack intellectual toughness, and be unwilling to work towards an improvement of her prose style which is at present anonymous, her novels are entertaining, and her characters quirkily alive. Her virtues and shortcomings can both be seen in *The Prime of Miss Jean Brodie* (1961), which is witty and accomplished, yet finally too slight for what it sets out to achieve. Her other novels include *The Ballad of Peckham Rye* (1960), *Girls of Slender Means* (1963), *The Mandelbaum Gate* (1965), and *The Public Image* (1968). In mid-career, Miss Spark's talent may appear to have hardened already into a certain mannerism, but it is still possible for her to develop in some quite new direction. She is secure in her reputation as an amusing and original, though sometimes verbally clumsy, novelist. [CO]

Collected Stories, i (1967); *Collected Poems*, i (1967).

Spasmodic School. The Scottish poet William ◊ Aytoun gave this title to a number of his contemporaries whose work was produced in what seemed to him uncontrolled verbose spurts. Those thus accused included Alexander ◊ Smith, Sydney ◊ Dobell, Philip ◊ Bailey and Gerald Massey. Dobell was the best poet of the Spasmodic School, a placing which contains little praise. Bailey, like Martin ◊ Tupper, was not really a poet at all and it was only the sheer size and weight of his *Festus* (1839) which induced his semi-literate public to take it seriously. Massey's voluminous works were forgiven, chiefly on the grounds that he was self-educated. Smith was accused of copying Tennyson. [RB]

M. A. Weinstein, *W. E. Aytoun and the Spasmodic Controversy* (1968).

Spence, James Lewis Thomas Chalmers (1874–1955). Scottish poet. A native of

Broughty Ferry outside Dundee, he studied dentistry at Edinburgh in the 1890s and imbibed from William ◊ Sharp, Patrick Geddes and their 'Scottish Renaissance' of the time a characteristic blend of patriotism, Francophilia and interest in the occult. After some years in journalism (including three years with the *L.itish Weekly*, the medium through which the ◊ 'Kailyard' novelists Barrie, John Watson and S. R. Crockett had reached the world ten years previously) Spence settled in Edinburgh and wrote substantial works on mythology and anthropology, with a special emphasis on South America. He was one of the poets who formed the Scottish Renaissance movement in the 1920s, and a founder of the Scottish National Party in 1929. His verses combine the aesthetic attitudes of his youth with a rather academic, unidiomatic Scots, drawn from the old 'aureate' tradition rather than from contemporary speech or less remote literary models. [A I]

Collected Poems (1953) (selection from his earlier volumes).
C. M. Grieve, *Contemporary Scottish Studies* (1926).

Spence, Joseph (1699–1768). Miscellaneous writer. Prebendary of Durham and Professor of Poetry at Oxford, he was the author of a number of learned and critical works. He is now chiefly remembered for his *Anecdotes*, long known and quoted, but unpublished until 1820 (ed. E. Malone, 1820; ed. S. W. Singer, 1820; ed. with notes and commentary J. M. Osborn, 1966), which preserve much useful information about his friend Pope and the contemporary literature. [A R]

A. Wright, *J.S. A Critical Biography* (Chicago, 1952).

Spencer, Herbert (1820–1903). Philosopher, sociologist and writer on education. The son of Methodist parents in Derby, Spencer received part of his early education (1833–6) from his uncle, Thomas Spencer, Rector of Hinton Charterhouse near Bath, where he later maintained he learned nothing of any significance. He then trained as a railway engineer, but soon gave up this profession to devote himself to journalism and philosophy. He was sub-editor of *The Economist* (1848–53). He came to know George Eliot through the publisher John Chapman and also met Thomas ◊ Huxley and Tindall. Ardently adopting the Dar-

winian theory of evolution, Spencer constructed a philosophy based on evolution as the ultimate principle both in the universe itself and in our knowledge of it. He went on to apply the same principle to sociology and ethics, attempting with limited success to develop an individualist utilitarianism from biological data (*The Data of Ethics*, forming part I of *Principles of Ethics*, 2 vols., 1892–3). Spencer also applied his evolutionary theory to aesthetics, deriving human aesthetic needs from the fact that human beings accumulate more energy than is necessary for survival. The increased efficiency of social adaptation made more unused energy available for art. This view is expressed in his *Principles of Psychology* (2 vols., 1870–2, first published 1855), which bases psychology on the principle of evolution and had considerable influence on William James and through him on American pragmatism. Spencer has proved most influential as an educational theorist. In 1859 in the first of 4 articles on education in the *Westminster Review* he asked 'What education is of most worth?' and replied that it was Science, which he argued was most efficient for all purposes – self-preservation, making a living, bringing up and disciplining children, the development of adequate political and social relationships, the pursuit of intellectual moral and religious disciplines, even in the enjoyment of art. In the other 3 essays he attacked the view that the teaching of the classics in schools was a sound intellectual discipline and minimized the importance of the arts in general, advocating instead education in the sciences. These articles were later published as *Education, Intellectual, Moral and Physical* (1861). Spencer's educational theories had world-wide influence, and had an important effect on the thinking and practice of Charles William Eliot, president of Harvard. His evolutionary philosophy had at one time considerable influence in Europe, America and the Far East, but it has not worn well, although Spencer is still esteemed in some quarters as a pioneer of sociology. Among his other works are *Social Statics* (1851, where his extreme individualism was first expressed), *Programme of a System of Synthetic Philosophy* (1860), *Principles of Biology* (2 vols., 1864–7), *The Classification of the Sciences* (1864), *The Study of Sociology* (1873), *Principles of Sociology* (3 vols., 1876–96), *Factors of Organic Evolution* (1887), *Man*

Versus the State (1884; originally 4 articles in the *Contemporary Review* arguing in favour of limiting the power of the State), *Autobiography* (2 vols., 1904). [D D]

D. Duncan, *The Life and Letters of H.S.* (1908); J. A. Thomson, *H.S.* (1906); R. C. K. Ensor, *Some Reflections on S.'s Doctrine* (1946); J. Rumney, *S.'s Sociology* (1934).

Spender, Stephen (Harold) (1909–). Poet, critic, editor, novelist and short-story writer. He is the son of Edward Harold Spender, a leading Liberal journalist, and Violet Hilda Schuster. He was educated at University College School and University College, Oxford. In 1936 he married Inez Pearn, from whom he was divorced, and in 1941 the pianist Natasha Litvin, by whom he has one son and one daughter. In the 1930s he and W. H. ◊ Auden were the most prominent of the group of left-wing or anti-Fascist poets which also included Louis ◊ MacNeice and C. ◊ Day Lewis. A Left Book Club publication, *Forward from Liberalism*, expressed his political development from the Liberal politics of his family, and for about a week he was a member of the Communist Party. His poems about the Spanish Civil War were more concerned with the horrors and distresses of war than with the rights and wrongs of the conflict, and his political development since about 1937 might be described as 'backwards to liberalism'. During the war, he served in the Auxiliary Fire Service and was also, with Cyril Connolly, co-editor of *Horizon* between 1940 and 1941; from 1953 to 1965 he was co-editor of *Encounter*. He remained on the editorial board of *Encounter* till 1967, when, along with the new co-editor, Professor Frank Kermode, he resigned on discovering that neither he nor Professor Kermode had been informed that the Congress for Cultural Freedom, which had originally subsidized *Encounter*, had originally been partly financed by the United States intelligence agency, the C.I.A. He is a prominent public literary figure and has lectured widely in Europe and Asia for the British Council.

There is an odd contrast between the prominent public roles which Spender has assumed or been thrust into throughout his life, and the nature of his poetic gift, which is essentially one of subjective lyrical meditation. Half German by ancestry, he has a strong feeling for German poets of the Romantic period like Hölderlin, and has a

gift for alternating very personal lyricism and subjective self-examination with direct public, moral or political, exhortation, which is German rather than English. In his critical writings – a very amusing and malicious review of F. R. Leavis's *Revaluation* in T. S. Eliot's *Criterion* has never been collected in a volume – there is often a slyness, amusingness, or acerbity, for which Spender finds little place in his poems. The tendency of his later poems, like *Poems of Dedication* (1947) and *The Edge of Being* (1949), is towards a kind of metaphysical rumination on the nature of existence rather than towards religious or political commitment of an orthodox sort. Since the publication of his *Collected Poems* (1955), he has published, whether or not he has written, very few new poems. His later poems are nevertheless often his profounder work. Uneven, often clumsy, but with moments of great lyrical beauty and emotional penetration, his poetry has perhaps attracted less critical attention, at least academic critical attention, than it deserves. It may be that, in Yeats's phrase in *A Vision*, he was born 'out of phase' and that the public roles to which he has yielded have interfered with his true inner development as a poet. His autobiography, *World within World* (1951), though it has the unevenness and slightly groping quality of all his writing, is a key document for the literary and intellectual history of the 1930s. He was made a C.B.E. in 1962. [G S F]

The Still Centre (1939); *Ruins and Visions* (1942); Criticism: *The Destructive Element* (1935); *The Creative Element* (1953); Stories: *The Burning Cactus* (1936).

G. S. Fraser, *Vision and Rhetoric* (1959).

Spenser, Edmund (1552?–1599). Poet. Born probably in East Smithfield, London, Spenser was the elder son of John Spenser, a gentleman by birth, of a Lancashire family, who had settled in London and become a journeyman of the Merchant Taylors' Company. Later in life the poet claimed kinship with the noble family of the Spencers of Althorpe, Northampton. From 1561 to 1569 he attended the recently founded Merchant Taylors' School, whose headmaster was the notable educationist Richard ◊ Mulcaster, a Renaissance humanist who was nevertheless enthusiastic about the English language and its potentialities as a literary medium. He had great respect for tradition and order, and considerable reverence for women. His ideas seem to have had some influence on Spenser, as they are echoed later in the poet's work. Already in his schooldays Spenser was writing verse; translations by him of some sonnets of Du Bellay and of parts of a translation by Marot of one of the canzoni of Petrarch appeared anonymously in John van der Noodt's *A Theatre wherein be Represented ... the Miseries ... that Follow the Voluptuous Worldlings* ... (1569). Spenser went as a sizar (or poor scholar) to Pembroke Hall, Cambridge, in 1569, taking his B.A. degree in 1573, and his M.A. in 1576. During his second year, Gabriel ◊ Harvey (1545?–1630), became a Fellow. A friendship developed between them, but basically their minds were very different, and Harvey's influence on Spenser was superficial. Whereas Spenser looked backwards to the medieval legends of chivalry and romance out of which to create the dreamlike visions and pageants of his characteristic poetry, Harvey, who was very much up-to-date and concerned to be forward-looking in his views, ridiculed the 'Elvish Queene', which he described as 'Hobgoblin runne away with the garland from Apollo'.

In 1578 Spenser became secretary to John Young, Bishop of Rochester, formerly Master of Pembroke, while in 1579, through Harvey's influence, he secured a place in the Earl of Leicester's household, and there became acquainted with Sir Philip ◊ Sidney, Leicester's nephew. His first important published work, *The Shepheardes Calender*, appeared in 1579, and is dedicated to Sidney. This consists of a series of eclogues or pastoral poems, one for each month of the year, together with a rather undiscerning gloss or commentary by one 'E.K.', possibly Edward Kirke of Pembroke Hall. The title is borrowed from a farmers' almanac, *The Kalender and Compost of Shepherds*, a translation of a 15th-century French original, which first appeared in 1503, and which ran into many subsequent editions. Renaissance critics like Vida recommended a young poet to begin with pastorals, as Virgil had done in his *Eclogues*, and Spenser, like Pope, begins in this form which needs comparatively slight experience of life. There is a long tradition behind Spenser's pastorals, stemming ultimately from Theocritus and Virgil, but also including the neo-Latin eclogues (1498) of Mantuan (Baptista Spagnuoli,

1448–1516), the English eclogues (*c.* 1515) of Alexander Barclay (1475?–1552), and the Italian *Arcadia* (1504) of Jacopo Sannazaro (*c.* 1456–1530), a series of poems connected by a prose narrative. Although written within a well-worn convention, Spenser's poems contain much that is fresh and individual. The eclogues may be divided into two large groups: first, those in the mellifluous idealizing manner of Sannazaro, and secondly, those in the harsher, more satirical manner of Mantuan and Barclay. In the first group are the eclogues for January, April, June, October, November and December; in the second are those for February, March, May, July and September, while that for August has elements of both. Some of the characters in the *Calender* stand for real people, as Colin Clout for Spenser himself, Hobbinol for Harvey and Algrind for Archbishop Grindal; while topics of contemporary interest such as the relative merits of Anglicanism and Roman Catholicism appear under pastoral disguise. However, there are also more universal elements. Throughout the series runs the theme of time and its effect on man, the growth from youth to maturity and the decline into age.

By 1580 Spenser had begun the major work of his life, *The Faerie Queene*, although he published none of it for ten years. In 1580, too, he became secretary to Lord Grey de Wilton, who was going to Ireland as Lord Deputy. Although Grey was recalled in 1582, Spenser remained in Ireland, becoming a landowner in 1586, getting the castle and estate of Kilcolman in County Cork. His prose work, *A Veue of the Present State of Ireland*, written 1595–7 but not published until 1633, gives a vivid if one-sided account of the disordered conditions there.

On the death of Sir Philip Sidney in 1586, Spenser wrote a pastoral elegy, *Astrophel*, in his memory. In 1589 he visited London with Sir Walter ◊ Ralegh and prepared books I–III of *The Faerie Queene* for the press; these appeared in 1590 together with a letter to Ralegh explaining the purpose and structure of the work. In 1591 Spenser returned to Ireland, and commemorated the event in the pastoral autobiographical poem *Colin Clouts Come Home Againe*, published in 1595. The favourable reception of the first 3 books of *The Faerie Queene* led Ponsonby the printer to issue the poet's juvenilia and minor poems in 1591, *Com-*

plaints, *Containing Sundrie Small Poems of the Worlds Vanitie*, which includes *The Ruines of Time*, another elegy on Sidney, dedicated to his sister the Countess of Pembroke, and the lively satire in the manner of the medieval beast-fable, *Mother Hubberds Tale*. In 1591 also appeared *Daphnaida*, an elegy on Lady Douglas Howard. Spenser's courtship of and marriage to his second wife, Elizabeth Boyle, are celebrated in *Amoretti* and *Epithalamion*, published in 1595. *Amoretti* is a distinguished sonnet-sequence reflecting the various stages of the courtship, while individuality is given by Spenser's characteristic union of courtly sentiment with praise for the institution of marriage, found too in *The Faerie Queene*. The style of the sonnets is musical and decorated, and the language at times shows traces of that archaism found more notably in *The Faerie Queene*. *Epithalamion* is in the style of a classical marriage ode, and shows many of Spenser's finest literary traits. In the celebration of his love he unites sensuousness with idealism; the whole is carefully constructed to follow the events of the marriage day, and the style is rich and harmonious throughout. Spenser wrote another marriage ode, *Prothalamion* (published 1596), to celebrate the double marriage of the daughters of the Earl of Worcester. Although smoothly flowing and brightly coloured, it has less emotional intensity than *Epithalamion*. Also in 1596 was issued *Foure Hymnes*, 2 dating from Spenser's youth, 'Of Love' and 'Of Beautie', showing the influence of the Renaissance neo-platonic attitudes to love and beauty; and 2 retractions of the earlier poems, 'Of Heavenly Love' and 'Of Heavenly Beautie'. It was too in 1596 that books I–III with revisions, together with books IV–VI of *The Faerie Queene* were published, Spenser being once more in London for the purpose. A fragment of another book, 'Two Cantos of Mutabilitie', part of the 'Legend of Constancie', were printed only in the posthumous 1609 edition of *The Faerie Queene*. Spenser returned to Ireland in 1597, but in October 1598 his castle of Kilcolman was burnt during an insurrection of the Irish. Spenser fled with his wife and children and it is likely that lost parts of *The Faerie Queene* were burnt in the castle. He died in London in distressed circumstances in 1599, and was buried in Westminster Abbey, the funeral being paid for by the Earl of Essex.

The Faerie Queene is Spenser's most im-

portant poem, and the basis of his claim to major status as a poet. The *Letter to Sir Walter Ralegh* prefixed to the 1590 edition is important for an understanding of the poem, although parts of it can mislead the reader. The poem is, Spenser tells us, 'a continued Allegory, or darke conceit', and his general intention in it is 'to fashion a gentleman or noble person in vertuous and gentle discipline'. In Prince Arthur (before he became king) he labours 'to pourtraict ... the image of a brave knight, perfected in the twelve private morall vertues, as Aristotle hath devised', and he hopes that if his work is well received, he may later 'frame the other part of polliticke vertues in [Arthur's] person after that hee came to be king'. Arthur has had a vision or dream of the Faerie Queene, and ravished by her beauty has gone to seek her in Fairyland. 'In that Faery Queene', writes Spenser, 'I meane glory in my generall intention, but in my particular, I conceive the most excellent and glorious person of our soveraine the Queene, and her kingdome in Faery land.' While Arthur is to represent in himself the perfection of virtue, or 'magnificence', other knights are to be made the patrons of particular virtues in the different books.

Of this scheme all that was completed were 6 books and the Mutability fragment, and the poem as we have it does not entirely fit the description in the *Letter*. The part of Arthur is not sufficiently prominent or realized in imaginative terms to bear all the weight of Spenser's intention, and the virtues which he deals with are not really Aristotelian (although Aristotle in Spenser's day was loosely credited with the writing of twelve moral virtues). Thus the poem consists of the legends of the quests and struggles of: book I, The Knight of the Red Crosse or of Holinesse; book II, Sir Guyon or of Temperaunce; book III, Britomart or of Chastitie; book IV, Cambel and Triamond or of Friendship; book V, Artegall or of Justice; book VI, Sir Calidore or of Courtesie; while the Mutability Cantos are part of a Legend of Constancie. Holinesse is placed first, as a kind of theological introduction, because according to the Anglican theology of Spenser's day no virtues may be truly acquired except in the converted Christian who has entered on the path of sanctification. Books III and IV deal with love in its various forms; the chastity of Britomart is not a negative asceticism, but a pure love leading to marriage. The stuff of the narratives of the books shows the influence of medieval legend and romance, of the Italian romantic epic, especially the *Orlando furioso* (1532) of Ludovico Ariosto (1474–1533), and also at times of the Italian Christian epic, *Gerusalemme liberata* (1581) of Torquato Tasso (1544–95). However the tone and atmosphere of the poem is Spenser's own, and the dreamlike ambience of Fairyland, created by a slow-moving, sonorous, somewhat archaic style, allows him to express in powerful imaginative terms the states of mind and heart which lie at the centre of his poem. Although the commentators fail to agree about the meaning of the details of the narrative, the main drift is always clear, and yields itself to sensitive reading. The central 'allegorical cores' (as C. S. Lewis puts it) of the books, which may well have been composed first, exercise an extremely profound effect upon the reader's sensibilities, and carry a meaning with them which seems to be partly below the level of conscious thought, as in the description of the Garden of Adonis in book II.

The moral allegory is of prime importance and it is wiser to give much less attention to the fugitive historical allegory, which is often difficult to disengage and identify. The verse form of the poem is Spenser's invention; known as the Spenserian stanza, it consists of 9 lines, 8 iambic pentameters with a final Alexandrine, rhyming *a b a b b c b c c*, and its slow-moving ampleness is peculiarly appropriate to his art. Although others have written in Spenserian stanzas, such as James Thomson in *The Castle of Indolence* (1748) or Byron in *Childe Harold* (1812–18), the effect is different; and it has not proved possible to recapture the peculiar magic of Spenser's own work.

The earlier critics were lavish in praise of Spenser, and Milton's testimony in *Areopagitica* (1644) has attained classical status: 'our sage and serious Poet *Spencer*, whom I dare be known to think a better teacher then *Scotus* or *Aquinas*'; although Ben Jonson was critical of the archaisms of style; '*Spencer* in affecting the Ancients writ no Language: Yet I would have him read for his matter' (*Timber: or Discoveries*, 1641). However, in the Romantic period Spenser's allegory was considered an irrelevance, and Hazlitt could write: 'The love of beauty . . . not of truth, is the moving principle of his mind, and he is guided in his fantastic

delineations by no rule but the impulse of an inexhaustible imagination' (*Lectures on the English Poets*, 1818). It has been left to the best modern critics, e.g. A. C. Hamilton, to recognize that we should accept both the varied surface of *The Faerie Queene*, the master-work of the 'poet's poet' (in Charles Lamb's phrase), and also attain to its depths of meaning in an inclusively imaginative reading. [JWB]

The Works. A Variorum Edition, ed. E. Greenlaw, C. G. Osgood, R. M. Padelford, and others (9 vols., Baltimore, 1932–49) (with full critical apparatus and commentary; index added in 1957); *The Poetical Works*, ed. J. C. Smith and E. de Selincourt (3 vols., 1909–10) (text without notes); *The Faerie Queene*, ed. K. M. Warren (6 vols., 1897–1900) (with introduction and notes); *The Minor Poems*, ed. with notes, W. L. Renwick (4 vols., 1928–34); *The Shepheardes Calender*, ed. with notes, C. H. Herford (1895); *The Shepherd's Calendar and Other Poems*, ed. P. Henderson (Everyman, 1932) (with some modernization of spelling); *Fowre Hymnes and Epithalamion*, ed. and intr. Enid Welsford 1(967); *The Faerie Queene*, ed. J. W. Hales (2 vols., Everyman, 1910); *Selections*, ed. W. L. Renwick (1923) (contains extracts from critics and notes); *Selected Poetry*, ed. A. C. Hamilton (1966) (with introduction and notes).
A. C. Judson, *Life*, in *Variorum Edition* (Baltimore, 1932–49); F. I. Carpenter, *Reference Guide to S.* (Chicago, 1923) (with supplements by D. F. Atkinson, 1937, W. F. McNeir and F. Provost, 1962); H. S. V. Jones, *S. Handbook* (New York, 1930); C. S. Lewis, *The Allegory of Love* (1936), *English Literature in the Sixteenth Century* (1954) and *Spenser's Images of Life* (ed. A. Fowler, 1967); M. Evans, *English Poetry in the Sixteenth Century* (1955; revised edn, 1967); W. L. Renwick, *E.S. An Essay on Renaissance Poetry* (1925) (for early poetry); J. W. Lever, *The Elizabethan Love Sonnet* (1956) (for 'Amoretti'); W. Nelson, *The Poetry of E.S.* (New York, 1963); ed. W. Nelson, *Form and Convention in the Poetry of Spenser* (New York, 1961); A. Fowler, *S. and the Numbers of Time* (1964); A. C. Hamilton, *Allegory in The Faerie Queene* (1961); Graham Hough, *A Preface to The Faerie Queene* (1961); M. P. Parker, *The Allegory of the Faerie Queene* (1960); K. Williams, *S.'s Faerie Queene. The World of Glass* (1966); P. J. Alpers, *The Poetry of the Faerie Queene* (Princeton, 1968).

Sprat, Thomas (1635–1713). Publicist and poet. Educated at Wadham College, Oxford, where he was an intimate of Wilkins and thus one of the group who founded the Royal Society. His interest was mathematical, but he also appeared as a poet, in company with Waller and Dryden, with a set of verses on the death of Cromwell. At the Restoration, he took orders and became a royal chaplain, consistently supporting the King, first Charles II and then James II, becoming Canon of Windsor (1680) and Bishop of Rochester and Dean of Westminster (1684). He was a member of James II's Ecclesiastical Commission; he permitted the Declaration of Indulgence to be read in the Abbey, but did not enjoin its observance; eventually he withdrew from the Commission. He regained popularity by being falsely accused of treason after the Revolution, and clearing himself. Sprat was a notable prose-writer, publishing sermons, but was best known as a publicist in his *History of the Royal Society* (1667; 1702, enlarged and 'corrected'; 1722; 1734; 1764), in which he more or less practised the 'close, naked, natural way of speaking – positive expressions, clear senses, a native easiness, bringing all things as near the mathematical plainness as they can, and preferring the language of artisans, countrymen, and merchants before wits and scholars', which he says the Society advocated. His other writings include a Life of his friend Abraham Cowley in Latin, prefixed to the latter's *Latin Works*, and in English to his *English Works* (1668). [AR]

Johnson, *Lives of the Poets*; R. F. Jones and others, *The Seventeenth Century: Studies by R. F. Jones and Others Writing in His Honour* (Stanford U.P., 1951).

Spring, (Robert) Howard (1889–1965). Novelist. Born in Cardiff, one of the nine children of a gardener, he left school at 11, started work as a message-boy with the *South Wales Daily News*, and became a reporter. He worked for the *Yorkshire Observer*, then the *Manchester Standard* (*Book Parade*, 1938, is a collection of his pieces). His first book was a collection of children's stories, *Darkie and Co.* (1932); his first novel, *Shabby Tiger*, appeared in 1934; and its sequel (also partly autobiographical), *Rachel Rosing*, in 1935. With the best-selling novel *O Absalom!* (1938; republished as *My Son, My Son,* and widely translated), he became famous. He thereafter went to live in Cornwall, which is frequently the setting of his later fiction. This includes: *Fame is the Spur* (1940); *Hard Facts* (1944); *The Houses in Between* (1951), a rather melodramatic historical panorama from the days of Victoria to 1948; *These*

Lovers Fled Away (1955); and *I Met a Lady* (1961). His tales are unhurried, and full of characters in a Dickensian way. [AR]

Heaven Lies about Us (1939); *In the Meantime* (1942); *And Another Thing* (1946) (autobiographies).

Squire, Sir John (Collings) (1884–1958). Journalist and poet. Born in Plymouth, Squire was educated at Blundell's School and Cambridge University. On leaving university he became a freelance journalist and enthusiastic Socialist, writing literary criticism under the pen-name of 'Solomon Eagle'. He was appointed literary editor of the *New Statesman* in 1913 and editor in 1917. From 1919 to 1934 he was the editor of the *London Mercury* which, on the demise of ◊ *Georgian Poetry* in 1922, became the unofficial organ of the Georgian poets. Because of what came to be regarded as the backward-looking image of the *Mercury* these later Georgian poets were often sneeringly referred to as the 'Squirearchy'. His many volumes of poetry include *The Three Hills* (1913), *Poems* (first series 1918; second series 1922) and *A Face in Candlelight* (1932). His *Collected Poems*, containing an introduction by John Betjeman, were published posthumously in 1959. A conventional poet, firmly in the Georgian tradition, he is seen at his best in his light verse on the subjects of architecture, rugby and cricket. His parodies, *Imaginary Speeches* (1912), *Steps to Parnassus* (1913), *Tricks of the Trade* (1917) and *Collected Parodies* (1921), show considerable wit and dexterity. He also published volumes of short stories, literary criticism, verse anthologies and a collection of autobiographical sketches, *The Honeysuckle and the Bee* (1937). He was knighted in 1933. [PJK]

Frank Swinnerton, *The Georgian Literary Scene* (1935); Patrick Howarth, S.: *Most Generous of Men* (1963).

Stanhope, Philip Dormer. ◊ Chesterfield, Philip Dormer Stanhope.

Stanley, Arthur Penrhyn (1815–81). Historian. The son of Edward Stanley, Bishop of Norwich, he was educated at Rugby, where he was the star pupil of Dr Thomas ◊ Arnold, of whom he wrote the rather stodgy *Life* (1844), one of his best-known books. It is indispensable for understanding the social and intellectual life of the period. Stanley went to University College, Oxford, where he became a Fellow; he took orders (1839). His ecclesiastical promotion was rapid: Canon of Canterbury (1851); Professor of Ecclesiastical History at Oxford (1856); Canon of Christ Church (1858); and Dean of Westminster (1864). In the Church controversies of the time he was a 'liberal', but he was charming and well-bred and had a ready pen. In 1868 he married Lady Augusta Bruce, one of the Queen's circle. He defended ◊ Colenso and supported the writers of *Essays and Reviews*, the seven 'liberal' churchmen of Jowett's group. His many rather superficial historical works are now forgotten, but he had an interest in the ecumenical movement and in the Orthodox Church in Russia, where he spent some time as royal emissary. [AR]

R. E. Prothero and G. G. Bradley, *Life and Correspondence of S.* (2 vols., 1893); F. Woodward, *The Doctor's Disciples* (1954).

Stark, Freya (Madeline) (1893–   ). Travel writer. Born in Paris, the daughter of Robert Stark, the sculptor, she was educated privately in Italy, and at Bedford College and the School of Oriental Studies in London. From 1927 she travelled widely in Syria, as well as in the less frequented area of Arabia (the Hadhramaut) and Persia, gaining many awards from geographical and academic bodies. During the Second World War, she worked as a propagandist for the British government in the Middle East. Her travel books are colourful and lively, and infectiously convey her love of the wild Arabian landscape (she is also a brilliant photographer) and its independent peoples. She has a wide and sympathetic knowledge of their speech and culture, in this continuing the tradition of well-informed and literate British reporters in that region started by ◊ Doughty and earlier Englishmen. Her books include: *The Valleys of the Assassins* (1934); *The Southern Gates of Arabia* (1936), which contains an interesting account of a serious illness and recovery in these wild regions; *Letters from Syria* (1942); *East is West* (1945), an account of her wartime experiences; *The Lycian Shore* (1956); *Alexander's Path* (1958); and *Rome on the Euphrates* (1966). She has also written poems and short stories. [AR]

Perseus in the Wind (1948); *Traveller's Prelude* (1950); *Beyond Euphrates* (1951); *The Journey's Echo* (1963) (autobiographies).

Steele, Sir Richard (1672–1729). Essayist and dramatist. Born in Dublin, the son of an attorney who died when his son was 'not quite five'. Steele was educated at Charterhouse School in London through the patronage of the Duke of Ormonde, and there he began his life-long friendship with Joseph ◊ Addison. He followed the latter to Oxford, though to Christ Church and Merton, but soon left and enlisted as a trooper in the Life Guards, later obtaining a commission in the Coldstreams by dedicating a bad poem to Lord Cutts, the colonel. He became a captain, in command of the Tower guard, and to improve the tone of his fellows wrote a moral tract, praising Christian virtue over Stoicism, *The Christian Hero* (1701; ed. and intr. R. Blanchard, 1932). He became a writer and a member of the Kit-Cat Club, and eventually left the army. From this period date his plays: *The Funeral, or Grief à la Mode* (1702), a comedy of manners but with a new strain of bourgeois respectable sentiment; *The Lying Lover* (1704), which was 'damned for its piety'; and *The Tender Husband* (1705), containing more sentiment, but with a better plot. Steele was a successful journalist, being in 1707 appointed Gazetteer, the official government writer. In 1709 he founded the *Tatler*, thus beginning his highly successful journalistic partnership with Addison. In starting it Steele had the assistance of Swift, from whom he borrowed the pseudonym of 'Isaac Bickerstaff' which he used in his editorial capacity. Though there had previously been periodicals mingling essays and news (such as the *Review* run by ◊ Defoe), the *Tatler* may be considered the real start of that prosperous and successful civilizing agent of 18th-century English culture. It appeared on Tuesday, Thursday and Saturday, the days the post left London for the country, so that it obviously aimed at a wide audience; the first four issues were free, thereafter it cost a penny. Each issue was a folio half sheet. It ran until 2 January 1711, and 271 numbers appeared, of which Steele wrote about 188 and Addison 42; in 36 they collaborated. Steele's writing, relaxed, intimate and engaging, was a hit with the public, and the contents became less various in each issue, with more papers 'from my own apartment'. The paper was also an important forerunner of the novel; it contained character drawing of real insight, deft conversation reporting and close observation of the passing scene.

From the fall of the administration he had worked for until the accession of George I Steele lost his government post as Gazetteer. On 1 March 1711, he launched another periodical, the *Spectator*, where he again acted as editor, but here Addison was the more important partner. Addison's writing is more remote, more polished and chillier than Steele's. Addison has a greater grasp of ideas and is more in touch with the periodical's role as a popularizer of ideas, but Steele is more human and at his best a greater *writer*. 555 numbers of the *Spectator* appeared before it stopped publication on 6 December 1712. There was a brief revival by Addison alone in 1714. The common assignment is 240 complete papers to Steele and 274 to Addison. The *Spectator* had more scope than the *Tatler* in morality, philosophy and criticism, but again it was Steele who introduced the attractive characters of the Club. The enlivening of morality with wit, and the tempering of wit with morality – Addison's statement of the paper's purpose in number 10 – was of a piece with Steele's previous literary and dramatic career. Though Steele was an active politician and pamphleteer, as was Addison, both papers avoided active political engagement. Steele also ran 2 political periodicals, the *Guardian. By Nestor Ironside* (175 numbers, 1713) and the 2 series of the *Englishmen* (95 numbers 1713–14 and 1715), as well as shorter-lived ventures such as the *Theatre* (28 numbers, 1720). After 1714, Steele was appointed to a number of offices, Justice of the Peace, Deputy Lieutenant for Middlesex, Governor of the Royal Stables, and a Commissioner for the forfeited estates in Scotland. In 1715, he was knighted and obtained a life-patent in Drury Lane Theatre, and was thus an important figure in the dramatic life of the time. He quarrelled with Addison and his financial difficulties increased. His last work was his best play, *The Conscious Lovers* (1722), which long held the stage as one of the best sentimental comedies. Steele died in Carmarthen in Wales after a paralytic stroke. [AR]

The Dramatic Works, ed. G. A. Aitken (Mermaid Series, 1894); *The Tatler* (4 vols., 1710–11) (essays); *The Spectator* (8 vols., 1712–15) (essays); *Essays*, ed. G. A. Aitken (8 vols., 1898; ed. G. Gregory Smith, Everyman, 5 vols., 1907) (various selections exist); *Letters*, ed. R. Blanchard (1941); *S.'s Periodical Journalism: 1714–16*, ed. R. Blanchard (1959). G. A. Aitken, *Life* (2 vols., 1889) (with bibliography); C. Winton, *Captain S. The Early*

Career of R.S. (Johns Hopkins U.P., 1964); W. Graham, *The Beginnings of English Literary Periodicals* (1926); F. W. Bateson, *English Comic Drama: 1700–1750* (1929); J. Loftis, *S. at Drury Lane* (1952); A. R. Humphreys, *S., Addison and their Periodical Essays* (WTW, 1959).

Stephen, Sir Leslie (1832–1904). Journalist, biographer and critic. Born in London, the son of Sir James Stephen (closely concerned as Under-Secretary of State for the Colonies with the abolition of slavery). The family was a member of the 'Clapham Sect', a group of practical Christians and benevolent philosophers, which in its turn was an ancestor of the ◊ 'Bloomsbury group'. The elder son of Sir James was Sir James Fitz-James Stephen, lawyer and philosopher and an important opponent of Mill's utilitarianism. Leslie Stephen was educated at Eton, King's College, London, and Trinity Hall, Cambridge. He took orders and became a 'muscular Christian' tutor. He was one of the pioneers of mountain-climbing as a neo-Wordsworthian refreshment for English intellectuals (editor of the *Alpine Journal*, 1868–71) and wrote essays on mountaineering (*The Playground of Europe*, 1871; ed. H. E. G. Tyndale, 1936). In 1870, when it became legally possible, he resigned his orders under the influence of ◊ Mill, Kant and Herbert ◊ Spencer, and after a struggle became an agnostic in typical 19th-century fashion (see his *Essays on Free Thinking and Plain Speaking*, 1873, and *Agnostic's Apology*, 1893). In 1864, he had come to London to make his way as a writer, by publishing in the *Saturday Review*, *Fraser's* and other magazines, critical essays which were collected as *Hours in a Library* (1874; 1876; 1879). He was editor of the *Cornhill Magazine* (1871–82).

Stephen turned his agnostic, rationalistic mind to a closer study of the 18th-century 'Enlightenment', and his most impressive work resulted, *English Thought in the Eighteenth Century* (1876–81). In it he has produced the most comprehensive study of the Deists, but since he regarded them as 'forerunners' of Victorian rationalists he is sometimes rather unsympathetic to other contributions they had to make. He is also fundamentally a reader who split up 'philosophy' and 'literature' into separate boxes. The work, however, remains valuable. A sequel (of less value), *English Utilitarians*, appeared in 1900 (reprinted

1950). His greatest labour was the editorship of the *Dictionary of National Biography*, which he held from 1882. The first 26 volumes were supervised by him and he contributed many of the articles, especially on 18th- and 19th-century figures. Stephen wrote a number of full-length biographies, including *Johnson* (1878), *Pope* (1880) and *Swift* (1882). They are informative, but vitiated by a lack of sympathy with the subject's full interests. Stephen is always worth reading, but in the Cambridge manner is a cold informant rather than a guide. His first wife was Thackeray's younger daughter, and he was the father of Virginia ◊ Woolf, who portrayed him as the father in her novel *To the Lighthouse*, and in her *The Captain's Deathbed and Other Essays* (1950). [AR]

Men, Books and Mountains, ed. O. A. Ullmann (U. of Minnesota P., 1956) (bibliography of periodical writings).
N. G. Annan, *L.S.: His Thought and Character in Relation to His Time* (1951); Q. D. Leavis, 'L.S.: Cambridge Critic', *Scrutiny*, VII (1939).

Stephens, Alfred George (1865–1933). Australian critic. Born at Toowoomba. After experience as a journalist in Queensland, he travelled in Europe and the U.S.A. in 1893. The next year he became sub-editor of the influential Sydney *Bulletin*. In 1896 he founded its Red Page, the literary section, which he edited until 1906. He knew most of the writers of the period and published the earliest work of many who became famous. Among those he encouraged were ◊ Furphy, ◊ Neilson and ◊ Brennan. He worked for a national literature without neglecting European tradition and standards. After 1906 he worked as a free-lance writer, literary agent and editor of the *Bookfellow*. He died in Sydney. Stephens' books are out of print, but Vance ◊ Palmer published a selection in *A. G. Stephens* (1941). [PT]

V. Palmer, *The Legend of the Nineties* (1954).

Stephens, James (1882–1950). Poet and novelist. Born in the slums of Dublin, he had no formal education and taught himself. While working as a clerk, he was discovered by ◊ 'Æ', who encouraged his writing and helped him to publish his first book of poems, *Insurrections* (1909). Stephens helped to found the *Irish Review* in 1911, and in its pages published his first novel, *The Charwoman's Daughter* (1911). His prose fantasy, *The Crock of Gold* (1912), won the Polignac Prize,' and henceforth he lived by his pen. Stephens was a student of Gaelic literature and art (he worked in the Dublin National Gallery), and tried to turn Irish mythology into an instrument of modern Irish imagination and nationalism, as in his romance, *Deirdre* (1923), which won the Irish Tailltean Gold Medal. He was a friend of James Joyce, who thought him the only man capable of finishing *Finnegans Wake*, if it was left uncompleted. Stephens' fiction is a mixture of ironic wit, nonsense, fantasy and philosophy, and he produced several volumes of short stories, such as *Here are Ladies* (1913) and *Etched in Moonlight* (1928), and a collection of *Irish Fairy Tales* (1920) for children. A Sinn Feiner, he also published a pamphlet *The Insurrection in Dublin* (1920). He published several volumes of clear and workmanlike poems, including *The Hill of Vision* (1912), *Songs from the Clay* (1915), *The Adventures of Seumas Beg* (1915), *Reincarnations* (1918) and *Kings and the Moon* (1938). [AR]

Collected Poems, revised and with additions (1954); *J.S.: A Selection*, ed. Lloyd Frankenburg, intr. Padraic Colum (1962).

Stern, G(ladys) B(ronwyn) (1890–   ). Novelist. Born in London and educated at Notting Hill High School, she left school at 16, travelled in Germany and Switzerland, and studied for two years at the London Academy of Dramatic Art. Her first novel, *Pantomime*, written when she was 20, appeared in 1914, and was followed by many others. The best known of these are probably the series of popular 'matriarch' stories of a Jewish family, based on the life of an aged great-aunt; they include *Tents of Israel* (1924), *A Deputy was King* (1926), *Mosaic* (1930) and *The Young Matriarch* (1942). She has also written (with Sheila Kaye-Smith) *Talking of Jane Austen* (1943) and *More Talk of Jane Austen* (1950); and on R. L. Stevenson in *No Son of Mine* (1948). Apart from her fiction, plays and short stories, she is publishing a racy series of autobiographies: *Monogram* (1936), *Another Part of the Forest* (1941), *Benefits Forgot* (1949), *A Name to Conjure With* (1953) and *All in Good Time* (1954), in which she recounts her conversion to Roman Catholicism. [AR]

Sterne, Laurence (1713–68). Novelist and sermon writer. Born at Clonmel in Tipperary, Ireland, the son of an army ensign. His mother and he followed the camp, in low financial circumstances, for some years, chiefly in Ireland. He was sent to school in Halifax, Yorkshire, from 1723 until his father's death in 1731, as a poor lieutenant in Jamaica. Thereafter Sterne idled until in 1733 he was entered as a sizar (a poor scholar) at Jesus College, Cambridge. There he made the acquaintance of John (Hall-) Stevenson of Skelton Hall, a young land-owner with a taste for pornography and fantastic wit. In 1737, Sterne became a B.A. and shortly afterwards took holy orders. Through family influence (his great-grandfather had been Archbishop of York and his uncle Jaques was an influential chapter pluralist) in 1738 he obtained the living of Sutton, near York, and a prebend in the cathedral. In 1741 he married, and through his wife's influence he got the neighbouring benefice of Stillington. From 1738 to 1759 he lived there, or in York, preaching his turn in the cathedral and in his churches, reading voraciously. His letters and works are used to describe his activities, but must clearly be taken very carefully. He wrote miscellaneous journalism for York periodicals, and his first book was *A Political Romance* (1759; *The History of a Good Warm Watch-Coat*, 1769). This allegory arose out of a chapter quarrel, and in it Sterne displays many of the qualities of his later fiction: layers of meaning, misleading use of learning, obscenity and rhetorical dexterity in the management of a tale. His wife suffered an attack of mental illness, and Sterne started work on a literary enterprise. He had read chapters of this to the coterie at Skelton Hall, and described it as 'taking in, not only the weak part of the sciences in which the true point of Ridicule lies, but every thing else which I find laugh-at-able'. This was *The Life and Opinions of Tristram Shandy* (vols. I and II, York, 1759 – a small edn – and London, 1760); vols. III and IV, 1761; vols. V and VI, 1762; vols. VII and VIII, 1765; vol. IX, 1767); it was several times reprinted with varying accuracy. He intended to issue *Tristram Shandy* in annual instalments until he died, so he said, and the way it was composed and issued has important consequences for the work, emphasizing the extemporary nature of the narrative and making room for the deliberately chaotic treatment of time. The first 2 volumes made him a celebrity and he visited London to be fêted. He got another

Yorkshire benefice from a friendly noble-man and he was able to travel abroad. His health had been bad for a long time (he was a consumptive), and thereafter he alternated bouts of being lionized in London with recuperative continental travels. He died in London while looking after the publication of *A Sentimental Journey* (1768), a pendant work to *Tristram Shandy*, in which he developed on its own account, and exploited, the vein of sentiment he had opened in the novel. In his last fevered visit to London, Sterne cultivated a platonic passion for the young wife of an official of the East India Company, then absent in Bombay. The letters he sent her, which cannibalized his previous correspondence, form the basis of his *Journal to Eliza* (*Letters from Yorick to Eliza*, 1773). The success of *Tristram Shandy* encouraged Sterne to publish *The Sermons of Mr Yorick* (vols. I and II, 1760; vols. III and IV, 1766; vols. V, VI and VII, 1769; all several times reprinted). These sermons are interesting only as being from the same pen as the novel, though they display quite sound preaching, heightened with an attempt to 'dramatize' points and stimulate the audience's feelings.

Sterne's life was not very satisfactory; he was temperamentally unsuited to the Church, then one of the few refuges for the ingenious poor man. Modern criticism of his work, however, concentrates on discussing the complexities of *Tristram Shandy* rather than, as formerly, probing Sterne's personal life or trying to excuse his novel as the work of a cleric, on the ground that he has created some amusing characters. Thus *Tristram Shandy* is seen to be one of the most remarkable works of the century. Starting with a saying of Epictetus, that 'not actions but opinions of actions are the concern of men', Sterne creates a Shandean world that leads the reader to explore the meeting in common life of thought, feeling and action. The two main actors, Walter Shandy, the pedant of thought, and Uncle Toby, the pedant of feeling, are displayed in a very complex rhetorical way by Tristram, the narrator, using gesture, the conventions of drama, Locke's theory of the association of ideas, obscenity and learning, all for Sterne's end, to show that thought without feeling is futile and feeling without reason is barren, too. There is a plan, a time scheme, and the usual documentation of a novel, all buried and the elements re-arranged to emphasize the continuity of experience. All of human life appears – love, war, trade, theology, science, economics, medicine – but in changed and comic form. There are failures from time to time, but even these are offered for the reader's use. Sterne's other works are monuments to the cult of sentiment that seized the latter part of the century. The leering and attitudinizing may be considered as the way in which Sterne offers the sentiment to the reader, to demand a careful consideration of it. [AR]

Works, ed. W. L. Cross (12 vols., New York, 1906); 'Shakespeare Head Edition' (7 vols., 1926–7); selection ed. D. Grant (Reynard Library, 1950); *Tristram Shandy*, ed. J. A. Work, annotated, with Hogarth's illustrations (1940); ed. with introduction S. Monk (New York, 1950); *Letters*, ed. L. P. Curtis (3 vols., 1935).

W. L. Cross, *Life and Times of S.* (2 vols., New Haven, Conn., revised 1929); P. Quennell, *Four Portraits* (1945); E. N. Dilworth, *The Unsentimental Journey of L.S.* (New York, 1948); J. Traugott, *Tristram Shandy's World* (Berkeley, Calif., 1954); A. H. Cash, *S.'s Comedy of Moral Sentiment* (Pittsburgh, 1966).

Stevenson, Robert Louis (originally Lewis) **Balfour** (1850–94). Novelist and essayist, Born in Edinburgh, son of a prosperous civil engineer who expected him to follow the family profession but finally agreed on law as a compromise, Stevenson studied law at Edinburgh University, and at the same time revolted violently against the Presbyterian respectability of the city's professional classes. There were painful clashes with his parents. Severe respiratory illness, which was to dog him all his life, afflicted him in his early twenties, and in 1873 – now determined to be a professional writer – he sought health in the French Riviera. In his next few years he travelled much in France and described two of his journeys in *An Inland Voyage* (1878) and *Travels with a Donkey in the Cevennes* (1879), agreeably mannered narratives in the tradition of romantic essay-writing. Through the 1870s he published essays in periodicals, trying out styles and improving his technique. While staying at Fontainebleau in 1876 Stevenson met the American Fanny Vandergrift Osbourne, an older married woman separated from her husband. Mrs Osbourne returned to California in 1878 and in August 1879 Stevenson followed her there, crossing the Atlantic and the American continent in difficult condi-

tions as an impoverished immigrant (recorded in *Across the Plains*, 1892, and *The Amateur Emigrant*, 1895). A period of poverty and illness in Monterey and San Francisco while waiting for Fanny to get her divorce ended in marriage and a honeymoon in a deserted miners' cabin on Mount St Helena on the Californian Coast Range (described in *The Silverado Squatters*, 1883; this work together with the two previously mentioned and other essays on California written at this period, including some hitherto unpublished material, ed. J. D. Hart, *From Scotland to Silverado*, Cambridge, Mass., 1966). A reconciliation with his parents followed and Stevenson returned to Scotland with Fanny in August 1880, to move soon afterwards, on medical advice, to Davos. The summer of 1881 was spent in Scotland, where Stevenson started *Treasure Island* (1883), under the original title *The Sea-Cook*, as a serial in the boys' paper *Young Folks* (1881–2). In 1881 he published *Virginibus Puerisque*, his first collection of essays, and in 1882 (back in Scotland after another spell in Davos) he produced 2 of his finest short stories, 'Thrawn Janet' and 'The Merry Men'. But the Scottish climate brought on lung haemorrhages, and Stevenson had to flee once more, this time to Hyères in southern France, where he worked on *Prince Otto* (1885) and his book of children's poems, *A Child's Garden of Verses* (1885).

A severe bout of illness in 1885 was followed by two fruitful years' residence in Bournemouth, when he became close friends with Henry James (see *Henry James and R. L. Stevenson*, ed. J. Adam Smith, 1948) and wrote *Kidnapped* (1886), a novel of the aftermath of the Jacobite rebellion, and his best-known work, *The Strange Case of Dr Jekyll and Mr Hyde* (1886), a melodramatic treatment of one of his favourite themes, the moral ambiguity of the individual. His reputation was now established, but even Bournemouth proved to have too severe a climate for him and in August 1887 the Stevensons left England for the last time, first for the United States (where he began one of his finest novels, *The Master of Ballantrae*, 1889), then for an extended period of sailing in the South Seas, finally settling in Samoa, where, the climate suiting him, he built himself a house and lived in patriarchal style with his wife, mother, stepson and stepdaughter. He developed a deep interest in South Seas politics and wrote descriptive and historical accounts of the area (*In the South Seas*, 1896; *A Footnote to History*, 1892). In his Samoan years he produced *Catriona* (American title, *David Balfour*, 1893), a sequel to *Kidnapped*, *The Ebb-Tide* (1894; based on a draft by his stepson Lloyd Osbourne), *The Beach of Falesá* (1892; a story based on his local knowledge of the South Seas), and the unfinished *Weir of Hermiston* (1896), his masterpiece, on which he was working when he died suddenly on 3 December 1894.

Stevenson's reputation has been erratic; he was first hero-worshipped as a brave invalid, then relegated to the nursery as a children's writer, then 'exposed' as a rake and bohemian. But modern biography and criticism shows him as a complex and troubled figure, whose 'optimism' was a wry acceptance of the inevitable and whose concern with moral ambiguities led him steadily towards greatness. *Treasure Island* is one of the finest adventure stories in the language; *Kidnapped* counterpoints history, psychology and topography in an impressive manner; *Weir of Hermiston*, set in Edinburgh and the Lowland hills at the end of the 18th century and dealing with a conflict between a grim Scottish judge and his idealistic son, has something of the Border ballads about its atmosphere and, fragmentary though it is, in theme, style and tone it establishes itself as a work of great power and originality. Stevenson was working towards a true maturing of his talents at the time of his sudden and premature death.

Stevenson's admirable letters give a vivid picture of his life (but play down the early conflict with his parents). These were edited by Sidney Colvin (4 vols., 1911), but with tactful omissions and editorial telescoping which makes the new complete edition now being prepared by Bradford Booth all the more necessary. The fascinating letters to his lifelong friend Charles Baxter were edited by De Lancey Ferguson and Marshall Waingrow (New Haven, 1956). The standard modern life is J. C. Furnas, *Voyage to Windward*, 1952, but the 'authorized' biography by Stevenson's cousin, Graham Balfour (2 vols., 1901) is still worth consulting. [DD]

D. Daiches, *R.L.S.* (1947); R. Kiely, *R.L.S. and the Fiction of Adventure* (Cambridge, Mass., 1964); E. M. Eigner, *R.L.S. and Romantic Tradition* (Princeton, 1966).

Stewart, Douglas (1913–   ). New Zealand poet, playwright and critic. Born in Eltham, New Zealand, and educated at Victoria University College, he worked as a journalist in New Zealand before crossing to Australia in 1938 to join the Sydney *Bulletin*. In 1941 he began a long spell as editor of its influential, literary Red Page (◊ Stephens, A. G.). *The Flesh and the Spirit* (1948) is a selection of his criticism. Stewart has shown a consistent interest in the Australian ballad. *The Dosser in Springtime* (1946) and *Glencoe* (1947) contain many examples of the enrichment of an old form by modern techniques. In 1955 he was joint-editor of an anthology of *Australian Bush Ballads*. He has published 7 further books of verse as well as several short stories, but his verse-plays are his best work.

Ned Kelly (1943), like *Shipwreck* (1947), was written for the stage. It presents its legendary hero as an equivocal revolutionary, a megalomaniac as well as a scourge of 'respectable' materialism. *The Fire on the Snow* (1944) with another fine radio-play, *The Golden Lover*, uses a sparer diction in its treatment of Scott and his Antarctic companions. It relies for its effects simply on the voices of five men and a narrator – and silence. *Fisher's Ghost* (1960) is a comedy based on an Australian legend. [PT]

Collected Poems 1936–1967 (1967).

A. A. Phillips, 'D.S.'s *Ned Kelly* and Australian Romanticism', *Meanjin*, XV, 3 (Spring, 1956); V. Smith, 'D.S.: Lyric Poet', *Meanjin*, XXVI 1 (1967).

Stewart, Dugald (1753–1828). Philosopher and editor. Professor of Moral Philosophy at Edinburgh University from 1785 until 1810, he was at once the eloquent popularizer and the literary heir of the first generation of the 18th-century Scottish 'Golden Age'. He transmitted many aspects of that culture to the Edinburgh Augustans of the early 19th century, to the *Edinburgh Review* and to the Whig statesmen of the Reform period; his pupils included James ◊ Mill, Lord ◊ Jeffrey, Lord ◊ Cockburn, ◊ Scott, ◊ Brougham, Palmerston, Russell and Sydney ◊ Smith. Stewart's philosophical work is forgotten, and it is significant of the trace of genteel shallowness in the culture he represented that, while he edited the works of Thomas ◊ Reid and wrote lives of Reid, Adam Smith and William ◊ Robertson, he ac-

quiesced in contemporary neglect and dis-
paragement of David Hume. [AI]

Works, ed. Sir W. Hamilton (1854–8) (last
volume includes a Life by J. Veitch).

Stewart, J(ohn) I(nnes) M(ackintosh) (1906–
). Historian of literature, and writer of
detective stories under the pseudonym
'Michael Innes'. Born in Edinburgh, the
son of the Director of Education there, and
educated at Edinburgh Academy and
Oriel College, Oxford. He taught English
at the University of Leeds (lecturer 1930–5),
at the University of Adelaide (professor
1935–45) and at the Queen's University,
Belfast (1946–8); he has been a Student
(Fellow) of Christ Church, Oxford, since
1949. His scholarly works include *Character
and Motive in Shakespeare* (1949) and
Eight Modern Writers (vol. XII of the
Oxford History of English Literature, 1963).
The latter is a change from the earlier
inclusive volumes, and is a cautious attempt
at interpreting an age by discussing the
works of eight major authors only. He has
also written several straightforward novels
under his own name, beginning with *Mark
Lambert's Supper* (1954). The best known is
The Man Who Won the Pools (1961). It is as
'Michael Innes', however, that he is most
widely known to readers, through his
popular detective fiction. This is in the
English tradition of genteel, 'literary'
puzzles, neatly written and held together
by a knowledge of stereotyped, middle-class
habits. His detective, Inspector Appleby, is
a 'university man'. These works include
Hamlet, Revenge! (1937), *The Hawk and the
Handsaw* (1948), *The New Sonia Wayward*
(1960), *A Connoisseur's Case* (1962) and
Money from Holme (1964). [AR]

Stoker, Bram (Abraham) (1847–1912).
Novelist. Born in Dublin, the son of a
Civil Servant, he was a semi-invalid as a
child, but became a well-known athlete at
Dublin University, where he had a distinguished career as a student of mathematics and was president of the Philosophical Society. From 1867 to 1877 he
was himself a Civil Servant in Dublin and
published *The Duties of Clerks of Petty
Sessions in Ireland* (1878). He wrote newspaper dramatic criticism, and in 1878 his
strong admiration for Henry Irving led
him to become the famous actor's touring
manager and secretary, an experience that
produced *Personal Reminiscences of Henry
Irving* (1906). Stoker wrote short stories
and novels, a book about America and the
amusing *Famous Imposters* (1910); he was
also on the staff of the *Daily Telegraph*.
None of Stoker's works (which include
The Mystery of the Sea, 1902, and *The
Lady of the Shroud*, 1909) are now remembered except his very successful story
Dracula (1897), the story told in journals
and letters of the vampire Hungarian,
Count Dracula, involving mesmerism,
hypnotism and other occult interests,
woven together with considerable narrative
skill. It sold over a million copies, and is
still selling in paperback form. Several
film versions and sequels have been made,
but none to equal the first, an early talkie
with Bela Lugosi, issued in 1931. A rather
poor sequel was printed from the novelist's
papers in 1914.

An interesting essay analysing *Dracula*
and relating it to Freud's speculations in
The Uncanny is in M. Richardson's 'The
Psychoanalysis of Ghost Stories', *Twentieth
Century*, CLXVI (December 1956). [AR]

H. Ludlam, *A Biography of Dracula: The Life
Story of B.S.* (New York, 1962).

Stow, John (*c.* 1525–1605). Historian and
antiquary. Originally a tailor, from
around 1560 he busied himself collecting
and transcribing manuscripts and in
writing chronicles, and was an early member of the Society of Antiquaries. He
published an edition of Chaucer (1561). *A
Summarie of Englyshe Chronicles* (1565) is in
the form of annals, but contains much new
material he had himself discovered. *The
Chronicles of England from Brut unto This
Present Year* (1580) was republished as the
Annals (1592). His greatest work, *A Survey
of London* (1598), was enlarged by him in
1603 and by others from 1618 onwards,
and is the most valuable source of London
traditions, and of the City's history. He
spent all his money on his historical
pursuits. [MJ]

D. Bush, *English Literature in the Earlier Seventeenth Century* (revised edn, 1962); C. S. Lewis,
English Literature in the Sixteenth Century
(1954).

Stow, Randolph (1935–   ). Australian
novelist and poet. Born at Geraldton and
educated at the University of Western
Australia. His interest in anthropology was
increased by visits to central Australia and
New Guinea. He taught English at Adelaide

University before joining the English Department of the University of Leeds. In 1964–5 he visited New Mexico before returning to Australia.

Stow's novels are intensified by his powerful sense of place. *The Bystander* (1957) is less ambitious than *A Haunted Land* (1946) or *To the Islands* (1958), and less flawed. The 'bystander' of the title is a retarded boy whose innocence and lack of awareness of his own past have a disruptive and finally tragic effect on the guilt-ridden, time-fearing members of an isolated Australian community. The novel is typical of Stow's work in its investigation of abnormal psychology and its dependence on archetypal symbol. He has published 2 books of verse, *Act One* (1957) and *Outrider* (1962). Like the novels they show remarkable powers of description and an informed application of myth. Stow's more recent novels, *Tourmaline* (1963), set in a dying town in the Australian desert, and *The Merry-Go-Round in the Sea* (1965), the story of a boy's growth in Western Australia during the forties, have not fully maintained his promise. [PT]

G. K. W. Johnston, 'The Art of R.S.', *Meanjin*, XX, 2 (Winter, 1961); D. Martin, 'White and S.', *Meanjin*, XVIII, 1 (Autumn, 1959).

Strachey, (Giles) Lytton (1880–1932). Essayist and biographer. Born in London, the son of a general who had also been an Indian administrator, he was educated at Leamington College, Liverpool University (where he read history) and Trinity College, Cambridge. At the latter he became a member of a group that included Keynes, E. M. ◊ Forster, Desmond ◊ MacCarthy, Leonard ◊ Woolf and Clive ◊ Bell. He went to London and wrote, mostly reviews, for the *Spectator*, then edited by John St L. Strachey, and for other periodicals. He was the centre of the so-called ◊ 'Bloomsbury Group', which included his Cambridge friends, and Vanessa Bell, Virginia Woolf, Roger Fry and Arthur Waley. They practised in common a devotion to art, with professions of rebellion against the middle-class society from which they sprang, and against the Victorian culture they unwillingly inherited. Strachey's first book was *Landmarks in French Literature* (Home University Library, 1912). He was a conscientious objector in the First World War and in 1918 appeared *Eminent Victorians*, a volume of biographical sketches of Dr

Arnold (pompous), Florence Nightingale (a busybody), General Gordon (a drunkard, allegedly) and Cardinal Manning (an ambitious prelate). It is a kind of 'debagging' of public figures. The method has merit, however, somewhat in the fashion of French 'inward' biographies. Strachey also writes with a witty, cynical irony that carries the intention off. He called his work 'psychography' and there is a rather loose connexion with the work of Freud which deals with the 'real' motivations of men's lives in the 'unconscious'. Strachey has also many of the gifts of the novelist, including vivid actualization and imagination. His other works are *Queen Victoria* (1921) and *Elizabeth and Essex* (1928). It is noticeable that he begins to be rather sentimental towards Victoria, a political nullity, while with Elizabeth, a person of real power, he is comparatively unsuccessful. He also published collections of smaller pieces: *Books and Characters: French and English* (1922), *Portraits in Miniature and other Essays* (1931) and *Characters and Commentaries* (1933). [AR]

Letters (to V. Woolf), ed. L. Woolf and J. Strachey (1956).

J. K. Johnstone, *The Bloomsbury Group* (1954) (with bibliography); R. A. Scott-James, *L.S.* (WTW, 1955); C. R. Sanders, *L.S., His Mind and Art* (Yale U.P., 1957) (with bibliography); M. Holroyd, *L.S.: A Critical Biography* (2 vols., 1967, 1968).

Strickland, Agnes (1796–1874). Historical writer. Born in London of a family of country gentry. She started out as a poet, but turned to popular semi-fictional history (as in *Historical Tales of Illustrious British Children*, 1833, and *Tales and Stories from History*, 1836). Her most ambitious works (in which she was assisted by her sister Elizabeth, whose name never appears) were *The Lives of the Queens of England from the Norman Conquest* (1840–8) and *The Lives of the Queens of Scotland, and English Princesses* (8 vols., 1850–9). She was a popularizer rather than an original writer, but her somewhat flat writings were extremely popular, perhaps because of their use in teaching. [AR]

U. Pope-Hennessy, *A.S.: Biographer of the Queens of England* (1940).

Strong, L(eonard) A(lfred) G(eorge) (1896–1958). Novelist, short-story writer and poet.

Born in Plymouth of an Irish family, Strong was educated at Brighton College and Oxford University. For several years he was a master at Summer Fields School, Oxford, before moving to London in 1930 to earn his living as a writer. His first novel, *Dewer Rides* (1929), was a melodramatic tale of rural life in the West Country. This was followed by *The Jealous Ghost* (1930), *The Garden* (1931), *The Brothers* (1932), *Sea Wall* (1933) and *Corporal Tune* (1934). A novelist of limited ability, his most characteristic work is set in Ireland and the West of England, which allows him fully to employ his considerable knowledge of dialect and his sympathetic understanding of rural life. These same qualities are also apparent in his short stories, *Doyle's Rock* (1925), *The English Captain* (1929), *Don Juan and the Wheelbarrow* (1932), *Travellers* (1945), *Sun on the Water* (1940) and *Darling Tom* (1952). He also published several volumes of poetry, collected as *The Body's Imperfection* (1957), an autobiography, *Green Memory* (1961), many books of common-sense criticism, and a study of James Joyce, *The Sacred River* (1949). Some later novels are *The Seven Arms* (1935), *The Unpractised Heart* (1942) and *The Director* (1944). [PJK]

R. L. Megroz, *Five Novelist Poets of To-Day* (1933).

Strype, John (1643–1737). Ecclesiastical historian and manuscript collector. He was educated at Jesus College, Cambridge, and made an extensive collection of documents, mostly of the Tudor period, which are now in the British Museum in the Harleian and Lansdowne manuscript collections. He was the author of a number of works written in a confused and unmethodical way, including *Cranmer* (1694), *Sir John Cheke* (1705), *Annals of the Reformation* (1709–31) and *Ecclesiastical Memorials* (1721). His use of original sources, however, makes some of his works still authoritative. [AR]

DNB.

Stubbes or **Stubbs, Philip** (*c.* 1555–91). Pamphleteer. After studying at Cambridge and Oxford, he became a printer, and wrote indifferent ballads before devoting himself to polemical writing. In 1583 he published *The Anatomy of Abuses*, a dialogue between Spudeus and Philoponus, a traveller recently returned after seven years in Ailgna (England), whose people have great possibilities but are wicked. The theatre is condemned amongst twenty-two profanations of the Sabbath, including May Games, bear-baiting, cock-fighting, dancing and pagan celebrations. The second part of the work attacks the professions for looseness and malpractice. *A Crystal Glass for Christian Women* (1590) was a eulogy on his wife whom he had lost in childbirth; it went through 20 editions. Stubbs is now remembered as one of several vociferous propagandists writing against the theatre in the years 1576 to 1583 of the kind who were later ridiculed by Jonson in the person of Rabbi Zeal-of-the-Land Busy in *Bartholomew Fair* (◊ Gosson, ◊ Lodge, ◊ Nashe, and – later – ◊ Prynne), but he was really a wide-ranging social critic, not a Puritan. [MK]

C. S. Lewis, *English Literature in the Sixteenth Century* (1954).

Sturt (**'Bourne'**), **George** (1863–1927). Wheelwright and writer. He was born into a family of wheelwrights at Farnham, Surrey (Cobbett's birthplace), and educated at the local grammar school, where he remained as a teacher until 1885, when he took charge of the family workshop. Some years later he went to live in a near-by village, The Bourne, from which he took his pen-name. In such books as *Change in the Village* (1912) and *The Wheelwright's Shop* (1923) he attempted to reconstruct village life as it had existed in former times. Although his vision of the 'organic community' may seem idealized, he produced valuable evidence of a still-surviving folk-culture (and showed moreover a subtle understanding of the many forms taken by 'culture'). Without advocating a return to a society based on traditional crafts and farming, Sturt suggests a challenging question: what equivalents or compensations does modern society provide for the close sense of involvement that men could have with their work and environment in the pre-industrial world? [NL]

The Bettesworth Book (1901); *Memoirs of a Surrey Labourer* (1907); *Lucy Bettesworth* (1913); *William Smith, Potter and Farmer* (1920); *A Farmer's Life* (1922); *The Journals of G.S.*, selected and ed. E. D. Mackerness (2 vols., 1967).
D. W. Harding, 'A Cure for Amnesia', *Scrutiny*, II (1933); F. R. Leavis and D. Thompson, *Culture and Environment* (1933).

Suckling, Sir John (1609–42). Cavalier poet and dramatist. He was descended from an ancient Norfolk family. After studying at Trinity College, Cambridge (from 1623), and Gray's Inn (1626–7), he travelled abroad, was knighted (1630), and went abroad again, this time to serve under Gustavus Adolphus. On his return to England in 1632 he lived the life of a courtier and man-about-town, talking brilliantly, giving sumptuous entertainments, gambling on a grand scale. In 1637 he put on his tragedy of *Aglaura*, paying for the gorgeous costumes out of his own pocket. To please the King, who disliked the bloody and indeed regicidal dénouement, he provided the play with an alternative, tragicomic ending. He wrote 2 more plays, and started another. His brisk *Account of Religion by Reason* was produced after a convivial trip to Bath.

In the first Bishops' War (1639) Suckling put himself at the King's disposal with a troop of 100 richly uniformed followers. In the second Bishops' War (1640) he served as a captain of carabineers. In the same year he sent a letter to his friend Henry Jermyn, suggesting a solution for the King's difficulties: the King was to gain the people's love by a gesture of overwhelming generosity – the granting of all popular demands, and more. As this advice was not taken, Suckling took part in the army plot (1641) and made active preparations to free Strafford from the Tower by force of arms. The plot was discovered, Suckling fled the country, and in 1642 he died in Paris. Aubrey credibly reports that he poisoned himself.

The majority of Suckling's poems are short pieces, either songs or occasional verses (there are a few epigrams); and they are directed at a courtly audience. The taste of this audience was for what French writers of the period called '*préciosité*' – the polished and highly elaborate expression of lofty but platonic passion. In a few of his poems Suckling is *précieux* (e.g. in 'Love's Representation'), but more often he is a *libertin* addressing a *précieux* audience. Much of the libertinism is couched in phrases and whole conceits borrowed from Donne; but his cynicism is far more genial than Donne's, whose frequent scorn for women he does not share. (In Suckling's hands, too, the Donne conceits are in every way simplified.) At times Suckling escapes altogether from the demands of *préciosité* by adopting a deliberately 'low' persona; thus 'A Session of Poets' seems to be spoken by a ballad-monger or a good fellow among drinking companions; while 'A Ballad upon a Wedding' purports to be spoken by a naïve country lad, whom the last stanza reveals to be thoroughly shrewd. Suckling is thus something rather more than 'a gentleman who writ with ease'. His peculiar combination of qualities – lucidity and conceited wit, polite language and down-to-earth sentiments – ensured his popularity in the Restoration and the Augustan age.

Suckling's plays are a great deal more *précieux* and less libertine than his poems. Not only are there among the female characters platonics and near-platonics, but much of the dialogue consists of elaborate debate, and expresses exalted sentiments. However, both in the tragedies (*Aglaura* and *The Discontented Colonel*, later revised as *Brennoralt*) and in his comedy *The Goblins*, there are anti-platonic characters who exercise their wit in mockery of the platonics. K. Lynch (*The Social Mode of Restoration Comedy*, New York, 1926) has pointed out that their similitude-contests provide a model for the conversation of Congreve's and Wycherley's 'false wits'.

The collected *Works* were published in 1676 and 1696, and three times more during the following century. H. Berry in 1960 published manuscript versions of some of the poems and letters (including 4 hitherto unpublished letters; he adds a very full commentary); his work, and that of L. R. Beaurline ('The Canon of Suckling's Poems'), show that a new edition of Suckling is needed. [TG]

Works, ed. W. C. Hazlitt (1874; revised edn, 1892); ed. A. H. Thompson (1910); *Aglaura* (1638); *The Discontented Colonel* (n.d.; ?1640); *Fragmenta Aurea* (1646) (poems, the plays, letters, *Account of Religion by Reason*); *The Last Remains of Suckling* (1659) (poems, letters, unfinished play *The Sad One*).
W. C. Hazlitt, *Life*, in *Complete Works* (1874); *DNB*; Aubrey, *Brief Lives*; R. Skelton, *The Cavalier Poets* (WTW, 1960).

Surrey, Earl of. ◇ Howard, Henry.

Surtees, Robert Smith (1805–64). Journalist and novelist. Born in County Durham of a family of country gentlemen, he practised unsuccessfully as a solicitor. Thereafter, with R. Ackermann, the younger, he started the *New Sporting Magazine*, which he edited (1831–6) and to which he contributed the prose sketches later collected as *Jorrocks's Jaunts and Jollities* (1838 ff.; revised and enlarged with illustrations by H. Allen, 1864). In these stories and several loosely constructed novels, he cultivated his own small garden, the 'sporting novel', infusing his pictures of English fox-hunting country society with an effective satire, amusing and coarse-grained, snobbish caricature and realistic social observation: *Handley Cross, or the Spa Hunt* (3 vols., 1843; expanded with illustrations by John Leech, the most famous sporting caricaturist of the day, 1854); *Hillingdon Hall, or the Cockney Squire* (1845; reprinted, intr. Siegfried Sassoon, 1931). The best of his work, apart from the *Jaunts*, is probably *Mr Sponge's Sporting Tour* (13 monthly parts, 1853). [AR]

Novels (10 vols., 1930).
H. Darton, *From S. to Sassoon* (1931); A. Steel, *Jorrocks's England* (1932); F. Watson, *R.S.S.: A Critical Study* (1933); R. L. Collison, *A Jorrocks Handbook* (1964).

Swift, Jonathan (1667–1745). Poet, satirist and priest. Born in Dublin after the death of his father. From about 1674 to 1682, he attended Kilkenny Grammar School with William Congreve, and entered Trinity College, Dublin, on 24 April 1682; he graduated as a B.A. there on 15 February 1686 in a category *speciali gratia*; the meaning of the phrase is unfavourable but not clear. Together with Swift's autobiographical notes compiled late in life, however, it has been taken to indicate that a turbulent and proud spirit made his college career frustrating. He continued at Trinity until the outbreak of the troubles following the abdication of James II in 1688, when he joined the stream of English refugees fleeing from the Catholic rebellion in Ireland. In 1689 he briefly lived with his mother in Leicestershire, and then became secretary to Sir William ◊ Temple at Moor Park in Surrey, where he also first met (and tutored) Esther Johnson ('Stella'), then 8 years old. In May 1690 he returned to Ireland, hoping to benefit from his family connexions in the aftermath of the unsuccessful rising. At the end of 1691, however, he again became Temple's secretary and companion. In 1692 he took an M.A. at Hart Hall, Oxford, as a preparation perhaps for hoped-for Church preferment in England. In these years he started writing poetry and he first appeared in print with a turgid, Cowleyesque 'Ode to the Athenian Society' (1692), but seems quickly to have abandoned that uncharacteristic and unprofitable mode. In 1694–5 he was ordained priest in the Anglican Church of Ireland, and appointed to the prebend of Kilroot, near Belfast. His isolation there, in a parish largely hostile to his Church, drove him back to Temple's service in May 1696 and he stayed at Moor Park until Temple's death in 1699. During this time he wrote perhaps his greatest work, the dangerously exuberant satire on the 'abuses of learning' and religious dissent *A Tale of a Tub* ('written for the Universal improvement of Mankind').

On Temple's death, Swift returned to Ireland as chaplain to Lord Berkeley, the King's representative in Ireland, who probably secured his presentation to the livings of Laracor and two other small parishes, as well as a prebend of St Patrick's Cathedral, Dublin. He returned to London with Berkeley in April 1701, and published his first political pamphlet, *A Discourse of the Contests and Dissensions between the Nobles and the Commons in Athens and Rome* (1701). This is, characteristically for Swift, anonymous, an oblique defence of Lord Somers and other ministers, who had been impeached by the House of Commons; it brought him, as designed, the favour of these powerful magnates of the low-Church oligarchy. He returned to Ireland in September, and in February 1702 took the degree of Doctor of Divinity at Dublin. It was at this period that Esther Johnson and her companion, Rebecca Dingley, settled in Ireland, and from then on formed an important part of Swift's life. In 1704 *A Tale of a Tub*, dedicated to Somers, was published along with *The Battle between the Ancient and Modern Books in St James' Library* (3 edns in that year; ed. A. Guthkelch and D. Nichol Smith, 1920). The latter was an excursion in defence of Temple into the 'ancients and moderns' controversy; it is important in understanding Swift's philosophical conservatism, as well as his powerful poetic imagination and sardonic wit.

In November 1707 he returned to London as the commissioner from the Irish clergy to the ministers (largely the group he had earlier defended) in order to ask for the remission of a royal tax on Church income. For complex political reasons, he did not succeed in this, nor was he more successful in gaining preferment in the Church of England, but he did become a literary celebrity. In 1708, he published the amusing *Bickerstaff Papers: Predictions for the Year 1708* (1708; several edns) and other contributions to the *Tatler*, and wrote poetry and politico-religious pamphlets. The latter included a powerful satire, *An Argument to Prove that the Abolishing of Christianity in England*, etc. (published 1711). After another brief spell in Ireland (June 1709 to September 1710), Swift returned to London for another attempt at his ecclesiastical embassy, and began four years of his most intensive political and journalistic work; his intimate letters to Esther Johnson, often written daily, are a fascinating record of his activity and states of mind (published as the *Journal to Stella*, ed. H. Williams, 2 vols., 1948). Shortly after his arrival in London, Swift began negotiating with the new chief minister, Robert Harley, the leader of the 'Tories', and thereafter supported this group; he became editor of their political journal the *Examiner* (1710–11; see vol. III of *Prose Works*, ed. H. Davis, 1940), and wrote many political pieces. The most famous of these is the skilfully argued work designed to prepare the public for Harley's policy of withdrawing from the War of the Spanish Succession and called *The Conduct of the Allies* (1711/12; 5 edns).

Swift had considerable power and influence as a public relations man, and also as an important member of a literary group of wits, of congenial political sympathies, which included Arbuthnot, Prior, Pope, Gay as well as Harley himself. *The Scriblerus Papers* (ed. P. Kerby Miller, Yale U.P., 1950) was one of the most important fruits of their collaboration. Swift eventually failed again in his reasonable hope of substantial preferment in the English Church, and had to content himself with the Deanery of St Patrick's in Dublin; he was installed on 13 June 1713, and returned to London in September. The death of the Queen (and the dismissal of his friends from power) ended his English career. He returned to Ireland in September 1714, where he spent the remainder of his life, in 1718, Swift became engaged in the political unrest in Ireland, caused by repressive English mercantilist economic measures; he emerged as a popular Irish patriot and most effective publicist. *A Proposal for the Universal Use of Irish*

Manufactures appeared in 1720, but his most effective works in this connexion were *The Drapier's Letters* (1724), in which, in the guise of a common-sensical Dublin tradesman, Swift presented a devastating indictment of a heartless and ineffective English policy. These works were anonymous, and a price was put on the author's head; everyone knew, including the English Government, who had written them, but Swift was never prosecuted. The most concentrated and powerful of all Swift's satires came out of this national preoccupation; this is *A Modest Proposal for Preventing the Children of Poor People from Becoming a Burthen to their Parents or Country, and for Making Them Beneficial to the Publick* (published 1729; several edns).

Sometime after his return to Ireland in 1714, Swift began work on his most famous book, *Travels into Several Remote Nations of the World by Lemuel Gulliver* (1726; ed. A. E. Case, New York, 1938; ed. L. A. Landa, Cambridge, Mass., 1960). This work was published in London on 28 October 1726, soon after Swift returned to Ireland after a brief stay of six months in England with Pope and Arbuthnot. He met Sir Robert Walpole, whom he cordially disliked, to discuss the state of Ireland, and also published a poem *Cadenus and Vanessa*, about his friendship with Esther Vanhomrigh who had died in June 1723. In 1727 he made a last short visit to his friends in England (April to September).

During his last years he continued to write a good deal, including 2 of his best poems: *Verses on the Death of Dr Swift* (composed 1731; published 1739) and *The Legion Club* (1736), a savage attack on the Irish House of Commons. As the 1730s closed, Swift's memory began to fail; his infirmities, the disease of the inner ear which he suffered from all his life, and old age began to oppress him more and more. On 17 August 1742 he was found 'of unsound mind and memory', and his affairs were entrusted to guardians; on 19 October 1745 he died, leaving the greater part of his estate to endow a hospital for the insane. Swift lies buried in his Cathedral, under the epitaph he composed for himself: *ubi saeva indignatio ulterius cor lacerare nequit* (He has gone where savage indignation can tear his heart no more).

One of the greatest satirists in the language, Swift's power as writer was created by the savage indignation he felt when he saw men behaving so far below their capacity as beings endowed with reason and created in God's image. His religious faith was profound, and this knowledge should act as a control on too easily interpreting his view as nihilistic pessimism. He was pessimistic, as all great moralists have been, when they consider that man misues his reason to aggravate his 'natural corruptions, and to acquire new ones, which Nature had not given him'. Swift published only one inconsiderable pamphlet under his own name; his characteristic tactic was to create a mask (such as the Dublin Drapier or Gulliver), and to present his moral judgements by complex and energetic argument and irony. Partly because of his religious and family upbringing, he was a traditionalist and a conservative in his historical writing, such as *The History of the Four Last Years of the Queen* (1758; vol. v of the *Prose Works*, ed. H. Davis, 1951), which deals with the period of his political activity in London. He sees events as determined, not by great impersonal forces, but by the motives of particular men. He is a considerable poet, who excelled in the anti-poetic uses of imagination. All his writing is marked by force, and a directness that masks a dangerous irony intended to trap the reader in argument. Swift is a witty writer with a serious purpose, whose most controlled work, *Gulliver's Travels*, has been misread and misunderstood by a too easy acceptance of the surface joking. On the other hand, psychological speculation has often produced elaborate profiles of his 'inner life' without noticeably assisting the reader to understand his works. In his own day, he was recognized as one of the greatest living writers in English. [AR]

Prose Works, general ed. H. Davis (14 vols., 1939 ff.) (in progress); *Poems*, ed. Sir H. Williams (3 vols.; 2nd edn, 1958); *Journal to Stella*, ed. Sir H. Williams (2 vols., 1948); *The Correspondence of S.*, ed. Sir H. Williams (5 vols., 1963).

H. Craik, *Life of S.* (2 vols., 1894); I. Ehrenpreis, *S.: The Man, His Works and the Age* (3 vols., 1962 ff.) (in progress); J. M. Bullitt, *J.S. and the Anatomy of Satire* (Harvard U.P., 1953); H. Davis, *J.S.: Essays on His Satire and Other Studies* (1964); M. Price, *S.'s Rhetorical Art* (Yale U.P., 1953); R. Quintana, *S.: An Introduction* (1955); K. Williams, *J.S. and the Age of Compromise* (U. of Kansas P., 1958); R. I. Cook, *J.S. as a Tory Pamphleteer* (U. of Washington P., 1967); ed. B. Vickers, *The World of J.S.* (1968); L. A. Landa and J. E. Tobin, *S.: A List of Critical Studies from 1895 to 1945* (New York, 1945).

Swinburne, Algernon Charles (1837–1909). Poet. Educated at Eton and Balliol College, Oxford, he came to know personally Rossetti and the Pre-Raphaelites, but developed an independent poetic idiom. His first important volume, *Atalanta in Calydon*, was published in 1865. Based on Greek tragic form, its choruses contain some of Swinburne's best-known lyrics, but it was in the following year that his most impressive volume, *Poems and Ballads*, appeared. He became interested in the struggles for independence in Europe, and particularly in Mazzini's cause in Italy, and produced *Songs before Sunrise* in their celebration. Swinburne led an anarchic and dissipated life, which finally made him seriously ill, and in 1879 he was taken under the wing of Theodore Watts-Dunton, who looked after him for the rest of his life.

Swinburne's inclination towards the deliberate and perverse attack on conventional moral attitudes dominated his poetry. It is irresistibly suggestive. He uses a powerful language of sensuality that, while not being at all precise in meaning, radiates waves of intoxicating sound. His swinging rhythms, too, are hypnotic in their repetitions of patterns of sound which help to convey the reader beyond the imprecision of language. In many of his lyrics Swinburne's syllables echo from one line to the next with such flow and rapidity that it is impossible to pause from the first word to the last.

Swinburne's suggestiveness and determination to scandalize frequently verge on extravagance, which is all the more suspect on account of his vagueness. He at times injects his sensuality with sadism, but does not create any complex or meaningful pattern of human emotion and action. There is nothing exploratory in his poems, which remain dim and suggestive statements of mood rather than particular expressions of emotion. Swinburne published a further 2 volumes of *Poems and Ballads* (1878 and 1889), several verse plays, a substantial amount of criticism and 2 novels, *Love's Cross Currents* (1905) and *Lesbia Brandon*, which was not published until 1952. There is no development or progress in Swinburne's poetry, and his first *Poems and Ballads* remain his highest achievement. Although he broke away from conventional Victorian thought there is little originality in his attitudes and it is not his aggressive stance that is of value. It is the splendid and unfaltering movement of his rhythms and the breathless resonance of his language that make his poetry impressive and unforgettable. [JRC]

Complete Works, ed. E. Gosse and T. Wise (20 vols., 1925–7); *The S. Letters*, ed. C. Y. Lang (6 vols., 1959–62); *The Best of S.*, ed. C. K. Hyder and L. Chase (1937); *Selected Poems*, ed. L. Binyon (World's Classics, 1939); *Poems and Prose*, ed. R. Church (Everyman, 1940); *Selected Poems*, ed. H. Treece (1948); *Selected Poems*, ed. H. Hare (1950); *Selected Poems*, E. Shanks (1950).

G. Lafou.cade, *S.: A Literary Biography* (1932); D. Bush, *Mythology and the Romantic Tradition* (1937); T. S. Eliot, 'S. as Poet', in *The Sacred Wood* (1920) (has had great influence); J. O. Fuller, *S. A Critical Biography* (1968).

Swinnerton, Frank (1884–   ). Novelist. He was born at Wood Green, London, the son of an engraver, and started work early as a proof-reader and later publisher's reader. He had published 5 novels before his best-known one, *Nocturne*, appeared in 1917. This was a virtuoso piece of writing, the result of a challenge issued by the publisher Martin Secker, and it established Swinnerton as a promising young writer. Since then he has written 35 more books, most of them moderately popular novels, of which the most successful were *Young Felix* (1923) and *Harvest Comedy* (1937). His latest work has been more substantial, comprising a quartet made up of the volumes *The Woman from Sicily* (1957), *A Tigress in Prothero* (1959), *The Grace Divorce* (1960) and *Quadrille* (1965), about four generations of an acting family, and *Death of a Highbrow* (1961), a study of an elderly writer. From 1937 to 1942 Swinnerton was chief novel reviewer on the *Observer*. He has also published 3 books of reminiscences, *Autobiography* (1937), *Background with Chorus* (1956) and *Figures in the Foreground* (1963), which are useful, if gossipy, guides to the literary scene both before and after the First World War. His work is unrelentingly cheerful and middle-brow. [JM]

Symonds, John Addington (1840–93). Art historian, critic and poet. Born in Bristol, the son of a leading physician there, he was educated at Harrow and Balliol College, Oxford, where he came under the influence of Jowett and gained distinction in classics. He won the Newdigate Poetry Prize and a fellowship at Magdalen, but developed consumption, a state of health that upset his mind and against which he struggled all his life. He travelled in Switzerland and Italy,

married, and returned to London in 1865, to study law; but his health forced him abroad for some years. In 1868 he started a career as a writer. His travels abroad had furnished him with essays which he had published in various magazines; these he collected as *Sketches in Italy and Greece* (1874; 1879), *Sketches and Studies in Italy* (1879) and a later volume, *Italian By-Ways* (1883). He did a little teaching, which produced *An Introduction to the Study of Dante* (1872; 1880) and *Studies of the Greek Poets* (2 vols., 1873, 1876). These were popular works, infusing a romantic love of Alpine and 'classical' scenery with the English idealized enthusiasm for the classical writers. In 1873 he was again abroad, and began his most famous work, *The Renaissance in Italy* (7 vols.: *The Age of the Despots*; *The Revival of Learning*; *The Fine Arts; Italian Literature*; *The Catholic Reaction;* 1875–86; abridged, 1893), in which, following ◊ Pater he stimulated one of the significant imaginative interests of the time. Symonds 'writes up' the Renaissance in his book is loosely put together, often inaccurate, but full of gusto. As might be expected, he tends to use the flowering of humanism as an escapist refuge from the gloom he felt in the Victorian literary and intellectual scene. Symonds was no philosopher and relies on his imagination to diagnose his problems.

In 1877, he had been forced abroad again, and thereafter lived chiefly at Davos in the Swiss Alps; an article on life there, published in the *Fortnightly* (1878), stimulated English Alpinism, and the creation of the little English colonies in the Engadine (see *Our Life in the Swiss Highlands*, 1892). Symonds produced a fair amount of literary journalism, including lives of Shelley (1878) and Sir Philip Sidney (1886), and *Shakespeare's Predecessors* (1884; 1900), as well as editions of various works. His criticism of English literature is not up to the highest standard of even his kind of classical dilettantism. He also wrote lives of Michelangelo (2 vols., 1893) and Boccaccio (1895). A study of Whitman (1893) arises from his enthusiasm for democracy. He published a number of translations, such as *Wine, Women and Song* (1884) from the Goliardic poets and *The Autobiography of Benvenuto Cellini* (1888). Symonds was an important popularizer of Italian culture in England, through his books and articles in the *Encyclopaedia Britannica*. He published several volumes of essays, characteristic of the imagination of his kind of classically educated English intellectual. *Essays Speculative and Suggestive* (1890) includes 'Evolution' and 'Elizabethan and Victorian Poetry'; *In the Key of Blue* (1893) includes 'Culture' and 'The Lyricism of Romantic Drama'. Symonds's volumes of poetry are *Many Moods* (1878), *New and Old* (1880), *Animi Figura* (sonnets) (1882) and *Vagabunduli Libellus* (which contains his sonnet-sequence *Stella Maris*, dealing with 'a passionate experience' in Venice, and the disillusionment that follows when he sees himself disloyal to 'his superior nature') (1884). In his verse his introspection often gets the better of him, and his poems tend to be overlaid with decorative allusion, virtuoso techniques and indirection, which his original genuine but slight imaginative power cannot control. [AR]

The Letters, ed. H. M. Schueller and R. L. Peters (1968 ff.).
H. F. Brown, *J.A.S.* (2 vols., 1903); Van Wyck Brooks, *J.A.S.* (New York, 1914); M. Symonds, *Out of the Past* (1925); P. L. Babington, *Bibliography of the Writings of J.A.S.* (1925); P. Grosskurth, *J.A.S.: A Biography* (1964).

Symons, Arthur (1865–1945). Poet and critic. Born in Wales, of Cornish parents, he was educated mostly at private schools abroad, and was fluent in French and Italian. He began writing religious and imitative verse, and on visits to London became a member of the Rhymers' Club and a friend of Wilde and ◊ Dowson. He was attracted to Baudelaire, Verlaine, Mallarmé and the French Symbolists, whose works by translation, imitation and criticism he helped to introduce to the English reader and poet. He shared rooms with Yeats; contributed to the ◊ *Yellow Book*; and in 1896 became editor of its successor, the *Savoy*, to whose pages with Yeats he added a certain Celtic tinge. Symons was also a prolific editor and literary journalist, with a specialized knowledge of Shakespeare and the Elizabethan dramatists. His poetry is characteristic of the work of the nineties, of the 'Decadence'. He imitates the Symbolists and shuns his own *milieu*, preferring to manipulate the suggestiveness of 'Javanese Dancers' or 'The Loom of Dreams'. His verse is sad and indefinite. He published a number of volumes of poems, from *Days and Nights* (1889), *Silhouettes* (1892), *London Nights*(1895), *Images of Good and Evil* (1899) to *Jezebel Mort and Other Poems* (1931). His *Poems* (2 vols., 1902) is a carefully selected edition. His later work is not different. As a critic, he was a disciple of ◊ Pater, who praised his work. He describes and 'realizes' books for his readers, and here too his ideas showed no great development. His important volume *The Symbolist Movement in Literature* (1899) is not really a history but a manifesto written after the work was done and its force spent. His criticism includes *Studies in Two Literatures* (Elizabethan drama, and contemporary writing, including J. A. ◊ Symonds) (1897), *Studies in Prose and Verse* (Gautier, De Quincey, Pater, Yeats, Dobson, etc.) (1904). He also wrote on contemporary, chiefly French, painting. *Confessions: A Study in Pathology* (New York, 1930) gives a fascinating account of his mental breakdown, severe amnesia and ill-treatment by the police, in Naples. He has had a certain continuing influence through his introductory essays to reprints and anthologies. [AR]

Collected Works (9 vols., 1924) (incomplete).
T. E. Welby, *Arthur Symons, a Critical Study* (1925) (with bibliography); R. Lhombréaud, *S., His Life and Letters* (1962) and *S.: A Critical Biography* (1963); J. Peck, 'Divergent Disciples of Walter Pater', in *Thought*, 23 (1948).

Synge, John Millington (1871–1909). Dramatist. Born into an old Anglo-Irish family at a time when the fortunes of the 'Ascendancy' class were in decline, he was, because of ill-health, educated mainly by private tutors before going to Trinity College, Dublin, where he distinguished himself in Hebrew and Irish. He almost made music his career, and studied the violin in Germany. He went to Paris in 1895, and for some years divided his time between Ireland and Europe, extending his knowledge of literature and languages, and trying to write poems and essays. It was in Paris in 1896 that he met W. B. ◊ Yeats and joined the Irish League. In 1898 at Yeats's suggestion he went to the Aran Islands (where he spent the following four summers also) to study the customs, language and lore of an isolated people. *The Aran Islands* did not at first find a publisher, but appeared with illustrations by Jack B. Yeats in 1907, by which time Synge had found his vocation as a dramatist. In Aran he first heard stories which gave him plots, and his emergence as a playwright coincided with, and furthered, the Irish dramatic revival. His third play was already begun when his first, *In the Shadow of the Glen*, was performed by the Irish National Theatre Society in Dublin in 1903. Synge was attacked for the way he presented the Irish peasantry, and for his theme – the husband who shams death to test his wife's fidelity. *Riders to the Sea*, the tragedy of a widow whose seafaring sons are all drowned, was acted in Dublin in 1904, and Synge's first 2 plays were liked by English critics when taken to London in that year. When, through Miss Horniman's munificence, the Abbey Theatre became the base of Lady Gregory's and Yeats's dramatic revival, Synge was at first a literary adviser and later a director, and his plays entered the repertory. *The Well of the Saints* was produced in 1905. His great comedy, *The Playboy of the Western World*, caused uproar and riots in Dublin in 1907, where audiences rejected the notion that Irish peasants would harbour and even hero-worship a self-advertising murderer. The play has subsequently achieved classic status and is constantly revived. Synge's last years were darkened by illness. His love for the actress Molly Allgood (Maire O'Neill), who played Pegeen Mike in *The Playboy*, inspired his one play on an Irish myth, *Deirdre of the Sorrows*, acted posthumously and in unfinished form in 1910.

The short *Autobiography* was reconstructed from manuscripts by A. Price (1965). [MJ]

Collected Works, general ed. R. Skelton (1962 ff.) (in progress); *The Plays and Poems*, ed. T. R. Henn (1963).

E. Coxhead, *J.M.S. and Lady Gregory* (1962); D. H. Greene and E. M. Stephens, *J.M.S., 1871–1909* (1959); A. Price, *S. and Anglo-Irish Drama* (1961).

T

Tagore, Rabindranath (1861–1941). Indian poet, playwright, novelist, painter, educator and musician. He wrote in Bengali. Tagore was an innovator in all these fields. He was born in Calcutta, the youngest child of a gifted Brahmin family (see *My Boyhood Days*, 1940). From 1878 to 1880 he was in England, the first of ten foreign voyages. He was both patriot and internationalist, influenced by Western and Indian literature. His prolific creativity was uninterrupted by his increasing social and political involvement after 1890. He wrote more than any other Indian writer of comparable stature.

During a visit to England in 1912 Tagore was surprised by the enthusiasm of Yeats and others over some half-serious translations of his own poems. *Gitanjali* was published in England the same year, and earned him the Nobel Prize in 1913. In translation the poems become devotional fragments in lyrical prose, sometimes tranquil, sometimes ecstatic, but always chiefly active beneath the surface. He defined his main literary theme as 'the joy of attaining the Infinite within the finite'. Objective observation, both here and in the plays, is used to extend the area of spiritual action. The year 1913 also saw the publication of the beautiful poems about children in *The Crescent Moon*, and the first translated play, *Chitra*. Tagore was knighted in 1917, but resigned his knighthood two years later in protest against British policy in India. In 1921 his ambitions for the educational settlement he had established at Santiniketan in 1901 culminated in the opening of Visva-Bharati University. *Collected Poems and Plays* appeared in 1936, and *A Tagore Reader* in 1961.

Tagore wrote no plays directly in English, and only one poem. His own translations are loose, and much of his work is still available only in Bengali. The final impression is of enormous receptiveness, sometimes leading too easily into expression. [P T]

My Reminiscences (1917) (autobiography).
K. Kripalani, *R.T.* (1962); *Visva-Bharati Quarterly*, xxvi, 3 and 4 (1962) (Tagore centenary issues); E. J. Thompson, *R.T., Poet and Dramatist* (1948).

Taliesin (fl. 6th cent.). Welsh poet. Of the poets named in Nennius's *Historia Britonum* (9th century), the work of two only has survived, namely ◊ Aneirin and Taliesin. Taliesin's poetry is contained in *Llyfr Taliesin* ('Book of Taliesin'), a manuscript of *c.* 1275 which is preserved at the National Library of Wales, Aberystwyth. Not all the poems in the collection which are ascribed to Taliesin can be so accepted. Sir Ifor Williams, the chief worker in the field of early Welsh poetry, has selected a hard kernel of a dozen poems which he confidently attributes to the 6th-century Taliesin on the basis of internal evidence relating to orthography, metre, rhyme, historical allusions, etc. The poems are addressed to Cynan ap Brochfael, king of Powys (perhaps Taliesin was a native of Powys), Urien Rheged and his son Owain, and Gwallawg. They are of the 'heroic' type to be expected of this period, with eulogy of the king at war or at peace, of his generosity on one hand and his bravery on the other. The king is 'anchor of his country'. The elegy to Owain ap Urien is a sincere lament for a leader who left his enemies lying dead with the light in their open eyes after being pursued like a flock of sheep driven by a pack of wolves.

The authenticity of these Taliesin poems has always rested on the possibility whether Welsh could have developed from British by the 6th century. No one now doubts this possibility, but of recent years the technical excellence of the poet's craft has been suspected to be rather too early for the 6th century. The probability is, however, that the historical poems which are attributed to Taliesin are really contemporaneous with him. But much detailed work remains to be done, particularly on the metres.

Taliesin also figures as a character in the later tale which was possibly evolved in the 9th century. In this Gwion Bach is swallowed by Ceridwen the witch and is reborn as a baby with a beautiful forehead (*taliesin*). This Taliesin is connected with personages like Elphin ap Gwyddno and Maelgwn Gwynedd. Taliesin was also credited with supernatural powers, and this gave rise to his supposed knowledge of Druidical teaching. [MR]

Canu Taliesin, ed. I. Williams (1960).
I. Williams, *Lectures on Early Welsh Poetry* (1944); R. Bromwich, 'The Character of the Early Welsh Tradition', in *Studies in Early British History*, ed. N. K. Chadwick (1954); J. Morris-Jones, *T.* (1918); J. E. Caerwyn Williams, *The Poems of T.* (1968).

Tannahill, Robert (1774–1810). Scottish poet. A Paisley weaver, he burned his manuscripts and drowned himself when Constable, his publisher, rejected an edition of his poems. His work, a pale and sentimental imitation of Burns's songs, shows the stereotyping of theme and form that led to the decline of Scottish poetry in the 19th century. [AI]

Poems and Songs, ed. D. Semple (1874).

Tate, Nahum (1652–1715). Dramatist and poetaster. Educated at Trinity College, Dublin, he moved to London, published a volume of poems, and had several plays acted, but is now chiefly infamous for his neo-classical alterations of Shakespeare. His version of *King Lear* which excised the Fool and had a happy ending in which Cordelia survives to marry Edgar replaced the original on the British stage until the middle of the 19th century. He was co-author with Dryden of the second part of *Absalom and Achitophel*, was made Poet Laureate in 1692 and historiographer-royal in 1702, and with Nicholas Brady he wrote *New Versions of the Psalms* (1696). [MJ]

A. Nicoll, *British Drama* (revised edn, 1962) and *History of English Drama, 1660–1900*, i (revised edn, 1952).

Tawney, Richard Henry (1880–1962). Social critic and historian. Born in Calcutta and educated at Rugby and Balliol, he taught at several universities before becoming Professor of Economic History at London (1931–49) and he was also associated with the W.E.A. as tutor, organizer and president, for over forty years. As a writer his standpoint was Socialist: moderately Fabian in method but morally stringent in judgement. His most important historical works are *Religion and the Rise of Capitalism* (1926) and *Business and Politics under James I* (1958), but his importance to literature lies in his other books where he writes as a moral critic of society – in the tradition of Arnold and Ruskin, but using the tools of the professional historian. His attack on the distortion of purpose in modern society, *The Acquisitive Society* (1921), was based on his identification of two major evils: industrialism regarded as an ideal, and the existence and approval of inequality. This second observation was expanded into a book which has since become a classic, *Equality* (1931), where a detailed exposition of economic history is developed into an analysis of the moral aim of society. This leads to an indictment of the two features, private education and inherited wealth, which preserve inequality, and the conclusion that such violent contrasts of opportunity within a nation prevent the establishment of a common humanitarian culture. His other main area of research has been public education where his work has contributed to the Socialist education policy in Britain. Although his style is often tortuous and unattractive, his thinking has been very influential, and his outstanding importance is that of a constructive social moralist. [JM]

The Radical Tradition (1964).
Raymond Williams, *Culture and Society* (1958); W. H. Nelson, in *Some Modern Historians of Britain*, for R. L. Schuyler (1951).

Taylor, Jeremy (1613–67). Preacher, devotional writer and theologian. Taylor was born in 1613 at Cambridge, son of a barber, and was educated at Gonville and Caius College, Cambridge, becoming a Fellow in 1633. Having been ordained, he went to London as a substitute preacher at St Paul's and attracted the notice of Archbishop Laud, who nominated him to a fellowship at All Souls College, Oxford, in 1635. Subsequently he became a chaplain to Laud and to Charles I. In 1638 he was appointed Rector of Uppingham, and married in 1639. He left in 1642 to become a chaplain in the Royalist army, and was taken prisoner when, in 1645, the Royalists were defeated before Cardigan Castle. After a short imprisonment, he retired to Golden Grove, Carmarthenshire, where he was chaplain to Lord Carbery. Most of his finest works were written there: *The Liberty of Prophesying* (1647), a plea for toleration; *The Rule and Exercises of Holy Living* (1650) and *The Rule and Exercises of Holy Dying* (1651), 2 notable devotional books; *The Golden Grove* (1655), a manual of daily prayers; and *Eniautos* (1653), a collection of sermons. Taylor went to Lisburn in Northern Ireland in 1658 as a lecturer, and after the Restoration in 1660 was appointed Bishop of Down and Connor and vice-chancellor of Dublin University. He published *Ductor Dubitantium* in 1660, a manual of moral theology, using in it both Protestant and Roman Catholic authorities on the subject. He became Bishop of Dromore in 1661, and published in 1664 *A Dissuasive from Popery*. Although he had written in praise of toleration, the intransigence of the Presbyterians in his diocese forced him to take harsh measures against them.

Taylor's main claim to fame rests on his devotional books and sermons. *Holy Living*, a handbook to the devout life, provides a good example of reasonable, temperate Anglican piety, and is written in a lucid, flowing style. *Holy Dying*, which is in the old *ars moriendi* tradition, is an elaboration of Christian and classical commonplaces on the theme of death, but it is touched by Taylor's personal grief for the deaths of his wife and Lady Carbery. It contains some famous 'purple patches' of rhetorical and imaginative prose, which together with similar passages in the sermons attracted the critics of the Romantic period, such as Coleridge, Lamb and Hazlitt, and these remain today the best-known parts of Taylor's writings. His most striking device is the use of long elaborate similes of real poetic power. He employs also, with great effect, shorter similes, usually drawn from familiar objects, such as birds, animals, the seasons and the varied phenomena of nature. Although at times Taylor's images tend somewhat to glamorize sin, in their context most of the decorative passages are apt and much enliven the presentation of the subject matter. Equally felicitous are his frequent references to the classics, the Bible and the Church Fathers, but it must be stressed that the staple of his prose remains clear and straightforward and that merely to read him in an anthology will give a false impression of over-richness of style. [JWB]

The Whole Works, ed. R. Heber (15 vols., 1822); revised edn, C. P. Eden (10 vols., 1847–54); *J.T.*, ed. M. Armstrong (1923) (anthology); *The Golden Grove*, ed. L. Pearsall Smith (1930). Coleridge, *Literary Remains*, iii (1838) and *Notes on English Divines*, i (1853); Hazlitt, *Dramatic Literature of the Age of Elizabeth* (Lecture 7); Arnold, 'The Literary Influence of Academies'

(*Essays in Criticism*, 1st series); E. Gosse, *J.T.* (English Men of Letters, 1903); W. Fraser Mitchell, *English Pulpit Oratory from Andrewes to Tillotson* (1932); C. J. Stranks, *The Life and Writings of J.T.* (1952); H. Ross Williamson, *J.T.* (1952); C. Smyth, *The Art of Preaching* (1940); D. Bush, *English Literature in the Earlier Seventeenth Century* (1945).

Taylor, John (1580–1653). The self-styled 'Water-Poet'. Born in Gloucester, Taylor began life as a waterman on the Thames, but the times were bad for watermen, and so, as W. Notestein puts it, he 'transformed himself into a traveller-to-order and a rhymer of sorts, and found himself at length the spoiled guest of gentlemen and magistrates'. He was a very prolific but uninspired writer in prose and verse, for instance with the accounts of his various journeys about the country. [DELC]

Works . . . Comprised in the Folio Edition of 1630 (3 vols., Publications of the Spenser Society, nos. 2–4, 1863–9); *Works . . . Not Included in the Folio Volume of 1630* (5 vols., Publications of the Spenser Society, nos. 7, 14, 19, 21, 25, 1870–8); *J.T.'s Wandering, to See the Wonders of the West*, ed. C. Hindley in *Miscellanea Antiqua Anglicana*, iii (1873) (facsimile reissue, reprinted privately in Newcastle, 1967).
W. Notestein, *Four Worthies* (1956).

Temple, Sir William (1628–99). Diplomat and essay writer. Educated at Emmanuel College, Cambridge, he travelled abroad during the Civil War. The letters addressed to him by Dorothy Osborne (whom he married in 1655) are one of the best expressions of private emotions in the language (*Dorothy Osborne's Letters to Temple*, Everyman, 1932; ed. G. C. Moore Smith, 1928). Temple lived in Ireland and was an M.P., but returning to England after the Restoration he was sent abroad as a diplomat, helped to draft the Triple Alliance (1688), and became ambassador at The Hague, where he arranged the marriage of William and Mary. In 1681 he retired from public life and, though he advised William III, refused further office. Though by no means an original thinker, he carefully developed a prose style of ease and dignity, which was admired by Swift (who published his *Memoirs*, 1709), Pope and Johnson. His longer works (on state affairs), such as *Observations upon the United Provinces* (1673), *Essay on the Advancement of Trade in Ireland* (1673) and the *Introduction to the History of England* (1695), are little read.

but his shorter essays, dealing mainly with private reflections, are anthologized. Among his *Miscellanea* (3 vols., 1680, 1690, 1701), *Upon the Gardens of Epicurus* popularized the ideas that informed the English landscape gardening which became popular in the 18th century; another piece, *Of Ancient and Modern Learning*, adopting a 'classical', anti-progressivist argument, stimulated the 'ancients and moderns' controversy. Swift was Temple's secretary in his retirement at Moor Park in Surrey, and defended him with *The Battle of the Books*. [AR]

Essays, ed. J. A. Nicklin (1911).
H. E. Woodbridge, *Sir W.T.: The Man and His Work* (1940); N. Pevsner and S. Lang, 'T. and Sharawaggi', in *Architectural Review*, CVI (1949) (T. and gardening).

Tennyson, Alfred, Lord (1809–92). Poet. Born in Somersby, Lincolnshire, son of a country rector whose large and varied library provided his earliest inspiration. He began writing poetry at the age of 8, and in 1827 he and his brother Charles published their first book, *Poems by Two Brothers*. The following year Tennyson went to Trinity College, Cambridge, but left before completing his degree. The year 1830 saw the publication of *Poems Chiefly Lyrical*, his first important book, although it was not well received by the critics. In 1833 his closest friend Arthur Hallam died in Vienna, and this had a lasting influence on his life and writing. For many years Tennyson had a difficult life financially, and he was not able to marry until 1850. The same year brought the publication of *In Memoriam*, a series of lyrics and speculations about mortality in tribute to Hallam, considered by many to be his most important work, and his appointment as Poet Laureate.

Tennyson's earliest adult poems reveal his skill at drawing from classical myth and medieval legend a general mood of melancholy and particular moral comment which was to remain characteristic throughout his career. The colour and richness of his imagery and descriptive writing shows the influence of Keats, but are made distinctive by Tennyson's rhythmic qualities. His superb metric manipulation was well developed by 1833, when 'Oenone', 'The Lady of Shallott' and 'The Lotus Eaters' were published in *Poems*. In these poems his use of language and metre to sustain the dream-like and tragic inability of his pro-

tagonists to act against the inevitability of their situations is expertly and sensitively controlled. He is at his most impressive when he uses the musical qualities of language as a means of deepening his rhythms and his meaning.

Tennyson frequently presented legendary heroes as spokesmen for his own moral attitudes, but he was also concerned to show the innate moral heroism of ordinary domestic life. This led him at times to destroy a pleasing theme by inappropriate sentiment, or to strangle a poem's natural energy by simultaneously overlaying it with moral significance and cautiously restraining the human activity, as in 'Enoch Arden' (1864). But it was poems such as this that were most popular, although not necessarily praised by the critics. His 'Idylls of the King' (1859) have often been criticized for their use of legend as a vehicle for Victorian moralizing. But Tennyson was genuinely concerned at the contradictions of Victorian Britain and was not able to reconcile the two sides of his sense of responsibility – the one that worried and the one that saw itself as prophet of the age. While being confident of progress and of the value of a humbly heroic stance, he remained deeply troubled by the unpredictability of human emotions and behaviour. In 1855, the year after the publication of his most jingoistic poem 'The Charge of the Light Brigade', he wrote 'Maud', an intense, almost breathless group of lyrics describing a tragic love affair. The violent rhythms and impassioned language completely override any impression of complacency or narrowmindedness that Tennyson suggests elsewhere. *In Memoriam*, which contains some of his finest writing, is damaged by the inability to move beyond almost arbitrary statements of faith.

Tennyson had an almost unflawed metrical understanding, and it enabled him to handle a wide variety of forms. He was equally happy with the rapid narrative of 'The Princess' (1847), a fable of female emancipation, and the short lyrics that he later added to the poem. In his lyrics he created, in language that is both precise and suggestive, an identity of mood and physical surroundings which represents Tennyson at his elegiac best. The nostalgia of 'Tears, Idle Tears', the insistent sadness of 'Break, Break, Break', products of rhythmic control as much as of language, infect to some degree most of his poetry.

Even in his prophetic optimism his melancholy is hovering near.

Tennyson was a careful poet, as his much-revised manuscripts show, and he never lost touch with his earliest attitudes. He returned again and again to the same themes and moods. But if he was limited in scope, and if his talents were hampered by public demand – for he was one of the most popular of major poets – and by his own sense of moral duty, his metrical skill remains quite breathtaking in its vigour and delicacy. [JRC]

Works, ed. H. Tennyson (Alfred's son) (9 vols., 1907–8; ed., in 1 vol., W. J. Rolfe, 1898); *Poetical Works, Including the Plays* (Oxford Standard Authors, 1953); *Poems*, ed. C. Ricks (1968).

H. Tennyson, *A. Lord T. A Memoir* (2 vols., 1897); Sir C. Tennyson, *A.T.* (1949); Sir H. Nicolson, *T.* (1923); J. H. Buckley, *T.: The Growth of a Poet* (1960): ed. J. Killham, *Critical Essays on the Poetry of T.* (1960); V. Pitt, *T. Laureate* (1962).

Tey, Josephine. ⟡ Mackintosh, Elizabeth.

Thackeray, William Makepeace (1811–63). Novelist. Only son of a prosperous officer in the East India Company's Civil Service, Thackeray was born in Calcutta and sent to England at the age of barely 6 to a private school in Southampton, 'a dreadful place' (as he later wrote), 'cold, chilblains, bad dinners, not enough victuals, and caning awful'. After an acutely miserable year there he was removed to a more reputable school, but remained unhappy until his mother, with her second husband, returned from India in 1820. He was then sent to Charterhouse and from there in 1829 he proceeded to Trinity College, Cambridge. He spent five terms at Cambridge idling and gambling and then after a winter at Weimar entered the Middle Temple. But journalism attracted him more than the law, and in 1833 he bought the weekly paper the *National Standard* for which he both wrote and drew until it shortly afterwards expired. Until now he had been a young man of private means, but the failure of a Calcutta agency house in 1833 lost him the bulk of his inheritance, and he settled in Paris at the end of 1833 to try and make his way as a painter. He drew caricatures and dabbled in journalism. In Paris too he met and married (in 1836) 19-year-old Isabella Shawe, who was to be the prototype of so many of his good, weak and helpless heroines. The couple settled in London in 1837 and Thackeray pushed his fortune as a journalist. His writing for periodicals at this time included *The Yellowplush Correspondence*, social satire written obliquely in the person of a footman, which appeared in *Fraser's Magazine* (1837–8) and later (1841) in book form. The death in infancy of his second daughter in 1839 and the birth of a third in 1840 at a time when Thackeray's work took him often away from home reduced the already helpless Isabella first to a state of profound depression and then to complete and permanent mental collapse. Throughout the rest of his life the memory of the brief happiness and then the sudden collapse of his marriage and the existence in the background of a mentally ill wife were a permanent and central part of Thackeray's consciousness. In the assumed character of Michael Angelo Titmarsh he wrote *The Paris Sketch-Book* and *The Great Hoggarty Diamond* for *Fraser's* in 1840–1. Much of Thackeray's early work deals with rogues and dupes who batten on society and with the hypocrisies and falsities that prevail in respectable society itself. *Catherine* (*Fraser's*, 1839–40) is a deliberately sordid account of the progress from fornication to murder of a self-seeking tavern maid of the 18th century. *The Luck of Barry Lyndon* (*Fraser's*, 1844; revised as *The Memoirs of Barry Lyndon, Esq.*, 1856) is the story of an ingenious rogue who tells his own life history in a tone of innocent-seeming self-congratulation. Thackeray's *Punch* series *The Snobs of England* (1847, republished 1855 as *The Book of Snobs*) attacked every deviation from a simple ideal of openness and integrity produced by the demands of society.

The first major phase of Thackeray's literary career culminates in his masterpiece, *Vanity Fair* (monthly parts, 1847–8), where his apprenticeship in rogue literature and in satirical and mock-heroic writing bore fruit in one of the great social-satirical novels in the language. Yet there is a certain timidity if not confusion in the novel, for by making his heroine Becky Sharp an unscrupulous self-seeking adventuress he minimizes his more devastating insight that society as it is organized all over the Western world puts a premium on hypocrisy and that the only way for someone without money and position to succeed in it is to violate all the ethical principles to which society pays lip service. Which is to blame, the adventuress or the society that makes adventurism necessary if the talented but penniless are going to avoid despair? The brilliance of the novel (for all the fatuity of its few 'good' characters, especially the women) cannot quite disguise the ultimate confusion of purpose. Becky is made to overreach herself and so fall out of good society – an awful warning of the fate of an unscrupulous if talented woman; yet the society in which she forfeits her position has already been shown up as 'vanity fair'. Society is evil, yet the rebel who knows it for what it really is and uses that knowledge to her own advantage is shown as a bad person to be punished. The moral implications of *Vanity Fair* are more disturbing than Thackeray seemed to have realized.

The social satire is never quite so central again in Thackeray's novels. *The History of Pendennis* (1848–50) takes us through the adventures of a well-meaning and intelligent young man and shows him being educated by experience; its plot is of little significance, and the novel's interest lies in the vivid realization of the dramatic moments of confrontation and the balancing against each other of social types and attitudes. Society is still vanity fair, but the social satire is less pointed and the contrast (found in *Vanity Fair*) between intelligent and unscrupulous villainy and mindless virtue less absolute. *The History of Henry Esmond, Esq.* (1852) is a virtuoso historical novel told throughout in an 18th-century style and again exploring the relation between pride and goodness, between the public face and the private reality. Again, the exposure of snobs and hypocrites is an important feature, but the main emphasis is on personal relations and on uncovering the moral reality of a situation involving a particular group of characters only. *The Newcomes* (1853–5) continues to explore the relations between virtue and success, between honest simplicity and self-interested calculation, but in a mood of greater emotional self-indulgence which tends to resolve the ultimate moral questions in sentimentality. *The Virginians* (1857–9) is a sequel to *Esmond* and, as well as exploring in a rather loose and genial manner Thackeray's usual themes, provides lively accounts of English and American society in the second half of the 18th century.

Throughout his career as a novelist Thackeray continued with miscellaneous writing. His 1851 lectures, *The English Humourists of the Eighteenth Century*, were published in 1853. He published many volumes of *Miscellanies* of both prose and verse. *The Four Georges: Sketches of Manners, Morals, Court and Town Life* first appeared in the *Cornhill Magazine*, 1860. (See also *Christmas Books*, 1857; *Rebecca and Rowena*, 1850, a comic-ironic sequal to Scott's *Ivanhoe*; and *Ballads*, 1855.) The ballads – comic, sentimental, reminiscent, descriptive, elegiac – are of very mixed quality but reflect interesting aspects of Thackeray's character and of the taste of his audience.

Thackeray became the first editor of the *Cornhill* in 1860, and in it he published his last 3 novels, *Lovel the Widower* (1860), *The Adventures of Philip* (1861–2) and *Denis Duval* (1864, unfinished).

Like Dickens, Thackeray moved to novel-writing from miscellaneous journalism. He began with great gifts as a narrator, together with a feeling for the mock-heroic and the picaresque. His sense of character and his use of the violently picturesque in character drawing can sometimes (in *Pendennis*, for example) remind us of Dickens, but he was never as wholly committed to the novel as edifying entertainment as his age and his great contemporary were. In his preface to *Pendennis* he wrote: 'Since the author of Tom Jones was buried, no writer of fiction among us has been permitted to depict to his utmost power a MAN. We must drape him, and give him a certain conventional simper. Society will not tolerate the Natural in our Art.' Unlike Dickens, Thackeray resented the limitations on frankness set by Victorian taste. In some ways he belonged to the 18th century. He has not Dickens's baroque energy or George Eliot's ethical and psychological subtlety. But where he succeeds in striking a balance between outrage and sentimentality he can (as in *Vanity Fair*) produce a kind of socio-satirical fiction of a power and vitality that is not easily matched in the 19th century. [DD]

The Letters and Private Papers, ed. Gordon Ray (4 vols., Cambridge, Mass., 1945–6).
Gordon Ray, *T.: The Uses of Adversity* (New York, 1955), *T.: The Age of Wisdom* (New York, 1958) and *The Buried Life, A Study of the Relation between T.'s Fiction and His Personal History* (1952); J. Y. T. Grieg, *T.: A Reconsideration* (1950); G. Tillotson, *T. the Novelist* (1954); *T.: The Critical Heritage*, ed. G. Tillotson and D. Hawes (1968) (19th-century essays and reviews on T.).

Thériault, Yves (1915–   ). French Canadian novelist. Thériault is unusual in French Canada, a writer with barely any formal education. It is to this and to his varied experience of life in his native province of Quebec that Thériault, the story-teller, owes his fresh, vigorous and natural style, his anti-conformism and the directness of his narrative. His faults – lack of variety in sentence pattern and occasional unrestrained sentimentality – can be accounted for in the same way; they are, however, absent from his best work. He is by far the most prolific of French Canadian novelists, publishing 10 novels since 1950 as well as several collections of stories and a large number of children's books. Several of his novels – *La fille laide* (1950), *Le dompteur d'ours* (1951) and *Le grand roman d'un petit homme* (1963) – are set in small French Canadian villages. Life in a small community is treated in these with gentle satire, though Thériault evidently respects those rare characters whose independent spirit makes them remain true to themselves in spite of the overwhelming pressures to conform. A second set of novels, *Aaron* (1954), *Ashini* (1960) and *Amour au goût de mer* (1961), choose as their central figures members of minority groups or representatives of dying cultures and can be seen as symbolic transpositions of the situation of the French Canadians, threatened by assimilation. *Ashini*, which has been called a poetical sermon, evokes the plight of the Indians in Canada; it shows Thériault's flair for the sensual qualities of words, particularly those of the Indian languages with which he is familiar. Thériault has some Indian ancestry and has worked for the Federal Government as adviser on Indian cultural affairs. *Agaguk* (1959), translated into half a dozen languages, the long eskimo novel for which Thériault is famous, belongs to this group but is much more than a documentary on a vanishing culture. It is a beautifully simple story about love and hatred, life and death, and it is recognizably Canadian in that there emerges gradually, as the story unfolds, the belief that a love of life is inadequate unless it is particularized and given an identity. [CRPM]

Thomas, Dylan (1914–53). Poet. Born in Swansea and educated at the local grammar school, Thomas worked for a time as a reporter on the *South Wales Evening Post*. His first volume, after some earlier verse had been printed in the *Sunday Referee*, was *Eighteen Poems* (1934). He was fortunate in being taken up, early in his career, by Edith ▷ Sitwell, and in thus finding himself the centre of critical attention while still very young. *Twenty-Five Poems* (1936) was followed by *The Map of Love* (1939), which included prose pieces as well as poetry. During the war Thomas worked for the B.B.C. His autobiographical sketches, *Portrait of the Artist as a Young Dog*, appeared in 1940. His most widely known, possibly his finest, volume of poems was *Deaths and Entrances* (1946).

Thomas's obsessive drinking and disorderly way of life, in which he unwittingly caricatured the bohemian temperament, were strong contributory causes to his tragically early death at 39 in a New York hospital during a lecture tour of the United States. He was, in his lifetime, widely regarded as one of the finest poets of his generation. The circumstances of his death have to some extent made it difficult to assess him fairly, but there can be no doubt that he was a poet of great power and a certain degree of originality. An apparently wilful obscurity was apt to disfigure Thomas's early verse, but by the time of *Deaths and Entrances* he had achieved, with the assurance he found in maturity, a simpler and more direct manner as well. His verse is rhetorical and large in scale. He explored the worlds of childhood and adolescence with a remarkable compound of superb precision and cunning theatrical effect. His imagery is bright, his rhythms new and compelling. The influence of Hopkins is strongly apparent in much of his verse.

Thomas's prose was uneven: much of what he wrote for broadcasting is ephemeral, and although the play he wrote for radio, *Under Milk Wood* (1954), was highly regarded when first heard, it has worn less well than the poems. It is self-consciously 'poetic' in a way that Thomas's finest poems are not. [CO]

Adventures in the Skin Trade (1955); *Selected Letters*, ed. C. FitzGibbon (1966).
J. Ackerman: *D.T.: His Life and Work* (1964); J. M. Brinnin, *D.T. in America* (1955); C. FitzGibbon, *The Life of D.T.* (1965); J. A. Rolph, *D.T.: A Bibliography* (1956).

Thomas, Edward (1878–1917). Poet and prose writer. Educated at Oxford, he wrote nature studies, of which *The South Country* and *The Heart of England* are the most enjoyed, and critical biographies, of which the books on Richard Jefferies, George Borrow and Swinburne are the best known. He was among the first recognizers of Ezra Pound. His destiny, to be a poet, came later. Influenced by Robert Frost, and with a prose training behind him, he delighted in a freer, shorter, more expressive form, but without afflatus. He wrote of landscape, rural life and values, fauna and flora, the weather, transience and endurance, and the involvement in these of his own striving for peace and integrity. He combines a fine feeling for detail with a power of emotional generalization. His poems make no demands upon life and thus discover, through their innate strength, and beyond the poet's own tensions, a quality of alert repose, often absent from 'nature poetry'. Thomas's *Collected Poems* (1920) have been constantly in print. The current edition is introduced by Walter de la Mare, who refers to his 'delicate yet vigorous intuition'. Thomas fell before Arras in 1917. [FG]

H. Coombes, *E.T.* (1956); H. Thomas, *As It Was* (1926) and *World without End* (1931); E. Farjeon, *E.T.: The Last Four Years* (1958); William Cooke, *E.T.: A Critical Biography* (1970).

Thomas, R(onald) S(tuart) (1913–   ). Poet and clergyman. He has since his first modest publications in the late 1940s, built up a reputation as one of the most honest and penetrating of living British poets. He is a clergyman of the Church of Wales, which, unlike the Church of England, is disestablished and is also the Church of a minority of the Welsh people. It is, however, the Welsh rural communities, hill farmers and shepherds, who have given him the subject matter of most of his poems, which resemble Robert Frost's in their plain clarity of diction and structure and in their handling of a pastoral theme without pastoral sentiment or idealism. He depicts a way of life which is bleak and hard, which narrows and cramps the character, but which also breeds staunchness and simplicity. In his Christian realism he has perhaps something in common with George Crabbe. Some of his more recent poems, without being militantly nationalist, have shown a strong dislike of the invasion of Wales by tourist caravanners. A recently published lecture, 'Words and the Poet', throws much

indirect light on his own poetic principles and practice.

Stones of the Field (1947); *Song at the Year's Turning* (1955); *Poetry for Supper* (1958); *Tares* (1961); *Words and the Poet* (1964).

Thomas, William (Islwyn) (1832–78). Welsh poet. Born at Ynys-ddu, in the Sirhywi valley, Monmouthshire, he was educated for the Calvinistic Methodist ministry and ordained in 1859. In early life his fiancée Ann Bowen died before they could get married, and this deeply and permanently affected Islwyn. By the time that he was beginning his poetic career the verse form known as the *pryddest* or long poem in the free metres was becoming acceptable as a main competition at the Eisteddfod, and this was later to result in the recognition of two poetic forms, the *awdl* in the strict classical metres as the Chair poem, and the *pryddest* as the Crown poem, a distinction which still holds good. The abstract, patriotic and biblical themes on which Islwyn wrote in his *awdlau* are typical of the period, and so is their diffuseness and prosiness. The special place which Islwyn holds is due to his *Storm*, a long unpublished poem which he began to write under the stress of losing Ann Bowen. The poem is completely formless and uneven. What plan there is revolves around the author's three personalities – poet, preacher and philosopher. He attempts to make a synthesis of his meditations on man and his soul, man and nature, man and God. This contemplative poetry, concerned with vast abstractions, led to the emergence of what was known as *Y Bardd Newydd* 'The New Poet' in the last decades of the 19th century, with their 'philosophical' approach to poetry. None of them however had sufficient poetic genius to transmute their meditations and raise them to an artistic level. The positive virtue of Islwyn's *Storm* is that it marked a change in the poets' attitude to poetry which had previously been purely descriptive. The influences on him must be found in earlier English poets like Edward ◊ Young, Alexander ◊ Smith and the Romanticists. [MR]

Gwaith Barddonol Islwyn, ed. O. M. Edwards (1897).

Thomas of Erceldoune (Thomas the Rhymer. True Thomas, or Thomas Learmonth) (fl. 13th cent.). Reputed poet and prophet,

Associated with Earlston in Berwickshire, he was apparently a historical figure, although no surviving poem or prophecy is demonstrably his. Neither *The Romance and Prophecies of Thomas Erceldoune* (ed. J. A. H. Murray, EETS, 1875), which tells how Thomas accompanied the Queen of Elfland to her country and received from her the gift of prophecy and many actual prophecies, some specifically referring to Bannockburn and Otterburn, others obscure and fabulous, nor the romance of *Sir Tristram* (ed. G. P. McNeill, STS, 1886), a version of the Tristan story also ascribed to Thomas, seems likely to have been composed in its present form by a Scotsman of Thomas's time. True Thomas is best known today through the ballad 'Thomas Rymer', based on the romance, but for many centuries he was remembered for the cryptic prophecies traditionally attached to his name. *The Whole Prophecies of Scotland, England, France, Ireland and Denmark*, first printed in 1603, continued in circulation as a chap-book until the early 19th century, and scraps of rhyme attributed to Thomas remained in oral circulation until recent times. [A I]

English and Scottish Popular Ballads, ed. F. J. Child, no. 37 (repr. 1957); R. Chambers, *Popular Rhymes of Scotland* (1826); W. P. Albrecht, *The Loathly Lady in 'Thomas of Erceldoune'* (Albuquerque, New Mexico, 1954).

Thomas of Hailes (fl. 1250). Early English poet. A Franciscan friar, presumably came from Hales in Gloucestershire. Some sermons at St John's College, Oxford, are ascribed to him, and the name appears in letters and documents of the mid-century. He is known for his poem, *A Luve Ron* (ed. C. Brown, *English Lyrics of the XIIIth Century*, 1932), composed at the request of a young nun. It deals, in 25 stanzas, with the vanity of human wishes, developing into an exhortation to the love of God, and is perhaps the finest English treatment of the universal medieval theme, *Ubi sunt qui ante nos fuerunt*. Thomas uses the names of heroes of history and romance to great effect in evoking the glories of the dead past; his strategy in turning the apparatus of the courtly love-lyric to religious ends is characteristic of the period, and especially of the Franciscan movement in literature. The poem was still remembered at the end of the 14th century. [A G]

B. Hill, 'The *Luve Ron* and Thomas de Hales', *M L R*, LIX (1965); R. M. Wilson, *Early Middle English Literature* (1939); R. Woolf, *English Religious Lyric in the Middle Ages* (1968).

Thompson, Francis (1859–1907). Poet and critic. Born at Preston, the son of a homeopath. His parents, and his father's brothers (of whom Edward Thompson was Professor of English at University College, Dublin), were converts to Roman Catholicism. Francis Thompson was educated at Ushaw College and given a strong classical training. The priesthood was thought of, but he went to Owens College, Manchester, to study medicine. He did badly in this uncongenial course and abandoned it after six years. In 1885, with vague notions of writing, he went to London but succumbed to the habit of taking opium, and ended up destitute selling matches. During this crisis, he developed a poetic talent. He wrote two poems, 'The Passion of Mary' and 'Dream Tryst', and an essay, 'Paganism Old and New', on some sheets of paper given to him by a shopkeeper; these were published by Wilfred Meynell in *Merry England* (April–June 1888). Meynell befriended him; he took a cure with the monks of Storrington Priory. His health was ruined, but the withdrawal symptoms of the drug cure also stimulated his writing. *Poems* (1893) contained his best-known poem, 'The Hound of Heaven', a rich and passionate result of his musing on the conflict between sacred and profane love. *Sister Songs* (poems for the Meynell children) (1895) and *New Poems* (1897) are his other volumes. Thompson's poetry is heavily influenced by ◊ Patmore's poetry among the modern and by ◊ Crashaw among older Roman Catholic writers. He seeks to unite in colourful poetry a sensuous appreciation of beauty with an ascetic self-abnegation; his revivals of old words, liturgical echoes in poetry and religious symbolism caused more trouble in his own day than they do now. Thompson is daring: to many readers, out of sympathy with his faith, he has seemed to succeed in only a handful of poems, but he has an authentic vision, however fragmented in its individual realization. From 1893 to 1897 he lived near the Franciscan monastery at Pantasaph in North Wales. He published a fair number of critical essays in the *Academy* and the *Athenaeum* as well as one or two religious works and saints' lives. [A R]

521

Works, ed. W. Meynell (3 vols., 1913) (vol. iii is a selection of early prose); *Poems* (1937; 1955); *Poems*, ed. T. L. Connolly (New York, revised edn, 1941) (with notes and bibliography); *Literary Criticisms: Newly Discovered and Collected*, ed. T. L. Connolly (New York, 1948). Margoliouth (1958); *Poems, Centuries, and Three Thanksgivings*, ed. Anne Ridler (1965). E. Meynell, *Life* (1913); R. L. Mégroz, *F.T., the Poet of Earth in Heaven* (1927); P. Danchin, *F.T., la vie et l'œuvre* (Paris, 1959) (with good bibliography); J. C. Reid, *F.T., Man and Poet* (1959); R. Van K. Thomson, *F.T.: A Critical Biography* (1961); P. H. Butter, *F.T.* (WTW, 1961).

Thomson, James (1700–48). Scottish poet. Thomson, the son of a Border minister, published poems in Edinburgh magazines while studying Divinity at Edinburgh University. A professor's criticism of his prose as too ornate for the Scottish pulpit impelled Thomson to seek his fortune in London (1725), where he became tutor to a nobleman and was introduced into Pope's circle by David ◊ Mallet. In 1726 he published *Winter*, a description of autumn and the onset of winter in what is clearly his native Border landscape; he expanded this into a complete series of *The Seasons* (1730), which by the time of his death he had elaborated into a tissue of descriptions of animals, plants and geological and meteorological phenomena, interspersed with discursive political and moral comment and sentimental tales. Stylistically, Thomson vulgarized Milton's diction and syntax into a poetic currency that served the 18th and early 19th centuries as an alternative to the pointed and urbane Augustan couplet. Coleridge, who disliked Thomson's style, acknowledged that the great popularity of *The Seasons* at all levels of society was 'true fame'. Critics of the 19th century found Thomson's 'feeling for Nature' a ground for treating him as a 'pre-Romantic' along with ◊ Akenside and ◊ Shenstone; more recently his 'Nature' has been seen as an Augustan blend of Newtonian science with the deistic optimism of ◊ Shaftesbury, and *The Seasons* has fallen into place beside the didactic pietism of ◊ Blair, ◊ Young and parts of ◊ Cowper.

Johnson, who praised the originality and comprehensiveness of *The Seasons* while regretting its incoherence, thought Thomson's later tragedies 'declamation rather than dialogue' and the patriotic poem *Liberty* (1735–6) unreadable, and these judgements have not been seriously disputed. *The Castle of Indolence* (1748; ed., with other poems, A. D. McKillop, 1961) however is a more unassuming and individual poem, incongruously caricaturing Thomson and his 18th-century circle through the idiom and conventions of Spenser. Thomson also wrote 'Rule Britannia' as a song in one of the patriotic stage entertainments that kept flowing the stream of sinecures and patronage by which, like his friend and rival Mallet, he lived. [A I]

Complete Poetical Works, ed. J. L. Robertson (1908).
A. D. McKillop, *The Background of T.'s Seasons* (1942); D. Grant, *T., Poet of the Seasons* (1951); A. M. Oliver, 'The Scottish Augustans', in *Scottish Poetry*, ed. J. Kinsley (1955).

Thomson, James (1834–82). Poet and essayist. He sometimes signed his work B.V. or Bysshe Vanolis – a pseudonym alluding to two of his favourite authors, Shelley and Novalis. He was born in Port-Glasgow, his parents moving to London when he was still a child. In 1842 he became a boarder in a school for sons of poor Scottish soldiers and sailors. After training at the Royal Military Asylum, Chelsea, he became an army schoolmaster in 1856. The fits of drinking that were to become increasingly characteristic of his life now first made their appearance. In 1862 he was discharged for a trivial offence. For a time he went to live in the household of Charles Bradlaugh, whose atheistic Republican and Malthusian weekly, the *National Reformer*, was one of the chief outlets for Thomson's verse and essays. His last years were spent in lodging-houses. *The City of Dreadful Night*, published in instalments in Bradlaugh's paper in 1874, and in a volume with other poems in 1880, attracted some attention. In this long work the city becomes a very modern symbol of man's isolation (it anticipates in some ways the Waste Land of T. S. Eliot), while the stock-imagery of the post-Romantics – abandoned churches, ruined statues, dead maidens and moonlight – feeds the nightmares and hallucinations of a man trying to come to terms with the fear of death and the pain of life in a Godless universe. The tone moves between horror, despair and acceptance. Thomson's feeling for rhythm is continually threatened (particularly in his other work) by conventional vocabulary and by undistinguished and sometimes heavy rhymes. It is not always easy to tell whether the borrowings in his verse are deliberate or not. 'Sunday at Hampstead' (1866) is interesting for the skilful use which is made of the rhythms of popular speech. The poets he admired and wrote about (often in obscure periodicals such as *Cope's Tobacco Plants*) included Jonson, Blake, Browning and Walt Whitman. He translated some of Leopardi's essays. [NL]

Poems and Some Letters, ed. and intr. Anne Ridler (1963); *The Speedy Extinction of Evil and Misery: Selected Prose of J.T.*, ed. W. D. Schaefer (1967).
B. Dobell, *The Laureate of Pessimism* (1910); I. Walker, *J.T.: A Critical Study* (1950); C. Vachot, *J.T.* (1964) (with bibliography).

Thrale, Mrs. ⟡ Piozzi, Hesther Lynch.

Tickell, Thomas (1686–1740). Poet. Educated at Queen's College, Oxford, where he became a Fellow, being dispensed from taking orders. His poetry is mostly occasional, correct and decorous. *On the Prospect of Peace* (1713), supporting the negotiations to dish the Dutch and sign the Peace of Utrecht, was very popular, running to 6 editions. He became a *protégé* of Addison's, contributed to the *Spectator* and wrote a fulsome poem on George I's accession. He also produced a good verse translation of the *Iliad*, Book I, which came out two days after Pope's version (first part), one of the grounds of Pope's antipathy to Addison, who was assumed to be the instigator. Addison took Tickell with him to Ireland, and made him his Under-Secretary of State; he later became Secretary to the Lords Justices in Ireland, a post he held till his death. He edited Addison's *Works*, and contributed a famous elegy on his patron (1721). There are several 18th- and early 19th-century editions of his poems. [AR]

R. E. Tickell, *T.T. and the Eighteenth Century Poets: 1685–1740* (1931) (life, letters and poems).

Tillotson, John (1630–94). Sermon-writer. Born in Yorkshire the son of a Presbyterian clothier, he was educated at Clare College, Cambridge. He conformed in 1662 and became a very popular preacher at Lincoln's Inn. He was made Dean of Canterbury (1672) and advocated wide comprehension for the Church of England. William III made him Archbishop of Canterbury (1691). His sermons, 'latitudinarian', reasonable and written in the lucid, simpler prose becoming fashionable, were widely read and influential. [AR]

Works, ed., with a Life, by T. Birch (1752).

Toland, John (1670–1722). Deist, theologian and political writer. He was born a Roman Catholic in Ireland, but having become a Protestant was educated at the Universities of Glasgow, Edinburgh and Leyden. Developing a rationalist train of thought, he gave up his intention of becoming a Dissenting minister and published his able *Christianity Not Mysterious* (1696). This work caused great controversy and was presented by the Grand Jury of Middlesex as atheistical and subversive, and burned by the common hangman in Dublin. He wrote much on political subjects, somewhat inconsistently, and was employed by Harley as his intelligence agent in Hanover. He is also remembered for the Life prefixed to his edition of Milton's *Prose Works* (1698). [AR]

L. Stephen, *History of English Thought in the Eighteenth Century* (1902).

Tolkien, J(ohn) R(onald) R(euel) (1892–   ). Philologist and romancer. Fellow of Merton College, Oxford, a Roman Catholic member of the Oxford wartime circle of C. S. ⟡ Lewis, Charles ⟡ Williams and others, and Merton Professor of English Language and Literature, he published some notable criticism (e.g. on *Beowulf*, and on fairy stories) while already turning his knowledge of Norse, Teutonic and Celtic myth and language to direct creation in *The Hobbit* (1937) and its sequel, the trilogy *The Lord of the Rings* (1954–5). The former has enjoyed the fame proper to a competently told fairy story: the latter has had an extraordinary success throughout the world, especially with the 'hippy' generation. It presents something of a critical problem. Its outline – the discovery of a ring which confers indefinite power, and which therefore must be destroyed because it leads to infinite corruption, and the journey to destroy it in the mountain where it was created by the Dark Lord, who having lost it needs it to subdue the world – is grand, and the world in which this takes place has a remarkable imaginative density and complexity: certain episodes and creatures (notably the Ents, conscious and thinking trees rumoured to be based on C. S. Lewis) are undoubtedly products of a powerful mythopoeic imagination. But

Tomlinson

other episodes seem rather to weaken than add to the fairy traditions which they imitate. Perhaps (as Roger Sale has indicated) the book's essence is the discovery by its central beings, the hobbits, of the variousness and majesty of the world which is fighting to keep alive against 'the darkness that threatens to obliterate the natural separateness of living things'. The writing is therefore good while the discovery is going on and while we see with the hobbits' perceptions; trite in, for example, the battle scenes, where we have only the general narrator's description. Thus, though some of the book's appeal lies in a simple reaction against the world of industrialism and impersonal social organization (a reaction symbolically reflected in it), it cannot be denied a probably enduring impressiveness of its own. But it will conceivably remain difficult to assess until the phase of culture against which it reacts is past. A further romance, *The Silmarillion*, is promised. [SM]

Beowulf, the Monsters and the Critics (1936); *Tree and Leaf* (1964).
Ed. N. D. Isaacs and R. A. Zimbardo, *Tolkien and the Critics* (1968) (in particular R. Sales's essay).

Tomlinson, H(enry) M(ajor) (1873–1958). Novelist and essayist. Born in London, the son of a radical non-conformist cooper, Tomlinson grew up among the East End docks and early developed an imaginative love for all things connected with the sea. On the death of his father in 1886 he was obliged to leave the local board school where he was a star pupil and take a job in a City office. In 1904 he joined the staff of the *Morning Leader* and as a journalist at last fulfilled his childhood ambition to travel. His first book, *The Sea and the Jungle* (1912), was a vivid account of a voyage up the Amazon River. During the First World War he was a newspaper correspondent in France and his bitter wartime experiences served to reinforce his already critical attitude towards English society. This comes out clearly in his novels, which are descriptive and discursive and often strongly autobiographical. They include: *Gallions Reach* (1927), *All Our Yesterdays* (1930), *The Snows of Helicon* (1933), *All Hands!* (1937), *Morning Light* (1946) and *The Trumpet Shall Sound* (1957). Tomlinson's best work is to be found in his essays, *Old Junk* (1918), *London River* (1921), *Out of Soundings* (1931) and *The Wind is Rising* (1941). Deeply felt and keenly

observed they deal with the subjects which perennially interested him – London, the sea, tropical countries and the futility of war. He also published the study *Norman Douglas* (1931); a record of his trip to the East Indies, *Tidemarks* (1924); and a collection of autobiographical sketches, *A Mingled Yarn* (1953). [PJK]

H.M.T., ed. Kenneth Hopkins (1953) (selection).
Frank Swinnerton, *The Georgian Literary Scene* (1935).

Tottel, Richard (d. 1594). Publisher, printer and bookseller. From 1553 until his death he conducted his business at The Hand and Star within Temple Bar, and was a member of the Stationers' Company from its foundation in 1557. Although he was principally a printer and publisher of law books, he issued More's *Dialogue of Comfort* (1553), Lydgate's *Fall of Princes* (1554), and Surrey's *Aeneid* (1557). His name recurs in English literary history through his publication in 1557 of *Songs and Sonnets Written by the Right Honourable Lord Henry Howard Late Earl of Surrey and Others*. Better known as *Tottel's Miscellany*, this collection of poems was frequently expanded and reissued (ed. H. E. Rollins, revised edn, 2 vols., 1965). By 1587 it contained 310 poems – 36 attributed to Surrey, 81 to Wyatt, and 40 to Nicholas Grimald; Tottel's 'Uncertain authors' include Chaucer, Sir John Cheke, William Gray, John Harington, John Heywood, Thomas Norton, Sir Antony St Leger, D. Sand, and Thomas Vaux. The *Miscellany* is the greatest gathering of 16th-century English sonnets and lyrics; its sales and influence were immense. [MJ]

C. S. Lewis, *English Literature in the Sixteenth Century* (1954).

Tourneur, Cyril (Turnour, Turner) (*c.* 1570/80–1626). Dramatist. As the vagueness about the date of his birth suggests, little is known of Tourneur's early life or his education. He spent many years in the service of the great families, the Veres and the Cecils. He saw military action in the Low Countries around 1614, and was employed on foreign service. His first known publication is a satire, *The Transformed Metamorphosis* (1600), a poem influenced by John ◊ Marston, and he is thought to have written *A Funerall Poeme upon the Death of the Most Worthie and True Soldier, Sir Francis*

524

Vere (1609). His *Character of Robert Earl of Salisbury* appeared in 1612, and the following year he wrote one of *Three Elegies on the Most Lamented Death of Prince Henrie*. His career in the theatre was brief and his reputation as a dramatist rests on 2 plays, *The Atheist's Tragedy* (printed 1611; ed. I. Ribner, 1964) and *The Revenger's Tragedy* (printed anonymously in 1607; ed. R. A. Foakes, 1966). Many critics now attribute the second play to Thomas ◊ Middleton. Other plays by Tourneur have been lost. He died in Ireland, in poverty.

Since *The Revenger's Tragedy* is the greater of the 2 plays usually thought of as his, Tourneur's ultimate standing as a dramatist depends on whether this work is his or some other's. It is a revenge tragedy, patterned like a morality play, in which the characterization is stylized and the court atmosphere of evil and corruption is vividly evoked in the poetic imagery. The revenger figure, Vendice, is a malcontent exposing the behaviour of the other characters, but himself entering their evil world. It was memorably revived by the Royal Shakespeare Company (Stratford, 1966; London 1969). [MJ]

Works, ed. A. Nicoll (1930).
M. C. Bradbrook, *Themes and Conventions of Elizabethan Tragedy* (1935); T. S. Eliot, 'Cyril Tourneur', in *Selected Essays* (enlarged edn, 1954); ed. G. Salgādo, Introduction to *Three Jacobean Tragedies* (1965); L. G. Salingar, '*The Revenger's Tragedy* and the Morality Tradition,' in *Scrutiny* VI (1938), and 'T. and the Tragedy of Revenge', in *Pelican Guide to English Literature*, ed. B. Ford, ii (1955).

Towneley Cycle. ◊ Miracle Plays.

Townshend, Aurelian (*c.* 1583–*c.* 1643). Dramatist and poet. Born in Norfolk, he was sent abroad by Sir Robert Cecil (later Earl of Salisbury) around 1600 as a preparation for a post as tutor, and may have been attached to his household at the time of Cecil's death in 1612. He married and had several children, and little is known of him until *c.* 1631 when he emerged as a writer of masques and poems, replacing Ben Jonson as author of court entertainments after the latter's quarrel with the designer Inigo Jones. In 1632 he collaborated with Jones on two masques, *Albion's Triumph* and *Tempe Restored*, in both of which scenery, music and dance far outshone the writing. His poems were not collected until 1912, but circulated in miscellanies and presumably in manuscript, and some of his lyrics are still

admired. He may have fallen into poverty and neglect, or may have lived at Knole under the protection of the Earl of Dorset until *c.* 1651. [MJ]
Poems and Masques, ed. E. K. Chambers (1912).

Toynbee, Philip (1916–   ). Novelist and critic. Born in Oxford, son of Arnold Toynbee, and educated at Rugby and Christ Church, Oxford. For a time he was a foreign correspondent but for some years has made a profession of literary journalism. As a novelist he is one of the very few experimentalists of any stature in modern English literature. He wrote his first novel, *The Savage Days* (1937), when he was 20. *The Barricades* (1943) contains strong autobiographical elements, dealing as it does with a schoolboy in 1937 who runs away from school in an attempt to join the International Brigade in Spain.

In *Tea with Mrs Goodman* (1947) and *The Garden to the Sea* (1953) Toynbee's urge to experiment with form and technique is given full rein. The prose is what might loosely be called poetic, characterization is fragmented and plot is buried beneath several layers of consciousness. The loss in surface clarity is more than compensated for by the intensity of the writing, and by the poetic beauty of much of Toynbee's imagery. Having, in these books, brought poetic insights and images to the prose of the novel, Toynbee then proceeded to attempt to infuse poetry with the exterior concerns and the narrative interest of the novel-form, and produced 2 novels in verse, *Pantaloon, or The Valediction* (1961), *Two Brothers* (1964) and *A Learned City* (1966). The first of these is refreshingly readable, but *Two Brothers* suffers from an obsessive concern with its form at the expense of its language. *Friends Apart* (1954) is a memoir of two of the author's friends of the thirties. It is also perhaps Toynbee's most formally satisfactory work to date. [CO]
The Fearful Choice (1958); *Comparing Notes* (1963) (with A. Toynbee).

Traherne, Thomas (1637–74). Poet. The son of a Hereford shoemaker, he was possibly left an orphan and seems to have been brought up and educated by Philip Traherne, a rich innkeeper who was twice mayor of Hereford. He went to Brasenose College, Oxford, in 1653, took his B.A. in 1656, and was made M.A. in 1661 and B.D. in 1669.

He was appointed by the Parliamentary Commissioners incumbent of Credenhill in 1657, but seems to have been prevented from taking up residence. In 1660 he was episcopally ordained, and resided at Credenhill as rector from 1661 to 1669. While there he became associated with a religious circle centring on Susanna Hopton at Kington, for whom he wrote the meditations now known as the *Centuries*. In 1669 he became chaplain to Sir Orlando Bridgeman, who was Lord Keeper from 1667 to 1672, and remained in Sir Orlando's household in London and at Teddington until his death in 1674.

Traherne's *Roman Forgeries* (on the forging of ecclesiastical documents by the Church of Rome) was published in 1673 and he prepared *Christian Ethicks* (1675; ed. Carol L. Marks and George Robert Guffey, Cornell U.P., 1968) for the press. Some of his meditations were published anonymously in 1699 and 1717. The chance finding of manuscripts on a London bookstall and the establishing by Bertram Dobell of Traherne as their author led to the publication of the *Poetical Works* in 1903 and the *Centuries of Meditations* (Dobell's title) in 1908. A manuscript of the *Poems of Felicity*, edited for the press by Traherne's brother, was subsequently discovered in the British Museum and published by H. I. Bell in 1910. Later discoveries have included a manuscript volume of meditations on the Church year and a notebook containing early poems.

Traherne's *Centuries* are a series of meditations turning on the recognition that as God's child he has access to all the riches of God manifest throughout creation, his conscious enjoyment of these being the fulfilment of their purpose, an expression of the mutual love between him and God, and the key to an unbounded felicity, itself the gift of God. The *Centuries* are written in a strong and manly but curiously worked prose which conveys a vivid sense of illumination and peace.

His poems are a less certain achievement. His complex stanza forms often cause distortion of the natural word order of English, his vocabulary tends to be generalized, abstract and sometimes trite, and there is in his poems a sparsity of vivid imagery and symbolism. His best poems, however, have a stark simplicity which is not without power; most of these, like many passages in the *Centuries*, deal with the unadulterated joy in the world which he experienced in childhood, and which he has refound in his mature vision of the world as the gleaming manifestation of God. 'Christendom', 'The Apostasy' and 'On News' are among his most successful poems. [PM]

Centuries, Poems, and Thanksgivings, ed. H. M. Margoliouth (1958; *Poems, Centuries, and Three Thankgivings*, ed. Anne Ridler (1965).

G. I. Wade, *T.T.* (2nd edn, revised, 1946); Louis L. Martz, *The Paradise Within: Studies in Vaughan, T., and Milton* (Yale U.P., 1964); Malcolm M. Day, 'T. and the Doctrine of Pre-existence', *SP*, 65 (1968).

Treece, Henry (William) (1911–). Poet and novelist. Treece was born in Staffordshire and educated at Wednesbury Grammar School and Birmingham University. On leaving university he became a schoolmaster and in the late thirties he was a founder member, together with J. F. ◊ Hendry, of the ◊ Apocalypse movement. From 1941 to 1946 he served as an Intelligence Officer in Bomber Command and after the war wrote verse dramas, short stories and scripts for the B.B.C. His volumes of poetry include *Towards a Personal Armageddon* (Illinois, 1940), *Invitation and Warning* (1942), *The Black Seasons* (1945), *Collected Poems* (New York, 1946), *The Haunted Garden* (1947) and *The Exiles* (1952). More recently he has written a great number of historical novels, mainly for children, the first of which, *The Dark Island* (1952), was set in Roman-occupied Britain. Later novels include *Don't Expect Any Mercy* (1958), *A Fighting Man* (1960), *Red Queen, White Queen* (1958), *Jason* (1961) and *Oedipus* (1964). He has also written a critical study of *Dylan Thomas* (1949), a volume of short stories *I Cannot Go Hunting Tomorrow* (1946), and has edited an anthology of articles on Herbert Read (1944). [PJK]

Trelawny, Edward John (1792–1881). Raconteur and biographer. Born in London, the son of an army officer, he joined the navy in 1805 but (according to his account) deserted and travelled adventurously in the East and Europe. He became an intimate of the Byron–Shelley circle on Lake Geneva, and was in Leghorn when Shelley was drowned, later (with Byron) witnessing the burning of his body. Thereafter he fought in the Greek War of Independence and travelled in America, finally settling in London, where he became a rather raffish diner-out on his picturesque reminiscences. He was the author of a fictionalized semi-autobiography *The Adventures of a Younger Son* (3 vols., 1831; ed. E. Garnett, 1890; ed. H. N. Brailsford, 1914; ed. E. C. Mayne, World's Classics, 1925), which has a Byronic hero and the very exotic backcloth of the popular romantic fiction of the time. Although unreliable where not corroborated, his mythcreating biographical works are valuable and certainly readable: *Recollections of the Last Days of Shelley and Byron* (1858. ff; ed. E. Dowden. 1906; ed. J. E. Morpurgo, 1952); *The Relations of P. B. Shelley with His Two Wives and a Comment on the Character of Lady Byron* (privately printed, 1920). [AR]

Letters, ed. H. Buxton Forman (1910).
H. J. Massingham, *The Friend of Shelley. A Memoir of E.J.T.* (1930); R. G. Grylls, *T.* (1950).

Trevelyan, G(eorge) M(acaulay) (1876–1962). Historian. He was the son of the historian Sir G. O. Trevelyan (whose Life he wrote), grand-nephew of Lord ◊ Macaulay, and related to a number of other English intellectuals. He was educated at Harrow and Trinity College, Cambridge, where he became a Fellow. In 1927, he was appointed Regius Professor of Modern History at Cambridge, and in 1940 Master of Trinity; he retired in 1951. Trevelyan's first large-scale historical writing was on the Italian *risorgimento*: *Garibaldi's Defence of the Roman Republic* (1907), *Garibaldi and the Thousand* (1909) and *Garibaldi and the Making of Italy* (1911). There is a plain connexion between his view of history and his Liberal principles. With his works on English history he became a well-known writer. His *History of England* (1926) was followed by his most substantial work: *Blenheim* (1930), *Ramillies and the Union with Scotland* (1932) and *The Peace and the Protestant Succession* (1934). In this work on England under Queen Anne he writes with an eye for vivid detail and clear narrative, though it is also well documented. These volumes, together with the even more popular *English Social History* (1942; and an illustrated edition, 4 vols., 1965) are the modern flower of 'Whig' history, in which the important progressive figures are invariably motivated by Liberal ideals, and the present state of affairs is seen as the product of necessary English change. His lively rhetoric is readable and traditional. His Clark Lectures on the English writing of the past which he has enjoyed were published as *A Layman's Love of Letters* (1954). [AR]

Autobiography and Other Essays (1949).
J. H. Plumb, *G.M.T.* (WTW, 1951).

Trevisa. ◊ John of Trevisa.

Trollope, Anthony (1815–82). Novelist and miscellaneous writer. Born in London, he was the son of a bankrupt barrister; his mother, Frances ◊ Trollope, was a prolific writer on whom the family depended. He was poorly educated at Harrow as a despised 'day-boy', and for a brief period at Winchester. In 1834 family influence obtained for him a clerkship in the General Post Office, where he did rather badly; from 1841 to 1859, however, he was mostly employed in Ireland and his career prospered. In 1858, he was sent first to Egypt and then to the West Indies. The latter visit produced a good travel book, *The West Indies and the Spanish Main* (1859). After his retirement from the Post Office in 1867, he travelled widely in Australia, New Zealand and South Africa; his series of 7 volumes of colonial observation are of some interest. During his Civil Service career, he is credited with the invention of the pillar box. He started writing to supplement his income, and his first 3 novels (2 realistic stories of Irish life in the manner of Charles ◊ Lever and a historical novel) were all failures. During a two-year tour of duty as a postal inspector in the West country, a mid-summer evening's stroll in Salisbury Cathedral Close suggested *The Warden* (1855). The first of his novels that enjoyed some success, it was succeeded by other Barsetshire novels. employing the same characters, Archdeacon Grantly, the worldly cleric, and the redoubtable Mrs Proudie, and the saintly warden. These novels are: *Barchester Towers* (1857), *Dr Thorne* (1858), *Framley Parsonage* (1861) and *The Last Chronicle of Barset* (1867) ('Barsetshire Novels', ed. F. Harrison, 8 vols., 1900 ff.; ed. M. Sadleir, 14 vols., 1929). This series is justly regarded as Trollope's masterpiece. He realizes a complete world; the stories are not so important, but the steady if moderate vision of Trollope himself is. The solidity of this world provides an escapist refuge, but the reader's interest is stimulated by Trollope's imaginative grasp of the great subject of 18th- and 19th-century English novels – property. In the Barsetshire novels, Trollope explores the interpenetration of property and established religion, with the pathos and the irony this produces. Tragedy and radical satire are excluded. He admires the ecclesiastical-rural side of the Establishment, not uncritically, yet from the inside. Another, political, series of novels, almost as good, shows property and politics reacting. Plantagenet Palliser and his wife Lady Glencora (the Duke and Duchess of Omnium), the Duke of St Bungay and other members of the political and professional Establishment people the wider world of *Can You Forgive Her?* (1864); *Phineas Finn* (1869); *The Eustace Diamonds* (1873); *Phineas Redux* (1874); *The Prime Minister* (1876); and *The Duke's Children* (1880). Trollope is a shrewd observer of the borderlands and sidelines of his chosen area of social and national life; he deals with the arrangements, the compromises, the just-missed realizations of individual action, in marriage, in belief, in political principle. He lacks the sharpest and most incisive art to realize his insight fully, but his achievement is considerable.

He wrote nearly 50 novels, as well as short stories, so that his point of view, his sensibility, is coarsely diffused. He sometimes writes sloppily, but is also capable here and there of fine turns of wit and some subtlety. His main weakness is a kind of tactical obtuseness in handling his story, obtruding his views of what is 'just a story'. *The Way We Live Now* (1875; a successful B.B.C. television serial in 1969) is his keenest satire. In the character of Augustus Melmotte, he attempts to explore the inroad of the speculative financier in English political and social life; that is the appearance of a new kind of property on the Establishment scene. His moral position is traditional, not very guarded or aware, but serviceable. Trollope unsuccessfully contested Beverley for Parliament in 1868, so that his knowledge of politics, like that of the Church, is an outsider's, an imaginative construction. Like Thackeray, he has an interesting fascination for the border-lines of gentility; the world of the shabby-genteel, of the desperate confidence-trick. He published his *Autobiography* in 1883 (ed. M. Sadleir, World's Classics, 1947; ed. J. B. Priestley, 1962); in it he makes much of his regular industry as a novelist and rather naïvely boasts of the income it brought him (a total of £68,939 17s. 5d.). This is a sidelight on how he sought to justify his life as an artist in middle-class English society. [AR]

The Oxford T., ed. M. Sadleir and F. Page (1948 ff.) (incomplete); *Novels* ('Shakespeare Head Edition'), ed. M. Sadleir (1929 ff.) (incomplete); *Letters*, ed. B. A. Booth (1951).

Henry James, *Partial Portraits* (1888; reprinted in different collections) (essay on T.); M. Sadleir, *T., a Commentary* (1927); A. O. Cockshut, *A.T.: A Critical Study* (1955); M. Praz, *The Hero in Eclipse in Victorian Fiction* (1956); B. A. Booth, *A.T.: Aspects of his Life and Art* (Indiana U.P., 1958); H. Sykes Davies, *T.* (W T W, 1960) (with bibliography); M. Sadleir, *T. A Bibliography* (1928); *Supplement* (1934) and additions in *Nineteenth Century Fiction* (1951).

Trollope, Frances (1780–1863). Novelist and prolific miscellaneous writer. Born Frances Milton, near Bristol, she married Thomas Trollope (1809), the third son of the marriage being Anthony ◊ Trollope. Financial misfortune drove her to take her family to Cincinnati in an unsuccessful bid to settle. Returning to England, she supported them by her pen. Possessed of a beady eye for social observation, an easily outraged English gentility and a caustic pen, she gave great offence (some of it justified) in America by her *Domestic Manners of the Americans* (1832). She wrote other travel books, and many novels (some anti-clerical, some dealing with fashionable life) which are now (though not without wit and power) read more because of the vogue enjoyed by her son's work; the best known are *The Widow Barnaby* (1838) and *The Vicar of Wrexhill* (1837). [AR]

M. Sadleir, *Anthony Trollope* (1945); E. Bigland, *The Indomitable Mrs T.* (1953).

Tudur Aled (fl. 1480–1526). Welsh poet. Born in the parish of Llansannan, Denbighshire, of a gentry family, he was a bardic pupil and nephew of Dafydd ab Edmwnd and was named chief bard and master at the Caerwys Eisteddfod of 1523. He died at Carmarthen in 1526 having taken the habit of a Grey Friar on his death-bed. Tudur Aled represents the finest flowering of the classical Welsh poets of the 14th–16th centuries (*Beirdd yr Uchelwyr*, 'poets of the gentry'). The tradition of eulogy and elegy had proved too strong even for the individuality of a master like ◊ Dafydd ap Gwilym, and the poets developed the *awdl* and especially the *cywydd* as a medium for praise of the nobility who gave them patronage and sustenance, although the other stock themes are also found (love and nature, religion, request poems, vaticination, etc.). The *cywydd* in its earlier period

(1350–1450) was full of parentheses and compound words, but during the middle and greatest period (1450–1550) a simpler form was evolved: ideas were set out in couplets as units, and *cynghanedd* became the vehicle for dignified and compressed expression.

Tudur Aled was distinguished for his ability in the handling of *cynghanedd* and for the smooth run of cogent and quotable couplets. He was well aware of the social changes which were taking place in Tudor Wales, and whereas his predecessors had laid stress on generosity and good Welsh breeding, Tudur saw the qualities of those Welsh gentry who were moving with the times and who were taking an ever greater part in the life and government of Wales, particularly under the new dynasty. He was not, however, blind to their faults, and his greatest poem is undoubtedly the famous 'Wheel of Peace' in which he chides the gentry for quarrelling among themselves because family ties were loosened and the only people to benefit were the English. Tudur Aled excelled in the genre of 'request' poems in which a gift is solicited and the giver is praised. His *cywydd* to Gwenfrewi, patron saint of Holywell, is a beautiful example of poems to saints. [MR]

Gwaith Tudur Aled, ed. T. Gwynn Jones (1926).

Tupper, Martin (Farquhar) (1810–89). Writer of verse and miscellaneous prose. Born in London and educated at Charterhouse and Christ Church, Oxford, he was called to the bar (1835), but made his living by writing many poems and ballads on current affairs (such as *Half a Dozen Ballads for Australian Emigrants*, 1853; *A Dozen Ballads for the Times about White Slavery*, 1854), full of a complacency and jingoism, which earned him popularity with a large section of the English public. His 4 series of *Proverbial Philosophy* (1838–76, various printings), presenting banal thoughts in a fatally loose, versified prose, have embedded him in amber, because he had the facility to write down the unspoken code of millions of prosperous citizens of the last century. These works had an enormous vogue in Britain and America and he is important as a social phenomenon: 'Choose thy friend discreetly, and see thou consider his station, / For the graduated scale of ranks accordeth with the ordinance of heaven.' His works were admired by Queen Victoria. [AR]

Complete Poems (Hartford, 1850); *Complete Prose Works* (Hartford, 1850); *Autobiography* (1886).
A. Lang, *Letters to Dead Authors* (1886) (a contemporary attack); D. Hudson, *M.T.: His Rise and Fall* (1949).

Tutuola, Amos (1920–   ). Nigerian fantast. Born of Christian parents in Abeokuta, Tutuola had only a few years' schooling. He has worked as a coppersmith, a government messenger in Lagos, and is now a storekeeper with Radio Nigeria in Ibadan. His best book was his first, *The Palm-Wine Drinkard* (1952), though there is evidence of renewed vitality in his fifth, *Feather Woman of the Jungle* (1962). His books defy categorization. They combine elements of myth, fairy-tale and tall story in a style that is oral and ungrammatical. Narrative energy puts pressure on the tangled, rhythmic sentences, and Gargantuan fantasy tumbles endearingly into empirical fact, or is illustrated by a startling analogy drawn from the apparatus of modern life. A grotesque exploitation of magic's scorn for probability, a perception of humour in horror, and an intuitive treatment of myth are the staple of his work, which is closer to epic than to the novel. [PT]

My Life in the Bush of Ghosts (1954); *Simbi and the Satyr of the Dark Jungle* (1955); *The Brave African Huntress* (1958); *Ajaiyi and His Inherited Poverty* (1967).
G. Moore, *Seven African Writers* (1962); H. R. Collins, 'The Ghost Novels of A.T.', in *Critique*, IV, 1 (Autumn/Winter, 1960–1); B. Lindfors, '*The Palm-Wine Drinkard* and Old Tradition', *Critique* XI, 1.

Tynan, Kenneth (1927–   ). Dramatic critic. From King Edward's School, Birmingham, he went to Magdalen College, Oxford, and won himself a dazzling reputation as a wit, controversialist, aesthete, theatrical director, dandy and dramatic reviewer. He was briefly director of a repertory company at Lichfield, and in 1950 published *He That Plays the King*, a collection of his undergraduate writings on the theatre. He was in rapid succession theatre critic on the *Spectator*, the *Evening Standard*, and the *Daily Sketch*, and gained journalistic notoriety for his savage wit and passion for the theatre. On the *Observer* from 1954 to 1963 he increasingly showed social, political and artistic commitment, championing new work and the English discovery of Brecht's plays. He also worked, without distinction, as script editor for Ealing Films (1955–7) and was visiting drama critic on the *New Yorker* (1958–60). He has published books on personalities and on bull-fighting, and 2 fine gatherings of theatrical reviews and critical journalism, *Curtains* (1961) and *Tynan Right and Left* (1967).

He became literary manager of the National Theatre in 1963, and since 1964 has written on films, sex and other topics in the *Observer*. An opponent of all censorship, he was influential in the campaign to abolish the Lord Chamberlain's powers in the British theatre, and was the deviser of the nude revue *Oh! Calcutta!* (New York, 1969; London, 1970). [MJ]

Tyndale, William (*c.* 1494–1536). Translator and theologian. Educated at Oxford and Cambridge, he was a Protestant and a humanist, zealous both to make the Bible available in the vernacular to the layman and to work scrupulously from original Greek and Hebrew texts. While chaplain and tutor in a private household in Gloucestershire, he became involved as preacher in disputes with the local clergy, and had to answer a charge of heresy before the Chancellor of his diocese, Worcester. He translated Erasmus's *Enchiridion militis christiani* at this time, and sought in vain the patronage of the Bishop of London for the translation of the New Testament which he had begun. He resumed this work at Hamburg and visited Luther in Wittenberg in 1524. The following year John Cochläus, a heretic-hunter, disclosed that Tyndale and his assistant, Roy, were supervising the printing in Cologne of the New Testament in English, and the collaborators had to flee to Worms whence copies of the translation were smuggled to England in 1526, and denounced by the bishops. Tyndale, too, was denounced, and hounded round Germany and the Netherlands. Sir Thomas ◊ More and he engaged in an acrimonious exchange of pamphlets. He also managed to produce a version of the Pentateuch and of Jonah, as well as revisions of his New Testament. He became a Zwinglian, and in 1528 published 2 treatises, *The Parable of the Wicked Mammon* and *The Obedience of a Christian Man*. In the second he stated two seminal principles of the English Reformation, the authority of Scripture within the Church, and the supremacy of the King within the State. His political theory and his doctrine of 'degree' match those of Shakespeare's history plays, and were approved by Henry VIII. His *Practice of Prelates* (1530) denounced the Roman Church and Henry's divorce proceedings. The King requested that the Emperor return him forcibly to England. Tyndale was forced to leave Antwerp but went back in 1533, all the while working on his biblical translation. He was betrayed to the imperial authorities and (despite the pleas of Thomas Cromwell) he was tried, condemned and strangled and burned as a heretic at Vilvorde. Ironically in 1537 a composite translation of the Bible, containing the work both of Tyndale and of Coverdale was issued with the Church's approval. This was prepared for publication by John Rogers, and it was attributed to Thomas Matthew, probably for diplomatic reasons.

Tyndale's significance in English literature is twofold: he was a powerful scholarly and stylistic influence on English biblical translation (including the Authorized Version, 1611) as well as being a leading force in the English Reformation and in the political thought of his time. (◊ Bible.) [MJ]

C. C. Butterworth, *The Literary Lineage of the King James Bible* (1941); D. Daiches, *The King James Bible: An Account of Its Development and Sources* (1941); C. S. Lewis, *English Literature in the Sixteenth Century* (1954); C. Morris, *Political Thought in England: T. to Hooker* (1953); J. F. Mozley, *W.T.* (1937).

Tytler, Alexander Fraser (Lord Woodhouselee) (1747–1813). Scottish essayist and critic. Educated in Edinburgh and London and called to the Scottish bar in 1770, Tytler became Professor of Universal History at Edinburgh University in 1780 and was made a judge in 1802. He contributed essays to Henry Mackenzie's *Mirror* and *Lounger*, published a sensible *Essay on the Principles of Translation* (1791) and one of the first translations of Schiller's *The Robbers* (1792), gave Burns detailed advice on his poems, and wrote *Memoirs of . . . Henry ◊ Home of Kames* and 'Remarks on the Genius and Writings of Allan Ramsay' (in *The Poems of Allan Ramsay*, ed. G.

Chalmers, 1800, and reprinted in many later editions). There he defends Ramsay's use of Scots and argues that one's immediate response to a work of literature, rather than one's theoretical position, is the true basis of criticism. His son Patrick Fraser Tytler (1791–1849) wrote at Scott's suggestion a *History of Scotland from 1249 to 1603* (1828–43). [AI]

A. Alison, *Memoir of the Life and Writings of A.F.T., Lord Woodhouselee* (1818).

Tytler, Patrick Fraser. ⟡ Tytler, Alexander Fraser.

U

Ua Brolchá(i)n, Máel Ísu (*c*. 1000–1086). Irish poet. A striking aspect of Irish cultural history in the late Middle Ages is the emergence of certain families of poets, historians and lawyers for whom learning was a hereditary profession. Already by the 11th century, for example, several members of the Ua Brolcháin family are mentioned. (The form *Ua* is a variant of *Ó*, 'grandson, descendant'.) One of these is Máel Ísu, described in the annals as the 'doyen and chief sage of Ireland', to whom a number of religious poems are attributed. These include a hymn to the Holy Spirit, which begins: 'May the Holy Spirit be about us, in us and with us; let the Holy Spirit, O Christ, come to us speedily'. Another example is the bilingual hymn beginning *Deus meus, adiuva me | Tuc dam do sheirc, a meic mo Dé* ('My God, help me / Give me love of thee, O son of my God'), in which the internal rhymes are close to those regularly found in the *amhrán* or stressed metres of modern times (compare *Lochlann*, ii, Oslo, 1962, 52). In yet another poem he prays 'Lest we carry any sin with us to the world beyond, lest we find torment awaiting us there, Give us tribulation which cleanses us, Son of the living God, King of mysteries'. He belonged to the North of Ireland, and was connected with a monastery at Inishowen in Co. Donegal, where, according to Colgan (*Acta Sanctorum Hiberniae*, Louvain, 1645, 108), traditions of him still survived in the 17th century. [SB]

G. Murphy, *Early Irish Lyrics* (1956).

Udall or **Uvedale, Nicholas** (1505–56). Dramatist. A native of Hampshire, he was successively a scholar at Winchester and at Corpus Christi College, Oxford, of which he became a fellow in 1524, and was soon after suspected of Lutheran tendencies. He published selections from Terence with English translations in 1533, when he also collaborated on the Coronation Triumph of Anne Boleyn. The following year he was made headmaster of Eton. Famous for his discipline and his flogging, he was dismissed in 1541, but Etonians may have been the original actors of his best-known work, the first English comedy. At Christmas 1553 he probably wrote *Respublica*, an anti-Protestant political morality-play, but he is important as the author of one of two English vernacular plays patterned after Plautus and Terence, which, with their 5-act structure and lively native touches, mark a significant stage in the evolution of English stage-comedy and an advance on the interludes of men like John ◊ Heywood. *Ralph Roister Doister*, the older comedy (*c*. 1552), is concerned with a braggart warrior and his courtship. Like William Stevenson's *Gammer Gurton's Needle* (*c*. 1552–63) it was intended to be acted by undergraduates – or earlier by schoolboys at Eton – and both show how vividly the classical mode of Terence and Plautus was domesticated in terms of English rural life.

Udall was a vicar for some years, before gaining further preferment, and published translations of the *Apophthegms* of Erasmus. He won the patronage first of Edward VI, for whom he wrote a reply to the Devonshire Catholics (1549), and later of Mary, whose play-writer he became. Despite his record at Eton, he ended his life as headmaster of Westminster. [MJ]

M. C. Bradbrook, *The Growth and Structure of Elizabethan Comedy* (1955); W. L. Edgerton, *N.U.* (New York, 1965); A. P. Rossiter, *English Drama from Early Times to the Elizabethans* (1950); F. P. Wilson, *The English Drama, 1485–1585* (1969).

University Wits. The name given to a group of Elizabethan writers who held themselves superior poets and dramatists for having been educated at Oxford or Cambridge. They were John ◊ Lyly, the leader of the Wits; George ◊ Peele, its most dissolute associate; Robert ◊ Greene, who was extra-proud, having travelled in Spain and Italy; Thomas ◊ Lodge, who was to turn against writing altogether and become a doctor; and Thomas ◊ Nashe, who wrote the first English picaresque novel. ◊ Marlowe, a Cambridge contemporary, is sometimes associated with the group. [RB]

Urquhart or **Urchard, Sir Thomas** (of Cromarty) (1611–60). Translator and miscellaneous writer. A Scottish Royalist imprisoned in the Tower after the battle of Worcester (1651), he was the last important translator in the Tudor tradition of John ◊ Florio and Sir Thomas ◊ North. His translation of the first 2 books of Rabelais' *Gargantua and Pantagruel* appeared in 1653, Urquhart's third book being published posthumously in 1693 by P. A. Motteux, who then translated the rest of the work himself (1694). Urquhart's cranky erudition expands and embroiders the original, blurring its satirical point but enhancing its raciness and fantasy (ed. D. B. Wyndham Lewis, Everyman, 1929; ed. C. Whibley, 1900). Urquhart also published eccentric excursions into mathematics, linguistics and genealogy; *Ekskybalauron, or The Discovery of a Most Exquisite Jewel* (1652) includes his famous account of the Renaissance paragon known as 'the admirable Crichton'. [AI]

Works, ed. T. Maitland (1834); *Selections*, ed. J. Purves (1942).

J. Willock, *Sir T.U.* (1899); F. C. Roe, *Sir T.U. and Rabelais* (1957); H. Miller, *Scenes and Legends of the North of Scotland* (1834); H. MacDiarmid, *Scottish Eccentrics* (1936).

Usk, Thomas (d. 1388). Author of *The Testament of Love*. Usk was a Londoner, in minor orders, and a Lollard sympathizer. He became tragically involved in politics and, though he changed sides successfully in 1387 and was made under-sheriff of London, he shared in the fall of his new leader, Nicholas Brembre, after the Duke of Gloucester's rebellion, and was executed in 1388. His only known work, once thought to be Chaucer's, is *The Testament of Love* (ed. W. W. Skeat, *Chaucerian Pieces*, 1894), which may well have been written in prison. It is a prose allegory, drawing very heavily on Chaucer's translation of Boethius. The Dreamer is visited in prison by a beautiful woman, Love, who listens to his self-justification, and teaches him the way to reconciliation. Usk's purpose is clearly to appease the religious and secular authorities, and he apparently hoped to enlist Chaucer's help by much fulsome praise.

As literature, the *Testament* is interesting in intention rather than execution. Usk is the first English writer to attempt a truly literary prose; there are some features which anticipate ◊ Lyly's *Euphues*, and he sometimes catches the alliterative rhythm, but his choice of a model was not happy, for the *Boece* is loose and diffuse. [AG]

C. S. Lewis, *The Allegory of Love* (1936).

V

Vanbrugh, Sir John (1664–1726). Dramatist and architect. Son of a London tradesman of Flemish parentage, he entered the army in 1686 and while imprisoned in the Bastille drafted his first comedy. On his return to London he saw ◊ Cibber's *Love's Last Shift* in 1696 and in six weeks wrote *The Relapse, or Virtue in Danger*, which developed out of the situation at the close of the earlier play, retaining several characters, including the splendid fop, Sir Novelty Fashion, Lord Foppington, whom Cibber again acted. Its success was such that Vanbrugh re-wrote his first play, *The Provok'd Wife*, for performance in 1697, and it had a continued success, Sir John Brute later being a great part of David Garrick's. His plays were censured for immorality by Jeremy Collier in 1698. Subsequent plays and adaptations were less notable. In 1705 he was architect of his own ornate and over extravagant theatre in the Haymarket, a disastrous speculation. He designed Castle Howard in 1701 and Blenheim Palace in 1705, as well as other country seats and public buildings. [MJ]

The Complete Works, ed. B. Dobrée and G. Webb (4 vols., 1927).
G. H. Lovegrove, *The Life, Works, and Influence of Sir J.V.* (1938); L. Whistler, *Sir J.V.* (1938); B. Dobrée, *Restoration Comedy* (1924); T. H. Fujimura, *The Restoration Comedy of Wit* (1952); N. N. Holland, *The First Modern Comedies* (1959).

Van der Post, Laurens (Jan) (1906–   ). South African novelist and traveller. Born in Philippolis, the son of a politician, he was associated with ◊ Campbell and ◊ Plomer in the journal *Voorslag*, for which he wrote in Afrikaans. After *Voorslag*'s virtual suppression in 1927, he went to Japan. His first novel, *In a Province* (1934), is on the theme of ignorant colour prejudice. Colonel van der Post served in the British Army during the Second World War. He was captured by the Japanese in Java in 1944 while commanding a guerrilla unit. Since returning to Britain in 1949 he has undertaken several government missions, including one to Nyasaland in 1949 (see *Venture to the Interior*, 1952) and one to the Kalahari in 1952

(see *The Lost World of the Kalahari*, 1958; and *The Heart of the Hunter*, 1961). *Flamingo Feather* (1955) is the best of his later fiction. *The Face Beside the Fire* (1953) and the 3 linked tales of the Japanese war in *The Seed and the Sower* (1963) are sometimes overloaded by an emphasis on psychological dualities and a presentation of time as mysterious. *Journey into Russia* was published in 1963 and the novel *The Hunter and the Whale* in 1967. [PT]

Vaughan, Henry (?1621/2–95). Poet. Born, with a twin brother, Thomas, at Llansantffread, Breconshire, he very probably went to Jesus College, Oxford, in 1638, but instead of remaining to take a degree, removed to London about 1640 to study law. The Civil War having interrupted his education, he became clerk to Judge Sir Marmaduke Lloyd, Chief Justice of the Brecon circuit, and appears also to have seen service in the Royal armies before South Wales finally came under Parliamentary control in 1646.

For a few years Vaughan's brother held the living of Llansantffread, but was ejected in 1650. Both brothers were interested in alchemy and the Hermetic philosophy. At some unknown date Vaughan began to support himself by practising medicine (he was referred to as M.D. in 1677, although no evidence of his having taken a degree in physic has come to light). He married about 1646; his first wife dying in 1653, he married her sister about 1655. There were four children by each marriage. In his later years Vaughan was involved in litigation with his children by his first marriage. He is buried in the churchyard at Llansantffread.

Vaughan attained no great fame in his own lifetime. His present reputation stems from the 19th century, when attention was at first paid to him as a pious writer rather than a considerable poet. The poems of his first book, dated 1646, are mostly competent conventional love poems in the manner of the followers of Ben Jonson. Publication of a further book was delayed, probably for political reasons; some of the poems from

534

it appeared, however, in *Olor Iscanus* (1651), a book which shows an increased emotional maturity and technical mastery, the consequences of the Royalist defeat and the deepened influence of Jonson's work.

In 1650 appeared the first version of Vaughan's now famous *Silex Scintillans*, a book of religious and mystical verse written in the Metaphysical manner. Many of the poems revolve round emblems of man's spiritual situation, allegorical journeys and dramatized allegorical situations. The poems are most successful when they centre firmly on Vaughan's own intuitions and least successful when they approach general allegory and didacticism; thus 'The Retreate', which is based on Vaughan's acute sense of a lost state of purity associated with childhood, successfully sustains a weight of general implication, whereas 'The World', despite its closely organized form and the superb immediacy of its opening, degenerates from convincing vision to reasoned allegory and loses something in emotional impact. 'The Sap' and 'I walkt the other day' are among the most successful poems in the book.

Silex Scintillans reappeared in 1655 with the addition of a preface and a second collection of poems. The preface claims that the book was the result of a religious awakening brought on by a severe illness and by the reading of Herbert's poetry. Spiritually and poetically the additional poems are a continuation and in some measure a fulfilment of the earlier part of the work. They are characterized by increased vividness, a stronger and more colloquial language, a more intense awareness (as opposed to intellectual knowledge) of the harmony of the external universe, a greater certainty of the grace of God and on occasion a new note of triumphant spiritual exultation. The Metaphysical techniques are handled with greater assurance; there is an ease and naturalness in the word order of many lines which seems to give spontaneous rise to dramatic contrasts and tensions. Such poems as 'The Proffer' illustrate Vaughan's new capacity to produce allegory which is convincingly incarnated on the physical level. 'They are all gone into the world of light' illustrates his increased facility of reference between the inner world of man and the outer macrocosm, while 'The Night', even if compared with such a good poem as 'The Sap' from the earlier part of the volume, shows an increased mastery and clarity in handling a complex symbol, or rather a group of complex symbols.

Neither Vaughan's religious thought nor its origins can be given precise and indisputable definition. His approach to Christianity was influenced by Hermeticism, but possibly also by many other of the mystical types of thought current in his age. He held that the soul is created pure, and associated clear mystical vision with childhood. He also accepted pre-existence, although it is not clear whether he attributes this to the individual soul as such, or to the most essential and divine element in it. Through the sensory experiences of physical life man grows oblivious of his divine origin, but the external world manifests God's harmony to the awakened eye of spiritual insight. It is from such manifestation and from the correspondences and bonds of sympathy between microcosm and macrocosm that Vaughan's most typical imagery arises. His spiritual aim is to regain the purity and vision of eternity associated with childhood and, 'when this dust falls to the urn / In that state I came return'. His poetic achievement is limited in range and somewhat unequal in quality, but his best poems successfully communicate a valuable and highly individual religious experience; on the strength of them he is reasonably ranked among the most important minor poets in English. [PM]

Works, ed. L. C. Martin (2nd revised edn, 1958); *The Complete Poetry*, ed. French Fogle (New York, 1964); *Poetry and Selected Prose*, ed. L. C. Martin (1963); *A Selection*, ed. Christopher Dixon (1967).

F. E. Hutchinson, *H.V. A Life and Interpretation* (1947); L. C. Martin, 'H.V. and the Theme of Infancy', in *Seventeenth Century Studies Presented to Sir Herbert Grierson* (1938); E. Holmes, *H.V. and the Hermetic Philosophy* (1932); R. Garner, *H.V.: Experience and the Tradition* (Chicago, 1959); E. C. Pettet, *Of Paradise and Light: A Study of V.'s Silex Scintillans* (1960) (best introduction); R. A. Durr, *The Mystical Poetry of H.V.* (Cambridge, Mass., 1962); E. L. Marilla, *A Comprehensive Bibliography of H.V.* (Tuscaloosa, Al., 1948).

Vaux, Thomas (2nd Baron Vaux of Harrowden) (1510–56). Poet. Son of a courtier and soldier who had served Henry VII and Henry VIII, he was educated at Cambridge and succeeded to his father's barony in 1523, and was himself a courtier and soldier, accompanying Cardinal Wolsey to France in 1527 and Henry VIII in 1532. At least 2, and possibly 4, of his poems appeared posthumously and anonymously in ◊ Tottel's *Miscellany* (1557) and 13 in a later collection of lyrics, *The Paradise of Dainty Devices* (1576). [MJ]

Ed. A. B. Grosart, *Fuller Worthies' Miscellanies* (vol. 4, 1872); ed. H. E. Rollins, *Tottel's Miscellany, 1557–1587* (revised edn, 1965).

Vere, Edward de (17th Earl of Oxford) (1550–1604). Poet. Educated at Cambridge, de Vere succeeded to his father's earldom in 1562 and for the next twenty years was a prominent figure at Queen Elizabeth's court. His bad temper and violence of manner brought him into disgrace with the court in 1582–3 and his extravagant habits lost him his fortune. His poems (ed. A. B. Grosart, with those of Lord Vaux, Robert Earl of Essex and Walter Earl of Essex, 1872; ed. J. T. Looney, 1921) show some slight talent, but for the most part they are, in C. S. Lewis's words, 'undistinguished and verbose'. They were not published in his lifetime. If he had not been claimed by some as the true author of Shakespeare's plays he would hardly have been remembered now as a writer. The Oxford theory of the authorship of Shakespeare's plays never had massive support and is not now often maintained. [DD]

Poetry of the English Renaissance, ed. J. W. Hebel and H. H. Hudson (New York, 1929) (selection).
J. T. Looney, *'Shakespeare'Identified in E. de V., 17th Earl of Oxford* (1920); Percy Allen, *Shakespeare and Chapman as Topical Dramatists* (1929), *The Case for E. de V., 17th Earl of Oxford as 'W. Shakespeare'* (1930) and *The Oxford–Shakespeare Case Corroborated* (1931); G. H. Rendall, *Shakespeare Sonnets and E. de V.* (1930) and *Shakespeare: Handwriting and Spelling* (1931); M. W. Douglas, *Lord Oxford was 'Shakespeare'* (1934); G. Bowen, *Shakespeare's Farewell* (1951); D. and C. Ogburn, *This Star of England: Shakespeare, Man of the Renaissance* (New York, 1952); W. Kittle, *E. de V.* (Washington, 1935); B. M. Ward, *The Seventeenth Earl of Oxford* (1928) (claims him as author of the songs in Lyly's plays).

Villiers, George (2nd Duke of Buckingham) (1628–87). Poet. Son of the court favourite of Charles I, he was brought up with the royal children and educated at Trinity College, Cambridge. Both before and after the Restoration he was continually involved in political and court intrigues. Inconsistent both in politics and religion, he was the Zimri of Dryden's *Absalom and Achitophel* (1681), and often figured in Augustan satirical verse. A dilettante scientist and a gardener, he also wrote satires, verse and works for the theatre including an adaptation of Fletcher's *The Chances*. His best play was the burlesque of heroic tragedy, *The Rehearsal* (ed. M. Summers, 1914), acted in 1671 but drafted in 1663 and revised as a particular attack upon Dryden. It was frequently staged in the 18th century by Cibber and Garrick and it provided the framework for Sheridan's *The Critic* (1779) and later satires about plays-in-rehearsal. [MJ]

Works, ed. T. Brown (2 vols., 1704).
D. F. Smith, *Plays about the Theatre in England* (1936).

W

Wace, Robert (*c.* 1100–84?). Poet. A pure Norman from Jersey, Wace was educated at Caen, where he spent most of his life as a *clerc lisant*. His early works were religious, but in 1155 he completed his most important poem, from an English point of view, the *Roman de Brut* (ed. I. Arnold, Paris, 1938–40). This is a free paraphrase, in rhyming couplets, of ◊ Geoffrey of Monmouth's *Historia*, and was for long the most influential literary form of the Arthurian material. ◊ Laȝamon, who tells us of its dedication to Queen Eleanor, and Robert ◊ Mannyng translated it into English, and it was the basis of many of the French cycles. Wace adds material from other sources, and though the poem is relaxed entertainment he preserves a pleasant scepticism, and some historical conscience. The *Roman de Brut* shows his gift for description and incident; the verse, though a little monotonous, is at once well-bred and colloquial.

Wace's finest work, *Le Roman de Rou*, a chronicle of the dukes of Normandy, has no place in English literature, despite its great historical interest. It was commissioned by Henry II, but the King's patience gave out before Wace could complete it. [A G]

R. Bezzola, *Origines et la formation de la littérature courtoise*, iii (Paris, 1963).

Wain, John (Barrington) (1925–). Novelist and poet. Born at Stoke-on-Trent, Staffordshire, Wain was educated at Newcastle High School and Oxford University. From 1946 to 1949 he was a Fellow of St John's College, Oxford, and from 1949 to 1955 a lecturer in English literature at Reading University. A dry, witty, at times rather self-consciously clever poet, he contributed to Robert Conquest's influential anthology, *New Lines* (1956), and has published 4 volumes of verse: *Mixed Feelings* (1951), *A Word Carved on a Sill* (1956), *Weep before God* (1961) and *Wildtrack* (1965). His first novel, *Hurry on Down* (1953), was an amusing and original work. In the traditional manner of picaresque fiction, it traced the adventures of a university graduate struggling to establish some kind of personal identity in the rapidly changing society of post-war Britain. It showed Wain to be a satirist of considerable verve and authority and remains his best novel. His later fiction includes *Living in the Present* (1955), *The Contenders* (1958), *A Travelling Woman* (1959), *Strike the Father Dead* (1962) and *The Young Visitors* (1965). *Nuncle* (1960) and *Death of the Hind Legs* (1966) are collections of short stories. He has also written literary criticism, *Preliminary Essays* (1957), *Essays on Literature and Ideas* (1963) and *The Living World of Shakespeare* (1964); a volume of autobiography, *Sprightly Running* (1962); and has edited a collection of critical essays, *Interpretations* (1955). [P J K]

John Lehmann, 'The Wain-Larkin Myth', *Sewanee Review*, LXVI (Winter, 1958); James Gindin, *Postwar British Fiction* (U. of California P., 1962).

Wakefield Cycle. ◊ Miracle Plays.

Walcott, Derek (1930–). West Indian poet and playwright. Born in Castries, St Lucia. As a schoolmaster he published *Twenty Five Poems* (1948) and was a regular contributor to Caribbean magazines. Though often derivative – 'Epitaph for the Young' exhibits the influence of Dylan Thomas – this early volume of a 19-year-old small islander is remarkably accomplished. After graduating from the University College of the West Indies in Jamaica, Walcott wrote a series of verse dramas, *Henri Christophe, The Sea at Dauphin, Ione, Ti Jean and His Brothers* and *Malcauchon*. The award of a Rockefeller Foundation Fellowship in 1957 enabled him to study the theatre in New York, and in 1958 he was commissioned to write *Drums and Colours*, a pageant for the opening of the first Federal Parliament. *The Sea at Dauphin* and *Six in the Rain* have been produced at the Royal Court Theatre in London.

West Indian magazines and the B.B.C.'s 'Caribbean Voices' remained the chief vehicles for his poetry until 1962, when *In a Green Night: Poems 1948–60* was published in England. The poems' peculiar dualism is the product of a sophisticated mind familiar with the fruits of civilization, which nevertheless retains the consciousness of an islander. The tension between Caribbean and English attachments is embodied in the infusion of West Indian dialect and rhythms into his beautiful English verse. Another collection, *The Castaway*, appeared in 1966.

Walcott's decision to remain in the Caribbean as a journalist with the *Trinidad Guardian* keeps him in contact with his natural sources of rhythm and image. [WAG]

Waley, Arthur (David) (1889–1966). Historian and translator of Chinese and Japanese literature. Born at Tunbridge Wells as A. D. Schloss, and educated at Rugby and King's College, Cambridge (of which he was an honorary Fellow). From 1912 to 1930 he was Assistant Keeper in the British Museum Department of Prints and Drawings, and he also lectured at the University of London School of Oriental Studies. He published many beautiful translations from the Chinese and Japanese. These include influential renderings of Chinese poetry in various volumes published between 1918 and 1946; *The Nō Plays of Japan* (1921); a translation of the great medieval Japanese novel by Lady Murasaki, *The Tale of Genji* (6 vols., 1925–32); Confucius's *Analects* (1938); and *Ballads and Stories from Tun Huang* (1960). His more general works include *Three Ways of Thought in Ancient China* (1939); *The Life and Times of Po Chü-i* (1949), a brilliant biography of an ancient Chinese poet and official: *The Opium War through Chinese Eyes* (1958); and *The Secret History of the Mongols* (1963). [AR]

Wallace, Edgar (1875–1932). Writer. He was born at Greenwich, the illegitimate son of an actress, and brought up by fosterparents. He left school at 12 and had a succession of jobs until he joined the army at 18. He was sent to South Africa, where he contributed poems to local journals; on his discharge in 1899 he became a correspondent with Reuters and later with the *Daily Mail*. His first best-selling novel, *The Four Just Men* (1905), was sold outright for a small sum. Later works, starting with his West African stories, such as *Sanders of the River* (1911) and *Bones* (1915), were more substantially successful. Thereafter his output was phenomenally prolific – 170 books in twenty-eight years. He is most widely known as the writer of thrilling detective stories, such as *Crimson Circle* (1922) and *Green Archer* (1923), based on a simple formula which his ingenuity was able to vary with success each time. But he also wrote plays for the West End theatre – one such was written over a weekend – and a daily flow of magazine and newspaper articles. He became immensely rich and spent lavishly. On his death (in Hollywood, where he had gone to write screenplays) he left a mountain of debts. Within two years royalties had paid them all off. [JM]

Margaret Lane, *E.W. The Biography of a Phenomenon* (1938).

Waller, Edmund (1606–87). Poet. The son of a wealthy country gentleman, after Eton and a brief sojourn at Cambridge he became a Member of Parliament at 16, and sat in most of the parliaments elected between that time and his death. A runaway match with an heiress who was a ward of court brought him fame and a great deal of wealth (1631). Two years after his wife's death in 1634 he began to court Lady Dorothy Sidney (his 'Sacharissa'), but to no effect. A brilliant parliamentary orator, Waller stood for constitutional Royalism, and in the first year of the Civil War remained in London and spoke for the King. But in 1643 he became involved in a plot for seizing some of the defences of the City of London and holding them until the King's army came; and when the plot was betrayed, Waller confessed everything. The rhetoric of his speech of confession and apology probably saved his life (two of his accomplices were hanged), and he escaped with a heavy fine and banishment. On his way to exile he remarried, and he spent seven years in France without apparently suffering undue hardship. In 1652 he returned and became an admirer and friend of Cromwell's. His poem 'Upon the Late Storm and the Death of His Highness [i.e. Cromwell] Ensuing' is one of his most impressive performances. After the Restoration he was re-elected to Parliament, where he continued to sit, an elder statesman in manner though not in influence, until near the end of his life. He spoke repeatedly for religious toleration. Outside Parliament he continued to move in elegant and learned circles (he joined the Royal Society in 1661). He died peacefully, surrounded by his children, and was buried at Beaconsfield.

Waller's output consists to a large extent of occasional verse, much of it of a complimentary nature. He differed from his immediate predecessors (Donne and Jonson for example) in many ways. More polite, less didactic, devoid of all emotional complexity, he was also less given than they to logical (or pseudo-logical) argument. His thoughts cohere by association of ideas, not by reasoning; his hyperboles are mere embellishments, not parts of the structure of his poems. As a result, his complimentary pieces are unambiguously complimentary, and they are about their subjects, not about Waller. He achieved, moreover, a new poetic diction, arrived at by the exclusion of all expressions too closely associated with the more down-to-earth aspects of ordinary life, and by a preference for the abstract or most general way of putting things. Yet words with emotional connotations play an important part in this language. Periphrases are often employed to avoid an inelegant bluntness of statement. In metre, Waller's reforms are even more striking. The limits of sentence, clause or phrase coincide, in the first place, with those of the couplet; almost as often with those of the line; and very often indeed with those of the half-line; and further, there are often symmetries of meaning between two lines of a couplet, or the two halves of a line. These are the most easily defined of his metrical reforms. The result is poetry which moves very evenly, but in which subtle variations of pace remain possible. Waller was thus understandably regarded by poets after 1660 as the great improver of English verse. (◊ Denham shared this honour with him. Waller's versification, in turn, was said to have been suggested by that of ◊ Fairfax's translation of Tasso.) His stock was very high throughout the later 17th century. The first edition of his *Poems* appeared as early as 1645 (3 editions in that year alone, and 5 more before the end of the century). His less interesting *Divine Poems* appeared in 1685, while *The Second Part of Mr Waller's Poems*, complete with an essay by Atterbury, appeared in 1690 and ran into a further 4 editions by 1722. A number of Waller's poems had meanwhile been published separately or in collections of songs. His *Instructions to a Painter* (1666) was to give rise to numerous imitations and parodies.

In the 18th century Waller's fame declined very slowly (Fenton's 1729 edition of his *Works*, including letters, speeches and copious editorial matter of great interest, was reprinted in 1730 and 1758; Stockdale's edition appeared in 1772), but he was increasingly seen as a pioneer to be honoured, rather than as a great poet in his own right. By the very standards that he had created he fell below Dryden and Pope. From the respectful neglect into which he had declined by the early 19th century he has never really recovered. Gilfillan edited him in 1857, and Thorn-Drury's Muses Library edition of 1893 (2nd edn, 1905) provides a good biographical introduction and a text which may well be a critical one, but which is offered without adequate apparatus. No modern critical text has as yet been published. [T G]

Johnson, *Life of W.* (1779); R. Wallerstein, in *PMLA* (1935) (study of W.'s metrics); B. Chew, in *The Bibliographer* (New York, 1902); A. W. Allison, *Toward an Augustan Poetic* (Kentucky, 1965).

Walpole, Horace or **Horatio** (4th Earl of Orford) (1717–97). Dilettante, connoisseur and letter-writer. Born in London, the youngest son of Sir Robert Walpole, and educated at Eton and King's College, Cambridge, he made the grand tour (1739–41) with his school and college friend the poet ◊ Gray. This tour of France and Italy was of the greatest importance in developing Walpole's sympathy with the 'picturesque', and in making him one of the most important 'taste-makers' of the mid 18th century. As a member of an important political family, he was an M.P. (1741–67) and had considerable backstairs influence. In 1747, he bought the villa at Twickenham, which he renamed Strawberry Hill. Remodelled, extended and embellished in the 'gothick' taste over two decades, this was the most famous of Walpole's achievements in his own day: it was full of his collections and became a popular tourist attraction, so that he was forced to issue tickets. In England Gothic building had never been completely forgotten, and antiquaries used the 'style' as an exotic element in domestic building, but Walpole made it modish. He also set up a press at Strawberry Hill, at which he printed first (1757) Gray's 2 'pindarick odes' ('The Progress of Poesy' and 'The Bard') and works by others as well as himself. The latter included his *Fugitive Pieces in Verse and Prose* (1758), and a tragedy (never staged), *The Mysteri-*

ous Mother (1768), which incorporates an incest story in medieval trappings. Walpole also published several of his non-fiction works there, including the *Catalogue of Royal and Noble Authors of England* (2 vols., 1758; several other 'enlarged' editions), a gossipy blend of antiquarianism and snobbery; *Historic Doubts on the Life and Reign of Richard III* (1768), an imaginative but slight piece of literary defence; and works based on the notebooks (which he had purchased) of the famous antiquary and engraver George Vertue, *Anecdotes of Painting in England* (2 vols., 1762; 3rd vol., 1763; 4th vol., 1771), *A Catalogue of Engravers who Have Been Born or Lived in England* (1763), several other editions of the *Anecdotes* (a fifth volume, *Anecdotes: 1760–95*, was edited by F. W. Hilles and P. B. Daghlian, Yale, N.J., 1937). These volumes are valuable in themselves, and of great importance in the history of taste. (There is an informative 'History of the Modern Taste in Gardening' annexed to volume 4, ed. I. W. U. Chase, Princeton, N.J. 1943).

The best known of Walpole's books is his 'gothick' novel, *The Castle of Otranto* ('A Story Translated by William Marshall, Gent. From the Original Italian of Onuphrio Muratto'), at first published anonymously, not at Strawberry Hill (1764), and many times reprinted (ed. Walter Scott, 1811; ed. M. Summers, 1924; ed. O. Doughty, 1929; Everyman, with *Rasselas* and *Vathek*, 1930). It is the prototype gothic novel and contains most of the obligatory themes – the supernatural, an Italian setting, crimes of passion and a wronged heir restored. The story is rather clumsy, but was extremely influential. Walpole was greatly interested in contemporary English history, which he saw in terms of politics and personalities (enemies and friends of his father's); his notes were published posthumously as *Memoirs of the Reign of King George the Third* (and the last ten of George II) (ed. G. F. R. Baker, 4 vols., 1894) and *Journal of the Reign of George the Third: 1771–83* (ed. A. F. Steuart, 2 vols., 1910). Perhaps his greatest monument, however, is the vast collection of his letters (3,000 of them), which in the mingling of his wide interests, the penetration, wit and inside knowledge they show, as well as his deftness of touch, gives one of the best pictures of life in 18th-century upper-class society, as well as a history of

contemporary taste. There is some reason to think that Walpole partly designed his correspondence as an *œuvre*, specializing in different topics with different correspondents (e.g. politics in the letters to Horace Mann, consul in Florence; and antiquarian talk to William Cole). In writing letters he constantly set himself against Mme de Sévigné, and with Gray and Cowper makes this period a great age of the flowering of letter-writing as an art-form. [A R]

Letters, ed. P. Cunningham (9 vols., 1857 and several reprints); ed. Mrs P. Toynbee (16 vols., 1903–5; and 3 supplementary vols., ed. P. Toynbee, 1918–25); *W.'s Correspondence* ('Yale Edition'), ed. W. S. Lewis et al. (1937 ff.) (24 vols. have appeared of about 50 projected); *Selected Letters*, ed. W. Hadley (Everyman, 1926); *A Selection of Letters*, ed. W. S. Lewis (2 vols. with illustrations, New York, 1926). R. W. Ketton-Cremer, *H.W., a Biography* (1940); W. S. Lewis, *H.W.* (1961); W. H. Smith, ed. *H.W., Writer, Politician and Connoisseur* (Yale U.P., 1968); A. T. Hazen, *A Bibliography of the Strawberry Hill Press* and *A Bibliography of W.* (Yale, 1942 and 1948).

Walpole, Sir Hugh (Seymour) (1884–1941). Novelist and critic. Born in Auckland, New Zealand; his father was an Anglican clergyman there, but returned to Britain, becoming principal of Bede College, Durham, and later Bishop of Edinburgh. The son was educated at King's School, Canterbury, and Emmanuel College, Cambridge. He taught briefly in a boys' preparatory school, a hateful experience which is the subject of his best book, the short but powerfully realistic story, *Mr Perrin and Mr Traill* (1911). He struggled for some years in London, trying to make a living as a writer and book reviewer; after three or four slow-starters, *Fortitude* (1913) and *The Duchess of Wrexe* (1914) brought him recognition and an income. During the First World War he worked with the Red Cross in Russia (1914–16) and was awarded the Order of St George for heroism. *The Dark Forest* (1916) is set in Russia, and *The Secret City* (1919; James Tait Black Memorial Prize) deals with the 1917 revolution. Walpole was a bachelor; he lived in London and had a country house in Keswick. He became a wealthy book-collector, particularly of Walter Scott material. He was a voluminous writer who produced several kinds of fiction. His strong suit was a close knowledge of upper-middle-class English life, and a feeling for this kind of society, though he had no particular analytical power. His early novels were intermittently realistic, but he gradually developed a very popular vein of fantastic, romantic, even mystical, imagination, chiefly in his most ambitious piece of work, a family 'saga' covering a hundred years: *The Herries Chronicle* (*Rogue Herries,* 1930; *Judith Paris,* 1931; *The Fortress,* 1932; and *Vanessa,* 1933). The taste for this kind of fiction has declined among serious readers of novels, and with it Walpole's reputation. He also wrote a series of works set in and around the Cornish town of Polchester (he was fond of large-scale projects of linked volumes), beginning with *The Cathedral* (1922; successfully dramatized 1932) and including *The Old Ladies* (1924) and *Harmer John* (1926). Another trilogy was based on his boyhood: *Jeremy* (1919), *Jeremy and Hamlet* (1923) and *Jeremy at Crale* (1927). Walpole was an uneven writer, probably because of the amount he wrote. He was an influential critic (through reviews, introductions to books, lectures and essays). His influence, in the English Book Society, was particularly important in the choice of what American writing was printed and valued in England; for example he was responsible for the early British success of Sinclair Lewis. Among his miscellaneous works are *Joseph Conrad* (1916), *Tendencies of the Modern Novel* (with others) (1934) and editions of Walter Scott's *Letters* and *Journals.* [A R]

F. Swinnerton, *The Georgian Literary Scene* (1935); R. Hart-Davis, *H.W.: A Biography* (1952) (with bibliography).

Walsh, William (1663–1708). Poet and critic. A man of family from Worcestershire, an M.P. and Gentleman of the Horse to Queen Anne. His poems, which consist of love songs, elegies and pastorals, were greatly overrated by his contemporaries. He had a coffee-house reputation as a critic, and was praised by Dryden (who freely commended his friends), but his greatest importance is probably as a very early friend and mentor of Pope, who honoured him in the *Essay on Criticism,* which Walsh probably encouraged. [A R]

Johnson, *Lives of the Poets*; *D N B.*

Walton, Izaak (1593–1683). Author. Born in Stafford, the son of an alehouse-keeper,

he was apprenticed to a sempster in London, and became a prosperous draper. He had many literary friends, and though writing did not come easily to him, perhaps because of his irregular education, his few prose works were highly prized. Sir Henry ◊ Wotton asked him to gather material for his own proposed life of John Donne, but died in 1639. Walton's life of Donne, hastily written, appeared in 1640, and was expanded in 1658. He published separate lives of three other churchmen, George Herbert, Richard Hooker and Robert Sanderson, and a memoir of Wotton. His collected *Lives* appeared in 1670. His ecclesiastical biographies are edifying, instructive, even hagiographic. Digressive in style, full of invented conversations, the *Lives* were frequently revised in the interests of greater accuracy. In 1653 appeared his greatest work, *The Compleat Angler,* a treatise on angling with dialogue which celebrates the countryside and the joys of fishing. It is *the* classic of piscatory literature. [M J]

The Complete Works, ed. G. L. Keynes (1929). M. Bottrall, *I.W.* (1955); D. Novarr, *The Making of W.'s Lives* (1958); S. Martin, *I.W. and His Friends* (2nd edn, 1904).

Warburton, William (1698–1779). Theologian, polemical writer and critic. He was educated (and practised briefly) as an attorney, but after private study took orders (1728) and eventually became Dean of Bristol (1757) and Bishop of Gloucester (1759). He first appeared as an ecclesiastical writer in *The Alliance between Church and State* (1736) but was best known in his own day for his powerful, paradoxical but overlong work *The Divine Legation of Moses* (1737–41). This shows Warburton's extensive learning and considerable intellect. The ensuing controversy with more orthodox divines gave him scope for his swashbuckling and arrogant ill-manners which, perhaps with his lack of university training, earned him a bad contemporary reputation, and consequently a worse modern press. He is chiefly remembered now, however, because of his friendship with Pope, in which he rather overawed the old poet, who made him his literary executor. Warburton's would-be definitive edition of Pope's *Works* (1751), by clumsy editing and insensitive 'improvements' in arrangement, did something to blight Pope's reputation. In 1747 Warburton published a peremptory edition of Shakespeare, which was severely criticized. [AR]

A. W. Evans, *W. and the Warburtonians* (1932).

Ward, Warde or **Wade, Arthur Sarsfield.** ◊ Rohmer, Sax.

Ward, E. R. ◊ Mac an Bhaird, E. R.

Ward, Mrs Humphry (*née* Mary Augusta Arnold) (1851–1920). Novelist and philanthropist. Circumstance and family connexions exposed her to some of the central intellectual controversies of the age. Thomas ◊ Arnold of Rugby was her grandfather, and Matthew ◊ Arnold her uncle. Her father had emigrated to Tasmania, where she was born, but in 1856, soon after becoming a Roman Catholic, he returned to England with his family, and for several years worked under ◊ Newman. Part of her childhood was spent in Westmorland (the setting of some well-drawn scenes in her novels), in the family home built by Thomas Arnold and still inhabited by her grandmother. From 1867 she lived in Oxford, and in 1872 married Thomas Humphry Ward, Fellow and tutor of Brasenose College. In 1881 the Wards moved to London, and Mrs Ward began her career as author, in the course of which she was to produce 28 novels. Although she was stimulated by the views and personalities of Newman, Pusey and other figures who had been associated with the Oxford Movement, her sympathies lay with the liberal and reforming forces in Oxford, and in particular with the social philosophy of T. H. ◊ Green, to whom she dedicated *Robert Elsmere* (1888), her second novel and a great popular success. This is a story about a young clergyman who loses his faith in the miraculous part of Christ's story, resigns his living, and establishes a quasi-religious foundation devoted to benevolent work in the East End of London. Here and in her other novels Mrs Ward was a popularizer of religious disputes about the historical and the essential meaning of Christianity, as of the social and political issues of the day. She has been rightly criticized for being snobbish and conventional; her standards are those of the cultivated rich. Nonetheless, her own philanthropic activities are worthy of respect, and she is besides a writer of considerable talent – as appears in her observation of nature and of society and in the psychology of her characters. The artist prevails over the didactic writer in *Bessie Costrell* (1895), a tale of greed and deception from which emerges a sense of the blindness of men to one another; the characters – agricultural labourers and their families – are presented with genuine tact. In *The Coryston Family* (1913), despite an anti-feminist thesis, she actually suggests that tyranny may be inherent in power and property. The later novels have little to offer. *A Writer's Recollections* (1918) contains interesting accounts of her family, acquaintances and friends (including Henry James). The introductions she wrote to the Haworth edition of *The Works of Charlotte Brontë and Her Sisters* (7 vols., 1899–1900) are the product of a perceptive and discriminating mind, well read in English and continental literature. After the death of her sister in 1908, she devoted much care to her nephews Julian ◊ Huxley and Aldous ◊ Huxley. [NL]

The History of David Grieve (1892); *Marcella* (1894); *Helbeck of Bannisdale* (1898); *Eleanor* (1900); *The Case of Richard Meynell* (1911). Stephen Gwynn, *Mrs H.W.* (1917); Janet Trevelyan, *The Life of Mrs H.W.* (1923).

Wardlaw, Lady Elizabeth (1677–1727). Balladist. The wife of a Fife landowner, she wrote the imitation ballad *Hardyknute*, printed without comment in 1719, embroidered by Allan Ramsay in *The Ever Green* (1724) and recognized for what it is by the time of Thomas ◊ Percy's *Reliques* (1765). *Hardyknute* helped to stimulate interest in the genuinely old Scottish ballads, but induced Robert ◊ Chambers to detect imagined revisions by Lady Wardlaw in almost all the known ballads. [AI]

DNB.

Warner, Rex (1905–   ). Novelist, poet, translator and critic. Born in Birmingham, and educated at St George's, Harpenden, and Wadham College, Oxford. For a period in the 1940s he was Director of the British Institute in Athens. His first published volume, *Poems*, appeared in 1937. His translations from the Greek successfully combine scholarship and elegance. The most important of them are Aeschylus's *Prometheus Bound* (1947), Xenophon's *Anabasis* (1949), and Euripides's *Hippolytus* (1949) and *Helen* (1951). It is, however, as a novelist that Warner is most likely to be remembered. *The Wild Goose Chase* (1937), *The Professor* (1938) and *The Aerodrome* (1941) are the novels he produced before turning his attention to classical studies. In technique and, to a certain extent, in the nature of the world he invents and describes, Warner can be classified as a follower of Kafka. But in the lack of ambiguity of his moral attitudes, he reveals that the influence of Kafka on his work is less important than that of Bunyan or Dickens. Warner's novels are those of a social moralist, warning against the evils of a capitalist society. His nightmarish allegories serve a quite definite, almost explicit extra-literary purpose.

Warner returned to fiction after his years of immersion in the classical world by writing 2 historical novels with a difference. In *The Young Caesar* (1958) and *Imperial Caesar* (1960) he cast his biographies of Julius Caesar into the form of fictionalized first-person autobiography. The result is a remarkable feat of sustained literary imagination and historical insight. He has continued along the same lines in *Pericles the Athenian* (1963) and *The Converts* (1967). Both as novelist and as translator, one of Warner's strongest attributes is his prose style, which possesses the classical virtues of clarity, mellifluousness and simplicity. [CO]

Warner, Sylvia Townsend (1893–). Novelist, short-story writer and poetess. Born in Middlesex, the daughter of a schoolmaster, Miss Warner was educated privately. A woman of wide-ranging intellectual and social interests, she was one of the editors of a 10-volume collection of Tudor Church music and is a well-known authority on all matters relating to the supernatural. In the thirties she took an active part in left-wing politics and for a while served in Spain during the Civil War. She began her writing career as a poet with *The Espalier* (1925) and this was followed by *Time Importuned* (1928) and *Opus 7* (1931), but later concentrated almost exclusively on fiction. Her novels and short stories, written in a simple graceful manner, explore a world of fantasy and semi-reality with great subtlety and skill. They include *Lolly Willowes* (1926), *Mr Fortune's Maggot* (1927), *Summer Will Show* (1936), *The Corner That Held Them* (1948) and *The Flint Anchor* (1954), novels; *The Salutation* (1932), *A Garland of Straw* (1943), *The Museum of Cheats* (1947), *The Cat's Cradle Book* (1960), *A Spirit Rises* (1962) and *A Stranger with a Bag* (1966), short stories. *Sketches from Nature* (1963) are childhood reminiscences, and she has also written a fine biography of T. H. White (1967). [PJK]

Warner, William (*c*. 1558–1609). Poet. A London attorney educated at Oxford, he published *Pan His Syrinx or Pipe*, 7 prose romances, in 1584 (ed. W. A. Bacon, Urbana, Ill., 1950); and a translation of the *Menaechmi* of Plautus in 1595. His principal work was a metrical history of Britain, *Albion's England*. Originally published in 4 books in 1586, extending from Noah to the Norman Conquest, it was successively enlarged until the sixth edition (1606) reached King James VI & I. To avoid the rambling quality of most such mythological-historical epics Warner devised a novel structure of separate, linked stories after the style of Ovid's *Metamorphoses*. Francis Meres, with characteristic lack of discrimination, ranked this work with Spenser's. [MJ]

C. S. Lewis, *English Literature in the Sixteenth Century* (1954).

Warton, Joseph (1722–1800). Critic and poet. The son of the Reverend Thomas Warton, the elder, who had been Professor of Poetry at Oxford. Joseph Warton was headmaster of Winchester (1766–93) and a prebendary of Winchester and St Paul's cathedrals. He published 2 volumes of somewhat placid *Odes* (1744 and 1746), in which like his friend ◊ Collins he cultivated 'imagination', and further developed the contemporary (sometimes primitivistic) interest in the country, rather than Pope's urban and social vision. This interest he partly derived, of course, from classical models (he published translations of Virgil's *Eclogues* and *Georgics*), though it is sometimes interpreted solely as 'pre-Romantic' pioneering. Warton was also an important critic, with a similar bias; his *Essay on the Writings and Genius of Pope* (i, 1756; ii, 1782) was treated against his own will as a hostile critique, and his last writing was an edition of Pope's works (1796). Like his brother, Thomas ◊ Warton, he was a member of Johnson's Literary Club. [AR]

The Three W.s: A Choice of Their Verse, ed. E. Partridge (1927).
H. Trowbridge, 'J. W. on the Imagination', *MP*, xxxv (1937); A. Ross, 'The Wartons Revisited', *Summary*, I (1970).

Warton, Thomas, the younger (1728–90). Critic, historian and poet. The son of the Reverend Thomas Warton, the elder, who had been Professor of Poetry at Oxford (1718–28). The son was Professor of Poetry there in his turn (1757–67), and later Camden Professor of History; he became Poet Laureate in 1785. Thomas Warton's rather timid poems were much in the same vein as those of his brother Joseph ◊ Warton, as can be seen in his first book *The Pleasures of Melancholy* (1747); but he also wrote some sprightly lyric verse, such as his *Panegyric on Oxford Ale*. His *Poems* (in which he includes his revivals of the sonnet form) were published in 1777. Warton is, however, best known as a critic with a vast store of historical knowledge. His *Observations on Spenser's Faery Queen* (1754) was one of the first critiques of an English poem written with the kind of solid learning hitherto thought worthy only of classical studies. His very learned *History of English Poetry* (1774; additions and revisions to 1781), which ends at the death of Queen Elizabeth, is significant in the development of modern appreciation of medieval literature, and contains memorable and influential discussions of myths and romances. [AR]

The Three W.s: A Choice of Their Verse, ed. E. Partridge (1927).
C. Rinaker, *T.W.: A Bibliographical and Critical Study* (U. of Illinois P., 1916); R. Wellek, *The Rise of English Literary History* (U. of North Carolina P., 1941).

Waterhouse, Keith (1929–   ). Novelist and dramatist. Born in Hunslet, Leeds, Waterhouse was educated at Osmond-thorpe Council School, which he left at 15 to work at various temporary jobs before becoming a journalist, at first in Yorkshire and then in London. His first novel was *There is a Happy Land* (1957). This was followed by *Billy Liar* (1959), which, adapted in collaboration with Willis Hall, was later successfully produced as both a play and a film, and *Jubb* (1963). A writer with a keen ear for dialogue (especially in the working-class scenes of his first 2 novels) and a fast-flowing, humorous style, his work as a whole is severely limited by the sociological self-consciousness that typifies many English novels of the fifties. Together with Willis Hall he has also written several plays and revues, including *Celebration* (1961), *England, Our England* (1962), *All Things Bright and Beautiful* (1962), *They Called the Bastard Stephen* (1964) and *Say Who You Are* (1965), and has written film scripts for *Whistle Down the Wind, A Kind of Loving, Man in the Middle* and *Torn Curtain*. [PJK]

Watson, John (1850–1907). Scottish ◊ 'Kailyard' novelist. He wrote under the pseudonym of 'Ian Maclaren'. Brought up at Perth and Stirling and educated at Edinburgh University (1866–70), Watson was successively a Free Church of Scotland minister in Perthshire and Glasgow and minister (from 1880) of Sefton Park Presbyterian Church, Liverpool. Anecdotes of his Perthshire experience, first published in the religious paper the *British Weekly* and collected in *Beside the Bonnie Brier Bush* (1894), shrewdly exploited the current vogue for pawky sentimental sketches of Scottish village and church life, and within a few years sold a quarter of a million copies in Great Britain and twice as many in the United States. Unlike his counterpart S. R. ◊ Crockett, Watson remained in the ministry. He helped to found Liverpool University and was made principal of a dissenters' theological college in Cambridge. Before moving there, however, he died while touring the United States for the third time with a combined programme of sermons and religious addresses and readings from his Scots dialect works. [AI]

W. R. Nicoll, *Life of the Reverend J.W.* (1908).

Watson, Thomas (*c.* 1557–92). Poet. Possibly educated at Oxford, he studied law in London and was a friend of Marlowe and of Sir Francis Walsingham. His scholarly interests are reflected in the Latin poems and Latin versions of Petrarch which he circulated in manuscript, in his translation of the *Antigone* of Sophocles into Latin (1581), and in the knowledge of French and Italian originals which his own poetry in English reveals. His *Hecatompathia, or Passionate Century of Love* (1582) consists of 18-line English poems (which he called 'sonnets'); *Meliboeus* (1590) is an elegy for Walsingham translated from the Latin; and *The Tears of Fancy* (1593) is a collection of 60 sonnets written at much the same time as Sidney's *Astrophel and Stella*. A minor poet, he was read by the greater sonneteers, and thus contributed to the Elizabethan vogue of Petrarch. [MJ]

J. W. Lever, *The Elizabethan Love Sonnet* (1956); C. S. Lewis, *English Literature in the Sixteenth Century* (1954).

Watson, Sir William (1858–1935). Poet. Born at Burley-in-Wharfedale, Yorkshire, the son of a grocer, and educated at Southport. Watson's first volume of verse, *The Prince's Quest and Other Poems*, appeared in 1880. Other volumes include *Wordsworth's Grave and Other Poems* (1890), *Lachrymae Musarum* (a collection of verses on the death of Tennyson) (1892), *Poems* (2 vols., intr. J. A. Spender, 1905), *Poems, 1878–1935* (1936). Watson's great strength was a certain turn for epigrammatic pith, best illustrated in his verses commemorating other poets (Burns, Wordsworth, Arnold, Tennyson). He was associated with John Lane's ◊ *Yellow Book*, but opposed the work of Beardsley. As an artist he looked backward to Tennyson and even Landor, but rather easily accepted the pale agnosticism and evolutionary complacency of Herbert ◊ Spencer. His opposition to the Boer War (see *For England. Poems Written during Estrangement*, 1904) cost him the Laureateship, but he was knighted in 1917. He had a true if slender talent. [AR]

Collected Poems, ed. J. A. Spender (1905); *I Was an English Poet* (selected by Lady Watson) (Ashville, 1941).
'W.: A Distinguished Poet', *TLS* (14 August 1935) (leading article and obituary); J. G. Nelson, *W.W.* (New York, 1966); J. L. May, *John Lane and the Nineties* (1936); H. K. Bett, 'The Poetry of W.', *London Quarterly*, XI (1936).

Watts, Isaac (1674–1748). Poet, hymnwriter and theologian. The son of a nonconformist schoolmaster, he was educated at the Dissenting Academy at Stoke Newington. He was minister of an Independent congregation in London, but a breakdown in health soon forced him to give up a regular ministry and he spent the last thirty years of his life in the house of Sir Thomas Abney, preaching and teaching only occasionally. Watts was the author of several theological and educational works, such as *The Christian Doctrine of the Trinity . . . Asserted and Prov'd* (1722) and *Logick; or the Right Use of Reason in Enquiry after Truth* (1725), which was used as a university and college text book, as was his influential *The Art of Reading and Writing English* (1721). He is now remembered for his

hymns and poems (chiefly sacred), of which he wrote over 500. Naturally in this large output much is flat, which made Johnson wish 'sprightliness and vigour' added to his great abilities. He can be, however, a poet of real standing, and, compared with that of minor Anglican and Catholic Metaphysical poets, his reputation seems to be adversely affected by the evangelical associations of his images; he has also suffered from his readers' familiarity with his works in early life. He experimented with different verse and stanza forms, and also produced metrical translations of the psalms. Also popular were his *Divine Songs Attempted in Easy Language for Children* (1715), containing such lines as ''Tis the voice of the Sluggard: I heard him complain' and 'How doth the little busy Bee'; after more than a century they were still being satirized by Carroll in *Alice in Wonderland*. Some of his hymns are still popular, among them 'Our God, our help in Ages past' and 'Jesus shall reign where'er the sun'. [AR]

Works, ed. G. Burder (1810–11; 1812–13).
Johnson, *Lives of the Poets*; A. P. Davis, *I.W.* (New York, 1943); T. Wright, *Lives of the British Hymn Writers*, iii (1914); J. Laird, *Philosophical Incursions into English Literature* (1946).

Watts-Dunton, Walter Theodore (1832–1914). Critic and miscellaneous writer. Born at St Ives in Huntingdonshire, he gave up his father's profession of solicitor after brief practice in London and, under the influence of his friendship with some of the Pre-Raphaelites, began to contribute to the *Athenaeum*; some of his contributions, on the Rossettis, Borrow, Tennyson and others, were reprinted as *Old Familiar Faces* (1916). His meeting with George Borrow in 1872 strengthened his interest in gypsies, who appear in several of his works, such as the title verse narrative in the volume *The Coming of Love, and Other Poems* (1898; 1899 with notes on gypsies etc.; revised and enlarged, 1906) and in his once-popular novel *Aylwin* (1899; with a long introduction, 1901; 1902). His other main work was *Poetry and the Renascence of Wonder* (1916), reprinting 2 encyclopedia essays of some note. He is best known now, however, as the guardian of the poet ◊ Swinburne in his old age. He took the patrician, dionysiac eccentric to live with him in his house, 'The Pines' in Putney, and over him exercised a friendly and tactful supervision, or stuffy bourgeois restraint, depending on the observer's point of view. [AR]

J. Douglas, *T.W.-D.: Poet, Critic, Novelist* (1904); A. C. Benson, 'T.W.-D.: Life and Letters', in *Twentieth Century Critical Essays* (World's Classics, 1933): L. Marchand, *The Athenaeum: A Mirror of Victorian Culture* (U. of North Carolina P., 1941); H. R. Angeli, 'W.-D. and Swinburne', *TLS*, 24 March 1950.

Waugh, Alexander Raban (Alec) (1898–). Novelist and travel writer. Waugh was born in Hampstead, London, the son of Arthur Waugh, editor and publisher, and elder brother of Evelyn ◊ Waugh. He was educated at Sherborne and Sandhurst. At 17, while waiting to go in the army, he wrote a novel attacking the public school system, *Loom of Youth* (1917), which brought him a certain amount of notoriety. During the First World War he served in France and was taken prisoner. After the war he worked as a reader for Chapman and Hall and in 1926 a journey to Tahiti inspired in him the love of tropical countries that was to reappear in many of his later books. A prolific writer, his most characteristic novels are *Island in the Sun* (1956) and *Fuel for the Flame* (1960), which treat of romance and intrigue in exotic settings. Other novels include *Kept* (1925), *No Truce with Time* (1941) and *Guy Renton* (1953). He has also written *Hot Countries* (1930), *The Sugar Islands* (1958), and a history of the West Indies, *A Family of Islands* (1964). *The Early Years of Alec Waugh* (1962) and *My Brother Evelyn and Other Profiles* (1967) are autobiographical. [PJK]

Waugh, Evelyn (Arthur St John) (1903–66). Novelist. Born in Hampstead, Waugh was the second son of Arthur Waugh, writer and publisher, and younger brother of Alexander ◊ Waugh. He was educated at a local school in Hampstead, Lancing College and Hertford College, Oxford, where he read Modern History. At Oxford, he paid little attention to his studies, gained a reputation for dandyism and led, in his own phrase, an 'idle, dissolute and extravagant' life. On leaving Oxford he studied for a short while at Heatherley's Art School in London, and then taught at two private schools, being dismissed from one of them for drunkenness. He then enrolled at a school of arts and crafts with the intention of becoming a cabinet-maker. In 1928 he married, and in the same year published a study of Rossetti and his first novel,

Decline and Fall. In the following year he separated from his wife, the marriage being annulled by decree of the Catholic Church in 1936. He married again in 1937 and went to live at Piers Court, a manor house in Gloucestershire. During the thirties he travelled widely in Europe, Africa, the Near East, West Indies and Mexico, and published records of his travels as well as novels and short stories. His travel books, *Labels: A Mediterranean Journal* (1930), *Remote People* (1931), *Ninety-Two Days* (1934), *Waugh in Abyssinia* (1936) and *Robbery under Law: The Mexican Object-Lesson* (1939), were later published in a one-volume abridged edition, *When the Going Was Good* (1946).

His second novel, *Vile Bodies* (1930), was his first financial success, and this was followed by *Black Mischief* (1932), *A Handful of Dust* (1934), *Mr Loveday's Little Outing and Other Sad Stories* (1936) and *Scoop* (1938), a total achievement which immediately established him as the most considerable comic novelist in England since Charles Dickens. Although he frequently rejected the description of himself as a social critic, these novels (at least on one of their many levels) do precisely convey the mood and tenor of upper-class life in England during the twenties and thirties, a way of life that both attracts and disgusts the author. Unique among English novelists of the 20th century in creating instantly memorable comic characters (Paul Pennyfeather, Basil Seal, Captain Grimes, Margot Beste-Chetwynde, Tony Last), he places them in a world seemingly devoid of law and order, and by a devastating use of biting satire, black comedy and pure farce transforms sociologically observed reality into complex ironic structures.

During the Second World War he served with the Royal Marines in the Middle East and in 1944 was a member of the British Military Mission to Yugoslavia. He continued to write fiction and published *Put Out More Flags* (1942), *Work Suspended* (1942) and his most romantic and controversial novel, *Brideshead Revisited* (1945). He had been received into the Roman Catholic Church in 1930 and even in the early novels there is observable a firm religious attitude emerging from the dominant atmosphere of social anarchism, but from *Brideshead Revisited* onwards the Catholic message in his work became intentionally more pronounced. Also more overtly expressed in the later novels is his profound distrust of modern life, a much vaunted reactionary attitude that is most clearly conveyed in *Scott-King's Modern Europe* (1947), *The Loved One: An Anglo-American Tragedy* (1948), his brilliantly macabre study of the American funeral industry, and *Love among the Ruins: A Romance of the Near Future* (1953). In 1957 he published *The Ordeal of Gilbert Pinfold*. A frankly autobiographical study of a middle-aged writer who suffers a nervous breakdown, it is a fine example of the lucid prose style that Waugh so painstakingly developed and is regarded by many critics as his best novel. His final work of fiction was *Sword of Honour* (1965), a recension of a trilogy of novels about the Second World War, *Men at Arms* (1952), *Officers and Gentlemen* (1955) and *Unconditional Surrender* (1961), in which the streak of arbitrary cruelty that flaws some of his earlier work is largely replaced by a more tolerant and sympathetic view of humanity. He also published a historical-religious novel, *Helena* (1950), 2 biographies, *Edmund Campion* (1935) and *Ronald Knox* (1959); 3 collected essays, *Holy Places* (1952); and the first volume of his autobiography, *A Little Learning* (1964). [PJK]

Sean O'Faolain, *The Vanishing Hero: Studies in the Novels of the Twenties* (1956); Christopher Hollis, *E.W.* (WTW, 1954); A. A. DeVitis, *Roman Holiday: The Catholic Novels of E.W.* (New York, 1956); Paul A. Doyle, 'E.W.: A Bibliography (1926–1956)', *Bulletin of Bibliography* (Boston, U.S.A.), XXII, 3 (May–August 1957); Frederick J. Stopp, *E.W.: Portrait of an Artist* (1958); Gilbert Highet, *The Anatomy of Satire* (1962); Malcolm Bradbury, *E.W.* (Writers and Critics, 1964); Stephen Jay Greenblatt, *Three Modern Satirists* (1965); Frances Donaldson, *E.W.: Portrait of a Country Neighbour* (1967); James F. Carens, *The Satiric Art of E.W.* (U. of Washington P., 1967); Alec Waugh, *My Brother Evelyn and Other Profiles* (1967).

Webb, Mary (Gladys) (*née* Meredith) (1881–1927). Novelist. She was born at Leighton, Shropshire, and educated at a school in Southport. In 1912 she married a school teacher, Henry Webb, and after living for two years in Weston-super-Mare they returned to Shropshire, where they tried to earn a living by running a market garden. It was during this period that she began seriously to write novels, publishing *The Golden Arrow* (1916), *Gone to Earth* (1917), *The House in Dormer Forest* (1920) and a collection of essays, *The Spring of Joy* (1917). These brought her little success and for most of her life she struggled with ill health and poverty. In 1921 the Webbs moved to London, where Mary wrote 2 further novels, *Seven for a Secret* (1922) and *Precious Bane* (1924), which was awarded the Prix Fémina for the best English novel of the year. Shortly before her death the Prime Minister, Stanley Baldwin, publicly praised *Precious Bane*, and his recommendation turned the book into a best-seller. *Armour Wherein He Trusted*, an uncompleted novel, was published posthumously in 1928 and *Fifty-One Poems* in 1946. Mary Webb was an unusual and original novelist about whom critical opinion is sharply divided. Her novels are set in her own invented county, Salop (Shropshire), which she brings alive by a skilful use of rural dialect, superstition and custom, but she was never able really to integrate these aspects of rural life into a totally satisfying pattern. Her novels have often been compared with those of Thomas Hardy, but there was a naïve primitive quality about her work which prevented it from ever attaining tragic stature. [PJK]

Stanley Baldwin, Introduction to *Precious Bane* (1928); Thomas Moult, *Life and Work of M.W.* (1933); W. Byford-Jones, *Shropshire Haunts of M.W.* (1948); Dorothy P. H. Wrenn, *Goodbye to Morning* (1964); Charles Sanders, 'M. W.: An Introduction and an Annotated Bibliography of Writings about Her', *English Literature in Transition*, IX, 3 (1966).

Webbe, William (fl. 1586–91). Prose writer. Educated at Cambridge, where he was a contemporary of Spenser, he was a tutor to families in Essex (1583–91). He published in 1586 a *Discourse of English Poetry, together with the Author's Judgment Touching the Reformation of Our English Verse*, a work which expresses his enthusiasm for new poets like Spenser (without always understanding their aims) and advocates Latin metres for English poems. Webbe's work has been variously pronounced 'attractive' and 'uniquely bad'. [MJ]

Ed. G. Gregory Smith, *Elizabethan Critical Essays*, i (1904); C. S. Lewis, *English Literature in the Sixteenth Century* (1954).

Webster, John (*c*. 1580–*c*. 1638). Dramatist. Almost nothing is known of Webster's life, though he may be the John Webster who was admitted to the Middle Temple in 1598. In 1602 the theatre manager, Philip ◊ Henslowe, recorded payments to Webster as author and part-author of various plays, now lost. In 1604 he wrote the Induction to *The Malcontent* by Marston and collaborated on *Westward Ho!* with ◊ Dekker. They later wrote *Northward Ho!* and *The Famous History of Sir Thomas Wyatt*. His high reputation rests on 2 tragedies, which have been admired by critics since the Romantic period and have occasionally been revived in the modern theatre. *The White Devil*, acted and published in 1612, was based on the recent Italian *cause célèbre* of the adulterous Vittoria Corombona; *The Duchess of Malfi*, performed around 1613, was also based on contemporary events. Both are revenge tragedies and have strong scenes and memorable speeches, the poetry often being full of literary borrowings. Both plays deal with violence and vividly evoke the corrosive power of evil in Renaissance courts. Some literary critics have found the plays less satisfactory as wholes.

Webster also wrote an elegy on the death of Prince Henry and contributed to the sixth edition of Overbury's *Characters*. His later plays included *The Devil's Law Case* (1616) and various collaborative works – *Anything for a Quiet Life* (with Middleton), *Appius and Virginia* (with Heywood), *A Cure for a Cuckold* (with Rowley), and the lost play *A Late Murder of the Son upon the Mother* (with Dekker, Ford and Rowley). Webster disliked the popular theatre and expressed in his prefaces the wish that he could have written in more classical forms. He died during the 1630s. [MJ]

The Complete Works, ed. F. L. Lucas (4 vols., 1927).

T. Bogard, *The Tragic Satire of J.W.* (Berkeley, Calif., 1955); M. C. Bradbrook, *Themes and Conventions of Elizabethan Tragedy* (1935); Rupert Brooke, *J.W. and the Elizabethan Drama* (1916); R. W. Dent, *J.W.'s Borrowings* (1960); C. Leech, *J.W.* (1951); G. Salgādo, Introduction to *Three Jacobean Tragedies* (PEL, 1965).

Wells, H(erbert) G(eorge) (1866–1946). Novelist, reformer and controversialist. Born in Bromley, Kent, the son of an unsuccessful shopkeeper. He too was educated to be a shopkeeper and apprenticed to a draper, but proved inattentive. He had read much on his own, and in 1880 he became a pupil-teacher in Somerset, then tried apprenticeship with a pharmacist and again with a draper, finally returning to pupil-teaching in Midhurst. He studied biology with T. H. ◊ Huxley, on a scholarship at the (later Royal) College of Science in South Kensington. His academic career had ups and downs, because he was liable to desert his scientific studies for literature, but he finally graduated in 1890. He taught in several schools and wrote scientific journalism, but when his short stories became saleable he turned professional writer. Wells wrote more than a hundred books, as well as pamphlets, plays for the radio and film scripts. His scientific study made him a passionate believer in the perfectibility of mankind through scientific advance, but as the millennium time and again eluded man's grasp, Wells tried in turn various short-cuts to realize his dream: politics (he was an undisciplined Fabian Socialist), religion, world government and various 'causes'. As he switched his attention from one to the other, his friendships turned to enmities, and frequently back again. He was a tireless and constantly frustrated working reformer. Wells's writings suffer from the restlessness which kept his astonishing talents from being completely and satisfactorily effective in any one direction. His performance remains a remarkable piece of social history rather than a part of living literature. He is perhaps best known now for his 'fantasies' or science-fiction, to which the term 'Wellsian' was, much to his annoyance, firmly attached. It denoted a kind of pseudo-scientific prediction; he maintained that his aim was political and social. In comparison with the sophisticated work now appearing in this genre, his own has declined in interest. *The Time Machine* (1895), *The Stolen Bacillus* (1895), *The Invisible Man* (1897), *In the Days of the Comet* (1906) and *The Shape of Things to Come* (1933) are examples of this kind of writing, in which he often made remarkable guesses about future events and discoveries, now so completely out-stripped in some directions that the once fascinating daring of imagination is lost.

He also wrote about the world of the shabby-genteel which he had personally experienced. Among these comedies of English class and society are his best works of fiction; they include *Love and Mr*

Lewisham (1900), *Kipps* (1905), *Tono-Bungay* (1909) and *The History of Mr Polly* (1910). In *Ann Veronica* (1909), he wrote a book which in its frankness about female sexuality caused an uproar. He followed up his ideas on free love and the impermanence of marriage in a political novel, *The New Machiavelli* (1911), and in *Marriage* (1912). To an increasing extent, Wells used fiction as a vehicle for his ideas and dogmas. So the novels became more argumentative; the characters talk interminably and often brilliantly, but (as in the plays of Shaw) as the ideas lose force the books now seem to flag. The art, too, became less well managed. *Mr Britling Sees It Through* (1916) was a justification of the war on religious grounds, as was *God the Invisible King* (1917), though Wells afterwards recanted his religious beliefs. *The World of William Clissold* (3 vols., 1926) is mostly 'ideas'.

Wells also wrote a number of influential books in which he did not fictionalize his ideas. Some of these works, like *The Outline of History* (1919; 1930), *The Science of Life* (1929) and *The Work, Wealth and Happiness of Mankind* (1932), are remarkable achievements, in which Wells's assumption of the role of world encyclopedist is not unwarranted. He became a kind of sage. He grew more and more pessimistic with age, and *The Fate of Homo Sapiens* (1939) is a very querulous work. The Second World War, which he had prophesied, depressed him immeasurably. Human nature in others betrayed Wells the reformer, and in himself Wells the artist. He was a stimulating and characteristic force in his day, but his own comment on his life is only too accurate: 'He was clever but not clever enough.' His own *Experiment in Autobiography* (2 vols., 1934), written from the point of view of an admiring observer, is, in its frankness, one of his most engaging works. [A R]

Works (26 vols., 'Atlantic Edition', 1925–7) (up to 1927 only); V. Brome, *H.G.W.* (1951); M. Belgion, *H.G.W.* (W T W, 1953); B. Bergonzi, *The Early H.G.W.: A Study of the Scientific Romances* (1961); I. Raknem, *H.G.W. and His Critics* (Oslo, 1963); L. Dickson, *H.G.W. His Turbulent Life and Times* (1969); H. G. Wells Society, *Bibliography* (1966).

Wesker, Arnold (1932–). Dramatist.

Born in the East End of London, of working-class Jewish parentage, he worked as a carpenter's mate, farm labourer and pastry-cook before taking a course in film-making, and writing a 2-act play, *The Kitchen* (produced privately, 1959; publicly, 1961). It presents one day behind-the-scenes in a large London restaurant, and mingles realistic and symbolic techniques. *Chicken Soup with Barley*, seen in Coventry and London in 1958, and his first play to be produced, is the story of an East End Jewish family in the thirties, forties and fifties – from Fascist demonstrations to the Welfare State. It is the first part of 'The Wesker Trilogy', which also contains *Roots* (1959) and *I'm Talking about Jerusalem* (1960). *Roots*, arguably Wesker's best play, shows the moral and political awakening of a country girl who returns from London and is dissatisfied with the restricted lives of the rural labouring class. *Jerusalem* dramatizes an experiment in Socialist community living. The 3 plays present significant aspects of contemporary Britain often neglected in the theatre, though the actual writing is of varying quality. *Chips With Everything* (1962) is simultaneously a fairly realistic picture of recruit-training in the Royal Air Force and a symbolic comment on the British class-war, the brutalization of the working classes by those in authority, and the decay of folk-culture.

Wesker, a political activist, passionately devoted himself to Centre 42, an organization he created to further working-class interest in the arts – and to enable artists to work in cooperation with the trade unions. Though his recent work, including a vision of the future, *Their Very Own and Golden City* (Marzotto Prize, 1964), has gained favour in Socialist states abroad, his British admirers have been disappointed. [M J]

Ed. W. A. Armstrong, *Experimental Drama* (1963); ed. J. R. Brown, *Modern British Dramatists* (New Jersey, 1968); ed. C. Marowitz, *Theatre at Work* (1967); H. U. Ribalow, *A.W.* (New York, 1965); J. Russell Taylor, *Anger and After* (revised edn, 1969).

Wesley, Charles (1707–88). Hymn writer.

Born at Epworth in Lincolnshire, eighteenth and youngest son of the rector, and brother of John ♢ Wesley, he was educated at Westminster School and Christ Church, Oxford. There he had a hand in founding the group of 'methodic' Christians, which his brother joined. Charles, too, kept a *Journal* (ed. T. Jackson, 2 vols., 1849) for some twenty years. He went to Georgia with his brother, and was associated with him in his itinerant preaching and organization of the Methodists, though his ideas differed significantly from his brother's. He retired from itinerant preaching in 1756, and thereafter lived in Bristol and London. He was the greatest of the good hymn writers of that time, and among his huge output for Methodist congregational singing are: 'Hark! the Herald angels sing', 'Love divine, all Loves excelling' and 'Oh, for a thousand tongues to sing'. [AR]

F. L. Wiseman, *C.W., Evangelist and Poet* (1933); R. N. Flew, *The Hymns of C.W.: A Study of Their Structure* (1953); J. Julian, *Dictionary of Hymnology* (revised edn, 1925).

Wesley, John (1703–91). Founder of Methodism, diarist and miscellaneous writer. Born of an old Puritan family, brother of Charles ◊ Wesley, and second son of Samuel Wesley, rector of Epworth in Lincolnshire. He was educated at Charterhouse and Christ Church, Oxford. A Fellow and tutor of Lincoln College, he took orders, and in 1729 became a member of the 'Holy Society' founded by his brother. The Wesleys, and other members of the university with the same feeling of dissatisfaction with contemporary un-evangelical religious life, sought mutual improvement in piety and self-dedication. Their corporate programme earned them the at first derogatory title of Methodists. The powerful personality of John soon made him the leading spirit of the group. The Wesleys were greatly influenced by the mystic William Law, and in 1735 John went on an evangelizing mission to the colonists and Indians of Georgia, where he parted from the Calvinists in the movement and cleaved to the Moravian Brethren there. He returned to London in 1738, and became an adherent of the Moravian chapel in Fetter Lane, visiting the mystic Zinzendorf in Germany. His views gradually excluded him as a preacher from the churches of the Anglican Establishment, and he developed his remarkable oratorical powers as a mass persuader by beginning his fantastic career as a field preacher. In the course of the rest of his life, he is reputed to have travelled nearly a quarter of a million miles on horseback all over England and preached more than forty thousand sermons, often several times a day. In 1740, he finished his connexion with the Moravians and opened a

'Methodist' chapel in Bristol. Both Wesleys wished to remain within the Anglican Church, but in 1784 John's was the driving force that finally cut Methodism off, when, against the advice of Charles, he ordained a minister for America, where there was a desperate and unfulfilled need for clergymen. With his preaching and proselytizing, John Wesley was perhaps the greatest single force in the 'revival of religion' that marked the latter part of the century; he also incurred great hostility, at times violent, both from the ecclesiastical and municipal authorities, and from the mob. Wesley, though arrogant and in controversy an implacable and ruthless antagonist, was an able organizer and with his gentlemanly address could inspire great loyalty. He wrote much on education and the Bible, and on theological controversy and produced a number of translations and editions of devotional works for the use of his followers. His greatest written monument is the remarkable *Journal* (21 parts, 1739–91; 4 vols., 1827; abridged, Everyman, 1902; ed. N. Ratcliff, 1940; the most complete edition by N. Curnock, 8 vols., 1909–16). This is a record of his own inner life, his work and his travels. For all students of the age, it is an indispensable document full of close observation of the social scene and the countryside, and sharp (even witty) judgement. He wrote hymns, like his brother Charles, with whom he often collaborated. [AR]

Works (32 vols., 1771–4); *Letters*, ed. J. Telford (8 vols., 1931); *Prayers*, ed. F. C. Gill (1951); *Hymns*, in J. Julian, *Dictionary of Hymnology* (2nd edn, 1907).
B. Dobrée, *W.* (1933); M. Schmidt, *J.W.* (Zurich, 1953 ff.); T. W. Herbert, *W. as Editor and Author* (1940); R. Green, *Bibliography of the Works of J. and Charles W.* (1896).

West, Rebecca (1892–). Novelist, journalist and critic. Born Cicily Isabel Fairfield in Co. Kerry, Ireland, Rebecca West was the daughter of an army officer. On the death of her father in 1902 the family moved to Edinburgh, where she was educated at George Watson's Ladies' College. She later studied at a London dramatic academy and was an actress for a short time. Her pen-name was taken from the heroine of Ibsen's *Rosmersholm*, one of the parts she played. In 1911 she joined the staff of the *Freewoman* and in the following year became a political writer on the

Clarion. Although, at this time, she was known mainly for her active participation in the fight for female suffrage and for her regular contributions to the left-wing press, her first book was a critical biography, *Henry James* (1915), which clearly indicated the wide-ranging intellectual curiosity that has distinguished all of her subsequent work. In 1918 she published her first novel, *The Return of the Soldier*, a study of the effects of shell-shock which showed, as did her next novel *The Judge* (1922), the impact of Freudian psychology upon her thinking. At irregular intervals, over a period of forty years, she has continued to publish finely written and psychologically penetrating novels which have been curiously neglected by critics. They include *Harriet Hume* (1929), *The Thinking Reed* (1936), *The Fountain Overflows* (1957) and *The Birds Fall Down* (1966). In 1937 a visit to Yugoslavia produced *Black Lamb and Grey Falcon* (2 vols., 1942), a strikingly individual work that begins as a travel diary and expands into a cultural and political examination of Balkan history. It anticipates her later book, *The Meaning of Treason* (1949), on the William Joyce trial which she reported for the *New Yorker*. Revised and brought up to date (1965), it is a classic study of the changing role of the intellectual, the scientist and the traitor in modern society. She has also written *D. H. Lawrence: An Elegy* (1930); *St Augustine* (1933); *A Train of Powder* (1955), reports of criminal cases including the Nuremberg trials; *The Court and the Castle* (1958), a study of the interactions of political and religious ideas in imaginative literature; and 2 volumes of collected articles, *The Strange Necessity* (1928) and *Ending in Earnest* (1931). She was awarded the C.B.E. in 1949 and the D.B.E. in 1959. [PJK]

'Westminster Review'. Published 1824–1914 and alternately appearing as *The London and Westminster Review* and *The Westminster and Foreign Quarterly Review*, it was founded by Jeremy ◊ Bentham, with the help of John Stuart ◊ Mill, as the journal of the philosophical radicals. John Bowring (1792–1872) was its first editor. It contained (1832) Mill's important essay showing his divergence from Benthamite utilitarianism. George ◊ Eliot became a contributor in 1850 and was assistant editor (under John Chapman) from 1851 to 1853. [RB]

Whetstone, George (*c.* 1544–87). Poet, prose-writer and dramatist. After having lost his inheritance on riotous living and on litigation, he distinguished himself as a soldier in the Low Countries and later sailed with Sir Humphrey Gilbert on his voyage to Newfoundland. He wrote in a bewildering variety of forms. His *Rock of Regard* (1576) includes verse narrative, a prose *novella*, poems addressed to friends and a burlesque. He published in 1577 a 'Remembrance' of George ◊ Gascoigne, which was followed by other such panegyrics. His unacted rhyming play *Promos and Cassandra* has a plot very similar to Shakespeare's *Measure for Measure*. His *Heptameron of Civil Discourses* (1582), a collection of tales, is significant in the history of Elizabethan fiction. His sententious prose pamphlets include the *Mirror for Magistrates of Cities* and *A Touchstone for the Time* (both 1584); the first holds up Henry VII and Alexander Severus as examples of good governors, while the second denounces those dissipations in which he is himself reputed to have indulged. [MJ]

T. C. Izard, *G.W.* (New York, 1942); C. S. Lewis, *English Literature in the Sixteenth Century* (1954).

Whibley, Charles (1859–1930). Critic and journalist. Born in Kent and educated in Bristol and at Jesus College, Cambridge, he worked for Cassells, the publishing firm, and wrote for W. E. ◊ Henley, who published the *Scots Observer* which became the *National Observer*, participating in attacks on Ruskin's aesthetic theories as artistic 'methodism'. In 1892, he collaborated with Henley in the Tudor Translations, and furnished introductory essays to many of the series' reprints of Elizabethan and Jacobean authors. He wrote for the *Pall Mall Gazette*, and (sent to Paris) was a member of Whistler's circle; he later married the painter's sister-in-law and was a friend of Mallarmé and Valéry. Returning to London, he contributed a series of monthly essays, 'Musings without Method', to *Blackwood's Magazine* for thirty years. His tendentious literary, political and other opinions in these pieces greatly influenced T. S. Eliot, who wrote of his work in 'Imperfect Critics', in *The Sacred Wood* (1920). Whibley also wrote for the *Spectator* and the *Daily Mail*, contributed to the *Cambridge History of English Literature*, and published several collections of essays including *A Book of Scoundrels* (1897), *Studies in Frankness* (1898), *The Letters of an Englishman* (1915) and *Political Portraits* (1917). He was a learned man, who practised the art of invective; he is an interesting link between the eighties and nineties and the Georgian poets and writers. [AR]

T. S. Eliot, *C.W., a Memoir* (1931) (English Association pamphlet); 'John Connell' (J. R. Robertson) W. E. Henley (1949).

White, Gilbert (1720–93). Naturalist. Educated with the ◊ Wartons and at Oriel College, Oxford, where he became a Fellow. He resigned in 1755 and settled as a curate in his native Selborne in Hampshire, where he lived unmarried until his death. He spent a retired life observing the scene around him and writing letters communicating his observations and reflections to men of kindred interests, especially Thomas Pennant and Daines Barrington. These letters were published in 1789 as *The Natural History and Antiquities of Selborne* (ed. B. C. A. Windle, Everyman, 1906), and many times reprinted. White's minute observation, steady reflection and love of his native scene together produced a minor masterpiece fusing literary imagination with the scientific temper. [AR]

E. A. Martin, *A Bibliography of G.W. with a Biography* (revised 1934); W. S. Scott, *W. of Selborne* (1950).

White, Patrick (Victor Martindale) (1912–). Australian novelist. Born in London and brought up in Sydney. After leaving Cheltenham College he worked for two years in Australia as a jackeroo before going to Cambridge University. His first published novel was the fourth he wrote (*Happy Valley*, 1939). During the war he served in the R.A.F. and published a second novel, *The Living and the Dead* (1942). After writing *The Aunt's Story* (1948), he returned to Australia and bought a farm near Sydney. *The Tree of Man* (1955) grew from this new encounter with the country. His latest novels, *Voss* (1957), *Riders in the Chariot* (1961) and *The Solid Mandala* (1966) are the peak of his achievement.

White's long and intricate novels are among the finest of the 20th century. Recognizing the realism of stream-of-consciousness writing, he has made it the basis of a challenging moral claim. His 'good' characters are those who insist, even through madness, on the authenticity of

their own experience. Theodora Goodman of *The Aunt's Story* is both mad and realistic. *Voss* shows greater control. It is an epic novel about a visionary explorer's encounter with Australia. White does not shirk the fact that Voss's honesty is dangerous. The world he sees is ill-prepared for realism. *Riders in the Chariot* is the completest statement of his theme and his clearest opposition of good and evil forces. The orthodox world destroys three of the protagonists, an exile, a lunatic and an illiterate. The only survivor of a 'pogrom' perpetrated according to accepted criteria is a woman of unreasonable, mundane kindness. White has supported his achievement on a prose style able to bear stresses more common to poetry. [PT]

The Burnt Ones (1964) (short stories); *Four Plays* (1965).
G. Dutton, *P.W.* (Australian Writers and Their Work, 1962); R. F. Brissenden, *P.W.* (WTW, 1966; J. Finch, *Bibliography of P.W.* (1966); B. Argyle, *P.W.* (1968).

White, T(erence) H(anbury) (1906–64). Novelist. White was born in Bombay, where his father was a District Superintendent of Police, and came to England in 1911. He was educated at Cheltenham College and Cambridge University. From 1930 to 1936 he was a schoolmaster, during which time he published a book of poetry and several novels, attaining his first critical success with a volume of autobiography, *England Have My Bones* (1936). He now devoted himself to writing and to studying the out-of-the-way subjects that were to provide the material for his books. By nature a recluse, he led a life that alternated between moods of wild bohemianism and intense self-destructive loneliness, and for long periods of time was isolated from human society, finding consolation in hunting, fishing and the strange collection of animals he kept as pets. From 1939 to 1945 he lived in Ireland and from 1946 to 1960 on the Channel Island of Alderney. He is best known for his quartet of novels *The Once and Future King* (1958), comprising *The Sword in the Stone* (1938), *The Queen of Air and Darkness*, first published as *The Witch in the Wood* (1940), *The Ill-Made Knight* (1941) and *The Candle in the Wind*. An idiosyncratic handling of the Arthurian cycle combining great knowledge of medieval life, colourful fantasy, casual brutality, deep pathos and modern slang, it is a children's book of genius. Adapted as a Broadway musical, *Camelot*, it made White a wealthy man in his final years. He also published books of social history, *The Age of Scandal* (1950) and *The Scandal-monger* (1952); a classic study of falconry, *The Goshawk* (1951); satirical works, *Burke's Steerage* (1939) and *The Elephant and the Kangaroo* (1947); and a further autobiographical volume, *The Godstone and the Blackymor* (1959). [PJK]

Stephen P. Dunn, 'Mr W., Mr Williams and the Matter of Britain', *Kenyon Review*, XXIV (Spring, 1962); J. R. Cameron, 'T.H.W. in Camelot: The Matter of Britain Revitalized', *Humanities Association Bulletin*, XV (Spring, 1965); Sylvia Townsend Warner, *T.H.W.* (1967).

White, William Hale. ◊ Rutherford, Mark.

Whiting, John (1917–63). Dramatist. After training at the Royal Academy of Dramatic Art, he had a pre- and post-war career as an actor before he gradually became known and accepted as a playwright. *Saint's Day*, written 1947–9, won a prize in 1951. Its performance was fiercely attacked by critics, but defended in *The Times* by leading members of the theatrical profession. It is an obscure, and at the end violent play, generating its own power in the theatre. *A Penny for a Song*, also produced in 1951, is a charming and original comedy set in Dorset at the time of the Napoleonic wars. *Marching Song* (1954) was a stylish and sombre post-war play in which a German general examined the motives for his past actions. Respected as a serious artist, Whiting failed to win a large audience in the theatre, and worked on several film-scripts before writing his impressive historical play *The Devils*. This study of the 'possessed' nuns at Loudun in the years 1623–34 is based on Aldous Huxley's *The Devils of Loudun*. Whiting was a dramatist of originality, integrity and great potential. [MJ]

The Collected Plays, ed. R. Hayman (2 vols., 1969); *The Art of the Dramatist: Uncollected Works*, ed. R. Hayman (1970). J. Russell Taylor, *Anger and After* (revised edn, 1969); K. Tynan, *Curtains* (1961).

Whythorne, Thomas (1528–96). Musician, poet and autobiographer. A chorister at Magdalen College School, Oxford, he went on to Magdalen College briefly, but family circumstances forced him to find employ-ment in London, where for three years he worked for Thomas ◊ Heywood as amanu-ensis. In the course of the next twenty years he was usually employed as music tutor and professional musician at a succession of great houses, but spent two years in conti-nental travel (*c.* 1554), and accompanied one pupil, the son of a rich merchant, William Bromfield, to Trinity College, Cambridge (1560–2).

Whythorne's literary importance rests on his autobiography, discovered in manu-script at Hereford in 1955, a quarter of which is in verse, along with some 200 poems, or rather words for songs of which the tunes are lost. The *Autobiography* (ed. J. M. Osborn, 1961; modern spelling edn, 1962), written about 1576, is the earliest English example of a sustained, intimate and revealing life-story. Since it remained in manuscript and unknown, it had no influence. Whythorne attempted a phonetic spelling, and the book has especial interest for phonologists. The American editor presented the manuscript to the Bodleian Library, Oxford. [MJ]

Wilde, Oscar (1854–1900). Dramatist, essayist, poet and wit. Born in Dublin, he was the son of Sir William Wilde, the eye-surgeon, and his formidable wife, who had published poems and prose under the name 'Speranza'. He was educated at Portora Royal School and at Trinity College, Dublin, where he excelled in classics. In 1874 he went up to Magdalen College, Oxford, on a demyship and took a first in Mods and in Greats, as well as carrying off the Newdigate Prize with a poem, *Ravenna*. After this brilliant scholastic start, Wilde, with his talent, charm, wit and instinct for publicity, quickly won himself a place in the literary world as an essayist and poet and in London society as a conversationalist, first-nighter and diner-out. His dandyism and conspicuous espousal of aestheticism attracted notice, so that in April 1881 when Gilbert and Sullivan's *Patience* was per-formed the character of Bunthorne, the Fleshly Poet (intended as a skit on Rossetti), was universally greeted as a caricature of Wilde. That summer he published *Poems*, a volume much influenced by Keats, Rossetti, Swinburne, Tennyson and others, which went into five editions. In January 1882 he arrived in New York ('I have nothing to declare except my genius') for a one-year tour of North America; his topics included

'Decorative Art in America' and 'The English Renaissance of Art'.

Early in 1883 Wilde visited Paris, where he met the leading writers of the day, and in the autumn returned to New York for the performance of his *Vera, or The Nihilists*. In 1884 he married Constance Lloyd, a lady of moderate fortune, by whom he had two sons, Cyril (born 1885) and Vyvyan (born 1886). Probably for them he wrote the delightful fairy-tales *The Happy Prince* (1888). In 1891 Wilde published *The Picture of Dorian Gray*, a novel about a beautiful hedonist who miraculously retains his youth while his portrait shows the ravages of time and unnamed dissipations. Influenced by J. K. Huysmans' *A Rebours* (1884), it seemed to commend the indulgence of rarefied taste, and was attacked by some critics as 'decadent', 'vicious' and 'unmanly'. Wilde was entering the period of his greatest creativity, and 1891 also saw the staging of *The Duchess of Padua* in New York, the appearance of the epigrammatic essay, influenced by Shaw, 'The Soul of Man under Socialism', and the publication of three books – a collection of essays *Intentions, Lord Arthur Savile's Crime and Other Stories*, and *The House of Pomegranates*.

Wilde, on the threshold of a glittering and lucrative career, was beginning to write plays for the leading personalities of the commercial theatre. But already in January 1891 he had met and become infatuated with ⟡ Lord Alfred Douglas ('Bosie'), the beautiful, talented and petulant son of the eighth Marquess of Queensberry: their relationship was to cause Wilde's ruin. In 1892 the first of Wilde's social dramas, *Lady Windermere's Fan*, was presented by George Alexander; in 1893 *A Woman of No Importance* was produced by Beerbohm Tree; and in 1895 *An Ideal Husband* was staged. All three are exercises in well-made society melodrama, but the conventional values of the 'good' characters which, in theory, prevail tend to be undermined by the elegant wit of the epigrammatic 'Wildean' dandies. These plays, unlike the early pieces, were hugely successful. *Salomé*, written in French, was being rehearsed in London in 1892 by the great Sarah Bernhardt when the Lord Chamberlain refused to licence a play depicting biblical characters. It was published in 1894 in a translation by Lord Alfred Douglas with provocative illustrations by Aubrey Beardsley. In

February 1895 George Alexander produced Wilde's masterpiece, *The Importance of Being Earnest*, 'a trivial comedy for serious people'. In this play Wilde abandoned sentimentality and sententiousness in favour of a frankly farcical and Gilbertian plot, brilliant and sparkling dialogue, and splendid acting parts for a team of polished actors.

Wilde's special claims for the artist and his quest for experience and sensation had led him into strange company. In the Victorian underworld he sought out grooms and stable boys. He seemed driven towards self-destruction ('It was like feasting with panthers. The danger was half the excitement'). He also lavished time and money travelling abroad with Alfred Douglas, whose father – enraged and unbalanced – sought energetically to discredit Wilde by uncovering his private life. Wilde was drawn into the Queensberry family's quarrels and in 1895, against all good advice, sued the Marquess for criminal libel. The Marquess was acquitted and the evidence he had exposed led to Wilde's own arrest on charges of homosexual practices. Wilde refused to flee the country, and, after the first jury disagreed, he was found guilty and sentenced to two years' hard labour. In prison he wrote a long, acrimonious letter to Douglas analysing their relationship and Bosie's hysterical provocation of his father. Its more general passages were printed in 1905 as *De Profundis*, but the full text was published only in *The Letters* of 1962. While serving his sentence Wilde was declared bankrupt, and from his release from prison in 1897 he lived in France and Italy, and wrote nothing except his most famous poem *The Ballad of Reading Gaol*, published in 1898. He lived mainly on the charity of those friends who remained loyal to him. The end came in Paris ('I am dying beyond my means') in 1900.

Wilde once told André Gide he had put his genius into his life and only his talent into his works; the biographical tragedy has usually obscured the assessment of Wilde's *literary* achievement. Critics have seen him variously as a self-destructive artist and as the sacrificial victim of Victorian hypocrisy. Plays and two films have been made on his life. His European reputation, created by the success of Max Reinhardt's production of *Salomé* (Berlin, 1903) and increased by the fame of Richard Strauss's operatic version (1905), has been out of all proportion. The early essays and poems are important documents in the history of the aesthetic movement, and his three society plays are assured of regular revival in the theatre. Two years after Wilde's death the London reviewers were proclaiming that *The Importance* had achieved classic status. It has survived.

The drama of the career has been the subject of a spate of books – some sympathetic, some hostile – by partisan writers including Lord Alfred Douglas, Frank Harris, R. H. Sherard, André Gide, and St John ◊ Ervine. While Richard Ellmann's projected biography is awaited the best introductions, among a welter of books, are: Rupert Hart-Davis's *Letters of O.W.* (1962), Hesketh Pearson's *The Life of O.W.* (1946), and Philippe Jullian's *O.W.* (Paris, 1967; translated 1969). The plays were discussed by James Agate in *The Masque*, No. 3 (1947), and one of the few literary studies is *The Art of O.W.* (1967) by Epifanio San Juan, Jr. No good collected edition of Wilde's work exists, but Stuart Mason's *Bibliography* (1912; reprinted 1967) remains useful. [MJ]

The Works of O.W. (1948); *The Artist as Critic: Critical Writings of O.W.*, ed. R. Ellmann (New York, 1969); *O.W.: A Collection of Critical Essays*, ed. R. Ellmann (New Jersey, 1969).
Vyvyan Holland, *Son of O.W.* (1954); H. Montgomery Hyde, *The Trials of O.W.* (1948) and *O.W.: The Aftermath* (1963); The Marquess of Queensberry, *O.W. and the Black Douglas* (1949); T. de Vere White, *The Parents of O.W.* (1967); ed. K. Beckson, *O.W.: The Critical Heritage* (1970).

Wilkie, William (1721–72). Scottish verse-writer. Wilkie, a man of peasant origin, eccentric habits and great erudition, became minister of Ratho, near Edinburgh, and was later Professor of Natural Philosophy (i.e. science) at St Andrews. His *Epigoniad* (1757), consisting of 9 books of heroic couplets in supposed imitation of Homer, was justly dismissed by London critics but was warmly defended, apparently for patriotic reasons, by David Hume. Wilkie's *Fables* (1768) include one piece in Lothian Scots, 'The Hare and the Partan'. [AI]

Poems, with a Life by R. A. Davenport (British Poets, vol. 71, 1822).

William of Malmesbury (*c.* 1090–*c.* 1143). Historian. Born in south-west England, he was educated at Malmesbury, where he subsequently became a monk. His main works, apart from biographies of Wulfstan and St Dunstan, are the *Gesta regum Anglorum*, written *c.* 1125 and later revised (ed. W. Stubbs, Rolls Series, 2 vols., 1887–9), the *Gesta pontificum Anglorum*, about contemporary bishops and monasteries (ed. N. E. S. A. Hamilton, Rolls Series, 1870), and the *Historia Novella*, which breaks off, presumably because of his death, in 1142 (ed. W. Stubbs, with the *Gesta regum*). These, though made lively both by his style and by the number of anecdotes included, are of less value to historians than they might be for two reasons: in the earlier sections he depends very largely on sources which have independently survived, and his treatment is, further, distinctly confused. The more recent history, in which he drew partly on his own knowledge, is dominated by foreign affairs. [ATH]

William of Newburgh (1136–98). Chronicler. Born at Bridlington, Yorkshire, he spent most of his life as an Augustinian canon at Newburgh in the same county. His *Historia rerum Anglicarum* covers English history of the period 1066–1198. His integrity and impartiality led Freeman to call him 'the father of historical criticism'.

Historia, ed. R. Howlett in *Chronicles of Stephen*, etc. (Rolls Series, i and ii, 1884–5); tr. J. Stevenson, in *Church Historians of England*, IV, 2 (1856).

Williams, Charles (1886–1945). Critic, novelist, playwright and essayist. Born in London. A prolific writer of romantic thrillers, poetry and works of theology, he spent most of his life working for Oxford University Press. He was a literary critic of no great stature, but achieved something of a cult status in Anglican literary circles. The most interesting aspect of his talents is to be found in the novels, which he wrote purely for financial reasons, but in which he made use of the half-mystical, half-supernatural ideas that he toyed with in his other and, to him, more serious writings. *Descent into Hell* (1937) is the most rewarding of these crypto-gothic novels. [CO]

Shadows of Ecstasy (1933); *All Hallows' Eve* (1945); *The Image of the City* (1958); *Collected Plays* (1963).
A. M. Hadfield, *An Introduction to C.W.* (1959); J. Heath-Stubbs, *C.W.* (1955).

Williams, David John (1885–1970). Welsh short-story writer and autobiographer. Born at Penrhiw, Llansawel, Carmarthenshire, he moved to Aber-nant, Rhydcymerau, and later worked on the land. He was successively a collier, an assistant teacher and a student at University College of Wales, Aberystwyth, followed by two years at Jesus College, Oxford. He taught for a short period at Pengam, and was appointed English (later Welsh) master at Fishguard Grammar School in 1919, from which post he retired in 1945. One of the founders of the Welsh Nationalist Party in 1925, he was imprisoned for his part in the burning of the Bombing School near Pwllheli in 1936.

In 1934 D. J. Williams published a series of character sketches based on his knowledge of rural Carmarthenshire (*Hen Wynebau*). In these, sympathy and understanding of his characters are linked with acute observation of their social background and material and intellectual culture. His prose, in common with that of other Welsh writers of the highest calibre, is redolent of his native dialect. His characters are not really odd or outstanding in themselves, and what makes them interesting and credible for the reader is Williams' absorbed interest in their personalities. This volume was a preparation for two collections of short stories, *Storiau'r Tir Glas* (1936) and *Storiau'r Tir Coch* (1941). These are more varied, some frankly humorous, others essentially serious but lightened by the author's geniality and ready sympathy. He is not as conscious a literary artist as Kate ◊ Roberts, and there is a certain lack of discipline in his sometimes too loosely knit stories. He later commenced his autobiography, and here his talents are given free rein. In *Hen Dŷ Ffarm* (1953) and *Yn Chwech ar Hugain Oed* (1959; tr. W. Williams, *The Old Farmhouse*, 1961) he describes the days of his youth in Llansawel and Rhydcymerau back as far as his grandfather's period and on to his experiences as a collier up to his first days at Aberystwyth (1911). He succeeded in performing a prodigious feat of memory in re-creating the life of an agricultural community and a semi-industrialized area at the end of the 19th century and the beginning of the 20th. [MR]

Williams, (George) Emlyn (1905–). Actor and dramatist. Born in Flintshire to poor parents, he won a scholarship to Christ Church, Oxford. In the thirties and forties he wrote several successful plays, in which he often appeared to great advantage,

notably as the baby-faced killer Danny in *Night Must Fall* (1935) and as the young miner whom a determined schoolmistress sends to Oxford in *The Corn is Green* (1938), a play which made use of his early background. *The Wind of Heaven* (1945) shows the Second Coming in a Welsh rural setting. He wrote, directed and appeared in *The Last Days of Dolwyn*, a film set in Wales. His more recent plays have not been so successful. In 1951 he re-created one of Charles Dickens's famous 'readings' and this 15,000-word solo performance led to other Dickens recitations and to a similar programme, *Dylan Thomas Growing Up*, in 1955.

He has acted in a wide range of plays and films but excels in sinister parts. His plays are the work of a theatrical craftsman, usually telling a strong story well, and often creating the same sinister atmosphere as his own acting. His dialogue has a rhetorical richness, impressive in performance. His autobiography, a theatrical success-story, is in progress. [MJ]

George: An Early Autobiography (1961).
R. Findlater, *E.W.* (1956).

Williams, Thomas Herbert Parry-. ◊ Parry-Williams, Thomas Herbert.

Williams, William or **Pantycelyn** (1717–91). Welsh poet and hymnist. Born in Llanfair-ar-y-bryn, Carmarthenshire, he was educated at Llwyn-llwyd Academy. He was converted by the preaching of Howel Harris at Talgarth, and entered the Church in 1740, serving as curate for Theophilus ◊ Evans at Llanwrtyd, Llanfihangel and Llanddewi Abergwesyn until 1743. After some trouble with his superiors he threw in his lot with the Methodist movement and was soon recognized as one of its great leaders. After his marriage in 1748 he went to live at his mother's old home, Pantycelyn, by which name he became familiarly known. He played a leading part in the formation and supervision of Methodist societies (*seiat*), and spent his life in preaching all over Wales.

Williams was a prolific, if uneven, writer, and his works include hundreds of hymns, the long poems *Golwg ar Deyrnas Crist* (1756) and *Bywyd a Marwolaeth Theomemphus* (1764), and many prose works (e.g. *Crocodil Afon yr Aipht, Tri wyr o Sodom, Ductor Nuptiarum*, etc.). He must be regarded primarily as the voice of the Welsh Methodist revival. His hymns achieved an astonishing popularity and they are still prime favourites, the best of them being the expression of an intense personal religious feeling and experience. His literary standards compared with his contemporary, Goronwy ◊ Owen, and judged by the canons of classical Welsh poetry were low and uncritical. He has been widely recognized as an early figure in the Romantic movement. His long poem *Theomemphus* repays psychological study as an exercise in the history of a religious conversion. [MR]

Holl Weithiau . . . W.W., ed. J. R. Kilsby Jones (1867).
J. Gwilym Jones, *W.W.*, *P.* (1969).

Wilmot, John. ◊ Rochester, John Wilmot, 2nd Earl of.

Wilson, Angus (1913–   ). Novelist and critic. Born in Dumfriesshire of a Scottish father and a South African mother, Wilson visited South Africa as a child with his parents. He was educated in England at Westminster School and Merton College, Oxford. In 1936 he went to work at the British Museum in the Department of Printed Books and remained there for nearly twenty years, apart from a spell at the Foreign Office during the war. It was while trying to emerge from a period of depression and near-breakdown that he began to write short stories in 1946, a collection of which, *The Wrong Set*, was published in 1949, followed by a second collection, *Such Darling Dodos* (1950). His next published works were *Emile Zola: An Introductory Study* and a novel, *Hemlock and After* (both 1952). In 1955 he resigned from the British Museum in order to devote his entire time to writing. A play, *The Mulberry Bush* (1956), produced by the English Stage Company, was intelligent and thought-provoking. If it appeared at the time to lack the liveliness, creative tension and unerring sense of social nuance that characterize his stories, this was due mainly to Wilson's unfamiliarity with stage technique. His other novels include *Anglo-Saxon Attitudes* (1956), *The Middle Age of Mrs Eliot* (1958), *The Old Men at the Zoo* (1961), *Late Call* (1964) and *No Laughing Matter* (1967). A further volume of short stories was published in 1957.

The early stories, brilliant and amusing satires though they are, hardly prepare one for the depth and assurance of *Hemlock and After*, which is almost Gidean in its scrupulously painstaking examination of human relationships. *Anglo-Saxon Attitudes*, Dickensian in its length and its multiplicity of characters, and *The Middle Age of Mrs Eliot*, in which the author continues his study of liberal humanists grappling with both their own motivation and an indifferent or hostile world, lead naturally to *The Old Men at the Zoo*, a piece of cold-eyed political satire set in the immediate future. *No Laughing Matter* is his most ambitious novel, a chronicle of a somewhat bohemian middle-class family in the years between the two world wars.

As a novelist, Wilson is noted less for his stylistic virtues than for his psychological insight into character and motive. He has acknowledged the strong influence of Freud: *The Wild Garden* (1963), based on his Ewing Lectures at the University of California, usefully and authoritatively examines the author's own fiction. [CO]

J. L. Halio, *A.W.* (1964).

Wilson, Ethel (1890–   ). Canadian novelist. Born in South Africa, she spent her early childhood in England but was orphaned at the age of 8 and went to live with a grandmother in Vancouver. She was a schoolteacher before her marriage to a doctor, with whom she has travelled widely. Wilson published her first novel, *Hetty Dorval*, in 1947. The plot is trite, but the book is typical of her work in its dependence on a deceptively casual style that allows her to tell us more than she appears to know about her heroine's mixed motives. The 2 short novels in *Equations of Love* (1952) are examples of the skilled manipulation of points of view, and a willingness to experiment, particularly in the handling of time, continues in *Swamp Angel* (1954) and *Love and Salt Water* (1956). Humour, based on the wicked innocence of a sidelong glance at men, women and manners, is never long absent from her work. The title-piece of *Mrs Golightly* (1961) and several of its stories are among the finest passages of Canadian humour. [PT]

D. Pacey, *E.W.* (1967).

Wilson, John. ◊ North, Christopher.

Wilson, John Burgess. ◊ Burgess, Anthony.

Winchilsea, Anne Finch, Countess of (1661–1720). Poet. Of the Hampshire family of Kingsmill, she was one of the maids-of-honour of the Duchess of York (1683) and in 1684 married Heneage Finch, later 6th Earl of Winchilsea. She possessed a genuine personal sensibility and, though an amateur, enough poetic talent and force to give it pleasing and at times beautiful expression. Her treatment of the pleasures of the country made Wordsworth exempt her from his wholesale condemnation in the propaganda essay prefixed to *Lyrical Ballads* (1801). She began as a writer of 'pindaricks' and experimented with other metres in her *Miscellany Poems* (1713; ed. with a Life, M. Reynolds, Chicago, 1903), in which appears her best-known work, 'Nocturnal Reverie'. Also quite well known is 'The Spleen' (ed. with other poems in *Minor Poets of the Eighteenth Century*, Everyman, 1930), which appeared with some other poems in 1701. [AR]

Virginia Woolf, *A Room of One's Own* (1929); R. A. Brower, 'Lady W. and the Poetic Tradition of the 17th Century', *SP* 42 (1945).

Wither, George (1588–1667). Poet. He was born at Bentworth in Hampshire and educated at Magdalen College, Oxford. In 1614 he was detained in the Marshalsea in consequence of a satiric poem, *Abuses Stript and Whipt* (1613), and while in prison he collaborated with William Browne in the composition of *The Shepherd's Pipe* (1614). His best work was produced in a similar pastoral mode, notably *The Shepherd's Hunting* (1615), *Fidelia* (1615) and *Fair Virtue* (1622). His love and pastoral poems were collected in *Juvenilia* (1622). But as he became a convinced Puritan he increasingly devoted himself to satiric and didactic verse (and to 'precautions', prophecies and petitions); some of them were felt to be sufficiently powerful to warrant further terms of imprisonment (in 1621–2, 1646–7 and again after the Restoration). *Heleluiah* (1641) rises above the general level of Wither's later work, while *The Scholar's Purgatory* (1629) is interesting for the information it provides on relations between writers and publishers. His versified tracts obscured his earlier reputation, and until the end of the 18th century when Percy reprinted some of his lyrics 'Wither' was a by-word for 'hack'. His talent for pastoral verse was redis-

covered, thanks in particular to Charles Lamb, and in the 19th century most of his works were reprinted by the Spenser Society. He used 7-syllabled rhyming couplets, his favourite form, with subtlety and flexibility. [NL]

The Poetry of G.W., ed. and intr. F. Sidgwick (2 vols., 1902).
Charles Lamb, 'The Poetical Works of G.W.', *Works* (1818).

Wodehouse, P(elham) G(renville) (1881–   ). Novelist. Born at Guildford in Surrey, the son of a Civil Servant, he was educated at Dulwich College. He worked briefly in a bank, but by 1903 had become successful enough as a freelance writer to strike out on his own. Since 1904 he has lived much in America, and he now lives permanently on Long Island. In 1910, after writing some boys' stories, he started to write the humorous novels and short stories for which he is now famous. For many years he wrote about 2 books a year. The cast of characters is set in a timeless English upper-class world; first Edwardian, it later moved into the twenties, where it has remained. Perhaps it was fortunate that Wodehouse moved to America; it allowed him to create a truly imagined world. The characters themselves are now classics: Bertie Wooster, his man Jeeves, his Aunt Agatha, Psmith, and assorted girls, peers, clergymen, gardeners and the like. Their farcical adventures, unchanging highly stylized slang, have been worked up by Wodehouse, with deft arrangement of a strictly limited set of plot materials, into a delicate art of nostalgic charm. The most famous of his many titles are *Leave it to Psmith* (1923), *Carry on, Jeeves* (1925) and *The Code of the Woosters* (1938), and recent additions to his long list are *Ice in the Bedroom* (1961), *Service with a Smile* (1962), *Frozen Assets* (1964) and *A Pelican at Blandings* (1969). When the Second World War broke out, Wodehouse was living in France; he was captured by the Germans, who treated him well enough to induce him to agree to broadcast from Berlin in their praise. Though there were some ugly motions towards making the apolitical writer a scapegoat, the matter was finally dropped. George Orwell in *Dickens, Dali and Others* (1941) characteristically defended him, and has an interesting evaluation of his work, seizing on its 'dated' charm, which has, however, become a much prized quality. Wodehouse has also written plays and musical comedy lyrics. [AR]

Performing Flea: A Self-Portrait in Letters (1953) and *Over Seventy* (1957) (autobiographies). R. Usborne, *W. at Work* (1961).

Wodrow, Robert (1679–1734). Historian. Librarian of Glasgow University from 1697 to 1701 and minister of Eastwood near Glasgow from 1703, he wrote a *History of the Sufferings of the Church of Scotland 1660–1688* (1721–22) and left *Analecta, or Materials for a History of Remarkable Providences* (published in 1842, the year before the Disruption of the Church of Scotland). Wodrow's works helped to form the popular impression of the persecuted Covenanters of the Restoration period which supplied much of the mystique of the Evangelical party in the 18th-century Scottish Church and of the Free Church of Scotland after the Disruption. [AI]

Correspondence, ed. T. McCrie (1842–3); *Early Letters, 1698–1709*, ed. L. W. Sharp (1937).

Wolcot, John (1738–1819). Satirist. Born in Devonshire, he wrote under the pseudonym of Peter Pindar. In 1767 he went to Jamaica as physician to a Governor, Sir George Trelawny, and, becoming ordained in 1769, doubled as a parson. He returned to England in 1772 on his patient's death and resumed his medical practice there. In 1778 he went to London with his protégé, Opie the painter, and started writing satires for Griffith's *Monthly Review*. Wolcot had a vein of rough, effective humour, strengthened by gross insensitivity. He attacked easy targets such as members of the Royal Academy, the Royal Family (in *The Lousiad*, 1785 and 1787 – the joke is obvious), Boswell and Bruce (the explorer of Abyssinia). His collected works (1812; and 1816 with a memoir) are unreadable; he is too often simply wrong and his shrewd points are mixed with tedious fooling; but J. H. P. Hunt edited lively *Selections, with a Critical Notice* (1890). [AR]

K. Hopkins, *Portraits in Satire* (1958).

Wolfe, Humbert (1886–1940). Poet, critic and Civil Servant. He combined a strenuous life of public service with a wide literary production which earned him many readers during his lifetime, but which on the whole has not lasted well today. Born in Milan, of an English-Jewish family, he was a good linguist and a great admirer of Heine, some of whose poems he translated effectively. Heine's mixture of tartness and playfulness with a certain affectation and sentimentality had a profound effect on his own style. His poems are always neat, clever productions, but rather self-consciously so, and tend to lack depth and spontaneity. His critical prose, though often very intelligent, is similarly spoiled by mannerism. [GSF]

London Sonnets (1920); *Kensington Gardens* (1924); *The Unknown Goddess* (1925); *Lampoons* (1925); *News of the Devil* (1926); *Requiem* (1927); *This Blind Rose* (1928); *Snow* (1931); *Kensington Gardens in War-Time* (1940); *Dialogues and Monologues* (1928) (essays); *Tennyson* (1930) (criticism); *George Moore* (1931) (criticism).

Wollstonecraft, Mary. ◊ Godwin, Mary (Wollstonecraft).

Wood or **à Wood, Anthony** (1632–95). Antiquary and biographer. He wrote on the city and university in which he was educated, Oxford; he was at Merton College. His most useful work is *Athenae Oxonienses* (1691–2), a biographical dictionary of Oxford writers and bishops which illustrates the same kind of interest as the *Brief Lives* of ◊ Aubrey and preserves much minute information mingled with testy judgements. His reference to the first Earl of Clarendon caused his expulsion from the University (1693). [AR]

Life and Times of A. à W., ed. A. Clark (Oxford Historical Society, 5 vols., 1891–1900).

Wood, Mrs Henry (Ellen Wood) (1814–87). Novelist. She was born at Worcester, the daughter of Thomas Price, a manufacturing glover. She suffered from a spinal disability and spent a studious childhood, marrying a rich banker, Henry Wood (1836), and thereafter living mostly in the French Riviera, returning to London in 1880. She published almost 50 volumes of fiction, novels and tales. All are now forgotten except her second novel, *East Lynne* (1861), which was a bestseller and repeatedly made into melodramas. In 1867, she bought the *Argosy*, a periodical collection of shorter fiction, which she edited and wrote for. She had a certain taste for realistic (and approving) portrayal of middle-class life. [AR]

C. W. Wood, *Memorials of Mrs H.W.* (1894); M. Elwin, *Victorian Wallflowers* (1934).

Woolf, Leonard (1880–1969). Historian and critic. Born in London, he was educated at St Paul's and Trinity College, Cambridge. He was in the Ceylon Civil Service from 1904 to 1911, and in 1912 he married Virginia Stephen, who achieved distinction as a novelist and essayist under the name Virginia ◊ Woolf. Woolf's earliest books were stories about Ceylon: *The Village in the Jungle* (1913), *The Wise Virgins* (1914) and *Stories of the East* (1916). *The Village in the Jungle* is still highly regarded, not least in Ceylon, as one of the rare successful works of fiction written by a European about Asia.

In 1916 Woolf became a member of the Fabian Society, and wrote 2 reports on international government. He and Virginia Woolf began the Hogarth Press in 1917. The greater part of his writings was in the field of political theory, and includes *Co-operation and the Future of Industry* (1918), *Mandates and Empire* (1920), *Socialism and Co-operation* (1921), *Fear and Politics* (1925) and *Imperialism and Civilization* (1928). But as early as 1927 he had written *Essays on Literature, History, Politics* which testifies to the breadth of his interests. His judgements were penetrating, fair and gracefully expressed, and the range of his literary sympathies were impressively wide. He and his wife were active in what came to be known as the ◊ Bloomsbury Group. He began an autobiography in several volumes, the first of which, *Sowing* (1960), deals only with his first twenty-five years of life, ending as he comes down from Cambridge. *Growing* (1961) deals with his years in Ceylon, and *Beginning Again* (1964) with the next seven years up to 1918. *Downhill All the Way* (1967) brings the story up to 1939. Before his death he had completed a fifth volume, *The Journey, not the Arrival, Matters* (1969), covering the years of the Second World War, the death of Virginia Woolf, and his own old age. [co]

Principia Politica (1953).

Woolf, Virginia (1882–1941). Novelist and critic. Born in London, daughter of Sir Leslie ◊ Stephen, Virginia Woolf from earliest childhood moved in an atmosphere of literary culture and was patted on the head as a girl by many an eminent Victorian. She grew up as a member of a large and talented family. On the death of her father in 1904 she settled with her sister Vanessa and her two brothers in Bloomsbury, be-

coming an important figure in the so-called ◊ 'Bloomsbury Group', which included ◊ Lytton Strachey, J. M. Keynes the economist, Roger Fry the art critic, and E. M. ◊ Forster. When Vanessa married the art critic Clive ◊ Bell in 1907 Virginia and her brother took another house in Bloomsbury and there they entertained their literary and artistic friends in evening gatherings where the consciously witty conversation reflected the general attitudes (nothing more specific, for the group had no precise programme) of the Bloomsbury Group – rebellion against Victorianism and rejection of its taboos (including its sexual taboos) and a belief in the importance of freely explored and developed personal relationships. In 1912 she married Leonard ◊ Woolf, also a member of the group, and together they founded the Hogarth Press in 1917, partly as a therapeutic measure for Virginia, who suffered from fits of acute depression and mental disturbance. The Hogarth Press has published some of the most interesting literature of the present century, including an early volume of the poems of T. S. Eliot and her own novels. In March 1941, when the Woolfs were living in their cottage at Rodmell, Sussex, Virginia, dissatisfied (as she always was immediately on finishing a work) with the novel *Between the Acts*, which she had just completed, and acutely depressed both because of this and because of the constant German bombing going on in the south of England, and, more important, convinced that she was about to have an incurable relapse into an earlier state of mental illness, committed suicide by drowning.

Virginia Woolf moved into literature easily and almost by natural right. Beginning as a critic, for *The Times Literary Supplement* and other journals (and she continued to write criticism all her life), she began the writing of fiction with *The Voyage Out* (1915), a novel which, while wholly traditional in structure and technique, nevertheless showed signs of its author's search for a more sensitive savouring of experience than traditional fictional techniques allowed. *Night and Day* followed in 1919; it is an elaborately thoughtful study of an intelligent upper-middle-class young woman passing from the rejection of one lover to the acceptance of another, and again its methods are traditional and seem unable to contain the insights she seeks to convey. There followed a series of experiments in which she explored techniques better able to convey the sensitive shades of individual experience. These stories and sketches, published as *Monday or Tuesday* in 1921, show her developing an impressionist prose and bringing some of the techniques of lyrical poetry into prose fiction. At the same time she explained her ideas about fiction in critical essays, notably 'Modern Fiction', in which she described Wells, Bennett and Galsworthy as 'materialists' for being concerned more with the material surface of life than with the subtleties of inward experience. In a lecture she gave at Cambridge in 1928 she defined reality as 'something very erratic, very undependable – now to be found in a dusty road, now in a scrap of newspaper in the street, now in a daffodil in the sun'. The novelist, she asserted, 'has the chance to live more than other people in the presence of this reality.' 'It is his business to collect it and communicate it to the rest of us.'

She was now ready to put her theory into practice in full-length novels marked by a sensitive use of the 'stream-of-consciousness' technique and a prose delicately condensed so as to reflect the subtle shifts of inward sensibility. *Jacob's Room* (1922) makes no attempt to preserve the firm outlines of chronological events, but breaks down experience into a series of rapidly dissolving impressions that merge yet are never drowned in total formlessness, because the author keeps firm control of structure and pattern, so that the total meaning emerges through the interaction of images and the impression of an organizing sensibility at work which they produce. *Mrs Dalloway* (1925) is the story of one day in the life of the heroine in which the impingement of the past on present consciousness enables her (as it enabled James Joyce, in *Ulysses*, a work which certainly influenced her) to tell the whole of Mrs Dalloway's past by naturally developing flashbacks within consciousness; the interaction of Mrs Dalloway's thoughts, feelings and behaviour with those of other characters, the most significant of whom have no overt connexion with her, establishes a rhythm and a meaning related to Virginia Woolf's characteristic themes of the relationship between the desirable inviolability of the individual personality and the apparently incompatible but equally important desire for community, and the counterpointing of fixity and flux. In *To the Lighthouse* (1927) she explored these themes further, and was also much involved with the theme of time and change and its relation to personality. The novel is in 3 sections, of which the middle section, entitled 'Time Passes', gives an impressionistic rendering of the effect of the passing of time on both people and things. The symbolic use of objects, gestures and situations is developed in this novel with a combination of precision and subtlety. Her next work, *Orlando, A Biography* (1928), which takes its hero-heroine from Elizabethan times to the modern world with a change of sex *en route*, is a *jeu d'esprit* of great liveliness and wit, showing the tart humour and high spirits of which Virginia Woolf was capable in conversation but which she rarely allowed into her fiction; it also throws light on her conception of the relation between the sexes and of bisexuality, a theme which weaves in and out of all her novels though often well below the surface. *The Waves* (1931) is the most stylized of her novels and the furthest removed from the rhythms and vocabulary of ordinary speech. In *The Years* (1937) she reverts in some degree to a more traditional technique, moving forward through a large tract of time in chronological order rather than depending on stream-of-consciousness flashbacks, but in *Between the Acts* (published posthumously in 1941) she develops her kind of quasi-poetic symbolic fiction to a new pitch.

Virginia Woolf has been attacked for her over-refinement of experience and for ignoring the coarse realities of life in favour of the exploitation of a leisured and self-indulgent sensibility, but her achievement is substantial and her place in modern fiction significant. She responded with intelligence and delicacy to the breakdown of a sense of public values which made the more robust techniques of the Victorian novelists inappropriate in rendering some characteristic 20th-century themes; her art, if limited, is real and her imagination genuinely exploratory. At her best she is a novelist *sui generis*. [DD]

The Common Reader (1925); The Common Reader: Second Series (1932); The Death of the Moth and Other Essays (New York, 1942); The Moment and Other Essays (1947); The Captain's Death Bed and Other Essays (1950); Granite and Rainbow: Essays (1958); Flush: A Biography (1933) (a biography of Elizabeth Barrett Browning's dog); Roger Fry: A Biography (1940); A Room of One's Own (1929) and Three Guineas (1938) (essays which throw im-

561

portant light on Virginia Woolf's eminism);
A Writer's Diary, ed. Leonard Woolf (1953)
(selection from her diary); *V.W. and Lytton
Strachey: Letters*, ed. Leonard Woolf and
James Strachey (1956).
D. Daiches, *V.W.* (revised edn, Norfolk, Conn.,
1963), and *The Novel and the Modern World*
(revised edn, Chicago, 1960); Bernard Black-
stone, *V.W.*, *A Commentary* (1949); Jean
Guiget, *V.W. et son œuvre* (Paris, 1962; tr. Jean
Stewart, *V.W. and Her Works*, 1965); Herbert
Marder, *Feminism and Art: A Study of Virginia
Woolf* (Chicago,1968); Leonard Woolf, *Sowing:
An Autobiography of the Years 1880–1904*
(1960), *Growing: An Autobiography of the Years
1904–1911* (1961), *Beginning Again: An Auto-
biography of the Years 1911–1918* (1964), and
*Downhill All the Way: An Autobiography of the
Years 1919–1939* (1967); Irma Rantavaara,
V.W. and Bloomsbury (1953); J. K. Johnstone,
The Bloomsbury Group (1954); Quentin Bell,
Bloomsbury (1968).

Wordsworth, Dorothy (1771–1855). Sister
and helper of William ◊ Wordsworth. She
is remembered chiefly for her sustaining
relationship with her brother, who called
her the 'sister of my soul' (*Prelude* XIII).
She shared his passionate response to
Nature – 'For she was Nature's inmate'
(*Prelude* XI), – 'She gave me eyes, she gave
me ears' ('The Sparrow's Nest'). Dorothy
was a continuous affirmation of the spirit
of life within William. At the time of his
breakdown after the failure of his hopes
from political revolution and his vain
attempt to remake himself out of Godwinian
reason, Dorothy, 'the beloved woman . . . /
Maintained for me a saving intercourse /
With my true self; . . . / She in the midst of
all, preserved me still / A Poet . . .' (*Prelude* x).

Her *Grasmere Journal* was a direct stimulus and inspiration to him for such poems as
'Beggars', 'Daffodils', and 'The Leech-
Gatherer'. Walking together by day, reading and talking at night, worrying over their
beloved Coleridge, copying out the many
revisions of the poems, the brother and
sister led an extraordinarily close life during
Wordsworth's most intensely creative
period. But the *Journal* is immortal in its own
right. it is precious not only for its amazingly
vivid descriptions of light, cloud, lakewater
and wild flowers on the hillside, but also as a
valuable source of social history. Dorothy
shared her brother's sympathetic interest in
the personal lives of the poor, so we learn
much more from her than from a Parson
Woodforde about the resilient vitality of an

old beggar or the tragic past of a woman
vagrant. Her *Collected Letters* also contain
much to interest a student of English
Romanticism. [SO]

The Journals of D.W., ed. E. de Sélincourt (2 vols.,
1941); *The Early Letters of D. and W. W.*,
1787–1805, ed. E. de Sélincourt (1935; revised
C. L. Shaver, 1966); *Home at Grasmere*, ed.
Colette Clark (1960).
E. de Sélincourt, *D.W.* (1933).

Wordsworth, William (1770–1850). Poet.
Born in Cumberland, Wordsworth went to
Hawkshead Grammar School, where he
was allowed considerable freedom to roam
the countryside and come close to the life of
country people. He went to Cambridge in
1787, and was in France in 1790, the year
after the fall of the Bastille. He was profoundly influenced by the French Revolution, and returned to France, where his
affair with Annette Vallon produced a child
but no marriage. Wordsworth was later tormented by guilt and confusion, increased by
the ensuing war between France and
England, which shook his political convictions. These feelings are at the root of much
of his poetry. With his sister Dorothy, who
was very close to him, Wordsworth settled
in Dorset. At this time he began his long and
intimate association with Coleridge, and in
1798 they published *Lyrical Ballads*, which
included Coleridge's 'Ancient Mariner' and
Wordsworth's 'Tintern Abbey', a meditative poem in which he relates his response to
nature to his past and present sensibilities,
as well as a number of lyrics and verse
anecdotes. This volume announced a
radically new approach to the writing of
poetry, which, although Wordsworth is
often considered to be the father of the
Romantic movement, bears little relation to
what is conventionally termed Romantic.
In the preface to the second edition (1800)
Wordsworth stated his belief that neither
the language nor the content of poetry
should be stylized or elaborate and that the
value of the poet was his ability to feel and
express the relation between man and
nature. In his own poetry this was worked
out in the calm remembrance of tumultuous
experiences, which resulted in drawing
from this discrepancy a resolution that
yielded universal perceptions of humanity
and the natural world.
In 1799 Wordsworth and Dorothy
returned to the Lake District to live in Dove

Cottage, Grasmere. Coleridge also settled in the district. Three years later Wordsworth married Mary Hutchinson. A long-drawn-out quarrel with Coleridge and a decline in Dorothy's health disturbed the security that came with middle age. His reputation had grown, and in 1813 he was appointed Stamp Distributor, a sinecure that guaranteed him an income while he wrote. He became Poet Laureate in 1843. His poetry is generally considered to have declined after 1807, when *Poems in Two Volumes* was published.

At his best he wrote with a power that came from his fresh clarity of diction, and from a moving directness in his grappling with experience. Some of his early ballads are marred by the inappropriate use of an essentially simple and narrative form which could not easily accommodate the compound of description and moral message that Wordsworth was presenting. But at times his simple statements of elemental emotions, as in 'The Idiot Boy', were startling in their effect. But he was more successful in poems such as 'Michael' (1800) or 'The Old Cumberland Beggar' (1800), both poems rooted in his sympathetic experience of the intrinsic strength of country people, where the more solemn rhythm and the language that is direct and unadorned without the bareness of some earlier poems lends a more measured and thoughtful tone to the writing. The result is both more intense and more suggestive. But even here there is an intrusive strain of moral comment, assumptions about the essential goodness of humility and resignation which disturb the poetical demonstration of the qualities, that indicates the vein of his later poetry in which language, rhyme and phrasing become heavy and distanced from experience. His sonnets and lyrical recollections in tranquillity are probably his best-known poems – 'Composed upon Westminster Bridge', 'The Solitary Reaper', 'I Wandered Lonely as a Cloud', all published in the 1807 volumes. They illuminate moments of particular perception with a general sense of universal meaning, while his famous ode, 'Intimations of Immortality from Recollections of Early Childhood' (1807), presents both an explanation and a representation of the balance of experience and reflection. This is a fuller and more directed treatment of the 'Tintern Abbey' theme. Wordsworth traces his developing personality and understanding from earliest childhood and draws from the relations to the natural world fundamental human truths, 'thoughts that do often lie too deep for tears'.

Wordsworth's long autobiographical poem, *The Prelude* (ed. E. de Sélincourt, 1928; revised H. Darbishire, 1959), often considered his masterpiece, was not published until after his death. He had begun it in 1798 and had revised it continually throughout his life. It had been intended as an introduction to a long philosophical poem called *The Recluse*, of which only one part, *The Excursion*, was completed. In *The Prelude* there are passages of sustained intensity and excitement, particularly in Book I, describing his childhood, which show Wordsworth at his best. Although much of the linking narrative is not on such an inspired level, the rhythmic energy and the variety of incidents and states of mind hold the reader's interest.

Wordsworth's critical writings are important documents in the history of critical thought. His preface to the second edition of *Lyrical Ballads* (1800) contains his famous account of the nature of poetry which he derives from his view of the psychology of the poet and the process of poetic composition. The poet is 'a man speaking to men', but a man 'endowed with more lively sensibility, more enthusiasm and tenderness, who has a greater knowledge of human nature, and a more comprehensive soul' than ordinary people. The poet also is particularly 'affected . . . by absent things as if they were present'. Wordsworth's view that the mind of man had because of its very structure a deep relationship with the forces at work in the world of external nature, and that those forces in the last analysis represented 'joy', gave him his particular kind of optimism in observing and recording both human and natural phenomena. It was his development of this view that sustained him after the collapse of his earlier political idealism as a result of his disillusion with rationalistic radicalism and with the course of the French Revolution. But the view, which nourished some of his best poetry, was based on moments of vision which rarely recurred after 1805. In his later years he became conservative and conventional and turned to a rhetorical moral poetry which only occasionally has real poetic power. [JRC]

Poetical Works, ed. E. de Sélincourt and H. Darbishire (5 vols., 1940–9); *The Letters of W. and Dorothy W.*, ed. E. de Selincourt

(6 vols., 1935–9; vol. 1 revised C. L. Shaver, 1966); *Selected Poems*, ed. D. Davie (1962).

G. M. Harper, *W.W.: His Life, Works and Influence* (2 vols., 1916, revised edn, 1929); E. C. Batho, *The Later W.* (1933); N. P. Stallknecht, *Strange Seas of Thought* (1945); H. Darbishire, *The Poet W.* (1950); H. M. Margoliouth, *W. and Coleridge* (1953); F. Bateson, *W.* (1956); J. Danby, *The Simple W.* (1960); C. Clarke, *Romantic Paradox* (1962).

Wotton, Sir Henry (1568–1639). Poet. Educated at Winchester and Oxford, he was a diplomat and the friend of Donne and Izaac ◊ Walton. He became Provost of Eton in 1624, in which year he published *Elements of Architecture*. He planned to write the life of Donne, a task later performed by Walton, whose memoir of Wotton prefaced *Reliquiae Wottonianae*, a posthumous collection of poems and other works, in 1651. His famous poems were 'Character of a Happy Life' and 'You Meaner Beauties of the Night', a lyric on the Queen of Bohemia. [MJ]

Poems, ed. J. Hannah (1845); *Life and Letters*, ed. L. P. Smith (2 vols., 1907).

A. W. Fox, *Book of Bachelors* (1899); Douglas Bush, *English Literature in the Earlier Seventeenth* Century (revised edn, 1962).

Wren, P(ercival) C(hristopher) (1885–1941). Novelist. He was born in Devonshire and educated at Oxford, after which he worked his way round the world as schoolmaster, journalist, farm-hand and soldier, etc., serving in both the British Army and the French Foreign Legion. For ten years he lived in India and during the First World War he was an officer in the Indian forces in East Africa. Afterwards he settled in London, where he looked and played the part of the retired officer, tall, erect, monocled. He wrote a large number of novels, beginning before the war with *Dew and Mildew* (1912) and *Snake and Sword* (1914), but he hit a winning streak in the twenties with his romantic adventure stories about the Foreign Legion: *Beau Geste* (1924), *Beau Sabreur* (1926), *Beau Ideal* (1928) and *Good Gestes* (1929). He continued writing his tales of action and romance until his death; later novels include *Valiant Dust* (1932) and *Fort in the Jungle* (1936). [JM]

Wright, Judith (1915–). Australian poet. Born near Armidale, New South Wales, she spent much of her childhood on her family's sheep station. Her interest in her pioneering ancestry can be seen in an historical memoir, *The Generations of Men* (1959), as well as in her poetic use of Australia's traditions and landscape. After graduating from Sydney University, she spent a year in Europe. She is married to the philosopher, J. P. McKinney. Most of her poetry has been written at Tamborine, in the mountains of Southern Queensland. She has written biographical and critical studies of Shaw ◊ Neilson and Henry ◊ Lawson.

Wright's first book, *The Moving Image* (1946), begins her persistent poetic search for something steady and reliable in a world that obstructs its discovery. The 'moving image' is Time. In *Woman to Man* (1949), her best single volume, the search centres on love. Strong intelligence is brought to work on feminine experience. *The Gateway* (1953) takes the search further into metaphysics and, with *The Two Fires* (1955), points the way of her later poetry. In 1956 she edited *A Book of Australian Verse* for the Oxford University Press. She is a fine visual imagist and an accomplished myth-maker. The deftness with which she draws simple objects or experiences towards symbol by the accumulation of associations raises her to a high level among contemporary lyric poets. A selection of her poems appears in *Five Senses* (1964), and later poems in *The Other Half* (1966). [PT]

W. Scott, *Focus on J.W.* (1967); V. Buckley, 'The Poetry of J.W.', *Essays in Poetry, Mainly Australian* (1957); T. Inglis Moore, 'The Quest of J.W.', *Meanjin*, XVII, 3 (Spring, 1958).

Wulfstan (d. 1023). Homilist. He was Archbishop of York from 1002 until his death, and in 1002–16 also held the see of Worcester. 53 homilies in the Bodleian manuscript, Junius 99, are described as *Sermones Lupi* (his Latin nickname) but only 4 are indisputably his. He held office during the worst ravages of the Danes, and it is fitting that his famous *Sermo Lupi ad Anglos* (ed. D. Whitelock, 1939) should dwell with vehemence on the evils of the times and the imminence of Judgement Day. This is by far the most forceful prose in Old English, composed by a master of oratory using all the devices of rhyme, assonance and alliteration. It is likely that we have the text of the homily (and perhaps of some of the others in the collection) exactly as it was delivered. [AG]

The Homilies, ed. D. Bethurum (1957).

R. W. Chambers, *On the Continuity of English Prose* (1932); A. McIntosh, 'W.'s Prose', in *Proceedings of the British Academy*, XXXV (1949); D. Bethurum, 'W.', in *Continuations and Beginnings: Studies in Old English Literature* (1966).

Wyatt, Sir Thomas (1503–42). Poet and courtier. Born at Allington Castle in Kent, after studying at St John's College, Cambridge he married at 17, but separated from his wife after a few years. After holding a number of court appointments he was sent on a diplomatic mission to France in 1526, and then to Italy. At some point between 1526 and 1532 he became involved with Anne Boleyn, and a contemporary report which seems fairly trustworthy alleges that he warned the King of this liaison when the latter began to woo Anne. At all events Wyatt was out of the country from 1528 to 1532, filling the office of marshal of Calais. In 1532 Henry VIII was married to Anne. Wyatt returned to England and was appointed Justice of the Peace in Essex. He was briefly imprisoned for brawling (1534).

When Anne's alleged paramours, and Anne herself, were arrested in 1536, Wyatt too was imprisoned, though on a different charge and not at the King's instance. From his cell window he witnessed the execution of the paramours; the horror of the event is recorded in one of his lyrics ('Who lyst his welthe and eas retayne'). However, no charges were pressed, and he was released, to occupy positions of trust once again. In 1537 he was sent to Spain as ambassador, and when he returned in 1539 he was soon off on further diplomatic missions to the continent. But in 1540 his patron Thomas Cromwell was executed and Wyatt was accused by his old enemy, Bishop Bonner, of various crimes ranging from treason to immorality. He defended himself against these charges with such vigour that he was released, on condition that he took his wife back. (He was living with Elizabeth Darrell, one of the Queen's maids of honour.) Restored to favour, and on the point of rising to even higher office, Wyatt died of a fever in 1542.

Wyatt's literary output consists of a prose translation from Plutarch (*Quyete of Mynde*, written 1527), sonnets, lyrics, satires, and some longer verse-translations, including the *Penitential Psalms*. None of his verse was published in his lifetime, but much of it was printed (in a somewhat altered form) by ◊ Tottel, in his *Songes and Sonets* (1557), better known as *Tottel's Miscellany*. The Elizabethans honoured him together with ◊ Surrey, the other major contributor to Tottel, but later ages found Surrey's smoother verse more acceptable. For a long time Wyatt was praised as an innovator; today he is recognized as a good and perhaps great poet.

Before we can judge Wyatt's achievement we have to be sure we know how to read his verse. Many of his lyrics present no problem: they are written in metres that are firmly adhered to from stanza to stanza, and we read them as we would any Elizabethan lyric. But this is not true of all the lyrics, while the great majority of the sonnets are quite strikingly 'irregular' in metre. Until quite recently it was thought that these poems in 'irregular' metre were the result of carelessness, lack of polish, or the sheer inability to write 'iambic pentameter' lines. In view of Wyatt's great skill in handling the metres of his strictly metrical lyrics, these views are implausible, and most modern critics find that a possible way of reading the 'irregular' poems is to give each line the rhythm demanded by sense and syntax. There are theoretical disagreements about the way these lines 'work' for the reader, and about the metrical principles underlying Wyatt's practice, but it seems to be generally agreed that, provided we do not expect successive lines to have the same metrical pattern, the poems 'work' rhythmically.

Wyatt's lines (and this is true of 'strict metre' poems as well as 'irregular line' ones) are generally composed of phrases and clauses of obvious grammatical structure. Even if we do not know precisely what they are about we can generally tell at once what stresses, phrases and intonation patterns they require. It is this which accounts for the impression of rhythmic vitality and for the 'personal voice' which readers feel they can hear in his lines.

The subject matter of the lyrics is love – unrequited, frustrated or betrayed. Most of the sonnets are translations or imitations from Petrarch and his followers: they, too, deal mainly with the pains of love. What gives these poems their interest is the intensity with which the poet speaks of his feelings, and the subtlety with which he modulates his tone from stanza to stanza and from line to line. In the lyrics he makes use of the most hackneyed metaphors, the most obvious clichés of love: but he uses them in such a way as to bring them to life. He does not show off his ingenuity (though ingenuity there is): we notice above all the seriousness and the passion. Wyatt is an exceedingly economical poet: descriptions are minimal (one telling detail is enough), narration is hinted at; metaphors are hardly stated in full.

In the sonnets, whether he is translating or imitating, Wyatt is committed by his Italian models to rather more elaborate figures of speech. The effect is, sometimes, a loss of force and immediacy. But the best of the sonnets (e.g. 'My galey charged with forgetfulness', 'Whoso list to hunt', 'Farewell Love') have all the qualities of his best lyrics, with an additional richness. The critics have, on the whole, underrated them.

Wyatt's *Satires* are conversational, relaxed pieces of writing. The first is a translation from Alamanni, the other two are apparently original. The *Penitential Psalmes* (written perhaps after the fall of Cromwell) are translated from an Italian paraphrase (with linking passages) by Aretino; they are competent, and sometimes beautiful, but they lack the economy and force of his best work.

All the earlier editions of Wyatt were based on Tottel; however, in 1816 Nott published an edition based on two manuscripts contemporary with the poet, and it was seen for the first time that Tottel or his editor had 'smoothed' Wyatt's lines in many instances. The manuscripts in question – Egerton MS 2711 and Devonshire MS Addit. 17492 – have high textual authority, particularly the Egerton MS, which contains corrections and complete poems in Wyatt's own hand. There are several other 16th-century manuscripts containing poems by Wyatt, including the Blage MS (poems from this were edited by Kenneth Muir: *Sir Thomas Wyatt and His Circle: Unpublished Poems*, 1961). The text of the Egerton MS was printed by Flügel in *Anglia* (1896, 1897). A. K. Foxwell (1913) was the first editor to realize that the Egerton MS had the highest authority. Unfortunately the biographical material in her edition is fanciful and the critical comment eccentric. It has in any case been superseded by Kenneth Muir's edition (1949; reissued 1963 with additional matter). [T G]

K. Muir, *Life and Letters of Sir T.W.* (1963); S. Baldi, *La poesia di Sir T.W.* (Florence, 1953) (for W.'s Italian sources); P. Thomson, *Sir T.W. and His Background* (1964); J. Stevens,

Music and Poetry in the Early Tudor Court (1961); H. A. Mason, *Humanism and Poetry in the Early Tudor Period* (1959) (for the *Psalms*); D. W. Harding, *Pelican Guide to English Literature*, i (1954); C. S. Lewis, *English Literature in the Sixteenth Century* (1954); D. W. Harding, *Scrutiny* (December 1946)(on metre); J. Thompson, *The Founding of English Metre* (1961); E. M. W. Tillyard, *Sir T.W.: A Selection and a Study* (1929); E. K. Chambers, *Sir T.W. and Some Collected Studies* (1933) (the 2 works largely responsible for the modern revival of W.).

Wycherley, William (1640–1716). Dramatist. A member of the Inner Temple, he was educated in France and, briefly, at Oxford, and had his first play, *Love in a Wood, or St James's Park*, acted in 1671. His robust plays are among the most famous of Restoration comedies and are sardonic, sometimes savage, pictures of a licentious and hedonistic London society. They include *The Gentleman Dancing Master* (1672), the entertaining and highly indecent *The Country Wife* (1675), and *The Plain Dealer* (1676), his adaptation of Molière's *Le misanthrope*. A lesser artist than Molière, he was a more serious critic of society than either of his contemporaries, ◊ Etherege and ◊ Congreve, and his comedies insist on the selfishness and animality of the characters, and on the realities behind the polished surface of Restoration civility. [M J]

Complete Plays, ed. G. Weales (1967).
W. Connely, *Brawny W.* (New York, 1930); R. Zimbardo, *W.'s Drama: A Link in the Development of English Satire* (1965); B. Dobrée, *Restoration Comedy* (1924); T. H. Fujimura, *The Restoration Comedy of Wit* (1952); N. N. Holland, *The First Modern Comedies* (1959).

Wyclif or **Wiclif** or **Wycliffe, John** (c. 1328–84). Priest and reformer. A Yorkshireman, Wyclif was educated at Oxford, and became Master of Balliol in 1360, obtaining the degree of Doctor of Theology in 1370. Two years later, he went to Bruges as Ambassador to the Papal delegates, and soon afterwards accepted the living of Lutterworth in Leicestershire, with which he is always associated. He played an important role as reformer and precursor of the Reformation and the same ideals led him to the use of English as a teaching medium. The precise extent of his own contribution to the *Lollard Bible* (translated from the Vulgate Latin into English) is still to be determined, though the inspiration is surely his. Despite its importance, however, it is not a literary success, but heavy, mechanical and awkward. Wyclif's own sermons have more clarity and life, though they owe more to his burning zeal than to his care for the art of composition. (◊ Bible.) [A G]

W.'s *English Works*, ed. F. D. Matthew (1880); *The W. Bible*, ed. J. Forshall and F. Madden (1850); *W. Select English Writings*, ed. H. E. Winn (1929).

M. Deanesley, *The Lollard Bible* (1920); G. Leff, 'W.: The Path to Dissent', *Proceedings of the British Academy*, 52 (1966); K. B. MacFarlane, *J.W. and the Beginnings of English Nonconformity* (1952); H. B. Workman, *J.W.* (1926).

Wynne, Ellis (1671–1734). Welsh cleric and prose writer. Born at Y Lasynys near Harlech, Merioneth, of a gentle family, he was educated at Jesus College, Oxford. He entered the Church in 1704 and obtained the living of Llandanwg (with Llanbedr), and later that of Llanfair-juxta-Harlech. He was married twice. He was active in Church matters and published a translation of Jeremy ◊ Taylor's *Holy Living* (*Rheol Buchedd Sanctaidd*, 1701), and was editor of the Welsh Book of Common Prayer (1710).

In his *Rheol Buchedd Sanctaidd* Ellis Wynne was in the full succession of classical Welsh prose which had its roots in the 16th-century translations of the Bible and other religious works. These translators took themselves and their work seriously and were masters of a dignified and worthy instrument. His most famous accomplishment, and the one which gives the modern reader unalloyed enjoyment is his *Gweledigaetheu y Bardd Cwsc* ('Visions of the Sleeping Bard') (1703; ed. J. Morris-Jones, 1898). The original Spanish *Sueños* of Francisco de Quevedo had been published in 1649, and an English translation by Sir Roger L'Estrange in 1667 (4th edn, 1671). This translation was very free and easy and marked by extensive use of colloquial London English, with the locale set in England. In the same way Ellis Wynne used the colloquial Welsh of his native Merioneth and set his visions in the contemporary Wales. The book reads like a completely original work. Wynne writes from the standpoint of a staunch Churchman of the middle road between Rome and Geneva, to whom both Catholicism and Dissent were anathema. Church and State were the bulwarks of Christian civilization. Wynne lashed out at all the forces which were likely to subvert the life which he knew and loved. He was influenced too by the strong element of prognostication in Welsh literature and by the use of the dream as a literary form. He must be set against the social background of the late 17th century for us to appreciate him fully as a satirist and a critic of social conditions, and to understand his conservatism and intolerance. But the great glory of *Bardd Cwsc* is its language – a skilful blend of the literary prose tradition and current colloquial speech, muscular, often coarse and indelicate, but vibrant with life, which sweeps the reader along in a series of word pictures of 18th-century types from the squire with his pedigree rolls to the strumpet with all her paraphernalia of perfumes and cosmetics. [M R]

Rheol Buchedd Sanctaidd (1701; reprinted 1928).

Wyntoun, Andrew of (1350?–1420?). Scots verse chronicler. A canon of St Andrews and Prior of St Serf's Inch, Loch Leven, from 1395, Wyntoun compiled a doggerel history of Scotland from the Creation to 1408. Like similar works it is reliable for its own period but not for the earlier one; significantly, however, Wyntoun does not mention the forty-four fabulous kings introduced by later and more imaginative chroniclers. The story of Macbeth, which reached Shakespeare through Hector ◊ Boece and ◊ Holinshed, first appeared in Wyntoun's *Original Chronicle* (ed. F. J. Amours, S T S, 6 vols., 1903–14). [A I]

Y

Yeats, William Butler (1865–1939). Irish poet, dramatist, autobiographer, critic, and occult philosopher. He was of Irish Protestant background, his father, John Butler Yeats, being a well-known artist, his mother's family merchants at Sligo on the Irish west coast. Yeats spent his early childhood between Dublin and Sligo but when he was 9 his parents moved to London. At 19 he attended an art school in Dublin but his central interest was already in writing. At 21, Yeats published his first book, *Mosada*, and then returned to London, where he helped to found the Rhymers' Club, a group of 'decadent' poets which included Ernest ◊ Dowson and Lionel ◊ Johnson. Interested in Far Eastern religion and in magic, Yeats became a disciple of Madame Blavastsky and later joined the Hermetic Students of the Golden Dawn. The interest in magic led him to an interest in Blake's symbolism. His love, never to be physically fulfilled, for a beautiful Irish nationalist, Maud Gonne, led him to take a prominent part in the cultural movement called the Celtic Revival, though he was never politically an active nationalist. Throughout the 1890s he published many volumes of poems and of prose, the verse decorative, symbolist in manner, and much concerned, like the prose, with Irish myth and folklore. Under the patronage of Lady Gregory, he settled in Ireland, gave himself up to the management of the Abbey Theatre (see below). During the first decade and a half of this century he had been hardening and chastening his early ornate style, and concerning himself in poetry less with dreams and more with political and psychological realities. The change is crystallized in the volume first published in 1914, *Responsibilities*, and in the tragic and ironic poem on the Irish Easter Rebellion, *Easter*, 1916.

In his early fifties, Yeats married a wife much younger than himself, Georgie Hyde-Lees. With her encouragement, he wrote his famous book of occult philosophy, *A Vision* (privately 1925; 1961), which works out in detail a theory, rather like Spengler's, of cyclical recurrences in history. The idea

of history as a tragic and elaborate recurrent dance, of men as spirits playing the same roles repeatedly in an endless play, dominate his later poetry. He felt that a Christian and democratic cycle of history was at an an end, and a pagan and aristocratic cycle was about to begin. The later poems are also very realistically concerned with sexual passion and with the tension between what Yeats called 'heart' and 'soul', the world of bodily desire and that of spiritual aspiration. The volumes of 1928 and 1929, *The Tower* and *The Winding Stair*, embodying these ideas and also memories of love and friendship and a generous response, but one tinged with doubt and irony, to the tragic violence of Irish history, are generally thought the peak of his achievement. He was writing poetry, prose, and drama of very high quality, however, almost up to the time of his death. He died in France, and his body was not brought home to Ireland till 1948. His tombstone in the graveyard of his grandfather's parish church at Sligo bears the epitaph he composed for himself: 'Cast a cold eye/On life, on death:/Horseman, pass by!'

He had enjoyed many honours in his later years, the Nobel Prize, and membership of the Irish Senate. On his death his pre-eminent greatness was saluted in verse by W. H. Auden and in prose by T. S. Eliot. A whole library of exposition and appreciation of Yeats by such scholars as Richard Ellmann, Thomas Parkinson, F. A. C. Wilson, and others, as well as many shorter critical studies, has been written about Yeats since his death. He is generally accepted as the greatest poet writing in the English language of his period.

Broadly speaking, it could be said that Yeats, who was writing excellent poetry continually for more than fifty years, moved from a lyrical, feminine way of writing to one which was masculine and dramatic, from dreams to reality, and from poetry of an extremely and consciously 'literary' kind to poetry immersed in, and emerging from, his response to his personal life and the political strivings of Ireland in his time. He was broadly, all through, a poet in the

Romantic tradition, but his later poetry incorporates a conceptual wit he learned from Donne and a verbal poise and decorum he learned from Irish Augustan writers like Swift and Goldsmith. Critics are not agreed on how far his more fantastic 'magical' ideas helped, how far hindered his poetry, how deep his religions and metaphysical insights were, or how seriously one should take his cult of aristocracy. They are agreed on his range of mind, his honesty and courage in making poetry of his inner struggles, and on his mastery of style and rhetoric. [G S F]

Yeats is also important as a dramatist. Although *Mosada*, his first published work, was a verse drama his early plays, vague in rhythm and imagery and technically imperfect, were rarely performed. Nevertheless, he nursed a growing ambition to restore poetic drama to popularity and, believing that Ireland would be peculiarly receptive to such an attempt, he founded in 1899 the Irish Literary Theatre with Lady Gregory and Edward Martyn. Martyn, an Ibsenite, soon left the project while Yeats became increasingly worried about the lack of Irish actors. Then, in 1902, he discovered a troupe of Dublin amateurs led by the Fay brothers and amalgamated with them to form the Irish National Theatre Company. This group became the Abbey Theatre Company when, in 1904, Miss A. E. Horniman bought and fitted out a small theatre on its behalf.

During the early years of the Abbey Yeats continued to work within a traditional form, although watching his plays in performance taught him to write more colloquial and sinewy verse and to improve his technique. Discontented with the commercialism of the contemporary theatre he and the Fays developed an 'Abbey style' of acting whereby the actors used no irrelevant movement and were trained to give verse its full rhythmic value. Scenery and costumes were kept unelaborate and undistracting. Yeats drew most of his themes from Irish history and legend but except for the powerfully nationalistic *Cathleen ni Houlihan* his work was not generally popular. His first play to be produced in Ireland, *The Countess Cathleen*, was denounced as heresy and the public found much that he wrote too far removed from life. The production of Synge's plays, especially that of *The Playboy of the Western World* in 1907, added new bitterness to the attacks on the

theatre, and this, together with the fact that Irish audiences obviously preferred realistic to poetic drama, led to his disillusionment with the Abbey.

No longer hoping for popular success, he turned in 1916 to what he described as an 'aristocratic form' – the Nō drama of Japan, which appealed to him on account of its simplicity, its traditional, almost ritualistic manner, and its passionate and symbolic subject matter. His first Nō play, *At the Hawk's Well*, approximates most closely to the Japanese model, which he thereafter modified to his own purposes. As a young man he had written of the need to get an audience into a religious mood and it can be argued that his experiments, especially with the Nō, had that end. Many of his later plays have a strong liturgical element, making much use of mime, the dance, masks and the incantatory effect of chorus. Ideologically, too, they explore neo-platonic themes and ideas mooted in *A Vision*. It is too early to say whether these plays will have any lasting effect on the development of drama but in his attempts to create a viable form for poetry on the modern stage Yeats produced works which, although strange when first seen, have, even then, great intensity and beauty. [J K]

Collected Poems (1950; variorum edn, ed. P. Allt and R. K. Alspach, 1957); *Collected Plays* (1952; collected edn, ed. R. K. and C. C. Alspach, 1966); *Essays and Introductions* (1961); *Explorations* (1962); *Autobiographies* (1955); *Letters*, ed. A. Wade (1954).
A. N. Jeffares, *A Commentary on the Collected Poems of W.B.Y.* (1968); J. Hone, *W.B.Y. 1865–1939* (1962); R. Ellmann, *Y., the Man and the Masks* (1948); N. Jeffares, *W.B.Y., Man and Poet* (1949); F. A. C. Wilson, *W.B.Y. and Tradition* (1958); ed. J. Hall and M. Steinmann, *The Permanence of Y.* (1950); ed. A. N. Jeffares and K. G. W. Cross, *In Excited Reverie* (1965).

'Yellow Book'. A quarterly, founded and published by John Lane of The Bodley Head. The *Yellow Book* first appeared in 1894 and 13 volumes came out before its demise in 1897. Its literary editor was an American author, Henry Harland (who had written novels under the name of Sydney Luska), while Aubrey Beardsley was the artistic editor (until the fourth number, after which he was forced to withdraw owing to public demands that his work be suppressed). The *Yellow Book* was an indiscriminate mixture of reviews, fiction and poetry, and some of the most colourful writing of the nineties appeared there. Among the writers who contributed to it were Lionel Johnson, Ernest Dowson, Max Beerbohm, Baron Corvo, Arnold Bennett, H. G. Wells, George Saintsbury, Henry James, Kenneth Graham, Arthur Symons, Edmund Gosse and John Buchan. [NL]

J. Lewis May, *John Lane and the Nineties* (1936); K. L. Mix, *A Study in Yellow* (1960).

Yonge, Charlotte Mary (1823–1901). Novelist and children's writer. Born near Winchester, the daughter of a country gentleman, who educated her at home. Under the influence of ◊ Keble, a neighbouring parson and one of the founders of the ◊ Oxford Movement, she put forward high Anglican views in her fiction (rather as Mrs ◊ Oliphant served the Dissenters). In the book which brought her fame, *The Heir of Redclyffe* (1853), she deals with that favourite Victorian situation: a wrong (concerning property) and its expiation. *The Daisy Chain* (1856) is more religious in tone. She wrote a number of historical romances (more romance than history) of which *The Prince and the Page* (1865) and *The Dove in the Eagle's Nest* (1866) are the best. She was the author of more than 150 books, and edited the *Monthly Packet* from 1851 to 1898, in which appeared her 'Cameos from English History'. She also wrote a *Life of Hannah More* (1888). [AR]

Q. D. Leavis, 'C.Y. and Christian Discrimination', *Scrutiny*, XII (1944); M. Mare and A. C. Percival, *Victorian Best-Seller: The World of C.Y.* (1948); G. Battiscombe and M. Laski, *A Chaplet for C.Y.* (1965) (bibliography); K. Tillotson, 'The Heir of Radclyffe', in *Mid-Victorian Studies* (1965).

York Cycle. ◊ Miracle Plays.

Young, Andrew (John) (1885–). Clergyman, poet and prose writer on flowers and topography. He was born in Scotland in 1885 and educated at the Royal High School, Edinburgh, and at Edinburgh University. He is Vicar of Stonegate in Sussex and since 1948 has been a Canon of Chichester Cathedral. He is best known for his shorter poems, which combine an extraordinarily vivid observation of nature with extreme terseness and elegance of form and a delightful ingenuity in the use of the metaphysical conceit. A long poem, an imaginary description of the experiences of the soul immediately after death, was published first in 1952 as *Into Hades* and then, in a revised and improved and enlarged version in 1958, as *Out of The World and Back*. It is an extremely impressive work, combining homeliness and exactness of diction and detail with a genuinely visionary quality. Canon Young has also written a number of very pleasant prose books on wild flowers and topography. He is an Hon. LL.D. of Edinburgh University (1961) and a Fellow of the Royal Society of Literature. [GSF]

A Prospect of Flowers (1945); *A Retrospect of Flowers* (1950); *Collected Poems* (1950); *A Prospect of Britain* (1956); *The Collected Poems* (1960).
Ed. L. Clark, *A.Y.: Prospect of a Poet* (1956).

Young, Arthur (1741–1820). Travel writer and agricultural theorist. Born in London, the son of a clergyman from Suffolk, in his early years he was an unsuccessful farmer and later an Irish land-agent. His fame rests on his writing on agriculture, which is based on close, knowledgeable observation and a grasp of social and political realities. He published his views in 3 *Tours* through the South, North and East of England (1768–70); in a *Tour in Ireland* (1780); and in the *Annals of Agriculture* (45 vols., 1784–1809). His various gifts produced one work of the greatest historical interest in his *Travels in France* (1792; ed. C. Maxwell, 1929). This record of his three journeys in France, 1787–90, is a devastating indictment of the *ancien régime*, and was popular at the time as being a powerful if oblique defence of the Revolution. Young wrote several other works of technical interest on agriculture and 'political arithmetic', and became Secretary of the new Board of Agriculture (1793). For the last decade of his life he was blind. He was a member of the ◊ Burney circle and is mentioned by Fanny Burney in her letters and *Diary*. [AR]

Autobiography, ed. M. Betham-Edwards (1898).
A. Defries, *Sheep and Turnips: Being the Life of Y.* (1938).

Young, Douglas Cuthbert Colquhoun (1913–). Scots poet and nationalist. A native of Tayport, he was educated in Edinburgh and at St Andrews and Oxford Universities; he taught Greek at Aberdeen University, was imprisoned in 1942 and 1944 for refusing to accept call-up papers issued by what he regarded as an alien government, and later lectured in classics in the Dundee college of St Andrews University. Young has edited the Saltire Modern Poets (with J. M. Lindsay, from 1947) and a selection of *Scottish Verse 1851–1951* (1952). His original poems and translations in Scots and other languages are collected in *Auntran Blads* (1943) and *A Braird o' Thristles* (1947). Young's most substantial achievement is 'The Kirkyaird by the Sea', a Scots rendering of Valéry's 'Le cimetière marin' included in his 1947 volume; beside this his later translations from Aristophanes (*The Puddocks*, 1957; *The Burdies,* 1959) appear as *divertissements*, and his original work as an effort of the will and the intellect rather than as an unforced creative response to his experience. [AI]

Young, Edward (1683–1765). Poet. Son of the Dean of Salisbury, he was educated at Winchester, and New College and Corpus Christi, Oxford (Bachelor of Civil Law, 1714; Doctor, 1719). Appearing early as a writer and poet, he sought unsuccessfully by this means some professional advancement as 'a ready celebrator'. He took orders in 1727, and was appointed a Royal Chaplain and Rector of Welwyn, but surprisingly received no further preferment in the Church despite his considerable fame as a writer. He was the author of many more or less feeble lyric poems, now never read. He also wrote tragedies of passion commonly ending in suicides, among them *Busiris* (1719) and *The Revenge* (1721), both rather successful on the stage. He wrote a popular series of 7 satires, *The Universal Passion: The Love of Fame* (1725–8), which are competent and in places lively, and would be better known but for the incomparably greater work of Pope. Young's fame as a poet rests on the influential *The Complaint, or Night Thoughts on Life, Death and Immortality* (1742–4), an original series of pieces in blank verse, which appealed to one side of the 18th-century reader, an interest in the possibilities of combining moralizing, passion, sorrow, melancholy and the sublime. This poem kept its place as a classic well into the 19th century (◊ Graveyard School). Young was also the author of the influential essay *Conjectures on Original Composition* (in a letter to Richardson) (1759; ed. E. Morley, 1918), which shows the shift of emphasis in 18th-century criticism away from discussion of the 'kinds', to the discussion of the artist and the nature of 'genius'. [AR]

Johnson, *Lives of the Poets*; H. C. Shelley, *Life and Letters of E.Y.* (1914); M. Bailey, 'E.Y.', in *The Age of Johnson: Essays Presented to C. B. Tinker* (New Haven, N.J., 1949).

Z

Zangwill, Israel (1864–1926). Novelist and Zionist. Born in London, the eldest son of a refugee from Russia, he was educated in Bristol and at the Jews' Free School at Spitalfields, London, and at London University. He was a schoolteacher for a few years but gave this up for journalism. His first fiction was a fantasy, *The Premier and the Painter* (1888), and he published short stories in a humour journal, *Ariel*, which he edited. In 1892 his best-known work, *Children of the Ghetto*, written for the Jewish Publication Society of America, appeared. This partly autobiographical work was the forerunner of several such Jewish novels; *Ghetto Tragedies* (1893) and *Dreamers of the Ghetto* (1898) are among them. Zangwill also published verse, and several plays of which *The Melting Pot*, a 'message' play about Jewish immigrants in America, was very successful. He was an active Zionist, and founded the Jewish Territorial Organisation. [AR]

J. Leftwich, *I.Z.* (1957); M. Wohlgelerther, *I.Z.: A Study* (Columbia U.P., 1964).

SELECT LIST OF BIBLIOGRAPHICAL, HISTORICAL AND BACKGROUND WORKS

BIBLIOGRAPHIES

The Cambridge Bibliography of English Literature, ed. F. W. Bateson (4 vols., 1940); *Supplement*, ed. G. Watson (1957); *Concise Cambridge Bibliography of English Literature*, ed. G. Watson (1958). (The whole work is in process of being revised and brought up to date, ed. G. Watson. Volume 3 of the revised edition appeared in 1969.)

F. W. Bateson, *A Guide to English Literature* (1965).

Bibliographies appended to the individual volumes of *The Oxford History of English Literature* (see below).

LITERARY HISTORIES

A. C. Baugh et al., *A Literary History of England* (revised edn, New York, 1967)

Hardin Craig et al., *A History of English Literature* (New York, 1950)

D. Daiches, *A Critical History of English Literature* (2 vols., 1960)

B. Dobrée, ed., *Introductions to English Literature*, includes the following volumes:
  E. C. Batho and B. Dobrée, *The Victorians and After* (revised edn, 1950)
  D. Daiches, *The Present Age* (1958)
  H. V. D. Dyson and J. Butt, *Augustans and Romantics* (revised edn, 1950)
  V. de S. Pinto, *The English Renaissance* (1938)
  W. L. Renwick and H. Orton, *The Beginnings to Skelton* (revised edn, 1952)

B. Ford, ed., *The Pelican Guide to English Literature* (7 vols., 1954–61)

F. P. Wilson, Bonamy Dobrée and Norman Davis, ed., *The Oxford History of English Literature*. 15 vols. are planned, of which the following have appeared:
  H. S. Bennett, *Chaucer and the Fifteenth Century* (1947)
  D. Bush, *The Earlier Seventeenth Century* (2nd edn, 1962)
  E. K. Chambers, *The Close of the Middle Ages* (1945)
  B. Dobrée, *The Early Eighteenth Century* (1959)
  I. Jack, *English Literature 1815–1832* (1963)
  C. S. Lewis, *English Literature in the Sixteenth Century* (excluding Drama) (1954)
  W. L. Renwick, *English Literature 1789–1815* (1963)
  J. I. M. Stewart, *Eight Modern Writers* (1963)
  J. Sutherland, *The Late Seventeenth Century* (1969)
  F. P. Wilson, *The English Drama 1485–1584* (1969)

GENRES

Drama

A. Nicoll, *British Drama* (revised edn, 1962)
  A History of English Drama 1600–1900 (6 vols., revised edn, 1952–9)

Bibliographical, Historical and Background Works

The Novel

Walter Allen, *The English Novel* (1954)
A. E. Baker, *History of the English Novel* (10 vols., 1924–39)
A. Kettle, *Introduction to the English Novel* (1952–3)
L. Stevenson, *The English Novel: A Panorama* (1960)

Poetry

W. J. Courthope, *A History of English Poetry* (6 vols., 1895–1910)
E. M. W. Tillyard, *The English Epic and Its Background* (1954)

Literary Criticism

D. Daiches, *Critical Approaches to Literature* (1956)
G. Saintsbury, *A History of English Criticism* (1911)
R. Wellek, *A History of Modern Criticism: 1750–1950* (1955 ff.)
  (4 vols. of projected 5 have been published)
W. K. Wimsatt Jr and C. Brooks, *Literary Criticism: A Short History* (New York, 1957)

SPECIAL PERIODS

Medieval

G. K. Anderson, *The Literature of the Anglo-Saxons* (Princeton, 1949)
S. Greenfield, *A Critical History of Old English Literature* (New York, 1965)
G. Kane, *Middle English Literature* (1951)
C. S. Lewis, *The Allegory of Love* (1936)
M. Schlauch, *English Mediaeval Literature and Its Social Foundations* (Warsaw, 1956)
J. E. Wells, *Manual of the Writings in Middle English, 1050-1400* (1916–45)
R. M. Wilson, *Early Middle English Literature* (1939)
C. L. Wrenn, *A Study of Old English Literature* (1967)

Renaissance

G. E. Bentley, *The Jacobean and Caroline Stage* (7 vols., 1941–68)
J. M. Berdan, *Early Tudor Poetry* (1920)
D. Bush, *Mythology and the Renaissance Tradition in English Poetry* (1932)
E. K. Chambers, *The Elizabethan Stage* (4 vols., 1923)
H. J. C. Grierson, *Cross-Currents in English Literature of the Seventeenth Century* (1929)
E. M. W. Tillyard, *The Elizabethan World Picture* (1943)
B. Willey, *The Seventeenth Century Background* (1934)
F. P. Wilson, *Elizabethan and Jacobean* (1945)

Restoration and Eighteenth Century

F. S. Boas, *An Introduction to Eighteenth Century Drama* (1953)
A. R. Humphreys, *The Augustan World: Life and Letters in Eighteenth Century England* (1954)

I. Jack, *Augustan Satire* (1952)

R. F. Jones et al., *The Seventeenth Century: Studies in the History of English Thought and Literature from Bacon to Pope* (Stanford, 1965)

A. O. Lovejoy, *Essays in the History of Ideas* (Baltimore, 1948)

J. R. Sutherland, *A Preface to Eighteenth Century Poetry* (1948)

I. Watt, *The Rise of the Novel* (1957)

B. Willey, *The Eighteenth Century Background* (1940)

The Nineteenth Century

M. H. Abrams, *The Mirror and the Lamp: Romantic Theory and the Critical Tradition* (New York, 1953)

E. Bernbaum, *Guide through the Romantic Movement* (revised edn, New York, 1948)

J. H. Buckley, *The Victorian Temper* (1951)

F. E. Faverty et al., *The Victorian Poets: A Guide to Research* (Cambridge, Mass., 1956)

G. Hough, *The Last Romantics* (1949)

W. E. Houghton, *The Victorian Frame of Mind* (New Haven, 1957)

M. Praz, *The Romantic Agony* (revised edn, 1952)

M. Sadleir, *Nineteenth Century Fiction: A Bibliographical Record* (2 vols., 1951)

L. Stevenson, ed., *Victorian Fiction: A Guide to Research* (Cambridge, Mass., 1964)

K. Tillotson, *Novels of the Eighteen-forties* (1954)

The Twentieth Century

W. Allen, *Tradition and Dream* (1964) (on the modern novel)

D. Daiches, *The Novel and the Modern World* (revised edn, Chicago, 1960)

G. S. Fraser, *The Modern Writer and His World* (revised edn, 1964)

F. R. Leavis, *New Bearings in English Poetry* (revised edn, 1950)

W. Y. Tindall, *Forces in Modern British Literature* (revised edn, New York, 1956)

IRISH LITERATURE

U. Ellis-Fermor, *The Irish Dramatic Movement* (1954)

R. Flower, *The Irish Tradition* (1947)

H. Howarth, *The Irish Writers 1880–1940* (1958)

D. Hyde, *A Literary History of Ireland*, new edn, intr. Brian Ó Cuív (1967)

B. Ó Cuív, ed., *A View of the Irish Language* (1969)

SCOTTISH LITERATURE

D. Craig, *Scottish Literature and the Scottish People* 1680–1930 (1961)

T. F. Henderson, *Scottish Vernacular Literature, A History* (1910)

J. Kinsley, ed., *Scottish Poetry: A Critical Survey* (1955)

J. H. Millar, *A Literary History of Scotland* (1903)

J. Speirs, *The Scots Literary Tradition* (new edn, 1962)

K. Wittig, *The Scottish Tradition in Literature* (1958)

Bibliographical, Historical and Background Works

COMMONWEALTH LITERATURE

E. K. Brown, *On Canadian Poetry* (Toronto, 1943)

V. Buckley, *Essays in Poetry, Mainly Australian* (1957)

C. F. Clinck, ed., *A Literary History of Canada* (Toronto, 1965)

H. M. Green, *A History of Australian Literature* (2 vols., Sydney, 1961)

R. C. Ingamells, *Handbook of Australian Literature* (Melbourne, 1949)

E. H. McCormick, *New Zealand Literature, A Survey* (1959)

E. M. Miller and F. T. Macartney, *Australian Literature* (1953)

G. M. Miller and H. Sergeant, *A Critical Survey of South African Poetry in English* (1957)

M. Nathan, *South African Literature* (1925)

V. B. Rhodenizev, *A Handbook of Canadian Literature* (Ottawa, 1930)

C. Roderick, *The Australian Novel* (Sydney, 1945)

E. M. Smith, *A History of New Zealand Fiction* (1939)

K. R. Srinivasa Iyengar, *Indian Writing in English* (1962)

UNITED STATES OF AMERICA

EDITORIAL FOREWORD

The editors have been allowed a full freedom in their selection of authors, and a word is needed about the principles of selection used and the emphasis of their interests. We have attempted to provide from our somewhat different cultural and critical standpoints, a broad coverage of the most important names in American writing from the early period of settlement through to the immediate present, including figures of historical as well as directly literary interest. We have, however, deliberately chosen to give particularly strong representation to twentieth-century writing. In this period American literature becomes markedly an international literature – and very much a *contemporary* international literature, influencing practice and attracting attention in many countries of the world. It is for this reason that we have laid special emphasis on including writers of the century and indeed of the immediate present who seem of interest, even though this has meant unequal coverage of minor figures – those of earlier periods are less fully represented (though we have attended throughout to minor figures who seem to us of cultural significance). The reader thumbing through the book may thus find in it many contemporary writers of whom he has probably not heard previously; indeed it could be read selectively through as a short guide to current developments and tendencies. Generally we have gone for liveliness rather than solemnity, and critical judgement rather than simple biographical record. So the reader might do well from time to time to check the author of an entry in the List of Contributors, since he has been encouraged to give a personal judgement.

In addition we have generally tried to suggest that American writing can be illuminated by seeing it in its cultural context. So influential American thinkers – Parrington and Veblen, William James and Marshall McLuhan, etc. – are included. So are figures of popular significance – McGuffey and Horatio Alger, Margaret Mitchell and James Whitcomb Riley, Zane Grey and Edgar Guest. There are also a small number of subject entries designed to suggest important features of American literary thought and experience – on the Connecticut Wits and the Transcendentalists, on Expatriates and the Lost Generation, on Realism, Naturalism and Veritism and on Little Magazines. Other non-author entries dealing with important publications – *The Bay Psalm Book*, *The Federalist,* etc. – are present.

We have normally followed the practice of dating works by their *first appearance,* whether in England or America. Many American works of the nineteenth century were first published in England to secure copyright advantages, just as certain colonial works appeared in London which still, despite the early appearance of American printing presses, remained as a central publishing capital. But, to avoid proliferating publishing details, we have thus diverged from the practice of the companion volumes in the series and have *not* given the place of a non-English publication *where it is American.*

The brief bibliography which concludes the section is intended to suggest where

5

the reader might discover a broad range of connections between the authors and topics of the Companion. Most of the works are well known and readable without sacrificing scholarship.

King's College, London ERIC MOTTRAM

University of East Anglia MALCOLM BRADBURY

PUBLISHER'S NOTE

Bibliographies

The bibliographies in small type which generally follow an entry are arranged as follows. The first paragraph lists editions of texts and translations of texts not already dealt with in the entry itself. The second paragraph lists critical works concerning the subject of the entry. In cases where only one paragraph occurs, it will be clear from the titles of the works listed whether they are texts or criticism.

The list of critical works is deliberately selective – further bibliographical information can usually be found in the listed works themselves.

The date of publication given is that of first publication. Thus such dates are those of publication in the U.S.A. unless the work was first published elsewhere.

Bibliographies have been compiled by the contributors of the relevant articles – their initials are placed before the bibliographies only for convenience.

Cross-references

Cross-references ($\Diamond$ = see, $\Diamond\!\!\!\Diamond$ = see also) from one article to another are made in the following cases: (a) when relevant information can be found in the articles cross-referred to; (b) when the writer cross-referred to is comparatively minor and the reader may wish to know who he is, even though he has not much relevance to the article in which cross-reference occurs. (A fruitless search is thus avoided – if a minor figure is not cross-referred to it can be assumed that there is no article under his name.)

CONTRIBUTORS

A A   Arline Anglade

A G   Arnold Goldman, Lecturer in English and American Studies, University of Sussex

A H   Andrew Hook, Lecturer in American Literature, University of Edinburgh

B B   Brand Blanshard, Sterling Professor of Philosophy Emeritus, Yale University

B P   Barry Phillips, Assistant Professor of English, Wellesley College, Massachusetts

B S   Barry Spacks, Associate Professor in Humanities, Massachusetts Institute of Technology

B W   Brian Way, Lecturer in English, University College of Swansea

C A   Charles Angoff, Professor of English, Farleigh Dickinson University, New Jersey

D C   Dan Curley, Professor of English, University of Illinois

D G   Dorothy Goldman, Extra-mural Tutor, Universities of Sussex and Southampton

D H   Mrs Deni Heyck

D K A   David K. Adams, Department of American Studies, University of Keele

E M   Eric Mottram, Lecturer in American Literature, King's College, University of London

G D   George Decker, Senior Lecturer in Literature, University of Essex

G W   Geoffrey Walton, Professor of English and Modern Languages, Ahmadu Bello University, Nigeria

H D   Howell Daniels, Secretary of the Institute of United States Studies, University of London

H B   Harold Beaver, Senior Lecturer, School of Literature, University of Warwick

J F   Jean Franco, Professor of Literature, University of Essex

J M C   J. M. Cohen

M A   Michael Allen, Lecturer in English Literature, University of Belfast

M B   Malcolm Bradbury, Professor of American Studies, University of East Anglia

M G   Michael Green, Lecturer in English Literature, University of Birmingham

R W B   R. W. Butterfield, Lecturer in Literature, University of Essex

UNITED STATES OF AMERICA

A

Adams, Brooks (1848–1927). Historian, social commentator. Born in Quincy, Massachusetts, a younger brother of Henry ◊ Adams, of a distinguished family whose tradition he evoked in his preface to Henry's 'Letter to American Teachers of History' in *The Degradation of the Democratic Dogma* (1919); he was a profound influence on political and intellectual life during the progressive era. His first book, *The Emancipation of Massachusetts* (1887), argued that the early colonial ministry held the people imprisoned in a narrow, theocratic ideology; it attempted, thereby, to portray the moulding forces of a civilization. This led towards the large-scale, cyclical theory of history embodied in his greatest work, *The Law of Civilization and Decay* (1895; repr. 1955), which holds that the law of history is the law of centralization; but the centralized state contains the seeds of its own decay, since it invariably disintegrates under stress of economic competition. Not surprisingly, he set the virtues of the military over the commercial mind; he was a staunch nationalist, and an admirer of Theodore ◊ Roosevelt, over whom he had a significant influence. His intellectual influence is, like that of his more famous brother, in the promotion of a theoretical history accounting for progress through impersonal forces. But *The New Empire* (1902; repr. 1967) proposes a close integration of history and economics with geographical surroundings. [D K A/M B]

A. F. Beringause, *Brooks Adams: A Biography* (1955); Charles Olson, 'Brooks Adams' "The New Empire"', in *Human Universe* (1965); W. Berthoff, *The Ferment of Realism* (1965).

Adams, Henry Brooks (1838–1918). American historian. Born in Boston, Massachusetts. Of the fourth generation of distinguished statesmen (two of whom, John and John Quincy Adams, were Presidents of the United States), Henry, a man of thought and feeling rather than action, turned the family genius inwards to scholarship and writing. His formal education was at Harvard and in Germany. A secretary to his father, Charles Francis Adams, minister to England during the Civil War, he contributed to the newspapers on foreign and domestic affairs. From this it was an easy step to political journalism, history, fiction and, finally, the two master works, *Mont Saint-Michel and Chartres* (1913; private publ. 1904), a study of unity in the religion, art and architecture of the 12th century, and *The Education of Henry Adams* (1918; private publ. 1906), a study of multiplicity in the modern world of politics, science and technology, and an ironic analysis of the culture which formed him.

Adams taught history at Harvard, studied politics at first hand in Washington, and after the suicide of his wife in 1885 travelled to the East with his friend John La Farge and to the Sierras with the geologist Clarence King. His world travels are strongly reflected in the *Education* and in writings on Tahiti and Buddhism. For many years he was thought of only as a historian because of his thoughtful and discerning *History of the United States of America during the Administrations of Thomas Jefferson and James Madison* (9 vols., 1884–9, 1889–91), his *Historical Essays* (1891) and his biographies, *Albert Gallatin* (1879) and *John Randolph* (1882). But recently, with the republication of his political and social novels, *Democracy* (1880) and *Esther* (1884), and the appearance of his lively, voluminous letters, the imaginative power of these and of *Mont Saint-Michel and Chartres* and *The Education of Henry Adams* has been increasingly recognized. Adams's 'dynamic theory of history', expounded in the latter, is elaborated in *The Degradation of the Democratic Dogma* (1919, intr. Brooks Adams). Combining a layman's insights into both science and art with the perspective of the historian, Adams provided, in the symbols of the Virgin and the Dynamo, an interpretation of the intellectual and emotional foundations of subsequent American literature. He was one of the first to expound clearly the 20th-century need to ascertain ways of living with stability in what he called the 'multiverse'. [E M]

Letters, ed. W. C. Ford (2 vols., 1930, 1938);

A Henry Adams Reader, ed. E. Stevenson (1956). E. Samuels, *The Young Henry Adams* (1948), *Henry Adams: The Middle Years* (1958), *Henry Adams: The Major Phase* (1964); J. C. Levenson, *The Mind and Art of Henry Adams* (1957).

Ade, George (1866–1944). Humorist, playwright. Born in Indiana. *The Blond Girl Who Married a Butcher Shop Man* (1898) established the popular formula for this Chicago *Morning News* journalist: daily-life characters, colloquialism, erratic capitals. The one-per-week tales, written for 10 years, were collected in *Fables in Slang* (1900), *More Fables* (1900), *Forty Modern Fables* (1901), etc. His style consists not so much of slang as of Indiana Americanisms, his own racy manner and a cunning redemption of cliché by capital letters. F. D. Roosevelt used to educate his cabinet with Ade's *Fables*. His most famous plays are *The County Chairman* (1903) and *The College Widow* (1904), a hilarious and rather shrewd comedy of academics and athletes in mid-West college life, still regularly performed, and made into a musical, *Leave It to Jane*, by Jerome Kern. [E M]

Ed. Jean Shepherd, *The America of George Ade* (1962).

Agassiz, Louis (1807–73). Scientific writer. Born in Switzerland, he went to America in 1846, already famous for his work on glaciers and fish. At Harvard he made a reputation as lecturer, founded his Cambridge museum and the Wood's Hole Marine Biological Laboratory (1872), and compiled his chief work, *Contributions to the Natural History of the United States* (4 vols., 1857–63). His ice-age mania and anti-evolutionism did not prevent him from being a great naturalist and an inspiring and revolutionary teacher (William ◊ James and Sir Charles Lyell were his pupils); and probably he was a major influence on the naturalism of Emerson. Today his zoological studies are increasingly respected, and his example finds a place in Ezra Pound's pantheon. [E M]

Edward Lurie, *Louis Agassiz: A Life in Science* (1960); ed. E. C. Agassiz, *Louis Agassiz: His Life and Correspondence* (2 vols., 1885); Guy Davenport, *The Intelligence of Louis Agassiz: A Specimen Book of Scientific Writings* (1963).

Agee, James (1909–55). Poet, novelist, film critic. Born in Knoxville, Tennessee, he attended Harvard, published a collection of poems, *Permit Me Voyage* (1934), and worked for several magazines: *Fortune, Time* (1939–43), and the *Nation*, for which he reviewed films (1942–8). After 1948 his work was mainly for motion pictures. His brilliant film reviews and screenplays appeared in 2 volumes called *Agee on Film* (1958, 1960). A *Fortune* assignment of 1936 led to the eventual appearance in 1941 of *Let Us Now Praise Famous Men*, an account (with photographs by Walker Evans) of the social and economic conditions of poor-white sharecroppers in the South, re-creating the daily living of three representative tenant families. Agee's deep feeling for the land and its people emerges in a unique style of bitterness and passionate sympathy. Two novels followed, the second not quite finished when he died – *The Morning Watch* (1951), a short work about a day in the life of a 12-year-old boy in a Tennessee church school, and *A Death in the Family* (1957), which reports in meticulous detail a single episode in the life of a middle-class family in Nashville, Tennessee, in 1915. The novel presents straightforward people in an ordinary world, with great insight and compassion. Particularly successful is the handling of the children in the family, involved in troubles they only confusedly understand. [A H]

Col'ected Poems, ed. Robert Fitzgerald (1968); *Collected Short Prose*, ed. Robert Fitzgerald (1968); *Letters of James Agee to Father Flye* (1962).
Dwight MacDonald, *Against the American Grain* (1962); J. A. and H. Levitt, *A Way of Seeing* (1965); Peter H. Ohlin, *Agee* (1966).

Aiken, Conrad (1889–). Poet, novelist. Born in Savannah, Georgia. Early in his life, after his father killed his mother and committed suicide, he lived with relations in Massachusetts. At Harvard in 1911 he was in the famous class which included T. S. ◊ Eliot, Walter ◊ Lippmann, Robert ◊ Benchley and Van Wyck ◊ Brooks. His earliest influences as a philosophical poet and novelist were the French symbolists, the ◊ Imagists, Freud, William ◊ James and Havelock Ellis. But his great American antecedent is Poe, in both his insistence on the music of poetry and his psychological materials. In England, where he lived for a time from 1923, he was a friend of John Gould ◊ Fletcher and other younger poets. His first poems, *Earth Triumphant* (1914), and his criticism of contemporary poets,

Scepticisms (1919), aim for a concept of abstract aesthetic beauty which makes for Pateresque vagueness. From *The Jig of Forslin* (1916) onwards, Aiken's poetry shows the same mixture of psychological analysis and mellifluous sounds, without much development, through *Preludes for Memnon* (1931), *And in the Human Heart* (1940, a sonnet sequence) and *The Kid* (1947), a sequence of 9 poems on the curious legend of William Blackstone. *Three* (1968) is a short long poem celebrating everything and focused on the poet. Aiken's poetry is intermittently elusive and diffuse, brilliant in constructing atmosphere but weak in concentration. The musical ritualism of his poems tends towards hypnotic generalizations; but *Ushant* (1952) is a more clearly focused autobiographical prose work, and the criticism collected in *Reviewer's ABC* (1958) is completely lucid and useful. His stories tend to be illustrations of psychological ideas (from *Bring, Bring!*, 1925, to *Among the Lost People*, 1934). Of his 5 novels, *Blue Voyage* (1927) is a Joycean meditation of a playwright, *King Coffin* (1935) a meditation on a murder not committed, and *Great Circle* (1933) an analysis of the Oedipal breakdown of a marriage. Aiken's prose and poetry always have the integrity of his intense subjectivity; but also the narcissism. [EM]

Selected Poems (1961); *Collected Novels* (1964); *Collected Short Stories* (1960).
F. J. Hoffman, *Conrad Aiken* (1962); Jay Martin, *Conrad Aiken: A Life and His Art* (1962).

Albee, Edward (1928–   ). Playwright. Born Washington, D.C., and educated at Columbia University. His early one-act plays are brilliant absurdist analyses of contemporary social and psychological tensions: *The Zoo Story* (1958), *The Sandbox* (1959), *Fam and Yam* (1960) and the finest, *The Death of Bessie Smith* (1960), on the hysterical nature of Southern sexuality and politics. The dislocations and rituals of the theatre of the absurd are cunningly used in his first full-length play, *Who's Afraid of Virginia Woolf?* (1962), for the mutual destruction and reconciliation games of a history professor and his wife, and in *Tiny Alice* (1964), a psychological fantasy of sexual desire and manipulation in high camp manner. Albee has also adapted Carson ◊ McCullers's *The Ballad of the Sad Café* (1963) and James ◊ Purdy's *Malcolm* (1965) for the theatre, both studies in adolescence and fantasy life. *A Delicate Balance* (1966) is in many ways the major synthesis of his dramatic talents for comic timing, masks and revels of relatively sinister threats to life, and the numbing agonies of the search for love within a family apparently bent on destruction. In 1968, Albee Americanized the British playwright Giles Cooper's *Everything in the Garden*, altering practically every word, turning a black comedy into his own form of tragicomedy. *Box-Mao-Box* (1968) is probably his most impressive work so far. It consists of 'Box', a monologue by an unseen speaker, with a menacing structure visible on stage, matching the criticism of contemporary American life, and 'Quotations from Chairman Mao Tse-Tung', a piece for four characters with differing points of view. Albee is one of the few American dramatists to have achieved a developing stature since the Second World War. [EM]

Christopher Bigsby, *Edward Albee* (1969); Richard E. Amacher, *Edward Albee* (1969).

Alcott, Amos Bronson (1799–1888). Philosopher, educator, poet. Brought up on a Connecticut farm, he had little schooling, worked in a clock factory, wanted to be a schoolmaster but in fact became a Yankee pedlar in Virginia and the Carolinas (1818–23). With the planters he found a range of books and manners unavailable in New England, and when he did become a teacher in Connecticut his methods – based on the 'self-realization' of the child by socratic dialogue, comfortable conditions, music and games – were radically opposed to Calvinist disciplines; but Boston allowed him to experiment. In 1830 he married (see the family of Louisa M. ◊ Alcott's *Little Women*) and in 1831 he was asked to found a school in Philadelphia, where he read Pestalozzi. He then began an infant school in Boston, the Temple School, where he put into practice the advanced but controversial theories outlined in *Record of a School, Exemplifying the General Principles of Spiritual Culture*, published in 1835 by his assistant Elizabeth Peabody, and in his *Conversations with Children on the Gospels* (2 vols., 1836–7). He refused to dismiss a Negro girl from the school and was then himself dismissed because of his abolitionist entanglements, his religious emphasis and his admission that he discussed human physiology with his pupils. By this time a leading ◊ Transcendentalist, an educational theorist admired by Emerson and W. E. ◊ Channing (II), and a spiritual citizen of Concord, he moved in fact to the town and failed at farming. But his *Orphic Sayings* (1840, in the *Dial*; ed. William P. Randel, 1939) embodied his faith in innocence, intuition and the organic unity of all life 'agitated by the omnipresent soul', and were an important source of Transcendentalist ideas. In 1842 he visited England, and Carlyle, who found him 'a venerable Don Quixote . . . all bent on saving the world by a return to acorns', and returned to organize the 'Con-Sociate Family' community experiment at Fruitlands, near Harvard (his daughter Louisa M. Alcott's *Transcendental Wild Oats* is a fictional account), which failed after seven months. Thereafter he lived in Concord, neighbour to Emerson, Hawthorne, and Thoreau, supported by his wife and daughter Louisa, especially after the success of the latter's *Little Women*; until in 1859 he became Concord's Superintendent of Schools and 'travelling conversationalist'. From this work grew the Concord School of Philosophy (1879–88), run by a disciple, William T. Harris, and an important influence on American education. Most of Alcott's writing – poetry, reminiscences, sayings, a book on Emerson – belongs to the end of his life. He is no stylist or systematic thinker, and his real strength lay in endless learned conversations rooted in extreme neo-Platonism (Emerson said: 'As pure intellect, I have never seen his equal . . . the moral benefit of such a mind cannot be told'); but *Tablets* (1868) and *Table-Talk* (1877) reproduce something of his psychology of complexions and theory of relapsed creation. *Concord Days* (1872), based on his journals, and *New Connecticut. An Autobiographical Poem* (1887) have been reissued fairly recently. [MG]

The Journals, ed. O. Shepard (1938).
Ralph Waldo Emerson, 'Alcott', in *New American Cyclopaedia* (1858); O. Shepard, *Pedlar's Progress: The Life of Bronson Alcott* (1937); D. McCluskey, *Bronson Alcott, Teacher* (1940).

Alcott, Louisa May (1832–88). Novelist. In 1830 Bronson ◊ Alcott married Abigail May; their daughters Elizabeth, Louisa, Anna and May were immortalized as Beth, Jo, Amy and Meg in Louisa's best-known work, the lastingly popular *Little Women*. Born in Pennsylvania while her father ran a school in Germanstown, educated at home (though she also got some instruction from Thoreau, Emerson and Theodore Parker), forced to do menial work to support the household, she determined to write. *Flower Fables*, written when she was 16, appeared six years later (1855); considerable success came with *Hospital Sketches* (1863), about her experience as a Civil War nurse; her first novel, *Moods*, appeared in 1865; but fame arrived with *Little Women: Or Meg, Jo, Beth and Amy* (two parts, 1868, 1869). She followed this with *An Old-Fashioned Girl* (1870), *Little Men* (1871, about her nephews), *Aunt Jo's Scrap-Bag* (6 vols., 1872–82), *Eight Cousins* (1875), *Rose in Bloom* (1876), *Under the Lilacs* (1878), *Jo's Boys* (1886), etc., some of them for children, others showing her reform and suffrage interests. She visited Europe, edited a children's magazine, and died in Boston the day her father was buried. All her fiction is autobiographical, and most of her books are still in print in several languages. Her sentimental masterpiece not only provides several archetypal figures of American folklore but gives a lively rendering of mid-century Boston–Concord life. [MG]

Louisa May Alcott: Her Life, Letters and Journals, ed. E. D. Cheney (1889; repr. 1928).
Katharine Anthony, *Louisa May Alcott* (1938); Madeleine B. Sterne, *Louisa May Alcott* (1950).

Aldrich, Thomas Bailey (1836–1907). Novelist, poet. Born in New Hampshire. He became editor of the *Home Journal* at 20, and achieved national fame with his poem 'The Ballad of Babie Bell' (1855). His 'Marjorie Daw' was a famous short story of New York society (*Marjorie Daw and Other People*, 1873). Among his other works, *The Stillwater Tragedy* (1880), a detective story involved in anti-labour materials, and some of his academic lyrics, were most admired. He edited the *Atlantic Monthly* (1881–1900). But he is mainly remembered today for *The Story of a Bad Boy* (1870), a delightful autobiographical novel of his boyhood in Portsmouth (New Hampshire) and New Orleans. [EM]

Charles E. Samuels, *Thomas Bailey Aldrich* (1965).

Alger, Horatio (1834–99). Writer of children's books. Born in Revere, Massachusetts. After attending Harvard and going to Paris to lead a Bohemian life, he returned to become a Unitarian minister and then chaplain to the Newsboy's Lodging House in Manhattan. Here he wrote more than 100 tales of youthful self-improvement, generally about bootblacks and newsboys who made good through effort, resisting temptation and aiding elderly ladies. Subscribing to both the Victorian self-improvement myth and the American dream of success, they sold enormously well; over 20 million copies of each of the *Ragged Dick* series (1867 ff.), the *Luck and Pluck* series (1869 ff.) and the *Tattered Tom* series (1871 ff.) were published. He also wrote inspirational lives of Lincoln and Garfield. [MB]

Herbert B. Mayes, *Horatio Alger: A Biography without a Hero* (1928); J. Seelye, 'Who was Horatio? The Alger Myth and American Scholarship', *American Quarterly*, Winter, 1965; Kenneth S. Lynn, *The Dream of Success* (1955).

Algren, Nelson (1909–   ). Novelist. Born in Detroit, he has lived mainly in or near Chicago, where much of his work is set. Graduating from the University of Illinois School of Journalism in 1931, at the bottom of the Depression, he wandered through the American South-west as a migratory worker, writing his first story from experiences as attendant at an unsuccessful, fraudulent Texas filling-station. He returned to Chicago, worked on a W.P.A. Writer's Project, and as venereal disease control worker for the Chicago Board of Health. He began systematically collecting material from the Polish neighbourhoods of the North-west Side, making friends with poverty-stricken workers and criminals, attending police line-ups for scraps of dialogue, reading local papers for stories. Out of this commitment emerge the novels *Somebody in Boots* (1935), *Never Come Morning* (1942) and *The Man with the Golden Arm* (1949); the short stories *The Neon Wilderness* (1947); and *Chicago: City on the Make* (1951), his impressions of the city. He gives a certain poetic intensity to the anonymous desolation of the American metropolis, especially in *Never Come Morning*; he also renders, with the nerve-racking force of the sophisticated thriller writer, a number of the violent situations fundamental to the American imagination – rapes, brutal police interrogations, stick-ups, street hoodlums, sport as aggression. All is suffused with a romantic nihilism suggested in Algren's admiration for Sartre and acknowledged debt to

Hemingway and Dostoyevsky. *The Man with the Golden Arm*, one of the first novels about drug addiction, brought him international fame.

This fiction all belongs to the pattern of tough Depression writing – the world of James T. ¢ Farrell – and it makes an occasional left-wing gesture (though nothing in it really suggests Algren's radical outspokenness as a citizen, as in his protest against the execution of the Rosenbergs). *A Walk on the Wild Side* (1956), which Algren himself calls a 'readers' book' rather than a book 'written for myself', is, however, a conscious and ill-judged attempt to write in a more up-to-date idiom and respond to the vogue of ¢ Beat Generation writers like Kerouac.

Algren writes best at moments and in episodes; his novels are structureless; his characters or situations rarely develop convincingly; the action moves in jerks from phase to phase. The style is uneven – sometimes genuinely poetic, or filled with the vitality of American speech, but often inflated with false romanticism. However, as a tough Chicago novelist he has a permanent though minor place in American literature. *Who Lost an American?* (1963) is a book of world travels, and *Notes from a Sea Diary* (1965) combines observations on Hemingway and his critics with anecdotes of a voyage to India and Hongkong. [BW]

Nelson Algren's Own Book of Lonesome Monsters (1963).
H. E. F. Donaghue, *Conversations with Nelson Algren* (1964); ed. Malcolm Cowley, *Writers at Work* (1958) (interviews with Alston Anderson and Terry Southern); Maxwell Geismar, *American Moderns* (1958).

Allen, Hervey (1889–1949). Novelist, poet, biographer. Born in Pittsburgh, educated at the U.S. Naval Academy and the University of Pittsburgh, he became a First Lieutenant of Infantry in the First World War, describing his experiences in an autobiographical novel, *Toward the Flame* (1926). He taught in high schools and at Vassar College. His novel *Anthony Adverse* (1933), a swashbuckling historical romance set in the Napoleonic era, enjoyed extraordinary success. It was followed by a Civil War novel, *Action at Aquila* (1938), and three novels about the New York state frontier collected together in *The City in the Dawn* (1950). Volumes of poetry included *Wampum and Old Gold* (1921), *Carolina Chansons* (1922) and *New Legends* (1929). But he will probably be best remembered for his excellent biography of Poe: *Israfel* (1926). [MG]

Allston, Washington (1779–1843). Painter, poet, novelist. Though best known as a painter of the romantic school, he produced work of great interest in verse, fiction and essays. He was born in South Carolina and graduated from Harvard, then studying painting in England and Rome. Two lengthy visits to England brought him close to the English romantics, including Wordsworth and Coleridge, who influenced his own romanticism in art and literature. His volume of poems *The Sylphs of the Seasons* appeared in London in 1813 and was republished in Boston; Coleridge praised it for its nature poetry. He wrote the first American novel set in Italy, *Monaldi* (completed 1822; published 1841); it is a Gothic revenge novel set among painters. Richard Henry ◊ Dana, Jr, a relative, edited the posthumous volume *Lectures on Art, and Poems* (1850), containing 4 theoretical essays, his poems, a story and some aphorisms. [MB]

Jared Flagg, *Life and Letters of Washington Allston* (1893); Edgar P. Richardson, *Washington Allston: A Study of the Romantic Artist in America* (1948); Nathalia Wright, *American Novelists in Italy: The Discoverers: Allston to James* (1965).

Alsop, Richard. ◊ Connecticut Wits.

Anderson, Maxwell (1888–1959). Playwright. The son of a Pennsylvanian Baptist minister, he graduated from the University of Dakota, and after teaching and journalism (from which he was sacked for his Christian pacifism) he went to New York in 1918 and began to write for the theatre. After his first play, *White Desert* (1923), he successfully collaborated with Laurence ◊ Stallings on *What Price Glory?* (1924), a disillusioned comment on the First World War whose fairly accurate language and decent debunking is spoiled by sentimentality. Neither of the following two collaborations was as successful as Anderson's own domestic comedy, *Saturday's Children* (1927), or his first blank-verse box-office seller, *Elizabeth the Queen* (1930). Subsequently hailed as America's leading dramatist, he joined the ◊ Playwrights

Company and won Pulitzer and Drama Critics' Prizes.

In *Elizabeth the Queen*, the interplay of Elizabeth and Essex is worked up to a certain richness by language intended to revive verse drama for modern audiences. The theme of conflict between public and private life appears in a contemporary Congress setting in *Both Your Houses* (1933), and in *Mary of Scotland* (1933) the nobility of the queen's faith is betrayed by the machinations of Elizabeth in a verse tragedy. The compromise idiom of ancient and modern is clever but unreal. *Winterset* (1935) is a second handling (*Gods of the Lightning*, 1928, came first) of the Sacco–Vanzetti materials, in which the son revenging his father's uncommitted crime is a Hamlet figure, averted from crime by love. After four lesser plays, *High Tor* (1936) again uses verse for a contemporary subject: allegory of American individualism in which the New York Dutch past competes with modern gangsters, and self-reliance is taken West by the defeated hero. In *Key Largo* (1939) a Spanish Civil War deserter sacrifices his life objectively, conforming to a theory expounded by Anderson in *The Essence of Tragedy* (1939), essays. Before his death he completed another nine plays, including a version of Alan Paton's *Cry, the Beloved Country* (1948), with music by Kurt Weill (with whom he wrote the musical *Knickerbocker Holiday*, 1938). Anderson's best plays have a seriousness of purpose and theme which raises them above the rut, but their very earnestness and self-conscious universalizing through verse is no more than service in an honourable cause. [EM]

Eleven Verse Plays (1940).
B. H. Clark, *Maxwell Anderson: The Man and His Plays* (1933); Mabel D. Bailey, *Maxwell Anderson: The Playwright as Prophet* (1957).

Anderson, Robert (1917–). Playwright. Born in New York City. He achieved fame with his first play, *Tea and Sympathy* (1953), on the problems of homosexuality and loneliness as they affect a New England schoolboy. Sex and sentiment also helped *All Summer Long* (1955) – the actual and symbolic flooding of a family in their riverside home – and *Silent Night, Lonely Night* (1959), in which husband and wife (not married to each other) find a Christmas Eve vigil strengthening. *You Know I Can't Hear You When the Water's Running* (1967) is four one-act plays with a sexual bias. [EM]

Anderson, Sherwood (1876–1941). Novelist, short-story writer. His fiction is auto-biographical, his autobiography – in *A Story-Teller's Story* (1924), etc. – no less fictional; and he saw both as expressing not only an individual truth but a national legend, a distinctively American experience. He was born into small-town life in an Ohio scarcely a generation from the first settling, when pioneer memories were strong; this world laid the foundations of a life-long suspicion of modern industrial society, and a respect for the imaginative individual craftsman. His own story was that of a Horatio ◊ Alger hero with a new ending. He found a talent for writing advertising copy, worked in a Chicago agency, then became manager of an Ohio paint factory. Meanwhile, growing dissatisfied with this life, he tried writing fiction; and, according to legend, he walked out of his factory and family and into his career as an artist. Whether this is true or not, he clearly felt it should be; and this is the one 'fact' universally known about him. He joined the active literary scene of Chicago; was briefly an expatriate in Paris, sitting at the feet of Gertrude Stein; then returned to New Orleans, where he encouraged Faulkner. He settled in Marion, Virginia, writing and editing newspapers.

His first novel was *Windy McPherson's Son* (1916), and thereafter in novel after novel the hero follows Anderson's steps from town to city, often to success greater than he ever achieved, then to disillusionment and rejection of the standard images of success, and finally to exploration of new ends and means. Often the discovery is of a kind of mindless communion with and acceptance by others. It is a semi-mystical vision, and at once the cause of his fictional successes and failures. Everything depends upon Anderson's finding an adequate place to stand to tell his story. Most of his novels fail through dead stretches of flat narrative summary and clogging patches of authorial comment. Only when he gets an adequate voice in the story – usually a first-person narrator – does he effectively express his insight, as in 'The Egg', 'Death in the Woods' and 'The Man Who Became a Woman', three stories involving an adult narrator looking back to the still-puzzling crucial events of his adolescence. *Poor White* (1920) is the best early novel; it exploits the personal legend but makes it into a broad and representative experience;

in later pages, however, the presentation of adult life and sexuality gives Anderson many problems he cannot quite solve. But best known is *Winesburg, Ohio* (1919), a series of interrelated tales of the thwarted lives of small-town people, men of one idea (he calls them 'grotesques') trapped in ignorance and intolerance, yet groping for life. In most of the tales appears the figure of George Willard, a young newspaper reporter, who finally rejects the town and sets out in search of the virtues he has seen dimly revealed . . . personal freedom, sexual vitality, lyric insight, blood brotherhood. At 51, Anderson returned to Winesburg – Virginia, not Ohio – having bought two country weeklies; between 1927 and 1931 he wrote personal essays in editorial form for them, character sketches and mood pieces edited by Ray Lewis White in *Return to Winesburg* (1967).

The *Portable Sherwood Anderson* (New York, 1949), with an introduction by Horace Gregory, contains most of Anderson's best (including *Poor White*) and enough of his worst to give a fair picture. Best individual volumes in addition to *Winesburg, Ohio* are *The Triumph of the Egg* (1921) and *Horses and Men* (1923), both collections of stories. [D C]

Letters, ed. H. M. Jones and W. B. Rideout (1953); *Memoirs* (1969); *Tar: A Midwest Childhood*, ed. R. L. White (1969).
Ed. R. L. White, *The Achievement of Sherwood Anderson* (1966); Irving Howe, *Sherwood Anderson* (1951).

Antoninus, Brother (William Everson) (1912–   ). Poet. Born in California. During his term in a work camp for conscientious objectors, he was a member of a group of writers whose Untide Press mimeographed influential protest poetry in the Second World War. *The Residual Years: Poems 1934–1948* (1968) is a collection of poems which originally appeared in *These are the Ravens* (1935), *San Joaquin* (1939), *The Masculine Dead* (1942), *The Residual Years* (1944), *A Privacy of Speech* (1949), *In the Fictive Wish* (1967), *The Blowing of the Seed* (1966), *The Springing of the Blade* (1968) and *In the Year's Declension* (1961) (the first three of these appeared in *Single Source*, intr. Robert Duncan, 1966). These poems are an impressive achievement of personal forms and rhythms intent on recording contact with landscape, experience of marriage, moral concern with Post-Depression America, and the years leading to a crisis of religious faith in 1949. The poet became a Catholic, was active in the Catholic Worker movement, and, in 1951, entered the Dominican Order as a lay brother. His monastic withdrawal ended in 1957 and he became a force in the San Francisco Renaissance of the 1950s (*Evergreen Review*, 2, 1957). *The Crooked Lines of God: Poems 1949–54* (1960) states directly the nature of his spiritual changes with exceptional honesty. *The Hazards of Holiness: Poems 1957–1960* (1962) delineate a dark night of the soul and recovery through prayer and renewed contact with that landscape of California as close to Antoninus as it was to Robinson Jeffers. The centre of *The Rose of Solitude* (1967) is his love for a young woman. *The City Does Not Die* (1969) is a poem commemorating the San Francisco earthquake. He left his order early in 1970. [EM]

David Kherdian, *Six San Francisco Poets* (1969).

Arendt, Hannah (1906–   ). The German-born scholar received her doctorate at Heidelberg, where she studied under Jaspers and Heidegger. She went to America in 1941, and has since taught at a number of universities and made a brilliant reputation with *The Origin of Totalitarianism* (1951, 1958; British title *The Burden of Our Time*), a superb account of imperialist and totalitarian systems, *The Human Condition* (1958), a vital revisionary rethinking of Marxism, *Between Past and Future* (1961), a collection of essays, *On Revolution* (1963), and the controversial *Eichmann in Jerusalem* (1963). *Men in Dark Times* (1969) contains essays on Rosa Luxemburg, Karl Jaspes, Walter Benjamin, Randall Jarrell, etc., and *On Violence* is a short book on power and rebellion. [EM]

Arthur, Timothy Shay (1809–85). Novelist. Born in Orange Co., N.Y., he wrote novels against gambling and drink and for the domestic virtues, but was not himself teetotal. One of his stories became a classic when it was made by William Pratt into a play, *Ten Nights in a Barroom and What I Saw There* (produced 1858). At one time even more in demand than *Uncle Tom's Cabin*, it contained the song of little Mary, 'Father, dear father, come home to me now', and is now produced regularly as burlesque. [EM]

Asch, Shalom (1880–1957). Novelist, playwright. One of the great figures of modern Yiddish literature. Though essentially cosmopolitan, and drawing on international subject matter, he has direct links with American life and letters as well as with a distinct racial culture. He was born in Poland and became resident in New York in 1910, writing for Yiddish newspapers and contributing to Yiddish-American literature. He has also lived elsewhere, in Berlin, Paris and London, and published his work in various countries. Most of his prolific writing was written in Yiddish or German, and much is still not translated into English; his works in Yiddish, collected in Warsaw in 1937, already ran to 28 volumes. His translated works include *Mottke, the Vagabond* (1917), retranslated by Edwin and Willa Muir as *Mottke, the Thief* (1935); *America* (1918); and *Kiddush Ha-Shem, An Epic of 1648* (1926), which has been regarded as a major contribution to modern Jewish literature. His *Three Cities: A Trilogy* (1933; again translated by the Muirs) deals with St Petersburg, Warsaw and Moscow in modern revolutionary periods, seen from a Jewish perspective. Another notable group of books were those that appeared in London in 1938 under the title of *Three Novels* – containing *Uncle Moses, Chaim Lederer's Return* and *Judge Not . . . .* A further major trilogy is the group which treats early Christianity in its Jewish context – *The Nazarene* (1939), *The Apostle* (1943) and *Mary* (1949). There are many other books to his name, but *East River* (1946), which deals with Jewish life in New York at the turn of the century, and explores the intermixture of American races, is an example of his use of American materials. He has also written numerous short stories, and the collection *From Many Countries* appeared in London in 1958. Native Jewish writing has played a large part in the growth of American literature, and also has found in American culture much of its modern material; Asch's work manifests both the contribution and the debt. Certainly his novels of Jewish life, both in the modern period and at the time of Jesus, etc., are classics of the Yiddish literature movement and have proved popular reading among much wider audiences. [MB]

Ashbery, John (1927–   ). Poet, playwright, art critic. Born in Rochester, N.Y., he studied at Harvard and Columbia, where he specialized in French literature, worked in publishing, and in 1955 he went to France, serving as art critic for the Paris *Herald Tribune* and writing on art for *Art News*, of which he later became an editor. He returned to New York in 1965. He was on the editorial panel for the 12 issues of *Art and Literature* (1964–7) and for the 5 issues of *Locus Solus* (1961–2), important magazines reflecting the work and interests of a group of mainly New York poets and artists which includes Kenneth ♢ Koch, Harry ♢ Mathews, James Schuyler and Frank ♢ O'Hara, and their younger friends and followers (including those associated with 'C' publications and the magazine *Mother*), including Ted ♢ Berrigan, John Perrault, Rod Padgett and Peter ♢ Schjeldahl. Ashbery's poems are highly original in their use of logical narrative, complex interlocking imagery and a sharp visual sense of landscape and town localities. His work has been one of the main channels for the employment of French surrealist poetry and prose in modern American poetry, although the compositional theories of Gertrude Stein are also involved. He has also written plays, including *The Compromise* (1955) and *The Heroes* (1950). His poems are in *Turandot and Other Poems* (1953), *Some Trees* (1956), *The Poems* (1960), *The Tennis Court Oath* (1962), *Rivers and Mountains* (1965) and *Double Dream of Spring* (1970). *Selected Poems* (1967) is a British edition of his work. *The Nest of Ninnies* (1969) is a shrewd, funny novel, written with James Schuyler. [EM]

Paul Carroll, *The Poem in Its Skin* (1968); Richard Howard, *Alone with America* (1969).

Asimov, Isaac (1920–   ). Science-fiction writer. Born in Russia, he received a Ph.D. from Columbia University. A professor of biochemistry, he has published many popular works, including the 2-volume *Intelligent Man's Guide to Science* (1960). Asimov's chief contribution to science fiction has been his use of robots, from the collection of stories *I, Robot* (1950) to *The Caves of Steel* (1954) and *The Naked Sun* (1957), both of which employ a robot detective, as does *Asimov's Mysteries* (1968), a collection which combines the science-fiction with the mystery story. His three laws of robotics, although crude, are now widely accepted by other writers in the genre. Under the pseudonym Paul

French he has also written for juveniles. Other works include *The Foundation Trilogy* (1963), a reprinting of three earlier novels, *Nine Tomorrows* (1959), a collection of tales, and *The Universe* (1967), a history of man's attitudes and discoveries within the cosmos from earliest times to the most recent. [HD]

Atherton, Gertrude (1857–1948). Novelist, biographer, historian. Born in San Francisco, she married a New Englander in 1876 and began her long, lively and very prolific career only in the late 1880s, after his death. Her extraordinarily diverse, patchy output includes a series of novels describing California from Spanish times to the present, the best known being *The Californians* (1898; rev. 1935) and *Before the Gringo Came* (1894; rev. 1902 as *The Splendid Idle Forties*); several society novels, typified by *Black Oxen* (1923), considered scandalous when it appeared; some international social fiction; and fictional, 'dramatized' biographies. That of Alexander Hamilton, *The Conqueror* (1902), was extremely successful, despite criticism that she had misrepresented the historical figures involved. An ardent feminist, she campaigned with verve in her novels against Puritanism, and was nominated a member of 'The Erotic School' (with Ellen Wheeler ♢ Wilcox) in a popular-newspaper phrase, *c.* 1868. In 1932 she produced a characteristically exuberant autobiography, *Adventures of a Novelist*. During the twenties she was reported in Europe as the most widely read contemporary American author. [MG]

Auchincloss, Louis (1917–   ). Novelist, short-story writer. Educated at Yale and the University of Virginia, in 1941 he became a lawyer in New York. His fiction displays his experience of law firms and the higher levels of New York society. Since *The Indifferent Children* (1947) he has been a prolific writer, publishing a novel or short-story collection almost annually, and the unfailing wit, elegance and subtlety of his work have often led reviewers to compare him with Edith Wharton, about whom he has written, and even Henry James. Among his novels, *Sybil* (1952) is notable for its powers of characterization, but perhaps his short stories contain his best work. Some of his collections, such as *The Romantic Egoists* (1954), have one unifying theme, and in others, such as *Powers* *of Attorney* (1963), the separate stories (here of a law firm) are so closely interrelated as almost to comprise a new form between short story and novel. [MG]

The Injustice Collectors (1951); *A Law for the Lion* (1953); *The Great World and Timothy Colt* (1956); *Venus in Sparta* (1958); *Pursuit of the Prodigal* (1959); *The House of Five Talents* (1960); *Edith Wharton* (1961) (criticism); *Reflections of a Jacobite* (1961) (criticism); *Portrait in Brownstone* (1962); *The Rector of Justin* (1964); *Pioneers and Caretakers* (1965) (criticism of 9 American woman novelists); *Tales of Manhattan* (1967); *A World of Profit* (1968).

Audubon, John James (1785–1851). Naturalist. Born in Santo Domingo, the son of a French navy captain, he spent his early life studying art in Louisiana, Pennsylvania and France; but when his father went bankrupt he opened a general store in Louisville, Kentucky, with a partner and a wife who let him travel in America on his real vocation, birds. His narratives and his paintings are equally fine: but he too went bankrupt, and was imprisoned at one time. *The Birds of North America* (1827–38) is a huge collection of plates whose text he published (with William MacGillivray) in 1831–9 as *Ornithological Biography*. The text for *The Viviparous Quadrupeds of North America* (1831–9) followed in 1846–54. His voluminous journals have been made into fascinating books, which include *Delineations of American Scenery and Character* (ed. F. H. Herrick, 1926) and *Journal of John James Audubon, Made during his Trip to New Orleans in 1820–21* (ed. H. Corning, 1929). Besides his beautiful bird drawings, he packed his journals with first-hand information about early American pioneers and the Indians. [EM]

The Journals (2 vols., 1960); *The Imperial Collection of Audubon Animals* (with J. Backman), ed. V. H. Cahalane (1968).
Alice Ford, *John James Audubon* (1965); Alexander B. Adams, *John James Audubon* (1966).

B

Babbitt, Irving (1865–1933). Critic, teacher. Born in Ohio, he worked as a newspaper seller and cowboy before eventually graduating from Harvard (1889). After further study in Paris he taught in Montana, and became Professor of Romance Languages at Harvard in 1894. He was an outstanding scholar and teacher, and the most cogent and articulate member of the ◊ New Humanism movement. His lifelong advocacy of reason and his sustained and vehement opposition to romantic spontaneity had a lasting influence on the work of T. S. Eliot, and many others, including Yvor ◊ Winters.

All his favourite themes are present in the severe, elegant prose of *Literature and the American College: Essays in Defence of the Humanities* (1908). He recommends patience and discipline in literature as in life, attacking 'the moral impressionism' of modern society. 'The classical spirit, in its purest form, feels itself consecrated to the service of a high, impersonal reason. Hence its sentiment of restraint and discipline, its sense of proportion and pervading law.' In *The New Laokoön* (1910) he analyses 'the romantic confusion in the arts': 'Many of the greatest of our modern artists, Hugo, Wagner, Ibsen . . . have been eleutheromaniacs. For over a century the world has been fed on a steady diet of revolt. Everybody is . . . taken up with his rights rather than with his duties. . . . We should have the courage to affirm . . . that a man may throw off the outer law only in the name of a higher law, and not in the name of universal sympathy.' In *Rousseau and Romanticism* (1919) he analyses with devastating force the characteristics of romantic literature, and despite much local unfairness the book remains a major study. Later came *Democracy and Leadership* (1924), his philosophy of modern civilization; *On Being Creative* (1932), contrasting classic imitation and romantic spontaneity; and a posthumous collection of essays, *Spanish Character* (1940, with a bibliography). Despite their rather wearisomely negative polemic, Babbitt's works are among the classics of modern criticism. [MG]

T. S. Eliot, 'The Humanism of Irving Babbitt' and 'Second Thoughts about Humanism', in *Selected Essays* (1932); R. P. Blackmur, *The Lion and the Honeycomb* (1955); Herbert Howarth, *Notes on Some Figures behind T. S. Eliot* (1965).

Baker, Dorothy (1907–68). Novelist. Born in Montana, she married the poet and teacher Howard ◊ Baker and lived in Paris, Cambridge, Massachusetts, and on her husband's orange farm in southern California. Her novels are clever and finished works, with an intensity of rendering and a concern with exactness of psychology that owe much to Hemingway but show the positive qualities of an individual style. Most of her books examine challenges to the aesthetic and emotional qualities of the young. *Young Man with a Horn* (1938), about a hero derived from Bix Biederbecke, deals intensively with the culture of the jazz world. *Trio* (1943), which has a university background, is a study of the influence of an authoritarian lesbian teacher on two young people, and *Our Gifted Son* (1948) concerns the problems of an artist of Mexican origin. *Cassandra at the Wedding* (1962), probably her best novel, reverts to exploring modern college and youth culture through a sensitive, strained heroine whose moral values are caught with superb precision. [MB]

Baker, George Pierce (1866–1935). Teacher, editor. Born in Providence, Rhode Island, he graduated from Harvard in 1887 and stayed on to become one of the most important teachers in America. In 1905 he opened his '47 Workshop' to teach young playwrights and allow them to see their works performed. The students eventually included ◊ O'Neill, ◊ Barry, ◊ Behrman, ◊ Howard, Robert Edmond Jones, ◊ Dos Passos, John Mason ◊ Brown, Rachel Field and Thomas ◊ Wolfe (who describes Baker, as Professor Hatcher, in *Of Time and the River*). But Harvard did not like him, and in 1925 Yale provided the facilities he needed to develop a graduate drama school. He edited *Plays of the 47 Workshop* (1918–25). [EM]

W. P. Kinne, *George Pierce Baker and the American Theatre* (1954).

Baker, Howard (1905–). Poet, novelist. He has lived much of his life in California, where he is now a fruit farmer, but has also lived in France and Greece, the locale of some of his verse. He has taught writing in universities, including Harvard and the University of California at Davis. His wife was the novelist Dorothy ◊ Baker. His *A Letter from the Country and Other Poems*, distinguished and finely finished poems, appeared in pamphlet form in 1941, and was recently reissued with some new verse as *Ode to the Sea and Other Poems* (1966). He is also author of a good novel, *Orange Valley* (1931), and a scholarly critical work, *Induction to Tragedy* (1939; repr. 1965). [M B]

Baldwin, James (1924–). Novelist, playwright, essayist. He was born in Harlem, New York City, and his earliest experiences of life and religion in the ghetto are memorably presented in his first novel, *Go Tell It On the Mountain* (1953), an important book in the renaissance of black American literature since the 1950s. Baldwin lived for a number of years in Paris, recovering from racialist America and discovering his Americanism. His second novel, *Giovanni's Room* (1956), partly and obliquely covers that ground, but it also reveals one of his constant themes, the redemptive features of sexual love. The destructive horror of racialism and the struggle for sexual stability are the interlocking themes of his third novel, *Another Country* (1961), which shows the penetration of the effect of the life and death of a jazz drummer on his New York friends, black and white alike. *Tell Me How Long the Train's Been Gone* (1968) marks a serious change in his methods: instead of poise and Jamesian continuities, his style is looser and discontinuous, to fit the themes of shocking sexual and intellectual waste: the centre is a Negro actor's self-establishment in the face of racialism in the theatre. Baldwin's great talent is more secure in his series of essays, analysing his own experience and every aspect of Negro life and literature with one of the finest prose styles of our time: *Notes of a Native Son* (1955), *Nobody Knows My Name* (1961) and *The Fire Next Time* (1963), one of the most powerful indictments of racial tyranny and confusion ever written. *Going to Meet the Man* (1965) is a collection of stories on his characteristic themes, and his two plays are *Amen Corner* (1955) and *Blues for Mr Charlie* (1965). (◊ Negro Literature.) [E M]

Robert Bone, *The Negro Novel in America* (revised 1965); H. M. Harper Jr, *Desperate Faith* (1967); F. M. Eckman, *The Furious Passage of James Baldwin* (1968).

Bancroft, George (1800–91). Historian. Born Worcester, Massachusetts. Between 1810 and 1830 American scholarship developed a new professionalism, emphasizing the importance of original documentary sources. American historians went to German universities (especially Göttingen) for advanced study, returning usually to Harvard to apply German research methods. Bancroft went in 1818, returned to preach, teach and become a tutor at Harvard, to publish his *Poems* (1823), and also to write, largely on German subjects, for American reviews. His 10-volume *History of the United States from the Discovery of the American Continent* (1834–74; abridged and ed. R. B. Nye, 1967) was hailed as a classic on the appearance of the first volume. It still remains of interest, despite evident faults. Its highly rhetorical style was muted in the 6-volume edition of 1883–5, but other flaws remain. Certainly he remains a 'Father of American History', using philosophical concepts and original manuscript materials for his work; but cavalier use of quotations makes him unreliable, and his Jacksonian bias is strong. In fact, the work is best read as an expression of Jacksonian America: it sees the history of the colonies as an inevitable progression towards the establishment of separate national identity, is committed on the side of democracy and nationalism, and believes in the superior virtue of the American people. Significantly, Bancroft was involved in political and social reform movements before the Civil War, and was during periods as Secretary of the Navy and acting Secretary of War an open supporter of Manifest Destiny. He was minister to England (1846–9) and to Berlin (1867–74). [D K A/M B]

M. A. De Wolfe Howe, *The Life and Letters of George Bancroft* (2 vols., 1908); Russel B. Nye, *George Bancroft: Brahmin Rebel* (1944); Harvey Wish, *The American Historian* (1960).

Barker, James Nelson (1784–1858). Playwright. Born in Philadelphia, he became its

mayor; later he worked in the Treasury
Department. He wrote a number of plays,
some of patriotic character, of which the
best known are *Tears and Smiles* (1808), a
comedy in which, in the manner of Royall ◊
Tyler, he draws the essential Yankee in his
'Nathan Yank'; *The Indian Princess, or La
Belle Sauvage* (1808), on the story of John ◊
Smith and Pocahontas; a stage adaptation
of Scott's *Marmion* (1816) and *Superstition,
or The Fanatic Father* (1826), on the Salem
Witch Trials. This last touches on the problem of mob-democracy and prefigures a
number of treatments of this theme, in
fiction by Hawthorne and others, in the
theatre by Arthur Miller and others. [MB]

Paul M. Musser, *James Nelson Barker, 1784–1858*
(1929).

Barlow, Joel (1754–1812). Poet. The son of
a Reading, Connecticut, farmer, he was
educated at Dartmouth College and Yale,
where he associated with the ◊ Connecticut
Wits but found himself less conservative. He
became an army chaplain in 1780, probably
as one way to keep writing poetry, but at the
end of the revolutionary war he returned to
law, edited the *American Mercury*, opened
a bookshop in Hartford and collaborated
with the Wits. He travelled to Europe as
agent for an Ohio land deal and when it
failed escaped to France, where he met the
radical republicans Joseph Priestley, Horne
Tooke, ◊ Paine, etc. and wrote the revolutionary tract *Advice to the Privileged
Orders* (1792–3), and *The Hasty Pudding*
(1796), three cantos on a Yankee dish, as
an excuse for celebrating American
agrarianism. In 1811 he negotiated a trade
agreement with Napoleon, followed the
Russian campaign, and then died of pneumonia during the retreat from Moscow.
His fame rests on *The Columbiad* (1807), an
expansion of his *Vision of Columbus* (1787),
a turgid epic on 'the consequences of the
discovery' of America whose 10 books
absorb the founding of the colonies, colonial
wars and the Yorktown surrender, as part
of a divine plan. It was criticized in England
for linguistic innovations like 'crass' and
'utilize'. [EM]

J. Woodress, *A Yankee's Odyssey: The Life of
Joel Barlow* (1958); T. Grieder, 'Joel Barlow's
"The Hasty Pudding": A Study in American
Neo-Classicism', *BAAS Bulletin*, December
1965.

Barnes, Djuna (1892–   ). Novelist, playwright. Born in New York, she has spent

many years in Europe. From the earliest
work her essentially poetic and introspective
imagination has created its own forms. *A
Book of Repulsive Women* (1911; repr. 1948)
combines poems and drawings. *A Book*
(1923, reissued with three new stories as *A
Night among the Horses*, 1929; British title
Spillway) contained plays, stories, and
poems analysing a variety of people temperamentally drawn more to animal than
to human life. *Ryder* (1928) developed a
monologue style with its close-patterned
tracking of one man's relationship with
mother, wife and mistress. The novel *Ladies'
Almanack* appeared in 1928. With *Nightwood* (1936), praised by T. S. Eliot as 'so
good a novel that only sensibilities trained on
poetry can wholly appreciate it', she first
won a public name; this story of five
psychopathic characters, knotted together,
moving irrevocably to their doom, has
an inner claustrophobia which relates it
to the suspense and horror of Jacobean
tragedy. Her most recent publication, *The
Antiphon* (1958), a poetic drama, seems to
derive its stylized verse mannerism as much
from the 17th century as the classics.

'In the acceptance of depravity,' the
doctor in *Nightwood* remarks, 'the sense of
the past is most fully captured. What is a
ruin but Time easing itself of endurance?
Corruption is the age of Time. . . . Crime
itself is the door to an accumulation, a way
to lay hands on the shudder of a past that
is still vibrating.' While belonging to the
experimental, expatriate twenties, Djuna
Barnes's mood is closer to the *fin de siècle*.
Her special contributions have been a
fascination with lesbian relationships, a
delight in baroque language to accompany
the tortured drama of innocence and guilt,
and a gust of macabre humour that sometimes recalls Webster's theatre. [HB]

U. Weisstein, 'Beast Doll and Woman: Djuna
Barnes's Human Bestiary', in *Renaissance*,
xv, i (Fall, 1962); A. Williamson, 'The Divided
Image. The Quest for Identity in the Works of
Djuna Barnes', in *Critique*, VII, i (Spring,
1944).

Barry, Philip (1896–1949). Playwright. Born
in Rochester, N.Y. After a brief trial
as a diplomat he attended George Pierce ◊
Baker's '47 Workshop' at Yale, where his
work led to the prize-winning *You and I*
(1922). He became one of America's most
brilliant writers of light comedy about
wealthy society: *White Wings* (1926), *Paris*

Bound (1927), *Holiday* (1929) and *Here Come the Clowns* (1938). *Hotel Universe* (1930) attempts the more solemn theme of a God–Freud figure handling a crowd of neurotics in the south of France villa. *The Animal Kingdom* (1932) returns to sophisticated comedy (mistress more of a wife than wife), and Barry's finest play, the perennially witty and critical *The Philadelphia Story* (1939), shows Tracy Lord throwing over the traces of upper-class traditions with a reporter on the eve of marriage number two, only to remarry husband number one, C. K. Dexter Haven. Barry's art here is a masterly replay of the eternal triangle, with social overtones which do not disturb any more than they penetrate below the glittering surface. [EM]

J. M. Brown, *Upstage* (1930); Gerald Hamm, *The Drama of Philip Barry* (1948).

Barth, John (1930–   ). Novelist. Born in Maryland, he was educated at Johns Hopkins University, and taught at Pennsylvania State University. He teaches now at the University of Buffalo. His short fiction has appeared in various journals including the *Kenyon Review* and *Esquire*. He has written four brilliant novels which have lately won him a high reputation among critics. *The Floating Opera* (1956) is a marvellously funny analysis of a nihilist who decides not to commit suicide; *The End of the Road* (1961) is an excellent Existential black comedy about a man who refuses definition and brings others to misfortune; and *The Sotweed Factor* (1960) builds a wild extravaganza, with, as usual, strong philosophical implications, around the supposed career of the real Ebenezer ◊ Cook, the Maryland Laureate, whose Marylandiad epic 'The Sot-Weed Factor' – i.e. the tobacco planter – provides part of the structure of this bulky, fanciful historical novel. *Giles Goat-Boy, or The Revised New Syllabus* (1966) is a brilliantly written, complex epic satire on the meanings of education, on the world as university and humanity as an infinitely malleable material. It includes a parody of Sophocles' *Oedipus the Tyrant*, elaborate Dantean allegories, and pagan and Christian myths about animals and gods. *Lost in the Funhouse* (1968) consists of stories and narratives set in the context of a brilliant fictive language game, with, though, a sometimes slightly ponderous working out. [MB]

Leslie Fiedler, in *On Contemporary Literature*, ed. R. Kostelanetz (1965); Robert Scholes, *The Fabulators* (1967).

Barthelme, Donald (1933–   ). Short-story writer. A Texan, he served in the army and now lives in New York. His *Come Back, Dr Caligari* (1964) is a collection of absurdist, surrealistic tales, with a satirical, black-humour approach. Most appeared originally in the *New Yorker*. Varied in quality, they are at best sharp and funny distillations of modern technological society. *Snow White* (1967) is a brilliant novel, with an elaborate satirical structure of deflated myths, dislocated contemporary ideologies and fads, and scepticism. These qualities are at their finest in *Unspeakable Practices, Unnatural Arts* (1968) and *City Life* (1970), important collections of stories in which surreal fragmentation and black humour are fully developed. [MB/EM]

Bartram, William (1739–1823). Botanist (like his father John). He was born in Philadelphia. A Quaker and an artist, he turned down ◊ Franklin's offer of a printing training, and, after a few years as a planter and merchant, accompanied his father on botanical expeditions (1773–7); it is his narrative of these journeys which constitutes his classic work of literary as well as scientific value, *Travels through North and South Carolina, Georgia, East and West Florida, the Cherokee Country, the Extensive Territories of the Muscogulges, or Creek Confederacy, and the Country of the Choctaws* (1791; repr. 1958). His scientific interests take shape within a love of American landscape and its life, and an elaborate prose Carlyle called 'a wondrous kind of floundering eloquence'. The *Travels* is in fact a work of primary romantic imagination. Chateaubriand read it, and there are traces in Wordsworth and Coleridge (see John L. Lowes, *The Road to Xanadu*, 1927). [EM]

John and William Bartram's America: Selections from the Writings, ed. H. G. Cruikshank (1957).

Basso, Hamilton (1904–   ). Novelist. Born in New Orleans, he began his writing career working there as a journalist, later joining the staff of the *New Yorker*. He has lived in South Carolina and also in Europe, and has drawn on both backgrounds for his fiction. Of his considerable number of novels, many have southern settings. They include *Courthouse Square* (1936), *Days be-*

fore Lent (1939), *The View from Pompey's Head* (1954), *The Light Infantry Ball* (1959) and *A Quota of Seaweed* (1960). These, particularly the more recent ones, have won him a considerable reputation in both England and America as a writer who explores interestingly and detachedly the social dimension and the character of community life. [MB]

Baum, L(yman) Frank (1856–1919). Novelist. Born in Chittenango, N.Y. His achievement is to have created the land of happiness and mystery called Oz and 14 best-selling books about it, from *The Wonderful Wizard of Oz* (1900) to *Glinda of Oz* (1920). Ostensibly for children, this impressive series is a serious and delightful American fairy tale, whose characters and adventures in Utopia dramatize, without terror, a dream rural America, and satirize chauvinism in this 'melting pot' of races. He wrote other children's books under various pseudonyms. [EM]

H. M. Littlefield, 'The Wizard of Oz: Parable on Populism', *American Quarterly*, Spring, 1964.

'Bay Psalm Book' (1640) (full title, *The Whole Booke of Psalmes Faithfully Translated into English Metre*). Undertaken in 1636, to ensure translations closer to the Hebrew, by 'thirty pious and learned ministers', and edited by Richard Mather, Thomas Welde and John Eliot, it is considered to be the first book printed in America (Cambridge, Mass.). The 1651 revised edition was used for over a century, in 27 editions, many of them in England and Scotland. It was the first American literature to be a success in the Old World. These metrical versions were to be sung to 'very neere fourty common tunes, as they are collected out of our chief musicians by Thos. Ravenscroft' – a basis of style in American music. [EM]

Beach, Sylvia (1887–1962). Bookseller, memoirist. Born in New Jersey, she kept a bookshop, Shakespeare and Co., at 12 rue de l'Odéon, in Paris, which became an important expatriate centre during the 1920s (◊ Lost Generation). It began in 1919 at a slightly different location, and at one point served as a publishing house, when no publisher could be found to print James Joyce's *Ulysses*. Her record of this period, *Shakespeare and Company* (1959), is a valuable document, and is usefully supp-

lemented by *Sylvia Beach: A Memorial Volume of Reminiscences* (1966) by 38 of her contemporaries. [MB]

Beard, Charles Austin (1874–1948). Political scientist, historian. Born in Indiana and a graduate of DePauw, he went to Oxford, where he helped to found Ruskin College. After teaching politics at Columbia University (1907–17), he resigned to write, his interests having shifted from European to American history. Though not accepting Frederick Jackson ◊ Turner's frontier thesis of American development, he admired and followed Turner's new emphasis on economic and social determinism. Beard was author or editor of over 50 books on history and government. The major theme of his *An Economic Interpretation of the Constitution of the United States* (1913) was that the Federalist sponsors of the new constitution of 1787 were the commercial, financial and manufacturing groups, and that there was a conflict of interest between these and the small farmers who constituted a majority of the population. *The Economic Origins of Jeffersonian Democracy* (1915) similarly analyses ◊ Jefferson's political support. His large-scale history of the U.S.A., written with his wife Mary Ritter Beard, began with *The Rise of American Civilization* (1927), and again stresses the importance throughout American history of the class of interest groups and – without denying the force of ideas or moral concepts – the fundamental relationship of economics and politics. In *The Idea of National Interest* (1934) Beard applied his economic interpretation to recent American foreign policy; increasingly he urged that international economic interests were tending to involve America in world tensions and even war. In *America in Mid-Passage* (*The Rise of American Civilization*, iii; with Mary Beard, 1939), he vigorously advocated 'continentalism', a version of isolationism. In *American Foreign Policy in the Making: 1932–1940* (1946) and more strongly still in his last book, *President Roosevelt and the Coming of the War: 1941* (1948), he held that though Roosevelt's public statements stressed peace his foreign policy led the U.S.A. into war; this view became the basis of the 'revisionist' interpretation of American participation in the Second World War. Beard's interpretations (and his movement from progressivism to conservatism) have been attacked; but many of his bold generalizations remain to influence and challenge modern historians. [DKA/MB]

Bernard C. Borning, *The Political and Social Thought of Charles A. Beard* (1962).

Beat Generation Writers. A group of writers active in the 1950s, centred around William ◊ Burroughs, Allen ◊ Ginsberg, Jack ◊ Kerouac, and later Lawrence ◊ Ferlinghetti, Gregory ◊ Corso and Peter Orlovsky. The term 'beat' was first used in its new way by Kerouac and recorded in 1952 in an article by John Clellon ◊ Holmes in the *New York Times*. Roughly speaking, the Beats were a criticism of American complacency under the Ike–Nixon regime, an expression of new forms of prose and poetry and an exploration of consciousness, which joined the dissent of existing Bohemias in ◊ Greenwich Village (New York), North Beach (San Francisco) and Venice West (Los Angeles) to produce a distinctive style of literature and living, based on disaffiliation, poverty, anarchic individualism and communal living. A relaxation of 'square' (puritan, middle-class, respectable) attitudes towards sex, drugs, religion and art became the opposing uniformity of 'beat' (later fused into 'hip'). The word 'beat' has a range of meanings including depressed (to the point of wild escape from conventional living); exhausted; holy in poverty and beatific in joy and mystic illumination (with literary references back to Whitman, Blake and Rimbaud, and jazz associations with Lester Young and Charlie Parker), and to catching the note of spontaneous living (with references to Zen Buddhism, Indian peyote cults and visionary experience). In literature, the key works were Ginsberg's poem 'Howl' (1955), Kerouac's novel *On the Road* (1957), Gary ◊ Snyder's poems *Riprap* (1959), the early poems of ◊ Whalen and ◊ McClure, Ferlinghetti's *Pictures from the Gone World* (1955) (as well as the other work emanating from his City Lights bookshop in San Francisco), Corso's poems in *Gasoline* (1958), and Burroughs' *Junkie* (1953) and *The Naked Lunch* (1959). But there were a number of other significant figures, both in New York and in San Francisco, publishing in a number of beat magazines. Hangers-on developed into 'beatniks', a generally denigratory term, apparently coined by Herb Caen in the San Francisco *Chronicle*, for a form of living and writing partly created by a frightened bourgeoisie and its sensation-seeking press. *The Beat* (ed. S. Krim, 1960) and *The New American Poetry* (ed. D. M. Allen, 1960) contained representative writings, and F. Rigney's *The Real Bohemia* (1961) attempted a sociological study of North Beach. [EM]

Lawrence Lipton, *The Holy Barbarians* (1959); ed. Thomas Parkinson, *A Casebook on the Beat* (1961); Ned Polsky, *Hustlers, Beats, and Others* (1967).

Beecher, Henry Ward (1813–87). Clergyman, editor, novelist, miscellaneous writer. Born in Litchfield, Connecticut. A graduate of Amherst College, he studied at a Cincinnati theological college of which his father, Lyman Beecher, a stern and rigorous Presbyterian, was president. Ordained in 1838, he became Congregational minister in Indianapolis (1839–47), then at Plymouth Church, Brooklyn. His success in New York as a vigorous preacher and as editor of the *Independent* (1861–4) and *The Christian Union* (1870–81) was later diminished by his involvement in a notorious adultery case (1874).

A strong anti-slavery spokesman, Beecher used extreme oratorical skill and a racy sense of humour in disseminating a mild, gentle and rather vague neo-Emersonian religion – he described God as 'one who loves a man in his sins for the sake of helping him out of them'. V. L. ◊ Parrington called him 'the high priest of emotional liberalism'; Thoreau, 'a magnificent pagan'. His aphoristic *Seven Lectures to Young Men* (1844) warned of temptations on the frontier; study of Darwin ensued in *Evolution and Religion* (1885). A novel *Norwood or Village Life in New England* (1867) contained pleasant descriptions of the New England landscape. He was a readable and intelligent essayist and also published lectures and sermons. He has no impartial biographer: Lyman Abbott published a laudatory *Henry Ward Beecher* (1903), and Paxton Hibben the hostile *Henry Ward Beecher: An American Portrait* (1927). [MG]

Autobiographical Reminiscences, ed. T. J. Ellinwood (1898).
Lionel G. Crocker, *Henry Ward Beecher's Art of Preaching* (1934); Robert Shapler, *Free Love and Heavenly Sinners* (1954).

Behrman, S(amuel) N(athaniel) (1893–). Playwright. Born in Worcester, Massachusetts. After working with George Pierce ◊ Baker's '47 Workshop' at Harvard (1916) his long theatre career began with the immediate success of *The Second Man* (1927), a comedy of two couple relationships, and he succeeded Philip ◊ Barry as the leading Broadway writer of high comedy in which wit and optimism overcome the corrupt pressures of the thirties. Of his huge output, the better pieces are *End of Summer* (1936) and *No Time for Comedy* (1939), which make laughter out of class shifts between 1900 and the Depression and the conflict of money and politics with creativity. He has also written *Duveen* (1952), a biography of the art dealer, and *Max* (1960), a study of Max Beerbohm, and worked on a number of famous Hollywood films, including Garbo's *Queen Christina* (1933). *The Worcester Account* (1954), stories, provides autobiography. *The Burning Glass* (1968), his first novel, is a social comedy of the thirties. [EM]

Belitt, Ben (1911–   ). Poet. Born in New York City, he was educated at the University of Virginia, worked editorially for the *Nation*, and now teaches at Bennington College. His poetry, collected in *The Five-Fold Mesh* (1938), *Wilderness Stair* (1955) and *The Enemy Joy* (1964), is erudite, intellectually complex, emotionally intense and occasionally apocalyptic. He writes about nature, myth and poetry itself. He has also translated from Spanish, Mexican and South American verse. [BP]

Bellamy, Edward (1850–98). Novelist. He was born and lived most of his life in Massachusetts. Abandoning his profession of law – no lawyers are allowed in his ideal commonwealth – he became a journalist in 1871. His early novels possess no great originality; after *Six to One: A Nantucket Idyll* (1878), he published two romances which, as the titles indicate, owe something to Hawthorne: *Dr Heidenhoff's Process* (1880) and *Miss Ludington's Sister* (1884). *The Duke of Stockbridge*, a novel of Shay's rebellion, appeared serially in 1879 and in book form in 1900 (intr. J. Schiffman, 1962).

Despite Bellamy's growing interest in social reform there was nothing in these works to indicate that his next book would be the famous *Looking Backward: 2000–1887* (1888). Indeed, the work was originally

intended to be a fantasy in the manner of his earlier productions. As he wrote, however, it became the 'vehicle of a definite scheme of industrial reorganization'. The new social and industrial order of the future is presented through the eyes of Julian West, a Bostonian who awakes 112 years after he has fallen into a mesmeric sleep in 1887. The action of the novel, strongly dependent on the vivid contrasting of past and future, has considerable dramatic tension; this, and the attractive imagery and style in which he advanced his theories, did much to ensure its phenomenal popularity and influence. A controlled yet savage attack on the existing social order, the book posited a unique American theory of state capitalism in a society from which economic individualism had been banished, with a consequent rise in the health and happiness of its members.

In order to disseminate Bellamy's views, over 150 'Nationalist' clubs were formed, and loosely linked to the Populist Party. Two journals, the *Nationalist* (1889–91) and Bellamy's own *New Nation* (1891–4), were additional organs of propaganda; but the movement was unable to exert any realistic political influence (*Talks on Nationalism*, 1938, reprints articles from the latter journal). Before his death Bellamy published a sequel to *Looking Backward*, *Equality* (1897), in which he vigorously attacked the profit motive; the book, however, lacked the verve of its predecessor and remained a rather dull economic tract. [HD]

Edward Bellamy Speaks Again: Articles, Public Addresses, Letters, intr. R. L. McBride (1937); *Edward Bellamy: Selected Writings on Religion and Society*, ed. J. Schiffman (1956).
Arthur E. Morgan, *Edward Bellamy* (1944); Sylvia E. Bowman, *The Year 2000* (1958); S. E. Bowman et al., *Edward Bellamy Abroad: An American Prophet's Influence* (1962).

Bellow, Saul (1915–   ). Novelist. Born in Quebec, Canada, of immigrant Jewish background. His family moved to Chicago when he was 9, and he attended Chicago, Northwestern and Wisconsin Universities. Author of seven novels, as well as plays, short stories and essays, he is critically regarded as one of the best post-war American novelists. He has explored the situation of urban democratic man with intense sociological and psychological awareness, through a variety of fictional modes. His subject is the need to come to some adequate conception of selfhood in a world in which the romantic supports have been removed – a world crowded under the pressure of democratic numbers, hence encouraging deterministic philosophies which view man as the suffering victim of his environment. His heroes are concerned with man's desire to take on the duties of his humanity and understand the nature of responsibility for others. *Dangling Man* (1944), his first novel, showing obvious analogies with contemporary European Existential fiction, explores a man deprived of the capacity for effective choice by his city circumstances and by a draft notice which offers him the cancellation of freedom. *The Victim* (1947) deals with the difficulty of defining responsibility for others in a modern democratic city where the consequences of one's actions disappear into the crowd, no man has a defined place, and mechanical arrangements prevail. *The Adventures of Augie March* (1953) has a larger canvas, a more picaresque approach, and a joyous euphoria of tone and language as the hero is followed in a comic attempt to define the level of his humanity. *Seize the Day* (1956), a short, concentrated novel, meets the same question, concentrating on the challenge of human mortality. *Henderson the Rain King* (1959) has a broad comic scale and a large, extravagant hero who seeks the truth about the human scale in a semi-mythical African landscape, a landscape for adventures of the mind. On the same scale, *Herzog* (1964) restores the urban landscape. Its hero, a scholar and intellectual, confronts in a gladiatorial combat the question of his connexion with his society and the whole intellectual history of the West, exploring romantic optimism, deterministic pessimism, measuring the degree to which man must be seen as a suffering creature. Bellow exploits the double comedy involved; the world about his later heroes, depressing the nature of man, turns the quests of his heroes into intellectual farce; they are the Superman as clown. Though sometimes accused of unearned optimism, Bellow has a real capacity to render suffering and typify the conditions of modern life. Indebted to ⋄ Dreiser and the Naturalists, he goes beyond them in intellectual and technical power, in his interpretation of society, and in his wry view of the new Superman. Among his contemporaries in the so-

called 'Jewish efflorescence' in post-war American fiction, he reveals an intellectual mastery and literary control that distinguish him clearly as a major writer. He has also written plays including *The Last Analysis* (1956) and *A Wen* (1965). His stories of the last 20 years are collected in *Mosby's Memoirs* (1969), in which a growing movement towards ironic reflection on man can be seen. *Mr Sammler's Planet* (1970) extends the ironic mode into a full-length novel. The book is centred around Mr Sammler, an ancient survivor of the pleasures (Bloomsbury) and the horrors (Auschwitz) of modern western civilization. He now lives out his last days amid the chaos and discordance of New York City in the moonshot age, with its cults of liberation and apocalypse, playing his one cold eye (the other was lost at Auschwitz) over modern vanities and reflecting whether man is in a state of self-destruction or moving toward a new state of being appropriate to its role in space: Sammler's wryness in this cool comedy of ideas is obviously Bellow's, too. [MB]

Tony Tanner, *Saul Bellow* (1965); K. M. Opdahl, *The Novels of Saul Bellow* (1968); Maxwell Geismar, *American Moderns* (1958); John J. Clayton, *Saul Bellow, In Defense of Man* (1968); Malcolm Bradbury, 'Saul Bellow and the Naturalist Tradition', *Review of English Literature*, October 1963.

Bemelmans, Ludwig (1898–1963). Novelist, essayist. He was the son of a Belgian painter and a Bavarian brewer's daughter. He is best known for his memoirs – humorous and elegantly caught observations on his Austrian youth, and his early days as a hotel waiter in the U.S.A. A writer for the *New Yorker* and other sophisticated journals, he specialized mainly in records of pre-war Europe and travel and gourmet pieces. Among his many books, *Life Class* (1938), *Hotel Splendide* (1941) and *The World of Bemelmans* (1955) best show his wit and charm, which also overflow into his fiction. Among his novels, *Dirty Eddie* (1947), a venture into the Hollywood novel, is a delightful spoof about a movie star pig; *Are You Hungry Are You Cold* (1960) tends to sentimentality. *On Board Noah's Ark* (1962) is a wry travelogue of the Mediterranean, and *The Street Where the Heart Lies* (1963) is an exotic tale of Americans in Paris. He has also written books for children. [MB]

Benchley, Robert (1889–1945). Humorist. Born in Massachusetts, educated at Harvard. He went into journalism, was managing editor of *Vanity Fair*, and then worked as drama critic for *Life* and the *New Yorker*. He is among the most hilarious and professional of modern American humorists; his main *forte* has been in the short essay, mostly written under the conditions of daily journalism. He commonly deals with ordinary situations, taking snippets of news or moral rules as a foil for his own incompetence and failures, or else his fantasies of power and prestige. One of his main comic techniques is the *non sequitur*, producing a nonsense method of writing evident in the titles of some of his books. He has published many collections of essays, including *Pluck and Luck* (1925), *20,000 Leagues under the Sea, or David Copperfield* (1928), *From Bed to Worse, or Comforting Thoughts about the Bison* (1934), *My Ten Years in a Quandary, and How They Grew* (1936), *Inside Benchley* (1942) and *Benchley Beside Himself* (1943). Various posthumous collections have been made, showing his continued popularity: *Chips off the Old Benchley* (1949) and *The Benchley Round-Up* (1954), etc. [M B]

Nathaniel Benchley, *Robert Benchley: A Biography* (1955).

Benét, Stephen Vincent (1898–1943). Poet, story writer, novelist. Born in Bethlehem, Pennsylvania. The son of an army officer, with whom he read history in widely scattered army quarters, he published his first book of poems before graduating from Yale (1919) and continued publishing successfully while a graduate student at Yale and the Sorbonne. Most of his major poetry and fiction was dedicated to exploring and understanding American national character, history and legend. Two long epic poems are among his best-known work – *John Brown's Body* (1928), exploring the Civil War, and *Western Star* (1943), unrevised at his death, dealing with American roots in the great 17th-century European migrations. Representative among his many short poems are 'The Hemp' (1918), a ballad depicting the destruction of a pirate at sea by an outraged Virginia planter; 'Ballad of William Sycamore' (1923), about a frontier character 'cradled on twigs of pine' at Plymouth; and the famous 'American Names' (1927), which compares European and American history by place-names (Salem, or Santa Cruz, or Sussex). He was a traditionalist in both his subjects and forms of expression (e.g. the ballad); but in these limits his craftsmanship was strikingly original. His fantasies and light verse are less impressive, though *King David* (1923) and numerous smaller poems reflect charming gifts of wit and satire.

Though his five novels are not particularly memorable, his short stories remain much admired, particularly those dealing with historical materials rather than contemporary life – 'Jacob and the Indians', a narrative tribute to the Jewish colonial-Americans,'The Devil and Daniel Webster', a comic folk-tale (made into an opera and a film) about the popular statesman who became legendary before his death, etc. In the depression and war years Benét became a literary defender of the democracies; and in speaking for his political and social liberalism over-exerted himself as lecturer and radio propagandist (see *We Stand United and Other Radio Scripts*, 1945). He wrote more and more on social themes – stories, articles and poems. *Burning City* (1936) interestingly represents the poetry of this phase. His writing continues to excite enthusiasm, though the only collection of his work is inadequate, and little of his criticism is reprinted. [R S]

Selected Works (2 vols., 1942); *Selected Letters*, ed. C. A. Fenton (1960).
Charles A. Fenton, *Stephen Vincent Benét: The Life and Times of an American Man of Letters* (1958).

Benét, William Rose (1886–1950). Poet, critic. Born in New York, elder brother of Stephen Vincent ◊ Benét; he married Elinor ◊ Wylie, whose poems he edited (1932). Active in magazine journalism, he helped found the *Saturday Review of Literature* in 1924; he also wrote for children. He was an exuberant and prolific poet; his volumes include *Merchants from Cathay* (1913), *The Falconer of God* (1914), *The Burglar of the Zodiac* (1918), *Moons of Grandeur* (1920), *Day of Deliverance* (1944) and *The Stairway of Surprise* (1947). The early work is high-spirited and romantic, whether the fantasy ranges to China or the prairies with cowboys and their ballads. Later he developed a free-verse medley of narrative, monologue, dialogue and lyric, seeking like his brother to catch semi-legendary meanings in daily experience. He also tried an experimental verse novel, *Rip*

Tide (1932), and a (Pulitzer Prize-winning) verse autobiography, *The Dust Which Is God* (1941). [HB]

Berenson, Bernard (1865–1959). Art critic, aesthetician. Born in Lithuania, he was brought to the United States as a boy and educated at Harvard. Sponsored by a group of Boston friends, he went to study in Europe and devote himself to connoisseurship. He spent most of his life near Florence, where his house I Tatti became an important artistic centre, not only for those interested in painting but also for writers. He was a dominant figure in shaping the modern attitude toward all the arts. An aesthetic philosopher, his notions of 'life enhancement' through art were widely influential and through books and conversations he established many themes in modern aesthetics. In addition to the famous volumes on Renaissance art – *Venetian Painters of the Renaissance* (1894), etc. – his books include *Aesthetics, Ethics and History* (1948), the autobiographical *Sketch for a Self-Portrait* (1949), the wartime diary *Rumor and Reflection* (1952), and *Sunset and Twilight: From the Diaries of 1947–1958* (1963). [MB]

Selected Letters, ed. A. K. McComb (1964); *The Bernard Berenson Treasury*, ed. Hannah Kiel (1962).
Sylvia Sprigge, *Berenson: A Biography* (1960).

Bergé, Carol (1928–). Poet. Born and educated in New York, she has worked in publishing and advertising, run a small art gallery (she is a painter herself), and co-founded Poetry Workshop in 1961. She appeared in *Four Young Lady Poets* (ed. LeRoi Jones, 1962) but her mature poems, finely made and deeply personal, appeared later in *Poems Made of Skin* (1968), *Circles, as in the Eye* (1969), *The Chambers* (1969), and, above all, in *An American Romance* (1969). *The Vancouver Report* (1965) is a useful account of a poetry conference involving some of the major contemporary American poets. [EM]

Berger, Thomas (1924–). Novelist. Born in Cincinnati, Ohio, he served in the Army in the Second World War, and has since lived in New York. His first novel, *Crazy in Berlin* (1958), established him as one of the most notable of contemporary ironists. Concerned with GIs in Germany,

its hero, Carlos Reinhart, reappeared in *Reinhart in Love* (1961), still moving through post-war western life as in a dream which is not his own. *Little Big Man* (1964) is a large-scale parody and serious appraisal of the Wild West and its myths and actuality. *Killing Time* (1967), his finest work to date, is a masterly dramatization of the confusions between law and criminality, normality and madness. In *Vital Parts* (1970) Reinhart encounters Bob Sweet, a shrewd caricature of the American as competitive individualist, a self-made monster who manipulates the younger generation with the skill of a sociologist and puts his main faith in cryonics, the science of freezing. Berger's dark humour and exceptional ability to create characters which represent the post-war scene are at the service of an ironical intelligence both debunking and alarmed. He is a major comic writer of the period. ([EM]

Berrigan, Ted (1934–). Poet. Born in Providence, Rhode Island, he joined the Army for three years in 1953, and then studied at the University of Tulsa, moving to New York in 1960. In 1963, he founded, with Lorenz Gude, '*C*' *Magazine*, whose 13 issues, along with the concurrent 'C' books, defined a new scene of poetry, centred on New York, and featuring such poets as Berrigan himself, Ron Padgett, Dick Gallup, Tom Veitch, Kenward Elmslie and Joe Ceravolo, and the artists Joe Brainard and George Schneeman. He has written for *Art News* and taught at the University of Iowa. *Sonnets* (1964) is a long and intricate set of interacting and permutated poems of considerable virtuosity; *Bean Spasms* (1967, with Ron Padgett) excellently represents the 'C' effect – parody, self-parody and an intense interest in procedure; *Many Happy Returns* (1968) collects his alternately introvertly wary and extrovertly exuberant recent poems. [EM]

Berry, Wendell (1934–). Poet, novelist. Born in Louisville, Kentucky. The south has been a basic part of the subject matter of his poetry and fiction. Graduated from the University of Kentucky, he taught at Stanford and New York University; now he teaches at the University of Kentucky, and farms. His precocious first novel, *Nathan Coulter* (1960), a study of a boy's coming-of-age in the tobacco-growing country, delicately evokes the way character develops from rural values and customs. In 1964 he published *November Twenty-Six, Nineteen Hundred Sixty-Three*, a long poem on the death of John F. Kennedy illustrated by Ben Shahn, and a first collection of verse, *The Broken Ground*. These poems, which show the same concern for land and roots in place and family as the novel, use a stark, imagistic approach to settings and subjects to catch carefully established subtleties of the spirit. His novel, *A Place on Earth* (1968), is a slow pastoral set in a sentimentalized Kentucky during the Second World War. In 1969 he published two books of poems, *Openings* and *Findings*, as well as a collection of social and political essays, *The Long-Legged House* [BS]

Berryman, John (1914–   ). Poet. Born in Oklahoma, he graduated from Columbia and Cambridge, and has taught at Princeton, Washington and Cincinnati Universities, while his distinctive poetry appeared, since the thirties in little magazines and in 1940 in *Five American Poets*. After *Poems* (1942) and *The Dispossessed* (1948), *Homage to Mistress Bradstreet* (1956) presented Berryman's special abilities in a long and intricate work moving from Anne ◊ Bradstreet's life and spirit in 17th-century New England towards the present. *77 Dream Songs* (1964) is the first part of a projected series of complex, highly wrought dramatic commentaries on the poet and his times. The second sequence, *History, His Dream, His Rest* (1968), continues the forms, but draws in a wider range of American life. *Berryman's Sonnets* (1968) is a sequence of 115 love sonnets, written in the 1940s and reflecting the poetic fashions of the time (Empson, Donne, Hopkins). He has also written short stories and *Stephen Crane* (1950), the first major critical and biographical work on ◊ Crane. [EM]

Beverley, Robert (*c.*1673–1722). Historian. As a boy he was educated in England, returned to his parents in Virginia to manage the large plantation he inherited, and became Jamestown's representative in the House of Burgesses. His *The History and Present State of Virginia* (1705, 1722; ed. L. B. Wright, 1947) is a fascinating, brilliantly observed record, written in good plain 17th-century style – a history of the colony, drawing critically on John ◊ Smith;

a description of the country, including a first-hand report on the Indians; and an account of the government. His eye for nature is excellent, his account of the Indians respectfully recognizes their autonomous civilization, and his defence of the state is persuasive. But he cannot see that slavery besmirches his Virginian Eden. [EM]

Bierce, Ambrose (1842–1914?). Short-story writer, wit. Born in Ohio, he fought as a youth in the Civil War and went as a journalist to California. In London (1872–6) he published several books of sketches and epigrams and then returned to California, later to Washington; he finally disappeared into Mexico during a Civil War. An elegant and finished writer, his satirical objects and his California context never quite served him well enough. *The Devil's Dictionary* (1906; original title *The Cynic's Word Book*), a delightful compendium of misanthropic definitions – 'happiness' is the contemplation of the misery of another – shows that in concentration he was at his best. His concern with style is expressed in *Write It Right* (1909). The two best-known collections are *Tales of Soldiers and Civilians* (1891), in a later edition entitled *In the Midst of Life* (1892; revised 1898) and *Can Such Things Be?* (1893) – macabre tales, centred on death, given to fantasy, with a strong *fin de siècle* flavour. Bierce has been rather underestimated. A kind of Oscar Wilde, unsupported by his culture, his essentially Bohemian sensibility is at once sophisticated and in some sense derived – perhaps from European models (◊ Bohemianism). He has interested English readers for some time (though his London visit was not entirely successful), and A. J. A. Symons edited *Ten Tales* in 1925. [MB]

Collected Works, ed. Walter Neal (12 vols., 1909–12); *The Collected Writings*, selected Clifton Fadiman (1946); *The Enlarged Devil's Dictionary*, ed. E. J. Hopkins (1968).
Richard O'Connor, *Ambrose Bierce: A Biography* (1967); Paul Fatout, *Ambrose Bierce: The Devil's Lexicographer* (1951).

Biggers, Earl Derr (1884–1933). Playwright, novelist. Born in Ohio. He survives in his Hawaii Chinese detective, Charlie Chan, the plump philosophical American descendant of the oriental sage tradition of the West. He first appeared in *The House without a Key* (1925) and became an international hero through films in which he was portrayed by Warner Oland (see *The Chinese Parrot*, 1926, *The Black Camel*, 1929, *Keeper of the Keys*, 1932, etc.). [EM]

Billings, Josh (Henry Wheeler Shaw) (1818–85). Humorist. Born in Lanesboro, Massachusetts, he was one of the Civil War generation of vernacular comic commentators which took the age by storm, won Lincoln's admiration, and created the atmosphere in which a figure like 'Mark Twain' could become a significant writer. Most of this group – like 'Artemus ◊ Ward' and 'Petroleum V. ◊ Nasby' – used a single comic personality who lectured, wrote and commented on events in the voice of the illiterate crackerbarrel philosopher; 'Mark ◊ Twain' broke the pattern by making the pseudonym into the complex persona of a remarkable writer. The flowering of the group created a satirical era where agrarian folk-wisdom played against follies, government corruption and eastern pretensions for a popular audience.

Shaw, born in Massachusetts, was explorer in the West, farmer, steamboat captain, auctioneer and real-estate dealer until he turned to writing as 'Josh Billings', a Yankee countryman, comic essays based on his multifarious experiences, Artemus Ward, puns and bad spelling. He took on the part and lectured throughout the country. His fame was enormous and his output prolific, from *Josh Billings: His Sayings* (1865) through *Josh Billings on Ice* (1868) to *Josh Billings' Spice Box* (1881). Between 1869 and 1880 he produced the famous parody annual the *Farmer's Allminax*. [MB]

The Complete Works of Josh Billings (1919); Uncle Sam's Uncle Josh, ed. Donald Day (1953).
Cyril Clemens, Josh Billings: Yankee Humorist (1932).

Bird, Robert Montgomery (1806–54). Novelist, playwright. Born in Delaware, he became a doctor in Philadelphia, turned to drama and then to novels: *The Hawks of Hawk-Hollow* (1835), about a Tory family in the Revolution, and *Nick of the Woods* (1837), about post-Revolution struggles with the Indians, focused on a split-personality figure who is a Quaker and an Indian-killer, are the two best known. [MB]

Bishop, Elizabeth (1911–). Poet. Born in New England, educated at Vassar,

she now lives in Brazil, the setting of some of her poems. She made her reputation with *North and South* (1946) and *Poems* (1955), a small body of striking and distinctive verse, more recently substantiated with *Questions of Travel* (1966), in which the indirectness and ironic understatement are even more prominent. Her work, often touched with fantasy, frequently suggests the mysterious operation of the universe and the terrifying face of its large cities ('Man-Moth', 'A Letter to N.Y.'). She sometimes celebrates nature, but can show its cruelty ('The Prodigal'); hence her verse has a pervasive sense of exile. Her poems are frequently long and carefully mannered, using elaborate rhyme or half-rhymes. An extraordinary meticulousness of craftsmanship marks all her work; exactitude of perception plays against inherently nostalgic or romantically tragic themes, to give great subtlety and toughness. [MB]

Selected Poems (1968): Complete Poems (1970).

Bishop, John Peale (1892–1944). Poet. Born in West Virginia, educated at Princeton, he settled on Cape Cod, where most of the poems collected in *Green Fruit* (1917), *Now With his Love* (1933) and *Minute Particulars* (1935) were written. At Princeton he first met Edmund ◊ Wilson, with whom he later collaborated on *The Undertaker's Garland* (1922). There are also stories, *Many Thousands Gone* (1931), and a novel, *Act of Darkness* (1935). He is said to be the prototype of Tom D'Invilliers, the radical young Princeton poet in his friend F. Scott Fitzgerald's first novel, *This Side of Paradise* (1920). He was very consciously the poet. With a controlled but gilded vocabulary he created neo-classic friezes – mothers by the seashore, a guilt-stricken Actaeon, a late Roman emperor retreating before Barbarians, a retiring senator, a sword dance, Hecuba in tears – as finely etched, but as evasive, as a Flaxman sculpture or a Robert Bridges lyric. His is a literature of literature, effectively muffling his own pulse. [HB]

Collected Essays (1948); Collected Poems (1948); Selected Poems (1960).
Ed. Allen Tate, A Southern Vanguard, The John Peale Bishop Memorial Volume (1947).

Blackburn, Paul (1926–). Poet, translator. He was born in Vermont, spent his youth in New Hampshire, South Carolina and New York, served in the U.S. army, and studied at New York University, Wisconsin and Toulouse, where he was a Fulbright teacher in 1955–6. During 1953–7 he spent a good deal of time in Spain, and in 1962 was poetry editor of the *Nation*. He has translated *El Cid Campeador* and his fine Spanish translations appear in *Proensa* (1953); he has recently completed an anthology of Provençal poetry in translation. His earlier poetry is in *The Dissolving Fabric* (1955), *Brooklyn–Manhattan Transit* (1960) and *The Nets* (1961). His style here is a personal version of the immediate tradition of William Carlos ◊ Williams and what is loosely called ◊ Black Mountain poetry, meaning derivatives from 'projective verse'. But *Sing-Song* (1966), *The Cities* (1967) and *In. On. Or About the Premises* (1968) show him to be a major original poet, with a masterly rhythmic technique, a humane but critical sense of humour, and a feeling for urban living which is compassionate, satirical and wittily observant. [EM]

Black Mountain College. Accompanied by a handful of supporters, John Andrew Rice left Rollins College, California – where his attempts to found a liberal educational centre in an illiberal town led to his dismissal – and in 1933 founded Black Mountain, in the midst of the Depression, and with little or no money, as a college experiment in American community education. This centre, near Asheville, North Carolina, became a focus for all those dissatisfied with academic methods and in need of teaching and being taught creatively. Among contributing teachers, students and visitors were John ◊ Dewey, Josef Albers (director in the 1940s), Charles ◊ Olson, Louis Adamic, Eric Bentley and John ◊ Cage; among the painters and sculptors, De Kooning, Kline, Stamos, Tworkov, Vicente, Motherwell, Rauschenberg and Guston; among writers Paul ◊ Goodman, Robert ◊ Duncan, Robert ◊ Creeley, Jonathan ◊ Williams, Fielding Dawson, John ◊ Wieners, Joel ◊ Oppenheimer; and among musicians and film-makers, Lou Harrison, John Cage and Stanley Vanderbeek. Their work, and that of Paul ◊ Blackburn and Denise ◊ Levertov, was published and considered in Cid Corman's *Origin* (1951–6) and *Black Mountain Review* (1954–7), edited by Creeley, with contributing editors Allen ◊ Ginsberg, Irving Layton, Olson, Jonathan Williams and Robert Hellman. Among those

printed were also ◊ Zukofsky, Borges, William Carlos ◊ Williams, Jack ◊ Kerouac, Philip ◊ Whalen, Ed ◊ Dorn, Gary ◊ Snyder, Hubert ◊ Selby, Michael ◊ McClure and Michael ◊ Rumaker. These writers have long since become a major part of 20th-century American literature. The college closed in 1956 but its work fertilized art and literature to a degree rare in the history of any culture. [EM]

Blackmur, R(ichard) P(almer) (1904–65). Literary critic, poet. Born in Springfield, Massachusetts. Partly self-educated, he became Professor of English at Princeton. Among the more important modern American speculative critics, he is generally associated with the tendency of the ◊ New Criticism. The title of one of his critical volumes – *Language as Gesture* (1952) – suggests this kinship; he sought to identify the character of literary language, and develop a sophisticated analysis of it. But he was also widely interested in the social context of literature, writing on such topics as literary expatriates and the development of the modern literary intelligentsia. His essay 'A Critic's Job of Work' – reprinted in the useful paperback collection of his writings, *Form and Value in Modern Poetry* (1957) – presents criticism as 'the formal discourse of an amateur', relevant in its resistance to ulterior motive, dependent finally on the critic's strength of mind. Though particularly interested in modern American poetry, Blackmur ranged widely in his objects of study. He edited the Prefaces of Henry James – by whom his criticism is influenced both in elegance and in its weighty aesthetic emphasis – and among his books are *The Double Agent: Essays in Craft and Elucidation* (1935), *The Lion and the Honeycomb: Essays in Solicitude and Critique* (1955) and *Eleven Essays in the European Novel* (1964). His poems – in various volumes, including *From Jordan's Delight* (1937) – are dignified and speculative, moving between a classical rhetoric and a lyricism drawn from song. [MB]

Blechman, Burt (1927–). Novelist. He was born in New York, graduated at Vermont University, and studied at Columbia and Chicago. He ran away from home to join the merchant navy at 16 and then supported himself with miscellaneous jobs. He travels a good deal and was in Cuba during the revolution. His fiction began with one of the best satires on consumer society in the sixties, *How Much?* (1962), adapted as a play, *My Father, My Mother and Me*, by Lillian ◊ Hellman. His second novel, *The War of Camp Omongo* (1963), exposes the middle-class through its children at a holiday camp. *Stations* (1964) is as uncompromising in its style and form as his satire in the earlier work. The homosexual theme is presented surrealistically as the life of Everyman in a universe of pain (he is influenced by Céline and Genet). *The Octopus Papers* (1965) satirizes the American cultural establishment with an anger comparable to that of Nathanael ◊ West. *Maybe* (1967) is another black-humour novel concerning a widow squandering her husband's estate in an effort to counter the despair of her boring life. Blechman is rightly considered one of the best of contemporary American satirists. [EM]

Bly, Robert (1926–). Poet, translator. Born in western Minnesota, he attended St Olaf's College and Harvard, went to Norway on a Fulbright award, and now lives on a farm in his native state. The poems in *Silence in a Snowy Field* (1962) are sparse, personal and observant, and repeatedly deal with the mysterious and affirming natural landscape of America, particularly of Minnesota, exploring silence, solitude and natural vigour in an immediate and modern idiom. In *The Light Around the Body* (1967) Bly responds in outrage to the warfare state, combining broad wit with a sense of the surreal hypocrisy of the Vietnam war. In an act of civil disobedience, he handed over the prize money from the National Book Award in 1968 to help young Americans 'defy the draft authorities'. As one of the founders and editors of the periodical magazine *The Fifties*, later called *The Sixties*, and of the Sixties Press, printing off-beat poetry and translations from little-known European and South American poets, Bly has been an important general influence in recent poetic movements. [BP/EM]

Richard Howard, *Alone with America* (1969).

Bodenheim, Maxwell (1893–1954). Poet, novelist, playwright. Born in Mississippi, he was associated with Chicago Bohemia until the 1920s, when he moved to New York and became an exotic if squalid figure in ◊ Greenwich Village circles. He published several volumes of poems, including *Minna*

and Myself (1918), *The Sardonic Arm* (1923), *Returning to Emotion* (1926), and *Selected Poems 1914–1944* (1946), sometimes anthologized but not easily available. His novels, cynical, 'shocking', often *romans à clef*, include *Crazy Man* (1924), *Replenishing Jessica* (1925) and *Naked on Roller Skates* (1931). He wrote plays with Ben ◊ Hecht. [MB]

Bogan, Louise (1897–1970). Poet. She belonged to what Yvor ◊ Winters has termed the 'reactionary generation', a group of brilliant minor poets who, though aware of the achievements of Pound, Eliot and Williams, chose traditional English forms and metres. Of this group, which included Winters himself, Allen ◊ Tate, and Hart ◊ Crane, she was probably the most accomplished metrist. Born and educated in New England (at Boston University), she moved to New York, where from 1931 she was the regular poetry reviewer for the *New Yorker*. Her first book of poems, *Body of This Death* (1923), sometimes reveals the influence of E. A. ◊ Robinson, a fellow New Englander transplanted to New York. Later poems show the too-obvious influence of Yeats. The catholic taste which made her a good reviewer, and her *Achievement in American Poetry 1900–1950* (1951), the best popular introduction to the subject, did some disservice to her poetry: there are too many tracks in the snow. Yet ten to twenty short lyrics in her *Collected Poems* (1954) are among the most perfect of their kind. Notable for their limpid diction, varied rhythms and dramatic structure, they are also important poems because of their intelligent preoccupation with such central human themes as sexual love and bodily decay. A fine technician, she quotes with approval Synge's dictum that 'the strong things of life are needed in poetry ...'. *The Blue Estuaries, Poems 1923–1968* (1968) is her finest book. She won the Bollingen Prize in 1955. Her *Selected Criticisms* appeared in 1958. [GD]

Elder Olson, 'Louise Bogan and Leonie Adams', *Chicago Review*, VIII, 70–87 (Fall, 1954).

Bohemianism. Literary Bohemianism was already a well-established style in European literature before Murger's *Scènes de la vie de Bohême* (1851) popularized and ritualized its life of riotous poverty; and it has long attracted American writers. Much of the *avant garde* character of American (particularly modern) writing, and much of the movement of American writers to cities like Chicago, San Francisco and New York – and indeed to Europe (◊ Expatriates) – has been due to a strong neo-Bohemian pattern in American letters. Bohemianism may roughly be defined as characteristic of societies in which the absence of fixed social roles for the writer encourages him to devise a distinctive life-pattern of his own and gather into groups and communities of his peers; this in turn – because the standards are set by other writers and because technical discussion tends to ensue – encourages experimental and *avant garde* literature. Bohemianism – as Albert Parry in *Garrets and Pretenders: A History of Bohemianism in America* (1933; revised edn, 1960) has shown – has been a strong movement in the U.S.A. from ◊ Poe onward, developing through the Pfaff's Broadway beer-cellar group, including Whitman, in the 1850s, to a fashionable movement in the 1880s and thereafter. The aesthetic and dandyish style had many famous adherents – ◊ Huneker, ◊ Bierce, ◊ Hovey and so on to Pound. The expatriation and cosmopolitanism of the 1920s had much to do with the well-established Bohemian connexion with Paris; and the aesthetic, symbolist strain is strongly evident in American letters throughout this period – as in the early Faulkner, Wallace Stevens, and many others. Before 1920 the attractions of Bohemianism had created numerous ex-patriates – Lafcadio ◊ Hearn, Stephen ◊ Crane, Henry ◊ Harland – while Stuart ◊ Merrill and Francis Viélé-Griffin became fully fledged French symbolists, writing in French. The strong beatnik strain in current American writing is a later phase of the same movement, while the respectable Bohemian tone survives in the *New Yorker*, a derivative of a whole tradition of outrageous Bohemian literary journals. The distinct Bohemian habitats of the late 19th and early 20th centuries – ◊ Greenwich Village, Chicago, San Francisco, Carmel – survive in their roles. One might say that today Bohemianism has become a universal youth-style, with the modern university campus as one of the most familiar locales. [MB]

Boker, George Henry (1823–90). Poet, dramatist. Of wealthy Philadelphia background, he wrote many verse plays, the most celebrated being the tragedy *Francesca da Rimini* (1855), as well as sonnets on love and on public issues. He was a minister to Turkey and to Russia. [MB]

E. S. Bradley, *George Henry Boker: Poet and Patriot* (1927).

Booth, Philip (1925–   ). Poet. Born in New Hampshire, educated at Dartmouth. He was an air force pilot in the Second World War, an experience that appears in his verse. Since then he has taught at various colleges, including Dartmouth and Wellesley, and produced a body of interesting personal poetry. *Letters from a Distant Island* (1957), *The Islanders* (1961) and *Weathers and Edges* (1967) have established him as a significant writer. [MB]

Booth, Wayne ◊ Chicago Aristotelians.

Boucicault, Dion (1820–90). Playwright. Born in Ireland, educated in England, he went to New York in 1853, already a famous actor-dramatist. He remained in the lead (with an occasional relapse) from 1853 to 1890. His most famous plays are *The Octoroon* (1859, on Mayne ◊ Reid's novel), *Rip Van Winkle* (1865, with Joseph Jefferson, on Irving's tale), and his Irish specialities – *The Colleen Bawn* (1860), with water spectacle, *Arrah-na-Pogue* (1864), in which 'The Wearing of the Green' was given new words and led to the shamrock business, and *The Shaughraun* (1874), all excellent melodramas. [EM]

Bourjaily, Vance (1922–   ). Novelist. Born in Ohio. He founded and edited *Discovery* with John Aldridge (1952). His earlier novels, *The End of My Life* (1947) and *The House of Earth* (1955), have only some of the power of *The Violated* (1958), a huge but excellently organized novel of the forties generation, and *Confessions of a Spent Youth* (1960), a semi-autobiographical novel. *The Unnatural Enemy* (1963) is a brilliant history of American hunting and its complexes. In *The Man Who Knew Kennedy* (1967), Bourjaily attempts to probe the sickness around the President's assassination and the American glamour of successful men. [EM]

Bourne, Randolph (1886–1918). Social and literary critic. Born in Bloomfield, N.Y., he was crippled and disfigured by a childhood accident. He studied at Columbia and in Europe, and became an educational and political radical, loathing war and American society so openly that his *New Republic* articles were suspended, in spite of their basically humanitarian protests for freedom. His major books are *Youth and Life* (1913), *The Gary Schools* (1916) and *Education and Living* (1917). Van Wyck ◊ Brooks posthumously edited *The History of a Literary Radical* (1920). Bourne's dissenting passion and clear prose, in the great tradition of ◊ Paine and ◊ Thoreau, is excellently represented in *War and the Intellectuals: Collected Essays 1915–1919* (ed. C. Resek, 1964). [EM]

Ed. L. Schlissel, *The World of Randolph Bourne* (1965); Sherman Paul, *Randolph Bourne* (U. of Minnesota Pamphlet, 1967).

Bowers, Edgar (1924–   ). Poet. Born in Georgia, he studied at the University of North Carolina and Stanford, and teaches at the University of California at Santa Barbara. His poetry is reflective but under an impressive control. He has published *The Form of Loss* (1956) and *The Astronomers* (1965), and has been represented in many anthologies, including *Five American Poets* (ed. Thom Gunn and Ted Hughes), published in England in 1963. [MB]

Richard Howard, *Alone with America* (1969).

Bowles, Jane (1918–   ). Novelist, short-story writer. She was born in New York City, married the novelist Paul ◊ Bowles in 1939, and wrote her first novel, *Two Serious Ladies* (1943), when she was 21. It describes the lives of two different women whose careers cross only twice, and is told in a prose style distinguished for its precision and poetry. Her play, *In the Summer House*, was produced in New York in 1953 and concerns an alcoholic woman maintaining her self-respect. All Jane Bowles's work shows 'the terrible strength of the weak' and their survival as failures. These works and 7 short stories make up *The Collected Works of Jane Bowles* (1967), which is introduced by Truman Capote. *Plain Pleasures* (1966) is the British title of her short stories. [EM]

Bowles, Paul (1910–   ). Novelist, short-story writer, translator, composer. He was born in New York, went to the University of Virginia because Poe had been there, and escaped from there to Paris, where his earliest poems had been published in *transi-*

tion. Returning to America, he took some lessons in musical composition from Aaron Copland, but soon returned to Europe. Gertrude Stein suggested Tangier to him in 1931, but he went to Africa permanently only after a spell as music critic for the *Herald Tribune* and writing theatre music (for two Tennessee Williams' plays, among others). In 1949 he went to Ceylon and now lives between there and Morocco. In 1941 he completed his opera *The Wind Remains* (libretto by García Lorca) in Mexico. He is married to the novelist Jane ◊ Bowles. Morocco is the locality for most of his fiction. *The Sheltering Sky* (1949) shows his remarkable feeling for the power of the African town and desert to generate existential fear and panic in characters exhausted and degenerated by western urban success and its values. He is a master of cruelty and isolation, and the ironies of the search for meaning in an inadequately understood environment. *Let It Come Down* (1952) again concerns the derangement of the senses of Europeans in an alien culture, moving towards an orgiastic climax: the hero is a young American committed to nothing but survival within corruption. Bowles's interests in the effects of kief and hashish are involved in the *dénouement*. *The Spider's House* (1955) again observes the effects of Africa on sophisticated westerners, but with more weight on the Moroccans themselves. This has been the direction of Bowles's career: the stories in *The Delicate Prey* (1950; British title *The Little Stone*) develop the theme of his novels, and contain some fine examples of controlled violence, like 'A Distant Episode', but in *A Life Full of Holes* (1964) he has tape-recorded and translated a story by an illiterate North African Moslem, Driss ben Hamed Charhadi, a moving life of stoic resignation to poverty. *Hundred Camels in the Courtyard* (1963), *Love with a Few Hairs* (1966), taped from Mohammed Mrabet, and *The Time of Friendship* (1967) all contain powerful insights into African sensibility and story-telling ability. *Up Above the World* (1967), a novel, is a black comedy exploiting his fascination with the darkness of sexual struggle, this time in Latin America, and the frontiers between reality and hallucination. In *Pages from Cold Point and Other Stories* (1968) the best stories are again located in North Africa, and *Their Heads are Green and Their Hands are Blue* (1963) is a collection of sharply observed travel notes.

Scenes (1968) is a small collection of poems from the 1940s. [E M]

C. E. Eisinger, *Fiction of the Forties* (1965).

Boyd, James (1888–1944). Novelist, poet. Energetic Philadelphian novelist of American history. His *Eighteen Poems* (1944) and *Old Pines and Other Stories* (1952) pale beside *Drums* (1925) – Johnny Fraser in the Revolutionary War – *Marching On* (1927) – a Civil War love story with descriptions of Antietam and Chancellorsville battles – and *Long Hunt* (1930), *Roll River* (1935) and *Bitter Creek* (1939). His historical localities are generally vivid and authentic. [E M]

Boyle, Kay (1903–). Novelist, short-story writer, poet. Born in Minnesota, her expatriate years in France before her return to the U.S.A. in 1941 provided her with much of the material for her fiction. Her interest in the international theme of Europe and America is matched, particularly in her early stories and novels, by an equally Jamesian interest in psychological character analysis. [A H]

Collections of stories: *Wedding Day* (1930); *First Lover* (1933); *The White Horses of Vienna* (1936); *The Crazy Hunter* (1940); *Thirty Stories* (1946); *The Smoking Mountain* (1951); *Nothing Breaks Except the Heart* (1966). Novels: *Plagued by the Nightingale* (1931); *Year before Last* (1932); *Gentlemen, I Address You Privately* (1933); *My Next Pride* (1934); *Death of a Man* (1936); *Monday Night* (1938); *The Youngest Camel* (1939); *Primer for Combat* (1942); *Avalanche* (1943); *A Frenchman Must Die* (1946); *His Human Majesty* (1949); *The Seagull on the Step* (1955); *Generation without Farewell* (1959). Poems: *A Glad Day* (1938); *American Citizen* (1944); *Collected Poems* (1962).
Richard C. Carpenter, 'Kay Boyle', *College English*, xv (November 1953); H. T. Moore, 'Kay Boyle's Fiction', *Kenyon Review*, Spring, 1960.

Brackenridge, Hugh Henry (1748–1816). Poet, novelist, political commentator. Born in Scotland, brought by Calvinist parents to Pennsylvania when he was 5, he was 15 when he began teaching in local schools. He attended Princeton with James Madison, and Philip ◊ Freneau, with whom he composed a satirical prose-tale, *Father Bombo's Pilgrimage to Mecca* (1770), and a famous Princeton commencement poem, *A Poem on the Rising Glory of America* (1772). Also with Freneau, he ran an academy in Maryland. He wrote two patriotic dramas and served as chaplain in Washington's army. He then founded the short-lived *United States Magazine*, read law and practised in Philadelphia and Pittsburgh, and entered on a promising career in politics which collapsed with the decline of Federalism and because of the complexity of his own political position. For services to the Republican party he became justice to the Pennsylvania Supreme Court in 1799 and in late life revised Blackstone for American conditions.

He is best remembered for two things: the Princeton commencement poem and his massive documentary novel *Modern Chivalry*, published in instalments between 1792 and 1815 (ed. C. M. Newlin, 1937). Picaresque in structure, derived from English and European models, it has no concluded plot, being an episodic series designed as 'a mixture of images drawn from high and low life, with painting serious and ludicrous', formed into a loose satirical 'fable' of the adventures of Captain Farrago and Teague O'Regan. This classic Cervantean pair, the backwoods chevalier and the ignorant, conceited companion, travel through the corruptions of modern democracy. In Part One their travels expose local government and satirize ◊ Franklin's American Philosophical Society, the idiocy of Indian treaties, fashionable sexuality, duelling, the theatre and the tax system. Teague is successful in the French Revolution, and the captain returns home enlightened by his pragmatic truths. In Part Two, they found a new state on the frontier, and the book becomes a series of topical discussions on government and law. Brackenridge's description of American types has an edge, vigour and indigenous awareness not found again until Mark Twain; and his faith in democracy, finally, is complex enough to hold. *Modern Chivalry* is that rare thing, a neglected comic-satirical masterpiece, and a central achievement in 18th-century American fiction. [E M]

Claude M. Newlin, *The Life and Writings of Hugh Henry Brackenridge* (1932).

Bradbury, Ray (1920–). Science-fiction writer and novelist. Born in Illinois but has now lived for some years in California where he also writes for the screen (most notably the script for John Huston's *Moby Dick*). A prolific writer of short stories, he began his career with a collection of macabre fantasies entitled *Dark Carnival* (1947), some of which were reprinted in *The October Country* (1955). Thereafter followed other collections of stories and several novels.

There is some doubt whether Bradbury may be considered a science-fiction writer proper. Many of his tales are perhaps best described as essays in fantasy, excursions into a subjective world peopled by grotesques and inspired by recollections of childhood summers in the mid-West (the protagonists of *Dandelion Wine* and *Something Wicked* are both young boys in that region). His greatest asset is an imagination which allows him to indulge in a poetic rather than a scientific treatment of extra-terrestrial reality, a quality most in evidence in *The Silver Locusts*, a haunting account of Mars at the beginning of the 21st century. Though his work is not entirely devoid of the customary concerns of science fiction (*Fahrenheit 451* is a cautionary fable of a book-burning society of the future), his world is essentially private and poetic. His deceptively simple lyrical prose often reveals a subtle ear for the sound as well as the meaning of words; but sometimes his 'sensitivity' degenerates into whimsy and sentimentality. Whether we classify him as a writer of science fiction or of fantasies, here is a considerable talent which has done much to make respectable a new genre of fiction that goes beyond the confines of realism. [HD]

Stories: *The Martian Chronicles* (1950; English title *The Silver Locusts*), *The Illustrated Man* (1951), *The Golden Apples of the Sun* (1953), *The Day It Rained Forever* (1959), *The Machineries of Joy* (1964). Novels: *Fahrenheit 451* (1953), *Dandelion Wine* (1957), *Something Wicked This Way Comes* (1962), *I Sing the Body Electric!* (1969).

Bradford, William (1590–1657). Colonizer, historian. Bradford was a member of the dissenting congregation of Scrooby, Nottinghamshire, which fled to the Netherlands in 1609. Conditions there being harder and more uncertain than had been expected, a group from the Leyden congregation decided to emigrate to America. These famous Pilgrim Fathers who sailed from Plymouth on the *Mayflower* in September 1620 included William Bradford. Reaching the New World far to the north of their intended destination they established a colony in New England which they called Plymouth. On the death in 1621 of John Carver, their first governor, Bradford was

elected his successor and held the office for 30 years. He began his history of the settlement in 1630 and probably finished it in 1650, but it remained unpublished until 1856. He tells the story of the exodus from Europe, the early years of hardship, and social and religious problems, and relations with the Indians as the history of a Chosen People. But the account, carefully checked, is accurate within its theological structure; hence it is a source for most later accounts of early settlement in New England, while its plain and eloquent prose makes it fine reading. [DKA/EM]

Of Plymouth Plantation, annotated S. E. Morison (1952).
Bradford Smith, *Bradford of Plymouth* (1951).

Bradstreet, Anne (1612?–1672). Poet. Born in England, she sailed in 1630 with her husband Simon and her father Thomas Dudley, former steward to the Earl of Lincoln. She settled in Ipswich and later North Andover, Massachusetts, her father and then her husband becoming Governors of the Massachusetts Bay Colony. She lived the life expressed in her poems – domestic, pious, alert to the quality of family life in a theocracy. Formally she hardly develops beyond her Elizabethan models, particularly Spenser and 'great Bartas', but her skill and feeling are her own. The first edition of her poems, *The Tenth Muse Lately Sprung Up in America* (1650), appeared in London without her supervision; the posthumous second edition, *Several Poems Compiled with a Great Variety of Wit and Learning* (1678), appeared in Boston, Massachusetts, with her corrections and a number of additions. The longer poems exploit her learning and include a dull versification of Ralegh's *History of the World*, a set of imitations of Du Bartas on the idea of fours (ages of man, seasons, etc.), and 'Contemplations', a typical long work in Spenserian stanzas on Spenserian themes (time, mutability, etc.). But there is an interesting domestic-provincial streak, which comes out finely in the shorter pieces – 'To My Dear and Loving Husband', 'Upon the Burning of Our House', etc. – which are significant contributions to metaphysical poetry. They are piously witty, informed by Puritanism, and reveal intense domestic emotions. Their merits still have fully to be recognized. Though her position as the first settler-writer of poetic imagination is secure, these introspective meditations on family life in a masculine, practical community need placing in an important 'domestic metaphysical' tradition in American letters. [MB]

Works, ed. J. Hensley (1967); *Works*, ed. J. H. Ellis (1867; reprinted 1962).
Helen S. Campbell, *Anne Bradstreet and Her Time* (1891); Josephine E. Piercy, *Anne Bradstreet* (1965).

Brautigan, Richard (1935–). Novelist, poet. He is above all a writer of the place in which he lives: the landscape and cities of the Pacific coast. His novels and stories are funny, quirkily original, and resist any categorization, just as his heroes are those whose freedom is anarchistic: *A Confederate General from Big Sur* (1964), *Trout Fishing in America* (1967), and *In Watermelon Sugar* (1968). His poems are collected in *The Pill versus the Springhill Mining Disaster* (1968). [EM]

Brinnin, John Malcolm (1916–). Poet, biographer, critic. He was born of American parents in Halifax, Nova Scotia, educated at the Universities of Michigan and Harvard, and has taught at various colleges, including Vassar and the University of California. His poetry is deft, often witty, with a wide range of voices from parody to philosophical meditation. Primarily a poet of occasions, he uses verse to comment upon prevailing issues and his own experience. His early volumes – *The Garden Is Political* (1942), *The Lincoln Lyrics* (1942), etc. – are chiefly political and show the influence of Auden. Later work, broader in theme and manner, is found in *The Sorrows of Cold Stone: Poems 1940–1950* (1951), while *Selected Poems* (1963) forms a useful introduction. He has been an important promoter of verse as Director of the Poetry Center of the New York Y.M.-Y.W.H.A., and as anthologist (e.g. the interesting *The Modern Poets: An American–British Anthology*, ed. with Bill Read, 1963). His memoir *Dylan Thomas in America* (1955) aroused controversy for its portrayal of Thomas's wildness; he also wrote a factually valuable biography of Gertrude Stein, *The Third Rose: Gertrude Stein and Her World* (1959), and a pamphlet on William Carlos Williams (1963). [MB]

'Phases of my Work', in *Contemporary American Poetry*, ed. H. Nemerov (1965).

Bromfield, Louis (1896–1956). Novelist, playwright, journalist. Born and raised on an Ohio farm, he went to Cornell and Columbia before service in the First World War interrupted his education; later he was a journalist and critic in New York, and a long-time expatriate in France. *Escape*, a highly praised tetralogy concerning men's efforts to free themselves from their background, began with *The Green Bay Tree* (1924), and continued with *Possession* (1925), *Early Autumn* (1926) and *A Good Woman* (1927). His work declined in quality with *The Strange Case of Miss Annie Spragg* (1928) and *Twenty-Four Hours* (1930), both studies of emotional stress, then fell off sharply in such novels as *Mrs Parkington* (1942). *Pleasant Valley* (1945) and *Out of the Earth* (1950) are excellent straight descriptions of life and work at Malabar, his highly advanced Ohio farm. In his later years, he became a well-known conservative spokesman. [MG]

Morrison Brown, *Louis Bromfield and His Books* (1956).

Brooks, Cleanth (1906–). Literary critic. A Southerner, born in Kentucky, educated at Vanderbilt and Tulane, then teacher of English at Louisiana State University (1932–47), he is now Professor of English at Yale (and was briefly cultural attaché at the American Embassy in London). During the 1930s (when with Robert Penn ◊ Warren he edited the *Southern Review*), he was closely associated with the movement of ◊ New Criticism, and the Southern literary revival. His many critical books and articles reveal a strongly 'structuralist' approach – an approach stressing the primacy of the text and the secondary nature of discussion of its origins or effects. *Modern Poetry and the Tradition* (1939) and *The Well-Wrought Urn: Studies in the Structure of Poetry* (1947) are documents of New Critical practice. The first, indebted to Eliot but possessing a strong practical criticism approach, distinguishes the characteristic poetic tradition as one of 'wit'; the second broadens the definition to consider the language of all poetry as that of paradox, and offers excellent close reading of a wide range of poems. But his criticism can have a strong social – almost a sociological – dimension, as more recently his *William Faulkner: The Yoknapatawpha County* (1963) has shown. His three text books *Understanding Poetry* (with Robert

Penn Warren, 1938), *Understanding Fiction* (with Warren, 1943), and *Understanding Drama* (with Robert Heilman, 1947), devoted to close reading, played a large part in introducing a critical approach into American teaching. His scholarly *Literary Criticism: A Short History* (1957), written with W. K. ◊ Wimsatt, with its exact analysis of critical concepts, is surely the best short general history available. [MB]

Stanley Edgar Hyman, *The Armed Vision: A Study in the Methods of Modern Literary Criticism* (1948).

Brooks, Gwendolyn. ◊ Negro Literature.

Brooks, Van Wyck (1886–1963). Literary historian, essayist. Born in Plainfield, New Jersey. He produced a monumental body of writing on American literary culture. In *America's Coming of Age* (1915), he outlined a concept of the autonomous nature of American literature and of the country's cultural reliance on its authors. Always biographical in nature, Brooks's work became increasingly popularized after the early thirties and increasingly conservative of a hypothetically pure American strain. Under the over-all title *Makers and Finders*, he produced a number of readable, if lightweight and unspecific, works, including *The Flowering of New England, 1815–1865* (1936), *New England: Indian Summer, 1865–1915* (1940) and *The Confident Years: 1885–1915* (1952). Brooks was not particularly hospitable to the work of immigrants later than the old Yankee stock. Earlier, he produced two influential studies, *The Ordeal of Mark Twain* (1920) and *The Pilgrimage of Henry James* (1925), which express his feeling for the harm done to these authors, by society and expatriation respectively. [AG]

Stanley Edgar Hyman, 'Van Wyck Brooks and Biographical Criticism', in *The Armed Vision* (1948); Gladys Brooks, *If Strangers Meet: A Memory* (1967); F. W. Dupee 'The Americanism of Van Wyck Brooks'; (*Partisan Review Reader*, 1946); W. Wasserstrom, *Van Wyck Brooks* (University of Minnesota Pamphlet, 1968).

Brossard, Chandler (1922–). Novelist. His first, under-estimated novel, *Who Walk in Darkness* (1952), explores, early, the sensibility of outsider withdrawal from American life, and is managed with great intelligence and fictional awareness. He

is also the author of two other novels, *The Bold Saboteurs* (1953) and *The Double View* (1960), and has edited a semi-sociological collection of essays about modern America. He has written a short book on Spain, *The Spanish Scene* (1968). He has worked as a journalist for *Look, Time* and the *American Mercury* and taught in various universities. [MB]

Broughton, James (1913–). Poet, film maker. Born in California. His finely formed and witty poems and films are part of the San Francisco Renaissance of the 1950s. His poems are in *The Playground* (1949), *Musical Chairs* (1950), *The Right Playmates* (1952), *An Almanac for Amorists* (1955) and *True and False Unicorn* (1957). His delightful films include *Mother's Day, Loony Tom, Adventures of Jimmy, Four in the Afternoon*, and *Pleasure Garden*. He has also written plays and revues. [EM]

Brown, Charles Brockden (1771–1810). Novelist. Born in a prosperous Philadelphia Quaker merchant family who fostered his early intellectuality while his health deteriorated. He came to loathe the law in which he was trained, as a mixture of 'endless tautologies' and 'lying assertions'. In the nationalism of his youth he contemplated the usual patriotic epics but found journalism more suitable, and his essays in the *Columbia Magazine* (1789) on the romantic solitary, the introspective 'rhapsodist' wandering in the American wilderness near his city, are a prelude to his later psychological fiction. In 1790 he met Elihu Smith, an extraverted medical student, who became his friend and with whose circle he founded the Society for the Attainment of Useful Knowledge. He visited Smith regularly in New York, to which he moved in 1796. He began to develop his fiction and that interest in psychosomatic phenomena which characterizes his work. In 1797, back in Philadelphia, he began the series of novels for which he should be famous, and, from 1799, his editing of the *Monthly Magazine and American Review*. His novels were decently received, but only his magazine work supported him. An importing business he was involved in failed in 1806 but a legacy kept him writing fiction, although it was now disappointingly conventional romances (*Clara Howard*, 1801, and *Jane Talbot*, 1801). Abandoning fiction, he edited a new magazine, and became increasingly depressed with the increase of his profits from Federalist journalism and the success of his *American Register* and his *Literary Magazine*. He married in 1804 and died six years later of 'pulmonary consumption'. *Wieland* (1798) is an important American transformation of the psychology of the European 'gothic' novel and concerns a German emigrant father, who explodes under some supposed divine judgement, and his son, who murders his family under the combined influences of religious mania and a ventriloquist under the power of a criminal philosophical aristocrat. *Ormond* (1799) is a variation on these themes, the central action being a campaign of seduction based on a philosophical system. Like the earlier novels, *Arthur Mervyn* (1799, 1800) has an astonishingly involved plot, this time the picaresque adventures of an American innocent in corrupt society. *Edgar Huntly* (1799), his finest work, uses American wilderness and Indian hostilities for a detection plot, with startling dream motivations and moral conclusions. Brown's novels are the first to use American landscape and natives, and his transformations of the 'gothic' began a long, important tradition in American fiction, from Poe and Hawthorne to Faulkner and Burroughs. [EM]

The Novels (1827, 7 vols; repr. 6 vols., 1887).
H. R. Warfel, *Charles Brockden Brown, American Gothic Novelist* (1949); D. L. Clark, *Charles Brockden Brown: Pioneer Voice of America* (1952).

Brown, John Mason (1900–   ). War correspondent, essayist, drama critic. Born in Kentucky, he worked on the *Theatre Arts Monthly*, New York newspapers and the *Saturday Review*. His criticism, some of the most perceptive to have appeared in America, is collected in various volumes, including *The Modern Theatre in Revolt* (1929) and *As They Appear* (1952). [EM]

Brown, Norman O. (1913–   ). Classical scholar, philosopher. Born in Mexico, educated at Oxford, Chicago and Wisconsin Universities, he has been professor of languages and classics in American universities and is now professor of humanities at the University of California, Santa Cruz. *Hermes the Thief* (1947) is an important study of the interrelation of Greek mythology and social

and economic history. In *Life against Death* (1959) he explores the radical revisions which should have followed Freud's model of human nature, especially in attitudes towards money, authority and sexuality. His analysis leads towards a revolutionary programme of 'polymorphous perversity' as a form of the resurrection of the body, and an end to the accumulation of wealth as a viable social aim. *Love's Body* (1968) is a superb collage of texts and opinions which clarify and extend the implications of *Life against Death*, towards a definition of freedom within what is known of human nature and the nature of the earth. These two works alone have made Brown a seminal figure of contemporary American thinking; he takes his place with John ◊ Cage, Buckminster ◊ Fuller, Marshall ◊ McLuhan and Noam ◊ Chomsky. His introduction to his translation of Hesiod's *Theogany* (1953) already provides precise mythical relevance for the study of such descriptive syntheses in our own time. [EM]

Browne, Charles Farrar. ◊ Ward, Artemus.

Brownell, W(illiam) C(rary) (1851–1928). Critic. Born in New York. Because of the moral and classical emphasis of his approach, he has been often associated with the ◊ New Humanism, though he precedes it and differs from it on many points. His critical volumes include *French Traits* (1889), *Victorian Prose Masters* (1901), *Criticism* (1914) and *Standards* (1917); the titles suggest his range and concern with principles. He stressed that criticism is an impersonal activity, concerned with the abstract forces behind concrete artistic expression; and that art is a rational activity to do with human enlightenment. Particularly important is his *American Prose Masters* (1909), recently reissued (1963) as a classic of criticism. Here his stress on the non-sensational, morally realistic quality of art prevents him from regarding highly the strong romance elements in American fiction, but he makes many usefully rigorous observations about Cooper, Hawthorne, Emerson, Poe, Henry James and others. [MB]

Morton Dawen Zabel, 'Introduction', *Literary Opinion in America* (3rd edn, 1962).

Brownson, Orestes A(ugustus) (1803–76). Journalist, novelist, writer on philosophy and theology. Born in Vermont, he passed through a series of religious denominations (Presbyterian, Universalist, Unitarian, etc.) and ended in 1844 as a Catholic convert, but was condemned for trying to found an individual 'American' Catholicism. His politics went through a similar series of individualisms in the grand New England manner; he was first a socialist, sending his son to Brook Farm (◊ Ripley) and joining up with Robert Owen, later a Democrat and later still a Republican. Despite these shifts his ideas were influential and in many ways representative; and both sides of his fascinating personality appeared in his *Boston Quarterly Review*, which he founded in 1838, and its successors, which attacked capitalism in tones like Marx's until he lost faith in the common people. (It was the first American journal popular in England.) He published many books on theological and general intellectual matters; *Charles Elwood, or The Infidel Converted* (1840) is a novel; and *The Convert, or Leaves from My Experience* (1857) describes his pragmatic changes of attitude. [MG]

Works, ed. H. F. Brownson (20 vols., 1882–1907); *The Brownson Reader*, ed. A. S. Ryan (1955).
H. F. Brownson, *Life* (3 vols., 1898–1900); Arthur M. Schlesinger, Jr, *Orestes A. Brownson: A Pilgrim's Progress* (1939); Theodore Maynard, *Orestes Brownson: Yankee, Radical Catholic* (1943); Americo D. Papati, *Orestes Brownson* (1965); C. Carroll Hillis, 'Brownson on Native New England', *New English Quarterly*, XL (1967).

Bryant, William Cullen (1794–1878). Poet, editor. His father was a country doctor in Massachusetts; he studied the classics and already imitated 18th-century poetic conventions at the age of 13, composing a satire against ◊ Jefferson; but the precocious Federalist and Calvinist later became a deistic democrat. He did not graduate but studied and practised law. At 16 he had produced one of his famous poems, 'Thanatopsis' (1817). In 1821 he married and delivered 'The Ages' as his Phi Beta Kappa poem at Harvard, and through his friendship with R. H. ◊ Dana, Sr, published his first *Poems* (1821). His literary reputation was high enough in 1825 for him to give up law and move to New York as an editor of the *New York Review*. From 1829 he edited the *Evening Post*, making it a redoubtable organ of liberalism. His poetic achievement was virtually complete by middle life with the 1832 collection of

Poems, though his later translations of Homer are of interest. 'Thanatopsis' characteristically contemplates the inevitability of death with that serenity which made Lowell refer to his 'supreme iceolation'. He believed poetry should provide 'direct lessons in wisdom' through 'truths which the mind instinctively acknowledges', and was strongly aware of the problem of literary relations with England; in his 1825 lectures he proclaimed 'all the materials for poetry exist in our own country, with all the ordinary encouragements and appointments for making use of them'. But his own poems are not especially American. His reading of Wordsworth is everywhere apparent. His poems on Indians, Africans, Greeks and 'William Tell' are typical of his humanitarian liberalism. His language is that of the transitional period between 18th-century diction and early-19th-century romanticism. His best poems philosophize about a carefully delineated natural object or scene – 'To a Waterfowl', 'The Snow Shower', 'The Song of the Sower' – and exemplify American literature's movement from New England puritanism to mild Republican, romantic transcendentalism. [EM]

The Poetical Works, ed. H. C. Sturges and R. M. Stoddard (1903); *William Cullen Bryant: Representative Selections*, ed. T. McDowell (1935).
H. H. Peckham, *Gotham Yankee: A Biography of William Cullen Bryant* (1950).

Bryce, James (1838–1922). Statesman, commentator on America. Born in Belfast, Ireland, the son of a Scottish schoolmaster; educated at Glasgow and Oxford Universities. His prize essay, *The Holy Roman Empire* (published in expanded form when he was 26), established him as a historian and scholar. From 1870 to 1893 he was professor of Civil Law at Oxford, and after being an M.P. for some years, he became Under-Secretary for Foreign Affairs in 1886 and, in 1905, Chief Secretary for Ireland. His interests in travel and politics combine in *Modern Democracies* (1921); his mountaineering ability was recognized by his presidency of the Alpine Club, his services to the state by a peerage, the presidency of the British Academy, and an O.M. in 1907. But it is as a student and interpreter – indeed as an admirer – of American life that Bryce is best remembered. He travelled extensively in America, and his insights were embodied in his classical book on American government, *The American Commonwealth* (1888), drawn largely from discussion with Americans and analysing political corruption, race prejudice and preoccupation with materialism as much as more positive qualities, summarized in his statement: 'America marks the highest level, not only of material well-being but of intelligence and happiness, which the race has yet attained'. He became a popular ambassador at Washington (1907–13). [BB]

H. A. L. Fisher, *James Bryce* (2 vols., 1927).

Buchwald, Art (1925–). Humorous columnist. He left the University of Southern California without a degree to live in Paris and become a journalist. His column for the *New York Herald Tribune*'s Paris edition, a light-hearted commentary on social and political matters, was soon syndicated in American newspapers. In 1962 he moved to Washington, D.C., to apply his techniques of commentary to affairs in the nation's capital. His writing, though usually personal and whimsical, mixes high-spirited fantasy with political *savoir faire*. Collections include: *Art Buchwald's Paris* (1954), *A Gift from the Boys* (1958), *How Much Is That in Dollars?* (1961) and (on Washington) *I Chose Capitol Punishment* (1963). [MB]

Buck, Pearl S(ydenstricker) (1892–). Novelist, story writer, biographer. Born in Hillsboro, Virginia. Her parents, Presbyterian missionaries to China, are portrayed in her fine biographies *Fighting Angel* (1936) and *The Exile* (1936), combined in 1937 as *The Spirit and the Flesh*. She grew up in China and returned for education at Randolph Macon College and Cornell University. After teaching psychology in Virginia, she returned to Nanking as an English teacher (1921–31). She has worked in a number of fields to encourage Chinese–American understanding. Her trilogy *The House of Earth* (1935), a saga of Chinese peasant life written in quasi-biblical prose, began with *The Good Earth* (1931, revised 1935; Pulitzer Prize, Howells Medal) and continued with *Sons* (1932) and *House Divided* (1935). In 1938 she became the first American woman to receive the Nobel Prize for Literature. Other novels include *East Wind – West Wind* (1930), *Dragon Seed* (1942), *Pavilion of Women* (1946) and *The Three Daughters of Madame Liang* (1969). She translated the Chinese classic

Shui Hu Chuan as *All Men are Brothers* (1933). [MG]

Bukowski, Charles (1920–). Poet. Born in Germany, he was brought to America at the age of 2. He lives in Los Angeles. His prolific output began when he was 35, is anti-literary, strongly autobiographical and self-consciously the record of an outsider. His strength is an ability to record his vigorously alienated life in direct language, with neither self-pity nor the jargon of psychology and ideology. *Notes of a Dirty Old Man* (1969) is a prose record of his underground life (also in *Confessions of a Man Insane Enough to Live with Beasts*, 1965). His best poems are in *At Terror Street and Agony Way* (1968) and *The Days Run Away like Wild Horses over the Hills* (1969), which collects works from six earlier books. [EM]

A Bukowski Sampler, ed. Dounglas Blazek (1969).
Ed. J. E. Webb, *The Outsider*, I, 3 (1963) (a Bukowski issue).

Burke, Kenneth (1897–). Philosopher, literary critic, poet. Born in Pittsburg, associated with various expatriate magazines in the 1920s, later music critic for the *Dial* and the *Nation*, he is one of the freest-ranging and most exciting of modern American critics. His literary criticism, which despite certain analogies is radically at odds with the theory of the ◊ New Criticism, starts from essential social premises and moves out to an extended consideration of formal procedures. His three earliest books, *Counter-Statement* (1931, revised 1953), *Permanence and Change: Anatomy of Purpose* (1935; revised 1954) and *Attitudes toward History* (1937), while largely philosophical and ethical in emphasis, explore the social location of art and begin to ascertain its central character. In *The Philosophy of Literary Form: Studies in Symbolic Action* (1941), his most literary critical work, he considers that a work of literature involves the adoption of 'strategies' for encompassing 'situations', and these are 'the dancing of an attitude'. Critical and imaginative works are answers to questions posed by the situation in which they arose. Burke's approach, a genetic one, makes him treat writings as working objects, operating both for writer and reader in a social context. Later works – *A Grammar of Motives*

(1945), *A Rhetoric of Motives* (1950) and *A Rhetoric of Religion* (1961) – take the argument about the nature of art and language further into the realm of human relations. Attentive to the text and yet at a distance from it, Burke's highly sophisticated use of insights from sociology, psychology, philosophy and linguistics makes him sometimes abstruse and grandiose. His importance lies in his capacity to make associations between disparate disciplines and obtain a complex philosophy of form from them. He is essentially a literary theoretician of the works of man as 'the symbol-using animal'. The chapter 'The Philosophy of Literary Form', in the book of that title, is the most convenient introduction to his idea. *Language as Symbolic Form* (1966) is a brilliant collection of essays from the 1950s and 1960s. He is also a poet (*Books of Moments: Poems 1915–54*, 1955 and *Collected Poems: 1915–1967*, 1968) and a short-story writer (*The White Oxen and Other Stories*, 1924). *Toward a Better Life* (1932) is described by its subtitle: 'A Series of Declamations or Epistles'. In *Perspectives by Incongruity* (1964) and *Terms for Order* (1964), Stanley Edgar ◊ Hyman has edited selections which represent all Burke's resourceful writings. [MB/EM]

Stanley Edgar Hyman, 'Kenneth Burke and His Criticism of Symbolic Action', in *The Armed Vision* (1948); Denis Donaghue, 'Enigma Variations', *New York Review*, XI, 1 (1968).

Burnett, Frances Eliza Hodgson (1849–1924). Novelist, children's writer. An Englishwoman who settled in Knoxville, Tennessee, in 1865, she became a leading sentimental novelist with books like *Editha's Burglar* (1888), *The Secret Garden* (1911), a charming and nostalgic classic, and *The White People* (1917), about the supernatural. Her first novel, *That Lass o' Lowrie's* (1877), is set in Lancashire industry; but she is remembered best for *Little Lord Fauntleroy* (1886); a generation of boys in long curls and velvet and lace cursed her portrait of the little lord, the American-educated and precociously charitable heir to an English earldom. The original, her son Vivian, wrote a biography of his mother, *The Romantick Lady* (1927). Her autobiography is *The One I Knew Best of All* (1893). She established, through a lawsuit, the American author's control over his own work in England. [MG]

Burnett, W(illiam) R(iley) (1899–). Novelist. Born in Ohio, he made a fortune out of a series of filmed best-selling toughies, including *Little Caesar* (1929) and *The Asphalt Jungle* (1949), first-rate gangster novels. He is also the author of several historical novels; and screenplays. [EM]

Burnham, James (1905–). Social critic. This important figure in American social debate studied at Princeton and Balliol, founded the journal *Symposium* (1931–5) and was Professor of Philosophy at New York University 1932–54. He broke with Marxism in 1939, was one of the editors of the politico-literary *Partisan Review* in the 1940s, and became an editor of the conservative *National Review* in 1955. His most influential work is his analysis of modern bureaucracy, *The Managerial Revolution* (1941); and his books include *The Struggle for the World* (1947), *The Machiavellians* (1943), *Containment or Liberation* (1953) and *Congress and the American Tradition* (1959). His most recent work, *Suicide of the West* (1965), is a criticism of liberalism from Locke to Arthur Schlesinger, Jr. [EM]

Burns, John Horne (1916–53). Novelist. Born in Massachusetts, he studied at Harvard and served in Africa and Italy in the Second World War. He returned to the U.S.A. to write, but later settled in Italy. He died at 36, and his reputation has grown posthumously. *The Gallery* (1947) is a series of passionately written sketches about G.I.s in Naples and the corrupt idealism of democracy at war. *Lucifer with a Book* (1949) is a satirical novel exposing an American 'outward bound' type of private school, and *A Cry of Children* (1952) concerns complex love between two ex-Catholics. A further novel, *The Stranger's Guise*, was not published. [EM]

Burroughs, Edgar Rice (1875–1950). Popular novelist. Born in Chicago. With a career as soldier, policeman, Sears Roebuck manager, gold-miner, cowboy and storekeeper behind him, he became a best-selling novelist with science fiction and Tarzan stories – the first was *Tarzan of the Apes* (1914). He incorporated himself and had two towns named after him, but never visited either Mars or Africa. Tarzan lived on after his death in novels and films: he was the son of an English aristocrat, abandoned in Africa as a child and reared by apes into animal strengths and linguistics. He survived his adventures, married and eventually became a grandfather. By 1940, more than 25 million copies in 56 languages had been sold. The first film of a long series was *Tarzan of the Apes* in 1918 (remade with sound 1930). In 1929 Tarzan became a comic-strip hero, but he was already an international folk-hero. Burroughs wrote over 60 books, which made him rich; he once said: 'Most of the stories I wrote were the stories I told myself before I went to sleep.' The Martian and Pellucidar books are rapidly gaining some of the popularity of Tarzan, for example, *A Princess of Mars* (1917), *A Fighting Man of Mars* (1930–1), *Pellucidar* (1923) and *Tanar of Pellucidar* (1930). Venus is the subject of *The Pirates of Venus* (1934), *Lost on Venus* (1935), etc. [EM]

R. W. Fenton, *The Big Swingers* (1967).

Burroughs, John (1837–1921). Naturalist, essayist. Born in the Catskills section of New York State, he was deeply influenced by Emerson, became a friend of Whitman, and a leading figure in American natural history and a nature-dweller at Slabsides, a cabin on the Hudson River at Riverby, N.Y. His work mixes Transcendentalism and scientific exactness. His collections include *Wake-Robin* (1871), *Birds and Poets* (1877) and *Riverby* (1894). A poet himself, he wrote (with Whitman) *Notes on Walt Whitman as Poet and Person* (1867), the first study, later expanded as *Walt Whitman: A Study* (1896). Later work like *Accepting the Universe* (1920) presents his (very 19th-century) belief; *My Boyhood* (1922) is autobiography. The most convenient collection is *John Burroughs' America: Selections*, ed. F. A. Wiley (1951). [MB]

Writings (23 vols., 1904–22); *The Heart of Burroughs' Journals*, ed. C. Barrus (1928).
Dallas Lore Sharp, *The Seer of Slabsides* (1921).

Burroughs, William (1914–   ). Novelist. Born in St Louis, he graduated from Harvard, worked through a number of jobs in Europe and America, and has since lived a semi-legendary life between Tangiers, London and Paris, creating a series of brilliant novels based on the international post-Second-World-War world of totalitarian Western states, their wars, homosexuality and addictions. In form and style his radical experiments extend certain methods of Joyce, Gertrude Stein and Dada into a new prose, which is the most influential among mid-century younger writers. *Junkie: Confessions of an Unredeemed Drug Addict* (1953, under the name 'William Lee') begins as a straightforward documentary of the underground life of the addict, but closes with materials on addiction, sex and the police which were to be permutated in his most important work to follow. *The Naked Lunch* (1959), *The Soft Machine* (1961, rewritten finally from two earlier versions 1968), *The Ticket That Exploded* (1962) and *Nova Express* (1964) is a brilliant tetralogy of novels whose importance is twofold: an extreme formal experimentation, using a range of techniques from conventional narrative to multispatial and temporal devices based on 'cut-up', 'fold-in', and permutational methods which extend 20th-century fictional innovations into a more thorough expressionist medium; and a radical and cosmically pessimistic analysis of his vision of the death of God and the universe given over to the licence of uncontrolled technological power groups. His presentation of parasitical sexuality, racialism, corporation capitalism, and medical and psychiatric tyranny is advanced in its satire and non-ideological scorn. His interest in the psychic action of drugs which extend consciousness informs *The Yage Letters* (1963, with Allen Ginsberg), letters written from South American travels in search of drugs. His literary and social revolutionary methods are demonstrated instructionally in *The Exterminator* (1960, with Brion Gysin) and *Minutes to Go* (1960, with Gysin, Gregory Corso and Sinclair Beiles). The rest of his voluminous work is scattered through innumerable *avant garde* magazines. *The Last Words of Dutch Schultz* (1970) is a film scenario on the gangster, and *The Job* (1970) is mainly an important interview on techniques. He is undoubtedly a major force in 20th-century literature. [EM]

'The Art of Fiction XXXVI: William Burroughs', *Paris Review* 35 (Fall, 1965); Ihab Hassan, 'The Subtracting Machine; The Work of William Burroughs', *Critique*, Spring, 1963; J. G. Ballard, 'Myth-Maker of the Twentieth Century', *New Worlds of Science Fiction*, May-June 1964; Mary McCarthy, 'Burroughs' Naked Lunch', *Encounter*, April 1963; Eric Mottram, *William Burroughs* (1970).

Butler, Bill (1934–   ). Poet. Born in
Washington, educated at Montana University, he has written most of his poetry
while living and running a bookshop in
England. It is highly wrought, complex
in both rhythm and organization of
materials, in the tradition of Hart Crane,
with a technical accomplishment and
range of vision unique in contemporary
American poetry. His major work is:
Capricorn (1963), *The Discovery of
America* (1966), *A Long Slow Waltz* (1968)
and *Byrne's Atlas* (1970). [EM]

Byles, Mather (1707–88). Poet and preacher.
The nephew of Cotton ♦ Mather, he inherited his famous library but not his
intellectual character. He was strongly
British and was therefore dismissed from
his Boston church in 1776. His poems are
fearfully witty (he tried to emulate Augustan
elegance, and actually corresponded with
Pope), but they end in dullness. His preaching was, however, celebrated for its satire
and word-play, rather unlike most Puritan
sermons. [EM]

Poems on Several Occasions (1744); *Poems by
Several Hands* (1775).

Bynner, Witter (1881–1968). Poet. He
published his first volume of verse in 1907.
After Harvard he travelled extensively, read
widely, assimilating a variety of literary
influences, and became active in the new
movement of modern poetry in America
(though he participated with Arthur Davidson Fricke in a famous hoax, their volume
Spectra, 'by Emanuel Morgan and Anne
Knish', which parodied ♦ Imagism and
kindred poetic styles, in 1916). An important feature of his work is a strong oriental
influence, and he travelled in the East
studying and collecting Chinese literature,
producing, with Dr Kian Kang-hu, *The Jade
Mountain* (1929), a translation of Chinese
poems from the Tang dynasty. Bynner's
work showed the clarity and economy of
the Chinese influence. Many of his early
poems have clear lyrical echoes of the
nineties; but, though a lyrical poet, the
grandiloquence of some of his early
influences gradually faded from his work.
Bynner's other writing includes distinguished translations from several languages, verse-plays and *Journey with Genius*
(1951), an account of his days with D. H.
Lawrence in New Mexico, where he settled

and where he sets many poems. He is a
poet of real interest and considerable
endurance, altering with half a century of
poetic modes and fashions yet retaining a
distinctive voice. *Selected Poems* (1936:
revised edn, 1943, ed. Robert Hunt, intr.
Paul Horgan) is a useful representative
volume, while *New Poems* (1960) provides
more recent work. [MB]

William Jay Smith, *The Spectra Hoax* (1961).

Byrd II, William (1674–1744). Planter.
politician, writer. William Byrd of Westover, on the James River in Virginia, was
in style a genuine aristocrat whose life
helped to create the myth of a widespread
Southern aristocracy. Virginia-born, English-educated (in the Middle Temple) he
was elected to the Royal Society and to the
House of Burgesses (at 18). As a businessman he was eminently successful, expanding
his family estates from 26,000 to 180,000
acres. As a public servant he served for 37
years on Virginia's Royal Council. He was
an amateur *littérateur* and scientist, and
assembled a private library of over 4,000
volumes. For many years he kept a diary,
written in an easy and attractive style,
which is a valuable source for the social
history of Virginia and for conditions in
London where he spent many years. His
*History of the Dividing Line betwixt
Virginia and North Carolina: A Journey to
the Land of Eden, A.D. 1733* (ed. W. K.
Byrd, 1929) draws a sharp distinction between the two colonies, christening the
undeveloped land to the south of his own
province 'Lubberland'. Byrd was a secular-minded rationalist whose observations on
the state of his times are of historical
interest, but the *History* is also a witty,
Smollettian book of anecdotes, aristocratic
attitudes to the poor ('many of them seem
to Grunt rather than Speak in ordinary
conversation') and a surprising advocacy
of English intermarriage with the Indians.
[EM]

The Prose Works, ed. L. B. Wright (1966); *The
Writings of 'Colonel William Byrd, of Westover
in Virginia'*, ed. J. S. Bassett (1901); *A Great
American Gentleman: William Byrd of Westover
in Virginia, His Secret Diary for the Years
1709–1712*, ed. L. B. Wright and M. Trinling
(1963).
Louis B. Wright, *The First Gentleman of Virginia*
(1940); R. C. Beatty, *William Byrd of Westover*
(1932).

C

Cabell, James Branch (1879–1958). Novelist. Born in Richmond, Virginia, a graduate of William and Mary College, he always stayed outside the mainstream of modern American fiction, allowing his imagination to flourish in idealistic romances. Most of these, set in the medieval myth-country of Poictesme, deal epically, in mannered prose, with Dom Manuel, an adventurer striving for ideals he pessimistically realizes to be unattainable, with his descendants, and with the legends that grow round him after death. Two critical volumes (*Beyond Life*, 1919, and *Straws and Prayer-Books*, 1924) are 'prologue' and 'epilogue' to his Poictesme cycle, whose action, including short stories and poems, is arranged in the following genealogical sequence: *Figures of Earth* (1921), *The Silver Stallion* (1926), *Domnei* (1920; originally published as *The Soul of Melicent*, 1913), *The Music from behind the Moon* (1926), *Chivalry* (1909), *Jurgen* (1919), *The Line of Love* (1905), *The High Place* (1923), *Gallantry* (1907), *Something about Eve* (1927), *The Certain Hour* (1916), *The Cords of Vanity* (1909), *From the Hidden Way* (1916), *The Jewel Merchants* (1921), *The Rivet in Grandfather's Neck* (1915), *The Eagle's Shadow* (1904) and *The Cream of the Jest* (1917; revised 1920).

Jurgen was the first book to win him a wide reputation, partly because of a charge of obscenity levelled against it. A story of search and initiation, subtitled a 'comedy of justice', it concerns a middle-aged pawnbroker who sets out to find his wife, vanished under the influence of a useful devil. His wit and scepticism resist a mythological world whose symbolic entities include centaurs, Queen Helen, the land of Cockaigne, Hell and God's throne. He regains his wife and his prosaic life but the novel is a criticism of conventional morality and its tyrannies, hence the charges against its eroticism. *The High Place* again opposes dream and reality, placing comment on America in a fictional medieval locality, but *The Cream of the Jest* is more complex: a Virginian writer enters the world of allegorical dreams of his own creation, more

exciting than his own life and the ageing of his own body. But his dreams cannot be sustained and he returns to his fate; and again the hero's erotic dream of an 'ageless, loveable and loving woman of whom all poets had been granted fitful broken glimpses' turns to chilly reality. The deliberately archaic apparatus of image, diction and symbol make the inner meanings of Cabell's novels difficult to interpret with security, and they have dated. But their summaries do not do justice to their search for ideal states, their charmingly precise detail and their appeal to the erotic dreamer in urban wastelands. [HB/EM]

Works (18 vols., 1927–30); *Between Friends: Letters of James Branch Cabell and Others*, ed. P. Colum and M. F. Cabell (1932).
A. R. Wells, *Jesting Moses* (1963); Carl Van Doren, *James Branch Cabell* (1932); Edmund Wilson, 'The James Branch Cabell Case Reopened', *New Yorker*, 21 April 1955.

Cable, George Washington (1844–1925). Story writer, novelist, historian. Born New Orleans, the son of a Virginia slaveholder, he served in the Confederate army from 1862, reporting the experience later in *The Cavalier* (1901). After the war illness turned him to writing; he produced a popular humorous column under the pseudonym 'Drop Shot' for the New Orleans *Picayune* and joined the paper as a reporter, leaving when his Calvinism prevented him from being theatre critic. He turned to accountancy and research into the history of New Orleans, writing exact, careful local colour stories collected as *Old Creole Days* (1879). Their success encouraged *The Grandissimes* (1880), a study of the Louisiana Creole Negroes; *Madame Delphine* (1881), a novelette about a quadroon woman's anxiety to conceal her daughter's mixed blood; *Dr Sevier* (1885); *Bonaventure* (1888); and *Bylow Hill* (1902), which narrates the unsuccessful marriage of a Southern girl to a New England clergyman.

His history *The Creoles of Louisiana* (1884) angered Creoles by its account of their past; he has also been accused of misrepresenting them in fiction (typical objections are contained in Grace King's *Memories of a Southern Woman of Letters*, 1932). Always an enemy of slavery, he now became a determined reformer and further angered Southerners. *The Silent South* (1885) collects studies advocating the abolition of contract labour, better conditions for Negroes, and prison reform. Increasing opposition forced his move to Massachusetts, where he wrote *The Negro Question* (1888) and *The Southern Struggle for Pure Government* (1890).

Cable created a new province of American literature. He captured to the full picturesque scenes in the old French–Spanish city of New Orleans and the doomed plantations, especially in *The Grandissimes*, with its rich texture and atmosphere of mystery, yet quite avoided the excesses of later writers on this subject. His description of the French dialect of Creole Negroes was meticulously accurate; a keen dislike of caste and class oppression displays itself even in his early fiction; and an attractive sense of humour underlies his delicate and whimsical prose. [MG]

The Negro Question, A Selection of Writings on Civil Rights in the South, ed. Arlin Turner (1958).
Lucy L. C. Biklé, *George W. Cable: His Life and Letters* (1928); Arlin Turner, *George W. Cable, a Biography* (1956); Edmund Wilson, 'The Ordeal of George Washington Cable', *New Yorker*, XXXII (1957); P. Butcher, 'George Washington Cable', *American Literary Realism 1870–1910*, No. 1 (1967).

Cage, John (1912–   ). Composer, writer, mycologist. Born in Los Angeles, he studied music with Adolph Weiss, Arnold Schoenberg and others, adopted Zen Buddhism under the instruction of Daisetz Suzuki, worked with the dancer Merce Cunningham, the painter Robert Rauschenberg and the pianist David Tudor, and created the first 'happening' at Black Mountain College in 1952. He is internationally celebrated as one of the most important composers of this century; his compositional procedures involving chance, the *I Ching* and indeterminacy are central to modern art in general. His writings on music and the arts, in a style initially owing something to Gertrude Stein's terseness, are becoming as influential as his music (*Silence*, 1961, and *A Year from Monday*, 1967). He wrote the musical section of *Virgil Thomson* (1959, with Kathleen Hoover) and in 1969 edited *Notations*, a large collection of instructions for the performance of music and other events. [EM]

Calvin Tomkins, *The Bride and the Bachelors* (1965); ed. Richard Kostelanetz, *The Theatre of Mixed Means* (1968), and *Master Minds* (1969).

Cahan, Abraham (1860–1951). Novelist, journalist. Born in Russia, he came to the United States in 1882 and took up journalism, finally becoming editor of the Socialist daily *Forward*. His first American novel was *Yekl: A Tale of the New York Ghetto* (1896), about the Americanization of a Jewish immigrant from Russia who adapts from being blacksmith to sewing-machine operator and changes wives in the process. But the classic treatment of the theme of Americanization occurs in his *The Rise of David Levinsky* (1917), an excellent, exemplary Jewish and immigrant novel, about a man who rises in the New World at considerable psychic and human loss. It is a prototype for many Jewish American novels since, and is his best-known book. [MB]

Cain, James M(allahan) (1892–   ). Novelist. Born in Annapolis, Maryland. His stories of violence and racketeering contributed to modern sensational realism and helped to produce a whole school of hard-boiled murder fiction. Born in Maryland, he was a newspaper reporter and screen-writer before producing his first, best-known and most influential novel, *The Postman Always Rings Twice* (1934), about a wife plotting with a hoodlum lover to murder her husband. His other novels likewise exploit the vividness and violence of life in a variety of settings; they include *Mildred Pierce* (1941); *Love's Lively Counterfeit* (1942), about racketeering in a mid-Western city; *Double Indemnity* (1943); *Past All Dishonor* (1946), a historical novel; *The Butterfly* (1947), about incest in Kentucky; and *The Magician's Wife* (1965). In prefaces to various books Cain has disclaimed the desire to be considered a 'tough' novelist, stressing rather his realism and the accuracy of his vernacular. [MB]

Cain X3: Three Novels (1969).

Caldwell, Erskine (1903–   ). Novelist. Born in Georgia, son of a Presbyterian home missionary, he came to early fame with vivid, humorous, strongly dramatized tales of Georgia share-croppers, tenant farmers and mill-hands, which seemed melodramatic to those sheltered from the violence of the South. The play of his novel *Tobacco Road* (1932) ran continuously on Broadway for over seven years: the economic poverty, social crudeness and degenerate sexuality are documented in such a way that the prurient could make the work, in either form, a success. The equally notorious novel *God's Little Acre* (1933) is again a powerful but entertaining indictment – there is this element of ambiguous intention in Caldwell's writing – of social conditions focused here on a cotton weavers' strike in Carolina. Both works brought censorship against Caldwell; the charges were dismissed, as they were against *Tragic Ground* (1944). Some of his best work is his earliest – the working-class novels *The Bastard* (1929) and *Poor Fool* (1930) – and here again, as in all his writing, the basis is first-hand experience. He has held a variety of jobs, including reporting, and the detail of his fiction is accurate. He is prolific: in 1949, for instance, it was estimated that 20 million copies of his books in all editions were in circulation. His novels about the South include *Journeyman* (1935), *Trouble in July* (1940), *This Very Earth* (1948), *A Place Called Estherville* (1949), *Episode in Palmetto* (1950) and *Close to Home* (1962), a brilliant study in relations between coloured women and white men. *Miss Mama Aimée* (1967) is a memorable collection of upper-class plantation grotesques. *The Weather Shelter* (1969) is a genre novel set in Tennessee. Among his novels set outside the South, *A Lamp for Nightfall* (1952) deals with Maine people and *All Night Long* (1942) with guerillas in Russia. Throughout his career he has written many short stories, most conveniently presented in *The Complete Short Stories of Erskine Caldwell* (1953); some of the best are in *Georgia Boy* (1943), *Certain Women* (1957) and *Men and Women* (1961). During his marriage with the photographer Margaret Bourke-White, they collaborated in a documentary book on Georgia share-croppers, *You Have Seen Their Faces* (1937). Further social criticism is contained in *Say! Is This the U.S.A.?* (1941) and *Around about America* (1964); *In Search of Bisco* (1965) is a humane and shrewd guide to Southern racialism, and *In the Shadow of the Steeple*

(1966) presents the Christian church in the South through the life of Caldwell's minister father. Caldwell's is a unique career combining social teaching (he lectured on Southern tenant farmers at the New School for Social Research – see his pamphlet *Tenant Farmer*, 1935), social documentary and fiction which ambivalently shocks with its picture of the ugliness and decay of American life. [HB/EM]

Calef, Robert (1648–1719). Polemicist. A cloth merchant who went to Boston in 1688, he attacked Cotton ◊ Mather's attitude towards witchcraft trials (*Wonders of the Invisible World*, 1693) in his *More Wonders of the Invisible World*. No Boston printer would handle it, so it appeared in London in 1700. Increase ◊ Mather had it burned in Harvard yard. [EM]

G. L. Burr, *Narratives of the Witchcraft Cases 1648–1706* (1914).

Calisher, Hortense (1911–). Novelist. Born in New York. She is a major novelist of the intense movement of 'our common unusualness', presented in great detail and exactness. Her field is the American bourgeoisie, and her master is Henry James. *Absence of Angels* (1951), *Tales for a Mirror* (1962) and *Extreme Magic* (1964) are collections of short stories, and her novels are *False Entry* (1961), *Textures of Life* (1963), *Journal from Ellipsin* (1966), *The Railway Police* (1966), *The Last Trolley Ride* (1966) and *The New Yorkers* (1969). [EM]

Calverton, V(ictor) F(rancis) (pseud. of George Goetz) (1900–40). Critic. Born in Baltimore, Maryland. He is important both in the development of sociological literary criticism in America and in the campaign to assert that there was a distinctive tradition of American literature. Of Baltimore working background, and a Marxist, he published both polemical historical criticism and social commentary. His books include *The Newer Spirit: A Sociological Criticism of Literature* (1925), *The New Grounds of Criticism* (1930), *American Literature at the Crossroads* (1931) and *The Liberation of American Literature* (1932). Along with Van Wyck ◊ Brooks, Granville ◊ Hicks, Max ◊ Eastman and others, he did much to assert American literature's 'coming of age' and to establish its history.

He edited an *Anthology of American Negro Literature* (1929); founded a magazine, *The Modern Quarterly*; and wrote a novel, *The Man Inside* (1935). [MB]

Charles I. Glicksberg, 'V. F. Calverton: Marxism without Dogma', *Sewanee Review*, XLVI (1938).

Capote, Truman (1924–   ). Novelist, story writer, reporter. Born in New Orleans, where he lived until 1942. Since then has lived in New York City and travelled widely. His early work was associated with the development of post-war Southern gothic literature, but he has written in different modes and styles; and though some of his writing is disquietingly chic he has emerged as an enormously talented and successful literary professional. His first novel, *Other Voices, Other Rooms* (1948), hailed as the work of a youthful prodigy, takes its Southern hero into the hallucinatory and sinister world of the decadent and leaves him there. *The Grass Harp* (1951), a short novel, is a more benign exploration of the sinister and uncanny, with a stronger social theme. The surrealistic quality of this early writing comes out strongly in a collection of stories of this period, *A Tree of Night* (1949). They exploit sinister, monstrous and ghostly elements in exploring loneliness and lovelessness, and range from the tragic to the macabre comic. With *Breakfast at Tiffany's* (1958), made into a successful film, Capote shifts locale to New York and works much closer to the comedy of manners, exploiting more the stylish and quaint. But his work was turning more in the direction of reportage, much of it for the *New Yorker*. The collection *Local Color* (1950) brought together travel sketches and articles on famous people (particularly notable is a profile of Marlon Brando); *The Muses Are Heard* (1956) is a funny and well-observed study of a State Department-supported tour of Russia made by an American company playing *Porgy and Bess*; and the reportage manner reached its greatest success (both financially and in terms of its literary possibilities) in *In Cold Blood* (1966), a 'non-fiction novel' about the slaughter of a respectable Kansas farming family by two wandering psychopaths. The horrifying murder was intensively researched by Capote, who also came close to the murderers before their execution. Though over-promoted, the book is both powerfully terrifying and fascinating for its inside account of two distinct elements in the American national psyche, the orderly and the anarchic. [MB]

Selected Writings (1963).
Irving Malin, *New American Gothic* (1962); interview with Pati Hill, *Paris Review*, 16 (Spring-Summer, 1967); A. Kazin, *Contemporaries* (1962); Lee Baxandall, 'The New Capote and the Old Soviet Advice', *Studies on the Left*, VI, 2 (March-April 1966).

Carman, (William) Bliss (1861–1929). Poet. Canadian-born and Harvard-educated, he left business to become with Richard ◊ Hovey one of the Bohemian 'vagabond' school who stirred American verse at the end of the century (◊ Bohemianism). His first book was *Low Tide on Grand Pré* (1893), lyrics. With Hovey he wrote *Songs from Vagabondia* (1894), *More Songs from Vagabondia* (1896) and *Last Songs from Vagabondia* (1901). Between 1894 and 1898 he edited the early 'little' magazine the *Chap-Book* (◊ Little Magazines), worked for other papers, and, though an American resident, became Canadian poet laureate. His later work leaves the Bohemian image behind but stays strongly lyrical. He produced over 20 volumes, including *By the Aurelian Wall and Other Elegies* (1898), *Pipes of Pan* (5 vols., 1902–5), and *Ballads and Lyrics* (1923). He also wrote essays on art and nature. [MB]

Poems (1931).
Odell Shepard, *Bliss Carman* (1923).

Carnegie, Andrew (1835–1919). Industrialist, writer. This famous Scots-born industrialist worked his way up from work in a Pennsylvania cotton factory to domination of the steel industry; bought out by U.S. Steel in 1901 he turned to philanthropy and writing, contributing to letters not only the Carnegie Libraries but *Triumphant Democracy* (1886); *The Gospel of Wealth* (1889), about the stewardship obligations of the industrial oligarchs; an *Autobiography* (1920), etc. [MB]

Matthew Josephson, *The Robber Barons* (1934).

Carnegie, Dale (1888–1955). Popular educator. This famous lecturer and author of self-improvement manuals expressed a fundamental American remedial philosophy in best-sellers like *How to Win Friends and Influence People* (1936), which has had a world-wide sale of over 5 million; *How to Stop Worrying and Start Living* (1948); etc. [MB]

Carter, Nick. The hero of millions of readers may have been based on Allan Pinkerton (1819–84), who established the first United States detection agency in Chicago in 1850; but he was invented by John R. Coryell (1848–1924), whose mass of pop fiction appeared under a maze of pseudonyms and who worked in a writing team with T. C. Harbaugh and F. Van Rensselare Dey. Nick's first performance came in *The Old Detective's Pupil* (1886), and his character appeared also in stories by other writers, including George C. Jenks (1850–1929), who created another legendary hero, Diamond Dick (e.g. *Diamond Dick's Decoy Duck*, 1891). [EM]

Cartwright, Peter (1785–1872). Preacher, memoirist. A Virginia clergyman who spent his youth in the Kentucky region of Rogues Harbour, but became a Methodist itinerant preacher at 17 and was famous later on the frontier for his sermons and his courage. In 1842 he moved into Illinois and the Ohio valley, and opposed Lincoln as candidate for Congress. His *Autobiography of Peter Cartwright, the Backwoods Preacher* (1856) and *Fifty Years as a Presiding Elder* (1871) are essential readings on the frontier and revivalism. [EM]

Caruthers, William Alexander (1800–46). A Virginia-born physician, he is remembered for 3 novels: *The Kentuckian in New York, or The Adventures of Three Southerners* (1834); *The Cavaliers of Virginia* (1835), a romance about Bacon's Rebellion; and *The Knights of the Horseshoe, A Traditional Tale of the Cocked Hat Gentry in the Old Dominion* (1845). [MB]

C. C. Davis, *Chronicler of the Cavaliers: A Life of Dr W. A. Caruthers* (1953).

Carver, Jonathan (1710–80). Travel writer. Amid the controversies over his life and writings, it is clear that he was born in Weymouth, Massachusetts, grew up in Connecticut, served in the British army during the French and Indian wars, undertook an exploration of the western Great Lakes area in 1766–7, and at his death had a wife on both sides of the Atlantic. The preface to the third edition of his *Travels through the Interior of Parts of North America* (1778) fakes an aristocratic ancestry, and the text steals from other documents of the region, but the book carries an authentic grand vision of the American West and some good accounts of the Plains Indians. It was admired and used by ◊ Bryant, Schiller, Chateaubriand, Wordsworth and Coleridge. [EM]

Cary, Phoebe (1824–71). Poet. She was born in Cincinnati and became, with her sister, a member of the New York circle of Horace Greeley and Rufus ◊ Griswold. Her poetry is thin, but her parodies are exceptionally good. [EM]

Poems and Parodies (1854).

Cather, Willa (1873–1947). Novelist, short-story writer, poet, journalist. Born in Virginia, she moved at 9 to Nebraska, still to some extent a pioneer community. Educated at the University of Nebraska, she became a teacher, later a journalist and finally a free-lance writer. Much of her best fiction is about immigrant and pioneer life in the agricultural West. But she is much more than simply a regional novelist; she is a complex and formal writer, who writes out of a deeply felt culture, and she must be regarded as among the important American writers of this century. Her collection of essays *Not under Forty* (1936) expresses her debt to a substantial tradition of fiction, particularly to Flaubert, Henry James, and Sarah Orne ◊ Jewett, whom she knew; and she exploits this tradition, the tradition of the socio-moral novel – and, in a sense, the European novel – in her fiction. Her pioneers are not primitives; nor are they devoid of traditional culture. She is often concerned with the threat to traditional – yet subtly presented – moral and spiritual standards that modern life has brought, and with the values of an old prairie aristocracy pursuing an idealistic and spiritual life in a materialist world. Her most admired heroes and heroines are deeply involved with life, and she conveys them to us with an intensity to the rendering of which her aesthetic was committed.

Willa Cather published a book of poems, *April Twilights*, in 1903 (revised 1933), a collection of stories, *The Troll Garden*, in 1905, and her first novel, *Alexander's Bridge*, in 1912. In 1912 she gave up regular journalism to write; and, advised by Sarah Orne Jewett to write from her knowledge of her own background, she went on to produce the pioneer and immigrant novels for which she is best known – *O Pioneers!* (1913), *The Song of the Lark* (1915), *My Àntonia* (1918) and *One of Ours* (1922;

Pulitzer Prize). All these books evoke, intensely, the life of men and women against the land and landscape of Nebraska, the mid-West and Colorado. In 1920 she collected some of her excellent short stories in *Youth and the Bright Medusa*. The next group of novels – *A Lost Lady* (1923), *The Professor's House* (1925) and *My Mortal Enemy* (1926) – is rather less well known, but these are in fact among her best work. In them, there is a change of manner, towards a growing delicacy of theme, a greater concern with the pressure of modern life upon traditional standards, and a developing symbolic mode of presentation. In her two next books, *Death Comes for the Archbishop* (1927) and *Shadows on the Rock* (1931), her Catholicism becomes more overt; both are historical chronicles of the early spiritual pioneering of the Catholic Church, in the first in New Mexico, in the second in Quebec. She is even here concerned with the notion of the good life, of Christianity as vitality. A further collection of stories, *Obscure Destinies*, containing some excellent work, appeared in 1932; and there are two later novels, *Lucy Gayheart* (1935) and *Sapphira and the Slave Girl* (1940). Her writings on literature are edited by B. Slote in *The Kingdom of Art: Willa Cather's First Principles and Critical Statements* (1967) [MB]

The Novels and Stories (1937-41); Early Stories, ed. Mildred R. Bennett (1957); Collected Short Fiction (1965).

E. K. Brown, Willa Cather: A Critical Biography (1953); ed. James Schroeter, Willa Cather and Her Critics (1967); J. H. Randall, The Landscape and the Looking Glass (1960); Mildred R. Bennett, The World of Willa Cather (1961).

Catton, Bruce (1899–). Journalist, historian. Born in Petoskey, Michigan. By training a newspaperman, he has lately emerged as a historian of particular gifts. His *Mr Lincoln's Army* (1951), *Glory Road: The Bloody Route from Fredericksburg to Gettysburg* (1952) and *A Stillness at Appomattox* (1953) together form a lavishly written and colourful 3-volume history of the army of the Potomac during the Civil War. More incisively written are *The Hallowed Ground* (1956), the story of the war from the viewpoint of the Northern armies, and *The Coming Fury* (1961), which was the first volume of *The Centennial History of the Civil War* (completed by *Terrible Swift Sword*, 1963, and *Never*

Call Retreat, 1965). Though his work has been criticized for its romanticism, its emphasis on personality, and its view of history as a crusade of ideals (rather than as a matter of economic factors and power conflicts) it represents popular history at a very high level of achievement. [DKA]

Chandler, Raymond (1888–1959). Mystery writer. Chicago-born, he went at 8 to England with his mother and was educated at Dulwich College. After a brief spell of journalism he left in 1912 for California, where after war-service he became a businessman associated with various oil companies. It was not until the Depression that he began, at 44, to write, publishing more than 20 stories between 1933 and 1939, most in *Black Mask*, then the leading vehicle for the hard-boiled school of detective fiction. Their success led him into the famous novels about racketeers, crooked cops and politicians. He lived in Southern California, the usual setting of his work, for most of his life, but was contemplating return to England when he died.

Chandler brought to the mystery novel the poetry of violence, a remarkable personal style, and an ability to develop character and situation dramatically. His essays in *The Simple Art of Murder* (1950) and the miscellany *Raymond Chandler Speaking* (1962) show his close concern for language and plot. The first novel, *The Big Sleep* (1939), was followed by *Farewell, My Lovely* (1940), *The High Window* (1942) and *The Lady in the Lake* (1943), these usually being considered his best works. The style of the later novels – *The Little Sister* (1949), *The Long Goodbye* (1954), *Playback* (1958) – becomes increasingly mannered, while his detective-hero Philip Marlowe is touched with sentimentality. This character, who first appears in *The Big Sleep*, owes something to the ruthless protagonists of other *Black Mask* writers, notably Dashiell ◊ Hammett; but he has a highly individual style and appeal. The Marlowe novels are extended morality plays, set in the finely depicted neon wilderness of Los Angeles, where the hero searches for a hidden truth without reference to either individual gain or abstract justice. The novels are collected in *The Raymond Chandler Omnibus* (1953) and *The Second Chandler Omnibus* (1962), the stories in *Killer in the Rain* (1964) and *The Smell of Fear* (1965). [HD]

Matthew J. Bruccoli, *Raymond Chandler: A*

Checklist (1968); Philip Durham, *Down These Mean Streets* (1963).

Channing, Edward Tyrell (1790–1856). Editor, lecturer. Born in Newport, Rhode Island, the younger brother of William Ellery ◊ Channing the Unitarian propagandist, he helped found and edit the *North American Review*, a major organ of Boston and America, the most important 19th-century American review. He is also important as a teacher, since as Boylston Professor of Rhetoric at Harvard he taught Emerson, Thoreau, Holmes, Lowell and R. H. ◊ Dana, Jr, who edited his *Lectures* (1856). [MB]

Channing, William Ellery, (I) (1780–1842). Clergyman, poet, essayist. Born in Newport, Rhode Island, he became tutor in a rich family in Virginia, where he read Rousseau, Wordsworth and Godwin – an introduction to European romanticism which modified his Christianity towards Transcendentalism (◊ Transcendentalists). A graduate of Harvard Divinity School, he was ordained a Congregational Minister in 1803. He visited Schiller, Goethe, Coleridge and Wordsworth and returned to his pulpit in Federal Street Church, Boston, as a man of 'no sectarian bonds', whose sermons brought together the Unitarian and Transcendental. His strong opposition to the Calvinist doctrine of human depravity came out in the ordination sermon for Jared Sparks and in two *Christian Examiner* articles in 1819, attacks which, added to previous work of Joseph Priestley and Henry Ware, encouraged the establishment of Unitarianism. He helped found and run *The Unitarian Church Register* (1821), founded the American Unitarian Association, and propagated a liberal religion which fed Transcendentalism and influenced Emerson, Longfellow, etc. He wrote four important works on slavery abolition between 1835 and 1842, and promoted the cause in the *Christian Examiner* and the *North American Review*. He told parishioners that 'justice is a greater good than property' but believed social advance could be furthered only through individual self-improvement, distrusting reform societies and arguing against the bureaucracy of charitable agencies.

Channing also won great reputation as a man of letters; he was one of the best-known literary figures of his day, famed particularly for his essays and reviews. His 'The Importance and Means of a National Literature' (1830) is the most cogent defence of cultural nationalism before Emerson's Phi Beta Kappa oration of 1837; it notes that while Americans protest against 'dependence on European manufacturers' they are content to import 'fabrics of the intellect'. But American faith in 'the essential quality of all human beings' favoured creative activity; hence the New World would beget 'great minds' and 'a nobler race of men'. [MG]

Works (6 vols., 1841–3; revised 1875; 1 vol. edn, 1886).
Arthur W. Brown, *Always Young for Liberty: A Biography of William Ellery Channing* (1956); David P. Edgell, *William Ellery Channing: An Intellectual Portrait* (1955); R. E. Spiller, 'A Case for W. E. Channing', *New England Quarterly*, III (1930).

Channing, William Ellery, (II) (1818–1901). Poet, biographer. Born in Boston. Nephew of the above, he left Harvard to go west and write poetry. He later moved to Concord to be near Emerson, who influenced him and also published him in the *Dial*; and became close to the members of that community, including Thoreau, of whom he wrote the first biography, *Thoreau, the Poet-Naturalist* (1873; revised 1902). A ◊ Transcendentalist, he published several volumes of verse, from *Poems* (1843) to *John Brown and the Heroes of Harper's Ferry* (1886). F. B. Sanbourn selected from his work in *Poems of Sixty-Five Years* (1902). [MB]

Chapman, John Jay (1862–1933). Critic, poet, playwright. New York born, he went to Harvard and became an adopted Bostonian, involving himself in the prevailing debates about literature, politics and religion. The influence of Emerson appears in *Emerson, and Other Essays* (1898). Other works include *Learning, and Other Essays* (1910), *Letters and Religion* (1924) and *New Horizons in American Life* (1932). One of his many plays was *The Treason and Death of Benedict Arnold* (1910); his poetry is in *Songs and Poems* (1919). For his involvement in Boston see his *Memories and Milestones* (1915) and his collected letters, a fascinating social document. [MB]

Collected Works (12 vols., 1970).
Mark A. De Wolfe Howe, *John Jay Chapman and His Letters* (1937); Richard B. Hovey, *John Jay Chapman: An American Mind* (1959).

Chase, Mary Ellen (1887–   ). Novelist, essayist, scholar. Born and educated in Maine, she taught English at the University of Minnesota and Smith College. Her novels *Mary Peters* (1934) and *Silas Crockett* (1935), describing the past and present life of Maine seafarers, are impressive contributions to modern regional literature and have some excellent characterizations of women; later fiction includes *Dawn in Lyonesse* (1938), *The Edge of Darkness* (1957) and *Lonely Ambitions* (1960). She wrote humorous and descriptive essays about England (*This England*, 1936); two guides to the Bible, *The Bible and the Common Reader* (1944) and *Life and Language in the Old Testament* (1955); and *A Goodly Heritage* (1932) and *A Goodly Fellowship* (1939), interesting autobiographies about her teaching career. [M G]

Perry Westbrook, *Mary Ellen Chase* (1965).

Chase, Richard (1914–66). Literary critic, teacher. A Professor of English at Columbia, he was an important voice in the post-war critical movement that advanced beyond the ◊ New Criticism to myth and symbol studies and cultural analysis. His excellent *The American Novel and Its Tradition* (1957) stresses the 'romance' tradition of American fiction, and has advanced a general reappraisal of the distinctive symbolist and abstract quality of much American writing. *Quest for Myth* (1949) and the broader study of American culture *The Democratic Vista* (1959) are also important, as are various uncollected contributions to literary quarterlies. [M B]

Herman Melville (1949); *Emily Dickinson* (1951); *Walt Whitman Reconsidered* (1955).

Chayefsky, Paddy (1923–   ). Playwright. A New Yorker, he began writing television plays about ordinary people's humdrum lives, the best of which is *Marty* (1953), the tale of a Bronx butcher's courtship of an old maid schoolteacher. His humorous, sympathetic realism continued in *The Bachelor Party* (1954) and *The Catered Affair* (1955). His first Broadway play was also originally a television script: *The Middle of the Night* (1956). His tape-recorder naturalism is modified towards stylization in *The Tenth Man* (1960), on the Jewish dybbuk theme, and *Gideon* (1961), in which a God-chosen man refuses even miracles as aids to belief. In *The Latent Homosexual* (1968) the poet hero, confronted by tax problems,

is manipulated back into circulation by a cunning lawyer. His *Television Plays* appeared in 1955. [E M]

Cheever, John (1912–   ). Short-story writer, novelist. Born in Quincy, Massachusetts. The author of 5 collections of short stories and 3 novels, *The Wapshot Chronicle* (1957), *The Wapshot Scandal* (1964) and *Bullet Park* (1969), he is a prime exponent of the poignant, well-made story of the *New Yorker* school, in which magazine many of his stories have appeared. His novels have exposed his talents on a larger scale: there he has detailed a picture of the passing of rural America and its replacement by the new America of supermarket, superhighway and computer technology. His tone is of nostalgic regard for the old and satire for the new. Latterly, his writing has become increasingly satirical, its settings increasingly mechanized, and there are evident connexions with the work of William ◊ Burroughs and Terry ◊ Southern. His career shows that the contemporary trend to baroque satire and bizarre, black humour, especially in *Bullet Park* (1969), can be fed by a writer who has been working in his own personal strain for years and who has approached 'hard' satire only gradually. [A G]

Collections of stories: *The Way Some People Live* (1943); *The Enormous Radio* (1953); *The House-breaker of Shady Hill* (1958); *The Brigadier and the Golf Widow* (1964).

Chesnutt, C. W. ◊ Negro Literature.

Chicago Aristotelians. A group of literary critics associated, from the 1940s on, with the University of Chicago and a major force in the development of modern American criticism. Their importance lies in their close philosophical analysis of criticism itself, and their challenges to the mechanical, over-simplified assumptions (about paradox, poetic language, symbols) of much modern critical writing. Their debt to Aristotle, a sophisticated one, derives from their approval of his pragmatic approach to the study of a text and his concern with poetics – with defining the structural parts of a work of art in terms of their relative importance. In particular, they are much concerned with defining 'plot' – the 'imitation of an action', and therefore that part of a work which subsumes all other parts of the imitation within itself.

The main statement of the group is to be found in *Critics and Criticism: Ancient and Modern* (1952; revised abridged paperback edn, 1957), edited by R. S. ⟡ Crane, and containing essays by Crane, W. R. Keast, Richard McKeon, Norman Maclean, Elder Olson and Bernard Weinberg, all of whom base their critical approach – which, they insist, 'is one critical method among others' – on learned and wide-ranging scholarship and philosophical clarity. Weinberg, a Professor of Romance Languages and Literature, has produced an excellent *History of Literary Criticism in the Italian Renaissance* (1961); Elder Olson, *The Poetry of Dylan Thomas* (1954) and a general study, *Tragedy and the Theory of Drama* (1961); Crane an excellent theoretical study, *The Languages of Criticism and the Structure of Poetry* (1953). Deriving from the group is a most significant contribution to the study of fiction, Wayne Booth's *The Rhetoric of Fiction* (1961). [MB]

W. K. Wimsatt, *The Verbal Icon* (1954); René Wellek, *Concepts of Criticism* (1963); George Watson, *The Literary Critics* (1962).

Chivers, Thomas Holley (1809–58). Poet. Born in Georgia on a wealthy plantation. He trained as a physician but grew increasingly absorbed by any cult or sect he could join – Swedenborgian, ⟡ Transcendentalist, Fourierist, Mesmerist, spiritualist, etc. His poems are unique; sometimes they have a curious free lyricism whose wild sounds and surreal juxtapositions have attracted poets ever since, however academics may scoff. His books, published at his own expense, include *The Lost Pleïad and Other Poems* (1845), *Memoralia, or Phials of Amber, Full of the Tears of Love* (1853), and *Virginalia, or Songs of My Summer Nights* (1853). Poe accused his *Eonchs of Ruby: A Gift of Love* (1851) of plagiarism, and the reverse was retorted. The correspondence of these mutual plagiarists is a fascinating study in shrewdness and misunderstanding. Chivers also wrote a theory of the unconscious, *Search after Truth, or a New Revelation of the Psycho-Physiological Nature of Man* (1848), and one of the earliest dramatizations of the Deirdre legend: *The Sons of Usna: Tragi-Apotheosis, in Five Acts* (1858). He is a poet of self-mesmerism, a linguistic swinger of great energy and perhaps mystic power. [EM]

S. Foster Damon, *Thomas Holley Chivers: Friend of Poe* (1930).

Chomsky, Noam (1928–   ). Linguist, political critic. Born and educated in Philadelphia, he studied at Harvard 1951–5, and since 1955 he has taught at the Massachusetts Institute of Technology, where he is professor of modern language and linguistics. His first reputation came in the field of linguistics, through both his lectures and his publications: *Syntactic Structures* (1957); *Current Issues in Linguistic Theory* (1964); *Aspects of the Theory of Syntax* (1965), an important work on transformational grammar; *Topics in the Theory of Generative Grammar* (1966); *Cartesian Linguistics* (1966); and *Language and Mind* (1968), a lucid statement of his philosophy of language. Chomsky's second reputation came through the effects of his radical Jewish background on his political opinions during the sixties. He is one of the American Establishment's most formidable critics. The political essays in his *American Power and the New Mandarins* (1969) includes 'The Responsibility of Intellectuals' and 'On Resistance', fine attacks on complacency and hidden power. Chomsky has transformed the status and relevance of theoretical linguistics in our time, and he goes on to make a remarkable connexion between the possibility of language as a biologically determined and transmitted structure, a criticism of extreme behaviourist psychology, and the responsibility of men of knowledge to challenge the authoritarian state in any of its agencies. [EM]

John Lyons, *Chomsky* (1970).

Chopin, Kate (1851–1904). Novelist, story writer. Born in St Louis, of part-French descent, she lived in New Orleans, then on a plantation, then again in St Louis after her husband's death. An admirer of Maupassant, she wrote stories, criticism and a play. Her stories are set largely among Creoles and Cajuns, and are to be found in *Bayou Folk* (1894) and *A Night in Acadie* (1897); they show great finesse and quality. Her novel *At Fault* (1890) is about the strain in sexual relations that occurs within the constraints of marriage – a theme vastly more successfully extended in her *The Awakening* (1899), a poised, textured book which Larzer Ziff has called 'a novel of the first rank'. It is about Edna Pontellier, a woman married with two children, well-to-do and intelligent, tempted into feeling, freedom and adultery. It was critically ill-received and she wrote little else. [MB]

Larzer Ziff, *The American 1890s* (1966).

Churchill, Winston (1871–1947). Novelist. Born in St Louis (no relation of the British statesman), he graduated from the Naval Academy at Annapolis in 1894 and immediately began to write successfully, spending most of his life in New Hampshire. *The Celebrity: An Episode* (1898), a satire on the flamboyant New York journalist Richard Harding Davis, was followed by his best-seller, *Richard Carvel* (1899), a romance set in the Revolutionary period. *The Crisis* (1901), concerned with St Louis at the time of the Civil War, enjoyed another huge success and typified the lengthy historical romances popular at the turn of the century. *The Crossing* (1904), a characteristically uneven work, described life on the frontier during the Revolution. Later came *Coniston* (1906), *Mr Crewe's Career* (1908), *A Far Country* (1915) and three novels about religion in modern society: *A Modern Chronicle* (1910), *The Inside of the Cup* (1913) and *The Dwelling-Place of Light* (1917). He described his religious convictions in *The Uncharted Way* (1940). [MG]

Charles C. Walcutt, *The Romantic Compromise in the Novels of Winston Churchill* (1951).

Ciardi, John (1916–). Poet. Born in Boston. He has taught at Kansas City University, Harvard, Rutgers and the Bread Loaf Writers Conference, and been poetry editor of the *Saturday Review*. His earliest collection is *Homeward to America* (1940), followed by eight further volumes of poems including *In Fact* (1963) and an excellent translation of Dante's *Divine Comedy* (1954, 1961). His poems are influenced by Eliot and Laforgue towards the humorous critical lyric. His latest book, *Person to Person* (1964), contains sharp images of contemporary America in rather literary poems. [EM]

Miller Williams, *The Achievement of John Ciardi* (1968).

Clapp, Henry (1814–75). Journalist, Bohemian. A leader of the group that gathered at Pfaff's beer-cellar on Broadway in the 1850s, known as 'King of Bohemia', he was born in Nantucket and promoted Whitman

(another Pfaff Bohemian) and Fourier with equal energy. He founded the *Saturday Press*, where Whitman praised himself and where Twain and Billings appeared. He wrote *The Pioneer, or Leaves from an Editor's Portfolio* (1846). (◊ Bohemianism.) [MB]

Clare, Ada (pseud. of Jane McElheney) (1836–74). Novelist, poet, actress, Bohemian. She was 'Queen of Bohemia' to Henry ◊ Clapp's 'King', and was a leading figure in the Pfaff's beer-cellar group. Born in South Carolina, cousin of the poet Paul Hamilton ◊ Hayne, she made her own reputation as poetess and 'Love-Philosopher', producing an illegitimate child by pianist and composer Louis Gottschalk. A visit to bohemian circles in France encouraged her promotion of this advanced artistic life-style. Her writings themselves are relatively slender, but she published verse in Clapp's *Saturday Press* and on the west coast in the *Golden Era*, and distilled her affairs and her experience in a novel called *Only a Woman's Heart* (1866). (◊ Bohemianism.) [MB]

Clark, Walter van Tilburg (1909–). Novelist, poet, short-story writer. Born in Maine but brought up in Nevada, he has always identified his literary spirit with the West and explored frontier themes – those of man struggling for survival in the natural world, of justice and law confronted by forces of evil and anarchy, and of human action set against the motives for it. *The Ox-Bow Incident* (1940), set in the Nevada cattle country, is concerned with a posse's lynching of three men wrongly suspected of murder, and the forces and motives involved. *The City of Trembling Leaves* (1945), a less economically written book, describes the adolescence of a sensitive boy growing up in Reno. *The Track of the Cat* (1949) is a striking and exciting novel about the hunting of a panther, told with a density of symbolic meaning. *The Watchful Gods* (1950) is a collection of stories. Clark has also written poetry and taught creative writing. [AH]

Chester E. Eisinger, 'The Fiction of Walter van Tilburg Clark: Man and Nature in the West', *Southwest Review*, XLIV (Summer, 1959), and *Fiction of the Forties* (1965).

Clark, William. ◊ Lewis, Meriwether.

Cleaver, Eldridge. ◊ Negro Literature.

Clemens, Samuel. ◊ Twain, Mark.

Clurman, Harold (1901–). Stage director, critic. Born in New York City. In the 1920s, enthusiastic over the theory and practice of Copeau and Stanislavski, he joined with Lee Strasberg on his return from France, and together they founded the ◊ Group Theatre, a centre of creative hope in the Depression period. This experience is told in his excellent *The Fervent Years* (1945); and *Lies Like Truth* (1959) collects his first-rate theatre criticism. *The Naked Image* (1966) reports his theatre-going in America, Europe and Japan. He is drama critic of the *Nation*. [E M]

Coates, Robert M. (1897–). Novelist, short-story writer. Born in New Haven, Connecticut, he published his first novel, *The Eater of Darkness* (1929; revised edn reissued 1960), with Robert ◊ McAlmon's Contact Press while he was an expatriate in Paris; an experimental surrealist novel of considerable interest. His more recent novels are rather more conventional in character (*Yesterday's Burdens,* 1933; *Wisteria Cottage,* 1948, etc.). He is the author of some very good short stories, including *All the Year Round* (1943), *The View from Here* (1960) and *The Man Just Ahead of You* (1964), 13 *New Yorker* stories, his finest collection. He is art critic for the *New Yorker.* [M B]

Coffin, Robert P(eter) Tristram (1892–1955). Poet, novelist, biographer. A ' New Englander by birth, by bringing-up, by spirit' (but also educated at Princeton and Oxford), he devoted his life to the description and praise of his native State, Maine. A novel, *Lost Paradise* (1934), re-creates his boyhood life on a Maine salt-water farm; but he was primarily an energetic and prolific poet, among his best volumes being *Ballads of Square-Toed Americans* (1933), *Strange Holiness* (1935; Pulitzer Prize), *Maine Ballads* (1938) and *Poems for a Son with Wings* (1945). A preface to his *Collected Poems* (1939; expanded edition 1948) describes poetry as 'the art of making people feel well about life'. He also published biographies, including those of Laud (1930) and the Dukes of Buckingham (1931), and two critical works: *New Poetry of New England: Frost and Robinson* (1938) and *The Substance That Is Poetry* (1942). [M G]

Collier, John (1901–). Novelist, short-story writer. Born in England, a former poetry editor of *Time and Tide,* he moved to the U.S.A. in 1942 to live in Virginia and California. His inventive, surrealist vein, already established in novels like *His Monkey Wife* (1930) and *Defy the Foul Fiend* (1934) and volumes of stories like *Variations on a Theme* (1935), turned to American subjects, as in *Fancies and Goodnights* (1951), stories. [M B]

Colman, Benjamin (1673–1747). Minister, theologian, poet. Born in England, he was made pastor of Brattle Street Church, Boston, a liberal congregation. He published more than 90 books, mostly sermons – one is revealingly called *The Government and Improvement of Mirth* (1707) – but also poems. [M B]

Combs, (Elisha) Tram(mell, Jr) (1924–). Poet. He left Alabama to study physical sciences at five different Northern universities, then became an air-force meteorologist and oil-company chemist. In 1951 he migrated from science and the U.S.A. to St Thomas, Virgin Islands, where, using his talents as bibliophile, linguist, historian and poet, he ran a bookshop specializing in Spanish-American literature and history. His poetry, quietly intense, is collected in *Pilgrim's Terrace* (1957), *Ceremonies in Mind* (1959), *But Never Mind* (1961) and *Saint Thomas* (1965). Metrically and typographically experimental, he alternates between biting social reflection and sombre metaphysical meditation. [B P]

Commager, Henry Steele (1902–). Historian. Born in Pittsburgh. He has been professor of history and American studies at Amherst since 1956, and held the Pitt Professorship at Cambridge in 1947–8 and the Harmsworth Professorship at Oxford in 1952–3. His large output includes: editions of de Tocqueville's *Democracy in America* (1946) and W. D. Howells (1950, selected writings), *The American Mind* (1950, 'an interpretation of American thought and character since the 1880s'), *Theodore Parker* (1947), *The Growth of the American Republic* (2 vols., 4th edn 1950, with S. E. Morison), *Freedom and Order: A Commentary on the American Political Scene* (1966), *The Search for a Usable Past* (1967) and *The Commonwealth of Learning* (1968), an evaluation of American education. He is also the editor of *The Rise of the American Nation* (50 vols., in progress). [EM]

Comstock, Anthony (1844–1915). Censor. A Connecticut man, he founded and became life secretary of the Society for the Suppression of Vice. His merciless campaigns secured the 1873 Act excluding 'immoral' articles from the mails. His own moral nature seems not to have been outwardly corrupted by the mass of obscenity he read and saw. [EM]

H. Broun and M. Leech, *Anthony Comstock, Roundsman of the Lord* (1927).

Condon, Richard (1915–   ). Novelist. He specializes in the morality of crime and violence presented as comedy thrillers with a high degree of sophisticated invention. But the breaking of men, which occurs in so many of his fictions, is not frivolous. Within his humour lies a painful, almost despairing, sense of permanent human conflicts. His 'bad taste' is a weapon of analysis as well as a form of entertainment. [EM]

The Oldest Confession (1959); *The Manchurian Candidate* (1960); *A Talent for Loving* (1961); *Some Angry Angel* (1961); *Any God Will Do* (1966); *An Infinity of Mirrors* (1966); *The Ecstasy Business* (1967); *Mile High* (1969).

Congdon, Kirby (1924–   ). Poet. Born in Pennsylvania and brought up in New England, he has since lived mostly in New York and Florida. He edits *Magazine*, through which he has promoted what he has termed 'the mimeograph revolution', a rapid means of printing and circulating literary work without waiting for the cautious big publishing firms. His poetry takes the form of lyrics of the embattled self in a city context: *Iron Ark* (1962), *A Century of Progress* (1962), *Icarus* (1963), *Icarus in Aipotu* (1963) and *Juggernaut* (1965), a remarkable set of poems on the motor-cycle cult. He edited *Interim Books* with Jay Socin. [EM]

Connecticut Wits. Also known as the 'Hartford Wits'. The first American school of poets, flourishing in the 1780s and 1790s. They were all born in the 1750s, educated at Yale, amateurs, conservatives (i.e. Federalists), Calvinists and neo-classicists, with the possible exception of ◊ Barlow, and revolutionary satirists, modelled on Butler and Churchill. They included ◊ Trumbull, Timothy ◊ Dwight and his brother Theodore, Lemuel Hopkins, David Humphreys, Richard Alsop and Elihu Hubbard Smith. Their group products include *The Anarchiad* (1786–7) and the verse satire in 20 instalments, *The Echo* (1791–1805). [EM]

Ed. V. L. Parrington, *The Connecticut Wits* (1926); L. Howard, *The Connecticut Wits* (1943).

Connell, Evan S(helby), Jr (1924–   ). Story writer, novelist. Born in Kansas City, Missouri, educated at Dartmouth, he has contributed finely written stories to many American magazines. Collections are *The Anatomy Lesson* (1957), *Mrs Bridge* (1958), a group of delightfully ironic sketches about a suburban matron, and *At the Crossroads* (1965). His novel *The Patriot* (1960) deals again ironically with an innocent hero in the air force during the Second World War. *Notes from a Bottle Found on the Beach at Carmel* (1963) is a long poem of 243 pages, dense with strange facts and lore. *The Diary of a Rapist* (1966) is a novelistic *tour de force* on the nature of sexual violence. To *Mrs Bridge* he has now added a companion, *Mr Bridge* (1969). [MB]

Connelly, Marc (1890–   ). Journalist, dramatist. From Philadelphia. His friendship with George S. ◊ Kaufman led to their successful collaborations in the theatre: *Dulcy* (1921) – in which a stupid woman ironically helps her husband's business career – *To the Ladies* (1922) – the same situation in verse – *Merton of the Movies* (1922) – a Hollywood satire – and *Beggar on Horseback* (1924) – a dream play against the industrialization of art. Connelly's own finest work is *The Green Pastures* (1930), based on Roark Bradford's *Ol' Man Adam an' His Chillun* (1928) – Old Testament myths enacted through the lives of Deep South Negroes treated with saccharine theatricality. His most recent books are *A Survivor from Qam* (1965), a novel and *Voices Offstage: A Book of Memoirs* (1968). [EM]

Conway, Moncure D(aniel) (1832–1907). Biographer, novelist. Born in Virginia, he shifted to abolitionism and Unitarianism, was clergyman, editor and expatriate. He wrote biographies of Carlyle, Emerson, Hawthorne and Thomas Paine, whose writings he edited. His best-known novel is *Pine and Palm* (1887), about the Civil War, and his *Autobiography* (1904) records beliefs and personalities. [MB]

Cook, Ebenezer (*c*.1672–1732). Satiric poet. He was probably an English gentleman who went to buy tobacco in Maryland and returned to pour his disgust with greedy colonists into his hudibrastic satire 'The Sot-Weed Factor; or A Voyage to Maryland' (1708), a coarse, funny and probably realistic poem, which he may have followed up with *Sotweed Redivivus* (1730), a verse treatise on tobacco and its over-production. He may have written a comic poem on Nathaniel Bacon's 1676 revolution. He may have been an American and made 'laureate' by Lord Baltimore. He is certainly the hero of John ◊ Barth's *The Sotweed Factor* (1960). [EM]

Cooke, John Esten (1830–86). Novelist, biographer. This prolific Southern writer, best remembered for his ante-bellum romances, was born into a leading – and literary – Virginia family: his brother, Philip Pendleton Cooke, published a well-received volume of verse and his cousin was John Pendleton ◊ Kennedy. Amongst his novels, *Leather Stocking and Silk, or Hunter John Myers and His Times* (1854) is modelled on Cooper and deals with Virginia society; *The Virginia Comedians, or Old Days in the Old Dominion* (1854) and its sequel deals with pre-Independence actresses and aristocrats; *Surry of Eagle's Nest* (1866) fictionalizes the career of Stonewall Jackson; and *The Heir of Gaymount* (1870) deals with the Civil War, in which Cooke served on the Confederate side, and the need for agrarian reconstruction. He wrote biographies of Jefferson and Lee, and *Virginia: A History of the People* (1883). [MB]

Cooper, James Fenimore (1789–1851). Novelist. Born Burlington, New Jersey. The son of an enterprising and intelligent land speculator, Judge William Cooper, he spent most of his childhood in the frontier community of Cooperstown in upstate New York. This community later served as the model for 'Templeton' in *The Pioneers*, which was the first of his Leatherstocking tales. As the affluent Judge could afford to give his son a good education, he was sent to a school in Albany, where he received an excellent classical training and formed life-long friendships with the sons of the aristocratic Rensselaer and Jay families. After being expelled from Yale because of a prank, he went to sea as an ordinary merchant seaman, then as a midshipman in the U.S. Navy. His naval career, though successful, was brief: he gave up the sea in order to win the hand of Susan Delancy, whose distinguished ancestors had been governors of New York Colony. At 21 he prepared to settle down as a gentleman farmer, republican in his political principles but aristocratic in his sympathies. Apparently destined to a life of comfortable conservative mediocrity, he had in fact already absorbed the experience of ocean and wilderness which were to provide him with the raw materials for some 21 of his 34 novels.

His first novel, *Precaution* (1820), a clumsy imitation of Jane Austen, was written in 1819 on a dare, but with a secret hope that it might be successful enough to repair declining family fortunes; and during the remaining 32 years of his life he continued to write in order to maintain himself and his family at the social level to which they were accustomed. Yet in his second and third novels, *The Spy* (1821) and *The Pioneers* (1823), this American Gentleman created two outstanding democratic heroes – the patriotic pedlar Harvey Birch and the old hunter Natty Bumppo. In these, as in most of his later novels, the ostensible heroes and heroines are genteel characters whose actions, emotions and language are as stereotyped as possible: they provide the conventional 'love interest'; the lower-class characters come alive. Written in frank imitation of the early Waverley novels, *The Spy* and *The Pioneers* were so successful that Cooper, soon known as 'the American Scott', embarked seriously on a career of professional authorship. In 1822 he had moved to New York City. In his second and third works he had been the first writer to make successful novelistic use of authentic American scenes and manners; now in his fourth work, *The Pilot* (1823), he created the first novel in which strictly nautical action was of central importance. In this and subsequent sea romances, such as *The Red Rover* (1828), *The Water-Witch* (1830), *The Two Admirals* (1842), *Wing-and-Wing* (1843) and *The Sea Lions* (1849), he exhibited descriptive powers so remarkable that he became more famous as a sea novelist than as the creator of Leatherstocking. It was in this capacity that he was admired by Melville and Conrad. But he seems to have sensed quite early that in Leatherstocking he had created a mythical character who evoked the profoundest aspirations and regrets of expansive 19th-century white American civilization. In *The Last of the Mohicans* (1826) he wrote the first of four sequels to *The Pioneers*. This series of novels tells the life story of Natty Bumppo from the period of early manhood in *The Deerslayer* (1841), maturity in *The Last of the Mohicans*, unsuccessful courtship in *The Pathfinder* (1840), old age in *The Pioneers*, to extreme old age and death in *The Prairie* (1827). Read in this order, the series forms an artistically defective, yet intensely moving, epic of the Westward Movement. Not until *Moby Dick* did any other American write a work of comparable scope and power.

After the publication of *The Last of the Mohicans*, with its seemingly authentic portraits of American Indians, he found himself a world-famous author. Hoping to improve his health he took his family to Europe in 1826, where they were welcomed by many of the great literary and political figures of the age. He wished to manage publishing affairs in England, and have his children educated by peripatetic studies. He made friends with Scott, but his friendship with Lafayette was probably the decisive influence on his development during the seven years he spent in Europe. He incorporated Lafayette's tour of America into *Notions of America* (1828). He soon became an active supporter of democratic movements in England, France and Poland; he began to align himself with the Jefferson–Jackson faction in American politics. Though an uneasy democrat as soon as he returned to America, he was such an ardent supporter of European popular movements that *The Bravo* (1831), with its frankly proletarian ethos, greatly offended the Whig press in America, not to mention the Tory reviewers in Britain. During the 1830s, in fact, Cooper ceased to be a popular writer as he turned from tales of adventure to works of contemporary social satire like *Homeward Bound* and *Home as Found* (1838). Even before he returned to America in 1833, he was convinced that the republic had deteriorated during his absence into a mobocracy controlled by a licentious press, which was in turn controlled by commercial interests. He wished to retire from writing,

but he could not afford to; in any case, he had to strike back at his detractors. He struck back in print, and then, when he grew weary of being libelled, he personally conducted a series of libel suits which eventually silenced the Whig press.

The last decade of his life was an odd combination of great human sweetness in such works as *Satanstoe* (1845) and the double novel *Afloat and Ashore* (1844) and gloomy misanthropy in *Jack Tier* (1848), *The Crater* (1847) and *The Sea Lions* (1849). *Satanstoe* is the first of the Littlepage trilogy, which dramatizes the problems of land tenure in America, from the colonial period to the 1840s. *The Chainbearer* (1845) involves the Revolutionary war, and, in *The Redskins* (1846), Indians rescue the Littlepage family from exploiting agents and lawyers. Increasingly conservative in his social and religious views, he spent much of his energy supporting such bad causes as the American attack on Mexico and the Rensselaer family's attempt to force poor tenants to pay back rents. Though the latter was a bad cause, it incited him to write the Littlepage trilogy (1845–6), the first family chronicle novel in American literature.

Cooper was usually a slovenly writer; his plots were often loosely constructed, his action improbable and his genteel characters dull or insufferable or both. Yet at least a dozen of his novels have great imaginative vitality. His best novel, probably, is *Satanstoe*, though many critics prefer *The Pioneers*, *The Prairie* or *The Deerslayer*. Certainly the Leatherstocking tales, taken as a group, are his greatest work. But, as Robert Spiller has demonstrated, Cooper must not be judged only by his novels: he was probably the most acute social critic of his age, as he was also the most morally courageous writer America has ever produced. [GD]

Letters and Journals, ed. J. F. Beard (1960–).
James Grossman, *James Fenimore Cooper* (1949); Yvor Winters, 'Fenimore Cooper and the Ruins of Time', in *In Defense of Reason* (1947); George Dekker, *James Fenimore Cooper the Novelist* (1967); Robert Spiller, *Fenimore Cooper, Critic of His Times* (1931); Kay S. House, *Cooper's Americans* (1965).

Coover, Robert (1932–). Novelist. Born in Iowa, he studied at Indiana and Chicago Universities, served in the U.S. Navy 1953–7, has taught philosophy in universities and now lives in England. *The*

Origin of the Brunists (1965) is a first-rate first novel and concerns the founding of a mystical religion after a mining disaster. *The Universal Baseball Association, Inc., J. Henry Waugh, Prop.* (1968) is an allegorical novel using the American religious sport. *Pricksongs and Descants* (1969) contains his short fictions. [EM]

Corso, Gregory (1930–   ). Poet. Born in Greenwich Village, New York, he lived with foster parents, and spent his youth in poverty and violence until he met Allen ◊ Ginsberg and other ◊ Beat Generation writers who encouraged his gift for poetry. From *The Vestal Lady of Brattle* (1955) and *Gasoline* (1958), he developed the power of the longer poems in *The Happy Birthday of Death* (1960), some of the most personal and moving poetry since the Second World War, and the internationally located lyrics of *Long Live Man* (1962). *The Geometric Poem* (1966) is a long work in calligraphy on Egyptian materials. *American Express* (1961) is an amusing prose memoir. He contributed experimental work to *Minutes to Go* (1960) with William Burroughs and Brion Gysin, and to interviews (with Allen Ginsberg and William Burroughs) in *Journal for the Protection of All Beings* (1961). His plays include *In This Hurry-Up Age* (1962). [EM]

Selected Poems (1962).
John Fuller, 'The Poetry of Gregory Corso', *London Magazine*, April 1961.

Cotton, John (1584–1652). Theologian. Born in England, he was Dean of Emmanuel College, Cambridge, highly reputed as an Anglican theologian and orator. Drawn to Puritanism, he became rector of St Botolph's in Boston, Lincolnshire, but Archbishop Laud's enmity drove him to the Bay Colony in 1633. He arrived in Boston, Massachusetts, in part named in his honour, with a fellow graduate of Emmanuel, Thomas ◊ Hooker, and, with Hooker and Richard ◊ Mather, became one of the Colony's most important spiritual leaders. His grandson, Cotton ◊ Mather, called him 'indeed a most universal scholar, and a living system of the liberal arts, and a walking library'. His antinomian theory of grace direct from God inspired Anne Hutchinson, but he became more orthodox later, for example in *Bloudy Tenent Washed and Made White in the Bloude of the Lamb* (1647), a defence of theocracy against Roger ◊ Williams. Most of his works are theological argument with political implications, interpreting the function of the colony and the priesthood in it (he thought it should precede the magistracy). The titles of some of them suggest his interests: *An Abstract of the Lawes of New England* (1641), *The Covenant of God's Free Grace* (1645), *The Controversy Concerning Liberty of Conscience in Matters of Religion* (1646). *Milk for Babes, Drawn out of the Breasts of Both Testaments, Chiefly for the Spiritual Nourishment of Boston Babes in either England* (1646) is a stylish Puritan primer. His biography, John Norton's *Abel Being Dead Yet Speaketh* (1657), is the first American biography: this suggests his importance. [MB]

L. Ziff, *The Career of John Cotton: Puritanism and American Experience* (1963); Moses Coit Tyler, *A History of American Literature during the Colonial Period* (1949; repr. 1962).

Cowley, Malcolm (1898–   ). Critic, poet. Born near Balsano, Pennsylvania. Closely associated with the ◊ 'Lost Generation' of expatriates in Paris in the 1920s, where he was editorially involved with *Secession* and *Broom* (◊ Little Magazines), he has provided one of the most interesting objective records of this period in *Exile's Return* (1934; revised 1951). A general literary critic and a cultural historian, his *After the Genteel Tradition: American Writers since 1910* (1937; repr. 1959) is a useful broad study of American writing; and *The Literary Situation* (1954) has some fascinating cultural material on the conditions of American literary production. Volumes of poems: *Blue Juanita* (1929; reissued with additions, 1968) and *Dry Season* (1941). He has also edited several important volumes such as *The Portable Faulkner*. *The Faulkner–Cowley File: Letters and Memoirs, 1944-1962* (1967) is an important piece of literary history, and *Think Back on Us* (1967) is a collection of his writings from the 1930s arranged as a chronicle of the period by H. D. Piper. [MB]

Cozzens, James Gould (1903–   ). Novelist. Born in Chicago. After attending Harvard, he published in the 1920s four minor novels, which may be taken as apprentice fiction, before announcing in *The Last Adam* (1933; British title *A Cure of Flesh*) his characteristic subject: the subtle examination of moral predicaments and problems of conscience among the professional classes, whom he tends to regard as the guardians of a settled and traditional society. This theme, with variations, provides the material of *Men and Brethren* (1936), *The Just and the Unjust* (1942), *Guard of Honor* (1948) and *By Love Possessed* (1957).

The controversy aroused by the publication of the last succeeded in focusing attention upon Cozzens's achievement in earlier, strangely neglected novels – their central values and their formal adherence to the unities of time and place were apparently unfashionable virtues for their period. The protagonists are usually professional men – doctors, lawyers, clergymen – who are circumscribed by obligations and duties, limited in their actions by an awareness of responsibility to themselves and the society in which they live. Undoubtedly the best of these works is the long and complex *Guard of Honor*, one of the outstanding American novels to deal with the Second World War; here the civilian community is exchanged for a military air base in Florida, a setting which lets Cozzens analyse the dilemmas of leadership during three September days in 1943. All the novels are carefully constructed and accurately reflect their author's preoccupation with order, discipline, stability and hierarchy in social organizations. His early work includes two fine short novels: *S.S. San Pedro* (1931), a vivid tale of the sea, and *Castaway* (1934), a macabre fantasy of the isolation of modern man. *Ask Me Tomorrow* (1940), the story of a European education with autobiographical echoes, is among the least satisfying of the later works. *Children and Others* (1964) is a collection of short stories. His latest work is *Morning, Noon and Night* (1968). [H D]

Frederick Bracher, *The Novels of James Gould Cozzens* (1959); Dwight MacDonald, 'By Cozzens Possessed', in *Against the American Grain* (1962); D. E. S. Maxwell, *Cozzens* (1964); Granville Hicks, *James Gould Cozzens* (1968).

Crane, Hart (1899–1932). Poet. Born in Garretsville, Ohio. His parents separated while he was a child; as his mother was in need of sanatorium treatment, he lived with his grandparents. He began to write poetry at 13, and in 1916 went with his mother to his grandfather's fruit plantation on the Isle of Pines, south of Cuba, a crucial experience of exotic wild nature which supplied symbols for this poetry to place

with his childhood misery. He set himself against the Crane family's business life, and his alienation increased when his parents divorced. Leaving Cleveland for New York, already with a wide reading of poetry behind him, he worked briefly in his father's sweet business, as a munitions worker, labourer, advertising man, and even manager of a teashop, as his poems appeared in ◊ little magazines. Their broody Elizabethanisms and French symbolist images recorded his tensions and his homosexuality. His great efforts to shape his poetic skills while he was poor and exhausted increased his alcoholism. Living in Brooklyn in 1924 he began to think of his great poem 'The Bridge' (1930), but, sick and poor, restlessly moving between New York, the Isle of Pines and Europe, he found his creative periods difficult to maintain, in spite of financial help from the banker Otto Kahn. His first book of poems, *White Buildings*, appeared in 1926. After 1930, his unsettled life, the death of his father, and estrangement from his mother and many of his friends, he went to Mexico to write a poem on Montezuma. Returning from Vera Cruz, he leaped into the sea to drown.

'For the Marriage of Faustus and Helen' (1922–3), the long major poem in *White Buildings*, is a meditation in three sections on beauty, love and renaissance from death, 'an answer to the cultural pessimism' of T. S. Eliot which translates the two myths into contemporary symbols and localities in the vision of the poet, always the unifying agent present in Crane's poetry. 'Voyages' and 'At Melville's Tomb' show his persistent use of the sea as a complex Rimbaudian image throughout his career. In 'The Bridge', he again attempted a reply to *The Waste Land* by conceiving the span of Brooklyn Bridge as the symbolic creative curve of recurrent life which finally is to symbolize America as a new Utopia of the future. This masterpiece is a huge symphonic structure of movements which state major American myths: Pocahontas, Rip Van Winkle, Melville, Poe, Whitman, Columbus, the subway, Atlantis. The gist is relatively clear, but in detail the metaphors fuse myth, history, childhood memories and sensuous experience and need an exegesis of their brilliance.

Crane is one of America's finest poets. His visionary daring and seriousness of purpose have been a major influence on post-1946 poetry, especially through the West Indian poems, which were first brought together in the edition of *Collected Poems* (1933) edited by Waldo ⟡ Frank. [EM]

Complete Poems and Selected Letters and Prose, ed. by Brom Weber (1966). L. Dembo, *Hart Crane's Sanskrit Charge: A Study of the Bridge* (1961); R. W. B. Lewis, *The Poetry of Hart Crane* (1967); H. A. Leibowitz, *Hart Crane: An Introduction to the Poetry* (1968); R. W. Butterfield, *The Broken Arc: A Study of Hart Crane* (1969); J. Unterecker, *Voyages, A Life of Hart Crane* (1969).

Crane, R(onald) S(almon) (1886–1967). Critic, scholar. The best-known of the University of Chicago group of critics called the ⟡ Chicago Aristotelians, Crane, a professor of English and an 18th-century scholar, made a signal statement of the need for criticism in literary studies in 'History versus Criticism in the University Study of Literature' (1935). But his view of criticism is that it is a mode of inquiry which always contains a covert aesthetic; hence the need is to expand the descriptive power of criticism, its 'poetics' element, so that it can account fully for the parts that make up the unity of a work. A classic example of his method is his famous essay 'The Concept of Plot and the Plot of *Tom Jones*', collected in *Critics and Criticism: Ancient and Modern* (1952; revised edn, 1957), a Chicago Aristotelian collection of essays which he edited. He is even more explicit in his Alexander Lectures at the University of Toronto, *The Languages of Criticism and the Structure of Poetry* (1953). For some subtle objections to his strong case, see W. K. ⟡ Wimsatt, *The Verbal Icon* (1954). [MB]

Crane, Stephen (1871–1900). Novelist, short-story writer, poet. The youngest son of a Methodist minister in New Jersey. He studied at a military academy, Lafayette College and Syracuse University, and immediately set out on a career in New York journalism. The slum background of his first novel, *Maggie: A Girl of the Streets* (1893), was known at first hand: the book had to be published on borrowed money and under a pseudonym. *The Red Badge of Courage* (1895), which brought him success, was written partly out of war correspondent experience in Cuba and Greece, and partly from Civil War readings. It gained him the praise of Howells, Conrad, James, and H. G. Wells. A book of poetry and two further novels on contemporary American life followed in 1895–7, and his shipwreck in 1896 on the way to Cuba gave him the basis of his short story, 'The Open Boat' (1898). His marriage to a lady who had run a sporting house in Florida caused him to be ostracized, and his health was ruined by hardship and slum experience when he returned to England. Conrad looked after him, and Henry James visited the Cranes in their Surrey home. He died of tuberculosis in a Black Forest health centre. His work was given its present high critical evaluation only after the First World War, though it was deeply admired by many practising writers, including Conrad and Henry James.

Maggie is a terrifying and beautifully told story of poverty, seduction and suicide on the Bowery. *The Red Badge of Courage*, one of the greatest war novels, concerns the initiation of Henry Fleming into manhood and his violent conversion from chivalric heroics to a comprehension of battle and the relationships of men and nature, told in a prose which ranges from brilliant symbols to the most direct narrative of action. Jimmie Trescott, the hero of *Whilomville Stories* (1900), is one of the good bad boys of American fiction. *George's Mother* (1896) is a study of fear in the squalor of the Bowery. Among Crane's short stories the finest are 'The Bride Comes to Yellow Sky' and 'The Blue Hotel', masterpieces of slanted narrative whose influence on American fiction and films continues, and 'The Open Boat', a vivid description of the fear of death at sea, marred by confused determinism. *The Black Riders and Other Lines* (1895) and *War Is Kind* (1899) contain poems of originality, terse, inventive and strongly governed by symbols of ironic indifferent destiny. Less well known are his final works: *Active Service* (1899), on the Greco-Turkish war, *The Third Violet* (1897), in which a group of American matrons destroys the reputation of a painter who yields finally to a cigarette-smoking Bohemienne, and 'The Clan of No Name', a short story in which a young officer in the Spanish war places himself in a trap to test the law of fate. Little of this reaches the level of *The Red Badge*, but his whole career is a brilliant epitome of the early-19th-century writer grappling with urban corruption, war, and deterministic philosophies. [EM]

Works, ed. Wilson Follett (12 vols., 1925–6);
Stephen Crane: An Omnibus, ed. R. W. Stallman (1952); *Letters*, ed. R. W. Stallman and
Lillian Gilkes (1960); *The War Dispatches*, ed.
R. W. Stallman and E. R. Hagemann (1964);
Uncollected Writings, ed. O. W. Fryckstedt
(1964); *Complete Short Stories and Sketches*,
ed. T. A. Gullason (1963); *The New York City
Sketches of Stephen Crane and Related Pieces*,
ed. R. W. Stallman and E. R. Hagemann (1968).
John Berryman, *Stephen Crane* (1950); Edwin H.
Cady, *Stephen Crane* (1962); E. Solomon,
Stephen Crane: From Parody to Realism (1966);
R. W. Stallman, *Stephen Crane: A Biography*
(1968).

Crawford, F(rancis) Marion (1854–1909).
Novelist. Born in Italy, the son of the
famous expatriate sculptor Thomas Crawford, he spent a considerable part of his
life in that country, where much of his
fiction is set; though extensive travels gave
him world-wide locales for his more than
40 novels. *Mr Isaacs, A Tale of Modern
India* (1882) established a popular following.
His view of fiction as entertainment has
diminished his reputation, but his narrative
art and his powers of evocation of other
lands and past history are considerable,
and he was extremely successful. He dealt
with romantic themes (as in *To Leeward*,
1884, *Pietro Ghisleri*, 1893, and *The White
Sister*, 1909, all set in Italy); with political
matters (as in *An American Politician*, 1884,
set in the States in the Gilded Age); and
with history (as in *Via Crucis*, 1899, about
the Crusades). [M B]

Larzer Ziff, *The American 1890s* (1966).

Creeley, Robert (1926–   ). Poet, novelist,
short-story writer. Born in Massachusetts,
he studied at Harvard, ◊ Black Mountain
College and New Mexico University. He
has travelled widely in India, Burma,
France and Spain, and lectured and read
his poems all over America. His poetry first
began to appear with *Le Fou* (1952), *The
Immoral Proposition* (1953), *The Kind of
Act of* (1953), *All That is Lovely in Men*
(1955), *If You* (1956) and *The Whip* (1957).
These issues mark the maturing of a terse,
spare style of poem, inimitable and suited
to his slow, deliberate explorations of the
tensions of love and the struggle of men to
ascertain what exactly they know. With *A
Form of Women* (1959) and *For Love,
Poems 1950–1960* (1962) this form seemed
to be complete. In *Words* (1967) some of the
poems are longer and more complex, but
Creeley had hardly made any new depar-

tures. *Pieces* (1969), however, shows a
new range of formal procedures shaped
into a continuous work of considerable
power. *The Charm* (1969) consists of early
and uncollected poems. His short stories
appeared in *The Gold Diggers* (1954, 1965),
and they are like extended versions of his
poetic themes, taking considerable risks
in their tortuousness. His novel, *The Island*
(1963), is a psychological study of married
life in a prose which veers towards that of
late Henry James. He co-edited *New
American Story* with Donald Allen in 1965,
introduced *The New Writing in the U.S.A.*
(1967) and edited and introduced *Selected
Writings of Charles Olson* (1966). [E M]

Ed. David Ossman, *The Sullen Art* (1963); Paul
Carroll, *The Poem in Its Skin* (1968).

Crèvecoeur, Hector St John de (Michel
Guillaume Jean de Crèvecoeur) (1735–
1813). Travel writer and social historian.
Born in Normandy, he received part of his
education in Salisbury (England), and as a
young man, while serving as lieutenant
under Montcalm in Canada, took part in a
map-making expedition to the Great
Lakes; and after the fall of Quebec and
Britain's annexation of Canada, he began
to live in various parts of Pennsylvania and
New York. In 1764 he became a citizen of
New York, bought a farm in Orange
County (1769) and married Mehetable
Tippet of Yonkers. In a time of revolution,
although he agreed with Franklin's independent artisan ideal, he retained an
aristocratic attitude in some ways and was
driven from his farm by 'patriots'. Leaving
his wife and two children, he placed himself
and his son under British protection, was
promptly imprisoned, and on release returned to France, where his American
experiences made him popular in society.
He returned in 1783, but his wife had died
and his children lived with a Boston merchant. He stayed as French consul in New
York, New Jersey and Connecticut until
1790 and came to believe in the Revolution
enough to devote himself to improving
Franco–American understanding and
American agriculture.

His reputation rests not with his large-
scale *Voyage dans la haute Pennsylvanie
et dans l'état de New York* (1801) but with
Letters from an American Farmer (1782)
and *Sketches of Eighteenth Century
America* (1925). The *Letters* are an early
and important answer to the question

'What is an American?' Crèvecoeur assumed that in an imperfect world the good society would weaken evil by having enough natural resources for subsidence, allowing men to work freely for self-interest and turn aggression into energetic productivity. America would fulfil this plan: men could be happy in this huge virgin territory where work had its immediate reward, where British government and Christian morality would be tempered to a liberal state, and restraint would prevent tyranny. He admired Quaker humanitarianism and the American farmer's independence, and loathed Virginian slavery. His ideal was the colonial freeholder whose environment bred a life without 'ancient prejudices and manners': 'here individuals of all nations are melted into a new race of men ... Americans are the western pilgrims, who are carrying along with them that great mass of arts, sciences, vigour, and industry which began long since in the east; they will finish the great circle'. Crèvecoeur's celebrated formulation of optimism is modified by warning against the lawless individualism of prosperity and he finally recommends the Indians as his model of peaceful community happiness, again with a warning against primitive regression. His images of agrarian freedom, self-reliance and the melting pot of nations have persisted into modern American thought. His understanding of the precise points at which law, community and freedom break down have a lasting relevance for America. [EM]

Letters from an American Farmer and *Sketches of Eighteenth Century America* (New American Library, 1963).
J. P. Mitchell, *St Jean de Crèvecoeur* (1916); M. Bewley, 'The Cage and the Prairie' in *The Hudson Review Anthology*, ed. F. Morgan (1961).

Crockett, Davy (1786–1836). Politician, story writer, legendary figure. This fabled comic hunter was actually born – in Tennessee. His rough childhood did include a little schooling, but his distinctions were dancing, singing and hunting bears. He won honour in the Creek War under General Jackson and turned politician, elected to the Tennessee legislature and then to Congress – 'the coonskin Congressman'. In 1829 he changed sides and became a Whig, and to right the confusion he wrote his *Narrative* (1834) and *An Account of*

Col. Crockett's Tour to the North and Down East (1835). He opposed Jackson on the national bank controversy and on the break with the Creek Indians. He died heroically fighting for Texas at the Alamo. His narrative is typical of his American frontier wit and boisterous yarning. In his own lifetime he was a legend, and the posthumous *Crockett Almanacs* (1835–56), ballads, J. K. ◊ Paulding's play *The Lion of the West* (1831), and many folk plays and books secured his myth down to the Davy Crockett song and the coonskin-cap fashion of the 1950s. [EM]

C. Rourke, *Davy Crockett* (1934).

Cullen, Countee (1903–46). Negro American poet. He was reared by foster parents in Harlem, N.Y., and graduated from New York University (1925), already a published poet before he took his graduate degree at Harvard. After his first book, *Colour* (1925), he produced *Copper Sun* (1927), *The Ballad of the Brown Girl* (1928), *The Black Christ* (1929, written in France on a Guggenheim scholarship), *The Medea and Some Poems* (1935) and the posthumous *On These I Stand* (1947). He edited the Negro magazine *Opportunity* and an anthology of Negro poets, *Caroling Dusk* (1927), and wrote one novel, *One Way to Heaven* (1931). He taught French in New York schools until his death, when he had become the living representative of the Negro poet struggling to write accurately about himself and his people without sentimentality, and yet to create poetry which was not only protest or description of a condition. His models were Keats and E. A. ◊ Robinson, but his themes were American, with poems like 'Heritage' showing his nostalgia for Africa. (◊◊ Negro Literature.) [EM]

Cummings, E(dward) E(stlin) (1894–1962). Poet, painter. His father was a teacher and a minister of the Old South Church in Boston, Massachusetts, and his boyhood was spent in the academic atmosphere and traditions of Cambridge and Harvard, where he received his B.A. in 1916 and against which he rebelled. In the First World War he served with the Norton Harjes Ambulance Service and through a grotesque bureaucratic error was imprisoned, for certain radical observations, in a French detention camp (*The Enormous Room*, 1922), where his sense of the individual against authority received its first practical reinforcement. After 1920, he painted and wrote poetry in Paris, and between 1923 and 1944 became a lively controversial poet with his 9 volumes (*Collected Poems*, 1938, and *Poems 1923–1954*, 1954). In 1925 he won the *Dial* award for distinguished services to literature and in 1952–3 gave the Charles Eliot Norton lectures at Harvard (*Six Non-Lectures*, 1953). He exhibited his paintings several times with the Society of Independent Artists in Paris, and in at least two shows in America (*CIOPW*, 1931, is a book of his drawings and paintings). His large output of poems over 40 years remained virtually unchanged in their themes, compressed language and syntax, and typographical layout. His song-like rhythms and lower-case and capitalized spatial patterns made his lyrics into reading-libretti in a modern baroque style which brought him a reputation for outrageous modernism. In fact his quirky individualism, his commonplace love themes, his satire against politicians, businessmen and salesmen, his sympathy with the underdog and his downright escapism were nothing if not reactionary, in a New England tradition stretching back to his real ancestor, Emerson.

Cummings is America's best popular poet, voicing self-reliant anarchism which is nearer Frost than Dada. *The Enormous Room* is a masterpiece of radical individualism and exuberant prose, and *EIMI* (1933) a first-rate critical book of travel in Russia. *Tom* (1935) is a satirical ballet burlesquing *Uncle Tom's Cabin*, and his plays, *Him* (1927) and *Santa Claus* (1946), mix fantasy, poetry and symbolism in a style which antedates Beckett and the absurdists. Read in bulk his poems tend to be a repetitious series on love, springtime, April and freedom, and hedonistic attacks on an amorphous 'Them'. Singly his works often have a lyrical tenderness and joy, or a scornful rejection of commercialism and humbug, which is altogether refreshing. [EM]

Complete Poems (2 vols., 1968); *Selected Letters*, ed. F. W. Dupee and G. Stade (1969); *A Miscellany Revised*, ed. and intr. G. J. Firmage (1965).
C. Norman, *The Magic-Maker: E. E. Cummings* (1958).

D

Dahlberg, Edward (1890–   ). Novelist, essayist. His youth is described in a series of remarkable autobiographical books beginning with *Bottom Dogs* (intr. D. H. Lawrence, 1930): the Cleveland orphanage, his mother an itinerant lady barber, the life of Kansas City, his hobo boxcar existence until 1919, and his later meetings in New York with Alfred Stieglitz and his circle of artists and writers, including ◊ Garland, ◊ Dreiser and Randolph ◊ Bourne, whose opinions he appraises in *Alms for Oblivion* (1964), a collection of essays that ride his hobby horses in great style. His fictionalized life continued in *From Flushing to Calvary* (1932), *Those Who Perish* (1934), *Do These Bones Live* (1941), *The Flea of Sodom* (1950) and most recently *Because I Was Flesh* (1964), perhaps the definitive account of himself and his mother, told in a unique style as the life of Hagar and Ishmael in the American wilderness of cities. *The Sorrows of Priapus* (1957) is Dahlberg's didactic prophecy for the times, in his best aphoristic manner (see also *Reasons of the Heart*, 1965, a book of aphorisms). Further essays are collected in *The Leafless American* (1967); *Cipango's Hinder Door* (1966) is a volume of poems; and *Epitaphs for Our Times* (1967) is a collection of letters edited by Edwin Seaver. *The Carnal Myth* (1968) shows his collage methods at their most concentrated. He is a vehement agrarian, a fine chronicler, a stringent critic and an American stylist without imitators. [EM]

The Edward Dahlberg Reader, ed. P. Carroll (1967).

J. Williams, 'Edward Dahlberg's Book of Lazarus', *Texan Quarterly*, Summer, 1963; V. Lipton, 'The Sorrows and Joys of Edward Dahlberg', *Kenyon Review*, Autumn, 1958; H. Billings, *Edward Dahlberg: American Ishmael of Letters* (1968).

Dana, Richard Henry, Jr (1815–82). Writer, reformer, lawyer. Son of R. H. ◊ Dana, Sr, he was born in Cambridge, Massachusetts, and educated at Harvard. In 1834, at the end of his second year, he left the university because of eye trouble and shipped as a sailor round the Horn to California. After more than a year on the Pacific coast, gathering and curing hides, he returned to Boston to complete his studies at the Harvard Law School. In 1840, the year he was admitted to the Massachusetts bar, he anonymously published *Two Years before the Mast*, a narrative of 'the life of a common sailor at sea as it really is' based on a diary he had kept of the 150-day voyage on the brig *Pilgrim*, with all its minutiae of routine and off-duty hours and conversations, of the shore life in Santa Barbara, San Diego, Monterey and San Francisco, and of the stormy return trip on the ship *Alert*. Not only does it give an early important account of California; it also roused men's consciences – a central incident is the flogging of two shipmates and his vow 'to redress the grievances and sufferings of that class of beings with whom my lot has so long been cast'. Already earlier, in 1839, he had published an article in the *American Jurist*, 'Cruelty to Seamen', and in 1841 followed *The Seaman's Friend* (British title *The Seaman's Manual*), designed to show sailors their legal rights and duties; but the immediate popularity of *Two Years before the Mast* was due to its realism, its many portraits of officers and sailors, its detail. Dana became a founder of the Free-Soil Party; he was active before and during the Civil War in the slaves' cause; he became editor of a standard textbook on international law and author of *To Cuba and Back* (1859); nevertheless he felt, 30 years later, that his life had been an anti-climax, for 'my great success – my book – was a boy's work, done before I came to the Bar'. Hurt by failure, he withdrew to Rome in 1878 to continue his researches in international law; there he died. Posthumously collected were *Speeches in Stirring Times* (1910) and *An Autobiographical Sketch* (1953). [HB]

Journal, ed. R. F. Lucid (3 vols., 1968).

Charles Francis Adams, *Richard Henry Dana, a Biography* (1890); H. W. L. Dana, *The Dana Saga* (1941); James D. Hart, 'The Education of Richard Henry Dana, Jr', *New England Quarterly* IX, 1 (1936).

Dana, Richard Henry, Sr (1787–1879).
Poet, journalist, editor. Born in Boston, he
was one of the founders of the *North
American Review*, the leading American
19th-century review; he wrote for many
other journals and published *Poems* (1827).
Much of his work was collected in *Poems
and Prose Writings* (2 vols., 1833; enlarged
1850). [M B]

Dannay, Frederic ◊ Queen, Ellery.

Davidson, Donald (1893–   ). Critic,
poet. Born in Tennessee, a teacher at
Vanderbilt University, he was a member of
the ◊ Fugitive group there, one of the
founders of the *Fugitive* magazine and
later a contributor to the famous collection of southern agrarian essays *I'll Take
My Stand* (1930). He has published four
books of poetry – *An Outland Piper* (1924),
The Tall Men (1927), *Lee in the Mountains
and Other Poems, Including The Tall Men*
(1938), and *The Long Street* (1961). *The
Attack on Leviathan: Regionalism and
Nationalism in the United States* (1938) is
a vehement defence of the traditional
Southern culture and economy, and a
violent attack on the modern, capitalist
state. *Still Rebels, Still Yankees* (1957) is
a collection of essays; *The Spyglass*
(1963) of views and reviews. *Southern
Writers in the Modern World* appeared in
1958. Of the Fugitives, Davidson has
become the most militant defender of
every aspect of the *status quo* in the South.
[A H]

Davis, Richard Harding (1864–1916). Journalist, novelist, playwright. Born in
Philadelphia, the son of Rebecca Harding
Davis, an early realist novelist, he became
a famous journalist on the New York *Sun*
and covered the Spanish–American war for
'he *Journal*, and thereafter became a leading
and wide-travelled correspondent covering
wars and making fact-finding tours.
Collections of journalism include *Our
English Cousins* (1894), *Cuba in War Time*
(1897) and *With the Allies* (1914). His novels
are sensational and sophisticated; they
include *Soldiers of Fortune* (1897), *The
King's Jackal* (1898) and *Vera the Medium*
(1908). He also published many successful
collections of stories, some of them providing the source of his more than 20 plays.
[M B]

Larzer Ziff, *The American 1890s* (1967).

70

Day, Clarence (1874–1935). Essayist, artist.
Born in New York City, the son of a Stock
Exchange broker, he went to Yale, served
in the navy during the Spanish–American
war, ran a glove business in New York, and
became a regular writer for the *New Yorker*.
In four witty and unusual books Day
immortalized his father as a typical representative of upper-class New York in the
19th century: they were *God and My Father*
(1932), *Life with Father* (1935; successfully
dramatized in 1939), *Life with Mother* (1937)
and *Father and I* (1940). Other books
include the delightful curiosity *This Simian
World* (1920), a study of the ape-like nature
of man with Day's own brilliant and
fantastic illustrations, and *In the Green
Mountain Country* (1934), an account of
President Coolidge's funeral. [M G]

De Forest, John W(illiam) (1826–1906)
Novelist, miscellaneous writer. Born in
Connecticut, he returned from extensive
foreign travel to serve three years as a
Union Captain in the Civil War. His novel
*Miss Ravenel's Conversion from Secession
to Loyalty* (1867; intr. G. S. Haight, 1939)
gave for the first time a harshly realistic
treatment of the conflict and is also notable
for its portrayal (without authorial retribution) of the spirited, independent and
profligate Mrs Larue. Later work included
Kate Beaumont (1872), about plantation
society in Charleston and the 'poor whites'
of South Carolina, and *Honest John Vane*
(1875), a satire on political corruption. His
war memoirs, *A Volunteer's Adventures*,
appeared in 1946, and James H. Croushore
and David Morris Potter edited *A Union
Officer in the Reconstruction* (1948).

De Forest's complex novels, with their
uncompromising though finally exhausting
realism, never received sufficient attention
in his lifetime, except from his constant
admirer William Dean ◊ Howells, who commented that 'finer, and stronger workmen
succeeded him, and a delicate realism, more
responsive to the claims and appeals of the
feminine oversoul, replaced his inexorable
veracity'. [M G]

H. E. Starr, 'De Forest', *Dictionary of American
Biography* (1930); W. D. Howells, *Atlantic
Monthly*, xx (1867) and xxix (1872) (reviews),
and *Heroines of Fiction*, ii (1901); Edmund
Wilson, *Patriotic Gore* (1962).

Dell, Floyd (1887–   ). Novelist, playwright, editor. Born of a poor Illinois

family, he worked as a factory hand, later became a journalist, first on a Davenport, Iowa, newspaper and then in Chicago, where he was associated with the mid-Western 'Chicago School' of writers, among them Carl ◊ Sandburg and Ben ◊ Hecht. He was a notable editor of the *Chicago Evening Post's Literary Review*. After 1914 he worked in New York, editing the socialist *Masses* (1914–17) and its successor *Liberation* (1918–24) (◊ Little Magazines). He received high praise for his first and best novel, *Moon-Calf* (1920), and its sequel, *The Briary-Bush* (1921). These were largely autobiographical studies of an idealistic youth who, frustrated by the atmosphere of a small Illinois town, seeks relief in Chicago, but returns to marry his first love after a hectic career in Chicago journalism. In *Janet March* (1923), *Runaway* (1925) and other novels he assumed his role of outspoken mouthpiece for Greenwich Village Bohemia and a confused twenties generation (◊ Bohemianism, Greenwich Village). He caused something of a sensation in 1930 with *Love in the Machine Age*, an account of his attitude towards sex. A humorous novel, *An Unmarried Father* (1927; dramatized 1928), gave a new phrase to the language; *Homecoming* (1933) was his autobiography. He and Paul Jordan Smith produced (1927) a fine text of Burton's *Anatomy of Melancholy*. [M G]

Demby, William (1922–   ). Novelist. Born in Pittsburgh, he studied at West Virginia State College for Negroes and Fisk University, and has written a fine Existentialist novel, *Beetlecreek* (1950), set in West Virginia, an important contribution to novels of racial rejection in America. *Catacombs* (1965) is a novel set in Rome and employing considerable technical innovation. [E M]

R. Bone, 'William Denby's *Dance of Life*', *TriQuarterly*, 15 (1969).

Dennie, Joseph (1768–1812). Essayist, editor. Born in Boston, he went to Harvard, became a lawyer, and then one of the leading essayists of his age, writing pseudonymously and adapting the tradition of Addison and Steele. One of a group of Federalists of Anglophile sympathy, he edited in New Hampshire the *Farmer's Weekly Museum*. He later moved to Philadelphia and became central figure of an important literary circle, the Tuesday Club, and founder of one of the leading American literary weeklies, the *Port Folio*, in 1801. His pseudonyms were 'The Lay Preacher' and 'Oliver Oldschool, Esq.', and in the provincial atmosphere of American letters at this time he deeply influenced taste. His manner was imitated by Washington ◊ Irving, particularly for *The Sketch Book*. *The Lay Preacher* (1796, 1817; reprinted 1943) is collected essays. [M B]

Milton Ellis, *Joseph Dennie and His Circle: A Study of American Literature from 1792 to 1812* (1915).

Deutsch, Babette (1895–   ). Poet, novelist, critic. Born in New York City, she began contributing to literary periodicals while studying at Barnard College. She was ◊ Veblen's secretary while he worked at the New School for Social Research, and active on the Committee for Cultural Freedom under John ◊ Dewey. She has taught in various New York colleges and translated Russian and German literature, particularly modern poetry and Yiddish writers, with her husband Avrahm Yarmolinsky, the Russianist. She is best known as a poet, her work being prolific, sophisticated and socially concerned (though not distinguished by a sensitive ear or memorable imagery), from the energies of *Banners* (1919), though the exhortation of *Epistle to Prometheus* (1931) to the lyrics of *Animal, Vegetable, Mineral* (1954), all included in *Collected Poems: 1919–1962* (1963). She has written 4 novels, including *In Such a Night* (1927), about Socrates, and *Rogue's Legacy* (1942), about François Villon; a book on Whitman (1941); a prose version of 15 Shakespeare plays; and some criticism. This includes *Poetry in Our Time* (1952), a good introductory study of modern poetry; and the very useful *Poetry Handbook: A Dictionary of Terms* (1957; revised 1961). [M B/E M]

Collected Poems (1969).

De Voto, Bernard (1897–1955). Editor, critical scholar. He edited the *Saturday Review of Literature* (1936–8) and worked on *Harper's Magazine* (1935–55). His finest work was for one writer: *Mark Twain's America* (1932, a famous reply to Van Wyck ◊ Brooks's *The Ordeal of Mark Twain*), *Mark Twain at Work* (1942) and *Mark Twain in Eruption* (1940), selections from Twain's autobiography. He left 5 books of essays, a number of historical works including *Across the Wide Missouri* (1947, about the 1830s exploration and destruction of the West), and novels and short stories. *The Hour* (1951) is a lyric fanfare for the martini and cocktail fad. [EM]

De Vries, Peter (1910–   ). Novelist. Born in Chicago. Drawing his material almost exclusively from the successful, middle-class, East-coast America that has become the happy hunting-ground of organization men, status-seekers, and commuters in grey flannel suits, he has become the comic laureate of suburbia. Decency, Conn., is the setting for most of his novels, which delineate with zest and vitality the grotesqueries and idiosyncrasies of such a stable community. His characters are individuals trapped by patterns of behaviour often absurd in themselves. But De Vries, a talented comedian, a sharp social observer, is only in a limited sense a satirist; his work has no Swiftian intensity or disgust; he writes from inside an exurban world which amuses rather than offends him. At his best he writes a sophisticated, witty and entertaining novel of manners; but the energy and the punning verbal dexterity sometimes, not surprisingly, flag. Perhaps this is the reason why he has recently written a different kind of novel. In 1938 he became associate editor, and in 1942 co-editor of the magazine *Poetry*, and since 1944 he has been on the editorial staff of the *New Yorker*. His first book, *But Who Wakes the Bugler* (1940), was, appropriately, illustrated by the *New Yorker* cartoonist Charles Addams. Then followed *The Handsome Heart* (1943), *Angels Can't Do Better* (1944), *No, But I Saw the Movie* (1952), *Tunnel of Love* (1954), *Comfort Me with Apples* (1956), *The Mackerel Plaza* (1958), one of his best novels, and *The Tents of Wickedness* (1959), which incorporates some hilariously accurate literary parodies and burlesques. *Through Fields of Clover* (1961) concerns a gag-writer and his comedian. *The Blood of the Lamb* (1962) marks a change of manner; it is still funny and excellently written, but it changes tone to tragic seriousness. Through the characters' madness, suicide and tuberculosis, De Vries attempts a high level of sincere comment on religious faith. The result is disappointingly pseudo-profound, quite unlike the serious satire and dark underside of his usual comedy. *Reuben, Reuben* (1964) combines the quali-

ties of both his manners – the comic exuberance and the critical – to present a Dylan Thomas sort of poet, or his myth. *Let Me Count the Ways* (1965) is a study in self-consciousness and its chaotic tendency to farce: again the tragi-comic manner shows De Vries's later form. *The Vale of Laughter* (1968) once again takes up his steady obsession with religion, with God's sport with man, with clowning as an expression of suffering. *The Cat's Pyjamas and Witch's Milk* (1968) are a pair of interrelated short novels. Throughout his career, he has developed a classic series of novels on the themes of religious comedy. [AH/EM]

Dewey, John (1859–1952). Philosopher. Born in Burlington, Vermont, Dewey studied at the University of Vermont and the new graduate school of Johns Hopkins University. He taught at the University of Michigan, then at the University of Chicago, where he established a famous experimental school to try out his ideas on education. From 1905 till his retirement in 1929 he was a professor of Philosophy at Columbia University.

An extremely prolific writer, he continued to pour out books and articles until his death at 93. His influence has been immense, partly because his pragmatic philosophy made a special appeal to the American mind, partly because he was the opposite of an ivory-tower philosopher: he had strong political interests – he was a liberal of socialist leanings – and was the leading educational reformer of his time. He gave the Gifford lectures (*The Quest for Certainty*) at Edinburgh in 1929; spent many months in Japan and China in 1918–20; and visited Turkey, Mexico and Russia, and in all these countries his educational influence was strong. In philosophy, he began as a Hegelian, but his studies of Darwin's biology led him to a new conception of the nature of thought, which he called 'instrumentalism'. Thinking, he said, is an activity of the organism, which, like swimming, walking and climbing, was generated as a means to adjustment and survival; it is an instrument brought into play when instinct and habit break down, in order to surmount obstacles in the way of behaviour. Hence its true test is practical – whether it succeeds in reaching the specific end for which it was adopted (*Studies in Logical Theory*, 1903). This insight required, he held, a reconstruction of philosophy. The speculative thought of the West since Plato had been dominated by a 'spectator view' of knowledge; the business of thought was to contemplate an eternal and changeless order. Repudiating this, Dewey substituted for contemplation 'creative intelligence', whose business was to transform the conditions of life so as to achieve the greatest practicable fulfilment for all. Since evolution implies continual change, our ideals themselves must be tentative; the ideal that is fixed and final tends to arrest advance (*Reconstruction in Philosophy*, 1920).

From his instrumentalism followed his views on education, politics and religion. If the right use of intelligence is no longer the pursuit of truth for its own sake, but rather as a preface to action, the old difference between cultural and vocational training is illusory. Throughout the United States progressive schools grew up in which children learned by doing – acquiring arithmetic by keeping store and studying literature by acting plays and stories. Dewey likewise held that only as citizens are encouraged to share the responsibilities of government will they become politically mature; hence his lifelong support of democracy (*Democracy and Education*, 1916). His philosophy demanded also reform in religion: for religion as the acceptance of creeds there should be substituted the religious attitude, conceived as dedication to the long-run good of mankind (*A Common Faith*, 1934). *Art as Experience* (1934) is an influential examination of formal structures and characteristic effects in all the arts. [BB]

S. Ratner, *Intelligence in the Modern World: John Dewey's Philosophy* (1939); ed. P. A. Schilpp, *The Philosophy of John Dewey* (1939); C. Wright Mills, *Sociology and Pragmatism* (1964).

Dickens, Charles (1812–70). English novelist. His famous tour of the United States (1842) produced later in the year *American Notes for General Circulation*, a series of descriptive sketches. He antagonized American readers by attacking slavery, certain penal systems and the absence of copyright protection. Later he rescued the failing *Life and Adventures of Martin Chuzzlewit* (1843–44) by dispatching his hero to the States, where Martin is ruthlessly cheated by the Eden Land Corporation (Cairo, Illinois). His swindlers delight in boasting of American success in 'the regeneration of man', and he hears several score people described as 'one of the most remarkable men in this country'. Dickens returned for a reading tour (1867–8). [MG]

William Clyde Williams, *Charles Dickens in America* (1911); Philip Collins, *Dickens and Crime* (1962); 'Dickens in America', *The Times Literary Supplement*, 9 January 1943; Harry Stone, 'Dickens' Use of His American Experience in "Martin Chuzzlewit"', in *Publications of the Modern Language Association of America*, LXXII (1957).

Dickey, James (1923–   ). Poet. Born in Atlanta, Georgia, he taught at Rice University and the University of Florida, and worked in advertising, He has published *Into the Stone and Other Poems* (1960), *Drowning with Others* (1962), *Helmets* (1964), *Two Poems of the Air* (1964), *Buckdancer's Choice* (1965) and *Babel to Byzantium* (1968). He is a lively critic and reviewer of poetry; a collection of essays, *The Suspect in Poetry*, appeared in 1964.

In verse he early found an individual voice, stylish yet deceptively conversational in tone. His poems frequently take natural settings as occasions for mystical contemplation. More recent verse reveals a stronger narrative element. He is a poet both of passion and subtle insight, often understating what are really complex effects. *Poems 1957–1967* (1968) widens his subject matter, socially but not politically, notably in 'The Firebombing' and 'Slave Quarters'. *The Eye-beaters, Blood, Victory, Madness, Buckhead and Mercy* (1970) shows a considerable development in form and language. His novel, *Deliverance* (1970), about an allegorical canoe-trip in Georgia, has become a remarkable best-seller. [BS]

Laurence Lieberman, *The Achievement of James Dickey* (1968); Richard Howard, *Alone with America* (1969).

Dickinson, Emily (1830–86). Poet. Under a Calvinist father, dominatingly kind, she began an outwardly uneventful life at Amherst, Massachusetts. Apart from brief periods at Amhurst Academy and Holyoke Female Seminary she ran the family home; she did not marry. She did send poems to a well-known literary man, Thomas Wentworth Higginson, but his criticism of their unorthodoxies in metre and style pushed her back into privacy. She hoarded her poems, among them love poems, apparently addressed to Benjamin Newton, a student in her father's office, with whom she corresponded until his death in 1853, and

Charles Wadsworth, a distinguished married clergyman who may have left America because of her. For the rest, and apart from a stay in Philadelphia, hers was a New England small-town puritan life in the atmosphere of the Civil War years. 'Pardon my sanity in a world insane', she wrote in a letter, a clue to her need to create a balanced life out of her passion and intellectual clarity.

In 1863 she probably wrote about 140 poems, and in 1864 nearly 200, the high point of her prolific output of about 1,775 poems, all written within the characteristic late-19th-century range of relationships between God, man and nature. Since she did not have the pressures of publication, her style is remarkably free, intense and idiosyncratic, the exact form of her complex personality. She may have dressed in white and enacted the role of subdued woman, but she concentrated on a 'lone orthography' which avoided genteel conventionality. Her weakness is a reliance on rhythmic cadences and metres from hymns and popular jingles. She was not a prosodic innovator, although her punctuation, derived from reading and pronunciation handbooks, looks odd, and her imagery continually startles with its freshness and penetration. Her modernity is her articulation of psychological experience and sceptical desire for faith.

Four years after her death her first volume was published, and augmented editions appeared in 1891 and 1896. A book of letters came out in 1894. But a true estimate of her genius began only after the First World War, and it was not until Thomas H. Johnson's magnificent editions of her poems and letters that a complete and accurate text was established. [EM]

The Poems, ed. T. H. Johnson (3 vols., 1958); *Letters*, ed. T. H. Johnson (3 vols., 1958).
G. F. Whicher. *This Was a Poet: A Critical Biography of Emily Dickinson* (1938); C. A. Anderson, *Emily Dickinson's Poetry: Stairway of Surprise* (1960); Richard Chase, *Emily Dickinson* (1951); T. H. Johnson, *Emily Dickinson: An Interpretative Biography* (1955); ed. C. R. Blake and C. F. Wells, *The Recognition of Emily Dickinson* (1964); R. B. Sewall, 'The Lyman Letters: New Light on Emily Dickinson and Her Family', *Massachusetts Review*, Autumn, 1965; R. W. Franklin, *The Editing of Emily Dickinson* (1968).

Dickinson, John (1732–1808). Born in Maryland, he studied law in London, and became a leader of the Revolutionary whigs. Rich and conservative, he refused to sign the Declaration of Independence, since he hoped for conciliation. His writings had a major influence at a crucial time: they include, besides his famous 'Liberty Song' (1768), and two sets of *Letters of Fabius* (1788, 1797), the important *Letters from a Farmer in Pennsylvania* (1767–8), which had several American, French and English editions in 1768. The 12 letters hold that the Anglo-American controversy was legally wrong, the government should support property rights, and that legal petition and commercial tactics should precede possible resort to arms. Burke and Voltaire admired them (see R. T. H. Halsey's 1903 edition). [EM]

Charles J. Stillé, *The Life and Times of John Dickinson: 1732–1808* (1891).

Dodson, Owen (1914–   ). Poet, novelist. Born in Brooklyn, he studied at Bates College, Maine, and Yale School of Drama. He is head of the drama department at Howard University. Besides his volume of poems, *Powerful Long Ladder* (1946), and a number of unpublished but acted plays, he is best known for his novel, *Boy at the Window* (1951). [EM]

Donleavy, J(ames) P(atrick) (1926–   ). Novelist, playwright. Born in Brooklyn, but studied at Trinity College, Dublin, and in recent years has lived in Ireland and England. His first novel, *The Ginger Man* (1955) – originally published in Paris, now reissued in England and the U.S.A. – mixes English-style social observation with anarchic American humour. Its hero, Sebastian Dangerfield, is a well-elaborated American comic figure, an arrogant sensualist who romps through Dublin and London violating middle-class susceptibilities. Also dramatized as a play, the novel has strong elements of fantasy and violence as well as of very funny farce. This fantasy is further developed in his neo-surrealist play *Fairy Tales of New York* (1961) and in later fiction: *A Singular Man* (1963), a lively novel about a wealthy man with a complicated psyche and a persecution complex; *Meet My Maker, the Mad Molecule* (1964), short stories in similar vein; and *The Saddest Summer of Samuel S.* (1966), a novel about a sexual pilgrimage through Vienna. Donleavy's main gift is his ability to mix a comic inventiveness with an intense sense of personal loneliness. [MB]

Donnelly, Ignatius (1831–1901). Politician, historian, novelist. Born in Philadelphia, he became a lawyer and then moved west to found an ideal emigrant community in Minnesota. He became a Congressman and a leading figure in Populist protest, and in 1900 was the Vice-Presidential candidate of the party. He was a powerful orator and a devotee of many theories, including that of Delia Bacon that Sir Francis Bacon wrote Shakespeare's plays. His literary importance lies in his novel *Caesar's Column* (1891), a utopian – or rather anti-utopian – novel about a 20th-century world in which a capitalist aristocracy enslaves the working classes and is overcome by a revolution that itself degenerates into brutality, the story being seen from the standpoint of a moral agrarianism and, in addition, a melo-dramatic romanticism. [MB]

Doolittle, Hilda (H. D.) (1886–1961). Poet, novelist, translator. She was born in Pennsylvania and educated in Philadelphia. At Bryn Mawr she met Marianne Moore and – from Pennsylvania University – Pound and William Carlos Williams, all four poets representing the early stages of ◊ Imagism in America. H.D. appeared in Pound's *Des Imagistes* in 1914, as well as in the *Imagist Anthology* of 1930. In 1911 she left America, and in 1913 married Richard Aldington. She lived in England and in Switzerland. Her first volume, *Sea Garden* (1916), appeared in England, although some of the poems had already been published in Harriet ◊ Monroe's *Poetry*. *Hymen* (1921) is a masque with Greek figures, and her later poetry, in *Heliodora and Other Poems* (1924), *Red Roses for Bronze* (1929), and the *Collected Poems* of 1925 and 1940, maintained classical images and thought in a generally limpid and visual style. But her Greece was really a world of dream perfection whose modern symbolism rejected the complexity of the modern world between the wars – in spite of the intelligence of her prose love poem *Tribute to Freud* (1956). Her shorter poems are economical but not austere, their moments of arrested time and intense response to a revelatory landscape or object carefully composed, for all their apparent licence. Her search for moments of beauty and love are not as reactionary as is sometimes said. Later collections include *The Walls Do Not Fall* (1944), a response to

wartime London, *Tribute to Angels* (1945), devotional poems, and *Flowering of the Rod* (1946). *By Avon River* (1949) is a miscellany inspired by Shakespeare. She translated choruses from Euripides' *Iphigenia in Aulis*, *Hippolytus* and *Ion*, and *Hippolytus Temporizes* is a verse tragedy. Her novels include *Palimpsest* (1922), which is intent on cutting across boundaries of time and culture, *Hedylus* (1928) and *Bid Me To Live* (1960), ostensibly a First World War novel with leading literary figures, but better described by words which appear in it: 'Past the danger point, past the point of any logic and of any meaning, and everything has meaning. Start superimposing, you get odd composites, nation on nation.' One of her latest and finest works is *Helen in Egypt* (1961, posthumous), a 300-page lyrical poem. The usual estimation of H.D. as an Imagist in the minor key, with a restricted and rather precious beauty, is being radically changed by American poets who, in the 1960s, are reading her concentrated lyricism with renewed attention. The chief of these is Robert ◊ Duncan, whose articles in little magazines (*Coyote's Journal*, *TriQuarterly, Aion, origin* and *Caterpillar*) are parts of his forthcoming *H.D. Book*. [EM]

T. B. Swann, *The Classical World of H.D.* (1962); Glenn Hughes, *Imagism and Imagists* (1960); H. Gregory and M. Zaturenska, *A History of American Poetry 1900–1940* (1946).

Dorn, Edward (1929–). Poet. He was born in Illinois, studied at Illinois University and ◊ Black Mountain College, and has taught at Idaho State University and the University of Essex. He edited the magazine *Wild Dog* from Pocatello, Idaho. His poetry first appeared in substantial form in Donald Allen's anthology *The New American Poetry* (1960), and then in *The Newly Fallen* (1961) and *Hands Up!* (1964). They show an individual voice, uncertain in structure but able to convey attachment to the land and complex intellectual arguments with skill. *From Gloucester Out* (1964) was a turning point, a poem in which 'projective verse' methods were extended personally beyond the obvious reference to Charles ◊ Olson. This skill with long poems of varied materials and complex free form is clear, too, in *Geography* (1965) and *The North Atlantic Turbine* (1967), which contains mature work examining the nature of commitment to a particular locality and culture. *Gunslinger* (1968–9) is an extended poem of wit, verve and philosophical complexity. Of his prose, *What I See in the Maximus Poems* (1960) concerns Olson's poetry. *The Rite of Passage* (1965) is a first-rate novel of life on the land in the North-west of America, and *The Shoshoneans* (1966) a personal discovery of the plight of the Indians of the Basin-Plateau. [E M]

Twenty-four Love Songs (1969).
Ed. David Ossman, *The Sullen Art* (1963).

Dos Passos, John (1896–1970). Novelist, social historian. Born in Chicago, of Portuguese descent; educated at Choate School and Harvard, graduating in 1916. In Spain studying architecture when America entered the First World War, he joined the Ambulance Corps (as did Hemingway, E. E. Cummings and other idealistic young Americans). His disillusion with the experience of war and its social implication is given fictional form in *One Man's Initiation: 1917* (1920; reissued in unbowdlerized complete form, 1969) and *Three Soldiers* (1921). His next few years were spent as newspaper correspondent and journalist, and in 1922 he published a volume of poetry, *A Pushcart at the Curb*, and *Rosinante to the Road Again*, a collection of essays which explore the Iberian immigrant element in himself as well as aspects of Spanish culture. His next novel, *Streets of Night* (1923), begun while he was a student, begins to examine, however clumsily, the waste in urban American lives, the theme of so much of his mature writing, first exemplified in *Manhattan Transfer* (1925), which takes megalopolitan New York as its subject. This is his first attempt at composing a collective novel by means of a multiplicity of characters and scenes. The city itself seems to be of more oppressive importance than its citizens, and this determinist atmosphere makes the book a prelude to Dos Passos's central achievement, the trilogy *U.S.A.* (1937), a prose epic comprising *The Forty-Second Parallel* (1930), *1919* (1932) and *The Big Money* (1936). It traces, through interwoven biographies, the history of America from the early 20th century to the onset of the Depression in 1929. Gradually the numerous body of characters, fictional figures and real historical persons, forms a composite picture of society, expounding America's post-war aims and potentials, its whoring

after false materialistic gods, and its political and social injustices, with the execution of Sacco and Vanzetti (two anarchists accused of robbery and murder in Massachusetts in 1921) forming a focal disenchantment. The trilogy is an anti-epic in that it celebrates the *disestablishment* of an order, but as 'polyphonic' as the Renaissance epic in its complex structuring of fictional narrative, biographies of strategic socio-cultural figures like Edison, Ford, ◊ Veblen, Frank Lloyd Wright, Valentino and William Randolph Hearst, the prose-poetry of the impressionist 'Camera Eye' sections, and the newspaper montages of the 'Newsreel' sections.

Dos Passos's second trilogy, *District of Columbia* (1952), covers ·American social history and opinion in the thirties and forties: *The Adventures of a Young Man* (1939) concerns the disillusion of a young leftist in the Spanish Civil War, after bitter experiences among the workers of America; *Number One* (1943), based on the career of the southern politician, Huey Long, is a novel of political corruption; and *The Grand Design* (1949) is a criticism of the Roosevelt regime. Earlier experimental methods have been abandoned in this work, which is less brilliant as literature but still forceful as social analysis. *Mid-Century* (1961) returns to something of the structure of *U.S.A.* and has a broader scope, including a wider variety of public figures. But it is sentimentally patriotic, attacks the younger generations and the leaders of labour with considerable vehemence, and returns to the earlier attack on financiers. The main onslaught is against power men in any form; the defect is an abstract morality inside a deadened prose.

During the thirties Dos Passos progressively disengaged himself from the political left, ceasing to regard it as a solution to America's socio-economic problems. He espoused 'Jeffersonian' democratic conservativism (◊ Jefferson), expressed in *The Head and Heart of Thomas Jefferson* (1954), and a series of fictional and socio-historical works in which his wistfulness about the American past and his depression about the present grow side by side: *The Ground We Stand On* (1941), *The Prospect Before Us* (1950), *Chosen Country* (1951), *The Theme is Freedom* (1956), *The Men Who Made the Nation* (1957), *Prospects of a Golden Age* (1959); this is where the bulk of his work lay after *District of Columbia*. He also wrote two volumes of reportage, and several plays, which include *The Garbage Man* (1926), *Airways, Inc.* (1928) and *Fortune Heights* (1933). His later work includes *Mr Wilson's War* (1963), which uses his early dramatic and epic methods to document the First World War, *The Best Times* (1967), an account of a 1921 journey in the Near East and acquaintances in America (including Cummings, Hemingway and Hart Crane), *Brazil on the Move* (1963), a further examination of his ancestral preoccupations as well as a glance at modern South America, and *Occasions and Protests* (1965), a collection of essays with one redeeming piece, 'Satire as a Way of Seeing'. In *The Portugal Story* (1969) Dos Passos, the grandson of a Portuguese immigrant, describes three centuries of Portuguese history. In spite of this large output, it is *U.S.A.* that lasts as a major work of fiction, a great collective novel which gains in significance for its slow and painful abandonment of hopes, combined with modern technical scale and scope. [A G/E M]

J. H. Wrenn, *John Dos Passos* (1961); Maxwell Geismar, 'John Dos Passos: Conversion of a Hero', in *Writers in Crisis* (1942); Jean-Paul Sartre, 'John Dos Passos', in *Literary and Philosophical Essays* (1955); Robert Gorham Davis, *John Dos Passos* (University of Minnesota Pamphlet, 1962); John D. Brantley, *The Fiction of John Dos Passos* (1968).

Douglas, Lloyd (1877–1951). Novelist. Born in Indiana, he was a Lutheran and later a Congregational clergyman, mostly in university districts. He turned to fiction in his fifties, with *The Magnificent Obsession* (1929), about a Christian brain surgeon, and became an international best-selling writer. Other novels followed, usually dealing with success through piety. His formula of sex and religion, plus happy endings, plus a dash of spiritual fascism, reached case-history dimensions in *The Robe* (1942), the adventures of Jesus's last garment. *The Big Fisherman* (1948), the life of St Peter, had almost as incredible a global success. [E M]

Drake, Joseph Rodman (1795–1820). Poet, satirist. Born in New York. Only his 'Croaker Papers', satirical skits written with Fitz-Greene ◊ Halleck, were published during his short life, but *The Culprit Fay and Other Poems* appeared posthumously (1835), the title poem a striking work in the romantic mode about a fairy who loved a mortal, with a Hudson River setting. He was one of the important New York 'Knickerbocker' group, which included ◊ Irving, ◊ Bryant and ◊ Paulding. [M B]

Frank L. Pleadwell, *The Life and Works of Joseph Rodman Drake* (1935).

Dreiser, Theodore (1871–1945). Novelist. Born in Terre Haute, Indiana, the ninth child of German-speaking parents. Memories of his childhood, one of extreme poverty in which the family was dominated by the harsh and bigoted father, appear in his later fiction. After some months at Indiana University, Dreiser became a newspaperman on the Chicago *Globe* and worked in St Louis and Pittsburgh before arriving in New York in 1894. His first novel, *Sister Carrie* (1900), was rejected by Harper but enthusiastically received by Frank ◊ Norris, then working for Doubleday. But the publisher's wife apparently objected to the book's rawness, and while it was not exactly suppressed, a small, unpublicized edition ensured its commercial failure and another period of poverty for its author. Later, as editor for a firm which published magazines for a predominantly female readership, Dreiser achieved a considerable degree of financial independence. His second novel, *Jennie Gerhardt* (1911), was followed by two volumes of the 'Cowperwood' trilogy, partly based on the career of the Chicago traction magnate Charles T. Yerkes: *The Financier* (1912; revised edn, 1927) and *The Titan* (1914). (The third volume, *The Stoic*, appeared posthumously in 1947.) Dreiser's other novels are *The 'Genius'* (1915), an autobiographical and in some ways lamentable study of the artistic temperament; *An American Tragedy* (1925), a long and detailed novel based upon an actual murder case of 1906; and *The Bulwark* (1946).

In 1927 Dreiser visited Russia and expressed his new faith in *Dreiser Looks at Russia* (1928) and in *Tragic America* (1931). Thereafter he retained a strong sympathy for communism and shortly before his death joined the Communist Party.

Since the publication of his first novel Dreiser has remained a controversial figure. His prose has often been attacked for stylistic crudities; his novels tend to be loosely constructed; his opinions are often inconsistent and over-simple; his reduction of the complexities of human behaviour and motives to mechanistic 'chemisms' is obviously open to assault; his naturalistic universe often relies heavily upon the operations of chance. But he remains a writer of enormous power. In novel after novel he presents compulsive analyses of American life tragically illustrating the manner in which individual aspirations are thwarted or misdirected because of the perversion of American energies and ideals; his books are a bleak and ironical inversion of the Horatio ◊ Alger myth.

Profoundly influenced by his youthful reading of such authors as Hardy, T. H. Huxley and, in particular, Herbert Spencer, whose views left him 'intellectually in bits', Dreiser is usually included with those naturalist writers whose works express the principal tenets of Social Darwinism. Yet his novels reveal a redeeming sense of wonder and awe before the splendid if appalling mystery of life, while the quest of his characters for significance and self-fulfilment in the ordinary processes of living often invests them with dignity and pathos.

These qualities are well displayed by the heroine of *Sister Carrie*, about which Dreiser wrote: 'It is not intended as a piece of literary craftsmanship, but as a picture of conditions done as simply and effectively as the English language will permit.' It broke new ground in the subject matter of the American novel and in the objectivity with which the unconventional subject was treated. This and *An American Tragedy* probably constitute Dreiser's best work, and show his principal asset as a novelist: the relentless accumulation of detail to convey a vivid impression of reality. In its skilful use of the elementary symbolism afforded by houses, clothes and colours, *An American Tragedy* goes beyond the traditional confines of naturalistic writing; metaphor and symbol, as well as monumental descriptive narrative, indict the tawdry nature of the 20th-century American dream by illuminating the life and death of one lonely, but representative, individual. By contrast, in the Cowperwood trilogy Dreiser, for all his diligent research, sometimes failed to dramatize effectively the Nietzschean role he assigned to his prototypical financier; his real success comes in the presentation of Cowperwood's human relationships, not his business affairs.

Other works include *The Hand of the Potter* (1918), a full-length play which anticipates the theme of *An American Tragedy*;

Twelve Men (1919), which contains an affectionate portrait of his brother Paul Dresser, the songwriter; and a series of autobiographical volumes – *A Traveler at Forty* (1913), *A Hoosier Holiday* (1916), *A Book about Myself* (1922; reissued as *Newspaper Days*, 1931) and *Dawn* (1931). Dreiser also published *Hey Rub-a-Dub-Dub* (1920), a collection of essays which comes as near to expressing his philosophy as any single book by him, and 3 volumes of short stories: *Free* (1918), *Chains* (1927) and *A Gallery of Women* (1929). [HD]

Letters, ed. R. H. Elias (3 vols., 1959).
Helen Dreiser, *My Life with Dreiser* (1951); F. O. Matthiessen, *Theodore Dreiser* (1951); ed. Alfred Kazin and Charles Shapiro, *The Stature of Theodore Dreiser* (1955); Charles Shapiro, *Theodore Dreiser: Our Bitter Patriot* (1964); W. A. Swanberg, *Dreiser* (1965); Ellen Moers, *Two Dreisers* (1969).

DuBois, William Edward Burghardt (1868–1963). Negro sociologist, writer and propagandist. Born in Great Barrington, Massachusetts, he was educated at Fisk University and Harvard; his doctoral thesis there, on the suppression of the African slave trade with the U.S.A., was the first volume in the Harvard Historical Series. He went on to become prominent through his series of sociological studies of the status of the Negro in the U.S.A. Rejecting the views of the Negro leader Booker T. ◊ Washington, who believed in slow development through vocational training, he claimed more immediate equality and full citizenship for Negroes, and between 1903 and 1905 he emerged as leader of a militant radical, Negro wing. His writing is filled with passionate emotional concern for the fortunes of his race. Among his best early books is *Souls of Black Folk* (1903; repr. 1953), a series of sketches of Negro life. In 1909 he resigned from the faculty of Atlanta University to become a founder of the National Association for the Advancement of Coloured People, with whose moderate politics he later became disillusioned. In 1935 appeared his book *Black Reconstruction* (repr. 1955), in 1940 the autobiographical *Dusk at Dawn*. In 1949 he became director of the Peace Information Center in New York and was accused of communist sympathies. In 1961 he joined the Communist Party and, as director of the *Encyclopaedia Africana*, moved to Ghana, taking out citizenship in the year of his death. (◊ Negro Literature.) [DKA/MB]

An ABC of Colour: Selections (1963); *Autobiography* (1968).
F. L. Broderick, *W. E. B. DuBois: Negro Leader in a Time of Crisis* (1959).

Dugan, Alan (1923–   ). Poet. Born in New York City, he graduated from Mexico City College, returning to New York to work as model-maker for a medical supply house. He has published *Poems* (1961), which won the National Book Award and the Pulitzer Prize for Poetry, *Poems 2* (1963) and *Poems 3* (1967). His manner is brittle and determinedly anti-rhetorical, his subjects and style direct and plain. He writes at his best with a wit variously caustic, despairing and ferocious. [BP]

Collected Poems (1969).
Richard Howard, *Alone with America* (1969).

Dunbar, Paul Laurence (1872–1906). Poet. A leading poet of the 'Harlem Renaissance', he was the son of former slaves, born in Ohio and discovered working an elevator in Dayton in 1893, the year of his privately printed *Oak and Ivy*, which with *Majors and Minors* (1895) prepared for the book which brought him wider recognition, *Lyrics of a Lowly Life* (1896). Dunbar was the first Negro poet with a national reputation since Phyllis ◊ Wheatley, but (like her) he suffered from tuberculosis during his brief life. Written in tune with current regionalism, and with a good use of dialect (he admired Burns), his poems have strong rhythms and skilful folk quality, often humorous, though his attitudes seem conventionally pathetic and optimistic compared with later Negro protest poetry. He wrote leniently and sentimentally except in 'Ode to Ethiopia' and 'We Wear a Mask', which reveal the pain beneath the popular singer. (◊ Negro Literature.) [EM]

The Complete Poems (1940).
V. Cunningham, *Paul Laurence Dunbar and His Song* (1947).

Duncan, Robert (1919–   ). Poet. Born in Oakland, California, he has been a leading poet of the important San Francisco circle, which included Robin Blaser, Jack ◊ Spicer, Kenneth ◊ Rexroth and Helen Adam, active since the 1940s. At ◊ Black Mountain College he worked with Charles ◊ Olson, Robert ◊ Creeley and Denise ◊ Levertov (see his own biographical note in *The New American Poetry 1945–1960*, 1960), and is associated with the discontinuities and spatial improvisations of Californian painters of the mid-century. His career is marked by a dedication to the vocation of poet which is rare. The turning point in his earlier poetry, collected in *Heavenly City, Earthly City* (1947) and *Selected Poems* (*1942–1950*) (1959), is with 'The Venice Poem', in which he turned 'from the concept of a dramatic form to a concept of musical form in poetry'. His complex poetry explores the metaphysics of consciousness, the platonic relationship of man and nature, and what he calls 'the structure of rime'. His procedures and imagery are as erudite and wide-ranging as they are cunning and elusive. His books include *The Opening of the Field* (1959), *Roots and Branches* (1964) and *Bending of the Bow* (1968), which contains the first batch of 'Passages', the continuous open-ended series of poems in which his work is now contained. *Writing Writing* (1953) is a collection of pieces in the modes of Gertrude Stein. His prose includes *The Sweetness and Greatness of Dante's Divine Comedy* (1965), *As Testimony* (1965), a commentary on two poems, parts of a book on H.D. (Hilda ◊ Doolittle) which have appeared in *avant garde* magazines, and the introduction to a reissue of earlier work as *The Years as Catches: First Poems (1939–1946)* (1966). Other poetry has appeared as the pamphlet *Fragments of a Disordered Devotion* (1966) and *Of the War* (1966), which constitutes 'Passages 22–27', and in a special number of *Audit* magazine (IV, 3, 1967). Two of his plays are *Faust Foutu* (1960) and *Medea at Kolchis: The Maiden Head* (1965). *Letters* (1958) combines verse and prose, and is important for statements about his work, as is the essay 'Towards an Open Universe' (*Contemporary American Poetry*, ed. Howard Nemerov, no date). [EM]

Selected Poems, i, *The First Decade, 1940–1950*, ii, *Derivations, 1950–1956* (1969).

Dunlap, William (1766–1839). Playwright. Born at Perth Amboy, New Jersey, he was one of the first American professional writers, certainly the first professional playwright. First a portrait painter, he studied in London with Benjamin West, and grew involved with the theatre. Back in America, he became playwright, adapter of continental dramas, producer and manager. He wrote or adapted some 60 plays, in a vast variety of modes, and set in a variety of locales throughout the world. His *The*

79

Father: or, American Shandyism (1788) draws on Royall ◊ Tyler's *The Contrast*. *André* (1798; *American Plays*, ed. A. G. Halline, 1935) is a powerful drama about the British officer captured by the Americans during the War of Independence and hanged (it was later revised as a musical spectacle under the title *The Glory of Columbia Her Yeomanry!*). Others of his plays have the patriotic dimension familiar in the early American theatre. Dunlap also wrote many prose works, including *The Life of Charles Brockden Brown* (1815) and *A History of the American Theatre* (London, 1832). His translation of Kotzebue's play *The Stranger* (1798) was widely known. His work, now hard to obtain, was well known in England, as in the U.S.A., in the 19th century. [M B]

Van Wyck Brooks, *The World of Washington Irving* (1945); Oral S. Coad, *William Dunlap: A Study* (1917; 1962).

Dunne, Finley Peter (1867–1936). Journalist. Born in Chicago, where he became a reporter for the *Herald* (1884) and other papers. In 1896 he became editor of the *Evening Journal*, in 1900 of the New York *Morning Telegraph*, and later (1918–19) of *Collier's Weekly*. From 1903 he was famous as the creator of Mr Dooley, a witty and sceptical Chicago-Irish barman whose thoughts on events of the day appeared weekly in the press. Dooley's observations to his silent and gloomy comrade Malachi Hennessey were widely cherished, and often occasioned anxiety to politicians. They were collected in *Mr Dooley in Peace and in War* (1898), *Mr Dooley in the Hearts of His Countrymen* (1898), *What Mr Dooley Says* (1899) and so through to *Mr Dooley on Making a Will* (1919). Dooley thought only three books interesting – Shakespeare, the Bible and 'Mike Ahearn's history in Chicago' – but remarked 'What I like about Kipling is that his pomes are right off th' bat. ... No col' storage pothry f'r Kipling. All lays laid this mornin'.' [M G]

Mr Dooley at His Best, ed. Elmer Ellis (1938); *Mr Dooley on Ivrything and Ivrybody*, ed. Robert Hutchinson (1963).
Elmer Ellis, *Mr Dooley's America: A Life of Finley Peter Dunne* (1941).

Duyckinck, Evert A. (1816–78) and **George L.** (1823–63). Editors, literary critics and historians. Born in New York, these brothers were central figures in the post-

Knickerbocker, mid-19th-century New York literary scene, active with new writers and movements. Evert, a graduate of Columbia, originally hoped to become professor of literature there, studying in Europe for the purpose in 1838–9. When this did not come about, he became an active literary personality, a sponsor of ◊ Melville, friend of ◊ Hawthorne, ◊ Bryant, ◊ Irving, ◊ Lowell, ◊ Simms, etc., and a promoter of writers. He and Cornelius Mathews ran the critical magazine *Arcturus: A Journal of Books and Opinion* (1840–2). Then with his brother George and others he edited the even more brilliant *Literary World* (1847–53), a weekly journal of society, literature and art with remarkable contributors (Melville's 'Hawthorne and His Mosses' appeared there). The most significant venture of all was the two brothers' *Cyclopaedia of American Literature: Embracing Personal and Critical Notices of Authors, and Selections from Their Writings, from the Earliest Period to the Present Day* (1855; suppl. 1866, etc.), a 2-volume anthology and critical study which had major influence in establishing the significance and the study of American literature. [M B]

Perry Miller, *The Raven and the Whale* (1956).

Dwight, Timothy (1752–1817). Poet, miscellaneous writer. A precocious fellow-student of John ◊ Trumbull at Yale, he was born in Massachusetts, became tutor at Yale and, like his friend, collaborated on 'The Meddler' essays and in introducing more literature into the theology-bound curriculum, although he did become Professor of Theology as well as president of the college. He was an authoritative preacher (grandson of Jonathan ◊ Edwards) and administrator in many fields, but his fame rests on his work as a ◊ Connecticut Wit: *The Conquest of Canaan* (1785), which he claimed to be the first religious epic in America, is part of the large literature which celebrates America by biblical analogy, a deadening rehandling of the Book of Joshua in 10,000 lines of heroic couplets in 11 books; *The Triumph of Infidelity* (1788), in which Satan's historical perversions – paganism, Catholicism, Voltaire, Hume, etc. – are given a stolid run-through; and his better poem, *Greenfield Hill* (1794), a long praise of Connecticut agrarian life contrasted with European depravity, worse apparently than the massacre of the Pequod Indians in Part Four. He engaged little in the satirical activities of the Wits, but published Federalist political argument, many sermons, and a book of *Travels in New England and New York, 1769–1815* which contains valuable historical information. [MB/EM]

C. E. Cunningham, *Timothy Dwight, 1752–1817, A Biography* (1942); Leon Howard, *The Connecticut Wits* (1943).

E

Eastlake, William (1917–   ). Novelist. Born in New York City, he was in the army and lives on a New Mexico ranch. His prose and fiction include *Go in Beauty* (1956), *The Bronc People* (1958), *Portrait of an Artist with Horses* (1963) and the outstanding *Castle Keep* (1965), a novel of an American garrison holding a 13th-century Ardennes castle. *The Bamboo Bed* (1969) is a satire based on his reports from the Vietnam war which appeared in the *Nation*. [E M]

Eastman, Max (1883–   ). Critic, poet. Born at Canandaigna, N.Y. One of the group of Marxist critics – others include V. F. ◊ Calverton, Waldo ◊ Frank and John ◊ Reed – who strongly influenced American criticism from the First World War onwards. He taught philosophy at Columbia before editing Marx, becoming editorially involved in two left-wing journals, the *Masses* (1911) and the *Liberator* (1917), and developing a deep interest in the social and scientific context of literature. His best-known books are *The Enjoyment of Poetry* (1913), *The Literary Mind: Its Place in an Age of Science* (1931), and then in 1934 two statements against totalitarian coercion of art: *Artists in Uniform: A Study of Literature and Bureaucratism* and *Art and the Life of Action*. He has produced some interesting works of memoirs (e.g. *Great Companions*, 1959), and his poetry is collected in *Poems of Five Decades* (1954). *Seven Kinds of Goodness* (1967) is a guide to Buddhism, Confucius, Socrates, Plato, Moses, Mohammed and Jesus. [M B]

Van Wyck Brooks, *Sketches in Criticism* (1932); Charles I. Glicksberg, 'Max Eastman: Literary Insurgent', *Sewanee Review*, XLIV (1936).

Eberhart, Richard (1904–   ). Poet, playwright. Born in Minnesota and educated at Dartmouth and Harvard, he tutored a Siamese prince, taught naval gunnery in the Second World War, worked with the Butcher Polish Company, served as poet-in-residence in universities, founded the Poet's Theatre, served the Library of Congress and National Culture Centre, and won the Bollingen Prize, with John Hall Wheelock,

in 1962. His first book of poems, *A Bravery of Earth* (1930), was followed by many others, including his *Selected Poems* (1951) and *Collected Poems* (1960). In his poems, the traditional religious moralist considers sin and war against a context of childhood wholeness and a mystical vision of Nature. A more direct and American speech emerged in *Burr Oaks* (1947) and reaches a high level of achievement in *Undercliff* (1953), his ninth book. His original explorations of baffling experience are as fine as ever in *Great Praises* (1957). His *Collected Verse Plays* (1962) tend to be undramatic discussions in a rather old-fashioned and extravagant idiom. *Thirty One Sonnets* (1967) was written 35 years earlier and put away, he says, 'as being too proud, too youthful, and too imitative'. His most recent work is *Shifts of Being* (1969). [E M]

Bernard F. Engel, *The Achievement of Richard Eberhart* (1968); Ralph J. Mills, *Richard Eberhart* (University of Minnesota Pamphlet, 1966).

Edmonds, Walter D. (1903–   ). Novelist. His native north-western New York State, with the Black River and the Erie Canal, is the stamping ground of an imagination which produced a series of energetic historical novels appearing since 1929, the most famous of which is *Drums along the Mohawk* (1936), a tale of Revolutionary rebels, British foes and Indian destruction, whose research he describes in *How You Begin a Novel* (1936). Other novels include *Rome Haul* (1929) and *Erie Water* (1933), about life on, and the building of, the Erie Canal; and *Young Ames* (1942), set in New York City in the 1830s. [E M]

Edwards, Jonathan (1703–58). Philosopher, scientist, theologian. Born in Connecticut, son and grandson of Puritan ministers. His boyhood sensitivity and precocity were curbed under a strict Calvinist education. The essays 'Of Insects' and 'Of the Rainbox', written at 11, already show his interest in natural science. At 13 he was studying at Yale, where he graduated at 16. His theological studies and experience of

Calvinist rigours were transformed into a sense of joy through mystical conversion and intellectually enriched through Locke's psychology and Newton's physics. The result was his firm belief in God's benevolence, expressed in two private works of self-examination and programmes for living, the 70 *Resolutions* and the *Personal Narrative*. He married Sarah Pierrepont in 1727, and in 1729 succeeded his grandfather in the ministry of Northampton, where the power of his sermons developed the religious revival known as the Great Awakening, which spread throughout New England in the 1730s and 1740s. Edwards' *Sinners in the Hands of an Angry God* (1741) is America's most celebrated sermon, insisting graphically on the realities of damnation and on the precariousness of life, which God holds like a spider 'or some loathsome insect over the fire'. His preaching terror and enthusiasm were opposed by religious rationalists, led by Charles Chauncey, minister in Boston, who stressed 'an enlightened Mind, and not raised Affections'. Edwards opposed the 'Half-Way Covenant' by which the Congregationalist bourgeoisie compromised between good living and the chance of damnation, and insisted that 'none ought to be admitted into the communion and privileges of members of the visible church of Christ in complete standing' unless they had experienced the 'sensible effect or sensation' of conversion or regeneration. On this issue he resigned and instead of forming a separatist movement moved to Stockbridge, Massachusetts, a frontier missionary church for the Mohawk and Housatonic Indians, where he expounded his organized philosophy in *Freedom of Will* (1754), *The Nature of True Virtue* (1765), *Concerning the End for which God Created the World* (1765) and *The Great Christian Doctrine of Original Sin Defended* (1758). Although his projected *History of the Work of Redemption* never materialized, his treatises gained him the presidency of the College of New Jersey (later Princeton University) in 1757; he died of smallpox inoculation after three months in office. *Freedom of Will* begins by opposing the idea of post-Adamite freedom to choose 'goodness' with the theory of God's choosing and rejecting whom he pleases. Edwards argues that will, like any effect, must have a cause and therefore cannot be 'free', since it is a consequence and therefore necessary. Will records only

choice made by a man's whole consciousness; a man has not freedom of will but of act; action not will must be morally judged, and man is morally responsible for his action. *Original Sin Defended* continues from these evasive but essential arguments on freedom, the great American cause, to announce man's two God-given principles, the one inferior – 'mere human nature' – and the other superior – 'spiritual, holy, man's divine nature'. But God is to be blamed for depriving man of the latter and he does inject his evolutionary creative urge or grace every now and then. It is at this point that Edwards' biology modified his theology. Adam, the American Adam, is the seed of the tree whose branches are later generations, and the finite universe can be resolved into sensations operating in the mind of both God and man. The types of the world are in moral correspondence with their anti-types in the spiritual world. It is the variations on freedom, determinism and the eternal Adam that make Edwards a significant American unifier of spirit and matter, of man's moral incapabilities with his scientific and literary endeavours. What Van Wyck ◊ Brooks termed his 'high-brow' legacy penetrated American thinking, the polar opposite of ◊ Franklin's self-reliant opportunism (see *America's Coming of Age* by Van Wyck Brooks). [EM]

Representative Selections, ed. C. H. Faust and T. H. Johnson (1935).
P. Miller, *Jonathan Edwards* (1949).

Eggleston, Edward (1837–1902). Novelist, historian, editor. He was educated in various Indiana country schools and brought up in the most rigid Methodism. At first a Methodist minister, he founded the creedless Church of Christian Endeavour in Brooklyn and became its minister (1874–9), also editing Sunday-school magazines. He campaigned enthusiastically for reform in many fields. He was responsive to the currents of literary realist and sociological thought of his time; and regional fiction makes an important advance in his varied, interesting novels, with their realistic descriptions of Indiana, the 'Hoosier State'. He seems to have written partly as a protest against the current literary obsession with New England, partly under the influence of Taine's remark in his *History of Art in the Netherlands* that 'the artist of originality will work courageously with the materials he finds in his own environment'. *The*

Hoosier School-Master (1871) describes adventures in a one-man village school, and reveals Eggleston's close study of Indiana dialect. *The End of the World* (1872) is an Indiana love story with a religious background; *The Circuit Rider* (1874), describing the confusion of a refined Methodist minister from the east when he meets religious ecstasies on the frontier, successfully captures the atmosphere of the frontier camps; and *Roxy* (1878) portrays a young woman against the setting of early-19th-century Indiana.

His two completed volumes of a projected *History of Life in the United States* (1896, 1900) are pioneering explorations of the country's social history; the second of these was reissued in 1933 as *The Transit of Civilization from England to America in the Seventeenth Century*, and has considerable analytical merits. [MG]

William Pierce Randel, *Edward Eggleston: Author of The Hoosier School-Master* (1946) and *Edward Eggleston* (1963).

Eliot, John (1604–90). Teacher and 'Apostle to the Indians'. Born in England, educated at Cambridge, he emigrated in 1631 and devoted himself to the conversion of the Massachusetts Indians. He established 'praying villages' and translated the Bible into the dialect of the Naticks, a branch of the Algonquins (1661, 1663). He wrote a variety of books about his mission and the Indians, some in their dialect; they include *The Glorious Progress of the Gospel among the Indians* (1649), *The Indian Primer* (1669) and *Up-Bookum Psalmes* (1663). Cotton ◊ Mather wrote his life (1691). [MB]

Eliot, T(homas) S(tearns) (1888–1965). Poet, critic, playwright. Though born and raised in St Louis, Missouri, he came from a Unitarian family whose roots were in New England: this twin heritage he was later to memorialize in 'The Day Salvages', the third section of his greatest poem, *Four Quartets* (1943). Harvard-educated, public-spirited and wealthy, the Eliot family made sure that he received an excellent classical training before he went up to Harvard in 1906. His mother, a gifted if very minor poetess, encouraged his early predilection for verse writing. Admirably prepared, he arrived at Harvard when it had much to offer: ◊ Santayana, Irving ◊ Babbitt and Barrett Wendell were among his teachers, and, as Herbert Howarth has shown in

Notes on Some Figures behind T. S. Eliot (1964), the influence of these men on the direction of Eliot's thought was decisive. From them, especially from Babbitt, he learned how the past could be used to measure, discipline and enrich the present. No less important during his Harvard days were his extracurricular studies: here he first read Dante, the poet whom he later considered the greatest permanent influence on his work. A more immediately utilizable discovery was Laforgue, whose wry ironic treatment of the modern urban landscape provided him with a voice which seemed and – in English – *was* strangely original and modern. His first attempts in verse have been published as *Poems Written in Early Youth* (1967; private edn, Stockholm, 1950). By 1911, at 23, he had completed 'The Love-Song of J. Alfred Prufrock', surely one of the most brilliantly precocious poems in the language. Already the master of the vivid sensuous imagery, the extraordinarily flexible tone, and the strongly expressive rhythms which were to be the chief characteristics of his mature poetry, he did not produce a comparable success again (though this is a disputable point) until 'Gerontion' (1920).

After obtaining his B.A. and M.A. degrees and embarking on doctoral study of the philosopher F. H. Bradley, and studying at Paris, Munich and Merton College, Oxford, he settled in London in 1915, where during the next few years he earned a precarious living by teaching, reviewing and working at Lloyds Bank. These were also the years when he wrote the remarkable satiric quatrain poems 'Whispers of Immortality' and 'Sweeney among the Nightingales', poems which, ostentatiously terse, grotesque and learned, had a programmatic significance for Eliot and his new mentor Pound, who wished to correct the delinquencies of the *vers libre* movement. *The Waste Land* (1922), written partly as a sequel to 'Gerontion', expressed what he took to be the spiritual and moral plight of post-war Europe. Abandoning (with Pound's help) the monologue form of 'Prufrock' and 'Gerontion', he created a poem in which an apparently random succession of images and points of view is presented, yet which is controlled (more or less) by a submerged symbolic narrative. The poem seemed to express the disillusionment of a generation, it was recognized by Pound and others as the chief masterpiece of the modern movement, and it established Eliot at once as the leading American poet of the day.

But it was as a critic that he first gained recognition among those in whose eyes poetic experimentation was suspect. Especially in his earlier criticism (*c*. 1917–25) he had an almost unprecedented gift for expressing with cogency and authoritative manner what others had often thought and said. Frequently muddled and contradictory as a theorist, and, compared with Johnson, Coleridge or Arnold, unoriginal and unadventurous as a practical critic, he has been perhaps the most successful dictator of literary taste in the history of English criticism. Thanks to his essays Milton and the romantics have been re-examined and revalued; the Metaphysical poets, the great Augustans, Dante and the French symbolists have gained a vastly larger and more appreciative audience. He did much, too, to encourage a popular awareness of the vitality of past literatures and the necessity to range outside English literature if one is to understand and evaluate it properly.

Eliot's interest in verse drama dated from the Harvard days, and the dramatic monologue, conceived partly as a development of the Jacobean soliloquy, was his favourite poetic form. This interest was extended during the early twenties by close study of the Senecan tradition, coupled with a perception that the Mass and the music hall might be exploited to help revive verse drama. The first result of this research was *Sweeney Agonistes* (1926–7), a brilliant fragment related in both tone and technique to the earlier quatrain poems. After 1927, when he was confirmed in the Church of England and shortly thereafter became a British citizen, he had powerful reasons to try to make contact with a larger community than his poetry could be expected to reach. True, two of his greatest poems, *Ash Wednesday* (1930) and *Four Quartets*, were yet to be written; and they, no less than *The Waste Land*, could be called coterie poems. But after 1927, it can be inferred from his critical writings, he was aiming at a much larger, if still a minority, public. *Murder in the Cathedral* (1935) was his first artistically successful play; to many critics it seems the only play he wrote (aside from *Sweeney*) in which Eliot the great poet is much in evidence. The later plays, however, show a more certain and

subtle command of dramatic technique; and they represent a serious attempt, as the two earlier plays do not, to deal with familiar contemporary society. Perhaps the best of these plays are *The Cocktail Party* (1950) and *The Confidential Clerk* (1954). He was awarded the Nobel Prize for Literature in 1948. [GD]

Donald Gallup, *T. S. Eliot; a Bibliography* (1953); Grover Smith, *T. S. Eliot's Poetry and Plays* (1956); ed. Hugh Kenner, *T. S. Eliot; a Collection of Critical Essays* (1962); Northrop Frye, *T. S. Eliot* (1963); ed. Allen Tate, *T. S. Eliot: The Man and His Work* (1966); George Williamson, *A Reader's Guide to T. S. Eliot* (1953); F. O. Matthiessen, *The Achievement of T. S. Eliot* (1935; 3rd edn 1958); Hugh Kenner, *The Invisible Poet* (1960).

Elkin, Stanley (1930–). Novelist. Born in St Louis. His first novel, *Boswell* (1964), is a black-humour tale of a teenager who becomes a wrestler and enters the top ranks of international society (including the Queen of England); it is a fine comedy of the pretensions of institutions and 'great names'. *Criers and Kibitzers, Kibitzers and Criers* (1966) is a collection of 9 stories with the same intelligence and imagination and similar themes of the destruction of illusions and the insanities of isolation. With *A Bad Man* (1967) Elkin penetrates into contemporary America through Leo Feldman, a man born with a homunculus inside him; he is the ultimate salesman who senses the madness of 'civilization' and operates his departmental store as a counter-organization. Elkin is one of the most important American novelists of the sixties. [EM]

Ellison, Ralph (1914–). Novelist. Born in Oklahoma. His *Invisible Man* (1952) is one of the most impressive post-war American novels. Its theme is that of much 20th-century literature: modern man's search for identity in an incomprehensible world. Its Negro hero emerges as an archetypal faceless underground man; denied any basis for self-definition by his world, he remains invisible. His forays into society, in both North and South, result in violent rejection; and he ends a figure of total isolation, one who has chosen to live underground. This theme is articulated with an impressive richness of naturalistic detail; but what emerges from the density of minute particulars, often violent and terrifying, is a myth of man's search for meaning in chaotic experience. 'And Hickman Arrives' is a fragment from a second novel (*Noble Savage I*, 1960). *Shadow and Act* (1964) is a collection of essays, on a wide variety of aspects of the Negro and Negro culture in America. (◊ Negro Literature.) [AH]

Robert A. Bone, *The Negro Novel in America* (1958); Marcus Klein, *After Alienation* (1962); Ellin Horowitz, 'The Rebirth of the Artist', in *On Contemporary Literature*, ed. R. Kostelanetz (1965).

Emerson, Ralph Waldo (1803–82). Philosopher, poet. One of America's most important writers and a leading Transcendentalist, he was born in Boston, Massachusetts, descended from generations of New England ministers. When his father died, leaving the large family in poverty, the mother's self-reliance and endurance enabled four sons to be educated at Harvard. Emerson was no great scholar but read widely, already trusting his instincts – as his later philosophy would assert. He became Pastor of the Old Second Church of Boston; but, guided by W. E. ◊ Channing's reformed Unitarianism, his brother William's experience of Göttingen Bible criticism, and his own reading of Swedenborg and Coleridge, he came to decline the ministry traditional in his family. After the shock of his new wife's death in 1831, the mental derangement of his younger brother (1828) and his own psychosomatic symptoms when he preached, he doubted his vocation and in 1832 sailed for Malta, travelled through Italy and Switzerland, and reached Paris, where the Jardin des Plantes inspired him to almost mystical naturalism, the transcendental unity of men and nature. Disappointed with the ageing Coleridge and Wordsworth's conservativism, he obtained more nourishment from Carlyle, but returned to America to create 'pale face', as he called himself, into the great lecturer and writer he was ready to be. He remarried, settled in Concord, and crystallized his ideas in *Nature* (1836), combining the needed part of Puritan and Unitarian religion with 19th-century romantic ideology. *The American Scholar* (1837) calls for a national literature, and the 'Divinity School Address' (1838) rejects formal religion for intuitional experience of the World Soul. His sociability and lecturing reputation increased as he lectured as far west as the frontier and Mississippi valley.

For materials he drew on his journals, and the final form appeared as *Essays: First Series* (1841) and *Second Series* (1844). Although he met with the Transcendentalist Club and edited the *Dial*, he refused to join Brook Farm (◊ Ripley) in the name of individualism and doubt as to the artificiality of group experiment. He supported ◊ Thoreau's Walden Act and the Abolition cause in the 1850s. In 1847 he lectured successfully in London and Oxford, and met Arnold and Clough and renewed the friendship with Carlyle. Back in America he published *Representative Men* (1850) and *Conduct of Life* (1860) and gradually became an establishment figure himself. But his optimism grew bewildered and assertive as the Civil War drew nearer, and his voice after the war sounded forced. He was buried in Sleepy Hollow Cemetery, Concord, beside Thoreau and Hawthorne. His essays can be represented by 'Self-Reliance' ('society is everywhere in conspiracy against the manhood of every one of its members', therefore 'whosoever would be a man must be a non-conformist'), 'Spiritual Laws' ('there is a soul at the centre of nature, and over the will of man, so that none of us can wrong the universe'), 'Circles' (a man's own circle of thought should enclose earlier and contemporary circles), 'Art' (the artist 'employs the symbols in use in his day and nation, to convey his enlarged sense to his fellow men'), and 'The Poet' ('the complete man' using 'symbolic language'). The titular *Representative Men* are Plato, Swedenborg, Montaigne, Shakespeare, Napoleon and Goethe: the types of great men of 'a rich and related existence'. Of the relationship between his poetry and his essays he said, 'I can breathe at any time, but I can only whistle when the right pucker comes'. He championed Whitman in 1855 and his own poems often take free-verse organic forms to delineate his man-and-nature themes ('The Rhodora', 'Ode Inscribed to W. H. Channing', 'Brahma', 'Two Rivers'). His experiments with line and sound were of major use in developing American poetry. Although his thought and vocabulary have penetrated American culture, he was a great articulator of liberal ideas rather than a great artist. In his *Journals* the record of inner tension and joy is often finer than the published work of his lifetime. [EM]

Complete Works, ed. E. W. Emerson (12 vols., 1903–4); *The Journals* ed. E. W. Emerson and W. E. Forbes (10 vols., 1909–14). Ralph L. Rusk, *The Life of Ralph Waldo Emerson* (1949); Sherman Paul, *Emerson's Angle of Vision: Man and Nature in American Experience* (1965); Stephen E. Whicher, *Freedom and Fate: An Inner Life of Ralph Waldo Emerson* (1953); Frederic I. Carpenter, *Emerson Handbook* (1953); W. M. Konvitz and S. Whicher, *Emerson: A Collection of Critical Essays* (1962).

Enslin, Theodore (1925–   ). Poet. Born and raised near Philadelphia, he has lived mostly on Cape Cod and in Maine. He studied music under Nadia Boulanger but gave it up for poetry. His considerable body of original work is published in *The Work Proposed* (1958), *The Place Where I am Standing* (1964), *New Sharon Prospect* (1966, which contains 'Pages from the Journals'), *This Do* (& the Talent) (1966), and *The Diabelli Variations* (1967). [E M]

Eshleman, Clayton (1935–   ). Poet. Born in Indianapolis, and educated at the local university, he lived often in Japan and South America, and now edits from New York *Caterpillar*, one of the most important little magazines of the sixties. In 1969 he published a major translation of the poetry of the Peruvian poet César Vallejo, *Poemas humanos/Human Poems*. His representative book of poems is *Indiana* (1969), which reads like the unhurried search of a man with more varied and complex experience than he can easily encompass. His projective verse forms are also worked out in *Walks* (1967), *Yellow River Record* (1969) and *The House of Ibuki* (1969). [E M]

Everett, Alexander Hill (1790–1847). Poet, essayist, editor. Born in Boston, Massachusetts, brother of E. ◊ Everett, he was a diplomat in Russia, Holland and Spain, where he assisted and befriended Washington ◊ Irving. Later he wrote the studies *Europe* (1822) and *America* (1827), and became a frequent contributor to, then editor of, the *North American Review* (1830–5), translating Goethe and encouraging attention to European romanticism. [M B]

Essays, Critical and Miscellaneous (1845–6).

Everett, Edward (1794–1865). Editor, essayist, orator, statesman. Brother of A. H. ◊ Everett, and like him an important figure in making American and Bostonian thought cosmopolitan. He was among the early group of Americans who studied at Göttingen and reformed and advanced American scholarship in theology, classics, history and European literature. First a Unitarian minister, then Professor of Greek at Harvard, he deeply influenced letters as editor of the important *North American Review* (1820–4) in one of its most cosmopolitan phases. He won great reputation as an orator, and his speeches, published as *Orations and Speeches on Various Occasions* (4 vols., 1853–68), had widespread popularity. Like his brother he turned to politics, and became in due course Minister to England and Secretary of State (1852–3). [M B]

Expatriates. The habit of literary expatriation, usually to Europe, is so well established in the history of American literature as to constitute a tradition. The circumstances of America's founding, as a colony intellectually dependent upon Europe, particularly on England, made this inevitable in the early days. Benjamin ◊ Franklin, who himself spent a large part of his life in England and France, observed that because Americans were not rich enough to encourage the fine arts 'our Geniuses all go to Europe'. During the 19th century many of the major writers – including Irving, Hawthorne, Cooper, James, Edith Wharton, Bret Harte and Stephen Crane – spent long periods in Europe. James became, at the end of his life, a British citizen. During this century the sentimental pilgrimage to what Hawthorne called 'our Old Home' developed; T. G. Appleton once spoke of the importance of Europe for the Yankee – 'it is the home of his protoplasm, of the long succession of forces which make him what he is.' In the early years of the present century, Ezra Pound and T. S. Eliot (who also became a British citizen) came to London to conduct their poetic revolution, and Gertrude Stein chose Paris as the city in which to seek 'glory'. Even after Van Wyck ◊ Brooks declared American literature officially of age, the pattern continued. A large part of the literary generation of the twenties, the so-called ◊ 'lost generation' – including Hemingway, Fitzgerald, Dos Passos, Katherine Anne ◊ Porter and Sylvia ◊ Beach – spent time in Paris, where a large American literary colony developed. A largish artistic colony still remains.

Expatriation became a conventional

mode of acquiring a literary apprenticeship, and later of expressing protest against
the provincialism or repression of American
life. At times – as with Theodore ◊ Roosevelt's complaints against 'hyphenated
Americans' – it came close to being a serious
political issue. There is a long debate about
it in American letters; it is much associated
with the literary dissatisfactions of American writers. At one time the essential opposition was between Europe's 'civilization'
and America's lack of it, but in the present
century the terms shift: it is Europe's
freedom, and the opportunities afforded
there for ◊ Bohemianism, that are contrasted with America's limitations. The
effect of such expatriation on American
letters is important; despite the repeatedly
expressed fears that this was leading to
intellectual servility and the Anglicization
or Europeanization of American writing,
its effect has been to make American letters
remarkably cosmopolitan and international, and the cosmopolitan ideal was
repeatedly expressed by expatriates like
James and Pound. Recently there have
been signs that the tide is flowing the other
way; from ◊ Nabokov, Auden, Isherwood
and the German refugees from Hitler onward, the expatriate from Europe has
played an important part in American
letters. [MB]

R. P. Blackmur, 'The American Literary Ex-
patriate' in *Foreign Influences in American Life:
Essays and Critical Bibliographies*, ed. D. F.
Bowers (1944); Malcolm Cowley, *Exile's Re-
turn* (1934); ed. Philip Rahv, *Discovery of
Europe: The Story of American Experience in
the Old World* (1947); Ernest Hemingway, *A
Moveable Feast* (1964).

F

Fair, A. A. ◊ Gardner, Erle Stanley.

Falkner, William C. (1825–79). Novelist. Now best known as the great-grandfather of William ◊ Faulkner (who changed the spelling of the family name), this Mississippi railroad builder, lawyer and soldier was once esteemed as the author of *The White Rose of Memphis* (1880), an exotic Southern romance. He also wrote, in reply to *Uncle Tom's Cabin*, *The Little Brick Church* (1882) and a travel book, *Rapid Ramblings in Europe* (1884). [M B]

Farrell, James (Thomas) (1904–   ). Novelist, short-story writer. Born on Chicago's South Side, he lived in that city until 1931. He attended classes at the University of Chicago (where he wrote the sketch that would eventually grow into his best-known work, the Studs Lonigan trilogy) and worked in various jobs, including advertising and undertaking. Since the early 1920s he has lived more or less continuously in New York City, writing and lecturing extensively. *It Has Come to Pass* (1958) records his visit to Israel in 1956.

Farrell's reputation rests upon three distinct yet related cycles of fiction: the Studs Lonigan trilogy, the Danny O'Neill pentalogy and the Bernard Carr trilogy. The first, comprising *Young Lonigan* (1932), *The Young Manhood of Studs Lonigan* (1934) and *Judgment Day* (1935), dispassionately records the brutalized Chicago life and pathetic death at 29 of Farrell's inarticulate hero. Danny O'Neill, who appears in *A World I Never Made* (1936), *No Star Is Lost* (1938), *Father and Son* (1940), *My Days of Anger* (1943) and *The Face of Time* (1953), succeeds in escaping the destructive forces of the family and the larger environment of Chicago. His literary aspirations are indirectly fulfilled in the Bernard Carr trilogy: *Bernard Clare* (1946), *The Road Between* (1949) and *Yet Other Waters* (1952). Among Farrell's other novels are *Gas-House McGinty* (1933) and *This Man and This Woman* (1951). *New Year's Eve 1929* (1968) is a short allegory of a woman's life and *Lonely for the Future*

(1966), a story of 1927 Chicago's clubs. *The Silence of History* (1963) inaugurates a new series based on another young man from Chicago; the second volume is *What Time Collects* (1964). *A Brand New Life* (1968) makes a return to his earlier vigour. A prolific writer of short stories, he has now published over 200, many of which were brought together in *The Short Stories of James T. Farrell* (1937) and *An Omnibus* (1956). His literary criticism and occasional essays are collected in *A Note on Literary Criticism* (1936), *The League of Frightened Philistines* (1945), *Literature and Morality* (1947), all exploring his proletarian-naturalist aesthetics, and *Reflections at Fifty* (1954). Luna Wolf has edited *Selected Essays* (1964).

Farrell's work has been unfashionable in literary circles, and critics tend to view his novels with an air of patronage. Since the early 1930s he has remained in his fiction very much an unreconstructed naturalist (though he professes allegiance to Sherwood ◊ Anderson rather than to ◊ Dreiser), exploiting the monotony, boredom, cruelty and violence of modern urban life, concentrating upon the relationship of the individual to the family unit and to the larger, frequently hostile environment in which the family finds itself. Certainly, Farrell's work tends to lack variety; so does his prose style, despite the stylistic experimentation of *Gas-House McGinty*. But if his achievement is limited, it still represents a positive, substantial contribution to modern American literature. The Bernard Carr trilogy (the name was changed after a libel suit) is less interesting and convincing than the earlier sequences; but it too forms part of Farrell's avowed overall intention to create 'as complete a story of America as I knew it, of the hopes, the shames, the aspirations'. In this sense much of his work is an immense *roman fleuve* which offers an effective, at times moving and indignant, history of 20th-century America. [H D]

Edgar M. Branch, *A Bibliography of James T. Farrell's Writings, 1921–1957* (1959); Edgar M. Branch, *James T. Farrell* (University of Minnesota Pamphlet, 1963); C. C. Walcutt, *American Naturalism: A Divided Stream* (1956); B. H. Gelfant, *The American City Novel* (1954); W. M. Frohock, *The Novel of Violence in America* (2nd edn, 1957); ed. S. J. Krause, *Essays on Determinism in American Literature* (1964).

Fast, Howard (1914–   ). Novelist. Born in New York City, he travelled through the States during the Depression, taking a variety of jobs, and became a leading American left-winger; his *The Naked God* (1957) is a famous document of disenchantment with the Communist Party, though not with the left. His writing, mostly historical, tends to deal with revolutionary situations, often touched with 'propaganda' emphasis. One group of his novels is concerned with the American Revolutionary war (*Two Valleys*, 1933, *The Unvanquished*, 1942, *The Proud and the Free*, 1950, etc.), while *Citizen Tom Paine* (1943) is a persuasive study of ◊ Paine as European-American revolutionary. He has also set novels in the Reconstruction period, in more contemporary American settings – *Clarkton* (1947), for instance, deals with a strike in a Massachusetts mill town – and in the biblical and Roman past. His romantic historical epics, some of them filmed, include *My Glorious Brothers* (1948), set in pre-Christian Israel; *Spartacus* (1952), set in Rome; *Moses, Prince of Egypt* (1958); and *Agrippa's Daughter* (1965). *Power* (1963) is a portrait of a labour leader, which includes an account of the origins of the coal miners' union, in the 1920s or 1930s. Fast can write sentimentally and splashily; but a sophistication not only political but historical invigorates his work. [MB]

S. Meistler, 'The Lost Drums of Howard Fast', in *A View of the Nations*, ed. H. M. Christian (1960).

Faulkner, William (1897–1962). Novelist, short-story writer, poet. Born in New Albany, Mississippi, and brought up in Oxford, seat of the University of Mississippi, he left school early, joined the Royal Flying Corps in Canada in the First World War (which ended before he had completed training), and studied briefly at the University in Oxford. Supporting himself with odd jobs, he began to write (writing was in the family and the fame of his great-grandson has renewed the reputation of William C. ◊ Falkner, the model for Faulkner's Colonel Sartoris). Faulkner's first book,

The Marble Faun (1924), is a collection of derivative (Keatsian, Georgian) pastoral verses of little distinction. (A second volume of poetry, *A Green Bough*, appeared in 1933.) The following year he was helped by Sherwood ◊ Anderson in New Orleans, wrote journalism, and began work on his first novel, *Soldiers' Pay* (1926), in which a wounded First World War soldier returns to the South. He returned from travel in Europe that year and thereafter spent most of his life in Oxford. *Mosquitoes* (1927), a mildly satirical novel of New Orleans literary Bohemia, was followed, on Sherwood ◊ Anderson's advice, by fiction about his home area, and *Sartoris* (1929) begins the series of novels and stories about life in north Mississippi, re-created as Yoknapatawpha County, in which his full creative powers were to develop. A world-weary, lost generation approach still impregnates *Sartoris*, but parts of it rise to that level of emotional and historical realism which the Yoknapatawpha work attains: *The Sound and the Fury* (1929), *As I Lay Dying* (1930), *Sanctuary* (1931), *Light in August* (1932), *Absalom, Absalom!* (1936), *Go Down, Moses* (1942), *Intruder in the Dust* (1948), the trilogy of *The Hamlet* (1940), *The Town* (1957) and *The Mansion* (1959), and *The Reivers* (1962), his last novel.

Although Faulkner renders the physical reality of Yoknapatawpha's inhabitants, soil, river, sand and brush country, Negro cabins, small farms, decaying mansions, small towns with their court-house, jail, stores, square and statue to the Confederate dead, he is not limited by this particularity of time, place and history: he is not simply a regional novelist. His fiction moves continually towards the condition of myth through which he is able to express and define an imaginative vision of human existence.

Faulkner's world, though often regarded as a compound of Jacobean horror and a naturalistic emphasis on the brutal and violent in human nature, does affirm the human values he spoke of in accepting the Nobel Prize (1950) – 'courage and honor and hope and pride and compassion and pity and sacrifice'. He reveals a tragic sense of man's failure to sustain these ideals, seen specifically in the failure of the South, buttressed by flawed notions of religion, to recognize the humanity of the Negro, and in his outrage at the existence of men, in both North and South, obsessed by the desire for self-aggrandizement, who fail even to know such ideals exist. Faulkner's key merits are regional, and idealistic, though formally his novels reveal a readiness for modernist experiment. He frequently employs such devices as Joycean stream of consciousness, scrambled chronology, mythic and biblical parallelism, and the manipulation within a single novel of apparently disparate narrative lines: *The Wild Palms* (1939), which consists of two wholly distinct stories printed in alternating chapters, provides the extreme example of this last technique. The style can be equally complex; though sometimes undisciplined and rhetorically extravagant, its page-long sentences, involuted and parenthetical, can often create a richly significant verbal texture. Structural and stylistic devices, however, are usually related to major thematic preoccupations: for example, Faulkner's frequent departures from standard narrative chronology have much to do with his idea of time, his sense that past events continue into the present.

The Sound and the Fury (1929) employs most of the devices mentioned to tell the history of the decline of the Compson family in Jefferson, Mississippi, due to its failure to love. The novel's four sections rehearse the story from the differing points of view of four characters, the first being a brilliant *tour de force* told by an idiot, Benjy. *As I Lay Dying* (1930), also technically complex, is the story of the poor-white Bundren family's journey to bury Addie Bundren in Jefferson – on a naturalistic level, grotesquely humorous, but ritualistic and symbolic in its elaborate telling. *Light in August* (1932), Faulkner's most penetrating and dramatic analysis of contemporary Southern society, tells the two stories of Joe Christmas, victim of the South's racial prejudice, and Lena Grove searching for the father of her unborn child; both come together to define the strength and weaknesses of the South's way of life, the clash between white and black finally seen in terms more universal than those of Southern racial conflict. *Absalom, Absalom!* (1936), also often of extraordinary rhetorical and structural complexity, is about Thomas Sutpen's doomed attempt to build up a plantation and found a family; his design founders on Southern racial prejudice and the inability to love; his fate becomes an emblem for the whole

South. In *Go Down, Moses* (1942), which includes the superb story 'The Bear', Faulkner brilliantly unites the idea of a promised land cursed by slavery and the destruction of America's pastoral wilderness – a recurring symbol in his work for man's urge to exploit and violate. In contrast, *The Unvanquished* (1938) relates his Southern preoccupations in a more conventional prose form. *Intruder in the Dust* is a good example of Faulkner's attempt to come to terms with his inheritance of Negro and white relations, and the short story 'Red Leaves' shows something of his interest in native American Indians and their declining culture. The *Hamlet–Town–Mansion* trilogy concerns the growth to power of the Snopes clan, Faulkner's image, at once realistic and grotesque, of greed and licence inherent in the development of the South. *Requiem for a Nun* (1951) develops material in *Sanctuary* concerning the nature of moral law, and includes some definitive statements about the history of Yoknapatawpha, complex prose passages placed between the dramatized main narrative. Of the novels not directly concerned with Yoknapatawpha, *Pylon* (1935) concerns the courage of aviators during a New Orleans Mardi Gras, and *A Fable* (1954) is a grandiose, verbose allegory of power based on mutinies on the Western front in the First World War.

Faulkner's many first-rate short stories appeared in *These Thirteen* (1931), *Doctor Martino and Other Stories* (1934), *Knight's Gambit* (1949), *Collected Stories* (1950) and *Faulkner's County* (1955; includes the Nobel address, *As I Lay Dying*, and extracts from the Yoknapatawpha novels). *The Portable Faulkner* (1946, ed. Malcolm Cowley) arranges selections of Yoknapatawpha fiction materials to form a chronological 'saga', for which Faulkner provided a map and a history of the Compson family. The generation of this important work is given in *The Faulkner–Cowley File* (1967). *New Orleans Sketches by William Faulkner* (1955) is a collection of his contributions to the *Times-Picayune* in 1925. His direct expressions of opinion are contained in *Essays, Speeches and Public Letters* (ed. J. B. Meriwether, 1967), *Faulkner at Nagano* (1956; included in *Lion in the Garden: Interviews with William Faulkner, 1926–1962*, ed. J. B. Meriwether and M. Millgate, 1968), *William Faulkner in the University* (1959) and *Faulkner at West Point* (1964). [AH/EM]

Michael Millgate, *The Achievement of William Faulkner* (1967); Cleanth Brooks, *William Faulkner: The Yoknapatawpha Country* (1963); Edmond L. Volpe, *A Reader's Guide to William Faulkner* (1964); C. H. Nilon, *Faulkner and the Negro* (1965); Dorothy Tuck, *A Handbook of Faulkner* (1965).

Fearing, Kenneth (1902–61). Poet, novelist. Born in Oak Park, Illinois. After the University of Wisconsin he worked at various jobs until he became a freelance writer in New York. His commercial work appeared under several pseudonyms while he wrote poetry for little magazines, collected in his first volume, *Angel Arms* (1929). His first novel was *The Hospital* (1939) and the best known is *The Big Clock* (1946). Fearing's poetry definitively concerns urban, mechanized society, in which faith and love are thinned away. His typical poem uses newspaper and police-report styles to document satirically some disgrace of bourgeois neglect and greed, or some city criminality. His use of city slang is as masterly as his handling of the accumulative line. [EM]

New and Selected Poems (1956).

'Federalist, The' (written by Alexander Hamilton, 1755–1804, John Jay, 1745–1829, and James Madison, 1751–1836). The constitution of 1781 under which the 13 newly emancipated colonies were held together in a loose union of States provided for a national congress to which the States delegated certain defined powers. Gradually the desire to establish a more effective and efficient national government grew, and in 1787 a convention was appointed in Philadelphia to propose such revision. As the debates progressed it became clear that what was emerging was not an amended constitution but an entirely new one setting up a tripartite national government with much more positive powers. The question of whether or not the new constitution would be ratified by the States dominated politics in 1787 and 1788. It was particularly controversial in New York State, where the governor, George Clinton, opposed ratification. After letters advocating non-ratification appeared in the New York press, an opposition series supporting the constitution appeared between 27 October 1787 and 4 April 1788 over the pen name 'Publius'. Some of these letters were published in book form on 22 March 1788; a complete collection appeared on 28 May 1788. The volume was called *The Federalist*, a name which had been assumed by the proponents of a new constitution. In 1792 it was revealed that 'Publius' was the collective pseudonym of Alexander Hamilton, John Jay and James Madison. Madison, a delegate to the Philadelphia convention, had probably contributed more to the drafting of the constitution than any other of the Founding Fathers. Hamilton, although a delegate, had missed many of the meetings, but he and Jay (who had not been at Philadelphia) were keenly interested in both ratification and the local political battles within New York State.

Of the 85 letters which make up *The Federalist*, Hamilton is credited with the authorship of 51, Madison with 27, and Jay with 5. Numbers 62 and 63 are disputed, but Professor B. F. Wright has recently attributed them to Madison. *The Federalist* is less a comprehensive work of political philosophy than a series of observations aimed at winning voter support by urging that the objects of government, which are assumed rather than analysed, can best be attained through stronger central government, and that the type of federalism advocated cannot, because of the system of checks and balances and separation of powers, become despotic. But inherent in the letters is a concept of property right and individual liberty. Society is believed to be composed of a collection of interest groups, and the main function of government is seen to be arbitration between these, since, man being essentially selfish, he must be persuaded that unrestricted pursuit of self-interest cannot but be prejudicial to society as a whole and thus eventually to himself. It is debatable whether *The Federalist* letters had much effect in winning support for the constitution of 1787, but since that time they have been acclaimed as a cogently argued and practical defence of the federal form of government. [DKA]

The Federalist, ed. B. J. Wright (1961).

Federal Theatre. The only American theatre nationally sponsored, as the Works Progress Administration, a project to rescue unemployed theatre artists and staff during the Depression and to bring their work to an American audience which had hardly experienced theatre at all. It was begun (1935) and directed by Hallie Flanagan, a pupil of George P. ◊ Baker, and a woman of outstanding knowledge of the theatre. She organized five regional theatres to provide work, a stage as an incentive to dramatists and technicians alike, and to encourage experiment in form and production, through such projects as a children's theatre, a Negro theatre, a marionette theatre, a topical 'Living Newspaper', a popular-price theatre for new authors, an experimental theatre and a try-out theatre. Hallie Flanagan understood that the Federal Theatre could continue its social purpose and survive only by becoming a national theatre. In four years, thousands of productions were created throughout the country in 31 States. By 1937 alone it had played to approximately 16 million people, at an average audience price of 30 cents. Productions included an all-Negro *Macbeth* and T. S. Eliot's *Murder in the Cathedral*, both of which were major successes; Labiche's *The Italian Straw Hat* (*Horse Eats Hat*, in America), directed by the then unknown Orson Welles, with music by Virgil Thomson; Blitzstein's important political musical *The Cradle Will Rock*; and on 27 October 1936, 21 simultaneous productions of Sinclair ◊ Lewis's and John C. Moffit's *It Can't Happen Here*, which concerned the establishment of a Fascist dictatorship in America. Accused of communism, this superb achievement was assassinated by Congress in 1939 in a disgraceful 'trial' without adequate evidence. [EM]

Hallie Flanagan, *Arena: The Story of the Federal Theatre* (1940); Jane De Hart Matthews, *The Federal Theatre, 1935–1939* (1968).

Feldman, Irving (1928–). Poet. Born and educated in New York City, he travelled and taught abroad and at Kenyon College and the State University of New York at Buffalo. His two books of poems, *Works and Days* (1961) and *The Pripet Marshes* (1965), employ Yiddish inflections, usually in short, quick run-on lines, to explore Old Testament themes as they are translated and transformed by the fate of Jewish civilization in the 20th century. [BP]

Ferber, Edna (1887–1968). Short-story writer, novelist, playwright. Born in Michigan, she was a reporter for newspapers in Wisconsin, Milwaukee and Chicago, and later a war correspondent,

before becoming a full-time writer. *Dawn O'Hara*, her first novel, concerns a newspaper woman in Milwaukee. Her early stories described with great success a new American type, the woman in business; they were collected in *Roast Beef, Medium* (1913), *Personality Plus* (1914) and *Emma McChesney and Co.* (1915). Women were also the protagonists in her early novels, *Fanny Herself* (1917); *The Girls* (1921), about three generations of a family; and *So Big* (1924; Pulitzer Prize), a study of a widowed school-mistress and mother in a rough rural community. Two big popular novels, *Show Boat* (1926), about a Mississippi river family, and *Cimarron* (1930), which concerned the Oklahoma land rush of 1889, were filmed. Later novels, though less successful, have tackled with relish an extraordinary variety of subjects; they include *American Beauty* (1931), *Come and Get It* (1935), *Saratoga Trunk* (1941), *Great Son* (1945) and *Ice Palace* (1958). Texans were enraged by the unflattering *Giant* (1952), and Edna Ferber comments on the book's reception and the making of a film version in the second of two lively autobiographies, *A Peculiar Treasure* (1939) and *A Kind of Magic* (1963). With George S. ◊ Kaufman she wrote a series of plays, among them *The Royal Family* (1927), a satire on the Barrymores; *Stage Door* (1936); and the famous *Dinner at Eight* (1932). [MG]

Ferlinghetti, Lawrence (1919–). Poet. Born in New York, he studied at Columbia and the Sorbonne, and with his poetry and his publishing centre the City Lights Bookshop helped to make San Francisco a by-word as a city of new literature during the 'San Francisco Renaissance' and the ◊ Beat Generation period of the fifties. His poems in *Pictures from The Gone World* (1955), *A Coney Island of the Mind* (1958) and *Starting from San Francisco* (1961) are partly finely made personal lyrics and partly long public poems – frequently written for declamation, with and without jazz. His public readings in the 1950s were part of the rejuvenation of spoken poetry on the West Coast. He has perfected a kind of public poem made up of topical and critical references, light-toned but serious satire, and literary references which is extremely effective in performance. He published some of his poems as broadsides, to facilitate their display and general availability:

these are included in *Starting from San Francisco* and continue in, for example, 'Berlin' (1961), 'Where is Vietnam' (1965) and 'Moscow in the Wilderness, Segovia in the Snow' (1967). Ferlinghetti has always been conscious of the need for direct statement and clear responsibility in poetry. *Unfair Arguments with Existence* (1962) is a collection of experimental plays, and *Routines* (1963) are scenarios for happenings. *Her* (1960) is a novel in the form of an interior and surreal monologue. *After the Cries of the Birds* (1967) is a poem with an essay on its genesis. *The Secret Meaning of Things* (1969) contains six long poems, and *Tyrannus Nix?* (1969) is the latest of his 'political-satirical tirades'; the target is President Nixon. [E M]

Fiedler, Leslie (1917–   ). Literary and social critic, novelist, storywriter. Born in Newark, New Jersey, he was head of the English Department at Montana State University until moving recently to the University of Buffalo. Most influential as a critic, he has combined sociological interests with concern with psychology and myth to produce eccentric but stimulating critical studies, mostly of American literature. He came to prominence with long essays on the Alger Hiss and the Rosenberg espionage cases and a piece on *Huckleberry Finn* attributing repressed homosexual emotion to Huck and Jim; these are collected in *An End to Innocence: Essays on Culture and Politics* (1955). This notion is expanded into a general theory of white American psychological inability to face up to 'coloured' races in its midst; of American literature and culture as a series of accommodations and rejections of 'love' for men of other races; of the cultural dominance of the white American female and the male attempt to escape it. *Love and Death in the American Novel* (1960), Fiedler's most connected work, is a bulky study of American literature seen in this light, concentrating on the Sentimental (love) and Gothic (death) traditions in the novel. A monograph, *The Jew in the American Novel* (1950), assimilates the Jew into his notion that 'outsider' groups like Indians and Negroes are akin to the major American writers who at their best produced works severely critical of American life – as argued in *No! in Thunder: Essays in Myth and Literature* (1960). *Waiting for the End* (1964) looks at modern American writing

in the light of cultural shifts from expatriate through Jewish to Negro mentality, and is depressed and apocalyptic. *The Return of the Vanishing American* (1968) develops the thesis that the Indians carry the sacred energies of America. His complex and elaborately constructed novels include *The Second Stone* (1963) and *Back to China* (1965); *Pull Down Vanity* (1962) and *The Last Jew in America* (1967) are collections of very lively stories. *Being Busted* (1970) concerns the implications of his being tried on narcotic charges in Buffalo. [A G]

Field, Eugene (1850–95). Poet, newspaperman, prankster. Born in St Louis, Missouri, he seems to have been expelled from three colleges for practical jokes. Working on papers in St Louis, Kansas City and Denver, he found his vocation in Chicago on the *Daily News*. His column made fun of current idiocies; his poetry churned out sentimentalities by the foot. His parodic *Tribune Primer* (1881) advised children to mutilate flies, eat lye, beat the baby, etc., but his normal target was Chicago philistinism. His range runs from Western ballads and hymns to corny children's verse. Most of it is awful. His fame may well rest with 'Wynken, Blynken and Nod' and 'Little Boy Blue'. [E M]

Fisher, Vardis (1895–   ). Novelist, poet. He was born in a Mormon family in Idaho and has taught English at Utah and New York Universities. During the Works Progress Administration years he directed the Federal Project for the *Idaho State Guide* (1937). As a novelist, his reputation began with a tetralogy about Vridar Hunter – *In Tragic Life* (1932), *Passions Spin the Plot* (1934), *We Are Betrayed* (1935) and *No Villain Need Be* (1936). *Children of God* (1939) is a historical novel about the early Mormons, and *Darkness and the Deep* (1943) begins his series of novels on the development of primitive man, continued in *Peace like a River* (1958), *My Holy Satan* (1959) and *Orphans in Gethsemane* (1960). His recent works include *Suicide or Murder: The Strange Death of Meriwether Lewis* (1962) and the novel *Mountain Man* (1965). His poems are found in *Sonnets to an Imaginary Madonna* (1927). [E M]

Fiske, John (1842–1901). Philosopher, historian. Born in Hartford, Connecticut. One of the leading intellectual figures of his day, he was a Christian evolutionist who promoted the views of Comte, Herbert Spencer and other neo-Darwinians in such books as the influential *Outlines of Cosmic Philosophy* (1875) and *Darwinism and Other Essays* (1879). He taught philosophy at Harvard and later history at Washington University, St Louis. He wrote numerous historical works, mostly dealing with the U.S.A., and including *The Beginnings of New England* (1889), *The American Revolution* (1891) and *How the United States Became a Nation* (1904). Both as evolutionary positivist and historian he was an eloquent popularizer rather than an originator; his skill in presentation, both as lecturer and writer, and his tendency to reconcile evolution with Christian providence – both seemed to work in favour of the U.S.A. – won him great general prestige. [MB]

Writings (24 vols., 1902).
J. S. Clark, *The Life and Letters of John Fiske* (2 vols., 1917); Thomas S. Perry, *John Fiske* (1906).

Fitch, Clyde (1865–1909). Dramatist. Born in Elmira, N.Y. His series of successes began with *Beau Brummel* (1890). His professionalism produced a large number of realistic social plays of topicality and caricatural detail, including *Barbara Frietchie* (1899), using Whitter's Civil War poem (and the basis of Romberg's musical *My Maryland*), *Captain Jinks of the Horse Marines* (1901) and *The Girl with Green Eyes* (1902), a melodrama of neurotic jealousy and some satire of New York society. [EM]

Fitts, Dudley (1903–   ). Poet, translator. Born in Boston, he was educated at Harvard and teaches at Philips Academy, Andover. *Poems: 1929–1936* (1937) collects some of his verse. Amongst his chief work have been his vigorous translations from the Greek – notably of Aristophanes (*Lysistrata*, 1954, *The Frogs*, 1955, etc.) and of Sophocles, whose *Oedipus* he translated with Robert Fitzgerald. [MB]

Fitzgerald, F. Scott (1896–1940). Novelist. Born in St Paul, Minnesota, with an ancestry from poor Irish and old Maryland. His family had become prosperous, and had included the author of 'The Star-Spangled Banner'. At Newman School, New Jersey, his tentative and aborted grooming as America's great Catholic writer began in the

hands of Father Fay. At Princeton he wrote for the Triangle Club, but literary success did not compensate for not being rich or an athletic hero. Nor did the army send him abroad in 1917, although he found time to write in camp *The Romantic Egoist*, rewritten as his first published novel, *This Side of Paradise* (1920), an autobiographical work using extracts from letters, episodes from his relations with Fr Fay, and his failed Princeton dreams. But his personal disillusion, his sense of youthful fling being all a man had, and his moral message of waste and the need for responsibility suited post-war urban America; the book became a best-seller and made him rich. He had described 'a generation grown up to find all Gods dead, all wars fought, all faiths in man shaken'; he defined the Jazz Age, the boom reaction to the First World War, and bitterly knew it was mistaken and doomed. He now lived like a hotel playboy, and *Flappers and Philosophy* (1920, stories) confirmed the image he and his wife Zelda projected, the decayed underside of which he described in *The Beautiful and the Damned* (1922), with its world of parties, petting, aesthetics and anxiety over money. But this novel's satirical gloom and noisy barrenness did not suit Fitzgerald's public. He and his wife now paraded through American and European hotel society on the cash he could make only through writing fiction as entertainment. The need for wealth is projected in 'The Diamond as Big as the Ritz' in *Tales of the Jazz Age* (1922). But during his wrangling life with Zelda he managed to write his masterpiece, *The Great Gatsby* (1925), and *All the Sad Young Men* (1926). In spite of praise from T. S. Eliot and Edmund Wilson, *Gatsby* had little success. Back in America Fitzgerald tried to write a Hollywood comedy, and lived in Delaware, but he returned to Europe in 1928. Zelda spent an increasing amount of time in asylums, for which he felt guilty, and he dramatized some of their experience in *Tender is the Night* (1934), a disordered novel written desperately after a long period of sterility and hackwork, and *Taps at Reveille* (1935), a last collection of stories. The breakdown he suffered in America he brilliantly recorded in three essays in *Esquire* in 1936 (see *The Crack-Up*, ed. Edmund Wilson, 1945). He died exhausted from Hollywood hackwork and a ruined constitution. But he had managed, during this final period, to

95

write 17 fine tales (*The Pat Hobby Stories*, 1962).

It is clear from his letters to his daughter that his understanding of capitalist society intensified as he read Marx: his sense of Western decay gives a dimension of the epic to his last and unfinished novel, *The Last Tycoon* (1941). His work as a whole is a serious analysis of the need for 'responsibility' of action between the wars and dramatizes how potential leaders fail from under-nourishment as they search for alternatives to capitalism, Catholicism and communism. The 'ability to function' is betrayed by materialism and ignorance. The hero of *The Great Gatsby* is a *nouveau riche* whose Prohibition loot corrupts an idealism based on American myths of self-reliance and endless opportunity. In spite of its structural flaws, the meticulous style and insights into the American class system make this one of the most gifted novels of the century. *Tender is the Night* is in some ways a profounder study of the talented man exhausted before maturity by the society which needs him. *The Last Tycoon* is a brilliant account of the misgivings of the last Hollywood producer with faith in the moral and social necessity of films. Fitzgerald, more than any other American novelist, presents understandingly the interior exhaustion and the decline of leadership in America during the inter-war years. His melancholy is the sadness of the breakdown of the American dream itself. [E M]

Letters, ed. Andrew Turnbull (1963); *The Apprentice Fiction*, ed. J. Kuehl (1969).

A. Mizener, *The Far Side of Paradise: A Biography of F. Scott Fitzgerald* (1951); Andrew Turnbull, *Scott Fitzgerald* (1962); *F. Scott Fitzgerald, The Man and His Work*, ed. Alfred Kazin (1951); H. D. Piper, *F. Scott Fitzgerald: A Critical Portrait* (1967).

Fitzgerald, Robert S. (1910–   ). Born in Geneva, N.Y., he studied at Trinity College, Cambridge, and Harvard, worked on the New York *Herald Tribune* and *Time*, and in 1946 began his distinguished university teaching career. Apart from his own work in *A Wreath for the Sea* (1943) and *In the Rose of Time* (1956), he has collaborated with Dudley ◊ Fitts on a magnificent translation of Sophocles' Oedipus plays (1939) and made a brilliant version of the *Odyssey* (1961). [E M]

Fletcher, John Gould (1886–1950). Poet. Born in Arkansas, of 'Mugwump' or

intellectual-populist background, he studied at Harvard during the lively period when the French symbolists and Chinese verse were being discussed. The receipt of an inheritance decided him to throw up his studies, pursue his aesthetic interests in these fields, and become a poet. In 1909 he settled in London, 'an interloper on the charmed circle of London literary life' – as he said in his interesting autobiography *Life Is My Song* (1937) – and produced a considerable quantity of poems, publishing five volumes at his own expense. He came under the influence of Pound and ◊ Imagism, but, disquieted by some of the more radical implications of the movement, linked himself with Amy ◊ Lowell's breakaway wing, with its more exotic and highly coloured poetry. In 1932, after long vacillation between Europe and America, he chose the U.S.A. and associated with the ◊ Fugitives, contributing to the Southern agrarian anthology *I'll Take My Stand.* Asserting more strongly his Southern heritage, Fletcher's later poetry – *The Epic of Arkansas* (1936), *The Burning Mountain* (1946), *Arkansas* (1947) – draws on national and regional themes.

As a poet, Fletcher participated in several modern movements, but he is primarily an impressionist. He was fascinated by the analogy between poetry and other arts, particularly painting; and his aesthetic speculations have real substance to them. With Amy Lowell he worked on 'polyphonic prose' and 'colour symphonies'. He was devoted to elaborate visual and rhythmic effects; the title of his best-known volume, *Irradiations: Sand and Spray* (London, 1915), suggests the kind of aesthetic texture he sought. There is a strong *chinoiserie* element in his verse, and if in the long run it seems touched with dilettantism it is never without real interest. He undoubtedly contributed to the development of Southern poetry, and his *Selected Poems* (1938) won him belatedly considerable admiration. [M B]

Amy Lowell, *Tendencies in Modern American Poetry* (1917); Glenn Hughes, *Imagism and the Imagists* (1931).

Foerster, Norman (1887–   ). Critic, editor, teacher. Born in Pittsburg, Pennsylvania, he has been Professor of English at the University of North Carolina (1914–30) and at the University of Iowa (1930–44) (where as Director of the School of Letters he recognized novels, poems and plays as work towards a Ph.D.). A leader of the ⟡ New Humanist movement, he edited its manifesto, *Toward Standards* (1930). His own most important book is *Nature in American Literature* (1923), which explores the development of the 'naturalistic movement in American literature from Bryant to Whitman and the typical essayists of the present century . . . at the same time, by studying the movement in relation to the Classical and Christian tradition which it has more and more supplanted, we may determine in some measure how far it has enriched man's life and how far it has tended to imperil his self-knowledge.' The characteristic values and concerns expressed here are also found in his other books: *American Criticism: A Study in Literary Theory from Poe to the Present* (1928); *The American Scholar* (1929); *The Humanities after the War* (1944) and *The Humanities and the Common Man* (1946). He has edited many anthologies. [MG]

Ford, J. H. ⟡ Negro Literature.

Frank, Waldo (1889–). Novelist, social commentator. Born in Long Branch, New Jersey, he co-founded and edited the magazine *Seven Arts* (1916–17), which sought a literary regeneration; and was active in *avant garde* and social reformist circles, gradually moving to Marxism. His revolutionary position and interest in sociology and economics are reflected in some of his many novels – *City Block* (1922), *Holiday* (1923), *The Bridegroom Cometh* (1938) etc. – though others have a more mystical or more poetic aspect. As a social commentator he wrote on Latin America (where he has a high reputation), Spain and Russia, as well as criticizing American life from a semi-Marxist position. His *Our America* (1919; British title *The New America*, 1922) was an influential item in the protest against American stuffiness and contempt for the arts that lay behind the expatriate movement of the twenties; it is one of many non-fiction books. He was Hart Crane's first editor. [MB]

Gorham B. Munson, *Waldo Frank: A Study* (1923); W. R. Bittner, *The Novels of Waldo Frank* (1958); R. L. Perry, *The Shared Vision of Waldo Frank and Hart Crane* (1963).

Franklin, Benjamin (1706–90). Printer, statesman, natural philosopher and miscellaneous writer. Born in Boston, he was the first fully self-made Man of the Enlightenment, American style. The son of a candlemaker, he went to Philadelphia at 17 and by the range and vigour of his activities helped to make that city the cosmopolitan capital of the infant republic that it later became. His *Do-good Papers* (1722) – essays modelled on the *Spectator* and Defoe, which praised the artisan class for their self-taught middle way of industriousness – appeared while he was a printer. Under the patronage of the governor of Pennsylvania he travelled to London (1724–6) and there formed his rational life plan based self-consciously on his balance of character, and wrote *A Dissertation on Liberty and Necessity, Pleasure and Pain* (1725), a conventional 18th-century tract. He returned to Philadelphia, married, opened his own shop in 1728, and by 1748 was rich and celebrated, living a career based on thirteen points conducive to prosperity, social comfort and the minimum disturbance to self-esteem. Through the annual 10,000 copies of *Poor Richard's Almanack* (1732–58), aphoristic prefaces and notes (including the last preface 'The Way to Wealth'), his ideas penetrated the populace via his mouthpiece, 'Poor Richard' Saunders, and his sayings or 'gleanings' were largely rephrased folk-sayings made from 'the sense of all Ages and Nations' (e.g. 'Love your neighbour; yet don't pull down your hedge', 'If you would be loved, love and. be loveable', and 'A plowman on his legs is higher than a gentleman on his knees'). He founded and supported the Junta (1727) for the self-improvement of artisans and tradesmen, the Library Company (1731), the American Philosophical Society (1744) and the Academy of Philadelphia (1749; later the University of Pennsylvania). One of his main publications was his *Pennsylvania Gazette*, which became the *Saturday Evening Post*. From local government posts he rose to be the State delegate to the Albany Convention, the first colonial move towards confederation, and in 1757 the Pennsylvania Assembly sent him to London to appeal through Parliament concerning the proprietorship of their territory. He returned to America in 1762, but was sent to England, returning only in 1775. His huge journalistic output records his interests in science and invention; his tall stories, whimsical *Bagatelles*, satires,

'Remarks Concerning the Savages of North America' (1784), his electrical experiments, his practical development of bifocal spectacles, a smokeless street-lamp globe, a stove, etc., all testify to his endless pragmatic curiosity and utilitarian habits. His scientific papers and international correspondence contain important contributions to knowledge and terminology (he seems to have pioneered 'armature', 'battery', 'conductor', 'electrician', 'charge' and 'discharge', and 'positive' and 'negative' for the language of electricity). From 1776 to 1784 he lived in France as colonial negotiator and ambassador, the living embodiment of America to the Europeans, a role he played with entertaining skill. But he died in Philadelphia; his tomb inscription reads: 'Benjamin Franklin, Printer'. He is best known in literature for his *Autobiography*, covering the years 1731–59, which was not fully published until 1868. His claim to literary distinction rests more on the style than on the usually utilitarian subjects of his essays; for his writing followed his interests, from men and manners through politics, education, religion, cultural institutions, science, military and maritime policies, spelling, swimming, and back to the more trivial amenities in old age. Combining wit and morality, ingenuity and clarity, force and fancy, the best of his essays are models of literary expression. A gift of mild irony lightens the heaviest subjects and gives weight to the lightest. As a political satirist, particularly during the period of debate with England on the rights of the colonies, he rivalled Swift and Voltaire and the best of his contemporaries, and his *Autobiography* deserves the reputation it has achieved for candour and insight; the record of a man's life, it is also a major document for the birth of the American republic. [E M]

Writings, ed. A. H. Smyth (10 vols., 1905–7); *Papers*, ed. L. W. Larabee, etc. (12 vols., 1960–   ); *Representative Selection*, ed. C. E. Jorgensen and F. L. Mott (revised edn 1962). Carl Van Doren, *Benjamin Franklin* (1938); I. Bernard Cohen, *Benjamin Franklin: His Contribution to the American Tradition* (1953); A. O. Aldridge, *Benjamin Franklin: Philosopher and Man* (1965); P. W. Connor, *Poor Richard's Politicks* (1965).

Frederic, Harold (1856–98). Newspaperman, novelist. Born in New York State, he became permanent London correspondent of the *New York Times* in 1884. He wrote nine novels, some of them historical, most dealing with New York State, mixing naturalism and romanticism. They include *Seth's Brother's Wife* (1887), a dramatic tale set in upper New York State; *The Lawton Girl* (1890); and *The Return of the O'Mahony* (1892). The work for which he is remembered is *The Damnation of Theron Ware* (1896; ed. Everett Carter, 1960; British title, *Illumination*). A friend and admirer of W. D. ◊ Howells, Frederic went well beyond Howells's limited realism in this frank account of a Methodist minister losing his faith. [H D]

Harold Frederic's Stories of New York State, ed. T. F. O'Donnell (1966). T. F. O'Donnell and H. C. Franchere, *Harold Frederic* (1961).

Freeman, Mary E(leanor) Wilkins (1852–1930). Novelist, story writer. Born in Randolph, Massachusetts. Her subject-matter was New England rural life, which she caught with a local-colourist's exactness and an objectivity that makes her comparable with Sarah Orne ◊ Jewett. Two collections of stories, *A Humble Romance and Other Stories* (1887) and *A New England Nun and Other Stories* (1891), with their ironies and their grim spinsters, are usually thought her best work. Among her novels, *The Portion of Labor* (1901), with its social analysis of a New England mill, is the most highly regarded. [M B]

Edward Foster, *Mary E. Wilkins Freeman* (1956).

Freneau, Philip (1752–1832). Poet. Born in New York City, he grew up in the New Jersey house he lived in for the rest of his life. As a Princeton student, he associated with such youthful revolutionary patriots as James Madison, H. H. ◊ Brackenridge and Aaron Burr, and his political nationalism began to form, although his earlier poems imitate 18th-century English pastoral and 'graveyard' verse, and Goldsmith. He and Brackenridge wrote a class poem for commencement called 'The Rising Glory of America' (1772) – as part of the British Empire, however, and he had to revise it later to suit his Americanism. After graduation in 1771, and a period of teaching and pamphleteering, in 1776 he became secretary to a West Indian planter for two years and wrote his early militant poems far from the bloodshed, together with exotic landscape and mutability poems, and the long 'gothic' 'The House of Night'. On his way home a British privateer captured and released him; he enlisted in the militia, served on American privateers, published patriotic verses, and was again captured by the British in 1780, an experience he described in 'The British Prison Ship' (1781). In the same year he pugnaciously edited the *Freeman's Journal* and wrote satires and eulogies for the republican cause ('Columbia shall never be ruled by an isle'), the most readable of which are 'The Political Balance' and 'To the Memory of the Brave American'. For health and fortune he became a sea captain; his poetic reputation increased and he now wrote against American money-grubbing, the neglect of poetry, and uncertain justice in the new democracy ('On the Emigration to America and Peopling of the Western Country'). He married, and from 1789 onwards edited ◊ Jefferson's *National Gazette*. His poems celebrated now the ideals of ◊ Paine's *Rights of Man*. Later he turned to nature poetry. Some of his most famous works of distinctly American quality are: 'The Wild Honey Suckle', 'The Indian Burying Ground' and 'The Dying Indian: Tomo Chequi'. The hero of the latter became his mouthpiece of noble savagery in *The Jersey Chronicle* (1795), a prose soliloquy of romantic primitivism and deism. Poverty sent him back to sea in 1803, but he continued his philosophical nature poems ('On the Religion of Nature', 'On a Honey Bee'). In 1809 he gave up the sea, published the third edition of his *Poems Written and Published during the American Revolutionary War*, and settled on the remains of his estate. The 1812 war roused him to poems like 'The Volunteer's March', but in 1815 his house was burned down; he began to drink ; he was found dying of exposure after a December snowstorm. Most of his poetry has lost its special appeal with the passing of the political occasion, but his work is the first body of professional journalism and poetry in American literature. His talents were turned towards polemics for a nation struggling for independence. He had little time to develop his art while fighting poverty, federalism and the British. [EM]

Poems, ed. Fred L. Pattee (3 vols., 1902–7; repr. 1963); *Poems*, ed. H. H. Clark (1929; repr. 1960) (selection).
Lewis Leary, *That Rascal Freneau: A Study in Literary Failure* (1941); Philip M. Marsh, *The Works of Philip Freneau: A Critical Study* (1968).

Friedman, Bruce Jay (1930–   ). Novelist. He was born in New York City, studied at the University of Missouri, and served in the air force. He has emerged as a leading figure in the satirical-fantasy genre and black-humour movement of the sixties, about which he has written. His novels are *Stern* (1962), about a melancholy urban Jew undergoing fantasies of comic paranoia and undermining persecution mania, and *A Mother's Kisses* (1964), which concerns a Jewish adolescent's struggles with college, mother and American mores. His short stories are collected in *Far from the City of Class* (1963), which includes '23 Pat O'Brien Movies' from which a play was made in 1966, and *Black Angels* (1966). *Scuba Duba* (1967) is a play farcically sending up the current fads of skin-diving, psychiatry and so on. He has also edited an anthology, with an important introduction, *Black Humor* (1965). [EM/MB]

Fromm, Erich (1900–   ). Psychoanalyst and philosopher. Born in Germany, he studied at Heidelberg, Munich and Berlin. From Frankfurt psycho-analytic and social research institutes he went to the International Institute of Social Research in New York in 1934. He has taught in many universities and written important books, mainly on his major theme: the correction of puritanism and authoritarianism. The most celebrated are *Escape from Freedom* (1941 ; British title *The Fear of Freedom*) a study of the meaning of freedom and authority, and *Man for Himself: Inquiry into the Psychology of Ethics* (1947). His later books include *The Forgotten Language* (1951, dreams, fairy tales, myths), *The Sane Society* (1955), *The Art of Loving* (1956), *Zen Buddhism and Psychoanalysis* (1960), *The Dogma of Christ* (1966) and *You Shall Be as Gods* (1966), a non-theistic interpretation of Jewish scriptures. [EM]

Frost, Robert (1874–1963). Poet. Born in San Francisco, he was brought to New England when he was 10, at his father's death. He went to Dartmouth College, married, studied at Harvard, and between 1900 and 1905 farmed in New Hampshire and worked in mills in Lowell, Massachusetts, and as editor and teacher. But although his first published poem appeared when he was 19 ('My Butterfly'), only 14 poems were printed before 1918, and *A Boy's Will*, his first book, published in England when he was 39. He had sold his farm, gone to London and cultivated the friendship of Edward Thomas. After three years and *North of Boston* (1914), he returned to America well known and settled in New Hampshire again. *New Hampshire* (1923) shows one of his few developments – towards politics and satire. *A Further Range* (1936) is more philosophically theoretical than earlier work, while the two *Masques* (1945, 1947) mark a third stage – concern with man's relations with God and ultimate metaphysical conditions. Frost by now had a wide public and numerous prizes and university posts and degrees, and was on the way to becoming America's unofficial laureate, tacitly acknowledged by his trips to Russia and Israel, and the invitation to read 'The Gift Outright' (1942) at President Kennedy's inauguration.

From first to last (*In the Clearing*, 1962) Frost did not experiment much with line and rhythm; *A Boy's Will* already includes 'Mowing' and 'The Pasture', which fix a part of his poetic character, unaltered in 'Mending Wall', 'The Death of the Hired Man' and 'After Apple Picking' (1914), 'The Witch of Coos', 'The Star-Splitter', and 'Stopping by Woods on a Snowy Evening' (1923), 'Design' (1936) and 'Directive' (1947). These poems take the even, Georgian movement and tune of Frost's English friends, such as Lascelles Abercrombie and Edward Thomas, and combine it with Emersonian and New England poetic and speech styles to project his characteristic assertive sentence of the Yankee farmer, sometimes wise, sometimes the anti-political village wiseacre, sometimes the broadly sceptical determinist. His finest lyrics and narrative poems create a non-urban relationship between man, landscape and sky, which is romantic and frequently uneasy inside the assured tone. The 'design of darkness' and the uncertainty of meaning and action which recur in his work and life were made bearable by the creative act and the stance of public poet. As recent volumes of his letters show (*Selected Letters of Robert Frost*, ed. L. Thompson, 1964, and *Letters of Robert Frost to Louis Untermeyer*, 1963), his 44 honorary degrees and national respect came at the end of a life of stoic loneliness, family misfortunes, fear of mental unbalance, and profound distrust of the 'deep shadow' of melancholy. As he once said, 'irony is simply a kind of guardedness' and 'humour is the most engaging cowardice'. Poetry was his 'momentary stay' against disaster, and he had made his readers feel his own need for 'a word of assurance'. [EM]

The Complete Poems (1951); *Selected Prose*, ed. H. Cox and E. C. Latham (1966).
Sidney Cox, *A Swing of Birches: A Portrait of Robert Frost* (1957); ed. J. M. Cox, *Robert Frost: A Collection of Critical Essays* (1963); Daniel Smythe, *Robert Frost Speaks* (1965); Reuben A. Brewer, *The Poetry of Robert Frost* (1963); Lawrance Thompson, *Robert Frost: The Early Years* (1966); ed. E. C. Latham, *Interviews with Robert Frost* (1966).

Frye, Northrop (1912–   ). Literary critic. Though Canadian-born and now principal of Victoria College in Toronto, Frye has taken a central place in the development of modern American criticism and is one of the most influential of post-war theoretical critics. His general position is stated in *Anatomy of Criticism* (1957): criticism is a species of humane studies, a form of organized knowledge that can work by general principles deriving from the theoretical classification of various fundamental elements. These elements are a mixture of traditional generic classifications and mythological universals – which can, nonetheless, be seen as related to the changing cultural context of literature. [MB]

Fables of Identity: Studies in Poetic Mythology (1963); *The Well-Tempered Critic* (1963); *Fearful Symmetry: A Study of William Blake* (1947); *T. S. Eliot* (1963); *A Natural Perspective: The Development of Shakespearean Comedy and Romance* (1965); *The Return of Eden: Five Essays on Milton's Epics* (1965); *Fools of Time: Studies in Shakespearean Tragedy* (1967); *The Modern Century* (1967).
Ed. M. Krieger, *Northrop Frye in Modern Criticism* (1966).

Fuchs, Daniel (1909–   ). Novelist. Born in New York City. In 1961 his early novels – *Summer in Williamsburg* (1934), *Homage to Blenholt* (1936) and *Low Company* (1937) – were republished as *Three Novels* and re-established his reputation as a realist of Jewish slum life in Brooklyn, a closed world seen with humour and without political comment. He has lived and worked in Hollywood since the thirties and received the 1955 Academy Award for his scenario of *Love Me or Leave Me*. [EM]

Fugitives, The. A group of Southern poets, contributors to the *Fugitive*, a poetry magazine, 19 numbers of which were published in Nashville, Tennessee, from April 1922 to December 1925. The group comprised Donald ◊ Davidson, James Marshall Frank, Sidney Mttron Hirsch, Stanley Johnson, John Crowe ◊ Ransom, Alec B. Stevenson, Allen ◊ Tate, Walter Clyde Curry, Merrill ◊ Moore, William Yandell Elliott, William Frierson, Jesse Wills, Ridley Wills, Robert Penn ◊ Warren, Laura ◊ Riding (Gottschalk) and Alfred Starr. Andrew ◊ Lytle and Cleanth ◊ Brooks became closely associated with the group at the time of the magazine's demise. With the exceptions of Hirsch, a playwright, Frank and Stevenson, Nashville businessmen, and Laura Riding, wife of a faculty member of the University of Louisville, Kentucky, all the contributors were associated with Nashville's Vanderbilt University, as either students or teachers.

The Fugitives represent the most talented, cohesive group of creative writers America produced since the ◊ Transcendentalists. After 1925, Ransom, Tate and Warren all went on to make major contributions to American poetry; a psychiatrist in Boston, Merrill Moore continued to produce his 'American sonnets' with fantastic facility; Tate and Warren also became important novelists, and with Brooks and Ransom became the founders of the so-called ◊ 'New Criticism', which transformed the formal teaching and study of literature in America and elsewhere. Curry and Frierson produced works of literary scholarship, Elliott of political science; Stanley Johnson published a novel, *The Professor* (1925), and Ridley Wills two novels: *Hoax* (1922) and *Harvey Landrum* (1924). Davidson remained most strongly pro-Southern, and has published poems and essays; Lytle has published four fine novels.

Despite its responsibility for the emergence of the New Criticism, the Fugitive movement, as its social and economic thinking most clearly reveals. was essentially a conservative one. Founded at a time when a rapid expansion of industrialism was widely seen as the answer to most of the South's problems, the group remained firmly committed to a traditional, regionalist, agrarian, Southern ideal. Ransom, Tate, Davidson, Warren and Lytle were among the 'Twelve Southerners' who defended an agrarian South in *I'll Take My Stand: The South and the Agrarian Tradition* (1930). The same group was joined by Brooks in the publication of a second agrarian volume, *Who Owns America? A Declaration of Independence* (1936). The Fugitive vision of a rural, non-industrial South reflected a wider philosophical conservatism. The Fugitive movement focused a rather Eliot-like reaction against many social, political and philosophical aspects of the modern world: progressive liberal optimism, Marxism, capitalism, philosophical relativism and rationalism. The campaign to preserve the agrarian tradition produced little effect; but by the end of the 1930s the movement's conservative ideology, touched with modernist overtones, had penetrated deeply into literary and intellectual circles in America.

The dominant tone of the poetry of the *Fugitive* was set by John Crowe Ransom. Ransom on the whole turned away from such contemporary doctrines as ◊ Imagism and free verse. His poems are classical in their attention to matters of formal discipline, metaphysical in their mannered verbal complexity and ironic wit. What they express with an elegance and sophistication of tone is a rather bleak view of the imperfect nature of the human condition. Fugitive criticism largely mirrors this kind of poetry, though it has dealt well and ably with modern literature and is influenced by some of its aesthetics. It finally arrives at a position of aesthetic formalism in which the work of literature is seen as autonomous – a complex verbal structure largely independent of any social, historical or philosophical background. The critic's work is the analysis of that independent verbal structure.

The Fugitive movement ended the idea that the South represented a cultural backwater; indeed its major figures launched that literary renaissance in the South which remains one of the most striking features of 20th-century American literature. [A H]

Fugitives, An Anthology of Verse (1928).
John M. Bradbury, *The Fugitives, A Critical Account* (1958); ed. R. R. Purdy, *Fugitives' Reunion: Conversations at Vanderbilt* (1959); Louise Conran, *The Fugitive Group: A Literary History* (1959); John L. Stewart, *The Burden of Time: The Fugitives and Agrarians* (1969).

Fuller, Henry Blake (1857–1929). Novelist. Born in Chicago. He wrote in a cosmopolitan vein that drew on numerous short visits to Europe and contributed important pieces of international fiction to American letters; but he is now best remembered, perhaps a little unfairly, as a 'realist'. Like several contemporaries he seesawed between realism and romance. His first two novels, *The Chevalier of Pensieri-Vani* (1890; written under the pseudonym 'Stanton Page') and *The Châtelaine of La Trinité* (1892), are historical romances set in Europe. His next two, *The Cliff-Dwellers* (1893), his best-known work, about workers in a skyscraper, and the excellent *With the Procession* (1895), were realist, with Chicago settings. Then followed other books of various kinds – *From the Other Side: Stories of Transatlantic Travel* (1898), which united his realistic American and his European materials; *The Last Refuge: A Sicilian Romance* (1900); *Under the Sky-lights* (1901), with a Chicago setting; *Waldo Trench and Others: Stories of Americans in Italy* (1908); *On the Stairs* (1918), which reverts to Chicago materials; *Not on the Screen* (1930), etc. A novelist of manners and a pioneer of the American city-novel, Fuller also wrote for Chicago newspapers and was closely involved with the Chicago magazine *Poetry* (◊ Little Magazines). [MB]

Fuller, Margaret (1810–50). Critic, Transcendentalist. She was educated by her father in her birthplace, Cambridgeport, Massachusetts, to a point where his will and possessiveness wrecked her childhood. She grew up a disturbed prodigy, with – as she said – 'a man's ambition with a woman's heart'. Emerson remarked that her friendships were 'chemical' in their demands. After her father's death she became a leading ◊ Transcendentalist, a friend of Emerson, Alcott's assistant, head teacher of a Providence school, and famous for her 'Conversations' and femininism. For two years she edited the *Dial*, an important collection of poetry, criticism, philosophy and translations of eastern literature. Her part in Brook Farm (◊ Ripley) is fictionalized in Hawthorne's *The Blithedale Romance. Summer on the Lakes* (1844) is a fascinating account of this gifted New England intellectual's confrontation with the frontier, the Indians in Oregon, and the immigrants in Milwau-

kee. *Woman in the Nineteenth Century* (1845) idealizes America as the redemptive centre of the world in which women would overcome man's tyranny and harmony would ensue. After her last job, writing first-rate criticism of American literature for Horace Greeley's New York *Tribune*, she sailed in 1846 for Europe, visited Wordsworth, Carlyle, Mazzini, George Sand, Chopin and, in Rome, the Marquis Ossoli, with whom she fell in love. The ship they and their son returned to America on was wrecked off Fire Island, and they were drowned. [EM]

Writings, ed. Mason Wade (1941).
Mason Wade, *Margaret Fuller: Whetstone of Genius* (1940); Madeleine B. Stern, *The Life of Margaret Fuller* (1942); ed. Perry Miller, *Margaret Fuller American Romantic* (1963).

Fuller, R. Buckminster (1895–   ). Engineer, poet, philosopher. Born in Milton, Massachusetts, he was educated at the U.S. Naval Academy and at Harvard, but received no academic degrees. His inventions are part of his life programme of intention to benefit mankind as directly as possible, and are too numerous to list completely; they include houses, an electric car, a world map, and geodesic and tensegrity structures. His first book, *Nine Chains to the Moon* (1938), contains most of his basic ideas for 'comprehensive anticipatory design science', the recycling of resources in order 'to do more with less', the rationalization of the Earth on a 'One Town World Plan', and the elimination of scarcity as the basis of both wretched human conditions and the philosophical basis of their perpetuation. His major works include: *Education Automation* (1962), *Untitled Epic Poem on the History of Industrialization* (1962), *No More Second Hand God* (1963), *Ideas and Integrities* (1963) and *Operating Manual for Spaceship Earth* (1969). *What I am Trying to Do* (1968) is a set of drawings with an introduction. Fuller's international influence has reached the prophetic stage. [EM]

Robert W. Marks, *The Dymaxion World of Buckminster Fuller* (1960); John McHale, *R. Buckminster Fuller* (1962); ed. James Meller, *The Buckminster Fuller Reader* (1970).

G

Gaddis, William (1922–   ). Novelist. His single major work is *The Recognitions* (1955), a large experimental, and elaborately organized novel on ruse and forgery rather in the manner of *Tristram Shandy*; it is based on the palindrome 'trade ye no mere moneyed art'. [E M]

Gale, Zona (1874–1938). Novelist, story writer, poetess, dramatist. Born in Portage, Wisconsin, she began a career in journalism which took her to New York. Her early stories reverted to mid-Western materials, treating them sentimentally in the local colourist manner, as titles like *Friendship Village* (1908) and *Heart's Kindred* (1915) suggest. But when she returned home with unpopular progressive and pacifist views she began to develop a more detached attitude to the region, and works like *Birth* (1918) and *Miss Lulu Bett* (1920), which she dramatized, reveal the repressiveness and middle-class conventionality of the mid-West and link her work with that of Sinclair ◊ Lewis. *When I Was a Little Girl* (1913) and *Portage, Wisconsin* (1928) are autobiography. Her later work, which includes the novel *Faint Perfume* (1923) and *Yellow Gentians and Blue* (1927), short stories, had great success. [M B]

August Derleth, *Still Small Voice: The Biography of Zona Gale* (1940).

Gardner, Erle Stanley (1889–1970). Detective-story writer. Born in Malden, Massachusetts. One of the literary phenomena of our time, he was for many years a prolific author of stylistically undistinguished but phenomenally successful novels which for the most part feature either the lawyer Perry Mason (*The Case of . . .*) or the District Attorney Douglas Selby (*The D.A. . . .*). Publishing also under the pseudonyms A. A. Fair and Charles J. Kenny, among others, Gardner, a lawyer, produced over 100 books since he first began writing in the early 1920s. Among his non-fictional works are several books about Baja California and *The Court of Last Resort* (1952), an account of his attempts to help men unjustly convicted of murder. [H D]

Alva Johnston, *The Case of Erle Stanley Gardner* (1947).

Garland, Hamlin (1860–1940). Novelist, story writer, memoirist. Born in West Salem, Wisconsin. An important voice in the mid-Western literary upsurge, and a significant spokesman for new realist techniques in writing, he grew up amid the hard realities of life in Iowa and South Dakota. He went to Boston, still a major literary centre, in 1884 to study, write and lecture, and here was influenced by the aesthetic theories of the realist William Dean ◊ Howells and the economic ideas of the reformer Henry ◊ George. He read in science, economics and social matters, as well as in American writing. The poverty and monotony of frontier life deeply affected him and, adopting a form of realism he called 'veritism', he wrote the tales in his first book, *Main-Travelled Roads: Six Mississippi Valley Stories*(1891), drawing on boyhood experience to explore the rural poor of the prairies and the social and economic forces behind agrarian hardship. Others in the same mood were collected in *Prairie Folks* (1893) and *Wayside Court-ships* (1897) – later combined as *Other Main-Travelled Roads* (1910). In the 1890s active in the reform movement, he wrote several novels illustrating Populist principles. *Jason Edwards: An Average Man* (1892) dramatizes George's single-tax theory; but the most sustained is *Rose of Dutcher's Coolly* (1895), a realistic narrative of a Wisconsin girl's attempt to escape the brutalizing drudgery of farm life. All these exemplified 'veritism', a theory made explicit in the essay-collection *Crumbling Idols* (1894; repr. 1960), a statement of his literary radicalism (◊ Realism).

In 1893 he moved back to the mid-West and associated with a Chicago group of writers, which included Henry Blake ◊ Fuller, interested in regional realism. He now began to travel widely through the West, writing articles, joining a gold rush; and in 1899 made his first trip to England (where he came to know Shaw and Zangwill) and France. Over this period he published – in addition to *Her Mountain Lover* (1901), caricaturing English society – many works of fiction, most of them popular, sentimental romances of the Far West. Late in life he published eight volumes of rambling reminiscences, marked by a fascinating neo-scientific approach to experience – four deal with his family background, the others with his literary acquaintances. The first, *A Son of the Middle Border* (1917), has claims to be considered with *Main-Travelled Roads* as his best work. *A Daughter of the Middle Border* (1921; Pulitzer Prize) deals with the early years of his marriage; *Trail-Makers of the Middle Border* (1926) with his father's migration from Maine to Wisconsin; *Back-Trailers from the Middle Border* (1928) with his literary career. *Roadside Meetings* (1930) and *Companions on the Trail: A Literary Chronicle* (1931) are the more interesting of the accounts of literary contemporaries.

Though the literary revolution he in part pioneered was taken further by others, he remains interesting for his literary mode and his strong regional flavour. The long-established view that he was a victim of the genteel tradition (symbolized by his transfer from the radical journal *The Arena* to the more conventional *Century*) is now being modified. ◊ Fuller's portrait of him as Abner Joyce in *Under the Skylights* (1901) offers too simple an explanation of his defection from early literary ideals. His reputation, however, still rests on the stories of frontier life and the re-creation of the background to them in the autobiography. Although the theories of *Crumbling Idols* – an ultimately disappointing book – were never fully incorporated into the fiction, the accuracy with which he presented little-publicized aspects of American life marks an important development in the history of American literary realism and naturalism, while the memoirs do constitute a valuable and still interesting record of a vanished era. [HD]

Diaries, ed. D. Pizer (1968).
Donald Pizer, *Hamlin Garland's Early Work and Career* (1960); Jean Holloway, *Hamlin Garland: A Biography* (1960); ed. L. A. Arvidson, *Centennial Tributes* (1962).

Garrigue, Jean (1914–   ). Poet. Born in Indiana, educated at the University of Chicago, she has taught at several colleges, including the University of Iowa and Bard, and travelled in Europe, where a number of

her poems are set. Though her range is not wide, and she deals usually with natural objects interfused with states of emotion, she is an able, convincing poet who works her material intensively, at length and with great vigour. Her best poems are probably those in which the background detail gives way to her argument, which is frequently in favour of hope or permanence found through love or poetry itself. Her volumes are *The Ego and the Centaur* (1947), *The Monument Rose* (1953), *A Water Walk by Villa d'Este* (1959), *Country without Maps* (1964), which contains some of her best poems to date, and *The Animal Hotel* (1966), a novel. [MB]

Gass, William (1924–   ). Novelist. Born in North Dakota, he teaches philosophy at Purdue University. Gass has emerged as a major fiction writer of the 1960s, with an exciting insight into provincial life and a prose style of considerable power: *Omensetter's Luck* (1966), *In the Heart of the Heart of the Country* (1968 – a set of excellent stories – and *Willie Master's Lonesome Wife* (1968) – a hilarious fiction in the manner of Sterne and Blast. [EM]

Gelber, Jack (1932–   ). Playwright. Born in Chicago. His reputation was made through the Living Theatre's New York production of *The Connection* (1959) by Julian Beck and Judith Malina, in which heroin addiction is the metaphor for other forms of social addiction and alienation. The jazz of Freddie Redd and Jackie McLean considerably helped the action. *The Apple* (1961), as the title implies, concerns temptation in New York, employing a variety of Brechtian and Absurd effects. *The Cuban Thing* (1968) uses the Castro revolution. *On Ice* (1964), his first novel, forsakes the inflexions of Pirandello and Charlie Parker for conventional picaresque meandering in New York. [EM]

George, Henry (1839–97). Political economist, editor. He was born in Philadelphia, left school at 14, and after various jobs became a compositor and editor in California. After years of near-poverty he became a journalist and essayist, a self-taught man making use of his experience to understand economic and social problems. What he termed his 'ecstatic vision' (in 1869), that land value is related to the growth of the community around it more than man's labour on it, inspired his *Our Land and Land Policy* (1871), a pamphlet attacking land grants for railway companies. His work as editor of the Oakland *Transcript*, experience of land speculation in California, and first-hand knowledge of economic inequalities led to his best-selling *Progress and Poverty* (1879), which gained him an international reputation. Its basis is the 'single-tax' argument that a tax on unearned increment from land would prevent the absorption of surplus wealth through land rents and en-able the community to reap the land's value according to their creation of its value. His now largely discounted ideas were helped into circulation by his vivid jargon-free prose. Clubs were established in support of his doctines, which influenced many reformist figures, including William Dean ◊ Howells, Hamlin ◊ Garland, Tolstoy and Bernard Shaw. [DKA/HD]

The Complete Works (10 vols., 1906–11).
George R. Geiger, *The Philosophy of Henry George* (1933); Charles A. Barker, *Henry George* (1955).

Gibson, William (1914–   ). Playwright. Born in New York. His *Two for the Seesaw* (1959) is a neat dialogue between a Bronx girl with ulcers and a mid-Western lawyer. *Dinny and the Witches* (1959), a fantasy, appeared off Broadway, and *The Miracle-Worker* (1960), the story of Helen Keller's early training, became an international success. *A Cry of Players*, originally written and produced in 1947, was revived in 1968. *A Mass for the Dead* (1968) is a prose autobiographical work. [EM]

Gilbert, Jack (1925–   ). Poet. He has spent most of his literary life on the West Coast and been involved in the recent movements in poetry there. He taught creative writing at the University of California and San Francisco State College. His one volume, *Views of Jeopardy* (1962), translates classical myth into a vision of the modern Orpheus singing obsessively to the unattentive hell of New York or San Francisco. [BP]

Ed. Howard Nemesov, *Poets on Poetry* (1967); *Genesis West*, I, 1 (1962).

Gilder, Richard Watson (1844–1909). Newspaperman, poet. He was born in New Jersey and went into newspapers there,

later becoming an influential figure as editor of *Scribner's Monthly* and *The Century Magazine*. He had great con-temporary fame as a poet for volumes such as *Five Books of Songs* (1900). [MB]

Gill, Brendan (1914–   ). Novelist, story writer. He was born in Hartford, Connecti-cut, and after graduating from Yale joined the editorial staff o the *New Yorker*, in which many of his stories have appeared. He is an elegant and amusing writer of social observation. His first novel, *The Trouble of One House* (1950), takes as its subject a dying woman, and *The Day the Money Stopped* (1957) is a delightful character comedy with a social point. [MB]

Ginsberg, Allen (1926–   ). Poet. Born in New Jersey, the son of the poet and teacher Louis Ginsberg; his mother was a Russian emigrant, active on the left, whom he laments in one of his finest poems, 'Kad-dish', in which he emotionally bridges the political gaps between the crucial American generations of the thirties and fifties. After school in Paterson and study at Columbia University, he worked at various jobs – café dish-washer, seaman, welder, night porter and book reviewer for *Newsweek*. Meanwhile he studied and absorbed the particular inspirations of his poetry, Blake and Whitman, and experimented with states of consciousness with drugs. He exploded into the literary scene with *Howl and Other Poems* (1956) as a major poet, and, with Kerouac and Burroughs, as the centre of the ◊ Beat Generation group. He consolidated his poetic art in *Kaddish and Other Poems* (1960), *Reality Sandwiches* (1963) and *Planet News* (1969). *Empty Mirror* (1960) is a collection of poems which are mostly preparations for his central achievement, and *The Change* (1963) is two poems written in India and Japan in 1963. 'Howl' is a lament for the sick-ness of urban America and for poets, artists and intellectuals in the Ike–Nixon era, written in long-breathed lines and high-ly wrought language developed from Blake, Whitman, Melville, William Carlos Williams and Hart Crane. Ginsberg's characteristic poems at this stage were either short, intensely personal lyrics or long rhapsodic celebrations of ecstasy, the search for the godhead, and the expansion of consciousness. His visionary ability to invite the reader to an open exchange of honesty and tenderness is valuable and extraordinary, both in his poetry and in his life generally. His more recent work develops a long, discursive and socially conscious and critical poem, partly based on transcriptions of verbal recording into a tape-recorder of ideas, images and responses while travelling. A good example is 'Wichita Vortex Sutra' (1966, in *Planet News*), and *TV Baby Poems* (1967) contains two such poems. The method is developed in *Ankor Wat* (1968) and *Airplane Dreams* (1968). From being a Beat Generation poet Ginsberg has responded to the America of his time to become an intensely political poet, a man active throughout the world in promoting the free life, and attacking authoritarianism in Czechoslovakia, Russia and America alike. [EM]

A Casebook on the Beat, ed. T. Parkinson (1961); *The Beats*, ed. S. Krim (1960).
E. Lucie-Smith, *Mystery in the Universe: Notes on an Interview with Allen Ginsberg* (1965); J. Clellon Holmes, *Nothing More to Declare* (1967); Lawrence Lipton, *The Holy Barbarians* (1959); *Paris Review* 37 (Spring, 1966) (interview with Thomas Clark); Jane Kramer, *Allen Ginsberg in America* (1969).

Glasgow, Ellen (1874–1945). Novelist, poet· Born in Richmond, Virginia, the Old Dominion to which she limited her fiction and which in her time was part of the post-Reconstruction South. As a child her health prevented her from attending school and her education came from her father's library and her later reading of the great European novelists and the British evolutionists. She did not marry. After destroying an adolescent novel, she published *The Descendant* (1897), a novel concerning a New York Bohemia she hardly knew. Although she often travelled, and did live in New York for a short time, Richmond was her home. She published a volume of poems, *The Freeman*, in 1902. *Virginia* (1913) brought her popular acclaim, and *Barren Ground* (1925) established her critical success. *In This Our Life* (1941) gained a Pulitzer Prize (1947). Besides her 19 novels she wrote short stories, essays, and an autobiography, *The Woman Within* (1954). Her fiction is an acute account of the old agrarian South invaded by industrialization, of a society dying under out-moded manners, opinions and methods, and of a woman's place in these changes. In *A Certain Measure* (1943) a collection of criticism, her 19th-century philosophy of nature against human nature insists on the courage of an inner integrity to carry a person through bad times. *The Voice of the People* (1900), *The Battle-Ground* (1902) and *The Deliverance* (1904) are social historical novels with this interior action. *Barren Ground* and *Vein of Iron* (1935), her finest novels, both present the survival of girls, from declining Southern families, by their stoicism of work and gritty selfhood. Ellen Glasgow's realism rejects both the despair and the arrogance of the South, and although approaching sexual relations rather drily, her delineation of family life is keen. [EM]

Collected Stories, ed. R. K. Meeker (1963); *Letters*, ed. B. Rouse (1958).
F. P. W. McDowell, *Ellen Glasgow and the Ironic Art of Fiction* (1960); Louis Auchincloss, *Ellen Glasgow* (University of Minnesota Pamphlet, 1964); M. Geismar, *Rebels and Ancestors: The American Novel 1890–1915* (1953).

Godfrey, Thomas (1736–63). Playwright, poet. Born in Philadelphia, he was the author of the first play by a native American to be acted professionally on the American stage. *The Prince of Parthia: A Tragedy*, written before 1763, published in 1765 and acted in Philadelphia in 1767, draws on Elizabethan and Jacobean dramatic conventions and language, and deals with passion and violence in oriental Parthia. Godfrey also published *The Court of Fancy: A Poem* (1762) and *Juvenile Poems on Various Subjects*, printed with *The Prince of Parthia* in 1765. [MB]

Goetz, George. ◊ Calverton, Victor Francis.

Goggan, John Patrick ◊ Patrick, John.

Gold, Herbert (1924–). Novelist. He was born in Ohio, studied in Paris and at Columbia, and lives in San Francisco, after finding New York 'too nervous' for a writer. He has taught in universities, received prizes, but remains a highly independent writer and critic. With his first five novels – *Birth of a Hero* (1951), *The Prospect before Us* (1954), *The Man Who Was Not with It* (1956), *The Optimist* (1959) and *Therefore Be Bold* (1960) – he established himself as a professional novelist of the anxieties and tensions of the fifties. His collected stories, written in the same racy, topical style, appear in *Love and Like* (1960).

His best novel to date is *Salt* (1963), a hectic account of New York middle-class degeneracy. *The Age of Happy Problems* (1962) is 18 sharp essays on American society. Gold's taut, highly metaphored style is the exact vehicle for that contemporary vision he shares with the writers in his shrewdly introduced collection, *Fiction of the Fifties* (1959). *Fathers* (1967) takes the form of a memoir novel about first- and second-generation Americans in this century. *The Great American Jackpot* (1970) adopts a sour attitude towards San Francisco in the 1960s. [E M]

Genesis West, II, 2 and 3 (1964) (interview).

Gold, Michael (pseud. of Irving Granich) (1894–). Novelist, playwright. Born on New York's Lower East Side, he was, under his pen-name, an important contributor to American 'proletarian realist' letters. One of the group of political radicals with literary interests that included Max ◊ Eastman and Floyd ◊ Dell, and gathered around the magazines the *Masses*, the *Liberator* and the *New Masses*, he edited the last in a particularly revolutionary phase (◊ Little Magazines). He was also associated with the ◊ Provincetown Players, along with John ◊ Reed, Dell and of course Eugene O'Neill, and wrote several plays. With the upsurge of literary-social criticism in the 1920s, he became, through his *New Masses* mouthpiece, an influential voice advancing virtually a Stalinist line, promoting socialist–communist theories of literature, attacking 'genteel' writing (Thornton Wilder was a famous victim). Plays include *Fiesta* (1925), set in Mexico, and *Battle Hymn* (1936; with Michael Blankfort), about John Brown. *120 Million* (1929) and *Change the World!* (1937) are articles. But his best-known work is a novel, *Jews without Money* (1935), drawing on the world of his childhood. [M B]

The Mike Gold Reader, ed. S. Sillen (1954); *Proletarian Literature in the United States*, ed. Granville Hicks (1935).
Daniel Aaron, *Writers on the Left* (1961).

Golden, Harry (1902–). Essayist, humorist. Of New York Jewish background, he moved to Charlotte, North Carolina, and started the *Carolina Israelite*, a monthly 'personal journal' written by himself and with a national circulation which unfortunately ceased publication in 1968. Four selections of his notes and essays from it

have appeared - *Only in America* (1958), *For 2c Plain* (1959), *Enjoy! Enjoy!* (1960) and *The Harry Golden Omnibus* (1962). Golden is the Jew as cracker-barrel philosopher, and exploits the irony of the mixture; his pieces are mainly nostalgic reminiscence or shrewd comic social commentary, but he excoriates segregation and supports the Negro struggle. He has also published a biography of Carl ◊ Sandburg. [M B]

The Right Time (1969) (autobiography).

Goldman, William (1931–). Novelist. *The Temple of Gold* (1957), an immensely popular novel on Fitzgerald themes transferred to the sixties, sympathetically explores adolescence and 'delinquency'. There followed *Your Turn to Curtsey, My Turn to Bow* (1958), *Soldier in the Rain* (1960) and *Boys and Girls Together* (1964), a highly successful novel on his familiar youth themes. But *No Way to Treat a Lady* (1964) treats themes of sexual violence and murder within a blandly innocent prose, very much part of the black humour of the sixties. *The Season* (1969) is a critical attack on Broadway and theatre critics. *Butch Cassidy and the Sundance Kid* (1969) is the screenplay of George Roy Hill's film. [E M]

Goodman, Paul (1911–). Novelist, poet, playwright, psychologist, philosopher. He was born in New York and studied at the City College and Chicago University. The range and quality of his work and his ability to speak directly without the obscuring jargon of his special fields has made him a figure of major importance in the revolutionary American situation of the fifties and sixties. Since his first work in *New Directions* in the forties his reputation as a comprehensive critic and creative writer has grown. *Drawing the Line*, which brings together his *May Pamphlet* and additional materials written in 1962, is the clearest statement of his anarchist principles and ·his attack on political and psychological ideologies and 'sociolatry', the fetishism of over-organized society and its theory. *Communitas* (1947, with his brother Percival Goodman) is a comprehensive study of comparative city planning, with concrete recommendations. *Gestalt Therapy* (1951, with F. S. Perls and Ralph Hefferline) is a textbook of psychology and analysis, influenced by the psychologist Wilhelm ◊ Reich. The highly influential *Growing Up Absurd* (1960) is a study of youth and delinquency, using materials from literature, psychology and political theory. *Utopian Essays and Proposals* (1962) is a collection of articles on subjects ranging from Reich to American *avant garde* writing. *The Community of Scholars* (1963) and *Compulsory Mis-Education* (1964) criticize, respectively, the idea and practice of the university in America, and the notion and effects of 'formal schooling' within a structure of compulsory education. The nonconformism, constructiveness and practicability of these materials is the basis of *People or Personnel* (1965), and the same radicalism, pacifism and clarity penetrates his plays: *The Cave of Machpelah* (1959), and those in *The Facts of Life* (1965) – *Faustina* (1949), *The Young Disciple* (1955) and *Jonah* (1965). His short stories are collected in *The Break-Up of Our Camp* (1949) and *Our Visit to Niagara* (1960). His very individual and rather didactic poems are in *The Lordly Hudson* (1962), *Hawkweed* (1967) and *North Percy* (1968). His criticism appears in *Art and Social Nature* (1946), *Kafka's Prayer* (1947) and *The Structure of Literature* (1954), a really useful study of plot structures. *The Empire City* (1959) is a large complex novel of New York from the thirties to the fifties, and comprises *The Grand Piano* (1942), *The State of Nature* (1964), *The Dead Spring of* (1950) and *The Holy Terror* (1959). *Making Do* (1963) is a novel about a group of unconventional young men and women whose behaviour challenges middle-class standards. *Five Years: Thoughts during a Useless Time* (1967) is a frank autobiographical study, and *Like a Conquered Province* (1967) a study of 'the moral ambiguity of America' through examinations of education, planning, ecology, decentralization and the media. Goodman is a prime example of fertile discontent and original thinking in America, part of a great tradition which includes Thoreau and other anarchists and rebels. His influence on contemporary dissent and reconstruction is inestimable. [EM]

Adam and His Works: Collected Stories (1968).

Gordon, Caroline (1895–). Novelist, short-story writer, critic. Born in Todd Co., Kentucky. Married Allen ⟡ Tate in 1924. A sense of failure and disintegration, both personal and social, and a consequent

search for salvation, characterize her fiction; hence the history of the South provides her with a powerful image for her vision of the human predicament. Her first four novels are set in the region around Clarksville, Tennessee, including part of Kentucky, where she grew up. *Penhally* (1931) relates the history of four generations of a Kentucky plantation family as an index of the disruption of a culture. *Aleck Maury, Sportsman* (1934) shows an individual's search to resolve this same disintegration of social values. *The Garden of Adonis* (1937), which confronts the social and economic conflicts of the changing South more directly, also shows another form of personal salvation, agrarian retreat, as inadequate. *None Shall Look Back* (1937) returns to the Penhally family and shows how the Civil War is largely responsible for the destruction of the social basis of its way of life. With *Green Centuries* (1941), she moves back to frontier North Carolina and Tennessee in the 18th century, bringing together European and Indian cultures to illuminate Western man's ultimately self-destructive drives. *The Woman on the Porch* (1944) once again employs a passionate, sensitive woman as the principal victim of life's failures. *The Forest of the South* (1946) and *Old Red and Other Stories* (1963) are fine collections of stories.

Her most recent novels, *The Strange Children* (1951) and *The Malefactors* (1956), show Miss Gordon's controlled, almost clinical, vision of individual disintegration leading her towards a religious definition of the meaning of salvation. *How to Read a Novel* (1957) is a valuable contribution to criticism of fiction; and with Allen Tate she edited *The House of Fiction; An Anthology of the Short Story* (1950). [AH]

Andrew Lytle, 'Caroline Gordon and the Historic Image', *Sewanee Review*, LVII (Autumn, 1949); Vivienne Koch, 'The Conservatism of Caroline Gordon', in *Southern Renascence*, ed. L. D. Rubin, Jr, and R. D. Jacobs (1953); F. P. W. McDowell, *Caroline Gordon* (U. of Minnesota Pamphlet, 1966).

Gover, Robert (1929–). Novelist. His first novel, *One Hundred Dollar Misunderstanding* (1962), won considerable attention for its relationship between Kitten, a 14-year-old Negro prostitute, and a college sophomore; his third novel, *Here Goes Kitten* (1964), returns to the same two characters with the same white liberal fun.

Between these two came *The Maniac Responsible* (1963), a highly wrought and rhetorical study of a murderer, and after them, *Poorboy at the Party* (1966). *J. C. Saves* (1968) is the third instalment of Kitten's adventure. Gover is skilful, amusing and culturally observant, but also sentimental. [MB]

Goyen, William (1915–   ). Novelist. Born in Texas, he went into the navy and later taught at the University of Houston, Texas, and the New School for Social Research, New York. His first novel, *The House of Breath* (1950), already showed his characteristically virtuoso poetic and mythic style in which the plot and characters are embedded. In his short stories *Ghost and Flesh* (1952) it is again the charged style which impresses; *The Faces of Blood Kindred* (1960) contains highly atmospheric stories of chance revelations of family connexions. His second novel, *In a Farther Country* (1955), is a series of stories centred on a Spanish-American woman and again written in a richly wrought manner, which recognizes the fact that the normal is frequently uncanny. *The Fair Sister* (1963), a novel expanded from an earlier story called 'Savata, My Fair Sister', shows Goyen firmly established in the body of Southern writers of the fantastically normal – Eudora ◊ Welty, Carson ◊ McCullers, Flannery ◊ O'Connor – with his poetic versions of local idiom and relish for warped intensities of life. But through the wrought-up prose the comic satire on the popular religion of camp meetings and preachers is clear. So is his old-fashioned condescension towards Negroes. [EM]

Granich, Irving. ◊ Gold, Michael.

Grau, Shirley Ann (1929–   ). Novelist, short-story writer. Born in New Orleans. Her early fiction is concerned with the primitive inhabitants of the coastal islands and bayous west of the mouth of the Mississippi River; these people, mixed French and Spanish in origin, isolated by geography, poverty and race, are well documented in *The Black Prince and Other Stories* (1955) and *The Hard Blue Sky* (1958), an episodic novel. Action and event are more prominent than psychological complexity, but characters and setting are observed with clarity. *The Hard Blue Sky* is particularly impressive for its sense of the subordination of human action to the power of the natural world. In *The House on Coliseum Street* (1961), a more introspective, psychological novel, the enervating heat and humidity of the New Orleans summer match the passivity and pointlessness of the life of the protagonist. *The Keepers of the House* (1964) is wider in scope than any of her earlier novels – the story of a Southern family destroyed by divisions within itself, but fighting back against a corrupt community. But here as previously a strain of over-simplifying primitive romanticism prevents her from the fullest exploration of the issues her novel raises. [AH]

Louise Y. Gossett, 'Primitives and Violence: Shirley Ann Grau', in *Violence in Recent Southern Fiction* (1965).

Green, Paul Eliot (1894–   ). Dramatist. From North Carolina, he has written conventional plays about his home State, including *Abraham's Bosom* (1926), a courageous work about race conflict in the South, *The House of Connelly* (1931), landowners and tenant farmers in conflict, and *Native Son* (1941; with Richard Wright). But his reputation rests with his open-air productions derived from legend, folklore and history, a native American theatre whose plays he calls 'symphonic drama'. His achievement, independent of Broadway, is a combination of ambitious experiment, poetic language and a real feeling for America's past. *The Lost Colony* (1937) uses music, dance, pageant and dialogue to present the origins of Roanoke Island, where it was played. *The Highland Call* (1939) does the same for the Scots North Carolina settlement of Cape Fear River Valley, and *The Common Glory* (1947) uses the history of Jefferson and Virginia, 1775–82. *The Founders* (1957) dramatizes the Jamestown colony. *Texas* (1966) is one of his most recent outdoor dramas. He also wrote the libretto for Kurt Weill's musical, *Johnny Johnson* (1936). [EM]

Five Plays of the South (1963).
Ed. R. Walser, *Paul Green of Chapel Hill* (1951).

Greenberg, Samuel (1843–1917). Poet. He was born in Austria and reached the U.S.A. when he was 7. He survived lower East Side New York squalor and, while suffering from tuberculosis in hospital, read poetry for the first time and began to write poems. Nothing was published in his lifetime, but the manuscripts reached Hart ◊ Crane, who was impressed enough with his sensuously powerful metaphors to use them and their method in his own work. [EM]

Poems: A Selection from the Manuscripts, intr. Allen Tate (1947).

Greenwich Village. A section of New York City in Lower Manhattan which has had long literary associations – with ◊ Paine, ◊ Poe, ◊ James, ◊ Whitman, ◊ Twain and others. From about 1910 onward it became a distinct artistic and literary community, because of its low rents, European flavour and literary associations; its cold-water flats and studios and its general freedom made it a centre of American ◊ Bohemianism. During the 1920s it became a stepping stone for expatriation (◊ Expatriates) and Paris, a movement encouraged by rising rents. Caroline Ware, in *Greenwich Village, 1920–1930: A Comment on American Civilization in the Post-War Years* (1935), gives an interesting sociological analysis of this phase. Again after the Second World War it became a thriving Bohemian centre, spreading outward from the now fashionable and expensive core, and its proliferation of coffee houses, jazz centres and off-Broadway playhouses gives it a distinctive pattern of life. Throughout this century it has abounded in ◊ little magazines and movements. The magazines include the *Little Review,* the *Masses,* the *Seven Arts* and the *Quill*; it also now produces an interesting paper, *Village Voice.* Those associated with it include Floyd ◊ Dell, Maxwell ◊ Bodenheim, Eugene ◊ O'Neill, Edna St Vincent ◊ Millay, E. E. ◊ Cummings, John ◊ Reed, Willa ◊ Cather and Max ◊ Eastman, and more recently many 'hip' and 'beat' writers including Norman ◊ Mailer, who has contributed important pieces to the *Village Voice.* Among its many theatre groups special mention should be made of the Greenwich Village Players, an outgrowth of the ◊ Provincetown Players. Reminiscences appear in Alfred Kreymbourg, *Troubador* (1925), Max Eastman, *Enjoyment of Living* (1948), Alyse Gregory, *The Day is Gone* (1948) and Henry W. Lanier, *Greenwich Village Today and Yesterday* (1949). The active and exciting post-Second-World-War phase is best reported in Albert Parry, *Garrets and Pretenders* (1960), and in two articles in the special New York number of *Dissent,* VIII (Summer, 1961). [MB]

Gregory, Horace (1898–   ). Poet, translator, critic. He was born in Milwaukee, Wisconsin, and after attending the university there became a writer in New York, publishing his first volume of poems, *Chelsea Rooming House,* in 1930 (it appeared in England as *Rooming House,* 1932). He then taught classics and modern poetry at Sarah Lawrence College, and has published many further volumes of poems, translations from the classics, literary criticism and essays on art. As a poet he is conveniently represented in *Poems 1930–1940* (1941), *Selected Poems* (1951) and *Collected Poems* (1964), which won the Bollingen Prize. Gregory's poetry has strongly marked social concerns and a strong vernacular element; at the same time there is a clarity and distillation drawn from his devotion to the classics. His excellent idiomatic translation of the *Odes of Catullus* (1931) shows the force of this influence. (He has also translated Ovid's *Metamorphoses,* 1958.) His literary criticism includes a sympathetic early book on D. H. Lawrence, *Pilgrim of the Apocalypse* (1933), a volume of essays on American poetry, *The Shield of Achilles* (1944), and *The Dying Gladiator* (1961). *The World of James McNeill Whistler* (1961) is the best biography of this painter. With his wife, Marya ◊ Zaturenska, he wrote the very useful *A History of American Poetry: 1900–1940* (1946). [MB]

Grey, Zane (1875–1939). Best-selling Western novelist. Born in Zanesville, Ohio. In the development of the Western into a convention with enormous popular appeal and distinct codes of chivalry and toughness, the novels of Zane Grey – originally an Ohio dentist – have played a great part. He produced over 60 books, selling over 15 million copies. His characters, heroes and villains, are usually cowboys. *The Last of the Plainsmen* (1908), an early book, is said by *aficionados* to be one of the best; but it was *Riders of the Purple Sage* (1912) that won him his first popular success, and thereafter came a wealth of others, many published posthumously. [MB]

Jean Kerr, *Zane Grey: Man of the West* (1950).

Griffin, John Howard (1902–   ). He was born in Texas, served in the Pacific in the Second World War, travelled in Europe, and has been a professional lecturer in music, aesthetics and history. He was blinded in the war and recovered his eyesight recently. His novel *The Devil Rides Outside* (1952) is outstanding, and he has since written *Nuni* (1956); but he is famous for his experiences, disguised as a Negro, through the South, which appeared in *Sepia* magazine and subsequently as *Black Like Me* (1961). [EM]

The John Howard Griffin Reader (1968).

Griswold, Rufus W(ilmot) (1815–57). Editor, anthologist. Born in Benson, Vermont. He replaced Edgar Allan ◊ Poe as editor of the famous and well-paying *Graham's Magazine* in Philadelphia, and through that, his editorship of the *International Literary Monthly*, and his famous anthologies – *The Poets and Poetry of America* (1842), *Prose Writers of America* (1847) and *Female Poets of America* (1848) – exercised great influence over mid-century taste. He promoted Poe but, as his literary executor and 'friend', presented him in a biography and a memoir to his edition of Poe's works (1850) as 'satanic' and corrupt. This and factual dishonesties in biography and editing have not endeared him to subsequent scholars and Poe-defenders. [MB]

Grossman, Alfred (1927–). Novelist. Grossman writes with confidence and panache of the milieu of New York City office-and-apartment life, though his well-shod heroes drop from time to time into the seedier world of delinquency and dereliction. His usual pattern, followed in each of his three novels – *Acrobat Admits* (1959), *Many Slippery Errors* (1963) and *Marie Beginning* (1964) – is to take a hero who feels constricted by the niceties and exigencies of his buttoned-down life and plunge him for a while into a more-or-less self-willed topseyturveydom. From his contact with the 'forbidden' and *outré*, the hero returns to the upper world more integrated. Recently, as his fiction has begun to approximate the 'black humour' of Terry ◊ Southern and Thomas ◊ Pynchon, he has shifted his focus on to the female guide-figures to his underworlds. [AG]

Group Theatre. An important association of actors, dramatists and producers, some from the ◊ Theatre Guild, who under Harold ◊ Clurman, Cheryl Crawford and Lee Strasberg formed their own organization for plays of 'social significance' in 1931. Their first success on Broadway was Paul ◊ Green's *The House of Connelly* (1931), and subsequently they offered 23 productions, including work by ◊ Anderson, ◊ Lawson, ◊ Kingsley, Irwin ◊ Shaw, ◊ Saroyan and ◊Odets. The Group was united in radical politics and Stanislavskian acting and production methods. After its dissolution in 1941, its method principles at least were continued into Strasberg's Actor's Studio. [EM]

H. Clurman, *The Fervent Years* (1945).

Guest, Edgar A(lbert) (1881–1959). Journalist, famous bad poet. Born in England, he came to the U.S.A. at 10. He wrote a daily poem for the Detroit *Free Press*, full of folksy morality. Among the many collections are *A Heap o' Livin'* (1916) ('It takes a heap o' livin' in a house t' make it home') and *Just Folks* (1917). *Collected Verse* appeared in 1934, though Guest had many, many more poems to come. [MB]

Gunther, John (1901–70). Journalist. Born in Chicago, he became a reporter on the Chicago *Daily News* in 1922 and gained a reputation particularly for his reports from Germany in the thirties. In 1936 he produced the first of his famous books, *Inside Europe*, which set the pattern of the series which followed: *Inside Asia* (1939), *Inside Latin America* (1941), *Inside USA*, (1947), *Inside Africa* (1955), *Inside Russia Today* (1958), *Inside Europe Today* (1961). These are digests of facts, entertainingly put together with a minimum of commitment. He also wrote *The High Cost of Hitler* (1940), *Roosevelt in Retrospect* (1950), *General Douglas McArthur* (1951), *President Eisenhower* (1952), *Death, Be Not Proud* (1949, on the brain cancer of his young son), and *A Fragment of Autobiography* (1962). [EM]

H

Hadas, Moses (1900–66). Scholar. Born in Georgia and educated at Emory University, the Jewish Theological Seminary and Columbia University, where he was Professor of Greek from 1953. His eminence as a Hellenist was famous through *Hellenistic Culture: Fusion and Diffusion* (1959), *Humanism* (1960) and many other volumes. He was also a scholar of Old Testament period culture and introduced and translated the delightful *Three Greek Romances* (1954). [EM]

Hale, Edward Everett (1822–1909). Popular author, clergyman, scholar. A Boston Unitarian clergyman, at one time chaplain to the United States Senate, he published widely in a variety of fields. Stories were collected in *If, Yes, and Perhaps* (1868), containing his famous tale 'The Man without a Country', about a naval officer who suffers from a wish never to see the States again. He wrote various kinds of social, historical, satirical and supernatural fiction; utopian and philanthropic promotion; and two excellent volumes of memoirs, *A New England Boyhood* (1893) and *Memories of a Hundred Years* (2 vols., 1902). [MB]

Edward Everett Hale, Jr, *The Life and Letters of Edward Everett Hale* (2 vols., 1917).

Hall, Donald (1928–   ). Poet. He was born in Connecticut, educated at Harvard and Oxford, where his poem 'Exile' won the Newdigate Prize and was published by the Fantasy Press. He has published several volumes – *To the Loud Wind and Other Poems* (1955), *Exiles and Marriages* (1955), *The Dark Houses* (1958) and *A Roof of Tiger Lilies* (1964). Like several young American poets he has united the ironical formalism of much post-war English poetry and the more speculative, subjective manner of much recent American verse. Some of Hall's poems reach out towards social themes, and towards overt discovery ('Man learns by love, and not by metaphor'); others are concerned with rendering the vigour of a thing, a relationship, a cultural heritage. He has also edited an encyclo-

pedia of modern poetry and several anthologies, including the Penguin *Contemporary American Verse* (1962). *String Too Short to Be Saved* (1962) is a series of reminiscences of boyhood holidays in New Hampshire. [MB]

Hall, James (1793–1868). Journalist, editor. The Philadelphian banker and lawyer was one of the first Americans to record frontier legends. His books include *Letters from the West* (1828), *Tales of the Border* (1835) and *Sketches of History, Life and Manners in the West* (2 vols., 1834–5). He founded and edited the *Illinois Monthly Magazine* (1830–2), the first Western literary journal, and the *Western Monthly Magazine* (1832–6). [EM]

J. T. Flanagan, *James Hall: Literary Pioneer of the Ohio Valley* (1950).

Hall, James N. ◊ Nordhoff, Charles.

Halleck, Fitz-Greene (1790–1867). Poet. Born in Guilford, Connecticut, he became an important figure in the lively literary scene of early-19th-century New York, in its 'Knickerbocker' period. A friend of Washington Irving and James Fenimore Cooper, he was first a clerk in a banking house, then personal secretary to John Jacob Astor, the merchant and a patron of literary men. In 1819 Halleck and Joseph Rodman ◊ Drake produced the famous 'Croaker' poems, a series of humorous and satirical odes printed anonymously in the New York *Evening Post*; in 1860 they appeared in book form as *The Croakers*. Halleck's other famous satire was *Fanny* (1821), which mocked contemporary *nouveaux riches*. A tour to Europe in 1822 produced two of his best poems, 'Alnwick Castle' and 'Burns', collected in *Alnwick Castle, with Other Poems* (1827). Campbell, Byron and Scott particularly influenced him, and he was an editor of Byron and of *Selections from the British Poets* (1840). His work shows ways in which English romanticism, both as a sensibility and as a literary technique, could be adapted by American writers to American materials –

as in 'Red Jacket' (1828), about an Indian chief, 'The Field of Grounded Arms' (1831), about the Battle of Saratoga, 'Young America' (1865), and the unfinished 'Connecticut'. A minor poet, highly regarded in his day, he undoubtedly helped to form a whole phase of American literary sensibility. *The Poetical Works* first appeared in 1847 and went through three revised editions in the poet's lifetime. [MB]

The Poetical Writings, ed. J. G. Wilson (1869).
James G. Wilson, *The Life and Letters of Fitz-Greene Halleck* (1869); Nelson F. Adkins, *Fitz-Greene Halleck: An Early Knickerbocker Wit and Poet* (1930).

Hammett, Dashiell (1894–1961). Detective-story writer. He served in the army in the First World War, and subsequently worked as a private detective for a Pinkerton Agency, in San Francisco, before he began to write his famous tough detective novels. He re-enlisted for the Second World War, and served in the Aleutians. His heroes, Sam Spade and the Thin Man, are universally known, and his reputation has been strong in intellectual as well as popular quarters (he was admired by Sinclair Lewis, Robert Graves, André Gide, etc.) because of his economical style and capacity to catch the tone of a cool American toughness. He helped to sketch a new American folk-hero, akin to the Hemingway hero, whose apotheosis came in film (for which Hammett wrote). His novels are *Red Harvest* (1929), now often considered the best, with its anonymous Continental Operative hero; *The Dain Curse* (1929); *The Maltese Falcon* (1930), which introduces Sam Spade and which had most influence on subsequent detective writers like Raymond ◊ Chandler; *The Glass Key* (1931); and *The Thin Man* (1932). Five of these were reissued by his friend Lillian ◊ Hellman in *The Novels of Dashiell Hammett* (1966). Hammett's detectives (particularly the Continental Operative), though tough, also use intelligence and observation to meet crime. Many of his stories and novels first appeared in the popular detective magazine *Black Mask*. Some of the stories appeared in *The Adventures of Sam Spade* (1944) and *The Creeping Siamese and Other Stories* (1950), and a selection with a biographical introduction by Lillian Hellman, *The Big Knockover* (1966), includes *Tulip*, an unfinished autobiographical novel. [MB]

Hansberry, H. ◊ Negro Literature.

Harland, Henry (1861–1905). Novelist, story writer, editor. Best remembered as an important figure in the Aesthetic movement in England, where he edited the *Yellow Book* (1894–7), his earlier career is fascinating and his biography confusing (most sources give it incorrectly). He claimed to have been born in St Petersburg, and later announced English aristocratic parentage; in fact he was born in New York of parents from Connecticut. He went to Paris and then briefly to the Harvard Divinity School, and in New York began writing under the pen-name 'Sidney Luska' realistic novels of New York Jewish life. This early work includes *As It Was Written: A Jewish Musician's Story* (1885), *Mrs Peixada* (1886), *My Uncle Florimund* (1888) and *A Latin Quarter Courtship and Other Stories* (1889). Several of these novels are touched with sensationalism and cosmopolitan matter, but it was not until he advocated intermarriage with Gentiles in *The Yoke of the Thorah* (1887) that his pretence of being Jewish was unmasked. Harland then moved to Paris and in 1889 to London with an introduction from his godfather, Edmund Clarence Stedman, to Henry James. He now became an aesthete and a Jamesian stylist, tempted by Paris Bohemia, and was converted to Catholicism. Thereafter came historical novels and Left-Bank romances – *Mademoiselle Miss and Other Stories* (1893), *Grey Roses* (1895), *Comedies and Errors* (1898) and two books which caught the full tide of historical fiction and have survived well, *The Cardinal's Snuff Box* (1900), his most successful novel, a romance about an Italian duchess, and *My Friend Prospero* (1904). James said of the fiction of his expatriate aesthete period that it was lost in a whimsical picturesque vision of palace secrets, rulers and pretenders, of the heavy air of Rome 'where Cardinals are part of the furniture'. [MB]

Henry James, 'The Story-Teller at Large: Mr Henry Harland', in *American Essays*, ed. Leon Edel (1956).

Harrington, Alan (1919–   ). No velis He was born in Massachusetts and graduated from Harvard in 1939; he has worked in public relations and advertising. *The Revelations of Doctor Modesto* (1955) is a highly entertaining novel satirizing philosophical universal panaceas. *Life in the Crystal Palace* (1959) takes on organization men in an American corporation, and *The Secret Swinger* (1966) tells of the disastrous adventures of a middle-aged man attempting to rejuvenate himself in young 'beat' circles and free himself from family and marriage with hip permissiveness. *The Immortalist* (1969) is a nonfiction account of salvation through medical engineering. [EM]

Harris, George W(ashington) (1814–69). Southern humorist. He was born in Pennsylvania, apprenticed to a jeweller, captained a Tennessee river-boat and wrote technological articles. Then he turned to sketches in the South-western tall-tale tradition and produced *Sut Lovingood: Yarns Spun by a 'Nat'ral Born Durn'd Fool'* (1867), frontier-dialect writing founded in Sut's practical joking and rough-neck humour. This kind of early pop-writing drew heavily on folklore. Mark Twain knew this work and was undoubtedly influenced. [MB]

Milton Rickels, *George Washington Harris* (1965).

Harris, Joel Chandler (1848–1908). Novelist, short-story writer. He was born in Georgia and as a boy began work in a printing shop. Work on a plantation gave him a contact with Negro folklore. He put this to profit in comic sketches for the *Atlanta Constitution*, which he joined in 1876 and where, in 1879, the first Uncle Remus story appeared: 'Negro Folklore. The Story of Mr Rabbit and Mr Fox, as Told by Uncle Remus' (the 1880 introductory story for *Uncle Remus, His Songs and His Sayings*). *Nights with Uncle Remus* (1883) maintained the popularity of the tales and introduced Daddy Jack, whose Gullah dialect of the Sea Islands made the stories less accessible. Where the earlier stories were post-Civil War, these concerned a generally affectionate master–slave relationship, although Uncle Remus is permitted shrewd individuality. After *Uncle Remus and His Friends* (1892) and *Mr Rabbit at Home* (1895), further volumes (1905 and 1910, posthumous) were backed with 5 children's books (1894–9) and many stories and novels not in the Uncle Remus series. *Mingo and Other Sketches in Black and White* (1884) concerns a faithful black Georgia servant and white class contrasts; *Sister Jane* (1896) deals with ante-bellum Georgia, *Free Joe, and Other Georgian Sketches* (1887), whose main story concerns the problems of an ex-slave, and *Gabriel*

Tolliver (1902) with the Reconstruction. *On the Plantation* (1892) is an autobiographical fiction of his early years.

The Uncle Remus tales preserve dialect, lore and attitudes of Southern 19th-century Negroes as seen by a white Southerner fascinated by the animal mythology through which they came to terms with their condition. Harris newly presented this material to Americans without black-faced minstrel crudeness. In his later stories he was more conscious of the international beast-folklore tradition of which the Afro-American oral tradition was part, but the Remus pattern stayed: the philosophical old Negro reciting to the 7-year-old son of 'Marse' John and 'Miss' Sally, or his descendant. Today the characters are part of American folklore, and Brer Rabbit is a major American, the cunning trickster who survives oppression by a craft which challenges physical domination. The European Reynard the Fox has become the Afro-American rabbit, accompanied by Brer Tarrypin, the hero of the cautious, who may often master the strong and crafty, Brer Fox, the predator who himself is preyed upon, and many more. Although Harris believed he was a transcriber, his tales are finished literary works, drawn, however, from plantation tradition. [EM]

Joel Chandler Harris: Miscellaneous Writings, ed. J. C. Harris (1931); *The Favorite Uncle Remus*, ed. G. Van Santvoord and A. C. Coolidge (1948).
Julia C. Harris, *The Life and Letters of Joel Chandler Harris* (1918); Alvin F. Harlow, *Joel Chandler Harris (Uncle Remus): Plantation Storyteller* (1941); Francis P. Gaines, *The Southern Plantation: A Study in the Development and the Accuracy of a Tradition* (1924); P. M. Cousins, *Joel Chandler Harris: A Biography* (1968).

Hart, Moss (1904–61). Playwright, librettist. He began his career in 1925, his first success being *Once in a Lifetime* (1930), written with George S. ◊ Kaufman, his collaborator in many future works. It is a typical comedy-farce, composed, like all his best work, with wit, speed and broad humanity. With Kaufman he also wrote *Merrily We Roll Along* (1934) and, one of their best, *You Can't Take It with You* (1936). There followed *I'd Rather Be Right* (1937) and *The American Way* (1939). *George Washington Slept Here* (1940), *Winged Victory* (1943), *Light Up the Sky* (1948) and *The Climate of Eden* (1952) are his own plays.

Best of all the collaborations with Kaufman is *The Man Who Came to Dinner* (1939), a caricature of Alexander ◊ Woolcott's career, superficial and funny. He wrote the librettos for Irving Berlin's *Face the Music* (1933) and Kurt Weill's *Lady in the Dark* (1941). His work with Kaufman epitomizes Broadway show business of the thirties at its finest. [EM]

Harte, Bret (1836–1902). Short-story writer. Born in Albany, New York, he went as a youth to California (1854) where he worked as an itinerant gold-miner, schoolmaster, Wells Fargo expressman, journalist and printer, gaining prominence through the prose sketches and verses he contributed to the *Golden Era* and the *Californian* (for which later, as editor, he engaged Mark Twain to write weekly articles). In 1863 he was appointed secretary of the U.S. branch mint in San Francisco. In 1867 appeared *The Lost Galleon*, a collection of his poems, and *Condensed Novels and Other Papers* (1867), clever satirical parodies of Dickens, Cooper, Victor Hugo and others, whose aptness suggests Harte's real qualities as a critic (he was an effective, sharp reviewer). A year later he helped to establish the famous *Overland Monthly*, a centre for western writing (including the work of Mark Twain). Harte edited the paper for two years, until 1870, and in it appeared some of his most famous work, stories of western life like 'The Luck of Roaring Camp', 'The Outcasts of Poker Flat', 'Tennessee's Partner', 'Brown of Calaveras', and the humorous ballad 'Plain Language from Truthful James', better remembered as 'The Heathen Chinee'.

Their collection in *The Luck of Roaring Camp and Other Sketches* (1870) had a triumphant reception, which he promptly followed up by resigning a professorship at the newly founded University of California and returning East to write for the *Atlantic Monthly*. He sought desperately to maintain his talents, collaborated with Twain, etc. But his life thereafter was to be a decline, though he made frequent contributions of stories to magazines and collected them in book form: *Mrs Skaggs's Husbands* (1873), *Tales of the Argonauts* (1875), *An Heiress of Red Dog* (1879), *A Sappho of Green Springs* (1891), *Colonel Starbottle's Client* (1892), as well as writing novels and plays. From 1878 to 1885 he was U.S. consul in Germany and Scotland,

spending the last years of his life in London. He never returned to the U.S.A.

A deceased prostitute's child who softens the hardened hearts of the miners so that, when the river rises, one of them drowns with the child in his arms; a gambler, two prostitutes and a thief snow-bound with an eloping couple whose true love thaws their hearts until all starve, die or shoot themselves in an effort to save the innocents; a faithful friend willing to give his entire mining stake in return for the life of a partner, captured as a highwayman, who had once eloped with his wife: out of such rhetorical contrasts of moral black and white Bret Harte captured the imagination of his Victorian reading audience. The formula is still effective. This brawling world of miners, prospectors, gamblers, robbers and prostitutes is perhaps even more attractive, a century after, to a generation brought up on Hollywood and the Wild West: while something of a young man's sharp ear and eye, stirred heart and mind, lives for ever in the bravado of these tales which an older Harte could never recapture. [HB]

Letters, ed. G. B. Harte (1926); *Representative Selections*, ed. G. B. Harrison (1941).
R. O'Connor, *Bret Harte: A Biography* (1966).

Hartford Wits. ◊ Connecticut Wits.

Hawkes, John (1925–). Novelist, dramatist. Born in Connecticut, he studied at Harvard and teaches creative writing at Brown University, Rhode Island. One of the few post-war American writers convincingly exploiting the experimental tradition of modern fiction, he has had a considerable cult reputation that has lately widened to broader acclaim. His surrealistic fiction is founded on a sense that nightmare consciousness reveals a fundamental mythology; and he is extraordinarily inventive in his creation of symbolic moments and nightmare landscapes. His novels, set in post-war Germany, in wartime England, in deserts, on islands, explore the elemental, grotesque experience of the psyche. The blurred settings, fantastic landscape, and use of powerful horror devices make for an extremely intense fiction. At times, however, the effect seems overworked and literary; in *The Lime Twig* (1960) he clearly derives his landscape and world, that of wartime England (a country he had not visited), from Graham Greene and others. His other books include *The Cannibal* (1949), *Chari-vari* (a novella, 1949), *The Beetle Leg* (1951), two short novels called *The Owl* and *The Goose on the Grave* (1953), and *Second Skin* (1964), which seems to mark a development in his work in that the hero finds a pattern of escape and rediscovery. *The Innocent Party* (1967) contains four of his plays. *Lunar Landscape* (1969) collects shorter fiction from the 1940s onwards. [M B]

S. K. Oberbeck, 'John Hawkes: The Smile Slashed by a Razor', in *Contemporary American Novelists*, ed. Harry T. Moore (1964); I. Malin, *New American Gothic* (1962); R. Scholes, *The Fabulators* (1967).

Hawthorne, Nathaniel (1804–64). Novelist, short-story writer. The Hawthornes of Salem, Massachusetts, declined from colonial prominence (one was a witch-trial judge) to Nathaniel's sea-captain father, who died on a voyage when his son was 4. While recovering from a leg injury, the boy took to reading and solitude in the remote Maine village to which his mother had removed when he was 12. When he returned to Salem from Bowdoin College (Longfellow was a classmate), he began to write professionally in a seclusion reflected in the hero of his 'gothic' first novel, *Fanshawe* (1828), unsold copies of which he burned; he wrote no more novels for 21 years. Nor did his tales, also anonymous, bring him reputation until the *Twice-Told Tales* of 1837. He worked in the Boston Custom House (1839–41) as salt and coal measurer, and when this political appointment ended bought a share in Brook Farm (◊ Ripley), later withdrawing from its impracticable utopian ends, disillusioned with agrarian ideology and liberal evasions about the nature of leadership and community – major materials of all his work. In 1842 he married and lived in the Old Manse, Concord, where Emerson had written *Nature*. He did know the ◊ Transcendentalist circle but did not share their optimism and reforming faith. *Mosses from an Old Manse* (1846) appeared the year he left for his Salem custom surveyorship, from which political change again removed him in 1848. In his freedom he wrote his 'hell-fired' masterpiece *The Scarlet Letter* (1850), on which his reputation grew. Living at Lenox, in the Berkshires, he was contacted by Melville, and brought out *The House of the Seven Gables* (1851), *A Wonder Book for Boys and Girls* (1851) and

The Snow Image and Other Thrice-Told Tales (1851). At West Newton he wrote *The Blithedale Romance* in 1852, the year he returned to Concord and published a campaign biography for his college friend Franklin Pierce, the Democratic presidential nominee. After election Pierce gave him the consulship at Liverpool (1853), where he served for four years before going to Italy in 1857, where he began *The Marble Faun* (1860). He returned to Concord in 1860, and after writing *Our Old Home* (1863) his creativity relaxed. Family ill health and the Civil War depressed him. The Abolitionist movement conflicted with his scepticism about reform. He died leaving three unfinished novels.

His masterworks are 'romances', by which he meant an imaginative fictional projection of moral life rather than detailed naturalism. One major group of his works translates 17th-century American life into 19th-century moral and political concerns. *The Scarlet Letter* takes the ancestral New England confrontation of witch and judge and delineates it as a 19th-century conflict of ideas and ways of living which include female emancipation, the nature of sexuality in marriage and adultery, the personal character of religious or philosophical vocation, and the ontology of psychological independence. The greatness of this novel is supported by a group of important short stories on related themes of guilt, intellectual pride, suppressed sensuousness and the heroism of speculative and emotional living. These dramatic moral fables include 'The Maypole of Merrymount' (the effects of the implantation of traditional paganism into the puritan New World), 'The Gray Champion' (the beginnings of independence in the colonies), 'The Minister's Black Veil' (the refusal of love and sympathy), 'Young Goodman Brown' (witchcraft as necessary parallel to puritanism), and 'My Kinsman Major Molineux' (a boy becoming a man at the time colonial America begins to throw off England). Another group of stories concerns intellectual power in the scientist and artist, the head's conflict with the heart, and Faustian hubris of challenge to established ideas and ways of living. 'Ethan Brand' deals with the 'unpardonable sin' of using another human being instrumentally, 'Rappacini's Daughter' and 'The Birthmark' with the scientific alteration of nature and human nature, and 'The Artist of the Beautiful' with the ways in which art and science cut a man off from the chain of common humanity. These are constant themes in Hawthorne's work as a whole and are deeply embedded in the nature of American literature and culture in the 19th century. In his other novels he begins with the conflict between social inheritance and the needs of the present. In *The House of the Seven Gables* two young people seek to be released from an archaic New England family whose tradition of public probity has become warped into criminal fraud and enfeebled amoral delicacy. Opposed to the ancient house and its ghosts are the technology of the railway and the daguerreotype, as well as the freedom symbolized by nature. *The Blithedale Romance* is a critique of the Brook Farm experiment and a superb analysis of the urge to Utopia, the corrupting effects of unexamined desires for leadership, and the undetermined and tragic effects of feminist emancipations. For his last completed novel, *The Marble Faun* (1860), Hawthorne places his action in Italy: the Italian count Donatello, the mysteriously European Miriam, and an American couple form a triangulation of his familiar themes. Apart from long passages of not unpleasant travelogue, it is a romance of crime and punishment, a myth of the fortunate and necessary fall from innocence to maturity, and the relative purity of New World youth in wicked old Europe. The stylization and dogma are far more schematic than in *The Scarlet Letter*, and earlier uncertainties of tone and address in his prose have a field day, but it is an important extension of his fundamental issues. Besides these major works various fragments were published after his death, including *Septimius Felton: or, The Elixir of Life* (1872), *The Dolliver Romance and Other Pieces* (1876) and *Doctor Grimshawe's Secret* (1883; ed. from manuscript 1954). Passages from his American, English, and French and Italian notebooks have been edited by Randall Stewart (1932 and 1941) and Sophia Hawthorne (1872) respectively. His letters have not yet been published in a reliable edition, but a collection of love letters appeared in 1907, and some letters to Ticknor, the publisher, in 1910. But the collected letters is being prepared, and an annotated Centenary Edition of all his works has been initiated by Ohio State University with *The House of the Seven Gables*,

The Blithedale Romance and *Fanshawe* (1966). This attention is justified for a great fiction writer whose career is at the centre of the American tradition of apprehension concerning the nature of permanent evil in a society dedicated to and capable of infinite progress. His influence extends powerfully through Henry James, especially in his treatment of the 'international theme' of the American in Europe, to William Faulkner and mid-20th-century 'gothic' novelists of the American power structure. [EM]

The Portable Hawthorne, ed. Malcolm Cowley (1948).

H. H. Waggoner, *Hawthorne: A Critical Study* (1955); Randall Stewart, *Nathaniel Hawthorne* (1948); E. Wagenknecht, *Nathaniel Hawthorne: Man and Writer* (1961); R. R. Male, *Hawthorne's Tragic Vision* (1957); ed. J. D. Crowley, *Hawthorne: The Critical Heritage* (1970).

Hay, John (1838–1905). Diplomat, historian, poet, novelist. Born Salem, Indiana, he grew up in the Illinois region of Pike County, setting of his famous ballads. After attending Brown University, he began to study law in an office next door to Abraham ◊ Lincoln's in Springfield, Illinois. On Lincoln's election to the Presidency, Hay went with him to Washington as an assistant private secretary. A posting to the American legation in Paris deflected him towards the arts. In 1870 he returned to America and to journalism. He published many poems and ballads, collecting them in *Pike County Ballads and Other Pieces* (1871). In 1878 he went to Washington as an assistant secretary of state and was the neighbour and friend of Henry ◊ Adams. He appears recurrently in Adams' *Education of Henry Adams*. Like Adams, Hay published a novel anonymously: *The Bread-Winners: A Social Study* (1884), which defended capitalism against labour and is notable for its expression of the post-Civil-War discontent of the 'dispossessed' upper class in the mercenary Gilded Age. In 1890 he published (with John Nicolay) the 10-volume *Abraham Lincoln: A History*. In the same year *Poems*, his collected verses, appeared. Afterwards American ambassador to England and, briefly, Secretary of State, he worked for peace on many fronts in his remaining years. But his literary fame rests firmly on his dialect poems of Pike County, such as 'Little Breeches' and 'Jim Bludso of the Prairie Bell'. [AG]

The Complete Poetical Works (1916).

117

William Roscoe Thayer, *The Life and Letters of John Hay* (2 vols., 1915); W. D. Howells, 'John Hay in Literature', *North American Review*, September 1905; T. Dennett, *John Hay: From Poetry to Politics* (1933).

Hayne, Paul Hamilton (1830–86). Poet. Born in Charleston, South Carolina, he was one of the important group of pre-Civil-War Southern writers who gathered in that city, others being William Gilmore ◊ Simms and Henry ◊ Timrod, whose works he edited. His elegant and reflective nature poetry appeared in the *Southern Literary Messenger*, and with Timrod he founded *Russell's Magazine*. *Poems* (1855) and *Sonnets and Other Poems* (1857) appeared before the Civil War, during the course of which he wrote patriotic Confederate verse. After the war, in difficult circumstances, he vowed to live by writing, and produced *Legends and Lyrics* (1872) and other poetry and biography. [M B]

Collected Poems (1882).
Kate H. Becker, *Paul Hamilton Hayne: His Life and Letters* (1951).

H. D. ◊ Doolittle, Hilda.

Hearn, Lafcadio (1850–1904). Novelist, travel-writer, translator. Though usually regarded as an American writer because he exerted most influence in the U.S.A., Hearn spent only a part of his life there. Born on the Ionian island of Santa Maria, son of a surgeon-major in the English army and a Greek mother, he was reared in Dublin by an aunt who sent him to Catholic schools and finally to America in 1869. He settled in Cincinnati and became a journalist. In 1877 he went on an assignment to New Orleans, where he studied Creole literature with George Washington ◊ Cable. He began translation from Gautier, Flaubert and Anatole France; his first book, *One of Cleopatra's Nights* (1882), translates six Gautier tales. A professed romantic, impressionist and hunter of the exotic, he began exploring through a variety of literatures, and *Stray Leaves from Strange Literature* (1884) consists of articles founded on literary exotica. He published two novels, *Chita* (1889), on the destruction of an island off Louisiana by a tidal wave, and *Youma* (1890), about slave rebellion in Martinique (see also *Two Years in the French West Indies*, 1890). Already interested in the orient – *Some Chinese Ghosts* (1887) is a collection of oriental legends – he went in 1890 to Japan on a commission from *Harper's*. He married a Japanese woman and settled there, becoming a citizen and a Buddhist, working as a teacher – for a time at Tokyo University – and an interpreter of Japanese life to the west.

Japan realized for Hearn his impressionism, mysticism and taste for the exotic, and it was in these lights that he interpreted it to American and English readers. Most of his later books are studies of the richer aspects of Japanese life – *Glimpses of Unfamiliar Japan* (2 vols., 1893), *Gleanings in Buddha Fields* (1897), *In Ghostly Japan* (1899), *Shadowings* (1900), *Japan: An Attempt at Interpretation* (1904), etc. – or else collections of stories and legends. His journalism and his lectures on literature, English, American, European and oriental, have been collected only since his death: *Occidental Gleanings* (2 vols., 1925), *Appreciations of Poetry* (1916), and *Life and Literature* (1922). The important *Leaves from the Diary of an Impressionist: Early Writings*, which states his aesthetic, was collected in 1911 by Ferris Greenslet. His Japanese wife, Setsuko Koizumi, wrote a memoir, *Reminiscences of Lafcadio Hearn* (1918); so did his son, Kazuo Koizumi, in *Father and I: Memories of Lafcadio Hearn* (1935). Yone Noguchi's *Lafcadio Hearn in Japan* (1910) contains a useful Japanese appreciation of the man.

Hearn's reputation is somewhat uncertain, not least because of the complications of his citizenship and his publishing history. His importance in international literature is that he made accessible the long-closed world of Japan and *japonisme* to the modern arts, he also led the way into much of the 20th-century interest in imagism and impressionism. His Bohemian sensibility (◊ Bohemianism), his taste for the exotic, his fascination with symbolism, make his aesthetic development important. His mind is highly sophisticated and critically interesting; and its cosmopolitanism (as Earl Miner shows in *The Japanese Tradition in British and American Literature*, 1958) gave many new hints to the poets of England and America from about 1910 onwards. His *Letters from the Raven* (1907) are an important source for his autobiography. [M B]

Writings (16 vols., 1922); *The Selected Writings*, ed. H. Goodman, intr. Malcolm Cowley (1949).
Vera McWilliams, *Lafcadio Hearn* (1946); Elizabeth Stevenson, *Lafcadio Hearn* (1961);

Albert Parry, *Garrets and Pretenders* (1960); Elizabeth Bisland, *The Life and Letters of Lafcadio Hearn* (2 vols., 1906).

Hecht, Anthony (1923–). Poet. A former student of John Crowe ♢ Ransom at Kenyon College and now a teacher, he won considerable poetic reputation both in the U.S.A. and England with *A Summoning of Stones* (1954), a collection of excellent verse. The book takes its title from Santayana's phrase suggesting that poetry's aim is to 'call the stones themselves to their ideal places, and enchant the very substance and skeleton of the world'. Hecht's verse is both witty and moralizing, and it ranges between poems of occasions and philosophical quandaries deriving from painfully felt experience. *The Hard Hours* (1967) confirms his talent and elegance, includes a nice parody 'The Dover Bitch' and extends the autobiographical tendency of the earlier book (some of whose poems are reprinted here). [MB]

Hecht, Ben (1893–1964). Novelist, dramatist journalist. Born in New York, he made his career in Chicago, beginning in the 'literary renaissance' there in the thirties. His first novel, *Erik Dorn* (1921), uses his reporter experience in Berlin (1918–19) as well as his admiration for Huysmans. From 1922, he wrote novels and stories, edited his *Literary Times*, and worked on plays and films: *The Front Page* (1920, with Charles MacArthur), *Wuthering Heights*, *Nothing Sacred*, *Scarface*, *Notorious* (1946), etc.; his plays include *The Scoundrel* (with Noël Coward). In the 1940s he advocated extreme forms of Zionism, and all his life remained a mid-Western radical journalist using all literary forms, including autobiography, with *A Child of the Century* (1954). [EM]

Heggen, Thomas (1919–49). Novelist, dramatist. Born in Iowa. He left the *Reader's Digest* to serve in the navy in the Pacific during the Second World War and put that experience to work in *Mister Roberts* (1946), a money-making novel, film and play, which is an uninhibited satire on the service, a study in boredom and revolt. He died of talented inertia in what Budd ♢ Schulberg called 'that gold-plated bear trap' of early success ('Taps at Reveille', in *Esquire*, November 1960). [EM]

Heinlein, Robert A(nson) (1907–). Science-fiction writer. Born at Butler, Missouri. A trained physicist, he began writing in 1939 and has since published many influential and widely translated novels and stories for juvenile as well as adult audiences. Several of his works are now accepted as classics of the genre; they include *Orphans of the Sky* (1951; originally published as a 2-part serial in 1941) and *Methuselah's Children* (1958; serial version, 1941), both of which form part of his 5-volume *History of the Future*. Others in the series are *The Man Who Sold the Moon* (1950) and *The Green Hills of Earth* (1951). His many works include *The Puppet Masters* (1951), *The Star Beast* (1954), *The Door into Summer* (1957), *Stranger in a Strange Land* (1961), *Glory Road* (1963) and *The Moon is a Harsh Mistress* (1966). [HD]

Heliczer, Piero (1937–). Poet. Born in Rome, he went to America at 10, studied at Harvard, was an expatriate in Paris, and has made films and written poems, both extremely individual in their imagery and form, in England and New York. His films include *Autumn Feast*, made in Brighton, Sussex, and the unfinished *Dirt*. His poems are included in *You Could Hear the Snow Melting and Dripping from the Deer's Mouth* (1958), *I Dreamt I Shot Arrows in my Amazon Bra* (1960) and *Second Battle of the Marne* (1961). *The Soap Opera* (1967) is his most mature work to date, and is illustrated by artists which include Andy Warhol and Jack Smith. Heliczer combines surrealist imagery, direct expressions of love and clear lyricism with a complexity of form partly derived from his training in music. [EM]

Heller, Joseph (1923–). Novelist. Born in Brooklyn, he studied literature at New York University, Columbia and Oxford. He has taught writing at Pennsylvania State College but spent more time in advertising, now heading the promotion department of *McCall's* magazine. In the Second World War a bombardier in the air force, he flew 60 combat missions from Corsica over Italy and France – an experience that lies behind his one novel, *Catch–22* (1961). Among the best novels to appear since the war, it is funny, compassionate, technically original and morally concerned, using the methods of black humour and the theatre of the absurd to satirize the army, the capitalist state and the host of doctors and psychiatrists modern living demands. His air force is less a fighting unit than a bureaucracy perpetuating itself through flagrant but persuasive use of authoritarian logic – Catch–22 – which constantly thwarts the hero Yossarian, a kind of *homme moyen sensuel*, in his attempts to enjoy life and survive. His play *We Bombed in New Haven* (1968) shows war as a game of role-playing and spectatorism. [B W]

Brian Way, 'Formal Experiment and Social Discontent: Joseph Heller's *Catch-22*', *Journal of American Studies* (October 1968).

Hellman, Lillian (1905–   ). Playwright. Born in New Orleans, she has lived mainly in New York. Her first important play with a Broadway run was *The Children's Hour* (1934). She visited Russia in 1936 and 1945, was active on several leftish organizations, and was therefore called before the House Un-American Activities Committee in 1952, but refused to testify against friends and colleagues. *The Children's Hour* concerns sexual scandal in a girl's boarding school and analyses abnormal psychology. In *The Little Foxes* (1939) she presents an Alabama aristocratic family in decline through a new rapacious social class, *The Watch on the Rhine* (1941) exposes pre-war complacency about Nazism, and *The Searching Wind* (1944) delineates the appeasement of fascism in the thirties. *Another Part of the Forest* (1946; the earlier chronicles of the *Little Foxes* family) and *Toys in the Attic* (1960) again concern the South in decline and neurosis. Her most recent work is a version of Burt ◊ Blechman's satirical novel *How Much?* called *My Mother, My Father and Me* (1963). All her plays are notable for their psychological intensity, strongly motivated violence and liberal critical attitudes. She also adapted Voltaire's *Candide* for Leonard Bernstein's musical, which had lyrics by Richard Wilbur, Dorothy Parker and John La Touche. *An Unfinished Woman* (1969) is autobiography oddly omitting her life in the theatre. [E M]

Hemingway, Ernest (1898–1961). Novelist. Born in Oak Park, Illinois. In boyhood he developed that passion for active outdoor pursuits which so deeply marked his life and fiction. He hunted and fished in the forests of the Great Lakes region, which still kept some of their frontier characteristics. His independence, and his compulsion to bury himself in the American wilderness, indeed to identify with the primitive everywhere,

can be traced to this time and place, and to his experiences with his father, who was a doctor, and with the Indians. After a stylistically formative spell as a journalist, he joined a volunteer ambulance unit (before America entered the war). Severely wounded near the Austrian frontier in 1918, he was awarded the Croce di Guerra. The wound altered his consciousness profoundly, bringing him face to face with death and terror of annihilation; he said that he 'ceased to be hard-boiled' and, discovering his own vulnerability (a feeling intensified by his father's suicide), he set out to exorcise his fears by confronting death or observing others confront it as often as he could. Hence his obsession with violence – bullfighting, boxing, safari, big-game hunting and war – and the skills of games and writing. At his most confident – as in the superb story 'The Undefeated' – he holds off terror with the virtues of the born fighter, courage and nobility in the face of death, a stoical resistance to pain, a perfect sympathy with one's physical environment. The hero is a Spanish bullfighter; his virtues are those of the idealized American redskin.

Sent after the war to Paris as correspondent for Hearst newspapers, he began to write under instruction from Gertrude ◊ Stein and Ezra ◊ Pound and emerged with Scott ◊ Fitzgerald as the most gifted of the ◊ 'Lost Generation' writers. Influenced by *Huckleberry Finn* and the discipline of journalism, he developed a distinctive fictional manner, vernacular, terse, unabstract, concerned with 'the real thing, the sequence of emotion and fact which make the emotion'. Apart from some privately printed ventures, his first book was *In Our Time* (1925), short stories using the expatriate perspective to define his sense of America, the central figure in the finest ones being Nick Adams, a young man shaped by the mid-West and the war. *The Torrents of Spring* (1926), a comic masterpiece, begins as a burlesque of Sherwood ◊ Anderson's *Dark Laughter*, and becomes a successful enterprise in self-mockery, a satire on the cult of American maleness. His more popular success came with *The Sun Also Rises* (1926; British title *Fiesta*), usually considered his best novel. Jake Barnes, an American, and Brett, an Englishwoman, cannot consummate their love because Jake is impotent, 'wounded in the war'. In the religion, bull-fighting and drinking of the fiesta at Pamplona they are forced to confront the emptiness of their lives, from which the pleasures of the expatriate round in Paris had protected them; they are sustained, if at all, only by that stoical fortitude in the face of the intolerable which is the last resort of the Hemingway hero. The novel conveys with equal brilliance the ritual or turbulence of the fiesta, the pleasures of fishing and drinking, and, through its dialogue, the flat surface of Paris lost-generation life. *Men without Women* (1927), his finest collection of stories, shows many such confrontations with death and emptiness; its heroes are soldiers, bull-fighters, boxers, gangsters; it evokes the feel of violent action with unequalled economy and force. *A Farewell to Arms* (1929) deals with a love-affair conducted against the background of the war in Italy. Its excellence lies in the delicacy with which it conveys a sense of the impermanence of the best human feelings; the unobtrusive force of its symbolism of mountain and plain; above all the vast scope of its vision of war – the retreat from Caporetto is one of the great war-sequences of literature.

After 1930, with the exception of a few stories and episodes, Hemingway reworks less and less successfully the situations of the earlier books. *Death in the Afternoon* (1932) and *Green Hills of Africa* (1935), about bull-fighting and safari, already contain much of the attitudinizing and simple-pretentious writing that mar later novels. *Winner Take Nothing* (1933) has one excellent story, 'A Clean Well-Lighted Place'. *To Have and Have Not* (1937), a short novel about a Caribbean smuggler, is marred by an inept attempt at fashionable social criticism; but *The Fifth Column and The First Forty-Nine Stories* (1938) contains, along with a play and the stories from the earlier collections, some fine new stories using recent African and Spanish experiences – the best work of the later years. His next novel, *For Whom the Bell Tolls* (1940), set in the Spanish Civil War, is impressive, his most ambitious book; but its moulded attitude to politics confuses its direction and its dialogue, attempting epic simplicity, is often portentously absurd.

Hemingway by now was living in Cuba; during the Second World War he took active part as correspondent and irregular soldier in France, experiences reflected in *Across the River and into the Trees* (1950), an unconscious parody of his earlier work

and his worst novel. *The Old Man and the Sea* (1952), a fable about a Cuban fisherman's struggle with a great marlin, though dignified and often beautiful, does not entirely succeed, though it won him the Nobel Prize. Work he left after his death is now appearing posthumously. As he aged, Hemingway found it growingly difficult to keep up the active life he loved and, after treatment for mental disturbance, he shot himself at Ketchum, Idaho, in 1961, just as his father had done many years before. *Islands in the Stream* (1970), though never properly revised, possesses some of the intensity of his best work, and the lonely, almost broken hero, Thomas Hudson, has the tragic qualities of the later Hemingway himself.

He is one of the great American writers, not only because he superbly evokes action and the surface of things, but even more because of the uncanny force with which his work asks ultimate questions about life and death. A nihilist for whom the emptiness of modern life was perhaps most adequately symbolized by modern war, a nightmare of darkness, blood, confusion and treachery, he still held an ideal of the decent life. A man may sustain himself with the ephemeral pleasures of physical sensation, such as sex, alcohol and sport; he may acquire skills that make him precise and controlled, may possess a stoical resistance to his fate, may take sustenance from organized religion. But when these fail, he may prefer the nothingness of death to the nothingness of life. No writer has so effectively expressed this tension between the extreme pleasures and extreme terrors of being alive. [B W]

Stewart Sanderson, *Hemingway* (1961); Philip Young, *Ernest Hemingway* (1952; revised edn, 1959); Carlos Baker, *Hemingway: The Writer as Artist* (1956: revised edn, 1963); Edmund Wilson, 'Hemingway: Gauge of Morale', in *The Wound and the Bow* (revised edn, 1952); W. William White, *By-Line: Ernest Hemingway* (1967); Carlos Baker, *Ernest Hemingway* (1969); ed. Carlos Baker, *Hemingway and His Critics* (1961).

Henry, O(liver) (pseud. of William Sidney Porter) (1862–1910). Short-story writer, humorist, journalist. One of the most prolific writers ever, he was born in North Carolina and, without much schooling and virtually orphaned, worked in his uncle's drugstore, gradually retreating into a shy, poverty-stricken world of fantasy escape. After two years on a Texas ranch, he ran through a series of unskilled jobs, developing talents for cartooning and singing. In 1894 he founded *The Rolling Stone*, a comic magazine which soon failed, and two years later he was charged with embezzlement of funds from an Austin, Texas, bank and fled to New Orleans and Honduras. He returned when his wife was dying and served a long sentence in the Federal Penitentiary, Colombus, Ohio. Here he began to write and publish as 'O. Henry', from 1899 onwards, his first story, 'Whistling Dick's Christmas Stocking', already concluding with the twist for which he became famous. On release, he worked in New York, gathering material from a detailed contact with every aspect of the city's life. Overwhelming success brought him a salaried contract with the *World* for a story a week. He became a central figure in this peak period of the American magazine short story. The fatalism of his stories penetrated his life as well, and he died in drunkenness.

Cabbages and Kings (1904), his first collection, is a linked series of South American yarns. The New York tales of *The Four Million* (1906) include some of his perfect stereotypes, in works such as 'The Skylight Room' and 'The Furnished Room'. *Heart of the West* (1907) is a Western collection, and the hero of *The Gentle Grafter* (1908) is Jeff Peters, a confidence man in a main American tradition. *Roads of Destiny* (1909) embodies strongly his crude notion of fate, the basis of his twist. His style is almost anonymous, his use of dialect completely authentic, and his range of locality wide and vivid. But to entertain he resorted to cheap suspense and caricature. His strength is the startling surfaces of paradox and the grotesque, combined with commendable skill at plotting irony. [EM]

The Collected Works, intr. H. Harrison (2 vols., 1953); *Best Short Stories of O. Henry*, ed. B. Cerf and Van H. Cartmell (1945).
G. Langford, *Alias O. Henry: A Biography of William Sidney Porter* (1957); E. H. Long, *O. Henry: The Man and His Work* (1949).

Hergesheimer, Joseph (1880–1954). Novelist. He studied art in his home town, Philadelphia, and in Italy, before returning first to Virginia, then Pennsylvania, to write. Like James Branch ◊ Cabell, whom he knew and who wrote a short book about him, he admired aristocracy and idealism, and his early novels like *Mountain Blood*

(1915), set in Virginia, *The Three Black Pennys* (1917), about several generations of a Pennsylvania ironmaster family, *Java Head* (1919), about Salem in its great days of the China trade, *Linda Condon* (1919), and *Balisand* (1924), about post-Revolution Virginia, are classics of twenties exoticism, based both on devotion to 'beauty' and on an evocative power derived from research or feeling for regional history. But it is usually agreed that the later romances – like *Tampico* (1926) and *The Limestone Tree* (1931) – lack the earlier finesse and convincing exoticism. He also produced accounts of travel and two interesting autobiographical volumes, *A Presbyterian Child* (1923) and *From an Old House* (1925). [MB]

R. E. Martin, *The Fiction of Joseph Hergesheimer* (1966).

Herrick, Robert (1868–1938). Teacher and novelist. Born in Cambridge, Massachusetts, he joined the English Department at the nascent University of Chicago in 1893 and taught there for 30 years. He thought highly of his self-styled 'idealistic' novels, which include *The Real World* (1901), *A Life for a Life* (1910), *The Healer* (1911) and *Clark's Field* (1914), but his best work is to be found in a series of realistic novels which examined the materialism and corruption of contemporary Chicago: *The Gospel of Freedom* (1898); *The Web of Life* (1900); *The Common Lot* (1904); and *The Memoirs of an American Citizen* (1905; reissued, intr. Daniel Aaron, 1963). [HD]

Blake Nevius, *Robert Herrick: The Development of a Novelist* (1962).

Hersey, John (1914–). Novelist, reporter. Born in China, once secretary to Sinclair Lewis, during the Second World War a correspondent with a literary flair, he made his reputation as a war novelist with *A Bell for Adano* (1944), dealing with peasant life in American-occupied Sicily. Then came a remarkable piece of reportage about the first atomic bomb explosion, *Hiroshima*, which occupied an entire issue of the *New Yorker* (31 August 1946) – for which Hersey had been a writer – before achieving vast circulation as a book. His later novels have a journalist's sense of relevance and efficiency of manner, and have sometimes moved towards a broadly allegorical purpose; they are *The Wall* (1950), *The Marmot Drive* (1953), *A Single Pebble* (1956), *The War Lover* (1959), *The*

Child Buyer (1960), and *Under the Eye of the Storm* (1967). *Too Far to Walk* (1966), a Faustian novel about university students, is his best yet. *The Algiers Motel Incident* (1969) documents police and National Guard killings in the black ghetto of Detroit in 1967. [MB]

Heyward, DuBose (1885–1940). Novelist, poet, playwright. His best-known work is his novel *Porgy* (1925), about Negro life in Catfish Row in old Charleston, South Carolina, his home town. He and his wife Dorothy Heyward, herself a well-known playwright and novelist, adapted it into a successful play (1927), which George Gershwin then adapted into the famous opera *Porgy and Bess* (1935). Heyward was at his best as a local-colour writer, exploiting his deep knowledge of regional conditions, local vernacular, humour 'and folk-philosophy. Earlier he had produced a romantic collection of poems with Hervey ◊ Allen, *Carolina Chansons* (1922), and he continued to publish verse. Other fiction includes *Mamba's Daughters* (1929), also about Charleston Negro life, and *Peter Ashley* (1932), about Charleston during the Civil War. [MB]

Frank Durham, *DuBose Heyward: The Man Who Wrote 'Porgy'* (1954).

Hicks, Granville (1901–). Literary critic. Until his famous resignation from the Communist Party in 1939, one of the group of literary radicals who interpreted American literature from a Marxist point of view – see, for instance, his *The Great Tradition: An Interpretation of American Literature since the Civil War* (1933, revised 1935) and also his *Figures of Transition* (1939) on late-19th-century English literature. He was the literary editor and staff critic of *New Masses*, edited the collection *Proletarian Literature in the United States* (1935), and wrote a study of John ◊ Reed. More recently he has written fiction and edited a good collection of criticism of fiction, *The Living Novel* (1957). *Part of the Truth* (1965) is a modest but essential account of his career, which now seems part of American intellectual history. [MB]

Hillyer, Robert (1895–1961). Poet, novelist, translator, critic. Born in East Orange, New Jersey, he graduated from Harvard and served in the ambulance corps and in the army during the First World War. He

taught at various American universities, including Harvard and Kenyon College. His poetry, with its links with the Georgians and an acknowledged debt to Robert Bridges, tends toward the romantic-pastoral: *Sonnets and Other Lyrics* (1917); *In Time of Mistrust* (1939); *Collected Verse* (1933); *Collected Poems* (1961). He also wrote novels and three useful volumes of criticism – *Some Roots of English Poetry* (1933), *First Principles of Verse* (1938) and *In Pursuit of Poetry* (1960). [MB]

Himes, Chester (1909–). Novelist. He was born in Missouri, studied at Ohio State University and worked on the Cleveland *Daily News*. He is one of the leading Negro novelists in America, in direct descent from Richard ◊ Wright. *If He Hollers Let Him Go* (1945) violently delineates the conflict of black and white in a wartime shipyard in California, with a hero whose neurotic race-consciousness is a stage beyond Wright's Bigger Thomas. *Lonely Crusade* (1947) concerns race discriminations in the labour unions and the betrayal of a black American by the Communists. *Cast the First Stone* (1952) is about prison life, with largely white characters. *The Third Generation* (1954) is a penetrating study of middle-class Negro experience and the Negro college. *The Primitive* (1955) concerns inter-racial sexuality, treated with tragic passion. *Pink-toes* (1965) is a funny and highly topical satire on the sexual levelling between black and white, and *Cotton Comes to Harlem* (1965) is again a serious treatment of his familiar themes in a comic form. *The Heat's On* (1966) is a Harlem detective novel and *Blind Man with a Pistol* (1969) combines all his effects into a high point of his career. (◊ Negro Literature.) [EM]

Hoffman, Charles Fenno (1806–84). Novelist, poet, travel-writer. Born in New York, editor of several journals including the *Knickerbocker Magazine*, and one of the Knickerbocker group that included ◊ Irving, he wrote two famous accounts of prairie travels, *A Winter in the West* (1835) and *Wild Scenes in the Forest and Prairie* (1839), and three volumes of poems, many with Hudson River settings, brought together in *The Poems of Charles Fenno Hoffman* (1873). Best known is his novel *Greyslaer: A Romance of the Mohawk* (1840), dealing with the struggles of Whigs and Tories during the Revolution. [MB]

Hofstadter, Richard (1916–70). Historian. Born in Buffalo, N.Y., he taught in New York City universities. One of the leading historians of American political, social and cultural thought, his *Social Darwinism in American Thought* (1944, 1960), *The American Political Tradition* (1948) and *The Age of Reform: From Bryan to F.D.R.* (1955) are definitive, excellently written works. *Anti-Intellectualism in American Life* (1963) is an important and pioneer book whose effect ought to be salutary. *The Paranoid Style in American Politics* (1965) is a collection of essays and *The Progressive Historians* (1968) concerns F. J. Turner, C. Beard and V. L. Parrington. [E M]

Hollander, John (1929–). Poet, critic. Born in New York, he teaches at Yale and is poetry editor of *Partisan Review*. His volumes of verse are *A Crackling of Thorns* (1958), *Movie-Going and Other Poems* (1962) and *Visions from the Ramble* (1965). His critical work, besides numerous articles, includes *The Untuning of the Sky: Ideas of Music in English Poetry, 1500–1700* (1961). His verse is usually reflective and philosophical, the steady rigorous analysis of a given situation, moving towards an abstract insight. [M B]

Holmes, John Clellon (1926–). Novelist. Born in Massachusetts. His novel *Go* (1952) described the ◊ Beat Generation at first hand before it became a popular subject. 'The Philosophy of the Beat Generation' is an important essay reprinted on the same matter, *The Horn* (1958) an interesting jazz novel, and *Get Home Free* (1964) a sophisticated bleak story of New York and Louisiana. He has also published poems, and *Nothing More to Declare* (1968), a personal account of writing in the last two decades, with portraits of Allan ◊ Ginsberg, Jack ◊ Kerouac, Gershon Legman, etc.: an essential document for understanding the Beat Generation. [E M]

The Beats, ed. S. Krim (1960) (anthology).

Holmes, Oliver Wendell (1809–94). Essayist, poet, humorist, scientist, teacher. A descendent of Anne ◊ Bradstreet, he was born in Cambridge, Massachusetts, and brought up among the upper-class Boston 'Brahmins' he described as 'the harmless, inoffensive, untitled aristocracy'. During his time at Harvard (graduated in 1829, celebrating his class in a long series of reunion poems), a group of Calvinists ousted his father Abiel from his Cambridge parish; Holmes was to attack Calvinism throughout his life, especially in his poem 'The Deacon's Masterpiece' (1858), in which he satirizes Calvinist reliance on logic and compares their theology to a 'one-hoss shay' which suddenly collapsed. Abandoning law for medicine, he received his Harvard M.D. in 1836, and was Professor of Anatomy at Dartmouth (1838–40), then at Harvard (1847–82), publishing between appointments his important *Homeopathy and Its Kindred Delusions* (1842) and *The Contagiousness of Puerperal Fever* (1843). His aesthetic delight in physiognomy was shown in such poetry as the excellent *The Stethoscope Song* (1849), *The Living Temple* (1858) and *La Griesette* (1863). His pioneering *The Physiology of Versification* (1883) tried to find a common law governing metre and the pulse rate. Three 'medicated novels' were revealed as early studies in psychiatry by Clarence P. Obendorf in his abridgement *The Psychiatric Novels of Oliver Wendell Holmes* (1944; revised 1946). The best, *Elsie Venner* (1861), is a penetrating study of a schizophrenic girl, and also a thrust at Calvinism; Holmes said he tried in it to 'test the doctrine of "original sin" and human responsibility'. *The Guardian Angel* (1867) analyses multiple personality and the possibility of conflict between heredity and environment; *A Mortal Antipathy* (1885) examines a severe phobia. Both are inferior as novels.

Meanwhile Holmes had become famous as a witty and stimulating lecturer, clubman and conversationalist. From two early papers he developed his mastery of anecdotes, stories and epigrams ('Do not put your trust in money, put your money in trust'; 'Man has his will, woman her way') into *The Autocrat of the Breakfast Table* (1858), a series of brilliant and wide-ranging conversations, and its successors *The Professor at the Breakfast Table* (1860), *The Poet at the Breakfast Table* (1872) and *Over the Teacups* (1891). Other essays, written for *Atlantic Monthly*, became *Soundings from the Atlantic* (1864) and *Pages from an Old Volume of Life* (1883).

His biographies of Motley (1879) and of Emerson (1885) were disappointing except, significantly, for a chapter on Emerson's verse; Holmes himself hoped to be remembered primarily as a poet. From the appearance of 'Old Ironsides' (1830), a widely reprinted poem opposing the destruction of the frigate *Constitution*, he was a prolific writer of occasional verse. His work is always skilful, but only a few of his poems are much read, among them 'The Ballad of the Oysterman' (1830), a parody on the romantic ballad; 'The Lost Leaf' (1831), a half-sentimental, half-satirical character study; and his own favourite, the mystical 'The Chambered Nautilus' (1858). [MG]

Complete Poetical Works, ed. H. E. Scudder (1895); *Works* (13 vols., 1892); *Oliver Wendell Holmes: Representative Selections*, ed. S. I. Hayakawa and H. M. Jones (1939).

John T. Morse, *The Life and Letters of Oliver Wendell Holmes* (1896); William L. Schroeder, *Oliver Wendell Holmes: An Appreciation* (1909); Mark A. de Wolfe Howe, *Holmes of the Breakfast Table* (1939); Miriam R. Small, *Oliver Wendell Holmes* (1962).

Hooker, Thomas (1586–1647). Theologian. An Emmanuel College, Cambridge, Congregational divine, he went to New England in 1633 and three years later removed his congregation from Massachusetts to Connecticut, founding the town of Hartford in moderate opposition to rigid Calvinism. *Survey of the Sum of Church Discipline* (1648; with John Cotton) summarizes his tolerant reconciliatory role in the discussion of theocracy. Most of his other works survive in shorthand versions by admirers. An important early American democrat, he believed in the abolition of property and religious tests for the franchise, and that 'the foundation of authority is laid in the free consent of the people'. [EM]

G. L. Walker, *Thomas Hooker, Preacher, Founder, Democrat* (1891).

Hooper, Johnson Jones (1815–62). Southern humorist. He was born in North Carolina, edited the Montgomery, Alabama, *Mail* until 1861, and made a name as a humorist chiefly with *Some Adventures of Captain Suggs, Late of the Tallapoosa Volunteers* (1846) about an early dialect picaro whose principle is that 'it is good to be shifty in a new country'. Hooper became secretary of the Provisional Congress of the Southern States in 1861. [EM]

Hopkins, Lemuel ◊ Connecticut Wits.

Hopkinson, Francis (1737–91). Poet, satirical novelist. Born in Philadelphia, where he became a lawyer and Federal judge. He was the first student at the Academy of Philadelphia (University of Pennsylvania) and

claimed to have been the first American-born composer (in 1781 he wrote the 'dramatic allegorical cantata' *The Temple of Minerva*). He also signed the Declaration of Independence as New Jersey's delegate and wrote for the Revolutionary cause. *Battle of the Kegs* (1778), his best-known work, is a satirical poem (to be sung to *Yankee Doodle*) based on the incident of the mechanical gunpowder kegs sent down the Delaware to blow up the British fleet (the British burned his home town in revenge), and *A Pretty Story* (1774) is a satirical allegory of revolutionary politics. Hopkinson designed New Jersey's State seal and helped to design the American flag. John Adams unfairly described him as 'one of your pretty, little, curious, ingenious men'. [EM]

Hovey, Richard (1864–1900). Poet. Born in Normal, Illinois, he graduated from Dartmouth College, where he wrote early verse, and studied art before finally committing himself, stylishly, to poetry. He was one of the underestimated group of American *fin de siècle* poets who prepared for the transition to 'modern' verse. Perhaps more significant for the kind of sensibility he expressed than for the quality of his writing, he was devoutly 'Bohemian', celebrating in life and verse the vagabond existence (◊ Bohemianism). In 1891–2 he visited Europe and came under strong influence from the French symbolists, then strongly affecting writing in English; he translated Mallarmé and eight plays of Maeterlinck, who stirred his dramatic ambitions.

Hovey's wandering-poet ideal is best revealed in the three series of *Songs from Vagabondia* (1894, 1896, 1901), written with the Canadian Bohemian poet Bliss ◊ Carman. He early planned a cycle of poetic dramas on the Arthurian legends which he did not live to complete, though several parts of the work appeared between 1891 and 1907 (the posthumous *Holy Grail*). Other work includes *Seaward* (1893), an elegy on a friend's death, and the collections *Along the Trail* (1898) and *To the End of the Trail* (1908). [MB]

Bruce Weirick, *From Whitman to Sandburg in American Poetry* (1924); A. H. Macdonald, *Richard Hovey: Man and Craftsman* (1957).

Howard, Sidney Coe (1891–1939). Playwright. Born in Oakland, California. He studied at the University of California and in George Pierce ◊ Baker's 47 Workshop at Harvard. After war service he produced his first play, a Renaissance melodrama, *Swords* (1921). He died at the height of his career through a tractor accident in Massachusetts. His first prize-winner was *They Knew What They Wanted* (1924; musical version, *The Most Happy Fella*, 1957), a sensational but tender and truthful social drama of an ageing Italian vine-grower in the Napa Valley, California, who marries a mail-order wife. *The Silver Cord* (1926) exposes neurotic mother-love in New England; *The Late Christopher Bean* (1932) satirizes the art-dealing world; and *Alien Corn* (1933) opposes the Babbitt personality with an émigré musician from Vienna. Howard's competent abilities and realistic dialogue correspond to the social observation fiction of ◊ Marquand. [EM]

Howe, Julia Ward (1819–1910). Biographer, poetess. A New Yorker by birth, she was a famous female suffrage leader, promoter of prison reform and international peace, biographer of Margaret ◊ Fuller, and composer of 'The Battle Hymn of the Republic' (1862) and a mass of other poems. [EM]

Howells, William Dean (1837–1920). Novelist, critic, playwright. Born in Ohio, entirely self-educated, he began work at 9 in the printing office of his father and by 15 was contributing essays and poems to Ohio newspapers. Two autobiographical volumes, *A Boy's Town* (1890) and *Years of My Youth* (1916), re-create these years, while *My Literary Passions* (1895) shows the phenomenal reading he undertook to become a writer (it equipped him later to become Professor of Modern Languages at Harvard). In 1860 he published *Poems of Two Friends* (with John J. Piatt) and a campaign biography of Lincoln, and visited Boston to meet Lowell, Fields, Emerson and Hawthorne, while Holmes prophetically spoke of 'the apostolic succession'. The Lincoln biography won him the Consulate at Venice (1861–5), where he spent a happy and fruitful period recorded in the engaging sketches of *Venetian Life* (1866), *Italian Journeys* (1867) and the more scholarly *Modern Italian Poets* (1887). He returned to work on the *Nation* and attained the eminence of editing the *Atlantic Monthly*. His move from Boston to New York in 1888 signalled a change in the relative

cultural power of the two centres and also in Howells's thought, bringing a Tolstoyan social concern into his later novels. A prolific writer of highly esteemed, successful and influential books, he was the close friend of many major writers, including Stephen Crane, Frank Norris and Henry James, finely discussed in *Literary Friends and Acquaintance* (1900). He became first president of the American Academy of Arts and Letters (1908); celebrations marked his seventy-fifth birthday; he achieved the rarely filled role of 'Dean of American letters', though a new generation of writers was often disrespectful – Mencken called him 'an Agnes Repplier in pantaloons'.

Howells deserved much better; he is an important novelist in a distinctive mode, a central figure in American social fiction, as well as a superb memoirist and a significant cultural figure. His first novel, *Their Wedding Journey* (1872), is pleasant but slight; but *A Chance Acquaintance* (1873), *A Foregone Conclusion* (1875), *The Lady of the Aroostook* (1879), *The Undiscovered Country* (1880), *A Fearful Responsibility* (1881) and *Dr Breen's Practice* (1881) strike a distinctive note in the history of American fiction. Howells used his European experiences to develop the new species of the international novel; he also began to create, with subtle psychological realism, a novel of manners entirely American in inspiration and setting. His work reaches great distinction with his two most successful novels, *A Modern Instance* (1881) and *The Rise of Silas Lapham* (1885), the latter a fascinating, deep-rooted analysis of the social and moral predicaments of a newly rich New England family.

With *Indian Summer* (1886) Howells became the acknowledged leader of the American 'realist' school. In later novels his irony shifts further away from love-relationships into crucial social issues. *Annie Kilburn* (1888) indicts labouring conditions and false philanthropy; *A Hazard of New Fortunes* (1890) shows the clash of labour and capital in a strike; *An Imperative Duty* (1892) introduces a heroine of Negro blood; and *A Traveler from Altruria* (1894), with its sequel *Through the Eye of a Needle* (1907), contrasts American society with a well-ordered Utopia. Of his last novels, some revert to earlier themes or to scenes of youth and childhood. The best are *The Landlord at Lion's Head* (1897) and *The Kentons* (1902), while *The Vacation of the Kelwyns* (1920), is a delightful idyll set in the Centennial summer of 1876. Most of Howells's works are now being reprinted in a series of authoritative texts.

Howells wrote plays, four volumes of indifferent poetry, and numerous works of criticism, travel and autobiography. For many years the leading exponent of realism in the U.S.A., his insistence on the 'smiling aspects' of American life and the weight of his statements in *Criticism and Fiction* (1891) separated him from younger writers. This was not timidity. He believed the commonplace and average were typical of America, and made for genuine democratic art. Unobtrusively his often underrated novels assert that 'fidelity to experience and probability of motive' which he thought the essential condition of imaginative literature, and his great sense of community makes him that rare thing, an American *social* novelist. [HD]

Complete Plays, ed. W. J. Meserve (1960); William Dean Howells, ed. Clara and Rudolph Kirk (1950) (selections); Selected Writings, ed. H. S. Commager (1950).
Edwin H. Cady, The Road to Realism: The Early Years, 1837–1885, of William Dean Howells (1956) and The Realist at War: The Mature Years, 1885–1920, of William Dean Howells 1958); Everett Carter, Howells and the Age of Realism (1954); G. N. Bennett, William Dean Howells: The Development of a Novelist (1959); ed. K. E. Eble, Howells: A Century of Criticism (1962); C. Marburg Kirk, William Dean Howells and Art in His Time (1965).

Howes, Barbara (1914–). Poet. Born in Boston, Massachusetts, she edited in New York the magazine *Chimera* and, after marrying the poet William Jay ◊ Smith, spent considerable time in Italy and France. Her poetry in *In the Cold Country* (1954) and *Light and Dark* (1959) is written in a cultivated tradition, developing occasions drawn from domestic settings, life in foreign lands, and paintings and works of art into a kind of mythological intensity. Concerned primarily with delicate shades and the intricate pathways of human love, she has been praised by Louise ◊ Bogan, who has influenced her. Her latest volume is *Looking Up at Leaves* (1967). [MB]

Hughes, Langston (1902–67). Poet, novelist satirist, playwright. Born in Joplin, Missouri. His boyhood was spent in mid-Western towns, and as a young man he taught in Mexico, worked his father's ranch

there, became a Staten Island farmer, a seaman, a Montmartre night-club cook and a bus-boy in a Washington hotel – where he got Vachel ◊ Lindsay to read his poems at a recital (see his autobiography in *The Big Sea*, 1940, and *I Wonder as I Wander*, 1956). His first book of poetry, *The Weary Blues* (1926), began a long and admirable career as one of America's leading men of letters and Negro poets. His blues, ballads and lyrics have appeared in at least 7 volumes. His plays include *Mulatto* (1936) and *The Prodigal Son* (1964), and he has written opera libretti, lyrics for musicals, and the cantata *The Ballad of the Brown King. Not without Laughter* (1936) is a novel, and *The Ways of White Folks* (1934) short stories. Hughes' satirical sketches, written originally for a Negro paper, have been collected in *Simple Speaks His Mind* (1950), *The Best of Simple* (1961) and *Simple's Uncle Sam* (1965), the wry, witty adventures of one of American literature's most endearing characters, Jesse B. Simple of Harlem, U.S.A. Throughout his career Hughes has created a body of Negro American writing in which he uses the tradition of Whitman, ◊ Lindsay, ◊ Sandburg and ◊ Dunbar for his own genial irony and caustic humours. The recording of his *Weary Blues* is one of the few jazz-and-poetry performances of any quality. (◊ Negro Literature.) [EM]

Selected Poems (1959); The Panther and the Lash (1969).

Humphrey, William (1924–). Novelist. Born in Clarksville, Texas, he has made the South-west the chief subject matter of his fiction. But though writing in the Southern tradition of novels concerned with communities and families responding to forces of change, he has a psychological and sociological awareness that makes him much more than a regionalist. His two novels, *Home from the Hill* (1958) and *The Ordways* (1965), set in contrast legends from the past and present-day Texas, the latter concerning the Southern diaspora following the Civil War and the changes in Texan life. Though sometimes sentimental, his accuracy of rendering and his scope make him a figure of considerable interest in the recent fictional scene. [MB]

Humphreys, David. ◊ Connecticut Wits.

Huneker, James Gibbons (1860–1921). Critic, novelist. Born in Philadelphia, he studied music in Paris and was music critic on Philadelphia and New York newspapers; in this role he became the leading spokesman of Impressionism and did much to promote European *avant garde* tendencies in the U.S.A. He was a glutton of the arts, was closely associated with the cosmopolitan-Bohemian phase of the late-19th-century American arts (◊ Bohemianism), and hence not only advanced American modernism but promoted a style of aestheticism that was to come through to the *Smart Set* and the *New Yorker*. ◊ Mencken, a later version of the same kind of sensibility, admired him as 'the chief man of the movement of the nineties on this side of the ocean'. His early books are chiefly on music. Then came *Iconoclasts: A Book of Dramatists* (1905) and *Egoists: A Book of Supermen* (1909) on the little-known modernists of the European theatre, etc. *Promenades of an Impressionist* (1910) conveys his aesthetics and his highly Parisian sensibility. He is a sharp and colourful critic, if in what is now a faded manner. Among other works are two volumes of stories, *Melomaniacs* (1902) and *Visionaries* (1905), and *Painted Veils* (1920), a highly elaborated, fanciful, 'daring' novel about the New York art world. *Steeplejack* (2 vols., 1920), his autobiography, asserts his commitment to all the arts. [M B]

Letters, ed. J. Huneker (1922); *Intimate Letters*, ed. J. Huneker (1924).
Arnold T. Schwab, *James Gibbons Huneker, Critic of the Seven Arts* (1963); Benjamin de Casseres, *James Gibbons Huneker* (1925); Alfred Kazin, *On Native Grounds* (1942); Albert Parry, *Garrets and Pretenders* (1960).

Hunter, Evan (1926–   ). Novelist. Born in New York, he has published several novels under his own name – including *The Blackboard Jungle* (1954), *Buddwing* (1964) and *Last Summer* (1968) – and consider-

ably more under the pseudonym Ed McBain. For the most part these are realistic and well-constructed accounts of crime and detection in the 87th Precinct of a large American city. Hunter has often been praised for the way in which his detailed knowledge of police procedure communicates a sense of reality. [H D]

Cop Hunter (1956); *Lady Killer* (1958); *King's Ransom* (1959); *Give the Boys a Great Big Hand* (1960); *The 87th Squad* (1960); *See Them Die* (1961); *The Empty Hours* (1962); *Axe* (1964); *Fuzz* (1968); *Shotgun* (1968); *Sons* (1969).

Hutchinson, Thomas (1711–80). He was born in Boston, went to Harvard at 12, and by the age of 21, having made money, entered public life. His Toryism helped George III appoint him a chief justice and, later, governor of Massachusetts. It was he who provoked James Otis to remark 'Taxation without representation is tyranny'. In 1774 martial law was proclaimed and he had to account for his failures in England: he never went back. His chief work was *A Collection of Original Papers Relative to the History of the Colony of Massachusetts* (1764, 1767, 1818), the best account of his times. [E M]

Hyman, Stanley Edgar (1919–70). Critic. He was born in New York City, graduated at Syracuse University and taught at Bennington. His original and wide-ranging criticism includes *The Armed Vision* (1948), an important analysis of modern critics (some of the basic texts he edited in *The Critical Performance*, 1956), *Poetry and Criticism* (1961), concerning literary taste, *Nathanael West* (1962), *The Tangled Bank: Darwin, Marx, Frazer and Freud as Imaginative Writers* (1962) and *The Promised End* (1963), collected essays and reviews, also assembled in *Standards: A Chronicle of Books of Our Times* (1966). [M B]

I

Ignatow, David (1914–   ). Poet. Author of *Poems* (1948), *Gentle Weight Lifter* (1955), *Say Pardon* (1961), *Figures of the Human* (1964) and *Rescue the Dead* (1968), he left college during the Depression and, until he turned to full-time teaching in 1965, worked as a businessman in his native New York City, lecturer at the New School for Social Research, editor of the *Beloit Poetry Journal* (1949–59) and poetry editor of the *Nation* (1962–3). His flat, colloquial style re-creates Brooklyn speech rhythms in the telling of concentrated episodes which suggest an ironic mythic vision of modern city life. *Poems 1934–1969* (1970) contains previously uncollected and unpublished poetry. [BP]

Imagism. A poetic movement flourishing in England and the United States between 1912 and 1917, and originating in the theories, expounded in London from 1908 onwards, of the anti-romantic aesthetician T. E. Hulme and the polyglot poetry reviewer F. S. Flint. Ezra ♢ Pound's *Ripostes* (1912) included five miniature poems by Hulme, his 'Complete Poetical Works', and during this year Pound coined the term 'Les Imagistes'. A platform for Imagism was found in Harriet ♢ Monroe's *Poetry* (Chicago), where in March 1913 Flint and Pound published a few definitions and principles (♢ Little Magazines). *Des Imagistes: An Anthology* (1914) included poems by Flint, Pound, Richard Aldington, H.D. (Hilda ♢ Doolittle), Ford Madox Ford, William Carlos ♢ Williams, and Amy ♢ Lowell, thus associating English and American poets. By then Pound's interest in the movement was waning, and after a row with Amy Lowell over the distribution of her financial resources, he dissociated himself from the group. *Some Imagist Poets* (1915) contained a new statement of Imagist doctrine by Aldington and Amy Lowell, and poems by Aldington, Lowell, Flint, H.D., John Gould ♢ Fletcher and D.H. Lawrence. These six poets were represented in similarly entitled anthologies issued in 1916 and 1917, after which by general consent no further collections appeared.

The brief history of Imagism is one of irascibility and recrimination, with Pound as the chief source of disturbance. However, the foremost Imagist theoreticians, Hulme, Flint, Pound and Aldington, were largely in agreement on the following principles: that Japanese *haiku* and *tanka*, certain lesser-known Greek and Latin writers, 19th-century French poetry and theory, and a few neglected English figures had more to teach the contemporary poet than most of the conventionally accepted 'great English poets'; that Victorian verbosity, heavy-handed didacticism, platitudinous ornamentation and fondness for ethereal abstractions were crimes against art; that the poetic virtues include precision, concentration, firmness of outline, freshness and clarity of vision, and the use of striking, arresting analogies; and that each emotion has its distinctive rhythm and need not pay heed to obsolete metrical rules, i.e. free verse, Flint's 'unrhymed cadence', is to be preferred.

To these purificatory rather than revolutionary postulates the ten poets most closely associated with Imagism remained for a very few years more or less loyal. Of these poets, Fletcher, Ford and Amy Lowell were always more impressionistic than imagistic; Lawrence and Williams were affected by the movement rather than dedicated to it; Flint and Hulme were more influential as theorists than as practitioners; and Aldington and Pound were either too adventurous or too versatile to be long fulfilled within the self-imposed limitations of Imagism. The purest, finest and most consistent application of Imagist principles is to be found in the poetry of H.D.

Imagism, as a self-proclaiming movement, died in 1917. Almost by definition it was a movement destined to produce minor poetry, and apart from H.D. all the chief Imagists soon went in search of broader horizons. But its influence upon subsequent poetry has nonetheless been considerable and for the most part salutary. Imagism was the first organized attack in this century upon sloppy approximation in description, rhythmic monotony, staleness of perception and cultural parochialism. Further, one of its most striking features was that it was Anglo-American in character, and for a time closely linked two poetic traditions. [R W B]

Glenn Hughes, *Imagism and the Imagists* (1960); Stanley K. Coffman, Jr, *Imagism* (1951).

Imlay, Gilbert (1754?–1828?). Novelist, propagandist. He was born in New Jersey, fought in the Revolution, and in 1783 involved himself in shady land sales in Kentucky. He fled the lawsuits and turned up in the 1790s in London and Paris radical circles with Joel ◊ Barlow and Tom ◊ Paine. In 1793 he was in the Girondist plot to seize Louisiana from Spain, and he fathered a boy on Mary Wollstonecraft. The next known fact is his burial on the island of Jersey. *A Topographical Description of the Western Territory of North America* (1792) takes the form of 11 enthusiastic letters to an English friend. *The Emigrants* (1793) is the first novel of the area between Pittsburg and the Mississippi, and an early version of the 'American innocence versus wicked Old Europe' myth, with its basis in 'natural rights', including the rights of women and divorce. America sustains men's natural goodness and is free from 'the commercial spirit', the class system and 'the tyranny of custom'. Imlay's epistolary novel is readable, psychologically fairly full in the Richardson manner, and designed to tempt Englishmen to America. [E M]

Inge, William (1913–   ). Playwright. He was born in Kansas, taught in Missouri and was general arts critic on the St Louis *Times* (1943). He produced his first play, *Farther Off from Heaven*, in 1947, inspired by Tennessee Williams' *The Glass Menagerie*. His very successful plays are psychodramas involving the solution of personal and social problems by introspection and togetherness among average mid-Westerners: *Come Back Little Sheba* (1950), *Picnic* (1953), *Bus Stop* (1955) and *The Dark at the Top of the Stairs* (1957). *A Loss of Roses* (1960), *Natural Affection* (1963) and *Where's Daddy?* (1966) show a distinct easing towards melodrama and routine. [E M]

R. Baird Shuman, *William Inge* (1965).

Irving, Washington (1783–1859). Short-story writer, historian. Born in New York City. His father was an ex-petty officer, a hardware dealer and a Calvinist deacon. Irving was very different and needed the less strict encouragement of his mother for the development of his sensibility, which preferred dreamy out-of-doors wandering to school. While he trained as a lawyer, his bookishness turned towards literature. His first and anonymous work was *The Letters of Jonathan Oldstyle, Gent* (1802–3) in the *Morning Chronicle*, followed by the *Salmagundi Papers* (1807–8), again a series of sketches and essays. In 1809 appeared his *History of New York,* called the 'Knicker-bocker History' after its supposed author; it begins as a comic parody of historical scholarship and ends as a straight account of Dutch colonization. Financial and critical success decided him on a literary career, slightly interrupted by war service in 1812. In 1815 he travelled to Europe and stayed 17 years; when he needed money he wrote *The Sketch Book of Geoffrey Crayon, Gent* (1819–20), published in instalments in New York and as a book in London (with the help of Scott). Irving's reputation as a gentleman of letters was established. *Bracebridge Hall* (1822), a dullish celebration of the English squire, and *Tales of a Traveller* (1824), a hack assemblage of stories, were blasted by critics, and he left for Spain and wrote a life of Columbus (1828), which swelled his patriotism, his reputation and his pocket. *The Conquest of Granada* (1829) is a wretched historical romance of the Moors in Spain but it gained him Spanish honours and a room in a palace where he wrote a better book, *The Alhambra* (1832). He reluctantly left Spain to become American Legation secretary in London, resigning in 1832 to return to America and be shocked by its 'all pervading commonplace'. But his extensive journeys made *Tours on the Prairies* (1835), and the Astors commissioned a fur-trade epic based on the family manuscripts: *Astoria* (1836, 1849) – after which he bought a Hudson valley cottage and decorated it with ivy from Scott's own house. He returned to Spain as ambassador in 1842 and back in New York wrote lives of Goldsmith, Washington and Astor before he died. The 32 pieces of his *Sketch Book* contain his best work. Embedded in whimsy and bland Anglicized stylishness in imitation of English essayists, and in sentimental landscape descriptions, are two famous tales, 'Rip Van Winkle', with a hero whose easy-going Dutch ancestors retain him in the Kaatskill mountains where he misses

20 years of American progress, and 'The Legend of Sleepy Hollow', in which a Yankee schoolmaster, Ichabod Crane, finds his belief in old New England witchcraft disables him before the supposed ghost of a headless Hessian left-over from the Revolutionary War, and loses him the hand of an heiress. Irving transformed the German originals of these tales into American myths. He encouraged American cultural life by his professional example. [EM]

Works (40 vols., 1910).
Pierre M. Irving, *The Life and Letters of Washington Irving* (4 vols., 1862–4); Stanley T. Williams, *The Life of Washington Irving* (2 vols., 1935); W. L. Hedges, *Washington Irving* (1965).

Jackson, Shirley (1919–65). Novelist. She was born in San Francisco, and after her marriage to Stanley Edgar ◊ Hyman settled in Vermont to a middle-class intellectual life she described in *Life among the Savages* (1953) and *Raising Demons* (1957). The dark obverse side to these humorous chronicles is her novels of mental morbidity and the supernatural in ordinary localities – *The Road through the Wall* (1948), *Hangsaman* (1951) and *The Bird's Nest* (1954). The personal nightmare penetrates the weird allegory of *The Lottery* (1949), *The Sundial* (1958), *The Haunting of Hill House* (1959) and *We Have Always Lived in the Castle* (1962). *The Witchcraft of Salem Village* (1956) is a children's account of the 1690 trials. *Come Along with Me* (1968) includes posthumous work and is edited by her husband. [EM]

The Magic of Shirley Jackson, ed. Stanley E. Hyman (1966).

James, Henry, Sr (1811–82). Philosopher. Of wealthy Albany, New York, background, he withdrew from Princeton Theological Seminary in revolt against Calvinism and in due course became a Swedenborgian with ◊ Transcendentalist overtones. A friend of many major European and American thinkers, including Emerson and Carlyle, he travelled in Europe and lectured widely in the States, while his own family became a remarkable community in itself (Henry ◊ James, William ◊ James). He was a complex social thinker and reformer, as books like his *Christianity the Logic of Creation* (1857), *Substance and Shadow* (1863) and *Society the Redeemed Form of Man* (1879) show. His influence on both his sons, the philosopher and the novelist, has come more and more to light. [MB]

F. O. Matthiessen, *The James Family* (1947); Austin Warren, *The Elder Henry James* (1934); Frederick H. Young, *The Philosophy of Henry James, Sr* (1951).

James, Henry (1843–1916). Novelist, short-story writer, playwright, critic, essayist. He was born in New York City, the second of the five children of Henry ◊ James, Sr, the

Swedenborgian philosopher, who later took his family to Europe in order that the children might receive a better 'sensuous education'. Henry was educated intermittently at schools in Geneva, Paris, Boulogne and Bonn; during 1862–3 he attended Harvard Law School. In 1869 he made his first extended adult trip to Europe, and the record of these months and the later period 1872–4, also spent abroad, is to be found in his first published books: *A Passionate Pilgrim and Other Tales* (1875) and *Transatlantic Sketches* (1875), travel essays which complement and interact with the fiction to present a young American's highly enthusiastic European impressions. For a year James lived in Paris, but in 1877 he decided to settle in London, where he remained, with the exception of frequent excursions to the continent and fewer to his native land, until 1896. During his last years he lived and wrote in Lamb House, Rye; from this period the famous 'legend of the master' takes its origin. Returning to London in 1912, he felt the advent of the First World War keenly, and in protest against what he considered to be American tardiness assumed British nationality in 1915. Next year he suffered a stroke ('So here it is at last, the distinguished thing', he is reported as saying), and on his death-bed received the Order of Merit.

It is customary and convenient to divide James's career into three periods. In the first he made his reputation as the originator of the international novel and story. His first published novel, *Roderick Hudson*, about the moral and artistic disintegration of an American in Rome, appeared in 1876; it was followed by *The American* (1877), the first self-conscious and consistently serious attempt to dramatize in fiction the social relationships between the Old World and the New; *The Europeans* (1878), a subtle examination of the impact of two slightly raffish Europeans upon their cousins in the rural Boston of the 1830s; *Washington Square* (1881); and such charming productions as 'Daisy Miller' (1879), probably James's most popular single work in his lifetime, and the witty tale 'An International

Episode' (1879). This period culminated in the undisputed masterpiece *The Portrait of a Lady* (1881), where the accepted contrasts of the international theme are subordinated to the psychological realization of the heroine's character in a way which foreshadows his later subject matter and experiments in technique; the central focus shifts to the single observing consciousness and to the growth of that moral consciousness as a result of the incompatibility of the demands of the individual and those of society. The novels and tales of these six years present James's fullest and most complex use of the international subject for primary rather than secondary effects. During this period he created the twin figures of the American girl and the American businessman in Europe, and also discovered, most notably in *The Portrait of a Lady*, the artistic possibilities offered by the Europeanized American. Manipulating his favourite theme for a variety of purposes and with differing emphasis, James eschews any easy preference for one civilization over another, allowing a hypothetical ideal combination of moral values to emerge from the interplay of two societies and the concomitant mixture of manners.

The themes of the second period, from the mid-1880s to 1897, are more specifically English, though earlier contrasts appear in such tales as 'Lady Barberina' (1884) and *The Reverberator* (1888). Major works of this decade are *The Bostonians* (1886) and *The Princess Casamassima* (1886), the one a satiric account of female emancipation in Boston, the other a richly observed novel of anarchists and aristocrats in London, which together effectively refute the charge that James was neither interested in nor capable of rendering immediate social concerns and actualities. During 1890–5 an intense preoccupation with the possibilities of the stage, which first emerges in *The Tragic Muse* (1890) and which lasted until the disastrous first night of *Guy Domville* in 1895, did not prevent him from writing an impressive group of stories centring on the nature and predicament of the creative artist. His unsuccessful experiments in dramatic technique nevertheless profoundly influenced the structure of his later novels.

The third period of James's literary career opens with *The Spoils of Poynton* (1897) and *What Maisie Knew* (1897), and includes such works as *The Turn of the Screw* (1898), *The Awkward Age* (1899) and *The Sacred Fount* (1901). If criticism is still undecided as to the merits of some of these last works, an even sharper division of opinion is observable in the case of the three novels *The Wings of the Dove* (1902), *The Ambassadors* (1903) and *The Golden Bowl* (1904), in which, it is sometimes claimed, an over-elaboration of motive is accompanied by an over-refinement in style. In them James develops most fully his commitment to the single point of view and his theories on 'scenic' progression in a subtle and intricate prose which is capable of reproducing every nuance of the fine moral intelligence with which he endows his characters. These novels have been praised and denigrated in a wide variety of interpretations, which ranges from their acceptance as moral fables of a high order to a consideration of them as James's reworkings of his father's Swedenborgian theology and ethics.

In 1904 James visited the United States for the first time since 1883. The result was *The American Scene* (1907), at once a fine travel book and James's farewell to a country he could not live in. On his return he began the prodigious task of revising his novels and tales for the selective 'New York' edition of his works (24 vols., 1907–9). Two posthumously published novels, *The Ivory Tower* (1917) and *The Sense of the Past* (1917), were later added.

James was also a remarkable critic who ranged widely in European and American literature. Throughout his career he was preoccupied with questions of form, from his early plea in the often reprinted essay 'The Art of Fiction' (included in *Partial Portraits*, 1888) to his final assessments in *Notes on Novelists* (1914). His prefaces to the volumes in the 'New York' edition, conveniently collected by R. P. Blackmur as *The Art of the Novel* (1934), established categories and principles which have deeply affected – and not always for the best – later developments in criticism. Among his many other works one may mention the biographies *Hawthorne* (1879) and *William Wetmore Story* (1903); his engaging travel essays, the best of which were issued as *The Art of Travel* (ed. M. D. Zabel, 1958); and the unfinished autobiography: *A Small Boy and Others* (1913), *Notes of a Son and Brother* (1914) and *The Middle Years* (1917), together edited by F. W. Dupee as *Henry James: Autobiography* (1956).

The 'New York' edition has been recently reprinted (1961–6), a text followed in *The Novels and Stories of Henry James* (35 vols., 1921–3) which includes all the fiction published in James's lifetime. Leon Edel has edited the *Complete Tales*, which reprints the 112 short stories (12 vols., 1962–7) and the *Complete Plays* (1949). Robert E. Spiller's excellent survey of James criticism up to 1954 appears in *Eight American Authors* (ed. Floyd Stovall, 1956); the revised edition of 1963 contains a check list covering 1955 to 1962. See also 'Criticism of Henry James: A Selected Checklist', *Modern Fiction Studies*, III (1957) and *Modern Fiction Studies*, XII (1966). [HD]

Letters, ed. Percy Lubbock (1920); *Selected Letters*, ed. L. Edel (1956); *The Notebooks*, ed. F. O. Matthiessen and K. Murdock (1947).
Leon Edel, *Henry James: The Untried Years, 1843–1870* (1953), *Henry James: The Conquest of London, 1870–1883* (1962), *Henry James: The Middle Years, 1884–1895* (1963), *Henry James: The Treacherous Years, 1895–1901* (1969); F. O. Matthiessen *Henry James: The Major Phase* (1946); ed. F. W. Dupee, *The Question of Henry James* (1945); Richard Poirier, *The Comic Sense of Henry James* (1960); Oscar Cargill, *The Novels of Henry James* (1961); Dorothea Krook, *The Ordeal of Consciousness in Henry James* (1962); Maxwell Geismar, *Henry James and His Cult* (1964); Douglas Jefferson, *Henry James and the Modern Reader* (1964); L. B. Holland, *The Expense of Vision* (1964); S. Gorley Putt, *A Reader's Guide to Henry James*; ed. Tony Tanner, *Henry James: Modern Judgements* (1968); ed. R. Gard, *Henry James: The Critical Heritage* (1968).

James, William (1842–1910). Philosopher, psychologist. James was born in New York City of a father, Henry ◊ James, Sr, himself a considerable philosopher, and rich enough to send his sons abroad for much of their education. In Paris, the young James conceived the ambition of being a painter; at Harvard, which he entered at 19, his interests shifted to biology, and in 1865 he went with ◊ Agassiz on a scientific expedition to Brazil, returning to Harvard to enter the Medical School, and taking his M.D. in 1870. In 1872 he began his teaching career of 35 years at Harvard as an instructor in physiology, but his interest gradually shifted again, first to psychology and finally to philosophy. In 1860 he published his *Principles of Psychology*, which is a classic in its field. In 1901–2, he gave the Gifford lectures in Edinburgh on *The Varieties of Religious Experience*. The

development of his pragmatic philosophy came late in his life; *Pragmatism* was published in the year of his retirement from Harvard in 1907, and *A Pluralistic Universe* in 1909. He died at his summer home in Chocorua, New Hampshire, on 26 August 1910. He was the elder brother of the novelist, Henry James.

Regarding James's achievements as a philosopher opinions vary, but there is no doubt that his thought was influential on writers as various as his brother Henry and Gertrude Stein and that he was a remarkable writer with a unique personality. He had an 'artistic temperament' whose ups and downs were accentuated by a life-long frailty of health. He was impatient of pedantry, of the formal side of teaching, and even of philosophy as a purely intellectual pursuit; he was impulsive, imaginative, deeply affectionate, unconventional in his tastes, sympathetic with spiritualism and mysticism, and broadly democratic in his feelings – 'a sort of Irishman among the Brahmins', as Santayana put it. These traits appear in his writing, and give it colour and vitality. *The Varieties of Religious Experience*, especially, is remarkable for its balance of rationality and sympathy for extreme religious experiences.

The leading idea running through James's thought is that of the will as the dominant factor in experience. His studies as a biologist suggested to him that man is an organism made for action. Even the emergence in our experience of distinct things and concepts is due to the attempt to satisfy practical needs. Life begins for the infant as 'a blooming, buzzing confusion', in which balls and bottles are slowly singled out because they satisfy some interest. When concepts are formed, they are usually fashioned in terms of utility; spoons are things to eat with and knives to cut with; 'the meaning of essence is teleological,' said James in the *Psychology*. His dynamic way of conceiving the mind appears again in the James-Lange theory of emotion: 'we feel sorry because we cry, angry because we strike, afraid because we tremble.' Some object sets up a reaction in us, and the emotion *is* our feeling of this reaction. The secret of emotional control is therefore the control of the bodily responses.

The most famous expression of James's view of primacy of the will is found, however, in his pragmatism. He did not believe that wholly disinterested thought was possible; a philosophy is accepted as much because it satisfies the heart's desire or is congenial to one's temperament as because it convinces the intellect. But James did not adopt his pragmatism all at once. *The Will to Believe* (1897) was a half-way house to the later doctrine. In that much-discussed essay, he held that, if probabilities were balanced and the doctors disagreed, we were justified in accepting the belief which worked best, in the sense of leading to the most satisfying results in practice. But he came to see that he could not stop there; if the practical consequences of a belief were really relevant to its truth in such a case, they must be so generally.

Pragmatism was essentially a doctrine of truth. Whereas philosophers of the past had held that the truth of a belief lay in its correspondence with fact or its coherence with experience as a whole, James held that 'the true . . . is only the expedient in our way of thinking'. If the belief in God or in immortality leads to lives of more courage, peace and happiness, it is, so far, true. This teaching was heard gladly by many persons concerned to hold their religious beliefs, but it has not worn well. It is in trouble, for example, when it comes to beliefs about the past or to those scientific beliefs which are without practical effects.

James was not afraid of the unconventional. He was an eager investigator of spiritualistic mediums. In religion he was inclined to the view of a finite and struggling Deity, warring like ourselves against evil; and in the *Varieties* he regards certain mystical experiences as probable revelations of a superhuman consciousness. In later life he developed an ingenious theory of the relation of the mental and physical realms. There existed only one neutral stuff, which became mental or physical according to context; tables and chairs when taken in the context of our thoughts and feelings were mental; taken merely in their relations of space and causality, they were physical. This theory of 'neutral monism' found an advocate for a time in Bertrand Russell.

Though not a rigorous thinker, James's insight into human nature, his power of describing it, and his capacity for friendship were extraordinary. Fortunately he has been made the subject of one of the best biographies of the century (see Perry, below). [BB]

Letters, ed. Henry James (2 vols., 1920); *The Writings*, ed. John McDermott (1968).
R. B. Perry, *The Thought and Character of William James* (2 vols., 1935); F. O. Matthiessen, *The James Family* (1947); G. W. Allen, *William James: A Biography* (1967).

Jarrell, Randall (1914–65). Poet, critic, novelist. He was born in Nashville, Tennessee, served in the air force in the Second World War, taught at a number of universities, was consultant in poetry at the Library of Congress 1956–8, and worked on the *Nation*. His distinguished poetry began with *Blood for a Stranger* (1942) and subsequently appeared in *Little Friend, Little Friend* (1945), *Losses* (1948), *The Seven-League Crutches* (1951), *Selected Poems* (1955), *The Woman at the Washington Zoo* (1960) and *The Lost World* (1965). His characteristic subjects were the victims of war and historical crisis as examples of the ineradicable human condition, only briefly and uncertainly ameliorated in childhood. Although his poems have the tight elliptical quality of much ◊ New Criticism verse, there is an unmistakable anguish and compassion entirely personal to him, as if the ills of the unstable and violent forties had penetrated into his own sensibility and had to be exorcized. Poems in the last two books have the additional poignancy of the self-irony of the poet whose own condition hardly seems to him to warrant his analysis and evaluation of his fellow men. The added intensity raised his freer forms to a fresh quality. Of his criticism, *Poetry and the Age* (1953) is incisive and generous, and is especially valuable for its estimations by careful quotation, and *A Sad Heart at the Supermarket* (1962) includes good studies of Kipling and Malraux and a classic essay in wry disillusionment with western chances of literacy. His novel of academic life, *Pictures from an Institution* (1954), is both hilariously funny and a comment on the hopeless condition of certain liberal arts colleges. Jarrell stood for a level of critical integrity and independent poetry which is rare in a culture which tended towards inimical groups. [EM]

The Complete Poems (1969); *The Third Book of Criticism* (1969).
Ed. Robert Lowell, Peter Taylor and Robert Penn Warren, *Randall Jarrell 1914–1965* (1967); S. Stepanchev, *American Poetry since 1945* (1965); M. L. Rosenthal, *The Modern Poets* (1960).

Jeffers, Robinson (1887–1962). Poet. He was born in Pittsburg, and as a boy, tutored by his father, a theologian and classical scholar, his education continued lengthily in Switzerland, Germany and America. When he was 16 the family settled in California; he graduated from Occidental College, California, in 1905. His studies in medicine, forestry and literature in various colleges resulted in that broad scholarly and geographical interest which penetrates his poetry. But he could not give his complete time to poetry until he received an inheritance and married a woman whose secure vitality warmed his own austerity. He settled in Carmel, on the Monterey coast of California, whose mountains over the Pacific and timeless, barbaric natural life are so active in his work – 'people living – amid magnificent unspoiled scenery – essentially as they did in the Idylls or the Sagas, or in Homer's Ithaca. Here life was purged of its ephemeral accretions.' At Point Sur he built a granite house and worked out his solitude in its tower.

His first two volumes of poetry, *Flagons and Apples* (1912) and *Californians* (1916), are most conventional, but *Tamar and Other Poems* (1924) marks the beginning of his impressively unique career. 'Tamar', based on Samuel 11:13 and Shelley's *The Cenci*, is his first long narrative poem, transposing the Old Testament story of cursed heredity, incest and revenge to California: it is representative of Jeffers's vision of mankind doomed with introspection and lust. 'The Tower beyond Tragedy' is a brilliant drama based on the *Oresteia*, and the title poem of *Roan Stallion* (1925) concerns a man killed by his horse, identified with a woman as a primitive god. His following volumes include *The Women at Point Sur* (1927), *Cawdor* (1928), *Dear Judas* (1929), *Descent to the Dead* (1931), *Thurso's Landing* (1932), *Give Your Heart to the Hawks* (1933), *Solstice* (1935), *Such Counsels You Gave Me* (1937), *Selected Poetry* (1938), *Be Angry at the Sun* (1941), *Medea* (1946), *The Double Axe* (1948), *Hungerfield* (1954) and a version of Euripides' *Hippolytus*.

Of the poems and plays in these, 'Cawdor' is an American Hippolytus myth, 'Thurso's Landing' a powerful poem of lust, impotence and insanity in Monterey, and 'Give Your Heart to the Hawks' the embodiment of his philosophy that humanity must develop the peace and endurance of rocks, the solitude of hawks, and respect for a God who is 'hardly a friend of humanity'. *Medea* (staged in New York in

1947 and 1965) is his greatest play. His shorter poems are elegies and conversations on similar themes: the steady background of nature, the pessimistic human foreground of men, a dark vision influenced by Nietzsche and Freud. His sensibility seems to look longingly away from human life towards the cold mysteries of nature, viewed from the heights of his own Sierras. He returned repeatedly to the theme of incest to embody his visionary drama of sterile life and inturned passion cut off from nature and inviting disaster. Merely to reject Christianity for a faith based on lust and energy, like the ranting of Dr Barclay in *The Women at Point Sur*, is to invite bloodshed and waste. Not anarchy of impulse, but 'to uncentre the human mind from itself' is what man needs. Jeffers's aim was 'to awake dangerous images and call the hawks'. His language and line reject modern symbolism and rhetoric, and speak directly and passionately in classical clarity. His brutality can be monotonous, but where his characters grow archetypal against monumental nature, his poems have a unique grandeur. [HB/EM]

The Selected Poetry (1959); *Selected Poems* (1965). L. C. Powell, *Robinson Jeffers: The Man and His Work* (revised edn, 1940); R. Squires, *The Loyalties of Robinson Jeffers* (1956).

Jefferson, Thomas (1743–1826). Reformer, third President of the United States. He was born in Virginia, graduated from William and Mary College in 1762, became a lawyer and was elected to the Virginia House of Burgesses in 1769. His paper *A Summary View of the Rights of British Americans*, sent to the Virginia convention in 1774, claimed 'natural rights' for emigrant settlement, the end of British taxation, and the need for a trade agreement with Britain. Its sane, clear, flexible prose illuminates the *Declaration of Independence* in 1776, drafted by Jefferson, with changes by John Adams and ◊ Franklin; it was partly indebted for ideas to John Locke's *Two Treatises of Civil Government* (1690) and *Letters Concerning Toleration* (1689, 1690, 1692), and influenced by George Mason's *Virginia Declaration of Rights* (1776). Jefferson was a member of the Virginia House of Delegates (1776–9) and governor of Virginia (1779–81), his main legislature concerning laws of inheritance and religious freedom. He tried to establish free education and the gradual abolition of slavery. In retirement at his magnificently designed Monticello he worked on his great *Notes on the State of Virginia* (1784–5). Where the *Declaration* set out a general philosophy of the Revolution and the reasons for colonial resistance, *Notes* places the idea of freedom in a wider context. After 7 chapters on the geography and resources of Virginia, 16 chapters delineate its social and political history, and through this scheme Jefferson set out to show that nature and man were not inferior in the New World, that America had already produced men of genius, and that the Indians themselves were 'formed in mind as well as in body on the same module' as Europeans. But he believed Negroes were inferior, although entitled to freedom and opportunity. The master–slave relationship was degrading; a Negro insurrection was to be feared; freedom was more expedient (Jefferson owned over 100 slaves). He also believed country workers were God's chosen people; towns bred vice as well as bad health. The independent farmer is the ideal: law and order are based on his property-owning self-reliance. Jefferson modified this view later ('our people have a decided taste for navigation and commerce'), but it is his agrarian opinions that have had a lasting effect on American belief.

Jefferson was elected to Congress in 1783 and in 1784 was appointed Franklin's assistant on the trade treaties with France. He observed the early French Revolution and deplored its later violence and imperialism. In Europe, he studied the classical architecture which became the basis of his plans for Virginia's state capitol and the subsequent national architectural style. After his appointment as first American secretary of state in 1790, he became the Republican leader in opposition to the Federalists under Alexander Hamilton, whom he suspected of monarchism, aristocracy and commercial industrialism. He was Vice-President under John Adams (one result was his *Manual of Parliamentary Practice*, 1801) and President in 1800, his main achievements being the Louisiana Purchase of 1803 and the subduing of pirates who had menaced shipping for some years past. The last years of his life he spent at Monticello, experimenting with agricultural methods, inventing and studying. He sold his large library to Congress in 1814 (the basis of the Library of Congress), to replace what the British had burned. Between 1811 and 1814 he carried on an important correspondence with John Adams.

The University of Virginia, founded on his plans and curriculum, opened in 1825. Jefferson's knowledge was extensive and utilitarian: he was an architect, a gardener and farmer, a mathematician and scientist, a lawyer, an inventor and a musician. As a deist, like Franklin and Paine, he believed in tolerance and the separation of church and state. As a founder of the Democratic Party, he advocated the abolition of slavery, freedom of the Press, States rights and isolationism. Apart from *Notes on Virginia*, his writings are mainly political pamphlets and papers, letters, and an *Autobiography* (1820; mostly on public life). All his writing is practical, since, as he said, 'literature is not yet a distinct profession with us ... the first object of young societies is bread and covering'. The standard edition of *The Papers of Thomas Jefferson* (Princeton, various editors) runs to nearly 20 volumes. [EM]

Life and Selected Writings, ed. A. Koch and W. Peden (Modern Library, 1944); *The Basic Writings*, ed. P. S. Foner (1944).

Claude G. Bowers, *The Young Jefferson* (1945), *Jefferson and Hamilton* (1925), *Jefferson in Power* (1936); Leonard W. Levy, *Jefferson and Civil Liberties: The Darker Side* (1963); Albert J. Nock, *Jefferson* (1961); Dumas Malone, *Jefferson and His Times* (3 vols., 1962).

Jewett, Sarah Orne (1849–1909). Novelist, story writer. Though she went to Berwick Academy, she seems to have derived her main education accompanying her doctor father on calls to farms and fishing villages around South Berwick, Maine, where she was born and about which she wrote. Early stimulated by Harriet Beecher Stowe's novels of New England life to describe the declining harbours and deserted farms of the Maine Coast, she published her first sketch at 19 in the *Atlantic Monthly*; it was republished in a series assembled as *Deephaven* (1877). Then followed *A Country Doctor* (1884), *A Marsh Island* (1885) and *A White Heron* (1886), tales of a New England girl declining marriage for a medical career, a planter's love for a farmer's daughter, and a girl's heart torn between a white heron and a predatory ornithologist. But her best book is *The Country of the Pointed Firs* (1896), a series of sketches written in a compact evocative style, modelled in part on Flaubert's, to catch (as in *Deephaven*) the spirit of the isolated Maine seaport of Dunnet ('more like one of the lazy English seaside towns ... not in the least American') as seen by a summer visitor. She hears landlady's gossip, meets the local characters (the Queen's twin, born in the same hour as Victoria; shy William Blackett, courting for 40 years a girl who lives with an invalid mother; poor fisherfolk, retired sea-captains old gentlefolk) and draws together the cross-threads of reminiscence till a delicately humorous fabric is woven of a people, a place and its past – making this her most successful attempt at conveying the atmosphere of loss, decay and regret haunting a coast once bustling with West Indian trade. Other books and stories include: *The King of Folly Island* (1888), *A Native of Winby* (1893), *The Life of Nancy* (1895), the historical romance *The Tory Lover* (1901) and the posthumously collected *Verses* (1916). Her life-long friend Annie Fields edited her *Letters* (1911); Willa ◊ Cather, who deeply admired and was much influenced by her work, edited her stories. [HB]

The Best Stories, ed. Willa Cather (2 vols., 1925; reissued as *The Country of the Pointed Firs and Other Stories*, 1 vol., 1955).
F. O. Matthiessen, *Sarah Orne Jewett* (1929); Richard Cary, 'Sarah Orne Jewett', *American Literary Realism 1870–1910*, No. 1 (1967).

Johnson, Edward (1598–1672). Historian. A Canterbury joiner, he went to Boston, Massachusetts, in 1630 with Winthrop and became distinguished in the colonial militia and government. In 1650 he began his history of the colony, *The Wonder-Working Providence of Sion's Saviour in New England* (published anonymously in 1654; ed. W. F. Poole, 1867), in which the structure of historical Providence takes the form of a military revolution of release from bondage organized by the forces of Christ. Its style is grandiose and bathetic, and includes doggerel praises of the Puritan leaders. But Johnson is good on daily life and on the Indians. [EM]

Johnson, James Weldon (1871–1938). Poet. Born in Jacksonville, Florida, he became one of the first Negroes admitted to the Florida bar since Reconstruction. As his fascinating autobiography, *Along This Way* (1933), records, he was a New York song-writer, a consul in Venezuela and Nicaragua, executive secretary of the NAACP, and professor of creative literature at Fisk University. The best of his poetry is in *God's Trombones* (1927), an important collection of folk

sermons. He also edited an anthology of Negro poetry and two books of spirituals. (◊ Negro Literature.) [EM]
Selected Poems (1935).

Jones, James (1921–). Novelist, short-story writer. He was born in Illinois, joined the regular army, and in 1945 submitted the manuscript of a novel to the editor Maxwell Perkins, who, although returning the book, backed his talent as he had backed Thomas Wolfe, Jones's own inspiration, years earlier. His first novel, *From Here to Eternity* (1951), was a best-seller, which, in spite of some weak love scenes, is a remarkably fine account of frustrated and fulfilled creativity, of authority in conflict with independence, within the heavily detailed army setting. Private Robert E. Lee Prewitt is outstanding amongst the fictional heroes of the fifties and sixties who fight the system. *Some Came Running* (1957) is another large novel which repeats some of the earlier materials, in a different form, before moving on to a study of Illinois small-town society. The naturalism tends to be obsessed with detail, but the characterization is excellent. *The Pistol* (1950) is a powerful short novel whose material – the consuming desire of a soldier to own his own pistol as a means to manhood – begins *The Thin Red Line* (1962), a large-scale novel about the war in the Pacific islands. Jones handles clearly and vividly a wide range of characters and a complex campaign, and has the courage and knowledge to describe with almost unique accuracy the nature of killing, fear and leadership. In *Go to the Widow-Maker* (1967) he returns once again to his themes of masculinity attained through war and war-substitutes, but this time the sexual scenes have some vigour, even if they are protracted and repetitious. Jones's handling of the excitement and neuroses of skin-diving and the exhaustion of urban literary life is first-rate. He is one of the few intelligent writers in his field. *The Ice-Cream Headache* (1968) is a collection of his short stories within a running commentary on his methods. [EM]

Jones, LeRoi (1934–). Playwright, novelist, editor. Born in New Jersey. His long education included scholarships to schools, studies at Rutgers, Howard and Columbia, air-force service as a gunner, and being a leading Negro thinker, speaker and writer during the revolution of the 1950s and 1960s. His plays – *Dutchman, The Slave* and *The Toilet* (1964) – and his poetry – *Preface to a Twenty Volume Suicide Note* (1961), *The Dead Lecturer* (1964) and *Black Art* (1966) – articulate the anger and anguish of an intelligent man faced with the violence of a segregated society. *Blues People: Negro Music in White America* (1963) is an insider's book on jazz as the social response of Negro America, and *The System of Dante's Hell* (1965) is both a passionate autobiographical novel and an exploration of post-Joyce, post-Kerouac prose styles. His *Yugen* magazine (1957) and Totem Press have encouraged a large number of contemporary poets. While he was director of the Black Arts repertory theatre in Harlem, financed by the HARYOU Act (a government anti-poverty programme), he produced a number of plays articulating 1965 definitions of Black Power: his own play *Slave Ship* (undated, duplicated typescript) is typical in its scorn for Uncle Toms and their white masters. *Home: Social Essays* (1966) collects his articles into the chronicle of his experience between visiting Cuba in 1960 and the death of Malcolm X in 1965. *Tales* (1967) is a collection of his short stories, and *Black Music* (1968) of articles on contemporary jazz. LeRoi Jones is an important writer: as a black American writer his significance is even greater. (◊ Negro Literature.) [EM]

Josephson, Matthew (1899–   ). Literary social critic. Born in Brooklyn, N.Y., he was one of the ◊ 'Lost Generation' expatriates in Paris in the 1920s, where he was editorially involved with *Secession, Broom,* and *transition* (◊ Little Magazines); he was later assistant editor of the *New Republic*. Strongly influenced by surrealism in the twenties, he made, like other writers, a transition to social interests in the thirties. His *Portrait of the Artist as American* (1930), an interesting piece of socio-literary criticism, gives a historical analysis of the American writer's instinct towards exile. Other books include *Zola and His Time* (1928), *Jean-Jacques Rousseau* (1931), a notable biography, and *Life among the Surrealists* (1962). His strongly social emphasis is best indicated by his lively left-wing analysis of the great Gilded Age American capitalists, *The Robber Barons* (1934). *Infidel in the Temple* (1967) is a lively account of personal and journalistic experience in the 1930s, vital for any estimate of this period. *Al Smith: Hero of Cities* (1970, with Hannah Josephson) is a study of the presidential candidate of 1928. There is an interesting portrait of Josephson in Malcolm Cowley's *Exile's Return* (1934; 1962). [MB]

Josselyn, John (fl.1638–75). Naturalist. An Englishman who spent 10 years in New England, mostly in Maine with his brother; they were shareholders in Sir Fernando Gorges' company, whose disputes with the Puritans caused some of the rancour in Josselyn's *An Account of Two Voyages to New England* (1674). His important work is *New England's Rarities Discovered in Birds, Fishes, Serpents and Plants of That Country* (1672), the earliest naturalist account of the area with any pretensions to science amid the fantasy. [EM]

Justice, Donald (1925–   ). Poet. Born in Florida, he has taught at the State University of Iowa. *The Summer Anniversaries* (1960), and *A Local Storm* (1963), show him to be a formalist, in the manner of Richard ◊ Wilbur or John Crowe ◊ Ransom. He has experimented with verse modes and shows a delicate feeling for language and a powerful musicality. His latest volume is *Night Light* (1967). [BS]

Richard Howard, *Alone with America* (1969).

K

Kanin, Garson (1912–   ). Actor, director, playwright. He was born in Rochester, N.Y., and has been active in Hollywood and on Broadway most of his adult life, and acted in a number of stage successes. In 1937 he joined Samuel Goldwyn's organization, and in 1947 he and the English film director Carol Reed made *The True Glory*, a documentary war film. His best-known play is *Born Yesterday* (1946), an archetypal drama of the not-so-dumb-blonde-and-her-gangster-friend sort of star vehicle. Among his other works are *A Double Life* (1948, with his wife, Ruth Gordon), his direction of the film *The Diary of Anne Frank* (1955), and a novel, *Blow Up a Storm* (1959). [E M]

Kantor, MacKinlay (1904–   ). Novelist. Born in Webster City, Iowa, a prolific writer of highly competent fiction, he is probably best known for his historical novels, particularly the group dealing with the American Civil War. His first novel, *Diversey* (1928), is set among Chicago gangsters, an early example of literary exploitation of the theme. The first Civil War novel was *The Jaybird* (1932), but great success came with *Long Remember* (1934), a detailed fictional treatment of the Battle of Gettysburg. *Arouse and Beware* (1936) and more recently *Andersonville* (1955) return to the same area of interest. Other books include *Gentle Annie* (1942), set in the Oklahoma of 1901; *Happy Land* (1943), touching on the Second World War; *Signal 32* (1950), about life in a New York police precinct; and *Spirit Lake* (1961). All are carefully researched, the wide range of subjects suggesting his professionalism. He has written for Hollywood, and published books for children and a childhood autobiography, *But Look, the Morn* (1947). [M B]

Kauffmann, Stanley (1916–   ). Novelist, playwright, critic. Born in New York, he was already writing for the theatre as a student at New York University. After working with the Washington Square Players and in publishing, he became a leading critic of film and theatre in such journals as *New Republic* and *Commentary* and is now the influential drama critic of the *New York Times*. His work, critical, theatrical, fictional, mixes professionalism with intelligence. His novels, which commonly deal with the world of writers, artists and musicians, and their moral and emotional problems, include *The King of Proxy Street* (1941), *This Time Forever* (1945), *The Hidden Hero* (1949), *A Change of Climate* (1954), *The Philanderer* (1954) – the subject of a famous obscenity case in the English courts – and *Man of the World* (1956). [M B]

Kaufman, Bob (?   –   ). Satirist, poet. He was born on the West Coast and, after spending 20 years in the merchant navy, was working in the Los Angeles Hilton when ◊ Kerouac and ◊ Ginsberg found him and he became part of the 'San Francisco Renaissance' of the 1950s. ◊ Ferlinghetti published his satires in *Abomunist Manifesto* (1959) and the prose poems *Second April* (1960) as City Lights broadsides. They are collected with interesting shorter pieces in *Solitudes Crowded with Loneliness* (1965). *Golden Sardine* (1967) contains poems and montage sequences which have some of the sardonic social criticism and lonely passion of Bob Dylan's lyrics. [E M]

Kaufman, George S(imon) (1889–1961). Playwright, columnist. Born in Pittsburg, he had a long list of popular plays to his name, mostly Broadway hits, mostly in collaboration with Moss ◊ Hart and Marc ◊ Connelly (including *Dulcy*, 1961), and *Merton of the Movies* (1922). Apart from his columns in the Washington *Mail* and the New York *World, Tribune* and *Times*, he collaborated on *The Royal Family* (1927), *Dinner at Eight* (1932) and *Stage Door* (1936) with Edna ◊ Ferber; *Of Thee I Sing* (1932) with Morris Ryskind and George Gershwin; *June Moon* (1929) with Ring ◊ Lardner; *The Solid Gold Cadillac* (1952) with Howard Teichmann. His film scripts include the Marx Brothers' *Animal Crackers* and *Coconuts,* and he collaborated with J. P. ◊ Marquand on the film script for this novelist's *The Late George Apley* (1946). [E M]

Kazin, Alfred (1915–   ). Autobiographer, critic. He writes excellently about his Brooklyn childhood in *A Walker in the City* (1951) and of his later literary life in *Starting Out in the Thirties* (1965). *On Native Grounds* (1942) is a standard critical discussion of American literature since 1900, and three further critical volumes maintain his usefulness: *The Inmost Leaf* (1955) and *Contemporaries* (1962), two collections of essays, and *F. Scott Fitzgerald* (1951). [EM]

Keast, W. R. ◊ Chicago Aristotelians.

Kees, Weldon (1914–55). Poet. Born in Nebraska, he worked on the Federal Works Project, became director of the Bibliographical Centre for the Rocky Mountain Region, wrote for *Time* in New York, made documentary films, and exhibited paintings in shows with De Kooning, Hofmann and the abstract expressionists. In 1951 he went to San Francisco, began to compose music, made more films and collaborated with Dr Jurgen Ruesch on *Non-Verbal Communication*, also contributing the magnificent photographs. His car was found abandoned on the approach to the Golden Gate Bridge on 18 July 1955, and he has not been seen since. The bitter, distinctively dislocating poems of this brilliant man appeared in *The Last Man* (1943), *The Fall of the Magicians* (1947), and *Poems 1947–1954* and have been republished as part of *Collected Poems*, edited by Donald Justice (1960). [EM]

Kelley, W. M. ◊ Negro Literature.

Kelly, Robert (1935–   ). Poet. Born in Brooklyn, he studied at the City College of New York and at Columbia, and launched the *Chelsea Review* and, with George Economou, *Trobar*, an important magazine of new verse (1960). He has taught at various colleges. With other poets he has been associated with *The Sixties* magazine, and with the subjective surrealism of 'deep image' poetry ('Notes on the Poetry of the Deep Image', *Trobar* 2, 1961). With seven other poets, he formed The Blue Yak, a poets' cooperative in New York in 1961. His earlier poems in *Armed Descent* (1961) and *Her Body against Time* (1963) are mainly short lyrical pieces, placing personal experience in intellectual and religious contexts. *Lunes* (1965) shows a masterly

handling of the extremely brief form. But it is with *Finding the Measure* (1968) that this poetry achieves its unique combination of experimental form, wide-ranging intellectual knowledge and a personal voice. He has since then published prolifically; *Sonnets* (1968), *Songs I–XXX* (1968), *The Common Shore, Books I–V* (1969), *A California Journal* (1969), and *Kali Yuga* (1970). His most carefully worded poetry is still *Axon Dendron Tree* (1967). [EM]

Kennedy, John Pendleton (1795–1870). Novelist, satirist, memoirist. He was born in Baltimore, practised law, served in Congress and was Speaker to the House and secretary of the navy (he organized the Perry expedition to Japan and Kane's second expedition to the Arctic). He sponsored Poe, was a friend of Irving and Holmes, and supplied Thackeray with material for *The Virginians*. Of his Southern romances the most important is *Swallow Barn* (1832), which eulogizes the Virginian planter in a tale of boundary disputes and love affairs between two families. *Horseshoe Robinson* (1835) concerns a backwoodsman in the Revolution, and *Rob of the Bowl* (1838) is a satire of Jacksonian democracy. [EM]

C. H. Bohner, *John Pendleton Kennedy: Gentleman from Baltimore* (1961).

Kennedy, X. J. (1929–   ). Poet. He was born in New Jersey, studied at Columbia and the Sorbonne, and has taught at several universities. His poems in *Nude Descending a Staircase* (1961) move easily between a world of bawdry, irreverent high spirits and apt contemporary reference, and one of traditional poetic elegance. He is a serious wit and a good poetic craftsman. A second collection of poems, *Growing into Love*, appeared in 1969. [BS]

Kerouac, Jack (1922–69). Novelist. He was born in Lowell, Massachusetts, studied in local Catholic schools and at Columbia University (1941), and began to write and live in the image of his early reading: Jack London, Hemingway, Saroyan, Wolfe and Joyce, and the free style of prose and living of his friend Neal Cassady, the Dean Moriarty of *On the Road*. With William ◊ Burroughs and ◊ Ginsberg in New York and San Francisco in the late 1940s and early 1950s, he practised the ◊ Beat Generation life, after a period in the merchant navy and bumming around America. After his first published novel, *The Town and the City* (1950), an excellent work in Wolfeian autobiographic style, *On the Road* (1957) soon came to represent his generation throughout the world: its record of a new Bohemian style of living, the 'spontaneous bop prosody' of its rapid physical movement, urgent absorption of experience and jazz sense, all contributed to a heady fiction which is still influencing young writers. Drink, sex, drugs and jazz again form the San Francisco life of *The Subterraneans* (1958); but *The Dharma Bums* (1958) includes more oriental philosophical practices and a direct contact with nature in the North-west mountains (see also *The Scripture of Golden Eternity*, 1960, an American *sutra*).

Doctor Sax (1959) is a *tour de force* of Kerouac's style, evoking boyhood experiences with unique exhilaration, and *Maggie Cassidy* (1959) and *Visions of Gerard* (1963) are simpler written memories of boyhood. *Tristessa* (1960) concerns Mexican experience, *Big Sur* (1962) returns to the earlier complex style to describe breakdowns of the self on the Californian coast, *Satori in Paris* (1966) is about the search for ancestral identity in Brittany, and *Desolation Angels* (1965) is a fine re-working of Beat Generation experiences in an apparently definitive if mournful and nostalgic tone. All these books constitute parts of the continuous *Duluoz Legend* series, whose most recent addition is *Vanity of Duluoz: An Adventurous Education, 1935–46* (1968), a disappointingly sentimental re-animation of the past: middle-age did not suit Kerouac, and he grew garrulous. As in Wolfe's case, his autobiographical passion makes for looseness of form and a prose of rhapsodic repetition; but his vision of the post-war world of youth is an authentic and tragically exuberant response in an original prose style. *Lonesome Traveller* (1960) is a collection of travel sketches, and *Book of Dreams* (1961) a book of his sources. *Mexico City Blues* (1959) is an influential volume of poetry experimenting with jazz forms, *Rimbaud* (1960), a broad-sheet poem, and *Pull My Daisy* (1961), the printed form of an ad-libbed commentary to film incorporating an unproduced play, and starring Allen Ginsberg, Gregory Corso, Peter Orlovsky and the painter Larry Rivers. [EM]

Ann Charters, *A Bibliography of the Works of*

Jack Kerouac (1967); ed. Thomas Parkinson, *A Casebook on the Beat* (1961); John Clellon Holmes, *Nothing More to Declare* (1968); *Paris Review* 43 (Summer, 1968) (interview with Ted Berigan).

Kesey, Ken (1935–   ). Novelist. He grew up in the timber country of Oregon, studied at the University of Oregon, where he was a champion wrestler, and came south to Stanford University to attend creative writing classes held by Wallace ◊ Stegner and Malcolm ◊ Cowley. He worked in a mental hospital for a time, and later became the centre of a new-style ◊ Bohemianism in the Bay Area of San Francisco, before being arrested, hunted from the country and re-arrested, and imprisoned, in 1966. His first novel, *One Flew over the Cuckoo's Nest* (1962), draws on his mental hospital experience for a brilliant, funny and mordant satire on the dehumanization of western society, one of the most important novels of the post-war years. His second, *Sometimes a Great Notion* (1964), concerns the conflicts and solidarities in a logging family in the North-west – a large, ambitious novel with the pretentions and scale of Thomas ◊ Wolfe. His messianic LSD scene is the subject of *The Electric Kool-Aid Acid Test* (1968) by Tom ◊ Wolfe. [EM]

Keyes, Frances Parkinson (1885–1970). Novelist, biographer. Born in Virginia, daughter of a Professor of Greek, Mrs Keyes was educated in Boston and Switzerland. A journalist, she was associate editor of *Good Housekeeping* (1923–35), editor of the *National Historical Magazine* (1937–9). Mrs Keyes won enormous success with a long series of novels, usually set in the South or New England. Among them are *The Ambassadress* (1938), *Queen Anne's Lace* (1930), *All That Glitters* (1941), *Dinner at Antoine's* (1948) and *Steamboat Gothic* (1952). She wrote two biographies: *Written in Heaven* (1937; rev. as *St Teresa of Lisieux,* 1950), and *The Sublime Shepherdess*, concerning Bernadette of Lourdes (1940; enlarged 1953). [MG]

Killens, J. O. ◊ Negro Literature.

Kingsley, Sidney (1906–   ). Actor, playwright. Born in New York, he gained his first prize on Broadway with *Men in White* (1933), probably the archetype of hospital soap-opera, with accurate details. But *Dead*

End (1935) is a good social drama (and an even better film, 1937) about the struggles of children in an East River slum, overshadowed by the rich and the gangster Baby Face Martin. Social purpose impregnated Kingsley's plays for all their sensationalism. His 'dead end kids' went into American mythology. His later career is best represented by *Ten Million Ghosts* (1936), a protest play against munitions profiteering and war; *Detective Story* (1949); and an adaptation of Koestler's *Darkness at Noon* (1951). *Night Life* (1962) is a Manhattan night-club melodrama in which the meek are supposed to inherit the earth, and die doing so. [EM]

Kinnell, Galway (1927–). Poet. Born in Rhode Island, educated at Princeton and the University of Rochester, he has taught in universities in the U.S.A. and abroad, and been a freelance writer. Lucid and at best finely detailed, his verse has tended toward the experimental, particularly in recent work. It is often concerned with semi-religious matter, as in the fascinating long poem 'The Avenue Bearing the Initial of Christ into the New World', in his first collection, *What a Kingdom It Was* (1960). He has since published *Flower Herding on Mount Monadnock* (1964), *Poems of the Night* (1968) and *Body Rags* (1969), and translated *The Poetry of François Villon* (1964). *Black Light* (1966) is a novel set in Persia. [MB]

Kizer, Carolyn (1925–). Poet. Born in Spokane, Washington, she has been associated with a group of poets residing in and around Seattle and publishing in *Poetry North-West*. Besides writing her own personal but tough-minded poetry, collected in *The Ungrateful Garden* (1961) and *Knock upon Silence* (1965), she has done a number of translations from the Chinese, particularly from the great 8th-century poet Tu Fu. The formal verse and violent imagery of her earlier poems have recently given way, perhaps via an influence from Chinese, to poems of quiet situation in which free verse and plain speech dominate. [BP]

Knight, Sarah Kemble (1666–1727). Travel writer. A merchant's daughter and sea-captain's widow who travelled from Boston, where she was born, to New York and back in 1704–5 and described her dif-

ficult and dangerous experiences on horseback in the *Journal* (ed. and pub. Theodore Dwight, 1825), a vivid, humorous and authoritative impression of the times and an image of early American self-reliance. [EM]

Koch, Kenneth (1925–). Poet, playwright, novelist. Born in Cincinnati, served in the army in the Pacific, studied at Harvard and Columbia. With John ◊ Ashbery and Frank ◊ O'Hara, with whom he was linked in the Poet's Theatre, he represents the American extension of modern French poetic methods, a group who with Edward Field, Barbara Guest, James Schuyler and Harry ◊ Mathews were associated with the Artist's Theatre, *Locus Solus* magazine, and New York abstract expressionist painters of the 1950s. His is a poetry and drama of witty juxtapositions, cubist and dadaist dislocations, and anti-symbolism, in direct line from Raymond Roussel and Gertrude Stein and influenced by Pierre Reverdy and Max Jacob. Koch's main work is in *Poems* (1953); *Ko, or A Season on Earth* (1959), an exhilarating multi-plotted novel in verse; *Thank You and Other Poems* (1962); the long and dazzling 'When the Sun Tries to Go on' (*The Hasty Papers* 1960; reissued with illustrations by Larry Rivers, 1969); *Poems from 1952 and 1953* (1968) and *The Pleasures of Peace* (1969). *Bertha and Other Plays* (1966) is a collection of 17 plays in 130 pages. [EM]

F. W. Dupee, 'Kenneth Koch's Poetry', *The King of the Cats* (1965); Richard Howard, *Alone with America* (1969).

Kopit, Arthur L. (1937–). Playwright *Oh Dad, Poor Dad, Mamma's Hung You in the Closet and I'm Feelin' So Sad* (1960) is a hilarious take-off of 'absurd' drama ending with the nice line 'What is the meaning of this?' Kopit has also published *The Day the Whores Came Out to Play Tennis* (1965), a collection of 6 expert plays, one of which, 'The Hero', has no dialogue, and *Indians* (1968), a satirical drama on the myths of the 'West'. [EM]

Krutch, Joseph Wood (1893–). Teacher, critic. Born in Knoxville, Tennessee. His main fields are represented by *The American Drama since 1918* (1938, 1957), *Edgar Allan Poe* (1926), an early psychological literary study, *The Modern Temper* (1929), an important analysis of 'meaninglessness' during the twenties, and *The Desert Year* (1952), reflections on man and nature. *More Lives Than One* (1962) is his entertaining autobiography. [EM]

The Best Nature Writings of Joseph Wood Krutch (1970).

Kunitz, Stanley (1905–). Poet. Born in Worcester, Massachusetts, he was educated at Harvard, served in the Second World War, and has taught in several universities. Though a volume, *Intellectual Things*, appeared in 1930 it is not until lately that he has received considerable notice. *Passport to the War* appeared in 1944. With *Selected Poems 1928–1958* (1958) he made a powerful impact on critics, other poets and a wider reading public (he won the Pulitzer Prize), perhaps because now a poetry made out of intense personal experience, and concerned with the intricacies and tensions of a man's relations with the world, was found more important. His poems have a strong metaphysical speculativeness coupled with great intellectual and rhythmic resource. Kunitz is a joyous, celebratory poet of great craft and real substance, capable of wisdom, wit and balance. [MB]

L

La Farge, Oliver (1901–   ). Novelist. The greatest American expert on the Indians. Born in New York City. At Harvard he specialized in anthropology and archaeology, and made expeditions to Arizona, Mexico and Guatemala for his universities. His understanding of Indian culture is complete, and he writes about it in a first-rate style in the form of novels and stories: *Laughing Boy* (1929), *Sparks Fly Upward* (1931), *The Year-Bearer's People* (1931), *Long Pennant* (1933) and *The Enemy Gods* (1937). *Behind the Mountains* (1956) concerns a New Mexico village, and *Raw Material* (1945) is an autobiography. [EM]

Ed. Winfield Townley Scott, *Oliver La Farge: The Man with the Calabash Pipe* (1966).

Lamantia, Philip (1927–   ). Poet. He was born in San Francisco and is one of the foremost contemporary poets of drug experience and the surreal image. His visionary poems appear mostly in ◊ little magazines, but his books include *Erotic Poems* (1946), *Narcotica* (1959), *Ekstasis* (1959), *Destroyed Works* (1962), *Touch of the Marvelous* (1966), a collection of early poems, and *Selected Poems 1943–1966* (1967), which includes new work. He was published at the age of 15 by *View* magazine and praised by André Breton. His poems have retained the essential surrealist quality of revealing inner life through explosive images and ecstatic vision. [EM]

Langer, Susanne K. (1895–   ). Philosopher. Born in New York City, she studied at Radcliffe and has taught in American universities. *The Practice of Philosophy* (1930) and *An Introduction to Symbolic Logic* (1937) preceded her more influential syntheses of aesthetics and symbolism in *Philosophy in a New Key* (1942) and *Feeling and Form* (1953), extensions of Emile Cassirer's and other modern theories of significant form, which she usefully supports with *Problems of Art* (1955) and *Reflections on Art* (1958), an extremely useful source book of writings by artists and critics. *Philosophical Sketches*

appeared in 1962, and *Mind: An Essay on Human Feeling* (1967) inaugurates a new 3-volume project. [EM]

Langland, Joseph T. (1917–   ). Poet. He was born in Spring Grove, Minnesota, and educated at the State University of Iowa; before turning to college teaching in 1941, he was a farmer and rural schoolteacher. *The Green Town* (1956) and *The Wheel of Summer* (1963) contain his poems; he has edited anthologies and been poetry editor of the *Massachusetts Review*. Much of his work is searching and ponderous, employing a great deal of verbal density; more recent poems have tended to be wryly observant and more relaxed. [BP]

Lanier, Sidney (1842–81). Poet, novelist, critic. Born in Georgia, he was the first significant poet of Southern experience. His family were not planter 'aristocrats' but urban middle class. In his lawyer father's library he found Scott, Froissart, Bulwer-Lytton and *Gil Blas* – the staple of 19th-century chivalric nostalgia in the South. Although he was an excellent musician he felt that God had made music 'so small a business in comparison with other things' that he refused his natural vocation. During the Civil War he fought for a romantic-medieval South he saw later as 'the conceit of a whole people'. Captured by the Union army, he spent 1864–5 in prison, where he resisted ill health enough to translate Heine and Herder. Finding a living in the ravaged post-war South was difficult for a sick poet and musician. He taught, served in his father's law office, and wrote a novel, *Tiger-Lilies* (1867), a farrago of romantic themes and war which at least enabled him to realize the inferior provincialism of the South; his best poems in the *Round Table*, in the late 1860s, present a broken society through his own uncertainty and instability. In 1873 he played in the Peabody Orchestra of Baltimore, a good career interrupted by sickness. 'Corn', published in *Lippincott's Magazine*, began his late reputation as a poet. He lectured at Johns Hopkins and at the end of his life wrote *The Science of English Verse* (1880), on the theory that poetry was basically music, and *The English Novel and the Principle of its Development* (1883), slightly wild but interesting works.

Whitman's physicality and directness, which he admired, might have corrected Lanier's extravagantly Keatsian imagery and musicality, but his achievement was skilful and perhaps heroic, considering his life and times. Poems like 'Tyranny' and 'Laughter in the Senate' criticize the Reconstruction, and 'Nirvana' is a lament for the war obstructions to his development. 'Corn' dramatizes the case for replacing cotton with corn to revive Southern economy: the imagery and rhythm are surprisingly effective and seem to have influenced the ◊ Fugitive poets of the 1930s. In 'The Symphony' (1875) textures and metaphors imitate musical instruments in a discussion of social themes and reconciliation through love, an ambitious affair. His lyrics are better, and his best poem is 'The Marches of Glyn' (1878), a Transcendentalist transformation of nature in Georgian swamps and live-oaks. Lanier's effort to write genuinely contemporary poetry during Civil War and Reconstruction is one of the most interesting causes in American literature. [E M]

Collected Works: Centennial Edition, ed. C. R. Anderson, etc. (10 vols., 1945).

A. H. Starke, *Sidney Lanier: A Biographical and Critical Study* (1933).

Lardner, Ring (1885–1933). Journalist, short-story writer. Born in Michigan, he was a reporter in South Bend, Indiana, and Chicago, before editing (1910–11) a St Louis baseball weekly. He covered sport for various newspapers and became a syndicated columnist, after which he lived in New York. He made his name as a satirist through publishing, in the Chicago *Tribune, You Know Me, Al: A Busher's Letters* (1916; revised edn, 1925), a series of letters by 'Jack Keefe', an imaginary newcomer to a professional baseball team, which revealed Lardner's keen sense of humour, unsparing accuracy of observation, and gift for rendering American vernacular speech which earned him the admiration and gratitude of H. L. ◊ Mencken. A collection of verse, *Bib Ballads* (1915), though not well received, again shows the satirist's delight in the comic

flaws of the average American which was to be developed in *Gullible's Travels* (1917; revised edn, 1925) and in several collections of short stories, the best of which are *How to Write Short Stories (with Samples)* (1924), and *The Love Nest and Other Stories* (1926), whose title story is perhaps his best single piece. In these and later volumes the stupidity and dullness of his protagonists – typists, barbers, sportsmen – are analysed with sardonic wit and a growing pessimism. Unlike Hemingway, he did not suffer from hero-worship: as a news-reporter he simply exposed ignorance and ineptitude without enjoying it. He won a large popular audience long before the critics discovered him.

Lardner's autobiography, *The Story of a Wonder Man* (1927), is characteristically ironic and entertaining. There is a full and accurate biography in Donald Elder's *Ring Lardner* (1956). [M G]

The Collected Short Stories (1941); *The Portable Ring Lardner*, ed. G. Seldes (1946).

John Berryman, 'The Case of Ring Lardner', *Commentary*, XXII (1956); W. Goldhurst, *F. Scott Fitzgerald and His Contemporaries* (1963).

Larner, Jeremy (1937–). Novelist. Born in Indianapolis, he studied at Brandeis and Berkeley. His novel *Drive, He Said* (1964), an excellent example of satirical humour and social criticism of the sixties, is the story of a college sportsman spoiled by grafting intellectual and business society. His second novel, *The Answer* (1968), deals with psychedelic trippers and their disillusion. *The Addict in the Street* (1964, with Ralph Tefferteller) is a documentary commenting on the statements of drug addicts; it is one of the best works of its kind. He has recently edited with Irving Howe a collection of essays, *Poverty: Views from the Left* (1968). *Nobody Knows* (1970) is a study of the 1968 Eugene McCarthy campaign. [E M]

Laurents, Arthur (1918–). Dramatist. Born in Brooklyn, N.Y. He first achieved recognition with *Home of the Brave* (1946), a penetrating war play. His work generally shows concern for the individual in oppressive environment and for experiments in dramatic form. *The Bird Cage* (1950) presents tyranny in the relations between a chorus girl and a night-club owner, both *The Time of the Cuckoo* (1953) and *A Clearing in the Woods* (1957) concern a woman's self-discovery, and *Invitation to a March* (1960) is a comic fantasy based on the Sleeping Beauty. Laurents is respected also for his film scripts, *Rope*, *Anastasia* and *The Snake Pit*, and his stories for musicals, including *West Side Story* (1957) and *Gypsy* (1959). [EM]

Lawson, John Howard (1895–). Playwright. He was born in New York City, served in the American ambulance service in the First World War, marched for Sacco and Vanzetti and became a communist as well as one of America's leading radical dramatists (at least since his early Freudian Expressionist play, *Roger Bloomer*, 1923). *Processional* (1925), a 'jazz symphony of American life', in which Dynamite Jim, the proletarian hero, is attacked by anti-Marxist forces in West Virginia during a coal strike, is his earliest typical work: the twenties bitterness is brilliantly alleviated by the sharp humour of racial and social types. Then came *Loud Speaker* (1927), again dealing with worker persecution and injustice, and *The International* (1928), in which love provides a surprisingly bourgeois solution to the class war. *Success Story* (1932) is more concerned with the individual than the communist class pattern, and after *Gentlewoman* (1934) Lawson revaluated his orthodoxy, organized his *Theory and Techniques of Playwriting and Screenwriting* (1936), and in 1937 wrote *Marching Song*, as a model revolutionary play whose collective hero is the Auto Workers Union. Then he went to Hollywood and wrote good film scripts (see *Film in the Battle of Ideas*, 1953). He was one of the Hollywood artists imprisoned by the House Un-American Activities Committee during its witch-hunting 1950s. Lawson's work is a lively dramatization of social power in America, even if some of his stereotypes age badly. His most recent work is *Film: The Creative Process* (1965). A neglected and most interesting work is *The Hidden Heritage* (1950), a radical appreciation of social and political ideas prior to the founding of America in the 17th century. [EM]

M. Y. Himelstein, *Drama Was a Weapon: The Left-Wing Theatre in New York 1929–1941* (1963); G. Rabkin, *Drama and Commitment: Politics in the American Theatre of the Thirties* (1964).

Leary, Timothy (1920–). Psychologist. Born in Springfield, Massachusetts, he studied classical psychology at Berkeley and was dismissed from the Harvard University Centre for Research in Personality in 1963, when the faculty discovered that he, his associates and volunteers had taken part in controlled experiments with psilocybin, the chemical derivative of a certain sacred mushroom. In 1960, Leary had been given the mushroom in Cuernavaca by a scientist from the University of Mexico. The illumination he experienced radically changed his attitude towards consciousness and the nature of traditional religious mysticisms. His teachings on expanded consciousness, the use of LSD and other drugs, and the transformation of Western society have a strongly religious bias. He has a large following both in America and beyond, through his lectures and his writings in *The Psychedelic Reader* (1965, with G. M. Weil and R. Metzner: articles from *The Psychedelic Review*), *The Psychedelic Experience* (1964, with R. Metzner and R. Alpert) and *The Politics of Ecstasy* (1969). *High Priest* (1969) is autobiographical, and *Psychedelic Prayers* (1966) draws on the Tao Te Ching to form a manual of preparation for psychedelic experience. [EM]

Lee, Manfred B. ◊ Dannay, Frederic.

Legman, Gershon (1919–). The most erudite scholar of erotic folklore alive, his career is marked by unique courage and persistence. *The Horn Book* (1964), a large-scale account of erotica and bawdy, is a standard work. *Love and Death* (1949) is a short, definitive study of censorship, and his other works include *Oragenitalism* (1940), *The Guilt of the Templars* (1964), *The Fake Revolt* (1967 – a severe criticism of the so-called sexual revolution) and *Rationale of the Dirty Joke* (1968, first series), a superb analysis of sexual humour using over 2,000 examples. He also edited *Neurotica*, an important journal which appeared between 1948 and 1951, and Robert Burns's *Merry Muses of Caledonia* (1965). An account of his life in New York is lovingly given in John Clellon ◊ Holmes's *Nothing More to Declare* (1968). [EM]

Leland, Charles Godfrey (1824–1903). Humorist. Born in Philadelphia; educated in New Jersey and Germany. He became an important figure in journalism, and a man of many learned interests; but he is best remembered for his Pennsylvania German dialect-humour, particularly for the Hans Breitmann ballads. His first work in this vein was *Meister Karl's Sketch-Book* (1855); then came *Hans Breitmann's Barty and Other Ballads* (1868). Leland continued to produce more of these comic mock-German poems, and they were collected in *Hans Breitmann's Ballads* (1914). [MB]

Lerner, Max (1902–). Critic, social commentator. Born in Russia, he belongs to the tradition of critical social analysis so active in America in the 1930s, a tradition less concerned for literature as such than for its expressive function in revealing the culture. His numerous books and articles include *It Is Later Than You Think* (1938) and the monumental, useful study *America as a Civilization: Life and Thought in the United States Today* (1957), which clearly shows his social-historical approach. Lerner has taught at Sarah Lawrence, Harvard and Brandeis Universities; recently he has become widely known as a newspaper columnist commenting on social and literary matters. [MB]

Levertov, Denise (1923–). Poet. She grew up in Ilford, Essex, but after marrying the American writer Mitchell Goodman moved to the U.S.A. in 1948. Though an early volume, *The Double Image*, appeared in London in 1946, it is in America that she has really formed her poetic manner. She employs that kind of concentrated pictorial approach bequeathed by the ◊ Imagists to both English and American poetry, but taken further in the U.S.A. Her incantatory quality and her visionary ecstatic dimension separate her from the British tradition and link her closely with the ◊ Beat Generation and ◊ Black Mountain poets. Like them, she has been influenced by William Carlos ◊ Williams in her concern with celebrating the life residing in particular things and responding innocently to 'authentic' experience. Her volumes include *Here and Now* (1957), *Overland to the Islands* (1958), *Jacob's Ladder* (1961), which contains some interesting pieces on the Eichmann trial and reprints poems from the 1958 volume, *O Taste and See* (1964), which includes her first published story, and *The Sorrow Dance* (1967). She translated *In Praise of Krishna: Songs from the Bengali* (1968) with E. C. Dimock. [MB]

Levin, Harry (1912–). Critic. He has been teaching at Harvard since 1934; his erudition and range are exceptional in a critical scholar. He has edited Jonson, Rochester and Flaubert, and the novelist himself praised his *James Joyce* (1941). His major works are *The Broken Column: A Study in Romantic Hellenism* (1931), *Toward Stendhal* (1945), *The Overreacher* (1952; on Marlowe), *The Power of Blackness: Hawthorne, Poe, Melville* (1958) and the essays in *Contexts of Criticism* (1957). *The Gates of Horn* (1963) is an important study of French fiction. His advocacy of comparative literature is a major contribution to a possible Atlantic culture. [EM]

Levin, Meyer (1905–). Novelist. A Chicago-born journalist, in his first novel, *Reporter* (1929), he dealt with newspaper life. He lived for a while in Europe, including Palestine; his novel *Yehuda* (1931) is about a Zionist community there, while *Golden Mountain* (1932) retells traditional Jewish folk-tales. His other novels, most of them realistic and reportorial in character, usually treat Jewish themes; they include *The Old Bunch* (1937), about Chicago immigrant children; *Citizens* (1940), about a strike; *Compulsion* (1956), based on the Leopold-Loeb case; and *The Fanatic* (1964), where he treats of such serious matters as Jewish experience under Hitler and anti-semitism in America, with characteristically false portentousness. *In Search* (1950) is autobiography. [MB]

Lewis, (Harry) Sinclair (1885–1951). Novelist. Born at Sauk Center, Minnesota. He attended Yale and held various jobs – he joined briefly in Upton ◊ Sinclair's Helicon Hall venture, and later sold plots to Jack ◊ London – before devoting his full time to writing from 1915. His first novel, *Our Mr Wrenn* (1914), was followed by *The Trail of the Hawk* (1915), *The Job* (1917) and *Free Air* (1919). With *Main Street* (1920) and *Babbitt* (1922) he rapidly established an international reputation, officially sealed by the award of the Nobel Prize in 1930, the first time it had gone to an American author. This marked the apogee of Lewis's literary career. In the melancholy period from *Ann Vickers* (1933) to the posthumously published *World So Wide* (1951) Lewis produced 10 novels which testified to the progressive decline in his creative powers. During his last years he wandered extensively in Europe, and after his death in Rome his ashes were appropriately returned to his birthplace.

A journalist rather than an artist, Lewis wrote too much too quickly, and his later work is mostly negligible. Yet, as his biographer has stated in a definitive survey, although Lewis was one of the worst important writers in modern American literature 'without his writing one cannot imagine modern American literature'. The authentic voice of the mid-West, he liberated new areas of experience for the American novelist. Again, rather in the manner of Cooper a century earlier, he gave to Europeans an image of the United States which they recognized and which, to a certain extent, they wanted. His novels are often confused in style and sprawling in structure, and he tended to indulge in caricature and not character. The strengths and weaknesses of his books derive ultimately from those in the man. Although he became known primarily as a satirist of the American scene, Lewis's own reaction to the vulgar materialism and cultural impoverishment of his time was ambivalent. The Gopher Prairie of *Main Street* may exhibit a provincial complacency, but the values which the culture-bearing Carol Kennicott attempts to impose upon the town are so jejune as to render her a fool as well as a prig. Similarly, in *Babbitt*, which with *Arrowsmith* (1925) is probably his best work, the satiric force of Lewis's portrait of Zenith tends to be dissipated by his recognition of the rebelliousness, albeit stifled, in George F. Babbitt himself. The victory for another businessman in *Dodsworth* (1929) is less equivocal; in a leisurely reworking of one of James's major themes and with a backward glance to his own first novel, Lewis presents the liberating effect of Europe upon Sam Dodsworth. These novels and *Elmer Gantry* (1927), a broad and vigorous satire on the excesses of American religion, constitute the most permanent of his sociological fictions. In them he offered, especially in his dialogue, a sharp and easily assimilated image of the American middle class; and, as a result of his concentration upon a single representative individual, who often stood in the same ambiguous relation to his society as he did himself, Lewis was able to define dramatically the best and the worst in that culture. Characteristically, in his novel *It Can't Happen Here* (1935), he examined the triumph of an American dictator without examining the nature of political power or the impotence of liberalism. [H D]

Mark Schorer, *Sinclair Lewis: An American Life* (1961); ed. Mark Schorer, *Sinclair Lewis: A Collection of Critical Essays* (1962); D. J. Dooley, *The Art of Sinclair Lewis* (1967).

Lewis, Meriwether (1774–1809). Soldier, explorer. Born in Albemarle, Virginia. In 1802 Thomas Jefferson sponsored an expedition to explore the headwaters of the Mississippi and to discover a water route to the Pacific. It would have to pass through French territory at a time when the Louisiana Purchase was being negotiated and the boundaries disputed with Britain. Command was given to Lewis, a Virginian who had served in the state militia during the Whiskey rebellion, in the regular army and as one of President ◊ Jefferson's private secretaries. He chose as his associate commander William Clark (1770–1838), an old Virginian friend who had resigned from the army in ill health in 1796. The expedition set out in 1804 and in 1805 reached the three forks of the Missouri, ascended the Jefferson to its source, and crossed to the Columbia river. They returned in 1806, and Lewis was rewarded with the governorship of Missouri territory, but he died, possibly by his own hand, possibly murdered, in 1809 (see Robert Penn ◊ Warren's *Brother to Dragons*). Clark was governor of Louisiana and the Missouri territories, and later superintendent of Indian affairs in St Louis from 1822 to his death. Both men kept extensive journals of their exploration but publication was delayed by their later duties and the death of Lewis. In 1810 Clark secured Nicholas Biddle to prepare an edition, and this too was delayed until 1814. The *Journals* stimulated interest in the West and encouraged the idea of a trans-continental trade route to the Pacific. [D K A/E M]

The Journals of Lewis and Clark, abridged and ed. Bernard De Voto (1953).
Ed. Elliott Cowes, *History of the Expedition under the Command of Lewis and Clark* (3 vols., 1965); Richard Dillon, *Meriwether Lewis: A Biography* (1965).

Lewisohn, Ludwig (1882–1955). Novelist, literary and social critic. Born of Jewish background in Berlin and brought to the U.S.A. as a child, he grew up in Charleston, South Carolina. After graduate work at

Columbia he taught European literature in various universities, including Wisconsin and Brandeis. He was a participant in American social debate and was for a time associate editor of the liberal periodical the *Nation*. At first a liberal idealist urging the America of the 1920s out of its Puritan phase – many of his novels and articles turn on emancipated human and social relationships – he later became a devout Zionist. Two volumes of autobiography, intense, strongly voiced documents, expose his background and position – *Up Stream* (1922) and *Mid-Channel: An American Chronicle* (1929). Both reveal his sense of being persecuted in the States for his German-Jewish background, particularly during the war, and a feeling that American culture is narrow and repressive. Among his numerous novels, some of them concerned with marital problems, are *The Broken Snare* (1908); *The Case of Mr Crump* (1926), first published in Paris and praised by European critics, only lately available in the U.S.A.; *The Island Within* (1928); *Stephen Escott* (1930); *An Altar in the Fields* (1934), about a couple sent by a psychiatrist to solve their marital problems in the African desert; and *Trumpet of Jubilee* (1937), touching on the experience of Jews under Hitler.

As a literary critic Lewisohn comments valuably and from an enlightened viewpoint on European literature in studies like *The Modern Drama* (1915), *The Spirit of Modern German Literature* (1916), *The Poets of Modern France* (1918), *The Creative Life* (1924) and on American literature in two highly useful studies, *Expression in America* (1932) and *The Story of American Literature* (1937). His concern with the Jewish problem appears in several books, including *Israel* (1925) and *The American Jew* (1950). [MB]

Liebling, A(bbott) J(oseph) (1904–63). Journalist, social commentator. Born in New York City. His early career was with various semi-popular newspapers whose shortcomings he later analysed in cultural critiques of the press in the *New Yorker*, to which journal he became a leading contributor. A stylist, humorist and writer of strong cultural opinions, he has documented not only the press (*The Wayward Pressman*, 1947, *The Press*, 1961), but also the war in Europe (*The Road Back to Paris*, 1944), boxing (*The Sweet Science*, 1956),

and Southern politics (*The Earl of Louisiana*, 1961). [MB]

Lincoln, Abraham (1809–65). The sixteenth President of the United States. He was born in Kentucky, grew up on the frontier in Illinois, where he learned Western storytelling and humorous rhetoric, and worked variously as storekeeper, surveyor, postmaster and army captain in the Black Hawk War (1832) before being elected in 1834 to four terms in the State legislature. After being called to the bar, he moved to Springfield in 1837 and married, following a problematic courtship. His lawyer reputation helped him to be elected in 1846 to Congress, where he voted against both Abolition and the Mexican War. He did not run for re-election. The Dred Scott case (1857) increased his feeling for the anti-slavery cause, and after his 1858 acceptance of Republican nomination for the Senate he engaged Stephen Douglas in a series of debates which made him nationally famous. It is in these and in the *Cooper Union Address* (1860) that Lincoln's mastery of persuasive language is first clear. When he was nominated for the presidency, his virtual silence during the campaign did not prevent his overwhelming victory. Then, in 1861, his *Farewell Address* at Springfield (perhaps revised later) again shows his rhetorical individuality – that combination of alliteration, rhythm, cadence and timing of clauses which has long since degenerated in the mouths of presidential imitators and others. In the *First Inaugural Address* (1861) Lincoln increased his power by making his chief concern the preservation of the Union, even at the expense of Abolition, although when the War of Secession came he refrained from employing a dictatorial manner even in the face of generals he could not approve of, a free press which abused him and a cabinet largely unsympathetic. His *Emancipation Proclamation* (1862), originally a war measure, became a foundation of the Reconstruction, and his *Gettysburg Address* (1863) is the standard Lincoln speech. Phrases from its 260 words are part of American folk-speech. The magic lies in the King James Bible rhythms and common American diction employed to carry unoriginal ideas with tremendous articulation of common feeling. The *Second Inaugural Address* (1865), delivered six weeks before his assassination, again includes no new ideas but is powerful in its directive of feeling based on 17th-century cadence and references to God and America in united action. The other side of the great man was the melancholy faced joker who admired Artemus ◊ Ward (see Lloyd Dunning's *Lincoln's Funnybone*, 1942), and inherited the tradition of Western humour (see Constance Rourke's *American Humour*, 1931). Among the hundreds of books on Lincoln and collections of his writings, a beginning may be made with Philip Van Doren's *Life and Writings of Abraham Lincoln* (1940), a comprehensive selection with notes, and R. P. Basler's *Abraham Lincoln: His Speeches and Writings* (1946), a large number of authentic texts with a useful analysis of his progress as a writer. [EM]

James G. Randall, *Lincoln the President* (4 vols., 1945–55); Allan Nevins, *The Emergence of Lincoln* (1950).

Lindsay, (Nicholas) Vachel (1879–1931)· Poet. Among the earliest writers of the modern American 'renaissance' of literature. He was born in Springfield, Illinois, and family associations made him early acquainted with the rural life of the mid-West, where devotion to Lincoln as Emancipator and Andrew Jackson as 'friend of the common man' merged with the moral earnestness of evangelical fundamentalism, its social philosopher William Jennings Bryan. Lindsay embraced the prevailing millennialism, but not his parents' ambition for him to enter the ministry. He left his college programme unfinished in 1900, and earned his way for several years while studying in art school in Chicago and New York. He taught social settlement and YMCA programmes, and while developing theories of community art prepared to become the prophet of those visionary Utopias which were to be expressed in later prose writings (for instance, *The Golden Book of Springfield*, 1920). At 30, still a poet without a subject, he began walking tours in which he played the mendicant minstrel, trading 'rhymes for bread', in poetry recitations through the eastern highlands and the South. Here indigenous myths and ballads gave him his effective inspirations, as did his search for an 'American' rhythm – which he related to the sounds of galloping herds and shrieking motors, Negro dancing and revival singing, and what he called 'vaudevilles' and 'circuses'.

With *General William Booth Enters into Heaven, and Other Poems* (1913) and *The Congo, and Other Poems* (1914) he won astonished attention for poetry. The two title poems established his mastery of a new – though not untraditional – ballad. With *The Chinese Nightingale and Other Poems* (1917), we find in the title poem an excellent example of his characteristic fantasy of contemporary common life – while such poems as 'The Ghost of the Buffaloes' and 'In Praise of Johnny Appleseed' continue his gift of transmitting living regional American folklore, as had the earlier Lincoln poems and 'The Santa-Fé Trail'. Famous first volumes by ◊ Masters and ◊ Sandburg were simultaneously advancing the growth of a new mid-West literature, celebrated and concentrated in the Chicago review *Poetry* (◊ Little Magazines). But beyond the accomplishment of these first three volumes, his *Collected Poems* (1923) added little – though some of his later poems about childhood and his poem-games retain a wistful charm. In the four negligible volumes of the later period sentimentality predominates. He supported himself by recitals of his own verse until the novelty of his spectacular dramatization wore thin; then as audiences and readers dwindled he suffered poverty and an emotional depression, which resulted in his suicide in 1931. [RS]

Selected Poems, ed. Mark Harris (1964).
Edgar Lee Masters, *Vachel Lindsay: A Poet in America* (1935); Eleanor Ruggles, *The West-Going Heart* (1959).

Lippmann, Walter (1889–   ). Columnist, social analyst. Born in New York. For a long time an influential, civilized voice in the American scene, Lippmann taught at Harvard, served in government under Woodrow Wilson and then, after writing for the *New Republic*, became the powerfully influential political columnist of the New York *Herald Tribune*. Lippmann remarkably mixes the insider's knowledge of government with the outsider's detachment and idealism. A radical moderate with a commonsense mind, he has the rare power to provide his readers with both inside analysis of contemporary issues and an ideal of a humane society (one of his books is called *The Good Society*, 1937). Among numerous other books and lectures are *A Preface to Morals* (1929), *Interpretations, 1933–1935* (1936), *The Cold War* (1947), the reflective *The Public Philosophy* (1955) and *The Communist World and Ours* (1959). [M B]

The Essential Lippmann, ed. Clinton Rossiter and James Lare (1963).

Literary Reviews. ◊ Little Magazines.

Little Magazines. In this century little magazines and small-circulation journals have played an important part in establishing the modern movement in literature and the consolidating movement in literary criticism which followed it. In *The Little Magazine: A History and a Bibliography* (1946) F. J. Hoffman, Charles Allen and Carolyn Ulrich argue that they 'have stood, since 1912 to the present, defiantly in the front ranks of the battle for a mature literature', and have done this by first publishing 'about 80 per cent of our most important post-1912 critics, novelists, poets, and story-tellers'. The growth of these magazines is in fact a fairly direct indication of the growth of a specialist or *avant garde* attitude towards literature, which has been very evident in this century, particularly in the U.S.A.; and during this century they have existed in very large numbers, deriving from Bohemian groups, expatriate groups, regional movements and even individuals (◊ Bohemianism, Expatriates, Lost Generation). The modern movement in literature, the experimental revival from about 1910 onwards, cosmopolitan, complex, often allusive and private, has depended on strong aesthetic motivations and the tendency of writers to form into movements and groups; this has been a feature of the American literary scene. Little magazines, flourishing in all parts of the U.S.A., and the expatriate centres of Europe (London, Paris, Rome, etc.), have presented these movements and *avant garde* tendencies. And more sober critical journals, often though not always centred on universities, also in terms of circulation and specialized interest 'little', have elaborated a new criticism as well as promoting many original poets and story writers – many of them also major critics (e.g. Allen ◊ Tate, John Crowe ◊ Ransom, Robert Penn ◊ Warren).

The early little magazines arose directly out of an atmosphere of experiment, renaissance, rebellion, often out of centres with active Bohemian movements. Early

models of the type are the *Chap-Book* (1894–8), from Chicago, printing Stephen ◊ Crane, Hamlin ◊ Garland, Henry James, William Vaughn ◊ Moody and others; *M'lle New York* (1895–9), involving James Gibbons ◊ Huneker and European experimental writers; and the *Lark* (1895–7), from San Francisco. But it was not until a strong vein of experimentalism established itself in American letters that the great journals began. In 1912 in Chicago Harriet ◊ Monroe began *Poetry: A Magazine of Verse*, which played a large part in establishing the new experimenters of the 1910s and 1920s, including Eliot, Vachel ◊ Lindsay, Amy ◊ Lowell, Edgar Lee ◊ Masters and Carl ◊ Sandburg, and is still alive. *The Masses* (1911–17) gradually began to turn into a ◊ Greenwich Village Bohemian journal, linking its founding socialist and pacificist attitudes with a strong interest in the arts. The Greenwich Village spirit promoted Alfred Kreymbourg's the *Glebe* (1913–14), which printed the first *Des Imagistes* anthology from Ezra Pound and others (1915–19); while the lively literary movement in Chicago, linked with the London expatriates through Pound, was the source of a second review, Margaret Anderson's *Little Review* (1914–29), printing Hart ◊ Crane, Pound, Eliot, Sherwood Anderson, Hemingway, and some of Joyce's *Ulysses*; it ended its days with Dada in Paris.

In such magazines many distinguished writers, young and experimental, began to gain attention – William Carlos ◊ Williams, Marianne ◊ Moore, Wallace ◊ Stevens, E. E. ◊ Cummings and Robert ◊ Frost should be added to the names already mentioned. At the same time Pound in London was tirelessly promoting their work among the little magazines there and providing them with international reputations, as well as acting as agent for English experimentalists with the American reviews. In America the number of reviews was growing, including *Bruno's Weekly*, *Contemporary Verse*, and the *Liberator*. From New York came the monthly *Seven Arts* (1916–17), edited by James Oppenheim, which spoke of a renaissance in American letters and printed much remarkable criticism supporting the view from Waldo ◊ Frank, Randolph ◊ Bourne, Van Wyck ◊ Brooks and others; Sherwood Anderson and Eugene O'Neill were among those who contributed fiction; Robert Frost, Carl

Sandburg and Amy Lowell were among the poets. It was later absorbed by the *Dial*, the famous review for which ◊ Emerson and Margaret ◊ Fuller had written; in 1916 it was taken over by new editors, including Randolph Bourne and Van Wyck Brooks; and from 1920, under Scofield Thayer, the *Dial* printed many new writers of importance, ranging from T. S. Eliot to Thomas Mann; later Marianne Moore became its editor.

In 1920, at the beginning of an even more exciting period, William Carlos Williams and Robert ◊ McAlmon produced *Contact* (1920–32), printing most of the writers already mentioned and Kenneth ◊ Burke, Yvor ◊ Winters and others. From New Orleans came the lively *Double-Dealer* (1921–6), which published important Southern writers like Tate, Ransom and Faulkner – as well as Hemingway, Anderson, Thornton Wilder and others – and so helped to promote the Southern renaissance. In 1922 appeared the *Fugitive* (◊ Fugitives). Other little magazines over this period were *Laughing Horse, S4N* and *Bozart*. But in the twenties, Paris became the new European centre, and many young writers went there (◊ Lost Generation), taking along or founding their reviews. Alfred Kreymbourg and Harold Loeb went to Italy, where costs were low, to produce *Broom*, which printed American and European experimentalists side by side (1921–4). Arthur Moss brought out *Gargoyle* (1921–2) in Paris, with surveys of Cubist art. Gorham B. ◊ Munson started *Secession* (1922–4), which printed Stevens, Marianne Moore, Matthew ◊ Josephson and Malcolm ◊ Cowley and pursued an expatriate flirtation with Surrealism and Dada. Ford Madox Ford had Hemingway as his assistant editor and a strong American contribution for his *transatlantic review* (1924–5), where Gertrude Stein, the experimentalists' folk-heroine, appeared with part of her *The Making of Americans*, along with Joyce, Ford himself, various young American writers and some English ones. Ernest Walsh's *This Quarter* (1925–32) brought out three issues containing Pound, Hemingway, Joyce, Yvor Winters, and others; then after the death of its editor it passed to Ernest Titus, who recast it and printed Williams, Cummings, Hemingway, Anderson, James T. ◊ Farrell and others.

In New York, H. L. ◊ Mencken and George Jean ◊ Nathan began the provocative, anti-expatriate, anti-aesthetic *American Mercury* (1924–33); it circulated fairly widely and had a popular-satirical tone which was very much Mencken's own, and it spoke for a new urban sophistication, attacking the 'booboisie' and other middle-class or provincial targets; Sinclair ◊ Lewis and Ernest Boyd were among the contributors. Also in New York, the *Masses* tradition was revived with *New Masses* (1926 on; various editors), preparing the way for the political interests of the 1930s. The vein of social criticism was strong in journals of this type (which include the *Freeman*, 1920–4, the *Nation*, the *New Republic* and V. F. ◊ Calverton's *Modern Quarterly*, 1923–40), but close connexions with literature were preserved; and *New Masses* in its early years printed some remarkable work by Robinson ◊ Jeffers, Sherwood Anderson, Floyd ◊ Dell, Carl Sandburg, Witter ◊ Bynner and others. The following year saw the *Hound and Horn* (1927–34) from Harvard, one of the earliest of the critical little magazines, printing Eliot, Kenneth ◊ Burke, R. P. ◊ Blackmur and Allen Tate as critics; fiction by Katherine Anne ◊ Porter, John ◊ Dos Passos, etc.; and verse by many important poets and now well established in the smaller journals. The number of regional reviews, many of them with a literary-critical flavour, was now growing; from Lincoln, Nebraska, for instance, came the *Prairie Schooner* (1927 onwards), university-centred but with a regional emphasis. The development of such journals became important in the thirties as the critical movement grew in force, as academic study of literature expanded, and as literary debate widened.

During the late twenties, another group of expatriate magazines developed in Paris and elsewhere; there was Pound's *Exile* (1927–8), printing Hemingway, McAlmon, Louis ◊ Zukofsky, etc., and some remarkable items by Pound himself; there was Eugene Jolas's remarkable *transition* (1927–38), printing Joyce's *Work in Progress*, Gertrude Stein, Hart Crane, Allen Tate, Kay ◊ Boyle, Harry Crosby, Horace ◊ Gregory, Archibald ◊ MacLeish and many other distinguished writers, and promoting the famous 'Revolution of the Word'; there was the *Tambour* (1928–30), and the *New Review* (1931–2), which printed Henry ◊ Miller. But by the 1930s the expatriate

153

movement was fading, the experimental-aesthetic impetus diminishing, and the new reviews tended either towards overtly political or literary critical perspectives. Some, in particular *Partisan Review* (1934 onwards), were both; beginning as a publication of the John Reed Club of New York, *Partisan Review* grew increasingly emancipated from the party line and published remarkably good criticism, usually with a sociological emphasis, from Lionel ◊ Trilling, Philip ◊ Rahv, Edmund ◊ Wilson, and Blackmur, as well as the poetry of Stevens, Tate, ◊ Jarrell, Karl ◊ Shapiro, etc., and the fiction of Delmore ◊ Schwartz, Saul ◊ Bellow, Katherine Anne Porter, etc. The experimental tradition found a new centre in James Laughlin's *New Directions in Prose and Poetry* (1936 onwards), printing most of the major moderns. From the South came Cleanth ◊ Brooks' and Robert Penn Warren's *Southern Review* (1935–42); in 1938 came John Crowe Ransom's excellent *Kenyon Review*, printing most of the major new critics and poetry by many important poets of both the experimental and a new semi-academic generation, as well as similar fiction; and from New Haven, Connecticut, came *Furioso* (1939 onwards), linking poetry with analytical criticism of it (poets printed include Marianne Moore, Stevens, Cummings, Horace Gregory, John Peale ◊ Bishop, Richard ◊ Eberhart). These critical reviews had from the 1930s on a powerful influence on American writing, rationalizing the position of the literary intellectual, now more likely to be on the university campus than in Bohemia.

By the 1940s and 1950s, the Bohemian-experimental and the critical phase tended to merge as the university became more Bohemian, the Bohemian centres more academic; and though the two groups have often battled they were closely linked. A typical situation was that of the *Chicago Review*, which from 1946 was produced from the University of Chicago, printing many new writers like J. F. ◊ Powers along with older ones like Kenneth ◊ Patchen and James T. Farrell; it gradually grew associated with the Beat Generation (at the same time holding a lively sociological interest) and fell out with the university appearing independently as *Big Table*. *Western Review*, *Folio*, the *Antioch Review*, the *Hudson Review*, as well as the old *Sewanee Review* (founded 1892) and the

Yale Review (1892), took on new importance in this phase; all came out of academic contexts and ranged from a strongly critical to an experimental emphasis. They virtually dominated the creative scene in the late 1940s and 1950s and are still important.

But in the 1950s there developed an increasing number of challengers. For example there was competition from the many magazines produced by the ◊ Beat Generation and the growing number of Bohemian and hippie literary enclaves, as well as from various experimental, free expression and liberation movements. *Evergreen Review* since its foundation in 1957 has been a major centre of new experimental writing, European as well as American, printing a lot of the best (as well as some spuriously sensational) work of the Beat writers, and has featured William ◊ Burroughs, Jack ◊ Kerouac, Gregory ◊ Corso, John ◊ Rechy and many others, though its quality has now declined severely. A strong competitor was the *Noble Savage* (1960 onwards; Saul Bellow was an editor), which published many important new writers. Both of these came from paperback publishers, and, seeing the small magazine as a good promotional device, other such publishers have produced *New World Writing* (1947 onwards), *Discovery*, and the *Anchor Review*, ranging in character from the experimental and academic to the slightly glossy. The important inheritor in this line is the *New American Review*. But the Beat Generation and other new forces produced in addition numerous smaller publications, such as those deriving from Jonathan ◊ Williams or from Lawrence ◊ Ferlinghetti's City Lights Bookshop. Some of these had a strong anarchist emphasis, like the *Journal for the Protection of All Beings*. More important were ventures like the *Black Mountain Review*, which was a centre of new experimental poetry by Robert ◊ Creeley, Charles ◊ Olson, etc.; Robert ◊ Bly's *The Sixties* (formerly *The Fifties*); and LeRoi ◊ Jones's *Yugen*. The tradition of dissent periodicals (*Dissent, Commentary*) was reinforced by a variety of ventures like Paul Krassner's *Realist*, printing writers like Terry Southern and Joseph Heller, and *Ramparts*. The expatriate tradition in the magazine continued too, most solidly with George Plimpton's *Paris Review* and J. F. McCrindle's *Transatlantic Review*; while with the coming into existence of a new reviewing newspaper with radical bias, the *New York Review of Books*, the entire balance of the media in relation to the literary scene was transformed.

In fact this phase saw a media explosion which has continued into the late sixties and played a large part in the expansive, radical cultural climate of this period. Through the 1960s the numbers of magazines went on increasing, but the forms of publication were changing significantly. What the poet-editor Kirby Congdon has called the 'mimeograph revolution' (indeed the general availability of cheap means of typographical reproduction) enabled poets and movements to issue their own magazines; publication has become far less a special achievement, and has lost the scarcity structure of editorial costs and selection; the capitalist market of narrowed enterprise has been relaxed as large numbers of magazines, printed regularly and circulated by a handful of booksellers but mainly by post, produced an expansive, creative climate. Then there is an underground newspaper press drawing in materials previously found in small journals; publications like *East Village Other, Los Angeles Free Press,* and *Rolling Stone* (there are scores more) provide a context for exploration of political protest, rock music, esoteric religion and relaxed sexuality, in the main line of American anarchism. Of more literary publications, with the demise of Lita Hornick's *Kulture* and *Art and Literature* (John ◊ Ashbery and others), two brilliant magazines, the best general magazines now are perhaps Charles Newman's *TriQuarterly* and Clayton Eshleman's *Caterpillar.* After the cessation of *C Magazine* (Ted ◊ Berrigan) and *Mother* (Peter ◊ Schjeldahl and Lewis MacAdams), the New York poetry scene is best seen in *Angel Hair* (Ann Waldman and Lewis Warsh) and *Adventures in Poetry* (Larry Fagin). For the more general scene: *Works* (John Hopper and Robert Brotherson), *Sumac* (Dan Gerber and Jim Harrison), *Some Thing* (Jerome ◊ Rothenberg and David Antin), *Floating Bear* (Diane di Prima), *The San Francisco Earthquake* (Jacob Herman and Claude Pelieu), etc. The best of the black literary magazines is David Henderson's *Umbra.* But selection is invidious in the extreme; the sheer vitality of the little magazine scene in 1970 is impossible to cover briefly. Today experimentalism is no longer an oddity, nor the

little magazine the place that harbours the writer too daring to sell. The climate of experimentalism has a general dominance in the literary and in the social scene; the clear categorization of the market which was once possible is no longer viable; the counter-culture so extensive and vigorous that the entire previous structure of the cultural scene is under challenge. [MB/EM]

Reed Whittemore, *Little Magazines* (U. of Minnesota Pamphlet, 1963); 'The Little Magazines', *Times Literary Supplement,* 25 April 1968; 'The Small Presses',*Works,* 11, i (1969); *Directory of Little Magazines,* ed. Leonard V. Fulton and Kavan McCarthy; James Gilbert, *Writers and Partisans* (1968).

Living Theatre, The. Founded in 1947 by Judith Malina and Julian Beck it has remained, with a few brief breaks, a centre of new theatre, first in America and later in Europe. In its initial New York centre, it put on experimental plays by Gertrude ◊ Stein, Paul ◊ Goodman, Kenneth ◊ Rexroth, T. S. ◊ Eliot, John ◊ Ashbery and William Carlos ◊ Williams, and Yeats, Brecht, Lorca, Strindberg, Jarry and Cocteau, thus injecting a variety of life into American theatre. The last productions before it left for Europe in 1963 included *The Connection* by Jack Gelber, Pound's version of Sophocles' *Women of Trachis,* and Kenneth Brown's *The Brig,* all strong works directly connected with the social and political protests against victimization which were to absorb the company in the sixties. Even when the acting and production standards may have been relaxed, the company generated a sense of commitment to the social function of theatre. In 1963 the Living Theatre was seized by the Internal Revenue Service for non-payment of taxes. The government showed no lenience and this seemed to fulfil the message gathering in the company's plays. The Becks, with 26 of their group, moved to Europe, where they developed the idea of a theatre company as creative political critics and emotional gurus. They became part of the radicalism of the late 1960s. Their major productions were Jean Genet's *The Maids,* the Sophocles Brecht *Antigone,* and three works which were created by the company as a group – *Frankenstein* (1965, partly based on Mary Shelley's character), *Mysteries and Smaller Pieces* (1966) and *Paradise Now* (1968). In 1964 and 1969 they performed in England,

and in 1968, as almost legendary heroes, returned triumphantly to America, and became part of both the new radicalism in politics and the developments in audience-participation and actor-activism in drama. The Becks' early work was aesthetic and poetic; their later theatre of revolution owes ideas to Antonin Artaud's 'theatre of cruelty', the pacifism and anarchism of Paul Goodman, Reich's psychology of sexual liberation, the epic theatre of Erwin Piscator, with whom Judith Malina studied in the late 1940s, and Hassidic Judaism, both the service and the mysticism. [E M]

'The Return of the Living Theatre', *Tulane Drama Review*, XIII, 3 (1969).

Lloyd, Henry Demarest (1847–1903). Journalist, reformer. Born in New York. After qualifying as a lawyer in 1869 he joined a New York group trying to reform Tammany Hall, the Democratic Party organization in the city. He then moved to Chicago and in the Chicago *Tribune*, part-owned by his father-in-law, pointed out the dangers of unrestrained big business and monopoly, and the unsavoury political practices of many large corporations. He investigated conditions among the miners in the Spring Valley, Illinois, coal strike, championed the demonstrators convicted after the Haymarket Riots of 1886, and in the early 1890s worked for the Populist party, becoming disillusioned later and turning to the Socialist-Labor party. In later life he held that socialism was the only sound alternative to the established American parties, though he believed firmly in a pragmatic, not a doctrinaire, approach to contemporary problems. His positive aims are expressed in *A Strike of Millionaires against Miners* (1890), an attempt to formulate the rights of labour, and in his most famous book, *Wealth against Commonwealth* (1894; ed. T. G. Cochran, 1963), he sought to produce a valid alternative to the prevailing concept of Social Darwinism. [D K A]

Daniel Aaron, *Men of Good Hope* (1951).

Locke, David Ross. ◊ Nasby, Petroleum Vesuvius.

Lockridge, Ross (1914–48). Novelist. Born in Indiana, he was educated at the Sorbonne and Harvard, and taught at Indiana University and Simmons College. By his early death he had completed one novel, the ambitious and extended *Raintree County* (1948), which takes in some of the great

political and social occasions of an imaginary Indiana county through the 19th century. Its scope and rhetoric link it with the work of Thomas ◊ Wolfe, whom the author admired. [M B]

Logan, John (1923–   ). Poet. Born in Iowa, educated at Coe College and the University of Iowa, he became editorial director of the Poetry Seminar in Chicago and a teacher at Notre Dame University. His volumes, which include *A Cycle for Mother Cabrini* (1955), *Ghosts of the Heart* (1960) and *Spring of the Thief* (1963), are marked by an extremely personal, vivid and erudite Catholicism. The earlier poetry is violent in imagery, coarse in diction; the latest volume shifts to a quieter, more assured and more directly personal kind of confessional poetry. [B P]

Paul Carroll, *The Poem in Its Skin* (1968).

London, Jack (John Griffith London) (1876–1916). Novelist. His father was an astrologer, his mother came from a comfortable Ohio family. In San Francisco he spent his boyhood on the waterfront and from the age of 15 worked in a cannery and became a fighting, drinking outlaw, and a voracious reader, beginning with Irving's *Alhambra* and working his way through the Oakland library with travel adventures, Smollett, Wilkie Collins, Kipling, Ouida, etc. He switched allegiance and became a government hero – see the stories in *Tales of the Fish Patrol* (1905) – and went to the Arctic in a sealing ship (material for *The Sea Wolf*, 1904). He returned in the 1893 depression, sank to the bottom of the labour scale, and joined Coxey's Army's march on Washington in 1894, just after winning first prize in a newspaper story competition. The four crucial elements of his youth were complete: heroic sea adventure, fiction of romance and exploration, the taste of success with his first story, and an understanding of the conditions of labour in America. Now he discovered the *Communist Manifesto*, enrolled at the University of California (he was 20) and became an active socialist. At Berkeley he read the 19th-century social evolutionists, and, in 1897, took off for the Klondike gold rush carrying Darwin, Haeckel and *Paradise Lost* in his bag.

His education in natural law, determinism and authority continued. His life was legendary. He now read Frazer, the 19th-century economists and Nietzsche, and was drawn to Shaw's philosopher-athlete in *Man and Superman*. In 1903 he wrote *The People of the Abyss*, an account of poverty in London's East End, and *The Call of the Wild*, an all-time best-seller. *The Sea Wolf* had an advance sale in America of 40,000. From 1900 to 1916, 50 books earned him over a million dollars, which he spent fast. *The War of the Classes* (1905) and *The Human Drift* (1917) work out his economic determinism and reformism, and *Martin Eden* (1909) dramatizes his own rise into the moneyed class as a betrayal of idealism, while *John Barleycorn* (1913) concerns his alcoholism. His travels ended on his ranch, Wolf House, in California: he died a public figure, exhausted and in despair.

In *The Call of the Wild* the transformation of a pet dog into leader of a Yukon wolf pack is the example of Darwinian survival, written in a swiftly moving style; *White Fang* (1906) is nearly as brilliant, telling the reverse story. *The Sea Wolf* concerns the career of Captain Wolf Larsen as he puts Spencer and Nietzsche into superman practice, defeated by symbolic blindness and the skill of an ex-dilettante pressed into his service. *The Iron Heel* (1907) is an early 20th-century nightmare Utopia, a warning against fascist dictatorship in Chicago. *The Assassination Bureau,* left unfinished, has recently been rescued and completed by R. L. Fish (1963); the plot concerns a millionaire socialist's scheme to kill the head of a bureau dedicated to eliminate enemies of society. In many ways London is the archetypal popular 20th-century novelist: his conflicts are still central. [EM]

Letters from Jack London, ed. K. Hendricks and I. Shepard (1965).

Ed. P. S. Foner, *Jack London: American Rebel* (1947); R. O. Connor, *Jack London: A Biography* (1965); Joan London, *Jack London and His Times* (1939; reissued with new introduction, 1968).

Longfellow, Henry Wadsworth (1807–82). Poet. One of the most popular poets who ever lived, he was born in the seaport and forest frontier of Portland, Maine, and educated with Hawthorne and the future president Pierce at Bowdoin. He modelled his early literary ambition on ⟡ Irving, who received him in Spain during his 1826–9 study journey. His linguistic abilities gained him a professorship at Bowdoin and, in 1834, at Harvard, after a second European trip to encounter Scandinavian and German romantic poetry, and Carlyle. The early death of his wife and child are reflected in the mild stoicism of his ensuing poetry and philosophy. He remarried in 1843 and lived in enough wealth to resign from Harvard in 1854, but in 1861 his wife died from burns: this ended a period of happiness during which most of his famous poems were written. His popularity in his own lifetime was great, unbroken by the Civil War, honoured by Oxford and Queen Victoria, and finally by Westminster Abbey. But 'A Psalm of Life' (1838) is typical, a work of melancholic cliché on mutability. *Ballads and Other Poems* (1842) includes 'The Wreck of the Hesperus', 'The Village Blacksmith', 'Excelsior' and 'The Rainy Day' – sentimental classics of bathetic rhetoric and self-pity raised by their readers to levels of myth, as was 'Evangeline' (1847), whose theme was intended to be American – the plight of the Acadian exile from Nova Scotia to Louisiana in slow, crude hexameters. *The Song of Hiawatha* (1855) versifies historical sources in hypnotic trochaic tetrameters, said to derive from the Finnish *Kalevala*. After his 'Indian Edda' appeared *The Courtship of Miles Standish* (1858), the last of his three 'epics', a New England courtship interrupted by Indian wars. *Tales of a Wayside Inn* (1863) includes 'Paul Revere's Ride', and his final poems included a poor translation of Dante (1865–7). The art of Longfellow is an outstanding example of popular taste. Recent efforts to raise him to the level of mythopoeic poetry have not been convincing, although his narrative poems are good fun. His synthetic folk-poems are internationally known but have little depth or linguistic talent. [EM]

Letters, ed. A. Hilen (2 vols., 1967); *Representative Selections*, ed. O. Shepard (1934).
Newton Arvin, *Longfellow: His Life and Work* (1933); E. Wagenknecht, *Longfellow: A Full-Length Portrait* (1955).

Longstreet, Augustus Baldwin (1790–1870). Born in Georgia, educated at Yale, he became a judge, a clergyman, a professional college president and a newspaper editor. But he is remembered for his comic tales and sketches in *Georgia Scenes* (1835), an entertaining collection of Georgia wit and folktales he apparently felt ashamed of later and tried to suppress. [EM]

J. D. Wade, *Augustus Baldwin Longstreet* (1924).

Loos, Anita (1893–   ). Novelist, playwright, film-script writer. Born in California, she was writing scenarios for D. W. Griffith at 15. Besides her screenplays of many well-known films, she has won fame and best-sellerdom for two celebrations of the female gold-digger in *Gentlemen Prefer Blondes* (1925), the witty, self-exposing narrative of Lorelei Lee, 'a Professional Lady', and its sequel *But Gentlemen Marry Brunettes* (1928). Both books are marked by an eye for the age, an ear for its speech and a sense of its values. More recently Miss Loos satirized Hollywood in *No Mother to Guide Her* (1961). Her plays include *Happy Birthday* (1947), *A Mouse Is Born* (1951) and the stage version of Colette's *Gigi*; her autobiographies are entitled *This Brunette Prefers Work* (1956) and *A Girl Like I* (1966), in which she describes her experiences in Hollywood and New York ('I reported Gertrude Stein as the most manly of the lot', is the level). [MB]

Lost Generation. 'You are all a lost generation': Gertrude Stein is credited with the remark in one of the epigraphs to Ernest Hemingway's *The Sun Also Rises* (1926). Though Hemingway subsequently regretted the phrase, and Gertrude Stein denied using it, it stuck as the description of the literary generation of the 1920s, particularly that part of it which expatriated to Paris (◊ Expatriates) and led a wild Bohemian-literary life. The phrase suggests the sense of alienation and philosophical uncertainty which has often been felt to be the defining characteristic of much American writing of the twenties; it also suggests the awareness of being a generation which existed among many of the writers of the period, and their sense that in a period of rapid change and uncertainty they had lost touch with the attitudes and norms of their parents. The generation was alienated, separated, lost (though all one needed do to find them was to go to Paris). There have been many chronicles of this 'mass-alienation', but few real explanations. The two best are by R. P. ◊ Blackmur in his essay 'The American Literary Expatriate' (in *Foreign Influences in American Life: Essays and Critical Bibliographies*, ed. David F. Bowers, 1944) and Malcolm ◊ Cowley in *Exile's Return* (1934; revised edn, 1951). Blackmur's semi-sociological argument is that this was the first time a country had attempted to detach its cultural capital from its political and economic capital, and that it was bound to lead to tension and failure. Cowley sees a pattern of development from the socially hostile art of the twenties to the socially committed art of the thirties; he regards the 'lost generation' as being detached both from previous generations and from the aims of their society, and sees them as involved in a rebellion whose character was not political but artistic. Their background was largely middle-class, and they regarded art as a traditional mode of escape from this class, because it was associated with Bohemianism, liberalism and radicalism. Lacking a strong social interest, having the middle-class sense of estrangement from power and its distrust of political action, they found France an appropriate centre for their creed, which was literary formalism. However, they found 'a crazy Europe in which the intellectuals of their own middle class were more defeated and demoralized than those at home', and this gradually turned them either towards political action or to extreme tension leading in a number of cases to suicide.

This was, nonetheless, a highly productive period for American letters, and this should not be forgotten in any account of it. Samuel Putnam, in *Paris Was Our Mistress: Memoirs of a Lost and Found Generation* (1947), stresses the disreputable quality of much of the activity, and also the remarkable size of the group present. But this included Hemingway, Fitzgerald, Ezra Pound, John Dos Passos and many others of importance; Hemingway distinguished between those who came to be Bohemians, and those who actually wrote. The strongly experimental atmosphere threw up numerous salons, magazines and small presses printing in English. Connexions were made with surrealism and Dada. A remarkable amount of important writing did emerge; this is the essential literary importance of the phase.

But it has another kind of significance in that it represents a phase in which the writer's life became – because of increased education and of the convenient economic arrangements which made Parisian Bohemian life extremely cheap for Americans – within the reach of a much larger group than previously; therefore the role of the writer changed. One aspect of the phenomenon was that a vastly enlarged generation of intellectuals found an attractive *modus vivendi* which however encouraged insecurity and tension. The result was that a very large group of writers and aspirants formed a kind of peer-group stimulating to technical advance and elaboration. The climate of the period is best evoked in Hemingway's *The Sun Also Rises* and Fitzgerald's *Tender Is the Night* (1934). Robert ◊ McAlmon's *Being Geniuses Together: An Autobiography* (1938) and Ernest Hemingway's *A Moveable Feast* (1964) give convenient pictures of lost-generation life, showing the personalities and famous occasions involved. [MB]

Lovingood, Sut ◊ Harris, George W.

Lowell, Amy Lawrence (1874–1925). Poet. Born in Brookline, Massachusetts, she was educated privately, and in her youth travelled much abroad. *A Dome of Many-Colored Glass* (1912) consists of poems conventional in form and sentimental in attitude, but after meeting Pound in London in 1913 she became an enthusiastic convert to ◊ Imagism, in whose anthologies she was liberally represented. Pound, having broken with the Imagist group, petulantly renamed the movement 'Amygism'. She died of a stroke after years of excessive literary industry and a series of operations.

Her collections of poetry include *Sword Blades and Poppy Seed* (1914), *Men, Women, and Ghosts* (1916), *Pictures of the Floating World* (1919) and *What's O'Clock?* (1925). Versatile rather than original, scintillating rather than substantial, her poetry lacks the firmness and concision advocated by Imagist theoreticians, and is in fact less Imagistic than impressionistic. Self-consciously exotic and extravagant, it is ablaze with flowers and rich fabrics. Although a devoted New Englander, she would often wander nostalgically to preRevolutionary France or to an oriental never-never land. She possessed an amazing facility for rhyming, but her characteristic form is an unrhymed free verse. She also experimented with polyphonic prose, an intermittently rhymed prose-poetry.

Her study of contemporary poetry, *Tendencies in Modern American Poetry* (1917), is less witty and succinct than *A Critical Fable* (1922), a similar survey in verse, modelled on *A Fable for Critics* by her relative James Russell ◊ Lowell. Just before her death she completed a massive, exuberant, but disorganized biography, *John Keats* (1925). Her *Complete Poetical Works* appeared in 1955. Richard Alding-

ton's estimate seems fair: 'In Amy there was something of an artist and a real aesthetic appreciation.' [RWB]

Stanley K. Coffman, Jr, *Imagism* (1951); S. Foster Damon, *Amy Lowell* (1935); Horace Gregory, *Amy Lowell* (1958).

Lowell, James Russell (1819–91). Poet, essayist, editor, diplomat. Born into a distinguished New England family, educated at Harvard, he came rapidly to prominence as a poet. His first book, *A Year's Life and Other Poems*, came out in 1841, and *Poems* in 1844, the year he married Martha White, who appears to have encouraged his interest in the Abolitionist cause and other liberal movements (he wrote many political essays and addresses). His liberal opinions had in them a distinct conservative strain, in that he was concerned with the survival of an 'exemplary' aristocracy. In 1848 his reputation as a poet increased with the publication *Poems: Second Series. A Fable for Critics*, a long satirical poem on his contemporaries, published anonymously (the title page describes it as 'By A Wonderful Quiz, who accompanies himself with a rub-a-dub-dub, full of spirit and grace, on the top of the tub'); *The Vision of Sir Launfal*, a Grail story in verse; and the first series of his famous *Biglow Papers*, Yankee dialect poems on contemporary issues, satirically treated, and attacking particularly American policy in the Mexican war. In 1855, two years after the death of his wife, he became Professor of Belles Lettres at Harvard; in 1857 he became editor of the *Atlantic Monthly*; and in 1867 he published the second series of *Biglow Papers*, which the Civil War stirred him to write. In the years after the war he continued to publish poetry, but grew increasingly well known as an essayist and literary critic. In two series of essays called *Among My Books* (1870, 1876), and elsewhere, he published studies of Chaucer, Dante, Spenser, Shakespeare, Keats, etc., which are still highly regarded. His *The English Poets: Lessing: Rousseau* (1888) circulated widely in England. By this time he had become American minister to the Court of Spain (1877–80); and then from 1880 to 1885 American minister in Britain (where he delivered his famous address 'Democracy'). To England he became closely attached, and he reveals in his later life a kind of fondness for the English social pattern which became a popular American nostalgia during these Gilded Age years.

The striking feature of his work is its range of manners and styles, a range so great that he later became convinced that he dissipated his gifts. Later criticism has tended to agree with his judgement. He has a variety of tones of voice, a variety of themes, the themes and voices of the wide-ranging Victorian intellectual. His interest in provincial vernacular, his exuberance, and his literary nationalism co-exist with a much more cosmopolitan vein, particularly evident in his substantial literary criticism. In his poetry, perhaps his most characteristic technique is descriptive or reflective, but he will move suddenly to exhortation, assailing poverty, tyranny and religious doubt. His satirical vein is important, but it often lacks direction and falls back on exuberance. A major figure, he is too varied to have produced any definitely major works. Probably his odes and longer poems – 'Commemoration Ode' (1865), 'The Cathedral' (1870) and 'Agassiz' (1874) – are among his best. [MB]

The Complete Writings, ed. Charles Eliot Norton (16 vols., 1904).

H. E. Scudder, *James Russell Lowell: A Biography* (2 vols., 1901); Leon Howard, *Victorian Knight-Errant: A Study of the Early Literary Career of James Russell Lowell* (1952); Martin Duberman, *James Russell Lowell* (1967).

Lowell, Robert (1917–). Poet. He was born in Boston, Massachusetts, and inherits New England introspection, dissent and spiritual exploration. After Harvard, he studied with John Crowe ◊ Ransom at Kenyon College, and with Robert Penn ◊ Warren and Cleanth ◊ Brooks at Louisiana State University. He became a Roman Catholic, and in 1943 was gaoled for conscientious objection to allied bombing of civilians. His training in the classics and with the ◊ New Criticism poets shows in his first two volumes of poetry, *Land of Unlikeness* (1944) and *Lord Weary's Castle* (1946). His international reputation began with *Poems 1938–1949* (1950). The title poem of *The Mills of the Kavanaughs* (1951) is a 20-page psychological novelette, and *Life Studies* (1959) consists of lengthy poems and a prose section concerned with his immediate family and his own experience of hospital, prison and married life in the 1940s and 1950s. *For the Union Dead* (1964) develops the forms of his later poetry

and shows an increased scope of social criticism. His free translations – *Phaedra* (1960) and *Imitations* (1962) – are among his finest work, and his three plays, based on stories by Hawthorne and Melville, *The Old Glory* (1965), have transformed the possibilities of verse drama. What Alfred Kazin called 'the elegantly turned tumult of style and evocation of Catholic glory and order' of his earlier poems is modified into the freer tradition of William Carlos ◊ Williams in the *Life Studies* poems of direct, non-exegetical confession, self-exposure and spoken-voice rhythms. Lowell's career, itself a remarkable achievement in poetic discipline, also reflects a crucial change in American poetry from academic verse to the renewal of the line from Whitman. But his nervous, slightly timid approach to contemporary affairs enervates the poems in *Now the Ocean* (1967), while his verse play treatment of the Aeschylean theme in *Prometheus Bound* (1967, with pictures by Sidney Nolan) is too oblique to be as politically effective as its intention seems to be. (Nolan also illustrates *The Voyage*, the Baudelaire poems from *Imitations*.) *Notebook 1967–8* (1969) is a remarkable poetic witness to the conflicts of the sixties. Lowell now reflects the American liberal intellectual's struggle to save what he can from increasing chaos. [EM]

H. B. Staples, *Robert Lowell: The First Twenty Years* (1962); Jerome Mazzaro, *The Poetic Themes of Robert Lowell* (1966).

Lowenfels, Walter (1897–). Poet. He was associated with many of the great American ◊ expatriate writers who lived in Paris after the First World War, publishing some half-dozen small volumes of poetry there. In 1934 he gave up Europe and poetry, returning to the States to be a journalist; in 1955, after his arrest during the McCarthyite purges, he returned to poetry, publishing recently *American Voices* (1959), *Song of Peace* (1959), *Some Deaths: Selected Poems, 1929–1962* (1964) and *Land of Roseberries* (1965). His important efforts to keep the spoken word alive on the page and the sometimes witty, sometimes poignant compassion he expresses for the victims of this world have won him the admiration of two different generations of the *avant garde*. In 1961 he edited the valuable *Walt Whitman's Civil War*, in 1964 *Poets of Today*, and in 1967 *Where is Vietnam? American Poets Respond. Thou Shalt not Kill* (1968) contains his peace poems. *We Are All Poets Really* (ed. Allen de Loach, 1967) and *The Portable Walter* (ed. Robert Gover, 1968) are collections of his work. *To an Imaginary Daughter* (1964) is a prose record of relationships between generations. [BP]

A. Guttman, 'Poetic Poetics', *Massachusetts Review*, Autumn, 1965.

Lowry, Robert (1919–). Novelist, story-writer. He is one of the group of vigorous realists produced by the experiences of the Second World War. He served in the army in Africa and Italy and drew on this for several novels – including *Casualty* (1946) and *Find Me in Fire* (1948) – and the Italian-set stories in *The Wolf That Fed Us* (1949). He is a vigorous and often a funny writer concerned with the horrors of war and the threat of modern experience to individual decency. [MB]

Luhan, Mabel Dodge (1879–1962). Patron-ess of the arts, memoirist. Born in Buffalo, N.Y. Her salons in different parts of the world linked her in many of the modern movements in American and European letters. In 1902, married to the architect Edward Dodge, she went to live in Florence, Italy; in 1913 she returned to New York and set up her salon on Fifth Avenue near Greenwich Village; in 1918 she settled in Taos, New Mexico, in an adobe house and married Antonio Luhan, a Pueblo Indian. Her various houses were literary centres, drawing important writers of each period; and she really participated in three distinct movements, one expatriate, the second New York revolutionary, the third Western. Gertrude Stein wrote a famous 'portrait' of her, 'Portrait of Mabel Dodge at the Villa Curonia', and she has been found to be the model for other characters in litera-ture. in the work of writers as different as Carl ◊ Van Vechten and D. H. Lawrence. Others associated with her include Bernard ◊ Berenson, John ◊ Reed, Max ◊ Eastman, Walter ◊ Lippmann, and E. A. ◊ Robinson. Her life is crucial for any understanding of intellectualism or feminism in the first half of this century.
Lorenzo in Taos (1932) is her record of her connexion in New Mexico with Law-rence, and gives insight into Indian culture and its artistic attraction. Her major work is *Intimate Memories*, four volumes of literary reminiscence which give important records of the whole period between about 1900 and 1935; the volumes are *Intimate Memories: Background* (1933), *European Experiences* (1935), *Movers and Shakers* (1936) and *Edge of the Taos Desert: An Escape to Reality* (1937). [MB]

Christopher Lasch, *The New Radicalism in America, 1889–1963* (1965).

Lynd, Robert S(taughton) (1892–1949) and **Helen M(errell)** (1896–). Teachers, sociologists. Born in Indiana and Illinois respectively. Their reputation was estab-lished with the classic studies of an American small town, *Middletown* (1929) and *Middletown Revisited* (1937). Robert Lynd became Professor of Sociology at Columbia in 1931, and his wife is Pro-fessor of Social Philosophy at Sarah Lawrence College. Her two major works are *England in the 1880s: Toward a Social Basis for Freedom* (1945) and the brilliant *On Shame and the Search for Identity* (1958). [EM]

Lytle, Andrew (1902–). Novelist, story-writer. Born in Tennessee, he graduated from Vanderbilt and associated there with the ◊ Fugitive group. He has taught at the University of Florida and the University of the South at Sewanee, Tennessee, where he now edits the *Sewanee Review* (◊ Little Magazines). He began, following the example of fellow-Fugitives ◊ Tate and ◊ Warren, by writing a biography with a Civil War setting, *Bedford Forrest and His Critter Company* (1931). Four novels followed – *The Long Night* (1936), a historical romance of the Civil War; *At the Moon's Inn* (1941), a more serious historical fiction dealing with DeSoto and the Spanish conquest of the Florida Indians; *A Name for Evil* (1947; reprinted in *A Novel, A Novella and Four Stories*, 1958), a fable of the clash between modern and traditional values; and his best work to date, *The Velvet Horn* (1957), superbly rendering a boy's initiation to manhood in the Civil War and after. All are in the Southern tradition, and the best resemble Faulkner in their concern with exploring a culture and creating a regional mythology. [AH]

M

McAlmon, Robert (1895–1956). Editor, publisher, novelist, poet, story writer. Born at Clifton, Kansas. An important figure among the ◊ Lost Generation in Paris in the 1920s, he left one of the best records of the period in his autobiography, *Being Geniuses Together* (1938). From Kansas, McAlmon went to New York and became co-editor with William Carlos ◊ Williams of the magazine *Contact* (◊ Little Magazines). Marriage to the English writer 'Bryher' brought him first to London and then to Paris, where he became deeply involved in expatriate life, helping James Joyce, editing magazines, and founding, in 1922 with William Bird, two small presses – Contact Editions and the Three Mountains Press – which became important centres of expatriate publishing (Hemingway, Williams, Pound, Stein and H.D. were among their authors). Several of McAlmon's own books appeared from these presses – the story-collections *A Hasty Bunch* (1922) and *A Companion Volume* (1923) and the novel *Post-Adolescence* (1923), etc. McAlmon's fiction, intensely realized, poetic, modern, has both the cosmopolitan and regional interests typical of expatriate writing – he writes, for instance, about Paris and the Riviera, and Kansas and childhood. For the latter, see particularly *Village: As It Happened Through a Fifteen-Year Period* (1924). His poetry, loosely ◊ Imagistic, appeared in several volumes, the most complete being *Not Alone Lost* (1937). [M B]

McBain, Ed. ◊ Hunter, Evan.

McCarthy, Mary (1912–   ). Novelist, critic, travel writer. She was born in Seattle, orphaned at the age of 6 and raised by relations of Catholic, Protestant and Jewish backgrounds. Her childhood complexities are carefully described in one of her best books, *Memories of a Catholic Girlhood* (1957). She graduated from Vassar in 1933 (see her novel *The Group*, 1963) and began her career as critic and reviewer on progressive magazines including the *Nation*, the *New Republic* and *Partisan Review*. She has taught at Bard and Sarah Lawrence (which provided material for *The Groves of Academe*, 1952), and has since lived in Paris. She has always been at the centre of sophisticated opinion in New York intellectual life, from her participation in the American left of the thirties, and her admiration for Trotsky, to her visit to Vietnam in the war of the 1960s. She began her literary career with *The Company She Keeps* (1942), which includes the well-known 'The Man in the Brooks Brothers Suit', the story of an intellectual woman's seduction by a businessman (Robert Penn ◊ Warren published her first story in the *Southern Review*). *The Oasis* (1949) is a satire on liberal utopians and *The Groves of Academe* (1952) shrewdly analyses a leftist academic's urge to martyrdom. *A Charmed Life* (1955) and her short stories collected in *Cast a Cold Eye* (1952) are sharply observant studies of contemporary manners, especially malicious towards intellectuals. *The Group* follows the lives of a set of young women who had known each other at college as they choose between emancipation, careers and family traditionalism. It is a smartly written novel, whose social and sexual analysis is not as superficial as the smooth style might suggest. *Venice Observed* (1956) and *The Stones of Florence* (1959) are highly personal travel books, containing critical information on the condition of Italy. *Sights and Spectacles* (1956) is a collection of surgical theatre reviews, and *On the Contrary: Articles of Belief 1946–1961* (1962) is a set of unevenly critical essays, travel pieces and estimations of classical authors. *The Writing on the Wall* (1970) is a collection of her literary criticism. *Vietnam* (1967) and *Hanoi* (1968) are critical reviews of America's war and its implications. She brings an independent eye and a sharp pen to everything she tackles, but her fiction does not have the qualities she admires in her criticism. [E M]

Doris Grumbach, *The Company She Kept* (1967); Irvin Stock, *Mary McCarthy* (U. of Minnesota Pamphlet, 1968).

McClure, Michael (1932–   ). Poet. He was born in Kansas but has lived most of his life in San Francisco. He is one of the most original and vital poets in America, developing some extreme personal forms of typographical, spatial and ejaculatory effects which combine ideas from both Antonin Artaud and Charles ◊ Olson (his and Robert ◊ Creeley's 'projective verse') and form a profoundly intimate poetry of love and transcendental experience. His extensive poetry in book form includes: *Passage* (1956), *For Artaud* (1959), *Hymns to St Geryon* (1959), *Dark Brown* (1961), which contains some uniquely open love poems, and *A New Book / A Book of Torture* (1961). *Ghost Tantras* (1964) combine words and phonetic phrases and are intended to be read and growled aloud. *Thirteen Mad Sonnets* (1964) is a printed version of handwritten poems, and ● (1966) is a set of poems completed by designs of the artist and filmmaker Bruce Connor. *Meat Science Essays* (1963) presents the philosophy of McClure's emergence from his 'dark night' into possession of his flesh and spirit, and *Love Lion Book* (1966, issued as *Writing II*) is a rather more overtly philosophical version of earlier poetic ideas, while *Poisoned Wheat* (1965) is a poetic blast against the warfare state. Among his plays the best known are *The Blossom, or Billy the Kid* (1967) and *The Beard* (1967), an extended erotic scene between Jean Harlow and Billy the Kid. *Freewheelin Frank, Secretary of the Angels* (1967), 'as told to Michael McClure by Frank Reynolds', concerns the Hell's Angels motorcycle gang of San Francisco. His recent works include *Hail Thee Who Play* (1968), *The Sermons of Jean Harlow and the Curses of Billy Kid* (1968) and *Little Odes and the Raptors* (1969). [E M]

Marshall Clements, *A Catalogue of the Works of Michael McClure* (1965).

McCullers, Carson (1917–67). Novelist, short-story writer, playwright. The world of her fiction is filled with violence, perversion and injustice, and deformed by conflict, frustration, pain and grief. She was born in a small town in Georgia, and such a town provides the unromantic setting for most of her work: long summers of glaring heat, drab houses, cafés and small factories, the smells of poverty and decay, an overpowering impression of bleak ugliness. Most of the inhabitants live locked in physical or spiritual isolation, suffering grotesque physical or psychological disfigurement as freaks, oddities, the dispossessed and outcast. Yet Carson McCullers does not create such a world to gain cheap, sensational effects; her central theme is love, its thwarting and failure, occasionally its grace. Without love, the human community disintegrates before the pressures of hatred and fear, social, racial and economic injustice, sexual violence and perversion.

The Heart is a Lonely Hunter (1940) explores the problems of isolation and communication as reflected in the central character, John Singer, a deaf-mute, whose loneliness focuses that of the four other main characters, who try to achieve some kind of communion with him. *Reflections in a Golden Eye* (1941) is more extravagantly scored by violence and perversion in a variety of forms within an army camp in the South, and its handling of characters owes too much to the psychologist's case-book. *Member of the Wedding* (1946) finely portrays the emotional anxieties and conflicts endured by an imaginative adolescent as she tries to come to terms with her maturing self. *The Ballad of the Sad Café* (1951) is a collection of stories which provides an excellent introduction to Carson McCullers' fictional world. *Clock without Hands* (1961), a novel more subdued in tone than most of her previous work, deals largely with the racial problems of Southern society, and states rather than dramatizes its solutions. Carson McCullers successfully dramatized *Member of the Wedding* in 1950; *The Square Root of Wonderful* (1958) is another play. [A H]

Ihab H. Hassan, 'Carson McCullers: The Alchemy of Love and Aesthetics of Pain', *Modern Fiction Studies*, v (Winter, 1959–60); Louise Y. Gossett, 'Dispossessed Love: Carson McCullers', in *Violence in Recent Southern Fiction* (1965); Oliver Evans, *Carson McCullers: Her Life and Work* (1965).

Macdonald, Dwight (1906–). Political writer. After graduating from Yale, he worked editorially on *Fortune* and *Partisan Review* (1944–9) and founded *Politics* (1944), an important journal of philosophical anarchism and pacifism, some of whose essays are contained with other political writings in *Memoirs of a Revolutionist* (1957). He has also written *Henry Wallace* (1948), *The Ford Foundation* (1956), *Against the American Grain* (1962), a collection of his essays including those on Mass Cult and Mid-Cult, Cozzens and Twain, and *The Ghost Conspiracy* (1965), a critique of the

Warren Commission report on the assassination of President Kennedy. He is one of the very few political and social thinkers since 1940 to have maintained independence of mind and a style uncorrupted by the editorial policies of the journals he has contributed to. [EM]

Hannah Arendt, 'He's All Dwight', *New York Review*, XI, 2 (1968).

McGinley, Phyllis (1905–). Poet. Oregon-born, she lives in New York. One of a school of sophisticated light-verse commentators more common in the U.S.A. than elsewhere, she is, along with Ogden ◊ Nash, among the most successful and satisfying. Her witty, satirical and urbane poems comment on the American scene with a variety of tones and subjects, contrasting urban and country life, observing commuters, patterns of taxation, fashions and foibles. Her work, published in the *New Yorker*, the *Saturday Review*, etc., has been collected in numerous volumes, including *A Pocketful of Wry* (1940), *Husbands Are Difficult* (1941) and the delightful and successful *Love Letters of Phyllis McGinley* (1954). *Times Three: Selected Verse from Three Decades* (1960) is a collection which shows the range of her work. She has also written books for children and a book on saints, *Saint-Watching* (1969). [MB]

McGrath, Thomas (1918–). Poet. Born in Dakota, he studied at three universities, served in the army in the Aleutians, and then worked and taught in a number of colleges. His power is revealed in long autobiographical poems such as *Letter from an Imaginary Friend* (1962), which evokes Dakota farm life of the twenties, the character of the I.W.W., and his youthful struggles during the Depression. He tends to be garrulous but it is out of exuberance and lack of interest in academic forms. His shorter poems, appearing since 1940, are represented in *New and Selected Poems* (1964). [EM]

McGuffey, William Holmes (1800–73). Teacher. Born in the Ohio wilderness, he graduated at Washington College with honours. His great linguistic gifts he used teaching at a number of universities; he became famous through his textbooks, which taught Americans how to read, a series opening in 1836 with his *First* and *Second Eclectic Readers* and continued in

1837, 1841 and 1857. These works, often written in collaboration with his brother, sold over 120 million copies, the most recent edition being in 1920. (One Wisconsin school board used the 1879 edition as late as 1961.) Harvey C. Minnick's *William Holmes McGuffey* (1936) shows how the *Readers* helped to release children from Calvinist Christian gloom and terror by creating a child's world of familiar toys, animals and friends. Richard V. D. Mosier's *Making the American Mind: Social and Moral Ideas in the McGuffey Readers* (1947) shows their moral and political purposes, strongly conservative within the Jefferson–Hamilton argument. [EM]

McKeon, Richard. ◊ Chicago Aristotelians.

Maclean, Norman. ◊ Chicago Aristotelians.

MacLeish, Archibald (1892–). Poet, playwright. Born at Glencoe, Illinois. His long public career began after he had graduated from Yale, returned from the First World War, and received his degree from Harvard, where he later taught law. *Tower of Ivory* (1917) was the first of many books of poems, collated in *Collected Poems 1917–1952* which gained three national awards. In 1923 he was an expatriate among the Paris ◊ Lost Generation; later he was an editor of *Fortune*, Librarian of Congress (1939–44), and in the United States government from 1941 to 1945 (finally becoming assistant secretary of state); he represented America in the organization of UNESCO. Naturally, his poetry concerns the interrelation of social and political action and the poet's responsibility. In his essay 'The Irresponsibles' (1940) he attacked his American contemporaries for their disillusioned disengagement from large American interests. He has served the state himself, and so his *Poetry and Experience* (1961) describes his theory that poetry must serve and be involved in society as a form of knowledge the state needs. In 1949 he became Boylston Professor at Harvard, and his poetry has always had about it a certain academic topicality. His early work is dominated by symbolism, Pound and Eliot (e.g. 'The Hamlet of A. MacLeish', 1928), and his professional skill did not conceal a certain superficiality. His best poems were meditative lyrics like 'You, Andrew Marvell'. *Conquistador* (1932), the result of a desire to use an American subject, concerns Cortez's conquests in New Spain. MacLeish pioneered the verse radio play with a message in *The Fall of the City* (1937) and *Air Raid* (1938), and *The Trojan Horse* (1952) is an interesting if ambiguous comment on the Red scare. His most successful verse play is *J.B.* (1958), in which Job, God and Satan enact conflict under the Big Top, while *Herakles* (1967) dramatizes the conflict between reason, work and science, and love of human life, the non-political, and the eternal feminine. All his work is eclectic, immediate and apprehensive; he has consistently worked out his idea of a public poetry. But his articulation of liberal uneasiness and the need for clear action suffers from the absence of risk in both form and content. *A Continuing Journey* (1968) is a collection of his essays and addresses on the American scene since the Second World War, poetry and art, libraries and teaching, and those men he has elegiacally memorialized. His latest poems are in *The Wild Old Wicked Man* (1968). [EM]

H. H. Waggoner, *The Heel of Elohim: Science and Values in Modern American Poetry* (1950); Signi Falk, *Archibald MacLeish* (1965).

McLuhan, Herbert Marshall (1911–   ). Critic. Born in Alberta, Canada, he studied at Manitoba University, and gained his Ph.D. at Cambridge University with a thesis on Thomas Nashe. He has taught at various American and Canadian universities, and returned to his Centre for Culture and Technology, University of Toronto, in 1969. He became a Catholic in 1937 and has taught only at Catholic institutions. His excellent literary criticism is collected in *The Literary Criticism of Marshall McLuhan, 1943–1962* (ed. E. McNamara, 1969), and with Richard J. Schoeck he has edited *Voices of Literature* (1964), a high school anthology. His popular reputation lies with a series of books (which overlap repetitiously, in spite of their concern with experimental format) concerning the media of communication. *The Mechanical Bride* (1951) is a warning analysis of advertising. *The Gutenberg Galaxy* (1962) is a brilliant study of the cultural effects due to the changes from script to print and to electronic circuitry. *Understanding Media* (1964), which first gained him an international fame, covers a wide range of communication and environmental matters, and is influential particularly for a controversial analysis

of the written and printed word in a society dominated by film and television. McLuhan uses a wide range of information from experts in various fields in order to state, aphoristically and trenchantly, a stream of ideas about technology and communications media, irrespective of overt content. His influence on business procedure and environmental studies is reflected in his *Dew-Line Newsletter*, designed largely for capitalist organizations. His work continues that of his predecessor, H. A. Innis, whose *The Bias of Communication* (1951) he introduced in an edition of 1964. In 1953, he founded, with Edmund S. Carpenter, the anthropologist, *Explorations*; some of the journal's essays, by various contributors, appear in *Explorations in Communication* (1960), and number 8 is reissued as *Verbi-Voco-Visual Explorations* (1967) – the title is from Joyce's *Finnegans Wake*, a major source for McLuhan. *The Medium is the Massage* (1967, with Quentin Fiore) is a collage of visual and typographical materials on environmental themes. *War and Peace in the Global Village* (1968, with Quentin Fiore) backs a programme for the elimination of current social and political disasters with apposite quotations from *Finnegans Wake*. *Through the Vanishing Point* (1968, with Harley Parker), one of his best works, is an analysis of space in poetry and painting. *Counter Blast* (1969, with Harley Parker), whose title acknowledges a typographical forerunner in Wyndham Lewis's *Blast* (1914), is another restatement of familiar materials. [EM]

Eric Mottram, etc., 'The World and Marshall McLuhan', *The Journal of Canadian Studies*, vol. 1, No. 2 (1966); ed. Gerald E. Stearn, *McLuhan Hot and Cool: A Critical Symposium* (1967); Sidney Finkelstein, *Sense and Nonsense of McLuhan* (1968); Richard Kostelanetz, *Master Minds* (1969).

Mailer, Norman (1923–   ). Novelist, short-story writer, poet, essayist, playwright. He was born in New Jersey, grew up in Brooklyn, graduated from Harvard in 1943, and served with the 112th Cavalry (San Antonio, Texas) in the Pacific campaign of the Second World War, as clerk and rifleman. The recurring image in his writings is a man on patrol against an enemy, moving warily and with as much intelligent appreciation of the terrain, whether jungle or city, as he can muster. His war experience went

165

primarily into his first novel, *The Naked and the Dead* (1948), a best-seller which also launched his critical reputation. Within the basic scheme of an operation on a Pacific island, Mailer provides a critical analysis of American society, through inset biographical sketches of main characters, in the manner of ◊ Dos Passos's *U.S.A.*, and an examination of authoritarian character and its place in recent Western history, through the character of General Cummings. The literary and social fame generated by this book rather dogged Mailer in the years that followed. His next two novels were radically misread and mistreated by the public and the critics, who wanted a repetition of his war novel and not risky explorations of a cancerous and plague-ridden society. Also his kind of public confessional openness and his sense of needing to be 'the champ' of his profession has not endeared him.

His first story appeared in 1941, and he wrote an early unpublished novel, *A Transit to Narcissus*, while awaiting draft into the army. His early work is contained in *Advertisements for Myself* (1959), in which short stories, essays and parts of novels are linked with an autobiographical commentary, designed as a therapeutical self-estimate and in fact a brilliant study of a talented writer growing up in the post-war scene. It includes 'The Man Who Studied Yoga', one of his finest stories, 'The Time of Her Time', an important section of what was then 'a novel in progress', and a key essay, 'The White Negro', a study of the hipster-outsider figure who represents significant aspects of the fifties and sixties and who is the heroic centre of Mailer's fiction and philosophy: the man who acts existentially, manufacturing his values in a world whose standards he largely rejects. *Barbary Shore* (1951), his second novel, is a Kafkaesque political allegory, elaborately written as a rehearsal of the struggle between socialism and the agents of capitalism. It is also a preparation for *The Deer Park* (1955), which dramatizes some of his existential ideas through the story of a film director in the thirties under pressure from the House Un-American Activities Committee, an air-force veteran trying to achieve some kind of life in post-war America, and Marion Faye, Mailer's most important single character, a philosophical pimp with Faustian ambitions. The scene is Hollywood and the Californian desert, whose failure of nourishment reflects a national sickness. *An Ameri-*

can *Dream* (1965) presents the diseased society in an advanced state in the form of a continuing battle between evil, both the supernatural and the Mafia, and those who at least partly understand the nature of spiritual and social decadence. *Why Are We in Vietnam?* (1967) takes the supernatural, Reichian psychological and existential themes a stage further: a hallucinated Texas disc-jockey pours out a complex story of a bear-hunt in Alaska, on which he accompanies his father and his friend. The nature of hunting, killing, exposure to the nature of the earth, and his future embarkation for Vietnam service are projected through a dazzling pyrotechnic prose. Parallel with these two novels, Mailer has written two volumes of essays, *The Presidential Papers* (1963), which includes a vision of President Kennedy as existential president-hero of America and a famous account of the Democratic Convention of 1960, 'Superman Comes to the Supermarket', and *Cannibals and Christians* (1966), which includes with political and literary essays his short science fiction, 'The Last Night'. *The Idol and the Octopus* (1968) collects his writings on the Kennedy and Johnson administrations. *The Deer Park* was successful as a play in New York in 1967, and his poems appear in *Deaths for the Ladies and Other Disasters* (1962). He has always been a politically committed writer and it is this moral energy that makes *The Armies of the Night* (1968) one of his finest books, an account of the march on Pentagon by various protest groups in which he took part with Robert ◊ Lowell, Dwight ◊ Macdonald and others in 1967. But *Miami and the Siege of Chicago* (1968) is often a strained piece of reporting, only intermittently penetrating. He has recently made his first films, *Wild 90* (1968) and *Beyond the Law* (1968). His work is as unevenly brilliant as one might expect from a writer who explores the possibilities of prose and form and is committed to an honesty made difficult by his knowledge of psychology and theology, politics and the history of the novel. His intelligence is intensely individual in its seriousness and completely characteristic of mid-century America. [EM]

The Short Fiction (1969).
Richard Foster, *Norman Mailer* (U. of Minnesota Pamphlet, 1968); D. L. Kaufman, *Norman Mailer: The Countdown* (1969); B. H. Leeds, *The Unstructured Vision of Norman Mailer* (1969).

Malamud, Bernard (1914–). Novelist, short-story writer. Born in Brooklyn; educated at City College, New York, and Columbia. He has been teaching in universities since 1939.

The Natural (1952), a remarkable first novel, tells of the brief glory and final ruin of Roy Hobbs, a baseball hero, through a mocking yet sympathetic exploration of the myth of American baseball and the legend of the Grail. In his novel *The Assistant* (1957), Malamud takes up the specifically Jewish themes with which he is most closely associated. Morris Bober, a 'good Jew', a man incapable of dishonesty or malice but imprisoned in a desperately poor grocery store, takes on a Frank Alpine, turned from hold-up man to remorseful assistant. When Morris dies, Frank succeeds him and becomes a Jew, accepting the exacting Jewish heritage of imprisonment and righteousness. Malamud's theme is redemption in a squalid world illuminated by extraordinary bursts of love. *A New Life* (1961) is a novel about a New Yorker who goes to teach at a land-grant college in the Pacific North-west looking for self-renewal. Malamud fails to avoid the two main clichés of the American academic novel: the lone liberal faculty crusader against a reactionary administration; and sexual adventures with students and faculty wives. *The Fixer* (1966), a novel, takes the theme of Jewish suffering back to the Tsarist Russia of pre-1914. It presents the ordeal of Yakov Bok, a poor Jewish handyman, falsely accused of the ritual murder of a Christian child. In spite of some moving passages, Malamud's handling of the material shows a certain woodenness and lack of warmth.

In the two short-story collections, *The Magic Barrel* (1958) and *Idiots First* (1963), the finest stories belong to the world of *The Assistant* or take the form of brilliant Jewish parables like 'The Magic Barrel' and 'The Jewbird'. The poorer ones are tales of academic life or Americans in Italy. *The Fixer* (1966) fictionalizes the notorious case of Mendel Beiliss, a Jewish Russian worker in Kiev, accused in an anti-semitic murder case in 1911. Malamud's theme here is the tribal solidarity of Jews and the individual Jew's solitariness. 'My short stories,' Malamud has said, 'acknowledge indebtedness specifically to Chekhov, James Joyce, Hemingway, Sherwood Anderson, and a touch perhaps of Sholem Aleichem and the films of Charlie Chaplin.' *Pictures of Fidelman* (1969), short stories, continues the theme of the American–Jewish artist in Italy.

Malamud's range is wide, his moral sensibility extraordinarily fine, and his humour complex and subtle. Although he can evoke actual places and atmospheres with unequalled force, his special talent is for the fable and the symbolic tale. With Saul ◊ Bellow, he is the most impressive figure among American urban Jewish writers. [B W]

A Malamud Reader, intr. Philip Rahv (1967). Jonathan Baumbach, 'The Economy of Love: the Novels of Bernard Malamud', *Kenyon Review*, Summer, 1963; Leslie Fiedler, 'Malamud: The Commonplace as Absurd', in *No! in Thunder* (1960); Marcus Klein, *After Alienation: American Novels in Mid-Century* (1962).

Maltz, Albert (1908–). Dramatist, fiction writer. Born in Brooklyn, N.Y. He was a member of George Pierce ◊ Baker's Yale workshop and wrote, with his fellow student George Sklar, *Merry-Go-Round* (1932), a celebrated play of New York City corruption, and the pacifist *Peace on Earth* (1933). His most powerful work is *Black Pit* (1935), a Marxist tragedy in which a miner, forced to spy and betray, is ostracized by his fellow workers. In *Private Hicks* (1936), the National Guard hero refuses to act as strike-breaker. Maltz's stories and novels have similar attitudes. Although two of his scripts became official Marine Corps and Navy films, he was thrown out of work by the Hollywood anti-Left bullying in the 1950s. [E M]

Marcuse, Herbert (1898–). Philosopher. Born in Berlin, he studied under Heidegger at Freiburg and wrote a doctoral thesis on Hegel. With the Nazis dominating Germany, in 1933 he left to teach in Geneva. From 1933 to 1934 he worked with the Institute of Social Research, which had emigrated from Frankfurt University to Columbia University, New York (its founders were T. W. Adorno and Max Horkheimer). Its journal, *Zeitschrift für Sozialforschung*, printed Marcuse's papers on Marx and Hegel. *Reason and Revolution: Hegel and the Rise of Social Theory* (1941; 2nd edn, with additional material 1954) concerns the bases of social freedom; Marcuse tries to exonerate Hegel from intellectual involvement in the pre-history of Nazism. In 1950, after a period with the government's Office of Intelligence Research, he returned to Columbia. The result of Russian studies both there and at Harvard became *Soviet Marxism* (1958). Marcuse has since taught at Brandeis and California universities and increasingly become a focus for the New Left in both America and Europe. *Eros and Civilization* (1955) attempts to make Freud usable for socialist sociology. *One Dimensional Man* (1964) concerns the dehumanizing effects of capitalist technology, and the essay entitled 'Repressive Tolerance', in *A Critique of Pure Tolerance* (1967, with R. P. Wolff and Barrington Moore), proposes 'the withdrawal of toleration in speech and assembly from groups and movements which promote aggressive policies, armament, chauvinism, racial and religious discrimination, or which oppose the extension of public services'. *Negations* (1968), which reprints essays from the thirties, shows the unresolved conflicts between philosophical universals and historical particulars in Marcuse's programme from the beginning. *An Essay on Liberation* (1969) tones down his radical despair with optimism based on the necessary operation of dialectical theory in the shape of the 'diffused rebellion among the youth and the intelligentsia'. Marcuse places his faith in a 'union of liberating art and liberating technology' but he is caught in a 19th-century web of Marxist and Freudian dogma and a 20th-century mystique of Youth and the New. [EM]

Marquand, J(ohn) P(hillips) (1893–1960). Novelist. Though born in Wilmington, Delaware, he spent his boyhood in Newburyport, Massachusetts, and after graduating from Harvard in 1915 served on the staff of the *Boston Transcript*. There he began writing popular romances – *The Unspeakable Gentleman* (1922), *The Black Cargo* (1925), *Warning Hill* (1930), *Ming Yellow* (1934) – and first won prominence with Mr Moto, the Japanese detective, in the *Saturday Evening Post*. It was not until 1937, with the publication of *The Late George Apley*, which won him the Pulitzer Prize, that his serious reputation was established for ironic comedies of New England and New York upper-class manners, There followed *Wickford Point* (1939), *H. M. Pulham Esq.* (1941), *So Little Time* (1943), *B.F.'s Daughter* (1946), *Point of No Return* (1949), *Melville Goodwin, U.S.A.* (1951), *Sincerely Willis Wayde* (1955), *Stopover:*

Tokyo (1957), *Life at Happy Knoll* (1957), and *Women and Thomas Harrow* (1958). *Lord Timothy Dexter* (1925) is the life of an 18th-century New England eccentric. *Thirty Years* (1954) contains his collected stories and articles.

Marquand's world, set among Boston Brahmins, New Englanders and the white-collar New York suburbanites, is similar to that of Galsworthy's *Forsyte Saga*; but whereas Galsworthy's Forsytes still lived with an effortless, unquestioning confidence in their inherited values, the inner drive of Marquand's heroes, recorded by him with wry realism, is at constant odds with the outer conformity and inherited manners of their caste. He ranged increasingly among the professional classes with stories of a failed doctor, a domineering industrialist's daughter, a middle-aged banker, an army officer, a businessman: all are frustrated; all are failures, at least to themselves; for the impulse of their private lives and of their careers separated long ago, leaving them shipwrecked in middle age, divided against themselves. Out of these conflicts of the inner man withdrawn from the outer code of his career, his class or his society, Marquand has created the satirical comedy of his best novels. [HB]

Philip Hamburger, *J. P. Marquand, Esquire* (1952); John J. Gross, *John P. Marquand* (1963); C. Hugh Holman, *John P. Marquand* (University of Minnesota Pamphlet, 1965).

Marquis, Don (1878–1937). Humorist, novelist, playwright. Born at Walnut, Illinois. As a columnist on various newspapers, particularly on the New York *Sun* and the New York *Tribune*, he produced vast amounts of short humorous commentary, much of it ephemeral; but several of the comic characters he invented are still remembered and still relevant. He satirized the pretensions of ◊ Greenwich Village 'advanced thought' through a little group of would-be advanced gossips, collected as *Hermione and Her Little Group of Serious Thinkers* (1916). His 'Old Soak', an inebriated social commentator and a one-man challenge to Prohibition, was commemorated in several books and a successful play, *The Old Soak* (1922). He wrote several novels, comic and serious, including *The Cruise of the Jasper B* (1916) and the semi-autobiographical *Sons of the Puritans* (1939). His plays include a serious drama on the life of Christ, *The Dark Hours* (1924).

But his best-known work is the whole sequence of books beginning with *archy and mehitabel* (1927), and consisting of the comic verse and prose of a cockroach, archy, who had a former existence as a *vers libre* bard. archy types with his head, to produce typographical oddities. The whole series has a virtuosity of style and a comic vigour that gives it a special value in his work. 'i see things from the under side now,' says archy, commenting on various social matters and on his relations with mehitabel, the alley cat, a reincarnation of Cleopatra ('toujours gai is ever her word'). Marquis interestingly demonstrates the way in which the newspaper columnist made a valuable contribution to the American comic and vernacular tradition. [MB]

Edward Anthony, *O Rare Don Marquis: A Biography* (1962).

Masters, Edgar Lee (1868–1950). Poet. Raised in rural Illinois, Masters practised as a Chicago lawyer before retiring to New York. From 1898 onwards he published over 50 volumes of poetry, fiction and biography. However, he found no individual voice until *Spoon River Anthology* (1915), a collection of casual free-verse epitaphs, spoken by the dead from their cemetery in a mid-Western town. Their stories interact to form a fragmentary history of a decaying community, which has forsaken the ideals of its founders and fallen prey to acquisitiveness and hypocrisy. In Spoon River, men of integrity are derided or persecuted by the complacent and the corrupt, thwarted lovers driven to drink or suicide, and the decent and industrious rewarded only with poverty or misfortune. The few tales of fulfilment are significantly less memorable than those of defeat and oppression. Conspicuous above all is man's egocentricity, the cause of life-long tragic misunderstandings. The virtues of the anthology rest in its concentration upon essentials and in the ironic humour that variegates this flat record of human failure.

Masters never repeated this success. His later verbose works include *The Domesday Book* (1920), *The New Spoon River* (1924), a Jeremiad against urbanization, and *The New World* (1937), a populist agrarian's outline for an epic of America. Among the several biographies he wrote is the hostile *Lincoln, the Man* (1931). Masters' poetic achievement is slight, but he is important because in *Spoon River Anthology* he dealt a death-blow to the more obtuse forms of sentimental regionalism and clarified some of the reasons for the disintegration of small communities and the collapse of traditional American values. *Spoon River Anthology* was made into a theatre entertainment in 1963. [RWB]

Bernard Duffey, *The Chicago Renaissance in American Letters* (1954); M. Yatron, *America's Literary Revolt* (1959).

Mather, Cotton (1663–1728). Minister, historian, scholar. He was born into the New England ministry, his father Increase ◊ Mather and his grandfathers Richard Mather and John ◊ Cotton being clergymen and central figures in New England affairs. He entered Harvard at 12, and at 22 became assistant to his father at the North Church in Boston, where he served until his death. His interests were multifarious; he was a man of monumental learning on a vast range of subjects, possessing a personal library that rivalled that of William ◊ Byrd of Westover for size. Though somewhat conservative in his religion at a time when an increasingly liberal tone was creeping into Puritan theology, and a believer in witchcraft at a time of scientific progress (his *The Wonders of the Invisible World,* 1693, analyses – yet with scientific detachment – the work of devils among the Salem witches), he was on some issues, such as his advocacy of inoculation for smallpox, well in advance of his age. Indeed his conservatism has been much exaggerated at the expense of his scientific curiosity. He was elected to the Royal Society in 1713, and was in close communication with men of learning throughout Europe.

He was a prolific writer; and though no collected edition of his work has been assembled some 450 items are traced to him. They include sermons, verse, history, comments on economic, educational and political matters, scientific commentary, folklore, etc. He often forsook Puritan 'plain style' for elegant writing, influenced – as in his *Political Fables* – by Jacobean elaboration and Restoration elegance. His most famous work, the *Magnalia Christi Americana* (1702), a learned and vastly documented history of New England, showed how God was at work in the new land. Mather considered it important enough to send it to London for publication, and its elegance and fineness make it clear it was to speak for New England to the world. The body and range of his work are a remarkable testament to New England learning and energy as well as to piety. [MB]

Selections, ed. Kenneth B. Murdock (1926; 1960); *On Witchcraft* (1956).

Perry Miller, *The New England Mind: From Colony to Province* (1953); Barrett Wendell, *Cotton Mather: The Puritan Priest* (1891; 1926); R. P. and L. Boas, *Cotton Mather* (1928).

Mather, Increase (1639–1723). Writer on theology, history and politics. He was the youngest son of Richard Mather (1596–1669), the first generation New England minister and one of the authors of the ◊ *Bay Psalm Book*. His son, continuing this important dynasty, was Cotton ◊ Mather, a powerfully influential figure of the next generation of Puritan divines. Increase was educated at Harvard, of which he later became president, and Trinity College Dublin, and later married John ◊ Cotton's daughter in Massachusetts. He became minister at North Church, Boston, the most influential centre of Puritan theocracy of which he was a leading theorist and preacher. In 1692, he gained the new charter for Massachusetts from England, an act which ironically weakened theocratic power by basing suffrage on property-ownership. During the witchcraft fears of the 1690s in Salem and elsewhere he warned the early Americans that the Devil was taking over New England, but he did not fully support the trials and some secularization seems to have alleviated his mind before his death. His large output (at least 102 works are known to be by him) includes *The Life and Death of . . . Richard Mather* (1670), *An Arrow against Profane and Promiscuous Dancing* (1684), histories of New England, *Cases of Conscience Concerning Evil Spirits Personating Men* (1693) and *An Essay for the Recording of Illustrious Providences* (1684), a strange amalgam of superstitious natural history and supernatural special pleading, but a valuable record of the 17th-century state of mind. [EM]

Kenneth B. Murdock, *Increase Mather: The Foremost American Puritan* (1925).

Mathew, Harry (1930–   ). Novelist, poet. He was born in New York and lives in Paris. He edited *Locus Solus* magazine with ◊ Ashbery, ◊ Koch and ◊ Schuyler, his poems appear in *avant garde* journals, and he has written two brilliant imaginative novels: *The Conversions* (1962), a highly

170

complex quest in the form of answers to a game, satires on contemporary opinions, and invented cults; and *Tlooth* (1966), again modelled somewhat on the puzzle structures of Raymond Roussel's fiction, but less surrealist, more consciously directed, and certainly as startling and gripping as any bizarre detective story ever written. [EM]

Matthews, Brander (1852–1929). Literary historian, critic. Born in New Orleans. He is significant here for his early contribution – along with the work of E. P. ◊ Whipple, Moses Coit ◊ Tyler, W. C. ◊ Brownell, etc. – to the study of American literature. His *An Introduction to the Study of American Literature* (1896), though brief, opens up the 19th century as a subject for study. Professor of Literature and Dramatic Literature at Columbia between 1892 and 1924, he also wrote several important books on drama, with a practical and theatrical emphasis – they include *The Development of the Drama* (1903), *Molière* (1910), *Shakespeare as a Playwright* (1913) and *The Principles of Playmaking* (1919). He also wrote three plays in collaboration, and some fiction – the novel *A Confident Tomorrow* (1899), etc. [MB]

Matthiessen, F(rancis) O(tto) (1902–50). Critic, scholar. Born in California, educated at Yale and Harvard, he taught at Yale for two years and at Harvard for most of his life, becoming famous for his tutorial work in literature. In 1947 he taught at the Salzburg Seminar and Charles University, Prague, an experience recorded impressively in *From the Heart of Europe* (1948). In 1949–50 he worked on his *Oxford Book of American Verse* (1950) and on *Theodore Dreiser* (1951), left unrevised at his death. He committed suicide, 'terribly oppressed by the present times', a profound and symbolic shock to his friends and colleagues. His life's work was 'to search for a usable tradition in American literature' (Malcolm Cowley), and his teaching always emphasized the social context of literature. His major work is *American Renaissance* (1941), subtitled 'Art and Expression in the Age of Emerson and Whitman' and consisting of a detailed examination of those two authors, together with Thoreau, Hawthorne and Melville, in relationship to the 17th-century English and American cultural inheritance, in order to establish the nature of the first great blossoming of a distinctively American literature. Matthiessen shows how the reformist spirit of the 1840s precedes and informs the masterpieces of the 1850s, and his basis is Pound's statement that 'the history of an art is the history of masterwork, not of failures or mediocrity'. *Sarah Orne Jewett* (1929) is a biographical and sociological study of the American writer, and after *Translation: An Elizabethan Art* (1931), he wrote *The Achievement of T. S. Eliot* (1935, revised 1947), a relatively aesthetic literary study placing the poet in the American tradition of Puritanism and Dante studies at Harvard, as well as the European line; *Henry James: The Major Phase* (1944), one of whose important and pioneering sources was James's then unpublished notebooks; and a fascinating study, *The James Family* (1947), based on the lives and works of Henry James, his father, and his brother William, the philosopher. *F. O. Matthiessen, 1902–1950: A Collective Portrait* (ed. P. M. Sweezy and L. Huberman, 1950) reprints the special edition of the *Monthly Review* (October 1950) devoted to recollections of his friends and colleagues. It is said that May ◊ Sarton's novel, *Faithful Are the Wounds* (1955), is partly a version of his last years. [EM]

Stanley Edgar Hyman, *The Armed Vision: A Study in the Methods of Modern Literary Criticism* (1948).

Mead, Margaret (1901–). Psychologist, anthropologist. Born in Philadelphia, she was a pupil of Franz Boas in 1923, and in 1925 studied adolescent girls in Samoa, before taking her Columbia doctorate. *Coming of Age in Samoa* (1928) was both good anthropology and a best-seller, beginning the pattern of her later books, *Growing Up in New Guinea* (1930), *Sex and Temperament in Three Primitive Societies* (1935) and books on Polynesian and Indian societies. Her most popular success was *Male and Female* (1949), an application of anthropological discoveries to the contemporary urban West. All her work has ultimately been devoted to developing 'a war-less world' through re-education for racial understanding, whether through her *Redbook* column or *New Lives for Old* (1956). [EM]

Meltzer, David (1937–). Poet. He was born in New York but left for Los Angeles at 14 and has since been associated with poetry in the 'San Francisco renaissance' of the

fifties. He took part in the efforts to read poetry to jazz, and was represented in Donald Allen's *The New American Poetry* (1960). His poems appeared in *Ragas* (1959), which uses oriental instances and references and is largely unified by intensely personal moods, *The Process* (1965), *We All Have Something to Say to Each Other: Being an Essay Entitled Patchen and Four Poems* (1962), which includes one of the very few good accounts of Kenneth ◊ Patchen's poetry, and *The Dark Continent* (1967), a less overtly experimental collection but substantial in its extension of subjects. *Yesod* (1969) and *Round the Poem Box* (1969) are his recent poetry. *Journal of a Birth* (1967) is a prose work which originally appeared in 1961. His novels include a trilogy of sexual madness and erotic organizations, *The Agency, The Agent,* and *How Many Blocks in the Pile?* (1968), the four books of *Brain-Plant* (1969), which concerns totalitarian eroticism, and two single novels, *Orb* and *The Martyrs* (1969). [EM]

David Kherdian, *David Meltzer: A Sketch and a Checklist* (1965), and *Six Poets of the San Francisco Renaissance* (1967).

Melville, Herman (1819–91). Novelist, poet, short-story writer. One of America's greatest writers, complex, original and profound. He was born in New York City, of Boston Calvinist and New York Dutch ancestry, into an atmosphere of security and comfort, well educated and socially happy. In 1830 his father went bankrupt and became the poor failure the American success ethic insists on for the financially fallen. He died insane from overwork and worn-out nerves. Melville worked as bank clerk, salesman, farm-hand and schoolteacher in New York and Massachusetts, tried an engineering and surveying course, began writing, but in 1839 signed on as cabin boy, a deeply shocking experience of menial squalor and crude vice, both at sea and in Liverpool, which he used in *Redburn* (1849). On his return he taught, travelled to Illinois and the Great Lakes and down the Mississippi to Cairo, and in 1841 sailed as seaman on the whaler *Acushnet* into the Pacific. After eighteen months he deserted in the Marquesas Islands and escaped from there in an Australian whaler whose crew mutinied: he was imprisoned in Tahiti for his share. From there he sailed for Hawaii, where he worked in a pin-bowling alley and in a store, and returned to Boston in 1844. Backed by extensive reading and research, these events were the shaping experience of his life and served as bases for the series of books beginning with *Typee* in 1846. In 1850 he lived with his wife in Pittsfield, Massachusetts, near Hawthorne. Deeply disturbed by the stupid reception of his complex political and religious allegory *Mardi* (1849), he turned to the sea stories with which he could attract the reading public (*White Jacket*, 1850, and *Redburn*), but *Moby-Dick* (1851) combines sea story and allegory into the central masterpiece of American literature, written partly under the inspiration of the parallel achievement by Hawthorne, whom he met in 1850 and on whom he wrote an important essay, 'Hawthorne and His Mosses' (1850).

But *Moby-Dick* was 'broiled in hell fire' and too difficult for critics and public in a sentimental time, nor could they read *Pierre* (1852), rebarbative in its psychological complexity and elaborate prose. Melville, dubbed mad and obscene, was not supported by his family and friends, and his sense of vocation cut him off from the readership he needed. In 1853–4 he wrote magazine stories. *Israel Potter* (1855) is an amusing historical and satirical burlesque, and *Piazza Tales* (1856) and *The Confidence Man* (1857) are superb works of his maturity. He failed to gain a possible consulship, and his family had increased, but in 1856 his father-in-law paid for a tour for his health in Europe and the Near East (*Clarel*, 1876, and *Journal of a Visit to Europe and the Levant, October 11, 1856 – May 6, 1857*). The poetry he wrote in his later New York years is collected in *Battle Pieces* (1866), *John Marr and Other Sailors* (1888) and *Timoleon* (1891), the last book published in his lifetime. In 1866 he was appointed deputy customs inspector in New York, a job that left him little time for writing until in the 1870s he worked on *Clarel*. He resigned in 1885, his literary reputation nearly vanished, his writing restricted to poems; he left *Billy Budd, Sailor: An Inside Story* in manuscript at his death.

Apparently diverse, Melville's career has a splendid singleness of complex design. *Typee* tells of entry into and escape from a Pacific island community whose customs deeply disturb the American bourgeois hero. *Omoo* (1847) is a sequel less interesting but containing important material on the Pacific islands. The next four novels constitute a huge exploration of the historical and psychological origins and development of self, society and the desire to create and destroy gods and heroes. *Mardi* is a detailed allegory of religion, government and philosophic principles. In *Moby-Dick* the religion and commercial acumen of the New England whaling industry and its captains is a metaphor of the hunt for absolute truth, heroic leadership and Faustian self-discovery. Ahab and Ishmael, captain and seaman, represent the opposites of doomed hubris and pacific survival on the *Pequod*, itself the symbol of American, and therefore universal, society. *Pierre* explores Oedipal relationships, the isolation of a man seeking integrity, and the American country–city hostility, and *The Confidence Man, His Masquerade* is a brilliant narrative of passengers on a Mississippi river-boat as the image of the inherent moral destructiveness of the Protestant ethic, demonstrated with complete scepticism. *Redburn, White Jacket* and *Billy Budd* (1924; ed. H. Hayford and M. M. Sealts, 1962) show the world of the ship as the power structure into which a young man is initiated for survival against social and sexual oppression; Billy Budd transcends the enacted ideas of both Paine and Burke to become a man-made god. The finest of Melville's short stories explore his themes of the isolated self, the failure of conventional worldly knowledge and the 'power of blackness' penetrating love ('Bartleby', 'Benito Cereno', 'The Paradise of Bachelors and the Tartarus of Maids', and 'The Encantadas'). In the 18,000 lines of octosyllabic couplets of *Clarel*, an American theological student explores Palestine in hopes of finding secure faith, and makes a final ambivalent plunge away from theology and introspection and towards the common people.

Melville's great career is capped by his highly original poems, small-scale forms for his large themes. He died virtually unnoticed. His genius, recognized and evaluated only since the 1930s, is part of the first great period of American literature, the flowering which includes Poe, Emerson, Hawthorne, Whitman and Thoreau. [EM]

The Complete Works (Hendricks House edition, in progress); *Writings* (Northwestern Newbery edition, 1967 ff.) (*Typee, Omoo* published).
Merlin Bowen, *The Long Encounter: Self and Experience in the Writings of Herman Melville* (1960); Leon Howard, *Herman Melville: A Biography* (1951); Howard P. Vincent, *The Trying-Out of Moby-Dick* (1949); W. Berthoff, *The Example of Melville* (1962); H. Bruce Franklin, *The Wake of the Gods* (1963).

Mencken, H(enry) L(ouis) (1880–1956). Editor, journalist, literary critic. Born in Baltimore, his home all his life, Mencken had little more than a high-school formal education, and while still in his late teens he plunged into newspaper work. He was reporter, editorial writer, columnist and editor for the Baltimore *Sunpapers* from 1906 till his death. He became literary editor of the *Smart Set* in 1908 and six years later co-editor with George Jean ◊ Nathan. In 1924 he and Nathan founded the *American Mercury*. Nathan left the following year, and thereafter Mencken edited the magazine till the end of 1933. Meanwhile he had been collecting his essays into volumes, chiefly into a series of six *Prejudices* (1919, 1920, 1922, 1924, 1926, 1927). In 1919 he published the *American Language*, a brisk journalistic survey of the differences between English English and American English, and also an attempt to present the richness of American English. The book went into three editions and was expanded into two *Supplements* (1945, 1948). The general reading public was overwhelmed by its scholarship, though professional linguists saw in it little more than a lively rewriting of their researches. Mencken's *Book of Prefaces* (1917), a selection of critical essays, was far more impressive.

As an editor Mencken was enormously industrious and daring, and he had a good eye for writers with original ideas, especially in the realms of sociology, history and biography, though for a while he also was hospitable to novelists and short-story writers beginning their careers. He did a great deal to wake America up to the values in the novels of Theodore Dreiser, Sinclair Lewis and Sherwood Anderson. He was surprisingly blind to the works of Ernest Hemingway, Thomas Wolfe and William Faulkner. As a critic of poetry he was almost totally ignorant and inept.

The depression of 1929 robbed him of his vast audience among college students and their younger professors, and he went into a decline. For a long time, while the breadlines were multiplying, he denied the reality of the Depression, calling it 'newspaper talk'. His books on politics (*Notes on Democracy,* 1926), religion (*A Treatise on the Gods,* 1930) and morals (*A Treatise on Right and Wrong,* 1934) are of little value. They reveal Mencken as more a night-school scandalizer than a genuine and original scholar. He gradually returned to public attention with the publi-cation of his 3 volumes of autobiography: *Happy Days* (1940), *Newspaper Days* (1941) and *Heathen Days* (1943). These volumes make pleasant reading, but since there are so many 'stretchers' in them they cannot be taken too seriously as autobiography or history. Mencken also wrote much on music in the *American Mercury* and the *Baltimore Sun*, but he was never more than an amateur musicologist.

Above all else, he was a superb editor. His editing of the *American Mercury* during its first five years, 1924–8, was historic in its influence. The other quality periodicals were never the same afterwards. He was also a superb newspaper man. His sheer good reporting, yet to be properly sifted and collected, was of a high order. Thus his influence as a journalist was great, and this influence will probably keep his memory alive longer than his more ambitious writings. Perhaps the best all-round selective anthology of his writings was made by himself in *A Mencken Crestomathy* (1949). [CA]

Charles Angoff, *H. L. Mencken: A Portrait from Memory* (1956); Ernest Boyd, *H. L. Mencken* (1925); Edgar Kemler, *The Irreverent Mr Mencken* (1950); ed. M. Moos, *A Carnival of Buncombe* (1957); Carl Bode, *Mencken* (1969).

Meredith, William (1919–   ). Poet. Born in New York City, he was educated at Princeton and has taught at various American universities. His books, which have won various literary awards, include *Love Letter from an Impossible Land* (1944), *Ships and Other Figures* (1948), *The Open Sea* (1958), *The Wreck of the Thresher* (1964) and translations from Apollinaire (1964). His naval experience in the Second World War and the Korean war provides an important theme – 'the sea schools us with terrible water'. But his most typical poems celebrate nature and domestic life, about which he writes with decorum, directness and wit. [BP]

Merrill, James (1926–   ). Poet, novelist, playwright. Born in New York, he studied at Amherst College, has travelled widely, particularly in Greece and Italy, and taught in American universities. Several volumes of his poems – including *The Black Swan and Other Poems* (1946), *The Country of a Thousand Years of Peace and Other Poems* (1958), *Water Street* (1962) and *Nights and Days* (1966) – have appeared; *Selected Poems* came out in 1961. Merrill has published a novel, *The Seraglio* (1957), and written a play, *The Immortal Husband* (1955). He is an elegant, intellectual and sometimes very elliptical writer, drawing on classical knowledge and cultural contrasts between other civilizations and his own. He can be witty and elegant and also excitably and exactingly involved in his matter; he has a considerable range of voice and artistic resource, not confined to poetry. [MB]

Richard Howard, *Alone with America* (1969).

Merrill, Stuart (1863–1915). Poet. Born in Hempstead, New York, and educated in France, his father being an American lawyer there. In this way he became a long-term expatriate, and is perhaps most properly located as one of the French symbolist movement. Nearly all his writing was produced in French and came out of the Parisian Bohemian literary context (◊ Bohemianism). He published two collections of good symbolist verse, *Les gammes* (1887) and *Les fastes* (1891), and a socialist poem about the oppressed, *Une voix dans la foule* (1909). His one work in English is a collection of translations from the prose-poems of French symbolists (Huysmans, Baudelaire, Mallarmé, etc.) called *Pastels in Prose* (1890), which appeared with an introduction by W. D. ◊ Howells. [MB]

Edmund Wilson, *Axel's Castle* (1931).

Merton, Thomas (1915–69). Poet, religious writer. Born in France of an English father and an American mother, his advanced education was at Cambridge University and Columbia, where he did graduate work. He became a Catholic, and in 1941 a Trappist monk, entering the Abbey of Gethsemane at Trappist, Kentucky. His writings, all subsequent to his religious experience, explore it in various forms of contemplation, spiritual autobiography, and study of theological and moral problems. An interesting figure of modern devotion, he was influenced by Blake as well as St Augustine. He published first as a poet: *Thirty Poems* (1944), *Man in the Divided Sea* (1946), *Figures for an Apocalypse* (1947), *Emblems of a Season of Fury* (1963), *Cables to the Ace* (1968) and *The Geography of Lograine* (1969). In 1948 his spiritual autobiography, *The Seven Storey Mountain*, became an American best-seller. He later published many volumes of meditation, often touching on current problems of philosophy

or conduct: *Seeds of Contemplation* (1949), *No Man Is an Island* (1955), *The Silent Life* (1956), *Secular Journals* (1959) and *Life and Holiness* (1963), etc. Merton's monastic experience did not close him to contemporary events and processes; and his studied, religious approach to such matters made him a valuable commentator – exemplified by his introduction to and essay in *Breakthrough to Peace* (1964), and his essays and fables in *Raids on the Unspeakable* (1964). *Zen and the Birds of Appetite* (1968) and *Mystics and Zen Masters* (1969) show the congruencies of Christian mysticism and Buddhism. His last work was *Contemplative Prayer* (1970), composed for the community. [RWB]

Merwin, W(illiam) S(tanley) (1927–). Poet, translator. After study at Princeton, he went to France and Spain and finally to England, where he first established a reputation as a poet. He has published several volumes of verse, including *A Mask for Janus* (1952), *The Dancing Bears* (1954), *Green with Beasts* (1956), *The Drunk in the Furnace* (1960), *Moving Target* (1963) and *Lice* (1967) and some important translations – notably of *The Cid* (1959) – many collected in *Selected Translations, 1964–1968* (1969). He now lives in the U.S.A. and France. His earlier poems resembled those of the English 'Movement', though he is more philosophical and enigmatic. He has a fondness for the curious and metaphysical turn of thought and image. His attitude to modern civilization is often satiric or despairing, yet always vigorous and passionate. His nature poems, particularly, show an exciting baroque energy – especially the ones about the great beasts of the animal world. He has had considerable influence on contemporaries, showing the possibilities of a dignified, elaborated poetry as a relevant means of dealing with modern subjects. [BS]

Mezey, Robert (1935–). Poet. He was born in Philadelphia and, in a classic pattern for many mid-century American poets, went to Kenyon College and the State University of Iowa, thereafter teaching in various American universities. *The Lovemaker* (1961) shows an assured manipulation of traditional verse forms that reflects the tutelage of John Crowe ◊ Ransom and Paul Engle; but at its best his verse displays very personal and unacademic concerns. [BP]

Michener, James A(lbert) (1907–). Novelist, short-story writer. He was born in New York and travelled widely in early life; during the Second World War he served in the South Pacific. Out of these experiences he wrote his widely known fiction. *Tales of the South Pacific* (1947), a collection of stories told by a naval officer about American servicemen and the inhabitants of the South Pacific islands, was made into a romping musical. Essentially the novelist as story-teller, Michener exploits colourful settings and the charm of places; other novels and stories, such as *Sayonara* (1954) and *Hawaii* (1959), deal colourfully with the South Pacific and Japan, though he also writes of home ground – *The Fires of Spring* (1949) is set in Pennsylvania. *Caravans* (1963) is a conventional search for a lost girl set in a detailed Afghanistan background. *Iberia* (1968) is a further instalment of the American intellectual flirtation with Spain. [MB]

A. Grove Day, *James A. Michener* (1964).

Miles, Josephine (1911–). Poet, literary scholar. She teaches English at the University of California at Berkeley. Her poetry is extremely intellectual, abstruse and witty, in a manner particularly associated with the 1930s, though it has been adapted in more recent work. Books of verse include *Lines at Intersection* (1939) and *Prefabrications* (1955), the most convenient representation being in *Poems 1930–1960* (1960), which selects from earlier volumes. *Kinds of Affection* (1968) has a less strenuous style, more direct and less filtered. Her literary studies have largely been devoted to the analysis of poetic vocabulary; these analyses, using word counts and statistical comparisons, have been of radical importance in systematic discussion of literary language. The several books devoted in different ways to this large-scale task include *The Vocabulary of Poetry* (1946), *The Continuity of Poetic Language* (1951) and *Eras and Modes in English Poetry* (1957). Also important is her study of the changing relationship between object and emotion in literature, *Pathetic Fallacy in the Nineteenth Century* (1942). [MB]

Millay, Edna St Vincent (1892–1950). Poet. Born in Rockland, Maine. She presented in her early volumes – of which the witty and rebellious collection *A Few Figs from Thistles* (1920) is a striking example – a woman writer's position in the twenties' revolt against conventionality. This Greenwich Village Bohemianism she soon outgrew. In 1923 *The Harp-Weaver and Other Poems* revealed the mature poet and recalled her first success in 1912, 'Renascence', a reflective poem still admired for its depth and lyric felicity. Its proponents provoked a controversy when it lost an award in competition with an established poet; but it gained her a sponsor who helped her to complete her college years at Vassar (1917). Her girlhood at Camden on the coast of Maine gave her intimate knowledge of the frugal living and intellectual energy then characteristic of that region, and enriched her natural imagery and shrewd knowledge of character.

Her writing increasingly reflected the sophistication of her literary environment and her married life. From the Elizabethan and Cavalier poets of England she discovered the roots of her own sensibility and won her freedom. Her style was independent and flexible, witty and brilliant if seldom profound, and nearly as precise as that of ◊ MacLeish, who surpassed her in imagination and depth. Like him and S. V. ◊ Benét, she participated prominently in the democratic literary propaganda of the war, of which her poem *The Murder of Lidice* (1942) was a noteworthy example. Following *The Harp-Weaver*, her best-accomplished work is found in *The Buck in the Snow and Other Poems* (1928) and *Fatal Interview* (1931), inspired by a love affair, but remarkable for its objective psychological interest. It is also uniquely a successful modern sonnet sequence, in the Elizabethan tradition. Her mastery of the sonnet was manifest from the beginnings, in form impeccable, but adapted to many moods, and to subjects as diverse as the logical paradigm, 'Euclid Alone . . .' and the passionate Endymion poem. With comparable success she maintained independent control of her swift-moving ballads without disguising their Pre-Raphaelite affinity. Her poetic dramas are remarkable for their survival in the little theatres, and one, *The King's Henchman* (1927), with a score by Deems Taylor, was performed by the Metropolitan Opera. After three volumes of declining appeal (1939–40) she virtually ceased publication during her last decade and she died in 1950. [RWB]

Collected Poems (1956) (comprises the bulk of *Collected Sonnets*, 1941, and *Collected Lyrics*,

1943); *Letters,* ed. A. R. MacDougall (1952). Elizabeth Atkins, *Edna St Vincent Millay and Her Times* (1936); Vincent Sheean, *The Indigo Bunting: A Memoir of Edna St Vincent Millay* (1951).

Miller, Arthur (1915–   ). Playwright. The most distinguished of contemporary liberal dramatists in America, he was born and educated in New York City. After his father's business failed in the Depression (he was a Jewish manufacturer and shop-owner), he worked at a number of prole-tarian jobs, studied journalism at Michigan University in 1934, and began to write plays and radio scripts which gained him prizes and a living. He worked briefly with the ◊ Federal Theatre project and during the war worked as a fitter in the Brooklyn navy yard and on an army training film (*Situation Normal,* 1944). In 1945 he published *Focus,* a novel on anti-semitism in American cities. His first performed play was *The Man Who Had All the Luck* (1944); it was not a success but here already were some of his major themes of the insecure relationships between a man's honour, his work and his family, and the nature of business ethics and personal ethics under capitalism. His life has always been public and committed. In 1960–1 John Huston filmed his script of *The Misfits,* a brilliant work concerning the end of cowboy masculinity and the Western pastoral myth. Miller's wife, Marilyn Monroe, played a leading role. In 1956 he refused to betray left-wing associates to the House Un-American Activities Com-mittee; in 1965 he was elected the first American international president of P.E.N. All these elements of his career appear in one form or another in his plays and stories. In 1968 he appeared in Paris as the leader of an American pacifist group with a plan for peace in Vietnam.

His plays all concern the nature of a man who, under pressure from his society's stated and assumed laws, is driven to actual or virtual suicide, whether in America or in Europe, today or in the 17th century. In *The Man Who Had All the Luck* the mechanism of determinism and luck is too obvious and philosophically confused. Business success or failure is again central in *All My Sons* (1947), with moral equivocations surround-ing betrayals of faith in public and family situations during the Second World War. Miller allows his businessman hero suicide after his cry 'a man can't be Jesus in this world!', but he has no idea how to change

'this world'. In *Death of a Salesman* (1947) the stocking salesman Willy Loman goes to his death bewildered by his failures and his sons' loss of respect for him, but the only positive is his wife's cry that 'attention must finally be paid to such a person'. Both plays were successful in the New York theatre. The basis of *The Crucible* (1953) is the 1690 witchcraft hunt and trial series in Salem, Massachusetts, related to the contemporary McCarthy hysteria. Again the hero, John Proctor, is confronted with a conflict be-tween laws of self-judgement and judgement by society, with the relationship between the man and his wife and family stretched to breaking point under social pressure. What survives is a man's integrity and the love of his wife. But the end is death. The stylization of language begun in *Death of a Salesman* is developed here, but Miller has returned to earlier naturalist settings; his characteristic combination of expressionist decor, semi-stylized language and thorough-ly naturalistic characterization is at its best in *A View from the Bridge* (1955; *A Memory of Two Mondays* was produced the same year but it is hardly a major part of Miller's career). Here the clash is between Sicilian law embodied in Eddie Carbone and his dockland slum community, and the law of the wider society of America. Eddie's 'good name' is lost in the confusion of values, and his death is part of the logic of ancient law. In *After the Fall* (1964) the centre of lost values and lost integrity is a liberal-leftist lawyer; the expressionist action takes place inside his head as an act of recovering his past. In *Incident at Vichy* (1964) a group of Frenchmen and an Austrian aristocrat are under interrogation as Jews in 1942; the arguments for self-sacrifice put forward are cynical and the writing is even looser than in the previous play. *The Price* (1968) still concerns guilt, responsibility and the con-flict between self and society, this time be-tween two brothers, a policeman and a surgeon, as they define their relationship with their dead father, their own innocence and their own moral superiority. Miller is a serious dramatist of the American liberal middle class, his post-ideological plays exactly representing the irresolution and worry of the post-war years. His many theoretical essays reinforce the delineation of family, personal honour and sexual in-security in his plays, themes and their method of exposition which he partly in-herits from Ibsen, a version of whose *An*

Enemy of the People he has made (1951), and O'Neill. His short stories are in *I Don't Need You Any More* (1968). *Collected Plays* (1957) contains five plays and an important introduction. *In Russia* (1969) combines his prose with Inge Morath's photographs. [EM]

Dennis Welland, *Arthur Miller* (1961); Robert Hogan, *Arthur Miller* (1964); S. Haftel, *Arthur Miller: The Burning Glass* (1965); J. Goode, *The Story of the Misfits* (1963); Edward Murray, *Arthur Miller: Dramatist* (1967).

Miller, Henry (1891–   ). Novelist. He was born in New York City of German ancestry, and brought up in Brooklyn. After attending the City College of New York for two months, he worked at various odd jobs before becoming employment manager of the messenger department of the Western Union Telegraph Company of New York. In 1924 he gave this up to write, and settled in Paris in 1930. Here he wrote *Tropic of Cancer* (1934), an American classic. Usually classed as a novel, it is, like many other books of Miller's, an intermediate form, fictional autobiography. The first-person narrator is clearly Miller, but the material is shaped into novelistic episodes, not left in the accidental order imposed by the actual chronology of events. *Cancer* records Miller's life in Paris as poverty-stricken artist, amorist, good companion and receptive soul. It is sharply anecdotal, with enormous comic verve, bringing together the traditions of European bawdry and of American humour. Its use of obscene words was revolutionary, reflecting with a new realism the ordinary callousness of male talk and the destructive potential of such words. When the sexual act is performed without love, Miller feels, it becomes an index of all human futility, and only obscene words can render its emptiness. *Black Spring* (1936) is a Parisian companion-piece to *Cancer* with important developments in prose style, and *Tropic of Capricorn* (1939) its American counterpart, with classic opening scenes in a telegraph company.

In 1939, Miller left Paris and visited Greece, publishing *The Colossus of Maroussi* (1941) in which he describes his transformation under the effects of ancient and modern forces. He returned to America in 1940, toured the country in 1941–2, and produced *The Air-Conditioned Nightmare*, recording his repudiation of modern American life and his championing of individual American artists and eccentrics. In 1944, he settled at

Big Sur on the Californian coast, where he has lived ever since. His main literary enterprise there has been the trilogy *The Rosy Crucifixion*, his most ambitious exercise in fictional autobiography, consisting of *Sexus* (1945), *Plexus* (1949) and *Nexus* (1960). But the sharp sense of life and the delightful humour of the Parisian books have given way to a philosophical examination of sexual experience, which tends to repetition and loose style. Besides the stories in *Nights of Love and Laughter* (1955), the rest of his large output consists of collections of essays and personal reminiscences: *Max and the White Phagocytes* (1938), *The Cosmological Eye* (1939), *The World of Sex* (1940), *The Wisdom of the Heart* (1941), *Sunday after the War* (1944), *Remember to Remember* (1947), *The Smile at the Foot of the Ladder* (1948), *Books in My Life* (1952), *Rimbaud* (1952), which became *Time of the Assassins* (1956), *Big Sur and the Oranges of Hieronymus Bosch* (1957) and *Stand Still Like the Hummingbird* (1962), which contains an important essay on Thoreau, who, with Lawrence, stands at the head of the major influences of Miller's explorations of sex and anarchistic liberty. *Just Wild about Harry* (1963) is a play, *The Michael Fraenkel–Henry Miller Correspondence Called Hamlet* (1939; repr. 1952), a fascinating clash of intelligences and styles of literary consideration. *The Red Notebook* (no date) is a reproduction of a notebook which he began while touring America prior to *The Air-Conditioned Nightmare* and which he finished in 1944 before going to live at Big Sur. *To Paint is to Love Again* (1960) is illustrated by his own paintings (he has had a number of exhibitions over the years). *Maurizius Forever* (1959) is analysis of crime, and he contributed an essay to the volume on tribute to *Joseph Delteil* (1962). *Order and Chaos Chez Hans Reichel* (1966), a memoir of friends, is a magnificently produced book from the Loujon Press, Tucson, Arizona, one of the great little presses of the world. Of Miller's huge correspondence 3 volumes have appeared: *Art and Outrage* (1959, with the major contributions by Alfred Perlès and Lawrence Durrell), *Lawrence Durrell and Henry Miller: A Private Correspondence* (1963) and *Letters to Anais Nin* (ed. Gunther Stuhlmann, 1965). Miller is the major 20th-century participant in the increasingly important American line of dissent and pacifist anarchism. His writing is mainly autobiographical, and this is both an advantage in its direct personal commitment and its tendency to garrulousness. His sexual frankness has been of positive value for readers, internationally, and his dedication to literature as an instrument of self-development has created for him a large following, especially among the dissenting generations of the fifties and sixties. [BW/EM]

The Henry Miller Reader, ed. Lawrence Durrell (1960).
Alfred Perlès, My Friend, Henry Miller (1955); William A. Gordon, The Mind and Art of Henry Miller (1967); Kingsley Widmer, Henry Miller (1967); George Orwell, 'Inside the Whale', in England, Your England, and Other Essays (1954).

Miller, Joaquin (Cincinnatus Hiner Miller) (1841–1913). Poet and dramatist. Born in Indiana, he was, like Bret Harte and to some extent Mark Twain, one of the literary figures who represented the pioneer West to the literary East. As a child he travelled the Oregon trail with his family, later became a cook in the California mines, and later still lived with the Digger Indians. He acquired some education and in 1860 was admitted to the bar, but after various other ventures he went to San Francisco with literary ambitions. But his success came when he went to London. He printed *Pacific Poems* (1871) at his own expense and won acclaim in many quarters, particularly among the Pre-Raphaelites, as 'the Byron of Oregon'. Rossetti helped him to revise his work to produce *Songs of the Sierras* (1871), and he acquired international reputation. His verse dramas and histories of his own past and of various parts of the country were only a part of his considerable later publication. Their documentary interest is damaged by literariness and exaggeration, but he draws on an evidently fascinating culture. Some of his poems, and his *Life among the Modocs* (1873), about living among Indians, have survival value. [MB]

Miller, Perry (1905–63). Scholar and critic. Born in Chicago, he left college in 1923 for three years of adventure as bum and seaman, discovered his vocation in the Congo, and began his teaching career at Harvard in 1931. His life-work was the study of the American puritans and their tradition in a series of important works beginning with *Orthodoxy in Massachusetts* (1933) and continuing with *The New England Mind: The Seventeenth Century*

(1939) and *From Colony to Province* (1953). His authoritative biographical study *Jonathan Edwards* (1949) was backed by an edition of *Images or Shadows of Divine Things* in 1948. *The Raven and the Whale* (1956) studies the backgrounds of Poe and Melville, and *Errand into the Wilderness* (1956) collects his best essays. He is one of America's greatest intellectual historians, and his final, unfinished work, *The Life of the Mind in America* (1965), is as masterly as ever. [EM]

Miller, Warren (1921–66). Novelist. Born in Pennsylvania, he studied at the University of Iowa, served in the U.S. Army in Europe in the Second World War, and lived his literary life in New York. Some of his books appeared under the pseudonym of Amanda Veil, and he also wrote children's books with Edward Sorel. But he is best known for novels under his own name: *The Cool World* (1959), a remarkable account of teenage Harlem gang activity; *Looking for the General* (1964), a satire; and *The Siege of Harlem* (1965), concerning the founding of Harlem as a separate state. [EM]

Mills, C(harles) Wright (1916–62). Sociologist. Born in Texas, he was professor at Columbia from 1945, writing some of the most influential political commentaries of the century in America. He was a polemicist for social change rather than an academic 'pure' sociologist. His earliest work (with H. H. Gerth) was *From Max Weber: Essays in Sociology* (1946), followed by a study of labour leaders, *The New Men of Power* (1948) and (with Clarence Senior and Rose Goldstein) *The Puerto Rican Journey* (1950). His wider public came with *White Collar* (1951), a brilliant and relentless penetrating analysis of American middle-class society, and *The Power Elite* (1956), which poses the three controlling power-groups in America: corporation capitalists, militarists and politicians. These were extended and followed up with *The Causes of World War Three* (1958), an acutely persuasive description of war momentum, and *Listen, Yankee* (1960), an outspoken commentary on the Cuban revolution. *The Marxists* (1962) is 'a primer on marxisms', written to educate Americans away from mere hearsay on some fundamental modern ideas. Mills' broader sociological works began with his dissertation *Sociology and*

Pragmatism (published in 1964), and included *Character and Social Structure* (1953, with H. H. Gerth), one of the best introductions to modern sociology, *The Sociological Imagination* (1959), a criticism of the methods and assumptions of modern sociologists, and *Power, Politics and People* (collected essays, ed. I. L. Horowitz, 1963). Mills' work has considerable influence with the New Left, both in America and Britain, and among the student revolutionaries in Europe in the 1960s. [EM]

Mitchell, Margaret (1900–49). Novelist. Born in Georgia, she became a journalist, and later world-famous as the author of *Gone with the Wind* (1936), the classic best-seller of the century. The novel is a variant on the tradition of Southern romance fiction, and is set in Georgia during the Civil War and Reconstruction. A historical romance with exciting characters and epic dimensions, more than 8 million copies were sold in 40 countries. Its action turns on the attempts of the exotic and mercenary heroine, Scarlett O'Hara, to restore Tara, the family plantation, and on her love-relationships: its ably presented sentimentality and its mixture of daring and morals made it an incredible success of great cultural significance. [MB]

Finis Farr, *Margaret Mitchell of Atlanta: The Author of Gone with the Wind* (1966); Frank Luther Mott, *Golden Multitudes: The Story of the Best-Seller in the United States* (1947).

Monroe, Harriet (1860–1936). Editor, poet, autobiographer. Born in Chicago. She is best known for founding and editing *Poetry: A Magazine of Verse*, which first appeared in Chicago in October 1912 and was thereafter one of the leading journals of the new movement in American poetry, printing most of the distinguished names of the poetic revolution – Pound, Eliot, H.D., Sandburg, Masters and Hart Crane, among others (◊ Little Magazines). Her selection was helped radically by Pound, the London editor, whose *Letters* (ed. D. D. Paige, 1950) show much about the review's development. Her own verse – collected in *Valeria and Other Poems* (1892), *You and I* (1914) and *Chosen Poems* (1935) – is not particularly distinguished; but her autobiography, *A Poet's Life: Seventy Years in a Changing World* (1937), is a fascinating document of the literary revolution of the early years of the century, also revealing

much about the Chicago revival of which she was part. [MB]

Moody, William Vaughn (1869–1910). Playwright, poet. A brilliant teacher at Harvard, and other colleges. His early poems were Elizabethan and Miltonic. But *Gloucester Moors* (1901) is an individual work of some originality on the theme of oppressive power, and *An Ode in Time of Hesitation* (1900) and *On a Soldier Fallen in the Philippines* (1900) are bitter attacks on American imperialism. His largest work is the verse trilogy *The Masque of Judgement* (1900), a play about American sin obsession written in high Miltonic language, *The Fire-Bringer* (1904), a promethean work with a celebrated lyric section, 'The Song of Pandora', and *The Death of Eve*, planned to complete the dramatic sequence by making woman the mediator between man and God, but never completed. His positivist romantic inheritance also comes out in his prose plays, *The Faith Healer* (1909), concerning mysticism, and *The Great Divide* (1909), which ran for a thousand performances in New York, contrasting Puritan New England with the Arizona West and featuring the ways to end guilty sexual repression. [MB/EM]

The Poems and Plays, ed. J. M. Manley (2 vols., 1912); *The Selected Poems*, ed. B. M. Lovett (1931).
David D. Henry, *William Vaughn Moody: A Study* (1934).

Moore, Julia A. (1847–1920). Poet. The 'Sweet Singer of Michigan' was a notoriously bad poetess whose *The Sweet Singer of Michigan Salutes the Public* (1876) – later called *The Sentimental Song Book* – had wide circulation and eventually became the subject of wide humorous commentary; Ogden Nash says he learned the possibilities of bad versifying from her work. It stands in American literary history as a cultural document – widely remembered, almost totally unread. [MB]

Moore, Marianne (1887–). Poet. Born in St Louis, she graduated from Bryn Mawr in 1909. After teaching stenography for five years, she began contributing poems to the English magazine of the ◊ Imagists, the *Egoist*. Her first volume of *Poems* (1921) was chosen from that magazine by friends without her knowledge. In the same year she became an assistant in the New York Public

Library. The second volume, *Observations* (1924), she prepared herself. From 1925 until its demise in 1929 she edited the *Dial*, the fortnightly literary review which had moved in 1918 from Chicago to New York, attracting such writers and associates as Conrad ◊ Aiken, Van Wyck ◊ Brooks, John ◊ Dewey, Thomas Mann and T. S. Eliot (◊ Little Magazines). Her *Selected Poems* (1935), introduced by T. S. Eliot, was followed by *The Pangolin, and Other Verse* (1936), *What Are Years?* (1941), *Nevertheless* (1944), and *Collected Poems*, which won the Pulitzer Prize in 1951. *Predilections* (1955) contains essays on her favourite writers. Her most recent publications are *The Fables of La Fontaine* (1954), a verse translation, *Like a Bulwark* (1956), *O To Be a Dragon* (1959), *The Arctic Fox* (1964) and *Tell Me, Tell Me* (1966).

'I tend to write', she has said, 'in a patterned arrangement, with rhymes . . . to secure an effect of flowing continuity.' Her line is long, gathering in its wake a host of observed detail and sharply drawn images, which she leaves to stir their own unaided ripples in the reader's imagination. Her mood is at once elegant and ironical, conversational yet restrained, the starting point of her meditations often being rare or fabulous animals – hippopotamus, wild ostrich, basilisk, pelican, buffalo, monkey, mongoose, octopus, unicorn or peacock. 'There is a great amount of poetry in unconscious/fastidiousness. Certain Ming/products', she writes, ' . . . are well enough in their way . . . ', but passes on to a puppy eating off a plate, a swan under the willows in Oxford, ants scurrying round an ant-heap. 'What is/there in being able/to say that one has dominated the stream in an attitude/of self-defence,' she ends, 'in proving that one has had the experience/of carrying a stick?' 'Self-reliant like the cat,' her father used to say, 'that takes its prey to privacy . . . the deepest feeling always shows itself in silence; not in silence, but restraint.' As much can be said of her poems. [HB]

The Complete Poems (1968).
Eugene P. Sheehy and Kenneth A. Lohf, *The Achievement of Marianne Moore: A Biography 1907–57* (1958).

Moore, Merrill (1903–57). Poet. Born in Tennessee, he was educated at Vanderbilt and associated there with the ◊ Fugitive Group. By profession a doctor and psychiatrist, he later taught at Harvard.

Throughout his life he wrote sonnets on a playfully prolific scale, even dictating them to a tape-recorder in his car. Over 100,000 are said to exist, only a small proportion in print – in volumes like *The Noise That Time Makes* (1929), *Six Sides to a Man* (1935), *M: One Thousand Autobiographical Sonnets* (1938), and *Case Record from a Sonnetarium* (1951). The high rate of production does not detract from their elegance and formal control; the Fugitive voice is there in the stylish accuracy of diction. The subjects, though usually simple, are carefully analysed with strong psychological awareness. [MB]

Henry W. Wells, *Poet and Psychiatrist: Merrill Moore, M.D.* (1955).

More, Paul Elmer (1864–1937). Critic, philosopher. He was born in St Louis, Missouri, and had a Calvinist upbringing. After graduating from Washington University in 1887 he taught for five years, then went to study at Harvard, where he met Irving ◊ Babbitt. He now abandoned his planned doctorate and conceived his task as 'the formulation of conscious and deliberate standards'; he thus became a leader in the ◊ New Humanism. A journalist and critic for many years, he edited the *Nation* (1909–14) before returning to lecture at Princeton in semi-retirement.

His chief work was the long series of *Shelburne Essays* (11 vols., 1904–21) and the later *New Shelburne Essays* (3 vols., 1928–36), from which selections were published in 1935. Most of these essays concern English and American literature, but he also wrote on other subjects and became virtually an equivalent of Matthew Arnold. He was a life-long student of the Upanishads, and a distinctive, curious blend of Platonism and mysticism runs through the series. His main concern is to show the qualities of classical writing and to scourge the modern value of romanticism, 'the infinitely craving personality'. This he did time and again, from *The Drift of Romanticism* (1913) to 1928, when his outburst against ◊ Dos Passos's *Manhattan Transfer* (which he described as 'an explosion in a cesspool' in his *Demon of the Absolute*, 1928) provoked serious attacks on New Humanism in general, and on More from an old foe, H. L. ◊ Mencken. [MG]

The Religion of Plato (1921); *The Christ of the New Testament* (1924); *Pages from an Oxford Diary* (1937); *The Greek Tradition* (5 vols., 1921–31).

Robert Shafer, *Paul Elmer Mőre and American Criticism* (1935); Arthur H. Dakin, *Paul Elmer More* (1960); Francis X. Duggan, *Paul Elmer More* (1966).

Morison, Samuel Eliot (1887–). Historian. Born in Boston. His major work derives from his passionate interests in early New England and the history and practice of seafaring, happily combined in *The Maritime History of Massachusetts* (1921), *Builders of the Bay Colony* (1930) and the brilliant *Admiral of the Ocean Sea* (2 vols., 1942), a full-scale study of Columbus's voyages. His most recent works have been a 15-volume *History of United States Naval Operations during World War II* (1947–62), *Freedom in Contemporary Society* (1956) and *The Oxford History of the American People* (1965). He has also notably contributed to literary history with his studies of the pattern of colonial New England intelligentsia, especially in *The Intellectual life of Colonial New England* (1956). [D K A/E M]

Morley, Christopher (1890–1957). Novelist, poet, essayist. Born in Pennsylvania, he was educated at Haverford College and, as a Rhodes Scholar, at Oxford, where he published a rare first volume of poems (*The Eighth Sin*, 1912). Oxford is the scene of his novel *Kathleen* (1920). He went on to become active in New York publishing and literary journalism. An intelligent and prolific writer, he was an influential columnist for various papers (notably the *Saturday Review of Literature*) and produced more than 50 books, many of them novels, all marked by charm, erudition and elegance. His witty, informal essays are brought together in *Shandygaff...* (1918), *Mince Pie* (1919), *Forty-Four Essays* (1925), etc.; *Essays* (1928) is a selection from earlier volumes. Among the novels are *Where the Blue Begins* (1922), and *Kitty Foyle* (1939); *Poems* (1929) is a collection of verse. [M B]

G. R. Lyle and H. T. Brown, Jr, *A Bibliography of Christopher Morley* (1952).

Morris, Wright (1910–). Novelist. The emptinesses of the great plains of Nebraska, where he was born, have had much to do with the qualities of his fiction; where objects are few those present gain a peculiar richness of meaning. His early novels reveal a tremendous sense that things, looked at closely, may show what life really is for those who made and used them. Hence *The In-*

habitants (1946) and *The Home Place* (1948), the story of a man who brings his family back to a Nebraska farm, combine text with photographs. Morris made his home more recently in Tamalpais Valley, California.

The later novels, in the main about personal and family relationships and cleavages in the mid-West, are equally concerned with revelation and reality. 'Objects' are replaced by characters and situations, actions and events, more publicly available. But the underlying preoccupation remains – the search for a genuine reality usually arrived at by an imaginative transformation momentarily produced by heroes or an act of heroism, or by the power of love, or by the creative consciousness itself. In *The World in the Attic* (1949) the imaginative attic world is more real than mundane reality outside; *Man and Boy* (1951) is about the struggle towards imaginative transformation of an empty, dry life; *The Works of Love* (1952) describes the quest for love and communion with others; *The Huge Season* (1954) concerns escape from limitation via an imaginative understanding of the meaning of the past – in this case the glamorous, heroic twenties. In *The Field of Vision* (1956) a bizarre group of American tourists in Mexico seek some kind of vision that will lead them out of the unreality of their lives. Other novels are *My Uncle Dudley* (1942), *The Man Who Was There* (1945), *The Deep Sleep* (1953), *Love among the Cannibals* (1957) and *Ceremony in Lone Tree* (1960). *What a Way to Go* (1962) makes a break with his earlier novels in that it deals, comically and sharply, with American and European tourists in Europe, and a middle-aged professor's encounter with the eternal feminine. *Cause for Wonder* (1963) isolates the awareness of his American characters once again in Europe, and *One Day* (1965), like its predecessor, concerns an individual's experience in time, but the plot deals with a small community near San Francisco. *In Orbit* (1967) shows Morris, with his next novel, still terse, oblique and deeply serious: it concerns the impact of a school drop-out on a university town of the South-west. Morris's novels are written in complex stream-of-consciousness structures but do not lose touch with human realities. With humour, wit and technical accomplishment, they evoke sensitively and poignantly the recent American past and present in the mid-West and South-west. His distinguished intelligence is acutely at work also in *The*

Territory Ahead (1958), critical essays on 19th- and 20th-century American writers. But *A Bill of Rites, A Bill of Wrongs, A Bill of Goods* (1968) is an angry and too sweepingly scornful indictment of American culture in the 1960s: the sense of doom has no sense of satirical direction. *God's Country and My People* (1968) links 85 photographs into an autobiographical statement. [A H/ E M]

Wright Morris: A Reader (1970).
David Madden, *Wright Morris* (1965); Wayne C. Booth, 'The Two Worlds in the Fiction of Wright Morris', *Sewanee Review*, L X V (Summer, 1957); Leon Howard, *Wright Morris* (U. of Minnesota Pamphlet, 1968).

Morton, Thomas (1575?–1647?). A wild London lawyer who arrived in New England as shareholder in Mount Wollaston, a Puritan settlement (later renamed Merrymount) which he managed to divert to atheism, maypole-dancing and licentious living, according to the Puritans, who also claimed he sold arms to the Indians and consorted with their women. Returning from banishment in 1643 he was imprisoned in Boston, and after release died a few years later in York, Maine. His Anglican settlement and commercial aplomb, in what is now Quincy, Massachusetts, are celebrated, and his enemies are satirized in *New English Canaan* (Amsterdam, 1637; ed. C. F. Adams, 1883). William Bradford's *History of Plymouth Plantation* is critical of Morton. Morton's experience is the basis of Hawthorne's 'The Maypole of Merrymount' (1836) and an opera by Howard Hanson and Richard Stokes (1934). Robert ◊ Lowell's play *Endecott and the Red Cross* (1965) treats him fairly. [E M]

Moss, Howard (1922–   ). Poet, critic. He was born in New York, taught at Vassar, and is now poetry editor of the *New Yorker*. He has published several volumes of verse – including *The Wound and the Weather* (1946), *A Swimmer in the Air* (1957), *A Winter Come, A Summer Gone: Poems 1946–1960* (1960), *Finding Them Lost* (1965) and *Poems* (1968) – as well as a critical work, *The Magic Lantern of Marcel Proust* (1962). His poems possess the power of making something close to light verse both dignified and revealing through skilful use of varied verse forms and elaborately detailed urban observation. [M B]

Motley, John Lothrop (1814–77). Historian, diplomat. Born at Dorchester, Massachusetts, the son of a prosperous New England family, he spent several years studying in Europe after graduating from Harvard in 1831. He published two fictional works, *Morton's Hope: or, The Memoirs of a Young Provincial* (1839), which was based on his experiences in Germany as a student at Göttingen, and *Merry-Mount: A Romance of the Massachusetts Colony* (1849). Later he was secretary of legation in St Petersburg, Minister to Austria, and Minister to Great Britain. His historical interests became focused on the Netherlands, and he published his best-known and most successful work, *The Rise of the Dutch Republic* (3 vols.), in 1856, following it with *The History of the United Netherlands* (1860–67) and *The Life and Death of John of Barneveld* (1874). His approach as a historian was chiefly political and religious; like his contemporary Prescott, he saw history as a branch of literature. But despite skilfully drawn portraits and a strong sympathy for his subject-matter his work is ponderously laden with reference and quotation, though his place in the history of American history is unquestioned. [D K A]

Motley, Willard (1912–65). Novelist. Born in Chicago, as a young man he worked his way across America as emigrant labourer, waiter, cook, ranch-hand, etc. His reputation began with his novel *Knock on Any Door* (1947), the story of a Chicago slum boy growing into a criminal in the corrupt pre-war city environment. In the forties, Motley had joined the Chicago writers of the thirties, and other city writers of America in condemning the urban environment which so much excited them. After this success, his big house on Wells Street became a Bohemian centre. He followed up with *We Fished All Night* (1951) and *Let No Man Write My Epitaph* (1958), which substantially and effectively covered the same ground, the chosen fields of ◊ Dreiser and ◊ Farrell before him. But the repetitions began to lack vitality. His experience as an American Negro living in Mexico, where he had been for 12 years before his death, went into *Let Noon Be Fair* (1966), which records the corruption of a fishing village by bored Americans and their money. It is a not successful study of triviality and hedonistic degradation. As Nelson ◊ Algren wrote: 'He was a Negro and a writer but he was not a Negro writer. His scene was always White Bohemia.' [EM]

Mumford, Lewis (1895–   ). Teacher, literary critic, writer on architecture, town planning and philosophy. Born in New York, he was educated at City College, Columbia and the New York School of Social Research, where he heard Thorstein ◊ Veblen. He helped to found the Regional Planning Association of America (1924), and taught at numerous universities. He is now best known for his lucid and stimulating essays on architecture and town planning, such as those collected in *From the Ground Up* (1956) and *The Highway and the City* (1963); but these are only a small part of his lifetime's work on the relations between man and his environment, a study greatly influenced by his early reading of Patrick Geddes, the Scottish biologist and city planner. A great American polymath, his early publications were *The Story of Utopias* (1922); *Sticks and Stones* (1924), a history of American civilization seen through its architecture; *Herman Melville* (1929), a critical biography with a strong psychological emphasis; and two valuable studies in 'American experience and culture' with special reference to literature, *The Golden Day* (1926), examining New England from 1830 to 1860, and *Brown Decades* (1931), surveying the arts between the Civil War and 1895. But his major work is a tetralogy, *Renewal of Life*, which presents his philosophy of modern civilization and is based on a study of Western cities from the 10th century; it consists of *Technics and Civilization* (1934), *The Culture of Cities* (1938), *The Condition of Man* (1944) and *The Conduct of Life* (1951), in which he stresses his plea that men should be sceptical of all 'systems'. His passionate concern with problems of metropolitan development has also produced *City Development: Studies in Disintegration and Renewal* (1945) and his most important single work, the classic *The City in History* (1961). His other works include *Green Memories* (1947), a biography of his son, *Art and Technics* (1954), *In the Name of Sanity* (1954), and *The Transformations of Man* (1956). *The Urban Prospect* (1968) is a collection of recent articles.

He has said: 'As time has gone on I have become more, rather than less, radical. Though brought up as an Episcopalian, my religion is that of the traditional American humanist, like Emerson or Whitman.' And: 'The issues that I raised have proved discussable; and the rigid methods and regimented goals that once seemed as inevitable as they were ominous, since they were based on the latest findings of science and technology, have begun to collapse like pricked balloons under rational examination.' These views receive their latest discussion in *The Myth of the Machine* (1967). [MG]

The Human Prospect, ed. Harry T. Moore and Karl W. Deutsch (1955) (selections).

Munson, Gorham B(ert) (1896–   ). Critic and editor. Born in Amityville, N.Y., he was, as an expatriate in the 1920s, editor of *Secession* (◊ Little Magazines, Lost Generation). Among his numerous books of criticism and economic commentary are *Waldo Frank* (1923); *Robert Frost: A Study in Sensibility and Good Sense* (1927), an early appreciation; *Destinations: A Canvas of American Literature since 1900* (1928), a useful survey; and some books on the teaching of creative writing, including *The Writer's Workshop Companion* (1951). [MB]

N

Nabokov, Vladimir (1899–   ). Novelist. One of the finest of present-day novelists, and now American by adoption, Nabokov was born in St Petersburg to an eminent Russian family whose fortunes collapsed in the Revolution: they went into exile in 1919. After finishing his education at Trinity College, Cambridge, he lived in England, Germany and France, writing in Russian and making his reputation in Russian émigré circles (about whom he has written considerably). During 20 years of this life he worked at a series of Russian novels, only later translated into English. In 1940 he went to America, began writing in English, became a citizen in 1945, taught at various colleges, used a research fellowship at Harvard in lepidoptera (his other main field), and spent an 11-year period as Professor of Russian at Cornell. He is now a full-time writer and lives in Switzerland.

The main springs of his fiction lie in the Russian and European literary tradition. In addition to an obvious debt to Gogol, on whom he wrote a curious study (1944), his style and sensibility are European, his aesthetic experiments emerging from those of the early 20th-century masters. His fiction is highly stylized, oblique in techniques, self-conscious in language, and playing elaborate jokes to present his materials with maximum indirection and to invent the maximum changes in form. Sartre said he has the exile's desire to knock down the material he has constructed. His work conveys a deep sense of loss and disintegration, exploiting the tension between his great capacity to re-create places, sensations and values, and his bold authorial detachment. Essentially a comic novelist, indulging in infallible wit and whimsy, he writes from penetrating political and cultural awareness. In 1923 he published two books of poetry and in 1926 his first novel, *Mashenka*; there followed *King, Queen, Knave* (1928; in English, 1968), a traditional romance parodied; *The Luzhin Defense* (1929; in English as *The Defense*, 1964), a chess novel; *The Eye* (1930; in English 1965), a nostalgic story of a Russian émigré in Berlin; *The*

Return of Chorb (1930), a collection of stories and poems; *The Exploit* (1931); *Camera Obscura* (1932; in English 1938); *Despair* (1934; in English 1966), a *doppelgänger* crime novel; and *Invitation to a Beheading* (1935; in English 1959).

Two plays, *The Event* and *The Waltz Invention*, appeared in 1938, and *The Gift* (1937; in English 1963), his last novel in Russian, shows his ability at its height in the story of another émigré in Berlin, this time a writer like Nabokov. In 1941 he published *The Real Life of Sebastian Knight* (written in English while he was still in Paris). Then came *Speak Memory: An Autobiography Revisited* (1967), originally pieces in the *New Yorker, Atlantic Monthly, Partisan Review* and *Harper's Magazine*, and appearing in earlier form as *Inconclusive Evidence* (1951). His second English novel was *Bend Sinister* (1948) and then followed his two 'American' novels: *Pnin* (1957), a superb comic novel about a teacher of Russian in an American college, and the novel that first established his reputation with a large audience, *Lolita* (1955 in Paris, 1958 in America), a *tour de force* of comic satire on sex and the American ways of life focused on the love of a middle-aged European for an American 'nymphet'. *Pale Fire* (1962) is a supreme example of Nabokov's formal games: a novel hidden in a poem and its commentary. *Ada or Ardor: A Family Chronicle* (1969) summarizes his life-long fascination with puzzles and games, and his obsession with family sexuality. *Nabokov's Dozen* (1958) is a collection of thirteen stories and *Nabokov's Quartet* (1967) collects four stories from between 1930 and 1959. *Nabokov's Congeries* (1968) is Page Stegner's selection from all his work. In 1964 appeared a translation (and commentary) of *Eugene Onegin* by Pushkin: of the 4 volumes' 2,000 odd pages, 228 are devoted to the translation. His work cannot be quickly summarized. He once urged that it is hard to judge work written in 'my untrammelled, rich, and infinitely docile Russian tongue' against the work written in a 'second-rate brand of English'. But his English writings show him to be an excellent and unique stylist. He is a major 20th-century novelist. [MB/EM]

Andrew Field, *Nabokov: His Life in Art* (1967); Page Stegner, *Escape into Aesthetics: The Art of Vladimir Nabokov* (1967); ed. L. S. Dembo, *Nabokov: The Man and His Work* (1968); Robert Scholes, *The Fabulators* (1967).

Nasby, Petroleum Vesuvius (pseud. of David Ross Locke) (1833–88). Humorist. Born in New York State, Locke was an itinerant printer and then a journalist in Ohio. It was in the Finlay, Ohio, *Jeffersonian* that 'Nasby' made his appearance as bigoted and illiterate Copperhead – a pro-Southern Northerner – during the Civil War years. In 1865 Locke went to the Toledo *Blade*, which he was to own, and produced more Nasby letters for the paper. Nasby is in the convention of ' Artemus ◊ Ward' and 'Josh ◊ Billings' and is presented with the usual grammatical illiteracies and vernacular spirit of this movement in humour. But Locke used Nasby ironically, to represent Southern white-supremacy views which he opposed, and he is, like other humorist-figures of the period, a congenital defector and rogue. *The Nasby Papers* (1864) first collected these newspaper pieces; other volumes followed including *Swingin' Round the Cirkle* (1867), *The Diary of an Office Seeker* (1881) and *Nasby in Exile: Or, Six Months of Travel* (1882), which, again typically, takes the character abroad. *The Nasby Letters* appeared posthumously in 1893. Locke also wrote novels – *A Paper City* (1879) satirizes land speculation, and *The Demagogues* (1881) political life. [MB]

Cyril Clemens, *Petroleum V. Nasby* (1936); James C. Austin, *Petroleum V. Nasby* (1965).

Nash, Ogden (1902–   ). Humorous poet. His verse, widely and internationally known, has been collected in numerous volumes, from the 1930s onwards, and includes *Versus* (1949), *Family Reunion* (1950), *Everyone But Thee and Me* (1962), and *Marriage Lines* (1964). Nash has confessed a debt to American 'bad' poetry, such as Julia A. ◊ Moore's; its clumsy prosody is at the heart of his method. But he is periodically very inventive and exploits many of the devices of modern poetry; his superbly ostentatious bad rhymes and his use of the long line have a 20th-century spirit, so much so that a number of serious poets confess to having learned from him. Nash's main themes are those of witty social commentary and the charming cele-bration of domestic life and domestic disaster. A poet to please children, he is like Belloc or Lear – which comic tradition he continues – more than a children's poet. Too genial and elegant to deserve the title of satirist, his books do often comment sharply on society; but his main persona in his poems is as husband and father or else as aphorist, questioning the world's platitudes, pieties and even grammar. Much of his work has appeared in the *New Yorker*, on which he has served editorially. [MB]

Collected Verse from 1929 On (1961).

Nathan, George Jean (1882–1958). Dramatic critic. A native of Indiana and a graduate of Cornell University, Nathan 'did time' on New York newspapers and popular magazines as a reporter and feature writer, but by the age of 30 he found himself and devoted the remainder of his life to dramatic criticism. He wrote for a variety of periodicals, but his name is chiefly associated with *Arts and Decoration*, *Vanity Fair*, the *Smart Set* and the *American Mercury*. His style was inclined to be slapstick, which prevented many people from noting the vast knowledge and extraordinary perception in his critical essays. He was probably the most learned, the most acute and the most influential dramatic critic the United States has yet produced. In the twenties and much of the thirties he could, pretty much, make or break a play or a playwright. He, more than any other individual critic, helped to educate the American public to look down upon the theatrical merchandise of the Belascos and to appreciate the full stature of Eugene O'Neill. He also laboured heroically to bring the works of Sean O'Casey, Molnar, Wedekind and Hauptmann to the attention of Broadway. Most of his two dozen books are collections of his critical reviews. He also wrote on morals, history, marriage, religion and politics, but what he had to say on these subjects is considerably inferior to his discussion of the theatre. His most representative and best books are *Mr George Jean Nathan Presents* (1917), *The Autobiography of an Attitude* (1925) and *The Theatre in the Fifties* (1953). [CA]

The World of George Jean Nathan, ed. C. Angoff (1952); *The Magic Mirror*, ed. T. Q. Curtiss (1960).

Charles Angoff, 'George Jean Nathan: A Candid Portrait', *Atlantic Monthly*, December 1962; Isaac Goldberg, *The Theatre of George Jean Nathan* (1926).

Neal, John (1793–1876). Novelist, essayist. A Maine Quaker. He wrote, quickly, a number of fairly melodramatic novels, including *Keep Cool* (1817) and *Randolph* (1823), and between 1824 and 1827 lived in London, where he contributed to *Blackwood's* a series of essays on American writers which did much to make American writing known in England. He asserted the need for a vernacular American literature and, in his later novels particularly, endeavoured to use native speech, themes and styles. His *Brother Jonathan* (1825), *Rachel Dyer* (1828) and other books drew on strongly Yankee materials. He settled again in Portland, Maine; founded *The Yankee*, a literary journal; and presented a record of his attitudes and experiences in his autobiography, *Wandering Recollections of a Somewhat Busy Life* (1869). [MB]

Negro Literature. 'Negro', like 'Indian', is a term invented by colonizing white Europeans to designate certain imported, or indigenous, human beings whom they intended to retain in subservient control. 'Negro' labelled a required stereotype, and most Negroes accepted this typification, under whatever duress, until nearly 350 years after the first importation of slaves into the New World in the 1620s (John Hope Franklin, *From Slavery to Freedom*, revised edn 1956). 'Negro' meant, and still does mean for many whites, a person who may be used as part of a cheap labour force because he can be considered as part of the myth of the Christianizing West that some men are nearer to beasts, can be called 'black' to associate them with darkness, the Devil and Hell, and may be lumped with that eternal underground force of the sexually potent and naturally wicked. The 'Negro' of mythical stereotype must therefore be kept down. But in the 1950s and 1960s black Americans, along with black people throughout the world, began to designate themselves 'black' without the malign connotations of the term. The movement of literature follows therefore the development from slavery to post-Civil War partial liberation, from incipient protest to full protest, and finally to the revolutionary 'black power' movement of the 1960s. The increase in information about black Americans grew considerably over this last period. The nature of slavery is documented in: Stanley Elkins, *Slavery, A Problem in American Institutional and Intellectual Life* (1959); D. P. Mannix and Malcolm Cowley, *Black Cargoes: A History of the Atlantic Slave Trade* (1962); and David Brion Davis, *The Problem of Slavery in Western Culture* (1966). In 1944 appeared Gunnar Myrdal's pioneering study, *An American Dilemma* (a useful condensed edition prepared by Arnold M. Rose, *The Negro in America*, 1948). The inadequate treatment of Negroes in books on history, economics, politics and sociology, and in school texts, is being slowly challenged by studies arguing the hypocrisies of democracy, including: Herbert Aptheker's pioneering *Documentary History of the Negro People in the United States* (2 vols., 1951); Howard Brotz, ed., *Negro Social and Political Thought, 1850–1920* (1966); and Leslie Fishel and Benjamin Quarles, *The Negro American: A Documentary History* (1967). Of the many works delineating the movement towards a less oppressed life, some of the more significant are: Booker T. ◊ Washington, *Up from Slavery* (1901); William E. B. ◊ DuBois, *Souls of Black Folk* (1903); *George Washington Carver: An American Biography* (1942); *Narrative of the Life of Frederick Douglass, An American Slave* (1845); Virginia Cunningham, *Paul Laurence Dunbar* (1947 – a life of the poet); James Weldon ◊ Johnson, *The Autobiography of an Ex-Coloured Man* (1912); Edwin P. Hoyt, *Paul Robeson* (1958); Constance Webb, *Richard Wright* (1968); R. G. B. Reisner, *The Legend of Charlie Parker* (1962); and Dick Gregory, *Nigger* (1964). The more general challenge to the Negro condition is documented in: M. Ahmann, ed., *The New Negro* (1961); Harold Isaacs, *The New World of Negro Americans* (1963); and Kenneth B. Clarke, *Dark Ghetto* (1965). Naturally, few Negroes have ever been able to achieve status as writers, rather than entertainers in the fields of sport, music and the stage. Only the freak sustained or transcended the compulsory physical labour, the enclosure in rural or city ghetto, the absence of education for self-realization and freedom and the deliberate condition for subordination from childhood onwards. Even black music, which until the 1960s always had a quality superior to black writing, was largely suppressed as racial expression throughout the 200 years before the Civil War, and in the years following either patronized as entertainment or used as a basis for sociology. The gap between rural and city folk music and blues, and compositions by artists such as Duke Ellington, Charles Parker, Ornette Coleman and Cecil Taylor, is exactly the gap between the permitted semi-anonymous artistry of the 'invisible' Negro and the public manifestations of important, sophisticated, minority art. The watershed between the two in literature occurs between the 1920s and 1960s, between the so-called Harlem Renaissance and the literature of Black Power, between literature which largely attempts to compete with and imitate general American forms and literature which focuses protest and revolt without necessarily being bound to those forms. This development has been hamstrung by the means of communication and production being in the hands of white publishing houses, theatres, television and radio networks. But since 1960, books on or about Negroes have become good business, and the amount of material published itself constitutes something of a revolution. As the novelist John A. Williams observes: 'the presence of black editors in large numbers would do as much for black writing as Jewish or Anglo-Saxon editors did for Jewish and Anglo-Saxon literature'. Black Americans are a minority and if their literature is to be differentiated from general American works, the problem of definition can only be made as part of the historical process of change in the Negro condition. This development is given in: August Meier, *Negro Thought in America 1880–1915* (1963), Leonard Broom and Norval Glenn, *Transformation of the Negro American* (1965) and the documentary and autobiographical writings of Negroes including Langston ◊ Hughes, James ◊ Baldwin, Ralph ◊ Ellison, LeRoi ◊ Jones and Martin Luther King Jr (*Stride Toward Freedom*, 1958, and *Why We Can't Wait*, 1964). The Black Muslim movement, so strong in the early 1960s, became considerably less powerful after the assassination of Malcolm X (E. Essien-Udom, *Black Nationalism*, 1962; Louis Lomas, *When the Word is Given*, 1963). The growth of the secular civil rights movement, both before and after Mrs Rosa Parks' refusal to step to the back of an Alabama bus in 1954 and the sit-ins of 1960, is documented in: John P. Roche, *The Quest for the Dream* (1963); Arthur I. Waskow, *From Race-Riot to Sit-In, 1919 to the 1960s* (1966); Ronald

Segal, *The Race War* (1966); and Louis E. Lomax, *The Negro Revolt* (1962). Detailed accounts of Negro culture in the crucial period of the 1960s are given in: Charles Silberman, *Crisis in Black and White* (1964); Harold Cruse, *The Crisis of the Negro Intellectual* (1967); and *In Black America* (ed. Pat Romero), a large volume of information and articles by leading black writers (1969). The development of the Black Power movement is given in: Joanne Grant, ed., *Black Protest: History, Documents and Analyses 1619 to the Present* (1968); Stokeley Carmichael and Charles V. Hamilton, *Black Power* (1967); and Floyd B. Barbour, ed., *The Black Power Revolt* (1968). The importance of the major black leader of the post Second World War period is given in his own excellent *Autobiography of Malcolm X* (1965) and George Breitman, *The Last Year of Malcolm X* (1967); *Malcolm X Speaks: Selected Speeches and Statements* (1965); A. Epps, ed., *The Speeches of Malcolm X at Harvard* (1969); and John Henrik Clarke, ed., *Malcolm X, The Man and His Times* (1969). The experience of the only man to inherit so far any of Malcolm's charisma is contained in Eldridge Cleaver's *Soul on Ice* (1968) and *Eldridge Cleaver: Post-Prison Writings and Speeches* (1969) – to which must be added a major influence on Negroes in America today, Frantz Fanon's *The Wretched of the Earth* (1963; tr 1965).

Negro slaves and their descendants had no choice but to live out their roles as stereotypes of Western imagination, 'an oversimplified clown, a beast or an angel', in Ralph Ellison's words, but always placed outside the 'democratic plan'. The plea of the black writer has always been, in the cry of J. Saunders Redding, 'I am tired of giving up my creative initiative to these demands' – of being a victim, a Negro, a type. LeRoi Jones speaks for the 1960s condition: 'The Negro writer can only survive by refusing to become a white man.' But M. B. ◊ Tolson speaks for those who wish to reach further: 'I, as a black poet, have absorbed the Great Ideas of the Great White World, and interpreted them in the melting-pot idiom of my people. My roots are in Africa, Europe and America.' Jupiter Hammon (1720–1800) was a slave poet praised for his verses by white critics; his 'Address' (1787) pleads for patience in the slave state. Phyllis ◊ Wheatley wrote in a similarly enchained condition. In 1789 appeared 'Negro Slavery by Othello, a Free Negro', a first protest against slavery. But the verbal creativity of Negroes was all the time going into the anonymous or semi-anonymous work-songs, ballads, blues and spirituals which did not need white praise (Newman I. White. *American Negro Folk-Songs*, 1928; Samuel Charters *The Poetry of the Blues*, 1963). The folk literature also included those stories handed on now through anthropological collections and the work of white men like Joel Chandler ◊ Harris. The most sophisticated Negro poets of the later nineteenth and early twentieth centuries – ◊ Dunbar, Johnson, Jean Toomer, Langston Hughes, Arna Bontemps, Gwendolyn Brooks, and many more – are good but not major poets. The main movement within Negro poetry lies between Johnson's preface to his *Book of American Negro Poetry* (1922) – the need to find 'a form that will express the racial spirit' – and ◊ Cullen's *Caroling Dusk: An Anthology of Verse by Negro Poets* (1927) – the need for universal rather than black poetry, 'the individual diversifying ego transcends the synthesizing hue'. This is the growing division in fiction and theatre as well. The first Negro novels were *Clotel, or The President's Daughter* (1853) by William Wells Brown and *Blake, or The Huts of America* (1859) by Martin Delany. After 1890 the numbers increased but were no better than the mass of American sentimental and naturalistic fiction. The fact of their being written by Negroes is their importance; the most representative include: Dunbar's *The Uncalled* (1898); Charles W. Chesnutt's *The Colonel's Dream* (1905); Claude McKay's *Home to Harlem* (1928); and Arna Bontemps' *Black Thunder* (1936). Jean Toomer's *Cane* (1923) is a rare affirmation of blackness written both passionately and complexly. From the 1930s onwards Negro fiction begins to take its place in the pattern of American writing, with outstanding work from Richard ◊ Wright, Chester ◊ Himes, Ralph Ellison and James Baldwin. (See also R. Boné, *The Negro Novel in America*, 1958; Margaret J. Butcher, *The Negro in American Culture*, 1956; J. Saunders Redding, *To Make a Poet Black*, 1939; ed. Seymour L. Gross and John E. Hardy, *Images of the Negro in American Literature*, 1966; ed. Herbert Hill, *Soon, One Morning*, 1963, and *Anger and Beyond* (1968.) The development of a Negro theatre is far

slower. At first it was restricted to Negroes playing their stereotypical roles in racial plays (and films later). Henry James remembered seeing the stage version of *Uncle Tom's Cabin* as a child, and Mrs Stowe dramatized her novel *Dred* in 1856, such entertainments were popular, and were, for white audiences, largely voyeuristic pleasures – for example, Dion Boucicault's *The Octoroon* (1959) and, as late as 1920, O'Neill's *The Emperor Jones*, and, more harmfully, the stage version of Thomas Dixon's *The Clansman* (1905). In the 1930s a handful of stage works presaged the changes in attitude to come: DuBose and Dorothy ◊ Heyward's novel *Porgy* (1927) made into a first-rate opera, *Porgy and Bess* (1935) by George Gershwin, and Marc Connelly's *The Green Pastures* (1930). The Federal Theatre encouraged Negro playwrights. But in 1958, Lorraine Hansberry's sentimental Negro family drama, *Raisin in the Sun*, was an exception on the New York stage, even if its characters were acceptable stereotypes. The crucial movement in Negro literature in the 1960s is from protest to revolution in its aims. James Baldwin's play *Blues for Mr Charlie* (1964) is a protest play for white audiences. LeRoi Jones's later plays are for black audiences and preach revolt, and therefore sharply differ from the general work of the Negro Ensemble Company of New York, whose style and programme is largely for bi-racial audiences. The New York Shakespeare Festival's Hamlet when asked what he is reading replies '*Ebony*, baby'; black actors have their television soap-opera series; and one of the 'hits' of Broadway in the 1960s was Howard Sackler's *The Great White Hope* (1968), largely based on the life of the boxer Jack Johnson. But the new black theatre is remote from any such games of entertainment. It uses modern theatre techniques to fire a black audience to action against white supremacy (Ed Bullins, *Five Plays*, 1969; Ed Bullins, *New Plays for the Black Theatre*, 1969; ed. William Couch, Jr, *New Black Playwrights*, 1969). The beginning was the Black Arts Repertory Theatre School (1964) and the Black Arts Alliance (1967) and what is termed 'guerrilla theatre', designed to awaken black audiences (*Tulane Drama Review*, Vol. 12, No. 4, 1968; *Black Theatre*; Loften Mitchell, *Black Drama: The Story of the American Negro in the Theatre*, 1969; Doris E. Abramson, *Negro*

Playwrights in the American Theatre 1925–1959, 1969). The tone is given in explicit statements by major black writers. John Oliver Killens: 'Everywhere Western man went on the earth, "Christianizing" and "civilizing", he made men into the "niggers", the better to conquer and exploit. And made men believe they were niggers. To deniggerize the earth is the black writer's challenge' ('The Black Writer and Revolution', *Tulane Drama Review,* op. cit.); LeRoi Jones: 'The Black Artist's role in America is to aid in the destruction of America as he knows it' (*Home*, 1968). As Calvin C. Hernton wrote in the 1966 edition of his polemical *Sex and Racism in America:* 'when racism disappears, the nature of the American political-economic system . . . will have changed '. The changes in poetry are registered in: LeRoi Jones and Larry Neal, ed., *Black Fire: An Anthology of Afro-American Writing*, 1968; Clarence Major, ed., *The New Black Poetry* (1969); and to some extent in Langston Hughes, ed., *New Negro Poets: USA* (1964). The African affinities, frequently stated in this period, can be found in Mercer Cook and Stephen E. Henderson, *The Militant Black Writer in Africa and the United States* (1969) and checked in Melville J. Herskovits, *The Myth of the Negro Past* (1941). A summary of the variety of opinions on Negro literature today may be read in Edward Margolies, *Native Sons* (1969), which examines a wide range of writers, from DuBois to LeRoi Jones, and Addison Gayle Jr, ed., *Black Expression: Essays by and about Black Americans in the Creative Arts* (1969). The new Negro fiction develops in: Paule Marshall's *Brown Girl Brownstones* (1959); William Melvin Kelley's *A Different Drummer* (1962), *A Drop of Patience* (1966) and *Dem* (1967); Earle Conrad's *The Premier* (1963); John Oliver Killens' *And Then We Heard the Thunder* (1963); Jesse Hill Ford's *The Liberation of Lord Byron Jones* (1965) and *The Feast of Saint Barnabas* (1969); Ishmael Reed's *The Freelance Pallbearers* (1967); and especially in the development of John A. Williams through *Night Song* (1961), *Sissie* (1963), *The Man who Cried I Am* (1967) and *Sons of Darkness, Sons of Light* (1969). Shorter fiction is collected usefully in: *American Negro Short Stories* (1967, ed. John Henrick Clarke) and *The Best Short Stories by Negro Writers* (1967, ed. Langston Hughes). Reference may be made to: *Negro American Literature Forum* (Indiana State University: quarterly) and *The Guide to African–American Books* (Negro Book Club). [E M]

Nemerov, Howard (1920–). Poet, novelist, critic. Born in New York and educated at Harvard. He edited the little magazine *Furioso*, and has taught at Hamilton College and Bennington. His poems in *The Image and the Law* (1947), *Guide to the Ruins* (1950), *The Salt Garden* (1955) and the useful collection *New and Selected Poems* (1960) have a considerable range of tone and manner, from an Eliot-like philosophical manner to something nearer light verse, where he responds more directly to immediate occasions or domestic experience. The intellectual moralist in Nemerov appears in his fiction. Besides his lively short stories in *A Commodity of Dreams and Other Stories* (1959), he has written novels dealing with the moral dilemmas of the intellectual in advertising and the academic among his students (*The Homecoming Game,* 1957). They include *The Melodramatist* (1949) and *Federigo, or the Power of Love* (1954). His criticism has appeared widely and is partly collected in *Poetry and Fiction: Essays* (1963). An impressive and interesting writer, with deep moral scruples, he can be ponderous and slight. *The Next Room of the Dream* (1963, poems and two plays) and *The Blue Swallows* (1968) contain too many conventional and dull 'serious' poems among the lighter ironical political pieces. *Journal of the Fictive Life* (1965) is a mixed bag of diary, sketches for novels, some uninteresting dreams and a few poems. [M B]

Peter Meinke, *Howard Nemerov* (U. of Minnesota Pamphlet, 1968).

Nevins, Allan (1890–). Historian. Born at Camp Point, Illinois. He rose to the highest ranks of the historical profession without having acquired the benediction of the doctorate; his first historical works were written while a practising journalist in New York City. Not until 1931, when he became Professor of American History at Columbia University, did he devote himself fully to teaching and research. His major work falls into two fields: biography, and a narrative history of the United States from 1847. All his work reflects an awareness of social and economic trends, and he is generally sympathetic to the rise of big business. His conservatism and preoccupation with character can be seen in his biographies *Grover Cleveland* (1932), subtitled 'A Study in Courage', and *Hamilton Fish* (1936). He rejects the muckraking interpretation of the rise of the corporation, stressing the qualities of leadership behind the huge personal fortunes of the late 19th and early 20th centuries. Particular application of his admiration for leadership in the economic sphere came with his 2-volume life *John D. Rockefeller: The Heroic Age of American Enterprise* (1940), revised and reissued as *Study in Power: John D. Rockefeller, Industrialist and Philanthropist* (1953) – in which emphasis was placed on the constructive aspects of economic consolidation. *Ford* (with F. E. Hill, 2 vols., 1954, 1957) also celebrates the heroic age of American business activity, showing Ford as an enlightened leader, though the authors criticize his increasingly autocratic ways during the inter-war years.

Nevins's history of the United States since 1847 began with *The Ordeal of the Union* (2 vols., 1947) and continued in *The Emergence of Lincoln* (2 vols., 1950) and *The War for the Union* (2 vols., 1959). This excellent, well-written narrative illustrates his belief that history should be seen whole, with the complete culture of the age displayed before the reader, and that only by an acknowledgement of the complexity of society can the historian hope to detach a satisfactory interpretation of climactic events. Nevins suggests that behind the slavery issue lay a race question; the crucial fact was not that the Negro was a slave, but that the slave was a Negro. However, he does not seem to accept the irrepressible conflict theory, feeling that had there been a series of strong instead of weak presidents during the 1850s some compromise solution might have been worked out to keep the union intact. [DKA]

New Criticism, The. A movement in American academic criticism starting in the 1920s, dominating most subsequent critical and educational approaches, and still influential. 'New Criticism' can be broadly characterized by its emphasis on the *autonomy* of a given literary work; it has made its purpose the 'close reading' of a single text, regarding biographical material, information about the writer's ideas, the work's reception, etc., as secondary. A work

of art is a concrete whole, a complete experience in itself, an unparaphrasable entity. It is also a *verbal* experience, a pattern of language working – unlike, say, science or discursive prose – by concentration, irony and ambiguity. The distinctiveness of literature lies in its capacity to be simultaneously particular and universal; hence it has a clear function (virtually an anti-scientific one) and great educational value in training responsiveness.

The movement's assumptions (and its philosophical emphasis) derive fairly directly from the criticism of Eliot and Pound and, through them, of Hulme and Bergson; particularly in its stress on the discreteness of literature. Hence it is closely linked with the modern movement in literature itself, and has certainly influenced much literary practice. Out of it has come some of the best of modern criticism, particularly of poetry – its emphasis on possessing a work as a sustained, complete experience, as an 'image', has made it rather less effective with fiction and drama. But the names associated with it – John Crowe ◊ Ransom, Allen ◊ Tate, Robert Penn ◊ Warren, Cleanth ◊ Brooks, R. P. ◊ Blackmur, Yvor ◊ Winters – are among the most important in modern criticism (some are also leading creative writers). Not all were totally united, and among the names mentioned there are clear differences of perspective (Blackmur and Winters particularly show clear temperamental and theoretical differences). But, like the *Scrutiny* group in England, the tendency profoundly influenced all critical practice; books like Brooks' and Warren's *Understanding Poetry* (1938) spread its influence widely, and its theories had great educational importance, replacing the prevailingly scholarly emphasis of literary study. Like Leavis, these critics had considerable concern with culture and tradition (many of them belonged to the ◊ Fugitives group and were Southerners), and also tended to prefer poetry created in metaphysical or 'concrete' traditions, hence distrusting romanticism.

The term 'the New Criticism' was used as the title for a book by Ransom (1941), one of the most explicit statements. The movement's general premises have been usefully questioned by W. K. ◊ Wimsatt and R. S. ◊ Crane, who represent dissenting but not entirely dissociated tendencies in modern American criticism. Its importance generally lies in its sophistication of practice and of theory; its remarkable critical integrity and insight, a condition of the very high quality of its exponents; and its general cultural influence – on writers, on the condition of letters, on education. Indeed it is because the movement existed that we can regard the 20th century as a great age of criticism.

For discussion of the movement and examples of its work, see *Critiques and Essays in Modern Criticism* (1949), ed. R. W. Stallman; *The Critic's Notebook* (1950), ed. R. W. Stallman; and *Essays in Modern Literary Criticism* (1952), ed. Ray B. West. [MB]

René Wellek, *Concepts of Criticism* (1963); S. E. Hyman, *The Armed Vision* (1948); George Watson, *The Literary Critics* (1962); ed. John Crowe Ransom, *The Kenyon Critics* (1967).

New Humanism, The. The name given to the literary and philosophical writings of a group of conservative critics, notably Irving ⟡ Babbitt, Norman ⟡ Foerster, Paul Elmer ⟡ More and Stuart Sherman, who drew together to defend and clarify their literary and moral principles when under attack in the late 1920s. Such common beliefs as the group possessed derived partly from their shared admiration for W. C. ⟡ Brownell (1851–1928), who in such works as *Victorian Prose Masters* (1901) advised writers to pay closer attention to the traditions of their culture, and emphasized the central importance of 'discipline' – both ideas central to the Humanist movement.

Probably the most significant common factor in Humanist writing is its stress on the distinctions between God, man and nature, and on man's unique possession of moral and ethical ideas. These interests underline More's long and widely read series, *Shelburne Essays* (1904–21), to which Foerster paid tribute in attempting his own definition: 'humanism should be confined to a working philosophy seeking to make a resolute distinction between man and nature and man and the divine'. The common Humanist attitudes consequent upon this 'philosophy' may be briefly stated. First, they believe man's true nature is that of a controlled and rational being, so that the individual's proper business is the discriminating cultivation of all his faculties. 'The humanist, then as opposed to the humanitarian, is interested in the perfecting of the individual rather than in schemes for the elevation of mankind as a whole, and although he allows largely for sympathy, he

insists that it be disciplined and tempered by judgement' (Babbitt). Second, they wish to encourage and inhabit a society based on reason and control. Babbit attacked contemporary society for its worship of 'the quantitative life' adulterated with 'moral impressionism', claiming that the word *humanitas* 'implies doctrine and discipline, and is applicable not to men in general but only to a select few – it is, in short, aristocratic and not democratic in its implication'. But few of this group would have supported More's notorious claim (in *Aristocracy and Justice*, 1915) that property rights were more important than the human right to life. Third, they believe that a literature which truly reflects and explores man's nature will be primarily ethical and concern itself with moral values, and not with the ideal of self-expression introduced by romanticism. More chronicled *The Drift of Romanticism* (1913), and in 1919 came Babbitt's polemical and scathing *Rousseau and Romanticism*. New Humanist critics unite in praising the restraint of classical writing and in lamenting nearly all modern literature. Fourth, they reassert the supreme value of literature and the study of moral experience in education, and oppose the fashionable rise of the natural sciences. 'The humanities need to be defended today against the encroachments of physical science, as they once needed to be against the encroachments of theology' (Babbitt). (Accounts of the particular qualities of More, Babbitt and Foerster will be found under their separate entries. The early works of Stuart Sherman (1881–1926) – *Matthew Arnold: How to Know Him* (1917) and *On Contemporary Literature* (1917), attacking 'the chaos of naturalism' – are in the Humanist mainstream. Later he took up different and more moderate standards.)

The central document of the movement is *Humanism and America: Essays on the Outlook of Modern Civilization*, edited by Norman Foerster in 1930, to which T. S. Eliot was a contributor. It immediately provoked vigorous and hostile replies in the same year from, among others, Kenneth ⟡ Burke, Malcolm ⟡ Cowley, Lewis ⟡ Mumford, Allen ⟡ Tate, Edmund ⟡ Wilson and Yvor ⟡ Winters in *The Critique of Humanism: A Symposium*, edited by C. Hartley Grattan. The intellectual force of these objections and the marked trend in the thirties towards criticism with a sociological or Marxist bias severely weakened

New Humanist influence; but a deeper reason may have been an ultimate contradiction behind their work. A statement such as this, by Babbitt, appeared to represent the misapplication of a religious ideal: 'The individual who is practising humanistic control is really subordinating to the part of himself which he possesses in common with other men that part of himself which is driving him apart from them.' In 1927 Eliot asked prophetically: 'Is it, in the end, a view of life that will work by itself, or is it a derivative of religion which will work only for a short time in history, and only for a few highly cultivated persons like Mr Babbitt – whose ancestral traditions, furthermore, are Christian, and who is, like many people, at the distance of a generation or so from definite Christian belief? Is it, in other words, durable beyond one or two generations?' [MG]

N. Foerster, *Towards Standards: A Study of the Present Critical Movement in American Letters* (1930); Louis J. A. Mercier, *The Challenge of Humanism* (1933) and *American Humanism and the New Age* (1948).

Nin, Anais (1914–   ). Novelist. Born in Paris, of French, Spanish, Danish and Cuban descent, she went to America at 11, and there began the journals – an experiment with language and a life-long confession, as well as the source of her fiction. Volumes 1, 2 (1967) and 3 (1970) are already recognized as masterpieces of self-absorption and analysis. Encouraged by the *avant garde* in Paris in the twenties and thirties (which included Henry ◊ Miller and Antonin Artaud) she began her unique series of novels with *Winter of Artifice* (1939). After a period in her other two professions, dancing and psychology, she returned to America in 1940 and continued to write books which, because publishers turned them down, she printed herself, until Dutton brought out *Ladders to Fire* (1946), a chronicle of erotic attachments among four women written in the form of a lyric series of streams of consciousness. *A Spy in the House of Love* (1954) has been filmed and *The House of Incest* (1949) set to music by Varese. Her other fiction includes *Under a Glass Bell and Other Stories* (1944), *This Hunger* (1945), *Children of the Albatross* (1947), *The Four-Chambered Heart* (1950), *Seduction of the Minotaur* (1961) and most recently *Collages* (1964), a series of portraits of actual people fused into the

life of a central fictional character, a young woman painter living in Los Angeles. *Cities of the Interior* (1959) is a collection of five of her fictions (including *Solar Barque*). She has also written *D. H. Lawrence: An Unprofessional Study* (1932) and *The Novel of the Future* (1969), on the theory and technique of fiction. Anais Nin is a master of the *roman fleuve*, whose central theme, she has said, is 'the quest of the self through the intricate maze of modern confusion'. She employs the methods of symbolism, surrealism, psychoanalysis and various kinds of painting, together with technical influences from Lawrence, Henry Miller and Djuna ◊ Barnes. [EM]

Oliver Evans, *Anais Nin* (1968).

Nordhoff, Charles (1887–1947). Novelist. Born in England of American parents. After studies at Stanford and Harvard, and ambulance and Lafayette Flying Corps service in France in the First World War, he and James N. Hall went in 1920 to live in Tahiti. Their most famous collaboration was the trilogy *Mutiny on the Bounty* (1932), *Men against the Sea* (1934) and *Pitcairn's Island* (1934). [EM]

Norris, Frank (1870–1902). Novelist. He was born in Chicago and lived there until 1884, when his family moved to San Francisco. He then studied art briefly in Paris, where the principal influence upon him was not Zola but Froissart: *Yvernelle*, a juvenile poem which reflects his interest at this time in the Middle Ages, was privately published in 1892. In 1890 he entered the University of California at Berkeley and began to contribute to periodicals and magazines; during a year spent at Harvard (1894–5) he began to write novels. As a war correspondent, he travelled to South Africa and Cuba, then became publisher's reader for Doubleday, where he strongly recommended ◊ Dreiser's *Sister Carrie*. His first published novel, *Moran of the Lady Letty* (1898), was followed by *McTeague* (1899), *Blix* (1899) and *A Man's Woman* (1900). At the time of his death from peritonitis he was engaged on a trilogy on the production, distribution and consumption of wheat; *The Octopus* appeared in 1901, *The Pit* posthumously in 1903, and the third volume was never written. Other posthumously published works were *The Responsibilities of the Novelist* (1903); two collections of tales, *A Deal in Wheat* (1903) and *The Third Circle* (1909); and *Vandover and the Brute* (1914), the manuscript of which was lost for several years. Oscar Lewis edited *Frank Norris of 'The Wave'* (1931), a collection of occasional contributions, and Donald Pizer collected *The Literary Criticism of Frank Norris* (1964).

Norris's first attempt at fiction have little to offer the reader today. *Moran of the Lady Letty* is a short and vigorous seastory with an improbable heroine engaged in improbable adventures, *Blix* a slight autobiographical tale. Of the two naturalist novels which Norris began at Harvard under Professor Lewis E. Gates, *McTeague* is superior to *Vandover and the Brute*. The latter, set in San Francisco, charts the social descent and final degradation of a lycanthropic artist-hero. It is a youthful and immature work. The downfall of McTeague, an enormous and slow-witted dentist, produces, despite its romantic elements, its melodrama and its overt symbolism, an interesting novel which comes close to being a textbook for naturalistic fiction (◇ Realism). McTeague himself is a living illustration of the naturalist thesis: a man of prodigious strength and low intelligence, he rapidly reverts to a primitive state when his carefully assembled world collapses about him, even developing a sixth sense which warns him of approaching danger.

Norris's most satisfying novel is *The Octopus*, a long and complex book based upon an actual clash in 1880 between farmers in the San Joaquin valley and the Southern Pacific Railroad, the octopus of the title. The vitality and sweep of the writing enable the characters to be more effectively realized than in the earlier works; they are no longer stiff embodiments of a typically naturalistic preoccupation with the forces of heredity, environment and economic determinism. Norris himself would seem to agree with the shadowy Shelgrim, the head of the railroad, who denies the significance of human effort in the inexorable struggle between the major forces of the Wheat and the Railroad. Though the vagueness of these affirmations may be related to Vanamee's mystical vision of the wheat as a dynamic and irresistible natural force, its equation with the man-made iniquities of monopoly produces an evasive rather than a persuasive conclusion. *The Pit* concentrates upon the distribution of the wheat, with the attempt of Curtis Jadwin to corner the market in Chicago.

Though Norris was influenced by Zola, his debt is technical rather than philosophical; there is a great deal in his work that belongs to the older American tradition of romantic protest. He was a consistent thinker, and his novels are often confused and contradictory, sometimes excessively reliant upon traditional devices such as coincidence or upon perversions of naturalist theories of behaviour. Although his criticism shares with his fiction enthusiasm and sincerity, the essays collected in *The Responsibilities of the Novelist* (1903) are finally disappointing. Despite the guarded treatment of sexual relationships and the modish elevation of the Anglo-Saxon in his work, despite the crudities of half-assimilated naturalist doctrines and rather naïve philosophizings, his writing is important in that it represents a sharp break with the genteel tradition in American literature and looks forward to the work of Theodore Dreiser and John Steinbeck. [HD]

Letters, ed. F. Walker.
Ed. K. Lohf and E. P. Sheehy, *Frank Norris: A Bibliography* (1959); Franklin Walker, *Frank Norris: A Biography* (1932); Ernest Marchand, *Frank Norris: A Study* (1942); Warren French, *Frank Norris* (1962); Donald Pizer, *The Novels of Frank Norris* (1966).

Norton, Charles Eliot (1827–1908). Editor, critic, translator: Son of the American biblical scholar Andrews Norton, he was an active figure in Cambridge, Massachusetts, during the period 1850–1900 when Boston/Cambridge was an important intellectual centre. Professor of Fine Art at Harvard, co-editor of the *North American Review*, critic of literature and art, translator of Dante, editor of Donne's poems, Carlyle's letters and many other volumes, he had close connexions with writers, intellectuals and scholars in the U.S.A., and throughout Europe, which he visited often (see, for instance, his *Notes of Travel and Study in Italy*, 1860). His *Letters* (2 vols., 1913), in addition to revealing his critical viewpoint on the arts, are a cultural record of the Cambridge intellectual aristocracy in its cosmopolitan phase (or, as its critics would say, at the height of the genteel tradition) and a valuable document. [MB]

Edward W. Emerson, *Charles Eliot Norton* (1912).

O

O'Brien, Fitz-james (*c.* 1828–62). Poet, fiction writer. He was born in Ireland and went to New York in 1852 to enter its Bohemian life and continue his prolific output of poems, stories and plays. He died in the Civil War at the battle of Bloomery Gap. His science fiction is imaginative and well written; three of the best tales are *The Diamond Lens*, *What Was It?* and *The Wondersmith*. [EM]

Poems and Stories, ed. W. Winter (1881).
Sam Moskowitz, *Explorers of the Infinite* (1963).

O'Connor, Edwin (1918–68). Novelist. Born in Providence, Rhode Island. A former radio announcer, O'Connor developed this experience into a sharp satirical novel about a broadcaster who moves toward demagoguery in *The Oracle* (1951). Another form of demagoguery provides the subject of his second novel, *The Last Hurrah* (1956), which treats Boston political life and the history of an Irish-American party-machine politician. Fascination with Irish-American locations is taken further in *The Edge of Sadness* (1961), a study of a Catholic priest in a decaying city parish. *I Was Dancing* (1964) is about a superannuated vaudeville performer resisting old age. *All in the Family* (1966) concerns the further life of Jack Kinsella, the secretary of the hero of *The Last Hurrah*, Frank Skeffington. [MB]

O'Connor, Flannery (1925–64). Novelist and short-story writer. She was born and died in Georgia, and studied in Writer's Workshop at the University of Iowa. She is usually said to be a Southern Gothic and/or Catholic writer. Both are probably true, subject to severe qualification. Her typical characters are indeed God-ridden but not in a way that appears to be uniquely Catholic. Rather they seem the essence of Protestantism, seeking an individual and immediate relationship with God. They stalk him, defy him, try to trick him into some sign by doing the things 'that people have quit doing – like boiling in oil or being a saint or walling up cats'. Even the psychopathic murderer of 'A Good Man Is Hard to Find' (*The Artificial Nigger*, 1957) commits his murders in an attempt to force God to reveal himself. But grace can be attained only through the kind of self-knowledge arrived at in *The Violent Bear It Away* (1960) by Rayber, who has his eyes burned clean and is able at last to look into his own heart and recognize his real place in the world. Love, however, is not the clue to a saving communion with the world as it is in so many writers. The clue is suffering, and Hazel Motes (*Wise Blood,* 1952) burns out his eyes with quicklime so that he can see better. It is only in the last story she wrote, 'Parker's Back' (*Everything That Rises Must Converge*, 1965), that the vision of harmony underlying all the grotesqueness and agony becomes visible and the wild humour achieves its tragic focus. O. E. Parker is unable to achieve in his own flesh the vision of beauty he once saw in a tattooed man in a circus. Each new tattoo only adds to the mess he is making of himself. Then he has a stern Byzantine Christ tattooed on his back, not for his own eyes this time, and suddenly his very soul becomes an arabesque. He can now confess his secret name, Obadiah, worshipper of God. Clearly Flannery O'Connor is religious if not clearly Catholic, and clearly she is Gothic, although the horror and outrage are subordinated to the God passion and are not ends in themselves. [DC]

S. E. Hyman, *Flannery O'Connor* (University of Minnesota Pamphlet, 1966); ed. M. J. Friedman and L. A. Lawson, *The Added Dimension: The Art and Mind of Flannery O'Connor* (1966); Robert Drake, *Flannery O'Connor* (1966).

Odets, Clifford (1906–63). Playwright. He was born in Philadelphia, grew up in New York City, and after high school and work in radio, as an actor, and with Theatre Guild, joined the ◊ Group Theatre in 1930. His early work is the epitome of the socially conscious drama of the thirties and the Stanislavski realism of the Group which he organized with Harold ◊ Clurman and Herbert Biberman. He joined the Communist Party in 1934 and left in 1935, the year of

194

his establishment as a leading dramatist. He left for Hollywood in 1936, an act which shocked the committed theatre of the time. In 1952 he testified before the House Un-American Activities Committee that he resigned from the C.P. when asked to write propaganda.

In 1935 he had four plays on Broadway: *Waiting for Lefty*, a brilliant short play on the New York taximen's strike, with a cele- brated agitprop ending and an influential use of European expressionist methods; *Till the Day I Die*, about a communist agent in Nazi Germany; *Paradise Lost*, in which the middle-class Gordon family is pushed by Depression degradation into social rebellion; and *Awake and Sing!*, his finest work, in which a poverty-ridden Jewish family are raised to the level of universal drama; the awakening of Ralph Berger develops through his family: the atheist Marxist grandfather, the mother obsessed by money and acquiescence in the present, Moe's bourgeois dream of para- dise, and so on. The Bronx speech and Odets's sentimental progressive optimism are still capable of moving. In *Golden Boy* (1937), the money-success theme is senti- mentally embodied in the story of a young boxer-violinist corrupted by the fight world. After these excellent plays appeared the less impressive *I Can't Sleep* (1936), *Night Music* (1940) and *Clash by Night* (1941). But *The Big Knife* (1948) is a first- rate play on success and failure in Holly- wood. The loneliness of *Rocket to the Moon* (1938) and so many of his plays is again the centre of *The Country Girl* (1950). *The Flowering Peach* (1954) re-creates the Noah story. Odets's best work concerns the loneliness enforced by people's efforts to succeed in the city. His plays act better than they read and have an authentic life which is unique in the social theatre of the thirties. [E M]

Golden Boy and Other Plays (Penguin Plays, 1963); *Six Plays* (Modern Library, 1939).
J. W. Krutch, *The American Drama since 1918* (1939).

O'Hara, Frank (1926–66). Poet. He was born in Baltimore, served in the navy 1944–6, studied at Harvard and Michigan, and lived and worked in New York most of his highly productive life. He joined the Museum of Modern Art in 1951, resigned to give more time to his writing, and re- joined it in 1955. As assistant curator he was responsible for the organization of major exhibitions of work by David Smith, Robert Motherwell, Reuben Nakian and Jackson Pollock; among his books on painting are *Jackson Pollock* (1959) and *Robert Mother- well* (1965). A number of his poems were published in collaboration with artists, for example *Odes* (1960), with serigraphs by Michael Goldberg. In 1956 he worked as playwright in residence at the Poet's Theatre, Cambridge, Massachusetts: his plays include *Love's Labour*, *Awake in Spain!*, *What Century?*, *Try! Try!* (in *Artist's Theatre*, ed. H. Machiz, 1960), and *The General Returns from One Place to Another* (in *Eight Plays from Off-Off Broadway*, ed. N. Orzel and M. Smith, 1966). His plays were produced in many *avant garde* theatres: his verse play *The Houses at Fallen Hanging* was played by the Living Theatre in 1956. His poetry is associated with that of Kenneth ◊ Koch and John ◊ Ashbery in Donald Allen's *The New American Poetry* (1960), as part of the 'New York Poets', but his poems have a decided originality of their own: *A City Winter and Other Poems* (1952), *Oranges* (1953), *Meditations in an Emergency* (1957), *Second Avenue* (a long poem issued as a pamphlet, 1960), *Odes* (1960), *Lunch Poems* (1964), and *Love Poems* (*Tentative Title*) (1965). His poems have a visual detail and accuracy which is the location of their ex- uberance and joy; but they contain a certain melancholy confronted with cruelty and callousness. His musical references are witty and surprising; his love poems are tender and inventive. His sense of New York is unique. His forms are elegant without being fussy, poised and sophisticated with- out being exhibitionist. His tragic death in an accident was a major loss to American poetry and painting. [E M]

Ed. M. Anania and C. Doria, *Audit-Poetry*, I V, 1 (1964).

Richard Howard, *Alone with America* (1969).

O'Hara, John (1905–70). Novelist. Born in Pittsburg, Philadelphia. He began as a journalist ('I have done everything . . . on the editorial side, from covering girls' field hockey to a Congressional investigation') and in 1964 his byline was still to be read in the weekend edition of the Long Island *Newsday*. His literary credo appears clearly in the preface to *Sermons and Soda Water* (1960), three novellas which are among his best work: 'I want to get it all down on paper while I can. . . . I want to record the way people talked and thought and felt, and to do it with complete honesty and variety.' His first short stories concerned the life of country clubs, bars and the theatre, and throughout his career he has turned out a huge number of stories, works where is best located what Lionel ◊ Trilling calls his 'exacerbated social awareness'. The volumes include *The Doctor's Son* (1935), *Files on Parade* (1939), *Pipe Night* (1945), *Hellbox* (1947), *Assembly* (1961), *The Cape Cod Lighter* (1962), *The Horse Knows the Way* (1964) and *Waiting for Winter* (1967). The last two volumes are notable for their refusal to glamorize the bleak lives they record and their understated style, tense with underground alienated life, either evaded or panicky. *Waiting for Winter* is an extraordinary series of studies in slow ageing and seedy frustration. *And Other Stories* (1968) is a cycle of 12 deftly told stories of wealthy misery.

O'Hara's novels include *Appointment in Samarra* (1934), *BUtterfield 8* (1935), of which the historian Allan Nevins has said no one could understand 1930s America without reading it, *Hope of Heaven* (1938), *A Rage to Live* (1949), *The Farmer's Hotel* (1951) and *Ten North Frederick* (1955). *From the Terrace* (1959) is an over-large novel with most of O'Hara's vices: heaped-up detail, soupy nostalgia and boring sexuality. *Elizabeth Appleton* (1963) is another college novel, redeemed by its nailing down of campus life, suburban sex and wretched small-town power drives. *The Big Laugh* (1962) is a good novel of Hollywood in its 1930s heyday, and *The Lockwood Concern* (1965) is O'Hara's best since 1934 – a large novel of four generations of business family in Pennsylvania, a plot typically packed with suicide, murder, big deals and romantic social and sexual power ploys. None of these novels moves technically into the 20th-century area of experimental forms: the nearest would be *Ourselves to Know* (1960), which builds the story of a respectable Pennsylvanian who shoots his girl wife from the narrator's interpretation of documents, letters and manuscripts. *Lovely Childs* (1969) is a late study of wild oats sown and happy marriage reaped. *Pal Joey* (1940), a series of letters from a night-club singer, dramatized by O'Hara with others, became a most successful musical comedy, one of the finest scripts of its kind. *Five Plays* appeared in 1961 and

Sweet and Sour (1954) is a collection of some of his literary journalism.

O'Hara's fiction is preoccupied with social distinctions, the social and sexual codes of the wealthy and not so wealthy, located in Gibbsville, and other fictional forms of the native Pennsylvania, which is his Yoknapatawpha. But he also mastered the environments of New York and Hollywood for characters which appear much the same in all his work. His tone is jaunty and ironic, the equivalent of his refusal to reach introspectively too far into the life which obsesses him. His theme is the ironic gap between social and private selves. His strength lies in excellent dialogue which embodies social differences and a shrewd knowledge of a class stratum shunned by most intellectuals and their novelists as untouchable. But his later novels cannot resist a sheer accumulation of details about the external lives of his privileged Americans and their squandered affluence. If America has reared the Trollope it deserves, O'Hara is just that. [HB/EM]

Edward R. Carson, *The Fiction of John O'Hara* (1961).

Olson, Charles (1910–   ). Poet, critic. He was born in Worcester, Massachusetts, and formally educated at the Universities of Yale, Harvard and Wesleyan. He taught at Clark, Harvard and at ◊ Black Mountain College (instructor and rector 1951–6), where he began his continuing influence on American poetry, both in his theories of form and content, and in his own extensive practice. His first publication was an essay, 'Lear and Moby Dick' (1938, in *Twice-a-Year*). In 1952 he studied Mayan hieroglyphics in Yucatan. Until recently he was a governing force in the Department of Further Studies at New York State University, Buffalo. Of his prose, *Call Me Ishmael* (1947) is a searching essay on the meaning of Melville's *Moby Dick*; *Mayan Letters* (1953), letters to Robert ◊ Creeley on Mayan remains, is also an initiatory part of his personal rhetoric and his creative anthropology, the bases of his poetic vocation as well; and *Human Universe and Other Essays* (1965) is a massive collection of important essays, issued since 1950. They include the highly influential article 'Projective Verse' (1950), a discussion of 'composition by field', form as extension of content, and the line as a structure of syllable and 'breath'. Some of Olson's ideas extend principles in Pound and E. F. Fenollosa, the oriental art critic, but also derive from the work done at Black Mountain College with other poets. In *Letters for Origin 1950–1956* (1969) Olson discusses his philosophy of form and the idea of a literary journal (*Origin* being the important magazine founded by the poet Cid Corman). His poetry is some of the finest written this century, and is included in *In Cold Hell, in Thicket* (1953) and *The Distances* (1961), poems which make precise statements of personal experience given meaning in a discriminated historical and geographical context, strongly critical of urban democratic capitalism and its depredations of basically agrarian life. This work receives its most complete form to date in *The Maximus Poems* (1–10, 1953; 11–22, 1956; combined in 1960; and *Maximus IV, V, VI,* 1968), a remarkable series of lyrical, sociological and formal experimental poems, which together with Pound's *Cantos* and William Carlos ◊ Williams's poetry makes up the basic poetics of a great deal of American poetry since the 1950s. *O'Ryan* (1965) is 10 witty poetic examinations of the myth punned in the title. *A Bibliography on America for Ed Dorn* (1964) extends Pound's methods out of Frobenius and Williams's *In the American Grain* to form a plan of the process of the formation of America – in 16 pages. *Proprioception* (1965) is another bibliographic reading plan, in Olson's characteristic rhetoric of prose and verse together. *West* (1966) does this for the Red Indian and the land, and *Stocking Cap* (1966) is a reprint of a short story of 1951. *Charles Olson Reading at Berkeley* (1966) is a rough transcription of a reading at the Poetry Conference of 1965, available on tape. In *Causal Mythology* (1969) he states the basis of his use of myth. [EM]

Selected Writings, ed. Robert Creeley (1966).
G. F. Butterwick and A. Glover, *A Bibliography of Works by Charles Olson* (1967); Ann Charters, *Olson/Melville: A Study in Affinity* (1968).

Olson, Elder. ◊ Chicago Aristotelians.

O'Neill, Eugene (1888–1953). Playwright. Born in New York City, America's greatest playwright was the son of actors James O'Neill and Ellen Quinlan. After Catholic and private schools, he took a year at Princeton in 1906, married in 1909,

divorced in 1912, and after a period of unsatisfying jobs became a seaman, a career which furnished him with subjects and characters for the rest of his life. A spell of acting and reporting ended when he entered a sanatorium after a breakdown; recovering there from tuberculosis, he read the great dramatists of the world, looked back into his sea life and his family's unstable complexities, and wrote his first play, *The Web* (1913–14). In 1914 he joined George Pierce ◊ Baker's 47 Workshop at Harvard. The Provincetown Players produced his first performed play, *Bound East for Cardiff*, in 1916, the date of the beginning of serious American theatre. They put on three more of his sea plays and produced ten of his works when the company moved to New York (1917–20). Between 1918 and 1929 he won the Pulitzer Prize for *Beyond the Horizon* (1920) and *Anna Christie* (1921), married again, divorced, and married Carlotta Monterey, who survived him. The great cycles of plays he worked at in the later thirties and forties were frustrated by Parkinson's disease and repeated suffering from alcoholism and family neuroses. For 12 years after *Days without End* (1934) he had no play on Broadway, although he won the Nobel Prize in 1936. The last and finest stage of his career began with *The Iceman Cometh* (1946).

O'Neill had no serious theatre tradition to work on: he created his own out of his reading and first-hand practice. He is part of the generation of Joyce and Eliot, deeply concerned with European expressionism (Strindberg in particular) and with modern psychology as an instrument to analyse the classical and biblical myths. Nietzschean philosophy reinforced his American need to explore the nature of self-reliance and heroic individualism. His experimental forms were the expression of this complexity. *The Emperor Jones* (1920) is the monologue of the Negro dictator of a West Indian state, declining Darwinianly to the accompaniment of accelerating drums and stage sets which symbolize his fears. In *The Hairy Ape* (1922), the stoker Yank, dislocated from nature and society, is crushed by a gorilla at the conclusion of a symbolic search for himself. This is the theme and manner of *Desire under the Elms* (1924), with its opened-house set, *All God's Chillun Got Wings* (1924), a high stylization of miscegenation problems, and *The Great God Brown* (1926), an extraordinary conflict

197

of private and external selves displayed through masks and Greek and Nietzschean references. In *Marco Millions* (1928) O'Neill transposes satire on American commercialism to the Venice of Marco Polo. The search for self, already treated through the Ponce de Leon story in *The Fountain* (1925), is best handled at this period in *Strange Interlude* (1928), a long psychological study of a woman, using a modern version of soliloquy to express inner life. The symbolism of *Dynamo* (1929) is too crude, the dynamo being 'science', which fills the gap left by 'religion'. *Lazarus Laughed* (1926), which O'Neill mistakenly believed was his best play, is a choral drama of huge forces and ecstatic affirmative laughter.

The masterpiece of his middle career is *Mourning Becomes Electra* (1931), a trilogy transposing the House of Atreus into the New England Mannon family during the Civil War, with Aeschylean fate reinterpreted through modern psychological destiny. *Ah, Wilderness!* (1933) and *Days without End* (1934) are family plays of less importance. Between 1934 and 1943 O'Neill planned and began to execute a cycle of one-act plays, *By Way of Orbit* (of which *Hughie*, 1942, is a small masterpiece), and a cycle of full-length plays, *A Tale of Possessors Dispossessed*, the dramatic developments of interrelated families. In what O'Neill managed to write, Sarah Harford appears as a girl in *A Touch of the Poet* (1958) and as a married woman in *More Stately Mansions* (1965); and the superb *Long Day's Journey into Night* (1956) and *A Moon for the Misbegotten* (1957) present members of the Tyrone family. To these magnificent achievements can be added *The Iceman Cometh* (1946), which deals simply and grandly with the illusions and disillusions of a group of men in an archetypal bar – the measure of the final climax of a long strenuous career.

O'Neill's best work has an intensity of passion and a sense of theatre action which his faults of rhetoric and symbolism can withstand. His courage and endless experiment created an American theatre out of nothing, a series of plays which represent American culture between the wars and which can be compared only with the finest poetry and novels. [EM]

A. and B. Gelb, *O'Neill* (1962); ed. O. Cargill, etc., *O'Neill and His Plays* (1962); Edwin A. Engel, *The Haunted Heroes of Eugene O'Neill*

(1953); B. H. Clark, *Eugene O'Neill: The Man and His Plays* (1947); L. Sheaffer, *O'Neill, Son and Playwright* (1968).

Oppen, George (1908–   ). Poet. He was born in New Rochelle, N.Y., and lives in Brooklyn. His first book of poems, *Discrete Series* (1934, repr. 1966), was prefaced by Ezra Pound, who wrote: 'I salute a serious craftsman.' It is the terse, concentrated quality of these short poems that impresses; they are an epitome of the Objectivist movement with which he was associated with Louis ◊ Zukofsky, Charles ◊ Reznikoff and others. His poems appeared in the *Objectivists Anthology*, *Active Anthology* (ed. Pound), *Poetry, Hound and Horn* and a number of little magazines of the thirties, and were part of the extension of ◊ Imagist and Objectivist precision of language and form which came to be of major importance in Pound, Williams and Zukofsky. In the forties his work appeared in the little magazines and finally in two important volumes, *The Materials* (1962) and *This Is Which* (1965), poetry whose craft and inquiring intelligence are a significant influence on contemporary American poetry. His finest book is his most recent: *Of Being Numerous* (1968). [EM]

Oppenheimer, Joel (1930–   ). Poet, playwright. He was born and educated in New York, studied at Cornell and Chicago Universities and went to ◊ Black Mountain College. He worked as a printer-typographer until recently, when he became programme director of a Federal arts project centred on St Mark's-in-the-Bowerie, New York. His first two books of poetry were published by Jonathan Williams's Jargon Press: *The Dancer* (1952) and *The Dutiful Son* (1956), personal lyrics deeply in the tradition of lyrical poetry of private life since the Provençal poets, and with the same wary respect for and challenge to women. This style is excellently developed in *The Love Bit* (1962). *A Treatise* (1966) is a long poem of social criticism. *The Great American Desert* (1966) is a collection of plays, the title drama being a brilliant short epitome of the Western myth. *Bad Times in Bummersville* was produced in 1968. Oppenheimer's strength lies in durably honest and drily passionate poems of love and friendship, and a witty critical eye for the urban-pastoral relationship. [EM]

P

Pack, Robert (1929–   ). Poet. Born in New York City and educated at Dartmouth College and Columbia University, he taught for a number of years at Barnard College. Besides four volumes of poetry – *The Irony of Joy* (1955), *A Stranger's Privilege* (1959), *Guarded by Women* (1963) and *Home from the Cemetery* (1970) – he has written a book on Wallace ◊ Stevens, translated Mozart's librettos, composed children's books and helped to edit the influential series *New Poets of England and America*. The metaphysical speculations of his own poetry depend largely on concentrated verbal effects. [BP]

Page, Thomas Nelson (1853–1922). Novelist. Born in Hanover, Virginia, he was a lawyer many of whose romantic works were devoted to a sentimental reconstruction and justification of the old South. From 1913 to 1919 he was ambassador to Italy. *Marse Chan*, a tale in dialect, was included in the collection *In Ole Virginia* (1887); his first novel was *On Newfound River* (1891). Among Page's most popular works were *Red Rock* (1898), a fictional account of Reconstruction from the Southern point of view, and *John Marvel, Assistant* (1909), the action of which is set in Chicago. [HD]

The Novels, Stories, Sketches and Poems (18 vols., 1906–18).
Rosewell Page, *Thomas Nelson Page* (1923); Jay B. Hubbell, 'Thomas Nelson Page', in *The South in American Literature* (1954).

Paine, Thomas (1737–1809). Political philosopher, revolutionary. Born in Thetford, England, he had little schooling and worked at a number of jobs, including tax collector. ◊ Franklin persuaded him to emigrate to America, where on his recommendation, he edited the *Pennsylvania Magazine* in Philadelphia (1775). His essays on rights for women and Negroes, international arbitration and copyright, and humanitarianism were original and much needed in America. He won Washington's respect during the 1776 retreat in New Jersey, when he wrote the first of his *The American Crisis* series of 13 pamphlets (1776–83), arousing new energy for the revolution. *Common Sense* (1776) had made him a major influence on the emerging republic, attacking monarchy and containing some famous words: 'Government, even in its best state, is but a necessary evil; in its worst state, an intolerable one'. In 1787 he returned to Europe, promoting his ironbridge invention and entering French Revolution politics. His international revolutionary principles caused him to break with ◊ Jefferson's moderate reform. In England his books were burned by the public hangman. In reply to Burke's *Reflections on the French Revolution* (1790) he wrote *The Rights of Man* (1791–2) and dedicated it to Washington. Escaping to France, he took part in drafting a constitution but voted against the king's execution and supported the moderates. Robespierre's own death just prevented Paine's execution. Part of *The Age of Reason* (1794, 1796) he wrote in prison. In 1802 he returned to America and lived in New York State, poor, ill, attacked unfairly. Although he asked to be buried on his farm, William Cobbett took the coffin to England, and was not permitted to bury it. The remains are lost. In spite of being defended by Lincoln, Whitman and others, Paine remained largely hated and feared in America for his extremism and so-called atheism (he was in fact an ordinary deist), only rehabilitated a little after Moncure D. Conway's biography in (1892) and collection of his writings (1894–6). Today his New Rochelle cottage is a memorial. His pamphlets, poems and books are many, but his masterpieces are clear and outstanding. *The Rights of Man* affirms natural rights, the right to choose government, and the need to reject hereditary ruling classes. *The Age of Reason* is a popularization of 18th-century rationalist ideas on religion and philosophy – 'divine' revelations are myths, God's beneficence is manifest in his creation, every man has the right to follow the worship he prefers, Christianity like all traditional religions is a preposterous tool of enslavement against science and learning. The principles of this courageous and outspoken man were always directed towards humanitarian relationships in the world at large, not towards nation or class alone. His writings are clear, and he trusted that reason would bring about freedom and justice. His influence on American revolutionary thought was incalculably deep, ever since Washington said 'I find *Common Sense* working a powerful change in the minds of men'. [EM]

Writings, ed. P. Foner (2 vols., 1945).
W. E. Woodward, *Thomas Paine: America's God-father* (1945).

Parker, Dorothy (1893–1967). Humorist, story writer, poet. Born at West End, New Jersey, she began her writing career with *Vogue* and reviewed for *Vanity Fair*, the *New Yorker* and *Esquire*. Famous for her spoken wit, she showed in reviews, poems and sketches the same note of trenchant commentary. Her cynicism and the concentration of her judgements were famous; and while she was not always a reliable critic or a wise judge of manners her contempt for the sentimental, the stupid and the provincial were always enlivening. Her poems, usually ironic commentaries on love and the relationship between the sexes, have been collected in the volume *Not So Deep as a Well* (1936). Her stories, many of them analogous to revue sketches, and often devastatingly pointed, are also collected, in *Here Lies* (1939). With Elmer ◊ Rice she wrote a play, *Close Harmony* (1924); and she was closely associated with the development of modern urbane humour. In 1944 the *Viking Portable Dorothy Parker* made available all her main work. [MB]

Parkman, Francis (1823–93). Historian. Son of a Boston 'Brahmin' minister, he became interested in Indians at Harvard and undertook an expedition to the frontier with his cousin Quincy Adams Shaw, recorded in his famous travel book, *The Oregon Trail* (1849), in which his 'tour of curiosity and amusement' turns into a taxing and dangerous journey. Its observations on the customs of behaviour of the Sioux and Pawnee Indians, its heroic conception of the journey, and its skill in catching the spirit of the rising West give it an almost Scott-like fictional intensity. Strained in health and going blind, Park-

man turned to horticulture, and became for a spell Professor in the subject at Harvard; but above all he went on to his main work as a historian, the magnificent history *France and England in North America* (9 vols., 1851–92). Conceived as an account of the French war in Canada, it extended to cover the whole conflict in America between France and Britain, and the struggle of both powers with the Indians. Of the eight separate works in the series, *Montcalm and Wolfe* (1884), about the climax of the imperial clash and the death of both leaders, won most contemporary acclaim and remains the classic account of the period; though all volumes have stood well and are still widely consulted.

Parkman saw history finally as the delayed triumph of progressive forces, but shared Scott's ambition to recapture the spirit of an era, and his favourite subject was (as for Scott and Cooper) the description of important battles amid magnificent natural scenes. 'I was haunted with wilderness images day and night,' he noted; but his complex story is a piece of superb construction, incorporating scenes and causes, particular facts and large historical movements, with the wilderness and the advent of civilization as his main theme. His epical dimensions sometimes lead him to be classed with literary historians, but he used carefully numerous manuscript sources in the U.S.A. and Europe, followed the paths of his heroes and armies and noted geographical features and oral traditions. Though there are clear prejudices on religious matters, notably about Catholicism, his sense of the interaction of individuals and groups, and his determinism mitigated by a sense of geographical, climatic and other factors also give his work historical strength. Parkman also wrote a novel, *Vassall Morton* (1856), and his *Journals* (ed. Mason Wade, 2 vols., 1947) are important memoirs. [MG/DKA]

Works (12 vols., 1922); *The Parkman Reader*, ed. S. E. Morison (1955).
Mason Wade, *Francis Parkman: Heroic Historian* (1942); Howard Doughty, *Francis Parkman* (1962); Otis A. Pease, *Francis Parkman's History: The Historian as Literary Artist* (1953).

Parrington, Vernon L(ouis) (1871–1929). Historian, critic. He is best known as the author of *Main Currents of American*

Thought: An Interpretation of American Literature from the Beginnings to 1920, first published in 3 volumes, two in 1927, the third posthumously and incomplete in 1930. Parrington, a Professor of English at the University of Washington, won a Pulitzer Prize and immediate renown with the book, the first attempt to write a large-scale intellectual history of colonial America and the United States round a general interpretative thesis. His introduction defines the aim as tracing in American letters the genesis of certain germinal ideas that are reckoned traditionally American, following 'the broad path of our political, economic, and social development, rather than the narrower belletristic'. The first volume discusses the rise of New England Puritanism and contrasts Jonathan Edwards and Roger Williams as representatives of authoritarianism and liberty, and then goes on to trace the emergence of agrarianism as a dominant national characteristic as settlement spread westwards. The second volume, covering 1800 to the Civil War, examines the impact of industrialization, seeing the 'coonskin Jacksonians' and the Southern 'Greek democracy' as attempts to prevent this change and maintain older agrarian values. The unfinished third volume relates literature to the post-Civil-War growth of reform movements that were trying to resist the development of a centralized capitalist state.

Brought up in Kansas, Parrington has a strong, confessedly liberal, Jeffersonian belief in an individualistic and agrarian free democracy. The book's weaknesses – such as its famous elevation of James Branch ◊ Cabell over Henry James, its stress on realism, etc. – are apparent; but its scholarly range and its exploitation of the cultural commitments of the period in which it was written make it both useful and a significant American monument. Though the patterns traced by Parrington no longer find general acceptance among historians, the approach did much to condition the outlook of the subsequent generation of scholars; it also influenced many literary critics towards an environmentalist, 'Taine-ian' approach. Lionel Trilling speaks of its deep impact on 'our conception of American culture', and points out some of the ways its influence has been harmful. [D K A/M B]

Lionel Trilling, 'Reality in America', *The Liberal*

Imagination (1950); Richard Hofstadter, *The Progressive Historians* (1968).

Passos, John Dos. ◊ Dos Passos, John.

Patchen, Kenneth (1911–   ). Poet, novelist, painter. He was born in Ohio, and after one year at Alexander Meiklejohn's Experimental College, University of Wisconsin, he worked at 17 in a steel mill, as his father did. He has since held many jobs while maintaining himself as a poet. His poetic language was from the first contemporary and his material leftist in its social criticism. For the poems in *The Dark Kingdom* (1942) he painted water-colours and he has frequently designed his poems as visual pages of script and image. His early work also included *Before the Brave* (1936), *First Will and Testament* (1939), *The Teeth of the Lion* (1942) and *Cloth of the Tempest* (1943). His forms include short lyrics, odes, prose poems and ballads; his reputation was built largely on his love poetry (some of the finest of the century) and his scathing satire. In 1941 came his prose *The Journal of Albion Moonlight,* a brilliant allegorical journey to H Roivas, written in a surreal style of certain originality, with a hero who takes his place among the triumphs of existential literature. The novel *Memoirs of a Shy Pornographer* (1945) is nearly as good, written as a series of satirical episodes and dialogues. His other prose includes *Sleepers Awake* (1946) and *See You in the Morning* (1948), a novel, and the prose pieces in *They Keep Riding Down All the Time* (1946). The poetry continued in *An Astonished Eye Looks Out of the Air* (1945), *Pictures of Life and of Death* (1946), *Panels for the Walls of Heaven* (1947, prose poems), *Red Wine and Yellow Hair* (1949), one of his finest and most representative volumes, and *To Say If You Love Someone* (1950). *Selected Poems* appeared in 1946 and in an enlarged edition in 1957; further selections appeared as *Poems of Humour and Protest* (1956) and *The Love Poems of Kenneth Patchen* (1960), useful paperback editions.

After years of serious illness, he suffered a major spinal operation in 1951, but in spite of his painful incapacitation, Patchen continues to pour out his abundant gifts, against the worst odds. The poetry appears in *Orchards, Thrones and Caravans* (1952), *Fables and Other Little Tales* (1954), *The Famous Boating Party* (1954, prose poems), *When We Were Here Together* (1957, includes *Orchards* . . .). *Doubleheader* (1966) reprints *Hurrah for Anything* (1957, poems and drawings), *Poemscapes* (1958, prose poems), *A Letter to God* (1946; repr. from the pamphlet by Henry Miller, *Patchen, Man of Anger and Light*). *Because It Is* (1960) is a remarkably free and exuberant series of surreal poems and drawings; the comparisons often made with Blake and Edward Lear are not at all inept. *Hallelujah Anyway* (1966) is a good collection of his picture poems (see also *Tri-Quarterly*, Fall, 1964). The first major English edition of his poems appeared in 1968 (*Selected Poems*, ed. Nathaniel Tarn). *Love and War Poems* (1967) is a first-rate selection which includes a useful collection of criticism of Patchen. He is a typically American poet in his native exuberance and freedom of form and in his inheritance from European lyrical and surrealist traditions. But finally he is unique in his passion and intensely personal character. [EM]

Collected Poems (1968).

Patrick, John (pseud. of John Patrick Goggan) (1905–). Playwright. After attending Harvard and Columbia and writing two relatively unnoticed Broadway plays, he made his name with *The Hasty Heart* (1945) which drew upon his experiences as an ambulance driver in the Second World War. *The Story of Mary Surratt* (1947) and *The Curious Savage* (1951) were among subsequent plays, but another big success came with his stage adaptation of Vern Schneider's novel *The Teahouse of the August Moon* (1953). This wartime comedy about American soldiers building a teahouse on Okinawa won various prizes, including the Pulitzer. More recently most of his work has been for the cinema, and his screenplays include *Three Coins in the Fountain* and *Love Is a Many-Splendored Thing*. [MB]

Paul, Elliot (1891–1958). Journalist, editor, novelist. Born in Malden, Massachusetts. He remained in Paris as a newspaperman after the First World War, was associated with several of the expatriate magazines, and with Eugene Jolas he edited the last and largest of them: *transition* (◊ Little Magazines). Although Paul published several novels in his early thirties, much of his work may be described as an extended autobiography, to which he himself gave the title 'Items on the Grand Account'. This

sequence begins with what is probably his best work, *The Life and Death of a Spanish Town* (1937), an account of his life in a village on Ibiza from 1931 to the irruption of the Spanish Civil War. Other works in this series which concern themselves with his native land are *Linden on the Saugus Branch* (1947), *Ghost Town on the Yellowstone* (1948), *My Old Kentucky Home* (1949) and *Desperate Scenery* (1954). The success of his parody *The Mysterious Mickey Finn* (1939) led him to write crime novels, including *Hugger-Mugger in the Louvre* (1940) and *The Black Gardenia* (1952).

Among Paul's most popular books are his two tributes to his adopted city: *The Last Time I Saw Paris* (1942; British title *A Narrow Street*) and its sequel *Springtime in Paris* (1950). These fictionalized accounts of his experiences exhibit Paul's strengths and weaknesses as a writer: a keen and perceptive observer of life, he was not entirely free from sentimentality when recording it, with the consequence that he will perhaps be remembered more for his role in the literary history of the United States than for any actual contribution towards its literature. [HD]

Paulding, James Kirke (1778–1860). Satirist, poet, playwright, essayist. He was born in New York State, a contemporary and friend of Washington ◊ Irving, with whom he collaborated on *Salmagundi* (1807–8). The second series of *Salmagundi* (1819–20), sketches on New York written in character in the manner of the 18th-century English essayists, was entirely his. Unlike Irving, Paulding stayed in the U.S.A., and his work is strongly patriotic; *The Diverting History of John Bull and Brother Jonathan* (1812) is a satire on the settlement and revolution of the United States. He parodied Scott in *The Lay of the Scottish Fiddle* (1813) and Anglo-American relations in *A Sketch of Old England* (1822) and *John Bull in America* (1825). He wrote plays (*The Bucktails; or Americans in England*, 1847, and *The Lion of the West*, 1831) and epic verse (*The Backwoodsman*, 1818) but turned more and more to tales and sketches, drawing largely on American materials – the New York Dutch, the woodsmen, the pioneers. *The Dutchman's Fireside* (1831) draws on the New York Dutch before the Revolution, *Westward Ho!* (1832) is set in Kentucky, and *The Old Continental* (1846) is about the revolution in New York.

Paulding – who was late in life Secretary of the Navy – is a fascinating representative of the American literary mind at the time of Irving and Cooper, to both of whom he has close similarities, and by both of whom he has been overshadowed. [MB]

Amos L. Herold, *James Kirke Paulding: Versatile American* (1926).

Payne, John Howard (1791–1852). Dramatist. He grew up in Boston, and, in 1805, as a New York merchant's clerk, was already publishing his *Thespian Mirror*, 'to promote the interests of American drama'. At 15 his first play, *Julia, or, The Wanderer*, was performed. Sent to college by backers, he left through lack of funds and became a successful actor. In 1813 he began a 20-year period in London and Paris as playwright and adaptor; he courted Mary Shelley unsuccessfully, and returned to America in 1832, broke. Theatre benefit performances brought him $10,000, and he was given a consulship at Tunis. His most famous play was *Brutus, or, The Fall of Tarquin* (1818) but his fame rests with his words for Sir Henry Bishop's 'Home, Sweet Home', a song in his play *Clari, The Maid of Milan* (1823). His best play is *Charles II* (1924), a comedy (with Irving; see A. H. Quinn: *Representative American Plays*, 1917). The best biography is by Grace Overmyer (1957). [EM]

America's Lost Plays, ed. C. Hislop and W. R. Richardson (vols. 5 and 6, 1940).

Peck, George Wilbur (1840–1916). Newspaperman. Born in Huderson, N.Y. His newspaper, *Sun*, was so popular he was elected mayor of Milwaukee and governor of the state (1890–4); he remains moderately famous for his humorous tales *Peck's Bad Boy and His Pa* (1883), a series of which thousands of copies were sold. The last was *Peck's Bad Boy with the Cowboys* (1907). [EM]

Peirce, Charles Sanders (1839–1914). Logician, metaphysician. Born in Cambridge, Massachusetts, the son of Benjamin Peirce, Professor of Astronomy and Mathematics at Harvard, he attended Harvard and spent his working life in the U.S. Coast Survey until 1891, when he retired to write. He maintained his connexion with advanced thought in Cambridge, and though never widely known during his lifetime, made many original contributions to journals, on metaphysics, logic and other scientific matters. The bulk of Peirce's writing was not published until 1931–51, in *The Collected Papers of Charles Sanders Peirce*, ed. C. Hartshorne, P. Weiss and A. W. Burks. Peirce coined the term 'pragmatism' as a name for his philosophy. The approach was popularized by William ◊ James, with whom it is more commonly associated, but Peirce could not (with some justice) recognize his thought in James's formulation, and renamed his philosophy 'pragmaticism' by way of distinction. The standardization of philosophical language, so that philosophy might one day be put on a scientific basis, was always one of his *desiderata*: it shows, perhaps, both the stressed objectivity of his work and a certain naïveté in respect of philosophical idiosyncrasy. Peirce's logical analysis was not conducted in the symbolic language of post-Russell and Whitehead logicians, but in the discursive *exempla* of previous centuries. This non-mathematical prose of his essays makes them a considerable index of cultural opinion. It would not be too much to say that we have here the most keenly and solidly analytic mind in America in the 19th century operating, if only by the way, on the material of his civilization. Certain distinctions, fashioned to explain logical functions, tell us as much about the major socio-cultural dimensions of his time (see the distinction between acting, thinking and being). [AG]

Ed. Justus Buchler, *The Philosophy of Peirce* (1956); W. B. Gallie, *Peirce and Pragmatism* (1952).

Penn, William (1644–1718). Founder of Pennsylvania. Expelled from Oxford in 1662 for his beliefs, he travelled in France and Italy, tried the navy, the law, and managing his father's estates in Ireland, where he was imprisoned for the Quakerism he later expounded in *No Cross, No Crown* (1669). *The Great Case of Liberty of Conscience* (1670) was written during one of his many prison spells. In 1671 he founded a Quaker society in Holland, married, and in 1672 settled in Hertfordshire. Having become a proprietor of part of America, he went to the colony and drew up a constitution for what became a Quaker settlement in West Jersey. In 1677 he recruited more Quakers in Germany for Germantown, the early name of Philadelphia. In 1681 he asked for and received from Charles II a tract of land in America in payment of a debt to his father; it became the future Pennsylvania, designed by Penn as a Quaker state (*A Brief Account of the Province of Pennsylvania*, 1682, and *A Further Account ...* , 1685). He made a famous pact with Indians whom in *Letter to the Committee of the Free Society of Trades* (1683), one of his many promotional tracts, he describes without sentimentality and conjectures their ancestors were the Lost Tribes of Israel. Absent on a final mission to Europe in 1686, he was removed from the governorship by the Council. In his retirement he wrote *Some Fruits of Solitude* (1693), a collection of maxims. Although his governorship was restored in 1694, he did not return until 1699, and made another Indian treaty, but was unable to abolish slavery. Again in 1701 he was forced out and he decided to give his colony back to England if the Quakers were protected, but a stroke spoiled his mind and he died with this scheme unfulfilled. In 1693–4 *The Present and Future Peace of Europe* appeared, a plan for a European parliament, one of the last schemes of a great and active humanitarian. [EM]

C. O. Peare, *William Penn: A Biography* (1957).

Perelman, S(idney) J(oseph) (1904–   ). Humorist. One of the funniest of modern American writers, he was born in New York and educated at Brown University, where he began writing for university and other humour magazines. His first book, *Dawn Ginsbergh's Revenge* (1929), was so successful he was taken up by Hollywood, where he became a script- and gag-writer, particularly for Marx Brothers films. From the 1930s onward, his work mainly took the form of books and essays, mostly for the *New Yorker*. He also wrote plays, and worked as a play-doctor; and he also posed as a farmer in agrarian Pennsylvania, a prey to the locals who lived off such cosmopolitan commuters; Perelman preyed back by making them the subject of humorous pieces. He now lives in London.

Perelman's manner is immediately identifiable. Its tone is vernacular; he exploits, to great comic effect, the wisecracking language of the New York Jew and of show business. He is an excellent parodist, mocking and celebrating the various manifestations of American mass-culture. Other pieces are autobiographical, and usually show the sophisticated Perelman wisecracking his way into defeat. His essays

often begin with some folly reported in the press, from which he builds up an absurd and extravagant playlet. As a social observer, Perelman is very sharp and also ambiguous; there is a kind of self-mocking foolishness about his denunciation – he ends up exposing all the potentially ridiculous features of himself. Yet all his works show an extreme literary sense, a quality that goes beyond simple craftsmanship; one can recognize the debt he has confessed to James Joyce. He is indeed an advanced absurdist, much admired by many serious writers. Among his numerous books are *Crazy Like a Fox* (1944), *Acres and Pains* (1947) and *Listen to the Mocking Bird* (1949). A useful approach to him is through *The Most of S. J. Perelman* (1958), a collection of his pieces across the years. [MB]

Phillips, John (1861–1949). Iowa publisher and editor. He co-founded (with Samuel S. McClure) *McClure's Magazine* (1886), which became the main organ of the 'muckraking' period of American journalism. His own book is *The Papers: Occasional Pieces* (1936). [EM]

Pike, Zebulon Montgomery (1779–1813). Travel writer. The son of a New Jersey army officer, he was commissioned in his father's company at 20, and in 1805 was directed by the governor of the Louisiana Territory to lead an exploration to the sources of the Mississippi. His second expedition (1806) reached into Kansas, Arkansas and Colorado, where he saw the peak which now bears his name. The Spaniards, intercepting him in New Mexico, forced him to abandon his journey. In the war of 1812 he was killed by an exploding powder magazine. His imagination and style in his account of his explorations (1810) are excellent – see Elliott Coues' edition of his *Account of an Expedition to the Sources of the Mississippi and through the Western Parts of Louisiana* (3 vols. with memoir and notes, 1895). [EM]

The Journal of Zebulon Montgomery Pike, ed. D. Jackson (2 vols., 1966).
W. E. Hollon, *The Lost Pathfinder: Zebulon Montgomery Pike* (1949).

Plath, Sylvia (1932–63). Poet. Born in Boston, Massachusetts, she was educated at Smith and (on a Fulbright award) Newnham, Cambridge. Here she met and married the English poet Ted Hughes and settled in England. Her early death cut short a growingly impressive poetic career; her two books, *The Colossus* (1960) and the posthumous *Ariel* (1965), show a remarkable development. The first is largely personal poetry, intense and delicately rendered, usually dealing with the relationship between the poet and a perceived object from which she seeks illumination, 'that rare, random descent'. It is controlled, serious verse, but her later work shows new strains and pressures at work in her, and becomes a poetry of anguished confession. Delicacy and control remain, but manage painful, suicidal materials. She is better known in England than in the U.S.A., but must surely be regarded as one of the most impressive of recent American poets. She also wrote a novel, *The Bell Jar* (1966). [MB]

Richard Howard, *Alone with America* (1969).

Playwrights Company, The. A group founded in 1938 by dramatists ◊ Anderson, ◊ Behrman, ◊ Howard, ◊ Rice and ◊ Sherwood to produce their plays in independence. [EM]

Plutzik, Hyam (1911–62). Poet. Brooklyn-born, he spent most of his early life in Connecticut, studying at Trinity College, Hartford, Connecticut and Yale. After the Second World War he taught at the University of Rochester. An intense, technically self-assured poet, he published *Death at the Purple Rim* (1941), *Aspects of Proteus* (1949), *Apples from Shinar* (1959) and a long narrative poem, *Horatio* (1961). Though his poems are usually short, they are ambitious in theme, dealing with the fact of suffering, the mystery of self, the meaning of nature, the effects of time and Plutzik's own Jewishness. [BP]

Podhoretz, Norman (1930–   ). Critic. He was born in New York and acquired three bachelor degrees before becoming editor of Looking Glass Library – and subsequently, in 1960, of *Commentary* magazine. His criticism, collected in *Doings and Undoings* (1964), can be characterized by its preferences: contemporaries to ancients and moderns, fiction to poetry and drama, and, frequently, non-fiction to fiction. *Making It* (1968) is an obsessive autobiography of success in the New York literary world. [BP]

Poe, Edgar Allan (1809–49). Poet, short-story writer, critic. Born in Boston. He began his literary career as a young man in Richmond, Virginia, writing verse modelled on that of Byron, Moore and other fashionable romantic poets. He published his first volume of poems in 1827, his second in 1829; by now he had spent one year at the University of Virginia, two in the U.S. Army, and was about to enter, and shortly afterwards to be dismissed from, the Military Academy at West Point. In 1831, he produced a volume of new and revised poems which showed him drawing more widely on the great romantic writers, yet finding a poetic voice of his own. Poems like the well-known 'To Helen', 'Israfel', and 'The City in the Sea' are clearly less self-engrossed and more formally controlled than 'Tamerlane' and 'Al Aaraaf', the most substantial poems of his earlier volumes. His poetic position was also more confident; the sophisticated critical introduction to this collection defends a poetry characterized by 'music' and 'indefiniteness'.

Meanwhile Poe was writing prose-tales and submitting them for money-prizes offered by newspapers, hoping for later book publication. Several are simply rather affected burlesques of the popular literature of the day, though there are signs he took them half-seriously. And 'Berenice' (1835), which he claimed to have written as a joke, was the first of those intense, melodramatic tales, culminating in 'Ligeia' (1838) and 'The Fall of the House of Usher' (1839), in which he states a prevailing theme, that of the neurotic intellectual hero confronted with 'the death of a beautiful woman' (Poe thought this 'the most poetical topic in the world'). 'William Wilson' (1839) definitively exploits the theme of the double. 'Hans Phaall' (1835), a cleverly fantastic piece of science fiction, also anticipates later stories – like 'The Balloon Hoax' (1844), 'Mesmeric Revelation' (1844) and 'Mellonta Tauta' (1849). The best of these early tales, 'MS. Found in a Bottle' (1833), also leads into later interests; it resembles his novel *The Narrative of Arthur Gordon Pym of Nantucket* (1838) in describing with considerable psychological depth a symbolic voyage of discovery.

By now well involved with the development of American literary journalism, Poe became in 1835 editor of the monthly

Southern Literary Messenger, an important focus for Southern writing published in Richmond, Virginia. He printed his own stories and poems, and in reviews showed himself capable of close critical analysis of prose style and original, if wild, theoretical criticism of poetry; his criticism, particularly his attacks on overrated popular novels, was found devastating. Now married to his 14-year-old cousin, Virginia, he moved to New York in 1837, Philadelphia in 1838, and back to New York in 1844, editing or contributing to various magazines, seeking a path for his serious interests in the prevailing pattern of American publishing. In 1840 and 1845 he published volumes of tales (*Tales of the Grotesque and Arabesque* and *Tales*), and in 1845 another volume of poems.

As he became more dependent on the mass-audience, he began to simplify the manner of his horror-stories, making their perverse protagonists less intellectual (see 'The Black Cat', 1843, 'The Cask of Amontillado', 1846, and 'Hop-Frog', 1849), though the detective stories, 'The Murders in the Rue Morgue' (1841), 'The Mystery of Marie Roget' (1842) and 'The Purloined Letter' (1844), contributed, through their hero Dupin, a quality of analytical seriousness, an intellectual and semi-scientific bent, to the genre. His speculations about the short story itself are of great importance; he provided the rationale for the formally economical modern tale in his review of Hawthorne's *Twice Told Tales* (1842), which is amongst his best criticism. His poetry was changing, too; some earlier work had been typical romantic obscurantism, but he now wrote several sonorous, clearly plotted pieces – 'The Raven' (1845), 'The Bells' (1849) and 'Annabel Lee' (1849). Though in his important 'The Philosophy of Composition' (1846) he said 'The Raven' had been deliberately constructed for popularity, he never lost his pretensions to learning. In the miscellaneous snippets of erudition he called 'Marginalia', in metaphysical dialogues like 'The Conversation of Eiros and Charmion' (1839), etc., he kept alive speculative ambitions which finally manifested themselves in *Eureka* (1848), his brilliantly egocentric attempt to explain the universe.

He was immensely versatile, a great assimilator and innovator, with many styles to suit various purposes. Yet the felicities of both verse and prose tend to emerge only momentarily from cadences or periods too mechanically contrived. His best short stories expose a disturbing strain of morbid feeling, but all his writing is permeated by a hint of theatrical vulgarity. He saw himself in numerous roles – as Byron, Coleridge, the quixotic yet violent Southern gentleman-scholar, as a great scientist, a superb journalistic manipulator of the American mass-audience, a promoter of a great American literary magazine – divisions which show clearly in his writings. In his work, conversation, and letters he liked to glamorize his past and his actions; he could express both the solipsistic intensity of extreme romanticism and pure opportunism, exploiting his romantic role for profit and prestige. Yet he could not catch the interest of the American public, except for occasional journalistic success. His literary executor, R. W. ◊ Griswold, won more permanent attention for him after his death by exaggerating his neurotic debility and inherited dipsomania to make him an almost Satanic figure. His subsequent reputation has been uncertain, yet generally high, especially since through the influence of his personality and writings on Baudelaire he contributed to the main stream of European symbolist literature. He has also been dominant in the development of American Southern literature. One cannot ignore the pretensions to greatness in his work; some, like Baudelaire, can accept these, but in others they provoke extreme hostility (see for instance Yvor Winters, *In Defense of Reason*, 1947). We should probably resist both tendencies, and place Poe somewhere beside Hawthorne, De Quincey and Wilkie Collins. [M A]

The Complete Works, ed. J. A. Harrison (17 vols., 1902); *Representative Selections*, ed. M. Alterton and H. Craig (1962); *The Centenary Poe*, ed. M. Slater (1949); *The Poems*, ed. F. Stovall (1965).

E. H. Davidson, *Poe: A Critical Study* (1957); A. H. Quinn, *Edgar Allan Poe: A Critical Biography* (1941); P. Quinn, *The French Face of Edgar Poe* (1957); Allen Tate, *The Forlorn Demon* (1953); ed. E. W. Carlson, *The Recognition of Edgar Allan Poe* (1967).

Pohl, Frederik (1919–). Science-fiction writer. Editor of one of the leading magazines in his field, he has been called (by Kingsley Amis) 'the most consistently able writer science fiction, in the modern sense, has yet produced'. In collaboration with the late Cyril M. Kornbluth he wrote a series of novels of which the best is undoubtedly *The Space Merchants* (1953), a satiric account of a future society dominated by rival advertising agencies which is not without relevance to our own times. Others include *Search the Sky* (1954), *Gladiator-at-Law* (1955), *Presidential Year* (1956) and *Wolfbane* (1960). Pohl has also edited several anthologies, and his own works include *Alternating Currents* (1956), *Slave Ship* (1957) and *Drunkard's Walk* (1960). [H D]

Kingsley Amis, *New Maps of Hell* (1960).

Porter, Gene Stratton (1863–1924). Novelist. She was born in Wabash, Indiana, south of which is the Limberlost Swamp where she began her naturalist studies as a girl and which is the scene of *Laddie* (1913), a novel of her childhood of which a million and a half copies were sold in the following 30 odd years. *Freckles* (1904) rather duplicates this material, and so does *A Girl of the Limberlost* (1909), the tale of a girl hunting moths in the swamp to earn money for education. These and her other five books were bought in millions. The naturalist detail sometimes just compensates for the astonishing sentimentality. [E M]

Porter, Katherine Anne (1890–   ). Storywriter, novelist. Born in Texas into a declining family proud of its descent from Daniel Boone, the 18th-century pioneering hero of Kentucky, she early rebelled against family and regional tradition and set out to find her own place; hence she had little formal education. She worked on a newspaper in Denver for three years, then lived as an expatriate in Mexico and Europe. Despite her rebellion, her best work is almost exclusively in those stories where she deals with a female protagonist of her own birth date and background, or where she uses the material of her Southern society, often that of her childhood. Thus she is unmistakeably a Southern writer, using the endlessly rich material of the defeated South with the social texture of a writer like Faulkner, yet with much more detachment than most of the Southern group of writers. The relationship of diminished present to glorious past allows her to achieve her finest effects – as in her excellent 'Miranda' stories. These interlinked tales, dealing with the human and social initiation of a girl who stands in

close relation to the author, exploit a delicate symbolist method and show the past as a powerful inward force, its workings traced from story to story until in 'Flowering Judas' we find the emancipated Miranda bereft of the power to love.

Katherine Anne Porter's first volume was *Flowering Judas* (1930), containing, in addition to the complex title story, at least three other first-rate pieces: 'Maria Concepcion', about a Mexican Indian woman, one of the few cases where she successfully abandons her usual background; 'The Cracked Looking Glass', a similar but less extreme example, the story of an Irish farm woman; and 'The Jilting of Granny Wetherall', the death-bed reverie of a Southern matriarch. The most uniformly successful volume is *Pale Horse, Pale Rider* (1939), containing Miranda novellas. The title story of *The Leaning Tower* (1944) deals with Nazi Germany, and here there is dissipation of focus and a rather too detached attempt at social commentary. These weaknesses grow the more obvious in her novel *Ship of Fools* (1962), which was 20 years in the writing; it is a mechanical allegory about a shipload of travellers to Germany in the 1930s, dealing with human and social follies, seeking to encompass the character of Nazism. But her high reputation is based on her stories, at least half of which deserve the highest attention as explorations of the private consciousness. [D C/M B]

Collected Essays and Occasional Writings (1970).
H. J. Mooney, Jr, *The Fiction and Criticism of Katherine Anne Porter* (1957); George Hendrick, *Katherine Anne Porter* (1965).

Porter, William Sidney. ◊ Henry, O(liver).

Pound, Ezra (1885–   ). Poet. Although this seminal figure in 20th-century American poetry left Hailey, Idaho, soon after his birth and never afterwards lived in the West, he seems to have inherited from his frontier forebears his restless optimistic individualism. This background contrasts strangely, yet, in America, not untypically, with his career as a student of Romance languages at Hamilton College and the University of Pennsylvania. Here he became a friend of William Carlos ◊ Williams and Hilda ◊ Doolittle, took his B.A. and M.A. degrees and began to write verse translations in the tradition of Rossetti and Swinburne. As a budding romantic medievalist he was also drawn to Browning, whose combination of erudition and optimistic energy made him a peculiarly congenial model. From this period, too, dates his awareness of Whitman's central importance – at first as an antagonist, eventually as the most pervasive and enduring influence on his poetry.

In 1908, after a brief, abruptly terminated career as a college teacher, he left stuffy provincial America to seek his fortune in the Old World. After publishing his first book of poetry, *A lume spento*, in Venice (1908), he moved to London, where he soon found a sympathetic publisher in Elkin Mathews and an influential friend in Ford Madox Ford. Thereafter, his rise was meteoric. Together with Hulme, H. D., and Richard Aldington, he founded ◊ Imagism; became the European correspondent of *Poetry* (Chicago); and undertook his rewarding studies of Anglo-Saxon (*The Seafarer*) and Chinese (*Cathay*, 1915). His connexion with *Poetry* (◊ Little Magazines) enabled him to promote such major, but then unrecognized, talents as Robert Frost, T. S. Eliot and Marianne Moore. As a young but persuasive propagandist for the new anti-poetical poetry, he was able to help W. B. Yeats discover his mature style. By 1914 he had abandoned Imagism in favour of Vorticism, an ism which, by bringing the arts of poetry (Pound), painting (Wyndham Lewis), and sculpture (Gaudier-Brzeska) into relation, led Pound to think of large-scale poetic organization in terms of contrasting masses and planes. Whatever the intrinsic merits of Vorticist aesthetics, they left behind them, in the works of Gaudier-Brzeska and in *The Cantos* (1925, 1928, 1930, 1934, 1937, 1940), durable monuments.

The Cantos were begun shortly before his Vorticist phase and apparently were intended to be a Browningesque compendium of his cultural adventures, an essay in the Liberal Arts for philistine America. This plan, however, was abandoned as he became increasingly disturbed by the events of 1914–18: though he remained behind in London, the Great War put an end to his political innocence, greatly enlarged his human sympathies, and awakened typically American isolationist theories that social evils were caused chiefly by international (usually Zionist) conspiracies.

At first he resisted the pressures to abandon his somewhat narrowly literary

preoccupations: *Homage to Sextus Propertius* (1917), his first major poem (in the form of a set of imitations from the Latin), explicitly repudiates the demand to write 'socially useful', 'engaged' poetry. But his next major poem, *Hugh Selwyn Mauberley* (1920), recognizes that the poet, if he is to survive as a poet, must abandon vulnerable 19th-century Aestheticist postures. By now he had moved to Paris, where he set about recasting *The Cantos*, composing operas and assisting the young American writers, notably Ernest Hemingway, who were congregating there (◊ Lost Generation). Too gregarious for his own good, in poor health, he virtually retired, in 1924, to Rapallo, Italy, where he was able to devote himself to research for, and the composition of, his major life-work, the epic *Cantos*. During the early thirties he grew convinced that Mussolini was the saviour of Italy, a constructive, inspiriting force that would sweep away poverty, disease and bloodshed. He held to this vision to the end, remaining in Italy after the American entry into the war, later to be captured and imprisoned by the U.S. military authorities in Pisa, where he wrote the first draft of his Bollingen Prize-winning *Pisan Cantos*. After being charged with treason for his Rome Radio broadcasts to American troops, he was declared insane and incarcerated in St Elizabeth's Hospital, Washington, D.C. There he completed the Pisan sequence (1948), the *Rock-Drill Cantos* (1955), and his greatest translation, *The Classic Anthology Defined by Confucius* (1954). In 1958, under pressure from a number of prominent public men, including the poet Robert Frost, the treason charges were withdrawn and he was allowed to return to Italy, where he now lives, still revising and adding to *The Cantos*.

After a half-century of labour, *The Cantos* is not far from a thousand pages in length: like *Leaves of Grass*, it is something more, and something less, than a poem, and of astonishingly uneven quality. The basis of the poem is a series of permutations of Greek, Chinese, early American, Renaissance and modern Italian, African and English legal materials. These are combined with autobiographical and lyrical sections to define a number of processes of political, economic and artistic values in action. Though notoriously difficult, many of the finest individual cantos (e.g. 1, 2, 13, 45, 47, 49) can be read without recourse to

John Edward's *Annotated Index to the Cantos* (1957). But the great Pisan sequence, to be understood adequately, requires patient investigation of secondary works and a good working knowledge of the previous cantos. *Drafts and Fragments of Cantos CX–CXVII* (1969) contains some of his most careful and serene poetry. Pound's earlier poetry, collected in *Personae* (1952), is more accessible, and it is here that his brilliant achievements as a prosodist can be most readily appreciated. His voluminous prose writings include *The Spirit of Romance* (1910; revised 1953), *Antheil and the Treatise on Harmony* (1924), *ABC of Reading* (1934), *Make It New* (1934), *Guide to Kulchur* (1938; revised 1951), *Patria Mia* (written 1913, publ. 1950) and *Impact: Essays on Ignorance and the Decline of American Civilization* (1960). A large selection of his prose is edited by T. S. Eliot in *The Literary Essays of Ezra Pound* (1954). His letters appear in *The Letters of Ezra Pound* (ed. D. D. Paige, 1950) and *Pound/Joyce: The Letters of Ezra Pound to James Joyce* (1968). Pound has done more than any other poet to advance the metrical revolution begun by Whitman. His cantos continue to appear in the little magazines and he continues to be a major influence on the development of American poetry. [GD]

Donald Gallup, *A Bibliography of Ezra Pound* (1963); Charles Norman, *Ezra Pound* (1960); Donald Davie, *Ezra Pound: Poet as Sculptor* (1964); G. S. Fraser, *Ezra Pound* (1961); Hugh Kenner, *The Poetry of Ezra Pound* (1951); ed. Lewis Leary, *Motive and Method in The Cantos of Ezra Pound* (1954); Julian Cornell, *The Trial of Ezra Pound* (1966).

Powell, Dawn (1897–1963). Novelist. She was born in Mount Gilead, Ohio, and the setting of her earlier novels is her native mid-West, but the main scene of her later and major fiction is ◊ Greenwich Village, New York, where she lived. She rejected her first novel in 1924 and considered *She Walks in Beauty* (1928) her first. Among her 14 novels are *The Bride's House* (1929), *Dance Night* (1931), *The Happy Island* (1938), *A Time to Be Born* (1942), *The Locusts Have No King* (1948), *The Wicked Pavilion* (1954) and *A Cage for Lovers* (1957). Her last novel, *The Golden Spur* (1962), a fine satire of city life focused on an old-fashioned bar-club and its clientele. As usual in her fiction, the characters are indelibly accurate and the wit emerges from one of America's unique styles. Her target is the middle class; she never softened. Edmund Wilson believes her novels to be 'among the most amusing being written, and in this respect quite on a level with those of Anthony Powell, Evelyn Waugh and Muriel Spark'. Her short stories appear in *Sunday, Monday and Always* (1952), and of her plays, the ◊ Group Theatre produced *By Night* in 1933 and ◊ Theatre Guild *Jig Saw* in 1934. [EM]

Edmund Wilson, *The Bit Between My Teeth* (1965).

Powers, J(ames) F(arl) (1917–). Novelist, short-story writer. Born in Jacksonville, Illinois, he studied at Northwestern University and taught at Marquette University. He has written two volumes of short stories, *Prince of Darkness* (1947) and *The Presence of Grace* (1956), and a novel, *Morte D'Urban* (1962), all having predominantly Catholic themes and pursuing ironically the contrast between the mediocrity of ordinary day-to-day American living with the traditional ideals of the religious life. Several of the stories deal with the lives and problems of Catholic priests in provincial American rectories; they are witty and stylized. Others touch on lynchings, social cruelties, problems of immigrants. Powers's qualities come out most strongly of all in his novel, a superbly funny and devastating study of an entrepreneurish Catholic priest, Father Urban, who attempts to advance the fortunes of his order, the Clementines, by businesslike methods and alliances with the rich. It is a very well observed and ironic comedy of American life and the conditions under which the modern life of faith must be lived. [MB]

Alfred Kazin, 'Gravity and Grace: The Stories of J. F. Powers', in *Contemporaries* (1962); F. W. Dupee, 'In the Power County', *The King of the Cats* (1965).

Prescott, W(illiam) H(ickling) (1796–1859). Historian. Family fortune enabled Prescott to spend two years in Europe after an undistinguished undergraduate career at Harvard. He had literary and historical tastes and gradually focused his interests on Spain. In 1838 he published a 3-volume *History of the Reign of Ferdinand and Isabella*. This was followed by the works for which he is best known: a *History of the Conquest of Mexico* (3 vols., 1843; abridged and ed. C. H.

Gardiner, 1967) and a *History of the Conquest of Peru* (2 vols., 1847). He intended to complete his study with a *History of the Reign of Philip II*, but only the first 3 volumes had appeared at the time of his death. Prescott saw himself as a story-teller and history as a branch of literature. He had little concern for economic, social or even constitutional problems and was content to recount the heroic deeds of the past. Within this framework, however, his use of manuscript sources is impeccable. [D K A]

The Literary Memoranda, ed. C. H. Gardiner (2 vols., 1961).

Price, Reynolds (1933–). Novelist, short-story writer. Born in Macon, North Carolina. A Rhodes Scholar at Oxford, he had previously graduated from Duke University, North Carolina, where he subsequently taught. His North Carolina childhood provides the major creative stimulus for his writing. Like many Southern writers he is constantly engaged in the discovery of the meaning of the present in the experience of the past, particularly the past of childhood. His best work brings together themes of family and the past, realized with a precision and delicacy never allowed to become indulgent or uncontrolled.

Set in the flat tobacco country of North Carolina, *A Long and Happy Life* – which won the 1962 William Faulkner Foundation award – is concerned with Rosacoke Mustian's gradual discovery of the responsibilities of love and is told with humour and humanity. The title story in *The Names and Faces of Heroes* (1963, short stories) is Price's most searching analysis of childhood family relationships; two other stories portray aged Negroes, and 'A Chain of Love' re-introduces Rosacoke Mustian. *A Generous Man* (1966) is a novel again concerning the Mustians but less restrained in symbolism and the mythic levels of what is really a simple tale. *Love and Work* (1968) overloads a novelist's efforts to justify his dead parents with nervous over-emphasis. [A H/E M]

Prokosch, Frederic (1908–). Novelist, poet, translator. Born in Madison, Wisconsin. He has studied and taught in America and England, and travelled extensively in Europe and Asia; he now lives in Paris. All his work shows a cosmopolitan range of subject matter and influence, and he has been considerably affected by the work of many English writers, especially by Yeats and the whole movement of the 1930s. He is a writer with a political sense, who frequently reverts to themes of exile and loss, to the world of refugees and of men losing their selfhood. He has spoken of his attempt to write 'internationally', and this has given his books a strong travel and adventure dimension. His verse, lyrical yet with a contemporary awareness, has appeared in several volumes, including *The Assassins* (1936), *The Carnival* (1938), *Death at Sea* (1940) and in the selection *Chosen Poems* (1944). He has been a prolific writer of novels, some contemporary, some historical, all exploiting a wide range of settings – Asia (as in *The Asiatics*, 1935, centred on a young American traveller), Africa (*Storm and Echo*, 1948), Portugal (*The Conspirators*, 1943) and Europe generally (as in *The Skies of Europe*, 1941). His best-known books are probably the very successful *The Asiatics*, *The Seven Who Fled* (1937), about demoralized Russian exiles; and *Age of Thunder* (1945). *The Seven Sisters* (1962) concerns the death throes of an aristocratic American family, spread throughout the world, and *The Missolonghi Manuscript* (1968) takes the form of a private Byronic memoir rescued for posterity. His very wide range of subject and approach makes him a writer difficult to characterize, but his intelligence and cosmopolitan perspective make him always striking. Among his translations are renderings of Hölderlin. [M B]

James Radcliffe Squires, Frederic Prokosch (1964).

Provincetown Players. An important theatre group who produced between 1915 and 1929 nearly 100 plays by 50 playwrights, and thereby fostered the beginnings of serious American drama. George Cram Cook and his wife Susan Glaspell began the group in Provincetown, Massachusetts, at the Wharf Theatre (1916), where O'Neill's first play was performed. Their New York home was the Playwrights' Theatre at 139 MacDougall Street, and later in the Provincetown Playhouse. In 1929 they moved uptown to the Garrick Theatre, but unsuccessfully. Besides O'Neill, they produced ◊ Dreiser, ◊ Millay, ◊ Anderson, Paul ◊ Green, ◊ Cummings and Edna ◊ Ferber. [E M]

H. Deutsch and S. Hanan, The Provincetown (1931).

Purdy, James (1923–). Novelist, story writer. Born in Ohio, he studied at Chicago and Madrid Universities. His first two books, *Colour of Darkness* (1957), short stories, including '63: Dream Palace' and *Malcolm* (1959), his first novel, brought him an immediate high reputation which has not declined. His theme is selfishness, lovelessness and alienation in small-town life; his mannered high-style supports a fantastic vision of character and time. *The Nephew* (1960), a novel, concerns the reconstruction of small-town life through an elderly spinster's writing a 'memorial' for her nephew killed in the Korean War. *Children Is All* (1962) contains 10 stories and 2 plays on accumulating themes of irrational fears and destructive eccentricities. His plays are more metaphysical than his fiction (Edward ◊ Albee adapted *Malcolm* for the stage in 1965). *Cabot Wright Begins* (1964) his third novel, is an ironic and fantastic story of the triumph of innocence in a man sentenced for 300 rapes. The satire on America, in the line of Nathanael ◊ West, explodes into sexual violence in *Eustace Chisholm and the Works* (1968), which concerns homosexuality in the Chicago of the thirties. Purdy connects the Depression with a wider collapse of personal life, and the controlled writing of the horror is strictly contemporary in both style and implication. *My Evening* (1968) contains a long story and 9 poems. [EM]

Jonathan Cott, in *On Contemporary Literature*, ed. R. Kostelanetz (1965).

Putnam, Phelps (1894–1948). Poet. Born in Boston, Massachusetts, he graduated from Yale, worked in an Arizona copper mine, served as associate editor on the *Atlantic Monthly,* and published two books of poetry, *Trinc* (1927) and *The Five Seasons* (1930). He left unfinished a long philosophical poem, 'The Earthly Comedy'. He has a distinctive personal voice in some of his lyrical and satirical poems. [EM]

Pynchon, Thomas (1937–). Novelist. Born in Long Island, he served in the navy, graduated from Cornell University in 1958, and after a spell in ◊ Greenwich Village moved to Seattle and then to Mexico. *V.* (1963) is a huge brilliant novel with two heroes – Profane, hero of a plot incorporating his quest for identity and the similar exploits of a neurotic intellectual band called the Whole Sick Crew, and Stencil, hero of a plot in which his quest for the meaning of his father's memoirs involves the history of Malta, German colonialism in South-West Africa, and much more. The diverse materials are united through the struggle of the human against the inanimate. *The Crying of Lot 49* (1966) is a shorter novel, equally complex and erudite, concerning communications theory and the organization of energy. His short story 'Entropy' (1960, repr. *12 from the Sixties,* ed. R. Kostelanetz, 1967) is a brief dazzling elaboration of science into fiction. His other, uncollected, stories are 'Low-Lands' and 'Under the Rose'. Pynchon is one of the few important literary talents of the 1960s. [EM]

S. E. Hyman, in *On Contemporary Literature*, ed. R. Kostelanetz (1965).

Q

Queen, Ellery (pseud. of Frederic Dannay) (1905–). Detective-story writer. With his cousin Manfred B. Lee (1905–) he has published approximately 100 books. Queen himself is the son of an inspector in the New York Police Department, and he and his father have appeared in a large number of stylistically unremarkable but usually well-constructed mysteries. Under the pseudonym Barnaby Ross, Dannay and Lee have also written novels which employ the detective Drury Lane, but many of these are now being issued under their more famous name. The highly successful *Ellery Queen's Mystery Magazine* began publication in 1941, and the University of Texas possesses the comprehensive Ellery Queen collection of detective fiction. [HD]

A. Boucher, *Ellery Queen: A Double Profile* (1951).

Quinn, Arthur Hobson (1875–1960). Critic. Born in Philadelphia, he spent most of his life as a distinguished teacher at the University of Pennsylvania. *Edgar Allan Poe* (1941) is an important critical exploration, but his major work is the immensely valuable *History of American Drama* (3 vols., 1923; revised 1943). [EM]

R

Rahv, Philip (1908–). Critic, editor. Born in Kupin, Russia, he teaches at Brandeis. He has written mainly on American and continental, particularly Russian, authors. In 1934 he was a founder of the *Partisan Review*, which he has co-edited for 30 years and helped to maintain as a journal of liberal-to-radical thought in both the literary and social spheres (◊ Little Magazines). In 1947 he edited *Discovery of Europe: The Story of American Experience in the Old World*. In a collection of his essays, *Image and Idea* (1949), he included 'Paleface and Redskin' and 'The Dark Lady of Salem', clever and incisive articles on the major dichotomies of the American literary imagination, torn between Eastern (and European) and Western (more specifically 'American') allegiances. *The Myth and the Powerhouse* (1965) is essays on European and American writers. He also edited two collections of essays from the *Partisan Review* and texts of various Russian writers. [A G]

Literature and the Sixth Sense (1969) (collected essays).

Rand, Ayn (1905–). Philosopher, novelist. Born in Russia. She is important for the powerful influence her 'objectivist' philosophy has had in the America of the 1950s and 1960s, particularly though not only among college students. Her views, for which she has strongly proselytized, are a variant on the superman theory: she urges the rational recognition of self-interest, the limitation of emotional and altruistic judgements, and the uses of enlightened selfishness. Her position has strong conservative overtones. Her novels, which are polemical and usually show heroes in industry or town planning standing out against the common herd, include *The Fountainhead* (1943), *Atlas Shrugged* (1957) and *We the Living* (1959). [M B]

Ransom, John Crowe (1888–). Critic and poet. Born in Tennessee and educated there at Vanderbilt University, where he taught for many years (1914–37). He subsequently went to Kenyon College, Ohio, founding there the *Kenyon Review*, one of the most important American academic critical and creative journals. He is associated with two major movements in American letters – the ◊ Fugitive group and the ◊ New Criticism. The latter took its name from the title of one of his books, and his critical position has been as influential as this suggests. As expressed in *God without Thunder* (1930), *The World's Body* (1938; revised 1969) and *The New Criticism* (1941), his approach, despite its practical-criticism emphasis, has large philosophical overtones and a considerable debt to Kant and probably to Bergson. He has a dominant concern with the 'ontological' discussion of a work; that is, with it as a thing in itself. This is in turn associated with an emphasis on concreteness, a distrust of abstraction, and a belief that art is essentially concerned with the act of perception as such, with showing that 'the object is perceptually or physically remarkable'. The position is in a sense an attempt to distinguish the language of literature from the language of science; its importance is that it has stressed the need for reading a text attentively and distinguishing its verbal procedures.

His poetry – contained in *Poems about God* (1919), *Chills and Fever* (1924), *Grace after Meat* (1924), *Two Gentlemen in Bonds* (1927), *Selected Poems* (1945), etc. – is, as his criticism might encourage us to suppose, metaphysically witty and presented with an enormous technical ability. What is surprising is its high style, its decorum; it is Southern, but Southern in its charm and aptness of language and form, rather than in its violence (cf. Robert Penn ◊ Warren). Many of the poems are elegies, a form in which Ransom is critically interested. Common themes are the contrast between the vigour of youth and the sad wisdom of age, the joy of summer and the reflective numbness of winter, themes that sometimes take a social dimension. Often opposites are held in a state of equilibrium in which we appreciate the intellectual and emotional complexity of a situation. Concepts of honour and tradition are presented with appreciative irony, so that we are conscious

213

as much of detachment as of commitment; yet finally a human appreciation usually brings the poet into his poem. The high language, with its biblical overtones, creates a stylized and indeed melodramatic world. As a poet Ransom is idiosyncratic and enormously impressive; his influence on subsequent poets has been as strong as his influence on critics. [MB]

Selected Poems (revised edn 1970).
René Wellek, *Concepts of Criticism* (1963); George Watson, *The Literary Critics* (1962); Vivienne Koch, in *Modern American Poetry*, ed. B. Rajan (1952); 'Homage to John Crowe Ransom', *Sewanee Review*, LVI (1948); ed. T. D. Young, *John Crowe Ransom: Critical Essays and a Bibliography* (1968).

Rawlings, Marjorie Kinnan (1896–1953). Novelist. Born in Washington, D.C., she settled in Florida after working as a journalist, and began to write fiction about the region. In her autobiographical *Cross Creek* (1942) the significance and the security of the old Florida wilderness is central. A simple but delicate writer, steeped in local material and dialect, deeply concerned with the virtue of wilderness and pioneer life, she has taken as her main subject the semi-pioneer period of Florida's development in the late 19th century. Her works include *South Moon Under* (1933), *Golden Apples* (1935) and *When the Whippoorwill* (1940), a collection of Florida stories. Her best-known work is *The Yearling* (1938), a delicate, attractive novel set in the Florida of the 1870s, the story of a young boy with a tame fawn. Knowledgeably and carefully written, her books are good examples of American regional fiction. [MB]

Realism (Veritism, Naturalism). Though these terms, particularly the first and last, have been variously used by critics, their main significance in American literature is that they were employed by certain late-19th and early-20th-century writers to describe a self-conscious and developing literary tendency that was held to be particularly American and democratic. Though this movement, part of a general Western tendency in literature, derives largely from European models, it undoubtedly did strike particularly hard in the U.S.A., where one of its most clear-cut phases can be seen. The reason may be that these writers found themselves dealing with materials unworked

by any earlier literary tradition (mid-Western city life, immigrant experience, etc.), that they were usually deeply affected by neo-Darwinian, neo-socialist or neo-Malthusian theories, taking a determinist approach to a society that seemed large, abstract and industrial and was run by others, and that they were conscious of the impersonal pressures of man upon man in a competitive environment. American realism, and the associated movements, can broadly be seen as a reaction against the eastern 'genteel tradition', and towards a more 'primitive' and scientistic literature, which was also a more modern literature. Certainly much modern American writing was ushered in by these movements.

REALISM: ◊ Howells emerged as the chief American spokesman of this tendency, pioneered by Flaubert, Balzac and Tolstoy in Europe, and encouraged by Taine's critical theories. Demanding that attention be paid not to literary tradition but to things as they are, he best expressed his principles – a mixture of emphasis on verisimilitude and an ethical-aesthetic standpoint – in *Criticism and Fiction* (1891), arguing that we must first ask of a work of the imagination 'Is it true? – true to the motives, the impulses, the principles that shape the life of actual men and women? This truth, which necessarily includes the highest morality and the highest artistry – this truth given, the book cannot be wicked and cannot be weak. ...' Various local-colour writers are associated with this movement and principle; so was Henry James, though for some he represented an opposite principle, a totally aesthetic standpoint.

VERITISM: This term was used by Hamlin ◊ Garland in his *Crumbling Idols* (1894) to assert a more scientific standpoint, in part a reaction against ◊ Howells' moralism and his emphasis on the 'smiling' aspects of life (which to Howells were the 'typically American' aspects). Garland, drawing on Darwin and social determinism, stressed that literature was democratic when it was scientific and engaged with social problems; this meant that realism had no inherent optimism or ethics. This description came much closer to what writers like Stephen ◊ Crane, Harold ◊ Frederic and Henry Blake ◊ Fuller were doing, though Garland was strongly opposed to the 'immoralism' of the Zola-esque tradition.

NATURALISM: Indebted to Zola, naturalism tended even further towards a determinist standpoint, drawing on economic and sociological analysis to show, normally, the effect of environment on the lower levels of society. Writers like ◊ Dreiser, ◊ London and ◊ Norris best exemplify this tendency, and it runs deep in 20th-century American fiction, particularly in proletarian writing. But in naturalism was also involved a franker and more psychologically determinist view of man's sexual and perhaps his violent impulses, and with what Dreiser called 'the clock of thought', the deeper-seated functions of will and desire.

Since it has long been characteristic for new movements in literature to assert the superior realism of their mode, and since 'reality' itself is a doubtful concept, these designations have only limited critical use; but in the specific usages of those who formulated them they show a steady realignment of aesthetic position. As used in the critical vocabulary of writers like ◊ Parrington (with his 'critical realists') and the neo-Marxists (with their 'social realists') this general area of terminology, though generally significant in modern aesthetics, is less enlightening than it is when used to denote the working principles of practising writers. [MB]

Alfred Kazin, *On Native Grounds* (1942, repr. 1956); Lars Åhnebrink, *The Beginnings of Naturalism in American Fiction* (1961); Charles C. Walcutt, *American Literary Naturalism: A Divided Stream* (1956).

Rechy, John (1934–   ). He was born in El Paso, Texas, studied at Texas Western College, and served in the army in Germany. He established himself as an original writer with *The City of Night* (1963), a study, written in ambitiously elaborate styles, in the form of linked stories, of miscellaneous homosexuality and narcissism in American cities. *Numbers* (1968) again chronicles the limbo of male sexuality with first-hand detail. [EM]

Reed, John (1887–1920). Journalist. He attended Harvard and later worked for the *American Magazine* and *The Masses*. His reports from Mexico and Europe for the *Metropolitan* were published as *Insurgent Mexico* (1914) and *The War in Eastern*

Europe (1916). His best-known work is *Ten Days That Shook the World* (1919), a product of his enthusiastic observation of events in Russia. On his return to America he was active in organizing the Communist Party there before being forced to leave for Russia, where he died of typhus in 1920. Reed, a flamboyant, romantic journalist, also published *Tamburlaine and Other Verses* (1917). Floyd ◊ Dell edited *Daughter of the Revolution and Other Stories* (1927), and John Stuart made a selection of his writings in *The Education of John Reed* (1955). [HD]

Granville Hicks, *John Reed: The Making of a Revolutionary* (1936); Richard O'Connor and Dale L. Walker, *The Last Revolutionary* (1965).

Reich, Wilhelm (1897–1957). Psychologist. He was born in Dobrzcynica, Galicia, into a German-speaking family which had largely relinquished its Jewish origins. His father, who was a prosperous farmer, and did not rear his children in the Jewish faith, died in 1914. Reich directed the farm and continued his schooling until the farm was destroyed in the war. In 1915, he joined the army of the declining Austro-Hungarian Empire. After the war, at the University of Vienna he first studied law and then changed to medicine, obtaining his M.D. in 1922 and taking graduate studies in neurology and psychiatry. He became First Clinical Assistant at Freud's Psychoanalytic Polyclinic in 1922 and its vice-director in 1928. In 1924 he joined the Austrian Socialist Party and began to consider the possibility of reconciling Freudian and Marxist ideas, convinced of the necessity of making psychoanalysis available to the working classes. In 1927 he published *The Function of the Orgasm*, in 1928 joined the Communist Party, and in 1929 opened the first sex hygiene clinics, for workers and employees, with his professional colleagues of the Socialist Society for Sex Consultation and Sexological Research. *The Mass Psychology of Fascism* (1933) explores political sociology and criticizes the party lines of both Communists and psychoanalysts. Reich's break with Freud was at least partly due to his double emphasis on socialism and the primary function of the orgasm in therapy. Between 1930 and 1937 he lectured in Berlin and then, to escape the Nazis, went to Denmark and Norway, until prejudice against his politics and his psychotherapy, together with his own recalcitrant personality, encouraged him to depart for America. He lectured as associate professor of Medical Psychology at the New School for Social Research in New York from 1939 to 1941, when his influence on American literature and sociology began. Reich's 'sex economy' and its sexual-political bases was bound to disturb the Establishment, since he worked *between* the dogmas and disciplines, stressed both the corruption of the Left and the puritanical cruelties of Western sexual repressions, and proclaimed a cosmic unity of all energy which appeared to be cranky. He had been expelled from the International Psychoanalytic Association in 1934, and the year before from the fascistic German Psychoanalytical Society. During this period and throughout the forties, he developed a highly original theory of the bioelectric nature of sexuality as the operative principle of the body, involving both the wide-ranging information of *Character Analysis* (1933) and the transformation of muscular energy by physical contact between patient and therapist which he termed 'vegetotherapy', a major development in psychosomatic medicine. His work in America was mainly forwarded through the Orgone Institute, founded in 1942, and established at Orgonon, Maine, in 1946, and the Wilhelm Reich Foundation, organized by students and friends in 1949. In 1940, Reich first used his orgone accumulator (a device for concentrating the universal energy element, the *bion*) on human beings, and it was this which caused the Federal Food and Drugs Administration to object to what they took to be a falsely offered cure and to bring an injunction against him. Reich was sentenced to two years' imprisonment and died in the Federal Penitentiary, Lewisburg, Pa. Since then his work has been developed considerably and his therapy become increasingly widespread. The effect of his writings, especially the model of the psychosomatic body and his terminology, have deeply influenced American writers since the forties, primarily Paul ◊ Goodman and certain writers of the Beat Generation (Allen ◊ Ginsberg and Jack ◊ Kerouac in particular), and William ◊ Burroughs. Besides works already mentioned, his books include *The Sexual Revolution* (1936), *Listen, Little Man!* (1948), *Ether, God and Devil* (1951), *Cosmic Superimposition* (1951), *The Murder of Christ* (1953), and *People in Trouble* (1953).

216

Documents of his relationship with Freud are contained in *Reich Speaks of Freud* (ed. M. Higgins and C. M. Raphael, 1967). [E M]

Wilhelm Reich: Selected Writings (1960).
Ilse Ollendorf Reich, *Wilhelm Reich: A Personal Biography* (1969); Michel Cattier, *La vie et l'œuvre du Docteur Wilhelm Reich* (1969); Philip Rieff, *The Triumph of the Therapeutic* (1966); Paul A. Robinson, *The Freudian Left* (1969).

Reid, Mayne (1818–83). Novelist. Born in Ireland, went to America about 1838, and served in the Mexican War. He was one of the most popular writers of romance on American frontier themes: *The Rifle Rangers* (1850), *The Castaways* (1870) and *Afloat in the Forest* (1866). He was a loyal friend of Poe's, and his *The Quadroon* (1856) was the basis of Dion ◊ Boucicault's popular play *The Octoroon* (1859). [E M]

Rexroth, Kenneth (1905–   ). Poet, critic, translator. Born in South Bend, Indiana, he spent his childhood and youth in the Middle West; orphaned at 13, he moved around the country working in a wide variety of casual labour, gradually picking up a personal knowledge of the arts and the world of radical politics. Apart from two years in school, his education began in the twenties, at the New School, the Arts Students League and the Chicago Art Institute. He moved to San Francisco in 1927 and has remained ever since. In the thirties he was active on the left and in the union movement. He has had several one-man shows of his paintings. His literary output is large, and as a teacher, translator, poet and critic his influence and encouragement has been radiating steadily since 1940. His early poems in *The Art of Worldly Wisdom* (1949) are surreal and experimental in the fashions of the twenties, but *The Phoenix and the Tortoise* (1944) has a maturity which shows the effect of his association with the Objectivists. There followed *The Signature of All Things* (1949), *Beyond the Mountains* (1951; 4 verse plays), and *The Dragon and the Unicorn* (1952), the verse journal of travel in Europe. *In Defence of the Earth* (1956) clearly shows the division in his work between the arguing and often irascible intellectual and the poet of quiet landscape and love. *Natural Numbers: New and Selected Poems* (1964) represents his poetry over 40 years, the newer poems having a personal, lyrical intensity. In 1957, the *Quarterly Review of Literature* issued his

'The Homestead Called Damascus' (in book form 1962), an autobiographical poem finished about 1926, one of his best works, and looking forward to *An Autobiographical Novel* (1966), an account of the first 21 years of his life, a small classic of anti-establishment experience. His other work includes *Original Sin*, a ballet performed in 1961, *The Minority of One* (1961), poems, *The Collected Shorter Poems* (1967) and *The Collected Longer Poems* (1968). His translations of classical, oriental and European poetry include the excellent *One Hundred Poems from the Chinese* (1956). His important critical essays are collected in *Bird in the Bush* (1959), which includes articles on ◊ Patchen, Henry ◊ Miller, and Martin Buber, and *Assays* (1962), with essays on contemporary poetry, Twain and William Carlos Williams. Rexroth fostered San Francisco literary life which blossomed between 1945 and the end of the fifties, and helped to pioneer the revival of jazz-and-poetry in the Bay Area and in New York. His life's work is a major contribution to American letters. [EM]

Lawrence Lipton, 'Notes towards an Understanding of Kenneth Rexroth . . .', *Quarterly Review of Literature*, IX, 2 (1957); Eric Mottram, *A Kenneth Rexroth Reader* (1970).

Reznikoff, Charles (1894–   ). Poet. He graduated in law but, though called to the bar, did not practise. He is the author of a number of volumes of poetry, dating from 1927 onwards, and novels and a volume of verse plays. He was, along with George ◊ Oppen, etc., one of the Objectivist poets of the 1930s – that movement, which had a strong debt to ◊ Imagism, being strongly supported by Ezra Pound. At the same time there is a strong opposing vein of Jewish lyricism and Jewish learning in his work. He has been long a lonely and relatively unknown poet, but in recent years his reputation has come into ascendancy with *By the Waters of Manhattan* (1962), which is a selection from his verse, and *Testimony: The United States 1885–1890* (1965), the first volume of a long· and documented poetic meditation on this period of American social economic and cultural history. *Family Chronicle* (1969) is a prose record of life in New York in the thirties. [EM/MB]

Rice, Elmer (1892–1967). Playwright, novelist. He was born in New York City, studied law at night school, but set out on a theatre career, which began with *On Trial* (1914), a mystery play of victimization told through expressionist flashback. But his next success did not come until *The Adding Machine* (1923), where his typical concern for the social victim is embodied in the fate of Mr Zero, a 'waste product' of mechanized society. In *Street Scene* (1929) a slice of slum life moves towards murder and frustrated love without solution (Langston ◊ Hughes and Kurt Weill made it into a musical in 1947). *Left Bank* (1931) concerns feckless expatriates, and *Counsellor-at-Law* (1931) the legal profession. In 1933 Rice protested against Depression conditions in *We the People*, a Marxist play with democratic ideals, and *Judgment Day* (1934) is a warning against Nazism based on the Dimitroff trial. *Not for Children* (1935) attacks the theatre's divorce from reality, and *American Landscape* (1938) reasserts national traditions of 'freedom and the common rights of humanity', as against *Between Two Worlds* (1934), which had contrasted the Soviet system with the less humane American world. In 1951 he defended his leftist friends and colleagues at a time of national hysteria. His later plays have not been too good (*Dream Girl*, 1946, and *Cue for Passion*, 1959), but his autobiography, *Minority Report* (1963), is a significant document of the last three decades. The utopian satire *A Voyage to Purilia* (1930) is the best of his novels. [EM]

R. Hogan, *The Independence of Elmer Rice* (1965).

Rich, Adrienne Cecile (1929–   ). Poet Born in Baltimore, educated at Radcliffe, and now lives in Cambridge, Massachusetts. Her volumes include *A Change of World* (1951), *The Diamond Cutters* (1955) and *Snapshots of a Daughter-in-Law* (1963). She also published a pamphlet of poems in the English Fantasy Poets series during a year spent in England on a Guggenheim award. Her early verse is marked by a delicacy of insight, but her precocious talent has deepened and darkened in recent years. Her themes are those of personal and family relationships, and the nature of the subjective life. The poems in *Necessities of Life* (1966) have an extraordinary brevity and compassion of feeling (this volume includes translations from Dutch poetry). [BS/EM]

Selected Poems (1967); *Leaflets* (1969).
Richard Howard, *Alone with America* (1969).

Richardson, Jack (1935–   ). Dramatist, fiction writer. He was born and works in

New York. *The Prodigal* (1960) showed the beginning of his highly intelligent wit in the theatre with its rehandling of the Agamemnon–Orestes story, and was followed by another play of conflicting idealism and opportunism, *Gallows Humor* (1961), a brilliant and funny satire on capital punishment. *Lorenzo* (1963) uses a Renaissance Italian touring actors' company to point the triumph of art-illusion over war-reality, but it is a less interestingly written play. His latest drama is *Christmas in Las Vegas* (1965). He has also written a novel, *The Prison Life of Harris Philmore* (1961). [E M]

Richter, Conrad (1890–1968). Novelist. Born in Pine Grove, Pennsylvania, he settled in the American South-west after a career in journalism, and began studying and writing about the past of the region. An interesting historical novelist, he is much concerned to convey the sensations and the texture of the imagined life of the past, and to show the growth of American attitudes and ambitions. His books include *The Sea of Grass* (1937), *Tacey Cromwell* (1942), *The Freeman* (1943), *Always Young and Fair* (1947) and the striking *The Water of Kronos* (1960). *The Awakening Land*, a pioneer trilogy, consists of *The Trees* (1940), *The Fields* (1946) and *The Town* (1950); the story of the Luckett family, who move into the Ohio wilderness, it follows the development of a new American liberal thought, and the movement from frontier to town culture. Richter comments interestingly on literary regionalism in *The Mountain on the Desert* (1955). In *The Grandfathers* (1964) a west Maryland mountain valley is the location of a 15-year-old girl's search for her father: a novel of unexpected humour and irony. [M B]

Riding, Laura (1901–   ). Poet, novelist, critic. She was born in New York City and was one of the Southern ◊ Fugitive Group, but finally became an expatriate in Majorca, England and Switzerland. She established the Seizin Press in Deyá, Majorca, in 1927, and there edited the literary magazine *Epilogue* (1935–8) with Robert Graves. Her poetry is confessedly a private poetry, not only because it is modernist but also because it is very much the work of sensibility. Her volumes, published in various countries, some under the name Laura Riding Gottschalk, include *The Close Chaplet* (1926), *Poems: A Joking Word* (1930) and *Poet: A Lying Word* (1933). With Robert Graves she

wrote a novel, *No Decency Left* (1932), under the name Barbara Riche; but better known are her novels *A Trojan Ending* (1937), on the Trojan war, and *Lives of Wives* (1939). It was also with Graves that she wrote the famous and useful critical *Survey of Modernist Poetry* (1927), and she has produced other critical books and essays, including *Contemporaries and Snobs* (1928). [M B]

Collected Poems (1938).

Riesman, David (1909–   ). Sociologist. Born in Philadelphia, he attended a Quaker school, graduated from Harvard in 1931, practised law, and moved his interests towards the social sciences through Erich ◊ Fromm and readings in psychology. After working in this field at Chicago, his researches on American society produced (in collaboration) *The Lonely Crowd* (1950) and *Faces in the Crowd* (1952), a classic contribution whose terminology has contributed to the language. He became Professor of Social Science at Harvard in 1954. Before this wide recognition, he had written *Civil Liberties in a Period of Transition* (1942) and *Democracy and Defamation* (1942). His later work includes *Thorstein Veblen: A Critical Interpretation* (1953), *Constraint and Variety in American Education* (1956, 1958), two books of occasional pieces, *Individualism Reconsidered* (1954) and *Abundance for What?* (1964), and *Conversations in Japan* (1967, in collaboration with his wife). *The Academic Revolution* (1968, with Christopher Jencks) is a detailed survey of American higher education: the 'revolution' is the increasing professionalism of graduate schools. [E M]

Riley, James Whitcomb (1849–1916). The 'Hoosier poet'. Born in Indiana. His popular Indiana dialect poems won him enormous reputation at the height of the 'local-colour' movement. He began writing them, under the name 'Benj. F. Johnson, of Boone', while working as a journalist on the *Indianapolis Journal*. They were collected in *'The Old Swimmin'-Hole', and 'Leven More Poems* (1883). Then followed numerous other volumes, including *Home-Folks* (1900), *Riley Songs O' Cheer* (1905) and *A Hoosier Romance* (1910). The *Homestead Edition of The Poems and Prose Sketches of James Whitcomb Riley* (1897–1914) runs to 16 volumes. His *Letters* were collected (1930); there are numerous memoirs; he drew, and still draws State and national pride. Riley wrote 'Little Orphant Annie'. [MB]

Jeanette C. Nolan, *James Whitcomb Riley, Hoosier Poet* (1941); Richard Crowder, *Those Innocent Years: The Legacy and Inheritance of a Hero of the Victorian Era, James Whitcomb Riley* (1957).

Rinehart, Mary Roberts (1876–1958). Novelist, detective-story writer. Born in Pittsburg, Pennsylvania, she began her long and prolific career in the then novel genre of literary detection with *The Circular Staircase* (1908; revised edn, 1935) and *The Man in Lower Ten* (1909). Her sixty-first book, *The Swimming Pool* (1952), was also a mystery. She was also the author of a popular series of stories centred on an old maid and her two friends, of which the first was *The Amazing Adventures of Letitia Carberry* (1911) and the last *The Best of Tish* (1955). A revised version of her autobiography, *My Story*, appeared in 1948. [HD]

Ripley, George (1802–80). Clergyman, editor, critic. From Greenfield, Massachusetts, and Harvard, he became a leading ◊ Transcendentalist Unitarian minister in Boston (from 1826). He instigated and organized the Brook Farm community experiment (1841–7), a utopian agrarian, self-supporting community of intellectuals and workers, in which ◊ Hawthorne, Theodore Parker, Margaret ◊ Fuller, and William Ellery ◊ Channing (I) among others, were associated. Its aim was 'to prepare a society of liberal, intelligent, and cultivated persons' who would resist 'the pressure of our competitive institutions'. It was not finally successful. Ripley also edited the *Harbinger* (1845–9), a magazine of the Fourierist ideas behind Brook Farm, and the Unitarian weekly, *Christian Register*. His important *Specimens of Foreign Standard Literature* (1838–52) introduced European writers to American readers. His *Discourses on the Philosophy of Religion* (1836) was attacked as heresy by Andrew Norton, and Ripley replied in *Letters on the Latest Form of Infidelity* (1840), a plea for religious tolerance. In 1841 he resigned his ministry, feeling he had lost his sense of vocation, became head of Brook Farm (see Hawthorne's novel which partly describes it, *The Blithedale Romance*), and later edited the *New American Cyclopaedia* (1858–63). He is the very type of the earnest, experimenting,

soul-searching New England intelligence of the mid 19th century. [EM/MG]

Selected Writings of the American Transcendentalists, ed. George Hochfield (1966).
O. B. Frothingham, *George Ripley* (1882); Katherine Burton, *Paradise Planters: The Story of Brook Farm* (1939).

Roberts, Elizabeth Madox (1886–1941). Southern novelist. She was born in Kentucky, and most of her novels deal with her home State, drawing on its history and folklore. Her interest in folk-speech and custom usually means that she is defined as a regionalist, but it is possible to see her as an interesting figure in that transitional phase of Southern fiction between Ellen ◊ Glasgow and writers like Faulkner and Robert Penn ◊ Warren. Her novels, sometimes set in the pioneer period, deal with violence but rather in the manner of the 'genteel tradition'. Among them are *The Time of Man* (1926), *My Heart and My Flesh* (1927), *The Great Meadow* (1930), and *Black Is My Truelove's Hair* (1938). She also produced 3 volumes of poetry. [MB]

H. M. Campbell and R. E. Forster, *Elizabeth Madox Roberts: American Novelist* (1956); Robert Penn Warren, 'Life is from Within', *Saturday Review*, 2 March 1963.

Roberts, Kenneth (1885–1957). Historical novelist, journalist. Born in Kennebunk, Maine. His novels have the reputation of being extremely well researched (he has also produced historical research and translations). Several of them deal with the historical development of Maine, his native State, and Canada, over the period of the Revolution. Among them are *Arundel* (1930), about Benedict Arnold's expedition against Quebec; *The Lively Lady* (1931); *Rabble in Arms* (1933); *Northwest Passage* (1937); and *Boon Island* (1956). His *I Wanted to Write* (1949) is revealing about his background and attitudes. [MB]

Robinson, Edwin Arlington (1869–1935). Poet. The major poet of his generation, he grew up in Gardiner, Maine, the 'Tilbury Town' of his poems. A precocious, delicate boy, he had to leave Harvard in 1893, after two years, because his father's health failed and the family's finances collapsed. His mother died suddenly of black diphtheria, and was buried hurriedly because the priest and doctor feared the disease. His father was a spiritualist who even experimented with his beliefs on his deathbed. Robinson referred to these events as a 'living hell' which 'cut my universe clean in half'. His brother's disasters and loss of family money and the poet's own serious ear trouble and fear of brain damage resulted in his regarding himself as an exhausted misfit, 'a tragedy from the beginning'.

He printed his first poems, *The Torrent and the Night Before* (1896), at his own expense: it contained some of his finest works (revised edn 1897 as *The Children of Night*). Living in New York from 1898, his lonely retreat from company increased; he drank and was nearly destitute. Public recognition came with his verse novel, *Captain Craig* (1902). He made his first of many summer visits to the MacDowell Colony in New Hampshire, his refuge until his death. *The Man against the Sky* (1916) established him firmly with a readership, and his verse novel *Tristram* (1927) was a best-seller. He died of cancer in New York.

His intelligence and careful forms rejuvenated American *fin de siècle* poetry with works of austere honesty and precision. His melancholy is not tragic but ironic and dry; it resists romantic sentimentalities. 'Luke Havergal' and 'Children of the Night' are poems of failure balanced by briefly sustaining hope and oncoming life. His response to small-town suffering is beautifully articulated in poems like 'Miniver Cheevy', 'Flammande', 'Eros Turannos' and 'Mr Flood's Party'. He is a master of long narrative poems ('The Man against the Sky' and 'Tasker Norcross'), although the passive gloom of the Tilbury world can be monotonous and intellectually thin. His infatuation with medieval gothicry produced his narrative poems 'Merlin' (1917), 'Launcelot' (1927) and 'Tristam' (1927), visions of the decline of the West. His Jamesian verse novels are a unique and often interesting achievement – 'Roman Bartholow' (1923), 'Cavender's House' (1929), 'The Glory of Nightingales' (1930), 'King Jasper' (1935) – this last an allegory of capitalist and communist conflicts. *Tilbury Town: Selected Poems of E. A. Robinson* (ed. L. Thompson, 1953) is a useful introduction to his work.

For a shy and pessimistic man, his huge output and intense concern with human relationships and solitude are an achievement of extraordinary affirmation, most of it thoroughly readable. [EM]

C. P. Smith, *Where the Light Falls* (1965); H. C.

Franchere, *E. A. Robinson* (1968); Louis O. Coxe, *E. A. Robinson: The Life of Poetry* (1969); ed. E. Barnard, *E. A. Robinson: Centenary Essays* (1970).

Roethke, Theodore (1908–63). Poet. He was born and spent his childhood in Saginaw, Michigan; he taught in American universities; but his poetry is deeply associated with the landscape of the North-west. Poems appearing in *Open House* (1941), *The Lost Son and Other Poems* (1948), *Praise to the End!* (1951) and *The Waking* (1953) were selected for an excellently representative volume, *Words for the Wind* (1958). After the conventionalities of his first book, Roethke developed a unique poetry out of his sense of the links between the unconscious and nature – Richard Eberhart called it his 'worms period' – with Yeats as his formal model. His floppy whimsical poems, often in a sort of baby talk, were exceptional in a poetic career of almost desperate stabilities. His strength lay in creating an interior landscape out of a crowded greenhouse or a river estuary which locates, with lyrical precision and a degree of splendour, a sense of alienation, madness and reconciliation which he strives to unify. His last book, *The Far Field* (1964), contains some of his finest poems, with a new control of the long meditative line and a less obtrusive Freudian idea of men's lives. *On the Poet and His Craft* (ed. R. J. Mills, 1965) is a collection of his occasional prose. [EM]

Collected Poems (1968); *The Notebooks*, ed. D. Wagoner (1970).
Karl Malkoff, *Theodore Roethke: An Introduction to the Poetry* (1967); ed. Arnold Stein, *Theodore Roethke: Essays on the Poetry* (1966); Allan Seager, *The Glass House: The Life of Theodore Roethke* (1968).

Rogers, Will(iam) (1879–1935). Humorist. This modern American folk hero was born in Oklahoma of part Indian blood. He turned from a Wild West cowboy act into a comedian, with the Ziegfeld Follies, then in motion-pictures and a newspaper column. He continued the wisecracking folk-humour tradition of men like Artemus ◊ Ward and Petroleum ◊ Nasby, and his eye often turned to modern political affairs. He took the name of the 'Cowboy Philosopher' and wrote *The Cowboy Philosopher on Prohibition* (1919), *The Cowboy Philosopher on the Peace Conference* (1919), *Will Rogers' Political Follies* (1929), etc. Donald Day's

The Autobiography of Will Rogers (1949) selects from the writings of this great comic personality. [MB]

Rølvaag, O(le) E(dvart) (1876–1931). Novelist. Born in Norway of seafaring background, he became a sailor, then in 1896 came to the U.S.A. to farm in South Dakota. He eventually became Professor of Norwegian at St Olaf College in Minnesota. He began writing in Norwegian about Scandinavian immigrants in the States; *Giants in the Earth* (1927), and the two novels consecutive to it, *Peder Victorious* (1929) and *Their Father's God* (1931), written in Norwegian and translated, are the best known of his novels. Many still remain untranslated, but of those that are, *Pure Gold* (1930) and *The Boat of Longing* (1933), which celebrates his native Norway, are particularly notable. Rølvaag is usually identified as an American regional novelist, but he is also in the tradition of Scandinavian fiction, with its emphasis on the titanic struggle of individual men with both the forces within themselves and the environment in which they live. Thus the trilogy beginning with *Giants in the Earth* deals with the political, social and religious scene, but it is essentially pastoral – as the subtitle says, it is a 'Saga of the Prairie'. Rølvaag was in fact able to contribute to both traditions. [MB]

Theodore Jorgensen and Nora O. Solum, *Ole Edvart Rølvaag: A Biography* (1939).

Roosevelt, Theodore (1858–1919). Reformer, politician, historian. Born in New York. After Harvard he served briefly as a Republican member of the New York State legislature, but following the death of his first wife in 1884 bought a ranch in the Dakota territory where he stayed for several years. From childhood he had believed in the virtue of strenuous outdoor activity and had improved his naturally poor health by sport and physical exercises. He had also, while at Harvard, begun work on his first book, a naval history of the war of 1812. During his years in Dakota he indulged both interests, following an active career as a rancher and working in his spare time on a history, *The Winning of the West* (4 vols., 1889–96). In 1889 he was called back to the East by the offer of a post on the Civil Service Commission; other offices quickly followed. In 1898 he resigned his assistant secretaryship of the navy in order to take part in the Spanish–American War as

colonel of his own troop of volunteer cavalry, the Rough Riders. Fame in this campaign led to his election as governor of New York in 1898; in 1901 he became vice-president of the United States and succeeded to the presidency on the assassination of McKinley. He was re-elected in 1904, and in 1912 unsuccessfully stood as candidate for the Progressive Party.

In his public career a moderate reformer and a believer in manifest destiny, Anglo-Saxon superiority and social Darwinism, he expressed his philosophy in *The New Nationalism* (1910). The same qualities were displayed in his historical writing, as in *The Winning of the West*. He was a literary historian with a great admiration for Francis ◊ Parkman, and a staunch moralist who believed that the historian should take sides and should use his imagination in order to make his material dramatically alive. He emphasized the value of the individual and accepted the validity of applying evolutionary theories to national and international history. He believed implicitly that Anglo-Saxon America represented the highest point of human development. His values and judgements no longer find general acceptance, but his use of sources was excellent, and he had a gift for narrative that makes his work highly readable and historically valuable. [DKA]

Autobiography, ed. Wayne Andrews (1958).

Rosenberg, Harold (1906–). Poet, critic, philosopher. He is a New Yorker, and in the thirties and forties began his reputation with work in *Poetry, Transition, The Symposium* and *View*. Later he wrote for *Partisan Review, Commentary*, the *Nation, Dissent* and *Les Temps Modernes*. He is a fine example of the art and literary critic completely dedicated to his profession of discrimination of contemporary culture. Merleau-Ponty asked him to write on Marx in *Les philosophes célèbres*, and his poetry has appeared in *Trance above the Streets* (1942) and in a number of little magazines. He has lectured at the New School for Social Research on literature and art. His major work consists of three highly important books of cultural analysis: *Arshile Gorky* (1962), the only significant study of the great Armenian-American painter; *The Tradition of the New* (1959), which demonstrates a tradition of art and poetry from Poe and Rimbaud through to American Action Painting (a term he himself coined),

Marxist judgements in the arts, Pop culture, etc.; and *The Anxious Object* (1964), a series of essays on art today and its audience, including pieces on De Kooning, Hofmann, Steinberg and Jasper Johns. *Art Works and Packages* (1969) continues his analysis of contemporary art. [EM]

Ross, Barnaby. ◊ Dannay, Frederic.

Ross, Leonard Q. ◊ Rosten, Leo Calvin.

Ross, Lillian (1898–   ). Reporter, novelist. Born in Syracuse. N.Y., she now lives in New York City and is on the staff of the *New Yorker*, where most of her work appears. Its main spirit is documentary, but her analytical talent also spreads towards fiction. *Picture* (1952) is a fictionalized true story and a classic study of Hollywood filmmaking. Her frank *Portrait of Hemingway* (1961) began as a *New Yorker* profile of the novelist. *The Player* (1962), written with Helen Ross, is a group portrait of 55 actors. Her first novel (best read as a series of short stories), *Vertical and Horizontal* (1963), is a marvellous detached analysis of contemporary New York, concentrating particularly on the world of medicine and psychoanalysis. *Talk Stories* (1966) is a collection of 60 interviews and descriptions (previously published in the *New Yorker* between 1958 and 1965) – the figures include Glenn Gould, Yehudi Menuhin, and Dag Hammerskjold – and *Reporting* (1966) reprints the account of John Huston in *Picture*, with six other pieces. [MB]

Rosten, Leo Calvin (1908–   ). Political scientist, sociologist, humorist. Born in Poland. Under this name he pursued his career as political scientist and sociologist, and published such books as his study of *Hollywood* (1941) and his *Guide to the Religions of America* (1955). But his sharp intellectual observation also shows in his writings as 'Leonard Q. Ross', author of *The Education of H*y*m*a*n K*a*p*l*a*n* (1937) and *The Return of H*y*m*a*n K*a*p*l*a*n* (1959). Kaplan is a somewhat dissident and confused student in the beginner's grade at the American Night Preparatory School for Adults, where immigrants encounter linguistic and social confusions of various kinds. 'Ross' is an enormously funny writer, and these stories, most of them from the *New Yorker*, are sometimes too readily placed in the tradition of American-Jewish humour. His subject gives him an accurate measure for treating some of the follies of American life with strong satirical and sociological observation. *The Joys of Yiddish* (1968) is 'a lexicon for readers of English'. [MB]

Roth, Henry (1907–   ): Novelist. He left New York City in 1945 and lives in Augusta, Maine, teaching mathematics. His reputation lies solely with *Call It Sleep* (1934), one of the finest novels of the century and one of the few in the thirties to survive ideological fashion, the story of immigrants in New York seen through the eyes of a boy. After its publication, he worked at a new novel, and although Maxwell Perkins believed it was brilliant, Roth destroyed it (a section did appear in *Partisan Review*). It concerned a worker who had lost an arm and become a Communist Party organizer. The reprinting of *Call It Sleep* in England in 1963, with a preface by Walter Allen, revived an excellent reputation and its author's interest in writing. [EM]

A. S. Knowles, 'The Fiction of Henry Roth', *Modern Fiction Studies*, Winter, 1965–6; W. B. Rideout, *The Radical Novel in the United States 1900–1954* (1956).

Roth, Philip (1933–   ). Novelist, story writer. He was born in Newark, New Jersey, educated at Bucknell University and the University of Chicago, and has taught at the latter and the University of Iowa. He is one of the most highly reputed of post-war Jewish writers and a brilliant delineator of Jewish mores and psychology. *Goodbye, Columbus* (1959) contains a novella and 5 stories and won the National Book Award; the stories are wittily distilled vignettes of modern Jewish life, the novella an analysis in depth of wealthy life-styles and the American way of life seen through the glow of a romantic love affair. Roth's capacity to create a dense social texture, explore manners with a witty but saddened perception and probe deeply into psychological problems shows even more sharply in his long novel *Letting Go* (1962). In part an academic novel about depressed graduate students, it spreads into an elaborate complex of relationships in modern American life, without attempting slick moral solutions. *When She was Good* (1967), a further study in urban behaviour and values, is one of the few radical attacks on the American small town to achieve power without cheap sensationalism. *Portnoy's Complaint* (1969) *is* sensational and lacks Roth's previous precision and control, as if the contemporary situation has devastated his moral poise. But it is marvellously funny – an extended variant on classic jokes about the sterilizing Jewish mother, and her masturbatory consequences, turned this time into a less certain if obviously now more anguished and confused myth about the American dream. But it has been a great commercial success and has, paradoxically, enlarged critical interest in this important novelist. [MB]

Rothenberg, Jerome (1931–   ). Poet. He was born in New York City, studied at the City College and the University of Michigan, and after two years in the army has lived in his home city, teaching, writing, translating and founding the Hawk's Well Press and the important magazine *Poems from the Floating World.* In discussion with Robert ⟡ Kelly, Armand Schwerner, Robert ⟡ Bly and other poets, and through studies of Blake, Rimbaud, Neruda, Whitman, modern German poets (see his translations in *New Young German Poets,* 1959) and American Indian texts, he developed the 'deep image' concept of poetry (see 'An Exchange: Deep Images and Modes', with Robert Creeley, in *Kulchur,* 6, 1962, and 'Why Deep Image?', in *Trobar,* 3, 1961, reprinted *Eleventh Finger No. 1,* 1965). His intention was to re-establish forms of visionary poetry for the modern world. His poetry includes *White Sun Black Sun* (1960), *The Seven Hells of Jigoku Zoshi* (1962), *Sightings I–IX* (1964), *The Gorky Poems* (1966), related to the works of the painter Arshile Gorky, *Ritual: A Book of Primitive Rites and Events* (1966), *Between: Poems 1960/63* (1967), *Further Sightings* (1967) and *The Flight of Quetzalcoatl* (1967). He also translated Rolf Hochhuth's *The Deputy* (1964) for the New York stage. Besides being an important poet in his own right, Rothenberg is part of a significant contemporary American effort to understand and incorporate world visionary literature. *Technicians of the Sacred* (1968) is a large and highly important collection of translations of ethnic poetry placed in the context of significant developments in 20th-century arts. [EM]

Rourke, Constance (1885–1941). Cultural historian. Born in Cleveland, Ohio, she taught English at Vassar, and after 1915 lived at Grand Rapids. She was a rare scholar of American literature, folklore and humour, and one of the first to write serious American cultural history with the bias away from formal literature (*The Roots of American Culture,* 1942). *American Humour: A Study of the National Character* (1931) is a standard work and concerns the relationships between Yankee, frontier and Negro humour, popular folklore and its figures, and writers like Henry James and Robert Frost. Her *Davy Crockett* (1934), *Audubon* (1936) and *Charles Sheeler* (1938) are permanent contributions to American studies. *Trumpets of Jubilee* (1927) consists of important pioneering studies of Lyman Beecher, Harriet Beecher ⟡ Stowe, Horace Greeley and P. T. Barnum. [EM]

Rowlandson, Mary (*c.* 1635–*c.* 1678). Born in Lancaster, Massachusetts. Her fame rests entirely on being captured, with her daughter, by Indians in 1675, during King Philip's War, and writing her *Captivity and Restoration* (1682). America's first bestseller by a woman, it records this Massachusetts minister's wife's seven weeks and five days with the native Americans. Although she writes in the facile context of 'God's judgement', she carefully relates the ordeal of 20 'removes' with her captors, the sufferings both she and they underwent, and offers a certain amount of field anthropology. Her courage and endurance come clearly through her simple style and shrewd attitudes. [EM]

Narratives of the Indian Wars, 1675–1699, ed. C. H. Lincoln (1913); *The Oxford Anthology of American Literature,* ed. W. R. Benét and N. H. Pearson (2 vols., 1939).

Rowson, Susanna (1762–1824). Novelist, poet, dramatist. She was born in England and spent much of her varied life in America, where her father, a naval lieutenant, had been based, in Massachusetts. Her first novels – *Victoria* (1786), *The Inquisitor* (1788) and *Mary, or, The Test of Honour* (1789) – were not too successful, nor were her *Poems on Various Subjects* (1788) and *A Trip to Parnassus* (1788). But her fourth, and first American novel, *Charlotte, A Tale of Truth* (1791), made her name; it is a sentimental, didactic tale of a young lady seduced by an English officer and a French governess, told with some realism and much poetic justice, in the English romantic fiction manner. The Rowsons staged her plays in England and America (*Slaves of Algiers,*

1794, *The Female Patriot,* 1795, etc.). But she left the stage and opened a girls' school in Boston (1797), edited a magazine, and wrote three more novels, including the inevitable sequel, *Charlotte's Daughter* (known as *Lucy Temple*) (1828). [E M]

Royce, Josiah (1855–1916). Philosopher. Born in a frontier village of California and educated at the newly founded State university. With the support of interested businessmen, he went to Germany to study philosophy at Leipzig and Göttingen, returning to take a doctorate at Johns Hopkins University in 1878. After four years as instructor in English at California, he went to Harvard, where for the rest of his life he was a leading light in a department of philosophy that included William ◊ James and ◊ Santayana. He was the first American appointed to the Gifford lectureship in Scotland, and his lectures *The World and the Individual* (publ. 1900–1), given at Aberdeen in 1899, proved to be his masterpiece. His interests were manifold. He was a pioneer of mathematical logic; he gave the Lowell lectures in Boston and the Hibbert lectures in Oxford (*The Problem of Christianity,* 1913); his *Philosophy of Loyalty* (1908) sketches a system of ethics; he even wrote an outline of psychology, a novel and a history of California. As a metaphysician he was considered James's superior, but not his equal as a writer. His style is wordy, and the hortatory tone and the archaisms that he sometimes affected do not commend him to current taste.

He was the most eminent of American idealists. He did not begin, as did the British idealists, with sensation, but with an examination of the nature of ideas. He conceived an idea as a purpose, a striving to realize in our experience the character of an object. This he called the internal meaning of the idea. But there was also an external meaning, the reference to something that lay beyond our experience. The advance of knowledge is the gradual approximation of the first to the second. What would experience be like if the one overtook the other? The answer lies in three characteristics of his thought. First, as an idealist, he believed that no matter how far we went we should never find anything but experience; reality *is* experience. Secondly, the real order is an intelligible order, that is one in which everything is necessarily related to everything else in the experience of one all-embracing mind. Thirdly, in this mind there is realized the complete fulfilment of man's strivings for goodness and beauty as well as truth. Finite mind is thus in its essence an attempt to realize an Absolute, which is the object at once of speculative search, of ethical striving and of religious worship. Such an idealism faces many problems, of which two proved particularly serious. Did not individuals lose their distinctness and simply disappear in this all-engulfing Absolute? And if the Absolute is perfect, does not this mean that the vast mass of suffering and injustice in the world must be accepted as part of the Divine goodness? Royce himself was troubled, since he took morality most seriously. As Santayana wrote of him: 'What calm could there be in the double assurance that it was really right that things should be wrong, but that it was really wrong not to strive to right them?' Royce's last days were unhappy, since in the First World War he felt compelled to turn bitterly against the Germany from whose teaching he had drawn his inspiration. [B B]

J. H. Muirhead, *The Platonic Tradition in Anglo-Saxon Philosophy* (1931); G. Santayana, *Character and Opinion in the United States* (1920) (essay on Royce).

Rukeyser, Muriel (1913–   ). Poet. Born and reared in New York City, a youth she writes about poignantly in *The Life of Poetry* (1949), an account of the wide social purposes for poetry and its connexions with science – a sense which permeates her poetry and prose. Her first poems, in *Theory of Flight* (1935), concern researches at the Roosevelt School of the Air, and *U.S.1.* (1938) projects her knowledge of working-class exploitation and her feeling for the thirties. As a young woman she had reported social conflict in America and in Spain; later in life, she developed her power to marshal a man's career through her own sensibility; the result is the magnificent *Willard Gibbs: American Genius* (1942) and the less detailed, more autobiographical *One Life* (1957), a study of Wendell Wilkie. *The Orgy* (1965) is an imaginative recreation of experiences at the Kerry 'Puck Fair'. *Waterlily Fire: Poems 1935–1961* selects from her previous 8 books of poetry; the title poem is a brilliant reflection on the processes of humanly controlled change. She has also translated *Selected Poems of Octavio Paz* (1961) and his long poem 'Sun Stone' (1961). Her most recent poetry, collected in *The Speed of Darkness* (1968), includes 'The Outer Banks', a fine long poem, published separately in 1967. *The Traces of Thomas Hariot* (1970) is a pioneering study of the great Elizabethan. [EM]

Rumaker, Michael (1932–). Story writer. He studied at ▷ Black Mountain College; his stories have appeared in *Black Mountain Review* and *Short Story 2*. His first book of fiction is *The Butterfly* (1962), and his *Gringos and Other Stories* (1967) includes the first-rate 'Exit 3', 'The Desert' and 'The Truck' (also in *Exit 3 and Other Stories*, 1966). [EM]

Runyon, Damon (1884–1946). Humorist, story writer. Born in Kansas, he grew up in Pueblo, Colorado, and had already been writing articles for local newspapers when he enlisted, at 14, for service in the Spanish-American war. He returned to work as a journalist on various Western newspapers, then became a sportswriter for the New York *American* in 1911. During the First World War he was a war correspondent for the Hearst newspapers, and after it was a regular Hearst columnist. His experiences in the world of New York sport fed into his best-known work – his many stories of Broadway characters, actors, petty crooks and athletes, first collected in *Guys and Dolls*, which did not appear until 1932. He had evolved a unique and bizarre style, a mixture of extravagant metaphor and racy slang, to describe intimately his particular world. A creator of types rather than stories, he belongs in the tradition of vernacular comedy exploited by many American writers. Other collections of his stories include *Blue Plate Special* (1934), *Take It Easy* (1938), and *Runyon on Broadway* (1950). Other selected collections are *The Best of Runyon* (1938), *Runyon à la Carte* (1944) and *Runyon First and Last* (1949). *Short Takes* (1946) is an entertaining selection of his newspaper columns. With Howard Linsay (1889–), the Broadway director and actor, he wrote his only play, a farce called *A Slight Case of Murder* (1935).

His work is identified by its distinct social world and its superb exploitation of its vernacular; his striking literary use of this has been called 'Runyonese'. His range is not large, and his stories develop simply, but they have both authenticity and an entertaining and distinctive extravagance. [MG/MB]

Ed Weiner, *The Damon Runyon Story* (1948); Edwin P. Hoyt, *A Gentleman of Broadway* (1964); Jean Wagner, *Runyonese: The Mind and Craft of Damon Runyon* (1965).

S

Salinger, J(erome) D(avid) (1919–). Novelist, short-story writer. Born in New York. After publishing 20 relatively undistinguished short stories, he 'found his subject' with the short novel *The Catcher in the Rye* (1951). In it, the teenage hero, Holden Caulfield, leaves his 'prep school' and spends a week-end in New York City. Salinger's sympathies seem largely with Holden, especially in the sardonic criticisms of the grown-up world of hypocrisy. The book's main theme is Holden's resistance to growing up into the world of 'phoniness' and the betrayal by adults of youthful integrity. The title implies Holden's desire to protect other, younger children from the blight of maturity. The book had enormous popular success, particularly among college students. It was followed by a collection of short stories, *Nine Stories* (1953; British title, *For Esmé, With Love and Squalor*) which encapsulated many of the themes later to be found in Salinger's linked series of works. Some of the characters from the short stories reappear in the longer stories of the fifties and sixties, all concerned with the members of the Glass family of New York, particularly the children of Les and Bessie Glass, a Jewish-Irish theatrical act. All are brilliant, former radio 'stars' on a programme called 'It's a Wise Child'. Seymour, the eldest, and *the* genius, dies in his thirties, a suicide. The problem that this act creates has become increasingly the covert subject of the Glass stories. It has fallen on the second son, 'Buddy' Glass, to explore the life of Seymour and his own relationship to his dead brother. In *Franny and Zooey* (1961), the youngest member of the family, Franny, breaks down in a religious/nervous crisis, and attempts to preserve herself by the obsessive repetition of a 'Jesus prayer' from the inanities of her college life. She is rescued by her brother Zachary (Zooey), who abases himself by citing the authority of his older brothers, whom he holds responsible for his sister's condition, and so ends her obsession. *Raise High the Roofbeam, Carpenters and Seymour: An Introduction* (1963) contains two stories,

narrated by Buddy – the first an account of his attempt to attend Seymour's wedding, the second a general 'essay' on Seymour. Most recently (June 1965), Salinger has added to the canon a letter home from summer camp by Seymour at the age of 7.

In the Glass family, Salinger has created an object of almost Janeite interest for some, while others have found the increasingly elliptical and qualificatory manner of writing and the air of total knowledgeability and of familial mutual appreciation distasteful. There is some justice in thinking that no real conflict or tension exist any more in the saga, since all potential 'evils', including Seymour's suicide, are now entirely welcome as 'magnificent' by whoever narrates the stories. [A G]

Ed. Henry A. Grunwald, *Salinger: A Critical and Personal Portrait* (1962); Frank Kermode, 'Fit Audience', in *Puzzles and Epiphanies* (1962); F. L. Gwynn and J. L. Blotner, *The Fiction of J. D. Salinger* (1958); ed. M. Laser and N. Freeman, *Studies in J. D. Salinger* (1963).

Saltus, Edgar (1855–1921). Novelist and writer. Born in New York City, educated at Columbia and in Germany, he set an influential, atheistic, hedonistic mood with two fashionable studies, *The Philosophy of Disenchantment* (1885) and *The Anatomy of Negation* (1886). It persists through into his novels. A number of these, like *Mr Incoul's Misadventure* (1887), touch on diabolism and sensationalism in exotic New York society settings; he bore marked resemblances to Oscar Wilde, about whom he wrote. Later novels turned to historical settings with erotic undertones, notably *Imperial Purple* (1892) and *The Imperial Orgy* (1920). [M B]

Sandburg, Carl (1878–1967). Poet. The son of Swedish immigrants in Illinois. Leaving school at 13 he took a series of jobs, wandered West, and served in Puerto Rico during the American War, returning to Lombard College for four years. During his newspaper days in Chicago he was encouraged by Harriet ◊ Monroe, through whose *Poetry* magazine his poems first received wide recognition in 1914. His first book was a pamphlet of poems, *In Reckless Ecstasy* (1904). In 1905 he married the photographer Edward Steichen's daughter. From 1910 to 1912 he was secretary to the first socialist mayor of Milwaukee. He first attracted attention with poems in *Poetry* in 1914. In 1916 *Chicago Poems* announced a new voice in poetry of free-verse urban speech rhythms harnessing the people and the tempo of the 20th-century American city. That popular line continued in *Cornhuskers* (1918), *Smoke and Steel* (1920) and, inspired by prairie rather than city, *Slabs of the Sunburnt West* (1922). In *Good Morning, America* (1928) his optimism is darkened by American poverty and distress, but in *The People, Yes* (1936) a rich variety of poetic forms sustains faith in an ideal America, the folk-concept implicit in *The American Songbag* (1927) and *The New American Songbag* (1950), important collections of folk-ballads.

In 1932 he moved to the Michigan lakeside and in 1946 from there to a farm in North Carolina; in later years he paid a visit to his forbears' relations in Sweden. He was a major poet of the mid-West and of urban Populist feelings. His earlier ◊ Imagism was augmented from popular idioms and forms; his range from brief images like 'Fog' to the rhetorical paragraphs of *The People, Yes* is singular and always socially conscious. Scorning the genteel, he was a sentimental and unanalytical socialist, confident in 'the people', conscious of the ephemerality of civilizations (his poems are full of images of decay), and quietist in his melancholy. He records rather than artistically shapes and elaborates his materials; his rhetoric is really a voice whose rhythms create a basic recurrent form. Consequently his verse has been most popular with a general readership rather than the sophisticated and academic. Besides his authoritative imaginative biography of Abraham Lincoln (*The Prairie Years*, 1926, *The War Years*, 1939), he wrote *Steichen the Photographer* (1929), four children's *Rootabaga Stories* collections (1922–30), a novel, *Remembrance Rock* (1948) and an account of his youth, *Always the Young Strangers* (1950). [E M/R W B]

Complete Poems (1950); The Letters, ed. H. Mitgang (1968).
K. W. Detzer, Carl Sandburg: A Study in Personality and Background (1941); William Carlos

Williams, *Selected Essays* (1954); H. W. Wells, *The American Way of Poetry* (1964).

Sanders, Ed (1939–). Poet. Born in Kansas City, Missouri, he went East in 1957 after reading Ginsberg's *Howl* and Pound's *Cantos*, and studied Greek at New York University. His classical and Egyptological interests are a main basis of his poetic vision. He edits *Fuck You/A Magazine of the Arts*, an important journal of poetry, and leads The Fugs, a counter-pop group concerned with anti-war protest, erotic freedom, and the musical setting of lyrics by Blake and Swinburne. Sanders' poetry moves with startling confidence in an area which combines sexual verve and mythological instances: *Poem from Jail* (1963), *Peace Eye* (1965; revised edn 1969), and *The Fugs Song Book* (1968), whose lyrics are attributed to Sanders, Tuli Kupferberg, Ken Weaver, William Blake and God. [E M]

Santayana, George (1863–1952). Philosopher. Born in Spain of Spanish parents, he came to the United States at the age of 8. He studied philosophy at Harvard under William ◊ James and ◊ Royce, and remained there as a teacher for some 25 years. But he never felt at home in America; he was repelled by its Puritanism and its commercialism alike; and he returned to Europe in 1912 to stay. He made his home in Oxford, then in Paris and in Spain; from 1920 on, his time was chiefly spent in Rome, where at the end he was cared for by the sisters in a Catholic convent.

Santayana is the most polished writer among American philosophers. His style deliberately avoids technical terms and prefers literary imprecision to pedantry. He published 2 volumes of poetry, a verse play, 5 commentaries on literature and contemporary culture, a work of fiction, *The Last Puritan* (1935), a 3-volume autobiography, and 18 substantial volumes of philosophy. His most important works are *The Life of Reason* (5 vols., 1905–6) and *The Realms of Being* (4 vols., 1940). *The Life of Reason* is a persuasive statement of naturalism; Santayana described himself as 'a decided materialist – apparently the only one living'. But he was not a behaviorist; consciousness was not for him a form of bodily behaviour, but a by-product of changes in the brain, 'a lyric cry in the midst of business'. His materialism lay in insisting that thought and emotion were produced by matter. Consciousness is the sole seat of value in the world, and the life of reason consists in such control of animal impulses as will lead to peace and satisfaction of mind. Brought up as a Catholic, he held that religious dogma was not fact but poetry, fabricated by the imagination and retained for its consoling power.

In *The Realms of Being*, the masterpiece of his old age, there is a notable shift of emphasis. Though our thoughts are controlled by our brains, their objects are not. And these objects are 'essences', a term that covers every quality and relation that we can be immediately aware of. Perception is the taking of some of these essences to exist in the object before us; if we are fortunate, our perceptions are 'true', although we can never be sure. Santayana is a sceptic who holds that all knowledge rests in the end on 'animal faith'.

In *Egotism in German Philosophy* (1916), he criticized idealism as contributing to German arrogance in the First World War. His main work on politics, *Dominations and Powers* (1950), hardly had a more promising theory to offer. Holding that there was no rational ground for preferring anything to anything else, nor therefore any rational way of settling international conflicts, he spoke scornfully of the United Nations. But his analyses of personal and national character were penetrating. In his *Character and Opinion in the United States* (1920), he etched vivid though rather acid portraits of James and Royce, and in his *Soliloquies in England* (1922), he pays a series of memorable tributes to the English temper. His studies in literature are often useful and perceptive: *Interpretations of Poetry and Religion* (1900) contains essays on Browning and Emerson; *Three Philosophical Poets* (1910) covers Lucretius, Dante and Goethe; and *Winds of Doctrine* (1913) includes pieces on Bertrand Russell and Shelley and 'The Genteel Tradition in American Philosophy'. [BB/EM]

Persons and Places (3 vols., 1944–53) (autobiography); *The Philosophy of Santayana*, ed. P. A. Schilpp (1940); *Selected Critical Writings*, ed. N. Henfrey (2 vols., 1969); *The Genteel Tradition*, ed. D. L. Wilson (1969); *The Birth of Reason and Other Essays*, ed. Daniel Cory (1969).
Ed. James Ballowe, *George Santayana's American: Essays on Literature and Culture* (1967); Daniel Cory, *Santayana: The Later Years* (1963).

Saroyan, William (1908–   ). Playwright, fiction writer. Born in California, he spent his early childhood in an orphanage. He left school at 12 to be a telegraph boy, and drifted from job to job until he became manager of a postal telegraph office in San Francisco. His first stories appeared in 1934, the year of his successful *The Daring Young Man on the Flying Trapeze*. He tells his life in *My Name is Aram* (1940), *Here Comes There Goes You Know Who* (1962), *After Thirty Years* (1962) and *One Day in the Afternoon of the World* (1964) with a boisterous self-assurance which is his main prose style. Novels and stories poured forth from California, his home since 1936. From 1939 to 1941 his main concern was drama; he refused a Pulitzer Prize (as bourgeois patronizing) for *The Time of Your Life* (1939). The Second World War seems to have tempered his exuberance a little in *The Human Comedy* (1942), a novel. His best work since 1945 is *The Assyrian and Other Stories* (1950), his autobiographies (including *Not Dying*, 1966, and *Don't Go But if You Must Say Hello to Everybody*, 1969), and *Boys and Girls Together* (1963), a novel exposing American married love with a surprising savagery. *The Daring Young Man* remains his typical best, stories reminiscent of Chaplin comedies or Joyce's *Dubliners*, with a range of poignant characters, creative sensitives caught in mass society. His stories are packed with America's racial and cultural outsiders, often treated sentimentally, but generally with sympathy and humanity. His plays demonstrate this faith in goodness over evil but without much moral reason, as he admits in the preface to *Don't Go Away Mad* (1949). In *The Time of Your Life* assorted types jostle for life in a San Francisco honkytonk, and *My Heart's in the Highlands* (1939) is a similar series of 'acts' which insist on slightly desperate vitality, dreams and frustrations. The motto of Saroyan is 'live – so that in that good time there shall be no ugliness or death for yourself or for any your life touches' – but his poverty-stricken Californians and outcasts generally hardly have the chance to find out how to. His bitter sentimentalities are not cynical or political in the twenties and thirties manner, but his derelicts and humble men and women struggle in the same Depression with a warmth which is heroic, on a small scale. He is a major writer of weakness and compensatory fantasy in a culture of success. [E M]

Howard R. Floan, *William Saroyan* (1966).

Sarton, May (1912–   ). Novelist, poet. Born in Belgium, she went to the U.S.A. when her father, George Sarton, chemist and historian of science, joined the Harvard faculty. Her poems, generally personal or else highly abstract, include the volumes *Encounter in April* (1937), *The Lion and the Rose* (1948) and *Cloud, Stone, Sun, Vine* (1961). Her novels tend to see through the eyes of sensitive females and be fictions of sensibility. *The Single Hound* (1938) and *The Bridge of Years* (1946) both draw on Belgian experience; but most of her later fiction uses New England settings and relationships; notably her two college novels – *Faithful Are the Wounds* (1955), a striking study of the life and suicide of a politically radical Harvard professor; and *The Small Room* (1961), exploring the life of a woman's college near Cambridge, Massachusetts. *I Knew a Phoenix* (1959) is sketches for an autobiography. [M B]

Schevill, James Erwin (1920–   ). Poet. Born in Berkeley, California, he graduated from Harvard and has worked in journalism and university teaching. An abstract and rhetorical poet who has often written of out-of-the-way subjects with learning and stylishness, he is also capable of very great intensity in dealing with the immediate world. He has spoken of his strong interest in bringing dramatic elements into lyric poetry, and his more recent verse has moved this way. Among his collections are *Tensions* (1947), *The American Fantasies* (1951), *The Right to Greet* (1955) and *Selected Poems, 1945–1959* (1960). He is most conveniently represented in the collection *Private Dooms and Public Destinations: Poems 1945–1962* (1962). *The Stalingrad Elegies* (1964), his best volume, is a sequence based on last letters from Stalingrad. He has also written plays and a biography of Sherwood ◊ Anderson (1951). [M B]

Schjeldahl, Peter (1942–   ). Poet. He was born in North Dakota, educated in Minnesota and New York, and later worked as a newspaper reporter. In 1964 he co-founded *Mother*, a poetry magazine, and has worked as art critic for *Art News* and *Village Voice*. His poetry belongs with that of Ted Berrigan, Ron Padgett and other writers associated with '*C*' *Magazine* Press. But his first book, *White Country* (1968), shows individual talent. [E M]

Schlesinger, Arthur Meier, Jr (1917–   ). Historian. He is both a professional historian and an active political figure within the Democratic Party and his published work has been mainly concerned with issues connected with his political leanings. In 1945 he received a Pulitzer Prize for a study of *The Age of Jackson*, in which he departed from the established interpretation relating the outburst of Jacksonian democracy to the expanding frontier, stressing instead the impact on national politics of the developing urban working class. He is at present engaged on a multi-volume series, *The Age of Roosevelt*, of which three volumes have so far appeared. *The Crisis of the Old Order* (1957) examines the Republican administrations of the 1920s, the onset of the Depression, and the election of Franklin D. Roosevelt in 1933. It is permeated by a faith in democracy; and by a rejection of *laisser-faire* individualism in favour of intervention by the state in the interests of the poorer sections of the community. Though supported by a formidable amount of research, the presentation is emotional and impressionistic: skilfully drawn pen portraits of individuals often take the place of analysis of issues. The early years of the Roosevelt administrations are described in *The Coming of the New Deal* (1959) and in *The Politics of Upheaval* (1960). These impressive volumes, more reserved in their technique, firmly establish Schlesinger as a major historian in the literary tradition. [E M]

Schorer, Mark (1908–   ). Novelist, critic. He was born in Wisconsin, studied at the University of Wisconsin, taught literature at Harvard and is now at the University of California at Berkeley. He is an excellent theoretical critic of the novel – two essays of his, 'Technique as Discovery' and 'Fiction and the "Matrix of Analogy"', are critical classics – and a fine practitioner, in *A House Too Old* (1935), *The Hermit Place* ('941) and *The Wars of Love* (1954). He has also published an important study of Blake (*William Blake: The Politics of*

Vision, 1946) and the key biography of Sinclair ◊ Lewis (*Sinclair Lewis: An American Life*, 1961). [MB]

The World We Imagine (1968) (collected essays).

Schulberg, Budd (1914–   ). Novelist. He was born in New York City but lived for many years in Hollywood, where his father was one of the first screenwriters and later a producer. He himself has written screenplays, including that of *On the Waterfront* (1954), published as the novel *Waterfront* (1955).

His principal works seem directly inspired by the American entertainment industry, and he may be described as a somewhat uneasy anatomist of the Hollywood dream of success. The title of his first novel, *What Makes Sammy Run?* (1941), has now become a conversational cliché in American usage. This terrifying portrait of the rise of Sammy Glick from a New York slum to the unstable heights of Hollywood remains his best work, despite the attempt to universalize Sammy's fortunately unique life into a 'blueprint of a way of life that was paying dividends in America in the first half of the twentieth century'. Neither *The Harder They Fall* (1947) nor *The Disenchanted* (1950) possesses the concentrated force and economy of this first novel. The former is an exposure of the way in which 'the fight game' may be manipulated for profit; *The Disenchanted* offers a thinly veiled portrait of an ageing Scott Fitzgerald, with whom Schulberg once worked on an abortive film script. In both, the ambivalent nature of Schulberg's commitment is reflected in an unsteady narrative focus which tends to evoke an equally blurred response. He has also published a collection of short stories, *Some Faces in the Crowd* (1953). *Sanctuary V* (1970), his most recent novel, describes the conflict between a revolutionary president and a popular hero. In 1965, following the riots in the Watts area of Los Angeles, he set up the Writer's Workshop in order to promote the exploration of the social scene by local talent. Plays, poetry and fiction emerged to fulfil his vision. [HD]

C. E. Eisinger, *Fiction of the Forties* (1963).

Schwartz, Delmore (1913–66). Poet, short-story writer, critic. Born in Brooklyn, N.Y. An important figure in the group of Jewish writers that emerged in American letters around the Second World War. His first volume of stories and poems, *In Dreams Begin Responsibilities* (1938), shows some characteristic features and themes; he speaks of the difficulty of breaking through from the essence of being into the outside world, of the need for joy and celebration. His next work was a translation of Rimbaud's *A Season in Hell* (1939); then followed a verse-play, *Shenandoah* (1941), and a collection of essays, *The Imitation of Life* (1941). In 1943 came *Genesis Book I*, a long poem about the growth of a Jewish boy in New York City, and in 1948 his excellent collection of short stories *The World is a Wedding*, intelligent poetic stories dealing often with the young Jew's pursuit of wealth or intellectual prowess. His later volumes include *Vaudeville for a Princess* (1950) and *Summer Knowledge: New and Selected Poems 1938–58* (1959), poems which continued his free self-revelation and lavish use of the European writers he loved. His last work was *Successful Love and Other Stories* (1961). He taught in a number of universities, lastly at Syracuse. In criticism he is associated with a reaction against 'academic' poetry. [MB]

Marius Bewley, *The Complex Fate* (1952).

Scott, Winfield Townley (1910–   ). Poet. Born in Haverhill, Massachusetts, educated at Brown University, he was for many years literary editor of the *Providence* (Rhode Island) *Journal* until in 1951 he resigned to live in Sante Fé, New Mexico, and write full-time. His poetry inherits the stoic romanticism of poets like Frost and Robinson, and many of its themes are of New England derivation, often using local vernacular. He frequently celebrates the virtues of individualism and solitary perception against the background of a meticulously observed landscape. Though his directness of statement sometimes comes close to folksy wisdom, he can be a very complex poet. Some of the poems (particularly the earlier ones) are comic episodes, often character pieces directly recalling ◊ Robinson or ◊ Sandburg. [MB]

Collected Poems 1937–1962 (1962); *Biography for Traman* (1937); *To Marry Strangers* (1945); *Mr Whittier and Other Poems* (1948); *Change of Weather* (1965); *Exiles and Fabrications* (1961) (essays).

Seidel, Frederick (1936–). Poet. Born in St Louis and educated at Harvard, he works and lives in New York. His first book, *Final Solutions* (1963), won him a reputation as a verse satirist. With ruthless calm, often employing dramatic monologue which leans on a kind of Jacobean ellipsis, he has attacked the largest social and political problems facing America in the sixties. [BP]

Selby, Hubert (1926–). He was born in Brooklyn, went to sea after school, and worked at a number of jobs while writing. His work has appeared in *Black Mountain Review*, *New Directions*, *Kulchur*, etc. His *Last Exit to Brooklyn* (1964) is one of the most searing and carefully written moral exposures of urban violence and degeneracy in American literature. [EM]

Seldes, Gilbert (1893–1970). One of America's first systematic students of the popular arts. He was born in New Jersey and began his career as music critic, foreign correspondent and editor on *Collier's* magazine and the *Dial*. Later he became director of television for C.B.S. His best-known book is *The Seven Lively Arts* (1924, 1957), a study of comic strips, films, vaudeville and other pop entertainment. *The Movies and Talkies* (1929), *The Movies Come from America* (1937), *Your Money or Your Life* (1937) and *The Great Audience* (1937) take up the sociology and technique of films, and *The Future of Drinking* (1930) and *Against Revolution, The Years of the Locust* (1932) are studies of Prohibition and the Depression. *The Public Arts* (1956) is an invaluable work. He also wrote a novel, detective stories (as 'Foster Johns'), radio and TV scripts, and *Writing for Television* (1952). [EM]

Seton, Anya (1916–). Popular novelist. Born in New York City, she is author of several historical novels, most with American settings, some best-sellers. They include *My Theodosia* (1941), about Aaron Burr's daughter; *Dragonwyck* (1944); *The Turquoise* (1946); *Foxfire* (1951); and *Katherine* (1954), which is about Chaucer's sister-in-law. [MB]

Sewall, Samuel (1652–1730). Born in England, he went to New England when he was 9, graduated from Harvard in divinity in 1671, and became a businessman and a judge. The richest man in Massachusetts, he became its chief justice in 1718. His *Diary* records his life (from 1674 to 1729) as a fairly humane secularist with considerable civic sense. As a private document its style is not literary but frank, with a detail which makes it a valuable record of an early American businessman who employed his worldly status, opposed witchcraft executions and slavery. *The Selling of Joseph* (1700) was the first anti-slavery tract printed in America. *Phaenomena quaedam Apocalyptica* (1697), 'a Description of the New Heaven', is an early celebration of American patriotism. [EM]

O. E. Winslow, *Samuel Sewall of Boston* (1964).

Sexton, Anne (1928–). Poet. She was born in Newton, Massachusetts, and after a time in Baltimore and San Francisco has now returned to the Boston area. Her 3 volumes, *To Bedlam and Part Way Back* (1960), *All My Pretty Ones* (1962) and *Live or Die* (1967) have had considerable attention, in England as well as the U.S.A. A student of Robert ◊ Lowell, and indebted to him, she writes poetry of a strongly 'confessional' cast. The occasions are frequently familial and domestic; but out of them she manages to invest many of her poems with a kind of psychological mythology. Her second volume shows a mastery and a purposefulness less evident in the first; and though she is sometimes obvious she is an interesting poet in a rewarding American tradition. [MB]

Shapiro, Karl (1913–). Poet, editor. Born in Baltimore, he made his first poetic reputation through his individual reactions to the crises of the 1940s, and to being a Jewish soldier in the American army (*V-Letter and Other Poems*, 1944). His review of American poetry and a theory of poetry appear in *Essay on Rime* (1945; in verse), *Beyond Criticism* (1953) and especially in the vigorously iconoclastic *In Defense of Ignorance* (1960), a challenge to academicism and 'criticism-poetry', augmented by *To Abolish Children*. He edited *Poetry* (1950–6) and taught at Johns Hopkins and Nebraska Universities. He edits *Prairie Schooner*. The poems in his first book, *Poems* (1935), are archaic in diction and form, but by *Person, Place and Thing* (1942) his style had clarified with his selection of social subjects. *Trial of a Poet*

(1947) defines his religious experience, and *Poems of a Jew* (1958) asserts a special identity; *White-Haired Love* (1968) is a set of erotic love poems. *The Bourgeois Poet* (1964) is a collection of freely associated sections of autobiography, polemics and illusions, designed to maintain relationships with the irrational and disjunctive. [EM]

Poems 1940–1953 (1953); *Selected Poems* (1968).

Shaw, Henry Wheeler. ◊ Billings, Josh.

Shaw, Irwin (1913–   ). Novelist, short-story writer, playwright. Born in Brooklyn, he took various jobs before graduating from Brooklyn College. Later he scripted radio serials and wrote screenplays in Hollywood. A one-act play, *Bury the Dead* (1936), was a macabre and surrealist plea for pacifism; a second, *The Gentle People: A Brooklyn Fable* (1939), a parable warning against the spread of fascist behaviour. Since *Retreat to Pleasure* (1940) and *Sons and Soldiers* (1944) he has turned from drama to fiction. *The Young Lions* (1948) is a long war novel, rather limitingly constructed around three characters – a bitter young Nazi, a New York stage manager, and a sympathetic liberal Jew – through whom Shaw condenses attitudes towards the Second World War. *The Troubled Air* (1951) is an interesting study of the American liberal and his dilemma at that time. He has continued to treat ambitious subjects with *Lucy Crown* (1956) and *Two Weeks in Another Town* (1960), a study of the film industry and its preoccupation with appearance and reality. He is a distinguished short-story writer, publishing *Sailor off the Bremen* (1939), *Act of Faith and Other Stories* (1946), *Mixed Company* (1950), *Tip on a Dead Jockey and Other Stories* (1957) and *Love on a Dark Street* (1965). [MG]

Selected Short Stories (1961).
C. E. Eisinger, *Fiction of the Forties* (1963).

Sherman, Stuart. ◊ New Humanism, The.

Sherwood, Robert (1896–1955). Playwright. Born in New Rochelle, N.Y. He began his career, after Harvard and war service on the Western Front, with an attack on militarism in *The Road to Rome* (1927). He had been drama critic (1919–20) and editor of *Life* (1920–8), and he continued to work in the theatre throughout a busy life elsewhere. During the thirties and forties he was active in trying to convince Americans of the dangers of totalitarianism, and F. D. Roosevelt, many of whose speeches he wrote, made him director of overseas operations in the Office of War Information (see his *Roosevelt and Hopkins: An Intimate History*, 1948). His playwriting eased off during this period, and latterly he wrote mostly for films and television, his most famous scenario being for William Wyler's *The Best Years of Our Lives* (1946). *Acropolis* (1933) excoriated Hitler, and *Idiot's Delight* (1936) is a pacifist set of arguments about the coming war and the decline of the West. *The Petrified Forest* (1935) takes place in an Arizona desert filling-station: a New England writer sacrifices his life to let a girl escape her desert environment. A certain slickness and simplification of motivation haunt Sherwood's work and make it more superficial than his grand themes might suggest. [EM]

John Mason Brown, *The Worlds of Robert E. Sherwood: Mirror to His Times* (1965).

Sigal, Clancy (1926–   ). Novelist, social commentator. Born in Chicago, he studied literature and film-making at the University of California. After army-service he worked as a reporter, then in film and television documentary in Hollywood. Recently he has lived in England and contributed articles on social and film matters to English and American periodicals. His first book, *Weekend in Dinlock* (1960), reportage about a Yorkshire mining village, was much praised for its sharp observations and its strong social sense. His novel *Going Away* (1962) is a detailed study of disillusion with the left and the Unions in America: one of the few major political novels since the Second World War. [MB/EM]

Simms, William Gilmore (1806–70). Novelist, poet, editor. Through his birth and youth in Charleston, South Carolina, he inherited an aristocratic tradition, although he was virtually an orphan and lacked the money to be a Southern gentleman. He resisted his 'discontented and ever-wandering' father's invitation to Mississippi and practised law at home, writing poetry, his early mistaken vocation. In 1832 he moved north to New England and New York and in 1833 published his first novel, *Martin Faber*, a crime story out of Godwin and Brockden ◊ Brown, followed by the first of his famous Southern romances,

Guy Rivers: A Tale of Georgia (1834). During the composition of over 80 books, mostly novels and intelligent without being outstanding, he became the foremost writer in the South. After his second marriage he became a planter, defended the slave-state, was ruined in the Civil War, and was neglected as a writer until the Southern Renaissance after the Second World War. He wrote many romances of the Revolution and the Indian wars, but his best and most celebrated novel is *The Yemassee* (1835), which dramatizes the encroachment of white settlements on the American Indians. Unlike Cooper, Simms shows in realistic detail the community life of the Indians, which he knew at first hand. The vanquishing of the Yemassees is an American tragedy paralleled by the confrontation of Puritan and Cavalier whites, the other major American theme. He produced a series of romance-novels about the Revolution, beginning with *The Partisan* (1835); a series of novels about colonial and 19th-century Southern life; some novels on Spanish history; and a body of short stories. He is deeply indebted to Scott and Cooper and helped to establish the relevance of these writers for Southern literature. He also wrote histories of South Carolina, a *Life of Captain John Smith* (1846), several other biographies, and 18 volumes of poetry. He edited the *Southern and Western Monthly Magazine and Review* and later the *Southern Quarterly Review*, and later still became involved with *Russell's Magazine* – all part of his task of promoting Southern literature. His literary criticism is in *Views and Reviews in American Literature, History and Fiction* (1845). Though much of his output is hack work, Simms is an important cultural figure, influentially active for Southern literature, a friend of Poe and other Southern writers, and helping to build a body of work which develops towards Ellen Glasgow and William Faulkner. [EM/MB]

J. V. Ridgely, *William Gilmore Simms* (1962); Jay B. Hubbell, *The South in American Literature 1607–1900* (1954); W. J. Cash, *The Mind of the South* (1941).

Simpson, Louis (1923–). Poet. Born and educated in Jamaica, a background on which some of his work draws, he then went to Columbia University, New York, and now teaches at the University of California at Berkeley. He is an impressive, inventive and often very witty poet, making close use of personal experience but also exploiting literary allusion and literary elegance. His volumes include *The Arrivistes: Poems 1940–1948* (1949) and *A Dream of Governors* (1959). *At the End of the Open Road* (1963) contains poems which experiment with freer forms. [MB]

Selected Poems (1966).
Richard Howard, *Alone with America* (1969).

Sinclair, Upton (1878–1968). Novelist. Born in Baltimore. While still under 20 he wrote with incredible facility and under a series of pseudonyms more than two million words a year for juvenile pulp fiction. Converted to socialism, he used the profits from his successful protest novel *The Jungle* (1906) to establish Helicon Hall, an experiment in cooperative living which ended in a disastrous fire. In California he was an unsuccessful candidate for the Senate, but his most audacious venture occurred during the Depression when he ran for the governorship of California on the EPIC platform – End Poverty in California. Something of a prophet without honour in his own country, his books – which number over 100 – have sold by the million; over 1,000 translations in over 50 languages have been noted. He told the story of the first 35 years of his life in *American Outpost* (1932) and incorporated this volume in his *Autobiography* (1962).

It is extraordinarily difficult to fit him into any of the established categories. In nearly all his novels the polemicist dominates the artist; even *The Jungle*, a nightmarish account of conditions in Chicago's Packingtown and probably his best single work, is to some extent vitiated by Jurgis's conversion to socialism. This work had been preceded by several novels, of which the best is *Manassas* (1904; revised as *Theirs Be The Guilt,* 1959), the first volume of a projected but never completed trilogy on the Civil War; he followed it with a lengthy series of artistically crude assaults upon the institutions and abuses of a capitalist society, from the operation of Wall Street in *The Money-changers* (1908) to the automobile industry in *The Flivver King* (1937). *King Coal* (1917) exposed the treatment of the striking Colorado miners; *Oil!* (1927), one of the most readable of his novels, skilfully depicts the corruption of the Harding era; *Boston* (1928) is a somewhat ponderous account of the trial and execution of Sacco and Vanzetti. At times he is undoubtedly a brisk and attractive narrator; but persistent socialist bias rarely allows his novels to rise above the

233

ideological treatise. A better medium for his combative talents and ideas on social reform was the vigorous series of polemics which he wrote between 1918 and 1927: *The Profits of Religion* (1918); *The Brass Check* (1919), on the press; *The Goose Step* (1923) and *The Goslings* (1924), on the American educational system; *Mammonart* (1925) and *Money Writes* (1927), on art and literature.

In 1940 he published the first of the 11 novels collectively known as *World's End*. Through his protagonist Lanny Budd, he offered a detailed investigation of the international scene from the beginning of the First World War. Stylistically undistinguished and, like most of his writings, wanting in the humorous and the sexual, frequently naïve and sometimes dull, this immense *roman fleuve* achieved great popularity which, it has been suggested, derived from the mass of information it purveyed in an age of tyrannical fact. At the age of 83, he published a romance, *Affectionately Eve* (1961), whose main interest is the behavioural pattern of small-town Georgia and big-city New York.

The Sinclair papers – over eight tons – now reside at the Lilly Library, Indiana University, and the commemorative catalogue (compiled by Ronald Gottesman) issued to accompany an exhibition in 1963 gives some indication of the range and variety of the extraordinary career of this extraordinary man. [H D]

My Lifetime in Letters (1960).

Floyd Dell, *Upton Sinclair: A Study in Social Protest* (1927); D. M. Chalmers, *The Social and Political Ideas of the Muckrakers* (1965).

Singer, Isaac Bashevis (1904–). Story writer, novelist. Born in Radzymin, Poland, and raised in a poor section of Warsaw. His father and grandfather were rabbis, and he was educated at the Warsaw Rabbinical Seminary. Warsaw at this time was a major centre of religious and cultural Jewish life and had already produced many major Jewish writers when Singer turned to a writing career in preference to the rabbinical. In 1935, anticipating Hitler's invasion of Poland, he emigrated to the U.S.A., and since then has worked as a regular journalist and columnist for the New York Jewish daily paper, the *Forward*, where he has printed fiction over his own name and journalism under the pen-name Warshofsky. Apart from some early work published in Warsaw, nearly all his fiction has been

written in Yiddish for this journal, and usually produced under the strain of regular journalism. It is only recently that it has been translated on any scale and that his merit, and the endurance of his writing, has been recognized by a general audience. His reputation with non-Jewish audiences is now higher than that of any other Yiddish writer.

He writes chiefly about the Yiddish communities of his native Poland, exploring the folk-traditions and a deep-seated communal life of the past. His work is undoubtedly much indebted to his precursors in the Yiddish tradition, such as Aleichem and ♢ Asch, but is much more modern in approach and has undoubtedly been shaped by his experience in America. His themes of witchcraft, mystery and legend draw on traditional sources and traditional life, but they are established in a modern and ironic way. Worked with a deep and humane wisdom and insight, rich in the details of Jewish peasant and town life, they are also concerned with the bizarre and the grotesque, with irrationality and sexuality, and are often structurally convoluted and daring. His first major work, *Satan in Goray*, a short novel about the ferment in a Polish town in the 17th century when a messianic sect takes over, appeared in Yiddish in 1935 (in English, 1955). Among other books now translated are the novels *The Family Moskat* (in English, 1950), about a Warsaw family between 1914 and 1939, *The Magician of Lublin* (1960), *The Slave* (1960), *The Manor* (1967), the first part of a longer work concerning the exodus from their Polish ghetto of Jews after the insurrection of 1863, and *The Estate* (1969). His stories, which probably show him at his very best, are to be found in *Gimpel the Fool* (1957), *The Spinoza of Market Street* (1961), *Short Friday* (1964), and *The Seance and Other Stories* (1968). In 1966, Singer published *In My Father's Court*, a sensitive memoir of his youth in Warsaw. [M B]

Irving Howe 'I. B. Singer', *Encounter*, xxvi, 3 (March 1966); Dan Jacobson, 'The Problem of Isaac Bashevis Singer', *Commentary*, February 1965.

Skinner, Cornelia Otis (1901–). Actress, humorist. She was born in Chicago, and wrote her first play, *Captain Fury*, in 1925. She became famous for her solo shows and her humorous books: *Tiny Garments* (1932), *Excuse It, Please* (1936), *The Ape in Me* (1959), etc. Her best-selling *Our Hearts*

Were Young and Gay (1942), with Emily Kimbrough, describes their European trip. She has also written a biography of Sarah Bernhardt. [EM]

Slaughter, Frank (1908–). Novelist. Born in Washington, D.C. He has written non-fiction works on surgery and psychosomatic medicine, but it is his medical novels that have been best-sellers since *That None Should Die* (1941). They include *Air Surgeon* (1943), *A Touch of Glory* (1945), *The Healer* (1955), *Epidemic* (1961) and *Surgeon's Choice* (1969). [EM]

Smith, Betty (1904–). Novelist. Born in Brooklyn, N.Y. After her early career as an actress she drew on her slum childhood for a best-selling novel, *A Tree Grows in Brooklyn* (1943). *Tomorrow Will Be Better* (1948) and *Maggie-Now* (1958) were only slightly less successful. [EM]

Smith, Elihu Hubbard. ◊ Connecticut Wits.

Smith, (Captain) John (1580?–1631). Soldier of fortune, explorer, chronicler. He was an Elizabethan adventurer before and after becoming governor of Virginia. He had travelled and lived in Poland, Russia, Transylvania and Turkey, returning to England in 1604 and, according to his own account, became one of the original promoters of the Virginia Company. He sailed with the first expedition to Virginia in 1605, helped to found the Jamestown settlement in the following spring, and was elected president of the colony. During important local explorations he established invaluable good relations with the Indians, securing food supplies which enabled the colonists to survive the first winter. His function was to consolidate the Virginia adventure on a business footing and substantiate semimythical geography. He was an enthusiast rather than a factual historian; his *A True Relation of . . . Virginia* (1608) is a business report raised by style to the level of literature, and it includes an account of the founding of Jamestown. He returned to England in 1609, revisiting America in 1614 to explore the coastline up to Maine and to trade for furs with the Indians. His series of maps and topographical accounts were to stimulate colonization, but his intelligent and explorative mind comes through clearly. *A Description of New England* (1616) is a valuable treatise urging the importance of fish and furs as economic bases, arguing that to hunt for gold in the New World was futile. Codfish were unglamorous but a foundation for prosperity (see Charles Olson, *The Maximus Poems*, 1960). His *General History of Virginia, New England, and the Summer Isles* (1624) combines writings by himself and others. Smith helped to create American myths of heroism and endurance, and, through the Indian princess Pocahontas, the romance which tended to hide the exploitation of the Indians. But his stories tend to be more plausible than fictitious, and certainly evoke the spirit of early settlers who were not Puritans. [DKA/EM]

Travels and Works, ed. W. Arber, intr. A. G. Bradley (2 vols., Edinburgh, 1910); *Captain John Smith's America: Selections from His Writings*, ed. J. Lankford (1967).
Bradford Smith, *Captain John Smith* (1953); Philip Barbour, *The Three Worlds of Captain John Smith* (1964).

Smith, Logan Pearsall (1865–1946). Critic, scholar. Born at Millville, New Jersey, he came from a famous Philadelphia Quaker family, and was educated at Harvard and Oxford. Enabled by an annuity to become an expatriate, he settled in England. Like his brother-in-law Bernard ◊ Berenson, he wished to pursue a life of connoisseurship and aestheticism. His writings include a series of books of elegant, witty aphorisms and essays – *Trivia* (1902), *More Trivia* (1921), etc.; and a good deal of biographical, lexicographical and bibliographical work, including a biography of Sir Henry Wootton. He attacked the denigration of Milton by Pound and Eliot in *Milton and His Modern Critics* (1941). *Words and Idioms* (1925) is an excellent collection of articles on language. His autobiography, *Unforgotten Years* (1938), has some fascinating, Anglophile comments on American letters and on the habit of literary expatriation among American writers. [MB]

Smith, William (1727–1803). Scottish clergyman, historian. He went to Long Island as a tutor in 1751. His *A General Idea of the College of Mirania* (1753) impressed ◊ Franklin into helping him become provost of the College of Philadelphia. His pro-British views (*Sermon on the Present Situation of American Affairs*, 1775) and criticism of the Quakers made him suspect and vulnerable, and in 1779 the college's charter was withdrawn. He founded Washington

College, Maryland, but returned to his Philadelphian college and remained until it became the University of Pennsylvania in 1791. The best account of this eminent if irascible teacher is A. F. Gegenheimer's *William Smith: Educator and Churchman* (1943). [EM]

Smith, William Gardner (1926–   ). Novelist. Born in Philadelphia and studied at Temple University. One of the most interesting Negro American writers. His novels include *Last of the Conquerors* (1948), *Anger at Innocence* (1950) and *The Stone Face* (1964). [EM]

Smith, William Jay (1918–   ). Poet. Born in Louisiana, he studied at Washington University, Columbia, and as a Rhodes Scholar at Oxford, and has taught at Wesleyan, Columbia and Williams. A member of the Vermont legislature, he is married to the poet Barbara ◊ Howes. His books include *Poems* (1947), *Celebration at Dark* (1950), *Poems 1947–1957* (1957) and *The Tin Can and Other Poems* (1966). He has written children's books and published translations of Laforgue and Valéry Larbaud. His verse ranges between concise and precise lyrical poems and, more recently, long-line poems of a newly expansive and explorative kind. *The Spectre Hoax* (1961) and *Herrick: Selections* (1969) are books of criticism. [MB]

Snodgrass, W(illiam) D(e Witt) (1926–   ). Poet. Born in Wilkinsburg, Pennsylvania, he won a high reputation on the strength of a single volume, *Heart's Needle*, published in America in 1959 and in England in 1960. It contains a number of poems written over the previous eight years, and the long title-sequence of poems to his daughter. The 'Heart's Needle' sequence shows his best qualities, particularly his power of using very indirectly connected images to link the central events of the poem – the birth of his child during the Korean War and his subsequent loss of contact with her after his divorce – with various social and political events and with the context of a bleak natural world. He studied at Geneva College and the State University of Iowa, and has taught at various American universities, including Cornell and Wayne State. The cosy domesticity and traditional cadences of the original poems in *After Experience:*

Poems and Translations (1968) are somewhat oppressive, but the translations from Rilke and others are excellent. [MB]

Paul Carroll, *The Poem in Its Skin* (1968).

Snyder, Gary (1930–   ). Poet. He was born in San Francisco and grew up in the North-west. He studied Japanese and Chinese at Berkeley and in Japan, took his B.A. in anthropology, and has worked as logger, forester, carpenter and seaman. Since 1956 he has lived mostly in Japan. All these elements of his life are used in his poetry, which can be seen as a series of relationships between western and eastern cultures, machine technology and wild nature in America, the city and the soil, history and contemporary society. His images draw on this wide range of concerns and experience. His diction is economical and pure, his syntax flexible and terse, and his excellent craftsmanship has a freshness and respect for shapeliness rare in modern poetry. His poetry shows the open-air American fused with the scholar of *haiku* and Indian lore. His work is included in *Riprap* (1959; repr. with 'Cold Mountain Poems', 1958, in 1965), *Myths and Texts, Six Sections from Mountains and Rivers Without End* (1965), *A Range of Poems* (1966, which includes the earlier poems and two other sections, 'Miyazawa' and 'The Back Country') and *The Back Country* (1967). *Earth House Hold* (1969) is an important collection of essays and journals. [EM]

David Kherdian, *Gary Snyder: A Biographical Sketch and Descriptive Checklist* (1965).

Sontag, Susan (1933–   ). Novelist, critic. Her first novel, *The Benefactor* (1963), is a semi-surrealistic analysis of inner consciousness. The title of *Death Kit* (1967), her second, refers to a death kit for the white race, which she described in an article as 'the cancer of human history'; the novel itself does not quite satisfy its experimental and symbolistic pretensions. Her influential essays on cultural matters have appeared in *Partisan Review, New York Review of Books,* etc., and show a sharp eye for cultural tendencies and great cleverness of manner; they are collected in *Against Interpretation* (1966). *Trip to Hanoi* (1969) is both reportage and an act of self-discovery. She has also published experimental short stories and *Styles of Radical Will* (1969). [MB]

Sorrentino, Gilbert (1929–). Poet. He was educated at Brooklyn College, founded the magazine *Neon*, and extends W. C. ◊ Williams' and ◊ Creeley's work in *The Darkness Surrounds Us* (1960) and *Black and White* (1964). *The Sky Changes* (1966) is a penetrating autobiographical novel. [EM]

Southern, Terry (1924–). Novelist, short-story writer. Born in Alvarado, Texas, he lives in New York City. His novel *Candy* written in collaboration with Mason Hoffenberg and published in Paris in 1955 under the pseudonym 'Maxwell Kenton', and in America in 1964, is a parody of *Candide* in which a naïve and innocent girl is subjected to an outrageous series of sexual advances in various contexts. The novel is also a parody of pornographic and salacious writing. Like *Candy*, Southern's *Flash and Filigree* (1958) contains parody of contemporary mores in its twin plots of persecuted medical specialist and college-level seduction. *The Magic Christian* (1959) is a short *conte* in which Guy Grand, a 'fabulous' billionaire, sets out to prove that everyone has his price and will perform any exploit, however scatological or malodorous, if you have the money to pay for it. Southern also collaborated on the film script of *Dr Strangelove: or, How I learned to Stop Worrying and Love the Bomb*. *Red Dirt Marijuana and Other Tastes* (1967) is a collection of short stories in excellent bad taste. [AG]

Arnold Goldman, 'What's New in American Fiction', *Views Quarterly* (Spring, 1965).

Spencer, Elizabeth (1921–). Novelist. Most of her fiction is set in Mississippi, where she was born. At Vanderbilt University, Nashville, she came under the influence of Donald Davidson, once a leading member of the ◊ Fugitive group, who helped her to publish her first novel, *Fire in the Morning* (1948). This and its successor, *This Crooked Way* (1952), show the influence of established Southern writers such as Eudora ◊ Welty and Carson ◊ McCullers. *The Voice at the Back Door* (1956) is an economically written novel about the problem of justice in the South. *The Light in the Piazza* (1960) is a short novel about an American woman and her mentally retarded daughter travelling in Italy. *Knights and Dragons* (1965) is an ambitious novel of blocked sensibilities, set in Rome. *No Place*

for an Angel (1967) describes a pair of American marriages, and succumbs to self-conscious time-effects. *Ship Island* (1968) is a collection of neat stories. [AH/EM]

Spicer, Jack (1925–65). Poet. Born in California, where he lived and worked most of his life, his work as research linguist is strongly felt in his poetry, which is a highly complex but humane series of exploits with language. In *After Lorca* (1957) he says 'a poet is a time mechanic not an embalmer': the translations, poems and letters construct a witty commentary on the Spanish poet. *Billy the Kid* (1959) is a long poem on this Western myth; *The Head of the Town up to the Aether* (1962) is a set of poems and commentaries of considerable wit and formal experiment; *Language* (1965) and *Book of Magazine Verse* (1966) develop Spicer's complex sense of his particular society and extend his poetics. His other volumes include: *Lament for the Makers* (1962), *The Holy Grail* (1964), *Vancouver Lectures* 1966) and *A Book of Music* (1969). [EM]

Spillane, Mickey (Frank Morrison Spillane) (1918–). Detective-story writer. The exponent of a debased form of the 'hard-boiled' school of crime fiction and the creator of Mike Hammer, the private detective who appears in a series of novels which offer a best-selling mixture of sex and sadism. Hammer's relationship with his secretary Velda may be said to invoke the principle of procrastinated rape. Spillane's works include *I, The Jury* (1947), *Vengeance Is Mine* (1950), *The Long Wait* (1951), *Kiss Me, Deadly* (1952) and, more recently, *The Deep* (1961), *The Girl Hunters* (1962) and *The Snake* (1964). With *The Twisted Thing* (1966) it has become clear that Spillane's formula is an accurate myth of American violence. [HD]

Stafford, Jean (1915–). Novelist, story writer. Born in California, she studied at the University of Colorado and in Germany. She was married to Robert ◊ Lowell and later to A. J. Leibling, and has lived in various parts of the U.S.A. A delicate, highly accomplished writer, she has won high regard for her fiction – a fiction of sensibility and texture that frequently turns to the study of the growth of maturity and insight. Her novels include *Boston Adventure* (1944), dealing with a girl of cosmopolitan background who works as a private secre-

tary to a woman in Boston; *The Mountain
Lion* (1947), which treats the experience of
two children living on a Colorado ranch;
and *The Catherine Wheel* (1951). She is
probably best known, however, as a short-
story writer, for her two collections *Children
Are Bored on Sunday* (1953) and *Bad
Characters* (1964), both remarkable ventures in a form well suited to her talent and
sensibility. Her non-fiction book on Lee
Harvey Oswald's mother, *A Mother in
History* (1966), captures a terrifying personality. [MB]

Collected Stories (1969).
C. E. Eisinger, *Fiction of the Forties* (1965).

Stafford, William (1914–   ). Poet. A
native of Kansas, educated at the Universities of Kansas, Wisconsin and Iowa. He
now teaches at Lewis and Clark College in
Oregon, and a good deal of his poetry –
collected in *West of Your City* (1960),
Travelling through the Dark (1962) and *The
Rescued Year* (1966) – is set in the un-
cluttered Western and West Coast landscape. A lucid but not a simple poet,
establishing his themes coolly and with
detachment, he often draws for his subject matter on the contrast between modern
mechanical civilization and more natural
and primitive cultures, between the turns
and ambiguities of our minds today and a
more direct apprehension of things. [MB]

Five American Poets, ed. Thom Gunn and Ted
Hughes (1963).

Stallings, Laurence (1894–   ). Novelist,
dramatist. Born in Georgia. His active early
life is told in his novel *Plumes* (1924). His
war experience went into his plays in collaboration with Maxwell ◊ Anderson, *What
Price Glory?* (1924), *First Flight* (1925; on
Andrew Jackson's youth), and *The Buccaneer* (1925; on Sir Henry Morgan). His
photographic record *The First World War*
(1933) was a best-seller, and he subsequently
wrote many scenarios and librettos, none of
them as popular as his early writings. His
Deep River (1926) was one of the first works
to use jazz in opera. His most famous film
was *The Big Parade* (1925), and in 1963 he
wrote *The Doughboys*, a first-rate account
of the American Expeditionary Force,
1917–18. [EM]

Starbuck, George (1931–   ). Poet. Born
in Columbus, Ohio, and studied at the
University of Chicago and at Harvard. His

stay in the Boston area produced some of
his best poems, which form a part of his
volume *Bone Thoughts* (1960). A poet of
striking versatility and range of interests, he
offers poems of a mordant whimsicality
along with fables, odes, personal confessions, and celebrations and satires of places
and their human populations. There is a
macabre strain to his work; he presents with
stylish vernacular effects the cruelty and
violence he finds in the modern world. His
most recent work is in *White Paper* (1966).
[MB]

Steffens, (Joseph) Lincoln (1866–1936).
Journalist. He was born in San Francisco
and became an important newspaper man
in New York, after a restless youth and
studying abroad. He is associated with what
President Theodore ◊ Roosevelt, in 1906,
termed the 'muckraking' movement, journalists who were trying to expose the widespread corruption of American public life.
He contributed a great deal to this cause
through his editorship of *McClure's* magazine (1902–6) and associate editorship of
the *American Magazine* (1906–11). His influence was the more considerable, coming
at a time when the reformist progressive
movement was increasing political strength.
His *McClure's* articles analysing civic
government in six major cities formed the
basis of *The Shame of the Cities* (1904).
There followed *The Struggle for Self-
Government* (1906), *Upbuilders* (1909) and
Out of Muck (1913). His rambling and readable *Autobiography* (1931) demonstrates his
political radicalism as well as his interest in
social reform. His articles were collected
posthumously in *Lincoln Steffens Talking*
(1936), and his *Letters* in 1938. [HD]

The World of Lincoln Steffens, ed. Ella Winter and
Herbert Shapiro (1962).
Ella Winter, *And Not To Yield* (1963).

Stegner, Wallace (1909–   ). Novelist,
short-story writer, journalist. He was born
in Iowa, and studied at Iowa and California
Universities. He has been a university
teacher, partly as a director of the creative
writing centre at Stanford. His writing
draws on wide first-hand and historical
knowledge of the West. His distinguished
novels of rural America include *Remembering Laughter* (1937), set on an Iowa farm,
On a Darkling Plain (1940), about Saskat-
chewan during the 1918 influenza epidemic,
The Big Rock Candy Mountain (1943), a

family's search for opportunity through the Western frontierlands, *The Preacher and the Slave* (1950), about Joe Hill the labour leader, and *A Shooting Star* (1961), about wealthy Californians. His finest novel is *Wolf Willow* (1962), which besides being a classic of survival by adaptation is an analysis of the last frontier of the Great Plains and contains much autobiographical material. *All the Little Things* (1967) concerns the search for paradise gardens on the West Coast by a retired editor, a hippy and a university ethnologist. All his fiction is factually detailed, packed with characters and richly planned and written. His short stories are included in *Women on the Wall* (1950) and *City of the Living* (1956). Stegner is at least as famous for his non-fiction: *One Nation* (1945), a polemical survey of national and religious tension, *The Central Northwest* (1947), *The Gathering of Zion* (1964), a fascinating study of the Mormon treks, and *The Writer's Art* (1950). *Beyond the Hundredth Meridian* (1954) is a fine biography of John Wesley Powell, the explorer and nature conservationist, and an important study of the non-mythical west. Essays, letters and memoirs are collected in *The Sound of Mountain Water* (1969). [EM/MB]

Stein, Gertrude (1874–1946). Novelist, poet. Born in Allegheny, Pennsylvania, she was educated at Harvard's Radcliffe College (for women) and Johns Hopkins University in Baltimore. Psychology and medicine were then her primary interests, and at Harvard she had come under the influence of William ◊ James. In 1903 she moved abroad where, except for a short visit, she remained for the rest of her life, making Paris her 'home town'. She championed various young painters, most notably Picasso, Braque and Juán Gris, all then unknown, and her salon at 27 rue de Fleurus, where she hung her *inaccrochables*, became famous. Expatriate and visiting American writers like Sherwood Anderson and Scott Fitzgerald always sought her out (◊ Expatriates, Lost Generation). Her relationship with Ernest Hemingway, who helped type the vast manuscript of her novel *The Making of Americans* (1925, but written almost 20 years before), is legendary: she came to think his vaunted courage a sham; in his posthumously published *A Moveable Feast*, Gertrude Stein's relation with Alice B. Toklas, her female companion who died in

1967, is impugned. Nevertheless, her experiments in prose – originating perhaps in her Harvard project on automatic writing – particularly in the simplification of syntax, influenced Hemingway and others. These experiments may be seen in various stages of development in *Three Lives* (1909), *Tender Buttons* (1914) and *Geography and Plays* (1922). These books gave her a reputation for extreme unintelligibility, and she became in the eyes of many the leader of the *avant garde* in American writing. Her syntactical manipulations perhaps blinded her first readers to the homespun quality of her feelings about place and country – she was perhaps the only modernist who was always 'patriotic' – and for all her interest in subconscious processes her analysis of motive is hardly Freudian. The really radical departure in her stylistic experimentation was her attempt to develop a 'cubist' literature, a prose independent of meaningful associations, relying merely on sound-orchestration. Why she felt that 'meaning' had to be abandoned to create a multi-dimensional art remains something of a mystery, and there is no doubt that many who find pleasure in her work do so against her express intention, by enjoying the meaning they can piece out. *The Making of Americans* is her most assuming work, an attempt to write a *total* history of America by reporting in infinite detail and repetition the history of the Hersland family; the work runs to over 900 pages. In 1933 she wrote an autobiographical fragment of her Paris life, entitling it *The Autobiography of Alice B. Toklas*. While influenced by her other experiments, *The Autobiography* is not itself experimental and gained for her a wider readership. This book, combined with her lecture tour of America in 1934 – out of which came her *Lectures in America* (1935) (*Everybody's Autobiography*, 1938, deals with this period of her life) – and her 'mothering' of American G.I.s in the Second World War, brought her into public prominence. Her writing took a turn for the lucid, and her naïve posture – which many had thought drollery – combined with a new lucidity made her a lost leader in the eyes of many more determinedly aesthetic intellectuals. In this last period, she enjoyed herself as never before, and this is clear in *Paris France* (1940) and *Wars I Have Seen* (1945). Her lifelong appreciation of painting is demonstrated in many essays and particularly in *Picasso* (1939). The two best introductory collections of her writings are Carl

Van Vechten's *Selected Writings of Gertrude Stein* (1946; intr. F. W. Dupee 1962) and Patricia Meyerowitz's *Gertrude Stein: Writing and Lectures 1911-1945* (1967). [A G]

The Yale Edition of the Unpublished Writings (8 vols., 1951 ff.).
Donald Sutherland, *Gertrude Stein: A Biography of her Work* (1951); J. M. Brinnin, *The Third Rose: Gertrude Stein and Her World* (1959); Allegra Stewart, *Gertrude Stein and the Present* (1967); B. L. Reid, *Art by Subtraction: A Dissenting Opinion of Gertrude Stein* (1958); Alice B. Toklas, *What Is Remembered* (1963).

Steinbeck, John (1902–68). Novelist, short-story writer. Born in California, he attended Stanford University, studying marine biology without taking a degree. After a series of labouring jobs, he began writing. Most of his best work is related to the California either of his childhood or of the 1930s, when the social and economic conflicts inherent in the earlier period erupted. Born into a society in flux, he has turned usually to proletarian subjects and made a major theme of the search for values in the face of increasing dehumanization. The objectivity of this search has drawn attack from all sides; by dealing with the unfortunate, and showing how food was allowed to rot while men starved (*In Dubious Battle*, 1936, *The Grapes of Wrath*, 1939), he won the hostility of the haves, while his view that human happiness was not of necessity linked with the competitive life but could reside in idyllic poverty (*Tortilla Flat*, 1935) was attacked by the militant left. Though he wrote extensively about labour troubles, and even developed a theory of group man, both his life-long interest in biological observation and his deep romanticism make him at once too objective and too lyric for a simple political classification. Even *In Dubious Battle*, entirely devoted to the story of a strike of migratory fruit-pickers in California, is primarily concerned with creating actuality, and engages us with the strikers on humane, not doctrinaire, ground. Even more famous in this respect is *The Grapes of Wrath*, a landmark in American culture; the epic migration of the Joad family from Oklahoma to California, hunting work, is seen as a remarkable human endeavour, as meaningful and moving as any of the earlier westward migrations. He uses the same kind of language to re-create this crossing as he does in 'The Leader of the People' to describe a wagon-train crossing: 'Every man wanted something for himself, but the big beast that was all of them wanted only westering.' The book is simultaneously realistic and lyrical, gaining its scope by a technique of interposed chapters of commentary.

He is often a novelist of large ambitions; *Tortilla Flat*, about the happy lower depths of Monterey society, attempts a whimsically heroic dimension by bringing in Arthurian overtones. Fortunately, here as elsewhere, the book can be read without too much attention to its over-elaborate intellectual framework, and it is, with the two books already mentioned, among his best work. *Of Mice and Men* (1937), about a simpleton farmhand, has not stood up, but *The Pastures of Heaven* (1932) – best read not as a novel but as a collection of loosely related stories – and *The Long Valley* (1938) have. The latter work includes the four magnificent 'Red Pony' stories, and could serve as an admirable introduction to Steinbeck, showing his characteristic interests – the tensions of town and country, of past and present, of labour and ownership, as well as the objectivity of biological observation and a sort of Lawrencean mystic concept of personal power.

The later books are less impressive. *Cannery Row* (1945) returns to the mood and locale of *Tortilla Flat*, but the tone is less consistent, often more sentimental (though some scenes, notably the celebrated frog hunt, stand out). *The Wayward Bus* (1947), *The Pearl* (1947), *Sweet Thursday* (1954; a sequel to *Cannery Row*) and *The Short Reign of Pippin IV* (1957), a political satire, are all professional but minor works which do not recapture his earlier strength. The most ambitious post-war novel is *East of Eden* (1952), a parable of the fall of man, of Cain and Abel, and of human possibility, showing many of the virtues of his best books, but touched with sentimentality, melodrama and intrusive commentary. *The Winter of Our Discontent* (1961) partly renews his ability to write topical social fiction – the scene has shifted from California to Long Island. The best of his non-fiction works is *Sea of Cortez* (1941, with Edward F. Ricketts) and *The Log of the Sea of Cortez* (1951); and of his three books from the Second World War, *Once There Was a War* (1958) selects well from his war-correspondent articles. The play and film of his novel of the Nazis in Scandinavia, *The Moon is Down* (1942), were popularly successful, and recently his rediscovery of America, *Travels with Charley* (1962), was a best-seller. In 1966 he wrote the text for a book of photographs, *America and Americans*, a further stage in his idiosyncratic search for a usable native land. His mixed career won the Nobel Prize in 1962. [D C]

Warren French, *John Steinbeck* (1961); F. W. Watt, *Steinbeck* (1962); Peter Lisca, *The Wide World of John Steinbeck* (1958).

Stern, Richard (1928–). Novelist, short-story writer. He was born in New York City, and studied at the Universities of North Carolina, Harvard and Iowa. He is Professor of English in the Department of General Studies in the Humanities at Chicago. *Golk* (1960), his first novel, is a satire on television through the career of a megalomaniac TV producer and his willingly duped assistants and audiences. *Europe or Up and Down with Baggish and Schreiber* (1961) describes the adventure of two Americans exploring Europe immediately after the last war. Then followed *In Any Case* (1963), a rather overwritten work, and *Teeth, Dying and Other Matters* (1964), which combined a collection of short stories, an essay on politics and a play, 'The Gamesman's Island'. *Stitch* (1965) concerns an advertising copy-writer who gives up his Chicago life and takes his family to Venice, unsuccessfully searching for answers to his perennial human problems. But the centre of the book is an American sculptor and his masterpiece, a stone garden, and Nina, a young poet, with Poundian ambitions. Stern has also edited an interesting anthology called *Honey and Wax: The Powers and Pleasures of Narrative* (1966). [E M]

Stevens, Wallace (1879–1955). Poet. Born in Reading, Pennsylvania. Now critically regarded as one of the greatest 20th-century American poets, he was an executive of a Hartford, Connecticut, insurance company, writing verse in his spare time. One of the experimental generation in modern poetry that appeared between 1910 and 1920, printing his verse in various little magazines, including *Poetry*, he published his first volume, *Harmonium*, in 1923. The volumes that followed – *Ideas of Order* (1935), *Owl's Clover* (1936), *The Man with the Blue Guitar* (1937), *Parts of a World* (1942), *Notes toward a Supreme Fiction* (1942), *Esthétique du Mal* (1945) and *The Auroras of Autumn* (1950) – show a continuous development in poetic thought and method. His chief concern as a poet – and as an aesthetician – has been with the central issue of post-romantic verse: the problem of how we perceive reality creatively in a universe in which God cannot be assumed to be pantheistically present. In a sense, he is the poet as philosopher, and his poems consistently deal with the way in which things outside the self resist meaningful definition, and how poetry and imagination, 'the supreme fiction', are primary and truthful instruments of comprehension – are, in fact, the highest way of knowing. Many of his poems deal, then, with the actual poetic act itself, and in this sense he is a modern romantic. Other poems demonstrate how the loss of Christian faith actually elevates poetry, affording the poet and indeed the ordinary man the clarity of the unencumbered imagination. Yet reality, particularly in a post-Christian universe, constantly changes; and it is the truthfulness and accuracy with which he pursues truthful accounting and truthful speculation – his basic themes throughout an extensive and continued body of work – that make him so major a poet.

His early reputation was as a dandy of poetry; much of his verse, particularly his early verse, was witty, balletic and comic in diction. He is well known for his use of recondite words; and his highly mannered style is the basis of the attraction he first exerts on his readers. But even the lightest and gayest and most colourful of his verse is consistent with his general line of speculation. To Coleridge, whom speculatively he resembles, such verse would show the operation of 'fancy', but, in a universe without basic revelatory symbols, fancy becomes important as a mode of creativity; the poet by loving the world enriches it. Stevens is concerned with the discovery of the universals operative in the world; but impressionism – and he *is* an impressionist – becomes very much more important to him than to the romantics. Yet reading through the body of his poetry, one finds a core of repeated, fundamental imagery – the imagery of the seasons, standing for different modes of imagining, different relations between perceiver and perceived; the imagery of colours; the images of harmony – central to the continued speculation. In his later poems, the ones usually preferred by his most dedicated followers, the gay enrichment of the world is less evident. These poems are much sparer than the early ones, and closer, in a sense, to the ideal relationship between the poet and his reality. But there are no conditions (and this point is essential to his aesthetics) in which the perfect relationship is fully attainable, because of the mutability of the world, and of the imagination. What he can propose is that there is an idea of order, a contained set of conditions (like the cycle of the seasons, which is a pattern of *predictable* change), within which the modern poet can work.

The problems of modern poetry make him a central figure of modern aesthetics. His essays, *The Necessary Angel* (1951), contain his prose speculations about the imagination, and make quite evident his relation to Coleridge and the romantics. His poetry is collected in two volumes, *Collected Poems* (1954) and *Opus Posthumous* (1957), which together with *The Necessary Angel* provide the body of his work. The *Letters of Wallace Stevens* (1967) is essential, but still leaves about 2,000 letters unpublished. [MB]

Frank Kermode, *Wallace Stevens* (1960); Robert Buttel, *Wallace Stevens: The Making of 'Harmonium'* (1967); John J. Enck, *Wallace Stevens: Images and Judgements* (1964); ed. R. H. Pearce and J. H. Miller, *The Act of Mind: Essays on the Poetry of Wallace Stevens* (1965).

Stewart, Donald Ogden (1894–   ). Humorist, dramatist. He began his career as an actor and then in the 1920s won a reputation as a humorist with books like *A Parody Outline of History* (1921) and *Mr and Mrs Haddock Abroad* (1924). In the 1930s and early 1940s he was one of the many interesting figures in the Hollywood movie colony, where he wrote a number of film scripts. His plays for Broadway included *How I Wonder* (1947). He now lives in London. [MB]

Stickney, Trumbull (1874–1904). Poet. Brought from Switzerland to America when he was 5, he was educated by his father well enough to enter Harvard. After graduation in 1895 he returned to Europe and became one of the first Americans to receive the *doctorat de lettres* from the Sorbonne. He taught at Harvard until his early death from a brain tumour. As poet he is associated with the neo-classicism of William Vaughn ◊ Moody. His *Prometheus Pyphoros* (1900) presents the Greek hero as hero of scientific progress in dramatic scenes influenced by his friend Henry ◊ Adams. His collected poems (1905) was issued by his friends posthumously. [EM]

Ed. James Reeves and S. Haldane, *Homage to Trumbull Stickney* (1968).

Stone, Irving (1903–   ). Novelist. Born in California, he studied at the University of California. Though he began his literary career by writing plays, he is best known as the author of a number of fictionalized biographies, the method of which is to present well-researched factual material while dramatizing – often very romantically – the thoughts and conversations of the characters. *Lust for Life* (1934) deals with Van Gogh; *The Agony and the Ecstasy* (1961) with Michelangelo. *Adversary in the House* (1947) takes as its subject Eugene V. Debs, the American labour leader, and *The Passionate Journey* (1949) John Noble, an American painter expatriate in Paris. *False Witness* (1940) explores the discord that breaks out in an idealistic California community in 1903. He has also written biographies of Jack London and Earl Warren. [MB]

Stout, Rex (1886–   ). Detective-story writer. Born in Noblesville, Indiana. He published several 'straight' novels before turning at 48 to detective fiction. Since *Fer-de-Lance* (1934) his massive private investigator, Nero Wolfe, has dominated a large number of novels and stories. A verbally and gastronomically fastidious man who delights in growing orchids, Wolfe rarely ventures out of his New York house; the essential facts in his cases are gathered by his assistant Archie Goodwin. Stout's more recent publications include *Champagne for One* (1958), *Too Many Clients* (1960), *Gambit* (1962) and *A Right to Die* (1964). In *The Doorbell Rang* (1965), his twenty-second Nero Wolfe novel, the hero traps the F.B.I. to the point when J. Edgar Hoover himself comes to the rescue. A profile of Stout by Alva Johnston appeared in the *New Yorker*, 16 and 23 July 1949. [HD]

W. S. Baring-Gould, *Nero Wolfe of West Thirty-Fifth Street* (1969).

Stowe, Harriet Beecher (1811–96). Novelist. She was born in Litchfield, Connecticut, daughter of a famous orthodox Calvinist minister and sister of five brothers who became ministers. Although educated at private schools and her sister's female academy, where she taught later, she also read the *Arabian Nights*, Scott's novels and Lord Byron, as well as Cotton ◊ Mather.

In 1832 the family dutifully took religion and culture to the mid-Western frontier town of Cincinnati, where Harriet learned about slavery and the 'Underground Railway' at first hand. In 1836 she married a teacher at her father's theological seminary and in 1850 returned east with him to Maine (where he was professor at Bowdoin College) with her seventh child. Up to 1852 her writings were religious, didactic or textbookish, but these and her temperance tales were at least practice for her masterpiece, *Uncle Tom's Cabin*, immediately inspired by the Fugitive Slave Law of 1850 and by a vision of Uncle Tom's death during a communion service in 1851. With the steady income due to his wife's celebrity, Calvin Stowe left Bowdoin, and the family went to live at Hartford, Connecticut, near Mark Twain; Harriet bought a plantation in Florida. One of her sons drowned in 1857, another became an ex-army drunkard, her twin daughters were old maids and another daughter a morphine addict. But Mrs Stowe managed to find time, in 1869, to defend Lady Byron, whom she had met in England, by charging the poet with incest.

Uncle Tom's Cabin was serialized in the *National Era* (1851–2) and in book form (1852) 300,000 copies were sold in six months and it became an international best-seller. It is not the simple sentimental tract it is often held to be but a powerful analysis of every aspect of racialism, including a good understanding of the sexuality of slavery and a fair range of Yankee and Southern slaveholders. Mrs Stowe knew exactly how slavery degenerates, even if her death of Little Eva is sentimental and her integratable Negro rather crude. Her book undoubtedly contributed to national resistances to slavery which led to the Civil War, as Lincoln himself recognized. Translated into every European language, it caused Russian and Siamese masters to liberate their slaves and Scotland to raise a penny 'emancipation fund'. In *A Key to Uncle Tom's Cabin* (1853) Mrs Stowe documented her materials, and in 1856 she again tackled the problem in *Dred: A Tale of the Great Dismal Swamp*. Her later fiction concerns New England life, for example *The Minister's Wooing* (1859), *The Pearl of Orr's Island* (1862) and, the best, *Oldtown Folks* (1869). [EM]

Edmund Wilson, *Patriotic Gore* (1962); Constance Rourke, *Trumpets of Jubilee* (1927); E. Wagenknecht, *Harriet Beecher Stowe: The Known and Unknown* (1965).

Strachey, William (fl.1609–18). Born in England, he was appointed secretary of the Jamestown colony (until 1611), but is otherwise known only through his writings. He wrote *History of Travel into Virginia Britannia* (printed 1849) and edited, and partly compiled, *For the Colony in Virginia: Laws Divine, Moral and Martial* (1612). *A True Repertory of the Wracks and Redemption of Sir Thomas Gates* tells of his experiences in *Sea Venture*, the flagship of a 1609 Virginia expedition wrecked in the Bermudas. After a pleasant nine months in the islands the 150 colonists sailed for Jamestown in two pinnaces built from the wreckage. Strachey's account is included in Samuel Purchas's *Hakluytus Posthumus, or, Purchas His Pilgrims* (1625). G. M. Gayley's *Shakespeare and the Founders of Liberty in America* (1917) discusses parallels with *The Tempest*. [EM]

C. R. Sanders, *The Strachey Family: Their Writings and Literary Associations* (1953).

Stribling, T(homas) S(igismund) (1881–). Novelist. From Tennessee. He has written a series of good tales of the South. *These Bars of Flesh* (1938), for example, attacks progressive education and New York trades unions, and *Teeftallow* (1926) was dramatized as *Rope* (1928). [EM]

Sturgeon, Theodore (Edward Hamilton Waldo) (1918–). Science-fiction writer. He began writing after a variety of occupations, including service as a merchant seaman. His works include *The Dreaming Jewels* (1950), *More Than Human* (1953), *E Pluribus Unicorn* (1953), *A Way Home* (a selection of stories edited by G. Conklin, 1955), *A Touch of Strange* (1958) and *Cosmic Rape* (1968). His best-known work is *More Than Human*, an account of the evolution of a group of disparate individuals into an entity which Sturgeon terms *Homo Gestalt*. [HD]

Sturgis, Howard Overing (1855–1920). Novelist. Born in London, he was the youngest son of an expatriate Boston banker, the half-brother of Julian Sturgis, a prolific Victorian novelist, and a cousin of George ♢ Santayana (whose Mario in *The Last Puritan* is said to have been based in part on Sturgis). Queen's Acre, the house near Windsor Great Park which

Sturgis occupied in 1889, for many years attracted a large number of British and American friends, among them Edith Wharton and Henry James, and was an important expatriate centre.

Sturgis never completely fulfilled the literary promise he was thought to possess. *Tim,* published anonymously in 1891, was aptly called by E. M. Forster 'an Etonian meditation'; *All That Was Possible* (1895) is a pallid account of a frustrated love affair. Both are concerned with the characteristically Jamesian theme of the conflict between the demands of the individual and those of society, a subject that achieves its best and fullest expression in *Belchamber* (1904). Though James dismissed the passive central figure as a 'poor rat', this novel remains a moving analysis of the plight of the suffering, sensitive individual in a corrupt and philistine society. *Belchamber* reveals a detailed knowledge of the habits and behaviour of the English upper classes; indeed, the degree of social criticism and sexual frankness alienated some friends and more readers. [HD]

Edith Wharton, *A Backward Glance* (1934); E. M. Forster, 'Howard Overing Sturgis', in *Abinger Harvest* (1936); Elmer Borklund, 'Howard Sturgis, Henry James, and *Belchamber*', *Modern Philology*, LVIII (May 1961).

Styron, William (1925–). Novelist. Born in Newport News, Virginia, he graduated at Duke University, North Carolina after military service as a Marine lieutenant, and attended Hiram Haydn's writing class at the New School for Social Research, where he began *Lie Down in Darkness* (1951), a massive novel about the disintegration of a Southern family with conscious overtones of Greek tragedy. It begins with analysis of the chaotic lives of Milton and Helen Loftis, the suicide of whose daughter, Peyton, focuses the family's tragedy and is seen as a consequence of that same loss of traditional Southern values of family order and stability by which her parents' weakness is defined. Styron's prose is rich, often rhetorical, sometimes extravagantly so.

The Long March (1952) is, in contrast, short, economically written, restricted in scope, raising issues rather than exploring them. An exhausting Marines route march provides the occasion for a breakdown of liberal ideals when confronted with military

values. *Set This House on Fire* (1960) partly returns to the broad scope and abundant prose of his first novel. It is a story of American expatriates in Italy, taking the form of an exploration of past violence in the search for understanding and self-discovery. Mason Flagg, a convincing embodiment of the evil that is only a twist away from American innocence, is placed in conflict with the tortured struggles of an artist, Cass Kinsolving, for personal salvation. Peter Leverett, who largely embodies the author's point of view, has a Southern background, and once again it is in the Southern past that acceptable human values seem best defined.

In 1967, he returned to a subject he had contemplated earlier, *The Confessions of Nat Turner*, based on the 1831 rebellion in Southern Virginia led by the Negro Nat Turner, whose 'confessions' (1831) form the ground of the novel. Styron's structure and style are more involuted and artificial as he imagines the interpretation and motive of this example of the American dilemma. The novel was a highly acclaimed bestseller in America, although some – including Negro – critics objected to both its composition and its attitudes. [EM]

Maxwell Geismar, 'William Styron: The End of Innocence', in *American Moderns* (1958); Louise Y. Gossett, 'The Cost of Freedom: William Styron', in *Violence in Recent Southern Fiction* (1965); ed. John H. Clark, *William Styron's Nat Turner: Ten Black Writers Respond* (1968).

Swados, Harvey (1920–). Novelist and story writer. Born in Buffalo, N.Y.; educated at the University of Michigan. Besides teaching at Sarah Lawrence, the University of Iowa and San Francisco State College, he has been active in journalism and in left-wing politics; a collection of polemical essays, *A Radical's America* (1962), explores his socialist position and his view of American society. His novels are *Out Went the Candle* (1955), an analysis of a scheming businessman in a struggling relationship with his children; *False Coin* (1959), a witty analysis of a Utopian writers' colony; and *The Will* (1963), another family novel, exploring the way an inheritance corrupts the lives of three brothers. An early collection of stories, *Nights in the Gardens of Brooklyn* (1951), has recently been reissued in England; *Out on the Line* (1957) contains stories interlinked by being about workers on a car-assembly line; and *A Story for*

Teddy (1965) brings together his recent short fiction. Though sometimes a ponderous writer, he has a strong social perception and a powerful capacity to render the complexities of modern experience. He has recently edited a first-rate collection of documents on the thirties, *The American Writer and the Great Depression* (1968). [MB]

Charles Shapiro, 'Harvey Swados: Private Stories and Public Fiction', in *Contemporary American Novelists*, ed. Harry T. Moore (1964).

Sward, Robert (1923–). Poet. Born in Chicago, he was educated at the Universities of Illinois and Iowa, went to the University of Bristol on a Fulbright award and has taught at Cornell University. Volumes of verse include *Advertisements* (1958), *Uncle Dog* (1962), *Kissing the Dancer* (1964) and *Thousand-Year-Old Fiancée* (1966). He is a poet of varied styles and great verbal self-consciousness. [BP]

Swenson, May (1927–). Poet. Born and educated in Utah. She now lives in New York, an editor for the publishing firm New Directions. Her collections include *Another Animal*, published in *Poets of Today, I* (1954); *A Cage of Spines* (1958); *To Mix with Time* (1963), which contains many new poems but also a substantial selection from the two earlier volumes; and *Half Sun Half Sleep* (1967). One block of her poems takes its occasions from European subjects; many others derive from rural and urban American subjects. Elaborate typography, grandiose metaphysics and high rhetorical intensity create many of her effects, and though the pitch is often shrill she certainly deals with problems of real importance for contemporary poetry. *Poems to Solve* (1966) consists of 35 poems in the form of riddles, allegories and extended metaphors, composed for children. [MB]

T

Tarkington, Booth (1869–1946). Novelist. Born in Indianapolis, educated at Philips Exeter Academy, Purdue and Princeton Universities. His first successful novel, *The Gentleman from Indiana* (1899), was a cheerful, realistic story of a newspaper's crusade against political corruption and cynicism; *In the Arena* (1905) developed a similar theme. In 1902–3 he was a Republican member of the Indiana legislature. His reputation was made with *Monsieur Beaucaire* (1900), a period whimsy. In a style deriving partly from William Dean ◊ Howells and Mark Twain, there followed a series of mid-Western novels, of which two won Pulitzer Prizes, *The Magnificent Ambersons* (1918) and *Alice Adams* (1921). *Growth* (1927) is the overall title of a city trilogy which includes *The Turmoil* (1915), *The Magnificent Ambersons* (1918) and *The Midlander* (1923). New wealth and social mobility are his dominant concern. *The Magnificent Ambersons* charts the decline through three generations of a family fortune made by real estate in the Gilded Age, to be supplanted at last in wealth and status by the founder of the local automobile plant. *Alice Adams* is a sad morality tale of a drugstore assistant's attempt, with his own formula, to open a glue factory, and his daughter's attempt, with a web of fabrications, to win the love of a rich stranger and rise in society. The Horatio ◊ Alger sermon of 'Luck and Pluck' is squarely turned upside down. Further novels, *The Conquest of Canaan* (1905), *The Plutocrat* (1927), *The Heritage of Hatcher Ide* (1941), *Kate Fennigate* (1943) and *The Image of Josephine* (1945), carry the Indiana setting through the Depression and war years.

His series of novels, *Penrod* (1914), *Penrod and Sam* (1916), *Penrod Jashber* (1929), *Seventeen* (1916), *Gentle Julia* (1922) and *Little Orvie* (1934), had a wide readership: Penrod is the rowdy middle-class boy, with a mongrel dog and assorted intimates including the Negro brothers Herman and Verman (principal performers in a circus he organizes): he is the traditional American good 'bad' boy.

Tarkington dramatized several of his novels as well as writing 25 plays, some in collaboration, and an autobiography, *The World Does Move* (1928). He is the epitome of the middle-brow American novelist. [H B]

Your Amiable Uncle: Letters to his Nephew (1949). R. C. Holliday, *Booth Tarkington* (1918); James Woodress, *Booth Tarkington, Gentleman from Indiana* (1955).

Tate, Allen (1899–   ). Poet, critic. He was born and educated in Kentucky, studied at Georgetown and Washington, and in 1922 graduated from Vanderbilt University, Tennessee, where with John Crowe Ransom, Robert Warren, Merrill Moore, Donald Davidson and Cleanth Brooks he was a member of the ◊ Fugitives group, dedicated to agrarianism, the ◊ New Criticism they were demonstrating, the South, and political conservativism (see *The Fugitive Magazine*, 1922–5, and the symposium, *I'll Take My Stand*, 1930). He lived in New York 1924–8, and in Paris, 1928–9, on a Guggenheim fellowship, taught in a number of American universities, edited *Hound and Horn* (1931–4), *Sewanee Review* (1944–6), with Herbert Agar, *Who Owns America?* (1936) and, with John Peale Bishop, *American Harvest* (1942). His important criticism, including essays on Hart Crane, Emily Dickinson, Poe and 'Tension in Poetry', appeared in *Reactionary Essays on Poetry and Ideas* (1936), *Reason in Madness* (1941) and *The Forlorn Demon* (1953). *Stonewall Jackson* (1928) documents aspects of the pre-Civil-War South and its myths, the subject also within his novel *The Fathers* (1938), in many ways his finest work. His poems, in *Mr Pope and Other Poems* (1928), *Poems 1928–1931* (1932) and *The Mediterranean and Other Poems* (1936), are tightly complex forms, embodying nostalgia for European culture, dedication to a vision of the viable South and a tradition of aristocratic experience. They need exegesis of their academic allusiveness and indirection, but the unravelling usually shows a distinguished intellect within its broadly religious moral orbit. [EM]

Collected Essays (1959); *Poems* (1960); *Essays of Four Decades* (1969).
J. C. Stewart, *The Burden of Time: The Fugitives and Agrarians* (1965).

Taylor, Bayard (1825–78). Novelist, travel-writer, poet, translator. Born in Pennsylvania, he was a member of the New York circle of the 1860s which included ◊ Aldrich, R. H. Stoddard and ◊ Howells. He worked on the *Saturday Evening Post* and the *Tribune*. He published his first volume of poems, *Ximena*, in 1844, and *Poems of the Orient* in 1854. His translation of Goethe's *Faust* (1870–1), for which he is perhaps best remembered, is in original metres, and serviceable. The first of his famous and popular travel books was *Views Afoot; or Europe Seen with Knapsack and Staff* (1846), a conventional touristic work. In 1849 he reported the Californian gold rush for the *Tribune*, and his experiences were recounted in *El Dorado; or Adventures in the Path of Empire* (1850), a useful record, frequently reprinted. He continued to travel and give popular lectures on his travels for audiences avid for news of the world. He worked for the diplomatic service in St Petersburg and in 1878 was appointed minister in Berlin. His poetry is the overripe obverse of his realistic journalism, but his novel *The Story of Kennett* (1866) treats country people with something of the detail of his travel works. [EM]

M. Hansen-Taylor and H. E. Scudder, *Life and Letters of Bayard Taylor* (2 vols., 1884); R. C. Beatty, *Bayard Taylor: Laureate of the Gilded Age* (1936); R. Cary, *The Genteel Circle: Bayard Taylor and His New York Friends* (1952).

Taylor, Edward (1645?–1729). Poet. He was born in Leicestershire and went to Boston, Massachusetts, in 1668. Samuel ◊ Sewall was his room-mate at Harvard, where he graduated in 1671, becoming a minister the same year. He ordered his poetry to be left unpublished. It was discovered in Yale library in 1937. The best colonial poetry of its kind, it is in fact characteristic English 17th-century devotional verse, with 'metaphysical' qualities and some significant New England linguistic usages. His ingenious metaphors and conceits dramatize abstract religious philosophy in original and attractive ways

which partly redeem *God's Determinations Touching His Elect*, a series of poems on the New England covenant dogma. His 217 'Sacramental Meditations' are a lifetime's application of the Bible to daily life. [EM]

The Poems, ed. D. E. Stanford (1960).
N. S. Grabo, *Edward Taylor* (1962).

Taylor, John (1753–1824). He was born in Virginia, studied at William and Mary College, practised law, and made a career as a soldier and, after the Revolution, as a plantation owner. His ◊ Jeffersonian beliefs in the self-reliant agrarian property-owner are set out in *The Arator* (1813; agricultural essays), *Tyranny Unmasked* (1822; a pamphlet supporting protective tariffs), *New Views of the Constitution* (1823; on states rights governmental philosophy), and many more essays and pamphlets. His major work is *An Inquiry into the Principles and Policy of the Government in the United States* (1814), a thorough and plodding treatise on agrarian liberalism. [EM]

Taylor, Peter (1917–   ). Novelist, short-story writer. Born in Nashville, Tennessee. His concern with the past, family and childhood gives a distinctively Southern quality to most of his fiction. Middle-class family life in the upper South provides his basic material, which is handled with subtlety and humour. His characteristic narrative method is one of careful reconsideration of event, distilled reminiscence rather than re-created dialogue and action. *A Long Fourth, and Other Stories* (1948), *The Widows of Thornton* (1954), *Happy Families are All Alike* (1960) and *Miss Leonora When Last Seen, and Fifteen Other Stories* (1963) are collections of stories. *A Woman of Means* (1950) is a short novel about the decay of a wealthy family in St Louis in the mid-twenties, told by an adult recollecting childhood experiences in the family. *The Death of a Kinsman* (1949) and *Tennessee Day in St Louis* (1957) are plays. [AH]

Collected Stories (1969).
Sewanee Review, LXX (Autumn, 1962) (three essays on his work).

Theatre Guild. Formed from among the Washington Square Players in 1918 'for drama, for beauty, for ideas' and the circumvention of commercialism in the theatre. Its first play was Jacinto Beneventi's *Bonds of Interest* (1919). The Guild Theatre itself opened in 1925 with Shaw's *Caesar and Cleopatra*. In 1931, many of the actors, playwrights and producers associated with Theatre Guild combined with others to produce plays of some social importance, the first important production of which was Paul ◊ Green's *The House of Connelly* (1931). [EM]

Thomas, Norman (1884–1969). Writer, politician. Born in Marion, Ohio, he graduated from Princeton in 1905 and was for some years a Presbyterian minister, until he resigned in order to devote himself to the causes of socialism and pacifism. Since the 1920s he unsuccessfully offered himself as a socialist candidate for most political offices, including that of the presidency. In 1918 he founded *World Tomorrow* and during 1921–2 was an editor of the *Nation*. His many publications include *The Challenge of War* (1925); *Socialism of Our Time* (1929); *The Choice before Us* (1934); *We Have a Future* (1941); *A Socialist's Faith* (1951); *Prerequisites for Peace* (1959); *The Great Dissenters* (1961); and *Socialism Re-Examined* (1964). [HD]

Harry Fleischman, *Norman Thomas: A Biography* (1964); M. B. Seidler, *Norman Thomas: Respectable Rebel* (1962).

Thoreau, Henry David (1817–62). As a child in Concord, Massachusetts, where he was born, he played the flute and shared his naturalist interests with his brother John. After Concord Academy, and Harvard (1833–7), he had a thorough training in mathematics, literature, classical languages, French and some Spanish and Italian. He also acquired some knowledge of Indian and Oriental literature. Through his friend Orestes Brownson, he came to ◊ Transcendentalism; Emerson encouraged him to keep the journals from which his books were made. In 1838, the Thoreau brothers opened a private school, together fell in love with Ellen Sewall, and made the trip which became the basis of Henry's first book, *A Week on the Concord and Merrimack Rivers* (1849). Ellen turned them both down, and Henry later wrote: 'It appears to be a law that you cannot have a deep sympathy with both man and nature.' After their school closed in 1841, he became Emerson's residential working companion. W. E. ◊ Channing (II) and Hawthorne became his friends. Needing to earn a self-

reliant living he tried tutoring in Emerson's brother's New York family, and had introductions to Horace Greeley and Henry James, Sr. But he needed to return to his Concord woods. He improved his father's pencil business by developing a graphite process, contributed to the *Dial*, and made himself 'self-appointed inspector of snow-storms, and rain-storms', 'surveyor of forest-paths and all across-lot routes', and guardian of 'wild stock'. In 1845 he began a two-year experiment in simple economy and creative leisure in a self-made cabin on Emerson's land at Walden Pond, occasionally visiting friends, and interrupting his isolation with a gaol sentence for refusing to pay poll tax to a government waging war in Mexico. *Civil Disobedience* appeared in the Transcendentalist *Aesthetic Papers* in 1849. On their return from England he settled with the Emersons again and remained until his death. He turned professional surveyor, developed his botany skills with Louis ◊ Agassiz, the great American botanist and zoologist, and in 1853 went north to the Maine woods to experience a more primitive nature. After the Fugitive Slave Law of 1850 he assisted escapes via the 'Underground Railway', attacked slavery in 'Slavery in Massachusetts'. and supported John Brown's Harper's Ferry raid. He travelled to Niagara and Mississippi, but found no cure for his health and died upright, murmuring 'moose' and 'Indian', a memory of his horrified witness of a slaughtering at Chesuncook in 1853.

Civil Disobedience asserts 'that government is best which governs least', enables men to let one another alone instead of serving the state as 'machines', and urges passive resistance to tyranny. Its international influence extended at least as late as Gandhi. The journeys in *A Week on the Concord* are the frame for a programme of self-reliance, criticism, reading, poetry and the recording of American myth and history: it is the form itself of Thoreau's philosophy of free choice in a natural landscape known at first hand without the intervention of dogma or religion. The form of his masterpiece, *Walden* (1854), is again the organic articulation of personal experience, delineating what 'a necessary life' and a fundamental economy of work and leisure might be for 'freedom and a prospect of success'. Every closely observed natural and human event is to lead towards the recovery of a life of 'universal laws'. Thoreau's *Journals* contain the minute record of his daily life presented less formally, with some of the meditative metaphysical quality of his best poems. He is one of the masters of prose style, an exemplary individualist, and a living inspiration to resisters and dissenters everywhere, including, at one time, Gandhi, Tolstoy and the British Labour Party. His anarchist opposition to state coercion, and refusal to pay taxes which might contribute to national war or enforce the slavery-economy, have a direct bearing on American dissent in the 1960s. His final support of violence against slavery, in direct contrast to his earlier belief in passive resistance, is prophetic of the course many liberals were forced to take a hundred years later. [EM]

Collected Poems, ed. C. Bode (1964); *Selected Journals*, ed. C. Bode (1967); *The Correspondence*, ed. W. Harding and C. Bode (1957); *The Portable Thoreau*, ed. C. Bode (1947).
Walter Harding, *The Thoreau Handbook* (1959) and *The Days of Henry Thoreau* (1965).

Thurber, James (1894–1961). Humorist. He grew up in Columbus, Ohio, amid an eccentric family portrayed in some of his best essays. After working as a newspaperman in Columbus, Paris and New York, he met Harold Ross, editor of the *New Yorker*, and joined that paper, for which most of his essays, short stories and drawings were produced. His manner, interests and distinctive tone were inseparable from it and shaped it; the connexion is recorded in his memoir *The Years with Ross* (1959).

His very distinctive humour is a definable phase in the development of American literary tone. Like his *New Yorker* colleague and collaborator, E. B. ◊ White, he was elegant, genteel, devoted to 'good style'. His work appeals to a sense of gentleness, order and control, having a literary delicacy distinguished from most American writing; and it has a clear moral concern, a sense of the growth of anarchy, folly and absurdity which the slightly affected gentility can bring clearly out. Many of the essays and stories deal with the triumph of moral innocence in the world of mass-media, psychoanalysis and sexual revolution. Besides comic essays he wrote elegant fantasies where, again, the kind of moral innocence he valued shows plainly. His many drawings have the same sophisticated simplicity. A central theme is the transition from the bourgeois and small-town America of the 1920s to the modern sophisticated society of the sex war, psychoanalysis and scientism. Though the approach has a vein of gentle mid-Western cracker-barrel philosophy, its great virtue is his capacity to place modernity and sophistication; as in his parody of pseudo-scientific sex articles, *Is Sex Necessary?* (1929, with E. B. White), and his spoof of psychoanalysis, *Let Your Mind Alone* (1937). A deft social commentator and inventor of superb comic locutions, he conveys strongly the atmosphere of America between the wars. The essays, short stories, cartoons and sequences of sketches are collected in *The Owl in the Attic and Other Perplexities* (1931), *The Seal in the Bedroom and Other Predicaments* (1932), *My Life and Hard Times* (1933), *Men, Women, and Dogs* (1943), *Alarms and Diversions* (1957), etc. With Elliot Nugent he wrote a stage comedy, *The Male Animal* (1940). *The Thurber Carnival* (1945) is a convenient English collection from his work over the years. [MB]

Timrod, Henry (1828–67). Poet. Born in Charleston, South Carolina, he lies in the chivalric, Keats-influenced tradition of Southern poetry deriving from Poe. One of the Russell's bookstore group, including William Gilmore ◊ Simms, Paul Hamilton ◊ Hayne and Basil Gildersleeve, who in 1867 founded in Charleston *Russell's Magazine* (an imitation of the English *Blackwood's*), he published poems and essays here and in other Southern journals. His earlier sentimental verse toughens as he encounters the experience of the Civil War, when he served in the Confederate Army and wrote loyal poetry, the two best-known poems being 'Ethnogenesis', which looks forward to the growth of a new stronger South, and his 'Ode Sung at the Occasion of Decorating the Graves of the Confederate Dead'. A Memorial edition of his poems, *Poems of Henry Timrod*, was issued in Boston in 1899; they can also be reached through the *American Writers Series, Southern Poets* (1936). [MB]

Jay B. Hubbell, *The South in American Literature 1607–1900* (1954).

Tocqueville, Alexis, Comte de (1805–59). French writer on America, politician. In 1831, a junior magistrate in Versailles, he was appointed to a commission of inquiry into American prisons and penitentiaries; and his work on *Du système pénitentiaire aux États-Unis et de son application en France* (1832) provided him with material for *De la démocratie en Amérique* (1835 and 1840), his lucid, concise and masterly analysis of American society and its institutions, in which he suggests that modern democracies will tend to sacrifice liberty to equality. Later a deputy and Minister for Foreign Affairs (June–October 1849), he was prevented by ill-health from completing his great *L'ancien régime et la révolution* (1856).

In Volume II, Book I, Chapters xɪ–xɪx of *Democracy in America* (tr. H. Reeve, ed. P. Bradley, 2 vols., 1945), he analyses with penetrating cogency the present and future condition of American literature, developing a characteristic general thesis that 'the relations which exist between the social and political condition of a people and the genius of its authors are always numerous'. He claims American authors are 'English in substance and still more so in form', irrelevantly apeing the culture of a foreign aristocracy: in consequence 'the only authors whom I acknowledge as American are the journalists'. Two main factors are likely to vitiate the prospects of an American literature: the absence of a leisured intellectual class, and the inherent tendency of democracies to 'make the taste for the useful predominate over the love of the beautiful in the heart of man'. American authors (and their heterogeneous audience) will find themselves in an intellectual vacuum: prose style 'will frequently be fantastic, incorrect, overburdened and loose, almost always bold. . . . The object . . . will be to astonish rather than to please'. American poetry, turning from the past, will 'prefer the delineation of passion and ideas to that of persons and achievements'. 'Haunted by visions of what will be' it will 'range at last to purely imaginary regions'. Hence he probably suggests social reasons for American literature's symbolist preoccupation. [MG]

J. P. Mayer, *Tocqueville: Prophet of the Mass Age* (1940); Janes Bryce, *The Predictions of Hamilton and Tocqueville* (1887); G. W. Pierson, *Tocqueville and Beaumont in America* (1938).

Tolson, M. B. (1898–   ). Poet. Born in Moberly, Missouri, he was educated at Fisk, Lincoln and Columbia, with considerable distinctions and prizes. He has taught in a number of colleges and is well known for his drama clubs and public readings. He has served four terms as mayor of Langstone, Oklahoma, where he directs the Dust Bowl Theatre and teaches creative literature. His reputation as a leading Negro poet began with 'Dark Symphony', dramatizing the Negro condition (in *Rendezvous with America*, 1944). His long psychological poem *E. & O.E.* won him a *Poetry* award in 1952, and Allen ◊ Tate introduced his *Libretto for the Republic of Liberia* in 1953 (part of it was a commission he received as poet laureate of Liberia in 1947). *Harlem Gallery: Book 1, The Curator* (1965) is one of the most important events in Negro American literature and is itself a remarkably fine poem; the 24 sections, in an original literary idiom, dramatize ironically and passionately the relationships between African, Negro America and Western culture. (◊ Negro Literature.) [EM]

Toomer, Jean. ◊ Negro Literature.

Totheroh, Dan (1895–   ). The San Francisco dramatist whose fame rests with *Wild Birds* (1922), a mid-Western tale of an orphan girl, a reform school boy and psychology. There are also extant *Distant Drums* (1932 – a neurotic lady in a caravan *en route* for Oregon), *Moor Born* (1934 – the Brontës), and *Live Life Again* (1943 – Hamlet on a Nebraska farm). [EM]

Tourgée, Albion W(inegar) (1838–1905). Novelist. Born in Ohio, a lawyer and a judge, he moved in 1865 to North Carolina, where his experiences as a carpetbagger provided material for his most important works. He returned north to New York State in 1879, and in 1897 was appointed American consul in Bordeaux. His outstanding novel is *A Fool's Errand* (1879), a semi-autobiographical account of the Reconstruction, where exciting narration is interspersed with lucid socio-political analysis, managed from a northern point of view. Tourgée supplemented later editions with 'The Invisible Empire', a famous essay on the Ku Klux Klan. Related novels are *Toinette* (1874) – later revised as *A Royal Gentleman* – and *Bricks without Straw* (1880). Other novels deal with racial problems; and his 'The South as a Field for Fiction', in *Forum* (1888), is a seminal investigation. [DG]

Otto H. Olson, *Carpetbagger's Crusade: The Life of Albion Winegar Tourgée* (1965); Roy F. Dibble, *Albion W. Tourgee* (1921).

Transcendentalists, The. A group of writers who articulated the decline of 18th-century Calvinism in Massachusetts, the advent of Unitarianism and rationalism, and the effects of European romanticism. The leaders included Emerson, Thoreau, Alcott, W. E. ◊ Channing (I) and George ◊ Ripley; associated were Margaret ◊ Fuller, Orestes ◊ Brownson, Jones ◊ Very, Theodore Parker and others. Their ideas included the ideal nature of reality, the immanence of God in nature and man, the presence of Soul in all things, the unity of all things, the need to transcend what the physical senses and science can know through the truth of intuition. They borrowed freely from versions of Kant's concepts through Coleridge and Schelling to establish what Ripley called 'an order of truths which transcends the sphere of external sense' and 'the operations of understanding' (Brownson), and ascertain the 'facts' of 'certain great primal intuitions of human nature' (Parker). Alcott once 'saw the world as one great spinal column'. They rejected formal worship or any interceding between soul and God. The Christian gospels, with Shakespeare, Socrates and all great writing, were part of the totality of human and therefore divine work. They expressed their ideas not only in literature but in individual living, the founding of schools and Utopias, and the practice of dietary regimes. Emerson's *Nature* (1836) is the nearest to systematic formulation of a Transcendentalist philosophy and his essay *The Transcendentalist* (1842) suggests some of the attitudes of the group. The Transcendental Club was formed by Ripley in 1836 to exchange views. The quarterly *Dial* (1842–4) was their outlet, under the successive editing of Margaret Fuller and Emerson. Brook Farm was their joint stock company utopian experiment, organized at West Roxbury, Massachusetts, in 1841. [EM]

The Transcendentalists: An Anthology, ed. P. Miller (1950); *Selected Writings of the American Transcendentalists*, ed. George Hochfield (1966). *Transcendentalism and Its Legacy*, ed. M. Simon and T. Parsons (1967).

Traven, Ben (1890–1969). Novelist. A Chicago-born fiction writer who died in Mexico City. His guarded anonymity gave rise to wild speculations on his identity, especially since his fiction shows experience of extreme human situations and his style is not only vigorously contemporary, but has a certain clumsiness which is retained in the translations from the German. He gave his first press interview in 1966, still insisting on the privacy of his life. Traven's novels are exciting and vividly visualized narratives, strongly critical of capitalist motives: *The Death Ship* (1934), *The Treasure of the Sierra Madre* (1935), *The Carreta* (1935), *Government* (1935), *The Bridge in the Jungle* (1938), *The Rebellion of the Hanged* (1952). *The Night Visitor and Other Stories* appeared in 1966. Kenneth Rexroth calls Traven 'the greatest novelist of total disengagement' and adds that he was 'an elderly I.W.W. of German ancestry', a statement that probably needs corroboration from Judy Stone's 'The Mystery of B. Traven' (*Ramparts*, September 1967) and his American editor, Bernard Smith's article in the *New York Times*, 22 November 1970. [EM]

Trilling, Lionel (1905–). Literary critic, novelist. He grew up in New York, and was educated there at Columbia University, where he is now Professor of English in the graduate school. He is one of the most influential of modern American critics. His critical writing, though founded on the ◊ New Criticism, has worked rather in the realm of advancing general ideas; it is notably informed by psychological, sociological and philosophical methods and insights. At its core is a deep concern with the totality of culture; he has urged the case for the liberal imagination of art as a primary social value. He is thus essentially a humanist and moralist, devoted to literature as an expression of the human mind in all its variousness and possibility, involved with the whole growth of human experience and judgement. Most of his criticism has been of romantic and post-romantic literature, and recently he has become concerned with the way this literature has, by adopting the pieties of alienation, tended to promote limited assumptions about our human nature.

He has written excellently on Arnold (*Matthew Arnold*, 1939) and Forster (*E. M. Forster*, 1943), in whose liberal humanist tradition he clearly lies. Essays on modern English and American fiction, romantic poetry and general socio-literary issues are collected in *The Liberal Imagination* (1950), *The Opposing Self* (1955), *A Gathering of Fugitives* (1956) and *Beyond Culture: Essays on Literature and Learning* (1965). He has also written a short study of Freud, *Freud and the Crisis of Our Culture* (1955). The *Experience of Literature* (1967) is an anthology from Sophocles to Ginsberg, with pedagogic commentary.

His one novel, *The Middle of the Journey* (1947), taking as its basic material the political development that the liberal mind in America went through in the 1930s and 1940s, puts political life to exacting moral examination. He has written two remarkable stories, widely reprinted but never collected together: 'Of this Time, of That Place', a classic story of the burden of responsibility a teacher bears for an eccentric student, and 'The Other Margaret', about a young girl initiated into consciousness of the moral and political inter-connectedness of people. [MB]

Trumbull, John (1750–1831). Poet. As a precocious Connecticut boy he passed the Yale entrance examinations at 7 and entered college at 13. With 'The Meddler' group of essayists he wrote *Spectator* imitations and stayed on as tutor, advocating a more liberal curriculum (e.g. introducing Augustan poetry) in *An Essay on the Uses and Advantages of the Fine Arts* (1770) and the long satirical poem *The Progress of Dulness* (1772–3). After 1773 he read law under John Adams, with whose Federalism he sympathized. Law and politics engrossed his later life and he died in Detroit having abandoned poetry and brief fame as a ◊ Connecticut Wit. *The Progress of Dulness* is a hudibrastic adventure of Tom Brainless, farmer's son, as he proceeds fecklessly through school, college, society and the ministry. Trumbull's better poem is the mock epic *M'Fingal* (1775–82), an extremely popular attack on the Loyalists, after Bulter and Macpherson. [EM]

A. Cowie, *John Trumbull, Connecticut Wit* (1936).

Tuckerman, Frederick Goddard (1821–73). Poet. Born in Boston, Massachusetts, he practised law in early life and then retired to Greenfield as a solitary observer of nature and a poet. His *Poems* (1860) is a collection of sonnets, highly regarded by poets and critics from Tennyson to Yvor ◊ Winters. Witter ◊ Bynner introduced his edition enthusiastically in 1931. Tuckerman's eccentric

phrasing and original imagery have a new following since N. Scott Momoday's *The Complete Poems* (1965). [EM]

S. A. Golden, *Frederick Goddard Tuckerman: An American Sonneteer* (1952).

Turner, Frederick Jackson (1861–1932). Historian. Born in Portage, Wisconsin, a frontier community, he was educated at Wisconsin University and Johns Hopkins University, where he was influenced by and reacted against Herbert Baxter Adams, a foremost exponent of the 'germ theory' of American development, which is primarily concerned with American institutions, tracing them back to primitive tribal Teutonic democracy at the time of the Roman empire. Turner maintained that exclusive concentration upon European origins distorted American experience. His own early experiences, Darwinian theory and the human geography of Friedrich Ratzel came together in his economic and social environmental theory of American history: the 'Turner thesis'. His 1893 paper, 'The Significance of the Frontier in American History', insisted that the characteristic of American history had been westward expansion and settlement into free land areas. Each settled locality evolved from primitive culture to more advanced and still individualized societies. Frontier conditions conditioned national legislation and distinctive values. These ideas were developed in *The Rise of the New West, 1819–29* (1906) into a theory of the sectional rather than state-political basis of national unity and common interests. *The United States 1830–50*, left unfinished at his death, was edited by Avery Craven, his former student, in 1935. In spite of his great influence, he wrote comparatively little, and his only other major books are two collections of essays, *The Frontier in American History* (1920) and *The Significance of Sections in American History* (1932). Since his death his theories have come under radical criticism (usefully summarized in *The Turner Thesis*, ed. G. R. Taylor, 1956). But he remains a monumental figure in American history and thought, although he is sometimes regarded as the founder of a myth rather than the discoverer of lasting historical facts. [DKA/EM]

Twain, Mark (Samuel Langhorne Clemens) (1835–1910). Novelist, humorist. He was the fifth of six children in a household with two slaves. His father was a Virginian lawyer working in Florida, Missouri, a frontier settlement on a tributary of the Mississippi. When Sam was 4 the family moved to Hannibal, on the great river itself (an idyllic boyhood told in the *Autobiography*, 1871). His father died when he was 12 and he was apprenticed to a printer, the beginning of his career of accurate reporting and entertaining sketches (written in the South-western humour tradition of ◊ Longstreet and George W. ◊ Harris). In 1857 he yielded to his boyhood ambition and trained with the great Horace Bixby as a river-boat pilot, a profession he loved 'better than any I have followed since' (*Life on the Mississippi*, 1883), a 'brief sharp schooling' during which he met 'all the different types of human nature that are to be found in fiction, biography or history'.

But the Civil War closed the river traffic and Twain's career terminated. His brief hilarious war experience is in 'The History of a Campaign That Failed'. He turned his hand to silver prospecting in Nevada, went back to journalism on the Virginia City *Enterprise*, and, in 1864, on the San Francisco *Morning Call* (*Roughing It*, 1872), and in 1865 published his first short story, 'The Celebrated Jumping Frog of Calaveras County'. After his 1865–6 voyage to Hawaii, he made the first of his hundreds of lecturing appearances. On his return from Europe and Palestine in 1867 (*Innocents Abroad*, 1869), he married and set up house in Hartford, Connecticut, his base until 1890. He began to play his Eastern, genteel present against his Western and wilder past, and thus became a major representative of post Civil War America entering the era of industrial expansion. His *The Gilded Age* (1873, with Charles D. Warner) is a novel exposing American business politics in the post Civil War era. He wrote a large number of short stories and essays, two travel books (*A Tramp Abroad*, 1880, and *Following the Equator*, 1897); he became a literary businessman, speculating in a publishing firm and over a hundred inventions, one of which, together with his extravagant living, bankrupted him. His daughter died tragically in 1896, and his writing reflects these disasters in its increasing irony and bitterness ('The Man That Corrupted Hadleyburg', 1900, 'What Is Man?', 1917 posth., and *The Mysterious Stranger*, 1916 posth.). His gusto as a public figure masked the private tensions which he wrote into pessimistic works relegated to a locked desk drawer for posthumous exhumation.

Mark Twain's career was a central, representative one in American letters. He made the already well-developed role of humorist (◊ Billings; Nasby; Ward) into a central post of social observation. His worldwide reputation was based on a gift for mixing boyish rascality and innocence in a naïve, vernacular vision, one complicated, however, by his darkening, bitter view of man as hypocrite, victim and self-deceiver. The contradictions spread several ways: much of his work was about the Mississippi valley world of his childhood, but angled through the eyes of one deeply in the rapidly industrializing Gilded Age phase and its base in Eastern capital and Northern morality. Many of his books turn on complex ironies deriving from this: romance is questioned by realism, boyhood idyll by manhood despair, the agrarian past by the industrial present, the slaveholding South by the Northern progressivism of the postbellum period. But the industrial and progressive present contains the highest irony of all: pretending to high morality, its real centre lies in money, machines and force. So, from the standpoint either of the wonderingly innocent childhood eye, or from that of an ironic disgust that holds that 'We have no *real* morals, but only artificial ones, morals created and preserved by the forced suppression of natural and healthy instincts,' Twain creates a world in which men are lost children or else bleak slaves to determinism.

The complexity and often inconsistency of the view; the fact that he often wrote carelessly or amateurishly; the instinct he felt to succeed at the most popular level of acclaim – all this meant his huge energies are not often raised to the level of major literature. He lacked the discipline of the persistent artist except in five great central works. Weakest are the historical novels: *The Prince and the Pauper* (1882) and *Personal Recollections of Joan of Arc* (1896). The Tom Sawyer books (1876; 1894; 1896), centred in his fascination with boyish play and imposture, are at times amusing, especially *The Adventures of Tom Sawyer* (1876), but thin stuff. His finest works are: *Life on the Mississippi* (1883), not a novel but a superbly evocative memoir, a brilliant account of pilotage and a criticism of the South; *A Connecticut Yankee in King Arthur's Court* (1889), which shifts Hank

Morgan, the machine-shop superintendent, into medieval England, which he promotes as an industrial American utopia and then destroys in a technological apocalypse; *The American Claimant* (1892), which resurrects Colonel Sellers, the confidence man of the earlier *Gilded Age; Pudd'nhead Wilson* (1894), a profoundly ironic work, drawing on Twain's recurring themes of exchanged identities and the paradox of slavery and freedom, that takes its story of the switched master and slave through to an ending of savage force; and the masterpiece *The Adventures of Huckleberry Finn* (1885), one of the world's great books. A deeply complex novel, it is at once the initiation of a 12-year-old boy into the hypocrisies of the Christian bourgeoisie, with its slavery, Southern feuds and money materialism, and a definition of morality learned empirically as the boy helps his Negro friend, Jim, down the Mississippi by raft. The multiple ironies, the vivid series of escape episodes, the variety of characters, and the brilliantly invented language of Huck's narrative make this an American classic and the triumph of Twain's special kind of humour. Twain's reputation is firmly based on these works. Year by year critical and biographical works about him pour from the universities, but he is worthy of such attention. [EM]

Letters from the Earth, ed. B. de Voto (1942); *The Autobiography*, ed. C. Neider (1961); *Mark Twain on the Damned Human Race*, ed. Janet Smith (1962).
H. N. Smith, *Mark Twain: The Development of a Writer* (1962); Walter Blair, *Mark Twain and Huck Finn* (1960); ed. Walter Blair, *Mark Twain: A Collection of Critical Essays* (1960); J. M. Cox, *Mark Twain: The Fate of Humour* (1967); J. Kaplan, *Mr Clemens and Mark Twain* (1967); S. J. Krause, *Mark Twain as Critic* (1968).

Tyler, Moses Coit (1835–1900). Literary historian. Born in Griswold, Connecticut. Important in the development of the syste-matic study of American literature, which took on impetus during the late 19th century, he helped – with John Seely Hart, Greenough White, E. P. ◊ Whipple, Brander ◊ Matthews and Albert Bigelow Paine – to establish the possibility of a serious study in the field. A sound and thorough scholar, his two great works on the Colonial and Revolutionary periods are still basic: *A History of American Literature, 1607–1765* (2 vols., 1878; abridged paperback edn, 1962) and *The Literary History of the American Revolution, 1763–1783* (2 vols., 1897). Tyler, who was Professor of English at the University of Michigan and then of American History at Cornell, also wrote *Three Men of Letters* (1895), on Joel ◊ Barlow, Timothy ◊ Dwight and Bishop Berkeley's three-year American visit. [MB]

Howard Mumford Jones *The Life of Moses Coit Tyler* (1933).

Tyler, Royall (1757–1826). Playwright. He wrote one of the most famous early American plays, *The Contrast*, first performed in 1787 (published 1790). The first American comedy, written in the manner of Sheridan, it exploited American vernacular on the stage for comic purposes, and showed the triumph of the decent American characters over an English cad. One of the American characters, Jonathan, a New England rustic, is drawn from a basic type-figure of American humour; and the play asserts its Americanness from prologue onward. Tyler, who fought in the Revolutionary War and worked in the law office of John Adams, wrote other plays; a novel with a foreign setting, *The Algerine Captive* (1797); and a series of fictional letters, *The Yankey in London* (1809), joking about American customs. *The Contrast* appears in various collections of American plays, including Arthur H. Quinn's *Representative American Plays* (1938). It was revised successfully at the National Playwrights Conference at Waterford, Connecticut, in 1966. [MB]

U

Updike, John (1932–   ). Novelist, short-story writer, poet. Born in Pennsylvania; educated at Harvard University and the Ruskin School of Drawing and Fine Art at Oxford. His poems and stories had appeared in the *New Yorker*, on which he worked, before his first book, *The Carpentered Hen and Other Tame Creatures* (1958), a collection of witty and satirical poems, was published. His prose and poetry have largely continued to reflect the polish and sophistication of the *New Yorker* at its best. *Hoping for a Hoopoe* (1959) and *Telephone Poles and Other Poems* (1963) are collections of poems; *The Same Door* (1959) is a collection of stories; and *The Poorhouse Fair* (1959) is a rather self-consciously bizarre novel about conflicts inside a poorhouse. *Assorted Prose* (1965) is a collection of parodies, autobiographical pieces and critical essays.

Updike's prose style is at all times precise and controlled. *Rabbit, Run* (1960) brilliantly evokes a world of total negation and moral confusion; the novel's protagonist is a man on the run from everything that might give him some kind of identity or definition as a human being. Some of the stories in *Pigeon Feathers and Other Stories* (1962), particularly those involving childhood recollections of Olinger, Pennsylvania, and expatriate days in England, have a greater sense of personal involvement than is common in his work. *The Centaur* (1963) is a more ambitious novel, linking the life of an Olinger teacher with the myth of Chiron, teacher of the Greek heroes. In 1964 appeared *Olinger Stories: A Selection*, and then came the books which have consolidated his career: *Of the Farm* (1965), a slow and over-written story of mother, son and son's wife during a farm weekend; *The Music School* (1966), short stories with bright surfaces; and *Couples* (1968), a novel on the topical matter of middle-class community sex. *Beck: A Book* (1970) dwells on writers' problems. His style still tends to replace character and clear motivation, but he is uncommonly readable. He has also written a children's book, *The Magic Flute* (1962). [AH/EM]

J. A. Ward, 'John Updike's Fiction', *Critique: Studies in Modern Fiction*, v (1962); D. D. Galloway, *The Absurd Hero in American Fiction* (1966).

V

'Van Dine, S. S.' ◊ Wright, Willard Huntington.

Van Doren, Mark (1894–   ). Poet, critic, novelist. Born in Hope, Illinois. He studied at the University of Illinois, then at Columbia University, New York, where he became Professor of Literature and a strong influence in the development of English studies. In the 1920s he was also literary editor of the important liberal weekly the *Nation*. A lucid, intelligent and very exact poet, his books of verse include *Spring Thunder* (1924), *Jonathan Gentry* (1931), a narrative poem, *The Last Look* (1937), *Seven Sleepers* (1944) and *The Country Year* (1946). In 1939 appeared *Collected Poems: 1922–1938*, which won the Pulitzer Prize. His novels include *The Transients* (1935), *Windless Cabins* (1940) and *Tilda* (1943); *Collected Stories* appeared in 1962. He has also written widely as scholar and critic, notably *Henry David Thoreau* (1916), *The Poetry of John Dryden* (1920; reissued 1946 as *John Dryden: A Study of His Poetry*), *Edwin Arlington Robinson* (1927), *Shakespeare* (1939) and *Nathaniel Hawthorne* (1949). *The Happy Critic* (1961) is a collection of essays, and he has edited several anthologies, including the *Oxford Book of American Prose*. [MB]

Collected and New Poems: 1924–1963 (1963); *Selected Poems* (1954); *Autobiography* (1958); *The Narrative Poems* (1965).

Van Druten, John (1901–57). English-born dramatist. His famous study of adolescence, *Young Woodley* (1925), was banned by the British censor, and Van Druten took it to New York and became American. His later plays are light work but good theatre and popular with actors: *Old Acquaintance* (1904), *The Voice of the Turtle* (1943), *I Remember Mama* (1944) and *Bell, Book and Candle* (1950). [EM]

Van Vechten, Carl (1880–1966). Novelist, critic. Born in Cedar Rapids, Iowa. Witty, elegant, under-rated, he wrote during the 1920s a number of delightful novels, in spirit a mixture of Firbank and Waugh. Most deal with artistic New York in the jazz age, and are notable both for their sense of prevailing fashion and their excellent comedy; *Nigger Heaven* (1926), set in Harlem, is rather different and is part of a new wave of interest in Negro culture, while *Spider Boy* (1928) satirizes Hollywood, and *The Tattooed Countess* (1924) deals with Iowa, Van Vechten's home state. *Peter Whiffle* (1922), *The Blind Bow-Boy* (1923), *Firecrackers* (1925) and *Parties* (1930) are jazz-age novels. His several volumes of criticism derive chiefly from his activities as a music and drama critic; he wrote various memoirs (e.g. *Sacred and Profane Memoirs*, 1932), including some (e.g. his Introduction to the Modern Library edition of Gertrude Stein's *Three Lives*) about his friendship with Miss ◊ Stein, some of whose posthumous papers he edited. [MB]

Bruce Kellner, *Carl Van Vechten and the Irreverent Decades* (1969).

Veblen, Thorstein (1857–1929). Economist, social commentator. Born to Norwegian parents in Cato Township, Wisconsin. One of the most enduring of American social thinkers, he has had much impact on 20th-century intellectual and literary thought. Educated at Charleton College, Johns Hopkins and Yale, he joined the new University of Chicago in 1891 as an instructor in economics. In 1899 he published his best-known book, *The Theory of the Leisure Class*, an acute and witty analysis of the social values of America and its caste system based on pecuniary emulation. This was followed by *The Theory of Business Enterprise* (1904) and a series of socio-economic analyses, including *The Instinct of Workmanship* (1914). As a progressive social thinker, Veblen was influential for his literary manner as well as his analysis. The most incisive economist of his day in America, he wrote with a mordant irony that has preserved his writing. Steadfastly refusing to identify the American future with yet more capitalism, he projected not the usual agrarian alternative, but a third force of 'technocrats', scientifically trained workers who would take over control from the mere politicians. The question of 'who is to rule America?' is the invisible force behind his seemingly objective but ironical prose. Unpopular in many quarters in his day, he has been influential in most of the intellectual critiques of the 20th-century. H. L. ◊ Mencken challenged him; ◊ Dos Passos admired him; and he is extensively read today. [A G]

David Riesman, *Thorstein Veblen: A Critical Interpretation* (1953); J. Dorfman, *Thorstein Veblen and His America* (1934); Bernard Rosenberg, *The Values of Veblen* (1956); ed. Carlton C. Qualey, *Thorstein Veblen* (1968).

Veil, Amanda ◊ Miller, Warren.

Veritism ◊ Realism.

Very, Jones (1813–80). Poet, essayist. He was born in Salem, Massachusetts, and spent much of his childhood at sea with his father, a sea-captain. But on graduation from Harvard (1836) he became a tutor in Greek, entered the Divinity School and became isolated by the intensity of his religious vision. He moved from Unitarianism to a submissive mysticism. Forced to resign, and later released from a madhouse, he was befriended by the ◊ Transcendentalists Emerson and James Freeman Clarke, and began to write while he preached. His *Essays and Poems* (1839), prepared under Emerson's guidance, and the only volume to appear in his lifetime, are a surprisingly formal expression of his absolute faith in universal law and God's immanence in nature. His sonnets, with their celebrated extra-footed last line, have the power of complete integration of belief and feeling which can be called 'metaphysical'. In *Maule's Curse* (1938; repr. in *In Defense of Reason*, 1947), Yvor Winters printed a selection of Very's poems and praised them as being 'as convincing, and within their limits as excellent, as are the poems of Blake, or Traherne, or George Herbert'. This was an excessive judgement but helped to rehabilitate some of the poet's earlier reputation. [E M/M B]

Poems and Essays, ed. J. F. Clarke (1886); *Selected Poems*, ed. Nathan Lyons (1966).
W. I. Bartlett, *Jones Very: Emerson's 'Brave Saint'* (1942); Edwin Gittleman, *Jones Very: The Effective Years* (1967).

Vidal, Gore (1925–). Novelist. Born in New York, he used his army service experience for the first of his 8 novels, *Williwaw* (1946). He has also written

mysteries as 'Edgar Box'. His stories are collected in *A Thirsty Evil and Other Stories* (1956). He ran for Congress as a democrat in 1960, gathering 25,000 votes more than J. F. Kennedy, an experience used in his neat play *The Best Man* (1960) and discussed in one of the excellent critical essays in *Rocking the Boat* (1962). *Reflections upon a Sinking Ship* (1969) is a second collection of essays. The title work of *Visit to a Small Planet and Other Television Plays* (1956) was rewritten as a Broadway success in 1957. Besides rewriting *Williwaw*, Vidal has rewritten or revised others of his novels: *The Judgement of Paris* (1952), *Messiah* (1954) and *The City and the Pillar* (1948), the first American novel to deal in detail with homosexuals and their world. *Julian* (1964) makes a novel out of the career of the apostate nephew of Constantine the Great: an erudite as well as an entertainingly physical book. In *Washington D.C.* (1967) the target is the corridor men of American power, the manipulations of a press lord and the game of the presidential elections. Behind the appalling picture of those who might control the world lies Vidal's disgust at the immoral procedures of government, and the same exacerbation propels *Myra Breckinridge* (1968), a novel of sexual interchange and doomed carnal America focused in the show-biz world. Vidal is today a leading satirist of pretentious, sophisticated America: in his latest play, *Weekend* (1968), he has a liberal senator insist that his son marry a black fiancée. *Two Sisters* (1970) is camp biography in the form of a novel. [E M]

Viereck, Peter (1916–). Poet, critic. Born in New York City, he studied at Harvard and Oxford. After war service in Europe he taught English and German at Harvard, and later became Professor of History at Mount Holyoke. His poetry, which ranges from the comic and ironic to the extremely self-analytic, is collected in *Terror and Decorum* (1948), which in part reflects the violence of his war experience, and won the Pulitzer Prize, *Strike Through the Mask!* (1950), *The First Morning* (1952), *The Persimmon Tree* (1956) and *New and Selected Poems, 1932–1967* (1967). *The Tree Witch* (1961), in form between a poem and a play, concerns the conflict between the spirit of man's lost sense of the earth and the forces of conformism. Although he has spoken of his 'conservative' poetics, his work is capable of considerable savagery, a mixture of terror and decorum, power and control. Its themes are also reflected in his strong polemic against some of the tendencies of American liberalism, in works of social commentary which include *Metapolitics: From the Romantics to Hitler* (1941), *Conservatism Revisited: The Revolt against Revolt* (1949), *Dream and Responsibility* (1953) and *The Shame and Glory of the Intellectuals* (1953). These books have added a useful astringency to modern debate. *The Education of a Poet* (1951) is a critical work containing some useful analysis of ◊ New Criticism ploys. [MB/EM]

John Lawlor, 'Peter Viereck, Poet and Critic of Values', *Études Anglaises*, July 1954.

Vonnegut, Kurt (1922–   ). Novelist. He was born in Indianapolis, was a prisoner of war in Germany, studied at Tennessee and Chicago Universities, and later began to write magazine short stories. His large reputation, established by *The Sirens of Titan* (1961) and *Cat's Cradle* (1963), was confirmed by *Slaughterhouse Five* (1969). Although he makes use of the apparatus of science fiction – *The Sirens of Titan* contains a good deal of what has been called 'wide-screen baroque' – Vonnegut's novels reflect a highly individual talent which revels in irony. *Cat's Cradle*, for instance, is among other things a satire on both science and religion. Not least among his virtues is a sense – and use – of humour in a genre which notoriously suffers from the lack of it. His first novel, *Player Piano* (1960), is satirical science fiction on automation fantasies. *God Bless You, Mr Rosewater, or Pearls before Swine* (1965) is a brilliant example of black humour in the form of surrealist humour and short comic-strip-like sections: the theme is 'how to love people who have no use'. *Mother Night* was reissued in hardcover in 1966, a measure of Vonnegut's increasing reputation. The neat introduction comments on its Nazi and anti-semitic materials, used with familiar humour. *Welcome to the Monkey House*, a collection of short stories 'sold in order to finance the writing of the novels', appeared in 1968, and *Slaughterhouse Five* (1969) continues his phosphorescent analysis of twentieth-century addiction to warfare. [HD/EM]

Robert Scholes, *The Fabulators* (1967).

W

Wakoski, Diane (1937–   ). Poet. She was born and educated in California, and lives in New York. She has evolved into a major poet of what she terms 'the completely personal expression'; her powerful, sometimes surrealistically intense work is contained in: *Coins and Coffins* (1961), *Discrepancies and Apparitions* (1966), *George Washington Poems* (1967), *Greed* (1968–9) and *Inside the Blood Factory* (1968). She appears in *Four Young Lady Poets* (ed. LeRoi Jones, 1962). [EM]

Waldo, Edward Hamilton. ◊ Sturgeon, Theodore.

Wallace, Lew (1827–1905). Novelist. Born in Indiana, he practised law in Indianapolis, and served as general in the Civil War and on the court martial which tried those involved in Lincoln's assassination. He was governor in New Mexico and minister to Turkey, and is remembered for his *Ben Hur: A Tale of the Christ* (1880), a multiple best-seller. Among his other writings are 'The Wooing of Mulkatoon' (poem, 1898), and *The Prince of India, or, Why Constantinople Fell* (1893), a 300,000-word novel suggested by President Garfield. [EM]

Wallant, Edward Lewis (1926–1962). Novelist. Born in New Haven, Connecticut, he studied art and eventually became art director for a large New York advertising agency. When he died at 36, he had already made an important and substantial contribution to fiction, as one of the most interesting of post-war Jewish writers. His novels are *The Human Season* (1960); *The Pawnbroker* (1961), his best work; *The Tenants of Moonbloom* (1963); and *The Children at the Gate* (1964). All are dramas of religious conversion, in which the heroes, turned in upon themselves by suffering or timidity, are forced into contact with life through some redeeming act of love. Thus Joseph Berman, the hero of *The Human Season*, a Jewish plumber, struggles with despair on the death of his wife, finally achieving a redeeming sense of the power and energy alive in ordinary existence. He evokes memorably the archetypal Jewish experiences – particularly the horrors of the concentration camp and the degradation of the 'mercantile heritage'. [BW]

Jonathan Baumbach, *The Landscape of Nightmare: Studies in the Contemporary American Novel* (1965).

Ward, Artemus (Charles Farrar Browne) (1834–67). Humorist. Born in Maine, he became a printer as a young man, sent his earliest writings to the *Carpet Bag* (Boston) and began his reputation as a humorist on Ohio newspapers. 'Artemus Ward' first appeared, in a letter to the Cleveland *Plain Dealer* (of which he was city editor) in 1858, as a shrewd showman with a Yankee dialect and weird spelling. Ward began as a comic adventurer, but was soon commenting iconoclastically on political matters and the social developments of his time, from the Civil War to the Mormon Church. He became nationally famous; some of his best work appeared in *Vanity Fair,* including a mock interview with Lincoln. Like his fellow-humorists known as much by his appearances as his writing, Browne/Ward lectured across the country, knew 'Mark Twain' (whom he helped launch) in Virginia City, and in 1886 made a great success in England as lecturer and editor of *Punch,* but died there the following year. He is an outstanding example of American popular humour (e.g. 'the pretty girls in Utah mostly marry Young,' which he thought his best joke) and along with 'Petroleum V. ◊ Nasby' and 'Josh ◊ Billings' who took up the mode, he represents an important movement in American vernacular comedy. Only two books appeared in his lifetime, *Artemus Ward: His Book* (1862), and *Artemus Ward: His Travels* (1865), but more appeared posthumously, including *Artemus Ward in London* (1867). [MB]

The Complete Works, ed. T. W. Robertson and E. P. Hingston (1903); *Selected Works*, ed. Albert J. Nock (1912; 1924).
Don C. Seitz, *Artemus Ward (Charles Farrar Browne): A Biography and a Bibliography* (1919).

Ward, Nathaniel (1568–1652). Excommunicated by Laud he arrived in New England in 1634, became a minister in Ipswich, Massachusetts and returned when Cromwell came to power, in 1648. His significant book is *The Simple Cobbler of Aggawam in America* (1647), a discussion of Puritan doctrine and a defence of Congregationalism written in one of the finest idiosyncratic prose styles of the 17th century. His attack on tolerance includes a spicy satire on female costume and 'the nuduistertian fashion' of 'nugiperous gentledames'. [EM]

M. C. Tyler, *A History of American Literature 1607–1765* (2 vols., 1878; repr. 1949).

Warner, Charles Dudley (1829–1900). Novelist, essayist, biographer. Born in Plainfield, Massachusetts. Now usually recalled as a collaborator with Mark ◊ Twain on *The Gilded Age* (1873). He also wrote essays, reminiscent and literary (*My Summer in a Garden*, 1871, *Fashions in Literature*, 1902, etc.); a fictional trilogy (*A Little Journey in the World*, 1889, *The Golden House*, 1894, and *That Fortune*, 1899), on the misuse of a great fortune; and several good travel-books, including *Our Italy* (1891). Editor of the 'American Men of Letters' series, he contributed the biographies of John Smith and Washington Irving. [MB]

Warren, Robert Penn (1905–   ). Novelist, poet, critic. He was born in Kentucky, educated at Vanderbilt, California and Yale, and was a Rhodes scholar at Oxford in 1930. He has taught in a number of universities in America. His student contributions to the *Fugitive* (1922–5) already showed his affinities with the Southern Agrarians and *John Brown, the Making of a Martyr* (1929) and his essay in *I'll Take My Stand* (1930) confirmed them. He co-edited the *Southern Review* (1935–42) and, with Cleanth ◊ Brooks, compiled three highly influential ◊ New Criticism volumes, *Understanding Poetry* (1938), *Understanding Fiction* (1943) and *Fundamentals of Good Writing* (1950). His literary criticism in *Selected Essays* (1958) includes important essays on Conrad, Faulkner and 'The Rime of the Ancient Mariner'. Warren's handling of the long narrative poem and the short, metaphysically complex lyric distinguish a large poetic output in *Selected Poems 1923–1943* (1944), *Promises, Poems 1954–6* (1957), *Selected Poems; New and Old, 1923–1966*

(1966) and *Incarnations* (1968). His characteristic themes of personal and social guilt receive extended treatment in *Brother to Dragons* (1953), a book-length dramatic narrative in verse centred on the family history and ideas of ◊ Jefferson, and *Circus in the Attic* (1948, short stories). In *Audubon: A Vision* (1969), the great naturalist becomes the Adamic hero of a long poem on the American wilderness.

His eight novels explore obsessively the conflicts of the South as universal problems, but his moral point of view and style are uncomplex enough to make him a popular novelist. His materials are always vividly local: *Night Rider* (1939) concerns the Kentucky tobacco war of the 1900s, *At Heaven's Gate* (1943) contemporary Southern capitalism and pretensions to culture, *All the King's Men* (1946) the rise and fall of a Louisiana demagogue and his entourage, *World Enough and Time* (1950), his finest and most elaborate work, a famous Kentucky 19th-century murder case, *Band of Angels* (1955) the tragedy of miscegenation, *The Cave* (1959) the social effects of a cave accident, *Wilderness* (1961) a Bavarian Jew in the Civil War, and *Flood* (1964) a Tennessee town about to vanish under federal dam waters. These novels constitute a record of serious fiction-making on important themes, a lifetime's thinking which is clear, too, in his two important considerations of the Negro problems: *Segregation* (1956) and *Who Speaks for the Negro?* (1965). [EM]

L. Casper, *Robert Penn Warren: The Dark and Bloody Ground* (1960); ed. J. W. Longley, Jr, *Robert Penn Warren: A Collection of Critical Essays* (1967).

Warshow, Robert (1917–55). Critic, social commentator. An editor of the New York Jewish review *Commentary*, he wrote outstanding essays on films, comics, theatre and other aspects of popular culture, posthumously collected in *The Immediate Experience* (1962). [MB]

Washington, Booker T(aliaferro) (1856–1915). Negro leader. Was the son of a slave and a white man. He began work at an early age in salt furnaces and coal mines in West Virginia, and educated himself at night school and Hampton Normal Agricultural Institute (1872–5). After a period of teaching and a return to Hampton for experimental work for Indians, he created the Tuskegee

Institute (1881), which later became a large and important centre of Negro education (see his *Tuskegee and Its People*, 1905), and organized the National Negro Business League in Boston (1901). His books are the foundation of Negro American aspiration at the turning point in its history: *Sowing and Reaping* (1900), *Character Building* (1902) and *Working with the Hands* (1904). *Up from Slavery* (1901), an autobiography, is a major document in the history of America (see also *The Story of the Negro*, 1909, *My Larger Education*, 1911, and *The Man Farthest Down*, 1912). His biography of Frederick Douglass (1907) is a pioneering work in this field. Washington's philosophy of expediency, gradualism and submission, best in his famous 1895 speech at the Cotton State and International Exposition in Atlanta, was vitally challenged by W. E. B. ⟡ DuBois in 1903, but he was the senior Negro leader for a quarter of a century. (⟡ Negro Literature.) [EM]

S. R. Spencer, *Booker T. Washington and the Negro's Place in American Life* (1955).

Webster, Daniel (1782–1852). Lawyer, statesman, orator. Born in Salisbury, New Hampshire, he studied at Dartmouth College, practised law, entered politics in 1813, was Massachusetts senator from 1827 to 1841 and Secretary of State 1841–3 and 1850–2, but never gained the presidency he frequently sought. His willingness to compromise on any issue which might split the Union made him distrusted by both Northern Abolitionists and Southern planters. Whittier attacked him in 'Ichabod' but, after the Civil War, came to understand him ('The Lost Occasion', 1880), and Oliver Wendell ⟡ Holmes wrote a similar pair of poems. Webster was New England capitalism's legal representative even while in public office. His special kind of eloquence and his dramatic appearance are celebrated in S. V. ⟡ Benét's 'The Devil and Daniel Webster' (1937), in a sentence in Hawthorne's 'The Great Stone Face', and elsewhere, and some of his own words are legendary; 'Liberty *and* Union, now and forever, one and inseparable', and 'Liberty exists in proportion to wholesome restraint', etc. [EM]

The Writings and Speeches, ed. J. W. McIntyre (18 vols., 1903); S. H. Adams, *The Godlike Daniel* (1933); ed. W. Lewis, *Speak for Yourself, Daniel: A Life of Webster in His Own Words* (1969).

Webster, Noah (1758–1843). Lexicographer. Born in Connecticut, he served with his father in the army against General Burgoyne, studied at Yale (1778), and became a teacher and a lawyer. *Sketches of American Policy* (1785) is one of several pamphlets he wrote promoting strong central government, and between 1793 and 1798 he wrote in support of Washington's and Adams' policies and edited the *American Minerva*. But together with national government his deep concern was national language – 'our honour requires us to have a system of our own, in language as well as in government' – and literature. His *Grammatical Institute of the English Language, Comprising an Easy, Concise, and Systematic Method in Education, Designed for the Use of English Schools in America* (1783) is a patriot's compendium, a major aid to standardizing American spelling and pronunciation, and a best-seller as *The American Speller*. Webster's broad interests in science, literature, politics and local government and social life undoubtedly aided his monumental 20 years of preparation for his greatest work, *An American Dictionary of the English Language* (1828), which he completed in 1825 and revised in 1841. In 1843, G. and C. Merriam took over the right to the editions that have been appearing ever since. The 1962 *Third New International Dictionary* also defines English and Commonwealth words. Webster's original *Dictionary* was not only one of the first major works of American scholarship: it struck a blow for definition by usage rather than by linguistic purities. [EM]

Noah Webster: On Being American. Selected Writings, 1783–1828, ed. H. D. Babbage, Jr (1967).

Weems, Mason Locke (1759–1825). Clergyman, bookseller, biographer. Born in Arundel, Maryland. Ordained in 1784, Weems's rationalist views and his admiration for Thomas ⟡ Paine alienated his fellow clergy and he left his parish to become an itinerant agent of the Philadelphia bookseller Mathew Carey. For 31 years he travelled throughout the sea-board states peddling 'improving' books. His fame lies in the moral tracts and biographies of revolutionary heroes which he himself wrote during this period. His famous life of George Washington (1800; ed. Marcus Cunliffe, 1962) embodied the virtues which he had consistently propagated. He portrayed

Washington as an almost impossibly moral, honest and wise leader, creating a folk myth which still lives. The work was continuously embroidered throughout successive editions, the famous story of the cherry tree and the hatchet appearing for the first time in the fifth edition of 1806. Parson Weems also wrote lives of Francis Marion (1809), Benjamin Franklin (1815) and William Penn (1822), but none achieved the great popular success of the earlier book. [EM]

Weidman, Jerome (1913–   ). Novelist, playwright. Born in New York, he studied there at City College and New York University. New York is a central part of his subject-matter. A witty observer of urban mores, particularly in the city's Jewish groups, he used his fiction to analyse ruthless business men, ambitious writers, tough newspaper-men and go-getting poor boys. *I Can Get it for You Wholesale* (1937), and it's sequel, *What's In It for Me?* (1938), novels about Harry Bogen, an ambitious clerk in the New York garment trade, were found upsetting when they appeared. *I'll Never Go There Any More* (1941) shows an outsider confronted with Manhattan mores; *Too Early to Tell* (1946) mocks governmental agencies with its Bureau of Psychological Combat. Other novels include *Your Daughter Iris* (1955), which contrasts the Bronx and England, *The Sound of Bow Bells* (1962) and *Word of Mouth* (1964). Weidman's short stories have been collected in *The Horse That Could Whistle 'Dixie'* (1939), *The Death of Dickie Draper* (1965), etc. Latterly he has had Broadway successes with *Fiorello!* (1959), about La Guardia, Mayor of New York, and *Tenderloin* (1961). [MB]

Weinberg, Bernard. ◊ Chicago Aristotelians.

Weiss, Theodore (1916–   ). Poet. Pennsylvania-born, he was educated at Muhlenberg College and Columbia University. He taught at the University of North Carolina and Yale before joining the faculty of Bard College, where he edits the *Quarterly Review of Literature*. Five books of his verse have appeared – *The Catch* (1951), *Outlanders* (1960), *Gunsight* (1962), *The Medium* (1965) and *The Last Day and the First* (1968) – revealing his interest in the long poem, his inclination toward rhetoric and philosophy, and his debt to William Carlos ◊ Williams. [MB]

Richard Howard, *Alone with America* (1969).

Welty, Eudora (1909–   ). Story writer, novelist. Born in Jackson, Mississippi, of Northern parents, she is at once saturated in the familiar details of Southern life and history and removed from any deep commitment to the specifically Southern myths. Though she attended university at Wisconsin and Columbia, and worked briefly in advertising in New York, she has spent most of her life in Jackson as a part of that Mississippi delta community out of which her best writing grows. Works like *Delta Wedding* (1946) are sometimes said to present a nostalgic view of the remnants of a decadent aristocracy; in fact her interest is in the inward awareness of the individual, rather than in any social case. And though she is superb at creating an atmosphere and the texture of a community, her best stories explore the theme of what she calls in one of them ('The Still Moment') 'Separateness' and the potential reconciliation of love. She shows each individual as an endless mystery, and the necessity of love to include that mystery. Her works vary considerably, in part because she is technically accomplished and is constantly answering new creative problems. She can be quaint, as in some of her character-stories and in some of her use of legend (*The Robber Bridegroom*, 1942); she can also be superbly comic and effectively bizarre.

Her first book, *A Curtain of Green* (1941), is a collection of varied stories, many dealing with Southern grotesques. Then came a fairy-tale novel, *The Robber Bridegroom* (1942), set in Mississippi in 1798. *The Wide Net* (1943), stories, is a sure, impressive volume; so are the novels that followed, *Delta Wedding* (1946), a child's approach to the mysterious adult world of love and experience, and *The Golden Apples* (1949), interlinked short stories set in a single town and exploring elaborate narrative methods. The more recent books, the splendidly funny novel *The Ponder Heart* (1954) and the experimental collection of stories *The Bride of the Innisfallen* (1954), seem to be the work of an artist in complete command of impressive powers keeping her hand in while meditating some more important move. *Losing Battle* (1970) is a long novel celebrating the cohesion of a Mississippi family. [DC/MB]

A. Appel, Jr, *A Season of Dreams: The Fiction of Eudora Welty* (1966).

Wescott, Glenway (1901–   ). Novelist,

poet, story writer. He grew up in Wisconsin and studied at the University of Chicago, then became an expatriate, living in England, Germany and for eight years in the South of France, associated with but not closely allied to the ◊ 'Lost Generation'. He settled in New Jersey in 1934. He has published two volumes of poems, *The Bitterns* (1920) and *Natives of Rock* (1926), but is better known for his fiction. He is a delicate and lyrical writer who in his best work has made strong use of his native Wisconsin materials. His novels include *The Apple of the Eye* (1924), about a young boy's growth to maturity in a Wisconsin farm setting; *The Grandmothers* (1927), about a pioneer Wisconsin family; *The Pilgrim Hawk* (1940), set in Paris; and *Apartment in Athens* (1945), about the Greek underground resistance to the Nazis. A volume of stories, *Goodbye Wisconsin* (1928), exploits the contrast between Wisconsin and expatriate life; other volumes are *Like a Lover* (1926) and *Babe's Bed* (1930). *Images of Truth* (1962) is a collection of portraits of authors, including Katherine Anne Porter and Thomas Mann. [MB]

William H. Ruecket, *Glenway Wescott* (1965).

West, Nathanael (Nathan Wallenstein Weinstein) (1904–40). Novelist. Born in New York City. Increasingly recognized as a great precursor of the black comedy manner, West, who was killed in a car crash at 37, wrote four short novels which add up to one of the most telling indictments of the U.S.A. produced by an American. The American dream of a new world of liberty and the pursuit of happiness is envisaged as a grotesque nightmare; the land of opportunity turns comically into a land of failure, disillusionment, boredom, inhumanity and suffering.

West's first novel *The Dream Life of Balso Snell* (1931) is untypical in being concerned with the disintegration of the isolated self, removed from any specific, social context; a surrealist dream story, it is a bitter, contemptuous exhibition of private despair. In his second, *Miss Lonelyhearts* (1933), the protagonist is the writer of a newspaper agony column gradually overcome by the weight of real suffering revealed by the halting letters he receives from his readers. His attempts both to evade and confront the immensities of pain in the world of which he is part end equally in failure. The story is told with economy and the intellectual exhibitionism of *Balso Snell* has gone; the result is a modern fable of disturbing power. *A Cool Million* (1934) is a more overt denunciation of modern America in social and political terms. The form of the story is uninhibited parody of the Horatio Alger success myth. The innocent hero, having lost teeth, eyes, a leg and his scalp, in a *laissez-faire* world, and having become the witless tool of both Communist and Fascist organizations, ironically ends as a heroic martyr. The book makes its satirical points unerringly, and the wholly fabulous narrative mode is comically rich – but lacks that rooting in immediate human reality which makes *Miss Lonelyhearts* so compelling. West's last novel, *The Day of the Locust* (1939), is set in Hollywood, where he worked writing screenplays for the last five years of his life. The bizarre life of Hollywood and Southern California comes to focus the dangerous, explosive boredom and meaninglessness of modern life. Society's suppressed violence and hatred boil over in the last pages in an account of a mob riot at a film première. Character-types, action and setting are superbly chosen to define and articulate his vision of a modern world that is brutal, mindless and unredeemed. [AH]

The Complete Works, intr. Alan Ross (1957).
Randall Reid, *The Fiction of Nathanael West* (1968); J. F. Light, *Nathanael West: An Interpretative Study* (1961); Victor Comerchero, *Nathanael West: The Ironic Prophet* (1964).

Wexley, John (1907–). New York dramatist, celebrated for his plays on social themes, *The Last Mile* (1930), a plea for prison reform, and *They Shall Not Die* (1934), an impressive dramatization of the Scottsboro trial. [EM]

Whalen, Philip (1923–). Poet. He was born in Oregon, served in the air force 1943–6, studied at Reed College, and became associated with the San Francisco poetry revival of the 1940s and 1950s. Since 1966 he has been living in Japan. His published poetry begins with *Three Satires* (1951) and is established characteristically with *Self-Portrait from Another Direction* (1960), already notable for its invention of typographical and spatial layout forms to articulate the motion of thinking and feeling down the page. *Like I Say* (1960) and *Memoirs of an Interglacial Age* (1960) develop his poetic strengths: the direct graphical presentation of immediate experience, the abstract expressionist form of poetic diary, and the sense of the poem as an example of the poet's situation at a given moment, into which his current interests – Buddhism, jazz, sex, painting, anything he is taking part in – are projected and unified. There followed *Monday in the Evening* (1964), *Every Day* (1965), which includes calligraphically drawn works, a form which is most developed in *Highgrade* (1966) in order to obtain the sense of the poem being immediately made on the page. *On Bear's Head* (1969) is a collection of most of his twenty years' work. *You Didn't Even Try* (1966) is an interesting domestic novel, with little of the experiment of his poetry. [EM]

Wharton, Edith (1862–1937). Novelist. Born Edith Newbold Jones into a very well-to-do New York family, she was educated by governesses, her own extensive reading in the family library, and travel abroad. She came out into New York Society very young and married a member of her mother's circle, Edward Wharton, years older than herself, in 1885. Her first full-length novel, *The Valley of Decision* (1902), was a reconstruction of 18th-century Italy. Then followed subjects closer to home: as a wife and hostess Edith Wharton belonged to Society, but as a novelist she analysed its customs and attitudes with increasing penetration and devastating irony. The New York novels present a changing society, made significant morally; a strong sense of human dignity and integrity supplies the ultimate standard behind the social conventions and forms. She presents as the background to her stories a running conflict between two distinct upper middle classes, the old 'patrician' American families such as her own and the new rich for whom traditional ideals of culture, morals and manners, though they pay assiduous lip-service to them, are losing their sanctity.

The earlier work focuses attention on the relationship, usually hostile, between the individual and the community. The first great novel, *The House of Mirth* (1905), which shocked contemporary Society by its inwardness and realism, is an ironically tragic treatment of this theme in the disastrous social career of Lily Bart. *The Custom of the Country* (1913), the story of Undine Spragg's pyrrhic victory over family

and Society at home and abroad, is a satiric comedy. Between writing these, Edith Wharton produced her contribution to 'muck-raking', *The Fruit of the Tree* (1907), on the evils of industrialism; and also *Ethan Frome* (1911), which deals with the plight rather than the rebellion of the individual in Puritan, lower-middle-class New England. Its strong sense of tragedy and its highly dramatic development make it somewhat exceptional in her work (though it bears resemblance to *Summer*, 1917, also set in New England). All these novels possess a solidity and richness that makes them comparable with the great early novels of Henry James. Physical detail and the details of social gradation and custom are much more precisely and thoroughly presented than in his work; the 'visibility' of characters was always as strong an artistic principle with Edith Wharton as selection of 'crucial moments' and careful planning. Always elegant, she increasingly developed a clear, richly concrete and sharply ironic manner, which gives her books their distinctive moral acerbity.

After 1907 she spent much of her life in Paris and, after her husband's nervous collapse, followed by separation and divorce, she settled there, an important figure in the American expatriate community. She had known James from her youth; latterly he regarded her as an artist of equal standing. Other friends close to her interests were Bernard ◊ Berenson, Logan Pearsall ◊ Smith, Howard ◊ Sturgis, Geoffrey Scott, Walter Berry, and Percy Lubbock, who wrote the valuable *Portrait of Edith Wharton* (1947). After the First World War she bought a minor showplace, the Pavillon Colombe near Paris, where she entertained many younger writers. She had exhausted herself with large-scale welfare activities during the war; the 1920s at first bewildered her. Her brilliant *The Age of Innocence* (1920), once again dealing with New York society, has the faint air of an escape to the world of her childhood. But in *Twilight Sleep* (1927) and *The Children* (1928) she found a suitably rough satiric mode for portraying the disintegrating Society of America and Europe; her theme is now the helplessness of individuals amid social anarchy. The revival of her powers continues into her autobiography, *A Backward Glance* (1934), a record both of her social and literary life and an important document, and her unfinished novel *The Buccaneers* (1938), where the search for social order is brought into the English aristocracy.

She wrote altogether 46 books, many others worthy of attention. There are many good short stories, several admirable travel books, and the critical (and useful) *The Writing of Fiction* (1925). A recognized master of her art during her lifetime, she has been unduly neglected since her death; she needs to be seen not merely as Henry James's heiress but as a major novelist in her own right – the critic of a phase of civilization, an upholder of the idea of human civilization itself. [GW]

Collected Short Stories (2 vols., 1968).

Louis Auchincloss, *Edith Wharton* (1961); ed. Irving Howe, *Edith Wharton: A Collection of Critical Essays* (1962); Henry James, 'The New Novel', in *The Art of Fiction*, ed. Morris Roberts (1948); Blake Nevius, *Edith Wharton* (1953); Grace Kellogg, *The Two Lives of Edith Wharton* (1965); Geoffrey Walton, *Edith Wharton: A Critical Interpretation* (1970).

Wheatley, Phyllis (*c*. 1753–84). Poet. She was born in Africa, sold as a slave in Boston at the age of 8 to John Wheatley, a tailor, who educated her in his family, and became a precocious student of English, Latin and Greek. Her poems were admired for their freakishness – Negro and juvenile as well as pietistic. But her small achievement is genuine and saddening. She came to London when she was 18, much admired in society, and returned to America, marrying unhappily with a free Negro, John Peters, and died of her struggle against poverty in Boston. *Memoir and Poems of Phyllis Wheatley* appeared in 1834 and her letters in 1864. Voltaire mentioned her once as 'une Négresse qui a fait de très bons vers anglais'. (◊ Negro Literature.) [EM]

M. Bacon, *Puritan Promenade* (1964).

Wheelwright, John (1897–1940). Poet. Born in a wealthy Boston suburb, he graduated from Harvard College and studied architecture at M.I.T. Until it was cut short by a drunken driver, his life was given half to poetry and architecture and half to Trotskyism: he was Boston's most elegant and legendary leftist. Except for the posthumous *Selected Poems* (1941), all of his poetry was privately published, and won him a reputation only among critics and

other poets. It is important minor poetry: often in the form of parable, metrically difficult, and displaying a relish for the particular and for the epigrammatic. [BP]

Whipple, Edwin Percy (1819–86), Critic. Born in Gloucester, Massachusetts. Like Moses Coit ◊ Tyler and Brander ◊ Matthews, he was important for his part in establishing American literature as a field of study. In his day he was regarded as an authoritative American critic and lecturer; a typical work is his *Lectures on Subjects Connected with Literature and Life* (1850). Though he gave most of his attention to European literature, his late *American Literature and Other Papers* (1887) represents his interests in native authors, particularly in Emerson. In 1963, Mark Schorer introduced a useful collection of his essays on American writers entitled *Spokesmen*. [MB]

White, E(ltoyn) B(rooks) (1899–). Humorist, critic. Important in a sometimes neglected tradition in modern American letters, the tradition of elegance, urbanity and formal concern, he exploited the traditional periodical essay-form and helped make it relevant for modern literary journalism. Associated from the 1920s with the *New Yorker*, he resembles ◊ Thurber – with whom he collaborated on *Is Sex Necessary?* (1929) – in exactness of style, satirical sharpness and response to the anti-humane tendency of much modern life. But if less euphoric than Thurber, he is more openly intelligent. His humorous commentary is to be found in such collections as *Alice through the Cellophane* (1933), *Quo Vadimus? or the Case for the Bicycle* (1939) and in the satirical stories of *The Second Tree from the Corner* (1954). Editorial commentaries from the *New Yorker*, etc., are collected in *The Wild Flag* (1946) and his essays in *The Points of My Compass* (1962). In addition to writing humour, he wrote a scholarly work on the popular religious literature of the 16th century; revised William Strunk Jr's classic little *The Elements of Style* (1959); published children's books and a volume of poems, *The Fox of Peapack* (1938); and compiled with his wife *A Sub-Treasury of American Humor* (1941). [MB]

Whitman, Walt (1819–92). Poet. The great poet's father was a Long Island carpenter, builder and radical who read ◊ Paine and Owen and admired the Quaker, Hicks, imparting to his son his own respect for democracy and the interior life of the soul. After a childhood period in the (then) country town of Brooklyn, apprenticed to a printer, he returned to 'fish-shaped Paumanok' and taught in schools from 1836 to 1841, at intervals working as printer and journalist and on his own paper, the *Long Islander*. His poetry showed little originality and his prose, including a temperance novel (1842), is slight and topical. At 23 he edited the Democratic *Aurora* in New York but was sacked after a few months, as he was from the Brooklyn *Eagle*, apparently for his independent, radical opinions. In 1848 he travelled to New Orleans to work on the *Crescent*, a trip which opened his provinciality to the Mississippi heartlands. His New York journalism ended. He had been prolific, conventional and rhetorical; his personal manner was dandified; he moved in the company of painters, opera buffs and Bohemians; he was excited by the international art and industry of the World's Fair; he had supported his family as a shrewd real estate man. Then at the age of 31 his image changed, as his notebooks show, towards his new prophetic, bardic role as poet of an ideal America. He grew a beard and became Walt, the poet of *Leaves of Grass* (1855), his name appearing only in small print in the copyright, the frontispiece portraying the new bard as 'an American, one of the roughs, a kosmos, disorderly fleshy and sensual . . . eating and drinking and breeding' (*Song of Myself*). This was not the language of genteel letters, and his poems were attacked for their free structure and physicality, although he was backed by Emerson and Thoreau. By 35, he embodied the mythical national poet he wanted to be. For the rest of his life he augmented the book of his personality until he received the ninth and final edition on his deathbed. The 1860 version contained 124 new poems and many revisions; the fifth edition (1872) includes the Civil War poems, *Drum Taps* and its sequel.

Whitman's workman's costume became less emblematic when the Depression left him poor in 1853. From 1857 to 1859 he edited the Brooklyn *Times*, his last journalistic job. The 1860 portrait for *Leaves* shows him more Byronic than rough. In the Civil War he demonstrated the comradely tenderness and love of his poems by tending the wounded in camp hospitals, offering his friendship to men suffering from war and primitive medicine (*Hospital Visits*, 'The Wound Dresser'). His poetry was enriched but his health was impaired: Matthew Brady's 1863 photograph shows him a white-haired old man at 44. Little critical attention was paid to *Drum Taps*; a shocked Secretary of the Interior sacked him from his Washington clerkship; and he resigned from the series of minor posts from ill-health in 1873. During this period he produced 'When Lilacs Last in the Dooryard Bloom'd', an elegy for Lincoln and a celebration of regenerative powers, *Democratic Vistas* (1871), a pamphlet on the nature of democracy, and 'Passage to India' (1868), representative of his later manner. By 1866 he had sufficient allegiance in America and England but recognized his descent from 'the high plateau of my life and capacity', a decline speeded by a paralysing stroke in 1873. He lived in Camden, New Jersey, wrote a few more poems, and *Specimen Days* (1882–3), and during a brief recovery of energy travelled to St Louis and the Rocky Mountains (1879). In 1884 he bought a little house in Camden where he lived well looked after until his death.

Leaves of Grass is a continuous performance maintaining the stance of the new American poet, inheritor of Emerson's self-reliance and ◊ Transcendental universalism: 'who touches this touches a man'. 'Out of the Cradle Endlessly Rocking' displays the poet's origins in the boy's intimations of loss of love and life, countered by the active sense of being part of universal processes of rejuvenation, that ebb and flow of oceanic energies which is Whitman's central philosophical image. His 'evangel-poems of comrades and love' are designed to reveal an ecstatic vision of diversified life exemplified by the Manifest Destiny of the United States, the opportunity for recovering Adam's innocence and 'a world primal again'. The fine erotic 'Calamus' poems are a central personal demonstration whose wider circle is an ideal Brotherhood of 'America' round the globe: 'One's self I sing, a single separate person, Yet utter the word Democratic, the word En-Masse'. 'Song of Myself' is a magnificent series of examples of exact individual, social and natural life unified through an organic linear form which itself is the shape of exuberant energy, that 'procreant urge of the world' the poem's philosophy contains. Whitman's greatness springs from his need to make a 'song of Sex and Amativeness, and even Animality' which is the song, too, of the 'libidinous' power of nature. His poetic forms appear to be loose, even rhetorically diffuse, but at their best their rhythms firmly articulate his naturally spreading genius. [EM]

Complete Poetry and Selected Prose, ed. E. Holloway (1938); *Leaves of Grass: Readers' Edition*, ed. H. Blodgett and S. Bradley (1964).
G. W. Allen, *The Solitary Singer: A Critical Biography* (1955); R. Chase, *Walt Whitman Reconsidered* (1955); ed. M. Hindus, *Leaves of Grass One Hundred Years After* (1955); ed. R. H. Pearce, *Whitman: A Collection of Critical Essays* (1962).

Whittemore, Reed (1919–). Poet. Born in New Haven, Connecticut, he attended Yale University. He served in Europe in the Second World War and now teaches English at Carleton College in Minnesota, where he edited two leading literary reviews, *Furioso* and its successor the *Carleton Miscellany*. In 1964–5 he was Poetry Consultant to the Library of Congress. A witty and critical commentator both in prose and verse, his criticism has stressed the need for poetry to emphasize its rational elements, and his own work, varied as it is in theme, is concerned with quality and accuracy of mind. His books of poems are *Heroes and Heroines* (1946), *An American Takes a Walk and Other Poems* (1956), and *The Self-Made Man and Other Poems* (1959). *The Boy from Iowa* (1962) contains essays as well as poems, and *The Fascination of the Abomination* (1963) brings together poems, essays and short stories. [MB]

Whittier, John Greenleaf (1807–92). Poet, journalist. Raised on his Quaker father's farm at East Haverhill, Massachusetts, he early became familiar with the poetry of Burns. In 1831, while he was working as an editor, he published *Legends of New-England*, early verse. From 1833 until the Emancipation of the slaves in 1865, his main concerns were political, and he was an extremely influential spokesman in the anti-slavery cause. His anti-slavery poems, collected in *Voices of Freedom* (1846), were declamatory 'trumpet calls', and he tended to justify himself as a poet on the grounds of his devotion to freedom and brother-

hood, his decent if homespun Quaker concern. In his later work his concern with his region turned him towards historical and legendary narratives and to what he called 'Yankee pastoral'. As a nature poet, despite his strong religious vein, he is by no means as convincing as his many 19th-century admirers thought, and his reputation has not really survived. Even so there is much of interest. The personal quality of *Snow-Bound* (1866), written after the death of his beloved sister Elizabeth and recalling his childhood, makes it an interesting and significant poem; it brought him poetic success. Some of his best work, including *Home Ballads* (1860), *In War Time* (1864; containing 'Barbara Frietchie'), *The Tent on the Beach* (1867) and *Among the Hills* (1869), appeared during and just after the Civil War, which he both criticized and celebrated in verse. The radical changes which the war brought in American society made his recollective nature-poetry, about the pastoral land-owning life of the Jeffersonian dream, seem nostalgic and therefore the more popular. Though conventional in its metrics, evidently excessive in its 'poetic diction', his verse remains worthy of interest. Widely circulated in England during the last century, it is to be found in numerous old editions. [MB]

Writings, ed. H. E. Scudder (7 vols., 1888–9); *The Poetical Works*, ed. W. G. Horder (1919).
Samuel T. Pickard, *Life and Letters of John Greenleaf Whittier* (1894); Edward Wagenknecht, *John Greenleaf Whittier* (1967).

Wieners, John (1934–). Poet. He was born in Boston, graduated from Boston College, studied at ◊ Black Mountain College, founded *Measure* magazine in 1961 with Robin Blaser and Stephen Jonas, and has recently been living and working in Buffalo. His plays, including *Anklesox* and *Jive Shoelaces* (1968), a lyrical work on drug addiction, have been produced by New York poets' theatres. His reputation was established immediately with *The Hotel Wentley Poems* (1958; 2nd edn, original versions, 1965), a series recording days and nights (dated) of experience. *Ace of Pentacles* (1964) develops his range of material rather than his technical ability. The poems in *Pressed Wafer* (1967), written in 1965, show a further extension of his delicate, edgy style. *Unlived* is a set of three variations. [EM]

Wigglesworth, Michael (1631–1705). Poet. He went from England to Connecticut when he was 7, graduated from Harvard in 1651 and became minister at Malden, Massachusetts, in 1656. Typically, he used his bad health to write his poem 'Meat Out of the Eater' (1669), on the uses of sickness. Fame arrived with two long poetic warnings of great popularity. *The Day of Doom* (1662) is the first American religiose bestseller, repeatedly reprinted, 224 stanzas of doggerel which allowed the faithful to enjoy the tortures of the non-elect in hell, their own smug depravity or self-righteousness, and the torment of damned children. *God's Controversy with New England* (1662, publ. 1871) laments the advent of secularism and celebrates a new love for New England as New Eden betrayed by carnality. A Harvard dormitory bears his name. His *Diary 1653–1657* (ed. E. S. Morgan, 1965) is a classic of Puritan introspection and criticism. [EM]

R. Crowder, *No Featherbed to Heaven: Wigglesworth, 1631–1705* (1962).

Wilbur, Richard (1921–   ). Poet, translator, critic. One of the best and most highly regarded of post-war American poets. He was born in New York and served in the army in Italy. He has studied and taught at Harvard and now teaches writing at Wesleyan College. His volumes include *The Beautiful Changes, and Other Poems* (1947), *Ceremony and Other Poems* (1950), *Advice to a Prophet* (1961), a collected volume, *The Poems of Richard Wilbur* (1963) and *Walking to Sleep* (1969). His elegance, fineness of manner and formality are the distinguishing features of his work, and have made him the target of those who speak for a rawer sort of poetry and who identify him as a leading figure among the 'academic' poets. He projects a sensibility in which the claims of aesthetic beauty are pitted against the difficulties of living authentically in an age of confused values. His way of universalizing particular experience is not that of Robert ◊ Lowell, the other major figure of the period; his is rather the attempt to create out of some impulse towards emotion a revelation of something 'lofty or long-standing', displaying the essential nature of experience. He has also written a number of light, extremely witty poems (e.g. the songs he wrote for the musical *Candide*). He has done some distinguished translations, particularly of Molière, and some striking criticism, particularly of Poe. [MB]

The Moment of Poetry, ed. Don Cameron Allen (1962).

Wilcox, Ella Wheeler (1850–1919). Poet. Born in Wisconsin. 'Laugh and the world laughs with you, Weep and you weep alone.' With this sort of verse she became one of the most influential and best-selling poets of the late 19th century in America and elsewhere. Now regarded as of the pokerwork school, she was thought an erotic poet in her time, and readers throbbed to her verses. Her *Drops of Water* volume (1872), her first, had a temperance emphasis; but with the daring *Poems of Passion* (1883) she disturbed America. Spiritualism and oriental metaphysics of vaguely erotic cast informed her more than 40 volumes, which included fiction and short stories. *The Worlds and I* (1918) is autobiographical. [MB]

Wilder, Thornton (1897–   ). Novelist, playwright. He was born in Wisconsin and grew up in China, graduated from Yale in 1920, studied archaeology in Rome, and took an M.A. in French at Princeton. Briefly a teacher, he began making a living from writing in 1928, but taught at Chicago University (1930–6). A best-selling novelist and Pulitzer Prize dramatist, he is one of the most successful professionals in the business, writing what he pleases out of a wide culture and yet captivating a popular audience. His first novel, *The Cabala* (1926), is an elaborate multilevelled analysis of a great European past. The manner of James and Proust is again apparent in *The Bridge of San Luis Rey* (1927), a philosophic novel of fate and chance. *The Woman of Andros* (1930) again concerns decadence before a new coming, in pre-Christian Greece in this case, and *Heaven's My Destination* (1934) deals satirically with the clash of salesmanship and evangelism in America. *The Ides of March* (1948) is an elaborate epistolary novel about Julius Caesar. *The Eighth Day* (1967), his first novel for nearly 20 years, is a large-scale structure built round a murder case in Southern Illinois. It is ambitious, inflated and impregnated with a facile optimism curiously remote from the American sixties. Wilder's first play was *The Trumpet Shall Sound* (1926) and collections of one-act plays appeared in 1928 and 1931. His most famous plays are *Our Town* (1938), an American pastoral without scenery, influenced by Gertrude Stein's ideas, and *The Skin of Our Teeth* (1942), a satirical morality on man's escapades with wife and mistress. Recently Jose Quintero produced three short plays as *Plays for Bleecker Street*.

Wilder's themes are philosophically weighty, but nothing disturbs very deeply and his forms are imitative, as he himself will admit; but he is a skilful entertainer, a tolerant philosopher without anguish, and totally undidactic. Life is cyclic, he says, man will prevail, there is no need to worry. This is the source of his comedy. [EM]

M. G. Goldstein, *The Art of Thornton Wilder* (1965).

Williams, Jonathan (1929–   ). Poet. He was born in Asheville, North Carolina, educated at Princeton, Chicago Institute of Design and ◊ Black Mountain College. His Jargon Press, founded in 1951, is one of the most important publishers of poetry and *avant garde* writing in America, making available for the first time a considerable number of now established American writers. His publications also set a particularly high standard of design and illustration. He has served as poet in residence at Aspen Institute for Humanistic Studies. His own poetry is some of the wittiest, most formally accomplished and original in America, with subjects ranging from baseball to the English Lake District, from American ecology to social injustice in the South. His early work appeared in *Red/Gray* (1951) and *Four Stoppages* (1953); his stature is clear in *The Empire Finals of Verona* (1959), a particularly fine volume with brilliant drawings and photocollages by Fielding Dawson. There followed *Amen/Huzza/Selah* (1961), *Elegies and Celebrations* (1962), with characteristic references to ◊ Olson, Sherwood ◊ Anderson, Thoreau, the painter Franz Kline, Whitman, Messiaen, the composers Charles Ives and Carl Ruggles – a Williams pantheon. *In England's Green &* (1962) partly shows his interest in curious flora and fauna; *Lullabies Twisters Gibbers Drags* (1963) contains satires worthy of ◊ Patchen and ◊ Cummings; *Lines about Hills above Lakes* (1964, intro John Wain) is an October postcard series, mainly in prose, sent in critical love from Cumberland and Westmorland. He has recently produced poems on *Mahler* (1965) with illustrations from R. B. Kitaj, and *The Lucidities* (1968), the latest in his books of epigrams on art and eccentricities. [EM]

An Ear in Bartram's Tree: Selected Poems 1957–1967 (1969).

Williams, John A. ◊ Negro Literature.

Williams, Roger (1603–83). Puritan dissenter. A London tradesman's son, he graduated at Cambridge and went to Boston, Massachusetts, in 1630, preaching in Plymouth and Salem as unordained minister because of his unorthodox theology. Banished in 1635, he founded Providence Plantation in 1636 on Narragansett Indian land – but he was the first New Englander to meet the indigenous Americans with understanding rather than exploitation and conversion: *A Key into the Language of America* (1643) mainly concerns Indian words and opinions. Williams is one of the greatest early dissenters, a man of educated intelligence who believed in the rights of Indians to their lands, in the spiritual freedom of the individual, and in a church freely joined by those truly converted. Cromwell granted him a charter for Rhode Island in 1643. He was the first to welcome Jews to a New World colony. *The Bloudy Tenent of Persecution, for Cause of Conscience* (1644) is a dialogue between Peace and Truth concerning freedom of conscience and authority: to John ◊ Cotton's famous reply, Williams himself replied with *The Bloudy Tenent Yet More Bloudy* (1652). *George Fox Digg'd out of His Burrowes* (1676) attacks Quakers for their self-righteous reliance upon 'inner light' infallibility. [EM]

The Puritans: A Sourcebook of Their Writings, ed. P. Miller and T. H. Johnson (1938, revised bibliography, 1963).
P. Miller, *Roger Williams: His Contribution to American Tradition* (1953).

Williams, Tennessee (1914–   ). Playwright. His grandfather was an episcopalian minister, his father a travelling salesman and his mother a Quaker. He was born in Columbus, Mississippi, but the family moved to St Louis when he was 12. During the Depression he worked in a shoe factory while writing short stories which did not sell, and eventually he reached Iowa University, graduated in 1940, and received a Rockefeller grant (1940) to work on a play, *Battle of Angels*. After its disastrous opening in Boston, his first success came with *The Glass Menagerie* (1945) in New York, and since then his reputation has become international. His novels and stories include *The Roman Spring of Mrs Stone* (1950), *Hard Candy* (1954), and *Three Players of a Summer Game* (1960), and his poems appeared in *In the Winter of Cities* (1956). *The Knightly Quest* (1967) is a novella and four short stories.

Central in his drama is the lonely vulnerable woman whose present hell of insecurity is sustained by a dream of the past or the future. Illusion is confronted by reality to bring about a violent climax associated with the young male intruder. These are the materials of *The Glass Menagerie, A Streetcar Named Desire* (1947), *Summer and Smoke* (1948) and *The Rose Tattoo* (1951), a tender and boisterous play about a Sicilian widow's remarriage. In *Camino Real* (1953), Williams experimented with expressionist methods to explore his own attitudes towards the artist's activity. His finest plays so far appeared between 1955 and 1959, the superb dramatic analysis of American conflicts in *Cat on a Hot Tin Roof, Orpheus Descending* (a reworking of *Battle of Angels*), *The Garden District,* and *Sweet Bird of Youth,* all plays set in the South and dealing with the attempts of sensitive trapped women to escape isolation. *Period of Adjustment* (1960) is a full-length domestic comedy, *Night of the Iguana* (1961) and *The Milk Train Doesn't Stop Here Any More* (1962) tend to repeat earlier formulas, and the latest are *Slapstick Tragedy* (1965) (2 plays, *The Mutilated* and *The Gnadiges Fräulein*), and *The Two Character Play* (1967), about two actors trying frantically to keep their life theatre going. *Kingdom of Earth* (1968) is the complete version of the play whose Broadway version was entitled *The Seven Descents of Myrtle. In the Bar of a Tokyo Hotel* (1969) is a lacerating study of a painter's life.

Although Williams is often attacked for violence, sexual neurosis and personal shock tactics, his plays are no more sensational than Jacobean tragedies of blood. The language of his best plays is consistently brilliant and careful, a clear and sometimes poetic vehicle for his vision of primitive violence which cuts through superficial civilization in the American South as elsewhere. His symbolic dramas are universally recognized as necessary allegories of rough conditions and as such have their beauty,

not always revealed in hysterical film and stage performances. [EM]

N. Tischler, *Tennessee Williams, Rebellious Puritan* (1961).

Williams, William Carlos (1883–1963). Poet, fiction writer. Began his long creative life as doctor and writer in Rutherford, New Jersey, where he was born. His father was English; his mother's family came from various Caribbean islands and contained French, Spanish and Jewish elements. After Swiss, Parisian and New York schools, he studied medicine at Pennsylvania University (where he met Pound and H.D.), taking his internship at hospitals in New York (where he met Wallace Stevens), and a year in pediatrics in Leipzig, before becoming a G.P. in Rutherford in 1909, the year of his first book, *Poems,* printed privately. In London, he had met Yeats, and throughout his busy life he never ceased to keep in touch with writers and painters among his friends and correspondents. The first book to show his poetic character, at least in embryo, was *The Tempers* (1913), and in *Spring and All* (1923) revealed a major poet, combining what he needed from Cubism (recorded in *A Novelette and Other Prose,* 1921–31), the surreal methods of his prose poems in *Kora in Hell* (1920), ◊ Imagism and Pound, and, finally, his own direct apprehension of common life in America. His elucidatory detail from everyday life and speech deliberately avoided the mandarin expatriate manners of Eliot and Pound and allied him with a group of thirties poets – including ◊ Reznikoff and ◊ Oppen – whose aims were stated in the 'Objectivist' number of *Poetry* (21 March 1931) and Louis ◊ Zukofsky's *Five Statements for Poetry.* Williams extended these principles in his prose and poetry through his own poetically guiding concept: 'No ideas but in things', the root of the four books of *Paterson* (1946–58) as well as his critical essays.

In 1926 he won the *Dial* award, in 1950 the National Book Award, and with ◊ MacLeish the Bollingen Prize in 1952, the year he was appointed consultant in poetry at the Library of Congress but prevented from serving because of alleged leftism. *A Voyage to Pagany* (1928) and the *Autobiography* (1951) provide some account of his personal life and opinions; *Selected Essays* (1954) and *Selected Letters* (1957) contain his criticism and a running commentary on his creative life in the context of contemporary literature. His fiction includes short stories (collected in *The Farmer's Daughters*, 1961) and documentaries (*The Knife of the Times*, 1932, and *Life along the Passaic River*, 1938), and the novel trilogy, *White Mule, In the Money* and *The Build-Up* (1937–52). His plays, some of them radically experimental, and a considerable influence on American drama, are collected in *Many Loves and Other Plays* (1961), and the poems in *Collected Earlier Poems* (1951), *Collected Later Poems* (1950) and *Pictures from Breughel* (1962), which includes *The Desert Music* (1954) and *Journey to Love* (1955).

In the American Grain (1925) is a prose account of the Americanness of America told through the works and lives of explorers and writers, an essential and beautifully written part of Williams' lifelong concern for the definition of a man and his cultural and topographical environment and heritage, and for the nature of being an American and a writer. The 4 books (a fifth in notes) of *Paterson* epically explore the life of a man in a city, experiencing the historical and contemporary in order to design his life productively but without religious or philosophical dogma. The variety of characterization, poetic skills and humane but discriminating sympathies make this poem a masterpiece. Throughout his life, Williams came near to despair only over the betrayal and waste of human natural resources in America. His superb ear and explorative linear controls articulate his essential unsentimental serenity. His work has been an endless source of formal inspiration to American poetry since 1950. [EM]

M. L. Rosenthal, *A William Carlos Williams Reader* (1966).

Alan Ostrom, *The Poetic World of William Carlos Williams* (1966); L. W. Wagner, *The Poems of William Carlos Williams* (1964); T. R. Whitaker, *William Carlos Williams* (1968); J. Guimond, *The Art of William Carlos Williams* (1969).

Wilson, Edmund (1895–). Critic, playwright, poet, novelist, short-story writer. He was born in Red Bank, New Jersey, studied at Princeton, where he edited the *Nassau Literary Magazine* and collaborated in *The Undertaker's Garland* (1922), a dull collection of dirges and epitaphs, reported for the New York *Sun*, and during the First World War worked in a French hospital and

for U.S. Intelligence. Returning to New York, he edited *Vanity Fair*, reviewed for the *New Republic* and the *New Yorker*, and became Edmund Wilson, the formidably erudite pundit. He has written a novel, *I Thought of Daisy* (1929), short stories of the New York suburban and educated, *Memoirs of Hecate County* (1946; slightly revised 1960), *Five Plays* (1954; his plays include *Discordant Encounters*, 1926, *This Room and This Gin and These Sandwiches*, 1937, *The Blue Light*, 1950, his best, and *The Duke of Palermo and Other Plays*, 1969) and neat collections of private prose and verse, *Note-Books of Night* (1942) and *Night Thoughts* (1961). He collected his friend Scott Fitzgerald's posthumous writings (*The Crack-Up*, 1945) and his own verse (*Poets, Farewell*, 1929). His travel reflections, sociological studies and autobiographical essays appeared as *The American Jitters: A Year of the Slump* (1932), *Travels in Two Democracies* (1936), about Russia and America, *Europe without Baedeker* (1947), 'sketches among the ruins of Italy, Greece and England' (reissued in 1967 with 'Notes from a Diary of 1963–64: Paris, Rome, Budapest'), *Apologies to the Iroquois* (1960) (with a study of 'The Mohawks in High Steel' by Joseph Mitchell), a personal ethnological exercise of considerable significance, and *The Cold War and the Income Tax* (1963), an attack on America's military expenditure. *Red Black Blond and Olive* (1956) is an important book of comparative cultural studies based on experiences among the Zuñi Indians in New Mexico, in Haiti, in Russia and in Israel, between 1935 and 1954. *The Scrolls from the Dead Sea* (1955) and *O Canada!* (1965) again testify to the extraordinary range of interest and application of intelligent research Wilson consistently shows as he penetrates other people's cultures. The training for this began with *To the Finland Station* (1940), a magnificent study of history in the making, through considerations of Michelet, Taine, Marx, Bakunin, Trotsky, Lenin and others. Of his literary criticism, *Axel's Castle* (1931) is a standard work on symbolist literature, *The Triple Thinkers* (1938; enlarged 1948) combines essays on American and European writers, and *The Wound and the Bow* (1941) is a study of the relationship between neurosis and literary imagination.

His analytical commentary and criticism of American and European literature, arts and politics appears as the superb and enlightening series *The Shock of Recognition* (1943), an annotated anthology of works concerning the recognition of an explicitly American literature, *Classics and Commercials* (1950), reviews of literature in the forties, *The Shores of Light* (1952), on the cultured life of the twenties and thirties, *The American Earthquake* (1958), *Patriotic Gore* (1962), prefaced by an attack on American militarism and concerned with Civil War literature, and *The Bit between My Teeth* (1965), covering 1950 to 1965. These works constitute a huge chronicle of responsive reading in literature written between the early 19th century and the 1960s, an intellectual biography of a scholar and critic of wide tastes, uncommon linguistic abilities and a few notoriously querky neglects, especially in 20th-century literature. The autobiographical materials in *A Piece of My Mind* (1956) and *A Prelude* (1967) offer circumspect and selective details about private life. Productive in so many fields of writing, Wilson is distinguished for his commitment, his exemplary absence of academic objectivity, and his ability to remain detached from political and psychological schools in a period beset by dogmatic theory and absurd abnegation before leaders. He is deeply American in his active sense of a free culture based on the continuous life of knowledge and research uninhibited by precedent. [EM]

Sherman Paul, *Edmund Wilson: A Study in Literary Vocation in Our Time* (1965).

Wilson, Sloan (1920–   ). Novelist. Born in Norwalk, Connecticut, he graduated from Harvard in 1942 and became a reporter on the *Providence Journal* (1946–7). Later he was an Assistant Director of the National Citizens Commission for Public Schools (1947–52), and Assistant Professor of English at the University of Buffalo (1952–5). Wilson achieved an early success with *The Man in the Gray Flannel Suit* (1944), a study of a business executive, and after *Voyage to Somewhere* (1946) produced four more best-selling novels about contemporary American manners: *A Summer Place* (1958), *A Sense of Values* (1961), *Georgie Winthrop* (1962) and *Janus Island* (1967). [MG]

Wimsatt, W(illiam) K(urty) (1907–   ). Critic, scholar. Educated at Georgetown

University, Washington, and then at Yale, where in 1939 he received his Ph.D. and became an instructor; in 1955 he was appointed Professor. His first book, *The Prose Style of Samuel Johnson* (1941), analyses the qualities of a good prose style – a subject almost ignored in modern criticism. A reviewer's criticism prompted him to rethink and develop one chapter as *Philosophic Words* (1948). Other work on the English 18th century includes his editions of *Alexander Pope, Selected Poetry and Prose* (1951), *Boswell for the Defence* (with F. A. Pottle, 1959) and *Samuel Johnson on Shakespeare* (1960).

His major work has been in theoretical literary criticism, where his rigorously philosophical approach has been coupled with a strong 'structuralist' theory stressing the distinctively metaphorical character of literary language. Though this has differentiated him from ◊ New Criticism, his stress on the need for criticism to be 'the general anatomy of verbal powers' links him in some respects. With Cleanth ◊ Brooks he wrote *Literary Criticism: A Short History* (1957) which again combines great learning with original insight. He is best known for his collection of articles *The Verbal Icon* (1954) which dismisses two 'fallacious' approaches to literature – the 'Intentional Fallacy' of judging not an author's achievement but his hopes, and the 'Affective Fallacy' of describing not 'the verbal object' but individual and collective reactions to it – and also examines the relation of poetry to morals, and to 'universal' rather than 'local' truth; and various problems of style. He develops his themes and approach further in *Hateful Contraries* (1965), more essays on criticism. No other book – save possibly Northrop ◊ Frye's *Anatomy of Criticism* – has defined so well the formidable problems facing the serious critic. [MG/MB]

Wingfield, Edward-Maria (*c*.1560–*c*.1620?). First governor of Jamestown. Elected president of the Council of Virginia on arrival, he was deposed later by the Virginia company councillors. Besides *A Map of Virginia* . . . (1612), he wrote *The Generall Historie of Virginia, New-England, and the Summer Isles* (1624), which includes work by other voyagers to America and elaborated Captain John ◊ Smith's version of the early days of the community, and *The True Travels, Adventures, and Observations of Captaine John Smith* (1630). [EM]

Winters, Yvor (1900–68). Poet, critic. Chicago-born and educated at the Universities of Chicago, Colorado and Stanford, he is one of the first notable poets of distinctively Western, particularly Californian, landscape and history, in verse which is severely restrained and patterned. A second major subject area of his poetry derives from his experience as a scholar and teacher at Stanford since 1927: 'The young are quick of speech./Grown middle-aged, I teach/Corrosion and distrust.' His critical work is best read as the effort of a poet to understand and thus free himself from past (romantic) and contemporary ('modernistic') ideas and techniques which interfered with his own poetic development. He is married to the American novelist Janet Lewis.

Winters' best critical work is as a metrical analyst and pioneer interpreter of American literary history. His defence of conventional metres, his essays on Poe, Cooper and Dickinson have classic status, heavily indebted in theory to Arnold and ◊ Babbitt. *In Defense of Reason* (1947) collects important essays on 19th- and 20th-century American writers, from Cooper to Hart Crane. *The Function of Criticism* (1957) includes major studies of Hopkins and Frost. *Forms of Discovery* (1967) is a set of essays on the short poem in English. *Yvor Winters on Modern Poets* (1959) is a useful paperback collecting six critical essays, prefaced by a short introduction by Keith McKean. [GD/EM]

Collected Poems (1963).
Alan Stephens, 'The Collected Poems of Yvor Winters', *Twentieth Century Literature*, October 1963; Denis Donoghue, 'The Black Ox', *New York Review of Books*, 29 February 1968.

Winthrop, John (1588–1649). Lawyer, colonial administrator, chronicler. A group of leading English Puritans obtained from Charles I in 1629 a charter for a colonizing venture called the Massachusetts Bay Company. Winthrop was elected their governor, and in 1630 the entire company transferred itself to America, founding Boston and a number of other settlements nearby. Winthrop became the first governor of the Massachusetts Bay Colony and continued in this office, or as deputy governor, for most of the time until his death in 1649. Under his guidance a theocratic commonwealth developed in which, despite restriction of the franchise to church members,

a system of representative institutions enabled the creation of a fairly democratic society. In addition to a number of religious works, Winthrop wrote a famous journal which recounted the migration from England and the story of his private and public life in the colony down to the year of his death. While less elegantly composed than William ◊ Bradford's history of Plymouth, it is a highly readable and historically valuable account of the early development of one of the most important of the New England colonies. [EM]

Winthrop's Journal: 'History of New England 1630–1649', ed. J. K. Hosmer (2 vols., 1908); ed. P. Miller and T. H. Johnson, *The Puritans: A Sourcebook of Their Writings* (1938; revised bibliography 1963).
Samuel Eliot Morison, *Builders of the Bay Colony* (1930).

Wise, John (1652–1725). Theologian. Born in Roxbury, Massachusetts, and Harvard-educated, he was one of the most courageous and witty ministers of his time. His base was Ipswich, Massachusetts, but he went as chaplain on two military expeditions. His leading protests against arbitrary colonial taxation, which brought him imprisonment, and his petition on behalf of the victims of the Salem Witch trials, are typical of his life. *The Churches Quarrel Espoused* (1710), a plea for independent churches against the ◊ Mathers' central organization proposals, was held in high regard by the pre-revolutionary patriots; it was reprinted in 1772. So was *A Vindication of the Government of New England Churches* (1717), proposing to replace Calvinist doctrines of election with ideas of equality; it influenced the writers of the Declaration of Independence. He also wrote *A Word of Comfort to a Melancholy Country* (1721). Wise's merits as a writer of prose are urged by Moses Coit ◊ Tyler in *A History of American Literature: 1607–1765* (1878, 1962), and his style of controversy is as humorous as it is humane. [MB/EM]

George Allan Cook, *John Wise: Early American Democrat* (1952).

Wister, Owen (1860–1938). Novelist. Born in Pennsylvania, he graduated from Harvard. Several trips to Wyoming provided material for *Lin McLean* (1898), a series of related stories of the Western cattle country; *The Jimmy-john Boss* (1900), short stories; and, easily his most popular work, *The Virginian* (1902), a classic Western novel,

273

featuring a prototype Western hero, ideally brave, handsome, honourable and chivalrous. *Lady Baltimore* (1906) is a romantic novel of life in Charleston, and *Philosophy 4* (1903) is a story with a Harvard background. [A H]

Writings (11 vols., 1928).
Larzer Ziff, *The American 1890s* (1967).

Wolfe, Thomas (1900–38). Novelist. His father was a stone-cutter in Asheville, North Carolina, and his mother, from the hill country around, ran a boarding-house. At 15 he went to North Carolina University where he developed his inclination to write plays, further mistakenly fostered in G. P. ◊ Baker's '47 Workshop' at Harvard (1922). He played the lead there in his own *The Return of Buck Gavin* (1924) and *Welcome to Our City* (1923), the city being the native 'Altamont' of his first novel, *Look Homeward, Angel* (1929). From 1924 to 1930 he taught English at New York University, wrote his play *Mannerhouse*, travelled in Europe, began writing his first novel in England (published by Maxwell Perkins at Scribner's), married Aline Bernstein, and commenced *Of Time and the River* (1935). He worked with Perkins on this latter novel until it was published and in that year settled in New York, famous and successful. In 1935–6 he travelled to the West Coast, the South, and to Germany, and in 1937 paid his first visit to Asheville since his first novel appeared. He had two operations for a brain infection after pneumonia in 1938. His last two novels and a second volume of short stories were edited after his death by Edward C. Aswell.

His four novels, and parts of the stories in *From Death to Morning* (1935) and *The Hills Beyond* (1941), are a continuous autobiographical fiction on a huge scale, the anguish of whose composition is partly told in 'The Story of a Novel' (1936). In *Look Homeward, Angel*, the hero is Eugene Gant, immersed in the tumultuous pressures of his exuberant family from which he escapes into literature and college. It is a great overflowing work with superb characterizations of Gant's parents, his sister Helen, and his brother Ben. *Of Time and the River* moves Gant to university, Europe and New York, and in *The Web and the Rock* (1939) he has become George Webber, experiencing his first love affair in New York (the first half parallels the first novel), and in *You Can't Go Home Again* (1940) he is a published novelist, lonely in the city and nostalgic for North Carolina. Wolfe's large scheme has the scope, massive detail and sense of space and time of an epic structure, but also the redundancy of its cyclic conception. The interest lies with the accurate dialogues, realistic descriptions and passages of poetic rhetoric sometimes of considerable power. Wolfe is neither a Southern writer nor a ◊ 'Lost Generation' expatriate: he reaches for a dimension beyond America and the contemporary 'wilderness of ugliness and provincialism', a degree of romantic ambition towards completely unified experience. [E M]

Letters, ed. E. Nowell (1956); *The Enigma of Thomas Wolfe: Biographical and Critical Selections*, ed. R. Walser (1953); *The Notebooks*, ed. R. S. Kennedy and P. Reeves (1970).
Andrew Turnbull, *Thomas Wolfe* (1968); R. S. Kennedy, *The Window of Being: The Literary Career of Thomas Wolfe* (1952); *Modern Fiction Studies*, Autumn, 1965 (Thomas Wolfe issue).

Wolfe, Tom (1931–). Critic. Born in Virginia, he took his doctorate in American studies at Yale, became a newspaper reporter, and after an award-winning report from Cuba, moved to the *New York Herald-Tribune*. The first piece in his celebrated pop style was for *Esquire* in 1963. Subsequent pieces built into *The Kandy-Kolored Tangerine-Flake Streamline Baby* (1965), a classic of American studies. In *The Electric Kool-Aid Acid Test* (1968) his baroque style of disc-jockey harangue plus acute observation of salient detail is used to present Ken Kesey and his Merry Pranksters, the world of psychedelia. *The Mid-Atlantic Man* (1969) explores the cults of the faddists on both sides of the ocean. [E M]

Woods, John (1926–). Poet. Born in Martinsville, Indiana, educated at the University of Indiana. During the years he has taught at Western Michigan University, at Kalamazoo, he has published *The Deaths at Paragon* (1955), *On the Morning of Color* (1961), *Cutting Edge* (1966) and *Keeping Out of Trouble* (1968). His best and most characteristic poems are terse, ironic, wittily cryptic statements of social concerns. [B P]

Woodworth, Samuel (1784–1842). Born in Massachusetts, he edited a children's magazine, *The Fly*, wrote plays and poems in New York, and became a successful editor and publisher. He is remembered for two popular poems, 'The Old Oaken Bucket' (1818) and 'The Hunters of Kentucky' (1821). [E M]

Woolcott, Alexander (1887–1943). Journalist, critic, story writer. He was born in the Utopia of the North American Phalanx in an 85-room building. He became a bank clerk, and a drama reporter on the New York *Times*. After the First World War, his fame exploded as a journalist, raconteur and make-or-break critic. His cruelty was sometimes witty and is accurately displayed in Kaufman and ◊ Hart's revenge, *The Man Who Came to Dinner* (1939), whose title role he absorbed by playing it himself. His journalism and tales are collected in 10 volumes. The glint shines somewhat in *The Portable Woolcott* (ed. J. Hennessy, 1946). [EM]

Woolman, John (1720–72). Preacher, mystic. He was born in New Jersey into a devout Quaker farming family, and became a tailor, shop assistant and preacher, teaching social reform, tolerance and anarchistic pacifism. He died in England, at York, of smallpox. His *Essay on Some Considerations on the Keeping of Negroes* (1754; second part, 1762) was an important early anti-slavery document and contributed towards the abandonment of this practice by the Quakers. His *Journal* (1774) is an important record of the spirit of American Quakerism and a classic of Quaker intimacy with God and insistent truth-telling. The account of his spiritual and mystical experiences have a simple lucidity, and yet there is also a concrete respect for work and a realistic confrontation which resembles the 19th-century ◊ Transcendentalists. The *Journal* was widely read in the 19th century; the Everyman edition appeared in 1910 and it is edited, with other works on social and religious matters, by A. M. Gummere in *The Journals and Essays of John Woolman* (1922), with a biographical introduction and bibliography. [MB/EM]

Janet Whitney, *John Woolman: American Quaker* (1942); Edwin Cady, *John Woolman* (1965); G. M. Trevelyan, 'John Woolman, the Quaker', in *Clio, a Muse and Other Essays* (1913).

Woolson, Constance Fenimore (1840–94). Novelist, story writer. Born in Claremont, New Hampshire, the grandniece of James Fenimore ◊ Cooper, she is usually associated by critics with the local colorist movement which flourished, notably among female writers, in the late-19th-century America. Her earlier novels, some historical, some contemporary, deal with various parts of the States. The sketches in *Castle Nowhere: Lake-Country Sketches* (1875) treat the French inhabitants of the Great Lakes region of the U.S.A. Those in *Rodman the Keeper: Southern Sketches* (1880) deal with Florida, also the setting of her novel *East Angels* (1886). *For the Major* (1883) has a North Carolina background. After 1879 she was attracted to Europe by 'that old-world feeling' and lived in Oxford, Florence and Venice. Her *Dorothy and Other Italian Stories* (1896) deals interestingly with Americans in Italy. She became a friend of Henry James, whom she idolized, and he represented her in 'The Aspern Papers'. [MB]

John D. Kern, *Constance Fenimore Woolson: Literary Pioneer* (1934).

Wouk, Herman (1915–). Novelist, playwright. Born in New York. Before the war a professional radio scriptwriter, he served in the navy in the Pacific and began writing fiction. His first two novels are comic – *Aurora Dawn* (1947) satirizes the world of radio and advertising with a stylish, 18th-century comic-novel approach; *The City Boy* (1948) treats the humour of a Bronx boyhood. Then came *The Caine Mutiny* (1951), a concentrated, tough, and well-managed treatment of a mutiny aboard a Second World War minesweeper. Wouk made from it a Broadway play, *The Caine Mutiny Court Martial*, which became a successful film. He has never quite regained this form. *Marjorie Morningstar* (1955) follows a Jewish girl through an elaborate love-life and show business ambitions to a final resting place in suburban security. *Slattery's Hurricane* (1956) reworks an earlier film-script. *Youngblood Hawke* (1962) shows a Thomas ◊ Wolfe-like Southern novelist destroyed by success and the big city. *Don't Stop the Carnival* (1965) has surface attractions in its Carribbean setting; for the rest it is matter for compulsive readers. [MB]

Wright, James (1927–). Poet. He studied at Kenyon College, in his native state Ohio, and at the University of Washington, and now teaches at the University of Minnesota. His elegant and excellently controlled poetry, with its strong moral concern, has won high reputation. It is collected in *The Green Well* (1957), *Saint Judas* (1959) and *Shall We Gather at the River* (1968). [MB]

Paul Carroll, *The Poem in Its Skin* (1968).

Wright, Richard (1908–60). Novelist, story writer, social critic, commentator. Nearly all his work is concerned with the role of the Negro in a white-dominated world. Born near Natchez, Mississippi, he began to write soon after moving to Chicago in 1934. In the early 1940s he lived mainly in Mexico; in 1946 he moved to Paris where he remained until his death. He joined the Communist Party in the early thirties, and remained a member until 1944.

The ironically titled *Uncle Tom's Children* (1938; enlarged, 1940) is a collection of stories all portraying Southern racial prejudice and brutality in harshly naturalistic style. *Native Son* (1940) describes the career of Bigger Thomas, a Negro boy raised in the Chicago slums. This powerful novel is written in the mode of social determinism; in his violence and cruelty Bigger Thomas is the inhuman product of an inhuman world. More interesting is the sense in which he emerges as an early existential hero; the way of violence becomes for him the only way towards self-consciousness and claiming his human rights. *The Outsider* (1953) is about an intellectual Negro's much more self-conscious search for identity and meaning in life; but the language in which the action, and the socio-political problems involved, is handled is shrill and over-pitched for the whole to be convincing. In *The Long Dream* (1958) Wright returns to the special problem of being a Negro in America. *Land Today*, written before *Native Son*, but published only in 1963, is a powerful documentary novel of Chicago's South Side during the Depression: its hero, Jake Jackson, is a classic of the insulted and injured black American.

Wright's other work includes *Black Boy* (1945), an autobiography; *12 Million Black Voices* (1941), a short text and picture folk-history of the American Negro; *Black Power* (1954), a rather unsympathetic account of Ghana; *The Color Curtain* (1956), a report on the Bandung Conference in Indonesia; *Pagan Spain* (1957), a severely critical account of Franco's Spain; *White Man, Listen!* (1957), a lecture on racial injustices; and *Eight Men* (1961), a fine collection of stories. (◇ Negro Literature.) [AH]

Robert A. Bone, *The Negro Novel in America* (1958), and *Richard Wright* (U. of Minnesota Pamphlet, 1969); Constance Webb, *Richard Wright: A Biography* (1968); James Baldwin, *Notes of a Native Son* (1955); Dan McCall, *The Example of Richard Wright* (1969).

Wright, Willard Huntington ('S.S. Van Dine') (1888–1939). Critic, detective-story writer. Born in Virginia, Wright became an influential critical journalist writing on art and drama. With H. L. ◇ Mencken and George Jean ◇ Nathan he edited the important periodical *The Smart Set* (1912–14), with them wrote *What Nietzsche Taught* (1914), and also published collections of critical essays and a novel, *The Man of Promise* (1916). An illness in 1923 started him writing detective stories, his detective being the learned dilettante Philo Vance. In 1926 appeared *The 'Benson' Murder Case*, a year later came *The 'Canary' Murder Case*, and thereafter came many more Philo Vance novels, all reaching a wide and varied public. [MB]

Wylie, Elinor (1885–1928). Poet, novelist. Born in New Jersey and educated in Philadelphia, Elinor Hoyt was married three times, secondly to Horace Wylie. Her literary career was short, but within one decade, the 1920s, she established a reputation equally as poet and novelist. After the early and anonymous *Incidental Numbers* (1912) she published *Nets to Catch the Wind* (1921), a collection of delicate, elegant poems about birds and animals. Similar work appeared in *Black Armour* (1923) and *Trivial Breath* (1928), and there were new elements of fantasy and mysticism in her *Angels and Earthly Creatures* (1928), which contained the interesting sonnet sequence, *One Person*. Her *Last Poems* appeared in 1943.

She wrote four historical novels; each could be described by the subtitle, 'A Sedate Extravaganza' of her first, *Jennifer Lorn* (1923), which concerned English aristocrats in India during the 18th century and was highly praised by Sinclair Lewis. *The Venetian Glass Nephew* (1925) was a fantastic parable. *The Orphan Angel* (1926; British title *Mortal Image*, 1927) imagined Shelley's escape from drowning and an enthusiastic visit to America; its successor *Mr Hodge and Mr Hazard* (1928) described England in the sober decade following the deaths of Byron and Shelley.

Her last husband, the poet William Rose ◇ Benét, edited her *Collected Poems* (1932) and *Collected Prose* (1933), and wrote a brief critical study, *The Poetry and Prose of Elinor Wylie* (1934). [MG]

Nancy Hoyt, *Elinor Wylie: The Portrait of an Unknown Lady* (1935).

Y

Yerby, Frank (1916–   ). Novelist, short-story writer. Born in Georgia. Educated at Paine College and at the Universities of Fisk and Chicago. After teaching in Southern argicultural colleges (1939–41) he worked in industry, and has since been a full-time writer, living in France and Spain. Yerby won national attention and the O. Henry Memorial Award with his first short story, 'Health Card' (1944), describing the brutal humiliation of a Negro couple by military policemen; but his first novel, *The Foxes of Harrow* (1946), was a romance about the South before the Civil War, and despite criticism from other Negro writers he has produced a long and immensely popular series of such works, including *The Golden Hawk* (1948), *The Saracen Blade* (1952), *Gillian* (1960), *The Old Gods Laugh* (1964) and *Judas, My Brother* (1968). *Speak Now* (1969) uses the black jazz life but the setting is romantic Paris. [MG]

Young, Stark (1881–   ). Critic. He was educated at the University of Mississippi and Columbia; he taught English at a number of universities, published poems, a verse drama, and a number of plays (after 1919) while he was drama editor of *The New Republic*. His serious essays on theatre appeared in *The Flower of Drama* (1923). In *I'll Take My Stand* (1930), he criticized the South's 'mad self-respect and honour complex' as well as its victimization by Washington government. His best work is the theatre criticism in *Immortal Shadows* (1948) and his translations of Chekhov. [EM]

Z

Zaturenska, Marya (1902–). Poet. Born in Russia, she came to the U.S.A. in 1909. She is married to Horace ◊ Gregory, with whom she wrote the important *History of American Poetry: 1900–1940* (1946). Her poems have been published regularly since 1924 and her latest book is *Terraces of Light* (1960). [EM]

Zukofsky, Louis (1904–). Poet. He was born on the lower East Side of Manhattan and has lived in New York City most of his life, for over 30 years in Brooklyn. He has taught at the University of Wisconsin, San Francisco State College and Brooklyn Polytechnic Institute. His poetry, one of the most magnificent bodies of work in American literature, is a long and persistent search for and achievement of accuracy and refinement of language and a continuous lyrical expression of faith in men and women. It appeared firstly in *An 'Objectivist's Anthology* (a *To* publication, 1932), in such little magazines as *Origin, Poetry, Black Mountain Review, Dial, Transition* and *Trobar,* and *First Half of 'A' – 9* (1934). After *55 Poems* (1941) there appeared a number of volumes, still published largely through the support of small publishers of poetry, who included Jonathan ◊ Williams, Cid Corman and Iain Hamilton Finlay: *Anew* (1946), *Some Time* (1956), *Barely and Widely* (1958), *'A' 1–12* (1959), *16 once published* (1962), *I's (pronounced eyes)* (1963), *After I's* (1964) and *Found Objects 1962–1926* (1964). *All: The Collected Short Poems 1923–1958* (1965) and *All: The Collected Short Poems 1956–64* (1967) are, as Zukofsky says, 'an autobiography: the words are my life', and an expression of 'the desirability of making order out of history as it is felt and conceived'. These aims are achieved through poems built mainly from short cadences of unique precision and frugality which control warmth of feeling in a delightfully spare objectivity. *'A' 1–12* (1959) and *'A' 13–21* (1969) are the first sections of the only long poem to compare with the *Cantos* of Pound and *Paterson* of Williams for intellectual scope, lyrical intensity, formal invention and poetic intelligence. *All* and *'A'* constitute a great onward-going major poetry constructed from 'historical and contemporary particulars', a 'process of active literary omission', a rejection of crude metaphor and symbolism, and a use of the poetic line and typography to demonstrate 'how the voice should sound' (see *Five Statements for Poetry*, 1958; original publication 1951 and repr. *Kulchur* 7, 8 and 10, 1962). His quietly incisive poetry is the form of a lifetime's regard for definition. *Catullus* (with Celia Zukofsky, 1969) is a large collection of translations. His criticism is in *Le Style Apollinaire* (1934), *A Test for Poetry* (1948), a book of documentation for his theory of poetry and good writing in general, and *Prepositions* (1967), a collection of critical essays. *It was* (1961) is fiction, issued complete as *Ferdinand* (1968). His finest prose work is *Bottom: On Shakespeare* (1963), volume 1 of which is a brilliant reading of Shakespeare out of a lifetime of study and research; volume 2 is a musical setting of *Pericles* by the poet's wife, Celia Zukofsky. *The Gas Age* (1969) transcribes some observations on poetry made at a reading, and *Autobiography* (1970) interposes brief personal prose statements between musical settings of his lyrics by Celia Zukofsky. [EM]

Ezra Pound, *Polite Essays* (1937); Robert Creeley, 'A Note on Louis Zukofsky', *Kulchur* 14 (1964); Cid Corman, *At: Bottom* (1966); ed. Charles Tomlinson, *Agenda*, III, 6 (1964) (Zukofsky issue).

RECOMMENDED READING

ANTHOLOGIES AND COLLECTIONS

Oscar Cargill, ed., *American Literature: A Period Anthology* (4 vols., revised edn, 1949).

Geoffrey Moore, ed., *American Literature* (1964).

Edmund Wilson, ed., *The Shock of Recognition: The Development of Literature in the United States Recorded by the Men Who Made It* (1943).

Philip Rahv, ed., *Literature in America* (1957).

G. W. Allen, W. B. Rideout and J. K. Robinson, eds, *American Poetry* (1965).

Donald M. Allen, *The New American Poetry: 1946–1960* (1960).

G. N. Grob and R. N. Beck, eds, *American Ideas: Some Readings in the Intellectual History of the United States* (2 vols., 1963).

Hennig Cohen, ed., *The American Experience* (1968) and *The American Culture* (1968).

BIBLIOGRAPHICAL, HISTORICAL AND CRITICAL WORKS

A Guide to the Study of the United States of America (1960).

Clarence Gohdes, *Bibliographical Guide to the Study of the Literature of the U.S.A.* (revised edn, 1963).

Alexis de Tocqueville, *Democracy in America* (1835; 1840; various modern edns).

Oscar Handlin, *The American People* (1963).

John Blum *et al.*, *The National Experience* (1963); English edition: *The American Experience*, 1963).

David M. Potter, *People of Plenty* (1954).

H. B. Parkes, *The American Experience* (1955).

D. W. Brogan, *The American Problem* (1944; repr. as *The American Character*, 1950).

Daniel J. Boorstin, *The Americans: The Colonial Experience* (1958); *The National Experience* (1965).

Robin M. Williams, *American Society* (revised edn, 1961).

W. J. Cash, *The Mind of the South* (1941).

Harvey Wish, *Society and Thought in Modern America: A Social and Intellectual History of the American People from 1865* (2 vols. 1950–52; v. 2. revised edn, 1962).

Henry F. May, *The End of American Innocence: A Study of the First Years of Our Own Time, 1912–1917* (1959).

Richard Hofstadter, *Anti-Intellectualism in American Life* (1963).

Marcus Cunliffe, *The Literature of the United States* (revised edn, 1970).

R. S. Spiller, W. Thorp, T. H. Johnson and H. S. Canby, eds, *Literary History of the United States* (revised edn, 1964).

Constance Rourke, *American Humor: A Study in National Character* (1931).

Oliver W. Larkin, *Art and Life in America* (revised edn, 1960).

279

Bernard Rosenberg and David M. White, eds, *Mass Culture: The Popular Arts in America* (1957).

Wilfrid Mellers, *Music in a New Found Land* (1964).

Henry Nash Smith, *Virgin Land: The American West as Symbol and Myth* (1950).

Leo Marx, *The Machine in the Garden: Technology and the Pastoral Ideal in America* (1964).

Howard Mumford Jones, *The Theory of American Literature* (1948).

Leon Howard, *Literature and the American Tradition* (1960).

R. W. B. Lewis, *The American Adam: Innocence, Tragedy and Tradition in the Nineteenth Century* (1955).

F. O. Matthiessen, *American Renaissance: Art and Expression in the Age of Emerson and Whitman* (1941).

Charles Feidelson, Jr, *Symbolism and American Literature* (1953).

Harry T. Levin, *The Power of Blackness: Hawthorne, Poe, Melville* (1958).

A. N. Kaul, *The American Vision: Actual and Ideal Society in Nineteenth Century Fiction* (1963).

Kenneth B. Murdock, *Literature and Theology in Colonial New England* (1949).

Edmund Wilson, *Patriotic Gore: Studies in the Literature of the American Civil War* (1962).

Larzer Ziff, *The American 1890's: Life and Times of a Lost Generation* (1966).

Malcolm Cowley, *Exile's Return: A Literary Odyssey of the 1920's* (revised edn, 1961).

Daniel Aaron, *Writers on the Left: Episodes in American Literary Communism* (1961).

Richard Chase, *The American Novel and its Tradition* (1957).

Marius Bewley, *The Complex Fate: Hawthorne, Henry James and Some Other American Writers* (1952); *The Eccentric Design* (1959).

Alfred Kazin, *On Native Grounds: An Interpretation of Modern American Prose Literature* (revised edn, 1956).

Leslie Fiedler, *Love and Death in the American Novel* (revised edn, 1966).

D. G. Hoffman, *Form and Fable in American Fiction* (1961).

Nelson Manfred Blake, *Novelists' America: Fiction as History, 1910–1940* (1969).

W. B. Rideout, *The Radical Novel in the United States, 1900–1954* (1956).

Ihab Hassan, *Radical Innocence: Studies in the Contemporary American Novel* (1961).

Richard Bridgman, *The Colloquial Style in America* (1966).

Richard Poirier, *A World Elsewhere: The Place of Style in American Literature* (1966).

Tony Tanner, *The Reign of Wonder: Naivety and Reality in American Literature* (1965); *City of Words: American Fiction 1950–1970* (1971).

Roy Harvey Pearce, *The Continuity of American Poetry* (1961).

C. Feidelson and P. Brodtkorb, eds, *Interpretations of American Literature* (1959).

S. L. Gross and J. E. Hardy, eds, *Images of the Negro in American Literature* (1966).